First edition for the United States, its territories and dependencies and Canada published in 2007 by Barron's Educational Series, Inc.

Copyright © Oxford University Press 2005

This Americanization of *Oxford School Dictionary & Thesaurus,* first edition originally published in English in 2005, published by arrangement with Oxford University Press.

All inquiries should be addressed to:
Barron's Educational Series, Inc.
250 Wireless Blvd.
Hauppauge, NY 11788
www.barronseduc.com

ISBN-13: 978-0-7641-3606-1
ISBN-10: 0-7641-3606-2

Library of Congress Control No.: 2006925200

Printed and bound in China

9 8 7 6 5 4 3 2 1

Dictionary and Thesaurus Features

Pronunciations are given for difficult words

Parts of speech (word classes) are given for all headwords and derivatives

plaintiff *NOUN* **plaintiffs** the person who brings a complaint against somebody else to a court of law COMPARE **defendant**

plaintive *ADJECTIVE* sounding sad • *a plaintive cry*

Cross-references are given to other words of interest

plait (plat) *VERB* **plaits, plaiting, plaited** weave three or more strands of hair or rope to form one length

Plurals of nouns are given

plait *NOUN* **plaits** a length of hair or rope that has been plaited

plan *NOUN* **plans** 1 a way of doing something thought out in advance 2 a drawing showing the arrangement of parts of something 3 a map of a town or district

Definitions are clear and accurate

plan *VERB* **plans, planning, planned** make a plan for something
▷ **planner** *NOUN*

plane[1] *NOUN* **planes** 1 an airplane 2 a tool for making wood smooth by scraping its surface 3 a flat or level surface

Headwords are numbered when they have different meanings or origins

Headwords in the dictionary and the thesaurus are on the same page to make access quick and easy

plane *VERB* **planes, planing, planed** smooth wood with a plane

plane *ADJECTIVE* flat or level • *a plane surface* USAGE Do not confuse with **plain**.

plane[2] *NOUN* **planes** a tall tree with broad leaves

planet *NOUN* **planets** one of the bodies that move in an orbit around the sun. The main planets are Mercury, Venus, Earth, Mars, Jupiter, Saturn, Uranus, and Neptune.
▷ **planetary** *ADJECTIVE*

Usage notes in the dictionary give grammar and language support

---

plan *NOUN* 1 (*informal*) *a plan of the building*
► chart, diagram, map, layout, blueprint, representation 2 *a clever plan for raising money*
► idea, proposal, project, program, strategy, suggestion, proposition

Register labels help users to select appropriate vocabulary

Over 100,000 synonyms are listed with the most appropriate listed first

plan *VERB* 1 *She began planning tomorrow's journey.* ► organize, arrange, figure out, think out, prepare 2 *some tips for anyone planning a new garden* ► design, devise, contrive, sketch out 3 *We plan to go abroad this year.* ► intend, propose, aim, mean, envisage, contemplate, be thinking of USAGE If you use any of the last three synonyms, you need to say *going* instead of *to go*, e.g., *We envisage going abroad this year.*

Usage notes in the thesaurus give language and grammar support

plane *NOUN* 1 *The plane rose gently in the air.*
► airplane, aircraft, jet, airliner, craft 2 *The thought that came to her now was on a more creative plane.* ► level, stage, degree, position

planet *NOUN* *the population of the planet*
► globe, world, orb

Up-to-date example sentences and phrases show how words are used in context

Aa

a ADJECTIVE (called the *indefinite article* and changing to an before most vowel sounds) **1** one (but not any special one) • *Can you lend me a book?* **2** each; per • *We see it once a day or once an hour.*

aback ADVERB
taken aback surprised
[from Old English *on baec* = backwards]

abacus (ab- a- kus) NOUN **abacuses** a frame used for counting with beads sliding on wires [from a Greek word *abax* meaning "slab." An early form of abacus was a slab of wood with a coating of dust, for writing on and adding up figures]

abandon VERB **abandons, abandoning, abandoned 1** give up • *We never abandoned hope.* **2** leave something without intending to return • *Abandon ship!*
▷ **abandonment** NOUN

abandon NOUN a careless and uncontrolled manner • *She was dancing with great abandon.*

abbey NOUN **abbeys 1** a monastery or convent **2** a church that was once part of a monastery • *Westminster Abbey*

abbot NOUN **abbots** the head of an abbey

abbreviate VERB **abbreviates, abbreviating, abbreviated** shorten something

abbreviation NOUN **abbreviations 1** a shortened form of a word or words, especially

one using the initial letters, such as GCSE, St., U.S. **2** abbreviating something [from Latin *brevis* = short]

abdicate VERB **abdicates, abdicating, abdicated 1** resign from a throne **2** give up an important responsibility
▷ **abdication** NOUN

abdomen (ab- dom- en) NOUN **abdomens 1** the lower front part of a person's or animal's body, containing the stomach, intestines, and other digestive organs **2** the rear section of an insect's body
▷ **abdominal** (ab- **dom**- in- al) ADJECTIVE

abduct VERB **abducts, abducting, abducted** take a person away illegally; kidnap
▷ **abduction** NOUN **abductor** NOUN

abhor VERB **abhors, abhorring, abhorred** (*formal*) hate something very much
▷ **abhorrent** ADJECTIVE **abhorrence** NOUN

abide VERB **abides, abiding, abided 1** (*old use; past tense* **abode**) remain or dwell somewhere **2** bear or tolerate • *I can't abide wasps.*
abide by keep a promise
[from Old English]

ability NOUN **abilities 1** being able to do something **2** cleverness or talent

ablaze ADJECTIVE blazing; on fire

able ADJECTIVE **1** having the power or skill or opportunity to do something **2** skillful or clever
▷ **ably** ADVERB

-able SUFFIX (also **-ble, -ible,** and **-uble**) forms adjectives (e.g. *readable, legible*) The nouns formed from these end in **-bility** (e.g. *readability, legibility*)

Thesaurus

abandon VERB **1** *The children had been abandoned in the war.* ► desert, leave behind, leave stranded, strand, forsake, leave in the lurch **2** *The car was abandoned near the highway.* ► leave, (*more informal*) dump, (*more informal*) ditch **3** *The entire project had to be abandoned.* ► cancel, drop, discontinue, (*more informal*) give up, (*more informal*) scrap, (*very informal*) ditch **4** *The company abandoned its claims to the money.* ► drop, give up, renounce, waive, (*more formal*) relinquish

abbreviate VERB *The medium is known as a digital versatile disc, usually abbreviated to DVD.* ► shorten

abhorrent ADJECTIVE *Racial abuse is abhorrent to most people.* ► hateful, loathsome, detested (by), detestable, repugnant, repellent, obnoxious, odious, offensive, horrifying, repulsive, revolting

abide VERB **1** *I cannot abide grown men walking around in sneakers.* ► bear, stand, endure, tolerate, (*more informal*) stomach, (*more*

informal) put up with **2 abide by** *The company expects its employees to abide by its rules.* ► obey, observe, follow, accept, keep to, carry out, conform to, stick to, adhere to, act in accordance with, stand by, submit to

ability NOUN **1** *An unexpected inheritance gave him the ability to travel the world.* ► power, resources, capability, capacity, means, opportunity, potential, wherewithal **2** *Jane's new employers had received good reports of her ability.* ► capability, competence, aptitude, expertise, proficiency, (*more informal*) know-how **3** *You have the ability to do well in life.* ► capacity, talent, intelligence, skill, aptitude, flair **4** *He has many unusual abilities.* ► talent, skill, accomplishment, gift, qualification

able ADJECTIVE **1** *a group of the most able students* ► talented, accomplished, proficient, efficient, gifted, capable, clever, skilled, competent, intelligent, effective AN OPPOSITE IS incompetent **2 able to** *Are you able to come?* ► allowed to, free to, prepared to, in a position to, (*more informal*) up to (coming)

A
B
C
D
E
F
G
H
I
J
K
L
M
N
O
P
Q
R
S
T
U
V
W
X
Y
Z

abnormal ADJECTIVE not normal; unusual
▷ **abnormally** ADVERB **abnormality** NOUN

aboard ADVERB, PREPOSITION on or into a ship or aircraft or train

abolish VERB abolishes, abolishing, abolished put an end to a law or custom, etc.
▷ **abolition** (ab- ol- **ish**- on) NOUN

abominable ADJECTIVE very bad or unpleasant
▷ **abominably** ADVERB **abomination** NOUN

aborigine (ab- er- **ij**- in- ee) NOUN aborigines one of the original inhabitants of a country
▷ **aboriginal** ADJECTIVE, NOUN
Aborigine one of the original inhabitants of Australia who lived there before the Europeans arrived
[from Latin *ab origine* = from the beginning]

abort VERB aborts, aborting, aborted put an end to something before it has been completed ● *They aborted the space flight because of problems.*

abortion NOUN abortions an operation to remove a fetus from the womb before it has developed enough to survive

abortive ADJECTIVE unsuccessful ● *an abortive attempt*

abound VERB abounds, abounding, abounded **1** be plentiful or abundant ● *Fish abound in the river.* **2** have something in great quantities ● *The river abounds in fish.*

about PREPOSITION **1** near in amount or size or time, etc. ● *It costs about $5.* ● *Come about two o'clock.* **2** on the subject of; in connection with ● *Tell me about your holiday.* **3** all around; in various parts of ● *They ran about the playground.*

about ADVERB **1** in various directions ● *They were running about.* **2** not far away ● *He is somewhere about.*
be about to be going to do something

above PREPOSITION **1** higher than **2** more than

above ADVERB at or to a higher place

abrasive ADJECTIVE **1** that scrapes things away ● *an abrasive wheel.* **2** harsh ● *an abrasive manner.*

abreast ADVERB **1** side by side **2** keeping up with something

abridge VERB abridges, abridging, abridged shorten a book, etc., by using fewer words ● *an abridged edition.*
▷ **abridgement** NOUN

abroad ADVERB in or to another country

abrupt ADJECTIVE **1** sudden or hasty ● *his abrupt departure* **2** rather rude and unfriendly; curt ● *She has quite an abrupt manner.*
▷ **abruptly** ADVERB **abruptness** NOUN

abscess (ab- ses) NOUN abscesses an inflamed place where pus has formed in the body

abscond VERB absconds, absconding, absconded go away secretly ● *The cashier had absconded with the money.*

absent ADJECTIVE not here; not present ● *absent from school*
▷ **absence** NOUN

absent (ab- sent) VERB absents, absenting, absented
absent yourself stay away

absentee NOUN absentees a person who is absent
▷ **absenteeism** NOUN

Thesaurus

abnormal ADJECTIVE **1** *The tests produced some abnormal results.* ► unusual, untypical, uncommon, extraordinary, exceptional, unrepresentative, aberrant, anomalous, freak **2** *He was surprised by her abnormal beliefs and behavior.* ► strange, peculiar, odd, weird, curious, eccentric, wayward, perverse, erratic, queer, bizarre AN OPPOSITE IS normal

abnormality NOUN **1** *The study gave evidence of some abnormality.* ► strangeness, peculiarity, irregularity, oddity, oddness, aberration, anomaly, deviation, eccentricity, idiosyncrasy, waywardness, singularity **2** *The baby was born with several abnormalities.* ► deformity, malformation

abolish VERB *a decision to abolish the community charge* ► end, cancel, put an end to, (*more informal*) get rid of, (*more informal*) do away with, (*technical*) abrogate, annul, repeal, remove, rescind, revoke, quash, suppress, terminate, eliminate, eradicate, overturn, withdraw AN OPPOSITE IS create

abominable ADJECTIVE *The revolt was suppressed with abominable cruelty.* ► atrocious, appalling, detestable, hateful, odious, vile, obnoxious, brutal, dreadful, abhorrent, diabolical, disgusting, repellent, horrifying AN OPPOSITE IS humane

abrupt ADJECTIVE **1** *She gave a cry and came to an abrupt halt.* ► sudden, hurried, unexpected, quick, hasty, rapid, swift, precipitate, unforeseen, unpredicted **2** *Beyond the cliff edge they could see an abrupt drop.* ► sheer, sharp, steep, precipitous AN OPPOSITE IS gradual **3** *He had a decidedly abrupt manner.* ► blunt, harsh, curt, terse, gruff, rude, offhand, brusque, insensitive, outspoken, plain-spoken OPPOSITES ARE polite, courteous

absent ADJECTIVE **1** *The man had been absent from work all week.* ► away, off, missing, (*more informal*) skiving AN OPPOSITE IS present **2** *Her eyes had an absent look.* ► distracted, dreamy, far-away, absorbed, inattentive, preoccupied, absent-minded OPPOSITES ARE attentive, alert

absent-minded ADJECTIVE having your mind on other things; forgetful

absolute ADJECTIVE complete; not restricted
• *absolute power*
▷ **absolutely** ADVERB

absolute zero NOUN the lowest possible temperature, calculated as -27.315°C

absolve VERB absolves, absolving, absolved
1 clear a person of blame or guilt **2** release a person from a promise or obligation

absorb VERB absorbs, absorbing, absorbed
1 soak up a liquid or gas **2** receive something and reduce its effects • *The buffers absorbed most of the shock.* **3** take up a person's attention or time
▷ **absorption** NOUN

absorbent ADJECTIVE able to soak up liquids easily • *absorbent paper*

abstain VERB abstains, abstaining, abstained
1 keep yourself from doing something; refrain

2 choose not to use your vote
▷ **abstention** NOUN

abstinence NOUN abstaining, especially from alcohol
▷ **abstinent** ADJECTIVE

abstract (ab- strakt) ADJECTIVE **1** concerned with ideas, not solid objects • *Truth, hope, and danger are all abstract.* **2** (said about a painting or sculpture) showing the artist's ideas or feelings, not showing a recognizable person or thing

absurd ADJECTIVE ridiculous or foolish
▷ **absurdly** ADVERB **absurdity** NOUN

abundance NOUN a large amount, plenty

abundant ADJECTIVE plentiful
▷ **abundantly** ADVERB

abuse (ab- yooz) VERB abuses, abusing, abused
1 use something badly or wrongly; misuse
2 hurt someone or treat them cruelly **3** say unpleasant things about a person or thing

Thesaurus

absent-minded ADJECTIVE *Stephen looked absent-minded as he hurried off.* ► forgetful, distracted, preoccupied, inattentive, absorbed, scatterbrained OPPOSITES ARE attentive, alert

absolute ADJECTIVE **1** *The house was an absolute mess.* ► complete, total, utter, sheer, perfect, downright, unmitigated **2** *The venture had been an absolute success.* ► complete, total, outright, categorical, out-and-out, unqualified **3** *Speak only the absolute truth.* ► definite, positive, categorical, undoubted, unquestioned **4** *The country had known only absolute rulers.*
► autocratic, despotic, dictatorial, tyrannical, omnipotent, sovereign, totalitarian, unrestricted, undemocratic

absolutely ADVERB *You are absolutely right.*
► completely, totally, utterly, perfectly, quite, unquestionably, unreservedly

absorb VERB **1** *Wood absorbs wetness and expands.* ► soak up, suck up, assimilate, take in AN OPPOSITE IS emit **2** *It is difficult to absorb so much information at once.* ► assimilate, take in, soak up, digest, comprehend **3** *Getting through the day absorbed all her energies.*
► consume, drain, exhaust, use up, take up, swallow up **4** *Special buffers absorb the impact.*
► cushion, deaden, soften, reduce, lessen
5 *The children were absorbed by their game.*
► preoccupy, engross, captivate, occupy, enthral, fascinate, interest, involve, rivet

abstain VERB abstain from *They agreed to abstain from violent action for the time being.*
► go without, give up, forgo, refrain from, eschew, avoid, reject, renounce, deny yourself, desist from AN OPPOSITE IS indulge (yourself)

abstemious ADJECTIVE *They lead an abstemious life.* ► frugal, temperate, austere, ascetic,

restrained, sparing, puritanical, strict, spartan, sober AN OPPOSITE IS self-indulgent

abstract ADJECTIVE **1** *Abstract concepts are hard to define.* ► theoretical, conceptual, hypothetical, academic, notional, metaphysical, philosophical, intangible, intellectual, indefinite AN OPPOSITE IS concrete **2** *The pieces are stitched together to form a large abstract design.* ► symbolic, nonpictorial, nonrepresentational AN OPPOSITE IS representational

abstruse ADJECTIVE *He had spent a lifetime poring over abstruse codes.* ► obscure, cryptic, complex, difficult, hard, puzzling, incomprehensible, perplexing, mysterious, unfathomable AN OPPOSITE IS obvious

absurd ADJECTIVE *It was an absurd suggestion.*
► ridiculous, preposterous, ludicrous, unreasonable, nonsensical, incredible, irrational, senseless, insane, mad, anomalous, silly, stupid, illogical, incongruous, meaningless, paradoxical, untenable, laughable, (more informal) crazy, (more informal) zany OPPOSITES ARE reasonable, sensible

abundant ADJECTIVE *Luckily, there was an abundant supply of things to do.* ► plentiful, copious, ample, liberal, profuse, generous, lavish, rich, bountiful, prolific, inexhaustible OPPOSITES ARE scarce, sparse

abuse VERB **1** *Players on both sides were abusing the referee.* ► insult, be rude to, curse, swear at, call someone names, malign, revile, defame, slander **2** *He was accused of abusing children.*
► mistreat, maltreat, ill-treat, (sexually) assault, molest, interfere with, batter, harm,

A

abuse (ab-*yooss*) NOUN **abuses** **1** a misuse • *the abuse of power.* **2** ill-treatment **3** physical harm or cruelty done to someone

abusive ADJECTIVE rude and insulting • *abusive remarks*

abysmal (ab-*iz*-mal) ADJECTIVE extremely bad • *abysmal ignorance*

abyss (ab-*iss*) NOUN **abysses** an extremely deep pit [from Greek *abyssos* = bottomless]

AC ABBREVIATION alternating current

academic ADJECTIVE **1** related to education or studying, especially at a school or college or university **2** theoretical; having no practical use • *an academic point*

academic NOUN **academics** a university or college teacher

academy NOUN **academies** **1** a school or college, especially one for specialized training **2** a society of scholars or artists • *The Royal Academy.* [from Greek *Akademeia*, the name of the garden where the Greek philosopher Plato taught his pupils. The garden was

named after *Akademos*, one of the ancient heroes of Athens.]

accelerate VERB **accelerates, accelerating, accelerated** make or become quicker; increase speed

acceleration NOUN **accelerations** **1** the rate at which the speed of something increases **2** the rate of change of velocity

accelerator NOUN **accelerators** **1** the pedal that a driver presses to make a motor vehicle go faster **2** a thing used to increase the speed of something

accent (ak-*sent*) NOUN **accents** **1** the way a person pronounces the words of a language • *She has a French accent.* **2** the main emphasis or stress in a word • *In 'strawberry', the accent is on 'straw-'.* **3** a mark placed over a letter to show how it is pronounced, e.g., in *fête*

accept VERB **accepts, accepting, accepted** **1** take a thing that is offered or presented **2** say yes to an invitation, offer, etc. ▷ **acceptance** NOUN
USAGE Do not confuse with **except**.

Thesaurus

hurt **3** *The judge had abused his authority in his directions to the jury.* ► misuse, misapply, exploit

abuse NOUN **1** *The action amounted to a serious abuse of authority.* ► misuse, misapplication **2** *No society can tolerate the abuse of children.* ► maltreatment, mistreatment, ill-treatment, misuse, (sexual) assault, molestation **3** *A group of mothers yelled abuse.* ► insults, invective, obscenities, curses, slanders

abusive ADJECTIVE *He was thrown out of the hall for yelling abusive remarks.* ► insulting, derogatory, rude, offensive, opprobrious, pejorative, defamatory, disparaging, scathing, hurtful, impolite, libellous, obscene, scurrilous, slanderous, vituperative OPPOSITES ARE friendly, polite

abysmal ADJECTIVE **1** *The service was abysmal.* ► poor, very bad, awful, appalling, dreadful, disgraceful, terrible, worthless **2** *the abysmal ignorance of science among students* ► profound, extreme, utter, complete, deep, unfathomable, immeasurable, incalculable, infinite

abyss NOUN *There is still a deep abyss to be crossed.* ► chasm, pit, void, gulf, crater, fissure, gap, hole, opening, rift

academic ADJECTIVE **1** *She had spent her entire life in an academic environment.* ► educational, scholastic, scholarly, pedagogical **2** *They are academic historians and not writers for the popular market.* ► scholarly, studious, learned, intellectual, erudite, educated, cultured, bookish, clever, highbrow, intelligent, well-

read, (more informal) brainy **3** *The point is of more than academic interest.* ► theoretical, notional, conceptual, conjectural, hypothetical, speculative AN OPPOSITE IS practical

academic NOUN *a group of visiting academics* ► scholar, intellectual, professor, lecturer, thinker, (more informal) egghead, (more informal) highbrow

academy NOUN *The students of the academy were involved in a project to catalog the papers.* ► college, educational institution, training establishment, conservatory, conservatoire, university, institute

accede VERB **accede to** *He acceded to all her demands.* ► agree to, consent to, accept, grant, comply with, concur with

accelerate VERB **1** *The vehicle accelerated sharply.* ► go faster, speed up, pick up speed, quicken speed OPPOSITES ARE decelerate, slow down **2** *The oil-producing countries have agreed to accelerate production.* ► increase, step up, stimulate, expedite, promote, spur on

accent NOUN **1** *She spoke with a distinct Southern accent.* ► pronunciation, intonation, inflection, tone, cadence, enunciation **2** *There is an accent on the first syllable.* ► stress, emphasis, accentuation, force **3** *The accent is on economy.* ► emphasis, stress

accept VERB **1** *I decided to accept the offer.* ► receive, take, welcome, (more informal) jump at **2** *The council does not accept responsibility.* ► admit, acknowledge, bear, assume, undertake **3** *Reluctantly, he had to accept the decision.* ► agree to, go along with,

acceptable ADJECTIVE good enough to accept; pleasing
▷ **acceptably** ADVERB **acceptability** NOUN

access (ak- sess) NOUN **1** a way to enter or reach something **2** the right to use or look at something

access VERB **accesses, accessing, accessed** find information that has been stored in a computer

accessible ADJECTIVE **1** able to be reached **2** able to be understood easily
▷ **accessibly** ADVERB **accessibility** NOUN

accessory (ak- sess- er- ee) NOUN **accessories 1** an extra thing that goes with something **2** a person who helps another with a crime

accident NOUN **accidents** an unexpected happening, especially one causing injury or damage
▷ **accidental** ADJECTIVE **accidentally** ADVERB

by accident by chance; without its being arranged in advance

acclaim VERB **acclaims, acclaiming, acclaimed** welcome or applaud
▷ **acclaim** NOUN **acclamation** NOUN

accommodate VERB **accommodates, accommodating, accommodated 1** provide somebody with a place to live, work, or sleep overnight **2** help by providing something
• We can accommodate you with skis.

accommodation NOUN somewhere to live, work, or sleep overnight

accompanist NOUN **accompanists** a pianist, etc., who accompanies a singer or another musician

accompany VERB **accompanies, accompanying, accompanied 1** go somewhere with somebody **2** be present with something • Thunder accompanied the storm.

Thesaurus

accede to, acquiesce in, defer to, comply with, consent to, concur with, abide by, acknowledge, be reconciled to, recognize, resign yourself to, submit to, yield to AN OPPOSITE IS reject

acceptable ADJECTIVE **1** The agreement was acceptable to the majority. ► welcome, agreeable, appreciated, gratifying, pleasant, pleasing, worthwhile **2** The courses fell below an acceptable standard. ► adequate, satisfactory, reasonable, tolerable, admissible, appropriate, passable, suitable AN OPPOSITE IS unacceptable

acceptance NOUN **1** The plan found wide acceptance. ► approval, consent, acquiescence, agreement, welcome AN OPPOSITE IS refusal **2** Their acceptance of the explanation came as some relief. ► belief (in), confidence (in)

access NOUN **1** The fans could not gain access to that end of the stadium. ► entry, admission, admittance, right of entry **2** The building has no access at the front. ► entrance, entry, way in, approach

accessible ADJECTIVE **1** The library has been made accessible for wheelchairs. ► reachable, within reach, at hand, available, convenient, (more informal) handy AN OPPOSITE IS inaccessible **2** Officials want to be more accessible. ► approachable, available, informal, welcoming

accessory NOUN **1** Accessories include a remote control. ► attachment, fitting, extra, addition, appendage, extension **2** He might be charged with being an accessory to the crime.
► accomplice, associate, collaborator (in)

accident NOUN **1** He died in an accident while working on his boat. ► misfortune, mishap, disaster, calamity, catastrophe, misadventure **2** She had witnessed a traffic accident. ► collision,

smash, (more informal) pile-up **3** It was pure accident that we met that day. ► chance, luck, coincidence, fate, a fluke
by accident I found it by accident. ► by chance, accidentally, fortuitously, unwittingly, coincidentally

accidental ADJECTIVE Make sure you avoid accidental erasure of the tape. ► unintentional, chance, coincidental, fortuitous, inadvertent, unintended, adventitious, arbitrary, casual, lucky, random AN OPPOSITE IS intentional

accidentally ADVERB We met accidentally. ► by accident, by chance, fortuitously, unintentionally, unwittingly AN OPPOSITE IS intentionally

acclaim VERB The film has been widely acclaimed in the press. ► praise, applaud, commend, cheer, congratulate, celebrate

acclimatize VERB They soon became acclimatized to their new surroundings. ► accustom, adjust, familiarize

accolade NOUN He received the accolade of a knighthood. ► praise, honor, tribute, recognition, admiration, acclamation, plaudits

accommodate VERB **1** We will do our best to accommodate your wishes. ► serve, help, aid, assist, supply, oblige, provide **2** The lodge accommodates nine residents. ► house, lodge, provide for, cater for, shelter, board, take in, hold, (more informal) put up

accommodating ADJECTIVE The local tourist office is very accommodating. ► helpful, obliging, cooperative, considerate

accommodation NOUN The cost includes three days' accommodation in Bruges. ► board, lodging, shelter, housing, rooms

accompany VERB **1** She regularly accompanied groups of her students. ► go with, escort, travel with, attend, follow, chaperone, look after,

a
b
c
d
e
f
g
h
i
j
k
l
m
n
o
p
q
r
s
t
u
v
w
x
y
z

A
B
C
D
E
F
G
H
I
J
K
L
M

3 play music, especially on a piano, that supports a singer or another player, etc.
▷ **accompaniment** NOUN

accomplice (a- käm- pliss) NOUN accomplices a person who helps another in a crime, etc.

accomplish VERB accomplishes, accomplishing, accomplished do something successfully
▷ **accomplishment** NOUN

accomplished ADJECTIVE skilled

accord NOUN agreement; consent
of your own accord without being asked or compelled

according ADVERB
according to 1 as stated by • *According to him, we are stupid.* **2** in relation to • *Price the apples according to their size.*

accordingly ADVERB **1** in the way that is required • *I've given you your instructions and I expect you to act accordingly.* **2** therefore

accordion NOUN accordions a portable musical instrument like a large concertina with a set of piano-type keys at one end, played by squeezing it in and out and pressing the keys

account NOUN accounts **1** a statement of money owed, spent, or received; a bill **2** an arrangement to keep money in a bank, etc.
3 a description or report
on account of because of **on no account** under no circumstances; certainly not take **something into account** consider or include it when making a decision or calculation

account VERB accounts, accounting, accounted
account for make it clear why something happens
[from early French *conter* = to count]

accountable ADJECTIVE responsible; having to explain why you have done something
▷ **accountability** NOUN

accountant NOUN accountants a person whose job is keeping or inspecting financial accounts
▷ **accountancy** NOUN

accumulate VERB accumulates, accumulating, accumulated pile up or increase
▷ **accumulation** NOUN

accurate ADJECTIVE correct or exact
▷ **accurately** ADVERB **accuracy** NOUN

Thesaurus

N
O
P
Q
R
S
T
U
V
W
X
Y
Z

partner, (*more informal*) tag along with **2** *A note accompanied the flowers.* ► go with, occur with, coincide with, be present with, coexist with, complement, belong with, supplement

accomplice NOUN *An accomplice stood at the door on lookout.* ► associate, partner, accessory, abetter, confederate, collaborator, co-conspirator

accomplish VERB *Brady believes his side can accomplish the awesome task.* ► achieve, fulfill, succeed in, realize, complete, conclude, bring off, carry out, discharge, attain, effect, execute, finish, perform

accomplished ADJECTIVE *Diana is an accomplished pianist.* ► expert, talented, able, skilled, gifted, capable, clever, competent, proficient

accomplishment NOUN *This was quite an accomplishment and she was duly rewarded.* ► achievement, attainment, ability, talent, skill, gift

account NOUN **1** *Write down a full account of what you saw.* ► description, report, statement, report, record, explanation, narrative, version, commentary, (*more informal*) write-up **2** *An account for the work has come in the mail.* ► invoice, statement, bill **3** *The damage done to the vehicles is of little account.* ► importance, significance, consequence, concern, moment, interest, worth, value, use
on account of *They stayed indoors on account of the bad weather.* ► because of, in view of,

owing to, due to, as a result of, as a consequence of, considering

account VERB *account for It is difficult to account for such a sudden change in their attitude.* ► explain, justify, clarify, elucidate, answer for, give reasons for, excuse, make excuses for, rationalize, vindicate

accountable ADJECTIVE *The senator is accountable to her constituents.* ► responsible, answerable, subject, liable

accrue VERB *Honor is supposed to accrue from being unpaid.* ► result, follow, ensue, arise, stem, spring, emanate, be produced

accumulate VERB **1** *He accumulated information from different sources.* ► gather, collect, amass, assemble, bring together, heap up, mass, pile up, hoard, store up, (*more informal*) stash away AN OPPOSITE IS disperse **2** *Leaves tend to accumulate in the gutters.* ► build up, increase, multiply, grow, accrue AN OPPOSITE IS decrease

accumulation NOUN *The book is an accumulation of work by many scholars.* ► collection, build-up, mass, store, supply, heap, pile, hoard, stock, conglomeration

accuracy NOUN *Can we trust the accuracy of these figures?* ► precision, correctness, exactness, validity, reliability

accurate ADJECTIVE **1** *It was an accurate account of what had happened.* ► faithful, factual, authentic, true, truthful, close, exact, precise, reliable **2** *She took accurate notes during the meeting.* ► exact, precise, correct, careful,

accuse VERB accuses, accusing, accused say that a person has committed a crime, etc.; blame
▷ **accusation** NOUN **accuser** NOUN

ace NOUN aces **1** a playing card with one spot **2** a very skillful person or thing **3** (in tennis) a serve that is too good for the other player to reach

ache NOUN aches a dull continuous pain

ache VERB aches, aching, ached have an ache

achieve VERB achieves, achieving, achieved succeed in doing or producing something
▷ **achievable** ADJECTIVE **achievement** NOUN

acid NOUN acids a chemical substance that contains hydrogen and neutralizes alkalis. The hydrogen can be replaced by a metal to form a salt
▷ **acidic** ADJECTIVE **acidity** NOUN

acid ADJECTIVE **1** sharp-tasting; sour **2** looking or sounding bitter • an acid reply
▷ **acidly** ADVERB

acid rain NOUN rain made acidic by mixing with waste gases from factories, etc.

acknowledge VERB acknowledges, acknowledging, acknowledged **1** admit that

something is true **2** state that you have received or noticed something • The college wrote back to acknowledge my letter. **3** express thanks or appreciation for something
▷ **acknowledgement** NOUN

acne (ak- nee) NOUN inflamed red pimples on the face and neck

acorn NOUN acorns the seed of the oak tree

acoustic (a- koo- stik) ADJECTIVE **1** to do with sound or hearing **2** (said about a musical instrument) not electronic • an acoustic guitar.
▷ **acoustically** ADVERB
[from Greek akouein = hear]

acoustics (a- koo- stiks) PLURAL NOUN **1** the qualities of a hall, etc., that make it good or bad for carrying sound **2** the properties of sound

acquaint VERB acquaints, acquainting, acquainted tell somebody about something • Acquaint him with the facts.
be acquainted with know slightly

acquaintance NOUN acquaintances **1** a person you know slightly **2** familiarity with someone or something

---

Thesaurus

---

faultless, errorless, error-free, meticulous, minute, perfect, scrupulous **3** His aim was steady and accurate. ► certain, unerring, sure AN OPPOSITE IS inaccurate

accusation NOUN There had been several accusations of cheating. ► allegation, charge, complaint, indictment, alleged offense

accuse VERB **1** accuse of The men were accused of disorderly behavior. ► charge with, blame for, put on trial for, take to court for, indict for **2** accuse of The banks are accused of creating confusion among customers. ► blame for, hold responsible for, criticize for, condemn for, denounce for AN OPPOSITE IS defend

accustomed ADJECTIVE Wars remove entire populations from their accustomed ways of life. ► normal, customary, familiar, habitual, established, usual, common, conventional, traditional, ordinary, regular, routine, set **become** OR **get accustomed to** The family soon became accustomed to life in the country. ► get used to, adapt to, adjust to, acclimatize to, become conditioned to, become inured to, familiarize yourself with, (more informal) feel at home in

ache NOUN A nagging stomachache spoiled the evening. ► pain, pang, soreness, hurt, discomfort, twinge

ache VERB His tooth was beginning to ache. ► hurt, smart, be painful, be sore, throb, sting

achieve VERB **1** Students who achieve their goals will be promised jobs. ► succeed in, accomplish,

fulfill, complete, carry out, attain, manage, bring about **2** They worked hard to achieve success. ► acquire, win, gain, earn, get, obtain, procure, reach, score

achievement NOUN **1** They are proud of their achievement. ► accomplishment, attainment, success, deed, exploit **2** We hoped for the achievement of all our aims. ► attainment, realization, accomplishment, fulfillment, reaching, gaining, winning, conclusion

acknowledge VERB **1** They acknowledged their obligation to their predecessors. ► admit, concede, accept, grant, recognize, allow AN OPPOSITE IS deny **2** No one has acknowledged my letter. ► answer, reply to, respond to, react to, notice **3** She acknowledged him with a nod. ► greet, salute, hail, recognize, respond to, (more informal) say hello to

acknowledgement NOUN **1** There was an acknowledgement of a need for action. ► admission, acceptance, agreement, realization, concession **2** Tom gave a smile of acknowledgement. ► greeting, recognition, welcome, (more formal) salutation

acquaint VERB be acquainted with Lorna is acquainted with several European languages. ► be familiar with, be conversant with, be versed in, be informed about AN OPPOSITE IS be ignorant of

acquaintance NOUN Philip was just a business acquaintance. ► associate, colleague, contact

A

acquire VERB acquires, acquiring, acquired obtain

acquisition NOUN something you have obtained

acquit VERB acquits, acquitting, acquitted decide that somebody is not guilty • *The jury acquitted her.*
▷ **acquittal** NOUN
acquit yourself well perform or do something well

acre (ay- ker) NOUN acres an area of land measuring 4,840 square yards or .405 hectares
▷ **acreage** NOUN
[from Old English *aecer* = field]

acrobat NOUN a person who performs spectacular gymnastic stunts for entertainment
▷ **acrobatic** ADJECTIVE **acrobatics** PLURAL NOUN

acronym (ak- ron- im) NOUN acronyms a word or name that is formed from the initial letters of other words and pronounced as a word in its own right • *Nato is an acronym of North Atlantic Treaty Organization.*

across PREPOSITION, ADVERB **1** from one side to the other • *Swim across the river.* • *Are you across yet?* **2** on the opposite side • *the house across the street*

acrylic (a- kril- ik) NOUN a kind of fiber, plastic, or resin made from an organic acid

act NOUN acts **1** something someone does **2** a pretense • *She is only putting on an act.* **3** one of the main divisions of a play or opera **4** each short performance in a program of entertainment • *a juggling act.* **5** a law passed by a legislature

act VERB acts, acting, acted **1** do something; perform actions **2** perform a part in a play or film etc. **3** function; have an effect

action NOUN actions **1** doing something **2** something done **3** a battle; fighting • *He was killed in action.* **4** a lawsuit
out of action not working or functioning
take action do something

activate VERB activates, activating, activated start something working
▷ **activation** NOUN **activator** NOUN

active ADJECTIVE **1** taking part in many activities; energetic **2** functioning or working; in operation • *an active volcano* **3** radioactive **4** (said about a form of a verb) used when the subject of the verb is performing the action. In "The shop *sells* videos" the verb is active; in "Videos *are sold* by the shop" the verb is passive.
▷ **actively** ADVERB **activeness** NOUN

Thesaurus

---

acquire VERB *His father had acquired some shares in a freight company.* ▸ obtain, get, receive, come by, gain, appropriate

acquit VERB *The jury acquitted all three of the accused.* ▸ absolve, clear, exonerate, find innocent, find not guilty, free, discharge, excuse, (*more informal*) let off

acrimonious ADJECTIVE *The meetings were acrimonious and badly managed.* ▸ bitter, hostile, abusive, peevish, acerbic, caustic, angry, petulant, bad-tempered, ill-tempered, ill-natured, venomous, biting, sharp AN OPPOSITE IS peaceable

acrobat NOUN *An acrobat performed a back somersault.* ▸ gymnast, tumbler, contortionist

act NOUN **1** *It needed an act of great courage.* ▸ deed, feat, action, exploit, undertaking, effort, enterprise, operation, proceeding **2** *The next act will be a juggler.* ▸ item, turn, performance, routine, sketch
put on an act ▸ pretend, dissemble, play a part

act VERB **1** *Jim was beginning to act strangely.* ▸ behave, conduct yourself **2** *The large table also acted as a work area. The medicine will soon begin to act.* ▸ function, operate, serve, work, take effect, have an effect **3** *He has always wanted to act the role of a villain.* ▸ play, portray, appear (as), perform, represent, assume the character of, characterize, enact,

impersonate **4** *It was obvious that they were only acting.* ▸ pretend, sham, fake, pose, (*more informal*) kid

action NOUN **1** *It was a decisive action and very effective.* ▸ act, deed, step, feat, exploit, endeavor, enterprise, proceeding, effort, measure, performance, process, undertaking **2** *Write a story with plenty of action.* ▸ activity, drama, excitement, vitality, movement, energy, liveliness, vigor **3** *The action of the play is set in medieval France.* ▸ story, plot, events, happenings, incidents **4** *The clock has a mechanical action.* ▸ working, works, mechanism, functioning, operation **5** *McLeish led his troops into action.* ▸ battle, engagement

activate VERB *The smaller button activates the reboot function.* ▸ operate, start, initiate, mobilize, actuate, trigger off, set in motion

active ADJECTIVE **1** *They were having an active time.* ▸ busy, lively, eventful, energetic, vivacious OPPOSITES ARE inactive, uneventful **2** *She is very active for her age.* ▸ energetic, agile, sprightly, lively, spry, frisky, (*more informal*) on the go OPPOSITES ARE inactive, lethargic **3** *Yvonne is an active member of the society.* ▸ diligent, hard-working, dedicated, enthusiastic, assiduous, industrious, committed, devoted, staunch, zealous OPPOSITES ARE inactive, unenthusiastic **4** *Part of the old factory was still active.* ▸ functional, functioning,

activist NOUN activists a person who is active and energetic, especially in politics

activity NOUN activities **1** an action or occupation • *outdoor activities* **2** being active or lively

actor NOUN actors a person who acts a part in a play or film, etc.

actress NOUN actresses a woman who acts a part in a play or film, etc.

actual ADJECTIVE real
▷ **actually** ADVERB **actuality** NOUN

acupuncture (ak- yoo- punk- cher) NOUN the insertion of needles into parts of the body to relieve pain or cure disease
▷ **acupuncturist** NOUN

acute ADJECTIVE **1** sharp or strong • *acute pain* **2** having a sharp mind
▷ **acutely** ADVERB **acuteness** NOUN
[from Latin *acus* = needle]

acute accent NOUN acute accents a mark over a vowel, as over *é* in *fiancé*

acute angle NOUN acute angles an angle of less than 90°

AD ABBREVIATION Anno Domini (Latin = in the year of Our Lord), used in dates counted from the birth of Jesus Christ

adamant (ad- am- ant) ADJECTIVE firm and not giving way to requests

adapt VERB adapts, adapting, adapted **1** change something so that it is suitable for a new purpose **2** to become used to a new situation
▷ **adaptable** ADJECTIVE **adaptation** NOUN

adaptor NOUN adaptors a device to connect pieces of electrical or other equipment

add VERB adds, adding, added **1** put one thing with another **2** make another remark
add up 1 make or find a total **2** (*informal*) make sense; seem reasonable

adder NOUN adders a small poisonous snake [from Old English; originally called *a nadder*, which became *an adder*. The same change happened to other Old English words, e.g. *apron*]

addict NOUN addicts a person who does or uses something that he or she cannot give up
▷ **addicted** ADJECTIVE **addiction** NOUN

addictive ADJECTIVE causing a habit that people cannot give up • *an addictive drug.*

Thesaurus

operative, working, in operation OPPOSITES ARE inactive, defunct

activity NOUN **1** *At weekends the house is always a scene of great activity.* ► liveliness, action, commotion, bustle, life, hustle, animation, movement, excitement **2** *Marketing is an activity in which all staff can be involved.* ► job, task, venture, enterprise, undertaking, project, scheme **3** *She enjoyed many leisure activities.* ► interest, pursuit, hobby, pastime, occupation

actor NOUN *He was the actor who played James Bond.* ► player, performer, stage performer, artist, (*female*) actress, (*female*) artiste

actual ADJECTIVE *Have you seen the actual damage done?* ► real, true, physical, genuine, definite, certain, concrete OPPOSITES ARE imaginary, supposed, notional, nonexistent

acute ADJECTIVE **1** *The pain was acute.* ► sharp, severe, stabbing, burning, intense, piercing, fierce AN OPPOSITE IS mild **2** *There is an acute shortage of teachers.* ► severe, drastic, extreme, serious, dire, grave AN OPPOSITE IS continual **3** *He was suffering from an acute illness.* ► critical, sudden **4** *Jenna has an acute mind.* ► sharp, keen, astute, shrewd, penetrating, perceptive, quick, discerning OPPOSITES ARE dull, stupid

adapt VERB **1** **adapt to** *The children have adapted well to their new surroundings.* ► adjust to, acclimatize yourself to, get used to, reconcile

yourself to **2** *The vans are all adapted to carry dangerous substances.* ► modify, alter, convert, change, rearrange, reorganize, reconstruct, customize, tailor, prepare, transform **3** *The story has been adapted for television.* ► edit, modify, prepare, alter

adaptable ADJECTIVE **1** *The tool is adaptable to many tasks.* ► adjustable, versatile, convertible **2** *Michael is always willing and very adaptable.* ► flexible, versatile, resilient, amenable

add VERB **1** *Add all the numbers in the first column.* ► add up, count, count up, calculate, total, find the sum of OPPOSITES ARE deduct, subtract **2** *A conservatory was added in the 1930s.* ► build on, attach, add on, integrate, join, (*more informal*) tack on OPPOSITES ARE remove, demolish **3** **add to** *Our shouts only added to the confusion.* ► increase, intensify, amplify, augment, enlarge, supplement
add up 1 *It was time to add up the scores.* ► count, count up, calculate, total, find the sum of **2** (*more informal*) *The story didn't add up.* ► make sense, be convincing, be reasonable, (*more informal*) hold water, (*more informal*) ring true **add up to** *The costs added up to many thousands.* ► total, amount to, come to, make

addiction NOUN *An addiction to cookies was putting cellulite on her thighs.* ► dependence, compulsion, craving, fixation, habit, obsession

a
b
c
d
e
f
g
h
i
j
k
l
m
n
o
p
q
r
s
t
u
v
w
x
y
z

A

addition NOUN additions **1** the process of adding **2** something added
▷ **additional** ADJECTIVE **additionally** ADVERB in addition also; as an extra thing

additive NOUN additives a substance added to another in small amounts for a special purpose, e.g., as a flavoring

address NOUN addresses **1** the details of the place where someone lives or of where letters, etc., should be delivered to a person or firm **2** (in computing) the part of an instruction that shows where a piece of information is stored in a computer's memory **3** a speech to an audience

address VERB addresses, addressing, addressed **1** write an address on a letter, etc. **2** make a speech or remark, etc., to somebody

adenoids PLURAL NOUN thick spongy flesh at the back of the nose and throat, which may hinder breathing

adept (a- dept) ADJECTIVE very skillful

adequate ADJECTIVE enough or good enough
▷ **adequately** ADVERB **adequacy** NOUN

adhere VERB adheres, adhering, adhered stick to something
▷ **adhesion** NOUN

adhesive ADJECTIVE sticky; causing things to stick together

adhesive NOUN adhesives a substance used to stick things together; glue

adjacent ADJECTIVE near or next to ● *I waited in an adjacent room.*

adjective NOUN adjectives a word that describes a noun or adds to its meaning, e.g., *big, honest, strange, our*
▷ **adjectival** ADJECTIVE **adjectivally** ADVERB

adjourn (a- jern) VERB adjourns, adjourning, adjourned **1** break off a meeting etc. until a later time **2** break off and go somewhere else ● *They adjourned to the library.*
▷ **adjournment** NOUN

adjudicate (a- joo- dik- ayt) VERB adjudicates, adjudicating, adjudicated act as judge in a competition, etc.
▷ **adjudication** NOUN **adjudicator** NOUN

adjust VERB adjusts, adjusting, adjusted **1** put a thing into its proper position or order **2** alter something so that it fits or is suitable
▷ **adjustable** ADJECTIVE **adjustment** NOUN

ad-lib VERB ad-libs, ad-libbing, ad-libbed say or do something without any rehearsal or preparation

Thesaurus

addition NOUN **1** *I'm not very good at addition.* ► adding, adding up, counting, calculating, totaling **2** *The porch is a nineteenth-century addition.* ► supplement, appendage, extension, attachment, afterthought, (*more informal*) add-on

additional ADJECTIVE *The railways need additional resources.* ► extra, added, further, supplementary, increased, more, new, other, spare

address NOUN **1** *They live at a fashionable address in town.* ► residence, location, locality, home, abode **2** *The president gave a short address to the press.* ► speech, talk, discourse, lecture, monologue, (*more formal*) oration, (*more formal*) disquisition

address VERB *A man came up and addressed me.* ► greet, hail, salute, speak to, talk to, accost, approach, engage in conversation, (*more informal*) buttonhole

adequate ADJECTIVE **1** *The work must be of an adequate standard.* ► satisfactory, acceptable, sufficient, suitable, tolerable, competent, fair, good enough, passable, presentable, respectable AN OPPOSITE IS inadequate **2** *The hospital lacks adequate resources.* ► sufficient, enough, suitable, appropriate

adhere VERB **1** *A piece of lint adhered to his collar.* ► stick, cling, be fixed, be fastened **2 adhere to** *We must adhere to our principles.* ► maintain, observe, follow, respect, stick to, abide by, stand by, comply with

adjacent ADJECTIVE **adjacent to** *the area adjacent to the fire station* ► adjoining, bordering, abutting, neighboring, alongside, touching, next to, close by, next door to, (*more formal*) contiguous with

adjoin VERB *The house adjoins an old warehouse.* ► be next to, abut, border on, connect with, link up with, be next door to, touch, (*more formal*) be contiguous with

adjourn VERB *The meeting was adjourned for a week.* ► suspend, break off, discontinue, defer, dissolve, postpone, interrupt, put off

adjournment NOUN *The reason for the adjournment of the meeting will become clear in time.* ► suspension, postponement, putting off, break (in), pause (in), interruption, discontinuation, deferment

adjust VERB **1** *You need to adjust the picture.* ► modify, alter, regulate, rectify, tune, vary, change, balance, amend, arrange, position, put right **2 adjust to** *The workforce have had to adjust to new procedures.* ► adapt to, acclimatize yourself to, accommodate yourself to, familiarize yourself with, get used to, reconcile yourself to, harmonize yourself with

ad-lib ADJECTIVE *The chairperson made a few ad-lib remarks.* ► impromptu, extempore, improvised, spontaneous, unplanned, unprepared, unrehearsed, made-up, (*more informal*) off the cuff, (*more informal*) off the top of your head

administer VERB administers, administering, administered **1** give or provide something • *He administered medicine.* **2** manage business affairs

admirable ADJECTIVE worth admiring; excellent
▷ **admirably** ADVERB

admiral NOUN admirals a naval officer of high rank [from Arabic *amir* = commander. The full title was *amir-al bahr* = commander of the sea (*bahr* = sea). Early Western writers thought that *amir-al* was one word meaning "commander," whereas it meant "commander of the"]

admire VERB admires, admiring, admired **1** look at something and enjoy it **2** think that someone or something is very good
▷ **admiration** NOUN **admirer** NOUN

admission NOUN admissions **1** admitting **2** the charge for being allowed to go in **3** a statement admitting something; a confession

admit VERB admits, admitting, admitted **1** allow someone or something to come in **2** state reluctantly that something is true;

confess • *We admit that the task is difficult.* • *He admitted his crime.*

admittance NOUN being allowed to go in, especially to a private place

admonish VERB admonishes, admonishing, admonished advise or warn someone firmly
▷ **admonition** NOUN

adolescent NOUN adolescents a young person at the age between being a child and being an adult
▷ **adolescence** NOUN **adolescent** ADJECTIVE

adopt VERB adopts, adopting, adopted **1** take someone into your family as your own child **2** accept something; take something and use it • *They adopted new methods of working.*
▷ **adoption** NOUN

adore VERB adores, adoring, adored love a person or thing very much
▷ **adorable** ADJECTIVE **adoration** NOUN

adorn VERB adorns, adorning, adorned decorate
▷ **adornment** NOUN

adrenalin (a- dren- al- in) NOUN a hormone that stimulates the nervous system, making

Thesaurus

ad-lib VERB *She ad-libbed a large part of her speech.* ► improvise, extemporize, make it up, (more informal) play it by ear

administer VERB **1** *The director administers an organization of two hundred people.* ► regulate, run, manage, direct, preside over, conduct the affairs of, control, supervise, govern, head, lead, look after, command, organize, oversee **2** *A nurse administered medicines throughout the ward.* ► dispense, hand out, deal out, give, provide, supply, apply, distribute, dole out, measure out, mete out (a punishment)

admirable ADJECTIVE *Their aims are admirable but will be difficult to achieve.* ► laudable, praiseworthy, worthy, fine, commendable, creditable, estimable, excellent, pleasing, exemplary, honorable, wonderful, marvelous, enjoyable, likeable AN OPPOSITE IS deplorable

admiration NOUN *Their achievement won much admiration.* ► esteem, acclaim, commendation, high regard, honor, praise, respect, appreciation, approval AN OPPOSITE IS contempt

admire VERB **1** *Jill is much admired for her efficiency.* ► applaud, approve of, respect, praise, revere, esteem, value, look up to, marvel at, think highly of, (more formal) laud AN OPPOSITE IS despise **2** *Come and admire the view.* ► enjoy, appreciate, be delighted by

admirer NOUN *He is a great admirer of Napoleon.* ► fan, devotee, supporter, adherent, enthusiast

admission NOUN **1** *Admission to the gallery is free.* ► entrance, entry, admittance, access

2 *The statement sounded like an admission of guilt.* ► confession, declaration, acknowledgment, profession, revelation, affirmation, avowal, acceptance AN OPPOSITE IS denial

admit VERB **1** *Some of the people were not admitted to the house.* ► let in, allow in, grant access, receive, take in AN OPPOSITE IS exclude **2** *She admitted she had been to the house that morning.* ► acknowledge, concede, confess, reveal, declare, disclose, divulge, agree, grant, accept, allow, own up, profess, recognize AN OPPOSITE IS deny

adolescence NOUN *The problems are the normal ones of adolescence and will pass in time.* ► puberty, teens, youth, boyhood, girlhood, growing-up

adopt VERB **1** *The blue shirt was adopted as the official uniform in the 1930s. He asked them to adopt a more professional approach.* ► take up, choose, support, follow, accept, approve, back, embrace, espouse, endorse, (more informal) go for **2** *She already knew that she had been adopted.* ► foster, take in

adorable ADJECTIVE *What an adorable little cat!* ► lovable, delightful, charming, appealing, enchanting

adore VERB **1** *Neil obviously still adores you.* ► love, be fond of, dote on, idolize, worship, cherish, admire **2** *We all adore shopping.* ► love, like OPPOSITES ARE hate, detest

adorn VERB *The room was adorned with tapestries.* ► decorate, embellish, enhance, beautify, furnish, trim the heart beat faster and increasing energy and the ability to move quickly

adrift ADJECTIVE, ADVERB drifting

adulation NOUN very great flattery

adult (ad- ult) NOUN **adults** a fully grown or mature person

adultery NOUN being unfaithful to one's wife or husband by having sexual intercourse with someone else
> ▷ **adulterer** NOUN **adulterous** ADJECTIVE

advance NOUN **advances 1** a forward movement; progress **2** an increase **3** a loan; payment made before it is due
in advance beforehand; ahead

advance VERB **advances, advancing, advanced 1** move forward; make progress **2** lend or pay money ahead of the proper time • *Can you advance me a month's salary?*
> ▷ **advancement** NOUN

advantage NOUN **advantages 1** something useful or helpful **2** the next point won after deuce in tennis
> ▷ **advantageous** ADJECTIVE
take advantage of use a person or thing profitably or unfairly

to advantage making a good effect • *The painting can be seen to its best advantage here.*
to your advantage profitable or helpful to you

Advent NOUN the period just before Christmas, when Christians celebrate the coming of Christ

advent NOUN the arrival of a new person or thing • *the advent of computers*

adventure NOUN **adventures 1** an exciting or dangerous experience **2** willingness to take risks
> ▷ **adventurer** NOUN **adventurous** ADJECTIVE

adverb NOUN **adverbs** a word that adds to the meaning of a verb or adjective or another adverb and tells how, when, or where something happens, e.g., *gently, soon*, and *upstairs*
> ▷ **adverbial** ADJECTIVE **adverbially** ADVERB

adversary (ad- ver- ser- ee) NOUN **adversaries** an opponent or enemy

adverse ADJECTIVE unfavorable or harmful
• *adverse effects.*
> ▷ **adversely** ADVERB

Thesaurus

adult ADJECTIVE *a medical problem associated with adult males* ► grown-up, of age, fully grown, full-grown, developed, mature AN OPPOSITE IS immature

advance NOUN *There has been a considerable advance in cancer treatments.* ► progress, development, improvement, headway, step, stride

advance VERB **1** *The column of soldiers began to advance.* ► move forward, go forward, proceed, press ahead, press on, progress, approach, come near, gain ground, forge ahead, make headway, make progress, (*more informal*) make strides, (*more informal*) push on AN OPPOSITE IS retreat **2** *Computer technology has advanced in the last few years.* ► develop, evolve, improve, increase, grow, thrive AN OPPOSITE IS regress **3** *Good qualifications will advance your career.* ► benefit, boost, further, promote, foster, assist, expedite, facilitate, accelerate AN OPPOSITE IS hinder **4** *The bank has agreed to advance the money.* ► lend, loan, pay in advance, provide, supply **5** *He advanced some interesting ideas.* ► present, propose, submit, suggest, adduce, cite, furnish, give

advanced ADJECTIVE **1** *Advanced techniques have solved many of these problems.* ► progressive, leading, modern, sophisticated, up-to-date, forward, latest AN OPPOSITE IS obsolete **2** *Their ideas were very advanced for the time.* ► forward-looking, innovative, pioneering, progressive, revolutionary, trend-setting, leading, futuristic, avant-garde, new, novel,

original AN OPPOSITE IS old-fashioned **3** *a course in advanced mathematics* ► higher, complex, complicated, difficult, hard AN OPPOSITE IS elementary **4** *Jamie appears quite advanced for his age.* ► mature, grown-up, sophisticated, well-developed

advantage NOUN *There is an advantage in having a bank account.* ► benefit, asset, help, assistance, aid, blessing, convenience, boon, favor, gain, use, service
take advantage of *His friends all took advantage of him.* ► exploit, make use of, utilize, profit by, manipulate

adventure NOUN **1** *His adventures had already turned him into a local hero.* ► exploit, escapade, venture, enterprise, undertaking, deed, feat **2** *They traveled the world together in search of adventure.* ► excitement, danger, interesting times, fun, stimulation

adventurous ADJECTIVE **1** *an adventurous child* ► daring, enterprising, bold, venturesome, heroic, intrepid, valiant **2** *an adventurous time* ► eventful, exciting, challenging, dangerous, perilous, risky AN OPPOSITE IS unadventurous

adverse ADJECTIVE **1** *The request brought an adverse response.* ► hostile, unfriendly, unfavorable, critical, antagonistic, negative, uncomplimentary, derogatory, disapproving, censorious **2** *The treatment can produce adverse side effects.* ► harmful, unfavorable, disadvantageous, unfortunate, inauspicious, uncongenial, unpropitious, contrary AN OPPOSITE IS favorable

adversity NOUN **adversities** trouble or misfortune

advert NOUN **adverts** (*informal*) an advertisement

advertise VERB **advertises, advertising, advertised 1** praise goods, etc., in order to encourage people to buy or use them **2** make something publicly known • *advertise a meeting* **3** ask or offer by a public notice • *advertise for a secretary*
▷ **advertiser** NOUN

advertisement NOUN **advertisements** a public notice or announcement, especially one advertising goods or services in newspapers, on posters, or in broadcasts

advice NOUN **1** telling a person what you think he or she should do **2** a piece of information • *We received advice that the goods had been dispatched.*
USAGE Do not confuse with the verb **advise.**

advisable ADJECTIVE to be recommended; sensible
▷ **advisability** NOUN

advise VERB **advises, advising, advised 1** give somebody advice; recommend **2** inform
▷ **adviser** NOUN **advisory** ADJECTIVE

aerial ADJECTIVE **1** in or from the air **2** to do with aircraft

aerial NOUN **aerials** a wire or rod, etc., for receiving or transmitting radio or television signals

aerobics PLURAL NOUN exercises to stimulate breathing and strengthen the heart and lungs
▷ **aerobic** ADJECTIVE

aerodrome NOUN **aerodromes** an airfield

aerodynamic ADJECTIVE designed to move through the air quickly and easily

aeronautics NOUN the study of aircraft and flying
▷ **aeronautic** ADJECTIVE **aeronautical** ADJECTIVE

aerosol NOUN **aerosols** a container that holds a liquid under pressure and can let it out in a fine spray

aesthetic (es- thet- ik) ADJECTIVE to do with the appreciation of beautiful things

afar ADVERB far away • *The din was heard from afar.*

affair NOUN **affairs 1** an event or matter • *The party was a grand affair.* **2** a temporary sexual relationship between two people who are not married to each other

affairs PLURAL NOUN the business and activities that are part of private or public life • *Keep out of my affairs* • *current affairs*

affect VERB **affects, affecting, affected 1** have an effect on; influence **2** pretend • *She affected ignorance.*
USAGE The word **affect** is a verb. Do not confuse it with the noun **effect.**

affectation NOUN **affectations** unnatural behavior that is intended to impress other people

affected ADJECTIVE pretended and unnatural

Thesaurus

adversity NOUN *Peter showed he was stable in adversity.* ▶ misfortune, bad luck, hardship, difficulty, affliction, tribulation, suffering, sorrow, misery, hard times

advertise VERB *The job will be advertised in national newspapers.* ▶ publicize, promote, make known, market, announce, broadcast, display, flaunt, show off, (*more informal*) push, (*more informal*) spotlight, (*more informal*) tout, (*more informal*) plug

advertisement NOUN **1** *There are far more advertisements on television now.* ▶ commercial, (*more informal*) ad **2** *Let's put an advertisement in the local newspaper.* ▶ announcement, notice, (*more informal*) ad **3** *There are advertisements all along the main road.* ▶ billboard, placard

advice NOUN *I could do with some advice.* ▶ guidance, counseling, counsel, directions, suggestions, recommendations, tips, pointers

advisable ADJECTIVE *It is advisable to arrive early.* ▶ wise, sensible, prudent, desirable, a good idea, recommended AN OPPOSITE IS inadvisable

advise VERB **1** *He advised her to go the police.* ▶ recommend, counsel, instruct, encourage, admonish, caution, warn, (*more formal*) enjoin,

(*more formal*) exhort **2** *The doctor advised a period of rest.* ▶ suggest, prescribe, urge, advocate **3** *Visitors are advised that the house will close at six o'clock.* ▶ inform, notify, warn

affair NOUN **1** *The meeting was an odd affair.* ▶ incident, event, happening, episode, occurrence, circumstance, occasion, (*more informal*) business **2** *She suspected her husband was having an affair.* ▶ relationship, love affair, romance, (*more informal*) fling **3 affairs** *They need to put their financial affairs in order.* ▶ business, activities, concerns, transactions, operations, undertakings, interests, matters

affect VERB **1** *Alcohol affects women and men differently.* ▶ have an effect on, have an impact on, influence, impinge on, modify, act on, alter, attack, change, transform, (*more informal*) hit **2** *The sad news affected all of us.* ▶ upset, disturb, trouble, concern, move, perturb, sadden, distress, agitate, grieve, impress, stir, touch **3** *The man affects a French accent.* ▶ assume, feign, put on

affected ADJECTIVE *He assumed an affected voice, as though coming from God.* ▶ artificial, sham, insincere, pretentious, assumed, (*more informal*) put-on

A

affection NOUN **affections** a strong liking for a person

affectionate ADJECTIVE showing affection; loving
▷ **affectionately** ADVERB

affirm VERB **affirms**, **affirming**, **affirmed** state something definitely or firmly
▷ **affirmation** NOUN

affirmative ADJECTIVE that says "yes" ● *an affirmative reply* COMPARE **negative**

afflict VERB **afflicts**, **afflicting**, **afflicted** cause somebody to suffer ● *He is afflicted with arthritis.*
▷ **affliction** NOUN

affluent (af- loo- ent) ADJECTIVE rich
▷ **affluence** NOUN

afford VERB **affords**, **affording**, **afforded**
1 have enough money to pay for something
2 have enough time or resources, etc., to do something **3** to be able to do something without a risk ● *We can't afford to complain.*

affront VERB **affronts**, **affronting**, **affronted** insult or offend someone

affront NOUN **affronts** an insult

afloat ADJECTIVE, ADVERB floating; on the sea

afraid ADJECTIVE frightened or alarmed
I'm afraid I regret ● *I'm afraid I'm late.*

afresh ADVERB again; in a new way ● *We must start afresh.*

African ADJECTIVE to do with Africa or its people

African NOUN **Africans** an African person

aft ADVERB at or toward the back of a ship or aircraft

after PREPOSITION **1** later than ● *Come after lunch.*
2 behind in place or order ● *Which letter comes after H?* **3** trying to catch; pursuing ● *Run after him.* **4** in spite of ● *We can come after all.* **5** in imitation or honor of ● *She is named after her aunt.* **6** about or concerning ● *He asked after you.*

after ADVERB **1** behind ● *Jill came tumbling lunch.* **2** later ● *It came a week after.*

afternoon NOUN **afternoons** the time from noon to evening

aftershave NOUN a pleasant-smelling lotion that men put on their skin after shaving

afterwards ADVERB at a later time

again ADVERB **1** another time; once more ● *try again.* **2** as before ● *You will soon be well again.*
3 besides; moreover

against PREPOSITION **1** touching or hitting ● *He leaned against the wall.* **2** in opposition to; not in favor of ● *They voted against the proposal.*
3 in preparation for ● *Protect them against the cold.*

age NOUN **ages 1** the length of time a person has lived or a thing has existed **2** a special period of history or geology ● *the ice age*
ages PLURAL NOUN (informal) a very long time
● *We've been waiting for ages.*
come of age reach the age at which you have an adult's legal rights and obligations (now at 18 years; formerly 21)

age VERB **ages**, **ageing**, **aged** make or become old

Thesaurus

---

affection NOUN *The friends show obvious affection for one another.* ► fondness, friendship, friendliness, attachment, devotion, tenderness, warmth, feeling, liking, love, (more informal) soft spot AN OPPOSITE IS hatred

affectionate ADJECTIVE *an affectionate smile*
► fond, loving, devoted, tender, friendly, kind, kind-hearted, warm-hearted, sympathetic

afflict VERB *The family has been afflicted by illness.* ► trouble, bother, torment, beset, burden, strike, distress, oppress, harass, vex, plague

affliction NOUN *He bore his affliction with great dignity.* ► suffering, distress, misfortune, hardship, misery, torment, ordeal, pain, trouble, tribulation, adversity

affluence NOUN *In recent years the country has shown signs of greater affluence.* ► wealth, prosperity, opulence, fortune, richness

affluent ADJECTIVE *The more affluent houses had compost heaps in their large gardens.*
► prosperous, rich, well-off, wealthy, opulent,

(more informal) flush OPPOSITES ARE poor, impoverished

afford VERB *We can't afford a vacation this year.*
► have enough money for, pay for, manage

afraid ADJECTIVE **1** *The younger children were afraid of the dark.* ► frightened, scared, terrified, alarmed (at, by), fearful, intimidated (by), anxious, nervous OPPOSITES ARE unafraid, brave, bold, confident **2** *I'm afraid all the food has gone.* ► sorry, regretful, unhappy **3** *Don't be afraid to ask.* ► reluctant, hesitant, shy, slow

age NOUN **1** *The grandparents were showing signs of age.* ► old age, senility, elderliness, decrepitude, dotage, decline AN OPPOSITE IS youth **2** *the Elizabethan age* ► era, period, epoch, days, generation, time, years **3** (more informal) *It's been an age since you were last here. We've had to wait for ages.* ► lifetime, long time, aeon

age VERB **1** *Frank had aged in the last few years.*
► decline, degenerate, look older, fade **2** *A good wine needs to age.* ► mature, mellow, ripen, develop, grow older

aged ADJECTIVE *an aged relative* ► elderly, old

aged ADJECTIVE **1** (ayjd) having the age of • *a girl aged 9* **2** (ay- jid) very old • *an aged man*

agency NOUN agencies **1** the office or business of an agent • *a travel agency* **2** the means by which something is done • *Flowers are pollinated by the agency of bees.*

agenda (a- jen- da) NOUN agendas a list of things to be done or discussed • *The agenda is rather long.*

agent NOUN agents **1** a person who organizes things for other people **2** a spy • *a secret agent*

aggravate VERB aggravates, aggravating, aggravated **1** make a thing worse or more serious **2** (*informal*) annoy
▷ **aggravation** NOUN
[from Latin *gravis* = heavy]

aggregate NOUN aggregates a total amount or score

aggression NOUN starting an attack or war, etc.; aggressive behavior

aggressive ADJECTIVE likely to attack people; forceful
▷ **aggressively** ADVERB **aggressiveness** NOUN **aggressor** NOUN

aggrieved (a- greevd) ADJECTIVE resentful because of being treated unfairly

aghast ADJECTIVE horrified

agile ADJECTIVE moving quickly or easily
▷ **agilely** ADVERB **agility** NOUN

agitate VERB agitates, agitating, agitated **1** make someone feel upset or anxious **2** stir up public interest or concern; campaign • *They agitated for a new bypass.* **3** shake something
▷ **agitation** NOUN **agitator** NOUN

agnostic (ag- nost- ik) NOUN agnostics a person who believes that it is impossible to know whether God exists
▷ **agnosticism** NOUN
[from *a-* = not + Greek *gnostikos* = knowing. The word was invented by the biologist Thomas Huxley in the 19th century. He based it on the word *gnostic*, which meant "relating to knowledge"]

ago ADVERB in the past • *long ago*

agog ADJECTIVE eager and excited

agony NOUN agonies extremely great pain or suffering
▷ **agonizing** ADJECTIVE

agree VERB agrees, agreeing, agreed **1** think or say the same as another person, etc.

Thesaurus

agent NOUN *When she became a writer she needed an agent.* ► representative, mediator, intermediary, broker, delegate, emissary, go-between, middleman, negotiator, trustee

aggravate 1 *The delays only aggravated the situation.* ► worsen, exacerbate, increase, intensify, magnify, add to, make more serious, make worse, augment, compound, heighten, inflame, exaggerate AN OPPOSITE IS alleviate **2** (*informal*) *Their flippant remarks aggravated us.* ► annoy, irritate, bother, exasperate, incense, vex, irk, anger, nettle, provoke, trouble, (*more informal*) needle, (*more informal*) peeve

aggravation NOUN *It's not worth all the aggravation.* ► bother, annoyance, nuisance, trouble, hassle, irritation, difficulty

aggression NOUN *an act of aggression* ► hostility, aggressiveness, provocation, militancy, violence

aggressive ADJECTIVE *Lily was in one of her aggressive moods.* ► hostile, provocative, pugnacious, antagonistic, militant, belligerent, bellicose, argumentative, quarrelsome, attacking, violent, warlike, assertive, bullying, (*more informal*) pushy, (*more informal*) macho AN OPPOSITE IS friendly

aggrieved ADJECTIVE *He sounded aggrieved and astonished.* ► offended, indignant, resentful, wronged, distressed, discontented, piqued, riled

aghast ADJECTIVE *They were aghast at the news.* ► horrified, appalled, shocked, dismayed, astounded, astonished, amazed

agile ADJECTIVE *The child was as agile as a monkey.* ► nimble, lithe, spry, deft, graceful, fleet, adroit, sprightly, supple, lively, acrobatic, active, limber, lissom, mobile, quick-moving, swift OPPOSITES ARE clumsy, slow

agitate VERB **1** *A special device agitates the clothes.* ► stir, disturb, shake, ruffle, stimulate, beat, churn, convulse, toss **2** *Her remark seemed to agitate her guest.* ► upset, alarm, rouse, unsettle, disquiet, disturb, excite, worry, confuse, trouble, disconcert, fluster, perturb, stir up AN OPPOSITE IS calm

agitated ADJECTIVE *She became agitated when they did not appear.* ► upset, unsettled, anxious, confused, disturbed, ruffled, edgy, excited, distraught, flustered, nervous, restive, restless, fidgety, feverish, (*more informal*) OPPOSITES ARE calm, relaxed

agonize VERB *We agonized for hours over the decision.* ► worry, fret, fuss, struggle, labor, suffer, wrestle, be anxious

agonizing ADJECTIVE *an agonizing pain* ► excruciating, acute, intense, severe, extreme, piercing, painful

agony NOUN *The victims died in agony.* ► pain, torment, torture, suffering, anguish, distress, suffering

agree VERB **1** *I'll have a word with your father, and I'm sure he'll agree.* ► approve, consent, be

agreeable ➡ air

A B C D E F G H I J K L M N O P Q R S T U V W X Y Z

2 consent • *She agreed to come.* **3** suit a person's health or digestion • *Curry doesn't agree with me.* **4** correspond in grammatical number, gender, or person. In "They were good teachers" *they* agrees with *teachers* (both are plural forms) and *were* agrees with *they*; *was* would be incorrect because it is singular.

agreeable ADJECTIVE **1** willing • *We shall go if you are agreeable.* **2** pleasant • *an agreeable place*
▷ **agreeably** ADVERB

agreement NOUN agreements **1** agreeing **2** an arrangement that people have agreed on

agriculture NOUN cultivating land on a large scale and rearing livestock; farming
▷ **agricultural** ADJECTIVE

aground ADVERB, ADJECTIVE stranded on the bottom in shallow water

ahead ADVERB **1** further forward; in front **2** forward • *Full steam ahead!*

aid NOUN aids **1** help **2** something that helps • *a hearing aid* **3** money, food, etc., sent to another country to help it • *overseas aid*
in aid of for the purpose of; to help something

aid VERB aids, aiding, aided help

Aids NOUN a disease that greatly weakens a person's ability to resist infections [from the initial letters of "acquired immune deficiency syndrome"]

ailing ADJECTIVE **1** ill; in poor health **2** in difficulties; not successful • *the ailing ship industry*

ailment NOUN ailments a slight illness

aim VERB aims, aiming, aimed **1** point a gun, etc. **2** throw or kick in a particular direction **3** try or intend to do something

aim NOUN aims **1** aiming a gun, etc. **2** a purpose or intention

aimless ADJECTIVE without a purpose
▷ **aimlessly** ADVERB

air NOUN airs **1** the mixture of gases that surrounds the earth and which everyone breathes **2** the open space above the earth **3** a tune or melody **4** an appearance or impression of something • *an air of mystery* **5** an impressive or haughty manner • *He puts on airs.*
by air in or by aircraft
on the air on radio or television

air VERB airs, airing, aired **1** put clothes, etc., in a warm place to finish drying **2** ventilate a room **3** express • *He aired his opinions.*

Thesaurus

willing **2** *You must agree to take six books in the first year of membership.* ► be willing, consent, undertake, promise **3** *I think we all agree on the action needed.* ► concur, be unanimous, be united, (*more informal*) see eye to eye **4** *No two versions of the story seem to agree.* ► match, accord, correspond, tally, coincide, conform, harmonize, fit OPPOSITES ARE disagree, conflict
agree on *We should agree on a price.* ► fix, settle, decide on, establish, choose
agree to *He agreed to their requests.* ► accept, consent to, acquiesce in, accede to, assent to, grant, allow
agree with *I don't agree with the decision to go to war.* ► support, advocate, defend, argue for, (*more informal*) back

agreeable ADJECTIVE *I spent an agreeable day with their family.* ► pleasant, likable, pleasing, delightful, congenial, appealing OPPOSITES ARE disagreeable, unpleasant

agreement NOUN **1** *There's a large measure of agreement between them.* ► accord, concord, concurrence, unanimity, consensus, harmony, unity, affinity, similarity, sympathy, conformity, consistency, correspondence AN OPPOSITE IS disagreement **2** *The two sides reached an agreement.* ► settlement, deal, compact, accord, pact, understanding, pledge, arrangement

aid NOUN *The project was largely financed from foreign aid.* ► help, support, assistance, relief, favor, patronage

aid VERB **1** *an agreement to aid the poorest countries* ► help, assist, support, sustain, relieve, subsidize **2** *These measures will aid the process.* ► encourage, support, promote, facilitate, expedite

aim NOUN *Our aim is to win the championship.* ► ambition, goal, objective, object, aspiration, plan, purpose, intention, target, wish, end, dream, hope, desire, design

aim VERB **1** *He aimed a gun at her.* ► point, direct, level, train, focus **2** *We aim to meet our targets in full next year.* ► intend, aspire, resolve, want, wish, seek, plan, strive, try, endeavor, attempt

aimless ADJECTIVE *an aimless existence* ► pointless, purposeless, undirected, haphazard, random, meaningless, senseless, fruitless

air NOUN **1** *the air around us* ► sky, atmosphere, ether, heavens, airspace **2** *Open the window and let some air in.* ► breeze, draft, breath of air, oxygen, waft, wind **3** *She showed an air of defiance.* ► appearance, look, aura, manner, impression, bearing, aspect, ambience, character, demeanor, effect, feeling

air VERB **1** *You will need to air the room.* ► ventilate, aerate, freshen **2** *an opportunity to air your opinions* ► express , voice, utter, disclose, divulge, vent, declare, make known

16

air bag NOUN air bags a safety device in a vehicle, which inflates in front of the driver or passenger to reduce the impact in a collision

air-conditioning NOUN a system for controlling the temperature, purity, etc., of the air in a room or building
▷ **air-conditioned** ADJECTIVE

aircraft NOUN aircraft an airplane, glider, or helicopter, etc.

aircraft carrier NOUN aircraft carriers a large ship with a long deck where aircraft can take off and land

airfield NOUN airfields an area equipped with runways, etc., where aircraft can take off and land

air force NOUN air forces the part of a country's armed forces that is equipped with aircraft

airline NOUN airlines a company that provides a regular service of transport by aircraft

airliner NOUN airliners a large aircraft for carrying passengers

airlock NOUN airlocks 1 a compartment with an airtight door at each end, through which people can go in and out of a pressurized chamber 2 a bubble of air that stops liquid flowing through a pipe

airmail NOUN mail carried by air

airman NOUN airmen a man who is a member of an air force or of the crew of an aircraft

airplane NOUN airplanes a flying machine with wings

airport NOUN airports a place where aircraft land and take off, with passenger terminals and other buildings

air raid NOUN air raids an attack by aircraft

airstrip NOUN airstrips a strip of ground prepared for aircraft to land and take off

airtight ADJECTIVE not letting air in or out

airy ADJECTIVE 1 with plenty of fresh air 2 light as air 3 vague and insincere • airy promises
▷ **airily** ADVERB

aisle (I'll) NOUN aisles 1 a passage between or beside rows of seats or pews 2 a side part of a church

ajar ADVERB, ADJECTIVE slightly open • Leave the door ajar.

akin ADJECTIVE related or similar to • a feeling akin to regret

alarm NOUN alarms 1 a warning sound or signal; a piece of equipment for giving this 2 a feeling of fear or worry 3 an alarm clock

alarm VERB alarms, alarming, alarmed make someone frightened or anxious
▷ **alarming** ADJECTIVE
[from Italian all' arme! = to arms!]

alarm clock NOUN alarm clocks a clock that can be set to make a sound at a fixed time to wake a sleeping person

alas INTERJECTION an exclamation of sorrow

albatross NOUN albatrosses a large seabird with very long wings

albino (al- bIn- oh) NOUN albinos a person or animal with no color in the skin and hair (which are white)

album NOUN albums 1 a book with blank pages in which to keep a collection of photographs, stamps, autographs, etc. 2 a collection of songs on a CD, record, or tape

alcohol NOUN 1 a colorless liquid made by fermenting sugar or starch 2 drinks containing this liquid (e.g., wine, beer, whisky), that can make people drunk [The original meaning was a powdered cosmetic, and it came from an Arabic word al-kuhul. The meaning changed to any powder and then to a refined liquid produced by purifying, as alcohol is.]

alcoholic ADJECTIVE containing alcohol

alcoholic NOUN alcoholics a person who is seriously addicted to alcohol
▷ **alcoholism** NOUN

ale NOUN ales beer

alert ADJECTIVE watching for something; ready to act
▷ **alertly** ADVERB **alertness** NOUN

Thesaurus

airy ADJECTIVE 1 The room was light and airy.
► fresh, well ventilated, spacious, roomy, breezy OPPOSITES ARE stuffy, airless, close, oppressive 2 He looked at them with an airy confidence. ► cheerful, cheery, light-hearted, nonchalant, lively OPPOSITES ARE serious, solemn

aisle NOUN The theater had several aisles.
► gangway, passage, passageway, corridor, lane

alarm NOUN 1 The woman looked around in alarm.
► fear, fright, panic, terror, trepidation, apprehension, consternation, dismay, anxiety, distress, nervousness, uneasiness 2 Suddenly the alarm sounded. ► signal, alarm signal, warning signal, distress signal, siren

alarm VERB The news had alarmed us ► frighten, scare, startle, unnerve, agitate, shock, disturb, fluster, surprise, terrify, upset, daunt, dismay, distress, panic AN OPPOSITE IS reassure

alert ADJECTIVE 1 We need to stay alert driving in the dark. ► attentive, vigilant, watchful, aware, circumspect, wide awake, on the lookout, on the ball, on your guard AN OPPOSITE IS inattentive 2 mentally alert
► sharp, quick-witted, alive, active, acute

A

alert NOUN alerts a warning or alarm **on the alert** on the lookout; watchful

alert VERB alerts, alerting, alerted warn someone of danger, etc.; make someone aware of something [from Italian *all' erta!* = to the watchtower!]

algae (al- jee) PLURAL NOUN plants that grow in water, with no true stems or leaves

algebra (al- jeb- ra) NOUN mathematics in which letters and symbols are used to represent quantities
▷ **algebraic** (al- jib- **ray**- ik) ADJECTIVE
[from Arabic *al-jabr* = putting together broken parts. It was part of the name of an Arabic mathematical work written in the 9th century.]

alias (ay- lee- as) NOUN aliases a false or different name

alias ADVERB also named • *Clark Kent, alias Superman.*

alibi (al- ib- I) NOUN alibis evidence that a person accused of a crime was somewhere else when it was committed

alien (ay- lee- en) NOUN aliens **1** a person who is not a citizen of the country where he or she is living; a foreigner **2** a being from another world

alien ADJECTIVE **1** foreign **2** unnatural • *Cruelty is alien to her nature.*

alienate (ay- lee- en- ayt) VERB alienates, alienating, alienated make a person become unfriendly or not willing to help you
▷ **alienation** NOUN

alight ADJECTIVE **1** on fire **2** lit up

alike ADJECTIVE, ADVERB like one another; in the same way • *The twins are very alike.* • *Treat them alike.*

alimony NOUN money paid by someone to their wife or husband after they are separated or divorced; maintenance

alive ADJECTIVE **1** living **2** alert • *Be alive to the possible dangers.*

alkali (alk- al- I) NOUN alkalis a chemical substance that neutralizes an acid to form a salt
▷ **alkaline** ADJECTIVE
[from Arabic *al-kali* = the ashes (because alkalis were first obtained from the ashes of seaweed)]

all ADJECTIVE the whole number or amount of • *All my books are here.* • *all day*

all NOUN **1** everything • *That is all I know.* **2** everybody • *All are agreed.*

all ADVERB **1** completely • *She was dressed all in white.* **2** to each team or competitor • *The score is fifteen all.*
all there (*informal*) having an alert mind
all the same in spite of this; making no difference • *I like him, all the same.*

Allah NOUN the Muslim name of God

all-around ADJECTIVE general; not specialized • *an all-around athlete*

allegation (al- ig- ay- shon) NOUN allegations a statement made without proof

allege (a- lej) VERB alleges, alleging, alleged say something without being able to prove it • *He alleged that I had cheated.*
▷ **allegedly** (a- lej- id- lee) ADVERB

Thesaurus

---

alert VERB *We alerted them to the problem.*
► warn (of), notify (of), tip off (about), inform (about)

alias NOUN *Jack was not his real name, only an alias.* ► pseudonym, false name, assumed name, (*said of a writer*) pen name, (*said of an actor*) stage name

alibi NOUN *She has a cast-iron alibi for that evening.* ► excuse, pretext, story, defense, explanation

alien ADJECTIVE **1** *an alien landscape* ► strange, unfamiliar, outlandish, exotic, foreign, remote **2** *alien beings* ► foreign, extraterrestrial, remote

alien NOUN *illegal aliens* ► foreigner, immigrant, stranger, outsider

alight ADJECTIVE *The house was truly alight.* ► on fire, ablaze, burning, blazing, in flames, ignited, lit up

alight VERB **1** *Three passengers alighted from the train.* ► get off, get down, descend, disembark, dismount **2** *The bird alighted on a branch.* ► land, settle, perch, come to rest, touch down, come down

align VERB **1** *The shelves are aligned in rows.* ► place in line, arrange in line, line up, straighten up **2** *He aligns himself with the workers.* ► associate, affiliate, side, sympathize, agree, ally, cooperate, join

alike ADJECTIVE *All the houses looked alike.* ► similar, identical, indistinguishable, the same, uniform, comparable, interchangeable

alive ADJECTIVE **1** *She was last seen alive a week ago.* ► living, live, breathing, animate, existing AN OPPOSITE IS dead **2** *Many of the old customs of the country are kept alive.* ► active, in existence, current, functioning, flourishing, surviving OPPOSITES ARE obsolete, inactive **3** *The company is alive to recent developments.* ► alert, sensitive, aware (of), conscious (of), apprised (of), cognizant (of)

allegation NOUN *There were the usual allegations of police brutality.* ► accusation, charge, claim, assertion, declaration, statement, testimony

allege VERB *She alleged that he had attacked her.* ► assert, affirm, maintain, claim, contend, declare, insist, state

Left margin: A B C D E F G H I J K L M N O P Q R S T U V W X Y Z

allegiance (a- lee- jans) NOUN **allegiances** loyalty

allegory (al- ig- or- ee) NOUN **allegories** a story in which the characters and events represent or symbolize a deeper meaning, e.g., to teach a moral lesson
▷ **allegorical** (al- ig- **o**- rik- al) ADJECTIVE

alleluia INTERJECTION praise to God

allergy (al- er- jee) NOUN **allergies** something that a person is sensitive to and that can make him or her ill • *He has an allergy to cats.*
▷ **allergic** (al- **er**- jik) ADJECTIVE

alley NOUN **alleys 1** a narrow street or passage **2** a place where you can bowl

alliance (a- leye- ans) NOUN **alliances** an association formed by countries or groups who wish to support each other

allied ADJECTIVE **1** joined as allies; on the same side **2** of the same kind

alligator NOUN **alligators** a large reptile of the crocodile family [from Spanish *el lagarto* = the lizard]

alliteration NOUN the repetition of the same letter or sound at the beginning of several words to make a special effect, e.g., in • *Whisper words of wisdom.*

allotment NOUN **allotments 1** a small rented piece of public land used for growing

vegetables, fruit, or flowers **2** allotting; the amount allotted

allow VERB **allows, allowing, allowed 1** permit • *Smoking is not allowed.* **2** permit someone to have something; provide with • *She was allowed $10 for books.* **3** agree • *I allow that you have been patient.*
▷ **allowable** ADJECTIVE

allowance NOUN **allowances** an amount of money that is given regularly for a particular purpose
make allowances be considerate; excuse • *Make allowances for his age.*

alloy NOUN **alloys** a metal formed by mixing two or more metals, etc.

all right ADJECTIVE, ADVERB **1** satisfactory **2** in good condition **3** as desired **4** yes, I consent

allude VERB **alludes, alluding, alluded** refer to something without naming it
▷ **allusion** NOUN
USAGE Do not confuse with elude.

allure VERB **allures, alluring, allured** attract or fascinate someone
▷ **allure** NOUN **alluring** ADJECTIVE

ally (al- eye) NOUN **allies 1** a country in alliance with another **2** a person who cooperates with another

ally VERB **allies, allying, allied** form an alliance

Thesaurus

allegiance NOUN *an oath of allegiance to the flag* ► loyalty, fidelity, obedience, devotion, duty, faithfulness, (*historical*) fealty

allergic ADJECTIVE **1** *If you are allergic to foods, you'll know what these are.* ► sensitive **2** (*more informal*) *I think I must be allergic to hard work.* ► averse, opposed, hostile, resistant, disinclined, antagonistic, unsympathetic, antipathetic

alleviate VERB *Medication can help alleviate the pain.* ► ease, relieve, calm, soothe, diminish, reduce, lessen, dull, assuage, moderate AN OPPOSITE IS aggravate

alliance NOUN **1** *a political alliance* ► association, confederation, federation, compact, league, bloc, treaty, pact **2** *a business alliance* ► partnership, relationship, consortium, affiliation

allocate VERB *Funds are allocated to each project.* ► allot, assign, apportion, grant, award, distribute, set aside (for), allow, dispense, give out, share out

allow VERB **1** *Smoking is only allowed in certain parts of the hotel.* ► permit, approve, authorize, tolerate, bear, (*more informal*) put up with AN OPPOSITE IS forbid **2** *The teacher allowed him to go home.* ► permit, let, authorize, give permission, enable **3** *We need to allow more time for the journey.* ► provide, set aside, grant, allot, allocate, give

allowance NOUN **1** *A weekly allowance is provided for each prisoner.* ► allocation, portion, measure, quota, ration, share, amount **2** *He received an allowance from his father.* ► remittance, payment, pocket money, subsistence, annuity, grant, stipend, pension **3** *The shop will offer you an allowance for your old appliance.* ► discount, rebate, reduction, deduction
make allowances for *You have to make allowances for possible delays on the journey.* ► take into account, consider, bear in mind, keep in mind, remember, have regard for

all right ADJECTIVE **1** *She seemed all right.* ► well, unhurt, unharmed, uninjured, in good health, safe, secure **2** *The food's all right, though not very exciting.* ► satisfactory, acceptable, adequate, reasonable, tolerable, passable OPPOSITES ARE unsatisfactory, unacceptable

allude VERB **allude to** *Several speakers alluded to the problem.* ► refer to, hint at, make an allusion to, mention, touch on, speak of, suggest

ally NOUN *a political ally* ► associate, colleague, collaborator, partner, companion, confederate, supporter, friend, helper, accomplice, helpmate AN OPPOSITE IS enemy

ally VERB *Bruce again allied himself with the English.* ► unite, join, band together, join

a
b
c
d
e
f
g
h
i
j
k
l
m
n
o
p
q
r
s
t
u
v
w
x
y
z

A

almighty ADJECTIVE **1** having complete power **2** (informal) very great • an almighty din

almond (ah- mond) NOUN **almonds** an oval edible nut

almost ADVERB close to being something but not quite • almost ready

alone ADJECTIVE without any other people or things; without help

along PREPOSITION following the length of something • Walk along the path.

along ADVERB **1** on or onward • Push it along. **2** accompanying somebody • I've brought my brother along.
along with as well as; together with

alongside PREPOSITION, ADVERB next to something; beside

aloof ADVERB apart; not taking part • We stayed aloof from their quarrels.

aloof ADJECTIVE distant and not friendly in manner • She seemed aloof.

aloud ADVERB in a voice that can be heard

alpha NOUN the first letter of the Greek alphabet, = a

alphabet NOUN **alphabets** the letters used in a language, usually arranged in a set order ▷ **alphabetical** ADJECTIVE **alphabetically** ADVERB [from *alpha* and *beta*, the first two letters of the Greek alphabet. The Hebrew names *aleph* and *beth* are related to the Greek words.]

already ADVERB by now; before now

Alsatian (al- say- shan) NOUN **Alsatians** a German shepherd dog

also ADVERB in addition; besides

altar NOUN **altars** a table or similar structure used in religious ceremonies
USAGE Do not confuse with the verb **alter**.

alter VERB **alters, altering, altered** make or become different; change
▷ **alteration** NOUN
USAGE Do not confuse with the noun **altar**.

alternate (ol- tern- at) ADJECTIVE **1** happening or coming one after the other • alternate layers of cake and filling **2** one in every two • We meet on alternate Fridays.
▷ **alternately** ADVERB
USAGE See the note at **alternative**.

alternate (ol- tern- ayt) VERB **alternates, alternating, alternated** use or come alternately
▷ **alternation** NOUN

alternating current NOUN **alternating currents** electric current that keeps reversing its direction at regular intervals

alternative ADJECTIVE available instead of something else
▷ **alternatively** ADVERB
USAGE Do not confuse **alternative** with **alternate**. If there are *alternative colors* it means that there is a choice of two or more colors, but *alternate colors* means that there is first one color and then the other.

alternative NOUN **alternatives** one of two or more possibilities
no alternative no choice

alternative energy NOUN any form of energy that does not use up the earth's resources or harm the environment

Thesaurus

forces, side, team up, form an alliance, make common cause

almighty ADJECTIVE **1** Almighty God ► all-powerful, omnipotent, supreme, preeminent **2** an almighty explosion ► huge, enormous, tremendous, mighty, overpowering, overwhelming, big

almost ADVERB The riders had almost reached her. He was earning almost a million a year by now. I was almost tempted to ask why they had come. ► nearly, not quite, practically, virtually, about, just about, all but, around, as good as, approximately

alone ADJECTIVE **1** The man was alone in the house at the time. ► on your own, by yourself, solitary, single, unaccompanied, apart, separate, solo **2** She said she often felt very alone. ► lonely, isolated, lonesome, solitary, friendless, forlorn, desolate

aloof ADJECTIVE Michele seemed aloof and oddly tense. ► distant, remote, haughty, supercilious, forbidding, cold, unfriendly, reserved, standoffish, austere, scornful, unsympathetic,

unforthcoming, inaccessible, detached
OPPOSITES ARE friendly, approachable

aloud ADVERB Madge read the letter aloud. ► out loud, audibly, clearly, distinctly, plainly, loudly
AN OPPOSITE IS silently

also ADVERB His married sister also lives nearby. ► too, additionally, in addition, as well, besides, furthermore, moreover

alter VERB The text of the speech had been altered to take account of the recent events. ► change, adjust, modify, vary, adapt, convert, transform, amend, re-form

alteration NOUN After a few alterations the typescript was ready for publication. ► change, modification, variation, adaptation, adjustment, amendment, reorganization, transformation

alternate VERB In a democratic system political parties alternate in office. ► take turns, interchange, act alternately, swap, replace each other, rotate

alternative NOUN There is no alternative. ► choice, option, other possibility, substitute, replacement

alternative medicine NOUN types of medical treatment that are not based on ordinary medicine

alternator NOUN alternators a dynamo that generates an alternating current

although CONJUNCTION though

altitude NOUN altitudes the height of something, especially above sea level

alto NOUN altos **1** an adult male singer with a very high voice **2** a contralto

altogether ADVERB **1** with all included; in total • *The outfit costs $20 altogether.* **2** completely • *The stream dries up altogether in summer.* **3** on the whole • *Altogether, it was a good concert.*
USAGE Do not confuse **altogether** and *all together*.

aluminum NOUN a lightweight silver-colored metal

always ADVERB **1** at all times **2** often • *You are always crying.* **3** whatever happens • *You can always sleep on the floor.*

Alzheimer's disease NOUN a serious disease of the brain which affects some old people and makes them confused and forgetful

a.m. ABBREVIATION before noon

amalgamate VERB amalgamates, amalgamating, amalgamated mix or combine ▷ **amalgamation** NOUN

amateur (am- at- er) NOUN amateurs a person who does something as a hobby, not as a professional

amateurish ADJECTIVE not done or made very well; not skillful

amaze VERB amazes, amazing, amazed surprise somebody greatly; fill with wonder ▷ **amazement** NOUN

amazing ADJECTIVE very surprising or remarkable

amazon NOUN amazons a strong or athletic woman [The Amazons were a mythical race of women warriors. The Greeks thought that the name came from *a-* = without + *mazos* = breast, believing that the Amazons used to cut off their right breast in order to hold a bow better.]

ambassador NOUN ambassadors a person sent to a foreign country to represent his or her own government

amber NOUN **1** a hard clear yellowish substance used for making ornaments **2** a yellow traffic light shown as a signal for caution, placed between red (= stop) and green (= go)

ambidextrous ADJECTIVE able to use either your left hand or your right hand equally well

ambiguous ADJECTIVE having more than one possible meaning; unclear ▷ **ambiguously** ADVERB **ambiguity** NOUN

ambition NOUN ambitions **1** a strong desire to achieve something **2** the thing desired

ambitious ADJECTIVE full of ambition

Thesaurus

altogether ADVERB *We are not altogether satisfied.* ▶ completely, entirely, fully, wholly, totally, perfectly, absolutely, quite, thoroughly, utterly

always ADVERB **1** *You are always late.* ▶ every time, constantly, repeatedly, habitually, invariably, regularly **2** *He is always complaining.* ▶ forever, constantly, incessantly, endlessly **3** *I will always remember you.* ▶ forever, permanently, perpetually, evermore

amateur ADJECTIVE *The band was made up entirely of amateur musicians.* ▶ unpaid, unqualified, untrained, inexperienced AN OPPOSITE IS professional

amateur NOUN *The players were all amateurs.* ▶ nonprofessional, layman, layperson, enthusiast, devotee, dabbler AN OPPOSITE IS professional

amateurish ADJECTIVE *There are some very poor amateurish productions around.* ▶ unskillful, incompetent, inept, inexpert, crude, bumbling AN OPPOSITE IS skilled

amaze VERB *It always amazes me how dirty the place is.* ▶ astonish, astound, surprise, stagger, startle, disconcert, dumbfound, shock,

flabbergast, perplex, stun, stupefy, bewilder, confound

amazing ADJECTIVE *an amazing sight* ▶ astonishing, astounding, extraordinary, remarkable, staggering, startling, stunning, breathtaking, fantastic, wonderful, magnificent, phenomenal, incredible AN OPPOSITE IS unimpressive

ambiguous ADJECTIVE *The replies were ambiguous and misleading.* ▶ confusing, obscure, enigmatic, ambivalent, uncertain, unclear, equivocal, indefinite, indeterminate, puzzling, vague, woolly AN OPPOSITE IS definite

ambition NOUN **1** *young people with a lot of ambition* ▶ drive, enthusiasm, enterprise, self-assertion, zeal, (*more informal*) push **2** *Her ambition is to become a model.* ▶ aim, dream, hope, goal, aspiration, objective, object, target, wish, desire, ideal, intention

ambitious ADJECTIVE **1** *an ambitious politician* ▶ aspiring, assertive, determined, enthusiastic, (*more informal*) pushy AN OPPOSITE IS apathetic. **2** *ambitious ideas* ▶ grand, grandiose, large-scale, big, far-reaching, unrealistic OPPOSITES ARE modest, realistic

a
b
c
d
e
f
g
h
i
j
k
l
m
n
o
p
q
r
s
t
u
v
w
x
y
z

A
B
C
D
E
F
G
H
I
J
K
L
M
N
O
P
Q
R
S
T
U
V
W
X
Y
Z

ambivalent (am- biv- al- ent) ADJECTIVE having mixed feelings about something (e.g. liking and disliking it)
▷ ambivalence NOUN

amble VERB ambles, ambling, ambled walk at a slow easy pace

ambulance NOUN ambulances a vehicle equipped to carry sick or injured people

ambush NOUN ambushes a surprise attack from troops, etc., who have concealed themselves

ambush VERB ambushes, ambushing, ambushed attack someone after lying in wait for them

amen INTERJECTION a word used at the end of a prayer or hymn, meaning "may it be so"

amend VERB amends, amending, amended alter something in order to improve it
▷ amendment NOUN
make amends make up for having done something wrong; atone

American ADJECTIVE 1 to do with the continent of America 2 to do with the United States of America
▷ American NOUN

amino acid (a- meen- oh) NOUN amino acids an acid found in proteins

amiss ADJECTIVE wrong or faulty • She knew something was amiss.

ammonia NOUN a colorless gas or liquid with a strong smell

ammunition NOUN a supply of bullets, shells, grenades, etc., for use in fighting

amnesia (am- nee- zee- a) NOUN loss of memory

amnesty NOUN amnesties a general pardon for people who have committed a crime

amoeba (a- mee- ba) NOUN amoebas a microscopic creature consisting of a single cell which constantly changes shape and can split itself in two

among PREPOSITION 1 surrounded by; in • There were weeds among the flowers. 2 between • Divide the candy among the children.

amount NOUN amounts 1 a quantity 2 a total

amount VERB amounts, amounting, amounted amount to 1 add up to 2 be equivalent to • Their reply amounts to a refusal.

amp NOUN amps 1 an ampere 2 (informal) an amplifier

ampere (am- pir) NOUN amperes a unit for measuring electric current

amphibian NOUN amphibians 1 an animal able to live both on land and in water, such as a frog, toad, or newt 2 a vehicle that can move on both land and water

amphibious ADJECTIVE able to live or move on both land and in water

ample ADJECTIVE 1 quite enough • ample provisions 2 large
▷ amply ADVERB

Thesaurus

ambivalent ADJECTIVE an ambivalent attitude toward the new technology ► equivocal, uncertain, hesitant, fluctuating, contradictory, inconsistent, vacillating, wavering, ambiguous, confused, muddled

ambush NOUN The fighters set up an ambush. ► surprise attack, trap, snare, ambuscade

ambush VERB The gang specialized in ambushing unsuspecting passers-by. ► waylay, pounce on, surprise, swoop on, trap, entrap, ensnare, intercept, attack

amends NOUN make amends to It's not too late to make amends to them for the trouble you caused. ► recompense, compensate, make it up to

amenity NOUN an old house with few amenities ► facility, service, benefit, provision

amiable ADJECTIVE an amiable old fellow ► friendly, amicable, agreeable, affable, likeable, pleasant, congenial

ammunition NOUN 1 The house was full of ammunition. ► bullets, cartridges, shells, bombs, missiles, shrapnel 2 The blunder provided ammunition for the opposition. ► evidence, arguments, material, information

amok or **amuck** ADVERB run amok Some of the animals had broken loose and run amok. ► go berserk, go on the rampage, go out of control, go crazy

amoral ADJECTIVE Guy was greedy, amoral, and obsessed with power. ► unprincipled, loose, lax, unethical AN OPPOSITE IS moral.

amorous ADJECTIVE Her employer had made amorous advances. ► sexual, romantic, lustful, erotic, carnal, passionate, impassioned OPPOSITES ARE unloving, frigid

amount NOUN 1 He wrote a check for the whole amount. ► quantity, sum, total, lot, whole 2 The program needs a large amount of computer memory. ► quantity, volume, bulk, lot, mass, expanse, extent, measure, supply

amount VERB amount to The cost amounted to several thousands. ► add up to, come to, total, aggregate, be equivalent to, equal, make

ample ADJECTIVE 1 an ample supply of books and magazines ► plentiful, abundant, copious, lavish, generous, liberal, rich AN OPPOSITE IS meager 2 ample space for several cars ► enough, adequate, sufficient, plenty of OPPOSITES ARE inadequate, insufficient

amplifier NOUN amplifiers a piece of equipment for making a sound or electrical signal louder or stronger

amplify VERB amplifies, amplifying, amplified **1** make a sound or electrical signal louder or stronger **2** give more details about something • *Could you amplify that point?*

amplitude NOUN **1** (in science) the strength of a sound wave or electronic signal **2** largeness or abundance

amputate VERB amputates, amputating, amputated cut off an arm or leg by a surgical operation
▷ **amputation** NOUN

amuse VERB amuses, amusing, amused **1** make a person laugh or smile **2** make time pass pleasantly for someone
▷ **amusing** ADJECTIVE

amusement NOUN amusements **1** being amused **2** a way of passing time pleasantly

an ADJECTIVE SEE a

anachronism (an-ak-ron-izm) NOUN anachronisms something wrongly placed in a particular historical period, or regarded as out of date • *Bows and arrows would be an anachronism in modern warfare.* [from Greek *chronos* = time]

anagram NOUN anagrams a word or phrase made by rearranging the letters of another • *'Trap' is an anagram of "part".*

anal (ay-nal) ADJECTIVE to do with the anus

analogy (a-nal-oj-ee) NOUN analogies a comparison between things that are alike in some ways • *the analogy between the human heart and a pump*
▷ **analogous** ADJECTIVE

analysis NOUN analyses **1** a separation of something into its parts **2** a detailed examination of something
▷ **analytic** ADJECTIVE **analytical** ADJECTIVE

analyze VERB analyzes, analyzing, analyzed **1** examine and interpret something • *The book analyzes the causes of the war.* **2** separate something into its parts

anarchist (an-er-kist) NOUN anarchists a person who believes that all forms of government are bad and should be abolished

anarchy (an-er-kee) NOUN **1** lack of government or control, resulting in lawlessness **2** complete disorder

anatomy (an-at-om-ee) NOUN the study of the structure of the bodies of humans or animals
▷ **anatomical** ADJECTIVE **anatomist** NOUN

ancestor NOUN ancestors anyone from whom a person is descended
▷ **ancestral** ADJECTIVE **ancestry** NOUN

Thesaurus

amplify VERB **1** *A good acoustic will amplify the sound.* ► louden, magnify, boost, intensify, heighten, increase, make louder, raise the volume of AN OPPOSITE IS decrease **2** *The following notes amplify the position.* ► expand, enlarge on, elaborate on, develop, supplement, augment, add to, flesh out, broaden AN OPPOSITE IS condense

amuse VERB *Their comments amused him.* ► entertain, delight, divert, enliven, gladden, cheer up, make laugh, raise a smile, (*more informal*) tickle
amuse yourself *He amused himself by writing postcards.* ► occupy yourself, pass the time, engage yourself, interest yourself, immerse yourself (in)

amusement NOUN **1** *We read the article with amusement.* ► mirth, hilarity, delight, merriment, enjoyment, laughter **2** *The theme park had a wide range of amusements for all the family.* ► entertainment, activity, leisure activity, recreation, diversion, interest, delight, distraction, enjoyment, game, hobby, pastime, sport

amusing ADJECTIVE *an amusing story* ► entertaining, enjoyable, witty, funny, diverting, pleasing

analogy NOUN *There is an analogy between the human brain and a computer.* ► similarity, parallel, resemblance, comparison, likeness, correspondence, correlation

analysis NOUN *an analysis of the unemployment figures* ► examination, breakdown, evaluation, study, scrutiny, research (into), inquiry (into), interpretation, investigation, test

analytical ADJECTIVE *an analytical approach to the problem* ► systematic, logical, methodical, rational, critical, rigorous, searching, inquiring, investigative, penetrating, questioning AN OPPOSITE IS unsystematic

analyze VERB *You need to analyze your motives.* ► examine, evaluate, review, scrutinize, consider, study, interpret, investigate

anarchy NOUN *The country is threatened with anarchy.* ► lawlessness, disorder, bedlam, disorganization, insurrection, chaos, confusion, misgovernment, misrule, mutiny, pandemonium, riot

ancestor NOUN *We can trace our ancestors back to the Stuarts.* ► forebear, forefather, antecedent, predecessor, progenitor AN OPPOSITE IS descendant RELATED ADJECTIVE ► atavistic

ancestry NOUN *The family has a Spanish ancestry.* ► lineage, origin, pedigree, roots, stock, pedigree, parentage, ancestors, forebears

a
b
c
d
e
f
g
h
i
j
k
l
m
n
o
p
q
r
s
t
u
v
w
x
y
z

A

B
C
D
E
F
G
H
I
J
K
L
M
N
O
P
Q
R
S
T
U
V
W
X
Y
Z

anchor NOUN anchors a heavy object joined to a ship by a chain or rope and dropped to the bottom of the sea to stop the ship from moving

anchor VERB anchors, anchoring, anchored **1** fix or be fixed by an anchor **2** fix something firmly

ancient ADJECTIVE **1** very old **2** belonging to the distant past • *ancient history*

and CONJUNCTION **1** together with; in addition to • *We had cakes and cookies.* **2** so that; with this result • *Work hard and you will pass.* **3** to • *Go and buy a pen.*

android NOUN androids (in science fiction) a robot that looks like a human being

anecdote NOUN anecdotes a short amusing or interesting story about a real person or thing

anemia (a- nee- mee- a) NOUN a poor condition of the blood that makes a person pale
▷ **anemic** ADJECTIVE

anesthetic (an- iss- thet- ik) NOUN anesthetics a substance or gas that makes you unable to feel pain
▷ **anesthesia** NOUN

anesthetist (an- ees- thet- ist) NOUN anesthetists a person trained to give anesthetics
▷ **anesthetize** VERB

angel NOUN angels **1** an attendant or messenger of God **2** a very kind or beautiful person
▷ **angelic** (an- **jel**- ik) ADJECTIVE
[from Greek *angelos* = messenger]

anger NOUN a strong feeling that you have toward someone who has done wrong or has done something you do not like

anger VERB angers, angering, angered make a person angry

angle NOUN angles **1** the space between two lines or surfaces that meet; the amount by which a line or surface must be turned to make it lie along another **2** a point of view

angle VERB angles, angling, angled **1** put something in a slanting position **2** present news, etc., from one point of view

angler NOUN anglers a person who fishes with a fishing rod and line
▷ **angling** NOUN

Anglican ADJECTIVE to do with the Church of England
▷ **Anglican** NOUN

Anglo-Saxon NOUN Anglo-Saxons **1** an English person, especially of the time before the Norman conquest in 1066 **2** the form of English spoken from about 700 to 1150; Old English

angry ADJECTIVE angrier, angriest feeling anger
▷ **angrily** ADVERB

Thesaurus

anchor VERB **1** *Several ships had anchored in the harbor.* ► berth, moor, tie up, make fast **2** *The lid was anchored to the sides with screws.*
► fasten, attach, fix

ancient ADJECTIVE **1** *the ancient buildings at Pompeii* ► old, historic, early, classical **2** *ancient civilizations* ► early, old, historic, prehistoric (= before the time of written records), archaic, bygone AN OPPOSITE IS modern

angel NOUN **1** *a depiction of angels with wings and beautiful faces* ► archangel, divine messenger, cherub, seraph **2** *She was an absolute angel during my illness.* ► dear, darling, treasure, gem

angelic ADJECTIVE **1** *angelic beings* ► heavenly, celestial, divine, ethereal **2** *an angelic expression* ► beautiful, lovely, heavenly, enchanting **3** *angelic behavior* ► innocent, virtuous, exemplary, pure, saintly, pious, unworldly AN OPPOSITE IS devilish

anger NOUN *Anger surged through him.*
► annoyance, irritation, crossness, exasperation, displeasure, fury, rage, indignation, temper, vexation, bitterness, hostility, outrage, resentment, passion, pique, (*more formal*) rancor, (*literary*) wrath, (*literary*) ire

anger VERB *Their rudeness angered all of us.*
► enrage, annoy, irritate, infuriate, exasperate, incense, vex, madden, aggravate, antagonize, displease, incite, inflame, make angry, (*more informal*) needle, (*more informal*) rile, (*more informal*) bug, (*more informal*) rub the wrong way OPPOSITES ARE pacify, placate, appease

angle NOUN **1** *a cupboard built into the angle of the two walls* ► corner, intersection, recess **2** *We need to look at the problem from another angle.* ► perspective, point of view, standpoint, viewpoint, position, slant, approach, outlook

angry ADJECTIVE *John looked angry and started to shout. She gave us all an angry look.* ► annoyed, enraged, cross, displeased, furious, irritated, irate, infuriated, incensed, indignant, outraged OPPOSITES ARE pleased, calm
become angry *Eventually the witch became angry.* ► lose your temper, go into a rage, fly into a rage, flare up, (*more informal*) see red, (*more informal*) fly off the handle, (*more informal*) hit the roof, (*more informal*) go off the deep end, (*very informal*) freak out, (*very informal*) go ballistic

anguish NOUN *a cry of anguish* ► agony, pain, distress, torment, torture, sorrow, suffering,

angular ADJECTIVE **1** having angles or sharp corners **2** (said about a person) bony, not plump

animal NOUN animals **1** a living thing that can feel and usually move around • *Horses, birds, fish, bees, and people are all animals.* **2** a cruel or uncivilized person

animate VERB animates, animating, animated make a thing lively
▷ animation NOUN

animated ADJECTIVE **1** lively and excited **2** (said about a film) made by photographing a series of still pictures and showing them rapidly one after another, so they appear to move

ankle NOUN ankles the part of the leg where it joins the foot

annihilate (an- I- il- ayt) VERB annihilates, annihilating, annihilated destroy something completely
▷ annihilation NOUN

anniversary NOUN anniversaries a day when you remember something special that happened on the same day in a previous year

announce VERB announces, announcing, announced make something known, especially by saying it publicly or to an audience
▷ announcement NOUN announcer NOUN

annoy VERB annoys, annoying, annoyed **1** make a person slightly angry **2** be troublesome to someone
▷ annoyance NOUN

annual ADJECTIVE **1** happening once a year • *her annual visit* **2** calculated over one year

Thesaurus

anxiety, grief, misery, tribulation, heartache, (*literary*) woe

animal NOUN **1** *Like many animals they hibernate in winter.* ► living being, creature, beast, being, brute **2** animals ► wildlife

animate VERB *A feeling of excitement animated the whole team.* ► invigorate, enliven, vitalize, revitalize, energize, stimulate, hearten, activate, revive, liven up, excite, encourage, exhilarate, fire, inspire, arouse, rejuvenate, galvanize, (*more informal*) buck up, (*more informal*) pep up, (*more informal*) give a buzz

animated ADJECTIVE *There was a sound of animated conversation in the next room.* ► lively, spirited, excited, enthusiastic, exuberant, heated, vivacious, high-spirited, passionate, impassioned OPPOSITES ARE lethargic, lifeless

animation NOUN *They arrived full of animation and determination.* ► liveliness, energy, vitality, spirit, enthusiasm, excitement, activity OPPOSITES ARE lethargy, inertia

animosity NOUN *There was a strong animosity between the two brothers.* ► hostility, ill-feeling, antagonism, enmity, acrimony, antipathy, rancor, bitterness, hate, hatred, loathing, venom OPPOSITES ARE goodwill, rapport, friendship

annihilate VERB *The army set about annihilating the whole population.* ► destroy, wipe out, eliminate, eradicate, exterminate, extinguish, obliterate, slaughter, raze, abolish, erase, liquidate, (*more formal*) extirpate, (*more informal*) kill off

announce VERB **1** *The government will announce its plans next week.* ► make public, make known, declare, reveal, disclose, divulge, publish, publicize, broadcast, advertise

OPPOSITES ARE conceal, suppress **2** *The presenter announced the next act.* ► introduce, present

announcement NOUN **1** *There will be an announcement from the president this afternoon.* ► statement, declaration, communiqué, pronouncement, proclamation, bulletin, dispatch **2** *We are still waiting for an announcement of the decision.* ► declaration, notification, intimation, disclosure

announcer NOUN *The announcer gave details of the program changes.* ► presenter, anchorman, anchorwoman, newscaster, newsreader, broadcaster, commentator, compère, master of ceremonies

annoy VERB *The comments had clearly annoyed her.* ► irritate, displease, anger, infuriate, enrage, exasperate, incense, vex, madden, aggravate, nettle, antagonize, inflame, make angry, (*more informal*) needle, (*more informal*) rile, (*more informal*) bug, (*more informal*) rub the wrong way OPPOSITES ARE please, gratify

annoyance NOUN **1** *Much to her annoyance, Mike had taken the car.* ► irritation, indignation, displeasure, exasperation, pique, chagrin, vexation **2** *The animals in the road proved quite an annoyance.* ► irritant, irritation, nuisance, bother, worry, (*more informal*) aggravation

annoyed ADJECTIVE *His mother was beginning to look annoyed.* ► irritated, angry, cross, displeased, vexed, peeved, infuriated, incensed, enraged, (*more informal*) miffed, (*more informal*) put out AN OPPOSITE IS pleased

annoying ADJECTIVE *His mouth curled into an annoying smile.* ► irritating, infuriating, exasperating, maddening, irksome, bothersome, tiresome OPPOSITES ARE pleasant, agreeable

a
b
c
d
e
f
g
h
i
j
k
l
m
n
o
p
q
r
s
t
u
v
w
x
y
z

A

• *our annual income* **3** living for one year or one season • *an annual plant*
▷ **annually** ADVERB

annual NOUN **annuals 1** a book that comes out once a year **2** an annual plant [from Latin *annus* = year]

anode NOUN **anodes** the electrode by which electric current enters a device COMPARE **cathode**

anoint VERB **anoints, anointing, anointed** put oil or ointment on something, especially in a religious ceremony

anon ADVERB (*old use*) soon • *I will say more about this anon.*

anon. ABBREVIATION anonymous

anonymous (an- on- im- us) ADJECTIVE without the name of the person responsible being known or made public • *an anonymous donor*
▷ **anonymously** ADVERB **anonymity** (an- on- im- it- ee) NOUN

anorak NOUN **anoraks** a thick warm jacket with a hood [from an Inuit word]

anorexia (an- er- eks- ee- a) NOUN an illness that makes a person so anxious to lose weight that he or she refuses to eat
▷ **anorexic** ADJECTIVE

another ADJECTIVE, PRONOUN a different or extra person or thing • *another day* • *choose another*

answer NOUN **answers 1** a reply **2** the solution to a problem

answer VERB **answers, answering, answered 1** give or find an answer to; reply **2** respond to a signal • *Answer the telephone.*
answer back reply rudely
answer for be responsible for
answer to correspond to • *This answers to the description of the stolen bag.*

ant NOUN **ants** a very small insect that lives as one of an organized group

antagonism (an- tag- on- izm) NOUN an unfriendly feeling; hostility
▷ **antagonist** NOUN **antagonistic** ADJECTIVE

antagonize VERB **antagonizes, antagonizing, antagonized** make a person feel hostile or angry

antelope NOUN **antelope** *or* **antelopes** a fast-running animal like a deer, found in Africa and parts of Asia

antenatal (an- tee- nay- tal) ADJECTIVE before birth; during pregnancy

antenna NOUN **1 antennae** a feeler on the head of an insect or crustacean **2 antennas** an aerial

anthem NOUN **anthems** a religious or patriotic song, usually sung by a choir or group of people

anthology NOUN **anthologies** a collection of poems, stories, songs, etc. in one book [from Greek *anthos* = flower + *logia* = collection: early collections of poems were regarded as

Thesaurus

anonymous ADJECTIVE **1** *The author was anonymous.* ► unnamed, nameless, incognito, unacknowledged, unidentified, unknown, unspecified, (*literary*) unsung **2** *an anonymous letter* ► unattributed, unsigned **3** *an anonymous way of writing* ► impersonal, nondescript, characterless, faceless, unremarkable

answer NOUN **1** *Our letter brought a quick answer.* ► reply, response, reaction, acknowledgment, riposte **2** *The answer to the question was far from clear.* ► solution, explanation **3** *Violence is no answer.* ► solution, remedy, way out **4** *his answer to the charge* ► defense, plea, vindication

answer VERB **1** *Please answer my question. Will nobody answer me?* ► reply to, respond to, acknowledge, give an answer to, react to **2** *'I'm not feeling well,' she answered.* ► rejoin, reply, respond, retort, return **3** *A good encyclopedia will answer your problem.* ► resolve, solve, explain **4** *The accused could answer all but one of the charges.* ► refute, rebut, defend yourself against **5** *We have enough money to answer our present needs.* ► satisfy, serve, fulfill, meet, correspond to, echo, fit, match up to,

suffice, suit **6** *The police have arrested a man answering the description.* ► match, fit, correspond to, conform to
answer someone back *It was unwise to answer the teacher back in those days, however provoked you felt.* ► talk back to, be impertinent to, be rude to, contradict

answerable ADJECTIVE *Senators are answerable to their constituents.* ► responsible, accountable, subject

antagonism NOUN *She was pleased, despite her antagonism to him.* ► hostility, ill-feeling, animosity, enmity, acrimony, antipathy, rancor, bitterness, hate, hatred, loathing, venom OPPOSITES ARE goodwill, rapport, friendship

antagonistic ADJECTIVE *The march threatened to attract an antagonistic rival mob.* ► hostile, opposed, ill-disposed, antipathetic

antagonize VERB *They seem to be trying to antagonize us.* ► alienate, provoke, make an enemy of, offend, anger, annoy, embitter, estrange, irritate, upset OPPOSITES ARE pacify, placate

anthology NOUN *an anthology of short stories* ► collection, selection, treasury, compilation, compendium, miscellany, digest including the "flowers," i.e., the most beautiful examples]

anthropoid ADJECTIVE like a human being
• Gorillas are anthropoid apes.

anthropology NOUN the study of human beings and their customs
▷ anthropological ADJECTIVE anthropologist NOUN

antibiotic NOUN antibiotics a substance (e.g., penicillin) that destroys bacteria or prevents them from growing

antibody NOUN antibodies a protein that forms in the blood as a defense against certain substances which it then attacks and destroys

anticipate VERB anticipates, anticipating, anticipated **1** take action in advance about something you are aware of • A good teacher learns to anticipate what students will ask. **2** act before someone else does • Others may have anticipated Columbus in discovering America. **3** expect • We anticipate that it will rain.
▷ anticipation NOUN anticipatory ADJECTIVE
USAGE Many people regard use 3 as incorrect; it is better to avoid it and use "expect."

anticlimax NOUN anticlimaxes a disappointing ending or result where something exciting had been expected

anticlockwise ADVERB, ADJECTIVE moving in the direction opposite to clockwise

antics PLURAL NOUN funny or foolish actions

anticyclone NOUN anticyclones an area where air pressure is high, usually producing fine settled weather

antidote NOUN antidotes something that acts against the effects of a poison or disease

antifreeze NOUN a liquid added to water to make it less likely to freeze

antihistamine NOUN antihistamines a drug that protects people against unpleasant effects when they are allergic to something

antimony NOUN a brittle silvery metal

antiquarian (an- ti- **kwair**- ee- an) ADJECTIVE to do with the study of antiques

antiquated ADJECTIVE old-fashioned

antique (an- **teek**) ADJECTIVE very old; belonging to the distant past

antique NOUN antiques something that is valuable because it is very old

antiquity (an- **tik**- wit- ee) NOUN ancient times

anti-Semitic (an- ti- sim- **it**- ik) ADJECTIVE hostile or prejudiced toward Jews
▷ anti-Semitism (an- ti- **sem**- it- izm) NOUN

antiseptic ADJECTIVE **1** able to destroy bacteria, especially those that cause things to become septic or to decay **2** thoroughly clean and free from germs

antiseptic NOUN antiseptics a substance with an antiseptic effect

antisocial ADJECTIVE unfriendly or inconsiderate toward other people

antler NOUN antlers the branching horn of a deer

Thesaurus

anticipate VERB **1** It was impossible to anticipate all the possible moves. ► forestall, preempt, intercept, prevent **2** I anticipate that the result will be a draw. ► expect, foresee, predict, forecast, foretell, hope

anticlimax NOUN After all the excitement, the journey proved to be rather an anticlimax. ► let-down, comedown, disappointment

antics PLURAL NOUN He was reminded of his childhood antics. ► foolery, tricks, capers, buffoonery, tomfoolery, clowning, escapades, fooling, pranks

antidote NOUN The poison has no known antidote. ► antitoxin, cure, remedy, neutralizing agent

antipathy NOUN He expressed his antipathy to institutions of any kind. ► hostility, ill-feeling, animosity, enmity, acrimony, antagonism, rancor, bitterness, hate, hatred, loathing, venom OPPOSITES ARE fondness, goodwill, liking

antiquated ADJECTIVE Their ideas seem antiquated these days. an antiquated typewriter
► old-fashioned, out-dated, outmoded, out-

of-date, obsolete, ancient, antediluvian, antique, archaic, dated, anachronistic, old, passé, (more informal) past it, (more informal) prehistoric, primitive, quaint, (humorous) superannuated, unfashionable OPPOSITES ARE up to date, modern, current, new

antique ADJECTIVE Amanda has an eye for good antique furniture. ► old, ancient, antiquarian, antiquated, historic, old-fashioned, traditional, veteran (car), vintage (car) OPPOSITES ARE modern, new

antique NOUN a sale of antiques ► collector's item, curio, curiosity, rarity

antiquity NOUN **1** The place had been a harbor in antiquity. ► ancient times, the ancient past, past times **2** a site of great antiquity ► age, oldness, elderliness

antisocial ADJECTIVE Most people show some signs of antisocial behavior. ► asocial, unsociable, unacceptable, objectionable, undisciplined, offensive, disorderly, disruptive, obnoxious, uncooperative, unfriendly, troublesome, unruly, alienated, anarchic, disagreeable, nasty, rebellious, rude OPPOSITES ARE friendly, sociable

A
B
C
D
E
F
G
H
I
J
K
L
M
N
O
P
Q
R
S
T
U
V
W
X
Y
Z

anus (ay- nus) NOUN **anuses** the opening at the lower end of the alimentary canal, through which solid waste matter is passed out of the body

anvil NOUN **anvils** a large block of iron on which a blacksmith hammers metal into shape

anxious ADJECTIVE **1** worried **2** eager • *She is anxious to please us.*
▷ **anxiously** ADVERB **anxiety** NOUN

any ADJECTIVE, PRONOUN **1** one or some • *Have you any wool?* • *There isn't any.* **2** no matter which • *Come any day you like.* **3** every • *Any fool knows that!*

any ADVERB at all; in some degree • *Is that any better?*

anybody NOUN, PRONOUN any person

anyhow ADVERB **1** anyway **2** (*informal*) carelessly • *He does his work anyhow.*

anyone NOUN, PRONOUN anybody

anything NOUN, PRONOUN any thing

anyway ADVERB whatever happens; whatever the situation may be

anywhere ADVERB in or to any place

anywhere PRONOUN any place • *Anywhere will do.*

aorta (ay- or- ta) NOUN **aortas** the main artery that carries blood away from the left side of the heart

apart ADVERB **1** away from each other; separately • *Keep your desks apart.* **2** into

pieces • *It fell apart.* **3** excluded • *Joking apart, what do you think of it?*
apart from excluding, other than

apartheid (a- part- hayt) NOUN the political policy that used to be practiced in South Africa, of keeping people of different races apart [Afrikaans, = being apart]

apartment NOUN **apartments 1** a set of rooms **2** (*American*) a flat

apathy (ap- ath- ee) NOUN not being interested in something or caring much about it
▷ **apathetic** (ap- a- thet- ik) ADJECTIVE

ape NOUN **apes** any of the four kinds of monkey (gorillas, chimpanzees, orangutans, and gibbons) that do not have a tail

ape VERB **apes, aping, aped** imitate or mimic

aperture NOUN **apertures** an opening

apex (ay- peks) NOUN **apexes** the tip or highest point

aplomb (a- plom) NOUN dignity and confidence • *She handled the press conference with aplomb.*

apologetic ADJECTIVE making an apology
▷ **apologetically** ADVERB

apologize VERB **apologizes, apologizing, apologized** make an apology

apology NOUN **apologies 1** a statement saying that you are sorry for having done something wrong or badly **2** something very poor • *this feeble apology for a meal*

Thesaurus

anxiety NOUN **1** *anxiety about money*
► concern, apprehension, unease, worry, disquiet, foreboding, nervousness, tension, distress, doubt, dread, fear, fretfulness, misgiving, qualm, scruple, strain, stress, uncertainty AN OPPOSITE IS calmness **2** *She showed a strong anxiety to please.* ► eagerness, enthusiasm, desire, keenness, impatience, willingness OPPOSITES ARE reluctance, unwillingness

anxious ADJECTIVE **1** *Anxious relatives were waiting for further news. Everyone is anxious about the next few weeks.* ► worried, concerned, nervous, apprehensive, fearful, uneasy, troubled, distressed, agitated, tense, restless AN OPPOSITE IS calm **2** *She always seems anxious to please.* ► eager, keen, enthusiastic, willing, impatient
be anxious *He was anxious about his work.*
► worry, fret

apart ADVERB *Their parents are now living apart.*
► separately, independently, on one's own
apart from *Everyone came apart from him.*
► except (for), but for, aside from, besides, excepting, excluding

apathetic ADJECTIVE *They seem apathetic about the whole idea.* ► uninterested (in), indifferent

(to), unconcerned, unenthusiastic, uncommitted, unfeeling, uninvolved, unmotivated (by) OPPOSITES ARE enthusiastic, eager, keen (on)

apathy NOUN *At the general election the voters showed more than usual apathy.* ► indifference, coolness, lack of interest, unconcern, lassitude, lethargy, listlessness, passivity, inertia, inactivity AN OPPOSITE IS enthusiasm

aperture NOUN *There was a strange windowlike aperture in one wall.* ► opening, hole, gap, slit, vent, fissure, (*technical*) orifice

apologetic ADJECTIVE *They don't sound very apologetic considering it was their fault.*
► regretful, repentant, sorry, contrite, penitent, remorseful, rueful OPPOSITES ARE unrepentant, defiant

apologize VERB *He apologized for his mistake.*
► say sorry, express regret, ask for forgiveness, be penitent, make an apology, repent

apology NOUN *We all owe you an apology.*
► expression of regret, acknowledgment, confession, explanation, justification, defence, excuse, plea

apoplexy (ap- op- lek- see) NOUN **1** (old use) sudden loss of the ability to feel and move, caused by the blocking or breaking of a blood vessel in the brain **2** (informal) rage or anger
▷ **apoplectic** ADJECTIVE

Apostle NOUN **Apostles** any of the twelve men sent out by Christ to preach the Gospel

apostrophe (a- poss- trof- ee) NOUN **apostrophes** the punctuation mark ' used to show that letters have been omitted (as in I can't = I cannot) or to show possession (as in the boy's book; the boys' books)

appalling ADJECTIVE shocking; very unpleasant

apparatus NOUN the equipment for a particular experiment or job, etc.

apparent ADJECTIVE **1** clear or obvious • His embarrassment was apparent to everyone. **2** seeming; appearing to be true but not really so • I could not understand her apparent indifference.
▷ **apparently** ADVERB

apparition NOUN **apparitions 1** a ghost **2** something strange or surprising that appears

appeal VERB **appeals, appealing, appealed 1** ask for something earnestly or formally • They appealed for funds. **2** ask for a decision to be changed • He appealed against the prison sentence. **3** seem attractive or interesting • Baseball doesn't appeal to me.

appeal NOUN **appeals 1** asking for something you badly need **2** asking for a decision to be changed **3** attraction or interest

appear VERB **appears, appearing, appeared 1** come into sight **2** seem **3** take part in a play, film, or show, etc.

appearance NOUN **appearances 1** appearing **2** what somebody looks like; what something appears to be

appease VERB **appeases, appeasing, appeased** calm or pacify someone, especially by giving in to demands
▷ **appeasement** NOUN

Thesaurus

appal VERB The level of violence appals most people. ► horrify, shock, alarm, outrage, dismay, scandalize, repel, offend, disgust, sicken, revolt

appalling ADJECTIVE **1** Their attitude was appalling in its callousness. ► horrifying, horrific, shocking, outrageous, revolting, repellent, repulsive, terrifying, terrible, dreadful, awful, unnerving, sickening, nauseating, horrible **2** an appalling piece of work ► dreadful, awful, terrible, atrocious, abysmal

apparatus NOUN **1** an apparatus for processing seawater ► device, appliance, gadget, instrument, machine, mechanism, system, tool, (usually disapproving) contraption, (more informal) setup **2** Laboratory apparatus can be extremely expensive. ► equipment, implements, materials, machinery, (more informal) tackle, (more informal) gear

apparent ADJECTIVE There was no apparent motive for the crime. A sense of relief was all too apparent. ► evident, discernible, ostensible, perceptible, recognizable, noticeable, observable, obvious, clear, manifest, conspicuous, detectable, overt, patent, visible, self-explanatory OPPOSITES ARE obscure, hidden, concealed

apparently ADVERB Apparently satisfied, the man leaned back. ► seemingly, evidently, ostensibly

appeal NOUN **1** The radio station broadcast an appeal for calm. ► call, request, cry, entreaty, petition, supplication, prayer **2** Packaging is an important part of a product's appeal. ► attraction, attractiveness, charm, allure, charisma, seductiveness, (more informal) pull

appeal VERB **1** appeal for Detectives are appealing for information about the incident. ► call for, cry out for, beg for, plead for, ask earnestly for, request, solicit **2** appeal to Hoskins said that at first the film role didn't appeal to him. ► attract, interest, please, entice, tempt

appealing ADJECTIVE The prospect of a whole day with Jemima was rather appealing. ► attractive, agreeable, engaging, captivating, charming, delightful, lovely, enchanting OPPOSITES ARE unappealing, disagreeable

appear VERB **1** A large building appeared in the distance. ► come into view, come into sight, be seen, arise, loom up OPPOSITES ARE disappear, vanish **2** By lunch time the twins still hadn't appeared. ► arrive, come, make an appearance, put in an appearance, (more informal) show your face, (more informal) show up, (more informal) turn up **3** A few problems have appeared since we last met. ► emerge, arise, develop, come to light, materialize, occur, (more informal) crop up, (more informal) turn up **4** The road did not appear to lead anywhere. ► seem, look, turn out **5** Jake's sister was appearing in the school play for the first time. ► perform, take part, act

appearance NOUN **1** His scruffy appearance took us by surprise. ► look, looks, aspect, bearing, demeanor, impression **2** an appearance of friendliness ► semblance, air, pretence, illusion, facade, guise, veneer

a
b
c
d
e
f
g
h
i
j
k
l
m
n
o
p
q
r
s
t
u
v
w
x
y
z

appendage ➡ appointment

appendage NOUN appendages something added or attached; a thing that forms a natural part of something larger

appendicitis NOUN inflammation of the appendix

appendix NOUN 1 appendixes a small tube leading off from the intestine 2 appendices a section added at the end of a book

appetite NOUN appetites 1 desire for food 2 an enthusiasm for something • *an appetite for violent films*

appetizing ADJECTIVE (said about food) looking and smelling good to eat

applaud VERB applauds, applauding, applauded show that you like something, especially by clapping your hands

applause NOUN clapping

apple NOUN apples a round fruit with a red, yellow, or green skin

appliance NOUN appliances a device or piece of equipment • *electrical appliances*

applicable (ap- lik- a- bul) ADJECTIVE able to be applied; suitable or relevant

applicant NOUN applicants a person who applies for a job or position

application NOUN applications 1 the action of applying 2 a formal request 3 the ability to apply yourself 4 (in computing) a program or piece of software designed for a particular purpose

applied ADJECTIVE put to practical use • *applied maths*

apply VERB applies, applying, applied 1 put one thing on another 2 start using something 3 concern; be relevant • *This rule does not apply to you.* 4 make a formal request • *apply for a job*
apply yourself give all your attention to a job; work diligently

appoint VERB appoints, appointing, appointed 1 choose a person for a job 2 arrange something officially • *They appointed a time for the meeting.*

appointment NOUN appointments 1 an arrangement to meet or visit somebody at a particular time 2 choosing somebody for a job 3 a job or position

Thesaurus

appetite NOUN 1 *A long walk will sharpen our appetites.* ► hunger, need for food, taste buds 2 *Her appetite for information was phenomenal.* ► craving, longing, yearning, eagerness, hankering (after), desire, passion, thirst, relish, zest, demand

appetizing ADJECTIVE *The woman brought in a large appetizing meal.* ► tasty, delicious, inviting, palatable, (more informal) mouth-watering

applaud VERB 1 *The audience applauded loudly.* ► clap, cheer, give an ovation, acclaim, show your approval, (more informal) bring the house down OPPOSITES ARE boo, hiss 2 *They were watching and applauding the youngsters' efforts.* ► acclaim, commend, praise, salute, congratulate, compliment, eulogize, extol, (more formal) laud AN OPPOSITE IS criticize

applause NOUN 1 *There was a great round of applause when the dance ended.* ► clapping, cheering, acclamation, (an) ovation, plaudits, approval 2 *The author wins universal applause from his followers.* ► praise, acclaim, approval, acclamation, plaudits, accolades, admiration

appliance NOUN 1 *There's no reason why you shouldn't use individual heating appliances.* ► device, apparatus, gadget, instrument, machine, mechanism, system, tool, (usually disapproving) contraption, (more informal) setup

applicant NOUN *The best applicant was a female graduate with fresh ideas.* ► candidate, contender, interviewee, competitor, entrant, participant, aspirant

application NOUN 1 *an application for a grant* ► request, appeal, claim 2 *the application of new solutions to old problems* ► implementation, employment, use, exercise

apply VERB 1 *Apply antiseptic cream to the cut.* ► administer, bring into contact, lay on, put on, spread 2 *Contestants will need to apply all their skill and experience.* ► employ, exercise, use, utilize, bring into use, implement, practise 3 **apply for** *More than a hundred people have applied for the job.* ► put in an application for, seek, request, (more informal) put in for 4 **apply to** *The rules only apply to England and Wales.* ► be relevant to, pertain to, refer to, relate to, appertain to, concern, affect, involve
apply yourself ► concentrate, exert yourself, be diligent, be assiduous, be industrious, work hard, make an effort, persevere, (more informal) buckle down

appoint VERB *Amanda had been appointed store manager.* ► name, nominate, designate, choose (to be), engage (as), take on (as), install (as)

appointment NOUN 1 *June had to rush to keep her five o'clock appointment.* ► engagement, assignation, arrangement, consultation, session, date, fixture, meeting, rendezvous, (in poetry) tryst 2 *the appointment of new members of staff* ► nomination, selection, choice, choosing, commissioning, election, naming 3 *Frank held an appointment at the University.* ► position, post, job, situation, office, place

apposition NOUN placing things together, especially nouns and phrases in a grammatical relationship. In "the reign of Elizabeth, the Queen," *the Queen* is in apposition to *Elizabeth*.

appreciable ADJECTIVE enough to be noticed or felt; perceptible
▷ **appreciably** ADVERB

appreciate VERB appreciates, appreciating, appreciated **1** enjoy or value something **2** understand **3** increase in value
▷ **appreciation** NOUN **appreciative** ADJECTIVE

apprehend VERB apprehends, apprehending, apprehended **1** seize or arrest someone **2** understand

apprehension NOUN **1** fear or worry **2** understanding **3** the arrest of a person

apprehensive ADJECTIVE anxious or worried

apprentice NOUN apprentices a person who is learning a trade or craft by a legal agreement with an employer
▷ **apprenticeship** NOUN

apprentice VERB apprentices, apprenticing, apprenticed place a person as an apprentice

approach VERB approaches, approaching, approached **1** come near **2** go to someone with a request or offer • *They approached me for help.* **3** set about doing something or tackling a problem

approach NOUN approaches **1** approaching **2** a way or road

appropriate (a- proh- pree- at) ADJECTIVE suitable
▷ **appropriately** ADVERB

appropriate (a- proh- pree- ayt) VERB appropriates, appropriating, appropriated take something and use it as your own
▷ **appropriation** NOUN

Thesaurus

appraisal NOUN *The article is an honest appraisal of the problems.* ► assessment, evaluation, estimation, valuation, review, rating, consideration, appreciation

appraise VERB *They stood back to appraise the work they had done.* ► assess, evaluate, estimate, review, consider, (*more informal*) size up

appreciable ADJECTIVE *an appreciable sum of money* ► considerable, substantial, significant, sizable, large, (*more informal*) tidy

appreciate VERB **1** *I'd appreciate any help you can give me.* ► be grateful for, value, welcome, prize, regard highly, esteem OPPOSITES ARE think little of, despise, disparage **2** *We appreciate good music.* ► enjoy, value, cherish, respect, treasure, like, think highly of OPPOSITES ARE despise, dislike **3** *I appreciate that you cannot stay long.* ► recognize, realize, understand, acknowledge, comprehend, know, apprehend, see OPPOSITES ARE be unaware of, disregard **4** *Most properties in the area have appreciated in value.* ► increase, gain, rise, go up, grow, improve, build up, escalate, mount, soar, strengthen OPPOSITES ARE depreciate, decrease, fall, go down, weaken

appreciation NOUN **1** *They showed their appreciation by taking us out to dinner.* ► gratitude, indebtedness, thanks, obligation, thankfulness **2** *an appreciation of good literature* ► enjoyment, understanding

apprehensive ADJECTIVE *Polly was apprehensive about going back up on deck.* ► anxious, worried, concerned, nervous, fearful, uneasy, troubled, distressed, agitated, tense, restless

approach NOUN **1** *Flowers in the park announced the approach of spring.* ► arrival, coming, advance, appearance, nearing, imminence, advent OPPOSITES ARE retreat, departure

2 *The most beautiful approach to the city is from the south.* ► access, passage, road, way in, entry, entrance, drive **3** *His approach was to try out new ideas on other people.* ► method, procedure, technique, way, system, course, manner, means, style, mode **4** *We need an international approach to problems such as global warming.* ► attitude, perspective, policy (for, regarding), outlook (on), point of view (on), viewpoint (on) **5** *I made an informal approach to the bank manager.* ► appeal, application, invitation, offer, overture, proposal, proposition

approach VERB **1** *A grinning dark-haired youth approached them, holding out his hand.* ► move toward, proceed toward, come toward, go toward, come near, draw near, advance on, bear down on, near **2** *The committee approached its task with determination.* ► set about, tackle, embark on, make a start on, begin, undertake, get down to **3** *Should we approach the bank manager about a loan?* ► contact , speak to, sound out, appeal to **4** *The likely cost was now approaching several millions.* ► border on, get near, get close to, verge on, approximate, (*more informal*) get on for

approachable ADJECTIVE *She looked younger and more approachable.* ► friendly, welcoming, well-disposed, congenial, cordial, agreeable, pleasant, obliging, communicative, accessible, affable, informal, kind, open, sociable, sympathetic, (*more informal*) unstuffy OPPOSITES ARE aloof, formal

appropriate ADJECTIVE **1** *This isn't an appropriate time to ask questions.* ► suitable, fitting, proper, apt **2** *The form should be completed with any appropriate comments.* ► relevant, apposite, pertinent, applicable, germane OPPOSITES ARE inappropriate, irrelevant

A

B
C
D
E
F
G
H
I
J
K
L
M
N
O
P
Q
R
S
T
U
V
W
X
Y
Z

approval NOUN approving somebody or something
on approval received by a customer to examine before deciding to buy

approve VERB approves, approving, approved
1 say or think that a person or thing is good or suitable **2** agree formally to something • *The committee has approved the expenditure.*

approximate (a- proks- im- at) ADJECTIVE almost exact or correct but not completely so
▷ **approximately** ADVERB

approximate (a- proks- im- ayt) VERB approximates, approximating, approximated make or be almost the same as something

apricot NOUN apricots a juicy orange-colored fruit with a pit in it [from Spanish or Portuguese]

April NOUN the fourth month of the year [from Latin *Aprilis*]

apron NOUN aprons **1** a piece of clothing worn over the front of the body, especially to protect other clothes **2** a hard-surfaced area on an airfield where aircraft are loaded and unloaded

apt ADJECTIVE **1** likely • *He is apt to be careless.* **2** suitable • *an apt quotation*
▷ **aptly** ADVERB **aptness** NOUN

aptitude NOUN a talent or skill • *an aptitude for languages*

aquarium NOUN aquariums a tank or building in which live fish and other water animals are displayed

aquatic ADJECTIVE to do with water • *aquatic sports*

aqueduct NOUN aqueducts a bridge carrying a water channel across low ground or a valley

Arab NOUN Arabs a member of a Semitic people living in parts of the Middle East and North Africa
▷ **Arabian** ADJECTIVE

Arabic ADJECTIVE to do with the Arabs or their language

Arabic NOUN the language of the Arabs

arabic numerals PLURAL NOUN the symbols 1, 2, 3, 4, etc. COMPARE **Roman numerals**

arable ADJECTIVE suitable for plowing or growing crops on • *arable land*

arbitrary (ar- bit- rer- ee) ADJECTIVE chosen or done on an impulse, not according to a rule or law • *an arbitrary decision.*
▷ **arbitrarily** ADVERB

arbitration NOUN settling a dispute by calling in someone from outside to make a decision
▷ **arbitrate** VERB **arbitrator** NOUN

Thesaurus

approval NOUN **1** *Jane looked at them with approval.* ► favor, approbation, admiration, support, appreciation, commendation, acclaim, acclamation, applause, respect, regard, esteem, liking OPPOSITES ARE disapproval, disfavor **2** *Congress had given final approval to the bill in October.* ► consent, assent, support, agreement, endorsement, acceptance, authorization, acquiescence, (*more informal*) blessing, (*more informal*) (the) go-ahead, (*more informal*) (the) green light, (*more informal*) OK, (*more informal*) thumbs up OPPOSITES ARE refusal, veto

approve VERB **1** *Some members are thought to have approved the plan.* ► support, accept, agree to, assent to, consent to, acquiesce in, accede to, endorse, back, subscribe to, authorize OPPOSITES ARE refuse, veto
2 approve of *Some parents and teachers still do not approve of the use of calculators.* ► welcome, favor, endorse, advocate, support, hold with, countenance, tolerate, recommend, (*more informal*) go along with OPPOSITES ARE disapprove of, condemn, reject

approximate ADJECTIVE *All measurements are approximate.* ► rough, estimated, close, inexact, near AN OPPOSITE IS exact

approximately ADVERB *Homework should last approximately an hour.* ► roughly, about, round about, around, more or less, nearly, in the region of, in the order of, approaching,
(*more informal*) something like, (*more informal*) ... or so, (*more informal*) ... or thereabouts, (*much more informal*) pushing

apt ADJECTIVE **1** *He tried to think of an apt reply.* ► appropriate , suitable, fitting, proper **2** *The old man is apt to fall asleep in the evening.* ► inclined, liable, prone, likely

aptitude NOUN *an aptitude for dancing* ► talent, gift, flair, ability, genius, faculty, capacity

arbitrary ADJECTIVE **1** *Decisions can appear arbitrary without all the information.* ► random, irrational, indiscriminate, capricious, unreasonable, unpredictable, whimsical, wilful, casual, chance, fanciful, illogical, subjective OPPOSITES ARE methodical, rational **2** *the exercise of arbitrary power* ► autocratic, despotic, dictatorial, absolute, unrestrained, high-handed, oppressive, repressive, imperious, summary, tyrannical, tyrannous

arbitrate VERB *The ambassador offered to arbitrate in the dispute.* ► adjudicate, judge, intercede, mediate, negotiate, pass judgment, referee, umpire, settle, make peace, decide the outcome

arbitration NOUN *The county court will automatically refer the matter to arbitration.* ► mediation, negotiation, conciliation, adjudication, judgment, settlement

arbor (ar- ber) NOUN **arbors** a shady place among trees

arc NOUN **arcs** 1 a curve; part of the circumference of a circle 2 a luminous electric current passing between two electrodes

arcade NOUN **arcades** a covered passage or area, especially for shopping

arch[1] NOUN **arches** 1 a curved structure that helps to support a bridge or other building etc. 2 something shaped like this

arch VERB **arches, arching, arched** form something into an arch; curve • *The cat arched its back and hissed.*

arch[2] ADJECTIVE pretending to be playful; mischievous • *an arch smile*
 ▷ **archly** ADVERB

archaeology (ar- kee- al- oj- ee) NOUN the study of ancient civilizations by digging for the remains of their buildings, tools, coins, etc., and examining them
 ▷ **archaeological** ADJECTIVE **archaeologist** NOUN

archaic (ar- kay- ik) ADJECTIVE belonging to former or ancient times

archangel NOUN **archangels** an angel of the highest rank

archbishop NOUN **archbishops** the chief bishop of a region

arch-enemy NOUN **arch-enemies** the chief enemy

archer NOUN **archers** a person who shoots with a bow and arrows

archery NOUN the sport of shooting at a target with a bow and arrows

archetype (ark- i- typ) NOUN **archetypes** the original form or model from which others are copied

archipelago (ark- i- pel- ag- oh) NOUN **archipelagos** a large group of islands, or the sea containing these

architect (ark- i- tekt) NOUN **architects** a person who designs buildings [from Greek *arch-* = chief + Greek *tekton* = builder]

architecture NOUN 1 the process of designing buildings 2 a particular style of building
 • *Elizabethan architecture*
 ▷ **architectural** ADJECTIVE

archives (ark- I'vz) PLURAL NOUN the historical documents, etc., of an organization or community

archway NOUN **archways** an arched passage or entrance

arc lamp or **arc light** NOUN **arc lamps** or **arc lights** a light using an electric arc

arctic ADJECTIVE very cold • *The weather was arctic.*

ardor (ar- der) NOUN enthusiasm or passion

arduous ADJECTIVE needing much effort; laborious
 ▷ **arduously** ADVERB

area NOUN **areas** 1 the measurement of a surface, or the amount of space a surface covers • *The area of the room is 150 square feet.* 2 a particular region or piece of land 3 a subject or activity

arena (a- reen- a) NOUN **arenas** the level area in the center of an amphitheatre or sports stadium [from Latin, = sand: the floors of Roman arenas were covered with sand to soak up the blood that was spilled in fighting between gladiators]

aren't (*mainly spoken*) are not
aren't I? (*informal*) am I not?

arguable ADJECTIVE possible but not certain
 ▷ **arguably** ADVERB

argue VERB **argues, arguing, argued** 1 say that you disagree; exchange angry comments 2 state that something is true and give reasons

---

Thesaurus

---

archaic ADJECTIVE 1 *archaic Greek sculpture*
 ▶ ancient, old, primitive 2 *He arrived in a top hat and coat, already a somewhat archaic form of fashion.* ▶ old-fashioned, antiquated, outmoded, obsolete

architect NOUN *Ictinus, architect of the Parthenon*
 ▶ builder, master builder, designer, planner

ardent ADJECTIVE *ardent admirers of good music*
 ▶ passionate, avid, fervent, zealous, eager, keen, enthusiastic

arduous ADJECTIVE *an arduous journey over the hills* ▶ exhausting, tiring, punishing, onerous, demanding, daunting, rigorous, tough
OPPOSITES ARE easy, effortless

area NOUN 1 *They came to an open area of land.*
 ▶ expanse, extent, stretch, patch, tract, sector, sheet, space, surface, width, breadth 2 *More*

money is needed for deprived urban areas.
 ▶ district, region, sector, locality, neighborhood, precinct, vicinity, zone, environment, environs, province, territory 3 *an area of study* ▶ field, domain, sphere, subject

arguable ADJECTIVE *It is arguable that the official figures exaggerate the unemployment problem.*
 ▶ possible, conceivable, tenable, credible, defensible

argue VERB 1 *The children do seem to argue a lot.*
 ▶ quarrel, squabble, wrangle, bicker, 2 *The group argued late into the night.* ▶ deliberate, discuss, debate, dispute 3 *Some people argue that all ownership is theft.* ▶ contend, maintain, postulate, assert, claim, submit, suggest, reason, insist, show, demonstrate, prove

argument NOUN arguments **1** a disagreement or quarrel **2** a reason or series of reasons put forward

argumentative ADJECTIVE fond of arguing

aria (ar- ee- a) NOUN arias a solo in an opera or oratorio

arid ADJECTIVE dry and barren

arise VERB arises, arising, arose, arisen **1** come into existence; come to people's notice
• *Problems arose.* **2** (old use) rise; stand up
• *Arise, Sir Francis.*

aristocracy (a- ris- tok- ra- see) NOUN people of the highest social rank; members of the nobility

aristocrat (a- ris- tok- rat) NOUN aristocrats a member of the aristocracy
▷ **aristocratic** ADJECTIVE

arithmetic NOUN the science or study of numbers; calculating with numbers
▷ **arithmetical** ADJECTIVE

ark NOUN arks **1** (in the Bible) the ship in which Noah and his family escaped the Flood **2** a wooden box in which the writings of the Jewish Law were kept

arm NOUN arms **1** either of the two upper limbs of the body, between the shoulder and the hand **2** a sleeve **3** something shaped like an arm or jutting out from a main part **4** the raised side part of a chair
▷ **armful** NOUN

arm VERB arms, arming, armed **1** supply someone with weapons **2** prepare for war

armada (ar- mah- da) NOUN armadas a fleet of warships
the Armada or Spanish Armada the warships sent by Spain to invade England in 1588

armadillo NOUN armadillos a small burrowing South American animal whose body is covered with a shell of bony plates

armature NOUN armatures the current-carrying part of a dynamo or electric motor

armchair NOUN armchairs a chair with arms

armed forces or **armed services** PLURAL NOUN a country's army, navy, and air force

armistice NOUN armistices an agreement to stop fighting in a war or battle

armor NOUN **1** a protective covering for the body, formerly worn in fighting **2** a metal covering on a warship, tank, or car to protect it from missiles
▷ **armored** ADJECTIVE

armpit NOUN armpits the hollow underneath the top of the arm, below the shoulder

arms PLURAL NOUN **1** weapons **2** a coat of arms
up in arms protesting vigorously

arms race NOUN competition between nations in building up supplies of weapons, especially nuclear weapons

army NOUN armies **1** a large number of people trained to fight on land **2** a large group

aroma (a- roh- ma) NOUN aromas a smell, especially a pleasant one
▷ **aromatic** (a- ro- mat- ik) ADJECTIVE

around ADVERB, PREPOSITION all around; about

Thesaurus

argument NOUN **1** *A fierce argument followed.*
► quarrel, disagreement, squabble, wrangle, altercation, difference, dispute, dissension, clash, controversy, feud, fight, remonstration, expostulation **2** *a long argument about politics*
► discussion, debate, consultation, deliberation **3** *No convincing argument has been offered.*
► case, line of reasoning, demonstration, hypothesis, defense, gist, idea, summary, synopsis, view **4** *the principal argument of the book* ► thesis, contention, theme, topic, plot

argumentative ADJECTIVE *He could be difficult and argumentative at times.* ► quarrelsome, combative, contentious, disputatious, truculent, aggressive

arid ADJECTIVE *an arid landscape* ► barren, parched, desert, dry, waste, waterless, infertile, lifeless, sterile, torrid, unproductive OPPOSITES ARE fertile, lush

arise VERB **1** *If any problems arise go and see your doctor.* ► emerge, develop, appear, come to light, materialize, occur, (more informal) crop up, (more informal) turn up **2** *The*

misunderstanding arose from poor communications.* ► result, originate, stem, derive, spring, follow, ensue, proceed

aristocrat NOUN *an aristocrat from an old family*
► noble, nobleman, noblewoman, lord, lady, peer, peeress, patrician, grandee, titled person, (more informal) toff, (more informal) nob

aristocratic ADJECTIVE *a member of an aristocratic family* ► noble, upper-class, high-born, titled, patrician, blue-blooded, lordly, princely, royal, courtly, élite, thoroughbred

arm VERB *The woman had gone downstairs, armed with an empty bottle.* ► equip, provide, protect, supply, fortify, furnish

army NOUN **1** *The king raised an army of ten thousand foot soldiers.* ► armed force, fighting force, force, militia, horde RELATED ADJECTIVE
► military **2** *an army of tourists* ► crowd, swarm, throng, horde, stream, mass, herd, host, multitude

aroma NOUN *an aroma of fresh coffee* ► smell, fragrance, odor, bouquet, perfume, scent, whiff

arouse VERB arouses, arousing, aroused **1** stir up a feeling in someone ● *You've aroused my curiosity.* **2** wake someone up

arpeggio (ar- pej- ee- oh) NOUN arpeggios the notes of a musical chord played one after the other instead of together

arrange VERB arranges, arranging, arranged **1** put things into a certain order; adjust **2** form plans for something ● *We arranged to be there.* **3** prepare music for a particular purpose
▷ arrangement NOUN

array NOUN arrays **1** a display **2** an orderly arrangement

arrears PLURAL NOUN **1** money that is owing and ought to have been paid earlier **2** a backlog of work, etc.
in arrears behind with payments

arrest VERB arrests, arresting, arrested **1** seize a person by authority of the law **2** stop a process or movement

arrest NOUN arrests **1** arresting somebody ● *The police made several arrests.* **2** stopping something

arrive VERB arrives, arriving, arrived **1** reach the end of a journey or a point on it **2** come ● *The great day arrived.*
▷ arrival NOUN

arrogant ADJECTIVE behaving in an unpleasantly proud way because you think you are superior to other people
▷ arrogantly ADVERB arrogance NOUN

arrow NOUN arrows **1** a pointed stick to be shot from a bow **2** a sign with an outward-pointing V at the end, used to show direction or position
▷ arrowhead NOUN
[from Old Norse]

arsenic NOUN a very poisonous metallic substance

arson NOUN the crime of deliberately setting fire to a house or building
▷ arsonist NOUN

Thesaurus

arouse VERB *The proposals aroused strong public hostility.* ► rouse, cause, kindle, prompt, provoke, instigate, spark, stimulate, stir up, (*more informal*) whip up AN OPPOSITE IS allay

arrange VERB **1** *It was time to arrange the seating for dinner.* ► organize, set out, lay out, sort out, put in order, plan, fix, order, spread out, dispose **2** *We hope to arrange an outing for next week.* ► organize, fix, fix up, plan, set up, make arrangements for, devise, schedule, contrive, coordinate, manage, prepare, see to, settle **3** *Ravel arranged the music for an orchestra.* ► adapt, score, set, harmonize, orchestrate

arrangement NOUN **1** *They've changed the arrangement of the furniture.* ► positioning, layout, placing, planning, spacing, disposition, distribution, organization, setting out, alignment, display, grouping, design **2** *an arrangement to share the costs* ► agreement, understanding, settlement, compact, contract, deal, pact, scheme, terms **3** *a musical arrangement* ► adaptation, setting, harmonization, orchestration, version

array NOUN *a gleaming array of vintage cars* ► arrangement, display, presentation, show, exhibition, parade, collection, muster, (*more informal*) line-up

arrest VERB **1** *Police arrested him for shoplifting.* ► apprehend, detain, take into custody, take in, (*more informal*) book, (*more informal*) pull in, (*more informal*) pick up, (*more informal*) nab

2 *Recent measures have arrested the spread of disease.* ► check, stop, end, halt, prevent, retard, slow, stem, impede, slow down, block, inhibit, interrupt, delay, hinder, obstruct

arrival NOUN **1** *A crowd awaited the president's arrival.* ► coming, appearance, approach, entrance, homecoming, landing, return, touchdown **2** *Pretty girls greeted the new arrivals.* ► comer, caller, newcomer, visitor

arrive VERB **1** *Guests started to arrive at around six o'clock.* ► come, come along, appear, enter, present yourself, (*more informal*) turn up, (*more informal*) roll up, (*more informal*) show up **2** (*informal*) *When they got the invitation they knew they had arrived.* ► succeed, be successful, reach the top, break through, (*more informal*) make it **3** arrive at *We arrived at the bus station.* ► reach, come to, get to, (*more informal*) make

arrogance NOUN *His arrogance took her breath away.* ► haughtiness, conceit, self-importance, high-handedness, condescension, disdain, insolence

arrogant ADJECTIVE *He was proud and had an arrogant manner.* ► haughty, conceited, self-important, high-handed, lordly, overbearing, boastful, scornful, condescending, supercilious, superior, bumptious, disdainful, cavalier, imperious, insolent, pompous, presumptuous, proud, snobbish, vain, (*more informal*) cocky, (*more informal*) high and mighty, (*more informal*) stuck-up AN OPPOSITE IS modest

a
b
c
d
e
f
g
h
i
j
k
l
m
n
o
p
q
r
s
t
u
v
w
x
y
z

A
B
C
D
E
F
G
H
I
J
K
L
M
N
O
P
Q
R
S
T
U
V
W
X
Y
Z

art NOUN arts **1** producing something beautiful, especially by painting or drawing; things produced in this way • *the art of sailing*

artery NOUN arteries **1** one of the tubes that carry blood away from the heart to all parts of the body COMPARE vein **2** an important road or route
▷ **arterial** (ar- **teer**- ee- al) ADJECTIVE

artesian well NOUN artesian wells a well that is bored straight down into a place where water will rise easily to the surface

artful ADJECTIVE crafty
▷ **artfully** ADVERB

arthritis (arth- ry- tiss) NOUN a disease that makes joints in the body stiff and painful
▷ **arthritic** (arth- **rit**- ik) ADJECTIVE

arthropod NOUN arthropods an animal of the group that includes insects, spiders, crabs, and centipedes

artichoke NOUN artichokes a kind of plant with a flower head used as a vegetable [from Arabic]

article NOUN articles **1** a piece of writing published in a newspaper or magazine **2** an object
definite article the word "the"
indefinite article the word "a" or "an"

articulate (ar- tik- yoo- lat) ADJECTIVE able to express things clearly and fluently

articulate (ar- tik- yoo- layt) VERB articulates, articulating, articulated **1** say or speak clearly **2** connect by a joint
▷ **articulation** NOUN

articulated ADJECTIVE (said about a vehicle) in two sections that are connected by a flexible joint • *an articulated bus*

artifact NOUN artifacts an object made by humans, especially one from the past that is studied by archaeologists

artificial ADJECTIVE not natural; made by human beings in imitation of a natural thing
▷ **artificially** ADVERB **artificiality** NOUN

artificial intelligence NOUN the use of computers to perform tasks normally requiring human intelligence, e.g. decision-making

artificial respiration NOUN helping somebody to start breathing again after their breathing has stopped

artillery NOUN **1** large guns **2** the part of the army that uses large guns

artist NOUN artists **1** a person who produces works of art, especially a painter **2** an entertainer
▷ **artistry** NOUN

artistic ADJECTIVE **1** to do with art or artists **2** having a talent for art
▷ **artistically** ADVERB

arts PLURAL NOUN subjects (e.g. languages, literature, or history) in which opinion and understanding are very important, as opposed to sciences where measurements and calculations are used
the arts painting, music, and writing etc., considered together

as ADVERB equally or similarly • *This is just as easy.*

as PREPOSITION in the function or role of • *Use it as a handle.*

as CONJUNCTION **1** when or while • *She slipped as she got off the bus.* **2** because • *As he was late, we missed the train.* **3** in a way that • *Leave it as it is.*
as for with regard to • *As for you, I despise you.*
as it were in a way • *She became, as it were, her own enemy.*
as well also

A/S ABBREVIATION advanced subsidiary level in GCSE

asbestos NOUN a fireproof material made up of fine soft fibres

ascend VERB ascends, ascending, ascended go up
ascend the throne become king or queen

Thesaurus

---

art NOUN **1** *She had taken an art course.* ► fine art, painting, sculpture, drawing, artistry, artwork, craft, craftsmanship, draftsmanship **2** *the art of writing* ► skill, craft, talent, technique, aptitude, gift, knack, expertise, facility, knack, proficiency, trick, cleverness, dexterity

article NOUN **1** *various household articles* ► object, item, thing, commodity, product, (in plural) goods **2** *I read an article on the subject.* ► essay, report, paper, study, feature, review, account, piece

artificial ADJECTIVE **1** *artificial light; artificial trees* ► synthetic, imitation, simulated, unnatural, manmade, manufactured, false, fake, substitute AN OPPOSITE IS natural **2** *an artificial smile* ► false, spurious, affected, fake,

feigned, assumed, pretended, bogus, contrived, counterfeit, factitious, pseudo, sham, simulated, unreal, (more informal) phoney, (more informal) put-on AN OPPOSITE IS genuine

artist NOUN **1** *The artist used a wide range of color.* ► painter, sculptor, craftsman, craftsperson, designer **2** *a music-hall artist* ► performer

artistic ADJECTIVE *Desktop publishing requires artistic skills. The designs looked very artistic.* ► creative, imaginative, aesthetic, decorative, ornamental, tasteful, stylish, elegant, beautiful, attractive, cultured OPPOSITES ARE crude, ugly

ascend VERB **1** *He ascended the stairs.* ► climb, climb up, go up, come up, mount, move up,

ascent NOUN ascents **1** ascending **2** a way up; an upward path or slope

ascertain (as- er- tayn) VERB ascertains, ascertaining, ascertained find something out by asking
▷ ascertainable ADJECTIVE

ascetic (a- set- ik) ADJECTIVE not allowing yourself pleasure and luxuries
▷ asceticism NOUN

ascribe VERB ascribes, ascribing, ascribed regard something as belonging to or caused by; attribute • *She ascribes her success to good luck.*

asexual ADJECTIVE (in biology) not involving sexual activity • *asexual reproduction*

ash[1] NOUN ashes the powder that is left after something has been burned
▷ ashy ADJECTIVE

ash[2] NOUN ashes a tree with silver-grey bark

ashamed ADJECTIVE feeling shame

Asian ADJECTIVE to do with Asia or its people

Asian NOUN Asians an Asian person

Asiatic ADJECTIVE to do with Asia

aside ADVERB **1** to or at one side • *pull it aside* **2** away; in reserve

aside NOUN asides words spoken so that only certain people will hear

ask VERB asks, asking, asked **1** speak so as to find out or get something **2** invite • *Ask her to the party.*

asleep ADVERB, ADJECTIVE sleeping

asparagus NOUN a plant whose young shoots are eaten as a vegetable

aspect NOUN aspects **1** one part of a problem or situation • *Violence was the worst aspect of the crime.* **2** a person's or thing's appearance • *The forest had a sinister aspect.* **3** the direction a house, etc., faces • *This room has a southern aspect.*

asphalt (ass- falt) NOUN a sticky black substance like tar, often mixed with gravel to surface roads, etc.

asphyxiate (ass- fiks- ee- ayt) VERB asphyxiates, asphyxiating, asphyxiated suffocate
▷ asphyxiation NOUN

aspidistra NOUN aspidistras a house plant with broad leaves

aspirate (asp- er- at) NOUN aspirates the sound of "h"

Thesaurus

scale **2** *The little plane began slowly to ascend.* ► rise, soar, take off, lift off, fly up **3** *An unmade road ascends to the church.* ► climb, slope up AN OPPOSITE IS descend

ascent NOUN *A gradual ascent made the walk more arduous.* ► rise, slope, gradient, hill, incline, climb, elevation, ramp AN OPPOSITE IS descent

ascertain VERB *The police had to ascertain whether Darren had actually entered the room.* ► find out, establish, confirm, determine, discover, learn, make certain, make sure, settle, verify, identify

ascribe VERB *The inquest ascribed his death to natural causes.* ► attribute, assign, put down, blame (on), connect (with), associate (with)

ashamed ADJECTIVE **1** *She was ashamed of her outburst of bad temper.* ► sorry (for), apologetic (about), remorseful (about), contrite (about), repentant (about), shamefaced (about), abashed (about), penitent (about), embarrassed (about), distressed (about), upset (about), conscience-stricken (about), discomfited (about), mortified (about), red-faced (about), chastened (about), rueful (about) OPPOSITES ARE unrepentant, unabashed **2** *He seemed too ashamed to admit his mistake.* ► reticent, reluctant, loath, unwilling, bashful, shy, diffident, hesitant,

embarrassed, modest, prudish, self-conscious, sheepish OPPOSITES ARE proud, shameless

ask VERB **1** *I'll ask him what he means.* ► inquire (of somebody), quiz (somebody about) **2** *They want to ask a few questions.* ► pose, put, raise, submit **3** *Ask them to get help.* ► entreat, request, implore, beg, solicit, exhort, urge, plead with, (*literary*) beseech, (*literary*) enjoin **4** *We could ask them to dinner.* ► invite, summon, (*more formal*) request the pleasure of the company of **5** *ask for Don't hesitate to ask for anything you need.* ► request, demand, seek **6** *ask for The remarks were asking for trouble.* ► look for, provoke, invite, attract, court, incite, tempt, cause, encourage, generate, (*more informal*) stir up

asleep ADJECTIVE *The girls were asleep in bed.* ► sleeping, slumbering, dozing, napping, (*more informal*) out like a light, (*more informal*) dead to the world

aspect NOUN **1** *The article describes every aspect of life in deprived areas.* ► feature, facet, characteristic, side, angle, respect, particular, circumstance, detail, standpoint **2** *Dark stone gave the facade a grim aspect.* ► appearance, look, air **3** *The house has a southern aspect.* ► outlook, view, prospect, exposure, orientation, direction, position, situation

aspiration NOUN aspirations ambition; strong desire

aspire VERB aspires, aspiring, aspired have an ambition to achieve something • *He aspired to be world champion.*

aspirin NOUN aspirins a medicinal drug used to relieve pain or reduce fever

ass NOUN asses **1** a donkey **2** (*informal*) a stupid person

assassin NOUN assassins a person who assassinates somebody [from Arabic *hashishi* = hashish-takers: the word was used as a name for a group of Muslims at the time of the Crusades, who were believed to use hashish before going out to kill Christian leaders]

assassinate VERB assassinates, assassinating, assassinated kill an important person deliberately and violently, especially for political reasons
▷ assassination NOUN

assault NOUN assaults a violent or illegal attack

assault VERB assaults, assaulting, assaulted make an assault on someone

assemble VERB assembles, assembling, assembled **1** bring or come together **2** fit or put together the parts of something
▷ assemblage NOUN

assembly NOUN assemblies **1** assembling **2** a regular meeting, such as when everybody in a school meets together **3** people who regularly meet for a special purpose; a legislature

assent VERB assents, assenting, assented consent; say you agree

assent NOUN consent or approval

assert VERB asserts, asserting, asserted state something firmly
▷ assertion NOUN
assert yourself use firmness or forcefulness

assertive ADJECTIVE acting forcefully and with confidence

Thesaurus

aspersions NOUN cast aspersions on *The remarks are not intended to cast any aspersions on your honesty.* ► criticize, disparage, denigrate, belittle, vilify, deprecate, decry, condemn, malign, discredit, stigmatize, denounce

aspire VERB aspire to *They aspired to be back in the city to which they belonged. We can aspire to a higher and fuller life.* ► aim to OR for, wish to OR for, want, yearn to OR for, strive (after), seek (to), long to OR for, desire to, crave to OR for, dream of, hope to OR for, pursue, set your sights on, have ambitions to OR for

aspiring ADJECTIVE *aspiring young writers* ► would-be, intending, aspirant, budding, hopeful, eager, potential

assault VERB *He was prosecuted for assaulting a police officer.* ► attack, hit, strike, set upon, beat up, fall on, molest, (*more informal*) rough up

assault NOUN *an assault on the enemy position* ► attack , onslaught, strike, offensive, raid, foray, sortie, charge

assemble VERB **1** *A crowd began to assemble.* ► gather, congregate, come together, collect, converge, convene, crowd together, rally, meet, flock together, join up, swarm, muster, accumulate **2** *We assembled our belongings in the hall. The general assembled his forces.* ► gather, collect together, bring together, amass, convene, get together, round up, marshal, mobilize, muster, pile up, rally OPPOSITES ARE disperse, scatter **3** *Few cars are now assembled in Britain.* ► build, construct, manufacture, produce, put together, erect, fabricate, fit together, make, piece together AN OPPOSITE IS dismantle

assembly NOUN **1** *a political assembly, an assembly of bishops* ► gathering, meeting, congress, convocation, assemblage, council, (church) synod **2** *An assembly of spectators waited at the gates.* ► crowd, gathering, throng, rally, meeting, (*literary*) multitude **3** *The special glue is used in the assembly of model aircraft.* ► construction, building, making, putting together, manufacture, erection (of buildings)

assent NOUN *Parents need to give their assent to attendance on field trips.* ► agreement, approval, consent, permission, authorization, blessing, (*more informal*) go-ahead AN OPPOSITE IS refusal

assert VERB **1** *She asserted that multinational companies should not be blamed for damage to the environment.* ► declare, maintain, contend, submit, insist, argue, proclaim, profess, claim, emphasize, affirm, allege, protest, state, stress **2** *It is not always easy for people to assert their rights.* ► insist on, claim, stand up for, make use of, uphold
assert yourself *Some of the newer committee members began to assert themselves at meetings.* ► be assertive, behave confidently, be resolute, make yourself felt, exert your influence, make demands, persist, stand firm, (*more informal*) stick to your guns

assertive ADJECTIVE *You will need to be assertive in this job.* ► forceful, determined, resolute, confident, decisive, firm, assured, self-assured, authoritative, strong-willed, bold, positive, aggressive, domineering, strong, (*usually disapproving*) pushy OPPOSITES ARE submissive, reticent, retiring

assess VERB assesses, assessing, assessed decide or estimate the value or quality of a person or thing
▷ **assessment** NOUN **assessor** NOUN

asset NOUN assets something useful

assets PLURAL NOUN a person's or company's property that could be sold to pay debts or raise money

assign VERB assigns, assigning, assigned **1** give or allot **2** appoint a person to perform a task

assignment NOUN assignments **1** assigning **2** something assigned; a task given to someone

assimilate VERB assimilates, assimilating, assimilated take in and absorb something, e.g., nourishment into the body or knowledge into the mind
▷ **assimilation** NOUN

assist VERB assists, assisting, assisted help
▷ **assistance** NOUN

assistant NOUN assistants **1** a person who assists another; a helper **2** a person who serves customers in a shop

assistant ADJECTIVE helping a person and ranking next below him or her • *the assistant manager*

associate VERB associates, associating, associated **1** connect things in your mind • *I don't associate Ryan with fitness and healthy living.* **2** spend time or have dealings with a group of people

associate NOUN associates a colleague or companion; a partner
▷ **associate** ADJECTIVE

association NOUN associations **1** an organization of people; a society **2** associating **3** a connection or link in your mind

assonance (ass- on- ans) NOUN similarity of vowel sounds, e.g., in *vermin* and *furnish*

assorted ADJECTIVE of various sorts put together; mixed • *assorted sweets*

assortment NOUN assortments a mixed collection of things

assume VERB assumes, assuming, assumed **1** accept (without proof or question) that something is true or sure to happen **2** take

Thesaurus

assess VERB **1** *The hospital used a scanner to assess the extent of their head injuries.*
► evaluate, gauge, judge, determine, review, reckon, estimate, appraise, calculate, figure out, value **2** *All pupils are assessed and graded at the end of their first term.* ► rate, judge, appraise, check, review

asset NOUN **1** *A good sense of humor can be an asset.* ► benefit, advantage, blessing, boon, strength, virtue, help, aid, support, good, (more informal) plus, (more informal) godsend **2** *assets The family's assets were estimated at over two million dollars.* ► capital, resources, possessions, reserves, property, estate, funds, goods, holdings, means, money, savings, securities, wealth, (more informal) worldly goods

assign VERB **1** *Tasks are assigned on the basis of experience.* ► allocate, distribute, allot, apportion, dispense, give out, hand over, share out **2** *Kathryn was told she would be assigned to the case.* ► appoint, consign, delegate, designate, nominate, put down, choose (for), select (for)

assignment NOUN **1** *I have a difficult assignment to finish.* ► task, piece of work, exercise, project, job, duty **2** *the assignment of responsibilities* ► allocation, issuing, granting

assist VERB *Could you assist us for a while?*
► help, aid, support, give a hand to, lend a (helping) hand to, oblige OPPOSITES ARE hinder, impede

assistance NOUN *They said they would not need any assistance.* ► help, support, aid,

encouragement, reinforcement, backing, collaboration, cooperation, contribution, patronage, sponsorship, subsidy AN OPPOSITE IS hindrance

assistant NOUN *The team leader has three assistants.* ► helper, subordinate, supporter, associate, deputy, colleague, underling, junior, ancillary, collaborator

associate VERB **1** *Stephen had been associating with dropouts and oddballs.* ► mix, keep company, go about, consort, socialize, fraternize, mingle AN OPPOSITE IS dissociate **2** *Patience was not a quality I associated at all with him.* ► connect, link, identify, equate, relate (to)

association NOUN **1** *They enjoyed several years of friendly association.* ► relationship, connection, link, bond, ties, friendship, attachment, union **2** *an association of sports clubs* ► organization, confederation, federation, coalition, society, league, partnership, alliance, syndicate, group

assorted ADJECTIVE *a collection of assorted objects*
► miscellaneous, mixed, different, sundry, varied, various, differing, diverse, diversified, heterogeneous, manifold, motley, multifarious, several

assortment NOUN *an assortment of dog-eared paperbacks* ► mixture, selection, collection, variety, array, miscellany, choice, diversity, medley, mélange

assume VERB **1** *I assumed the book was a gift.*
► presume, suppose, infer, deduce, take for granted, surmise, conjecture, reckon, imagine,

on; undertake • *She assumed the extra responsibility.* **3** put on • *He assumed an innocent expression.*
▷ **assumption** NOUN
assumed name a false name

assurance NOUN assurances **1** a promise or guarantee that something is true or will happen **2** a kind of life insurance **3** confidence in yourself

assure VERB assures, assuring, assured **1** tell somebody confidently; promise **2** make certain

asterisk NOUN asterisks a star-shaped sign * used to draw attention to something

asteroid NOUN asteroids one of the small planets found mainly between the orbits of Mars and Jupiter

asthma (az- ma) NOUN a disease that makes breathing difficult
▷ **asthmatic** ADJECTIVE, NOUN

astonish VERB astonishes, astonishing, astonished surprise somebody greatly
▷ **astonishment** NOUN

astound VERB astounds, astounding, astounded astonish; shock somebody greatly

astray ADVERB, ADJECTIVE away from the right path or place or course of action
go astray be lost or mislaid
lead astray make someone do something wrong

astride ADVERB, PREPOSITION with one leg on each side of something

astringent ADJECTIVE **1** causing skin or body tissue to contract **2** harsh or severe
• *astringent criticism*

astrology NOUN the study of how the stars and planets may influence people's lives
▷ **astrologer** NOUN **astrological** ADJECTIVE

astronaut NOUN astronauts a person who travels in a spacecraft
▷ **astronautics** NOUN

astronomical ADJECTIVE **1** to do with astronomy **2** extremely large • *The restaurant's prices are astronomical.*

astronomy NOUN the study of the stars and planets and their movements
▷ **astronomer** NOUN

astute ADJECTIVE clever and good at understanding situations quickly; shrewd
▷ **astutely** ADVERB **astuteness** NOUN

asylum NOUN asylums **1** refuge and safety offered by one country to political refugees from another **2** (*old use*) a hospital for mentally ill people

asymmetrical (ay- sim- et- rik- al) ADJECTIVE not symmetrical
▷ **asymmetrically** ADVERB

at PREPOSITION This word is used to show **1** position (*at the top*), **2** time (*at midnight*), **3** condition (*Stand at ease*), **4** direction towards something (*Aim at the target*), **5** level or price etc. (*Sell them at $1 each*), **6** cause (*We were annoyed at his failure*)
at all in any way
at it doing or working at something
at once 1 immediately **2** at the same time
• *It all came out at once.*

atheist (ayth- ee- ist) NOUN atheists a person who believes that there is no God
▷ **atheism** NOUN

Thesaurus

come to the conclusion, guess, suspect, believe, imagine, deduce, expect, think, understand, (*more informal*) have a hunch **2** *The children should be encouraged to assume responsibilities.* ► take on, undertake, accept, embrace **3** *To play the part she had to assume a Scottish accent.* ► adopt, put on, feign, acquire

assumption NOUN *The assumption is that prices will stay the same.* ► supposition, presumption, conjecture, expectation, belief, guess, hypothesis, premise, surmise, theory

assurance NOUN *She had an air of complete assurance.* ► confidence, composure, self-confidence, poise, aplomb, level-headedness, self-possession, self-reliance

assure VERB **1** *He assured me he would arrive in time.* ► promise, reassure, convince, persuade, satisfy **2** *The win assured them a place in the finals.* ► ensure, secure, guarantee, make certain, confirm, establish

assured ADJECTIVE *an assured manner*
► confident, self-confident, self-assured,

positive, assertive, composed, collected, calm, level-headed

astonish VERB *We were astonished at how much the place had changed.* ► amaze, astound, surprise, stagger, startle, disconcert, dumbfound, shock, flabbergast, perplex, stun, stupefy, bewilder

astound VERB *His arrogance astounded her.*
► astonish, amaze, surprise, stagger, startle, disconcert, dumbfound, shock, flabbergast, perplex, stun, stupefy, bewilder

astray ADVERB *Several missiles had gone astray and hit civilian targets.* ► off course, adrift, amiss, awry, lost, wide of the mark

astute ADJECTIVE *an astute manager, some astute remarks* ► shrewd, sharp, acute, canny, prudent, clever, intelligent, quick-witted, perceptive, discerning, crafty, wily AN OPPOSITE IS stupid

asylum NOUN *Spain refused to hand over four men who had sought asylum in the embassy.*
► haven, shelter, refuge, retreat, safety, sanctuary

athlete NOUN athletes a person who is good at sports, especially athletics

athletic ADJECTIVE **1** physically strong and active **2** to do with athletes
▷ **athletically** ADVERB

athletics PLURAL NOUN physical exercises and sports, e.g., running, jumping, and throwing

atlas NOUN atlases a book of maps [named after Atlas, a giant in Greek mythology who was punished for taking part in a revolt against the gods by being made to support the sky on his shoulders. *Atlas* was used as the title of a 17th-century Flemish book of maps which had a picture of Atlas at the front.]

atmosphere NOUN atmospheres **1** the air around the earth **2** a feeling or mood given by surroundings • *the happy atmosphere of the fairground* **3** (in science) a unit of pressure, equal to the pressure of the atmosphere at sea level
▷ **atmospheric** ADJECTIVE

atom NOUN atoms the smallest particle of a substance [from Greek *atomos* = indivisible: people used to think that an atom could not be divided]

atom bomb or **atomic bomb** NOUN atom bombs or atomic bombs a bomb that explodes from the energy produced by splitting atoms

atomic ADJECTIVE **1** to do with an atom or atoms **2** to do with the energy produced by splitting atoms

atomic number NOUN atomic numbers (in science) the number of protons in the nucleus of the atom of a chemical element

atrocity (a- tross- it- ee) NOUN atrocities something extremely bad or wicked; wickedness

attach VERB attaches, attaching, attached **1** fix or join to something else **2** think that something is an important part of something else • *We attach great importance to fitness.*
▷ **attachment** NOUN
attached to fond of

attack NOUN attacks **1** a violent attempt to hurt or overcome somebody **2** a piece of strong criticism **3** sudden illness or pain **4** an attempt to score a goal in a game

Thesaurus

athletic ADJECTIVE *an athletic physique*
► muscular, fit, well-built, powerful, strong, sturdy, acrobatic, active, energetic, robust, sinewy, vigorous, wiry, (more informal) sporty, (more informal) strapping OPPOSITES ARE frail, weak

atmosphere NOUN **1** *Harmful gases are escaping into the atmosphere.* ► air, sky, ether, (literary) heavens **2** *the warm cosy atmosphere of the kitchen* ► ambience, aura, environment, surroundings, quality, character, climate, mood, feeling, (more informal) vibes

atom NOUN *There is not an atom of truth in the story.* ► scrap, speck, spot, trace, morsel, bit, crumb, grain, iota, jot, molecule, particle

atrocious ADJECTIVE *They were guilty of atrocious brutality.* ► abominable, appalling, brutal, vicious, detestable, hateful, odious, detestable, vile, obnoxious, dreadful, abhorrent, diabolical, disgusting, repellent, horrifying AN OPPOSITE IS humane

atrocity NOUN *Further atrocities have been reported.* ► outrage, enormity, cruelty, act of brutality

attach VERB **1** *The brackets are attached to the wall with a pair of small screws.* ► fix, fasten, secure, affix, join, link, stick, bond, couple, anchor, connect, tie, add, append OPPOSITES ARE detach, remove **2** *We attach great importance to punctuality.* ► attribute, ascribe, assign, apply, put (on), place (on), associate (with), impute

attached ADJECTIVE **attached to** *The sisters seem very attached to each other.* ► fond of, close to, devoted to, dear to, affectionate to OR towards, friendly to OR towards, loving to OR towards, loyal to OR towards, warm to OR towards

attack NOUN **1** *An attack on the enemy was planned for the next day.* ► assault, onslaught, strike, offensive, raid, charge, ambush, foray, sortie, rush, blitz, bombardment, broadside, cannonade, counter-attack **2** *Their attack on her honesty upset her very much.* ► criticism (of), tirade (against), outburst (against), vilification (of), abuse (of), censure (of), denunciation (of), diatribe (against), revilement (of), invective (against) **3** *an attack of coughing* ► fit, bout, spasm, convulsion, outbreak, paroxysm, seizure, stroke, (more informal) turn

attack VERB **1** *We attack the enemy position at dawn.* ► charge, bombard, assault, ambush, raid, rush, descend on, storm, strike at, (more informal) blast, (more informal) pitch into, (more informal) wade into **2** *Someone attacked him in the street on his way home.* ► assault, mob, mug, pounce on, ambush, set about, set on, jump on, (more informal) beat up, (more informal) do over, (more informal) lay into **3** *The clergy regularly attack government policy.* ► criticize, find fault with, censure, denounce, condemn, impugn, vilify, inveigh against, malign, round on, snipe at AN OPPOSITE IS defend **4** *We need to attack the problem of poverty.* ► confront, address, focus on, attend to, apply yourself to, deal with

attack VERB attacks, attacking, attacked make an attack
▷ **attacker** NOUN

attain VERB attains, attaining, attained accomplish; succeed in doing or getting something
▷ **attainable** ADJECTIVE **attainment** NOUN

attempt VERB attempts, attempting, attempted make an effort to do something; try

attempt NOUN attempts an effort to do something; a try

attend VERB attends, attending, attended **1** give care and thought to something; look and listen • *Why don't you attend to your teacher?* **2** be present somewhere; go often to a place **3** look after someone; be an attendant
▷ **attendance** NOUN

attendant NOUN attendants a person who helps or accompanies someone

attention NOUN **1** giving concentration and careful thought • *Pay attention to what I'm*

saying. **2** a position in which a soldier etc. stands with feet together and arms straight downwards

attentive ADJECTIVE giving attention to something
▷ **attentively** ADVERB **attentiveness** NOUN

attic NOUN attics a room in the roof of a house

attitude NOUN attitudes **1** the way a person thinks or behaves **2** the position of the body; posture

attract VERB attracts, attracting, attracted **1** get someone's attention or interest; seem pleasant to someone **2** pull something by an invisible force • *Magnets attract metal pins.*

attraction NOUN **1** something that attracts visitors • *a tourist attraction* **2** what is pleasant or appealing about something • *City life has many attractions.*

attractive ADJECTIVE **1** pleasant or good-looking **2** interesting or appealing • *an attractive plan*
▷ **attractively** ADVERB **attractiveness** NOUN

Thesaurus

attacker NOUN **1** *The little force fought bravely against its attackers.* ► aggressor, assailant, invader, opponent, raider, enemy **2** *The attacker ran off empty-handed.* ► assailant, mugger, aggressor, intruder, rapist **3** *The journal agreed to publish a defense against her attackers.* ► critic, detractor, persecutor, opponent, enemy

attain VERB *He did not attain this honor until the reign of Queen Victoria.* ► achieve, accomplish, obtain, gain, win, earn, get, acquire, secure, reach, (*more informal*) clinch, (*more informal*) carry off, (*more informal*) pull off

attempt NOUN *a brave attempt* ► try, effort, endeavor, venture, (*more informal*) shot

attempt VERB **1** *We attempted to visit all three sites in one day.* ► try, endeavor, aim, aspire, strive, undertake, set out, make an effort OR every effort, do your best, do your utmost, venture, seek, (*more informal*) take a stab (at), (*more informal*) bend over backwards **2** *Candidates should attempt three questions.* ► undertake, try, choose, answer

attend VERB **1** *Frances had to attend an interview the following week.* ► go to OR for, present yourself at, appear at, be present at **2** *The bride was attended by two bridesmaids.* ► escort, assist, accompany, chaperone, follow, guard, usher, wait on **3** *attend to A nurse attended to the injured.* ► look after, care for, tend, treat, help, deal with, (*more formal*) minister to **4** *attend to Frank said he would attend to the details of the trip.* ► deal with, take care of, look after, see to, manage, organize, make

arrangements for, take responsibility for **5** *attend to Please attend to what I say.* ► listen to, pay attention to, heed, mark, mind, concentrate on, follow carefully, hear, note, notice, observe, think about

attendant NOUN *The Queen had three attendants.* ► assistant, aide, retainer, companion, escort, servant, bodyguard

attention NOUN *Please give the matter your full attention.* ► concentration, observation, regard, consideration, scrutiny, notice, thought, concern, care, diligence, heed, recognition

attentive ADJECTIVE **1** *Julian was standing silent and attentive in the shadows.* ► alert, vigilant, watchful, aware, circumspect, wide awake, on the lookout, on the ball, on your guard **2** *Helen was patient and attentive, holding my hand to calm me.* ► thoughtful, considerate, kind, caring, understanding, tender, devoted

attitude NOUN *a positive, joyful attitude* ► outlook, approach, air, manner, demeanor, disposition, inclination, position, bearing, frame of mind, mien, mood, posture, stance, behavior

attract VERB **1** *The recent lecture attracted a good turnout.* ► draw, bring, bring in, produce, cause, generate **2** *They were attracted by the beauty of the place.* ► enchant, entrance, excite, captivate, lure, entice, allure, tempt, charm, fascinate, beguile, bewitch AN OPPOSITE IS repel

attractive ADJECTIVE **1** *an attractive young woman* ► good-looking, nice-looking, pretty, striking, fetching, beautiful, gorgeous, lovely,

attribute (a- trib- yoot) VERB attributes, attributing, attributed regard something as belonging to or created by • *We attribute his success to hard work.*
▷ **attribution** NOUN

attribute (at- rib- yoot) NOUN attributes a quality or characteristic • *Kindness is one of his attributes.*

attributive (a- trib- yoo- tiv) ADJECTIVE expressing an attribute and placed before the word it describes, e.g. *old* in *the old dog*
COMPARE predicative
▷ **attributively** ADVERB

auburn ADJECTIVE (said about hair) reddish-brown

auction NOUN auctions a public sale where things are sold to the person who offers the most money for them

auction VERB auctions, auctioning, auctioned sell something by auction
▷ **auctioneer** NOUN

audacious (aw- day- shus) ADJECTIVE bold or daring
▷ **audaciously** ADVERB **audacity** NOUN

audible ADJECTIVE loud enough to be heard
▷ **audibly** ADVERB **audibility** NOUN

audience NOUN audiences **1** people who have gathered to hear or watch something **2** a formal interview with an important person

audio NOUN reproduced sounds

audio-visual ADJECTIVE using both sound and pictures to give information

audit NOUN audits an official examination of financial accounts to see that they are correct

audit VERB audits, auditing, audited make an audit of accounts
▷ **auditor** NOUN

audition NOUN auditions a test to see if an actor or musician is suitable for a job
▷ **audition** VERB

auditorium NOUN auditoriums the part of a theater or hall where the audience sits

August NOUN the eighth month of the year [named after Augustus Caesar, the first Roman emperor]

aunt NOUN aunts the sister of your father or mother; your uncle's wife

au pair (oh pair) NOUN au pairs a person from abroad, usually a young woman, who works for a time in someone's home

aura (or- a) NOUN auras a general feeling surrounding a person or thing • *an aura of happiness*

aural (or- al) ADJECTIVE to do with the ear or hearing
▷ **aurally** ADVERB
USAGE Do not confuse with oral.

aurora (aw- raw- ra) NOUN auroras bands of colored light appearing in the sky at night, the aurora borealis (bor- ee- a- liss) in the Northern Hemisphere and the aurora australes (aw- stray- less) in the Southern Hemisphere

auspices (aw- spiss- eez) PLURAL NOUN protection or support • *under the auspices of the Red Cross*

auspicious (aw- spish- us) ADJECTIVE fortunate or favorable • *an auspicious start*

austere (aw- steer) ADJECTIVE very simple and plain; without luxuries
▷ **austerely** ADVERB **austerity** NOUN

Thesaurus

charming, engaging, appealing, delightful, glamorous, stunning AN OPPOSITE IS repulsive **2** *an attractive offer* ► appealing, agreeable, tempting, interesting, difficult to resist OR refuse

attribute VERB *A cool head is not the first quality I would attribute to the colonel.* ► ascribe, associate (with), connect (with), assign, put down, blame (on)

audacious ADJECTIVE *an audacious decision* ► bold, daring, brave, courageous, adventurous, enterprising

audacity NOUN **1** *His sheer audacity was enough to carry the day.* ► bravery, daring, boldness, courage, enterprise **2** (*usually disapproving*) *Then they had the audacity to ask for money.* ► effrontery, nerve, boldness, temerity, impertinence, impudence, insolence, presumptuousness, shamelessness

audible ADJECTIVE *Her words were hardly audible above the noise of the traffic.* ► perceptible, discernible, recognizable, clear, distinct, detectable, high, loud, noisy, strong AN OPPOSITE IS inaudible

audience NOUN *There was a more lively audience on the Saturday.* ► spectators, onlookers, crowd, gathering, turnout, (*television*) viewers, (*radio*) listeners

austere ADJECTIVE **1** *Their lives tended to be short and austere.* ► severe, sober, frugal, strict, spartan, restrained, abstemious, ascetic, temperate, simple, chaste OPPOSITES ARE indulgent, elaborate **2** *She seemed austere but had a great deal of charm, once you got to know her.* ► stern, severe, strict, grave, solemn, forbidding, dour, formal, remote, distant, aloof AN OPPOSITE IS genial **3** *Dark windows gave the house an austere appearance.* ► stark, grim, bleak, forbidding OPPOSITES ARE bright, ornate

authentic ADJECTIVE genuine • *an authentic signature*
▷ **authentically** ADVERB **authenticity** NOUN

author NOUN **authors** the writer of a book, play, poem, etc.
▷ **authorship** NOUN

authoritative ADJECTIVE having proper authority or expert knowledge; official

authority NOUN **authorities** 1 the right or power to give orders to other people 2 a person or organization with the right to give orders 3 an expert; a book, etc., that gives reliable information • *an authority on spiders*

authorize VERB **authorizes**, **authorizing**, **authorized** give official permission for something
▷ **authorization** NOUN

autistic (aw- **tist**- ik) ADJECTIVE having a disability that makes someone unable to communicate with other people or respond to surroundings
▷ **autism** NOUN

autobiography NOUN **autobiographies** the story of a person's life written by himself or herself
▷ **autobiographical** ADJECTIVE

autocrat NOUN **autocrats** a ruler with unlimited power
▷ **autocratic** ADJECTIVE **autocratically** ADVERB

autograph NOUN **autographs** the signature of a famous person

autograph VERB **autographs**, **autographing**, autographed sign your name in a book, etc.

automatic ADJECTIVE 1 working on its own without continuous attention or control by people 2 done without thinking
▷ **automatically** ADVERB

automation NOUN making processes automatic; using machines instead of people to do jobs

automaton (aw- tom- at- on) NOUN **automatons** 1 a robot 2 a person who seems to act mechanically without thinking

autonomy (aw- ton- om- ee) NOUN 1 self-government 2 the right to act independently without being told what to do
▷ **autonomous** ADJECTIVE

autumn NOUN **autumns** the season between summer and winter
▷ **autumnal** ADJECTIVE

auxiliary ADJECTIVE giving help and support • *auxiliary services.*

auxiliary NOUN **auxiliaries** a helper

auxiliary verb NOUN **auxiliary verbs** a verb such as *do*, *have*, and *will*, which is used to form parts of other verbs, e.g., *have* in *I have finished*

Thesaurus

authentic ADJECTIVE 1 *an authentic painting by Rembrandt* ► actual, bona fide, certain, genuine, legitimate, original, real, true, valid AN OPPOSITE IS fake 2 *an authentic story* ► accurate, authoritative, dependable, factual, honest, reliable, truthful, veracious AN OPPOSITE IS false

author NOUN 1 *modern American authors* ► writer, novelist, dramatist, composer, creator, playwright, poet, scriptwriter 2 *the author of the plan* ► originator, creator, initiator, instigator, architect, producer, begetter, designer, inventor

authoritative ADJECTIVE 1 *an authoritative edition of the text* ► definitive, authorized, classic, standard 2 *an authoritative source of information* ► reliable, dependable, sound, authentic, trustworthy

authority NOUN 1 *The salesperson does not always have the authority to deal with a complaint.* ► authorization, power, right, prerogative, consent, license, mandate, permission 2 *I was convinced that she would never accept a challenge to her authority.* ► power, sovereignty, control, jurisdiction, domination, supremacy, charge, command, force, influence, might, prerogative, right,

sway, weight 3 *He is the world's foremost authority on the subject.* ► expert, specialist, pundit, connoisseur (of)
the authorities *The matter was reported to the authorities.* ► officials, officialdom, government, management, administration, people in charge, (*more informal*) the powers that be

authorize VERB *The government has authorized a further billion dollars of spending on health.* ► approve, permit, allow, agree to, enable, sanction, back, accede to, consent to, (*more informal*) OK, ratify, (*more informal*) rubber-stamp, (*more informal*) give the go-ahead for

automatic ADJECTIVE 1 *His reaction was automatic.* ► instinctive, spontaneous, involuntary, unconscious, reflex, unthinking, unintentional, natural, mechanical, habitual, impulsive 2 *automatic windows* ► mechanical, automated, computerized, programmed, robotic, self-regulating, unmanned

autonomous ADJECTIVE *an autonomous nation* ► independent, self-governing, sovereign, free, self-ruling, self-determining AN OPPOSITE IS subject

auxiliary ADJECTIVE 1 *an auxiliary power supply* ► supplementary, additional, ancillary, reserve, secondary, spare, subsidiary, emergency, extra, (*more informal*) back-up

avail NOUN
to no avail without any success

available ADJECTIVE ready or able to be used; obtainable
▷ **availability** NOUN

avalanche NOUN **avalanches** a mass of snow or rock falling down the side of a mountain

avenge VERB **avenges, avenging, avenged** take vengeance for something done to harm you
▷ **avenger** NOUN

avenue NOUN **avenues** 1 a wide street 2 a road with trees along both sides

average NOUN **averages** 1 the value obtained by adding several quantities together and dividing by the number of quantities 2 the usual or ordinary standard

average ADJECTIVE 1 determined as an average • Their average age is ten. 2 of the usual or ordinary standard

average VERB **averages, averaging, averaged** work out, produce, or amount to as an average

aversion NOUN a strong dislike

avert VERB **averts, averting, averted** 1 turn something away • People averted their eyes from the accident. 2 prevent • We averted a disaster.

aviary NOUN **aviaries** a large cage or building for keeping birds

aviation NOUN the flying of aircraft
▷ **aviator** NOUN

avocado (av- ok- **ah**- doh) NOUN **avocados** a pear-shaped tropical fruit [via Spanish from Nahuatl (a Central American language)]

avoid VERB **avoids, avoiding, avoided** 1 keep yourself away from someone or something 2 keep yourself from doing something; refrain from • Avoid rash promises.
▷ **avoidable** ADJECTIVE **avoidance** NOUN

avoirdupois (av- wah- dew- **pwah**) NOUN a system of weights using the unit of 16 ounces = 1 pound

await VERB **awaits, awaiting, awaited** wait for

awake VERB **awakes, awaking, awoke, awoken** wake up

awake ADJECTIVE not asleep

Thesaurus

available ADJECTIVE Camping facilities will be available on site. ► obtainable, accessible, procurable, ready, at OR on OR to hand, to be had, usable, disposable AN OPPOSITE IS unavailable

avenge VERB We shall avenge their deaths a thousand times. ► take revenge for, take vengeance for, punish, exact punishment for, exact retribution for, repay, (more informal) get your own back for

average ADJECTIVE 1 Few of us have any idea how much water we use on an average day. ► typical, normal, ordinary, usual, regular, standard 2 He is only an average golfer. ► mediocre, undistinguished, unremarkable, indifferent, unexceptional, run-of-the-mill, second-rate, passable, tolerable, mainstream OPPOSITES ARE exceptional, outstanding 3 The average summer temperature is 78 degrees. ► mean, medial, standard

average NOUN Prices of new cars will rise by an average of 3 percent. ► mean, median, midpoint

avid ADJECTIVE avid fans of the movies ► eager, enthusiastic, ardent, passionate, fervent, devoted, dedicated, zealous OPPOSITES ARE uninterested, apathetic

avoid VERB 1 I try to avoid arguments. ► refrain from, stay clear of, steer clear of, eschew, circumvent OPPOSITES ARE seek, confront 2 You cannot avoid responsibility for the decision. ► evade, escape, dodge, shirk, sidestep, (more informal) get out of, (more informal) duck AN OPPOSITE IS face up to 3 She had to swerve to avoid a collision. ► prevent, avert, circumvent

4 There was a woman at the party he was anxious to avoid. ► ignore, shun, keep away from, hide from, stay clear of, steer clear of AN OPPOSITE IS seek out 5 Women should avoid alcohol during pregnancy. ► refrain from, desist from, abstain from, eschew AN OPPOSITE IS indulge in

awake ADJECTIVE They are often not awake until ten or eleven. She felt too awake to go back to sleep again. ► conscious, alert, sleepless, wakeful, wide awake, lively, restless AN OPPOSITE IS asleep

awake VERB 1 The alarm awoke her at six. ► wake (up), waken, awaken, rouse, arouse 2 James awoke with a start. ► wake (up), waken, awaken, stir, come to 3 The accident awoke old fears about passenger safety. ► awaken, waken, rouse, arouse, stir up, revive, stimulate, trigger, bring back USAGE The normal word to use for the main meanings is wake or wake up. There are three other words, awake, awaken, and waken, but you cannot use up with any of these. All four words can be transitive (i.e., can take an object, as in the first example in this entry) or intransitive (i.e., can have no object, as in the second example). Awaken and waken are rather more formal or literary in effect than awake and wake.

awaken VERB 1 The noise outside awakened us. We awakened early. ► wake (up), waken, awake, stir, come to 2 The incident awakened strong feelings in her. ► awake, waken, rouse, arouse, stir up, revive, stimulate, trigger, bring back

award VERB awards, awarding, awarded give something officially as a prize, payment, or penalty

award NOUN awards something awarded, such as a prize or a sum of money

aware ADJECTIVE knowing or realizing something • Were you aware of the danger?
▷ awareness NOUN

away ADVERB 1 to or at a distance; not at the usual place 2 out of existence • The water had boiled away. 3 continuously or persistently • We worked away at it.

away ADJECTIVE played on an opponent's ground • an away match

awe NOUN fearful or deeply respectful wonder • The mountains always fill me with awe.
▷ awed ADJECTIVE awesome ADJECTIVE
awestricken ADJECTIVE awestruck ADJECTIVE

awful ADJECTIVE 1 very bad • an awful accident. 2 (informal) very great • That's an awful lot of money.
▷ awfully ADVERB

awkward ADJECTIVE 1 difficult to use or deal with; not convenient 2 clumsy; not skillful
▷ awkwardly ADVERB awkwardness NOUN
[from Old Norse afugr = turned the wrong way]

awning NOUN awnings a rooflike shelter made of canvas, etc.

axe NOUN axes 1 a tool for chopping things 2 (informal) being axed
have an axe to grind have a personal interest in something and want to take care of it

axe VERB axes, axing, axed 1 cancel or abolish something 2 reduce something greatly

axis NOUN axes 1 a line through the center of a spinning object 2 a line dividing a thing in half 3 the horizontal or vertical line on a graph

Thesaurus

award NOUN 1 By his third year he had won three awards. ► prize, trophy, decoration, medal 2 an award of $5,000 ► payment, subsidy, subvention, bursary 3 the award of an honor ► granting, bestowal, conferment, conferral

award VERB 1 U.S. senators plan to award themselves a four percent pay rise. Referee Hart did not even award a free kick. ► grant, give, present, accord, allot, assign 2 The college awarded her a scholarship. ► grant, present, (more formal) endow, (more formal) confer, (more formal) bestow
USAGE If you use present or endow, you say The college presented (or endowed) her with a scholarship. If you use bestow or confer, you say They bestowed (or conferred) a scholarship on her. These words are much more formal in effect and are mainly used in official language.

aware ADJECTIVE aware of The children were aware of the dangers. ► conscious of, acquainted with, alive to, appreciative of, mindful of, informed about, knowledgeable about, sensitive to, familiar with, attentive to, conversant with, heedful of, observant of, responsive to OPPOSITES ARE unaware, ignorant, insensitive (to)

awe-inspiring ADJECTIVE The stained-glass windows were awe-inspiring in gold and blue. ► awesome, breathtaking, dramatic, stunning, stupendous, spectacular, astonishing, grand, imposing, impressive, magnificent, amazing, marvelous, overwhelming, wonderful, fearsome, (poetic) wondrous OPPOSITES ARE insignificant, unimpressive

awful ADJECTIVE 1 awful weather ► bad, terrible, dreadful, atrocious, appalling, frightful, poor, (more informal) lousy OPPOSITES ARE wonderful, lovely 2 an awful smell ► unpleasant, disgusting, nasty, dreadful, terrible, horrible, horrid, foul, frightful, obnoxious OPPOSITES ARE pleasant, lovely 3 awful news, an awful illness ► grave, serious, bad, terrible, dreadful AN OPPOSITE IS excellent 4 I felt awful for losing my temper. ► guilty, remorseful, regretful, ashamed, sorry

awkward ADJECTIVE 1 The case was an awkward object to carry. ► cumbersome, bulky, unmanageable, unwieldy, inconvenient AN OPPOSITE IS convenient 2 He ran with awkward movements. ► clumsy, ungainly, inept, inexpert, unskillful, uncoordinated, graceless, blundering, bungling, gauche, gawky, ham-fisted, maladroit OPPOSITES ARE skillful, dexterous, adroit 3 This is an awkward situation to be in. ► difficult, troublesome, trying, vexatious, vexing, annoying, perplexing AN OPPOSITE IS straightforward 4 There was an awkward pause in the conversation. ► embarrassing, uncomfortable, uneasy, delicate, tricky, unwelcome AN OPPOSITE IS comfortable 5 He thought she was being extremely awkward. ► unreasonable, unhelpful, uncooperative, stubborn, obstinate, perverse, tiresome, exasperating, wayward OPPOSITES ARE cooperative, obliging, amenable

axe VERB The company will axe thousands of jobs. ► terminate, discontinue, eliminate, cut, cancel, drop, get rid of, remove, withdraw

axis NOUN The earth spins on its axis once a day. ► center line, central line, pivot

axle *NOUN* axles the rod through the center of a wheel, on which the wheel turns

ayatollah (I- a- tol- a) *NOUN* ayatollahs a Muslim religious leader in Iran

aye (I) *ADVERB* yes

azure *ADJECTIVE* sky-blue

Thesaurus

axle *NOUN* Something had broken the car's back axle. ► rod, shaft, spindle

Bb

babble VERB **babbles, babbling, babbled**
1 talk very quickly without making sense
2 make a murmuring sound
▷ **babble** NOUN **babbler** NOUN

baboon NOUN **baboons** a kind of large
monkey from Africa and Asia. Baboons have
long muzzles and short tails.

baby NOUN **babies** a very young child or animal
▷ **babyish** ADJECTIVE

babysitter NOUN **babysitters** someone who
looks after a child while the parents are out

bachelor NOUN **bachelors** a man who has not
married
Bachelor of Arts or **Science** a person who has
taken a first degree in arts or science

back NOUN **backs** 1 the part that is farthest
from the front 2 the back part of the body
from the shoulders to the buttocks 3 the part
of a chair, etc., that your back rests against
4 a defending player near the goal in
football, hockey, etc.

back ADJECTIVE 1 placed at or near the back
2 to do with the back ● back pain

back ADVERB 1 to or toward the back 2 to the
place you have come from ● Go back home.
3 to an earlier time or position ● Put the clocks
back one hour.

back VERB **backs, backing, backed** 1 move
backward 2 give someone support or help
3 bet on something 4 cover the back of
something ● Back the rug with canvas.
▷ **backer** NOUN

back out refuse to do what you agreed to do

back up 1 give support or help to a person or
thing 2 (in computing) make a spare copy of
a file or data **backup** NOUN

backbone NOUN **backbones** the column of
small bones down the center of the back; the
spine

backfire VERB **backfires, backfiring, backfired**
1 if a car backfires, it makes a loud noise,
caused by an explosion in the exhaust pipe
2 if a plan backfires, it goes wrong

background NOUN 1 the back part of a
picture, scene, or view, etc. 2 the conditions
influencing something 3 a person's family,
upbringing, and education
in the background not noticeable or obvious

backing NOUN 1 support 2 material that is
used to line the back of something 3 musical
accompaniment

Thesaurus

baby NOUN 1 *The woman was holding a baby.*
► infant, toddler, child 2 *a baby car*
► miniature, mini, small-scale, midget,
diminutive

babyish ADJECTIVE *Older children are usually told
that it is babyish to cry.* ► childish, juvenile,
puerile, immature, infantile AN OPPOSITE IS
mature

back NOUN 1 *a person's back* ► spine, backbone,
spinal column RELATED ADJECTIVE ► dorsal
(upper side of an animal), lumbar (lower back)
2 *the back of the vehicle* ► end, rear, tail-end
AN OPPOSITE IS front 3 *the back of the building*
► rear, rear side OPPOSITES ARE front, facade
4 *the back of the ship* ► stern OPPOSITES ARE
front, bow 5 *the back of an envelope* ► reverse,
verso AN OPPOSITE IS front 6 *the back of an
animal* ► rear, tail, hindquarters, posterior AN
OPPOSITE IS front

back ADJECTIVE 1 *the back door* ► rear AN
OPPOSITE IS front 2 *an animal's back legs*
► rear, hind, hindmost AN OPPOSITE IS front
3 *the back row of the hall* ► end, rearmost AN
OPPOSITE IS front 4 *a bird's back feathers;
the back fin of a fish* ► (technical) dorsal 5 *back
issues of a journal* ► past, previous OPPOSITES
ARE forthcoming, future

back VERB 1 *He decided to back his van into the
space. The car backed slowly up the drive.*
► reverse, go backward, move back 2 *We
would like them to back our plan.* ► support,

endorse, approve of, stand behind, sponsor,
patronize 3 *He backed a horse at 3-1.* ► bet on,
place a bet on, put money on

back down *The government has had to back
down on tax increases.* ► withdraw, concede,
yield, give way, retreat, change your mind,
(more informal) do a U-turn

back out of *Mr. James wanted to back out of the
deal.* ► withdraw from, give up, pull out of

backbone NOUN 1 *She has an injured backbone.*
► spine, spinal column, vertebrae RELATED
ADJECTIVE ► spinal 2 *The backbone of a good
team is a good manager.* ► mainstay,
foundation, cornerstone, chief support
3 *Drivers need to have some backbone to sustain
pole position.* ► courage, nerve, spirit, mettle,
determination, strength of character, firmness
of purpose

backfire VERB *The plan backfired.* ► miscarry,
misfire, fail, flop, rebound

background NOUN 1 *You can see a steeple in the
background.* ► distance, (on the) horizon AN
OPPOSITE IS foreground 2 *the background to the
war* ► circumstances (of), context (of), history,
(informal) lead-up 3 *students from different
backgrounds* ► environment, social
circumstances, breeding, culture, (formal)
milieu, tradition, upbringing

backing NOUN 1 *We need the backing of the
unions.* ► support, agreement, endorsement,

backlash NOUN backlashes a violent reaction to an event

backlog NOUN backlogs an amount of work that should have been finished but is still waiting to be done

backstroke NOUN a way of swimming lying on your back

backward ADJECTIVE 1 going backward 2 slow at learning or developing
▷ **backwardness** NOUN

backward ADVERB 1 to or towards the back 2 with the back end going first 3 in reverse order • *Count backwards.*
backward and forward in each direction alternately; to and fro

bacon NOUN smoked or salted meat from the back or sides of a pig

bacterium NOUN bacteria a microscopic organism that can cause disease
▷ **bacterial** ADJECTIVE
USAGE Note that it is a mistake to use the plural form **bacteria** as if it were the singular. It is incorrect to say "a bacteria" or "this bacteria"; correct usage is *this bacterium* or *these bacteria*.

bad ADJECTIVE worse, worst 1 not having the right qualities; not good 2 wicked or evil 3 serious or severe • *a bad accident* 4 ill or unhealthy 5 harmful • *Sweets are bad for your teeth.* 6 decayed or rotten • *This meat has gone bad.*
▷ **badness** NOUN
not bad quite good

badge NOUN badges a button or sign that you wear to show people who you are or what school or club, etc., you belong to

badger NOUN badgers a grey burrowing animal with a black and white head

badger VERB badgers, badgering, badgered keep asking someone to do something; pester

badly ADVERB worse, worst 1 in a bad way; not well 2 severely; causing much injury • *He was badly wounded.* 3 very much • *She badly wanted to win.*

baffle VERB baffles, baffling, baffled puzzle or confuse somebody
▷ **bafflement** NOUN

bag NOUN bags a container made of a soft material, for holding or carrying things
bags (*informal*)plenty • *bags of room*

Thesaurus

---

assistance, encouragement, help 2 *financial backing* ► support, funding, patronage, subsidy, sponsorship 3 *a musical backing* ► accompaniment, orchestration, scoring

backward ADJECTIVE 1 *a backward movement* ► reverse, rearward, regressive, retrograde, retrogressive AN OPPOSITE IS forward 2 *Don't be backward if you need to ask for help.* ► reticent, bashful, coy, diffident, shy, timid, unforthcoming, hesitant, inhibited, afraid, modest, reluctant, reserved, self-effacing AN OPPOSITE IS confident 3 *The decision was a backward step.* ► retrograde, regressive, negative 4 *a backward learner* ► subnormal, (*offensive*) retarded

bad ADJECTIVE 1 *bad work* ► poor, inferior, substandard, second-rate, unsatisfactory, inadequate, deficient, awful, terrible, dreadful, (*more informal*) shoddy OPPOSITES ARE excellent, outstanding, good 2 *a bad driver* ► incompetent, poor, awful, terrible, dreadful 3 *a bad effect* ► harmful, damaging, detrimental, injurious, undesirable OPPOSITES ARE beneficial, good 4 *leading a bad life* ► wicked, sinful, immoral, depraved, degenerate, dissolute OPPOSITES ARE virtuous, good 5 *a bad child* ► naughty, badly behaved, disobedient, mischievous OPPOSITES ARE well behaved, good 6 *bad language* ► vulgar, crude, foul, coarse, indecent, offensive, profane, blasphemous 7 *bad news* ► unpleasant, disagreeable, unwelcome OPPOSITES ARE good, welcome 8 *a bad time to buy a house* ► unsuitable, inappropriate,

difficult, unfavorable, unfortunate, inauspicious OPPOSITES ARE favorable, suitable, good 9 *a bad accident, a bad toothache* ► serious, severe, acute, grave, critical OPPOSITES ARE minor, slight 10 *the meat is bad* ► rotten, off, putrid, decomposing, decomposed, moldy, contaminated, sour (milk), rancid (butter) AN OPPOSITE IS fresh 11 *feeling bad* ► unwell, ill, sick OPPOSITES ARE well, healthy 12 *a bad leg* ► injured, wounded, diseased 13 *I felt bad after losing my temper.* ► guilty, remorseful, ashamed, conscience-stricken OPPOSITES ARE proud, unrepentant

bad-tempered ADJECTIVE *She was a thoroughly selfish, bad-tempered little girl.* ► irritable, irascible, grumpy, testy, grouchy, touchy, crotchety, cantankerous, peevish, fractious, cross OPPOSITES ARE good-tempered, good-humored, affable

baffle VERB *Her answer baffled him.* ► perplex, bewilder, puzzle, mystify, confuse, bemuse, disconcert, confound, (*more informal*) floor

baffling ADJECTIVE *a baffling response* ► puzzling, bewildering, perplexing, confusing, mystifying, mysterious, inexplicable, inscrutable, insoluble, unfathomable, extraordinary, frustrating OPPOSITES ARE clear, straightforward, comprehensible

bag NOUN 1 *I'll put these things in a bag.* ► container, carrier bag, carrier 2 *We'd better go and pack our bags* ► case, suitcase 3 *She always carried a bag.* ► handbag, shoulder bag

A
B
C
D
E
F
G
H
I
J
K
L
M
N
O
P
Q
R
S
T
U
V
W
X
Y
Z

bag VERB bags, bagging, bagged **1** (*informal*) catch or claim something **2** put something into bags

baggage NOUN luggage

baggy ADJECTIVE (said about clothes) large and loose

bagpipes PLURAL NOUN a musical instrument in which air is squeezed out of a bag into pipes. Bagpipes are played especially in Scotland.

bail[1] NOUN money that is paid or promised as a guarantee that a person who is accused of a crime will return for trial if he or she is released in the meantime

bail VERB bails, bailing, bailed provide bail for a person

bail[2] VERB bails, bailing, bailed scoop out water that has got into a boat

bailiff NOUN bailiffs **1** a law officer who serves writs and performs arrests **2** an official who takes people's property when they owe money

bait NOUN **1** food that is put on a hook or in a trap to catch fish or animals **2** something that is meant to tempt someone

bait VERB baits, baiting, baited **1** put bait on a hook or in a trap **2** try to make someone angry by teasing them

baize NOUN the thick green cloth that is used for covering pool tables

bake VERB bakes, baking, baked **1** cook in an oven **2** make or become very hot **3** make a thing hard by heating it

baker NOUN bakers a person who bakes and sells bread or cakes
▷ **bakery** NOUN

balance NOUN balances **1** a steady position, with the weight or amount evenly distributed **2** a person's feeling of being steady **3** a device for weighing things, with two containers hanging from a bar **4** the difference between money paid into an account and money taken out **5** the amount of money that someone still has to pay

balance VERB balances, balancing, balanced make or be steady or equal

balcony NOUN balconies **1** a platform that sticks out from an outside wall of a building **2** the upstairs part of a theater or cinema

bald ADJECTIVE **1** without hair on the top of the head **2** with no details; blunt • *a bald statement*
▷ **baldly** ADVERB **baldness** NOUN

ball[1] NOUN balls **1** a round object used in many games **2** anything that has a round shape • *a ball of string*

Thesaurus

4 *The walkers had bags on their backs.*
▶ backpack, rucksack

bag VERB **1** *You need to get there early and bag a good seat.* ▶ secure, obtain, reserve, acquire, get **2** *He bagged four pheasants.* ▶ catch, shoot, kill, capture

baggage NOUN *She put her baggage in and climbed aboard.* ▶ luggage, bags, cases, suitcases, trunks, belongings, paraphernalia, (*informal*) gear, (*informal*) stuff

bait NOUN *The offer was meant to be a bait.*
▶ enticement, inducement, lure, bribe, allurement, attraction

bait VERB *The boys wouldn't stop baiting her.*
▶ tease, torment, annoy, goad, persecute, pester, provoke, hound, jeer at, (*more informal*) needle

bake VERB *The hot sun was baking the earth.*
▶ scorch, burn, parch, sear

balance NOUN **1** *You can weigh the fruit in the balance.* ▶ scales, weighing machine **2** *It is easy to stumble and lose your balance.*
▶ equilibrium, stability, equipoise, poise, steadiness **3** *a balance between fairness and firmness* ▶ parity, correspondence, symmetry, evenness, equality, equivalence **4** *a sense of personal balance* ▶ composure, self-assurance, equanimity, self-possession **5** *The balance of the payment is due in July.* ▶ remainder, difference, rest, residue

on balance On balance it is a good plan.
▶ overall, all in all, by and large

balance VERB **1** *If I carry one bag in each hand, they balance each other.* ▶ counteract, counterbalance, neutralize, offset, equalize, match, stabilize, steady **2** *He tried to eat by balancing a plate on his knee.* ▶ support, keep, keep balanced, steady **3** *You have to balance the advantages and disadvantages.* ▶ weigh, weigh up, compare, assess, appraise, consider, estimate

balanced ADJECTIVE **1** *a balanced view of the issues* ▶ fair, objective, impartial, equitable, even-handed, impartial, disinterested OPPOSITES ARE partial, biased **2** *a balanced individual* ▶ level-headed, equable, sensible, sane, stable, practical OPPOSITES ARE unbalanced, neurotic **3** *a balanced diet* ▶ mixed, varied, well-planned, healthy OPPOSITES ARE unbalanced, unhealthy

bald ADJECTIVE **1** *a bald man* ▶ bald-headed, hairless, (*euphemistic*) thin on top **2** *bald tires* ▶ bare, smooth **3** *a bald statement* ▶ plain, direct, forthright, plain, simple, stark, straightforward, unadorned, uncompromising

ball[1] **1** *a ball of string, The little animal curled itself into a ball.* ▶ sphere, globe, globule, orb, spheroid **2** *a ball of food* ▶ pellet, globule, slug **3** *a fancy-dress ball* ▶ dance, party, disco, social

ball of the foot the rounded part of the foot at the base of the big toe

ball² NOUN **balls** a formal party where people dance

ballad NOUN **ballads** a simple song or poem that tells a story

ballast (bal- ast) NOUN heavy material that is carried in a ship to keep it steady

ball bearings PLURAL NOUN small steel balls rolling in a groove on which machine parts can move easily

ballerina (bal- er- **een**- a) NOUN **ballerinas** a female ballet dancer

ballet (bal- ay) NOUN **ballets** a stage entertainment that tells a story with dancing, mime, and music

ballistic missile NOUN **ballistic missiles** a missile that is initially powered and guided and then falls under gravity on its target

balloon NOUN **balloons** 1 a bag made of thin rubber that can be inflated and used as a toy or decoration 2 a large round bag inflated with hot air or light gases to make it rise in the air, often carrying a basket for passengers to ride in 3 an outline around spoken words in a cartoon

ballot NOUN **ballots** 1 a secret method of voting, usually by making a mark on a piece of paper 2 a piece of paper on which a vote is made

ballot VERB **ballots, balloting, balloted** invite people to vote for something by a ballot

ballpoint pen NOUN **ballpoint pens** a pen with a tiny ball round which the ink flows

balm NOUN 1 a sweet-scented ointment 2 something that soothes you

balmy ADJECTIVE 1 sweet-scented like balm 2 soft and warm • *a balmy breeze*

bamboo NOUN **bamboos** 1 a tall plant with hard hollow stems 2 a stem of the bamboo plant

ban VERB **bans, banning, banned** forbid something officially

ban NOUN **bans** an order that bans something

banana NOUN **bananas** a long curved fruit with a yellow or green skin

band¹ NOUN **bands** 1 a strip or loop of something 2 a range of values, wavelengths, etc.

band² NOUN **bands** 1 an organized group of people doing something together • *a band of robbers* 2 a group of people playing music together

band VERB **bands, banding, banded** form an organized group

bandage NOUN **bandages** a strip of material for binding up a wound
▷ **bandage** VERB

bandit NOUN **bandits** a member of a gang of robbers who attack travelers

bandwagon NOUN
jump *or* **climb on the bandwagon** join other people in something that is successful

bandy VERB **bandies, bandying, bandied** if a word or story is bandied about, it is mentioned or told by a lot of different people

bane NOUN a cause of trouble or worry etc.
• *Exams are the bane of our lives!*

bang NOUN **bangs** 1 a sudden loud noise like that of an explosion 2 a sharp blow or knock

Thesaurus

ballot NOUN *a ballot for the party leadership*
▶ election, vote, poll, plebiscite, referendum

ban NOUN *a ban on smoking* ▶ embargo, prohibition, bar, moratorium, veto

ban VERB *The government wants to ban some blood sports.* ▶ prohibit, forbid, bar, disallow, proscribe, suppress, make illegal, stop, restrict OPPOSITES ARE permit, allow

banal ADJECTIVE *a banal image of the perfect married couple* ▶ trite, hackneyed, commonplace, stereotypical, stock, humdrum, clichéd, dull, unimaginative, tired, boring, tedious, (*more informal*) corny OPPOSITES ARE original, interesting

band NOUN 1 *red with a blue band along the top* ▶ strip, stripe, streak, belt, line, loop, ribbon, ring 2 *a band of followers* ▶ troop, body, company, group, gang, horde, party, association, clique, club, crew, flock, herd, society 3 *A band was playing.* ▶ orchestra, ensemble, group

band VERB **band together** *The village banded together to repel their attackers.* ▶ gather, group, unite, cooperate, join together, work together, fight together, collaborate

bandage NOUN *The nurse put a bandage on his wound.* ▶ dressing, plaster, gauze, lint

bandit NOUN *The camp was attacked by bandits.* ▶ robber, brigand, thief, outlaw, desperado, gangster, gunman, marauder, highwayman, pirate, hijacker

bang NOUN 1 *He got a bang on the head.* ▶ blow, hit, smack, knock, thump, rap, clout, punch, whack, cuff, bump, collision, slam, stroke, (*more informal*) wallop 2 *Suddenly there was a loud bang.* ▶ blast, report, boom, crack, thud, thump, explosion, clap, crash, pop

bang VERB *He banged the table with his fist.* ▶ hit, thump, strike, whack, (*more informal*) bash, (*more informal*) clout

a
b
c
d
e
f
g
h
i
j
k
l
m
n
o
p
q
r
s
t
u
v
w
x
y
z

A
B
C
D
E
F
G
H
I
J
K
L
M
N
O
P
Q
R
S
T
U
V
W
X
Y
Z

bang VERB bangs, banging, banged **1** hit or shut something noisily **2** make a sudden loud noise

bang ADVERB **1** with a bang; suddenly **2** (informal) exactly • bang in the middle

banish VERB banishes, banishing, banished **1** punish a person by ordering them to leave a place **2** drive away doubts or fears
▷ **banishment** NOUN

banisters PLURAL NOUN a handrail with upright supports beside a staircase

banjo NOUN banjos an instrument like a guitar with a round body

bank[1] NOUN banks **1** a slope **2** a long piled-up mass of sand, snow, cloud, etc. **3** a row of lights or switches, etc.

bank VERB banks, banking, banked **1** build or form a bank **2** tilt sideways while changing direction • The plane banked as it prepared to land.

bank[2] NOUN banks **1** a business that looks after people's money **2** a reserve supply • a blood bank

bank VERB banks, banking, banked put money in a bank
bank on rely on

banker NOUN bankers a person who runs a bank

bank holiday NOUN bank holidays a public holiday, when banks are officially closed

bankrupt ADJECTIVE unable to pay your debts
▷ **bankruptcy** NOUN

banner NOUN banners **1** a flag **2** a strip of cloth with a design or slogan on it, carried on a pole or two poles in a procession or demonstration

banquet NOUN banquets a formal public meal
▷ **banqueting** NOUN

banter NOUN playful teasing or joking
▷ **banter** VERB

baptism NOUN baptisms the ceremony of baptizing someone

Baptist NOUN Baptists a member of a group of Christians who believe that a person should not be baptized until he or she is old enough to understand what baptism means

baptize VERB baptizes, baptizing, baptized receive a person into the Christian Church in a ceremony in which he or she is sprinkled with or dipped in water, and usually given a name or names

bar[1] NOUN bars **1** a long piece of something hard • a gold bar **2** a counter or room where refreshments, especially alcoholic drinks, are served **3** a barrier or obstruction **4** one of the small equal sections into which music is divided • three beats to the bar
the Bar lawyers

bar VERB bars, barring, barred **1** fasten something with a bar or bars **2** block or obstruct • A man with a dog barred the way. **3** forbid or ban

barb NOUN barbs the backward-pointing spike of a spear, arrow, or fish hook, which makes the point stay in

Thesaurus

banish VERB **1** The authorities banished him as a traitor. ► exile, expel, deport, send away, eject, evict, expatriate, outlaw, ship away, transport **2** Her look banished any remaining fears. ► dispel, remove, dismiss, disperse, allay, scatter, dissipate, drive away OR out

bank NOUN **1** a grassy bank ► slope, rise, incline, earthwork, embankment, mound, ridge, dike, rampart **2** the bank of the lake ► edge, border, margin, shore, side, brink **3** a steep bank on the curve ► camber, gradient, incline, slope, tilt, ramp, rise, (formal) declivity **4** a bank of dials and switches ► array, row, panel, tier, console, collection, series, display, file, group, line **5** a blood bank ► store, reserve, stock, supply, fund, depository

bank VERB **1** The little plane banked to the left. ► tilt, lean, slant, pitch, tip, incline, cant, heel, list, slope **2** Bank the check immediately. ► deposit, pay in

bankrupt ADJECTIVE **1** The business was soon bankrupt. ► insolvent, failed, ruined, in liquidation, (more informal) bust AN OPPOSITE IS solvent

banner NOUN A banner was flying from a tall building. ► flag, pennant, pennon, standard, streamer, ensign, colors (plural)

banter NOUN good-humored banter ► joking, jesting, repartee, badinage, raillery, ribbing, jocularity, teasing, word play, chaffing, pleasantry

bar NOUN **1** an iron bar ► rod, pole, stake, shaft, batten, stick, strut, beam, girder, rail, railing **2** a bar of chocolate, a bar of soap ► block, slab, cake, tablet, chunk, wedge, piece, hunk, ingot, lump, nugget **3** a bar to progress ► obstacle, barrier, obstruction, hindrance, impediment, block, hurdle, check, deterrent, barricade **4** eating and drinking at bars ► pub, public house, saloon, cafe, tavern

bar VERB **1** The people were barred from entering the country. ► ban, prohibit, forbid, exclude, debar, forbid to enter, prevent from entering, keep out **2** An angry crowd barred the way. ► block, obstruct, hinder, impede, check, halt, prevent, stop, thwart

barbarian NOUN barbarians an uncivilized or brutal person

barbaric ADJECTIVE savage and cruel
▷ **barbarity** NOUN **barbarism** NOUN

barbecue NOUN barbecues **1** a metal frame for grilling food over an open fire outdoors **2** a party where food is cooked in this way

barbecue VERB barbecues, barbecuing, barbecued cook food on a barbecue [via American Spanish from a Caribbean word. It originally meant a wooden frame for drying fish and meat.]

barbed ADJECTIVE **1** having a barb or barbs **2** a barbed comment or remark is deliberately hurtful

barbed wire NOUN wire with small spikes in it, used to make fences

barber NOUN barbers a men's hairdresser

bar chart NOUN bar charts a diagram that shows amounts as bars of varying width or height

bar code NOUN bar codes a set of black lines that are printed on goods, library books, etc., and can be read by a computer to give information about the goods, books, etc.

bard NOUN bards a poet or traveling singer [from a Celtic word used in Scottish, Irish, and Welsh]

bare ADJECTIVE **1** without clothing or covering **2** empty • The cupboard was bare. **3** plain; without details • the bare facts **4** only just enough • the bare necessities of life
▷ **bareness** NOUN

bare VERB bares, baring uncover or reveal • The dog bared its teeth in a snarl.

barely ADVERB only just; with difficulty • We barely reached home in time.

bargain NOUN bargains **1** an agreement about buying or selling or exchanging something **2** something that you buy cheaply

bargain VERB bargains, bargaining, bargained argue over the price to be paid or what you will do in return for something
bargain for be prepared for or expect • He got more than he bargained for.

barge NOUN barges a long flat-bottomed boat used on canals

barge VERB barges, barging, barged push or knock against roughly
barge in rush into a room rudely

baritone NOUN baritones a male singer with a voice between a tenor and a bass

barium (bair- ee- um) NOUN a soft silvery-white metal

bark[1] NOUN barks the short harsh sound made by a dog or fox
▷ **bark** VERB
[from Old English beorc, imitating the sound]

bark[2] NOUN the outer covering of a tree's branches or trunk

barley NOUN a cereal plant from which malt is made

Thesaurus

barbaric ADJECTIVE a barbaric attack
▶ barbarous, brutal, cruel, cold-blooded, inhuman, primitive, savage, uncivilized, wild OPPOSITES ARE civilized, humane

bare ADJECTIVE **1** bare flesh ▶ naked, unclothed, uncovered, nude, stark-naked, exposed, stripped, unclad, undressed, bald OPPOSITES ARE clothed, covered **2** a bare landscape ▶ barren, bleak, desolate, exposed, featureless, treeless, stark, empty, open, windswept OPPOSITES ARE lush, fertile **3** bare trees ▶ leafless, defoliated AN OPPOSITE IS leafy **4** a bare room ▶ empty, unfurnished, vacant, cleared, plain, simple, austere **5** a bare wall ▶ blank, clean, uncovered, unadorned, undecorated, unmarked, stripped **6** the bare facts ▶ straightforward, plain, simple, basic, pure, essential, fundamental, hard, bald, literal, unadorned, unambiguous, unembellished, unconcealed, undisguised **7** the bare necessities ▶ basic, essential, minimum, mere, just adequate, just sufficient

bare VERB She bared her arm for the injection.
▶ uncover, expose, unclothe, strip

bargain NOUN **1** The government has made a bargain with the other parties. ▶ agreement, deal, understanding, arrangement, pact, pledge, compact, contract, negotiation, promise, settlement, transaction, treaty **2** a bargain at $12.99 ▶ good buy, good value, (more informal) snip, (more informal) steal

bargain VERB The union is trying to bargain with the employers. ▶ negotiate, do a deal, barter, discuss terms, hold talks, argue, haggle
bargain on OR **for** The crush at the doors was something I hadn't bargained for. ▶ expect, foresee, imagine, plan for, allow for, reckon on, anticipate, be prepared for, contemplate, consider

bark VERB **1** The dog barked. ▶ woof, yap, yelp **2** The sergeant barked an order. ▶ shout, snap, growl, snarl

bark NOUN the dog's bark ▶ woof, yap, yelp

barmy ADJECTIVE (informal) You must be barmy. a barmy idea ▶ mad, crazy, foolish

a
b
c
d
e
f
g
h
i
j
k
l
m
n
o
p
q
r
s
t
u
v
w
x
y
z

bar mitzvah NOUN bar mitzvahs a religious ceremony for Jewish boys aged 13

barn NOUN barns a farm building for storing hay or grain, etc.
▷ **barnyard** NOUN

barnacle NOUN barnacles a shellfish that attaches itself to rocks and the bottoms of ships

barometer (ba- rom- it- er) NOUN barometers an instrument that measures air pressure, used in forecasting the weather

baron NOUN barons 1 a member of the lowest rank of noblemen 2 a powerful owner of an industry or business • *a newspaper baron*
▷ **barony** NOUN **baronial** (ba- roh- nee- al) ADJECTIVE

baroness NOUN baronesses a female baron or a baron's wife

baronet NOUN baronets a nobleman ranking below a baron but above a knight
▷ **baronetcy** NOUN

baroque (ba- rok) NOUN an elaborately decorated style of architecture used in the 17th and 18th centuries

barracks NOUN a large building or group of buildings for soldiers to live in

barrage (ba- rahzh) NOUN barrages 1 a dam built across a river 2 heavy gunfire 3 a large amount of something • *a barrage of questions*

barrel NOUN barrels 1 a large rounded container with flat ends 2 the metal tube of a gun, through which the shot is fired

barrel organ NOUN barrel organs a musical instrument which you play by turning a handle

barren ADJECTIVE 1 (said about a woman) not able to have children 2 (said about land) not fertile

barricade NOUN barricades a barrier, especially one put up hastily across a street or door

barricade VERB barricades, barricading, barricaded block a street or door with a barricade

barrier NOUN barriers 1 a fence or wall that prevents people from getting past 2 something that stops you doing something

barrister NOUN barristers a lawyer who represents people in the higher lawcourts

barrow NOUN barrows 1 a wheelbarrow 2 a small cart that is pushed or pulled by hand

barter VERB barters, bartering, bartered trade by exchanging goods for other goods, not for money
USAGE This word does not mean "to bargain".

barter NOUN the system of bartering

basalt (bas- awlt) NOUN a kind of dark volcanic rock

base[1] NOUN bases 1 the lowest part of something; the part on which a thing stands 2 a starting point or foundation; a basis 3 a headquarters 4 each of the four corners that must be reached by a runner in baseball 5 a substance that can combine with an acid to form a salt 6 the number in terms of which other numbers can be expressed in a number system; 10 is the base of the decimal system and 2 is the base of the binary system

base VERB bases, basing, based use something as a starting point or foundation • *The story is based on facts.*

base[2] ADJECTIVE 1 dishonorable • *base motives* 2 not of great value • *base metals*
▷ **basely** ADVERB **baseness** NOUN

baseball NOUN baseballs 1 an American game in which runs are scored by hitting a ball and running around a series of four bases 2 the ball used in this game

basement NOUN basements a room or rooms below ground level

Thesaurus

---

barn NOUN *The farm vehicles were kept in a barn.*
► shed, outbuilding

barrage NOUN 1 *a barrage across a river* ► dam, barrier, embankment, wall 2 *a barrage of gunfire* ► bombardment, salvo, battery, cannonade, fusillade, storm, volley, assault, attack, onslaught 3 *a barrage of criticism* ► stream, deluge, flood, onslaught, torrent, shower, mass

barrel NOUN *a barrel of beer* ► cask, butt, keg, tub, tun, drum, canister, hogshead, water-butt

barren ADJECTIVE 1 *barren desert* ► infertile, lifeless, arid, parched, desert, dry, waste, waterless, sterile, torrid, unproductive OPPOSITES ARE fertile, lush 2 *a barren woman* ► infertile, sterile, childless, sterilized AN OPPOSITE IS fertile

barricade NOUN *barricades across the road*
► barrier, obstruction, obstacle, blockade, bulwark, fence, palisade, stockade

barrier NOUN 1 *Police put up barriers to keep out the crowd.* ► barricade, fence, obstacle, obstruction, railing, fencing, wall, bar, hurdle 2 *a barrier to progress* ► obstacle, hindrance, impediment, check, drawback, handicap, limitation, restriction, stumbling block

base NOUN 1 *the base of the tower* ► foot, bottom, foundation, pedestal 2 *The hut was used as a base for the expedition.*
► headquarters, center, station, camp, depot, post

base VERB 1 *The company is based in Paris.*
► locate, establish, set up, station 2 *Base your story on events in the news.* ► build, construct, establish, found, ground

bash VERB bashes, bashing, bashed hit hard

bash NOUN bashes **1** a hard hit **2** (*informal*) a try ● *Have a bash at it.*

bashful ADJECTIVE shy and self-conscious
▷ **bashfully** ADVERB

basic ADJECTIVE forming a basis or starting point ● *Bread is a basic food.*

basin NOUN basins **1** a deep bowl **2** a washbasin **3** a sheltered area of water for mooring boats **4** the area from which water drains into a river ● *the Amazon basin*

basis NOUN bases something to start from or add to; the main principle or ingredient

bask VERB basks, basking, basked sit or lie comfortably warming yourself in the sun

basket NOUN baskets a container for holding or carrying things, made of strips of flexible material or wire woven together

basketball NOUN basketballs **1** a game in which goals are scored by putting a ball through high nets **2** the ball used in this game

bass (bayss) ADJECTIVE deep-sounding; the bass part of a piece of music is the lowest part

bass NOUN basses **1** a male singer with a very deep voice **2** a bass instrument or part

bassoon NOUN bassoons a bass woodwind instrument

bastard NOUN bastards **1** (*old use*) an illegitimate child **2** (*slang*) an unpleasant or difficult person or thing
▷ **bastardy** NOUN

bat[1] NOUN bats **1** a shaped piece of wood used to hit the ball in baseball, cricket, etc. **2** a batsman ● *their opening bat*
off your own bat without help from other people

bat VERB bats, batting, batted use a bat in baseball etc.

bat[2] NOUN bats a flying animal that looks like a mouse with wings

batch NOUN batches a set of things or people dealt with together

bath NOUN baths **1** washing your whole body while sitting in water **2** a large container for water in which to wash your whole body; this water ● *Your bath is getting cold.* **3** a liquid in which something is placed ● *an acid bath*

bath VERB baths, bathing, bathed wash in a bath

bathe VERB bathes, bathing, bathed **1** go swimming **2** wash something gently
▷ **bathe** NOUN **bather** NOUN **bathing suit** NOUN

bathroom NOUN bathrooms a room containing a bath

baths PLURAL NOUN **1** a building with rooms where people can bath **2** a public swimming pool

batsman NOUN batsmen a player who uses a bat in cricket etc.

battalion NOUN battalions an army unit containing two or more companies

batten VERB battens, battening, battened fasten something down firmly

batter VERB batters, battering, battered hit hard and often

batter NOUN batters **1** a beaten mixture of flour, eggs, and milk, used for making pancakes etc. **2** a player who is batting in baseball

battery NOUN batteries **1** a device for storing and supplying electricity **2** a set of similar pieces of equipment; a group of large guns **3** the act of battering or beating

Thesaurus

bash VERB **1** *She could hardly avoid bashing him in the stomach.* ► hit, strike, knock, smack, clout, (*more informal*) biff **2** **bash into** *The car bashed into a lamp post.* ► collide with, crash into, run into, bang into, bump into

bashful ADJECTIVE *Men tend to be bashful about their feelings.* ► shy, coy, reserved, diffident, embarrassed, inhibited, modest, self-conscious, hesitant, timid, reserved, retiring OPPOSITES ARE assertive, forward, bold, confident

basic ADJECTIVE **1** *You must first learn the basic principles of the subject.* ► fundamental, chief, main, key, crucial, principal, central, primary, elementary AN OPPOSITE IS secondary
2 *Washing facilities at the camp are very basic.* ► plain, simple, crude, modest, stark, sparse, spartan, unsophisticated OPPOSITES ARE elaborate, sophisticated

basin NOUN *She poured some water into the basin.* ► bowl, dish, sink, stoup

basis NOUN *The accusations had no factual basis.* ► foundation, justification, support, rationale, base

basket NOUN *a basket of fruit* ► hamper, pannier, creel, punnet, trug

bass ADJECTIVE *a bass note* ► low, deep, bottom

batch NOUN *a batch of cakes* ► consignment, group, quantity, assortment, lot, set

bath NOUN **1** *I'm going to have a bath.* ► wash, jacuzzi (*trademark*) , sauna, shower, (*more informal*) soak

bathe VERB **1** *Vacationers were bathing in the sea.* ► swim, paddle, plunge, (*more informal*) take a dip **2** *The wound must be carefully bathed.* ► cleanse, clean, wash, rinse, immerse, moisten, soak, steep, swill

batter VERB **1** *Someone battered on the door.* ► pound, beat, knock **2** *Winds were battering the waterfront.* ► pound, buffet, lash, pummel **3** *He was battered into submission.* ► beat, pummel, thump

a
b
c
d
e
f
g
h
i
j
k
l
m
n
o
p
q
r
s
t
u
v
w
x
y
z

A
B
C
D
E
F
G
H
I
J
K
L
M
N
O
P
Q
R
S
T
U
V
W
X
Y
Z

battle NOUN **battles** **1** a fight between two armies **2** a struggle
▷ **battlefield** NOUN **battleground** NOUN

battle VERB **battles, battling, battled** fight or struggle

battlements PLURAL NOUN the top of a castle wall, often with gaps from which the defenders could fire at the enemy

battleship NOUN **battleships** a heavily armed warship

bawl VERB **bawls, bawling, bawled** **1** shout **2** cry noisily

bay[1] NOUN **bays** a place where the shore curves inwards

bay[2] NOUN **bays** a compartment or small area set aside for something ● *a parking bay*

bay[3] NOUN **bays** the long deep cry of a hunting hound or other large dog
at bay cornered but defiantly facing attackers ● *a stag at bay*
keep at bay prevent something from coming near or causing harm ● *We need laws to keep poverty at bay.*

bayonet NOUN **bayonets** a blade that can be fixed to the end of a rifle and used for stabbing

bay window NOUN **bay windows** a window that sticks out from the main wall of a house

bazaar NOUN **bazaars** **1** a market place in an Eastern country **2** a sale to raise money for a charity, etc.

BBC ABBREVIATION British Broadcasting Corporation

BC ABBREVIATION before Christ (used with dates counting back from the birth of Jesus Christ)

be VERB **am, are, is; was, were; being, been** **1** exist; occupy a position ● *The shop is on the corner.* **2** happen; take place ● *The wedding is tomorrow.* This verb is also used **1** to join subject and complement (*He is my teacher*) **2** to form parts of other verbs (*It is raining. He was killed*)
have been have gone to or come to as a visitor, etc. ● *We have been to Rome.*

beach NOUN **beaches** the part of the seashore nearest to the water

beacon NOUN **beacons** a light or fire used as a signal or warning

bead NOUN **beads** **1** a small piece of a hard substance with a hole in it for threading with others on a string or wire, e.g., to make a necklace **2** a drop of liquid ● *a bead of sweat* [from Old English *gebed*. The original meaning was "prayer": people kept count of the prayers they said by moving the beads on a rosary, to which the meaning of *bead* was transferred.]

beady ADJECTIVE (said about eyes) small and bright

beak NOUN **beaks** the hard horny part of a bird's mouth [via early French from Latin *beccus*]

beaker NOUN **beakers** **1** a tall drinking mug, often without a handle **2** a glass container used for pouring liquids in a laboratory

beam NOUN **beams** **1** a long thick bar of wood or metal **2** a ray or stream of light or other radiation **3** a happy smile

Thesaurus

battered ADJECTIVE *help for battered wives* ► beaten, abused, assaulted, maltreated, victimized

battle NOUN **1** *The battle took place a few miles north of the city.* ► fight, engagement, action, clash, encounter, conflict **2** *a legal battle for ownership of the club* ► conflict, struggle, dispute **3** *a battle to save the library from closure* ► campaign, crusade

battle VERB *They battled to control the fire.* ► fight, struggle, strive

baulk VERB *baulk at Some farmers baulk at using pesticides.* ► resist, (more formal) eschew, be reluctant to

bawdy ADJECTIVE *bawdy stories* ► rude, indecent, crude, ribald, naughty, improper, risqué, lewd, vulgar, obscene

bawl VERB **1** *The child sat on its bed bawling.* ► cry, sob, weep, blubber **2** *"Get out," she bawled.* ► yell, shout, roar, bellow, shriek, scream

bay NOUN **1** *a large bay on the coast* ► cove, inlet, gulf, bight **2** *a loading bay* ► recess, alcove, booth, compartment, niche, nook, opening

bazaar NOUN *the church bazaar* ► sale, fair, fête, market, auction, swap meet

be VERB **1** *There was a young family next door.* ► exist, live *After he'd been there a while he ordered a drink.* ► remain, stay, wait, linger, (more informal) hang on **3** *The next performance of the play will be tomorrow.* ► take place, occur, happen, come about

beach NOUN *a picnic on the beach* ► shore, sand, sands, seashore, coast, (poetic) strand

beacon NOUN *a beacon on the hill* ► flare, signal, bonfire, beam

bead NOUN *beads of sweat* ► drop, droplet, globule, blob, drip, pearl

beaker NOUN *a beaker of water* ► mug, tumbler, goblet, cup, glass, jar, tankard

beam NOUN **1** *a house with wooden beams* ► timber, joist, girder, spar, bar, plank, post, rafter, support, stanchion, boom **2** *a beam of light* ► ray, shaft, gleam, stream

beam VERB beams, beaming, beamed **1** smile happily **2** send out a beam of light or other radiation

bean NOUN beans **1** a kind of plant with seeds growing in pods **2** its seed or pod eaten as food **3** the seed of coffee

bear[1] NOUN bears a large heavy animal with thick fur and large teeth and claws

bear[2] VERB bears, bearing, bore, borne **1** carry or support **2** have or show a mark, etc. • *She still bears the scar.* **3** endure or stand • *I can't bear this pain.* **4** produce or give birth to • *She bore him two sons.*
▷ **bearer** NOUN
bear in mind remember something and take it into account
bear out support or confirm

bearable ADJECTIVE able to be endured; tolerable

beard NOUN beards hair on a man's chin
▷ **bearded** ADJECTIVE

beard VERB beards, bearding, bearded come face to face with a person and challenge him or her boldly

bearing NOUN bearings **1** the way a person stands, walks, behaves, etc. **2** relevance • *My friendship with Tom has no bearing on his selection for the team.* **3** the direction or position of one thing in relation to another **4** a device for preventing friction in a machine • *ball bearings*
get your bearings work out where you are in relation to things

beast NOUN beasts **1** any large four-footed animal **2** (*informal*) a cruel or vicious person
▷ **beastly** ADJECTIVE

beat VERB beats, beating, beat, beaten **1** hit often, especially with a stick **2** shape or flatten something by beating it **3** stir vigorously **4** make repeated movements • *His heart beat faster.* **5** do better than somebody; overcome
▷ **beater** NOUN

beat NOUN beats **1** a regular rhythm or stroke • *the beat of your heart* **2** emphasis in rhythm; the strong rhythm of pop music **3** a policeman's regular route

beautiful ADJECTIVE attractive to your senses or your mind
▷ **beautifully** ADVERB

a
b
c
d
e
f
g
h
i
j
k
l
m
n
o
p
q
r
s
t
u
v
w
x
y
z

Thesaurus

beam VERB **1** *Satellites beam radio waves to rooftop aerials.* ► broadcast, transmit, direct, emit, radiate, send out, aim **2** *Daphne beamed happily.* ► smile, grin OPPOSITES ARE glower, frown

bear VERB **1** *The rope would no longer bear his weight.* ► support, carry, hold, sustain, prop up, take **2** *The document bore a signature.* ► display, possess, show, exhibit, have **3** *The postman arrived, bearing a large parcel.* ► carry, bring, convey, transport, deliver, fetch, move, take, transfer **4** *I cannot bear pain. We found the noise hard to bear.* ► put up with, endure, tolerate, stand, stomach, abide, accept, cope with, live with, suffer, sustain, undergo, brook **5** *The woman bore a child.* ► give birth to, produce, mother, bring forth
bear down on *A huge vehicle was bearing down on them.* ► approach, advance on, close in on
bear out *The report bears out what I was saying.* ► confirm, endorse, corroborate

bearable ADJECTIVE *The pain was only just bearable.* ► tolerable, endurable, acceptable

bearing NOUN **1** *The Baroness had a regal bearing.* ► demeanor, air, manner, look, appearance, behavior, presence, carriage, deportment, mien, poise, posture, style **2** *The discovery could have some bearing on the mystery.* ► connection (with), relevance (to), significance (for), import (for), pertinence (to), reference (to), relationship (with)

bearings PLURAL NOUN *When it got dark we began to lose our bearings.* ► sense of direction,

orientation, whereabouts, position, situation, way

beast NOUN **1** *the roars of wild beasts* ► animal, creature, brute **2** *Her husband was a beast.* ► brute, monster, fiend, demon RELATED ADJECTIVE ► bestial

beastly ADJECTIVE *Derek had been beastly to them.* ► unkind, cruel, mean, nasty, horrible, spiteful

beat NOUN **1** *music with a strong beat* ► rhythm, pulse, throb, accent, stress **2** *a policeman's beat* ► circuit, rounds, route, itinerary, journey, path, way

beat VERB **1** *The man was beating a dog with a stick.* ► hit, strike, thrash, whip, attack, assault, (*more informal*) wallop, (*more informal*) whack **2** *Molly was beating eggs for her omelette.* ► whip, agitate, blend, froth up, mix, stir **3** *His heart was beating faster.* ► pound, pulsate, race, thump, flutter, palpitate **4** *William of Normandy beat the English at the Battle of Hastings. The visitors beat the home team decisively.* ► defeat, overcome, conquer, vanquish, subdue, crush, overpower, overwhelm, rout, trounce, win against, get the better of, (*more informal*) thrash
beat around the bush *Let's not beat around the bush.* ► prevaricate, vacillate, hedge
beat up *They went into town and got beaten up.* ► assault, attack

beautiful ADJECTIVE *a beautiful young woman, a beautiful garden* ► attractive, pretty, good-looking, nice-looking, lovely, glamorous, gorgeous, stunning AN OPPOSITE IS ugly

beautify ➡ before

beautify VERB beautifies, beautifying, beautified make someone beautiful
▷ **beautification** NOUN

beauty NOUN beauties **1** a quality that gives pleasure to your senses or your mind **2** a person or thing that has beauty **3** an excellent example of something

beaver NOUN beavers an animal with soft brown fur and strong teeth; it builds its home in a deep pool which it makes by damming a stream

beaver VERB beavers, beavering, beavered work hard • *He's beavering away on the computer.*

because CONJUNCTION for the reason that
because of for the reason of • *He limped because of his bad leg.*

beck NOUN
at someone's beck and call always ready and waiting to do what he or she asks

beckon VERB beckons, beckoning, beckoned make a sign to a person asking him or her to come

become VERB becomes, becoming, became, become **1** come or grow to be; begin to be • *It became dark.* **2** be suitable for; make a person look attractive
become of happen to • *What became of it?*

bed NOUN beds **1** a piece of furniture that you sleep or rest on, especially one with a mattress and coverings **2** a piece of a garden where plants are grown **3** the bottom of the sea or of a river **4** a flat base; a foundation **5** a layer of rock or soil

bedclothes PLURAL NOUN sheets, blankets, etc.

bedpan NOUN bedpans a container for use as a lavatory by a bedridden person

bedraggled (bid-rag-eld) ADJECTIVE very untidy; wet and dirty

bedridden ADJECTIVE too weak or ill to get out of bed

bedrock NOUN solid rock beneath soil

bedroom NOUN bedrooms a room for sleeping in

bedtime NOUN bedtimes the time for going to bed

bee NOUN bees a stinging insect with four wings that makes honey

beech NOUN beeches a tree with smooth bark and glossy leaves

beef NOUN meat from an ox, bull, or cow [via early French from Latin *bos bovis* = head of cattle]

beefy ADJECTIVE having a solid muscular body
▷ **beefiness** NOUN

beehive NOUN beehives a box or other container for bees to live in

beeline NOUN
make a beeline for go straight or quickly toward something

beer NOUN beers an alcoholic drink made from malt and hops
▷ **beery** ADJECTIVE

beet NOUN beet or beets a plant with a thick root used as a vegetable or for making sugar

beetle NOUN beetles an insect with hard shiny wing covers

beet NOUN beets a dark red root vegetable

before ADVERB at an earlier time • *Have you been here before?*

Thesaurus

beauty NOUN *the beauty of the scene*
▶ attractiveness, prettiness, loveliness, charm, allure, magnificence, radiance, splendor, appeal, glamor, glory, grace, handsomeness AN OPPOSITE IS ugliness RELATED ADJECTIVE
▶ aesthetic

because CONJUNCTION
because of *He missed most of the season because of injury.* ▶ on account of, owing to, due to, as a result of, as a consequence of, in view of

beckon VERB *She beckoned him to go over to her.*
▶ signal, gesture, motion, gesticulate, invite

become VERB **1** *Caterpillars become butterflies.*
▶ grow into, turn into, change into, develop into **2** *The family soon became rich.* ▶ grow, come to be, turn **3** *She wants to become the first woman president.* ▶ be appointed, be elected, be chosen, be made **4** *Dark colors become you.*
▶ suit, flatter, befit, grace, set off, enhance, harmonize with

becoming ADJECTIVE *The dress is very becoming.*
▶ attractive, elegant, fetching, pretty, comely

bed NOUN **1** *A cat lay on the bed.* ▶ divan, bunk, couch **2** *a flower bed* ▶ plot, patch, area **3** *the bed of a river* ▶ bottom, floor, course **4** *posts set in a bed of concrete* ▶ base, foundation, support, setting

bedraggled ADJECTIVE *The heavy rain had left him looking bedraggled.* ▶ disheveled, unkempt, untidy, sodden, messy, scruffy, dirty, soiled, stained, wet OPPOSITES ARE neat, clean, spruce

bee NOUN *Bees hovered around the flowers.*
▶ drone, worker, bumblebee, honeybee, queen
a bee in your bonnet *He had a bee in his bonnet about traffic.* ▶ obsession, preoccupation, fixation, compulsion, (more informal) hang-up

beefy ADJECTIVE *A beefy man sat at the bar.*
▶ muscular, brawny, burly, hefty, stocky, fat, portly

before PREPOSITION, CONJUNCTION **1** earlier than • *I was here before you!* **2** in front of • *He came before the judge.*

beforehand ADVERB earlier; in readiness

befriend VERB befriends, befriending, befriended make friends with someone

beg VERB begs, begging, begged **1** ask to be given money, food, etc. **2** ask formally or desperately

beg the question argue in an illogical way by relying on the result that you are trying to prove

go begging be available

I beg your pardon I apologize; I did not hear what you said

beggar NOUN beggars **1** a person who lives by begging **2** (*informal*) a person • *You lucky beggar!*
▷ **beggary** NOUN

begin VERB begins, beginning, began, begun **1** do the earliest or first part of something; start speaking **2** come into existence • *The problem began last year.* **3** have something as its first part • *The word begins with B.*

beginner NOUN beginners a person who is just beginning to learn a subject

beginning NOUN beginnings the start or first part of something

begrudge VERB begrudges, begrudging, begrudged resent having to give or allow something; grudge

beguile (big- I'll) VERB beguiles, beguiling, beguiled **1** amuse or fascinate **2** deceive

behalf NOUN
on behalf of for the benefit of someone else or as their representative • *We are collecting money on behalf of cancer research.*
on my behalf for me
USAGE Do not use *on behalf of* (= for someone else) when you mean *on the part of* (= by someone). For example, do not say: *This was the worst performance on behalf of Arsenal that I can remember.*

behave VERB behaves, behaving, behaved **1** act in a particular way • *They behaved badly.* **2** show good manners • *Behave yourself!*
▷ **behavior** NOUN **behavioral** ADJECTIVE

behead VERB beheads, beheading, beheaded cut the head off a person or thing; execute a person in this way

behind ADVERB **1** at or to the back; at a place people have left • *Don't leave it behind.* **2** not making good progress; late • *I'm behind with my rent.*

behind PREPOSITION **1** at or to the back of; on the further side of **2** having made less progress than • *He is behind the others in French.* **3** supporting; causing • *What is behind all this trouble?*
behind a person's back kept secret from him or her deceitfully
behind the times out of date

behind NOUN behinds (*informal*) a person's bottom

behindhand ADVERB, ADJECTIVE late or slow in doing something

Thesaurus

before ADVERB *She had called the day before.*
▶ earlier, in advance, previously, sooner

befriend VERB *He had tried to befriend the new boy.* ▶ make friends with, get to know, look after, stand by, help, support, take under your wing

beg VERB **1** *A man on the pavement was begging.* ▶ ask for money, solicit money, (*more informal*) cadge, (*more informal*) scrounge **2** *Do we have to beg for a favor?* ▶ plead, entreat, implore, ask, beseech, crave, importune, petition, pray, request, (*formal*) supplicate

beggar NOUN *He always gave money to beggars he met in the street.* ▶ tramp, vagrant, destitute person, down-and-out, homeless person, (*more formal*) mendicant, pauper, poor person

begin VERB **1** *We will begin work tomorrow.*
▶ start, embark on, set about, get down to, (*more formal*) commence AN OPPOSITE IS finish **2** *The interviewer began with a few quick questions.* ▶ start, start off, open, lead off, get going AN OPPOSITE IS conclude **3** *Where did the rumor begin?* ▶ start, originate, spring up, emerge, (*more formal*) commence AN OPPOSITE IS end RELATED ADJECTIVE ▶ incipient

beginner NOUN **1** *The course is for beginners.*
▶ novice, initiate, learner, starter, new recruit, trainee, apprentice, tiro

beginning NOUN **1** *the beginning of a new era*
▶ birth, dawn, start, starting point, inception, establishment, origin, onset, emergence **2** *She had been opposed to the idea from the beginning*
▶ outset, start **3** *the beginning of the story*
▶ opening, start, prelude

begrudge VERB *Kate didn't seem to begrudge Harry all his wealth.* ▶ resent, grudge, mind, object to, be bitter about, covet, envy, be jealous of, be envious of

behave VERB **1** *The children worked hard and behaved well.* ▶ conduct yourself, act, react, respond, run, acquit yourself **2 behave yourself** *Try to behave yourself.* ▶ be good, act correctly, be on your best behavior

behavior NOUN *Their behavior was disgusting.*
▶ conduct, manners, attitude, demeanor, deportment, bearing

behead VERB *The king was beheaded.*
▶ decapitate, execute, guillotine

a
b
c
d
e
f
g
h
i
j
k
l
m
n
o
p
q
r
s
t
u
v
w
x
y
z

A
B
C
D
E
F
G
H
I
J
K
L
M
N
O
P
Q
R
S
T
U
V
W
X
Y
Z

beige (bayzh) NOUN, ADJECTIVE a very light brown color

being NOUN beings **1** existence **2** a creature

belated ADJECTIVE coming very late or too late
▷ **belatedly** ADVERB

belch VERB belches, belching, belched **1** send out wind from your stomach through your mouth noisily **2** send out fire or smoke, etc., from an opening
▷ **belch** NOUN

belief NOUN beliefs **1** believing **2** something a person believes

believe VERB believes, believing, believed think that something is true or that someone is telling the truth
▷ **believable** ADJECTIVE **believer** NOUN
believe in think that something exists or is good or can be relied on

belittle VERB belittles, belittling, belittled make something seem of little value • Do not belittle their success.
▷ **belittlement** NOUN

bell NOUN bells **1** a cup-shaped metal instrument that makes a ringing sound when struck by the clapper hanging inside it **2** any device that makes a ringing or buzzing sound to attract attention **3** a bell-shaped object

belligerent (bil- ij- er- ent) ADJECTIVE **1** aggressive; eager to fight **2** fighting; engaged in a war
▷ **belligerently** ADVERB **belligerence** NOUN

bellow NOUN bellows **1** the loud deep sound made by a bull or other large animal **2** a deep shout

bellow VERB bellows, bellowing, bellowed give a deep shout

belly NOUN bellies the abdomen; the stomach

belong VERB belongs, belonging, belonged have a proper place • The pans belong in the kitchen.
belong to be the property of; be a member of • We belong to the same club.

belongings PLURAL NOUN a person's possessions

beloved ADJECTIVE dearly loved

below ADVERB at or to a lower position; underneath • There's fire down below.

below PREPOSITION lower than; under • The temperature was ten degrees below zero.

belt NOUN belts **1** a strip of cloth or leather, etc., worn around the waist **2** a band of flexible material used in machinery **3** a long narrow area • a belt of rain

Thesaurus

being NOUN **1** She loves him with all her being. ► existence, soul, spirit, essence, actuality, life, living, reality, solidity, substance **2** a mortal being ► person, creature, individual, animal, entity

belch VERB **1** Laurence belched behind his hand. ► burp, emit wind **2** The vehicle was belching black smoke. ► emit, give out, discharge, send out, smoke, spew out, erupt, fume, gush

belief NOUN **1** She had a strong belief that he was innocent. ► conviction, confidence, opinion, certainty, credence, sureness OPPOSITES ARE disbelief, doubt **2** a belief in the benefits of a good diet ► trust, reliance on, credence **3** religious belief ► faith, ideology, principle, creed, dogma AN OPPOSITE IS scepticism

believe VERB **1** I find that hard to believe. ► accept, be certain about, be convinced by, regard as true, (more informal) swallow AN OPPOSITE IS disbelieve RELATED ADJECTIVE ► credible **2** I believe several people have cheated. ► think, consider, maintain, conclude, be of the opinion, think it likely, feel, imagine, judge, suppose, take it for granted

believer NOUN a religious believer ► devotee, disciple, follower, adherent, fanatic, proselyte, supporter, upholder, zealot OPPOSITES ARE sceptic, agnostic, atheist

bell NOUN I can hear the bell. ► chime, gong, alarm, carillon, knell, peal, signal

belligerent ADJECTIVE **1** She stared in a belligerent manner. ► aggressive, hostile, antagonistic, confrontational, argumentative, quarrelsome, militant, combative, provocative, contentious, pugnacious **2** a belligerent nation ► warlike, bellicose, militant, militaristic, violent AN OPPOSITE IS peaceable

bellow VERB He bellowed something in her ear. ► shout, yell, bawl, roar, boom, shriek

belly NOUN He stood scratching his belly. ► stomach, abdomen, middle, (usually disapproving) paunch, (more informal) tummy, (much more informal) tum

belong VERB **1** belong to The house belongs to his mother. ► be owned by, be the property of **2** belong to I belong to a sports club. ► be a member of, be affiliated with, be connected with **3** They felt they did not belong there. ► feel welcome, have a place, be at home **4** The book belongs on the top shelf. ► be located, have a place, go

belongings PLURAL NOUN Remember to take all your belongings with you. ► possessions, property, personal effects, (more informal) stuff

beloved ADJECTIVE her beloved father ► dear, dearest, darling, loved, much loved, cherished

belt NOUN **1** a raincoat tied with a belt ► girdle, sash, strap, waistband, (of a man's tuxedo)

belt VERB belts, belting, belted **1** put a belt around something **2** (slang) hit or beat **3** (slang) rush along

bench NOUN benches **1** a long seat **2** a long table for working at **3** the seat where judges or magistrates sit; the judges or magistrates hearing a lawsuit

bend VERB bends, bending, bent **1** change from being straight **2** turn downward; stoop • She bent to pick it up.

bend NOUN bends a place where something bends; a curve or turn • a bend in the road

beneath PREPOSITION **1** under **2** unworthy of • Cheating is beneath you.

beneath ADVERB underneath

benefactor NOUN benefactors a person who gives money or other help

beneficial ADJECTIVE having a good or helpful effect; advantageous

beneficiary (ben- if- ish- er- ee) NOUN beneficiaries a person who receives benefits, especially from a will

benefit NOUN benefits **1** something that is helpful or profitable **2** a payment to which a person is entitled from government funds or from an insurance policy

benefit VERB benefits, benefiting, benefited **1** do good to a person or thing **2** receive a benefit

benevolent ADJECTIVE **1** kind and helpful **2** formed for charitable purposes • a benevolent fund
▷ **benevolently** ADVERB **benevolence** NOUN

benign (bin- I'n) ADJECTIVE **1** kindly **2** favorable **3** (said about a disease) mild, not malignant
▷ **benignly** ADVERB

benignant (bin- ig- nant) ADJECTIVE kindly

bent ADJECTIVE curved or crooked
bent on intending to do something

bent NOUN a talent for something

bequeath VERB bequeaths, bequeathing, bequeathed leave something to a person, especially in a will

bequest NOUN bequests something left to a person, especially in a will

bereaved ADJECTIVE extremely sad because a relative or friend has died
▷ **bereavement** NOUN

berry NOUN berries any small round juicy fruit without a stone

berserk (ber- serk) ADJECTIVE
go berserk become uncontrollably violent

Thesaurus

cummerbund **2** a spindle driven by a belt ► band, loop, circle **3** a belt of woodland ► strip, stretch, area, tract, zone, region, district, line, swathe

belt VERB **belt along** (informal) They all belted along to the bus station. ► hurry, rush, speed

bemused ADJECTIVE She sat there with a bemused expression. ► bewildered, confused, distracted, puzzled, muddled, baffled, perplexed

bench NOUN The children sat in a row on a bench. ► pew, long seat, form, stall

bend NOUN We came to a bend in the road. ► curve, turn, angle, corner, twist, zigzag

bend VERB **1** You can bend the pipe around the tank. ► curve, curl, angle, turn **2** The road bends ahead. ► curve, turn, veer, deviate, twist
bend down He bent down to pick up the piece of paper. ► stoop, bow, crouch, duck, kneel, lean

beneficial ADJECTIVE A good diet is beneficial to health. ► good (for), advantageous, favorable, useful, valuable, helpful, salutary, wholesome AN OPPOSITE IS harmful

benefit NOUN **1** the benefits of a healthy diet ► advantage, reward, strength, blessing, convenience, gain, asset, service AN OPPOSITE IS disadvantage **2** We are doing it for your benefit. ► good, sake, interest, welfare, advantage **3** the unemployed who are on benefit ► social security, welfare, assistance, allowance, income support

benefit VERB The tax cuts will benefit those on a low income. ► help, advantage, assist, aid, advance, be beneficial to, do good to, profit, serve AN OPPOSITE IS hinder

benevolence NOUN The hospital is dependent on the benevolence of local businesses. ► kindness, generosity, goodness, goodwill, consideration, charity, magnanimity

benevolent ADJECTIVE She smiled a benevolent smile. ► kind, generous, helpful, caring, benign, friendly, magnanimous, sympathetic, considerate, philanthropic AN OPPOSITE IS unkind

benign ADJECTIVE **1** a benign smile ► friendly, kind, benevolent **2** a benign influence ► favorable, beneficial, advantageous, propitious

bent ADJECTIVE **1** a bent nail ► crooked, twisted, misshapen, angled, buckled, distorted, folded, looped, warped AN OPPOSITE IS straight **2** a man with a bent back ► crooked, hunched, arched, bowed, curved **3** (informal) bent politicians ► corrupt, criminal, dishonest, fraudulent, immoral, untrustworthy, wicked AN OPPOSITE IS honest

berserk ADJECTIVE **go berserk** reports of a man who went berserk in the street and was hit by a car ► go crazy, go mad, become demented, become frantic, become hysterical, go out of your mind, rave, become deranged, run amok, (more informal) freak out

berth NOUN berths **1** a sleeping place on a ship or train **2** a place where a ship can moor give a wide berth to keep at a safe distance from a person or thing

berth VERB berths, berthing, berthed moor in a berth

beseech VERB beseeches, beseeching, beseeched or besought ask earnestly; implore

beside PREPOSITION **1** by the side of; near **2** compared with
be beside himself or herself etc be very excited or upset

besides PREPOSITION, ADVERB in addition to; also • Who came besides you? • And besides, it's the wrong color.

besiege VERB besieges, besieging, besieged **1** surround a place in order to capture it **2** crowd round • Fans besieged the singer after the concert.

besotted ADJECTIVE too fond of something; fond in a silly way

besought past tense of beseech

best ADJECTIVE of the most excellent kind; most able to do something

best ADVERB **1** in the best way; most **2** most usefully; most wisely • We had best go.

best man NOUN the bridegroom's chief attendant at a wedding

bestow VERB bestows, bestowing, bestowed present to someone
▷ bestowal NOUN

best-seller NOUN best-sellers a book that sells in large numbers

bet NOUN bets **1** an agreement that you will receive money if you are correct in choosing the winner of a race, game, etc., or in saying something will happen, and will lose money if you are not correct **2** the money you risk losing in a bet

bet VERB bets, betting, bet or betted **1** make a bet **2** (informal) think most likely; predict • I bet he will forget.

beta (bayt- a) NOUN the second letter of the Greek alphabet, = b

betray VERB betrays, betraying, betrayed **1** be disloyal to a person or country, etc. **2** reveal something without meaning to
▷ betrayal NOUN betrayer NOUN

betrothed ADJECTIVE (formal) engaged to be married
▷ betroth VERB betrothal NOUN

better ADJECTIVE **1** more excellent; more satisfactory **2** recovered from illness

better ADVERB **1** in a better way; more **2** more usefully; more wisely • We had better go.
get the better of defeat or outwit

better VERB betters, bettering, bettered **1** improve something **2** do better than
▷ betterment NOUN

between PREPOSITION, ADVERB **1** within two or more given limits • between the walls **2** connecting two or more people, places, or things • The train runs between New York and Boston. **3** shared by • Divide this money between you. **4** separating; comparing • Can you tell the difference between them?

Thesaurus

besiege VERB **1** Alexander besieged the city for two years. ► lay siege to, blockade, surround, encircle, confine, beleaguer, (old use) invest **2** She spent a whole day besieged by reporters outside her New York home. ► surround, mob, plague, harass, pester, overwhelm

best ADJECTIVE **1** one of the best bookshops in town ► foremost, leading, top, finest, pre-eminent, supreme, premier, optimum, outstanding, unsurpassed, unequalled, unrivalled AN OPPOSITE IS worst **2** Do whatever you think best. ► most suitable, most appropriate, most fitting, most sensible

bestow VERB The college bestowed a scholarship on her. ► award, confer, endow, (less formal) present, (less formal) give
USAGE If you use award, you say The college awarded her a scholarship. This is a much less formal and more ordinary word. If you use present or endow, you say The college presented (or endowed) her with a scholarship. If you use confer, you say The college conferred a scholarship on her.

bet NOUN **1** a $10 bet ► gamble, wager, (informal) punt **2** My bet is they won't come. ► opinion, forecast, prediction, feeling, hunch

bet VERB **1** She bet all her savings and won. ► wager, gamble, stake, risk **2** (informal) I bet I'm right. ► (less informal) be sure, (less informal) be confident, (less informal) be convinced, (less informal) expect

betray VERB **1** We trusted him and he betrayed us. ► let down, break your promise to, be unfaithful to, double-cross, deceive **2** They were betrayed to the authorities. ► inform on, denounce **3** Please don't betray my secret. He found it hard not to betray his feelings. ► reveal, give away, manifest, show, indicate, disclose, divulge, expose, let out, let slip, tell

better ADJECTIVE **1** We are looking for better facilities. ► superior, finer, preferable **2** Are you feeling better? ► healthier, fitter, stronger, recovered, (more informal) on the mend

better VERB The idea cannot be bettered. ► improve on, surpass, outdo

USAGE The preposition **between** should be followed by the object form of the pronoun (me, her, him, them, or us). The expression "between you and I" is incorrect; say *between you and me.*

beverage NOUN beverages any kind of drink

bewail VERB bewails, bewailing, bewailed mourn for something

beware VERB be careful • *Beware of pickpockets.*

bewilder VERB bewilders, bewildering, bewildered puzzle someone hopelessly
▷ **bewilderment** NOUN

bewitch VERB bewitches, bewitching, bewitched **1** put a magic spell on someone **2** delight someone very much

beyond PREPOSITION, ADVERB **1** further than; further on • *Don't go beyond the fence.* **2** outside the range of; too difficult for • *The problem is beyond me.*

bias NOUN biases **1** a feeling or influence for or against someone or something; a prejudice **2** a tendency to swerve **3** a slanting direction

biased ADJECTIVE prejudiced

bib NOUN bibs **1** a cloth or covering put under a baby's chin during meals **2** the part of an apron above the waist

Bible NOUN Bibles the sacred book of the Jews (the Old Testament) and of the Christians (the Old and New Testament) [from Greek *biblia* = books. The word originally meant rolls of papyrus from Byblos, a port now in Lebanon.]

biblical ADJECTIVE to do with or in the Bible

bibliography (bib-lee-og-ra-fee) NOUN bibliographies **1** a list of books about a subject or by a particular author **2** the study of books and their history
▷ **bibliographical** ADJECTIVE

bicentenary (by-sen-ten-er-ee) NOUN bicentenaries a 200th anniversary
▷ **bicentennial** (by-sen-ten-ee-al) ADJECTIVE

biceps (by-seps) NOUN biceps the large muscle at the front of the arm above the elbow

bicker VERB bickers, bickering, bickered quarrel over unimportant things; squabble

bicycle NOUN bicycles a two-wheeled vehicle driven by pedals
▷ **bicyclist** NOUN

bid[1] NOUN bids **1** the offer of an amount you are willing to pay for something, especially at an auction **2** an attempt

bid VERB bids, bidding, bid make a bid
▷ **bidder** NOUN

bid[2] VERB bids, bidding, bid or (old use) bade, bid or bidden **1** say as a greeting or farewell • *I bid you all good night.* **2** command • *Do as you are bid* or *bidden*

bidding NOUN if you do someone's bidding, you do what they tell you to do

bide VERB bides, biding, bided bide your time wait patiently for the right time to do something

biennial NOUN biennials a plant that lives for two years, flowering and dying in the second year

bier (beer) NOUN biers a movable stand on which a coffin or a dead body is placed before it is buried

bifocal (by-foh-kal) ADJECTIVE (said about lenses for glasses) made in two sections, with the upper part for looking at distant objects and the lower part for reading

bifocals PLURAL NOUN bifocal glasses

Thesaurus

beware VERB **1** *There are landmines in the fields so beware.* ► watch out, look out, be careful, take care, be on the lookout, be on the alert **2** *Beware of the dog.* ► watch out for, mind, avoid, steer clear of

bewilder VERB *His remarks had bewildered her.* ► puzzle, perplex, baffle, mystify, confuse, bemuse, disconcert, confound, (more informal) flummox, (more informal) floor

bewildered ADJECTIVE *Harry looked quite bewildered.* ► puzzled, perplexed, baffled, mystified, confused, bemused, disconcerted, (more informal) flummoxed

bewitch VERB *We were bewitched by the beauty of the place.* ► captivate, charm, enchant, entrance, enthral, delight, mesmerize AN OPPOSITE IS repel

bias NOUN *The management was accused of bias.* ► prejudice, partiality, discrimination, unfairness, injustice, partisanship, favoritism, bigotry, intolerance, chauvinism, racism, sexism

biased ADJECTIVE *The judge was clearly biased.* ► prejudiced, partial, one-sided, partisan, subjective, bigoted, chauvinistic, racist, sexist OPPOSITES ARE unbiased, impartial

bicker VERB *I don't want to stand here all day bickering about it.* ► quarrel, squabble, wrangle, argue, scrap, row

bid NOUN **1** *a bid of $5,000* ► offer, tender, proposal, price, proposition **2** *a bid to discover the truth* ► attempt, effort, endeavor, try (at), (informal) go (at), (informal) crack (at)

bid VERB *A buyer bid a record price at the auction.* ► offer, make an offer of, put in a bid of, tender, proffer, propose

biff VERB (informal) *He had biffed her by mistake.* ► hit, strike, knock, smack, bash, clout

big ADJECTIVE bigger, biggest **1** large **2** important • *the big match* **3** more grown-up; elder • *my big sister*

bigamy (big- a- mee) NOUN the crime of marrying a person when you are already married to someone else
▷ **bigamous** ADJECTIVE **bigamist** NOUN

bigot NOUN bigots a bigoted person

bigoted ADJECTIVE narrow-minded and intolerant
▷ **bigotry** NOUN

bike NOUN bikes (*informal*) a bicycle or motorcycle

bikini NOUN bikinis a woman's two-piece swimsuit [named after the island of Bikini in the Pacific Ocean, where an atomic bomb test was carried out in 1946, at about the time the bikini was first worn (both caused great excitement)]

bilateral ADJECTIVE **1** of or on two sides **2** between two people or groups • *a bilateral agreement*

bile NOUN a bitter liquid produced by the liver, helping to digest fats

bilingual (by- ling- wal) ADJECTIVE **1** able to speak two languages well **2** written in two languages

bilious ADJECTIVE feeling sick; sickly
▷ **biliousness** NOUN

bill[1] NOUN bills **1** a written statement of charges for goods or services that have been supplied **2** a poster **3** a list; a program of entertainment **4** the draft of a proposed law to be discussed by Congress **5** a banknote **bill of fare** a menu

bill[2] NOUN bills a bird's beak

billabong NOUN billabongs (in Australia) a backwater

billboard NOUN billboards a tall fence or hoarding for advertisements

billiards NOUN a game in which three balls are struck with cues on a cloth-covered table (billiard table)

billion NOUN billions **1** a thousand million (1,000,000,000)
▷ **billionth** ADJECTIVE, NOUN
USAGE Although the word originally meant a million million, nowadays it means a thousand million.

billow NOUN billows a huge wave

bin NOUN bins a large or deep container, especially one for garbage or litter [via Old English from a Celtic word]

binary (by- ner- ee) ADJECTIVE involving sets of two; consisting of two parts

binary digit NOUN binary digits either of the two digits (0 and 1) used in the binary system

binary system or **binary notation** NOUN (in computing) a system of expressing numbers by using the digits 0 and 1 only

bind VERB binds, binding, bound **1** fasten material around something **2** fasten the pages of a book into a cover **3** tie up or tie together **4** make somebody agree to do something
▷ **binder** NOUN
bind a person over make him or her agree not to break the law

bind NOUN (*slang*) a nuisance; a bore

binding NOUN bindings something that binds, especially the covers, glue, etc., of a book

binding ADJECTIVE (said about an agreement or promise) that must be carried out or obeyed

binge NOUN binges (*slang*) a time spent eating a lot of food

bingo NOUN a game using cards on which numbered squares are crossed out as the numbers are called out at random

binoculars PLURAL NOUN a device with lenses for both eyes, making distant objects seem nearer

Thesaurus

big ADJECTIVE **1** *a big house. The bill was very big.* ► large, great, huge, enormous, colossal, immense **2** *a big difference* ► significant, important, substantial, considerable, sizable **3** *big ideas* ► ambitious, grand, grandiose, far-reaching **4** *That was big of you.* ► generous, considerate, magnanimous, kind, gracious

bigoted ADJECTIVE *He disliked people who held such bigoted views.* ► prejudiced, biased, partial, intolerant, narrow-minded
USAGE Note that *bigoted* is a much stronger word than the alternatives given here.

bill NOUN **1** *The bill came to over a thousand dollars.* ► account, invoice, statement, list of charges **2** *a bill advertising a sale* ► poster, notice, advertisement, placard, sheet, leaflet,

broadsheet, circular, handout, bulletin **3** *a bill in parliament* ► draft law, proposed law

billow VERB **1** *Her dress billowed out in the wind.* ► balloon, blow, puff, swell, bulge **2** *Smoke billowed from the chimney.* ► pour, swirl, spiral

bin NOUN *a row of storage bins* ► container, canister, receptacle, drum

bind VERB **1** *I'll bind the two pieces with string.* ► fasten, tie, secure, attach, clamp, stick, connect, join, lash, link, rope, strap, truss, hitch **2** *A nurse bound their wounds.* ► bandage, dress, cover, wrap, swathe **3** *They were bound by a solemn oath not to reveal their secret.* ► oblige, require, compel, constrain, force, necessitate **4** *Their sufferings had bound them together.* ► unite, join, draw, hold

biochemistry NOUN the study of the chemical composition and processes of living things
▷ **biochemical** ADJECTIVE **biochemist** NOUN

biodegradable ADJECTIVE able to be broken down by bacteria in the environment • *All our packaging is biodegradable.*

biography (by- og- ra- fee) NOUN **biographies** the story of a person's life
▷ **biographical** ADJECTIVE **biographer** NOUN

biology NOUN the study of the life and structure of living things
▷ **biological** ADJECTIVE **biologist** NOUN

bionic (by- on- ik) ADJECTIVE (said about a person or parts of the body) operated by electronic devices

biopsy (by- op- see) NOUN **biopsies** examination of tissue from a living body

biped (by- ped) NOUN **bipeds** a two-footed animal

birch NOUN **birches 1** a deciduous tree with slender branches **2** a bundle of birch branches for flogging people

bird NOUN **birds 1** an animal with feathers, two wings, and two legs **2** (*slang*) a young woman
bird's-eye view a view from above

bird of prey NOUN **birds of prey** a bird that feeds on animal flesh, such as an eagle or hawk

birth NOUN **births 1** the process by which a baby or young animal comes out from its mother's body **2** origin; parentage • *He is of noble birth.*

birth control NOUN ways of avoiding conceiving a baby

birthday NOUN **birthdays** the anniversary of the day a person was born

birth rate NOUN **birth rates** the number of children born in one year for every 1,000 people

birthright NOUN a right or privilege to which a person is entitled through being born into a particular family or country

biscuit NOUN biscuits a small flat kind of cake that has been baked until it is crisp [from Latin *bis* = twice + *coctus* = cooked: originally they were baked and then dried out in a cool oven to make them keep longer]

bisect (by- sekt) VERB **bisects, bisecting, bisected** divide something into two equal parts
▷ **bisection** NOUN **bisector** NOUN

bishop NOUN **bishops 1** an important member of the clergy in charge of all the churches in a city or district **2** a chess piece shaped like a bishop's miter

bismuth NOUN a greyish-white metal

bison (by- son) NOUN **bison** a wild ox found in North America and Europe, with a large shaggy head

bit[1] NOUN **bits 1** a small piece or amount of something **2** the metal part of a horse's bridle that is put into its mouth **3** the part of a tool that cuts or grips things when twisted
a bit 1 a short distance or time • *Wait a bit.* **2** slightly • *I'm a bit worried.*
bit by bit gradually

bit[2] past tense of **bite**

bit[3] NOUN **bits** the smallest unit of information in a computer, expressed as a choice between two possibilities

bitch NOUN **bitches 1** a female dog, fox, or wolf **2** (*vulgar*) a spiteful woman
▷ **bitchy** ADJECTIVE

bite VERB **bites, biting, bit, bitten 1** cut or take something with your teeth **2** penetrate; sting **3** accept bait • *The fish are biting.*
bite the dust die or be killed

bite NOUN **bites 1** an act of biting • *She took a bite.* **2** a wound or mark made by biting • *an insect bite* **3** a snack

Thesaurus

birth NOUN **1** *the birth of a child* ► delivery, childbirth, (*technical*) parturition RELATED ADJECTIVE ► natal **2** *of noble birth* ► ancestry, descent, origin, parentage, lineage, pedigree, breeding, background, blood, extraction, family, genealogy, line, race, stock, strain **3** *the birth of socialism* ► beginning, origin, emergence, advent, dawn

bit NOUN *a bit of chocolate, a bit of stone* ► piece, portion, chunk, lump, hunk, fragment, morsel, particle, slice
a bit *That was a bit hard.* ► rather, fairly, slightly, somewhat, a little, (*more informal*) pretty
a bit of *a bit of a shame* ► rather
bit by bit *Bit by bit she began to understand.* ► gradually, slowly, little by little

bite NOUN **1** *a bite on the arm* ► nip, sting, pinch, wound **2** *a bite to eat* ► mouthful, snack, morsel, bit, nibble, piece, taste

bite VERB **1** *He bit a chunk out of an apple.* ► munch, nibble, chew, crunch, gnaw, nip, champ, (*formal*) masticate **2** *She had been bitten by an insect.* ► sting, pierce **3** *Tax increases will begin to bite in the new tax year.* ► take effect, have an effect, take hold **4** **bite into** *Acid starts to bite into the metal.* ► eat into, corrode, erode, wear away

biting ADJECTIVE **1** *a biting wind* ► bitterly cold, bitter, freezing, icy, raw, piercing, perishing, arctic **2** *a biting remark* ► caustic, harsh, cutting, incisive, bitter, penetrating, stinging, hurtful, cruel, sharp

a
b
c
d
e
f
g
h
i
j
k
l
m
n
o
p
q
r
s
t
u
v
w
x
y
z

bitter ➡ blancmange

bitter ADJECTIVE **1** tasting sharp, not sweet **2** feeling or causing mental pain or resentment • *a bitter disappointment* **3** very cold
▷ **bitterly** ADVERB **bitterness** NOUN

bivalve NOUN bivalves a shellfish (e.g., an oyster) that has a shell with two hinged parts

bizarre (biz- ar) ADJECTIVE very odd in appearance or effect

black NOUN blacks **1** the very darkest color, like coal or soot **2** a person with a very dark or black skin

black ADJECTIVE **1** of the color black **2** (said about a person) having dark skin **3** dismal; not hopeful • *The outlook is black.* **4** hostile; disapproving • *He gave me a black look.* **5** very dirty **6** (said about coffee or tea) without milk
▷ **blackly** ADVERB **blackness** NOUN

black VERB blacks, blacking, blacked make a thing black
black out 1 cover windows, etc., so that no light can penetrate **2** faint, lose consciousness

blackberry NOUN blackberries a sweet black berry

blackbird NOUN blackbirds a European songbird, the male of which is black

blackboard NOUN blackboards a dark board for writing on with chalk

black box NOUN black boxes a flight recorder

blacken VERB blackens, blackening, blackened make or become black

black eye NOUN black eyes an eye with a bruise round it

blackguard (blag- erd) NOUN blackguards (*old use*) a wicked person

black hole NOUN black holes a region in outer space with such a strong gravitational field that no matter or radiation can escape from it

black ice NOUN thin transparent ice on roads

blacklist VERB blacklists, blacklisting, blacklisted put someone on a list of those who are disapproved of

blackmail VERB blackmails, blackmailing, blackmailed demand money, etc., from someone by threats
▷ **blackmail** NOUN **blackmailer** NOUN

black market NOUN black markets illegal trading

black sheep NOUN a member of a family who behaves badly or has a bad reputation

blacksmith NOUN blacksmiths a person who makes and repairs iron things, especially one who makes and fits horseshoes

black spot NOUN black spots a dangerous place

bladder NOUN bladders **1** the bag-like part of the body in which urine collects **2** the inflatable bag inside a football

blade NOUN blades **1** the flat cutting edge of a knife, sword, axe, etc. **2** the flat wide part of an oar, spade, propeller, etc. **3** a flat narrow leaf • *blades of grass* **4** a broad flat bone • *shoulder blade*

blame VERB blames, blaming, blamed **1** say that somebody or something has caused what is wrong • *They blamed me.* **2** find fault with someone • *We can't blame them for wanting a vacation.*

blame NOUN responsibility for what is wrong

blancmange (bla- monj) NOUN blancmanges a jellylike pudding made with milk

---
Thesaurus
---

bitter ADJECTIVE **1** *a bitter taste* ► sour, sharp, acid, acrid, tart, harsh OPPOSITES ARE mild, sweet **2** *The decision was seen as a bitter disappointment.* ► cruel, distressing, painful, unpleasant **3** *bitter remarks* ► harsh, cutting, caustic, incisive, biting, penetrating, stinging, hurtful, cruel, sharp **4** *She felt bitter about what had happened.* ► resentful, embittered, cynical, aggrieved, disgruntled **5** *a bitter quarrel* ► acrimonious, rancorous, angry, vitriolic **6** *a bitter wind* ► biting, freezing, icy, raw, piercing, perishing, bitterly cold, arctic AN OPPOSITE IS gentle

bizarre ADJECTIVE *a bizarre story of survival in wartime* ► strange, weird, odd, extraordinary, eccentric, peculiar, curious, queer, unusual, grotesque AN OPPOSITE IS ordinary

black ADJECTIVE **1** *black ink* ► jet-black, coal-black **2** *a black night* ► dark, unlit, moonless, starless, gloomy **3** *hands black from mending*

the mower ► filthy, dirty, grimy, grubby, soiled AN OPPOSITE IS spotless **4** *in a black mood* ► melancholy, miserable, glum, wretched, unhappy, despondent

black VERB *I blacked my shoes.* ► blacken, polish

blacken VERB *She decided to blacken her hair.* ► darken, make black

blame NOUN **1** *They were cleared of all blame.* ► responsibility, guilt, liability, culpability **2** *Who got the blame for it?* ► criticism, censure, condemnation, (*more informal*) rap

blame VERB *The report blamed the driver for the accident.* ► hold responsible, hold accountable, condemn, censure, criticize, reprove, reprimand, accuse (of), charge (with) AN OPPOSITE IS excuse

blameless ADJECTIVE *a blameless life* ► innocent, guiltless, faultless, exemplary, irreproachable, upright, virtuous, unblemished OPPOSITES ARE blameworthy, guilty

bland ADJECTIVE **1** having a mild flavor rather than a strong one **2** lacking any interesting features or qualities • *a bland manner*
▷ **blandly** ADVERB **blandness** NOUN

blank ADJECTIVE **1** not written or printed on; unmarked **2** without interest or expression • *a blank look*. **3** empty of thoughts • *My mind's gone blank.*
▷ **blankly** ADVERB **blankness** NOUN

blank NOUN **blanks 1** an empty space **2** a blank cartridge

blanket NOUN **blankets 1** a warm cloth covering used on a bed, etc. **2** any thick soft covering • *a blanket of snow*

blanket ADJECTIVE covering all cases or instances • *a blanket ban*

blank verse NOUN poetry without rhyme, usually in lines of ten syllables

blare VERB **blares, blaring, blared** make a loud harsh sound
▷ **blare** NOUN

blaspheme (blas- feem) VERB **blasphemes, blaspheming, blasphemed** talk or write irreverently about sacred things

blasphemy (blas- fim- ee) NOUN **blasphemies** irreverent talk about sacred things
▷ **blasphemous** ADJECTIVE

blast NOUN **blasts 1** a strong rush of wind or air **2** a loud noise • *the blast of the trumpets*

blast VERB **blasts, blasting, blasted** blow up with explosives
blast off launch by the firing of rockets **blast-off** NOUN

blatant (blay- tant) ADJECTIVE very obvious • *a blatant lie*
▷ **blatantly** ADVERB

blaze NOUN **blazes** a very bright flame, fire, or light

blaze VERB **blazes, blazing, blazed 1** burn or shine brightly **2** show great feeling • *He was blazing with anger.*

blazer NOUN **blazers** a kind of jacket, often with a badge or in the colors of a school or team etc.

bleach VERB **bleaches, bleaching, bleached** make or become white

bleach NOUN **bleaches** a substance used to bleach things

bleak ADJECTIVE **1** bare and cold • *a bleak hillside* **2** dreary or miserable • *a bleak future*
▷ **bleakly** ADVERB **bleakness** NOUN

bleary ADJECTIVE watery and not seeing clearly • *bleary eyes*
▷ **blearily** ADVERB

bleat NOUN **bleats** the cry of a lamb, goat, or calf

bleat VERB **bleats, bleating, bleated** make a bleat

bleed VERB **bleeds, bleeding, bled 1** lose blood **2** draw blood or fluid from

blemish NOUN **blemishes** a flaw; a mark that spoils a thing's appearance
▷ **blemish** VERB

blench VERB **blenches, blenching, blenched** flinch

Thesaurus

bland ADJECTIVE **1** *a bland taste* ► insipid, uninteresting, dull, weak, nondescript, watery, mild, boring, flat OPPOSITES ARE sharp, strong **2** *a bland personality, bland remarks* ► dull, tedious, uninteresting, unexciting, monotonous, drab, dreary, feeble, vapid, weak, (informal) wishy-washy OPPOSITES ARE interesting, stimulating

blank ADJECTIVE **1** *a blank page* ► empty, unused, unfilled, clear, bare, void, unmarked AN OPPOSITE IS used **2** *a blank look* ► expressionless, featureless, impassive, vacant, deadpan, inscrutable, unresponsive AN OPPOSITE IS expressive

blanket NOUN *a blanket of fog* ► covering, layer, film, shroud, cloak, mantle, mask, sheet, cover

blare VERB *Sirens were blaring.* ► blast, resound, screech, shriek

blast NOUN **1** *a blast of cold air* ► gust, rush, blow, draught, squall **2** *Hundreds were injured in the blast.* ► explosion, discharge, shock

blast VERB **1** *A series of missiles blasted the building.* ► blow up, bomb, demolish, raze

2 *radios blasting out rock music* ► blare, boom, roar, thunder, bellow

blatant ADJECTIVE *a blatant lie* ► flagrant, brazen, barefaced, glaring, shameless, unconcealed AN OPPOSITE IS inconspicuous

blaze NOUN **1** *It took firefighters all night to control the blaze.* ► fire, flames **2** *a blaze of light* ► burst, flash, gleam, streak, beam, glitter

blaze VERB **1** *The fire began to blaze.* ► burn, flare up, be alight **2** *Lights blazed from the top floor.* ► shine, beam, flare, flash, gleam, glitter

bleak ADJECTIVE *a bleak landscape* ► bare, barren, desolate, exposed, featureless, treeless, stark, empty, open, windswept

bleary ADJECTIVE *bleary eyes, bleary vision* ► blurred, blurry, unfocused, clouded, cloudy, fogged, foggy, hazy, murky AN OPPOSITE IS clear

bleed VERB *The wound began to bleed.* ► lose blood, hemorrhage, weep, seep

blemish NOUN *a beautiful rose bloom without a single blemish* ► imperfection, flaw, fault, defect, spot, mark, stain, speck, taint

a
b
c
d
e
f
g
h
i
j
k
l
m
n
o
p
q
r
s
t
u
v
w
x
y
z

blend ➡ blob

blend VERB blends, blending, blended mix smoothly or easily

blend NOUN blends a mixture

blender NOUN blenders an electric machine used to mix food or turn it into liquid

bless VERB blesses, blessing, blessed 1 make sacred or holy 2 bring God's favor on a person or thing

blessing NOUN blessings 1 a prayer that blesses a person or thing; being blessed 2 something that people are glad of

blight NOUN blights 1 a disease that makes plants wither 2 something that does a lot of harm • *Vandalism is a blight on our community.*

blight VERB blights, blighting, blighted 1 affect with blight 2 spoil or damage something • *Injuries have blighted his career.*

blind ADJECTIVE 1 without the ability to see 2 without any thought or understanding • *blind obedience.* 3 (said about a tube, passage, or road) closed at one end
▷ **blindly** ADVERB **blindness** NOUN

blind VERB blinds, blinding, blinded make a person blind

blind NOUN blinds 1 a screen for a window 2 a deception; something used to hide the truth • *His journey was a blind.*

blind date NOUN blind dates a date between a man and woman who have not met before

blindfold NOUN blindfolds a strip of cloth tied round someone's eyes so that they cannot see

blindfold VERB blindfolds, blindfolding, blindfolded cover someone's eyes with a blindfold

blind spot NOUN blind spots a subject that you do not understand or know much about

blink VERB blinks, blinking, blinked shut and open your eyes rapidly
▷ **blink** NOUN

bliss NOUN perfect happiness
▷ **blissful** ADJECTIVE **blissfully** ADVERB

blister NOUN blisters a swelling like a bubble, especially on skin
▷ **blister** VERB

blizzard NOUN blizzards a severe snowstorm

bloated ADJECTIVE swollen by fat, gas, or liquid

blob NOUN blobs a small round mass of something • *blobs of paint*

Thesaurus

blend NOUN *a blend of several ingredients*
► mixture, mix, combination, mingling, amalgam, fusion, synthesis

blend VERB 1 *Blend the ingredients carefully.*
► mix, combine, mingle, merge, stir together, beat, fold in, integrate, whip, whisk 2 *The colors blend well.* ► harmonize, match, fit

bless VERB *The couple was blessed with a child.*
► favor, grace, endow

blessed ADJECTIVE *a blessed place* ► holy, sacred, sanctified, adored, divine, hallowed, revered

blessing NOUN 1 *The priest gave a blessing.*
► benediction, grace, prayer 2 *The manager gave the scheme his blessing.* ► approval, backing, support, consent, approbation, leave, permission AN OPPOSITE IS disapproval 3 *Central heating is a blessing in the winter.*
► benefit, advantage, asset, boon, comfort, convenience, godsend, help AN OPPOSITE IS affliction

blight NOUN 1 *potato blight* ► disease, rot, decay, (more formal) infestation 2 *the blight of traffic noise* ► affliction, curse, plague, menace, nuisance, tribulation, trial, misfortune AN OPPOSITE IS blessing

blight VERB *Their lives were blighted by troublesome neighbors.* ► ruin, wreck, spoil, afflict, shatter, disrupt

blind ADJECTIVE 1 *She had been blind from birth.*
► sightless, unsighted, visually impaired, partially sighted, unseeing 2 *blind to all dangers* ► oblivious, imperceptive, heedless (of), unaware (of), inattentive, indifferent,

insensible, insensitive, ignorant (of), blinkered (from) OPPOSITES ARE aware, perceptive 3 *showing a blind acceptance of criticism*
► uncritical, reckless, impulsive, indiscriminate, unreasoning, mindless 4 *a blind corner* ► concealed, hidden, obscure, obstructed

blind NOUN *She pulled down a blind.* ► screen, shade, cover, curtain, shutter

blind VERB 1 *The light blinded her for a few moments.* ► dazzle 2 *They are trying to blind us all with science.* ► confuse, deceive, overawe, intimidate, disconcert, unsettle, (more informal) put off

blink VERB *A light on the control panel began to blink.* ► flash, wink, flicker, twinkle, flutter, gleam, glimmer

bliss NOUN *a life of bliss* ► joy, delight, pleasure, rapture, ecstasy, euphoria, felicity, gladness, happiness, heaven, paradise AN OPPOSITE IS misery

blissful ADJECTIVE *They spent a blissful week together.* ► ecstatic, joyful, rapturous, euphoric, elated, happy AN OPPOSITE IS miserable

blizzard NOUN *They were kept indoors by blizzards.* ► snowstorm, squall

bloated ADJECTIVE *a bloated stomach* ► swollen, dilated, distended, enlarged, inflated OPPOSITES ARE shrunken, shrivelled

blob NOUN *a blob of ice cream* ► drop, droplet, globule, lump

block NOUN blocks **1** a solid piece of something **2** an obstruction **3** a large building divided into flats or offices **4** a group of buildings

block VERB blocks, blocking, blocked obstruct; prevent something from moving or being used
▷ **blockage** NOUN

blockade NOUN blockades the blocking of a city or port etc. in order to prevent people and goods from going in or out

blockade VERB blockades, blockading, blockaded set up a blockade of a place

block letters PLURAL NOUN plain capital letters

blond or **blonde** ADJECTIVE fair-haired; fair

blonde NOUN blondes a fair-haired girl or woman

blood NOUN **1** the red liquid that flows through veins and arteries **2** family relationship; ancestry • *He is of royal blood.* **in cold blood** deliberately and cruelly

blood bank NOUN blood banks a supply of blood and plasma for transfusions

bloodbath NOUN bloodbaths a massacre

blood donor NOUN blood donors a person who gives blood for use in transfusions

blood group NOUN blood groups any of the classes or types of human blood

bloodhound NOUN bloodhounds a large dog that tracks people by their scent

bloodshed NOUN the killing or wounding of people

bloodshot ADJECTIVE (said about eyes) streaked with red

blood sport NOUN blood sports a sport that involves wounding or killing animals

bloodstream NOUN the blood circulating in the body

bloodthirsty ADJECTIVE eager for bloodshed

blood vessel NOUN blood vessels a tube carrying blood in the body; an artery, vein, or capillary

bloody ADJECTIVE bloodier, bloodiest **1** bloodstained **2** with much bloodshed • *a bloody battle*

bloom NOUN blooms **1** a flower **2** the fine powder on fresh ripe grapes, etc.

bloom VERB blooms, blooming, bloomed produce flowers

blossom NOUN blossoms a flower or mass of flowers, especially on a fruit tree

blossom VERB blossoms, blossoming, blossomed **1** produce flowers **2** develop into something • *She blossomed into a fine singer.*

blot NOUN blots **1** a spot of ink **2** a flaw or fault; something ugly • *a blot on the landscape*

blot VERB blots, blotting, blotted **1** make a blot or blots on something **2** dry with blotting paper
blot out 1 cross out thickly **2** obscure • *Fog blotted out the view.*

Thesaurus

block NOUN **1** *a block of chocolate, a block of stone* ► chunk, hunk, slab, bar, brick, cake, lump, mass, piece **2** *The pipe had a block in it.* ► blockage, obstruction, stoppage **3** *Lack of funds proved a block to progress.* ► barrier, hindrance, impediment, obstacle

block VERB **1** *The drain was blocked with leaves* ► (*informal*) bung up, choke, clog, close, congest, constrict, dam, fill, jam, obstruct, plug, stop up **2** *A parked van was blocking access to the house.* ► obstruct, bar, impede, inhibit, restrict, limit **3** *The scheme was blocked by the directors.* ► stop, prevent, halt, thwart

blockage NOUN *The drain has a blockage.* ► obstruction, stoppage, block, constriction, jam, obstacle, resistance, barrier, bottleneck, congestion

blond, blonde ADJECTIVE blond hair ► fair, flaxen, golden, light, yellow, bleached

blood NOUN *a person of noble blood* ► ancestry, descent, origin, parentage, lineage, pedigree, breeding, background, birth, extraction, family, genealogy, line, race, stock, strain

bloodshed NOUN *The government were anxious to avoid further bloodshed.* ► killing, slaughter, carnage, butchery, violence

bloody ADJECTIVE **1** *a bloody wound* ► bleeding, blood-stained, raw, gaping **2** *a bloody battle* ► fierce, gory, bloodthirsty, violent

bloom NOUN **1** *rose blooms* ► blossom, flower, bud **2** *the bloom of youth* ► prime, peak, glow, flush, acme

bloom VERB **1** *The roses have all bloomed now.* ► blossom, flower, open AN OPPOSITE IS fade **2** *The children had bloomed in the country air.* ► flourish, thrive, prosper, blossom, develop

blossom NOUN *apple blossom* ► blooms, buds, florets, flowers

blossom VERB **1** *The trees have started to blossom.* ► bloom, flower, open AN OPPOSITE IS fade **2** *The plan can blossom with the right support.* ► flourish, thrive, prosper, bloom, develop

blot NOUN **1** *a blot of ink* ► spot, blotch, mark, smear, smudge, stain, splodge, blob **2** *a blot on the landscape* ► eyesore, blemish, defect, fault, flaw

blot VERB *Ink blotted the page.* ► smudge, mark, spoil, spot, stain, bespatter, mar
blot out *A tall building blotted out the view.* ► conceal, hide, mask, obliterate, obscure, cover, delete, eclipse, erase, expunge, rub out, wipe out, cancel

a
b
c
d
e
f
g
h
i
j
k
l
m
n
o
p
q
r
s
t
u
v
w
x
y
z

A
B
C
D
E
F
G
H
I
J
K
L
M
N
O
P
Q
R
S
T
U
V
W
X
Y
Z

blotch NOUN blotches an untidy patch of color
▷ **blotchy** ADJECTIVE

blotting paper NOUN absorbent paper for soaking up ink from writing

blouse NOUN blouses a loose piece of clothing like a shirt, worn by women

blow¹ VERB blows, blowing, blew, blown **1** send out a current of air **2** move in or with a current of air • *His hat blew off.* **3** make or sound something by blowing • *blow bubbles* • *blow the whistle* **4** melt with too strong an electric current • *A fuse has blown.*
blow up 1 inflate **2** explode **3** shatter by an explosion

blow NOUN blows the action of blowing

blow² NOUN blows **1** a hard knock or hit **2** a shock; a disaster

blowlamp or **blowtorch** NOUN blowlamps or blowtorches a device used for directing a very hot flame at a surface

blubber NOUN the fat of whales

bludgeon (bluj- on) NOUN bludgeons a short stick with a thickened end, used as a weapon

bludgeon VERB bludgeons, bludgeoning, bludgeoned hit someone several times with a heavy stick or other object

blue NOUN blues the color of a cloudless sky
out of the blue unexpectedly

blue ADJECTIVE **1** of the color blue **2** unhappy; depressed • *feeling blue* **3** indecent; obscene • *blue films*
▷ **blueness** NOUN

bluebottle NOUN bluebottles a large bluish fly

blueprint NOUN blueprints a detailed plan

blues NOUN a slow sad jazz song or tune
the blues a very sad feeling; depression

bluff¹ VERB bluffs, bluffing, bluffed deceive someone, especially by pretending to be someone else or to be able to do something

bluff NOUN bluffs the act of bluffing; a threat that you make but do not intend to carry out

bluff² ADJECTIVE frank and hearty in manner
▷ **bluffness** NOUN

blunder NOUN blunders a stupid mistake

blunder VERB blunders, blundering, blundered **1** make a blunder **2** move clumsily and uncertainly

blunt ADJECTIVE **1** not sharp **2** speaking in plain terms; straightforward • *a blunt refusal*
▷ **bluntly** ADVERB **bluntness** NOUN

Thesaurus

blotch NOUN *The walls had damp blotches down them.* ► patch, smudge, speck, speckle, blot, mark

blotchy ADJECTIVE *a blotchy skin* ► spotty, spotted, blemished, marked, patchy, smudged, uneven

blow NOUN **1** *a blow on the head* ► knock, bang, hit, thump, smack **2** *The news was a terrible blow.* ► shock, surprise, reverse, setback, upset, disappointment, calamity, disaster

blow VERB **1** *The storm blew the ship on the rocks.* ► drive, sweep, force, blast, fling, whisk **2** *Leaves were blowing across the drive.* ► drift, flutter, whirl, stream
blow out *The heater blows out hot air.* ► puff out, blast out, exhale, breathe, fan, waft
blow up 1 *I'll blow up the tires.* ► inflate, pump up, fill, dilate, expand OPPOSITES ARE let down, deflate **2** *The photograph can be blown up.* ► enlarge **3** *A bomb blew up the building.* ► bomb, blast, detonate, dynamite, explode **4** (informal) *When he heard what we had done he blew up.* ► grow angry, lose your temper, rage

blue ADJECTIVE **1** *a pretty blue color* ► sky-blue, turquoise, ultramarine, aquamarine, azure, cerulean, cobalt, indigo, navy, sapphire **2** *a blue movie* ► indecent, coarse, obscene, salacious, risqué **3** (informal) *Jake was feeling blue that day.* ► sad, depressed, dejected

blueprint NOUN **1** *blueprints of the new aircraft* ► design, plan, drawing, draft, outline,

pattern, layout, prototype **2** *a blueprint for political reform* ► model, plan, framework, basis, pattern, guide, proposal

blues PLURAL NOUN **the blues** *I woke up with the blues just like you did.* ► depression, sadness, melancholy, dejection, despondency, low spirits, misery, gloom

bluff NOUN *The offer is regarded as a crude bluff.* ► deception, subterfuge, sham, pretense, fake, fraud, ruse, artifice, trick

bluff VERB **1** *We think they must be bluffing us.* ► deceive, delude, mislead, hoodwink, trick **2** *I am sure they are only bluffing.* ► pretend, sham, put on an act, lie, (more informal) kid

blunder NOUN *Harry shook his head at his own blunder.* ► mistake, error, gaffe, slip, faux pas, (more informal) howler

blunder VERB **1** *The security officer had blundered by letting the men into the building.* ► make a mistake, bungle, err, be in error, misjudge, miscalculate, slip up, (more informal) put your foot in it, (more informal) goof, (much more informal) screw up

blunt ADJECTIVE **1** *a blunt knife* ► dull, rounded, thick, unpointed, unsharpened AN OPPOSITE IS sharp **2** *a blunt reply* ► abrupt, harsh, curt, terse, gruff, rude, offhand, brusque, insensitive, outspoken, plain-spoken
OPPOSITES ARE polite, tactful

blunt VERB blunts, blunting, blunted make a thing blunt

blur VERB blurs, blurring, blurred make or become indistinct or smeared

blur NOUN blurs an indistinct appearance
• *Without his glasses on, everything was a blur.*

blurt VERB blurts, blurting, blurted say something suddenly or tactlessly • *He blurted it out.*

blush VERB blushes, blushing, blushed become red in the face because you are ashamed or embarrassed

blush NOUN blushes reddening in the face

bluster VERB blusters, blustering, blustered **1** blow in gusts; be windy **2** talk loudly and aggressively
▷ **blustery** ADJECTIVE

BMX ABBREVIATION a kind of bicycle for use in racing on a dirt track

boar NOUN boars **1** a wild pig **2** a male pig

board NOUN boards **1** a flat piece of wood **2** a flat piece of stiff material, e.g., a chessboard **3** daily meals supplied in return for payment or work • *board and lodging.* **4** a committee
on board on or in a ship, aircraft, etc.

board VERB boards, boarding, boarded **1** go on board a ship, etc. **2** give or get meals and accommodation
board up block with fixed boards

boarder NOUN boarders **1** a student who lives at a boarding school during the term **2** a lodger who receives meals

boarding school NOUN boarding schools a school where students live during the term

boast VERB boasts, boasting, boasted **1** speak with great pride and try to impress people **2** have something to be proud of • *The town boasts a fine park.*
▷ **boaster** NOUN **boastful** ADJECTIVE **boastfully** ADVERB

boast NOUN boasts a boastful statement

boat NOUN boats a vehicle built to travel on water and carry people, etc.
in the same boat in the same situation; suffering the same difficulties

bob VERB bobs, bobbing, bobbed move quickly up and down

bobsled or **bobsleigh** NOUN bobsleds or bobsleighs a sled with two sets of runners

bodice NOUN bodices the upper part of a dress

bodily ADJECTIVE to do with your body • *bodily functions*

bodily ADVERB by taking hold of someone • *He was picked up bodily and thrown into a car.*

body NOUN bodies **1** the structure consisting of bones and flesh, etc., of a person or animal; the main part of this apart from the head and limbs **2** a corpse **3** the main part of something **4** a group or quantity regarded as a unit • *the school's governing body* **5** a distinct object or piece of matter • *Stars and planets are heavenly bodies.*
▷ **bodily** ADJECTIVE, ADVERB

Thesaurus

---

blunt VERB *A series of snacks blunted my appetite.* ► dull, reduce, dampen, take the edge off, weaken OPPOSITES ARE sharpen, intensify

blur VERB *The steam had blurred her glasses.* ► cloud, fog, mask, obscure, befog, blear, dim, smear

blurred ADJECTIVE *When he lifted his head everything looked blurred.* ► indistinct, blurry, bleary, fuzzy, hazy, misty

blush VERB *She blushed as he kissed her hand.* ► go red, flush, glow, color

board NOUN **1** *a wooden board* ► plank, panel, beam, length of timber, lath **2** *the board of directors* ► committee, council, panel

board VERB **1** *Passengers may now board the aircraft.* ► get on, go on board, enter, embark, ascend **2** *His wife boarded students in a spare room.* ► accommodate, house, lodge, put up, billet, quarter

boast VERB *His mother had been boasting about how clever he was.* ► brag, crow, bluster, swank, show off, gloat, sing someone's praises, (*more informal*) talk big

boastful ADJECTIVE *He was constantly boastful of all his achievements.* ► bragging, conceited,
big-headed, bumptious, proud, puffed-up, swaggering, swollen-headed, vain, egotistical, (*informal*) cocky, (*informal*) swanky AN OPPOSITE IS modest

boat NOUN *boats in the little harbor* ► craft, vessel, ship

bob VERB *Little boats were bobbing in the water.* ► bounce, move up and down, dance, toss about, skip about, oscillate
bob up *A woman at the back bobbed up to ask a question.* ► jump up, leap up, spring up, rise (up), appear

bodily ADJECTIVE *bodily contact* ► physical, corporeal

body NOUN **1** *the human body* ► frame, figure, form, physique, shape, anatomy, being, build RELATED ADJECTIVES ► corporal, somatic **2** *a blow to the body* ► trunk, torso **3** *a body floating in the river* ► corpse, cadaver, carcass, mortal remains, (*more informal*) stiff **4** *the managing body* ► committee, company, association, corporation, society, band **5** *a large body of evidence* ► quantity, collection, volume, mass, accumulation, agglomeration, corpus

a
b
c
d
e
f
g
h
i
j
k
l
m
n
o
p
q
r
s
t
u
v
w
x
y
z

bodyguard NOUN bodyguards a guard to protect a person's life

bog NOUN bogs an area of wet spongy ground
▷ **boggy** ADJECTIVE
bogged down stuck and unable to make any progress

bogus ADJECTIVE not real; sham

boil¹ VERB boils, boiling, boiled **1** make or become hot enough to bubble and give off steam **2** cook or wash something in boiling water **3** be very hot

boil NOUN boiling point • *Bring the milk to the boil.* [via early French *boillir* from Latin *bullire* = to bubble]

boil² NOUN boils an inflamed swelling under the skin

boiler NOUN boilers a container in which water is heated

boisterous ADJECTIVE noisy and lively

bold ADJECTIVE **1** confident and courageous **2** impudent **3** (said about colors, designs, etc.) strong and bright
▷ **boldly** ADVERB **boldness** NOUN

bolster NOUN bolsters a long pillow for placing across a bed under other pillows

bolster VERB bolsters, bolstering, bolstered add extra support

bolt NOUN bolts **1** a sliding bar for fastening a door **2** a thick metal pin for fastening things together **3** a sliding bar that opens and closes the breech of a rifle **4** a shaft of lightning **5** an arrow shot from a crossbow **6** the action of bolting
a bolt from the blue a surprise, usually an unpleasant one
bolt upright quite upright

bolt VERB bolts, bolting, bolted **1** fasten with a bolt or bolts **2** run away or escape **3** swallow food quickly

bomb NOUN bombs an explosive device
the bomb an atomic or hydrogen bomb

bomb VERB bombs, bombing, bombed attack a place with bombs

bombard VERB bombards, bombarding, bombarded **1** attack with gunfire or many missiles **2** direct a large number of questions or comments, etc., at somebody
▷ **bombardment** NOUN

bomber NOUN bombers **1** someone who plants or sets off a bomb **2** an airplane from which bombs are dropped

Thesaurus

bog NOUN *The ground became wetter, and eventually they were on the edge of a bog.*
► marsh, marshland, swamp, mire, morass, fen, quicksands, mudflats, quagmire
bogged down *bogged down with all the work*
► encumbered, hindered, impeded, slowed down, in difficulties, stuck, sunk

bogey NOUN *bogies and other beings of the night*
► evil spirit, ghost, spectre, phantom

bogus ADJECTIVE *The man had given a bogus address.* ► fake, false, spurious, fraudulent, counterfeit, pretended

boil NOUN *a boil on the skin* ► swelling, pustule, pimple, abscess, blister, spot, tumor

boil VERB **1** *Boil the potatoes in water.* ► bring to boiling point, bring to the boil, cook, heat, simmer **2** *The water was beginning to boil.*
► bubble, effervesce, foam, seethe, steam
3 *She was boiling with anger.* ► seethe, be angry, lose your temper, go into a rage, fly into a rage, flare up, (*more informal*) see red

boisterous ADJECTIVE *a boisterous beach game*
► lively, spirited, animated, exuberant, rough, rowdy OPPOSITES ARE restrained, calm

bold ADJECTIVE **1** *a bold move, a bold traveller*
► brave, courageous, daring, adventurous, audacious, confident, dauntless, enterprising, fearless, forceful, gallant, heroic, intrepid, self-confident, valiant, valorous, venturesome, (*more informal*) plucky AN OPPOSITE IS cowardly **2** *bold remarks* ► brazen, forward, cheeky, brash, impertinent, impudent, insolent,

presumptuous, fresh, pert, rude, saucy, shameless, unashamed OPPOSITES ARE polite, reticent **3** *a bold pattern, bold colors* ► striking, strong, bright, clear, conspicuous, eye-catching, prominent, pronounced, showy, vivid AN OPPOSITE IS inconspicuous

bolt NOUN **1** *The door bolt was stuck.* ► catch, bar, latch, lock, fastening **2** *Put a nut on the bolt.* ► pin, rivet, rod, screw
a bolt from the blue ► shock, surprise, (*more informal*) bombshell

bolt VERB **1** *We'd better bolt the door.* ► fasten, latch, lock, secure, bar **2** *She bolted from the room.* ► dash, dart, flee, fly, rush, hurry, sprint, run, escape **3** *He was in such a rush he had to bolt his food.* ► gobble, gulp, wolf, guzzle, stuff, scoff down

bomb NOUN *The building was destroyed by bombs.*
► explosive, missile

bomb VERB *The city was bombed for days on end.*
► bombard, drop bombs on, shell

bombard VERB **1** *Offshore ships bombarded the city all night.* ► shell, pound, blast, strafe, assault, attack, beset, bomb, fire at, pelt, shoot at, assail **2** *The speaker was bombarded with questions.* ► overwhelm, inundate, swamp, flood, deluge, pester, plague

bombardment NOUN *The city was practically demolished by the bombardment.* ► barrage, blast, shelling, attack, cannonade, discharge, fusillade, hail, salvo, volley

bombshell NOUN bombshells a great shock

bonanza (bon- an- za) NOUN bonanzas sudden great wealth or luck

bond NOUN bonds **1** a close friendship or connection between two or more people **2** bonds ropes or chains used to tie someone up **3** a document stating an agreement

bond VERB bonds, bonding, bonded become closely linked or connected

bondage NOUN slavery; captivity

bone NOUN bones one of the hard parts that make up the skeleton of a person's or animal's body

bone VERB bones, boning, boned remove the bones from meat or fish

bonfire NOUN bonfires an outdoor fire to burn garbage or celebrate something [originally bone fire = a fire to dispose of people's or animals' bones]

bonnet NOUN bonnets **1** a hat with strings that tie under the chin **2** a Scottish beret **3** the hinged cover over a car engine

bonus (boh- nus) NOUN bonuses **1** an extra payment in addition to a person's normal wages **2** an extra benefit

bony ADJECTIVE **1** with large bones; having bones with little flesh on them **2** full of bones **3** like bones

boo VERB boos, booing, booed shout "boo" in disapproval
▷ **boo** NOUN

booby NOUN boobies a babyish or stupid person

booby prize NOUN booby prizes a prize given as a joke to someone who comes last in a contest

booby trap NOUN booby traps something designed to hit or injure someone unexpectedly

book NOUN books a set of sheets of paper, usually with printing or writing on them, fastened together inside a cover
▷ **bookseller** NOUN **bookshop** NOUN **bookstall** NOUN

book VERB books, booking, booked **1** reserve a place in a theater, hotel, train, etc. **2** enter a person in a police record • The police booked him for speeding.

bookcase NOUN bookcases a piece of furniture with shelves for books

bookkeeping NOUN recording details of the money that is spent and received by a business
▷ **bookkeeper** NOUN

booklet NOUN booklets a small thin book

bookmaker NOUN bookmakers a person whose business is taking bets

bookmark NOUN bookmarks something to mark a place in a book

bookworm NOUN bookworms a person who loves reading

boom VERB booms, booming, boomed **1** make a deep hollow sound **2** be growing and prospering • Business is booming.

boom NOUN booms **1** a deep hollow sound **2** prosperity; growth

boomerang NOUN boomerangs a curved piece of wood that can be thrown so that it returns to the thrower, originally used by

Thesaurus

bond NOUN **1** There was a close bond between the two brothers. ► attachment, connection, tie, link, relationship, affinity, unity, affiliation **2** By running away he had broken his bond. ► promise, pledge, word, agreement, compact, contract, covenant, guarantee **3 bonds** The prisoner struggled to undo his bonds. ► chains, fetters, manacles, shackles, restraints, fastenings

bonus NOUN **1** no Christmas bonus this year ► extra payment, handout, reward **2** A meal out was an unexpected bonus. ► benefit, extra, addition, advantage, (informal) plus

bony ADJECTIVE a bony figure ► thin, angular, gawky, lanky, gaunt, emaciated, gangling, lean, scraggy, scrawny, skinny AN OPPOSITE IS plump

book NOUN a book to read and enjoy ► volume, tome, publication, tract, booklet

book VERB **1** On his way to the hospital he was booked for speeding. ► arrest, take your name, write down details **2** We booked tickets for the concert. ► reserve, order, arrange for, prearrange, buy **3** Will you book a club for the party? ► engage, organize, sign up, arrange

booklet NOUN a booklet of travel advice ► pamphlet, brochure, leaflet, paperback

boom NOUN **1** Suddenly there was the boom of the one o'clock gun. ► bang, reverberation, roar, sound, blast **2** a boom in trade ► upturn, upsurge, upswing, boost, growth, improvement, expansion, increase, spurt AN OPPOSITE IS slump

boom VERB **1** The guns began to boom. ► rumble, thunder, crash, reverberate, resound, echo **2** Business is booming. ► thrive, prosper, flourish, do well, (more informal) pick up OPPOSITES ARE decline, slump

boon NOUN Cheap travel is such a boon. ► benefit, blessing, help, asset, advantage, (more informal) piece of luck

A
B
C
D
E
F
G
H
I
J
K
L
M
N
O
P
Q
R
S
T
U
V
W
X
Y
Z

Australian Aborigines [from an Australian Aborginal word]

boor NOUN boors an ill-mannered person
▷ **boorish** ADJECTIVE

boost VERB boosts, boosting, boosted **1** increase the strength, value, or reputation of a person or thing **2** push something upwards
▷ **booster** NOUN

boost NOUN boosts **1** an increase **2** an upward push

boot NOUN boots **1** a shoe that covers the foot and ankle or leg
▷ **booted** ADJECTIVE

boot VERB boots, booting, booted **1** kick hard **2** switch on a computer

booty NOUN valuable goods taken away by soldiers after a battle

booze VERB boozes, boozing, boozed (slang) drink alcohol

booze NOUN (slang) alcoholic drink

border NOUN borders **1** the boundary of a country; the part near this **2** an edge **3** something placed round an edge to strengthen or decorate it **4** a strip of ground around a garden or part of it

border VERB borders, bordering, bordered put or be a border to something

borderline ADJECTIVE only just belonging to a particular group or category ● a borderline case

bore[1] VERB bores, boring, bored **1** drill a hole **2** get through by pushing

bore[2] VERB bores, boring, bored make somebody feel uninterested by being dull

bore NOUN bores a boring person or thing
▷ **boredom** NOUN

bore[3] past tense of bear[2]

bored ADJECTIVE weary and uninterested because something is so dull

boring ADJECTIVE dull or tedious

born ADJECTIVE **1** having come into existence by birth (See the note on borne) **2** having a certain natural quality or ability ● a born leader

borne past participle of bear[2]
USAGE The word **borne** is used before **by** or after **have**, **has**, or **had**, e.g., children borne by Eve; she had borne him a son. The word **born** is used, e.g., in a son was born.

bosom NOUN bosoms a woman's breasts

boss NOUN bosses (informal) a manager; a person whose job is to give orders to workers, etc.

boss VERB bosses, bossing, bossed (informal) order someone about

---

Thesaurus

---

boost NOUN **1** a boost to morale ► impetus, stimulus, lift, uplift, (more informal) shot in the arm **2** a boost in sales ► increase, expansion, growth, improvement, boom, upturn, upsurge, upswing, spurt OPPOSITES ARE decrease, decline

boost VERB The award boosted everyone's morale. ► raise, uplift, heighten, stimulate, bolster, increase, enhance OPPOSITES ARE depress, hinder

boot NOUN He had lost his left boot in the mud. ► gumboot

booth NOUN a telephone booth, a voting booth ► cubicle, kiosk, stall, compartment, enclosure, carrel, hut, stand

booze NOUN (informal) Lunch had to include lots of booze. ► alcohol, drink, alcoholic drink, liquor, spirits

booze VERB (informal) They had been boozing all night. ► drink, have a drink, indulge, imbibe, (also informal) tipsy

border NOUN **1** the border of a tablecloth; the border of a lake ► edge, margin, perimeter, fringe, verge **2** the border between Italy and Slovenia ► frontier, boundary, borderline

border VERB The park borders a housing estate. ► skirt, adjoin, be adjacent to, be alongside, abut on, join, share a border with, touch

borderline ADJECTIVE a borderline case

► marginal, indeterminate, uncertain, ambivalent

bore VERB **1** You need to bore a hole in the wall. ► drill, punch, cut, pierce, sink **2** Long films tend to bore him. ► weary, tire, (more informal) turn off OPPOSITES ARE interest, entertain

bore NOUN What a bore to have to wait another hour. ► nuisance, bother, annoyance, (more informal) drag, (more informal) pain, (more informal) pest

boring ADJECTIVE What a boring book. The work turned out to be very boring. ► tedious, dull, monotonous, dreary, humdrum, routine, uninteresting, unexciting, insipid, vapid, jejune OPPOSITES ARE interesting, stimulating

born ADJECTIVE a born comic ► natural, untaught, instinctive, genuine

borrow VERB I need to borrow a pen. ► loan, have use of, obtain, acquire, (more informal) cadge, (more informal) scrounge AN OPPOSITE IS lend

bosom NOUN **1** The dress was cut high over her bosom. ► bust, chest, breasts **2** The family took her into its bosom. ► care, protection, shelter

boss NOUN (informal) The boss would be away all that week. ► head, chief, manager, leader

boss VERB You have no right to boss me about like this. ► order, dictate to, push around, lord it over, bully, domineer

bossy ADJECTIVE fond of ordering people about
▷ **bossiness** NOUN

botany NOUN the study of plants
▷ **botanical** ADJECTIVE **botanist** NOUN

both ADJECTIVE, PRONOUN the two; not only one
● *Are both films good?* ● *Both are old.*

both ADVERB
both … and not only … but also ● *The house is both small and ugly.*

bother VERB bothers, bothering, bothered
1 cause somebody trouble or worry; pester
2 take trouble; feel concern ● *Don't bother to reply.*

bother NOUN trouble or worry

bottle NOUN bottles **1** a narrow-necked container for liquids

bottle VERB bottles, bottling, bottled put or store something in bottles
bottle up if you bottle up your feelings, you keep them to yourself
[via early French *botaille* from Latin *buttis* = cask]

bottle bank NOUN bottle banks a large container in which used glass bottles are collected for recycling

bottleneck NOUN bottlenecks a narrow place where something, especially traffic, cannot flow freely

bottom NOUN bottoms **1** the lowest part; the base **2** the part furthest away ● *the bottom of the garden* **3** a person's buttocks

bottom ADJECTIVE lowest ● *the bottom shelf*

bough NOUN boughs a large branch coming from the trunk of a tree

boulder NOUN boulders a very large smooth stone

bounce VERB bounces, bouncing, bounced
1 spring back when thrown against something **2** make a ball, etc., bounce **3** (said about a check) be sent back by the bank because there is not enough money in the account **4** jump suddenly; move in a lively manner

bounce NOUN bounces **1** the action or power of bouncing **2** a lively confident manner ● *full of bounce*
▷ **bouncy** ADJECTIVE

bound[1] VERB bounds, bounding, bounded jump or spring; run with jumping movements ● *The dogs were bounding along.*

bound NOUN bounds a bounding movement

bound[2] *past tense* of bind

Thesaurus

---

bossy ADJECTIVE *Why do you treat us in such a bossy manner?* ► domineering, officious, overbearing, high-handed, imperious, dictatorial, authoritarian, autocratic, aggressive, bullying, despotic, lordly, oppressive, peremptory, tyrannical AN OPPOSITE IS submissive

botch VERB *They managed to botch the next job as well.* ► bungle, make a mess of, mismanage, mishandle, do badly, spoil, mess up, (*more informal*) screw up AN OPPOSITE IS succeed in

bother NOUN **1** *There was some bother at the bar.* ► disorder, trouble, disturbance, difficulty, fuss, (*more informal*) hassle **2** *It was a bother to keep the food hot.* ► nuisance, annoyance, irritation, inconvenience, palaver, pest, trouble, worry, trial, job

bother VERB **1** *We found a quiet spot where no one would be able to bother us.* ► disturb, trouble, pester, molest, annoy, vex, worry, concern, dismay, exasperate, harass, (*informal*) hassle, inconvenience, irk, irritate, nag, plague, upset **2** *The accident was too minor to bother about.* ► concern yourself, be concerned, be worried, care, mind

bottle NOUN **1** *a bottle of wine; water in bottles* ► flask, carafe, decanter, flagon, jar, pitcher

bottle VERB bottle up *He had bottled up his problems for too long.* ► suppress, repress, hold in, keep in, stifle

bottleneck NOUN *There was a bottleneck ahead at the old bridge.* ► blockage, hold-up, traffic jam, tailback

bottom ADJECTIVE **1** *the bottom rung of a ladder* ► deepest, lowest AN OPPOSITE IS top
2 *bottom marks* ► least, minimum AN OPPOSITE IS top

bottom NOUN **1** *the bottom of the stairs* ► foot, base AN OPPOSITE IS top **2** *the bottom of the wall* ► foot, base, foundation AN OPPOSITE IS top **3** *the bottom of the car* ► underside, underneath AN OPPOSITE IS topside **4** *the bottom of the sea* ► bed, depths, floor AN OPPOSITE IS surface **5** *They were at the bottom of their fortunes.* ► lowest point, nadir AN OPPOSITE IS peak **6** *It is very hard to get to the bottom of the problem.* ► origin, root, source, heart, essence, grounds **7** *She said she had a tattoo on her bottom.* ► buttocks, rear, rump, seat, (*more informal*) behind, (*more informal*) backside, (*formal or humorous*) posterior

bounce VERB *The ball hit the ground and bounced up.* ► rebound, spring up, bob up, bound, leap up, recoil, ricochet

bounce NOUN *She was exhausted and had lost much of her bounce.* ► vitality, energy, vigor, liveliness, vivacity, verve, exuberance

bound ADJECTIVE **1** *Our friends are bound to help.* ► certain, sure, very likely, liable, obliged, destined, fated **2** *bound by an oath* ► obligated, committed, obliged, duty-bound,

A
B
C
D
E
F
G
H
I
J
K
L
M
N
O
P
Q
R
S
T
U
V
W
X
Y
Z

bound ADJECTIVE
bound to certain to • *He is bound to fail.*
bound up with closely connected with
• *Happiness is bound up with success.*

bound³ ADJECTIVE going towards something
• *We are bound for Spain.*

bound⁴ VERB bounds, bounding, bounded
limit; be the boundary of • *Their land is bounded by the river.*

boundary NOUN boundaries **1** a line that marks a limit

bounds PLURAL NOUN limits • *This was beyond the bounds of possibility.*
out of bounds where you are not allowed to go

bouquet (boh- kay) NOUN bouquets a bunch of flowers

bout NOUN bouts **1** a boxing or wrestling contest **2** a period of exercise or work or illness • *a bout of flu*

boutique (boo- teek) NOUN boutiques a small shop selling fashionable clothes

bow¹ (rhymes with go) NOUN bows **1** a strip of wood curved by a tight string joining its ends, used for shooting arrows **2** a wooden rod with horsehair stretched between its ends, used for playing a violin etc. **3** a knot made with loops

bow² (rhymes with cow) VERB bows, bowing, bowed **1** bend your body forwards to show respect or as a greeting **2** bend downward
• *bowed by the weight*

bow NOUN bows bowing your body

bow³ (rhymes with cow) NOUN bows the front part of a ship

bowels PLURAL NOUN the intestines

bowl¹ NOUN bowls **1** a rounded deep container for food or liquid **2** the rounded part of a spoon or tobacco pipe, etc.

bowl² NOUN bowls a ball used in the game of bowls or in bowling, when heavy balls are rolled toward bowling pins

bowl VERB bowls, bowling, bowled **1** send a ball to be played by a batsman **2** get a batsman out by bowling **3** send a ball, etc., rolling

bow-legged ADJECTIVE having legs that curve outwards at the knees; bandy

bowling NOUN **1** the game of bowling **2** the game of knocking down objects with a heavy ball

bow tie NOUN bow ties a man's necktie tied into a bow

bow window NOUN bow windows a curved window

box¹ NOUN boxes **1** a container made of wood, cardboard, etc., usually with a top or lid **2** a rectangular space to be filled in on a form, computer screen, etc. **3** a compartment in a theater, court, etc. • *the witness box* **4** a hut or shelter • *a sentry box* **5** a small evergreen shrub
the box (*informal*) television

box² VERB boxes, boxing, boxed fight with the fists as a sport

boxer NOUN boxers **1** a person who boxes **2** a dog that looks like a bulldog

---

Thesaurus

---

pledged, compelled **3** *His wrists and ankles were bound with rope.* ► tied, tied up, shackled, fettered, secured, trussed up, strapped
4 bound for *a train bound for the north* ► going to, heading for, making for, off to, traveling toward

bound VERB *A dog bounded across the lawn.*
► leap, jump, skip, spring, bounce, gambol, bob, caper, frisk

boundary NOUN **1** *A wire fence marks the boundary.* ► border, frontier, borderline, dividing line **2** *the boundary of the estate*
► bounds, confines, circumference, perimeter, extremity, outer edge, fringe, limit, margin

boundless ADJECTIVE *The boys seemed to have boundless energy.* ► unlimited, limitless, unbounded, untold, endless, immeasurable, incalculable, inexhaustible, infinite, unflagging, vast AN OPPOSITE IS limited

bouquet NOUN **1** *a bouquet of flowers* ► bunch, spray, posy, sprig, nosegay, corsage, garland
2 *The white wine had a sweet bouquet.* ► aroma, fragrance, nose, scent

bourgeois ADJECTIVE *a bourgeois family*
► middle-class, suburban, conventional, traditional, conservative

bout NOUN **1** *a bout of coughing* ► attack, fit, spasm, outburst, burst, convulsion **2** *a boxing bout* ► contest, match, round, fight, encounter, engagement, struggle, combat, competition

bow VERB (rhymes with cow) **1** *The man bowed his head.* ► incline, lower, bend **2** *In the end they had to bow to pressure.* ► yield, succumb, submit, surrender, give way, give in

bow NOUN (rhymes with cow)*the bow of a ship*
► front, prow, fore-end

bow NOUN (rhymes with go)*She tied the ribbon into a neat bow.* ► loop, knot

bowl NOUN *a bowl of soup* ► dish, basin, tureen, vessel

bowl VERB *He bowled three fast balls in a row.*
► throw, toss, fling, hurl, pitch, lob

box NOUN *a box of colored pencils* ► carton, pack, packet, case, casket, chest

Boxing Day NOUN the first weekday after Christmas Day

box office NOUN box offices an office for booking seats at a theater or cinema

boy NOUN boys **1** a male child **2** a young man
▷ **boyhood** NOUN **boyish** ADJECTIVE

boycott VERB boycotts, boycotting, boycotted refuse to use or have anything to do with
• They boycotted the buses when the fares went up.
▷ **boycott** NOUN

boyfriend NOUN boyfriends a person's regular male companion in a romantic or sexual relationship

bra NOUN bras a piece of underwear worn by women to support their breasts

brace VERB braces, bracing, braced support; make a thing firm against something

bracelet NOUN bracelets an ornament worn round the wrist

braces PLURAL NOUN straps to hold trousers up, passing over the shoulders

bracing ADJECTIVE making you feel refreshed and healthy • the bracing sea breeze.

bracken NOUN a type of large fern that grows in open country; a mass of these ferns

bracket NOUN brackets **1** a mark used in pairs to enclose words or figures • There are round brackets ( ) and square brackets [ ]. **2** a support attached to a wall etc. **3** a group or range between certain limits • a high income bracket.

bracket VERB brackets, bracketing, bracketed **1** enclose in brackets **2** put things together because they are similar

brahmin NOUN brahmins a member of the highest Hindu class, originally priests

Braille (rhymes with mail) NOUN a system of representing letters, etc., by raised dots which blind people can read by feeling them

brain NOUN brains **1** the organ inside the top of the head that controls the body **2** the mind; intelligence

brainwash VERB brainwashes, brainwashing, brainwashed force a person to give up one set of ideas or beliefs and accept new ones; indoctrinate

brainwave NOUN brainwaves a sudden bright idea

brainy ADJECTIVE clever; intelligent

brake NOUN brakes a device for slowing or stopping something

brake VERB brakes, braking, braked use a brake

bramble NOUN brambles a blackberry bush or a prickly bush like it

bran NOUN ground-up seed coats of grain

branch NOUN branches **1** a woody arm-like part of a tree or shrub **2** a part of a railway, road, or river, etc., that leads off from the main part **3** a shop or office, etc., that belongs to a large organization

branch VERB branches, branching, branched form a branch
branch out start something new

brand NOUN brands a particular make of goods

Thesaurus

boy NOUN He loved reading as a boy. ► lad, youngster, (more informal) kid

boyish ADJECTIVE He had a boyish sense of fun. ► youthful, childlike, young, (disapproving) childish, (disapproving) puerile OPPOSITES ARE manly, mature, adult

bracing ADJECTIVE The sea air is very bracing. ► invigorating, stimulating, refreshing, exhilarating, fortifying AN OPPOSITE IS debilitating

brag VERB He was bragging about all the friends he had. ► boast, crow, bluster, swank, show off, gloat, sing someone's praises, (more informal) talk big

brain NOUN **1** You need brains to succeed in this job. ► intelligence, intellect, sense, common sense, understanding, a good mind, a good head, (informal) gray matter **2** the brains of the family ► intellectual, clever one, clever person, mastermind, (more informal) egghead RELATED ADJECTIVE ► cerebral

brainwash VERB He likes to brainwash people into thinking they need help. ► indoctrinate, condition, re-educate

brainy ADJECTIVE a brainy child ► intelligent, clever, bright, gifted, brilliant, intellectual, highbrow, (more informal) smart OPPOSITES ARE stupid, unintelligent

brake VERB She saw a child step out and braked quickly. ► slow down, reduce speed, put on the brakes, (more formal) decelerate AN OPPOSITE IS accelerate

branch NOUN **1** a branch of a tree ► bough, limb, arm, offshoot, sprig **2** the executive branch of government ► department, section, division, subdivision, wing, part **3** The firm has closed several overseas branches. ► office, bureau, agency

branch VERB The road branches ahead. ► divide, fork
branch out She wanted to branch out into another career. ► diversify, develop, expand, extend, enlarge, broaden out

brand NOUN a new brand of margarine ► make, kind, type, variety, brand-name, trademark, label, line, sort

brand VERB **1** The cattle are branded with hot irons. ► mark, stamp, burn, identify, label, scar

A

B

C

D

E

F

G

H

I

J

K

L

M

N

O

P

Q

R

S

T

U

V

W

X

Y

Z

brandish VERB brandishes, brandishing, brandished wave something about

brand new ADJECTIVE completely new

brandy NOUN brandies a strong alcoholic drink, usually made from wine

brash ADJECTIVE 1 impudent 2 reckless

brass NOUN brasses 1 a metal that is an alloy of copper and zinc 2 wind instruments made of brass, e.g., trumpets and trombones
▷ **brass** ADJECTIVE

brassy ADJECTIVE brassier, brassiest 1 resembling brass in color 2 loud or showy

bravado (brav- ah- doh) NOUN a display of boldness

brave ADJECTIVE having or showing courage
▷ **bravely** ADVERB, **bravery** NOUN

brave VERB braves, braving, braved face and endure something bravely

brawl NOUN brawls a noisy quarrel or fight

brawl VERB brawls, brawling, brawled take part in a brawl

brawny ADJECTIVE strong and muscular

brazen VERB brazens, brazening, brazened brazen it out behave as if there is nothing to be ashamed of when you have done wrong

breach NOUN breaches 1 the breaking of an agreement or rule, etc. 2 a broken place; a gap

bread NOUN breads a food made by baking flour and water, usually with yeast
▷ **breadcrumbs** PLURAL NOUN

breadth NOUN width; broadness

break VERB breaks, breaking, broke, broken 1 divide or fall into pieces by hitting or pressing 2 damage; stop working properly 3 fail to keep a promise or law, etc. 4 stop for a time; end • She broke her silence. 5 change • the weather broke 6 (said about waves) fall in foam 7 go suddenly or with force • They broke through. 8 appear suddenly • Dawn had broken.
▷ **breakage** NOUN

break a record do better than anyone else has done before

break down 1 stop working properly 2 collapse

break out 1 begin suddenly 2 escape

break the news make something known

break up 1 break into small parts

break NOUN breaks 1 a broken place; a gap 2 an escape; a sudden dash 3 a short rest from work 4 a number of points scored continuously in pool, etc. 5 (informal) a piece of luck; a fair chance • Give me a break.

break of day dawn

Thesaurus

2 The men are all branded as troublemakers.
▶ stigmatize, vilify, censure, denounce, discredit, disgrace, taint, give (someone) the reputation of

brash ADJECTIVE a group of brash youths
▶ brazen, forward, insolent, (more informal) cocky OPPOSITES ARE meek, shy

brave ADJECTIVE He was a good fighter and a brave man. They put up a brave fight. ▶ courageous, valiant, daring, audacious, spirited, intrepid, plucky, adventurous, fearless AN OPPOSITE IS cowardly

bravery NOUN Everyone praised their bravery.
▶ courage, audacity, boldness, daring, nerve, gallantry, determination, fearlessness, fortitude, heroism, (more informal) bottle, (more informal) grit, (more informal) guts, (more informal) pluck, (much more informal) spunk AN OPPOSITE IS cowardice

brawl NOUN The argument rapidly grew into a drunken brawl. ▶ fight , affray, melee, wrangle, altercation, fracas, clash, fray, scrap, scuffle, tussle, (informal) punch-up, (more informal) set-to, (more informal) bust-up

brawl VERB grown men brawling in the street
▶ fight, scuffle, scrap, tussle, wrestle, exchange blows

brazen ADJECTIVE a brazen lie ▶ blatant, barefaced, flagrant, shameless, unashamed,

unabashed, audacious, cheeky, defiant, impertinent, impudent, insolent, rude OPPOSITES ARE modest, shamefaced

breach NOUN 1 a breach of the rules ▶ breaking, infringement, violation, contravention, offence (against), transgression 2 a breach between the king and his chancellor ▶ rift, break, split, difference, disagreement, drifting apart, estrangement, quarrel, separation, alienation 3 a breach in the sea wall ▶ break, split, fissure, gap, crack, fracture, rupture, aperture, chasm, hole, opening

bread NOUN 1 She was responsible for keeping a roof over their heads and bread in their mouths.
▶ food, nourishment, sustenance, subsistence

break NOUN 1 a break in a pipe ▶ breach, split, fissure, gap, crack, fracture, rupture, aperture, chasm, hole, opening 2 a break in work
▶ pause, respite, rest, breathing space, intermission, interval, hiatus, interlude, (informal) let-up, lull, (informal) breather 3 He had listened to thirty new songs without a break.
▶ interruption, disruption, halt, stop, lapse, suspension

break VERB 1 The cup fell to the floor and broke.
▶ shatter, smash, crack, split, fragment, splinter, (more informal) bust 2 He broke the stick into three pieces. ▶ split, cut, divide, sever, (more informal) bust OPPOSITES ARE repair, mend 3 It would be unwise to break the law.

breakdown NOUN **breakdowns** **1** breaking down; failure • *the breakdown of law and order* **2** a period of mental illness caused by anxiety or depression **3** an analysis of accounts or statistics **4** a sudden failure to work, especially by a car • *We had a breakdown on the highway.*

breakfast NOUN **breakfasts** the first meal of the day

breakneck ADJECTIVE dangerously fast • *He had to drive at breakneck speed to get there on time.*

breakthrough NOUN **breakthroughs** an important advance or achievement

breast NOUN **breasts** **1** one of the two fleshy parts on the upper front of a woman's body that produce milk to feed a baby **2** a person's or animal's chest

breastplate NOUN **breastplates** a piece of armor covering the chest

breath (breth) NOUN **breaths** **1** air drawn into the lungs and sent out again **2** a gentle blowing • *a breath of wind*

out of breath panting
take your breath away surprise or delight you greatly
under your breath in a whisper

breathalyzer NOUN **breathalyzers** a device for measuring the amount of alcohol in a person's breath
▷ **breathalyze** VERB

breathe (breeth) VERB **breathes, breathing, breathed** **1** take air into the body and send it out again **2** speak or utter • *Don't breathe a word of this.*

breather (bree-ther) NOUN **breathers** a pause for rest • *Let's take a breather.*

breathless ADJECTIVE out of breath

breed VERB **breeds, breeding, bred** **1** produce young creatures **2** keep animals in order to produce young ones from them **3** bring up or train **4** create or produce • *Poverty breeds illness.*
▷ **breeder** NOUN

Thesaurus

▶ contravene, violate, disobey, flout, infringe OPPOSITES ARE obey, respect, abide by **4** *Let's break for lunch.* ▶ pause, stop, take a break, (*more informal*) knock off **5** *She was determined to break the power of the unions.* ▶ subdue, tame, defeat, crush, smash, suppress, undermine

break down **1** *The car broke down near the border.* ▶ stop working, go wrong, (*more informal*) pack up, (*more informal*) conk out **2** *Negotiations broke down without an agreement.* ▶ fail, collapse, fall through, come to nothing

break in **1** *His mother then broke in with a question about the arrangements.* ▶ interrupt, butt in, intrude **2** *Thieves had broken in during the night.* ▶ commit burglary, force your way in, make a raid

break off *It was hard to break off before finishing the chapter.* ▶ discontinue, pause, stop

break out of *Several prisoners were able to break out of the detention center.* ▶ escape from, abscond from, break loose from

break up **1** *A dump where they break up old cars.* ▶ demolish, dismantle, take apart **2** *The meeting broke up after several hours.* ▶ adjourn, finish, end, come to an end, (*more informal*) terminate **3** *The crowd began to break up.* ▶ disperse, scatter, disband, go their separate ways **4** *Jane and her boyfriend had recently broken up.* ▶ separate, split up, stop living together, get divorced

breakdown NOUN **1** *The system has experienced a complete breakdown.* ▶ malfunction, failure, collapse **2** *a breakdown in the peace talks*

▶ failure, collapse **3** *a breakdown of the figures* ▶ analysis, classification, itemization

break-in NOUN *a break-in at the bank* ▶ burglary, robbery, theft, raid

breakneck ADJECTIVE *driving at breakneck speed* ▶ headlong, dangerous, reckless, fast, hasty, suicidal

breakthrough NOUN *a breakthrough in the search for a cure* ▶ advance, leap forward, discovery, development, revolution, progress, find, improvement, innovation, invention, success

breast NOUN *a woman's breast* ▶ bosom(s), bust, chest, front RELATED ADJECTIVE ▶ mammary

breath NOUN **1** *Take a deep breath.* ▶ gulp of air, (*technical*) inhalation **2** *a breath of wind* ▶ puff, waft, whiff, whisper, breeze, sigh

breathe VERB **1** *It is lovely to breathe fresh air again.* ▶ inhale, exhale, respire, puff, pant **2** *Try not to breathe a word of what happened.* ▶ speak, whisper, hint, let out

breathless ADJECTIVE *They arrived breathless and red in the face.* ▶ out of breath, gasping, panting, puffing, tired out, wheezy, exhausted

breathtaking ADJECTIVE *The view was breathtaking.* ▶ spectacular, magnificent, stunning, amazing, astonishing, astounding, staggering, startling, fantastic, wonderful, phenomenal AN OPPOSITE IS unimpressive

breed NOUN **1** *a rare breed of dog* ▶ variety, type, kind, sort, strain, family, pedigree **2** *a new breed of writer* ▶ type, kind, sort, class, variety, genre, order

breed NOUN breeds a variety of animals with qualities inherited from their parents

breeze NOUN breezes a wind
▷ **breezy** ADJECTIVE

brevity NOUN shortness; briefness

brew VERB brews, brewing, brewed **1** make beer or tea **2** develop • *Trouble is brewing.*

brew NOUN brews a brewed drink

brewery NOUN breweries a place where beer is brewed

bribe NOUN bribes money or a gift offered to a person to influence him or her

bribe VERB bribes, bribing, bribed give someone a bribe
▷ **bribery** NOUN

brick NOUN bricks **1** a small hard block of baked clay, etc., used to build walls **2** a rectangular block of something

brick VERB bricks, bricking, bricked close something with bricks • *We bricked up the gap in the wall.*

bricklayer NOUN bricklayers a worker who builds with bricks

bride NOUN brides a woman on her wedding day
▷ **bridal** ADJECTIVE

bridegroom NOUN bridegrooms a man on his wedding day

bridesmaid NOUN bridesmaids a girl or unmarried woman who attends the bride at a wedding

bridge[1] NOUN bridges **1** a structure built over and across a river, railway, or road, etc., to allow people to cross it **2** a high platform above a ship's deck, for the officer in charge **3** the bony upper part of the nose **4** something that connects things

bridge VERB bridges, bridging, bridged make or form a bridge over something

bridge[2] NOUN a card game

bridle NOUN bridles the part of a horse's harness that fits over its head

bridleway or **bridle path** NOUN bridleways or bridle paths a road suitable for horses but not for vehicles

brief ADJECTIVE short
▷ **briefly** ADVERB **briefness** NOUN
in brief in a few words

brief NOUN briefs instructions and information given to someone, especially to a barrister

Thesaurus

breed VERB **1** *Rabbits have a reputation for breeding rapidly.* ► reproduce, produce young, bear young, multiply, procreate, increase **2** *Familiarity breeds contempt.* ► produce, cause, create, arouse, engender, foster, cultivate, develop, generate, induce, nourish, nurture, occasion

breeze NOUN *A slight breeze made the tall grass tremble.* ► gentle wind, breath of air, puff of air, flurry

breezy ADJECTIVE **1** *a breezy afternoon* ► windy, blowy, fresh, brisk, airy, drafty, fresh OPPOSITES ARE still, windless **2** *She walked in with a breezy air.* ► cheerful, jaunty, lively, bright, animated, carefree, light-hearted OPPOSITES ARE sombre, serious

brevity NOUN *Everyone who had to read it welcomed the brevity of the report.* ► conciseness, shortness, succinctness, economy, briefness, compression, incisiveness, pithiness, terseness, crispness, curtness OPPOSITES ARE verbosity, long-windedness

brew NOUN *a strong brew made with fruit juices* ► mixture, blend, concoction, compound, infusion, potion, preparation, punch, drink, liquor

brew VERB **1** *He just can't brew good beer.* ► ferment, make **2** *Christopher and Francis disappeared to brew coffee.* ► make, prepare, heat **3** *Someone is brewing mischief for us.* ► plot, stir up, foment, threaten, concoct, contrive, hatch, plan, prepare, scheme, (more informal) cook up **4** *Trouble is brewing.* ► develop, loom, build up, threaten, gather

bribe NOUN *He was accused of accepting bribes.* ► inducement, enticement, incentive, (more informal) sweetener, (more informal) backhander, (more informal) carrot

bribe VERB *They tried to bribe an official.* ► offer a bribe to, buy off, pay off, corrupt, entice, influence, pervert, (more formal) suborn

brick NOUN *an outhouse made of bricks* ► block, building block, breeze-block

bridge NOUN *a bridge over the river* ► viaduct, aqueduct (carrying water), arch, crossing, span, way over

bridge VERB *A footpath bridged the thruway.* ► span, cross, straddle, traverse, go over, extend across, reach across

brief ADJECTIVE **1** *a brief visit* ► short, cursory, fleeting, passing, quick, hasty, limited, little, momentary, sharp, short-lived, temporary, transient OPPOSITES ARE long, prolonged **2** *a brief account of the incident* ► short, concise, succinct, pithy, crisp, incisive, compact, condensed, curt, terse, thumbnail OPPOSITES ARE wordy, verbose, lengthy

brief NOUN **1** *Here is a detailed brief for the assignment.* ► (set of) instructions, (set of) orders, (set of) directions, (set of) guidelines, set of information, outline, plan **2** *a lawyer's*

brief VERB briefs, briefing, briefed **1** give a brief to a barrister **2** instruct or inform someone concisely in advance

briefcase NOUN briefcases a flat case for carrying documents etc.

briefing NOUN briefings a meeting to give someone concise instructions or information

briefs PLURAL NOUN very short underpants

brigade NOUN brigades **1** a large unit of an army **2** a group of people organized for a special purpose • *the fire brigade*

bright ADJECTIVE **1** giving a strong light; shining **2** clever **3** cheerful
▷ **brightly** ADVERB **brightness** NOUN

brighten VERB brightens, brightening, brightened make or become brighter

brilliant ADJECTIVE **1** very bright; sparkling **2** very clever
▷ **brilliantly** ADVERB **brilliance** NOUN

brim NOUN brims **1** the edge of a cup, etc. **2** the bottom part of a hat that sticks out

brim VERB brims, brimming, brimmed be full to the brim
brim over overflow

brimful ADJECTIVE full to the brim

bring VERB brings, bringing, brought cause a person or thing to come; lead; carry
bring about cause to happen
bring off achieve; do something successfully
bring up 1 look after and train growing children **2** mention a subject **3** vomit **4** cause to stop suddenly

Thesaurus

brief ► case, defense, argument, dossier, summary

brief VERB *Staff will be briefed about the changes.*
► inform, advise, direct, instruct, prime, apprise of, give the facts, guide, prepare, (*more informal*) fill in, (*more informal*) put in the picture

briefs PLURAL NOUN *He stood in the doorway in nothing but briefs.* ► underpants, pants, panties, shorts, trunks

brigand NOUN *The travelers were robbed by brigands.* ► bandit, robber, thief, outlaw, desperado, gangster, gunman, marauder, highwayman, footpad, pirate, hijacker

bright ADJECTIVE **1** *bright colors; bright sunshine*
► shining, luminous, brilliant, vivid, radiant, dazzling, glaring, blazing, sparkling, twinkling OPPOSITES ARE dark, dull **2** *a bright morning*
► sunny, fine, fair, clear, cloudless OPPOSITES ARE dull, cloudy **3** *a bright manner* ► cheerful, jaunty, lively, breezy, animated AN OPPOSITE IS subdued **4** *a bright student* ► clever, intelligent, gifted, sharp, quick, quick-witted, smart, brilliant OPPOSITES ARE dull, stupid, unintelligent

brighten VERB *The weather brightened*
► become sunny, become bright, clear up, lighten AN OPPOSITE IS darken
brighten up *Some pictures will brighten the place up.* ► cheer up, smarten up, embellish, enhance, enliven, gladden, illuminate, light up, revitalize AN OPPOSITE IS darken

brilliant ADJECTIVE **1** *brilliant light* ► blazing, bright, dazzling, glaring, gleaming, glittering, glorious, resplendent, scintillating, shining, showy, sparkling, splendid, vivid AN OPPOSITE IS dull **2** *a brilliant student* ► clever, intelligent, outstanding, gifted, sharp, quick, quick-witted, smart, bright OPPOSITES ARE dull, stupid **3** (*informal*) *a brilliant game*
► excellent, marvelous, wonderful, superb, exceptional

brim NOUN *full to the brim* ► top, rim, edge, limit, lip, brink, circumference, margin, perimeter, periphery

bring VERB **1** *She brought me a mug of tea.*
► fetch, carry, convey, bear, deliver, take, transfer, transport **2** *Bring your friends into the garden.* ► escort, accompany, conduct, guide, lead, usher **3** *Their success brought a great deal of great attention.* ► draw, attract, produce, cause, engender, generate
bring about *The new manager brought about many changes.* ► cause, effect, achieve, create, engineer, manage
bring in 1 *The appeal brought in a huge response.* ► result in, lead to, realize, yield, earn, gross **2** *The company is bringing in a new product.* ► introduce, initiate, start, make available
bring off *It was a difficult play to bring off.*
► achieve, accomplish, be successful in, do successfully, succeed in
bring on *The shock brought on his asthma.*
► cause, give rise to, induce, trigger, lead to, precipitate, provoke, aggravate
bring out 1 *The publishers are to bring out a new edition.* ► publish, release, issue, produce, print **2** *The description brings out the comical side of the story.* ► emphasize, accentuate, underline, highlight, stress, dwell on, feature, make obvious, play up, point up, show clearly, spotlight
bring up 1 *As a young child she was brought up in Poland.* ► raise, rear, educate, care for, look after, nurture, teach, train **2** *The baby brought up his dinner.* ► vomit, sick up **3** *There's a small matter I want to bring up.* ► mention, raise, broach, touch on, refer to

brink NOUN **1** *The children stood at the brink staring into the water.* ► edge, verge, margin, bank, brim, border **2** *We were on the brink of a major discovery.* ► verge, point, threshold, start

a
b
c
d
e
f
g
h
i
j
k
l
m
n
o
p
q
r
s
t
u
v
w
x
y
z

brisk ADJECTIVE quick and lively
▷ **briskly** ADVERB **briskness** NOUN

bristle NOUN bristles **1** a short stiff hair **2** one of the stiff pieces of hair, wire, or plastic, etc., in a brush
▷ **bristly** ADJECTIVE

bristle VERB bristles, bristling, bristled **1** (said about an animal) raise its bristles in anger or fear **2** show indignation
bristle with be full of • *The roof bristled with aerials.*

brittle ADJECTIVE hard but easy to break or snap
▷ **brittleness** NOUN

broad ADJECTIVE **1** large across; wide **2** full and complete • *broad daylight* **3** in general terms; not detailed • *We are in broad agreement.* **4** strong and unmistakable • *a broad hint* • *a broad accent*
▷ **broadly** ADVERB **broadness** NOUN

broad bean NOUN broad beans a bean with large flat seeds

broadcast NOUN broadcasts a program sent out on the radio or on television

broadcast VERB broadcasts, broadcasting, broadcast send out a program on the radio or on television
▷ **broadcaster** NOUN

broaden VERB broadens, broadening, broadened make or become broader

broad-minded ADJECTIVE tolerant; not easily shocked

broccoli NOUN broccoli a kind of cauliflower with greenish flower heads

brochure (broh- shoor) NOUN brochures a booklet or pamphlet containing information

broke ADJECTIVE (informal) having spent all your money

broken-hearted ADJECTIVE extremely sad or upset about something

broken home NOUN broken homes a family lacking one parent through divorce or separation

bronchitis (bronk- I- tiss) NOUN a disease with bronchial inflammation, which makes you cough a lot

Thesaurus

brisk ADJECTIVE **1** *walking at a brisk pace* ▸ quick, rapid, fast, lively, energetic, speedy, swift, hurried OPPOSITES ARE leisurely, slow **2** *brisk exercise* ▸ vigorous, energetic, bracing, refreshing **3** *The hotel was doing a brisk trade.* ▸ busy, bustling, lively, hectic, good OPPOSITES ARE quiet, slack

bristle NOUN *John rubbed a hand over his bristles.* ▸ stubble, facial hair, whisker, prickle, spine, wire

brittle ADJECTIVE *brittle bones* ▸ breakable, fragile, frail, delicate, splintery, crackly OPPOSITES ARE flexible, resilient

broad ADJECTIVE **1** *They were walking along a broad path.* ▸ wide, large, big, ample, capacious, expansive, extensive, great, large, open, roomy, spacious, sweeping, vast OPPOSITES ARE narrow, small **2** *a broad sweep of countryside* ▸ wide, spacious, ample, extensive, vast, rolling **3** *the broad outline of the story* ▸ general, rough, vague, loose, imprecise, indefinite, inexact, undetailed OPPOSITES ARE detailed, precise **4** *She had broad tastes in music* ▸ comprehensive, eclectic, catholic, wide-ranging, all-embracing, encyclopedic, universal OPPOSITES ARE restricted, limited, narrow **5** *broad humor* ▸ coarse, earthy, racy, ribald, indecent, vulgar, indelicate, bawdy, suggestive, improper, impure, (more informal) blue **6** *a broad local accent* ▸ pronounced, strong, marked, noticeable **7** *You'll need to drop a broad hint.* ▸ clear, direct, obvious, unmistakable

broadcast NOUN *a radio broadcast* ▸ transmission, relay, program

broadcast VERB **1** *The concert was broadcast worldwide on television.* ▸ transmit, relay, send out, televise, show, (more informal) screen, (more informal) air **2** *This is sensitive information and should not be broadcast too widely.* ▸ report, publicize, circulate, spread, make known, make public, proclaim, advertise, announce, (more formal) disseminate, (more formal) promulgate

broad-minded ADJECTIVE *Their language would offend the most broad-minded of people.* ▸ liberal, tolerant, enlightened, permissive, forbearing, open-minded, unbiased, receptive OPPOSITES ARE narrow-minded, intolerant

broke ADJECTIVE (informal) *He reached home completely broke.* ▸ impoverished, penniless, poor, insolvent, destitute, ruined

broken ADJECTIVE **1** *A waitress was picking up the broken plates.* ▸ smashed, shattered, cracked, split OPPOSITES ARE whole, unbroken **2** *The television is broken.* ▸ faulty, defective, out of order, not working, (more formal) inoperative OPPOSITES ARE working, fixed **3** *The failure of the company left him a broken man.* ▸ defeated, crushed, beaten, overwhelmed **4** *a broken marriage* ▸ failed, ended **5** *a few hours of broken sleep* ▸ interrupted, disturbed, disrupted, fitful, troubled OPPOSITES ARE continuous, uninterrupted

broken-hearted ADJECTIVE *The little girl was broken-hearted at the loss of her doll.* ▸ heartbroken, inconsolable, devastated, grief-stricken, desolate, despairing AN OPPOSITE IS happy

bronze NOUN bronzes **1** a metal that is an alloy of copper and tin **2** something made of bronze **3** a bronze medal, awarded as third prize **4** yellowish-brown
▷ **bronze** ADJECTIVE

Bronze Age NOUN the time when tools and weapons were made of bronze

brooch NOUN brooches an ornament with a hinged pin for fastening it on to clothes

brood NOUN broods young birds that were hatched together

brood VERB broods, brooding, brooded **1** sit on eggs to hatch them **2** keep thinking and worrying about something

brook NOUN brooks a small stream

broom NOUN brooms **1** a brush with a long handle, for sweeping **2** a shrub with yellow, white, or pink flowers

broomstick NOUN broomsticks the handle of a broom

broth NOUN broths a kind of thin soup

brother NOUN brothers **1** a son of the same parents as another person **2** a man who is a fellow member of a Church, trade union, etc.
▷ **brotherly** ADJECTIVE
[from Old English]

brother-in-law NOUN brothers-in-law the brother of a married person's husband or wife; the husband of a person's sister

brow NOUN brows **1** an eyebrow **2** the forehead **3** the ridge at the top of a hill; the edge of a cliff

brown NOUN browns the color of earth

brown ADJECTIVE **1** of the color brown **2** having a brown skin; suntanned

Brownie NOUN Brownies a member of a junior branch of the Girl Scouts

browse VERB browses, browsing, browsed **1** read or look at something casually **2** feed on grass or leaves **3** (in computing) to look through files or data, especially on the Internet

browser NOUN browsers (in computing) a program for searching the Internet

bruise NOUN bruises a dark mark made on the skin by hitting it

bruise VERB bruises, bruising, bruised give or get a bruise or bruises

brunette NOUN brunettes a woman with brown hair

brunt NOUN the chief impact or strain • *They bore the brunt of the attack.*

brush NOUN brushes **1** an implement used for cleaning or painting things or for smoothing the hair, usually with pieces of hair, wire, or plastic, etc., set in a solid base **2** a fox's bushy tail **3** brushing • *Give it a good brush.* **4** a short fight • *They had a brush with the enemy.*

brush VERB brushes, brushing, brushed **1** use a brush on something **2** touch gently in passing
brush up revise a subject

brusque (bruusk) ADJECTIVE curt and offhand in manner
▷ **brusquely** ADVERB

Brussels sprouts PLURAL NOUN the edible buds of a kind of cabbage

Thesaurus

brood NOUN **1** *a mother hen and her brood*
► young, offspring, clutch, family **2** *Felicity was the eldest of a large brood.* ► family, household

brood VERB **1** *A hen was brooding her eggs.*
► hatch, incubate, sit on **2** *It's a mistake to brood over past mistakes.* ► dwell (on), agonize, muse (on), ponder, reflect (on), think (about), sulk (about), fret, meditate (on), mope, mull over

brother NOUN *Freddie was Margaret's brother.*
► sibling RELATED ADJECTIVE ► fraternal

brow NOUN *the brow of the hill* ► peak, crest, summit, crown, top OPPOSITES ARE foot, bottom

brown ADJECTIVE **1** *brown hair* ► brunette, auburn, bronze, chestnut, chocolate-colored **2** *a brown coat* ► fawn, beige, buff, tan, tawny, biscuit, terracotta, dun, khaki, ochre, russet, sepia, umber

browse VERB **1** *I was browsing in a book.* ► flick through, leaf through, look through, scan,

skim, thumb through, dip in, (*more formal*) peruse **2** *Cattle browsed in a field.* ► graze, pasture, crop grass, feed, eat

bruise NOUN *He had a bruise on his leg.*
► swelling, bump, contusion, lesion, discoloration

bruise VERB *The blow bruised her arm.* ► mark, discolor, injure, hurt

brush NOUN **1** *Use a brush to sweep up.* ► broom, besom **2** *a brush with the law* ► clash, encounter, altercation, quarrel, wrangle

brush VERB *Wait while I brush my hair.* ► tidy, comb, groom
brush aside *The minister tried to brush aside the objections.* ► discount, dismiss, disregard, ignore, shrug off, put aside, (*more informal*) pooh-pooh
brush off *He was trying to be friendly but they brushed him off.* ► spurn, rebuff, snub, cold-shoulder, reject, disregard, ignore, slight
brush up *Are you going to brush up your French?*
► revise, improve, read up, go over, refresh your memory of, relearn, study

brutal ➡ budget

brutal ADJECTIVE very cruel
▷ **brutally** ADVERB **brutality** NOUN

brute NOUN brutes **1** a brutal person **2** an animal
▷ **brutish** ADJECTIVE

BSE ABBREVIATION bovine spongiform encephalopathy; a fatal disease of cattle that affects the nervous system. BSE is sometimes known as "mad cow disease."

bubble NOUN bubbles **1** a thin transparent ball of liquid filled with air or gas **2** a small ball of air in something
▷ **bubbly** ADJECTIVE

bubble VERB bubbles, bubbling, bubbled **1** send up bubbles; rise in bubbles **2** show great liveliness

buccaneer NOUN buccaneers a pirate

buck NOUN bucks a dollar, a male deer, rabbit, or hare

buck VERB bucks, bucking, bucked (said about a horse) jump with its back arched
buck up (informal) **1** hurry **2** cheer up

bucket NOUN buckets a container with a handle, for carrying liquids, etc.
▷ **bucketful** NOUN

buckle NOUN buckles a device through which a belt or strap is threaded to fasten it

buckle VERB buckles, buckling, buckled fasten something with a buckle

bud NOUN buds a flower or leaf before it opens

Buddhism (buud- izm) NOUN a faith that started in Asia and follows the teachings of the Indian philosopher Siddhartha Gautama, who lived in the 5th century BC
▷ **Buddhist** NOUN

budge VERB budges, budging, budged if you cannot budge something, you cannot move it at all

budgerigar NOUN budgerigars an Australian bird often kept as a pet in a cage [from Australian Aboriginal budgeri = good + gar = cockatoo]

budget NOUN budgets **1** a plan for spending money wisely **2** an amount of money set aside for a purpose
▷ **budgetary** ADJECTIVE
the Budget the government's statement of plans to raise money (e.g., by taxes) [via early French bougette = little leather bag, from Latin bulga = leather bag. In the 18th

---

Thesaurus

---

brutal ADJECTIVE a brutal attack ► savage, cruel, vicious, fierce, ferocious, barbaric, callous, heartless, cold-blooded, pitiless, ruthless, merciless, vile, sadistic, brutish OPPOSITES ARE gentle, humane

brutality NOUN The crime was committed with staggering brutality. ► savagery, cruelty, viciousness, ferocity, barbarity, callousness, heartlessness, cold-bloodedness, ruthlessness AN OPPOSITE IS gentleness

brute NOUN He began behaving like the brute he was. ► beast, animal, monster, fiend, demon

brute ADJECTIVE brute force ► physical, crude, rough, unthinking

bubble NOUN **1** bubbles rising to the ceiling ► globule, ball, blister, hollow, (more formal) vesicle **2** bubbles soap bubbles ► foam, froth, lather, suds **3** bubbles bubbles of champagne ► effervescence, fizz

bubble VERB The water was bubbling. ► boil, gurgle, seethe, sparkle

bubbly ADJECTIVE **1** a bubbly drink ► fizzy, carbonated, foaming, seething, sparkling, effervescent OPPOSITES ARE still, flat **2** a bubbly personality ► vivacious, animated, spirited, vibrant, lively AN OPPOSITE IS dull

buck VERB The horse began to buck. ► jump, leap, prance, bound, jerk, spring
buck up (informal) **1** We'll have to buck up if we're going to catch the train. ► hurry, speed up, get a move on **2** She did her best to buck me up

but I still felt miserable. ► cheer up, encourage, rally, hearten, enliven, inspire, make cheerful, please, revitalize, revive

bucket NOUN a bucket of water ► pail, can, tub, pitcher

buckle NOUN a belt buckle ► clasp, clip, fastener, fastening, hasp, catch

buckle VERB **1** He quickly buckled his coat. ► fasten, do up, clasp, hook up, secure, clip **2** The bridge began to buckle under the weight. ► bend, warp, twist, crumple, distort, fold, bulge, collapse, contort, curve, dent

budding ADJECTIVE a budding young singer ► promising, aspiring, developing, (informal) hopeful, inexperienced, intending, new, potential, (more informal) would-be OPPOSITES ARE established, experienced

budge VERB **1** The window was stuck and wouldn't budge. ► give way, move, shift, change position **2** The solution is a compromise but no one will budge. ► change your mind, give way, yield, compromise, influence, move, persuade, propel, push, remove, shift, sway **3** They are much too stubborn and won't be be budged. ► persuade, influence, sway, induce, cajole

budget NOUN The hospital had not spent all its budget for the year. ► allowance, allocation of funds, quota, estimate, resources, funds, means century, the Chancellor presented his statement by "opening the budget."]

buffalo NOUN buffalo or buffaloes a large ox; different kinds are found in Asia, Africa, and North America (where they are also called bison)

buffer NOUN buffers **1** something that softens a blow, especially a device on a railroad engine or wagon or at the end of a track **2** (in computing) a memory in which text or data can be stored for a time

buffet[1] (buu- fay) NOUN buffets **1** a cafe at a station **2** a meal where guests serve themselves to food

buffet[2] (buf- it) NOUN buffets a hit, especially with the hand

buffet VERB buffets, buffeting, buffeted hit or knock • *Strong winds buffeted the aircraft.*

buffoon NOUN buffoons a person who plays the fool
▷ **buffoonery** NOUN

bug NOUN bugs **1** an insect **2** an error in a computer program that prevents it working properly **3** (*informal*) a germ or virus **4** (*informal*) a secret hidden microphone

bug VERB bugs, bugging, bugged (*informal*) **1** fit with a secret hidden microphone **2** annoy

bugbear NOUN bugbears something that you fear or dislike

buggy NOUN buggies a stroller for young children

build VERB builds, building, built make something by putting parts together

build in include
build up 1 establish gradually **2** accumulate **3** cover an area with buildings **4** make stronger or more famous • *build up a reputation*

build NOUN builds the shape of someone's body • *of slender build*

builder NOUN builders someone who puts up buildings

building NOUN buildings **1** the process of making houses and other structures **2** a structure with walls and a roof that people can go into

bulb NOUN bulbs **1** a thick rounded part of a plant from which a stem grows up and roots grow down **2** a rounded part of something • *the bulb of a thermometer* **3** a glass globe that produces electric light
▷ **bulbous** ADJECTIVE

bulge NOUN bulges a rounded swelling; an outward curve
▷ **bulgy** ADJECTIVE

bulge VERB bulges, bulging, bulged form or cause to form a bulge

bulimia (buu- lim- ia) NOUN an illness that makes someone eat too much and then too little. People who suffer from bulimia often makes themselves vomit after eating.
▷ **bulimic** ADJECTIVE

bulk NOUN bulks **1** the size of something, especially when it is large **2** the greater

Thesaurus

buffet VERB *The sea front was buffeted by the wind and spray.* ► batter, pound, lash, dash

buffoon NOUN *She thought her cousin was a complete buffoon.* ► fool, idiot, clown, ass, dolt, blockhead, (*more informal*) prat, (*more informal*) halfwit, (*more informal*) chump

bug NOUN **1** *The plants were covered in tiny bugs.* ► insect, pest, mite **2** *a stomach bug* ► illness, disease, upset, ailment, complaint, disorder **3** *The computer software developed a bug.* ► fault, error, defect, flaw, (*more informal*) gremlin

bug VERB **1** *The telephone had been bugged.* ► intercept, tap, interfere with, listen in to **2** (*informal*) *Her constant whining was bugging me.* ► annoy, irritate, anger, infuriate, needle, rile

build VERB **1** *There are plans to build a new apartment house on the site.* ► construct, erect, raise, put up, set up, assemble, fabricate OPPOSITES ARE demolish, destroy
build up 1 *He has built up a thriving business.* ► establish, develop, create, enlarge, expand, raise, accumulate, amass, assemble, begin,

bring together, collect **2** *Traffic is building up in the city center.* ► increase, intensify, escalate, grow, mount up, strengthen, rise, augment

build NOUN *a man of slim build* ► physique, form, frame, body

building NOUN *a large grim building with few windows* ► structure, construction, premises, erection, establishment, place, piece of architecture, (*more formal*) edifice, (*more informal*) pile

buildup NOUN *a steady military buildup on the border* ► increase, growth, escalation, expansion, development, accumulation, proliferation

bulge NOUN *There was a strange bulge at the bottom of the bed.* ► bump, swelling, protuberance, hump, lump, projection, (*more formal*) protrusion

bulge VERB *The sheets bulged in the breeze.* ► swell, billow, puff out, balloon out, dilate, distend, expand, belly, enlarge, project, protrude, stick out

bulk NOUN **1** *The sheer bulk of the containers was staggering.* ► size, volume, dimensions,

bulk ➡ bunch

portion; the majority • *The bulk of the population voted for it.*
in bulk in large amounts

bulk VERB bulks, bulking, bulked increase the size or thickness of something • *bulk it out*

bulky ADJECTIVE bulkier, bulkiest taking up a lot of space
▷ **bulkiness** NOUN

bull NOUN bulls **1** a fully grown male of the cow family **2** an adult male seal, whale, or elephant

bulldog NOUN bulldogs a dog of a powerful courageous breed with a short thick neck

bulldozer NOUN bulldozers a powerful tractor with a wide metal blade or scoop in front, used for shifting soil or clearing ground

bullet NOUN bullets a small piece of metal shot from a rifle or revolver

bulletin NOUN bulletins **1** a brief news report on radio or television **2** a regular letter or report giving information

bullfight NOUN bullfights a public entertainment in which bulls are tormented and killed in an arena
▷ **bullfighter** NOUN

bullock NOUN bullocks a young castrated bull

bullseye NOUN bullseyes the center of a target

bully VERB bullies, bullying, bullied **1** use strength or power to hurt or frighten a

weaker person **2** start play in hockey, when two opponents tap the ground and each other's stick • *bully off*

bully NOUN bullies someone who bullies people

bulwark NOUN bulwarks a wall of earth built as a defence; a protection

bumblebee NOUN bumblebees a large bee with a loud hum

bump VERB bumps, bumping, bumped **1** knock against something **2** move along with jolts
bump into (*informal*) meet by chance
bump off (*slang*) kill

bump NOUN bumps **1** the action or sound of bumping **2** a swelling or lump
▷ **bumpy** ADJECTIVE

bumper NOUN bumpers a bar along the front or back of a motor vehicle to protect it in collisions

bumper ADJECTIVE unusually large or plentiful • *a bumper crop*

bumpkin NOUN bumpkins a country person with awkward manners

bun NOUN buns **1** a small round sweet cake **2** hair twisted into a round bunch at the back of the head

bunch NOUN bunches a number of things joined or fastened together

Thesaurus

proportions, extent, magnitude, mass, substance, amplitude, body, immensity, largeness **2** *We did the bulk of the work ourselves.* ► most, best part, most part, greater part, preponderance, majority

bulky ADJECTIVE *a bulky parcel* ► sizable, large, substantial, cumbersome, unwieldy, massive, immense, enormous OPPOSITES ARE small, compact, manageable

bulletin NOUN **1** *a television news bulletin* ► report, statement, announcement, communication, communiqué, dispatch, message, newsflash, notice, proclamation **2** *The club's monthly bulletin* ► newsletter, gazette

bully NOUN *the well-known school bullies* ► tormentor, persecutor, oppressor, thug, tough, (*more informal*) heavy

bully VERB *Some of the other children used to bully him.* ► persecute, torment, intimidate, oppress, tyrannnize, (*more informal*) push around

bump NOUN **1** *The man fell on the floor with a bump.* ► thud, thump, smack, crash, bang, blow, collision, hit, knock, smash **2** *When he got up he had a bump on the head.* ► swelling,

lump, bulge, (*technical*) contusion, protuberance

bump VERB **1** *Chris bumped his head while snorkeling.* ► hit, strike, knock, bang **2** *bump into A bus had bumped into a parked car.* ► collide with, run into, crash into, bang into, smash into, knock into, knock, hit, ram, slam, strike **3** *We were bumping up and down on the rough road.* ► bounce, shake, jerk, jolt
bump off (*informal*) *He became president by bumping off all his rivals.* ► kill, murder, assassinate, eliminate

bumpy ADJECTIVE **1** *a bumpy ride* ► bouncy, rough, jerky, jolting, lurching **2** *a bumpy surface* ► uneven, rough, irregular, pitted, knobbly, lumpy OPPOSITES ARE even, smooth

bunch NOUN **1** *a bunch of carrots; a bunch of keys* ► bundle, cluster, clump, collection, heap, batch, set, lot, number, quantity **2** *a bunch of flowers* ► bouquet, posy, spray, garland **3** *a friendly bunch of people* ► group, set, circle, band, (*more informal*) gang, (*more informal*) crowd

bunch VERB *The friends had bunched together in a corner.* ► gather, assemble, cluster, huddle, collect, congregate, crowd, flock, group, herd AN OPPOSITE IS scatter

bundle NOUN bundles a number of things tied or wrapped together

bundle VERB bundles, bundling, bundled **1** make a number of things into a bundle **2** push hurriedly or carelessly • *They bundled him into a taxi.*

bungalow NOUN bungalows a house without any upstairs rooms [from Hindi *bangla* = to do with Bengal, where there were houses of this kind]

bungle VERB bungles, bungling, bungled make a mess of doing something
▷ **bungler** NOUN

bunion NOUN bunions a swelling at the side of the joint where the big toe joins the foot

bunk NOUN bunks a bed built like a shelf

bunker NOUN bunkers **1** a container for storing fuel **2** a sandy hollow built as an obstacle on a golf course **3** an underground shelter

bunny NOUN bunnies (*informal*) a rabbit

Bunsen burner NOUN Bunsen burners a small gas burner used in scientific work

bunting[1] NOUN buntings a kind of small bird

bunting[2] NOUN strips of small flags hung up to decorate streets and buildings

buoy (boi) NOUN buoys a floating object anchored to mark a channel or underwater rocks, etc.

buoyant (boi- ant) ADJECTIVE **1** able to float **2** lighthearted; cheerful
▷ **buoyantly** ADVERB **buoyancy** NOUN

bur NOUN burs a different spelling of burr (see case)

burden NOUN burdens **1** a heavy load that you have to carry **2** something troublesome that you have to bear • *Exams are a burden.*
▷ **burdensome** ADJECTIVE

burden VERB burdens, burdening, burdened cause someone work or trouble

bureau (byer- oh) NOUN bureaux **1** a writing desk **2** a business office • *They will tell you at the Information Bureau.*

bureaucracy (byer- ok- ra- see) NOUN the use of too many rules and forms by officials, especially in government departments
▷ **bureaucratic** (bewr- ok- **rat**- ik) ADJECTIVE

burger NOUN burgers a hamburger

burglar NOUN burglars a person who breaks into a building in order to steal things
▷ **burglary** NOUN

burgle VERB burgles, burgling, burgled rob a place as a burglar

burial NOUN burials burying somebody

burlesque (ber- **lesk**) NOUN burlesques a comical imitation

burly ADJECTIVE burlier, burliest having a strong heavy body

Thesaurus

bundle NOUN *a bundle of papers* ► bunch, sheaf, carton, collection, pack, package, packet, parcel, bag, bale

bundle VERB **1** *He quickly bundled up the remaining papers.* ► tie, bind, wrap, bale, truss, fasten, pack, roll **2** *The kidnappers bundled their victim into the back of the car.* ► hustle, jostle, shove, sweep

bungle VERB *Two prisoners bungled an escape after running on either side of a lamppost while handcuffed.* ► mishandle, mismanage, botch, ruin, spoil, fluff, muff, mess up, make a mess of, (*much more informal*) screw up OPPOSITES ARE succeed in, bring off

buoyant ADJECTIVE **1** *a buoyant material* ► floating, light **2** *in a buoyant mood* ► cheerful, happy, cheery, carefree, light-hearted, lively, optimistic, animated, sunny OPPOSITES ARE depressed, pessimistic

burden NOUN **1** *donkeys carrying heavy burdens* ► load, weight, encumbrance, pack, bundle, cargo **2** *a large financial burden* ► responsibility, obligation, liability, duty, onus, charge, affliction, anxiety, worry, care, handicap, problem, millstone

burden VERB *For years she was burdened by family worries.* ► afflict, oppress, bother, beset, torment, distress, strain, tax, trouble, worry, encumber, hamper, handicap, load (with), (*informal*) lumber (with), (*informal*) saddle (with)

bureau *an information bureau* ► agency, office, service, department, organization, counter

bureaucracy NOUN *hampered by regulations and bureaucracy* ► administration, government, officialdom, paperwork, (*more informal*) red tape

burglar NOUN *Burglars stole jewelry worth thousands of dollars.* ► housebreaker, robber, thief, intruder

burglary NOUN *Barry had been convicted of burglary.* ► housebreaking, breaking and entering, robbery, theft, forcible entry, larceny, pilfering, stealing, thieving, break-in

burial NOUN *a burial service* ► burying, entombment, funeral, interment, obsequies

burly ADJECTIVE *a burly figure* ► hefty, beefy, sturdy, well-built, strapping, brawny, hulking, muscular, powerful, stocky, stout, athletic, big, heavy OPPOSITES ARE slight, thin

A
B
C
D
E
F
G
H
I
J
K
L
M
N
O
P
Q
R
S
T
U
V
W
X
Y
Z

burn VERB **burns, burning, burned 1** blaze or glow with fire; produce heat or light by combustion **2** damage or destroy something by fire, heat, or chemicals **3** be damaged or destroyed by fire, etc. **4** feel very hot

burn NOUN **burns 1** a mark or injury made by burning **2** the firing of a spacecraft's rockets

burning ADJECTIVE **1** intense • *a burning ambition* **2** very important; hotly discussed • *a burning question*

burr NOUN **burrs 1** a plant's seed case or flower that clings to hair or clothes **2** a whirring sound **3** a soft country accent

burrow NOUN **burrows** a hole or tunnel dug by a rabbit or fox, etc., as a dwelling

burrow VERB **burrows, burrowing, burrowed 1** dig a burrow **2** push your way through or into something; search deeply • *She burrowed in her handbag.*

bursar NOUN **bursars** a person who manages the finances and other business of a school or college

burst VERB **bursts, bursting, burst 1** break or force apart **2** come or start suddenly • *It burst into flame.* • *They burst out laughing.* **3** be very full • *bursting with energy*

burst NOUN **bursts 1** a split caused by something bursting **2** something short and forceful • *a burst of gunfire*

bury VERB **buries, burying, buried 1** place a dead body in the earth, a tomb, or the sea **2** put underground; cover up

bus NOUN **buses** a large vehicle for passengers to travel in

bush NOUN **bushes 1** a shrub **2** wild uncultivated land, especially in Africa and Australia
▷ **bushy** ADJECTIVE

bushel NOUN **bushels** a measure for grain and fruit (8 gallons or 4 pecks)

business (biz- niss) NOUN **businesses 1** a person's concern or responsibilities • *Mind your own business.* **2** an affair or subject • *I'm tired of the whole business.* **3** a shop or firm **4** buying and selling things; trade
▷ **businessman** NOUN **businesswoman** NOUN

bust NOUN **busts 1** a sculpture of a person's head, shoulders, and chest **2** the upper front part of a woman's body

bustle VERB **bustles, bustling, bustled** hurry in a busy or excited way

Thesaurus

burn VERB **1** *The bonfire burned all day.* ► be alight, be on fire, be ablaze, flare, blaze, flicker, glow, smoke, smoulder **2** *An incinerator will burn anything.* ► ignite, kindle, incinerate, cremate, consume **3** *The heat began to burn our skin.* ► scald, scorch, blister, brand, toast, char, sear, singe, sting

burning ADJECTIVE **1** *a burning building* ► blazing, flaming, glowing, ablaze, afire, alight, incandescent, lit up, on fire, raging, smoldering **2** *a burning pain* ► scalding, searing, acute, stinging, biting **3** *a burning desire* ► intense, extreme, fervent, passionate, eager, ardent, profound, consuming **4** *a burning question* ► urgent, crucial, vital, essential, pressing, important, pertinent, relevant

burrow VERB *A rabbit could burrow under the fence.* ► tunnel, excavate, dig, mine, delve

burst VERB **1** *The impact cause a tire to burst.* ► rupture, split open **2** *Water burst through the hole.* ► gush, surge, stream, pour, spurt, cascade **3** *A man suddenly burst into the room.* ► rush, run, charge, plunge, shove your way

bury VERB **1** *The dog buried its bone in the ground.* ► hide, conceal, cover, sink, embed AN OPPOSITE IS uncover **2** *The dead are buried in the local cemetery.* ► inter, lay to rest, entomb **3** *She buried herself in her work.* ► absorb, engross, engage, occupy, immerse

business NOUN **1** *It proved to be quite a tricky business.* ► matter, affair, issue, problem, point, question, concern **2** *What sort of business do you want to go into?* ► work, job, occupation, employment, career, line of work, profession, pursuit, trade, vocation, calling, craft, industry **3** *The new supermarket has taken a lot of business from the local shops.* ► trade, trading, buying and selling, selling, merchandising, transactions, commerce, dealings, industry, marketing **4** *He wants to run his own business.* ► firm, company, establishment, enterprise, organization, concern, venture, corporation, practice, (more informal) outfit, (more informal) set-up

businesslike ADJECTIVE *The office was run in a businesslike way.* ► efficient, professional, competent, methodical, well organized, systematic, practical, pragmatic, orderly

businessman, businesswoman NOUN *a shrewd businesswoman* ► entrepreneur, executive, industrialist, dealer, financier, manager, merchant, trader, tycoon, magnate

bust NOUN *a woman's bust* ► bosom, chest, breast, breasts

bust VERB *Be careful with that or you'll bust it.* ► break, snap, crack, split, burst

bustle VERB *People were bustling about looking for their friends.* ► rush, dash, scurry, scamper, scuttle, hurry, hustle, dart, fuss, move busily, scramble, whirl, hasten, (more informal) tear

bustle NOUN hurried or excited activity

busy ADJECTIVE busier, busiest **1** having a lot to do; occupied **2** full of activity **3** (said about a telephone line) engaged
▷ **busily** ADVERB **busyness** NOUN

busy VERB busies, busying, busied
busy yourself occupy yourself; keep busy

busybody NOUN busybodies a person who meddles or interferes

but CONJUNCTION however; nevertheless • *I wanted to go, but I couldn't.*

but PREPOSITION except • *There is no one here but me.*

but ADVERB only; no more than • *We can but try.*

butcher NOUN butchers **1** a person who cuts up meat and sells it **2** a person who kills cruelly or needlessly
▷ **butchery** NOUN

butcher VERB butchers, butchering, butchered kill cruelly or needlessly

butler NOUN butlers a male servant in charge of other servants in a large private house [from early French *bouteillier* = someone who carried the bottles]

butt[1] NOUN butts **1** the thicker end of a weapon or tool **2** a stub • *cigarette butts*

butt[2] NOUN butts a large cask or barrel

butt[3] NOUN butts a person or thing that is a target for ridicule or teasing • *He was the butt of their jokes.*

butt VERB butts, butting, butted **1** push or hit with the head as a ram or goat does **2** place the edges of things together
butt in interrupt or meddle

butter NOUN a soft fatty food made by churning cream
▷ **buttery** ADJECTIVE

buttercup NOUN buttercups a wild plant with bright yellow cup-shaped flowers

butterfly NOUN butterflies **1** an insect with large white or colored wings **2** a swimming stroke in which both arms are lifted at the same time

buttock NOUN buttocks either of the two fleshy rounded parts of your bottom

button NOUN buttons **1** a knob or disc sewn on clothes as a fastening or ornament **2** a small knob pressed to work an electric device

button VERB buttons, buttoning, buttoned fasten something with a button or buttons

buttonhole NOUN buttonholes **1** a slit through which a button passes to fasten clothes **2** a flower worn on a lapel

buttonhole VERB buttonholes, buttonholing, buttonholed stop somebody so that you can talk to him or her

buttress NOUN buttresses a support built against a wall

buy VERB buys, buying, bought get something by paying for it
▷ **buyer** NOUN

buy NOUN buys something that is bought

Thesaurus

bustle NOUN *The air terminal was full of bustle.*
► activity, hustle, commotion, stir, excitement, flurry, fuss, haste, hurry, movement, restlessness, scurry, agitation

busy ADJECTIVE **1** *Are you very busy at work?*
► active, occupied, hard-pressed, (*more informal*) rushed off your feet AN OPPOSITE IS idle **2** *She's a very busy person.* ► active, energetic, diligent, industrious OPPOSITES ARE lazy, idle **3** *The manager is busy at the moment but can see you this afternoon.* ► engaged, unavailable, occupied, (*more informal*) tied up AN OPPOSITE IS free **4** *Her mother leads a busy life.* ► active, hectic, lively, strenuous, demanding, exacting **5** *The committee members are busy organizing the next conference.*
► occupied (with), working (at), engaged (in), hard at work (on), wrapped up (in) **6** *The shopping malls were busy all day.* ► crowded, hectic, lively, teeming, bustling, swarming, thronging, frantic, full of people AN OPPOSITE IS quiet

busybody NOUN *Pry was an inquisitive busybody.*
► meddler, interferer, gossip, scandalmonger, snooper, eavesdropper

butch ADJECTIVE (*informal*) *a butch builder*
► masculine, manly, virile OPPOSITES ARE effeminate, feminine

butt NOUN **1** *the butt of a rifle* ► stock, shaft, shank, handle, hilt, haft **2** *a water butt*
► barrel, cask, keg, vat **3** *a cigarette butt*
► stub, end, stump, remnant **4** *the butt of a joke* ► target, victim, object, subject, mark

butt VERB *He butted her playfully with his head.*
► hit, ram, bump, knock, jab, prod, poke
butt in *Nick didn't want to butt in, so he waited patiently.* ► interrupt, break in, cut in, (*more informal*) chip in

buttocks PLURAL NOUN *He knelt with his heels against his buttocks.* ► bottom, behind, backside, rear, rump, seat, haunches, hindquarters, (*more informal*) bum, (*usually humorous*) posterior

buy VERB **1** *I will buy the drinks.* ► get, pay for, obtain, acquire, (*more formal*) purchase AN OPPOSITE IS sell **2** *a man who could not be bought*
► bribe, buy off, suborn, corrupt

buy NOUN *A well-looked-after used car can be a good buy.* ► acquisition, deal, bargain, (*more formal*) purchase

buzz *NOUN* buzzes a vibrating humming sound

buzz *VERB* buzzes, buzzing, buzzed **1** make a buzz **2** threaten an aircraft by deliberately flying close to it

by *PREPOSITION* This word is used to show **1** closeness (*Sit by me*), **2** direction or route (*We got here by a short cut*), **3** time (*They came by night*), **4** manner or method (*cooking by gas*), **5** amount (*You missed it by inches*)
by the way incidentally
by yourself alone; without help

by *ADVERB* **1** past • *I can't get by.* **2** in reserve; for future use • *Put it by.*
by and by soon; later on
by and large on the whole

by-election *NOUN* by-elections an election to replace a legislator who has died or resigned

bygone *ADJECTIVE* belonging to the past
let bygones be bygones forgive and forget

bypass *NOUN* bypasses **1** a road taking traffic round a city or congested area **2** a channel that allows something to flow when the main route is blocked

bypass *VERB* bypasses, bypassing, bypassed avoid something by means of a bypass

by-product *NOUN* by-products something useful produced while something else is being made

byroad *NOUN* byroads a minor road

bystander *NOUN* bystanders a person standing near but taking no part when something happens

byte *NOUN* bytes a fixed number of bits (= binary digits) in a computer, often representing a single character

byword *NOUN* bywords a person or thing spoken of as a famous example • *Their firm became a byword for quality.*

Thesaurus

bypass *VERB* **1** *To speed things up we can bypass the usual checking process.* ► ignore, omit, avoid, circumvent, sidestep, neglect, find a way around, get out of, go around, dodge, evade

by-product *NOUN* *Temporary deafness was a by-product of her illness.* ► side effect, consequence, repercussion, result,

complement, corollary, (*more informal*) knock-on effect, (*more informal*) spin-off (from), (*more informal*) fallout (from)

bystander *NOUN* *The man had assaulted a bystander and smashed windows.* ► onlooker, passerby, observer, spectator, watcher, witness, eyewitness

Cc

cab NOUN cabs **1** a taxi **2** a compartment for the driver of a train, bus, or crane

cabaret (kab- er- ay) NOUN cabarets an entertainment provided for the customers in a restaurant or nightclub [from early French *cabaret* = wooden inn or hut]

cabbage NOUN cabbages a vegetable with green or purple leaves [from early French *caboche* = head]

cabin NOUN cabins **1** a hut or shelter **2** a room for sleeping on a ship **3** the part of an aircraft in which passengers sit **4** a driver's cab

Cabinet NOUN the group of chief ministers, chosen by a president or prime minister, who meet to decide government policy

cabinet NOUN cabinets a cupboard or container with drawers or shelves

cable NOUN cables **1** a thick rope of fiber or wire; a thick chain **2** a covered group of wires laid underground for transmitting electrical signals **3** a telegram sent overseas

cable television NOUN a system of television programs transmitted by cables to people who have paid for themd

cackle NOUN cackles **1** a loud silly laugh **2** noisy chatter **3** the loud clucking noise a hen makes
▷ **cackle** VERB

cactus NOUN cacti a fleshy plant, usually with prickles, from a hot dry climate

cad NOUN cads a dishonorable man

cadaverous (kad- av- er- us) ADJECTIVE pale and gaunt

caddie NOUN caddies a person who carries a golfer's clubs during a game

cadence (kay- denss) NOUN cadences **1** rhythm; the rise and fall of the voice in speaking **2** the final notes of a musical phrase

cadenza (ka- den- za) NOUN cadenzas an elaborate passage for a solo instrument or singer, to show the performer's skill

cadet NOUN cadets a young person being trained for the armed forces or the police

cadge VERB cadges, cadging, cadged get something by begging for it
▷ **cadger** NOUN

cadmium NOUN a metal that looks like tin

Caesarean or **Caesarean section** (siz- air- ee- an) NOUN Caesareans or Caesarean sections a surgical operation for taking a baby out of the mother's womb

cafe (kaf- ay) NOUN cafes a small restaurant

caffeine (kaf- een) NOUN a stimulant substance found in tea and coffee

cage NOUN cages **1** a container with bars or wires, in which birds or animals are kept **2** the enclosed platform of an elevator

cairn NOUN cairns a pile of loose stones set up as a landmark or monument

cajole VERB cajoles, cajoling, cajoled persuade someone to do something by flattering them; coax

cake NOUN cakes **1** a baked food made from a mixture of flour, eggs, sugar, etc. **2** a shaped or hardened mass • *a cake of soap* • *crab cakes*

caked ADJECTIVE covered with dried mud etc.

calamine NOUN a pink powder used to make a soothing lotion for the skin

calamity NOUN calamities a disaster
▷ **calamitous** ADJECTIVE

Thesaurus

cabaret NOUN *a cabaret at a nightclub in town*
► floor show, revue, entertainment

cabin NOUN **1** *a cabin by the river* ► hut, lodge, chalet, shack, shanty, shed, shelter **2** *a cabin on the lower deck* ► berth, compartment, sleeping quarters **3** *the driver's cabin* ► cab, compartment

cabinet NOUN *a glass-fronted cabinet for china*
► cupboard, dresser, closet, chest

cable NOUN **1** *The ship was moored by means of thick cables.* ► rope, cord, hawser, line, chain, mooring **2** *Watch out for the power cable.*
► wire, lead, line

cache NOUN *a cache of weapons; a cache of gold*
► hoard, store, stock, stockpile, depot, dump, repository, storehouse, supply

cafe NOUN *We could have a snack at a local cafe.*
► snack bar, cafeteria, coffee bar, coffee shop, tea shop, buffet, canteen, bistro

cage NOUN *an animal's cage* ► enclosure, pen, pound, coop, hutch USAGE A large cage for birds is called an *aviary*

cagey ADJECTIVE *He was being very cagey about what he had been up to.* ► secretive, guarded, cautious, tight-lipped, reticent, evasive, wary, chary OPPOSITES ARE open, frank

cake NOUN **1** *There is a cake for tea today.* ► bun, gateau **2** *a cake of soap* ► bar, tablet, block, lump, piece, slab

cake VERB *Finn's shoes were caked with mud.*
► cover, coat, clog, encrust

calamity NOUN *Disobedience will bring calamity on the nation.* ► disaster, catastrophe, tragedy, misfortune, affliction, blow, cataclysm, tribulation, mishap

a
b
c
d
e
f
g
h
i
j
k
l
m
n
o
p
q
r
s
t
u
v
w
x
y
z

A
B
C
D
E
F
G
H
I
J
K
L
M
N
O
P
Q
R
S
T
U
V
W
X
Y
Z

calcium NOUN a chemical substance found in teeth, bones, and lime

calculate VERB calculates, calculating, calculated **1** figure something out by using mathematics **2** plan something deliberately; intend • *Her remarks were calculated to hurt me.*
▷ **calculable** ADJECTIVE **calculation** NOUN

calculator NOUN calculators a small electronic device for making calculations

calculus NOUN mathematics for figuring out problems about rates of change

calendar NOUN calendars a chart or set of pages showing the dates of the month or year

calf¹ NOUN calves a young cow, whale, seal, etc.

calf² NOUN calves the fleshy back part of the leg below the knee

caliber (kal- ib- er) NOUN calibers **1** the diameter of a tube or gun barrel, or of a bullet etc. **2** ability; importance • *someone of your caliber*

call NOUN calls **1** a shout or cry **2** a visit **3** telephoning somebody **4** a summons

call VERB calls, calling, called **1** shout or speak loudly, e.g., to attract someone's attention **2** telephone somebody **3** name a person or thing • *They've decided to call the baby Alexander.* **4** tell somebody to come to you; summon **5** make a short visit
▷ **caller** NOUN
call a person's bluff challenge a person to do what was threatened, and expose the fact that it was a bluff
call for 1 come and collect **2** require • *The scandal calls for an investigation.*
call off cancel or postpone
call up summon to join the armed forces

calligraphy (kal- ig- raf- ee) NOUN the art of beautiful handwriting

calling NOUN callings an occupation; a profession or trade

callous (kal- us) ADJECTIVE hard-hearted; unsympathetic
▷ **callously** ADVERB **callousness** NOUN

calm ADJECTIVE **1** quiet and still; not windy **2** not excited or agitated
▷ **calmly** ADVERB **calmness** NOUN

Thesaurus

---

calculate VERB *Interest on the loan is calculated monthly.* ► figure out, compute, reckon, assess, count, determine, add up

caliber NOUN *People of this caliber are not something you come across every day.* ► quality, ability, distinction, excellence, capacity, standard, talent, stature, character

call VERB **1** *"Come here!," she called.* ► cry, cry out, shout, yell, exclaim **2** *I'll call you this evening.* ► phone, telephone, ring, ring up, give someone a call **3** *What did they call him?* ► baptize, christen, dub, name **4** *Why did you call your cat Albert?* ► name **5** *His mother said she would call him early next morning.* ► wake, wake up, waken, awaken, get someone up, arouse, rouse **6** *The principal called me to her office.* ► summon, invite, order **7** *We'd better call the doctor.* ► send for, fetch, summon, ask to come **8** *We need to call a meeting.* ► convene, organize, gather **9** *Harriet's mother called the next day.* ► visit, pay a visit, (more informal) drop in, (more informal) drop by
call for 1 *The assignment calls for careful planning.* ► require, need, demand, necessitate, make necessary, involve, entail, warrant **2** *Shall we call for you about six o'clock?* ► fetch, pick up, come for, collect
call off *The barbecue was called off because of bad weather.* ► cancel, abandon, postpone, adjourn, discontinue, drop, end, halt USAGE You use *cancel* if you mean calling off for good, and *postpone* if you mean calling off until a later date. You often use *abandon* to refer to things that have been started but cannot be completed.

call on *I might call on my friends this afternoon.* ► visit, go and see, (more informal) drop in on, (more informal) look up

call NOUN **1** *a call for help* ► cry, exclamation, shout, yell, scream **2** *a call for strike action* ► appeal, plea, summons, demand, request **3** *He decided to pay a call on his old father.* ► visit, stop **4** *There's little call for caviar here.* ► demand, market, need **5** *There's no call for that kind of talk.* ► need, necessity, occasion, reason, justification, excuse

calling NOUN *He thought that the law was the right calling.* ► profession, career, line of work, occupation, vocation, business, employment, walk of life, job, trade, work

callous ADJECTIVE *a callous remark* ► heartless, hard-hearted, unfeeling, uncaring, indifferent, insensitive, cruel, brutal, ruthless OPPOSITES ARE kind, considerate

calm ADJECTIVE **1** *a calm sunny day* ► still, tranquil, quiet, peaceful, balmy OPPOSITES ARE stormy, windy **2** *The sea was calm.* ► smooth, tranquil, still, flat, waveless **3** *He remained calm despite the difficulties.* ► composed, collected, self-possessed, cool, poised, dispassionate, unperturbed, imperturbable, unruffled, unflustered, unbothered, untroubled, unemotional, (more informal) unflappable, (more informal) laid-back OPPOSITES ARE anxious, upset, excited **4** *a calm temperament* ► serene, placid, phlegmatic, tranquil, relaxed

calm VERB calms, calming, calmed make or become calm

calorie NOUN calories a unit for measuring an amount of heat or the energy produced by food
▷ **calorific** ADJECTIVE

calypso NOUN calypsos a West Indian song about current happenings, made up as the singer goes along

calyx (kay- liks) NOUN calyces a ring of leaves (sepals) forming the outer case of a bud

camcorder NOUN camcorders a combined video camera and sound recorder

camel NOUN camels a large animal with a long neck and either one or two humps on its back, used in desert countries for riding and for carrying goods

cameo (kam- ee- oh) NOUN cameos 1 a small hard piece of stone carved with a raised design in its upper layer 2 a short part in a play or film, usually one played by a well-known actor

camera NOUN cameras a device for taking photographs, films, or television pictures
▷ **cameraman** NOUN
in camera in a judge's private room; in private

camouflage (kam- off- lahzh) NOUN a way of hiding things by making them look like part of their surroundings

camouflage VERB camouflages, camouflaging, camouflaged hide by camouflage

camp NOUN camps a place where people live in tents or huts, etc.

camp VERB camps, camping, camped have a holiday in a tent
▷ **camper** NOUN

campaign NOUN campaigns 1 a series of battles in one area or with one purpose 2 a planned series of actions, usually to arouse interest in something • *an advertising campaign*

campaign VERB campaigns, campaigning, campaigned take part in a campaign
▷ **campaigner** NOUN
[via French from Latin *campania* = a piece of open ground (where armies camped and had exercises)]

camphor NOUN a strong-smelling white substance used in medicine, mothballs, and making plastics
▷ **camphorated** ADJECTIVE

campsite NOUN campsites a place where people can have a camping holiday

campus NOUN campuses the grounds of a university or college

can[1] NOUN cans 1 a sealed tin in which food or drink is preserved 2 a metal or plastic container for liquids

can VERB cans, canning, canned preserve in a sealed can
▷ **canner** NOUN

can[2] AUXILIARY VERB *past tense* could 1 be able to
• *He can play the violin.* 2 have permission to
• *You can go.*
USAGE Some people object to can being used with the meaning "have permission to" and insist that you should only use *may* for this meaning. *Can* is widely used in this meaning, however, and in most situations there is little reason to prefer *may*. *May* is appropriate, though, in formal or official writing.

canal NOUN canals 1 an artificial river cut through land so that boats can sail along it or so that it can drain or irrigate an area 2 a tube through which something passes in the body • *the alimentary canal*

canary NOUN canaries a small yellow bird that sings

cancel VERB cancels, canceling, canceled 1 say that something planned will not be done or will not take place 2 stop an order or instruction for something 3 mark a stamp or ticket etc. so that it cannot be used again
▷ **cancellation** NOUN

Thesaurus

calm NOUN 1 *the calm of a summer afternoon*
► tranquillity, calmness, quietness, stillness, peace, quiet, quietude AN OPPOSITE IS storm 2 *I had to admire her calm.* ► composure, calmness, self-possession, equanimity

calm VERB *He was so upset it was impossible to calm him.* ► soothe, placate, quieten, mollify, pacify, settle down, sober down, tranquilize, appease, compose, control, cool down, lull OPPOSITES ARE agitate, upset

camouflage NOUN 1 *The foliage made good camouflage.* ► disguise, concealment, cover, screen, veil, blind, cloak, front, guise, mask 2 *an animal's camouflage* ► protective coloring

3 *Their friendly manner was only camouflage.*
► facade, front, disguise, mask, pretence

camp NOUN *an army camp* ► encampment, camping ground, campsite, base

campaign NOUN 1 *a military campaign*
► operation, offensive, action, engagement, advance, battle, drive 2 *a campaign to save the environment* ► crusade, movement, drive, effort, struggle, fight, push

can NOUN *a can of orange juice* ► tin, canister, jar

cancel VERB 1 *The family had to cancel their vacation.* ► call off, abandon, drop, end, (*more informal*) axe 2 *They agreed to cancel the debt.*
► revoke, annul, nullify, rescind, erase, expunge, set aside, withdraw

A
B
C
D
E
F
G
H
I
J
K
L
M
N
O
P
Q
R
S
T
U
V
W
X
Y
Z

cancel out stop each other's effect • *The good and harm cancel each other out.*

cancer NOUN **cancers 1** a disease in which malignant growths form in the body **2** a tumor, especially a harmful one
▷ **cancerous** ADJECTIVE

candid ADJECTIVE frank and honest
▷ **candidly** ADVERB **candour** NOUN

candidate NOUN **candidates 1** a person who wants to be elected or chosen for a particular job or position, etc. **2** a person taking an examination
▷ **candidacy** NOUN **candidature** NOUN

candle NOUN **candles** a stick of wax with a wick through it, giving light when burning
▷ **candlelight** NOUN

candyfloss NOUN **candyflosses** a fluffy mass of very thin strands of spun sugar

cane NOUN **canes 1** the stem of a reed or tall grass etc. **2** a thin stick

cane VERB **canes, caning, caned** beat someone with a cane

canine (kayn- I'n) ADJECTIVE to do with dogs
canine tooth a pointed tooth at the front of the mouth

canine NOUN **canines 1** a dog **2** a canine tooth

canker NOUN a disease that rots the wood of trees and plants or causes ulcers and sores on animals

cannabis NOUN hemp, especially when smoked as a drug

cannibal NOUN **cannibals 1** a person who eats human flesh **2** an animal that eats animals of its own kind
▷ **cannibalism** NOUN

cannon NOUN **1** cannon a large heavy gun **2** cannons the hitting of two balls in billiards by the third ball

cannon VERB **cannons, cannoning, cannoned** bump into something heavily
USAGE Do not confuse with **canon.**

cannon ball NOUN **cannon balls** a large solid ball fired from a cannon

cannot can not

canoe NOUN **canoes** a narrow lightweight boat, moved forwards with paddles

canoe VERB **canoes, canoeing, canoed** travel in a canoe
▷ **canoeist** NOUN

canon NOUN **canons 1** a general principle or rule **2** a clergyman of a cathedral
USAGE Do not confuse with **cannon.**

canopy NOUN **canopies 1** a hanging cover forming a shelter above a throne, bed, or person, etc. **2** the part of a parachute that spreads in the air

cant NOUN **1** insincere talk **2** jargon

can't (*mainly spoken*) cannot

cantankerous ADJECTIVE bad-tempered

canteen NOUN **canteens 1** a restaurant for workers in a factory, office, etc. **2** a case or box containing a set of cutlery **3** a soldier's or camper's water flask

canter NOUN a gentle gallop

canter VERB **canters, cantering, cantered** go or ride at a canter

cantilever NOUN **cantilevers** a beam or girder fixed at one end only and used to support a bridge, etc.

canvas NOUN **canvases 1** a kind of strong coarse cloth **2** a piece of canvas for painting on; a painting

canvass VERB **canvasses, canvassing, canvassed** visit people to ask them for their support, especially in an election
▷ **canvasser** NOUN

canyon NOUN **canyons** a deep valley, usually with a river running through it

cap NOUN **caps 1** a soft hat without a brim but often with a peak **2** a special headdress, e.g., that worn by a nurse **3** a cap showing membership of a sports team **4** a caplike cover or top **5** something that makes a bang when fired in a toy pistol

Thesaurus

cancel out *One small mistake could cancel out all our hard work.* ► counterbalance, neutralize, wipe out, offset, outweigh, make up for, compensate for

candid ADJECTIVE *a candid reply* ► frank, honest, open, sincere, straightforward, blunt, truthful, outspoken, forthright, unequivocal OPPOSITES ARE insincere, guarded, devious

canny ADJECTIVE *a canny businessman* ► shrewd, astute, sharp, acute, perceptive, clever, prudent USAGE *Canny* is a generally favorable word. Other words that are less favorable, because they imply a kind of dishonesty, are *cunning*, *crafty*, and *wily*.

cantankerous ADJECTIVE *The heat had made him especially cantankerous.* ► bad-tempered, irritable, irascible, grumpy, testy, grouchy, touchy, crotchety, peevish, fractious, cross OPPOSITES ARE good-tempered, good-humored, affable

canteen NOUN *Let's have a quick lunch in the canteen.* ► snack bar, cafeteria, cafe, coffee bar, coffee shop, tea shop, buffet, bistro

canyon NOUN *The army moved through a deep canyon.* ► gorge, ravine, defile

cap VERB *The mountains were capped with snow.* ► cover, top, crown, blanket

cap VERB caps, capping, capped **1** put a cap or cover on something; cover **2** award a sports cap to someone chosen to be on a team **3** do better than something ● *Can you cap that joke?*

capable ADJECTIVE able to do something
▷ **capably** ADVERB **capability** NOUN

capacious (ka- pay- shus) ADJECTIVE roomy; able to hold a large amount

capacity NOUN capacities **1** the amount that something can hold **2** ability; capability **3** the position that someone occupies ● *In my capacity as your guardian I am responsible for you.*

cape[1] NOUN capes a cloak

cape[2] NOUN capes a large piece of high land that sticks out into the sea

caper VERB capers, capering, capered jump or run about playfully

caper NOUN capers **1** jumping about playfully **2** (*slang*) an activity or adventure

capillary (ka- pil- er- ee) NOUN capillaries any of the very fine blood vessels that connect veins and arteries

capital ADJECTIVE **1** important **2** (*informal*) excellent

capital NOUN capitals **1** a capital city **2** a capital letter **3** the top part of a pillar **4** money or property that can be used to produce more wealth

capital city NOUN capital cities the most important city in a country

capitalism (kap- it- al- izm) NOUN an economic system in which trade and industry are controlled by private owners for profit, and not by the state COMPARE communism

capitalist (kap- it- al- ist) NOUN capitalists **1** a person who has a lot of wealth invested; a rich person **2** a person who is in favor of capitalism

capitalize (kap- it- al- I'z) VERB capitalizes, capitalizing, capitalized **1** write or print as a capital letter **2** change something into capital; provide something with capital (= money)
▷ **capitalization** NOUN
capitalize on profit by something; use it to your own advantage ● *You could capitalize on your skill at drawing.*

capital letter NOUN capital letters a large letter of the kind used at the start of a name or sentence

capital punishment NOUN punishing criminals by putting them to death

capitulate VERB capitulates, capitulating, capitulated admit that you are defeated and surrender
▷ **capitulation** NOUN

capricious (ka- prish- us) ADJECTIVE deciding or changing your mind in an impulsive way
▷ **capriciously** ADVERB **capriciousness** NOUN

capsize VERB capsizes, capsizing, capsized overturn ● *The boat capsized.*

capsule NOUN capsules **1** a hollow pill containing medicine **2** a plant's seed case that splits open when ripe **3** a compartment of a spacecraft that can be separated from the main part

---

Thesaurus

---

capable ADJECTIVE *a capable young woman*
► competent, able, accomplished, proficient, efficient, talented, gifted, clever, skilled, intelligent, effective AN OPPOSITE IS incompetent
be capable of *He's capable of doing any of these tasks.* ► have the ability (to do), be competent (to do), be adept (at doing), be equal (to doing) AN OPPOSITE IS be incapable of

capacity NOUN **1** *The tank's capacity is 30 gallons.* ► size, volume, magnitude, extent, space **2** *You need the capacity to motivate yourself.* ► ability, power, potential, capability, competence, aptitude, faculty, skill, talent **3** *He acted in his capacity as commander-in-chief of the army.* ► position, function, role, office

cape NOUN **1** *She was wearing a waterproof cape.* ► cloak, mantle, shawl, wrap, stole **2** *The ship rounded the cape at dawn.* ► headland, promontory, head, point, foreland

caper VERB *The children capered about the room.* ► skip, bound, dance, leap, cavort, jump, spring, bounce, gambol, bob, frisk

capital ADJECTIVE **1** *a capital city* ► chief, principal, leading, main, first, foremost **2** *in capital letters* ► upper-case, large, big, block

capital NOUN **1** *Rome is the capital of Italy.* ► chief city, first city, seat of government, center of government **2** *In three years he had enough capital to start his own business.* ► funds, finance, money, cash, assets, savings, means, wherewithal

capitalize VERB **capitalize on** *The opposition capitalized on the government's mistakes.* ► exploit, take advantage of, profit from, make capital out of

capitulate VERB *The enemy capitulated after a siege of ten months.* ► surrender, give in, submit, succumb, admit defeat, yield, (*more informal*) throw in the towel OPPOSITES ARE resist, hold out

capsize VERB *Some of the boats capsized.* ► overturn, tip over, turn over, turn upside down, flip over, keel over, (*more informal*) turn turtle

a
b
c
d
e
f
g
h
i
j
k
l
m
n
o
p
q
r
s
t
u
v
w
x
y
z

A
B
C
D
E
F
G
H
I
J
K
L
M
N
O
P
Q
R
S
T
U
V
W
X
Y
Z

captain NOUN captains **1** a person in command of a ship or aircraft **2** the leader in a sports team **3** an army officer ranking next below a major; a naval officer ranking next below a commodore
▷ **captaincy** NOUN

caption NOUN captions **1** the words printed with a picture to describe it **2** a short title or heading in a newspaper or magazine

captious (kap- shus) ADJECTIVE pointing out small mistakes or faults

captivate VERB captivates, captivating, captivated charm or delight someone
▷ **captivation** NOUN

captive NOUN captives someone taken prisoner

captive ADJECTIVE taken prisoner; unable to escape
▷ **captivity** NOUN

capture VERB captures, capturing, captured **1** take someone prisoner **2** take or obtain by force, trickery, skill, or attraction • *He captured her heart.* **3** (in computing) put data in a form that can be stored in a computer

capture NOUN taking or obtaining by force; capturing

car NOUN cars **1** a motor car **2** a carriage of a train • *the dining car*

caramel NOUN caramels **1** a kind of toffee tasting like burned sugar **2** burned sugar used for coloring and flavoring food

carat NOUN carats **1** a measure of weight for precious stones **2** a measure of the purity of gold • *Pure gold is 24 carats.*

caravan NOUN caravans **1** a vehicle towed by a car and used for living in **2** a group of people travelling together across desert country
▷ **caravanning** NOUN

carbohydrate NOUN carbohydrates a compound of carbon, oxygen, and hydrogen (e.g., sugar or starch)

carbolic NOUN a kind of disinfectant

carbon NOUN carbons **1** a substance that is present in all living things and that occurs in its pure form as diamond and graphite **2** carbon paper **3** a carbon copy

carbonate NOUN carbonates a compound that gives off carbon dioxide when mixed with acid

carbon dioxide NOUN a gas formed when things burn, or breathed out by humans and animals

carburetor NOUN carburetors a device for mixing fuel and air in an engine

carcass NOUN carcasses **1** the dead body of an animal **2** the bony part of a bird's body after the meat has been eaten

carcinogen NOUN carcinogens any substance that produces cancer

card NOUN cards **1** thick stiff paper or thin cardboard **2** a small piece of stiff paper for writing or printing on, especially to send messages or greetings or to record information **3** a small, oblong piece of plastic issued to a customer by a bank or credit union, giving details of their account and allowing them to use cash machines, etc. **4** a playing card
cards PLURAL NOUN a game using playing cards
in the cards likely; possible

Thesaurus

captain NOUN **1** *the captain of the winning team* ► leader, chief player, head, boss **2** *the ship's captain* ► commander, master, officer in charge, skipper **3** *a captain of industry* ► magnate, mogul, tycoon, mandarin, baron

captivate VERB *The beauty of the scene captivates all visitors.* ► charm, enchant, delight, entrance, enthrall, fascinate, bewitch, beguile, engross, excite, mesmerize OPPOSITES ARE repel, disgust

captive ADJECTIVE **1** *captive animals* ► confined, caged, captured, incarcerated, chained, detained, enslaved, ensnared, fettered, gaoled, imprisoned, jailed, restricted, secure, taken prisoner **2** *The men had been held captive for several weeks.* ► locked up, imprisoned, jailed, detained, under lock and key AN OPPOSITE IS free

captive NOUN *The captives all wore handcuffs.* ► prisoner, convict, detainee, inmate, internee, hostage

captivity NOUN *Years of captivity had ruined his health.* ► imprisonment, confinement, internment, incarceration, detention, custody AN OPPOSITE IS freedom

capture VERB **1** *He was captured boarding a ship for France.* ► catch, arrest, apprehend, seize, take prisoner, take into custody, (*more informal*) nab, (*more informal*) pull in, (*much more informal*) nick **2** *The building was captured by stormtroopers.* ► occupy, take, seize, secure

car NOUN *A lot of the students arrived in cars.* ► motor car, automobile, motor, vehicle

card NOUN **1** *a piece of stiff card* ► cardboard, pasteboard, board **2** *Let's play cards.* ► card game, game of cards
USAGE *Card* is often short for *playing card*, *greeting* (or *birthday* or *Christmas*) *card*, and *credit card*
in the cards (*informal*) *A marriage was always in the cards.* ► possible, a possibility, likely, a likelihood, probable, a probability, in the offing AN OPPOSITE IS out of the question

cardboard NOUN a kind of thin board made of layers of paper or wood fiber

cardiac (**kard**- ee- ak) ADJECTIVE to do with the heart

cardigan NOUN cardigans a knitted sweater fastened with buttons down the front [named after the Earl of Cardigan, a commander in the Crimean War in the 19th century, whose troops wore this kind of sweater]

cardinal NOUN cardinals a senior priest in the Roman Catholic Church

cardinal ADJECTIVE 1 chief; most important ● *the cardinal features of our plan* 2 deep scarlet (like a cardinal's cassock)

cardinal number NOUN cardinal numbers a number for counting things, e.g., one, two, three, etc. COMPARE ordinal number

cardinal points PLURAL NOUN the four main points of the compass (North, South, East, and West)

care NOUN cares 1 serious attention and thought ● *Plan your holiday with care.* 2 caution to avoid damage or loss ● *Glass -*

handle with care. 3 protection or supervision ● *Leave the child in my care.* 4 worry or anxiety ● *freedom from care*
take care be especially careful
take care of look after

care VERB cares, caring, cared 1 feel interested or concerned 2 feel affection
care for 1 have in your care 2 be fond of

career NOUN careers a series of jobs that mark a person's progress in the profession or work they choose to do ● *a career in journalism*

career VERB careers, careering, careered rush along wildly

carefree ADJECTIVE without worries or responsibilities

careful ADJECTIVE 1 giving serious thought and attention to something 2 avoiding damage or danger, etc.; cautious
▷ **carefully** ADVERB **carefulness** NOUN

careless ADJECTIVE not careful
▷ **carelessly** ADVERB **carelessness** NOUN

caress NOUN caresses a gentle loving touch

Thesaurus

cardboard NOUN *a cardboard cutout* ► card, pasteboard

care NOUN 1 *We need to proceed with care.* ► caution, carefulness, vigilance, watchfulness, awareness, prudence, circumspection, concentration, attention, concern, diligence, heed AN OPPOSITE IS carelessness 2 *The job needs to be done with great care.* ► discretion, thought, attention, thoroughness, meticulousness, concentration 3 *You need to escape from all your cares.* ► worry, anxiety, trouble, concern, burden, problem, difficulty, hardship, responsibility, sorrow, stress, tribulation, vexation, woe AN OPPOSITE IS joy 4 *She left the baby in the care of a sitter.* ► charge, safekeeping, keeping, custody, control, supervision, protection

care VERB care about *She obviously cares about her staff.* ► interest yourself in, concern yourself about, mind about , bother about, worry about, be troubled by
care for 1 *The hospice cares for sick children.* ► look after, take care of, tend, attend to, provide for, nurse, supervise, watch over, (*more informal*) keep an eye on 2 *He cares for his grandchildren.* ► love, be fond of, adore, cherish, hold dear, dote on, think the world of 3 *I don't really care for those biscuits.* ► like, fancy, feel like, enjoy, want

career NOUN *a career in teaching* ► profession, occupation, job, calling, position

carefree ADJECTIVE 1 *a carefree young girl* ► unworried, untroubled, cheerful, cheery, lighthearted, easygoing, casual, relaxed, (*more informal*) laid-back OPPOSITES ARE anxious,

tense 2 *a carefree time* ► relaxing, restful, trouble-free, untroubled, peaceful, quiet OPPOSITES ARE hectic, nerve-racking

careful ADJECTIVE 1 *Be careful walking through the park at night.* ► alert, vigilant, heedful, attentive, watchful AN OPPOSITE IS careless 2 *You must be careful with your spending.* ► prudent, cautious, circumspect, economical, thrifty, canny OPPOSITES ARE careless, extravagant, reckless 3 *Such a long journey needs careful planning.* ► detailed, thorough, meticulous, conscientious, scrupulous 4 *She's a very careful driver.* ► attentive, diligent, conscientious OPPOSITES ARE careless, inattentive

careless ADJECTIVE 1 *a careless driver; careless remarks* ► inattentive, thoughtless, inconsiderate, negligent, absentminded, heedless, irresponsible, reckless OPPOSITES ARE careful, attentive 2 *There is no excuse for careless work.* ► slipshod, shoddy, slapdash, slovenly, inaccurate, scrappy, incorrect OPPOSITES ARE careful, accurate 3 *She has always been rather careless about money.* ► extravagant, reckless OPPOSITES ARE careful, prudent

carelessness NOUN *The accident was caused by carelessness.* ► inattention, inattentiveness, absentmindedness, negligence, recklessness, irresponsibility, slovenliness, thoughtlessness, untidiness, haste, (*more informal*) sloppiness OPPOSITES ARE care, carefulness

A
B
C
D
E
F
G
H
I
J
K
L
M
N
O
P
Q
R
S
T
U
V
W
X
Y
Z

caress VERB caresses, caressing, caressed touch lovingly

caretaker NOUN caretakers a person employed to look after a school, apartment building, etc.

cargo NOUN cargoes goods carried in a ship or aircraft

Caribbean ADJECTIVE to do with or from the Caribbean Sea, a part of the Atlantic Ocean east of Central America

caricature NOUN caricatures an amusing or exaggerated picture of someone

carnage NOUN the killing of many people

carnival NOUN carnivals a festival, often with a procession in fancy dress [from Latin *carnis* = of flesh: originally this meant the festivities before Lent, when meat was given up until Easter]

carnivorous (kar- niv- er- us) ADJECTIVE meat-eating COMPARE **herbivorous**
▷ **carnivore** NOUN

carol NOUN carols a Christmas hymn
▷ **caroler** NOUN **caroling** NOUN

carp[1] NOUN carp an edible freshwater fish

carp VERB carps, carping, carped keep finding fault

car park NOUN car parks an area where cars may be parked

carpenter NOUN carpenters a person who makes things out of wood
▷ **carpentry** NOUN

carpet NOUN carpets a thick soft covering for a floor
▷ **carpeted** ADJECTIVE **carpeting** NOUN
[from early Italian *carpita*, from Latin *carpere* = to pluck]

carriage NOUN carriages **1** one of the separate parts of a train, where passengers sit **2** a passenger vehicle pulled by horses **3** carrying goods from one place to another; the cost of carrying goods • *Carriage is extra.* **4** a moving part carrying or holding something in a machine

carrier NOUN carriers a person or thing that carries something

carrot NOUN carrots a plant with a thick orange-colored root used as a vegetable

carry VERB carries, carrying, carried **1** take something from one place to another **2** support the weight of something **3** take an amount into the next column when adding figures **4** be heard a long way away • *Sound carries in the mountains.* **5** if a proposal at a meeting is carried, it is approved by most people at the meeting • *The motion was carried by ten votes to six.*
be carried away be very excited
carry on 1 continue **2** (*informal*) behave excitedly **3** (*informal*) complain
carry out put into practice

cart NOUN carts an open vehicle for carrying loads

cart VERB carts, carting, carted **1** carry in a cart **2** (*informal*) carry something heavy or tiring • *I've carted these books all around the school.*

carthorse NOUN carthorses a large strong horse used for pulling heavy loads

cartilage NOUN tough white flexible tissue attached to a bone

carton NOUN cartons a cardboard or plastic container

Thesaurus

---

caretaker NOUN *the caretaker at the village hall* ► janitor, warden, custodian, attendant, keeper, porter, superintendent, watchman

cargo NOUN *a ship's cargo* ► freight, load, haul, payload, consignment, merchandise, shipment, goods

caricature VERB *She caricatured the movements of a ballerina.* ► parody, mimic, imitate, lampoon, mock, ridicule, satirize, burlesque, make fun of, exaggerate, (*more informal*) send up, (*more informal*) take off

carnival NOUN *the town's annual carnival* ► festival, gala, jamboree, fiesta, fete, fair, celebration, revelry

carriage NOUN *a railway carriage* ► coach, wagon

carry VERB **1** *We will have to carry our own luggage.* ► convey, take, transfer, bring, fetch, haul, lift, handle, move, remove, shoulder, (*more informal*) lug **2** *The channel ships carry passengers and freight.* ► transport, convey, handle, ferry, ship **3** *Telegraph wires carry signals.* ► communicate, relay, transmit **4** *The*

bridge would not carry the weight of a large vehicle. ► support, bear, hold up **5** *The job carries many responsibilities.* ► demand, entail, involve, require, lead to, result in
carry on 1 *We carried on for as long as we could.* ► persevere, persist, continue, go on, keep on, last, remain, stay, (*informal*) stick it out **2** *She has been carrying on her own business for several years.* ► run, engage in, maintain, manage, operate, administer **3** (*informal*) *Tell them to stop carrying on like that!* ► misbehave, behave badly, cause trouble
carry out *They were just carrying out orders.* ► obey, follow, discharge, implement, execute, finish, perform, complete

cart NOUN *The fruit was taken to the barns in carts.* ► barrow, wheelbarrow, handcart, trolley, truck

cart VERB (*informal*) *The books were too bulky to cart around.* ► carry, move, take, haul, (*informal*) lug

cartoon NOUN cartoons **1** an amusing drawing **2** a series of drawings that tell a story; a comic strip **3** an animated film
▷ **cartoonist** NOUN

cartridge NOUN cartridges **1** a case containing the explosive for a bullet or shell **2** a container holding film for a camera, ink for a pen, etc. **3** the device that holds the stylus of a record player

cartwheel NOUN cartwheels **1** the wheel of a cart **2** a handstand balancing on each hand in turn with arms and legs spread like spokes of a wheel

carve VERB carves, carving, carved **1** make something by cutting wood or stone, etc. **2** cut cooked meat into slices
▷ **carver** NOUN

case[1] NOUN cases **1** a container **2** a suitcase

case[2] NOUN cases **1** an example of something existing or occurring; a situation • *In every case we found that someone had cheated.* **2** something investigated by police, etc., or by a court • *a murder case* **3** a set of facts or arguments to support something • *She put forward a good case for equality.* **4** the form of a word that shows how it is related to another word. *Fred's* is the possessive case of *Fred; him* is the objective case of *he.*
in any case anyway
in case because something may happen

cash NOUN **1** money **2** immediate payment for goods, etc.

cash VERB cashes, cashing, cashed change a check, etc. for cash

cashew NOUN cashews a small kidney-shaped nut [via Portuguese from Tupi (a South American language)]

cashier NOUN cashiers a person who takes in and pays out money in a bank or takes payments in a shop

cash machine or **cash dispenser** NOUN cash machines or cash dispensers a machine, usually outside a bank or building society, from which people can draw out cash by using a bank card

cash register NOUN cash registers a machine that records and stores the money received in a shop

casing NOUN casings a protective covering

casino NOUN casinos a public building or room for gambling

cask NOUN casks a barrel

casket NOUN caskets a small box for jewelry, etc.

casserole NOUN casseroles **1** a covered dish in which food is cooked and served **2** food cooked in a casserole

cassette NOUN cassettes a small sealed case containing recording tape, film, etc.

cast VERB casts, casting, cast **1** throw **2** shed or throw off **3** make a vote **4** make something of metal or plaster in a mold **5** choose performers for a play or film, etc.

cast NOUN casts **1** a shape made by pouring liquid metal or plaster into a mold **2** all the performers in a play or film

castaway NOUN castaways a shipwrecked person

caste NOUN castes (in India) one of the social classes into which Hindus are born

Thesaurus

cartoon NOUN **1** *The story is in the form of a cartoon.* ► comic strip, drawing, caricature, sketch **2** *a film cartoon* ► animation **3** *a political cartoon* ► caricature, parody, lampoon

carve VERB **1** *It was time to carve the meat.* ► cut, slice, chop **2** *a tool for carving wood* ► chisel, hew, sculpt, fashion, form, shape

case NOUN **1** *She hurriedly threw a few clothes into a case.* ► suitcase, bag, travel bag, trunk **2** *The books were still in their packing cases.* ► box, chest, canister, carton, crate, container **3** *The videotape was spilling out of its case.* ► shell, cartridge, cassette, container, capsule, cover **4** *The china was kept in a handsome display case.* ► cabinet, cupboard, showcase, sideboard **5** *a classic case of misunderstanding* ► instance, example, occurrence, occasion, manifestation, illustration **6** *If that's the case we'll have to think of an another way.* ► situation, position, state of affairs, event, circumstances **7** *Police from several forces are involved in the case.*
► investigation, inquiry **8** *The lawyers agreed it was a difficult case.* ► lawsuit, action, legal action, suit, trial

cash NOUN *a purse full of cash* ► money, notes, banknotes, coins, change, ready money

cash VERB *I need to cash a check.* ► exchange, change, get money for, get cash for
cash in on *I don't like to cash in on your bad luck.* ► take advantage of, profit by, exploit

casing NOUN *The hard disk has its own protective casing.* ► case, shell, cover, sheath, housing, sleeve

cask NOUN *a cask of wine* ► barrel, keg, butt, vat, tun, hogshead, firkin

cast VERB **1** *He cast a coin into the fountain.* ► throw, toss, fling, flip, sling, (*more informal*) chuck, hurl **2** *The statue is cast entirely in bronze.* ► mold, form, shape, model, sculpture
cast down *They all felt cast down at the news.* ► downcast, dejected, depressed, saddened, upset, disheartened

a
b
c
d
e
f
g
h
i
j
k
l
m
n
o
p
q
r
s
t
u
v
w
x
y
z

casting vote NOUN casting votes the vote that decides which group wins when the votes on each side are equal

castle NOUN castles **1** a large old fortified building **2** a piece in chess, also called a rook
castles in the air daydreams

castor NOUN castors a small wheel on the leg of a table, chair, etc.

castor sugar NOUN finely ground white sugar

castrate VERB castrates, castrating, castrated remove the testicles of a male animal
COMPARE spay
▷ **castration** NOUN

casual ADJECTIVE **1** happening by chance; not planned **2** not careful; not methodical **3** informal; suitable for informal occasions
• *a casual clothes* **4** not permanent • *casual work*
▷ **casually** ADVERB **casualness** NOUN

casualty NOUN casualties **1** a person who is killed or injured in war or in an accident **2** a department of a hospital that deals with emergency patients

cat NOUN cats **1** a small furry domestic animal **2** a wild animal of the same family as a domestic cat, e.g., a lion, tiger, or leopard **3** (*informal*) a spiteful girl or woman
let the cat out of the bag reveal a secret

cataclysm (kat- a- klizm) NOUN cataclysms a violent upheaval or disaster

catalog or **catalogue** NOUN catalogs, catalogues **1** a list of things (e.g., of books in a library), usually arranged in order **2** a book containing a list of things that can be bought
• *a Christmas catalog*

catalogue VERB catalogs, cataloging, cataloged; catalogues, cataloguing, catalogued enter something in a catalog

catalyst (kat- a- list) NOUN catalysts **1** (in science) something that starts or speeds up a chemical reaction **2** something that causes a change

catalytic converter NOUN catalytic converters a device fitted to a car's exhaust system, with a catalyst for converting pollutant gases into less harmful ones

catapult NOUN catapults **1** a device with elastic for shooting small stones **2** an ancient military weapon for hurling stones etc.

catapult VERB catapults, catapulting, catapulted hurl or rush violently

cataract NOUN cataracts **1** a large waterfall or rush of water **2** a cloudy area that forms in the eye and prevents a person from seeing clearly

catastrophe (ka- tass- trof- ee) NOUN catastrophes a sudden great disaster
▷ **catastrophic** (kat- a- strof- ik) ADJECTIVE catastrophically ADVERB

catch VERB catches, catching, caught **1** take and hold something **2** arrest or capture **3** overtake **4** be in time to get on a bus or train etc. **5** be infected with an illness **6** hear

Thesaurus

casual ADJECTIVE **1** *a casual encounter with an old friend* ► chance, unexpected, unforeseen, unintentional, unplanned, fortuitous, accidental, random OPPOSITES ARE deliberate, intentional **2** *a casual remark* ► offhand, spontaneous, impromptu, unconsidered, random OPPOSITES ARE committed, enthusiastic **3** *a casual acquaintance* ► slight, vague OPPOSITES ARE close, intimate **4** *a casual approach to life* ► relaxed, nonchalant, lackadaisical, indifferent, carefree, easygoing, offhand, apathetic, flippant, (*more informal*) laid-back OPPOSITES ARE concerned, serious **5** *He gave her a casual glance.* ► cursory, fleeting, passing, hasty, quick, perfunctory OPPOSITES ARE thorough, careful **6** *casual clothes* ► informal AN OPPOSITE IS formal

casualty NOUN *The bombing led to many casualties.* ► death, fatality, injury, loss, victim, (*in plural*) dead and wounded

cat NOUN *People thought he was odd for talking to his cat.* ► tom, tomcat, tabby, kitten, (*more informal*) pussy RELATED ADJECTIVE ► feline

catalog, catalogue NOUN **1** *a library catalog* ► inventory, list, record, register, directory, index, roll, schedule, table **2** *a catalog of mistakes* ► series, sequence, string, long list

catastrophe NOUN *The floods were a catastrophe for the area.* ► calamity, tragedy, misfortune, mishap, tragedy, affliction, cataclysm, blow

catch VERB **1** *Josh caught the ball.* ► seize, grab, take hold of, grip, clutch, intercept **2** *They hadn't managed to catch any fish.* ► hook, net, land, trap **3** *Do you think they will catch the thief?* ► capture, arrest, apprehend **4** *We have a train to catch.* ► board, be in time for, get to, reach **5** *He caught a rare virus on a business trip.* ► contract, be infected with, develop, get, go down with, become sick with, become ill with **6** *She caught them in the act.* ► discover, detect, find, find out, surprise, expose **7** *A trip to Paris caught their fancy.* ► capture, attract, appeal to, seize, win, absorb, engross **8** *I didn't catch what you said.* ► hear, perceive, discern, make out, recognize
catch up *If we hurry we can catch up.* ► reach, overtake, draw level with

catch NOUN **1** *The fishermen returned with their catch over their shoulders.* ► haul, net, bag, booty, prize **2** *The price is so good there must be a catch.* ► snag, disadvantage, difficulty,

• *I didn't catch what he said.* **7** discover someone doing something wrong • *They were caught smoking in the playground.* **8** make or become fixed or unable to move; entangle • *I caught my dress on a nail.* **9** hit; strike • *The blow caught him on the nose.*

catch fire start burning

catch it (*informal*) be scolded or punished

catch on (*informal*) **1** become popular **2** understand

catch out discover someone in a mistake

catch NOUN catches **1** catching something **2** something caught or worth catching **3** a hidden difficulty **4** a device for fastening something

catching ADJECTIVE infectious

catchment area NOUN catchment areas **1** the area from which a school takes pupils or a hospital takes patients **2** the whole area from which water drains into a river or reservoir

catchphrase NOUN catchphrases a popular phrase

catchy ADJECTIVE easy to remember; soon becoming popular • *a catchy tune*

category NOUN categories a set of people or things classified as being similar to each other

cater VERB caters, catering, catered **1** provide food, especially for a lot of people **2** provide what is needed
▷ **caterer** NOUN

caterpillar NOUN caterpillars the creeping wormlike creature that will turn into a butterfly or moth

cathedral NOUN cathedrals the most important church of a district, usually containing the bishop's throne

Catherine wheel NOUN Catherine wheels a firework that spins round

cathode NOUN cathodes the electrode by which electric current leaves a device COMPARE anode

Catholic ADJECTIVE **1** belonging to the Roman Catholic Church **2** of all Christians • *the Holy Catholic Church*
▷ **Catholicism** NOUN

Catholic NOUN Catholics a Roman Catholic

catholic ADJECTIVE including most things • *Her taste in literature is catholic.*

cattle PLURAL NOUN animals with horns and hoofs, kept by farmers for their milk and beef

catty ADJECTIVE cattier, cattiest speaking or spoken spitefully

catwalk NOUN catwalks a long platform that models walk along at a fashion show

cauldron NOUN cauldrons a large deep pot for boiling things

cauliflower NOUN cauliflowers a cabbage with a large head of white flowers

cause NOUN causes **1** a person or thing that makes something happen or produces an effect **2** a reason • *There is no cause for worry.* **3** a purpose for which people work; an organization or charity

cause VERB causes, causing, caused be the cause of; make something happen

causeway NOUN causeways a raised road across low or marshy ground

Thesaurus

drawback, obstacle, problem, trap, trick **3** *He tried to slip the catch on the window.* ► latch, lock, fastener, fastening, bolt, clasp

catching ADJECTIVE *Fortunately the disease is not catching.* ► infectious, contagious, communicable, transmittable, spreading

catchy ADJECTIVE *a catchy tune* ► memorable, tuneful, haunting, attractive, popular, singable

categorical ADJECTIVE *a categorical assurance* ► absolute, unqualified, unconditional, unequivocal, unreserved, outright, complete, definite, express

category NOUN *There is a maximum penalty for each category of offense. Nonfiction books fall into several categories.* ► class, type, classification, kind, sort, division, group, grade, heading

cater VERB **1** cater for *The hotel will cater for vegetarians.* ► provide for, make arrangements for, supply, feed, cook for **2** cater to *A simple*

barrow will cater to most of your gardening needs. ► serve, satisfy, answer, provide for, cope with, take care of

cause NOUN **1** *Police are still trying to find the cause of the explosion.* ► source, origin, root, basis, reason (for), beginning, genesis, grounds, motivation, motive, occasion, spring, stimulus **2** *The older boys were the cause of much of the trouble.* ► initiator, instigator, originator, producer, agent **3** *There is no cause for alarm.* ► reason, grounds, justification, call, need, necessity, occasion, excuse, pretext **4** *a worthy cause* ► purpose, object, end, aim, ideal, undertaking, enterprise

cause VERB **1** *The bad weather has caused many delays.* ► bring about, result in, give rise to, lead to, produce, generate, create, precipitate, induce, entail, stimulate **2** *Poor health caused him to give up work.* ► force, compel, lead, encourage, induce, make

A B **C** D E F G H I J K L M N O P Q R S T U V W X Y Z

caustic ADJECTIVE **1** able to burn or wear things away by chemical action **2** sarcastic
▷ **caustically** ADVERB

caution NOUN **1** care taken in order to avoid danger, etc. **2** a warning

caution VERB cautions, cautioning, cautioned warn someone

cautionary ADJECTIVE giving a warning

cautious ADJECTIVE showing caution
▷ **cautiously** ADVERB **cautiousness** NOUN

Cavalier NOUN Cavaliers a supporter of King Charles I in the English Civil War (1642-9)

cavalry NOUN soldiers who fight on horseback or in armored vehicles COMPARE infantry

cave NOUN caves a large hollow place in the side of a hill or cliff, or underground

cave VERB caves, caving, caved
cave in **1** fall inward **2** give way in an argument

cavern NOUN caverns a large cave
▷ **cavernous** ADJECTIVE

cavity NOUN cavities a hollow or hole

cavort (ka- vort) VERB cavorts, cavorting, cavorted jump or run about excitedly

caw NOUN caws the harsh cry of a crow, etc.

cc ABBREVIATION cubic centimeter(s)

CCTV ABBREVIATION closed circuit television, a security device

CD ABBREVIATION compact disc

CD-ROM ABBREVIATION compact disc read-only memory; a compact disc on which large amounts of data can be stored and then displayed on a computer screen

cease VERB ceases, ceasing, ceased stop or end

cease NOUN
without cease not ceasing

ceasefire NOUN ceasefires a signal to stop firing

ceaseless ADJECTIVE not ceasing

cedar NOUN cedars an evergreen tree with hard fragrant wood
▷ **cedarwood** NOUN

cedilla (sid- il- a) NOUN cedillas a mark under c in certain languages to show that it is pronounced as s, e.g. in façade

ceiling NOUN ceilings **1** the flat surface under the top of a room **2** the highest limit that something can reach

celebrate VERB celebrates, celebrating, celebrated **1** do something special or enjoyable to show that a day or event is important **2** perform a religious ceremony
▷ **celebrant** NOUN **celebration** NOUN

celebrated ADJECTIVE famous

celebrity NOUN celebrities **1** a famous person **2** fame; being famous

Thesaurus

caustic ADJECTIVE **1** a caustic substance
► corrosive, acid, astringent, burning **2** caustic remarks ► sharp, sarcastic, scathing, hurtful, acid, acerbic, cutting, bitter, spiteful, vicious, abrasive

caution NOUN **1** Drivers were advised to proceed with extreme caution. ► care, alertness, attentiveness, carefulness, wariness, watchfulness, vigilance, restraint, discretion, circumspection, heed, heedfulness, prudence AN OPPOSITE IS recklessness **2** A first offender is usually let off with a caution. ► reprimand, warning, admonition

cautious ADJECTIVE **1** He was a cautious man and avoided risks. ► careful, attentive, vigilant, circumspect, heedful, alert, prudent, scrupulous, watchful OPPOSITES ARE careless, reckless **2** Their response was cautious.
► guarded, discreet, wary, chary, tactful OPPOSITES ARE forthright, impetuous

cave NOUN There are caves at the foot of the cliffs.
► cavern, grotto, hollow, cavity, underground chamber, den, hole, pothole

cave VERB **1** cave in The roof caved in ► collapse, fall in, give way, disintegrate, crumble **2** cave in The government refused to cave in to the protesters' demands. ► yield, surrender, comply (with)

cavity NOUN a secret cavity in the wall ► space, chamber, hollow, hole, pit, cave, crater, dent

cavort VERB The children cavorted about the room.
► skip, bound, dance, leap, caper, jump, spring, bounce, gambol, bob, frisk

cease VERB Hostilities will cease at midnight. Both armies have ceased military activity. ► end, stop, finish, halt, come OR bring to an end, conclude, terminate AN OPPOSITE IS commence

ceaseless ADJECTIVE ceaseless activity
► continuous, continual, constant, incessant, endless, unceasing, interminable, nonstop OPPOSITES ARE temporary, intermittent

celebrate VERB **1** They celebrated with a bottle of champagne. ► enjoy yourself, have fun, have a good time, make merry **2** The couple celebrate their golden wedding this week.
► commemorate, observe, mark, recognize, honor, remember, keep

celebration NOUN **1** a birthday celebration
► party, function, festivity, (more informal) binge **2** a cause for celebration ► festivities, jollification, merrymaking, enjoying yourself, partying

celebrity NOUN **1** a team made up of celebrities
► star, famous person, public figure, dignitary, idol, personality, luminary **2** The

celery NOUN a vegetable with crisp white or green stems

celestial (sil- est- ee- al) ADJECTIVE **1** to do with the sky **2** to do with heaven; divine celestial bodies PLURAL NOUN stars, etc.

cell NOUN cells **1** a small room where a prisoner is locked up **2** a small room in a monastery **3** a microscopic unit of living matter **4** a compartment of a honeycomb **5** a device for producing electric current chemically **6** a small group or unit in an organization etc.

cellar NOUN cellars an underground room

cello (chel- oh) NOUN cellos a musical instrument like a large violin, placed between the knees of a player
▷ **cellist** NOUN

cellular ADJECTIVE **1** consisting of living cells **2** (said about a mobile telephone system) using a number of short-range radio stations to cover the area it serves

cellulose NOUN **1** tissue that forms the main part of all plants and trees **2** paint made from cellulose

Celsius (sel- see- us) ADJECTIVE measuring temperature on a scale using 100 degrees, where water freezes at 0° and boils at 100° [named after A. Celsius, a Swedish astronomer, who invented it]

Celtic ADJECTIVE to do with the Celts, a group of peoples living in parts of Europe and Asia before Roman times, or to the languages spoken by them, including Irish, Scottish Gaelic, and Welsh

cement NOUN **1** a mixture of lime and clay used in building, to join bricks together, etc. **2** a strong glue

cement VERB cements, cementing, cemented **1** put cement on something **2** join firmly; strengthen

cemetery (sem- et- ree) NOUN cemeteries a place where people are buried

censor NOUN censors a person who examines films, books, letters, etc., and removes or bans

anything that seems harmful
▷ **censor** VERB **censorship** NOUN
USAGE Do not confuse with censure.

censure (sen- sher) NOUN strong criticism or disapproval of something
▷ **censure** VERB
USAGE Do not confuse with censor.

census NOUN censuses an official count or survey of the population of a country or area

cent NOUN cents a coin worth one-hundredth of a dollar

centenary (sen- ten- er- ee) NOUN centenaries a 100th anniversary
▷ **centennial** (sen- ten- ee- al) ADJECTIVE

center NOUN centers **1** the middle point or part **2** an important place ● a center of the film industry **3** a building or place for a special purpose ● a sports center

center VERB centers, centering, centered place something at the center
center on or center around **1** be concentrated in **2** have as its main subject or concern

center of gravity NOUN centers of gravity the point in an object around which its mass is perfectly balanced

centigrade ADJECTIVE measuring temperature on a scale using 100 degrees, where water freezes at 0° and boils at 100° Celsius

centimeter NOUN centimeters one-hundredth of a meter, about four-tenths of an inch

centipede NOUN centipedes a small crawling creature with a long body and many legs

central ADJECTIVE **1** to do with or at the center **2** most important
▷ **centrally** ADVERB

central heating NOUN a system of heating a building from one source by circulating hot water or hot air or steam in pipes or by linked radiators

century NOUN centuries **1** a period of one hundred years

ceramic ADJECTIVE to do with or made of pottery

Thesaurus

group seemed to be enjoying their celebrity.
▶ fame, stardom, prominence, popularity, glory, reputation, renown

cell NOUN **1** a prison cell ▶ room, cubicle, chamber, compartment, enclosure, unit **2** cells of a honeycomb ▶ compartment, cavity, chamber, hollow, section **3** a terrorist cell ▶ unit, group, faction, caucus, section, arm, wing

censure NOUN Her voice had a note of censure.
▶ criticism, disapproval, reproach, rebuke, condemnation, reproof

censure VERB Shareholders censured the bank.
▶ criticize, reprimand, condemn, rebuke, reproach

center NOUN **1** the center of a circle ▶ middle, mid-point, heart, core, eye, bullseye **2** the center of the city ▶ middle, heart, nucleus

central ADJECTIVE **1** the central chamber of the temple ▶ innermost, inner, interior, middle, focal **2** the central issues ▶ chief, key, main, essential, pivotal, primary, principal, vital, fundamental, crucial, major, overriding, important AN OPPOSITE IS peripheral

a
b
c
d
e
f
g
h
i
j
k
l
m
n
o
p
q
r
s
t
u
v
w
x
y
z

A
B
C
D
E
F
G
H
I
J
K
L
M
N
O
P
Q
R
S
T
U
V
W
X
Y
Z

cereal NOUN cereals **1** a grass producing seeds which are used as food, e.g., wheat, barley, or rice **2** a breakfast food made from these seeds
USAGE Do not confuse with serial.

cerebral (se- rib- ral) ADJECTIVE to do with the brain

cerebral palsy NOUN a condition caused by brain damage before birth that makes a person suffer from spasms of the muscles and jerky movements

ceremonial ADJECTIVE to do with or used in a ceremony; formal
▷ **ceremonially** ADVERB

ceremonious ADJECTIVE full of ceremony; elaborately performed

ceremony NOUN ceremonies the formal actions carried out on an important occasion, e.g., at a wedding or a funeral

certain ADJECTIVE sure; without doubt a certain person or thing a person or thing that is known but not named
▷ **certainly** ADVERB

certainty NOUN certainties **1** something that is sure to happen **2** being sure

certificate NOUN certificates an official written or printed statement giving information about a person, etc. • a birth certificate

certitude NOUN a feeling of certainty

cervix NOUN cervices (ser- vis- ees) the entrance to the womb
▷ **cervical** ADJECTIVE

cesspit or **cesspool** NOUN cesspits or cesspools a covered pit where liquid waste or sewage is stored temporarily

CFC ABBREVIATION chlorofluorocarbon; a gas containing chlorine and fluorine that is thought to be harmful to the ozone layer in the Earth's atmosphere

chaff[1] NOUN husks of corn or grain, separated from the seed

chaff VERB tease someone

chain NOUN chains **1** a row of metal rings fastened together **2** a connected series of things • a chain of mountains • a chain of events **3** a number of shops, hotels, or other businesses owned by the same company

chain VERB chains, chaining, chained fasten something with a chain or chains

chain letter NOUN chain letters a letter that you are asked to copy and send to several other people, who are supposed to do the same

chain reaction NOUN chain reactions a series of happenings in which each causes the next

chain store NOUN chain stores one of a number of similar shops owned by the same firm

chair NOUN chairs **1** a movable seat, with a back, for one person **2** the person in charge at a meeting

chair VERB chairs, chairing, chaired be in control of a meeting • Who will chair this meeting?

chairman NOUN chairmen the person who is in control of a meeting
▷ **chairmanship** NOUN

Thesaurus

cereal NOUN farmers who prefer cereal production to livestock ▸ corn, grain

ceremony NOUN **1** a wedding ceremony ▸ rite, ritual, service, observance, celebration **2** a grand occasion with all due ceremony
▸ formality, pomp, protocol, propriety, ritual, solemnity

certain ADJECTIVE **1** I was certain they did it. ▸ sure, confident, positive, convinced, assured, satisfied OPPOSITES ARE uncertain (whether), doubtful (whether) **2** It is certain that there will be reprisals. ▸ definite, undeniable, indubitable, unquestionable, clear, plain, evident, obvious, conclusive OPPOSITES ARE uncertain (whether), doubtful **3** She faced certain failure. ▸ inevitable, assured, inescapable, unavoidable **4** They are certain to win. ▸ sure, bound, assured (of winning) AN OPPOSITE IS unlikely **5** A certain person has been here. ▸ particular, specific, definite, unnamed, individual

certainly ADVERB It was certainly a beautiful building. ▸ undoubtedly, unquestionably, surely, undeniably, definitely, without question, without doubt

certainty NOUN **1** The answers may never be known with certainty. ▸ assurance, assuredness, confidence, conviction, certitude OPPOSITES ARE uncertainty, doubt **2** A high-scoring match seemed a certainty. ▸ inevitability, certain fact, foregone conclusion, matter of course, necessity, (more informal) sure thing AN OPPOSITE IS impossibility

certify VERB You have to sign the form to certify that the information is true. ▸ verify, guarantee, confirm, affirm, testify, warrant, declare, demonstrate

chain NOUN **1** The prisoners were held in chains. ▸ fetters, shackles, bonds, irons, manacles, coupling, handcuffs, links **2** a chain of events ▸ series, sequence, succession, string, course, train, progression **3** a chain of supermarkets ▸ group, firm, series

chain VERB The bicycle was chained to a fence. ▸ tie, fasten, secure, hitch, tether, manacle, fetter

USAGE The word **chairman** may be used of a man or of a woman; they are addressed formally as *Mr. Chairman* and *Madam Chairman*.

chairperson NOUN chairpersons a chairman

chalk NOUN chalks **1** a soft white or colored stick used for writing on blackboards or for drawing **2** soft white limestone
▷ **chalky** ADJECTIVE

challenge NOUN challenges **1** a call to someone to take part in a contest **2** a task or activity that is new and exciting but also difficult

challenge VERB challenges, challenging, challenged **1** make a challenge to someone **2** be a challenge to someone **3** question whether something is true or correct
▷ **challenger** NOUN

chamber NOUN chambers **1** (*old use*) a room **2** a hall used for meetings of a legislature, etc.; the members of the group using it **3** a compartment in machinery, etc.

chambermaid NOUN chambermaids a woman employed to clean bedrooms at a hotel, etc.

chamber music NOUN classical music for a small group of players

chamber pot NOUN chamber pots a receptacle for urine, etc., used in a bedroom

chameleon (kam- ee- lee- on) NOUN chameleons a small lizard that can change its colour to that of its surroundings

champagne (sham- **payn**) NOUN a bubbly white wine, especially from the Champagne region in France

champion NOUN champions **1** a person or thing that has defeated all the others in a sport or competition, etc. **2** someone who supports a cause by fighting, speaking, etc.
▷ **championship** NOUN

champion VERB champions, championing, championed support a cause by fighting or speaking for it

chance NOUN chances **1** an opportunity or possibility ● *Now is your chance to escape.* **2** the way things happen without being planned ● *I met her by chance.*
take a chance take a risk

chancellor NOUN chancellors **1** an important government or legal official **2** the chief minister of the government in some European countries
Chancellor of the Exchequer the government minister in charge of a country's finances
[from Latin *cancellarius* = secretary]

change VERB changes, changing, changed **1** make or become different **2** exchange **3** put on different clothes **4** go from one train or bus, etc., to another **5** give smaller units of money, or money in another currency, for an amount of money ● *Can you change $20?*

change NOUN changes **1** changing; a difference in doing something **2** coins or notes of small values **3** money given back to the payer when the price is less than the

Thesaurus

challenge VERB **1** *The woman had challenged an intruder.* ► accost, confront, take on **2** *It was a job that would challenge their abilities.* ► test, tax, try, stretch **3** *He challenged one of the men to a duel.* ► dare, summon, invite, defy, provoke **4** *We will have to challenge the decision.* ► dispute, oppose, object to, protest against, query, question, disagree with, argue against, dissent from

champion NOUN **1** *the world champion* ► title-holder, victor, conqueror, winner **2** *a champion of reform* ► supporter, advocate, defender, upholder, patron, backer, guardian, protector

champion VERB *a charity championing the rights of the poor* ► support, promote, uphold, defend, campaign for, fight for, stand up for, advance, espouse, protect

chance ADJECTIVE *a chance discovery* ► accidental, fortuitous, coincidental, casual, incidental, unintentional, unforeseen, random OPPOSITES ARE intentional, planned

chance NOUN **1** *There is a slight chance of snow.* ► possibility, likelihood, probability, prospect,

risk, danger **2** *Give them a chance to answer.* ► opportunity, time, turn, occasion **3** *We were taking an awful chance.* ► risk, gamble **by chance** *I found the earring by chance.* ► by accident, accidentally, fortuitously, inadvertently, unwittingly

chancy ADJECTIVE (*informal*) *It was chancy taking a shortcut across the meadow in the dark.* ► risky, dangerous, hazardous, unsafe, precarious, insecure, tricky, uncertain, unpredictable, (*more informal*) dicey OPPOSITES ARE safe, predictable

change NOUN **1** *a change of plan* ► alteration, modification, variation, revision, amendment (to), replacement (for) **2** *We'd like a change.* ► diversion, novelty, innovation, variety **3** *I've got no change for the bus.* ► coins, small change, loose change

change VERB **1** *These events have changed the world forever.* ► alter, make different, transform, modify, reshape, refashion, reorder **2** *Things have changed a lot since we were last here.* ► alter, become different, develop, fluctuate, (*more informal*) move on **3** *I need to change my library book.* ► exchange, swap, substitute, switch, replace amount handed over **4** a fresh set of clothes **5** a variation in routine • *Let's walk home for a change.*

changeable ADJECTIVE likely to change; changing frequently • *changeable weather*

channel NOUN channels **1** a stretch of water connecting two seas **2** a broadcasting wavelength **3** a way for water to flow along **4** the part of a river or sea, etc., that is deep enough for ships

channel VERB channels, channelling, channelled **1** make a channel in something **2** direct something through a channel or other route

chant NOUN chants **1** a tune to which words with no regular rhythm are fitted, especially one used in church music **2** a rhythmic call or shout

chant VERB chants, chanting, chanted **1** sing **2** call out words in a rhythm

chaos (kay- oss) NOUN great disorder
▷ **chaotic** ADJECTIVE **chaotically** ADVERB
[from Greek, = vast chasm or pit]

chap NOUN chaps (*informal*) a man

chapatti NOUN chapattis a flat cake of unleavened bread, used in Indian cookery

chapel NOUN chapels **1** a small building or room used for Christian worship **2** a section

of a large church, with its own altar [via early French *chapele* from Latin *capella* = little cloak: the first chapel had as a relic the cloak of St. Martin]

chaplain NOUN chaplains a member of the clergy who regularly works in a college, hospital, prison, regiment, etc.

chapped ADJECTIVE with skin split or cracked from cold, etc.

chapter NOUN chapters **1** a division of a book **2** the clergy of a cathedral or members of a monastery. The room where they meet is called a chapter house.

character NOUN characters **1** a person in a story, film, or play **2** all the qualities that make a person or thing what he, she, or it is **3** a letter of the alphabet or other written symbol

characteristic NOUN characteristics a quality that forms part of a person's or thing's character

characteristic ADJECTIVE typical of a person or thing
▷ **characteristically** ADVERB

charade (sha- rayd) NOUN charades **1** a scene in the game of charades, in which people try to guess a word from other people's acting **2** a pretense

Thesaurus

changeable ADJECTIVE *The weather is very changeable.* ► variable, unsettled, unpredictable, unreliable, temperamental, volatile

channel NOUN **1** *a water channel* ► duct, conduit, gully, gutter, furrow, flume **2** *a channel of communication* ► medium, avenue, means, route, path, way **3** *a television channel* ► station, waveband, wavelength

chaos NOUN *When we arrived on the scene there was total chaos.* ► confusion, disorder, mayhem, muddle, bedlam, pandemonium, anarchy, disorganization, lawlessness, shambles, tumult AN OPPOSITE IS order

chaotic ADJECTIVE **1** *A good party is a chaotic jumble of noise and movement.* ► disorderly, confused, disorganized, disordered, topsy-turvy, uncontrolled, muddled, tumultuous OPPOSITES ARE organized, orderly **2** *The country was in a chaotic state for years.* ► anarchic, lawless, unruly, uncontrolled AN OPPOSITE IS orderly

chap NOUN (*informal*) *Some chap gave it to me.* ► man, boy, individual

chapter NOUN **1** *a chapter of a book* ► section, part, division **2** *a new chapter in the nation's history* ► stage, phase, period, era, epoch

character NOUN **1** *Jane has a forceful character.* ► personality, temperament, nature, temper

2 *The trees and parks add a special character to the town.* ► distinctiveness, individuality, uniqueness, stamp, feature **3** *He was acquitted without a stain on his character.* ► reputation, name, standing, stature, position **4** (*informal*) *The new doctor is a charming character.* ► person, individual, being, sort, type, fellow, (*more informal*) chap **5** (*informal*) *Her father is something of a character.* ► eccentric, oddity, (*more informal*) oddball, (*more informal*) case **6** *a woman of character* ► integrity, honor, quality **7** *She has played several characters in the same play.* ► part, role **8** *The sign was printed in Greek characters.* ► letter, figure, symbol

characteristic ADJECTIVE *He spoke with his characteristic eloquence.* ► typical, distinctive, usual, normal, particular, singular, special, individual, peculiar, recognizable, specific, unique, distinguishing, essential, idiosyncratic

characteristic NOUN *The building has some interesting characteristics.* ► feature, peculiarity, trait, attribute, distinguishing feature, property, aspect, hallmark, idiosyncrasy

characterize VERB **1** *The film characterizes the king as a cruel dictator.* ► portray, depict, represent, describe, categorize, delineate, draw, present **2** *The period after the war was characterized by great social hardship.* ► distinguish, mark, identify, set apart, brand, differentiate, individualize, recognize, typify

charcoal NOUN a black substance made by burning wood slowly. Charcoal can be used for drawing.

charge NOUN **charges 1** the price asked for something **2** a rushing attack **3** the amount of explosive needed to fire a gun, etc. **4** electricity in something **5** an accusation that someone has committed a crime **6** a person or thing in someone's care **in charge** in control; deciding what shall happen to a person or thing

charge VERB **charges, charging, charged 1** ask a particular price **2** rush forward in an attack **3** give an electric charge to something **4** accuse someone of committing a crime **5** entrust someone with a responsibility or task

chariot NOUN **chariots** a horse-drawn vehicle with two wheels, used in ancient times for fighting, racing, etc.
▷ **charioteer** NOUN

charity NOUN **charities 1** an organization set up to help people who are poor, ill, or disabled or have suffered a disaster **2** giving money or help to the needy **3** kindness and sympathy towards others; being unwilling to think badly of people
▷ **charitable** ADJECTIVE **charitably** ADVERB

charm NOUN **charms 1** the power to please or delight people; attractiveness **2** a magic spell **3** a small object believed to bring good luck **4** an ornament worn on a bracelet, etc.

charm VERB **charms, charming, charmed 1** give pleasure or delight to people **2** put a spell on someone; bewitch
▷ **charmer** NOUN

chart NOUN **charts 1** a map for people sailing ships or flying aircraft **2** an outline map showing special information • *a weather chart* **3** a diagram, list, or table giving information in an orderly way
the charts a list of the records that are most popular

chart VERB **charts, charting, charted** make a chart of something; map

charter NOUN **charters 1** an official document giving somebody certain rights **2** chartering an aircraft, ship, or vehicle

charter VERB **charters, chartering, chartered 1** hire an aircraft, ship, or vehicle **2** give a charter to someone

charwoman NOUN **charwomen** a woman employed as a cleaner

Thesaurus

charge NOUN **1** *Our charges will increase from next April.* ► fee, price, cost, tariff **2** *The children were left in their sister's charge.* ► care, protection, custody, keeping, surveillance, command, control, responsibility, safe-keeping, trust **3** *The company's directors face criminal charges.* ► accusation, allegation, indictment, imputation **4** *The infantry suffered heavy casualties in the charge.* ► assault, attack, onslaught, offensive, rush, sortie, raid
in charge of *He was in charge of the factory during his father's absence.* ► responsible for, in control of, managing, running, looking after

charge VERB **1** *What do they charge for a coffee?* ► ask for, ask in payment, make you pay, exact, levy, require **2** *They charged him with producing a video of the event.* ► entrust, burden, saddle, tax, empower **3** *The witness was later charged with perjury.* ► accuse (of), prosecute (for), indict (for), put on trial (for) **4** *The mounted cavalry charged the enemy line.* ► attack, storm, rush, assault, assail, fall on, set on

charitable ADJECTIVE **1** *a charitable activity* ► philanthropic, humanitarian, benevolent **2** *a charitable attitude* ► generous, magnanimous, friendly, liberal, benign, considerate, compassionate, understanding, broad-minded

charity NOUN **1** *Show some charity towards those in need.* ► goodwill, generosity, consideration, kindness, sympathy, compassion, fellow feeling AN OPPOSITE IS selfishness **2** *The church depends on the charity of parishioners.* ► financial assistance, generosity, donations, contributions, subsidies, patronage

charm NOUN **1** *As he relaxed, his charm and humor returned.* ► attractiveness, appeal, allure, lure, charisma, desirability, fascination, enchantment **2** *magical charms* ► spell, incantation, **3** *a lucky charm* ► trinket, talisman, amulet, mascot, idol

charm VERB *He charmed everyone with his stories.* ► delight, please, captivate, bewitch, enchant, entrance, enthral, mesmerize OPPOSITES ARE repel, disgust

charming ADJECTIVE *My mother tells me that I was a charming baby.* ► delightful, attractive, pleasant, pleasing, endearing, alluring, disarming, likable

chart NOUN **1** *a flow chart* ► diagram, graph, plan, table **2** *a weather chart* ► map

chary ADJECTIVE *She was chary about lending him any more money.* ► wary, cautious, doubtful, dubious, careful, hesitant, guarded AN OPPOSITE IS heedless

a
b
c
d
e
f
g
h
i
j
k
l
m
n
o
p
q
r
s
t
u
v
w
x
y
z

chase VERB chases, chasing, chased go quickly after a person or thing in order to capture or catch them up or drive them away
▷ **chase** NOUN

chasm (kazm) NOUN chasms a deep opening in the ground

chassis (shas- ee) NOUN chassis the framework under a car, etc., on which other parts are mounted

chaste ADJECTIVE not having sexual intercourse at all, or only with the person you are married to
▷ **chastity** NOUN

chat NOUN chats a friendly conversation

chat VERB chats, chatting, chatted have a friendly conversation

chatter VERB chatters, chattering, chattered **1** talk quickly about unimportant things; keep on talking **2** (said about the teeth) make a rattling sound because you are cold or frightened
▷ **chatterer** NOUN

chatter NOUN chattering talk or sound

chauvinism (shoh- vin- izm) NOUN **1** prejudiced belief that your own country is superior to others **2** the belief of some men that men are superior to women
▷ **chauvinist** NOUN **chauvinistic** ADJECTIVE

cheap ADJECTIVE **1** low in price; not expensive **2** of poor quality; of low value
▷ **cheaply** ADVERB **cheapness** NOUN

cheapen VERB cheapens, cheapening, cheapened make cheap

cheat VERB cheats, cheating, cheated **1** try to do well in an examination or game by breaking the rules **2** trick or deceive somebody so they lose something

cheat NOUN cheats a person who cheats

check[1] VERB checks, checking, checked **1** make sure that something is correct or in good condition **2** make something stop or go slower **3** in chess, put an opponent's king in check

check NOUN checks **1** checking something **2** stopping or slowing; a pause **3** a receipt; a bill in a restaurant **4** in chess, the situation in which a king is threatened with capture [via early French from a Persian word meaning "king": the chess meaning is the oldest]

check[2] NOUN checks a pattern of squares
▷ **checked** ADJECTIVE

check[3] NOUN checks a printed form on which you write instructions to a bank to pay out money from your account

checkmate NOUN the winning situation in chess
▷ **checkmate** VERB

Thesaurus

chase VERB *The farmer chased the intruders across a field.* ▶ pursue, run after, track, trail, drive, follow, hound, hunt
chase around *I've been chasing around all morning trying to finish my work.* ▶ rush, hurry, bustle, scamper

chat VERB *We spent hours chatting about nothing in particular.* ▶ talk, gossip, chatter, (more informal) jabber, (more informal) babble
chat up (informal) *He tried to chat Jenny up while waiting for the bus.* ▶ flirt with, make up to, make advances to

chat NOUN *I needed to have a chat with her.* ▶ talk, conversation, chatter, (more informal) natter

chatter VERB *Some of the people stayed chattering at one end of the room.* ▶ talk, gossip, chat, (more informal) jabber, (more informal) babble

chatty ADJECTIVE (informal) *She seemed to be in a chatty mood.* ▶ talkative, communicative, effusive, expansive, open, friendly

cheap ADJECTIVE **1** *a cheap edition of Shakespeare's works* ▶ inexpensive, economical, low-priced, affordable, reasonable **2** *racks of cheap digital watches* ▶ inferior, second-rate, shoddy, vulgar, tawdry, (more informal) tatty, (more informal) tacky **3** *cheap tabloid journalism* ▶ mean, despicable, low, contemptible, tasteless **4** *They made us feel cheap.* ▶ ashamed, embarrassed, humiliated, degraded

cheat VERB *Some dealers are cheating their customers.* ▶ swindle, defraud, deceive, exploit, hoodwink, short-change, dupe, (more informal) con, (more informal) rip off

cheat NOUN **1** *He called his brother a cheat.* ▶ swindler, deceiver, fraud, charlatan, impostor, (more informal) phoney **2** *The scheme was really a bit of a cheat.* ▶ deception, deceit, fraud, pretence, hoax, trick, (more informal) racket, (more informal) fiddle

check VERB **1** *Police were checking vehicles at roadblocks.* ▶ examine, inspect, test, look over, scrutinize, scan, investigate **2** *I'll check the answers against this list.* ▶ verify, confirm, test, compare **3** *He checked an impulse to look round.* ▶ resist, control, suppress, restrain, curb, repress, stifle **4** *Extensive flooding checked their progress.* ▶ hinder, obstruct, hamper, impede, restrict, inhibit, frustrate

check NOUN **1** *There will be an official check of documents at the border.* ▶ inspection, examination, scrutiny, perusal, investigation **2** *a check on the abuse of power* ▶ curb, restraint, control

A B C D E F G H I J K L M N O P Q R S T U V W X Y Z

checkout NOUN checkouts a place where goods are paid for in a self-service shop

checkup NOUN checkups a routine medical or dental examination

cheek NOUN cheeks **1** the side of the face below the eye **2** rude or disrespectful behavior; impudence

cheeky ADJECTIVE rude or disrespectful; impudent
▷ **cheekily** ADVERB **cheekiness** NOUN

cheer NOUN cheers **1** a shout of praise or pleasure or encouragement **2** cheerfulness
• *full of good cheer*

cheer VERB cheers, cheering, cheered **1** give a cheer **2** gladden or encourage somebody
cheer up make or become cheerful

cheerful ADJECTIVE **1** looking or sounding happy **2** pleasantly bright or colorful
▷ **cheerfully** ADVERB **cheerfulness** NOUN

cheerless ADJECTIVE gloomy or dreary

cheery ADJECTIVE bright and cheerful

cheese NOUN cheeses a solid food made from milk

cheetah NOUN cheetahs a large spotted animal of the cat family that can run extremely fast

chemical ADJECTIVE to do with or produced by chemistry

chemical NOUN chemicals a substance obtained by or used in chemistry

chemist NOUN chemists **1** a person who makes or sells medicines **2** a shop selling medicines, cosmetics, etc. **3** an expert in chemistry

chemistry NOUN **1** the way that substances combine and react with one another **2** the study of substances and their reactions, etc.

chemotherapy NOUN the treatment of disease, especially cancer, by the use of chemical substances

cherish VERB cherishes, cherishing, cherished **1** look after a person or thing lovingly **2** be fond of

cherry NOUN cherries a small soft round fruit with a pit

chess NOUN a game for two players with sixteen pieces each (called chessmen) on a board of 64 squares (a chessboard)

chest NOUN chests **1** the front part of the body between the neck and the waist **2** a large strong box for storing things in

chestnut NOUN chestnuts **1** a tree that produces hard brown nuts **2** the nut of this tree **3** an old joke or story

chest of drawers NOUN chests of drawers a piece of furniture with drawers for storing clothes, etc.

chew VERB chews, chewing, chewed grind food between the teeth
▷ **chewy** ADJECTIVE

chewing gum NOUN a sticky flavored type of sweet for chewing

chick NOUN chicks a very young bird

Thesaurus

checkup NOUN *The car goes for a checkup next week.* ► check, inspection, examination, overhaul

cheek NOUN (*informal*) *He had the cheek to tell me to leave.* ► audacity, effrontery, nerve, temerity, impertinence, impudence, insolence, presumptuousness, shamelessness, (*more informal*) sauce

cheeky ADJECTIVE *A cheeky boy from down the road called after him.* ► impudent, impertinent, insolent, impolite, disrespectful, brazen, audacious, forward, pert

cheer VERB **1** *We'll be there to cheer our team.* ► applaud, acclaim, clap, shout **2** *The good news cheered them a great deal.* ► comfort, console, gladden, delight, encourage, uplift, exhilarate, make cheerful, please, solace AN OPPOSITE IS sadden
cheer up *As I reached home I began to cheer up.* ► take heart, become more cheerful, perk up, brighten, rally, revive

cheer NOUN *The spectators gave her a cheer.* ► hurrah, cry of approval, shout of approval, ovation, acclamation, applause, encouragement

cheerful ADJECTIVE *They arrived looking cheerful. It was a cheerful occasion.* ► happy, jolly, glad, joyful, joyous, lively, elated, animated, contented, buoyant, good-humoured, light-hearted, chirpy OPPOSITES ARE sad, dejected

cheerless ADJECTIVE *The town was a nondescript cheerless place.* ► dreary, dull, gloomy, bleak, dismal, grim, sombre, dingy, drab, stark, desolate AN OPPOSITE IS cheerful

cheery ADJECTIVE *She answered the phone with a cheery "Good morning."* ► cheerful, jolly, merry, spirited, jaunty, carefree, happy, sunny, joyful, joyous

cherish VERB **1** *His friends all cherished him.* ► adore, love, be devoted to, be fond of, hold dear, care for, foster, keep safe, look after, nourish, nurse, protect **2** *I shall cherish this gift all my life.* ► treasure, value, prize

chest NOUN **1** *The ball hit him in the chest.* ► breast, ribcage RELATED ADJECTIVE
► pectoral **2** *a large chest of tools* ► case, crate, box, casket, coffer, strongbox, trunk

chew VERB *Claire was chewing a piece of bread.* ► eat, munch, nibble, champ, bite, crunch, gnaw, (*more formal*) masticate

chicken ➡ chip

chicken NOUN chickens **1** a young hen **2** a hen's flesh used as food

chicken ADJECTIVE (slang) afraid to do something; cowardly

chicken VERB chickens, chickening, chickened **chicken out** (slang) not take part in something because you are afraid

chickenpox NOUN a disease that produces red spots on the skin

chief NOUN chiefs **1** a leader or ruler of a people, especially of a Native American tribe **2** a person with the highest rank or authority

chief ADJECTIVE most important; main
▷ **chiefly** ADVERB

chieftain NOUN chieftains the chief of a tribe or clan

child NOUN children **1** a young person; a boy or girl **2** someone's son or daughter

childhood NOUN childhoods the time when a person is a child

childish ADJECTIVE **1** like a child; unsuitable for a grown person **2** silly and immature
▷ **childishly** ADVERB

chili NOUN chilies the hot-tasting pod of a red pepper [via Spanish from Nahuatl (a Central American language)]

chill NOUN chills **1** unpleasant coldness **2** an illness that makes you shiver

chill VERB chills, chilling, chilled make a person or thing cold

chilly ADJECTIVE **1** rather cold **2** unfriendly • We got a chilly reception.
▷ **chilliness** NOUN

chime NOUN chimes a series of notes sounded by a set of bells each making a different musical sound

chimney NOUN chimneys a tall pipe or structure that carries smoke away from a fire

chimney pot NOUN chimney pots a pipe fitted to the top of a chimney

chimpanzee NOUN chimpanzees an African ape, smaller than a gorilla

chin NOUN chins the lower part of the face below the mouth

china NOUN thin delicate pottery

chink NOUN chinks **1** a narrow opening • a chink in the curtains **2** a chinking sound

chink VERB chinks, chinking, chinked make a sound like glasses or coins being struck together

chip NOUN chips **1** a thin piece cut or broken off something hard **2** a fried oblong strip of potato **3** a place where a small piece has been knocked off something **4** a small counter used in games **5** a microchip
a chip off the old block a child who is very like their father or mother
have a chip on your shoulder feel resentful or defensive about something

chip VERB chips, chipping, chipped **1** knock small pieces off something **2** cut a potato into chips

Thesaurus

chief ADJECTIVE **1** Money was the chief problem.
► main, principal, primary, prime, most important, overriding, foremost, fundamental, key, crucial, central, paramount, predominant, basic, essential **2** the chief cook ► head, senior, principal, leading

chief NOUN He is the chief of a merchant bank.
► head, principal, president, chairman, chief executive

chiefly ADVERB Dogs were chiefly to blame for the damage. ► mainly, mostly, primarily, principally, predominantly, especially, essentially

child NOUN **1** She was only a child when I last saw her. ► youngster, girl (or boy), baby, infant, little one, (more informal) kid, (more informal) tot RELATED ADJECTIVE ► juvenile **2** She is the child of Greek parents. ► offspring, progeny, daughter (or son), descendant, heir, issue

childish ADJECTIVE It was childish of him to say that. ► immature, babyish, puerile, infantile, juvenile, silly, foolish AN OPPOSITE IS mature
USAGE Note that childish is normally an unfavorable word, whereas childlike is favorable or neutral in tone.

childlike ADJECTIVE a world of childlike simplicity ► innocent, naive, artless, guileless, ingenuous, trusting OPPOSITES ARE artful, disingenuous

chill NOUN **1** We felt a distinct chill in the air.
► coldness, chilliness, coolness, crispness, rawness, bite, nip **2** She decided to stay at home because of her chill. ► cold, flu

chill VERB The drinks need to be chilled. ► cool, refrigerate, ice, freeze, make cold AN OPPOSITE IS warm

chilly ADJECTIVE **1** a chilly evening in March ► cold, crisp, sharp, fresh, cool, frosty, icy, raw, (more informal) nippy AN OPPOSITE IS warm **2** You may get a chilly reception.
► unfriendly, cool, lukewarm, unwelcoming, frigid, hostile, unsympathetic, reserved, aloof, (informal) standoffish OPPOSITES ARE warm, friendly, enthusiastic

chip NOUN **1** a chip of wood ► fragment, piece, bit, sliver, splinter, slice, flake, fleck, scrap, shaving **2** The cup had a chip in it. ► crack, nick, flaw, scratch, gash, notch, snick

chip VERB Someone had chipped the teapot.
► crack, nick, scratch, splinter, notch, damage

chipolata NOUN chipolatas a small spicy sausage

chiropody (ki- rop- od- ee) NOUN medical treatment of the feet, e.g., corns
▷ **chiropodist** NOUN

chirp VERB chirps, chirping, chirped make short sharp sounds like a small bird
▷ **chirp** NOUN

chisel NOUN chisels a tool with a sharp end for shaping wood, stone, etc.

chisel VERB chisels, chiseling, chiseled shape or cut something with a chisel

chivalrous (shiv- al- rus) ADJECTIVE being considerate and helpful towards people less strong than yourself
▷ **chivalry** NOUN

chlorine (klor- een) NOUN a greenish-yellow gas used to disinfect water etc.

chloroform (klo- ro- form) NOUN a liquid that gives off a vapor that makes people unconscious

chlorophyll (klo- ro- fil) NOUN the substance that makes plants green

chock-full ADJECTIVE crammed full

chocolate NOUN chocolates 1 a solid brown food or powder made from roasted cacao seeds 2 a drink made with this powder 3 a sweet made of or covered with chocolate [via French or Spanish from Nahuatl (a Central American language)]

choice NOUN choices 1 choosing between things 2 the range of things from which someone can choose • *There is a wide choice of holidays.* 3 a person or thing chosen

choice ADJECTIVE of the best quality • *choice bananas*

choir NOUN choirs a group of people trained to sing together, especially in a church
▷ **choirboy** NOUN **choirgirl** NOUN

choke VERB chokes, choking, choked 1 cause somebody to stop breathing properly 2 be unable to breathe properly 3 clog

choke NOUN chokes a device controlling the flow of air into the engine of a motor vehicle

cholera (kol- er- a) NOUN an infectious disease that is often fatal

cholesterol (kol- est- er- ol) NOUN a fatty substance that can clog the arteries

choose VERB chooses, choosing, chose, chosen decide which you are going to take from among a number of people or things
▷ **choosy** ADJECTIVE

chop VERB chops, chopping, chopped cut or hit something with a heavy blow

chop NOUN chops 1 a chopping blow 2 a small thick slice of meat, usually on a rib

choppy ADJECTIVE choppier, choppiest (said about the sea) not smooth; full of small waves
▷ **choppiness** NOUN

chopsticks PLURAL NOUN a pair of thin sticks used for lifting Chinese and Japanese food to your mouth

choral ADJECTIVE to do with or sung by a choir or chorus

chord[1] (kord) NOUN chords a number of musical notes sounded together

chord[2] (kord) NOUN chords a straight line joining two points on a curve
USAGE Do not confuse with **cord**.

Thesaurus

chirpy ADJECTIVE *She came in with a chirpy grin.*
► cheerful, happy, jolly, glad, joyful, joyous, lively, elated

chivalrous ADJECTIVE *He treated everyone in the same chivalrous manner.* ► gallant, courteous, polite, honorable, considerate, gracious, thoughtful OPPOSITES ARE dishonourable, rude

chivalry NOUN *Where is your sense of chivalry Roger?* ► gallantry, courtesy, politeness, consideration, graciousness, thoughtfulness

choice NOUN *We have no other choice now.*
► option, alternative, possibility, answer 2 *the viewers' choice of programs* ► selection, choosing, preference, election 3 *Write in with your choice.* ► decision, selection, vote, nomination 4 *a wide choice of good food*
► range, variety, selection, array, assortment, display

choke VERB 1 *The dust was nearly choking them.*
► suffocate, asphyxiate, smother, stifle
2 *There was a danger of the necklace choking her to death.* ► strangle, throttle, suffocate,

asphyxiate 3 *Oliver choked and had to be thumped on the back.* ► gag, gasp, retch, suffocate 4 *The motorways are constantly choked with traffic.* ► clog, congest, constrict, block, obstruct

choke back *Sandra choked back the tears as she tried to answer.* ► stifle, suppress, fight back, hold back

choose VERB 1 *We chose a quiet spot by the river.*
► pick, pick out, select, opt for, plump for, go for, settle on, fix on, decide on 2 *Mark chose to go in first.* ► decide, elect, make up your mind, determine, prefer, resolve, see fit

chop VERB 1 *He was in the yard chopping wood.*
► cut, hew 2 *Chop the vegetables into small chunks.* ► cut up, slice, split, dice
chop down *The tree should be chopped down.*
► cut down, fell
chop off *His arm had been chopped off in an accident.* ► sever, amputate, detach, lop off

chopper NOUN *He cut up the logs with a chopper.*
► axe, cleaver

chore (chor) NOUN chores a regular or dull task

choreography (ko- ree- og- ra- fee) NOUN the art of writing the steps for ballets or stage dances
▷ **choreographer** NOUN

chorus NOUN choruses **1** the words repeated after each verse of a song or poem **2** music sung by a group of people **3** a group singing together

chorus VERB choruses, chorusing, chorused sing or speak in chorus

christen VERB christens, christening, christened **1** baptize **2** give a name or nickname to a person or thing
▷ **christening** NOUN

Christian NOUN Christians a person who believes in Jesus Christ and his teachings

Christian ADJECTIVE to do with Christians or their beliefs
▷ **Christianity** NOUN

Christian name NOUN Christian names a name given to a person at his or her christening; a person's first name

Christmas NOUN Christmases the day (25 December) when Christians commemorate the birth of Jesus Christ; the days around it

Christmas pudding NOUN Christmas puddings a dark pudding containing dried fruit, etc., eaten at Christmas

Christmas tree NOUN Christmas trees an evergreen or artificial tree decorated at Christmas

chromatic (krom- at- ik) ADJECTIVE to do with colors
chromatic scale NOUN a musical scale going up or down in semitones

chromium (kroh- mee- um) NOUN a shiny silvery metal

chromosome (kroh- mos- ohm) NOUN chromosomes a tiny threadlike part of an animal cell or plant cell, carrying genes

chronic ADJECTIVE lasting for a long time • a chronic illness
▷ **chronically** ADVERB

chronicle NOUN chronicles a record of events in the order that they happened

chronology (kron- ol- oj- ee) NOUN the order of events in the sequence in which they happened, e.g., in history
▷ **chronological** ADJECTIVE

chrysalis NOUN chrysalides the hard cover a caterpillar makes round itself before it changes into a butterfly or moth

chrysanthemum NOUN chrysanthemums a garden flower that blooms in autumn

chubby ADJECTIVE chubbier, chubbiest plump
▷ **chubbiness** NOUN

chuckle NOUN chuckles a quiet laugh

chuckle VERB chuckles, chuckling, chuckled laugh quietly

chum NOUN chums (informal) a friend
▷ **chummy** ADJECTIVE

chunk NOUN chunks a thick piece of something
▷ **chunky** ADJECTIVE

church NOUN churches **1** a public building for Christian worship **2** a religious service in a church • I will see you after church. **3** a particular Christian religion, e.g., the Church of England

churlish ADJECTIVE ill-mannered and unfriendly; surly

churn NOUN churns **1** a large can in which milk is carried from a farm **2** a machine in which milk is beaten to make butter

churn VERB churns, churning, churned **1** make butter in a churn **2** stir or swirl vigorously
churn out produce something in large quantities

Thesaurus

---

chore NOUN I spent the day cooking and doing household chores. ► task, job, duty, burden, errand

chorus NOUN **1** The chorus sang well. ► choir, choral group, choral society, vocal ensemble **2** Everyone can join in the choruses. ► refrain, response

christen VERB **1** The church in which Tania was christened. ► baptize, name **2** His friends christened him "The King." ► name, dub, style, designate

chronic ADJECTIVE **1** a chronic illness ► persistent, long-standing, lifelong, lingering, incurable OPPOSITES ARE acute, temporary **2** chronic food shortages ► constant, persistent, continuous, continual

chubby ADJECTIVE a chubby little baby ► plump, tubby, round, dumpy, portly, rotund, stout, buxom

chuck VERB (informal) I'll chuck the letter in the bin. ► throw, toss, fling, hurl, dump, sling
chuck out There are a lot of old clothes to chuck out. ► throw away, discard, dispose of, reject, scrap

chuckle VERB Andrew chuckled as he left the room. ► chortle, snigger, giggle, laugh

chunk NOUN little chunks of cheese on a plate; a chunk of wood ► lump, hunk, block, wedge, piece, portion, slab

churn VERB churn up The propellers churned up the water. ► agitate, stir up, disturb
churn out When he was young he churned out poem after poem. ► produce, turn out

chute (shoot) NOUN chutes a steep channel for people or things to slide down

chutney NOUN chutneys a strong-tasting mixture of fruit, peppers, etc., eaten with meat [from Hindi *chatni*]

cider NOUN ciders an alcoholic drink made from apples

cigar NOUN cigars a roll of compressed tobacco leaves for smoking

cigarette NOUN cigarettes a small roll of shredded tobacco in thin paper for smoking

cinder NOUN cinders a small piece of partly burned coal or wood

cinema NOUN cinemas **1** a place where films are shown **2** the business or art of making films

cipher (sy- fer) NOUN ciphers **1** a kind of code **2** the symbol 0, representing zero

circle NOUN circles **1** a perfectly round flat shape or thing **2** a number of people with similar interests **3** the balcony of a cinema or theater

circle VERB circles, circling, circled move in a circle; go around something

circuit (ser- kit) NOUN circuits **1** a circular line or journey **2** a track for motor racing **3** the path of an electric current

circular ADJECTIVE **1** shaped like a circle; round **2** moving around a circle
▷ **circularity** NOUN

circular NOUN circulars a letter or advertisement etc. sent to a number of people

circulate VERB circulates, circulating, circulated **1** go around something continuously • *Blood circulates in the body.* **2** pass from place to place **3** send something round to a number of people

circulation NOUN circulations **1** the movement of blood around the body **2** the number of copies of each issue of a newspaper or magazine that are sold or distributed

circumcise VERB circumcises, circumcising, circumcised cut off the fold of skin at the tip of the penis
▷ **circumcision** NOUN

circumference NOUN circumferences the line or distance around something, especially around a circle

circumflex accent NOUN circumflex accents a mark over a vowel, as over *e* in *fête*

circumnavigate VERB circumnavigates, circumnavigating, circumnavigated sail completely around something
▷ **circumnavigation** NOUN

circumscribe VERB circumscribes, circumscribing, circumscribed **1** draw a line around something **2** limit or restrict something • *Her powers are circumscribed by many regulations.*

circumspect ADJECTIVE cautious and watchful
▷ **circumspection** NOUN

circumstance NOUN circumstances a fact or condition connected with an event or person or action

circumstantial (ser- kum- **stan**- shal) ADJECTIVE consisting of facts that strongly suggest something but do not actually prove it
• *circumstantial evidence*

circus NOUN circuses a traveling show usually performed in a tent, with clowns, acrobats, and sometimes trained animals [from Latin, = ring; related to *circle*]

cistern NOUN cisterns a tank for storing water

Thesaurus

circle NOUN **1** *The children stood in a circle.*
► ring, round RELATED ADJECTIVE ► circular **2** *He has a new circle of friends.* ► group, set, band, body, company, society, association, gang, party

circle VERB **1** *The birds circled over his head.*
► wheel, fly around, spiral **2** *Satellites circle the earth.* ► orbit, go round, circumnavigate, revolve round **3** *The grass was circled by trees.*
► surround, enclose, encircle, ring, skirt, girdle, hem in

circuit NOUN **1** *two circuits of the playing field*
► lap, turn, round, revolution **2** *a racing circuit* ► track, course

circular ADJECTIVE *a circular window* ► round, disc-shaped, ring-shaped USAGE You can also use *oval* and *elliptical* to describe a shape that is nearly circular but slightly flattened.

circular NOUN *an advertising circular*
► advertisement, leaflet, letter, notice, pamphlet

circulate VERB *We circulated a notice about our sale.* ► send around, distribute, issue, publicize, publish, spread about, disseminate

circulation NOUN **1** *air circulation* ► flow, motion, movement, course **2** *the circulation of information* ► dissemination, distribution, spread, transmission, broadcasting **3** *a newspaper's circulation* ► distribution, readership, sales figures

circumstances PLURAL NOUN **1** *the right economic circumstances* ► situation, conditions, state of affairs, factors, position, background **2** *The police wanted to know all the circumstances.*
► facts, details, particulars, incidents, events

a
b
c
d
e
f
g
h
i
j
k
l
m
n
o
p
q
r
s
t
u
v
w
x
y
z

A
B
C
D
E
F
G
H
I
J
K
L
M
N
O
P
Q
R
S
T
U
V
W
X
Y
Z

citizen NOUN citizens a person belonging to a particular city or country
▷ **citizenship** NOUN

citrus fruit NOUN citrus fruits a lemon, orange, grapefruit, or other sharp-tasting fruit

city NOUN cities a large important town, usually with special rights given by a charter

civic ADJECTIVE 1 to do with a city or town 2 to do with citizens

civil ADJECTIVE 1 polite and courteous 2 to do with citizens 3 to do with civilians; not military • civil aviation
▷ **civilly** ADVERB

civilian NOUN civilians a person who is not serving in the armed forces

civility NOUN civilities politeness

civilization NOUN civilizations 1 a society or culture at a particular time in history • ancient civilizations 2 a developed or organized way of life • We were far from civilization.

civilize VERB civilizes, civilizing, civilized bring culture and education to a primitive community

Civil Service NOUN people employed by the government in various departments other than the armed forces

civil war NOUN civil wars war between groups of people of the same country

claim VERB claims, claiming, claimed 1 ask for something to which you believe you have a right 2 declare; state something without being able to prove it
▷ **claimant** NOUN

claim NOUN claims 1 claiming 2 something claimed 3 a piece of ground claimed or assigned to someone for mining, etc.

clairvoyant NOUN clairvoyants a person who is said to be able to predict future events or communicate mentally with people who are dead or far away
▷ **clairvoyance** NOUN

clamber VERB clambers, clambering, clambered climb with difficulty

clammy ADJECTIVE damp and slimy

clamor NOUN clamors 1 a loud confused noise 2 an outcry; a loud protest or demand
▷ **clamorous** ADJECTIVE

clamor VERB clamors, clamoring, clamored make a loud protest or demand

clamp NOUN clamps a device for holding things tightly

clamp VERB clamps, clamping, clamped 1 fix something with a clamp 2 fix something firmly
clamp down on become stricter about something or put a stop to it

clan NOUN clans a group sharing the same ancestor

clang NOUN clangs a loud ringing sound
▷ **clang** VERB

clank NOUN clanks a sound like heavy pieces of metal banging together
▷ **clank** VERB

Thesaurus

---

citizen NOUN 1 an American citizen ► subject, national, taxpayer, voter RELATED ADJECTIVES ► civic, civil, civilian 2 the citizens of Glasgow ► inhabitant, resident, native, townsperson, householder

city NOUN a large city north of the river ► town, metropolis, conurbation RELATED ADJECTIVES ► civic, urban

civil ADJECTIVE 1 I know you don't like her but try to be civil. ► polite, respectful, well mannered, courteous, considerate, affable, civilized, refined, obliging OPPOSITES ARE impolite, rude 2 a civil wedding ► secular, nonreligious 3 civil rights ► social, state, communal, national, public 4 civil politics ► domestic, home, internal, national, local

civilization NOUN 1 ancient civilizations ► culture, society, people 2 advances in civilization ► human development, human achievements, human attainments, enlightenment

civilized ADJECTIVE 1 a civilized nation ► advanced, developed, enlightened, cultured, refined AN OPPOSITE IS uncivilized 2 civilized behaviour ► polite, orderly

claim VERB 1 You can claim a refund at the office. ► ask for, request, demand, collect, require, take 2 He claimed the witness had been lying. ► allege, maintain, contend, assert, avow, protest, insist

claim NOUN 1 a claim for damages; an insurance claim ► application, demand, request 2 Their claim is hardly credible. ► assertion, allegation, contention, declaration

clammy ADJECTIVE 1 They sat waiting with clammy hands for an hour and a half. ► moist, sticky, sweaty, damp 2 The atmosphere was cold and clammy. ► dank, humid, damp, moist, muggy, slimy, sticky

clamp VERB Each shelf is clamped to three brackets. ► fasten, fix, secure, attach, clip
clamp down on a plan to clamp down on illegal parking ► reduce, suppress, end, stop, eradicate, get tough on, crack down on

clap VERB claps, clapping, clapped **1** strike the palms of the hands together loudly, especially as applause **2** slap in a friendly way • *She clapped him on the shoulder.* **3** put quickly

clap NOUN claps **1** a sudden sharp noise • *a clap of thunder.* **2** a round of clapping • *Give the winners a clap.* **3** a friendly slap

claret NOUN clarets a kind of red wine

clarify VERB clarifies, clarifying, clarified make something clear or easier to understand
▷ **clarification** NOUN

clarinet NOUN clarinets a woodwind instrument
▷ **clarinetist** NOUN

clarity NOUN clearness

clash VERB clashes, clashing, clashed **1** make a loud sound like that of cymbals banging together **2** conflict **3** (said about two or more events) happen inconveniently at the same time **4** (said about colors) look unpleasant together
▷ **clash** NOUN

clasp NOUN clasps **1** a device for fastening things, with parts that lock together **2** a tight grasp

clasp VERB clasps, clasping, clasped **1** grasp or hold tightly **2** fasten with a clasp

class NOUN classes **1** a group of children, students, etc., who are taught together **2** a group of similar people, animals, or things **3** people of the same social or economic level **4** level of quality • *first class*

class VERB classes, classing, classed arrange things in classes or groups; classify

classic ADJECTIVE generally agreed to be excellent or important

classic NOUN classics a classic book, film, writer, etc.

classical ADJECTIVE **1** to do with ancient Greek or Roman literature, art, or history **2** serious or conventional in style • *classical music*

classified ADJECTIVE **1** put into classes or groups **2** (said about information) declared officially to be secret and available only to certain people

---

Thesaurus

---

clap VERB **1** *The audience clapped her performance.* ► applaud, cheer, acclaim **2** *Someone clapped me on the shoulder.* ► slap, hit, pat, smack

clap NOUN **1** *a clap of thunder* ► crash, crack, boom, bang, thunderclap **2** *a clap on the shoulder* ► slap, thump, smack, blow

claptrap NOUN (*informal*) *He was speaking claptrap.* ► nonsense, trash, gibberish, drivel

clarify VERB *To clarify matters, let us ask some basic questions.* ► explain, throw light on, elucidate, make clear, gloss, illuminate, define AN OPPOSITE IS confuse

clarity NOUN *She explained the problem with great clarity.* ► clearness, lucidity, transparency, intelligibility, simplicity, precision, coherence

clash NOUN **1** *There was a metallic clash as the two vehicles came together.* ► crash, striking, bang **2** *Clashes followed between students and riot police.* ► fight, conflict, hostilities, collision **3** *a clash between the president and his secretary of state* ► disagreement, altercation, argument, quarrel, exchange

clash VERB **1** *The cymbals clashed.* ► crash, strike, resound, bang **2** *The violence began outside a bike shop, when rival gangs clashed.* ► disagree, conflict, quarrel, wrangle, fight **3** *The interview clashes with my vacation.* ► coincide, conflict, come at the same time (as)

clasp NOUN **1** *The bracelet needs a strong clasp.* ► fastener, fastening, catch, hook, buckle, clip, hasp, pin **2** *His clasp loosened a bit, but he didn't let her go.* ► hold, grasp, grip, embrace, squeeze, hug, cuddle

clasp VERB **1** *John clasped the woman in his arms.* ► hug, hold, embrace, squeeze, cling to, clutch, enfold, grasp, grip **2** *Before leaving she clasped his hand for a few moments.* ► grasp, hold, grip, clutch

class NOUN **1** *Our hotel is quite good for its class.* ► category, grade, classification, group, section, division, status **2** *a new class of medicine* ► type, kind, sort, genre, species, genus **3** *discrimination on the basis of social class* ► status, standing, position, station, caste, grouping **4** *a history class* ► form, set, group, stream

class VERB *Her performance was classed as a distinction.* ► classify, categorize, group, grade, designate, rank, label

classic ADJECTIVE **1** *the classic book on the subject; classic works of literature* ► definitive, outstanding, established, best, ideal, time-honored, abiding, enduring **2** *a classic example of how a good idea has gone wrong* ► typical, characteristic, quintessential, archetypal, perfect

classic NOUN *The film has good points but is certainly not a classic.* ► masterpiece, masterwork, model

classical ADJECTIVE **1** *classical civilizations* ► ancient, Greek and Roman **2** *a classical style* ► traditional, simple, pure, restrained, elegant, well-proportioned **3** *classical music; classical ballet* ► traditional, established, harmonious, highbrow AN OPPOSITE IS modern

a b **c** d e f g h i j k l m n o p q r s t u v w x y z

115

A
B
C
D
E
F
G
H
I
J
K
L
M
N
O
P
Q
R
S
T
U
V
W
X
Y
Z

classify VERB classifies, classifying, classified arrange things in classes or groups
▷ **classification** NOUN

classroom NOUN classrooms a room where a class of children or students is taught

clatter VERB clatters, clattering, clattered make a sound like hard objects rattling together
▷ **clatter** NOUN

clause NOUN clauses 1 a single part of a treaty, law, or contract 2 part of a complex sentence, with its own verb ● *There are two clauses in "We choose what we want."*

claustrophobia NOUN fear of being inside an enclosed space

claw NOUN claws 1 a sharp nail on a bird's or animal's foot 2 a clawlike part or device used for grasping

clay NOUN a kind of stiff sticky earth that becomes hard when baked, used for making bricks and pottery
▷ **clayey** ADJECTIVE

clean ADJECTIVE 1 without any dirt or marks or stains 2 fresh; not yet used 3 honorable; not unfair ● *a clean fight* 4 not indecent 5 a clean catch is one made skilfully with no fumbling
▷ **cleanness** NOUN

clean VERB cleans, cleaning, cleaned make a thing clean

clean ADVERB completely ● *I clean forgot*

clear ADJECTIVE 1 transparent; not muddy or cloudy 2 easy to see or hear or understand; distinct 3 free from obstacles or unwanted things 4 free from guilt ● *a clear conscience* 5 complete ● *Give three clear days' notice.*
▷ **clearly** ADVERB **clearness** NOUN

clear ADVERB 1 distinctly; clearly ● *We heard you loud and clear.* 2 completely ● *He got clear away.* 3 apart; not in contact ● *Stand clear of the doors.*

clear VERB clears, clearing, cleared 1 make or become clear 2 show that someone is innocent or reliable 3 jump over something

---

Thesaurus

---

classification NOUN *the classification of volcanoes into active, dormant, and extinct; a system of classification* ▶ categorization, division, grading, ordering, organization, codification, taxonomy

classify VERB *We can classify the plants according to the shape of their leaves.* ▶ categorize, class, group, organize, grade, sort, catalog, order

classy ADJECTIVE *a classy outfit* ▶ stylish, elegant, smart, chic, sophisticated, fashionable, high-class, (*more informal*) posh, (*more informal*) snazzy

clatter VERB *Something in the engine began to clatter.* ▶ rattle, clank, clunk

clause NOUN *There is an extra clause in the new contract.* ▶ section, article, condition, provision, proviso, subsection, paragraph, item, part, passage

claw NOUN 1 *a bird's claws* ▶ talon, nail 2 *a crab's claw* ▶ pincer, nipper

clean ADJECTIVE 1 *She went in to put on clean clothes.* ▶ washed, cleaned, laundered, pristine 2 *Keep the wound clean.* ▶ sterile, sterilized, healthy, uncontaminated 3 *Write your details on a clean sheet of paper.* ▶ blank, unused, empty, plain, fresh, bare 4 *The air is clean in the mountains.* ▶ pure, clear, fresh, untainted 5 *The family all led a clean life.* ▶ virtuous, honest, moral, decent, respectable, exemplary, blameless, upright, pure, innocent 6 *We hope for a clean fight.* ▶ fair, honest, sporting 7 *Make a clean cut with a sharp knife.* ▶ smooth, neat, tidy, straight, accurate 8 *I decided to make a clean break with the place.* ▶ complete, total, thorough, decisive, final

clean VERB 1 *I'll go and clean the car.* ▶ wash, sponge, hose down, shampoo, polish 2 *We'll have to clean the bathroom floor.* ▶ wash, wipe,

sponge, scrub, sweep, mop, swab 3 *Put out the clothes you want to be cleaned.* ▶ launder, dry-clean 4 *The whole room needs cleaning.* ▶ dust, brush, spruce up 5 *Make sure you clean the wound.* ▶ cleanse, wash, bathe, disinfect, sanitize, purify

clear ADJECTIVE 1 *clear instructions* ▶ plain, understandable, easy, direct, logical 2 *It was clear we would have to wait; a clear case of discrimination* ▶ evident, obvious, plain, apparent, patent, blatant, glaring, manifest 3 *a pool of clear water* ▶ transparent, translucent, crystalline 4 *a clear blue sky* ▶ bright, cloudless, unclouded, sunny, fair, fine 5 *a clear complexion* ▶ fresh, unblemished 6 *a clear voice* ▶ clear, distinct 7 *The motorway was clear again by the afternoon.* ▶ open, unobstructed, unblocked, unrestricted, passable 8 *a clear conscience* ▶ untroubled, undisturbed, easy, calm, guiltless, blameless 9 *a clear month's notice* ▶ full, whole, entire, complete, total

clear VERB 1 *The weather seemed to be clearing.* ▶ brighten, become brighter, turn fine, lighten OPPOSITES ARE darken, get worse 2 *Rain will slowly clear from the south.* ▶ disappear, fade out, dwindle, disperse, recede, diminish, peter out, wear off, dry out 3 *We should clear the backlog of work by Friday.* ▶ complete, eliminate, deal with, get rid of 4 *a special tool for clearing drains* ▶ unblock, unclog, free, loosen AN OPPOSITE IS block 5 *I have cleared most of the weeds.* ▶ tidy, remove, get rid of, eliminate, disentangle 6 *Staff were told to clear the building immediately.* ▶ evacuate, empty, leave 7 *The ball cleared the bar easily.* ▶ go over, pass over, go above without touching it **4** get approval or authorization for something • *Clear this with the headmaster.*

clear away remove used plates, etc., after a meal

clear off or out (*informal*) go away

clear up 1 make things tidy **2** become better or brighter **3** solve • *clear up the mystery*

clearing NOUN clearings an open space in a forest

clef NOUN clefs a symbol on a stave in music, showing the pitch of the notes • *treble clef* • *bass clef*

cleft NOUN clefts a split in something

clemency NOUN gentleness or mildness; mercy

clench VERB clenches, clenching, clenched close your teeth or fingers tightly

clergy NOUN the people who have been ordained as priests or ministers of the Christian Church
▷ **clergyman** NOUN **clergywoman** NOUN

clerical ADJECTIVE **1** to do with the routine work in an office, such as filing and writing letters **2** to do with the clergy

clerk NOUN clerks a person employed to keep records or accounts, deal with papers in an office, etc.

clever ADJECTIVE **1** quick at learning and understanding things **2** skilful
▷ **cleverly** ADVERB **cleverness** NOUN

cliché (klee- shay) NOUN clichés a phrase or idea that is used so often that it has little meaning

click NOUN clicks a short sharp sound
▷ **click** VERB

client NOUN clients a person who gets help or advice from a professional person such as a lawyer, accountant, architect, etc.; a customer

cliff NOUN cliffs a steep rock face, especially on a coast

climate NOUN climates the regular weather conditions of an area
▷ **climatic** (kly- mat- ik) ADJECTIVE

climax NOUN climaxes the most interesting or important point of a story, series of events, etc.

climb VERB climbs, climbing, climbed **1** go up or over or down something **2** grow upwards **3** go higher
▷ **climb** NOUN **climber** NOUN
climb down admit that you have been wrong

clinch VERB clinches, clinching, clinched **1** settle something definitely • *We hope to clinch the deal today.* **2** (said about boxers) be clasping each other
▷ **clinch** NOUN

cling VERB clings, clinging, clung hold on tightly

Thesaurus

8 *The appeal judges are expected to clear him this week.* ► acquit, exonerate, free AN OPPOSITE IS condemn

clear up 1 *I'll stay here and clear up the mess.* ► tidy (up), clean (up) **2** *I'm glad we've cleared up the misunderstanding.* ► resolve, explain, straighten out, get to the bottom of

clearly ADVERB **1** *Clearly we will need to make some changes.* ► obviously, evidently, surely, plainly, undoubtedly, patently **2** *It is important to write clearly.* ► legibly, distinctly, intelligibly

clench VERB **1** *She clenched her hands to stop them shaking.* ► squeeze (tightly), press (together) **2** *He looked ridiculous, clenching a rose in his teeth.* ► hold, clasp, grasp, grip

clergyman or **clergywoman** NOUN *an elderly clergyman in a cassock* ► cleric, churchman, churchwoman, man OR woman of God, minister, priest, vicar, pastor, parson, chaplain USAGE Special ranks of clerics include *canon, curate, deacon, dean, rector.*

clever ADJECTIVE *a clever young student; It was clever of you to work that out.* ► intelligent, bright, gifted, brilliant, intellectual, talented, capable, (*more informal*) smart

climate NOUN **1** *countries with a temperate climate* ► weather, weather conditions, weather pattern **2** *a changed political climate* ► atmosphere, mood, spirit, ambience, temper, trend, environment, feeling

climax NOUN *The appointment marked the climax of her career.* ► peak, summit, acme, zenith, highlight, high point, head AN OPPOSITE IS nadir

climb VERB **1** *She climbed the stairs.* ► ascend, go up, mount, move up, scale, clamber up **2** *The plane climbed to 30,000 feet.* ► rise, ascend, fly up, soar **3** *The road climbs steeply into the hills.* ► rise, ascend, slope up **4** *They climbed the mountain in three days.* ► conquer, reach the top of

climb down *The government has had to climb down on the issue.* ► give way, back down, yield, retreat, capitulate

clinch VERB *eager to clinch a deal* ► conclude, agree, settle, sign, close, ratify, confirm, decide, make certain of, shake hands on, verify

cling VERB **1** *cling to Climbing plants cling to the walls.* ► adhere to, fasten on, stick to **2** *cling to Charles took her hand and clung to it.* ► clasp, clutch, embrace, grasp, hug **3** *cling to I still cling to the hope that I'm mistaken.* ► adhere to, stand by, abide by, have faith in, cherish

a
b
c
d
e
f
g
h
i
j
k
l
m
n
o
p
q
r
s
t
u
v
w
x
y
z

clinic NOUN clinics a place where people see doctors, etc., for treatment or advice

clinical ADJECTIVE **1** to do with the medical treatment of patients **2** coldly efficient or aloof

clink NOUN clinks a thin sharp sound like glasses being struck together
▷ **clink** VERB

clip[1] NOUN clips a fastener for keeping things together, usually worked by a spring

clip VERB clips, clipping, clipped fasten with a clip

clip[2] VERB clips, clipping, clipped **1** cut with shears or scissors, etc. **2** (informal) hit

clip NOUN clips **1** a short piece of film shown on its own **2** (informal) a hit on the head

clippers PLURAL NOUN an instrument for cutting hair

clique (kleek) NOUN cliques a small group of people who stick together and keep others out

cloak NOUN cloaks a sleeveless piece of outdoor clothing that hangs loosely from the shoulders

cloak VERB cloaks, cloaking, cloaked cover or conceal

cloakroom NOUN cloakrooms **1** a place where people can leave outdoor clothes, luggage, etc. **2** a toilet

clock NOUN clocks **1** a device that shows what the time is **2** a measuring device with a dial or digital display

clock VERB clocks, clocking, clocked

clock in or out register the time you arrive at work or leave work
clock up reach a certain speed

clockwise ADVERB, ADJECTIVE moving round a circle in the same direction as a clock's hands

clockwork NOUN a mechanism with a spring that has to be wound up
like clockwork very regularly

clod NOUN clods a lump of earth or clay

clog NOUN clogs a shoe with a wooden sole

clog VERB clogs, clogging, clogged block up

cloister NOUN cloisters a covered path along the side of a church or monastery, etc., around a courtyard

clone NOUN clones an animal or plant made from the cells of another animal or plant and therefore exactly like it

clone VERB clones, cloning, cloned produce a clone of an animal or plant

close[1] (klohss) ADJECTIVE **1** near **2** detailed or concentrated • with close attention **3** tight; with little empty space • a close fit **4** in which competitors are nearly equal • a close contest **5** stuffy
▷ **closely** ADVERB **closeness** NOUN

close ADVERB closely • close behind

close NOUN closes **1** a street that is closed at one end **2** an enclosed area, especially round a cathedral

close[2] (klohz) VERB closes, closing, closed **1** shut **2** end
close in **1** get nearer **2** if the days are closing in, they are getting shorter

Thesaurus

clip NOUN **1** He undid the clip and opened the case. ► fastener, clasp, catch, hook **2** a clip from a film ► excerpt, extract, section, fragment

clip VERB **1** It's my job to clip the hedge. ► cut, trim, snip, prune, crop **2** Clip the coupon and send it to the address below. ► cut out, remove, detach, tear out **3** She clipped him on the head and made him yell. ► slap, smack, hit, cuff

cloak NOUN **1** She threw her cloak over her shoulder. ► cape, wrap, mantle, coat, cope, robe **2** a cloak of secrecy ► screen, mask, shield, cover, veneer

clog VERB Wet leaves had clogged the drains. ► block, bung up, stop up, obstruct, choke

close ADJECTIVE **1** close to A large proportion of the world's population lives close to rivers. ► near, near to, adjacent to, alongside, not far from, in the vicinity of, within reach of **2** close to He seemed to be close to tears as he told the story. ► near to, on the verge of, on the brink of, on the point of **3** The house is fairly close. ► near, nearby **4** At last an agreement seemed close. ► imminent, impending, at hand **5** It

was a very close contest. ► even, level, evenly matched, evenly balanced, hard-fought **6** The aircraft were flying in a close formation. ► tight, dense, concentrated, compact **7** They are close friends. ► intimate, dear, devoted, loving, constant **8** The problem needs our close attention. ► careful, thorough, fixed, concentrated, keen, intense **9** The weather had become somewhat close. ► humid, muggy, stuffy, airless, heavy, sticky, clammy, oppressive

close VERB **1** Come in and close the door. ► shut, lock, secure, fasten, bolt **2** The road was closed at the far end. ► block off, cordon off, bar, barricade, obstruct **3** The chairman closed the meeting at this point. ► conclude, end, finish, stop, terminate, discontinue, wind up, complete **4** The hole had been closed with a wad of paper. ► fill, stop, seal, plug, bung **5** a plan to close the gap between rich and poor ► narrow, reduce, lessen, shorten, fill, make smaller

close NOUN At the close of polling, the votes are collected in a central area. ► end, finish, completion, conclusion, cessation, termination

close NOUN end • *at the close of play*

close-up NOUN close-ups a photograph or piece of film taken at close range

closure NOUN closures closing

clot NOUN clots 1 a small mass of blood, cream, etc., that has become solid 2 (*slang*) a stupid person

clot VERB clots, clotting, clotted form clots

cloth NOUN cloths 1 woven material or felt 2 a piece of this material 3 a tablecloth

clothes PLURAL NOUN things worn to cover the body

clothing NOUN clothes

cloud NOUN clouds 1 a mass of condensed water vapor floating in the sky 2 a mass of smoke, dust, etc., in the air

cloudy ADJECTIVE cloudier, cloudiest 1 full of clouds 2 not transparent • *The liquid became cloudy.*
▷ **cloudiness** NOUN

clover NOUN a small plant usually with three leaves on each stalk
in clover in ease and luxury

clown NOUN clowns 1 a performer who does amusing tricks and actions, especially in a circus 2 a person who does silly things

cloying ADJECTIVE sickeningly sweet

club NOUN clubs 1 a heavy stick used as a weapon 2 a stick with a shaped head used to hit the ball in golf 3 a group of people who meet because they are interested in the same thing; the building where they meet 4 a playing card with black clover leaves on it 5 a nightclub

club VERB clubs, clubbing, clubbed hit with a heavy stick
club together join with other people in order to pay for something • *club together to buy a boat*

cluck VERB clucks, clucking, clucked make a hen's throaty cry
▷ **cluck** NOUN

clue NOUN clues something that helps a person to solve a puzzle or a mystery
not have a clue (*informal*) be stupid or helpless

clump NOUN clumps 1 a cluster or mass of things 2 a clumping sound

clump VERB clumps, clumping, clumped 1 form a cluster or mass 2 walk with a heavy tread

clumsy ADJECTIVE clumsier, clumsiest 1 heavy and ungraceful; likely to knock things over or drop things 2 not skillful; not tactful • *a clumsy apology*
▷ **clumsily** ADVERB **clumsiness** NOUN

Thesaurus

clot NOUN 1 *a clot of blood* ► lump, mass, (*in an artery or vein*) embolism, thrombosis 2 (*informal*) *I felt a real clot.* ► fool, idiot

clot VERB *a substance to make the blood clot* ► coagulate, congeal, set, thicken, solidify, stiffen

cloth NOUN *a length of cloth* ► fabric, material, textile

clothe VERB 1 *Despite the war she was able to clothe herself well.* ► dress, fit out, attire 2 *be clothed in* He was clothed in a long striped garment. ► be dressed in, be attired in, wear

clothes PLURAL NOUN *She wore lovely clothes, beautifully made from fine materials.* ► clothing, garments, attire, garb, dress, (*more informal*) gear RELATED ADJECTIVE ► sartorial

cloud NOUN 1 *Visibility was affected by cloud.* ► haze, vapor, mist 2 *a cloud of steam* ► mass, billow, haze, mist, puff

cloud VERB 1 *A light haze clouded the view.* ► obscure, shade, hide, conceal, shroud, mist, dim 2 *Anger clouded their judgment.* ► confuse, obscure, blur, muddle, obfuscate

cloudy ADJECTIVE 1 *a cloudy sky* ► overcast, dull, gray, gloomy, hazy, leaden OPPOSITES ARE clear, bright 2 *The water became cloudy.* ► hazy, milky, murky, muddy AN OPPOSITE IS clear

clout VERB *His mother clouted him on the ear.* ► hit, slap, thump, bash, box, smack, cuff, strike

clout NOUN *She threatened him with another clout on the ear.* ► slap, smack, thump, bash

clown NOUN *They regarded him as the clown of the group.* ► joker, jester, comedian, comic, fool, funny man OR woman, buffoon

club NOUN 1 *He had been hit with a heavy club.* ► cosh, cudgel, bat, bludgeon, truncheon, baton, stick 2 *She belonged to a local book club.* ► society, association, circle, group, union, organization, league, set

club VERB *The man had been clubbed almost to death.* ► beat, batter, cosh, cudgel, hit, strike, (*more informal*) clobber

clue NOUN 1 *Give me a clue what it's all about.* ► hint, indication, sign, pointer, inkling, tip, idea, suggestion, key 2 *Police are looking for clues in the immediate area of the crime.* ► piece of evidence, lead, evidence
not have a clue (*informal*) *I didn't have a clue what to do next.* ► have no idea, be baffled, be completely stuck, be at a loss, (*more informal*) not have the faintest idea

clump NOUN 1 *a clump of trees* ► cluster, group, mass, thicket, bunch, bundle, collection 2 *a clump of grass* ► tuft, bundle, bunch 3 *a clump of earth* ► lump, clod, mass

clumsy ADJECTIVE 1 *She was clumsy and spilled most of the milk.* ► inept, bungling, bumbling, blundering, fumbling, uncoordinated, unskillful OPPOSITES ARE careful, adroit 2 *His*

a
b
c
d
e
f
g
h
i
j
k
l
m
n
o
p
q
r
s
t
u
v
w
x
y
z

A
B
C
D
E
F
G
H
I
J
K
L
M
N
O
P
Q
R
S
T
U
V
W
X
Y
Z

cluster NOUN clusters a small close group

cluster VERB clusters, clustering, clustered form a cluster

clutch VERB clutches, clutching, clutched grasp tightly

clutch NOUN clutches **1** a tight grasp **2** a device for connecting and disconnecting the engine of a motor vehicle from its gears

clutter NOUN things lying about untidily

clutter VERB clutters, cluttering, cluttered fill with clutter • *Piles of papers cluttered her desk.*

Co. ABBREVIATION Company

c/o ABBREVIATION care of

co- PREFIX **1** together, jointly (as in *coexistence, cooperate*) **2** joint (as in *copilot*)

coach NOUN coaches **1** a bus used for long journeys **2** a carriage of a railway train **3** a large horse-drawn carriage with four wheels **4** an instructor in sports **5** a teacher giving private specialized tuition

coach VERB coaches, coaching, coached instruct or train somebody, especially in sports

coagulate VERB coagulates, coagulating, coagulated change from liquid to semi-solid; clot
▷ **coagulation** NOUN

coal NOUN coals a hard black mineral substance used for burning to supply heat; a piece of this

coalesce (koh- a- less) VERB coalesces, coalescing, coalesced combine and form one whole thing
▷ **coalescence** NOUN

coalition NOUN coalitions a temporary alliance, especially of two or more political parties in order to form a government

coarse ADJECTIVE **1** not smooth or delicate; rough **2** composed of large particles **3** not refined; vulgar
▷ **coarsely** ADVERB **coarseness** NOUN

coarsen VERB coarsens, coarsening, coarsened make or become coarse

coast NOUN coasts the seashore or the land close to it
▷ **coastal** ADJECTIVE **coastline** NOUN
the coast is clear there is no chance of being seen or hindered

coastguard NOUN coastguards a person whose job is to keep watch on the coast, detect or prevent smuggling, etc.

coat NOUN coats **1** a piece of clothing with sleeves, worn over other clothes **2** the hair or fur on an animal's body **3** a covering layer • *a coat of paint*

coat VERB coats, coating, coated cover something with a coating

coating NOUN coatings a thin covering or layer

coat of arms NOUN coats of arms a design on a shield, used as an emblem by a family or institution

coax VERB coaxes, coaxing, coaxed persuade someone gently or patiently

cobalt NOUN a hard silvery-white metal

cobble NOUN cobbles a rounded stone used for paving streets, etc.
▷ **cobbled** ADJECTIVE **cobblestone** NOUN

cobra (koh- bra) NOUN cobras a poisonous snake that can rear up

Thesaurus

movements looked clumsy. ► awkward, ungainly, graceless, ungraceful, gawky, gangling, fumbling OPPOSITES ARE graceful, elegant

cluster NOUN **1** *a cluster of buildings* ► group, bunch, collection **2** *a cluster of people* ► crowd, group, gathering, body, throng, assembly

clutch VERB *They were all clutching beer mugs.* ► grip, grasp, clasp, hold

clutter NOUN *It's difficult to work with all this clutter around.* ► mess, muddle, confusion, untidiness, disorder, jumble, junk, litter, lumber, mix-up, odds and ends, rubbish

clutter VERB *Bits of broken machinery cluttered the yard.* ► litter, fill, cover, bestrew, mess up

coach NOUN **1** *The coach takes the motorway.* ► bus, motor coach **2** *a railway coach* ► carriage, wagon, van **3** *a sports coach* ► trainer, instructor, teacher

coach VERB *Michael coached her to an international standard.* ► train, instruct, tutor, teach, prepare

coalition NOUN *a coalition from the three main political parties* ► combination, alliance, union, partnership

coarse ADJECTIVE **1** *coarse sand; coarse cloth* ► rough, unrefined, unprocessed, lumpy, gritty OPPOSITES ARE fine, soft **2** *coarse language* ► crude, vulgar, offensive, bawdy, lewd, foul, dirty, smutty, indecent, indelicate, improper, obscene, ribald OPPOSITES ARE refined, polite

coast NOUN *a house by the coast* ► seaside, seashore, sea, shore, beach, coastline, seaboard

coat NOUN **1** *Put on a coat if you go out.* ► overcoat, jacket **2** *the coat of an animal* ► fur, hair, hide, pelt, skin, fleece **3** *a coat of paint* ► layer, coating, covering, veneer

coat VERB *Coat the surface with varnish.* ► cover, paint, glaze, varnish, laminate, smear

coax VERB *It was impossible to coax them back home.* ► persuade, tempt, cajole, allure, entice, induce, wheedle, beguile, inveigle, woo

cobweb NOUN cobwebs the thin sticky net made by a spider to trap insects

cocaine NOUN a drug made from the leaves of a tropical plant called *coca*

cock NOUN cocks **1** a male chicken **2** a male bird **3** a stopcock **4** a lever in a gun

cock VERB cocks, cocking, cocked **1** make a gun ready to fire by raising the cock **2** turn something upward or in a particular direction • *The dog cocked its ears.*

cockatoo NOUN cockatoos a crested parrot

cockerel NOUN cockerels a young male chicken

cocker spaniel NOUN cocker spaniels a kind of small spaniel

cockpit NOUN cockpits the compartment where the pilot of an aircraft sits

cockroach NOUN cockroaches a dark brown beetlelike insect, often found in dirty houses

cocksure ADJECTIVE very sure; too confident

cocoa NOUN cocoas **1** a hot drink made from a powder of crushed cacao seeds **2** this powder

coconut NOUN coconuts **1** a large round nut that grows on a kind of palm tree **2** its white lining, used in sweets and cookery

cocoon NOUN cocoons **1** the covering round a chrysalis **2** a protective wrapping

cod NOUN cod a large edible sea fish

code NOUN codes **1** a word or phrase used to represent a message in order to keep its meaning secret **2** a set of signs used in sending messages by machine, etc. • *the Morse code* **3** a set of numbers that represents an area in telephoning • *Do you know the code for Boston?* **4** a set of laws or rules • *the Highway Code*

code VERB codes, coding, coded put a message into code

coeducation NOUN educating boys and girls together
▷ **coeducational** ADJECTIVE

coefficient NOUN coefficients a number by which another number is multiplied; a factor

coexist VERB coexists, coexisting, coexisted exist together or at the same time
▷ **coexistence** NOUN **coexistent** ADJECTIVE

coffee NOUN coffees **1** a hot drink made from the roasted ground seeds (coffee beans) of a tropical plant **2** these seeds

coffin NOUN coffins a long box in which a body is buried or cremated

cog NOUN cogs one of a number of toothlike parts round the edge of a wheel, fitting into and pushing those on another wheel

cogent (koh- jent) ADJECTIVE convincing • *a cogent argument*

cogitate VERB cogitates, cogitating, cogitated think deeply about something
▷ **cogitation** NOUN

coherent (koh- heer- ent) ADJECTIVE clear, reasonable, and making sense
▷ **coherently** ADVERB

coil NOUN coils something wound into a spiral

coil VERB coils, coiling, coiled wind something into a coil

coin NOUN coins a piece of metal, usually round, used as money

coin VERB coins, coining, coined **1** manufacture coins **2** invent a word or phrase

coincide VERB coincides, coinciding, coincided **1** happen at the same time as something else **2** be in the same place **3** be the same • *My opinion coincided with hers.*

Thesaurus

---

code NOUN **1** *a code of conduct; a social code* ► system, set of rules, set of principles **2** *The message was written in code.* ► cipher, secret language

coerce VERB *He was coerced into signing an agreement.* ► pressure, pressurize, force (to), compel (to), constrain (to), bully, browbeat, intimidate

coercion NOUN *Some form of coercion is needed to get them to start work.* ► compulsion, pressure, force, constraint, intimidation, duress, harassment

coherent ADJECTIVE *a coherent argument* ► logical, reasonable, rational, lucid, clear, sound, cogent, compelling, persuasive OPPOSITES ARE incoherent, illogical

coil NOUN *coils of rope* ► loop, twist, ring, spiral, roll, turn

coil VERB *He coiled her hair around his finger.* ► curl, wind, twine, loop, roll

coin NOUN **1** *a pile of silver coins* ► piece, bit **2** *large quantities of coin* ► change, loose change, small change, coppers, silver

coin VERB **1** *The city began to coin silver money at this time.* ► mint, make, mold, stamp RELATED ADJECTIVE ► numismatic **2** *A Czech writer coined the word "robot."* ► invent, devise, make up, create, originate, think up, conceive

coincide VERB **1** *It was a nuisance that the two programs coincided.* ► come together, occur simultaneously, happen at the same time, overlap, clash **2** *coincide with His life coincides with the decline of the empire.* ► clash, coexist, fall together, happen together, synchronize **3** *Your interests and ours do not always coincide.* ► correspond, tally, agree, match, accord, harmonize

coincidence ➡ collect

coincidence NOUN **coincidences** the happening of similar events at the same time by chance

colander NOUN **colanders** a bowl-shaped container with holes in it, used for straining water from vegetables, etc., after cooking

cold ADJECTIVE **1** having a low temperature; not warm **2** not friendly or loving; not enthusiastic
▷ **coldly** ADVERB **coldness** NOUN
get cold feet have doubts about doing something bold or ambitious
give someone the cold shoulder be deliberately unfriendly

cold NOUN **colds 1** lack of warmth; low temperature; cold weather **2** an infectious illness that makes your nose run, your throat sore, etc.

cold-blooded ADJECTIVE **1** having a body temperature that changes according to the surroundings **2** callous; deliberately cruel

collaborate VERB **collaborates, collaborating, collaborated** work together on a job
▷ **collaboration** NOUN **collaborator** NOUN

collapse VERB **collapses, collapsing, collapsed 1** break or fall to pieces; fall in **2** become very weak or ill **3** fold up

collapse NOUN **collapses 1** collapsing **2** a breakdown

collapsible ADJECTIVE able to be folded up • *a collapsible bed*

collar NOUN **collars 1** the part of a piece of clothing that goes round your neck **2** a band that goes round the neck of a dog, cat, horse, etc.

colleague NOUN **colleagues** a person you work with

collect (kol- ekt) VERB **collects, collecting, collected 1** bring people or things together from various places **2** obtain examples of things as a hobby • *She collects stamps.* **3** come together **4** ask for money or contributions etc. from people **5** fetch • *Collect your coat from the cleaners.*
▷ **collector** NOUN

Thesaurus

coincidence NOUN *The resemblance was just a coincidence.* ► accident, chance, fluke, luck, providence

coincidental ADJECTIVE *Any resemblance is purely coincidental.* ► accidental, fortuitous, by chance, unintentional

cold ADJECTIVE **1** *a cold day; cold weather* ► chilly, cool, fresh, freezing, icy, raw, bitter, biting, perishing, wintry, (*more informal*) nippy, (*more informal*) parky AN OPPOSITE IS hot **2** *I was feeling cold.* ► chilly, chilled, shivery, freezing, frozen AN OPPOSITE IS hot **3** *a cold reception* ► unfriendly, unsympathetic, unwelcoming, cool, frosty, lukewarm, forbidding, indifferent, unenthusiastic OPPOSITES ARE warm, friendly

cold NOUN *We all feel the cold in winter.* ► coldness, chill, chilliness

cold-blooded ADJECTIVE *cold-blooded murder* ► cruel, brutal, savage, barbaric, callous, inhuman, pitiless, merciless, sadistic AN OPPOSITE IS humane

collaborate VERB **1** *Several companies have collaborated to develop a new vaccine.* ► cooperate, combine, unite, work together, join forces, team up **2** *Several villagers were accused of collaborating with the enemy.* ► conspire, fraternize, collude, consort, cooperate

collaboration NOUN **1** *The work was done in collaboration with a British firm.* ► association, cooperation, partnership, combination, alliance, tandem **2** *collaboration with the enemy* ► collusion, connivance, conspiring

collaborator NOUN **1** *She wrote the book with the help of a collaborator.* ► associate, colleague, partner, coworker, coauthor **2** *After the war he was accused of being a collaborator.* ► traitor, fraternizer, colluder, defector, quisling

collapse VERB **1** *Part of the floor collapsed.* ► fall in, cave in, fall down, give way, crumble, crumple, tumble down, buckle, disintegrate **2** *People were collapsing in the heat.* ► faint, pass out, lose consciousness, black out, keel over, (*more informal*) flake out **3** *Harriet collapsed exhausted in her chair.* ► fall, sink, slump **4** *The banking system was about to collapse.* ► fail, break down, founder, come to grief

collapse NOUN **1** *the collapse of part of the floor* ► cave-in, disintegration, subsidence **2** *the collapse of peace talks* ► breakdown, failure, foundering

collect VERB **1** *He collected data from over fifty countries.* ► accumulate, gather, assemble, amass, accrue, bring together **2** *The squirrels scurried around collecting nuts.* ► gather, heap, hoard, lay up, pile up, put by, reserve, save, scrape together, stockpile, store AN OPPOSITE IS scatter **3** *People collected to watch the fireworks.* ► assemble, gather, come together, congregate, crowd around, convene, converge, flock, group, muster AN OPPOSITE IS disperse **4** *We are collecting money for charity.* ► raise, appeal for, ask for, seek, solicit **5** *I must collect the children from school.* ► fetch, get, meet, go and get, bring, call for OPPOSITES ARE take, drop off

collection NOUN collections **1** collecting **2** things collected **3** money collected for a charity, etc.

collective noun NOUN collective nouns a noun that is singular in form but refers to many individuals taken as a unit, e.g. *army*, *herd*

college NOUN colleges a place where people can continue learning something after they have left high school

collide VERB collides, colliding, collided crash into something
▷ **collision** NOUN

colloquial (col- oh- kwee- al) ADJECTIVE suitable for conversation but not for formal speech or writing
▷ **colloquially** ADVERB **colloquialism** NOUN

colon[1] NOUN colons a punctuation mark (:), often used to introduce lists

colon[2] NOUN colons the largest part of the intestine

colonel (ker- nel) NOUN colonels an army officer in charge of a regiment

colonial ADJECTIVE to do with a colony

colonize VERB colonizes, colonizing, colonized establish a colony in a country
▷ **colonist** NOUN **colonization** NOUN

colony NOUN colonies **1** an area of land that the people of another country settle in and control **2** the people of a colony **3** a group of people or animals of the same kind living close together

color NOUN colors **1** the effect produced by waves of light of a particular wavelength **2** the use of various colors, not only black and white **3** the color of someone's skin **4** a substance used to color things **5** the special flag of a ship or regiment

color VERB colors, coloring, colored **1** put color on; paint or stain **2** blush **3** influence what someone says or believes
▷ **coloring** NOUN

color-blind ADJECTIVE unable to see the difference between certain colors

colored ADJECTIVE **1** having color **2** having a dark skin
USAGE The word **colored**, used to describe people, is often considered to be insulting. It is better to use **black**.

colorful ADJECTIVE **1** full of color **2** lively; with vivid details

Thesaurus

collection NOUN **1** *a collection of strange objects* ► assortment, accumulation, hoard, array, cluster, conglomeration, heap, mass, pile, supply, stock, set, stack **2** *a collection of people outside the ground* ► group, crowd, gathering, band, accumulation **3** *a collection of poems* ► anthology, selection, compilation, treasury, miscellany

college NOUN *a college of art* ► school, academy, institute, conservatory

collide VERB **1** collide with *A van collided head-on with the stolen vehicle.* ► crash into, smash into, hit, strike **2** *The two vehicles collided head-on.* ► crash, hit each other, run into each other, meet

collision NOUN *a collision on the motorway* ► crash, accident, smash, pile-up

colloquial ADJECTIVE *colloquial language* ► informal, conversational, everyday, casual, vernacular AN OPPOSITE IS formal

colony NOUN **1** *Britain's former colonies in the region* ► territory, possession, dependency, dominion, protectorate, province, settlement, outpost **2** *the British colony in New York* ► population, community

color NOUN **1** *You can choose from over thirty beautiful colors.* ► hue, shade, tint, tone, tinge, pigment, tincture, coloring **2** *The exercise put some color back in her cheeks.* ► bloom, redness, pinkness, glow, rosiness, ruddiness **3** colors

the team's new colors ► strip, kit, uniform, livery, outfit **4** colors *the regimental colors* ► banner, ensign, flag, standard

color VERB **1** *Why not color it blue?* ► paint, tint, tinge, dye, stain, shade, colorwash **2** *Her face began to color.* ► blush, flush, redden, go red OPPOSITES ARE fade, go pale **3** *The experience had colored his judgment.* ► influence, affect, prejudice, sway, impinge on, slant, bias, distort, pervert

colorful ADJECTIVE **1** *a colorful bunch of flowers* ► brilliant, bright, showy, radiant, vibrant, gaudy, iridescent, multicolored, psychedelic OPPOSITES ARE colorless, dull **2** *a colorful account of the incident* ► graphic, vivid, dramatic, picturesque, animated, exciting, stimulating, striking, florid, picturesque, rich OPPOSITES ARE dull, plain **3** *music and colorful dancing* ► lively, flamboyant, glamorous, energetic, dashing, vigorous, flashy AN OPPOSITE IS restrained

colorless ADJECTIVE **1** *a bottle of colorless liquid* ► transparent, uncolored, neutral, watery **2** *a colorless complexion* ► pale, pallid, wan, anaemic, sickly **3** *a colorless personality* ► dull, uninteresting, unexciting, boring, tedious, insipid, dismal, drab, characterless, dreary, vapid, lackluster, monotonous AN OPPOSITE IS colorful

colossal ➡ come

colossal ADJECTIVE immense; enormous [from *colossus* = huge statue, from the bronze statue of Apollo at Rhodes, called the *Colossus of Rhodes*]

column NOUN columns **1** a pillar **2** something long or tall and narrow • *a column of smoke* **3** a vertical section of a page • *There are two columns on this page.* **4** a regular article in a newspaper
▷ **columnist** NOUN

coma (koh- ma) NOUN comas a state of deep unconsciousness, especially in someone who is ill or injured [from Greek *koma* = deep sleep]

comb NOUN combs **1** a strip of wood or plastic, etc., with teeth, used to tidy hair or hold it in place **2** something used like this, e.g., to separate strands of wool **3** the red crest on a fowl's head **4** a honeycomb

comb VERB combs, combing, combed **1** tidy hair with a comb **2** search thoroughly

combat NOUN, VERB combats, combating, combated fight
▷ **combatant** (kom- ba- tant) NOUN

combination NOUN combinations
1 combining **2** a number of people or things that are combined
combination lock a lock that is opened by using a special sequence of numbers or letters

combine (komb- I'n) VERB combines, combining, combined join or mix together

combustion NOUN the process of burning, a chemical process (accompanied by heat) in which substances combine with oxygen in air

come VERB comes, coming, came, come
1 move toward somewhere • *Come here!*
2 arrive at or reach a place or condition or result • *They came to a city.* • *We came to a decision.* **3** happen • *How did you come to lose it?* **4** occur or be present • *It comes on the next page.* **5** result • *That's what comes of being careless.*
come by obtain
come in for receive a share of
come to 1 amount to **2** become conscious again
come to pass (old use) happen

Thesaurus

colossal ADJECTIVE *a colossal building* ► huge, massive, enormous, gigantic, immense, vast, giant, towering, mammoth, monumental, elephantine AN OPPOSITE IS tiny

column NOUN **1** *The temple stood on massive columns.* ► pillar, support, pilaster, post, upright **2** *His sister writes a column in the local newspaper.* ► article, report, feature, review, editorial **3** *a column of figures* ► list, line, string **4** *The troops advanced in three columns.* ► line, row, rank

comb VERB **1** *He looked for a mirror to comb his hair.* ► groom, tidy, neaten, arrange, smarten up, smooth out, untangle **2** *Police combed the house and garden for signs of a struggle.* ► search, scour, explore, rake, ransack, hunt, sweep

combat NOUN *Many men were killed in the combat that followed.* ► action, battle, fight, fighting, hostilities, warfare, engagement, encounter, armed conflict, contest, clash

combat VERB *new measures to combat crime* ► fight, battle against, tackle, contest, counter, contend against, stand up to, strive against, struggle against, withstand, face up to, grapple with, oppose, resist

combination NOUN **1** *a combination of luck and good judgment* ► blend, mixture, amalgamation, fusion, synthesis **2** *The evidence was considered in combination with other factors.* ► conjunction, association

combine VERB **1** *His father combines a social visit with a trip to the market.* ► merge, amalgamate, join (to) **2** *Several drivers combined to get everyone home.* ► cooperate, collaborate, join forces, pool resources, come together, get together, link up, unite

come VERB **1** *Our friends came last night.*
► arrive, appear, visit, (more informal) turn up **2** *Spring came early this year.* ► occur, happen **3** **come to** *Eventually they came to a river.*
► reach, arrive at, get to, come across, happen on, approach, near **4** **come to** *The shirt came to his knees.* ► reach, extend to
come about ► happen, occur, (more formal) come to pass
come across *I came across an old friend.* ► find, encounter, discover, chance upon, meet, (more informal) bump into
come apart *One of my shoes came apart.*
► disintegrate, fall to pieces, break up
come around *It took nearly an hour for her to come around after the operation.* ► recover, wake, awake
come clean *You'd better come clean before they find out.* ► confess, own up
come out with *Goodness knows what he'll come out with next.* ► say, let out, utter, disclose
come up *Something has come up and she has had to leave.* ► arise, occur, happen, crop up
come upon *He came upon a little hut in the woods.* ► find, discover, (more informal) bump into

comedian NOUN comedians someone who entertains people by making them laugh

comedy NOUN comedies 1 a play or film, etc., that makes people laugh 2 humor [from Greek *komos* = noisy fun + *oide* = song]

comet NOUN comets an object moving across the sky with a bright tail of light

comfort NOUN comforts 1 a comfortable feeling or condition 2 soothing somebody who is unhappy or in pain 3 a person or thing that gives comfort

comfort VERB comforts, comforting, comforted make a person less unhappy; soothe

comfortable ADJECTIVE 1 (said about a person) physically relaxed and feeling good 2 making someone physically relaxed • *a comfortable chair*
  ▷ **comfortably** ADVERB

comic ADJECTIVE making people laugh
  ▷ **comical** ADJECTIVE **comically** ADVERB
comic strip a series of drawings telling a story, especially a funny one

comic NOUN comics 1 a paper full of comic strips 2 a comedian

comma NOUN commas a punctuation mark (,) used to mark a pause in a sentence or to separate items in a list

command NOUN commands 1 a statement telling somebody to do something; an order 2 authority; control 3 ability to use something; mastery • *She has a good command of Spanish.*

command VERB commands, commanding, commanded 1 give a command to somebody; order 2 have authority over 3 deserve and get • *They command our respect.*
  ▷ **commander** NOUN

commandeer VERB commandeers, commandeering, commandeered take or seize something for military purposes or for your own use

commandment NOUN commandments a sacred command, especially one of the Ten Commandments given to Moses

commando NOUN commandos a soldier trained for making dangerous raids

commemorate VERB commemorates, commemorating, commemorated be a celebration or reminder of some past event or person, etc.
  ▷ **commemoration** NOUN **commemorative** ADJECTIVE

Thesaurus

comeback NOUN *The band has achieved an amazing comeback.* ► recovery, revival, resurgence, rally, upturn

comedian NOUN *a well-known television comedian* ► comic, entertainer, humorist, wit, jester, buffoon, clown, fool, joker, wag

comedy NOUN *The show contained a great deal of comedy.* ► humor, farce, wit, jesting, facetiousness, clowning, satire, slapstick, fun, joking, buffoonery, hilarity

comfort NOUN 1 *They like to live in comfort.* ► ease, tranquillity, luxury, opulence, prosperity, relaxation, well-being OPPOSITES ARE discomfort, hardship 2 *We tried to offer the unfortunate woman some words of comfort.* ► consolation, sympathy, condolence, commiseration, encouragement, moral support, reassurance, solace, succor, support, aid, help OPPOSITES ARE misery, grief

comfort VERB *Her sister tried to comfort her.* ► console, soothe, cheer, assuage, hearten, encourage, reassure, solace, sympathize with

comfortable ADJECTIVE 1 *a comfortable chair; a comfortable house* ► snug, cosy, relaxing, convenient, pleasant, easy, enjoyable, roomy, plush, soft, well furnished, warm, (more *informal*) comfy AN OPPOSITE IS uncomfortable 2 *comfortable shoes* ► well fitting, well made, snug 3 *a comfortable lifestyle* ► prosperous, affluent, pleasant, well off, luxurious, agreeable

comic ADJECTIVE *The effect of the speech was almost comic.* ► comical, humorous, funny, amusing, entertaining, diverting, laughable, facetious, hilarious, absurd, ridiculous, ludicrous

comic NOUN 1 *The show included a rather feeble comic.* ► comedian, entertainer, jester, clown, humorist 2 *A girl was buying a comic to read on the train.* ► magazine, cartoon paper

command NOUN 1 *Officers shouted commands.* ► order, instruction, directive, direction, requirement 2 *He has twenty men under his command.* ► authority, control, direction, charge, leadership, supervision, jurisdiction 3 *She has a good command of French and German.* ► knowledge, mastery, grasp, understanding, comprehension, grip, fluency (in)

command VERB 1 *He commanded his men to advance.* ► order, instruct, direct, tell, call on, require, bid 2 *Meredith commands a squadron.* ► be in charge of, be in command of, have charge of, lead, head, manage, supervise, rule, control, govern

commander NOUN *Army commanders were discouraged from getting involved in politics.* ► chief , leader, officer, general, head, captain, commanding officer

commemorate VERB *The ceremony commemorated those who died in war.* ► celebrate, honor, salute, remember, be a memorial to, be a reminder of, pay respects to, pay tribute to

A
B
C
D
E
F
G
H
I
J
K
L
M
N
O
P
Q
R
S
T
U
V
W
X
Y
Z

commence VERB commences, commencing, commenced begin
▷ **commencement** NOUN

commend VERB commends, commending, commended **1** praise • *He was commended for bravery.* **2** entrust • *We commend him to your care.*
▷ **commendation** NOUN

comment NOUN comments an opinion given about an event, etc., or to explain something

comment VERB comments, commenting, commented make a comment

commentary VERB commentaries a description of an event by someone who is watching it, especially for radio or television
▷ **commentate** VERB **commentator** NOUN

commercial ADJECTIVE **1** to do with commerce **2** paid for by companies, etc., whose advertisements are included • *commercial radio* **3** profitable
▷ **commercially** ADVERB

commercial NOUN commercials a broadcast advertisement

commiserate VERB commiserates, commiserating, commiserated sympathize
▷ **commiseration** NOUN

commission NOUN commissions **1** a task formally given to someone • *a commission to paint a portrait* **2** an appointment to be an officer in the armed forces **3** a group of people given authority to do or investigate something **4** payment to someone for selling your goods, etc.

commission VERB commissions, commissioning, commissioned give a commission to a person or for a task, etc.

commit VERB commits, committing, committed **1** do or perform • *commit a crime* **2** place in someone's care or custody • *He was committed to prison.* **3** promise that you will make your time, etc., available for a particular purpose • *Don't commit all your spare time to helping him.*

commitment NOUN commitments something you have agreed to do or to be involved in; an obligation

Thesaurus

commence VERB **1** *Work will commence in the spring.* ► begin, start, get under way **2** *He has now commenced his contract with an Italian club.* ► begin, start, inaugurate, launch, open, get under way

commend VERB **1** *The committee commended her for a thorough and useful report.* ► praise, compliment, congratulate, applaud, salute, acclaim AN OPPOSITE IS criticize **2** *They have done well and I commend them unreservedly.* ► recommend, endorse, support, vouch for

comment NOUN **1** *I have had some very positive comments about it.* ► remark, opinion, criticism, observation, reference, statement, mention **2** *He added a few comments at the end of the paper.* ► note, annotation, footnote, gloss **3** *The news caused a lot of comment in the press.* ► discussion, debate, interest, consideration

comment VERB comment on *The article commented on the problems of travel in the area.* ► mention, discuss, refer to, allude to, remark on, touch on, speak about

commentary NOUN **1** *a commentary on the test match* ► description, report, narration, account **2** *The second part contains a commentary on the text.* ► analysis, criticism, critique, explanation, review, interpretation, treatise, discourse, elucidation, notes

commerce NOUN *Settlers came to Gaul for the sake of commerce.* ► trade, trading, buying and selling, business, dealing, traffic, (old-fashioned) merchandising

commercial ADJECTIVE **1** *The ships were built for commercial use.* ► trading, trade, business,

economic, financial, mercantile **2** *She turned to writing as a commercial venture.* ► business, monetary, financial, profitable, profit-making, viable, lucrative

commission NOUN **1** *a commission to paint the family's portraits* ► assignment, appointment, contract, order, mandate, charge, instruction, project, undertaking, task

commission VERB *They went on to commission him to build a palace for the queen.* ► appoint, engage, contract, recruit, employ, hire, retain, delegate, select, nominate

commit VERB **1** *He swore he had not committed any crime.* ► carry out, be guilty of, be responsible for, perform, perpetrate, do, effect, enact, execute, (more informal) pull off **2** *The child was committed to her care.* ► entrust, consign, hand over, give over, turn over, deliver, deposit
commit yourself to *Tenants often have to commit themselves to long leases on apartments.*
► undertake, pledge, guarantee, promise, contract

commitment NOUN **1** *The contract included a commitment to complete the work by the end of the year.* ► promise, pledge, undertaking, guarantee, assurance, liability, duty **2** *The team felt a commitment to continue the search.*
► determination, resolution, obligation, responsibility, dedication, devotion **3** *There are only a few commitments this week.*
► engagement, duty, appointment

committee NOUN committees a group of people appointed to deal with something

commodity NOUN commodities a useful thing; a product

commodore NOUN commodores **1** a naval officer ranking next below a rear admiral **2** the commander of part of a fleet

common ADJECTIVE **1** ordinary; usual; found or occurring frequently • *a common weed* **2** of all or most people • *They worked for the common good.* **3** shared • *Music is their common interest.* **4** vulgar

▷ **commonly** ADVERB **commonness** NOUN

in common shared by two or more people or things

Common Market NOUN a group of European countries that trade freely together

commonplace ADJECTIVE ordinary; usual

common sense NOUN normal good sense in thinking or behavior

commonwealth NOUN **1** a group of countries cooperating together **2** a country

made up of an association of states • *the Commonwealth of Australia*

the Commonwealth 1 an association of Britain and various other countries that used to be part of the British Empire, including Canada, Australia, and New Zealand **2** the republic set up in Britain by Oliver Cromwell, lasting from 1649 to 1660

commotion NOUN an uproar; a fuss

commune (kom- yoon) NOUN communes **1** a group of people living together and sharing everything **2** a district of local government in France and some other countries

communicate VERB communicates, communicating, communicated **1** pass news, information, etc., to other people **2** (said about rooms, etc.) have a connecting door

communication NOUN communications **1** communicating **2** something communicated; a message **communications** PLURAL NOUN links between places (e.g., roads, railways, telephones, or radio)

communicative ADJECTIVE willing to talk

Thesaurus

committee NOUN *A committee will be set up to supervise the project.* ► board, panel, council, supervisory body, advisory group, task force

common ADJECTIVE **1** *This is a common question. Accidents are quite common on this stretch of road.* ► frequent, regular, usual, normal, habitual, customary, familiar, standard, typical, routine, everyday **2** *Her parents had thought some of her friends were too common for her.* ► inferior, low-class, ill-bred, vulgar, coarse, crude **3** *There is a common belief in these superstitions.* ► widespread, general, popular, universal, prevalent, conventional, established, accepted **4** *working for the common good* ► collective, communal, public, shared, joint

commonplace ADJECTIVE **1** *a commonplace occurrence* ► common, regular, normal, typical, familiar, routine, standard, everyday, typical, unremarkable AN OPPOSITE IS unusual **2** *a commonplace style of writing* ► ordinary, plain, simple, unremarkable, undistinguished, average, indifferent, humdrum, pedestrian, prosaic OPPOSITES ARE remarkable, original

commotion NOUN *She was distracted by the commotion across the street.* ► disturbance, uproar, racket, tumult, hullabaloo, hubbub, rumpus, fracas, furor, upheaval, agitation, excitement

communal ADJECTIVE *communal washing facilities* ► collective, shared, joint, common, public, general, mutual, open AN OPPOSITE IS private

commune NOUN *She lived for several years in a commune in California.* ► community,

collective, settlement, colony, fellowship, kibbutz

communicate VERB **1** *Somebody has to communicate the bad news to her.* ► convey, announce, report, reveal, declare, disclose, impart, pass on, relate USAGE You can also say *Somebody has to tell her the bad news,* or *Somebody has to inform her of the bad news,* or *Somebody has to acquaint her with the bad news* **2** *communicate with Parents and teachers need to communicate with one another regularly.* ► speak to, talk to, make contact with, liaise with **3** *communicate with Each bedroom communicates with its own bathroom.* ► connect with, adjoin, lead to **4** *It is possible to communicate the disease through ordinary contact.* ► transmit, pass on, infect someone with, spread, transfer, give

communication NOUN **1** *She received an official communication from the tax office.* ► message, letter, correspondence, advice **2** *There has been little communication between them for several years.* ► contact, dealings, association, relations, correspondence, intercourse **3** *The newsletters are used for the communication of information.* ► transmission, imparting, disclosure, dissemination, reporting, imparting, passing on

communicative ADJECTIVE *They are always friendly and communicative.* ► forthcoming, outgoing, informative, candid, uninhibited, frank, open, sociable, talkative OPPOSITES ARE uncommunicative, secretive

communion ➡ comparison

A B C D E F G H I J K L M N O P Q R S T U V W X Y Z

communion NOUN the act of sharing thoughts or feelings
Communion or **Holy Communion** the Christian ceremony in which consecrated bread and wine are given to worshippers

communism NOUN a political system where the state controls property, production, trade, etc. COMPARE **capitalism**
▷ **communist** NOUN

community NOUN communities 1 the people living in one area 2 a group with similar interests or origins

commute VERB commutes, commuting, commuted 1 travel a fairly long way by train, bus, or car to and from your daily work 2 alter a punishment to something less severe

commuter NOUN commuters a person who commutes to and from work

compact ADJECTIVE 1 closely or neatly packed together 2 concise
▷ **compactly** ADVERB **compactness** NOUN

compact NOUN compacts a small flat container for face powder

compact disc NOUN compact discs a small plastic disc on which music, information, etc., is stored as digital signals and is read by a laser beam

companion NOUN companions 1 a person you spend time with or travel with 2 one of a matching pair of things 3 (in book titles) a guidebook or reference book • *The Oxford Companion to Music*
▷ **companionship** NOUN

company NOUN companies 1 a number of people together 2 a business firm 3 having people with you; companionship 4 visitors • *We've got company.* 5 a section of a battalion

comparative ADJECTIVE comparing a thing with something else • *They live in comparative comfort.*
▷ **comparatively** ADVERB

comparative NOUN comparatives the form of an adjective or adverb that expresses "more" • *The comparative of "big" is "bigger."*

compare VERB compares, comparing, compared put things together so as to tell in what ways they are similar or different
compare notes share information
compare with 1 be similar to 2 be as good as • *Our art gallery cannot compare with Tate Modern.*
USAGE When **compare** is used with an object, it can be followed by either *to* or *with*. Traditionally *to* is used when you are showing the similarity between two things: *She compared me to a pig.* *With* is used when you are looking at the similarities and differences between things: *Just compare this year's profits with last year's.*

comparison NOUN comparisons the act of comparing things

Thesaurus

community NOUN 1 *He had the interests of the community in mind.* ► population, populace, society, people, residents, inhabitants, local people, general public 2 *a small farming community in the Borders* ► district, region, locality, neighborhood 3 *a community of gay men* ► group, colony, commune, coterie, band, society

commute VERB 1 *The death sentence will be commuted to life imprisonment.* ► reduce, lessen, cut, lighten, remit, moderate, adjust 2 *Her husband commutes to the city every day.* ► travel, journey, shuttle

compact ADJECTIVE 1 *a compact machine that will fit in a small suitcase* ► small, little, petite, portable 2 *a compact encyclopedia* ► concise, succinct, condensed, brief

companion NOUN *He turned to speak to his companions.* ► friend, associate, comrade, colleague, partner, mate, escort

company NOUN 1 *I miss her company.*
► companionship, fellowship, society, presence, friendship 2 *We are expecting company tomorrow evening.* ► visitors, guests, callers 3 *He works for an insurance company.*
► firm, business, corporation, establishment, concern, enterprise, office, bureau 4 *a*

performance by the local theater company
► group, troupe, society, ensemble, association 5 *a company of friends* ► group, circle, community, band, gang, gathering

comparable ADJECTIVE *Customers will look elsewhere for better service at comparable prices. Interest rates are not comparable to those in Europe.* ► similar, equivalent, corresponding, proportionate, commensurate (with), analogous, parallel, compatible (with), equal, related AN OPPOSITE IS dissimilar

compare VERB 1 *We have to compare this year's results with last year's.* ► check (against), contrast, correlate, juxtapose, set side by side, weigh, draw parallels between, make connections between, match, relate 2 *You can't compare the book to the video.* ► liken, equate, draw a parallel between (the book and the video), regard (the book) as the same as (the video) 3 *compare with Our achievements hardly compare with yours.* ► match, equal, compete with, emulate, rival, vie with

comparison NOUN 1 *There is no comparison between the two versions of the story.*
► resemblance, likeness, similarity, correspondence, parallel, correlation, equivalence, analogy 2 *The conclusions are based on a comparison of Chicago and New York.*

compartment NOUN compartments **1** one of the spaces into which something is divided; a separate room or enclosed space **2** a division of a railway carriage

compass NOUN compasses a device that shows direction, with a magnetized needle pointing to the north

compasses or pair of compasses a device for drawing circles, usually with two rods hinged together at one end

compassion NOUN pity or mercy
▷ compassionate ADJECTIVE compassionately ADVERB

compel VERB compels, compelling, compelled force somebody to do something

compensate VERB compensates, compensating, compensated **1** give a person money etc. to make up for a loss or injury **2** have a balancing effect ● *This victory compensates for our earlier defeats.*
▷ compensation NOUN compensatory ADJECTIVE

compete VERB competes, competing, competed take part in a competition

competent ADJECTIVE able to do a particular thing
▷ competently ADVERB competence NOUN

competition NOUN competitions **1** a game or race or other contest in which people try to win **2** competing **3** the people competing with yourself
▷ competitive ADJECTIVE

competitor NOUN competitors someone who competes; a rival

compile VERB compiles, compiling, compiled put things together into a list or collection, e.g., to form a book
▷ compiler NOUN compilation NOUN

complacent ADJECTIVE smugly satisfied with the way things are, and feeling that no change or action is necessary
▷ complacently ADVERB complacency NOUN

complain VERB complains, complaining, complained say that you are annoyed or unhappy about something

---

Thesaurus

► analysis, collation, correlation, juxtaposition, contrast

compartment NOUN **1** *He then discovered that the case had a secret compartment.* ► section, space, pocket, cavity, recess **2** *The shed has a small compartment at the back for tools.*
► alcove, space, niche, cubby hole, chamber, division

compel VERB **1** *The court could compel him to give evidence.* ► force, oblige, coerce, constrain, order, pressure, pressurize **2** be compelled to *In the end Jem was compelled to admit the truth.*
► have to, be obliged to, be bound to, have no choice but to

compensate VERB **1** *If you have lost money you will be compensated for it.* ► recompense, repay, reimburse, pay back, remunerate **2** compensate for *Nothing can compensate for such a dreadful loss.* ► make up for, make amends for, balance, offset, counteract, cancel out, neutralize, redress, atone for

compensation NOUN **1** *You will receive compensation for any loss.* ► reparation, recompense, reimbursement, repayment, restitution, amends **2** *The balmy evening was some compensation for the unpleasantness of the day.* ► consolation, recompense, comfort

compete VERB **1** *The boys were competing in a five-day tournament.* ► take part, participate, perform, enter, go in for **2** *You will have to compete with children over twice your age.* ► contend, vie **3** compete with *No one can compete with him when he's on good form.* ► match, rival, compare with, equal, challenge, emulate, keep up with

competent ADJECTIVE **1** *a competent builder* ► capable, proficient, accomplished, qualified, able, skillful, efficient, adept AN OPPOSITE IS incompetent **2** *a competent performance* ► adequate, satisfactory, acceptable, decent, reasonable

competition NOUN **1** *We face some fierce competition this year.* ► opposition, rivalry, contention, struggle, contest **2** *Lisa came third in the competition.* ► contest, match, tournament, game, championship, race

competitive ADJECTIVE **1** *a competitive sport* ► combative, contentious, aggressive, antagonistic **2** *a competitive player* ► ambitious, aggressive, combative **3** *Banking is a highly competitive business.* ► ruthless, aggressive, contentious, fierce, cutthroat **4** *top quality at competitive prices* ► reasonable, moderate, affordable, economical OPPOSITES ARE exorbitant, uncompetitive

competitor NOUN **1** *Every competitor has to take a blood test.* ► candidate, contestant, entrant, participant, contender **2** *We have to improve on our business competitors.* ► rival, challenger, adversary, opponent

complacent ADJECTIVE *We are doing a good job but we must not be complacent.* ► smug, self-satisfied, overconfident, oversatisfied, pleased with yourself, self-congratulatory, self-righteous, unconcerned, contented, untroubled AN OPPOSITE IS dissatisfied

complain VERB **1** *We'll wait until we get home before complaining.* ► protest, make a complaint, grumble **2** complain about *The neighbors complained about the noise.* ► protest about, grumble about, make a fuss about,

A
B
C
D
E
F
G
H
I
J
K
L
M
N
O
P
Q
R
S
T
U
V
W
X
Y
Z

complaint NOUN complaints **1** a statement complaining about something **2** an illness

complement NOUN complements **1** the quantity needed to fill or complete something • *The ship had its full complement of sailors.* **2** the word or words used after verbs such as *be* and *become* to complete the sense. In *She was brave* and *He became king of England*, the complements are *brave* and *king of England* USAGE Do not confuse with compliment.

complementary ADJECTIVE completing; forming a complement

complementary angle NOUN complementary angles either of two angles that add up to 90°

complete ADJECTIVE **1** having all its parts **2** finished **3** thorough; in every way • *a complete stranger* ▷ **completely** ADVERB completeness NOUN

complete VERB completes, completing, completed make a thing complete; add what is needed ▷ **completion** NOUN

complex ADJECTIVE **1** made up of parts **2** complicated ▷ complexity NOUN

complex NOUN complexes **1** a set of buildings made up of related parts • *a sports complex* **2** a group of feelings or ideas that influence a person's behavior, etc. • *a persecution complex*

complexion NOUN complexions **1** the natural color and appearance of the skin of the face **2** the way things seem • *That puts a different complexion on the matter.*

complicated ADJECTIVE **1** made up of many parts **2** difficult to understand or do

complication NOUN complications **1** something that complicates things or adds difficulties **2** a complicated condition

compliment NOUN compliments something said or done to show that you approve of a person or thing • *He paid me a compliment.* compliments PLURAL NOUN formal greetings given in a message

——— Thesaurus ———

object to, carp about, find fault with, criticize, condemn, (more informal) whinge about, (more informal) go on about

complaint NOUN **1** *After a series of complaints about his behavior he was sent back home.* ► protest, objection (to), criticism (of), accusation, grumble, censure, fault-finding, (more informal) gripe **2** *Supporters have little cause for complaint.* ► grievance, dissatisfaction, disapproval, criticism, grumbling, fuss **3** *Her breathing difficulty was due to a lung complaint.* ► disorder, disease, illness, infection, sickness, upset, affliction, ailment, indisposition, malady, malaise

complement VERB *The restaurant's wine list complements its good food perfectly.* ► accompany, complete, go with, round off, enhance, make complete, make perfect USAGE Do not confuse complement with compliment

complete ADJECTIVE **1** *The complete report will be published tomorrow.* ► whole, full, entire, unabridged, unedited, unexpurgated, total, unabbreviated AN OPPOSITE IS incomplete **2** *The exercise is now complete.* ► completed, finished, concluded, ended, accomplished, achieved AN OPPOSITE IS incomplete **3** *He was acting like a complete fool.* ► absolute, utter, out-and-out, thorough, thoroughgoing, outright OPPOSITES ARE qualified, partial **4** *The story was complete trash.* ► utter, absolute, downright, sheer, pure, total, unqualified, unmitigated

complete VERB **1** *She will complete her training in two years.* ► finish, end, conclude,

terminate, finalize, fulfill, round off, accomplish, achieve, carry out, clinch, close, do, perfect, perform, (informal) wind up **2** *Please complete the application form attached.* ► fill in, fill out, fill up, answer

completely ADVERB *He was completely honest about what happened.* ► totally, absolutely, utterly, entirely, perfectly, quite

completion NOUN *the completion of the project* ► finish, conclusion, realization, achievement, fulfillment

complex ADJECTIVE *a complex subject* ► complicated, intricate, involved, elaborate, convoluted, tortuous, tangled, diverse, manifold OPPOSITES ARE simple, straightforward

complexion NOUN **1** *a young girl with a pale complexion* ► coloring, color, appearance, skin, skin color **2** *The latest revelation put a new complexion on things.* ► perspective, angle, slant **3** *political views of different complexions* ► type, kind, sort, nature, character

complicated ADJECTIVE *a complicated story; a complicated set of rules* ► complex, intricate, involved, elaborate, convoluted, tortuous, tangled, diverse, manifold OPPOSITES ARE simple, straightforward

complication NOUN **1** *Patients can leave the hospital after three days if no complications occur.* ► problem, setback, repercussion, difficulty, drawback, snag, complexity, ramification **2** *the complication of modern city life* ► intricacy, complexity, confusion

compliment NOUN *She blushed at the unexpected compliment.* ► praise, flattery,

compliment ➡ compress

compliment VERB compliments, complimenting, complimented pay someone a compliment; congratulate
USAGE Do not confuse with **complement**.

complimentary ADJECTIVE 1 expressing a compliment 2 given free of charge
• *complimentary tickets*

component NOUN components each of the parts of which a thing is made up

compose VERB composes, composing, composed 1 form or make up • *The class is composed of 20 students.* 2 write music or poetry etc. 3 arrange in good order 4 make calm • *compose yourself*

composer NOUN composers a person who composes music etc.

composite (kom- **poz**- it) ADJECTIVE made up of a number of parts or different styles

composition NOUN compositions
1 composing 2 something composed,

especially a piece of music 3 an essay or story written as a school exercise 4 the parts that make something • *the composition of the soil*

compost NOUN 1 decayed leaves and grass etc. used as a fertilizer 2 a soil-like mixture for growing seedlings, cuttings, etc.

composure NOUN calmness of manner

compound ADJECTIVE made of two or more parts or ingredients

compound NOUN compounds a compound substance

compound VERB compounds, compounding, compounded put together; combine

comprehensible ADJECTIVE understandable

comprehensive ADJECTIVE including all or many kinds of people or things

compress (kom- **press**) VERB compresses, compressing, compressed press together or into a smaller space
▷ **compression** NOUN **compressor** NOUN

Thesaurus

tribute, accolade, approval, eulogy, (*more informal*) pat on the back AN OPPOSITE IS insult
USAGE Do not confuse **compliment** with **complement**. *Flattery* usually means insincere praise.

compliment VERB *He complimented her on the performance.* ► praise, applaud, commend, congratulate, flatter OPPOSITES ARE criticize, insult USAGE See the note at the previous entry.

complimentary ADJECTIVE 1 *The comments were all complimentary.* ► appreciative, approving, favorable, congratulatory, laudatory, admiring, commendatory, eulogistic, flattering, fulsome, generous, rapturous, supportive OPPOSITES ARE critical, insulting 2 *You get a complimentary lunch on the day of arrival.* ► free, gratis, courtesy

comply VERB comply with *He was anxious to comply with their wishes.* ► abide by, accede to, observe, obey, follow, fulfill, acquiesce in, submit to, yield to, agree to, assent to, conform to, consent to, defer to, fall in with, perform, satisfy OPPOSITES ARE ignore, defy

component NOUN *a store full of components for computers* ► part, piece, bit, constituent part, spare part, unit, element, ingredient, item, (*more informal*) spare

compose VERB 1 *The village was composed of small huts.* ► build, compile, constitute, construct, fashion, form, frame, make, put together 2 *That year he composed mainly film music. She sat down to compose a letter.* ► write, create, arrange, devise, imagine, make up, produce 3 **compose yourself** *He began to tremble and tried to compose himself.* ► calm

down, control yourself, settle down, pull yourself together
be composed of *The government was composed of individuals rather than parties.* ► consist of, comprise, contain, embody, incorporate, involve, comprehend, embrace, include

composition NOUN 1 *the composition of the new team* ► structure, makeup, formation, constitution, content, establishment, formulation 2 *the composition of a group of poems* ► writing, creation, devising, production 3 *a musical composition* ► piece, work, (*technical*) opus

composure NOUN *She acted with great composure.* ► self-control, dignity, calmness, coolness, tranquillity, (*more informal*) cool

compound VERB *The bad weather compounded our difficulties.* ► aggravate, exacerbate, intensify, increase, worsen, complicate

comprehend VERB *I tried to comprehend what he was saying.* ► understand, grasp, conceive, fathom, make sense of, appreciate, discern, fathom, follow, perceive

comprehensive ADJECTIVE *a comprehensive account of the topic* ► inclusive, complete, full, broad, exhaustive, compendious, wide-ranging, detailed, extensive, all-embracing, thorough, total, universal, encyclopedic
OPPOSITES ARE selective, partial

compress VERB 1 *The activities can be compressed into an eight-hour day.* ► squeeze, press, squash, jam 2 *The text has been compressed into a mere ten pages.* ► condense, abridge, shorten, cut, summarize

compromise ➡ conceive

A
B
C
D
E
F
G
H
I
J
K
L
M
N
O
P
Q
R
S
T
U
V
W
X
Y
Z

compromise (kom- prom- I'z) NOUN
compromises an agreement reached by each
side accepting less than it asked for

compromise VERB compromises,
compromising, compromised **1** settle a
dispute by a compromise **2** expose someone
to danger or suspicion, etc. • *His confession
compromises his sister.*

compulsion NOUN compulsions a strong and
uncontrollable desire to do something

compulsory ADJECTIVE required by law or rule;
not optional • *Wearing seat belts is compulsory.*

compunction NOUN a guilty feeling • *She felt
no compunction about hitting the burglar.*

compute VERB computes, computing,
computed calculate
▷ **computation** NOUN

computer NOUN computers an electronic
machine for making calculations, storing and
analyzing information put into it, or
controlling machinery automatically

comrade NOUN comrades a companion who
shares in your activities
▷ **comradeship** NOUN

concave ADJECTIVE curved like the inside of a
ball or circle (The opposite is convex)
▷ **concavity** NOUN

conceal VERB conceals, concealing, concealed
hide; keep something secret
▷ **concealment** NOUN

concede VERB concedes, conceding, conceded
1 admit that something is true **2** grant or
allow something • *They conceded us the right to
cross their land.* **3** admit that you have been
defeated

conceit NOUN being too proud of yourself;
vanity
▷ **conceited** ADJECTIVE

conceive VERB conceives, conceiving,
conceived **1** become pregnant; form a baby
in the womb **2** form an idea or plan; imagine
• *I can't conceive why you want to come.*

Thesaurus

---

comprise VERB *The building comprises several
apartments.* ► consist of, contain, be
composed of, include, incorporate, embody,
embrace, involve

compromise NOUN *Eventually the two sides
reached a compromise.* ► understanding,
accommodation, settlement, agreement,
middle course, middle way

compromise VERB **1** *In the end we had to
compromise.* ► make concessions, meet
halfway, strike a balance, concede a point,
negotiate, settle **2** *The scandal has severely
compromised his reputation.* ► undermine,
discredit, jeopardize, weaken, prejudice, risk,
dishonour, imperil

compromising ADJECTIVE *Before he left he tore
up the compromising letter.* ► embarrassing,
damaging, scandalous, discreditable,
dishonorable, improper

compulsion NOUN **1** *There is no compulsion to
go.* ► obligation, necessity, constraint,
pressure **2** *She felt a strong compulsion to tell the
whole story.* ► urge, impulse, desire, longing,
obsession

compulsive ADJECTIVE **1** *He felt a compulsive
urge to jump out.* ► irresistible, uncontrollable,
overpowering, overwhelming, besetting,
compelling, driving, involuntary, powerful
2 *Not all fat people are compulsive overeaters.*
► habitual, obsessive, addicted, persistent,
incorrigible, incurable

compulsory ADJECTIVE *Each exam paper has one
compulsory question. Carrying an identity card is
now compulsory.* ► obligatory, mandatory,
binding, required, stipulated, unavoidable, de
rigueur, imperative, imposed, incumbent,
inescapable, official AN OPPOSITE IS optional

con NOUN *The offer proved to be just a con.*
► trick, cheat, swindle, deception, fraud

con VERB *They conned the couple out of their life
savings.* ► trick, cheat, swindle, dupe, deceive,
inveigle, hoodwink, (more informal) bamboozle

conceal VERB **1** *She concealed the device in her
camera. A mass of cloud concealed the sun.*
► hide, cover up, disguise, secrete, blot out,
mask, obscure, screen, veil, bury, cloak,
envelop, camouflage OPPOSITES ARE reveal,
expose, uncover **2** *He could barely conceal his
frustration.* ► hide, suppress, keep secret, hush
up, keep dark, keep quiet AN OPPOSITE IS
reveal

concealed ADJECTIVE *The house stood behind a
concealed entrance.* ► hidden, invisible,
camouflaged, disguised, secret, cloaked,
furtive, unobtrusive OPPOSITES ARE obvious,
visible

concede VERB **1** *I conceded that I might have
been wrong.* ► admit, acknowledge, accept,
grant, agree, recognize, allow, confess AN
OPPOSITE IS deny **2** *The country conceded some of
the territory to its neighbor.* ► surrender, yield,
give up, relinquish, cede, hand over, submit

conceit NOUN *She said it without conceit, simply
as a fact.* ► vanity, arrogance, pride, boastfulness

conceited ADJECTIVE *Without sounding conceited,
I think we offer the best service.* ► vain, boastful,
immodest, arrogant, haughty, self-satisfied,
proud, complacent, (more informal) cocky AN
OPPOSITE IS modest

conceive VERB **1** *She was unable to conceive.*
► get pregnant, become pregnant, have a
baby **2** *The plan was conceived after the war.*
► think up, devise, originate, create, form,
formulate, invent, design **3** *It is hard to*

concentrate VERB concentrates, concentrating, concentrated **1** give your full attention or effort to something **2** bring or come together in one place **3** make a liquid, etc., less dilute

concentration NOUN concentrations **1** concentrating **2** the amount dissolved in each part of a liquid

concentric ADJECTIVE having the same center
• concentric circles

concept NOUN concepts an idea

conception NOUN conceptions **1** the conceiving of a baby **2** an idea

concern VERB concerns, concerning, concerned **1** be important to or affect somebody **2** worry somebody **3** be about; have as its subject • The story concerns a group of rabbits.

concern NOUN concerns **1** something that concerns you; a responsibility **2** worry **3** a business

concert NOUN concerts a musical entertainment

concerto (kon- chert- oh) NOUN concertos a piece of music for a solo instrument and an orchestra

concession NOUN concessions **1** conceding **2** something conceded **3** a reduction in price for a certain category of person
▷ **concessionary** ADJECTIVE

conciliate VERB conciliates, conciliating, conciliated **1** win over an angry or hostile person by friendliness **2** help people who disagree to come to an agreement
▷ **conciliation** NOUN

concise ADJECTIVE brief; giving much information in a few words
▷ **concisely** ADVERB **conciseness** NOUN

conclude VERB concludes, concluding, concluded **1** bring or come to an end **2** decide; form an opinion by reasoning • The jury concluded that he was guilty.

conclusion NOUN conclusions **1** an ending **2** an opinion formed by reasoning

---

Thesaurus

---

conceive what it must have been like for them.
► imagine, envisage, visualize, picture, appreciate, comprehend, apprehend, grasp

concentrate VERB **1** concentrate on Sharon was concentrating on the video. ► pay attention to, keep your mind on, put your mind to, apply yourself to, focus on, be engrossed in, be absorbed in, attend to, think about **2** Troops concentrated on the border. ► gather, mass, collect, congregate, converge, crowd, accumulate AN OPPOSITE IS disperse **3** We need to concentrate our efforts on improving public services. ► focus, direct (to), aim (at), intensify OPPOSITES ARE reduce, dilute

concentrated ADJECTIVE **1** concentrated fruit juice ► condensed, undiluted, reduced, rich, dense, strong, evaporated AN OPPOSITE IS diluted **2** making concentrated efforts ► intense, strenuous, intensive, concerted, vigorous, committed, thorough, hard, (more informal) all-out AN OPPOSITE IS half-hearted

concept NOUN It's not an easy concept to grasp. ► idea, notion, principle, theory, thought, hypothesis, image, conception

concern VERB **1** What I have to say concerns everyone. ► affect, involve, apply to, refer to, relate to, be relevant to, be important to, interest, matter to, (more formal) pertain to **2** The book concerns various aspects of the subject. ► deal with, be about, treat, describe, review, relate to **3** Her news concerned us deeply. ► worry, disturb, upset, trouble, distress, bother

concern NOUN **1** concern for others ► regard, consideration, thought, care, attention (to), interest (in) **2** It's no concern of ours. ► affair,

business, matter, responsibility, problem **3** a cause for great concern ► anxiety, worry, disquiet, unease, distress, apprehension **4** a publishing concern ► company, firm, business, enterprise, establishment, organization, corporation

concerned ADJECTIVE **1** His parents looked concerned. ► worried, anxious, troubled, bothered, disturbed, distressed, fearful, upset AN OPPOSITE IS unconcerned **2** If you want more information, talk to the people concerned. ► connected, interested, involved, relevant

concise ADJECTIVE a concise account of events in the war ► brief, succinct, compact, short, condensed, concentrated, compressed, abridged, abbreviated, pithy, terse OPPOSITES ARE lengthy, diffuse

conclude VERB **1** Hostilities concluded at midnight. ► finish, end, stop, cease, terminate, be over, come to a close, be brought to an end OPPOSITES ARE start, commence **2** The jury concluded that the witness had been lying. ► infer, deduce, decide, gather, judge, suppose, think, reckon, surmise, assume **3** an attempt to conclude a treaty ► negotiate, agree, come to terms on, arrange, effect, bring about, broker

conclusion NOUN **1** A few gentle jokes formed the conclusion of her speech. ► end, finish, close, completion, termination, culmination, finale, rounding-off, peroration **2** The court's original conclusion in the case has been proved correct. ► deduction, decision, judgment, verdict, opinion, interpretation, inference, resolution, belief, conjecture, assumption, presumption, surmise

A
B
C
D
E
F
G
H
I
J
K
L
M
N
O
P
Q
R
S
T
U
V
W
X
Y
Z

conclusive ADJECTIVE putting an end to all doubt
▷ **conclusively** ADVERB

concoct VERB concocts, concocting, concocted **1** make something by putting ingredients together **2** invent • *We'll have to concoct an excuse.*
▷ **concoction** NOUN

concord NOUN friendly agreement or harmony

concrete NOUN cement mixed with sand and gravel, used in building

concrete ADJECTIVE **1** able to be touched and felt; not abstract **2** definite • *We need concrete evidence, not theories.*

concurrent ADJECTIVE happening or existing at the same time

concussion NOUN a temporary injury to the brain caused by a hard knock
▷ **concussed** ADJECTIVE

condemn VERB condemns, condemning, condemned **1** say that you strongly disapprove of something **2** convict or sentence a criminal • *He was condemned to death.* **3** make someone suffer something unpleasant • *They were condemned to a life of poverty.* **4** declare that houses, etc., are not fit to be used
▷ **condemnation** NOUN

condense VERB condenses, condensing, condensed **1** make a liquid denser or more compact **2** put something into fewer words **3** change from gas or vapor to liquid • *Steam condenses on windows.*
▷ **condensation** NOUN **condenser** NOUN

condescend VERB condescends, condescending, condescended **1** behave in a way which shows that you feel superior to others **2** allow yourself to do something that seems unsuitable for a person of your high rank
▷ **condescension** NOUN

condition NOUN conditions **1** the state or fitness of a person or thing • *This bicycle is in good condition.* **2** the situation or surroundings that affect something • *working conditions* **3** something required as part of an agreement on condition that only if; on the understanding that something will be done

condition VERB conditions, conditioning, conditioned **1** put something into a good or proper condition **2** train someone to behave in a particular way or become used to a particular situation

conditional ADJECTIVE depending on a condition or requirement being met • *a conditional offer*
▷ **conditionally** ADVERB

Thesaurus

conclusive ADJECTIVE *It will be difficult to provide conclusive proof.* ► decisive, definitive, definite, indisputable, incontrovertible, irrefutable, unequivocal, unambiguous, unarguable, convincing, persuasive, unanswerable AN OPPOSITE IS inconclusive

concoct VERB *She didn't have much time to concoct her story.* ► make up, think up, invent, fabricate, contrive, formulate, prepare, devise, create, develop, (*more informal*) cook up

concrete ADJECTIVE **1** *concrete objects* ► solid, physical, material, palpable, substantial, tactile, touchable, visible **2** *The case lacks concrete evidence. The proposals are not yet concrete.* ► firm, solid, objective, tangible, material, physical, factual, real, actual, definite, existing OPPOSITES ARE abstract , theoretical

condemn VERB **1** *He condemned all forms of violence.* ► deplore, denounce, castigate, criticize, censure OPPOSITES ARE commend, approve of **2** *The committee condemned them for their behavior.* ► criticize, censure, denounce, reprehend, deprecate, disparage, berate, revile **3** *After a lengthy trial the court finally condemned them.* ► convict, find guilty, sentence, pass judgment, prove guilty, punish, judge AN OPPOSITE IS acquit

condense VERB **1** *She condensed the ten episodes into a single hour-long drama.* ► shorten, reduce, abridge, compress, cut, contract, telescope, summarize AN OPPOSITE IS expand **2** *The liquid is slowly condensed.* ► distill, reduce, concentrate, solidify, thicken AN OPPOSITE IS dilute

condescend VERB *Eventually an official condescended to see us.* ► deign, consent, see fit, vouchsafe, stoop, lower yourself

condescending ADJECTIVE *She narrowed her eyes at us in a condescending manner.* ► superior, supercilious, disdainful, patronizing, haughty, imperious, lofty, (*more informal*) snooty

condition NOUN **1** *Check that your vehicle is in good condition.* ► order, state, shape, (*more informal*) trim USAGE If you use *state* you have to say *in a good state* **2** *She was told she had a medical condition.* ► disorder, illness, disease, complaint, ailment, infirmity **3** *There are some conditions attached to membership.*
► requirement, proviso, term, qualification, restriction, stipulation, limitation, obligation

conditional ADJECTIVE *The offer of a place was a conditional one.* ► provisional, qualified, dependent, limited, restricted AN OPPOSITE IS unconditional

condom NOUN condoms a rubber sheath worn on the penis during sexual intercourse as a contraceptive and as a protection against disease

condone VERB condones, condoning, condoned forgive or ignore wrongdoing • *We do not condone violence.*

conduct (kon- dukt) VERB conducts, conducting, conducted **1** lead or guide **2** be the conductor of an orchestra or choir **3** manage or direct something • *conduct an experiment* **4** allow heat, light, sound, or electricity to pass along or through **5** behave • *They conducted themselves with dignity.*

conduction NOUN the conducting of heat or electricity, etc.

conductor NOUN conductors **1** a person who directs the performance of an orchestra or choir by movements of the arms **2** a person who collects the fares on a bus, etc. **3** something that conducts heat or electricity, etc.
  ▷ **conductress** NOUN

cone NOUN cones **1** an object that is circular at one end and narrows to a point at the other end **2** an ice cream cone **3** the dry cone-shaped fruit of a pine, fir, or cedar tree

confectionery NOUN sweets, cakes, and cookies

confederate ADJECTIVE allied; joined by an agreement or treaty

confederate NOUN confederates **1** a member of a confederacy **2** an ally; an accomplice

confederation NOUN confederations **1** the process of joining in an alliance **2** a group of people, organizations, or states joined together by an agreement or treaty

conference NOUN conferences a meeting for holding a discussion

confess VERB confesses, confessing, confessed say openly that you have done something wrong or have a weakness; admit

confession NOUN confessions saying that you have done something wrong

confetti NOUN tiny pieces of colored paper thrown by wedding guests at the bride and bridegroom

confide VERB confides, confiding, confided **1** tell someone a secret • *I decided to confide in my sister.* **2** entrust something to someone

confidence NOUN confidences **1** firm trust **2** a feeling of certainty or boldness; being sure that you can do something **3** something told confidentially
in confidence as a secret
in a person's confidence trusted with his or her secrets

Thesaurus

condone VERB *We cannot condone this sort of behavior.* ► tolerate, endorse, disregard, overlook, pardon, forgive, ignore, allow, connive at, excuse, let someone off OPPOSITES ARE condemn, punish

conduct NOUN **1** *good conduct* ► behavior, demeanor, attitude, bearing, manner, ways, actions **2** *the conduct of the nation's affairs* ► management, direction, handling, organization, running, supervision, administration, control, discharge

conduct VERB **1** *Visitors are conducted around the building in small groups.* ► escort, guide, accompany, take, usher, lead, convey, shepherd **2** *The group conducted a survey into children's eating habits.* ► organize, administer, coordinate, carry out, manage, direct, run, handle, preside over
conduct yourself *He conducted himself in a typically high-handed manner.* ► behave, act, carry on, acquit yourself

confer VERB **1** *The king conferred a knighthood on him.* ► bestow, award, accord, give, grant, honor with, invest USAGE Note that with all the alternatives apart from *bestow*, you say (for example) *The king awarded him a knighthood.* If you use *bestow* you follow the same pattern as for *confer*. **2** *He asked for a pause to confer with his colleagues.* ► consult,

discuss things, have a discussion, speak, communicate, deliberate

conference NOUN **1** *an international conference on the environment.* ► congress, convention, meeting, symposium, summit **2** *They gathered around the table for a conference.* ► discussion, consultation, deliberation, exchange of views, talks

confess VERB **1** *Several of the suspects later confessed.* ► admit guilt, plead guilty, own up, accept blame, (*more informal*) come clean **2** *She confessed that she had broken the man's window.* ► own up, admit, acknowledge, concede **3** *I confess I agree with all they have said.* ► admit, concede, grant, allow

confession NOUN *The interrogators failed to get a confession out of him.* ► admission of guilt, acknowledgment of guilt, declaration, disclosure, profession, revelation

confide VERB *He confided his fears to his wife.* ► reveal, disclose, divulge, admit, declare
confide in *He is not easy to confide in.* ► unburden yourself to, tell all to, trust in

confidence NOUN **1** *We can face the future with confidence. She shows a lot of confidence.* ► optimism, assurance, positiveness, conviction, certainty, credence, faith, hope, reliance, trust OPPOSITES ARE doubt, scepticism, diffidence

confidence trick NOUN confidence tricks swinging a person after persuading him or her to trust you

confident ADJECTIVE showing or feeling confidence; bold
▷ **confidently** ADVERB

confidential ADJECTIVE meant to be kept secret
▷ **confidentially** ADVERB **confidentiality** NOUN

confine VERB confines, confining, confined **1** keep something within limits; restrict
• *Please confine your remarks to the subject being discussed.* **2** keep somebody in a place

confirm VERB confirms, confirming, confirmed **1** prove that something is true or correct **2** make a thing definite • *Please write to confirm your booking.* **3** make a person a full

member of the Christian Church
▷ **confirmation** NOUN **confirmatory** ADJECTIVE

confiscate VERB confiscates, confiscating, confiscated take something away as a punishment
▷ **confiscation** NOUN

conflagration NOUN conflagrations a great and destructive fire

conflict (**kon-** flikt) NOUN conflicts a fight, struggle, or disagreement

conflict (kon-**flikt**) VERB conflicts, conflicting, conflicted have a conflict; differ or disagree

conform VERB conforms, conforming, conformed keep to accepted rules, customs, or ideas
▷ **conformist** NOUN **conformity** NOUN

Thesaurus

---

have confidence in *They have confidence in your abilities.* ► trust, believe in, be sure of

confident ADJECTIVE **1** *We are confident that the money can be found.* ► optimistic, hopeful, sure, certain, convinced, sanguine, positive, trusting AN OPPOSITE IS doubtful **2** *She lifted her head in a confident gesture.* ► self-assured, self-confident, assertive, assured, self-possessed, self-reliant, positive, bold, composed, definite, fearless, secure, unafraid AN OPPOSITE IS diffident

confidential ADJECTIVE **1** *All conversations are strictly confidential.* ► secret, top secret, private, personal, classified, restricted, suppressed, intimate, (more informal) hush-hush, (more informal) off the record **2** *a confidential secretary* ► personal, private, trusted

confine VERB **1** *She confined her writing to poems and short stories.* ► restrict, limit, keep **2** *During the winter months the animals are confined in a small field near the buildings. He was confined in jail to await his trial.* ► enclose, imprison, keep, shut, close, fence, box, cage, incarcerate, intern, isolate

confinement NOUN **1** *a period of confinement* ► imprisonment, incarceration, detention, internment, custody, captivity, restraint OPPOSITES ARE freedom, liberty **2** *She was admitted to the hospital for her confinement.* ► labor, delivery, childbirth

confirm VERB **1** *What happened the next day confirmed her suspicions about the place.* ► support, corroborate, back up, upheld, validate, approve, give credence to, substantiate OPPOSITES ARE contradict, disprove **2** *The hotel will need a deposit to confirm the reservation.* ► verify, guarantee, clinch, endorse, validate, ratify, formalize, make legal, make official AN OPPOSITE IS cancel **3** *I confirm that I will be arriving on*

Saturday. ► affirm, assert, assure you, give an assurance

confirmation NOUN **1** *The DNA evidence provided confirmation of his guilt.* ► proof, corroboration, verification, testimony, substantiation **2** *Confirmation of the appointment will follow shortly.* ► ratification, endorsement, approval, validation, formalization

conflict NOUN **1** *conflict between management and workers* ► dispute, disagreement, discord, contention, confrontation, dissension, antagonism, hostility, friction, strife, clash AN OPPOSITE IS harmony **2** *a military conflict* ► war, struggle, confrontation, contest, clash, campaign, encounter, engagement, action, battle, combat, feud, fight, quarrel, skirmish, warfare

conflict VERB *This fact conflicts with statements made back in September.* ► clash, disagree, differ (from), be incompatible, be inconsistent, be at variance, be at odds OPPOSITES ARE support, agree with

conform VERB **1** *I conform because I think it gives a good impression.* ► comply, acquiesce, follow convention, fit in, obey the rules, play by the rules, keep in step OPPOSITES ARE rebel, disobey, differ **2** *conform to You have to conform to strict rules of etiquette.* ► comply with, follow, obey, abide by, accept, accede to, fit in with, uphold, fulfil **3** *conform to Our experiences do not always conform to our beliefs.* ► match, fit, suit, correspond to, agree with, tally with, harmonize with, accord with, compare with, square with

conformity NOUN *There is a lot of conformity among young people.* ► conventionality, orthodoxy, uniformity, compliance, obedience, submission OPPOSITES ARE eccentricity, rebellion

confound VERB confounds, confounding, confounded **1** astonish or puzzle someone **2** confuse

confront VERB confronts, confronting, confronted **1** come or bring face to face, especially in a hostile way **2** be present and have to be dealt with • *Problems confront us.*
▷ **confrontation** NOUN

confuse VERB confuses, confusing, confused **1** make a person puzzled or muddled **2** mistake one thing for another
▷ **confusion** NOUN

confute VERB confutes, confuting, confuted prove a person or statement to be wrong
▷ **confutation** NOUN

congeal (kon- jeel) VERB congeals, congealing, congealed become jellylike instead of liquid, especially in cooling • *congealed blood*

congenital (kon- jen- it- al) ADJECTIVE existing in a person from birth
▷ **congenitally** ADVERB

congested ADJECTIVE crowded or blocked up • *congested streets* • *congested lungs*
▷ **congestion** NOUN

conglomeration NOUN conglomerations a mass of different things put together

congratulate VERB congratulates, congratulating, congratulated tell a person that you are pleased about his or her success or good fortune
▷ **congratulation** NOUN **congratulatory** ADJECTIVE

congregate VERB congregates, congregating, congregated assemble; flock together

congregation NOUN congregations a group of people who have come together to take part in religious worship

Congress NOUN the legislature of the U.S.

congruent ADJECTIVE congruent triangles have exactly the same shape and size
▷ **congruence** NOUN

conic ADJECTIVE to do with a cone

conical ADJECTIVE cone-shaped
▷ **conically** ADVERB

conifer (kon- if- er) NOUN conifers an evergreen tree with cones
▷ **coniferous** ADJECTIVE

conjecture NOUN conjectures guesswork or a guess
▷ **conjecture** VERB **conjectural** ADJECTIVE

conjugate VERB conjugates, conjugating, conjugated give all the different forms of a verb
▷ **conjugation** NOUN

conjunction NOUN conjunctions **1** a word that joins words or phrases or sentences, e.g., *and*, *but* **2** combination or union • *The four armies acted in conjunction.*

conjure VERB conjures, conjuring, conjured perform tricks that look like magic
▷ **conjuror** NOUN

Thesaurus

---

confront VERB **1** *He confronted an intruder in the hallway.* ► challenge, accost, approach, stand up to, take on, tackle, defy, face, meet, oppose, withstand, argue with, brave AN OPPOSITE IS avoid **2** *He realized he had to confront his problems and sort himself out.* ► tackle, face up to, address, deal with, cope with

confrontation NOUN *a serious confrontation with the authorities* ► conflict, dispute, disagreement, discord, contention, dissension, antagonism, hostility, friction, strife, clash

confuse VERB **1** *All these comments only confuse the issue.* ► complicate, muddle, obscure, cloud, obfuscate **2** *Too much detail will confuse us.* ► bewilder, perplex, baffle, puzzle, mystify, bemuse, disconcert, confound, (*more informal*) flummox, (*more informal*) floor

confused ADJECTIVE **1** *The children were very confused about what was happening.* ► bewildered, perplexed, baffled, puzzled, mystified, bemused, disconcerted, confounded, (*more informal*) flummoxed AN OPPOSITE IS clear **2** *Her clothes lay in a confused pile on the floor.* ► untidy, disorderly, disorganized, muddled, jumbled OPPOSITES

ARE tidy, organized **3** *confused accounts of the incident* ► vague, muddled, unclear, indistinct AN OPPOSITE IS clear

confusion NOUN **1** *a lot of confusion about which system to buy* ► uncertainty, indecision, misunderstanding, hesitation, doubt, ignorance **2** *People were wandering about in confusion.* ► bewilderment, perplexity, bafflement, mystification, shock **3** *The kitchen was in a terrible state of confusion.* ► disorder, disorganization, untidiness, clutter, chaos, mayhem, disarray, muddle, jumble, mess, shambles

congratulate VERB *I must congratulate Freda on her success.* ► praise, compliment, commend, applaud, acclaim

congratulations PLURAL NOUN **1** *We sent our congratulations on their wedding.* ► compliments, good wishes, greetings, felicitations **2** *You all deserve warm congratulations on the success of the enterprise.* ► praise, commendation, applause

congregate VERB *A large crowd had congregated in the town square.* ► gather, assemble, come together, collect, converge, convene, crowd together, rally, rally round, meet, flock together, join up, swarm, muster, throng round, accumulate

conjure up produce in your mind • *Mention of the Arctic conjures up visions of snow.*

connect VERB **connects, connecting, connected** **1** join together; link **2** think of things or people as being associated with each other

connection NOUN **connections** **1** a point where two things are connected; a link • *We all know there is a connection between smoking and cancer.* **2** a train, bus, etc., that leaves a station soon after another arrives, so that passengers can change from one to the other

connoisseur (kon- a- ser) NOUN **connoisseurs** a person with great experience and appreciation of something • *a connoisseur of wine*

conquer VERB **conquers, conquering, conquered** defeat or overcome
▷ **conqueror** NOUN

conquest NOUN **conquests** **1** a victory over someone **2** conquered territory

conscience (kon- shens) NOUN **consciences** knowing what is right and wrong, especially in your own actions

conscientious (kon- shee- en- shus) ADJECTIVE careful and honest about doing your work properly
▷ **conscientiously** ADVERB

conscientious objector NOUN **conscientious objectors** a person who refuses to serve in the armed forces because he or she believes it is morally wrong

conscious (kon- shus) ADJECTIVE **1** awake and knowing what is happening **2** aware of something • *I was not conscious of the time.* **3** done deliberately • *a conscious decision*
▷ **consciously** ADVERB **consciousness** NOUN

conscript (kon- skript) VERB **conscripts, conscripting, conscripted** make a person join the armed forces
▷ **conscription** NOUN

conscript (kon- skript) NOUN **conscripts** a conscripted person

consecrate VERB **consecrates, consecrating, consecrated** officially say that a thing, especially a building, is holy
▷ **consecration** NOUN

consecutive ADJECTIVE following one after another
▷ **consecutively** ADVERB

consensus NOUN **consensuses** general agreement; the opinion of most people

consent NOUN agreement to what someone wishes; permission

Thesaurus

connect VERB **1** *The speakers are connected to a powerful amplifier.* ► link, attach, couple, join, fasten AN OPPOSITE IS disconnect. **2** *Police believe the two crimes could be connected.*
► associate, link, relate, couple, compare, tie up, bracket together, put together AN OPPOSITE IS dissociate

connection NOUN *There is a connection between money and power.* ► relationship, link, association, correlation, correspondence, bond, affinity, coherence, contact, interrelationship, join, unity, (*more informal*) tie-up AN OPPOSITE IS distinction

conquer VERB **1** *Napoleon's attempt to conquer Europe* ► seize, capture, overrun, occupy, invade, take possession of, subjugate, take, win, annex, subject **2** *William of Normandy conquered the English at the Battle of Hastings.*
► defeat, beat, overcome, conquer, vanquish, subdue, crush, overpower, rout **3** *With a great effort she conquered her fears.* ► overcome, suppress, master, control, curb, surmount, prevail over

conqueror NOUN *He entered the capital of Bengal as a conqueror.* ► victor, subjugator, defeater, winner, champion, master

conquest NOUN *Alexander's conquest of the Persian Empire* ► defeat, subjection, subjugation, capture, invasion, occupation, annexation, appropriation, overthrow,

triumph (over), victory (over), (*more informal*) takeover

conscience NOUN **1** *His conscience forced him to admit the truth in the end.* ► moral sense, principles, morals, ethics, standards **2** *Large organizations have no conscience about getting rid of people.* ► scruples, compunction, misgivings, qualms, reservations

conscientious ADJECTIVE *a conscientious worker* ► hardworking, diligent, industrious, painstaking, thorough, meticulous, punctilious, accurate, attentive, dedicated, rigorous, careful, dutiful, unflagging, assiduous, scrupulous OPPOSITES ARE careless, irresponsible, lazy

conscious ADJECTIVE **1** *Despite the blow to his head, he remained conscious.* ► awake, aware, alert, compos mentis, sensible AN OPPOSITE IS unconscious **2** *It was a conscious attempt to deceive us.* ► deliberate, intended, intentional, calculated, knowing, planned, premeditated, studied, wilful AN OPPOSITE IS accidental

consecutive ADJECTIVE *Interest rates have remained unchanged for six consecutive months.* ► continuous, successive, uninterrupted, running (*six months running*), in succession (*six months in succession*), in a row (*six months in a row*)

consent VERB **1** *In the end she consented to do something about it.* ► agree, be willing, undertake OPPOSITES ARE refuse, decline

consent VERB consents, consenting, consented say that you are willing to do or allow what someone wishes

consequence NOUN consequences
1 something that happens as the result of an event or action **2** importance • *It is of no consequence.*

consequent ADJECTIVE happening as a result
▷ **consequently** ADVERB

conservation NOUN conserving; preservation, especially of the natural environment
▷ **conservationist** NOUN

conservative ADJECTIVE **1** liking traditional ways and disliking changes **2** moderate or cautious; not extreme • *a conservative estimate*
▷ **conservatively** ADVERB **conservatism** NOUN

Conservative NOUN Conservatives a person who supports the Conservative Party, a political party that favors private enterprise and freedom from state control
▷ **Conservative** ADJECTIVE

conserve VERB conserves, conserving, conserved prevent something valuable from being changed, spoiled, or wasted

consider VERB considers, considering, considered **1** think carefully about or give attention to something, especially in order to make a decision **2** have an opinion; think to be • *Consider yourself lucky.*

considerable ADJECTIVE fairly great • *a considerable amount*
▷ **considerably** ADVERB

considerate ADJECTIVE taking care not to inconvenience or hurt others
▷ **considerately** ADVERB

consideration NOUN considerations **1** being considerate **2** careful thought or attention **3** a fact that must be kept in mind **4** payment given as a reward
take into consideration allow for

considering PREPOSITION taking something into consideration • *The car runs well, considering its age.*

consist VERB consists, consisting, consisted be made up or composed of • *The apartment consists of three rooms.*

Thesaurus

---

2 consent to *He said the girl had consented to his advances.* ► agree to, allow, approve, concede, grant, authorize, permit, comply with
OPPOSITES ARE refuse, forbid

consent NOUN *The authorities refused their consent.* ► agreement, assent, permission, authorization, approval, backing, endorsement, (more informal) go-ahead

consequence NOUN **1** *Cooling of the stratosphere was seen as a consequence of the greenhouse effect.* ► result, effect, outcome, aftermath, by-product, corollary, repercussion, sequel, side effect, upshot **2** *These small losses are of little consequence.* ► importance, significance, account, concern, moment, note, value, weight

conservation NOUN *the conservation of energy and resources* ► preservation, protection, safeguarding, saving, careful management, economy, maintenance, upkeep AN OPPOSITE IS destruction

conservative ADJECTIVE **1** *conservative ideas; his conservative father* ► traditional, conventional, orthodox, reactionary, old-fashioned, die-hard, hidebound, moderate, narrow-minded, sober, unadventurous OPPOSITES ARE progressive, radical **2** *the conservative section of the party* ► right-wing, right-of-center, reactionary, traditionalist OPPOSITES ARE radical, socialist **3** *Fifty dollars is a conservative estimate.* ► cautious, moderate, reasonable, understated, unexaggerated AN OPPOSITE IS extreme

conserve VERB *It is important to conserve energy.* ► save, preserve, protect, sustain, maintain, safeguard, be economical with, use sparingly, keep, look after, store up OPPOSITES ARE waste, squander

consider VERB **1** *Donna paused to consider the possibilities.* ► think about, contemplate, ponder, reflect on, weigh, mull over, cogitate, deliberate, muse, meditate on, discuss, examine, ruminate, study, (informal) turn over **2** *I consider it a privilege.* ► regard (as), deem, count, think, judge, reckon, believe (to be)

considerable ADJECTIVE *There was a considerable amount of traffic on the road. He had inherited a considerable sum from his grandparents.*
► substantial, sizable, appreciable, significant, reasonable, respectable, tolerable, worthwhile, large, comfortable, noteworthy, noticeable, perceptible AN OPPOSITE IS negligible

considerate ADJECTIVE *We are encouraged to be polite, modest, and considerate to others.* ► kind, thoughtful, attentive, helpful, caring, obliging, generous, sensitive, accommodating OPPOSITES ARE inconsiderate, selfish

consideration NOUN *The matter needs careful consideration.* ► thought, attention, deliberation, reflection, examination, contemplation, meditation, scrutiny, review

consist VERB **consist of** *Audiences consist of very different types of people.* ► be composed of, comprise, be made of, include, contain, incorporate, involve

A
B
C
D
E
F
G
H
I
J
K
L
M
N
O
P
Q
R
S
T
U
V
W
X
Y
Z

consistency NOUN consistencies **1** being consistent **2** thickness or stiffness, especially of a liquid

consistent ADJECTIVE **1** keeping to a regular pattern or style; not changing **2** not contradictory
▷ **consistently** ADVERB

consolation NOUN consolations **1** consoling **2** something that consoles someone

console[1] (kon- sohl) VERB consoles, consoling, consoled comfort someone who is unhappy or disappointed

console[2] (kon- sohl) NOUN consoles a panel or unit containing the controls for equipment

consolidate VERB consolidates, consolidating, consolidated **1** make or become secure and strong **2** combine two or more organizations, funds, etc., into one
▷ **consolidation** NOUN

consonant NOUN consonants a letter that is not a vowel ● *b, c, d, f, etc. are consonants.*

conspicuous ADJECTIVE easily seen; noticeable
▷ **conspicuously** ADVERB **conspicuousness** NOUN

conspiracy NOUN conspiracies planning with others to do something illegal; a plot
▷ **conspirator** NOUN

constable NOUN constables a police officer of the lowest rank

constant ADJECTIVE **1** not changing; happening all the time **2** faithful or loyal
▷ **constantly** ADVERB **constancy** NOUN

constant NOUN constants **1** a thing that does not vary **2** (in science and mathematics) a number or value that does not change

constellation NOUN constellations a group of stars

constipated ADJECTIVE unable to empty the bowels easily or regularly
▷ **constipation** NOUN

constituency NOUN constituencies a district represented by a legislator elected by the people who live there

constituent NOUN constituents **1** one of the parts that form a whole thing **2** someone who lives in a particular constituency
▷ **constituent** ADJECTIVE

constitute VERB constitutes, constituting, constituted make up or form something
● *Twelve months constitute a year.*

constitution NOUN constitutions **1** the group of laws or principles that state how a country is to be organized and governed **2** the nature

Thesaurus

consistent ADJECTIVE **1** *a consistent pattern of behavior* ► steady, uniform, stable, regular, even, uniform, constant, unchanging, unvarying, dependable, reliable, predictable, unfailing **2** *The theory is consistent with recent research.* ► compatible, in accordance, in agreement, in harmony AN OPPOSITE IS inconsistent

consolation NOUN *I tried to offer her some consolation for her loss.* ► comfort, solace, sympathy, commiseration, compassion, reassurance, support, succor, encouragement, cheer, ease, help, relief

console VERB *His friends tried to console him.* ► comfort, solace, hearten, encourage, relieve, soothe, sympathize with, calm, cheer

consolidate VERB **1** *attempts to consolidate their reputation in Canada* ► strengthen, reinforce, fortify, enhance, stabilize, make secure, make strong AN OPPOSITE IS weaken **2** *All the resources need to be consolidated.* ► amalgamate, combine, integrate, merge, unify, bring together, fuse

consort VERB consort with *consorting with the opposition* ► associate with, socialize with, have dealings with, befriend, fraternize with, keep company with, mix with, be friends with, be seen with

conspicuous ADJECTIVE **1** *Her bright clothes made her conspicuous.* ► prominent, distinct, clearly visible, easily seen, noticeable,

apparent, perceptible AN OPPOSITE IS inconspicuous **2** *The infantry showed conspicuous bravery that day.* ► obvious, manifest, evident, outstanding, exceptional, marked, pronounced, unmistakable

conspiracy NOUN *They were involved in a conspiracy to kill the king.* ► plot, scheme, intrigue, machination, plan, stratagem

conspire VERB *They twice conspired to overthrow the dictatorship.* ► plot, scheme, intrigue, plan, hatch a plot, collude, connive, collaborate, consort, be in league

constant ADJECTIVE **1** *the constant hum of traffic on the bypass* ► continuous, continual, persistent, ceaseless, incessant, endless, unending OPPOSITES ARE changeable, irregular **2** *The wheel should turn at a constant speed* ► steady, regular, stable, uniform, even, invariable, fixed **3** *She proved to be a constant friend.* ► faithful, loyal, devoted, staunch, true, firm, dependable, reliable, dedicated OPPOSITES ARE fickle, unreliable

constantly ADVERB *The train times are constantly changing.* ► always, continually, repeatedly, all the time, forever

constitute VERB **1** *Their attitude constitutes a form of discrimination.* ► amount to, be equivalent to, be tantamount to, compose, comprise, form, make up **2** *A Scottish Parliament was constituted in 1999.* ► establish, set up, inaugurate, create, found, appoint

of the body in regard to health • *She has a strong constitution.* **3** constituting **4** the composition of something
▷ **constitutional** ADJECTIVE

constrict VERB **constricts, constricting, constricted** squeeze or tighten something by making it narrower
▷ **constriction** NOUN

construct VERB **constructs, constructing, constructed** make something by placing parts together; build
▷ **constructor** NOUN

construction NOUN **constructions** **1** constructing **2** something constructed; a building **3** two or more words put together to form a phrase or clause or sentence **4** an explanation or interpretation • *They put a bad construction on our refusal.*

constructive ADJECTIVE helpful and positive • *constructive suggestions*

consult VERB **consults, consulting, consulted** go to a person or book, etc., for information or advice
▷ **consultation** NOUN

consultant NOUN **consultants** a person who is qualified to give expert advice

consume VERB **consumes, consuming, consumed** **1** eat or drink something **2** use up • *Much time was consumed in waiting.* **3** destroy • *Fire consumed the building.*

consumer NOUN **consumers** a person who buys or uses goods or services

consummate (kon- **sum**- at) ADJECTIVE perfect; highly skilled • *a consummate artist*

consumption NOUN **1** consuming **2** (*old use*) tuberculosis of the lungs

contact NOUN **contacts** **1** touching **2** being in touch; communication **3** a person to communicate with when you need information or help

contact VERB **contacts, contacting, contacted** get in touch with a person

contact lens NOUN **contact lenses** a tiny lens worn against the eyeball, instead of glasses

contagious ADJECTIVE spreading by contact with an infected person • *a contagious disease*

contain VERB **contains, containing, contained** **1** have inside • *The box contains chocolates.* **2** consist of • *A gallon contains 8 pints.* **3** restrain; hold back • *Try to contain your laughter.*

Thesaurus

constraint NOUN *Political constraints prevented him from speaking his mind.* ► restriction, restraint, limitation, inhibition, control, hindrance, check

constriction NOUN *He felt a constriction in his throat.* ► tightening, tightness, narrowing, pressure, stricture

construct VERB **1** *The local council wants to construct a new bridge over the railway line.* ► build, erect, put up, set up, assemble **2** *We must construct a new form of society.* ► create, devise, develop, formulate, fashion, design, invent

construction NOUN **1** *In 1858 the construction of the present church was begun.* ► building, erection, assembly, creation, establishment, putting-up, setting-up, erecting **2** *The new building was a mainly timber construction.* ► building, edifice, erection, structure, framework

constructive ADJECTIVE *The talks proved to be helpful and constructive.* ► positive, useful, worthwhile, beneficial, advantageous, creative, helpful, practical, valuable AN OPPOSITE IS destructive

consult VERB **1** *He wanted to consult the workforce before introducing any changes.* ► speak to, confer with, refer to, seek advice from, debate with, discuss matters with, exchange views with **2** *Consult your doctor before attempting these exercises.* ► see, ask, get

advice from, refer to **3** *He consulted a list pinned to the wall.* ► refer to, turn to, look something up in

consume VERB **1** *A lot of food and drink was consumed that day.* ► eat, drink, devour, digest, swallow, feast on, (*more informal*) gobble up **2** *The factory consumes tons of tons of fuel each year.* ► use, use up, utilize, expend, absorb, swallow up, deplete, drain, eat into, employ, exhaust **3** *Fire consumed a row of buildings.* ► destroy, demolish, devastate, wipe out, annihilate, wreck, ravage, ruin **4** *George was consumed by guilt.* ► overcome, overwhelm, preoccupy, obsess, absorb

contact NOUN **1** *He had been avoiding physical contact with her all day.* ► touch, touching, proximity **2** *Contact between Europe and Africa can be traced back hundreds of years.* ► communication, connection, association **3** *Make sure all electrical contacts are secure.* ► connection, join **4** *I will ask one of my contacts in Los Angeles.* ► associate, connection, acquaintance, liaison

contact VERB *I'll contact them when I have more information.* ► notify, communicate with, get in touch with, get hold of, approach, correspond with, call, call on, phone, ring, speak to, talk to, (*more informal*) drop a line to

contain VERB **1** *The box contained bottles of red wine.* ► hold, accommodate **2** *The atlas contains photographs taken from space.* ► include, incorporate, comprise, consist of,

a b **c** d e f g h i j k l m n o p q r s t u v w x y z

container ➡ contented

A
B
C
D
E
F
G
H
I
J
K
L
M
N
O
P
Q
R
S
T
U
V
W
X
Y
Z

container NOUN containers **1** a box or bottle, etc., designed to contain something **2** a large boxlike object of standard design in which goods are transported

contaminate VERB contaminates, contaminating, contaminated make a thing dirty or impure or diseased, etc.; pollute
▷ contamination NOUN

contemplate VERB contemplates, contemplating, contemplated **1** look at something thoughtfully **2** consider or think about doing something • We are contemplating a visit to my sister's.
▷ contemplation NOUN contemplative ADJECTIVE

contemporary ADJECTIVE **1** belonging to the same period • Dickens was contemporary with Thackeray. **2** modern; up-to-date
• contemporary furniture

contemporary NOUN contemporaries a person who is contemporary with another or who is about the same age • She was my contemporary at college.

contempt NOUN a feeling of despising a person or thing

contemptible ADJECTIVE deserving contempt
• Hurting her feelings like that was a contemptible thing to do.

contemptuous ADJECTIVE feeling or showing contempt • She gave me a contemptuous look.
▷ contemptuously ADVERB

content¹ (kon- tent) ADJECTIVE contented
▷ contentment NOUN

content² (kon- tent) NOUN or **contents** PLURAL NOUN what something contains

contented ADJECTIVE happy with what you have; satisfied
▷ contentedly ADVERB

Thesaurus

---

be composed of **3** You will have to contain your impatience. ► restrain, curb, suppress, control, hold back, keep back, repress, check, stifle, limit

container NOUN a watertight container
► receptacle, vessel, holder, repository, canister, case

contaminate VERB Farming contaminates waterways every day. ► pollute, adulterate, defile, infect, poison, foul, soil, taint AN OPPOSITE IS purify

contemplate VERB **1** He contemplated her over his glasses. ► look at, view, observe, regard, survey, watch, eye, gaze at, stare at, (in literature) behold **2** She could not even contemplate what might happen. ► think about, consider, cogitate, deliberate, examine, mull over, plan, reflect on, study, work out **3** He contemplated leaving. ► consider, think about, envisage, have in mind, intend (to), propose **4** She sat quietly and contemplated. ► ponder, reflect, ruminate, think, meditate, muse

contemporary ADJECTIVE **1** The historical information comes from contemporary accounts.
► contemporaneous, concurrent, synchronous, coinciding, simultaneous, coexistent, of the time **2** a concert of contemporary music ► modern, current, present-day, recent, fashionable, the latest, newest

contempt NOUN She had nothing but contempt for them. ► disgust, scorn, disdain, loathing, abhorrence, derision, disparagement, detestation, dislike, disrespect, hatred, ridicule AN OPPOSITE IS admiration
feel OR **show contempt for** He felt contempt for their extreme views. ► despise, spurn, revile, detest

contemptible ADJECTIVE a contemptible insult
► despicable, shameful, disgraceful, detestable, hateful, deplorable, ignominious, loathsome, odious, mean, vile, low, cheap AN OPPOSITE IS admirable

contemptuous ADJECTIVE a contemptuous tone of voice ► scornful, disdainful, scathing, disrespectful, insulting, derisive, dismissive, supercilious, condescending, insolent, haughty, mocking, withering, arrogant AN OPPOSITE IS admiring
be contemptuous of ► denigrate, disparage, revile, malign, belittle, decry, impugn, abuse

contend VERB **1** political parties contending for power ► compete, struggle, vie, strive, fight, grapple, oppose one another, rival one another, contest, dispute **2** She contended that she had been given bad advice. ► claim, declare, maintain, aver, hold, assert, allege, argue, affirm, plead **3** contend with They have a lot to contend with. ► cope with, deal with, put up with, sort out, manage, organize

content ADJECTIVE He seems content now that he has his way. ► happy, contented, satisfied, pleased, gratified, glad, cheerful, smug

content NOUN **1** The article is admired more for its content than its style. ► subject matter, subject, theme, substance, argument, message **2** Butter has a high fat content. ► element, ingredient, substance **3** She smiled with content. ► happiness, contentment, satisfaction, pleasure

content VERB The answer seemed to content him.
► satisfy, please, placate, appease, pacify, soothe

contented ADJECTIVE a contented feeling
► happy, content, satisfied, pleased, gratified, glad, cheerful, smug OPPOSITES ARE discontented, dissatisfied

contest (kon- test) NOUN contests a competition; a struggle in which rivals try to obtain something or to do best

contestant NOUN contestants a person taking part in a contest; a competitor

context NOUN contexts 1 the words that come before and after a particular word or phrase and help to fix its meaning 2 the background to an event that helps to explain it

continent NOUN continents one of the main masses of land in the world ● *The continents are Europe, Asia, Africa, North America, South America, Australia, and Antarctica.*
▷ **continental** ADJECTIVE
the Continent the mainland of the United States

continual ADJECTIVE happening all the time, usually with breaks in between ● *Stop this continual quarreling!*
▷ **continually** ADVERB
USAGE Do not confuse with **continuous**. Continual is used to describe something that happens very frequently (*there were continual interruptions*) while continuous is used to describe something that happens without a pause (*there was continuous rain all day*).

continue VERB continues, continuing, continued 1 do something without stopping 2 begin again after stopping ● *The game will continue after lunch.*
▷ **continuation** NOUN

continuous ADJECTIVE going on and on; without a break
▷ **continuously** ADVERB **continuity** NOUN
USAGE See note at **continual**.

contort VERB contorts, contorting, contorted twist or force out of the usual shape or meaning
▷ **contortion** NOUN

contortionist NOUN contortionists a person who can twist his or her body into unusual positions

contour NOUN contours 1 a line on a map joining the points that are the same height above sea level 2 an outline

contraband NOUN smuggled goods

contraception NOUN a way of preventing pregnancy; birth control

contraceptive NOUN contraceptives a substance or device that prevents pregnancy

contract (kon- trakt) NOUN contracts 1 a formal agreement to do something 2 a document stating the terms of an agreement

Thesaurus

contention NOUN *Her contention is that the action would be illegal.* ► argument, claim, opinion, view, assertion, submission, belief, position

contentious ADJECTIVE 1 *a contentious issue* ► controversial, debatable, disputed, disputable, vexed 2 *a contentious group of people* ► quarrelsome, argumentative, disputatious, difficult

contentment NOUN *They achieved contentment in the country.* ► happiness, well-being, comfort, pleasure, content, contentedness, gratification, satisfaction, peace of mind, tranquillity, ease, fulfillment, relaxation, serenity OPPOSITES ARE dissatisfaction, unhappiness

contest NOUN 1 *a song contest; a boxing contest* ► competition, tournament, match, bout, encounter, fight, battle, dispute 2 *a contest for the leadership* ► struggle, challenge, confrontation, duel

contest VERB 1 *Seven candidates will contest the election.* ► enter, compete in, take part in, participate in, contend in, fight in, (*informal*) make a bid for, strive for, struggle for, take up the challenge of, vie for 2 *They decided to contest the decision.* ► oppose, challenge, dispute, object to, argue against, take issue with, query, refute, resist, debate, doubt, question

context NOUN *The events have to be put in their historical context.* ► background, circumstances, surroundings, framework, situation, ambience, frame of reference, milieu, position

continual ADJECTIVE *She needed continual reassurance. The service is affected by continual breakdowns.* ► constant, repeated, frequent, regular, perpetual, ceaseless, incessant, persistent OPPOSITES ARE occasional, sporadic

continuation NOUN 1 *He returned to the clinic for the continuation of his treatment.*
► resumption, maintenance, continuing, continuance, carrying on, extension, prolongation 2 *the continuation of a story*
► sequel, supplement, addition, appendix, postscript

continue VERB 1 *Police continued the search until dark.* ► carry on, maintain, keep up, keep going, persevere with, proceed with, prolong, pursue, (*more informal*) stick at 2 *Shall we continue after lunch?* ► resume, restart, begin again, recommence 3 *Talks continued all week.* ► last, carry on, go on, endure, persist, keep on, linger, live on, remain, stay, survive

continuous ADJECTIVE *three days of continuous rain* ► uninterrupted, unbroken, constant, steady, ceaseless, endless, incessant, persistent, nonstop OPPOSITES ARE intermittent, sporadic

contract NOUN *A contract is legally binding.*
► agreement, settlement, covenant, compact, commitment, deal, bond, pact, concordat,

contract ➡ contribute

contract (kon- trakt) VERB contracts, contracting, contracted **1** make or become smaller **2** make a contract **3** get an illness • *She contracted measles.*

contraction NOUN contractions **1** contracting **2** a shortened form of a word or words. *Can't is a contraction of cannot.*

contractor NOUN contractors a person who makes a contract, especially for building

contradict VERB contradicts, contradicting, contradicted **1** say that something said is not true or that someone is wrong **2** say the opposite of • *These rumors contradict previous ones.*
▷ **contradiction** NOUN **contradictory** ADJECTIVE

contraflow NOUN contraflows a flow of road traffic traveling in the opposite direction to the usual flow and close beside it

contralto NOUN contraltos a female singer with a low voice

contraption NOUN contraptions a strange-looking device or machine

contrary ADJECTIVE **1** (kon- tra- ree) of the opposite kind or direction, etc.; opposed; unfavorable **2** (kon- trair- ee) awkward and obstinate

contrary (kon- tra- ree) NOUN the opposite on the contrary the opposite is true

contrast NOUN contrasts **1** a difference clearly seen when things are compared **2** something showing a clear difference

contrast VERB contrasts, contrasting, contrasted **1** compare or oppose two things in order to show that they are clearly different **2** be clearly different when compared

contravene VERB contravenes, contravening, contravened act against a rule or law
▷ **contravention** NOUN

contribute VERB contributes, contributing, contributed **1** give money or help along with

---
Thesaurus
---

bargain, indenture, lease, treaty, understanding, undertaking

contract VERB **1** *The glass contracts as it cools. Labor markets contracted in this area.* ► shrink, lessen, diminish, reduce, become smaller, condense, shrivel, decrease, dwindle, wither, close up, draw together, fall away, narrow, slim down, thin out OPPOSITES ARE expand, enlarge **2** *The company contracted to build an extension to the house.* ► sign an agreement, undertake, covenant, make a deal, promise, agree, arrange **3** *The woman might have contracted smallpox.* ► develop, catch, get, become infected by, be taken ill with

contraction NOUN **1** *a contraction of overseas markets* ► shrinking, shrivelling, diminution, decline, decrease **2** *"Goodbye" is a contraction of "God be with you."* ► abbreviation, diminutive, short form, shortened form

contradict VERB **1** *I didn't like to contradict him but I really didn't agree.* ► disagree with, challenge, oppose, speak against, impugn **2** *The new evidence contradicts earlier conclusions.* ► conflict with, be at odds with, be inconsistent with, run counter to, challenge, disprove **3** *The statement was later contradicted by the president.* ► deny, repudiate, rebut, dispute, counter AN OPPOSITE IS confirm

contradictory ADJECTIVE *The two points of view are completely contradictory.* ► opposite, opposed, conflicting, contrary, incompatible, inconsistent, irreconcilable, different, discrepant, antithetical OPPOSITES ARE consistent, compatible

contraption NOUN *Above his head was a contraption consisting of springs and wires.* ► device, contrivance, gadget, apparatus, mechanism, invention, machine

contrary ADJECTIVE **1** (with the stress on *con*) *Other may take the contrary view.* ► opposite, opposing, opposed, contradictory, conflicting, contrasting, reverse, converse, different, other AN OPPOSITE IS similar **2** (with the stress on -*trary*, pronounced like *Mary*) *a contrary child* ► perverse, awkward, difficult, uncooperative, obstinate, unhelpful, tiresome, disobedient, vexatious AN OPPOSITE IS cooperative **3 contrary to** *The result was contrary to all expectations.* ► in conflict with, at odds with, at variance with, counter to

contrast NOUN *a noticeable contrast between what they say and what they do* ► difference, dissimilarity, disparity, variance, divergence, contradiction, opposition AN OPPOSITE IS similarity

contrast VERB **1** *People contrast the two brothers.* ► differentiate, distinguish, make distinctions between, discriminate between, compare **2** *contrast with Her fair hair contrasted with her dark dress.* ► set off, complement, clash with

contrasting ADJECTIVE *contrasting colors; contrasting opinions* ► complementary, conflicting, different, opposing, opposite AN OPPOSITE IS similar

contribute VERB **1** *Employers have to contribute a set amount to the fund.* ► give, subscribe, donate, provide, put up, supply, add, grant, bestow **2 contribute to** *The weather contributed to the success of the occasion.* ► play a part in, add to, be a factor in, have a hand in, make

other people **2** write something for a newspaper or magazine, etc. **3** help to cause something • *Tiredness contributed to the accident.*
▷ **contribution** NOUN **contributor** NOUN **contributory** ADJECTIVE

contrite ADJECTIVE very sorry for having done wrong

contrive VERB contrives, contriving, contrived plan cleverly; find a way of doing or making something

control VERB controls, controlling, controlled **1** have the power to make someone or something do what you want **2** hold something, especially anger, in check; restrain
▷ **controller** NOUN

control NOUN controlling a person or thing; authority
in control having control of something
out of control no longer able to be controlled

controls PLURAL NOUN the switches, etc., used to control a machine

controversial ADJECTIVE causing controversy

controversy (kon- tro- ver- see, kon- **trov**- er-see) NOUN controversies a long argument or disagreement

conundrum NOUN conundrums a riddle; a hard question

convalesce VERB convalesces, convalescing, convalesced be recovering from an illness
▷ **convalescence** NOUN **convalescent** ADJECTIVE, NOUN

convection NOUN the passing on of heat within liquid, air, or gas by circulation of the warmed parts

convenience NOUN conveniences **1** being convenient **2** something that is convenient **3** a public toilet
at your convenience whenever you find convenient; as it suits you

convenient ADJECTIVE easy to use or deal with or reach
▷ **conveniently** ADVERB

a
b
c
d
e
f
g
h
i
j
k
l
m
n
o
p
q
r
s
t
u
v
w
x
y
z

Thesaurus

---

for, enhance, help, reinforce, support, encourage

contribution NOUN *All income comes from charitable contributions.* ▶ donation, benefaction, payment, gift, subscription, allowance, endowment, grant, offering, sponsorship, (*more informal*) handout

contributor NOUN **1** *The charity has acquired several new contributors.* ▶ donor, benefactor, subscriber, supporter, patron, sponsor, giver, backer, helper **2** *a regular contributor to the magazine* ▶ writer, columnist, correspondent, freelance, journalist, reporter

contrivance NOUN *The blinds were opened by a strange contrivance at the side.* ▶ device, contraption, gadget, apparatus, mechanism, invention, machine

control NOUN **1** *this theme of giving back control over civic affairs to the local people* ▶ jurisdiction, administration, management, regulation, authority, charge, power, government, supervision, command, direction, oversight, organization, guidance, influence **2** *He needs to exercise a little more control and not lose his temper so much.* ▶ restraint, self-control, self-command, self-possession, composure **3** *Some of the controls were difficult to reach.* ▶ switch, knob, button, lever, handle, dial
gain control of *The Portuguese had gained control of the Indian Ocean a century earlier.*
▶ take over, dominate, usurp, win, annex, seize, steal

control VERB **1** *You have to be able to control all the resources.* ▶ be in charge of, manage, administer, have authority over, supervise,

govern, oversee, run, operate, look after **2** *He found it hard to control his temper.* ▶ restrain, check, contain, curb, confine, keep in check, master, repress, subdue, suppress

controversial ADJECTIVE *He wrote a controversial article on the death penalty.*
▶ contentious, controvertible, debatable, disputable, questionable, doubtful, polemical, problematical, arguable OPPOSITES ARE uncontroversial, straightforward

convene VERB **1** *The chairman convened a meeting.* ▶ call, summon, assemble, bring together, (*more formal*) convoke **2** *The committee convened at two o'clock.* ▶ assemble, meet, gather, come together

convenient ADJECTIVE **1** *He asked when it would be convenient to interview her.* ▶ suitable, appropriate, opportune, fitting, agreeable, neat, timely, usable OPPOSITES ARE inconvenient, awkward **2** *Fast foods are often the most convenient option.* ▶ practical, handy, useful, helpful, labor-saving **3** *There is a regular bus service and convenient shops.*
▶ nearby, accessible, handy, at hand, available **4** convenient for *The house was so convenient for New York City.* ▶ accessible to, within easy reach of, well situated for, handy for AN OPPOSITE IS inconvenient

convention NOUN **1** *All these social conventions can become tedious.* ▶ custom, practice, tradition, rule, protocol, canon, formality, matter of form, matter of etiquette **2** *political conventions* ▶ conference, meeting, congress, assembly, symposium **3** *a convention signed by all the countries of the area* ▶ agreement, treaty, accord, compact, understanding

145

conventional ➡ convulsion

A
B
C
D
E
F
G
H
I
J
K
L
M
N
O
P
Q
R
S
T
U
V
W
X
Y
Z

conventional ADJECTIVE **1** done or doing things in the accepted way; traditional **2** (said about weapons) not nuclear
▷ **conventionally** ADVERB **conventionality** NOUN

conversation NOUN conversations talk between people
▷ **conversational** ADJECTIVE

convert (kon- vert) VERB converts, converting, converted **1** change **2** cause a person to change his or her beliefs
▷ **converter** NOUN **conversion** NOUN

convex ADJECTIVE curved like the outside of a ball or circle (The opposite is concave)
▷ **convexity** NOUN

convey VERB conveys, conveying, conveyed **1** transport **2** communicate a message or idea etc.
▷ **conveyor** NOUN

conveyor belt NOUN conveyor belts a continuous moving belt for moving objects from one place to another

convict (kon- vikt) VERB convicts, convicting, convicted prove or declare that a certain person is guilty of a crime

convict (kon- vikt) NOUN convicts a convicted person who is in prison

conviction NOUN convictions **1** convicting or being convicted of a crime **2** being convinced **3** a firm opinion or belief
carry conviction be convincing

convince VERB convinces, convincing, convinced make a person feel certain that something is true

convoy NOUN convoys a group of ships traveling together

convulsion NOUN convulsions **1** a violent movement of the body **2** a violent upheaval

Thesaurus

conventional ADJECTIVE **1** *He was willing to follow conventional ideas.* ▶ orthodox, established, traditional, customary, prevalent, mainstream, commonplace, routine, unoriginal, hackneyed OPPOSITES ARE unconventional, unorthodox **2** *Kevin was a conventional man.* ▶ conservative, hidebound, traditional, traditionalist, conformist, formal, correct, proper, bourgeois, stereotyped, unadventurous, unimaginative, unoriginal, (more informal) stuffy, (more informal) fuddy-duddy OPPOSITES ARE unconventional, radical **3** *A conventional telephone can be a lot less complicated than many cell phones.* ▶ standard, normal, regular, traditional, ordinary

converge VERB *The light rays converge to form a sharp image.* ▶ merge, combine, meet, join, come together, coincide OPPOSITES ARE separate, diverge

conversation NOUN *The rest of the conversation was in French.* ▶ discussion, talk, discourse, dialogue, exchange, consultation, (more informal) chat

conversion NOUN **1** *the conversion of waste into forms of energy* ▶ change, changing, turning, transformation **2** *The house has had a loft conversion.* ▶ adaptation, alteration, renovation, reconstruction, rebuilding, modification

convert VERB **1** *We plan to convert the loft into a workroom. Most of her novels have now been converted into films.* ▶ adapt, change, turn, rebuild, reconstruct, renovate, modify, reorganize **2** *a device for converting digital data into audio signals* ▶ turn, change, transform, translate

convey VERB **1** *A shuttle service conveys passengers from the city to the suburbs.*

▶ transport, carry, take, transfer, deliver, bring, fetch, move **2** *The dancer's movements can convey a variety of meanings.*
▶ communicate, signify, indicate, impart, disclose, relate, imply, mean, reveal, put across, get across

convict NOUN (with the stress on con-) *He looked like a convict in his striped pajamas.* ▶ prisoner, criminal, condemned person

convict VERB (with the stress on -vict) *A jury had earlier convicted Duncan of assault.* ▶ condemn, declare guilty, find guilty OPPOSITES ARE acquit, clear

conviction NOUN **1** *He spoke with complete conviction.* ▶ confidence, assurance, certainty, sureness, positiveness, firmness AN OPPOSITE IS uncertainty **2** *She has keenly felt political convictions.* ▶ belief, opinion, view, principle, persuasion, creed, faith, tenet

convince VERB *It will be difficult to convince them. She tried to convince herself that nobody would have heard her.* ▶ persuade, assure, prove to, reassure, satisfy, sway, win over, bring round

convincing ADJECTIVE **1** *a convincing argument* ▶ strong, powerful, conclusive, cogent, decisive, compelling, definite, persuasive, unambiguous, unarguable, unequivocal AN OPPOSITE IS inconclusive **2** *a convincing victory* ▶ decisive, conclusive, resounding, emphatic, impressive

convoy NOUN *a convoy of ships* ▶ group, fleet, armada, procession

convulsion NOUN **1** *The convulsions stopped and Charles lay back exhausted.* ▶ fit, seizure, spasm, attack, paroxysm **2** *seismic convulsions; a political convulsion* ▶ upheaval, disturbance, tremor, turbulence, eruption, outburst

146

coo VERB coos, cooing, cooed make a dove's soft murmuring sound
▷ **coo** NOUN

cook VERB cooks, cooking, cooked make food ready to eat by heating it
cook up (*informal*) if you cook up a story or plan, you invent it

cook NOUN cooks a person who cooks

cookery NOUN the skill of cooking food

cool ADJECTIVE **1** fairly cold; not hot or warm **2** calm; not enthusiastic
▷ **coolly** ADVERB **coolness** NOUN

cool VERB cools, cooling, cooled make or become cool
▷ **cooler** NOUN

cooped up ADJECTIVE having to stay in a place which is small and uncomfortable

cooperate VERB cooperates, cooperating, cooperated work helpfully with other people
▷ **cooperation** NOUN **cooperative** ADJECTIVE

coordinate VERB coordinates, coordinating, coordinated organize people or things to work properly together
▷ **coordination** NOUN **coordinator** NOUN

coordinate NOUN coordinates either of the pair of numbers or letters used to fix the position of a point on a graph or map

cope VERB copes, coping, coped manage or deal with something successfully

copious ADJECTIVE plentiful; in large amounts
▷ **copiously** ADVERB

copper NOUN coppers **1** a reddish-brown metal used to make wire, coins, etc. **2** a reddish-brown color **3** a coin made of copper or metal of this color
▷ **copper** ADJECTIVE

copse NOUN copses a small group of trees

copulate VERB copulates, copulating, copulated have sexual intercourse with someone
▷ **copulation** NOUN

Thesaurus

convulsive ADJECTIVE *convulsive movements* ► spasmodic, jerky, shaking, uncontrolled, uncoordinated, violent, (*more informal*) twitchy

cook NOUN *the hotel's new cook* ► chef

cook VERB *She cooked them both a romantic dinner.* ► prepare, make, get, put together, (*more informal*) fix RELATED ADJECTIVE ► culinary
cook something up *He cooked up an idea for getting her to go with him.* ► concoct, devise, contrive, plot, scheme

cool ADJECTIVE **1** *the cool air of early morning* ► fresh, bracing, crisp, brisk, chilly, chilled, (*more informal*) nippy OPPOSITES ARE warm, balmy **2** *We got a cool response.* ► unfriendly, chilly, lukewarm, unwelcoming, frigid, hostile, unsympathetic, reserved, aloof, (*informal*) standoffish OPPOSITES ARE warm, friendly, enthusiastic **3** *He was determined to keep cool in the crisis.* ► calm, composed, collected, clear-headed, self-controlled, self-possessed, unflustered, unruffled **4** (*informal*) *She seems to think she's so cool.* ► fashionable, trendy, stylish, sophisticated, chic **5** (*informal*) *It's a cool song.* ► good, excellent, super, superb

cool NOUN *He finally lost his cool and started shouting.* ► composure, self-control, self-possession, calm, calmness

cool VERB **1** *He threw open the shutters to cool the room.* ► chill, make cooler, lower the temperature of **2** *Cool the mixture in the fridge for about an hour.* ► chill, refrigerate, make cold **3** *Their enthusiasm had begun to cool. Recent events had cooled their enthusiasm.* ► lessen, reduce, moderate, dampen, diminish, abate, take the edge off OR lose its edge

cooped up ADJECTIVE *She doesn't like being cooped up at home all day.* ► confined, shut in,

shut up, caged, trapped, locked up, imprisoned, incarcerated

cooperate VERB **1** *Several police forces cooperated in the operation.* ► collaborate, combine, unite, work together, join forces, team up **2** *cooperate with He absolutely refused to cooperate with them.* ► assist, help, support, work with

cooperation NOUN **1** *wise cooperation between management and workers* ► collaboration, coordination, joint action, teamwork, unity, mutual support OPPOSITES ARE conflict, rivalry **2** *She thanked them all for their cooperation.* ► assistance, help, helpfulness, support, backing

cooperative ADJECTIVE **1** *The staff was pleasant and cooperative.* ► helpful, obliging, accommodating, supportive, constructive, willing, keen AN OPPOSITE IS uncooperative **2** *The project was achieved by a cooperative effort.* ► joint, combined, collective, concerted, coordinated, corporate, shared, communal AN OPPOSITE IS individual

coordinate VERB *A committee will coordinate all the sporting activities.* ► harmonize, organize, bring together, synchronize, systematize

cope VERB **1** *She is too old now to cope by herself.* ► manage, survive, carry on, get by, fend for yourself, make do **2** *cope with We found so many problems at once difficult to cope with.* ► deal with, handle, manage, contend with, endure, tolerate

copious ADJECTIVE *They sat listening and writing copious notes. A long breakfast of bagels and copious coffee* ► plenty of, abundant, plentiful, extensive, substantial, profuse, lavish, generous, ample, numerous, full OPPOSITES ARE sparse, meager

copy NOUN **copies 1** a thing made to look like another **2** something written or typed out again from its original form **3** one of a number of specimens of the same book or newspaper, etc.

copy VERB **copies, copying, copied 1** make a copy of something **2** do the same as someone else; imitate

copyright NOUN the legal right to print a book, reproduce a picture, record a piece of music, etc.

coral NOUN **1** a hard red, pink, or white substance formed by the skeletons of tiny sea creatures massed together **2** a pink color

cord NOUN **cords 1** a long thin flexible strip of twisted threads or strands **2** a piece of flex **3** a cordlike structure in the body • *the spinal cord* **4** corduroy
USAGE Do not confuse with **chord**.

cordial ADJECTIVE warm and friendly
▷ **cordially** ADVERB **cordiality** NOUN

corduroy NOUN cotton cloth with velvet ridges

core NOUN **cores 1** the part in the middle of something **2** the hard central part of an apple or pear, etc., containing the seeds

corgi NOUN **corgis** a small dog with short legs and upright ears

cork NOUN **corks 1** the lightweight bark of a kind of oak tree **2** a stopper for a bottle, made of cork or other material

cork VERB **corks, corking, corked** close something with a cork

corkscrew NOUN **corkscrews 1** a device for removing corks from bottles **2** a spiral

corn[1] NOUN **1** the seed of wheat and similar plants **2** a plant, such as wheat, grown for its grain

corn[2] NOUN **corns** a small hard painful lump on the foot

cornea NOUN **corneas** the transparent covering over the pupil of the eye
▷ **corneal** ADJECTIVE

corner NOUN **corners 1** the angle or area where two lines or sides or walls meet or where two streets join **2** a free hit or kick from the corner of a hockey or soccer field **3** a region • *a quiet corner of the world*

corner VERB **corners, cornering, cornered 1** drive someone into a corner or other position from which it is difficult to escape **2** travel around a corner **3** obtain possession of all or most of something • *corner the market*

cornet NOUN **cornets 1** a cone-shaped wafer, etc., holding ice cream **2** a musical instrument rather like a trumpet

cornflakes PLURAL NOUN toasted maize flakes eaten as a breakfast cereal

cornucopia NOUN **1** a horn-shaped container overflowing with fruit and flowers **2** a plentiful supply of good things

corny ADJECTIVE **cornier, corniest** (*informal*) **1** repeated so often that people are tired of it • *a corny joke.* **2** sentimental

corollary (kar-o-ler-ee) NOUN **corollaries** a fact, etc., that logically results from another • *The work is difficult and, as a corollary, tiring.*

coronary NOUN **coronaries** short for **coronary thrombosis**, blockage of an artery carrying

---

Thesaurus

---

copy NOUN **1** *Keep a copy of your letter.*
► duplicate, photocopy, (*trademark*) Xerox, facsimile, transcript, clone, double, pattern, print, representation, tracing **2** *The painting is only a copy.* ► reproduction, replica, imitation, likeness, model, fake, forgery, twin USAGE You use *fake* or *forgery* when you mean a copy that is intended to deceive people. AN OPPOSITE IS original

copy VERB **1** *Copy the passage from the book.*
► write out, reproduce, make a copy of, duplicate, repeat **2** *He copied several drawings by Hogarth.* ► reproduce, make a copy of, forge, fake, plagiarize, counterfeit, crib, follow USAGE You use *fake* or *forge* or *counterfeit* when you mean make a copy that is intended to deceive people. **3** *A lot of musicians have tried to copy their sound.* ► imitate, mimic, reproduce, emulate, ape, impersonate, parrot, poach

cord NOUN *I tightened the cord on the hood of my jacket.* ► string, thread, strap, tape, rope, strand, cable

core NOUN **1** *the earth's core* ► center, nucleus, heart, middle, inside **2** *the core of the problem* ► heart, essence, crux, nub, central issue, kernel, (*more informal*) nitty-gritty

corn NOUN *a field of corn* ► grain, cereal, cereal crop, wheat, barley

corner NOUN **1** *Turn left at the corner.* ► bend, curve, turning **2** *Three women sat in a corner of the room.* ► nook, niche, recess, alcove **3** *Stuart felt he was in a bit of a corner.*
► predicament, plight, quandary, dilemma, awkward situation, mess, (*more informal*) spot, (*more informal*) scrape, (*more informal*) stew around the corner *The shops are around the corner.* ► nearby, close at hand, not far away, within reach

corner VERB *The animal had cornered its prey.*
► trap, shut in, bring to bay, run to ground, capture, catch

corny ADJECTIVE *corny jokes* ► hackneyed, banal, stereotyped, stale, feeble, tired

A B **C** D E F G H I J K L M N O P Q R S T U V W X Y Z

blood to the heart [from Latin *corona* = crown: the coronary arteries encircle the heart like a crown]

coronation NOUN coronations the crowning of a king or queen

corporal NOUN corporals a soldier ranking next below a sergeant

corporal punishment NOUN punishment on the body, such as spanking or caning

corps (kor) NOUN corps (korz) **1** a special army unit • *the Medical Corps* **2** a large group of soldiers **3** a set of people doing the same job • *the diplomatic corps* [from French, from Latin *corpus* = body]

corpse NOUN corpses a dead body

corpuscle NOUN corpuscles one of the red or white cells in blood

correct ADJECTIVE **1** true; accurate; without any mistakes **2** proper; done or said in an approved way
▷ **correctly** ADVERB **correctness** NOUN

correct VERB corrects, correcting, corrected **1** make a thing correct by altering or adjusting it **2** mark the mistakes in something **3** point out or punish a person's faults
▷ **correction** NOUN **corrective** ADJECTIVE

correspond VERB corresponds, corresponding, corresponded **1** write letters to each other **2** agree; match • *Your story corresponds with his.* **3** be similar or equivalent • *Their assembly corresponds to our legislature.*

correspondence NOUN **1** letters; writing letters **2** similarity; agreement

corridor NOUN corridors a passage in a building

corroborate VERB corroborates, corroborating, corroborated help to confirm a statement, etc.
▷ **corroboration** NOUN

corrode VERB corrodes, corroding, corroded destroy metal gradually by chemical action
▷ **corrosion** NOUN **corrosive** ADJECTIVE

corrugated ADJECTIVE shaped into alternate ridges and grooves • *corrugated iron*

corrupt ADJECTIVE **1** dishonest; accepting bribes **2** wicked **3** decaying

Thesaurus

corporation NOUN **1** *a business corporation* ► company, firm, organization, concern, enterprise **2** *a city corporation* ► council, town council, local authority

corpse NOUN *Police found the corpse under the floorboards.* ► body, dead body, remains, cadaver, carcass, skeleton

correct ADJECTIVE **1** *What is the correct time? Not all the information proved correct.* ► right, accurate, exact, true, precise, genuine, authentic, reliable, factual, faithful, faultless, flawless, strict OPPOSITES ARE inaccurate, wrong **2** *She wanted to know the correct course of action.* ► right, proper, appropriate, fitting, suitable, acceptable, just OPPOSITES ARE inappropriate, wrong **3** *correct behavior* ► proper, decent, well mannered, tactful, unexceptionable

correct VERB **1** *Please correct your mistakes.* ► rectify, put right, make good, amend, remedy, cure, redress, adjust, alter, repair, right **2** *Your work will be corrected within two days.* ► mark, assess, evaluate, appraise **3** *She corrected him for his rudeness.* ► scold, admonish, rebuke, chastise, punish

correction NOUN *the correction of errors* ► rectification, righting, putting right, resolution, adjustment, amendment

correspond VERB **1** correspond to *The translator must choose words that correspond to the sense of the original.* ► match, fit, conform to, accord with, agree with, be consistent with, parallel, concur with, harmonize with, square with, tally with, convey **2** *Emma and I corresponded for many years.* ► communicate, exchange letters, write to each other

correspondence NOUN **1** *a collection of the composer's published correspondence* ► letters, communications, memoranda, notes **2** *There is some correspondence between the two ideas.* ► correlation, similarity, resemblance, comparability, agreement

corresponding ADJECTIVE *Climate change brings a corresponding change in average temperature.* ► matching, equivalent, commensurate, related, analogous, appropriate, complementary, parallel

corrupt ADJECTIVE **1** *The government is accused of being corrupt and incompetent.* ► dishonest, dishonorable, unprincipled, unscrupulous, untrustworthy, underhand, disreputable, discreditable, bribable, unsound, false, (more informal) bent OPPOSITES ARE honest, reputable **2** *They were involved in some form of corrupt practice.* ► dishonest, crooked, criminal, fraudulent, unethical **3** *Some people say society is getting more corrupt.* ► sinful, immoral, decadent, degenerate, depraved, dissolute, debauched, rotten, wicked, evil, iniquitous, low, perverted, profligate, venal AN OPPOSITE IS moral

corrupt VERB **1** *Some firms even try to corrupt local officials.* ► bribe, suborn, buy off, pay off, influence, (more informal) fix **2** *Pornography corrupts the innocent.* ► pervert, deprave, debauch, lead astray, make corrupt, contaminate, degrade, tempt, seduce

a
b
c
d
e
f
g
h
i
j
k
l
m
n
o
p
q
r
s
t
u
v
w
x
y
z

A
B
C
D
E
F
G
H
I
J
K
L
M
N
O
P
Q
R
S
T
U
V
W
X
Y
Z

corrupt VERB corrupts, corrupting, corrupted **1** cause someone to become dishonest or wicked **2** spoil; cause something to decay ▷ **corruption** NOUN **corruptible** ADJECTIVE

cosine NOUN cosines (in a right-angled triangle) the ratio of the length of a side adjacent to one of the acute angles to the length of the hypotenuse COMPARE sine

cosmetic NOUN cosmetics a substance (e.g., face powder or lipstick) put on the skin to make it look more attractive

cosmetic surgery NOUN surgery carried out to make people look more attractive

cosmic ADJECTIVE **1** to do with the universe **2** to do with outer space • *cosmic rays*

cosmopolitan ADJECTIVE from many countries; containing people from many countries

cosmos (koz- moss) NOUN the universe

cost NOUN costs **1** the amount of money needed to buy, do, or make something **2** the effort or loss needed to achieve something **at all costs** or **at any cost** no matter what the cost or difficulty may be

cost VERB costs, costing, cost **1** have a certain amount as its price or charge **2** cause the loss of • *This war has cost many lives.* **3** (*past tense* is costed) estimate the cost of something

costly ADJECTIVE costlier, costliest expensive ▷ **costliness** NOUN

costume NOUN costumes clothes, especially for a particular purpose or of a particular place or period

cosy ADJECTIVE cosier, cosiest warm and comfortable ▷ **cosily** ADVERB **cosiness** NOUN

cot NOUN cots a small bed with high sides [from Hindi *khat* = framework of a bed]

cottage NOUN cottages a small simple house, especially in the country

cotton NOUN **1** a soft white substance covering the seeds of a tropical plant; the plant itself **2** thread made from this substance **3** cloth made from cotton thread

cotton wool NOUN soft fluffy material originally made from cotton

couch NOUN **1** a long soft seat like a sofa **2** a sofa or settee

couch VERB couches, couching, couched express in words of a certain kind • *The request was couched in polite terms.*

cough (kof) VERB coughs, coughing, coughed send out air from the lungs with a sudden sharp sound

cough NOUN coughs **1** the act or sound of coughing **2** an illness that makes you cough

could past tense of can²

couldn't (*mainly spoken*) could not

council NOUN councils a group of people chosen or elected to organize or discuss something, especially those elected to organize the affairs of a town or county USAGE Do not confuse with counsel.

councillor NOUN councillors a member of a town or county council

council tax NOUN council taxes a tax paid to a local authority to pay for local services, based on the estimated value of someone's house or apartment

counsel NOUN counsels **1** advice • *give counsel* **2** a lawyer or group of lawyers representing someone in a lawsuit

Thesaurus

corruption NOUN **1** *He was found guilty of treason, espionage, and corruption.* ► dishonesty, deception, misconduct, bribery, fraud AN OPPOSITE IS honesty **2** *all kinds of moral corruption* ► sin, immorality, degradation, depravity, degeneracy, impurity OPPOSITES ARE morality, purity

cosmopolitan ADJECTIVE **1** *a large city with a cosmopolitan atmosphere* ► international, multicultural, sophisticated AN OPPOSITE IS provincial **2** *cosmopolitan attitudes* ► worldly, well traveled, sophisticated, urbane, liberal

cost NOUN **1** *The cost of a ticket has increased.* ► price, charge (for), expense, amount, payment (for), levy (on), tax (on), outlay (on), expenditure (on), rate (for), value, fare, figure **2** *The cost in human lives is too great.* ► sacrifice, loss, penalty, price, suffering

cost VERB **1** *Each item on this shelf costs a dollar.* ► be priced at, sell for, go for, come to, fetch, realize, (*more informal*) set you back

costly ADJECTIVE *The five-star service is very costly.* ► expensive, dear, overpriced, exorbitant, (*more informal*) pricey

costume NOUN *a prize for the best costume* ► outfit, dress, ensemble, clothing, suit, attire, (*informal*) get-up

cosy ADJECTIVE *They lived in a cosy little house.* ► snug, comfortable, warm, homely, restful, secure, intimate, reassuring, relaxing, soft, (*more informal*) comfy AN OPPOSITE IS uncomfortable

cottage NOUN *a cottage in the country* ► little house, bungalow, cabin, chalet

couch NOUN *A cat sat next to her on the couch.* ► sofa, settee, chesterfield, ottoman, divan

council NOUN **1** *The council is responsible for maintaining the roads.* ► local authority, legislature, corporation, assembly **2** *a meeting of the society's administrative council* ► board, committee, commission, panel

counsel ➡ courage

take counsel with consult
USAGE Do not confuse with council.

counsel VERB counsels, counselling, counselled give advice to someone; recommend

count[1] VERB counts, counting, counted **1** say numbers in their proper order **2** find the total of something by using numbers **3** include in a total • *There are six of us, counting the dog.* **4** be important • *It's what you do that counts.* **5** regard; consider • *I should count it an honor to be invited.*
count on rely on

count NOUN counts **1** counting **2** a number reached by counting; a total **3** any of the points being considered, e.g., in accusing someone of crimes • *guilty on all counts*

count[2] NOUN counts a foreign nobleman

countdown NOUN countdowns counting numbers backward to zero before an event, especially the launching of a space rocket

counter[1] NOUN counters **1** a flat surface over which customers are served in a shop, bank, etc. **2** a small round playing piece used in board games **3** a device for counting things

counter[2] VERB counters, countering, countered **1** counteract **2** counterattack; return an opponent's blow by hitting back

counteract VERB counteracts, counteracting, counteracted act against something and reduce or prevent its effects
▷ **counteraction** NOUN

counterbalance NOUN counterbalances a weight or influence that balances another
▷ **counterbalance** VERB

counterfeit (**kownt**- er- fit) ADJECTIVE fake; not genuine

counterfeit VERB counterfeits, counterfeiting, counterfeited forge or make an imitation of something

counterfoil NOUN counterfoils a section of a check or receipt, etc., that is torn off and kept as a record

counterpart NOUN counterparts a person or thing that corresponds to another • *Their prime minister is the counterpart of our president.*

countless ADJECTIVE too many to count

country NOUN countries **1** the land occupied by a nation **2** all the people of a country **3** the countryside

countryside NOUN an area with fields, woods, villages, etc., away from towns

county NOUN counties each of the main areas that a country is divided into for local government

coup (koo) NOUN coups a sudden action taken to win power; a clever victory

couple NOUN couples two people or things considered together; a pair

couple VERB couples, coupling, coupled fasten or link two things together

couplet NOUN couplets a pair of lines in rhyming verse

coupon NOUN coupons a piece of paper that gives you the right to receive or do something

courage NOUN the ability to face danger or difficulty or pain even when you are afraid; bravery
▷ **courageous** ADJECTIVE

Thesaurus

count VERB **1** *He was counting the number of cars parked along the street.* ► add up, total, calculate, work out, reckon, check, (*more informal*) tot up **2** *It's important for people to feel that they count.* ► matter, be important, have significance, signify **3** **count on** *You can count on my support.* ► rely on, depend on, bank on, be sure of, trust, believe in, expect, have faith in

counteract VERB *new laws to counteract terrorism* ► prevent, resist, oppose, curb, forestall, fight against, act against, work against, thwart, frustrate, foil, reduce, neutralize, withstand

countless ADJECTIVE *They have to make countless decisions every day.* ► innumerable, untold, myriad, numerous, numberless, unnumbered, endless, immeasurable, incalculable, infinite, many, measureless, limitless AN OPPOSITE is few

country NOUN **1** *a country of warlike people* ► nation, land, state, territory, realm **2** *They could return to their own country at last.*

► homeland, home, native land, native soil, mother country, country of origin, birthplace **3** *The president would appeal to the country in an election.* ► people, nation, public, populace, population, community **4** *You drive through wide open country.* ► terrain, landscape, countryside, scenery, surroundings, environment RELATED ADJECTIVE ► rural

couple NOUN **1** *A couple was dancing on the balcony.* ► pair, twosome, partners, duo, husband and wife **2** *Let me know if you see him in the next couple of days.* ► few, two or three
USAGE You can also say *in the next day or so.*

couple VERB *A second car is coupled to the train at Boston.* ► connect, attach, join, link, fasten, hitch, yoke, unite (with), combine (with), pair

coupon NOUN **1** *The offer includes money-saving coupons.* ► voucher, token, ticket, certificate **2** *For more information fill in the coupon below.* ► form, tear-off slip, slip

courage NOUN *It needs courage to argue with them.* ► bravery, audacity, boldness, daring,

a
b
c
d
e
f
g
h
i
j
k
l
m
n
o
p
q
r
s
t
u
v
w
x
y
z

A
B
C
D
E
F
G
H
I
J
K
L
M
N
O
P
Q
R
S
T
U
V
W
X
Y
Z

courier (koor- ee- er) NOUN **couriers 1** a messenger **2** a person employed to guide and help a group of tourists

course NOUN **courses 1** the direction in which something goes; a route ● *the ship's course* **2** a series of events or actions, etc. ● *Your best course is to start again.* **3** a series of lessons, exercises, etc. **4** part of a meal ● *the dinner course* **5** a racecourse **6** a golf course of course without a doubt; as we expected

court NOUN **courts 1** the royal household **2** a court of law; the judges, etc., in a court **3** an enclosed area for games such as tennis or netball **4** a courtyard

court VERB **courts, courting, courted** try to win somebody's love or support [from early French, from Latin *cohors* = a crowd of people]

courteous (ker- tee- us) ADJECTIVE polite
▷ **courteously** ADVERB **courtesy** NOUN

courtier NOUN **courtiers** (old use) one of a king's or queen's companions at court

courtly ADJECTIVE dignified and polite

courtship NOUN **1** courting someone, especially a boyfriend or girlfriend **2** the mating ritual of some birds and animals

courtyard NOUN **courtyards** a space surrounded by walls or buildings

cousin NOUN **cousins** a child of your uncle or aunt

cover VERB **covers, covering, covered 1** place one thing over or around another; conceal **2** travel a certain distance ● *We covered ten miles a day.* **3** aim a gun at somebody ● *I've got you covered.* **4** protect by insurance or a guarantee ● *These goods are covered against fire or theft.* **5** be enough money to pay for something ● *$10 should cover my fare.* **6** deal with or include ● *The book covers all kinds of farming.*
▷ **coverage** NOUN
cover up conceal something, especially an awkward fact or piece of information

cover NOUN **covers 1** a thing used for covering something else; a lid, wrapper, envelope, etc. **2** the binding of a book **3** something that hides or shelters or protects you

cow NOUN **cows** the fully grown female of cattle or of certain other large animals (e.g., elephant, whale, or seal)

Thesaurus
---

nerve, pluck, gallantry, determination, fearlessness, fortitude, heroism, (more informal) bottle, (more informal) grit, (more informal) guts, (much more informal) spunk AN OPPOSITE IS cowardice

courageous ADJECTIVE *It was a courageous attempt against all the odds.* ► brave, valiant, daring, audacious, spirited, intrepid, plucky, adventurous, fearless AN OPPOSITE IS cowardly

course NOUN **1** *a beginner's course in German* ► program of study, course of study, educational program, classes, lessons, studies **2** *The aircraft had changed its course again.* ► direction, route, way, tack, path, flight path, bearing, itinerary **3** *an event that changed the course of history* ► progress, progression, development, advance, evolution, flow, unfolding, future **4** *the best course to adopt* ► plan, plan of action, procedure, approach, method, programme, policy **5** *They had only just started the main course.* ► dish, part of a meal, menu item **6** *six laps of the course* ► track, circuit, ground, stadium

court NOUN **1** *The court acquitted them all.* ► court of law, bench, tribunal **2** *entertainment for the Queen's court* ► entourage, followers, royal household, establishment **3** *a court for basketball games* ► enclosure, playing area, ground, field

courteous ADJECTIVE *The staff are always helpful and courteous.* ► polite, civil, obliging,

considerate, respectful, well mannered, affable, civilized, refined

courtesy NOUN *Everyone is entitled to the same level of courtesy.* ► politeness, consideration, civility, respect, attention

cover NOUN **1** *The computer screen has its own plastic cover.* ► covering, envelope, wrapper, case **2** *Lift the cover and look inside.* ► lid, top, cap **3** *The book has a blue cover.* ► jacket, dust jacket, dust cover, wrapper **4** *a thick cover of snow* ► covering, layer, coat, coating, blanket, carpet, cloak, overlay **5** *The trees provide some sort of cover.* ► shelter, protection, refuge, shield, haven, defense **6** *The business is a cover for spying activities.* ► front, facade, pretext, disguise, screen

cover VERB **1** *She covered her knees with a blanket.* ► envelop, enclose, protect, overlay USAGE You can also say *She put* (or *placed*) *a blanket over her knees.* **2** *The car was covered in mud.* ► coat, cake, encrust, plaster, smother, spread **3** *The book covers most of the main topics.* ► deal with, treat, consider, include, contain, comprise, encompass, embrace, provide for, incorporate **4** *The money should cover most of our needs.* ► cater for, be enough for, meet, suffice for, pay for

covering NOUN *a light covering of snow* ► cover, layer, coat, coating, blanket, carpet, cloak, overlay

coward NOUN cowards a person who has no courage and shows fear in a shameful way
▷ **cowardice** NOUN **cowardly** ADJECTIVE

cowboy NOUN cowboys a man in charge of grazing cattle on a ranch

cower VERB cowers, cowering, cowered crouch or shrink back in fear

coy ADJECTIVE pretending to be shy or modest; bashful
▷ **coyly** ADVERB **coyness** NOUN

crab NOUN crabs a shellfish with ten legs, the first pair being a set of pincers

crab apple NOUN crab apples a small sour apple

crack NOUN cracks **1** a line on the surface of something where it has broken but not come completely apart **2** a narrow gap **3** a sudden sharp noise **4** a knock • *a crack on the head* **5** (*informal*) a joke; a wisecrack **6** a drug made from cocaine

crack ADJECTIVE (*informal*) first-class • *He is a crack investigator.*

crack VERB cracks, cracking, cracked **1** make or get a crack; split **2** make a sudden sharp noise **3** break down • *He cracked under the strain.*
crack a joke tell a joke
crack down on (*informal*) stop something that is illegal or against rules
get cracking (*informal*) get busy

cracker NOUN crackers **1** a paper tube that bangs when pulled apart **2** a thin biscuit

crackle VERB crackles, crackling, crackled make small cracking sounds • *The fire crackled in the grate.*
▷ **crackle** NOUN

cradle NOUN cradles **1** a small bed for a baby **2** a supporting framework

cradle VERB cradles, cradling, cradled hold gently

craft NOUN crafts **1** a job that needs skill, especially with the hands **2** skill **3** cunning; trickery **4** craft a ship or boat; an aircraft or spacecraft

craftsman NOUN craftsmen a person who is good at a craft
▷ **craftsmanship** NOUN

Thesaurus

coward NOUN *He accused them of being cheats and cowards.* ► weakling, faint-heart, (*more informal*) chicken, (*more informal*) wimp AN OPPOSITE IS hero

cowardice NOUN *Her husband had been executed for cowardice.* ► cowardliness, faint-heartedness, spinelessness, timorousness, timidity OPPOSITES ARE bravery, courage

cowardly ADJECTIVE *The thieves ran off, showing how cowardly they are. The decision was feeble and cowardly.* ► faint-hearted, lily-livered, spineless, craven, weak, timid, pusillanimous, (*more informal*) gutless, (*more informal*) yellow OPPOSITES ARE brave, courageous

coy ADJECTIVE *Don't be coy: come and be introduced* ► shy, bashful, reserved, diffident, embarrassed, inhibited, self-conscious, hesitant, timid, retiring OPPOSITES ARE assertive, forward, bold

crack NOUN **1** *a plate with a crack in it* ► break, chip, chink, split, fracture, fissure, gap **2** *a crack on the head* ► blow, bang, knock, smack, hit, punch, (*more informal*) bash **3** *the crack of a rifle; a crack of thunder* ► bang, report, crash, explosion, burst, snap, pop **4** *a cheap crack* ► joke, jest, quip, wisecrack, gibe, dig, (*more informal*) gag **5** *have a crack at it* ► try, attempt, (*more informal*) go, (*more informal*) shot, (*more informal*) stab

crack VERB **1** *She dropped a cup and cracked it.* ► break, split, shatter, splinter, chip, fracture **2** *Guns cracked in the distance.* ► burst, bang, go bang, explode, thump, boom, pop, crackle,

crash **3** *She cracked him in the head.* ► strike, smack, thump, slap, hit, (*more informal*) bash, (*more informal*) whack **4** *The problem proved hard to crack.* ► solve, resolve, work out, puzzle out, fathom, decipher, break **5** *A suspect finally cracked and confessed.* ► break down, give in, give way, collapse, yield
crack down on *a drive to crack down on street crime* ► reduce, suppress, end, stop, eradicate, get tough on, clamp down on
crack up (*informal*) **1** *I'm so anxious I could be cracking up.* ► break down, have a breakdown, lose control, go to pieces, go mad, go crazy **2** *The remark made everyone want to crack up.* ► burst out laughing, roar with laughter, laugh uncontrollably

crackle VERB *The fire began to crackle.* ► sizzle, fizzle, crack, fizz, hiss, sputter

cradle NOUN *a baby's cradle* ► crib, bed

craft NOUN **1** *the traditional craft of hand weaving* ► handicraft, trade, business, pursuit, activity, occupation, profession, work, job **2** *Pete demonstrated the blacksmith's craft.* ► skill, art, technique, expertise, mastery, talent, ability **3** *The harbor was teeming with river craft.* ► vessels, ships, boats

craftsman NOUN *Passersby could watch the craftsmen at work.* ► artisan, artist, craftsperson, master

craftsmanship NOUN *an age when craftsmanship in building reached a peak* ► skill, technique, expertise, workmanship, artistry,

A
B
C
D
E
F
G
H
I
J
K
L
M
N
O
P
Q
R
S
T
U
V
W
X
Y
Z

crafty ADJECTIVE craftier, craftiest cunning
▷ **craftily** ADVERB **craftiness** NOUN

crag NOUN crags a steep piece of rough rock
▷ **craggy** ADJECTIVE **cragginess** NOUN
[from a Celtic word]

cram VERB crams, cramming, crammed 1 push many things into something so that it is very full 2 learn as many facts as you can in a short time just before an examination

cramp NOUN cramps pain caused by a muscle tightening suddenly

cramp VERB cramps, cramping, cramped hinder someone's freedom or growth, etc.

cramped ADJECTIVE in a space that is too small or tight

crane NOUN cranes 1 a machine for lifting and moving heavy objects 2 a large wading bird with long legs and neck

crane VERB cranes, craning, craned stretch your neck to try to see something

crank NOUN cranks 1 an L-shaped part used for changing the direction of movement in machinery 2 a person with strange or fanatical ideas
▷ **cranky** ADJECTIVE

cranny NOUN crannies a crevice

crash NOUN crashes 1 the loud noise of something breaking or colliding 2 a violent collision or fall 3 a sudden drop or failure

crash VERB crashes, crashing, crashed 1 make or have a crash; cause to crash 2 move with a crash 3 (said about a computer) stop working suddenly

crash ADJECTIVE intensive • a crash course

crash helmet NOUN crash helmets a padded helmet worn by cyclists and motorcyclists to protect the head

crass ADJECTIVE 1 very obvious or shocking; gross • crass ignorance 2 very stupid

crate NOUN crates 1 a packing case made of strips of wood 2 an open container with compartments for carrying bottles

crater NOUN craters 1 the mouth of a volcano 2 a bowl-shaped cavity or hollow caused by an explosion or impact

craving NOUN cravings a strong desire; a longing

crawl VERB crawls, crawling, crawled 1 move with the body close to the ground or other surface, or on hands and knees 2 move slowly 3 be covered with crawling things
▷ **crawler** NOUN

crawl NOUN 1 a crawling movement 2 a very slow pace 3 an overarm swimming stroke

crayon NOUN crayons a stick or pencil of colored wax, etc., for drawing

craze NOUN crazes a temporary enthusiasm

Thesaurus

ability, dexterity, handiwork, (more informal) know-how

crafty ADJECTIVE That's a crafty way of avoiding the problem. ► cunning, clever, shrewd, ingenious, wily, artful, canny

cram VERB 1 They were busy cramming burgers into their mouths. The shelves were crammed with books. ► stuff, force, press, squeeze, jam, pack, overfill 2 I'll never know how we managed to cram into such a tiny car. ► crowd, crush, squeeze, pack 3 Many of the students are still cramming for tomorrow's exam. ► study hard

cramped ADJECTIVE It was hard to sleep in the cramped quarters of the submarine. ► restricted, confined, constricted, narrow, tight, uncomfortable AN OPPOSITE IS roomy

crash NOUN 1 There was a loud crash in the kitchen. ► bang, smash, clash, clatter, clang, racket, thump, thud, boom 2 She had been injured in a car crash. ► accident, collision, smash, bump, pile-up, derailment, disaster, impact, knock, wreck 3 a stock-market crash ► collapse, failure, depression, fall, ruin

crash VERB 1 crash into The car crashed into a tree. ► hit, strike, smash into, collide with, bump into, knock into, lurch into, pitch into

2 The company had crashed in the recession. ► fail, collapse, fold, go under, founder, become bankrupt 3 Parts of the roof crashed to the ground. ► collapse, fall, plunge, topple, hurtle

crate NOUN Three crates of books stood by the door. ► case, packing case, box, carton, tea chest

crave VERB The chapel might provide the privacy she craved. ► long for, yearn for, hunger for, dream of, hanker after, desire, seek

craving NOUN the body's natural craving for food ► longing, desire, hankering, hunger, thirst, appetite

crawl VERB 1 He escaped by crawling out of the back of the house. ► creep, edge, inch, slither, clamber 2 (informal) You can get their support without having to crawl to them all the time. ► grovel, pander, kowtow, fawn (over), be obsequious, (more informal) suck up
be crawling with The place is crawling with visitors in the summer months. ► be full of, be overrun by, be teeming with, be packed with, be crowded with

craze NOUN the latest craze to sweep the country ► fad, trend, vogue, fashion, rage, mania,

crazy ADJECTIVE **crazier, craziest 1** insane **2** very foolish • *this crazy idea*
▷ **crazily** ADVERB **craziness** NOUN

creak NOUN **creaks** a harsh squeak like that of a stiff door hinge
▷ **creaky** ADJECTIVE

creak VERB **creaks, creaking, creaked** make a creak

cream NOUN **creams 1** the fatty part of milk **2** a yellowish-white color **3** a food containing or looking like cream • *chocolate cream* **4** a soft substance • *face cream* **5** the best part
▷ **creamy** ADJECTIVE

cream VERB **creams, creaming, creamed** make creamy; beat butter, etc., until it is soft like cream

crease NOUN **creases 1** a line made in something by folding, pressing, or crushing it

crease VERB **creases, creasing, creased** make a crease or creases in something

create VERB **creates, creating, created 1** bring into existence; make or produce, especially something that no one has made before **2** (*slang*) make a fuss; grumble
▷ **creation** NOUN **creator** NOUN

creative ADJECTIVE showing imagination and thought • *a creative use of language*
▷ **creativity** NOUN

creature NOUN **creatures** a living being, especially an animal

crèche (kresh) NOUN **crèches** a place where babies and young children are looked after while their parents are at work

credentials PLURAL NOUN documents showing a person's identity, qualifications, etc.

credible ADJECTIVE able to be believed; convincing
▷ **credibly** ADVERB **credibility** NOUN
USAGE Do not confuse with **creditable** or **credulous**.

Thesaurus

diversion, enthusiasm, infatuation, novelty, obsession, passion, pastime

crazy ADJECTIVE *It was crazy to expect them to agree.* ► absurd, ridiculous, ludicrous, preposterous, foolish, idiotic, stupid, foolhardy, unwise **2** *She was going crazy with all the work.* ► mad, insane, out of your mind, off your head, unbalanced, demented, deranged **3** *The whole family is crazy about golf.* ► mad, passionate, devoted (to), smitten (with), taken (with)

creak VERB *The door began to creak.* ► squeak, grate, groan, scrape, grind, rasp

cream NOUN **1** *Rub in some skin cream.* ► lotion, ointment, rub, salve, moisturizer **2** *the cream of the country's jockeys* ► pick, elite, choice, finest, best AN OPPOSITE IS dregs

creamy ADJECTIVE *The powder makes a creamy paste when mixed with water.* ► smooth, thick, rich, velvety, milky, oily

crease NOUN *The cloth was full of creases and would have to be ironed.* ► wrinkle, crinkle, pucker, fold, furrow, groove, line, pleat, ridge, ruck, tuck, corrugation

crease VERB *I tried not to crease my clothes.* ► crumple, crinkle, wrinkle, pucker, crush, crimp, rumple, ruck, fold, furrow, pleat, ridge

create VERB **1** *A new job had to be created from scratch.* ► produce, make, generate, develop, compose, devise, design **2** *His father created the business fifty years before.* ► set up, start, begin, found, establish, institute, initiate **3** *The appointment created a lot of resentment.* ► cause, bring about, lead to, engender, prompt, produce, result in, give rise to

creation NOUN **1** *the creation of a modern industrial society* ► making, formation, foundation, fashioning, establishment, institution, conception, birth, development, origination, production OPPOSITES ARE disintegration, destruction **2** *The decor was entirely her creation.* ► work, effort, conception, invention, design, devising, achievement, handiwork, brainchild, product, work of art

creative ADJECTIVE *Students need to be creative in their thinking.* ► imaginative, inventive, expressive, resourceful, original, productive, fertile, artistic, positive, ingenious, clever, inspired, talented, visionary AN OPPOSITE IS destructive

creator NOUN **1** *the creator of many good novels* ► writer, author, producer, composer, designer, deviser, initiator, inventor, maker, manufacturer, parent **2** *the creators of the Assyrian Empire* ► architect, builder, originator, begetter

creature NOUN **1** *Whales are the largest living creatures.* ► animal, living thing, beast, being, brute **2** *The poor creature had been out in the rain all night.* ► fellow, individual, person, wretch, beggar

credibility NOUN *The details give credibility to the story.* ► plausibility, conviction, integrity, believability, reliability, probability, trustworthiness

credible ADJECTIVE *The man was unable to give any credible explanation for his presence there.* ► believable, plausible, reasonable, tenable, conceivable, possible, convincing, imaginable, likely, persuasive AN OPPOSITE IS incredible

a
b
c
d
e
f
g
h
i
j
k
l
m
n
o
p
q
r
s
t
u
v
w
x
y
z

credit ➡ crib

credit NOUN **credits 1** a source of pride or honor • *a credit to the school* **2** praise or acknowledgment given for some achievement or good quality • *I must give you credit for persistence.* **3** an arrangement trusting a person to pay for something later on **4** an amount of money in an account at a bank, etc., or entered in a financial account as paid in COMPARE **debit 5** belief or trust • *I put no credit in this rumor.*

credits a list of people who have helped to produce a film or television program

credit VERB **credits, crediting, credited 1** believe **2** attribute; say that a person has done or achieved something • *Columbus is credited with the discovery of America.* **3** enter something as a credit in a financial account COMPARE **debit**

creditable ADJECTIVE deserving praise
USAGE Do not confuse with **credible** or **credulous.**

credit card NOUN **credit cards** a card authorizing a person to buy on credit

creditor NOUN **creditors** a person to whom money is owed

credulous ADJECTIVE too ready to believe things; gullible
USAGE Do not confuse with **credible** or **creditable.**

creed NOUN **creeds** a set or formal statement of beliefs

creep VERB **creeps, creeping, crept 1** move along close to the ground **2** move quietly **3** come gradually **4** prickle with fear • *It makes my flesh creep*

creep NOUN **creeps 1** a creeping movement **2** (*informal*) an unpleasant person, especially one who seeks to win favor

the creeps (*informal*) a nervous feeling caused by fear or dislike

creeper NOUN **creepers** a plant that grows along the ground or up a wall

creepy ADJECTIVE **creepier, creepiest** frightening and sinister

cremate VERB **cremates, cremating, cremated** burn a dead body to ashes
▷ **cremation** NOUN

crematorium NOUN **crematoria** a place where dead bodies are cremated

crescendo (krish- end- oh) NOUN **crescendos** a gradual increase in loudness

crescent NOUN **crescents 1** a narrow curved shape coming to a point at each end **2** a curved street

cress NOUN a plant with hot-tasting leaves, used in salads and sandwiches

crest NOUN **crests 1** a tuft of hair, skin, or feathers on an animal's or bird's head **2** the top of a hill or wave etc. **3** a design used on notepaper etc.
▷ **crested** ADJECTIVE

crestfallen ADJECTIVE disappointed or dejected

crevasse (kri- vass) NOUN **crevasses** a deep open crack, especially in a glacier

crevice NOUN **crevices** a narrow opening, especially in a rock or wall

crew[1] NOUN **crews 1** the people working in a ship or aircraft **2** a group working together • *the camera crew*

crew[2] past tense of **crow**[2]

crib NOUN **cribs 1** a baby's cot **2** a framework holding fodder for animals **3** a model representing the Nativity of Jesus Christ **4** something cribbed **5** a translation for use by students

Thesaurus

credit NOUN **1** *Gary helped him with his chemistry and deserves a lot of the credit for the good grades he got.* ► praise, acclaim, approval, recognition, acknowledgment, commendation, distinction, prestige, merit, esteem, fame, glory, honor, (*more informal*) kudos, reputation, status AN OPPOSITE IS dishonour **2** *Kate had better taste than she'd been given credit for.* ► recognition, acknowledgment, approval

credit VERB **1** *It is difficult to credit such an unlikely story.* ► accept, believe, subscribe to, trust, have confidence in, have faith in, rely on, depend on, count on, endorse, reckon on, (*more informal*) swallow, (*informal*) buy AN OPPOSITE IS disbelieve **2** *The idea is credited to Aristotle.* ► attribute to, ascribe to, assign to, attach to, associate (with)

creditable ADJECTIVE *The team were on good form and put on a creditable performance.*
► commendable, laudable, respectable,

estimable, admirable, praiseworthy, worthy, excellent, good, honorable, meritorious, well thought of AN OPPOSITE IS unworthy

creep VERB **1** *She watched him creep under the table.* ► crawl, slither, slink, wriggle, worm your way, writhe, edge, inch, move slowly **2** *Gilly packed a suitcase and crept down the stairs.* ► slip, sneak, steal, move quietly, tiptoe

creepy ADJECTIVE *The place gave her creepy feelings.* ► frightening, eerie, spooky, scary, weird, sinister, uncanny, unearthly, macabre, ominous AN OPPOSITE IS pleasant

crest NOUN **1** *a bird with a bright crest* ► plume, tuft, comb **2** *We reached the crest of the hill.* ► peak, crown, brow, ridge, summit, top, apex **3** *the royal crest* ► insignia, regalia, emblem, badge, seal, sign, symbol

crew NOUN **1** *a ship's crew* ► company, complement, sailors, seamen **2** *a road-mending crew* ► team, gang, unit, party, squad

156

crib VERB **cribs, cribbing, cribbed** copy someone else's work

crick NOUN **cricks** painful stiffness in the neck or back

cricket[1] NOUN a game played outdoors between teams with a ball, bats, and two wickets
▷ **cricketer** NOUN

cricket[2] NOUN **crickets** a brown insect like a grasshopper

crime NOUN **crimes 1** an action that breaks the law **2** lawbreaking

criminal NOUN **criminals** a person who has committed a crime or crimes
▷ **criminal** ADJECTIVE **criminally** ADVERB

crimson ADJECTIVE deep-red
▷ **crimson** NOUN

cringe VERB **cringes, cringing, cringed** shrink back in fear; cower

cripple NOUN **cripples** a person who is permanently lame

cripple VERB **cripples, crippling, crippled 1** make a person lame **2** weaken or damage something seriously

crisis NOUN **crises** an important and dangerous or difficult situation

crisp ADJECTIVE **1** very dry so that it breaks with a snap **2** fresh and stiff • *a crisp $5 note* **3** cold and dry • *a crisp morning* **4** brisk and sharp • *a crisp manner*
▷ **crisply** ADVERB **crispness** NOUN

crisp NOUN **crisps** a very thin fried slice of potato, usually sold in packets

crisscross ADJECTIVE, ADVERB with crossing lines

criterion (kry- teer- ee- on) NOUN **criteria** a standard by which something is judged or decided

critic NOUN **critics 1** a person who gives opinions on books, plays, films, music, etc. **2** a person who criticizes

critical ADJECTIVE **1** criticizing **2** to do with critics or criticism **3** to do with or at a crisis; very serious
▷ **critically** ADVERB

Thesaurus

---

crime NOUN **1** *The report shows a decrease in street crime.* ▶ lawbreaking, lawlessness, delinquency, wrongdoing, transgression, misconduct, dishonesty, illegality **2** *Blackmail is a serious crime.* ▶ offence, misdeed, misdemeanour, transgression, illegal act, unlawful act, (*more informal*) racket, (*old use*) felony

criminal NOUN *His friends were criminals, working with the smugglers.* ▶ lawbreaker, offender, villain, wrongdoer, delinquent, miscreant, convict, culprit, (*more informal*) crook

criminal ADJECTIVE *Hardship can never justify criminal behavior.* ▶ illegal, unlawful, illicit, dishonest, corrupt, nefarious, (*more informal*) crooked, (*more informal*) bent OPPOSITES ARE legal, honest

cringe VERB **1** *The old man cringed, his hands shaking.* ▶ cower, shrink back, draw back, recoil, flinch, shy away, quail, tremble, crouch, quiver, dodge, duck, grovel **2** *I cringe when I hear those songs these days.* ▶ wince, blench, squirm, blush

cripple VERB **1** *The car hit her, crippling her for life.* ▶ disable, incapacitate, maim, injure, lame, damage, paralyze **2** *Industry was crippled by a series of strikes.* ▶ ruin, destroy, crush, paralyse, scupper, bring to a standstill, put out of action, spoil

crippled ADJECTIVE **1** *His crippled right leg is bent back at the knee.* ▶ disabled, deformed, lame, incapacitated, physically impaired, injured, maimed, paralyzed, handicapped, hurt,

invalid, mutilated **2** *Witnesses watched the crippled car being winched onto the tow truck.* ▶ immobilized, damaged, incapacitated, out of action, sabotaged, useless

crisis NOUN **1** *Events in Europe were reaching a crisis.* ▶ climax, critical point, turning point, moment of truth **2** *The following year there was another economic crisis.* ▶ emergency, predicament, problem, danger, difficulty

crisp ADJECTIVE **1** *crisp cookies* ▶ crunchy, crispy, brittle, crackly, fragile, crumbly AN OPPOSITE IS soft **2** *a crisp morning in November* ▶ fresh, brisk, bracing, exhilarating, refreshing **3** *a crisp style of writing* ▶ terse, incisive, pithy, succinct, sparing, laconic

critic NOUN **1** *the most famous music critic of the time* ▶ commentator, reviewer, authority, expert, pundit, judge, analyst **2** *a major critic of government policy* ▶ detractor, attacker

critical ADJECTIVE **1** *a critical assessment of the available literature* ▶ analytical, objective, evaluative, discerning, perceptive **2** *He is highly critical of American foreign policy.* ▶ disapproving, censorious, derogatory (about), disparaging (about), scathing (about), uncomplimentary (about) OPPOSITES ARE appreciative, complimentary (about) **3** *He only escaped death by moving his head at the critical moment.* ▶ crucial, vital, decisive, essential, all-important **4** *She was taken to the hospital where her condition was described as critical.* ▶ serious, grave, dangerous, precarious AN OPPOSITE IS safe

a
b
c
d
e
f
g
h
i
j
k
l
m
n
o
p
q
r
s
t
u
v
w
x
y
z

A
B
C
D
E
F
G
H
I
J
K
L
M
N
O
P
Q
R
S
T
U
V
W
X
Y
Z

criticism NOUN criticisms **1** criticizing; pointing out faults **2** the work of a critic

criticize VERB criticizes, criticizing, criticized say that a person or thing has faults

croak NOUN croaks a deep hoarse sound like that of a frog
▷ **croak** VERB

crockery NOUN household china

crocodile NOUN crocodiles **1** a large tropical reptile with a thick skin, long tail, and huge jaws **2** a long line of schoolchildren walking in pairs
crocodile tears sorrow that is not sincere (so called because the crocodile was said to weep while it ate its victim)

crocus NOUN crocuses a small plant with yellow, purple, or white flowers

crony NOUN cronies a close friend or companion

crook NOUN crooks **1** a shepherd's stick with a curved end **2** something bent or curved **3** (informal) a person who makes a living dishonestly

crooked ADJECTIVE **1** bent or twisted; not straight **2** dishonest

croon VERB croons, crooning, crooned sing softly and gently

crop NOUN crops **1** something grown for food ● a good crop of wheat **2** a whip with a loop instead of a lash **3** part of a bird's throat **4** a very short haircut

crop VERB crops, cropping, cropped **1** cut or bite off ● Sheep were cropping the grass. **2** produce a crop
crop up happen unexpectedly

croquet (kroh- kay) NOUN a game played with wooden balls and mallets

cross NOUN crosses **1** a mark or shape made like + or x **2** an upright post with another piece of wood across it, used in ancient times for crucifixion; **(the Cross)** the cross on which Christ was crucified, used as a symbol of Christianity **3** a mixture of two different things

cross VERB crosses, crossing, crossed **1** go across something **2** draw a line or lines across something **3** make the sign or shape of a cross ● Cross your fingers for luck. **4** produce something from two different kinds
cross out draw a line across something because it is unwanted, wrong, etc.

cross ADJECTIVE **1** annoyed or bad-tempered **2** going from one side to another ● There were cross winds on the bridge.
▷ **crossly** ADVERB **crossness** NOUN

Thesaurus

---

criticism NOUN **1** The management has received a lot of criticism. ► disapproval, blame, censure, disparagement, fault-finding, reproach, stricture, tirade, verbal attack, (more informal) flak **2** Their work will be submitted for criticism. ► evaluation, assessment, appraisal, analysis, judgment, appreciation

criticize VERB **1** Police criticized motorists for using cell phones while driving. ► condemn, censure, find fault with, denounce, blame, castigate, disparage, denigrate, deprecate, (more informal) knock, (more informal) slam, (more informal) pan AN OPPOSITE IS praise **2** a review criticizing the work of four modern poets ► appraise, assess, evaluate, analyze, judge, review

crockery NOUN The table had been laid and the crockery brought out. ► dishes, plates, tableware, china, crocks, earthenware, porcelain, pottery, ceramics

crook NOUN **1** His head was lying in the crook of her arm. ► bend, curve, angle **2** She accused them of being crooks. ► criminal, lawbreaker, villain, wrongdoer

crooked ADJECTIVE **1** The picture looks slightly crooked. ► askew, awry, lopsided, off-centre, slanting, angled **2** The garden was a maze of crooked paths. ► winding, twisting, tortuous, twisty, zigzag **3** She put a crooked finger to her lips. ► bent, misshapen, deformed, bowed,

curved, curving **4** Several officials were probably crooked. ► criminal, dishonest, corrupt, nefarious, (more informal) bent

crop NOUN My crop of Brussels sprouts are ready to eat. ► harvest, yield, produce, gathering

crop VERB **1** Sheep cropped grass in the fields. ► graze on, browse on, eat, nibble, bite off **2** She had to crop her long blonde hair. ► cut short, cut, clip, trim, snip, shear
crop up The same names keep cropping up over the years. ► occur, arise, appear, come up, turn up, emerge, spring up, happen

cross ADJECTIVE Dad got cross and said I was setting a bad example. ► angry, annoyed, testy, tetchy, upset, vexed, irate, bad-tempered, cantankerous, crotchety, ill-tempered, irascible, irritable, peevish, short-tempered, (more informal) grumpy AN OPPOSITE IS good-humored

cross NOUN **1** a difficult cross to bear ► burden, problem, difficulty, misfortune, trial, tribulation, trouble, worry, grief, sorrow, affliction **2** a cross between a yak and a cow ► hybrid, cross-breed, amalgam (of), blend (of), combination (of), halfway house, mixture (of)

cross VERB **1** The roads cross north of the town. ► intersect, intertwine, meet **2** There is only one place you can cross the river. ► go across, pass over, ford, traverse **3** It's better not to cross the road in the dark. ► go across, walk across,

crossbar NOUN crossbars a horizontal bar, especially between two uprights

cross-breed VERB cross-breeds, cross-breeding, cross-bred breed by mating an animal with one of a different kind
▷ cross-breed NOUN COMPARE hybrid

cross-examine VERB cross-examines, cross-examining, cross-examined cross-question someone, especially in a lawcourt
▷ cross-examination NOUN

cross-eyed ADJECTIVE with eyes that look or seem to look toward the nose

crossing NOUN crossings a place where people can cross a road or railway

cross-legged ADJECTIVE, ADVERB with ankles crossed and knees spread apart

cross-question VERB cross-questions, cross-questioning, cross-questioned cross-question someone carefully in order to test answers given to previous questions

cross-reference NOUN cross-references a note telling people to look at another part of a book, etc., for more information

crossroads NOUN crossroads a place where two or more roads cross one another

cross-section NOUN cross-sections 1 a drawing of something as if it has been cut through 2 a typical sample

crossword NOUN crosswords a puzzle in which words have to be guessed from clues and then written into the blank squares in a diagram

crotchet NOUN crotchets a quarter note in music, which usually represents one beat (written ♩)

crouch VERB crouches, crouching, crouched lower your body, with your arms and legs bent

crow[1] NOUN crows a large black bird *as the crow flies* in a straight line

crow[2] VERB crows, crowing, crowed or crew 1 make a shrill cry as a rooster does 2 boast; be triumphant
▷ crow NOUN

crowbar NOUN crowbars an iron bar used as a lever

crowd NOUN crowds a large number of people in one place

crowd VERB crowds, crowding, crowded 1 come together in a crowd 2 cram; fill uncomfortably full

crown NOUN crowns 1 an ornamental headdress worn by a king or queen 2 (often Crown) the sovereign • *This land belongs to the Crown.* 3 the highest part • *the crown of the road*
Crown Prince or Crown Princess the heir to the throne

crown VERB crowns, crowning, crowned 1 place a crown on someone as a symbol of royal power or victory 2 form or cover or decorate the top of something 3 reward; make a successful end to something • *Our efforts were crowned with victory.* 4 (slang) hit someone on the head

crucial (kroo- shal) ADJECTIVE most important
▷ crucially ADVERB

crucifix NOUN crucifixes a model of the Cross or of Jesus Christ on the Cross

Thesaurus

traverse 4 *A stone bridge crossed the stream.*
▶ span, bridge, arch, go across, extend across, pass across 5 *He blew up if anyone crossed him.*
▶ oppose, annoy, defy, argue with, obstruct, thwart
cross out *He crossed out part of the sentence and rewrote it.* ▶ delete, strike out, erase, cancel

crouch VERB *The boys crouched behind a large tree.* ▶ squat, kneel, stoop, bend, bob down, bow down, cower, cringe, duck, hunch, huddle

crowd NOUN 1 *The crowd dispersed quickly.*
▶ throng, multitude, mob, masses, horde, gathering, company, rabble, crush 2 *a large crowd at the ground* ▶ gate, attendance, audience, spectators

crowd VERB 1 *Some of them had crowded around a vending machine.* ▶ gather, collect, cluster, congregate, huddle, muster, mass, swarm, surge 2 *The guests were crowding into the dining room.* ▶ stream, push, pile, pack, squeeze, swarm, flock, surge, jostle

crowded ADJECTIVE *It was hard to find a space on the crowded beach.* ▶ packed, congested, overcrowded, swarming, teeming, thronging, cramped, full, busy, jammed, jostling, overflowing OPPOSITES ARE empty, deserted

crown NOUN 1 *The queen was wearing her crown.*
▶ coronet, diadem, tiara 2 *He paused at the crown of the hill.* ▶ brow, crest, top, summit, peak, ridge, head, apex

crown VERB 1 *William was crowned in Westminster Abbey on Christmas Day.* ▶ install, enthrone, anoint 2 *He crowned his career with a diplomatic post in Spain.* ▶ cap, round off, top off, complete, conclude, consummate, fulfil, finish off, perfect

crucial ADJECTIVE 1 *Police investigation plays a crucial role in the criminal process.* ▶ major, central, pivotal, decisive, critical, important, momentous, serious OPPOSITES ARE minor, unimportant 2 *Secrecy is crucial in this matter.*
▶ paramount, essential, vital, critical, indispensable

crucify VERB crucifies, crucifying, crucified put a person to death by nailing or binding the hands and feet to a cross
▷ **crucifixion** NOUN

crude ADJECTIVE **1** in a natural state; not yet refined • *crude oil* **2** not well finished; rough • *a crude carving* **3** vulgar
▷ **crudely** ADVERB **crudity** NOUN

cruel ADJECTIVE crueler, cruelest causing pain or suffering
▷ **cruelly** ADVERB **cruelty** NOUN

cruise NOUN cruises a pleasure trip in a ship

cruise VERB cruises, cruising, cruised **1** sail or travel at a moderate speed **2** have a cruise

cruiser NOUN cruisers **1** a fast warship **2** a large motor boat

crumb NOUN crumbs a tiny piece of bread

crumble VERB crumbles, crumbling, crumbled break or fall into small fragments
▷ **crumbly** ADJECTIVE

crumpet NOUN crumpets a soft flat cake made with yeast, eaten toasted with butter

crumple VERB crumples, crumpling, crumpled **1** crush or become crushed into creases **2** collapse loosely

crunch VERB crunches, crunching, crunched crush something noisily, for example between your teeth

crunch NOUN crunches a crunching sound
▷ **crunchy** ADJECTIVE
the crunch (*informal*) a crucial event or turning point

Crusade NOUN Crusades a military expedition made by Christians in the Middle Ages to win Palestine from the Muslims
▷ **Crusader** NOUN

crusade NOUN crusades a campaign against something bad

crush VERB crushes, crushing, crushed **1** press something so that it gets broken or harmed **2** squeeze tightly **3** defeat

crush NOUN crushes **1** a crowd of people pressed together **2** a drink made with crushed fruit

crust NOUN crusts **1** the hard outer layer of something, especially bread **2** the rocky outer layer of the earth

crustacean (krust- ay- shon) NOUN crustaceans an animal with a shell, e.g., a crab, lobster, or shrimp

---

Thesaurus

---

crude ADJECTIVE **1** *increased production of crude oil* ► unrefined, unpurified, unprocessed, natural, raw AN OPPOSITE IS refined **2** *a crude method of counting votes* ► primitive, simple, basic, rudimentary, rough, makeshift, improvised, homespun, clumsy, unrefined, amateurish, awkward, inelegant, inept OPPOSITES ARE sophisticated, advanced **3** *He went in for a very crude type of humor.* ► coarse, indecent, vulgar, bawdy, lewd, offensive, obscene USAGE Obscene is a very strong word and often implies an intention to offend or corrupt people.

cruel ADJECTIVE **1** *Their opponents were huge cruel men. Hunting is widely regarded as a cruel sport.* ► brutal, savage, vicious, fierce, ferocious, barbaric, callous, heartless, cold-blooded, pitiless, ruthless, merciless, vile, sadistic, brutish OPPOSITES ARE gentle, humane, kind, compassionate **2** *Her father's sudden death was a cruel blow.* ► severe, harsh, bitter, grim, painful OPPOSITES ARE mild, gentle

cruelty NOUN *The rebellion was put down with great cruelty.* ► brutality, savagery, viciousness, ferocity, barbarity, callousness, heartlessness, cold-bloodedness, ruthlessness

crumb NOUN *crumbs of bread; a small crumb of comfort* ► fragment, grain, morsel, scrap, bit, speck, particle, shred

crumble VERB **1** *The damaged buildings were beginning to crumble.* ► disintegrate, break up, collapse, fall apart, fall down, decay, decompose, deteriorate **2** *He crumbled the soil into a fine powder.* ► crush, grind, pound, powder, pulverize, break into pieces, fragment

crumple VERB *It's hard not to crumple your clothes in such a tiny car.* ► crease, crush, crinkle, wrinkle, squash

crunch VERB **1** *She sat there crunching chips.* ► munch, chomp, champ, masticate, devour **2** *He was fed up with getting his head crunched in football matches.* ► crush, pound, pulverize, grind, smash

crush VERB **1** *He nearly crushed his arm in the elevator doors.* ► squash, squeeze, mangle, crunch, scrunch, compress, mash, break, bruise, grind **2** *She was afraid she would crush her dress.* ► crease, crumple, crinkle, wrinkle, squash **3** *The army crushed the rebellion in a short time.* ► suppress, subdue, quell, quash, put down, defeat, vanquish, overcome

crush NOUN *There was quite a crush by the doors.* ► crowd, throng, congestion, jam, press, multitude, mob

crust NOUN *The paint left in the pot had formed a hard crust.* ► covering, skin, surface, shell, exterior, outside

crusty ADJECTIVE **1** *a meal of dry crusty bread and cheese* ► crisp, crispy, brittle, crunchy **2** *He seems so crusty these days.* ► irritable, grumpy, gruff, grouchy, tetchy, testy, bad-tempered, irascible, fractious

cry VERB **1** *Debbie looked upset and about to cry.* ► weep, shed tears, sob, howl, whimper,

crutch NOUN crutches a support like a long walking stick for helping a lame person to walk

cry NOUN cries **1** a loud wordless sound expressing pain, grief, joy, etc. **2** a shout **3** crying ● *Have a good cry.*

cry VERB cries, crying, cried **1** shed tears; weep **2** call out loudly

cryptic ADJECTIVE hiding its meaning in a puzzling way
▷ **cryptically** ADVERB

crystal NOUN crystals **1** a transparent colorless mineral rather like glass **2** very clear high-quality glass **3** a small solid piece of a substance with a symmetrical shape ● *ice crystals*
▷ **crystalline** ADJECTIVE

crystallize VERB crystallizes, crystallizing, crystallized **1** form into crystals **2** become definite in form
▷ **crystallization** NOUN

cub NOUN cubs a young lion, tiger, fox, bear, etc.

Cub or **Cub Scout** NOUN Cubs or Cub Scouts a member of the junior branch of the Boy Scouts

cubby hole NOUN cubby holes a small compartment

cube NOUN cubes **1** an object that has six equal square sides, e.g., a box or dice **2** the number produced by multiplying something by itself twice ● *The cube of 3 is 3 x 3 x 3 = 27.*

cube VERB cubes, cubing, cubed **1** multiply a number by itself twice ● *4 cubed is 4 x 4 x 4 = 64.* **2** cut something into small cubes

cube root NOUN cube roots the number that gives a particular number if it is multiplied by itself twice ● *The cube root of 27 is 3.*

cubic ADJECTIVE three-dimensional cubic metre, cubic foot, *etc*, the volume of a cube with sides one meter, foot, etc., long, used as a unit of measurement for volume

cubicle NOUN cubicles a compartment of a room

cuckoo NOUN cuckoos a bird that makes a sound like "cuck-oo"

cucumber NOUN cucumbers a long green-skinned vegetable eaten raw or pickled

cuddle VERB cuddles, cuddling, cuddled put your arms closely round a person or animal that you love
▷ **cuddle** NOUN

cuddly ADJECTIVE pleasantly soft and plump; nice to cuddle

cue[1] NOUN cues something said or done that acts as a signal for an actor, etc., to say or do something

cue[2] NOUN cues a long stick for striking the ball in billiards or snooker

cuff NOUN cuffs **1** the end of a sleeve that fits round the wrist **2** hitting somebody with your hand; a slap
off the cuff without rehearsal or preparation

cuff VERB cuffs, cuffing, cuffed hit somebody with your hand

cul-de-sac NOUN cul-de-sacs a street with an opening at one end only; a dead end

cull VERB culls, culling, culled **1** pick out and kill surplus animals from a flock **2** select and use ● *I've culled lines from several poems.*
▷ **cull** NOUN

culpable ADJECTIVE deserving blame

culprit NOUN culprits the person who has done something wrong

cult NOUN cults **1** a religious sect **2** a film, TV program, rock group, etc. that is very popular with a particular group of people

cultivate VERB cultivates, cultivating, cultivated **1** use land to grow crops **2** grow or develop things by looking after them
▷ **cultivation** NOUN **cultivator** NOUN

Thesaurus

snivel, blubber, bawl, wail USAGE The last six synonyms are unfriendly or disapproving, and *sob* means to cry uncontrollably and unattractively. *Weep* and *shed tears* are more neutral in tone, although *weep* is more literary. **2** *"Come on!" cried Sam.* ► call, yell, exclaim, shout, shriek, scream, bawl
cry out *Somebody was crying out in the darkness.* ► call out, yell, scream, screech, shout, shriek

cry NOUN **1** *a cry of pain* ► call, shout, yell, shriek, scream, screech, roar, bellow **2** *a cry for help* ► appeal, plea, entreaty

cuddle VERB *So far he had only kissed and cuddled her.* ► hug, caress, embrace, hold, clasp, pet, fondle, huddle against, snuggle against

culprit NOUN *New evidence showed that he was not the culprit after all.* ► guilty party, person responsible, offender, criminal, wrongdoer, miscreant, transgressor

cultivate VERB **1** *Peasants cultivated the land.* ► farm, till, dig, work, plough **2** *They helped with cultivating food crops.* ► grow, raise, rear, sow, plant, tend, produce **3** *We need to cultivate a better attitude to work.* ► develop, foster, nurture, encourage, promote, pursue, try to achieve, cherish, further, improve

A
B
C
D
E
F
G
H
I
J
K
L
M
N
O
P
Q
R
S
T
U
V
W
X
Y
Z

culture NOUN cultures **1** appreciation and understanding of literature, art, music, etc. **2** the customs and traditions of a people • *West Indian culture* **3** (in science) a quantity of bacteria or cells grown for study **4** improvement by care and training • *physical culture* **5** cultivating things
▷ **cultural** ADJECTIVE

cumbersome ADJECTIVE clumsy to carry or manage

cumulative ADJECTIVE accumulating; increasing by continuous additions

cunning ADJECTIVE **1** clever at deceiving people **2** cleverly designed or planned

cunning NOUN **1** skill in deceiving people; craftiness **2** skill or ingenuity [originally = clever, skillful: perhaps from an Old Norse word meaning "knowledge"]

cup NOUN cups **1** a small bowl-shaped container for drinking from **2** anything shaped like a cup **3** a goblet-shaped ornament given as a prize
▷ **cupful** NOUN

cup VERB cups, cupping, cupped form into the shape of a cup • *cup your hands*

cupboard NOUN cupboards a piece of furniture with a door, for storing things

cur NOUN curs a scruffy or bad-tempered dog

curate NOUN curates a member of the clergy who helps a vicar

curator (kewr- ay- ter) NOUN curators a person in charge of a museum or other collection

curb VERB curbs, curbing, curbed restrain • *You need to curb your impatience.*

curb NOUN curbs a restraint • *Put a curb on spending*
USAGE Do not confuse with kerb.

curd NOUN or **curds** PLURAL NOUN a thick substance formed when milk turns sour

curdle VERB curdles, curdling, curdled form into curds
make someone's blood curdle horrify or terrify them

cure VERB cures, curing, cured **1** get rid of someone's illness **2** stop something bad **3** treat food in order to preserve it

cure NOUN cures **1** something that cures a person or thing; a remedy **2** curing; being cured • *We cannot promise a cure.*

curfew NOUN curfews a time or signal after which people must remain indoors until the next day

curiosity NOUN curiosities **1** being curious **2** something unusual and interesting

Thesaurus

cultural ADJECTIVE *a country's cultural heritage*
► artistic, intellectual, aesthetic, educational, elevating, enlightening, improving

culture NOUN **1** *modern popular culture*
► civilization, society, intellectual activity, arts, traditions, customs, education, learning **2** *a person of culture* ► intellectual awareness, achievement, enlightenment, education, discernment, good taste

cultured ADJECTIVE *a pleasant, cultured man*
► cultivated, educated, well educated, well read, enlightened, civilized, erudite, artistic, refined, urbane, highbrow, knowledgeable, scholarly AN OPPOSITE IS ignorant

cumbersome ADJECTIVE *The suitcases were cumbersome rather than heavy.* ► unwieldy, awkward, bulky, clumsy, hefty, burdensome

cunning ADJECTIVE **1** *a cunning plan* ► crafty, wily, artful, sly, devious, knowing, guileful, disingenuous, machiavellian OPPOSITES ARE ingenuous, guileless **2** *The crime was solved by cunning detective work.* ► skillful, clever, shrewd, astute, adroit, subtle, ingenious

cunning NOUN *The defense counsel will need quite a bit of cunning.* ► guile, craftiness, artfulness, shrewdness, astuteness, adroitness, deviousness

cup NOUN **1** *They were drinking tea from pretty cups.* ► teacup, coffee cup, mug, tankard **2** *a silver cup for the winner* ► trophy, award, prize

cupboard NOUN *The tools and nails were kept in a cupboard.* ► cabinet, closet, locker, dresser, (for clothes) wardrobe, (for food) pantry

curb VERB *He tried to curb his temper.* ► restrain, suppress, control, contain, check, hold back, stifle AN OPPOSITE IS release

cure VERB **1** *A long period of rest will cure his ailment.* ► heal, remedy, treat, alleviate, counteract, ease, help, palliate, relieve OPPOSITES ARE aggravate, worsen **2** *The fault may be difficult to cure.* ► correct, rectify, mend, repair, put right, solve, (more informal) fix

cure NOUN **1** *a cure for cancer* ► remedy, treatment, antidote, medicine, prescription, restorative, panacea, palliative, therapy **2** *Her unexpected cure amazed the doctors.* ► recovery, healing, restoration to health

curiosity NOUN **1** *I found it hard to contain my curiosity.* ► inquisitiveness, interest, nosiness, prying, meddling, snooping USAGE The last four synonyms are unfavorable in tone, whereas the first two are neutral. **2** *He had an elephant's head displayed as a curiosity in his house.* ► novelty, oddity, curio, rarity, collector's item

curious ADJECTIVE **1** wanting to find out about things; inquisitive **2** strange; unusual
▷ **curiously** ADVERB

curl NOUN curls a curve or coil, e.g., of hair

curl VERB curls, curling, curled form into curls **curl up** sit or lie with your knees drawn up

curly ADJECTIVE having curls

currant NOUN currants **1** a small black dried grape used in cookery **2** a small round red, black, or white berry
USAGE Do not confuse with current.

currency NOUN currencies **1** the money in use in a country **2** the general use of something
• *Some words have no currency now.*

current ADJECTIVE happening now; used now
▷ **currently** ADVERB

current NOUN currents **1** water or air, etc., moving in one direction **2** the flow of electricity along a wire etc. or through something
USAGE Do not confuse with currant.

curriculum NOUN curricula a course of study in a school or university

curry[1] NOUN curries food cooked with spices that taste hot
▷ **curried** ADJECTIVE

curry[2] VERB curries, currying, curried **curry favour** seek to win favor by flattering someone

curse NOUN curses **1** a call or prayer for a person or thing to be harmed; the evil produced by this **2** something very unpleasant **3** an angry word or words

curse VERB curses, cursing, cursed **1** make a curse **2** use a curse against a person or thing **be cursed with something** suffer from it

cursor NOUN cursors a movable indicator, usually a flashing light, on a computer screen, showing where new data will go

curt ADJECTIVE brief and hasty or rude • *a curt reply*
▷ **curtly** ADVERB **curtness** NOUN

curtain NOUN curtains **1** a piece of material hung at a window or door **2** the large cloth screen hung at the front of a stage

curtsy NOUN curtsies a movement of respect made by women and girls, putting one foot behind the other and bending the knees

curtsy VERB curtsies, curtsying, curtsied make a curtsy

curvature NOUN curvatures curving; a curved shape

Thesaurus

---

curious ADJECTIVE **1** *I was curious about the reason for this unexpected visit.* ► inquisitive, intrigued, interested, puzzled, eager to know, agog OPPOSITES ARE incurious, unconcerned, indifferent. **2** *He walked off with a curious jerking motion.* ► strange, odd, peculiar, queer, funny, bizarre, unusual, extraordinary, eccentric AN OPPOSITE IS normal

curl NOUN **1** *Her hair was a mass of curls.* ► ringlet, wave, coil, loop, kink **2** *a pattern with repeated curls* ► loop, spiral, swirl, twist, bend, circle, curve, scroll, turn **3** *There was a curl of smoke in the distance.* ► spiral, coil, swirl, twirl, whorl, corkscrew

curl VERB **1** *Smoke curled from the tall chimney.* ► coil, spiral, twirl, swirl, furl **2** *The path curls around old tree trunks.* ► wind, twist, curve, meander, snake, writhe, zigzag **3** *Sarah curled an arm around his waist.* ► wind, twine, entwine, wrap, twist **4** *a treatment to curl the hair* ► crimp, wave, frizz, perm

curly ADJECTIVE *thick curly hair* ► wavy, curled, curling, crinkly, kinky, frizzy, fuzzy, crimped, permed AN OPPOSITE IS straight

currency NOUN *The euro simplifies the business of getting foreign currency in Europe.* ► money, legal tender, coinage, cash, coins, banknotes

current ADJECTIVE **1** *keeping abreast of current events* ► modern, contemporary, present-day, topical AN OPPOSITE IS past **2** *The opinion is still current.* ► common, prevalent, prevailing,

widespread, popular, accepted AN OPPOSITE IS obsolete **3** *a current driver's license* ► valid, usable, up to date OPPOSITES ARE out of date, expired **4** *the current administration in the White House* ► present, incumbent, existing, extant, reigning OPPOSITES ARE past, former

current NOUN **1** *a current of air* ► stream, flow, draught, jet, course **2** *The girls were in danger from the strong currents.* ► tide, undertow, drift

curse NOUN **1** *John caught his finger in the door and let out a curse.* ► swear word, oath, expletive, profanity, obscenity, blasphemy, exclamation **2** *The witch had put a curse on them.* ► malediction, imprecation, jinx **3** *the curse of unemployment* ► affliction, blight, scourge, plague, bane, misfortune, torment, evil

curse VERB *I listened to him cursing and shouting.* ► swear, utter profanities, blaspheme, damn, fulminate
be cursed with *The family was cursed for years with sickness and poverty.* ► be afflicted with, be blighted with, be plagued with, be troubled by, be burdened with

curt ADJECTIVE *Carl dismissed the idea with a curt grunt.* ► abrupt, blunt, harsh, terse, gruff, rude, offhand, brusque, insensitive, outspoken, plain-spoken OPPOSITES ARE polite, courteous

curtain NOUN *Clive closed the curtains.* ► drape, drapery, hanging, blind, screen

A
B
C
D
E
F
G
H
I
J
K
L
M
N
O
P
Q
R
S
T
U
V
W
X
Y
Z

curve VERB curves, curving, curved bend
smoothly

curve NOUN curves a curved line or shape
▷ **curvy** ADJECTIVE

cushion NOUN cushions **1** a bag, usually of
cloth, filled with soft material so that it is
comfortable to sit on or lean against
2 anything soft or springy that protects or
supports something • *The hovercraft travels on a
cushion of air.*

cushion VERB cushions, cushioning, cushioned
protect from the effects of a knock or shock,
etc. • *A pile of boxes cushioned his fall.*

custard NOUN custards **1** a sweet yellow sauce
made with milk **2** a pudding made with
beaten eggs and milk

custody NOUN **1** care and supervision;
guardianship **2** imprisonment
take into custody arrest
[from Latin *custos* = guardian]

custom NOUN customs **1** the usual way of
behaving or doing something **2** regular
business from customers

customary ADJECTIVE according to custom;
usual
▷ **customarily** ADVERB

customer NOUN customers a person who uses
a shop, bank, or other business

customs PLURAL NOUN **1** taxes charged on
goods brought into a country **2** the place at a
port or airport where officials examine your
luggage

cut VERB cuts, cutting, cut **1** divide or wound
or separate something by using a knife, axe,
scissors, etc. **2** make a thing shorter or
smaller; remove part of something • *They are
cutting all their prices.* **3** divide a pack of
playing cards **4** hit a ball with a chopping
movement **5** go through or across something
6 switch off electrical power or an engine, etc.
7 (in a movie) move to another shot or scene
8 make a sound recording
cut a corner pass around it very closely
cut and dried already decided
cut in interrupt

cut NOUN cuts **1** cutting; the result of cutting
2 a small wound **3** (*slang*) a share
be a cut above something be superior

Thesaurus

---

curve NOUN **1** *a series of curves in the road*
► bend, turn, twist, loop **2** *a tall window with
a curve at the top* ► arch, arc, bow, crescent

curve VERB *The river curved to the west.* ► bend,
twist, wind, loop, snake, turn, swerve

curved ADJECTIVE **1** *a tall building with a curved
roof* ► arched, bowed, rounded, humped,
crescent, vaulted, convex, bent OPPOSITES ARE
flat, straight **2** *The road was narrow and curved.*
► twisty, twisted, sinuous, meandering,
serpentine, sweeping AN OPPOSITE IS straight

cushion NOUN **1** *She put a cushion behind her
and leaned back.* ► pillow, bolster, headrest,
hassock, pad, beanbag **2** *a cushion against
inflation* ► protection, buffer, shield, defence

custom NOUN **1** *local customs dating back to the
thirteenth century* ► tradition, practice, usage,
institution, convention, procedure,
observance, form, habit, way, etiquette,
manner, formality, routine **2** *It is our custom to
visit relatives on the weekends.* ► practice, habit,
routine, way, rule, policy, wont **3** *The shop
offers discounts to attract custom* ► business,
trade, customers, buyers, patronage, support

customary ADJECTIVE **1** *It is customary to stand
during the playing of the anthem; the customary
rules of behavior* ► traditional, normal, usual,
common, conventional, established, expected,
general, ordinary, popular, prevailing, routine,
fashionable AN OPPOSITE IS unusual **2** *Dr. Ali
fell once again into his customary silence.* ► usual,
accustomed, regular, wonted, habitual, typical

customer NOUN *The business is trying to attract
younger customers.* ► shopper, buyer,
purchaser, client, consumer, patron AN
OPPOSITE IS seller

cut NOUN **1** *He had a cut on his hand.* ► gash,
wound, injury, nick, incision, scratch, graze
USAGE *Scratch* and *graze* do not normally
involve breaking of the skin and escape of
blood. **2** *She had to accept a small cut in pay.*
► reduction, decrease, lowering (of), lessening
(of) **3** *The leader of the gang demanded a higher
cut.* ► share, portion, slice, (*more informal*)
whack

cut VERB **1** *He had cut his finger with a kitchen
knife.* ► gash, pierce, wound, injure, slash,
nick, incise, scratch, graze USAGE *Scratch* and
graze do not normally involve breaking of the
skin and escape of blood. **2** *Cut the vegetables
into small pieces.* ► slice, chop, dice, cube,
divide, pare **3** *She was going to have her hair
cut. It will soon be time to start cutting the grass
again.* ► trim, clip, crop, mow **4** *The
supermarkets have cut prices on a wide range of
goods.* ► reduce, lower, lessen, (*more informal*)
slash **5** *Parts of the story were cut to make the
film version.* ► omit, remove, delete, excise,
take out, edit out **6** *You will have to cut your
essay by about a third.* ► shorten, abridge,
condense, reduce, precis, truncate **7** *The
remarks were spiteful and cut her deeply.* ► hurt,
offend, upset, wound

cut down 1 *Men are cutting the trees down.*

cute ADJECTIVE (informal) **1** attractive **2** clever
▷ **cutely** ADVERB **cuteness** NOUN

cutlass NOUN cutlasses a short sword with a broad curved blade

cutlery NOUN knives, forks, and spoons

cutlet NOUN cutlets a thick slice of meat for cooking

cutting NOUN cuttings **1** a steep-sided passage cut through high ground for a road or railway **2** something cut out of a newspaper or magazine **3** a piece cut from a plant to form a new plant

cycle NOUN cycles **1** a bicycle or motorcycle **2** a series of events that are regularly repeated in the same order
▷ **cyclic** ADJECTIVE **cyclical** ADJECTIVE

cycle VERB cycles, cycling, cycled ride a bicycle or tricycle
▷ **cyclist** NOUN

cyclone NOUN cyclones a wind that rotates round a calm central area
▷ **cyclonic** ADJECTIVE

cygnet (sig- nit) NOUN cygnets a young swan

cylinder NOUN cylinders an object with straight sides and circular ends
▷ **cylindrical** ADJECTIVE

cymbal NOUN cymbals a percussion instrument consisting of a metal plate that is hit to make a ringing sound
USAGE Do not confuse with **symbol**.

cynic (sin- ik) NOUN cynics a person who believes that people's reasons for doing things are selfish or bad
▷ **cynical** ADJECTIVE **cynically** ADVERB **cynicism** NOUN
[from Greek *kynikos* = surly: probably from the name *Kynosarges*, the gymnasium where the Greek philosopher Aristotle taught, but popularly associated with the Greek word *kuon* = dog]

cypress NOUN cypresses an evergreen tree with dark leaves

Thesaurus

▶ fell, hew, lop **2** *I'm trying to cut down some of these expenses.* ▶ reduce, decrease, lower, lessen
cut in *Tessa cut in with a remark that made everyone laugh.* ▶ interrupt, butt in, break in, interject, intervene, intrude
cut off **1** *The blade nearly cut off her finger.* ▶ sever, chop off, amputate, hack off, remove **2** *The Gas Company threatened to cut off the supply.* ▶ disconnect, discontinue, interrupt, suspend OPPOSITES ARE restore, reconnect **3** *Storms cut off the village for several days.* ▶ isolate, separate, seclude **4** *Her family had cut her off without a penny.* ▶ disinherit, disown, reject, repudiate, cast aside
cut out *The report mentioned several ways in* which we could cut out inefficiencies. ▶ remove, eliminate, excise, get rid of
cut up *Cut up the meat into small cubes.* ▶ chop, slice, dice, carve

cute ADJECTIVE *When I was young I had a cute little collie dog.* ▶ appealing, lovely, delightful, attractive, pretty, endearing, adorable, engaging

cycle NOUN *a cycle of growth and decline lasting 75 years* ▶ pattern, sequence, round, circle, series, era, period, revolution, rotation

cynical ADJECTIVE *I may be unduly cynical in thinking they are only in it for the money.* ▶ sceptical, distrustful, suspicious, disbelieving, pessimistic, negative, doubting, questioning AN OPPOSITE IS optimistic

a
b
c
d
e
f
g
h
i
j
k
l
m
n
o
p
q
r
s
t
u
v
w
x
y
z

A
B
C
D
E
F
G
H
I
J
K
L
M
N
O
P
Q
R
S
T
U
V
W
X
Y
Z

Dd

dab NOUN dabs **1** a quick gentle touch, usually with something wet **2** a small lump • *a dab of butter*

dab VERB dabs, dabbing, dabbed touch something quickly and gently

dabble VERB dabbles, dabbling, dabbled **1** splash something about in water **2** do something as a hobby • *dabble in chemistry*

dachshund (daks- huund) NOUN dachshunds a small dog with a long body and very short legs

daffodil NOUN daffodils a yellow flower that grows from a bulb

daft ADJECTIVE (*informal*) silly or stupid

dagger NOUN daggers a pointed knife with two sharp edges, used as a weapon

daily ADVERB, ADJECTIVE every day

dainty ADJECTIVE daintier, daintiest small, delicate, and pretty
▷ **daintily** ADVERB **daintiness** NOUN

dairy NOUN dairies a place where milk, butter, etc. are produced or sold

daisy NOUN daisies a small flower with white petals and a yellow center

dam[1] NOUN dams a wall built to hold water back

dam VERB dams, damming, dammed hold water back with a dam

dam[2] NOUN dams the mother of a horse or dog etc. COMPARE sire

damage NOUN harm or injury done to something

damage VERB damages, damaging, damaged harm or spoil something

damages PLURAL NOUN money paid as compensation for an injury or loss

Dame NOUN Dames the title of a woman who has been given the equivalent of a knighthood

dame NOUN dames a comic middle-aged woman in a pantomime, usually played by a man

damn VERB damns, damning, damned curse or condemn

damnation NOUN being condemned to hell

damned ADJECTIVE hateful or annoying

damp ADJECTIVE slightly wet; not quite dry
▷ **damply** ADVERB **dampness** NOUN

damp NOUN moisture in the air or on a surface or all through something

damp course NOUN damp courses a layer of material built into a wall to prevent dampness in the ground from rising

dampen VERB dampens, dampening, dampened **1** make something damp **2** reduce the strength of something

damsel NOUN damsels (*old use*) a young woman

dance VERB dances, dancing, danced move about in time to music

Thesaurus

dab VERB *He dabbed paint on the scratch.* ▶ pat, daub, touch, apply (to)

dabble VERB **1** *The children dabbled their feet in the water.* ▶ dip, paddle, splash, wet **2** *dabble in She began to dabble in astrology.* ▶ toy with, dip into, tinker with, trifle with

daft ADJECTIVE *a daft idea* ▶ silly, stupid, absurd, foolish, crazy, unwise, idiotic

daily ADJECTIVE *a daily occurrence* ▶ everyday, day-to-day, regular

dainty ADJECTIVE **1** *a dainty lace handkerchief* ▶ delicate, elegant, exquisite, neat, charming, fine, graceful, pretty OPPOSITES ARE clumsy, crude **2** *a dainty eater* ▶ fastidious, choosy, fussy, finicky, discriminating, careful AN OPPOSITE IS gross

dally VERB *There's not enough time to dally.* ▶ dawdle, delay, linger, loiter, waste time, idle, loaf, play about, procrastinate, (*more informal*) hang about, (*informal*) dilly-dally, (*literary*) tarry

damage NOUN *Fortunately the thieves caused little damage.* ▶ harm, injury, destruction, devastation, havoc, hurt, mutilation

damage VERB *High winds damaged properties along the sea front.* ▶ harm, hurt, injure, spoil, wreck, blemish, disfigure, deface, mutilate

damn VERB **1** *The voices damned him to hell.* ▶ curse, put a curse on, (*more formal*) execrate **2** *They had been damned for something that was not their fault.* ▶ condemn, censure, blame, abuse, revile, criticize, denounce, castigate, reprove

damp ADJECTIVE **1** *Someone had applied a damp cloth to her head.* ▶ moist, dampened, moistened, wet, wetted, soggy **2** *The air was damp and cold.* ▶ wet, drizzly, muggy, humid

dampen VERB **1** *Dampen a soft cloth.* ▶ moisten, wet, damp **2** *Nothing could dampen their enthusiasm now.* ▶ lessen, diminish, deaden, dull, stifle, muffle, restrain, smother, discourage, dishearten

dance NOUN *He was going to take her to the dance next week.* ▶ ball, disco, (*more informal*) hop

dance NOUN dances **1** a set of movements used in dancing **2** a piece of music for dancing to **3** a party or gathering where people dance
▷ **dancer** NOUN

dandelion NOUN dandelions a yellow wild flower with jagged leaves

dandruff NOUN tiny white flakes of dead skin in a person's hair

danger NOUN dangers **1** something that is not safe or could harm you **2** the possibility of suffering harm or death

dangerous ADJECTIVE likely to kill or harm you
▷ **dangerously** ADVERB

dangle VERB dangles, dangling, dangled hang or swing loosely

dappled ADJECTIVE marked with patches of a different color

dare VERB dares, daring, dared **1** be brave or bold enough to do something **2** challenge a person to do something risky

dare NOUN dares a challenge to do something risky

dark ADJECTIVE **1** with little or no light **2** not light in color • *a dark suit* **3** having dark hair **4** sinister or evil
▷ **darkly** ADVERB **darkness** NOUN

dark NOUN **1** absence of light • *Cats can see in the dark.* **2** the time when darkness has come • *She went out after dark.*

darken VERB darkens, darkening, darkened make or become dark

darling NOUN darlings someone who is loved very much; a term of endearment

darn VERB darns, darning, darned mend a hole by weaving threads across it

darn NOUN darns a place that has been darned

dart NOUN darts **1** an object with a sharp point, thrown at a target **2** a darting movement **3** a tapering tuck stitched in something to make it fit

dart VERB darts, darting, darted run suddenly and quickly

darts NOUN a game in which darts are thrown at a circular board (dartboard)

Thesaurus

RELATED ADJECTIVE ► choreographic RELATED NOUN ► choreography

dance VERB *Children danced around playfully.*
► caper, cavort, frisk, frolic, skip, prance, leap, gambol, hop, jig, jump

danger NOUN **1** *There is a danger of flooding on low ground.* ► risk, threat, chance, probability, possibility, likelihood, prospect, liability **2** *The contamination could become a danger to public health.* ► threat, hazard, menace, risk **3** *There was a real sense of danger about the place.*
► insecurity, vulnerability, uncertainty, precariousness **4** *Their very lives were in danger.*
► peril, jeopardy, (at) risk AN OPPOSITE IS safety

dangerous ADJECTIVE **1** *Building at such a height can be dangerous work.* ► hazardous, perilous, risky, unsafe, precarious, insecure, tricky **2** *He was charged with dangerous driving.* ► reckless, careless **3** *a dangerous criminal* ► ruthless, violent, vicious, desperate

dangle VERB **1** *There were curtains dangling above my head.* ► hang, droop, swing, flap, sway, trail, be suspended, wave about **2** *She dangled the keys in his face.* ► wave, swing, brandish, flourish, hold

dare VERB **1** *No one dared to say anything.*
► have the courage, be brave enough, take the risk (of), take a chance, venture **2** *She dared him to jump.* ► challenge, defy, provoke, goad, taunt

daring ADJECTIVE *a daring attack* ► bold, brave, courageous, adventurous, audacious, intrepid,

gallant, confident, dauntless, enterprising, heroic, valiant, (more informal) plucky AN OPPOSITE IS timid

dark ADJECTIVE **1** *a dark room* ► dim, dingy, dull, gloomy, unlit, unilluminated, shadowy OPPOSITES ARE light, bright **2** *a dark night* ► black, pitch-black, starless, moonless, unlit, unilluminated OPPOSITES ARE light, bright **3** *a dark color* ► deep, strong, heavy OPPOSITES ARE pale, light **4** *a dark secret* ► mysterious, enigmatic, hidden, obscure, impenetrable, cryptic **5** *dark thoughts* ► pessimistic, gloomy, sinister, sombre, grim, dismal, bleak, cheerless, fatalistic AN OPPOSITE IS optimistic

dark NOUN *afraid of the dark* ► darkness, blackness, gloom, night, night-time AN OPPOSITE IS light

darken VERB **1** *The sky darkened.* ► become dark, become overcast, cloud over OPPOSITES ARE lighten, brighten **2** *These fears darkened his life for many years.* ► overshadow, shadow, blacken, threaten, dim, make gloomy OPPOSITES ARE lighten, brighten

darling ADJECTIVE *his darling wife* ► dear, dearest, beloved, adored, cherished, treasured

darling NOUN **1** *Jane had always been his darling.*
► beloved, loved one, love, sweetheart, dear, dearest **2** *the darling of the gods* ► favorite, pet, idol

dart VERB *Children were darting about everywhere.*
► dash, rush, hurtle, leap, shoot, spring, bound, flit, fly, move suddenly, (more informal) whiz, (more informal) zip

dash VERB dashes, dashing, dashed **1** run quickly; rush **2** throw a thing violently against something • *The storm dashed the ship against the rocks.*

dash NOUN dashes **1** a short quick run; a rush **2** energy or liveliness **3** a small amount • *Add a dash of brandy.* **4** a short line (-) used in writing or printing

dashboard NOUN dashboards a panel fitted in a vehicle in front of the driver, with dials and controls

dashing ADJECTIVE lively and showy

data (day- ta) NOUN pieces of information
USAGE Strictly speaking, this word is a plural noun (the singular is *datum*), so it should be used with a plural verb: *Here are the data.* However, the word is widely used nowadays as if it were a singular noun and most people do not regard this as wrong: *Here is the data.*

database NOUN databases a store of information held in a computer

date[1] NOUN dates **1** the time when something happens or happened or was written, stated as the day, month, and year (or any of these) **2** an appointment to meet someone, especially someone of the opposite sex

date VERB dates, dating, dated **1** give a date to something **2** have existed from a particular time • *The church dates from 1684.* **3** seem old-fashioned

date[2] NOUN dates a small sweet brown fruit that grows on a kind of palm tree

daub VERB daubs, daubing, daubed paint or smear something clumsily
▷ **daub** NOUN

daughter NOUN daughters a girl or woman who is someone's child

daughter-in-law NOUN daughters-in-law a son's wife

daunt VERB daunts, daunting, daunted make somebody afraid or discouraged
▷ **daunting** ADJECTIVE

dawdle VERB dawdles, dawdling, dawdled go slowly and lazily
▷ **dawdler** NOUN

dawn NOUN dawns the time when the sun rises

dawn VERB dawns, dawning, dawned **1** begin to grow light in the morning **2** begin to be realized • *The truth dawned on them.*

day NOUN days **1** the 24 hours between midnight and the next midnight **2** the light part of this time **3** a particular day • *sports day* **4** a period of time • *in Grandpa's day*

daybreak NOUN dawn

daydream NOUN daydreams pleasant thoughts of something you would like to happen

daydream VERB daydreams, daydreaming, daydreamed have daydreams

day-to-day ADJECTIVE ordinary; happening every day

dazed ADJECTIVE unable to think or see clearly
▷ **daze** NOUN
[from Old Norse *dasathr* = weary]

Thesaurus

dash NOUN *They made a dash for the door.* ► rush, bolt, leap, sprint, spurt, race, run, chase

dash VERB **1** *We dashed home as soon as we could.* ► rush, race, bolt, tear, hasten, hurry, speed, shoot, run, sprint, chase, dart, fly, hasten, (*informal*) zoom **2** *He dashed the plate against the wall.* ► smash, crash, hurl, strike, throw, knock

data NOUN *a group collecting data on teenage pregnancies* ► information, details, particulars, facts and figures, statistics, evidence, material

date NOUN **1** *coins and pottery from a very early date* ► time, age, era, period **2** *She was in danger of missing her date with Paul.* ► meeting, appointment, rendezvous, engagement, assignation, fixture **3** *Mary was his date for the evening.* ► partner, escort, girlfriend (or boyfriend)

dawdle VERB *Ruth dawdled back through the wood, reluctant to return.* ► linger, dally, take your time, delay, idle, (*more informal*) dilly-dally **AN OPPOSITE IS** hurry

dawn NOUN **1** *We got up at dawn.* ► daybreak, sunrise, break of day, first light, (*more informal*) first thing **AN OPPOSITE IS** dusk **2** the

dawn of modern civilization ► beginning, start, birth, origin, genesis, advent, emergence

day NOUN **1** *He looked after Lucy during the day while I was at work.* ► daytime, daylight **AN OPPOSITE IS** night **2** *The girls are required to plan their own day.* ► working day, working time, work time, period of work **3** *He was the leading musician of the day.* ► age, period, time, era, epoch

daydream NOUN *She tried to shake off her daydreams.* ► reverie, fantasy, trance, fancy, dream, vision, imagining, absent-mindedness, meditation, musing, illusion, pipe dream

daydream VERB *He went out, leaving me to dress and daydream.* ► fantasize, dream, muse, meditate, be lost in thought, imagine

daylight NOUN *Until eight o'clock there is no daylight in our room.* ► sunlight, light of day, natural light

daze VERB **1** *The fall dazed him for a few minutes.* ► stun, stupefy, shock **2** *She was dazed by the news.* ► astound, amaze, astonish, startle, dumbfound, bewilder, stagger

dazzle VERB dazzles, dazzling, dazzled **1** make a person unable to see clearly because of too much bright light **2** amaze or impress a person by a splendid display

DC ABBREVIATION direct current

de- PREFIX **1** removing (as in *defrost*) **2** down, away (as in *descend*) **3** completely (as in *denude*)

dead ADJECTIVE **1** no longer alive **2** not lively **3** not functioning; no longer in use **4** exact or complete • *a dead loss*

deaden VERB deadens, deadening, deadened make pain or noise etc. weaker

dead end NOUN dead ends **1** a road or passage with one end closed **2** a situation where there is no chance of making progress

dead heat NOUN dead heats a race in which two or more winners finish exactly together

deadline NOUN deadlines a time limit [originally this meant a line around an American military prison. If prisoners went beyond it they could be shot.]

deadlock NOUN deadlocks a situation in which no progress can be made

deadly ADJECTIVE deadlier, deadliest likely to kill

deaf ADJECTIVE **1** unable to hear **2** unwilling to hear
▷ **deafness** NOUN

deafen VERB deafens, deafening, deafened make somebody become deaf, especially by a very loud noise
▷ **deafening** ADJECTIVE

deal VERB deals, dealing, dealt **1** hand something out; give **2** give out cards for a card game **3** do business; buy and sell • *He deals in scrap metal.*
▷ **dealer** NOUN
deal with 1 be concerned with • *This book deals with words and meanings.* **2** do what is needed • *I'll deal with the cleanup.*

deal NOUN deals **1** an agreement or bargain **2** someone's turn to deal at cards
a good deal or **a great deal** a large amount

Thesaurus

dazzle VERB **1** *The sunlight burst through the window and dazzled him.* ► daze, blind **2** *The beauty of the place dazzled her.* ► overpower, overwhelm, overawe, impress, amaze, astonish

dead ADJECTIVE **1** *Both her parents were dead.* ► deceased, departed, passed on, gone OPPOSITES ARE alive, living **2** *There was a dead animal on the road.* ► lifeless, killed, inanimate **3** *Latin is a dead language.* ► extinct, obsolete, defunct, disused, died out AN OPPOSITE IS existing **4** *My feet were dead with cold.* ► numb, deadened, insensitive, paralyzed, without feeling AN OPPOSITE IS sensitive **5** *The battery was dead.* ► flat, unresponsive, defunct, inoperative, not working, burnt out, used up, useless, worn out AN OPPOSITE IS operational **6** *When Sheila picked up the phone again the line was dead.* ► not working, inoperative, out of order, unresponsive **7** *The place is dead on a Friday night.* ► lifeless, dreary, uninteresting, boring, dull, moribund, slow OPPOSITES ARE lively, exciting **8** (*informal*) *He felt dead by the time he got home.* ► exhausted, worn out, drained, tired **9** *He is the dead image of his brother.* ► exact, absolute, perfect, complete, utter, downright

dead ADVERB *The road ahead was dead straight.* ► completely, absolutely, perfectly, utterly

deaden VERB **1** *Mufflers deaden the noise.* ► muffle, soften, mute, damp, reduce, quieten, smother, stifle, suppress, weaken, cushion, lessen, check, hush OPPOSITES ARE amplify, sharpen **2** *A local anaesthetic will deaden the pain.* ► numb, stifle, dull, blunt, suppress, alleviate, soothe, desensitize, anesthetize OPPOSITES ARE intensify, aggravate

deadly ADJECTIVE **1** *a deadly poison* ► lethal, noxious, harmful, mortal, dangerous AN OPPOSITE IS harmless **2** *a deadly disease* ► terminal, fatal, life-threatening, destructive

AN OPPOSITE IS mild **3** (*informal*) *The party turned out to be deadly.* ► dull, boring, dreary, tedious, unexciting, uninteresting OPPOSITES ARE lively, exciting **4** *He fired an arrow with a deadly aim.* ► unerring, unfailing, true, perfect

deaf ADJECTIVE **1** *By this time he was deaf and nearly blind.* ► hard of hearing **2** *They were deaf to all our pleas.* ► indifferent to, unmoved by, heedless of, oblivious to, unconcerned with

deafening ADJECTIVE *a deafening roar* ► loud, noisy, piercing, ear-splitting, booming, thunderous, overpowering

deal NOUN **1** *He was good at business deals and not much more.* ► agreement, arrangement, negotiation, transaction, settlement, contract, bargain, understanding **2** *Shoppers should look around for the best deal.* ► buy, bargain, transaction
a good deal OR **a great deal** *We have already achieved a great deal.* ► a lot, much, plenty, a large amount, a large quantity

deal VERB **1** *She dealt the cards for another round.* ► give out, distribute, share out, dispense, apportion, allot, assign, divide, (*informal*) dole out **2** *The man dealt him a blow on the head.* ► deliver, inflict, give, administer, apply, mete out **3** *He deals in stocks and shares.* ► trade, do business, buy and sell, traffic **4** *deal with a difficult issue to deal with* ► handle, manage, tackle, cope with, attend to, come to grips with, resolve, control, consider, grapple with, look after, see to, sort out, take action on **5** *deal with The book deals with several important topics.* ► be concerned with, treat, cover, tackle, explain

dealer NOUN *an antique dealer; a dealer in second-hand cars* ► trader, supplier, merchant, wholesaler, retailer, merchandiser, shopkeeper, tradesman

dear ➡ decay

dear ADJECTIVE **1** loved very much **2** a polite greeting in letters • *Dear Sir* **3** expensive
▷ **dearly** ADVERB

death NOUN deaths dying; the end of life

debatable ADJECTIVE questionable; that can be argued against

debate NOUN debates a formal discussion

debate VERB debates, debating, debated hold a debate
▷ **debater** NOUN

debilitating ADJECTIVE causing weakness

debit NOUN debits an entry in an account showing how much money is owed

debit VERB debits, debiting, debited enter something as a debit in a financial account [from Latin *debitum* = something owed]

debris (deb- ree) NOUN scattered fragments or wreckage

debt (det) NOUN debts something that you owe someone

in debt owing money, etc.
[from Latin *debitum* = something owed]

debtor (det- or) NOUN debtors a person who owes money to someone

decade (dek- ayd) NOUN decades a period of ten years

decadent (dek- a- dent) ADJECTIVE falling to lower moral standards, especially in order to enjoy pleasure
▷ **decadence** NOUN

decaffeinated ADJECTIVE (said about coffee or tea) with the caffeine removed

decapitate VERB decapitates, decapitating, decapitated cut someone's head off; behead
▷ **decapitation** NOUN

decathlon NOUN decathlons an athletic contest in which each competitor takes part in ten events

decay VERB decays, decaying, decayed **1** go bad; rot **2** become less good or less strong
▷ **decay** NOUN

Thesaurus

dear ADJECTIVE **1** *They soon became dear friends.*
► beloved, close, intimate, lovable, loved, valued, darling AN OPPOSITE IS hated **2** *Fruit is dear at this time of year.* ► expensive, costly, high-priced, overpriced, exorbitant, (*more informal*) pricey AN OPPOSITE IS cheap

dear NOUN *Everyone agrees he's a dear.* ► darling, lovable person, treasure, pet

dearly ADVERB *She loved Simon dearly.* ► deeply, intensely, profoundly, fondly, tenderly, very much, a great deal

death NOUN **1** *Charles phoned to tell her of her uncle's death.* ► dying, passing, passing away, end RELATED ADJECTIVE ► mortal **2** *The disaster caused many deaths.* ► casualty, fatality RELATED ADJECTIVE ► fatal **3** *The news meant the death of all their dreams.* ► end, ending, finish, collapse, ruin, destruction, termination, cessation
put to death *The king put all the conspirators to death.* ► execute, kill, have killed

debatable ADJECTIVE *It is debatable whether the public wants this sort of sensationalism.*
► arguable, questionable, disputable, doubtful, dubious, a moot point, open to doubt, open to question, contentious, controversial, controvertible, problematical, uncertain AN OPPOSITE IS indisputable

debate NOUN *a debate about personal freedom*
► discussion, argument, exchange of views, controversy, deliberation, contention, dialogue, dispute, (*more formal*) dialectic, (*more formal*) disputation

debate VERB **1** *Congress will debate plans for reducing traffic in cities.* ► discuss, consider, deliberate, confer about, exchange views on,

dispute, argue, weigh up **2** *I am debating whether to get in touch with them.* ► consider, think over, ponder, deliberate, contemplate, reflect, (*more informal*) mull over

debris NOUN **1** *There was debris all around from the collapsed buildings.* ► rubbish, rubble, ruins, remains, wreckage **2** *Use rubber gloves to clean out debris from the gutters.* ► waste, remains, detritus, refuse, litter, bits, dregs, scraps

debt NOUN **1** *It is easy for students to build up large debts.* ► money owed, arrears, financial obligation, financial commitment, bill **2** *I owe you a great debt for your kindness.* ► duty, indebtedness, obligation
in debt *By the end of the year he was heavily in debt.* ► owing money, in arrears, insolvent
in someone's debt *I shall be forever in your debt.* ► grateful to, indebted to, obliged to, beholden to

debtor NOUN *Debtors who fail to pay their hotel bill are not usually sent to prison any more.*
► bankrupt, defaulter

decadent ADJECTIVE *a decadent society*
► immoral, dissolute, degenerate, dissipated, corrupt, depraved, declining AN OPPOSITE IS moral

decay VERB **1** *The skulls were in good condition but the bones had decayed.* ► decompose, rot, putrefy, go bad, waste away, perish, deteriorate, degrade, disintegrate **2** *Inner cities had been allowed to decay.* ► decline, deteriorate, degenerate, crumble, corrode, disintegrate, wither, fall apart, go downhill

decay NOUN **1** *Today I found a dead blackbird in an advanced state of decay.* ► decomposition, rotting, festering, putrefaction **2** *Television is often blamed for the so-called decay in social*

deceased ADJECTIVE dead

deceit (dis- eet) NOUN deceits making a person believe something that is not true
▷ **deceitful** ADJECTIVE **deceitfully** ADVERB

deceive VERB deceives, deceiving, deceived make a person believe something that is not true
▷ **deceiver** NOUN

December NOUN the twelfth month of the year [from Latin *decem* = ten, because it was the tenth month of the ancient Roman calendar]

decent ADJECTIVE **1** respectable and honest **2** reasonable or adequate **3** (*informal*) kind
▷ **decently** ADVERB **decency** NOUN

deception NOUN deceptions deceiving someone
▷ **deceptive** ADJECTIVE **deceptively** ADVERB

decibel (dess- ib- el) NOUN decibels a unit for measuring the loudness of sound

decide VERB decides, deciding, decided **1** make up your mind; make a choice **2** settle a contest or argument
▷ **decider** NOUN

decided ADJECTIVE **1** having clear and definite opinions **2** noticeable • *a decided difference*
▷ **decidedly** ADVERB

deciduous (dis- id- yoo- us) ADJECTIVE a deciduous tree is one that loses its leaves in autumn

decimal ADJECTIVE using tens or tenths

decimal NOUN decimals a decimal fraction

decimal currency NOUN decimal currencies a currency in which each unit is ten or one hundred times the value of the one next below it

decimal fraction NOUN decimal fractions a fraction with tenths shown as numbers after a dot ($\frac{1}{3}$ is 0.3; $1\frac{1}{2}$ is 1.5)

decimal point NOUN decimal points the dot in a decimal fraction

decipher (dis- I- fer) VERB deciphers, deciphering, deciphered **1** work out the meaning of a coded message **2** work out the meaning of something written badly
▷ **decipherment** NOUN

decision NOUN decisions **1** deciding; what you have decided **2** determination

decisive (dis- I- siv) ADJECTIVE **1** that settles or ends something • *a decisive battle* **2** able to make decisions quickly and firmly
▷ **decisively** ADVERB **decisiveness** NOUN

Thesaurus

values. ► deterioration, decline, degradation, collapse, fall, disintegration

deceit NOUN *They achieved much by lies and deceit.* ► deception, duplicity, trickery, pretense, cheating, misrepresentation, fraud, guile, subterfuge, artifice, ruse OPPOSITES ARE honesty, openness

deceitful ADJECTIVE *George got used to the fact that I was deceitful and irresponsible.*
► dishonest, untruthful, insincere, untrustworthy, deceptive, duplicitous, underhand, false, fraudulent, (*more informal*) two-faced

deceive VERB *It had not been too difficult to deceive him.* ► trick, fool, mislead, hoodwink, delude, dupe, cheat, swindle, (*more informal*) take in

decent ADJECTIVE **1** *Mother always said it wasn't decent to watch people undress.* ► proper, respectable, appropriate, suitable, fitting, seemly, becoming, nice, modest, decorous, tasteful AN OPPOSITE IS indecent **2** *Apart from that, he seemed a decent enough guy.* ► obliging, courteous, honest, trustworthy, reliable, dependable, upright, polite, honorable **3** *It was her first decent meal of the day.* ► good, satisfactory, nice, pleasant, agreeable AN OPPOSITE IS unsatisfactory

deception NOUN *For a spy, I'm not very good at deception.* ► deceit, duplicity, trickery, pretense, cheating, misrepresentation, fraud,

guile, subterfuge, artifice, ruse OPPOSITES ARE honesty, openness

deceptive ADJECTIVE **1** *Similarities can be deceptive.* ► misleading, illusory, false, unreliable, delusive, fallacious, fraudulent, insincere, specious, spurious, treacherous AN OPPOSITE IS genuine **2** *deceptive practices*
► dishonest, deceitful, fraudulent, underhand, duplicitous, sham, bogus AN OPPOSITE IS honest

decide VERB **1** *He decided to become a journalist.* ► resolve, determine, make up your mind, choose, reach a decision, opt, plan, aim **2** *We don't have enough evidence to decide the issue.* ► determine, judge, adjudicate on, make a judgment on, pronounce on

decision NOUN **1** *the jury's decision on damages* ► verdict, finding, ruling, conclusion, judgment, pronouncement, adjudication **2** *The king agreed with this decision.* ► resolution, conclusion, outcome, result, recommendation, resolve, determination

decisive ADJECTIVE **1** *The car's faster speed proved to be a decisive advantage.* ► conclusive, definite, significant, crucial, critical, positive, deciding, determining, convincing, final, influential OPPOSITES ARE inconclusive, insignificant **2** *His decisive no-nonsense manner had given him quite a reputation. They showed themselves capable of decisive action.* ► resolute, determined, firm, strong-willed, strong-

a b c **d** e f g h i j k l m n o p q r s t u v w x y z

A
B
C
D
E
F
G
H
I
J
K
L
M
N
O
P
Q
R
S
T
U
V
W
X
Y
Z

deck NOUN decks **1** a floor on a ship or bus **2** a pack of playing cards **3** a turntable on a record player

deckchair NOUN deckchairs a folding chair with a canvas or plastic seat

declaim VERB declaims, declaiming, declaimed make a speech, etc., loudly and dramatically
▷ **declamation** NOUN

declare VERB declares, declaring, declared **1** say something clearly or firmly **2** tell customs officials that you have goods on which you ought to pay duty
▷ **declaration** NOUN
declare war announce that you are starting a war against someone

decline VERB declines, declining, declined **1** refuse **2** become weaker or smaller **3** slope downward **4** state the forms of a noun, pronoun, or adjective that correspond to particular cases, numbers, and genders

decline NOUN declines a gradual decrease or loss of strength

decode VERB decodes, decoding, decoded figure out the meaning of something written in code
▷ **decoder** NOUN

decompose VERB decomposes, decomposing, decomposed decay or rot
▷ **decomposition** NOUN

decorate VERB decorates, decorating, decorated **1** make something look more beautiful or colorful **2** put fresh paint or paper on walls **3** give somebody a medal
▷ **decoration** NOUN **decorator** NOUN **decorative** ADJECTIVE

decorous (dek- er- us) ADJECTIVE polite and dignified
▷ **decorously** ADVERB

decoy (dee- koi) NOUN decoys something used to tempt a person or animal into a trap or into danger

decoy (dik- oi) VERB decoys, decoying, decoyed tempt a person or animal into a trap, etc.

decrease VERB decreases, decreasing, decreased make or become smaller or fewer

Thesaurus

minded, forceful, forthright, unhesitating, incisive, decided, definite OPPOSITES ARE indecisive, hesitant

declaration NOUN **1** a joint declaration by the four heads of state ► announcement, proclamation, notification, promulgation, edict, manifesto **2** a declaration of trust in the government ► affirmation, assertion, acknowledgment, profession, confirmation, pledge, avowal

declare VERB **1** Both sides declared their intentions. ► announce, proclaim, express, voice, affirm, reveal, divulge **2** He declared that he was ready to do a deal. ► assert, insist, maintain, announce, aver, state, claim, certify, vow, avow

decline NOUN **1** a decline in profits ► reduction, decrease, drop, fall, downturn, falling off, recession, slump, diminution (of), loss (of), failing (of) **2** a decline in their fortunes ► deterioration, degeneration, worsening (of)

decline VERB **1** He declined all our invitations. ► refuse, reject, dismiss, turn down, pass up, forgo AN OPPOSITE IS accept **2** After the accident her health declined. ► worsen, deteriorate, weaken, degenerate, flag, die away, fail, fall off, sink, wane, wilt AN OPPOSITE IS improve **3** Profits have declined for the third year in succession. ► decrease, diminish, be reduced, lessen, go down, drop away, dwindle, ebb

decode VERB The messages were quickly decoded. ► decipher, unscramble, interpret, make sense of, understand, construe, solve, read, (more

informal) crack, (more informal) make out, (more informal) figure out OPPOSITES ARE code, encode

decorate VERB **1** a nursery chair decorated with little rabbits ► adorn, ornament, embellish, trim, beautify, enhance **2** We will decorate the house before moving in. ► paint, renovate, smarten up, refurbish, redecorate, paper, wallpaper, (more informal) do up **3** He was decorated for bravery at the end of the war.
► honor, reward, give a medal to, mention in dispatches

decoration 1 a tall ceiling with elaborate decoration ► ornamentation, adornment, embellishment, trimmings, filigree, tracery, frill, scroll **2** a decoration for bravery ► award, badge, medal, ribbon, star, (more informal) gong

decorative ADJECTIVE a decorative mirror in a frame ► ornamental, ornate, fancy, adorning, embellishing, enhancing, elaborate, non-functional AN OPPOSITE IS functional

decoy NOUN They set up a decoy to distract our attention. ► lure, bait, trap, enticement

decoy VERB His enemies had decoyed him to another part of the country. ► lure, entice, induce, inveigle, ensnare, seduce, tempt, bait, draw, lead

decrease NOUN a decrease in crime levels ► reduction, decline, lessening (of), falling off, drop, downturn AN OPPOSITE IS increase

decrease NOUN decreases decreasing; the amount by which something decreases

decree NOUN decrees an official order or decision

decree VERB decrees, decreeing, decreed make a decree

decrepit (dik- rep- it) ADJECTIVE old and weak
▷ **decrepitude** NOUN

dedicate VERB dedicates, dedicating, dedicated **1** devote all your time or energy to something • She dedicated her life to nursing. **2** name a person as a mark of respect, e.g., at the beginning of a book
▷ **dedication** NOUN

deduce VERB deduces, deducing, deduced work something out by reasoning from facts that you know are true
▷ **deducible** ADJECTIVE

deduct VERB deducts, deducting, deducted subtract part of something

deduction NOUN deductions **1** deducting; something deducted **2** deducing; something deduced

deed NOUN deeds **1** something that someone has done; an act **2** a legal document

deep ADJECTIVE **1** going a long way down or back or in • a deep well • deep cupboards **2** measured from top to bottom or front to back • a hole six feet deep **3** intense or strong • deep colors • deep feelings **4** low-pitched, not shrill • a deep voice
▷ **deeply** ADVERB **deepness** NOUN

deepen VERB deepens, deepening, deepened make or become deeper

deer NOUN deer a fast-running graceful animal, the male of which usually has antlers

deface VERB defaces, defacing, defaced spoil the surface of something, e.g., by scribbling on it
▷ **defacement** NOUN

default VERB defaults, defaulting, defaulted fail to do what you have agreed to do, especially to pay back a loan
▷ **defaulter** NOUN

default NOUN defaults **1** failure to do something **2** (in computing) what a computer does unless you give it another command
by default because something has failed to happen

Thesaurus

decrease VERB **1** We need to decrease our costs. ► reduce, lessen, lower, cut, cut down, curtail AN OPPOSITE IS increase **2** The aircraft's speed was rapidly decreasing. ► diminish, lessen, reduce, fall off, dwindle AN OPPOSITE IS increase

decree NOUN a presidential decree banning all protest meetings ► order, edict, command, mandate, proclamation, dictum, enactment

decree VERB The law decreed that Sunday should be a day of rest. ► order, command, declare, prescribe, ordain, proclaim, pronounce, direct, rule, decide, determine, dictate

decrepit ADJECTIVE **1** He lived in a decrepit old cottage. ► dilapidated, battered, ramshackle, tumbledown, worn out, broken down, derelict **2** a decrepit old woman ► feeble, frail, weak, infirm

dedicated ADJECTIVE a dedicated musician ► devoted, committed, keen, staunch, steadfast, fervent, loyal, enthusiastic, zealous, wholehearted, single-minded, faithful

dedication NOUN **1** She appreciated all his hard work and dedication. ► devotion, commitment, allegiance, faithfulness, loyalty, adherence, single-mindedness **2** The book bore a dedication to his wife. ► inscription

deduce VERB He deduced that she must be a good cook. ► conclude, come to the conclusion, reason, work out, gather, infer, surmise, glean

deduct VERB The cost of the breakage will be deducted from his allowance. ► subtract, knock off, take away, debit (to) OPPOSITES ARE add (to), credit (to)

deduction NOUN **1** USAGE from the verb **deduct** Income is subject to the deduction of tax. ► subtraction, taking away, taking off, removal, stoppage **2** USAGE from the verb **deduce** Her deduction was quite correct. ► conclusion, inference, reasoning

deed NOUN a heroic deed ► act, action, feat, exploit, endeavor, enterprise, achievement, adventure, effort, performance, undertaking

deep ADJECTIVE **1** The well is deep. ► bottomless, fathomless, cavernous, yawning AN OPPOSITE IS shallow **2** a deep disappointment ► intense, profound, extreme, serious **3** a deep mystery ► obscure, secret, mysterious, unfathomable, fathomless, arcane **4** deep affection ► intense, heartfelt, fervent, ardent, deep-seated **5** a deep thinker ► wise, intelligent, profound, perceptive, learned, discerning **6** They were deep in conversation. ► rapt, absorbed, engrossed, immersed, preoccupied, riveted **7** a deep sound ► low, low-pitched, bass, resonant, booming **8** a deep color ► dark, rich, vivid, strong, intense

deepen VERB **1** Their love had deepened over the years. ► increase, intensify, grow, grow stronger **2** The hole had been deepened. ► dig out, make deeper, hollow, scoop out

a
b
c
d
e
f
g
h
i
j
k
l
m
n
o
p
q
r
s
t
u
v
w
x
y
z

defeat ➡ defile

defeat VERB defeats, defeating, defeated
1 win a victory over someone **2** baffle; be too difficult for someone

defeat NOUN defeats **1** defeating someone **2** being defeated; a lost game or battle

defect (dee- fekt) NOUN defects a flaw

defect (dif- ekt) VERB defects, defecting, defected desert your own country, etc., and join the enemy
▷ **defection** NOUN **defector** NOUN

defective ADJECTIVE having defects; incomplete
▷ **defectiveness** NOUN

defend VERB defends, defending, defended **1** protect, especially against an attack **2** try to prove that a statement is true or that an accused person is not guilty
▷ **defender** NOUN

defendant NOUN defendants a person accused of something in a lawcourt

defense NOUN defenses **1** defending something **2** something that defends or protects **3** a reply put forward by a defendant

defensive ADJECTIVE used or done for defense; protective
▷ **defensively** ADVERB
on the defensive ready to defend yourself

defer[1] VERB defers, deferring, deferred postpone
▷ **deferment** NOUN **deferral** NOUN

defer[2] VERB defers, deferring, deferred give way to a person's wishes or authority; yield

deference (def- er- ens) NOUN polite respect
▷ **deferential** (def- er- en- shal) ADJECTIVE **deferentially** ADVERB

defiant ADJECTIVE defying; openly disobedient
▷ **defiantly** ADVERB **defiance** NOUN

deficiency NOUN deficiencies **1** a lack or shortage **2** a defect
▷ **deficient** ADJECTIVE

defile VERB defiles, defiling, defiled make a thing dirty or impure
▷ **defilement** NOUN

Thesaurus

defeat NOUN **1** *the defeat of Napoleon at Waterloo* ► conquest, subjugation, overthrow, beating, victory (over) **2** *The home side faced defeat.* ► failure, loss, setback, humiliation, disappointment, reverse, trouncing AN OPPOSITE IS victory

defeat VERB **1** *The French army defeated the enemy in a long engagement.* ► overcome, beat, conquer, overpower, subdue, vanquish, subjugate, quell, rout **2** *The complexity of the task defeated them.* ► confound, baffle, frustrate

defect NOUN (with the stress on *de-*) *The machinery showed several defects.* ► fault, flaw, imperfection, deficiency, weakness, failing, inadequacy, blemish, error, (*more informal*) bug

defect VERB (with the stress on *-fect*) *Politicians might defect to other parties.* ► desert, go over, change sides, revolt

defective ADJECTIVE *The car's brakes were defective.* ► faulty, out of order, deficient, broken, malfunctioning, inoperative

defend VERB **1** *An air squadron helped to defend the country against enemy attack.* ► protect, guard, safeguard, secure, shield, shelter, screen, cover **2** *He found it hard to defend his actions.* ► justify, vindicate, make a case for

defense NOUN **1** *Several friends spoke in defense of his actions.* ► support, vindication, justification, endorsement **2** *a defense against attack* ► protection, resistance (to), shield, deterrent, barricade, bulwark

defensive ADJECTIVE **1** *The aircraft formed a defensive circle.* ► defending, protective, protecting, guarding AN OPPOSITE IS aggressive **2** *Her attitude seemed nervous and defensive.* ► wary, watchful, cautious, apologetic, self-justifying AN OPPOSITE IS assertive

defer VERB **1** *She had decided to defer unpacking to the following day.* ► postpone, put off, delay, adjourn, hold over, suspend, (*more informal*) shelve **2** *defer to He agreed to defer to his parents' wishes.* ► yield to, submit to, respect, accede to, give way to, agree to, surrender to

defiance NOUN *Her dark eyes were ablaze with defiance.* ► opposition, confrontation, resistance, challenge, audacity, bravado, contempt

defiant ADJECTIVE *He remained defiant in spite of the threats.* ► obstinate, determined, intransigent, resistant, confrontational, recalcitrant, unyielding OPPOSITES ARE cooperative, apologetic

deficiency NOUN *a vitamin deficiency* ► insufficiency, shortage, inadequacy, lack, deficit, shortfall

deficient ADJECTIVE **1** *a diet deficient in vitamins* ► lacking, wanting, defective, inadequate, insufficient OPPOSITES ARE adequate, excessive **2** *deficient leadersip* ► defective, flawed, faulty, unsound, imperfect, inadequate, (*more informal*) duff AN OPPOSITE IS perfect

deficit NOUN *a deficit in the budget* ► loss, shortfall, deficiency, lack AN OPPOSITE IS surplus

define VERB **1** *We can define evidence as information about whether a particular thing is true or not.* ► explain, interpret, clarify, formulate, give the meaning of **2** *The fence defines the boundary of the estate.* ► mark, mark

define VERB defines, defining, defined
1 explain what a word or phrase means
2 show clearly what something is; specify
3 show a thing's outline
▷ **definable** ADJECTIVE

definite ADJECTIVE **1** clearly stated; exact • *Fix a definite time.* **2** certain or settled • *Is it definite that we are to move?*

definite article NOUN definite articles (in grammar) the word "the"

definitely ADVERB certainly; without doubt

definition NOUN definitions **1** a statement of what a word or phrase means or of what a thing is **2** being distinct; clearness of outline (e.g., in a photograph)

deflate VERB deflates, deflating, deflated
1 let out air from a tire or balloon, etc.
2 make someone feel less proud or less confident **3** reduce or reverse inflation
▷ **deflation** NOUN **deflationary** ADJECTIVE

deflect VERB deflects, deflecting, deflected make something turn aside
▷ **deflection** NOUN **deflector** NOUN

deforest VERB deforests, deforesting, deforested clear away the trees from an area
▷ **deforestation** NOUN

deform VERB deforms, deforming, deformed spoil a thing's shape or appearance
▷ **deformation** NOUN

deft ADJECTIVE skilful and quick
▷ **deftly** ADVERB **deftness** NOUN

defuse VERB defuses, defusing, defused
1 remove the fuse from a bomb so that it cannot explode **2** make a situation less dangerous or tense

defy VERB defies, defying, defied **1** resist something openly; refuse to obey • *They defied the law.* **2** challenge a person to do something you believe cannot be done • *I defy you to prove this.* **3** prevent something being done • *The door defied all efforts to open it.*

degenerate (di- jen- e- rayt) VERB degenerates, degenerating, degenerated become worse or lower in standard
▷ **degeneration** NOUN

degenerate (di- jen- e- ret) ADJECTIVE having become immoral or bad
▷ **degeneracy** NOUN

degrade VERB degrades, degrading, degraded
1 humiliate or dishonor someone **2** reduce to a simpler molecular form
▷ **degradation** (deg- ra- **day**- shon) NOUN

degree NOUN degrees **1** a unit for measuring temperature **2** a unit for measuring angles **3** extent • *to some degree* **4** an award to someone at a university or college who has successfully finished a course

Thesaurus

out, indicate, set, determine, demarcate, outline

definite ADJECTIVE **1** *She came to some definite conclusions.* ► clear, clear-cut, explicit, express, precise, established, fixed, concrete, plain, hard AN OPPOSITE IS indefinite **2** *There are definite signs of improvement.* ► distinct, clear, plain, discernible, obvious, perceptible, noticeable, positive, unmistakable, marked, pronounced, apparent AN OPPOSITE IS imperceptible

definitely ADVERB *She definitely hadn't been there before.* ► certainly, positively, surely, unquestionably, beyond doubt, assuredly, for certain, indubitably, doubtless, without doubt, without fail

definition NOUN **1** *It is hard to write a good definition of "left" and "right."* ► explanation, description, elucidation, interpretation, meaning **2** *The photograph lacked definition.* ► clarity, clearness, sharpness, precision, focus

definitive ADJECTIVE **1** *the definitive film guide* ► authoritative, standard, classic, recognized, accepted, official, ultimate, complete, reliable **2** *a definitive reply* ► decisive, conclusive, categorical, final AN OPPOSITE IS provisional

deflate VERB **1** *Someone had deflated two of the tires.* ► let down, let the air out of, flatten AN

OPPOSITE IS inflate. **2** *The news deflated him.* ► subdue, humble, humiliate, dishearten, dispirit, dismay, chasten, mortify OPPOSITES ARE encourage, boost

deflect VERB *He managed to deflect the blow.* ► divert, turn aside, parry, fend off, intercept, avert, head off, prevent, ward off

deformed ADJECTIVE *He was so deformed the gods took pity on him.* ► misshapen, contorted, crippled, crooked, distorted, disfigured, twisted, malformed, maimed, bent, warped, mutilated, buckled, mangled, defaced, gnarled, grotesque, ugly

defy VERB **1** *He was arrested for defying a court order to hand over the property.* ► disobey, refuse to obey, flout, disregard, violate, contravene, infringe, breach, resist AN OPPOSITE IS obey **2** *She defied Robin to admit the truth.* ► challenge, dare **3** *The situation defied all attempts at rational explanation.* ► elude, escape, defeat, frustrate, thwart, resist

degree NOUN *The work involves a high degree of trust.* ► level, order, measure, extent, range, stage, intensity, standard
to some degree *The risk will still be present to some degree.* ► partly, to some extent, up to a point

a
b
c
d
e
f
g
h
i
j
k
l
m
n
o
p
q
r
s
t
u
v
w
x
y
z

dehydrated ➡ delicate

A
B
C
D
E
F
G
H
I
J
K
L
M
N
O
P
Q
R
S
T
U
V
W
X
Y
Z

dehydrated ADJECTIVE dried up, with all moisture removed
▷ **dehydration** NOUN

deity (dee- it- ee, day- it- ee) NOUN **deities** a god or goddess

dejected ADJECTIVE sad or depressed
▷ **dejectedly** ADVERB **dejection** NOUN

delay VERB delays, delaying, delayed **1** make someone or something late **2** postpone

delay NOUN delays delaying; the time for which something is delayed • *a two-hour delay*

delegate (del- ig- at) NOUN delegates a person who represents others and acts on their instructions

delegate (del- ig- ayt) VERB **delegates, delegating, delegated 1** give someone a task or duty to do on your behalf • *I'm going to delegate this job to my assistant.* **2** appoint someone as a delegate • *We delegated Jones to represent us.*

delegation (del- ig- **ay**- shon) NOUN **delegations 1** delegating **2** a group of delegates

delete (dil- eet) VERB **deletes, deleting, deleted** cross out or remove something written or printed or stored on a computer
▷ **deletion** NOUN

deliberate (dil- ib- er- at) ADJECTIVE **1** done on purpose; intentional **2** slow and careful
▷ **deliberately** ADVERB

deliberate (dil- ib- er- ayt) VERB **deliberates, deliberating, deliberated** discuss or think carefully
▷ **deliberation** NOUN

delicacy NOUN **delicacies 1** being delicate **2** a delicious food

delicate ADJECTIVE **1** fine and graceful • *delicate embroidery* **2** fragile and easily damaged **3** pleasant and not strong or intense **4** becoming ill easily **5** using or needing great care • *a delicate situation*
▷ **delicately** ADVERB **delicateness** NOUN

Thesaurus

---

deign VERB *She practiced all the things she would say to him when he deigned to contact her.*
► condescend, see fit, consent, descend, stoop

dejected ADJECTIVE *Lisa was looking dejected.*
► downcast, depressed, despondent, dispirited, disheartened, downhearted, unhappy, fed up, sad, down, glum, melancholy, miserable, cast down OPPOSITES ARE cheerful, happy

delay NOUN **1** *Traffic is subject to long delays.*
► hold-up, wait, waiting period, stoppage, obstruction **2** *A delay in the proceedings followed.* ► deferment, postponement, suspension

delay VERB **1** *Heavy traffic delayed many of the guests.* ► detain, hold up, make late, hamper, impede **2** *We might have to delay the start of the game.* ► postpone, put off, defer, suspend, adjourn, hold over OPPOSITES ARE advance, bring forward **3** *There is no time to delay.*
► linger, dally, take your time, (more formal) procrastinate, (more informal) drag your feet, (more informal) hang about

delegate VERB **1** *The council delegated a member to speak to the press.* ► appoint, authorize, commission, nominate, designate, empower, mandate **2** *She delegates routine tasks to an assistant.* ► assign, entrust, pass on, hand over, devolve, consign

delegation NOUN *There was a delegation from Nigeria.* ► deputation, commission, legation, delegacy, mission, representative group, contingent

delete VERB *One paragraph was deleted from the article.* ► remove, cut out, take out, erase, expunge, cross out

deliberate ADJECTIVE **1** *The disaster may have been an accident rather than deliberate sabotage.*
► intentional, calculated, conscious, planned, culpable, premeditated, wilful OPPOSITES ARE unplanned, accidental, fortuitous **2** *She could hear the slow deliberate footsteps.* ► careful, measured, steady, cautious, unhurried, considered, methodical AN OPPOSITE IS hasty

delicacy NOUN **1** *lacework of great delicacy*
► fineness, exquisiteness, daintiness, fragility, intricacy, precision, accuracy, care **2** *It was an unpleasant matter that called for some delicacy.*
► sensitivity, subtlety, tact, discrimination, finesse **3** *Several plates of delicacies were brought in.* ► titbit, rarity, speciality, treat

delicate ADJECTIVE **1** *The tablecloths were made of beautiful, delicate fabrics.* ► fine, exquisite, elegant, intricate, graceful, flimsy, fragile OPPOSITES ARE coarse, crude **2** *He awoke feeling somewhat delicate, after his night on the town.*
► unwell, sickly, ill, unfit, poorly, frail, weak OPPOSITES ARE healthy, fit, robust **3** *The old clock had a delicate mechanism.* ► precise, intricate, accurate, exact **4** *a delicate shade of blue* ► subtle, muted, soft, pale, gentle, pastel, subdued **5** *Angie made a tiny, delicate gesture with her hand.* ► gentle, deft, adroit, neat, skilful **6** *The next issue to come up was delicate, to put it mildly.* ► difficult, tricky, sensitive, awkward, embarrassing, problematical **7** *The matter called for delicate handling.* ► sensitive, careful, discriminating **8** *It would not be easy to cater for their delicate taste in food.* ► fastidious, discriminating, fussy, (more informal) choosy, (more informal) faddy, (more informal) picky

delicious ➡ demand

delicious ADJECTIVE tasting or smelling very pleasant
▷ **deliciously** ADVERB

delight VERB delights, delighting, delighted **1** please someone greatly **2** take great pleasure in something

delight NOUN delights great pleasure
▷ **delightful** ADJECTIVE **delightfully** ADVERB

delinquent (dil- ing- kwent) NOUN delinquents a young person who breaks the law
▷ **delinquent** ADJECTIVE **delinquency** NOUN

delirious (di- li- ri- us) ADJECTIVE **1** affected with delirium **2** extremely excited or enthusiastic
▷ **deliriously** ADVERB

delirium (dil- iri- um) NOUN **1** a state of mental confusion and agitation during an illness **2** wild excitement

deliver VERB delivers, delivering, delivered **1** take letters or goods, etc., to someone's house or place of work **2** give a speech or lecture etc. **3** help with the birth of a baby

4 aim or strike a blow or an attack **5** rescue; set free
▷ **deliverer** NOUN **deliverance** NOUN **delivery** NOUN

delta NOUN deltas a triangular area at the mouth of a river where it spreads into branches

delude VERB deludes, deluding, deluded deceive or mislead someone

deluge NOUN deluges **1** a large flood **2** a heavy fall of rain **3** something coming in great numbers ● *a deluge of questions*

deluge VERB deluges, deluging, deluged overwhelm by a deluge

delusion NOUN delusions a false belief

demagogue (dem- a- gog) NOUN demagogues a leader who wins support by making emotional speeches rather than by careful reasoning

demand VERB demands, demanding, demanded **1** ask for something firmly or forcefully **2** need ● *This work demands great skill*

Thesaurus

delicious ADJECTIVE *You can have a delicious meal at the local bar.* ► tasty, appetizing, palatable, delectable, enjoyable, luscious, succulent, choice, savory, (*more informal*) mouth-watering, (*more informal*) scrumptious, (*more informal*) yummy OPPOSITES ARE unpleasant, uneatable

delight NOUN *Florence laughed with delight.* ► pleasure, happiness, joy, enjoyment, bliss, rapture, ecstasy

delight VERB **1** *She delighted her father by singing for him.* ► please, charm, thrill, gratify, enchant, captivate, enthral, entrance, amuse, (*more informal*) bowl over OPPOSITES ARE displease, disgust **2 delight in** *Fran delighted in the flowers he gave her.* ► relish, enjoy, love, savor, revel in OPPOSITES ARE hate, dislike, loathe

delighted ADJECTIVE *He was delighted to see that Jenny had arrived.* ► pleased, happy, glad, thrilled, overjoyed, gratified, excited, ecstatic OPPOSITES ARE dismayed, disappointed

delightful ADJECTIVE *He told Julie how delightful it had been to meet her.* ► pleasant, lovely, enjoyable, pleasing, pleasurable, gratifying, satisfying, marvelous, wonderful

delinquency NOUN *attacking the root causes of delinquency* ► crime, wrongdoing, criminality, lawbreaking, misconduct, misbehavior

delinquent ADJECTIVE *She was quite good with delinquent adolescents.* ► lawless, lawbreaking, errant, unruly, offending, criminal, unmanageable, uncontrollable

delinquent NOUN *It was not fair to label them delinquents.* ► offender, lawbreaker,

wrongdoer, young offender, criminal, hooligan, hoodlum, miscreant

delirious ADJECTIVE **1** *The illness made Luke delirious for days on end.* ► demented, raving, incoherent, hysterical, irrational, feverish, frenzied **2** *She was delirious with joy.* ► ecstatic, elated, thrilled, beside yourself, exultant, wild

deliver VERB **1** *The books will be delivered to your address within the next week.* ► send, convey, transport, bring, supply, take, dispatch **2** *The court delivered its verdict.* ► utter, give, make, read, announce, declare, pronounce, speak **3** *He delivered a powerful blow to the back of the head.* ► administer, deal, launch, aim, strike, hit **4** *The hostages were all delivered from their captors.* ► rescue, save, set free, liberate, release, redeem, ransom

delivery NOUN **1** *There is a daily delivery of fresh vegetables.* ► consignment, batch, shipment, distribution **2** *The delivery of the message was timed at 3:30.* ► dispatch, transmission, conveyance

delude VERB *You are deluding yourself if you think that.* ► deceive, mislead, fool, take in, hoodwink, beguile, bamboozle, trick

demand NOUN **1** *She refused to give way to their demands.* ► request, requirement, claim, ultimatum, stipulation, insistence **2** *There is much less demand for hardcover books.* ► call, market, need, necessity

demand VERB **1** *The workers demanded a 10% pay rise.* ► call for, ask for, claim, want, insist on, require, request, expect **2** *"Where are they?" he demanded.* ► ask, inquire, challenge, question

A B C D E F G H I J K L M N O P Q R S T U V W X Y Z

demand NOUN **demands 1** a firm or forceful request **2** a desire to have or buy something • *There is a great demand for computers* in demand wanted or needed

demanding ADJECTIVE needing a lot of effort or attention • *a demanding job;* • *a demanding child*

demarcation (dee- mar- **kay**- shon) NOUN marking the boundary or limits of something

demented ADJECTIVE driven mad; crazy

demigod NOUN **demigods** a partly divine being

democracy NOUN **democracies 1** government of a country by representatives elected by the people **2** a country governed in this way
▷ **democrat** NOUN **democratic** ADJECTIVE **democratically** ADVERB

Democrat NOUN **Democrats** a member of the Democratic Party

demolish VERB **demolishes, demolishing, demolished 1** knock a building down and break it up **2** destroy something completely
▷ **demolition** NOUN

demon NOUN **demons 1** a devil; an evil spirit **2** a fierce or forceful person
▷ **demonic** (dim- **on**- ik) ADJECTIVE

demonstrate VERB **demonstrates, demonstrating, demonstrated 1** show or prove something **2** take part in a demonstration
▷ **demonstrator** NOUN

demonstration NOUN **demonstrations 1** demonstrating; showing how to do or work something **2** a march or meeting held to show everyone what you think about something

demonstrative (dim- on- **strat**- iv) ADJECTIVE **1** showing or proving something **2** showing feelings or affections openly **3** (in grammar) pointing out the person or thing referred to. *This, that, these,* and *those* are demonstrative adjectives and pronouns.
▷ **demonstratively** ADVERB **demonstrativeness** NOUN

demoralize VERB **demoralizes, demoralizing, demoralized** dishearten someone; weaken someone's confidence or morale
▷ **demoralization** NOUN

demote VERB **demotes, demoting, demoted** reduce a person to a lower position or rank
▷ **demotion** NOUN

demure ADJECTIVE shy and modest
▷ **demurely** ADVERB **demureness** NOUN

den NOUN **dens 1** a lair **2** a person's private room **3** a place where something illegal happens • *a gambling den*

Thesaurus

demanding ADJECTIVE **1** *a demanding child* ► insistent, trying, tiresome, importunate, nagging **2** *a demanding task* ► difficult, challenging, testing, exacting, taxing, hard, tough, onerous, arduous, formidable

demeanor NOUN *an anxious and nervous demeanor* ► attitude, bearing, manner, disposition

demise NOUN *the demise of the Assyrian Empire* ► downfall, collapse, end, disappearance, failure

democratic ADJECTIVE *a democratic government* ► elected, elective, popular, representative, chosen, egalitarian AN OPPOSITE IS undemocratic

demolish VERB *The explosion demolished a row of houses.* ► destroy, wreck, flatten, level, knock down, tear down, break down, obliterate, reduce to ruins OPPOSITES ARE construct, assemble

demolition NOUN *The houses face demolition.* ► destruction, dismantling, levelling, pulling down, flattening, clearance

demon NOUN *demons from hell* ► devil, fiend, spirit, goblin, imp

demonstrate VERB **1** *The evidence demonstrates a major change in the role of women.* ► show, indicate, establish, display, exhibit, point to, prove, substantiate, verify, exemplify, illustrate, manifest, represent **2** *People demonstrated in the streets.* ► protest, rally, hold a rally, lobby, march, parade, picket

demonstration NOUN **1** *a demonstration of skill and creativity* ► display, exhibition, manifestation, indication, revelation, expression, presentation, embodiment **2** *a demonstration against the war* ► protest, (informal) demo, rally, march, parade, sit-in, vigil

demoralize VERB *Poor pay demoralized the staff.* ► discourage, dishearten, depress, deject, dispirit, disconcert

den NOUN *He worked all evening in his den upstairs.* ► study, retreat, sanctum, hideaway, hideout, lair, sanctuary, private place, secret place

denial NOUN **1** *Reports of a threatened strike met with a firm denial.* ► contradiction, renunciation, repudiation, disavowal, dismissal, abnegation, disclaimer, negation, rejection AN OPPOSITE IS admission **2** *the denial of rights to certain minorities* ► refusal, withholding, withdrawal, veto

denote VERB *A snort from the corner denoted disagreement.* ► indicate, mean , express, signify, stand for, represent, symbolize, be the sign for

denial NOUN denials denying or refusing something

denim NOUN a kind of strong, usually blue, cotton cloth used to make jeans, etc.

denomination NOUN denominations **1** a name or title **2** a religious group with a special name • *Baptists, Methodists, and other denominations* **3** a unit of weight or of money • *coins of small denomination*

denominator NOUN denominators the number below the line in a fraction, showing how many parts the whole is divided into, e.g., 4 in $\frac{1}{4}$ COMPARE **numerator**

denounce VERB denounces, denouncing, denounced speak strongly against something; accuse • *They denounced him as a spy.*
▷ **denunciation** NOUN

dense ADJECTIVE **1** thick; packed close together • *dense fog* • *dense crowds* **2** (*informal*) stupid
▷ **densely** ADVERB

density NOUN densities **1** thickness **2** (in science) the proportion of mass to volume

dent NOUN dents a hollow left in a surface where something has pressed or hit it

dent VERB dents, denting, dented make a dent in something

dental ADJECTIVE to do with the teeth or with dentistry

dentist NOUN dentists a person who is trained to treat teeth, fill or extract them, fit false ones, etc.
▷ **dentistry** NOUN

denture NOUN dentures a set of false teeth

denude VERB denudes, denuding, denuded make bare or naked; strip something away
▷ **denudation** NOUN

denunciation NOUN denunciations denouncing

deny VERB denies, denying, denied **1** say that something is not true **2** refuse to give or allow something • *deny a request*

deodorant (dee- oh- der- ant) NOUN deodorants a substance that removes smells

depart VERB departs, departing, departed go away; leave
▷ **departure** NOUN
[from early French *départir* = separate]

department NOUN departments one section of a large organization or shop
▷ **departmental** ADJECTIVE

depend VERB depends, depending, depended depend on **1** rely on • *We depend on your help.* **2** be controlled by something else • *It all depends on the weather.*

Thesaurus

denounce VERB *He denounced them for their dishonesty.* ► condemn, censure, find fault with, criticize, blame, castigate, disparage, denigrate, deprecate, (*more informal*) knock, (*more informal*) slam, (*more informal*) pan

dense ADJECTIVE **1** *a dense crowd; dense undergrowth* ► thick, closely packed, tightly packed, impenetrable, massed AN OPPOSITE IS sparse **2** *dense smoke* ► thick, heavy, concentrated OPPOSITES ARE thin, light **3** *too dense to understand the point* ► stupid, foolish, crass, dull, slow, slow-witted, unintelligent OPPOSITES ARE clever, intelligent

dent NOUN *There were several small dents in the side of the vehicle.* ► indentation, dint, dimple, dip, concavity, depression, hollow, pit

dent VERB **1** *He dropped the saucepan and dented it.* ► make a dent in, push in, knock in, buckle, depress **2** *Nothing much could dent her confidence.* ► diminish, reduce, impair, damage, harm, affect

deny VERB **1** *The story was denied by the senator's office. The accused denied all the charges.* ► contradict, repudiate, rebut, reject, dismiss, contest, oppose, refute USAGE Note that *refute* means "to disprove by using arguments" **2** *The authorities have denied them their basic rights.* ► refuse, forbid, withhold

depart VERB **1** *The officials departed after lunch.* ► leave, go, go away, go off, withdraw, make off, retire, quit, (*old-fashioned*) take your leave, (*old-fashioned*) decamp AN OPPOSITE IS arrive **2** *At this point the speaker departed from his notes.* ► deviate, digress, differ, diverge, drift AN OPPOSITE IS stick to

department NOUN **1** *He works in a government department.* ► division, section, sector, unit, branch, subdivision, office, bureau, agency, ministry **2** (*informal*) *I'm afraid travel arrangements are not my department.* ► domain, responsibility, business, affair, concern, field, area, sphere, line, province, function, job, specialty

departure NOUN **1** *Our departure has been delayed by half an hour.* ► leaving, setting off, going, exit, withdrawal, disappearance, embarkation, escape, exodus, retirement, retreat AN OPPOSITE IS arrival **2** *The book represents a departure from the author's familiar style.* ► change, change of direction, deviation, digression, shift, variation, innovation, branching out

depend VERB **1 depend on** *Choice of university can depend a lot on expected exam grades.* ► be dependent on, hinge on, hang on, rest on, revolve around **2 depend on** *I shall depend on you to help me.* ► rely on, count on, need, bank on, trust

dependent ➡ depraved

A
B
C
D
E
F
G
H
I
J
K
L
M
N
O
P
Q
R
S
T
U
V
W
X
Y
Z

dependent NOUN dependents a person who depends on another, especially financially
• She has two dependents.

dependent ADJECTIVE depending • She has two dependent children. • they are dependent on her
▷ **dependence** NOUN

deplore VERB deplores, deploring, deplored be very upset or annoyed by something
▷ **deplorable** ADJECTIVE **deplorably** ADVERB

deport VERB deports, deporting, deported send an unwanted foreign person out of a country
▷ **deportation** NOUN

depose VERB deposes, deposing, deposed remove a person from power

deposit NOUN deposits **1** an amount of money paid into a bank, etc. **2** money paid as a first instalment **3** a layer of solid matter in or on the earth

deposit VERB deposits, depositing, deposited **1** put something down **2** pay money as a deposit
▷ **depositor** NOUN

depot (dep- oh) NOUN depots **1** a place where things are stored **2** a place where buses or trains are kept and repaired **3** a headquarters

depraved ADJECTIVE behaving wickedly; of bad character
▷ **depravity** NOUN

Thesaurus

dependable ADJECTIVE She looked at Roland: so strong and dependable. ► reliable, trustworthy, faithful, true, loyal, constant, unswerving, sensible, responsible, conscientious, sound, steady, unfailing AN OPPOSITE IS unreliable

dependence NOUN **1** Trevor was determined to reduce his dependence on his family. ► reliance, need (for), trust (in), confidence (in) **2** a rise in drug dependence ► addiction, dependency, reliance, craving, abuse

dependent ADJECTIVE **1** dependent on A lot is dependent on their decision. ► conditional on, contingent on, connected with, controlled by, determined by, liable to, relative to, subject to, vulnerable to AN OPPOSITE IS independent **2** dependent on Prisoners remain dependent on what visitors bring for them. ► reliant on, supported by, sustained by, needful of **3** dependent on Some of these people are dependent on drugs. ► addicted to, reliant on, enslaved by, (more informal) hooked on

depict VERB **1** The painting depicts a village in winter. ► show, portray, represent, picture, illustrate, reproduce, delineate, describe, draw, narrate, outline, paint, sketch **2** The author depicts his own childhood in the story.
► describe, relate, narrate, recount, present, record, outline, delineate, portray, characterize

deplete VERB Local wars have depleted the food supply. ► exhaust, use up, consume, expend, reduce, decrease, lessen, drain, cut OPPOSITES ARE increase, augment, boost

deplorable ADJECTIVE **1** Their behavior had been deplorable. ► disgraceful, shameful, inexcusable, unforgivable, disreputable, lamentable, shocking, blameworthy, discreditable, reprehensible, scandalous, unfortunate, unworthy OPPOSITES ARE admirable, praiseworthy **2** The troops lived in deplorable conditions. ► lamentable, regrettable, awful, wretched, terrible, miserable, atrocious

deplore VERB **1** We deplore all forms of violence. ► condemn, disapprove of, denounce, abhor, decry, deprecate **2** He deplored the past difficulties and promised a brighter future.
► regret, lament, bemoan, express regret for

deploy VERB **1** The government deployed troops to prevent demonstrations. ► position, station, post, install, establish, bring into action **2** You will need to deploy all your personal and social skills. ► use, make use of, utilize, employ, exploit, take advantage of

deport VERB Illegal immigrants were deported.
► expel, banish, exile, expatriate, transport, extradite

depose VERB A military coup deposed the government. ► overthrow, overturn, bring down, oust, get rid of, remove, displace, (more informal) topple AN OPPOSITE IS enthrone

deposit NOUN **1** You will need to pay a deposit to keep the reservations. ► down payment, advance payment, part payment, security, retainer, first payment **2** a thick deposit of mud ► layer, covering, coating, accumulation, sediment, silt, sludge, dregs, lees, precipitate **3** a deposit at the bottom of the bottle
► sediment, accumulation, dregs, silt

deposit VERB **1** She deposited a pile of papers on the desk. ► put down, set down, lay down, place, leave, (more informal) dump, (more informal) stick, (more informal) plonk, (more informal) park **2** The money is deposited each Friday. ► pay in, bank, lodge, save **3** The flood water deposited layers of mud. ► precipitate, wash up

depot NOUN **1** a military depot ► store, storehouse, base, cache, depository, arsenal, dump, hoard **2** a bus depot ► garage, station, terminus, headquarters

depreciate VERB The value of property is not likely to depreciate. ► drop, fall, become less, lessen, lower, reduce, decrease, go down, deflate, slump, weaken AN OPPOSITE IS appreciate

depress VERB depresses, depressing, depressed **1** make somebody sad **2** lower the value of something • *Threat of war depressed prices.* **3** press down • *Depress the lever.*
▷ **depressive** ADJECTIVE

depression NOUN depressions **1** a feeling of great sadness or hopelessness **2** a long period when trade is very slow because many people cannot afford to buy things, with widespread unemployment **3** a shallow hollow in the ground or on a surface **4** an area of low air pressure which may bring rain **5** pressing something down

deprive VERB deprives, depriving, deprived take or keep something away from somebody
▷ **deprival** NOUN **deprivation** NOUN

depth NOUN depths **1** being deep; how deep something is **2** the deepest or lowest part in depth thoroughly
out of your depth **1** in water that is too deep to stand in **2** trying to do something that is too difficult for you

deputation NOUN deputations a group of people sent as representatives of others

deputy NOUN deputies a person appointed to act as a substitute for another

deranged ADJECTIVE insane
▷ **derangement** NOUN

derby NOUN derbies a sport between two teams from the same city or area [from the name of the Earl of Derby, who in 1780 founded the famous horse race called the Derby which is run at Epsom in Surrey]

derelict (derri- likt) ADJECTIVE abandoned and left to fall into ruin
▷ **dereliction** NOUN

deride VERB derides, deriding, derided laugh at with contempt or scorn; ridicule
▷ **derision** NOUN

derive VERB derives, deriving, derived **1** obtain something from a source • *She derived great enjoyment from music.* **2** form or originate from something • *Some English words are derived from Latin words.*
▷ **derivation** NOUN **derivative** ADJECTIVE

——— Thesaurus ———

depress VERB **1** *The latest news depressed everyone.* ► sadden, deject, dishearten, dispirit, upset, discourage, grieve, lower the spirits of, oppress, make sad AN OPPOSITE IS cheer **2** *Aid tends to depress local markets.* ► undermine, weaken, impair, inhibit, check, make less active, slow down, bring down, push down, deflate AN OPPOSITE IS boost

depressed ADJECTIVE *Sam looked tired and depressed.* ► dejected, downcast, despondent, dispirited, disheartened, downhearted, disconsolate, unhappy, sad, down, glum, melancholy, miserable, cast down OPPOSITES ARE cheerful, happy

depressing ADJECTIVE **1** *Tuesday was a cold, depressing day.* ► gloomy, bleak, dreary, dismal, grim, drab, somber, dingy, cheerless **2** *He tried to get rid of all such depressing thoughts.* ► dispiriting, disheartening, upsetting, distressing, melancholy, painful, morbid

depression NOUN **1** *A sudden feeling of depression took hold of him.* ► sadness, dejection, melancholy, sorrow, despondency, unhappiness, low spirits, glumness, desolation, despair, pessimism, (more informal) the blues, (more informal) the dumps AN OPPOSITE IS cheerfulness **2** *an economic depression* ► recession, slump, decline, downturn, slowdown, stagnation, hard times AN OPPOSITE IS boom **3** *a meteorological depression* ► area of low pressure, cyclone, low AN OPPOSITE IS anticyclone **4** *The wheel hit a depression in the ground.* ► hollow, indentation, dent, cavity, hole, pothole, dip, dimple, concavity OPPOSITES ARE bump, protuberance

deprive VERB deprive of *The war deprived her of her income.* ► deny, dispossess of, rob of, divest of, strip of, take away, starve of, refuse, prevent from having

deprived ADJECTIVE *deprived sections of society* ► disadvantaged, underprivileged, needy, poor, badly off, destitute

depth NOUN **1** *They tried to measure the depth of the water.* ► deepness, distance to the bottom, vertical extent, drop **2** *The orchestra's playing showed a great depth of feeling.* ► extent, degree, range, breadth, scope

deputy NOUN *During her absence her duties are done by a deputy.* ► second in command, number two, substitute, assistant, stand-in, representative, understudy USAGE Note that *understudy* normally means an actor who takes the place of the main actor when he or she is ill or indisposed.

derelict ADJECTIVE *The car passed a row of derelict buildings.* ► dilapidated, ramshackle, run down, tumbledown, ruined, deserted, abandoned, neglected, broken down, decrepit

derivation NOUN **1** *the derivation of the word "posh"* ► origin, etymology, root, provenance, source **2** *a family of noble derivation* ► ancestry, origin, genealogy, descent, provenance

derive VERB **1** *She derived some comfort from the fact that she knew the truth.* ► gain, receive, obtain, draw, acquire, get **2** *The family's wealth derives from oil.* ► originate (in), stem, arise, spring, flow, emanate **3** be derived from *The word "yacht" is derived from Dutch.* ► come from, originate in, stem from, descend from

a
b
c
d
e
f
g
h
i
j
k
l
m
n
o
p
q
r
s
t
u
v
w
x
y
z

descend ➡ design

descend VERB descends, descending, descended go down
▷ **descent** NOUN
be descended from have as an ancestor; come by birth from a certain person or family

descendant NOUN descendants a person who is descended from someone

describe VERB describes, describing, described
1 say what someone or something is like
2 draw in outline; move in a pattern • *The orbit of the Earth around the Sun describes an ellipse.*
▷ **description** NOUN **descriptive** ADJECTIVE

desert (dez- ert) NOUN deserts a large area of dry often sandy land

desert (diz- ert) VERB deserts, deserting, deserted leave a person or place without intending to return
▷ **deserter** NOUN **desertion** NOUN

desert island NOUN desert islands an uninhabited island

deserve VERB deserves, deserving, deserved have a right to something; be worthy of something
▷ **deservedly** ADVERB

design NOUN designs 1 a drawing that shows how something is to be made 2 the way something is made or arranged 3 lines and shapes that form a decoration; a pattern 4 a mental plan or scheme
have designs on plan to get hold of

Thesaurus

descend VERB 1 *The little plane descended toward the runway.* ► come down, go down, drop, subside, fall, move down, sink, dive, plummet OPPOSITES ARE ascend, climb 2 *The road descends to a small village.* ► slope, dip, drop, fall, incline, slant AN OPPOSITE IS ascend
be descended from *We are descended from an Italian family.* ► come from, originate in, spring from, stem from
descend from *He watched her descend from the train.* ► get off, alight from, disembark from, dismount from
descend on *A bachelor party descended on the local bar.* ► engulf, overwhelm, invade
descend to *In the end they descended to trickery.* ► condescend to, stoop to, lower yourself to, resort to, be reduced to, go as far as

descendants PLURAL NOUN *descendants of J. S. Bach* ► line, lineage, heirs, family, successors, offspring, progeny, children, issue, posterity AN OPPOSITE IS ancestors

descent NOUN 1 *the descent into the Grand Canyon* ► way down, drop, incline, dip, declivity, slant, slope, fall AN OPPOSITE IS ascent 2 *a person of French descent* ► ancestry, parentage, origin, lineage, extraction, heredity, blood, pedigree, genealogy, background, derivation, family, stock, strain

describe VERB 1 *A witness described the incident in detail.* ► report, narrate, relate, set out, explain, recount 2 *describe as I would never describe him as "charming."* ► call, speak of, refer to, classify, categorize, characterize as, portray, present, represent 3 *The pencil described a circle.* ► draw, mark out, trace

description NOUN 1 *She launched into a detailed description of her day.* ► account, explanation, report, narration, commentary (on) 2 *The room was crammed with furniture of every description.* ► sort, kind, variety, type, category, class, order

descriptive ADJECTIVE *an exercise using descriptive language* ► expressive, graphic,
colorful, detailed, pictorial, vivid, striking, explanatory, illustrative

desert NOUN (with the stress on *des-*) *lost in the desert* ► wasteland, wilderness, waste, wilds

desert ADJECTIVE (with the stress on *des-*)
1 *desert conditions* ► arid, dry, waterless, parched, barren, infertile, sterile, uncultivated, wild AN OPPOSITE IS fertile 2 *a desert island* ► uninhabited, solitary, lonely, desolate, isolated, unfrequented AN OPPOSITE IS inhabited

desert VERB (with the stress on *-sert*) 1 *Her husband had deserted her.* ► abandon, leave, strand, forsake, give up, jilt, renounce, betray, (more informal) dump, (more informal) walk out on, (more informal) leave in the lurch 2 *He had decided to desert the party and join the opposition.*
► renounce, abandon, leave, quit, disavow, forsake, (more informal) have done with
3 *Soldiers were deserting in large numbers.*
► abscond, defect, decamp, make off, go absent, turn tail, run away

deserted ADJECTIVE 1 *a deserted village*
► uninhabited, empty, unoccupied, evacuated, neglected, desolate, vacant 2 *a deserted wife* ► abandoned, stranded, forsaken, jilted, cast off, betrayed

deserve VERB 1 *You deserve a vacation.* ► be entitled to, be worthy of, have earned, have a right to, be good enough for 2 *The work deserves the highest praise.* ► merit, justify, warrant, rate

design NOUN 1 *a design for the new building*
► plan, blueprint, drawing, outline, pattern, prototype, sketch, draft, model 2 *furniture of a fresh bright design* ► pattern, style, form, composition, arrangement, configuration
3 *His design was to travel and enjoy life.*
► intention, ambition, aim, aspiration, goal, object, objective, purpose, end, scheme

design VERB 1 *Wren designed several churches.*
► plan, draw plans of, map out, outline, draw, sketch 2 *an engineer who designed a new*

design VERB designs, designing, designed **1** draw a design for something **2** plan or intend something for a special purpose
▷ **designer** NOUN

desirable ADJECTIVE **1** causing people to desire it; worth having **2** worth doing; advisable
▷ **desirability** NOUN

desire NOUN desires a feeling of wanting something very much
▷ **desirous** ADJECTIVE

desire VERB desires, desiring, desired have a desire for something

desk NOUN desks **1** a piece of furniture with a flat top and often drawers, used when writing or doing work **2** a counter at which a cashier or receptionist sits

desktop ADJECTIVE suitable to be used on a desk ● *a desktop computer*

desolate ADJECTIVE **1** lonely and sad **2** uninhabited
▷ **desolation** NOUN

despair NOUN a feeling of hopelessness

despair VERB despairs, despairing, despaired feel despair

desperate ADJECTIVE **1** extremely serious or hopeless ● *a desperate situation* **2** having a great need or desire for something ● *She is desperate to get a ticket* **3** reckless and ready to do anything
▷ **desperately** ADVERB **desperation** NOUN

despise VERB despises, despising, despised think someone or something is inferior or worthless

despite PREPOSITION in spite of

despondent ADJECTIVE sad or gloomy
▷ **despondently** ADVERB **despondency** NOUN

dessert (diz- ert) NOUN desserts fruit or a sweet food served as the last course of a meal

destination NOUN destinations the place to which a person or thing is traveling

destined ADJECTIVE having as a destiny; intended

destiny NOUN destinies what will happen or has happened to somebody or something; fate

Thesaurus

kind of engine ► create, invent, develop, devise, originate, conceive, think up

desirable ADJECTIVE **1** *a very desirable woman* ► attractive, beautiful, alluring, appealing, (*more informal*) sexy **2** *It would be desirable for them to express their support.* ► advantageous, advisable, helpful, beneficial, worthwhile, preferable, sensible, prudent

desire NOUN **1** *Ed has always had a desire to travel.* ► wish, longing, yearning, craving, inclination, eagerness, enthusiasm, impulse, appetite (for), (*more informal*) yen **2** *She saw that his eyes were dark with desire.* ► lust, passion, ardor, lasciviousness, libido, love

desire VERB **1** *We all desire peace.* ► want, wish for, yearn for, long for, covet, crave, need, hanker after, hunger for, thirst for, pine for, ache for, fancy, like, prefer, (*informal*) set your heart on, (*informal*) itch for, (*informal*) have a yen for **2** *He knew he desired him.* ► be attracted to, be captivated by, be infatuated by, lust after, (*more informal*) have a crush on

desolate ADJECTIVE **1** *They reached a desolate spot near the coast.* ► deserted, uninhabited, abandoned, barren, bare, bleak, gloomy, dismal, dreary, godforsaken **2** *Feeling desolate, she asked him to forgive her.* ► miserable, sad, unhappy, forlorn, depressed, dejected, downcast, despondent, disconsolate AN OPPOSITE IS cheerful

despair NOUN *Stephen was in a state of despair.* ► hopelessness, desperation, despondency, anguish, pessimism, melancholy, gloom, misery, wretchedness, dejection, depression AN OPPOSITE IS hope

despair VERB *At times like this you can easily despair.* ► lose hope, give up hope, lose heart, be demoralized AN OPPOSITE IS hope

desperate ADJECTIVE **1** *He tried not to listen to the desperate cries outside.* ► despairing, hopeless, anguished, inconsolable, distraught, distressed, miserable, wretched **2** *There was a desperate shortage of food.* ► acute, critical, severe, serious, grave, dire, urgent **3** *a band of desperate criminals* ► violent, wild, dangerous, reckless, impetuous

desperation NOUN **1** *In desperation, she decided to go back to Chicago to find him.* ► despair, hopelessness, anguish, despondency, distress **2** *The robbery seemed like an act of desperation.* ► recklessness, rashness, impetuosity, foolhardiness, frenzy

despicable ADJECTIVE *guilty of despicable crimes* ► contemptible, loathsome, hateful, vile, shameful, detestable, abhorrent

despise VERB *She despised the methods he used in business.* ► scorn, disdain, look down on, deride, condemn, deplore, revile, detest, loathe, feel contempt for AN OPPOSITE IS admire

despondent ADJECTIVE *Perhaps he was feeling despondent about his exam results.* ► disheartened, dejected, depressed, downhearted, downcast, gloomy, upset, down, miserable, sad

destiny NOUN **1** *Destiny had intervened to help them.* ► fate, fortune, chance, luck, providence, karma **2** *He seemed once more in control of his destiny.* ► future, fortune, fate, lot

a
b
c
d
e
f
g
h
i
j
k
l
m
n
o
p
q
r
s
t
u
v
w
x
y
z

destitute ADJECTIVE left without anything; living in extreme poverty
▷ **destitution** NOUN

destroy VERB destroys, destroying, destroyed ruin or put an end to something
▷ **destruction** NOUN **destructive** ADJECTIVE

destroyer NOUN destroyers a fast warship

detach VERB detaches, detaching, detached unfasten or separate
▷ **detachable** ADJECTIVE **detachment** NOUN

detached ADJECTIVE **1** separated **2** (said about a house) not joined to another **3** impartial; not involved in something

detail NOUN details **1** a very small part of a design or plan or decoration, etc. **2** a small piece of information
▷ **detailed** ADJECTIVE

in detail describing or dealing with everything fully

detain VERB detains, detaining, detained **1** keep someone waiting **2** keep someone at a place

detect VERB detects, detecting, detected discover
▷ **detection** NOUN **detector** NOUN

detective NOUN detectives a person who investigates crimes

detention NOUN detentions **1** detaining; being detained **2** being made to stay late in school as a punishment

deter VERB deters, deterring, deterred discourage or prevent a person from doing something

Thesaurus

destitute ADJECTIVE He had left her destitute with two children to care for. ► penniless, impoverished, poverty-stricken, impecunious, homeless, indigent, deprived, down and out, insolvent, needy, poor AN OPPOSITE IS wealthy

destroy VERB **1** A bomb had destroyed the building. ► demolish, ruin, wreck, obliterate, devastate, shatter, blow up **2** Disease destroyed all hopes of an economic recovery. ► wreck, ruin, spoil, obliterate, disrupt, upset, put an end to, frustrate, thwart, undermine OPPOSITES ARE raise, revive **3** Their intention was to destroy the enemy. ► kill, slaughter, annihilate, slay, eradicate

destruction NOUN **1** Fires caused widespread destruction. ► devastation, damage, demolition, ruination, havoc **2** much wildlife faces destruction ► annihilation, obliteration, elimination, extinction, extermination

destructive ADJECTIVE **1** a destructive storm ► devastating, damaging, ruinous, catastrophic, violent, ravaging **2** destructive criticism ► hostile, antagonistic, vicious, negative, fierce, disparaging AN OPPOSITE IS constructive

detach VERB You can detach the printing head for cleaning. ► remove, unfasten, disconnect, take off, separate, disengage, unfix, free AN OPPOSITE IS attach

detached ADJECTIVE **1** detached houses set back from the road ► freestanding, separate, unconnected **2** Her face expressed detached amusement. ► dispassionate, disinterested, impartial, aloof, distant, objective AN OPPOSITE IS committed

detachment NOUN **1** He regarded the matter with detachment. ► dispassion, objectivity, disinterest, impartiality, neutrality, unconcern, aloofness, remoteness **2** a detachment of soldiers ► unit, squad, force, troop, corps, brigade, task force

detail NOUN **1** The copy of the painting was accurate in every detail. ► feature, particular, aspect, characteristic, circumstance, respect, item, point, factor, specific, fact, ingredient USAGE You can also use minutiae, which is a Latin plural word meaning "details." **2** She has an eye for detail. ► precision, exactness, accuracy, rigor, thoroughness
in detail They commented on the proposals in detail. ► in depth, thoroughly, closely, methodically, minutely, meticulously, point by point, item by item

detail VERB **1** An appendix details the sources used in the book. ► describe, list, present, explain, recount, spell out **2** The head boy was detailed to look after the visitors. ► appoint, assign, delegate, commission, nominate, choose

detailed ADJECTIVE a detailed description of the scene ► precise, exact, comprehensive, complete, elaborate, exhaustive, minute, intricate, specific OPPOSITES ARE general, summary

detain VERB **1** The authorities wanted to detain them for questioning. ► hold, arrest, apprehend, hold in custody, confine, restrain, intern, imprison, gaol, capture AN OPPOSITE IS release **2** Something must have detained them. ► delay, hold up, impede, hinder, keep, check, prevent, keep waiting, retard, slow, stop, waylay

detect VERB **1** We detected slight patches of rust. ► notice, become aware of, perceive, discern, make out, recognize, identify, spot **2** The crime was detected with the help of DNA evidence. ► discover, uncover, expose, reveal, unearth, find out, root out, unmask, track down

deter VERB **1** It was mainly the expense that deterred them. ► discourage, put off, inhibit, dissuade, intimidate, prevent, exclude AN OPPOSITE IS encourage **2** measures to deter

detergent NOUN detergents a substance used for cleaning or washing things

deteriorate (dit- eer- ee- er- ayt) VERB deteriorates, deteriorating, deteriorated become worse
▷ deterioration NOUN

determination NOUN **1** the firm intention to achieve what you have decided to achieve **2** determining or deciding something

determine VERB determines, determining, determined **1** decide • *determine what is to be done* **2** find out; calculate • *determine the height of the mountain*

determined ADJECTIVE full of determination; with your mind firmly made up

determiner NOUN determiners (in grammar) a word (such as *a, the, many*) that modifies a noun

deterrent NOUN deterrents something that deters people, such as a powerful weapon or a threat of punishment

detest VERB detests, detesting, detested dislike something very much; loathe
▷ detestable ADJECTIVE detestation NOUN

detonate (det- on- ayt) VERB detonates, detonating, detonated explode or cause something to explode
▷ detonation NOUN detonator NOUN

detour (dee- toor) NOUN detours a roundabout route instead of the normal one

detriment (det- rim- ent) NOUN harm or disadvantage • *She worked long hours, to the detriment of her health.*

detrimental (det- rim- en- tal) ADJECTIVE harmful or disadvantageous
▷ detrimentally ADVERB

deuce NOUN deuces a score in tennis where both sides have 40 points and must gain two consecutive points to win

devalue VERB devalues, devaluing, devalued **1** reduce a thing's value **2** reduce the value of a country's currency in relation to other currencies or to gold
▷ devaluation NOUN

devastate VERB devastates, devastating, devastated **1** ruin or cause great destruction to something **2** cause great shock or grief to someone
▷ devastating ADJECTIVE devastation NOUN

develop VERB develops, developing, developed **1** make or become bigger or

Thesaurus

crime ► prevent, stop, check, put a stop to, reduce, discourage, counteract

deteriorate VERB **1** *His health deteriorated rapidly after his wife's death.* ► worsen, weaken, decline, lapse, fail, fade, fall off, get worse, relapse, slip, collapse, depreciate, (*more informal*) go downhill AN OPPOSITE IS improve **2** *These materials deteriorate if they are not stored correctly.* ► decay, degenerate, disintegrate, decompose, crumble

determination NOUN **1** *His determination to win grew stronger.* ► resolution, resolve, will, strength of will, intentness **2** *You will need a lot of determination.* ► resolve, firmness of purpose, tenacity, persistence, dedication, drive

determine VERB **1** *It can be difficult to determine the sex of pandas.* ► find out, discover, ascertain, decide, establish, identify, verify **2** *Certain chromosomes determine the sex of an embryo.* ► control, regulate, decide, direct, dictate, govern, influence, affect

determined ADJECTIVE **1** *He is determined he will have his way.* ► adamant, resolute, insistent, convinced, bent (on having), resolved (to have), intent (on having) AN OPPOSITE IS doubtful **2** *a determined young woman* ► resolute, purposeful, strong-willed, single-minded, strong-minded, steadfast, tenacious, dogged AN OPPOSITE IS irresolute

deterrent NOUN *Penalties need to serve as a deterrent to those tempted to offend.*
► discouragement, disincentive, impediment, warning, caution, brake, check, curb, obstacle, restraint, threat, (*more informal*) turn-off AN OPPOSITE IS encouragement

detest VERB *I detest that kind of talk.* ► hate, abhor, loathe, despise, dislike, deplore, recoil from

devastate VERB **1** *Storms have devastated the region.* ► destroy, damage severely, ravage, demolish, flatten, ruin, wreck, lay waste, level, overwhelm, raze **2** *He was clearly devastated by the news.* ► shatter, shock, dismay, stun, distress, overwhelm, upset

develop VERB **1** *Our plans have developed rapidly in the last few weeks.* ► progress, advance, evolve, grow, flourish, get better, improve, mature, thrive, move on AN OPPOSITE IS regress **2** *An argument developed.* ► arise, ensue, result, emerge, start, begin, erupt, come about, (*informal*) blow up **3** *The company wants to develop its overseas business.* ► expand, extend, diversify, build up, enlarge, increase, swell **4** *Children develop their reading skills at this age.* ► evolve, expand, advance, cultivate, acquire **5** *Let's see if we can develop these ideas.* ► amplify, augment, elaborate, enlarge on **6** *People were developing the disease at an early age.* ► contract, catch, get, succumb to, be infected with, come down with

a b c **d** e f g h i j k l m n o p q r s t u v w x y z

deviate ➡ devour

A
B
C
D
E
F
G
H
I
J
K
L
M
N
O
P
Q
R
S
T
U
V
W
X
Y
Z

better **2** come gradually into existence
• *Storms developed.* **3** begin to have or use
• *They developed bad habits.* **4** use an area of
land for building houses, shops, factories, etc.
5 treat photographic film with chemicals so
that pictures appear
▷ **developer** NOUN **development** NOUN

deviate (dee- vee- ayt) VERB **deviates,
deviating, deviated** turn aside from a course
or from what is usual or true
▷ **deviation** NOUN

device NOUN **devices 1** something made for a
particular purpose • *a device for opening cans*
2 a design used as a decoration or emblem
leave someone to their own devices leave
them to do as they wish

devil NOUN **devils 1** an evil spirit **2** a wicked,
cruel, or annoying person
▷ **devilish** ADJECTIVE **devilry** NOUN

devilment NOUN mischief

devious (dee- vee- us) ADJECTIVE **1** roundabout;
not direct • *a devious route* **2** not
straightforward; underhand
▷ **deviously** ADVERB **deviousness** NOUN

devise VERB **devises, devising, devised** invent
or plan

devoid ADJECTIVE lacking or without something
• *His work is devoid of merit.*

devolution NOUN handing over power from
central government to local or regional
government

devolve VERB **devolves, devolving, devolved**
pass or be passed to a deputy or successor

devote VERB **devotes, devoting, devoted** give
completely • *He devoted his time to sport.*

devoted ADJECTIVE very loving or loyal

devotee (dev- o- tee) NOUN **devotees** a person
who is devoted to something; an enthusiast

devotion NOUN great love or loyalty

devotions PLURAL NOUN prayers

devour VERB **devours, devouring, devoured**
eat or swallow something hungrily or greedily

Thesaurus

development NOUN **1** *the development of a
national road network* ▸ evolution, growth,
advance, furtherance, expansion, spread,
enlargement, promotion, improvement
2 *Congress met to discuss recent developments in
the Middle East.* ▸ event, happening,
occurrence, outcome, result, change, incident
3 *The land has been set aside for industrial
development.* ▸ exploitation, building,
conversion, use

deviate VERB *politicians who deviate from the
party policy* ▸ diverge, depart, digress, drift,
stray, wander, turn aside, differ, part, veer,
vary, err

deviation NOUN *Any deviation from the normal
routine caused chaos.* ▸ departure, divergence,
digression, variation, variance, deflection,
alteration, fluctuation, change, shift, disparity

device NOUN **1** *a device for converting digital
data into audio signals* ▸ implement,
apparatus, appliance, contraption,
contrivance, tool, utensil, gadget, instrument,
invention, machine **2** *a device to avoid
prosecution* ▸ ploy, tactic, plan, ruse, scheme,
stratagem, maneuver, contrivance, trick, stunt,
expedient, wile, gambit, gimmick, (*more
informal*) dodge **3** *a shield with a device showing
the family arms* ▸ emblem, symbol, motif,
badge, crest, insignia, seal, figure, logo

devil NOUN **1** *a sermon on the Devil and his works*
▸ Satan, Lucifer, the Evil One, the Prince of
Darkness, the Adversary **2** *a painting with
green-skinned devils holding tridents* ▸ demon,
fiend, imp, spirit **3** *The poor devil looked frozen
and soaked through.* ▸ wretch, fellow, soul

4 *impudent young devils* ▸ rascal, rogue,
monkey, scamp

devious ADJECTIVE **1** *a devious route around the
hills* ▸ circuitous, indirect, winding, rambling,
meandering, tortuous, roundabout, erratic,
deviating, wandering, crooked AN OPPOSITE IS
direct **2** *devious methods; a devious person*
▸ underhand, deceitful, dishonest, scheming,
calculating, cunning, treacherous, evasive,
insincere, misleading, sly, sneaky, wily AN
OPPOSITE IS straightforward

devise VERB *Devise a history project that includes
role play.* ▸ conceive, think up, think out, work
out, invent, make up, plan, form, prepare,
design, concoct, contrive, scheme, formulate,
imagine, plot

devote VERB *He claimed he wanted to devote
more time to his family.* ▸ set aside, dedicate,
assign, allot, commit, give yourself

devoted ADJECTIVE *a devoted wife and mother*
▸ loyal, faithful, dedicated, staunch, fond,
loving, caring, committed, devout, steadfast,
true

devotion NOUN **1** *her devotion to her family*
▸ loyalty, dedication, commitment,
faithfulness, staunchness, steadfastness,
fondness (for) **2** *a life of religious devotion*
▸ piety, spirituality, devoutness, holiness,
sanctity

devour VERB **1** *She watched him as he devoured
his meal.* ▸ eat, consume, guzzle, gobble, wolf
down, bolt down, (*more informal*) scoff, (*more
informal*) demolish **2** *Flames devoured the barn.*
▸ destroy, consume, engulf, envelop,
demolish, ravage, wreck, dispatch

186

devout ➜ dictate

devout ADJECTIVE earnestly religious or sincere
  ▷ **devoutly** ADVERB **devoutness** NOUN

dew NOUN tiny drops of water that form during the night on surfaces of things in the open air
  ▷ **dewdrop** NOUN **dewy** ADJECTIVE

dexterity (deks- terri- tee) NOUN skill in handling things

dhoti NOUN **dhotis** the loincloth worn by male Hindus

diabetes (dy- a- bee- teez) NOUN a disease in which there is too much sugar in a person's blood
  ▷ **diabetic** (dy- a- bet- ik) ADJECTIVE, NOUN

diabolical ADJECTIVE **1** like a devil; very wicked **2** very clever or annoying

diadem (dy- a- dem) NOUN **diadems** a crown or headband worn by a royal person

diagnose VERB **diagnoses, diagnosing, diagnosed** find out what disease a person has or what is wrong
  ▷ **diagnosis** NOUN **diagnostic** ADJECTIVE

diagonal (dy- ag- on- al) NOUN **diagonals** a straight line joining opposite corners
  ▷ **diagonal** ADJECTIVE **diagonally** ADVERB

diagram NOUN **diagrams** a kind of drawing or picture that shows the parts of something or how it works

dial NOUN **dials** a circular object with numbers or letters round it

dial VERB **dials, dialing, dialed** telephone a number by turning a telephone dial or pressing numbered buttons

dialect NOUN **dialects** the words and pronunciations used by people in one district but not in the rest of a country

dialogue NOUN **dialogues** **1** the words spoken by characters in a play, film, or story **2** a conversation

dialysis (dy- al- iss- iss) NOUN a way of removing harmful substances from the blood by letting it flow through a machine

diameter (dy- am- it- er) NOUN **diameters** **1** a line drawn straight across a circle or sphere and passing through its center **2** the length of this line

diametrically ADVERB completely
  • *diametrically opposite*

diamond NOUN **diamonds** **1** a very hard precious stone, a form of carbon, that looks like clear glass **2** a shape with four equal sides and four angles that are not right angles **3** a playing card with red diamond shapes on it

diaper NOUN **diapers** a baby's undergarment

diaphanous (dy- af- an- us) ADJECTIVE (said about fabric) almost transparent

diaphragm (dy- a- fram) NOUN **diaphragms** **1** the muscular layer inside the body that separates the chest from the abdomen and is used in breathing **2** a dome-shaped contraceptive device that fits over the cervix

diarist NOUN **diarists** a person who keeps a diary

diarrhea (dy- a- ree- a) NOUN too frequent and too watery emptying of the bowels

diary NOUN **diaries** a book in which someone writes down what happens each day

diatribe NOUN **diatribes** a strong verbal attack

dice NOUN (strictly this is the plural of **die**[2], but it is often used as a singular, plural **dice**) a small cube marked with dots (1 to 6) on its sides, used in games

dice VERB **dices, dicing, diced** **1** cut meat, vegetables, etc. into small cubes **2** gamble or take risks with • *dice with death*

dictate VERB **dictates, dictating, dictated** **1** speak or read something aloud for someone

Thesaurus

devout ADJECTIVE *a devout Muslim* ▶ pious, devoted, dedicated, reverent, faithful, dutiful, true

diabolical ADJECTIVE **1** *The soldiers showed diabolical cruelty.* ▶ outrageous, appalling, atrocious, wicked, vile, shocking, fiendish, devilish **2** (*informal*) *The standard of driving was diabolical.* ▶ dreadful, awful, frightful, terrible, poor, bad

diagnose VERB *The consultant diagnosed a tumor.* ▶ identify, detect, recognize, spot, determine, isolate, distinguish, find, pinpoint

diagnosis NOUN *The original diagnosis proved to be incorrect.* ▶ identification, explanation, pronouncement, opinion, verdict, analysis, conclusion, interpretation

diagram NOUN *a diagram showing the workings of the digestive system* ▶ chart, plan, drawing,

outline, representation, sketch, schematic representation, figure, table, flowchart, graph, illustration, picture

diary NOUN **1** *She kept a diary from the age of ten.* ▶ journal, chronicle, daily record, log **2** *Put the date in your diary.* ▶ appointment book, engagement book, organizer, personal organizer

dicey ADJECTIVE (*informal*) *Crossing the bridge can be dicey in high winds.* ▶ risky, chancy, dangerous, hazardous, unsafe, precarious, insecure, tricky, uncertain, unpredictable AN OPPOSITE IS safe

dictate VERB **1** *He dictated a letter to his secretary.* ▶ read out, say aloud, recite, utter **2** *She wasn't going to let him dictate how she wore her hair.* ▶ prescribe, lay down, direct, order, ordain, impose, command, decree, enforce,

a b c d e f g h i j k l m n o p q r s t u v w x y z

187

else to write down **2** give orders in a bossy way
▷ **dictation** NOUN

dictates (dik- tayts) PLURAL NOUN orders or commands

dictator NOUN dictators a ruler who has unlimited power
▷ **dictatorial** (dik- ta- **tor**- ee- al) ADJECTIVE
dictatorship NOUN

diction NOUN **1** a person's way of speaking words • *clear diction* **2** a writer's choice of words

dictionary NOUN dictionaries a book that contains words in alphabetical order so that you can find out how to spell them and what they mean

didactic (dy- **dak**- tik) ADJECTIVE having the manner of someone who is lecturing people
▷ **didactically** ADVERB

diddle VERB diddles, diddling, diddled (*slang*) cheat or swindle

didn't (*mainly spoken*) did not

die[1] VERB dies, dying, died **1** stop living or existing **2** stop burning or functioning • *The fire had died down.*
be dying for or **to** (*informal*) want to have or do something very much • *We are all dying to see you again.*

die[2] NOUN singular of **dice**

die[3] NOUN dies a device that stamps a design on coins, etc., or that cuts or molds metal

diehard NOUN diehards a person who obstinately refuses to give up old ideas or policies

diesel (dee- zel) NOUN diesels **1** an engine that works by burning oil in compressed air **2** fuel for this kind of engine

diet[1] NOUN diets **1** special meals that someone eats in order to be healthy or to lose weight **2** the sort of foods usually eaten by a person or animal

diet VERB diets, dieting, dieted keep to a diet

diet[2] NOUN diets the legislature of certain countries (e.g., Japan)

dietitian (dy- it- ish- an) NOUN dietitians an expert in diet and nutrition

differ VERB differs, differing, differed **1** be different **2** disagree

difference NOUN differences **1** being different; the way in which things differ **2** the remainder left after one number is subtracted from another • *The difference between 8 and 3 is 5.* **3** a disagreement

different ADJECTIVE unlike; not the same
▷ **differently** ADVERB

Thesaurus

give orders about, make the rules about, (*informal*) lay down the law about **3** dictate to *He does rather tend to dictate to his friends.* ▶ order about, boss, tyrannize, bully, domineer, lord it over, (*more informal*) push around, (*more informal*) walk all over

dictator NOUN *what I would do if I were dictator for a day* ▶ tyrant, despot, autocrat, oppressor, (*more informal*) Big Brother

dictatorial ADJECTIVE *a dictatorial regime* ▶ autocratic, authoritarian, (*informal*) bossy, despotic, totalitarian, tyrannical, domineering, oppressive, absolute, intolerant, overbearing, repressive, undemocratic AN OPPOSITE IS democratic

dictionary NOUN *a word that was not in their dictionary* ▶ lexicon, glossary, vocabulary, wordbook, wordfinder, thesaurus

die VERB **1** *He was sixteen when his father died.* ▶ pass away, pass on, lose your life, meet your end, breathe your last, expire, (*more formal*) decease, (*more informal*) snuff it, (*more informal*) bite the dust, (*more informal*) kick the bucket **2** *Hopes of a peaceful settlement are dying.* ▶ fade, dwindle, sink, disappear, vanish, wither, melt away, dissolve **3** *The engine spluttered and died.* ▶ fail, cut out, stall

diet NOUN **1** *You need a healthy diet.* ▶ nutrition, nourishment, nutriment, food, fare **2** *His doctor put him on a diet.* ▶ dietary regime, regimen, abstinence, fast

differ VERB **1** *Opinions on the matter differed.* ▶ vary, diverge, be different **2** *Our beliefs differ from those of other religious groups.* ▶ diverge, vary, deviate, be different, contrast (with) AN OPPOSITE IS conform (to) **3** *The ministers differed about what to do next.* ▶ disagree, argue, dispute, dissent, clash, conflict, be at odds, oppose each other, contradict each other, fall out, quarrel AN OPPOSITE IS agree

difference NOUN *There is a big difference in their ages.* ▶ dissimilarity, divergence, contrast, disparity, discrepancy, distinction, diversity, gap, variety, inconsistency, incompatibility, differential, differentiation, incongruity AN OPPOSITE IS similarity

difference of opinion *The brothers were trying to resolve their difference of opinion.* ▶ disagreement, misunderstanding, dispute, argument, clash, conflict, controversy, debate, disharmony, dissent, quarrel, strife, tiff, wrangle

different ADJECTIVE **1** *There were many different answers to the question.* ▶ dissimilar, unlike, unalike, diverging, divergent, varying, deviating, opposed, inconsistent, incompatible, contradictory, contrary, clashing OPPOSITES ARE identical, similar **2** *Everything about the house looked different.* ▶ changed, altered, transformed, strange, unfamiliar AN OPPOSITE IS unchanging **3** *We want to try something different.* ▶ unusual, unorthodox,

a
b
c
d
e
f
g
h
i
j
k
l
m
n
o
p
q
r
s
t
u
v
w
x
y
z

USAGE It is regarded as more acceptable to say *different from* rather than *different than*, which is common in less formal use.

differential NOUN differentials **1** a difference in wages between one group of workers and another **2** a differential gear

differential gear NOUN differential gears a system of gears that makes a vehicle's driving wheels revolve at different speeds when going round corners

differentiate VERB differentiates, differentiating, differentiated **1** be a difference between things; make one thing different from another • *What are the features that differentiate one breed from another?* **2** distinguish; recognize differences • *We do not differentiate between them.*
▷ **differentiation** NOUN

difficult ADJECTIVE needing a lot of effort or skill; not easy

difficulty NOUN difficulties **1** being difficult **2** something that causes a problem

diffident (dif- id- ent) ADJECTIVE shy and not self-confident; hesitating to put yourself or your ideas forward
▷ **diffidently** ADVERB **diffidence** NOUN

diffract VERB diffracts, diffracting, diffracted break up a beam of light, etc.
▷ **diffraction** NOUN

diffuse (dif- yooz) VERB diffuses, diffusing, diffused **1** spread something widely or thinly
• *diffused lighting* **2** mix slowly • *diffusing gases*
▷ **diffusion** NOUN

diffuse (dif- yooss) ADJECTIVE **1** spread widely; not concentrated **2** using many words; not concise
▷ **diffusely** ADVERB **diffuseness** NOUN

dig VERB digs, digging, dug **1** break up soil and move it; make a hole or tunnel by moving soil **2** poke something in • *Dig a knife into it.* **3** seek or discover by investigating
• *We dug up some facts.*
▷ **digger** NOUN

dig NOUN digs **1** a piece of digging, especially an archaeological excavation **2** a poke **3** a critical remark

digest (dy- jest) VERB digests, digesting, digested **1** soften and change food in the stomach, etc., so that the body can absorb it **2** take information into your mind and think it over
▷ **digestible** ADJECTIVE **digestion** NOUN

digest (dy- jest) NOUN digests a summary of news, information, etc.

Thesaurus

uncommon, new, fresh, original, unconventional, unique, abnormal, extraordinary, irregular AN OPPOSITE IS conventional **4** *Every person's fingerprint is different.* ► distinct, unique, distinctive, individual, special, peculiar, personal, particular, specific OPPOSITES ARE identical, indistinguishable

differentiate VERB *It was hard to differentiate fact from fiction.* ► distinguish, tell apart, tell the difference between, discriminate between

difficult ADJECTIVE **1** *a difficult problem*
► complicated, complex, hard, intricate, involved, intractable, abstruse, obscure, advanced, perplexing, problematical, baffling, deep, enigmatic, (more informal) thorny, (more informal) tricky OPPOSITES ARE easy, straightforward **2** *a difficult climb; a difficult task* ► hard, arduous, laborious, demanding, strenuous, tough, formidable, wearisome, burdensome, exacting, challenging OPPOSITES ARE easy, light **3** *difficult neighbors; a difficult child* ► unmanageable, troublesome, trying, tiresome, uncooperative, intractable, unruly, unhelpful, perverse OPPOSITES ARE manageable, tractable, accommodating

difficulty NOUN **1** *They found themselves in some difficulty.* ► trouble, distress, hardship, adversity, need, predicament, embarrassment, (more informal) fix, (more informal) mess **2** *The*

cost of the vacation might be a difficulty.
► problem, complication, snag, obstacle, hindrance, stumbling block, hurdle, pitfall, (more informal) headache, (more informal) hiccup

diffidence NOUN *She replied with some diffidence.* ► reserve, shyness, bashfulness, timidity, modesty, humility, hesitancy, uncertainty, unassertiveness, self-consciousness

diffident ADJECTIVE *a diffident smile* ► shy, coy, reserved, bashful, sheepish, inhibited, embarrassed, modest, self-conscious, hesitant, timid, retiring OPPOSITES ARE assertive, forward, bold, confident

dig VERB **1** *The little dog was digging a hole in the garden.* ► burrow, excavate, scoop, tunnel, gouge out, hollow out, mine, quarry, delve **2** *Dinah dug him in the ribs.* ► poke, prod, jab, nudge, shove

dig up 1 *The police dug up the remains.*
► disinter, extricate, exhume **2** *Can you dig up some more information?* ► uncover, find out, discover

digest VERB **1** *The food is heavy and difficult to digest.* ► absorb, assimilate, process, dissolve, break down **2** *There is a lot of information to digest.* ► take in, consider, absorb, ponder, study, understand

189

A
B
C
D
E
F
G
H
I
J
K
L
M
N
O
P
Q
R
S
T
U
V
W
X
Y
Z

digestive ADJECTIVE to do with digestion • *the digestive system*

digit (dij- it) NOUN digits **1** any of the numbers from 0 to 9 **2** a finger or toe

digital ADJECTIVE **1** to do with or using digits **2** (said about a watch or clock) showing the time with a row of figures **3** (said about a computer, recording, etc.) storing the data or sound as a series of binary digits

dignified ADJECTIVE having dignity

dignitary NOUN dignitaries an important official

dignity NOUN a calm and serious manner **beneath your dignity** not considered worthy enough for you to do

dilapidated ADJECTIVE falling to pieces
▷ **dilapidation** NOUN

dilemma (dil- em- a) NOUN dilemmas a situation where someone has to choose between two or more possible actions, each of which will bring difficulties
USAGE Do not use **dilemma** to mean simply a problem or difficult situation. There should be some idea of choosing between two (or perhaps more) things.

diligent (dil- ij- ent) ADJECTIVE hard-working
▷ **diligently** ADVERB **diligence** NOUN

dilute VERB dilutes, diluting, diluted make a liquid weaker by adding water or other liquid
▷ **dilution** NOUN

dilute ADJECTIVE diluted • *a dilute acid*

dim ADJECTIVE dimmer, dimmest **1** not bright or clear; only faintly lit **2** (*informal*) stupid
▷ **dimly** ADVERB **dimness** NOUN

dim VERB dims, dimming, dimmed make or become dim
▷ **dimmer** NOUN

dimension NOUN dimensions **1** a measurement such as length, width, area, or volume **2** size or extent
▷ **dimensional** ADJECTIVE

diminish VERB diminishes, diminishing, diminished make or become smaller
▷ **diminution** NOUN

diminutive (dim- in- yoo- tiv) ADJECTIVE very small

Thesaurus

digit NOUN **1** *Add up the digits.* ► numeral, figure, number, integer **2** *We tried to bring the blood back to our frozen digits.* ► finger, toe, extremity

dignified ADJECTIVE *Dr. McNab combined an air of authority with a calm and dignified manner.* ► stately, solemn, noble, majestic, imposing, distinguished, honorable, becoming, august, proper, grand, grave, decorous, sedate AN OPPOSITE IS undignified

dignity NOUN **1** *They accepted their misfortune with great dignity.* ► calmness, decorum, gravity, propriety, self-respect, eminence **2** *the dignity of a state occasion* ► majesty, grandeur, formality, solemnity, stateliness, magnificence, glory, greatness, honor, importance, nobility, pride, respectability, seriousness

digs PLURAL NOUN (*informal*) *My father paid for my digs in New York.* ► lodgings, room(s), accommodation, living quarters, apartment, (*more informal*) place, (*more informal*) pad

dilapidated ADJECTIVE *a row of dilapidated Victorian houses* ► rundown, ramshackle, decrepit, tumbledown, rickety, derelict, broken down, crumbling, neglected, ruined, decayed, tottering, uncared for OPPOSITES ARE smart, well maintained

dilemma NOUN *The need to earn money while still studying placed him in a dilemma.* ► quandary, difficulty, predicament, awkward situation, (*more informal*) catch-22

diligent ADJECTIVE *She had been diligent about her piano lessons.* ► conscientious, industrious, hard-working, painstaking, thorough, meticulous, punctilious, accurate, attentive, dedicated, rigorous, careful, dutiful, unflagging, assiduous, scrupulous OPPOSITES ARE careless, irresponsible, lazy

dim ADJECTIVE **1** *dim shapes in the distance; dim memories of their childhood* ► vague, indistinct, shadowy, unclear, fuzzy, blurred OPPOSITES ARE distinct, clear **2** *a dim room* ► dark, somber, dingy, gloomy, murky, dismal AN OPPOSITE IS bright **3** (*informal*) *You probably think I'm awfully dim.* ► stupid, dense, obtuse, (*more informal*) thick

dim VERB **1** *The sky slowly dimmed.* ► grow dark, darken, blacken, dull, cloud over **2** *He insisted on dimming the lights.* ► turn down, fade, lower, dip, shade, obscure OPPOSITES ARE turn up, brighten

dimensions PLURAL NOUN *a palace of huge dimensions* ► proportions, magnitude, size, scale, capacity, extent, scope

diminish VERB **1** *His angry feelings diminished in time.* ► decrease, reduce, lessen, decline, subside, wane, become less, depreciate, dwindle, peter out, shrink, shrivel, contract AN OPPOSITE IS increase **2** *We must not diminish their achievement.* ► belittle, disparage, demean, minimize, undervalue, devalue OPPOSITES ARE exaggerate, magnify

dimple NOUN dimples a small hollow or dent, especially in the skin
▷ **dimpled** ADJECTIVE

din NOUN a loud annoying noise

dine VERB dines, dining, dined (formal) have dinner
▷ **diner** NOUN

dinghy (ding- ee) NOUN dinghies a kind of small boat [from Hindi dingi = a small river boat]

dingy (din- jee) ADJECTIVE dirty-looking
▷ **dingily** ADVERB **dinginess** NOUN

dinner NOUN dinners **1** the main meal of the day, either at midday or in the evening **2** a formal evening meal in honor of something

dinosaur (dy- noss- or) NOUN dinosaurs a prehistoric reptile, often of enormous size

diocese (dy- oss- iss) NOUN dioceses a district under the care of a bishop

dioxide NOUN an oxide with two atoms of oxygen to one of another element • carbon dioxide

dip VERB dips, dipping, dipped put down or go down, especially into a liquid

dip NOUN dips **1** dipping **2** a downward slope **3** a quick swim **4** a substance into which things are dipped

diploma NOUN diplomas a certificate awarded by a college, etc., for skill in a particular subject

diplomacy NOUN **1** the work of making agreements with other countries **2** skill in dealing with people and gently persuading them to agree to things; tact

diplomat NOUN diplomats **1** a person employed in diplomacy on behalf of his or her country **2** a tactful person
▷ **diplomatic** ADJECTIVE

direct ADJECTIVE **1** as straight as possible **2** going straight to the point; frank **3** exact
• the direct opposite

direct VERB directs, directing, directed **1** tell someone the way **2** guide or aim in a certain direction **3** control or manage **4** order • He directed his troops to advance.

direct current NOUN electric current flowing only in one direction

direction NOUN directions **1** directing **2** the line along which something moves or faces
▷ **directional** ADJECTIVE

Thesaurus

dimple NOUN Her smile produced an instant dimple in each cheek. ► hollow, dip, depression, dint, cleft

din NOUN It was hard to hear anything above the din. ► uproar, racket, rumpus, commotion, hubbub, clamor, tumult, hullabaloo, noise, outcry, pandemonium, row, shouting

dingy ADJECTIVE The front door opened on to a dingy hallway. ► gloomy, dismal, dim, dreary, somber, dark, drab, dull, murky OPPOSITES ARE bright, cheerful

dip VERB **1** She dipped her hand in the water. ► immerse, lower, plunge, submerge, douse, dunk, drop, duck **2** The path dips towards the village. ► descend, slope down, go down, subside, dive, slump **3** He would just smile and dip his head a little. ► lower, drop

dip NOUN **1** We reached a dip in the ground. ► slope, incline, depression, declivity, dent, hollow, fall, hole, concavity **2** There will be a dip in sales after Christmas. ► decrease, fall, decline, downturn, falling off **3** He likes a quick dip in the river. ► bathe, swim, dive, plunge, splash, paddle

diplomacy NOUN **1** They gave up the war and tried diplomacy. ► negotiation, discussion, consultation, dialogue, statesmanship, statecraft **2** Her answer combined honesty and diplomacy. ► tact, tactfulness, sensitivity, politeness, discretion, delicacy

diplomatic ADJECTIVE He tried to be diplomatic but the news was not good. ► tactful, sensitive, considerate, discreet, subtle, polite, understanding, politic, careful, delicate, judicious, prudent, thoughtful OPPOSITES ARE tactless, outspoken

dire ADJECTIVE **1** The economy was in a dire state. ► terrible, dreadful, awful, appalling, disastrous, catastrophic **2** a dire warning ► ominous, portentous, dreadful, gloomy, grim **3** in dire need of help ► urgent, desperate, pressing, sore, serious, grave

direct ADJECTIVE **1** Travel by the direct route. ► straight, undeviating, shortest, quickest, nonstop, unswerving AN OPPOSITE IS indirect **2** We want a direct answer. ► straightforward, honest, frank, candid, unequivocal, sincere, blunt AN OPPOSITE IS evasive **3** The sisters are direct opposites in character. ► absolute, exact, complete, diametrical, downright, thorough, utter, head-on, (informal) out-and-out

direct VERB **1** Earlier in her career she directed a child-growth project. ► manage, run, administer, be in charge of, be responsible for, control, preside over, lead, organize **2** An official directed them to the meeting room. ► show the way, tell the way, indicate the way, give directions to, guide, point, route **3** The books are mainly directed at teenagers. ► target, aim, point, design (for), orient (toward) **4** The judge directed the jury to return a verdict of not guilty. ► instruct, order, tell, command, require, advise, charge, bid, enjoin

direction NOUN **1** She left an hour later and went off in another direction. ► route, way, course,

A
B
C
D
E
F
G
H
I
J
K
L
M
N
O
P
Q
R
S
T
U
V
W
X
Y
Z

directly ADVERB immediately; by a direct route

direct object NOUN direct objects the word that receives the action of the verb In 'she hit him', 'him' is the direct object

director NOUN directors **1** a person who is in charge of something **2** a person who decides how a movie, program, or play should be made or performed

directory NOUN directories a book containing a list of people with their telephone numbers, addresses, etc.

direct speech NOUN someone's words written down exactly in the way they were said

dirge NOUN dirges a slow sad song

dirt NOUN earth, soil; anything that is not clean [from an Old Norse word meaning "excrement"]

dirty ADJECTIVE dirtier, dirtiest **1** not clean; soiled **2** unfair; dishonorable ● *a dirty trick* **3** indecent; obscene
▷ **dirtily** ADVERB **dirtiness** NOUN

dis- PREFIX (changing to dif- before words beginning with *f*, and to di- before some consonants) **1** not; the reverse of (as in *dishonest*) **2** apart; separated (as in *disarm*, *disperse*)

disabled ADJECTIVE unable to use part of your body properly because of illness or injury
▷ **disability** NOUN **disablement** NOUN

disadvantage NOUN disadvantages something that hinders or is unhelpful

disagree VERB disagrees, disagreeing, disagreed **1** have or express a different opinion from someone **2** have a bad effect ● *Rich food disagrees with me.*
▷ **disagreement** NOUN

disagreeable ADJECTIVE unpleasant

Thesaurus

line, bearing, orientation **2** (directions) *The nursing staff receive regular directions on new medicines.* ► instructions, guidelines, guidance, indications, briefing, plans, orders

directly ADVERB **1** *She will join us directly.* ► immediately, at once, instantly, right away, straight away, in a moment, forthwith, presently **2** *You can fly directly from here to Montreal.* ► straight, immediately, by a direct route

director NOUN *the directors of the main London museums* ► head, chief, manager, administrator, principal, (more informal) boss

dirt NOUN **1** *The area in front of the house was covered in dirt.* ► grime, filth, muck, refuse, garbage, rubbish, dust, slime, sludge, mess, mire, pollution **2** *Chickens were scratching in the dirt.* ► earth, soil, mud, loam, clay

dirty ADJECTIVE **1** *a dirty room; dirty clothes* ► filthy, grimy, grubby, soiled, stained, mucky, dingy, unwashed, squalid AN OPPOSITE IS clean **2** *dirty water* ► impure, muddy, murky, polluted, untreated, cloudy AN OPPOSITE IS pure **3** *dirty tricks* ► corrupt, dishonest, illegal, mean, treacherous, unfair, ungentlemanly, unsporting, (more informal) low-down OPPOSITES ARE honest, sporting **4** *a dirty joke* ► rude, indecent, obscene, coarse, crude, smutty, suggestive, improper, risqué, offensive, vulgar AN OPPOSITE IS clean **5** *a dirty look* ► angry, hostile, resentful, peeved, black

dirty VERB *Try not to dirty the towels.* ► soil, stain, mess up, spoil, taint, tarnish AN OPPOSITE IS clean

disability NOUN *A disability can make the most routine tasks extremely difficult.* ► handicap,

incapacity, infirmity, disablement, impairment, affliction, complaint, abnormality, weakness

disable VERB **1** *The injury disabled her for several months.* ► incapacitate, injure, immobilize, cripple, debilitate, enfeeble, handicap, impair, lame, maim, paralyze, weaken, (informal) hamstring **2** *The army succeeded in disabling the device.* ► incapacitate, put out of action, deactivate, disarm, make useless, stop working OPPOSITES ARE restore, repair

disabled ADJECTIVE *The house caters well for disabled visitors.* ► handicapped, physically handicapped, physically impaired, incapacitated, immobilized, bedridden, crippled, deformed, lame, paralysed AN OPPOSITE IS able-bodied

disadvantage NOUN *Heavy traffic is a major disadvantage of road travel.* ► drawback, snag, downside, inconvenience, weakness, nuisance, handicap, hardship, liability, privation, trouble, hindrance, impediment, (more informal) minus

disagree VERB **1** *We constantly disagree.* ► dissent, differ, argue, conflict, clash, fall out, quarrel, squabble, wrangle, bicker AN OPPOSITE IS agree **2** *disagree with She disagrees with everything he says.* ► oppose, contradict, counter, argue with, dissent from, object to, take issue with, be at variance with, deviate from **3** *disagree with Onions disagree with me.* ► make ill, make unwell, upset

disagreeable ADJECTIVE *a disagreeable taste; a disagreeable person* ► unpleasant, nasty, horrible, horrid, offensive, repugnant, revolting, repellent

disagreement NOUN **1** *The two brothers had a disagreement.* ► argument, altercation, clash, quarrel, dispute, contretemps,

disappear VERB disappears, disappearing, disappeared stop being visible; vanish
▷ **disappearance** NOUN

disappoint VERB disappoints, disappointing, disappointed fail to do what someone hopes for
▷ **disappointment** NOUN

disapprove VERB disapproves, disapproving, disapproved have an unfavorable opinion of something; not approve
▷ **disapproval** NOUN

disarm VERB disarms, disarming, disarmed **1** reduce the size of armed forces **2** take away someone's weapons **3** overcome a person's anger or doubt • *Her friendliness*

disarmed their suspicions.
▷ **disarming** ADJECTIVE

disarmament NOUN reduction of a country's armed forces or weapons

disaster NOUN disasters **1** a very bad accident or misfortune **2** a complete failure
▷ **disastrous** ADJECTIVE **disastrously** ADVERB

disbelief NOUN refusal or unwillingness to believe something
▷ **disbelieve** VERB

disc NOUN discs **1** any round flat object **2** a layer of cartilage between vertebrae in the spine **3** a CD or record

discerning ADJECTIVE perceptive; showing good judgment

Thesaurus

misunderstanding, squabble, wrangle, (*more informal*) tiff, (*more informal*) fight AN OPPOSITE IS agreement **2** *There is some disagreement between the two versions of the story.* ▶ difference, disparity, variance, dissimilarity, discrepancy, incompatibility, divergence

disappear VERB **1** *The crowd rapidly disappeared.* ▶ vanish, disperse, recede, clear, evaporate, fade, melt away, wane, dissolve, dwindle, cease to exist, ebb **2** *She disappeared around a corner.* ▶ go, pass, withdraw, run away, walk away, depart, retire, escape, flee, fly AN OPPOSITE IS appear **3** *a way of life that has almost disappeared* ▶ die out, become extinct, vanish, perish OPPOSITES ARE emerge, appear

disappoint VERB **1** *We will try not to disappoint you.* ▶ let down, fail, dissatisfy, disillusion, disenchant, dishearten AN OPPOSITE IS satisfy **2** *In the end their hopes were disappointed.* ▶ thwart, frustrate, dash, defeat, foil

disappointed ADJECTIVE *I was disappointed when you didn't come.* ▶ saddened, unhappy, upset, let down, dissatisfied, dejected, despondent, downcast, downhearted, crestfallen, discontented, disenchanted, disgruntled, disillusioned, frustrated OPPOSITES ARE satisfied, contented

disappointment NOUN **1** *She could not hide her feeling of disappointment.* ▶ regret, sorrow, sadness, displeasure, dissatisfaction, disapproval, dismay, disillusionment, discontent **2** *The exam result had been a disappointment.* ▶ let-down, setback, misfortune, blow, anticlimax

disapproval NOUN *Her face clearly showed her disapproval.* ▶ dislike, displeasure, dissatisfaction, criticism, anger, disapprobation, disfavor, dissent, reproach, hostility, censure, condemnation, reprimand AN OPPOSITE IS approval

disapprove VERB disapprove of *They disapprove of gambling.* ▶ dislike, condemn,

deplore, deprecate, object to, frown on, look askance at, be displeased by, take exception to, reject, criticize, denounce, censure, disparage, make unwelcome, regret, (*more informal*) take a dim view of AN OPPOSITE IS approve of

disarray NOUN *The room was by now in some disarray. The opposition parties were in disarray.* ▶ disorder, confusion, chaos, mess, muddle

disaster NOUN **1** *the world's worst air disaster* ▶ catastrophe, calamity, tragedy, misfortune, mishap, affliction, cataclysm, blow **2** (*informal*) *It would be a complete disaster for him if she came back.* ▶ failure, fiasco, catastrophe, setback, reversal AN OPPOSITE IS success

disastrous ADJECTIVE *a disastrous fire; a disastrous choice* ▶ catastrophic, calamitous, cataclysmic, devastating, ruinous, terrible, tragic, crippling, destructive, dire, dreadful, fatal, bad OPPOSITES ARE fortunate, successful

disband VERB *The team disbanded once the work was done.* ▶ break up, disperse, scatter, separate, part company, go your own way

disbelief NOUN *He looked at her in disbelief.* ▶ incredulity, distrust, scepticism, doubt, mistrust, suspicion OPPOSITES ARE belief, credence

disbelieve VERB *He disbelieved everything we said.* ▶ doubt, mistrust, reject, suspect, discount, discredit, have no faith in, be sceptical of AN OPPOSITE IS believe

disc NOUN **1** *the disc of the sun* ▶ circle, round, ring **2** *a new disc from the same band* ▶ CD, compact disc, record, album, single

discard VERB *I decided to discard some old clothes.* ▶ get rid of, dispose of, dispense with, throw away, cast off, reject, eliminate, jettison, scrap, shed, dump, (*more informal*) chuck away, (*more informal*) ditch

discern VERB *We discerned a tower in the distance.* ▶ perceive, spot, make out, pick out,

discharge ➡ discount

discharge VERB discharges, discharging, discharged **1** release a person **2** send something out • *discharge smoke* **3** pay or do what was agreed • *discharge the debt*

disciple NOUN disciples **1** a person who accepts the teachings of another whom he or she regards as a leader **2** any of the original followers of Jesus Christ

discipline NOUN disciplines **1** orderly and obedient behavior **2** a subject for study
▷ disciplinary (**dis**- ip- lin- er- ee) ADJECTIVE

disc jockey NOUN disc jockeys a person who plays recorded music on the radio or at a disco or nightclub

disco NOUN discos a place where CDs or records are played for dancing

discolor VERB discolors, discoloring, discolored spoil a thing's color; stain
▷ discoloration NOUN

disconcert (dis- kon- sert) VERB disconcerts, disconcerting, disconcerted make a person feel uneasy

disconnect VERB disconnects, disconnecting disconnected break a connection; detach
• *The phone has been disconnected.*
▷ disconnection NOUN

disconsolate (dis- **kon**- sol- at) ADJECTIVE disappointed

discontent NOUN lack of contentment; dissatisfaction
▷ discontented ADJECTIVE discontentment NOUN

discontinue VERB discontinues, discontinuing, discontinued put an end to something

discord NOUN discords **1** disagreement; quarrelling **2** musical notes sounded together and producing a harsh or unpleasant sound
▷ discordant ADJECTIVE

discount NOUN discounts an amount by which a price is reduced

discount VERB discounts, discounting, discounted ignore or disregard something
• *We cannot discount the possibility.*

Thesaurus

---

detect, recognize, distinguish, become aware of

discernible ADJECTIVE *His face was clearly discernible to her all the time.* ► visible, perceptible, observable, noticeable, distinct, manifest, conspicuous

discharge VERB **1** *Factories along the river were discharging thick smoke.* ► emit, give out, pour out, give off, exude, belch, release, secrete, produce, send out, eject, expel **2** *He discharged the gun by accident.* ► fire, shoot, detonate, let off, explode **3** *Three employees were discharged on the same day.* ► dismiss, fire, make redundant, remove, throw out **4** *The authorities discharged him from prison on a Sunday.* ► release, liberate, free, allow to leave, dismiss, excuse

discharge NOUN **1** *discharge from prison* ► release, liberation **2** *the discharge of a duty* ► accomplishment, execution, completion, fulfilment, achievement

disciple NOUN *a disciple of Aristotle* ► follower, pupil, adherent, devotee, student, supporter, acolyte, admirer, apostle

discipline NOUN **1** *Good financial discipline is important.* ► control, regulation, order, authority, orderliness, management, self-control, strictness, system, training, obedience **2** *Their mother had been responsible for administering discipline.* ► punishment, chastisement, correction. **3** *Sociology is a fairly new discipline.* ► field of study, field, branch of knowledge, speciality

discipline VERB **1** *Families have different ways of disciplining their children.* ► train, control, instruct, educate, restrain, break in, drill

2 *Several staff members have been disciplined.* ► punish, reprimand, reprove, penalize, chasten, chastise

disclaim VERB *The company disclaimed all responsibility for the pollution.* ► deny, reject, renounce, repudiate, disown, forswear OPPOSITES ARE acknowledge, accept, admit

disclose VERB *This information should not be disclosed to anyone outside this room.* ► divulge, reveal, communicate, make known, pass on

discomfort NOUN *Her arm felt numb but she managed to hide the discomfort.* ► pain, soreness, ache, irritation, distress, hardship AN OPPOSITE IS comfort

disconcerting ADJECTIVE *He answered all the questions with disconcerting honesty.* ► unsettling, unnerving, off-putting, confusing, disturbing, perplexing, upsetting, worrying AN OPPOSITE IS reassuring

disconnect VERB **1** *The power company had disconnected the supply.* ► cut off, break off, stop OPPOSITES ARE reconnect, restore **2** *The engine was disconnected at Crewe.* ► uncouple, detach, disengage, decouple, separate OPPOSITES ARE attach, connect **3** *Televisions should be disconnected at night.* ► unplug, deactivate OPPOSITES ARE connect, plug in

disconnected ADJECTIVE *a disconnected argument* ► incoherent, disjointed, garbled, confused, disorganized, rambling, uncoordinated OPPOSITES ARE coherent, logical

discount NOUN *a $5 discount on the sticker price* ► reduction, deduction, concession, cut, allowance, rebate, (*more informal*) markdown

discourage VERB discourages, discouraging, discouraged **1** take away someone's enthusiasm or confidence **2** try to persuade someone not to do something
▷ **discouragement** NOUN

discover VERB discovers, discovering, discovered **1** find or find out **2** be the first person to find something
▷ **discoverer** NOUN **discovery** NOUN

discredit VERB discredits, discrediting, discredited **1** cause something to be doubted **2** damage someone's reputation

discredit NOUN damage to someone's reputation
▷ **discreditable** ADJECTIVE

discreet ADJECTIVE **1** not giving away secrets **2** not showy
▷ **discreetly** ADVERB
USAGE Do not confuse with discrete.

discrepancy (dis- **krep**- an- see) NOUN discrepancies lack of agreement between things which should be the same ● *There are several discrepancies in the two accounts.*

discrete ADJECTIVE separate; distinct from each other
USAGE Do not confuse with discreet.

discretion (dis- **kresh**- on) NOUN **1** being discreet; keeping secrets ● *I hope I can count on your discretion.* **2** freedom to decide things and take action according to your own judgement ● *You can use your discretion.*

Thesaurus

---

discount VERB *We discounted all these rumors.*
▶ disregard, reject, disbelieve, overlook, ignore

discourage VERB **1** *The audience was discouraged from asking questions.* ▶ deter, dissuade, restrain, prevent, hinder, put off, warn off **2** *Her cool response discouraged them.*
▶ dishearten, dispirit, demoralize, disappoint, dismay, depress, unnerve, intimidate

discouragement NOUN *Strong police presence is a discouragement to crime.* ▶ deterrent, disincentive, constraint, hindrance, impediment, restraint, obstacle, setback, (*informal*) damper (on) AN OPPOSITE IS encouragement

discouraging ADJECTIVE *The latest news is discouraging.* ▶ depressing, dispiriting, disheartening, demoralizing, disappointing, daunting

discourse NOUN (with the stress on *dis-*) **1** *They continued their discourse well into the night.*
▶ conversation, disquisition, literature, speech **2** *a discourse on semantics* ▶ dissertation, essay, treatise, monograph, thesis, paper

discourse VERB (with the stress on *-course*) *He likes to discourse on his favorite topics.* ▶ speak, hold forth, expatiate, pontificate

discourteous ADJECTIVE *It would be discourteous to refuse.* ▶ rude, impolite, bad-mannered, ill-mannered, disrespectful, uncivil, churlish, ungracious, boorish

discourtesy NOUN *He had committed the grave discourtesy of not turning up for the speech.*
▶ rudeness, bad manners, ill manners, disrespect, incivility, churlishness

discover VERB **1** *The children had discovered a secret door at the bottom of the garden.* ▶ find, locate, come across, uncover, chance on, stumble on **2** *We discovered that he had been lying.* ▶ find out, learn, realize, come to know,

come to realize, work out, perceive **3** *Faraday discovered electricity.* ▶ originate, develop, pioneer, invent USAGE Note that *discover* and *invent* do not mean quite the same: you discover something natural that was always there (e.g., electricity), and you invent something new that did not exist before (e.g., television)

discovery NOUN **1** *a major new discovery*
▶ invention, innovation, revelation, breakthrough, disclosure, exploration, (*more informal*) find **2** *the discovery of the body*
▶ finding, location, locating, detection, uncovering, unearthing

discredit VERB **1** *His enemies are looking for information that might discredit him.*
▶ disparage, defame, disgrace, smear, slander, dishonor, ruin the reputation of, slur, vilify **2** *The new evidence discredits the witness's story.*
▶ disprove, prove false, invalidate, challenge, refute, raise doubts about, (*more informal*) explode, (*more informal*) show up

discreet ADJECTIVE USAGE Do not confuse this word with *discrete*, which means "distinct" or "separate." *I made a few discreet enquiries.*
▶ careful, circumspect, cautious, guarded, wary, tactful, judicious, prudent, considerate, delicate, diplomatic, sensitive, thoughtful, polite, politic OPPOSITES ARE indiscreet, rash

discrepancy NOUN *There is a discrepancy between the two versions of the story.*
▶ inconsistency, difference, disparity, variance, conflict, dissimilarity, divergence, incompatibility, incongruity AN OPPOSITE IS similarity

discrete ADJECTIVE USAGE Do not confuse this word with *discreet*, which means "careful" or "cautious." *teaching the course in discrete units*
▶ distinct, separate, individual, detached

discretion NOUN **1** *The police conducted their inquiries with discretion.* ▶ diplomacy, tact, sensitivity, good sense, judgment, maturity,

discriminate VERB discriminates, discriminating, discriminated **1** notice the differences between things; distinguish; prefer one thing to another **2** treat people differently or unfairly, e.g., because of their race, sex, or religion
▷ discrimination NOUN

discus NOUN discuses a thick heavy disc thrown in athletic contests

discuss VERB discusses, discussing, discussed talk with other people about a subject
▷ discussion NOUN

disease NOUN diseases an unhealthy condition; an illness
▷ diseased ADJECTIVE

disembark VERB disembarks, disembarking, disembarked get off a ship or aircraft
▷ disembarkation NOUN

disentangle VERB disentangles, disentangling, disentangled free from tangles or confusion

disfigure VERB disfigures, disfiguring, disfigured spoil the appearance of a person or thing
▷ disfigurement NOUN

disgrace NOUN **1** shame; loss of approval or respect **2** something that causes shame
▷ disgraceful ADJECTIVE disgracefully ADVERB

disgrace VERB disgraces, disgracing, disgraced bring disgrace on someone

disguise VERB disguises, disguising, disguised **1** make a person or thing look different in order to deceive people **2** conceal your feelings

disguise NOUN disguises something used for disguising

Thesaurus

prudence, responsibility, wisdom AN OPPOSITE IS indiscretion **2** *Payment of interest is at the bank's discretion.* ► choice, option, judgement, will, wish, preference

discriminate VERB **1** *It is hard to discriminate between the two theories.* ► differentiate, distinguish, make a distinction, tell the difference **2** *Some employment practices still discriminate against women.* ► be biased, be prejudiced, show discrimination, be intolerant (towards)

discriminating ADJECTIVE *a discriminating art collector* ► discerning, perceptive, astute, judicious, fastidious, critical, particular, selective, (*more informal*) choosy AN OPPOSITE IS undiscriminating

discrimination NOUN **1** *She shows discrimination in her choice of music.*
► discernment, good taste, insight, judgment, perceptiveness, refinement, selectivity, subtlety, taste **2** *victims of discrimination*
► prejudice, bias, bigotry, intolerance, chauvinism, favoritism, male chauvinism, racism, sexism, unfairness AN OPPOSITE IS impartiality

discuss VERB *It was good to discuss other people's problems.* ► debate, consider, talk about, confer about, consult about, deliberate, examine, deal with

discussion NOUN *a lively discussion about funding universities* ► debate, deliberation, conference, dialogue, consultation, conversation, argument, discourse, consideration, examination, exchange of views, symposium, talk

disease NOUN *suffering from a disease; a country afflicted by disease* ► illness, sickness, bad health, ailment, malady, disorder, infirmity RELATED ADJECTIVE ► morbid

disentangle VERB **1** *The cord had a knot that was difficult to disentangle.* ► untangle, undo, untie, untwist, sort out, straighten, unknot, unravel AN OPPOSITE IS entangle **2** *She disentangled his hand from her twisted clothing.*
► free, release, extricate, extract, remove, disengage, liberate, separate AN OPPOSITE IS enmesh

disfigure VERB *A new highway will disfigure the landscape.* ► mar, scar, deface, deform, mutilate, spoil, damage OPPOSITES ARE enhance, beautify

disgrace NOUN **1** *the public disgrace of being prosecuted for shoplifting* ► dishonor, shame, humiliation, ignominy, degradation, slur, stain, stigma, discredit, embarrassment, opprobrium, scandal AN OPPOSITE IS honor **2** (*informal*) *The local facilities for children were a disgrace.* ► outrage, scandal, affront, insult OPPOSITES ARE credit, asset

disgrace VERB *He very nearly disgraced his friends by reciting an improper poem.* ► shame, bring shame on, defame, humiliate, scandalize

disgraceful ADJECTIVE *Their behavior had been disgraceful.* ► shameful, deplorable, shocking, dreadful, despicable, dishonorable, reprehensible, appalling, bad

disguise NOUN *She looked quite convincing in her nun's disguise.* ► costume, outfit, impersonation, camouflage, concealment, pretense, cloak, cover, fancy dress, makeup, front, mask, (*more informal*) get-up

disguise VERB **1** *Her long sleeves disguised her burns.* ► hide, conceal, cover, mask, screen, shroud, veil, camouflage, dress up, make inconspicuous **2** *He made no attempt to disguise his anger.* ► hide, conceal, cover up, gloss over, misrepresent
disguise yourself as *I changed my identity and disguised myself as one of the locals.* ► dress up

disgust ➡ disinterested

disgust NOUN a feeling that something is very unpleasant or disgraceful

disgust VERB disgusts, disgusting, disgusted give someone a feeling of disgust
▷ disgusted ADJECTIVE disgusting ADJECTIVE

dish NOUN **1** a plate or bowl for food **2** food prepared for eating **3** a satellite dish

dish VERB dishes, dishing, dished (*informal*) dish out give out portions of something to people

disheveled (dish- ev- eld) ADJECTIVE ruffled and untidy
▷ dishevelment NOUN

dishonest ADJECTIVE not honest
▷ dishonestly ADVERB dishonesty NOUN

dishonor VERB dishonors, dishonoring, dishonored disgrace someone
▷ dishonor NOUN dishonorable ADJECTIVE

disillusion VERB disillusions, disillusioning,

disillusioned get rid of someone's wrong beliefs
▷ disillusionment NOUN

disinclined ADJECTIVE unwilling to do something

disinfect VERB disinfects, disinfecting, disinfected destroy the germs in something
▷ disinfection NOUN

disinfectant NOUN disinfectants a substance used for disinfecting things

disintegrate VERB disintegrates, disintegrating, disintegrated break up into small parts or pieces
▷ disintegration NOUN

disinterested ADJECTIVE impartial; not influenced by the hope of gaining something yourself • *She gave us some disinterested advice.* USAGE It is not accepted as part of standard English to use this word as if it meant "not interested" or "bored." If this is what you mean, use uninterested.

Thesaurus

as, impersonate, pretend to be, pose as, counterfeit, imitate, mimic, (*more informal*) take off

disgust NOUN *I couldn't hide my disgust at his behavior.* ► revulsion, repugnance, repulsion, abhorrence, distaste, aversion, antipathy, contempt, loathing, detestation, nausea, dislike, hatred OPPOSITES ARE liking, relish

disgust VERB *The hospital food disgusted me.* ► revolt, nauseate, offend, appall, repel, sicken, be distasteful to, displease, horrify, outrage, put off, shock, (*more informal*) turn your stomach OPPOSITES ARE please, appeal to

disgusting ADJECTIVE *The smell was disgusting. They showed disgusting bigotry.* ► revolting, nauseating, offensive, sickening, loathsome, repugnant, repulsive, unpleasant OPPOSITES ARE pleasant, appealing, attractive

dish NOUN **1** *He tipped the pasta into a dish.* ► plate, bowl, platter **2** *a nutritious vegetarian dish* ► food, recipe

dish VERB (*informal*)
dish out *The children helped by dishing out piles of books.* ► distribute, give out, hand out, deal out, issue
dish up *Shirley was busy dishing up burgers and hot dogs.* ► serve, serve up, provide, dispense

dishearten VERB *The result disheartened them so much they almost gave up.* ► discourage, dispirit, dismay, depress, disappoint, deter, put off, sadden OPPOSITES ARE hearten, encourage

disheveled ADJECTIVE *She ran a hand through her disheveled hair.* ► untidy, bedraggled, disordered, unkempt, scruffy, disarranged, tangled, ruffled, rumpled, slovenly, tousled, uncombed, messy OPPOSITES ARE neat, tidy

dishonest ADJECTIVE *Their solicitor proved to be dishonest. a dishonest statement* ► deceitful,

untruthful, lying, fraudulent, false, double-dealing, cheating, swindling, corrupt, underhand, untrustworthy, (*more informal*) crooked OPPOSITES ARE honest, truthful

dishonesty NOUN *a charge of dishonesty against former colleagues* ► corruption, fraud, fraudulence, cheating, deceit, deception, deviousness, lying, falsity, falsehood, (*more informal*) crookedness, (*more informal*) shadiness AN OPPOSITE IS honesty

dishonor NOUN *I have no wish to bring dishonor on you or your family.* ► disgrace, shame, discredit, degradation, humiliation, ignominy, stigma, opprobrium, indignity OPPOSITES ARE honor, credit

dishonorable ADJECTIVE *It would be dishonorable to refuse to pay.* ► disgraceful, shameful, discreditable, ignominious, contemptible, reprehensible

disinfect VERB *An aromatic plant is used to disinfect houses where malaria is present.* ► sterilize, sanitize, clean, cleanse, purify, fumigate OPPOSITES ARE infect, contaminate

disinfectant NOUN *She wiped the surface down with disinfectant.* ► antiseptic, sterilizer, germicide, carbolic, cleaner

disintegrate VERB *The aircraft caught fire and disintegrated in the air.* ► break up, fall apart, fall to pieces, explode, come apart, decompose

disinterested ADJECTIVE *Her advice would always be disinterested.* ► impartial, neutral, unbiased, unprejudiced, dispassionate, open-minded, even-handed AN OPPOSITE IS biased USAGE Note that *disinterested* means "impartial" and does not mean the same as *uninterested.*

A
B
C
D
E
F
G
H
I
J
K
L
M
N
O
P
Q
R
S
T
U
V
W
X
Y
Z

disjointed ADJECTIVE (said about talk or writing) not having parts that fit together well and so difficult to understand

disk NOUN disks a computer storage device consisting of magnetically coated plates

dislike VERB dislikes, disliking, disliked not like somebody or something

dislocate VERB dislocates, dislocating, dislocated **1** move or force a bone from its proper position in one of the joints **2** disrupt ● *Fog dislocated the traffic.*
▷ **dislocation** NOUN

dislodge VERB dislodges, dislodging, dislodged move or force something from its place

disloyal ADJECTIVE not loyal
▷ **disloyally** ADVERB **disloyalty** NOUN

dismal ADJECTIVE **1** gloomy **2** of poor quality
▷ **dismally** ADVERB

dismantle VERB dismantles, dismantling, dismantled take something to pieces

dismay NOUN a feeling of surprise and discouragement
▷ **dismayed** ADJECTIVE

dismiss VERB dismisses, dismissing, dismissed **1** send someone away **2** tell a person that you will no longer employ him or her **3** put something out of your thoughts because it is not worth thinking about
▷ **dismissal** NOUN **dismissive** ADJECTIVE

dismount VERB dismounts, dismounting, dismounted get off a horse or bicycle

disobey VERB disobeys, disobeying, disobeyed not obey; disregard orders
▷ **disobedient** ADJECTIVE **disobedience** NOUN

Thesaurus

---

disjointed ADJECTIVE *She turned her disjointed thoughts over in her mind.* ► disconnected, incoherent, confused, disordered, unconnected, disorganized, jumbled, rambling, fitful, erratic AN OPPOSITE IS coherent

dislike VERB *She dislikes me because I won't do what she says.* ► not like, detest, hate, object to, abhor, disapprove of, despise AN OPPOSITE IS like

dislike NOUN *He had a fear and dislike of big cities.* ► aversion (to), distaste (for), antagonism (to), antipathy (to), contempt (for), disgust (for), revulsion (from), detestation, disapproval, hatred, loathing AN OPPOSITE IS liking

dislodge VERB *Several stones had been dislodged, causing a hazard to passersby.* ► displace, disarrange, dislocate, disturb, misplace, move, shift, remove, knock out of place, knock out of position

disloyal ADJECTIVE *His colleagues criticized him for being disloyal in his comments.* ► unfaithful, faithless, treacherous, subversive, seditious, dissident, false, traitorous OPPOSITES ARE loyal, faithful

disloyalty NOUN *She felt a sense of guilt, of disloyalty.* ► unfaithfulness, infidelity, betrayal, duplicity, faithlessness, falseness, inconstancy, perfidy, treachery, treason, double-dealing AN OPPOSITE IS loyalty

dismal ADJECTIVE **1** *She led them into a dismal little room.* ► gloomy, dingy, dim, dreary, sombre, dark, drab, dull, murky OPPOSITES ARE bright, cheerful **2** (*informal*) *a row of dismal performances* ► dreadful, awful, terrible, feeble, disgraceful **3** *We looked at the dismal faces around us.* ► glum, gloomy, sad, miserable, melancholy, somber, forlorn, despondent, downcast, sorrowful, mournful, woeful

dismantle VERB *Before they left, the soldiers dismantled the row of huts.* ► take apart, take to pieces, take down, knock down, break up, demolish, strip down OPPOSITES ARE assemble, build

dismay NOUN *Laura gave a yelp of dismay as she caught sight of the time on her watch.* ► alarm, shock, surprise, consternation, concern, distress, apprehension, agitation, trepidation, fright, horror

dismay VERB *You should not be dismayed by these comments.* ► alarm, daunt, horrify, shock, appal, discourage, dishearten, dispirit, distress, deject, depress, devastate, disappoint, unnerve, frighten, scare AN OPPOSITE IS encourage

dismiss VERB **1** *Elaine dismissed her husband with a wave of her hand.* ► send away, discharge, free, let go, release **2** *Three employees were dismissed on the spot.* ► give someone notice, discharge, lay off, (*more informal*) fire **3** *She had dismissed Nina's allegations as lies.* ► reject, discount, disregard, set aside, repudiate, discard, spurn, drop, get rid of, give up, shelve, wave aside, (*more informal*) pooh-pooh **4** *He tried to dismiss these thoughts from his mind.* ► banish, dispel, remove, reject, shrug off

disobedience NOUN *They were punished for their disobedience.* ► insubordination, naughtiness, misbehavior, bad behavior, misconduct, unruliness, rebelliousness, wilfulness

disobedient ADJECTIVE *The children had been disobedient and demanding.* ► badly behaved, insubordinate, troublesome, naughty, disorderly, disruptive, fractious, rebellious, unruly, wayward, intractable, obstreperous, wilful, contrary AN OPPOSITE IS obedient

disobey VERB **1** *The queen was angry that so many people had disobeyed her orders.* ► defy,

disorder NOUN disorders **1** untidiness **2** a disturbance **3** an illness
▷ **disorderly** ADJECTIVE

disorganized ADJECTIVE muddled and badly organized
▷ **disorganization** NOUN

dispatch VERB dispatches, dispatching, dispatched **1** send off to a destination **2** kill

dispatch NOUN dispatches **1** dispatching **2** a report or message sent **3** promptness; speed

dispel VERB dispels, dispelling, dispelled drive away; scatter • *Wind dispels fog.*

dispensary NOUN dispensaries a place where medicines are dispensed

dispense VERB dispenses, dispensing, dispensed **1** distribute; deal out **2** prepare medicine according to prescriptions
▷ **dispensation** NOUN

dispense with do without something

dispenser NOUN dispensers a device that supplies a quantity of something • *a cash dispenser*

disperse VERB disperses, dispersing, dispersed scatter
▷ **dispersal** NOUN **dispersion** NOUN

displace VERB displaces, displacing, displaced **1** shift from its place **2** take a person's or thing's place
▷ **displacement** NOUN

display VERB displays, displaying, displayed show; arrange something so that it can be clearly seen

display NOUN displays **1** the displaying of something; an exhibition **2** something displayed **3** (in computing) an electronic device for visually presenting data

---

Thesaurus

---

flout, rebel against, contravene, disregard, ignore, infringe, break, resist, transgress, violate **2** *Remember never to disobey.* ► be disobedient, rebel, revolt AN OPPOSITE IS obey

disorder NOUN **1** *They were arrested for acts of public disorder.* ► disturbance, unrest, agitation, disruption, upheaval, tumult, insurrection, rebellion OPPOSITES ARE order, peace **2** *The house is in total disorder.* ► untidiness, disarray, disorganization, confusion, chaos, a jumble, a mess, a muddle, a shambles OPPOSITES ARE order, tidiness

disorderly ADJECTIVE **1** *behaving in a disorderly manner* ► unruly, rowdy, rebellious, disruptive, undisciplined, disobedient, boisterous, rough, wild OPPOSITES ARE orderly, disciplined **2** *a disorderly arrangement* ► untidy, disorganized, messy, muddled, confused, chaotic OPPOSITES ARE orderly, tidy

disorganized ADJECTIVE **1** *The room looked completely disorganized.* ► untidy, disorderly, messy, muddled, confused, chaotic OPPOSITES ARE neat, systematic **2** *I was accused of being careless and disorganized.* ► unmethodical, slapdash, slovenly, absent-minded, scatterbrained, inefficient

disown VERB *Her family disowned her when she married Jem.* ► reject, renounce, repudiate, cast off, abandon, end relations with

dispatch NOUN *A messenger brought dispatches.* ► bulletin, communiqué, letter, message, report

dispatch VERB **1** *Reminders will be dispatched next week.* ► send, post, transmit, consign, convey, forward **2** *In the movie the good guy has to dispatch a host of vicious villains.* ► kill, put an end to, put to death, dispose of, finish off

dispense VERB **1** *Waiters were there to dispense drinks.* ► distribute, give out, pass around, mete out, provide, allocate, allot, apportion,

deal out, dole out, share **2** *The local pharmacist dispenses medicines.* ► supply, prepare, make up **3** *dispense with We can dispense with the formalities.* ► waive, disregard, ignore, forgo, do without, pass over, drop, omit, cancel, dispose of, get rid of

disperse VERB **1** *Troops arrived to disperse the demonstrators.* ► break up, split up, separate, scatter, drive away, send away, disband, dispel, dismiss OPPOSITES ARE assemble, collect **2** *The crowd dispersed quickly.* ► break up, split up, disband, separate, scatter, dissolve, disappear, vanish, melt away OPPOSITES ARE collect, gather, assemble **3** *Birds disperse the seed.* ► scatter, spread, disseminate, distribute, strew AN OPPOSITE IS centralize

dispirited ADJECTIVE *He felt tired and dispirited.* ► disheartened, depressed, dejected, downcast, despondent, downhearted, disconsolate, unhappy, sad, down, glum, melancholy, miserable, cast down OPPOSITES ARE cheerful, happy

displace VERB **1** *The winds have displaced many roof tiles.* ► dislodge, disarrange, dislocate, disturb, misplace, move, shift, remove, knock out of place, knock out of position **2** *The recent land reforms have displaced thousands of people.* ► force out, drive out, eject, expel, oust, remove, supplant

display NOUN *an air display a display of horsemanship* ► exhibition, demonstration, show, spectacle, pageant, presentation, parade

display VERB **1** *A room will be built to display the marbles.* ► exhibit, show, put on show, present **2** *He displayed a good knowledge of the subject.* ► show, reveal, demonstrate, manifest, flaunt, produce, betray, air, evince

displease VERB *The decision clearly displeased him.* ► annoy, irritate, infuriate, incense,

A
B
C
D
E
F
G
H
I
J
K
L
M
N
O
P
Q
R
S
T
U
V
W
X
Y
Z

disposable ADJECTIVE made to be thrown away after it has been used • *disposable diapers*

dispose VERB disposes, disposing, disposed **1** make a person ready or willing to do something • *I feel disposed to help him.* **2** place in position; arrange • *Dispose your troops in two lines.*
be well disposed be friendly
dispose of get rid of

disposition NOUN dispositions **1** a person's nature or qualities **2** arrangement

disproportionate ADJECTIVE out of proportion; too large or too small

disprove VERB disproves, disproving, disproved show that something is not true

dispute VERB disputes, disputing, disputed **1** argue; debate **2** quarrel **3** raise an objection to • *We dispute their claim.*

dispute NOUN disputes **1** an argument or debate **2** a quarrel
in dispute being argued about

disqualify VERB disqualifies, disqualifying, disqualified bar someone from a competition, etc., because he or she has broken the rules or is not qualified to take part
▷ **disqualification** NOUN

disregard VERB disregards, disregarding, disregarded ignore

disregard NOUN the act of ignoring something

disrepair NOUN bad condition caused by not doing repairs • *The old mill is in a state of disrepair.*

disreputable ADJECTIVE not respectable

disrespect NOUN lack of respect; rudeness
▷ **disrespectful** ADJECTIVE **disrespectfully** ADVERB

disrupt VERB disrupts, disrupting, disrupted put into disorder; interrupt a continuous flow • *Fog disrupted traffic.*
▷ **disruption** NOUN **disruptive** ADJECTIVE

dissatisfied ADJECTIVE not satisfied
▷ **dissatisfaction** NOUN

Thesaurus

---

anger, enrage, vex, exasperate, madden, aggravate, antagonize, inflame, make angry, (*more informal*) needle, (*more informal*) rile, (*more informal*) bug, (*more informal*) rub up the wrong way

disposal NOUN **1** *the disposal of troops for battle* ► arrangement, disposition, order, grouping, mustering **2** *the disposal of radioactive waste* ► removal, elimination, discarding, destruction, riddance

dispose VERB **1** *A general disposes his troops for battle.* ► arrange, array, group, place, position, set out **2** *dispose of Equipment was needed to dispose of soiled diapers.* ► deal with, get rid of, destroy, discard, jettison, scrap, sell, throw away, (*more informal*) dump
be disposed to *Brian was not disposed to question this idea.* ► be inclined to, be ready to, be willing to, be liable to, be likely to

disproportionate ADJECTIVE *Small tasks can take up a disproportionate amount of time.* ► undue, uneven, unequal, unreasonable, inordinate, excessive, unbalanced OPPOSITES ARE proportional, reasonable

disprove VERB *New evidence has disproved the original verdicts.* ► invalidate, refute, overturn, confute, contradict, controvert, discredit, negate, rebut, expose, (*more informal*) explode OPPOSITES ARE prove, confirm

dispute NOUN *a matter of great dispute* ► debate, discussion, controversy, contention, argument, disagreement, conflict, dissension

dispute VERB **1** *We disputed with them deep into the night.* ► debate, argue, contend, exchange views, quarrel **2** *No one can dispute their claim.* ► challenge, contest, question, oppose, deny,

doubt, contradict, controvert, impugn, argue against, quarrel with AN OPPOSITE IS accept

disqualify VERB *He was disqualified from entering the game.* ► ban, bar, debar, prohibit, forbid (to drive), preclude

disregard VERB *Anne tried to disregard the noise.* ► ignore, take no notice of, pay no attention to, discount, overlook, pass over, make light of, brush aside AN OPPOSITE IS heed

disrespectful ADJECTIVE *He was often disrespectful toward his elders.* ► rude, discourteous, impertinent, impolite, insolent, impudent OPPOSITES ARE respectful, polite

disrupt VERB *A strike of air-traffic controllers has disrupted holiday travel.* ► interrupt, break up, dislocate, disturb, upset, interfere with, throw into disorder, break the routine of

dissatisfaction NOUN *There is widespread dissatisfaction with the quality of service.* ► discontent, discontentment, disappointment, disquiet, disgruntlement, frustration, annoyance, irritation, unhappiness, displeasure, anger, exasperation, chagrin, dismay, regret AN OPPOSITE IS satisfaction

dissatisfied ADJECTIVE *They were clearly dissatisfied with our answer.* ► discontented, disappointed, unsatisfied, unhappy, disgruntled, displeased, aggrieved (by), disaffected (by), frustrated (by), (*more informal*) fed up, unfulfilled OPPOSITES ARE satisfied, contented

dissimilar ADJECTIVE **1** *a wide range of dissimilar tasks* ► different, differing, diverse, distinct, unrelated, varying, unlike, disparate, heterogeneous **2** *dissimilar to This catfish*

dissect (dI- sekt) VERB dissects, dissecting, dissected cut something up in order to examine it
▷ **dissection** NOUN

dissent NOUN disagreement over an idea, proposal, etc.

dissent VERB dissents, dissenting, dissented disagree

dissident NOUN dissidents a person who disagrees, especially someone who opposes their government
▷ **dissident** ADJECTIVE **dissidence** NOUN

dissolute ADJECTIVE having an immoral way of life

dissolution NOUN dissolutions **1** putting an end to a marriage or partnership, etc. **2** the formal ending of an assembly

dissolve VERB dissolves, dissolving, dissolved **1** mix something with a liquid so that it becomes part of the liquid **2** make or become liquid; melt **3** put an end to a marriage or partnership, etc. **4** formally end an assembly or other gathering • *Parliament was dissolved and a general election was held.*

dissuade VERB dissuades, dissuading, dissuaded persuade somebody not to do something
▷ **dissuasion** NOUN

distance NOUN distances the amount of space between two places
in the distance far away but visible

distant ADJECTIVE **1** far away **2** not friendly; not sociable **3** not closely related • *distant cousins*
▷ **distantly** ADVERB

distaste NOUN dislike

distasteful ADJECTIVE unpleasant

distemper NOUN **1** a disease of dogs and certain other animals **2** a kind of paint

distil VERB distils, distilling, distilled purify a liquid by boiling it and condensing the vapor
▷ **distillation** NOUN **distiller** NOUN

distinct ADJECTIVE **1** easily heard or seen; noticeable **2** clearly separate or different
▷ **distinctly** ADVERB **distinctness** NOUN
USAGE See the note at distinctive.

distinction NOUN distinctions **1** a difference **2** excellence or honor **3** an award for excellence; a high mark in an examination

Thesaurus

shows a parental care not dissimilar to that of the cuckoo. ► unlike, different from OR to, unrelated to AN OPPOSITE IS similar

dissociate VERB *We decided to dissociate ourselves from the more extravagant claims being made.* ► break away, back away, detach, distance, separate , cut off, divorce, isolate AN OPPOSITE IS associate

dissolve VERB **1** *The acids dissolve in water.* ► liquefy, become liquid, diffuse, disperse, melt, deliquesce, disappear, disintegrate **2** *Dissolve salts in the water to keep it pure.* ► liquefy, melt, disintegrate, disperse **3** *His anger began to dissolve.* ► disappear, vanish, evaporate, dissipate, subside, disperse OPPOSITES ARE grow, develop **4** *The Army was dissolved after the revolution.* ► disband, terminate, abolish, close down, suspend, break up, dismiss, end, bring to an end, cancel, (more informal) wind up

dissuade VERB dissuade from *He dissuaded his colleagues from taking strike action.* ► discourage from, prevent from, deter from, divert from, disincline (to take), talk out of, urge against, advise against, persuade not (to take) AN OPPOSITE IS persuade (to)

distance NOUN **1** *the distance between the two vehicles* ► space, interval, gap, extent, length, range, reach, separation **2** *She keeps her distance.* ► aloofness, reserve, detachment, reticence, coolness, remoteness, coldness AN OPPOSITE IS closeness

in the distance *a church spire visible in the distance* ► far away, far off, in the background, on the horizon, yonder

distant ADJECTIVE **1** *distant countries* ► far-off, faraway, remote, outlying, isolated AN OPPOSITE IS close **2** *a distant memory* ► vague, dim, faint, indistinct, obscure, indefinite **3** *a distant manner* ► aloof, detached, impersonal, reserved, reticent, unfriendly, withdrawn, cool OPPOSITES ARE friendly, warm

distaste NOUN **1** *George looked with distaste at the man sitting opposite.* ► disgust, revulsion, abhorrence, repugnance, disdain, disfavor, dislike **2** *a distaste for politics* ► dislike (of), aversion (to), repugnance (for), disapproval (of)

distasteful ADJECTIVE *The day was hot and their work distasteful.* ► unpleasant, disagreeable, offensive, repulsive, objectionable, unappealing, unpalatable, repugnant, abhorrent, unsavory

distinct ADJECTIVE **1** *four distinct categories* ► discrete, separate, individual, detached OPPOSITES ARE indistinct, fuzzy **2** *a distinct improvement* ► clear, definite, marked, sharp, decided, unmistakable, obvious, plain

distinction NOUN **1** *There is a clear distinction between politicians and the rest of us.* ► difference, contrast, dissimilarity, divergence, variance, variation, differentiation, discrimination, distinctiveness AN OPPOSITE IS similarity **2** *a writer of distinction* ► importance, significance, note, consequence, account, greatness, renown,

a
b
c
d
e
f
g
h
i
j
k
l
m
n
o
p
q
r
s
t
u
v
w
x
y
z

A
B
C
D
E
F
G
H
I
J
K

distinctive ADJECTIVE that distinguishes one thing from another or others • *The school has a distinctive uniform.*
▷ **distinctively** ADVERB
USAGE Do not confuse this word with **distinct**. A distinct mark is a clear mark; a distinctive mark is one that is not found anywhere else.

distinguish VERB distinguishes, distinguishing, distinguished **1** make or notice differences between things **2** see or hear something clearly **3** bring honor to • *He distinguished himself by his bravery.*
▷ **distinguishable** ADJECTIVE

distinguished ADJECTIVE **1** important and famous **2** dignified in appearance

distort VERB distorts, distorting, distorted **1** pull or twist out of its normal shape **2** misrepresent; give a false account of something • *distort the truth*
▷ **distortion** NOUN

distract VERB distracts, distracting, distracted take a person's attention away from something

distraction NOUN distractions **1** something that distracts attention **2** an amusement **3** great worry or distress

distress NOUN distresses great sorrow, pain, or trouble

distribute VERB distributes, distributing, distributed **1** deal or share out **2** spread or scatter
▷ **distribution** NOUN **distributor** NOUN

district NOUN districts part of a town or country

distrust NOUN lack of trust; suspicion
▷ **distrustful** ADJECTIVE

distrust VERB distrusts, distrusting, distrusted have little trust in

Thesaurus

L
M
N
O
P
Q
R
S
T
U
V
W
X
Y
Z

celebrity, eminence, fame, reputation, repute, prestige, honor AN OPPOSITE IS mediocrity **3** *treating people without distinction of race, age, creed, or sex* ► differentiation, discrimination (between) **4** *He served with distinction in the war.* ► honor, credit, merit, courage, valor

distinctive ADJECTIVE *This duck has a distinctive white neck.* ► distinguishing, characteristic, typical, individual, peculiar, unique, special, singular, different, original, idiosyncratic, unusual

distinguish VERB **1** *the capacity to distinguish between good and bad in literature* ► differentiate, discriminate, decide, tell the difference, pick out (good and bad), determine (what is good and bad) **2** *We could distinguish a line of trees in the darkness.* ► make out, identify, discern, perceive, recognize, observe, notice, glimpse

distinguished ADJECTIVE *a distinguished statesman* ► eminent, famous, prominent, well known, celebrated, acclaimed, renowned, illustrious, famed, notable, noteworthy, esteemed, respected, honored, outstanding

distort VERB **1** *His face was distorted with pain.* ► twist, contort, warp, deform, misshape, bend, wrench **2** *That explanation distorts the truth.* ► twist, misrepresent, pervert, slant, falsify, misstate, garble, put a slant on, (*more informal*) put a spin on

distorted ADJECTIVE *a distorted version of the events* ► twisted, slanted, perverted, colored, false, biased, one-sided, prejudiced, inaccurate

distract VERB **1** *A noise across the street distracted him.* ► divert, sidetrack, disturb **2** *Helen appeared to be distracted by the back of the cereal packet.* ► puzzle, bewilder, disconcert, confuse, perplex, trouble, worry

distraction NOUN **1** *the distractions of life in a big city* ► amusement, entertainment, diversion, pleasure, recreation, enjoyment, fun, interest, pastime **2** *The baby's crying drove her to distraction.* ► frenzy, distress, insanity, madness, delirium

distraught ADJECTIVE *The poor woman looked distraught.* ► upset, overwrought, distressed, distracted, agitated, frantic, (*more informal*) beside yourself

distress NOUN **1** *She put her hand over her mouth to hide her distress.* ► anguish, suffering, misery, torment, discomfort, wretchedness, unhappiness, disquiet, despair, desolation, agony, grief OPPOSITES ARE happiness, comfort **2** *the distress of extreme poverty* ► hardship, adversity, tribulation, destitution, privation, trial AN OPPOSITE IS prosperity

distress VERB *I was distressed by the fact that everyone seemed to turn against him.* ► upset, perturb, disturb, trouble, bother, worry, sadden, afflict, torment OPPOSITES ARE comfort, soothe

distribute VERB **1** *They spent the day distributing pamphlets.* ► circulate, issue, spread, disperse, hand out, make available **2** *The house was sold and the money distributed among his heirs.* ► share out, divide up, apportion, allocate **3** *The seed should be distributed evenly.* ► scatter, spread, disperse, strew, disseminate, arrange

district NOUN *the shopping district of the town* ► area, region, quarter, locality, zone, neighborhood, sector, vicinity, part

distrust VERB *On the whole the public distrusts politicians.* ► mistrust, suspect, be suspicious of, be sceptical about, have misgivings about,

disturb VERB disturbs, disturbing, disturbed **1** spoil someone's peace or rest **2** cause someone to worry **3** move a thing from its position
▷ **disturbance** NOUN

disuse NOUN the state of being no longer used
▷ **disused** ADJECTIVE

ditch NOUN ditches a trench dug to hold water or carry it away, or to serve as a boundary [from Old English]

ditto NOUN (used in lists) the same again

dive VERB dives, diving, dived **1** go under water, especially head first **2** move down quickly
▷ **dive** NOUN

diverse (dy- verss) ADJECTIVE varied; of several different kinds
▷ **diversity** NOUN

diversify VERB diversifies, diversifying, diversified make or become varied; involve yourself in different kinds of things
▷ **diversification** NOUN

diversion NOUN diversions **1** diverting something from its course **2** an alternative route for traffic when a road is closed **3** a recreation or entertainment

divert VERB diverts, diverting, diverted **1** turn something aside from its course **2** entertain or amuse
▷ **diverting** ADJECTIVE

divide VERB divides, dividing, divided **1** separate from something or into smaller parts; split up **2** find how many times one number is contained in another • *Divide six by three (6 ÷ 3 = 2)*
▷ **divider** NOUN

divine ADJECTIVE **1** belonging to or coming from God **2** like a god **3** (*informal*) excellent; extremely beautiful
▷ **divinely** ADVERB **divinity** NOUN

division NOUN divisions **1** dividing **2** a dividing line; a partition **3** one of the parts into which something is divided
▷ **divisional** ADJECTIVE

Thesaurus

have qualms about, be wary of, disbelieve, doubt, question AN OPPOSITE IS trust

disturb VERB **1** *He crept into the house quietly so as not to disturb his sleeping parents.* ► bother, annoy, interrupt, intrude on, disrupt, upset, alarm, wake **2** *Try not to disturb the books and papers.* ► mix up, disarrange, disorganize, confuse, muddle

disturbance NOUN *People were injured in violent disturbances in the capital.* ► commotion, uproar, racket, tumult, hullabaloo, hubbub, rumpus, fracas, furor, upheaval, agitation, excitement

ditch NOUN *Some sheep had fallen into a ditch and had to be rescued.* ► trench, channel, gully, watercourse, conduit, dike, drain, gutter, moat

ditch VERB (*informal*) *We will have to ditch that idea.* ► abandon, drop, scrap, jettison, throw out, shelve, discard, forget, (*more informal*) dump, (*more informal*) pull the plug on

dither VERB *He dithered over which suit to wear that day.* ► hesitate, waver, be in two minds, vacillate

dive VERB **1** *A young girl dived into the water.* ► plunge, leap, jump, drop **2** *The hawk dived rapidly towards its prey.* ► swoop, plunge, plummet, descend, nose-dive, drop, pitch

diverge VERB **1** *The roads diverged at this point.* ► separate, divide, part, split, branch, deviate, fork OPPOSITES ARE converge, come together, join **2** *Clearly our opinions diverge.* ► differ, disagree, clash, be different OPPOSITES ARE agree, coincide

diverse ADJECTIVE *information from diverse sources* ► various, varying, different, sundry,

assorted, miscellaneous, mixed, distinct, (*more formal*) manifold

diversion NOUN **1** *a traffic diversion* ► detour, deviation, alternative route **2** *a large city with plenty of diversions* ► entertainment, amusement, recreation, relaxation, distraction, pastime, game, hobby, play, sport

diversity NOUN *a great diversity of fruit and vegetables* ► variety, assortment, miscellany, mixture, range, array, multiplicity OPPOSITES ARE uniformity, similarity

divert VERB **1** *The plane was diverted to another airport.* ► redirect, reroute, deflect, turn aside, switch **2** *We tried to divert them with funny stories.* ► amuse, entertain, distract, occupy, interest, cheer up, delight, keep happy, regale

divide VERB **1** *The river divides north of the city. We divided into two groups.* ► separate, diverge, split, split in two, fork, branch AN OPPOSITE IS converge **2** *We divided the food between us* ► share out, allocate, allot, apportion, distribute, pass round **3** *We divide the eggs according to size.* ► sort, classify, grade, group, arrange, organize, categorize, sort out, separate, subdivide AN OPPOSITE IS combine

divine ADJECTIVE **1** *divine worship* ► holy, sacred, religious **2** *a divine being* ► supernatural, godlike, superhuman, heavenly, spiritual, immortal

division NOUN **1** *divisions in modern society* ► split, disunity, rupture, breach, disunion, schism, disagreement, conflict **2** *the division of Germany after the war* ► dividing, splitting, partitioning, separation **3** *the overseas division of the company* ► department, branch, arm, sector, office, bureau, subsidiary **4** *the division*

a
b
c
d
e
f
g
h
i
j
k
l
m
n
o
p
q
r
s
t
u
v
w
x
y
z

A
B
C
D
E
F
G
H
I
J
K
L
M
N
O
P
Q
R
S
T
U
V
W
X
Y
Z

divisive (div- I- siv) ADJECTIVE causing disagreement within a group

divorce NOUN divorces the legal ending of a marriage

divorce VERB divorces, divorcing, divorced **1** end a marriage by divorce **2** separate; think of things separately

Diwali (di- **wah**- lee) NOUN a Hindu religious festival at which lamps are lit, held in October or November

DIY ABBREVIATION do-it-yourself

dizzy ADJECTIVE dizzier, dizziest having or causing the feeling that everything is spinning around; giddy
▷ **dizzily** ADVERB **dizziness** NOUN

DJ ABBREVIATION disc jockey

DNA ABBREVIATION deoxyribonucleic acid; a substance in chromosomes that stores genetic information

do VERB does, doing, did, done This word has many different uses, most of which mean performing or dealing with something (*Do your best. I can't do this. She is doing well at school.*) or being suitable or enough (*This will do.*) The verb is also used with other verbs **1** in questions (*Do you want this?*), **2** in statements with "not" (*He does not want it.*), **3** for emphasis (*I do like nuts.*), **4** to avoid repeating a verb that has just been used (*We work as hard as they do.*)
do away with get rid of
do up 1 fasten • *Do your coat up.* **2** repair or redecorate • *Do up the spare room.*

dock[1] NOUN docks a part of a harbor where ships are loaded, unloaded, or repaired

dock VERB docks, docking, docked **1** bring or come into a dock **2** when two spacecrafts dock, they join together in space

dock[2] NOUN an enclosure for the prisoner on trial in a lawcourt

dock[3] NOUN a weed with broad leaves

dock[4] VERB docks, docking, docked **1** cut short an animal's tail **2** reduce or take away part of someone's wages or supplies, etc.

docker NOUN dockers a laborer who loads and unloads ships

doctor NOUN doctors **1** a person who is trained to treat sick or injured people **2** a person who holds an advanced degree (a doctorate) at a university • *Doctor of Music*

doctrine NOUN doctrines a belief held by a religious, political, or other group
▷ **doctrinal** ADJECTIVE

Thesaurus

of the spoils ▶ distribution, dividing up, sharing out, allocation, apportionment, allotment

divorce NOUN *One in three marriages ends in divorce.* ▶ separation, annulment, (*more informal*) break-up, (*more informal*) split-up

divorce VERB *Her parents divorced last year.* ▶ separate, end a marriage, (*more informal*) split up

divulge VERB *The article did not divulge the whereabouts of the individuals.* ▶ disclose, reveal, communicate, make known, pass on

dizzy ADJECTIVE *All that spinning made her feel dizzy.* ▶ giddy, faint, shaky, wobbly, light-headed, (*more informal*) woozy

do VERB **1** *I have a lot of work to do.* ▶ carry out, undertake, perform, achieve, fulfill, complete, discharge **2** *You can do as you please.* ▶ behave, act, conduct yourself **3** *If there's no tea, a glass of water will do.* ▶ suffice, satisfy, serve, be enough, be adequate **4** *Shall I do the lunch now?* ▶ prepare, make, get ready, fix, organize, provide **5** *She went upstairs to do her hair.* ▶ arrange, groom, style, brush, comb, wash, fix **6** *He will be doing languages at university.* ▶ study, read, learn, take a course in **7** *She has been doing very well in the new job.* ▶ get on, progress, succeed
do away with 1 *We want to do away with*

outdated practices. ▶ abolish, get rid of, discontinue, put an end to, dispense with, terminate, suppress **2** *I was afraid his enemies might want to do away with him.* ▶ kill, murder, put to death, assassinate, eliminate, exterminate

do up 1 *He stopped to do up his laces.* ▶ tie, fasten, secure **2** *They have bought an old farmhouse to do up.* ▶ renovate, restore, refurbish, decorate, revamp, (*more informal*) make over

do without *I cannot do without my eight hours' sleep.* ▶ forgo, dispense with, give up, renounce, abstain from

docile ADJECTIVE *Hannah has a docile nature.* ▶ gentle, compliant, meek, mild, obedient, amenable, cooperative, submissive, deferential

dock NOUN *The boat was moored at the end of the dock.* ▶ harbor, quay, wharf, jetty, landing stage, marina, dockyard, boatyard, waterfront

dock VERB **1** *The ship docked the next morning.* ▶ moor, berth, tie up, put in, anchor, drop anchor **2** *The dog's tail had been docked.* ▶ cut short, cut off, crop, shorten **3** *The company will dock your wages for any misdemeanor.* ▶ reduce, cut, lessen, decrease

doctor NOUN *Jane is sick and should see a doctor.* ▶ GP, physician, medical officer, consultant, (*more informal*) medic RELATED ADJECTIVE medical

document NOUN documents a written or printed paper giving information or evidence about something
▷ **documentation** NOUN

documentary ADJECTIVE **1** consisting of documents ● *documentary evidence* **2** showing real events or situations

documentary NOUN documentaries a movie giving information about real events

dodge VERB dodges, dodging, dodged move quickly to avoid someone or something

dodge NOUN dodges **1** a dodging movement **2** (*informal*) a trick; a clever way of doing something

dodgy ADJECTIVE (*informal*) **1** awkward or tricky **2** not working properly **3** dishonest

dodo NOUN dodos a large heavy bird that used to live on an island in the Indian Ocean but has been extinct for over 200 years

doe NOUN does a female deer, rabbit, or hare

doesn't (*mainly spoken*) does not

dog NOUN dogs a four-legged animal that barks, often kept as a pet

dog VERB dogs, dogging, dogged follow closely or persistently ● *Reporters dogged his footsteps.* [from Old English]

dog-eared ADJECTIVE (said about a book) having the corners of the pages bent from constant use

dogged (dog- id) ADJECTIVE persistent or obstinate
▷ **doggedly** ADVERB

dogma NOUN dogmas a belief or principle that a Church or other authority declares is true and must be accepted

dogmatic ADJECTIVE expressing ideas in a very firm authoritative way
▷ **dogmatically** ADVERB

do-it-yourself ADJECTIVE suitable for an amateur to do or make at home

dole VERB doles, doling, doled
dole out distribute

dole NOUN (*informal*) money paid by the state to unemployed people

doll NOUN dolls a toy model of a person

dollar NOUN dollars a unit of money in the U.S. and some other countries

dolphin NOUN dolphins a sea animal like a small whale with a beak-like snout [via early French from Greek *delphis*]

domain (dom- ayn) NOUN domains **1** a kingdom **2** an area of knowledge, interest, etc.

dome NOUN domes a roof shaped like the top half of a ball
▷ **domed** ADJECTIVE

domestic ADJECTIVE **1** to do with the home or household **2** (said about animals) kept by people, not wild
▷ **domestically** ADVERB **domesticated** ADJECTIVE

Thesaurus

document NOUN *a legal document* ► paper, certificate, contract, deed, record, charter, (*technical*) instrument

dodge NOUN (*informal*) *a clever dodge* ► ruse, ploy, trick, device, scheme, tactic, maneuver, stratagem, (*informal*) wheeze

dodge VERB **1** *He flicked his head to one side as if dodging a blow.* ► avoid, duck, fend off, evade, move out of the way of, swerve away from, turn away from, veer away from **2** *The senator may try to dodge the issue.* ► avoid, evade, shun, equivocate over, get out of, fudge, sidestep, (*more informal*) duck **3** *He managed to dodge between parked cars.* ► dart, dive, duck, leap, swerve, jump

dodgy ADJECTIVE*informal*) **1** *Avoid dodgy travel agents at all costs.* ► dishonest, suspect, unreliable, underhand **2** *He took out a dodgy-looking sausage sandwich.* ► suspicious, suspect, dubious, unappealing, inferior, nasty

dog NOUN *She was walking her dog along the beach.* ► hound, mongrel, pedigree, pup, puppy, whelp, bitch, dingo

dogged ADJECTIVE *She was found again by the dogged efforts of her father.* ► determined,

persistent, resolute, persevering, tenacious, steadfast, single-minded, unflagging, relentless

dogma NOUN *religious dogma* ► belief, creed, doctrine, teaching, tenet, principle, conviction, orthodoxy, set of beliefs

dogmatic ADJECTIVE *He was far too dogmatic to argue with.* ► opinionated, doctrinaire, assertive, peremptory, insistent, arrogant, categorical, overbearing AN OPPOSITE IS open-minded

dole NOUN (*informal*) *He lived on the dole for three years.* ► unemployment benefit, state benefit, benefit, social security, income support, in Great Britain

dole VERB
dole out *Mother started doling out cornflakes.* ► distribute, give out, share out, hand around, dish up, issue

domain NOUN **1** *the king's domain* ► realm, kingdom, empire, dominion, territory, country **2** *the domain of science education* ► field, sphere, area, concern, speciality, department

domestic ADJECTIVE **1** *fuel for domestic use* ► household, home, family, private AN

A
B
C
D
E
F
G
H
I
J
K
L
M
N
O
P
Q
R
S
T
U
V
W
X
Y
Z

dominate VERB dominates, dominating, dominated **1** control by being stronger or more powerful **2** be conspicuous or prominent ● *The mountain dominated the whole landscape.*
▷ **dominant** ADJECTIVE **dominance** NOUN **domination** NOUN

domineer VERB domineers, domineering, domineered behave in a dominating way
▷ **domineering** ADJECTIVE

dominion NOUN dominions **1** authority to rule others; control **2** an area over which someone rules; a domain

domino NOUN dominoes a small flat oblong piece of wood or plastic with dots (1 to 6) or a blank space at each end, used in the game of dominoes

donkey NOUN donkeys an animal that looks like a small horse with long ears

donor NOUN donors someone who gives something ● *a blood donor*

don't (*mainly spoken*) do not

doom NOUN a grim fate that you cannot avoid, especially death or destruction ● *a sense of impending doom*

doomed ADJECTIVE destined to fail or be destroyed

door NOUN doors a movable barrier on hinges (or one that slides or revolves), used to open or close an entrance
▷ **doorknob** NOUN **doormat** NOUN

doorstep NOUN doorsteps the step or piece of ground just outside a door

doorway NOUN doorways the opening into which a door fits

dope NOUN dopes **1** (*informal*) a drug, especially one taken or given illegally **2** (*informal*) a stupid person
▷ **dopey** ADJECTIVE

dope VERB dopes, doping, doped (*informal*) give a drug to a person or animal [from Dutch *doop* = sauce]

dormant ADJECTIVE **1** sleeping **2** living or existing but not active; not extinct ● *a dormant volcano*

dormitory NOUN dormitories a room for several people to sleep in, especially in a school or institution

dormouse NOUN dormice an animal like a large mouse that hibernates in winter

dose NOUN doses an amount of medicine, etc., taken at one time

dot NOUN dots a tiny spot

dot VERB dots, dotting, dotted mark something with dots

Thesaurus

OPPOSITE IS public **2** *goods for the domestic market* ► national, inland, internal, local, state AN OPPOSITE IS foreign **3** *a domestic type of person* ► home-loving, homely, domesticated

domesticated ADJECTIVE *domesticated animals* ► tame, tamed, domestic, house-trained, trained AN OPPOSITE IS wild

dominant ADJECTIVE **1** *She was the dominant member of the partnership.* ► leading, primary, prime, main, principal, foremost, uppermost, prominent, preeminent **2** *The leader plays a dominant role.* ► controlling, leading, authoritative, powerful, influential, assertive **3** *the dominant feature of the landscape* ► conspicuous, prominent, imposing

dominate VERB *London no longer dominates the British arts scene.* ► control, monopolize, govern, rule, direct, overshadow, predominate in

domineering ADJECTIVE *He had a domineering mother.* ► overbearing, authoritarian, autocratic, tyrannical, dictatorial, despotic, oppressive, harsh, strict

donation NOUN *The organization depends on voluntary donations.* ► gift, contribution, subscription, benefaction

donor NOUN *a large gift from an anonymous donor* ► benefactor, contributor, philanthropist, provider, sponsor, giver AN OPPOSITE IS recipient

doom NOUN *There was a feeling of doom about the place.* ► ruin, downfall, catastrophe, destruction, disaster

doomed ADJECTIVE *The project seemed doomed from the start.* ► ill-fated, ill-omened, condemned, damned, fated, cursed, jinxed, hopeless, hapless

doomsday NOUN *He kept bomb-making equipment for a doomsday scenario.* ► apocalypse, end of the world, judgment day

door NOUN *She walked out through the door.* ► doorway, entrance, exit

dope NOUN **1** (*informal*) *smuggling dope* ► drugs, narcotics, cannabis, heroin **2** (*informal*) *He must have looked a real dope.* ► fool, idiot, dolt, dimwit, nincompoop

dopey ADJECTIVE (*informal*) *He grew dopey and fell asleep.* ► dazed, groggy, befuddled, drowsy

dose NOUN *a dose of cough mixture* ► measure, prescribed amount, dosage, portion, quantity

dot NOUN *The picture consists of tiny dots.* ► spot, speck, point, mark, particle

double ADJECTIVE **1** twice as much; twice as many **2** having two things or parts that form a pair • *a double-barrelled gun* **3** suitable for two people • *a double bed*
▷ **doubly** ADVERB

double NOUN doubles **1** a double quantity or thing **2** a person or thing that looks exactly like another

double VERB doubles, doubling, doubled **1** make or become twice as much or as many **2** bend or fold in two **3** turn back sharply • *The fox doubled back on its tracks.* [via early French from Latin *duplus*]

double bass NOUN double basses a musical instrument with strings, like a large cello

double-cross VERB double-crosses, double-crossing, double-crossed deceive or cheat someone who thinks you are working with them

double-decker NOUN double-deckers a bus with two floors, one above the other

doubt NOUN doubts a feeling of not being sure about something

doubt VERB doubts, doubting, doubted feel doubt
▷ **doubter** NOUN

doubtful ADJECTIVE **1** feeling doubt **2** making you feel doubt
▷ **doubtfully** ADVERB

dough NOUN **1** a thick mixture of flour and water used for making bread, pastry, etc.

2 (slang) money
▷ **doughy** ADJECTIVE

doughnut NOUN doughnuts a round bun that has been fried and covered in sugar

dour (dow- er) ADJECTIVE stern and gloomy-looking
▷ **dourly** ADVERB

dove NOUN doves a kind of pigeon

dovetail NOUN dovetails a wedge-shaped joint used to join two pieces of wood

dovetail VERB dovetails, dovetailing, dovetailed **1** join pieces of wood with a dovetail **2** fit neatly together • *My plans dovetailed with hers.*

dowager NOUN dowagers a woman who holds a title or property after her husband has died • *the dowager duchess*

dowdy ADJECTIVE dowdier, dowdiest shabby; unfashionable
▷ **dowdily** ADVERB

down[1] ADVERB **1** to or in a lower place or position or level • *She fell down.* **2** to a source or place, etc. • *Track them down* **3** in writing • *Take down these instructions.* **4** as a payment • *We will pay $5 down and the rest later.* **5** unhappy or depressed
be down on disapprove of • *She is down on smoking.*

down PREPOSITION downward through or along or into • *Pour it down the drain.*

down[2] NOUN very fine soft feathers or hair
▷ **downy** ADJECTIVE

Thesaurus

double ADJECTIVE *double yellow lines on the road*
► dual, twin, duplicate, matched, matching, twofold, duple AN OPPOSITE IS single

double NOUN *It was either you or your double.*
► lookalike, clone, replica, spitting image

double VERB *We must double our efforts.*
► increase, multiply, magnify, enlarge, repeat
double back *He doubled back, crossed the bridge, and reached home.* ► turn back, backtrack, retrace your steps, return
double up *She doubled up with pain.* ► collapse, crumple up, fold over, fold up, bend over

double-cross VERB *He was double-crossing his friends.* ► cheat, betray, deceive, defraud, (more informal) two-time

doubt NOUN **1** *There was some doubt about the identity of the father.* ► uncertainty, hesitation, confusion, difficulty **2** *I was plagued by doubt.* ► indecision, uncertainty, misgiving, lack of confidence, distrust, mistrust, suspicion, reservation, qualm

doubt VERB **1** *I doubt whether they will be there.* ► question, think it unlikely **2** *I do not doubt their motives.* ► disbelieve, distrust, question, query, suspect

doubtful ADJECTIVE **1** *At first I was doubtful about taking him with me. The woman sounded doubtful.* ► hesitant, uncertain, unsure, undecided, dubious, irresolute, ambivalent, wavering, tentative, sceptical, in two minds OPPOSITES ARE confident, assured **2** *It was doubtful whether the witness would back him up.* ► dubious, uncertain, questionable, debatable, in doubt, open to question AN OPPOSITE IS certain **3** *We are very doubtful of the conclusions they reached.* ► suspicious, distrustful, mistrustful, cautious, wary, uneasy (about), sceptical, unsure OPPOSITES ARE confident, trusting **4** *The chances of success are fairly doubtful.* ► unlikely, improbable, uncertain, dubious, remote OPPOSITES ARE probable, likely

down ADJECTIVE *He felt down all day.*
► depressed, dejected, sad, unhappy, miserable, downcast, despondent, dispirited, disheartened, disconsolate, glum, melancholy, cast down OPPOSITES ARE cheerful, happy

down and out ADJECTIVE *down and out in the streets of a big city* ► destitute, homeless, penniless, vagrant, living rough OPPOSITES ARE prosperous, affluent, well off

a
b
c
d
e
f
g
h
i
j
k
l
m
n
o
p
q
r
s
t
u
v
w
x
y
z

A
B
C
D
E
F
G
H
I
J
K
L
M
N
O
P
Q
R
S
T
U
V
W
X
Y
Z

down[3] NOUN downs a grass-covered hill • *the South Downs*
▷ **downland** NOUN

downhill ADVERB, ADJECTIVE down a slope

download VERB downloads, downloading, downloaded transfer data from a large computer system to a smaller one

downpour NOUN downpours a heavy fall of rain

downright ADVERB & ADJECTIVE complete or completely • *a downright lie*

Down's syndrome NOUN a medical condition caused by a chromosome defect that causes intellectual impairment and physical abnormalities such as short stature and a broad flattened skull

down-to-earth ADJECTIVE sensible and practical

downward ADJECTIVE, ADVERB going towards what is lower
▷ **downwards** ADVERB

dowry NOUN dowries property or money brought by a bride to her husband when she marries him

doze VERB dozes, dozing, dozed sleep lightly

doze NOUN a light sleep
▷ **dozy** ADJECTIVE

dozen NOUN dozens a set of twelve
USAGE Correct use is *ten dozen* (not *ten dozens*).

drab ADJECTIVE drabber, drabbest **1** not colorful **2** dull or uninteresting • *a drab life*
▷ **drably** ADVERB **drabness** NOUN

draft[1] NOUN drafts **1** a rough sketch or plan **2** a written order for a bank to pay out money

draft[2] (drahft) NOUN drafts **1** a current of usually cold air indoors **2** the depth of water needed to float a ship **3** a swallow of liquid
▷ **drafty** ADJECTIVE

draft (drahft) ADJECTIVE (said about beer) served from a cask or barrel rather than a bottle or can

draft VERB drafts, drafting, drafted **1** prepare a draft **2** select for a special duty • *She was drafted to our office in Paris.*

drag VERB drags, dragging, dragged **1** pull something heavy along **2** search a river or lake etc. with nets and hooks **3** continue slowly and tediously

drag NOUN **1** something that is tedious or a nuisance **2** (*slang*) women's clothes worn by men

dragon NOUN dragons **1** a mythological monster, usually with wings and able to breathe out fire **2** a fierce person, especially a woman

dragonfly NOUN dragonflies an insect with a long thin body and two pairs of transparent wings

drain NOUN drains **1** a pipe or ditch, etc., for taking away water or other liquid

Thesaurus

downcast ADJECTIVE *Their mother often looked downcast.* ► dejected, depressed, despondent, dispirited, disheartened, downhearted, unhappy, sad, down, glum, melancholy, miserable, cast down OPPOSITES ARE cheerful, happy

downhearted ADJECTIVE *Steve tried not to look too downhearted.* ► dejected, depressed, despondent, dispirited, disheartened, downcast, unhappy, sad, down, glum, melancholy, miserable, cast down OPPOSITES ARE cheerful, happy

downpour NOUN *On the way home we were caught in a downpour.* ► rainstorm, cloudburst, deluge

downright ADJECTIVE *They were telling half-truths and downright lies.* ► utter, absolute, total, complete, out-and-out, outright, positive, categorical, sheer, unmitigated

doze VERB *He began to doze by the fire.* ► sleep lightly, nap, catnap, drowse, (*more informal*) snooze, (*more informal*) have a snooze, (*more informal*) have forty winks

doze NOUN *She needed a short doze before her guests arrived.* ► nap, catnap, light sleep,

siesta, (*more informal*) snooze, (*more informal*) forty winks

drab ADJECTIVE *The room had a few pieces of drab furniture.* ► dowdy, shabby, dreary, dingy, dull, shabby, somber, lackluster, unattractive, uninteresting, (*more informal*) tatty OPPOSITES ARE bright, colourful

draft NOUN *a draft of a speech* ► outline, sketch, abstract, first version, rough version, plan

draft NOUN **1** *The draft made her shiver.*
► current of air, puff, wind, breeze **2** *He took another draft of his beer.* ► drink, gulp, swallow, mouthful, (*more informal*) swig

drag VERB **1** *She dragged another chair over to the table.* ► pull, draw, haul, heave, (*more informal*) yank AN OPPOSITE IS push **2** *Time began to drag.* ► become tedious, crawl, go slowly, move slowly, pass slowly OPPOSITES ARE fly, pass quickly

drag NOUN (*informal*) *Working six days a week can become a drag.* ► bore, nuisance, bother, pest, annoyance, trial, (*informal*) pain in the neck

drain NOUN *The drain had become clogged with leaves.* ► channel, conduit, culvert, pipe, drainpipe, outlet, duct, gutter, sewer, watercourse

2 something that takes away strength or resources
▷ **drainpipe** NOUN

drain VERB drains, draining, drained **1** take away water, etc., through a drain **2** flow or trickle away **3** empty liquid out of a container **4** take away strength, etc.; exhaust
▷ **drainage** NOUN

drake NOUN drakes a male duck

drama NOUN dramas **1** a play **2** writing or performing plays **3** a series of exciting events
▷ **dramatic** ADJECTIVE **dramatist** NOUN **dramatize** VERB
[from Greek *drama*, from *dran* = to do, to act]

drape VERB drapes, draping, draped hang cloth etc. loosely over something

draper NOUN drapers (*old use*) a shopkeeper who sells cloth or clothes
▷ **drapery** NOUN

drastic ADJECTIVE having a strong or violent effect
▷ **drastically** ADVERB

draw VERB draws, drawing, drew, drawn **1** produce a picture or outline by making marks on a surface **2** pull **3** take out • *draw water* **4** attract • *The fair drew large crowds.*

5 end a game or contest with the same score on both sides **6** move or come • *The ship drew nearer.* **7** write out a check to be cashed **draw a conclusion** form an opinion about something by thinking about the evidence

draw NOUN draws **1** the drawing of lots (SEE lot) **2** the drawing out of a gun, etc. • *He was quick on the draw.* **3** an attraction **4** a drawn game

USAGE Do not confuse this word with drawer.

drawback NOUN drawbacks a disadvantage

drawbridge NOUN drawbridges a bridge over a moat, hinged at one end so that it can be raised or lowered

drawer NOUN drawers **1** a sliding box-like compartment in a piece of furniture **2** a person who draws something **3** someone who draws (= writes out) a check

drawing NOUN drawings a picture or outline drawn

drawing room NOUN drawing rooms a sitting room

drawl VERB drawls, drawling, drawled speak very slowly or lazily

drawl NOUN drawls a drawling way of speaking

Thesaurus

drain VERB **1** *There is a tap to drain water from the tank.* ▶ draw off, empty, remove, bleed, clear, take off **2** *Lisa drained the cocoa from her mug.* ▶ empty, drink up, quaff, gulp, swallow, finish off, polish off **3** *The water drains through into the river.* ▶ seep, leak out, ooze, strain, trickle **4** *The color had drained from her face.* ▶ fade, vanish, disappear, wane, evaporate **5** *The expense drained all my funds.* ▶ exhaust , consume, deplete, use up, sap, spend

drama NOUN **1** *Ruth is studying drama.* ▶ acting, dramatics, dramatic art, the theater, the stage, stagecraft **2** *Hardly a day goes by without some family drama or other.* ▶ scene, incident, excitement, spectacle, crisis, commotion, disturbance, fracas

dramatic ADJECTIVE **1** *a dramatic production* ▶ theatrical, stage **2** *a dramatic rescue at sea* ▶ exciting, striking, thrilling, stirring OPPOSITES ARE unexciting, routine **3** *a dramatic change in the weather* ▶ substantial, significant, marked, pronounced AN OPPOSITE IS insignificant

dramatize VERB **1** *The novel has been dramatized for television.* ▶ adapt, make into a play, rewrite **2** *He tends to dramatize small difficulties.* ▶ exaggerate, overplay, overstate, overdo, make too much of

drastic ADJECTIVE *drastic measures to reduce pollution* ▶ extreme, harsh, severe, radical, rigorous, draconian, desperate, dire

draw NOUN *She won a prize in the office draw.* ▶ raffle, lottery

draw VERB **1** *Neil drew a shape on his paper.* ▶ sketch, depict, trace, outline, mark out, pencil, map out, (*more formal*) delineate **2** *The secretary drew another chair up to the desk.* ▶ pull, drag, haul, heave, (*more informal*) yank **3** *His aunt went over to draw the curtains.* ▶ close, shut, pull together, open, part USAGE Note that *draw* can mean either "close" or "open" when referring to curtains. **4** *By Saturday the show was drawing huge audiences.* ▶ attract, bring in, win, entice, allure, persuade **5** *That is the conclusion I drew.* ▶ reach, arrive at, deduce, infer **6** *The teams drew after extra time.* ▶ tie, be even, be equal **draw out** *We could draw out the conversation for hours.* ▶ prolong, extend, protract, stretch, lengthen **draw up** **1** *The lawyers will draw up a contract.* ▶ formulate, compose, prepare, write, draft **2** *A car drew up outside the house.* ▶ stop, pull up, come to a halt, come to a standstill

drawback NOUN *The weather was rather a drawback.* ▶ disadvantage, snag, hitch, nuisance, weakness, (*more informal*) fly in the ointment OPPOSITES ARE advantage, benefit

drawing NOUN *She made drawings of the children.* ▶ sketch, picture , illustration, study, portrayal, design, outline

A
B
C
D
E
F
G
H
I
J
K
L
M
N
O
P
Q
R
S
T
U
V
W
X
Y
Z

dread NOUN great fear

dread VERB dreads, dreading, dreaded fear something very much

dreadful ADJECTIVE very bad • *dreadful weather*
▷ **dreadfully** ADVERB

dreadlocks PLURAL NOUN hair worn in many ringlets or plaits, especially by Rastafarians

dream NOUN dreams **1** a series of pictures or events in a sleeping person's mind **2** something imagined; an ambition or ideal
▷ **dreamy** ADJECTIVE **dreamily** ADVERB

dream VERB dreams, dreaming, dreamed or dreamt **1** have a dream or dreams **2** have an ambition **3** think something might happen • *I never dreamed she would leave.*
▷ **dreamer** NOUN

dream up invent or imagine a plan, idea, etc.

dreary ADJECTIVE drearier, dreariest **1** dull or boring **2** gloomy
▷ **drearily** ADVERB **dreariness** NOUN

dredge VERB dredges, dredging, dredged drag something up, especially by scooping at the bottom of a river or the sea
▷ **dredger** NOUN

dregs PLURAL NOUN the last drops of a liquid at the bottom of a glass, barrel, etc., together with any sediment

drench VERB drenches, drenching, drenched make wet all through; soak

dress NOUN dresses **1** a woman's or girl's piece of clothing with a bodice and skirt **2** clothes; costume • *fancy dress*

dress VERB dresses, dressing, dressed **1** put clothes on **2** arrange a display in a window, etc.; decorate • *dress the shop windows* **3** prepare food for cooking or eating **4** put a dressing on a wound
▷ **dresser** NOUN

dresser NOUN dressers a sideboard with shelves at the top for dishes, etc.

dressing NOUN dressings **1** a bandage, plaster, or ointment, etc., for a wound **2** a sauce of oil, vinegar, etc., for a salad **3** manure or other fertilizer for spreading on the soil

dressing gown NOUN dressing gowns a loose garment for wearing when you are not fully dressed

dress rehearsal NOUN dress rehearsals a rehearsal at which the cast wear their costumes

dribble VERB dribbles, dribbling, dribbled **1** let saliva trickle out of your mouth **2** (said about a liquid) flow in drops **3** move the ball forward in soccer or hockey with slight touches of your feet or stick

drift VERB drifts, drifting, drifted **1** be carried gently along by water or air **2** move along

---

Thesaurus

---

dread VERB *He dreaded the telephone call that might take her away from him.* ► fear, be afraid of, shrink from, be anxious about, worry about

dread NOUN *With a mounting feeling of dread I went to answer the door.* ► fear, trepidation, apprehension, foreboding, anxiety

dreadful ADJECTIVE **1** *a dreadful accident; a dreadful mistake* ► terrible, frightful, horrible, awful, fearful, ghastly, hideous, shocking, frightening, terrifying **2** *a dreadful person* ► unpleasant, disagreeable, nasty, awful, deplorable

dream NOUN **1** *I had a dream about lizards.* ► fantasy, nightmare, delusion, vision, hallucination, illusion, reverie, trance **2** *She was walking around in a dream.* ► daydream, reverie, trance, daze **3** *It had always been his dream to run a country inn.* ► ambition, wish, desire, yearning, aspiration, pipedream, daydream, ideal

dream VERB **1** *She dreamed she was on a journey.* ► have a dream, imagine, fantasize **2** *I have always dreamed of playing baseball.* ► long (to play), yearn (to play), hanker (after), fantasize (about)

dream up *There's not much time to dream up an excuse.* ► invent, devise, think up, concoct, contrive, work out

dreary ADJECTIVE **1** *a dreary story* ► dull, uninteresting, drab, tedious, boring, monotonous, unexciting OPPOSITES ARE exciting, interesting **2** *dreary countryside* ► gloomy, dismal, bleak, drab, somber, murky

dress NOUN **1** *Guests must wear formal dress.* ► clothes, clothing, costume, attire, apparel, garb, garments, ensemble, outfit, (more informal) gear RELATED ADJECTIVE ► sartorial **2** *She wore a beautiful red dress.* ► frock, gown, robe, shift USAGE A *robe* is usually a long dress, and a *shift* is usually a short one.

dress VERB **1** *She had to dress her disabled husband.* ► clothe, provide clothes for, put clothes on AN OPPOSITE IS undress **2** *He dressed quickly and left the house.* ► put on clothes, get dressed **3** *A nurse dressed the wound.* ► bandage, put a dressing on, bind up, tend, treat, attend to

dribble VERB **1** *A dog lay in the hearth dribbling.* ► drool, slaver, slobber, salivate **2** *Water dribbled from the end of the hose.* ► trickle, seep, drip, ooze, flow, leak, run

slowly and casually **3** live casually with no definite objective
▷ **drifter** NOUN

drift NOUN drifts **1** a drifting movement **2** a mass of snow or sand piled up by the wind **3** the general meaning of what someone says

driftwood NOUN wood floating on the sea or washed ashore by it

drill NOUN drills **1** a tool for making holes; a machine for boring holes or wells **2** repeated exercises, e.g., in military training

drill VERB drills, drilling, drilled **1** make a hole, etc., with a drill **2** teach someone to do something by making them do repeated exercises

drink VERB drinks, drinking, drank, drunk **1** swallow liquid **2** drink a lot of alcoholic drinks
▷ **drinker** NOUN

drink NOUN drinks **1** a liquid for drinking; an amount of liquid swallowed **2** an alcoholic drink

drip VERB drips, dripping, dripped fall or let something fall in drops

drip NOUN drips **1** liquid falling in drops; the sound it makes **2** apparatus for dripping liquid into the veins of a sick person

drip-dry ADJECTIVE made of material that dries easily and does not need ironing

dripping NOUN fat melted from roasted meat and allowed to set

drive VERB drives, driving, drove, driven **1** make something or someone move **2** operate a motor vehicle or a train, etc. **3** force or compel someone to do something • *Hunger drove them to steal* **4** force someone into a state • *She is driving me crazy.* **5** rush; move rapidly • *Rain drove against the window.*
▷ **driver** NOUN

drive NOUN drives **1** a journey in a vehicle **2** a hard stroke in golf, etc. **3** the transmitting of power to machinery • *four-wheel drive* **4** energy or enthusiasm **5** an organized effort • *a sales drive* **6** a track for vehicles through the grounds of a house

drive-in ADJECTIVE that you can use without getting out of your car

drivel NOUN silly talk; nonsense

drizzle NOUN very fine rain

drone VERB drones, droning, droned **1** make a deep humming sound **2** talk in a boring voice

drone NOUN drones **1** a droning sound **2** a male bee

drool VERB drools, drooling, drooled dribble **drool over** be very emotional about liking something

Thesaurus

drift NOUN **1** *a drift of deep snow* ► pile, heap, bank, mass, mound, ridge, accumulation **2** *the drift of the story* ► gist, essence, core, substance, thrust, import, tenor, purport

drift VERB **1** *The boat began to drift downstream.* ► be carried, float, stray, coast, move slowly **2** *People drifted out into the gardens.* ► wander, ramble, stray, meander, move casually, dawdle, potter **3** *The snow had drifted across the road.* ► pile up, bank up, heap up, accumulate, gather, form drifts

drill NOUN **1** *three months of military drill* ► training, instruction, discipline, exercise, practice **2** *Everyone knows the drill.* ► routine, procedure, system

drill VERB **1** *He filed the edges and drilled a series of holes.* ► bore, make, pierce, penetrate **2** *A sergeant was drilling the new recruits.* ► train, instruct, coach, teach, exercise

drink NOUN **1** *She had another drink of her coffee.* ► sip, swallow, gulp, swill, (*more informal*) swig **2** *In the end he turned to drink.* ► alcohol, liquor, alcoholic drink, strong drink, (*more informal*) booze

drink VERB **1** *She drank her tea.* ► swallow, sip, gulp down, quaff, swill **2** *an upright citizen who never drank* ► take alcohol, indulge, (*more informal*) booze

drip NOUN **1** *You could hear the drips from the blocked gutters.* ► drop, dribble, splash, plop, trickle **2** (*informal*) *He thought he must have seemed a complete drip.* ► weakling, idiot, (*informal*) ninny, (*informal*) wimp, (*informal*) weed, (*informal*) wally

drip VERB *Water was dripping on the floor.* ► drop, plop, splash, dribble, leak, drizzle, fall in drips, sprinkle, trickle

drive NOUN **1** *a short drive into town* ► trip, run, ride, excursion, journey, outing, jaunt **2** *a young woman with plenty of drive* ► motivation, ambition, initiative, enterprise, determination, enthusiasm, energy, keenness, persistence, zeal, (*more informal*) push **3** *a drive to recruit blood donors* ► campaign, crusade, effort, appeal

drive VERB **1** *I'll drive them to the station.* ► take, transport, ferry, carry **2** *Can you drive a tractor?* ► operate, control, manage, handle **3** *She drives everywhere.* ► go by car, travel by car, (*old-fashioned*) motor **4** *Most teachers drove their students very hard.* ► work, push, urge, direct **5** *Poverty drove them to crime.* ► force, compel, urge, push **6** *He drove a nail into the wall.* ► hammer, bang, ram

drive at *What was he driving at?* ► imply, suggest, intimate, insinuate, allude to, refer to, hint at, (*more informal*) get at

droop ➡ dry

droop VERB droops, drooping, drooped hang down weakly

drop NOUN drops **1** a tiny amount of liquid **2** a fall or decrease **3** a descent **4** a small round candy

drop VERB drops, dropping, dropped **1** fall **2** let something fall **3** become lower or less **4** put down a passenger, etc. • *Drop me at the station*
drop in visit someone casually

dropout NOUN dropouts a person who has dropped out of society or a course of study

droppings PLURAL NOUN the dung of animals or birds

drought (drout) NOUN droughts a long period of dry weather

drown VERB drowns, drowning, drowned **1** die or kill by suffocation under water **2** flood or drench **3** make so much noise that another sound cannot be heard

drowsy ADJECTIVE sleepy
▷ **drowsily** ADVERB **drowsiness** NOUN

drudge NOUN drudges a person who does hard or tedious work
▷ **drudgery** NOUN

drug NOUN drugs **1** a substance used in medicine **2** a substance that affects your senses or your mind, especially one causing addiction

drug VERB drugs, drugging, drugged give a drug to someone, especially to make them unconscious

drum NOUN drums **1** a musical instrument made of a cylinder with a skin or parchment stretched over one or both ends **2** a cylindrical object or container • *an oil drum*

drum VERB drums, drumming, drummed **1** play a drum or drums **2** tap repeatedly on something
▷ **drummer** NOUN
drum into drive a lesson, facts, etc., into a person's mind by constant repetition

drumstick NOUN drumsticks **1** a stick for beating a drum **2** the lower part of a cooked bird's leg

drunk ADJECTIVE not able to control your behavior through drinking too much alcohol

drunk NOUN drunks a person who is drunk

drunkard NOUN drunkards a person who is often drunk

drunken ADJECTIVE **1** drunk • *a drunken man* **2** caused by drinking alcohol • *a drunken brawl*

dry ADJECTIVE drier, driest **1** without water or moisture **2** thirsty **3** boring or dull **4** (said about remarks or humor) said in a matter-of-fact or ironical way • *dry wit*
▷ **drily** ADVERB **dryness** NOUN

Thesaurus

droop VERB *The flowers began to droop.*
► wither, wilt, flop, sag, slump, go limp, hang, bend, dangle, fall

drop NOUN **1** *a drop of water* ► droplet, drip, globule, bead, bubble **2** *It needs a drop of glue.* ► dash, spot, dab, trace, pinch, small amount **3** *a drop of 100 meters* ► descent, fall, dive, plunge **4** *She walked to the edge of the cliff and peered at the drop below her.* ► precipice, chasm, gorge, abyss, slope **5** *a drop in prices* ► reduction, decrease, cut, falling off, downturn, slump AN OPPOSITE IS rise

drop VERB **1** *A maid had dropped a tray in the hallway.* ► let fall, let go of **2** *They all dropped to their knees.* ► sink, fall, go down **3** *The union decided to drop some of its claims.* ► abandon, give up, relinquish, discontinue **4** *She dropped many of her friends after leaving university.* ► desert, abandon, renounce, give up, disown, reject, discard **5** *Many outlets have dropped their prices.* ► reduce, lower, cut **6** *He was dropped from the team.* ► exclude, leave out (of), discard, expel **7** *The airplane dropped a thousand feet.* ► descend, fall, plunge, plummet, dive, nosedive, sink

drown VERB **1** *He fell into the water and nearly drowned.* ► submerge, sink, go under **2** *Noises*

from the street drowned our conversation.
► overwhelm, overpower, drown out, engulf, make inaudible, silence

drowsy ADJECTIVE *We became drowsy in the heat.*
► sleepy, dozy, lethargic, somnolent, (more informal) snoozy

drug NOUN **1** *Her doctor prescribed a new drug.*
► medicine, medication, medicament, remedy, potion **2** *under the influence of drugs* ► narcotic, hallucinogen, stimulant, (more informal) dope, junk

drug VERB *The victim seems to have been drugged before being driven off.* ► anesthetize, knock out, stupefy, (more informal) dope

drum NOUN *a drum of oil* ► barrel, canister, cask, butt, keg, tub, tun

drunk ADJECTIVE *The men got drunk and waved bottles around.* ► intoxicated, inebriated, tipsy, drunken, under the influence, (more informal) plastered, (more informal) tight, (more informal) sloshed

dry ADJECTIVE **1** *Ahead lay miles of dry desert.*
► arid, parched, barren, waterless, desiccated, scorched, torrid **2** *a dry story* ► dull, tedious, boring, dreary, monotonous **3** *dry humor* ► droll, ironic, wry, sardonic, subtle

dry VERB *It wasn't easy drying clothes in such a wet climate.* ► get dry, make dry

dry ➡ dumb

dry VERB dries, drying, dried make or become dry

dry cleaning NOUN a method of cleaning clothes, etc., using a liquid that evaporates quickly

dual carriageway NOUN dual carriageways a road with a dividing strip between lanes of traffic in opposite directions

dub VERB dubs, dubbing, dubbed change or add new sound to the soundtrack of a film or to a recording

dubious (dew- bee- us) ADJECTIVE doubtful
▷ **dubiously** ADVERB

duchess NOUN duchesses a duke's wife or widow

duck NOUN ducks **1** a swimming bird with a flat beak; the female of this **2** a ducking movement

duck VERB ducks, ducking, ducked **1** bend down quickly to avoid something **2** go or push quickly under water **3** dodge; avoid doing something

duckling NOUN ducklings a young duck

duct NOUN ducts a tube or channel through which liquid, gas, air, or cables can pass

ductile ADJECTIVE (said about metal) able to be drawn out into fine strands

due ADJECTIVE **1** expected; scheduled to do something or to arrive • The train is due in ten minutes. **2** owing; needing to be paid **3** that ought to be given; rightful • Treat her with due respect.
due to as a result of

USAGE Traditionally, correct use is as in His lateness was due to an accident. Some people object to the use of "due to" without a preceding noun (e.g., "lateness") to which it refers. However, such uses as He was late, due to an accident are nowadays widely regarded as acceptable. But if you prefer, you can use because of or owing to instead.

due ADVERB exactly • We sailed due east.

due NOUN dues **1** something you deserve or have a right to; proper respect • Give him his due. **2** a fee • harbor dues

duel NOUN duels a fight between two people, especially with pistols or swords
▷ **duelling** NOUN **duellist** NOUN

duet NOUN duets a piece of music for two players or singers

duffel coat NOUN duffel coats a thick overcoat with a hood

duffer NOUN duffers a person who is stupid or not good at doing something

duke NOUN dukes a member of the highest rank of noblemen
▷ **dukedom** NOUN
[via early French from Latin dux = leader]

dull ADJECTIVE **1** not bright or clear • dull weather **2** stupid **3** boring • a dull concert **4** not sharp • a dull pain; • a dull thud
▷ **dully** ADVERB **dullness** NOUN

dumb ADJECTIVE **1** without the ability to speak **2** silent **3** (informal) stupid
▷ **dumbly** ADVERB **dumbness** NOUN

Thesaurus

---

dubious ADJECTIVE **1** I was dubious about the idea. ► doubtful, hesitant, uncertain, unsure, undecided, irresolute, ambivalent, wavering, tentative, sceptical, in two minds OPPOSITES ARE confident, assured **2** a dubious excuse ► suspect, suspicious, untrustworthy, unreliable, (more informal) fishy, (more informal) shady

duck VERB **1** The boys ducked behind a bush. ► crouch, stoop, bob down **2** I ducked to avoid an overhanging branch. ► dodge, sidestep, bend, swerve, bob down **3** They ducked him in the river. ► dip, immerse, plunge, submerge, lower

dud ADJECTIVEinformal) The light bulb was dud. ► faulty, defective, useless

dud NOUNinformal) Some of the fireworks were duds. ► failure, flop, disappointment

due ADJECTIVE **1** Your subscription is due this week. ► owing, owed, payable, outstanding **2** She drove with due care. ► proper, rightful, fitting, appropriate, necessary, suitable, adequate

3 the respect due to an eminent statesman ► deserved (by), merited (by), earned (by), fitting, appropriate, suitable (for)
due to **1** Death was due to a heart attack. ► caused by, the result of, attributable to **2** The game was cancelled due to bad weather. ► owing to, because of, on account of, as a consequence of, as a result of, in view of, thanks to

due NOUN We must give them their due. ► deserts, entitlement, rightful treatment, rights, merits, reward

dull ADJECTIVE **1** dull colors ► drab, dreary, somber, dark, lackluster AN OPPOSITE IS bright **2** a dull winter morning ► gloomy, overcast, dark, dim, dismal, bleak, murky, sunless OPPOSITES ARE sunny, bright **3** The report makes dull reading. ► boring, tedious, uninteresting, unexciting, monotonous, tiresome, insipid OPPOSITES ARE interesting, exciting **4** a dull pupil ► stupid, slow, unintelligent, dim, slow-witted, dense OPPOSITES ARE clever, bright

dumb ADJECTIVE **1** He kept dumb while the others argued. ► mute, silent, speechless, tongue-tied, unable to speak **2** (informal) He's not as

213

A
B
C
D
E
F
G
H
I
J
K
L
M
N
O
P
Q
R
S
T
U
V
W
X
Y
Z

dumbfound VERB dumbfounds, dumbfounding, dumbfounded astonish; strike a person dumb with surprise

dummy NOUN dummies 1 something made to look like a person or thing

dump NOUN dumps 1 a place where something (especially garbage) is left or stored 2 (*informal*) a dull or unattractive place

dump VERB dumps, dumping, dumped 1 get rid of something that is not wanted 2 put something down carelessly

dumpling NOUN dumplings a lump of dough cooked in a stew, etc., or baked with filling inside

dumpy ADJECTIVE short and fat

dunce NOUN dunces a person who is slow at learning [from John Duns Scotus, a Scottish philosopher in the Middle Ages. His opponents said that his followers could not understand new ideas.]

dune NOUN dunes a mound of loose sand shaped by the wind

dung NOUN solid waste matter excreted by an animal

dungarees PLURAL NOUN overalls made of thick strong cloth [from Hindi *dungri* = the cloth they were made of]

dungeon (dun- jon) NOUN dungeons an underground cell for prisoners

duo (dew- oh) NOUN duos a pair of people, especially playing music

duodenum (dew- o- deen- um) NOUN duodenums the part of the small intestine that is just below the stomach
▷ **duodenal** ADJECTIVE

dupe VERB dupes, duping, duped deceive

duplicate (dyoop- lik- at) NOUN duplicates 1 something that is exactly the same as something else 2 an exact copy

duplicate (dyoop- lik- ayt) VERB duplicates, duplicating, duplicated make or be a duplicate
▷ **duplication** NOUN **duplicator** NOUN

duplicity (dew- plis- it- ee) NOUN deceitfulness

durable ADJECTIVE strong and likely to last
▷ **durably** ADVERB **durability** NOUN

during PREPOSITION while something else is going on

dusk NOUN dusks twilight in the evening

dust NOUN tiny particles of earth or other solid material

dust VERB dusts, dusting, dusted 1 wipe away dust 2 sprinkle with dust or something powdery

dustbin NOUN dustbins a bin for household trash

dustpan NOUN dustpans a pan into which dust is brushed from a floor

dusty ADJECTIVE dustier, dustiest 1 covered with dust 2 like dust

dutiful ADJECTIVE doing your duty; obedient
▷ **dutifully** ADVERB

duty NOUN duties 1 what you ought to do or must do 2 a task that must be done 3 a tax charged on imports and on certain other things
on *or* **off duty** actually doing (or not doing) what is your regular work

Thesaurus

dumb as he makes out. ► stupid, unintelligent, foolish, slow-witted, dull, dim

dumbfounded ADJECTIVE *I gazed back at him, dumbfounded.* ► astonished, astounded, amazed, surprised, staggered, startled, nonplussed, disconcerted, speechless, shocked, flabbergasted, perplexed, stunned, stupefied, bewildered, (*more informal*) thunderstruck

dummy NOUN 1 *The gun was only a dummy.*
► imitation, fake, sham, substitute, toy, copy, model, counterfeit 2 *a ventriloquist's dummy*
► doll, puppet, mannequin, figure

dummy ADJECTIVE *a dummy attack* ► simulated, pretended, trial, mock, practice, bogus, (*more informal*) pretend

dump NOUN 1 *We've a lot to take to the dump.*
► tip, refuse dump, garbage heap, junkyard 2 *an ammunition dump* ► cache, depot, hoard, store

dump VERB 1 *Worn-out cars had been dumped at the side of the road.* ► dispose of, discard, get rid of, jettison, reject, scrap, (*more informal*) ditch 2 *She dumped her shopping by the door.*

► put down, set down, throw down, deposit, drop, tip, place, unload, (*more informal*) park

duplicate ADJECTIVE *The manager opened his room with a duplicate key.* ► matching, identical, twin, second, alternative, copied, corresponding

duplicate NOUN *The document in the file is a duplicate.* ► copy, facsimile, photocopy, carbon copy, reproduction, replica

dust NOUN *The surfaces were covered in dust.*
► dirt, grime, grit, filth, smut, particles, powder

dusty ADJECTIVE 1 *The tables were dusty.* ► dirty, filthy, grubby 2 *a light dusty substance*
► powdery, chalky, crumbly, granular, sandy

duty NOUN 1 *He felt a strong sense of duty.*
► responsibility, loyalty, obligation, allegiance, faithfulness, obedience, service 2 *One of his duties was to make lunch.* ► job, role, task, assignment, function, (*more informal*) chore 3 *an increased duty on cigarettes*
► tax, levy, tariff, excise, toll, dues

duvet (doo- vay) NOUN **duvets** a kind of quilt used instead of other bed linens

DVD ABBREVIATION digital versatile disc (formerly digital videodisc); a disc used for storing large amounts of audio or video information, especially films

dwarf NOUN **dwarfs** or **dwarves** a very small person or thing

dwarf VERB **dwarfs, dwarfing, dwarfed** make something seem small by contrast • *The ocean liner dwarfed the tugs that were towing it.*

dwelling NOUN **dwellings** a house, etc., to live in

dwindle VERB **dwindles, dwindling, dwindled** get smaller gradually

dye VERB **dyes, dyeing, dyed** color something by putting it into a liquid
▷ **dyer** NOUN

dye NOUN **dyes** a substance used to dye things

dynamic ADJECTIVE **1** energetic or forceful **2** (said about a force) producing motion
▷ **dynamically** ADVERB

dynamics NOUN the scientific study of force and motion

dynamite NOUN **1** a powerful explosive **2** something likely to make people very excited or angry

dynamo NOUN **dynamos** a machine that makes electricity

dynasty (din- a- stee) NOUN **dynasties** a line of rulers or powerful people all from the same family
▷ **dynastic** ADJECTIVE

dyslexia (dis- leks- ee- a) NOUN special difficulty in being able to read and spell, caused by a brain condition
▷ **dyslexic** ADJECTIVE

dystrophy (dis- trof- ee) NOUN a disease that weakens the muscles

Thesaurus

dwarf ADJECTIVE *a dwarf cactus* ► miniature, small, little, undersized, diminutive

dwarf VERB *The tower blocks dwarf the old cathedral.* ► dominate, tower over, overshadow

dwell VERB **dwell in** *Hermits used to dwell in these caves.* ► inhabit, live in, populate, lodge in, (more formal) reside in

dwindle VERB *After the war the population dwindled.* ► decrease, decline, diminish, shrink, contract, peter out, wane, fall off, die out

dye NOUN *a yellow dye* ► coloring, colorant, pigment, stain, tint, tinge

dye VERB *She dyed the curtains to match the new paint.* ► color, tint, stain, pigment, color-wash

dynamic ADJECTIVE *The country needs dynamic leadership.* ► energetic, vigorous, forceful, spirited, positive, effective, bold, vital, active

dynasty NOUN *The ruling dynasty went back to medieval times.* ► family, house, line, bloodline, succession, regime

a
b
c
d
e
f
g
h
i
j
k
l
m
n
o
p
q
r
s
t
u
v
w
x
y
z

Ee

A
B
C
D
E
F
G
H
I
J
K
L
M
N
O
P
Q
R
S
T
U
V
W
X
Y
Z

E. *ABBREVIATION* east; eastern

each *ADJECTIVE, PRONOUN* every; every one • *each child;* • *each of you*
USAGE In standard English, the pronoun each should be used with a singular verb and singular pronouns: *Each has chosen her own outfit.*

eager *ADJECTIVE* strongly wanting to do something; enthusiastic
▷ **eagerly** *ADVERB* **eagerness** *NOUN*

eagle *NOUN* eagles a large bird of prey with very strong sight

ear¹ *NOUN* ears **1** the organ of the body that is used for hearing **2** hearing ability • *She has a good ear for music.*

ear² *NOUN* ears the spike of seeds at the top of a stalk of corn

eardrum *NOUN* eardrums a membrane in the ear that vibrates when sounds reach it

earl *NOUN* earls a British nobleman
▷ **earldom** *NOUN*

early *ADJECTIVE, ADVERB* earlier, earliest **1** before the usual or expected time **2** near the beginning • *early in the book*
▷ **earliness** *NOUN*

earmark *VERB* earmarks, earmarking, earmarked put something aside for a particular purpose

earn *VERB* earns, earning, earned get something by working or in return for what you have done

earnest *ADJECTIVE* showing serious feelings or intentions
▷ **earnestly** *ADVERB* **earnestness** *NOUN*
in earnest **1** more seriously or with more determination • *We began to shovel the snow in earnest.* **2** meaning what you say

earshot *NOUN* the distance within which a sound can be heard

earth *NOUN* earths **1** the planet (Earth) that we live on **2** the ground; soil **3** the hole where a fox or badger lives **4** connection to the ground to complete an electrical circuit

earth *VERB* earths, earthing, earthed connect an electrical circuit to the ground

earthenware *NOUN* pottery made of coarse baked clay

earthly *ADJECTIVE* concerned with life on earth rather than with life after death

earthquake *NOUN* earthquakes a violent movement of part of the earth's surface

earthy *ADJECTIVE* like earth or soil

earwig *NOUN* earwigs a crawling insect with pincers at the end of its body [called this because it was thought to crawl into people's ears]

ease *NOUN* freedom from trouble or effort or pain • *She climbed the tree with ease.*
at ease relaxed

Thesaurus

eager *ADJECTIVE* **1** *It was good to see smiling, eager faces.* ► keen, enthusiastic, avid, fervent, zealous OPPOSITES ARE apathetic, unenthusiastic **2** *They were eager to find a seat near the front.* ► keen, anxious, determined **3** *The young ones are eager for more adventure.* ► longing, yearning, intent (on)

eagerness *NOUN* *Her eyes shone with eagerness.* ► enthusiasm, keenness, fervor, ardor, earnestness, excitement, intentness, longing, passion OPPOSITES ARE apathy, indifference

ear *NOUN* *He had the ear of the president.* ► attention, heed, notice, consideration, regard RELATED ADJECTIVE ► aural

early *ADJECTIVE* **1** *early symptoms of the disease* ► initial, first, advance, preliminary, forward AN OPPOSITE IS late **2** *early civilizations* ► ancient, primitive, prehistoric USAGE Note that *prehistoric* means "before the time of written records." *Primitive* means "early in history," but can also mean "not advanced, simple," and so it is not always a good choice for the meaning shown here.

earn *VERB* **1** *She earns a six-figure salary.* ► receive, be paid, make, (more informal) bring

in, (more informal) take home **2** *They have all earned our gratitude.* ► deserve, merit, warrant, justify, be worthy of, gain, secure, obtain OPPOSITES ARE lose, forfeit

earnest *ADJECTIVE* **1** *an earnest attempt to help* ► committed, determined, resolute, conscientious, devoted, diligent, purposeful, eager, industrious, involved OPPOSITES ARE casual, flippant **2** *He was an earnest, church-going man.* ► serious, serious-minded, thoughtful, solemn, grave, sober, staid, humorless OPPOSITES ARE casual, half-hearted

earnings *PLURAL NOUN* *He looked for ways to supplement his earnings.* ► income, pay, salary, wages, remuneration

earth *NOUN* **1** *life on earth* ► this world, the planet, the globe RELATED ADJECTIVE ► terrestrial **2** *The fork turned the soft earth.* ► soil, topsoil, loam, clay, sod, ground, humus, land

ease *NOUN* **1** *Most people can recognize road symbols with ease.* ► effortlessness, straightforwardness, no trouble, no problem, facility, simplicity AN OPPOSITE IS difficulty **2** *Notice the ease with which he completed the task.*

ease VERB eases, easing, eased **1** make less painful or less tight or troublesome **2** move gently into position **3** become less severe • *The pressure eased.*

easel NOUN easels a stand for supporting a blackboard or a painting

easily ADVERB **1** without difficulty; with ease **2** by far • *easily the best* **3** very likely • *He could easily be lying.*

east NOUN **1** the direction where the sun rises **2** the eastern part of a country, city, etc.

east ADJECTIVE, ADVERB towards or in the east; coming from the east
▷ **easterly** ADJECTIVE **eastern** ADJECTIVE **easterner** NOUN **easternmost** ADJECTIVE

Easter NOUN the Sunday (in March or April) when Christians commemorate the resurrection of Christ; the days around it

eastward ADJECTIVE, ADVERB towards the east
▷ **eastwards** ADVERB

easy ADJECTIVE easier, easiest able to be done or used or understood without trouble
▷ **easiness** NOUN

easy ADVERB with ease; comfortably • *Take it easy!*

eat VERB eats, eating, ate, eaten **1** chew and swallow as food **2** have a meal • *When do we eat?* **3** use up; destroy gradually • *Extra expenses ate up our savings.* [from Old English]

eaves PLURAL NOUN the overhanging edges of a roof

eavesdrop VERB eavesdrops, eavesdropping, eavesdropped listen secretly to a private conversation
▷ **eavesdropper** NOUN

ebb NOUN ebbs **1** the movement of the tide when it is going out, away from the land **2** a low point • *Our courage was at a low ebb.*

Thesaurus

► skill, dexterity, facility, naturalness, deftness, mastery, cleverness **3** *a life of ease* ► affluence, comfort, contentment, enjoyment, relaxation, luxury, leisure, wealth, prosperity AN OPPOSITE IS stress

ease VERB **1** *The medicine will ease the pain.* ► relieve, alleviate, mitigate, soothe, assuage, allay, lessen, deaden, dull, calm, lighten, moderate, quell, comfort OPPOSITES ARE aggravate, worsen **2** *measures taken to ease the tension* ► reduce, relax, decrease, slacken, take off AN OPPOSITE IS increase **3** *He eased the cork out of the bottle.* ► guide, slide, slip, edge, inch, maneuver, move gradually
ease off *The rain eased off.* ► abate, subside, let up, slacken off, die out, lessen

easily ADVERB **1** *She is easily the brightest student of her year.* ► by far, without doubt, undoubtedly, indubitably, indisputably, undeniably, definitely, certainly, patently **2** *In the end I managed the work easily.* ► effortlessly, comfortably, with ease, simply, straightforwardly, with no difficulty

easy ADJECTIVE **1** *an easy task* ► straightforward, undemanding, effortless, light, pleasant, painless, (*more informal*) cushy OPPOSITES ARE difficult, heavy **2** *easy instructions to follow* ► simple, straightforward, elementary, clear, uncomplicated, understandable, plain, user-friendly, foolproof, manageable OPPOSITES ARE complicated, difficult **3** *an easy manner* ► relaxed, easy-going, affable, natural, friendly, tolerant, informal, open, docile, amenable, accommodating, undemanding, (*more informal*) laid-back OPPOSITES ARE difficult, intolerant **4** *I long for an easy life.*

► comfortable, carefree, untroubled, leisurely, peaceful, restful, serene, relaxed, contented, cosy, tranquil AN OPPOSITE IS stressful

easy-going ADJECTIVE *Despite his easygoing nature he was extraordinarily energetic.* ► relaxed, easy, affable, natural, friendly, tolerant, informal, open, docile, amenable, accommodating, undemanding, (*more informal*) laid-back

eat VERB **1** *The condemned man ate a hearty breakfast.* ► consume, devour, swallow, (*more informal*) put away, (*more informal*) scoff, (*more informal*) polish off, (*more informal*) get stuck into RELATED ADJECTIVE ► edible **2** *Where shall we eat tonight?* ► have a meal, have dinner, dine, (*more informal*) feed **3** *eat into Rust was eating into the bodywork.* ► corrode, erode, wear away, wear through, rot, decay

eatable ADJECTIVE *The food is a little overcooked, but still eatable.* ► palatable, wholesome, edible, fit to eat, safe to eat, digestible OPPOSITES ARE uneatable, inedible USAGE Note that *edible* does not mean quite the same as *eatable*. You say that something is *edible* when you mean it is suitable as food and is not (for example) poisonous, whereas you use *eatable* about food that is good enough to eat and not (for example) burned or undercooked.

ebb VERB **1** *The tide ebbed late in the morning.* ► go out, recede, fall back, flow back, retreat AN OPPOSITE IS come in **2** *Her strength was beginning to ebb.* ► dwindle, decline, fade, wane, diminish, disappear, vanish, weaken OPPOSITES ARE increase, revive

A
B
C
D
E
F
G
H
I
J
K
L
M
N
O
P
Q
R
S
T
U
V
W
X
Y
Z

eccentric (ik- sen- trik) ADJECTIVE behaving strangely
▷ **eccentrically** ADVERB **eccentricity** (ek- sen- triss- it- ee) NOUN

ecclesiastical (ik- lee- zee- ast- ik- al) ADJECTIVE to do with the Church or the clergy

echo NOUN echoes a sound that is heard again as it is reflected off something

echo VERB echoes, echoing, echoed **1** make an echo **2** repeat a sound or saying

eclair (ay- klair) NOUN eclairs a finger-shaped cake of pastry with a creamy filling

eclipse NOUN eclipses the blocking of the sun's or moon's light when the moon or the earth is in the way

ecology (ee- kol- o- jee) NOUN the study of living things in relation to each other and to where they live
▷ **ecological** ADJECTIVE **ecologically** ADVERB **ecologist** NOUN

economic (ee- kon- om- ik) ADJECTIVE **1** to do with economy or economics **2** profitable

economical ADJECTIVE using as little of something as possible
▷ **economically** ADVERB

economics NOUN the study of how money is used and how goods and services are provided and used
▷ **economist** NOUN

economize VERB economizes, economizing, economized be economical; use or spend less
• *We need to economize on fuel.*

economy NOUN economies **1** a country's or household's income (e.g., from what it sells or earns) and the way this is spent (e.g., on goods and services) **2** being economical **3** a saving • *You need to make economies.*

ecstasy (ek- sta- see) NOUN **1** a feeling of great delight **2** an illegal drug that makes people feel very energetic and can cause hallucinations
▷ **ecstatic** (ik- stat- ik) ADJECTIVE **ecstatically** ADVERB

eddy NOUN eddies a swirling patch of water or air or smoke etc.

Thesaurus

eccentric ADJECTIVE *His eccentric behavior was worrying.* ▶ unconventional, abnormal, irregular, odd, strange, peculiar, weird, bizarre, extraordinary, idiosyncratic, capricious, quirky, erratic OPPOSITES ARE ordinary, conventional

eccentric NOUN *She had a reputation as an eccentric.* ▶ individualist, nonconformist, oddity, (*more informal*) oddball, (*more informal*) weirdo, (*more informal*) crackpot

echo NOUN *The mountains are full of strange echoes.* ▶ reverberation, reiteration, reflection of sound

echo VERB **1** *The slightest sound echoes across the hall. The words echoed in Isabel's head.*
▶ reverberate, resound, ring, resonate **2** *These thoughts were echoed by another speaker.*
▶ repeat, reiterate, reproduce, say again, ape, copy, imitate, mimic

eclipse VERB **1** *The sun is eclipsed by the moon.*
▶ blot out, block out, obscure, veil, cloud, cover, shade, darken, extinguish **2** *This achievement eclipsed all previous attempts.*
▶ overshadow, outshine, surpass, excel, outdo, put into the shade, dim

economic ADJECTIVE USAGE The main meanings of *economic* are "to do with economics or use of money" (the first meaning below) and "providing good value or profit" (the second meaning below). If you mean "careful in using money" you should use *economical* or its synonyms. **1** *an outline of the government's economic policies* ▶ financial, monetary,

commercial, fiscal, budgetary, business, money-making, trading **2** *The railroad line was closed because it was no longer economic.*
▶ profitable, lucrative, fruitful, productive

economical ADJECTIVE USAGE See the note at the entry for *economic*. **1** *It may be more economical to use an alternative form of fuel.*
▶ inexpensive, cost-effective, reasonable OPPOSITES ARE wasteful, expensive **2** *She is very economical with what money she has.* ▶ thrifty, careful, prudent, provident, sensible, canny AN OPPOSITE IS extravagant

economize VERB *One way of economizing is to grow your own vegetables.* ▶ save, save money, cut back, cut costs, cut expenditure, spend less, (*more informal*) tighten your belt AN OPPOSITE IS be extravagant

economy NOUN **1** *You can enjoy life and still exercise economy.* ▶ thrift, frugality, prudence, parsimony, providence AN OPPOSITE IS wastefulness **2** *To avoid debt we had to make some economies.* ▶ saving, cut **3** *the country's economy* ▶ financial system, wealth, budget

ecstasy NOUN *He ran out in ecstasy, doing cartwheels across the grass.* ▶ rapture, bliss, joy, delight , elation, euphoria, exultation

ecstatic ADJECTIVE *They were ecstatic as they returned with the good news.* ▶ elated, rapturous, exultant, delighted, euphoric, enraptured, joyful, overjoyed, blissful, delirious, gleeful, happy, (*more informal*) over the moon, (*more informal*) on top of the world

edge NOUN edges **1** the part along the side or end of something **2** the sharp part of a knife or axe or other cutting instrument **be on edge** be tense and irritable

edgy ADJECTIVE tense and irritable
▷ **edginess** NOUN

edible ADJECTIVE suitable for eating, not poisonous ● *edible fruits*

edit VERB edits, editing, edited **1** be the editor of a newspaper or other publication **2** make written material ready for publishing **3** choose and put the parts of a film or tape recording, etc., into order

edition NOUN editions **1** the form in which something is published ● *a paperback edition* **2** all the copies of a book, etc., issued at the same time ● *the first edition* **3** an individual television or radio program in a series

editor NOUN editors **1** the person in charge of a newspaper or a section of it **2** a person who edits something

editorial ADJECTIVE to do with editing or editors

editorial NOUN editorials a newspaper article giving the editor's comments on something

educate VERB educates, educating, educated provide people with education
▷ **educative** ADJECTIVE **educator** NOUN

educated ADJECTIVE showing a high standard of knowledge and culture, as a result of a good education

education NOUN the process of training people's minds and abilities so that they acquire knowledge and develop skills
▷ **educational** ADJECTIVE **educationally** ADVERB **educationist** NOUN

EEC ABBREVIATION European Economic Community (= the Common Market)

eel NOUN eels a long fish that looks like a snake

eerie ADJECTIVE eerier, eeriest strange in a frightening or mysterious way
▷ **eerily** ADVERB **eeriness** NOUN

effect NOUN effects **1** a change that is produced by an action or cause; a result **2** an impression that is produced by something ● *a cheerful effect*
USAGE Do not confuse with **affect**.

effective ADJECTIVE **1** producing the effect that is wanted **2** impressive and striking
▷ **effectively** ADVERB **effectiveness** NOUN

Thesaurus

edge NOUN **1** *We sat by the edge of the lake.* ► border, bank, fringe, extremity, verge, perimeter **2** *They now have the edge over their competitors.* ► advantage, upper hand, superiority

edge VERB **1** *a dress edged with lace* ► trim, decorate, finish, fringe, border **2** *She edged closer to the table.* ► creep, inch, slink, steal, sidle, move stealthily

edible ADJECTIVE USAGE See the note at the entry for *eatable. The decorations on the tree were all edible.* ► fit to eat, safe to eat, eatable, wholesome AN OPPOSITE IS inedible

edict NOUN *a royal edict* ► decree, order, command, mandate, proclamation, dictum, enactment

educate VERB *They hired a tutor to educate the children at home.* ► teach, tutor, instruct, coach, train, drill, cultivate, school

educated ADJECTIVE *an educated woman named Fiona* ► learned, knowledgeable, cultivated, cultured, well read, informed, refined, enlightened, civilized, erudite, literate, numerate, sophisticated AN OPPOSITE IS uneducated

education NOUN *He had received a first-class education.* ► schooling, training, teaching, instruction, tuition, coaching, curriculum, enlightenment, guidance

eerie ADJECTIVE *an eerie silence* ► weird, strange, uncanny, sinister, frightening, (more informal)

spooky, (more informal) creepy, (more informal) scary

effect NOUN **1** *The effect of all these announcements was to confuse everyone.* ► result, consequence, upshot, outcome, conclusion **2** *Sandy and I were feeling the effect of our long day.* ► consequence, repercussion, result, influence, aftermath **3** *The violence of those years had a profound effect on people.*
► impression, impact **4** *The drug was losing its effect.* ► effectiveness, efficacy, power, potency **in effect** *He was now in effect a figurehead with little real power.* ► in fact, effectively, really, actually, in truth, to all intents and purposes **take effect** *The change takes effect next April.*
► come into force, be effective, become operative, become valid, be implemented AN OPPOSITE IS lapse

effect VERB USAGE Do not confuse this word, which means "to achieve or bring about," with *affect*, which means "to cause a change in." *We need to effect a compromise.* ► achieve, accomplish, bring about, carry out, initiate, make, put into effect, cause, create, execute, implement

effective ADJECTIVE **1** *There is no effective alternative.* ► useful, workable, successful, fruitful, productive, worthwhile, potent, powerful, effectual, real, strong, (more formal) efficacious AN OPPOSITE IS ineffective **2** *The government still lacks an effective opposition.* ► capable, competent, able, proficient, useful **3** *He produced several effective*

effeminate ➡ elastic

A B C D **E** F G H I J K L M N O P Q R S T U V W X Y Z

effeminate ADJECTIVE (said about a man) having qualities that are thought to be feminine
▷ **effeminacy** NOUN

efficient ADJECTIVE doing work well; effective
▷ **efficiently** ADVERB **efficiency** NOUN

effort NOUN efforts **1** the use of energy; the energy used **2** something difficult or tiring **3** an attempt • *This painting is a good effort.*

e.g. ABBREVIATION for example
USAGE Do not confuse with i.e.

egg¹ NOUN eggs **1** a more or less round object produced by the female of birds, fish, reptiles, and insects, which may develop into a new individual if fertilized **2** a hen's or duck's egg used as food **3** an ovum

egg² VERB eggs, egging, egged encourage someone with taunts or dares • *We egged him on.*

ego (eeg- oh) NOUN egos a person's self or self-respect

Eid (eed) NOUN a Muslim festival marking the end of the fast of Ramadan

eiderdown NOUN eiderdowns a quilt stuffed with soft material

eight ADJECTIVE, NOUN eights the number 8
▷ **eighth** ADJECTIVE, NOUN

eighteen ADJECTIVE, NOUN the number 18
▷ **eighteenth** ADJECTIVE, NOUN

eighty ADJECTIVE, NOUN eighties the number 80
▷ **eightieth** ADJECTIVE, NOUN

either ADJECTIVE, PRONOUN **1** one or the other of two • *Either team can win.* • *either of them* **2** both of two • *There are fields on either side of the river.*

either ADVERB also; similarly • *If you won't go, I won't either.*

either CONJUNCTION (used with or) the first of two possibilities • *He is either ill or drunk.* • *Either come right in or go away.*

ejaculate VERB ejaculates, ejaculating, ejaculated **1** (said about a man) produce semen from the penis **2** (formal) suddenly say something
▷ **ejaculation** NOUN

eject VERB ejects, ejecting, ejected **1** send something out forcefully **2** force someone to leave **3** (said about a pilot) be thrown out of an aircraft in a special seat in an emergency
▷ **ejection** NOUN **ejector** NOUN

elaborate (il- ab- er- at) ADJECTIVE having many parts or details; complicated
▷ **elaborately** ADVERB **elaborateness** NOUN

elaborate (il- ab- er- ayt) VERB elaborates, elaborating, elaborated explain or work something out in detail
▷ **elaboration** NOUN

elastic NOUN cord or material woven with strands of rubber, etc., so that it can stretch

elastic ADJECTIVE able to be stretched or squeezed and then go back to its original length or shape
▷ **elasticity** NOUN

Thesaurus

arguments. ► convincing, cogent, persuasive, compelling, telling, striking, meaningful OPPOSITES ARE weak, unconvincing **4** *The changes will be effective from midnight.* ► operative, in force, valid OPPOSITES ARE inoperative, invalid

efficient ADJECTIVE **1** *The housekeeping was extremely efficient.* ► methodical, systematic, well organized, cost-effective AN OPPOSITE IS inefficient **2** *She was lucky to have found such an efficient young assistant.* ► capable, competent, proficient, able, well-organized, businesslike

effort NOUN **1** *We will make an effort to complete the task in time.* ► attempt, endeavor, try, (more informal) shot, (more informal) stab **2** *It took considerable effort to get the boiler working again.* ► exertion, energy, trouble, force, application, pains **3** *It was a tremendous team effort.* ► achievement, accomplishment, performance, feat, undertaking, success

egg VERB egg on *One of the group was egging the others on.* ► urge, goad, drive, provoke, incite, encourage

eject VERB **1** *Two heavy bouncers arrived to eject him from the club.* ► expel, throw out, evict, remove, dismiss, (more informal) kick out **2** *A*

tall chimney was ejecting black smoke. ► emit, discharge, send out, pour out, spew out, give off, belch, disgorge

elaborate ADJECTIVE **1** *elaborate schemes to raise money* ► complicated, complex, intricate, detailed, extensive, well worked out, involved AN OPPOSITE IS simple **2** *elaborate wood carvings* ► ornate, decorative, ornamental, intricate, fancy, baroque, rococo, showy OPPOSITES ARE simple, plain

elastic ADJECTIVE **1** *An elastic cord is tied to an ankle.* ► flexible, plastic, pliable, pliant, rubbery, bendy, ductile, yielding, (more informal) bouncy, (more informal) springy, (more informal) stretchy AN OPPOSITE IS rigid **2** *The arrangements can be made more elastic if you wish.* ► flexible, adaptable, adjustable, variable, accommodating OPPOSITES ARE rigid, fixed

elated ADJECTIVE *Her huge win left her feeling elated.* ► thrilled, exhilarated, ecstatic, exultant, delighted, euphoric, overjoyed, (more informal) over the moon, (more informal) on top of the world

elbow NOUN **elbows** the joint in the middle of the arm

elbow VERB **elbows, elbowing, elbowed** push with the elbow

elder[1] ADJECTIVE older • *my elder brother*

elder NOUN **elders 1** an older person • *Respect your elders!* **2** an official in certain Churches

elder[2] NOUN **elders** a tree with white flowers and black berries
▷ **elderberry** NOUN

elderly ADJECTIVE rather old

eldest ADJECTIVE oldest

elect VERB **elects, electing, elected 1** choose by voting **2** choose to do something; decide

election NOUN **elections** electing; the process of electing legislators

electorate NOUN **electorates** all the electors

electric ADJECTIVE **1** to do with or worked by electricity **2** causing sudden excitement • *The news had an electric effect.*
▷ **electrical** ADJECTIVE **electrically** ADVERB

electric chair NOUN an electrified chair used for capital punishment in the U.S.

electrician NOUN **electricians** a person whose job is to deal with electrical equipment

electricity NOUN a form of energy carried by certain particles of matter (electrons and protons), used for lighting and heating and for making machines work

electrify VERB **electrifies, electrifying, electrified 1** give an electric charge to something **2** supply something with electric power; cause something to work with electricity **3** thrill with sudden excitement
▷ **electrification** NOUN

electrocute VERB **electrocutes, electrocuting, electrocuted** kill by electricity
▷ **electrocution** NOUN

electrode NOUN **electrodes** a solid conductor through which electricity enters or leaves a vacuum tube

electromagnet NOUN **electromagnets** a magnet worked by electricity
▷ **electromagnetic** ADJECTIVE

electron NOUN **electrons** a particle of matter with a negative electric charge

electronic ADJECTIVE produced or worked by a flow of electrons
▷ **electronically** ADVERB

electronic mail NOUN a system of sending messages and data from one computer to another by means of a network

electronics NOUN the use or study of electronic devices

elegant ADJECTIVE graceful and dignified
▷ **elegantly** ADVERB **elegance** NOUN

element NOUN **elements 1** each of the parts that make up a whole thing **2** each of about 100 substances composed of atoms that have the same number of protons **3** a basic or elementary principle • *the elements of algebra* **4** a wire or coil that gives out heat in an electric fire or cooker **5** the environment or circumstances that suit you best • *Karen is really in her element at parties.*
the elements the forces of weather, such as rain, wind, and cold

elementary ADJECTIVE dealing with the simplest stages of something; easy

elephant NOUN **elephants** a very large animal with a trunk and tusks

Thesaurus

elderly ADJECTIVE *the increase in the number of elderly people* ► aged, aging, old, senile

elect VERB *The Party elects a leader every four years.* ► choose, select, vote for, pick, adopt, appoint, decide on, name, nominate

election NOUN **1** *the election of a president* ► selection, choosing, ballot (for), poll (for), vote (for) **2** *She became a senator in the 1997 election.* ► poll, vote, ballot RELATED NOUN ► psephology

electric ADJECTIVE *The atmosphere in the room was electric.* ► electrifying, exciting, dramatic, thrilling, tense, charged

electrifying ADJECTIVE *an electrifying performance* ► thrilling, exciting, astounding, hair-raising, stimulating, amazing, astonishing, electric

elegant ADJECTIVE **1** *Fire destroyed an elegant building in the Old Town.* ► handsome, stylish, graceful, gracious, smart, tasteful AN OPPOSITE IS inelegant **2** *A tall elegant woman walked in.* ► graceful, fashionable, beautiful, chic, smart **3** *an elegant solution to an awkward problem* ► neat, ingenious, clever, deft, effective

element NOUN **1** *That is only one element of the situation.* ► component, factor, part, ingredient, constituent, piece, strand, aspect **2** *There is an element of truth in the story.* ► trace, hint, touch, suspicion, smattering, soupçon **3** *James was in his element when working on old cars.* ► environment, domain, habitat, sphere
the elements *We could brave the elements in our parkas.* ► the weather, the wind and rain

elementary ADJECTIVE **1** *an elementary math course* ► basic, rudimentary, fundamental, introductory, primary AN OPPOSITE IS advanced **2** *The answer to the question is elementary.* ► simple, easy, straightforward, uncomplicated

a
b
c
d
e
f
g
h
i
j
k
l
m
n
o
p
q
r
s
t
u
v
w
x
y
z

elevate VERB elevates, elevating, elevated lift or raise something to a higher position
▷ **elevation** NOUN

eleven ADJECTIVE, NOUN elevens the number 11
▷ **eleventh** ADJECTIVE, NOUN

elicit (ill- iss- it) VERB elicits, eliciting, elicited draw out information by reasoning or questioning

eligible (el- ij- ib- ul) ADJECTIVE qualified or suitable for something
▷ **eligibility** NOUN

eliminate VERB eliminates, eliminating, eliminated get rid of something
▷ **elimination** NOUN

elision (il- lizh- on) NOUN omitting part of a word in pronouncing it, e.g., in saying *I'm* for *I am*

elite (ay- leet) NOUN a group of people given privileges which are not given to others

ellipse (il- ips) NOUN ellipses an oval shape

elliptical (il- ip- tik- al) ADJECTIVE **1** shaped like an ellipse **2** with some words omitted • *an elliptical phrase*
▷ **elliptically** ADVERB

elm NOUN elms a tall tree with rough leaves

elocution (el- o- kew- shon) NOUN the art of speaking clearly and correctly

elongated ADJECTIVE made longer; lengthened
▷ **elongation** NOUN

elope VERB elopes, eloping, eloped run away secretly to get married
▷ **elopement** NOUN

eloquent ADJECTIVE speaking fluently and expressing ideas vividly
▷ **eloquently** ADVERB **eloquence** NOUN

else ADVERB **1** besides; other • *Nobody else knows.* **2** otherwise; if not • *Run or else you'll be late.*

elsewhere ADVERB somewhere else

elude (il- ood) VERB eludes, eluding, eluded avoid being caught by someone • *The fox eluded the hounds.*
▷ **elusive** ADJECTIVE
USAGE Do not confuse with **allude**.

email NOUN electronic mail
▷ **email** VERB

emancipate (im- an- sip- ayt) VERB emancipates, emancipating, emancipated set free from slavery or other restraints
▷ **emancipation** NOUN

embalm VERB embalms, embalming, embalmed preserve a dead body from decay by using spices or chemicals

embankment NOUN embankments a long bank of earth or stone to hold back water or support a road or railway

embargo NOUN embargoes an official ban, especially on trade with a country

embark VERB embarks, embarking, embarked put or go on board a ship or aircraft
▷ **embarkation** NOUN
embark on begin • *They embarked on a dangerous exercise.*

embarrass VERB embarrasses, embarrassing, embarrassed make someone feel awkward or ashamed
▷ **embarrassment** NOUN

embassy NOUN embassies **1** an ambassador and his or her staff **2** the building where they work

Thesaurus

elevated ADJECTIVE **1** *an elevated highway*
▶ raised, overhead, high **2** *elevated discussions*
▶ grand, dignified, noble, superior, exalted, lofty

eligible ADJECTIVE be eligible for *You would be eligible for tax relief on donations.* ▶ be entitled to, qualify for, be allowed, be permitted AN OPPOSITE IS ineligible

eliminate VERB **1** *We can eliminate sabotage as a cause of the accident.* ▶ exclude, discount, disregard, remove **2** *The junta went on to eliminate many of their opponents.* ▶ get rid of, do away with, eradicate, exterminate, kill, murder, stamp out

eloquent ADJECTIVE *After dinner he made an eloquent speech.* ▶ expressive, articulate, fluent, moving, stirring, forceful, potent, persuasive, powerful, unfaltering AN OPPOSITE IS inarticulate

embark VERB **1** *Passengers may embark from eight o'clock this evening.* ▶ board, go aboard, go on board OPPOSITES ARE disembark, land

2 embark on *He was ready to embark on a career in medicine.* ▶ begin, start, enter on, commence, undertake, take up, set about

embarrass VERB *He gazed at her until he realized he was embarrassing her.* ▶ make (someone) uncomfortable, make (someone) feel embarrassed, disconcert, distress, upset, shame, mortify, fluster, nonplus, humiliate

embarrassed ADJECTIVE *Geoff's outspoken remarks left him feeling embarrassed.*
▶ awkward, self-conscious, disconcerted, uncomfortable, abashed, mortified, ashamed, confused, distressed, flustered, nonplussed, humiliated, shamed, upset, (more informal) red in the face

embarrassing ADJECTIVE *She was afraid of making an embarrassing mistake.* ▶ awkward, humiliating, shaming, shameful, disconcerting, distressing, mortifying, upsetting

embarrassment NOUN *Jane tried to hide her embarrassment.* ▶ awkwardness, self-consciousness, discomfort, unease, mortification, humiliation, distress

embellish VERB embellishes, embellishing, embellished ornament something; add details to it
▷ **embellishment** NOUN

embers PLURAL NOUN small pieces of glowing coal or wood in a dying fire

embezzle VERB embezzles, embezzling, embezzled take dishonestly money that was left in your care
▷ **embezzlement** NOUN

emblem NOUN emblems a symbol that represents something ● *The crown is a royal emblem.*
▷ **emblematic** ADJECTIVE

embody VERB embodies, embodying, embodied **1** express principles or ideas in a visible form ● *The house embodies our idea of a modern home.* **2** include or contain ● *Parts of the old treaty are embodied in the new one.*
▷ **embodiment** NOUN

embrace VERB embraces, embracing, embraced **1** hold someone closely in your arms **2** include a number of things **3** accept or adopt a cause or belief

embrace NOUN embraces a hug

embroider VERB embroiders, embroidering, embroidered **1** decorate cloth with needlework **2** add made-up details to a story to make it more interesting
▷ **embroidery** NOUN

embryo (em- bree- oh) NOUN embryos **1** a baby or young animal as it starts to grow in the womb; a young bird growing in an egg

2 anything in its earliest stages of development
▷ **embryonic** (em- bree- **on**- ik) ADJECTIVE

emend VERB emends, emending, emended remove errors from a piece of writing

emerald NOUN emeralds **1** a bright-green precious stone **2** its color

emerge VERB emerges, emerging, emerged **1** come out or appear **2** become known
▷ **emergence** NOUN **emergent** ADJECTIVE

emergency NOUN emergencies a sudden serious happening needing prompt action

emigrate VERB emigrates, emigrating, emigrated leave your own country and go and live in another
▷ **emigration** NOUN **emigrant** NOUN
USAGE People are *emigrants* from the country they leave and *immigrants* in the country where they settle.

eminent ADJECTIVE **1** famous and respected **2** outstanding and conspicuous
▷ **eminently** ADVERB **eminence** NOUN

emit VERB emits, emitting, emitted send out light, heat, fumes, etc.
▷ **emission** NOUN

emotion NOUN emotions a strong feeling in the mind, such as love or hate
▷ **emotional** ADJECTIVE **emotionally** ADVERB

emperor NOUN emperors a man who rules an empire

emphasis (em- fa- sis) NOUN emphases **1** special importance given to something **2** stress put on a word or part of a word
▷ **emphasize** VERB

Thesaurus

emblem NOUN *America's national emblem, the bald eagle* ► symbol, sign, token, mark, insignia, badge, crest, device, image, regalia, seal

embrace VERB **1** *The old man got up and embraced his son.* ► hug, clasp, hold, cuddle, grasp, squeeze **2** *Imelda could not embrace the idea of life without a husband.* ► accept, espouse, welcome, take on, receive **3** *The county embraces the best part of two national parks.* ► comprise, embody, include, incorporate, bring together, contain, assimilate, take in

emerge VERB **1** *A cyclist emerged from the entrance.* ► come out, appear, come into view, issue, emanate AN OPPOSITE IS disappear **2** *Another version of the story later emerged.* ► become known, become evident, be revealed, come to light, surface, unfold, (more informal) crop up

emergency NOUN *She offered a helping hand in an emergency.* ► crisis, danger, difficulty, predicament, urgent situation, extremity, (more informal) tight spot

eminent ADJECTIVE *an eminent scientist and scholar* ► distinguished, famous, prominent, well known, celebrated, acclaimed, renowned, illustrious, famed, notable, noteworthy, esteemed, respected, honored, outstanding

emission NOUN *carbon dioxide emissions* ► discharge, release, issue, outpouring, emanation

emit VERB *Vehicle exhausts emit hydrocarbons.* ► discharge, release, give off, give out, pour out, radiate

emotion NOUN *He spoke with a voice full of emotion.* ► feeling, passion, sentiment, intensity, warmth, agitation, excitement, fervor AN OPPOSITE IS indifference

emotional ADJECTIVE **1** *an emotional tribute* ► poignant, passionate, impassioned, intense, moving, touching, warm-hearted **2** *an emotional woman* ► passionate, demonstrative, fervent, sensitive, temperamental, excitable, romantic

emphasis NOUN *This year there is a special emphasis given to creative writing.*

A
B
C
D
E
F
G
H
I
J
K
L
M
N
O
P
Q
R
S
T
U
V
W
X
Y
Z

emphatic (im- fat- ik) ADJECTIVE using emphasis
▷ **emphatically** ADVERB

empire NOUN **empires** 1 a group of countries controlled by one person or government 2 a large business organization controlled by one person or group

employ VERB **employs, employing, employed** 1 pay a person to work for you 2 make use of
• *Our doctor employs the most modern methods.*
▷ **employment** NOUN

employee NOUN **employees** a person employed by someone

employer NOUN **employers** a person or organization that employs people

empress NOUN **empresses** 1 a woman who rules an empire 2 an emperor's wife

empty ADJECTIVE 1 with nothing in it 2 with nobody in it 3 with no meaning or no effect
• *empty promises*
▷ **emptily** ADVERB **emptiness** NOUN

empty VERB **empties, emptying, emptied** make or become empty

emulsion NOUN **emulsions** 1 a creamy or slightly oily liquid 2 a kind of water-based paint 3 the coating on photographic film which is sensitive to light

enable VERB **enables, enabling, enabled** give the means or ability to do something

enamel NOUN **enamels** 1 a shiny substance for coating metal 2 paint that dries hard and shiny 3 the hard shiny surface of teeth

encamp VERB **encamps, encamping, encamped** settle in a camp

encampment NOUN **encampments** a camp

enchant VERB **enchants, enchanting, enchanted** 1 put someone under a magic spell 2 fill someone with intense delight
▷ **enchanter** NOUN **enchantment** NOUN **enchantress** NOUN

encircle VERB **encircles, encircling, encircled** surround
▷ **encirclement** NOUN

enclose VERB **encloses, enclosing, enclosed** 1 put a wall or fence round; shut in on all sides 2 put something into a box or envelope, etc.

enclosure NOUN **enclosures** 1 enclosing 2 an enclosed area 3 something enclosed with a letter or parcel

encore (on- kor) NOUN **encores** an extra item performed at a concert, etc., after previous items have been applauded

encounter VERB **encounters, encountering, encountered** 1 meet someone unexpectedly 2 experience • *We encountered some difficulties.*

Thesaurus

► importance, significance, prominence, priority, urgency, weight, stress, attention

emphasize VERB *The spokesman emphasized the need to remain calm.* ► stress, underline, focus on, highlight, point up, draw attention to, play up, make a point of OPPOSITES ARE understate, play down

emphatic ADJECTIVE *an emphatic refusal* ► absolute, firm, forceful, vehement, vigorous, definite, unequivocal, direct, positive, energetic, out-and-out

employ VERB 1 *The business employs over a hundred people.* ► engage, hire, pay, take on, retain, use the services of, give work to, have on the payroll 2 *This medical practice employs the most modern techniques.* ► use, utilize, apply

employee NOUN *He was an employee of his own brother's bank.* ► worker, member of staff, member of the workforce
employees *measures to improve working conditions for the employees* ► staff, workforce

employer NOUN 1 *His employer was younger than he was.* ► boss, manager, proprietor, chief executive, head 2 *The government is the country's largest employer.* ► business, management, company, organization

employment NOUN *She found employment as a bank clerk.* ► work, a job, a post, a position, a situation, a livelihood

empty ADJECTIVE 1 *The house had been empty for years.* ► vacant, unoccupied, uninhabited, abandoned, deserted 2 *Without him her life felt empty.* ► aimless, futile, worthless, purposeless, unimportant, hollow 3 *These warnings were not just empty threats.* ► vain, idle, meaningless, ineffectual

empty VERB 1 *No one had troubled to empty the washing machine.* ► unload, unpack, clear OPPOSITES ARE fill, load 2 *He emptied the glass for a second time.* ► drain, exhaust, drink up AN OPPOSITE IS fill

enable VERB 1 *The new law will enable individuals to own shares in these companies.* ► authorize, permit, allow, qualify, empower, equip, aid, assist 2 *Wells took time off work to enable him to train twice a day.* ► allow, permit, let, help, make it possible for, provide the means for AN OPPOSITE IS prevent

enchant VERB *The scenery never ceased to enchant me.* ► delight, please, captivate, bewitch, charm, entrance, enthral, mesmerize OPPOSITES ARE repel, disgust

enclose VERB 1 *A tall fence enclosed the garden.* ► surround, circle, encircle, bound, border, skirt, encompass, shut in, fence in, confine, contain 2 *Please enclose payment with your order.* ► include, insert, put in

encounter VERB 1 *One day, they encountered their friends.* ► meet, run into, come across,

encounter NOUN **encounters 1** an unexpected meeting **2** a battle

encourage VERB **encourages, encouraging, encouraged 1** give confidence or hope; hearten **2** try to persuade; urge **3** stimulate; help to develop • *We need to encourage healthy eating.*
▷ **encouragement** NOUN

encroach VERB **encroaches, encroaching, encroached** intrude upon someone's rights; go further than the proper limits • *The extra work would encroach on their free time.*
▷ **encroachment** NOUN

encrust VERB **encrusts, encrusting, encrusted** cover with a crust or layer
▷ **encrustation** NOUN

encumber VERB **encumbers, encumbering, encumbered** be a burden to; hamper
▷ **encumbrance** NOUN

encyclopedia NOUN **encyclopedias** a book or set of books containing all kinds of information
▷ **encyclopedic** ADJECTIVE

end NOUN **ends 1** the last part or extreme point of something **2** the half of a sports field or court defended or occupied by one team or player **3** destruction or death **4** a purpose • *She did it to gain her own ends.*

end VERB **ends, ending, ended** bring or come to an end

endanger VERB **endangers, endangering, endangered** cause danger to

endless ADJECTIVE **1** never stopping **2** with the ends joined to make a continuous strip for use in machinery, etc. • *an endless belt*
▷ **endlessly** ADVERB

endow VERB **endows, endowing, endowed 1** provide a source of income to establish something • *She endowed a scholarship.* **2** provide with an ability or quality • *He was endowed with great talent.*
▷ **endowment** NOUN

endure VERB **endures, enduring, endured 1** suffer or put up with pain or hardship etc. **2** continue to exist; last
▷ **endurable** ADJECTIVE **endurance** NOUN

enemy NOUN **enemies 1** one who hates and opposes or seeks to harm another **2** a nation or army etc. at war with another

Thesaurus

chance on, (*more informal*) bump into **2** *You may encounter a few problems.* ► experience, be faced with, come up against, suffer, undergo

encourage VERB **1** *The cries of support encouraged the players.* ► hearten, cheer, inspire, buoy up, uplift, motivate, stimulate, animate, invigorate, spur, rally, reassure **2** *The government is eager to encourage small businesses.* ► support, promote, endorse, stimulate, aid, advance, assist, foster, strengthen **3** *Clever marketing encourages sales.* ► promote, increase, boost, generate, foster, further, be conducive to, be an incentive to, engender, help, induce **4** *Her mother encouraged her to take up medicine.* ► persuade, prompt, urge, invite AN OPPOSITE IS discourage

encouragement NOUN *All they need is a little encouragement.* ► reassurance, support, inspiration, stimulation, cheering up

encouraging ADJECTIVE *The first results were very encouraging.* ► reassuring, heartening, promising, favorable, gratifying, hopeful, auspicious, cheering, comforting, optimistic

end NOUN **1** *The shed was at the end of the garden.* ► extremity, edge, boundary, limit **2** *The end of the story is confusing.* ► conclusion, ending, culmination, climax, denouement AN OPPOSITE IS beginning **3** *His end came when he contracted pneumonia.* ► death, demise, passing on, expire, downfall **4** *The plan was just a means to achieve an end.* ► aim, goal, purpose, objective

end VERB **1** *The program ends at midnight. The bus route ends at this point.* ► finish, conclude, terminate, come to an end, close OPPOSITES ARE start, begin **2** *He wanted to end his relationship with Greta.* ► break off, stop, halt, discontinue, wind up OPPOSITES ARE maintain, continue **3** *The government plans to end the benefit next year.* ► abolish, terminate, finish, extinguish, put an end to

ending NOUN *The story has an exciting ending.* ► end, conclusion, finish, close, resolution, completion, climax, denouement

endless ADJECTIVE **1** *an endless source of good ideas* ► boundless, infinite, unlimited, unbounded **2** *He sipped endless cups of strong coffee.* ► ceaseless, countless, innumerable, constant, perpetual, interminable, eternal

endurance NOUN **1** *The race is a test of endurance.* ► stamina, staying power, fortitude, perseverance, determination, tenacity, resoluteness, resolution, strength, (*more informal*) grit **2** *Such suffering is beyond anyone's endurance.* ► toleration, tolerance, bearing, sufferance, forbearance

endure VERB **1** *The pain is greater than anyone could endure.* ► tolerate, bear, withstand, suffer, cope with, undergo, submit to **2** *Their love will endure for ever.* ► last, survive, abide, persist, prevail, continue, remain, stay

enemy NOUN *The country faces a new and more dangerous enemy.* ► foe, adversary, opponent, antagonist, opposition OPPOSITES ARE friend, ally

a
b
c
d
e
f
g
h
i
j
k
l
m
n
o
p
q
r
s
t
u
v
w
x
y
z

A
B
C
D
E
F
G
H
I
J
K
L
M
N
O
P
Q
R
S
T
U
V
W
X
Y
Z

energetic ADJECTIVE full of energy
▷ **energetically** ADVERB

energy NOUN energies **1** strength to do things, liveliness **2** the ability of matter or radiation to do work. Energy is measured in joules. **3** power obtained from fuel and other resources and used for light and heat, the operation of machinery, etc.

enforce VERB enforces, enforcing, enforced compel people to obey a law or rule
▷ **enforcement** NOUN **enforceable** ADJECTIVE

engage VERB engages, engaging, engaged **1** arrange to employ or use • *Engage a typist.* **2** occupy the attention of • *They engaged her in conversation.* **3** begin a battle with • *We engaged the enemy.*

engaged ADJECTIVE **1** having promised to marry somebody **2** in use; occupied

engagement NOUN engagements **1** engaging somebody **2** a promise to marry somebody **3** an arrangement to meet somebody or do something **4** a battle

engaging ADJECTIVE attractive or charming

engine NOUN engines **1** a machine that provides power **2** a vehicle that pulls a railway train; a locomotive [from old French: it originally meant "cleverness" and is related to *ingenious*]

engineer NOUN engineers an expert in engineering

engineer VERB engineers, engineering, engineered plan and construct or cause to happen • *He engineered a meeting between them.*

engineering NOUN the design and building or control of machinery or of structures such as roads and bridges

engrave VERB engraves, engraving, engraved carve words or lines on a surface
▷ **engraver** NOUN **engraving** NOUN

enigma (in- ig- ma) NOUN enigmas something very difficult to understand; a puzzle

enigmatic (en- ig- mat- ik) ADJECTIVE mysterious and puzzling
▷ **enigmatically** ADVERB

enjoy VERB enjoys, enjoying, enjoyed get pleasure from something
▷ **enjoyable** ADJECTIVE **enjoyment** NOUN

Thesaurus

energetic ADJECTIVE **1** *an energetic young person* ► dynamic, active, lively, spirited, animated, enthusiastic, indefatigable, tireless, unflagging OPPOSITES ARE inactive, lethargic, lazy **2** *energetic exercises* ► strenuous, vigorous, rigorous, arduous, brisk **3** *an energetic sales promotion* ► forceful, vigorous, aggressive, determined, powerful OPPOSITES ARE feeble, half-hearted

energy NOUN **1** *She felt full of energy.* ► vitality, vigor, drive, liveliness, spirit, verve, zest, zeal, exuberance, strength, (more informal) zip AN OPPOSITE IS lethargy **2** *new and cleaner sources of energy* ► power, fuel

engage VERB **1** engage in *She is always eager to engage in conversation.* ► participate in, take part in, become involved in, go in for, enter into, share in **2** *They decided to engage a nanny for the younger children.* ► employ, hire, recruit, take on, appoint, retain **3** *These activities do not always engage the imagination very well.* ► occupy, absorb, engross, attract, interest, capture, captivate, grip **4** *The infantry engaged the enemy early the next day.* ► fight, do battle with, clash with, encounter, enter into battle with **5** *The lowest gear did not engage properly.* ► connect, mesh, interlock

engaged ADJECTIVE **1** *an engaged couple* ► betrothed, affianced, attached **2** *He was engaged in his work.* ► occupied, busy, engrossed, absorbed, immersed, preoccupied

engagement 1 *They have broken off their engagement.* ► betrothal, promise to marry

2 *He had a business engagement that afternoon.* ► appointment, arrangement, commitment, obligation, meeting, date **3** *A series of military engagements followed.* ► battle, conflict, encounter, fight, clash, skirmish, offensive

engaging ADJECTIVE *an engaging little girl* ► charming, attractive, appealing, delightful, lovely, pleasing, likable, lovable

engine NOUN **1** *a car engine* ► motor, power unit, mechanism **2** *a train engine* ► locomotive

engineer NOUN *the engineer's drawings* ► designer, planner, inventor, architect

engraving NOUN *an engraving of the two younger children* ► etching, print, impression, woodcut, carving

engrossed ADJECTIVE *Fran was engrossed in her book.* ► absorbed, immersed, involved, interested, engaged, preoccupied (by), gripped (by), captivated (by), occupied (by), enthralled (by), fascinated (by), riveted (by)

enhance VERB *These successes enhanced his reputation.* ► improve, further, increase, heighten, reinforce, boost, intensify, strengthen, build up

enjoy VERB **1** *We all enjoy our outings. She enjoyed playing the piano.* ► like, love, appreciate, be fond of, be keen on, be pleased by, take pleasure from OR in, delight in, indulge in, rejoice in, relish, revel in, savor OPPOSITES ARE dislike, hate **2** *Visitors enjoy many privileges.* ► benefit from, have the benefit of, have the advantage of, experience, use

enlarge VERB enlarges, enlarging, enlarged
make bigger
▷ **enlargement** NOUN

enlighten VERB enlightens, enlightening,
enlightening give more knowledge or
information to a person
▷ **enlightenment** NOUN

enlist VERB enlists, enlisting, enlisted **1** join
the armed forces **2** obtain someone's support
or services etc. • *enlist their help*
▷ **enlistment** NOUN

enmity NOUN being somebody's enemy;
hostility

enormous ADJECTIVE very large; huge
▷ **enormously** ADVERB **enormousness** NOUN

enough ADJECTIVE, NOUN, ADVERB as much or as
many as necessary • *enough food* • *I have had
enough.* • *Are you warm enough?*

enrage VERB enrages, enraging, enraged
make someone very angry

enrich VERB enriches, enriching, enriched
make richer
▷ **enrichment** NOUN

enroll VERB enrolls, enrolling, enrolled
1 become a member of a society, etc. **2** make
someone into a member
▷ **enrollment** NOUN

ensemble (on- **sombl**) NOUN ensembles **1** a
group of things that go together **2** a group
of musicians **3** a matching outfit of clothes

enslave VERB enslaves, enslaving, enslaved
make a slave of someone; force someone into
slavery
▷ **enslavement** NOUN

ensure VERB ensures, ensuring, ensured make
certain of; guarantee • *Good food will ensure
good health.*
USAGE Do not confuse with **insure**.

entail VERB entails, entailing, entailed make a
thing necessary; involve • *This plan entails
danger.*
▷ **entailment** NOUN

entangle VERB entangles, entangling,
entangled tangle
▷ **entanglement** NOUN

enter VERB enters, entering, entered **1** come
in or go in **2** put something in a list or
book **3** type something into a computer
4 register as a competitor

Thesaurus

---

enjoy yourself ► have fun, have a good time,
celebrate, (*informal*) have a ball, (*informal*) let
your hair down

enjoyable ADJECTIVE *You can have a good meal in
enjoyable surroundings.* ► agreeable, pleasant,
delightful, gratifying, likeable, satisfying,
delicious, pleasurable, rewarding,
entertaining, amusing OPPOSITES ARE
unpleasant, disagreeable

enlarge VERB **1** *The new emperor sought to
enlarge his territory to the east.* ► increase,
expand, augment, develop, add to, stretch
2 enlarge on *He didn't want to enlarge on his
remarks.* ► elaborate on, expand on, amplify,
develop, broaden, supplement, flesh out

enlightened ADJECTIVE *an enlightened attitude
to funding the arts* ► informed, educated,
liberal, sophisticated, knowledgeable,
civilized, cultivated, refined, open-minded

enlist VERB **1** *Arafat enlisted thousands of young
people in his army.* ► recruit, enrol, conscript,
engage, muster **2 enlist in** *The brothers enlisted
in the Royal Engineers.* ► enrol in, sign up for,
join, enter, join up for, volunteer (for) **3** *In
Paris, he enlisted the aid of an influential
American physician.* ► obtain, secure, procure,
engage, win

enmity NOUN *people who live in a state of enmity
with one another* ► hostility, antagonism,
animosity, strife, opposition (towards),
antipathy (towards), acrimony (towards) AN
OPPOSITE IS friendship

enormity NOUN **1** *the enormities of the Nazi
years* ► atrocity, outrage, horror, crime,
abomination, wickedness **2** *the enormity of the
task* ► immensity, hugeness, magnitude,
vastness, seriousness, enormousness USAGE
Note that *enormity* is not correct when the
reference is simply to physical size, e.g., *the
enormity of the building.* It's better to say *the
huge size of the building* or use one of the
synonyms given above.

enormous ADJECTIVE *An enormous insect crept
across the floor.* ► huge, gigantic, immense,
massive, colossal, (*more informal*) whopping,
(*more informal*) ginormous

enough ADJECTIVE *Do you have enough food?*
► sufficient, adequate, ample, as much (food)
as you need

enrage VERB *Such a casual attitude enraged her.*
► anger, annoy, irritate, exasperate,
incense, vex, madden, aggravate, antagonize,
displease, incite, inflame, make angry, (*more
informal*) needle, (*more informal*) rile, (*more
informal*) bug, (*more informal*) rub up the
wrong way OPPOSITES ARE pacify, placate

ensure VERB USAGE Note that *ensure* means "to
make sure" whereas *insure* means "to take out
insurance." *A mild sedative ensured a good
night's sleep.* ► guarantee, make sure, secure,
confirm, make certain

enter VERB **1** *Soldiers entered the building.* ► go
in OR into, come in OR into, gain access to, set
foot in, pass into AN OPPOSITE IS leave **2** *While*

A
B
C
D
E
F
G
H
I
J
K
L
M
N
O
P
Q
R
S
T
U
V
W
X
Y
Z

enterprise NOUN **enterprises** **1** being enterprising; adventurous spirit **2** an undertaking or project **3** business activity
• *private enterprise*

enterprising ADJECTIVE willing to undertake new or adventurous projects

entertain VERB **entertains, entertaining, entertained** **1** amuse **2** have people as guests and give them food and drink **3** consider
• *He refused to entertain the idea.*
▷ **entertainer** NOUN

entertainment NOUN **entertainments** **1** entertaining; being entertained **2** something performed before an audience to amuse or interest them

enthusiasm NOUN **enthusiasms** a strong liking, interest, or excitement
▷ **enthusiast** NOUN **enthusiastic** ADJECTIVE

entire ADJECTIVE whole or complete
▷ **entirely** ADVERB

entirety (int- I- rit- ee) NOUN the whole of something
in its entirety in its complete form

entitle VERB **entitles, entitling, entitled** give the right to have something • *This coupon entitles you to a ticket.*
▷ **entitlement** NOUN

entitled ADJECTIVE having as a title • *a short poem entitled 'Spring'*

entomology (en- tom- ol- o- jee) NOUN the study of insects
▷ **entomologist** NOUN

entrance[1] (en- trans) NOUN **entrances** **1** the way into a place **2** entering • *Her entrance is the signal for applause.*

Thesaurus

the sign is up please do not enter. ► go in, come in AN OPPOSITE IS leave **3** *A bullet had entered his chest.* ► penetrate, pierce, puncture, perforate, make a hole in **4** *That year the Americans entered the war.* ► join, take part in, participate in **5** *I'm going to enter a competition.* ► go in for, become a contestant in, enrol for **6** *Please enter your details on the form.* ► record, register, note, write down

enterprise NOUN **1** *a dangerous enterprise* ► undertaking, endeavor, venture, pursuit, operation, project, adventure, business, effort **2** *a charitable enterprise* ► organization, business, establishment, company, firm **3** *Success in the job calls for considerable enterprise.* ► initiative, resourcefulness, resource, adventurousness, spirit, drive, determination, imagination

enterprising ADJECTIVE *An enterprising buyer can get quite a bargain at this time of year.* ► adventurous, resourceful, daring, bold, enthusiastic, energetic, imaginative, inventive, creative AN OPPOSITE IS unadventurous

entertain VERB **1** *He told stories to entertain his children.* ► amuse, divert, delight, gladden, cheer up, make laugh, raise a smile, (*more informal*) tickle **2** *We will be entertaining friends this Christmas.* ► receive, play host to, cater for, welcome **3** *She refused to entertain the idea.* ► consider, contemplate, countenance, accept, agree to

entertainer NOUN *a television entertainer* ► performer, artiste, artist

entertaining ADJECTIVE *an entertaining story* ► amusing, enjoyable, witty, funny, diverting, pleasing

entertainment NOUN *The holiday includes free evening entertainment.* ► amusement, diversion, enjoyment, recreation, pastime, play, fun, pleasure, sport, distraction

enthralling ADJECTIVE *They watched an enthralling series of singles matches.* ► exciting, fascinating, engrossing, captivating, dazzling

enthusiasm NOUN **1** *They will take on their new role with enthusiasm. He has a new-found enthusiasm for the game.* ► eagerness, excitement, keenness, ardor, relish, commitment, zeal, zest, fervor, ambition, drive, panache, spirit, verve AN OPPOSITE IS apathy **2** *Their latest enthusiasm is swimming.* ► interest, pursuit, pastime, diversion, hobby, passion, craze, (*informal*) fad

enthusiast NOUN *an amateur radio enthusiast* ► devotee, fan, fanatic, aficionado, follower, lover, (*more informal*) buff

enthusiastic ADJECTIVE *The visitors got an enthusiastic reception; a group of enthusiastic supporters* ► eager, ardent, fervent, devoted, passionate, fervent, wholehearted OPPOSITES ARE unenthusiastic, apathetic

entice VERB *A friend of mine enticed me to go to a club with him.* ► persuade, tempt, lure (into going), induce, coax

entire ADJECTIVE **1** *He spent his entire life on the island.* ► whole, complete, total, full **2** *The arch of one of the gates is entire.* ► intact, complete, undamaged

entirely ADVERB *I entirely agree with you.* ► completely, absolutely, fully, totally, utterly, thoroughly

entitle VERB **1** entitle to *The voucher entitles you to free entrance to the gallery.* ► qualify for, authorize to, allow, permit, warrant **2** *The story is entitled "A Day in the Life of My Dog."* ► call, name, title, designate

entrance NOUN **1** *The main entrance to the building is around the corner.* ► entry, way in, access, door, doorway, gateway, approach **2** *At the entrance of the hosts a silence fell on the room.* ► entry, appearance, arrival, approach,

entrance[2] (in- trahns) VERB **entrances, entrancing, entranced** fill with intense delight; enchant

entrant NOUN **entrants** someone who enters for an examination or contest etc.

entrench VERB **entrenches, entrenching, entrenched 1** fix or establish firmly • *These ideas are entrenched in his mind.* **2** settle in a well-defended position
▷ **entrenchment** NOUN

entrust VERB **entrusts, entrusting, entrusted** place a person or thing in someone's care

entry NOUN **entries 1** an entrance **2** something entered in a list, diary, or reference book **3** something entered in a competition • *Send your entries to this address.*

entwine VERB **entwines, entwining, entwined** twine round

enumerate VERB **enumerates, enumerating, enumerated** count; list one by one

envelop (en- vel- op) VERB **envelops, enveloping, enveloped** cover or wrap round something completely

envelope (en- vel- ohp) NOUN **envelopes** a wrapper or covering, especially a folded cover for a letter

envious ADJECTIVE feeling envy
▷ **enviously** ADVERB

environment NOUN **environments 1** surroundings, especially as they affect people's lives **2** the natural world of the land, sea, and air
▷ **environmental** ADJECTIVE **environmentally** ADVERB

environmentalist NOUN **environmentalists** a person who wants to protect or improve the environment

environmentally friendly ADJECTIVE not harmful to the environment

envy NOUN **1** a feeling of discontent you have when someone possesses things that you would like to have for yourself **2** something causing this • *Their car is the envy of all their friends.*

envy VERB **envies, envying, envied** feel envy towards someone

enzyme NOUN **enzymes** a kind of substance that assists chemical processes

epic NOUN **epics 1** a long poem or story about heroic deeds or history **2** a spectacular film

epicentre NOUN **epicentres** the point where an earthquake reaches the earth's surface

epidemic NOUN **epidemics** an outbreak of a disease that spreads quickly among the people of an area

epigram NOUN **epigrams** a short witty saying

epilepsy NOUN a disease of the nervous system, causing convulsions
▷ **epileptic** ADJECTIVE, NOUN

epilogue (ep- il- og) NOUN **epilogues** a short section at the end of a book or play, etc.

episode NOUN **episodes 1** one event in a series of happenings **2** one program in a radio or television serial

epitaph NOUN **epitaphs** words written on a tomb or describing a person who has died

Thesaurus

coming in, going in, (*more formal*) ingress **3** *Several people were refused entrance.*
► admission, admittance, entry, access

entrust VERB **1** *She entrusted her brother with the task.* ► charge, give responsibility for, put in charge of, trust, (*more informal*) saddle **2** *She entrusted the task to her brother.* ► assign, allocate, commit, delegate, confer (on), turn over

entry NOUN **1** *The entry to the grounds was closed.* ► entrance, way in, access, door, doorway, gateway, approach **2** *They were allowed entry on production of a passport.* ► admission, admittance, entrance, access **3** *the entry in the diary* ► item, record, statement, note, insertion **4** *an entry in a competition* ► candidate, competitor, contender, contestant, entrant, participant, player

envelop VERB *A poison gas enveloped the place.* ► cover, surround, enfold, blanket, enwrap, engulf, cloak, cocoon

envelope NOUN *He put the money in an envelope.* ► wrapper, wrapping, cover, sleeve

enviable ADJECTIVE *She has the enviable job of entertaining celebrities.* ► attractive, desirable, favorable

envious ADJECTIVE *He was envious of his brother's success.* ► jealous, resentful, grudging, begrudging, bitter (about), covetous, dissatisfied, (*more informal*) green with envy (about OR over)

environment NOUN **1** *a natural environment for wild birds* ► habitat, location, setting, surroundings, conditions, situation, milieu, territory **2** the environment *industrial activities that threaten the environment* ► the natural world, the earth, the planet, the world we live in

envy NOUN *He could not help feeling envy at her good luck.* ► jealousy, bitterness, resentment, covetousness, cupidity, dissatisfaction, ill-will

envy VERB *He envied her success.* ► be jealous of, be envious of, begrudge, grudge, resent

episode NOUN **1** *a happy episode in my life* ► incident, event, occurrence, happening, occasion, circumstance **2** *the final episode of the series* ► installment, part, section, program

a b c d e f g h i j k l m n o p q r s t u v w x y z

A B C D **E** F G H I J K L M N O P Q R S T U V W X Y Z

epithet NOUN epithets an adjective; words expressing something special about a person or thing, e.g., "the Great" in *Alfred the Great*

equal ADJECTIVE **1** the same in amount, size, or value etc. **2** having the necessary strength, courage, or ability, etc. • *She was equal to the task.*
▷ **equally** ADVERB

equal NOUN equals a person or thing that is equal to another • *She has no equal*

equal VERB equals, equaling, equaled **1** be the same in amount, size, or value **2** match or be as good as • *No one has yet equaled this score.*

equality NOUN being equal

equalize VERB equalizes, equalizing, equalized make things equal
▷ **equalization** NOUN

equation NOUN equations (in mathematics) a statement that two amounts are equal, e.g., $3 + 4 = 2 + 5$

equator NOUN equators an imaginary line around the Earth at an equal distance from the North and South Poles

equatorial (ek-wa-tor-ee-al) ADJECTIVE to do with or near the equator

equilateral (ee-kwi-lat-er-al) ADJECTIVE (said about a triangle) having all sides equal

equilibrium (ee-kwi-lib-ree-um) NOUN **1** a balance between different forces, influences, etc. **2** a balanced state of mind

equinox (ek-win-oks) NOUN equinoxes the time of year when day and night are equal in length (about 20 March in spring, about 22 September in autumn)
▷ **equinoctial** ADJECTIVE

equip VERB equips, equipping, equipped supply with what is needed

equipment NOUN the things needed for a particular purpose

equivalent ADJECTIVE equal in importance, meaning, value, etc.
▷ **equivalence** NOUN

-er[1] and **-ier** SUFFIX can form the comparative of adjectives and adverbs (e.g., *high/higher, lazy/lazier*)

-er[2] SUFFIX can form nouns meaning "a person or thing that does something" (e.g., *farmer, computer*)

era (eer-a) NOUN eras a period of history

eradicate VERB eradicates, eradicating, eradicated get rid of something; remove all traces of it
▷ **eradication** NOUN

erase VERB erases, erasing, erased **1** rub something out **2** wipe out a recording on magnetic tape
▷ **eraser** NOUN

erect ADJECTIVE standing straight up

erect VERB erects, erecting, erected set up or build something
▷ **erection** NOUN **erector** NOUN

erosion NOUN the wearing away of the earth's surface by the action of water, wind, etc.

erotic ADJECTIVE arousing sexual feelings
▷ **erotically** ADVERB

Thesaurus

equal ADJECTIVE **1** *a row of houses of equal size* ▸ identical, similar, uniform, the same, like, corresponding, comparable, commensurate OPPOSITES ARE unequal, different, varying **2** *an equal contest* ▸ even, balanced, level, evenly matched OPPOSITES ARE unequal, uneven **3** equal to *We thought he was equal to the task.* ▸ capable of, fit for, adequate for, good enough for, suitable for, suited for AN OPPOSITE IS incapable of

equal NOUN *They treated him as their equal.* ▸ peer, equivalent, counterpart, fellow

equal VERB **1** *Her performance almost equaled the world record.* ▸ match, reach, be as good as, compete with, rival **2** *Three and ten equals thirteen.* ▸ total, amount to

equality NOUN **1** *an equality of supply and demand* ▸ evenness, similarity, balance (between), parity, uniformity, correspondence, identity **2** *equality before the law* ▸ fairness, justice, equal rights, impartiality

equalize VERB **1** *The law equalizes pay for men and women.* ▸ balance, make equal, level, match, even up, (more informal) square **2** *The score equalized after ten minutes.* ▸ level the score, draw level

equip VERB **1** *Each seat is equipped with a set of headphones.* ▸ provide, supply, furnish, fit, fit up **2** *qualifications that will equip you for your careers* ▸ qualify, prepare

equipment NOUN *equipment needed to record the concert* ▸ apparatus, appliances, tools, gear

equivalent ADJECTIVE *a degree or an equivalent qualification* ▸ comparable, similar, identical, corresponding

era NOUN *a new era of peace* ▸ age, period, epoch

erase VERB *They erased a sentence that might cause offense.* ▸ delete, remove, rub out

erect ADJECTIVE *an erect posture* ▸ upright, rigid, stiff

erect VERB *They will erect a walkway to join the two buildings.* ▸ build, construct, assemble, put up

erode VERB *Rainwater has eroded the soil.* ▸ wear away, wear down, eat away, corrode

erotic ADJECTIVE *erotic art* ▸ sensual, sexual, amatory, carnal, titillating, (disapproving) pornographic, (disapproving) salacious, (disapproving) lewd, (disapproving) suggestive

errand NOUN errands a short journey to take a message or fetch goods, etc.

erratic (ir- at- ik) ADJECTIVE **1** not regular **2** not reliable
> ▷ **erratically** ADVERB

error NOUN errors a mistake

erupt VERB erupts, erupting, erupted **1** burst out **2** when a volcano erupts, it shoots out lava
> ▷ **eruption** NOUN

escalate VERB escalates, escalating, escalated make or become greater, more serious, or more intense ● *The riots escalated into a war.*
> ▷ **escalation** NOUN

escalator NOUN escalators a staircase with an endless line of steps moving up or down

escapade (es- ka- **payd**) NOUN escapades a reckless adventure

escape VERB escapes, escaping, escaped **1** get yourself free; get out or away **2** avoid something ● *He escaped punishment.* **3** be forgotten by someone ● *Her name escapes me for the moment.*

escape NOUN escapes **1** escaping **2** a way to escape

escapism NOUN escaping from the difficulties of life by thinking about or doing more pleasant things
> ▷ **escapist** ADJECTIVE

escort (ess- kort) NOUN escorts a person or group accompanying a person or thing, especially to give protection

escort (iss- kort) VERB escorts, escorting, escorted act as an escort to somebody or something

esophagus (e- sof- a- gus) NOUN esophagi (e- sof- a- gI) the tube leading from the throat to the stomach; the gullet

especially ADVERB **1** in particular **2** to a great extent

espionage (ess- pee- on- ah*zh*) NOUN spying

espresso NOUN espressos coffee made by forcing steam through ground coffee beans

Esq. ABBREVIATION (short for **Esquire**) a title written after a man's surname where no title is used before his name

-ess SUFFIX forms feminine nouns (e.g. *lioness, princess*)

essay (ess- ay) NOUN essays **1** a short piece of writing in prose **2** an attempt

Thesaurus

err VERB **1** *The authorities had erred in not making the information known.* ► be wrong, make a mistake, misjudge, miscalculate, blunder, slip up **2** *They were punished if they erred.*
► misbehave, do wrong, be bad, be naughty, disobey, transgress

errand NOUN *They did errands for their parents.*
► task, job, duty, assignment, commission, mission

erratic ADJECTIVE *It is hard to explain such erratic behavior.* ► changeable, unpredictable, inconstant, irregular, unstable, variable OPPOSITES ARE consistent, stable

error NOUN *The report contained many factual errors.* ► mistake, inaccuracy, slip, blunder, fault, flaw, miscalculation

erupt VERB **1** *Lava continued to erupt from the volcano.* ► spew, spout, spurt, gush, issue, pour out, shoot out, belch, be discharged, be emitted, be expelled **2** *Violence erupted on the streets of the city.* ► break out, flare up

eruption NOUN **1** *an eruption of Vesuvius; an eruption of violence* ► outbreak, outburst, discharge, burst, explosion **2** *a skin eruption* ► rash, inflammation

escalate VERB *The dispute might escalate into an all-out war.* ► grow, develop, build up, heighten, intensify, accelerate

escapade NOUN *a dangerous escapade*
► adventure, exploit, prank, caper, mischief, romp, antic, spree, fling, scrape, stunt, (*more informal*) lark

escape NOUN **1** *an escape from prison*
► breakout, getaway, absconding, bolt, flight, flit, retreat, running away **2** *an escape of gas*
► leak, leakage, emission, seepage, discharge **3** *an escape from life's troubles* ► distraction, diversion, relief, avoidance, relaxation

escape VERB **1** *They must have had help to escape.*
► get away, break free, break out, break loose, run away, abscond, make a break for it **2** *Oil was escaping from a crack in the hull.*
► leak, seep, ooze, discharge, drain, pour out, run out **3** *The passengers all escaped serious injury. We managed to escape a lot of the work.*
► avoid, evade, elude, dodge, miss

escort NOUN **1** *The police provided an escort.*
► guard, guide, bodyguard, convoy **2** *a royal escort* ► attendant, entourage, train, retinue

escort VERB *A representative will escort you to your seat.* ► accompany, conduct, guide, lead, take, show, usher

especially ADVERB **1** *Property is especially expensive in the central area of the city.*
► particularly, exceptionally, extremely, peculiarly, extraordinarily, remarkably, uncommonly **2** *Patients, especially those with head injuries, become disoriented.* ► chiefly, mainly, principally, particularly, in particular, above all, primarily

essay NOUN *I have to write an essay by the end of the week.* ► article, piece of writing, composition, assignment, study

a
b
c
d
e
f
g
h
i
j
k
l
m
n
o
p
q
r
s
t
u
v
w
x
y
z

A
B
C
D
E
F
G
H
I
J
K
L
M
N
O
P
Q
R
S
T
U
V
W
X
Y
Z

essence NOUN essences **1** the most important quality or element of something **2** a concentrated liquid

essential ADJECTIVE not able to be done without
▷ **essentially** ADVERB

essential NOUN essentials an essential thing

-est or **-iest** SUFFIX can form the superlative of adjectives and adverbs (e.g., high/highest, lazy/laziest)

establish VERB establishes, establishing, established **1** set up a business, government, or relationship, etc., on a firm basis **2** show something to be true; prove • He established his innocence.
the established Church a country's national Church, officially recognized as such by law

establishment NOUN establishments **1** establishing something **2** a business firm or other institution
the Establishment people who are established in positions of power and influence

estate NOUN estates **1** an area of land with a set of houses or factories on it **2** a large area of land owned by one person **3** all that a person owns when he or she dies **4** (old use) a condition or status • the holy estate of matrimony

estate agent NOUN estate agents a person whose business is selling houses and land

esteem VERB esteems, esteeming, esteemed think that a person or thing is excellent

esteem NOUN respect and admiration

estimable ADJECTIVE worthy of esteem

estimate (ess- tim- at) NOUN estimates a rough calculation or guess about an amount or value

estimate (ess- tim- ayt) VERB estimates, estimating, estimated make an estimate
▷ **estimation** NOUN

estrogen (es- tro- jen) NOUN a hormone which develops and maintains female sexual and physical characteristics

estuary (ess- tew- er- ee) NOUN estuaries the mouth of a river where it reaches the sea and the tide flows in and out

etc. ABBREVIATION (short for et cetera) and other similar things; and so on

etch VERB etches, etching, etched **1** engrave a picture with acid on a metal plate, especially for printing **2** if something is etched on your mind or memory, it has made a deep impression and you will never forget it
▷ **etcher** NOUN

eternal ADJECTIVE lasting for ever; not ending or changing
▷ **eternally** ADVERB **eternity** NOUN

Thesaurus

essence NOUN **1** The essence of good detective work is patience. ► nature, substance, quintessence, core, kernel, basis, crux, essential part **2** Add a little vanilla essence. ► extract, concentrate

essential ADJECTIVE The leaflet provides essential travel information. ► necessary, basic, vital, important, indispensable, crucial, fundamental, principal, key, primary, requisite, main AN OPPOSITE IS inessential

establish VERB **1** The new evidence established their guilt. ► prove, demonstrate, substantiate, confirm, indicate, affirm, verify, certify, authenticate **2** The bank aims to establish branches throughout the world. ► set up, install, found, initiate, institute, organize, inaugurate, create, base

established ADJECTIVE an established practice ► accepted, confirmed, orthodox, traditional, customary, prevailing, well known, well tried, familiar, entrenched, long-standing, routine

establishment NOUN **1** the establishment of a new republic ► creation, institution, introduction, constitution, formation, foundation, inauguration, inception, composition **2** an old publishing establishment ► business, concern, enterprise, venture, undertaking, company

estate NOUN **1** The family lived in a housing estate. ► development, area, land **2** Her grandfather had left an estate worth several millions. ► assets, possessions, wealth, property, belongings, holdings

esteem NOUN She was held in high esteem by all her friends. ► respect, admiration, favor, honor, regard, opinion, acclaim, estimation, credit, reverence, veneration

estimate NOUN **1** Our estimate of the situation is fairly dire. ► assessment, appraisal, evaluation, estimation, judgment, opinion, view **2** The painter will let us have an estimate. ► price, quotation, reckoning, specification, valuation, calculation

estimate VERB The agents estimated the selling price of the house at over a million dollars.
► reckon, consider, assess, evaluate, calculate, gauge, work out

eternal ADJECTIVE **1** eternal happiness
► everlasting, never-ending, unending, undying, enduring, abiding, timeless, infinite OPPOSITES ARE transient, ephemeral **2** I'm tired of your eternal complaining. ► constant, continual, interminable, ceaseless, unceasing, incessant, everlasting, never-ending, perpetual, persistent, unremitting OPPOSITES ARE occasional, intermittent

ether (ee- ther) NOUN **1** a colorless liquid that evaporates easily into fumes that are used as an anaesthetic **2** the upper air

ethereal (ith- eer- ee- al) ADJECTIVE light and delicate
▷ **ethereally** ADVERB

ethical (eth- ik- al) ADJECTIVE **1** to do with ethics **2** morally right; honorable
▷ **ethically** ADVERB

ethics (eth- iks) PLURAL NOUN standards of right behavior; moral principles

ethnic ADJECTIVE belonging to a particular racial group within a larger set of people

ethnic cleansing NOUN the mass expulsion or killing of one ethnic group by another in an area

etiquette (et- ik- et) NOUN the rules of correct behavior

etymology (et- im- ol- o- jee) NOUN etymologies **1** an account of the origin of a word and its meaning **2** the study of the origins of words
▷ **etymological** ADJECTIVE

EU ABBREVIATION European Union

eucalyptus (yoo- kal- ip- tus) NOUN eucalyptuses **1** a kind of evergreen tree **2** a strong-smelling oil obtained from its leaves

Eucharist (yoo- ker- ist) NOUN the Christian sacrament in which bread and wine are consecrated and swallowed, commemorating the Last Supper of Christ and his disciples

eulogy (yoo- loj- ee) NOUN eulogies a piece of praise for a person or thing

euphemism (yoo- fim- izm) NOUN euphemisms a mild word or phrase used instead of an offensive or frank one; "to pass away" is a euphemism for "to die."
▷ **euphemistic** ADJECTIVE **euphemistically** ADVERB

euro NOUN euros or euro the currency which replaced the national currencies of several EU states in 2002

European ADJECTIVE to do with Europe or its people
▷ **European** NOUN

euthanasia (yooth- an- ay- zee- a) NOUN causing somebody to die gently and without pain, especially when they are suffering from a painful incurable disease

evacuate VERB evacuates, evacuating, evacuated **1** move people away from a dangerous place **2** make a thing empty of air or other contents
▷ **evacuation** NOUN

evacuee NOUN evacuees a person who has been evacuated

evade VERB evades, evading, evaded avoid a person or thing by cleverness or trickery

evaluate VERB evaluates, evaluating, evaluated estimate the value of something; assess
▷ **evaluation** NOUN

evaporate VERB evaporates, evaporating, evaporated **1** change from liquid into steam or vapor **2** cease to exist • *Their enthusiasm had evaporated.*
▷ **evaporation** NOUN

evasion NOUN evasions **1** evading **2** an evasive answer or excuse

evasive ADJECTIVE trying to avoid answering something; not frank or straightforward
▷ **evasively** ADVERB **evasiveness** NOUN

even ADJECTIVE **1** level and smooth **2** not varying **3** calm; not easily upset • *an even*

Thesaurus

---

eternity NOUN **1** *the eternity after death*
► afterlife, eternal life, infinity, perpetuity, immortality **2** *an eternity* (*informal*) *We waited an eternity for a train.* ► ages, hours, a long time, for ever

ethics PLURAL NOUN *the ethics of medical research*
► morality, moral code, morals, principles, propriety, standards, values, ideals, rights and wrongs

ethnic ADJECTIVE **1** *people with different ethnic backgrounds* ► cultural, national, indigenous, genetic, tribal, racial **2** *men and women in ethnic dress* ► local, traditional, national, folk

evacuate VERB **1** *It is essential to evacuate everybody from the building.* ► remove, clear, move out, send away **2** *Police decided to evacuate the area.* ► vacate, leave, quit, relinquish, withdraw from, abandon, decamp from, desert, empty

evacuation NOUN **1** *the evacuation of buildings*
► clearance, vacation, abandonment **2** *the evacuation of civilians* ► removal, clearance, eviction

evade VERB **1** *Charlie was clearly guilty of evading his responsibilities.* ► avoid, shirk, shun, dodge, duck, sidestep, steer clear of, turn your back on AN OPPOSITE IS accept **2** *They did all they could do to evade capture.* ► avoid, elude, escape, escape from, fend off, circumvent

evaluate VERB *A panel of doctors will evaluate the treatment.* ► assess, value, gauge, appraise, rate, calculate

evaporate VERB **1** *The water quickly evaporates.*
► disperse, dry up, vaporize AN OPPOSITE IS condense **2** *With this news all their hopes evaporated.* ► disappear, fade, vanish, melt away, come to an end, dissolve, dissipate AN OPPOSITE IS materialize

even ADJECTIVE **1** *an even surface* ► flat, smooth, level, flush, true, unbroken AN OPPOSITE IS rough **2** *an even temperament* ► calm, stable, equable, even-tempered, placid, composed,

a b c d **e** f g h i j k l m n o p q r s t u v w x y z

temper **4** equal • *Our scores were even.* **5** able to be divided exactly by two • *Six and fourteen are even numbers* . COMPARE **odd**
▷ **evenly** ADVERB **evenness** NOUN
get even take revenge

even VERB evens, evening, evened make or become even

even ADVERB (used to emphasize a word or statement) • *She ran even faster*
even so although that is correct

even-handed ADJECTIVE fair and impartial

evening NOUN evenings the time at the end of the day before most people go to bed

event NOUN events **1** something that happens, especially something important **2** a race or competition that forms part of a sports contest

eventful ADJECTIVE full of happenings

eventual ADJECTIVE happening at last • *his eventual success*
▷ **eventually** ADVERB

ever ADVERB **1** at any time • *the best thing I ever did* **2** always • *ever hopeful* **3** (informal, used for emphasis)• *Why ever didn't you tell me?*

evergreen ADJECTIVE having green leaves all the year
▷ **evergreen** NOUN

every ADJECTIVE each without any exceptions
• *We enjoyed every minute*
every one each one
every other day or week, etc., each alternate one; every second one
USAGE Follow with a singular verb, e.g., *Every one of them is growing* (not "are growing").

everybody PRONOUN every person

everyday ADJECTIVE ordinary; usual • *everyday clothes*

everyone PRONOUN everybody

everything PRONOUN **1** all things; all **2** the only or most important thing • *Beauty is not everything.*

everywhere ADVERB in every place

evict VERB evicts, evicting, evicted make people move out from where they are living
▷ **eviction** NOUN

evidence NOUN **1** anything that gives people reason to believe something **2** statements made or objects produced in a lawcourt to prove something

evident ADJECTIVE obvious; clearly seen
▷ **evidently** ADVERB

Thesaurus

serene, steady OPPOSITES ARE moody, excitable **3** *the even ticking of the clock*
► steady, regular, constant, uniform, unvarying AN OPPOSITE IS irregular **4** *The scores were even.* ► level, equal, identical, balanced, the same AN OPPOSITE IS unequal

even VERB
even out *I tried to even out the wrinkled carpet.*
► smooth, straighten, flatten, level
even up *Another point will even up the scores*
► level, balance, equalize, (more informal) square

evening NOUN *It was evening when we reached home.* ► dusk, sunset, sundown, nightfall, twilight, (poetic) eventide, (poetic) gloaming

event NOUN **1** *an annual event* ► occurrence, happening, occasion, affair, episode, experience, activity, function, business, circumstance, contingency, eventuality, incident, chance **2** *a sports event* ► game, match, competition, tournament
in the event *In the event, the plan was abandoned.* ► as it turned out, as it happened, in the end, in actual fact, as a result, as a consequence

eventful ADJECTIVE *It had been a long and eventful week.* ► busy, lively, active, full, action-packed, remarkable, noteworthy, momentous OPPOSITES ARE routine, uneventful, dull

eventual ADJECTIVE *We will have to wait for the eventual verdict.* ► final, ultimate, ensuing, resulting, prospective, future

eventually ADVERB *Eventually they agreed.* ► in the end, by and by, finally, at length

everlasting ADJECTIVE *The gift would be an everlasting reminder of her evening.* ► eternal, never-ending, unending, undying, enduring, abiding, timeless, infinite OPPOSITES ARE transient, ephemeral

everyday ADJECTIVE *Road accidents were an everyday occurrence.* ► commonplace, common, frequent, ordinary, regular, familiar

everyone PRONOUN *She was afraid everyone would know by now.* ► everybody, the whole world, every person, one and all, (more informal) every Tom, Dick, and Harry

everywhere ADVERB *He looked everywhere for his keys.* ► all over, in every place, far and wide, high and low

evidence NOUN **1** *evidence of life on other planets* ► confirmation, verification, proof, corroboration, substantiation, authentication **2** *Her evidence helped convict all four of them.* ► testimony, statement, information

evident ADJECTIVE *It was evident that he didn't like her.* ► obvious, apparent, clear, plain, noticeable, observable, transparent, discernible AN OPPOSITE IS unclear

evil ADJECTIVE morally bad; wicked
▷ **evilly** ADVERB

evil NOUN evils **1** wickedness **2** something unpleasant or harmful

evolution (ee- vol- oo- shon) NOUN **1** gradual change into something different **2** the development of animals and plants from earlier or simpler forms
▷ **evolutionary** ADJECTIVE

evolve VERB evolves, evolving, evolved develop gradually or naturally

ewe (yoo) NOUN ewes a female sheep

ex- PREFIX (changing to ef- before words beginning with f; shortened to e- before many consonants) **1** out; away (as in *extract*) **2** up, upwards; thoroughly (as in *extol*) **3** formerly (as in *ex-president*)

exact ADJECTIVE **1** correct **2** clearly stated; giving all details ● *exact instructions*
▷ **exactly** ADVERB **exactness** NOUN

exact VERB exacts, exacting, exacted insist on something and obtain it ● *He exacted obedience from the recruits*
▷ **exaction** NOUN

exaggerate VERB exaggerates, exaggerating, exaggerated make something seem bigger, better, or worse, etc., than it really is
▷ **exaggeration** NOUN

examination NOUN examinations **1** a test of a person's knowledge or skill **2** examining something; an inspection ● *a medical examination*

examine VERB examines, examining, examined **1** test a person's knowledge or skill **2** look at something closely or in detail
▷ **examiner** NOUN

example NOUN examples **1** anything that shows what others of the same kind are like or how they work **2** a person or thing good enough to be worth imitating

exasperate VERB exasperates, exasperating, exasperated annoy someone
▷ **exasperation** NOUN

Thesaurus

evil ADJECTIVE **1** *an evil act; the most evil person he had met* ► wicked, bad, wrong, sinful, vile, immoral, depraved OPPOSITES ARE good, virtuous **2** *An evil smell came from the drains.* ► nasty, foul, noxious, unpleasant, offensive, unspeakable, vile, pestilential, poisonous, troublesome AN OPPOSITE IS pleasant **3** *an evil influence* ► harmful, hurtful, pernicious, destructive, deadly, poisonous

evil NOUN **1** *a crime of the utmost evil* ► wickedness, wrong, sinfulness, depravity, immorality, vileness, vice, iniquity **2** *a great social evil* ► catastrophe, affliction, disaster, enormity, calamity, curse, misfortune

evoke VERB *The scene evoked memories of her childhood.* ► arouse, stir up, summon up, bring to mind, call to mind, call up, raise, stimulate, inspire, awaken, conjure up, elicit, excite, kindle, produce, provoke, suggest

evolution NOUN *the evolution of scientific methods* ► development, emergence, growth, improvement, maturing, progress, unfolding

evolve VERB *The plan evolved from quite a simple idea.* ► develop, grow, derive, progress, mature, emerge, expand

exact ADJECTIVE **1** *Stacey likes to be exact in her work.* ► careful, precise, accurate, meticulous, methodical, painstaking, rigorous **2** *These are the exact measurements of the room.* ► precise, accurate, correct, definite **3** *Is this an exact copy?* ► identical, faithful, close

exactly ADVERB **1** *She looks exactly like her mother at that age.* ► precisely, entirely, absolutely,

completely, totally, utterly, every inch **2** *Describe the scene exactly.* ► accurately, precisely, faithfully, in detail

exaggerate VERB *The press reports exaggerated the scale of the fire.* ► overstate, overemphasize, overestimate, overstress, overdo, inflate, magnify, make too much of, amplify, enlarge, maximize, (more informal) play up OPPOSITES ARE understate, underestimate

examination NOUN **1** *the annual examination of the accounts* ► inspection, scrutiny, study, scanning, analysis, appraisal **2** *a written examination in history* ► exam, test, paper **3** *a medical examination* ► checkup, check, inspection, review

examine VERB **1** *The Fraud Squad will examine the company accounts for the last ten years.* ► inspect, scrutinize, study, investigate, check, analyse, review, scan, probe **2** *Students are examined at the end of each year.* ► test, assess, appraise **3** *The defense attorney will examine the witness tomorrow.* ► cross-examine, interrogate, cross-question

example NOUN **1** *a fine example of a Tudor building* ► specimen, sample, case, exemplar, illustration, instance, occurrence **2** *We ought to follow their example.* ► precedent, model, pattern, ideal, standard **3** *They were convicted as an example to others.* ► warning, lesson, deterrent, caution

exasperate VERB *This stupid behavior exasperated us.* ► infuriate, incense, anger, annoy, irritate, enrage, vex, (more informal) rile

a
b
c
d
e
f
g
h
i
j
k
l
m
n
o
p
q
r
s
t
u
v
w
x
y
z

A
B
C
D
E
F
G
H
I
J
K
L
M
N
O
P
Q
R
S
T
U
V
W
X
Y
Z

excavate VERB excavates, excavating, excavated dig out; uncover by digging
▷ **excavation** NOUN **excavator** NOUN

exceed VERB exceeds, exceeding, exceeded **1** be greater than; surpass **2** do more than you need or ought to do; go beyond a thing's limits ● *He has exceeded his authority.*

excel VERB excels, excelling, excelled be better than others at doing something

Excellency NOUN Excellencies the title of high officials such as ambassadors and governors

excellent ADJECTIVE extremely good
▷ **excellently** ADVERB **excellence** NOUN

except PREPOSITION excluding; not including
● *They all left except me.*

except VERB excepts, excepting, excepted exclude; leave out ● *I blame you all, no one is excepted.*
USAGE Do not confuse with **accept**.

exception NOUN exceptions a person or thing that is left out or does not follow the general rule

take exception raise objections to something
with the exception of except

exceptional ADJECTIVE **1** very unusual **2** outstandingly good
▷ **exceptionally** ADVERB

excess NOUN excesses too much of something
in excess of more than

excessive ADJECTIVE too much or too great
● *Do not use excessive force.*
▷ **excessively** ADVERB

exchange VERB exchanges, exchanging, exchanged give something and receive something else for it
▷ **exchangeable** ADJECTIVE

exchange NOUN exchanges **1** exchanging **2** a place where things (especially stocks and shares) are bought and sold ● *a stock exchange* **3** a place where telephone lines are connected to each other when a call is made

exchequer NOUN exchequers in Great Britain, a national treasury into which public funds (such as taxes) are paid

Thesaurus

excavate VERB **1** *Moles had excavated tunnels under the grass.* ▶ dig, bore, burrow, hollow out **2** *A coin hoard was excavated from the ancient site.* ▶ unearth, dig up, uncover, discover, reveal

exceed VERB **1** *Total luggage weight must not exceed 300 lbs.* ▶ be more than, be greater than, go over **2** *Police stopped her for exceeding the speed limit.* ▶ break, go beyond, go faster than **3** *The amount exceeded all our expectations.* ▶ surpass, beat, outstrip, better, outdo, excel, pass, top

exceedingly ADVERB *an exceedingly good meal* ▶ extremely, exceptionally, especially, supremely, outstandingly, immensely, amazingly, unusually, extraordinarily, tremendously, really, very

excel VERB **1** *One choir excelled all the others and was invited back for next year.* ▶ surpass, outdo, outclass, outstrip, do better than, beat, exceed **2** *He excels at most things he turns his hand to.* ▶ shine, do well, be good, stand out, be outstanding

excellent ADJECTIVE *an excellent idea; The book is excellent.* ▶ outstanding, very good, first-class, first-rate, superlative, superb, remarkable, exceptional, splendid, wonderful, marvellous, tremendous

except PREPOSITION *The restaurant is open every evening except Monday.* ▶ excluding, except for, apart from, other than, besides

exception NOUN *Most countries are represented, although there are a few exceptions.* ▶ abnormality, irregularity, oddity, peculiarity, deviation, anomaly, departure, eccentricity, special case, freak, quirk, rarity

take exception to *She takes exception to people smoking in the house.* ▶ object to, disapprove of, complain about, demur at, resent, be offended by

exceptional ADJECTIVE **1** *a woman of exceptional ability* ▶ outstanding, excellent, very good, first-class, first-rate, superlative, superb, remarkable **2** *exceptional weather patterns* ▶ unusual, abnormal, untypical, extraordinary, strange, irregular, peculiar, freakish

excess NOUN **1** *an excess of vitamin E* ▶ surplus, surfeit, superfluity, oversufficiency, superabundance, abundance, glut OPPOSITES ARE scarcity, deficit **2** *a lifestyle characterized by excess* ▶ extravagance, overindulgence, intemperance, lavishness, prodigality

excessive ADJECTIVE **1** *excessive drinking* ▶ immoderate, inordinate, extreme, extravagant, disproportionate, superfluous **2** *The cost proved excessive.* ▶ unreasonable, exorbitant, inordinate, (more informal) steep

exchange NOUN **1** *The two sides agreed to an exchange of prisoners.* ▶ switch, interchange, replacement, substitution, (informal) swap **2** *This misunderstanding led to a series of bitter exchanges.* ▶ argument, altercation, recrimination, war of words **3** *Archaeological evidence points to an exchange of goods between the two areas.* ▶ trade, traffic, barter, dealing

exchange VERB **1** *The players exchanged shirts at the end of the game.* ▶ swap, change, switch, interchange **2** *I exchanged my old bike for a new one.* ▶ swap, barter, trade, substitute

excitable ➡ executive

excitable ADJECTIVE easily excited

excite VERB **excites, exciting, excited** **1** make someone eager and enthusiastic about something • *The thought of finding gold excited them.* **2** cause a feeling or reaction • *The invention excited great interest.*
▷ **excited** ADJECTIVE **excitedly** ADVERB

excitement NOUN **excitements** a strong feeling of eagerness or pleasure

exclaim VERB **exclaims, exclaiming, exclaimed** shout or cry out in eagerness or surprise

exclamation NOUN **exclamations**
1 exclaiming **2** a word or words cried out expressing joy or pain or surprise, etc.

exclamation mark NOUN **exclamation marks** the punctuation mark (!) placed after an exclamation

exclude VERB **excludes, excluding, excluded**
1 keep somebody or something out **2** leave something out • *Do not exclude the possibility of rain.*
▷ **exclusion** NOUN

exclusive ADJECTIVE **1** allowing only certain people to be members • *an exclusive club* **2** not shared with others • *This newspaper has an exclusive report.*
▷ **exclusively** ADVERB **exclusiveness** NOUN exclusive of excluding, not including • *This is the price exclusive of meals.*

excrement (eks- kri- ment) NOUN waste matter from the body

excrete VERB **excretes, excreting, excreted** get rid of waste matter from the body
▷ **excretion** NOUN **excretory** ADJECTIVE
[from ex- = out + Latin *cretum* = separated]

excruciating (iks- **kroo**- shee- ayt- ing) ADJECTIVE extremely painful; agonizing
▷ **excruciatingly** ADVERB
[from ex- = out + Latin *cruciatum* = tortured]

excursion NOUN **excursions** a short journey made for pleasure [from ex- = out + Latin *cursus* = course]

excuse (iks- **kewz**) VERB **excuses, excusing, excused** **1** forgive **2** allow someone not to do something or to leave a room, etc. • *Please may I be excused from swimming?*

excuse (iks- **kewss**) NOUN **excuses** a reason given to explain why something wrong has been done

execute VERB **executes, executing, executed** **1** put someone to death as a punishment **2** perform or produce something • *She executed the somersault perfectly.*
▷ **execution** NOUN
[from Latin *executare* = to carry out, to punish]

executive (ig- **zek**- yoo- tiv) NOUN **executives** a senior person with authority in a business or government organization

Thesaurus

excite VERB *The prospect of a day out excited them.* ► thrill, exhilarate, elate, enliven, stimulate AN OPPOSITE IS bore

excited ADJECTIVE *The children were becoming excited.* ► animated, stimulated, worked up, boisterous, lively, elated, restless, overwrought, vivacious

excitement NOUN *They could hardly conceal their excitement.* ► enthusiasm, exhilaration, agitation, elation, eagerness, stimulation **2** *There will be a lot of excitement at the party this afternoon.* ► commotion, activity, adventure

exciting ADJECTIVE *an exciting story* ► thrilling, stirring, exhilarating, rousing, stimulating, invigorating, enthralling, gripping, dramatic, sensational OPPOSITES ARE dull, boring

exclaim VERB *He exclaimed that he had never been there.* ► cry, cry out, call, yell, shout, shriek, scream

exclamation NOUN *With an exclamation of horror she rushed upstairs.* ► cry, yell, call, shout, shriek, interjection, (old-fashioned) ejaculation

exclude VERB **1** *They were anxious to exclude the inevitable partycrashers from the house.* ► keep out, deny access to, ban, disallow, prevent, prohibit, deter, debar, reject **2** *He excluded his own name from the list.* ► omit, leave out, miss

out, fail to include, rule out **3** *These figures exclude any allowance for inflation.* ► omit, be exclusive of, not include

exclusive ADJECTIVE **1** *The room is for your exclusive use.* ► sole, unique, private, unshared, undivided, unrestricted **2** *one of Miami's most exclusive clubs* ► select, elite, fashionable, restrictive, private, premier, (more informal) classy, (more informal) posh

excursion NOUN *an excursion to the beach* ► trip, outing, jaunt, journey, expedition, day out, drive, run

excuse NOUN **1** *He trotted out the usual feeble excuses.* ► defence, pretext, explanation, alibi, plea, reason **2** *There is no excuse for what you did.* ► justification, vindication

excuse VERB **1** *We cannot excuse bad behavior.* ► justify, defend, condone, tolerate, overlook, ignore, sanction, mitigate **2** *She found it hard to excuse them this time.* ► forgive, pardon, absolve

execute VERB **1** *The maneuver is particularly hard to execute in heavy traffic.* ► carry out, implement, perform, complete, accomplish, achieve, do, effect **2** *The state no longer executes convicted murderers.* ► put to death, apply the death penalty to, hang, behead, electrocute

A
B
C
D
E
F
G
H
I
J
K
L
M
N
O
P
Q
R
S
T
U
V
W
X
Y
Z

exempt ADJECTIVE not having to do something that others have to do ● *Charities are exempt from paying tax.*
▷ **exemption** NOUN

exercise NOUN exercises **1** using your body to make it strong and healthy **2** a piece of work done for practice

exercise VERB exercises, exercising, exercised **1** do exercises **2** give exercise to an animal etc. **3** use ● *You must exercise more patience.*

exert VERB exerts, exerting, exerted use power or influence ● *He exerted all his strength.*
▷ **exertion** NOUN
exert yourself make an effort

exhale VERB exhales, exhaling, exhaled breathe out
▷ **exhalation** NOUN

exhaust VERB exhausts, exhausting, exhausted **1** make somebody very tired **2** use up something completely
▷ **exhaustion** NOUN

exhaust NOUN exhausts **1** the waste gases or steam from an engine **2** the pipe etc. through which they are sent out

exhaustive ADJECTIVE thorough; trying everything possible ● *We made an exhaustive search.*
▷ **exhaustively** ADVERB

exhibit VERB exhibits, exhibiting, exhibited show or display something in public
▷ **exhibitor** NOUN

exhibit NOUN exhibits something on display in a gallery or museum

exhibition NOUN exhibitions a collection of things put on display for people to look at

exhilarate (ig- **zil**- er- ayt) VERB exhilarates, exhilarating, exhilarated make someone very happy and excited
▷ **exhilaration** NOUN

exhort (ig- **zort**) VERB exhorts, exhorting, exhorted try hard to persuade someone to do something
▷ **exhortation** NOUN

exile VERB exiles, exiling, exiled banish

exile NOUN exiles **1** having to live away from your own country ● *He was in exile for ten years.* **2** a banished person

Thesaurus

exercise NOUN **1** *Regular exercise will keep you fit.* ► physical activity, working out, exertion, training **2** *the exercise of authority* ► use, application, practice **3** *exercises* army exercises ► operations, manoeuvres

exercise VERB **1** *She exercises every day.* ► work out, do exercises, keep fit **2** *Please exercise a little patience.* ► use, have, employ, apply **3** *The problem continues to exercise us.* ► trouble, worry, bother, make anxious

exert VERB **1** *She exerts a considerable influence on the children.* ► exercise, wield, bring to bear, apply **2** *exert yourself He exerted himself to get the job done on time.* ► strive, endeavor, try hard, make an effort, go to some trouble

exhaust VERB **1** *We exhausted the fuel supply after only a week.* ► use up, consume, drain, empty, deplete, dry up, finish off, go through, spend, sap, void **2** *Her day out had exhausted her.* ► tire out, wear out, fatigue, weary, tax, strain

exhausted ADJECTIVE **1** *They went to bed exhausted that night.* ► tired out, worn out, weary, fatigued, (more informal) shattered, (more informal) dead tired, (more informal) played out, (more informal) washed out **2** *exhausted money reserves* ► depleted, used up, spent

exhausting ADJECTIVE *an exhausting journey* ► tiring, wearying, fatiguing, wearing, arduous, strenuous, taxing, gruelling, demanding, laborious, punishing, sapping, difficult, hard, severe AN OPPOSITE IS refreshing

exhaustion NOUN *He had to stop from sheer exhaustion.* ► fatigue, weariness, tiredness, debility, weakness AN OPPOSITE IS vigor

exhibit VERB **1** *The gallery will exhibit a collection of new paintings.* ► show, display, put on display, present, set up **2** *He exhibited great pride in his family.* ► show, reveal, display, demonstrate, manifest, disclose, express OPPOSITES ARE hide, conceal

exhibition NOUN *an exhibition of Greek sculpture* ► display, presentation, show, showing, demonstration

exhilarated ADJECTIVE *The day's events left them feeling exhilarated.* ► excited, elated, thrilled, animated, stimulated, worked up AN OPPOSITE IS dejected

exhilarating ADJECTIVE *The ride was an exhilarating experience.* ► exciting, thrilling, stirring, rousing, stimulating, invigorating, enthralling, gripping, dramatic, sensational OPPOSITES ARE dull, boring

exhilaration NOUN *a feeling of exhilaration* ► excitement, enthusiasm, elation, eagerness, stimulation

exile NOUN **1** *The poet was punished with exile.* ► banishment, expulsion, deportation, expatriation, extradition **2** *a group of political exiles* ► émigré, exiled person, displaced person, deportee, expatriate, outcast, refugee

exile VERB *The new regime immediately exiled the dictators.* ► expel, banish, deport, drive out, eject, expatriate, send away

exist VERB exists, existing, existed **1** be present as part of what is real • *Do ghosts exist?* **2** stay alive • *We cannot exist without food.*
▷ **existence** NOUN **existent** ADJECTIVE

exit NOUN exits **1** the way out of a building **2** going off the stage • *The actress made her exit.*

exit VERB (in stage directions) he or she leaves the stage [from Latin *exit*, = he or she goes out]

exorcize VERB exorcizes, exorcizing, exorcized drive out an evil spirit
▷ **exorcism** NOUN **exorcist** NOUN

exotic ADJECTIVE **1** very unusual • *exotic clothes* **2** from another part of the world • *exotic plants*
▷ **exotically** ADVERB

expand VERB expands, expanding, expanded make or become larger or fuller
▷ **expansion** NOUN **expansive** ADJECTIVE

expect VERB expects, expecting, expected **1** think or believe that something will happen or that someone will come **2** think that something ought to happen • *She expects obedience.*

expectant ADJECTIVE **1** expecting something to happen; hopeful **2** an expectant mother is a woman who is pregnant
▷ **expectantly** ADVERB **expectancy** NOUN

expectation NOUN expectations **1** expecting something; being hopeful **2** something you expect to happen or get

expedient (iks- pee- dee- ent) ADJECTIVE **1** suitable or convenient **2** useful and practical though perhaps unfair
▷ **expediently** ADVERB **expediency** NOUN

expedient NOUN expedients a means of doing something, especially when in difficulty

expedition NOUN expeditions **1** a journey made in order to do something • *a climbing expedition* **2** speed or promptness
▷ **expeditionary** ADJECTIVE

expel VERB expels, expelling, expelled **1** send or force something out • *This fan expels stale air.* **2** make a person leave a school or country, etc.

expendable ADJECTIVE able to be sacrificed or got rid of in order to gain something

expenditure NOUN expenditures the spending or using up of money or effort, etc.

Thesaurus
---

exist VERB **1** *animals that no longer exist* ► occur, be alive, be in existence **2** *They had to exist for years on a meager income.* ► survive, subsist, live, hold out, keep going, continue, endure, last

existence NOUN **1** *The new law threatens the very existence of these old institutions.* ► survival, continuance, continuation, being, actuality, life, living, reality AN OPPOSITE IS non-existence **2** *a dreary existence in a remote part of the country* ► way of life, livelihood, lifestyle

existing ADJECTIVE *The existing arrangements were proving inadequate.* ► current, present, available, prevailing, actual, existent, extant USAGE You can also say *the arrangements already in place* or *the arrangements already in force.*

exit NOUN **1** *A passage on the right leads to the exit.* ► way out, door, doorway, egress, gate, gateway AN OPPOSITE IS entrance **2** *They made a quick exit.* ► departure, withdrawal, retreat, leaving, exodus OPPOSITES ARE entrance, arrival **3** *Take the exit marked New Haven.* ► turning, turn-off, turn, road

exotic ADJECTIVE **1** *exotic places in the Far East* ► faraway, distant, remote, foreign, romantic, unfamiliar, alien AN OPPOSITE IS familiar **2** *an exhibition of exotic birds* ► foreign, non-native, tropical, alien, unnaturalized, imported AN

OPPOSITE IS native **3** *exotic dress* ► colorful, striking, unusual, unfamiliar, unconventional, outlandish AN OPPOSITE IS conventional

expand VERB **1** *a good opportunity to expand the business* ► develop, enlarge, extend, broaden, build up, diversify, increase, amplify, augment, elaborate, fill out, make bigger OPPOSITES ARE contract, reduce **2** *Metal expands when heated.* ► increase in size, become larger, swell, dilate, grow, stretch, thicken, widen AN OPPOSITE IS contract

expansive ADJECTIVE *After a few drinks he became quite expansive.* ► talkative, communicative, forthcoming, outgoing, sociable, unreserved, uninhibited, voluble, conversational, open OPPOSITES ARE curt, unfriendly

expect VERB **1** *We expect a large number of visitors this year.* ► hope for, look for, look forward to, envisage, predict, anticipate, await, bank on **2** *We expect complete discretion.* ► demand, insist on, require, call for, count on, rely on, want **3** *I expect they missed the train.* ► suppose, assume, presume, imagine, believe, guess, judge, think, (more informal) reckon

expel VERB **1** *He was expelled from the country.* ► banish, exile, deport, drive out, throw out, cast out, evict, expatriate **2** *The machinery was expelling thick smoke.* ► discharge, emit, let out, release, disgorge, spew out

a
b
c
d
e
f
g
h
i
j
k
l
m
n
o
p
q
r
s
t
u
v
w
x
y
z

A
B
C
D
E
F
G
H
I
J
K
L
M
N
O
P
Q
R
S
T
U
V
W
X
Y
Z

expense NOUN expenses the cost of doing something

expensive ADJECTIVE costing a lot
▷ **expensively** ADVERB **expensiveness** NOUN

experience NOUN experiences **1** what you learn from doing or seeing things **2** something that has happened to you

experience VERB experiences, experiencing, experienced have something happen to you

experienced ADJECTIVE having great skill or knowledge from much experience

experiment NOUN experiments a test made in order to find out what happens or to prove something
▷ **experimental** ADJECTIVE **experimentally** ADVERB

experiment VERB experiments, experimenting, experimented carry out an experiment
▷ **experimentation** NOUN

expert NOUN experts a person with great knowledge or skill in something

expert ADJECTIVE having great knowledge or skill
▷ **expertly** ADVERB **expertness** NOUN

expire VERB expires, expiring, expired **1** come to an end; stop being usable ● *Your season ticket has expired.* **2** die **3** breathe out air
▷ **expiration** NOUN **expiry** NOUN

explain VERB explains, explaining, explained **1** make something clear to somebody else; show its meaning **2** account for something
● *That explains his absence.*
▷ **explanation** NOUN

Thesaurus

expense NOUN **1** *the increasing expense of driving a car* ► cost, price, spending **2** *unexpected expenses* ► expenditure, outlay, charges, outgoings, overheads, payment

expensive ADJECTIVE *an expensive vacation* ► costly, dear, high-priced, extravagant, lavish, exorbitant, (*more informal*) pricey OPPOSITES ARE cheap, inexpensive

experience NOUN **1** *You learn by experience* ► practice, involvement, participation, familiarity, observation, taking part **2** *Salary will depend partly on experience.* ► skill, knowledge, background, understanding, (*more informal*) know-how **3** *a terrifying experience* ► incident, event, episode, affair, happening, occurrence, ordeal, adventure

experience VERB *She experienced some harassment at work.* ► meet, encounter, undergo, face, run into, suffer

experienced ADJECTIVE **1** *an experienced actor* ► expert, skilled, skilful, qualified, trained, practiced, knowledgeable, professional, specialized, well versed AN OPPOSITE IS inexperienced **2** *an experienced man of the world* ► mature, seasoned, sophisticated, worldly wise, knowing, wise OPPOSITES ARE innocent, naive

experiment NOUN **1** *She conducted experiments using laser technology.* ► test, investigation, trial, inquiry, demonstration, observation, analysis, piece of research **2** *The new library hours are an experiment.* ► trial, trial run, try-out

experiment VERB experiment with *You need to experiment with the camera's different settings.* ► test, try out, investigate, explore, do tests on, conduct an experiment on, do research on

experimental ADJECTIVE **1** *The new designs are still at an experimental stage.* ► exploratory, investigatory, provisional, tentative, preliminary, speculative, trial, test **2** *experimental forms of music* ► innovative, innovatory, radical, avant-garde, original

expert ADJECTIVE **1** *You can get independent expert advice quite cheaply.* ► skilled, professional, qualified, specialized **2** *I am an expert swimmer.* ► skillful, skilled, accomplished, proficient, competent, talented, outstanding, exceptional, formidable

expert NOUN **1** *You need to get advice from an expert.* ► specialist, professional, authority, (*more informal*) pro **2** *He is an expert at board games.* ► authority, master, past master, connoisseur, genius, virtuoso, (*more informal*) ace, (*more informal*) whizz, (*more informal*) wizard, (*disapproving*) know-all AN OPPOSITE IS novice

expertise NOUN *A high level of expertise is required.* ► skill, competence, proficiency, ability, knowledge, capability, professionalism

expire VERB **1** *The animals were expiring in the heat.* ► die, perish, pass away **2** *Our television license has expired.* ► run out, become invalid, lapse, finish

explain VERB **1** *I will try to explain the problem.* ► describe, clarify, make clear, spell out, elucidate, interpret, demonstrate, express, put into words **2** *It is hard to explain such stupidity.* ► account for, justify, excuse, defend, vindicate, give reasons for, make excuses for, rationalize

explanation NOUN **1** *I owe you an explanation for what happened.* ► justification, reason, account, excuse, defense, rationale **2** *What on earth can the explanation be?* ► cause, motive, reason **3** *The summary at the end gives a brief explanation of the ideas discussed.* ► account, clarification, elucidation, interpretation, demonstration

explicit (iks- **pliss**- it) ADJECTIVE stated or stating something openly and exactly
COMPARE implicit
▷ **explicitly** ADVERB

explode VERB explodes, exploding, exploded
1 burst or suddenly release energy with a loud noise **2** cause a bomb to go off **3** increase suddenly or quickly

exploit (iks- **ploit**) VERB exploits, exploiting, exploited **1** use or develop resources **2** use a person or thing selfishly
▷ **exploitation** NOUN

explore VERB explores, exploring, explored **1** travel through an area in order to learn about it **2** examine a subject or idea carefully • We explored the possibilities.
▷ **exploration** NOUN **explorer** NOUN **exploratory** ADJECTIVE

explosion NOUN explosions **1** the exploding of a bomb, etc.; the noise made by exploding **2** a sudden great increase

explosive ADJECTIVE able to explode

explosive NOUN explosives an explosive substance

exponent NOUN exponents **1** a person who puts forward an idea **2** someone who is good at an activity **3** (in mathematics) the raised number etc. written to the right of another

(e.g., 3 in 2^3) showing how many times the first one is to be multiplied by itself; the index

export VERB exports, exporting, exported send goods abroad to be sold
▷ **exportation** NOUN **exporter** NOUN

export NOUN exports **1** exporting things **2** something exported

expose VERB exposes, exposing, exposed **1** reveal or uncover **2** allow light to reach a photographic film so as to take a picture
▷ **exposure** NOUN

express ADJECTIVE **1** going or sent quickly **2** clearly stated • This was done against my express orders.

express NOUN expresses a fast train stopping at only a few stations

express VERB expresses, expressing, expressed **1** put ideas, etc., into words; make your feelings known **2** press or squeeze out

expression NOUN expressions **1** the look on a person's face that shows his or her feelings **2** a word or phrase, etc. **3** a way of speaking or of playing music, etc., so as to show your feelings **4** expressing • this expression of opinion

expressive ADJECTIVE full of expression

expulsion NOUN expulsions expelling or being expelled

Thesaurus

---

explicit ADJECTIVE **1** The advance party had received explicit instructions to turn back. ► clear, plain, direct, definite, express, precise, distinct, exact, emphatic, specific, positive, categorical, unambiguous, unmistakable, unequivocal AN OPPOSITE IS vague **2** The film contains a number of sexually explicit scenes. ► candid, open, direct, frank, unreserved, undisguised, plain OPPOSITES ARE implicit, suggestive

explode VERB **1** A bomb exploded in the center of the city. ► go off, blow up, detonate **2** The findings explode a number of myths about cancer treatment. ► disprove, rebut, refute, expose, debunk, discredit, destroy, put an end to

exploit NOUN (with the stress on ex-) Their exploits gave them a fearsome reputation. ► feat, deed, adventure, accomplishment, achievement

exploit VERB (with the stress on -ploit) **1** The newcomers exploited the land's mineral resources. ► make use of, utilize, use, take advantage of, draw on, benefit from, capitalize on **2** They are accused of exploiting an impoverished workforce. ► take advantage of, mistreat, ill-treat, abuse, oppress, manipulate, cheat, swindle, (more informal) fleece

explore VERB **1** an outing to explore the neighborhood ► tour, travel through, reconnoiter, survey, inspect, take a look at

2 We'd like to explore the possibility of working together. ► investigate, examine, look into, consider, study, review, probe, analyze

explosion NOUN A loud explosion shook the building. ► blast, bang, boom, burst, crash, report, detonation, discharge

explosive ADJECTIVE **1** explosive substances ► volatile, inflammable, combustible, unstable **2** an explosive situation ► tense, highly charged, critical, fraught, hazardous, dangerous, perilous, sensitive AN OPPOSITE IS stable

expose VERB **1** The investigation exposed many faults. ► reveal, uncover, bring to light, disclose, unveil, unmask **2** expose someone to They were exposed to serious danger. ► put at risk of, subject to, lay open to

express VERB They expressed their wishes clearly. ► communicate, articulate, utter, convey, voice, vent, give vent to, release, air, phrase, put into words, ventilate

express ADJECTIVE **1** It was his express wish. ► explicit, clear, plain, direct, definite, precise, distinct, exact, emphatic, specific, positive, categorical, unambiguous, unmistakable, unequivocal **2** an express train ► fast, rapid, high-speed, non-stop

expression NOUN **1** He liked to use old-fashioned expressions. ► phrase, idiom, statement, saying,

exquisite ➡ extract

exquisite (eks- kwiz- it) ADJECTIVE very beautiful
▷ **exquisitely** ADVERB

extend VERB extends, extending, extended
1 stretch out **2** make something become longer or larger **3** offer or give • *Extend a warm welcome to our friends.*
▷ **extendible** ADJECTIVE

extension NOUN extensions **1** extending or being extended **2** something added on; an addition to a building **3** one of a set of telephones in an office or house

extensive ADJECTIVE covering a large area or range • *extensive gardens*
▷ **extensively** ADVERB **extensiveness** NOUN

extent NOUN extents **1** the area or length over which something extends **2** the amount, level, or scope of something • *the full extent of his power*

exterior ADJECTIVE outer

exterior NOUN exteriors the outside of something

exterminate VERB exterminates, exterminating, exterminated destroy or kill all the members or examples
▷ **extermination** NOUN **exterminator** NOUN

external ADJECTIVE outside
▷ **externally** ADVERB

extinct ADJECTIVE **1** not existing any more • *The dodo is an extinct bird.* **2** not burning; not active • *an extinct volcano*

extinction NOUN **1** making or becoming extinct **2** being extinguished

extinguish VERB extinguishes, extinguishing, extinguished **1** put out a fire or light **2** put an end to; destroy • *Our hopes of victory were extinguished.*

extort VERB extorts, extorting, extorted obtain something by force or threats
▷ **extortion** NOUN

extortionate ADJECTIVE charging or demanding far too much

extra ADJECTIVE additional; more than is usual • *extra strength*

extra ADVERB more than usually • *extra strong*

extra NOUN extras **1** an extra person or thing **2** a person acting as part of a crowd in a film or play

extract (iks- trakt) VERB extracts, extracting, extracted take out; remove
▷ **extractor** NOUN

extract (eks- trakt) NOUN extracts **1** a passage taken from a book, speech, film, etc. **2** a substance separated or obtained from another

Thesaurus

turn of phrase, phraseology, wording, cliché, formula, remark, term **2** *She had a puzzled expression.* ► look, countenance, aspect, air, face, appearance, mien **3** *She read the letter without expression.* ► emotion, feeling, passion, intensity, poignancy, sensibility, sensitivity, sympathy, understanding **4** *The regime forbids the expression of opposing ideas.* ► utterance, uttering, voicing, assertion

exquisite ADJECTIVE **1** *a ring with exquisite little jewels* ► beautiful, lovely, delicate, dainty **2** *She always showed exquisite taste.* ► refined, discriminating, discerning, sensitive, impeccable

extend VERB **1** *The emperor sought to extend his power.* ► expand, enlarge, develop, build up, broaden, spread AN OPPOSITE IS reduce **2** *The meeting was extended to allow for questions.* ► prolong, lengthen, continue, protract, draw out, make longer **3** *We extend our thanks to all contributors.* ► offer, proffer, advance, bestow, confer, hold out, present, accord **4** *The fields extend as far as the river.* ► reach, go, continue, carry on, spread

extension NOUN **1** *The new owners built a huge extension to the house.* ► addition, annex, wing **2** *We needed an extension of the deadline.* ► postponement, deferral, delay **3** *the extension of the territories; the extension of knowledge* ► enlargement, increase, expansion, broadening, development, growth

extent NOUN **1** *The estate is about three acres in extent.* ► area, size, expanse, scope, dimensions, spread, distance **2** *It was only later that we saw the extent of the damage.* ► degree, scale, scope, size, magnitude, amount, measure, quantity, range

external ADJECTIVE *an external surface* ► outer, outside, exterior, outermost

extinct ADJECTIVE **1** *an extinct volcano* ► inactive, extinguished OPPOSITES ARE active, dormant **2** *an extinct species* ► lost, vanished, defunct, died out, dead, destroyed, obsolete, exterminated OPPOSITES ARE extant, living, surviving

extra ADJECTIVE **1** *She had a second job to bring in extra money.* ► additional, more, further, added, increased, supplementary, fresh **2** *There was a lot of extra food in the house.* ► spare, excess, surplus, superfluous, unused, leftover **3** *The large stores take on extra staff before Christmas.* ► temporary, ancillary, auxiliary, supernumerary

extra ADVERB *He worked extra hard just before the exams.* ► especially, exceptionally, particularly, extremely, unusually

extra NOUN *The Monday holiday was a welcome extra.* ► addition, supplement, bonus, extension

extract VERB **1** *The dentist extracted her tooth.* ► pull out, take out, draw out, remove, withdraw AN OPPOSITE IS insert **2** *It was difficult to extract any information from them.*

extraction NOUN **1** extracting **2** someone's descent • *He is of Chinese extraction.*

extraordinary ADJECTIVE very unusual or strange
▷ **extraordinarily** ADVERB

extrasensory ADJECTIVE outside the range of the known human senses

extraterrestrial ADJECTIVE from beyond the earth's atmosphere; from outer space

extraterrestrial NOUN extraterrestrials a being from outer space

extravagant ADJECTIVE spending or using too much
▷ **extravagantly** ADVERB **extravagance** NOUN

extreme ADJECTIVE **1** very great or intense • *extreme cold* **2** furthest away • *the extreme north* **3** going to great lengths in actions or opinions; not moderate
▷ **extremely** ADVERB

extreme NOUN extremes **1** something extreme **2** either end of something

extricate (eks- trik- ayt) VERB extricates, extricating, extricated free someone or something from a difficult position or situation
▷ **extrication** NOUN

extrovert NOUN extroverts a person who is generally friendly and likes company (The opposite is introvert.)

exuberant (ig- zew- ber- ant) ADJECTIVE very lively and cheerful
▷ **exuberantly** ADVERB **exuberance** NOUN

exude VERB exudes, exuding, exuded **1** give off moisture, a smell, etc. **2** display a feeling or quality openly • *She exuded confidence.*

exult VERB exults, exulting, exulted rejoice greatly
▷ **exultant** ADJECTIVE **exultation** NOUN

eye NOUN eyes **1** the organ of the body that is used for seeing **2** the power of seeing • *She has sharp eyes.* **3** the small hole in a needle **4** the center of a storm

eye VERB eyes, eyeing, eyed look at something with interest [from Old English]

eyeball NOUN eyeballs the ball-shaped part of the eye inside the eyelids

eyebrow NOUN eyebrows the fringe of hair growing on the face above the eye

eyelash NOUN eyelashes one of the short hairs that grow on an eyelid

eyelid NOUN eyelids either of the two folds of skin that can close over the eyeball

eyepiece NOUN eyepieces the lens of a telescope or microscope that you put to your eye

eyesight NOUN the ability to see

eyewitness NOUN eyewitnesses a person who actually saw an accident or crime

Thesaurus

▶ obtain, wrest, draw, glean, elicit, derive, gather, get

extraordinary ADJECTIVE *What an extraordinary story! Their behavior was quite extraordinary.* ▶ remarkable, exceptional, amazing, astonishing, astounding, wonderful, startling, staggering, stunning, breathtaking, fantastic, phenomenal, incredible AN OPPOSITE IS ordinary

extravagance NOUN *The new outfit was bought in a fit of extravagance.* ▶ indulgence, lavishness, prodigality, profligacy, excess, squandering, improvidence, wastefulness AN OPPOSITE IS thrift

extravagant ADJECTIVE *an extravagant lifestyle* ▶ indulgent, lavish, spendthrift, improvident, squandering, wasteful AN OPPOSITE IS thrifty

extreme ADJECTIVE **1** *a sure sign of extreme tiredness* ▶ great, intense, exceptional, extraordinary, utter, acute, downright AN OPPOSITE IS slight **2** *The situation called for extreme measures.* ▶ drastic, serious, radical, dire, desperate, severe, tough, harsh, strict AN OPPOSITE IS mild **3** *in the extreme north of the country* ▶ farthest, furthest, far-off, distant, remotest, faraway **4** *a person of extreme*

political opinions ▶ radical, extremist, fanatical, diehard, zealous AN OPPOSITE IS moderate

extreme NOUN *These theories go from one extreme to the other. An attitude pushed to its extreme* ▶ limit, extremity, height, end

extremity NOUN **1** *at the southern extremity of the island* ▶ limit, edge, end, tip, boundary, margin

extrovert NOUN *Most of the volunteers are extroverts by nature.* ▶ socializer, outgoing person, mixer AN OPPOSITE IS introvert

extrovert ADJECTIVE *an extrovert personality* ▶ outgoing, extroverted, sociable, gregarious, positive, active, confident AN OPPOSITE IS introvert

eye NOUN **1** *He has a sharp eye.* ▶ eyesight, vision, power of sight, visual perception RELATED ADJECTIVES ▶ ocular, ophthalmic **2** *Not much escaped her attentive eye.* ▶ watch, observation, vigilance, notice **3** *eyes It was a dreadful mistake in our eyes.* ▶ opinion, view, judgment, way of thinking, viewpoint, (to our) mind
an eye for *an eye for detail* ▶ an appreciation of, an awareness of, an understanding of, a perception of, a sensitivity for, an instinct for

eye VERB *He eyed the visitors carefully.* ▶ look at, watch, observe, view, gaze at, glance at, scrutinize, examine

a b c d e f g h i j k l m n o p q r s t u v w x y z

A
B
C
D
E
F
G
H
I
J
K
L
M
N
O
P
Q
R
S
T
U
V
W
X
Y
Z

Ff

fable NOUN **fables** a short story that teaches about behavior, often with animals as characters [from Latin *fabula* = story]

fabric NOUN **fabrics** 1 cloth 2 the basic framework of something, especially the walls, floors, and roof of a building

fabricate VERB **fabricates, fabricating, fabricated** 1 construct or manufacture something 2 invent • *fabricate an excuse*
▷ **fabrication** NOUN

fabulous ADJECTIVE 1 wonderful 2 incredibly great • *fabulous wealth* 3 told of in fables and myths
▷ **fabulously** ADVERB

façade (fas- **ahd**) NOUN **façades** 1 the front of a building 2 an outward appearance, especially a deceptive one

face NOUN **faces** 1 the front part of the head 2 the expression on a person's face 3 the front or upper side of something 4 a surface • *A cube has six faces.*

face VERB **faces, facing, faced** 1 look or have the front towards something • *Our room faced the sea.* 2 meet and have to deal with something; encounter • *Explorers face many*

dangers. 3 cover a surface with a layer of different material

facetious (fas- **ee**- shus) ADJECTIVE trying to be funny at an unsuitable time • *facetious remarks*
▷ **facetiously** ADVERB

facilitate (fas- **il**- it- ayt) VERB **facilitates, facilitating, facilitated** make something easier to do
▷ **facilitation** NOUN

facility (fas- **il**- it- ee) NOUN **facilities** 1 something that provides you with the means to do things • *There are sports facilities.* 2 ease or skill in doing something • *She reads music with great facility.*

facsimile (fak- **sim**- il- ee) NOUN **facsimiles** 1 an exact reproduction of a document, etc. 2 a fax

fact NOUN **facts** something that is certainly true **the facts of life** information about how babies are conceived

faction NOUN **factions** a small united group within a larger one, especially in politics

factor NOUN **factors** 1 something that helps to bring about a result • *Hard work was a factor in her success.* 2 a number by which a larger number can be divided exactly • *2 and 3 are factors of 6.*

factory NOUN **factories** a large building where machines are used to make things

Thesaurus

fable NOUN *the fable of the fox and the crow* ► story, tale, parable, moral tale

fabric NOUN 1 *Special fabrics are often used for the seats.* ► cloth, material, stuff, textile 2 *The bomb did some damage to the fabric of the building.* ► structure, framework, frame, construction, makeup

fabricate VERB *The witness had fabricated his evidence.* ► invent, falsify, make up, concoct, trump up

fabulous ADJECTIVE 1 *They had a fabulous time in Morocco.* ► wonderful, marvelous, fantastic, splendid, magnificent 2 *fabulous places you read about in stories* ► legendary, mythical, imaginary, fictitious, fantastic

face NOUN 1 *She has a lovely face.* ► features, countenance, visage, profile, physiognomy 2 *His face became angry.* ► expression, look, appearance, manner, bearing, countenance 3 *A cube has six faces.* ► side, surface, plane, aspect 4 *the north face of the house* ► aspect, façade 5 *He put on a brave face for the sake of his visitors.* ► front, show, display, act

face VERB 1 *The hotel faces the lake.* ► overlook, be opposite (to), front, give on to 2 *You will face a lot of criticism.* ► meet, encounter, experience, confront

face up to *She faced up to all her obligations.* ► accept, come to terms with, recognize, acknowledge, deal with, cope with

facet NOUN *every facet of the situation* ► aspect, feature, characteristic, detail, particular

facility NOUN 1 *She has a great facility for singing.* ► aptitude, talent, flair, faculty, adeptness, skill (in), expertise (in) 2 *This facility is used for copying music to a CD.* ► function, device, provision 3 **facilities** *the use of a sauna and sports facilities* ► amenities, resources, services, equipment, provisions

fact NOUN *It is a fact that car use has risen steeply in the last decade.* ► reality, truth, actuality, certainty, fait accompli AN OPPOSITE IS fiction **the facts** *The jury has to take all the facts into account.* ► evidence, information, details, data, circumstances, particulars, aspects

factor NOUN *Cost was a key factor in the decision.* ► circumstance, element, feature, component, ingredient, influence, aspect, determinant

factory NOUN *I worked in a factory that made parts for tractors.* ► manufacturing plant, workshop, works, assembly line

faculty NOUN **faculties** **1** any of the powers of the body or mind (e.g., sight, speech, or understanding) **2** a department teaching a particular subject in a university or college • *the faculty of music*

fad NOUN **fads** **1** a person's particular like or dislike **2** a temporary fashion or craze ▷ **faddy** ADJECTIVE

fade VERB **fades**, **fading**, **faded** **1** lose color or freshness or strength **2** disappear gradually **3** make a sound, etc., become gradually weaker (*fade it out*) or stronger (*fade it in* or *up*)

Fahrenheit ADJECTIVE measuring temperature on a scale where water freezes at 32° and boils at 212° [named after G. D. Fahrenheit, a German scientist, who invented the mercury thermometer]

fail VERB **fails**, **failing**, **failed** **1** try to do something but be unable to do it **2** become weak or useless; break down • *The brakes failed.* **3** not do something • *He failed to warn me.* **4** not get enough marks to pass an examination **5** judge that someone has not passed an examination

fail NOUN **without fail** for certain; whatever happens

failing NOUN **failings** a weakness or a fault

failure NOUN **failures** **1** not being able to do something **2** a person or thing that has failed

faint ADJECTIVE **1** pale or dim; not distinct **2** weak or giddy; nearly unconscious **3** slight • *a faint hope* ▷ **faintly** ADVERB **faintness** NOUN

faint VERB **faints**, **fainting**, **fainted** become unconscious for a short time USAGE Do not confuse with feint.

fair[1] ADJECTIVE **1** right or just; according to the rules • *a fair fight* **2** (said about hair or skin) light in color; (said about a person) having fair hair **3** (*old use*) beautiful **4** fine or favorable • *fair weather* **5** moderate; quite good • *a fair number of people* ▷ **fairness** NOUN

Thesaurus

---

factual ADJECTIVE *a factual description of the events* ► truthful, accurate, historical, authentic, genuine, realistic, faithful, objective

faculty NOUN **1** *the faculty of speech* ► power, capability, capacity, facility **2** *a faculty for settling disputes* ► aptitude, talent, facility, flair, adeptness, skill (in), expertise (in) **3** **faculties** ► senses, wits, intelligence, reason, powers

fad NOUN *Rap music was not just a passing fad.* ► craze, fashion, trend, vogue, whim, passion, enthusiasm, obsession, compulsion, (*more informal*) rage, (*more informal*) thing

fade VERB **1** *The light has faded the colors.* ► blanch, bleach, discolor, whiten AN OPPOSITE IS brighten **2** *The music began to fade.* ► weaken, decline, decrease, diminish, dwindle, dim, wane, disappear, evanesce, fail, melt away, pale, vanish AN OPPOSITE IS intensify **3** *The flowers had faded by now.* ► wither, wilt, droop, flag, perish, shrivel AN OPPOSITE IS bloom **4** *Their enthusiasm was fading.* ► decline, diminish, dwindle, fail, flag, sink, disappear

fail VERB **1** *In the end all attempts failed.* ► be unsuccessful, go wrong, miscarry, fall through, come to grief, collapse AN OPPOSITE IS succeed **2** *The business had failed and the family faced ruin.* ► collapse, founder, go under, go bankrupt, (*more informal*) fold AN OPPOSITE IS prosper **3** *She was angry with her daughter who had failed to contact her.* ► neglect, forget, omit **4** *Her health was failing.* ► deteriorate, decline, weaken, sink, collapse AN OPPOSITE IS improve **5** *They believe we have failed them.* ► let down, disappoint, betray, desert AN OPPOSITE IS support **6** *He failed one of his exams.* ► be unsuccessful in, not pass AN OPPOSITE IS pass

failing NOUN *She loved him despite his failings.* ► fault, weakness, shortcoming, flaw, defect OPPOSITES ARE strength, strong point

failure NOUN **1** *The negotiations ended in failure.* ► disappointment, lack of success, defeat, disaster **2** *The plan proved to be a failure.* ► disaster, catastrophe, fiasco, debacle, blunder, mistake, (*more informal*) flop **3** *a failure in the power supply* ► breakdown, fault, malfunction **4** *To do nothing might be regarded as a failure of duty.* ► dereliction, neglect, omission, deficiency

faint ADJECTIVE **1** *There was a faint smell of gas.* ► slight, indistinct, vague, weak AN OPPOSITE IS strong **2** *The sky had a faint pink color.* ► pale, light, hazy, weak AN OPPOSITE IS bright **3** *We heard a faint cry from the next room.* ► quiet, muted, muffled, feeble, weak AN OPPOSITE IS loud **4** *There is a faint possibility of an improvement in the weather.* ► slight, slim, slender, remote, small, vague, doubtful AN OPPOSITE IS strong **5** *She was feeling faint and had to lie down.* ► dizzy, giddy, light-headed, weak, (*more informal*) woozy

faint VERB *He grew pale and seemed about to faint.* ► pass out, lose consciousness, black out, collapse, (*literary*) swoon

fair ADJECTIVE **1** *It doesn't seem fair to blame the children.* ► just, equitable, reasonable, honorable AN OPPOSITE IS unfair **2** *They gave a fair assessment of the situation.* ► honest, impartial, reasonable, objective, dispassionate, neutral, evenhanded OPPOSITES ARE unreasonable, biased **3** *She believes she has a*

a
b
c
d
e
f
g
h
i
j
k
l
m
n
o
p
q
r
s
t
u
v
w
x
y
z

fair ADVERB fairly • *Play fair!*

fair² NOUN fairs **1** a group of outdoor entertainments such as roundabouts, sideshows, and stalls **2** an exhibition or market
▷ **fairground** NOUN

fairly ADVERB **1** justly; according to the rules **2** moderately • *It is fairly hard.*

fairy NOUN fairies an imaginary very small creature with magic powers
▷ **fairyland** NOUN **fairy tale** NOUN

faith NOUN faiths strong belief or trust **in good faith** with honest intentions

faithful ADJECTIVE **1** loyal and trustworthy **2** true to the facts • *a faithful account* **3** sexually loyal to one partner
▷ **faithfully** ADVERB **faithfulness** NOUN
Yours faithfully see **yours**

fake NOUN fakes something that looks genuine but is not; a forgery

fake VERB fakes, faking, faked **1** make something that looks genuine, in order to deceive people **2** pretend to have or be something • *He used to fake illness to miss games.*
▷ **faker** NOUN

falcon NOUN falcons a kind of hawk often used in the sport of hunting other birds or game
▷ **falconry** NOUN

fall VERB falls, falling, fell, fallen **1** come or go down without being pushed or thrown **2** decrease; become lower • *Prices fell.* **3** be captured or overthrown • *The city fell.* **4** die in battle **5** happen • *Silence fell.* **6** become • *She fell asleep.*
fall back retreat
fall back on use for support or in an emergency
fall for 1 be attracted by a person **2** be taken in by a deception

Thesaurus

fair chance of success. He had achieved a fair result in his exams. ► moderate, reasonable, average, satisfactory, adequate, acceptable, tolerable, respectable, decent OPPOSITES ARE excellent, outstanding **4** *There was a fair amount of traffic going past.* ► considerable, moderate, average **5** *She had blue eyes and fair hair.* ► blond(e), light, pale, yellow **6** *It was a good match played in fair weather.* ► fine, dry, bright, clear, sunny, warm OPPOSITES ARE bad, wet, inclement

fair NOUN **1** *a country fair* ► fête, gala, carnival, funfair, festival **2** *an antiques fair* ► market, sale, mart, bazaar **3** *a book fair* ► exhibition, display, show, presentation

fairly ADVERB *The news is fairly good.* ► reasonably, moderately, tolerably, quite, rather, somewhat, *(more informal)* pretty AN OPPOSITE IS extremely

fairy tale or **fairy story** NOUN *fairy tales about witches and dragons* ► folk tale, legend, myth, story

faith NOUN **1** *His employers had complete faith in him.* ► trust, confidence, hope, belief, reliance **2** *Her faith is very precious to her.* ► religion, belief, religious conviction

faithful ADJECTIVE **1** *He wondered if Clara had a faithful partner waiting for her at home.* ► loyal, devoted, constant, dependable, dutiful, reliable, staunch, steadfast, trusty, trustworthy, close, consistent, unswerving OPPOSITES ARE unfaithful, disloyal **2** *He kept a faithful record of the events of that day.* ► accurate, true, truthful, precise, exact, authentic AN OPPOSITE IS inaccurate

fake ADJECTIVE **1** *You could tell the diamonds were fake.* ► imitation, artificial, simulated, synthetic, unreal, false, bogus, sham, *(more*

informal) phoney **2** *He brought out a wad of fake currency.* ► counterfeit, forged, false, sham, bogus, fraudulent, *(more informal)* phoney AN OPPOSITE IS genuine

fake NOUN **1** *One of the paintings was a fake.* ► forgery, copy, imitation, reproduction, replica, duplicate, hoax, sham, simulation, *(more informal)* phoney **2** *The man who claimed to be a surgeon is a fake.* ► fraud, charlatan, impostor, cheat, *(more informal)* quack, *(more informal)* phoney

fake VERB *They would have to fake a death certificate.* ► forge, fabricate, counterfeit, falsify, *(more informal)* fiddle

fall VERB **1** *He stumbled and fell.* ► tumble, fall over, topple, trip over, keel over, collapse AN OPPOSITE IS get up **2** *Flood levels began to fall at last.* ► drop, go down, subside, recede AN OPPOSITE IS rise **3** *Bombs continued to fall all night.* ► drop, descend, plummet, rain down **4** *Prices are expected to fall soon.* ► go down, decrease, decline, diminish OPPOSITES ARE rise, increase **5** *The Empire in the East did not fall for several more centuries.* ► decline, collapse, disintegrate, deteriorate AN OPPOSITE IS flourish **6** *Thousands fell in the war.* ► die, be killed, be lost, lose your life, perish, *(literary)* be slain **7** *Her birthday falls on a Saturday this year.* ► occur, come, happen, take place

fall apart *The sheds fell apart in the high winds.* ► collapse, disintegrate, break up, fragment, crumble, fall to pieces, shatter

fall asleep *She couldn't help falling asleep.* ► doze off, drop off, go to sleep, *(more informal)* nod off

fall in *The roof has fallen in.* ► collapse, come down, cave in

fall out quarrel
fall through fail • *plans fell through*
fall NOUN **falls 1** the action of falling
2 autumn, when leaves fall
fallacy (fal- a- see) NOUN **fallacies** a false or
mistaken idea or belief
▷ **fallacious** (fal- **ay**- shus) ADJECTIVE
Fallopian tube NOUN **Fallopian tubes** one of
the two tubes in a woman's body along which
the eggs travel from the ovaries to the uterus
fallout NOUN particles of radioactive material
carried in the air after a nuclear explosion
false ADJECTIVE **1** untrue or incorrect **2** not
genuine; artificial • *false teeth* **3** treacherous
or deceitful
▷ **falsely** ADVERB **falseness** NOUN **falsity** NOUN
falter VERB **falters, faltering, faltered**
1 hesitate when you move or speak
2 become weaker; begin to give way • *His
courage began to falter.*
fame NOUN being famous
▷ **famed** ADJECTIVE

familiar ADJECTIVE **1** well known; often seen or
experienced **2** knowing something well • *Are
you familiar with this book?* **3** very friendly
▷ **familiarly** ADVERB **familiarity** NOUN

family NOUN **families 1** parents and their
children, sometimes including grandchildren
and other relations **2** a group of things that
are alike in some way **3** a group of related
plants or animals • *Lions belong to the cat
family.*

family planning NOUN birth control

family tree NOUN **family trees** a diagram
showing how people in a family are related

famine NOUN **famines** a very bad shortage of
food in an area

famished ADJECTIVE very hungry

famous ADJECTIVE known to very many people

famously ADVERB (*informal*) very well • *They
get on famously.*

Thesaurus

fall off *Demand for these products has fallen off
lately.* ► decline, slacken, decrease, lessen,
drop off
fall out *They fell out over money.* ► quarrel,
argue, disagree, fight, squabble, bicker, clash
fall through *In the end the plan fell through.*
► come to nothing, fail, miscarry, founder,
collapse OPPOSITES ARE go ahead, succeed
fall NOUN **1** *He was hurt in a fall.* ► tumble, spill,
topple, stumble **2** *Economists expect a fall in
house prices.* ► drop, decline, fall-off, decrease,
dip, lessening, reduction, slump OPPOSITES ARE
rise, increase **3** *an epic poem on the fall of Troy*
► surrender, capitulation, submission, defeat
4 *the fall of the Roman Empire* ► downfall,
collapse, ruin, failure, demise, destruction
false ADJECTIVE **1** *a false alibi* ► untrue,
fictitious, invented, concocted, fabricated,
invalid, spurious AN OPPOSITE IS genuine **2** *a
false friend* ► unfaithful, disloyal, unreliable,
dishonorable, untrustworthy AN OPPOSITE IS
faithful **3** *false hair* ► artificial, unreal,
imitation, synthetic, simulated, fake, sham AN
OPPOSITE IS real **4** *a false belief* ► incorrect,
erroneous, mistaken, fallacious, wrong AN
OPPOSITE IS correct
falter VERB **1** *The country must not falter in the
face of such danger.* ► hesitate, waver, delay,
vacillate, flinch, hold back, lose confidence, be
indecisive, get cold feet AN OPPOSITE IS
persevere **2** *He faltered for a moment over an
awkward name.* ► stammer, stumble, stutter
fame NOUN *Their fame spread all over the world.*
► renown, celebrity, stardom, popularity,
notability, prestige, reputation, glory, name,
stature, standing, prominence

familiar ADJECTIVE **1** *The room was full of familiar
faces.* ► well known, recognizable,
accustomed, everyday, commonplace **2** *a
familiar friend* ► close, intimate, dear **3** *The
atmosphere in the house was friendly and familiar.*
► informal, casual, relaxed, natural, open,
unreserved, free and easy, unceremonious

familiarity NOUN **1** *A familiarity with at least
one European language is needed.*
► acquaintance, knowledge (of),
understanding (of) **2** *They spoke to one another
with a great deal of familiarity.* ► informality,
intimacy, closeness, friendliness, naturalness,
casualness

family NOUN **1** *a large house divided to
accommodate two families* ► household **2** *She
sends a yearly newsletter to family and friends.*
► relatives, relations, kin, kinsmen, clan
USAGE *Kin* and *kinsmen* are words you
normally find only in stories and literature.
3 *parents clearly devoted to their family*
► children, offspring, sons and daughters

famine NOUN *a country constantly threatened by
famine* ► hunger, malnutrition, scarcity,
shortage, starvation, dearth, want AN
OPPOSITE IS plenty

famous ADJECTIVE *a famous singer* ► well
known, celebrated, renowned, acclaimed,
admired, prominent, revered, distinguished,
honored, eminent, exalted, illustrious, great,
notable, noted OPPOSITES ARE unknown,
obscure

a
b
c
d
e
f
g
h
i
j
k
l
m
n
o
p
q
r
s
t
u
v
w
x
y
z

fan[1] *NOUN* **fans** an object or machine for making air move about so as to cool people or things

fan *VERB* **fans, fanning, fanned** send a current of air on something

fan out spread out in the shape of a fan

fan[2] *NOUN* **fans** an enthusiastic admirer or supporter

fanatic *NOUN* **fanatics** a person who is very enthusiastic or too enthusiastic about something
▷ **fanatical** *ADJECTIVE* **fanatically** *ADVERB* **fanaticism** *NOUN*

fanciful *ADJECTIVE* **1** imagining things **2** imaginary

fancy *NOUN* **fancies 1** a liking or desire for something **2** imagination

fancy *ADJECTIVE* decorated or elaborate; not plain

fancy *VERB* **fancies, fancying, fancied 1** have a liking or desire for something **2** imagine **3** believe ● *I fancy it's raining.*

fantastic *ADJECTIVE* **1** (*informal*) excellent **2** strange or unusual **3** designed in a very fanciful way
▷ **fantastically** *ADVERB*

fantasy *NOUN* **fantasies** something imaginary or fantastic

far *ADVERB* **1** at or to a great distance ● *We didn't go far.* **2** much; by a great amount ● *This is far better.*

far *ADJECTIVE* distant or remote ● *On the far side of the river.*

farce *NOUN* **farces 1** an exaggerated comedy **2** a situation or series of events that is ridiculous or a pretence ● *The trial was a complete farce.*
▷ **farcical** *ADJECTIVE*

fare *NOUN* **fares 1** the price charged for a passenger to travel **2** food and drink ● *There was only very plain fare.*

farewell *INTERJECTION, NOUN* **farewells** goodbye

farm *NOUN* **farms 1** an area of land where someone grows crops or keeps animals for food or other use **2** the farmer's house
▷ **farmhouse** *NOUN* **farmyard** *NOUN*

farm *VERB* **farms, farming, farmed 1** grow crops or keep animals for food, etc., **2** use land for growing crops; cultivate

farmer *NOUN* **farmers** a person who owns or manages a farm

farther *ADVERB, ADJECTIVE* at or to a greater distance; more distant
USAGE **Farther** and **farthest** are used only in connection with distance (e.g., *She lives farther from the school than I do*), but even in such cases many people prefer to use **further**. Only **further** can be used to mean "additional," e.g., in *We must make further inquiries.* If you are not sure which is right, use **further**.

farthest *ADVERB, ADJECTIVE* at or to the greatest distance; most distant
USAGE See the note at **farther**.

farthing *NOUN* **farthings** a former British coin worth one-quarter of a penny

fascinate *VERB* **fascinates, fascinating, fascinated** be very attractive or interesting to somebody
▷ **fascination** *NOUN* **fascinator** *NOUN*

Thesaurus

fan *NOUN* **1** *a fan of rock music* ▸ devotee, enthusiast, admirer, lover, fanatic, addict, aficionado, (*more informal*) freak **2** *A ceiling fan cooled the room.* ▸ ventilator, blower, extractor, air conditioner

fanatic *NOUN* **1** *a religious fanatic* ▸ extremist, zealot, militant, activist, diehard **2** *a fitness fanatic* ▸ enthusiast, devotee, admirer, lover, fan, addict, aficionado, (*more informal*) freak

fanciful *ADJECTIVE* full of fanciful ideas ▸ unrealistic, far-fetched, fantastic, imaginary, whimsical, illusory, visionary, romantic

fancy *ADJECTIVE* **1** *The belts are decorated with fancy patterns.* ▸ elaborate, decorative, ornamental, ornate **2** *They don't like wearing fancy clothes.* ▸ showy, ostentatious, gaudy

fancy *NOUN* **1** *The little cottage caught our fancy.* ▸ imagination, ingenuity, whim **2** *I had a fancy they might be there.* ▸ notion, idea, belief, impression, suspicion, hunch

fancy *VERB* **1** *I fancied I could see a light in the sky.* ▸ imagine, think, suppose, believe, suspect **2** *I fancy a doughnut.* ▸ feel like, wish for, want, desire **3** *This was the boy she had fancied for so long.* ▸ be attracted to, find attractive, have a crush on, desire, want

fantastic *ADJECTIVE* **1** *We had a fantastic time.* ▸ wonderful, marvelous, fabulous, splendid, magnificent **2** *It's a fantastic idea.* ▸ fanciful, extraordinary, incredible, unbelievable

fantasy *NOUN* a fantasy about living on a desert island ▸ dream, daydream, pipe dream, delusion, fancy

far *ADJECTIVE* He'd been to many far places. ▸ distant, faraway, far off, remote, out of the way, outlying

fare *NOUN* a standard-class train fare ▸ price, charge, cost, payment, fee

farm *NOUN* a farm of 200 acres ▸ smallholding, farmstead, estate, grange

fascinate *VERB* Most people are fascinated by the way words change their meaning. ▸ interest (in), engross, captivate, enthral, absorb, beguile, entrance, attract, charm

fascist NOUN fascists someone who believes in or practices very oppressive and nationalistic forms of government
▷ **fascism** NOUN
[from *fasces*, the rods of office in ancient Rome, used as an emblem by the Italian Fascist party in the 1920s]

fashion NOUN fashions **1** the style of clothes or other things that most people like at a particular time **2** a way of doing something ● *Continue in the same fashion.*

fashionable ADJECTIVE following the fashion of the time; popular
▷ **fashionably** ADVERB

fast[1] ADJECTIVE **1** moving or done quickly; rapid **2** allowing fast movement ● *a fast road* **3** showing a time later than the correct time ● *Your watch is fast* **4** firmly fixed or attached **5** not likely to fade ● *fast colors*
▷ **fastness** NOUN

fast ADVERB **1** quickly ● *Run fast!* **2** firmly ● *His leg was stuck fast in the mud.*
fast asleep in a deep sleep

fast[2] VERB fasts, fasting, fasted go without food
▷ **fast** NOUN

fasten VERB fastens, fastening, fastened fix one thing firmly to another
▷ **fastener** NOUN **fastening** NOUN

fat NOUN fats **1** the white greasy part of meat **2** oil or grease used in cooking
the fat of the land the best food

fat ADJECTIVE fatter, fattest **1** having a very thick round body **2** thick ● *a fat book* **3** full of fat
▷ **fatness** NOUN

fatal ADJECTIVE causing death or disaster ● *a fatal accident*
▷ **fatally** ADVERB

fate NOUN fates **1** a power that is thought to make things happen **2** what will happen or has happened to somebody or something; destiny [from Latin *fatum* = what has been spoken]

father NOUN fathers **1** a male parent **2** the title of certain priests
▷ **fatherly** ADJECTIVE
[from Old English]

father-in-law NOUN fathers-in-law the father of a married person's husband or wife

Thesaurus

fascinating ADJECTIVE *a fascinating book about the invention of the camera* ► interesting, engrossing, intriguing, captivating, enthralling, absorbing, beguiling, entrancing, attractive, charming

fashion NOUN **1** *the fashion for long dresses* ► trend, vogue, craze **2** *She was behaving in a very odd fashion.* ► way, manner, mode, method

fashionable ADJECTIVE *a fashionable hotel in New York* ► stylish, popular, chic, elegant, modish, (more informal) trendy AN OPPOSITE IS unfashionable

fast ADJECTIVE *She drives a fast car. The race was run at a fast pace. Delivery is always fast.* ► quick, rapid, speedy, swift, brisk, lively, sprightly, flying, high-speed, (more informal) nippy AN OPPOSITE IS slow

fast ADVERB **1** *The train was traveling fast toward the tunnel.* ► quickly, rapidly, swiftly, speedily, at full speed, at full tilt, briskly AN OPPOSITE IS slowly **2** *The wheels were stuck fast in the mud.* ► tightly, securely, immovably **3** *By now she was fast asleep.* ► deeply, sound, completely

fast VERB *a month in which many people are fasting* ► go without food, abstain, deny yourself AN OPPOSITE IS overeat

fasten VERB **1** *a sleeveless jacket that you fasten at the back* ► do up, tie, close, button up OPPOSITES ARE unfasten, undo **2** *We were told to fasten all windows.* ► close, secure, lock, bolt AN OPPOSITE IS unfasten **3** *Brackets are fastened to the wall.* ► fix, attach, secure, bolt AN OPPOSITE IS remove

fat ADJECTIVE **1** *A fat woman came into the room.* ► chubby, plump, stout, large, overweight, corpulent, rotund, podgy, obese, tubby, portly OPPOSITES ARE thin, slim **2** *He was reading a fat book.* ► thick, bulky, chunky, substantial **3** (informal) *A fat check arrived just before Christmas.* ► large, substantial, sizeable, generous

fat NOUN *He has a lot of fat to get rid of.* ► fatness, obesity, blubber, (technical) adipose tissue, (more informal) flab

fatal ADJECTIVE **1** *He delivered a fatal blow with the axe.* ► deadly, mortal, lethal **2** *She contracted a fatal illness in the Far East.* ► deadly, terminal, mortal, incurable, malignant **3** *That decision proved to be a fatal mistake.* ► disastrous, catastrophic, calamitous, destructive

fate NOUN **1** *I am ready for whatever fate has to offer.* ► destiny, chance, providence, fortune, the future, luck, the stars, karma, kismet **2** *He was to meet a terrible fate.* ► death, demise, end, ruin, doom

fated ADJECTIVE *They were fated not to meet again.* ► destined, doomed, predestined, preordained, predetermined, meant, bound, certain, intended

father NOUN *His father was now living in Boston.* ► male parent, (more informal) dad, (more informal) daddy, (more informal) pop, (old-fashioned) pater RELATED ADJECTIVE ► paternal

a b c d e **f** g h i j k l m n o p q r s t u v w x y z

A
B
C
D
E
F
G
H
I
J
K
L
M
N
O
P
Q
R
S
T
U
V
W
X
Y
Z

fatigue NOUN **1** tiredness **2** weakness in metals, caused by stress
▷ **fatigued** ADJECTIVE

fatten VERB fattens, fattening, fattened make or become fat

fatty ADJECTIVE like fat; containing fat

fatuous ADJECTIVE silly or foolish
▷ **fatuously** ADVERB **fatuousness** NOUN **fatuity** NOUN

fault NOUN faults **1** anything that makes a person or thing imperfect; a flaw or mistake **2** the responsibility for something wrong • *It wasn't your fault.* **3** a break in a layer of rock, caused by movement of the earth's crust
▷ **faulty** ADJECTIVE
at fault responsible for a mistake or failure

fault VERB faults, faulting, faulted find faults in something

fauna NOUN the animals of a certain area or period of time COMPARE flora

favor NOUN favors **1** a kind or helpful act **2** friendly support or approval • *The visitors soon won the favor of the local people.*
be in favor of like or support

favor VERB favors, favoring, favored be in favor of something; show favor to a person

favorable ADJECTIVE **1** helpful or advantageous **2** showing approval
▷ **favorably** ADVERB

favorite ADJECTIVE liked more than others

favorite NOUN **1** a person or thing that someone likes most **2** a competitor that is generally expected to win

fax NOUN faxes **1** a machine that sends an exact copy of a document electronically **2** a copy produced by this

fax VERB faxes, faxing, faxed send a copy of a document using a fax machine [a shortening of *facsimile*]

fear NOUN fears a feeling that something unpleasant may happen

fear VERB fears, fearing, feared feel fear; be afraid of somebody or something

fearful ADJECTIVE **1** feeling fear; afraid **2** causing fear or horror • *a fearful monster* **3** (*informal*) very great or bad
▷ **fearfully** ADVERB

fearsome ADJECTIVE frightening

Thesaurus

fatty ADJECTIVE *fatty food* ► greasy, oily, fat, (*technical*) oleaginous

fault NOUN **1** *a fault in the manufacturing process* ► defect, deficiency, failure, failing, flaw, weakness, imperfection, shortcoming, blemish, malfunction, snag **2** *There is a fault in their argument.* ► flaw, error, fallacy, inaccuracy, miscalculation, mistake **3** *He had his faults, but carelessness was not one of them.* ► failing, weakness, shortcoming, flaw, defect OPPOSITES ARE strength, strong point **4** *The problem was my fault.* ► responsibility, liability, mistake, error

faulty ADJECTIVE *The light bulb was faulty.* ► broken, defective, not working, malfunctioning, inoperative, out of order, deficient

favor NOUN **1** *She regards us with great favor.* ► approval, approbation, commendation, goodwill, kindness, friendliness, benevolence, esteem OPPOSITES ARE disfavor, disapproval **2** *Could you do me a favor?* ► good turn, benefit, kindness, kind act, courtesy, indulgence, good deed

favor VERB **1** *I favor casual clothes.* ► prefer, choose, opt for, approve of, like **2** *The government favors a policy of peace.* ► recommend, support, back, subscribe to, promote, advocate, espouse, endorse, champion

favorable ADJECTIVE **1** *CDs at favorable prices* ► advantageous, beneficial, competitive, convenient **2** *a favorable assessment of their ability* ► positive, encouraging, enthusiastic, complimentary, sympathetic, approving, agreeable

favorite ADJECTIVE *John was her favorite nephew.* ► best-loved, most-liked, preferred, favored, treasured, dearest, special, chosen, pet

favorite NOUN *Sarah had always been one of his favorites.* ► first choice, preference, darling, pet, idol, apple of your eye

fear NOUN **1** *I remember the shock of fear when I heard her scream.* ► terror, fright, horror, alarm, panic, dread, trepidation **2** *He found it hard to overcome his fears.* ► anxiety, concern, foreboding, unease, misgiving

fear VERB **1** *They all feared Ted and kept away from him.* ► be afraid of, be scared of, dread, be terrified of, tremble at, worry about **2** *We fear a bad outcome. I fear you may be right.* ► suspect, expect, foresee, anticipate

fearful ADJECTIVE **1** *The generals were fearful of enemy reprisals.* ► afraid, frightened, scared, nervous, apprehensive (about), anxious (about), uneasy (about), (*more informal*) jittery (about) *She felt a fearful pain in her leg.* ► terrible, dreadful, frightful, horrible, awful **3** (*informal*) *There would be a fearful fight if anyone found out.* ► major, very great, dreadful, terrible, awful

feasible ADJECTIVE **1** able to be done; possible **2** likely or probable • *a feasible explanation*
▷ feasibly **feasibility** NOUN
USAGE The use of **feasible** to mean "likely or probable" has not become generally accepted in standard English, so it is better to avoid it in writing or formal situations.

feast NOUN feasts **1** a large splendid meal **2** a religious festival
▷ feast VERB
[from old French; related to *fête*]

feather NOUN feathers one of the very light coverings that grow from a bird's skin
▷ feathery ADJECTIVE

feather VERB feathers, feathering, feathered cover or line something with feathers

feature NOUN features **1** any part of the face (e.g., the mouth, nose, or eyes) **2** an important or noticeable part; a characteristic **3** a special newspaper article or program that deals with a particular subject **4** the main film in a cinema program

February NOUN the second month of the year [named after *februa*, the ancient Roman feast of purification held in this month]

feces (fee- seez) PLURAL NOUN solid waste matter passed out of the body

fed past tense of **feed**
fed up (*informal*) discontented

federal ADJECTIVE to do with a system in which several states are ruled by a central government but are responsible for their own internal affairs

federation NOUN federations a group of federal states

fee NOUN fees a charge for something

feeble ADJECTIVE weak; without strength
▷ feebly ADVERB **feebleness** NOUN

feed VERB feeds, feeding, fed **1** give food to a person or animal **2** take food **3** supply something to a machine etc.
▷ feeder NOUN

feed NOUN food for animals or babies

feedback NOUN **1** the response you get from people to something you have done **2** the harsh noise produced when some of the sound from an amplifier goes back into it

feel VERB feels, feeling, felt **1** touch something to find out what it is like **2** be aware of something; have an opinion **3** experience an emotion **4** give a certain sensation • *the sand feels warm*
feel like want

feeler NOUN feelers **1** a long thin projection on an insect's or crustacean's body, used for feeling; an antenna **2** a cautious question or suggestion to test people's reactions

---

Thesaurus

---

feasible ADJECTIVE *With luck the plan might be feasible.* ► practicable, practical, workable, achievable, realizable, attainable, possible, viable OPPOSITES ARE impractical, impossible

feast NOUN *a feast fit for a king* ► banquet, meal, dinner, (*more formal*) repast, (*more informal*) spread, (*more informal*) binge

feat NOUN *a feat of great daring* ► deed, exploit, act, accomplishment, achievement, undertaking, action, attainment, performance

feature NOUN **1** *This latest incident has some notable features.* ► characteristic, circumstance, aspect, point, facet, detail, peculiarity, quality, trait **2** *a magazine feature* ► article, report, story, item, piece, column
features *Her curly hair accentuated her fine features.* ► face, countenance, expression, lineaments, look, (*more formal*) physiognomy

fed up ADJECTIVE **1** (*informal*) *You look tired and fed up.* ► depressed, dejected, dispirited, despondent, disheartened, miserable, cast down, sad, down, glum **2** (*informal*) **be fed up with** *I was totally fed up with all their whining.* ► be sick of, be tired of, be weary of, have had enough of

feeble ADJECTIVE **1** *My feeble attempts to protest were ignored.* ► weak, ineffective, inadequate, tame, poor, flimsy, shallow **2** *The illness left him too feeble to stand.* ► weak, weakened, frail, delicate, sickly, poorly, infirm,

incapacitated, helpless **3** *Her brother was a feeble character.* ► spineless, timid, weak, ineffective, ineffectual

feed VERB **1** *She has a large family to feed.* ► nourish, sustain, provide for, cater for **2** *He was feeding information to the enemy.* ► supply, provide, deliver, present **3** *They spend all their time feeding and sleeping.* ► eat, take food, have a meal, dine **4 feed on** *The local wildlife feeds on these plants.* ► eat, live on, exist on, consume, devour

feel VERB **1** *He felt the back of his head with his hand.* ► touch, stroke, finger, handle, caress, fondle **2** *She felt a hand on her shoulder.* ► sense, perceive, detect, be aware of, be conscious of, discern **3** *Did you feel any pain?* ► experience, suffer, undergo, endure, go through **4** *We feel you should apologize to her.* ► believe, think, consider, consider it right, reckon, judge **5** *The fabric feels soft.* ► seem, appear, strike you as
feel for *She had a bad time and I felt for her.* ► feel sorry for, sympathize with, pity, commiserate with
feel like *Do you feel like a drink?* ► fancy, wish for, want, desire

feel NOUN **1** *The wood had a warm feel.* ► texture, quality, surface, touch, impression **2** *She has a good feel for the music.* ► aptitude, flair, talent, gift, knack

A B C D E F G H I J K L M N O P Q R S T U V W X Y Z

feeling NOUN **feelings** **1** the ability to feel things; the sense of touch **2** what a person feels in the mind; emotion • *I didn't mean to hurt your feelings.* **3** what you think about something • *I have a feeling that we are going to win.*

feint (faynt) NOUN **feints** a pretended attack or punch meant to deceive an opponent

feint VERB **feints, feinting, feinted** make a feint
USAGE Do not confuse with **faint**.

fell[1] *past tense of* **fall**

fell[2] VERB **fells, felling, felled** make something fall; cut or knock down • *They were felling the trees.*

fellow NOUN **fellows** **1** a friend or companion; one who belongs to the same group **2** a man or boy **3** a member of a learned society

fellow ADJECTIVE of the same group or kind • *Her fellow teachers supported her.*

fellowship NOUN **fellowships** **1** friendship **2** a group of friends; a society

felt[1] *past tense of* **feel**

felt[2] NOUN a thick fabric made of fibers of wool or fur etc. pressed together

female ADJECTIVE of the sex that can bear offspring or produce eggs or fruit

female NOUN **females** a female person, animal, or plant

feminine ADJECTIVE **1** to do with or like women; suitable for women **2** (in some languages) belonging to the class of words which includes the words referring to women
▷ **femininity** NOUN

feminist NOUN **feminists** a person who believes that women should have the same rights and status as men
▷ **feminism** NOUN

fence NOUN **fences** **1** a barrier made of wood or wire, etc., around an area **2** a structure for a horse to jump over **3** a person who buys stolen goods and sells them again

fence VERB **fences, fencing, fenced** **1** put a fence around or along something **2** fight with long narrow swords (called **foils**) as a sport
▷ **fencer** NOUN

fend VERB **fends, fending, fended**
fend for yourself take care of yourself
fend off keep a person or thing away from you

ferment (fer- ment) VERB **ferments, fermenting, fermented** bubble and change chemically by the action of a substance such as yeast
▷ **fermentation** NOUN

ferment (fer- ment) NOUN **1** fermenting **2** an excited or agitated condition

fern NOUN **ferns** a plant with feathery leaves and no flowers

ferocious ADJECTIVE fierce or savage
▷ **ferociously** ADVERB **ferocity** NOUN

ferry VERB **ferries, ferrying, ferried** transport people or things, especially across water

ferry NOUN **ferries** a boat or ship used for transporting people or things across a short stretch of water

---

Thesaurus

feeling NOUN **1** *They enjoyed the feeling of power and superiority.* ► sensation, sense, awareness, consciousness, perception **2** *I had a feeling she wouldn't be coming.* ► suspicion, inkling, notion, idea, hunch, fancy, premonition **3** *There was a friendly feeling about the place.* ► atmosphere, aura, air, ambience, climate, quality, mood **4** *She spoke with great feeling.* ► emotion, passion, intensity, concern, tenderness, warmth, ardor **5** *He had lost all feeling in his arm.* ► sensation, perception, sense of touch

fell VERB **1** *A guard felled him with a single blow.* ► knock down, knock over, bring down, flatten, prostrate, (more informal) floor **2** *Dead trees have to be felled fairly quickly.* ► chop down, cut down

fellow NOUN *He's a decent fellow, always ready to help out.* ► chap, man, boy, individual, (more informal) bloke, (more informal) guy

fence NOUN *The area was surrounded by a tall fence.* ► railing, enclosure, barrier, wall, paling, hedge

fence VERB

fence in *You will need to fence in the hens.* ► confine, pen in, coop up, shut in, close in, hedge in

fence off *More land would be fenced off.* ► enclose, surround, encircle, separate off, section off, partition off, cut off

fend VERB

fend for yourself *They can fend for themselves for a few days.* ► look after yourself, care for yourself, take care of yourself, manage, cope, (more informal) get by

fend off *A small force might not be enough to fend off an attack.* ► repel, repulse, resist, ward off, beat off, fight off, hold back, thwart

ferocious ADJECTIVE *He was the victim of a ferocious attack.* ► fierce, brutal, violent, savage, cruel, vicious, barbaric, callous, heartless, cold-blooded, pitiless, ruthless, merciless, vile, sadistic, brutish OPPOSITES ARE gentle, humane

ferocity NOUN *The police were surprised by the ferocity of the attack.* ► savagery, brutality, cruelty, viciousness, fierceness, barbarity, callousness, heartlessness, cold-bloodedness, ruthlessness AN OPPOSITE IS gentleness

fertile ADJECTIVE **1** producing good crops • *fertile soil* **2** able to produce offspring **3** able to produce ideas • *a fertile imagination* ▷ **fertility** NOUN

fertilize VERB **fertilizes, fertilizing, fertilized 1** add substances to the soil to make it more fertile **2** put pollen into a plant or sperm into an egg or female animal so that it develops seed or young ▷ **fertilization** NOUN

fertilizer NOUN **fertilizers** chemicals or manure added to the soil to make it more fertile

fervent ADJECTIVE strongly passionate

festival NOUN **festivals 1** a time of celebration, especially for religious reasons **2** an organized series of concerts, films, performances, etc., especially one held every year

festivity NOUN **festivities** a festive occasion or celebration

festoon NOUN **festoons** a chain of flowers or ribbons, etc., hung as a decoration

festoon VERB **festoons, festooning, festooned** decorate something with ornaments

fetch VERB **fetches, fetching, fetched 1** go for and bring back • *fetch some milk* • *fetch a*

doctor **2** be sold for a particular price • *The chairs fetched $20.*

fête (fayt) NOUN **fêtes** an outdoor entertainment with stalls and sideshows

fetter NOUN **fetters** a chain or shackle put around a prisoner's ankle

fetus (fee- tus) NOUN **fetuses** a developing embryo, especially an unborn human baby ▷ **fetal** ADJECTIVE [from Latin, = offspring]

feud (fewd) NOUN **feuds** a long-lasting quarrel, especially between two families

feudal (few- dal) ADJECTIVE to do with the system used in the Middle Ages in which people could farm land in exchange for work done for the owner ▷ **feudalism** NOUN

fever NOUN **fevers 1** an abnormally high body temperature, usually with an illness **2** excitement or agitation ▷ **fevered** ADJECTIVE **feverish** ADJECTIVE **feverishly** ADVERB

few ADJECTIVE not many

few NOUN a small number of people or things **quite a few** or **a good few** a fairly large number USAGE See the note at less.

Thesaurus

fertile ADJECTIVE **1** *fertile soil* ► fruitful, productive, prolific, rich, fecund AN OPPOSITE IS infertile **2** *a fertile mind* ► imaginative, inventive, creative, resourceful, ingenious

fervent ADJECTIVE **1** *a fervent hope that we can be friends* ► heartfelt, earnest, eager, intense, keen, strong **2** *a fervent cricket supporter* ► eager, ardent, passionate, impassioned, avid, zealous, keen, enthusiastic

festival NOUN *The city has a music festival in the spring.* ► jubilee, pageant, carnival, gala, fête, jamboree, celebration, festivities, anniversary

festive ADJECTIVE *A festive atmosphere encourages the children to have a good time.* ► jolly, joyous, joyful, happy, merry, cheerful, cheery, jubilant, convivial, celebratory, gay, gleeful, jovial, light-hearted OPPOSITES ARE gloomy, somber

festivities PLURAL NOUN *The family returned home in time for the New Year festivities.* ► celebrations, revels, revelry, festival, party, entertainments, amusements, fun, jollification

fetch VERB **1** *She went to fetch a bucket from the cupboard.* ► get, bring, collect, pick up, retrieve, obtain, bear, call for, carry, convey, import, transfer, transport **2** *Will you fetch your brother from the station?* ► collect, pick up, transport, bring, get, convey, conduct **3** *We had better fetch the doctor.* ► send for, call for, summon, go for, get, bring **4** *By this time he reckoned the house might fetch a cool million.*

► sell for, be sold for, be bought for, raise, realize, bring in, earn, go for, make, produce

fête NOUN *a village fête* ► gala, fair, festival, pageant, bazaar, garden party, jubilee, carnival

feud NOUN *The family feud came to a head this week.* ► vendetta, dispute, conflict, rivalry, strife, quarrel , antagonism, hostility, enmity, animosity

fever NOUN **1** *He caught some sort of fever and never got over it.* ► feverishness, high temperature, delirium **2** *We were in a fever of impatience waiting for them to return.* ► frenzy, ferment **3** *World Cup football fever* ► excitement, agitation, passion, frenzy

feverish ADJECTIVE **1** *She looked flushed and feverish.* ► fevered, burning, hot, febrile, inflamed, delirious **2** *The house was a scene of feverish activity.* ► frenzied, frantic, frenetic, excited, hectic, agitated, hurried, hasty, impatient, restless OPPOSITES ARE calm, gentle

few ADJECTIVE **1** *Few details are available about the crash. A few people had gathered at the gates.* ► not many, hardly any, a small number of, a handful of AN OPPOSITE IS many **2** *Buses are few at this time of night.* ► scarce, scant, meager, in short supply, few and far between

few NOUN *I only have a few left.* ► small number, handful, sprinkling, couple, one or two AN OPPOSITE IS lot

a b c d e **f** g h i j k l m n o p q r s t u v w x y z

A
B
C
D
E
F
G
H
I
J
K
L
M
N
O
P
Q
R
S
T
U
V
W
X
Y
Z

fiancé (fee- ahn- say) NOUN **fiancés** a man who is engaged to be married

fiancée (fee- ahn- say) NOUN **fiancées** a woman who is engaged to be married

fiasco (fee- as- koh) NOUN **fiascos** a complete failure

fiber NOUN **fibers** 1 a very thin thread 2 a substance made of thin threads 3 indigestible material in certain foods that stimulates the action of the intestines
  ▷ **fibrous** ADJECTIVE

fiberglass NOUN 1 fabric made from glass fibers 2 plastic containing glass fibers

fickle ADJECTIVE constantly changing; not loyal to one person or group etc.
  ▷ **fickleness** NOUN

fiction NOUN **fictions** 1 writings about events that have not really happened; stories and novels 2 something imagined or untrue
  ▷ **fictional** ADJECTIVE

fiddle NOUN **fiddles** 1 a violin 2 (informal) a swindle

fiddle VERB **fiddles, fiddling, fiddled** 1 play the violin 2 fidget or tinker with something, using your fingers 3 (informal) alter accounts or records dishonestly
  ▷ **fiddler** NOUN

fidget VERB **fidgets, fidgeting, fidgeted** make small restless movements
  ▷ **fidgety** ADJECTIVE

field NOUN **fields** 1 a piece of land with grass or crops growing on it 2 an area of interest

or study • recent advances in the field of genetics 3 those who are taking part in a race or outdoor game, etc.

field VERB **fields, fielding, fielded** 1 stop or catch the ball 2 be on the side not batting in baseball or cricket 3 put a team into a match, contest, etc. • They fielded their best players for the final.
  ▷ **fielder** NOUN **fieldsman** NOUN

fieldwork NOUN practical work or research done in various places, not in a library or museum or laboratory

fiend (feend) NOUN **fiends** 1 an evil spirit; a devil 2 a very wicked or cruel person 3 an enthusiast • a fresh-air fiend

fiendish ADJECTIVE 1 very wicked or cruel 2 extremely difficult or complicated
  ▷ **fiendishly** ADVERB

fierce ADJECTIVE 1 angry and violent or cruel 2 intense • fierce heat
  ▷ **fiercely** ADVERB **fierceness** NOUN

fifteen ADJECTIVE, NOUN 1 the number 15 2 the first point scored in tennis
  ▷ **fifteenth** ADJECTIVE, NOUN

fifth ADJECTIVE, NOUN **fifths** next after the fourth
  ▷ **fifthly** ADVERB

fifty ADJECTIVE, NOUN **fifties** the number 50
  ▷ **fiftieth** ADJECTIVE, NOUN

fifty-fifty ADJECTIVE, ADVERB 1 shared equally between two people or groups • We'll split the money fifty-fifty. 2 evenly balanced • a fifty-fifty chance

Thesaurus

fib NOUN (informal) It was obvious that he was telling fibs. ► lie, untruth, story, falsehood

fiber NOUN 1 The fibers are then spun, either by hand or by machine. ► thread, strand, hair, filament 2 clothes in natural fibers ► cloth, fabric, stuff, material, substance 3 a diet low in fat and high in fiber ► roughage, bulk, fibrous material 4 a person of great moral fiber ► character, backbone, toughness, courage, determination, spirit, tenacity

fickle ADJECTIVE His fickle supporters soon deserted him. ► changeable, disloyal, unfaithful, inconstant, changing, erratic, faithless, variable, unreliable, unstable, vacillating, volatile, unpredictable OPPOSITES ARE loyal, faithful, constant

fiction NOUN 1 a course in twentieth-century fiction ► novels, stories, creative writing AN OPPOSITE IS nonfiction 2 The allegations were a total fiction. ► invention, fabrication, concoction, deception, fantasy, figment, flight of fancy, pack of lies, (more informal) tall story OPPOSITES ARE fact, truth

fiddle NOUN 1 a group of fiddle players ► violin 2 (informal) He was involved in a huge tax fiddle. ► fraud, swindle, cheat, trick

fiddle VERB 1 fiddle with Stephen was fiddling with the CD player. ► tinker with, play about with, tamper with, meddle with, twiddle, finger 2 (informal) The auditors will find out if anyone has fiddled the accounts. ► falsify, misrepresent, rig, alter, interfere with, tamper with, (more informal) doctor, (more informal) cook

fidget VERB The heat in the room made me fidget. ► wriggle, twitch, jiggle, shuffle, be jittery

field NOUN 1 There was a bull in the next field. ► enclosure, paddock, pasture 2 The field was too wet to play on. ► pitch, ground, sports field, playing field, (more informal) park 3 great names in the field of medicine ► sphere, domain, area, speciality, subject, discipline 4 The house lay outside our field of vision. ► range, scope, extent

fierce ADJECTIVE 1 a fierce dog ► ferocious, vicious, savage, wild, brutal OPPOSITES ARE gentle, tame 2 fierce competition ► strong, intense, powerful, keen, aggressive, cutthroat AN OPPOSITE IS mild 3 fierce resentment ► passionate, ardent, intense, strong, powerful 4 a fierce pain ► acute, severe, strong, powerful, intense

fig NOUN figs a soft fruit full of small seeds

fight NOUN fights **1** a struggle against somebody using hands, weapons, etc. **2** an attempt to achieve or overcome something • *the fight against poverty*

fight VERB fights, fighting, fought **1** have a fight **2** attempt to achieve or overcome something
▷ **fighter** NOUN

figure NOUN figures **1** the symbol of a number **2** an amount or value **3** a diagram or illustration **4** a shape **5** the shape of a person's, especially a woman's, body **6** a person **7** a representation of a person or animal in painting, sculpture, etc.

figure VERB figures, figuring, figured appear or take part in something • *She figures in some of the stories about King Arthur.*
figure out work something out

figurehead NOUN figureheads **1** a carved figure decorating the prow of a sailing ship **2** a person who is head of a country or organization but has no real power

figure of speech NOUN figures of speech a word or phrase used for special effect and not intended literally, e.g., "*a flood of letters*"

filament NOUN filaments a thread or thin wire, especially one in a light bulb

file¹ NOUN files a metal tool with a rough surface that is rubbed on things to shape them or make them smooth

file VERB files, filing, filed shape or smooth something with a file

file² NOUN files **1** a folder or box for keeping papers in order **2** a collection of data stored under one name in a computer **3** a line of people one behind the other

file VERB files, filing, filed **1** put something into a file **2** walk in a file • *They filed out.*

filings PLURAL NOUN tiny pieces of metal rubbed off by a file • *iron filings*

fill VERB fills, filling, filled **1** make or become full **2** block up a hole or cavity **3** hold a position, or appoint a person to a vacant post
▷ **filler** NOUN

fill NOUN enough to fill a person or thing • *We ate our fill.*

Thesaurus

fiery ADJECTIVE **1** *a fiery furnace* ► burning, blazing, flaming, raging, glowing, scorching, red-hot **2** *She remained calm, despite her fiery temperament.* ► passionate, ardent, fervent, excitable, spirited, lively, volatile, explosive, violent, hot-headed **3** *The sky was a fiery red.* ► bright, vivid, brilliant, intense, vibrant, rich, strong

fight NOUN **1** *He had got into a fight on the way home.* ► brawl, fracas, tussle, struggle **2** *She hated having fights with her boyfriend.* ► quarrel, argument, squabble, wrangle, contretemps, altercation, difference of opinion, (*more informal*) bust-up **3** *the fight for women's rights* ► struggle, battle, campaign, effort **4** *a championship fight* ► contest, match, bout, meeting, fixture

fight VERB **1** *Some men were fighting in the street.* ► brawl, tussle, struggle, grapple, wrestle, have a fight, exchange blows **2** *Her sons all fought in the war.* ► serve, be a soldier, join up, take up arms **3** *She and her boyfriend are always fighting.* ► quarrel, argue, row, squabble, wrangle **4** *The unions will fight any proposals to cut jobs.* ► oppose, resist, contest, challenge, defy, object to, combat, withstand **5** *women who fought for their basic freedoms* ► campaign, battle, strive, crusade

fighter NOUN *an enemy fighter* ► soldier, combatant, fighting man, fighting woman, warrior

figure NOUN **1** *The final figure was higher than last year.* ► total, sum, amount, number **2** *The*

third figure is an eight. ► digit, numeral, character, number **3** *It's hard to put an exact figure on it.* ► amount, price, cost, sum **4** *Jane has a lovely figure.* ► shape, physique, build, proportions, body, frame **5** *By now she had become a public figure.* ► personality, character, celebrity, dignitary, person, individual, personage **6** *He did not want to be seen as a figure of fun.* ► symbol, personification, embodiment, epitome

figure VERB *an animal that figures in many ancient myths* ► feature, appear, play a role, have a place

file NOUN **1** *He keeps his business letters in A4 files.* ► folder, binder, portfolio, wallet, sleeve **2** *There is a file on these people at headquarters.* ► dossier, record, set of notes **3** *A file of soldiers was walking up the road.* ► line, column, string, train, procession, convoy, stream

file VERB **1** *Completed forms are filed by year in the top drawer.* ► classify, arrange, organize, put in order, enter, store, keep, archive **2** *She was sitting filing her nails.* ► smooth, shape, rub, polish **3** *The children filed through the door into the sunshine.* ► stream, troop, march, parade, walk in a line, proceed in a line

fill VERB **1** *She soon filled a suitcase with the things she needed.* ► pack, load **2** *Fill the holes and gaps before you start wallpapering.* ► plug, stop, stop up, block up, seal **3** *With thirty guests we will fill the house.* ► crowd, throng, pack, pack into, congest **4** *A smell of coffee filled the room.* ► spread through, pervade, permeate, penetrate **5** *Recruits will fill the new posts by the*

A
B
C
D
E
F
G
H
I
J
K
L
M
N
O
P
Q
R
S
T
U
V
W
X
Y
Z

filling station NOUN filling stations a place where gas is sold from pumps

film NOUN films **1** a movie, such as those shown in theaters or on television **2** a rolled strip or sheet of thin plastic coated with material that is sensitive to light, used for taking photographs or making a movie **3** a very thin layer ● *a film of grease*

film VERB films, filming, filmed record something on film; make a film of a story etc.

filter NOUN filters **1** a device for holding back dirt or other unwanted material from a liquid or gas etc. that passes through it **2** a system for filtering traffic

filter VERB filters, filtering, filtered **1** pass through a filter **2** move gradually ● *They filtered into the hall.* ● *News began to filter out.* **3** (said about traffic) move in a particular direction while other traffic is held up

filth NOUN disgusting dirt

filthy ADJECTIVE filthier, filthiest **1** disgustingly dirty **2** obscene or offensive
▷ **filthiness** NOUN

fin NOUN fins **1** a thin flat part sticking out from a fish's body, that helps it to swim **2** a small part that sticks out on an aircraft or rocket etc., for helping its balance

final ADJECTIVE **1** coming at the end; last **2** that puts an end to an argument etc. ● *You must go, and that's final!*
▷ **finally** ADVERB **finality** NOUN

final NOUN finals the last in a series of contests

finalist NOUN finalists a competitor in a final

finance NOUN **1** the use or management of money **2** the money used to pay for something
▷ **financial** ADJECTIVE
finances PLURAL NOUN money resources; funds

finance VERB finances, financing, financed provide the money for something
▷ **financier** NOUN

find VERB finds, finding, found **1** get or see something by looking for it or by chance **2** learn something by experience ● *He found that digging was hard work.* **3** decide and give a verdict ● *The jury found him guilty.*
find out get or discover some information

Thesaurus

---

end of the year. ► occupy, take up, be appointed to, move into **6** *A bank loan will fill their needs for now.* ► fulfill, satisfy, meet, supply, furnish
fill in 1 *You have to fill in this form.*
► complete, fill out, answer **2** *I am filling in for Shirley while she is away.* ► deputize, cover, stand in, substitute **3** *Ken will fill us in on the details.* ► brief, inform (of), advise (of), apprise (of)

filling NOUN *The cushion was losing its filling.*
► stuffing, padding, wadding, insides, contents

filling ADJECTIVE *a filling meal* ► satisfying, nourishing, nutritious, ample, square, solid, substantial

film NOUN **1** *There was a film of dust on the table.*
► layer, covering, coat, coating, dusting, patina, sheet, veil, skin, screen **2** *The boys are going to see a film this evening.* ► movie, picture, feature, (old-fashioned) motion picture

filth NOUN *I needed a hose to get the filth off my boots.* ► dirt, muck, grime, mud, slime, sludge, garbage, excrement

filthy ADJECTIVE **1** *The house was filthy.* ► dirty, grubby, mucky, squalid, uncleaned, unwashed AN OPPOSITE IS clean **2** *Everyone agreed it was a filthy trick.* ► nasty, mean, vile, despicable, contemptible, disgusting, shabby **3** *They were accused of using filthy language.* ► rude, indecent, coarse, vulgar, lewd, improper, obscene OPPOSITES ARE clean, polite **4** *He was in a filthy mood.* ► bad, foul, bad-tempered, irritable

final ADJECTIVE **1** *the final month of their course* ► last, closing, concluding, finishing, end OPPOSITES ARE first, initial **2** *the final minutes of the match* ► last, closing, dying **3** *The judges' decision is final.* ► irrevocable, definitive, absolute, indisputable, unalterable, decisive, incontrovertible

finalize VERB *We can now finalize the arrangements for the trip.* ► complete, conclude, settle, clinch, resolve, decide, confirm, (more informal) wrap up

finally ADVERB *The bank finally agreed to loan the money.* ► eventually, ultimately, in the end, at length, at last

finance NOUN **1** *He needs to learn more about finance.* ► economics, money management, accounting, banking, fiscal matters **2** *The company is seeking longer-term finance.*
► funding, funds, capital, assets, revenue, income, financial backing **3** *His finances are in a fairly good state.* ► resources, assets, financial affairs, money affairs

finance VERB *Private sponsors will finance the venture.* ► fund, back, subsidize, support, provide money for, invest in, underwrite, pay for, sponsor

financial ADJECTIVE *financial affairs*
► monetary, fiscal, pecuniary, economic

find VERB **1** *I found some old coins in the cupboard.* ► discover, locate, retrieve, track down, come across, chance on, unearth, uncover **2** *We found it odd that there were so many complaints.* ► consider, think, believe, reckon, see as, regard as, look on as, view as

find NOUN finds something found

findings PLURAL NOUN the conclusions reached from an investigation

fine[1] ADJECTIVE **1** of high quality; excellent **2** dry and clear; sunny • *fine weather* **3** very thin; consisting of small particles **4** in good health; well • *I'm fine*
▷ **finely** ADVERB **fineness** NOUN

fine ADVERB **1** finely • *chop it fine* **2** (*informal*) very well • *That will suit me fine.*

fine[2] NOUN fines money which has to be paid as a punishment

fine VERB fines, fining, fined make somebody pay a fine

finger NOUN fingers **1** one of the separate parts of the hand **2** a narrow piece of something • *chicken fingers*

finger VERB fingers, fingering, fingered touch or feel something with your fingers

fingernail NOUN fingernails the hard covering at the end of a finger

fingerprint NOUN fingerprints a mark made by the tiny ridges on the fingertip, used as a way of identifying someone

finish VERB finishes, finishing, finished bring or come to an end

finish NOUN finishes **1** the last stage of something; the end **2** the surface or coating on woodwork

finite (fy- nyt) ADJECTIVE limited; not infinite • *We have only a finite supply of coal.*

finicky ADJECTIVE very fussy

fir NOUN firs an evergreen tree with needlelike leaves, that produces cones

fire NOUN fires **1** the process of burning that produces light and heat **2** coal and wood, etc., burning in a grate or furnace to give heat **3** a device using electricity or gas to heat a room **4** the shooting of guns • *Hold your fire!*
on fire burning
set fire to start something burning

fire VERB fires, firing, fired **1** set fire to **2** bake pottery or bricks in a kiln **3** shoot a gun; send out a bullet or missile **4** (*informal*) dismiss someone from a job **5** excite • *fire them with enthusiasm*
▷ **firer** NOUN

firearm NOUN firearms a small gun; a rifle, pistol, or revolver

fire brigade NOUN fire brigades a team of people organized to fight fires

fire engine NOUN fire engines a large vehicle that carries firefighters and equipment to put out large fires

Thesaurus

3 *You will find that it's helpful to number each paragraph.* ► realize, discover, learn, perceive, notice, become aware **4** *I hope you find the success you deserve.* ► achieve, attain, win, obtain, acquire, reach, secure, get
find out 1 *At last we will find out what happened.* ► learn, ascertain, discover, perceive **2** *The culprits were soon found out.* ► reveal, expose, unmask, uncover, (*more informal*) rumble

find *An ancient ship burial was among the exciting finds.* ► discovery, acquisition

fine ADJECTIVE **1** *It was a fine achievement.* ► excellent, outstanding, admirable, remarkable, exceptional, commendable, first-class, good **2** *The next day was fine.* ► bright, fair, dry, clear, sunny, warm, cloudless OPPOSITES ARE bad, wet, inclement **3** *He brought out the fine china.* ► delicate, fragile **4** *A pen with a fine tip.* ► thin, narrow, slender, slim **5** *a beach of fine warm sand* ► powdery, minute **6** *He likes fine clothes.* ► elegant, stylish, smart, chic, fashionable **7** *The mechanism needs a fine adjustment.* ► small, minor, subtle **8** *It's fine to write to me here.* ► all right, acceptable, suitable, agreeable

fine NOUN *He got a parking fine.* ► penalty, charge

finger VERB *He fingered the ring on his finger.* ► touch, feel, handle, stroke, rub, fondle, caress, twiddle

finish NOUN **1** *The race had an exciting finish.* ► ending, end, close, last stage, conclusion, result **2** *They went out to celebrate the finish of the work.* ► completion, conclusion, end, cessation, termination **3** *Mix the paint well for an even finish.* ► appearance, surface, texture, lustre, polish, shine, gloss, smoothness

finish VERB **1** *We have to finish the work today.* ► complete, conclude, end, finalize **2** *They never seem to finish complaining.* ► stop, cease, end **3** *We've finished the biscuits.* ► use up, eat, consume, devour, (*more informal*) polish off **4** *The film finishes at ten.* ► end, conclude, terminate **5** *Another year of losses will finish the company.* ► destroy, ruin, overwhelm, overpower

fire NOUN **1** *The building was destroyed in a fire.* ► blaze, conflagration, inferno, flames, burning, combustion, holocaust, pyre **2** *She spoke with fire in her eyes.* ► passion, feeling, enthusiasm, intensity, vigor, fervor, ardor, dynamism, exuberance

fire VERB **1** *The engine began to fire.* ► ignite, start, catch, (*more informal*) get going **2** *The guerrillas fired a rocket.* ► launch, discharge, shoot, detonate, set off, let off, let fly with

fire escape NOUN fire escapes a special staircase by which people may escape from a burning building

fire extinguisher NOUN fire extinguishers a metal cylinder from which water or foam can be sprayed to put out a fire

firefighter NOUN firefighters a member of a fire brigade

fireplace NOUN fireplaces an open structure for holding a fire in a room

firewood NOUN wood for use as fuel

firework NOUN fireworks a device containing chemicals that burn or explode attractively and noisily

firing squad NOUN firing squads a group of soldiers given the duty of shooting a condemned person

firm NOUN firms a business organization

firm ADJECTIVE **1** not giving way when pressed; hard or solid **2** steady; not shaking or moving **3** definite and not likely to change • *a firm belief*
▷ **firmly** ADVERB **firmness** NOUN

firm VERB firms, firming, firmed make something become firm

first ADJECTIVE coming before all others in time or order or importance
▷ **firstly** ADVERB

first ADVERB before everything else • *Finish this work first.*

first aid NOUN treatment given to an injured person before a doctor comes

first-class ADJECTIVE **1** using the best class of a service • *first-class post* **2** excellent

fish NOUN fish or fishes an animal with gills and fins that always lives and breathes in water

fish VERB fishes, fishing, fished **1** try to catch fish **2** search for something; try to get something • *He is only fishing for compliments.* [from Old English]

fisherman NOUN fishermen a person who tries to catch fish

fishmonger NOUN fishmongers a shopkeeper who sells fish

fishy ADJECTIVE fishier, fishiest **1** smelling or tasting of fish **2** (*informal*) causing doubt or suspicion • *a fishy excuse*
▷ **fishily** ADVERB **fishiness** NOUN

fission NOUN **1** splitting something **2** splitting the nucleus of an atom so as to release energy

fist NOUN fists a tightly closed hand with the fingers bent into the palm

fit[1] ADJECTIVE fitter, fittest **1** suitable or good enough • *a meal fit for a king* **2** healthy, in good physical condition • *Keep fit!* **3** ready or likely • *They worked till they were fit to collapse.*
▷ **fitness** NOUN

fit VERB fits, fitting, fitted **1** be the right size and shape for something; be suitable **2** put

---

Thesaurus

3 *The idea fired their imagination.* ► excite, stimulate, arouse, inspire, enliven, stir up **4** (*informal*) *They fired him for misconduct.* ► dismiss, discharge, sack, give someone notice, lay off

firm ADJECTIVE **1** *The ground is fairly firm at this point.* ► hard, solid, unyielding, hardened, compact, compressed, resistant, stable AN OPPOSITE IS soft **2** *The house lacked firm foundations.* ► secure, steady, strong, sturdy, fast, fixed, stable, tight, anchored **3** *Firm action is essential.* ► resolute, determined, decided, steadfast, adamant, dogged, obstinate, persistent, unshakeable, unwavering, unflinching **4** *We need a firm commitment.* ► definite, agreed, settled, unchangeable **5** *Sally was a firm friend of hers.* ► devoted, constant, faithful, loyal, reliable, dependable

firm NOUN *Dave joined an accountancy firm.* ► company, establishment, organization, business, concern, corporation

first ADJECTIVE **1** *Our first attempts didn't work.* ► initial, opening, preliminary **2** *The first inhabitants were hunters.* ► original, earliest, oldest, primeval, primitive **3** *The first consideration is the welfare of the children.*

► principal, prime, paramount, primary, main, chief, key, foremost, supreme, overriding

firstly ADVERB *Firstly, we must learn each other's names.* ► first, to begin with, to start with, at the outset, as a start

fishy ADJECTIVE (*informal*) *The price was so low it all seemed a bit fishy.* ► suspicious, dubious, doubtful, suspect, peculiar, strange, odd, queer, funny

fit ADJECTIVE **1** *She looked remarkably fit for a seventy-two-year-old.* ► healthy, well, able-bodied, robust, hale and hearty, in good form OPPOSITES ARE unfit, unhealthy **2** *The vehicles are all fit for commercial use.* ► suitable, appropriate, prepared, equipped, ready, proper, right, correct OPPOSITES ARE unfit, unsuitable **3** *Do you think he is fit to be a parent?* ► competent, able, capable (of being), qualified, worthy OPPOSITES ARE unfit, incapable

fit NOUN **1** *He might have an epileptic fit at any time.* ► seizure, convulsion, paroxysm, spasm, attack **2** *She was having a fit of hysterics.* ► outbreak, outburst, spell, bout, attack, explosion

fit VERB **1** *It takes a long time to fit all the pieces together.* ► arrange, assemble, build, construct,

something into place ● *Fit a lock on the door.*
3 alter something to make it the right size and shape **4** make suitable for something ● *His training fits him for the job.*
▷ **fitter** NOUN

fit NOUN the way something fits ● *a good fit*

fit[2] NOUN **fits 1** a sudden illness, especially one that makes you move violently or become unconscious **2** an outburst ● *a fit of rage*

fitful ADJECTIVE happening in short periods, not steadily
▷ **fitfully** ADVERB

fitting ADJECTIVE proper or appropriate ● *This statue is a fitting memorial to an extraordinary woman.*

five ADJECTIVE, NOUN **fives** the number 5

fix VERB **fixes, fixing, fixed 1** fasten or place firmly **2** make permanent and unable to change **3** decide or arrange ● *We fixed a date for the party.* **4** repair; put into working condition ● *He is fixing my bike.*
▷ **fixer** NOUN
fix up arrange or organize something

fix NOUN **fixes 1** (*informal*) an awkward situation ● *I'm in a fix* **2** finding the position of something, by using a compass, radar, etc. **3** (*informal*) an addict's dose of a drug

fixedly ADVERB with a fixed expression

fixture NOUN **fixtures 1** something fixed in its place **2** a sports event planned for a particular day

fizz VERB **fizzes, fizzing, fizzed** make a hissing or spluttering sound; produce a lot of small bubbles

fizzy ADJECTIVE (said about a drink) having a lot of small bubbles
▷ **fizziness** NOUN

flabby ADJECTIVE fat and soft, not firm
▷ **flabbily** ADVERB **flabbiness** NOUN

flag[1] NOUN **flags 1** a piece of cloth with a colored pattern or shape on it, used as a sign or signal **2** a small piece of paper or plastic that looks like a flag
▷ **flagpole** NOUN **flagstaff** NOUN

flag VERB **flags, flagging, flagged 1** become weak; droop **2** signal with a flag or by waving

flag[2] NOUN **flags** a flat slab of stone used for paving

flagrant (flay- grant) ADJECTIVE very bad and noticeable ● *flagrant disobedience*
▷ **flagrantly** ADVERB **flagrancy** NOUN

flagship NOUN **flagships 1** a ship that carries an admiral and flies his flag **2** a company's best or most important product, store, etc.

Thesaurus

dovetail, install, interlock, join, match, position, put in place, put together **2** *Make the punishment fit the crime.* ► suit, match, accord with, be appropriate to, correspond with OR to, be fitting for, conform with

fitted ADJECTIVE **1** *He clearly isn't fitted for the job.* ► suited, suitable, right, equipped, appropriate **2** *It was a modern house with fitted cupboards everywhere you looked.* ► built-in, integral, incorporated, customized

fitting ADJECTIVE *The concert was a fitting tribute to a fine singer.* ► suitable, apt, appropriate, apposite, proper, timely, felicitous OPPOSITES ARE inappropriate, unsuitable

fittings PLURAL NOUN *The bathroom fittings were cheap and flimsy.* ► fixtures, fitments, equipment, accessories, furnishings

fix VERB **1** *You can fix the notice to a lamppost.* ► fasten, tie, pin, attach, affix, secure **2** *The farmer had fixed posts into the ground.* ► set, embed, cement, place, position **3** *I can fix it for you to get an invitation.* ► arrange, organize, manage **4** *Let's fix a date to meet.* ► set, decide on, agree on, arrange, settle, determine **5** *The television needs to be fixed.* ► mend, repair, put right

fix NOUN (*informal*) *I'm in a bit of a fix.* ► difficulty, predicament, mess, plight,

dilemma, (*informal*) hole, (*informal*) jam, quandary, corner

fixed ADJECTIVE *The license is for a fixed period.* ► set, definite, decided, established, settled, predetermined, firm

fizz VERB *She dropped in a tablet and the water fizzed.* ► bubble, effervesce, foam, froth, fizzle, sizzle, hiss

fizzy ADJECTIVE *There are fizzy drinks in the garden.* ► sparkling, effervescent, bubbly, carbonated, foaming AN OPPOSITE IS still

flabbergasted ADJECTIVE *He just stood there, flabbergasted.* ► astonished, amazed, astounded, surprised, staggered, startled, disconcerted, dumbfounded, speechless, shocked, perplexed, stunned, stupefied, bewildered, (*more informal*) thunderstruck

flabby ADJECTIVE *When he took her hand in his, it was soft and flabby.* ► slack, limp, loose, floppy, flaccid, weak, feeble OPPOSITES ARE firm, stiff

flag NOUN *The route was decorated with flags.* ► banner, standard, ensign, pennant, pennon, streamer, bunting, colors

flag VERB *Our energy was beginning to flag.* ► fade, fail, decline, diminish, dwindle, sink, disappear

A
B
C
D
E
F
G
H
I
J
K
L
M
N
O
P
Q
R
S
T
U
V
W
X
Y
Z

flair NOUN a natural ability or talent • *Ian has a flair for languages.*
USAGE Do not confuse with flare.

flake NOUN flakes 1 a very light thin piece of something 2 a small flat piece of falling snow
▷ **flaky** ADJECTIVE

flamboyant ADJECTIVE very showy in appearance or manner

flame NOUN flames a tongue-shaped portion of fire or burning gas

flame VERB flames, flaming, flamed 1 produce flames 2 become bright red

flamingo NOUN flamingoes a wading bird with long legs, a long neck, and pinkish feathers

flammable ADJECTIVE able to be set on fire
▷ **flammability** NOUN
USAGE See note at inflammable.

flank NOUN flanks the side of something, especially an animal's body or an army

flannel NOUN flannels 1 a soft cloth 2 a soft woollen material

flap VERB flaps, flapping, flapped 1 wave about 2 (*informal*) panic or fuss about something

flap NOUN flaps 1 a part that is fixed at one edge to something else, often to cover an opening 2 the action or sound of flapping 3 (*informal*) a panic or fuss • *Don't get in a flap.*

flare VERB flares, flaring, flared 1 blaze with a sudden bright flame 2 become angry suddenly 3 become gradually wider • *flaring nostrils*

flare NOUN flares 1 a sudden bright flame or light, especially one used as a signal 2 a gradual widening, especially in skirts or trousers
USAGE Do not confuse with flair.

flash NOUN flashes 1 a sudden bright flame or light 2 a device for making a sudden bright light for taking photographs 3 a sudden display of anger, wit, etc. 4 a short item of news

flash VERB flashes, flashing, flashed 1 make a flash 2 appear suddenly; move quickly • *The train flashed past us.*

flashback NOUN flashbacks going back in a film or story to something that happened earlier

flashy ADJECTIVE gaudy or showy

flask NOUN flasks 1 a bottle with a narrow neck 2 a vacuum flask

flat ADJECTIVE flatter, flattest 1 with no curves or bumps; smooth and level 2 spread out; lying at full length • *Lie flat on the ground.* 3 (said about a tyre) with no air inside 4 (said about feet) without the normal arch underneath 5 absolute • *a flat refusal* 6 dull; not changing 7 (said about a drink) no longer fizzy 8 (said about a battery) unable to produce any more electric current 9 (in music) one semitone lower than the natural note • *E flat*
▷ **flatly** ADVERB **flatness** NOUN

Thesaurus

flair NOUN 1 *He has a flair for games.* ► talent, aptitude, gift, ability, genius, faculty, capacity, adeptness 2 *She dresses with great flair.* ► style, elegance, taste, discernment, panache, finesse

flake NOUN *First remove any loose flakes of old paint.* ► scale, sliver, chip, splinter, shaving, bit, leaf, slice, wafer

flamboyant ADJECTIVE *He was well known for his flamboyant appearance.* ► ostentatious, showy, colorful, gaudy, brilliant, resplendent, extravagant

flap VERB 1 *The washing was flapping in the wind.* ► flutter, sway, swing, quiver, wave about 2 *The swan flapped its wings angrily.* ► beat, flutter, shake, agitate, quiver, thrash 3 (*informal*) *He tried hard to avoid flapping.* ► panic, fuss, become agitated, become flustered

flare VERB *The match flared in his cupped hands.* ► blaze, flame, flash, burn, erupt, sparkle
flare up 1 *This border war could flare up at any time.* ► break out, burst out, erupt, blow up, recur 2 *They annoyed her and she flared up at*

them. ► lose your temper, lose control, fly into a rage, become angry

flash VERB *Lights flashed in the distance.* ► shine, blaze, flare, gleam, beam, glint, sparkle, spark

flash NOUN 1 *a flash of light* ► blaze, burst, flare, glare, gleam, glint, sparkle, flicker, twinkle, ray 2 *a flash of inspiration* ► burst, wave, surge, rush

flashy ADJECTIVE *Lily held out her hand with a flashy ring on one finger.* ► showy, gaudy, ostentatious, vulgar, (*more informal*) tacky

flat ADJECTIVE 1 *a flat surface* ► level, smooth, even, horizontal, plane OPPOSITES ARE bumpy, uneven 2 *She lay flat on the bed.* ► outstretched, prostrate, spread out, recumbent 3 *a flat sea* ► calm, still, smooth, waveless, tranquil OPPOSITES ARE rough, choppy 4 *His voice was flat and lifeless.* ► dull, monotonous, uninteresting, unexciting, tedious, boring, bland, dreary, insipid, colorless, featureless, unexpressive, weak AN OPPOSITE IS emotional 5 *The request met with a flat refusal.* ► outright, direct, straight, plain, absolute, positive

flat ➤ flesh

flat NOUN flats **1** (in music) a note one semitone lower than the natural note; the sign (♭) that indicates this **2** a punctured tire

flatten VERB flattens, flattening, flattened make or become flat

flatter VERB flatters, flattering, flattered **1** praise somebody more than he or she deserves **2** make a person or thing seem better or more attractive than they really are ▷ **flatterer** NOUN **flattery** NOUN

flaunt VERB flaunts, flaunting, flaunted display something proudly in a way that annoys people; show it off ● *He liked to flaunt his expensive clothes and cars.*
USAGE Do not confuse this word with **flout**, which has a different meaning.

flavor NOUN flavors the taste of something

flavor VERB flavors, flavoring, flavored give something a flavor; season it ▷ **flavoring** NOUN

flaw NOUN flaws something that makes a person or thing imperfect ▷ **flawed** ADJECTIVE

flea NOUN fleas a small jumping insect that sucks blood

fleck NOUN flecks **1** a very small patch of color **2** a particle; a speck ● *flecks of dirt* ▷ **flecked** ADJECTIVE

fledged ADJECTIVE (said about young birds) having grown feathers and able to fly **fully-fledged** ADJECTIVE fully trained ● *a fully-fledged engineer*

fledgeling NOUN fledgelings a young bird that is just fledged

fleece NOUN fleeces **1** the woolly hair of a sheep or similar animal **2** a warm piece of clothing made from a soft fabric ▷ **fleecy** ADJECTIVE

fleece VERB fleeces, fleecing, fleeced **1** shear the fleece from a sheep **2** swindle a person out of some money

fleet NOUN fleets a number of ships, aircraft, or vehicles owned by one country or company

fleeting ADJECTIVE passing quickly; brief

flesh NOUN **1** the soft substance of the bodies of people and animals, consisting of muscle and fat **2** the body as opposed to the mind or soul **3** the pulpy part of fruits and vegetables ▷ **fleshy** ADJECTIVE

Thesaurus

flatten VERB **1** *Tom flattened the crumpled paper against his knee.* ► smooth, press, even out, iron out, level out, roll OPPOSITES ARE roughen, crumple **2** *People had walked over the beds and flattened the plants.* ► squash, trample, crush, compress, run over **3** *The hurricane had flattened hundreds of buildings.* ► demolish, destroy, devastate, knock down, level, raze **4** (informal) *He's quite capable of flattening you with a single blow.* ► knock down, knock over, fell, prostrate, (informal) floor, (informal) lay out

flatter VERB **1** *He enjoyed teasing and flattering her.* ► praise, compliment, humor, fawn on, play up to, (more informal) sweet-talk, (more informal) butter up USAGE Note that to *flatter* is to compliment someone in an insincere way, whereas to *praise* is to pay genuine compliments. **2** *She wore a dress that flattered her small figure.* ► suit, enhance, set off, look good on, show to advantage

flattering ADJECTIVE **1** *flattering remarks* ► complimentary, favorable, appreciative, adulatory, effusive, obsequious, fawning, fulsome, ingratiating OPPOSITES ARE insulting, sincere **2** *a flattering outfit* ► becoming, fetching, enhancing

flattery NOUN *We succumb to flattery because it makes us feel good.* ► praise, compliments, adulation, blandishments, admiration, fawning, obsequiousness, servility

USAGE Note that *flattery* is always insincere, whereas *praise* is usually genuine.

flavor NOUN **1** *The food had a spicy flavor.* ► taste, tang, savor **2** *a story with an oriental flavor* ► character, quality, atmosphere, aura, ambience, mood, feel, style, feeling, aspect

flavor VERB *You can flavor the stew with mixed herbs.* ► season, spice, enliven, liven up, enrich

flavoring NOUN *Add some gentle flavoring.* ► seasoning, additive, spice, essence, extract

flaw NOUN *There is a flaw in this reasoning; a glass with a tiny flaw you can hardly see* ► defect, blemish, fault, imperfection, deficiency, weakness, failing, shortcoming

flawed ADJECTIVE *The argument was obviously flawed.* ► defective, unsound, faulty, imperfect, weak, deficient

flawless ADJECTIVE *Her skin was flawless.* ► perfect, faultless, immaculate, unblemished, unmarked, spotless

flee VERB *She left the others and fled to her room.* ► run off, bolt, fly, take off, clear off, hurry off, escape, disappear

fleet NOUN *A large fleet of ships sailed out.* ► flotilla, armada, naval force, convoy, navy, squadron, task force

flesh NOUN *an animal's flesh* ► meat, muscle, tissue, carrion, fat USAGE Note that *carrion* is the decaying flesh of a dead animal.

a b c d e **f** g h i j k l m n o p q r s t u v w x y z

A
B
C
D
E
F
G
H
I
J
K
L
M
N
O
P
Q
R
S
T
U
V
W
X
Y
Z

flex VERB flexes, flexing, flexed bend or stretch something that is flexible • *Try flexing your muscles*

flex NOUN flexes flexible insulated wire for carrying electric current

flexible ADJECTIVE **1** easy to bend or stretch **2** able to be changed or adapted • *Our plans are flexible.*
▷ **flexibility** NOUN

flick NOUN flicks a quick light hit or movement

flick VERB flicks, flicking, flicked hit or move with a flick

flicker VERB flickers, flickering, flickered **1** burn or shine unsteadily **2** move quickly to and fro

flicker NOUN flickers a flickering light or movement

flight[1] NOUN flights **1** flying **2** a journey in an aircraft **3** a series of stairs **4** a group of flying birds or aircraft **5** the feathers or fins on a dart or arrow

flight[2] NOUN flights fleeing; an escape

flight recorder NOUN flight recorders an electronic device in an aircraft that records technical information about its flight. It is used after an accident to help find the cause

flimsy ADJECTIVE flimsier, flimsiest made of something thin or weak
▷ **flimsily** ADVERB **flimsiness** NOUN

flinch VERB flinches, flinching, flinched move or shrink back because you are afraid; wince
▷ **flinch** NOUN

fling VERB flings, flinging, flung throw something violently or carelessly

fling NOUN flings **1** a short time of enjoyment • *a final fling before the exams* **2** a brief romantic affair **3** a vigorous dance • *the Highland fling*

flint NOUN flints **1** a very hard kind of stone **2** a piece of flint or hard metal used to produce sparks
▷ **flinty** ADJECTIVE

flip VERB flips, flipping, flipped **1** flick **2** (*slang*) become crazy or very angry

flip NOUN flips a flipping movement

flippant ADJECTIVE not showing proper seriousness
▷ **flippantly** ADVERB **flippancy** NOUN

flirt VERB flirts, flirting, flirted behave as though you are sexually attracted to someone to amuse yourself
▷ **flirtation** NOUN

flirt NOUN flirts a person who flirts
▷ **flirtatious** ADJECTIVE **flirtatiously** ADVERB

float VERB floats, floating, floated **1** stay or move on the surface of a liquid or in air **2** make something float **3** launch a business by getting financial support from the sale of shares
▷ **floater** NOUN

float NOUN floats **1** a device designed to float **2** a vehicle with a platform used for delivering milk or for carrying a display in a parade **3** a

Thesaurus

flex NOUN *a flex for an electric iron* ► cable, lead, wire

flexible ADJECTIVE **1** *flexible working practices* ► adaptable, adjustable, variable, fluid, open OPPOSITES ARE inflexible, rigid **2** *a flexible rod used as an aerial* ► bendable, pliable, pliant, malleable, stretchable OPPOSITES ARE rigid, fixed

flick VERB *He flicked a finger lightly against her cheek.* ► stroke, wag, brush, wave, sweep, flip, jerk

flick NOUN **1** *The king dismissed his page with a flick of his head.* ► jerk, toss, flip, sweep **2** *He gave the table a few flicks with a duster.* ► dab, touch, brush, swipe, stroke

flight NOUN **1** *a short history of flight* ► flying, aviation, aeronautics, air travel **2** *the flight of a missile* ► path, trajectory, track **3** *the king's flight to safety* ► escape , getaway, retreat, fleeing

flimsy ADJECTIVE **1** *He moved the flimsy barrier and walked past.* ► fragile, rickety, shaky, makeshift, insubstantial, frail, weak AN OPPOSITE IS substantial **2** *She wore a flimsy nightgown.* ► light, lightweight, thin, fine, diaphanous, silky, filmy **3** *We heard the usual*

flimsy excuses. ► feeble, weak, poor, thin, unconvincing, implausible

flinch VERB *She flinched as he put out his hand.* ► wince, recoil, start, shrink, pull back, draw back, shy away, shrink back
flinch from *He never flinches from his duty.* ► shrink from, shirk, avoid, evade, balk at

fling VERB *He flung the rope over the wall.* ► throw, hurl, toss, sling, cast, pitch, heave

flip VERB **1** *He flipped a coin in the air.* ► toss, flick, spin, throw **2** *The beetle flipped on to its back.* ► turn, spin, tip, topple **3** *flip through She was flipping through the pages of a magazine.* ► flick through, thumb through, skim through, scan, peruse

flirt VERB flirt with **1** *He loves flirting with the girls.* ► tease, trifle with, lead on, make up to, (*more informal*) chat up **2** *an idea I had been flirting with for some time* ► consider, entertain, toy with, trifle with, dabble in

flit VERB *insects flitting from plant to plant* ► dart, flip, fly, flutter, whisk, skim, dance

float VERB **1** *little boats floating on the water* ► sail, bob, drift **2** *A cloud floated across the sun.* ► drift, glide, hover, slip, slide, waft **3** *We want to float a few ideas.* ► suggest, propose, small amount of money kept for paying small bills or giving change

flock NOUN flocks a group of sheep, goats, or birds

flock VERB flocks, flocking, flocked gather or move in a crowd

flog VERB flogs, flogging, flogged **1** beat a person or animal hard with a whip or stick as a punishment **2** (slang) sell
▷ **flogging** NOUN

flood NOUN floods **1** a large amount of water spreading over a place that is usually dry **2** a great amount • a flood of requests **3** the movement of the tide when it is coming in towards the land

flood VERB floods, flooding, flooded **1** cover with a flood **2** come in great amounts • Letters flooded in

floodlight NOUN floodlights a lamp that makes a broad bright beam to light up a stage, stadium, important building, etc.
▷ **floodlit** ADJECTIVE

floor NOUN floors **1** the part of a room that people walk on **2** a story of a building; all the rooms at the same level

floor VERB floors, flooring, floored **1** put a floor into a building **2** knock a person down **3** baffle somebody [from Old English]

flop VERB flops, flopping, flopped **1** fall or sit down clumsily **2** hang or sway heavily and loosely **3** (informal) be a failure
▷ **floppy** ADJECTIVE

floppy disk NOUN floppy disks a flexible disc holding data for use in a computer

flora NOUN the plants of a particular area or period COMPARE **fauna**

florist NOUN florists a shopkeeper who sells flowers

floss NOUN **1** silky thread or fibers **2** a soft medicated thread pulled between the teeth to clean them
▷ **flossy** ADJECTIVE

flotsam NOUN wreckage or cargo found floating after a shipwreck
flotsam and jetsam odds and ends

flounce VERB flounces, flouncing, flounced go in an impatient or annoyed manner • She flounced out of the room.
▷ **flounce** NOUN

flounder VERB flounders, floundering, floundered **1** move clumsily and with difficulty **2** make mistakes or become confused when trying to do something

flour NOUN a fine powder of wheat or other grain, used in cooking
▷ **floury** ADJECTIVE

flourish VERB flourishes, flourishing, flourished **1** grow or develop strongly **2** be

Thesaurus

put forward, submit, raise, present, come up with, moot **4** The company was floated on the stock market. ► launch, set up, promote, initiate, offer

flock NOUN **1** a flock of sheep ► herd, drove, group **2** a flock of birds ► flight, group **3** a flock of anxious relatives ► crowd, throng, horde, gathering, bunch, huddle, mob, mass

flock VERB People flocked from all quarters.
► gather, collect, assemble, come together, congregate, crowd, convene, converge, muster

flog VERB The executioner flogged the woman on her back. ► whip, beat, flay, lash, scourge, thrash, flagellate, birch, cane

flood NOUN **1** The flood cut off several villages.
► inundation, deluge, torrent, downpour **2** a flood of protests ► succession, torrent, barrage, spate, storm, volley, excess, abundance, profusion, plethora AN OPPOSITE IS trickle

flood VERB **1** The dam burst, flooding the town.
► inundate, swamp, submerge, engulf, overwhelm, drown, deluge, immerse **2** Light flooded the room. ► fill, swamp, saturate **3** The bathtub flooded yesterday. ► overflow, run over, brim over **4** The press flooded back into the courtroom. ► pour, stream, surge, swarm, flock, crowd, throng

floor NOUN **1** The floor was sopping wet.
► ground, flooring, base **2** Take the lift to the third floor. ► level, story, stage, landing

flop VERB **1** His white hair flopped over his eyes.
► dangle, droop, hang down, slump, flag, sag, wilt **2** All she wanted was to flop into a chair. ► drop, fall, sink, slump, collapse, tumble **3** (informal) The idea flopped spectacularly. ► fail, founder, misfire, be unsuccessful, fold

flop NOUN (informal) The show was a flop.
► failure, disaster, debacle, fiasco, (more informal) washout

floppy ADJECTIVE a girl in pigtails, wearing a large floppy woolen hat ► limp, droopy, drooping, dangling, loose, saggy, sagging, hanging AN OPPOSITE IS stiff

flounder VERB The infantry floundered in the swampy ground. He was floundering in a situation of his own making. ► struggle, falter, grope, wallow, stumble, fumble, stagger

flourish VERB **1** Plants flourish in this good soil. The farmers flourished, aided by good weather.
► thrive, prosper, bloom, blossom, succeed, boom, be strong, be vigorous, progress **2** She went out, flourishing an umbrella. ► brandish, wave, wield, swirl, swing, flaunt

a
b
c
d
e
f
g
h
i
j
k
l
m
n
o
p
q
r
s
t
u
v
w
x
y
z

263

flourish ➡ flurry

successful; prosper **3** wave something about dramatically

flourish NOUN flourishes a showy or dramatic sweeping movement, curve, or passage of music

flout VERB flouts, flouting, flouted disobey a rule or instruction openly and scornfully • *She shaved her head one day just because she loved to flout convention.*
USAGE Do not confuse this word with flaunt, which has a different meaning.

flow VERB flows, flowing, flowed **1** move along smoothly or continuously **2** gush out • *Water flowed from the tap* **3** hang loosely • *flowing hair* **4** (said about the tide) come in toward the land

flow NOUN flows **1** a flowing movement or mass **2** a steady continuous stream of something • *a flow of ideas* **3** the movement of the tide when it is coming in towards the land • *the ebb and flow of the tide*

flower NOUN flowers **1** the part of a plant from which seed and fruit develops **2** a blossom and its stem used for decoration, usually in groups

flower VERB flowers, flowering, flowered produce flowers

flowery ADJECTIVE **1** full of flowers **2** (said about language) elaborate, full of ornamental phrases

flu NOUN influenza

fluctuate VERB fluctuates, fluctuating, fluctuated rise and fall; vary • *Prices fluctuated.*
▷ **fluctuation** NOUN

fluent (floo- ent) ADJECTIVE **1** skillful at speaking clearly and without hesitating **2** able to speak a foreign language easily and well
▷ **fluently** ADVERB **fluency** NOUN

fluff NOUN a fluffy substance

fluffy ADJECTIVE having a mass of soft fur or fibers
▷ **fluffiness** NOUN

fluid NOUN fluids a substance that is able to flow freely as liquids and gases do

fluid ADJECTIVE **1** able to flow freely **2** not fixed • *My plans for Christmas are fluid.*
▷ **fluidity** NOUN

fluke NOUN flukes a success that you achieve by unexpected good luck

fluorescent (flo- er- ess- ent) ADJECTIVE creating light from radiation • *a fluorescent lamp*
▷ **fluorescence** NOUN

fluoridation NOUN adding fluoride to drinking water in order to help prevent tooth decay

fluoride NOUN a chemical substance that is thought to prevent tooth decay

flurry NOUN flurries **1** a sudden whirling gust of wind, rain, or snow **2** a short period of activity or excitement

Thesaurus

flout VERB *He had no intention of flouting a court order.* ► disobey, defy, violate, contravene, infringe, break, spurn, scorn OPPOSITES ARE respect, observe

flow VERB **1** *Water was flowing through the pipes.* ► run, stream, spurt, trickle, ooze, spurt, squirt, gush, flood, cascade **2** *Several issues flow from these proposals.* ► result, proceed, follow, arise, spring, emerge, emanate

flow NOUN **1** *Alcohol increases the flow of blood to the brain.* ► movement, circulation, stream, motion, course, current, passage, surge **2** *a steady flow of correspondence* ► stream, current, deluge, cascade, flood, gush, spate

flower NOUN **1** *Mandy picked flowers from the garden.* ► bloom, blossom, floret, bud **2** *the flower of a nation's youth* ► finest, best, pick, cream, choice, elite

fluctuate VERB *Their income fluctuates from year to year.* ► vary, change, alter, shift, differ, rise and fall

fluent ADJECTIVE **1** *She is fluent in five European languages.* ► articulate, able to speak **2** *It is important to speak in a fluent and interesting manner.* ► articulate, natural, expressive,

eloquent, effortless, flowing, polished, ready, smooth, unhesitating, (*disapproving*) glib, (*disapproving*) facile AN OPPOSITE IS inarticulate

fluffy ADJECTIVE *She padded into the bedroom wrapped in a big fluffy towel.* ► furry, woolly, fleecy, fuzzy, downy, velvety, soft

fluid ADJECTIVE **1** *fluid substances* ► liquid, aqueous, flowing, watery, running, gaseous, liquefied, melted, molten, (*more informal*) runny AN OPPOSITE IS solid **2** *fluid movements* ► graceful, flowing, smooth **3** *My plans are still fairly fluid.* ► flexible, adaptable, adjustable, variable, open, changeable, unstable, indefinite, unsettled OPPOSITES ARE firm, fixed, definite USAGE Be careful when you use changeable or indefinite, because they have other meanings.

fluid NOUN *Drink lots of fluids and eat fiber-rich foods.* ► liquid, juice

fluke NOUN *By a lucky fluke she came along at that moment.* ► chance, accident, piece of luck, stroke of luck

flurry NOUN **1** *a snow flurry* ► swirl, whirl, gust **2** *a flurry of activity* ► spate, wave, burst, spell, stir, spurt, outbreak, commotion

flush[1] VERB flushes, flushing, flushed 1 blush 2 clean or remove something with a fast flow of water

flush NOUN flushes 1 a blush 2 a fast flow of water 3 (in card games) a hand of cards of the same suit

flush[2] ADJECTIVE 1 level with the surrounding surface • *The doors are flush with the walls.* 2 (informal) having plenty of money

fluster VERB flusters, flustering, flustered make somebody nervous and confused
▷ **fluster** NOUN

flute NOUN flutes a musical instrument consisting of a long pipe with holes that are stopped by fingers or keys

flutter VERB flutters, fluttering, fluttered 1 flap wings quickly 2 move or flap quickly and irregularly

flutter NOUN flutters 1 a fluttering movement 2 a nervously excited condition

fly[1] NOUN flies 1 a small flying insect with two wings 2 a real or artificial fly used as bait in fishing

fly VERB flies, flying, flew, flown 1 move through the air by means of wings or in an aircraft 2 travel through the air or through space 3 wave in the air • *Flags were flying.* 4 make something fly • *They flew model aircraft.* 5 move or pass quickly • *Time flies.*
▷ **flyer** NOUN

fly[2] NOUN flies the front opening of a pair of trousers

flying saucer NOUN flying saucers a mysterious saucer-shaped object reported to have been seen in the sky and believed by some people to be an alien spacecraft

flyleaf NOUN flyleaves a blank page at the beginning or end of a book

flyover NOUN flyovers a bridge that carries one road or railway over another

flywheel NOUN flywheels a heavy wheel used to regulate machinery

foal NOUN foals a young horse

foam NOUN 1 a white mass of tiny bubbles on a liquid; froth 2 a spongy kind of rubber or plastic
▷ **foamy** ADJECTIVE

foam VERB foams, foaming, foamed form bubbles or froth

fob VERB fobs, fobbing, fobbed
fob off get rid of someone by an excuse or a trick

focal ADJECTIVE to do with or at a focus

focus NOUN focuses or foci 1 the distance from an eye or lens at which an object appears clearest 2 the point at which rays, etc., seem to meet 3 something that is a center of interest or attention
in focus appearing clearly
out of focus not appearing clearly

focus VERB focuses, focusing, focused 1 adjust the focus of your eye or a lens so that objects appear clearly 2 concentrate • *She focused her attention on the screen.*

fodder NOUN food for horses and farm animals

fog NOUN thick mist
▷ **foggy** ADJECTIVE

foghorn NOUN foghorns a loud horn for warning ships in fog

a
b
c
d
e
f
g
h
i
j
k
l
m
n
o
p
q
r
s
t
u
v
w
x
y
z

Thesaurus

flush ADJECTIVE 1 *He had just been paid and was feeling flush.* ► rich, wealthy, well off, prosperous 2 *The opening needs to be flush with the wall.* ► level, flat, even, square, true

flush VERB 1 *Nancy flushed with embarrassment.* ► blush, go red, redden, color, glow 2 *Fruit helps flush toxins from the body.* ► cleanse, rinse out, wash out, swill 3 *The police tried to flush the suspects out.* ► chase out, drive out, expel, send up

flustered ADJECTIVE *She looked shocked and flustered.* ► confused, bewildered, bemused, perplexed, baffled, puzzled, mystified, disconcerted, confounded

fly VERB 1 *A flock of birds flew past.* ► glide, flit, flutter, hover, soar, wing 2 *A gull flew into the air.* ► rise, soar, ascend, mount 3 *He refused to fly the aircraft until it had been checked.* ► pilot, operate, take off in, travel in 4 *A flag was flying at half mast.* ► flutter, flap, wave 5 *The ship was flying a neutral flag.* ► display, show, exhibit

fly at *Charley flew at him, shaking his fist.* ► attack, assault, go for, set upon, weigh into, let fly at, hit out at, lash out at

foam NOUN 1 *The sea looked like white crests of foam.* ► froth, spume, surf, spray, lather, scum, suds 2 *There was at least an inch of foam on his beer.* ► head, bubbles, effervescence

foam VERB *The water heaved and foamed.* ► froth, fizz, seethe, ferment, bubble, effervesce, lather, boil

focus NOUN 1 *Get the camera into focus.* ► clarity, correct adjustment, sharpness 2 *The television has become a main focus of the living room.* ► center, focal point, heart, hub, core, pivot

focus VERB *focus on* We need to focus on the events of this coming week.* ► concentrate on, direct attention to, fix attention on, home in on, zero in on, spotlight, think about, aim at, center on, look mainly at

foggy ADJECTIVE *Outside it was dull and foggy.* ► misty, smoggy, hazy, murky, gloomy, dingy, dim AN OPPOSITE IS clear

A
B
C
D
E
F
G
H
I
J
K
L
M
N
O
P
Q
R
S
T
U
V
W
X
Y
Z

foil[1] NOUN foils **1** a very thin sheet of metal • *cooking foil* **2** a person or thing that makes another look better in contrast

foil[2] NOUN foils a long narrow sword used in the sport of fencing

foil[3] VERB foils, foiling, foiled prevent something from being successful • *We foiled his evil plan*

foist VERB foists, foisting, foisted make a person accept something inferior or unwelcome • *They foisted the job on me.*

fold VERB folds, folding, folded bend or move so that one part lies on another part

fold NOUN folds a line where something is folded

folder NOUN folders a folding cover for loose papers

folk NOUN people

folk dance NOUNS folk dances a dance in the traditional style of a country

folklore NOUN old beliefs and legends

folk song NOUN folk songs a song in the traditional style of a country

follow VERB follows, following, followed **1** go or come after **2** do a thing after something else **3** take a person or thing as a guide or example **4** take an interest in the progress of events or a sport or team, etc. **5** understand • *Did you follow what he said?* **6** result from something
▷ **follower** NOUN

following PREPOSITION after, as a result of • *Following the burglary, we had new locks fitted.*

folly NOUN follies foolishness; a foolish action etc.

fond ADJECTIVE **1** loving or liking a person or thing **2** foolishly hopeful • *fond hopes*
▷ **fondly** ADVERB **fondness** NOUN

fondle VERB fondles, fondling, fondled touch or stroke lovingly

food NOUN foods any substance that a person or animal can eat in order to grow and be healthy

food chain NOUN food chains a series of plants and animals each of which serves as food for the one above it in the series

Thesaurus

foil VERB *She foiled their efforts by walking in at the wrong moment.* ► thwart, frustrate, obstruct, impede, hamper, hinder, baffle, scotch, check, prevent, stop

fold VERB **1** *Fold the sheets and put them in a drawer.* ► double, double over, turn over, bend, tuck, overlap, crease, pleat **2** *She stood there, folding her arms.* ► clasp, wrap, cradle, enfold, enclose, embrace, entwine, envelop, hug **3** *I'll fold the chair and put it away.* ► close, collapse, let down, put down **4** *The business folded during the recession.* ► fail, collapse, crash, founder, close down

fold NOUN **1** *Neatly arrange the folds in the curtains.* ► pleat, crease, tuck, furrow, bend **2** *a fold for sheep* ► enclosure, pen, paddock, compound

folder NOUN *I need a folder for these papers.* ► file, binder, portfolio, wallet, sleeve

folk or **folks** PLURAL NOUN **1** *It was good news for the folk back home.* ► people, individuals, citizens, inhabitants **2** *She would visit her folks at the weekend.* ► family, parents, relatives, people, kinsfolk

follow VERB **1** *He followed them as far as the corner.* ► go after, come after, walk behind, tread on the heels of, trace the footsteps of **2** *She hoped to follow her father as chief executive of the company.* ► succeed, replace, take the place of, take over from, supplant, supersede, step into someone's shoes **3** *An undercover police officer followed him everywhere.* ► pursue,

stalk, track, shadow, trail, go after, (more informal) tail **4** *Make sure you follow the instructions on the packet.* ► observe, comply with, adhere to, carry out, obey, note, heed, conform to, keep to **5** *Many benefits followed from their membership of the community.* ► result, ensue, emanate, arise, develop **6** *I found it hard to follow his meaning.* ► understand, comprehend, grasp, fathom, take in, catch **7** *Which team do you follow?* ► support, be a fan of

following ADJECTIVE *She went home on the following day.* ► next, ensuing, subsequent, succeeding OPPOSITES ARE preceding, previous

folly NOUN *It would be an act of folly to start a war.* ► foolishness, stupidity, senselessness, recklessness, silliness, madness, lunacy, idiocy

fond ADJECTIVE **1** *her fond father* ► loving, adoring, devoted, doting, caring, attentive, kind **2** *a fond hope* ► foolish, unrealistic, naive, vain, empty **3** *be fond of* *She's fond of dancing. I'm very fond of Jo.* ► be partial to, be attached to, like, love, (more informal) be hooked on, (more informal) be wild about, (more informal) be crazy about

fondle VERB *He stooped down to fondle the cat.* ► stroke, caress, pat, pet, cuddle, play with

food NOUN **1** *He had gone a week without food.* ► nourishment, sustenance, nutriment, subsistence RELATED ADJECTIVE ► alimentary **2** *Have you brought any food?* ► provisions, refreshments, eatables, something to eat, (old use) victuals, (more informal) grub

fool NOUN **fools** **1** a stupid person; someone who acts unwisely **2** a jester or clown • *Stop playing the fool.* **3** a creamy pudding with crushed fruit in it • *raspberry fool*
fool's errand a useless errand
fool's paradise happiness that comes only from being mistaken about something

fool VERB **fools, fooling, fooled** **1** behave in a joking way; play about **2** trick or deceive someone

foolish ADJECTIVE without good sense or judgment; unwise
▷ **foolishly** ADVERB **foolishness** NOUN

foolproof ADJECTIVE easy to use or do correctly

foot NOUN **feet** **1** the lower part of the leg below the ankle **2** any similar part, e.g., one used by certain animals to move or attach themselves to things **3** the lowest part • *the foot of the hill* **4** a measure of length, 12 inches or about 30 centimeters • *a ten-foot pole*; • *it is ten feet long* **5** a unit of rhythm in a line of poetry, e.g., each of the four divisions in *Jack / and Jill / went up / the hill.*
on foot walking

foot-and-mouth disease NOUN a serious contagious disease that affects cattle, sheep, and other animals

football NOUN **footballs** **1** a game played by two teams which try to kick an inflated leather ball over a goal line or into their opponents' goal **2** the ball used in this game
▷ **footballer** NOUN

foothill NOUN **foothills** a low hill near the bottom of a mountain or range of mountains

foothold NOUN **footholds** **1** a place to put your foot when climbing **2** a small but firm position from which further progress can be made

footing NOUN **1** having your feet placed on something; a foothold • *He lost his footing and slipped.* **2** the status or nature of a relationship • *We are on a friendly footing with that country.*

footlights PLURAL NOUN a row of lights along the front of the floor of a stage

footnote NOUN **footnotes** a note printed at the bottom of the page

footpath NOUN **footpaths** a path for pedestrians

footprint NOUN **footprints** a mark made by a foot or shoe

footstep NOUN **footsteps** **1** a step taken in walking or running **2** the sound of this

for PREPOSITION This word is used to show **1** purpose or direction (*This letter is for you; we set out for home.*), **2** distance or time (*Walk for six miles or two hours*), **3** price or exchange (*We bought it for $2; new lamps for old*), **4** cause (*She was fined for speeding*), **5** defense or support (*He fought for his country; are you for us or against us?*), **6** reference (*For all her wealth, she is bored.*), **7** similarity or correspondence (*We took him for a fool.*)
forever for all time; always

for CONJUNCTION because • *They hesitated, for they were afraid.*

forbear VERB **forbears, forbearing, forbore, forborne** **1** refrain from something • *We forbore to mention it.* **2** be patient or tolerant
▷ **forbearance** NOUN

forbid VERB **forbids, forbidding, forbade, forbidden** **1** order someone not to do

Thesaurus

fool NOUN **1** *He was acting like a fool.* ► idiot, ass, halfwit, dimwit, blockhead, dunderhead, nincompoop, imbecile, moron, clown, buffoon, clot, chump, (*more informal*) dope, (*more informal*) jerk, (*more informal*) ninny, (*more informal*) twit, (*more informal*) twerp **2** (*old-fashioned*) *a fool at the court of the king* ► jester, clown, buffoon, comic, stooge

fool VERB **1** *We easily fooled him.* ► deceive, trick, hoodwink, hoax, dupe **2** *I thought you were just fooling.* ► pretend, joke, jest, tease, make believe, put on an act
fool about *Some children were fooling around.* ► play about, lark about, misbehave USAGE You can use *around* instead of *about* in all these synonyms.

foolish ADJECTIVE *a foolish remark; She had been extremely foolish.* ► stupid, silly, ill-advised, unwise, crazy, mad, insane, (*more informal*) daft OPPOSITES ARE wise, sensible

foolishness NOUN *They shook their heads at her foolishness in going back to France.* ► stupidity, folly, senselessness, recklessness, silliness, madness, lunacy, idiocy

foolproof ADJECTIVE *The system is foolproof if you follow the instructions carefully.* ► infallible, unfailing, dependable, straightforward, simple, (*more informal*) idiot-proof

foot NOUN **1** *The animal had hurt its foot.* ► paw, hoof, trotter, claw **2** *The house was at the foot of the hill.* ► bottom, base

footprint NOUN *There were huge footprints in the snow.* ► footmark, footstep, track, print, trace, spoor USAGE You use *spoor* only when referring to an animal.

forbid VERB *She forbids the use of calculators in this exercise.* ► ban, prohibit, bar, disallow, rule out, exclude, proscribe, veto, outlaw, refuse, preclude OPPOSITES ARE permit, allow something **2** refuse to allow • *We shall forbid the marriage.*

forbidding ADJECTIVE looking stern or unfriendly

force NOUN **forces 1** strength or power **2** (in science) an influence, which can be measured, that causes something to move **3** an organized group of police, soldiers, etc.
in *or* **into force** in or into effectiveness • *The new law comes into force next week.*
the forces a country's armed forces

force VERB **forces, forcing, forced 1** use force in order to get or do something, or to make somebody obey **2** break something open by force **3** cause plants to grow or bloom earlier than is normal • *You can force them in a greenhouse.*

forceful ADJECTIVE strong and vigorous
▷ **forcefully** ADVERB

forcible ADJECTIVE done by force; forceful
▷ **forcibly** ADVERB

ford NOUN **fords** a shallow place where you can walk across a river

ford VERB **fords, fording, forded** cross a river at a ford

fore ADJECTIVE, ADVERB at or towards the front • *fore and aft*

fore NOUN the front part
to the fore to or at the front; in or to a prominent position

forearm NOUN **forearms** the arm from the elbow to the wrist or fingertips

forearm VERB **forearms, forearming, forearmed** prepare in advance against possible danger

forecast NOUN **forecasts** a statement that tells in advance what is likely to happen

forecast VERB **forecasts, forecasting, forecast** make a forecast
▷ **forecaster** NOUN

forefinger NOUN **forefingers** the finger next to the thumb

foregone conclusion NOUN **foregone conclusions** a result that can be foreseen easily or is bound to happen

foreground NOUN the part of a scene, picture, or view that is nearest to you

forehand NOUN **forehands** a stroke made in tennis etc. with the palm of the hand turned forwards

forehead (for- hed, forrid) NOUN **foreheads** the part of the face above the eyes

foreign ADJECTIVE **1** belonging to or in another country **2** not belonging naturally to a place or to someone's nature • *Lying is foreign to her nature.*

foreigner NOUN **foreigners** a person from another country

foreman NOUN **foremen 1** a worker in charge of a group of other workers **2** a member of a jury who is in charge of the jury's discussions and who speaks on its behalf

Thesaurus

forbidden ADJECTIVE *Ball games are forbidden on the grass outside the building.* ► banned, prohibited, barred, disallowed, proscribed, illegal, against the law, outlawed, unauthorized, unlawful AN OPPOSITE IS permissible **2** *This part of the house is forbidden to them.* ► out of bounds, restricted, closed

forbidding ADJECTIVE *The house has a dark, forbidding appearance.* ► grim, ominous, menacing, threatening, gloomy, stern, unfriendly, uninviting, unwelcoming AN OPPOSITE IS friendly

force NOUN **1** *It needed some force to get the door open.* ► strength, might, vigor, effort, energy, muscle, power, drive, pressure, weight **2** *The force of the explosion was felt for miles.*
► intensity, impact, effect, shock, momentum **3** *They used force to get their way.* ► violence, coercion, compulsion, aggression, constraint, duress **4** *I could see the force of the argument.*
► strength, cogency, effectiveness, validity, persuasiveness, weight, rightness **5** *a peace-keeping force* ► body, group, corps, unit, team, detachment, troops, army

force VERB **1** *If necessary we will force them to do it.* ► compel, make, oblige, coerce, constrain, pressure, pressurize, order, impel, bulldoze, drive, press-gang **2** *The intruders had to force a door.* ► break open, burst open, prise open, smash, use force on, wrench **3** *They tried to force their opinions on us.* ► impose, inflict, thrust

forceful ADJECTIVE **1** *a forceful personality*
► strong, dynamic, powerful, assertive, commanding, self-assured, energetic **2** *forceful arguments* ► strong, cogent, compelling, convincing, potent, plausible, effective

foreign ADJECTIVE **1** *I like travelling to foreign countries.* ► overseas, distant, remote, exotic, faraway, far-flung **2** *the company's foreign branches* ► overseas, international, external AN OPPOSITE IS domestic **3** *Jealousy is foreign to her nature.* ► unknown, familiar, alien, strange AN OPPOSITE IS natural

foreigner NOUN *Many foreigners come to live in this city.* ► overseas visitor, visitor, immigrant, alien, outsider, newcomer, stranger AN OPPOSITE IS native

foremost ADJECTIVE, ADVERB first in position or rank; most important

forensic (fer-en-sik) ADJECTIVE to do with or used in lawcourts

forensic medicine NOUN medical knowledge used in legal matters or in solving crimes

forerunner NOUN forerunners a person or thing that comes before another; a sign of what is to come

foresee VERB foresees, foreseeing, foresaw, foreseen realize what is going to happen

foreshadow VERB foreshadows, foreshadowing, foreshadowed be a sign of something that is to come

foreshorten VERB foreshortens, foreshortening, foreshortened show an object in a drawing etc. with some lines shortened to give an effect of distance or depth

foresight NOUN the ability to foresee and prepare for future needs

forest NOUN forests trees and undergrowth covering a large area
▷ **forested** ADJECTIVE

forestry NOUN planting forests and looking after them
▷ **forester** NOUN

foretaste NOUN foretastes an experience of something that is to come in the future

foretell VERB foretells, foretelling, foretold tell in advance; prophesy

forethought NOUN careful thought and planning for the future

foreword NOUN forewords a preface

forfeit (for-fit) VERB forfeits, forfeiting, forfeited pay or give up something as a penalty
▷ **forfeiture** NOUN

forfeit NOUN forfeits something forfeited

forge NOUN forges a place where metal is heated and shaped; a blacksmith's workshop

forge[1] VERB forges, forging, forged 1 shape metal by heating and hammering 2 copy something in order to deceive people
▷ **forger** NOUN **forgery** NOUN

forge[2] VERB forges, forging, forged forge ahead move forward by a strong effort

forget VERB forgets, forgetting, forgot, forgotten 1 fail to remember 2 stop thinking about • *Forget your troubles.*
forget yourself behave rudely or thoughtlessly

forgetful ADJECTIVE tending to forget
▷ **forgetfully** ADVERB **forgetfulness** NOUN

forgive VERB forgives, forgiving, forgave, forgiven stop feeling angry with somebody about something
▷ **forgiveness** NOUN

fork NOUN forks 1 a small device with prongs for lifting food to your mouth 2 a large device with prongs used for digging or lifting things 3 a place where something separates into two or more parts • *a fork in the road*

fork VERB forks, forking, forked 1 lift or dig with a fork 2 form a fork by separating into two branches 3 follow one of these branches • *Fork left.*
fork out (*informal*) pay out money

Thesaurus

foremost ADJECTIVE *the foremost musicians of the day* ▶ leading, principal, chief, main, greatest, supreme, primary

foresight NOUN *She had the foresight to write a will.* ▶ forethought, prudence, perspicacity, farsightedness, prescience, vision, circumspection, preparedness AN OPPOSITE IS improvidence

forge VERB 1 *The blacksmith forged swords and knives for the army.* ▶ work, cast, make, mold, shape, hammer out, beat into shape 2 *He would have a go at forging the signature.* ▶ fake, falsify, counterfeit, imitate, copy, reproduce 3 *He had been highly successful in forging a strong team.* ▶ build, create, develop, establish, set up
forge ahead *The Persians forged ahead through Thrace.* ▶ advance, make progress

forgery NOUN *He thinks they sold him a forgery.* ▶ fake, copy, imitation, reproduction, replica, duplicate, hoax, sham, simulation, (*more informal*) phoney

forget VERB 1 *I forgot my passport.* ▶ leave behind, overlook, mislay AN OPPOSITE IS remember 2 *She forgot to lock the door.* ▶ omit,

neglect, fail AN OPPOSITE IS remember 3 *This is not something we can easily forget.* ▶ ignore, disregard, overlook, dismiss, think no more of, stop thinking about

forgetful ADJECTIVE *As he grew older he became more forgetful.* ▶ absentminded, inattentive, neglectful, abstracted, oblivious, vague, dreamy, lax, heedless

forgive VERB 1 *He found it hard to forgive them.* ▶ excuse, pardon, exonerate, absolve, let off, spare, (*more informal*) exculpate 2 *We cannot forgive such rudeness.* ▶ excuse, condone, overlook, ignore, disregard

forgiveness NOUN *He begged their forgiveness.* ▶ pardon, absolution, exoneration, understanding, tolerance, mercy

forgo VERB *They would have to forgo their morning swim.* ▶ do without, go without, miss, give up, sacrifice, eschew, abandon, renounce

fork VERB 1 *The road forks at the bottom of the hill.* ▶ branch, split, separate
fork out (*informal*) *If necessary they would just have to fork out the money.* ▶ pay, produce, (*informal*) cough up

A
B
C
D
E
F
G
H
I
J
K
L
M
N
O
P
Q
R
S
T
U
V
W
X
Y
Z

fork-lift truck NOUN fork-lift trucks a truck with two metal bars at the front for lifting and moving heavy loads

forlorn ADJECTIVE left alone and unhappy • forlorn hope the only faint hope left

form NOUN forms **1** the shape, appearance, or condition of something **2** the way something exists • Ice is a form of water. **3** a class in school **4** a bench **5** a piece of paper with spaces to be filled in

form VERB forms, forming, formed **1** shape or construct something; create **2** come into existence; develop • Icicles formed.

formal ADJECTIVE **1** strictly following the accepted rules or customs; ceremonious • a formal occasion • formal dress **2** rather serious and stiff in your manner
▷ **formally** ADVERB

format NOUN formats **1** the shape and size of something **2** the way something is arranged or organized **3** (in computing) the way data is organized for processing or storage by a computer

formation NOUN formations **1** the act of forming something **2** a thing formed **3** a special arrangement or pattern • flying in formation

former ADJECTIVE of an earlier time
▷ **formerly** ADVERB
the former the first of two people or things just mentioned

formidable (for- mid- a- bul) ADJECTIVE **1** difficult to deal with or do • a formidable task **2** fearsome or frightening
▷ **formidably** ADVERB

formula NOUN formulae **1** a set of chemical symbols showing what a substance consists of **2** a rule or statement expressed in symbols or numbers **3** a list of substances needed for making something **4** a fixed wording for a ceremony etc. **5** one of the groups into which racing cars are placed according to the size of their engines • Formula One

formulate VERB formulates, formulating, formulated express an idea or plan clearly and exactly
▷ **formulation** NOUN

fort NOUN forts a fortified building

forth ADVERB **1** out; into view **2** onward or forward • from this day forth
and so forth and so on

forthcoming ADJECTIVE **1** happening soon • forthcoming events **2** made available when

Thesaurus

form NOUN **1** a form of blackmail ► kind, type, sort, class, order, variety **2** the human form ► body, frame, shape, figure, build **3** They wanted to know the correct form for these occasions. ► etiquette, custom, protocol, usage, procedure, convention **4** There is a form to fill in. ► document, questionnaire, sheet **5** Her son moved into a new form at school. ► class, year, grade, set, group, stream **6** The form of the landscape has hardly changed for centuries. ► appearance, shape, formation, configuration, structure, outline, silhouette **7** He exercised hard to get into good form. ► condition, shape, health, fettle, fitness

form VERB **1** We must form a plan. ► devise, formulate, develop, prepare, draw up, put together, work out, conceive **2** The pots were formed from clay. ► make, fashion, shape, model **3** The decided to form a club. ► set up, establish, found, launch, institute, begin **4** Ice was forming on the windows. ► materialize, appear, take shape, develop, emerge, grow **5** Six players form a team. ► make up, constitute, compose, comprise

formal ADJECTIVE **1** a formal manner ► aloof, prim, staid, stiff, starchy, punctilious **2** a formal occasion ► solemn, official, ceremonious, conventional, dignified **3** a formal education ► prescribed, conventional, institutional

formality NOUN **1** He behaved towards her with greater formality. ► aloofness, remoteness, staidness, correctness, decorum, ceremony **2** formalities Certain formalities have to be observed. ► procedures, conventions, rules, customs, protocol

former ADJECTIVE **1** She met her former husband in town. ► ex-, past, one-time, previous, late **2** The fields were a lake in former times. ► earlier, past, bygone, ancient

formerly ADVERB The work had formerly been done by volunteers. ► previously, in the past, at one time, once, earlier, hitherto

formula NOUN **1** a legal formula ► form of words, phrase, rubric **2** a formula for success ► recipe, prescription, blueprint, procedure, method, rule, way

formulate VERB The party formulated a ten-point program. ► form, devise, develop, prepare, draw up, put together, work out, conceive

fort NOUN A small army was left to defend the fort. ► fortress, fortification, stronghold, castle, citadel, tower

forthcoming ADJECTIVE **1** He would be a candidate in the forthcoming election. ► imminent, impending, approaching, coming, future, next **2** She is not always particularly forthcoming. ► communicative, talkative, expansive, informative, voluble, chatty, sociable AN OPPOSITE IS uncommunicative **3** No reply was forthcoming.

needed • *Money for the trip was not forthcoming.*
3 willing to give information

forthright ADJECTIVE frank and outspoken

fortification NOUN **fortifications 1** fortifying something **2** a wall or building constructed to make a place strong against attack

fortify VERB **fortifies, fortifying, fortified 1** make a place strong against attack, especially by building fortifications **2** strengthen

fortnight NOUN **fortnights** a period of two weeks
▷ **fortnightly** ADVERB, ADJECTIVE

fortress NOUN **fortresses** a fortified building or town

fortunate ADJECTIVE lucky
▷ **fortunately** ADVERB

fortune NOUN **fortunes 1** luck, especially good luck **2** a great amount of money
tell someone's fortune predict what will happen to them in the future

forty ADJECTIVE, NOUN **forties** the number 40
▷ **fortieth** ADJECTIVE, NOUN
forty winks a short sleep; a nap

forward ADJECTIVE **1** going forward **2** placed in the front **3** having made more than the

normal progress **4** too eager or bold
▷ **forwardness** NOUN

forward ADVERB forwards

forward NOUN **forwards** a player in the front line of a team in football, hockey, etc.

forwards ADVERB **1** to or toward the front **2** in the direction you are facing

fossil NOUN **fossils** the remains or traces of a prehistoric animal or plant that has been buried in the ground for a very long time and become hardened in rock
▷ **fossilized** ADJECTIVE

fossil fuel NOUN **fossil fuels** a natural fuel such as coal or gas formed in the geological past

foster VERB **fosters, fostering, fostered 1** bring up someone else's child as if he or she was your own **2** help to grow or develop
▷ **foster child** NOUN **foster parent** NOUN

foul ADJECTIVE **1** disgusting; tasting or smelling unpleasant **2** (said about weather) rough; stormy **3** unfair; breaking the rules of a game **4** very disagreeable or unpleasant • *a foul mood*
▷ **foully** ADVERB **foulness** NOUN

foul NOUN **fouls** an action that breaks the rules of a game

Thesaurus

▶ available, ready, on offer, at hand AN OPPOSITE IS unavailable

fortify VERB **1** *The knights fortified the citadel.* ▶ strengthen, reinforce, secure, defend, protect, garrison **2** *She fortified herself with a strong drink.* ▶ strengthen, support, sustain, invigorate, hearten, reassure, encourage, boost, cheer OPPOSITES ARE weaken, subdue

fortuitous ADJECTIVE *It was fortuitous that they arrived on the same day.* ▶ accidental, coincidental, unintentional, chance

fortunate ADJECTIVE **1** *He was fortunate not to be shown a red card.* ▶ lucky, favored **2** *These events provided them with a fortunate opportunity.* ▶ favorable, advantageous, auspicious, providential, welcome, happy, lucky

fortune NOUN **1** *a major change of fortune* ▶ fate, destiny, luck **2** *By good fortune he was able to take up the offer.* ▶ chance, luck, accident, providence **3** *She decided she would leave her fortune to charity.* ▶ wealth, riches, property, possessions, (*more informal*) pile

fortune-teller NOUN *He had the solemn voice of a fortune-teller.* ▶ clairvoyant, crystal-gazer, soothsayer, palmist, prophet

forward ADJECTIVE **1** *The animal's long legs enable a fast forward movement.* ▶ onward, advancing, frontal, front, leading, progressive AN OPPOSITE IS backward **2** *forward planning*

▶ advance, future, early, prospective, forward-looking AN OPPOSITE IS retrospective. **3** *His manner on the phone had been a little too forward.* ▶ bold, brazen, barefaced, brash, audacious, daring, presumptuous, familiar, uninhibited, precocious, assertive, over-confident, cheeky, (*more informal*) fresh, (*more informal*) pushy OPPOSITES ARE shy, diffident

forward VERB **1** *Will you forward my letter?* ▶ send on, redirect **2** *The goods are forwarded by air.* ▶ dispatch, send, transport, transmit, convey, carry **3** *I will try to forward my plans during my visit.* ▶ advance, progress, develop, expedite, promote

forward or **forwards** ADVERB *The car shot forward.* ▶ ahead, in front, onward

foster VERB **1** *activities that foster good health* ▶ encourage, promote, cultivate, stimulate, nurture, advance, further **2** *The couple had fostered several children.* ▶ bring up, rear, raise, care for, take care of, look after, nurture, parent, mother USAGE You can also use *adopt*, but it has a special legal meaning.

foul ADJECTIVE **1** *You can recognize the animal from its foul smell.* ▶ nasty, horrible, unpleasant, disgusting, revolting, repulsive, repellent, dreadful, terrible, vile AN OPPOSITE IS pleasant **2** *There was a foul mess on the floor.* ▶ dirty, filthy, unclean, nasty, mucky AN OPPOSITE IS clean **3** *He had committed a foul crime.* ▶ wicked, evil, vile, contemptible, despicable,

a b c d e f g h i j k l m n o p q r s t u v w x y z

A
B
C
D
E
F
G
H
I
J
K
L
M
N
O
P
Q
R
S
T
U
V
W
X
Y
Z

foul VERB **fouls, fouling, fouled 1** make or become foul ● *Smoke had fouled the air* **2** commit a foul against a player in a game

found[1] *past tense of* find

found VERB **founds, founding, founded 1** establish; provide money for starting ● *They founded a hospital* **2** base ● *This novel is founded on fact*

foundation NOUN **foundations 1** the solid base on which a building is built up **2** the basis for something **3** the founding of something **4** a fund of money set aside for a charitable purpose
▷ **foundation stone** NOUN

founder[1] NOUN **founders** a person who founds something ● *the founder of the hospital*

founder[2] VERB **founders, foundering, foundered 1** fill with water and sink ● *The ship foundered* **2** stumble or fall **3** fail completely ● *Their plans foundered*

fountain NOUN **fountains** an ornamental structure in which a jet of water shoots up into the air

four ADJECTIVE, NOUN **fours** the number 4
on all fours on hands and knees

fourteen ADJECTIVE, NOUN the number 14
▷ **fourteenth** ADJECTIVE, NOUN

fourth ADJECTIVE next after the third
▷ **fourthly** ADVERB

fourth NOUN **fourths 1** the fourth person or thing **2** one of four equal parts; a quarter

fowl NOUN **fowls** a bird, especially one kept on a farm etc. for its eggs or meat

fox NOUN **foxes** a wild animal that looks like a dog with a long furry tail
▷ **foxy** ADJECTIVE

fraction NOUN **fractions 1** a number that is not a whole number, e.g., ½, 0.5 **2** a tiny part
▷ **fractional** ADJECTIVE **fractionally** ADVERB

fracture NOUN **fractures** the breaking of something, especially of a bone

fracture VERB **fractures, fracturing, fractured** break

fragile ADJECTIVE easy to break or damage
▷ **fragility** NOUN

fragment NOUN **fragments 1** a small piece broken off **2** a small part
▷ **fragmentary** ADJECTIVE **fragmentation** NOUN **fragmented** ADJECTIVE

Thesaurus

obnoxious, shameful, abhorrent, repellent, loathsome AN OPPOSITE IS pleasant **4** *She had been subjected to taunts and foul language.* ► obscene, indecent, coarse, vulgar, offensive, crude, lewd AN OPPOSITE IS mild **5** *The game was spoiled by a series of foul tackles.* ► illegal, unfair, prohibited OPPOSITES ARE legal, fair **6** *The weather was foul all day.* ► unpleasant, bad, vile, disagreeable, inclement AN OPPOSITE IS fine **7** *He apologized for having been so foul to her.* ► unkind, unfriendly, unpleasant, disagreeable, bad-tempered OPPOSITES ARE kind, friendly

foul VERB **1** *Chemical waste was fouling the water.* ► pollute, contaminate, dirty, soil, sully, stain **2** *Silt was fouling the river mouth.* ► clog, choke, block, obstruct, stop up **3** *The ship had fouled its own nets.* ► entangle, snarl, catch, ensnare, twist

found VERB **1** *He founded the business in the 1880s.* ► establish, set up, start, create, begin, institute, inaugurate, initiate, organize, endow, fund **2** *Democracy is founded on the principle of free speech.* ► base, build, ground, construct, erect

foundation NOUN **1** *the foundation of the company in the eighteenth century* ► founding, establishment, institution, inauguration, initiation, setting up, starting, beginning **2** *There was no foundation for the claim.* ► basis, grounds, reason, justification, rationale **3** **foundations** *The building had weak foundations.* ► base, substructure, footing, underpinning, basis, bottom, cornerstone,

bedrock **4** **foundations** *the foundations of the subject* ► fundamentals, rudiments, basic principles, elements, essentials, origins

founder NOUN *His grandfather had been the founder of the college.* ► originator, creator, initiator, benefactor

founder VERB *The scheme foundered for lack of money.* ► fail, collapse, miscarry, come to grief, come to nothing, (*more informal*) fold

fountain NOUN *The fountains are switched off in the cold months.* ► jet, spout, spray, spring, fount

fox VERB *The question completely foxed them.* ► baffle, confuse, perplex, bemuse, disconcert, confound, (*more informal*) flummox, (*more informal*) floor

fragile ADJECTIVE **1** *She put away her fragile china.* ► breakable, brittle, delicate, weak, easily damaged AN OPPOSITE IS strong **2** *The fragile ceasefire was barely holding.* ► precarious, tenuous, insecure, flimsy, vulnerable, (*more informal*) dodgy

fragment NOUN (with the stress on *frag-*) *Fragments of broken pottery lay around.* ► piece, bit, particle, chip, sliver, scrap, shiver, shred, remnant, snippet, speck, atom, crumb, part

fragment VERB (with the stress on *-ment*) *The impact made the glass fragment.* ► break, shatter, splinter, split, disintegrate, shiver, crumble, come to pieces

fragmentary ADJECTIVE *They couldn't tell much from the fragmentary information available.* ► scrappy, incomplete, piecemeal, partial,

fragrant ADJECTIVE having a pleasant smell
▷ **fragrance** NOUN

frail ADJECTIVE **1** (said about people) not strong or healthy • *a frail old man* **2** (said about things) fragile
▷ **frailty** NOUN

frame NOUN **frames 1** a holder that fits around the outside of a picture **2** a rigid structure that supports something **3** a human or animal body • *He has a small frame.* **4** a single exposure on a cinema film
frame of mind the way you think or feel for a while

frame VERB **frames, framing, framed 1** put a frame on or around **2** construct or form • *They framed the question badly.* **3** make an innocent person seem guilty by arranging false evidence

framework NOUN **frameworks 1** a frame supporting something **2** a basic plan or system

franc NOUN **francs** a unit of money used in many countries and replaced in some by the euro in 2002

frank ADJECTIVE making your thoughts and feelings clear to people; candid
▷ **frankly** ADVERB **frankness** NOUN

frantic ADJECTIVE wildly agitated or excited
▷ **frantically** ADVERB

fraud NOUN **frauds 1** the crime of swindling people **2** a dishonest trick **3** an impostor; a person or thing that is not what he, she, or it pretends to be
▷ **fraudulent** ADJECTIVE **fraudulently** ADVERB **fraudulence** NOUN

fray NOUN **frays** a fight or conflict • *ready for the fray*

fray VERB **frays, fraying, frayed 1** make or become ragged so that loose threads show **2** (said about tempers or nerves) become strained or upset

freak NOUN **freaks** a very strange or abnormal person, animal, or thing
▷ **freakish** ADJECTIVE

freckle NOUN **freckles** a small brown spot on the skin
▷ **freckled** ADJECTIVE
[from Old Norse]

free ADJECTIVE **freer, freest 1** able to do what you want to do or go where you want to go

Thesaurus

disconnected, disjointed, bitty USAGE Be careful when you use *partial*, because it has other meanings.
frame NOUN **1** *The vehicle has a strong lightweight frame.* ► framework, shell, skeleton, chassis, structure, construction, bodywork **2** *a portrait in a gilt frame* ► surround, mount, mounting, border, setting, edging
frame VERB **1** *The artists frame their own pictures.* ► mount, surround, encase, set **2** *The lawyers will frame the proposals.* ► compose, formulate, draw up, plan
frank ADJECTIVE *At least he is frank about his opinions.* ► honest, candid, sincere, genuine, direct, open, forthright, ingenuous, straightforward, straight, truthful, unequivocal OPPOSITES ARE insincere, disingenuous
frantic ADJECTIVE **1** *Her parents were frantic about her safety.* ► anxious, agitated, worried, distraught, fraught, overwrought, (*more informal*) beside yourself OPPOSITES ARE calm, composed **2** *There were frantic attempts to locate the luggage.* ► hectic, feverish, frenzied, wild AN OPPOSITE IS calm
fraud NOUN **1** *He was accused of fraud.* ► fraudulence, swindling, cheating, sharp practice, deceit, deception **2** *The offer turned out to be a fraud.* ► swindle, deception, trick, hoax, sham **3** *They exposed him as a fraud.* ► impostor, charlatan, cheat, trickster, (*more informal*) phoney

fraudulent ADJECTIVE *fraudulent dealings on the stock exchange* ► dishonest, illegal, unlawful, illicit, corrupt, criminal, bogus, (*more informal*) crooked AN OPPOSITE IS honest
fraught ADJECTIVE *By the end of the day she looked tired and fraught.* ► anxious, apprehensive, agitated, tense, worried, concerned, nervous, fearful, uneasy, troubled, distressed AN OPPOSITE IS calm
freak ADJECTIVE *The south of the country was battered by freak storms.* ► unusual, exceptional, abnormal, untypical, anomalous, unpredictable, extraordinary AN OPPOSITE IS normal
freak NOUN **1** *The animal is a genetically engineered freak.* ► oddity, aberration, abnormality, irregularity, anomaly, quirk, monster, monstrosity, mutant, malformation **2** (*informal*) *a weight-training freak* ► fanatic, devotee, enthusiast, admirer, lover, fan, addict, aficionado
free ADJECTIVE **1** *Tickets to the concert are free.* ► without charge, free of charge, gratis, complimentary, gratuitous, on the house AN OPPOSITE IS to be paid for **2** *The people longed to be free.* ► independent, self-governing, autonomous, emancipated OPPOSITES ARE subjugated, dependent **3** *The wanted man is still free.* ► at liberty, on the loose, at large, unrestrained AN OPPOSITE IS captive **4** *We don't have much free time.* ► spare, available, idle, unused **5** *The bathroom is free now.* ► vacant, unoccupied, empty, available, not in

A
B
C
D
E
F
G
H
I
J
K
L
M
N
O
P
Q
R
S
T
U
V
W
X
Y
Z

2 not costing anything **3** not fixed • *Leave one end free.* **4** not having or being affected by something • *The harbor is free of ice.* **5** available; not being used or occupied **6** generous • *She is very free with her money.*
▷ **freely** ADVERB

free VERB **frees, freeing, freed** set free

freedom NOUN **freedoms** being free; independence

freehand ADJECTIVE (said about a drawing) done without a ruler or compasses, or without tracing it • *Draw a circle freehand.*

free-range ADJECTIVE **1** free-range hens are not kept in small cages but are allowed to move about freely **2** free-range eggs are ones laid by these hens

freewheel VERB **freewheels, freewheeling, freewheeled** ride a bicycle without pedalling

freeze VERB **freezes, freezing, froze, frozen** **1** turn into ice; become covered with ice **2** make or be very cold **3** keep wages or prices etc. at a fixed level **4** suddenly stand completely still

freezer NOUN **freezers** a refrigerator in which food can be frozen quickly and stored

freezing point NOUN **freezing points** the temperature at which a liquid freezes

French window NOUN **French windows** a long window that serves as a door on an outside wall

frenzy NOUN wild excitement or agitation
▷ **frenzied** ADJECTIVE **frenziedly** ADVERB

frequency NOUN **frequencies** **1** being frequent **2** how often something happens **3** the number of vibrations made each second by a wave of sound, radio, or light

frequent (freek- went) ADJECTIVE happening often
▷ **frequently** ADVERB

frequent (frik- went) VERB **frequents, frequenting, frequented** be in or go to a place often • *They frequented the club*

fresh ADJECTIVE **1** newly made or produced or arrived; not stale • *fresh bread* **2** not tinned or preserved • *fresh fruit* **3** cool and clean • *fresh air* **4** (said about water) not salty
▷ **freshly** ADVERB **freshness** NOUN

Thesaurus

---

use OPPOSITES ARE occupied, engaged **6** *She is very free with her money.* ► generous, lavish, liberal, unstinting, bounteous OPPOSITES ARE mean, tight **7** *Are you free on Friday?* ► available, unoccupied, able to come AN OPPOSITE IS busy **8** *They are free to choose.* ► able, allowed, permitted, in a position, at leisure AN OPPOSITE IS unable **9** *free of We are free of any commitments now.* ► relieved of, unaffected by, unencumbered by, unhindered by, lacking, without AN OPPOSITE IS encumbered by **10** *the free movement of people and goods* ► unrestricted, unimpeded, unobstructed, unhindered, unlimited, clear, open AN OPPOSITE IS obstructed

free VERB **1** *The new government freed all political prisoners.* ► release, liberate, set free, set at liberty, let loose, set loose, turn loose, deliver OPPOSITES ARE confine, lock up **2** *The jury freed all three accused.* ► acquit, clear, exonerate, absolve, discharge, pardon AN OPPOSITE IS condemn **3** *Firefighters managed to free the trapped victims.* ► rescue, release, extricate, remove, pull out, pull free **4** *She struggled hard to free her hand.* ► clear, loose, extricate, disentangle, disengage, untie, untangle AN OPPOSITE IS tangle

freedom NOUN **1** *The prisoners longed for their freedom.* ► liberty, liberation, release, deliverance OPPOSITES ARE captivity, confinement **2** *Only a revolution would give the country its freedom.* ► independence, self-government, self-determination AN OPPOSITE IS dependence **3** *Parents should have the freedom*

to choose the education for their children. ► ability, opportunity, chance, facility, power, licence, scope, leeway AN OPPOSITE IS restriction

freely ADVERB *He found it hard to talk freely.* ► openly, candidly, frankly, plainly, honestly

freeze VERB **1** *In winter the river freezes.* ► ice over, become ice, become solid, solidify, harden **2** *We had no fire and were beginning to freeze.* ► feel cold, go numb with cold **3** *If you have too much fruit you can freeze it.* ► deep-freeze, dry-freeze, refrigerate, chill, preserve **4** *a government plan to freeze prices* ► fix, peg, hold, curb, limit, keep as they are

freight NOUN **1** *a mixture of passenger and freight services* ► cargo, goods, merchandise **2** *Air freight charges are extremely high.* ► transportation, shipment, carriage, conveyance

frenzy NOUN **1** *The audience was in a state of frenzy.* ► hysteria, fever, delirium, turmoil, agitation, mania, derangement **2** *a frenzy of anger* ► fit, spasm, outburst, paroxysm, ferment

frequent ADJECTIVE **1** *An airport bus leaves at frequent intervals.* ► regular, numerous, repeated, constant, recurring, continual **2** *Claire is a frequent visitor here.* ► habitual, constant, regular, common

fresh ADJECTIVE **1** *Good eating habits include fresh fruit and vegetables.* ► natural, raw **2** *The party needs new members and fresh ideas.* ► new, original, innovative, novel, recent, up-to-date **3** *The army has a batch of fresh recruits.* ► young, youthful, inexperienced, callow

freshen VERB freshens, freshening, freshened make or become fresh

fret VERB frets, fretting, fretted worry about something
▷ **fretful** ADJECTIVE **fretfully** ADVERB

fret NOUN frets a bar or ridge on the fingerboard of a guitar etc.

friar NOUN friars a man who is a member of a Roman Catholic religious order and has vowed to live a life of poverty
▷ **friary** NOUN

friction NOUN **1** rubbing of one thing against another **2** bad feeling between people; quarrelling
▷ **frictional** ADJECTIVE

Friday NOUN the day of the week following Thursday [from Old English *Frigedaeg* = day of Frigga, a Norse goddess]

fridge NOUN fridges a refrigerator

friend NOUN friends **1** a person you like who likes you **2** a helpful or kind person

friendly ADJECTIVE friendlier, friendliest behaving like a friend
▷ **friendliness** NOUN

friendship NOUN friendships being friends

frieze (freez) NOUN friezes a strip of designs or pictures around the top of a wall

fright NOUN frights **1** sudden great fear **2** a person or thing that looks ridiculous

frighten VERB frightens, frightening, frightened make someone afraid
be frightened of be afraid of

frightful ADJECTIVE awful; very great or bad
▷ **frightfully** ADVERB

frill NOUN frills **1** a decorative gathered or pleated trimming on a dress, curtain, etc. **2** something extra that is pleasant but unnecessary • *a simple life with no frills*
▷ **frilled** ADJECTIVE **frilly** ADJECTIVE

fringe NOUN fringes **1** a decorative edging with many threads hanging down loosely **2** a straight line of hair hanging down over the forehead **3** the edge of something
▷ **fringed** ADJECTIVE

frisk VERB frisks, frisking, frisked **1** jump or run about playfully **2** search somebody by running your hands over his or her clothes

frisky ADJECTIVE playful or lively
▷ **friskily** ADVERB **friskiness** NOUN

Thesaurus

4 *Next day was fresh and bright.* ► cool, crisp, refreshing, clear **5** *She was feeling fresh after her shower.* ► refreshed, rested, restored, revived, invigorated **6** *They walked out to a fresh wind.* ► cold, brisk, bracing, invigorating **7** *He told him not to get fresh.* ► impudent, impertinent, insolent, cheeky, saucy, familiar, disrespectful, forward

friend NOUN *He can stay with a friend while his parents are away.* ► acquaintance, companion, associate, (*more informal*) mate, (*more informal*) pal, (*more informal*) buddy, (*more informal*) chum

friendliness NOUN *They liked him for his friendliness and humor.* ► kindness, sociability, goodwill, hospitality, warmth

friendly ADJECTIVE **1** *The staff are very friendly and helpful.* ► pleasant, agreeable, kind, amiable, kindly, kind-hearted, well disposed, likeable, genial, congenial, sympathetic, approachable, receptive, sociable, outgoing **2** *Volunteers are on hand to give friendly advice. The hotel is small with a friendly atmosphere.* ► cordial, good-natured, sympathetic, amicable, warm, welcoming **3** *The girls had been friendly since their childhood.* ► close, affectionate, intimate, familiar, (*more informal*) chummy, (*more informal*) pally, (*more informal*) matey

friendship NOUN **1** *He thanked his colleagues for their friendship and support.* ► friendliness, affection, goodwill, comradeship, cordiality OPPOSITES ARE hostility, enmity **2** *Their friendship grew over the coming months.* ► relationship, affection, intimacy, closeness, love, attachment

fright NOUN **1** *The blast gave everyone a fright.* ► scare, shock, surprise, start, turn, jolt **2** *Amy was overcome by fright.* ► fear, alarm, terror, trepidation, consternation, horror, dismay, dread, panic

frighten VERB *The noises outside began to frighten them.* ► scare, startle, alarm, terrify, shock, agitate, disturb, fluster, panic, intimidate, disconcert AN OPPOSITE IS reassure

frightened ADJECTIVE *The children were tired and frightened.* ► scared, afraid, alarmed, terrified, petrified, fearful, shaken, shocked, panicky

frightening ADJECTIVE *a frightening experience* ► terrifying, alarming, fearsome, daunting, (*more informal*) scary

frightful ADJECTIVE **1** *We had to eat frightful food.* ► awful, terrible, dreadful, ghastly, appalling, horrible **2** *a scene of frightful devastation* ► shocking, horrible, terrible, gruesome, harrowing, hideous, grisly, horrid, macabre

frigid ADJECTIVE **1** *the frigid northern climate* ► bitter, bitterly cold, freezing, frozen, icy, arctic **2** *Leo glared back in frigid indignation.* ► stiff, stony, formal, unfeeling, austere, distant, aloof

frill NOUN **1** *a skirt with deep frills* ► fringe, ruff, ruffle, flounce **2** *a small hotel with no frills* ► extra, luxury, embellishment, extravagance

fringe NOUN **1** *a fringe around the edge of a curtain* ► border, edging, flounce, frill, gathering, trimming, valance **2** *on the fringe of the town* ► edge, outskirts, limits, periphery, perimeter, borders, margin AN OPPOSITE IS center

A
B
C
D
E
F
G
H
I
J
K
L
M
N
O
P
Q
R
S
T
U
V
W
X
Y
Z

fritter NOUN fritters a slice of meat or fruit or potato, etc., coated in batter and fried

fritter VERB fritters, frittering, frittered waste something gradually; spend money or time on trivial things

frivolous ADJECTIVE seeking pleasure in a light-hearted way; not serious
▷ **frivolously** ADVERB **frivolity** NOUN

frizzy ADJECTIVE (said about hair) in tight curls
▷ **frizziness** NOUN

fro ADVERB
to and fro backwards and forwards

frock NOUN frocks a girl's or woman's dress

frog NOUN frogs a small jumping animal that can live both in water and on land
a frog in your throat hoarseness

frolic NOUN frolics a lively cheerful game or entertainment
▷ **frolicsome** ADJECTIVE

frolic VERB frolics, frolicking, frolicked play about in a lively cheerful way

from PREPOSITION This word is used to show **1** starting point in space or time or order (*We flew from London to Paris; we work from 9 to 5 o'clock; count from one to ten.*), **2** source or origin (*Get water from the tap*), **3** separation or release (*Take the gun from him; she was freed from prison.*), **4** difference (*Can you tell margarine from butter?*), **5** cause (*I suffer from headaches.*).

frond NOUN fronds a leaflike part of a fern, palm tree, etc.

front NOUN fronts **1** the part or side that comes first or is the most important or furthest forward **2** a road or promenade along the seashore **3** the place where fighting is happening in a war **4** (in weather systems) the forward edge of an approaching mass of air
▷ **frontal** ADJECTIVE

front ADJECTIVE of the front; in front

frontier NOUN frontiers the boundary between two countries or regions

frontispiece NOUN frontispieces an illustration opposite the title page of a book

frost NOUN frosts **1** powdery ice that forms on things in freezing weather **2** weather with a temperature below freezing point

frosted ADJECTIVE covered with frost

frostbite NOUN harm done to the body by very cold weather
▷ **frostbitten** ADJECTIVE

frosty ADJECTIVE frostier, frostiest **1** cold with frost **2** unfriendly and unwelcoming • *a frosty look*
▷ **frostily** ADVERB

froth NOUN a white mass of tiny bubbles on a liquid
▷ **frothy** ADJECTIVE

frown VERB frowns, frowning, frowned wrinkle your forehead because you are angry or worried

frown NOUN frowns a frowning movement or look

Thesaurus

fritter VERB *He frittered away all the money he had been given.* ► squander, waste, misspend, dissipate, get through

frivolous ADJECTIVE *They often made frivolous comments.* ► flippant, facetious, trivial, trifling, silly, shallow, stupid, foolish, jocular, flighty, ridiculous, superficial, unimportant, vacuous AN OPPOSITE IS serious

frock NOUN *a red cotton frock* ► dress, gown, shift, robe

frolic VERB *Lambs frolicked in the fields.* ► play, cavort, frisk, caper, leap, jump, sport, spring, bounce, gambol, skip, bound

front NOUN **1** *the front of the house* ► façade, facing, exterior AN OPPOSITE IS back **2** *the front of a boat* ► prow, bow, forepart OPPOSITES ARE back, stern **3** *the front of a car* ► nose, forepart AN OPPOSITE IS rear **4** *the front of the queue* ► head, start, beginning, lead OPPOSITES ARE back, end **5** *Young recruits were sent to the front.* ► front line, battle line, combat zone **6** *He managed to keep up a brave front.* ► appearance, manner, show, pose, bearing

front ADJECTIVE *The front runners came into view.* ► first, leading, foremost, most advanced AN OPPOSITE IS back

frosty ADJECTIVE **1** *a frosty autumn morning* ► freezing, bitter, ice-cold, crisp **2** *I'm afraid we'll get a frosty reception.* ► unfriendly, unwelcoming, unsympathetic, cool, stony

froth NOUN **1** *Claude wiped the champagne froth from his moustache.* ► foam, bubbles, effervescence, head **2** *He shook his hand in the water to make a froth.* ► lather, suds, foam

frown VERB *The woman frowned at them.* ► scowl, glower, glare, grimace, knit your brow, look sullen, (*more informal*) give a dirty look
frown on *They frown on bad language.* ► disapprove of, view with disfavor, look askance at, object to, disfavor, dislike, discourage

frozen ADJECTIVE **1** *The lake is frozen.* ► iced over, ice-covered, ice-bound, solidified **2** *She felt frozen in the keen wind.* ► freezing, very cold, numbed

fruit ➡ fumble

fruit NOUN fruits for fruit **1** the seed container that grows on a tree or plant and is often used as food **2** the result of doing something • *the fruits of his efforts*
▷ **fruity** ADJECTIVE

fruit VERB fruits, fruiting, fruited produce fruit

fruitful ADJECTIVE producing good results • *fruitful discussions*
▷ **fruitfully** ADVERB

fruitless ADJECTIVE producing no results
▷ **fruitlessly** ADVERB

frustrate VERB frustrates, frustrating, frustrated prevent somebody from doing something; prevent something from being successful • *A lack of money has frustrated our plans.*
▷ **frustration** NOUN

fry VERB fries, frying, fried cook something in very hot fat
▷ **fryer** NOUN

fudge NOUN a soft sugary sweet

fuel NOUN fuels something that is burnt to produce heat or power

fuel VERB fuels, fueling, fueled supply something with fuel

fugitive (few- jit- iv) NOUN fugitives a person who is running away from something

fulcrum NOUN fulcrums or fulcra the point on which a lever rests

fulfill VERB fulfills, fulfilling, fulfilled **1** do what is required; satisfy; carry out • *You must fulfill your promises* **2** make something come true • *It fulfilled an ancient prophecy.* **3** give you satisfaction
▷ **fulfillment** NOUN

full ADJECTIVE **1** containing as much or as many as possible **2** having many people or things • *full of ideas* **3** complete **4** the greatest possible • *at full speed* **5** fitting loosely; with many folds • *a full skirt*
▷ **fully** ADVERB **fullness** NOUN
in full with nothing left out • *We have paid in full*

full ADVERB completely and directly • *It hit him full in the face.* [from Old English]

full-blown ADJECTIVE fully developed

full moon NOUN full moons the moon when you can see the whole of it as a bright disc

full stop NOUN full stops the dot used as a punctuation mark at the end of a sentence or an abbreviation

fully ADVERB completely

fumble VERB fumbles, fumbling, fumbled hold or handle something clumsily

Thesaurus

fruitful ADJECTIVE **1** *a fruitful crop* ► abundant, copious, productive, rich, prolific, fertile, plenteous, profuse AN OPPOSITE IS unproductive **2** *Talks have proved fruitful.* ► successful, productive, beneficial, profitable, useful, effective, worthwhile, gainful, rewarding AN OPPOSITE IS fruitless

fruitless ADJECTIVE *three days of fruitless negotiations* ► futile, vain, abortive, unsuccessful, unfruitful, unproductive, profitless, unavailing, pointless, useless, disappointing, unprofitable, unrewarding AN OPPOSITE IS fruitful

frustrate VERB **1** *The lack of progress was clearly frustrating them.* ► exasperate, discourage, dispirit, irritate OPPOSITES ARE satisfy, please **2** *Bad weather frustrated all attempts at a rescue.* ► thwart, foil, defeat, forestall, inhibit, prevent

fuel NOUN **1** *Vehicles were running out of fuel in the traffic jams.* ► petrol, propellant, diesel oil **2** *The inspectors' report added fuel to the war cause.* ► encouragement, provocation, incentive

fulfill VERB **1** *She was fulfilling her life's ambition of seeing the world.* ► achieve, realize, carry out, accomplish, succeed in, attain, effect, perform **2** *They have to work twelve hours a day to fulfill their obligations.* ► meet, complete, implement, execute, comply with, satisfy, respond to, answer, conform to OPPOSITES ARE fail in, neglect

full ADJECTIVE **1** *His glass was still full.* ► filled, loaded, topped up AN OPPOSITE IS empty **2** *The trains would be full on a Friday afternoon.* ► crowded, packed, crammed, congested, thronged, teeming, swarming, stuffed, mobbed, (more informal) jam-packed AN OPPOSITE IS empty **3** *By the end of the meal they were too full to talk.* ► well fed, satisfied, satiated, replete, sated, (more informal) bursting **4** *The bureau can give you a full list of local hotels and guest houses.* ► complete, comprehensive, exhaustive, thorough, copious **5** *The article did not tell the full story.* ► entire, complete, total, unabridged, unexpurgated **6** *She had led a full life and was looking forward to a period of quiet.* ► exciting, eventful, interesting, busy, lively, hectic **7** *The new piano had a full sound.* ► rich, resonant, sonorous, full-bodied, deep

fully ADVERB *We fully accept that there must be changes. I don't think you fully understand.* ► completely, entirely, wholly, totally, thoroughly, quite, altogether, positively, without reserve AN OPPOSITE IS partially

fumble VERB **1** *He fumbled for his wallet.* ► grope, feel about, fish, delve **2** *Without any light she could only fumble about.* ► stumble, blunder, flounder, lurch, stagger, totter **3** *Then, unfortunately, the quarterback fumbled the ball.* ► mishandle, miss, drop, fail to catch, fail to keep

A
B
C
D
E
F
G
H
I
J
K
L
M
N
O
P
Q
R
S
T
U
V
W
X
Y
Z

fume NOUN or **fumes** PLURAL NOUN strong-smelling smoke or gas

fume VERB fumes, fuming, fumed **1** give off fumes **2** be very angry

fumigate (few- mig- ayt) VERB fumigates, fumigating, fumigated disinfect something by fumes
▷ **fumigation** NOUN

fun NOUN amusement or enjoyment
make fun of make people laugh at a person or thing

function NOUN functions **1** what somebody or something is there to do • *The function of a knife is to cut things.* **2** an important event or party **3** a basic operation in a computer or calculator **4** a variable quantity whose value depends on the value of other variable quantities • *X is a function of Y and Z.*

function VERB functions, functioning, functioned perform a function; work properly

fund NOUN funds **1** money collected or kept for a special purpose **2** a stock or supply

fund VERB funds, funding, funded supply with money

fundamental ADJECTIVE basic
▷ **fundamentally** ADVERB

funeral NOUN funerals the ceremony when a dead person is buried or cremated

fungus NOUN fungi (fung- I) a plant without leaves or flowers that grows on other plants

or on decayed material, such as mushrooms and toadstools [from Latin]

funnel NOUN funnels **1** a metal chimney on a ship or steam engine **2** a tube that is wide at the top and narrow at the bottom to help you pour things into a narrow opening [from Latin *fundere* = pour]

funny ADJECTIVE funnier, funniest **1** making you laugh or smile **2** strange or odd • *a funny smell*
▷ **funnily** ADVERB

fur NOUN furs **1** the soft hair that covers some animals **2** animal skin with the fur on it, used for clothing; fabric that looks like animal fur

furious ADJECTIVE **1** very angry **2** violent or intense • *furious heat*
▷ **furiously** ADVERB

furnace NOUN furnaces a device in which great heat can be produced, e.g., for melting metals or making glass

furnish VERB furnishes, furnishing, furnished **1** provide a place with furniture **2** provide or supply with something

furniture NOUN tables, chairs, and other movable things that you need in a house or school or office

furrow NOUN furrows **1** a long cut in the ground made by a plow or other implement **2** a groove **3** a deep wrinkle in the skin

furry ADJECTIVE like fur; covered with fur

Thesaurus

fumes PLURAL NOUN *fumes from an old tractor*
► exhaust, smoke, gases, vapor, fog, pollution, smog

fuming ADJECTIVE *Dad was pacing back and forth, fuming.* ► angry, furious, enraged, seething, raging, incensed

fun NOUN *After their exams they just wanted some fun.* ► enjoyment, entertainment, amusement, recreation, diversion, distraction, relaxation, jollity, play

function NOUN **1** *The organization has several functions.* ► role, responsibility, obligation, purpose, concern, use, job, task **2** *I had seen him at an official function.* ► event, occasion, party, gathering, reception, dinner, (*more informal*) do

function VERB **1** *To stop the machine functioning, switch it off.* ► work, operate, run, perform **2** *function as an advice center.* ► act as, serve as, operate as, constitute, form, have the role of

fund NOUN **1** *an emergency fund for refugees*
► pool, kitty, Store, reserve, cache, source, supply **2** *funds Funds are running low.*
► money, cash, capital, finances, assets, reserves, savings

fund VERB *Private capital will help fund the railways.* ► pay for, finance, capitalize, sponsor, subsidize, back, endow, maintain

fundamental ADJECTIVE *fundamental political principles* ► basic, elementary, essential, primary, underlying, axiomatic, key, prime, principal, important, main, necessary
OPPOSITES ARE secondary, inessential

funny ADJECTIVE **1** *a funny story* ► amusing, humorous, comic, comical, witty, hilarious, facetious, droll, entertaining, silly, absurd, ridiculous AN OPPOSITE IS serious **2** *a funny coincidence* ► peculiar, strange, odd, curious, puzzling, queer, weird, bizarre

furious ADJECTIVE *She was furious when she found out.* ► angry, enraged, infuriated, incensed, fuming, annoyed, cross, displeased, irritated, irate, indignant, outraged OPPOSITES ARE pleased, calm

furnish VERB *They have furnished the rooms tastefully.* ► decorate, appoint, fit out, fit up, equip

furniture NOUN *After the fire they had to buy new furniture.* ► furnishings, fitments, fittings, effects, household goods, equipment, movables, possessions

further ADVERB, ADJECTIVE **1** at or to a greater distance; more distant **2** more; additional ● *We made further inquiries.*
USAGE See the note at **farther**.

further VERB furthers, furthering, furthered help something to progress ● *This success will further your career.*
▷ **furtherance** NOUN

further education NOUN education for people above school age

furthest ADVERB, ADJECTIVE at or to the greatest distance; most distant

fury NOUN furies wild anger; rage

fuse[1] NOUN fuses a safety device containing a short piece of wire that melts if too much electricity is passed through it

fuse VERB fuses, fusing, fused **1** stop working because a fuse has melted **2** blend together, especially through melting

fuse[2] NOUN fuses a length of material that burns easily, used for setting off an explosive

fusion NOUN **1** the action of blending or uniting things **2** the uniting of atomic nuclei, usually releasing energy

fuss NOUN fusses **1** unnecessary excitement or bustle **2** an agitated protest
make a fuss of treat someone with great kindness and attention

fuss VERB fusses, fussing, fussed make a fuss about something

fussy ADJECTIVE fussier, fussiest **1** fussing; inclined to make a fuss **2** choosing very carefully; hard to please **3** full of unnecessary details or decorations
▷ **fussily** ADVERB **fussiness** NOUN

future NOUN **1** the time that will come; what is going to happen then **2** (in grammar) the tense of a verb that indicates something happening in the future, expressed by using "shall," "will," or "be going to"

future ADJECTIVE belonging or referring to the future

fuzz NOUN something fluffy or frizzy

fuzzy ADJECTIVE **1** like fuzz; covered with fuzz **2** blurred; not clear
▷ **fuzzily** ADVERB **fuzziness** NOUN

Thesaurus

---

further ADJECTIVE *We need further information* ► more, additional, extra, fresh, new, supplementary

fury NOUN **1** *She could not hide her fury.* ► anger, rage, wrath, passion **2** *The storm hit the town with immense fury.* ► force, ferocity, fierceness, violence, turbulence, severity, savagery

fuss NOUN **1** *There was a lot of fuss about the missing money.* ► commotion, agitation, excitement, confusion, upset, worry **2** *He wanted to get the job done with as little fuss as possible.* ► bother, trouble, difficulty, inconvenience, effort, (more informal) hassle

fuss VERB *He begged her not to fuss.* ► fret, worry, get worked up, agitate, bother, complain, (more informal) flap

fussy ADJECTIVE **1** *They are both fussy about their food.* ► finicky, fastidious, particular, choosy, (more informal) picky **2** *The menu is a little fussy and over-rich.* ► fancy, elaborate, ornate, florid, detailed

futile ADJECTIVE *In the end the rebels abandoned the futile struggle.* ► fruitless, pointless, vain, ineffectual, unsuccessful, useless, abortive, unavailing, unproductive, barren AN OPPOSITE IS fruitful

future NOUN **1** *There is a bright future for them.* ► outlook, prospects, expectations, destiny **2** *our plans for the future* ► time to come, time ahead AN OPPOSITE IS past

future ADJECTIVE *Future generations may find themselves living on a warmer planet.* ► later, following, coming, succeeding, subsequent, prospective, approaching, forthcoming, impending AN OPPOSITE IS past

fuzzy ADJECTIVE **1** *The baby had a large fuzzy head.* ► downy, frizzy, fluffy, woolly, fleecy, velvety, feathery **2** *good sound but a fuzzy picture* ► blurred, bleary, unfocused, ill-defined, indistinct, vague, hazy, shadowy, unclear, cloudy, dim, faint, misty OPPOSITES ARE clear, sharp

a
b
c
d
e
f
g
h
i
j
k
l
m
n
o
p
q
r
s
t
u
v
w
x
y
z

A
B
C
D
E
F
G
H
I
J
K
L
M
N
O
P
Q
R
S
T
U
V
W
X
Y
Z

Gg

gabble VERB gabbles, gabbling, gabbled talk so quickly that it is difficult to know what is being said

gadget NOUN gadgets any small useful tool
▷ **gadgetry** NOUN
[probably from French *gâchette*, = lock mechanism]

Gaelic (gay- lik) NOUN the Celtic languages of Scotland and Ireland

gag NOUN gags 1 something put into a person's mouth or tied over it to prevent them from speaking 2 a joke

gag VERB gags, gagging, gagged 1 put a gag on a person 2 prevent someone from making comments • *We cannot gag the press* 3 retch

gaggle NOUN gaggles a flock of geese

gaiety NOUN 1 cheerfulness 2 brightly colored appearance

gaily ADVERB in a cheerful way

gain VERB gains, gaining, gained 1 get something that you did not have before; obtain 2 a clock or watch gains when it becomes ahead of the correct time 3 reach; arrive at • *At last we gained the shore*
gain on come closer to a person or thing when chasing them or in a race

gain NOUN gains something gained; a profit or improvement
▷ **gainful** ADJECTIVE

galaxy NOUN galaxies a very large group of stars
▷ **galactic** (ga- lak- tik) ADJECTIVE

gale NOUN gales a very strong wind

gallant (gal- lant) ADJECTIVE 1 brave or heroic • *a gallant effort* 2 (gal- lant, ga- lant) courteous towards women
▷ **gallantly** ADVERB **gallantry** NOUN

gallery NOUN galleries 1 a room or building for showing works of art 2 a platform jutting out from the wall in a church or hall 3 the highest balcony in a theater 4 a long room or passage

gallon NOUN gallons a unit used to measure liquids, 8 pints or 4.546 liters

Thesaurus

gadget NOUN *a kitchen full of gadgets* ► tool, utensil, appliance, contraption, contrivance, device, implement, machine, invention, instrument

gaffe NOUN *Anne was taking a day off trying to forget her gaffe.* ► mistake, blunder, error, slip, indiscretion

gag NOUN *His latest gag was quite funny for a change.* ► joke, jest, quip, funny remark, witticism, wisecrack

gag VERB 1 *The food had a strange taste that made her gag.* ► retch, choke, heave 2 *The regime found effective ways of gagging the press.* ► silence, muzzle, stifle, keep quiet, suppress, smother, restrain, prevent from speaking

gaiety NOUN 1 *There was gaiety in her voice.* ► cheerfulness, cheer, joy, happiness, merriment, jollity, delight 2 *They headed for the gaiety of the bar.* ► festivity, fun, celebration, revelry, jollification

gaily ADVERB 1 *She waved gaily back.* ► merrily, cheerfully, cheerily, happily, joyfully, blithely OPPOSITES ARE sadly, drearily 2 *She wore a gaily colored sari.* ► brightly, brilliantly, flamboyantly AN OPPOSITE IS drably 3 *There was Ben, gaily waving the traffic past.* ► casually, nonchalantly, heedlessly, airily, breezily, lightly, unthinkingly, uncaringly AN OPPOSITE IS anxiously

gain VERB 1 *She gained a huge income from her investments.* ► earn, gross, clear, bring in, obtain, acquire, procure 2 *They gained a wide*
reputation from the publicity. ► earn, achieve, acquire, win, secure 3 *Trevor raised his head to gain a better view.* ► get, achieve, attain 4 *The car began to gain speed.* ► increase, gather, pick up USAGE You can also say *the car began to accelerate.*
gain on *We were gaining on the vehicle in front.* ► catch up with, draw nearer to, narrow the gap between, creep up on, approach

gain NOUN 1 *We are all motivated by the prospect of financial gain. There was no personal gain in it for me.* ► profit, earnings, income, advantage, benefit, return, reward, proceeds, yield, acquisition, asset, attainment, dividend, increase, winnings AN OPPOSITE IS loss 2 *gain* OR *gains The Democrats made modest gains in the local elections in the spring.* ► advances, progress, advancement, headway

gala NOUN *the annual summer gala* ► festival, carnival, jamboree, fête, fair, fiesta, celebration, revelry, party

gale NOUN 1 *Rain and gales are frequent.* ► storm, squall, high wind, hurricane 2 *She collapsed in gales of laughter.* ► outburst, burst, eruption, paroxysm, fit, peal, howl, hoot, roar

gallant ADJECTIVE 1 *a gallant band of soldiers* ► brave, courageous, valiant, daring, fearless, intrepid, heroic, noble, manly AN OPPOSITE IS cowardly 2 *A gallant gentleman at the next table came over to help her.* ► courteous, chivalrous, respectful, considerate, obliging, gracious OPPOSITES ARE discourteous, rude

gallop NOUN **gallops 1** the fastest pace that a horse can go **2** a fast ride on a horse

gallop VERB **gallops, galloping, galloped** go or ride at a gallop

gallows NOUN **gallows** a framework with a noose for hanging criminals

galoshes PLURAL NOUN a pair of waterproof shoes worn over ordinary shoes

galvanize VERB **galvanizes, galvanizing, galvanized 1** stimulate someone into sudden activity **2** coat iron with zinc to protect it from rust
▷ **galvanization** NOUN

gambit NOUN **gambits 1** a kind of opening move in chess **2** an action or remark intended to gain an advantage

gamble VERB **gambles, gambling, gambled 1** bet on the result of a game, race, or other event **2** take great risks in the hope of gaining something
▷ **gambler** NOUN

gamble NOUN **gambles 1** a bet or chance • *a gamble on the lottery* **2** a risky attempt

gambol VERB **gambols, gambolling, gambolled** jump or skip about in play

game NOUN **games 1** a form of play or sport, especially one with rules • *a game of football;* • *a computer game* **2** a section of a long game such as tennis or whist **3** a scheme or plan; a trick • *Whatever his game is, he won't succeed.* **4** wild animals or birds hunted for sport or food
give the game away reveal a secret

game ADJECTIVE **1** able and willing to do something • *"Shall we swim to the island?" "I'm game!"* **2** brave
▷ **gamely** ADVERB

gamekeeper NOUN **gamekeepers** a person employed to protect game birds and animals, especially from poachers

gamma NOUN the third letter of the Greek alphabet, = g

gamma rays PLURAL NOUN very short X-rays emitted by radioactive substances

gander NOUN **ganders** a male goose

gang NOUN **gangs 1** a group of people who do things together **2** a group of criminals

gang VERB **gangs, ganging, ganged** join in a gang • *gang together*
gang up on form a group to fight or oppose someone

gangling ADJECTIVE tall, thin, and awkward-looking

gangplank NOUN **gangplanks** a plank placed so that people can walk into or out of a boat

gangrene (gang- green) NOUN decay of body tissue in a living person

gangster NOUN **gangsters** a member of a gang of violent criminals

gangway NOUN **gangways 1** a gap left for people to pass between rows of seats or through a crowd **2** a movable bridge placed so that people can walk on to or off a ship

gaol (jayl) NOUN **gaols** a different spelling of jail
▷ **gaol** VERB **gaoler** NOUN

gap NOUN **gaps 1** a break or opening in something continuous such as a hedge or fence **2** an interval **3** a wide difference in ideas

gape VERB **gapes, gaping, gaped 1** have your mouth open **2** stare with your mouth open **3** be open wide

Thesaurus

gallop VERB *A horse galloped past.* ▸ race, run, canter, rush, dash, speed, sprint

gambit NOUN *It was a daring gambit and might just work.* ▸ plan, stratagem, tactic, ruse, move, manoeuvre, trick

gamble VERB **1** *He drinks and gambles and chases women.* ▸ bet, game, risk money, wager, (more informal) have a flutter **2** *We gambled and were lucky.* ▸ take a risk, take a chance, try your luck, speculate, venture

game NOUN **1** *The children were playing a new game.* ▸ pastime, diversion, amusement, entertainment, sport, activity **2** *I know how to deal with his little game.* ▸ scheme, trick, plot, plan, dodge **3** *It was the big game on Saturday.* ▸ match, contest, tournament, competition, event, meeting **4** *They were just playing a game on us.* ▸ joke, trick, prank, hoax

gang NOUN **1** *a gang of teenagers* ▸ band, group, crowd, pack, mob **2** *a gang working on*

the road ▸ team, squad, troop, shift, detachment, working party **3** *I was never a part of his gang.* ▸ circle, set, group, ring, clan, clique

gang VERB **gang together** OR **up** *They always gang up to get their way.* ▸ combine, conspire, cooperate, work together, team up

gaol NOUN, VERB another spelling of jail

gap NOUN **1** *a gap in a wall* ▸ opening, breach, break, chink, space, hole, cleft, crack, cranny, crevice, rift, void **2** *a gap in the fighting* ▸ pause, break, interruption, lull, intermission, interval *the gap between rich and poor* ▸ divide, gulf, rift, chasm, disparity, imbalance

gape VERB *He gaped at her in surprise.* ▸ stare, gaze, goggle, (more informal) gawk, (more informal) gawp

a b c d e f **g** h i j k l m n o p q r s t u v w x y z

A
B
C
D
E
F
G
H
I
J
K
L
M
N
O
P
Q
R
S
T
U
V
W
X
Y
Z

garage (ga- rah*zh*) NOUN **garages 1** a building in which a motor vehicle or vehicles may be kept **2** a place where motor vehicles are repaired or serviced and where petrol is sold

garbage NOUN rubbish, especially household rubbish

garble VERB **garbles, garbling, garbled** give a confused account of a story or message so that it is misunderstood

garden NOUN **gardens** a piece of ground where flowers, fruit, or vegetables are grown
▷ **gardener** NOUN **gardening** NOUN

gargle VERB **gargles, gargling, gargled** hold a liquid at the back of the mouth and breathe air through it to wash the inside of the throat
▷ **gargle** NOUN

gargoyle NOUN **gargoyles** an ugly or comical face or figure carved on a building, especially on a water spout

garland NOUN **garlands** a wreath of flowers worn or hung as a decoration
▷ **garland** VERB

garlic NOUN a plant with a bulb divided into smaller bulbs (**cloves**), which have a strong smell and taste and are used for flavoring food

garment NOUN **garments** a piece of clothing

garnish VERB **garnishes, garnishing, garnished** decorate something, especially food

garnish NOUN something used to decorate food or give it extra flavor

garret NOUN **garrets** an attic

garrison NOUN **garrisons 1** troops who stay in a town or fort to defend it **2** the building they occupy
▷ **garrison** VERB

garter NOUN **garters** a band of elastic to hold up a sock or stocking

gas[1] NOUN **gases 1** a substance that (like air) can move freely and is not liquid or solid at ordinary temperatures **2** a gas that can be burned, used for lighting, heating, or cooking

gas VERB **gasses, gassing, gassed 1** kill or injure someone with gas **2** (*informal*) talk idly for a long time

gas[2] NOUN gasoline

gaseous (gas- ee- us) ADJECTIVE in the form of a gas

gash NOUN **gashes** a long deep cut or wound

gash VERB **gashes, gashing, gashed** make a gash in something

gasoline NOUN (*American*) petrol

gasp VERB **gasps, gasping, gasped 1** breathe in suddenly when you are shocked or surprised **2** struggle to breathe with your mouth open when you are tired or ill **3** speak in a breathless way
▷ **gasp** NOUN

gassy ADJECTIVE fizzy

gastric ADJECTIVE to do with the stomach

gastronomy (gas- tron- om- ee) NOUN the art or science of good eating
▷ **gastronomic** ADJECTIVE

gastropod NOUN **gastropods** an animal (e.g., a snail) that moves by means of a fleshy "foot" on its stomach

gate NOUN **gates 1** a movable barrier, usually on hinges, used as a door in a wall or fence **2** a barrier for controlling the flow of water in a dam or lock **3** a place where you wait before you board an aircraft **4** the number of people attending a football game, etc.

gatecrash VERB **gatecrashes, gatecrashing, gatecrashed** go to a private party without being invited
▷ **gatecrasher** NOUN

gateway NOUN **gateways 1** an opening containing a gate **2** a way to reach something ● *The gateway to success*

gather VERB **gathers, gathering, gathered 1** come or bring together **2** collect; obtain gradually ● *We've been gathering information.* **3** collect as harvest; pluck ● *Gather the corn*

Thesaurus

garage NOUN **1** *The house had a large garage, which the new owner turned into a study.* ▶ car-port **2** *She had stopped to fill up the tank at a local garage.* ▶ filling station, service station, gas station

garbled ADJECTIVE *The story seems garbled and may be nonsense.* ▶ confused, muddled, mixed up, twisted, jumbled, scrambled AN OPPOSITE IS clear

garden NOUN **1** *a house with a garden* ▶ plot, allotment, patch, yard **2** *gardens a walk through the gardens* ▶ grounds, park RELATED ADJECTIVE ▶ horticultural RELATED NOUN ▶ horticulture

gash NOUN *Blood was pouring from a gash on his head.* ▶ cut, slash, wound, injury, slit, laceration, abrasion

gash VERB *Frank gashed his hand on a broken glass.* ▶ cut, slash, lacerate, wound, injure, gouge

gasp VERB *She gasped and sat back, her face pale.* ▶ catch your breath, pant, choke, gulp, blow

gasp NOUN *The boy fell back with a gasp.* ▶ pant, heave, wheeze, puff, blow

gate NOUN *Some children came through the gate.* ▶ gateway, doorway, door, entrance, entry, exit, (*poetic*) portal

gather VERB **1** *A crowd gathered near the entrance.* ▶ assemble, collect, come together, congregate, crowd around, convene, converge, flock, group, muster AN OPPOSITE IS disperse **2** *She spent some time gathering her books.* ▶ collect, assemble, accumulate, bring together, heap up **3** *They went into the garden to gather flowers and berries.* ▶ pick, pluck, when it is ripe. ● *gather flowers* **4** understand or learn ● *I gather you've been on vacation.* **5** pull cloth into folds by running a thread through it gather speed move gradually faster

gathering NOUN **gatherings** an assembly or meeting of people; a party

gaudy ADJECTIVE too showy and bright
▷ **gaudily** ADVERB **gaudiness** NOUN

gauge (gayj) NOUN **gauges** **1** a standard measurement **2** the distance between a pair of rails on a railroad **3** a measuring instrument

gauge VERB **gauges, gauging, gauged** **1** measure **2** estimate; form a judgment

gaunt ADJECTIVE (said about a person) lean and haggard
▷ **gauntness** NOUN

gauntlet[1] NOUN **gauntlets** a glove with a wide cuff covering the wrist
throw down the gauntlet offer a challenge

gauntlet[2] NOUN
run the gauntlet have to suffer continuous severe criticism or risk

gauze NOUN **1** thin transparent woven material **2** fine wire mesh
▷ **gauzy** ADJECTIVE

gay ADJECTIVE **1** homosexual **2** cheerful **3** brightly colored
▷ **gayness** NOUN
USAGE Nowadays the most common meaning of **gay** is "homosexual." The older meanings "cheerful" and "brightly colored" can still be used but are becoming less and less common in everyday use. ● *Gayness* is the noun from meaning 1 of **gay**. The noun that relates to the other two meanings is **gaiety**.

gaze VERB **gazes, gazing, gazed** look at something steadily for a long time

gaze NOUN **gazes** a long steady look

gazetteer (gaz- it- eer) NOUN **gazetteers** a list of place names

GCSE ABBREVIATION General Certificate of Secondary Education

gear NOUN **gears** **1** a cogwheel, especially one of a set in a motor vehicle that turn power from the engine into movement of the wheels **2** equipment or apparatus ● *camping gear*

gear VERB **gears, gearing, geared**
gear to make something match or be suitable for something else ● *Health care should be geared to people's needs, not to whether they can pay.*
gear up get ready for ● *We were all geared up to play baseball, but then it rained.*

Geiger counter (gy- ger) NOUN **Geiger counters** an instrument that detects and measures radioactivity

gel NOUN **gels** a jellylike substance, especially one used to give a style to hair

gelatine NOUN a clear jellylike substance made by boiling animal tissue and used to make jellies and other foods and in photographic film
▷ **gelatinous** (jil- at- in- us) ADJECTIVE

gem NOUN **gems** **1** a precious stone **2** an excellent person or thing

gender NOUN **genders** **1** the group in which a noun is classed in the grammar of some languages, e.g. masculine, feminine, or neuter **2** a person's sex ● *Jobs should be open to all, regardless of race or gender.*

Thesaurus

garner, harvest **4** *I gather you have been unwell.*
► understand, believe, be told, be given to understand, learn, hear, be informed, deduce, infer, surmise **5** *You can gather the dress at the waist.* ► pleat, fold, crimp, ruffle, pucker

gaudy ADJECTIVE *She wore dull clothes, nothing gaudy.* ► garish, lurid, flashy, loud, glaring, vulgar OPPOSITES ARE sober, dull

gauge NOUN **1** *He checked the pressure gauge.*
► meter, instrument, dial, reading **2** *The track was the wrong gauge for the new rolling stock.*
► size, width, measure, standard **3** *The local elections will be seen as a gauge of public opinion.*
► measure, indicator, test, guide (to), touchstone, benchmark

gauge VERB **1** *A special scoring table will gauge which competitor does best.* ► assess, evaluate, appraise, calculate, reckon **2** *Instruments can gauge the distance precisely.* ► measure, calculate, compute, quantify, determine

gaunt ADJECTIVE *His arms were wrapped around his gaunt body.* ► haggard, drawn, lank,

emaciated, wasted, skinny, scrawny, shrivelled, skeletal, cadaverous

gawky ADJECTIVE *She had been a thin, gawky adolescent.* ► awkward, ungainly, inelegant, ungraceful, graceless, gangling, gauche, inept, lumbering, bumbling, maladroit, uncoordinated AN OPPOSITE IS graceful

gay ADJECTIVE **1** *a club for gay people*
► homosexual, (*female*) lesbian **2** *He was so gay and lively.* ► cheerful, happy, carefree, lively, merry, jolly, jovial, glad

gaze VERB *He continued to gaze out of the window.*
► stare, look, gape

gear NOUN (*informal*) *You can put your gear in here.* ► equipment, paraphernalia, belongings, possessions, stuff, things, tackle

gem NOUN **1** *a tiara made of gems and pearls*
► jewel, precious stone, gemstone **2** *The anthology contains some real gems.* ► pearl, wonder, treasure, masterpiece, outstanding example

A B C D E F G H I J K L M N O P Q R S T U V W X Y Z

gene (jeen) NOUN **genes** the part of a living cell that controls which characteristics (such as the color of hair or eyes) are inherited from parents

genealogy (jeen- ee- al- o- jee) NOUN **genealogies 1** a list or diagram showing how people are descended from an ancestor **2** the study of family history and ancestors
▷ **genealogical** (jeen- ee- a- loj- ik- al) ADJECTIVE

genera (jen- e- ra) PLURAL NOUN plural of **genus**

general ADJECTIVE **1** to do with or involving most people or things • *This drug is now in general use.* **2** not detailed; broad • *I've got the general idea.* **3** chief or head • *the general manager*
in general as a general rule; usually

general NOUN **generals** a senior army officer

general election NOUN **general elections** an election of legislators for the whole country

generally ADVERB **1** usually **2** in a general sense; without regard to details • *I was speaking generally.*

general practitioner NOUN **general practitioners** a doctor who treats all kinds of diseases. He or she is the first doctor that people see when they are ill.

generate VERB **generates, generating, generated** produce or create

generation NOUN **generations 1** generating **2** a single stage in a family • *Three generations were included: children, parents, and grandparents.* **3** all the people born at about the same time • *our parents' generation*

generator NOUN **generators 1** an apparatus for producing gases or steam **2** a machine for converting mechanical energy into electricity

generous ADJECTIVE **1** willing to give things or share them **2** given freely; plentiful • *a generous helping*
▷ **generously** ADVERB **generosity** NOUN

genetic (jin- et- ik) ADJECTIVE **1** to do with genes **2** to do with characteristics inherited from parents or ancestors
▷ **genetically** ADVERB
genetically modified (said about an animal or plant) containing genes that have been artificially altered

genetics NOUN the study of genes and genetic behavior

genial (jee- nee- al) ADJECTIVE kindly and cheerful
▷ **genially** ADVERB **geniality** (jee- nee- al- it- ee) NOUN

genital (jen- it- al) ADJECTIVE to do with animal reproduction or reproductive organs

genitals (jen- it- alz) PLURAL NOUN external sexual organs

genius NOUN **geniuses 1** an unusually clever or creative person **2** a very great natural ability • *He has a real genius for music*

genocide (jen- o- syd) NOUN deliberate extermination of a race of people

gentle ADJECTIVE **1** mild or kind; not rough **2** not harsh or severe • *a gentle breeze*
▷ **gently** ADVERB **gentleness** NOUN

Thesaurus

general ADJECTIVE **1** *The idea is sound in general terms.* ► broad, rough, sweeping, vague, loose, indefinite AN OPPOSITE IS specific **2** *This model is more suitable for general use.*
► widespread, universal, popular, regular, typical, normal, ordinary, everyday, conventional OPPOSITES ARE specialized, restricted **3** *a general pay increase*
► comprehensive, inclusive, overall, universal

generally ADVERB *It is generally a mistake to ignore these factors.* ► normally, as a rule, by and large, on the whole, broadly, mainly, mostly, in the main, predominantly, usually

generate VERB *a move to generate more business* ► create, produce, bring about, make, cause, give rise to, propagate, engender, beget, breed, (more informal) whip up

generation NOUN **1** *people of an earlier generation* ► age, age group **2** *the generation of new jobs* ► creation, production, origination, initiation, genesis

generosity NOUN *Thanks to the generosity of sponsors the games can continue.* ► kindness,

munificence, liberality, philanthropy, benevolence, bounty, charity, largesse

generous ADJECTIVE **1** *a person of a good and generous nature* ► kind, kindhearted, magnanimous, benevolent, unselfish, charitable, bighearted, beneficent, philanthropic **2** *She was always generous on the children's birthdays.* ► bountiful, liberal, lavish, munificent, indulgent, bounteous **3** *a generous helping of pudding* ► large, lavish, ample, copious, plentiful, abundant

genius NOUN **1** *They have a genius for getting attention.* ► talent, gift, flair, aptitude, bent, intellect, knack **2** *It doesn't take a genius to work out his little game.* ► mastermind, great thinker, great brain, prodigy, past master, expert, intellectual

gentle ADJECTIVE **1** *The mild, gentle face looked back at him.* ► kind, kindly, tender, sympathetic, compassionate, warm-hearted, softhearted, placid, calm OPPOSITES ARE unkind, harsh **2** *A gentle breeze was blowing.*
► light, faint, soft OPPOSITES ARE strong, fierce **3** *There was a gentle slope up to the house.*
► gradual, slight, easy AN OPPOSITE IS steep

gentleman NOUN **gentlemen** **1** a well-mannered or honorable man **2** a man of good social position **3** (in polite use) a man

genuine ADJECTIVE real; not faked or pretending
▷ **genuinely** ADVERB **genuineness** NOUN

genus (jee- nus) NOUN **genera** (jen- er- a) a group of similar animals or plants • Lions and tigers belong to the same genus.

geography (jee- og- ra- fee) NOUN the study of the earth's surface and of its climate, peoples, and products
▷ **geographer** NOUN **geographical** ADJECTIVE **geographically** ADVERB
[from geo- = earth + -graphy = description]

geology (jee- ol- o- jee) NOUN the study of the structure of the earth's crust and its layers
▷ **geological** ADJECTIVE **geologically** ADVERB **geologist** NOUN

geometry (jee- om- it- ree) NOUN the study of lines, angles, surfaces, and solids in mathematics
▷ **geometric** ADJECTIVE **geometrical** ADJECTIVE **geometrically** ADVERB

gerbil (jer- bil) NOUN **gerbils** a small brown rodent with long hind legs, often kept as a pet

geriatric (je- ree- at- rik) ADJECTIVE to do with the care of old people and their health [from Greek geras = old age + iatros = doctor]

germ NOUN **germs** **1** a micro-organism, especially one that can cause disease **2** a tiny living structure from which a plant or animal may develop **3** part of the seed of a cereal plant [from Latin germen = seed or sprout]

German measles NOUN rubella

German shepherd dog NOUN **German shepherd dogs** a large strong dog, often used by the police

germinate VERB **germinates, germinating, germinated** when a seed germinates, it begins to develop, and roots and shoots grow from it
▷ **germination** NOUN

gesticulate (jes- tik- yoo- layt) VERB **gesticulates, gesticulating, gesticulated** make expressive movements with your hands and arms
▷ **gesticulation** NOUN

gesture (jes- cher) NOUN **gestures** **1** a movement that expresses what a person feels **2** an action that shows goodwill • It would be a nice gesture to send her some flowers

gesture VERB **gestures, gesturing, gestured** tell a person something by making a gesture • She gestured me to be quiet.

get VERB **gets, getting, got** or **gotten** This word has many different uses, including: **1** obtain or receive • She got first prize **2** become • Don't get angry! **3** reach a place • We got there by midnight. **4** put or move • I can't get my shoe on. **5** prepare • Will you get the tea? **6** persuade or order • Get him to wash up. **7** catch or suffer from an illness **8** (informal) understand • Do you get what I mean?
get away with **1** escape with something **2** avoid being punished for what you have done
get by (informal) manage
get on **1** make progress **2** be friendly with somebody
get over recover from an illness, etc.
get up **1** stand up **2** get out of your bed in the morning **3** prepare or organize • We got up at the concert.

Thesaurus

genuine ADJECTIVE **1** A genuine Picasso hung on the wall. ► authentic, original, bona fide, actual, real, true, authenticated AN OPPOSITE IS fake **2** She's a very genuine person. ► sincere, honest, unaffected, frank, truthful, devout, candid, earnest, true AN OPPOSITE IS insincere

germ NOUN **1** the germ of a great idea ► beginning, nucleus, seed, start, genesis, embryo, cause, origin **2** a cleaner that also kills germs ► microbe, micro-organism, bacterium, (more informal) bug, virus

get VERB **1** She got her degree at St Andrews. ► obtain, receive, acquire, come by, achieve, procure **2** It's getting cold. ► become, turn, grow **3** We'll get there soon. ► arrive, reach, come to **4** Will you get my book? ► fetch, bring, collect, pick up **5** I got a cold. ► catch, come down with, develop
get across It's hard to get the idea across. ► communicate, convey, impart, transmit

get ahead people who want to get ahead ► succeed, prosper, flourish, get on well
get along **1** They do seem to get along with each other. ► agree, see eye to eye, be friendly, be compatible **2** We are getting along quite well now. ► manage, cope, get on, make out, progress, advance
get at What are you getting at? ► suggest, imply, intend, insinuate, mean
get away Tom and Fiona wanted to get away for the weekend. ► escape, leave, (more informal) make off
get back We won't get our money back. ► recover, recoup, regain, retrieve
get by (informal) We have enough money to get by. ► survive, manage, cope, make do, muddle through
get down All the talk of war got them down. ► depress, deject, dishearten, dispirit, sadden
get in The train gets in at 7 o'clock. ► arrive, come

A
B
C
D
E
F
G
H
I
J
K
L
M
N
O
P
Q
R
S
T
U
V
W
X
Y
Z

get your own back (*informal*) have your revenge
have got to must

geyser (gee- zer, gy- zer) NOUN **geysers 1** a
natural spring that shoots up columns of hot
water **2** a kind of water heater [from **Geysir**
= gusher, the name of a geyser in Iceland]

ghastly ADJECTIVE **1** very unpleasant or bad
2 looking pale and ill
▷ **ghastliness** NOUN
[from Old English *gaestan* = terrify]

ghost NOUN **ghosts** the spirit of a dead person
that appears to the living
▷ **ghostly** ADJECTIVE

ghoulish (gool- ish) ADJECTIVE enjoying things
that are grisly or unpleasant
▷ **ghoulishly** ADVERB **ghoulishness** NOUN
[from Arabic *gul* = a demon that eats dead
bodies]

giant NOUN **giants 1** (in myths or fairy tales) a
creature like a huge man **2** a man, animal, or
plant that is much larger than the usual size
[via early French from Greek *gigas*]

gibberish (jib- er- ish) NOUN meaningless
speech; nonsense

gibbet (jib- it) NOUN **gibbets 1** a gallows **2** an
upright post with an arm from which a
criminal's body was hung after execution, as a
warning to others

gibbon NOUN **gibbons** a small ape from southeast Asia. Gibbons have very long arms to
help them swing through the trees where
they live.

giddy ADJECTIVE **1** feeling that everything is
spinning around and that you might fall
2 causing this feeling ● *We looked down from
the giddy height of the cliff.*
▷ **giddily** ADVERB **giddiness** NOUN

gift NOUN **gifts 1** a present **2** a natural talent
● *She has a gift for music.*

gifted ADJECTIVE having a special talent

gig NOUN **gigs** (*informal*) a live performance by
a musician, comedian, etc.

gigabyte (gi- ga- byt, ji- ga- byt) NOUN
gigabytes (in computing) a unit of
information equal to one thousand million
bytes, or (more precisely) 2^{30} bytes

gigantic (jy- **gan**- tik) ADJECTIVE extremely
large; huge

Thesaurus

---

get on 1 *We'd better get on the bus.* ► board,
embark, mount, ascend **2** *How did they get on
during their holiday?* ► cope, manage, fare, get
along, make out

get out *Some of the prisoners had got out.*
► escape, break out, break free, get away, flee

get over 1 *She's just gotten over the flu.*
► recover from, shake off, survive **2** *difficulties
that we can never get over* ► overcome,
surmount, deal with

get around 1 *a problem they tried to get around*
► avoid, evade, overcome, get the better of
2 *He always got around his mother when he
needed something.* ► persuade, cajole, prevail
on, win over, beguile

get together *Let's get together next week.*
► meet, meet up, see one another

get up 1 *She got up from her chair.* ► rise,
stand, stand up **2** *They would have to get up
early to leave for the airport.* ► rise, get out of
bed

getaway NOUN *a quick getaway* ► escape,
breakout, breakaway

ghastly ADJECTIVE **1** *a ghastly murder* ► terrible,
frightful, horrible, horrific, horrifying,
gruesome **2** *a ghastly time* ► unpleasant,
disagreeable, nasty, horrid, revolting AN
OPPOSITE IS lovely

ghost NOUN **1** *They say there's a ghost in the
house.* ► phantom, specter, spirit, wraith,
vision **2** *a ghost of a smile* ► trace, hint,
suggestion, glimmer, semblance, shadow

ghostly ADJECTIVE *The ghostly figure seemed to*

belong to a dream. ► unearthly, spectral, eerie,
phantom, uncanny, weird, supernatural,
(*informal*) spooky, (*informal*) creepy, (*informal*)
scary

giant NOUN *A giant of a man stood in the
doorway.* ► monster, colossus, titan, Goliath,
ogre AN OPPOSITE IS dwarf

giant ADJECTIVE *The thrust from the four giant
engines pushed him back in his seat.* ► huge,
enormous, gigantic, colossal, immense,
massive, mighty, vast, large, elephantine,
gargantuan, mammoth, monstrous,
prodigious, titanic, (*more informal*) whopping,
(*more informal*) jumbo, (*more informal*) king-
size OPPOSITES ARE tiny, miniature

giddy ADJECTIVE *The heat of the sun made her
giddy.* ► dizzy, faint, weak, light-headed,
unsteady, wobbly, (*more informal*) woozy

gift NOUN **1** *He made the library a generous gift.*
► present, donation, benefaction,
contribution, largesse, handout, offering,
grant, gratuity, bequest, endowment **2** *a gift
for languages* ► talent, flair, aptitude, capacity,
genius, knack, ability, bent, capability

gifted ADJECTIVE *a gifted young musician*
► talented, able, accomplished, capable,
skilful, skilled

gigantic ADJECTIVE *a gigantic old building*
► huge, enormous, colossal, immense,
massive, mighty, vast, large, giant, (*more
informal*) whopping, (*more informal*) jumbo,
(*more informal*) king-size

giggle VERB giggles, giggling, giggled laugh in a silly way

giggle NOUN giggles **1** a silly laugh **2** (*informal*) something amusing; a bit of fun

gild VERB gilds, gilding, gilded cover something with a thin layer of gold or gold paint

gills PLURAL NOUN the part of the body through which fish and certain other water animals breathe

gilt NOUN a thin covering of gold or gold paint

gimmick NOUN gimmicks something unusual or silly done or used just to attract people's attention

gin NOUN a colorless alcoholic drink flavored with juniper berries

ginger NOUN **1** the hot-tasting root of a tropical plant, or a flavoring made from this root, used especially in drinks and Asian cooking **2** liveliness or energy **3** a reddish-yellow color
▷ **ginger** ADJECTIVE

ginger VERB gingers, gingering, gingered make something more lively ● *This will ginger things up!* [via Old English, Latin, and Greek from Dravidian (a group of languages spoken in southern India)]

gingerly ADVERB cautiously

giraffe NOUN giraffe or giraffes an African animal with long legs and a very long neck, the world's tallest mammal [from Arabic]

girder NOUN girders a metal beam supporting part of a building or a bridge

girdle NOUN girdles **1** a belt or cord worn around the waist **2** a woman's elastic corset covering from the waist to the thigh

girl NOUN girls **1** a female child **2** a young woman
▷ **girlhood** NOUN **girlish** ADJECTIVE

girlfriend NOUN girlfriends a person's regular female companion in a romantic or sexual relationship

giro (jy- roh) NOUN a system of sending money directly from one bank account or post office account to another

gist (jist) NOUN the essential points or general sense of what someone says

give VERB gives, giving, gave, given **1** let someone have something **2** make or do something ● *He gave a laugh.* **3** be flexible or springy; bend or collapse when pressed
▷ **giver** NOUN
give in acknowledge that you are defeated; yield
give up 1 stop trying **2** end a habit

given ADJECTIVE named or stated in advance ● *All the people in a given area.*

glacial (glay- shal) ADJECTIVE icy; made of or produced by ice
▷ **glacially** ADVERB

glacier (glas- ee- er) NOUN glaciers a mass of ice that moves very slowly down a mountain valley

glad ADJECTIVE **1** pleased; expressing joy **2** giving pleasure ● *We brought the glad news.*
▷ **gladly** ADVERB **gladness** NOUN
glad of grateful for or pleased with something

gladden VERB gladdens, gladdening, gladdened make a person glad

glade NOUN glades an open space in a forest

gladiator (glad- ee- ay- ter) NOUN gladiators a man trained to fight for public entertainment in ancient Rome
▷ **gladiatorial** (glad- ee- at- or- ee- al) ADJECTIVE [from Latin *gladius* = sword]

Thesaurus

---

giggle VERB *The silly hat made them giggle.*
► snigger, titter, chuckle, laugh

girdle NOUN *They wore girdles around their waists.*
► belt, sash, band, waistband, corset

girl NOUN *a pretty little girl* ► lass, daughter, female child, (*literary*) maid, (*literary*) maiden

give VERB **1** *He would give them another hundred pounds.* ► provide with, present with, supply with, allow, award, bestow on, donate, make over **2** *Will you give her a message?* ► pass on, convey, communicate, transmit, send, deliver **3** *three brothers who had given their lives in the Great War* ► sacrifice, lose, relinquish, devote **4** *a note giving details of Christmas opening times* ► show, list, provide, display **5** *The boys gave no trouble.* ► cause, make, create, start **6** *The right herbs will give your food a better flavor.* ► afford, produce, yield, lend **7** *We are going to give a party.* ► hold, lay on, organize, arrange **8** *He saw her and gave a shout.* ► utter,

emit, let out **9** *The roof was giving under the weight.* ► collapse, yield, break, fall in **10** *She would give them a warning.* ► issue, deliver, administer, impose on

give away *She tried not to give away their secret.*
► reveal, disclose, divulge, betray

give in *They had to give in after a while.*
► submit, surrender, capitulate, yield, succumb, comply

give off *The fire gave off grey fumes.* ► produce, emit, send out, discharge, exude, release

give out 1 *Please give out the books.* ► hand out, hand around, distribute, dole out, deal out **2** *The money gave out after four days.* ► run out, be used up, be exhausted, dry up

give up *Don't give up now.* ► quit, stop, concede defeat, admit defeat, resign, despair

glad ADJECTIVE **1** *I am glad you came.* ► pleased, happy, delighted, thrilled, overjoyed **2** *They were glad to help.* ► pleased, willing, eager, keen

A
B
C
D
E
F
G
H
I
J
K
L
M
N
O
P
Q
R
S
T
U
V
W
X
Y
Z

glamorous ADJECTIVE excitingly attractive

glamor NOUN an attractive and exciting quality

glance VERB glances, glancing, glanced **1** look at something briefly **2** strike something at an angle and slide off it • *The ball glanced off his bat.*
▷ **glance** NOUN

gland NOUN glands an organ of the body that separates substances from the blood so that they can be used or secreted (passed out of the body)
▷ **glandular** ADJECTIVE

glare VERB glares, glaring, glared **1** shine with a bright or dazzling light **2** stare angrily or fiercely
▷ **glare** NOUN

glasnost NOUN the open reporting of news or giving of information, especially in the former Soviet Union [from Russian, = openness]

glass NOUN glasses **1** a hard brittle substance that is usually transparent **2** a container made of glass for drinking from **3** a mirror **4** a lens
▷ **glassy** ADJECTIVE

glasses PLURAL NOUN **1** a pair of lenses in a frame, worn over the eyes to help improve eyesight **2** binoculars

glaze VERB glazes, glazing, glazed **1** fit a window or building with glass **2** give a shiny surface to something **3** (said of a person's eyes) lose brightness and animation

gleam NOUN gleams **1** a beam of soft light, especially one that comes and goes **2** a small amount of hope, humor, etc.

gleam VERB gleams, gleaming, gleamed shine brightly, especially after cleaning or polishing

glee NOUN great delight
▷ **gleeful** ADJECTIVE **gleefully** ADVERB

glen NOUN glens a narrow valley, especially in Scotland [from Scottish Gaelic or Irish]

glib ADJECTIVE speaking or writing readily but not sincerely or thoughtfully
▷ **glibly** ADVERB **glibness** NOUN

glide VERB glides, gliding, glided **1** move along smoothly **2** fly without using an engine **3** birds glide when they fly without beating their wings
▷ **glide** NOUN

glider NOUN gliders an aircraft without an engine that flies by floating on warm air currents called thermals

glimmer NOUN glimmers **1** a faint light **2** a small sign or trace of something • *a glimmer of hope*

glimmer VERB glimmers, glimmering, glimmered shine with a faint, flickering light

glimpse NOUN glimpses a brief view

glimpse VERB glimpses, glimpsing, glimpsed see something briefly

Thesaurus

glamorous ADJECTIVE **1** *a glamorous woman* ► beautiful, elegant, captivating, alluring, gorgeous, smart, lovely, entrancing, stylish, fashionable USAGE Be careful when you use *smart*, because it has another important meaning. **2** *a glamorous lifestyle* ► exciting, colorful, dazzling, glittering, alluring, smart

glamor NOUN **1** *She offered that extra bit of glamor.* ► beauty, attractiveness, elegance, style, charm, seductiveness **2** *the glamor of living in a big city* ► appeal, excitement, attraction, allure, glitter, luster, magic

glance VERB **1** *She glanced at her watch.* ► look, peek, peep, take a look at **2** glance at OR through *I only had time to glance at the article.* ► scan, skim, read quickly, run your eye over

glance NOUN *He gave us a quick glance.* ► look, peek, peep, glimpse

glare VERB **1** *She glared at him.* ► stare angrily, glower, scowl, frown **2** *The lights of oncoming cars glared in the darkness.* ► dazzle, blaze, be blinding, flare, beam

glare NOUN **1** *an angry glare* ► stare, scowl, glower, frown, black look **2** *the glare of the lights* ► dazzle, shine, blaze, brilliance, beam, flare

glaring ADJECTIVE *a glaring error* ► obvious, conspicuous, blatant, flagrant, patent, plain, overt, inescapable

gleam VERB *The brass door knob gleamed in the moonlight.* ► glimmer, glint, glow, shine, flash, glisten, glitter, sparkle, shimmer

gleam NOUN *the gleam of lights in the distance* ► glimmer, glint, glow, glitter, sparkle, shimmer

glide VERB **1** *A boat glided past.* ► slide, move smoothly, slip, sail, coast, skim **2** *The gulls were gliding overhead.* ► drift, soar, wheel, hover, sail, float, fly

glimmer VERB *The moonlight glimmered on the great sweep of lawn.* ► gleam, glint, glow, shine, flash, glisten, glitter, sparkle, shimmer, twinkle

glimmer NOUN *There was a faint glimmer in his eyes.* ► gleam, glint, glow, glitter, sparkle, shimmer, twinkle

glimpse VERB *I glimpsed Auntie sitting on the bottom stair.* ► spot, spy, catch sight of, make out

glimpse NOUN *I caught a quick glimpse of the house.* ► glance, peep, look, sight, sighting, view, (more informal) squint

glint NOUN glints a very brief flash of light

glint VERB glints, glinting, glinted shine with a flash of light

glisten (glis- en) VERB glistens, glistening, glistened shine like something wet or oily

glitter VERB glitters, glittering, glittered shine with tiny flashes of light; sparkle

glitter NOUN tiny sparkling pieces used for decoration

gloat VERB gloats, gloating, gloated be pleased in an unkind way that you have succeeded or that someone else has been hurt or upset

global ADJECTIVE **1** to do with the whole world; worldwide **2** to do with the whole of a system
▷ **globally** ADVERB

global warming NOUN the increase in the temperature of the earth's atmosphere, caused by the greenhouse effect

globe NOUN globes **1** something shaped like a ball, especially one with a map of the whole world on it **2** the world • *She has traveled all over the globe* **3** a hollow round glass object

gloom NOUN **1** darkness **2** sadness or despair

gloomy ADJECTIVE gloomier, gloomiest **1** almost dark **2** depressed or depressing
▷ **gloomily** ADVERB **gloominess** NOUN

glorify VERB glorifies, glorifying, glorified **1** give great praise or great honor to **2** make a thing seem more splendid or attractive than it really is • *It is a film that glorifies war.*
▷ **glorification** NOUN

glorious ADJECTIVE splendid or magnificent
▷ **gloriously** ADVERB

glory NOUN glories **1** fame and honor **2** praise **3** beauty or magnificence

glory VERB glories, glorying, gloried rejoice; pride yourself • *They gloried in victory.*

gloss[1] NOUN glosses the shine on a smooth surface

gloss VERB glosses, glossing, glossed make a thing glossy

gloss[2] VERB glosses, glossing, glossed gloss over mention a fault or mistake etc. only briefly to make it seem less serious than it really is

glossary NOUN glossaries a list of difficult words with their meanings explained

glossy ADJECTIVE glossier, glossiest smooth and shiny
▷ **glossily** ADVERB **glossiness** NOUN

glove NOUN gloves a covering for the hand, usually with separate divisions for each finger and thumb
▷ **gloved** ADJECTIVE

glow NOUN **1** brightness and warmth without flames **2** a warm or cheerful feeling • *We felt a glow of pride*

a b c d e f **g** h i j k l m n o p q r s t u v w x y z

Thesaurus

glint VERB *Her blue eyes glinted like ice.* ► gleam, glow, shine, flash, glisten, glitter, sparkle, shimmer

glint NOUN *a glint in the mirror* ► gleam, glimmer, glow, glitter, sparkle, shimmer

global ADJECTIVE **1** *global communications* ► worldwide, international, world, intercontinental, universal **2** *a global solution to the problem* ► total, comprehensive, general, all-inclusive, wide-ranging

globe NOUN **1** *people from all over the globe* ► world, earth, planet **2** *the shape of a globe* ► ball, orb, sphere, round

gloom NOUN **1** *They peered out into the gloom.* ► darkness, dimness, semi-darkness, murk, murkiness, shade, shadow, twilight, cloudiness, dullness, dusk, obscurity **2** *Her feeling of gloom lifted.* ► depression, dejection, despondency, low spirits, melancholy

gloomy ADJECTIVE **1** *They walked through the front door into a gloomy hall.* ► dark, dingy, dim, dismal, dreary, dull, shadowy, sombre, cheerless AN OPPOSITE IS bright **2** *a gloomy expression* ► miserable, downcast, downhearted, dejected, dispirited, glum, unhappy OPPOSITES ARE cheerful, happy **3** *a gloomy outlook for the economy* ► pessimistic, unfavorable, unpromising, depressing, bleak, downbeat OPPOSITES ARE optimistic, upbeat

glorious ADJECTIVE **1** *a glorious victory* ► magnificent, splendid, illustrious, celebrated, acclaimed, distinguished, renowned, great **2** *a glorious view across the hills* ► wonderful, spectacular, magnificent, superb, beautiful, stunning

glory NOUN **1** *the glory of competing for your country; successes that bring much glory* ► distinction, honor, renown, prestige, kudos, fame, credit, triumph, success **2** *glory to God* ► adoration, homage, praise, thanksgiving, veneration, worship **3** *the glories of New England in the autumn* ► beauty, magnificence, grandeur, majesty, radiance, splendor

gloss NOUN *The new paint has a fine gloss.* ► shine, sheen, brightness, brilliance, luster, burnish, polish

glossy ADJECTIVE *a glossy tiled floor* ► bright, burnished, glassy, glazed, gleaming, lustrous, polished, reflective, shiny, silky, sleek, smooth AN OPPOSITE IS dull

glow VERB **1** *Lights glowed from the windows.* ► shine, gleam, glimmer, flicker, flare **2** *She glowed with pleasure at having said the right thing.* ► shine, flush, blush, color, redden

A
B
C
D
E
F
G
H
I
J
K
L
M
N
O
P
Q
R
S
T
U
V
W
X
Y
Z

glow VERB **glows, glowing, glowed** shine with a soft, warm light

glue NOUN **glues** a sticky substance used for joining things together
▷ **gluey** ADJECTIVE

glue VERB **glues, gluing, glued** 1 stick with glue 2 attach or hold closely ● *His ear was glued to the keyhole*

glum ADJECTIVE miserable or depressed
▷ **glumly** ADVERB **glumness** NOUN

glut NOUN **gluts** an excessive supply

glutinous (gloo- tin- us) ADJECTIVE gluelike or sticky

glutton NOUN **gluttons** a person who eats too much
▷ **gluttonous** ADJECTIVE **gluttony** NOUN
glutton for punishment a person who seems to enjoy doing something difficult or unpleasant

gm ABBREVIATION gram

GMT ABBREVIATION Greenwich Mean Time

gnarled (narld) ADJECTIVE twisted and knobbly, like an old tree

gnash (nash) VERB **gnashes, gnashing, gnashed** grind your teeth together

gnat (nat) NOUN **gnats** a tiny fly that bites

gnaw (naw) VERB **gnaws, gnawing, gnawed** keep on biting something hard so that it wears away

gnome (nohm) NOUN **gnomes** a kind of dwarf in fairy tales, usually living underground

go VERB **goes, going, went, gone** This word has many uses, including: 1 move from one place to another ● *Where are you going?* 2 leave ● *I must go.* 3 lead from one place to another ● *The road goes to town.* 4 become ● *The milk has gone sour.* 5 make a sound ● *The gun went bang.* 6 belong in some place or position ● *Plates go on that shelf.* 7 be sold ● *The house went very cheaply.*
go off 1 explode 2 become stale or decayed 3 stop liking something
go on continue
go out stop burning or shining
go through experience something unpleasant or difficult

Thesaurus

---

glow NOUN 1 *the glow of the street lights* ► shine, gleam, glimmer, radiance, luminosity, brilliance 2 *There was a distinct glow in her cheeks.* ► flush, blush, rosiness, pinkness, warmth 3 *We felt a glow of excitement.* ► ardor, fervor, enthusiasm, feeling, intensity, passion

glowing ADJECTIVE 1 *glowing street lights* ► bright, shining, luminous, radiant 2 *glowing cheeks* ► bright, rosy, red, pink, blushing, flushed 3 *a glowing report* ► complimentary, enthusiastic, highly favorable, fervent, admiring, eulogistic, ecstatic

glue NOUN *a tube of glue* ► adhesive, paste, gum, fixative, sealant, cement

glue VERB *Glue the pieces together.* ► fix, stick, fasten, affix, paste, cement, bond, gum, seal

glum ADJECTIVE *Tony looked glum.* ► miserable, downcast, downhearted, dejected, dispirited, gloomy, unhappy OPPOSITES ARE cheerful, happy

go VERB 1 *She started to go towards the entrance.* ► move, advance, proceed, walk, make your way, progress 2 *We are going to Houston on Friday.* ► travel, journey, make a trip 3 *Several of the guests had already gone.* ► leave, depart, go away, withdraw, make off, (*more informal*) clear off 4 *My purse had gone.* ► disappear, vanish, be taken, be stolen 5 *The path goes to the village.* ► lead, take you, continue, extend, stretch 6 *All the money goes to charity.* ► be given, be donated, be granted, be presented 7 *All our money has gone.* ► be used up, be spent, be exhausted 8 *His hair had gone grey.* ► turn, become, grow 9 *I hope things go well*

for them. ► work out, turn out, develop 10 *The coat and hat don't go.* ► match, harmonize, blend, suit one another 11 *The car won't go.* ► start, work, function, operate, run 12 *Where do these books go?* ► belong, be placed, be kept, have a place 13 *Has the bell gone?* ► sound, ring, chime, peal 14 *The time will go quickly.* ► pass, go by, elapse, lapse

go ahead *The plan will go ahead.* ► begin, proceed, continue, take place

go away *She wanted them all to go away.* ► leave, depart, (*more informal*) clear off

go back *I'll have to go back and look for it.* ► return, turn around

go down *Prices are expected to go down.* ► fall, drop, decrease, get lower

go for 1 *Which one will you go for?* ► choose, take, favor, prefer 2 *He went for her with a hammer.* ► attack, assault, set on, lunge at

go in for *We are going in for a competition.* ► enter, take part in, participate in

go into *The lawyers will go into it in detail.* ► discuss, consider, think about, investigate, probe, delve into, review

go off 1 *A bomb went off.* ► explode, detonate, blow up 2 go bad, go sour, turn

go on 1 *The program went on for over two hours.* ► continue, extend, carry on, run 2 *She went on about how lucky we were.* ► chatter, witter, ramble, (*more informal*) rabbit

go over *Shall we go over the figures?* ► study, check, review, examine, analyse, scrutinize, investigate

go through *It's hard to comprehend what they*

go NOUN **goes** **1** a turn or try • *May I have a go?* **2** (*informal*) energy or liveliness • *She is full of go.*
make a go of make a success of something
on the go active; always working or moving

goad NOUN **goads** a stick with a pointed end for prodding cattle to move onwards

goad VERB **goads**, **goading**, **goaded** stir in action by being annoying • *He goaded me into fighting.*

goal NOUN **goals** **1** the place where a ball must go to score a point in soccer, hockey, etc. **2** a point scored in this way **3** something that you are trying to reach or achieve

goalkeeper NOUN **goalkeepers** the player who stands in the goal to try and keep the ball from entering

goat NOUN **goats** a mammal with horns and a beard, closely related to the sheep. Domestic goats are kept for their milk [from Old English]

gobble VERB **gobbles**, **gobbling**, **gobbled** eat quickly and greedily [from early French *gober* = to swallow]

go-between NOUN **go-betweens** a person who acts as a messenger or negotiator between others

God NOUN the creator of the universe in Christian, Jewish, and Muslim belief

god NOUN **gods** a male being that is worshipped • *Mars was a Roman god.*

godchild NOUN **godchildren** a child that has a godparent
▷ **god-daughter** NOUN **godson** NOUN

goddess NOUN **goddesses** a female being that is worshipped

godparent NOUN **godparents** a person at a child's christening who promises to see that the child has a religious education
▷ **godfather** NOUN **godmother** NOUN

godsend NOUN **godsends** a piece of unexpected good luck

goggle VERB **goggles**, **goggling**, **goggled** stare with wide open eyes

going *present participle* of **go**
be going to do something be ready or likely to do it

gold NOUN **golds** **1** a precious yellow metal **2** a deep yellow color **3** a gold medal, awarded as first prize
▷ **gold** ADJECTIVE

golden ADJECTIVE **1** made of gold **2** colored like gold **3** precious or excellent • *a golden opportunity*

golden wedding NOUN **golden weddings** a couple's fiftieth wedding anniversary

goldfish NOUN **goldfish** a small red or orange fish, often kept as a pet

golf NOUN an outdoor game played by hitting a small white ball with a club into a series of holes on a specially prepared ground (a **golf course** or **golf links**) and taking as few strokes as possible
▷ **golfer** NOUN **golfing** NOUN

gong NOUN **gongs** a large metal disc that makes an echoing sound when it is hit

good ADJECTIVE **better**, **best** **1** having the right qualities; of the kind that people like • *a good book* **2** kind • *It was good of you to help us.* **3** well behaved • *Be a good boy.* **4** skilled or talented • *a good pianist* **5** healthy; giving benefit • *Exercise is good for you.* **6** thorough • *Give it a good clean.* **7** large; considerable • *It's a good distance from the shops.*

Thesaurus

must have gone through. ► suffer, experience, undergo, endure, withstand
go with **1** *Will you go with them?*
► accompany, escort **2** *I'm not sure this tie goes with my shirt.* ► match, suit, harmonize with, blend with

goal NOUN *The overall goal is to promote the use of good English.* ► aim, objective, object, ambition, intention, purpose, target, aspiration, design, end

gobble VERB *He stopped talking to gobble his food.* ► guzzle, devour, bolt, gulp, eat

god or **goddess** NOUN *the gods and goddesses of ancient Olympus* ► deity, divinity, divine being, immortal RELATED ADJECTIVE ► divine

golden ADJECTIVE **1** *a golden carriage* ► gilt, gilded **2** *golden hair* ► blond, blonde, yellow **3** *a golden opportunity* ► excellent, unique, special, promising, auspicious, propitious

good ADJECTIVE **1** *She is basically a good person.* ► virtuous, exemplary, righteous, moral, honest, upright, worthy, trustworthy OPPOSITES ARE bad, wicked, immoral **2** *Can you recommend a good hotel?* ► fine, high-quality, satisfactory, acceptable, excellent, superb, outstanding AN OPPOSITE IS poor **3** *The children were exceptionally good all evening.* ► well behaved, obedient, well mannered AN OPPOSITE IS naughty **4** *That would be a good thing to do.* ► proper, right, correct, appropriate, auspicious AN OPPOSITE IS inappropriate **5** *He is not a good swimmer. She has always been good at music.* ► capable, able, proficient, accomplished, talented, skilled OPPOSITES ARE poor, inept **6** *She was a good friend.* ► true, loyal, close, dear, trusty, reliable, trustworthy, dependable AN OPPOSITE IS distant **7** *It was a good party.* ► enjoyable, pleasant, agreeable, pleasing **8** *Tom gave the*

a b c d e f **g** h i j k l m n o p q r s t u v w x y z

good ➡ gouge

A
B
C
D
E
F
G
H
I
J
K
L
M

good NOUN **1** something good • *Do good to others.* **2** benefit • *It's for your own good.*
for good for ever
no good useless
USAGE In standard English, **good** cannot be used as an adverb. You can say *She's a good player* but not *She played good.* The adverb that goes with good is **well**.

goodbye INTERJECTION a word used when you leave somebody or at the end of a phone call

goods PLURAL NOUN **1** things that are bought and sold **2** things that are carried on trains or lorries

goose NOUN geese a long-necked water bird with webbed feet, larger than a duck

gooseberry NOUN gooseberries **1** a small green fruit that grows on a prickly bush **2** (*informal*) an unwanted extra person

goose pimples or **goosebumps** PLURAL NOUN skin that has turned rough with small bumps on it because a person is cold or afraid

gorge NOUN gorges a narrow valley with steep sides

gorge VERB gorges, gorging, gorged eat greedily; stuff with food

gorgeous ADJECTIVE magnificent or beautiful
▷ **gorgeously** ADVERB

gorilla NOUN gorillas a large powerful African ape, the largest of all the apes
USAGE Do not confuse with **guerrilla**, which can be pronounced in the same way.

gospel NOUN
the Gospels the first four books of the New Testament, telling of the life and teachings of Jesus Christ

gospel music NOUN a fervent style of black American religious singing

gossip VERB gossips, gossiping, gossiped talk a lot about other people

gossip NOUN gossips **1** talk, especially rumors, about other people **2** a person who enjoys gossiping
▷ **gossipy** ADJECTIVE

got *past tense* of get
have got possess • *Have you got a car?*

Gothic NOUN the style of building common in Europe in the 12th-16th centuries, with pointed arches and much decorative carving

gouge (gowj) VERB gouges, gouging, gouged scoop or force out by pressing

---

Thesaurus

N
O
P
Q
R
S
T
U
V
W
X
Y
Z

car a good clean. ► thorough, complete **9** *a good number of people* ► considerable, substantial, appreciable, sizeable, fair, ample **10** *It is good of you to come.* ► kind, generous, considerate, obliging AN OPPOSITE IS unkind **11** *When is a good time to call?* ► convenient, suitable, appropriate, opportune, fitting OPPOSITES ARE bad, unsuitable **12** *food that is good for you* ► healthy, wholesome, nutritious, nourishing OPPOSITES ARE bad, unhealthy **13** *a diner that serves good food* ► delicious, appetizing, tasty **14** *There are several good reasons for going.* ► valid, genuine, cogent, real, convincing AN OPPOSITE IS poor

goodbye NOUN *Roddy said goodbye and left us.* ► farewell, (*more informal*) cheerio, (*French*) adieu, (*French*) au revoir, (*Italian*) ciao, (*Spanish*) adios

good-humored ADJECTIVE *He was patient and good-humored.* ► genial, affable, cordial, congenial, amiable, easygoing AN OPPOSITE IS ill-humored

good-looking ADJECTIVE *a good-looking woman* ► attractive, handsome, nice-looking, presentable, beautiful, pretty, lovely AN OPPOSITE IS ugly

good-natured ADJECTIVE *He had a blunt good-natured face.* ► kind, kindly, gentle, warm-hearted, amiable, friendly, neighborly, benevolent AN OPPOSITE IS ill-natured

goodness NOUN *There is a lot of goodness in*

these people, criminals though they are. ► virtue, good, uprightness, generosity, goodwill, honesty AN OPPOSITE IS wickedness

goods PLURAL NOUN **1** *the supply of goods and services* ► merchandise, produce, products, articles, stock **2** *The dead man's goods did not amount to much.* ► property, possessions, effects, chattels

good-tempered ADJECTIVE *He remained patient and good-tempered despite the difficulties.* ► calm, placid, equable, unflustered, composed, self-possessed, tranquil AN OPPOSITE IS bad-tempered

goodwill NOUN *People come here full of goodwill and good intentions.* ► kindness, benevolence, generosity, friendliness, consideration OPPOSITES ARE hostility, ill will

gorgeous ADJECTIVE **1** *a gorgeous young woman* ► beautiful, lovely, glamorous, dazzling, pretty, stunning, striking **2** *a gorgeous view* ► magnificent, spectacular, splendid, superb, glorious

gossip NOUN **1** *He liked gossip and knew something about everybody.* ► idle talk, tittle-tattle, tattle, prattle, rumor, hearsay, chatter, scandal **2** *The sisters were both dreadful gossips.* ► scandalmonger, gossipmonger, talebearer, busybody, tattler

gossip VERB *The landlord was busy gossiping to the other customers.* ► chat, chatter, prattle, spread stories, (*informal*) natter, (*informal*) tattle

gourmet (goor- may) NOUN **gourmets** a person who understands and appreciates good food and drink

govern VERB **governs, governing, governed** be in charge of the public affairs of a country or region

governess NOUN **governesses** a woman employed to teach children in a private household

government NOUN **governments 1** the group of people who are in charge of the public affairs of a country **2** the process of governing
▷ **governmental** ADJECTIVE

governor NOUN **governors 1** a person who governs a state or a colony **2** a member of the governing body of a school or other institution **3** the person in charge of a prison

gown NOUN **gowns 1** a woman's long dress **2** a loose robe worn by lawyers, members of a university, etc.

GP ABBREVIATION general practitioner

grab VERB **grabs, grabbing, grabbed** take hold of something firmly or suddenly

grace NOUN **1** beauty, especially of movement **2** goodwill or favor **3** dignity or good manners • *At least he had the grace to apologize.* **4** a short prayer of thanks before or after a meal **5** the title of a duke, duchess, or archbishop • *His Grace the Duke of Kent.*

grace VERB **graces, gracing, graced** bring honour or dignity to something • *The mayor himself graced us with his presence.*

graceful ADJECTIVE beautiful and elegant in movement or shape
▷ **gracefully** ADVERB **gracefulness** NOUN

gracious ADJECTIVE behaving kindly and honorably
▷ **graciously** ADVERB **graciousness** NOUN

grade NOUN **grades 1** a step in a scale of quality or value or rank **2** a mark showing the quality of a student's work

grade VERB **grades, grading, graded** sort or divide into grades

gradient (gray- dee- ent) NOUN **gradients** a slope or the steepness of a slope

gradual ADJECTIVE happening slowly but steadily
▷ **gradually** ADVERB

graduate (grad- yoo- at) NOUN **graduates** a person who has a university or college degree

graduate (grad- yoo- ayt) VERB **graduates, graduating, graduated** be awarded a university or college degree

graffiti NOUN words or drawings scribbled or sprayed on a wall
USAGE Strictly speaking, this word is a plural noun (the singular is *graffito*), so it should be used with a plural verb: *There are graffiti all over the wall.* However, the word is widely used nowadays as if it were a singular noun and

Thesaurus

govern VERB **1** *A coalition was formed to govern the country.* ► run, rule, administer, be in charge of, conduct the affairs of, direct, manage, preside over **2** *the rules that govern the way we treat each other* ► regulate, determine, control, direct, affect, influence, shape

government NOUN **1** *The new government takes office next week.* ► administration, executive, regime, ministry **2** *a country that badly needs a period of stable government* ► rule, direction, leadership, management, guidance, regulation

governor NOUN **1** *a prison governor* ► administrator, director, principal, superintendent **2** *the governor of a state* ► leader ruler, overseer, viceroy, commissioner, administrator

grab VERB **1** *She grabbed him by his arm.* ► seize, grasp, catch, grip, take hold of, clutch at **2** *Someone grabbed her credit card while she wasn't looking.* ► snatch, steal, take, (*more informal*) nab, (*more informal*) pinch

grace NOUN **1** *The dancers moved with considerable grace.* ► elegance, poise, gracefulness, refinement **2** *He conceded the point with good grace.* ► courtesy, civility, decorum, decency, charm, generosity **3** *They*

did not want to see another president fall from grace. ► favor, approval, esteem, regard, support **4** *by the grace of the monarch* ► generosity, favor, benevolence, indulgence, goodwill

graceful ADJECTIVE *Mary's clothes were light and graceful.* ► elegant, flowing, stylish, tasteful, smooth, beautiful

grade NOUN **1** *She is trying for a higher grade in the exam.* ► mark, score, level, grading, assessment, standard **2** *a hotel in the top grade* ► class, category, classification **3** *officers in the lower grades* ► rank, level, status, echelon, step

grade VERB **1** *Eggs are graded according to size.* ► sort, classify, categorize, differentiate, group, range, arrange, rank **2** *An external examiner will grade the coursework.* ► mark, assess, evaluate, rank, rate

gradual ADJECTIVE **1** *a gradual change in the weather* ► steady, slow, moderate, progressive, continuous, regular, step-by-step AN OPPOSITE IS sudden **2** *a gradual slope* ► gentle, moderate, slight, easy AN OPPOSITE IS steep

gradually ADVERB *The colors fade gradually in the sunlight. Gradually she eased the drawer back in its place.* ► slowly, little by little, steadily, gently, cautiously, progressively, imperceptibly most people do not regard this as wrong: *There is graffiti all over the wall.*

graft NOUN **grafts 1** a shoot from one plant or tree fixed into another to form a new growth **2** a piece of living tissue transplanted by a surgeon to replace what is diseased or damaged ● *a skin graft*

graft VERB **grafts, grafting, grafted** insert or transplant as a graft

grain NOUN **grains 1** a small hard seed or similar particle **2** cereal plants when they are growing or after being harvested **3** a very small amount ● *a grain of truth* **4** the pattern of lines made by the fibres in a piece of wood or paper
▷ **grainy** ADJECTIVE

gram NOUN **grams** a unit of mass or weight in the metric system

grammar NOUN **grammars 1** the rules for using words correctly **2** a book about these rules
▷ **grammatical** ADJECTIVE

grammar school NOUN **grammar schools** a secondary school for children with academic ability

grand ADJECTIVE **1** splendid and impressive **2** most important or highest-ranking **3** including everything; complete
▷ **grandly** ADVERB **grandness** NOUN

grandchild NOUN **grandchildren** the child of a person's son or daughter
▷ **granddaughter** NOUN **grandson** NOUN

grandeur (grand- yer) NOUN impressive beauty; splendor

grandfather NOUN **grandfathers** the father of a person's father or mother

grandiose (grand- ee- ohss) ADJECTIVE large and impressive; trying to seem impressive

grandmother NOUN **grandmothers** the mother of a person's father or mother

grandparent NOUN **grandparents** a grandfather or grandmother

grand piano NOUN **grand pianos** a large piano with the strings fixed horizontally

grandstand NOUN **grandstands** a building with a roof and rows of seats for spectators at a racecourse or sports ground

grand total NOUN the sum of other totals

granite NOUN a very hard kind of rock used for building

grant VERB **grants, granting, granted 1** give or allow someone what they have asked for ● *We have decided to grant your request.* **2** admit; agree that something is true
take for granted assume that something is true or will happen

grant NOUN **grants** something granted, especially a sum of money

Granth (grunt) NOUN the sacred scriptures of the Sikhs

grape NOUN **grapes** a small green or purple berry that grows in bunches on a vine. Grapes are used to make wine

grapefruit NOUN **grapefruit** a large round yellow citrus fruit

grapevine NOUN **grapevines 1** a vine on which grapes grow **2** a way by which news spreads unofficially, with people passing it on from one to another

graph NOUN **graphs** a diagram showing how two quantities or variables are related

graphic ADJECTIVE **1** to do with drawing or painting ● *a graphic artist* **2** giving a lively description
▷ **graphically** ADVERB

grapple VERB **grapples, grappling, grappled 1** struggle or wrestle **2** seize or hold firmly

---

Thesaurus

---

grain NOUN **1** *a good grain harvest* ► corn, cereal, seed **2** *grains of sand* ► granule, particle, speck, crumb, fragment **3** *not a grain of truth in the story* ► trace, hint, ounce, scrap **4** *wood with a strong grain* ► texture, marking, surface, pattern

grand ADJECTIVE **1** *a grand palace*
► magnificent, splendid, majestic, glorious, stately, imposing **2** *a grand old lady*
► distinguished, illustrious, august, eminent, prominent, celebrated **3** (*informal*) *They are doing a grand job.* ► excellent, very good, fine, splendid, first-class, first-rate

grandeur NOUN *the grandeur of the royal ceremonies* ► splendor, magnificence, glory, resplendence, stateliness

grant VERB **1** *The award body can grant you a scholarship.* ► give, award, allow, confer on you, pay, provide you with **2** *The court granted*

her request. ► allow, consent to, accede to, permit **3** *We grant that the difference is small.* ► admit, concede, acknowledge, agree, accept, confess

grant NOUN **1** *They were given a local authority grant to repair their roof.* ► award, allowance, subsidy, subvention, endowment, contribution, donation, allocation **2** *a student grant* ► bursary, scholarship, sponsorship, loan

graph NOUN *a graph showing the rise in house prices* ► table, chart, diagram, grid, pie chart, column graph

graphic ADJECTIVE *a graphic description of the accident* ► vivid, explicit, striking, forceful, dramatic, lurid, detailed, colorful AN OPPOSITE IS vague

grapple VERB **1** *They grappled for the gun on the wet grass.* ► struggle, wrestle, tussle, scuffle,

3 try to deal with a problem etc. • *I've been grappling with this essay all day.*

grasp VERB grasps, grasping, grasped **1** seize and hold firmly **2** understand

grasp NOUN **1** a person's understanding of something • *a good grasp of electronics* **2** a firm hold

grasping ADJECTIVE greedy for money or possessions

grass NOUN grasses **1** a plant with green blades and stalks **2** ground covered with grass; lawn
▷ **grassy** ADJECTIVE

grasshopper NOUN grasshoppers a jumping insect that makes a shrill noise

grass roots PLURAL NOUN the ordinary people in a political party or other group

grate NOUN grates **1** a metal framework that keeps fuel in a fireplace **2** a fireplace

grate VERB grates, grating, grated **1** shred something into small pieces by rubbing it on a rough surface **2** make an unpleasant noise by rubbing **3** sound harshly
grate on have an irritating effect

grateful ADJECTIVE feeling or showing that you are thankful for something that has been done for you
▷ **gratefully** ADVERB

gratify VERB gratifies, gratifying, gratified **1** give pleasure **2** satisfy a feeling or desire

• *May we gratify our curiosity and have a look?*
▷ **gratification** NOUN

grating NOUN gratings a framework of metal bars placed across an opening

gratitude NOUN being grateful

grave NOUN graves the place where a dead body is buried

grave ADJECTIVE serious or solemn
▷ **gravely** ADVERB

grave accent (rhymes with *starve*) NOUN grave accents a backward-sloping mark over a vowel, as in *vis-à-vis*

gravel NOUN small stones mixed with coarse sand, used to make paths
▷ **gravelled** ADJECTIVE **gravelly** ADJECTIVE

graveyard NOUN graveyards a burial ground

gravity NOUN **1** the force that pulls all objects in the universe towards each other **2** the force that pulls everything towards the earth **3** seriousness

gravy NOUN a hot brown sauce made from meat juices

gray NOUN grays the color between black and white, like ashes or dark clouds
▷ **gray** ADJECTIVE **grayness** NOUN

Thesaurus

brawl, fight **2 grapple with** *The President has a major problem to grapple with.* ► contend with, tackle, attend to, cope with, deal with, manage, handle, come to grips with, engage with, get involved with, try to solve, (*more informal*) have a go at AN OPPOSITE IS avoid

grasp VERB **1** *He got up and grasped her hand.* ► grip, clasp, clutch, grab, seize, catch, snatch, hold, get hold of, hang on to **2** *He got impatient if they failed to grasp a point.* ► understand, comprehend, follow, take in, apprehend, perceive, master, learn, realize, (*more informal*) cotton on to

grasp NOUN **1** *She managed to escape his grasp.* ► grip, hold, clutch, embrace, control **2** *His ultimate goal was within his grasp.* ► reach, power, command **3** *They now have a good grasp of the subject.* ► understanding, comprehension, perception, mastery, familiarity (with)

grass NOUN *A notice told them to keep off the grass.* ► lawn, turf, green

grate VERB **1** *She started to grate some cheese.* ► shred, grind, cut up, mince **2** *His whining voice began to grate.* ► irritate, jar, rankle, be irksome

grateful ADJECTIVE *The families are grateful for all the support they have received.* ► thankful,

appreciative (of), indebted, obliged AN OPPOSITE IS ungrateful

gratitude NOUN *His letter expressed gratitude for the help he had been given.* ► thanks, appreciation (of), acknowledgement (of), indebtedness

grave ADJECTIVE **1** *a grave error; grave matters* ► serious, important, significant, crucial, critical, momentous, vital, acute, weighty AN OPPOSITE IS unimportant **2** *a grave offense* ► criminal, indictable, punishable AN OPPOSITE IS minor **3** *a grave expression* ► serious, solemn, somber, earnest, severe, subdued, dignified, gloomy, thoughtful, unsmiling, grim, long-faced AN OPPOSITE IS happy

gravity NOUN **1** *the gravity of the situation* ► seriousness, severity, acuteness, magnitude, momentousness, danger, importance **2** *the gravity of his manner* ► solemnity, dignity, sobriety, earnestness, ceremony, pomp, sedateness **3** *the force of gravity* ► gravitation, pull, weight, heaviness, downward force

gray ADJECTIVE **1** *His gray beard had grown very long.* ► silver, silvery, slate-gray, whitish, graying, grizzled, grizzly, hoary **2** *Her face was gray with worry.* ► pale, ashen, leaden, wan, sallow, pasty, drawn **3** *The day began gray and dull.* ► cloudy, overcast, gloomy, dismal, dreary, bleak

graze VERB grazes, grazing, grazed **1** feed on growing grass **2** scrape your skin slightly • *I grazed my elbow on the wall.* **3** touch something lightly in passing

graze NOUN grazes a raw place where skin has been scraped

grease NOUN **1** any thick oily substance **2** melted fat
▷ **greasy** ADJECTIVE

grease VERB greases, greasing, greased put grease on something

great ADJECTIVE **1** very large; much above average **2** very important or talented • *a great composer* **3** (*informal*) very good or enjoyable • *It's great to see you again.* **4** older or younger by one generation • *great-grandfather*
▷ **greatly** ADVERB **greatness** NOUN

greed NOUN being greedy

greedy ADJECTIVE greedier, greediest wanting more food, money, or other things than you need
▷ **greedily** ADVERB **greediness** NOUN

green NOUN greens **1** the color of grass, leaves, etc. **2** an area of grassy land • *the village green* • *a putting green*

green ADJECTIVE **1** of the color green **2** concerned with protecting the natural environment **3** inexperienced and likely to make mistakes
▷ **greenness** NOUN

green belt NOUN green belts an area kept as open land around a city

greenery NOUN green leaves or plants

greengrocer NOUN greengrocers a person who keeps a shop that sells fruit and vegetables
▷ **greengrocery** NOUN

greenhouse NOUN greenhouses a glass building where plants are protected from cold

greenhouse effect NOUN the warming of the earth's surface when heat from the sun is trapped in the earth's atmosphere by gases such as carbon dioxide and methane

greens PLURAL NOUN green vegetables, such as cabbage and spinach

Greenwich Mean Time (gren- ich) NOUN the time on the line of longitude which passes through Greenwich in London, used as a basis for calculating time throughout the world

greet VERB greets, greeting, greeted **1** speak to a person who arrives **2** receive • *They greeted the song with applause.* **3** present itself to • *A strange sight greeted our eyes.*

greeting NOUN greetings words or actions used to greet somebody

---

Thesaurus

---

graze VERB **1** *She fell and grazed her knee.*
► scrape, cut, scratch, scuff, abrade **2** *Cattle grazed in the fields.* ► feed, browse, crop, ruminate, pasture

graze NOUN *a graze on his elbow* ► cut, abrasion, laceration, raw spot

greasy ADJECTIVE **1** *She had greasy hair and worried about her weight.* ► oily, shiny, waxy AN OPPOSITE IS dry **2** *His hand left greasy fingerprints on the glass.* ► fatty, oily, smeary, slimy, buttery

great ADJECTIVE **1** *A great hill rose before them.*
► large, huge, big, enormous, gigantic, massive, colossal AN OPPOSITE IS small **2** *Speaking a foreign language is a great advantage. She is a person of great courage.*
► considerable, special, much, extreme OPPOSITES ARE small, little **3** *He read through the list of great statesmen.* ► famous, eminent, celebrated, distinguished, honored, renowned, acclaimed, prominent, revered, exalted, illustrious OPPOSITES ARE unknown, obscure **4** *The invasion proved a great mistake; a talk on the great advances in medicine*
► important, significant, crucial, critical, big, vital OPPOSITES ARE insignificant, unimportant **5** (*informal*) *We went to a great party.*
► excellent, enjoyable, marvelous, wonderful, fantastic, first-rate AN OPPOSITE IS poor

greed NOUN **1** *I ate my supper with undisguised greed.* ► hunger, gluttony, ravenousness, overeating, overindulgence **2** *Material greed is not one of their faults.* ► avarice, acquisitiveness, covetousness, rapacity, cupidity, craving, desire, selfishness **3** *He was clearly motivated by a greed for power.* ► appetite, desire, urge, need, lust, longing, craving

greedy ADJECTIVE **1** *a greedy eater* ► gluttonous, ravenous, voracious, insatiable **2** *greedy for money* ► avaricious, covetous, acquisitive, mercenary, grasping **3** *greedy for power* ► eager, avid, longing, craving, (*more informal*) itching

green ADJECTIVE **1** *a green garden* ► leafy, grassy, verdant OPPOSITES ARE barren, bare **2** *green with envy* ► envious, covetous, jealous, resentful **3** *a green recruit* ► inexperienced, raw, naive, innocent, immature, untried, credulous, gullible OPPOSITES ARE experienced, worldly-wise **4** *green issues* ► environmental, ecological, conservationist

greet VERB *She greeted her visitors one by one.*
► welcome, say hello to, acknowledge, receive, give a greeting to, hail, salute

greeting NOUN **1** *She called out a greeting.*
► hello, salutation, welcome **2** *greetings birthday greetings* ► good wishes, best wishes, congratulations, compliments

greyhound NOUN greyhounds a slender dog with smooth hair, used in racing

grid NOUN grids **1** a framework or pattern of bars or lines crossing each other **2** a network of cables or wires for carrying electricity over a large area

grid reference NOUN grid references a set of numbers that allows you to describe the exact position of something on a map

grief NOUN deep sorrow, especially at a person's death
come to grief suffer a disaster

grievance NOUN grievances something that people are discontented about

grieve VERB grieves, grieving, grieved **1** feel deep sorrow, especially at a person's death **2** make a person feel very sad

grill NOUN grills **1** a heated element on a cooker, for sending heat downwards **2** food cooked under this **3** a grille

grill VERB grills, grilling, grilled **1** cook on a grill **2** question closely and severely ● *The police grilled him for an hour.*

grim ADJECTIVE grimmer, grimmest **1** stern or severe **2** unpleasant or unattractive ● *a grim prospect*
▷ **grimly** ADVERB **grimness** NOUN

grimace (grim- ayss, grim- as) NOUN grimaces a twisted expression on the face made in pain or disgust

grimace VERB grimaces, grimacing, grimaced make a grimace

grime NOUN dirt in a layer on a surface or on the skin
▷ **grimy** ADJECTIVE

grin NOUN grins a broad smile showing your teeth

grin VERB grins, grinning, grinned smile broadly showing your teeth

grind VERB grinds, grinding, ground **1** crush something into tiny pieces or powder **2** sharpen or smooth something by rubbing it on a rough surface **3** rub harshly together
● *He ground his teeth in fury.*
▷ **grinder** NOUN
grind to a halt stop suddenly with a loud noise

grip VERB grips, gripping, gripped **1** hold something firmly **2** hold a person's attention ● *The opening chapter really gripped me.*

grip NOUN grips **1** a firm hold **2** a handle, especially on a sports racket, bat, etc. **3** a traveling bag **4** control or power ● *The country is in the grip of lottery fever.*
get to grips with begin to deal with successfully

gristle NOUN tough rubbery tissue in meat
▷ **gristly** ADJECTIVE

grit NOUN **1** tiny pieces of stone or sand **2** courage and endurance
▷ **gritty** ADJECTIVE **grittiness** NOUN

grit VERB grits, gritting, gritted **1** spread a road or path with grit **2** clench your teeth when in pain or trouble

grizzled ADJECTIVE streaked with grey hairs

Thesaurus

gregarious ADJECTIVE *He is cheerful, hard-working, and gregarious.* ► sociable, outgoing, extrovert, friendly, convivial, companionable, affable

grid NOUN **1** *He had broken the stone to which the iron grid was fixed.* ► grating, grille, lattice, mesh, framework **2** *The information is shown in the form of a grid.* ► graph, matrix, network

grief NOUN *His letters made her grief for her mother more bearable.* ► sadness, sorrow, mourning, bereavement, unhappiness, distress, misery, affliction, desolation AN OPPOSITE IS joy

grieve VERB **1** *She grieved for her mother constantly.* ► mourn, sorrow, lament, weep, cry **2** *They were deeply grieved by the unkind newspaper reports.* ► hurt, wound, upset, sadden, distress

grim ADJECTIVE **1** *His face bore a grim expression.* ► stern, severe, harsh, dour, forbidding, sullen, morose, gloomy OPPOSITES ARE cheerful, pleasant **2** *the grim knowledge that she might die* ► unpleasant, dreadful, terrible,

grisly, gruesome, macabre, distressing, fearsome, horrid, shocking **3** *a grim little mining town* ► dreary, bleak, dismal, gloomy, dingy

grimy ADJECTIVE *The other office was dark and grimy.* ► dirty, grubby, filthy, messy, smutty, soiled

grin VERB *She grinned at us and left the room.* ► smile, beam, smirk

grin NOUN *He had a silly grin on his face.* ► smile, smirk

grind VERB **1** *He ground the coffee into a fine powder.* ► crush, pound, grate **2** *The kitchen had a wheel for grinding knives.* ► sharpen, whet, hone, file

grip VERB **1** *He gripped Helen's hand.* ► grasp, clasp, clutch, grab, seize, catch, snatch, hold, get hold of, hang on to **2** *The story gripped everyone.* ► engross, enthral, absorb, captivate, fascinate, rivet, mesmerize

grip NOUN *She kept a firm grip on the back of the chair.* ► hold, grasp, clasp, clutch

a
b
c
d
e
f
g
h
i
j
k
l
m
n
o
p
q
r
s
t
u
v
w
x
y
z

grizzly bear NOUN grizzly bears a large fierce bear of North America

groan VERB groans, groaning, groaned **1** make a long deep sound in pain, distress, or disapproval **2** creak loudly under a heavy load
▷ **groan** NOUN **groaner** NOUN

grocer NOUN grocers a person who keeps a shop that sells food and household goods

groceries PLURAL NOUN goods sold by a grocer

groom NOUN grooms **1** a person whose job is to look after horses **2** a bridegroom

groom VERB grooms, grooming, groomed **1** clean and brush a horse or other animal **2** make something neat and trim **3** train a person for a certain job or position • Evans is being groomed for the position.

groove NOUN grooves a long narrow furrow or channel cut in the surface of something
▷ **grooved** ADJECTIVE

grope VERB gropes, groping, groped feel about for something you cannot see

gross (grohss) ADJECTIVE **1** fat and ugly **2** very obvious or shocking • gross stupidity **3** having bad manners; vulgar **4** (informal) disgusting **5** total; without anything being deducted • our gross income (COMPARE net [2])
▷ **grossly** ADVERB **grossness** NOUN

gross NOUN gross twelve dozen (144) of something • ten gross = 1440

grotesque (groh-tesk) ADJECTIVE fantastically ugly or very strangely shaped
▷ **grotesquely** ADVERB **grotesqueness** NOUN [from Italian pittura grottesca = painting like one found in a grotto]

grotto NOUN grottoes a small pretty cave, especially an artificial one [from Italian]

ground past tense of grind

ground NOUN grounds **1** the solid surface of the earth **2** a sports field **3** land of a certain kind • marshy ground **4** the amount of a subject that is dealt with • The course covers a lot of ground

ground VERB grounds, grounding, grounded **1** prevent a plane from flying • All aircraft are grounded because of the fog. **2** stop a child from going out, as a punishment **3** give a good basic training to someone • Ground them in the rules of spelling. **4** base • This theory is grounded on reliable evidence.

grounds PLURAL NOUN **1** the gardens of a large house **2** solid particles that sink to the bottom • coffee grounds **3** reasons • There are grounds for suspicion.

group NOUN groups **1** a number of people, animals, or things that come together or belong together in some way **2** a band of musicians

group VERB groups, grouping, grouped put together or come together in a group or groups

grouse NOUN grouse a bird with feathered feet, hunted as game

grouse VERB grouses, grousing, groused (informal) grumble or complain
▷ **grouse** NOUN **grouser** NOUN

grove NOUN groves a group of trees; a small wood

grovel VERB grovels, grovelling, grovelled **1** crawl on the ground, especially in a show of

Thesaurus

groan VERB She heard him groaning in his sleep. ► moan, cry out, sigh, wail

groan NOUN He let out a weary groan. ► moan, sigh, cry, wail

groove NOUN The water had worn a groove in the rock. ► channel, furrow, hollow, rut, indentation, slot, track

gross ADJECTIVE **1** a gross exaggeration ► extreme, blatant, flagrant, glaring, obvious, conspicuous, sheer, outright **2** gross indecency ► coarse, vulgar, crude, obscene, lewd, improper **3** He looked gross and he knew it. ► obese, fat, corpulent, overweight, big **4** gross income ► total, inclusive, overall, aggregate, whole, full **5** gross misshapen versions of the human form ► disgusting, repellent, abhorrent, loathsome, sickening

ground NOUN **1** The ground was wet and spongy. ► earth, terrain, soil, turf, loam **2** The little plane slowly rose from the ground. ► land, surface **3** grounds a large house in its own grounds ► land, estate, gardens, surroundings

groundless ADJECTIVE Their fears proved to be groundless. ► baseless, needless, unfounded, unjustified, unwarranted, unsubstantiated, uncalled for, false, gratuitous, imaginary, irrational AN OPPOSITE IS justifiable

group NOUN **1** Divide the children into groups for a game. ► set, circle, section **2** The reading group meets once a month. ► club, circle, society, association **3** a small group of islands off the northeast coast ► cluster, collection, formation, bunch, mass, clump **4** A group of fans waited at the stage door. ► crowd, band, body, gathering, flock, assembly, gang, pack **5** They sorted the books into different groups. ► category, class, type, sort, kind, set

group VERB group together **1** Farmers began to group together to form cooperatives. ► unite, join together, join forces, team up, come together **2** Comfortable chairs are grouped around coffee tables. ► arrange, organize, dispose, assemble, collect, cluster **3** We group the books according to their size. ► classify, categorize, sort, range, band

fear or humility **2** act in an excessively humble way, for example by apologizing a lot
▷ **groveller** NOUN

grow VERB **grows, growing, grew, grown**
1 become bigger or greater **2** develop
3 cultivate; plant and look after • *She grows roses.* **4** become • *He grew rich.*
▷ **grower** NOUN
grow up become an adult

growl VERB **growls, growling, growled** make a deep angry sound in the throat
▷ **growl** NOUN

grown-up NOUN **grown-ups** an adult person
▷ **grown-up** ADJECTIVE

growth NOUN **growths 1** growing or developing **2** something that has grown **3** a lump that has grown on or inside a person's body; a tumor

grub NOUN **grubs 1** a tiny wormlike creature that will become an insect; a larva **2** (*slang*) food

grub VERB **grubs, grubbing, grubbed 1** dig up

by the roots **2** turn things over or move them about while looking for something; rummage

grubby ADJECTIVE **grubbier, grubbiest** rather dirty
▷ **grubbiness** NOUN

grudge NOUN **grudges** a feeling of resentment or ill will • *She isn't the sort of person who bears a grudge.*

grudge VERB **grudges, grudging, grudged** resent having to give or allow something

gruff ADJECTIVE having a rough or unfriendly voice or manner
▷ **gruffly** ADVERB **gruffness** NOUN

grumble VERB **grumbles, grumbling, grumbled** complain in a bad-tempered way
▷ **grumble** NOUN **grumbler** NOUN

grunt VERB **grunts, grunting, grunted 1** make a pig's gruff snort **2** speak or say gruffly
▷ **grunt** NOUN

guarantee NOUN **guarantees** a formal promise to do something or to repair something you have sold if it breaks or goes wrong

---

Thesaurus

---

grow VERB **1** *The baby grew fast.* ➤ get bigger, get larger, increase in size, fill out, put on growth **2** *Their debts are growing.* ➤ increase, mount up, multiply AN OPPOSITE IS decrease **3** *She grows roses in her garden.* ➤ cultivate, produce, propagate, farm **4** *At about 4 o'clock it grows dark.* ➤ become, turn, come to be **5** *The business was growing.* ➤ expand, develop, flourish, thrive, prosper, succeed, boom OPPOSITES ARE decline, fail

growl VERB *The dog growled at him.* ➤ snarl, snap, yap

grown-up ADJECTIVE *Chris has a grown-up sister.* ➤ adult, fully grown, mature

grown-up NOUN *He wants to be treated like a grown-up.* ➤ adult, grown person, mature person, grown man OR woman

growth NOUN **1** *a steady growth in population* ➤ increase, expansion, development OPPOSITES ARE decline, decrease **2** *hormones that aid growth* ➤ growing, development, maturing **3** *measures to increase economic growth* ➤ expansion, development, progress, advance AN OPPOSITE IS decline **4** *She has to have a growth removed.* ➤ tumor, lump, swelling, cyst

grub NOUN *The fruit was riddled with grubs.* ➤ larva, maggot, caterpillar

grubby ADJECTIVE *He had not yet changed out of his grubby overalls.* ➤ dirty, filthy, grimy, soiled, messy

grudge NOUN *The letter was written by someone with a grudge.* ➤ grievance, resentment, umbrage, pique, bitterness, rancour, bad feelings

grudge VERB *He grudged the money he would have to pay out.* ➤ resent, begrudge, object to, be angry about

grueling ADJECTIVE *a grueling journey back from the Himalayas* ➤ exhausting, arduous, tiring, wearying, exacting, demanding, punishing, hard, taxing, strenuous, laborious, (*more informal*) killing AN OPPOSITE IS easy

gruesome ADJECTIVE *The gruesome remains had to be analyzed.* ➤ grisly, gory, ghastly, bloody, horrific, repulsive, frightful, hideous, macabre, revolting, repellent

gruff ADJECTIVE **1** *His voice was gruff in the darkness.* ➤ harsh, rough, hoarse, husky, throaty **2** *his unique gruff manner* ➤ abrupt, brusque, curt, blunt, bad-tempered, churlish

grumble VERB *Everyone was grumbling about the heat.* ➤ complain, carp, protest, whine, grouch, moan, (*informal*) whinge, (*more informal*) bellyache, (*more informal*) gripe

grumble NOUN *constant grumbles about the weather* ➤ complaint, moan, groan, protest, objection

grumpy ADJECTIVE *I'm always grumpy early in the morning.* ➤ bad-tempered, irritable, irascible, testy, grouchy, touchy, crotchety, cantankerous, peevish, fractious, cross OPPOSITES ARE good-humored, good-tempered

guarantee NOUN **1** *Used cars come with a six-month guarantee.* ➤ warranty, warrant, covenant **2** *We cannot give a guarantee that these measures will succeed.* ➤ assurance, pledge, promise, commitment, surety, oath

guarantee ➡ guillotine

guarantee VERB guarantees, guaranteeing, guaranteed **1** give a guarantee; promise **2** make it certain that something will happen
• *Money does not guarantee happiness.*
▷ **guarantor** NOUN

guard VERB guards, guarding, guarded **1** protect; keep safe **2** watch over and prevent from escaping
guard against try to prevent something happening

guard NOUN guards **1** guarding; protection
• *Keep the prisoners under close guard.*
2 someone who guards a person or place **3** a group of soldiers or police officers etc. acting as a guard **4** a railway official in charge of a train **5** a protecting device • *a fireguard*
on guard alert for possible danger or difficulty

guardian NOUN guardians **1** someone who guards **2** a person who is legally in charge of a child whose parents cannot look after him or her
▷ **guardianship** NOUN

guerrilla (ger- il- a) NOUN guerrillas a member of a small unofficial army who fights by making surprise attacks
USAGE Do not confuse with **gorilla**.

guess NOUN guesses an opinion or answer that you give without making careful calculations or without certain knowledge

guess VERB guesses, guessing, guessed make a guess
▷ **guesser** NOUN

guesswork NOUN something you think of or work out by guessing

guest NOUN guests **1** a person who is invited to visit or stay at another's house **2** a person staying at a hotel **3** a person who takes part in another's show as a visiting performer

guidance NOUN **1** guiding **2** advising or advice on problems

guide NOUN guides **1** a person who shows others the way or points out interesting sights **2** a book giving information about a place or subject

guide VERB guides, guiding, guided show someone the way or how to do something

guidebook NOUN guidebooks a book of information about places that tourists visit

guide dog NOUN guide dogs a dog trained to lead a blind person

guile (rhymes with *mile*) NOUN craftiness

guillotine (gil- ot- een) NOUN guillotines a machine with a heavy blade for beheading criminals, formerly used in France [named after Dr. Guillotin, who suggested its use in France in 1789]

Thesaurus

---

guarantee VERB **1** *He could not guarantee that they would keep their jobs.* ► promise, swear, pledge, assure, certify, give a guarantee, give your word, vouch, vow **2** *You need a reservation to guarantee a seat.* ► secure, ensure, make sure of

guard VERB **1** *Troops guarded the house.*
► protect, stand guard over, watch over, shield, safeguard, defend, cover **2** *An escort guarded the prisoners.* ► supervise, watch over, control **3 guard against** *Take care to guard against over-tiredness in the first few weeks.*
► beware of, be alert to, try to prevent

guard NOUN **1** *We were turned back by the guards at the border.* ► sentry, sentinel, custodian, lookout, patrol, watchman **2** *He felt the guard's hand on his shoulder.* ► jailer, prison officer, warder, warden
off your guard OR **off guard** *He was caught off guard for a moment and the water surged over him.* ► unprepared, unready, unsuspecting
on your guard *Thieves are operating in this area, so be on your guard.* ► alert, watchful, vigilant, heedful, circumspect, chary

guarded ADJECTIVE *Their reaction was guarded and unfriendly.* ► cautious, wary, chary, unenthusiastic, noncommittal, discreet

guess VERB **1** *You have to guess the weight of a large cake.* ► estimate, reckon, judge, predict, gauge, determine **2** (*informal*) *I guess I should say sorry.* ► suppose, believe, think, imagine, expect, assume, consider, reckon

guess NOUN *My guess was he would head for the motorway.* ► theory, hypothesis, prediction, feeling, belief, opinion, conjecture, supposition, notion, idea, intuition

guest NOUN **1** *They joined their guests for dinner.*
► visitor, company, caller **2** *The hotel could take up to thirty guests.* ► resident, patron, client, lodger, boarder, customer, tenant

guidance NOUN *His supervisor offered him guidance.* ► advice, direction, instruction, help, counsel, teaching, support, pointers, guidelines

guide VERB **1** *I asked her to guide me back to the town.* ► lead, direct, show, show the way, take, accompany, escort, conduct **2** *The students have to be guided carefully through this stage of their work.* ► advise, counsel, direct, supervise, instruct, teach

guide NOUN **1** *Your guide will show you the way.*
► escort, leader, courier, navigator, pilot, attendant **2** *The sample is only meant to be a guide.* ► model, indication, example, gauge, guideline, pointer

guilt NOUN **1** the fact that you have committed an offense **2** a feeling that you are to blame for something that has happened

guilty ADJECTIVE **1** having done wrong • *He was found guilty of murder* **2** feeling or showing guilt • *a guilty conscience*
▷ **guiltily** ADVERB

guinea pig NOUN **guinea pigs** **1** a small furry animal without a tail **2** a person who is used as the subject of an experiment

guitar NOUN **guitars** a musical instrument played by plucking its strings
▷ **guitarist** NOUN

gulf NOUN **gulfs** **1** a large area of the sea that is partly surrounded by land **2** a wide gap; a great difference

gull NOUN **gulls** a seagull [a Celtic word]

gullible ADJECTIVE easily deceived

gulp VERB **gulps, gulping, gulped** **1** swallow hastily or greedily **2** make a loud swallowing noise, especially because of fear

gulp NOUN **gulps** **1** the act of gulping **2** a large mouthful of liquid

gum¹ NOUN **gums** the firm flesh in which your teeth are rooted

gum² NOUN **gums** **1** a sticky substance produced by some trees and shrubs, used as glue **2** a sweet made with gum or gelatine • *a fruit gum* **3** chewing gum **4** a gum tree
▷ **gummy** ADJECTIVE

gum VERB **gums, gumming, gummed** cover or stick something with gum

gum tree NOUN **gum trees** a eucalyptus

gun NOUN **guns** **1** a weapon that fires shells or bullets from a metal tube **2** a starting pistol **3** a device that forces a substance out of a tube • *a grease gun*
▷ **gunfire** NOUN **gunshot** NOUN

gun VERB **guns, gunning, gunned**
gun down shoot someone with a gun

gunpowder NOUN an explosive made from a powdered mixture of potassium nitrate, charcoal, and sulphur

gurgle VERB **gurgles, gurgling, gurgled** make a low bubbling sound
▷ **gurgle** NOUN

guru NOUN **gurus** **1** a Hindu religious leader **2** an influential teacher; a mentor

gush VERB **gushes, gushing, gushed** **1** flow suddenly or quickly **2** talk too enthusiastically or emotionally
▷ **gush** NOUN

gust NOUN **gusts** a sudden rush of wind, rain, or smoke
▷ **gusty** ADJECTIVE **gustily** ADVERB

gust VERB **gusts, gusting, gusted** blow in gusts

gut NOUN **guts** the lower part of the digestive system; the intestine

---

Thesaurus

---

guilt NOUN **1** *The jury was quite sure of his guilt.* ► guiltiness, culpability, liability, responsibility, blame, blameworthiness, wrongfulness, criminality AN OPPOSITE IS innocence **2** *There is no need to feel guilt about it.* ► shame, remorse, self-reproach, self-accusation, bad conscience, penitence, contrition, dishonor, guilty feelings, regret AN OPPOSITE IS virtue

guilty ADJECTIVE **1** *Brown was found guilty of assault.* ► culpable, blameworthy, at fault, liable, responsible, blameable, in the wrong, reprehensible AN OPPOSITE IS innocent **2** *She felt guilty about deceiving her friends.* ► ashamed, remorseful, sorry, repentant, regretful, contrite, penitent, conscience-stricken, shamefaced, sheepish AN OPPOSITE IS unrepentant

gulf NOUN **1** *Here ships turn into the gulf.* ► bay, inlet, creek, estuary, sound **2** *the gulf between rich and poor* ► gap, contrast, chasm, divergence, divide, rift, split, division

gullible ADJECTIVE *Wayne is very gullible when he's had too much to drink.* ► credulous, over-trusting, trustful, suggestible, easily taken in OPPOSITES ARE suspicious, astute

gulp VERB *Brian gulped his beer and stood to leave.* ► swallow, swill down, (*more informal*)

swig, (*more informal*) knock back AN OPPOSITE IS sip

gulp NOUN *She finished her juice in one gulp.* ► swallow, mouthful, (*more informal*) swig

gum NOUN *You can stick the pictures in with gum.* ► glue, adhesive, paste

gum VERB *The photos were gummed to the page.* ► stick, glue, paste, fix

gun NOUN *He threatened her with a gun.* ► firearm, weapon, pistol, revolver, rifle, shotgun, (*more informal*) shooter

gush VERB **1** *Blood gushed from the wound in his head.* ► pour, spurt, squirt, stream, flow, rush, cascade, spout, surge OPPOSITES ARE trickle, ooze **2** *They gushed all afternoon about their holiday plans.* ► enthuse, rave, effuse, chatter, jabber, (*more informal*) go on

gush NOUN *Turning the tap slightly produced a gush of scalding water.* ► rush, spurt, surge, stream, torrent, cascade, flood, flow, jet, spout, squirt, burst

gut NOUN **1** gut or guts (*informal*) *He felt a sharp pain in his gut.* ► stomach, belly, bowels, intestines, innards, insides RELATED ADJECTIVE ► visceral **2** guts (*informal*) *It takes guts to say what you think.* ► courage, nerve, bravery, audacity, boldness, daring, (*informal*) bottle

a
b
c
d
e
f
g
h
i
j
k
l
m
n
o
p
q
r
s
t
u
v
w
x
y
z

A
B
C
D
E
F
G
H
I
J
K
L
M
N
O
P
Q
R
S
T
U
V
W
X
Y
Z

gut VERB **guts, gutting, gutted** **1** remove the guts from a dead fish or other animal **2** remove or destroy the inside of something ● *The fire gutted the factory.*

guts PLURAL NOUN **1** the digestive system; the insides of a person or thing **2** (*informal*) courage

gutted ADJECTIVE (*informal*) extremely disappointed or upset

gutter NOUN **gutters** a long narrow channel at the side of a street, or along the edge of a roof, for carrying away rainwater

gutter VERB **gutters, guttering, guttered** a candle gutters when it burns unsteadily so that melted wax runs down

guttural (gut- er- al) ADJECTIVE throaty and harsh-sounding ● *a guttural voice*

guy[1] NOUN **guys** **1** (*informal*) a man **2** a figure representing Guy Fawkes, burned on 5 November in memory of the Gunpowder Plot which planned to blow up the British Parliament on that day in 1605

guy[2] or **guy-rope** NOUN **guys** or **guy-ropes** a rope used to hold something in place, especially a tent

gym (jim) NOUN **gyms** (*informal*) **1** a gymnasium **2** gymnastics

gymkhana (jim- kah- na) NOUN **gymkhanas** a series of horseriding contests and other sports events [from Urdu]

gymnasium NOUN **gymnasia** or **gymnasiums** a place equipped for gymnastics [from Greek *gymnasion*, from *gymnos* = naked (because Greek men exercised naked)]

gymnastics PLURAL NOUN exercises performed to develop the muscles or to show the performer's agility
▷ **gymnastic** ADJECTIVE

Gypsy NOUN **Gypsies** a member of a community of people, also called travelers, who live in caravans or similar vehicles and travel from place to place [from *Egyptian*, because gypsies were originally thought to have come from Egypt]

gyrate (jy- rayt) VERB **gyrates, gyrating, gyrated** revolve; move in circles or spirals
▷ **gyration** NOUN

gyroscope (jy- ro- skohp) NOUN **gyroscopes** a device used in navigation, which keeps steady because of a heavy wheel spinning inside it [from Greek *gyros* = a ring or circle + *skopein* = to look at (because gyroscopes were once used to study the earth's rotation)]

Thesaurus

---

gut ADJECTIVE *I had a gut feeling Eric was the right man for us.* ► instinctive, intuitive, deep-seated, spontaneous, innate, reflex

guy NOUN (*informal*) *He's a clever guy.*
► (*informal*) man, boy, individual, bloke, chap, fellow

guzzle VERB *They came in and guzzled all the food.* ► gobble, gobble up, wolf, wolf down, devour, (*more informal*) scoff, (*more informal*) tuck into, (*more informal*) polish off

Hh

haberdashery NOUN small articles used in sewing, e.g., ribbons, buttons, and thread
▷ **haberdasher** NOUN

habit NOUN **habits** **1** something that you do without thinking because you have done it so often; a settled way of behaving **2** something that is hard to give up • *a smoking habit* **3** the long dress worn by a monk or nun
▷ **habitual** ADJECTIVE **habitually** ADVERB

habitat NOUN **habitats** where an animal or plant lives naturally

habitation NOUN **habitations** **1** a place to live in **2** inhabiting a place

hack VERB **hacks, hacking, hacked** **1** chop or cut roughly **2** (*informal*) break into a computer system
▷ **hacker** NOUN

hackles PLURAL NOUN
make someone's hackles rise make someone angry or indignant

haddock NOUN **haddock** a sea fish like cod but smaller, used as food

hadn't (*mainly spoken*) had not

hag NOUN **hags** an ugly old woman

haggard ADJECTIVE looking ill or very tired

haggis NOUN **haggises** a Scottish food made from sheep's offal

hail[1] NOUN frozen drops of rain
▷ **hail** VERB **hailstone** NOUN **hailstorm** NOUN

hail[2] INTERJECTION (*old use*) an exclamation of greeting

hail VERB **hails, hailing, hailed** call out to somebody
hail from come from • *He hails from Ireland.*

hair NOUN **hairs** **1** a soft covering that grows on the heads and bodies of people and animals **2** one of the strands that make up this covering
▷ **hairbrush** NOUN **haircut** NOUN **hairstyle** NOUN
keep your hair on (*informal*) do not lose your temper
split hairs make petty or unimportant distinctions of meaning

hairdresser NOUN **hairdressers** a person whose job is to cut and arrange people's hair

hairpin NOUN **hairpins** a U-shaped pin for keeping hair in place

hairpin turn NOUN **hairpin turns** a sharp bend in a road

hair-raising ADJECTIVE terrifying

hairy ADJECTIVE **1** with a lot of hair **2** (*informal*) dangerous or risky

hajj NOUN the pilgrimage to Mecca which all Muslims are expected to make at least once

halal NOUN meat prepared according to Muslim law

halcyon (hal- see- on) ADJECTIVE happy and peaceful • *halcyon days*

half NOUN **halves** one of the two equal parts or amounts into which something is or can be divided

half ADVERB partly; not completely • *This meat is only half cooked.*
not half (*slang*) extremely • *Was she cross? Not half!*

half brother NOUN **half brothers** a brother to whom you are related by one parent but not by both parents

halfhearted ADJECTIVE not very enthusiastic
▷ **half-heartedly** ADVERB

half-life NOUN **half-lives** the time taken for the radioactivity of a substance to fall to half its original value

Thesaurus

habit NOUN **1** *healthy eating habits* ► practice, custom, pattern, routine, tendency, way, rule **2** *her habit of twirling her hair as she spoke* ► mannerism, quirk, trick, gesture, custom, practice **3** *They stole money to fund their drug habit.* ► addiction, dependence, craving, fixation, compulsion, obsession, weakness **4** *a nun's habit* ► costume, robe, garment, outfit, attire, garb
in the habit of *He was in the habit of practicing his flute before he went to bed.* ► used to, accustomed to, given to, inclined to

habitat NOUN *the panda's natural habitat* ► environment, surroundings, element, territory, terrain, haunt, domain

habitual ADJECTIVE **1** *She expected his habitual response to such suggestions.* ► usual, customary,

normal, regular, characteristic, typical, fixed, routine, accustomed, established AN OPPOSITE IS unaccustomed **2** *their habitual criticism of everything we did* ► constant, persistent, continual, recurrent, incessant, interminable, unremitting, endless, relentless AN OPPOSITE IS infrequent **3** *habitual smokers* ► confirmed, regular, addicted, persistent, inveterate, hardened, compulsive, chronic AN OPPOSITE IS occasional

hair NOUN **1** *She ran her hand through her hair.* ► locks, tresses, curls, (*more informal*) mop **2** *a dog with short hair* ► coat, fur, hide

hairy ADJECTIVE *His shirt was open, revealing a hairy chest.* ► shaggy, fuzzy, bristly, downy, hirsute, fleecy, furry, long-haired, stubbly, woolly OPPOSITES ARE hairless, smooth-skinned

half mast *NOUN* a point about halfway up a flagpole, to which a flag is lowered as a mark of respect for a person who has died

halfpenny (hayp- nee) *NOUN* **halfpennies** for separate coins, **halfpence** for a sum of money a former British coin worth half a penny

half sister *NOUN* **half sisters** a sister to whom you are related by one parent but not by both parents

halfway *ADJECTIVE, ADVERB* between two others and equally distant from each

hall *NOUN* **halls** **1** a space or passage just inside the front entrance of a house **2** a very large room or building used for meetings, concerts, etc. **3** a large country house

Halloween *NOUN* October 31, traditionally a time when ghosts and witches are believed to appear

hallucination *NOUN* **hallucinations** something you think you can see or hear that is not really there
▷ **hallucinate** *VERB*

halo *NOUN* **haloes** a circle of light round something, especially around the head of a saint in paintings

halt *VERB* **halts, halting, halted** stop

halt *NOUN* **halts** **1** a stop or standstill ● *Work came to a halt.* **2** a small stopping place on a railway

halve *VERB* **halves, halving, halved** **1** divide something into halves **2** reduce something to half its size

ham *NOUN* **hams** **1** meat from a pig's leg **2** (*informal*) an actor who overacts **3** (*informal*) someone who operates a radio to send and receive messages as a hobby

hamburger *NOUN* **hamburgers** a flat round cake of chopped meat served fried, often in a bread roll

hammer *NOUN* **hammers** a tool with a heavy metal head used for driving nails in, breaking things, etc.

hammer *VERB* **hammers, hammering, hammered** **1** hit something with a hammer **2** knock loudly ● *Someone was hammering on the door.* **3** (*informal*) defeat

hammock *NOUN* **hammocks** a bed made of a strong net or piece of cloth hung by cords [via Spanish from Taino (a South American language)]

hamper *NOUN* **hampers** a large box-shaped basket with a lid

hamper *VERB* **hampers, hampering, hampered** hinder; prevent from moving or working freely

hamster *NOUN* **hamsters** a small furry animal with cheek pouches for carrying grain

hamstring *NOUN* **hamstrings** any of the five tendons at the back of a person's knee

hand *NOUN* **hands** **1** the end part of the arm below the wrist **2** a pointer on a clock or dial **3** a worker; a member of a ship's crew ● *All hands on deck!* **4** the cards held by one player in a card game **5** side or direction ● *the right-hand side* ● *on the other hand* **6** help or aid ● *Give me a hand with these boxes.*
at hand near
by hand using your hand or hands
give *or* **receive a big hand** applaud or be applauded
hands down winning easily
in good hands in the care or control of someone who can be trusted
in hand in your possession; being dealt with

Thesaurus

hall *NOUN* **1** *The meeting will be in the village hall.* ► assembly hall, meeting room, auditorium, concert hall, theatre **2** *You can leave your coat in the hall.* ► hallway, entrance hall, lobby, foyer, corridor, passage, vestibule

halt *VERB* **1** *A series of strikes halted production for several weeks.* ► stop, terminate, obstruct, arrest, impede, block, check, curb OPPOSITES ARE start, continue **2** *Traffic halted on the bridge.* ► stop, wait, come to a halt, come to rest, draw up, pull up OPPOSITES ARE start, continue **3** *Work on the building halted during the holiday period.* ► cease, stop, break off, end, terminate OPPOSITES ARE start, resume

halt *NOUN* **1** *The train came to a halt.* ► stop, standstill, break, interruption, pause, stoppage **2** *a halt in the output of spare parts* ► stoppage, cessation, break, interruption, pause

halve *VERB* **1** *Halve the pears and remove the cores.* ► cut in half, split in two, divide in two, bisect **2** *Their income halved over the next year.* ► lessen by half OR by fifty percent, decrease by half OR by fifty percent

hammer *NOUN* *He hit the nail with a hammer.* ► mallet, gavel

hammer *VERB* *The soldiers hammered on the door.* ► beat, batter, bash, pummel, pound, strike, knock

hamper *VERB* **1** *Bad weather hampered the rescue operation.* ► obstruct, hinder, hold up, interfere with, restrict, thwart, prevent, curb, curtail, foil AN OPPOSITE IS facilitate **2** *Her bandaged hand hampered her.* ► hinder, encumber, impede, restrain, entangle, handicap, hold back AN OPPOSITE IS aid

hand *NOUN* **1** *a person's hand* ► fist, palm RELATED ADJECTIVE ► manual **2** *the hand of a gauge* ► pointer, indicator **3** *The factory took on more hands.* ► worker, employee, laborer **4 hands** *The property came into his sister's hands.*

on hand available
out of hand out of control

hand VERB hands, handing, handed give or
pass something to somebody ● *Hand it over.*
hand down pass something from one
generation to another

handbag NOUN handbags a small bag for
holding a purse and personal articles

handbook NOUN handbooks a small book
that gives useful facts about something

handcuff NOUN handcuffs one of a pair of
metal rings linked by a chain, for fastening a
prisoner's wrists together

handcuff VERB handcuffs, handcuffing,
handcuffed fasten with handcuffs

handful NOUN handfuls **1** as much as can be
carried in one hand **2** a few people or things
3 (*informal*) a troublesome person or task

handicap NOUN handicaps **1** a disadvantage
2 a physical or mental disability
▷ **handicapped** ADJECTIVE

handkerchief NOUN handkerchiefs a small
square of cloth for wiping the nose or face

handle NOUN handles the part of a thing by
which it is held, carried, or controlled

handle VERB handles, handling, handled
1 touch or feel something with your hands
2 deal with; manage ● *Will you handle the
catering?*
▷ **handler** NOUN

handlebar NOUN or **handlebars** PLURAL NOUN
the bar, with a handle at each end, that steers
a bicycle or motorcycle, etc.

handsome ADJECTIVE **1** good-looking
2 generous ● *a handsome offer*
▷ **handsomely** ADVERB

handstand NOUN handstands balancing on
your hands with your feet in the air

handwriting NOUN writing done by hand; a
person's style of writing
▷ **handwritten** ADJECTIVE

handy ADJECTIVE handier, handiest
1 convenient or useful **2** good at using the
hands
▷ **handily** ADVERB **handiness** NOUN

hang VERB hangs, hanging, hung **1** fix the top
or side of something to a hook or nail; be

Thesaurus

▶ possession, control, charge, custody, power,
responsibility
at OR **on** OR **to hand** ▶ close by, handy,
accessible, available, present, waiting, within
reach **give somebody a hand** *Let me give you a
hand with the dinner.* ▶ help, assist

hand VERB *He handed her a letter.* ▶ give, offer,
pass, present (her with a letter), submit (a
letter to her), convey, deliver
hand down *The family property is handed down
from one generation to the next.* ▶ pass down,
pass on, bequeath, leave as a legacy, will **hand
out** OR **round** *A flight attendant handed out
forms.* ▶ distribute, circulate, give out, deal
out, share out **hand over 1** *She handed over a
large sum.* ▶ pay, donate, tender, surrender
2 *The prisoners were handed over to the local
police.* ▶ deliver up, entrust, turn over

handful NOUN *a handful of complaining letters*
▶ small number, smattering, sprinkling, trickle

handicap NOUN *Their poor French was a
handicap when traveling.* ▶ disadvantage,
difficulty, drawback, shortcoming, hindrance,
inconvenience, limitation, encumbrance,
stumbling block, restriction, obstacle, problem,
nuisance OPPOSITES ARE advantage, benefit

handicap VERB *They were handicapped by the
fact that they had not been taught science.*
▶ hamper, impede, limit, disadvantage,
restrict, hinder, hold back AN OPPOSITE IS help

handle NOUN *The head flew off the handle and
cracked our only mirror.* ▶ haft, shank, stock,
shaft, grip

handle VERB **1** *A notice asked visitors not to
handle the exhibits.* ▶ touch, feel, finger,
fondle, pick up, grip, grasp **2** *It would not be
easy to handle such a tense meeting. He was used
to handling temperamental singers.* ▶ manage,
deal with, cope with, control, tackle, contend
with **3** *The firm handles a lot of overseas business.*
▶ deal in, trade in, market **4** *He needed a
smaller car that he could handle more easily.*
▶ control, drive, maneuver, operate, steer

handsome ADJECTIVE **1** *a handsome man*
▶ good-looking, nice-looking, attractive,
comely, personable, (*more informal*) dishy
OPPOSITES ARE ugly, unattractive **2** *a handsome
building* ▶ elegant, striking, imposing, stately,
well-proportioned, attractive OPPOSITES ARE
ugly, hideous **3** *a handsome profit* ▶ large, big,
sizeable, substantial, considerable, ample AN
OPPOSITE IS meager **4** *a handsome offer*
▶ generous, gracious, liberal, magnanimous,
munificent AN OPPOSITE IS mean

handy ADJECTIVE **1** *The brush is handy for cleaning
up stubborn dust.* ▶ useful, convenient,
practical, helpful, effective **2** *He's handy with a
screwdriver.* ▶ skillful, adept, dexterous,
proficient, practical, able, deft **3** *Keep your
timer handy.* ▶ accessible, available, ready, at
OR to hand, close by, nearby

hang VERB **1** *Baskets of flowers hung from the
lamp posts.* ▶ be suspended, dangle, swing,
sway **2** *Rich exotic curtains hang from every
window.* ▶ drape, drop, droop, cascade, trail
3 *Make sure you hang the pictures at eye level.*
▶ fix, attach, fasten, display, suspend, stick

A
B
C
D
E
F
G
H
I
J
K
L
M
N
O
P
Q
R
S
T
U
V
W
X
Y
Z

supported in this way **2** stick wallpaper to a wall **3** decorate with drapery or hanging ornaments • *The tree was hung with lights.* **4** droop or lean • *People hung over the gate.* **5** remain in the air or as something unpleasant • *Smoke hung over the city.* • *The threat is still hanging over him.* **6** (with *past tense & past participle* **hanged**) execute someone by hanging them from a rope that tightens around the neck • *He was hanged in 1950.*
hang about (*informal*) **1** loiter **2** not go away
hang back hesitate to go forward or to do something
hang on 1 hold tightly **2** (*informal*) wait
hang up end a telephone conversation by putting back the receiver
hang NOUN
get the hang of (*informal*) learn how to do or use something

hang-glider NOUN hang-gliders a framework in which a person can glide through the air
▷ **hang-gliding** NOUN

hangover NOUN hangovers an unpleasant feeling after drinking too much alcohol

hank NOUN hanks a coil or piece of wool, thread, etc.

hanker VERB hankers, hankering, hankered feel a longing for something

haphazard ADJECTIVE done or chosen at random, not by planning

happen VERB happens, happening, happened **1** take place; occur **2** do something by chance • *I happened to see him.*

happy ADJECTIVE happier, happiest **1** pleased or contented **2** fortunate • *a happy coincidence* **3** willing • *I'd be happy to help.*
▷ **happily** ADVERB **happiness** NOUN

harangue (ha- rang) VERB harangues, haranguing, harangued make a long aggressive speech to somebody
▷ **harangue** NOUN

harass (ha- ras) VERB harasses, harassing, harassed trouble or annoy somebody often
▷ **harassment** (ha- ras- ment) NOUN

harbor NOUN harbors a place where ships can shelter or unload

harbor VERB harbors, harboring, harbored **1** give shelter to somebody, especially a criminal **2** keep a strong or hostile thought in your mind • *I think she still harbors a grudge against them.*

Thesaurus

---

4 *A damp mist hung in the air.* ► float, hover, drift, linger, cling, remain
hang about (*informal*) *Don't hang about if you want to take advantage of this offer.* ► delay, wait, procrastinate **hang around** (*informal*) *small groups hanging around coffee bars* ► linger in, loiter in, frequent, haunt **hang back** *He hung back, afraid to go in.* ► hesitate, demur, hold back, recoil, shy away **hang on** *If they can hang on a few more days it will help us.* ► stay, persevere, remain, continue, carry on, persist **hang on to** *If you have cash, hang on to it.* ► keep, hold on to, retain, preserve **hang out** (*informal*) *She enjoyed hanging out with members of the band.* ► associate, mix, spend time, keep company, fraternize, socialize

hang-up NOUN (*informal*) *Wally has a hang-up about his appearance.* ► fixation, obsession, neurosis, inhibition, anxiety, (*more informal*) thing

haphazard ADJECTIVE *the haphazard spray of machine-gun fire strewn things about in a haphazard fashion* ► random, indiscriminate, arbitrary, chaotic, disorderly, disorganized, casual, irregular, unmethodical AN OPPOSITE IS orderly

happen VERB **1** *The collision happened as the pursuing boat tried to turn. Something strange was happening that day.* ► occur, take place, come about, arise, result, ensue, transpire

2 happen to *We never knew what happened to her.* ► become of, befall

happening NOUN *There is a record of all the happenings of that week.* ► event, incident, occurrence, circumstance, episode, affair

happiness NOUN *A feeling of great happiness filled her.* ► contentment, joy, joyfulness, gladness, pleasure, bliss, elation, ecstasy OPPOSITES ARE unhappiness, sorrow

happy ADJECTIVE **1** *a room full of happy faces* ► contented, cheerful, joyful, jolly, delighted, merry, smiling **2** *I will be happy to help.* ► pleased, glad, willing, disposed, delighted **3** *By a happy chance a film crew were there to record the scene.* ► fortunate, lucky, felicitous, favorable, fitting

harass VERB *The men continued to harass her.* ► pester, torment, badger, hound, persecute, trouble, harry, (*informal*) hassle, annoy, vex

harassed ADJECTIVE *good news for harassed moms and dads* ► stressed, harried, worn, troubled, exhausted AN OPPOSITE IS carefree

harbor NOUN *Boats bobbed up and down in the harbor.* ► port, dock, marina, mooring, quay, waterfront

harbor VERB **1** *He was arrested for harboring a criminal.* ► hide, protect, shelter, conceal, shield, give refuge to, give asylum to, give sanctuary to **2** *Better not to harbor a grudge.* ► bear, hold, nurse, nurture, entertain, foster, cling to

hard *ADJECTIVE* **1** firm or solid; not soft
2 difficult • *hard sums* **3** severe or stern
4 causing suffering • *hard luck* **5** using great
effort • *a hard worker* **6** hard drugs are strong
and addictive ones
▷ **hardness** NOUN
hard of hearing slightly deaf
hard up (*informal*) short of money

hard *ADVERB* **1** so as to be hard • *The ground
froze hard.* **2** with great effort; intensively
• *We worked hard.* • *It is raining hard.* **3** with
difficulty • *hard-earned*

hard disk NOUN hard disks a disk fixed inside
a computer, able to store large amounts of
data

harden *VERB* hardens, hardening, hardened
make or become hard
▷ **hardener** NOUN

hardly *ADVERB* only just; only with difficulty
• *She can hardly walk.*
USAGE It is not acceptable in standard English
to use "not" with **hardly**, as in "she can't
hardly walk."

hardship NOUN hardships difficult conditions
that cause discomfort or suffering • *a life of
hardship*

hardware NOUN **1** metal implements and
tools etc.; machinery **2** the machinery of a
computer as opposed to the software
COMPARE **software**

hard water NOUN water containing minerals
that prevent soap from making much lather

hardy *ADJECTIVE* hardier, hardiest able to
endure cold or difficult conditions
▷ **hardiness** NOUN

hare NOUN hares an animal like a rabbit but
larger

harm *VERB* harms, harming, harmed damage
or injure

harm NOUN damage or injury
▷ **harmful** *ADJECTIVE* **harmless** *ADJECTIVE*

harmonica NOUN harmonicas a mouth organ

harmonious *ADJECTIVE* **1** combining together
in a pleasant, attractive, or effective way
2 sounding pleasant **3** peaceful and friendly

harmony NOUN harmonies **1** a pleasant
combination, especially of musical notes
2 being friendly to each other

Thesaurus

hard *ADJECTIVE* **1** *The ground is too hard to play on.*
► solid, firm, unyielding, hardened, tough,
compact AN OPPOSITE IS soft **2** *three weeks of
hard work* ► strenuous, arduous, exhausting,
fatiguing, demanding AN OPPOSITE IS easy **3** *a
hard problem to solve* ► difficult, complicated,
complex, involved, knotty, baffling, puzzling
AN OPPOSITE IS simple **4** *a hard taskmaster*
► strict, harsh, firm, stern, demanding, severe
OPPOSITES ARE mild, easygoing **5** *a hard blow*
► heavy, forceful, strong, powerful, violent
AN OPPOSITE IS light

hard *ADVERB* **1** *She works hard at school.*
► diligently, industriously, steadily, earnestly,
energetically **2** *It has been raining hard.*
► heavily, steadily, (*more informal*) cats and
dogs **3** *She looked hard at them.* ► intently,
intensely, closely, attentively, keenly

harden *VERB* **1** *The cement hardens after two
hours.* ► set, solidify, become hard, stiffen
2 *These experiences hardened their determination
to continue.* ► strengthen, reinforce, increase,
intensify, fortify, toughen

hardly *ADVERB* **1** *It is hardly surprising that so
many people have considered leaving.* ► not at
all, by no means, barely, scarcely **2** *John said he
hardly knew her.* ► scarcely, barely, only just,
only slightly, only faintly

hardship NOUN *Drought caused the population
much hardship.* ► suffering, privation, misery,
misfortune, adversity, affliction, austerity,
destitution, difficulty, need, trouble,
unhappiness, want

hard-wearing *ADJECTIVE* *outdoor clothes that are
hard-wearing* ► durable, strong, tough,
resilient, lasting, sturdy, well made, stout
OPPOSITES ARE flimsy, delicate

hardy *ADJECTIVE* *a good expedition for hardy
walkers* ► fit, robust, sturdy, hearty, healthy,
tough, vigorous, strong, resilient, rugged
OPPOSITES ARE tender, delicate

harm *VERB* **1** *If they harmed any of the hostages
the police would have to go in.* ► hurt, injure,
maltreat, mistreat, ill-treat, wound, molest,
abuse, (*more informal*) lay a finger on
2 *chemicals that harm the environment*
► damage, spoil, ruin, hurt, do damage to, do
harm to

harm NOUN **1** *a way of dealing with waste without
causing any harm to the public* ► injury,
damage, suffering, hurt, detriment,
inconvenience AN OPPOSITE IS benefit **2** *We
can't see any harm in their idea.* ► wrong,
disadvantage, snag

harmful *ADJECTIVE* *the harmful effects of smoking*
► damaging, detrimental, injurious,
dangerous, noxious, destructive, unhealthy
OPPOSITES ARE harmless, beneficial

harmless *ADJECTIVE* **1** *a harmless substance*
► safe, innocuous, nontoxic, nonpoisonous,
benign AN OPPOSITE IS harmful **2** *It was just a
bit of harmless fun.* ► safe, inoffensive,
innocuous, unobjectionable, gentle AN
OPPOSITE IS objectionable

harmony NOUN **1** *different ethnic groups living
in harmony* ► friendship, agreement, concord,

harness NOUN harnesses the straps put around a horse's head and neck for controlling it

harness VERB harnesses, harnessing, harnessed **1** put a harness on a horse **2** control and use something • *Could we harness the power of the wind?*

harp NOUN harps a musical instrument with strings stretched across a frame and plucked by the fingers
▷ **harpist** NOUN

harpoon NOUN harpoons a spear attached to a rope, used for catching whales
▷ **harpoon** VERB

harrowing ADJECTIVE very upsetting or distressing

harsh ADJECTIVE **1** rough and unpleasant **2** severe or cruel
▷ **harshly** ADVERB **harshness** NOUN

harvest NOUN harvests **1** the time when farmers gather in the corn, fruit, or vegetables that they have grown **2** the crop that is gathered in

hash NOUN a mixture of small pieces of meat and vegetables, usually fried
make a hash of (*informal*) make a mess of something; bungle

hasn't (*mainly spoken*) has not

haste NOUN a hurry
make haste act quickly

hasten VERB hastens, hastening, hastened hurry

hasty ADJECTIVE hurried; done too quickly
▷ **hastily** ADVERB **hastiness** NOUN

hat NOUN hats a covering for the head, worn out of doors
keep something under your hat keep it a secret

hatch NOUN hatches an opening in a floor, wall, or door, usually with a covering

hatch VERB hatches, hatching, hatched **1** break out of an egg **2** keep an egg warm until a baby bird comes out **3** plan • *They hatched a plot.*

hatchet NOUN hatchets a small axe

hate VERB hates, hating, hated dislike very strongly

hate NOUN extreme dislike

hatred NOUN extreme dislike

haughty ADJECTIVE haughtier, haughtiest proud of yourself and looking down on other people
▷ **haughtily** ADVERB **haughtiness** NOUN

Thesaurus

peace, amity, fellowship, goodwill, unity OPPOSITES ARE disagreement, enmity **2** *musical harmony* ► tunefulness, euphony, concord, melody AN OPPOSITE IS discord

harsh ADJECTIVE **1** *He spoke in a high, harsh voice.* ► shrill, grating, strident, grasping **2** *harsh measures to combat street crime* ► severe, punitive, strict, draconian **3** *They exchanged harsh words.* ► sharp, bitter, unfriendly, unkind **4** *the harsh rule of a tyrant* ► cruel, savage, brutal, despotic, hard, strict, intolerant

harvest NOUN *a bumper harvest* ► crop, yield, produce, return

harvest VERB *crops that have to be harvested by hand* ► gather, reap, take in, bring in, collect, garner, mow, pick

hassle NOUN **1** (*informal*) *It's always such a hassle trying to park.* ► bother, nuisance, inconvenience, struggle, difficulty **2** (*informal*) *She started getting hassle from the kids coming to her.* ► harassment, trouble, annoyance, argument, (*more informal*) aggravation

hassle VERB (*informal*) *Some of the passengers were hassling the driver.* ► harass, pester, badger, trouble, harry, annoy

haste NOUN *He was working with great haste.* ► speed, hurry, urgency, swiftness, rapidity, promptness, impetuosity

hasten VERB **1** *The girl hastened back from her office.* ► hurry, rush, speed, make haste **2** *A*

rise in interest rates will hasten the ruin of many small businesses. ► quicken, accelerate, speed up, bring nearer, precipitate

hasty ADJECTIVE **1** *They made a hasty retreat back to the house.* ► hurried, swift, rapid, brisk, quick, headlong **2** *The decision seemed hasty.* ► rash, precipitate, impulsive, imprudent, impetuous, reckless

hate VERB **1** *The brothers hated each other.* ► loathe, detest, abhor, dislike, abominate, (*more informal*) can't bear, (*more informal*) can't stand **2** *I hate to bother them.* ► be sorry, hesitate, regret, be reluctant

hate NOUN **1** *feelings of hate* ► hatred, loathing, detestation, dislike, distaste, revulsion, abhorrence **2** *They made a list of their pet hates.* ► dislike, bugbear, bane, bête noire

hateful ADJECTIVE *I'll never come back to this hateful country.* ► detestable, loathsome, horrible, horrid, awful, nasty AN OPPOSITE IS lovable

hatred NOUN *The war left a legacy of fear and hatred.* ► hate, loathing, detestation, revulsion, repugnance, hostility, enmity, bad feeling OPPOSITES ARE love, liking

haughty ADJECTIVE *He walked out with a haughty toss of his head.* ► proud, arrogant, self-important, supercilious, disdainful, contemptuous, scornful, superior, lofty, overbearing AN OPPOSITE IS modest

A
B
C
D
E
F
G
H
I
J
K
L
M
N
O
P
Q
R
S
T
U
V
W
X
Y
Z

haul VERB hauls, hauling, hauled pull or drag with great effort
▷ **haulage** NOUN

haul NOUN hauls **1** hauling **2** the amount obtained by an effort; booty • *The thieves' haul came to $2 million.* **3** a distance to be covered • *a long haul*

haunt VERB haunts, haunting, haunted **1** (said about ghosts) appear often in a place or to a person **2** visit a place often **3** stay in your mind • *The memory haunts me still.*
▷ **haunted** ADJECTIVE

haunt NOUN haunts a place that you often visit • *my favourite haunt*

have VERB has, having, had This word has many uses, including: **1** possess or own • *We have two dogs.* **2** contain • *This tin has candy in it.* **3** be obliged to do something • *We have to go now.* **4** experience • *He had a shock.* **5** allow • *I won't have him bullied.* **6** receive or accept • *Will you have a chocolate?* **7** get something done • *I'm having my watch mended.* **8** (slang) cheat or deceive • *We've been had!*
have somebody on (informal) fool him or her

have AUXILIARY VERB used to form the past tense of verbs, e.g., *he has gone.*

haven NOUN havens a safe place or refuge

haven't (mainly spoken) have not

havoc NOUN great destruction or disorder
play havoc with disrupt something completely

hawk NOUN hawks a bird of prey with very strong eyesight

hawthorn NOUN hawthorns a thorny tree with small red berries (called haws)

hay NOUN dried grass for feeding to animals

hay fever NOUN irritation of the nose, throat, and eyes, caused by pollen or dust

hazard NOUN hazards **1** a danger or risk **2** an obstacle
▷ **hazardous** ADJECTIVE

hazy ADJECTIVE **1** misty **2** vague or uncertain
▷ **hazily** ADVERB **haziness** NOUN

he PRONOUN **1** the male person or animal being talked about **2** a person (male or female) • *He who hesitates is lost*

head NOUN heads **1** the part of the body containing the brains, eyes, and mouth **2** your brains; intelligence • *Use your head!* **3** a talent or ability • *She has a good head for figures.* **4** the side of a coin on which someone's head is shown • *Heads or tails?* **5** a person • *It costs $2 per head.* **6** the top or front of something • *a pinhead* • *at the head of the procession* **7** the chief; the person in charge **8** a headteacher

Thesaurus

haul VERB *A special locomotive is needed to haul these trains. She hauled him up from the floor.*
► pull, drag, heave, tug, tow AN OPPOSITE IS push

haunt VERB **1** *He likes to haunt old junk shops.*
► frequent, spend time in, keep returning to, visit frequently, (more informal) hang around in **2** *Her words came back to haunt her.* ► obsess, torment, trouble, worry, prey on

haunting ADJECTIVE *haunting and lyrical poetry*
► evocative, touching, emotive, memorable, poignant, nostalgic, wistful, plaintive AN OPPOSITE IS unmemorable

have VERB **1** *They have a house in France.* ► own, possess, be the owner of, keep, enjoy AN OPPOSITE IS lack **2** *We have coffee at eleven.*
► drink, take **3** *What did you have for lunch?*
► eat, consume **4** *She had a letter from her boyfriend.* ► receive, get, be sent, obtain, acquire OPPOSITES ARE send, reject **5** *They are having a party next door.* ► hold, give, organize, arrange, throw, provide, lay on **6** *The apartment has five rooms.* ► contain, comprise, consist of, include, incorporate, be made up of **7** *We had trouble parking.*
► experience, encounter, undergo, meet with, run into, suffer, face **8** *I have a bad cold.* ► be suffering from, be afflicted by, be affected by, be troubled by **9** *The boys had a lot of fun.*
► enjoy, experience, go through **10** *Mike had*

guests at the weekend. ► entertain, receive, be host to, cater for, invite **11** *Julia had her baby.*
► give birth to, bear, produce, be delivered of, bring into the world

haven NOUN **1** *a haven for ships on the north coast* ► harbor, port, anchorage, mooring **2** *a safe haven in time of trouble* ► refuge, retreat, shelter, sanctuary, asylum

hazard NOUN *a serious health hazard* ► risk, threat, danger, menace

hazard VERB **1** *a business that is too risky to hazard money on* ► risk, chance, jeopardize **2** *I wouldn't want to hazard a guess about that.*
► offer, put forward, venture, advance

hazardous ADJECTIVE *He knew how hazardous the road could be in the dark.* ► dangerous, risky, perilous, precarious, uncertain, unpredictable, unsafe, chancy, (more informal) dicey
OPPOSITES ARE safe, secure

hazy ADJECTIVE **1** *The weather was good, if a little hazy.* ► misty, cloudy, foggy, smoky **2** *hazy memories of childhood* ► vague, indistinct, blurred, fuzzy, unclear, faint, dim

head NOUN **1** *He hit his head on a beam.* ► skull, crown, cranium, (more informal) nut, (more informal) bonce RELATED ADJECTIVE ► cephalic **2** *the head of a publishing firm* ► chief, chairman, chief executive, president, principal **3** *You need a good head for this work.* ► brain, intellect, intelligence, wit **4** *She has quite a*

A
B
C
D
E
F
G
H
I
J
K
L
M
N
O
P
Q
R
S
T
U
V
W
X
Y
Z

come to a head reach a crisis point
keep your head stay calm
off the top of your head without preparation or thinking carefully

head VERB **heads, heading, headed 1** be at the top or front of something **2** hit a ball with your head **3** move in a particular direction • *We headed for the coast.* **4** force someone to turn aside by getting in front of them • *Let's see if we can head him off.* [from Old English]

headache NOUN **headaches 1** a pain in the head **2** (*informal*) a worrying problem

heading NOUN **headings** a word or words put at the top of a piece of printing or writing

headland NOUN **headlands** a large piece of high land that sticks out into the sea

headlight NOUN **headlights** a powerful light at the front of a car, engine, etc.

headline NOUN **headlines** a heading in a newspaper
the headlines the main items of news

headlong ADVERB, ADJECTIVE **1** falling head first **2** in a hasty or thoughtless way

headmaster NOUN **headmasters** a male headteacher or principal

headmistress NOUN **headmistresses** a female headteacher or principal

head-on ADVERB, ADJECTIVE with the front parts colliding • *a head-on collision*

headquarters NOUN the place from which an organization is controlled

headstrong ADJECTIVE determined to do as you want

headteacher NOUN **headteachers** the person in charge of a school

headway NOUN
make headway make progress

heal VERB **heals, healing, healed 1** make or become healthy flesh again • *The wound healed slowly.* **2** (*old use*) cure • *healing the sick*

health NOUN **1** the condition of a person's body or mind • *His health is bad.* **2** being healthy • *in sickness and in health*

healthy ADJECTIVE **healthier, healthiest 1** being well; free from illness **2** producing good health • *Fresh air is healthy.*
▷ **healthily** ADVERB **healthiness** NOUN

heap NOUN **heaps** a pile, especially an untidy one
heaps PLURAL NOUN (*informal*) a great amount; plenty • *There's heaps of time.*

heap VERB **heaps, heaping, heaped 1** make things into a heap **2** to load heavily with • *She heaped the plate with food.*

hear VERB **hears, hearing, heard 1** take in sounds through the ears **2** receive news or information, etc. **3** listen to and try a case in a lawcourt
▷ **hearer** NOUN
hear! hear! (in a debate) I agree

Thesaurus

---

head for figures. ► aptitude, gift, talent, bent, knack
lose your head *Connie lost her head and ran off.* ► panic, lose control, go to pieces, (*more informal*) lose your cool
off your head (*informal*) *He was quite off his head, spouting complete nonsense.* ► mad, crazy, insane, out of your mind, unbalanced, demented, deranged

head ADJECTIVE *the head chef* ► chief, senior, principal, leading

head VERB **1** *She headed a team of researchers.* ► lead, be in charge of, be at the head of, manage, direct, oversee, supervise **2** *head for They were heading for the station.* ► go OR move towards, make for, aim for, point to

heading NOUN **1** *He turned the page and read the chapter heading.* ► title, headline, caption, rubric **2** *The subject is discussed under several headings.* ► category, division, section, class, group

heal VERB **1** *Madra's wounds began to heal.* ► get better, recover, knit, mend, unite **2** *an ointment to heal her injured finger* ► make better, cure, treat, remedy, restore **3** *The rift between father and son was never completely*

healed. ► mend, repair, put right, settle, remedy, reconcile, patch up

health NOUN **1** *He is now in excellent health and back at work.* ► condition, shape, form, fettle, constitution **2** *Hormone levels are important to health.* ► fitness, well-being, healthiness, good health RELATED ADJECTIVE ► sanitary

healthy ADJECTIVE **1** *We try to promote a healthy lifestyle.* ► health-giving, wholesome, beneficial, bracing, invigorating **2** *I think I am fit, healthy, and looking good again.* ► well, in good health, in good condition, in good shape, in good trim **3** *a healthy respect for the opposite sex* ► sound, strong

heap NOUN **1** *a heap of old newspapers* ► pile, stack, mass, mound, mountain, collection, hoard **2** **heaps** (*informal*) *We've got heaps of time.* ► plenty, a lot, a great deal, (*more informal*) lots, (*more informal*) masses, (*more informal*) piles

heap VERB **1** *She heaped more cakes on their plates.* ► pile, stack, mass, bank, collect **2** *The praise heaped on them was well deserved.* ► lavish, shower, bestow, confer

hear VERB **1** *You can hear the traffic in the distance.* ► make out, catch, listen to, perceive, discern, detect USAGE Note that all these

not hear of refuse to allow something • *He wouldn't hear of my paying for it.*

hearing NOUN **hearings 1** the ability to hear **2** a chance to be heard; a trial in a court of law

hearing aid NOUN **hearing aids** a device to help a deaf person to hear

heart NOUN **hearts 1** the organ of the body that makes the blood circulate **2** a person's feelings or emotions; sympathy **3** enthusiasm; courage • *Take heart.* **4** the middle or most important part **5** a curved shape representing a heart **6** a playing card with red heart shapes on it
break someone's heart make someone very unhappy
by heart memorized

heart attack NOUN **heart attacks** a sudden failure of the heart to work properly, which results in great pain or sometimes death

hearten VERB **heartens, heartening, heartened** make a person feel encouraged

heartfelt ADJECTIVE felt deeply

hearth NOUN **hearths** the floor of a fireplace, or the area in front of it

heartless ADJECTIVE without pity or sympathy

hearty ADJECTIVE **1** strong and vigorous **2** enthusiastic and sincere • *hearty congratulations* **3** (said about a meal) large
▷ **heartily** ADVERB **heartiness** NOUN

heat NOUN **heats 1** hotness or (in scientific use) the form of energy causing this **2** hot weather **3** strong feeling, especially anger **4** a race or contest to decide who will take part in the final
on heat (said about a female mammal) ready for mating

heat VERB **heats, heating, heated** make or become hot

heathen NOUN **heathens** a person who does not believe in any of the world's chief religions

heather NOUN an evergreen plant with small purple, pink, or white flowers

heatwave NOUN **heatwaves** a long period of hot weather

Thesaurus

words, except for *listen to*, can also be used about seeing, and so you might need to make the meaning clear by saying, for example, *You can make out the sound of traffic in the distance.* Note also that *listen to* implies something you try to do, whereas *hear* can refer to sounds that you might be aware of by chance.
RELATED ADJECTIVE ▶ audible **2** *I heard that you were leaving.* ▶ be told, be informed, learn, gather, find out, discover **3** *A female judge heard the case.* ▶ try, judge, sit in judgment on

hearing NOUN **1** *He made the comment out of our hearing.* ▶ earshot, range, reach RELATED ADJECTIVE ▶ acoustic **2** *a judicial hearing* ▶ trial, court case, inquiry, investigation, tribunal, review, proceedings

heart NOUN **1** *His heart had stopped beating.* ▶ organ of circulation, (*more informal*) ticker RELATED ADJECTIVE ▶ cardiac **2** *an air link into the heart of the city* ▶ center, middle, nucleus, core, hub, inside, kernel **3** *the heart of the problem* ▶ essence, nub, crux, root, focus **4** *He won't allow his heart to rule his head.* ▶ feelings, emotion, sentiment **5** *The lack of support made them lose heart.* ▶ enthusiasm, eagerness, courage, bravery, resolution, determination **6** *She may be stern but she has a lot of heart.* ▶ compassion, feeling, sympathy, tenderness, understanding, affection, humanity, kindness, love

heartbreaking ADJECTIVE *heartbreaking sobs from the bedroom* ▶ distressing, harrowing,

pitiful, saddening, tragic, grievous, heart-rending

heartbroken ADJECTIVE *He was heartbroken at having to sell his home.* ▶ broken-hearted, inconsolable, devastated, grief-stricken, desolate, despairing AN OPPOSITE IS happy

hearty ADJECTIVE **1** *The remark brought a loud hearty laugh.* ▶ enthusiastic, sincere, warm, jovial, cordial, exuberant, cheerful, uninhibited **2** *Beth always had a hearty appetite.* ▶ big, healthy, strong, robust, vigorous **3** *They looked forward to a hearty meal and a good night's sleep.* ▶ substantial, generous, sizable, solid, large, ample, wholesome

heat NOUN **1** *The fire gave out a lot of heat.* ▶ warmth, hotness, glow RELATED ADJECTIVE ▶ thermal, calorific **2** *The summer heat was exhausting.* ▶ hot weather, warmth, humidity, sultriness, swelter **3** *There is too much heat in these arguments.* ▶ passion, intensity, ardor, warmth, vehemence, anger, fury

heat VERB **1** *You can heat the food in the oven, if you prefer.* ▶ cook, heat up, reheat **2** *The room has two external walls and is difficult to heat.* ▶ keep warm, warm up

heated ADJECTIVE **1** *The discussion soon became heated.* ▶ passionate, vehement, animated, impassioned, bitter, tempestuous OPPOSITES ARE dispassionate, calm **2** *Rachel grew heated as she talked about her ordeal.* ▶ excited, roused, worked up, keyed up, animated, impassioned AN OPPOSITE IS calm

a b c d e f g h i j k l m n o p q r s t u v w x y z

heave ➡ helix

A
B
C
D
E
F
G
H
I
J
K
L
M
N
O
P
Q
R
S
T
U
V
W
X
Y
Z

heave VERB heaves, heaving, heaved **1** lift or move something heavy **2** (*informal*) throw **3** rise and fall **4** (said about the stomach) feel uncomfortable, making you want to vomit
▷ **heave** NOUN
heave a sigh utter a deep sigh

heaven NOUN heavens **1** the place where God and angels are thought to live **2** a very pleasant place or condition
the heavens the sky

heavy ADJECTIVE heavier, heaviest **1** weighing a lot; difficult to lift or carry **2** great in amount or force etc. • *heavy rain* • *a heavy penalty* **3** needing much effort • *heavy work* **4** full of sadness or worry • *with a heavy heart*
▷ **heavily** ADVERB **heaviness** NOUN

heavyweight NOUN heavyweights **1** a heavy person **2** a boxer of the heaviest weight
▷ **heavyweight** ADJECTIVE

Hebrew NOUN the language of the Jews in ancient Palestine and modern Israel

hectare (hek- tair) NOUN hectares a unit of area equal to 10,000 square meters or nearly 2 acres

hedge NOUN hedges a row of bushes forming a barrier or boundary

hedgehog NOUN hedgehogs a small animal covered with long prickles

heed NOUN
take or pay heed give attention to something
▷ **heedful** ADJECTIVE **heedless** ADJECTIVE

heel NOUN heels **1** the back part of the foot **2** the part around or under the heel of a sock or shoe
take to your heels run away

hefty ADJECTIVE heftier, heftiest large and strong
▷ **heftily** ADVERB

height NOUN heights **1** how high something is; the distance from the base to the top or from head to foot **2** a high place **3** the highest or most intense part • *at the height of the holiday season*

heighten VERB heightens, heightening, heightened make or become higher or more intense

heir (say as air) NOUN heirs a person who inherits something

heiress (air- ess) NOUN heiresses a female heir, especially to great wealth

heirloom (air- loom) NOUN heirlooms a valued possession that has been handed down in a family for several generations

helicopter NOUN helicopters a kind of aircraft with a large horizontal propeller or rotor [from Greek *helix* = coil + Greek *pteron* = wing]

helium (hee- lee- um) NOUN a light colorless gas that does not burn

helix (hee- liks) NOUN helices (hee- liss- eez) a spiral [from Greek, = coil]

Thesaurus

heave VERB *Two men heaved back the great iron gates.* ► haul, drag, pull, throw, draw, tow, tug, hoist, lift, lug, raise

heaven NOUN **1** *You might get your reward in heaven, if you are lucky.* ► paradise, the next world, the hereafter, the afterlife **2** *In that heat a cool drink was absolute heaven.* ► ecstasy, bliss, joy, rapture, delight AN OPPOSITE IS hell **3** the heavens *The moon caused a glow in the heavens.* ► the sky, the skies, the firmament, the blue RELATED ADJECTIVE ► celestial

heavenly ADJECTIVE **1** *the sound of joyful, heavenly music* ► beautiful, celestial, divine, angelic, blissful, exquisite OPPOSITES ARE devilish, infernal **2** *They had a heavenly time.* ► delightful, marvelous, wonderful, lovely, pleasant

heavy ADJECTIVE **1** *too heavy to lift* ► weighty, massive, bulky, hefty **2** *a heavy man* ► large, fat, corpulent, overweight **3** *heavy smoking* ► excessive, immoderate, intensive, uncontrolled **4** *a heavy meal* ► substantial, hearty, filling, sizable, solid, stodgy **5** *a heavy blow* ► hard, forceful, violent, powerful, hefty **6** *heavy losses; a heavy fine* ► large, substantial, considerable **7** *a heavy burden of responsibility* ► onerous, demanding, formidable,

challenging, severe **8** *heavy work* ► arduous, strenuous, taxing **9** *heavy reading* ► serious, tedious, dull **10** *heavy rain* ► strong, intense, teeming, torrential

hectic ADJECTIVE *We spent three hectic days getting the house in order.* ► busy, frantic, feverish, frenzied, manic, chaotic OPPOSITES ARE leisurely, quiet

hefty ADJECTIVE *A hefty young man stood in their way.* ► burly, beefy, sturdy, well built, strapping, brawny, hulking, muscular, powerful, stocky, stout, athletic, big, heavy OPPOSITES ARE slight, thin

height NOUN **1** *We wanted to know the height of the tower.* ► tallness, highness, vertical measurement, elevation, altitude **2** *heights reaching the mountain heights* ► summit, top, peak, crest, crown, tip **3** *They were at the height of their fame.* ► peak, high point, acme, climax, zenith OPPOSITES ARE nadir, low point

heighten VERB **1** *The architects proposed heightening the roof levels.* ► raise, make higher, lift up, elevate, build up AN OPPOSITE IS lower **2** *The presence of police heightened their sense of alarm.* ► increase, magnify, intensify, add to, sharpen, strengthen, augment, boost, enhance AN OPPOSITE IS lessen

hell NOUN **1** a place where, in some religions, wicked people are thought to be punished after they die **2** a very unpleasant place or experience

hell for leather (*informal*) at high speed [from Old English]

hello INTERJECTION a word used to greet somebody or to attract their attention

helmet NOUN helmets a strong covering worn to protect the head

help VERB helps, helping, helped **1** do part of another person's work for him or her **2** benefit; make something better or easier • *This will help you to sleep.* **3** if you cannot help doing something, you cannot avoid doing it • *I can't help coughing.* **4** serve food, etc., to somebody • *just help yourself*
▷ **helper** NOUN **helpful** ADJECTIVE **helpfully** ADVERB

help NOUN **1** helping somebody **2** a person or thing that helps [from Old English]

helping NOUN helpings a portion of food

helpless ADJECTIVE not able to do things
▷ **helplessly** ADVERB **helplessness** NOUN

helpline NOUN helplines a telephone service giving advice on problems

hem NOUN hems the edge of a piece of cloth that is folded over and sewn down

hem VERB hems, hemming, hemmed put a hem on something

hem in surround and restrict

hemisphere NOUN hemispheres **1** half a sphere **2** half the earth • *Australia is in the southern hemisphere.*
▷ **hemispherical** ADJECTIVE

hemoglobin (heem- a- **gloh**- bin) NOUN the red substance that carries oxygen in the blood

hemophilia (heem- o- **fil**- ee- a) NOUN a disease that causes people to bleed dangerously from even a slight cut
▷ **hemophiliac** NOUN

hemorrhage (**hem**- er- ij) NOUN bleeding, especially inside a person's body

hen NOUN hens **1** a female bird **2** a female fowl

hence ADVERB **1** henceforth **2** therefore **3** (*old use*) from here

henchman NOUN henchmen a trusty supporter

her PRONOUN the form of she used as the object of a verb or after a preposition

her ADJECTIVE belonging to her • *her book*

herald NOUN heralds an official in former times who made announcements and carried messages for a king or queen

heraldry NOUN the study of coats of arms
▷ **heraldic** (hir- **al**- dik) ADJECTIVE

herb NOUN herbs a plant used for flavoring or for making medicine
▷ **herbal** ADJECTIVE

herbivorous (her- **biv**- er- us) ADJECTIVE plant-eating COMPARE **carnivorous**
▷ **herbivore** NOUN

Thesaurus

hell NOUN **1** *religions that believe in a hell*
► netherworld, eternal punishment, infernal regions, lower regions AN OPPOSITE IS heaven RELATED ADJECTIVE ► infernal **2** *Living with Patrick must be hell.* ► agony, torture, a misery, a nightmare, an ordeal, a torment

hellish ADJECTIVE *It was a hellish experience they wanted never to repeat.* ► dreadful, ghastly, horrible, terrible, frightful

help VERB **1** *Will you help me move this bed?*
► assist, aid, lend a hand **2** *I couldn't help laughing.* ► prevent yourself, restrain yourself from, refrain from, resist **3** *A small donation will help those in need.* ► support, contribute to, encourage, promote **4** *Foreign visits will help your languages.* ► improve, enhance, bolster **5** *She took aspirin to help her headache.*
► relieve, reduce, ease, soothe, alleviate, remedy, lessen

help NOUN **1** *We could do with some help.*
► assistance, support, aid, guidance, cooperation, advice AN OPPOSITE IS hindrance **2** *Would a screwdriver be of help?* ► use, service, benefit, utility

helper NOUN **1** *A chain of helpers passed buckets of water along.* ► supporter, volunteer, worker **2** *All her helpers were away that day.* ► assistant, colleague, collaborator, subordinate, associate, coworker

helpful ADJECTIVE **1** *The shop assistant was friendly and helpful.* ► obliging, willing, cooperative, thoughtful, considerate, sympathetic, eager to please, friendly **2** *A hammer might be helpful. A sceptical attitude won't be helpful.* ► useful, of use, beneficial, worthwhile, profitable, productive, constructive, valuable

helping NOUN *a good helping of pudding*
► portion, serving, plateful, bowlful, share, amount, ration, (*more informal*) dollop

helpless ADJECTIVE *She felt helpless and frustrated.*
► powerless, impotent, incapable, dependent, weak, forlorn, vulnerable, defenceless, destitute

hem NOUN *She lowered the hem of her skirt.*
► hemline, edge, border, fringe

hem VERB **hem in** *We were hemmed in by a group of tourist buses.* ► shut in, close in, box in, enclose, surround, confine, restrict

A
B
C
D
E
F
G
H
I
J
K
L
M
N
O
P
Q
R
S
T
U
V
W
X
Y
Z

herd NOUN **herds 1** a group of cattle or other animals that feed together **2** a mass of people; a mob
▷ **herdsman** NOUN

herd VERB **herds, herding, herded 1** gather or move or send in a herd • *We all herded into the dining room.* **2** look after a herd of animals

here ADVERB in or to this place etc.
here and there in various places or directions

hereby ADVERB by this act or decree

hereditary ADJECTIVE **1** inherited • *a hereditary disease* **2** inheriting a position • *The queen is a hereditary monarch.*

heredity (hir- ed- it- ee) NOUN the process of inheriting physical or mental characteristics from parents or ancestors

heresy (herri- see) NOUN **heresies** an opinion that disagrees with the beliefs generally accepted by the Christian Church or other authority

heretic (herri- tik) NOUN **heretics** a person who supports a heresy
▷ **heretical** (hi- ret- ik- al) ADJECTIVE

heritage NOUN the things that someone has inherited

hermetically ADVERB so as to be airtight
• *The tin is hermetically sealed.*

hermit NOUN **hermits** a person who lives alone and keeps away from people

hero NOUN **heroes 1** a man or boy who is admired for doing something very brave or great **2** the chief male character in a story
▷ **heroic** ADJECTIVE **heroically** ADVERB **heroism** NOUN

heroin NOUN a very strong drug, made from morphine

heroine NOUN **heroines 1** a woman or girl who is admired for doing something very

brave or great **2** the chief female character in a story etc.

heron NOUN **herons** a wading bird with long legs and a long neck

herring NOUN **herring** or **herrings** a sea fish used as food

hers POSSESSIVE PRONOUN belonging to her • *Those books are hers*
USAGE It is incorrect to write *her's*.

herself PRONOUN she or her and nobody else. The word is used to refer back to the subject of a sentence (e.g., *she cut herself*) or for emphasis (e.g., *she herself has said it*)
by herself alone; on her own

hertz NOUN **hertz** a unit of frequency of electromagnetic waves, = one cycle per second

hesitate VERB **hesitates, hesitating, hesitated** be slow or uncertain in speaking, moving, etc.
▷ **hesitant** ADJECTIVE **hesitation** NOUN

heterogeneous (het- er- o- jeen- ee- us) ADJECTIVE composed of people or things of different kinds

heterosexual ADJECTIVE attracted to people of the opposite sex; not homosexual
▷ **heterosexual** NOUN

hexagon NOUN **hexagons** a flat shape with six sides and six angles
▷ **hexagonal** ADJECTIVE

hibernate VERB **hibernates, hibernating, hibernated** spend the winter in a state like deep sleep
▷ **hibernation** NOUN
[from Latin *hiberna* = winter quarters]

hiccup NOUN **hiccups 1** a high gulping sound made when your breath is briefly interrupted **2** a brief hitch or setback
▷ **hiccup** VERB **hicups, hicupping, hicupped**

Thesaurus

herd NOUN **1** *herds of farm animals* ► drove, pack, flock **2** *She cut her way through the herd of lunchtime drinkers.* ► crowd, mass, throng, horde, crush

herd VERB **1** *They herded the sheep into the pens.* ► drive, lead, guide, round, gather, collect **2** *We all herded into a meeting room.* ► crowd, pack, throng, flock, huddle, squash

hero NOUN **1** *His father had been decorated as a war hero.* ► champion, brave man **2** *James had always been her hero.* ► idol, star, ideal, paragon, favorite, darling **3** *The story had no real hero.* ► principal character, lead character, protagonist

heroic ADJECTIVE *All his heroic efforts might come to nothing.* ► brave, courageous, noble, valiant, bold, daring, gallant, intrepid AN OPPOSITE IS cowardly

heroine NOUN *the heroine of the film* ► leading OR principal female character, female lead, female star, leading lady

hesitant ADJECTIVE *They were hesitant about what to do next. He took a hesitant step back.*
► uncertain, tentative, cautious, faltering, doubtful, halfhearted, irresolute, indecisive, undecided, dithering OPPOSITES ARE decisive, resolute

hesitate VERB *She hesitated before searching in her bag for her keys.* ► pause, delay, falter, dither, hold back, vacillate, waver, wait, have second thoughts

hesitation NOUN *He answered without any hesitation.* ► pause, delay, equivocation, reluctance, vacillation, misgivings, second thoughts, qualms, reservation, doubt, uncertainty

hide VERB **hides, hiding, hid, hidden** **1** get into a place where you cannot be seen **2** keep a person or thing from being seen **3** keep a thing secret

hide NOUN **hides** an animal's skin

hide-and-seek NOUN a game in which one person looks for others who are hiding

hideous ADJECTIVE very ugly or unpleasant
▷ **hideously** ADVERB

hiding[1] NOUN being hidden • *She went into hiding.*
▷ **hiding place** NOUN

hiding[2] NOUN **hidings** a thrashing or beating

hierarchy (hyr- ark- ee) NOUN **hierarchies** an organization that ranks people one above another according to the power or authority that they hold

hieroglyphics (hyr- o- glif- iks) PLURAL NOUN pictures or symbols used in ancient Egypt to represent words

hi-fi NOUN **hi-fis** (*informal*) **1** high fidelity **2** equipment for reproducing recorded sound with very little distortion

higgledy-piggledy ADVERB, ADJECTIVE completely mixed up; in great disorder

high ADJECTIVE **1** reaching a long way upward • *high hills* **2** far above the ground or above sea level • *high clouds* **3** measuring from top to bottom • *two meters high* **4** above average level in importance, quality, amount, etc. • *high rank* • *high prices* **5** (said about meat) beginning to go bad **6** (*informal*) affected by a drug
it is high time it is already the time for something to happen • *It's high time we left.*

high ADVERB at or to a high level or position etc. • *They flew high above us.*

highbrow ADJECTIVE intellectual

higher education NOUN education at a university or college

high fidelity NOUN reproducing recorded sound with very little distortion

high jump NOUN an athletic contest in which competitors try to jump over a high bar

highlight NOUN **highlights** **1** the most interesting part of something • *The highlight of the holiday was the trip to Pompeii.* **2** a light area in a painting etc. **3** a light-colored streak in a person's hair

highly ADVERB **1** extremely • *highly amusing* **2** very favorably • *We think highly of her.*

Highness NOUN **Highnesses** the title of a prince or princess

high road NOUN **high roads** the main road

high school NOUN **high schools** a secondary school

Thesaurus

hidden ADJECTIVE **1** *a hidden entrance*
▸ concealed, secret, unseen, invisible, disguised, camouflaged, covered **2** *The message may have a hidden meaning.*
▸ unknown, obscure, cryptic, secret, abstruse, mysterious, ulterior

hide VERB **1** *Sam hid in a cupboard.* ▸ conceal yourself, take cover, keep hidden, lie low, keep out of sight **2** *Where did they hide the jewels?* ▸ conceal, secrete, store away, bury, (*more informal*) stash AN OPPOSITE IS expose **3** *Richard tried to hide his disapproval.*
▸ disguise, conceal, keep hidden, suppress, repress, mask OPPOSITES ARE disclose, flaunt **4** *Passing clouds hid the moon.* ▸ obscure, shadow, block out, conceal, obstruct AN OPPOSITE IS reveal

hide NOUN *an animal's hide* ▸ skin, pelt, coat, fur, leather

hideous ADJECTIVE **1** *His mouth was twisted in a hideous grin.* ▸ ugly, unsightly, repulsive, repellent, revolting, gruesome, disgusting, macabre AN OPPOSITE IS beautiful **2** *It is one of the most hideous experiences we have had in our lives.* ▸ horrible, ghastly, horrific, terrible, appalling, shocking, sickening, dreadful, frightful, grim, grisly, odious

hiding NOUN *I was given a good hiding.*
▸ beating, thrashing, caning, spanking, belting, whacking

high ADJECTIVE **1** *a high mountain; a high building* ▸ tall, lofty, elevated, towering OPPOSITES ARE low, short **2** *a high position in the government* ▸ senior, prominent, high-ranking, top-ranking, leading, distinguished, important, influential, powerful OPPOSITES ARE junior, low-ranking **3** *high moral principles* ▸ noble, lofty, honorable, high-minded AN OPPOSITE IS base **4** *high prices* ▸ inflated, excessive, exorbitant, top, costly AN OPPOSITE IS low **5** *the high notes* ▸ high-pitched, soprano, treble, shrill, sharp, piercing OPPOSITES ARE low, bass **6** *the highest standards* ▸ excellent, outstanding, exceptional, exemplary OPPOSITES ARE low, poor **7** *high winds* ▸ strong, powerful, violent, stiff, blustery AN OPPOSITE IS gentle **8** *I have a high opinion of them.* ▸ favorable, positive, good, approving OPPOSITES ARE low, unfavorable

highbrow ADJECTIVE *highbrow tastes in music* ▸ intellectual, sophisticated, cultivated, cultured, serious

highly ADVERB *a form of waste that is highly toxic* ▸ very, extremely, considerably, exceedingly, distinctly, decidedly, immensely

high street NOUN high streets a town's main street

high tea NOUN a meal eaten in the late afternoon or early evening

highway NOUN highways a main road or route

highwayman NOUN highwaymen a man who robbed travellers on highways in former times

hijack VERB hijacks, hijacking, hijacked seize control of an aircraft or vehicle during a journey
▷ hijack NOUN hijacker NOUN

hike NOUN hikes a long walk
▷ hike VERB hiker NOUN

hilarious ADJECTIVE very funny
▷ hilariously ADVERB hilarity NOUN

hill NOUN hills a piece of land that is higher than the ground around it
▷ hillside NOUN hilly ADJECTIVE

hilt NOUN hilts the handle of a sword, dagger, or knife
to the hilt completely

him PRONOUN the form of he used as the object of a verb or after a preposition

himself PRONOUN he or him and nobody else
COMPARE herself

hind ADJECTIVE at the back • the hind legs

hinder VERB hinders, hindering, hindered get in someone's way or make things difficult for them
▷ hindrance NOUN

hindquarters PLURAL NOUN an animal's hind legs and rear parts

hindsight NOUN looking back on an event with knowledge or understanding that you did not have at the time

Hindu NOUN Hindus a person who believes in Hinduism, which is one of the religions of India

hinge NOUN hinges a joining device on which a lid or door etc. turns when it opens

hinge VERB hinges, hinging, hinged 1 fix something with a hinge 2 depend
• Everything hinges on this meeting.

hint NOUN hints 1 a slight indication or suggestion • Give me a hint of what you want.
2 a useful idea or piece of advice • household hints

hint VERB hints, hinting, hinted make a hint

hip[1] NOUN hips the bony part at the side of the body between the waist and the thigh

hip[2] NOUN hips the fruit of the wild rose

hippopotamus NOUN hippopotamuses a very large African animal that lives near water

hire VERB hires, hiring, hired 1 pay to borrow something 2 lend something for payment
• He hires out bicycles.
▷ hirer NOUN

hire NOUN hiring something • bikes for hire

hire purchase NOUN a system of buying something by paying for it in instalments

his ADJECTIVE, POSSESSIVE PRONOUN belonging to him
• That is his book. • That book is his.

hiss VERB hisses, hissing, hissed make a sound like an s • The snakes were hissing.
▷ hiss NOUN

Thesaurus

hijack VERB A man was charged with hijacking a Russian plane to Stockholm. ► seize, commandeer, take over, skyjack, expropriate

hike VERB They hiked across the moors for several miles. ► trek, go on foot, walk , ramble, tramp, trudge, traipse, slog

hike NOUN a twenty-mile hike ► trek, walk, ramble, tramp, trudge, slog

hilarious ADJECTIVE A group clustered around a hilarious puppet show. ► comical, funny, amusing, entertaining, uproarious, riotous, (more informal) hysterical, (more informal) side-splitting

hill NOUN 1 the house at the top of the hill ► high ground, elevation, hillock, ridge, peak, mount 2 The car stalled on a steep hill. ► slope, rise, gradient, incline, ascent

hinder VERB Power failures have hindered production. ► hamper, hold up, interfere with, obstruct, restrict, thwart, prevent, curb, curtail, foil AN OPPOSITE IS facilitate

hindrance NOUN Our presence might be as much a hindrance to you as a help. ► impediment, obstacle, obstruction, encumbrance, handicap,

restriction, limitation, restraint, inconvenience, complication, disadvantage, drawback AN OPPOSITE IS help

hinge VERB Everything hinges on next month's elections. ► depend, rest, hang, revolve, turn

hint NOUN 1 She would drop a few casual hints about leaving. I can take a hint that I'm not wanted. ► clue, sign, signal, indication, reminder, inkling, intimation 2 His father kept turning up to offer handy hints. ► tip, piece of advice, pointer 3 There was a hint of sadness in her voice. ► trace, tinge, touch, suggestion

hint VERB 1 He hinted that a new project was being considered. ► suggest, imply, indicate, intimate 2 I'm not sure what she was hinting at. ► allude to, refer to, imply, suggest

hire VERB 1 We could hire a car and drive to Boston. ► rent, lease, book, charter 2 The new bosses want to hire more freelance workers.
► employ, engage, recruit, appoint

hiss VERB 1 She turned the tap until she heard the gas hiss. ► fizz, fizzle, whistle 2 The audience hissed and threw things on the stage. ► jeer, boo, catcall

histogram NOUN histograms a chart showing amounts as rectangles of varying sizes

historian NOUN historians a person who writes or studies history

historic ADJECTIVE famous or important in history; likely to be remembered • *a historic town* • *a historic meeting*
USAGE Do not confuse with **historical**.

historical ADJECTIVE **1** to do with history **2** that actually existed or took place in the past • *The novel is based on historical events.*
USAGE Do not confuse with **historic**.

history NOUN histories **1** what happened in the past **2** study of past events **3** a description of important events [from Greek *historia* = learning or finding out]

hit VERB hits, hitting, hit **1** come forcefully against a person or thing; knock or strike **2** have a bad effect on • *Famine has hit the poor countries.* **3** reach • *I can't hit that high note.*
hit on discover something by chance

hit NOUN hits **1** hitting; a knock or stroke **2** a shot that hits the target **3** a success **4** a successful song, show, etc.

hitch VERB hitches, hitching, hitched **1** raise or pull with a slight jerk **2** fasten with a loop or hook etc. **3** hitchhike

hitch NOUN hitches **1** a slight difficulty causing delay **2** a hitching movement **3** a knot

hitchhike VERB hitchhikes, hitchhiking, hitchhiked travel by getting rides from passing vehicles
▷ **hitch-hiker** NOUN

hi-tech ADJECTIVE using the most advanced technology, especially electronic devices and computers

hither ADVERB to or toward this place

hitherto ADVERB until this time

HIV ABBREVIATION human immunodeficiency virus; a virus that causes Aids

hive NOUN hives **1** a beehive **2** the bees living in a beehive
hive of industry a place full of people working busily

hoard NOUN hoards a carefully saved store of money, treasure, food, etc.

hoard VERB hoards, hoarding, hoarded store something away
▷ **hoarder** NOUN
USAGE Do not confuse with **horde**.

hoarding NOUN hoardings a tall fence covered with advertisements

hoar frost NOUN a white frost

hoarse ADJECTIVE having a rough or croaking voice
▷ **hoarsely** ADVERB **hoarseness** NOUN

hoax VERB hoaxes, hoaxing, hoaxed deceive somebody as a joke
▷ **hoax** NOUN **hoaxer** NOUN

Thesaurus

historic ADJECTIVE *a historic meeting of the heads of state* ► famous, notable, epoch-making, celebrated, momentous, significant, important AN OPPOSITE IS unimportant

historical ADJECTIVE *a story based on historical events* ► real, real-life, true, actual, authentic, documented, attested, verifiable OPPOSITES ARE fictitious, fictional

history NOUN **1** *their interest in history* ► the past, former times, days of old, antiquity **2** *a history of the civil wars* ► chronicle, record, narrative

hit VERB **1** *He hit the tree with his fist.* ► strike, smack, slap, thump, whack, (*more informal*) slug **2** *Several buses hit the central barrier.* ► crash into, run into, collide with, smash into **3** *The industry has been hit by lightning strikes.* ► affect, hurt, harm, damage **4** *It suddenly hit me that I should have confirmed the reservation.* ► strike, occur to, dawn on, come to, cross your mind **5** *Contributions should hit the million mark.* ► reach, achieve

hit NOUN **1** *He got a hit on the head.* ► blow, punch, thump, knock, smack, slap, whack **2** *The party had been a huge hit.* ► success, triumph, winner, best-seller, (*more informal*) knockout

hitch NOUN *The moves all went without any hitch.* ► problem, difficulty, snag, setback, hindrance

hitch VERB **1** *The farmer hitched a tractor to the cart.* ► fasten, attach, hook, couple, connect **2** *Diana hitched up her skirts and entered the water.* ► pull, lift, raise, hoist, jerk, (*more informal*) hike

hoard NOUN *The tomb contained a huge hoard of jewelry.* ► cache, store, stock, pile, stockpile, heap, supply, treasure trove

hoard VERB *The refugees had hoarded their supplies.* ► store, amass, accumulate, mass, put by, save, stockpile, pile up, collect, gather, keep, lay up, treasure, (*more informal*) stash away AN OPPOSITE IS squander

hoarse ADJECTIVE *a voice that was hoarse from shouting* ► rough, harsh, gruff, husky, throaty, rasping, croaking, grating, gravelly, growling, raucous

hoax NOUN *The virus warning was a hoax.* ► joke, practical joke, prank, trick, spoof, deception, fake, fraud, imposture, cheat, swindle, (*more informal*) leg-pull, (*more informal*) con

A
B
C
D
E
F
G

H

I
J
K
L
M
N
O
P
Q
R
S
T
U
V
W
X
Y
Z

hobble VERB hobbles, hobbling, hobbled limp or walk with difficulty

hobby NOUN hobbies something you do for pleasure in your spare time

hobby horse NOUN hobby horses **1** a stick with a horse's head, used as a toy **2** a subject that a person likes to talk about whenever he or she gets the chance

hobgoblin NOUN hobgoblins a mischievous or evil spirit

hockey NOUN a game played by two teams with curved sticks and a hard ball

hoe NOUN hoes a tool for scraping up weeds

hoe VERB hoes, hoeing, hoed scrape or dig with a hoe

hog NOUN hogs **1** a male pig **2** (informal) a greedy person
go the whole hog (informal) do something completely or thoroughly

Hogmanay NOUN New Year's Eve in Scotland [perhaps from early French aguillanneuf = a gift at new year]

hoist VERB hoists, hoisting, hoisted lift something up, especially by using ropes or pulleys

hold VERB holds, holding, held **1** have and keep, especially in your hands **2** have room for ● The jug holds two pints. **3** support ● This plank won't hold my weight. **4** stay the same; continue ● Will the fine weather hold? **5** believe or consider ● We shall hold you responsible. **6** cause something to take place ● hold a meeting **7** restrain someone or stop them getting away ● The police are holding three men for the robbery.
hold forth make a long speech
hold out refuse to give in
hold up **1** hinder **2** stop and rob somebody by threats or force
hold your tongue (informal) stop talking

hold NOUN holds **1** holding something; a grasp **2** something to hold on to for support **3** the part of a ship where cargo is stored, below the deck
get hold of **1** grasp **2** obtain **3** make contact with a person

holdup NOUN holdups **1** a delay **2** a robbery with threats or force

hole NOUN holes **1** a hollow place; a gap or opening **2** a burrow **3** one of the small holes into which you have to hit the ball in golf **4** (informal) an unpleasant place
▷ **holey** ADJECTIVE
in a hole in an awkward situation

Thesaurus

---

hobby NOUN Kevin took up fishing as a hobby.
► pastime, leisure activity, leisure pursuit, recreation, diversion, interest, relaxation

hoist VERB The crew hoisted more cargo on deck.
► raise, lift, pull up, heave, winch up

hoist NOUN a hand-operated pneumatic hoist
► crane, jack, pulley, winch, lift, lifting gear, block and tackle, davit, windlass, derrick

hold VERB **1** He was holding a black briefcase.
► clasp, clutch, grip, cling to, cling on to **2** I wanted to hold her in my arms. ► hug, embrace, clasp, fold, cradle **3** Visitors must hold a valid passport. ► possess, bear, have, own **4** The society holds a general meeting in March. ► call, convene, summon, conduct, assemble **5** Police are holding him pending further investigation.
► detain, keep in custody, imprison, lock up, arrest **6** She held a senior position in a bank.
► occupy, fill, (more informal) hold down **7** The house holds six to eight people. ► take, accommodate, have room for, have space for, contain **8** The sect holds that killing animals is a sin. ► believe, consider, maintain, contend, think, take the view **9** I hope the good weather will hold. ► continue, last, carry on, persist, endure
hold back **1** Joe held back his anger.
► suppress, control, restrain, curb, check, keep back, hold in AN OPPOSITE IS release **2** The lack of information held us back. ► hinder, hamper, inhibit, impede, thwart, restrain AN OPPOSITE

IS help **3** There is no need to hold back if you have things to say. ► hesitate, pause, desist, shrink AN OPPOSITE IS proceed
hold forth Ivor was holding forth about his adventures. ► discourse, declaim, speak at length, spout, rant
hold off **1** The rain held off until lunch time.
► stay away, desist **2** He held the attackers off as long as he could. ► resist, fend off, ward off, stave off, repel, rebuff
hold out **1** Supplies will not hold out much longer. ► last, remain, continue AN OPPOSITE IS run out **2** The garrison held out for a whole month. ► resist, persevere, stand fast, hang on OPPOSITES ARE give in, yield
hold up **1** The bridge is held up by concrete columns. ► support, bear, shore up, carry, raise **2** Work on the roof was held up by bad weather.
► delay, detain, hinder, impede AN OPPOSITE IS facilitate

hold NOUN **1** She released her hold on the handle.
► grip, grasp, clutch **2** Tim had some kind of hold over them. ► influence, power, control, sway, (more informal) clout

holder NOUN **1** She put the knife back in its holder. ► case, container, receptacle, casing, cover, sheath, stand, rest **2** holders of U.S. passports ► bearer, possessor, owner

hole NOUN **1** The work gang dug a large hole in the road. ► opening, orifice, trench, ditch **2** There were holes in the plaster caused by water.

hole VERB holes, holing, holed **1** make a hole or holes in something **2** hit a golf ball into one of the holes

holiday NOUN holidays **1** a day or week when people do not go to work or to school **2** a time when you go away to enjoy yourself

holiness NOUN being holy or sacred
His Holiness the title of the Pope

hollow ADJECTIVE with an empty space inside; not solid
▷ **hollowly** ADVERB

hollow NOUN hollows a hollow or sunken place

hollow VERB hollows, hollowing, hollowed make a thing hollow

holly NOUN hollies an evergreen bush with shiny prickly leaves and red berries

holocaust NOUN holocausts an immense destruction, especially by fire • *the nuclear holocaust*
the Holocaust the mass murder of the Jews by the Nazis from 1939 to 1945

hologram NOUN holograms a type of photograph made by laser beams that produces a three-dimensional image

holy ADJECTIVE holier, holiest **1** belonging or devoted to God **2** consecrated • *holy water*
▷ **holiness** NOUN

homage NOUN homages an act or expression of respect or honor • *We paid homage to his achievements.*

home NOUN homes **1** the place where you live **2** the place where you were born or where you feel you belong **3** a place where those who need help are looked after • *an old people's home* **4** the place to be reached in a race or in certain games

home ADJECTIVE **1** to do with your own home or country • *home industries* **2** played on a team's own ground • *a home match*

home ADVERB **1** to or at home • *Is she home yet?* **2** to the point aimed at • *Push the bolt home.*
bring something home to somebody make him or her realize it

home VERB homes, homing, homed make for a target • *The missile homed in.*

home economics NOUN the study of cookery and how to run a home

homeless ADJECTIVE having no home

homely ADJECTIVE simple and ordinary • *a homely meal*
▷ **homeliness** NOUN

homemade ADJECTIVE made at home, not bought from a shop

homeopathy NOUN the treatment of disease by tiny doses of drugs that in a healthy person would produce symptoms of the disease
▷ **homeopathic** ADJECTIVE

Thesaurus

▶ gap, split, cavity, crack, fissure, pit, puncture, hollow, depression, tear **3** *The animal crawled out of its hole.* ▶ burrow, lair, retreat **4** (*informal*) *We were out of money and in a bit of a hole.* ▶ predicament, mess, difficulty, tight corner, quandary, plight, crisis, emergency

holiday NOUN **1** *Her doctor told her she needed a holiday.* ▶ vacation, break, rest, time off, leave **2** *Monday is a public holiday.* ▶ bank holiday, festival, feast day

holiness NOUN *Her holiness affected everyone who saw her.* ▶ sanctity, devoutness, spirituality, piety, saintliness, godliness, righteousness

hollow ADJECTIVE **1** *a hollow space* ▶ empty, concave, sunken, deep, depressed AN OPPOSITE IS solid **2** *a hollow laugh* ▶ dull, low, flat, muffled, muted **3** *a hollow promise* ▶ insincere, artificial, false, empty, deceptive AN OPPOSITE IS sincere **4** *a hollow victory* ▶ worthless, futile, vain, meaningless, pointless, pyrrhic AN OPPOSITE IS worthwhile

hollow NOUN *an ancient theater built in the hollow of a hillside* ▶ depression, cavity, dimple, dip, crater, hole, indentation, bowl, concavity, dent, dint, dish

holy ADJECTIVE **1** *holy men and women* ▶ saintly, godly, pious, devout, religious, spiritual, virtuous, pure **2** *a holy place* ▶ sacred, hallowed, consecrated, sanctified, revered, venerated

homage NOUN *an act of homage to the king* ▶ respect, recognition, acknowledgment, devotion, tribute, honor, admiration, esteem, deference, veneration
pay homage to *He paid homage to all who had sacrificed their lives in the war.* ▶ honor, praise, salute, acclaim, applaud

home NOUN **1** *People were forced to leave their homes.* ▶ house, dwelling, place of residence, address, accommodation RELATED ADJECTIVE ▶ domestic **2** *They had traveled thousands of miles from home.* ▶ native land, homeland, birthplace, motherland, fatherland **3** *He refused to go into a home.* ▶ institution, nursing home, residential home, hospice, shelter

homeless ADJECTIVE *increasing numbers of homeless people* ▶ destitute, vagrant, down-and-out, outcast, unhoused, wandering, evicted, forsaken, abandoned, itinerant, nomadic

homely ADJECTIVE *The hotel offers a warm welcome and a homely atmosphere.* ▶ friendly, informal, relaxed, easygoing, familiar, intimate, congenial, comfortable, cosy, natural, simple, unaffected, unpretentious AN OPPOSITE IS formal

a b c d e f g h i j k l m n o p q r s t u v w x y z

A
B
C
D
E
F
G
H
I
J
K
L
M
N
O
P
Q
R
S
T
U
V
W
X
Y
Z

home page NOUN home pages the first page of an Internet website, with a summary of all the information it gives

homesick ADJECTIVE sad because you are away from home
▷ **homesickness** NOUN

homeward ADJECTIVE, ADVERB going towards home
▷ **homewards** ADVERB

homework NOUN school work that has to be done at home

homicide NOUN homicides the killing of one person by another
▷ **homicidal** ADJECTIVE

homogeneous (hom- o- **jeen**- ee- us) ADJECTIVE formed of people or things of the same kind

homograph NOUN homographs a word that is spelled like another but has a different meaning or origin, e.g., *bat* (a flying animal) and *bat* (for hitting a ball)

homonym (hom- o- nim) NOUN homonyms a homograph

homophone NOUN homophones a word with the same sound as another, e.g., *son, sun*

Homo sapiens NOUN human beings regarded as a species of animal [Latin, = wise man or person]

homosexual ADJECTIVE attracted to people of the same sex
▷ **homosexual** NOUN **homosexuality** NOUN

honest ADJECTIVE not stealing or cheating or telling lies; truthful
▷ **honestly** ADVERB **honesty** NOUN

honey NOUN a sweet sticky food made by bees

honeycomb NOUN honeycombs a wax structure of small six-sided sections made by bees to hold their honey and eggs

honeycombed ADJECTIVE with many holes or tunnels

honeymoon NOUN honeymoons a holiday spent together by a newly married couple [from **honey** + **moon** (because the first intensely passionate feelings gradually wane like the moon)]

honeysuckle NOUN a climbing plant with fragrant yellow or pink flowers

honk NOUN honks a loud sound like that made by a goose or an old-fashioned car horn
▷ **honk** VERB

honorary ADJECTIVE **1** given or received as an honor ● *an honorary degree* **2** unpaid ● *the honorary treasurer of the club*
USAGE Do not confuse with **honorable**.

honor NOUN honors **1** great respect or reputation **2** a person or thing that brings honor **3** something a person is proud to do ● *It is an honor to meet you.* **4** honesty and loyalty ● *a man of honor* **5** an award for distinction
in honor of as an expression of respect for

honor VERB honors, honoring, honored **1** feel or show honor for a person **2** keep to the terms of an agreement or promise

---

Thesaurus

---

honest ADJECTIVE **1** *He's a fair and honest man.* ► upright, honorable, virtuous, law-abiding, high-minded, scrupulous, moral, decent, principled, upstanding AN OPPOSITE IS dishonest **2** *business practices that are barely honest* ► legal, lawful, ethical, legitimate, above-board, (*more informal*) on the level AN OPPOSITE IS dishonest **3** *It was an honest mistake.* ► genuine, real, authentic, legitimate AN OPPOSITE IS deliberate **4** *Let us have your honest opinion. I've tried to be perfectly honest with you.* ► sincere, objective, candid, direct, open, frank, truthful, impartial, unbiased, unprejudiced, balanced OPPOSITES ARE insincere, untruthful, biased

honestly ADVERB **1** *He said he had come by the money honestly.* ► fairly, legally, lawfully, legitimately, honorably **2** *She could honestly say she had had nothing to do with the incident.* ► frankly, sincerely, truthfully, genuinely

honesty NOUN **1** *She demanded complete honesty from her staff.* ► truthfulness, trustworthiness, integrity, goodness, morality, honor, uprightness, veracity, fairness, probity, rectitude, reliability, scrupulousness AN

OPPOSITE IS dishonesty **2** *They were encouraged to speak with complete honesty.* ► sincerity, candor, directness, frankness, straightforwardness, bluntness, outspokenness, plainness AN OPPOSITE IS insincerity

honor NOUN **1** *He defended the president, calling him a man of honor.* ► honesty, integrity, morality, principle, distinction, decency, probity **2** *She received many honors from the film industry.* ► award, accolade, tribute, distinction, commendation, acknowledgment, recognition **3** *I appreciate the honor of speaking at this assembly.* ► privilege, distinction, cachet, kudos **4** *They were received with honor by the king.* ► praise, acclaim, homage, admiration, adulation

honor VERB **1** *a grand parade to honor the distinguished visitors* ► praise, applaud, acclaim, salute, celebrate, commend, pay homage to **2** *They intend to honor their commitment to the peace process.* ► fulfil, respect, observe, carry out, keep, discharge

honorable ADJECTIVE deserving honor; honest and loyal
  ▷ **honorably** ADVERB
  USAGE Do not confuse with honorary.

hood NOUN **hoods** 1 a covering of soft material for the head and neck 2 a folding roof or cover
  ▷ **hooded** ADJECTIVE

hoodwink VERB **hoodwinks, hoodwinking, hoodwinked** deceive

hoof NOUN **hoofs** or **hooves** the horny part of the foot of a horse etc.

hook NOUN **hooks** a bent or curved piece of metal etc. for hanging things on or for catching hold of something

hook VERB **hooks, hooking, hooked** 1 fasten something with or on a hook 2 catch a fish, etc., with a hook 3 hit a ball in a curving path **be hooked on something** (slang) be addicted to it

hooked ADJECTIVE hook-shaped

hooligan NOUN **hooligans** a rough and violent young person
  ▷ **hooliganism** NOUN

hoop NOUN **hoops** a ring made of metal or wood

hoot NOUN **hoots** 1 the sound made by an owl or a vehicle's horn or a steam whistle 2 a cry of scorn or disapproval 3 an outburst of laughter 4 (informal) something funny
  ▷ **hoot** VERB **hooter** NOUN

hop VERB **hops, hopping, hopped** 1 jump on one foot 2 (said about an animal) spring from all feet at once 3 (informal) move quickly ● Here's the car-hop in! **hop it** (informal) go away

hop[1] NOUN **hops** a hopping movement

hop[2] NOUN **hops** a climbing plant used to give beer its flavor

hope NOUN **hopes** 1 the feeling of wanting something to happen, and thinking that it will happen 2 a person or thing that gives hope ● You are our only hope.

hope VERB **hopes, hoping, hoped** feel hope; want and expect something

hopeful ADJECTIVE 1 feeling hope 2 likely to be good or successful

hopefully ADVERB 1 it is to be hoped; I hope that 2 in a hopeful way
  USAGE Some people say it is incorrect to use **hopefully** to mean "I hope that" or "let's hope," and say that it should only be used to mean "in a hopeful way." This first use is very common in informal language but you should avoid it when you are writing or speaking formally.

Thesaurus

honorable ADJECTIVE 1 No one doubted that her motives were entirely honorable; honorable people who were fighting for the common good
  ▶ honest, sincere, reputable, noble, worthy, just, straight, trustworthy, principled, virtuous, upright, proper 2 a respected politician who has done honorable service in the Treasury
  ▶ distinguished, illustrious, eminent, great

hoodwink VERB The man had hoodwinked him into parting with a large sum of money.
  ▶ deceive, trick, dupe, cheat, swindle, fool, mislead, delude, (more informal) take in

hook NOUN 1 He hung his coat on one of the hooks. ▶ peg, nail 2 a dress fastened at the back with a hook and eye ▶ fastener, fastening, clasp, clip, hasp 3 a fishing hook ▶ barb, snare

hook VERB 1 David hooked a 64-pound carp.
  ▶ catch, take, land, net, bag 2 He hooked a trailer to the car. ▶ hitch, fasten, attach, couple, connect

hoop NOUN a hoop of metal ▶ band, loop, ring, round, circle, circlet, girdle

hoot VERB 1 An owl hooted. ▶ screech, call, 2 The driver became impatient and hooted.
  ▶ beep, toot, honk, sound the horn 3 The audience hooted in derision. ▶ shout, shriek, yell, jeer, call out

hoot NOUN 1 the hoot of an owl ▶ screech, call 2 hoots of laughter ▶ shriek, shout, scream, yell, jeer

hop VERB He hopped along beside her. She hopped on a bus and went home. ▶ jump, leap, skip, spring, trip, bound, dance, flit, prance, caper

hope VERB 1 I hope to answer all your questions.
  ▶ aim, intend, plan, have it in mind, aspire
  2 hope for We are hoping for a quick response.
  ▶ expect, look for, wish for, want USAGE It is better to avoid anticipate in this sense, because it has other meanings.

hope NOUN 1 She has the hope of being in the national team. ▶ ambition, aspiration, expectation, dream, desire, wish 2 There's some hope of a better future. ▶ prospect, expectation, likelihood, optimism, assumption

hopeful ADJECTIVE 1 We are still hopeful about avoiding a conflict. ▶ optimistic, confident, positive, expectant, sanguine AN OPPOSITE IS pessimistic 2 hopeful signs of an economic recovery ▶ promising, encouraging, favorable, heartening, reassuring, propitious, auspicious, cheering AN OPPOSITE IS discouraging

hopefully ADVERB 1 "Are we going back?" she asked hopefully. ▶ expectantly, optimistically, confidently, with hope AN OPPOSITE IS pessimistically 2 Hopefully the work will be completed next week. ▶ all being well, most likely, with luck, conceivably, probably

a b c d e f g h i j k l m n o p q r s t u v w x y z

A
B
C
D
E
F
G
H
I
J
K
L
M
N
O
P
Q
R
S
T
U
V
W
X
Y
Z

hopeless ADJECTIVE **1** without hope **2** very bad at something
▷ **hopelessly** ADVERB **hopelessness** NOUN

hopscotch NOUN a game of hopping into squares drawn on the ground

horde NOUN hordes a large group or crowd
USAGE Do not confuse with hoard.

horizon NOUN horizons the line where the earth and the sky seem to meet

horizontal ADJECTIVE level, so as to be parallel to the horizon; going across from left to right (The opposite is vertical)
▷ **horizontally** ADVERB

hormone NOUN hormones a substance produced by glands in the body and carried by the blood to stimulate other organs in the body
▷ **hormonal** ADJECTIVE

horn NOUN horns **1** a hard substance that grows into a point on the head of a bull, cow, ram, etc. **2** a pointed part **3** a brass instrument played by blowing **4** a device for making a warning sound
▷ **horned** ADJECTIVE **horny** ADJECTIVE

horoscope NOUN horoscopes an astrologer's forecast of future events

horrendous ADJECTIVE extremely unpleasant

horrible ADJECTIVE **1** horrifying **2** very unpleasant or nasty
▷ **horribly** ADVERB

horrid ADJECTIVE horrible
▷ **horridly** ADVERB

horrify VERB horrifies, horrifying, horrified **1** make somebody feel very afraid or disgusted **2** shock

horror NOUN horrors **1** great fear or disgust **2** a person or thing causing horror

horse NOUN horses **1** a large four-legged animal used for riding on and for pulling carts, etc. **2** a framework for hanging clothes on to dry
on horseback mounted on a horse

horse chestnut NOUN horse chestnuts a large tree that produces dark-brown nuts (conkers)

horsepower NOUN a unit for measuring the power of an engine, equal to 746 watts

horseshoe NOUN horseshoes a U-shaped piece of metal nailed to a horse's hoof

horticulture NOUN the art of cultivating gardens
▷ **horticultural** ADJECTIVE

hose NOUN hoses **1** (also hosepipe) a flexible tube for taking water to something **2** (old use) breeches ● doublet and hose

hospitable ADJECTIVE welcoming; liking to give hospitality
▷ **hospitably** ADVERB

Thesaurus

hopeless ADJECTIVE **1** He looked at her in hopeless bewilderment. ► despairing, desperate, dejected, downhearted, downcast, wretched, pessimistic **2** The doctors regarded his case as hopeless. ► impossible, incurable, irremediable, beyond hope, beyond recovery, lost, unattainable **3** The situation seemed hopeless, now that the food had run out. ► desperate, critical, serious, dire, impossible, beyond hope, useless, futile **4** He is hopeless at board games.
► incompetent, ineffective, ineffectual, poor, inept, (more informal) pathetic, (more informal) useless

horde NOUN A horde of journalists waited outside the house. ► crowd, throng, pack, mob, swarm, band, gang, group

horizon NOUN A ship was visible on the horizon.
► skyline, vista, range of view

horrible or **horrid** ADJECTIVE **1** a horrible accident on the bypass ► dreadful, horrific, horrifying, horrendous, frightful, fearful, terrible, ghastly, hideous, sickening **2** Saturday was a wet, horrible day. The smell was horrid.
► unpleasant, nasty, disagreeable, awful, beastly, dreadful, ghastly, revolting, terrible
OPPOSITES ARE pleasant, agreeable **3** Nora was a horrible person. The teachers were horrid to him.
► nasty, disagreeable, odious, objectionable,

loathsome, hateful, offensive OPPOSITES ARE nice, kind

horrific ADJECTIVE He died from horrific head injuries. ► dreadful, appalling, horrifying, horrendous, frightful, fearful, terrible, hideous, ghastly, sickening

horrify VERB **1** He wrote stories that horrified his readers. ► terrify, frighten, scare, alarm, petrify, terrorize **2** The news would have horrified her. ► shock, appal, outrage, scandalize, offend, sicken, disgust, revolt, nauseate, unnerve, alarm OPPOSITES ARE please, delight

horror NOUN **1** People screamed in horror.
► terror, fear, fright, alarm **2** Public opinion reacted with horror. ► shock, outrage, disgust, revulsion, repugnance, consternation AN OPPOSITE IS delight **3** Newspaper reports described the full horror of the attack.
► ghastliness, awfulness, frightfulness, hideousness, savagery, barbarity

horse NOUN a woman on a horse ► (for riding) mount, (small breed) pony, (adult male) stallion, (young male) colt, (large and strong) cob, (adult female) mare, (young female) filly, (newborn horse) foal RELATED ADJECTIVES ► equestrian, equine

hospitable ADJECTIVE a kind, hospitable family
► friendly, sociable, welcoming, congenial,

hospital NOUN hospitals a place providing medical and surgical treatment for people who are ill or injured

hospitality NOUN welcoming guests or strangers and giving them food and entertainment

host[1] NOUN hosts **1** a person who has guests and looks after them **2** the presenter of a television or radio program [from Latin *hospes*]

host[2] NOUN hosts a large number of people or things [from Latin *hostis* = enemy or army]

host[3] NOUN hosts the bread consecrated at Holy Communion [from Latin *hostia* = sacrifice]

hostage NOUN hostages a person who is held prisoner until the holder's demands are met

hostel NOUN hostels a building where travelers, students, or other groups can stay or live

hostess NOUN hostesses a woman who has guests and looks after them

hostile ADJECTIVE **1** unfriendly • *a hostile glance* **2** opposed to something **3** to do with an enemy • *hostile aircraft*
▷ **hostility** NOUN

hot ADJECTIVE hotter, hottest **1** having great heat or a high temperature **2** giving a

burning sensation when tasted **3** passionate or excitable • *a hot temper*
▷ **hotly** ADVERB **hotness** NOUN
in hot water (*informal*) in trouble or disgrace

hotel NOUN hotels a building where people pay to have meals and stay for the night

hound NOUN hounds a dog used in hunting or racing [from Old English]

hour NOUN hours **1** one twenty-fourth part of a day and night; sixty minutes **2** a time • *Why are you up at this hour?*
hours PLURAL NOUN a fixed period for work • *Office hours are 9 a.m. to 5 p.m.*

hourly ADVERB, ADJECTIVE every hour

house (howss) NOUN houses **1** a building made for people to live in, usually designed for one family **2** a building or establishment for a special purpose • *the opera house* **3** a building for a government assembly; the assembly itself • *the House of Representatives* **4** a family or dynasty • *the royal house of Tudor*

house (howz) VERB houses, housing, housed provide accommodation or room for someone or something [from Old English]

household NOUN households all the people who live together in the same house [from house + an old sense of hold = possession]

Thesaurus

cordial, convivial, amicable, generous, gracious, receptive OPPOSITES ARE inhospitable, unfriendly

hospital NOUN *Joe was lying in a bed in the hospital.* ► infirmary, clinic, nursing home, sanatorium, medical institution, convalescent home, hospice

hospitality NOUN **1** *We needed hospitality for the night.* ► accommodation, catering, entertainment **2** *Thank you for your hospitality.* ► kindness, friendliness, sociability, welcome, conviviality, warm reception

host NOUN **1** *A host of people headed for the town.* ► crowd, throng, band, horde, swarm, group **2** *The host of the restaurant welcomed his guests.* ► proprietor, landlord **3** *the host of a television program* ► presenter, anchorman, anchorwoman, announcer, link person, compère

hostage NOUN *The hijackers released some of the hostages.* ► captive, prisoner, detainee

hostile ADJECTIVE **1** *a hostile crowd; a hostile attack* ► aggressive, antagonistic, belligerent, confrontational, bellicose, pugnacious, angry, militant, unfriendly, malevolent, ill-disposed, warlike AN OPPOSITE IS friendly **2** *a hostile climate* ► harsh, unfavorable, adverse, inhospitable, bad, contrary, unpropitious AN OPPOSITE IS favorable **3** hostile to *They are hostile to the idea.* ► opposed to, averse to, unsympathetic to, antagonistic to, against

hostility NOUN **1** *They reacted with hostility.* ► antagonism, enmity, animosity, opposition, malice, hatred, ill will AN OPPOSITE IS friendship **2** *their hostility to our suggestion* ► opposition, antipathy, disapproval (of), aversion, antagonism

hot ADJECTIVE **1** *hot weather* ► warm, balmy, summery, boiling, blazing, roasting, scorching, sweltering, sultry OPPOSITES ARE cold, chilly **2** *What we need is a hot meal.* ► cooked, heated, piping, sizzling **3** *a hot dish with peppers* ► spicy, peppery, piquant, pungent AN OPPOSITE IS mild **4** *a hot temper* ► fierce, angry, raging, intense, violent, passionate

hotel NOUN *We stayed in a hotel by the river.* ► guest house, boarding house, inn, pension, motel

hound VERB *The reporters went on hounding her.* ► harass, pursue, harry, (*informal*) hassle, pester, persecute, trouble

house NOUN **1** *a row of terraced houses* ► home, dwelling, abode, residence **2** *the house of Stuart* ► dynasty, clan, family, tribe

house VERB *The cabins housed twenty people.* ► accommodate, provide room for, lodge, quarter, shelter, take in, billet, board, (*more informal*) put up

household NOUN *a large household with lots of children* ► family, home, ménage, establishment, (*more informal*) set-up

a b c d e f g **h** i j k l m n o p q r s t u v w x y z

A B C D E F **G H** I J K L M N O P Q R S T U V W X Y Z

householder NOUN householders a person who owns or rents a house

housekeeper NOUN housekeepers a person employed to look after a household

housekeeping NOUN **1** looking after a household **2** (informal) the money for a household's food and other necessities

housemaid NOUN housemaids a woman servant in a house, especially one who cleans rooms

house-proud ADJECTIVE very careful to keep a house clean and tidy

house-trained ADJECTIVE (said about an animal) trained to be clean in the house

housewife NOUN housewives a woman who does the housekeeping for her family

housework NOUN the cleaning and cooking done in housekeeping

housing NOUN housings **1** accommodation; houses **2** a stiff cover or guard for a piece of machinery

housing estate NOUN housing estates a set of houses planned and built together in one area

hovel NOUN hovels a small shabby house

hover VERB hovers, hovering, hovered **1** stay in one place in the air **2** wait about near someone or something

hovercraft NOUN hovercraft a vehicle that travels just above the surface of land or water, supported by a strong current of air sent downward from its engines

how ADVERB **1** in what way; by what means • How did you do it? **2** to what extent or amount • How high can you jump? **3** in what condition • How are you?

how about would you like • How about a game of football?

how do you do? a formal greeting

however ADVERB **1** in whatever way; to whatever extent • You will never catch him, however hard you try. **2** all the same; nevertheless • Later, however, he decided to go.

howl NOUN howls a long loud sad-sounding cry or sound, such as that made by a dog or wolf

howl VERB howls, howling, howled **1** make a howl **2** weep loudly

howler NOUN howlers (informal) a foolish mistake

HQ ABBREVIATION headquarters

hub NOUN hubs **1** the central part of a wheel **2** the central point of interest or activity

hubbub NOUN a loud confused noise of voices

huddle VERB huddles, huddling, huddled **1** crowd together with other people, often for warmth **2** curl your body closely
▷ **huddle** NOUN

huff NOUN
in a huff offended or sulking about something • She went away in a huff.
▷ **huffy** ADJECTIVE

hug VERB hugs, hugging, hugged **1** clasp someone tightly in your arms **2** keep close to something • The ship hugged the shore.

hug NOUN hugs a tight embrace

huge ADJECTIVE extremely large; enormous
▷ **hugely** ADVERB **hugeness** NOUN

Thesaurus

housing NOUN an acute need for better housing
▶ accommodation, houses, homes, habitation, shelter

hovel NOUN The little cottage was not much better than a hovel. ▶ shack, shanty, shed, slum, hut

hover VERB **1** A police helicopter hovered above the crowd. ▶ float, hang, flutter, drift, fly **2** He hovered outside the room waiting to be called in. ▶ linger, dally, pause, wait about, waver, loiter, hesitate, (informal) hang about

howl VERB A dog howled in the distance. ▶ yowl, bay, cry

howl NOUN howls of laughter ▶ shriek, hoot, roar, gale, scream, yell

hub NOUN **1** He gripped the hub of the rear wheel. ▶ center, middle, pivot, axis **2** The foyer will be the hub of activity in this part of the building. ▶ focus, focal point, heart, pivot, nucleus

huddle VERB **1** They huddled together in twos and threes. ▶ crowd, gather, cluster, squeeze, pack, throng, flock, herd, pile, press AN OPPOSITE IS scatter **2** He huddled under the duvet. ▶ cuddle, curl up, nestle, snuggle

hue NOUN **1** gloss paint in a range of hues ▶ color, shade, tone, tint, tinge **2** people of all political hues ▶ complexion, kind, type, nature, character

huffy ADJECTIVE They didn't have an answer and became huffy when we asked. ▶ irritable, irritated, annoyed, unfriendly, grumpy, prickly, piqued, testy, petulant AN OPPOSITE IS friendly

hug VERB Mary was kissed and hugged by her friends. ▶ embrace, clasp, cuddle, squeeze, cling to, enfold, fold in your arms, hold close, nurse, snuggle against

hug NOUN They met with tears and hugs. ▶ embrace, clasp, cuddle, squeeze

huge ADJECTIVE a huge building; a huge tax increase ▶ enormous, gigantic, immense, massive, colossal, vast, large, big, great, giant, (more informal) whopping, (more informal) ginormous AN OPPOSITE IS tiny

hulk NOUN hulks **1** the body or wreck of an old ship **2** a large clumsy person or thing
▷ **hulking** ADJECTIVE

hull NOUN hulls the framework of a ship

hullabaloo NOUN hullabaloos an uproar

hum VERB hums, humming, hummed **1** sing a tune with your lips closed **2** make a low continuous sound like that of a bee

human ADJECTIVE to do with human beings

human being NOUN human beings a man, woman, or child

humane (hew- mayn) ADJECTIVE kind-hearted and merciful
▷ **humanely** ADVERB

humanitarian ADJECTIVE concerned with people's welfare and the reduction of suffering
▷ **humanitarian** NOUN

humanity NOUN **1** human beings; people **2** being human **3** being humane
humanities PLURAL NOUN arts subjects such as history, literature, and music, not sciences

humble ADJECTIVE **1** modest; not proud or showy **2** of low rank or importance
▷ **humbly** ADVERB **humbleness** NOUN

humbug NOUN humbugs **1** insincere or dishonest talk or behavior **2** a hard peppermint sweet

humdrum ADJECTIVE dull and not exciting; commonplace

humid (hew- mid) ADJECTIVE (said about air) moist and damp
▷ **humidity** NOUN

humiliate VERB humiliates, humiliating, humiliated make a person feel disgraced or ashamed
▷ **humiliation** NOUN

humility NOUN being humble

hummingbird NOUN hummingbirds a small tropical bird that makes a humming sound by beating its wings rapidly

humor NOUN **1** being amusing; what makes people laugh **2** the ability to enjoy comical things ● *a sense of humor* **3** a mood ● *in a good humor*

humor VERB humors, humoring, humored keep a person contented by doing what he or she wants

humorous ADJECTIVE full of humor; amusing

Thesaurus

hum VERB *The engine was still humming.* ► purr, whirr, drone, murmur, throb, vibrate

human ADJECTIVE **1** *the human race* ► anthropoid **2** *They are only human and make mistakes.* ► mortal, fallible, imperfect, weak **3** *a very human reaction to the problem* ► compassionate, humane, kind, considerate, understanding, sympathetic, merciful, philanthropic AN OPPOSITE IS inhuman
human beings ► men and women, humankind, humanity, mortals, people, folk

humane ADJECTIVE *a humane way to control the fox population* ► kind, compassionate, considerate, understanding, sympathetic, merciful

humanity NOUN **1** *If they have a shred of humanity in them they will hand over the suspects.* ► compassion, understanding, sensitivity, fellow feeling, sympathy, tolerance **2** *a decision that could affect the whole of humanity* ► humankind, the human race, mankind, mortals, people

humble ADJECTIVE **1** *He acted in a humble and contrite manner.* ► meek, self-effacing, unassuming, deferential, respectful, submissive AN OPPOSITE IS proud **2** *I live in a humble house in the suburbs.* ► modest, simple, plain, ordinary, unpretentious, unostentatious OPPOSITES ARE grand, pretentious **3** *She comes from a humble background.* ► lowly, undistinguished, poor, common, ordinary OPPOSITES ARE distinguished, noble

humid ADJECTIVE *a hot and humid day* ► muggy, clammy, sultry, sticky, damp, dank, moist, steamy, sweaty AN OPPOSITE IS fresh

humiliate VERB *He liked to humiliate them with constant reminders of their mistakes.* ► embarrass, humble, mortify, demean, shame, put to shame

humiliating ADJECTIVE *Rome inflicted a humiliating defeat on its neighbor.* ► embarrassing, mortifying, ignominious, degrading, demeaning, humbling, chastening, crushing, inglorious, discreditable, dishonorable, shaming, undignified AN OPPOSITE IS glorious

humiliation NOUN *At immigration he suffered the humiliation of a body search.* ► embarrassment, indignity, ignominy, mortification, shame, disgrace, degradation, dishonor

humility NOUN *I'm not sure I have the humility to admit my mistakes.* ► modesty, deference, humbleness, meekness, self-effacement, unpretentiousness, lowliness AN OPPOSITE IS pride

humor NOUN **1** *a conversation spiced with humor* ► wit, jocularity, badinage, repartee, jokes, jesting, hilarity, comedy, drollery **2** *in a bad humor* ► mood, temper, frame of mind, state of mind, disposition, spirits

humorous ADJECTIVE *a love story with humorous episodes* ► amusing, funny, comic, comical, jocular, hilarious, entertaining

a
b
c
d
e
f
g
h
i
j
k
l
m
n
o
p
q
r
s
t
u
v
w
x
y
z

A
B
C
D
E
F
G
H
I
J
K
L
M
N
O
P
Q
R
S
T
U
V
W
X
Y
Z

hump NOUN humps **1** a rounded lump or mound **2** an abnormal outward curve at the top of a person's back

humpback bridge NOUN humpback bridges a small bridge that curves steeply upwards in the middle

humus (hew- mus) NOUN rich earth made by decayed plants

hunch NOUN hunches a feeling that you can guess what is going to happen

hunch VERB hunches, hunching, hunched bend your shoulders upward so that your back is rounded

hunchback NOUN hunchbacks someone with a hump on their back
▷ **hunchbacked** ADJECTIVE

hundred NOUN, ADJECTIVE hundreds the number 100
▷ **hundredth** ADJECTIVE, NOUN

hundredweight NOUN hundredweight a unit of weight equal to 112 pounds (about 50.8 kilograms)

hunger NOUN the feeling that you have when you have not eaten for some time; need for food

hunger strike NOUN hunger strikes refusing to eat, as a way of making a protest

hungry ADJECTIVE hungrier, hungriest feeling hunger
▷ **hungrily** ADVERB

hunk NOUN hunks **1** a large piece of something **2** (informal) a muscular, good-looking man

hunt VERB hunts, hunting, hunted **1** chase and kill animals for food or as a sport **2** search for something
▷ **hunter** NOUN **huntsman** NOUN

hurdle NOUN hurdles **1** an upright frame to be jumped over in hurdling **2** an obstacle or difficulty

hurdling NOUN racing in which the runners jump over hurdles
▷ **hurdler** NOUN

hurl VERB hurls, hurling, hurled throw something with great force

hurray or **hurrah** INTERJECTION a shout of joy or approval; a cheer

hurricane NOUN hurricanes a storm with violent wind

hurry VERB hurries, hurrying, hurried **1** move quickly; do something quickly **2** try to make somebody or something be quick
▷ **hurried** ADJECTIVE **hurriedly** ADVERB

hurry NOUN hurrying; a need to hurry

hurt VERB hurts, hurting, hurt **1** cause pain or injury to someone **2** suffer pain ● *My leg hurts.* **3** upset or offend ● *I'm sorry if I hurt your feelings.*

hurt NOUN physical or mental pain or injury
▷ **hurtful** ADJECTIVE

Thesaurus

hump NOUN *a hump in the road* ► bump, protuberance, bulge, mound, rise, curve, knob, lump, swelling

hunch NOUN *The theory was no more than a hunch.* ► feeling, intuition, inkling, guess, impression, suspicion, idea

hunch VERB *He sat in a corner and hunched his shoulders.* ► arch, curve, bend, hump, shrug, huddle, curl up

hunger NOUN **1** *She had no feelings of hunger that day.* ► appetite, desire for food **2** *He grew faint with hunger.* ► lack of food, malnutrition, starvation, deprivation, famine **3** *a hunger for knowledge* ► desire, yearning, longing, craving, appetite, thirst

hungry ADJECTIVE *I was hungry again by 3 o'clock.* ► in need of food, ravenous, famished, starving, (more informal) peckish

hunk NOUN *a hunk of bread* ► lump, chunk, block, wedge, piece, portion, slab

hunt NOUN *the hunt for clues* ► search, quest, pursuit (of), chase

hunt VERB **1** *They hunt foxes and deer.* ► chase, give chase to, stalk, track, trail, course, pursue **2** *She spent ages hunting for her keys.* ► search, look, rummage, scour, root around

hurdle NOUN **1** *He hit the last hurdle and fell.*
► fence, jump, barrier, obstacle **2** *There was one more hurdle to overcome before they could claim success.* ► obstacle, difficulty, handicap, problem, snag, stumbling block

hurl VERB *She hurled a book at Roger.* ► throw, fling, toss, cast, pitch, heave

hurried ADJECTIVE **1** *hurried attempts to change the venue* ► hasty, hectic, rushed, speedy, precipitate, swift, rapid **2** *He gave the paper a hurried read.* ► brief, cursory, superficial, swift, rapid

hurry VERB **1** *If I don't hurry I'll be late.* ► be quick, hurry up, hasten, make speed, move faster, (more informal) buck up, (more informal) shift, (more informal) step on it AN OPPOSITE IS dawdle **2** *Sarah hurried to the library.* ► rush, hasten, dash, speed, chase, hurtle, hustle, move quickly, (more informal) belt OPPOSITES ARE go slowly, amble **3** *She hurried the children into the bathroom.* ► hustle, hasten, push on, urge on, drive AN OPPOSITE IS delay

hurry NOUN *In our hurry we forgot the food.* ► haste, bustle, confusion, urgency, agitation

hurt VERB **1** *My arm hurts.* ► be sore, be painful, ache, throb, sting **2** *Derek hurt his leg.* ► injure, wound, maim, bruise, damage,

hurtle VERB hurtles, hurtling, hurtled move rapidly ● *The train hurtled along.*

husband NOUN husbands the man to whom a woman is married [from Old Norse *husbondi* = master of the house]

hush VERB hushes, hushing, hushed make or become silent or quiet
hush up prevent something from becoming generally known

husk NOUN husks the dry outer covering of some seeds and fruits

husky ADJECTIVE huskier, huskiest **1** hoarse **2** big and strong; burly
▷ **huskily** ADVERB **huskiness** NOUN

hustle VERB hustles, hustling, hustled **1** hurry **2** push or shove rudely
▷ **hustle** NOUN **hustler** NOUN

hut NOUN huts a small roughly made house or shelter

hutch NOUN hutches a box-like cage for a pet rabbit, etc.

hybrid NOUN hybrids **1** a plant or animal produced by combining two different species or varieties **2** something that combines parts or characteristics of two different things

hydrant NOUN hydrants a special water tap to which a large hose can be attached for fire-fighting or street-cleaning

hydraulic ADJECTIVE worked by the force of water or other fluid ● *hydraulic brakes*

hydrochloric acid NOUN a colorless acid containing hydrogen and chlorine

hydroelectric ADJECTIVE using water power to produce electricity
▷ **hydroelectricity** NOUN

hydrogen NOUN a lightweight gas that combines with oxygen to form water

hydrogen bomb NOUN hydrogen bombs a very powerful bomb using energy created by the fusion of hydrogen nuclei

hyena NOUN hyenas a wild animal that looks like a wolf and makes a shrieking howl

hygiene (hy- jeen) NOUN keeping things clean in order to remain healthy and prevent disease
▷ **hygienic** ADJECTIVE **hygienically** ADVERB

hymn NOUN hymns a religious song, usually one praising God
▷ **hymn book** NOUN

hype NOUN (*informal*) extravagant publicity or advertising

hyperactive ADJECTIVE unable to relax and always moving about or doing things

hyperbola (hy- per- bol- a) NOUN hyperbolas a kind of curve

hyphen NOUN hyphens a short dash used to join words or parts of words together (e.g., in *half-life*)

hypnosis (hip- noh- sis) NOUN a condition like a deep sleep in which a person's actions may be controlled by someone else

Thesaurus

disable **3** *The criticism hurt her deeply.* ► upset, distress, offend, grieve

hurt NOUN *She loved him in spite of the hurt he had caused her.* ► distress, suffering, pain, wrong, sadness, anguish, torment

hurt ADJECTIVE **1** *A hurt animal lay in the road.* ► injured, wounded, maimed, bruised, scarred **2** *He felt hurt by the words she had used.* ► upset, pained, distressed, wounded

hurtful ADJECTIVE *She forgot all the hurtful remarks and remembered the good times.* ► upsetting, distressing, unkind, spiteful, mean, cruel, malicious, wounding, painful OPPOSITES ARE kind, comforting

hurtle VERB *A train was hurtling toward them.* ► speed, rush, race, career, charge, dash, fly, tear, chase, shoot **2** *The plane hurtled to the ground.* ► plunge, plummet, nosedive, drop

husband NOUN *Their husbands had taken their cars to the rally.* ► spouse, partner, (*more formal*) consort, (*more informal*) man, (*more informal*) mate, (*more informal*) better half

hush NOUN *A hush fell on the room.* ► silence, quiet, quietness, calm, stillness, tranquillity OPPOSITES ARE noise, clamor

hush VERB *She wanted to hush their fears.* ► calm, soothe, allay, ease, assuage, quieten
hush up *The government is accused of hushing up the dangers.* ► conceal, cover up, keep secret, keep quiet, hide, stifle, suppress

hush-hush ADJECTIVE *The news is still rather hush-hush.* ► secret, confidential, restricted, classified, (*more informal*) under wraps

hut NOUN *a hut in the woods* ► cabin, shack, shed, shelter, shanty, den, hovel

hybrid NOUN *a hybrid of two species* ► cross, crossbreed, mixed breed, blend, amalgam, combination, composite, compound, mixture, fusion

hybrid ADJECTIVE *hybrid roses* ► crossbred, composite, mixed, compound, mongrel AN OPPOSITE IS purebred

hygiene NOUN *acceptable standards of hygiene* ► cleanliness, sanitariness, sanitation, health, wholesomeness RELATED ADJECTIVE ► sanitary

hygienic ADJECTIVE *Hygienic conditions are essential.* ► sanitary, clean, germ-free, sterilized, sterile, aseptic, disinfected, healthy, pure, salubrious, unpolluted, wholesome OPPOSITES ARE unhygienic, insanitary, dirty

a
b
c
d
e
f
g
h
i
j
k
l
m
n
o
p
q
r
s
t
u
v
w
x
y
z

A
B
C
D
E
F
G
H
I
J
K
L
M
N
O
P
Q
R
S
T
U
V
W
X
Y
Z

hypnotize VERB hypnotizes, hypnotizing, hypnotized produce hypnosis in somebody
▷ **hypnotism** NOUN **hypnotic** ADJECTIVE **hypnotist** NOUN

hypochondriac (hy- po- kon- dree- ak) NOUN hypochondriacs a person who constantly imagines that he or she is ill
▷ **hypochondria** NOUN

hypocrite (hip-o- krit) NOUN hypocrites a person who pretends to be more virtuous than he or she really is
▷ **hypocrisy** (hip- ok- riss- ee) NOUN **hypocritical** ADJECTIVE

hypodermic ADJECTIVE injecting something under the skin • *a hypodermic syringe*

hypotenuse (hy- pot- i- newz) NOUN

hypotenuses the side opposite the right angle in a right-angled triangle

hypothermia NOUN the condition of having a body temperature well below normal

hypothesis (hy- poth- i- sis) NOUN hypotheses a suggestion or guess that tries to explain something

hypothetical (hy- po- thet- i- kal) ADJECTIVE based on a theory or possibility, not on proven facts

hysteria NOUN wild uncontrollable excitement, panic, or emotion
▷ **hysterics** NOUN

hysterical ADJECTIVE **1** in a state of hysteria **2** (*informal*) extremely funny
▷ **hysterically** ADVERB

Thesaurus

---

hypnotize VERB *She was hypnotized by the flames of the camp fire.* ➤ mesmerize, bewitch, entrance, captivate, enthral, transfix, fascinate, dominate, magnetize, stupefy

hysterical ADJECTIVE **1** *The fans were screaming and hysterical.* ➤ overwrought, frenzied,

uncontrollable, uncontrolled, crazed, berserk, delirious, demented, frantic, wild, raving, distraught **2** (*informal*) *A dog set off the security alarm with hysterical results.* ➤ hilarious, crazy, comical, funny, amusing, uproarious, (*informal*) killing, (*informal*) side-splitting

Ii

I *PRONOUN* a word used by a person to refer to himself or herself

-ible *SEE* **-able**

ice *NOUN* **ices 1** frozen water, a hard transparent solid substance **2** an ice cream

ice age *NOUN* **ice ages** a period in the past when most of the earth's surface was covered with ice

iceberg *NOUN* **icebergs** a large mass of ice floating in the sea with most of it under water [from Dutch *ijs* = ice + *berg* = hill]

ice cream *NOUN* **ice creams** a sweet creamy frozen food

ice hockey *NOUN* a form of hockey played on ice

ice rink *NOUN* **ice rinks** a place made for skating

icicle *NOUN* **icicles** a pointed hanging piece of ice formed when dripping water freezes

icing *NOUN* a sugary substance for decorating cakes

icon (I- kon) *NOUN* **icons 1** a sacred painting of a holy person **2** a small symbol or picture on a computer screen

icy *ADJECTIVE* **icier, iciest 1** covered with ice **2** very cold
  ▷ **icily** *ADVERB* **iciness** *NOUN*

idea *NOUN* **ideas 1** a plan or thought formed in the mind **2** an opinion or belief **3** a feeling that something is likely [from Greek, = form, pattern]

ideal *ADJECTIVE* perfect; completely suitable
  ▷ **ideally** *ADVERB*

ideal *NOUN* **ideals** a person or thing regarded as perfect or a standard worth trying to achieve

identical *ADJECTIVE* exactly the same
  ▷ **identically** *ADVERB*

identify *VERB* **identifies, identifying, identified 1** recognize as being a certain person or thing **2** treat something as being identical to something else • *Don't identify wealth with happiness.* **3** think of yourself as sharing someone's feelings. • *We can identify with the hero of this play.*
  ▷ **identification** *NOUN*

identity *NOUN* **identities 1** who or what a person or thing is **2** being identical; sameness **3** distinctive character

Thesaurus

icy *ADJECTIVE* **1** *An icy blast of air hit Dad full in the face.* ► freezing, biting, bitter, frosty, arctic, cold **2** *Few people had braved the icy streets.* ► frozen, frozen over, ice-covered, glacial, glassy, slippery, (*more informal*) slippy **3** *She looked at him with an icy stare.* ► unfriendly, hostile, cold, frosty, stony

idea *NOUN* **1** *The idea of an afterlife appeals to him.* ► concept, notion, conception, image, perception, hypothesis **2** *Our idea is to go abroad this year.* ► plan, intention, scheme, object, objective, aim, goal, proposal, project **3** *I have other ideas on that subject.* ► view, thought, opinion, viewpoint, theory, feeling **4** *Did you have an idea this might happen?* ► suspicion, feeling, fancy, inkling, impression, notion **5** *We need some idea of the cost.* ► estimate, estimation, approximation, guess, (*more informal*) guesstimate

ideal *ADJECTIVE* **1** *The conditions for skiing were ideal.* ► perfect, excellent, optimum, exemplary, suitable, best, classic, faultless, model **2** *Such things are only possible in an ideal world.* ► Utopian, visionary, unattainable, hypothetical, imaginary, unreal, impractical

ideal *NOUN* **1** *an ideal to aim at* ► model, example, pattern, standard, yardstick, epitome, paradigm, archetype **2** *a person of high ideals* ► principle, standard, value, belief, conviction

identical *ADJECTIVE* **1** *The two houses looked identical.* ► alike, similar, the same, indistinguishable **2** *Successive tests produced identical results.* ► the same, corresponding, matching, equal, equivalent

identification *NOUN* **1** *The bank will need to see your identification.* ► ID, proof of identity, identity card, papers, credentials, documents **2** *An early identification of problems is important.* ► recognition, detection, diagnosis, discovery, classification, establishment **3** *their identification with independence struggles in Africa* ► association, sympathy, empathy, involvement, rapport, fellow feeling

identify *VERB* **1** *The suspect was identified by three witnesses.* ► recognize, pick out, single out, name **2** *The report identifies three areas for action.* ► establish, determine, recognize, diagnose, detect, discover, distinguish, pinpoint, spot
identify with *Readers can easily identify with the chief character in the story.* ► empathize with, relate to, feel for, sympathize with, (*informal*) put yourself in the shoes of

identity *NOUN* **1** *There was nothing to show the owner's identity.* ► name, ID **2** *a case of mistaken identity* ► identification, recognition, picking out **3** *She might lose her identity if she married him.* ► individuality, character, personality, selfhood, uniqueness, distinctiveness, singularity

a b c d e f g h **i** j k l m n o p q r s t u v w x y z

329

A
B
C
D
E
F
G
H
I
J
K
L
M
N
O
P
Q
R
S
T
U
V
W
X
Y
Z

idiom NOUN **idioms** a phrase that means something different from the meanings of the words in it, e.g., *in hot water* (= in disgrace), *hell to pay* (= dire consequences)
▷ **idiomatic** ADJECTIVE **idiomatically** ADVERB [from Greek *idios* = your own]

idiosyncrasy (id- ee- o- **sink**- ra- see) NOUN **idiosyncrasies** one person's own way of behaving or doing something [from Greek *idios* = your own + *syn-* = together + *krasis* = mixture]

idiot NOUN **idiots** a stupid or foolish person
▷ **idiocy** NOUN **idiotic** ADJECTIVE **idiotically** ADVERB
[from Greek *idiotes* = private citizen, uneducated person]

idle ADJECTIVE **1** doing no work; lazy **2** not in use • *The machines were idle.* **3** useless; with no special purpose • *idle gossip*
▷ **idly** ADVERB **idleness** NOUN

idol NOUN **idols 1** a statue or image that is worshipped as a god **2** a famous person who is widely admired [from Greek *eidolon* = image]

idolize VERB **idolizes, idolizing, idolized** admire someone greatly

i.e. ABBREVIATION that is • *The world's highest mountain (i.e., Mount Everest) is in the Himalayas.* USAGE Do not confuse with e.g.

-ier SEE **-er**

if CONJUNCTION **1** on condition that; supposing that • *He will do it if you pay him.* **2** even though • *I'll finish this job if it kills me.* **3** whether • *Do you know if dinner is ready?* **if only** I wish • *If only I were rich!*

ignite VERB **ignites, igniting, ignited** catch fire, or set on fire

ignition NOUN **ignitions 1** igniting **2** the part of a motor engine that starts the fuel burning

ignominious ADJECTIVE humiliating; bringing disgrace
▷ **ignominy** NOUN

ignorant ADJECTIVE **1** not knowing about something **2** knowing very little
▷ **ignorantly** ADVERB **ignorance** NOUN

ignore VERB **ignores, ignoring, ignored** take no notice of a person or thing

ilk NOUN
of that ilk (*informal*) of that kind

ill ADJECTIVE **1** unwell; in bad health **2** bad or harmful • *There were no ill effects.*

Thesaurus

---

idiom NOUN **1** *He uses "spiffing" and other outdated idioms.* ► expression, phrase, turn of phrase, choice of words, manner of speaking, colloquialism, usage **2** *the poet's idiom* ► language, mode of expression, style, usage, phraseology

idiomatic ADJECTIVE *idiomatic expressions* ► colloquial, natural, well phrased

idiot NOUN *The mistake made him feel an idiot.* ► fool, ass, dolt, imbecile, simpleton, blockhead, ignoramus, dunderhead, dunce, halfwit, moron, cretin, (*more informal*) dope, (*more informal*) dimwit, (*more informal*) nitwit, (*more informal*) chump, (*more informal*) ninny

idiotic ADJECTIVE *How idiotic it seemed for a man of his age to fall in love.* ► stupid, silly, foolish, absurd, senseless, nonsensical, (*more informal*) daft AN OPPOSITE IS sensible

idle ADJECTIVE **1** *The chief problem with Jack was that he was idle.* ► lazy, indolent, slothful, work-shy **2** *The computers had been idle all day.* ► out of use, unused, dormant, out of service, inoperative **3** *She refused to indulge in idle speculation.* ► futile, pointless, aimless, vain, meaningless, trivial, frivolous, fatuous

idle VERB **1** *Jane idled across the park.* ► saunter, amble, dawdle, wander **2** *Richard had finished his work and idled until it was time to go home.* ► do nothing, laze, take it easy, kill time, loaf, slack **3** *A car was idling in the driveway.*
idle away *We idled away an hour or two.*
► fritter away, while away, pass, spend

idol NOUN **1** *a temple in which idols were worshipped* ► image, icon, statue, deity, god **2** *the newest pop idols* ► star, superstar, icon, hero, heroine, favourite

ignorance NOUN **1** *She seemed amused by Rashid's obvious ignorance of the subject.* ► unawareness, unfamiliarity (with), incomprehension, lack of knowledge, inexperience OPPOSITES ARE knowledge, familiarity (with) **2** *They could not hide their ignorance.* ► foolishness, unintelligence, naivety, stupidity

ignorant ADJECTIVE **1** *He called the man an ignorant peasant.* ► uneducated, illiterate, unread, unschooled, untaught, untutored, simple, stupid **2** *We are hopelessly ignorant of events in this part of the world.* ► unaware, uninformed (about), unenlightened (about), oblivious, (*more informal*) clueless (about)

ignore VERB **1** *The complaints are too serious to ignore.* ► disregard, overlook, take no notice of, neglect, pass over, set aside **2** *Helen had ignored him, out of spite.* ► snub, spurn, shun, give the cold shoulder to

ill ADJECTIVE **1** *Jenny began to feel ill in the taxi home.* ► sick, unwell, poorly, out of sorts, off color, indisposed, ailing, peaky, queasy, nauseous **2** *She suffered no ill effects from her night out.* ► harmful, damaging, adverse

ill ADVERB badly • *She was ill-treated.*
  ill at ease uncomfortable or embarrassed

illegal ADJECTIVE not legal; against the law
  ▷ **illegally** ADVERB **illegality** NOUN

illegible ADJECTIVE impossible to read
  ▷ **illegibly** ADVERB **illegibility** NOUN

illegitimate ADJECTIVE born of parents who are not married to each other
  ▷ **illegitimately** ADVERB **illegitimacy** NOUN

illiterate ADJECTIVE unable to read or write
  ▷ **illiterately** ADVERB **illiteracy** NOUN

illness NOUN **illnesses 1** being ill **2** a particular form of bad health; a disease

illogical ADJECTIVE not logical; not reasoning correctly
  ▷ **illogically** ADVERB **illogicality** NOUN

illuminate VERB **illuminates, illuminating, illuminated 1** light something up **2** decorate streets, etc., with lights **3** decorate a manuscript with colored designs **4** clarify or help to explain something
  ▷ **illumination** NOUN

illusion NOUN **illusions 1** something that seems to be real or actually happening but is not, especially something that deceives the eye **2** a false idea or belief COMPARE **delusion**
  ▷ **illusive** ADJECTIVE **illusory** ADJECTIVE

illustrate VERB **illustrates, illustrating, illustrated 1** show something by pictures, examples, etc. **2** put illustrations in a book
  ▷ **illustrator** NOUN

illustration NOUN **illustrations 1** a picture in a book etc. **2** illustrating something **3** an example that helps to explain something

illustrious ADJECTIVE famous and distinguished

image NOUN **images 1** a picture or statue of a person or thing **2** the appearance of something as seen in a mirror or through a lens, etc. **3** a person or thing that is very much like another • *He is the image of his father.* **4** a word or phrase that describes something in an imaginative way **5** a person's public reputation

imaginary ADJECTIVE existing only in the imagination; not real

imagination NOUN **imaginations** the ability to imagine things, especially in a creative or inventive way
  ▷ **imaginative** ADJECTIVE

imagine VERB **imagines, imagining, imagined 1** form pictures or ideas in your mind **2** suppose or think • *I don't imagine there'll be any tickets left.*

Thesaurus

---

illegal ADJECTIVE *Under-age drinking is illegal.*
  ▶ unlawful, prohibited, criminal, wrong, forbidden, barred OPPOSITES ARE legal, lawful, permitted

illegible ADJECTIVE *The signature was illegible.*
  ▶ unreadable, indecipherable, unintelligible, indistinct, obscure, unclear OPPOSITES ARE legible, readable

illness NOUN *The doctors were unsure of the exact nature of the illness.* ▶ disease, disorder, sickness, infirmity, complaint, indisposition, ailment, malady, affliction

illogical ADJECTIVE *The conclusion, however illogical it seems, was correct.* ▶ irrational, unreasonable, fallacious, invalid, unsound, absurd, inconsequential, inconsistent, senseless AN OPPOSITE IS logical

illusion NOUN **1** *an illusion created by mirrors* ▶ hallucination, apparition, mirage, deception, delusion, fantasy, figment of the imagination, trick **2** *We have no illusions about the difficulty of the task.* ▶ delusion, misapprehension, misconception, fantasy

illustrate VERB **1** *The book is illustrated with photographs and drawings.* ▶ decorate, adorn, embellish **2** *A few examples will illustrate the argument.* ▶ clarify, elucidate, throw OR shed light on, illuminate, clear up, enlighten, explain

illustration NOUN **1** *a children's book with beautiful illustrations* ▶ picture, drawing, plate, sketch, photograph, figure, depiction **2** *a good illustration of the difficulties involved* ▶ example, instance, specimen, demonstration, case

image NOUN **1** *There were images of the saints along the church walls.* ▶ picture, portrait, representation, likeness, icon, effigy, figure **2** *The image on the screen was a little fuzzy.* ▶ picture, reproduction **3** *The image the company gives is one of ruthless profiteering.* ▶ impression, perception, conception, idea, notion

imaginary ADJECTIVE *a story set in an imaginary country* ▶ imagined, fictitious, fictional, invented, made-up, make-believe, fanciful, unreal, nonexistent, hypothetical, mythical, fabulous OPPOSITES ARE real, actual

imagination NOUN *The writing shows a great deal of imagination.* ▶ creativity, inventiveness, originality, inspiration, vision, ingenuity, insight, sensitivity, resourcefulness, artistry, cleverness, fancy, thought

imaginative ADJECTIVE *an imaginative dramatization for television* ▶ creative, inventive, original, inspired, ingenious, resourceful, enterprising, fanciful, clever AN OPPOSITE IS unimaginative

imagine VERB **1** *Can you imagine life on a desert island?* ▶ visualize, envisage, picture, conceive, conceptualize **2** *I imagine you'd like us to pay you now.* ▶ suppose, assume, presume, expect, take it

A
B
C
D
E
F
G
H
I
J
K
L
M
N
O
P
Q
R
S
T
U
V
W
X
Y
Z

imitate VERB imitates, imitating, imitated copy or mimic something
▷ **imitation** NOUN **imitator** NOUN **imitative** ADJECTIVE

immaculate ADJECTIVE **1** perfectly clean; spotless **2** without any fault or blemish
▷ **immaculately** ADVERB

immature ADJECTIVE not mature
▷ **immaturity** NOUN

immediate ADJECTIVE **1** happening or done without any delay **2** nearest; with nothing or no one between • *our immediate neighbors*
▷ **immediately** ADVERB **immediacy** NOUN

immense ADJECTIVE exceedingly great; huge
▷ **immensely** ADVERB **immensity** NOUN

immersion heater NOUN immersion heaters a device that heats up water by means of an electric element in the water in a tank

immigrate VERB immigrates, immigrating, immigrated come into a country to live there
▷ **immigration** NOUN **immigrant** NOUN
USAGE See the note at emigrate.

imminent ADJECTIVE likely to happen at any moment • *an imminent storm*
▷ **imminence** NOUN

immobilize VERB immobilizes, immobilizing, immobilized stop a thing from moving or working
▷ **immobilization** NOUN

immoral ADJECTIVE morally wrong
▷ **immorally** ADVERB **immorality** NOUN

immortal ADJECTIVE **1** living forever; not mortal **2** famous for all time
▷ **immortal** NOUN **immortality** NOUN
immortalize VERB

immune ADJECTIVE safe from danger or attack, especially from disease • *immune from* (or *against* or *to*) *infection*
▷ **immunity** NOUN

immunize VERB immunizes, immunizing, immunized make a person immune from a disease, e.g., by vaccination
▷ **immunization** NOUN

impact NOUN impacts **1** a collision; the force of a collision **2** an influence or effect • *the impact of computers on our lives*

impale VERB impales, impaling, impaled pierce or fix something on a sharp pointed object

Thesaurus

imitate VERB **1** *June liked to imitate her mother's social life.* ► copy, emulate, follow, model yourself on, echo **2** *He was good at imitating politicians.* ► mimic, impersonate, do an impression of, parody, caricature, send up, spoof

imitation NOUN **1** *a good imitation of the human voice* ► impersonation, impression, parody, travesty **2** *The stolen jewels turned out to be imitations.* ► copy, reproduction, replica, duplicate, fake, counterfeit

imitation ADJECTIVE *The weapon was an imitation firearm.* ► fake, artificial, simulated, sham, counterfeit, dummy, mock, model
OPPOSITES ARE real, genuine

immature ADJECTIVE *an immature young man behaving in a silly way* ► childish, babyish, inexperienced, callow

immediate ADJECTIVE **1** *We need to take immediate action.* ► instant, instantaneous, prompt, urgent, speedy, swift, quick, rapid, direct, pressing, top-priority OPPOSITES ARE delayed, low-priority **2** *our immediate neighbors* ► nearest, closest, close, near, adjacent, next AN OPPOSITE IS remote

immediately ADVERB **1** *I went back to L.A. immediately.* ► straight away, at once, directly, forthwith, instantly, promptly, right away, unhesitatingly **2** *The wall has a damp patch immediately below the window.* ► directly, exactly, precisely, squarely, dead, close

immense ADJECTIVE *a cathedral with two immense towers* ► huge, great, enormous, gigantic, massive, colossal, vast, giant, (*more informal*) whopping, (*more informal*) ginormous AN OPPOSITE IS tiny

immerse VERB *You need to immerse your hair in warm water.* ► plunge, submerge, submerse, bathe, dip, dunk, drench, douse, duck, lower

immersed ADJECTIVE *I was immersed in my work.* ► absorbed, engrossed, preoccupied (by), occupied (by), busy (with), involved, wrapped up, interested, engaged

imminent ADJECTIVE *An invasion of Crete seemed imminent.* ► close, near, at hand, in the offing, in the air, impending, threatening, about to happen, approaching, looming, coming, foreseeable

immoral ADJECTIVE *immoral behavior* ► wrong, unethical, morally wrong, wrongful, disreputable, degenerate, sinful, wicked, unscrupulous, unprincipled, evil, bad AN OPPOSITE IS moral

immortal ADJECTIVE *She might place her immortal soul in deadly peril.* ► eternal, undying, everlasting, ageless, timeless, deathless, endless, perpetual, unchanging AN OPPOSITE IS mortal

impact NOUN **1** *She suffered a broken ankle in the impact.* ► crash, collision, smash, clash, blow, jolt, bump, bang, knock **2** *High street technology is having a huge impact on modern life.* ► effect, influence, impression, repercussions, consequences (for)

impartial ADJECTIVE not favoring one side more than the other; not biased
▷ **impartially** ADVERB **impartiality** NOUN

impatient ADJECTIVE not patient; in a hurry
▷ **impatiently** ADVERB **impatience** NOUN

impel VERB impels, impelling, impelled **1** urge or drive someone to do something • *Curiosity impelled her to investigate.* **2** drive forward; propel

impending ADJECTIVE soon to happen; imminent

impenetrable ADJECTIVE **1** impossible to get through **2** incomprehensible

imperative ADJECTIVE **1** expressing a command **2** essential • *Speed is imperative.*

imperative NOUN imperatives a command; the form of a verb used in making commands (e.g., "come" in *Come here!*)

imperceptible ADJECTIVE too small or gradual to be noticed

imperfect ADJECTIVE **1** not perfect **2** (said about a tense of a verb) showing a continuous action, e.g. *She was singing*
▷ **imperfectly** ADVERB **imperfection** NOUN

imperial ADJECTIVE **1** to do with an empire or its rulers **2** (said about weights and measures) formerly fixed by British law; nonmetric
▷ **imperially** ADVERB

imperious ADJECTIVE haughty and bossy

impermeable ADJECTIVE not allowing liquid to pass through it

impersonal ADJECTIVE **1** not affected by personal feelings; showing no emotion **2** not referring to a particular person
▷ **impersonally** ADVERB

impersonal verb NOUN impersonal verbs a verb used only with "it," e.g., in *It is raining.*

impertinent ADJECTIVE insolent; not showing proper respect
▷ **impertinently** ADVERB **impertinence** NOUN

imperturbable ADJECTIVE not excitable; calm
▷ **imperturbably** ADVERB

impervious ADJECTIVE **1** not allowing water, heat, etc., to pass through • *impervious to water* **2** not able to be affected by something • *impervious to criticism*

impetuous ADJECTIVE acting hastily without thinking

impetus NOUN **1** the force that makes an object start moving and that keeps it moving **2** the influence that causes something to develop more quickly • *The cease-fire gave an impetus to peace talks.*

implacable ADJECTIVE not able to be placated; relentless
▷ **implacably** ADVERB

Thesaurus

impartial ADJECTIVE *Counselors are on hand to give you free and impartial advice.* ► objective, unbiased, disinterested, dispassionate, balanced, detached, neutral, nonpartisan, open-minded, equitable, evenhanded, fair, fair-minded, just, unprejudiced AN OPPOSITE IS biased

impatience NOUN **1** *There was a tremor of impatience in her voice.* ► irritability, agitation, shortness, intolerance, brusqueness, frustration, nervousness **2** *his impatience to start work* ► eagerness, keenness, haste

impatient ADJECTIVE **1** *As time passed Michael grew impatient.* ► restless, agitated, fretful, irritated, tetchy, testy, anxious, ill at ease, keyed up, jumpy **2** *The army was impatient to engage the enemy.* ► anxious, eager, keen, avid

imperceptible ADJECTIVE *The movement was slow and imperceptible.* ► indiscernible, undetectable, indistinguishable, unnoticeable, infinitesimal, insignificant, negligible, slight, small, subtle AN OPPOSITE IS noticeable
USAGE You can also use *inaudible* when you are referring to sounds, and *invisible* when you are referring to sight.

imperfect ADJECTIVE *The goods were imperfect and had to be sent back.* ► faulty, defective, deficient, flawed, damaged, broken, incomplete AN OPPOSITE IS perfect

imperfection NOUN *She handed over her work, hoping they would not notice its many imperfections.* ► defect, fault, deficiency, shortcoming, weakness, flaw, failing, blemish, inadequacy AN OPPOSITE IS perfection

imperil VERB *He did not wish to imperil their chances of success.* ► endanger, harm, risk, jeopardize, threaten, compromise

impersonal ADJECTIVE *His manner was brusque and impersonal.* ► detached, aloof, distant, formal, unemotional, unfriendly, unsympathetic, businesslike, remote, cold, cool AN OPPOSITE IS friendly

impertinence NOUN *They were unclear whether the remark was a joke or a piece of impertinence.* ► rudeness, insolence, impudence, effrontery, audacity, impoliteness, discourtesy, disrespect AN OPPOSITE IS politeness

impertinent ADJECTIVE *A question like that would seem impertinent from anyone else.* ► rude, impolite, insolent, impudent, disrespectful, audacious, brazen OPPOSITES ARE respectful, polite

impetus NOUN **1** *Their enthusiasm began to lose impetus.* ► momentum, force, power, drive, motivation, stimulus, energy, impulse, incentive, push, spur **2** *A new product would give the sales campaign an added impetus.* ► boost, stimulus, inducement, incentive, push, spur

a b c d e f g h **i** j k l m n o p q r s t u v w x y z

A
B
C
D
E
F
G
H
I
J
K
L
M
N
O
P
Q
R
S
T
U
V
W
X
Y
Z

implant VERB implants, implanting, implanted insert; fix something in
▷ **implantation** NOUN

implant NOUN implants an organ or piece of tissue inserted in the body

implement NOUN implements a tool

implicate VERB implicates, implicating, implicated involve a person in a crime, etc.; show that a person is involved • *His evidence implicates his sister.*

implication NOUN implications **1** implicating **2** implying; something that is implied

implicit (im- **pliss**- it) ADJECTIVE **1** implied but not stated openly COMPARE **explicit** **2** absolute; unquestioning • *She expects implicit obedience.*
▷ **implicitly** ADVERB

implore VERB implores, imploring, implored beg somebody to do something

imply VERB implies, implying, implied suggest something without actually saying it
▷ **implication** NOUN

impolite ADJECTIVE not polite

import VERB imports, importing, imported bring in goods etc. from another country

import NOUN imports **1** importing; something imported **2** (*formal*) meaning or importance • *The message was of great import.*

important ADJECTIVE **1** having or able to have a great effect **2** having great authority or influence
▷ **importantly** ADVERB **importance** NOUN

impose VERB imposes, imposing, imposed put or inflict • *It imposes a strain upon us.*
impose on somebody put an unfair burden on him or her

imposing ADJECTIVE impressive

imposition NOUN impositions **1** something imposed; an unfair burden or inconvenience **2** imposing something

impossible ADJECTIVE **1** not possible **2** (*informal*) very annoying; unbearable • *He really is impossible!*
▷ **impossibly** ADVERB **impossibility** NOUN

Thesaurus

implausible ADJECTIVE *The suggestion seemed implausible.* ► unconvincing, improbable, unlikely, questionable, unreasonable, doubtful, dubious, far-fetched, incredible, fanciful, suspect, flimsy, weak, feeble AN OPPOSITE IS plausible

implication NOUN **1** *He did not like the implication that he had been dishonest.* ► suggestion, insinuation, intimation, imputation, innuendo USAGE Strictly, *inference* means "a conclusion you draw" rather than "a conclusion you suggest," so it is better to use one of the other words given here. **2** *They are suspected of implication in the crime.* ► involvement, association, connection, entanglement, incrimination

implore VERB *His family implored him to come home.* ► beg, entreat, urge, appeal to, call on, exhort, (*literary*) beseech

imply VERB **1** *He seemed to imply that we were wrong.* ► suggest, hint, insinuate, intimate, indicate USAGE You will sometimes see *infer* used as a synonym of *imply*, but *infer* properly means "to draw a conclusion" rather than "to suggest a conclusion," so it is better to use one of the other words given here. **2** *The traffic measures imply a need for better public transport.* ► entail, involve, point to, indicate, suggest, signify, necessitate

impolite ADJECTIVE *It would have been impolite to leave the party so early.* ► rude, bad-mannered, discourteous, disrespectful, inconsiderate, ungracious

importance NOUN **1** *an event of the greatest importance* ► significance, consequence,

seriousness, import, substance, gravity, urgency **2** *a person of importance* ► power, influence, authority, prominence, status, distinction, eminence

important ADJECTIVE **1** *an important decision* ► significant, momentous, crucial, critical, vital, far-reaching, consequential, historic **2** *It is important to get there early.* ► crucial, vital, essential **3** *an important person* ► powerful, influential, prominent, distinguished, eminent

impose VERB *The library will impose a fine on the late return of books.* ► exact, enforce, introduce, fix, inflict, levy, prescribe, set, place
impose on *They were afraid they might be imposing on us.* ► intrude on, presume on, inconvenience, encroach on, obtrude on, force yourself on, take advantage of

imposing ADJECTIVE *an imposing building* ► grand, stately, impressive, magnificent, majestic, splendid, distinguished, striking, dignified, grandiose OPPOSITES ARE unimposing, modest

imposition NOUN **1** *the imposition of a windfall tax* ► introduction, levying, charging, exacting, enforcing, fixing, setting **2** *Asking for help might seem an imposition.* ► intrusion, encroachment, presumption, liberty, burden, encumbrance

impossible ADJECTIVE **1** *The tears made speaking impossible.* ► impractical, hopeless, inconceivable, unthinkable, out of the question, unachievable **2** *They had succeeded against impossible odds.* ► unrealistic, hopeless, overwhelming, insurmountable, implausible, unbelievable, preposterous, ludicrous, unattainable AN OPPOSITE IS possible

impostor ➡ improper fraction

impostor NOUN **impostors** a person who dishonestly pretends to be someone else

impotent ADJECTIVE **1** powerless; unable to take action **2** (said about a man) unable to have sexual intercourse
▷ **impotently** ADVERB **impotence** NOUN

impoverish VERB **impoverishes, impoverishing, impoverished 1** make a person poor **2** make a thing poor in quality • *impoverished soil*
▷ **impoverishment** NOUN

impracticable ADJECTIVE not able to be done in practice

impractical ADJECTIVE not practical

imprecise ADJECTIVE not precise

impregnable ADJECTIVE strong enough to be safe against attack

impregnate VERB **impregnates, impregnating, impregnated 1** fertilize; make pregnant **2** saturate; fill throughout • *The air was impregnated with the scent.*
▷ **impregnation** NOUN

impress VERB **impresses, impressing, impressed 1** make a person admire something or think it is very good **2** fix something firmly in the mind • *He impressed*

on them the need for secrecy. **3** press a mark into something

impression NOUN **impressions 1** an effect produced on the mind • *The book made a big impression on me.* **2** a vague idea **3** an imitation of a person or a sound **4** a reprint of a book

impressionable ADJECTIVE easily influenced or affected

impressive ADJECTIVE making a strong impression; seeming to be very good

imprison VERB **imprisons, imprisoning, imprisoned** put someone in prison; shut someone up in a place
▷ **imprisonment** NOUN

improbable ADJECTIVE unlikely
▷ **improbably** ADVERB **improbability** NOUN

impromptu ADJECTIVE, ADVERB done without any rehearsal or preparation

improper ADJECTIVE **1** unsuitable or wrong **2** indecent
▷ **improperly** ADVERB **impropriety** (im- pro-pry- it- ee) NOUN

improper fraction NOUN **improper fractions** a fraction that is greater than 1, with the numerator greater than the denominator, e.g., $\frac{7}{5}$

Thesaurus

impostor NOUN *The official turned out to be an impostor.* ► impersonator, masquerader, charlatan, fraud, cheat, hoaxer, trickster, (*more informal*) phoney

imprecise ADJECTIVE *an imprecise description* ► vague, loose, inexact, inaccurate, hazy, woolly, equivocal OPPOSITES ARE precise, exact

impress VERB **1** *This evidence did not impress the jury.* ► move, stir, influence, affect, excite, make an impression on, have an impact on, (*more informal*) grab **2** *impress on We must impress on Chris what good work he has done.* ► emphasize, bring home to, instill in, inculcate in

impression NOUN **1** *We got the impression they were hiding something.* ► feeling, sense, suspicion, conviction, awareness, notion, idea, hunch, inkling **2** *The experience left a good impression on him.* ► effect, impact, influence **3** *He had formed a favorable impression of them.* ► opinion, view, perception, assessment, estimation, judgment, verdict **4** *She did a good impression of Cher.* ► imitation, impersonation, parody, caricature, (*more informal*) send-up **5** *The mug had left a circular impression in the cloth.* ► indentation, dent, hollow, stamp, mark, print, outline

impressive ADJECTIVE **1** *She has made an impressive concert debut.* ► striking, accomplished, masterly, first-class, exciting, stirring AN OPPOSITE IS insignificant **2** *The conference is held in an impressive building near the university.* ► magnificent, imposing, splendid, grand, stately, monumental

imprison VERB *The judge imprisoned him for five years.* ► jail, incarcerate, send to prison, put in prison, detain, lock up, confine, (*more informal*) put away, (*more informal*) send down

imprisonment NOUN *The penalty is life imprisonment.* ► incarceration, internment, detention, confinement, custody

improbable ADJECTIVE *The excuse was most improbable.* ► unlikely, implausible, incredible, doubtful, questionable, far-fetched, unbelievable, unconvincing, preposterous AN OPPOSITE IS probable

improper ADJECTIVE **1** *It would be improper to accept payment.* ► wrong , inappropriate, unsuitable, irregular, out of place, unacceptable, unprofessional, incorrect, inopportune, uncalled for, unwarranted **2** *In those days such behavior would have been thought improper.* ► indecent, unseemly, indecorous, unbecoming, unfitting, shocking, vulgar AN OPPOSITE IS proper

a b c d e f g h **i** j k l m n o p q r s t u v w x y z

A
B
C
D
E
F
G
H
I
J
K
L
M
N
O
P
Q
R
S
T
U
V
W
X
Y
Z

improve VERB improves, improving, improved make or become better
▷ **improvement** NOUN

improvise VERB improvises, improvising, improvised **1** compose or perform something without any rehearsal or preparation **2** make something quickly with whatever is available
▷ **improvisation** NOUN

imprudent ADJECTIVE unwise or rash

impudent ADJECTIVE disrespectful or rude
▷ **impudently** ADVERB **impudence** NOUN

impulse NOUN impulses **1** a sudden desire to do something • *I did it on impulse.* **2** a push or impetus **3** (in science) a force acting for a very short time • *electrical impulses*

impulsive ADJECTIVE done or acting on impulse, not after careful thought
▷ **impulsively** ADVERB **impulsiveness** NOUN

impure ADJECTIVE not pure
▷ **impurity** NOUN

in PREPOSITION This word is used to show position or condition, e.g. **1** at or inside; within the limits of something (*in a box; in two hours*), **2** into (*He fell in a puddle.*), **3** arranged as; consisting of (*a serial in four parts*), **4** occupied with; a member of (*He is in the army.*), **5** by means of (*We paid in cash.*)
in all in total number; altogether

in ADVERB **1** so as to be in something or inside (*Get in*) **2** inward (*The top caved in.*) **3** at home; indoors (*Is anybody in?*) **4** in action **5** having arrived (*The train is in.*)
in for likely to get • *You're in for a shock*
in on (*informal*) aware of or sharing in • *I want to be in on this project.*

in- PREFIX (changing to il- before l, im- before b, m, p, ir- before r) **1** in; into; on; toward (as in *include, invade*) **2** not (as in *incorrect, indirect*)

inability NOUN being unable

inaccessible ADJECTIVE not able to be reached

inaccurate ADJECTIVE not accurate

Thesaurus

---

improve VERB **1** *We are always looking for ways to improve the service.* ► make better, better, enhance, reform, upgrade, develop **2** *Relations between the employers and unions have improved markedly.* ► get better, progress, advance, develop, make headway, rally, (*more informal*) look up **3** *Reduce the dose as soon as the patient begins to improve.* ► recover, get better, recuperate, regain strength **4** *They are hoping to improve their offer shortly.* ► increase, raise, supplement, enlarge, augment, top up
improve on *It will be hard to improve on work of that quality.* ► surpass, outdo, do better than, exceed

improvement NOUN **1** *The weather showed a little improvement; an improvement in East-West relations* ► recovery, advance, upturn, progress, enhancement, amelioration, development, rectification, betterment, gain, rally, reformation **2** *We have carried out a lot of improvements to the house.* ► renovation, alteration, extension, modernization, modification, (*informal*) face-lift

impudence NOUN *They soon forgave him his impudence.* ► cheek, insolence, impertinence, effrontery, audacity, rudeness, impoliteness, discourtesy, disrespect AN OPPOSITE IS politeness

impudent ADJECTIVE *She thought him an impudent bully.* ► rude, insolent, impertinent, impolite, disrespectful, audacious, brazen OPPOSITES ARE respectful, polite

impulse NOUN **1** *His first impulse was to call the police.* ► instinct, urge, inclination, compulsion, whim, caprice, desire **2** *His actions were so often governed by impulse.* ► impetuosity, spontaneity, rashness,

recklessness **3** *Emotion is one of the main impulses of poetry.* ► stimulus, inspiration, motivation

impulsive ADJECTIVE *With an impulsive gesture she bounded out of the room.* ► impetuous, spontaneous, rash, reckless, hasty, uninhibited, instinctive, passionate AN OPPOSITE IS deliberate

impure ADJECTIVE **1** *The water was found to be impure.* ► contaminated, polluted, tainted, unclean, foul, defiled, dirty, filthy, infected, unhygienic, unwholesome, adulterated **2** *impure thoughts* ► immoral, indecent, unclean, corrupt, wicked, degenerate

impurity NOUN **1** *An instrument measured the impurity of the air.* ► contamination, pollution, dirtiness, uncleanliness, foulness, filthiness **2** *water full of impurities* ► contaminant, pollutant, adulterant, foreign matter

inability NOUN *their inability to agree on a single point* ► incapacity, incapability, impotence, powerlessness, lack of ability

inaccessible ADJECTIVE *More of the countryside is becoming inaccessible.* ► unreachable, cut off, out of reach, isolated, remote, godforsaken, hard to find, out-of-the-way, in the middle of nowhere, in the back of beyond, secluded, unfrequented AN OPPOSITE IS accessible

inaccuracy NOUN *The information is marred by inaccuracies.* ► mistake, error, miscalculation, blunder, imprecision, fault, defect, flaw, slip, oversight OPPOSITES ARE accuracy, precision

inaccurate ADJECTIVE *The road map is very inaccurate.* ► inexact, imprecise, incorrect, erroneous, faulty, imperfect, defective, unsound

inadequate ADJECTIVE **1** not enough **2** not able to cope or deal with something
▷ **inadequately** ADVERB **inadequacy** NOUN

inadvisable ADJECTIVE not advisable

inanimate ADJECTIVE **1** not living **2** showing no sign of life

inappropriate ADJECTIVE not appropriate

inarticulate ADJECTIVE **1** not able to speak or express yourself clearly • *inarticulate with rage* **2** not expressed in words • *an inarticulate cry*

inaudible ADJECTIVE not able to be heard
▷ **inaudibly** ADVERB **inaudibility** NOUN

inaugurate VERB inaugurates, inaugurating, inaugurated **1** start or introduce something new and important **2** formally establish a person in office • *inaugurate a new president*
▷ **inaugural** ADJECTIVE **inauguration** NOUN **inaugurator** NOUN

inborn ADJECTIVE present in a person or animal from birth • *an inborn ability*

inbred ADJECTIVE **1** inborn **2** produced by inbreeding

inbreeding NOUN breeding from closely related individuals

incalculable ADJECTIVE not able to be calculated or predicted

incandescent ADJECTIVE giving out light when heated; shining
▷ **incandescence** NOUN

incantation NOUN incantations a spoken spell or charm; the chanting of this

incapable ADJECTIVE not able to do something • *They seem incapable of understanding.*

incapacitate VERB incapacitates, incapacitating, incapacitated make a person or thing unable to do something; disable

incarnate ADJECTIVE having a body or human form • *a devil incarnate*
▷ **incarnation** NOUN
the Incarnation the embodiment of God in human form as Jesus Christ

incautious ADJECTIVE rash

incendiary ADJECTIVE starting or designed to start a fire • *an incendiary bomb*

incentive NOUN incentives something that encourages a person to do something or to work harder

incest NOUN sexual intercourse between two people who are so closely related that they cannot marry each other
▷ **incestuous** ADJECTIVE

inch NOUN inches a measure of length, one-twelfth of a foot (about 2 centimeters)

inch VERB inches, inching, inched move slowly and gradually • *I inched along the ledge.* [from Old English]

incident NOUN incidents an event

incidental ADJECTIVE happening as a minor part of something else • *incidental expenses*

incidentally ADVERB by the way

incinerate VERB incinerates, incinerating, incinerated destroy something by burning
▷ **incineration** NOUN

incinerator NOUN incinerators a device for burning trash

incision NOUN incisions a cut, especially one made in a surgical operation

incisive ADJECTIVE clear and sharp • *incisive comments*

incisor (in- sy- zer) NOUN incisors each of the sharp-edged front teeth in the upper and lower jaws

Thesaurus

inactive ADJECTIVE **1** *Illness left me inactive for several weeks.* ► idle, immobile, inert, lethargic, listless, sluggish **2** *The alarm was inactive at the time of the break-in.* ► inoperative, idle, non-functioning, turned off, out of action, out of use

inappropriate ADJECTIVE *The police decided a prosecution would be inappropriate.*
► unsuitable, out of place, inapt, ill-suited, unfitting, untimely, ill-timed, improper, incongruous OPPOSITES ARE appropriate, suitable

inaudible ADJECTIVE *From that distance the voices were inaudible.* ► indistinct, hard to hear, unclear, quiet, silent, weak, undetectable, unidentifiable, muted, faint, low, muffled, mumbled AN OPPOSITE IS audible

incapable ADJECTIVE *Those who feel incapable in their work can get advice.* ► incompetent, ineffective, ineffectual, inadequate, impotent, inept, unable, useless, weak AN OPPOSITE IS capable

incessant ADJECTIVE *incessant noise from the road works outside* ► continuous, continual, constant, ceaseless, endless, unceasing, interminable, non-stop OPPOSITES ARE temporary, intermittent

incident NOUN **1** *He recalled an amusing incident from his childhood.* ► event, episode, occurrence, happening, occasion, affair, experience, activity, business, circumstance **2** *Police were called to an incident in the centre of town.* ► disturbance, commotion, fracas, scene, brawl, rumpus, fight

a
b
c
d
e
f
g
h
i
j
k
l
m
n
o
p
q
r
s
t
u
v
w
x
y
z

A
B
C
D
E
F
G
H
I
J
K
L
M
N
O
P
Q
R
S
T
U
V
W
X
Y
Z

incite VERB incites, inciting, incited urge a person to do something; stir up • *They incited a riot*
  ▷ **incitement** NOUN

inclination NOUN inclinations **1** a tendency **2** a liking or preference **3** a slope or slant

incline VERB inclines, inclining, inclined **1** lean or slope **2** bend the head or body forward, as in a nod or bow **3** cause or influence • *Her frank manner inclines me to believe her.*
  be inclined have a tendency or willingness • *The door is inclined to bang.* • *I'm inclined to agree with you.*

include VERB includes, including, included make or consider something as part of a group of things
  ▷ **inclusion** NOUN

inclusive ADJECTIVE including everything; including all the things mentioned • *Read pages 20 to 28 inclusive.*

incoherent ADJECTIVE not speaking or reasoning in an orderly way

income NOUN incomes money received regularly from doing work or from investments

income tax NOUN tax charged on income

incomparable ADJECTIVE without an equal; not surpassed • *incomparable beauty*

incompatible ADJECTIVE not able to exist or be used together

incompetent ADJECTIVE not able or skilled enough to do something properly

incomplete ADJECTIVE not complete

incomprehensible ADJECTIVE not able to be understood
  ▷ **incomprehension** NOUN

incongruous ADJECTIVE out of place or unsuitable
  ▷ **incongruously** ADVERB **incongruity** NOUN

inconsiderate ADJECTIVE not considerate toward other people

Thesaurus

inclination NOUN **1** *He showed no inclination to leave.* ► readiness, desire, impulse, wish, disposition, predisposition, predilection AN OPPOSITE IS disinclination **2** *She had no inclination for work that day.* ► liking, partiality, appetite, taste, fondness, penchant AN OPPOSITE IS dislike

incline VERB *The uprights incline slightly to the right.* ► lean, slant, tilt, tip, slope, veer
  be inclined *We are inclined to believe him.* ► be disposed, be minded, be willing, be ready

include VERB **1** *Sports activities include swimming and aerobics.* ► incorporate, involve, comprise, contain, embrace, encompass, consist of, take in, make room for, subsume **2** *The package includes flights, hotels costs, and all outings.* ► cover, allow for, take into account, add in AN OPPOSITE IS exclude

incoherent ADJECTIVE *The letter was long and incoherent.* ► unclear, confused, muddled, unintelligible, disorganized, incomprehensible, inarticulate, garbled, rambling, hard to follow, disjointed, disordered, illogical OPPOSITES ARE coherent, intelligible

income NOUN **1** *Her income has gone up significantly in the last year.* ► earnings, salary, pay, remuneration, wages, money **2** *taxes on business income* ► revenue, receipts, takings, profits, gains, proceeds, takeover OPPOSITES ARE expenditure, payments

incompetent ADJECTIVE *They were all either too lazy or too incompetent to do an honest day's work.* ► inept, incapable, unqualified, inefficient, unskilful, unfit, inadequate, unproficient, bungling, blundering, clumsy, ineffectual AN OPPOSITE IS competent

incomplete ADJECTIVE *They have to move into the house even though it's still incomplete.* ► unfinished, uncompleted, half-finished, not finished, unready

incomprehensible ADJECTIVE **1** *She made some incomprehensible remark.* ► unintelligible, incoherent, unfathomable, baffling, confusing, perplexing, obscure, cryptic, opaque, mysterious, inscrutable, enigmatic AN OPPOSITE IS comprehensible **2** *The writing was incomprehensible.* ► illegible, indecipherable, unintelligible OPPOSITES ARE intelligible, legible

inconceivable ADJECTIVE *It was inconceivable that the king would agree to these demands.* ► unimaginable, unthinkable, implausible, incredible, unbelievable, undreamed of, (more informal) mind-boggling OPPOSITES ARE conceivable, credible

inconclusive ADJECTIVE *The opinion polls are inconclusive.* ► unconvincing, indefinite, undecided, ambiguous, equivocal, indecisive, indeterminate, uncertain, unsettled, open AN OPPOSITE IS conclusive

incongruous ADJECTIVE *the incongruous sound of an electric doorbell* ► inappropriate, out of place, discordant, unsuitable, ill-suited, incompatible, inconsistent, conflicting, odd, clashing, contrasting, ill-matched, uncoordinated, irreconcilable AN OPPOSITE IS appropriate

inconsiderate ADJECTIVE *inconsiderate behavior; It was very inconsiderate of them.* ► thoughtless, insensitive, unthinking, uncaring, unkind, discourteous, impolite, unconcerned, tactless

inconsistent ➡ incubate

inconsistent ADJECTIVE not consistent
  ▷ **inconsistently** ADVERB **inconsistency** NOUN
inconspicuous ADJECTIVE not conspicuous
  ▷ **inconspicuously** ADVERB
incontinent ADJECTIVE not able to control the
bladder or bowels
  ▷ **incontinence** NOUN
incontrovertible ADJECTIVE unable to be
denied; indisputable
inconvenience NOUN inconveniences being
inconvenient
inconvenience VERB inconveniences,
inconveniencing, inconvenienced cause
inconvenience or slight difficulty to someone
inconvenient ADJECTIVE not convenient
incorporate VERB incorporates,
incorporating, incorporated include
something as a part of something larger
  ▷ **incorporation** NOUN
incorporated ADJECTIVE (said about a business
firm) formed into a legal corporation
incorrect ADJECTIVE not correct
  ▷ **incorrectly** ADVERB

incorruptible ADJECTIVE **1** not able to decay
2 not able to be bribed
increase VERB increases, increasing, increased
make or become larger or more
increase NOUN increases increasing; the
amount by which a thing increases
incredible ADJECTIVE unbelievable
  ▷ **incredibly** ADVERB **incredibility** NOUN
  USAGE Do not confuse with **incredulous**.
incredulous ADJECTIVE not believing
somebody; showing disbelief
  ▷ **incredulously** ADVERB **incredulity** NOUN
  USAGE Do not confuse with **incredible**.
incriminate VERB incriminates, incriminating,
incriminated show a person to have been
involved in a crime, etc.
  ▷ **incrimination** NOUN
incubate VERB incubates, incubating,
incubated **1** hatch eggs by keeping them
warm **2** cause bacteria or a disease, etc., to
develop
  ▷ **incubation** NOUN

Thesaurus

inconsistent ADJECTIVE **1** *Their attitudes are inconsistent and hard to understand.*
  ▶ changeable, unreliable, erratic, capricious, unstable, variable, fickle, inconstant, unpredictable, (*more informal*) up-and-down **2** *There are several inconsistent versions of the legend.* ▶ conflicting, contradictory, incompatible, irreconcilable, discrepant, incongruous, at variance, clashing, contrasting, different AN OPPOSITE IS consistent

inconsolable ADJECTIVE *Lisa was inconsolable when she arrived back from the accident.*
  ▶ heartbroken, broken-hearted, devastated, grief-stricken, desolate, despairing

inconspicuous ADJECTIVE **1** *The building is small and inconspicuous.* ▶ unobtrusive, undistinguished, unremarkable, unostentatious, camouflaged, hidden, out of sight, insignificant, ordinary, invisible **2** *Jane did her best to remain inconspicuous.* ▶ retiring, self-effacing, unassuming, modest, restrained OPPOSITES ARE conspicuous, noticeable

inconvenience NOUN *The roadworks have caused a great deal of inconvenience.* ▶ trouble, bother, difficulty, disruption, awkwardness, nuisance, hindrance, irritation, fuss, upset, annoyance, disadvantage, drawback, encumbrance AN OPPOSITE IS convenience

inconvenience VERB *We hope the delay will not inconvenience you too much.* ▶ trouble, bother, disturb, put out, incommode, annoy, irritate, disadvantage, embarrass, (*informal*) put you out

inconvenient ADJECTIVE *Shirley arrived at an extremely inconvenient moment.* ▶ awkward, difficult, unsuitable, inappropriate, inopportune, untimely, ill-timed, embarrassing, annoying, bothersome, irritating, troublesome AN OPPOSITE IS convenient

incorporate VERB **1** *The peace treaty incorporated the region into Italy.* ▶ absorb, merge, assimilate, subsume, embody, include (in), contain (in) **2** *The leaflet incorporates a sponsorship form.* ▶ include, contain, embrace

incorrect ADJECTIVE *The next three answers were incorrect.* ▶ wrong, erroneous, mistaken, inaccurate, imprecise, inexact, false, untrue

increase NOUN *an increase in size an increase in demand* ▶ growth, rise, development, enlargement, expansion, swelling, intensification, upsurge, upturn AN OPPOSITE IS decrease

increase VERB **1** *Applications for jobs have increased.* ▶ rise, grow, swell, multiply, expand, spread, proliferate OPPOSITES ARE decrease, decline **2** *Prosperity increases consumer demand.* ▶ raise, heighten, boost, enhance, add to, strengthen, intensify, develop, expand, escalate, augment OPPOSITES ARE reduce, lower

incredible ADJECTIVE **1** *an incredible feat of engineering* ▶ magnificent, marvelous, spectacular, remarkable, wonderful, extraordinary, amazing, astounding **2** *Their story is incredible.* ▶ unbelievable, implausible, far-fetched, improbable, unlikely, questionable, unreasonable, doubtful, dubious AN OPPOSITE IS credible

a
b
c
d
e
f
g
h
i
j
k
l
m
n
o
p
q
r
s
t
u
v
w
x
y
z

A
B
C
D
E
F
G
H
I
J
K
L
M
N
O
P
Q
R
S
T
U
V
W
X
Y
Z

incubator NOUN **incubators 1** a device in which a baby born prematurely can be kept warm and supplied with oxygen **2** a device for incubating eggs, etc.

incur VERB **incurs, incurring, incurred** bring something on yourself • *I hope you don't incur too much expense.*

indebted ADJECTIVE owing money or gratitude to someone

indecent ADJECTIVE not decent; improper
▷ **indecently** ADVERB **indecency** NOUN

indecisive ADJECTIVE not decisive

indeed ADVERB **1** really; truly • *I am indeed surprised*; (used to strengthen a meaning) • *very nice indeed* **2** admittedly • *It is, indeed, his first attempt.*

indefensible ADJECTIVE unable to be defended or justified • *an indefensible decision*

indefinite ADJECTIVE not definite; vague

indefinite article NOUN **indefinite articles** (in grammar) the word "a" or "an"

indefinitely ADVERB for an indefinite or unlimited time

indelible ADJECTIVE impossible to rub out or remove
▷ **indelibly** ADVERB

indelicate ADJECTIVE **1** slightly indecent **2** tactless
▷ **indelicacy** NOUN

independent ADJECTIVE **1** not dependent on any other person or thing for help, money, or support **2** (said about a country) governing

itself **3** (said about broadcasting) not financed by money from licences
▷ **independently** ADVERB **independence** NOUN

indestructible ADJECTIVE unable to be destroyed
▷ **indestructibility** NOUN

indeterminate ADJECTIVE not fixed or decided exactly; left vague

index NOUN **1 indexes** an alphabetical list of things, especially at the end of a book **2 indexes** a number showing how prices or wages have changed from a previous level **3 indices** (in mathematics) the raised number etc. written to the right of another (e.g., 3 in 2^3) showing how many times the first one is to be multiplied by itself

Indian ADJECTIVE **1** to do with India or its people **2** to do with Native Americans
▷ **Indian** NOUN
USAGE The preferred term for the descendants of the original inhabitants of North and South America is *Native American. American Indian* is usually acceptable but the term *Red Indian* is now regarded as offensive and should not be used.

india rubber NOUN **india rubbers** a rubber

indicate VERB **indicates, indicating, indicated 1** point something out or make it known **2** be a sign of **3** when drivers indicate, they signal which direction they are turning by using their indicators
▷ **indication** NOUN

Thesaurus

incur VERB *actions that might incur a penalty*
► earn, sustain, attract, provoke, run up, suffer, get, expose you to, bring on yourself

incurable ADJECTIVE **1** *an incurable illness*
► untreatable, inoperable, irremediable, irreparable, terminal, fatal, chronic, hopeless AN OPPOSITE IS curable **2** *Jenny is an incurable romantic.* ► inveterate, incorrigible, hardened, dyed-in-the-wool

indecision NOUN *She wanted to act, but indecision prevented her.* ► hesitation, irresolution, indecisiveness, uncertainty, doubt, ambivalence, vacillation, equivocation OPPOSITES ARE decisiveness, resolution

indecisive ADJECTIVE **1** *He came across as an indecisive leader.* ► hesitant, irresolute, tentative, equivocating, uncertain, weak, dithering **2** *The result of the tests was indecisive.* ► uncertain, doubtful, unsure

indefinite ADJECTIVE **1** *The inspectors are here for an indefinite period.* ► unspecified, unknown, uncertain, unlimited AN OPPOSITE IS definite **2** *a word like "get," with an indefinite meaning* ► vague, unclear, unspecific, imprecise, hazy

indelible ADJECTIVE **1** *indelible ink*
► permanent, ineradicable, fixed, lasting, fast,

ingrained **2** *The experience left an indelible impression on her.* ► unforgettable, ineradicable, lasting, enduring AN OPPOSITE IS erasable.

independence NOUN **1** *The country gained its independence in the 1950s.* ► self-government, autonomy, freedom, individualism, liberty, nonconformity AN OPPOSITE IS dependence **2** *The judges must be able to act with complete independence.* ► impartiality, neutrality, disinterest, detachment, objectivity, freedom

independent ADJECTIVE **1** *an independent country* ► autonomous, sovereign, self-governing **2** *an independent person* ► free, unconstrained, self-reliant, self-sufficient, free-thinking, liberated AN OPPOSITE IS dependent **3** *an independent opinion* ► impartial, unbiased, disinterested, objective

indicate VERB **1** *A linesman raised his flag to indicate a goal.* ► signify, denote, register, record, designate **2** *Good sales indicate the book's popularity.* ► show, demonstrate, be a sign of, testify to, suggest, imply, attest **3** *Indicate your choice of prize on the form.*
► specify, point out

indicative ADJECTIVE giving an indication

indicative NOUN the form of a verb used in making a statement (e.g., "he said" or "he is coming"), not in a command or question, or wish

indicator NOUN indicators **1** a thing that indicates or points to something **2** a flashing light used to signal that a motor vehicle is turning **3** (in science) a chemical compound, such as litmus, that changes color in the presence of a particular substance or condition

indifferent ADJECTIVE **1** not caring about something; not interested **2** not very good
• *an indifferent participant*
▷ **indifferently** ADVERB **indifference** NOUN

indigenous (in- dij- in- us) ADJECTIVE growing or originating in a particular country; native
• *The koala bear is indigenous to Australia.*

indigestible ADJECTIVE difficult or impossible to digest

indigestion NOUN pain or discomfort caused by difficulty in digesting food

indignant ADJECTIVE angry at something that seems unfair or wicked
▷ **indignantly** ADVERB **indignation** NOUN

indignity NOUN indignities treatment that makes a person feel undignified or humiliated; an insult

indirect ADJECTIVE not direct
▷ **indirectly** ADVERB

indirect speech NOUN someone's words given in a changed form reported by someone else, as in *He said that he would come* (reporting the words "I will come")

indiscreet ADJECTIVE **1** not discreet; revealing secrets **2** not cautious; rash
▷ **indiscreetly** ADVERB **indiscretion** NOUN

indiscriminate ADJECTIVE showing no discrimination; not making a careful choice
▷ **indiscriminately** ADVERB

indispensable ADJECTIVE not able to be dispensed with; essential
▷ **indispensability** NOUN

indisputable ADJECTIVE undeniable

indistinct ADJECTIVE not distinct
▷ **indistinctly** ADVERB **indistinctness** NOUN

indistinguishable ADJECTIVE not able to be told apart; not distinguishable

individual ADJECTIVE **1** of or for one person **2** single or separate • *Count each individual word.*
▷ **individually** ADVERB

Thesaurus

indication NOUN **1** *His secretary could give no clear indication of when he was expected back.*
► clue, hint, inkling, intimation, suggestion, explanation **2** *Pain may be an indication of injury.* ► sign, indicator, symptom, mark, evidence, manifestation

indifference NOUN *He reacted with complete indifference to their predicament.* ► unconcern, apathy, coolness, disregard, nonchalance, inattention

indifferent ADJECTIVE **1** *His voice showed how indifferent he was.* ► unconcerned, apathetic, uncaring, nonchalant **2** *After an indifferent meal he went off to bed.* ► mediocre, ordinary, inferior, unexceptional, average

indignant ADJECTIVE *The newspaper received indignant letters from outraged readers.* ► irate, angry, affronted, aggrieved, incensed, outraged, resentful, offended, vexed, piqued, heated, furious, fuming

indignation NOUN *The false accusations filled him with indignation.* ► anger, fury, resentment, outrage, affront, umbrage, vexation

indirect ADJECTIVE **1** *The convoy took a quieter indirect route.* ► roundabout, circuitous, meandering, out-of-the-way **2** *It was an insult, if only an indirect one.* ► disguised, ambiguous,

equivocal, oblique, implicit, implied, inexplicit AN OPPOSITE IS direct

indiscreet ADJECTIVE *Her mother would never have done anything so indiscreet.* ► imprudent, unwise, injudicious, tactless, ill-advised, ill-considered, ill-judged, unthinking, impolite, impolitic, undiplomatic, careless, incautious, unguarded OPPOSITES ARE discreet, careful

indisputable ADJECTIVE *Charles returned in triumph, indisputable king of Aquitaine.*
► incontrovertible, incontestable, acknowledged, undeniable, indubitable, unassailable, unequivocal OPPOSITES ARE questionable, debatable

indistinct ADJECTIVE **1** *In the photocopies, some of the letters were indistinct.* ► blurred, fuzzy, unclear, out of focus, ill-defined, dim, faint, hazy, misty, obscure, vague, shadowy, bleary **2** *She murmured, but her voice was indistinct.*
► muffled, muted, faint, weak, inaudible, slurred AN OPPOSITE IS distinct

indistinguishable ADJECTIVE *The boys are indistinguishable.* ► identical, interchangeable, alike, the same AN OPPOSITE IS different

individual ADJECTIVE **1** *music with an individual style* ► characteristic, distinctive, distinct, particular, special, specific, unique, peculiar, exclusive, idiosyncratic, private, personal

A
B
C
D
E
F
G
H
I
J
K
L
M
N
O
P
Q
R
S
T
U
V
W
X
Y
Z

individual NOUN individuals one person, animal, or plant

individuality NOUN the things that make one person or thing different from another; distinctive identity

indivisible ADJECTIVE not able to be divided or separated
▷ **indivisibly** ADVERB

indoctrinate VERB indoctrinates, indoctrinating, indoctrinated fill a person's mind with particular ideas or beliefs, so that they come to accept them without thinking
▷ **indoctrination** NOUN

indomitable ADJECTIVE not able to be overcome or conquered

indoor ADJECTIVE used or placed or done, etc., inside a building • *indoor games*

indoors ADVERB inside a building

induce VERB induces, inducing, induced **1** persuade **2** produce or cause • *Some substances induce sleep.* **3** if a pregnant woman is induced, labor is brought on artificially with drugs
▷ **induction** NOUN

indulge VERB indulges, indulging, indulged allow a person to have or do what they want
▷ **indulgence** NOUN **indulgent** ADJECTIVE

indulge in allow yourself to have or do something that you like

industrial ADJECTIVE to do with industry; working or used in industry
▷ **industrially** ADVERB

industrial action NOUN ways for workers to protest, such as striking or working to rule

industrialized ADJECTIVE (said about a country or district) having many industries
▷ **industrialization** NOUN

Industrial Revolution NOUN the rapid expansion of British industry by the use of machines during the late 18th and early 19th centuries

industrious ADJECTIVE working hard
▷ **industriously** ADVERB

industry NOUN industries **1** making or producing goods, etc., especially in factories **2** a particular branch of this, or any business activity • *the motor industry;* • *the tourist industry* **3** being industrious

ineffective ADJECTIVE not effective; inefficient
▷ **ineffectively** ADVERB

ineffectual ADJECTIVE not achieving anything

inefficient ADJECTIVE not efficient
▷ **inefficiently** ADVERB **inefficiency** NOUN

Thesaurus

2 *Individual countries can make their own decisions.* ► separate, single, discrete AN OPPOSITE IS collective

individual NOUN *In the corner sat a strange individual.* ► person, being, human being, soul, mortal

indoctrinate VERB *With their psychological techniques they were able to indoctrinate large numbers of people.* ► brainwash, propagandize, re-educate, instruct, train, teach

induce VERB **1** *Their leaders induced them to continue fighting.* ► persuade, convince, prevail upon, press, urge, encourage **2** *Conversations like these induce close friendship.* ► bring about, cause, create, effect, instigate, engender, develop, produce, lead to, give rise to, arouse, kindle

inducement NOUN *Paying off student loans is an inducement to join the profession.* ► incentive, encouragement, enticement, stimulus, motivation, spur, lure, bait

indulge VERB **1** *She decided to indulge her passion for music.* ► satisfy, gratify, fulfill, pander to, go along with, humor **2** *She could not be accused of indulging her children.* ► spoil, pamper, cosset, coddle

indulge in *Here we stopped and indulged in a iced tea.* ► enjoy, revel in

indulgent ADJECTIVE *He could see the looks of indulgent amusement on their faces.* ► tolerant, compliant, patient, permissive, easygoing,

lenient, liberal, overgenerous, fond, genial, kind AN OPPOSITE IS strict

industrious ADJECTIVE *an industrious and studious youth* ► diligent, hardworking, conscientious, assiduous, enterprising, painstaking, energetic, active, keen, productive, zealous, sedulous, tireless OPPOSITES ARE lazy, indolent

industry NOUN **1** *the American oil industry* ► business, trade, commerce, manufacturing **2** *The garden looked like a hive of industry.* ► activity, hard work, industriousness, diligence, effort, toil, energy, vigor, application, commitment, determination, labor, perseverance, persistence, tirelessness, zeal OPPOSITES ARE laziness, indolence

ineffective ADJECTIVE **1** *The protests were quite ineffective.* ► unsuccessful, unproductive, useless, futile, vain, fruitless, unavailing, worthless OPPOSITES ARE effective, fruitful **2** *an ineffective leader* ► inadequate, ineffectual, weak, feeble, inept, incompetent AN OPPOSITE IS effective

inefficient ADJECTIVE **1** *He must be the world's most inefficient gardener.* ► ineffective, ineffectual, unproductive, disorganized, incompetent, inept, inexpert **2** *The wood stoves are extremely inefficient for cooking food.* ► uneconomical, unproductive, extravagant, wasteful, awkward, clumsy AN OPPOSITE IS efficient

inept ADJECTIVE lacking any skill; clumsy
  ▷ **ineptly** ADVERB **ineptitude** NOUN

inert ADJECTIVE not moving or reacting
  ▷ **inertly** ADVERB

inert gas NOUN inert gases a gas that almost never combines with other substances

inertia (in- er- sha) NOUN **1** inactivity; being inert or slow to take action **2** the tendency for a moving thing to keep moving in a straight line

inevitable ADJECTIVE unavoidable; sure to happen
  ▷ **inevitably** ADVERB **inevitability** NOUN

inexhaustible ADJECTIVE so great that it cannot be used up completely ● Ben has an inexhaustible supply of jokes.

inexorable (in- eks- er- a- bul) ADJECTIVE **1** relentless **2** not able to be persuaded by requests or entreaties
  ▷ **inexorably** ADVERB

inexperience NOUN lack of experience
  ▷ **inexperienced** ADJECTIVE

infallible ADJECTIVE **1** never wrong **2** never failing ● an infallible remedy
  ▷ **infallibly** ADVERB **infallibility** NOUN

infancy NOUN **1** early childhood; babyhood **2** an early stage of development

infant NOUN infants a baby or young child

infantile ADJECTIVE **1** to do with infants **2** very childish

infantry NOUN soldiers who fight on foot
  COMPARE **cavalry**

infatuated ADJECTIVE filled with foolish or unreasoning love
  ▷ **infatuation** NOUN

infect VERB infects, infecting, infected pass on a disease or bacteria to a person, animal, or plant

infection NOUN infections **1** infecting **2** an infectious disease or condition

infectious ADJECTIVE **1** (said about a disease) able to be spread by air or water, etc.
  COMPARE **contagious 2** quickly spreading to others ● His fear was infectious.

inferior ADJECTIVE less good or less important; low or lower in position, quality, etc.
  ▷ **inferiority** NOUN

inferior NOUN inferiors a person who is lower in position or rank than someone else

infernal ADJECTIVE **1** to do with or like hell ● the infernal regions **2** (informal) detestable or tiresome ● that infernal noise
  ▷ **infernally** ADVERB

inferno NOUN infernos a raging fire

infertile ADJECTIVE not fertile
  ▷ **infertility** NOUN

infest VERB infests, infesting, infested (said about pests) be numerous and troublesome in a place
  ▷ **infestation** NOUN

infidelity NOUN unfaithfulness

infiltrate VERB infiltrates, infiltrating, infiltrated get into a place or organization gradually and without being noticed
  ▷ **infiltration** NOUN **infiltrator** NOUN

Thesaurus

inevitable ADJECTIVE There have been the inevitable delays. ► unavoidable, inescapable, obligatory, mandatory, ineluctable

inexperienced ADJECTIVE Inexperienced people often get entry-level jobs. ► inexpert, untrained, unskilled, unpracticed, unaccustomed, immature, callow, amateur, fresh, green, raw AN OPPOSITE IS experienced

infallible ADJECTIVE **1** The idea works well, but it is not infallible. ► foolproof, unfailing, guaranteed, perfect, certain AN OPPOSITE IS fallible **2** Kate always adopted her infallible routine. ► dependable, reliable, unerring, accurate

infant NOUN an age at which infants are learning to walk ► baby, child, tot, (informal) toddler

infect VERB **1** The organism may infect the eye of the infant with a "sticky eye." ► cause an infection in, spread disease to **2** The water supply had become infected. ► contaminate, pollute, poison, taint, blight **3** Her cheerful

humor infects every one she meets. ► affect, influence, inspire, animate, touch

infection NOUN **1** a bladder infection ► disease, virus, disorder, complaint **2** The dressing will keep the wound free of infection.
  ► contamination, contagion, bacteria, poisoning

infectious ADJECTIVE **1** the conquest of infectious diseases ► contagious, communicable, catching, transmissible, transmittable, spreading **2** infectious laughter ► contagious, irresistible, spreading

infer VERB What can we infer from the table of results? ► conclude, deduce, extrapolate, reason, gather, assume, figure out, guess, understand USAGE See the note at imply.

inferior ADJECTIVE **1** inferior rank ► lesser, lower, subsidiary, subordinate, junior, secondary, second-class, ancillary, low, humble **2** inferior quality ► poor, mediocre, substandard, shoddy, tawdry, bad, cheap, indifferent

a
b
c
d
e
f
g
h
i
j
k
l
m
n
o
p
q
r
s
t
u
v
w
x
y
z

A
B
C
D
E
F
G
H
I
J
K
L
M
N
O
P
Q
R
S
T
U
V
W
X
Y
Z

infinite ADJECTIVE **1** endless; without a limit **2** too great to be measured
▷ **infinitely** ADVERB

infinitesimal ADJECTIVE extremely small
▷ **infinitesimally** ADVERB

infinitive NOUN infinitives (in grammar) the form of a verb that does not change to indicate a particular tense or number or person, in English used with or without to, e.g., *go* in "Let him go" or "Allow him to go"

infinity NOUN an infinite number or distance or time

inflame VERB inflames, inflaming, inflamed **1** produce strong feelings or anger in people **2** cause redness, heat, and swelling in a body part

inflammable ADJECTIVE able to be set on fire
USAGE This word means the same as **flammable**. If you want to say that something is not able to be set on fire, use **non-flammable**.

inflammation NOUN painful redness or swelling in a part of the body

inflate VERB inflates, inflating, inflated **1** fill something with air or gas so that it expands **2** increase something too much **3** raise prices or wages etc. more than is justifiable

inflation NOUN **1** inflating **2** a general rise in prices and fall in the purchasing power of money
▷ **inflationary** ADJECTIVE

inflect VERB inflects, inflecting, inflected **1** change the ending or form of a word to show its tense or its grammatical relation to other words, e.g. *sing* changes to *sang* or *sung*; *child* changes to *children* **2** alter the voice in speaking

inflection NOUN inflections an ending or form of a word used to inflect, e.g. -ed

inflexible ADJECTIVE not able to be bent or changed or persuaded
▷ **inflexibly** ADVERB **inflexibility** NOUN

influence NOUN influences **1** the power to produce an effect **2** a person or thing with this power

influence VERB influences, influencing, influenced have influence on a person or thing

influential ADJECTIVE having great influence

influenza NOUN an infectious disease that causes fever, catarrh, and pain

inform VERB informs, informing, informed give information to somebody
▷ **informant** NOUN

informal ADJECTIVE not formal
▷ **informally** ADVERB **informality** NOUN

Thesaurus

infinite ADJECTIVE **1** *You will need infinite patience in detailed work like this.* ► endless, limitless, boundless, immeasurable, unlimited, incalculable, immense, prodigious OPPOSITES ARE limited, finite **2** *Along the roofs were infinite numbers of chimneys.* ► countless, innumerable, numberless, incalculable OPPOSITES ARE limited, finite

inflammation NOUN *inflammation of the skin* ► swelling, redness, soreness, burning, tenderness, infection

inflate VERB **1** *We have ten minutes to inflate fifty balloons.* ► pump up, blow up, puff up, dilate, distend, swell **2** *News reports have greatly inflated the number of casualties.* ► exaggerate, magnify, overstate, overplay, overdramatize

inflict VERB **1** *He was determined to inflict some sort of penalty on them.* ► impose, administer (to), mete out (to), deal out (to), apply (to), perpetrate, wreak, enforce, force **2** *No one really wants an elderly relative inflicted on them for months.* ► impose, foist, thrust, saddle someone (with), burden someone (with)

influence NOUN *The local organizations can have a large influence on the party at national level.* ► effect, impact, control, sway, hold, pressure, pull, power (over), direction (over), authority (over), dominance (over)

influence VERB **1** *Parents influence their children enormously in the first few years.* ► affect, have an effect on, guide, exert an influence on, direct, control **2** *There had been several attempts to influence the jury.* ► sway, bias, coerce, pressurize, prejudice, suborn, lead astray, bribe, corrupt

influential ADJECTIVE **1** *a respected and influential politician* ► important, authoritative, leading, powerful, dominant OPPOSITES ARE uninfluential, insignificant **2** *a piece of writing that has been highly influential* ► significant, persuasive, pivotal, seminal, crucial, effective, far-reaching, telling OPPOSITES ARE uninfluential, unimportant

inform VERB **1** *I'll inform them that we are ready to leave.* ► tell, notify, advise, let someone know, send word to, apprise **2** *inform on No one wants to inform on a friend.* ► denounce, betray, report, incriminate, tell on, (more informal) shop

informal ADJECTIVE **1** *We were having an informal conversation.* ► casual, relaxed, natural, easy-going **2** *The style of the article was very informal.* ► colloquial, idiomatic, vernacular, demotic, popular **3** *You can wear informal clothes.* ► casual, everyday, comfortable, leisure

information ➡ inhuman

a b c d e f g h i j k l m n o p q r s t u v w x y z

USAGE In this dictionary, words marked *informal* are used in talking but not when you are writing or speaking formally.

information NOUN facts told or heard or discovered, or put into a computer, etc.

informative ADJECTIVE giving a lot of useful information

informed ADJECTIVE knowing about something

infrared ADJECTIVE below or beyond red in the color spectrum

infuriate VERB infuriates, infuriating, infuriated make a person very angry

ingenious ADJECTIVE **1** clever at inventing things **2** cleverly made or thought out
▷ **ingeniously** ADVERB **ingenuity** NOUN

ingrained ADJECTIVE **1** (said about dirt) marking a surface deeply **2** (said about feelings or habits) firmly fixed

ingratiate VERB ingratiates, ingratiating, ingratiated
ingratiate yourself get yourself into favor with someone, especially by flattering them or always agreeing with their ideas or opinions
▷ **ingratiation** NOUN

ingratitude NOUN lack of gratitude

ingredient NOUN ingredients one of the parts of a mixture; one of the things used in a recipe

inhabit VERB inhabits, inhabiting, inhabited live in a place
▷ **inhabitant** NOUN

inhale VERB inhales, inhaling, inhaled breathe in
▷ **inhalation** NOUN

inhaler NOUN inhalers a device used for relieving asthma, etc., by inhaling

inherent (in- her- ent) ADJECTIVE existing in something as one of its natural or permanent qualities
▷ **inherently** ADVERB **inherence** NOUN

inherit VERB inherits, inheriting, inherited **1** receive money, property, or a title, etc., when its previous owner dies **2** get certain qualities etc. from parents or predecessors
▷ **inheritance** NOUN **inheritor** NOUN

inhibition NOUN inhibitions a feeling of embarrassment or worry that prevents you from doing something or expressing your emotions
▷ **inhibited** ADJECTIVE

inhospitable ADJECTIVE **1** unfriendly to visitors **2** (said about a place) not giving any shelter or good weather

inhuman ADJECTIVE cruel; without pity or kindness
▷ **inhumanity** NOUN

Thesaurus

information NOUN *You can get more information from the website.* ► details, particulars, facts, data, guidance, material, documentation, advice, knowledge, (*more informal*) info

informative ADJECTIVE *The two-day course is too short to be informative.* ► instructive, useful, helpful, communicative, enlightening, revealing, illuminating, factual OPPOSITES ARE uninformative, uncommunicative

informed ADJECTIVE *She seems highly informed on the subject.* ► knowledgeable, enlightened, conversant (with), familiar (with), abreast (of), au fait (with) OPPOSITES ARE ill-informed, ignorant

infuriate VERB *His stubborn refusal began to infuriate her.* ► anger, enrage, exasperate, incense, annoy, irritate, vex, madden, aggravate, antagonize, displease, make angry, (*more informal*) needle, (*more informal*) rile OPPOSITES ARE placate, appease, please

ingenious ADJECTIVE *an ingenious solution to the difficulty* ► inventive, imaginative, creative, clever, original, cunning, resourceful, astute, shrewd, inspired, skilful, subtle AN OPPOSITE IS unimaginative

inhabit VERB *a cave complex that hermits used to inhabit* ► live in, occupy, dwell in, people, populate, settle in

inhabitant NOUN *the inhabitants of the town* ► resident, citizen, native, local, occupant, dweller, (*plural*) population, (*plural*) townsfolk

inherit VERB *His son will inherit the business on his death.* ► receive, be left, be bequeathed, succeed to

inheritance NOUN *She bought a house with her inheritance.* ► legacy, bequest, estate, fortune, heritage

inhibited ADJECTIVE *He felt inhibited about discussing money.* ► shy, reticent, embarrassed, awkward, self-conscious, reserved, diffident, bashful, (*more informal*) hung-up

inhibition NOUN **1** *The state places no inhibition on press freedom.* ► restraint, bar, check, barrier, interference, impediment
2 inhibitions *Not everyone can overcome their inhibitions so easily.* ► shyness, reticence, diffidence, reserve, self-consciousness, insecurity, repression, (*informal*) hang-ups

inhuman ADJECTIVE *the inhuman treatment of political prisoners* ► inhumane, brutal, cruel, barbaric, barbarous, harsh, callous, bestial, savage, merciless, pitiless, ruthless, unnatural, bloodthirsty, diabolical, fiendish, heartless OPPOSITES ARE humane, compassionate

inhumane ADJECTIVE *It would be inhumane to take away their freedom.* ► cruel, inhuman, harsh, callous, sadistic, barbaric, barbarous, uncivilized AN OPPOSITE IS humane

A
B
C
D
E
F
G
H
I
J
K
L
M
N
O
P
Q
R
S
T
U
V
W
X
Y
Z

inimitable *ADJECTIVE* impossible to imitate

initial *NOUN* initials the first letter of a word or name

initial *ADJECTIVE* at the beginning • *the initial stages*
▷ **initially** *ADVERB*

initiative (in- ish- a- tiv) *NOUN* **1** the power or right to get something started **2** the ability to make decisions and take action on your own without being told what to do
take the initiative take action to start something happening

inject *VERB* injects, injecting, injected **1** put a medicine or drug into the body by means of a syringe **2** add a new quality • *Inject some humor into the story.*
▷ **injection** *NOUN*

injure *VERB* injures, injuring, injured harm or hurt someone
▷ **injury** *NOUN* **injurious** (in- joor- ee- us) *ADJECTIVE*

injustice *NOUN* injustices **1** lack of justice **2** an unjust action or treatment

ink *NOUN* inks a black or colored liquid used in writing and printing

inkling *NOUN* inklings a slight idea or suspicion • *I had no inkling of your artistic talents.*

inky *ADJECTIVE* **1** stained with ink **2** black like ink • *inky darkness*

inland *ADJECTIVE, ADVERB* in or towards the interior of a country; away from the coast

in-laws *PLURAL NOUN* (informal) relatives by marriage

inlet *NOUN* inlets a strip of water reaching into the land from a sea or lake

inmost *ADJECTIVE* most inward

inn *NOUN* inns a hotel or public house, especially in the country
▷ **innkeeper** *NOUN*

innards *PLURAL NOUN* the internal organs of a person or animal; the inner parts of a machine

inner *ADJECTIVE* inside; nearer to the center
▷ **innermost** *ADJECTIVE*

innings *NOUN* innings the time in baseball when each team gets to bat

innocent *ADJECTIVE* **1** not guilty **2** not wicked; lacking experience of evil **3** harmless
▷ **innocently** *ADVERB* **innocence** *NOUN*

innocuous *ADJECTIVE* harmless

innovation *NOUN* innovations **1** introducing new things or new methods **2** a newly introduced process or way of doing things
▷ **innovative** *ADJECTIVE* **innovator** *NOUN*

innumerable *ADJECTIVE* countless

inoculate *VERB* inoculates, inoculating, inoculated inject or treat someone with a vaccine or serum as a protection against a disease
▷ **inoculation** *NOUN*
USAGE Note the spelling of this word. It has one *n* and one *c*.

inoffensive *ADJECTIVE* harmless

inorganic *ADJECTIVE* not of living organisms; of mineral origin

input *NOUN* what is put into something, especially data put into a computer
▷ **input** *VERB* inputs, inputting, inputted

Thesaurus

initial *ADJECTIVE* **1** *Their initial reaction was one of anger.* ► first, original, provisional, earliest OPPOSITES ARE final, eventual **2** *an initial payment of $100* ► opening, preliminary, starting, commencing, inaugural, introductory OPPOSITES ARE final, closing

initiative *NOUN* **1** *Employers are looking for initiative in candidates for jobs.* ► enterprise, resourcefulness, drive, inventiveness, innovativeness, energy, dynamism, leadership, originality, ambition **2** *We are in danger of losing the initiative.* ► advantage, upper hand, edge, lead **3** *a new initiative for peace* ► proposal, plan, scheme, strategy, measure

injure *VERB* **1** *He was injured in a street fight.* ► hurt, harm, wound , maim, cripple, disfigure **2** *She injured her arm.* ► hurt, damage, break, crush

injury *NOUN* **1** *His hand injury had fully recovered.* ► wound, cut, damage, fracture, lesion **2** *The suit will protect you from personal injury.* ► harm, hurt, suffering

injustice *NOUN* **1** *He shook his head at the cruel injustice of the world.* ► unfairness, unjustness, inequality, inequity, oppression, discrimination, dishonesty, partiality, wrongness AN OPPOSITE IS justice **2** *She felt her treatment to be a grave injustice.* ► wrong, injury, affront, grievance, offence, crime, iniquity, outrage

inner *ADJECTIVE* **1** *the inner part of the building* ► interior, central, innermost, internal, inside AN OPPOSITE IS outer **2** *She kept her inner feelings to herself.* ► private, secret, personal, intimate

innocent *ADJECTIVE* **1** *He always swore that he was innocent.* ► guiltless, blameless, free from blame AN OPPOSITE IS guilty **2** *At her age she looked so innocent.* ► pure, virtuous, chaste, fresh, childlike, trusting, guileless, artless **3** *They claimed it had just been innocent fun.* ► harmless, innocuous, inoffensive

input *NOUN* *They went to the meeting armed with input from their survey.* ► information, data, facts and figures, statistics

inquest NOUN inquests an official inquiry to find out how a person died

inquire VERB inquires, inquiring, inquired **1** investigate something carefully **2** ask for information

inquiry NOUN inquiries **1** an official investigation **2** a question

inquisitive ADJECTIVE always asking questions or trying to find out things
  ▷ **inquisitively** ADVERB

inroads PLURAL NOUN make inroads on or into use up large quantities of supplies or resources

insane ADJECTIVE not sane; mad
  ▷ **insanely** ADVERB **insanity** NOUN

insanitary ADJECTIVE unclean and likely to be harmful to health

insatiable (in- **say**- sha- bul) ADJECTIVE impossible to satisfy • an insatiable appetite

inscribe VERB inscribes, inscribing, inscribed write or carve words, etc., on something

inscription NOUN inscriptions words written or carved on a monument, coin, stone, etc., or written in the front of a book

insect NOUN insects a small animal with six legs, no backbone, and a body divided into three parts (head, thorax, abdomen)

insecticide NOUN insecticides a substance for killing insects

insectivorous ADJECTIVE feeding on insects and other small invertebrate creatures
  ▷ **insectivore** NOUN

insecure ADJECTIVE **1** not secure or safe **2** lacking confidence about yourself
  ▷ **insecurely** ADVERB **insecurity** NOUN

inseminate VERB inseminates, inseminating, inseminated insert semen into the womb
  ▷ **insemination** NOUN

insensitive ADJECTIVE not sensitive or thinking about other people's feelings
  ▷ **insensitively** ADVERB **insensitivity** NOUN

inseparable ADJECTIVE **1** not able to be separated **2** liking to be constantly together
  • inseparable friends
  ▷ **inseparably** ADVERB

insert VERB inserts, inserting, inserted put a thing into something else
  ▷ **insertion** NOUN

inside NOUN insides the inner side, surface, or part
  inside out with the inside turned to face outwards
  insides (informal) the organs in the abdomen; the stomach and bowels

inside ADVERB, PREPOSITION on or to the inside of something; in • Come inside. • It's inside that box.

insider NOUN insiders a member of a certain group, especially someone with access to private information

insight NOUN insights being able to perceive the truth about things; understanding

insignificant ADJECTIVE not important or influential
  ▷ **insignificance** NOUN

insincere ADJECTIVE not sincere
  ▷ **insincerely** ADVERB **insincerity** NOUN

Thesaurus

inquire VERB inquire into The committee will inquire into all these matters. ▶ investigate, look into, examine, probe, scrutinize, explore

inquiry NOUN The government has set up a formal inquiry into the incident. ▶ investigation, inquest, scrutiny, inquisition, inspection

inquisitive ADJECTIVE Gareth possessed a sharp and inquisitive mind. ▶ curious, questioning, inquiring, interested, probing, prying

insane ADJECTIVE **1** She was declared insane on the recommendation of two doctors. ▶ mentally ill, mad, deranged, crazy, demented **2** It would be insane to think they could do the journey in a day. ▶ crazy, foolish, stupid, senseless, ludicrous, absurd, mad

insanity NOUN **1** Insanity ran in the family. ▶ mental disorder, mental illness, madness, derangement, lunacy, dementia **2** A loan at such a high rate of interest would be insanity. ▶ folly, foolishness, stupidity, madness, lunacy

insect NOUN Some insects are disguised as a leaf or a twig. ▶ bug, pest, (more informal) creepy-crawly

insecure ADJECTIVE **1** Police warned that the house was insecure. ▶ unsafe, unprotected, ill-protected, vulnerable, exposed, ill-defended, defenceless **2** All this bold talk made him feel insecure. ▶ anxious, worried, concerned, unconfident, diffident

insert VERB He inserted new film in the camera. ▶ put, place, push, slip, install, locate

inside ADJECTIVE The inside walls of the house were damp. ▶ inner, interior, internal, innermost, indoor OPPOSITES ARE outside, outer, exterior

inside NOUN The inside of the box should be lined with silver paper. ▶ interior, inner surface, inner part, core

insignificant ADJECTIVE The differences are mostly insignificant. ▶ unimportant, negligible, trivial, trifling, small, footling, inconsequential, inconsiderable, irrelevant, meaningless AN OPPOSITE IS significant

insincere ADJECTIVE He flashed a gleaming, insincere smile. ▶ false, deceitful, dishonest, disingenuous, pretended, feigned, hypocritical, devious AN OPPOSITE IS sincere

a
b
c
d
e
f
g
h
i
j
k
l
m
n
o
p
q
r
s
t
u
v
w
x
y
z

A
B
C
D
E
F
G
H
I
J
K
L
M
N
O
P
Q
R
S
T
U
V
W
X
Y
Z

insinuate VERB insinuates, insinuating, insinuated **1** hint something unpleasant **2** introduce a thing or yourself gradually or craftily into a place
▷ **insinuation** NOUN

insist VERB insists, insisting, insisted be very firm in saying or asking for something • *I insist on seeing the manager.*
▷ **insistent** ADJECTIVE **insistence** NOUN

insolent ADJECTIVE very rude and insulting
▷ **insolently** ADVERB **insolence** NOUN

insoluble ADJECTIVE **1** impossible to solve • *an insoluble problem* **2** impossible to dissolve
▷ **insolubility** NOUN

insomnia NOUN being unable to sleep
▷ **insomniac** NOUN

inspect VERB inspects, inspecting, inspected examine something carefully and critically
▷ **inspection** NOUN

inspector NOUN inspectors **1** a person whose job is to inspect or supervise things **2** a police officer ranking next above a sergeant

inspiration NOUN inspirations **1** a sudden brilliant idea **2** inspiring; an inspiring influence

inspire VERB inspires, inspiring, inspired fill a person with enthusiasm or creative feelings or ideas • *The applause inspired us with confidence.*

install VERB installs, installing, installed **1** put something in position and ready to use • *They installed central heating.* **2** put a person into an important position with a ceremony • *He was installed as chairman.*
▷ **installation** NOUN

installment NOUN installments each of the parts in which something is given or paid for over a period of time • *an installment of a serial* • *You can pay by installments.*

instance NOUN instances an example • *a serious instance of corruption*
for instance for example

instant ADJECTIVE **1** happening immediately • *instant success* **2** (said about food) designed

---

Thesaurus

---

insist VERB *He insisted he had done everything they had asked.* ► maintain, contend, assert, hold, aver, claim, declare, state, stress
insist on *parents who insist on an early bedtime* ► demand, enforce, require, stipulate

insistence NOUN **1** *her insistence that they should go with her* ► demand, requirement, entreaty, urging **2** *Jane's insistence that she loved him* ► assertion, declaration, contention, claim, avowal

insistent ADJECTIVE *There were insistent requests for financial support.* ► persistent, demanding, unrelenting, unremitting, urgent, emphatic, relentless, repeated, forceful, assertive

insolence NOUN *She accused him of insolence.* ► impertinence, impudence, effrontery, audacity, rudeness, impoliteness, discourtesy, disrespect

insolent ADJECTIVE *The boy was constantly insolent.* ► rude, impolite, impertinent, impudent, disrespectful, audacious, brazen OPPOSITES ARE respectful, polite

insoluble ADJECTIVE *one of the world's insoluble problems* ► unsolvable, unresolvable, inexplicable, unanswerable, unfathomable, incomprehensible, mysterious, mystifying, baffling, enigmatic, puzzling AN OPPOSITE IS soluble

inspect VERB *The houses had been inspected by a surveyor.* ► check, examine, investigate, scrutinize, supervise, oversee

inspection NOUN *The machinery needs a regular inspection.* ► examination, check, checkup, investigation, review, scrutiny, survey

inspector NOUN *Inspectors are sent out each week to assess the work done.* ► examiner, investigator, supervisor, tester, controller, official, superintendent

inspiration NOUN **1** *writing that relies on inspiration* ► creativity, imagination, inventiveness, ingenuity, enthusiasm, genius, influence **2** *The success proved an inspiration to everyone involved in the project.* ► stimulus, spur, motivation, boost **3** *Emma had a sudden inspiration.* ► idea, thought, brainwave, revelation

inspire VERB *a simple tune that inspired him to write a musical* ► stimulate, influence, motivate, prompt, encourage, enthuse, galvanize, spur, stir, animate, arouse, (more informal) egg on

install VERB **1** *We want to install central heating on all floors.* ► put in, establish, fix, introduce, set up **2** install yourself *She installed herself in a sofa by the fire.* ► ensconce yourself, settle, place yourself, plant yourself, (more informal) park yourself

installment NOUN **1** *You can pay for your license in monthly installments.* ► payment, part **2** *a serial in four installments* ► episode, part, section

instance NOUN *We could not find a single instance of discrimination.* ► example, occurrence, case, illustration, sample

instant ADJECTIVE *The web site gives you instant access to the information you need.* ► immediate, instantaneous, on-the-spot, prompt, fast, quick, rapid, speedy, direct, swift

to be prepared quickly and easily • *instant coffee*
▷ **instantly** ADVERB

instant NOUN instants a moment • *not an instant too soon*

instantaneous ADJECTIVE happening immediately
▷ **instantaneously** ADVERB

instead ADVERB in place of something else

instinct NOUN instincts a natural tendency or ability • *Birds fly by instinct.*
▷ **instinctive** ADJECTIVE **instinctively** ADVERB

institute NOUN institutes a society or organization; the building used by this

institution NOUN institutions **1** an institute; a public organization, e.g., a hospital or university **2** a habit or custom **3** instituting something
▷ **institutional** ADJECTIVE

instruct VERB instructs, instructing, instructed **1** teach a person a subject or skill **2** inform **3** tell a person what he or she must do
▷ **instructive** ADJECTIVE **instructor** NOUN

instruction NOUN instructions **1** teaching a subject or skill **2** an order or piece of information • *Follow the instructions carefully.*

instrument NOUN instruments **1** a device for producing musical sounds **2** a tool used for delicate or scientific work **3** a measuring device

instrumental ADJECTIVE **1** performed on musical instruments, without singing **2** being the means of doing something • *She was instrumental in getting me a job.*

insubordinate ADJECTIVE disobedient or rebellious
▷ **insubordination** NOUN

insufferable ADJECTIVE unbearable

insular ADJECTIVE **1** to do with or like an island **2** narrow-minded

insulate VERB insulates, insulating, insulated cover or protect something to prevent heat, cold, or electricity etc. from passing in or out
▷ **insulation** NOUN **insulator** NOUN

insulin NOUN a substance that controls the amount of sugar in the blood. The lack of insulin causes diabetes

insult (in- sult) VERB insults, insulting, insulted hurt a person's feelings or pride

insult (in- sult) NOUN insults an insulting remark or action

Thesaurus

instant NOUN *The incident was over in an instant.*
► moment, second, minute, flash, split second, (*more informal*) tick, (*more informal*) twinkling

instantly ADVERB *He fell asleep instantly.*
► immediately, at once, straight away, right away, there and then, directly

instinct NOUN *Her instinct was to find out more about them.* ► impulse, inclination, intuition, hunch, feeling, presentiment, sixth sense, tendency, urge

instinctive ADJECTIVE *Their instinctive reaction is to find someone to blame.* ► intuitive, natural, innate, automatic, reflex OPPOSITES ARE deliberate, conscious

institution NOUN **1** *the institution of a new language course* ► introduction, establishment, setting up, formation, creation, launching, inauguration, inception, initiation, founding, opening **2** *He did not want to spend the rest of his life in an institution.* ► home, hospital, asylum **3** *an academic institution*
► establishment, school, academy, college **4** *A spring holiday has become a family institution.* ► custom, convention, tradition, routine, practice, ritual, habit

instruct VERB **1** *A private tutor instructed the children in French.* ► coach, educate, train, drill,

ground, teach **2** *The officials instructed us to wait.* ► order, direct, command, require, call on, advise

instruction NOUN **1** *It is important to listen out for instructions.* ► direction, directive, order, command, guidance **2** *basic instruction in mathematics* ► education, tuition, teaching, schooling, coaching, tutoring, grounding

instrument NOUN *a sharp instrument*
► implement, tool, device, utensil, contrivance, contraption, apparatus, appliance, equipment, gadget, machine, mechanism

insult NOUN (with the stress on in-) *The two men threw insults at each other.* ► affront, abuse, indignity, slight, snub AN OPPOSITE IS compliment

insult VERB (with the stress on -sult) *She put her head out of the window to insult passersby.*
► abuse, affront, malign, revile, offend, mock, snub, vilify, sneer at AN OPPOSITE IS compliment

insulting ADJECTIVE *They directed their insulting remarks at anyone they happened to see.*
► abusive, rude, offensive, disparaging, contemptuous, deprecatory, scornful, scurrilous, slanderous, insolent, condescending, mocking, patronizing, (*more informal*) snide OPPOSITES ARE polite, complimentary

insuperable ADJECTIVE unable to be overcome
• *an insuperable difficulty*

insurance NOUN an agreement to compensate someone for a loss, damage, or injury, etc., in return for a payment (called a **premium**) made in advance

insure VERB insures, insuring, insured protect with insurance • *Is your jewelry insured?* USAGE Do not confuse with ensure.

intact ADJECTIVE not damaged; complete [from Latin *intactum* = not touched]

intake NOUN intakes **1** taking something in **2** the number of people or things taken in • *We have a high intake of students this year.*

integer NOUN integers a whole number (e.g. 0, 3, 19), not a fraction

integral (in- tig- ral) ADJECTIVE **1** being an essential part of a whole thing • *An engine is an integral part of a car.* **2** whole or complete

integrate VERB integrates, integrating, integrated **1** make parts into a whole; combine **2** bring people together harmoniously into a single community
▷ **integration** NOUN

integrity (in- teg- rit- ee) NOUN honesty

intellect NOUN intellects the ability to think and work things out with the mind

intellectual ADJECTIVE **1** to do with or using the intellect **2** having a good intellect and a liking for knowledge
▷ **intellectually** ADVERB

intellectual NOUN intellectuals an intellectual person

intelligence NOUN **1** being intelligent **2** information, especially of military value; the people who collect and study this information

intelligent ADJECTIVE able to learn and understand things; having great mental ability
▷ **intelligently** ADVERB

intend VERB intends, intending, intended **1** have something in mind as what you want to do **2** plan that something should be used or understood in a particular way

intense ADJECTIVE **1** very strong or great **2** feeling things very strongly and seriously • *He's a very intense young man.*
▷ **intensely** ADVERB **intensity** NOUN

intent NOUN intents intention

Thesaurus

---

intact ADJECTIVE *Several buildings remained intact despite heavy bombing.* ► whole, undamaged, untouched, unharmed, complete, entire

integral ADJECTIVE *Speech is an integral part of human interaction.* ► essential, constituent, indispensable, intrinsic, irreplaceable, necessary, requisite AN OPPOSITE IS incidental **2** *The equipment is sold as an integral system.* ► complete, integrated, combined, indivisible, whole

integrity NOUN *No one doubts their integrity.* ► honesty, honor, morality, sincerity, reliability, virtue, fidelity, uprightness, honorableness, righteousness, goodness, incorruptibility, loyalty, principle AN OPPOSITE IS dishonesty

intellect NOUN *a story that appeals to the intellect rather than the emotions* ► mind, reason, intelligence, judgement, wits

intellectual ADJECTIVE **1** *intellectual powers* ► mental, cerebral, rational, cognitive, conceptual **2** *an intellectual person* ► intelligent, academic, cultured, scholarly, studious, thoughtful, highbrow

intellectual NOUN *Opposition to the regime is strongest among intellectuals.* ► academic, scholar, highbrow, thinker, member of the intelligentsia, intelligent person

intelligence NOUN **1** *a person of great intelligence* ► intellect, brainpower, powers of reasoning, perceptiveness, acumen, wisdom, wits, understanding, comprehension, (more informal) nous AN OPPOSITE IS stupidity

2 *constant intelligence regarding terrorist attacks* ► information, report, warning, news, notification, data, facts, knowledge, (more informal) tip-off

intelligent ADJECTIVE *She is a highly intelligent writer.* ► clever, bright, acute, sharp, perceptive, profound, shrewd

intelligible ADJECTIVE *The message was barely intelligible.* ► understandable, comprehensible, coherent, decipherable, legible, clear, lucid, meaningful OPPOSITES ARE unintelligible, incomprehensible

intend VERB **1** *I intend to apply for a grant.* ► propose, mean, plan, have it in mind, have a mind, aim, contemplate (applying), determine, purpose **2** *The book is intended for learners of English.* ► design, destine, mean

intense ADJECTIVE *She was suffering from intense pain. The experience rouses intense emotions.* ► extreme, acute, severe, fierce, sharp, strong, powerful, profound, potent OPPOSITES ARE moderate, mild

intensify VERB **1** *The dizzy feeling in his head intensified.* ► increase, strengthen, grow, escalate AN OPPOSITE IS weaken **2** *We must intensify our efforts.* ► increase, escalate, step up, reinforce, sharpen, concentrate AN OPPOSITE IS reduce

intensive ADJECTIVE *Police have made an intensive search of the area.* ► thorough, exhaustive, comprehensive, rigorous, detailed, complete, full, all-out, concentrated

intent ADJECTIVE **1** *She was intent on visiting her friends in Spain.* ► keen (to), resolved (to),

intent _ADJECTIVE_ with concentrated attention; very interested
▷ **intently** _ADVERB_
intent on eager or determined to do something

intention _NOUN_ intentions what a person intends; a purpose or plan

intentional _ADJECTIVE_ deliberate, not accidental
▷ **intentionally** _ADVERB_

interact _VERB_ interacts, interacting, interacted have an effect upon one another
▷ **interaction** _NOUN_

interactive _ADJECTIVE_ (in computing) allowing information to be sent immediately in either direction between a computer system and its user

interbreed _VERB_ interbreeds, interbreeding, interbred breed with each other; cross-breed

intercept _VERB_ intercepts, intercepting, intercepted stop or catch a person or thing that is going from one place to another
▷ **interception** _NOUN_

interchange _VERB_ interchanges, interchanging, interchanged **1** put each of two things into the other's place **2** exchange things **3** alternate

▷ **interchangeable** _ADJECTIVE_

interchange _NOUN_ interchanges
1 interchanging **2** a road junction where vehicles can move from one highway, etc., to another

intercourse _NOUN_ **1** communication or dealings between people **2** sexual intercourse

interdependent _ADJECTIVE_ dependent upon each other

interest _NOUN_ interests **1** a feeling of wanting to know about or help with something **2** a thing that interests somebody ● _Science fiction is one of my interests._ **3** an advantage or benefit ● _She looks after her own interests._ **4** money paid regularly in return for money lent or deposited

interest _VERB_ interests, interesting, interested attract a person's interest
▷ **interested** _ADJECTIVE_ **interesting** _ADJECTIVE_

interface _NOUN_ interfaces (in computing) a connection between two parts of a computer system

interfere _VERB_ interferes, interfering, interfered **1** take part in something that has nothing to do with you **2** get in the way; obstruct
▷ **interference** _NOUN_

Thesaurus

determined (to), bent, fixed AN OPPOSITE IS reluctant **2** _He had an intent look on his face._
► attentive, engrossed, absorbed, preoccupied, steadfast OPPOSITES ARE vacant, blank

intention _NOUN_ _Our intention is to accept the offer._ ► aim, purpose, objective, object, plan, ambition, design, end, goal

intentional _ADJECTIVE_ _The remarks were intentional._ ► deliberate, premeditated, intended, planned, calculated, conscious, considered, meant, designed, prearranged, wilful AN OPPOSITE IS unintentional

interaction _NOUN_ _the interaction of two influences_ ► effect on each other, exchange, (_informal_) give and take, interplay, reciprocal effect, (_informal_) to and fro

interest _NOUN_ **1** _a matter of great interest to both of them_ ► importance, significance, consequence, moment, note, value **2** _Her interests include rock-climbing._ ► activity, pursuit, hobby, pastime, diversion, preoccupation
show interest in _John was showing interest in the idea._ ► take notice of, pay attention to, be concerned about, be curious about, have regard for, show involvement in, show commitment to

interest _VERB_ _an idea that interests me_ ► appeal to, attract, excite, fascinate, intrigue, engage, engross, concern, stimulate, arouse the

curiosity of, capture the imagination of, divert, entertain, involve, (_more informal_) turn on AN OPPOSITE IS bore

interested _ADJECTIVE_ **1** _None of them appeared to be interested._ ► curious, enthusiastic, excited, responsive, fascinated, absorbed, attentive, engrossed, intent AN OPPOSITE IS uninterested. **2** _At the meeting various problems were explained to the interested parties._ ► affected, involved, concerned, connected AN OPPOSITE IS disinterested
be interested in _The owners were interested in the idea of selling off part of the land._ ► like, be attracted by, fancy

interesting _ADJECTIVE_ _an interesting idea_
► attractive, appealing, engrossing, stimulating, exciting, intriguing, fascinating, thought-provoking

interfere _VERB_ **1** _interfere in She did not wish to interfere in her friends' lives._ ► intervene, intrude in, meddle in, butt into, pry into, snoop into, encroach on **2** _interfere with A headache interfered with his thoughts._ ► inhibit, hinder, hamper, impede, get in the way of

interference _NOUN_ _He would not tolerate any interference._ ► intrusion, intervention, meddling, snooping, involvement

interfering _ADJECTIVE_ _She blamed his interfering brother._ ► meddlesome, meddling, nosy, prying, snooping, intrusive

a
b
c
d
e
f
g
h
i
j
k
l
m
n
o
p
q
r
s
t
u
v
w
x
y
z

interior *ADJECTIVE* inner

interior *NOUN* interiors the inside of something; the central or inland part of a country

interjection *NOUN* interjections a word or words exclaimed expressing joy or pain or surprise, such as *oh!* or *wow!* or *good heavens!*

interlude *NOUN* interludes **1** an interval **2** something happening in an interval or between other events

intermediate *ADJECTIVE* coming between two things in time, place, or order

interminable *ADJECTIVE* seeming to be endless; long and boring
▷ interminably *ADVERB*

intermission *NOUN* intermissions an interval, especially between parts of a film

intermittent *ADJECTIVE* happening at intervals; not continuous
▷ intermittently *ADVERB*

internal *ADJECTIVE* inside
▷ internally *ADVERB*

internal-combustion engine *NOUN* internal-combustion engines an engine that produces power by burning fuel inside the engine itself

international *ADJECTIVE* to do with or belonging to more than one country; agreed between nations
▷ internationally *ADVERB*

international *NOUN* internationals **1** a sports contest between teams representing different countries **2** a sports player who plays for his or her country

Internet *NOUN* a computer network that allows users all over the world to communicate and exchange information [from *inter* = among, between + *net*]

interplanetary *ADJECTIVE* between planets

interpolate *VERB* interpolates, interpolating, interpolated **1** interject a remark in a conversation **2** insert words; put terms into a mathematical series
▷ interpolation *NOUN*

interpose *VERB* interposes, interposing, interposed place something between two things

interpret *VERB* interprets, interpreting, interpreted **1** explain what something means **2** translate what someone says into another language orally **3** perform music etc. in a way that shows your feelings about its meaning
▷ interpretation *NOUN* interpreter *NOUN*

interrogate *VERB* interrogates, interrogating, interrogated question someone closely or formally
▷ interrogation *NOUN* interrogator *NOUN*

interrogative *ADJECTIVE* questioning; expressing a question
▷ interrogatory *ADJECTIVE*

interrupt *VERB* interrupts, interrupting, interrupted **1** break in on what someone is saying by inserting a remark **2** prevent something from continuing
▷ interruption *NOUN*

intersect *VERB* intersects, intersecting, intersected **1** divide a thing by passing or lying across it **2** (said about lines or roads, etc.) cross each other
▷ intersection *NOUN*

interval *NOUN* intervals **1** a time between two events or parts of a play, etc. **2** a space between two things

---

Thesaurus

---

internal *ADJECTIVE* **1** *The house was built around an internal courtyard.* ▸ inner, interior, inside, central AN OPPOSITE IS external **2** *the country's internal affairs* ▸ domestic, home, interior, local, civil

international *ADJECTIVE* *the growth of fast international travel* ▸ global, worldwide, intercontinental, universal

interrogate *VERB* *The secret police wanted to interrogate them.* ▸ question, cross-examine, examine, investigate, (more informal) grill, (more informal) quiz

interrogation *NOUN* *The police interrogation continued all morning.* ▸ questioning, cross-examination, investigation, examination, (more informal) grilling

interrupt *VERB* **1** *He opened his mouth to interrupt.* ▸ butt in, break in, cut in, intervene **2** *People at the back of the hall began to interrupt her.* ▸ heckle, disrupt, butt in on, cut in on **3** *The news from home led them to interrupt their vacation.* ▸ suspend, break off, discontinue, delay, postpone, put off, defer **4** *The new building will interrupt the view.* ▸ break, break up, divide, disturb

interruption *NOUN* **1** *There were several interruptions during the speech.* ▸ intervention, intrusion, disruption, cutting in, disturbance **2** *A note in the mailbox warned of interruptions in the water supply.* ▸ break, disruption, suspension, pause, check, hiatus, stop

interval *NOUN* **1** *There will be an interval of 20 minutes halfway through the show.* ▸ intermission, interlude, break, pause **2** *The next class will be in a week's time and you can revise in the interval.* ▸ interim, meantime, meanwhile, pause, delay

at intervals with some time or distance between each one
[from Latin *intervallum* = space between the ramparts of a fortification, from *vallum* = rampart]

intervene VERB intervenes, intervening, intervened **1** come between two events ● *in the intervening years* **2** interrupt a discussion or fight etc. to try and stop it or change its result
▷ intervention NOUN

interview NOUN interviews a formal meeting with someone to ask him or her questions or to obtain information

interview VERB interviews, interviewing, interviewed hold an interview with someone
▷ interviewer NOUN

intestine NOUN intestines the long tube along which food passes while being absorbed by the body, between the stomach and the anus
▷ intestinal ADJECTIVE

intimate (in- tim- at) ADJECTIVE **1** very friendly with someone **2** private and personal ● *intimate thoughts* **3** detailed ● *an intimate knowledge of the country*
▷ intimately ADVERB intimacy NOUN

intimidate VERB intimidates, intimidating, intimidated frighten a person by threats into doing something
▷ intimidation NOUN

into PREPOSITION used to express **1** movement to the inside (*Go into the house.*), **2** change of condition or occupation etc. (*It broke into pieces; she went into politics.*), **3** (in division) *4 into 20* = 20 divided by 4

intolerable ADJECTIVE unbearable
▷ intolerably ADVERB

intoxicate VERB intoxicates, intoxicating, intoxicated make a person drunk or very excited
▷ intoxication NOUN

intransitive ADJECTIVE (said about a verb) used without a direct object after it, e.g., *hear* in *we can hear* (but not in *we can hear you*)
COMPARE transitive
▷ intransitively ADVERB

intravenous (in- tra- veen- us) ADJECTIVE directly into a vein

intricate ADJECTIVE very complicated
▷ intricately ADVERB intricacy NOUN

intrigue (in- treeg) VERB intrigues, intriguing, intrigued **1** interest someone very much ● *The subject intrigues me* **2** plot with someone in an underhand way

introduce VERB introduces, introducing, introduced **1** bring an idea or practice into use **2** make a person known to other people **3** announce a broadcast, speaker, etc.

Thesaurus

intimate ADJECTIVE **1** *an intimate friendship* ► close, loving, affectionate, personal, familiar, friendly, informal, sexual **2** *an intimate atmosphere* ► friendly, welcoming, warm, informal, relaxed, cosy **3** *intimate thoughts* ► personal, private, secret, confidential **4** *an intimate knowledge of the area* ► detailed, exhaustive, profound, deep, in-depth

intimidate VERB *He wanted to get his way without appearing to intimidate them.*
► threaten, bully, frighten, coerce, browbeat, menace, persecute, scare, terrify, terrorize, cow, daunt, hector, make afraid

intolerable ADJECTIVE *The noise had become intolerable.* ► unbearable, unendurable, unacceptable, insufferable, insupportable, excruciating, impossible OPPOSITES ARE tolerable, bearable

intolerant ADJECTIVE *He was extremely intolerant about religion.* ► bigoted, dogmatic, narrow-minded, opinionated, prejudiced, chauvinistic, illiberal AN OPPOSITE IS tolerant

intrepid ADJECTIVE *The four intrepid climbers had to turn back because of fierce winds.* ► bold, courageous, daring, brave, gallant, fearless, plucky, valiant

intricate ADJECTIVE *intricate designs; intricate relationships* ► complex, elaborate, ornate, detailed, complicated, convoluted, tangled, delicate, involved, sophisticated, tortuous AN OPPOSITE IS simple

intrigue NOUN **1** *a leader vulnerable to jealousy and intrigue* ► conspiracy, plotting, scheming, machination, trickery, subterfuge **2** *a family abuzz with romantic intrigues* ► affair, liaison, amour, flirtation, dalliance, intimacy

intrigue VERB **1** *These stories have always intrigued young children.* ► interest, fascinate, engross, captivate, enthral, absorb, beguile **2** *The men were suspected of intriguing against the king.* ► plot, conspire, scheme, connive, maneuver

intriguing ADJECTIVE *an intriguing account of a trip around the world* ► interesting, fascinating, engrossing, captivating, enthralling, absorbing, beguiling

introduce VERB **1** *Jane introduced us to her husband.* ► present, make known, acquaint **2** *The new owners have introduced some new features.* ► bring in, institute, initiate, establish, set up, start, begin, create, offer, propose, suggest, pioneer **3** *a new star to introduce the show* ► present, host, compère, announce

a
b
c
d
e
f
g
h
i
j
k
l
m
n
o
p
q
r
s
t
u
v
w
x
y
z

introduction NOUN introductions **1** introducing somebody or something **2** an explanation put at the beginning of a book or speech etc.
▷ **introductory** ADJECTIVE

introvert NOUN introverts a shy person who does not like to talk about his or her own thoughts and feelings with other people (The opposite is extrovert)

intrude VERB intrudes, intruding, intruded come in or join in without being wanted
▷ **intrusion** NOUN **intrusive** ADJECTIVE

intruder NOUN intruders **1** someone who intrudes **2** a burglar

intuition NOUN the power to know or understand things without having to think hard or without being taught
▷ **intuitive** ADJECTIVE **intuitively** ADVERB

Inuit (in- yoo- it) NOUN Inuit **1** a member of a people living in northern Canada and Greenland **2** the language of the Inuit
USAGE This name is now preferred to Eskimo.

inundate VERB inundates, inundating, inundated flood or overwhelm a place • We've been inundated with letters about the program.
▷ **inundation** NOUN

invade VERB invades, invading, invaded **1** attack and enter a country or area **2** crowd into a place • Tourists invade Cape Cod in summer.
▷ **invader** NOUN

invalid (in- va- lid) NOUN invalids a person who is ill or who is weakened by illness
▷ **invalidity** NOUN

invalid (in- val- id) ADJECTIVE not valid • This passport is invalid [from in- = not + Latin validus = strong or powerful]

invaluable ADJECTIVE having a value that is too great to be measured; extremely valuable

invariable ADJECTIVE not variable; never changing
▷ **invariably** ADVERB

invasion NOUN invasions attacking and entering a country or area

invent VERB invents, inventing, invented **1** be the first person to make or think of a

---

Thesaurus

---

introduction NOUN **1** the introduction of a democratic government ► institution, establishment, foundation, inauguration, beginning, development **2** The author thanks his friends in the book's introduction.
► foreword, preface, preamble, front matter, opening

introvert NOUN He enjoyed a social life despite being an introvert. ► shy person, reserved person AN OPPOSITE IS extrovert USAGE For other synonyms see the words in the next entry.

introverted ADJECTIVE a quiet and introverted character ► shy, reserved, retiring, introspective, inward-looking, thoughtful, meditative, withdrawn, contemplative, pensive, self-contained, unsociable AN OPPOSITE IS extrovert

intrude VERB intrude on No one has the right to intrude on a person's privacy in this way.
► encroach on, break in on, interrupt, interfere with, butt in on, eavesdrop on, intervene in, gatecrash

intruder NOUN Intruders left the house in a mess.
► trespasser, interloper, invader, burglar, housebreaker, prowler, robber, thief, raider

intuition NOUN **1** He relied on his intuition to get him out of the difficulty. ► instinct, intuitiveness, sixth sense, insight **2** What you say confirms all my intuitions. ► feeling, gut feeling, hunch, suspicion, premonition

invade VERB The allies invaded the country from the south. ► march into, occupy, enter,

penetrate, overrun, raid, subdue, violate, attack, descend on, encroach on

invalid ADJECTIVE (With the stress on -val-) **1** His license would be invalid in England. ► void, unacceptable, unusable, worthless, null and void AN OPPOSITE IS valid **2** It was not difficult to prove the idea invalid. ► false, fallacious, unfounded, unreasonable, unsound, incorrect, untrue, illogical, irrational, unconvincing, unscientific AN OPPOSITE IS valid

invalid ADJECTIVE (With the stress on in-) Kate has an invalid husband. ► sick, ailing, infirm, disabled, incapacitated, bedridden

invaluable ADJECTIVE James is an invaluable member of the team. ► crucial, indispensable, irreplaceable, precious, priceless, useful, valuable, incalculable, inestimable AN OPPOSITE IS worthless USAGE Note that invaluable is not the opposite of valuable: for this you should use valueless.

invasion NOUN **1** an air invasion of the island ► attack (on), occupation, incursion, seizure, annexation, overrunning, onslaught, raid **2** the annual invasion of tourists ► influx, incursion, inundation, flood, horde, spate, stream, swarm, throng, infestation

invent VERB **1** He invented a new board game.
► create, devise, conceive, formulate, improvise, originate **2** They invented any excuse to avoid going near the swimming pool. ► make up, concoct, fabricate, manufacture, (more informal) cook up

A B C D E F G H I J K L M N O P Q R S T U V W X Y Z

particular thing **2** make up a false story • *She had to make an excuse.*
▷ **invention** NOUN **inventor** NOUN **inventive** ADJECTIVE

invertebrate NOUN **invertebrates** an animal without a backbone
▷ **invertebrate** ADJECTIVE

invest VERB **invests, investing, invested 1** use money to make a profit, e.g., by lending it in return for interest to be paid, or by buying stocks and shares or property **2** give somebody an honor, medal, or special title in a formal ceremony
▷ **investment** NOUN **investor** NOUN

investigate VERB **investigates, investigating, investigated** find out as much as you can about something; make a systematic inquiry
▷ **investigation** NOUN **investigator** NOUN **investigative** ADJECTIVE

invigilate VERB **invigilates, invigilating, invigilated** supervise candidates at an examination
▷ **invigilation** NOUN **invigilator** NOUN

invigorate VERB **invigorates, invigorating, invigorated** give a person strength or courage
COMPARE **vigour**

invincible ADJECTIVE not able to be defeated
▷ **invincibly** ADVERB **invincibility** NOUN

invisible ADJECTIVE not visible; not able to be seen
▷ **invisibly** ADVERB **invisibility** NOUN

invite VERB **invites, inviting, invited 1** ask a person to come or do something **2** be likely to cause something to happen • *You are inviting disaster*
▷ **invitation** NOUN

invoice NOUN **invoices** a list of goods sent or work done, with the prices charged

involuntary ADJECTIVE not deliberate; unintentional
▷ **involuntarily** ADVERB

involve VERB **involves, involving, involved 1** have as a part; make a thing necessary • *The job involves hard work.* **2** make someone share or take part in something • *They involved us in their charity work.*
▷ **involvement** NOUN

Thesaurus

invention NOUN **1** *the invention of printing* ► development, origination, creation, devising, innovation, pioneering **2** *writing that shows a lot of invention* ► originality, creativity, imagination, ingenuity, inventiveness, resourcefulness, inspiration **3** *The excuse was pure invention.* ► fabrication, fantasy, fiction, deceit, concoction

inventor NOUN *the inventor of the telephone* ► creator, originator, designer, discoverer, architect, author, maker

invert VERB *A storm inverted the little boat.* ► overturn, reverse, turn upside down, upset, capsize

investigate VERB *Police are investigating the discovery of a body.* ► inquire into, look into, follow up, probe, examine, explore, consider, study, gather evidence about, scrutinize, (*more informal*) go into

investigation NOUN *The problem needs further investigation. There will have to be an official investigation.* ► examination, inquiry, research, scrutiny, study, survey, inspection, inquisition, (*informal*) probing

invincible ADJECTIVE *the invincible power of the invading armies* ► unbeatable, unassailable, indestructible, indomitable, unconquerable, invulnerable, mighty

invisible ADJECTIVE *The house was invisible in the dark.* ► hidden, obscured, concealed, undetectable, unnoticeable, imperceptible, unnoticed, unseen, out of sight, covered, disguised, inconspicuous AN OPPOSITE IS visible

invitation NOUN **1** *an invitation to attend the conference* ► call, summons, request **2** *An open door is an invitation to any passing thief.* ► temptation, encouragement, enticement, lure, provocation, inducement

invite VERB **1** *They've invited us to dinner on Saturday.* ► ask, request the company of, welcome, summon **2** *Using emotive language might invite trouble.* ► provoke, cause, generate, engender, include, embrace, elicit

inviting ADJECTIVE *the inviting sight of a buffet lunch* ► attractive, appealing, welcome, pleasant, enticing, agreeable, appetizing, seductive

involuntary ADJECTIVE *She gave an involuntary shudder.* ► reflex, automatic, unconscious, spontaneous, unthinking, unintentional, conditioned, impulsive, instinctive AN OPPOSITE IS deliberate

involve VERB **1** *Her job involves a lot of travel.* ► necessitate, entail, require, demand, mean **2** *These are decisions that involve everybody.* ► affect, concern, interest, include, embrace, take in, touch **3** *The project involved them in community work.* ► occupy, engage, absorb, engross **4** *A drug habit can rapidly involve them in crime.* ► implicate, associate, embroil, entangle

involved ADJECTIVE **1** *a long and involved story* ► complex, complicated, convoluted, elaborate, intricate, tangled, confusing, difficult, (*more informal*) knotty AN OPPOSITE IS straightforward **2** *She is totally involved in her work.* ► occupied, engrossed, absorbed, engaged, preoccupied, caught up, committed (to), dedicated (to) AN OPPOSITE IS uninvolved

involvement NOUN **1** *her involvement in charity work.* ► interest, participation, activity **2** *There was no doubting their involvement in the plot.* ► complicity, connivance, participation, entanglement, association

a b c d e f g h **i** j k l m n o p q r s t u v w x y z

A
B
C
D
E
F
G
H
I
J
K
L
M
N
O
P
Q
R
S
T
U
V
W
X
Y
Z

inward ADJECTIVE **1** on the inside **2** going or facing inwards

inward ADVERB toward the inside

iodine NOUN a chemical substance used as an antiseptic

ion NOUN ions an electrically charged particle

ionosphere (I- on- os- feer) NOUN a region of the upper atmosphere, containing ions

IQ ABBREVIATION intelligence quotient; a number showing how a person's intelligence compares with that of an average person

IRA ABBREVIATION Irish Republican Army

iridescent ADJECTIVE showing rainbowlike colors
  ▷ **iridescence** NOUN

iron NOUN irons **1** a hard grey metal **2** a device with a flat base that is heated for smoothing clothes or cloth **3** a tool made of iron • *a branding iron*
  ▷ **iron** ADJECTIVE

iron VERB irons, ironing, ironed smooth clothes or cloth with an iron

iron out sort out a difficulty or problem

Iron Age NOUN the time when tools and weapons were made of iron

ironic (I- ron- ik) ADJECTIVE using irony; full of irony
  ▷ **ironical** ADJECTIVE **ironically** ADVERB

ironmonger NOUN ironmongers a shopkeeper who sells tools and other metal objects
  ▷ **ironmongery** NOUN

irony (I- ron- ee) NOUN ironies **1** saying the opposite of what you mean in order to emphasize it, e.g., saying "What a lovely day" when it is pouring rain **2** an oddly contradictory situation • *The irony of it is that I tripped while telling someone else to be careful.*

irrational ADJECTIVE not rational; illogical
  ▷ **irrationally** ADVERB

irregular ADJECTIVE **1** not regular; uneven **2** against the rules or usual custom **3** (said about troops) not in the regular armed forces
  ▷ **irregularly** ADVERB **irregularity** NOUN

irrepressible ADJECTIVE unable to be repressed; always lively and cheerful
  ▷ **irrepressibly** ADVERB

irreproachable ADJECTIVE blameless or faultless
  ▷ **irreproachably** ADVERB

irresistible ADJECTIVE too strong or attractive to be resisted
  ▷ **irresistibly** ADVERB

irrespective ADJECTIVE not taking something into account • *Prizes are awarded to winners, irrespective of age.*

irresponsible ADJECTIVE not showing a proper sense of responsibility
  ▷ **irresponsibly** ADVERB **irresponsibility** NOUN

Thesaurus

---

irate ADJECTIVE *The helpline has to deal with hundreds of irate callers.* ► angry, enraged, furious, incensed, infuriated, indignant, displeased, outraged

ironic ADJECTIVE **1** *The tone of Sarah's voice was sharply ironic.* ► sarcastic, ironical, satirical, wry, derisive, double-edged, mocking **2** *It is ironic that after criticizing New York so much he should end up living there.* ► paradoxical, strange, peculiar, odd, weird, incongruous

irrational ADJECTIVE *an irrational fear of flying* ► illogical, baseless, unreasonable, senseless, arbitrary, unsound, absurd AN OPPOSITE IS rational

irregular ADJECTIVE **1** *an irregular surface* ► uneven, rough, coarse, bumpy, pitted **2** *an irregular heartbeat; an irregular pattern* ► variable, fluctuating, erratic, fitful, haphazard, unsystematic, intermittent **3** *Her appointment was most irregular.* ► improper, abnormal, unorthodox, anomalous, unconventional, against the rules

irrelevant ADJECTIVE *Don't waste time on irrelevant details.* ► inappropriate, unnecessary, inessential, extraneous, peripheral, immaterial, inapplicable, pointless,

unconnected, unrelated AN OPPOSITE IS relevant

irreparable ADJECTIVE *A power failure can cause irreparable damage.* ► permanent, irretrievable, irreversible, irremediable, unrectifiable, lasting, irrecoverable, unalterable, incurable AN OPPOSITE IS reparable

irreplaceable ADJECTIVE *a work of art that is irreplaceable* ► unique, inimitable, indispensable, matchless, priceless, rare OPPOSITES ARE replaceable, common

irresistible ADJECTIVE **1** *The temptation to laugh was irresistible.* ► overpowering, overwhelming, inescapable, inexorable, powerful, seductive, unavoidable, compelling, persuasive **2** *She has an irresistible laugh.* ► attractive, appealing, enticing, alluring, seductive, fetching, captivating, beguiling

irresponsible ADJECTIVE **1** *an irresponsible attitude* ► reckless, rash, inconsiderate, thoughtless, careless, immoral, selfish, shiftless AN OPPOSITE IS responsible **2** *They sometimes behave like irresponsible teenagers.* ► immature, unreliable, feckless, unthinking, untrustworthy

irrigate VERB irrigates, irrigating, irrigated supply land with water so that crops can grow
▷ **irrigation** NOUN

irritable ADJECTIVE easily annoyed; bad-tempered
▷ **irritably** ADVERB **irritability** NOUN

irritate VERB irritates, irritating, irritated **1** annoy **2** cause itching
▷ **irritation** NOUN **irritant** ADJECTIVE, NOUN

Islam NOUN the religion of Muslims
▷ **Islamic** ADJECTIVE

island NOUN islands **1** a piece of land surrounded by water **2** something that resembles an island because it is isolated or detached • a traffic island

isn't (mainly spoken) is not

isobar (I- so- bar) NOUN isobars a line on a map connecting places that have the same atmospheric pressure

isolate VERB isolates, isolating, isolated place a person or thing apart or alone; separate
▷ **isolation** NOUN

isosceles (I- soss- il- eez) ADJECTIVE an isosceles triangle has two sides of equal length

isotope NOUN isotopes (in science) a form of an element that differs from other forms in the structure of its nucleus but has the same chemical properties as the other forms

ISP ABBREVIATION Internet service provider, a company providing individual users with a connection to the Internet

issue VERB issues, issuing, issued **1** come or go out; flow out **2** supply; give out • We issued one blanket to each refugee. **3** send out • They issued a gale warning **4** put out for sale; publish **5** come or go out; flow out

issue NOUN issues **1** a subject for discussion or concern • What are the real issues? **2** a particular edition of a newspaper or magazine • The December issue of Vogue **3** issuing something • The issue of passports is held up. **4** (formal) heirs • He died without issue. **take issue with** disagree with

isthmus (iss- mus) NOUN isthmuses a narrow strip of land connecting two larger pieces of land

IT ABBREVIATION information technology

it PRONOUN **1** the thing being talked about **2** the player who has to catch others in a game **3** used in statements about the weather or about circumstances, etc. • It is raining. • It is six miles to New York. **4** used as an indefinite object • Run for it! **5** used to refer to a phrase • It is unlikely that she will fail.

italic (it- al- ik) ADJECTIVE printed with sloping letters (called italics) like this.

Thesaurus

irreverent ADJECTIVE an irreverent approach to authority ▶ disrespectful, discourteous, disdainful, insolent, impertinent, impudent, scornful, flippant, casual, rude OPPOSITES ARE reverent, respectful

irrevocable ADJECTIVE an irrevocable decision ▶ unalterable, unchangeable, irreversible, immutable, binding, final, firm, fixed, settled, hard and fast AN OPPOSITE IS reversible

irritable ADJECTIVE Harry sat back with an irritable look on his face. ▶ bad-tempered, irascible, grumpy, testy, grouchy, touchy, tetchy, crotchety, cantankerous, peevish, fractious, cross, (more informal) stroppy, (more informal) shirty OPPOSITES ARE good-tempered, good-humored, affable

irritate VERB I was letting silly things irritate me. ▶ annoy, displease, anger, infuriate, enrage, exasperate, incense, peeve, vex, madden, aggravate, antagonize, inflame, make angry, (more informal) needle, (more informal) rile, (more informal) bug, (more informal) rub up the wrong way OPPOSITES ARE please, gratify

irritation NOUN It was hard to hide our irritation at such rudeness. ▶ annoyance, indignation, displeasure, exasperation, pique, chagrin, vexation

isolate VERB **1** Their extreme political views tended to isolate them from their contemporaries. ▶ separate, set apart, keep apart, cut off, segregate, detach, insulate, seclude, alienate, exclude, single out **2** Sophisticated cameras can easily isolate offending vehicles. ▶ identify, recognize, pick out, single out, pinpoint, distinguish

isolated ADJECTIVE **1** an isolated town in eastern Malaysia ▶ remote, outlying, secluded, solitary, inaccessible, out of the way, deserted AN OPPOSITE IS accessible **2** an isolated occurrence ▶ unique, special, exceptional, untypical, abnormal

issue NOUN **1** The society debates political issues. ▶ matter, concern, subject, topic, affair, point, question, argument, controversy, dispute, problem **2** a special issue of the magazine ▶ edition, number, installment, publication, printing

issue VERB **1** Smoke issued from the top of the building. ▶ emerge, emanate, erupt, flow out, rise, appear, come out, gush, leak, spring **2** The ambassador issued a formal statement. ▶ publish, publicize, release, circulate, distribute, give out, print, produce, send out

itch ➡ -ize

itch VERB **itches, itching, itched** **1** have or feel a tickling sensation in the skin that makes you want to scratch it **2** long to do something

item NOUN **items** **1** one thing in a list or group of things **2** one piece of news or article, etc., in a newspaper or bulletin

its POSSESSIVE PRONOUN belonging to it ● *The cat hurt its paw.*
USAGE Do not put an apostrophe into *its* unless you mean "it is" or "it has" (see the next entry).

it's (*mainly spoken*) **1** it is ● *It's very hot.* **2** it has ● *It's broken all records.*
USAGE Do not confuse with *its.*

itself PRONOUN it and nothing else by itself on its own; alone

ivory NOUN **1** the hard creamy-white substance that forms elephants' tusks **2** a creamy-white color

ivy NOUN **ivies** a climbing evergreen plant with shiny leaves

-ize or **-ise** SUFFIX forms verbs meaning "bring or come into a certain condition" (e.g., *civilize*), or "treat in a certain way" (e.g., *pasteurize*), or "have a certain feeling" (e.g., *sympathize*)

Thesaurus

itch NOUN **1** *I have an itch on my back.* ► itchiness, tickle, tingling, irritation, need to scratch **2** *She felt an itch to start painting.* ► desire, hankering, longing, yearning, urge, wish, impulse, lust, need, ache, impatience, restlessness, (*more informal*) yen

itch VERB **1** *The warmth made my skin itch.* ► tickle, tingle, be irritated **2** *They were itching to leave.* ► long, hanker, yearn, be eager, be keen

item NOUN **1** *an item of equipment* ► article, bit, object, component, ingredient **2** *a news item* ► report, article, account, feature, notice, piece **3** *several items on the agenda* ► topic, subject

Jj

jab *VERB* jabs, jabbing, jabbed poke roughly; push a thing into something

jack *NOUN* jacks **1** a device for lifting something heavy off the ground **2** a playing card with a picture of a young man **3** a small white ball aimed at in bowls
jack of all trades someone who can do many different kinds of work

jackdaw *NOUN* jackdaws a kind of small crow

jacket *NOUN* jackets **1** a short coat, usually reaching to the hips **2** a cover to keep the heat in a water tank, etc. **3** a paper wrapper for a book **4** the skin of a potato that is baked without being peeled

jackpot *NOUN* jackpots an amount of prize money that increases until someone wins it
hit the jackpot **1** win a large prize **2** have remarkable luck or success

Jacuzzi (ja-koo-zi) *NOUN* Jacuzzis (*trademark*) a large bath in which underwater jets of water massage the body

jagged (jag-id) *ADJECTIVE* having an uneven edge with sharp points

jaguar *NOUN* jaguars a large fierce South American animal rather like a leopard [via Portuguese from Tupi (a South American language)]

jail *NOUN* jails a prison

Jain (jayn) *NOUN* Jains a believer in an Indian religion that has similarities to Buddhism

jam *NOUN* jams **1** a sweet food made of fruit boiled with sugar until it is thick **2** a lot of people, cars, or logs, etc., crowded together so that movement is difficult
in a jam in a difficult situation

jam *VERB* jams, jamming, jammed **1** make or become fixed and difficult to move ● *The window has jammed.* **2** crowd or squeeze into a space **3** push something forcibly ● *jam the brakes on* **4** block a broadcast by causing interference with the transmission

jamboree *NOUN* jamborees a large party or celebration

jangle *VERB* jangles, jangling, jangled make a loud harsh ringing sound
▷ **jangle** *NOUN*

janitor *NOUN* janitors a caretaker

January *NOUN* the first month of the year [named after *Janus*, a Roman god of gates and beginnings, usually shown with two faces that look in opposite directions]

jar¹ *NOUN* jars a container made of glass or pottery

jar² *VERB* jars, jarring, jarred **1** cause an unpleasant jolt or shock **2** sound harshly ● *Her voice really jars me.*
jar *NOUN* jars a jarring effect

jargon *NOUN* words or expressions used by a profession or group that are difficult for other people to understand ● *computer jargon*

jaunt *NOUN* jaunts a short trip

jaunty *ADJECTIVE* jauntier, jauntiest lively and cheerful
▷ **jauntily** *ADVERB* **jauntiness** *NOUN*

Thesaurus

jab *VERB* He laughed and jabbed his friend in the ribs. ► poke, prod, dig, nudge, elbow, shove

jack *VERB* jack up He got a passerby to help him jack up the car and change the tire. ► lift, raise, hoist, lever up

jagged *ADJECTIVE* He gashed his head against a jagged branch. ► spiky, uneven, broken, irregular, ragged, rough, toothed, serrated, zigzag OPPOSITES ARE even, smooth

jail *NOUN* a building that used to be the town jail ► prison, jailhouse, guardhouse, (*more informal*) clink

jail *VERB* If he's found guilty he'll be jailed. ► send to prison, put in prison, imprison, give a custodial sentence to

jam *NOUN* **1** a long jam on the highway ► tailback, hold-up, obstruction, blockage, bottleneck **2** We're in a bit of a jam. ► predicament, quandary, embarrassment, difficulty, dilemma, tight corner, trouble, plight, (*more informal*) fix, (*more informal*) hole **3** Have some homemade jam. ► preserve, conserve, jelly, marmalade

jam *VERB* **1** They try to jam too many people in the elevators. ► cram, pack, squeeze, stuff, crowd, crush, ram, squash **2** Protesters jammed one side of the highway. ► block, clog, obstruct, congest **3** I'll jam the door open with a newspaper. ► prop, stick, wedge **4** The window has jammed. ► stick, become stuck, become wedged, become lodged, seize

jangle *VERB* He jangled his keys as he walked to the door. Bracelets jangled on her wrists. ► jingle, clink, tinkle, clang

jar *NOUN* a jar of honey ► pot, drum, glass, crock, container

jar *VERB* **1** jar on His whining voice jarred on me. ► grate on, annoy, irritate, irk, exasperate, set your teeth on edge **2** The fall jarred her whole body. ► jolt, jerk, shake, shock, vibrate

jargon *NOUN* The instructions are full of difficult jargon. ► technical language, parlance, idiom, (*more informal*) gobbledegook

jaunt *NOUN* a jaunt around the old city ► trip, outing, excursion, tour, expedition, journey

javelin NOUN javelins a lightweight spear

jaw NOUN jaws **1** either of the two bones that form the framework of the mouth **2** the lower part of the face **3** something shaped like the jaws or used for gripping things **4** (slang) talking

jazz NOUN a kind of music with strong rhythm, often improvised
  ▷ **jazzy** ADJECTIVE

jealous ADJECTIVE **1** unhappy or resentful because you feel that someone is your rival or is better or luckier than yourself **2** careful in keeping something • He is very jealous of his own rights.
  ▷ **jealously** ADVERB **jealousy** NOUN

jeans PLURAL NOUN trousers made of strong cotton fabric

Jeep NOUN Jeeps (trademark) a small sturdy motor vehicle with four-wheel drive, especially one used in the army

jeer VERB jeers, jeering, jeered laugh or shout at somebody rudely or scornfully
  ▷ **jeer** NOUN

jelly NOUN jellies **1** a soft transparent food **2** any soft slippery substance
  ▷ **jellied** ADJECTIVE

jellyfish NOUN jellyfish a sea animal with a body like jelly

jerk VERB jerks, jerking, jerked **1** make a sudden sharp movement **2** pull something suddenly

jerk NOUN jerks **1** a sudden sharp movement **2** (slang) a stupid person
  ▷ **jerky** ADJECTIVE **jerkily** ADVERB

jerkin NOUN jerkins a sleeveless jacket

jersey NOUN jerseys **1** a pullover with sleeves **2** a plain machine-knitted material used for making clothes

jest NOUN jests a joke [from Middle English gest = a story]

jester NOUN jesters a professional entertainer at a royal court in the Middle Ages

jet NOUN jets **1** a stream of water, gas, flame, etc., shot out from a narrow opening **2** a spout or nozzle from which a jet comes **3** an aircraft driven by engines that send out a high-speed jet of hot gases at the back

jet lag NOUN extreme tiredness that a person feels after a long flight between different time zones

jettison VERB jettisons, jettisoning, jettisoned **1** throw something overboard **2** get rid of something that is no longer wanted **3** release or drop something from an aircraft or spacecraft in flight

jetty NOUN jetties a small landing stage

Thesaurus

---

jazzy ADJECTIVE **1** jazzy music ▸ animated, lively, rhythmic, spirited, syncopated **2** a jazzy color scheme ▸ bright, bold, colorful, gaudy, showy, loud, flashy OPPOSITES ARE sober, dull

jealous ADJECTIVE **1** Jason was jealous of her ability to come up with good ideas. ▸ envious, resentful, grudging, covetous, desirous OPPOSITES ARE proud, admiring **2** the story of a beautiful woman who is locked away by her jealous lover ▸ suspicious, distrustful, possessive, protective, dominating AN OPPOSITE IS trusting **3** They are very jealous of their privileges. ▸ protective, defensive, watchful, mindful AN OPPOSITE IS unconcerned (about)

jealousy NOUN **1** He was overcome by jealousy at their good fortune. ▸ envy, resentment, bitterness, discontent, covetousness **2** She could no longer stand her lover's jealousy. ▸ suspicion, distrust, mistrust, possessiveness

jeer VERB The demonstrators were jeering the police. ▸ mock, taunt, scoff, deride, sneer at, abuse, insult, barrack, heckle AN OPPOSITE IS cheer

jeer NOUN comments that brought jeers from his schoolmates ▸ taunt, sneer, jibe, insult, boo, hiss, ridicule, disapproval AN OPPOSITE IS cheer

jeopardize VERB He wouldn't jeopardize his career by taking risks now. ▸ threaten, endanger, put at risk, compromise, harm, imperil, expose

jeopardy NOUN in jeopardy With the country at war the empire was in jeopardy ▸ in danger, in peril, at risk, vulnerable, under threat AN OPPOSITE IS secure

jerk VERB **1** She jerked her hand from his and turned away. ▸ pull, tug, pluck, wrench, yank, tweak **2** The car jerked forward. ▸ jolt, lurch, bump, bounce

jerk NOUN **1** He pulled away his hand with a jerk. ▸ tug, pull, wrench, yank, twitch **2** The bus stopped with a jerk. ▸ jolt, lurch, start, bump, shock

jerky ADJECTIVE Her voice had grown jerky and breathless. ▸ fitful, spasmodic, convulsive, shaky, twitchy, jumpy, uncoordinated, incoherent OPPOSITES ARE steady, smooth

jest NOUN The men talked and exchanged jests. ▸ joke, witticism, quip, banter

jest VERB He admitted that he had been jesting. ▸ joke, fool, hoax, tease, (more informal) kid

jet NOUN **1** a jet of water ▸ stream, spurt, squirt, gush, spout, spray, flow, fountain, rush **2** He pointed the jet at the flames. ▸ nozzle, sprinkler

Jew NOUN Jews a member of a people descended from the ancient tribes of Israel, or who practices the religion of this people
▷ **Jewish** ADJECTIVE

jewel NOUN jewels **1** a precious stone **2** an ornament containing precious stones
▷ **jeweled** ADJECTIVE
[from early French]

jewelry NOUN jewels and similar ornaments for wearing

jigsaw NOUN jigsaws **1** a picture cut into irregular pieces which are then shuffled and fitted together again for amusement **2** a saw that can cut curved shapes

jilt VERB jilts, jilting, jilted abandon a boyfriend or girlfriend, especially after promising to marry him or her

jingle VERB jingles, jingling, jingled make or cause to make a tinkling sound

jingle NOUN jingles **1** a jingling sound **2** a very simple verse or tune, especially one used in advertising

jitters PLURAL NOUN (informal) a feeling of extreme nervousness
▷ **jittery** ADJECTIVE

job NOUN jobs **1** work that someone does regularly to earn a living **2** a piece of work to be done **3** (informal) a difficult task • You'll have a job to lift that box.

jockey NOUN jockeys a person who rides horses in races

jodhpurs (jod- perz) PLURAL NOUN pants for horse riding, fitting closely from the knee to the ankle [named after Jodhpur, a city in India, where similar trousers are worn]

jog VERB jogs, jogging, jogged **1** run or trot slowly, especially for exercise **2** give something a slight push
▷ **jogger** NOUN
jog someone's memory help someone to remember something

jogtrot NOUN a slow steady trot

join VERB joins, joining, joined **1** put or come together; fasten or connect **2** take part with others in doing something • We all joined in the chorus. **3** become a member of a group or organization • join the navy
join up enlist in the armed forces

joint NOUN joints **1** a place where two things are joined **2** the place where two bones fit

Thesaurus

jewel NOUN **1** a tiara encrusted with jewels
► gem, gemstone, precious stone **2** His girlfriend was a jewel. ► treasure, angel, paragon, pearl, wonder

jewelry NOUN A street fair was selling ethnic jewelry. ► gems, jewels, ornaments, (more informal) sparklers

jilt VERB Hugh had done her a favor by jilting her.
► reject, desert, discard, abandon, (more informal) ditch

jingle NOUN **1** He could hear the jingle of her bracelet. ► jangle, clink, tinkle **2** An advertising jingle kept coming into his head. ► slogan, song, catchline, ditty, refrain

jingle VERB The coins jingled in their pockets.
► jangle, clink, tinkle, clang

jinx NOUN They wondered whether the jinx would strike again. ► curse, spell, evil eye, bad luck

jinxed ADJECTIVE It was almost as if the house was jinxed. ► cursed, bewitched, bedevilled, under a spell

jitters PLURAL NOUN (informal) a fit of jitters
► nervousness, nerves, anxiety, agitation, tension, edginess, restlessness

jittery ADJECTIVE He felt jittery about meeting her again. ► nervous, anxious, agitated, tense, edgy, fretful, restless, ill at ease

job NOUN **1** The job involves some weekend work.
► occupation, employment, position, situation, post, work, career **2** Painting the house will be a long job. ► task, piece of work, undertaking, operation, assignment, project,

chore **3** It's my job to lock up in the evenings.
► responsibility, duty, task, concern, role, function **4** (informal) We had a job finding the house. ► problem, difficulty, difficult task, hard time, struggle

jobless ADJECTIVE Two percent of the population is jobless. ► unemployed, out of work, laid off, redundant OPPOSITES ARE employed, in work

jocular ADJECTIVE a few jocular remarks
► humorous, funny, witty, comical, amusing, droll, joking AN OPPOSITE IS serious USAGE Remember that funny can mean "peculiar" as well as "jocular," and it is sometimes better to use another word.

jog VERB **1** He jogged her elbow as he walked past.
► nudge, prod, jolt, jar, bump, jostle **2** I need a clue to jog my memory. ► prompt, stir, arouse, stimulate, remind **3** They were jogging through the park. ► trot, run, jogtrot

join VERB **1** Join the two pieces together.
► connect, fasten, attach, couple, merge, stick, tie, glue **2** Her son wanted to join the army. ► enlist in, enrol in, sign up in, enter, volunteer for, become a member of **3** We joined the peace march along the route. ► follow, go along with, tag along with, accompany **4** The two roads join here. ► meet, come together, converge

join NOUN You have to look hard to see the join.
► joint, connection, seam, knot, link, mend

joint NOUN the joint between the wall and the flat roof ► join, connection, junction, seam

joint ➡ jubilee

together **3** a large piece of meat cut ready for cooking **4** (*informal*) a cannabis cigarette

joint ADJECTIVE shared or done by two or more people, nations, etc. • *a joint project*
▷ **jointly** ADVERB

joke NOUN **jokes** something said or done to make people laugh

joke VERB **jokes, joking, joked 1** make jokes **2** tease someone or not be serious • *I'm only joking*

joker NOUN **jokers 1** someone who jokes **2** an extra playing card with a jester on it

jolly ADJECTIVE **jollier, jolliest** cheerful and good-humored
▷ **jollity** NOUN

jolly ADVERB (*informal*) very • *jolly good*

jolt VERB **jolts, jolting, jolted 1** shake or dislodge something with a sudden sharp movement **2** move along jerkily, e.g., on a rough road **3** give someone a shock

jolt NOUN **jolts 1** a jolting movement **2** a shock

jostle VERB **jostles, jostling, jostled** push roughly, especially in a crowd

jot VERB **jots, jotting, jotted** write something quickly • *Let me jot down that phone number.*

jotter NOUN **jotters** a notepad or notebook

joule (jool) NOUN **joules** a unit of work or energy

journal NOUN **journals 1** a newspaper or magazine **2** a diary

journalist NOUN **journalists** a person who writes for a newspaper or magazine
▷ **journalism** NOUN **journalistic** ADJECTIVE

journey NOUN **journeys 1** going from one place to another **2** the distance or time taken to travel somewhere • *two days' journey*

journey VERB **journeys, journeying, journeyed** make a journey

jovial ADJECTIVE cheerful and good-humored
▷ **jovially** ADVERB **joviality** NOUN

joy NOUN **joys 1** a feeling of great pleasure or happiness **2** a thing that causes joy
▷ **joyful** ADJECTIVE **joyfully** ADVERB **joyfulness** NOUN **joyous** ADJECTIVE **joyously** ADVERB

joyride NOUN **joyrides** a drive in a stolen car for amusement
▷ **joyrider** NOUN **joyriding** NOUN

joystick NOUN **joysticks 1** the control lever of an aircraft **2** a device for moving a cursor or image on a VDU screen, especially in computer games

JP ABBREVIATION Justice of the Peace

jubilant ADJECTIVE rejoicing or triumphant
▷ **jubilantly** ADVERB **jubilation** NOUN

jubilee (joo- bil- ee) NOUN **jubilees** a special anniversary: *silver* (25th), *golden* (50th), and *diamond* (60th) *jubilee*

Thesaurus

joint ADJECTIVE *The two artists are holding a joint exhibition.* ► combined, shared, common, collaborative, coordinated, cooperative, collective, communal, concerted, united, mutual OPPOSITES ARE separate, discrete, individual

joke NOUN *They sat all evening telling each other jokes.* ► funny story, jest, witticism, wisecrack, pleasantry, quip, (*more informal*) crack, (*more informal*) gag

joke VERB **1** *He laughed and joked with his friends.* ► tell jokes, crack jokes, jest, clown, have a laugh, be facetious **2** *From the look on her face I'd say she was only joking.* ► fool, tease, hoax, (*more informal*) kid

joker NOUN *She seems quite a joker, but she has her serious side.* ► jester, comedian, comic, humorist, wag, wit, clown

jolly ADJECTIVE *We had a jolly time. He was in a jolly mood when he came back.* ► cheerful, merry, cheery, happy, jovial, exuberant, hearty

jolt VERB **1** *The car jolted along the rough roads.* ► bump, bounce, jerk, jog, shake, shudder **2** *The fierceness of his remarks jolted her.* ► startle, surprise, shock, disturb, disconcert, upset, discompose, astonish, nonplus

jot VERB **jot down** *The man jotted down my details.* ► write down, note down, take down, scribble, make a note of

journal NOUN **1** *an academic journal* ► periodical, publication, magazine, gazette, digest **2** *She kept a journal of the voyage.* ► diary, log, record, chronicle, account

journalist NOUN *A journalist wanted to hear his story.* ► reporter, correspondent, columnist, feature-writer, contributor, writer

journey NOUN *The journey takes you through three countries.* ► trip, route, itinerary, travels, voyage, peregrination USAGE You normally use *voyage* to mean a long journey by sea.

joy NOUN *There was a look of joy on her face.* ► delight, bliss, pleasure, happiness, gladness, ecstasy, elation, joyfulness, exultation, rapture, euphoria, exuberance OPPOSITES ARE sorrow, misery

joyful ADJECTIVE *Kate set off with joyful enthusiasm.* ► cheerful, happy, joyous, jubilant, bright, sunny, lively, elated, animated, contented, buoyant, good-humored, lighthearted, chirpy AN OPPOSITE IS sad

jubilant ADJECTIVE *Jubilant fans surged on to the pitch.* ► delighted, joyful, overjoyed, exultant, joyous, elated, ecstatic, thrilled

jubilee NOUN *a royal jubilee* ► anniversary, celebration, festival, gala, carnival, commemoration

Judaism (joo- day- izm) NOUN the religion of the Jewish people

judge NOUN judges **1** a person appointed to hear cases in a lawcourt and decide what should be done **2** a person deciding who has won a contest or competition **3** someone who is good at forming opinions or making decisions • *She's a good judge of character.*

judge VERB judges, judging, judged **1** act as a judge **2** form and give an opinion **3** estimate • *He judged the distance carefully*

judgment NOUN judgments **1** judging **2** the decision made by a lawcourt **3** someone's opinion **4** the ability to judge wisely **5** something considered as a punishment from God • *It's a judgment on you!*

judicial ADJECTIVE to do with lawcourts, judges, or judgments • *the U.S. judicial system*
▷ **judicially** ADVERB
USAGE Do not confuse with **judicious**.

judicious (joo- dish- us) ADJECTIVE having or showing good sense or good judgement
▷ **judiciously** ADVERB
USAGE Do not confuse with **judicial**.

judo NOUN a Japanese method of self-defence without using weapons [from Japanese *ju* = gentle + *do* = way]

jug NOUN jugs a container for holding and pouring liquids, with a handle and a lip

juggernaut NOUN juggernauts a huge truck [named after a Hindu god whose image was dragged in procession on a huge wheeled vehicle]

juggle VERB juggles, juggling, juggled **1** toss and catch a number of objects skillfully for entertainment, keeping one or more in the air

at any time **2** rearrange or alter things skillfully or in order to deceive people
▷ **juggler** NOUN

jugular ADJECTIVE to do with the throat or neck • *the jugular veins*

juice NOUN juices **1** the liquid from fruit, vegetables, or other food **2** a liquid produced by the body • *the digestive juices*
▷ **juicy** ADJECTIVE

jukebox NOUN jukeboxes a machine that automatically plays a record you have selected when you put a coin in

July NOUN the seventh month of the year [named after Julius Caesar, who was born in this month]

jumble VERB jumbles, jumbling, jumbled mix things up into a confused mass

jumble NOUN a confused mixture of things; a muddle

jumbo NOUN jumbos **1** something very large; a jumbo jet **2** an elephant

jumbo jet NOUN jumbo jets a very large jet aircraft

jump VERB jumps, jumping, jumped **1** move up suddenly from the ground into the air **2** go over something by jumping • *The horse jumped the fence.* **3** pass over something; miss out part of a book, etc. **4** move suddenly in surprise **5** pass quickly to a different place or level
jump at (*informal*) accept something eagerly
jump on (*informal*) start criticizing someone
jump the gun start before you should
jump the queue not wait your turn

Thesaurus

judge NOUN **1** *The judges could not agree on a winner.* ▸ adjudicator, arbiter, arbitrator, assessor, moderator, referee, umpire **2** *a good judge of art* ▸ connoisseur, authority (on), expert (on), critic

judge VERB **1** *A magistrate will judge the case.* ▸ try, hear, sit in judgment on, adjudicate on, decide **2** *A panel of experts will judge the ten best entries.* ▸ assess, appraise, decide, evaluate, review, examine **3** *We judged that she had been misled.* ▸ conclude, decide, consider, believe, think, reckon, determine, come to the view, form the opinion

judgment NOUN **1** *the judgment of the court* ▸ verdict, decision, adjudication, ruling, finding, pronouncement, sentence **2** *He showed a lack of judgment.* ▸ understanding, discernment, perception, wisdom, sense, common sense, acumen, prudence **3** *my judgment of the situation* ▸ assessment,

appraisal, evaluation, estimate, analysis, view, opinion, belief

jug NOUN *a jug of water* ▸ pitcher, carafe, flagon, ewer, crock, vessel

juice NOUN *Add the juice of a lemon.* ▸ liquid, fluid, extract, essence

juicy ADJECTIVE **1** *a juicy pear* ▸ succulent, tender, moist, soft, ripe AN OPPOSITE IS dry **2** *a juicy piece of gossip* ▸ interesting, lurid, spicy, colourful, racy

jumble NOUN *Clothes lay on the floor in a jumble.* ▸ muddle, hotchpotch, mess, clutter, chaos, confusion, disorder

jumble VERB *I'll try not to jumble the photographs.* ▸ muddle, disorganize, mix up, shuffle, confuse, disarrange, (*more informal*) mess up AN OPPOSITE IS organize

jump VERB **1** *A dog jumped off the chair.* ▸ leap, spring, bound, bounce, hop **2** *All the horses jumped the first fence.* ▸ vault, clear **3** *The children were jumping about in the garden.*

jump ➡ juvenile delinquent

jump NOUN jumps **1** a jumping movement **2** an obstacle to jump over **3** a sudden rise or change

jumpy ADJECTIVE nervous and edgy

junction NOUN junctions **1** a join **2** a place where roads or railway lines meet

June NOUN the sixth month of the year [named after the Roman goddess Juno]

jungle NOUN jungles a thick tangled forest, especially in the tropics
▷ **jungly** ADJECTIVE
[from Hindi]

junior ADJECTIVE **1** younger **2** for younger children • *a junior high school* **3** lower in rank or importance • *junior officers* [from Latin, = younger]

junk NOUN rubbish; things of no value

junk food NOUN food that is not nourishing

junk mail NOUN unwanted advertising material sent by post

jury NOUN juries a group of people (usually twelve) appointed to give a verdict about a case in a lawcourt
▷ **juryman** NOUN **jurywoman** NOUN
[from Latin *jurare* = take an oath]

just ADJECTIVE **1** giving proper consideration to everyone's claims **2** deserved; right in amount • *a just reward*
▷ **justly** ADVERB **justness** NOUN

just ADVERB **1** exactly • *It's just what I wanted.* **2** only; simply • *I just wanted to see him.* **3** barely; by only a small amount • *just below the knee* **4** at this moment or only a little while ago • *She has just gone.*

justice NOUN justices **1** being just; fair treatment **2** legal proceedings • *a court of justice* **3** a judge or magistrate [via early French from Latin *jus* = law]

justify VERB justifies, justifying, justified show that something is fair, just, or reasonable
▷ **justifiable** ADJECTIVE **justification** NOUN

jut VERB juts, jutting, jutted stick out

jute NOUN fibre from tropical plants, used for making sacks etc.

juvenile ADJECTIVE to do with or for young people

juvenile NOUN juveniles a young person, not old enough to be legally considered an adult

juvenile delinquent NOUN juvenile delinquents a young person who has broken the law

--- **Thesaurus** ---

▶ skip, dance, frolic, prance, cavort **4** *A noise made him jump.* ▶ start, jerk, jolt, flinch, recoil **5** *Attendance had jumped by more than 20 percent.* ▶ rise, increase, leap, go up, escalate

jump NOUN **1** *With a jump he reached the other side.* ▶ leap, bound, spring, vault, hop **2** *The horse cleared the last jump comfortably.* ▶ fence, hurdle, ditch, barrier, obstacle, gap, gate **3** *a huge jump in house prices* ▶ rise, increase, escalation, upturn **4** *She woke up with a jump.* ▶ start, jerk, jolt, shock, shudder, lurch

jumpy ADJECTIVE *He was tired and jumpy.* ▶ nervous, edgy, jittery, tense, anxious, agitated, apprehensive

junior ADJECTIVE *a junior official* ▶ low-ranking, lower-ranking, subordinate, subsidiary, younger, lesser, minor, secondary AN OPPOSITE IS senior

junk NOUN *a cupboard full of old junk* ▶ rubbish, clutter, oddments, odds and ends, garbage, refuse, scrap, trash, waste

just ADJECTIVE **1** *a just ruler; a just settlement* ▶ fair, equitable, fair-minded, honorable, evenhanded, unprejudiced, unbiased, neutral, nonpartisan AN OPPOSITE IS unjust **2** *a just punishment* ▶ fair, fitting, deserved, merited, appropriate, suitable, reasonable, legitimate OPPOSITES ARE undeserved, unfair

justice NOUN **1** *He appealed to their sense of justice.* ▶ fairness, justness, fair play, integrity, equity, honesty, impartiality, legality, right AN OPPOSITE IS injustice **2** *the administration of justice* ▶ the law, legal proceedings

justifiable ADJECTIVE *a justifiable reaction* ▶ reasonable, justified, valid, legitimate, defensible, excusable, well founded, understandable, warranted, acceptable AN OPPOSITE IS unjustifiable

justification NOUN **1** *There is no justification for such callousness.* ▶ excuse, reason, grounds, basis, warrant, foundation **2** *Such extreme measures call for some justification.* ▶ explanation, defence, vindication, argument, rationalization

justify VERB *Tiredness cannot justify this kind of reckless behavior.* ▶ excuse, defend, absolve, mitigate, account for, vindicate, exonerate, warrant, validate, uphold, support

jut VERB jut out *A set of shelves jutted out on one wall.* ▶ project, protrude, stick out, extend, overhang, poke out

juvenile ADJECTIVE **1** *juvenile behavior* ▶ immature, childish, babyish, infantile, puerile AN OPPOSITE IS mature **2** *juvenile novels* ▶ adolescent, young, youthful

juvenile NOUN *The people involved were all juveniles.* ▶ youth, young person, minor, under-age person

Kk

kaleidoscope (kal- I- dos- kohp) *NOUN*
kaleidoscopes a tube that you look through
to see brightly colored patterns which change
as you turn the end of the tube
▷ **kaleidoscopic** *ADJECTIVE*

kangaroo *NOUN* kangaroos an Australian
animal that jumps along on its strong hind
legs (see marsupial) [an Australian Aboriginal
word]

karaoke *NOUN* (ka- ree- oh- ki) a form of
entertainment in which people sing well-
known songs against a pre-recorded backing
[from Japanese, = empty orchestra]

karate (ka- rah- tee) *NOUN* a Japanese method
of self-defense in which the hands and feet
are used as weapons [from Japanese *kara* =
empty + *te* = hand]

KB or **Kb** *ABBREVIATION* kilobyte(s)

keel *NOUN* keels the long piece of wood or
metal along the bottom of a boat
on an even keel steady

keel *VERB* keels, keeling, keeled
keel over fall down or overturn ● *The ship
keeled over.*

keen *ADJECTIVE* **1** alert or astute **2** sharp ● *a
keen edge* **3** piercingly cold ● *a keen wind*
▷ **keenly** *ADVERB* **keenness** *NOUN*

keep *VERB* keeps, keeping, kept **1** have
something and look after it or not get rid of
it **2** stay or cause to stay in the same
condition etc. ● *keep still;* ● *keep it hot* **3** do
something continually ● *She keeps laughing.*
4 last without going bad ● *How long will this
milk keep?* **5** respect and not break ● *keep a
promise* **6** make entries in ● *keep a diary*

keep to observe or respect
keep up 1 make the same progress as others
2 continue something

keep *NOUN* keeps **1** maintenance; the food,
etc., that you need to live ● *She earns her keep.*
2 a strong tower in a castle
for keeps (*informal*) permanently; to keep ● *Is
this football mine for keeps?*

keeper *NOUN* keepers **1** a person who looks
after an animal, building, etc. ● *the zookeeper*

keeping *NOUN* care; looking after something
● *in safe keeping*

keg *NOUN* kegs a small barrel

kelvin *NOUN* kelvins the SI unit of
thermodynamic temperature

kennel *NOUN* kennels a shelter for a dog

kerb *NOUN* kerbs the edge of a pavement

kernel *NOUN* kernels the part inside the shell
of a nut, etc.

ketchup *NOUN* a thick sauce made from
tomatoes and vinegar etc. [probably from
Chinese *k'e chap* = tomato juice]

kettle *NOUN* kettles a container with a spout
and handle, for boiling water in

kettledrum *NOUN* kettledrums a large drum
shaped like a bowl

key *NOUN* keys **1** a piece of metal shaped so
that it will open a lock **2** a device for winding
up a clock or clockwork toy, etc. **3** a small
lever to be pressed by a finger, e.g., on a
piano, typewriter, or computer **4** a system of
notes in music ● *the key of C major* **5** a fact or
clue that explains or solves something ● *the
key to the mystery* **6** a list of symbols used in a
map or table, showing what they mean

key *VERB* keys, keying, keyed
key in type information into a computer using
a keyboard

keyboard *NOUN* keyboards the set of keys on
a piano, typewriter, computer, etc.

Thesaurus

keen *ADJECTIVE* **1** *a knife with a keen cutting edge*
► sharp, sharp-edged, razor-sharp, honed
2 *Patience, nimble fingers, and keen eyesight are
needed to operate the tool.* ► sharp, acute, clear,
sensitive, strong, powerful **3** *She still displays a
keen sense of humor.* ► sharp, piercing, incisive,
penetrating, pungent, trenchant

keep *VERB* **1** *an in-flight magazine for you to read
and keep* ► retain, hold on to, hang on to,
possess **2** *They did their best to keep quiet.*
► remain, stay, continue to be, carry on being
3 *He keeps twitching his ears.* ► persist in, go
on, continue, carry on **4** *We'll try not to keep
you too long.* ► detain, delay, hold up, keep
waiting **5** *These problems shouldn't keep you
from continuing.* ► deter, constrain, hinder,
impede, obstruct **6** *You must keep your promise.*
► observe, fulfill, comply with, obey, respect,

keep faith with **7** *Where do you keep the coats?*
► store, put, stow, house **8** *Keeping a family
can be expensive.* ► support, maintain, provide
for, look after, care for, be responsible for

keeper *NOUN* **1** *the keeper of the museum*
► curator, custodian, administrator,
superintendent **2** *the prisoners and their keeper*
► jailer, warden, guard, custodian **3** *He said
he was not his brother's keeper.* ► guardian,
protector, minder

key *NOUN* **1** *the key to a problem* ► clue,
indicator, pointer, lead, secret, solution,
answer, interpretation **2** *a key to a map*
► guide, legend, index, table, explanation,
glossary

key *ADJECTIVE* *the key question* ► fundamental,
crucial, vital, critical, essential, important

a b c d e f g h i j **k** l m n o p q r s t u v w x y z

A
B
C
D
E
F
G
H
I
J
K
L
M
N
O
P
Q
R
S
T
U
V
W
X
Y
Z

keyhole NOUN keyholes the hole through which a key is put into a lock

keyhole surgery NOUN surgery carried out through a very small cut in the patient's body, using special instruments

keypad NOUN keypads a small keyboard or set of buttons used to operate a telephone, television, etc.

kg ABBREVIATION kilogram(s)

khaki NOUN a dull yellowish-brown color, used for military uniforms [from Urdu *khaki* = dust-colored]

kibbutz NOUN kibbutzim a commune in Israel, especially for farming [from Hebrew *qibbus* = gathering]

kick VERB kicks, kicking, kicked **1** hit or move a person or thing with your foot **2** move your legs about vigorously **3** (said about a gun) recoil when fired
kick off 1 start a football game **2** (*informal*) start doing something
kick out get rid of; dismiss
kick up (*informal*) make a noise or fuss

kick NOUN kicks **1** a kicking movement **2** the recoiling movement of a gun **3** (*informal*) a thrill **4** (*informal*) an interest or activity • *He's on a health kick*

kick-off NOUN kick-offs the start of a football match

kid NOUN kids **1** (*informal*) a child **2** a young goat **3** fine leather made from goatskin

kidnap VERB kidnaps, kidnapping, kidnapped take someone away by force, especially in order to obtain a ransom
▷ **kidnapper** NOUN

kidney NOUN kidneys either of the two organs in the body that remove waste products from the blood and excrete urine into the bladder

kill VERB kills, killing, killed **1** make a person or thing die **2** destroy or put an end to something
▷ **killer** NOUN
kill time occupy time idly while waiting

killing NOUN killings an act causing death

kilo NOUN kilos a kilogram

kilogram NOUN kilograms a unit of mass or weight equal to 1,000 grams (about 22 pounds)

kilometer (kil- o- meet- er, kil- **om**- it- er) NOUN kilometers a unit of length equal to 1,000 metres (about a mile)

kilowatt NOUN kilowatts a unit of electrical power equal to 1,000 watts

kilt NOUN kilts a kind of pleated skirt worn especially by Scotsmen
▷ **kilted** ADJECTIVE

kin PLURAL NOUN a person's family and relatives

kind NOUN kinds a class of similar things or animals; a sort or type
in kind (said about payment) made in goods or services and not in money
kind of (*informal*) in a way, to some extent • *I felt kind of sorry for him.*

Thesaurus

kick NOUN **1** *He gave the television a kick.* ▶ hit, boot, blow **2** (*informal*) *Some people might get a kick out of crossing the Atlantic in an old boat.* ▶ thrill, excitement, (*informal*) buzz

kick VERB **1** *Merv kicked the ball out.* ▶ boot, hit , drive, send, punt, heel **2** (*informal*) *a habit I have to kick* ▶ give up, quit, break, abandon, cease, desist from

kid VERB (*informal*) **1** *I think they were only kidding.* ▶ tease, fool, bluff, lie **2** *Are you kidding me?* ▶ hoodwink, pull your leg, have you on, deceive

kidnap VERB *The group was allegedly preparing to kidnap a businessman.* ▶ abduct, capture, seize, carry off, run away with, snatch

kill VERB **1** *The gang would not hesitate to kill the prisoners.* ▶ murder, put to death, slay, slaughter, dispatch, eliminate, exterminate, assassinate, (*more informal*) bump off USAGE You use *assassinate* to refer to an important person, especially a statesman or stateswoman. *Slay* and *dispatch* are literary words. **2** *The war killed all hopes of continuing archaeological investigation at the site.* ▶ end, destroy, put an end to, dash, extinguish, finish

3 *Take aspirin to kill the pain.* ▶ soothe, alleviate, assuage, deaden, suppress, dull, blunt, reduce, stifle, extinguish **4** (*informal*) *She complained that her back was killing her.* ▶ hurt, pain, torment, torture, give discomfort to, give pain to **5** *We arrived early and had an hour to kill.* ▶ occupy, fill up, while away, pass, spend **6** (*informal*) *She nearly killed herself getting the work finished in time.* ▶ exhaust, wear out, tire out, sap, debilitate

killer NOUN *A witness was able to identify the killers.* ▶ murderer, assassin, gunman, (*more informal*) hitman

killing NOUN *a brutal killing that shocked the community* ▶ murder, assassination, slaughter, massacre, execution USAGE Note that *slaughter* and *massacre* refer to the killing of a large number of people.

kind ADJECTIVE *A kind friend helped him home. It was kind of her to ring.* ▶ caring, good, kindhearted, kindly, considerate, sympathetic, thoughtful, obliging, tender-hearted, benevolent OPPOSITES ARE unkind, unfriendly

kind NOUN *a new kind of rock music* ▶ sort, type, style, form, variety, category, genre

USAGE Correct use is *this kind of thing* or *these kinds of things* (not "these kind of things").

kind ADJECTIVE friendly and helpful; considerate ▷ **kind-hearted** ADJECTIVE **kindness** NOUN

kindergarten NOUN **kindergartens** a school or class for very young children

kindle VERB **kindles, kindling, kindled 1** start a flame; set light to something **2** begin burning

kinetic ADJECTIVE to do with or produced by movement • *kinetic energy*

king NOUN **kings 1** a man who is the ruler of a country through inheriting the position **2** a person or thing regarded as supreme • *the lion is the king of beasts* **3** the most important piece in chess **4** a playing card with a picture of a king
▷ **kingly** ADJECTIVE **kingship** NOUN [from Old English]

kingdom NOUN **kingdoms 1** a country ruled by a king or queen **2** a major division of the natural world • *the animal kingdom*

kingfisher NOUN **kingfishers** a small bird with blue feathers that dives to catch fish

kink NOUN **kinks 1** a short twist in a rope, wire, piece of hair, etc. **2** a peculiarity

kinky ADJECTIVE involving peculiar sexual behavior

kiosk NOUN **kiosks 1** a telephone box **2** a small hut or stall where newspapers, sweets, etc. are sold

kiss NOUN **kisses** touching somebody with your lips as a sign of affection

kiss VERB **kisses, kissing, kissed** give somebody a kiss

kit NOUN **kits 1** equipment or clothes for a particular occupation **2** a set of parts sold ready to be fitted together

kitchen NOUN **kitchens** a room in which meals are prepared and cooked

kite NOUN **kites 1** a light framework covered with cloth, paper, etc., and flown in the wind on the end of a long piece of string **2** a large hawk

kitten NOUN **kittens** a very young cat

kiwi NOUN **kiwis** a New Zealand bird that cannot fly [from a Maori word]

kleptomania NOUN an uncontrollable urge to steal things
▷ **kleptomaniac** NOUN

km ABBREVIATION kilometre(s)

knack NOUN a special skill • *There's a knack to putting up a deckchair.*

knapsack NOUN **knapsacks** a bag carried on the back by soldiers, hikers, etc.

knave NOUN **knaves 1** (*old use*) a dishonest man; a rogue **2** a jack in playing cards

knead VERB **kneads, kneading, kneaded** press and stretch something soft (especially dough) with your hands

knee NOUN **knees** the joint in the middle of the leg

kneecap NOUN **kneecaps** the small bone covering the front of the knee joint

kneel VERB **kneels, kneeling, knelt** be or get yourself in a position on your knees

knickers PLURAL NOUN short pants worn by women and girls

knife NOUN **knives** a cutting instrument consisting of a sharp blade set in a handle

Thesaurus

kindle VERB **1** *Bonfires are kindled on Halloween.* ► light, burn, ignite, fire, set fire to **2** *These events kindled strong feelings.* ► stir up, stimulate, arouse, give rise to, evoke, induce, inflame, call forth

kindly ADJECTIVE *a kindly old man* ► kind, kind-hearted, benevolent, caring, good, considerate, sympathetic, thoughtful, obliging, tenderhearted

kindness NOUN *She had shown them much kindness over many years.* ► consideration, thoughtfulness, generosity, goodwill, benevolence, favor, understanding

king NOUN *After the war the country expelled its king.* ► ruler, monarch, sovereign, crowned head RELATED ADJECTIVES ► regal, royal

kingdom NOUN *a small kingdom in Asia Minor* ► monarchy, realm, dominion

kink NOUN **1** *a kink in the road* ► bend, corner, angle **2** *kinks in the line* ► twist, curl, loop, knot, tangle

kiss VERB *She stooped to kiss the little boy.* ► caress, embrace, (*more informal*) peck

kiss NOUN *He gave her a long kiss.* ► caress, embrace, (*more informal*) peck, (*more informal*) snog

kit NOUN **1** *a tool kit* ► equipment, gear, implements, appliances, tackle **2** *They made the furniture from kits.* ► outfit, set of parts, self-assembly set, flatpack **3** *a football kit* ► outfit, strip, colors, clothes

knack NOUN *He has a knack of hitting the nail on the head.* ► gift, flair (for), talent (for), instinct (for), ability (to hit), skill (for)

kneel VERB *She knelt by the bed to pray.* ► bend, bow, crouch, stoop, squat, fall to your knees, genuflect

knife VERB *The victim had been knifed repeatedly.* ► stab, gash, slash, pierce, cut, wound

a
b
c
d
e
f
g
h
i
j
k
l
m
n
o
p
q
r
s
t
u
v
w
x
y
z

knight ➡ knowledge

knight NOUN **knights 1** a man who has been given the rank that allows him to put "Sir" before his name **2** (in the Middle Ages) a warrior of high social rank, usually mounted and in armor **3** a piece in chess, with a horse's head
▷ **knighthood** NOUN

knit VERB **knits, knitting, knitted** or **knit** make something by looping together wool or other yarn, using long needles or a machine
▷ **knitter** NOUN **knitting needle** NOUN
knit your brow frown

knob NOUN **knobs 1** the round handle of a door, drawer, etc. **2** a round lump on something **3** a round button or switch on a dial or machine **4** a small round piece of something ● *a knob of butter*
▷ **knobbly** ADJECTIVE **knobby** ADJECTIVE

knock VERB **knocks, knocking, knocked 1** hit a thing hard or so as to make a noise **2** produce by hitting ● *We need to knock a hole in the wall.* **3** (*informal*) criticize unfavorably ● *People are always knocking this country.*
knock off 1 (*informal*) stop working **2** deduct something from a price **3** (*informal*) steal
knock out make a person unconscious, especially by a blow to the head

knockout NOUN **knockouts 1** knocking someone out **2** a contest in which the loser in each round has to drop out **3** (*informal*) an amazing person or thing

knot NOUN **knots 1** a place where a piece of string, rope, or ribbon is twisted round itself or another piece **2** a tangle or lump **3** a round spot on a piece of wood where a branch joined it **4** a cluster of people or things **5** a unit for measuring the speed of ships and aircraft, equal to 2,025 yards (= 1,852 meters or 1 nautical mile) per hour

knot VERB **knots, knotting, knotted 1** tie or fasten with a knot **2** entangle

know VERB **knows, knowing, knew, known 1** have something in your mind that you have learned or discovered **2** recognize or be familiar with a person or place ● *I've known him for years.* **3** understand ● *She knows how to please us.*

knowing ADJECTIVE showing that you know something ● *a knowing look*

knowingly ADVERB **1** in a knowing way **2** deliberately

knowledge NOUN **1** knowing **2** all that a person knows **3** all that is known
to my knowledge as far as I know

Thesaurus

---

knit VERB **knit together** *The new arrangements took a few months to knit together.* ▶ unite, become unified, come together, combine, connect

knob NOUN **1** *He held the door knob as he looked into the room.* ▶ handle **2** *The gnarled old tree was covered with knobs.* ▶ bump, lump, bulge, swelling, boss, projection, protuberance

knock VERB **1** *He swore as he knocked his knee on the edge of the desk.* ▶ bump, hit, strike, bang, crack, rap **2** *The man knocked on the door and waited.* ▶ bang, rap, tap, thump, pound
knock down 1 *They are going to knock down the entire row of houses.* ▶ demolish, level, raze, destroy **2** *He knocked her down with one blow.* ▶ fell, topple, flatten, floor
knock off (*informal*) **1** *We knock off early tonight.* ▶ finish work, go home **2** *Someone had knocked off the vicar's car.* ▶ steal, take, (*informal*) pinch, (*informal*) nick
knock out 1 *I hit him and knocked him out.* ▶ stun, strike unconscious **2** (*informal*) *The long walk knocked us out.* ▶ exhaust, tire out, wear out **3** (*informal*) *music that knocked me out* ▶ overwhelm, amaze, astound

knock NOUN *The car has taken a few knocks.* ▶ blow, bump, bang, shock, collision, smash

knockout NOUN *The event was a knockout.* ▶ success, sensation, triumph, winner, hit

knot NOUN **1** *a knot in a rope* ▶ tie, twist, splice, hitch **2** *a knot of people* ▶ cluster, bunch, clump, group

knot VERB *She knotted a scarf around her neck.* ▶ tie, secure, bind, fasten, do up, entwine
OPPOSITES ARE unknot, untie

know VERB **1** *Does she know we are here?* ▶ realize, be aware, understand, appreciate **2** *I speak French but don't know any German.* ▶ understand, speak, have knowledge of, be familiar with, be conversant with, have a grasp of **3** *Gerry knows me from our student days.* ▶ be acquainted with, have met, be friendly with, have had dealings with **4** *He had known much better times.* ▶ experience, live through, go through, undergo

know-it-all NOUN *He's such a know-it-all he's bound to be able to tell us.* ▶ (*informal*) smart alec, (*informal*) wise guy, show-off, wiseacre, expert, pundit

know-how NOUN (*informal*) *technical know-how* ▶ expertise, knowledge, skill, proficiency, understanding

knowing ADJECTIVE **1** *She gave a knowing look.* ▶ meaningful, expressive, significant, suggestive, eloquent, shrewd, artful AN OPPOSITE IS innocent **2** *a knowing young woman* ▶ clever, astute, crafty, cunning

knowledge NOUN **1** *an extensive knowledge of the local history* ▶ understanding, comprehension, mastery, command, grasp **2** *technical knowledge* ▶ expertise, skill, proficiency, understanding, (*more informal*) know-how **3** *I have no knowledge of these people.* ▶ acquaintance (with), familiarity (with)

knowledgeable *ADJECTIVE* well informed
  ▷ **knowledgeably** *ADVERB*
knuckle *NOUN* knuckles a joint in the finger
knuckle *VERB* knuckles, knuckling, knuckled
  knuckle down begin to work hard
  knuckle under yield or submit
koala (koh- **ah**- la) *NOUN* koalas an Australian
  animal that looks like a small bear [an
  Australian Aboriginal word]

Koran (kor- **ahn**) *NOUN* the sacred book of
  Islam, written in Arabic, believed by Muslims
  to contain the words of Allah revealed to the
  prophet Muhammad
kosher *ADJECTIVE* keeping to Jewish laws about
  the preparation of food • *kosher meat*
kw *ABBREVIATION* kilowatt(s)

Thesaurus
---

4 *people with a wide range of knowledge*
  ► learning, education, erudition, scholarship
knowledgeable *ADJECTIVE* **1** *a knowledgeable
man* ► educated, erudite, learned, well

informed **2** *knowledgeable about modern art*
  ► well informed, versed (in), acquainted
(with), conversant (with), familiar (with), au
fait (with) AN OPPOSITE IS ignorant

A
B
C
D
E
F
G
H
I
J
K
L
M
N
O
P
Q
R
S
T
U
V
W
X
Y
Z

Ll

label NOUN **labels** a small piece of paper, cloth, or metal, etc., fixed on or beside something to show what it is or what it costs, or its owner or destination, etc.

label VERB **labels, labeling, labeled** put a label on something

laboratory NOUN **laboratories** a room or building equipped for scientific experiments

laborious ADJECTIVE **1** needing or using a lot of hard work **2** explaining something at great length and with obvious effort
  ▷ **laboriously** ADVERB

labor NOUN **labors 1** hard work **2** a task **3** working people **4** the contractions of the womb when a baby is being born

labor VERB **labors, laboring, labored 1** work hard **2** explain or discuss something at great length and with obvious effort ● *I will not labor the point.*

laborer NOUN **laborers** a person who does hard manual work, especially outdoors

laburnum NOUN **laburnums** a tree with hanging yellow flowers

labyrinth NOUN **labyrinths** a complicated arrangement of passages or paths; a maze

lace NOUN **laces 1** netlike material with decorative patterns of holes in it **2** a piece of thin cord or leather for fastening a shoe

lack NOUN being without something

lack VERB **lacks, lacking, lacked** be without something ● *He lacks courage.*

lacquer NOUN a hard glossy varnish
  ▷ **lacquered** ADJECTIVE

lacrosse NOUN a game in which players use a stick with a net on it (a **crosse**) to catch and throw a ball

lacy ADJECTIVE made of lace or like lace

lad NOUN **lads** a boy or youth

ladder NOUN **ladders 1** two upright pieces of wood or metal and crosspieces (**rungs**), used for climbing up or down **2** a vertical ladderlike flaw in a pair of tights, etc., where a stitch has become undone

ladle NOUN **ladles** a large deep spoon with a long handle, used for lifting and pouring liquids

lady NOUN **ladies 1** a well-mannered woman **2** a woman of good social position **3** (in polite use) a woman
  ▷ **ladylike** ADJECTIVE **ladyship** NOUN
  Lady NOUN the title of a noblewoman

Thesaurus

label NOUN **1** *Always read the label on the packet.* ► tag, tab, sticker, ticket, docket, marker **2** *a new independent record label* ► brand, company, organization

label VERB *The authorities were too ready to label people as troublemakers.* ► identify, mark, categorize, class, classify, define, describe, regard, name, stamp, brand, call

laborious ADJECTIVE *Restoring your data is a long and laborious process.* ► arduous, hard, heavy, difficult, stiff, tough, exhausting, fatiguing, gruelling, wearisome, onerous, strenuous, burdensome, back-breaking, tiresome, uphill OPPOSITES ARE easy, straightforward

labor NOUN **1** *Keeping the place clean involved a lot of labor.* ► work , toil, effort, exertion, industry, drudgery, donkey work, (*more informal*) grind, (*more informal*) sweat **2** *The company took on extra labor to cope with the seasonal rush.* ► staff, workers, employees, workforce, (*more informal*) hands **3** *Agnes went into labor about lunchtime.* ► childbirth, labor pains, contractions, delivery, (*technical*) parturition

labor VERB **1** *Levin labored day and night on the project.* ► work, work hard, toil, drudge, grind, exert yourself, (*more informal*) beaver, (*more informal*) slave, (*more informal*) sweat **2** *As he labored to get back on course another blast threw the boat lopsided.* ► struggle, strive, endeavor,

work, do your utmost, go all out **3** *We have made our point and there is no need to labor it.* ► overdo, overemphasize, dwell on, elaborate, exaggerate, make heavy weather of

lace NOUN **1** *a cloth trimmed with lace* ► lacework, openwork, filigree, net, tatting **2** *One shoe had a lace missing.* ► shoelace, bootlace, shoestring, cord, string, thong

lace VERB **1** *He laced his shoes.* ► fasten, do up, tie up, secure **2** *She laced her fingers into his.* ► twine, entwine, intertwine, interweave

lack NOUN *suffering from a lack of vitamins* ► deficiency, shortage, want, scarcity, absence, dearth, paucity, deprivation, need, privation, famine OPPOSITES ARE sufficiency, abundance

lack VERB *The film lacks drama.* ► be without, be short of, be deficient in, miss, want, need, require

lacking ADJECTIVE **1** *a relationship lacking in affection* ► wanting, needing, without, missing, short of, weak in, deficient in, inadequate in, defective in **2** *Convincing arguments are lacking.* ► absent, missing, unavailable, nonexistent

lad NOUN *a young lad of ten* ► boy, youth, youngster, schoolboy, fellow, (*more informal*) kid, (*more informal*) guy [from Old English *hlaefdige* = person who makes the bread (compare **lord**)]

ladybird NOUN ladybirds a small flying beetle, usually red with black spots

lag[1] VERB lags, lagging, lagged go too slowly and fail to keep up with others

lag[2] VERB lags, lagging, lagged wrap pipes or boilers etc. in insulating material (**lagging**) to prevent loss of heat

lager (lah- ger) NOUN lagers a light beer

lagoon NOUN lagoons a saltwater lake separated from the sea by sandbanks or reefs

laid past tense of lay

laid-back ADJECTIVE (*informal*) relaxed and calm

lain past participle of lie[2]

lair NOUN lairs a sheltered place where a wild animal lives

lake NOUN lakes a large area of water entirely surrounded by land [from Latin *lacus* = pool, lake]

lamb NOUN lambs 1 a young sheep 2 meat from a lamb
▷ **lambswool** NOUN

lame ADJECTIVE 1 unable to walk normally 2 weak; not convincing • *a lame excuse*
▷ **lamely** ADVERB **lameness** NOUN

lament NOUN laments a statement, song, or poem expressing grief or regret

lament VERB laments, lamenting, lamented express grief or regret about something
▷ **lamentation** NOUN

lamentable (lam- in- ta- bul) ADJECTIVE regrettable or deplorable

lamp NOUN lamps a device for producing light from electricity, gas, or oil
▷ **lamplight** NOUN **lampshade** NOUN

lamp post NOUN lamp posts a tall post in a street with a lamp at the top

lance NOUN lances a long spear

lance corporal NOUN lance corporals a soldier ranking between a private and a corporal

land NOUN lands 1 the part of the earth's surface not covered by sea 2 the ground or soil; an area of country • *forest land* 3 the area occupied by a nation; a country

land VERB lands, landing, landed 1 arrive or put on land from a ship or aircraft, etc. 2 reach the ground after jumping or falling 3 bring a fish out of the water 4 obtain • *She landed an excellent job.* 5 arrive or cause to arrive at a certain place or position, etc. • *They landed up in jail.* 6 present with a problem • *He landed me with this task.* [from Old English]

landing NOUN landings 1 the level area at the top of a flight of stairs 2 bringing or coming to land • *The pilot made a smooth landing.* 3 a place where people can get on and off a boat

landing stage NOUN landing stages a platform on which people and goods are taken on and off a boat

landlady NOUN landladies 1 a woman who lets rooms to lodgers 2 a woman who runs a pub

landlord NOUN landlords 1 a person who lets a house, room, or land to a tenant 2 a person who runs a pub

landmark NOUN landmarks 1 an object that is easily seen in a landscape 2 an important event in the history or development of something

Thesaurus

lag VERB 1 *Some of the runners were lagging behind.* ► straggle, trail, fall behind, drop behind, hang back, linger, dally, dawdle, bring up the rear, come last, idle OPPOSITES ARE keep up, take the lead 2 *material for lagging water pipes* ► insulate, wrap up

laid-back ADJECTIVE (*informal*) *He took a laid-back attitude despite the difficulties.* ► relaxed, unruffled, nonchalant, philosophical, casual, easygoing, at ease, informal OPPOSITES ARE tense, uptight

lair NOUN 1 *an animal's lair* ► den, burrow, haunt, hole, earth 2 *a criminal's lair* ► hideaway, hideout, hiding place, refuge, retreat, shelter, sanctuary

lame ADJECTIVE 1 *The horse was lame and would not race that day.* ► crippled, limping 2 *As excuses went, this one was pretty lame.* ► feeble, weak, flimsy, thin, unconvincing, implausible, hard to believe OPPOSITES ARE convincing, persuasive

land NOUN 1 *a large house with several acres of land* ► grounds, ground, estate, property, farmland, open space 2 *Egypt is a land steeped in history.* ► country, nation, state, region 3 *The ship reached land at last.* ► dry land, terra firma, shore

land VERB 1 *Allied troops landed in Kuwait.* ► disembark, debark, go ashore, alight, arrive, berth, come ashore, dock, end a journey, reach landfall AN OPPOSITE IS embark 2 *The ship will land at Calais.* ► dock, berth, moor, anchor, reach shore OPPOSITES ARE set sail, put to sea 3 *The plane landed ten minutes ahead of schedule.* ► touch down, come in to land AN OPPOSITE IS take off

landmark NOUN 1 *The church steeple was a landmark visible for miles around.* ► feature, sight, spectacle, marker, high point 2 *a landmark in history* ► turning point, milestone, watershed, new era

land mine NOUN land mines an explosive mine laid on or just under the surface of the ground

landowner NOUN landowners a person who owns a large amount of land

landscape NOUN landscapes **1** a view of a particular area of countryside or town **2** a picture of the countryside

landslide NOUN landslides **1** a huge mass of soil and rocks sliding down a slope **2** an overwhelming victory in an election • *She won the general election by a landslide.*

lane NOUN lanes **1** a narrow road, especially in the country **2** a strip of road for a single line of traffic **3** a strip of track or water for one runner, swimmer, etc., in a race

language NOUN languages **1** words and their use **2** the words used in a particular country or by a particular group of people **3** a system of signs or symbols giving information, especially in computing

languid ADJECTIVE slow because of tiredness, weakness, or laziness
▷ **languidly** ADVERB **languor** NOUN

languish VERB languishes, languishing, languished **1** live in miserable conditions; be neglected • *He has been languishing in prison for three years.* **2** become weak or listless

lank ADJECTIVE (said about hair) long and limp

lanky ADJECTIVE lankier, lankiest awkwardly thin and tall
▷ **lankiness** NOUN

lantern NOUN lanterns a transparent case for holding a light and shielding it from the wind

lap NOUN laps **1** the level place formed by the front of the legs above the knees when a person is sitting down **2** going once round a racecourse **3** one section of a journey • *the last lap*

lap[1] VERB laps, lapping, lapped overtake another competitor in a race to become one or more laps ahead

lap[2] VERB laps, lapping, lapped **1** take up liquid by moving the tongue, as a cat does **2** make a gentle splash against something • *Waves lapped the shore*

lapel (la- **pel**) NOUN lapels a flap folded back at the front edge of a coat or jacket

lapse NOUN lapses **1** a slight mistake or failure • *a lapse of memory* **2** an amount of time elapsed • *after a lapse of six months*

lapse VERB lapses, lapsing, lapsed **1** pass or slip gradually • *He lapsed into unconsciousness.* **2** be no longer valid, through not being renewed • *My insurance policy has lapsed.*

laptop NOUN laptops a portable computer for use while travelling

larch NOUN larches a tall deciduous tree that bears small cones

lard NOUN a white greasy substance prepared from pig fat and used in cooking

larder NOUN larders a cupboard or small room for storing food

large ADJECTIVE of more than the ordinary or average size; big
▷ **largeness** NOUN
at large **1** free to roam about, not captured • *The escaped prisoners are still at large.* **2** in

Thesaurus

landscape NOUN **1** *the landscape of the Scottish Highlands.* ► scenery, countryside, topography, terrain, environment, rural scene, scene **2** *a landscape painting* ► panorama, vista, view, outlook, prospect

lane NOUN *a country lane* ► road, byroad, byway, track, trail, path

language NOUN **1** *the language of the media* ► vocabulary, usage, style, speech **2** *The forms are written in plain language.* ► wording, phraseology, phrasing **3** *the grammar of language* ► speech, writing, communication, utterance, discourse **4** *How many languages do you know?* ► tongue RELATED ADJECTIVE ► linguistic

lanky ADJECTIVE *a lanky young man* ► tall, gangling, gaunt, gawky, lean, spindly, scraggy

lap NOUN **1** *A cat was sitting on her lap.* ► knee OR knees, thighs **2** *They managed three laps of the track.* ► circuit, round, orbit, circle, loop, stretch, course

lap VERB **1** *Waves lapped against the rocks.* ► wash, splash, dash, beat, strike, surge, rush

2 *The dog lapped a bowl of water.* ► drink, sip, lick, slurp, gulp

lapse NOUN **1** *a temporary lapse of attention* ► failure, error, weakness, relapse, failing, fault, slip, mistake, omission, flaw, shortcoming **2** *a lapse into crime* ► decline, descent, fall, falling, deterioration **3** *The friends got back in touch after a lapse of ten years.* ► interval, gap, pause, break, interruption

lapse VERB **1** *They soon lapsed into their bad old habits.* ► slide, slip, drop, fall, decline, deteriorate, degenerate **2** *Membership will lapse at the end of the month.* ► expire, run out, finish, stop, terminate, become invalid

large ADJECTIVE **1** *a large house; elected with a large majority* ► big, great, huge, sizeable, substantial, enormous, gigantic, immense, massive, colossal, vast, giant, *(more informal)* whopping, *(more informal)* ginormous **2** *a large man* ► big, burly, hefty, bulky, stocky, hulking, strapping **3** *a large supply of food* ► plentiful, abundant, copious, generous, lavish, profuse, ample, liberal **4** *large areas of*

general, as a whole • *She is respected by the country at large.*
[from Latin *largus* = abundant or generous]

largely ADVERB to a great extent • *You are largely responsible for the accident.*

lark[1] NOUN larks a small sandy-brown bird; the skylark

lark[2] NOUN larks (*informal*) something amusing; a bit of fun • *We did it for a lark.*

larva NOUN larvae an insect in the first stage of its life, after it comes out of the egg
▷ **larval** ADJECTIVE
[from Latin, = ghost or mask]

laser NOUN lasers a device that makes a very strong narrow beam of light or other electromagnetic radiation [from the initials of "light amplification by stimulated emission of radiation"]

lash NOUN lashes **1** a stroke with a whip or stick **2** the cord or cordlike part of a whip **3** an eyelash

lash VERB lashes, lashing, lashed **1** strike with a whip; beat violently **2** tie with cord, etc. • *Lash the sticks together.*
lash down (said about rain) pour or beat down forcefully
lash out **1** speak or hit out angrily **2** spend money extravagantly

lass NOUN lasses a girl or young woman
▷ **lassie** NOUN

lasso NOUN lassoes or lassos a rope with a sliding noose at the end, used for catching cattle etc. [via Spanish *lazo* from Latin *laqueus* = noose]

last ADJECTIVE, ADVERB **1** coming after all others; final **2** latest; most recent • *last night* **3** least likely • *She is the last person I'd have chosen.*
the last straw a final thing that makes problems unbearable

last NOUN **1** a person or thing that is last **2** the end • *He was brave to the last.*
at last or at long last finally; after much delay

last VERB lasts, lasting, lasted **1** continue; go on existing or living or being usable **2** be enough for • *The food will last us for three days.*

lasting ADJECTIVE able to last for a long time • *a lasting peace.*

lastly ADVERB in the last place; finally

latch NOUN latches a small bar fastening a door or gate, lifted by a lever or spring
▷ **latchkey** NOUN

latch VERB latches, latching, latched fasten with a latch
latch onto **1** meet someone and follow them around all the time **2** understand something

late ADJECTIVE, ADVERB **1** after the usual or expected time **2** near the end • *late in the afternoon* **3** recent • *the latest news* **4** who has died recently • *the late king*
of late recently

lately ADVERB recently

latent heat NOUN the heat needed to change a solid into a liquid or vapor, or a liquid into a vapor, without a change in temperature

lathe (layth) NOUN lathes a machine for holding and turning pieces of wood while they are being shaped

Thesaurus

conifers ► widespread, extensive, wide-ranging, large-scale

largely ADVERB *She was largely responsible for getting us into this mess.* ► mainly, chiefly, principally, primarily, mostly, to a large extent

lark NOUN (*informal*) *It all seemed just a lark to them.* ► prank, bit of fun, joke, laugh, game, escapade, amusement

lash VERB **1** *Driving rain lashed down.* ► beat against, dash against, batter, pound **2** *She lashed the poor donkey with a belt.* ► whip, beat, thrash, lash out at **3** *The speaker lashed out at his critics.* ► attack, condemn, denounce, lambaste, castigate, censure

last ADJECTIVE **1** *There was none of the violence associated with the last protest.* ► previous, preceding, recent, former **2** *She realized she was still the last person in the line.* ► final, rearmost, endmost OPPOSITES ARE first, leading **3** *She decided to have one last look.* ► final, concluding, ultimate OPPOSITES ARE initial, opening *I am the last person to complain.* ► least likely, most unlikely OPPOSITES ARE first, most likely

last VERB *The storm lasted all night.* ► continue, carry on, keep on, persist, endure, linger, remain, stay, hold, hold out, live, survive
OPPOSITES ARE stop, cease, fade

lasting ADJECTIVE *The reforms will produce lasting change.* ► permanent, enduring, continuing, long-lasting, long-standing, unceasing, undying, unending, long-term, long-lived, durable, indestructible, indissoluble, lifelong, stable, abiding AN OPPOSITE IS temporary

late ADJECTIVE **1** *The train was over an hour late.* ► overdue, delayed, slow, behind-hand, belated, dilatory, tardy, unpunctual AN OPPOSITE IS early **2** *her father, the late king* ► deceased, dead, departed, former **3** *He had taken part in the late conflict.* ► recent, previous, preceding, former

later ADJECTIVE *The issue would be dealt with at a later meeting.* ► subsequent, future, following, succeeding

later ADVERB *We will meet you later.* ► afterwards, in a while, subsequently, eventually, next

a
b
c
d
e
f
g
h
i
j
k
l
m
n
o
p
q
r
s
t
u
v
w
x
y
z

A
B
C
D
E
F
G
H
I
J
K
L
M
N
O
P
Q
R
S
T
U
V
W
X
Y
Z

lather NOUN a mass of froth
lather VERB lathers, lathering, lathered
1 cover with lather **2** form a lather
Latin NOUN the language of the ancient Romans
Latin America NOUN the parts of Central and South America where the main language is Spanish or Portuguese
latitude NOUN latitudes **1** the distance of a place from the equator, measured in degrees **2** freedom from restrictions on what people can do or believe
latrine (la- treen) NOUN latrines a lavatory in a camp or barracks, etc.
latter ADJECTIVE later • *the latter part of the year* **the latter** the second of two people or things just mentioned COMPARE former
lattice NOUN lattices a framework of crossed laths or bars with spaces between
laudable ADJECTIVE deserving praise
▷ **laudably** ADVERB
laugh VERB laughs, laughing, laughed make the sounds that show you are happy or think something is funny
laugh NOUN laughs the sound of laughing
laughable ADJECTIVE deserving to be laughed at
laughing stock NOUN laughing stocks a person or thing that is the object of ridicule and scorn
laughter NOUN the act, sound, or manner of laughing

launch VERB launches, launching, launched
1 send a ship from the land into the water
2 send a rocket, etc., into space **3** set a thing moving by throwing or pushing it **4** make a new product available for the first time • *Our new model will be launched in April.* **5** start into action • *launch an attack*
launch[2] NOUN launches a large motor boat
launderette NOUN launderettes a place fitted with washing machines that people pay to use
laundry NOUN laundries **1** a place where clothes are washed and ironed for customers **2** clothes needing to be washed or after being washed
laureate (lorri- at) ADJECTIVE
Poet Laureate a person appointed to write poems for national occasions
laurel NOUN laurels an evergreen shrub with smooth shiny leaves
lava NOUN molten rock that flows from a volcano; the solid rock formed when it cools
lavatory NOUN lavatories **1** a toilet **2** a room containing a toilet
lavender NOUN **1** a shrub with sweet-smelling purple flowers **2** a light-purple color
lavish ADJECTIVE **1** generous **2** plentiful
▷ **lavishly** ADVERB **lavishness** NOUN
law NOUN laws **1** a rule or set of rules that everyone must obey **2** the profession of lawyers **3** (*informal*) the police **4** a scientific

Thesaurus

latter ADJECTIVE *There are more games in the latter part of the month.* ► later, closing, concluding, last, recent, second AN OPPOSITE IS former
laugh VERB *Joe's antics began to make them laugh.* ► giggle, chuckle, chortle, snigger, titter, guffaw, (*more informal*) scream with laughter
laugh at *I didn't say anything in case the others laughed at me.* ► mock, ridicule, make fun of, scoff at, deride, jeer
laugh NOUN **1** *She gave a loud laugh.* ► chuckle, chortle, snigger, titter, guffaw **2** *Being with Henry was always a laugh.* ► joke, piece of fun, adventure, (*more informal*) scream
laughable ADJECTIVE **1** *The money they were offering was laughable.* ► absurd, ridiculous, ludicrous, preposterous, risible, derisory **2** *laughable attempts to steer the boat* ► funny, comic, comical, amusing, hilarious, farcical
laughter NOUN *sounds of conversation and laughter from the next room* ► laughing, mirth, laughs, chuckling, sniggering, hilarity, tittering, giggling, guffaws, merriment, (*more informal*) hysterics
launch VERB **1** *In its heyday the dockyard launched a ship every year.* ► float, set afloat,

put in the water **2** *It was decided to launch the shuttle from a different site.* ► fire, propel, send off, blast off, set off **3** *The enemy launched a counteroffensive. A new business will be launched next year.* ► begin, start, initiate, open, set up, embark on, establish, found, inaugurate

lavatory NOUN *There's another lavatory downstairs.* ► toilet, cloakroom, convenience, (*more informal*) loo, (*old-fashioned*) WC

lavish ADJECTIVE *After the show there will be a lavish supper.* ► sumptuous, elaborate, copious, extravagant, luxurious, generous, liberal, abundant, plentiful, bountiful, munificent, opulent, unstinting AN OPPOSITE IS meagre

law NOUN **1** *a new law closing tax loopholes* ► regulation, statute, act, bill, ruling, rule, enactment, edict USAGE Note that a *bill* is a government's proposal for a law, and an *act* is the bill after it has been passed and received the royal assent. RELATED ADJECTIVE ► legal, judicial **2** *the laws of logic* ► rule, principle, precept, prescription, guideline, tenet, maxim, doctrine **3** (*informal*) *on the run from the law* ► police, authorities

statement of something that always happens
• *the law of gravity*

law-abiding ADJECTIVE obeying the law

law court NOUN law courts a room or building in which a judge or magistrate hears evidence and decides whether someone has broken the law

lawful ADJECTIVE allowed or accepted by the law
▷ **lawfully** ADVERB

lawless ADJECTIVE **1** not obeying the law **2** without proper laws • *a lawless country*
▷ **lawlessly** ADVERB **lawlessness** NOUN

lawn NOUN lawns an area of closely cut grass in a garden or park

lawnmower NOUN lawnmowers a machine for cutting the grass of lawns

lawn tennis NOUN tennis played on an outdoor grass or hard court

lawsuit NOUN lawsuits a dispute or claim that is brought to a lawcourt to be settled

lawyer NOUN lawyers a person who is qualified to give advice in matters of law

laxative NOUN laxatives a medicine that stimulates the bowels to empty

lay[1] VERB lays, laying, laid **1** put something down in a particular place or way **2** arrange

things, especially for a meal • *Can you lay the table?* **3** place • *He laid the blame on his sister.* **4** form or prepare • *We laid our plans.* **5** produce an egg

lay off 1 stop employing somebody for a while **2** (*informal*) stop doing something

lay on supply or provide

lay out 1 arrange or prepare **2** (*informal*) knock a person unconscious **3** prepare a dead body for burial

USAGE Do not confuse lay/laid/laying = "put down," with lie/lay/lain/lying = "be in a flat position." Correct uses are as follows: • *Go and lie down.* • *She went and lay down.* • *Please lay it on the floor.* "Go and lay down" is incorrect.

lay[2] past tense of **lie**[2]

lay ADJECTIVE **1** not belonging to the clergy • *a lay preacher* **2** not professionally qualified • *a lay magistrate*

layer NOUN layers a single thickness or coating

layman NOUN laymen **1** a person who does not have specialized knowledge or training (e.g., as a doctor or lawyer) **2** a person who is not ordained as a member of the clergy

layout NOUN layouts an arrangement of parts of something according to a plan

Thesaurus

law-abiding ADJECTIVE *law-abiding citizens*
▸ well-behaved, respectable, honest, decent, orderly, peaceable, peaceful, compliant, disciplined, good, obedient OPPOSITES ARE lawless, criminal

lawful ADJECTIVE **1** *The police were making a lawful arrest.* ▸ legal, legitimate, permissible, permitted, allowable, allowed, just, right **2** *people going about their lawful business* ▸ legitimate, rightful, proper, valid, recognized, authorized, regular, legal, documented, prescribed AN OPPOSITE IS illegal

lawless ADJECTIVE *a lawless rabble* ▸ disorderly, unruly, riotous, mutinous, wild, rowdy, rebellious, disruptive, undisciplined, seditious, reckless, anarchic, anarchical, chaotic AN OPPOSITE IS law-abiding

lawyer NOUN *This is a matter for the lawyers.* ▸ solicitor, legal practitioner, legal adviser, barrister, advocate, attorney

lax ADJECTIVE *lax discipline in schools* ▸ slack, slipshod, casual, easygoing, lenient, permissive, careless, loose, neglectful, negligent, remiss, vague AN OPPOSITE IS strict

lay VERB **1** *He laid the map on the seat beside him.* ▸ put, place, set, set down, spread, deposit, leave **2** *We began to lay plans for a spring holiday.* ▸ form, make, devise, prepare, work out, hatch, concoct **3** *Be careful where you lay the blame for this.* ▸ assign, attach, attribute,

ascribe, allot, apportion, fix, impute **4** *The landlady laid a table for breakfast.* ▸ arrange, set out, organize

lay in *The men laid in a supply of beer.* ▸ stock up with, put aside, put by, collect, store

lay into (*informal*) *His father laid into him when he got home.* ▸ scold, rebuke, berate, castigate, criticize, censure

lay off 1 (*informal*) *You really should lay off smoking.* ▸ give up, stop, cut out **2** *Over a hundred staff were laid off just before Christmas.* ▸ make redundant, dismiss, discharge, release, (*more informal*) sack

lay out 1 *Richard laid out the plans on the table.* ▸ arrange, set out, spread, display **2** (*informal*) *The blow laid him out for an hour.* ▸ knock out, make unconscious, flatten

layabout NOUN *It's odd for such a lively boy to have a layabout for a brother.* ▸ idler, loafer, good-for-nothing, sluggard, (*more informal*) slob, (*more informal*) couch potato OPPOSITE IS hard worker

layer NOUN **1** *an extra layer of paint* ▸ coating, coat, covering, surface, film, sheet, skin, thickness **2** *a layer of rock* ▸ seam, stratum, substratum

layout NOUN *The layout of the house takes some getting used to.* ▸ arrangement, organization, design, plan, disposition, (*more informal*) set-up

a
b
c
d
e
f
g
h
i
j
k
l
m
n
o
p
q
r
s
t
u
v
w
x
y
z

lazy ADJECTIVE lazier, laziest not wanting to work; doing little work
▷ **lazily** ADVERB **laziness** NOUN

lead[1] (leed) VERB leads, leading, led **1** take or guide someone, especially by going in front **2** be winning in a race or contest, etc.; be ahead **3** be in charge of a group of people **4** be a way or route • *This path leads to the beach.* **5** play the first card in a card game **6** live or experience • *He leads a dull life.*
lead to result in; cause

lead (leed) NOUN leads **1** a leading place or part or position • *She took the lead on the final bend.* **2** guidance or example • *We should be taking a lead on this issue.* **3** a clue to be followed **4** a strap or cord for leading a dog or other animal **5** an electrical wire attached to something

lead[2] (led) NOUN leads **1** a soft heavy grey metal **2** the writing substance (graphite) in a pencil
▷ **lead** ADJECTIVE

leader NOUN leaders **1** the person in charge of a group of people; a chief **2** the person who is winning **3** a newspaper article giving the editor's opinion
▷ **leadership** NOUN

leaf NOUN leaves **1** a flat, usually green, part of a plant, growing out from its stem, branch, or root **2** the paper forming one page of a book **3** a very thin sheet of metal • *gold leaf* **4** a flap that makes a table larger
▷ **leafy** ADJECTIVE **leafless** ADJECTIVE
turn over a new leaf make a fresh start and improve your behavior

leaflet NOUN leaflets a piece of paper printed with information

league[1] NOUN leagues **1** a group of teams who compete against each other for a championship **2** a group of people or nations who agree to work together
in league with working or plotting together

league[2] NOUN leagues an old measure of distance, about 3 miles

leak NOUN leaks **1** a hole or crack, etc., through which liquid or gas accidentally escapes **2** the revealing of secret information
▷ **leaky** ADJECTIVE

leak VERB leaks, leaking, leaked **1** get out or let out through a leak **2** reveal secret information
▷ **leakage** NOUN

Thesaurus

---

laze VERB *Young girls lazed in the sun.* ► relax, idle, loaf, lounge, loll AN OPPOSITE IS work

laziness NOUN *His report mentioned lateness and laziness.* ► idleness, indolence, slothfulness, sloth, lethargy, loafing, lounging about, dilatoriness, inactivity, slowness, sluggishness AN OPPOSITE IS industry

lazy ADJECTIVE **1** *No one can accuse them of being lazy after all they've achieved.* ► idle, indolent, slothful, inactive, lethargic, slack AN OPPOSITE IS industrious **2** *They headed for a lazy weekend in the country.* ► quiet, relaxing, peaceful

lead NOUN **1** *The older students provide a lead for the younger ones.* ► example, guidance, leadership, direction **2** *Detectives are following an important new lead.* ► clue, hint, tip, tip-off, line of inquiry **3** *One of the Ferrari team took the lead.* ► first place, front position, spearhead, vanguard **4** *She will play the lead in his new film.* ► principal role, chief part, starring role, title role **5** *The toaster needs a new lead.* ► cable, flex, wire **6** *He let the dog off the lead.* ► leash, tether, rein, chain, strap, cord

lead VERB **1** *She led her guests out on the terrace.* ► conduct, guide, show, escort, usher, marshal, shepherd, steer, pilot AN OPPOSITE IS follow **2** *Smith was appointed to lead the delegation.* ► head, be in charge of, be the leader of, preside over, direct, manage, command, govern, supervise, rule **3** *The Harvard boat was leading for most of the distance.*

► be in front, be in the lead, head the field AN OPPOSITE IS trail **4** *They have led a very happy life.* ► pass, spend, have, experience, undergo
lead to *Asking awkward questions might lead to trouble.* ► cause, bring about, result in, give rise to, produce, generate, create, precipitate, induce, stimulate
lead on *She was accused of leading them on.* ► mislead, deceive, entice, beguile, hoodwink, string along

leader NOUN **1** *the leader of the marketing team* ► head, chief, director, manager, principal, superior, (more informal) boss **2** *one of the country's former leaders* ► ruler, chief, governor

leading ADJECTIVE *The book is acknowledged as the leading authority on the subject.* ► principal, foremost, chief, major, key, main, primary, pre-eminent, outstanding, dominant, important, inspiring, prominent, well known

league NOUN **1** *The countries came together to form a league.* ► association, alliance, federation, confederation, confederacy, syndicate **2** *On Saturday they face the league leaders.* ► group, class, championship

leak VERB **1** *Oil was leaking from the tank.* ► seep, escape, ooze, spill, trickle, drip, exude **2** *We still haven't discovered who leaked the information.* ► reveal, disclose, divulge, pass on, give away, let out, make known

leak NOUN **1** *several leaks in the roof* ► hole, opening, crack, drip, perforation, puncture

lean ADJECTIVE **1** with little or no fat • *lean meat* **2** thin • *a lean body*

lean VERB leans, leaning, leaned **1** bend your body towards or over something **2** put or be in a sloping position **3** rest against something **4** rely or depend on someone for help

leaning NOUN leanings a tendency or preference

leap VERB leaps, leaping, leaped or leapt jump vigorously
▷ **leap** NOUN

leapfrog NOUN a game in which each player jumps with legs apart over another who is bending down

leap year NOUN leap years a year with an extra day in it (29 February)

learn VERB learns, learning, learned **1** get knowledge or skill through study or training **2** find out about something
USAGE It is not acceptable in standard English to use learn to mean "to teach."

learned (ler- nid) ADJECTIVE having much knowledge obtained by study

learner NOUN learners a person who is learning something

learning NOUN knowledge obtained by study

lease NOUN leases an agreement to allow someone to use a building or land, etc., for a fixed period in return for payment
▷ **leaseholder** NOUN
a new lease of life a chance to be healthy, active, or usable again

lease VERB leases, leasing, leased allow or obtain the use of something by lease

leash NOUN leashes a dog's lead

least ADJECTIVE, ADVERB very small in amount etc. • *the least bit;* • *the least expensive bike*
at least **1** not less than what is mentioned • *It will cost at least $40.* **2** anyway • *He's at home, or at least I think he is.*

leather NOUN material made from animal skins
▷ **leathery** ADJECTIVE

leave VERB leaves, leaving, left **1** go away from a person or place **2** stop belonging to a group or stop working somewhere **3** cause or allow something to stay where it is or as it is • *You left the door open.* **4** go away without taking something • *I left my book at home.* **5** let someone deal with something • *Leave the cleanup to me* **6** put something to be collected or passed on • *Would you like to leave a message?*
leave off cease
leave out omit; not include

Thesaurus

2 *a gas leak* ► escape, seepage, discharge **3** *a leak of information* ► disclosure, divulgence, revelation

leaky ADJECTIVE *a leaky roof* ► leaking, dripping, cracked, holed, perforated, punctured AN OPPOSITE IS watertight

lean ADJECTIVE **1** *a tall lean figure* ► thin, spare, skinny, slender, slim, gaunt, lanky, wiry, bony, emaciated AN OPPOSITE IS fat **2** *a lean harvest* ► meagre, scanty, sparse, poor, mean, barren, inadequate

lean VERB **1** *The trees were leaning in the wind.* ► slant, incline, bend, tilt, tip, bank, heel over, list, loll, slope **2** *Mary leaned against the fence.* ► rest, support yourself, prop yourself up, recline
lean toward *We lean toward a peaceful solution.* ► favor, prefer, tend toward, incline toward

leap VERB **1** *The dog leapt over the gate.* ► jump, spring, vault, bound **2** *Claire leapt to her feet* ► spring, jump **3** *Prices have leapt in the last few months.* ► soar, rise, rocket, surge, increase OPPOSITES ARE tumble, plummet, fall
leap at *He leapt at the opportunity.* ► seize, grasp, accept eagerly, (more informal) go for OPPOSITES ARE turn down, reject

learn VERB **1** *It is important to learn the language when living in a foreign country.* ► master, acquire a knowledge of, acquire, understand, assimilate, pick up **2** *If I want to learn a poem I*

stick it on the fridge. ► memorize, learn by heart, know

learned ADJECTIVE *a learned piece of writing* ► scholarly, erudite, intellectual, academic, cultured, educated, highbrow

learner NOUN *At this stage he is just a learner.* ► beginner, novice, apprentice, pupil, starter, newcomer, cadet, trainee, tiro

learning NOUN *a person of great learning* ► scholarship, erudition, knowledge, culture, education, schooling, wisdom, information

least ADJECTIVE **1** *I haven't the least idea what he means.* ► slightest, smallest, tiniest AN OPPOSITE IS greatest **2** *Choose a place that involves the least travel.* ► minimum, minimal, smallest amount of OPPOSITES ARE maximum, most

leave VERB **1** *It is time to leave now.* ► depart, set off, go, go away, go out, take your leave, withdraw, retire, say goodbye, (more informal) disappear AN OPPOSITE IS arrive **2** *She left the house that afternoon.* ► depart from, quit, vacate **3** *His wife has left him.* ► desert, abandon, forsake **4** *He's going to leave his job at the end of the month.* ► quit, give up, resign from, relinquish **5** *I've left my briefcase on the train.* ► lose, mislay, leave behind **6** *Leave it to me to sort out.* ► entrust, refer, hand over, consign **7** *When he died he left them the house.* ► bequeath, will, endow

leave ➡ leisure

leave NOUN **1** permission **2** official permission to be away from work; the time for which this permission lasts • *three days' leave* [from Old English]

lecture NOUN **lectures 1** a talk about a subject to an audience or a class **2** a long serious warning or reprimand given to someone

lecture VERB **lectures, lecturing, lectured** give a lecture
▷ **lecturer** NOUN
[from Latin *lectura* = reading, or something to be read]

led *past tense of* lead[1]

ledge NOUN **ledges** a narrow shelf • *a window ledge* • *a mountain ledge*

ledger NOUN **ledgers** an account book [probably from Dutch]

leech NOUN **leeches** a small blood-sucking worm that lives in water

leek NOUN **leeks** a long green and white vegetable of the onion family

leer VERB **leers, leering, leered** look at someone in a sly or unpleasant way
▷ **leer** NOUN

leeway NOUN **1** extra space or time available **2** a drift to leeward or off course
make up leeway make up lost time; regain a lost position

left ADJECTIVE, ADVERB **1** on or toward the west if you think of yourself as facing north **2** (said about political groups) in favor of socialist or radical views
▷ **left-hand** ADJECTIVE

left NOUN the left-hand side or part [from Old English *lyft* = weak]

left *past tense of* leave

left-handed ADJECTIVE using the left hand in preference to the right hand

leg NOUN **legs 1** one of the limbs on a person's or animal's body, on which it stands or moves **2** the part of a piece of clothing covering a leg **3** each of the supports of a chair or other piece of furniture **4** one part of a journey **5** one of a pair of matches between the same teams [from Old Norse]

legacy NOUN **legacies 1** something left to a person in a will **2** something that results from what people have done in the past • *a legacy of distrust*

legal ADJECTIVE **1** lawful **2** to do with the law or lawyers
▷ **legally** ADVERB **legality** NOUN

legend NOUN **legends 1** an old story handed down from the past, which may or may not be true COMPARE **myth 2** a very famous person
▷ **legendary** ADJECTIVE
[from Latin *legenda* = things to be read]

legible ADJECTIVE clear enough to read
▷ **legibly** ADVERB **legibility** NOUN
[from Latin *legere* = to read]

legion NOUN **legions 1** a division of the ancient Roman army **2** a group of soldiers or former soldiers

legislate VERB **legislates, legislating, legislated** make laws
▷ **legislation** NOUN **legislator** NOUN

legitimate ADJECTIVE **1** lawful **2** born when parents are married to each other
▷ **legitimately** ADVERB **legitimacy** NOUN

leisure NOUN time that is free from work, when you can do what you like
▷ **leisured** ADJECTIVE **leisurely** ADJECTIVE

Thesaurus

leave NOUN **1** *The judge granted him leave to appeal against the verdict.* ► permission, consent, authorization, approval, liberty **2** *Greg was having some leave from the army.* ► free time, time off, holiday, absence, sabbatical, vacation

lecture NOUN **1** *a lecture on modern poetry* ► talk, discourse, speech, address, lesson **2** *He got a stern lecture about being late.* ► reprimand, scolding, rebuke, harangue

lecture VERB **1** *Anna lectures at the university.* ► teach, give lectures, give lessons, take students **2** *Professor Jones will lecture on advances in genetics.* ► give a lecture, speak, talk, discourse, (*more informal*) hold forth **3** *She lectured us on our bad manners.* ► reprimand, scold, rebuke, admonish, chide

leg NOUN **1** *the first leg of the journey* ► stage, part, phase, stretch, lap, step **2** *a table leg* ► support, upright, prop

legal ADJECTIVE **1** *legal advice* ► judicial, judiciary **2** *activity that is not legal* ► lawful, legitimate,

licit, permissible, authorized, permitted, above board, allowable, allowed, rightful, proper, constitutional, valid AN OPPOSITE IS illegal

legend NOUN *legends from the past* ► myth, story, folk tale, fable, tradition

legible ADJECTIVE *The writing was barely legible.* ► readable, clear, decipherable, intelligible, distinct, neat, plain AN OPPOSITE IS illegible

legitimate ADJECTIVE **1** *They have legitimate reasons for the action they took.* ► valid, sound, cogent, admissible, well-founded, acceptable, justifiable **2** *The Duke lacked a legitimate heir.* ► lawful, legal, rightful, acknowledged, true, proper

leisure NOUN **1** *They lead a life of leisure.* ► ease, relaxation, enjoyment, inactivity, pleasure, amusement, recreation, retirement **2** *She never had enough leisure to do the things she wanted.* ► free time, spare time, time off, freedom, liberty, rest

leisurely ADJECTIVE *a leisurely stroll through the park* ► slow, gentle, unhurried, relaxed,

at leisure having leisure; not hurried

at your leisure when you have time

lemming NOUN lemmings a small mouselike animal of Arctic regions that migrates in large numbers and is said to run headlong into the sea and drown

lemon NOUN lemons **1** an oval yellow citrus fruit with a sour taste **2** a pale yellow color

lemonade NOUN a lemon-flavoured drink

lemur (lee- mer) NOUN lemurs a monkeylike animal

lend VERB lends, lending, lent **1** allow a person to use something of yours for a short time **2** provide someone with money that they must repay, usually in return for payments (called **interest**) **3** give or add a quality • *She lent dignity to the occasion.*
▷ **lender** NOUN
lend a hand help somebody
USAGE Do not use **lend** to mean **borrow**.

length NOUN lengths **1** how long something is **2** a piece of cloth, rope, wire, etc., cut from a larger piece **3** the distance of a swimming pool from one end to the other **4** the amount of thoroughness in an action • *They went to great lengths to make us comfortable.*
at length 1 after a long time **2** taking a long time; in detail

lengthen VERB lengthens, lengthening, lengthened make or become longer

lengthy ADJECTIVE going on for a long time
▷ **lengthily** ADVERB

lenient (lee- nee- ent) ADJECTIVE merciful; not severe
▷ **leniently** ADVERB **lenience** NOUN

lens NOUN lenses **1** a curved piece of glass or plastic used to focus things **2** the transparent part of the eye, immediately behind the pupil [Latin, = lentil (because of its shape)]

Lent NOUN a time of fasting and penitence observed by Christians for about six weeks before Easter
▷ **Lenten** ADJECTIVE
[from Old English *lencten* = the spring]

lent past tense of lend

lentil NOUN lentils a kind of small bean

leopard (lep- erd) NOUN leopards a large spotted mammal of the cat family, also called a panther
▷ **leopardess** NOUN

leper NOUN lepers a person who has leprosy

leprosy NOUN an infectious disease that makes parts of the body waste away
▷ **leprous** ADJECTIVE

lesbian NOUN lesbians a homosexual woman [named after the Greek island of Lesbos (because Sappho, a poetess who lived there about 600 BC, wrote poetry about love between women)]

less ADJECTIVE, ADVERB smaller in amount; not so much • *Make less noise.* • *It is less important.*
USAGE Do not use **less** when you mean **fewer**. You should use **fewer** when you are talking about a number of individual things, and **less** when you are talking about a quantity or mass of something: • *The less batter you make, the fewer pancakes you'll get.*

less NOUN a smaller amount

less PREPOSITION minus; deducting • *She earned $100, less tax.*

-less SUFFIX forms adjectives meaning "without" (e.g. *colorless*) or "unable to be ..." (e.g. *countless*)

lesser ADJECTIVE not so great as the other • *the lesser evil*

lesson NOUN lessons **1** an amount of teaching given at one time **2** something to be learnt by a pupil **3** an example or experience from

Thesaurus

relaxing, restful, sedate, comfortable, easy, lingering, peaceful OPPOSITES ARE brisk, hurried

lend VERB *He asked me to lend him the money.*
► loan, advance, let someone have AN OPPOSITE IS borrow

length NOUN **1** *The snakes grew to a length of twenty feet or more.* ► extent, measurement, stretch, distance **2** *People began to grumble about the length of the wait.* ► duration, extent, protractedness, period, time

lengthen VERB **1** *The days begin to lengthen in March.* ► grow longer, get longer, draw out, stretch, enlarge, elongate, expand, extend, increase, prolong, pull out AN OPPOSITE IS shorten **2** *You will need to lengthen the cooking time.* ► extend, increase, prolong, continue AN OPPOSITE IS shorten

lengthy ADJECTIVE *The family faced a lengthy journey.* ► long, protracted, drawn out, tedious, extended OPPOSITES ARE short, brief

lenient ADJECTIVE *He always said his mother had been too lenient with him.* ► soft, easygoing, tolerant, softhearted, indulgent, merciful, forgiving, mild, kind OPPOSITES ARE strict, severe

lessen VERB **1** *He took an aspirin to lessen the pain.* ► reduce, lower, decrease, deaden, alleviate, assuage, mitigate, make less, minimize, tone down **2** *Her love for him would never lessen.* ► diminish, decrease, abate, fade, dwindle, weaken, grow less, recede, shrink AN OPPOSITE IS increase

lesson NOUN **1** *a French lesson* ► class, period, lecture, seminar, tutorial, instruction **2** *The experience might be a lesson to all of them.*
► example, warning, deterrent, moral

A
B
C
D
E
F
G
H
I
J
K
L
M
N
O
P
Q
R
S
T
U
V
W
X
Y
Z

which you should learn • *Let this be a lesson to you!* **4** a passage from the Bible read aloud as part of a church service

lest CONJUNCTION (old use) so that something should not happen • *Remind us, lest we forget.*

let VERB lets, letting, let **1** allow somebody or something to do something; not prevent or forbid • *Let me see it.* **2** cause to • *Let us know what happens.* **3** allow or cause to come or go or pass • *Let me out!* **4** allow someone to use a house or building in return for payment (rent) **5** leave • *Let it alone.*

let down 1 deflate **2** disappoint somebody
let off 1 cause to explode **2** excuse somebody from a duty or punishment, etc.
let on (informal) reveal a secret
let up (informal) relax

lethal (lee- thal) ADJECTIVE deadly; causing death
▷ **lethally** ADVERB

lethargy (leth- er- jee) NOUN extreme lack of energy or vitality
▷ **lethargic** (lith- ar- jik) ADJECTIVE

letter NOUN letters **1** a symbol representing a sound used in speech **2** a written message, usually sent by post
to the letter paying strict attention to every detail

letter box NOUN letter boxes **1** a slot in a door, through which letters are delivered **2** a postbox

lettering NOUN letters drawn or painted

lettuce NOUN lettuces a garden plant with broad crisp leaves used in salads

leukemia (lew- kee- mee- a) NOUN a disease in which there are too many white corpuscles in the blood [from Greek *leukos* = white + *haima* = blood]

level ADJECTIVE **1** flat or horizontal **2** at the same height or position as something else

level NOUN levels **1** height, depth, position, or value, etc. • *Fix the shelves at eye level.* **2** a level surface **3** a device that shows whether something is level
on the level (informal) honest

level VERB levels, leveling, leveled **1** make or become level **2** aim a gun or missile **3** direct an accusation at a person

level crossing NOUN level crossings a place where a road crosses a railway at the same level

lever NOUN levers **1** a bar that turns on a fixed point (the **fulcrum**) in order to lift something or force something open **2** a bar used as a handle to operate machinery etc. • *a gear lever*

lever VERB levers, levering, levered lift or move something by means of a lever

---

Thesaurus

let VERB **1** *His parents wouldn't let him go on the trip.* ► allow, permit, give permission, authorize, consent to, agree to USAGE If you use *allow, permit,* or *authorize* you have to add to, e.g. *His parents wouldn't allow him to go.* If you use *give permission,* you have to say *His parents wouldn't give him permission to go* or *His parents wouldn't give permission for him to go.* If you use *consent* or *agree* you have to say *His parents wouldn't agree or consent to his (or him) going.* OPPOSITES ARE prevent, forbid **2** *The landlord will let rooms for six months.* ► rent out, lease out, hire out AN OPPOSITE IS intensify
let down *They felt the manager had let them down.* ► fail, disappoint, betray, abandon, desert
let off *They decided to let him off with a warning.* ► pardon, forgive, excuse, spare, release
let up *The rain let up for a while.* ► ease, subside, abate, slacken, diminish

lethal ADJECTIVE *execution by lethal injection* ► deadly, fatal, mortal, poisonous

letter NOUN **1** *She wrote a letter to her senator.* ► message, note, communication, dispatch, missive, (more formal) epistle RELATED ADJECTIVE ► epistolary **2** *The wall was daubed with large letters.* ► character, figure, sign, symbol, device

level ADJECTIVE **1** *Make sure the surface is level before spreading the paper on it.* ► flat, even, smooth, uniform, flush, regular, horizontal, plane AN OPPOSITE IS uneven **2** *The scores were level at half time.* ► equal, even, matching, balanced, the same, (more informal) neck-and-neck

level NOUN **1** *Soon she was promoted to a senior level.* ► rank, status, position, class, echelon **2** *There is a high level of absenteeism.* ► amount, quantity, extent, degree, proportion **3** *The water rose to a dangerous level.* ► height, elevation, altitude **4** *There are offices on this level of the building.* ► floor, story, tier

level VERB **1** *He piled on the earth, leveling it with his hands.* ► smooth, even out, flatten, rake **2** *A series of violent tremors leveled the area.* ► raze, demolish, destroy, devastate, knock down, lay low **3** *His hand was shaking, making it difficult to level the gun.* ► aim, point, direct, train

level-headed ADJECTIVE *Belinda was too level-headed to fool herself in this way.* ► sensible, balanced, practical, prudent, realistic, self-possessed, commonsensical, judicious

lever NOUN *You push the lever down and leave it there.* ► switch, handle, knob, bar

lever VERB *He picked up a crowbar and levered open the window.* ► prise, force, wrench, heave

leverage NOUN **1** the force you need when you use a lever **2** influence

levity NOUN being humorous, especially at an unsuitable time

levy VERB levies, levying, levied impose or collect a tax or other payment by the use of authority or force

levy NOUN levies an amount of money paid in tax

liability NOUN liabilities **1** being legally responsible for something **2** a debt or obligation **3** a disadvantage or handicap

liable ADJECTIVE **1** likely to do or suffer something • *She is liable to colds.* • *The cliff is liable to crumble.* **2** legally responsible for something

liaison (lee- ay- zon) NOUN liaisons **1** communication and cooperation between people or groups **2** a person who is a link or go-between **3** a sexual affair

liar NOUN liars a person who tells lies

libel (ly- bel) NOUN libels an untrue written, printed, or broadcast statement that damages a person's reputation COMPARE **slander**
▷ **libelous** ADJECTIVE

libel VERB libels, libeling, libeled make a libel against someone

liberal ADJECTIVE **1** giving generously **2** given in large amounts **3** not strict; tolerant
▷ **liberally** ADVERB **liberality** NOUN

liberate VERB liberates, liberating, liberated set free
▷ **liberation** NOUN **liberator** NOUN

liberty NOUN liberties freedom
take liberties behave too casually or in too familiar a way

librarian NOUN librarians a person in charge of or working in a library
▷ **librarianship** NOUN

library (ly- bra- ree) NOUN libraries **1** a place where books are kept for people to use or borrow **2** a collection of books, records, films, etc.

lice plural of louse

license NOUN licenses **1** an official permit to do or use or own something • *a driving license* **2** special freedom to avoid the usual rules or customs

license VERB licenses, licensing, licensed give a licence to a person; authorize • *We are licensed to sell tobacco.*

lichen (ly- ken, lich- en) NOUN lichens a dry-looking plant that grows on rocks, walls, trees, etc.

lick VERB licks, licking, licked **1** move your tongue over something **2** (said about a wave

Thesaurus

liability NOUN **1** *The driver of the other car admitted liability for the accident.*
► responsibility, blame, culpability, accountability **2** *Taking the dog with us could prove a liability.* ► nuisance, inconvenience, encumbrance, hindrance, burden, handicap, drawback, (more informal) drag

liable ADJECTIVE **1** *The company is not liable for any damage that might be caused.* ► responsible, accountable, answerable, to blame AN OPPOSITE IS exempt (from) **2** *The shaft is liable to break under pressure.* ► likely, apt, prone, inclined, given (to breaking), disposed, predisposed, ready AN OPPOSITE IS unlikely

liar NOUN *Parkin was either a coward or a liar, or both.* ► deceiver, fabricator, falsifier, (more informal) storyteller, (more informal) fibber

libel NOUN *He said the newspaper article amounted to libel.* ► defamation of character, misrepresentation, an insult, a slur, a smear USAGE You can also use slander when the insult is spoken rather than printed.

libelous ADJECTIVE *Lawyers check whether there is anything libelous in the writing.* ► defamatory, derogatory, false, insulting USAGE You can also use slanderous when the insult is spoken rather than printed.

liberal ADJECTIVE **1** *a liberal supply of liquid refreshment* ► copious, generous, plentiful,

lavish, abundant, ample, bounteous, bountiful, munificent, unstinting AN OPPOSITE IS mean **2** *liberal social attitudes* ► broad-minded, tolerant, enlightened, moderate, easygoing, magnanimous, lenient, unbiased, unprejudiced, permissive, free AN OPPOSITE IS narrow-minded **3** *liberal political views* ► progressive, radical, forward-looking AN OPPOSITE IS conservative

liberate VERB *the intention to liberate all people from every kind of slavery* ► free, set free, release, discharge, deliver, rescue, save, emancipate, unfetter, loose, ransom, untie OPPOSITES ARE enslave, subjugate

liberty NOUN *You can enjoy the liberty to follow your own interests.* ► freedom, independence, emancipation, liberation, release
at liberty 1 *The escaped prisoners were at liberty for three months.* ► free, on the run, on the loose **2** *She is at liberty to use her money as she wishes.* ► free, entitled, permitted, allowed, authorized AN OPPOSITE IS forbidden

license NOUN **1** *I needed a license to play music in my shop.* ► permit, certificate, document, authorization, warrant **2** *the license to act as you see fit* ► authority, authorization, permission, entitlement, prerogative, privilege

lick VERB **1** *Tessa was licking a lollipop.* ► suck, taste **2** (more informal) *They licked the visiting*

A
B
C
D
E
F
G
H
I
J
K
L
M
N
O
P
Q
R
S
T
U
V
W
X
Y
Z

or flame) move like a tongue; touch lightly **3** (*slang*) defeat
a lick of paint a light covering of paint
at a lick (*informal*) at a fast pace

licorice (lick- er- ish) NOUN **1** a black substance used in medicine and as a sweet **2** the plant from whose root this substance is obtained

lid NOUN **lids 1** a cover for a box or pot, etc. **2** an eyelid

lie NOUN **lies** a statement that the person who makes it knows to be untrue

lie[1] VERB **lies, lying, lied** tell a lie or lies; be deceptive

lie[2] VERB **lies, lying, lay, lain 1** be or get in a flat or resting position ● *He lay on the grass.* ● *The cat has lain here all night.* **2** be or remain ● *The island lies near the coast.* ● *The machinery lay idle.*
lie low keep yourself hidden
USAGE See the note at **lay**[1].

lieutenant (lef- ten- ant) NOUN **lieutenants 1** an officer in the army or navy **2** a deputy or chief assistant

life NOUN **lives 1** the period between birth and death **2** being alive and able to function and grow **3** living things ● *Is there life on Mars?* **4** liveliness ● *full of life* **5** a biography **6** the length of time that something exists or functions ● *The battery has a life of two years.*

lifebelt NOUN **lifebelts** a ring of material that will float, used to support someone's body in water

lifeboat NOUN **lifeboats** a boat for rescuing people at sea

life cycle NOUN **life cycles** the series of changes in the life of a living thing

lifeguard NOUN **lifeguards** someone whose job is to rescue swimmers who are in difficulty

life insurance NOUN insurance that pays out a sum of money when the insured person dies

life jacket NOUN **life jackets** a jacket of material that will float, used to support someone's body in water

lifeless ADJECTIVE **1** without life **2** unconscious
▷ **lifelessly** ADVERB

lifelike ADJECTIVE looking exactly like a real person or thing

lifestyle NOUN **lifestyles** the way of life of a person or a group of people

lifetime NOUN **lifetimes** the time for which someone is alive

lift VERB **lifts, lifting, lifted 1** raise or pick up something **2** rise or go upwards **3** remove or abolish something ● *The ban has been lifted.* **4** (*informal*) steal

lift NOUN **lifts 1** lifting **2** a device for taking people or goods from one floor or level to another in a building **3** a free ride in somebody else's vehicle ● *Can you give me a lift to the station?* [from Old Norse]

Thesaurus

side 4-0. ► beat, defeat, overcome, trounce, rout, thrash **3** *By now the flames were licking the ceiling.* ► touch, reach, brush, flicker round, dance round

lid NOUN *The lid was stuck to the jar.* ► top, cap, stopper, cover, covering

lie NOUN *He can't help telling lies.* ► untruth, falsehood, falsification, fabrication, deception, invention, falsity, deceit, fiction, (*more informal*) fib OPPOSITES ARE truth, fact

lie VERB **1** *He lied about where he'd been.* ► tell an untruth, invent a story, dissemble, (*more informal*) fib **2** *She was lying on the bed.* ► recline, stretch out, rest, lounge, sprawl **3** *The town lies twenty miles from the coast.* ► be situated, be located, be placed, be found, be sited

life NOUN **1** *The joy of giving life* ► existence, breath, being **2** *Their dog still looked full of life.* ► vitality, energy, liveliness, vigor, verve, spirit, vivacity, zest, activity, (*more informal*) go **3** *I'm reading a life of John Lennon.* ► biography, autobiography, life story **4** *The contract covers the life of the project.* ► duration, course, span, extent

lifeless ADJECTIVE **1** *The lifeless body fell into the grave.* ► dead, deceased, inanimate, defunct, comatose, inert AN OPPOSITE IS living **2** *a lifeless desert* ► barren, arid, bare, sterile AN OPPOSITE IS fertile **3** *The voice was dull and lifeless.* ► lackluster, lethargic, unexciting, apathetic, tedious, boring, flat, slow AN OPPOSITE IS animated

lifelike ADJECTIVE *The new portrait was unusually lifelike.* ► realistic, true to life, authentic, natural, graphic, convincing, photographic AN OPPOSITE IS unrealistic

lift VERB **1** *She lifted the twins into their special chairs.* ► raise, pick up, hoist, heave OPPOSITES ARE lower, drop **2** *The plane lifted off the ground.* ► rise, ascend, go up, soar OPPOSITES ARE land, touch down **3** *The sight of the sea lifted their spirits.* ► raise, boost, buoy up, revive, enliven, perk up OPPOSITES ARE lower, subdue **4** *The six-month ban has now been lifted.* ► cancel, revoke, rescind, remove, withdraw AN OPPOSITE IS impose **5** *By now the mist had lifted.* ► clear, disperse, disappear, vanish, dissolve, rise OPPOSITES ARE come down, appear

lift NOUN *She took the lift to the top floor.* ► elevator, escalator, hoist

ligament NOUN **ligaments** a piece of the tough flexible tissue that holds your bones together [from Latin *ligare* = bind]

light NOUN **lights 1** radiation that stimulates the sense of sight and makes things visible **2** something that provides light, especially an electric lamp **3** a flame
bring or **come to light** make or become known

light ADJECTIVE **1** full of light; not dark **2** pale • *light blue*

light VERB **lights, lighting, lit** or **lighted 1** start a thing burning; begin to burn **2** provide light for something
light up 1 put lights on, especially at dusk **2** make or become light or bright
USAGE Say *He lit the lamps; the lamps were lit* (not "lighted"), but *She carried a lighted torch* (not "a lit torch").

light ADJECTIVE **1** having little weight; not heavy **2** small in amount or force etc. • *light rain* • *a light punishment* **3** needing little effort • *light work* **4** cheerful, not sad • *with a light heart* **5** not serious or profound • *light music*
▷ **lightly** ADVERB **lightness** NOUN

light ADVERB lightly; with only a small load • *We were travelling light* [from Old English *liht*]

lighten[1] VERB **lightens, lightening, lightened** make or become lighter or brighter

lighten[2] VERB **lightens, lightening, lightened** make or become lighter or less heavy

lighthearted ADJECTIVE **1** cheerful and free from worry **2** not serious

lighthouse NOUN **lighthouses** a tower with a bright light at the top to guide or warn ships

lightning NOUN a flash of bright light produced by natural electricity during a thunderstorm
like lightning with very great speed

lightning conductor NOUN lightning conductors a metal rod or wire fixed on a building to divert lightning into the earth

light year NOUN **light years** the distance that light travels in one year (about 95 million million km)

like VERB **likes, liking, liked 1** think a person or thing is pleasant or satisfactory **2** wish • *I'd like to come.*

like ADJECTIVE similar; having some or all of the qualities of another person or thing • *They are as like as two peas.*

like NOUN a similar person or thing • *We shall not see his like again.*

like PREPOSITION **1** similar to; in the manner of • *He swims like a fish.* **2** in a suitable state for • *It looks like rain.* • *I feel like a cup of tea.*

likelihood NOUN being likely; probability

Thesaurus

light ADJECTIVE **1** *a light load* ► slight, lightweight, portable, insubstantial, weightless, flimsy, feathery AN OPPOSITE IS heavy **2** *a light blue* ► pale, faint, pastel, fair AN OPPOSITE IS dark **3** *a light meal* ► modest, frugal, simple, skimpy, insubstantial OPPOSITES ARE heavy, rich **4** *light music; a little light reading* ► entertaining, lightweight, diverting, undemanding, easy **5** *She looked light on her feet.* ► nimble, deft, agile, graceful

light NOUN **1** *The gas lamp did not give out much light.* ► brightness, illumination, radiance, luminescence, glow, luster **2** *There was a light on in the bedroom.* ► lamp, lantern, torch, bulb **3** *She saw the problem in a new light.* ► aspect, complexion, angle, standpoint, point of view, slant, approach USAGE With the last five synonyms you use *from* instead of *in*, e.g., *She saw the problem from a new standpoint.* **4** *In an hour they would be working in the light.* ► daylight, light of day, daytime, sunlight

light VERB **1** *The boys wanted to light a fire.* ► kindle, ignite, set alight, set burning, put a match to, set fire to, switch on OPPOSITES ARE put out, extinguish **2** *Hundreds of searchlights lit the sky.* ► illuminate, light up, lighten, brighten, irradiate, floodlight, cast light on, shed light on, shine on AN OPPOSITE IS darken

lighten VERB **1** *Pale streaks lightened the sky.* ► light, light up, illuminate, brighten, irradiate AN OPPOSITE IS darken **2** *The sky lightened in the east.* ► brighten, grow lighter AN OPPOSITE IS darken **3** *The gift lightened their financial burden.* ► ease, reduce, relieve, alleviate, mitigate, moderate OPPOSITES ARE increase, intensify

lighthearted ADJECTIVE *His light-hearted banter had a serious side.* ► cheerful, carefree, jolly, playful, jovial, bright

likable ADJECTIVE *The person appointed needs to be likable and a good mixer.* ► pleasant, personable, nice, friendly, attractive, charming, congenial, pleasing, endearing AN OPPOSITE IS hateful

like VERB **1** *I have always liked Rosamund.* ► be fond of, be attached to, care for, adore, admire, respect, esteem, (old-fashioned) hold dear, (more informal) have a soft spot for, (more informal) take a shine to, (more informal) fancy **2** *Do you like dancing?* ► enjoy, care for, appreciate, be keen on, be partial to, (more informal) love, (more informal) fancy

like ADJECTIVE *The cousins are very like each other.* ► similar to, the same as, identical AN OPPOSITE IS unlike

likely ADJECTIVE likelier, likeliest **1** probable; expected to happen or be true, etc. ● *Rain is likely.* **2** expected to be suitable or successful ● *a likely spot*

liken VERB likens, likening, likened compare ● *He likened the human heart to a pump.*

likeness NOUN likenesses **1** a similarity in appearance; a resemblance **2** a portrait

liking NOUN a feeling that you like something ● *She has a liking for ice cream.*

lilac NOUN **1** a bush with fragrant purple or white flowers **2** pale purple

lilt NOUN lilts a light pleasant rhythm in a voice or tune
▷ **lilting** ADJECTIVE

lily NOUN lilies a garden plant with trumpet-shaped flowers, growing from a bulb

limb NOUN limbs **1** a leg, arm, or wing **2** a large branch of a tree
out on a limb isolated; without any support

limber VERB limbers, limbering, limbered limber up do exercises in preparation for an athletic activity

lime[1] NOUN a white chalky substance (calcium oxide) used in making cement and as a fertilizer

lime[2] NOUN limes **1** a green fruit like a small round lemon **2** a drink made from the juice of this fruit

lime[3] NOUN limes a tree with yellow flowers

limelight NOUN
in the limelight receiving a lot of publicity and attention

limerick NOUN limericks a type of amusing poem with five lines [named after Limerick, a town in Ireland, possibly because people sang "will you come up to Limerick" as a refrain]

limestone NOUN a kind of rock from which lime (calcium oxide) is obtained

limit NOUN limits **1** a line, point, or level where something ends **2** the greatest amount allowed ● *the speed limit*

limit VERB limits, limiting, limited **1** keep something within certain limits **2** be a limit to something
▷ **limitation** NOUN

limited company NOUN limited companies a business company whose shareholders would have to pay only some of its debts if it went bankrupt

limp VERB limps, limping, limped walk lamely

limp NOUN limps a limping walk

limp ADJECTIVE **1** not stiff or firm **2** without strength or energy
▷ **limply** ADVERB **limpness** NOUN

limpet NOUN limpets a small shellfish that attaches itself firmly to rocks

line NOUN lines **1** a long thin mark **2** a row or series of people or things; a row of words **3** a length of rope, string, wire, etc. used for a special purpose ● *a fishing line* **4** a railway; a line of railway track **5** a company operating a transport service of ships, aircraft, or buses **6** a way of doing things or behaving; a type of business **7** a telephone connection
in line **1** forming a straight line
2 conforming

Thesaurus

likely ADJECTIVE **1** *It was likely that there would be an inquiry.* ► probable, possible, expected, foreseeable, envisaged, (*more informal*) odds-on **2** *Try to think of a more likely explanation.* ► credible, believable, plausible, convincing, reasonable **3** *It was a likely place for them to meet.* ► suitable, appropriate, proper, apposite, promising, hopeful

likeness NOUN **1** *The painting was a good likeness of their mother.* ► representation, image, depiction, portrayal, picture, portrait, copy, replica **2** *The brothers' likeness is remarkable.* ► resemblance, similarity, affinity, correspondence AN OPPOSITE IS dissimilarity

liking NOUN *a liking for rock music* ► fondness, partiality, taste, desire, attraction, weakness, penchant, predilection, fancy OPPOSITES ARE dislike (of), aversion (to)

limber VERB limber up *She was limbering up for the next race.* ► warm up, loosen up, work out, prepare, get ready, exercise

limit NOUN **1** *There was a limit to what they could do to help. There is a limit of ten thousand tickets for away supporters.* ► restriction, maximum,

ceiling, cut-off point, curb, restraint, limitation **2** *They drove out as far as the city limits.* ► boundary, border, edge, perimeter, confines

limit VERB *The organizers have to limit numbers in the interests of safety.* ► restrict, curb, put a limit on, restrain, check, control, circumscribe, demarcate, confine, fix

limited ADJECTIVE *Resources are limited.* ► restricted, circumscribed, finite, short, controlled, rationed, defined, determinate, fixed, inadequate, insufficient, narrow, reduced, small OPPOSITES ARE unlimited, limitless

limp ADJECTIVE *The man held out a limp hand.* ► soft, loose, flabby, drooping, slack, weak, sagging, wilting, bendy, flexible, pliable, yielding, floppy OPPOSITES ARE firm, rigid

limp VERB *She limped back into the house.* ► hobble, hop, falter, shuffle, stumble, totter

line NOUN **1** *A line of cars was waiting at the lights.* ► row, file, column, procession, chain, string **2** *He drew a line under his signature. From their window they could see lines in the sand.* ► stroke, rule, underline, strip, band, bar,

line[1] VERB lines, lining, lined **1** mark something with lines • *Use lined paper.* **2** form something into a line or lines • *Line them up.*

line[2] VERB lines, lining, lined cover the inside of something

lineage (lin- ee- ij) NOUN lineages ancestry; a line of descendants from an ancestor

linear (lin- ee- er) ADJECTIVE **1** arranged in a line **2** to do with a line or length

linen NOUN **1** cloth made from flax **2** shirts, sheets, and tablecloths, etc. (which were formerly made of linen)

liner NOUN liners a large passenger ship

linger VERB lingers, lingering, lingered stay for a long time, as if unwilling to leave; be slow to leave

lingerie (lan- zher- ee) NOUN women's underwear

linguistics NOUN the study of languages
▷ linguistic ADJECTIVE

lining NOUN linings a layer that covers the inside of something

link NOUN links **1** one of the rings or loops of a chain **2** a connection or relationship

link VERB links, linking, linked join things together; connect
▷ linkage NOUN

links PLURAL NOUN a golf course, especially one near the sea

linoleum NOUN a stiff shiny floor covering

linseed NOUN the seed of flax, from which oil is obtained

lint NOUN a soft material for covering wounds

lion NOUN lions a large strong flesh-eating animal of the cat family found in Africa and India
▷ lioness NOUN

lip NOUN lips **1** either of the two fleshy edges of the mouth **2** the edge of something hollow, such as a cup or crater **3** the pointed part at the top of a jug, etc., from which you pour things

lip-read VERB lip-reads, lip-reading, lip-read understand what a person says by watching the movements of their lips, not by hearing

lipstick NOUN lipsticks a stick of a waxy substance for coloring the lips

liqueur (lik- yoor) NOUN liqueurs a strong sweet alcoholic drink

liquid NOUN liquids a substance like water or oil that flows freely but (unlike a gas) has a constant volume

liquid ADJECTIVE **1** in the form of a liquid; flowing freely **2** easily converted into cash • *the firm's liquid assets*
▷ liquidity NOUN

Thesaurus

---

streak **3** *As she grew older the lines on her face increased.* ► crease, wrinkle, furrow, groove **4** *They walked in a straight line across the field.* ► direction, path, route, course, track **5** *The courts are taking a tough line with repeat offenders. Cabinet members are obliged to support the government line.* ► approach, course, course of action, procedure, policy, position, stance, tactic **6** *There aren't many opportunities in my line.* ► field, line of work, occupation, business, calling, speciality, trade, work, province, domain **7** *Mark attached a line to the post.* ► cord, rope, string, cable, wire, thread, flex **8** *the handsome lines of a classical building* ► shape, contour, profile, figure, features, silhouette **9** *The ball had not crossed the line.* ► limit, boundary, border, edge, demarcation **10** *She comes from a noble line related to the royal family.* ► ancestry, family, descent, lineage, extraction, pedigree, genealogy, stock, background

line VERB **1** *She lined the cat's box with blankets.* ► cover, face, pad, stuff, reinforce **2** *The drive was lined with trees.* ► border, edge, fringe, bound, skirt

line up *The children lined up by the door.* ► form a line, fall in

linger VERB **1** *Most of the crowd leave promptly but some tend to linger.* ► wait around, lag

behind, loiter, dally, tarry, hang on, stay put, delay **2** *An aroma of coffee lingered all morning.* ► persist, last, continue, remain, endure, stay

lining NOUN *a coat with a thick lining* ► padding, inner layer, interfacing, inlay, liner, interlining

link NOUN **1** *She fostered links between the two families.* ► bond, tie, relationship, attachment **2** *a rail link between the city center and the airport* ► connection, communication, line **3** *an important link in the organization* ► element, component, constituent, piece **4** *a chain of hardened steel links* ► loop, ring, connector, connection

link VERB **1** *Police are linking this crime with a series of other robberies.* ► connect, associate, relate (to), draw a connection between **2** *The two trains were linked together.* ► couple, join, connect, attach, fasten

lip NOUN *Coffee poured over the lip of the jug.* ► rim, brim, brink, mouth, edge

liquid NOUN *The doctor says he can only take liquids for a few days.* ► fluid, liquid substance, juice, drink, solution

liquid ADJECTIVE *The pudding had become liquid in the heat.* ► runny, fluid, thin, watery, sloppy, sloshy, wet, aqueous, molten, running, flowing AN OPPOSITE IS solid

liquor ➡ live

liquor NOUN **1** alcoholic drink **2** juice produced in cooking; liquid in which food has been cooked

lisp NOUN lisps a fault in speech in which s and z are pronounced like th
▷ **lisp** VERB

list NOUN lists a number of names, items, or figures, etc., written or printed one after another

list VERB lists, listing, listed make a list of people or things

listen VERB listens, listening, listened pay attention in order to hear something
▷ **listener** NOUN

listless ADJECTIVE too tired to be active or enthusiastic
▷ **listlessly** ADVERB **listlessness** NOUN

lit past tense of light

literacy NOUN the ability to read and write

literal ADJECTIVE **1** meaning exactly what is said, not metaphorical or exaggerated **2** word for word • *a literal translation*

literally ADVERB really; exactly as stated • *The noise made me literally jump out of my seat.*

literature NOUN books and other writings, especially those considered to have been written well

litigation NOUN litigations a lawsuit; the process of carrying on a lawsuit

litmus NOUN a blue substance that is turned red by acids and can be turned back to blue by alkalis

litmus paper NOUN paper stained with litmus

liter NOUN liters a measure of liquid, about 1.75 pints

litter NOUN litters **1** trash or untidy things left lying about **2** the young animals born to one mother at one time **3** absorbent material put down on a tray for a cat to urinate and defecate in indoors **4** a kind of stretcher

litter VERB litters, littering, littered make a place untidy with litter

little ADJECTIVE less, least small in amount or size or intensity, etc.; not great or big or much a little **1** a small amount • *Have a little sugar.* **2** slightly • *I'm a little tired.*
little by little gradually; by a small amount at a time

little ADVERB not much • *He was little known in this country.*

live (rhymes with give) VERB lives, living, lived **1** have life; be alive **2** have your home • *She lives in Glasgow.* **3** pass your life in a certain way • *He lived as a hermit.*
live down if you cannot live down a mistake

Thesaurus

list NOUN *I had a list of over 7,000 names.*
▸ register, inventory, catalog, index, file, roll, roster, schedule

list VERB **1** *We have listed names of contributors in alphabetical order.* ▸ record, register, itemize, enter, index, file, enumerate, catalogue **2** *The ship was listing in the heavy seas.* ▸ tilt, lean, lean over, tip, heel, pitch, keel over

listen VERB *I don't think they were listening.*
▸ pay attention, take notice
listen to *a doctor who listens to what his patients tell him* ▸ pay attention to, take notice of, hear, heed, attend to, concentrate on, (old-fashioned) hark AN OPPOSITE IS ignore

listless ADJECTIVE *a young woman clutching a pale, listless child* ▸ lethargic, sluggish, enervated, lackadaisical, torpid, inert, apathetic, unenthusiastic AN OPPOSITE IS lively

literal ADJECTIVE **1** *a literal translation* ▸ word-for-word, verbatim, faithful, strict, exact, close, plain, prosaic, unimaginative **2** *the literal truth of the Bible* ▸ strict, plain, bare, exact, precise, straightforward, unvarnished, narrow

literary ADJECTIVE **1** *a collection of literary works* ▸ written, printed, published, dramatic, poetic, imaginative **2** *a literary style of writing* ▸ formal, stylish, ornate, polished, sophisticated, imaginative, recognized as literature **3** *a group of literary friends*

▸ cultured, educated, literate, scholarly, refined, well read, widely read, erudite, learned

literature NOUN **1** *a class in English literature* ▸ writings, books **2** *We can pick up some literature about the place from the tourist office.* ▸ brochures, leaflets, pamphlets, handouts, circulars

litter NOUN **1** *It took days to clear up all the litter.* ▸ trash, rubbish, refuse, junk, waste, debris, clutter, garbage, mess, scraps, bits and pieces, odds and ends, jumble **2** *a litter of puppies* ▸ brood, family, (more formal) progeny

little ADJECTIVE **1** *a little book* ▸ small, tiny, minute, miniature, mini, petite, (more informal) teeny **2** *a little person* ▸ small, slight, short, diminutive **3** *in a little while* ▸ short, brief, fleeting **4** *We have a little problem.* ▸ minor, trivial, unimportant, insignificant, inconsequential, negligible
a little *Add a little water.* ▸ some, a small amount of, a bit of, a touch of, a spot of, a taste of

little NOUN *You only need a little.* ▸ bit, dash, pinch, small amount, touch, modicum

little ADVERB *The singers are little known in this country.* ▸ scarcely, barely, hardly, slightly, not much

live VERB **1** *We live in Dallas.* ▸ reside, have a home, dwell, lodge **2** *He hardly earns enough to*

386

or embarrassment, you cannot make people forget it

live on use something as food; depend on for your living

live (rhymes with *hive*) ADJECTIVE **1** alive **2** connected to a source of electric current **3** broadcast while it is actually happening, not from a recording **4** burning ● *live coals*

livelihood NOUN livelihoods a way of earning money or providing enough food to support yourself

lively ADJECTIVE livelier, liveliest full of life or action; vigorous and cheerful
▷ **liveliness** NOUN

liver NOUN livers **1** a large organ of the body, found in the abdomen, that processes digested food and purifies the blood **2** an animal's liver used as food

livestock NOUN farm animals

livid ADJECTIVE **1** bluish-grey ● *a livid bruise* **2** furiously angry

living NOUN **1** being alive **2** the way that a person lives ● *a good standard of living* **3** a way

of earning money or providing enough food to support yourself

living room NOUN living rooms a room for general use during the day

lizard NOUN lizards a reptile with a rough or scaly skin, four legs, and a long tail

llama NOUN llamas a South American animal with woolly fur [via Spanish from Quechua (a South American language)]

load NOUN loads **1** something carried; a burden **2** the quantity that can be carried **3** the total amount of electric current supplied **4** (*informal*) a large amount ● *It's a load of nonsense.* ● *You could earn loads of money.* **loads** (*informal*) plenty ● *We've got loads of time.*

load VERB loads, loading, loaded **1** put a load in or on something **2** fill heavily **3** weight with something heavy ● *loaded dice* **4** put a bullet or shell into a gun; put a film into a camera **5** enter programs or data into a computer

Thesaurus

live on. ► exist, subsist, survive, endure, stay alive **3** *I'm not sure these plants will live much longer.* ► last, survive, stay alive **4** *She has led a happy life.* ► pass, spend, experience, undergo

live ADJECTIVE **1** *live animals* ► living, alive, breathing, animate **2** *a live show* ► real-time, actual, unrecorded **3** *a live rail* ► electrified, charged, powered, connected **4** *a live issue* ► topical, current, relevant, pertinent, contemporary, vital, controversial

livelihood NOUN *The printing business was his main livelihood.* ► income, source of income, means of support, living, subsistence, occupation, employment

lively ADJECTIVE **1** *The bars are lively late in the evening.* ► busy, hectic, bustling, crowded, swarming OPPOSITES ARE quiet, dead **2** *an attractive and lively young woman* ► vivacious, high-spirited, exuberant, animated, alert, active, spirited, exciting, cheerful OPPOSITES ARE lifeless, dull **3** *a lively colour scheme* ► bright, vivid, colorful, striking, bold OPPOSITES ARE dull, bland

liven VERB **liven up** *The room needed a few pictures to liven it up.* ► brighten up, animate, cheer up, vitalize, put life into, (*more informal*) perk up, (*more informal*) pep up

livery NOUN **1** *the pageboys in their blue livery* ► uniform, costume, outfit, suit, regalia, garb, (*more informal*) get-up **2** *railway coaches repainted in their old maroon livery* ► colors, color scheme, paintwork

livid ADJECTIVE **1** *A row of livid bruises began to form on his skin.* ► bluish-grey, purplish, dark,

discolored **2** *He was livid with me.* ► furious, angry, fuming, seething, raging, enraged, infuriated

living ADJECTIVE *all living creatures* ► live, alive, breathing, animate, existing, vital, active, sentient, surviving, vigorous OPPOSITES ARE dead, extinct

living NOUN *He was washing cars for a living.* ► livelihood, income, source of income, means of support, subsistence, occupation, employment

living room NOUN *Music was playing in the living room.* ► sitting room, drawing room, lounge, reception room

load NOUN **1** *a load of goods* ► cargo, consignment, freight, vanload, truckload, shipment, boatload, (*more formal*) lading **2** *a heavy load of work* ► burden, commitment, obligation, weight
a load of (*informal*) *a load of garbage* ► a lot of, a great deal of, a wealth

load VERB **1** *We loaded the luggage into the car.* ► pack, stow, store, stack, cram, heap, pile AN OPPOSITE IS unload (from) **2** *They've loaded me with more responsibilities.* ► burden, encumber, weigh down, saddle AN OPPOSITE IS relieve (of)

loaded ADJECTIVE **1** *He had a loaded gun in his hand.* ► primed, charged, filled, ready **2** *A loaded bus trundled up the platform.* ► full, filled, laden, burdened, inundated, piled high, weighed down, crammed **3** *a loaded argument* ► one-sided, biased, tendentious, prejudiced, unfair, distorted, emotive, partial **4** (*informal*) *Their parents are loaded and can easily afford the*

loaf NOUN loaves a shaped mass of bread baked in one piece
use your loaf (*informal*) think; use common sense
[from Old English]
loaf VERB loafs, loafing, loafed spend time idly; loiter or stand about
▷ **loafer** NOUN

loam NOUN rich soil containing clay, sand, and decayed leaves etc.
▷ **loamy** ADJECTIVE

loan NOUN loans 1 something lent, especially money 2 lending; being lent • *These books are on loan from the library.*

loathe (rhymes with *clothe*) VERB loathes, loathing, loathed feel great hatred and disgust for something
▷ **loathing** NOUN

loathsome ADJECTIVE making you feel great hatred and disgust; repulsive

lob VERB lobs, lobbing, lobbed throw, hit, or kick a ball etc. high into the air, especially in a high arc

lobby NOUN lobbies 1 an entrance hall 2 a group that lobbies Congress • *the anti-hunting lobby*

lobby VERB lobbies, lobbying, lobbied try to persuade a Congressman or other person to support your cause, by speaking to them in person or writing letters

lobster NOUN lobsters a large shellfish with eight legs and two long claws

local ADJECTIVE belonging to a particular place or a small area
▷ **locally** ADVERB

local NOUN locals (*informal*) 1 someone who lives in a particular district 2 a pub near a person's home [from Latin *locus* = a place]

local anesthetic NOUN local anesthetics an anesthetic affecting only the part of the body where it is applied

localized ADJECTIVE restricted to a particular place • *localized showers*

locate VERB locates, locating, located discover where something is • *I have located the fault.* be located be situated in a particular place • *The theater is located on Broadway.*

location NOUN locations 1 the place where something is situated 2 discovering where something is; locating
on location filmed in natural surroundings, not in a studio

lock¹ NOUN locks 1 a fastening that is opened with a key or other device 2 a section of a canal or river fitted with sluice gates so that boats can be raised or lowered to the level beyond each gate 3 the distance that a

Thesaurus

fees. ► wealthy, well-off, rich, affluent, prosperous, moneyed
loaf VERB *He can't go on loafing around any longer.* ► laze, idle, lounge, waste time, kill time OPPOSITES ARE work, toil
loafer NOUN (*informal*) *education that produces a generation of loafers* ► layabout, idler, lounger, shirker, wastrel, (*informal*) skiver, (*informal*) lazybones, (*informal*) good-for-nothing
loan NOUN *A bank loan would help develop the business.* ► advance, credit, mortgage
loan VERB 1 *We will loan you the money for a period of 5 years.* ► lend, advance, credit 2 *The gallery loans pictures all over the world.* ► lend, give on loan, provide on loan
loathe VERB *She loathed living in the suburbs.* ► hate, detest, abhor, abominate, dislike, despise OPPOSITES ARE love, like, adore
loathing NOUN *Loathing for the other woman rose in her chest.* ► hatred, detestation, abhorrence, repugnance (for), revulsion (for) AN OPPOSITE IS love
loathsome ADJECTIVE *a loathsome crime* ► detestable, horrible, horrid, awful, nasty OPPOSITES ARE pleasant, likable
lob VERB *He lobbed the ball in the air.* ► throw, toss, hurl, pitch, fling, loft, shy, bowl, cast, chuck, sling

local ADJECTIVE 1 *the local library* ► nearby, neighborhood, neighboring 2 *Try the local cuisine.* ► regional, district, provincial, community OPPOSITES ARE national, global 3 *a local infection* ► confined, restricted, limited, localized, circumscribed AN OPPOSITE IS general
local NOUN (*informal*) *The restaurant is filled with locals.* ► inhabitant, resident, parishioner, native
locality NOUN 1 *There are several good schools in the locality.* ► region, area, neighborhood, vicinity, location, district, community, parish 2 *new housing in an attractive locality* ► position, location, setting, situation, place
locate VERB 1 *He located the skylight window he had noticed from the outside.* ► find, discover, identify, pinpoint, track down, detect, light on 2 *The boiler room is located in the basement.* ► situate, site, position, place
location NOUN *The firm is moving to a new location.* ► position, site, locality, locale, place, point, situation, spot, venue, whereabouts
lock NOUN 1 *a lock on a door* ► fastening, latch, clasp 2 *a lock of hair* ► curl, tress, tuft
lock VERB *We lock the door at night.* ► fasten, secure, shut, bolt, close, seal

vehicle's front wheels can turn **4** a wrestling hold that keeps an opponent's arm or leg from moving

lock, stock, and barrel completely

lock VERB **locks, locking, locked 1** fasten or secure something by means of a lock **2** store something away securely **3** become fixed in one place; jam

lock[2] NOUN **locks** a clump of hair

locker NOUN **lockers** a small cupboard or compartment where things can be stowed safely

locket NOUN **lockets** a small ornamental case for holding a portrait or lock of hair, etc., worn on a chain around the neck

locks PLURAL NOUN a person's hair

locomotive NOUN **locomotives** a railway engine

locomotive ADJECTIVE to do with movement or the ability to move • *locomotive power*
  ▷ **locomotion** NOUN

locus (loh- kus) NOUN **loci** (loh- ky) **1** (in mathematics) the path traced by a moving point, or made by points placed in a certain way **2** the exact place of something

locust NOUN **locusts** a kind of grasshopper that travels in large swarms which eat all the plants in an area

lodge NOUN **lodges 1** a small house, especially at the gates of a park **2** a porter's room at the entrance to a college, factory, etc. **3** a beaver's or otter's lair

lodge VERB **lodges, lodging, lodged 1** stay somewhere as a lodger **2** provide a person with somewhere to live temporarily **3** become stuck or caught somewhere • *The ball lodged in the tree.*

lodge a complaint complain formally

lodger NOUN **lodgers** a person who pays to live in another person's house

lodgings PLURAL NOUN a room or rooms, not in a hotel, rented for living in

loft NOUN **lofts** a room or storage space under the roof of a house or barn, etc.

lofty ADJECTIVE **1** tall **2** noble **3** haughty
  ▷ **loftily** ADVERB **loftiness** NOUN

log[1] NOUN **logs 1** a large piece of a tree that has fallen or been cut down; a piece cut off this **2** a detailed record kept of a voyage or flight, kept in a logbook

log VERB **logs, logging, logged** enter facts in a log

log in (*or* **on**) start using a computer

log out (*or* **off**) finish using a computer

log[2] NOUN **logs** a logarithm • *log tables*

logarithm NOUN **logarithms** one of a series of numbers set out in tables which make it possible to do sums by adding and subtracting instead of multiplying and dividing

loggerheads PLURAL NOUN

at loggerheads disagreeing or quarrelling

logic NOUN **1** reasoning; a system or method of reasoning **2** the principles used in designing a computer; the circuits involved in this

logical ADJECTIVE using logic; reasoning or reasoned correctly
  ▷ **logically** ADVERB **logicality** NOUN

logo (loh- goh) NOUN **logos** a printed symbol used by a business company, etc. as its emblem

loiter VERB **loiters, loitering, loitered** linger or stand about idly
  ▷ **loiterer** NOUN

lollipop NOUN **lollipops** a large round hard sweet on a stick

lonely ADJECTIVE **lonelier, loneliest 1** sad because you are on your own **2** solitary **3** far from inhabited places; not often visited or used • *a lonely road*
  ▷ **loneliness** NOUN

Thesaurus

lock up *He was locked up for causing criminal damage.* ▶ jail, imprison, put behind bars

lodge NOUN *a hunting lodge* ▶ cabin, cottage, hut, chalet

lodge VERB **1** *The family lodged at a guest house for a few weeks.* ▶ board, stay, live, reside **2** *I will lodge a formal complaint.* ▶ submit, register, enter, place, present

lodger NOUN *Her husband had once been a lodger of hers.* ▶ boarder, paying guest, tenant, resident, inmate, guest

logic NOUN *We accept the logic of your case.* ▶ reasoning, rationale, sense, validity, argumentation, rationality, cogency

logical ADJECTIVE *The conclusions are logical.* ▶ rational, reasonable, cogent, coherent, clear, sound, valid, consistent, intelligent,

methodical, sensible, systematic AN OPPOSITE IS illogical

loiter VERB *With so much to do there was no time to loiter in the shopping malls.* ▶ linger, dally, potter, dawdle, tarry, (*more informal*) loaf about, (*more informal*) mooch about

lone ADJECTIVE *a lone cyclist; a lone tree* ▶ solitary, single, solo, isolated, individual, unaccompanied, separate

lonely ADJECTIVE **1** *I walked through the garden feeling very lonely.* ▶ alone, solitary, friendless, abandoned, lonesome, neglected, forlorn AN OPPOSITE IS popular **2** *The cart drove along the lonely road* ▶ deserted, unfrequented, remote, secluded, isolated, abandoned, desolate, forsaken, out of the way, uninhabited,

a b c d e f g h i j k **l** m n o p q r s t u v w x y z

A
B
C
D
E
F
G
H
I
J
K
L
M
N
O
P
Q
R
S
T
U
V
W
X
Y
Z

long ADJECTIVE **1** measuring a lot from one end to the other **2** taking a lot of time • *a long holiday* **3** having a certain length • *The river is 10 miles long.*

long ADVERB **1** for a long time • *Have you been waiting long?* **2** at a long time before or after • *They left long ago.* **3** throughout a time • *all night long*

as long as or **so long as** provided that; on condition that
before long soon
no longer not any more

long VERB **longs, longing, longed** feel a strong desire

long division NOUN dividing one number by another and writing down all the calculations

longing NOUN **longings** a strong desire

longitude NOUN **longitudes** the distance east or west, measured in degrees, from the Greenwich meridian

long jump NOUN an athletic contest in which competitors jump as far as possible along the ground in one leap

long wave NOUN a radio wave of a wavelength above one kilometer and a frequency less than 300 kilohertz

long-winded ADJECTIVE talking or writing at great length

look VERB **looks, looking, looked 1** use your eyes; turn your eyes in a particular direction **2** face in a particular direction **3** have a certain appearance; seem • *You look sad.*

look after 1 protect or take care of someone **2** be in charge of something

look down on despise

look forward to be waiting eagerly for something you expect

look into investigate

look out be careful

look up 1 search for information about something **2** improve in prospects • *Things are looking up.*

look up to admire or respect

look NOUN **looks 1** the act of looking; a gaze or glance **2** appearance • *I don't like the look of this place*

Thesaurus

(*informal*) off the beaten track AN OPPOSITE IS crowded

long ADJECTIVE **1** *long blonde hair* ► flowing, shoulder-length, waist-length AN OPPOSITE IS short **2** *a long wait* ► lengthy, prolonged, extended, extensive, long-lasting OPPOSITES ARE short, brief

long VERB *long for We longed for the holidays.* ► yearn for, crave, dream of, hanker after, hunger for, pine for

longing NOUN *He felt a longing for his home.* ► yearning, hankering (after), craving desire, hunger, need, thirst, urge, wish, (*informal*) yen

long-lasting ADJECTIVE *We need long-lasting solutions to these problems.* ► enduring, abiding, long-running, durable, permanent, prolonged

long-standing ADJECTIVE *a long-standing arrangement* ► well-established, long-established, time-honored, firm

look VERB **1** *Everywhere you look there are trees.* ► see, observe, regard, survey, glance, scrutinize, scan **2** *Things looked difficult that day.* ► seem, appear

look after *Jane had to look after her father during his last illness.* ► take care of, care for, tend, attend to, provide for, mind, nurse, supervise, watch over, (*more informal*) keep an eye on

look at *I knew if I looked at her we'd both start laughing.* ► glance at, watch, observe

look down on *The family looked down on all their neighbors.* ► despise, disdain, scorn, hold in contempt, sneer at, (*more informal*) look down your nose at

look for 1 *I was still looking for my wallet.* ► search for, hunt for, seek, try to find **2** *Behavior like that is looking for trouble.* ► ask for, provoke, invite, attract, court, incite, tempt, cause, encourage, generate, (*more informal*) stir up

look into *The official said he would look into the complaint.* ► investigate, find out about, inquire into, study, explore, examine

look out *A ball can easily hit you if you don't look out.* ► beware, watch out, be careful, be vigilant, pay attention, keep your eyes open

look up 1 *You can look up the answer in an encyclopedia.* ► find, search for, research, track down **2** (*informal*) *We can look up some friends on our way home.* ► visit, call on, stop by, (*informal*) drop in on, (*informal*) look in on **3** *Things were beginning to look up.* ► improve, progress, show an improvement, revive

look up to *Susan looked up to her father.* ► admire, respect, esteem, revere, have a high regard for, have a high opinion of, think highly of

look NOUN **1** *We had a look at the house.* ► glance, glimpse, peek, peep, sight (of), observation (of), view (of), (*informal*) squint **2** *You could see he was angry from the look on his face.* ► expression, mien **3** *a house with a Tudor look* ► appearance, aspect, façade, guise, quality, atmosphere, semblance **4** *this year's new look* ► fashion, vogue, style, trend, craze, rage

looks *All the sisters enjoyed stunning good looks.* ► appearance, features

looking glass NOUN looking glasses a glass mirror

lookout NOUN lookouts **1** looking out or watching for something **2** a place from which you can keep watch **3** a person whose job is to keep watch **4** a future prospect • *It's a poor lookout for us.* **5** (*informal*) a person's own fault or concern • *If he wastes his money, that's his lookout.*

loom NOUN looms a machine for weaving cloth

loom VERB looms, looming, loomed appear suddenly; seem large or close and threatening • *An iceberg loomed up through the fog.*

loop NOUN loops the shape made by a curve crossing itself; a piece of string, ribbon, wire, etc., made into this shape

loophole NOUN loopholes a way of avoiding a law or rule or promise etc. without actually breaking it

loose ADJECTIVE **1** not tight; not firmly fixed • *a loose tooth* **2** not tied up or shut in • *There's a lion loose!* **3** not packed in a box or packet **4** not exact • *a loose translation*
▷ **loosely** ADVERB **looseness** NOUN
at a loose end with nothing to do
on the loose escaped or free

loosen VERB loosens, loosening, loosened make or become loose or looser

loot NOUN stolen things; goods taken from an enemy

loot VERB loots, looting, looted **1** rob a place or an enemy, especially in a time of war or disorder **2** take something as loot
▷ **looter** NOUN
[from a Hindi word, = to rob]

lop VERB lops, lopping, lopped cut away branches or twigs; cut off

lopsided ADJECTIVE with one side lower or smaller than the other

lord NOUN lords **1** a nobleman, especially one who is allowed to use the title "Lord" in front of his name **2** a master or ruler
▷ **lordly** ADJECTIVE **lordship** NOUN
[from Old English *hlaford* = person who keeps the bread (compare **lady**)]

lose VERB loses, losing, lost **1** be without something that you once had, especially because you cannot find it **2** fail to keep or obtain something • *We lost control.* **3** be defeated in a contest or argument, etc.
4 cause the loss of • *That one mistake lost us the game.* **5** (said about a clock or watch) become behind the correct time
▷ **loser** NOUN
be lost or lose your way not know where you are or which is the right path
lose your life be killed
lost cause an idea or policy, etc., that is failing

Thesaurus

---

look-alike NOUN *a Madonna look-alike*
▶ double, twin, exact likeness, spitting image, replica, clone

lookout NOUN **1** *a lookout on the bridge*
▶ sentry, guard, sentinel, scout, watchman **2** *It might not work but that's their lookout.*
▶ concern, responsibility, business, affair, problem

loom VERB **1** *The cathedral loomed above them.*
▶ soar, tower, rise, appear, rear up **2** *Blurred shapes loomed out of the mist.* ▶ appear, emerge, come into view, reveal itself **3** *Without action, big problems loom.* ▶ threaten, impend, be imminent, menace, overshadow

loop NOUN *He slipped a loop of wire over the handle and pulled it tight.* ▶ coil, noose, ring, twist, curl, hoop, turn, bend, circle, kink

loop VERB *Loop a rope round the animal's neck.*
▶ coil, wind, twist, bend, curl, entwine, turn

loophole NOUN *a loophole in the regulations*
▶ means of escape, ambiguity, flaw, (*more informal*) get-out, (*more informal*) let-out

loose ADJECTIVE **1** *a loose screw* ▶ insecure, unfastened, untied, unfixed, wobbly OPPOSITES ARE tight, secure **2** *a wild animal loose in the grounds* ▶ free, at large, unconfined, on the loose, at liberty AN OPPOSITE IS confined **3** *loose pants* ▶ baggy,

slack, loose-fitting, roomy OPPOSITES ARE tight, close-fitting **4** *a loose translation* ▶ free, imprecise, vague, inexact OPPOSITES ARE literal, exact

loosen VERB **1** *He tried to loosen the knots.*
▶ ease, free, slacken, undo, untie, unfasten, release **2** *She loosened her grip.* ▶ weaken, relax, lessen AN OPPOSITE IS tighten

loot NOUN *a bag full of the thieves' loot* ▶ booty, spoils, plunder, haul, (*more informal*) swag

loot VERB *Soldiers looted the deserted buildings.*
▶ raid, plunder, pillage, ransack, rifle, rob, steal from

lopsided ADJECTIVE *a tractor pulling a lopsided load* ▶ uneven, unbalanced, tilting, askew, asymmetrical, crooked, (*more informal*) cock-eyed

lord NOUN **1** *the lord of the manor* ▶ master, overlord, leader, chief, prince **2** *He has been made a lord.* ▶ peer, noble, baron, earl, duke

lordly ADJECTIVE **1** *lordly titles* ▶ noble, aristocratic, princely, courtly **2** *He spoke in a lordly manner.* ▶ haughty, imperious, disdainful, condescending, domineering, overbearing, high-handed

lose VERB **1** *I've lost my passport.* ▶ mislay, misplace, lose track of, forget AN OPPOSITE IS find **2** *We've already lost a lot of time. They lost money on the deal.* ▶ waste, use up, squander,

a
b
c
d
e
f
g
h
i
j
k
l
m
n
o
p
q
r
s
t
u
v
w
x
y
z

loss ➡ love

A B C D E F G H I J K **L** **M N O P Q R S T U V W X Y Z**

loss NOUN losses **1** losing something **2** something lost
be at a loss not know what to do or say

lot NOUN lots **1** a large number or amount • *You have a lot of friends.* • *There's lots of time.* **2** one of a set of objects used in choosing or deciding something by chance • *We drew lots to see who should go first.* **3** a person's share or fate **4** something for sale at an auction **5** a piece of land
a lot very much • *I feel a lot better.*
the lot or the whole lot everything; all

lotion NOUN lotions a liquid for putting on the skin

lottery NOUN lotteries a way of raising money by selling numbered tickets and giving prizes to people who hold winning numbers, which are chosen by a method depending on chance COMPARE lot (2)

loud ADJECTIVE **1** easily heard; producing much noise **2** unpleasantly bright; gaudy • *loud colors*
▷ **loudly** ADVERB **loudness** NOUN

loudspeaker NOUN loudspeakers a device that changes electrical signals into sound, for reproducing music or voices

lounge NOUN lounges a sitting room

lounge VERB lounges, lounging, lounged sit or stand in a lazy and relaxed way

louse NOUN lice a small insect that lives as a parasite on animals or plants

lousy ADJECTIVE lousier, lousiest **1** full of lice **2** (informal) very bad or unpleasant

lout NOUN louts a bad-mannered man

lovable ADJECTIVE easy to love

love NOUN loves **1** great liking or affection **2** sexual affection or passion **3** a loved person; a sweetheart **4** (in tennis) no score; nil
in love feeling strong love
make love have sexual intercourse

love VERB loves, loving, loved feel love for a person or thing
▷ **lover** NOUN **lovingly** ADVERB
[from Old English]

Thesaurus

dissipate, forfeit, exhaust OPPOSITES ARE gain, make **3** *The home side lost 3-0.* ▶ be beaten, be defeated, fail, suffer defeat AN OPPOSITE IS win

loser NOUN **1** *There are many losers and few winners in this game.* ▶ runner-up AN OPPOSITE IS winner **2** (informal) *He's a complete loser.* ▶ failure, non-achiever, nobody, (informal) no-hoper

loss NOUN **1** *The loss of all his money ruined the holiday.* ▶ losing, theft, deprivation, disappearance **2** *The loss of her husband devastated her.* ▶ death, demise, passing, decease **3** *The company faced a huge loss.* ▶ deficit, debit, debt, lack of profit **4** *Loss of the game was a major blow.* ▶ defeat (in), failure (in), forfeiture **5** *The army suffered heavy losses.* ▶ casualty, fatality, mortality, victim

lost ADJECTIVE **1** *The lost keys never turned up.* ▶ missing, mislaid, misplaced, vanished **2** *I became lost in the complications of the plot.* ▶ confused, baffled, bewildered, perplexed **3** *many lost opportunities* ▶ missed, neglected, wasted, squandered **4** *She appeared to be lost in thought.* ▶ absorbed, engrossed, preoccupied

lot NOUN **1** a lot of OR lots of *She has a lot of friends. We need lots of money.* ▶ many, plenty of, a large amount OR number of, a great deal of **2** *On Monday a new lot of tourists arrives.* ▶ set, collection, group, batch, crowd **3** *He was not at all happy with his lot.* ▶ fate, destiny, fortune, future **4** *The money was divided into three lots.* ▶ share, portion, allocation, quota

lottery NOUN *She won a thousand dollars in a lottery.* ▶ draw, raffle, sweepstake, sweep, gamble

loud ADJECTIVE **1** *loud music* ▶ noisy, blaring, deafening, booming, thunderous AN OPPOSITE IS quiet **2** *loud colors* ▶ gaudy, garish, bold, lurid, flashy, showy AN OPPOSITE IS subdued

lounge VERB *Miranda lounged on the sofa all morning.* ▶ laze, loll, recline, relax, sprawl, slump, slouch, luxuriate, idle, waste time

lounge NOUN *We will have our drinks in the lounge.* ▶ living room, sitting room, drawing room, day room

lousy ADJECTIVE (informal) *He had been a lousy father.* ▶ awful, terrible, dreadful, atrocious, appalling, frightful, poor, bad OPPOSITES ARE wonderful, lovely

lout NOUN *a group of drunken louts* ▶ troublemaker, hoodlum, ruffian, (more informal) yob

loutish ADJECTIVE *loutish behavior* ▶ uncouth, rude, ill-mannered, coarse, crude, vulgar

lovable ADJECTIVE *a lovable little kitten* ▶ adorable, dear, sweet, charming, appealing, likable, attractive, cuddly, enchanting, endearing, engaging, lovely, pleasing, taking, winning AN OPPOSITE IS hateful

love VERB **1** *She told him she loved him.* ▶ care for, feel deeply for, adore, cherish, hold dear, treasure OPPOSITES ARE hate, loathe, detest **2** *We all love the holidays.* ▶ like, like very much, enjoy, take pleasure in, appreciate, desire, look forward to, (more informal) fancy AN OPPOSITE IS dislike

love NOUN **1** *He gave her flowers to show his love.* ▶ fondness, affection, adoration, devotion, admiration, ardor, desire, friendship, infatuation, liking, passion **2** *Emma was his*

love affair NOUN love affairs a romantic or sexual relationship between two people in love

lovely ADJECTIVE lovelier, loveliest **1** beautiful **2** very pleasant or enjoyable
▷ **loveliness** NOUN

lover NOUN lovers **1** a person who someone is having a sexual relationship with but is not married to **2** someone who loves something • *an art lover*

lovesick ADJECTIVE longing for someone you love, especially someone who does not love you

low ADJECTIVE **1** only reaching a short way up; not high **2** below average in importance, quality, amount, etc. • *low prices* • *of low rank* **3** unhappy • *I'm feeling low.* **4** not high-pitched; not loud • *low notes* • *a low voice*
▷ **lowness** NOUN

low ADVERB at or to a low level or position, etc. • *The plane was flying low*

lower ADJECTIVE, ADVERB less high

lower VERB lowers, lowering, lowered make or become lower

loyal ADJECTIVE always firmly supporting your friends or group or country, etc.
▷ **loyally** ADVERB **loyalty** NOUN

lozenge NOUN lozenges **1** a small flavored tablet, especially one containing medicine **2** a diamond shape

Ltd. ABBREVIATION limited

lubricant NOUN lubricants a lubricating substance

lubricate VERB lubricates, lubricating, lubricated oil or grease something so that it moves smoothly
▷ **lubrication** NOUN

lucid ADJECTIVE **1** clear and easy to understand **2** thinking clearly; not confused in your mind
▷ **lucidly** ADVERB **lucidity** NOUN

luck NOUN **1** the way things happen without being planned; chance **2** good fortune • *It will bring you luck.*

lucky ADJECTIVE luckier, luckiest having or bringing or resulting from good luck
▷ **luckily** ADVERB

ludicrous ADJECTIVE ridiculous or laughable
▷ **ludicrously** ADVERB

Thesaurus

true love. ► beloved, loved one, darling, dear, dearest, lover
in love with He had been in love with her all his life. ► devoted to, enamored with, fond of, infatuated with RELATED ADJECTIVES
► amatory, erotic

loveless ADJECTIVE a loveless marriage
► passionless, unloving, unfeeling, heartless, unresponsive, cold, frigid, undemonstrative AN OPPOSITE IS loving

lovely ADJECTIVE **1** a lovely young woman; You look lovely. ► beautiful, attractive, good-looking, exquisite, pretty, enchanting, charming, delightful, appealing OPPOSITES ARE unattractive, hideous, ugly **2** a lovely spring morning ► pleasant, delightful, glorious, wonderful, fine OPPOSITES ARE horrible, unpleasant

lover NOUN There is a rumor that she has a secret lover. ► admirer, sweetheart, boyfriend, girlfriend, man friend, lady friend

loving ADJECTIVE He adored her loving nature. ► affectionate, tender, fond, friendly, kind, warm, amorous, ardent, demonstrative, devoted, doting, passionate AN OPPOSITE IS loveless

low ADJECTIVE **1** a low wall ► short, small, squat, shallow AN OPPOSITE IS high **2** Prices are now low. ► reasonable, cheap, inexpensive OPPOSITES ARE high, exorbitant **3** Supplies were getting low. ► sparse, scarce, meagre, inadequate, depleted, paltry OPPOSITES ARE plentiful, abundant **4** He was feeling low that

day. ► depressed, dispirited, downcast, unhappy AN OPPOSITE IS happy **5** a low trick ► mean, base, despicable, shameful, contemptible AN OPPOSITE IS admirable **6** a low rumbling sound ► muted, soft, deep AN OPPOSITE IS loud

lower VERB **1** The soldier lowered the flag. ► bring down, drop, let down, take down OPPOSITES ARE raise, hoist **2** a need to lower interest rates ► reduce, decrease, bring down, lessen OPPOSITES ARE raise, increase

loyal ADJECTIVE a loyal friend ► faithful, true, devoted, steadfast, staunch, constant, dependable, reliable, sincere AN OPPOSITE IS disloyal

loyalty NOUN His first loyalty was to his family. ► allegiance, faithfulness, fidelity, devotion, constancy, dependability, fealty, honesty, patriotism, reliability, staunchness, steadfastness, trustworthiness AN OPPOSITE IS disloyalty

luck NOUN **1** They could not believe their luck. ► good fortune, good luck, success **2** She hopes her luck will change. ► fate, fortune, lot, destiny **3** It was luck that brought them here. ► chance, accident, serendipity

lucky ADJECTIVE **1** a lucky chance; a lucky guess ► fortunate, auspicious, providential, opportune, expedient, timely **2** He is lucky to have such a good friend as you. ► fortunate, blessed, favored, advantaged

ludicrous ADJECTIVE a ludicrous suggestion ► absurd, ridiculous, laughable, incredible,

A
B
C
D
E
F
G
H
I
J
K
L
M
N
O
P
Q
R
S
T
U
V
W
X
Y
Z

luggage NOUN suitcases and bags holding things for taking on a journey

lukewarm ADJECTIVE **1** only slightly warm; tepid **2** not very enthusiastic • *lukewarm applause*

lull VERB lulls, lulling, lulled soothe or calm; send someone to sleep

lull NOUN lulls a short period of quiet or inactivity

lullaby NOUN lullabies a song that is sung to send a baby to sleep

lumbago NOUN pain in the muscles of the lower back

lumber NOUN **1** unwanted furniture, etc.; junk **2** timber

lumber VERB lumbers, lumbering, lumbered **1** leave someone with an unwanted or unpleasant task **2** move in a heavy clumsy way

luminous ADJECTIVE glowing in the dark
▷ **luminosity** NOUN

lump NOUN lumps **1** a solid piece of something **2** a swelling
▷ **lumpy** ADJECTIVE

lump¹ VERB lumps, lumping, lumped put or treat things together in a group because you regard them as alike in some way

lump² VERB lumps, lumping, lumped **lump it** (*informal*) put up with something you dislike

lump sum NOUN lump sums a single payment, especially one covering a number of items

lunacy NOUN lunacies insanity or great foolishness

lunatic NOUN lunatics an insane person
▷ **lunatic** ADJECTIVE

lunch NOUN lunches a meal eaten in the middle of the day
▷ **lunch** VERB

lung NOUN lungs either of the two parts of the body, in the chest, used in breathing

lunge VERB lunges, lunging, lunged thrust the body forward suddenly
▷ **lunge** NOUN

lupine NOUN lupines a garden plant with tall spikes of flowers

lurch VERB lurches, lurching, lurched stagger; lean suddenly to one side
▷ **lurch** NOUN

lurch NOUN
leave somebody in the lurch leave somebody in difficulties

lure VERB lures, luring, lured tempt a person or animal into a trap; entice
▷ **lure** NOUN

lurid (**lewr**- id) ADJECTIVE **1** in very bright colors; gaudy **2** sensational and shocking • *the lurid details of the murder*
▷ **luridly** ADVERB **luridness** NOUN

Thesaurus

farcical, preposterous, risible, foolish, idiotic, (*more informal*) crazy, (*more informal*) daft, (*more informal*) barmy, (*more informal*) zany
OPPOSITES ARE reasonable, sensible

lug VERB *He lugged his old suitcase up the hill.*
▶ drag, pull, haul, carry, heave, hump

luggage NOUN *Trevor put his luggage on the rack.*
▶ bags, cases, baggage, things, paraphernalia, belongings

lukewarm ADJECTIVE **1** *She pulled a face over her lukewarm tea.* ▶ tepid, warm **2** *a lukewarm response* ▶ unenthusiastic, indifferent, half-hearted, offhand, cool, apathetic

lull NOUN *a lull in the fighting* ▶ pause, respite, break, calm, gap, interval, rest, (*more informal*) let-up

lull VERB *The singing lulled her to sleep.* ▶ soothe, calm, subdue, hush, pacify, quell, quieten, tranquillize AN OPPOSITE IS agitate

lumber VERB **1** (*informal*) *We were lumbered with paying the bill.* ▶ saddle, burden, encumber, load **2** *Henry lumbered down the stairs.* ▶ shamble, trudge, tramp, plod, shuffle, blunder, move clumsily

lump NOUN **1** *a lump of bread* ▶ chunk, hunk, block, wedge, piece, portion, slab, wad **2** *The blow left a lump on his head.* ▶ swelling, bump, growth, protuberance

lump VERB **1 lump together** *The newspaper reports lumped together several stories.*
▶ combine, amalgamate, merge, bunch **2 lump it** (*informal*) *We're not going and we'll just have to lump it.* ▶ accept it, put up with it, tolerate it, endure it

lunacy NOUN **1** *a scene of despair and lunacy* ▶ insanity, madness, mental disorder, mental illness, derangement, dementia **2** *It would be lunacy to try a rescue in this weather.* ▶ folly, foolishness, stupidity, madness, insanity

lunatic NOUN *a dangerous lunatic* ▶ maniac, madman, madwoman, (*more informal*) loony

lunge VERB *The man lunged at him.* ▶ thrust, charge, pounce, rush, throw yourself, dash, dive, lurch

lurch VERB *James lurched into the bathroom.* ▶ stagger, stumble, totter, reel, roll, list, lunge, sway, pitch, heave, lean, plunge, wallow

lure VERB *Advertising can lure people into debt.* ▶ tempt, entice, attract, induce, coax, seduce, draw, inveigle, invite, lead on, persuade

lurid ADJECTIVE **1** *window blinds of lurid colors* ▶ garish, gaudy, flashy, loud, glaring, vulgar OPPOSITES ARE sober, dull **2** *The report included all the lurid details.* ▶ sensational,

lurk VERB lurks, lurking, lurked wait where you cannot be seen

luscious (lush- us) ADJECTIVE delicious
▷ **lusciously** ADVERB **lusciousness** NOUN

lush ADJECTIVE **1** growing thickly and strongly • *lush grass* **2** luxurious
▷ **lushly** ADVERB **lushness** NOUN

lust NOUN lusts powerful desire, especially sexual desire
▷ **lustful** ADJECTIVE

lust VERB lusts, lusting, lusted have a powerful desire for a person or thing • *people who lust after power*

lusty ADJECTIVE lustier, lustiest strong and vigorous
▷ **lustily** ADVERB **lustiness** NOUN

lute NOUN lutes a stringed musical instrument with a pear-shaped body, popular in the 14th-17th centuries

luxuriant ADJECTIVE growing abundantly
USAGE Do not confuse with **luxurious**.

luxurious ADJECTIVE expensive and comfortable
▷ **luxuriously** ADVERB
USAGE Do not confuse with **luxuriant**.

luxury NOUN luxuries **1** something expensive that you enjoy but do not really need **2** expensive and comfortable surroundings • *a life of luxury* [from Latin *luxus* = plenty]

-ly SUFFIX forms **1** adjectives (e.g. *friendly, heavenly, sickly*), **2** adverbs from adjectives (e.g. *boldly, sweetly, thoroughly*)

Lycra NOUN (*trademark*) a thin stretchy material used especially for sports clothing

lying *present participle* of lie[1] and lie[2]

lynch VERB lynches, lynching, lynched join together to execute or punish someone violently without a proper trial, especially by hanging them

lyric (li- rik) NOUN lyrics **1** a short poem that expresses thoughts and feelings **2** the words of a song
▷ **lyrical** ADJECTIVE **lyrically** ADVERB

Thesaurus

melodramatic, graphic, salacious, gruesome, macabre

lurk VERB *lions lurking in shadows* ► skulk, loiter, lie in wait, lie low, crouch, hide

luscious ADJECTIVE *luscious fruit hanging from the trees* ► delicious, juicy, succulent, mouth-watering, appetizing

lush ADJECTIVE **1** *lush vegetation* ► rich, luxuriant, abundant, profuse, exuberant, prolific, flourishing **2** *a lush penthouse* ► luxurious, sumptuous, grand, opulent, lavish

lust NOUN *a lust for power* ► greed, desire, craving, longing, hunger, appetite, itch

luxurious ADJECTIVE *luxurious surroundings* ► sumptuous, grand, opulent, lavish, comfortable, lush, magnificent, plush, splendid OPPOSITES ARE austere, simple, spartan

luxury NOUN *They led a life of luxury.* ► opulence, sumptuousness, splendor, affluence, extravagance, comfort, ease, enjoyment, indulgence, pleasure, relaxation, self-indulgence

lying ADJECTIVE *He was just a lying schemer.* ► deceitful, dishonest, double-dealing, two-faced, false, untrustworthy, untruthful AN OPPOSITE IS truthful

lying NOUN *She was no good at lying, even to save her own skin.* ► falsehood, untruthfulness, deceit, dishonesty, mendacity, (*more formal*) perjury

Mm

MA ABBREVIATION Master of Arts

mac NOUN macs (informal) a mackintosh

macaroni NOUN pasta in the form of short tubes [via Italian from Greek *makaria* = food made from barley]

macaroon NOUN macaroons a small sweet cake or cookie made with ground almonds

machine NOUN machines something with parts that work together to do a job

machine gun NOUN machine guns a gun that can keep firing bullets quickly one after another

machinery NOUN 1 machines 2 the moving parts of a machine 3 an organized system for doing something • *the machinery of local government*

mackerel NOUN mackerel a sea fish used as food

mackintosh NOUN mackintoshes a raincoat

mad ADJECTIVE madder, maddest 1 having something wrong with the mind; insane 2 extremely foolish 3 very keen • *He is mad about football.* 4 (informal) very excited or annoyed
▷ **madly** ADVERB **madness** NOUN **madman** NOUN

like mad (informal) with great speed, energy, or enthusiasm

madam NOUN a word used when speaking politely to a woman • *Can I help you, madam?*

mad cow disease NOUN BSE

madden VERB maddens, maddening, maddened make a person mad or angry
▷ **maddening** ADJECTIVE

mafia NOUN 1 a large organization of criminals in Italy, Sicily, and the United States 2 any group of people believed to act together in a sinister way

magazine NOUN magazines 1 a paper-covered publication that comes out regularly, with articles, stories, or features by several writers 2 the part of a gun that holds the cartridges 3 a store for weapons and ammunition or for explosives 4 a device that holds film for a camera or slides for a projector [from Arabic *makhazin* = storehouses]

magenta (ma-jen-ta) NOUN a color between bright red and purple [named after Magenta, a town in north Italy, where Napoleon III won a battle in the year when the dye was discovered (1859)]

maggot NOUN maggots the larva of some kinds of fly
▷ **maggoty** ADJECTIVE

magic NOUN 1 the art of making things happen by supernatural powers 2 mysterious

Thesaurus

macabre ADJECTIVE *the macabre business of the switched bodies* ► gruesome, grisly, grim, gory, morbid, eerie, weird, lurid, dreadful, horrible, ghoulish

machine NOUN *The machine started to make a noise.* ► apparatus, appliance, contrivance, device, contraption, instrument, tool, gadget, mechanism RELATED ADJECTIVE ► mechanical

machinery NOUN 1 *a factory equipped with modern machinery* ► equipment, machines, plant, instruments, hardware, gear 2 *the agreed machinery for resolving disputes* ► procedure, organization, structure, system, constitution, method

macho NOUN *macho jobs like bricklaying* ► manly, male, masculine, virile, (more informal) butch

mad ADJECTIVE 1 *He thought he was going mad.* ► insane, mentally ill, deranged, demented, crazy, (more informal) out of your mind, (more informal) off your head, (more informal) potty, (more informal) nutty, (more informal) nuts 2 *It was a mad idea but they liked it.* ► foolish, crazy, insane, absurd, senseless, wild, preposterous 3 (informal) *Is she still mad with you for ditching her?* ► angry, cross, furious,

enraged, infuriated, irate 4 *mad about* (informal) *Jenny is mad about jazz.* ► keen on, crazy about, enthusiastic about, eager for, devoted to, addicted to

madden VERB *It's their pretence that maddens me most.* ► infuriate, exasperate, anger, enrage, incense, annoy, craze, irritate, vex, provoke

maddening ADJECTIVE *The traffic moved with maddening slowness.* ► infuriating, exasperating, irritating, annoying, vexing, irksome

madness NOUN 1 *There was a gleam of madness in his eyes.* ► insanity, dementia, lunacy, delirium, frenzy, hysteria, derangement, eccentricity, mania, mental illness, psychosis 2 *It is madness to let children roam about after dark.* ► foolishness, folly, stupidity, insanity, lunacy

magazine NOUN 1 *a pile of magazines on the dining room table* ► journal, periodical, color supplement, weekly, monthly, comic 2 *a magazine of weapons* ► arsenal, ammunition dump, storehouse, depot

magic NOUN 1 *It was so real it had to be magic.* ► sorcery, wizardry, witchcraft, devilry, the black arts, the supernatural 2 *No children's party is complete without the magic.* ► conjuring,

tricks performed for entertainment **3** a mysterious and enchanting quality ● *the magic of the East*
▷ **magic** *ADJECTIVE* **magical** *ADJECTIVE* **magically** *ADVERB*

magician *NOUN* **magicians 1** a person who does magic tricks **2** a wizard

magistrate *NOUN* **magistrates** an official who hears and judges minor cases in a local court
▷ **magistracy** *NOUN*
[from Latin *magister* = master]

magnanimous (mag- **nan**- im- us) *ADJECTIVE* generous and forgiving, not petty-minded
▷ **magnanimously** *ADVERB* **magnanimity** *NOUN*

magnate *NOUN* **magnates** a wealthy influential person, especially in business

magnesium *NOUN* a silvery-white metal that burns with a very bright flame

magnet *NOUN* **magnets** a piece of iron or steel that can attract iron and that points north and south when it is hung up
▷ **magnetism** *NOUN*

magnetic *ADJECTIVE* **1** having the powers of a magnet **2** having the power to attract people ● *a magnetic personality*
▷ **magnetically** *ADVERB*

magnetize *VERB* **magnetizes, magnetizing, magnetized 1** make into a magnet **2** attract like a magnet
▷ **magnetization** *NOUN*

magneto (mag- **neet**- oh) *NOUN* **magnetos** a small electric generator using magnets

magnificent *ADJECTIVE* **1** grand or splendid in appearance, etc. **2** excellent
▷ **magnificently** *ADVERB* **magnificence** *NOUN*
[from Latin *magnificus* = splendid]

magnify *VERB* **magnifies, magnifying, magnified** make something look or seem bigger than it really is
▷ **magnification** *NOUN* **magnifier** *NOUN*

magnifying glass *NOUN* **magnifying glasses** a lens that magnifies things

magnitude *NOUN* **magnitudes 1** size or extent **2** importance

magpie *NOUN* **magpies** a noisy bird with black and white feathers, related to the crow [from Mag (short for Margaret) + an old word *pie* = magpie]

mahogany *NOUN* a hard brown wood

maid *NOUN* **maids 1** a female servant **2** (*old use*) a girl
▷ **maidservant** *NOUN*

maiden *NOUN* **maidens** (*old use*) a girl
▷ **maidenhood** *NOUN*

maiden *ADJECTIVE* **1** not married ● *a maiden aunt* **2** first ● *a maiden voyage*

maiden name *NOUN* **maiden names** a woman's family name before she married

maiden over *NOUN* **maiden overs** a cricket over in which no runs are scored

mail[1] *NOUN* letters and parcels sent by post

mail[2] *NOUN* armour made of metal rings joined together ● *a suit of chain mail*

mailing list *NOUN* **mailing lists** a list of names and addresses of people to whom an organization sends information from time to time

mail order *NOUN* a system for buying and selling goods by post

maim *VERB* **maims, maiming, maimed** injure a person so that part of their body is made useless

Thesaurus

conjuring tricks, illusion, sleight of hand, (*technical*) prestidigitation **3** *The place had lost none of its magic.* ► charm, fascination, appeal, allure, glamour

magic *ADJECTIVE* *a magic spell* ► supernatural, magical, miraculous

magical *ADJECTIVE* *They would remember this magical day for the rest of their lives.*
► wonderful, marvellous, extraordinary, delightful, enchanting

magician *NOUN* *A magician would finish off the day's entertainment.* ► conjuror, entertainer, illusionist, wizard, sorcerer

magnificent *ADJECTIVE* **1** *a magnificent view*
► spectacular, splendid, impressive, imposing, noble, glorious, gorgeous, sumptuous **2** *a magnificent achievement* ► brilliant, masterly, superb, marvellous, wonderful, very fine

magnify *VERB* **1** *The device magnifies the image.*
► enlarge, maximize, amplify, make larger, augment, expand, increase, intensify, (*more*

informal) blow up AN OPPOSITE IS reduce **2** *It is easy to magnify the difficulties involved.*(*informal*) ► exaggerate, inflate, maximize, overdo, overestimate, overstate, make too much of, blow up out of all proportion, dramatize AN OPPOSITE IS minimize.

magnitude *NOUN* **1** *They realized the magnitude of the task* ► size, immensity, vastness, hugeness, extent, enormousness **2** *events of tragic magnitude* ► importance, significance, consequence, import, moment

maid *NOUN* *A maid cleared the room.* ► servant, serving girl, maidservant, domestic

mail *NOUN* *The letter came with the morning mail.*
► post, letters, delivery, packages, packets, parcels, correspondence

mail *VERB* *I'll mail you the package tomorrow.*
► post, send, dispatch, forward

maim *VERB* *Many people were killed or maimed in the attack.* ► injure, disable, mutilate, wound, disfigure, cripple, handicap

main ➡ make

main *ADJECTIVE* largest or most important

main *NOUN* **1** the main pipe or cable in a public system carrying water, gas, or (usually called mains) electricity to a building **2** *(old use)* the seas • *Drake sailed the Spanish main.*
in the main for the most part; on the whole

main clause *NOUN* main clauses a clause that can be used as a complete sentence COMPARE subordinate clause

mainland *NOUN* the main part of a country or continent, not the islands round it

mainly *ADVERB* **1** chiefly **2** almost completely **3** usually

mainstream *NOUN* the most widely accepted ideas or opinions about something • *Fascism is not in the mainstream of U.S. politics.*

maintain *VERB* maintains, maintaining, maintained **1** cause something to continue; keep in existence **2** keep a thing in good condition **3** provide money for a person to live on **4** state that something is true

maintenance *NOUN* **1** maintaining or keeping something in good condition **2** money for food and clothing **3** money to be paid by a husband or wife to the other partner after a divorce

maize *NOUN* a tall kind of corn with large seeds on cobs

majestic *ADJECTIVE* **1** stately and dignified **2** imposing
▷ **majestically** *ADVERB*

majesty *NOUN* majesties **1** the title of a king or queen • *Her Majesty the Queen* **2** being majestic

major *ADJECTIVE* **1** greater; very important • *major roads* **2** of the musical scale that has a semitone after the 3rd and 7th notes COMPARE minor

major *NOUN* majors an army officer ranking next above a captain [from Latin, = larger, greater]

majority *NOUN* majorities **1** the greatest part of a group of people or things COMPARE minority **2** the amount by which the winner in an election beats the loser • *She had a majority of 25 over her opponent.* **3** the age at which a person becomes an adult according to the law (now usually 18) • *He has attained his majority.*

make *VERB* makes, making, made **1** bring something into existence, especially by putting things together **2** cause or compel • *Make him repeat it.* **3** gain or earn • *She makes $25,000 a year.* **4** achieve or reach • *He made 25 runs* • *The swimmer just made the shore.* **5** reckon • *What do you make the time?* **6** result in or add up to • *4 and 6 make 10* **7** perform

---

Thesaurus

---

main *ADJECTIVE* *These are the main issues.* ▶ chief, principal, primary, prime, most important, overriding, foremost, fundamental, key, crucial, central, paramount, predominant, basic, essential

mainly *ADVERB* *The staff are mainly trainees.* ▶ chiefly, primarily, principally, mostly, predominantly, especially, essentially

maintain *VERB* **1** *The villagers pay to maintain the private road.* ▶ keep up, preserve, service, look after, take care of **2** *We need to maintain our links with industry.* ▶ sustain, continue, keep up, conserve, retain, preserve, prolong **3** *They maintain that they were never there.* ▶ assert, claim, affirm, insist, make out, declare, contend, argue

maintenance *NOUN* **1** *The buildings need a good deal of regular maintenance.* ▶ upkeep, repairs, preservation, care, servicing, conservation, looking after **2** *Absent fathers have to pay maintenance.* ▶ financial support, subsistence, alimony, allowance

majestic *ADJECTIVE* *a majestic range of mountains* ▶ magnificent, grand, spectacular, splendid, impressive, imposing, noble, glorious, gorgeous, sumptuous

majesty *NOUN* **1** *The procession continued with great majesty.* ▶ dignity, stateliness, solemnity, glory, splendor, grandeur, nobility **2** *the*

Queen's majesty ▶ sovereignty, royalty, dominion, authority

major *ADJECTIVE* *a major achievement* ▶ important, considerable, significant, noteworthy, substantial, sizable, appreciable

majority *NOUN* **1** *The majority of older people are poor.* ▶ greater number, preponderance, bulk **2** *the age of majority* ▶ adulthood, coming of age, manhood, maturity, womanhood AN OPPOSITE IS minority
be in the majority ▶ predominate, preponderate, be greater, dominate, outnumber, prevail

make *VERB* **1** *He makes reproduction furniture.* ▶ build, construct, assemble, put together, manufacture, produce **2** *She made me tell her the whole story.* ▶ force, coerce, oblige, compel, prevail on, pressure, urge USAGE You need to use the word *to* after all these synonyms, e.g., *She forced me to tell her the whole story.* If you use *prevail* you have to say *She prevailed on me to tell her the whole story.* **3** *The animals make such a noise.* ▶ cause, create, generate, engender, give rise to **4** *She made a little bow.* ▶ perform, execute, give, do, effect, carry out **5** *The town made him their mayor.* ▶ appoint, name, designate, nominate, elect, vote **6** *We seem to have made some mistakes.* ▶ commit, an action etc. • *make an effort* **8** arrange for use • *make the beds* **9** cause to be successful or happy • *Her visit made my day.*

make do manage with something that is not what you really want

make for go towards

make love 1 have sexual intercourse **2** (*old use*) try to win someone's love

make off go away quickly

make out 1 manage to see, hear, or understand something **2** claim or pretend that something is true

make up 1 build or put together **2** invent a story etc. **3** be friendly again after a disagreement **4** compensate for something **5** put on makeup

make up your mind decide

make NOUN **makes 1** making; how something is made **2** a brand of goods; something made by a particular firm

makeshift ADJECTIVE improvised or used because you have nothing better • *We used a box as a makeshift table.*

makeup NOUN **1** cosmetics **2** the way something is made up **3** a person's character

maladjusted ADJECTIVE unable to fit in or cope with other people or your own circumstances

malapropism NOUN **malapropisms** a comical confusion of words, e.g., using **hooligan** instead of **hurricane**

malaria NOUN a feverish disease spread by mosquitoes
▷ **malarial** ADJECTIVE

male ADJECTIVE **1** belonging to the sex that reproduces by fertilizing egg cells produced by the female **2** of men • *a male voice choir*

male NOUN **males** a male person, animal, or plant

male chauvinist NOUN **male chauvinists** a man who thinks that women are not as good as men

malevolent (ma- lev- ol- ent) ADJECTIVE wishing to harm people
▷ **malevolently** ADVERB **malevolence** NOUN

malfunction NOUN **malfunctions** faulty functioning • *a malfunction in the computer*

malfunction VERB **malfunctions**, **malfunctioning**, **malfunctioned** fail to work properly

Thesaurus

perpetrate, be responsible for, be guilty of **7** *The plan is bound to make money.* ► earn, bring in, gain, acquire AN OPPOSITE IS lose **8** *James's mother went out to make the lunch.* ► prepare, get ready, cook, put together, concoct **9** *I make the total over $500.* ► estimate, calculate, work out USAGE You need to use the word at after all these synonyms, e.g., *I estimate the total at over $500.* **10** *We must make a decision.* ► reach, come to, arrive at, settle on **11** *I think she'll make a good leader.* ► be, constitute, act as, serve as

make off *The thieves made off with the money.* ► escape, run off, get away, leave, bolt, (*more informal*) clear off

make out 1 *We could make out a tower in the distance.* ► see, discern, distinguish, perceive, detect, recognize, catch sight of, glimpse **2** *They made out we owed them money.* ► maintain, assert, claim, affirm, insist, declare, contend, argue **3** *How did you make out at the interview?* ► manage, get on, get along, do, cope, (*more formal*) fare **4** *The old man had made out a will.* ► draw up, write, complete

make up 1 *Such a story is not something anyone could make up.* ► invent, fabricate, contrive, concoct, think up, devise, create, (*more informal*) cook up **2** *They decided to kiss and make up.* ► be friends again, make peace, settle your differences, bury the hatchet, mend fences AN OPPOSITE IS quarrel

make up for *The fine acting made up for all the problems with the production.* ► compensate for, offset, counterbalance, counteract, make amends for, redress

make NOUN *a new make of car* ► brand, model, sort, kind, type, variety

make-believe NOUN *The secret garden was only make-believe.* ► fantasy, pretence, fiction, fancy, illusion, invention, imagination AN OPPOSITE IS reality

make-believe ADJECTIVE *a make-believe world of elves and fairies* ► imaginary, fanciful, pretended, sham, simulated, unreal, feigned, made-up, mock, (*more informal*) pretend AN OPPOSITE IS real

maker NOUN *a maker of toy cars* ► manufacturer, producer, creator, designer, originator, constructor, builder

makeshift ADJECTIVE *He arranged a row of chairs to form a makeshift bed.* ► temporary, standby, rough-and-ready, improvised, stopgap, pernicious, hurtful

make-up NOUN **1** *Ambition is an important part of his make-up.* ► character, nature, temperament, constitution, disposition **2** *Her make-up started to run.* ► cosmetics, powder, paint

malevolent ADJECTIVE *the malevolent gaze of his eyes* ► malicious, hostile, spiteful, baleful, malign, vindictive, malignant, pernicious, hurtful, offensive, venomous

a
b
c
d
e
f
g
h
i
j
k
l
m
n
o
p
q
r
s
t
u
v
w
x
y
z

399

malice NOUN the desire to harm other people
▷ **malicious** ADJECTIVE **maliciously** ADVERB

malign (mal- I'n) ADJECTIVE **1** harmful • *a malign influence* **2** showing malice
▷ **malignity** (mal- **ig**- nit- ee) NOUN

malignant ADJECTIVE **1** (said about a tumor) growing uncontrollably **2** full of malice
▷ **malignantly** ADVERB **malignancy** NOUN

malleable ADJECTIVE **1** able to be pressed or hammered into shape **2** easy to influence; adaptable
▷ **malleability** NOUN

mallet NOUN **mallets** **1** a large hammer, usually made of wood **2** an implement with a long handle, used in croquet or polo for striking the ball

malnutrition NOUN bad health because you do not have enough food or the right kind of food
▷ **malnourished** ADJECTIVE

malt NOUN dried barley used in brewing, making vinegar, etc.
▷ **malted** ADJECTIVE

maltreat VERB **maltreats**, **maltreating**, **maltreated** ill-treat
▷ **maltreatment** NOUN

mammal NOUN **mammals** any animal of which the female gives birth to live babies which are fed with milk from her own body
▷ **mammalian** (mam- **ay**- lee- an) ADJECTIVE

mammoth NOUN **mammoths** an extinct elephant with a hairy skin and curved tusks

mammoth ADJECTIVE huge

man NOUN **men** **1** a grown-up male human being **2** an individual person **3** mankind **4** a piece used in chess or other board games

man VERB **mans**, **manning**, **manned** supply with people to work something • *Man the pumps!* [from Old English]

manacle NOUN **manacles** a fetter or handcuff

manacle VERB **manacles**, **manacling**, **manacled** fasten with manacles

manage VERB **manages**, **managing**, **managed** **1** be able to cope with something difficult **2** be in charge of a business or part of it, or a group of people
▷ **manageable** ADJECTIVE

management NOUN **1** managing **2** managers; the people in charge

manager NOUN **managers** a person who manages something
▷ **manageress** NOUN **managerial** (man- a- **jeer**- ee- al) ADJECTIVE

Thesaurus

malice NOUN *actions prompted by malice*
► malevolence, ill will, spite, spitefulness, animosity

malicious ADJECTIVE *malicious remarks*
► malevolent, hostile, spiteful, baleful, malign, vindictive, malignant, mischievous, pernicious, offensive, hurtful, venomous OPPOSITES ARE benevolent, kind

malignant ADJECTIVE **1** *a malignant disease* ► fatal, incurable, terminal, virulent, destructive **2** *a malignant growth* ► cancerous, poisonous, non-benign, spreading AN OPPOSITE IS benign **3** *a malignant stare* ► malevolent, hostile, spiteful, baleful, malign, pernicious, offensive, hurtful, venomous OPPOSITES ARE benevolent, kind

maltreat VERB *He was a bully and often maltreated his wife.* ► ill-treat, mistreat, abuse, misuse, harm, injure, molest, (more informal) knock about

mammoth ADJECTIVE *It would be a mammoth task getting the house to rights again.* ► huge, enormous, gigantic, immense, massive, colossal, vast, large, big, giant, (more informal) whopping, (more informal) ginormous AN OPPOSITE IS tiny

man NOUN **1** *a man in a smart suit* ► male, gentleman, fellow, (more informal) chap, (more informal) bloke **2** *All men are fallible.* ► person, individual, human being **3** *the evolution of modern man* ► humanity, humankind,

mankind, the human race, humans, Homo sapiens **4** *The men have gone on strike.*
► worker, employee RELATED ADJECTIVES
► male, masculine

man VERB *We need to man the reception desk from 8 until 5.* ► staff, provide personnel for, provide staff for, occupy

manage VERB **1** *She manages a team of 20.* ► be in charge of, run, head, lead, supervise, oversee, control **2** *a course in managing money* ► organize, administer, deal with, regulate **3** *I could only just manage the extra work I had to do.* ► undertake, accomplish, achieve, finish, complete, carry out **4** *I don't know how we'll manage without her.* ► cope, get along, survive, fare, make do **5** *a horse that's difficult to manage* ► control, handle, master, cope with, deal with

manageable ADJECTIVE **1** *a manageable task* ► achievable, doable, practicable, feasible, reasonable, attainable, viable AN OPPOSITE IS awkward **2** *a manageable horse* ► controllable, obedient, tractable, compliant, amenable, disciplined, docile OPPOSITES ARE unmanageable, disobedient

management NOUN **1** *The local movie theater is under new management.* ► administration, control, direction, supervision, charge, care **2** *The union is in dispute with the management.*

manager NOUN *a meeting of departmental managers* ► director, administrator, head, executive, supervisor, principal, controller, boss, chief

mandarin NOUN **mandarins 1** an important official **2** a kind of small orange

mane NOUN **manes** the long hair on a horse's or lion's neck

maneuver (man- oo- ver) NOUN **maneuvers** a difficult or skillful or cunning action

maneuver VERB **maneuvers, maneuvering, maneuvered** move carefully and skillfully
▷ **maneuverable** ADJECTIVE

manganese NOUN a hard brittle metal

manger NOUN **mangers** a trough in a stable for horses or cattle to feed from

mangle VERB **mangles, mangling, mangled** damage something by crushing or cutting it roughly

mango NOUN **mangoes** a tropical fruit with yellow pulp

manhandle VERB **manhandles, manhandling, manhandled** treat or push roughly

manhole NOUN **manholes** a space or opening, usually with a cover, by which a person can get into a sewer or boiler, etc., to inspect or repair it

manhood NOUN **1** the condition of being a man **2** manly qualities

mania NOUN **manias 1** violent madness **2** great enthusiasm • *a mania for sport*
▷ **maniac** NOUN **manic** ADJECTIVE

manicure NOUN **manicures** care and treatment of the hands and nails
▷ **manicure** VERB **manicurist** NOUN

manifest ADJECTIVE clear and obvious
▷ **manifestly** ADVERB

manifesto NOUN **manifestos** a public statement of a group's or person's policy or principles

manifold ADJECTIVE of many kinds; very varied

manipulate VERB **manipulates, manipulating, manipulated 1** handle or arrange something skilfully **2** get someone to do what you want by treating them cleverly
▷ **manipulation** NOUN **manipulator** NOUN

mankind NOUN human beings in general

manly ADJECTIVE **1** suitable for a man **2** brave and strong
▷ **manliness** NOUN

manner NOUN **1** the way something happens or is done **2** a person's way of behaving **3** a sort or type • *all manner of things*

mannerism NOUN **mannerisms** a person's own particular gesture or way of speaking

manners PLURAL NOUN how a person behaves with other people; politeness

manor NOUN **manors 1** a manor house **2** the land belonging to a manor house
▷ **manorial** ADJECTIVE
[from early French, related to **mansion**]

manor house NOUN **manor houses** a large important house in the country

manpower NOUN the number of people who are working or needed or available for work on something

mansion NOUN **mansions** a large stately house
[from Latin *mansio* = a place to stay, a dwelling]

manslaughter NOUN killing a person unlawfully but without meaning to

Thesaurus

maneuver NOUN **1** *She parked the car with a deft maneuver.* ► movement, move, action, operation **2** *a diplomatic maneuver* ► stratagem, strategy, tactic, move, plan, plot, ploy, ruse, dodge, gambit, trick **3** *military maneuvers* ► exercise, movement, operation, training

maneuver VERB *He maneuvered the trunk down the stairs.* ► manipulate, negotiate, move, engineer, guide, navigate, pilot, steer

mangle VERB *Henry was staring at the man's mangled hand.* ► maul, mutilate, maim, crush, damage, disfigure, injure, wound, lacerate, squash, tear

maniac NOUN *a homicidal maniac* ► lunatic, madman OR madwoman, psychopath, (*more informal*) loony

manipulate VERB **1** *You need to know how to manipulate all the machine's knobs and levers.* ► operate, work, wield, control, negotiate, twiddle **2** *Governments try to manipulate the economy before elections.* ► influence, control, exploit **3** *It is not difficult to manipulate the data to get the result you want.* ► alter, distort,

falsify, doctor, massage, tinker with, fiddle with, fudge, rig, (*more informal*) cook

mankind NOUN *They want to save nature from mankind.* ► humanity, humankind, the human race, humans, man, Homo sapiens

manly ADJECTIVE **1** *a manly physique* ► virile, masculine, muscular, sturdy, robust, well-built **2** *manly deeds* ► brave, courageous, bold, heroic, valiant, gallant, chivalrous

manmade ADJECTIVE *a manmade fiber* ► synthetic, artificial, manufactured, simulated, imitation AN OPPOSITE IS natural

manner NOUN **1** *They dealt with the problem in a very efficient manner.* ► way, fashion, style, method, means, procedure, process, mode **2** *I don't much like his unfriendly manner.* ► attitude, demeanour, disposition, air, look, bearing, behavior, character, conduct, mien **3** *We've seen all manner of things there.* ► kind, sort, type, variety, category, class **4** *manners He needs to learn some manners.* ► politeness, refinement, civility, courtesy, etiquette, good behavior, good conduct, breeding, gentility

mantelpiece NOUN mantelpieces a shelf above a fireplace

mantle NOUN mantles **1** a cloak **2** a covering • *a mantle of snow*

manual ADJECTIVE worked by or done with the hands • *a manual typewriter; manual work*
▷ **manually** ADVERB

manual NOUN manuals a handbook containing instructions etc.

manufacture VERB manufactures, manufacturing, manufactured make things, especially on a large scale
▷ **manufacture** NOUN **manufacturer** NOUN

manure NOUN fertilizer, especially dung

manuscript NOUN manuscripts something written or typed but not printed

Manx ADJECTIVE to do with the Isle of Man

many ADJECTIVE more, most great in number; numerous • *many people*

many NOUN many people or things • *Many were found.*

Maori (rhymes with *flowery*) NOUN Maoris **1** a member of the aboriginal people of New Zealand **2** their language

map NOUN maps a diagram of part or all of the earth's surface or of the sky

map VERB maps, mapping, mapped make a map of an area
map out plan the details of something

marathon NOUN marathons a long-distance running race, especially one covering 26 miles 385 yards (42.195 km) [named after Marathon in Greece, from which a messenger is said to have run to Athens (about 40 kilometers) to announce that the Greeks had defeated the Persian army]

March NOUN the third month of the year [named after Mars, the Roman god of war]

marauding ADJECTIVE going about in search of plunder or prey
▷ **marauder** NOUN

marble NOUN marbles **1** a small glass ball used in games **2** a kind of limestone polished and used in sculpture or building

march VERB marches, marching, marched **1** walk with regular steps **2** make somebody walk somewhere • *He marched them up the hill.*
▷ **marcher** NOUN

march NOUN marches **1** marching **2** music suitable for marching to

mare NOUN mares a female horse or donkey

margarine (mar- ja- rin) NOUN a substance used like butter, made from animal or vegetable fats

margin NOUN margins **1** an edge or border **2** the blank space between the edge of a page and the writing or pictures etc. on it **3** the difference between two scores or prices, etc. • *She won by a narrow margin.*

marginal ADJECTIVE **1** in a margin • *marginal notes* **2** very slight • *a marginal difference*
▷ **marginally** ADVERB

marine (ma- reen) ADJECTIVE to do with the sea; living in the sea

marine NOUN marines a member of the troops who are trained to serve at sea as well as on land

marionette NOUN marionettes a puppet worked by strings or wires

marital ADJECTIVE to do with marriage

maritime ADJECTIVE **1** to do with the sea or ships **2** found near the sea

Thesaurus

manual ADJECTIVE *manual work* ► laboring, physical, by hand

manual NOUN *a training manual* ► handbook, guide, guidebook, reference book

manufacture VERB *The country could manufacture a nuclear weapon within five years.* ► make, construct, create, build, prefabricate, assemble, fabricate, mass-produce, process, (*informal*) turn out

many ADJECTIVE *There are many reasons.* ► a lot of, plenty of, numerous, countless, various, copious, profuse, innumerable, umpteen, (*more informal*) lots of AN OPPOSITE IS few

map NOUN *a map of Europe* ► chart, diagram, plan RELATED ADJECTIVE ► cartographic
RELATED NOUN ► cartography

map VERB *Aircraft were used to map the region.* ► chart, survey
map out *We mapped out a plan.* ► outline, set out, formulate, detail

mar VERB *His good looks were marred by stubble and red eyes.* ► spoil, impair, disfigure, ruin, deface, detract from, tarnish

march VERB *A company of soldiers marched past.* ► file, troop, parade, stride, pace, walk

march NOUN **1** *a three-day march* ► trek, hike, tramp, slog **2** *a protest march* ► procession, rally, demonstration, parade, (*more informal*) demo **3** *the march of time* ► advance, progress, progression, passage, evolution

margin NOUN **1** *the margin of the lake* ► edge, border, boundary, verge, perimeter, side **2** *They won by a narrow margin.* ► difference, gap, surplus

marginal ADJECTIVE *The extra cost is marginal.* ► negligible, minimal, insignificant, unimportant, borderline OPPOSITES ARE significant, important

mark[1] NOUN **marks 1** a spot, dot, line, or stain, etc., on something **2** a number or letter, etc., put on a piece of work to show how good it is **3** a distinguishing feature **4** a sign or symbol • *They all stood as a mark of respect.* **5** a target
on your marks! a command to runners to get ready to begin a race
up to the mark of the normal or expected standard

mark VERB **marks, marking, marked 1** put a mark on something **2** give a mark to a piece of work **3** pay attention to something • *Mark my words!* **4** keep close to an opposing player in football etc.
▷ **marker** NOUN
mark time 1 march on the spot without moving forward **2** occupy your time without making any progress

mark[2] NOUN **marks** a German unit of money replaced by the euro in 2002

marked ADJECTIVE noticeable • *a marked improvement*
▷ **markedly** ADVERB

market NOUN **markets 1** a place where things are bought and sold, usually from stalls in the open air **2** demand for things • *Is there a market for typewriters now?*
▷ **marketplace** NOUN
on the market offered for sale

market research NOUN the study of what people need or want to buy

marksman NOUN **marksmen** an expert in shooting at a target
▷ **marksmanship** NOUN

marmalade NOUN jam made from oranges, lemons, or other citrus fruit

maroon VERB **maroons, marooning, marooned** abandon or isolate somebody in a deserted place; strand

marquee (mar- kee) NOUN **marquees** a large tent used for a party or exhibition, etc.

marquis NOUN **marquises** a nobleman ranking next above an earl

marriage NOUN **marriages 1** the state of being married **2** a wedding

marrow NOUN **marrows 1** a large gourd eaten as a vegetable **2** the soft substance inside bones

marry VERB **marries, marrying, married 1** become a person's husband or wife **2** join two people as husband and wife; be in charge of a marriage ceremony

marsh NOUN **marshes** a low-lying area of very wet ground
▷ **marshy** ADJECTIVE

marshal NOUN **marshals 1** an official who supervises a contest or ceremony, etc. **2** an officer of very high rank • *a field marshal*

Thesaurus

mark NOUN **1** *a dirty mark* ► spot, stain, blot, blotch, smudge, blemish **2** *a mark of respect* ► sign, token, symbol, indication, proof, evidence, gesture **3** *Donations have passed the million mark.* ► stage, point, level **4** *a comment that hit the mark* ► target, objective, purpose, aim **5** *He got a better mark for French than for German.* ► grade, grading, score, assessment, evaluation

mark VERB **1** *She took great care not to mark her white dress.* ► stain, blemish, smudge, dirty, discolor, blot **2** *All possessions should be clearly marked.* ► label, tag **3** *The capture of the rebel stronghold marked a new stage in the war.* ► represent, signify, herald, denote, identify, characterize **4** *a festival to mark the Golden Jubilee* ► celebrate, recognize, observe, commemorate, remember **5** *Mark my words carefully.* ► heed, note, mind, take notice of, listen to, regard **6** *She had exam papers to mark that evening.* ► assess, grade, correct, evaluate, appraise

marked ADJECTIVE *a marked improvement in health* ► distinct, noticeable, decided, pronounced, plain, clear, emphatic, palpable AN OPPOSITE IS slight

market NOUN **1** *The local market is every Saturday.* ► bazaar, fair, sale, marketplace

2 *The market for second-hand cars is thriving.* ► demand, call, need, requirement

market VERB *The firm markets reproduction furniture.* ► sell, trade in, merchandise, retail

maroon VERB *a story about a group of boys marooned on a desert island* ► strand, cast away, abandon, isolate, leave, desert, forsake

marriage NOUN **1** *The couple will celebrate their 50 years of marriage.* ► matrimony, wedlock, partnership, union **2** *The marriage took place in the local register office.* ► wedding, wedding ceremony, match, nuptials RELATED ADJECTIVES ► conjugal, marital, matrimonial, nuptial

marry VERB **1** *They never married.* ► get married, wed, (more informal) tie the knot OPPOSITES ARE separate, divorce **2** *He married Jessica in Italy.* ► wed, (more informal) get hitched to OPPOSITES ARE separate from, divorce **3** *The exhibition marries information with entertainment.* ► combine, unite, link, merge, connect, join, ally

marsh NOUN *The car had plunged into a marsh.* ► swamp, bog, marshland, wetland, mire, morass, quagmire, quicksand, fen

marshal VERB *The king marshaled a huge army. The police marshaled their evidence with great care.* ► gather, assemble, collect, organize, muster, set out, deploy, draw up, group, line up, arrange OPPOSITES ARE disperse, scatter

a b c d e f g h i j k l **m** n o p q r s t u v w x y z

403

A B C D E F G H I J K L M N O P Q R S T U V W X Y Z

marshmallow NOUN marshmallows a soft spongy sweet, usually pink or white

marsupial (mar- soo- pee- al) NOUN marsupials an animal such as a kangaroo or wallaby The female has a pouch on the front of its body in which its babies are carried

martial ADJECTIVE to do with war; warlike

martial arts PLURAL NOUN fighting sports, such as judo and karate

martial law NOUN government of a country by the armed forces during a crisis

martyr NOUN martyrs a person who is killed or made to suffer because of his or her beliefs
▷ **martyrdom** NOUN

marvel NOUN marvels a wonderful thing
▷ **marvelous** ADJECTIVE

marzipan NOUN a soft sweet food made of ground almonds, eggs, and sugar

mascot NOUN mascots a person, animal, or thing that is believed to bring good luck

masculine ADJECTIVE 1 to do with men 2 typical of or suitable for men 3 (in some languages) belonging to the class of words which includes the words referring to men, such as *garçon* and *livre* in French
▷ **masculinity** NOUN

mash VERB mashes, mashing, mashed crush into a soft mass

mask NOUN masks a covering worn over the face to disguise or protect it

masochist (mas- ok- ist) NOUN masochists a person who enjoys things that seem painful or tiresome
▷ **masochism** NOUN

mason NOUN masons a person who builds or works with stone

masonry NOUN 1 the stone parts of a building; stonework 2 a mason's work

masquerade NOUN masquerades a pretence

masquerade VERB masquerades, masquerading, masqueraded pretend to be something ● *He masqueraded as a policeman.*

Mass NOUN Masses the Communion service in a Roman Catholic church

mass NOUN masses 1 a large amount 2 a heap or other collection of matter 3 (in science) the quantity of physical matter that a thing contains

mass ADJECTIVE involving a large number of people ● *mass murder*

massacre NOUN massacres the killing of a large number of people
▷ **massacre** VERB

massage (mas- ah*zh*) VERB massages, massaging, massaged rub and press the body to make it less stiff or less painful
▷ **massage** NOUN **masseur** NOUN **masseuse** NOUN

massive ADJECTIVE large and heavy; huge

Thesaurus

marvel VERB marvel at *Everyone marveled at their courage.* ► admire, be amazed by, wonder at, applaud, praise, appreciate, respect, be astonished by, be surprised by

marvelous ADJECTIVE 1 *a marvelous achievement* ► remarkable, amazing, extraordinary, wonderful, magnificent, astonishing, astounding AN OPPOSITE IS ordinary 2 *We had a marvellous time.* ► excellent, wonderful, fantastic, splendid, lovely, delightful, smashing, (*more informal*) terrific OPPOSITES ARE awful, dreadful

masculine ADJECTIVE 1 *She wore a masculine shirt with rolled-up sleeves.* ► male, man's OR men's, manlike AN OPPOSITE IS feminine 2 *a powerfully masculine man* ► manly, virile, muscular, well-built, strapping, vigorous OPPOSITES ARE weak, timid

mash VERB *Mash the potatoes and put them on top.* ► crush, pulp, cream, purée, pulverize, pound, smash, squash, grind, mangle, beat

mask NOUN *They wore masks to hide their faces.* ► disguise, veil, camouflage, cover, screen, shield, façade

mask VERB *A row of trees masked the view.* ► conceal, cover, obscure, screen, shield, hide,

shroud, veil, blot out, camouflage, cloak, disguise

mass NOUN 1 *a mass of wet leaves* ► pile, heap, load, accumulation, collection, conglomeration 2 *a mass of cars heading for the coast* ► multitude, throng, crowd, troop, mob, quantity, large number 3 *The mass of people declined to vote at all.* ► majority, greater part, bulk, body 4 *an object having a large mass* ► weight, size, magnitude, bulk

mass ADJECTIVE *a mass protest* ► wholesale, universal, large-scale, widespread, comprehensive, general, popular AN OPPOSITE IS small-scale

mass VERB *Spectators massed under the trees during the downpour.* ► gather, assemble, collect, flock

massacre NOUN *the massacre of innocent civilians* ► slaughter, killing, mass murder, extermination, butchery, carnage, annihilation

massacre VERB *The army massacred most of the population.* ► slaughter, butcher, exterminate, annihilate, murder, liquidate, eliminate

massive ADJECTIVE *a massive building; massive debts* ► huge, enormous, gigantic, immense, colossal, vast, large, big, giant, (*more informal*) whopping, (*more informal*) ginormous AN OPPOSITE IS tiny

mass media NOUN the main media of news information, especially newspapers and broadcasting

mass production NOUN manufacturing goods in large quantities
▷ **mass-produced** ADJECTIVE

mast NOUN masts a tall pole that holds up a ship's sails or a flag or an aerial

master NOUN masters **1** a man who is in charge of something **2** a male teacher **3** a great artist, composer, sportsman, etc. **4** something from which copies are made **5** (old use) a title put before a boy's name

masterful ADJECTIVE **1** domineering **2** very skilful
▷ **masterfully** ADVERB

master key NOUN master keys a key that will open several different locks

masterly ADJECTIVE very skilful

Master of Arts NOUN Masters of Arts a person who has taken the next degree after Bachelor of Arts

master of ceremonies NOUN masters of ceremonies a person who introduces the speakers at a formal event, or the entertainers at a variety show

Master of Science NOUN Masters of Science a person who has taken the next degree after Bachelor of Science

masterpiece NOUN masterpieces **1** an excellent piece of work **2** a person's best piece of work

mastery NOUN complete control or thorough knowledge or skill in something

mastiff NOUN mastiffs a large kind of dog

masturbate VERB masturbates, masturbating, masturbated get sexual pleasure by rubbing your genitals
▷ **masturbation** NOUN

mat NOUN mats **1** a small carpet **2** a doormat **3** a small piece of material put on a table to protect the surface

matador NOUN matadors a bullfighter who fights on foot

match[1] NOUN matches a small thin stick with a head made of a substance that gives a flame when rubbed on something rough
▷ **matchbox** NOUN **matchstick** NOUN

match[2] NOUN matches **1** a game or contest between two teams or players **2** one person or thing that matches another **3** a marriage

match VERB matches, matching, matched **1** be equal or similar to another person or thing **2** put teams or players to compete against each other **3** find something that is similar or corresponding

Thesaurus

master NOUN **1** *He became master of the country after a bloody coup.* ► ruler, chief, head, lord, overlord, governor **2** *a dog's master* ► owner, keeper **3** *a master of disguises* ► expert (at), genius, past master, maestro, virtuoso

master VERB **1** *He managed to master his feelings.* ► control, restrain, check, contain, curb, confine, curb, keep in check, repress, subdue, suppress **2** *She mastered the language after a few months.* ► learn, grasp, take in, be expert in, (more informal) get the hang of

masterful ADJECTIVE USAGE Do not confuse this word with *masterly*, which has a different meaning. *The most masterful sovereign in English history* ► authoritative, commanding, powerful, domineering, overbearing, arrogant, dictatorial, tyrannical, bossy

masterly ADJECTIVE USAGE Do not confuse this word with *masterful*, which has a different meaning. *A masterly survey of the subject* ► expert, skilful, adept, adroit, accomplished, consummate, intelligent, fine

mastermind NOUN *the mastermind behind the robbery* ► originator, planner, creator, engineer, prime mover, architect, inventor, manager, (more informal) brain, (more informal) brains

mastermind VERB *They brought him back to mastermind the new operation.* ► control, direct, plan, organize, coordinate, conduct, supervise, carry through

mastery NOUN **1** *a mastery of languages* ► command, knowledge, grasp, comprehension, understanding, proficiency (in) **2** *work done with great mastery* ► proficiency, capability, expertness, skill, adroitness, dexterity

match NOUN **1** *a cricket match* ► game, contest, competition, fixture, test match, tie, tournament **2** *The dress and shoes are a good match.* ► combination, pair **3** *She found a match for the tall vase.* ► copy, replica, complement, counterpart, duplicate, twin **4** *The enemy tanks were no match for ours in speed and range.* ► equal, rival, equivalent, counterpart **5** *a love match* ► marriage, union, friendship, partnership, relationship, alliance

match VERB **1** *The hat matches her dress.* ► go with, suit, harmonize with, tone with, blend with, complement **2** *The two versions of the story don't match.* ► agree, correspond, tally **3** *No one can match him at Scrabble.* ► equal, rival, compete with

matching ADJECTIVE *The curtains have a matching duvet cover.* ► corresponding, coordinating, equivalent, harmonizing,

a
b
c
d
e
f
g
h
i
j
k
l
m
n
o
p
q
r
s
t
u
v
w
x
y
z

A
B
C
D
E
F
G
H
I
J
K
L
M
N
O
P
Q
R
S
T
U
V
W
X
Y
Z

mate[1] NOUN **mates 1** a companion or friend **2** each of a mated pair of birds or animals **3** an officer on a merchant ship

mate VERB **mates, mating, mated 1** come together or bring two together in order to breed **2** put things together as a pair or because they correspond

mate[2] NOUN, VERB (in chess) checkmate

material NOUN **materials 1** anything used for making something else **2** cloth or fabric

materialize VERB **materializes, materializing, materialized 1** become visible; appear • *The ghost didn't materialize.* **2** become a fact; happen • *The trip did not materialize.*
▷ **materialization** NOUN

maternal ADJECTIVE **1** to do with a mother **2** motherly
▷ **maternally** ADVERB

maternity NOUN motherhood

maternity ADJECTIVE to do with having a baby • *a maternity ward*

mathematics NOUN the study of numbers, measurements, and shapes
▷ **mathematical** ADJECTIVE **mathematically** ADVERB **mathematician** NOUN
[from Greek *mathema* = science, from *manthanein* = to learn]

matriarch (may- tree- ark) NOUN **matriarchs** a woman who is head of a family or tribe COMPARE **patriarch**
▷ **matriarchal** ADJECTIVE **matriarchy** NOUN

matrix (may- triks) NOUN **matrices** (may- tri-seez) **1** (in mathematics) a set of quantities arranged in rows and columns **2** a mould or

framework in which something is made or allowed to develop

matron NOUN **matrons 1** a mature married woman **2** a woman in charge of nursing in a school etc. or (formerly) of the nursing staff in a hospital
▷ **matronly** ADJECTIVE

matted ADJECTIVE tangled into a mass

matter NOUN **matters 1** something you can touch or see, not spirit or mind or qualities etc. **2** a substance • *Peat consists mainly of vegetable matter.* **3** things of a certain kind • *printed matter.* **4** something to be thought about or done • *It's a serious matter.* **5** a quantity • *in a matter of minutes*
a matter of course the natural or expected thing • *I always lock my bike, as a matter of course.*
as a matter of fact in fact
no matter it does not matter
what is the matter? what is wrong?

matter VERB **matters, mattering, mattered** be important

matter-of-fact ADJECTIVE keeping to facts; not imaginative or emotional • *She talked about death in a very matter-of-fact way.*

mattress NOUN **mattresses** soft or springy material in a fabric covering, used on or as a bed

mature ADJECTIVE **1** fully grown or developed **2** grown-up
▷ **maturely** ADVERB **maturity** NOUN

mature VERB **matures, maturing, matured** make or become mature

Thesaurus

toning, complementing AN OPPOSITE IS incongruous

mate NOUN **1** *a plumber's mate* ► assistant, helper, apprentice, colleague **2** *He went to see a film with his mates.* ► friend, pal, chum, companion **3** *He's still looking for his ideal mate.* ► partner, wife OR husband, spouse, lover, consort

mate VERB *The zoo is trying to get the pandas to mate.* ► breed, copulate, couple

material NOUN **1** *material for making curtains* ► fabric, cloth, textile, stuff **2** *organic material* ► matter, substance, stuff **3** *We are collecting material for an article on surfing.* ► data, information, facts, statistics, evidence, particulars

material ADJECTIVE **1** *the material world as distinct from the spiritual world* ► physical, corporeal, tangible, earthly, concrete OPPOSITES ARE spiritual, abstract **2** *information that is material to our enquiries* ► relevant, pertinent, applicable, germane OPPOSITES ARE irrelevant, immaterial

matter NOUN **1** *Excess vegetable matter can be kept in a separate waste bin.* ► material, substance, stuff **2** *The last sentence of his statement goes to the heart of the matter.* ► affair, business, subject, topic, issue, concern **3** *It's of little matter now.* ► importance, consequence, significance, moment

matter VERB *Does it matter what I wear?* ► make a difference, be important, count, signify

mature ADJECTIVE **1** *a mature woman* ► adult, grown-up, grown, full-grown, advanced, well-developed OPPOSITES ARE immature, adolescent **2** *He seems very mature for his age.* ► responsible, sensible, dependable, reliable OPPOSITES ARE immature, childish **3** *mature cheese; mature fruit* ► mellow, ready, ripened, seasoned AN OPPOSITE IS unripe

mature VERB **1** *Bella had matured into a beautiful young woman.* ► grow, grow up, develop, blossom **2** *Their friendship matured rapidly.* ► develop, grow, blossom, bloom, flourish, thrive

maul VERB mauls, mauling, mauled injure by handling or clawing • *He was mauled by a lion.*

mauve (mohv) NOUN pale purple

maxim NOUN maxims a short saying giving a general truth or rule of behavior, e.g., "Waste not, want not"

maximize VERB maximizes, maximizing, maximized increase something to a maximum

maximum NOUN maxima or maximums the greatest possible number or amount (The opposite is **minimum**)

May NOUN the fifth month of the year [named after Maia, a Roman goddess]

may AUXILIARY VERB may, might used to express **1** permission (*You may go now*), **2** possibility (*It may be true*), **3** wish (*Long may she reign*), uncertainty (*whoever it may be*) USAGE See note at **can**.

may NOUN hawthorn blossom

maybe ADVERB perhaps; possibly

mayfly NOUN mayflies an insect that lives for only a short time, in spring

mayhem NOUN violent confusion or damage • *The mob caused mayhem.*

mayonnaise NOUN a creamy sauce made from eggs, oil, vinegar, etc., usually eaten with salad or in sandwiches

mayor NOUN mayors the person in charge of the council in a town or city
▷ **mayoral** ADJECTIVE **mayoress** NOUN
[from early French, related to **major**]

maze NOUN mazes a network of paths, especially one designed as a puzzle in which to try and find your way

Mb ABBREVIATION megabyte(s)

MD ABBREVIATION Doctor of Medicine

me PRONOUN the form of I used as the object of a verb or after a preposition

meadow (med- oh) NOUN meadows a field of grass

meager ADJECTIVE scanty in amount; barely enough • *a meager diet*

meal[1] NOUN meals food served and eaten at one sitting [from Old English *mael*]

meal[2] NOUN coarsely ground grain
▷ **mealy** ADJECTIVE
[from Old English *melu*]

mean VERB means, meaning, meant (ment) **1** have as an equivalent or explanation • *"Maybe" means "perhaps"* **2** have as a purpose; intend • *I mean to win.* **3** indicate • *Dark clouds mean rain.* **4** have as a result • *It means I'll have to get the early train.*

mean ADJECTIVE meaner, meanest **1** not generous; miserly **2** unkind or spiteful • *a*

Thesaurus

maul VERB **1** *He pulled me to the ground and started mauling me on my back and neck.*
► savage, attack, claw, manhandle, molest, maltreat, ill-treat, mutilate, lacerate **2** *The new production was mauled by the critics.* ► criticize, attack, savage, pillory, lambaste, (*more informal*) hammer, (*more informal*) slam

maximum ADJECTIVE *a maximum speed of 80 mph* ► greatest, highest, top, full, utmost, extreme, fullest, largest, most, biggest, supreme AN OPPOSITE IS minimum

maximum NOUN *Production has reached its maximum.* ► upper limit, limit, peak, ceiling, highest point, pinnacle, top level AN OPPOSITE IS minimum

mayhem NOUN *I decided I'd caused enough mayhem for one day.* ► confusion, chaos, disorder, muddle, bedlam, pandemonium, anarchy, disorganization, lawlessness, shambles, tumult AN OPPOSITE IS order

maze NOUN *a maze of rooms and corridors*
► labyrinth, warren, network, web, tangle, confusion

meadow NOUN *sheep grazing in a meadow*
► field, paddock, pasture, (*poetic*) mead, (*poetic*) lea

meager ADJECTIVE **1** *He had a few coins in his pocket, his meager earnings for the day.* ► paltry, scanty, scant, sparse, negligible, pitiful,

miserable, modest, (*more informal*) mingy, (*more informal*) measly OPPOSITES ARE plentiful, abundant **2** *a tall, meager youth* ► thin, lean, skinny, scrawny, scraggy, lanky

meal NOUN *A meal would be waiting for them when they got home.* ► bite to eat, (*literary*) repast, (*more informal*) spread, (*more informal*) feed RELATED ADJECTIVE ► prandial

mean ADJECTIVE **1** *He was too mean to leave a tip.* ► miserly, niggardly, stingy, parsimonious, (*more informal*) mingy, (*more informal*) tight-fisted, (*more informal*) penny-pinching **2** *It was mean of them to leave her like that.* ► unkind, nasty, shameful, unpleasant, callous, cruel, spiteful **3** *His room was a cold mean affair.* ► squalid, shabby, wretched, dismal, humble, lowly

mean VERB **1** *The sign means you have to stop.* ► indicate, signify, denote, convey, show **2** *What do you think they mean by these remarks?* ► intend, suggest, imply **3** *I mean to find him come what may.* ► intend, plan, aim, want, wish, propose, purpose, aspire **4** *Her promotion meant a lot more travel.* ► involve, entail, necessitate, lead to, result in **5** *Your help means a lot to me.* ► matter, be important, have importance

meaning NOUN **1** *I didn't understand the meaning of her remarks.* ► significance, sense,

A
B
C
D
E
F
G
H
I
J
K
L
M
N
O
P
Q
R
S
T
U
V
W
X
Y
Z

mean trick **3** poor in quality or appearance • *a mean little house*
▷ **meanly** ADVERB **meanness** NOUN

mean NOUN means a point or number midway between two extremes; the average of a set of numbers

mean ADJECTIVE midway between two points; average

meander (mee- an- der) VERB meanders, meandering, meandered take a winding course; wander
▷ **meander** NOUN
[named after the Maeander, a river in south-west Turkey (now Mendere or Menderes)]

meaning NOUN meanings what something means
▷ **meaningful** ADJECTIVE **meaningless** ADJECTIVE

means NOUN a way of achieving something or producing a result • *a means of transport*
by all means certainly
by means of by this method; using this
by no means not at all

means PLURAL NOUN money or other wealth
live beyond your means spend more than you can afford

meantime NOUN
in the meantime in the time between two events or while something else is happening

meanwhile ADVERB in the time between two events or while something else is happening

measles NOUN an infectious disease that causes small red spots on the skin

measure VERB measures, measuring, measured **1** find the size, amount, or extent of something by comparing it with a fixed unit or with an object of known size **2** be a certain size • *The room measures 3 x 4 meters.*
▷ **measurable** ADJECTIVE **measurement** NOUN

measure NOUN measures **1** a unit used for measuring • *A kilometer is a measure of length.* **2** a device used in measuring **3** the size or quantity of something **4** something done for a particular purpose • *We took measures to stop vandalism.*

meat NOUN meats animal flesh used as food
▷ **meaty** ADJECTIVE

mechanic NOUN mechanics a person who maintains or repairs machinery

mechanical ADJECTIVE **1** to do with machines **2** produced or worked by machines **3** done or doing things without thought
▷ **mechanically** ADVERB

mechanics NOUN **1** the study of movement and force **2** the study or use of machines

mechanism NOUN mechanisms **1** the moving parts of a machine **2** the way a machine works **3** the process by which something is done

---

Thesaurus

---

import, implication, force, thrust, connotation **2** *Some words have several meanings.* ► sense, definition, denotation, explanation **3** *Life has little meaning for them now.* ► value, worth, point, purpose, significance

meaningless ADJECTIVE **1** *a meaningless compliment* ► empty, worthless, insincere, hollow, fatuous, nonsensical AN OPPOSITE IS meaningful **2** *Life seemed meaningless.* ► pointless, senseless, worthless, inconsequential, insignificant

means NOUN **1** *modern means of communication* ► method, mode, way, medium, channel, vehicle, instrument, course **2** *I don't have the means for such a lifestyle.* ► resources, funds, money, wherewithal, income, finance **3** *a person of means* ► wealth, riches, substance, property

measly ADJECTIVE (informal) *All he could find was a measly penny.* ► meager, paltry, scanty, scant, sparse, negligible, pitiful, miserable, modest, (more informal) mingy AN OPPOSITE IS generous

measure NOUN **1** *These successes earned them a measure of glory. Add three measures of liquid.* ► share, portion, amount, allocation, quota, ration **2** *personal income as a measure of success* ► gauge, criterion, yardstick, standard,

touchstone, meter, test **3** *special measures to monitor noise levels* ► step, action, procedure, process, means, control, operation

measure VERB **1** *It's not easy to measure the effects of such a disaster.* ► evaluate, assess, gauge, appraise, determine, fathom **2** **measure up to** *attempts to measure up to the expected standards* ► achieve, meet, satisfy, match, comply with

measurement NOUN **1** *Measurements are given in metric units.* ► dimension, size, extent, proportions **2** *an instrument used in the measurement of air speed* ► calculation, computation, mensuration, evaluation, assessment

mechanical ADJECTIVE **1** *a mechanical doll* ► mechanized, automated, machine-driven, motor-driven, automatic AN OPPOSITE IS manual **2** *The voice sounded detached and mechanical.* ► unemotional, unfeeling, matter-of-fact, perfunctory, unthinking, cold, inhuman, lifeless, routine, soulless AN OPPOSITE IS thoughtful

mechanism NOUN **1** *A trigger mechanism activates the bolt.* ► apparatus, machine, device, appliance, system, tool **2** *Mechanisms are in place for correcting mistakes.* ► procedure, process, system, means, channel, structure

medal NOUN medals a piece of metal shaped like a coin, star, or cross, given to a person for bravery or for achieving something

meddle VERB meddles, meddling, meddled **1** interfere **2** tinker • *Don't meddle with it.*
▷ **meddler** NOUN **meddlesome** ADJECTIVE

media plural of **medium** NOUN the media newspapers, radio, and television, which convey information and ideas to the public (See medium)
USAGE This word is a plural. Although it is commonly used with a singular verb, this is not generally approved of. Say *The media are* (not "is") *very influential.* It is incorrect to speak of one of them (e.g., television) as "this media."

mediate VERB mediates, mediating, mediated negotiate between the opposing sides in a dispute
▷ **mediation** NOUN **mediator** NOUN

medical ADJECTIVE to do with the treatment of disease
▷ **medically** ADVERB

medicine NOUN medicines **1** a substance, usually swallowed, used to try to cure a disease **2** the study and treatment of diseases
▷ **medicinal** (med- **iss**- in- al) ADJECTIVE **medicinally** ADVERB

medieval (med- ee- **ee**- val) ADJECTIVE belonging to or to do with the Middle Ages

mediocre (mee- dee- **oh**- ker) ADJECTIVE not very good; of only medium quality
▷ **mediocrity** NOUN

meditate VERB meditates, meditating, meditated think deeply and quietly
▷ **meditation** NOUN **meditative** ADJECTIVE

Mediterranean ADJECTIVE to do with the Mediterranean Sea (which lies between Europe and Africa) or the countries round it

medium ADJECTIVE neither large nor small; moderate

medium NOUN media **1** a thing in which something exists, moves, or is expressed • *Air is the medium in which sound travels.* • *Television is used as a medium for advertising.* (see media) **2** mediums a person who claims to be able to communicate with the dead

medium wave NOUN a radio wave of a frequency between 300 kilohertz and 3 megahertz

meek ADJECTIVE meeker, meekest quiet and obedient
▷ **meekly** ADVERB **meekness** NOUN

meet VERB meets, meeting, met **1** come together from different places • *We all met in London.* **2** get to know someone • *We met at a party.* **3** come into contact; touch **4** go to receive an arrival • *We will meet your train.* **5** pay a bill or the cost of something **6** satisfy or fulfill • *I hope this meets your needs.*

Thesaurus

medal NOUN *Their son had won a medal for bravery.* ► medallion, honor, decoration, award, reward, trophy, prize

meddle VERB *We don't want them meddling in our affairs.* ► interfere, pry, intrude, poke, nose, snoop, (more informal) stick your nose in

medicine NOUN **1** *examples of how modern medicine has helped to prolong life* ► medical science, healing, surgery, therapeutics, treatment of diseases **2** *He poured a dose of the medicine into the glass.* ► medication, medicament, remedy, cure, drug, prescription, treatment RELATED ADJECTIVES ► clinical, pharmaceutical

mediocre ADJECTIVE *Fred turned a mediocre business into one that was thriving.* ► ordinary, commonplace, indifferent, average, undistinguished, middle-of-the-road, run-of-the-mill, unexceptional, middling, passable, tolerable, second-rate OPPOSITES ARE exceptional, outstanding

meditation NOUN *He fell silent for a while, as if in meditation.* ► contemplation, prayer, reflection, yoga

medium ADJECTIVE *She is of medium height.* ► average, middling, middle, normal, ordinary, standard, usual, intermediate, midway, moderate

medium NOUN **1** *Television is a powerful medium of communication.* ► method, means, channel, mode, way, vehicle, instrument, course **2** *a happy medium between quality and quantity* ► average, midpoint, middle way, middle ground, compromise **3** *I went to see a medium and she told me I would be rich one day.* ► clairvoyant, spiritualist, psychic

meek ADJECTIVE *She seemed meek but could be fiercely passionate.* ► gentle, mild, demure, submissive, compliant, modest, docile, unassuming, self-effacing, unassertive, forbearing AN OPPOSITE IS assertive

meet VERB **1** *She met an old friend in town.* ► encounter, come across, run across, run into, chance on , stumble on **2** *I'll meet you at the airport.* ► collect **3** *They met the challenge bravely.* ► face, undergo, encounter, experience, endure, suffer **4** *The equipment does not meet our requirements.* ► satisfy, fulfill, answer, measure up to, match up to, conform to **5** *The board meets every month.* ► gather, assemble, come together, convene, hold a meeting **6** *The two roads meet north of the city.* ► join, converge, merge, come together, connect, intersect

a b c d e f g h i j k l **m** n o p q r s t u v w x y z

meet NOUN **meets** a gathering of riders and hounds for a hunt

meeting NOUN **meetings** **1** coming together **2** a number of people who have come together for a discussion, contest, etc.

megabyte NOUN **megabytes** (in computing) a unit of information roughly equal to one million bytes

megalomania NOUN an exaggerated idea of your own importance
▷ **megalomaniac** NOUN

megaphone NOUN **megaphones** a funnel-shaped device for amplifying a person's voice

melancholy ADJECTIVE sad; gloomy

melancholy NOUN sadness or depression [from Greek *melas* = black + *chole* = bile Black bile in the body was once thought to cause this feeling]

mellow ADJECTIVE **mellower, mellowest** **1** not harsh; soft and rich in flavor, color, or sound **2** having become more kindly and sympathetic with age
▷ **mellowness** NOUN

mellow VERB **mellows, mellowing, mellowed** make or become mellow

melodious ADJECTIVE like a melody; pleasant to listen to

melodrama NOUN **melodramas** a play full of dramatic excitement and emotion
▷ **melodramatic** ADJECTIVE

melody NOUN **melodies** a tune, especially a pleasing tune

melt VERB **melts, melting, melted** **1** make or become liquid by heating **2** disappear slowly

• *The crowd just melted away.* **3** soften • *a pudding that melts in the mouth*

melting pot NOUN **melting pots** a place where people of many different races and cultures live and influence each other

member NOUN **members** **1** a person or thing that belongs to a particular society or group **2** a part of something
▷ **membership** NOUN

membrane NOUN **membranes** a thin skin or similar covering
▷ **membranous** ADJECTIVE

memoir (mem- wahr) NOUN **memoirs** a biography, especially one written by someone who knew the person

memorable ADJECTIVE **1** worth remembering **2** easy to remember
▷ **memorably** ADVERB

memorandum NOUN **memoranda** or **memorandums** **1** a note to remind yourself of something **2** a note from one person to another in the same firm

memorial NOUN **memorials** something to remind people of a person or event • *a war memorial*
▷ **memorial** ADJECTIVE

memorize VERB **memorizes, memorizing, memorized** get something into your memory

memory NOUN **memories** **1** the ability to remember things **2** something that you remember **3** the part of a computer where information is stored
in memory of in honor of a person or event remembered

Thesaurus

meeting NOUN **1** *He rushed back to be in time for the meeting.* ► gathering, assembly, conference, forum, convention **2** *He adored her from their very first meeting.* ► encounter, rendezvous, contact, assignation, get-together, date **3** *The town stands at the meeting of three mighty rivers.* ► convergence, coming together, junction, confluence, union, concourse

melancholy ADJECTIVE **1** *melancholy music* ► sad, sorrowful, mournful, reflective **2** *a melancholy mood* ► unhappy, downhearted, despondent, gloomy, dispirited, depressed, dejected, downcast OPPOSITES ARE joyful, happy, elated

melancholy NOUN *a feeling of melancholy* ► sadness, sorrow, dejection, unhappiness, depression, dejection, despondency, gloom OPPOSITES ARE joy, happiness, elation

mellow ADJECTIVE **1** *a mellow voice* ► smooth, melodious, dulcet, tuneful, sweet **2** *a mellow temperament* ► easygoing, tolerant, amiable, good-natured, affable, kindhearted **3** *mellow fruit* ► ripe, mature, juicy, tender, sweet

melt VERB *The sun soon melted the snow. The ice was beginning to melt.* ► thaw, unfreeze, defrost, liquefy, soften, dissolve
melt away *The crowds rapidly melted away.* ► disperse, dissolve, dwindle, vanish, evaporate, disappear, fade

member NOUN *new members of the sports club* ► associate, subscriber, fellow, adherent

memorial NOUN *a memorial to victims of the war* ► monument, remembrance, shrine, cenotaph, plaque, tablet

memorize NOUN *Long numbers are hard to memorize.* ► remember, commit to memory, learn by heart, retain AN OPPOSITE IS forget

memory NOUN **1** *My mother always had a good memory.* ► recall, retention, ability to remember, recollection **2** *happy memories of a lovely occasion* ► reminiscence, recollection, remembrance, reminder, souvenir, impression **3** *a plaque in memory of local writers* ► commemoration, remembrance, tribute, honor, recognition

menace NOUN menaces **1** a threat or danger **2** a troublesome person or thing

menace VERB menaces, menacing, menaced threaten with harm or danger

mend VERB mends, mending, mended **1** repair **2** make or become better; improve
▷ **mender** NOUN

mend NOUN mends a repair
on the mend getting better after an illness

menopause NOUN the time of life when a woman gradually ceases to menstruate

menstruate VERB menstruates, menstruating, menstruated bleed from the womb about once a month, as girls and women normally do from their teens until middle age
▷ **menstruation** NOUN **menstrual** ADJECTIVE

-ment SUFFIX used to make nouns, as in *amusement* and *oddments*

mental ADJECTIVE **1** to do with or in the mind **2** (*informal*) mad
▷ **mentally** ADVERB

mentality NOUN mentalities a person's mental ability or attitude

mention VERB mentions, mentioning, mentioned speak or write about a person or thing briefly; refer to

mention NOUN mentions an example of mentioning something • *Our school got a mention in the local paper.*

menu (men- yoo) NOUN menus **1** a list of the food available in a restaurant or served at a meal **2** (in computing) a list of possible actions, shown on a screen, from which you decide what you want a computer to do

mercenary ADJECTIVE working only for money or some other reward

mercenary NOUN mercenaries a soldier hired to serve in a foreign army

merchandise NOUN goods for sale

merchant NOUN merchants a person involved in trade

merchant navy NOUN the ships and sailors that carry goods for trade

merciful ADJECTIVE showing mercy
▷ **mercifully** ADVERB

mercury NOUN a heavy silvery metal that is usually liquid, used in thermometers
▷ **mercuric** ADJECTIVE

mercy NOUN mercies **1** kindness or pity shown in not punishing a wrongdoer severely or not harming a defeated enemy, etc. **2** something to be thankful for
at the mercy of completely in the power of

mere ADJECTIVE not more than • *He's a mere child.*

merely ADVERB only; simply

merge VERB merges, merging, merged combine or blend

Thesaurus

---

menace NOUN **1** *a menace to society* ► danger, threat, hazard, risk **2** *That child is a menace.* ► nuisance, pest, annoyance **3** *a situation full of menace* ► threat, ominousness, intimidation

mend VERB **1** *An electrician was mending faulty wiring.* ► repair, fix, restore, renovate AN OPPOSITE IS break **2** *a pile of socks to mend* ► patch, repair, darn **3** *a quarrel that a few kind words can mend* ► put right, resolve, sort out, straighten out, remedy, rectify, redress AN OPPOSITE IS make worse

menial ADJECTIVE *Someone has to do the menial tasks.* ► humble, lowly, routine, unskilled, low-grade, humdrum, inferior, degrading, demeaning OPPOSITES ARE skilled, important

mental ADJECTIVE **1** *The work calls for considerable mental concentration.* ► intellectual, cerebral, abstract, rational, cognitive, theoretical **2** *Your mental attitude affects your behavior.* ► psychological, temperamental, emotional, subjective

mentality NOUN *They seem to have an ostrich-like mentality.* ► attitude, way of thinking, outlook, predisposition, disposition, frame of mind, character, temperament, personality, (*more informal*) make-up

mention VERB **1** *Nick mentioned that he would be here next week.* ► state, say, remark, observe, reveal, indicate, disclose, divulge **2** *Better not to mention the score.* ► refer to, allude to, touch on, speak about, comment on, disclose, hint at, let out, reveal, (*more informal*) let drop

merciful ADJECTIVE *They believe in a merciful God.* ► compassionate, forgiving, humane, gracious, understanding, sympathetic, generous, beneficent OPPOSITES ARE merciless, cruel

merciless ADJECTIVE *a leader who was merciless to his enemies* ► cruel, pitiless, ruthless, heartless, unsparing, unforgiving, unrelenting, harsh, severe AN OPPOSITE IS merciful

mercy NOUN **1** *The prisoners begged for mercy.* ► clemency, compassion, leniency, pity, sympathy, forbearance, forgiveness, understanding AN OPPOSITE IS cruelty **2** *It is a mercy that more people weren't killed.* ► blessing, godsend, boon, favor, piece of good fortune

merge VERB **1** *It seems a good idea to merge the two organizations.* ► combine, amalgamate, integrate, unite, join together, consolidate, coalesce, blend, fuse, link up, put together **2** *The two parties have agreed to merge.* ► unite, join together, combine, amalgamate, unify, combine **3** *The highways merge ahead.* ► join, meet, converge OPPOSITES ARE split, separate

a
b
c
d
e
f
g
h
i
j
k
m
n
o
p
q
r
s
t
u
v
w
x
y
z

merger NOUN mergers the combining of two business companies etc. into one

meridian NOUN meridians a line on a map or globe from the North Pole to the South Pole The meridian that passes through Greenwich is shown on maps as 0° longitude.

meringue (mer- ang) NOUN meringues a crisp cake made from egg white and sugar

merit NOUN merits **1** a quality that deserves praise **2** excellence
▷ **meritorious** ADJECTIVE

mermaid NOUN mermaids a mythical sea creature with a woman's body but with a fish's tail instead of legs
▷ **merman** NOUN

merry ADJECTIVE merrier, merriest cheerful and lively
▷ **merrily** ADVERB **merriment** NOUN

merry-go-round NOUN merry-go-rounds a roundabout at a fair

mesh NOUN meshes **1** the open spaces in a net, sieve, or other criss-cross structure **2** material made like a net

mesmerize VERB mesmerizes, mesmerizing, mesmerized **1** (old use) hypnotize **2** fascinate or hold a person's attention completely
▷ **mesmerism** NOUN **mesmeric** ADJECTIVE

mess NOUN messes **1** a dirty or untidy condition or thing **2** a difficult or confused situation; trouble **3** (in the armed forces) a dining room
make a mess of bungle

mess VERB messes, messing, messed
mess about behave stupidly or idly
mess up **1** make a thing dirty or untidy **2** bungle or spoil • They've messed up our plans.
mess with interfere or tinker with
[from early French mes = a portion of food]

message NOUN messages **1** a piece of information sent from one person to another **2** the main theme or moral of a book, film, etc.

messenger NOUN messengers a person who carries a message

Messiah (mis- I- a) NOUN Messiahs **1** the savior of the world expected by the Jewish people **2** Jesus Christ, who Christians believe to be this savior
▷ **Messianic** ADJECTIVE
[from Hebrew mashiah = anointed]

messy ADJECTIVE messier, messiest dirty and untidy
▷ **messily** ADVERB **messiness** NOUN

metabolism (mit- ab- ol- izm) NOUN the process by which food is built up into living material in a plant or animal, or used to supply it with energy
▷ **metabolic** ADJECTIVE **metabolize** VERB

metal NOUN metals a chemical substance, usually hard, that conducts heat and electricity and melts when it is heated, e.g., gold, silver, copper, iron, and uranium
▷ **metallic** ADJECTIVE

metamorphosis (met- a- mor- fo- sis) NOUN metamorphoses (met- a- mor- fo- seez) a

Thesaurus

merit NOUN writers of merit ► excellence, goodness, value, virtue, worth, importance, quality, credit, eminence

merit VERB The idea certainly merits consideration. ► deserve, warrant, be worth, be worthy of, be entitled to, justify, rate, earn, incur

merriment NOUN They could hear bursts of laughter and ripples of merriment. ► jollity, enjoyment, cheerfulness, mirth, festivity, conviviality, amusement, revelry, high spirits OPPOSITES ARE misery, gloom

merry ADJECTIVE merry crowds of holidaymakers; a merry ringing of bells ► jolly, cheerful, light-hearted, carefree, joyful, joyous, festive, happy, gleeful

mess NOUN **1** There's quite a mess in the kitchen. ► muddle, untidiness, disarray, jumble, confusion, clutter, shambles **2** It was a mess of his own making and he would have to find a way out. ► predicament, quandary, difficulty, trouble, (more informal) fix
make a mess of I'm afraid I've made a mess of the assignment. ► ruin, spoil, botch, bungle, mishandle, mismanage, fluff, muff, mess up, (much more informal) screw up OPPOSITES ARE succeed in, bring off

mess VERB mess about OR around They need to stop messing around and get on with something. ► fool about or around, play about or around, (more informal) muck about or around
mess up **1** They had messed up the garden in less than ten minutes. ► jumble, muddle, make a mess of, dirty, dishevel, disrupt, disarrange **2** A new assignment: try not to mess this one up. ► ruin, spoil, botch, bungle, mishandle, mismanage, fluff, muff, make a mess of, (more informal) make a hash of, (much more informal) cock up, (much more informal) screw up

message NOUN Sarah sent a message with her brother. ► communication, note, letter, word, memo, dispatch, missive

messenger NOUN A messenger brought the news. ► courier, emissary, go-between, envoy, runner, dispatch rider

messy ADJECTIVE **1** All these jobs can be messy and produce a lot of debris. ► dirty, filthy, mucky, grubby, grimy **2** The bathroom had become very messy. Her hair was tangled and messy. ► untidy, dishevelled, unkempt, disorganized, chaotic, sloppy OPPOSITES ARE tidy, neat, organized

metal NOUN a lump of metal ► ingot, nugget

change of form or character, especially one made by a living thing
▷ **metamorphose** VERB

metaphor NOUN **metaphors** using a word or phrase in a way that is not literal, e.g., "The pictures of starving people *touched our hearts.*"
▷ **metaphorical** ADJECTIVE **metaphorically** ADVERB

meteor (meet- ee- er) NOUN **meteors** a piece of rock or metal that moves through space and burns up when it enters the earth's atmosphere

meteorite NOUN **meteorites** the remains of a meteor that has landed on the earth

meter[1] NOUN **meters** a device for measuring something, e.g., the amount supplied • *a gas meter*
▷ **meter** VERB

meter[2] NOUN **meters 1** a unit of length in the metric system, about 39 inches **2** rhythm in poetry

methane (mee- thayn) NOUN an inflammable gas produced by decaying matter

method NOUN **methods 1** a procedure or way of doing something **2** methodical behavior; orderliness

methodical ADJECTIVE doing things in an orderly or systematic way
▷ **methodically** ADVERB

methylated spirit or **spirits** NOUN a liquid fuel made from alcohol

metric ADJECTIVE **1** to do with the metric system **2** to do with metre in poetry
▷ **metrically** ADVERB

metric system NOUN a measuring system based on decimal units (the meter, liter, and gram)

metric ton NOUN **metric tons** 1,000 kilograms

metronome NOUN **metronomes** a device that makes a regular clicking noise to help a person keep in time when practicing music

mew VERB **mews, mewing, mewed** make a cat's cry
▷ **mew** NOUN

mice plural of mouse

microbe NOUN **microbes** a microorganism

microchip NOUN **microchips** a very small piece of silicon etc. made to work like a complex wired electric circuit

microcosm NOUN **microcosms** a world in miniature; something regarded as resembling something else on a very small scale

microfilm NOUN a length of film on which written or printed material is photographed in greatly reduced size

micron NOUN **microns** a unit of measurement, one millionth of a metre

microphone NOUN **microphones** an electrical device that picks up sound waves for recording, amplifying, or broadcasting [from Greek *mikros* = small + *phone* = sound]

microprocessor NOUN **microprocessors** the central processing unit of a computer, consisting of one or more microchips

microscope NOUN **microscopes** an instrument with lenses that magnify tiny objects or details [from Greek *mikros* = small + *skopein* = to look at]

microscopic ADJECTIVE **1** extremely small; too small to be seen without the aid of a microscope **2** to do with a microscope

microwave NOUN **microwaves 1** a very short electromagnetic wave **2** a microwave oven

microwave oven NOUN **microwave ovens** an oven that uses microwaves to heat or cook food very quickly

mid ADJECTIVE in the middle of • *mid-July* • *He's in his mid thirties*

midday NOUN the middle of the day; noon

middle NOUN **middles 1** the place or part of something that is at the same distance from all its sides or edges or from both its ends **2** someone's waist
in the middle of during or halfway through a process or activity • *I'm just in the middle of cooking.*

middle ADJECTIVE **1** placed or happening in the middle **2** moderate in size or rank, etc.

middle-aged ADJECTIVE aged between about 40 and 60

Middle Ages NOUN the period in history from about 1000 to 1400

Thesaurus

method NOUN *a new method of gathering vital data* ► way, approach (to), procedure (for), manner, mode, technique (for), style, plan (for)

methodical ADJECTIVE *a methodical approach to working* ► organized, orderly, systematic, meticulous, painstaking, efficient, businesslike, meticulous, logical, tidy, precise, neat
OPPOSITES ARE disorganized, inefficient

meticulous ADJECTIVE *He continued his meticulous inspection of the machine.* ► careful,

methodical, scrupulous, diligent, painstaking, systematic, thorough, rigorous

middle ADJECTIVE *Remove the middle pin.*
► central, midway, mean, medial, median, half-way, inner, inside

middle NOUN **1** *There was a large table in the middle of the room.* ► center, midpoint
OPPOSITES ARE edge, border **2** *a journey to the middle of the earth* ► center, core, heart, kernel
OPPOSITES ARE surface, circumference

middle class or **classes** NOUN the class of people between the upper class and the working class, including business and professional people such as teachers and lawyers
▷ **middle-class** ADJECTIVE

Middle East NOUN the countries from Egypt to Iran inclusive

Middle English NOUN the English language from about 1150 to 1500

middle school NOUN middle schools a school for children aged from about 9 to 13

middling ADJECTIVE of medium size or quality

middling ADVERB fairly or moderately

midge NOUN midges a small insect like a gnat

midget NOUN midgets an extremely small person or thing
▷ **midget** ADJECTIVE

midland ADJECTIVE **1** to do with the middle part of a country **2** to do with the Midlands

Midlands PLURAL NOUN the central part of England

midnight NOUN twelve o'clock at night

midst NOUN
in the midst of in the middle of or surrounded by
in our midst among us

midsummer NOUN the middle of summer, about 21 June in the northern hemisphere

midway ADVERB halfway

midwife NOUN midwives a person trained to look after a woman who is giving birth to a baby
▷ **midwifery** (mid- wif- ri) NOUN

might NOUN great strength or power
with all your might using all your strength and determination

might AUXILIARY VERB used **1** as the past tense of may (We told her she might go), **2** to express possibility (It might be true)

mighty ADJECTIVE very strong or powerful
▷ **mightily** ADVERB **mightiness** NOUN

migraine (mee- grayn, my- grayn) NOUN migraines a severe kind of headache

migrate VERB migrates, migrating, migrated **1** leave one place or country and settle in another **2** (said about birds or animals) move periodically from one area to another
▷ **migration** NOUN **migratory** ADJECTIVE

mild ADJECTIVE milder, mildest **1** gentle; not harsh or severe **2** (said about weather) quite warm and pleasant **3** (said about food) not strongly flavored
▷ **mildly** ADVERB **mildness** NOUN

mildew NOUN a tiny fungus that forms a white coating on things kept in damp conditions
▷ **mildewed** ADJECTIVE

mile NOUN miles a measure of distance equal to 1,760 yards (about 16 kilometers) [from Latin mille = thousand; a Roman mile was reckoned as 1,000 paces]

milestone NOUN milestones **1** a stone of a kind that used to be fixed beside a road to mark the distance between towns **2** an important event in life or history

militant ADJECTIVE **1** eager to fight **2** forceful or aggressive ● a militant protest
▷ **militant** NOUN **militancy** NOUN

military ADJECTIVE to do with soldiers or the armed forces
the military a country's armed forces

milk NOUN **1** a white liquid that female mammals produce in their bodies to feed their babies **2** the milk of cows, sheep, or goats used as food by human beings **3** a milky liquid, e.g. that in a coconut

milk VERB milks, milking, milked get the milk from a cow or other animal [from Old English]

milkman NOUN milkmen a man who delivers milk to customers' houses

milkshake NOUN milkshakes a cold frothy drink made from milk whisked with sweet fruit flavoring

Thesaurus

middling ADJECTIVE She speaks middling to good Japanese. ► average, medium, fair, ordinary, moderate, everyday, modest, passable

midget ADJECTIVE a midget car ► miniature, baby, dwarf, small

miffed ADJECTIVE (informal) She felt miffed at being ignored. ► annoyed, irritated, angry, cross, displeased, vexed, infuriated, incensed, enraged, (more informal) put out

might NOUN I hit it with all my might. ► strength, force, power, energy, vigor

mighty ADJECTIVE a mighty blow to the head ► powerful, forceful, violent, vigorous, ferocious, hefty, savage AN OPPOSITE IS weak

mild ADJECTIVE **1** She spoke in a mild voice. ► gentle, soft, tender, calm, tenderhearted, easygoing, sympathetic AN OPPOSITE IS harsh **2** The weather turned mild. ► warm, calm, fair, temperate OPPOSITES ARE severe, cold

militant ADJECTIVE militant opponents of the regime ► belligerent, active, aggressive, combative, assertive, positive OPPOSITES ARE restrained, peaceful

military ADJECTIVE a military command; military units ► fighting, service, armed, martial, belligerent, enlisted, uniformed AN OPPOSITE IS civilian

milk VERB Unscrupulous moneylenders can milk unwary clients. ► exploit, take advantage of, cash in on, squeeze, bleed

milky ADJECTIVE milkier, milkiest **1** like milk **2** white

Milky Way NOUN the broad band of stars formed by our galaxy

mill NOUN mills **1** machinery for grinding corn to make flour; a building containing this machinery **2** a grinding machine • *a pepper mill* **3** a factory for processing certain materials • *a paper mill*

millennium NOUN millenniums a period of 1,000 years

millennium bug NOUN a fault in older computer systems that made it impossible for programs to deal with dates later than 1999

million NOUN millions one thousand thousand (1,000,000)
▷ **millionth** ADJECTIVE, NOUN

millionaire NOUN millionaires a person who has at least a million pounds or dollars; an extremely rich person

millipede NOUN millipedes a small crawling creature with many legs

millstone NOUN millstones either of a pair of large circular stones between which corn is ground
a millstone around someone's neck a heavy responsibility or burden

mimic VERB mimics, mimicking, mimicked imitate someone, especially to amuse people
▷ **mimicry** NOUN

mimic NOUN mimics a person who mimics others

mince VERB minces, mincing, minced **1** cut into very small pieces in a machine **2** walk in an affected way with short quick steps
▷ **mincer** NOUN
not to mince matters speak bluntly

mince NOUN minced meat

mincemeat NOUN a sweet mixture of currants, raisins, apple, etc., used in pies

mince pie NOUN mince pies a pie containing mincemeat, traditionally eaten at Christmas

mind NOUN minds **1** the ability to think, feel, understand, and remember, originating in the brain **2** a person's thoughts, opinion, or intention • *Have you made your mind up?* • *I changed my mind*
in two minds not able to decide
out of your mind insane

mind VERB minds, minding, minded **1** look after • *He was minding the baby.* **2** be careful about • *Mind the step.* **3** be sad or upset about something; object to • *We don't mind waiting.*
▷ **minder** NOUN

mindless ADJECTIVE done without thinking; stupid or pointless

---

Thesaurus

---

milky ADJECTIVE **1** *her beautiful milky skin* ► pale, white, cream, creamy **2** *a milky liquid* ► cloudy, chalky, misty, opaque, whitish AN OPPOSITE IS clear RELATED ADJECTIVE ► lactic

mill NOUN **1** *a paper mill* ► factory, plant, processing plant, works, workshop **2** *a pepper mill* ► grinder, crusher, roller

mill VERB *The wheat is milled into flour.* ► grind, crush, roll, pulverize, powder

mill about OR **around** *Outside, people were still milling about.* ► throng, swarm, stream, surge, wander about, move aimlessly

mime VERB *She mimed a telephone conversation.* ► act out, mimic, simulate, gesture, impersonate

mimic VERB *She could mimic anyone after a few minutes listening to them.* ► imitate, impersonate, copy, ape, caricature, do an impression of, parody, parrot, pretend to be, simulate, (more informal) take off

mimic NOUN *He was entertaining and a good mimic.* ► impersonator, impressionist, imitator

mince VERB **1** *He took the meat and minced it.* ► grind, chop, dice, crumble, cube **2** not mince words *She doesn't mince her words when she's angry.* ► speak plainly, speak straight, get to the point, not pull your punches

mind NOUN **1** *people with brilliant minds* ► brain, intellect, intelligence, sense, wits, understanding, mentality, power of reasoning, (more informal) grey matter RELATED ADJECTIVE ► mental **2** *It's hard to keep my mind on my work.* ► attention, concentration, thinking **3** *I couldn't get her words out of my mind.* ► memory, recollection, remembrance **4** *I've a mind to go and complain.* ► inclination, wish, desire, fancy, intention, disposition, tendency

mind VERB **1** *I'll mind your bags while you're gone.* ► look after, watch, guard, take care of, attend to, (more informal) keep an eye on **2** *You'd better mind what they say.* ► be careful of, beware of, heed, pay attention to, look out for, watch out for, take notice of, note, remember **3** *Would you mind if I eat my lunch?* ► care, object, bother, disapprove, grumble, take offence, worry, be resentful, complain

mindful ADJECTIVE mindful of *Rob flew with care, mindful of the lives of his crew.* ► aware of, conscious of, heedful of, alive to, attentive to, careful of OPPOSITES ARE heedless of, oblivious to

mindless ADJECTIVE **1** *The occasion was spoiled by incidents of mindless violence.* ► senseless, wanton, gratuitous, thoughtless **2** *People are reduced to mindless automatons, unable to think for themselves.* ► stupid, idiotic, brainless, witless, foolish

A
B
C
D
E
F
G
H
I
J
K
L
M
N
O
P
Q
R
S
T
U
V
W
X
Y
Z

mine *POSSESSIVE PRONOUN* belonging to me

mine *NOUN* mines **1** a place where coal, metal, precious stones, etc., are dug out of the ground **2** an explosive placed in or on the ground or in the sea etc. to destroy people or things that come close to it

mine *VERB* mines, mining, mined **1** dig from a mine **2** lay explosive mines in a place

minefield *NOUN* minefields **1** an area where explosive mines have been laid **2** something with hidden dangers or problems

miner *NOUN* miners a person who works in a mine

mineral *NOUN* minerals **1** a hard inorganic substance found in the ground **2** a cold fizzy nonalcoholic drink

mingle *VERB* mingles, mingling, mingled mix or blend

mingy *ADJECTIVE* mingier, mingiest (*informal*) not generous; mean

miniature *ADJECTIVE* **1** very small **2** copying something on a very small scale ● *a miniature railway*

miniature *NOUN* miniatures **1** a very small portrait **2** a small-scale model

minim *NOUN* minims a note in music, lasting twice as long as a crotchet (written ♩)

minimize *VERB* minimizes, minimizing, minimized make something as small as possible

minimum *NOUN* minima or minimums the lowest possible number or amount (The opposite is **maximum**)
▷ **minimal** *ADJECTIVE*

minister *NOUN* ministers **1** a person in charge of a government department **2** a member of the clergy
▷ **ministerial** *ADJECTIVE*

ministry *NOUN* ministries **1** a government department ● *the ministry of Defense* **2** the work of the clergy

minnow *NOUN* minnows a tiny freshwater fish

minor *ADJECTIVE* **1** not very important, especially when compared to something else **2** to do with the musical scale that has a semitone after the second note COMPARE **major**

minor *NOUN* minors a person under the age of legal responsibility

minority *NOUN* minorities **1** the smallest part of a group of people or things **2** a small group that is different from others COMPARE **majority**

minstrel *NOUN* minstrels a traveling singer and musician in the Middle Ages

---

Thesaurus

---

mine *NOUN* **1** *a coal mine* ► pit, colliery, coalfield, deposit, mineshaft **2** *He was killed by a mine.* ► landmine, explosive **3** *The book is a mine of information.* ► store, wealth, fund, treasury, repository, hoard, rich supply

mine *VERB* *Gold is mined in these hills.*
► excavate, extract, quarry, dig for, remove

mingle *VERB* **1** *Guests mingled in the gardens.*
► socialize, circulate, get together, merge, mix, fraternize, associate, move about, rub shoulders, intermingle **2** *Open air smells mingled with the aroma of food cooking.*
► combine, merge, fuse, unite, join, coalesce

mingy *ADJECTIVE* (*informal*) *All I got was a mingy five dollars.* ► meager, measly, paltry, miserable, scanty, scant, sparse, negligible, pitiful, modest, (*informal*) moldy AN OPPOSITE IS generous

miniature *ADJECTIVE* *a miniature village* ► tiny, small-scale, scaled-down, diminutive, minute, baby, model

minimal *ADJECTIVE* *Increases in rent this year have been minimal.* ► very little, negligible, slight, least, smallest, minimum, token, nominal

minimize *VERB* **1** *They banned smoking to minimize the danger of fire.* ► reduce, keep down, cut down, lessen, curtail, diminish OPPOSITES ARE maximize, increase **2** *He should not minimizes the value of their contribution.*
► underestimate, gloss over, make light of, play down OPPOSITES ARE maximize, exaggerate

minimum *ADJECTIVE* *The pay is well above the minimum wage.* ► lowest, least, smallest, minimal, bottom

minimum *NOUN* *Costs are kept to a minimum.*
► lower limit, limit, base, lowest point, bottom level AN OPPOSITE IS maximum

minister *NOUN* **1** *a minister of the church*
► clergyman, clergywoman, cleric, parson, priest, vicar, preacher **2** *a government minister*
► official, officeholder, executive, secretary of state USAGE In England, a *secretary of state* is a head of a government department (such as transport) and a member of the cabinet; not all ministers are secretaries of state.

minor *ADJECTIVE* *minor alterations to the treaty*
► small, trivial, unimportant, insignificant, inconsequential, negligible, secondary, lesser, trifling, petty AN OPPOSITE IS major

minority *NOUN* *A minority voted for a return to work.* ► small number, lesser number, smaller number
be in a minority ► be outnumbered, be less, be the smaller number

mint[1] NOUN **mints 1** a plant with fragrant leaves that are used for flavoring things **2** peppermint or a sweet flavored with this [from Latin *mentha* = mint]

mint[2] NOUN **mints** the place where a country's coins are made

in mint condition in perfect condition, as though it had never been used

mint VERB **mints, minting, minted** make coins [from Latin *moneta* = money]

minus PREPOSITION with the next number or thing subtracted ● *Ten minus four equals six (10 - 4 = 6)*

minus ADJECTIVE less than zero ● *temperatures of minus ten degrees (-10°)* [from Latin, = less]

minute (min- it) NOUN **minutes 1** one-sixtieth of an hour **2** a very short time; a moment **3** a particular time ● *Come here this minute!* **4** one-sixtieth of a degree (used in measuring angles)

minute (my- newt) ADJECTIVE **1** very small ● *a minute insect* **2** very detailed ● *a minute examination*
▷ **minutely** ADVERB

minutes PLURAL NOUN a written summary of what was said at a meeting

miracle NOUN **miracles** something wonderful and good that happens, especially something believed to have a supernatural or divine cause
▷ **miraculous** ADJECTIVE **miraculously** ADVERB

mirage (mi- rah*zh*) NOUN **mirages** an illusion; something that seems to be there but is not, especially when a lake seems to appear in a desert

mirror NOUN **mirrors** a device or surface of reflecting material, usually glass

mirror VERB **mirrors, mirroring, mirrored** reflect in or like a mirror

mis- PREFIX badly or wrongly COMPARE **amiss**

misbehave VERB **misbehaves, misbehaving, misbehaved** behave badly
▷ **misbehavior** NOUN

miscalculate VERB **miscalculates, miscalculating, miscalculated** calculate incorrectly
▷ **miscalculation** NOUN

miscarriage NOUN **miscarriages 1** the birth of a baby before it has developed enough to live **2** failure to achieve the right result ● *a miscarriage of justice*

miscellaneous (mis- el- ay- nee- us) ADJECTIVE of various kinds; mixed
▷ **miscellany** (mis- el- an- ee) NOUN

Thesaurus

mint ADJECTIVE *in mint condition* ► brand new, pristine, immaculate, perfect, new, unblemished, unmarked, unused, fresh

mint NOUN *(informal) They made a mint from the deal.* ► fortune, heap, *(informal)* packet, *(informal)* pile, *(informal)* stack

mint VERB *Special coins were minted to celebrate the jubilee.* ► strike, cast, manufacture, stamp out, coin, forge, make

minute ADJECTIVE *a minute insect* ► tiny, minuscule, infinitesimal, diminutive, miniature

minute NOUN *I'll only be a minute.* ► moment, short while, second, *(more informal)* tick

miracle NOUN *a miracle of modern technology* ► marvel, wonder, sensation, phenomenon, feat

miraculous ADJECTIVE *a miraculous escape* ► amazing, astounding, astonishing, extraordinary, unbelievable, incredible, inexplicable, marvellous, wonderful, mysterious

mirage NOUN *The lake turned out to be a mirage.* ► illusion, optical illusion, hallucination, vision, delusion

mirror NOUN **1** *She took a quick look in the mirror on her way out.* ► looking glass, glass, reflector

2 *art as a mirror of life* ► reflection, image, likeness, copy, double

mirror VERB *Jody's views mirrored her own.* ► reflect, correspond to, match, imitate, copy, echo

mirth NOUN *sounds of mirth from the terrace* ► merriment, amusement, revelry, jollity, enjoyment, cheerfulness, festivity, conviviality, high spirits OPPOSITES ARE misery, gloom

misbehave VERB *Little Mary was misbehaving again.* ► behave badly, be naughty, be disobedient, *(more informal)* play up, *(more informal)* fool about

misbehavior NOUN *In those days any form of misbehavior was punished.* ► bad behavior, misconduct, naughtiness, disobedience, indiscipline, insubordination, mischief, mischief-making, wrongdoing

miscalculate VERB *We miscalculated the amount of fuel we would need.* ► misjudge, make a mistake over, get wrong, underestimate OR overestimate, blunder over

miscalculation NOUN *The problem arises from miscalculations by officials.* ► mistake, error, error of judgment, blunder

miscellaneous ADJECTIVE *He made money from gardening and miscellaneous jobs.* ► various, varied, different, assorted, mixed, sundry, multifarious

a
b
c
d
e
f
g
h
i
j
k
l
m
n
o
p
q
r
s
t
u
v
w
x
y
z

A
B
C
D
E
F
G
H
I
J
K
L

M

N
O
P
Q
R
S
T
U
V
W
X
Y
Z

mischief NOUN **1** naughty or troublesome behavior **2** trouble caused by this
▷ **mischievous** ADJECTIVE **mischievously** ADVERB

misconception NOUN misconceptions a mistaken idea

misconduct NOUN bad behavior by someone in a responsible position • *professional misconduct*

miser NOUN misers a person who hoards money and spends as little as possible
▷ **miserly** ADJECTIVE **miserliness** NOUN

miserable ADJECTIVE **1** full of misery; very unhappy, poor, or uncomfortable **2** disagreeable or unpleasant • *miserable weather*
▷ **miserably** ADVERB

misery NOUN miseries **1** great unhappiness or discomfort or suffering, especially lasting for a long time **2** (*informal*) a person who is always unhappy or complaining

misfire VERB misfires, misfiring, misfired **1** fail to fire **2** fail to function correctly or to have the required effect • *The joke misfired.*

misfit NOUN misfits a person who does not fit in well with other people or who is not well suited to his or her work

misfortune NOUN misfortunes **1** bad luck **2** an unlucky event or accident

misgiving NOUN misgivings a feeling of doubt or slight fear or mistrust

misguided ADJECTIVE guided by mistaken ideas or beliefs

mishap (mis- hap) NOUN mishaps an unlucky accident

misinterpret VERB misinterprets, misinterpreting, misinterpreted interpret incorrectly
▷ **misinterpretation** NOUN

mislay VERB mislays, mislaying, mislaid lose something for a short time because you cannot remember where you put it

Thesaurus

mischief NOUN **1** *He was always plotting some mischief with his brother.* ► misbehavior, naughtiness, bad behavior, mischievousness, misconduct, disobedience, pranks **2** *A faulty fuel pipe can cause much mischief.* ► trouble, difficulty, harm, damage, injury, bother, nuisance

mischievous ADJECTIVE **1** *mischievous children* ► naughty, badly behaved, misbehaving, disobedient, insubordinate, troublesome, vexatious **2** *There was a mischievous grin on his face.* ► playful, impish, roguish, teasing **3** *The house was full of mischievous rumors.* ► malicious, malevolent, hostile, unfriendly, spiteful, vicious, pernicious

miser NOUN *an old miser who kept his money hidden under the floorboards* ► scrooge, penny-pincher, hoarder, niggard, (*informal*) skinflint AN OPPOSITE IS spendthrift

miserable ADJECTIVE **1** *She was too miserable to eat.* ► unhappy, sad, dejected, despondent, downcast, downhearted, down, disheartened, disconsolate, glum, melancholy, cast down **2** *The house was cramped and miserable.* ► dreary, dismal, gloomy, cheerless, joyless, squalid **3** *It was a miserable way to treat people.* ► contemptible, despicable, disgraceful, deplorable, shameful **4** *They kept us waiting for hours and all we got was a miserable cup of tea.* ► measly, paltry, meager, wretched, niggardly, pitiful, (*more informal*) mingy, (*more informal*) mouldy

miserly ADJECTIVE *He was miserly for all his life and died rich as a result.* ► mean, niggardly, penny-pinching, parsimonious, tight, stingy AN OPPOSITE IS generous

misery NOUN **1** *the misery of unemployment* ► hardship, suffering, privation, affliction, distress, misfortune, tribulation, anguish **2** *She put her hands to her face in silent misery.* ► unhappiness, distress, wretchedness, despair, grief, suffering **3** (*more informal*) *He can be fun but a lot of the time he's a real misery.* ► spoilsport, killjoy, pessimist, (*more informal*) wet blanket

misfire VERB *The plan had misfired.* ► fail, fall through, founder, miscarry, go wrong, (*more informal*) flop AN OPPOSITE IS succeed

misfit NOUN *a bunch of misfits and weirdos* ► eccentric, nonconformist, maverick, dropout, individualist, (*more informal*) oddball

misfortune NOUN *Bruce had the misfortune to break a bone in his wrist. The family had suffered several generations of misfortune* ► bad luck, mischance, mishap, trouble, setback, tribulation, hardship AN OPPOSITE IS good luck

misgiving NOUN *We agreed to the proposal with several misgivings.* ► doubt, reservation, qualm, scruple, diffidence AN OPPOSITE IS confidence

misguided ADJECTIVE *a misguided policy on immigration* ► mistaken, misconceived, erroneous, fallacious, unsound, unfounded, ill-judged, ill-considered

mishap NOUN *an unfortunate mishap in the kitchen* ► accident, misfortune, misadventure, setback, problem, difficulty

misjudge VERB *He misjudged the distance and hit a parked car.* ► miscalculate, overestimate, underestimate, get wrong, guess wrongly, make a mistake about, misinterpret, misunderstand

mislay VERB *I seem to have mislaid my passport.* ► lose, misplace, lose track of, forget

mislead VERB misleads, misleading, misled give somebody a wrong idea or impression deliberately

misnomer NOUN misnomers an unsuitable name for something

misogynist (mis- oj- in- ist) NOUN misogynists a man who hates women
▷ misogyny NOUN

misplaced ADJECTIVE 1 placed wrongly 2 inappropriate • *misplaced loyalty*
▷ misplacement NOUN

misprint NOUN misprints a mistake in printing

misrepresent VERB misrepresents, misrepresenting, misrepresented represent in a false or misleading way
▷ misrepresentation NOUN

Miss NOUN Misses a title put before a girl's or unmarried woman's name [short for mistress]

miss VERB misses, missing, missed 1 fail to hit, reach, catch, see, hear, or find something 2 be sad because someone or something is not with you 3 notice that something has gone miss out 1 leave out 2 not get the benefit

miss NOUN misses missing something • *Was that shot a hit or a miss?*

misshapen ADJECTIVE badly shaped

missile NOUN missiles a weapon or other object for firing or throwing at a target

missing ADJECTIVE 1 lost; not in the proper place 2 absent

mission NOUN missions 1 an important job that somebody is sent to do or feels they must do 2 a place or building where missionaries work 3 a military or scientific expedition

missionary NOUN missionaries a person who is sent to another country to spread a religious faith

misspell VERB misspells, misspelling, misspelt or misspelled spell a word wrongly

mist NOUN mists 1 damp cloudy air near the ground 2 condensed water vapour on a window, mirror, etc.
▷ mist VERB

mistake NOUN mistakes 1 something done wrongly 2 an incorrect opinion

mistake VERB mistakes, mistaking, mistook, mistaken 1 misunderstand • *Don't mistake my meaning.* 2 choose or identify wrongly • *We mistook her for her sister.*

mistaken ADJECTIVE 1 incorrect 2 having an incorrect opinion

mister NOUN (*informal*) a form of address to a man

mistletoe NOUN a plant with white berries that grows as a parasite on trees

mistress NOUN mistresses 1 a woman who is in charge of something 2 a woman who is a man's lover but not his wife 3 a woman teacher 4 the woman owner of a dog or other animal

Thesaurus

mislead VERB *Colin had evidently tried to mislead her.* ► deceive, delude, fool, hoodwink, take in, misguide, misinform, lead astray

misleading ADJECTIVE *a misleading answer* ► confusing, deceptive, equivocal, ambiguous, evasive, dishonest, unreliable

mismanage VERB *The redundancies had been badly mismanaged.* ► mishandle, bungle, botch, ruin, spoil, fluff, muff, mess up, make a mess of, (*more informal*) make a hash of, (*much more informal*) cock up, (*much more informal*) screw up

miss VERB 1 *The bullet missed him by inches.* ► fail to hit, fall short of 2 *It was an easy catch but he still missed it.* ► drop, fumble, fail to catch, let slip, mishandle 3 *If we're not careful we'll miss the last train.* ► be too late for, fail to catch 4 *He was ill and had to miss the party.* ► be absent from, skip 5 *I will miss Debbie terribly.* ► pine for, long for, yearn for, feel the loss of 6 *He swerved and managed to miss an oncoming car.* ► avoid, dodge, evade, escape, circumvent 7 *Don't miss your chance.* ► let slip, let go, forfeit, pass by, pass up, disregard

missing ADJECTIVE *A few books are still missing.* ► lost, mislaid, misplaced, gone astray, straying, unaccounted for, absent, disappeared

mission NOUN 1 *a mission to Africa* ► expedition, assignment, operation, exploration, journey, sortie, voyage 2 *his mission in life* ► calling, vocation, goal, aim, purpose, function

mist NOUN 1 *The sun was breaking through the early morning mist.* ► haze, fog, vapor, cloud, mistiness 2 *She wiped a hole to peep through the mist on the windows.* ► condensation, film, steam

mistake NOUN *It's easy to make mistakes when you are tired.* ► error, slip, blunder, lapse, misjudgment, miscalculation, oversight, (*more informal*) gaffe

mistake VERB *I mistook the meaning of the instruction.* ► misunderstand, misinterpret, confuse, get wrong, misjudge, misread, misconstrue, (*informal*) get the wrong end of the stick about, mix up

mistaken ADJECTIVE *These conclusions are mistaken, in our view.* ► wrong , incorrect, erroneous, misguided, unfounded, unsound, ill-judged, inappropriate

mistreat VERB *Some of the prisoners had been mistreated.* ► ill-treat, maltreat, abuse, misuse, harm, injure, molest, (*more informal*) knock about

a b c d e f g h i j k l **m** n o p q r s t u v w x y z

A
B
C
D
E
F
G
H
I
J
K
L
M
N
O
P
Q
R
S
T
U
V
W
X
Y
Z

mistrust VERB mistrusts, mistrusting, mistrusted feel no trust in somebody or something
▷ **mistrust** NOUN

misty ADJECTIVE mistier, mistiest **1** full of mist **2** not clear or distinct
▷ **mistily** ADVERB **mistiness** NOUN

misunderstand VERB misunderstands, misunderstanding, misunderstood get a wrong idea or impression of something
▷ **misunderstanding** NOUN

misuse (mis- yooz) VERB misuses, misusing, misused **1** use incorrectly **2** treat badly
▷ **misuse** (mis- yooss) NOUN

mitten NOUN mittens a kind of glove without separate parts for the fingers

mix VERB mixes, mixing, mixed **1** put different things together so that they are no longer distinct; blend or combine **2** (said about a person) get together with others
▷ **mixer** NOUN

mix up 1 mix thoroughly **2** confuse

mix NOUN mixes a mixture

mixed ADJECTIVE containing two or more kinds of things or people

mixture NOUN mixtures **1** something made of different things mixed together **2** the process of mixing

mnemonic (nim- on- ik) NOUN mnemonics a verse or saying that helps you to remember something [from Greek *mneme* = memory]

moan VERB moans, moaning, moaned **1** make a long low sound of pain or suffering **2** grumble
▷ **moan** NOUN

moat NOUN moats a deep wide ditch round a castle, usually filled with water
▷ **moated** ADJECTIVE

mob NOUN mobs **1** a large disorderly crowd **2** a gang

mobile ADJECTIVE moving easily
▷ **mobility** NOUN

Thesaurus

mistrust VERB *I mistrust their intentions.*
► distrust, suspect, be suspicious of, be sceptical about, have misgivings about, have qualms about, be wary of, disbelieve, doubt, question AN OPPOSITE IS trust

misty ADJECTIVE **1** *misty weather* ► hazy, foggy, murky, cloudy AN OPPOSITE IS clear **2** *a misty window* ► misted, clouded **3** *misty memories* ► indistinct, vague, hazy, unclear, obscure, nebulous OPPOSITES ARE sharp, distinct

misunderstand VERB *I must have misunderstood; I thought you were coming with us.* ► make a mistake, misapprehend, misinterpret, mishear, get it wrong, (more informal) get hold of the wrong end of the stick

misunderstanding NOUN **1** *The suggestion was based on a misunderstanding of the issues.* ► misapprehension, misconception, misinterpretation, misjudgment, false impression, delusion (about), (informal) mix-up **2** *It wasn't a fight, just a slight misunderstanding.* ► difference of opinion, disagreement, dispute, quarrel , squabble, argument, contretemps

misuse NOUN **1** *the misuse of confidential information* ► wrong use, misappropriation, misapplication, exploitation **2** *the misuse of innocent people* ► ill-treatment, maltreatment, mistreatment **3** *the misuse of drugs* ► abuse, careless use, ill-use, mishandling

misuse VERB **1** *He was accused of misusing public money.* ► misapply, misemploy, embezzle, put to wrong use **2** *She had been misused by successive partners.* ► ill-treat, maltreat, mistreat, abuse, harm, injure, molest, (more informal) knock about

mix VERB **1** *Mix the ingredients together. Oil and water don't mix.* ► blend, mingle, combine, merge, fuse, unite, coalesce, amalgamate **2** *He mixes with all sorts of people.* ► associate, consort, fraternize, socialize, mingle, (more informal) hang about with

mix up *I've mixed up the two dates.* ► confuse, muddle, muddle up, jumble up, mistake

mixed ADJECTIVE **1** *a mixed collection* ► assorted, varied, diverse, miscellaneous, heterogeneous, different **2** *mixed ingredients* ► combined, integrated, amalgamated, united, composite, hybrid, joint **3** *Their reactions were mixed.* ► ambivalent, equivocal, uncertain, unsure, confused, muddled, ambiguous

mixture NOUN *a strange mixture of people* ► assortment, variety, medley, combination, blend, miscellany, jumble, hotchpotch, assemblage, gathering

moan VERB **1** *The injured man was moaning with pain.* ► groan, cry, howl, whimper **2** *Everyone moaned about the food.* ► complain, grumble, grouse, grouch, carp, whine, (more informal) whinge

moan NOUN **1** *moans of pain* ► groan, cry, howl, whimper **2** *moans about the awful food* ► complain, grumble, grouse, grouch, carping, whining, (more informal) whinging

mob NOUN (informal) *An angry mob gathered at the gate.* ► crowd, throng, mass, horde, rabble, swarm, bunch, gang, group, herd, pack, riot

mob VERB *Her fans mobbed her all the way to her car.* ► crowd around, swarm around, throng around, jostle, surround, besiege, hem in, harass, hassle

mobile ADJECTIVE **1** *She was soon mobile again after her operation.* ► moving, walking, able to

mobile NOUN **mobiles 1** a decoration for hanging up so that its parts move in currents of air **2** a mobile phone

mobile home NOUN **mobile homes** a large trailer permanently parked and used for living

mobile phone NOUN **mobile phones** a phone you can carry about that uses a cellular radio system

mobilize VERB **mobilizes, mobilizing, mobilized** assemble people or things for a particular purpose, especially for war
▷ **mobilization** NOUN

mock VERB **mocks, mocking, mocked 1** make fun of a person or thing **2** imitate someone or something to make people laugh
▷ **mockery** NOUN

mock ADJECTIVE imitation, not real • mock exams

mock-up NOUN **mock-ups** a model of something, made in order to test or study it

mode NOUN **modes 1** the way a thing is done **2** what is fashionable

model NOUN **models 1** a copy of an object, usually on a smaller scale **2** a particular design **3** a person who poses for an artist or displays clothes by wearing them **4** a person or thing that is worth copying

model VERB **models, modeling, modeled 1** make a model of something **2** design or plan something using another thing as an example **3** work as an artist's model or a fashion model

modem (moh- dem) NOUN **modems** a device that links a computer to a telephone line for transmitting data

moderate ADJECTIVE **1** medium; not extremely small or great or hot, etc. • a moderate climate **2** not extreme or unreasonable • moderate opinions
▷ **moderately** ADVERB

moderate (mod- er- ayt) VERB **moderates, moderating, moderated** make or become moderate
▷ **moderation** NOUN
in moderation in moderate amounts

modern ADJECTIVE **1** belonging to the present or recent times **2** in fashion now
▷ **modernity** NOUN

modernize VERB **modernizes, modernizing, modernized** make a thing more modern
▷ **modernization** NOUN

modest ADJECTIVE **1** not vain or boastful **2** moderate in size or amount • a modest income **3** not showy or splendid **4** behaving or dressing decently or decorously
▷ **modestly** ADVERB **modesty** NOUN

Thesaurus

move **2** The village is visited by a mobile library once a week. ► traveling, itinerant, peripatetic, roving, wandering **3** It helps to be mobile in furthering a career. ► adaptable, flexible, versatile, adjustable

mobilize VERB **1** The army was mobilized to fight the rebels. ► summon, assemble, call up, enlist, levy, marshal, muster **2** The spin doctors mobilize support for government policy. ► rally, generate, activate, stir up, stimulate, promote, galvanize, organize

mock VERB Her brother had grinned and mocked her behind her back. ► ridicule, jeer, make fun of, laugh at, taunt, scorn, sneer at, deride, disparage, tease

mock ADJECTIVE He shook his head in mock disbelief. ► pretend, imitation, simulated, false, fake, sham, feigned

mockery NOUN **1** There was a note of mockery in her voice. ► ridicule, derision, contempt, scorn, sarcasm, disdain **2** The trial was a mockery of justice. ► travesty, parody, caricature, sham

model ADJECTIVE **1** a model train ► miniature, toy, replica **2** a model pupil ► ideal, perfect, exemplary, impeccable, faultless

model NOUN **1** a working model of a high-speed train ► replica, copy, representation, facsimile, imitation **2** a model of good behavior ► ideal, paragon, epitome, personification **3** laws based on the American model ► pattern, example, type, standard, paradigm, prototype, version, mold

model VERB **1** The artist modeled the figure in bronze. ► form, make, fashion, mold, sculpt, design **2** Characters who are modeled on real life. ► base, draw (from), derive (from)

moderate ADJECTIVE **1** a moderate success ► average, modest, mediocre, tolerable, passable **2** a moderate drinker; Prices are moderate this year. ► reasonable, sensible, restrained, controlled, modest, fair

moderate VERB **1** The wind has moderated. ► abate, die down, ease off, subside, decrease, become less extreme **2** Can we do something to moderate the noise? ► control, curb, check, reduce, lessen, mitigate, alleviate, allay, subdue

modern ADJECTIVE **1** modern art ► contemporary, present-day, current **2** She wears very modern clothes. ► fashionable, stylish, modish, voguish, advanced

modernize VERB (informal) The factory needs to modernize its production methods. ► update, renovate, refurbish, regenerate, improve, rebuild

modest ADJECTIVE **1** a modest increase in income ► moderate, reasonable, limited, slight, small AN OPPOSITE IS large **2** He is always modest about his achievements. ► unassuming, unpretentious, humble, reserved, discreet, retiring, bashful AN OPPOSITE IS boastful

modesty NOUN She shows admirable modesty about her abilities. ► humility, reserve, reticence, discretion, self-effacement, shyness, lack of pretension

modify VERB modifies, modifying, modified **1** change something slightly **2** describe a word or limit its meaning • *Adjectives modify nouns.*
▷ **modification** NOUN

modulate VERB modulates, modulating, modulated **1** adjust or regulate **2** vary in pitch or tone etc. **3** alter an electronic wave to allow signals to be sent
▷ **modulation** NOUN **modulator** NOUN

module NOUN modules **1** an independent part of a spacecraft, building, etc. **2** a unit; a section of a course of study
▷ **modular** ADJECTIVE

moist ADJECTIVE slightly wet
▷ **moistly** ADVERB **moistness** NOUN

moisten VERB moistens, moistening, moistened make or become moist

moisture NOUN water in the air or making a thing moist

moisturizer NOUN a cream used to make the skin less dry

mold[1] NOUN molds a hollow container of a particular shape, in which a liquid or soft substance is put to set into this shape

mold VERB molds, molding, molded make something have a particular shape or character

mold[2] NOUN a furry growth of very small fungi
▷ **moldy** ADJECTIVE

molder VERB molders, moldering, moldered rot away or decay into dust

mole[1] NOUN moles **1** a small furry animal that burrows under the ground **2** a spy working within an organization and passing information to another organization or country

mole[2] NOUN moles a small dark spot on skin

molecule NOUN molecules the smallest part into which a substance can be divided without changing its chemical nature; a group of atoms
▷ **molecular** (mo- lek- yoo- ler) ADJECTIVE

molehill NOUN molehills a small pile of earth thrown up by a burrowing mole

molest VERB molests, molesting, molested **1** annoy or pester **2** attack or abuse someone sexually

mollusk NOUN mollusks any of a group of animals including snails, slugs, and mussels, with soft bodies, no backbones, and sometimes external shells

molt VERB moults, moulting, moulted shed feathers, hair, or skin, etc., while a new growth forms

molten ADJECTIVE melted; made liquid by great heat

moment NOUN moments **1** a very short time **2** a particular time • *Call me the moment she arrives.*

momentary ADJECTIVE lasting for only a moment
▷ **momentarily** ADVERB

momentous (mo- ment- us) ADJECTIVE very important

Thesaurus

modify VERB *These events have led us to modify our views.* ► change, alter, amend, adapt, revise, adjust, reform

moist ADJECTIVE *He dug into the dark moist earth.* ► damp, soggy, clammy, wet, watery

moisten VERB *Moisten the compost if it becomes dry.* ► dampen, wet, damp, soak, moisturize, make moist, humidify AN OPPOSITE IS dry

moisture NOUN *The windows were covered in moisture.* ► dampness, condensation, damp, humidity, liquid, steam, vapour, wetness, wet

mold NOUN **1** *The cheese had mold on it.* ► mildew, fungus, must, growth **2** *The molten metal is poured into a mold.* ► cast, die, form, matrix, template

mold VERB **1** *The figures are molded in bronze.* ► shape, form, fashion, forge, model, create, sculpt **2** *Education helps to mold your character.* ► form, shape, influence, determine, direct

moldy ADJECTIVE **1** *a hunk of moldy bread* ► mildewed, mildewy, moldering, decaying,

musty, rotten, stale **2** (*informal*) *The prize was just a moldy book token.* ► measly, paltry, miserable, meager, wretched, niggardly, pitiful, (*informal*) mingy

molest VERB *The woman had been molested by a group of men.* ► harass, pester, beset, torment, persecute, harry

moment NOUN **1** *She waited for a moment before going in.* ► minute, second, little while, short time **2** *We can leave the moment the rain stops.* ► instant, minute, second, point **3** *These matters are of little moment to most people.* ► importance, import, significance, consequence, interest, weight, value

momentary ADJECTIVE *He had a momentary glimpse of her face.* ► brief, fleeting, passing, quick, temporary, transient, transitory AN OPPOSITE IS permanent

momentous ADJECTIVE *a momentous decision* ► important, significant, fateful, epoch-making, historic, critical, crucial, decisive AN OPPOSITE IS unimportant

a
b
c
d
e
f
g
h
i
j
k
l
m
n
o
p
q
r
s
t
u
v
w
x
y
z

momentum NOUN **1** the ability something has to keep moving or developing **2** (in science) the quantity of motion of a moving object, measured as its mass multiplied by its velocity

monarch NOUN monarchs a king, queen, emperor, or empress ruling a country
▷ **monarchic** ADJECTIVE

monarchy NOUN monarchies a country ruled by a monarch
▷ **monarchist** NOUN

monastery NOUN monasteries a building where monks live and work
▷ **monastic** ADJECTIVE

Monday NOUN the day of the week following Sunday [from Old English *monandaeg* = day of the moon]

monetary ADJECTIVE to do with money

money NOUN **1** coins and banknotes **2** wealth

mongrel (mung- rel) NOUN mongrels a dog of mixed breeds

monitor NOUN monitors **1** a device for watching or testing how something is working **2** a screen that displays data and images produced by a computer **3** a pupil who is given a special responsibility in a school

monitor VERB monitors, monitoring, monitored watch or test how something is working

monk NOUN monks a member of a community of men who live according to the rules of a religious organization COMPARE **nun**

monkey NOUN monkeys **1** an animal with long arms, hands with thumbs, and often a tail **2** a mischievous person, especially a child

monocle NOUN monocles a lens worn over one eye, like half of a pair of glasses

monogram NOUN monograms a design made up of a letter or letters, especially a person's initials
▷ **monogrammed** ADJECTIVE

monolith NOUN monoliths a large single upright block of stone

monolithic ADJECTIVE **1** to do with or like a monolith **2** huge and difficult to move or change

monologue NOUN monologues a long speech by one person

monopolize VERB monopolizes, monopolizing, monopolized take the whole of something for yourself ● *One girl monopolized my attention.*
▷ **monopolization** NOUN

monopoly NOUN monopolies the exclusive right to own something or to provide a service

monosyllable NOUN monosyllables a word with only one syllable
▷ **monosyllabic** ADJECTIVE

monotone NOUN a level unchanging tone of voice in speaking or singing

monotonous ADJECTIVE boring because it does not change ● *monotonous work*
▷ **monotonously** ADVERB **monotony** NOUN

monsoon NOUN monsoons **1** a strong wind in and near the Indian Ocean, bringing heavy rain in summer **2** the rainy season brought by this wind

monster NOUN monsters **1** a large frightening creature **2** a huge thing **3** a wicked or cruel person

monster ADJECTIVE huge

monstrosity NOUN monstrosities a monstrous thing

monstrous ADJECTIVE **1** like a monster; huge **2** very shocking or outrageous

Thesaurus

momentum NOUN *The car began to gain momentum. a momentum for change* ► impetus, force, velocity, power, impulse, incentive, thrust

money NOUN **1** *I don't have enough money to buy it.* ► cash, means, funds, capital, finance, change, (*more informal*) dosh **2** *How much money shall we take on holiday?* ► currency, cash
RELATED ADJECTIVES ► financial, monetary, pecuniary

monotonous ADJECTIVE *a monotonous piece of work* ► boring, tedious, dull, dreary, uninteresting, tiresome, wearisome, repetitive, repetitious OPPOSITES ARE interesting, varied

monotony NOUN *the monotony of their working lives* ► dullness, boredom, tedium, sameness, repetitiveness, repetitiousness, weariness, dreariness, routine, uniformity

monster NOUN **1** *a huge monster of a man* ► giant, colossus, mammoth, leviathan **2** *He was behaving like a monster.* ► beast, brute, fiend, savage, ogre

monster ADJECTIVE *She came in eating a monster ice cream. The film was a monster hit.* ► huge, enormous, massive, colossal, gigantic, immense, (*informal*) ginormous

monstrous ADJECTIVE **1** *A monstrous wave loomed over the ship.* ► huge, enormous, massive, colossal, gigantic, immense, (*informal*) ginormous **2** *a monstrous winged creature* ► grotesque, hideous, gruesome, horrible, grisly, repulsive **3** *a monstrous injustice* ► appalling, dreadful, shocking, outrageous, abominable, disgraceful, scandalous, hideous, wicked, vile, foul, evil

month NOUN months each of the twelve parts into which a year is divided

monthly ADJECTIVE, ADVERB happening or done once a month

monument NOUN monuments a statue, building, or column, etc., put up as a memorial of some person or event

monumental ADJECTIVE 1 built as a monument 2 very large or important

moo VERB moos, mooing, mooed make the low deep sound of a cow
▷ moo NOUN

mood NOUN moods the way someone feels • She is in a cheerful mood.

moody ADJECTIVE moodier, moodiest 1 gloomy or sullen 2 having sudden changes of mood for no apparent reason
▷ moodily ADVERB moodiness NOUN

moon NOUN moons 1 the natural satellite of the earth that can be seen in the sky at night 2 a satellite of any planet
▷ moonbeam NOUN moonlight NOUN moonlit ADJECTIVE

moor NOUN moors an area of rough land covered with heather, bracken, and bushes
▷ moorland NOUN

moor VERB moors, mooring, moored fasten a boat, etc., to a fixed object by means of a cable

mooring NOUN moorings a place where a boat can be moored

mop NOUN mops 1 a bunch or pad of soft material fastened on the end of a stick, used for cleaning floors, etc. 2 a thick mass of hair

mop VERB mops, mopping, mopped clean or wipe with a mop, etc.
mop up 1 wipe or soak up liquid 2 deal with the last parts of something • The army is mopping up the last of the rebels.

mope VERB mopes, moping, moped be sad

moped (moh- ped) NOUN mopeds a kind of small motorcycle

moral ADJECTIVE 1 connected with what is right and wrong in behavior 2 good or virtuous
▷ morally ADVERB morality NOUN
moral support help in the form of encouragement

moral NOUN morals a lesson in right behavior taught by a story or event
USAGE Do not confuse with morale.

morale (mor- ahl) NOUN the level of confidence and good spirits in a person or group of people • Morale was high after the victory.
USAGE Do not confuse with moral.

morals PLURAL NOUN standards of behavior

morbid ADJECTIVE 1 thinking about gloomy or unpleasant things 2 (in medicine) unhealthy
• a morbid growth
▷ morbidly ADVERB morbidity NOUN

more ADJECTIVE (comparative of much and many) greater in amount, etc.

Thesaurus

---

monument NOUN 1 a monument to local heroes
► memorial, obelisk, statue, shrine, mausoleum 2 a monument over his grave
► gravestone, headstone, tombstone 3 The book is a monument to years of research.
► testament, record, token, evidence

monumental ADJECTIVE 1 a monumental plaque
► commemorative, memorial 2 a monumental task ► huge, great, enormous, immense, awesome, grand, impressive

mood NOUN 1 He was in a bad mood for most of the day. ► temper, humor, disposition, spirit, frame of mind, state of mind, vein 2 The music sets the right mood for the story. ► atmosphere, feeling, tone, spirit, ambience

moody ADJECTIVE Charles was quiet and moody, and this worried her. ► changeable, temperamental, volatile, unpredictable, sulky, sullen, gloomy, morose

moon NOUN by the light of a full moon RELATED ADJECTIVE ► lunar

mop VERB A man was mopping the floor. ► wash, clean, sponge, wipe

mope VERB She realized it was no use moping.
► brood, fret, sulk, pine, be miserable, grieve

moral ADJECTIVE 1 moral issues ► ethical, social, behavioural 2 a very moral person ► good, honest, virtuous, upright, principled, honorable, decent, proper, pure, blameless, upstanding, responsible, trustworthy AN OPPOSITE IS immoral 3 moral support
► emotional, psychological

moral NOUN There's a clear moral to this story.
► lesson, message, meaning, point, significance, import, principle

morality NOUN standards of morality ► ethics, morals, ideals, principles, integrity, honesty, goodness, propriety, conduct, behavior, manners AN OPPOSITE IS immorality

morbid ADJECTIVE 1 a morbid obsession with death
► macabre, ghoulish, unhealthy, gruesome, grisly, unwholesome 2 The thought of old age made her morbid. ► gloomy, depressed, dejected, melancholy, downhearted, pessimistic AN OPPOSITE IS cheerful

more ADJECTIVE They want more money.
► additional, extra, further, added, increased, fresh, supplementary, other AN OPPOSITE IS less

more NOUN a greater amount

more ADVERB **1** to a greater extent • *more beautiful* **2** again • *once more*
more or less **1** approximately **2** nearly or practically

moreover ADVERB besides; in addition to what has been said

Mormon NOUN Mormons a member of a religious group founded in the U.S.

morning NOUN mornings the early part of the day, before noon or before lunchtime

moron NOUN morons (*informal*) a very stupid person
▷ **moronic** ADJECTIVE

morose (mo- rohss) ADJECTIVE bad-tempered and miserable
▷ **morosely** ADVERB **moroseness** NOUN

Morse code NOUN a signaling code using short and long sounds or flashes of light (dots and dashes) to represent letters

morsel NOUN morsels a small piece of food

mortal ADJECTIVE **1** not living forever • *All of us are mortal.* **2** causing death; fatal • *a mortal wound* **3** deadly • *mortal enemies*
▷ **mortally** ADVERB **mortality** NOUN

mortal NOUN mortals a human being, as compared to a god or immortal spirit

mortar NOUN mortars **1** a mixture of sand, cement, and water used in building to stick bricks together **2** a hard bowl in which substances are pounded with a pestle **3** a short cannon for firing shells at a high angle

mortgage (mor- gij) NOUN mortgages an arrangement to borrow money to buy a house, with the house as security for the loan

mortgage VERB mortgages, mortgaging, mortgaged offer a house, etc., as security in return for a loan

mortify VERB mortifies, mortifying, mortified humiliate someone or make them feel very ashamed
▷ **mortification** NOUN

mortuary NOUN mortuaries a place where dead bodies are kept before being buried or cremated

mosaic (mo- zay- ik) NOUN mosaics a picture or design made from small colored pieces of stone or glass

mosque (mosk) NOUN mosques a building where Muslims worship

mosquito NOUN mosquitoes a kind of gnat that sucks blood

moss NOUN mosses a plant that grows in damp places and has no flowers
▷ **mossy** ADJECTIVE

most ADJECTIVE(superlative of much and many) greatest in amount or degree • *Most people came by bus.*

most NOUN the greatest amount • *Most of the food was eaten.*

most ADVERB **1** to the greatest extent; more than any other • *most beautiful* **2** very or extremely • *most impressive*

mostly ADVERB mainly

motel NOUN motels a hotel providing accommodation for motorists and their cars

moth NOUN moths an insect rather like a butterfly, that usually flies at night

mother NOUN mothers a female parent
▷ **motherhood** NOUN

mother VERB mothers, mothering, mothered look after someone in a motherly way [from Old English]

mother-in-law NOUN mothers-in-law the mother of a married person's husband or wife

Thesaurus

morning NOUN *It was nearly morning when they finally reached home.* ► daybreak, dawn, daylight, sunrise, first light

morose ADJECTIVE *Back home, Dad was looking very morose.* ► sullen, gloomy, bad-tempered, ill-tempered, glum, sour, surly, moody, tetchy, crabby AN OPPOSITE IS cheerful

morsel NOUN *a few morsels of food* ► bite, mouthful, nibble, taste, fragment, piece, scrap, crumb, titbit

mortal ADJECTIVE **1** *The coffins contained the mortal remains of the victims.* ► physical, bodily, corporeal, earthly, worldly, perishable **2** *She struck him a mortal blow.* ► deadly, fatal, lethal **3** *mortal enemies* ► deadly, bitter, irreconcilable **4** *living in mortal fear*
► extreme, intense, grave, dire

mortal NOUN *a tale of mortals battling with divine forces* ► human being, human, mortal creature, individual, person, man OR woman, earthling

mostly ADVERB *She reads books all day, mostly novels.* ► mainly, chiefly, predominantly, primarily, principally, normally, typically, usually, generally, largely OPPOSITES ARE rarely, hardly

mother NOUN *Her mother picked her up every day from school.* ► female parent, (*more informal*) mom, (*more informal*) mommy, (*more informal*) ma, (*old-fashioned*) mater RELATED ADJECTIVE
► maternal

mother VERB *She was fond of mothering the residents when they were sick.* ► look after, care for, nurse, comfort, pamper, protect, cherish, fuss over

a
b
c
d
e
f
g
h
i
j
k
l
m
n
o
p
q
r
s
t
u
v
w
x
y
z

A
B
C
D
E
F
G
H
I
J
K
L
M
N
O
P
Q
R
S
T
U
V
W
X
Y
Z

motherly ADJECTIVE kind and gentle like a mother
▷ **motherliness** NOUN

motion NOUN **motions 1** a way of moving; movement **2** a formal statement to be discussed and voted on at a meeting

motion VERB **motions, motioning, motioned** signal by a gesture • *She motioned him to sit beside her.*

motivation NOUN what gives a person a reason for doing something
▷ **motivate** VERB

motive NOUN **motives** what makes a person do something • *a motive for murder*

motor NOUN **motors** a machine providing power to drive machinery, etc.; an engine

motor VERB **motors, motoring, motored** go or take someone in a car

motorcycle or **motorbike** NOUN **motorcycles** or **motorbikes** a two-wheeled road vehicle with an engine
▷ **motorcyclist** NOUN

motorist NOUN **motorists** a person who drives a car

motorway NOUN **motorways** a wide road for fast long-distance traffic

motto NOUN **mottoes 1** a short saying used as a guide for behavior • *Their motto is "Who dares, wins." ***2** a short verse or riddle, etc., found inside a cracker

mound NOUN **mounds 1** a pile of earth or stones etc. **2** a small hill

mount NOUN **mounts 1** a mountain • *Mount Everest ***2** something on which an object is mounted **3** a horse etc. for riding [from Latin *mons* = mountain]

mount VERB **mounts, mounting, mounted 1** climb or go up; ascend **2** get on a horse or bicycle etc. **3** increase in amount • *Our costs mounted. ***4** place or fix in position for use or display • *Mount your photos in an album.*

mountain NOUN **mountains 1** a very high hill **2** a large heap or pile or quantity
▷ **mountainous** ADJECTIVE

mountaineer NOUN **mountaineers** a person who climbs mountains
▷ **mountaineering** NOUN

mounted ADJECTIVE serving on horseback
• *mounted police*

mourn VERB **mourns, mourning, mourned** be sad, especially because someone has died
▷ **mourner** NOUN

Thesaurus

---

motherly ADJECTIVE *a motherly woman*
► maternal, protective, caring, kind, loving

motion NOUN *The motion of the bus made her queasy.* ► movement, moving, action, shifting, progress RELATED ADJECTIVES ► dynamic, kinetic

motionless ADJECTIVE **1** *The traffic ahead was motionless.* ► static, stationary, immobile, still, at a standstill, at rest AN OPPOSITE IS moving **2** *They stood motionless for several minutes, neither wanting to speak first.* ► still, stock-still, immobile, unmoving, paralysed, rooted to the spot, frozen, inert OPPOSITES ARE moving, active

motivate VERB *Money is what motivated them most.* ► prompt, drive, urge, stimulate, provoke, influence, activate, incite, persuade, impel

motivation NOUN *the motivation to learn*
► incentive, stimulus, impulse, drive, inspiration, inducement, encouragement, spur

motive NOUN *The police could not establish any motive for the attacks.* ► reason, grounds, rationale, motivation, object, intention, purpose, thinking, aim, cause

motto NOUN *Their guiding motto was "You scratch my back, and I'll scratch yours."* ► saying,

maxim, watchword, dictum, proverb, adage, precept, slogan, axiom

mound NOUN **1** *a mound of dirty socks* ► pile, heap, stack **2** *The common had several mounds to climb.* ► hill, hillock, hummock, rise, ridge, embankment

mount VERB **1** *The gallery mounts a special exhibition every year.* ► put on, organize, present, display, show, exhibit **2** *June mounted her pony. The guest of honor mounted the platform.* ► climb on to, jump on to, get on, get up on, get astride OPPOSITES ARE get off, climb down from **3** *Our savings were mounting at last.* ► grow, increase, accumulate, pile up OPPOSITES ARE dwindle, decrease

mountain NOUN **1** *several mountains to climb in the area* ► peak, summit, height RELATED ADJECTIVE ► alpine **2** *a mountain of work to get through* ► heap, pile, load, mound, stack, mass, great deal, backlog

mountainous ADJECTIVE **1** *mountainous country* ► hilly, craggy, rocky, alpine, highland, precipitous **2** *mountainous waves* ► huge, enormous, gigantic, colossal, immense, towering, (*more informal*) ginormous

mourn VERB **1** *He hid himself away, mourning his dead wife.* ► grieve for, sorrow over, lament for, weep for, pine for **2** *We all mourn the loss of so many precious artefacts.* ► regret, deplore, bewail AN OPPOSITE IS rejoice over

mournful *ADJECTIVE* sad and sorrowful
 ▷ **mournfully** *ADVERB*

mouse *NOUN* **mice 1** a small animal with a long thin tail and a pointed nose **2 mouses** or **mice** a small device which you move around on a mat to control the movements of a cursor on a computer screen
 ▷ **mousetrap** *NOUN* **mousy** *ADJECTIVE*

mousse (mooss) *NOUN* **mousses 1** a creamy pudding flavored with fruit or chocolate **2** a frothy creamy substance put on the hair so that it can be styled more easily

moustache (mus- tahsh) *NOUN* **moustaches** hair allowed to grow on a man's upper lip

mouth *NOUN* **mouths 1** the opening through which food is taken into the body **2** the place where a river enters the sea **3** an opening or outlet
 ▷ **mouthful** *NOUN*

mouth organ *NOUN* **mouth organs** a small musical instrument that you play by blowing and sucking while passing it along your lips

mouthpiece *NOUN* **mouthpieces** the part of a musical instrument or other device that you put to your mouth

move *VERB* **moves, moving, moved 1** take or go from one place to another; change a person's or thing's position **2** affect a person's feelings • *Their sad story moved us deeply.* **3** put forward a formal statement (**a motion**) to be discussed and voted on at a meeting
 ▷ **mover** *NOUN*

move *NOUN* **moves 1** a movement or action **2** a player's turn to move a piece in chess or other games
 get a move on (*informal*) hurry up
 on the move moving or making progress

movement *NOUN* **movements 1** moving or being moved **2** a group of people working together to achieve something **3** one of the main divisions of a symphony or other long musical work

mow *VERB* **mows, mowing, mowed, mown** cut down grass, etc.
 ▷ **mower** *NOUN*
 mow down knock down and kill

MP *ABBREVIATION* Member of Parliament

Mr. (mist- er) *NOUN* **Messrs.** a title put before a man's name

Mrs. (mis- iz) *NOUN* **Mrs.** a title put before a married woman's name

Ms. (miz) *NOUN* a title put before a woman's name
 USAGE You put **Ms.** before the name of a woman if she does not wish to be called "Miss" or "Mrs.," or if you do not know whether she is married.

M.Sc. *ABBREVIATION* Master of Science

Mt. *ABBREVIATION* mount or mountain

Thesaurus

mournful *ADJECTIVE* mournful music; a mournful cry ► sad, sorrowful, melancholy, unhappy, doleful, desolate, heartbroken, tragic, somber

mouth *NOUN* **1** He opened his mouth. ► jaws, lips, (more informal) gob RELATED ADJECTIVE ► oral **2** the mouth of the cave ► entrance, opening, entry, aperture **3** the mouth of a river ► outfall, outlet, estuary, firth

mouth *VERB* Thank you, I answered, mouthing the words carefully. ► utter, enunciate, pronounce, articulate, form, say

mouthful *NOUN* **1** a mouthful of food ► bite, taste, morsel, nibble, gobbet, spoonful, swallow **2** a mouthful of water ► gulp, draft, sip, swallow, (more informal) swig

move *VERB* **1** He got up and moved to the bench under the tree. ► go, walk, march, proceed, advance, stroll, amble **2** The traffic moved slowly forward. ► edge, creep, crawl, slide **3** I'll move the chair closer to the table. ► carry, take, shift, transport **4** We need to move quickly to secure a place. ► act, take action, take steps, make a move, take the initiative **5** At long last things are starting to move. ► progress, make progress, make headway, develop, (more informal) get somewhere **6** She moved from New York to the country last year. ► relocate, move house, move home, migrate, decamp,

depart **7** The beautiful performance moved them deeply. ► touch, affect, impress, disturb, agitate **8** The language course moved her to find out about living abroad. ► prompt, stimulate, motivate, persuade, rouse, impel, induce, inspire

move *NOUN* **1** The group got together to talk over their next move. ► step, action, initiative, tactic, ploy, ruse **2** It's your move. ► turn, go, opportunity, chance

movement *NOUN* **1** the movement of goods and animals ► transportation, carrying, relocation, conveyance, transferal, repositioning **2** She joined a left-wing political movement in her student days. ► party, organization, faction, group, grouping, campaign **3** A movement in the bushes caught his eye. ► motion, move, activity, action **4** There has been little movement on our grant application. ► progress, change, advance **5** a movement towards equal pay for men and women ► trend, tendency, swing, current

moving *ADJECTIVE* **1** a moving train ► traveling, mobile, active, on the move, under way OPPOSITES ARE stationary, motionless **2** a moving story ► touching, affecting, poignant, emotive, stirring, emotional, heartwarming, inspiring, exciting, stimulating AN OPPOSITE IS unemotional

a b c d e f g h i j k l **m** n o p q r s t u v w x y z

A
B
C
D
E
F
G
H
I
J
K
L
M
N
O
P
Q
R
S
T
U
V
W
X
Y
Z

much ADJECTIVE more, most existing in a large amount • *much noise*

much NOUN a large amount of something

much ADVERB **1** greatly or considerably • *much to my surprise* **2** approximately • *It is much the same.*

muck NOUN **1** farmyard manure **2** (*informal*) dirt or filth **3** (*informal*) a mess
▷ **mucky** ADJECTIVE

muck VERB
muck about (*informal*) mess about
muck out clean out the place where an animal is kept
muck up (*informal*) **1** make dirty **2** make a mess of; spoil
[probably from a Scandinavian language]

mud NOUN wet soft earth
▷ **muddy** ADJECTIVE **muddiness** NOUN

muddle VERB muddles, muddling, muddled **1** jumble or mix things up **2** confuse
▷ **muddler** NOUN

muddle NOUN muddles a muddled condition or thing; confusion or disorder

mudguard NOUN mudguards a curved cover over the top part of the wheel of a bicycle, etc., to protect the rider from the mud and water thrown up by the wheel

muff NOUN muffs a short tube-shaped piece of warm material into which the hands are pushed from opposite ends

muffin NOUN muffins **1** a flat bun eaten toasted and buttered **2** a small cake, usually containing fruit, chocolate chips, etc.

muffle VERB muffles, muffling, muffled **1** cover or wrap something to protect it or keep it warm **2** deaden the sound of something • *a muffled scream*

muffler NOUN mufflers a warm scarf

mug NOUN mugs **1** a kind of large cup with straight sides **2** (*slang*) a fool; a person who is easily deceived **3** (*slang*) a person's face

mug VERB mugs, mugging, mugged attack and rob somebody in the street
▷ **mugger** NOUN

mule NOUN mules an animal that is the offspring of a donkey and a mare, known for being stubborn
▷ **mulish** ADJECTIVE

Thesaurus

much NOUN *We don't have much to do.* ▶ a lot, a great deal, plenty

much ADJECTIVE *Do you need much help?* ▶ a lot of, a great deal of, plenty of, considerable, substantial

muck NOUN **1** *He went out to clean the muck off the windows.* ▶ dirt, grime, filth, slime, sludge, mess, mud, (*more informal*) gunge **2** *spreading muck in the fields* ▶ manure, dung

muck VERB **muck about** OR **around** (*informal*) *John was mucking about with an old engine.* ▶ fool about OR around, play about OR around, tinker, (*informal*) mess about OR around

mucky ADJECTIVE *She took off her mucky shoes.* ▶ dirty, messy, muddy, filthy, grubby, soiled, foul, grimy AN OPPOSITE IS clean

mud NOUN *He slipped and fell in the mud.* ▶ sludge, slime, slurry, clay, soil, dirt, mire, muck, ooze, silt

muddle NOUN **1** *a muddle over the time of the train* ▶ confusion, misunderstanding, mistake, mix-up **2** *Look at the muddle in the kitchen.* ▶ mess, shambles, jumble, clutter, chaos, untidiness, disorder, tangle

muddle VERB **1** *Her explanation merely muddled him.* ▶ confuse, bewilder, mix up, perplex, puzzle, disorientate, mislead AN OPPOSITE IS enlighten **2** *Don't muddle the papers on the desk.* ▶ disorganize, disarrange, mix up, mess up, jumble up, make a mess of, disorder OPPOSITES ARE tidy, clear up

muddled ADJECTIVE *He felt muddled and couldn't think what to do.* ▶ confused, disorganized, bewildered, mixed up, perplexed, puzzled, disorientated

muddy ADJECTIVE **1** *They came in to change their muddy boots.* ▶ dirty, messy, mucky, filthy, grubby, soiled, foul, grimy AN OPPOSITE IS clean **2** *The ground was wet and muddy.* ▶ waterlogged, boggy, marshy, sodden, soft, spongy, sloppy **3** *The water looked muddy.* ▶ cloudy, misty, opaque, messy AN OPPOSITE IS clear

muffle VERB **1** **muffle up** *She went out, muffling herself up against the cold.* ▶ wrap up, cover up, envelop, swathe, enclose **2** *He muffled the sound of the gun with cushions.* ▶ deaden, dull, dampen, smother, soften, suppress, muzzle

muffled ADJECTIVE *a muffled cry* ▶ faint, indistinct, muted, deadened, dull, unclear OPPOSITES ARE distinct, loud

mug NOUN **1** *We drank beer from mugs.* ▶ beaker, cup **2** *He was rather a mug to drive so fast.* ▶ fool, simpleton, idiot, clot

mug VERB *They were mugged on their way home.* ▶ attack, assault, molest, rob, steal from, set on, jump on

muggy ADJECTIVE *muggy weather* ▶ humid, close, clammy, sultry, oppressive, sticky, stuffy, airless

mull[1] VERB mulls, mulling, mulled heat wine or beer with sugar and spices, as a drink ● *mulled ale*

mull[2] VERB mulls, mulling, mulled mull something over think about something carefully; ponder

multicultural ADJECTIVE made up of people of many different races, religions, and cultures

multilateral ADJECTIVE (said about an agreement or treaty) made between three or more people or countries, etc.

multimedia ADJECTIVE using more than one medium ● *a multimedia show with pictures, lights, and music*

multimedia NOUN a computer program with sound and still and moving pictures linked to the text

multimillionaire NOUN multimillionaires a person with a fortune of several million pounds or dollars

multinational NOUN multinationals a large business company which works in several countries

multiple ADJECTIVE having many parts or elements

multiple NOUN multiples a number that contains another number (a **factor**) an exact amount of times with no remainder ● *8 and 12 are multiples of 4.*

multiple sclerosis NOUN a disease of the nervous system which makes a person unable to control their movements, and may affect their sight

multiply VERB multiplies, multiplying, multiplied **1** take a number a given quantity of times ● *Five multiplied by four equals twenty (5 x 4 = 20).* **2** make or become many; increase
▷ **multiplication** NOUN **multiplier** NOUN

multiracial ADJECTIVE consisting of people of many different races

multitude NOUN multitudes a great number of people or things
▷ **multitudinous** ADJECTIVE

mumble VERB mumbles, mumbling, mumbled speak indistinctly so that you are not easy to hear
▷ **mumble** NOUN **mumbler** NOUN

mumbo-jumbo NOUN talk that sounds mysterious but has no real meaning

mummy NOUN mummies a corpse wrapped in cloth and treated with oils, etc., before being buried so that it does not decay, as was the custom in ancient Egypt
▷ **mummify** VERB

mumps NOUN an infectious disease that makes the neck swell painfully

munitions PLURAL NOUN military weapons, ammunition, and equipment

mural ADJECTIVE on or to do with a wall

mural NOUN murals a picture painted on a wall

murder VERB murders, murdering, murdered kill a person unlawfully and deliberately
▷ **murderer** NOUN **murderess** NOUN

murder NOUN murders the murdering of somebody
▷ **murderous** ADJECTIVE

Thesaurus

mull VERB mull over *a few suggestions to mull over* ► consider, ponder, think about, contemplate, reflect on, weigh up, turn over in your mind

multiply VERB **1** *The problems began to multiply.* ► increase, proliferate, grow, mount up, spread, become numerous OPPOSITES ARE decrease, diminish **2** *The rabbits multiplied rapidly.* ► breed, propagate, reproduce, procreate

multitude NOUN *a multitude of people; a multitude of questions to answer* ► mass, host, myriad, swarm, throng, lots, large number, legion

mumble VERB *She walked off, mumbling quietly.* ► mutter, murmur, whisper, burble

mumbo-jumbo NOUN *The form was covered in mumbo-jumbo.* ► jargon, gobbledegook, gibberish, nonsense

munch VERB *The children waited, munching their rolls.* ► chomp, crunch, eat, bite, chew, gnaw

mundane ADJECTIVE *She hoped such mundane matters would keep him occupied for a while.*
► everyday, routine, commonplace, day-to-day, humdrum, tedious, dull, boring, unexceptional OPPOSITES ARE extraordinary, exceptional

murder NOUN *Reports are coming in of a brutal murder.* ► killing , homicide, slaughter (= killing of many people), assassination (= killing of an important person), fratricide (= killing of a brother), infanticide (= killing of a child), matricide (= killing of a mother), parricide (= killing of a parent or close relative), patricide (= killing of a father), regicide (= killing of a king or queen)

murder VERB *A gang had tried to murder him.* ► kill, put to death, assassinate

murderer NOUN *The murderer was never caught.* ► killer, assassin

murderous ADJECTIVE *a murderous assault* ► homicidal, deadly, lethal, brutal, bloodthirsty, barbarous, savage, ferocious, vicious

A
B
C
D
E
F
G
H
I
J
K
L
M
N
O
P
Q
R
S
T
U
V
W
X
Y
Z

murky ADJECTIVE murkier, murkiest dark and gloomy
▷ **murk** NOUN **murkiness** NOUN

murmur VERB murmurs, murmuring, murmured **1** make a low continuous sound **2** speak in a soft voice
▷ **murmur** NOUN

muscle NOUN muscles **1** a band or bundle of fibrous tissue that can contract and relax and so produce movement in parts of the body **2** the power of muscles; strength
▷ **muscular** ADJECTIVE **muscularity** NOUN

museum NOUN museums a place where interesting, old, or valuable objects are displayed for people to see [from Greek *mouseion* = place of the Muses, the goddesses of the arts and sciences]

mush NOUN soft pulp
▷ **mushy** ADJECTIVE

mushroom NOUN mushrooms an edible fungus with a stem and a dome-shaped top

music NOUN **1** a pattern of pleasant or interesting sounds made by instruments or by the voice **2** printed or written symbols which stand for musical sounds [from Greek *mousike tekhne* = art of the Muses (see museum)]

musical ADJECTIVE **1** to do with music **2** producing music **3** good at music or interested in it
▷ **musically** ADVERB

musical NOUN musicals a play or film containing a lot of songs

musician NOUN musicians someone who plays a musical instrument

Muslim NOUN Muslims a person who follows the religious teachings of Muhammad (who lived in about 570-632), set out in the Koran

must AUXILIARY VERB used to express **1** necessity or obligation (*You must go*), **2** certainty (*You must be joking!*)

mustard NOUN a yellow paste or powder used to give food a hot taste
mustard and cress small green plants eaten in salads

muster NOUN musters an assembly of people or things
pass muster be up to the required standard

mustn't (*mainly spoken*) must not

musty ADJECTIVE mustier, mustiest smelling or tasting mouldy or stale
▷ **mustiness** NOUN

mutation NOUN mutations a change in the form of a living creature because of changes in its genes
▷ **mutate** VERB **mutant** NOUN

mute ADJECTIVE **1** silent; not speaking or able to speak **2** not pronounced ● *The g in "gnat" is mute.*
▷ **mutely** ADVERB **muteness** NOUN

mutilate VERB mutilates, mutilating, mutilated damage something by breaking or cutting off part of it
▷ **mutilation** NOUN

mutineer NOUN mutineers a person who mutinies

mutiny NOUN mutinies rebellion against authority, especially refusal by members of the armed forces to obey orders
▷ **mutinous** ADJECTIVE **mutinously** ADVERB

mutiny VERB mutinies, mutinying, mutinied take part in a mutiny

mutter VERB mutters, muttering, muttered **1** speak in a low voice **2** grumble
▷ **mutter** NOUN

mutton NOUN meat from a sheep [from early French, probably from Celtic]

mutual (mew- chew- al) ADJECTIVE **1** given or done to each other ● *mutual destruction* **2** shared by two or more people ● *a mutual friend*
▷ **mutually** ADVERB

muzzle NOUN muzzles **1** an animal's nose and mouth **2** a cover put over an animal's nose and mouth so that it cannot bite **3** the open end of a gun

muzzle VERB muzzles, muzzling, muzzled **1** put a muzzle on an animal **2** silence; prevent a person from expressing opinions

---

Thesaurus

murky ADJECTIVE *The sky was murky and drizzle was falling.* ► gloomy, gray, dark, overcast, leaden, misty, dim, dull, cloudy, foggy, sombre AN OPPOSITE IS clear

murmur VERB *He murmured an apology and left.* ► mutter, mumble, whisper, burble

muscular ADJECTIVE *He's tall and muscular.* ► brawny, muscly, athletic, strong, well built, beefy, strapping, sinewy

musical ADJECTIVE *musical sounds* ► tuneful, melodic, melodious, euphonious, harmonious, lyrical, pleasant, sweet-sounding AN OPPOSITE IS discordant

musician NOUN *A small group of musicians were playing on the terrace.* ► performer, player, instrumentalist

mutiny NOUN *a mutiny on board ship*
► rebellion, revolt, protest, uprising, insurrection

mutiny VERB *The troops mutinied over pay.*
► rebel, revolt, rise up, protest, go on strike

mutter VERB *Her husband mutters in his sleep.*
► mumble, murmur, whisper, burble

mutual ADJECTIVE *an agreement based on mutual trust* ► joint, shared, reciprocal, reciprocated, common, complementary

my ADJECTIVE belonging to me

myself PRONOUN I or me and nobody else

mysterious ADJECTIVE full of mystery; puzzling
▷ **mysteriously** ADVERB

mystery NOUN mysteries something that cannot be explained or understood; something puzzling [from Greek *mysterion* = a secret thing or ceremony]

mystic ADJECTIVE **1** having a spiritual meaning **2** mysterious and filling people with wonder
▷ **mystical** ADJECTIVE **mystically** ADVERB **mysticism** NOUN

mystic NOUN mystics a person who seeks to obtain spiritual contact with God by deep religious meditation [from Greek *mystikos* = secret]

mystify VERB mystifies, mystifying, mystified puzzle or bewilder
▷ **mystification** NOUN

myth (mith) NOUN myths **1** an old story containing ideas about ancient times or about supernatural beings COMPARE **legend 2** an untrue story or belief

mythical ADJECTIVE imaginary; found only in myths • *a mythical animal*

mythology NOUN myths or the study of myths
▷ **mythological** ADJECTIVE

Thesaurus

mysterious ADJECTIVE *His friends had disappeared in mysterious circumstances.*
► strange, puzzling, odd, peculiar, curious, weird, obscure, baffling, unexplained, unknown AN OPPOSITE IS straightforward

mystery NOUN **1** *Their disappearance remains a mystery.* ► puzzle, enigma, riddle, conundrum **2** *events surrounded in mystery* ► secrecy, obscurity, uncertainty, ambiguity

mystify VERB *The work he did mystified his contemporaries.* ► puzzle, perplex, baffle, bewilder, bamboozle, confuse

mythical ADJECTIVE *a story based on mythical events* ► legendary, mythological, imaginary, fabled, fabulous, fictional, invented, fanciful, make-believe AN OPPOSITE IS real

mythological ADJECTIVE *mythological gods and heroes* ► mythical, fabled, legendary, traditional

mythology NOUN *creatures in mythology*
► legend, myth, tradition, folklore

a
b
c
d
e
f
g
h
i
j
k
l
m
n
o
p
q
r
s
t
u
v
w
x
y
z

Nn

N. ABBREVIATION **1** north **2** northern

nag VERB **nags, nagging, nagged 1** pester a person by keeping on criticizing, complaining, or asking for things **2** keep on hurting or bothering you • *a nagging pain*

nail NOUN **nails 1** the hard covering over the end of a finger or toe **2** a small sharp piece of metal hammered in to fasten pieces of wood etc. together

nail VERB **nails, nailing, nailed 1** fasten with a nail or nails **2** (*informal*) catch; arrest

naked ADJECTIVE **1** without any clothes or coverings on **2** obvious; not hidden • *the naked truth*
▷ **nakedly** ADVERB **nakedness** NOUN

naked eye NOUN the eye when it is not helped by a telescope or microscope etc.

name NOUN **names 1** the word or words by which a person, animal, place, or thing is known **2** a person's reputation

name VERB **names, naming, named 1** give a name to **2** state the name or names of **3** say

what you want something to be • *Name your price.*
name the day decide when something, especially a wedding, is to take place or happen • *Have you two named the day yet?*

namely ADVERB that is to say • *My two favorite subjects are sciences, namely chemistry and biology.*

nanny NOUN **nannies** a woman employed to look after young children

nap NOUN **naps** a short sleep
catch a person napping catch a person unprepared for something or not alert

napkin NOUN **napkins 1** a piece of cloth or paper used at meals to protect your clothes or for wiping your lips or fingers **2** (*old use*) a nappy

narcotic NOUN **narcotics** a drug that makes a person sleepy or unconscious
▷ **narcotic** ADJECTIVE **narcosis** NOUN
[from Greek *narke* = numbness]

narrative NOUN **narratives** a spoken or written account of something

narrow ADJECTIVE **1** not wide or broad **2** uncomfortably close; with only a small margin of safety • *a narrow escape*
▷ **narrowly** ADVERB

narrow-minded ADJECTIVE not tolerant of other people's beliefs and ways

---

Thesaurus

nab VERB (*informal*) *A police car nabbed him on his way home.* ► catch, arrest, apprehend, take into custody

nag VERB *He's been nagging me about it for weeks.* ► harass, badger, pester, chivvy, hound, (*more informal*) keep on at, (*more informal*) go on at, (*more informal*) moan at

nail NOUN **1** *The nail's fallen out so I'll have to use a screw.* ► tack, pin, stud **2** *He broke his nail opening a carton.* RELATED ADJECTIVE ► ungual

nail VERB *Nail it to the wall.* ► hammer, pin, tack, fasten, attach, secure, fix

naive ADJECTIVE *I was very naive in those days but I've learned a lot since then.* ► innocent, ingenuous, unsophisticated, inexperienced, credulous, artless, raw, green OPPOSITES ARE sophisticated, experienced, knowing

naked ADJECTIVE **1** *a naked statue* ► nude, bare, unclothed, uncovered, undressed, unclad AN OPPOSITE IS clothed **2** *the naked truth* ► plain, undisguised, unadorned, unvarnished, simple, bald, unmitigated

name NOUN *His name is Carl.* ► first name, forename, (*more formal*) denomination, (*more formal*) appellation RELATED ADJECTIVES ► nominal, onomastic

name VERB **1** *Her father had wanted to name her Clio.* ► call, dub, style, christen, baptize **2** *The*

victim will not be be named until relatives have been notified. ► identify, specify **3** *The king has to name a successor.* ► choose, designate, nominate, decide on, specify, appoint

nameless ADJECTIVE *pictures by a nameless artist* ► unnamed, unidentified, anonymous, unheard of

nap NOUN *He was on the sofa, having a nap.* ► snooze, doze, sleep, rest, lie-down, (*more informal*) forty winks

narrate VERB *The story is narrated by the governess.* ► tell, relate, recount, report, describe, unfold, detail, relay, chronicle

narrative NOUN *a chronological narrative of the events of the last five years* ► account, summary, narration, commentary, description, sketch

narrow ADJECTIVE **1** *a narrow path; She was elected by a narrow majority.* ► slim, thin, slender, fine **2** *a narrow space* ► tight, close, confined, cramped, enclosed, limited, constricting AN OPPOSITE IS wide **3** *a narrow point of view* ► narrow-minded, intolerant, conservative, illiberal, insular, parochial, small-minded, bigoted OPPOSITES ARE broad-minded, open-minded, tolerant

narrow-minded ADJECTIVE *a narrow-minded outlook* ► small-minded, intolerant, narrow, bigoted, conservative, illiberal, insular, parochial, short-sighted OPPOSITES ARE broad-minded, open-minded, tolerant

A B C D E F G H I J K L M N O P Q R S T U V W X Y Z

nasal _ADJECTIVE_ to do with the nose [from Latin _nasus_ = nose]

nasty _ADJECTIVE_ nastier, nastiest **1** unpleasant **2** unkind
▷ **nastily** _ADVERB_ **nastiness** _NOUN_

nation _NOUN_ nations a large community of people most of whom have the same ancestors, language, history, and customs, and who usually live in the same part of the world under one government
▷ **national** _ADJECTIVE, NOUN_ **nationally** _ADVERB_

national anthem _NOUN_ national anthems a nation's official song, which is played or sung on important occasions

national curriculum _NOUN_ an official list of the subjects that must be taught by state schools

nationalist _NOUN_ nationalists **1** a person who is very patriotic **2** a person who wants his or her country to be independent rather than being part of another country • _Scottish nationalists_
▷ **nationalism** _NOUN_ **nationalistic** _ADJECTIVE_

nationality _NOUN_ nationalities the condition of belonging to a particular nation • _What is his nationality?_

nationalize _VERB_ nationalizes, nationalizing, nationalized put an industry or business under state ownership or control
▷ **nationalization** _NOUN_

national park _NOUN_ national parks an area of natural beauty which is protected by the government and which the public may visit

nationwide _ADJECTIVE & ADVERB_ over the whole of a country

native _NOUN_ natives a person born in a particular place • _He is a native of Sweden._

native _ADJECTIVE_ **1** belonging to a person because of the place of his or her birth • _my native country_ **2** grown or originating in a particular place • _a plant native to China_ **3** natural; belonging to a person by nature • _native ability_

Native American _NOUN_ Native Americans one of the original inhabitants of North and South America
USAGE See note at **Indian.**

natural _ADJECTIVE_ **1** produced or done by nature, not by people or machines **2** normal; not surprising **3** having a quality or ability that you were born with • _a natural leader_ **4** (said about a note in music) neither sharp nor flat
▷ **naturally** _ADVERB_ **naturalness** _NOUN_

natural _NOUN_ naturals **1** a person who is naturally good at something **2** a natural note in music; a sign (♮) that shows this

natural history _NOUN_ the study of plants and animals

naturalist _NOUN_ naturalists an expert in natural history

natural science _NOUN_ the study of physics, chemistry, and biology

natural selection _NOUN_ Darwin's theory that only the plants and animals suited to their surroundings will survive and breed

nature _NOUN_ natures **1** everything in the world that was not made by people **2** the characteristics of a person or thing • _She has a_

Thesaurus

nasty _ADJECTIVE_ **1** _The dish had a nasty taste._
► unpleasant, disagreeable, disgusting, horrible, repellent OPPOSITES ARE pleasant, nice, lovely **2** _He can be very nasty at times._
► unkind, unfriendly, unpleasant, disagreeable, malicious, mean, spiteful, vindictive **3** _The weather turned nasty._
► unpleasant, rough, squally OPPOSITES ARE fine, pleasant

nation _NOUN_ **1** _The president will broadcast to the nation._ ► people, population, country, community, society **2** _the nations of the world_
► country, people, civilization, land, power, race, state RELATED ADJECTIVE ► ethnic

national _ADJECTIVE_ **1** _a national strike_
► nationwide, countrywide, general, widespread **2** _national costume_ ► ethnic, popular, domestic

national _NOUN_ _an Italian national_ ► citizen, subject, native, resident, inhabitant

nationalism _NOUN_ _the surge of nationalism in Europe_ ► patriotism, (_disapproving_) chauvinism,

(_disapproving_) jingoism, (_disapproving_) xenophobia

native _ADJECTIVE_ **1** _native inhabitants_ ► original, aboriginal, indigenous **2** _a native instinct for politics_ ► innate, inherent, inborn, inbred, natural, congenital, hereditary, inherited

native _NOUN_ _a native of New York_ ► inhabitant, resident, citizen, national

natter _VERB_ _They nattered on for hours._
► chatter, chat, prattle, blather, burble, talk

natural _ADJECTIVE_ **1** _a natural tendency to self-preservation_ ► innate, inborn, instinctive, intuitive, inherent **2** _Her manner is fresh and natural._ ► genuine, sincere, unaffected, uninhibited, ingenuous, open **3** _It was natural for them to want more information._
► understandable, reasonable, logical, unsurprising, predictable **4** _Kim proved to be a natural leader._ ► born, spontaneous, untaught **5** _The bay forms a natural port on this side of the island._ ► ready-made

nature _NOUN_ **1** _the beauties of nature_ ► the natural world, the living world, the

A
B
C
D
E
F
G
H
I
J
K
L
M
N
O
P
Q
R
S
T
U
V
W
X
Y
Z

loving nature. **3** a kind or sort of thing • *He likes things of that nature.*

naughty ADJECTIVE **naughtier, naughtiest 1** badly behaved or disobedient **2** slightly rude or indecent • *naughty pictures*
▷ **naughtily** ADVERB **naughtiness** NOUN

nausea (naw- zee- a) NOUN a feeling of sickness or disgust
▷ **nauseous** ADJECTIVE **nauseating** ADJECTIVE

nautical ADJECTIVE to do with ships or sailors

nautical mile NOUN **nautical miles** a measure of distance used at sea, equal to 2,025 yards (1852 kilometers)

naval ADJECTIVE to do with a navy [from Latin *navis* = ship]

navel NOUN **navels** the small hollow in the centre of the abdomen, where the umbilical cord was attached [from Old English]

navigate VERB **navigates, navigating, navigated 1** sail in or through a river or sea, etc. • *The ship navigated the Suez Canal.* **2** make sure that a ship, aircraft, or vehicle is going in the right direction
▷ **navigation** NOUN **navigator** NOUN

navy NOUN **navies 1** a country's warships and the people trained to use them **2** (also navy blue) a very dark blue, the color of naval uniform

Nazi (nah- tsee) NOUN **Nazis** a member of the National Socialist Party in Germany in Hitler's time, with fascist beliefs
▷ **Nazism** NOUN

NB ABBREVIATION take note that (Latin *nota bene* = note well)

NE ABBREVIATION **1** northeast **2** northeastern

near ADVERB, ADJECTIVE not far away
nearby not far away • *They live nearby.*

near PREPOSITION not far away from • *near the shops*

nearby ADJECTIVE near • *a nearby house*

nearly ADVERB almost • *We have nearly finished.*

neat ADJECTIVE **neater, neatest 1** simple and clean and tidy **2** skilful **3** undiluted • *neat whisky*
▷ **neatly** ADVERB **neatness** NOUN

neaten VERB **neatens, neatening, neatened** make or become neat

nebula NOUN **nebulae** a bright or dark patch in the sky, caused by a distant galaxy or a cloud of dust or gas

nebulous ADJECTIVE indistinct or vague • *nebulous ideas*

necessary ADJECTIVE not able to be done without; essential
▷ **necessarily** ADVERB

Thesaurus
---

environment, the countryside, the landscape **2** *It's not in his nature to make complaints.*
► character, personality, temperament, disposition, constitution, makeup **3** *decisions that by their nature cause resentment* ► essence, characteristics **4** *coins, medals, and things of that nature* ► kind, type, sort, category, description

naughty ADJECTIVE *a naughty child* ► badly behaved, mischievous, misbehaving, disobedient, insubordinate, troublesome, vexatious

nausea NOUN *He had a bad headache and a feeling of nausea.* ► sickness, queasiness, biliousness, retching, vomiting

nauseating ADJECTIVES *She disliked his nauseating self-importance.* ► sickening, disgusting, revolting, repulsive, repellent, loathsome, offensive

nautical ADJECTIVE *eating seafood in a nautical atmosphere* ► maritime, naval, marine, seafaring, seagoing

navy NOUN *an officer in the navy* ► fleet, armada, convoy, flotilla, naval force

near ADJECTIVE **1** *She is a near neighbor of ours.* ► nearby, close, adjacent, adjoining, next-door, bordering, connected, neighbouring OPPOSITES ARE distant, faraway **2** *A decision is near.* ► close, approaching, imminent, coming,

forthcoming, impending, (*more informal*) around the corner **3** *near relatives* ► close, dear, familiar, intimate AN OPPOSITE IS distant

nearby ADVERB *Her children all live nearby.*
► close by, not far away, at hand, within reach, in the vicinity

nearly ADVERB *The work is nearly finished.*
► almost, practically, virtually, about, more or less, as good as, just about, around

neat ADJECTIVE **1** *The room was neat and newly decorated.* ► tidy, orderly, trim, spick-and-span, spruce, immaculate OPPOSITES ARE untidy, messy **2** *hair tied in a neat bun at the back*
► compact, elegant, trim, well formed, simple OPPOSITES ARE clumsy, awkward **3** *neat writing*
► regular, precise, well formed, elegant **4** *a neat solution to the problem* ► clever, ingenious, adroit, deft, inventive, resourceful, slick AN OPPOSITE IS inept **5** *a glass of neat whisky*
► undiluted, straight, pure, unmixed, unadulterated AN OPPOSITE IS diluted

necessary ADJECTIVE *necessary repairs to the bridge* ► essential, indispensable, vital, unavoidable, requisite, needed, needful, obligatory, imperative, compulsory, mandatory AN OPPOSITE IS unnecessary

necessitate VERB *Measures as drastic as these would necessitate legislation.* ► require, involve, entail, demand, call for, mean, compel

necessity NOUN **necessities 1** need • *the necessity of buying food and clothing* **2** something necessary

neck NOUN **necks 1** the part of the body that joins the head to the shoulders **2** the part of a garment around the neck **3** a narrow part of something, especially of a bottle neck and neck almost exactly together in a race or contest

necklace NOUN **necklaces** an ornament worn round the neck

necktie NOUN **neckties** a strip of material worn passing under the collar of a shirt and knotted in front

need VERB **needs, needing, needed 1** be without something you should have; require • *We need two more chairs.* **2** (as an *auxiliary verb*) have to do something • *You need not answer.*

need NOUN **needs 1** something needed; a necessary thing **2** a situation where something is necessary • *There is no need to cry.* **3** great poverty or hardship
▷ **needful** ADJECTIVE **needless** ADJECTIVE

needle NOUN **needles 1** a very thin pointed piece of steel used in sewing **2** something long and thin and sharp • *a knitting needle* • *pine needles* **3** the pointer of a meter or compass

needlework NOUN sewing or embroidery

needy ADJECTIVE **needier, neediest** very poor; lacking things necessary for life
▷ **neediness** NOUN

negative ADJECTIVE **1** that says "no" • *a negative answer* **2** looking only at the bad aspects of a situation • *Don't be so negative.* **3** showing no sign of what is being tested for • *Her pregnancy test was negative.* **4** less than nought; minus **5** (in science) to do with the kind of electric charge carried by electrons
▷ **negatively** ADVERB
USAGE The opposite of sense 1 is **affirmative**, and of senses 2, 3, 4 **positive**.

negative NOUN **negatives 1** a negative statement **2** a photograph on film with the dark parts light and the light parts dark, from which a positive print (with the dark and light or colors correct) can be made

neglect VERB **neglects, neglecting, neglected 1** not look after or pay attention to a person or thing **2** not do something; forget • *He neglected to shut the door.*

neglect NOUN neglecting or being neglected
▷ **neglectful** ADJECTIVE

negligence NOUN lack of proper care or attention; carelessness
▷ **negligent** ADJECTIVE **negligently** ADVERB

Thesaurus

---

necessity NOUN **1** *A mobile phone is now regarded as a necessity by most people.*
► essential, requirement, prerequisite **2** *Necessity compelled thousands to emigrate.*
► need, poverty, hardship, destitution, penury, deprivation **3** *the necessity for caution*
► need, demand, indispensability (of)

need VERB **1** *The room needs redecorating.*
► require, want, be in need of, demand, call for **2** *We need more milk.* ► require, want, be short of, lack **3** *He needed her so much now.*
► yearn for, long for, pine for, crave, depend on, rely on **4** *Do we need to come?*
► have to, be obliged to, be required to, be compelled to, be under an obligation to

need NOUN **1** *There is no need to say anything.*
► necessity, obligation, call, requirement **2** *basic human needs like food and water*
► requirement, essential, necessity, want, prerequisite

needless ADJECTIVE *a lot of needless expense*
► unnecessary, unwanted, inessential, unneeded, gratuitous, superfluous, pointless

needy ADJECTIVE *day centers for the frail and needy* ► poor, deprived, destitute, impoverished, underprivileged, penniless

negate VERB *The decision negates years of hard work.* ► nullify, invalidate, undo, reverse, cancel, neutralize, abrogate, countermand

negative ADJECTIVE **1** *a negative response*
► dissenting, saying "no," rejecting, refusing OPPOSITES ARE affirmative, positive **2** *They have been criticized for their negative attitudes.*
► pessimistic, unenthusiastic, uncooperative, defeatist, dismissive, antipathetic AN OPPOSITE IS positive

neglect VERB **1** *He'd been neglecting his work for the past week.* ► pay no attention to, ignore, let slide, shirk, skip, disregard, overlook, forget, leave alone AN OPPOSITE IS concentrate on **2** *She neglected her son and had a succession of boyfriends.* ► fail to take care of, fail to look after, abandon, spurn, forsake AN OPPOSITE IS look after **3** *He was being neglected by all his friends.* ► ignore, disregard, abandon, rebuff, disdain, slight AN OPPOSITE IS appreciate

neglect NOUN *The building had suffered from years of neglect.* ► negligence, carelessness, dereliction of duty, inattention, indifference, slackness OPPOSITES ARE attention, care

neglected ADJECTIVE **1** *The back of the house overlooked a neglected garden.* ► untended, uncared for, derelict, dilapidated, run-down, ramshackle, overgrown

negligible ADJECTIVE *The difference in price is negligible.* ► tiny, trifling, trivial, insignificant, unimportant, inconsequential, imperceptible,

A
B
C
D
E
F
G
H
I
J
K
L
M
N
O
P
Q
R
S
T
U
V
W
X
Y
Z

negligible ADJECTIVE not big enough or important enough to be worth bothering about

negotiable ADJECTIVE able to be changed after being discussed • *The salary is negotiable.*

negotiate VERB negotiates, negotiating, negotiated **1** bargain or discuss with others in order to reach an agreement **2** arrange after discussion • *They negotiated a treaty.* **3** get over an obstacle or difficulty
▷ **negotiation** NOUN **negotiator** NOUN

neigh VERB neighs, neighing, neighed make the high-pitched cry of a horse
▷ **neigh** NOUN

neighbor NOUN neighbors a person who lives next door or near to another
▷ **neighboring** ADJECTIVE **neighborly** ADJECTIVE
[from Old English *neahgebur* = near dweller]

neighborhood NOUN neighborhoods **1** the surrounding district or area **2** a part of a town where people live • *a quiet neighborhood*

neither (ny- *ther*, nee- *ther*) ADJECTIVE, PRONOUN not either
USAGE Correct use is *Neither of them likes it. Neither he nor his children like it.* Use a singular verb (e.g., *likes*) unless one of its subjects is plural (e.g., *children*).

neither ADVERB, CONJUNCTION
neither ... nor not one thing and not the other • *She neither knew nor cared.*
USAGE Say *I don't know that either* (not "neither").

neolithic (nee- o- lith- ik) ADJECTIVE belonging to the later part of the Stone Age

neon NOUN a gas that glows when electricity passes through it, used in glass tubes to make illuminated signs

nephew NOUN nephews the son of a person's brother or sister

nerve NOUN nerves **1** any of the fibers in the body that carry messages to and from the brain, so that parts of the body can feel and move **2** courage; calmness in a dangerous situation • *Don't lose your nerve* **3** impudence • *You've got a nerve!*
get on someone's nerves irritate someone
nerves PLURAL NOUN nervousness

nerve VERB nerves, nerving, nerved give strength or courage to someone

nervous ADJECTIVE **1** easily upset or agitated; excitable **2** slightly afraid; timid **3** to do with the nerves • *a nervous illness*
▷ **nervously** ADVERB **nervousness** NOUN

nervous breakdown NOUN nervous breakdowns a state of severe depression and anxiety, so that the person cannot cope with life

nervous system NOUN nervous systems the system, consisting of the brain, spinal cord, and nerves, which sends electrical messages from one part of the body to another

-ness SUFFIX forming nouns from adjectives (e.g., *kindness, sadness*)

nest NOUN nests **1** a structure or place in which a bird lays its eggs and feeds its young **2** a place where some small creatures (e.g., mice or wasps) live **3** a set of similar things that fit inside each other • *a nest of tables*

Thesaurus

---

inconsiderable, minor, slight, small OPPOSITES ARE considerable, significant

negotiate VERB **1** *We would like to negotiate a better deal.* ► work out, hammer out, agree on, reach agreement on, settle, transact **2** *The other side refused to negotiate.* ► consult, confer, discuss terms, deal, talk, parley **3** *The road has several sharp bends to negotiate.* ► get round, clear, pass around, deal with, overcome

negotiation NOUN *The negotiations will begin in Rome next week.* ► discussion, consultation, bargaining, arbitration, mediation, conciliation, transaction, debate, diplomacy

neighborhood NOUN *a quiet neighborhood* ► district, area, locality, vicinity, region, place, community, environs, surroundings, zone

neighboring ADJECTIVE *The neighboring buildings have parking facilities.* ► nearby, adjacent, adjoining, nearest, closest, next-door, bordering, close OPPOSITES ARE distant, remote

neighborly ADJECTIVE *a neighborly offer of help* ► friendly, amiable, obliging, considerate, kind, helpful, genial, sociable, companionable

nerve NOUN **1** *The maneuver takes some nerve and a good sense of timing. He lost his nerve at the last moment and couldn't go through with it.* ► courage, bravery, boldness, daring, gallantry, determination, fearlessness, fortitude, heroism, (*more informal*) bottle, (*more informal*) grit, (*more informal*) guts, (*more informal*) pluck, (*much more informal*) spunk **2** *They had the nerve to ask for more money.* ► cheek, audacity, effrontery, temerity, impertinence, impudence, insolence, presumptuousness, shamelessness, (*more informal*) sauce **3** *the nerves in your body* RELATED ADJECTIVE ► neural

nervous ADJECTIVE **1** *a nervous girl who always wore black* ► high strung, nervy, anxious, excitable **2** *He was getting a little nervous out there, all by himself.* ► anxious, worried, apprehensive, agitated, concerned, (*more informal*) jumpy, (*more informal*) jittery

nest VERB nests, nesting, nested **1** have or make a nest **2** fit inside something

nest egg NOUN nest eggs a sum of money saved up for future use

nestle VERB nestles, nestling, nestled curl up comfortably

net NOUN nets **1** material made of pieces of thread, cord, or wire, etc., joined together in a crisscross pattern with holes between **2** something made of this
the Net the Internet

net VERB nets, netting, netted cover or catch with a net

net ADJECTIVE remaining when nothing more is to be deducted • *The net weight, without the box, is 100 grams.* COMPARE **gross**

net VERB nets, netting, netted obtain or produce as net profit

netball NOUN a game in which two teams try to throw a ball into a high net hanging from a ring

netting NOUN a piece of net

nettle NOUN nettles a wild plant with leaves that sting when they are touched

nettle VERB nettles, nettling, nettled annoy or provoke someone

network NOUN networks **1** a netlike arrangement or pattern of intersecting lines or parts • *the railway network* **2** an organization with many connecting parts that work together • *a spy network* **3** a group of radio or television stations which broadcast the same programs **4** a set of computers which are linked to each other

neuron NOUN neurons a cell that is part of the nervous system and sends impulses to and from the brain

neurotic (newr- ot- ik) ADJECTIVE always very worried about something

neuter ADJECTIVE **1** neither masculine nor feminine **2** (in some languages) belonging to the class of words which are neither masculine nor feminine, such as *Fenster* in German

neuter VERB neuters, neutering, neutered remove an animal's sex organs so that it cannot breed

neutral ADJECTIVE **1** not supporting either side in a war or quarrel **2** not very distinctive • *a neutral color such as gray* **3** neither acid nor alkaline
▷ **neutrally** ADVERB **neutrality** NOUN

neutral gear NOUN a gear that is not connected to the driving parts of an engine

neutron NOUN neutrons (in science) a particle of matter with no electric charge

never ADVERB **1** at no time; not ever **2** not at all

nevertheless ADVERB, CONJUNCTION in spite of this; although this is a fact

new ADJECTIVE not existing before; just made, invented, discovered, or received, etc.
▷ **newly** ADVERB **newness** NOUN

new ADVERB newly • *newborn;* • *new-laid*

newcomer NOUN newcomers a person who has arrived recently

newfangled ADJECTIVE disliked because it is new in method or style

newly ADVERB **1** recently **2** in a new way

new moon NOUN new moons the moon at the beginning of its cycle, when only a thin crescent can be seen

news NOUN **1** information about recent events or a broadcast report of this **2** a piece of new information • *That's news to me.*

Thesaurus

nestle VERB *The children nestled together in the back of the car.* ► huddle, cuddle, nuzzle, snuggle, curl up, lie comfortably

net NOUN *The gardener put nets on the trees to catch falling fruit.* ► mesh, netting, webbing, lattice

nettle VERB *remarks that began to nettle him* ► annoy, irritate, displease, anger, infuriate, enrage, exasperate, incense, vex, madden, aggravate, antagonize, inflame, make angry, (*more informal*) needle, (*more informal*) rile, (*more informal*) bug, (*more informal*) rub up the wrong way

network NOUN **1** *a network of tiny tubes* ► web, grid, mesh, net, netting, crisscross pattern, labyrinth, lattice, maze, tracery **2** *a computer network; the rail network* ► system, complex, organization

neutral ADJECTIVE **1** *He would be the perfect neutral umpire.* ► impartial, unbiased, objective, disinterested, unprejudiced, even-handed OPPOSITES ARE biased, prejudiced **2** *neutral colors* ► dull, indefinite, indeterminate, intermediate, characterless, colorless, middle AN OPPOSITE IS distinctive

new ADJECTIVE **1** *new ways of beating crime* ► modern, recent, up-to-date, advanced **2** *We need some new ideas.* ► fresh, original, innovative, novel, creative, different **3** *The school has had some new labs built.* ► additional, extra, more, further, supplementary, fresh **4** *After the operation I felt a new person.* ► changed, improved, restored, revived, invigorated

news NOUN *The news of his death stunned his colleagues.* ► report, announcement, story, account, tidings, information (about), disclosure (about), statement, revelation

A
B
C
D
E
F
G
H
I
J
K
L
M
N
O
P
Q
R
S
T
U
V
W
X
Y
Z

newsagent NOUN newsagents a shopkeeper who sells newspapers

newspaper NOUN newspapers **1** a daily or weekly publication on large sheets of paper, containing news reports, articles, etc. **2** the sheets of paper forming a newspaper • *Wrap it in newspaper.*

newt NOUN newts a small animal similar to a lizard, that lives near or in water [from Old English: originally *an ewt*]

newton NOUN newtons a unit for measuring force

New Year's Day NOUN January 1

next ADJECTIVE nearest; coming immediately after • *on the next day*

next ADVERB **1** in the next place **2** on the next occasion • *What happens next?*

next door ADVERB, ADJECTIVE in the next house or room

nib NOUN nibs the pointed metal part of a pen

nibble VERB nibbles, nibbling, nibbled take small, quick, or gentle bites

nice ADJECTIVE nicer, nicest **1** pleasant or kind **2** precise or careful • *Dictionaries make nice distinctions between meanings of words.*
▷ **nicely** ADVERB **niceness** NOUN

nick NOUN nicks **1** a small cut or notch **in good nick** (*informal*) in good condition **in the nick of time** only just in time

nickel NOUN nickels **1** a silvery-white metal **2** a 5-cent coin

nickname NOUN nicknames a name given to a person instead of his or her real name

nicotine NOUN a poisonous substance found in tobacco [from the name of J. Nicot, who introduced tobacco into France in 1560]

niece NOUN nieces the daughter of a person's brother or sister

niggardly ADJECTIVE mean or stingy
▷ **niggardliness** NOUN

night NOUN nights **1** the dark hours between sunset and sunrise **2** a particular night or evening • *the first night of the play*

nightclub NOUN nightclubs a place that is open at night where people go to drink and dance

nightgown NOUN nightgowns a loose dress that girls or women wear in bed

nightingale NOUN nightingales a small brown bird that sings sweetly

nightmare NOUN nightmares **1** a frightening dream **2** an unpleasant experience • *The journey was a nightmare.*
▷ **nightmarish** ADJECTIVE
[from night + Middle English *mare* = an evil spirit thought to lie on people asleep and suffocate them]

nil NOUN nothing or nought

nimble ADJECTIVE able to move quickly; agile
▷ **nimbly** ADVERB

nine ADJECTIVE, NOUN nines the number 9
▷ **ninth** ADJECTIVE, NOUN

nineteen NOUN, ADJECTIVE the number 19
▷ **nineteenth** ADJECTIVE, NOUN

ninety ADJECTIVE, NOUN nineties the number 90
▷ **ninetieth** ADJECTIVE, NOUN

nip VERB nips, nipping, nipped **1** pinch or bite quickly **2** (*informal*) go quickly

nip NOUN nips **1** a quick pinch or bite **2** sharp coldness • *There's a nip in the air.* **3** a small drink of a spirit • *a nip of brandy*

nippers PLURAL NOUN pincers

Thesaurus

next ADJECTIVE **1** *Her friend lived in the next street.*
▸ adjacent, neighboring, adjoining, connecting, closest, nearest AN OPPOSITE IS distant **2** *The next train is not for another hour.*
▸ following, soonest, succeeding, subsequent AN OPPOSITE IS previous

nibble VERB *She nibbled her sandwich while she waited.* ▸ munch, pick at, gnaw, eat

nice ADJECTIVE **1** *We had a nice time in Greece.*
▸ pleasant, agreeable, enjoyable, marvelous, wonderful, delightful, splendid **2** *They are such nice people.* ▸ pleasant, likable, agreeable, personable, friendly, congenial, genial

nick VERB **1** *He had nicked his skin while shaving.*
▸ cut **2** (*informal*) *Someone nicked my pen.*
▸ steal, take, (*informal*) pinch

nick NOUN **1** *a nick in the wood* ▸ cut, notch, chip, groove, scar **2** (*informal*) *The car is in good nick.* ▸ condition, shape, repair, order, trim, fettle

nickname NOUN *Her nickname is "Posh."* ▸ pet name, sobriquet, tag, alias

night NOUN *It had rained in the night.* ▸ night-time, dark RELATED ADJECTIVE ▸ nocturnal

nightmare NOUN **1** *After the accident he had a series of nightmares.* ▸ bad dream **2** *Getting the tire fixed had been a nightmare.* ▸ ordeal, trial, torment

nimble ADJECTIVE *He was surprisingly light and nimble on his feet.* ▸ agile, lithe, lively, sprightly, deft, quick, graceful, (*informal*) nippy

nip VERB **1** *The dog nipped her leg.* ▸ bite, peck, snap at, pinch, tweak **2** (*informal*) *I'll nip around and see how he's getting on.* ▸ go, dash, drop, (*informal*) pop

nippy ADJECTIVE **1** (*informal*) *She drives a nippy two-seater.* ▸ speedy, fast, nimble, quick, rapid **2** (*informal*) *The weather's quite nippy for June.*
▸ chilly, cold, raw

nipple *NOUN* nipples the small part that sticks out at the front of a person's breast, from which (on mothers) babies suck milk

nirvana *NOUN* (in Buddhism and Hinduism) the highest state of knowledge and understanding, achieved by meditation [from Sanskrit]

nit *NOUN* nits a parasitic insect or its egg, found in people's hair

nit-picking *NOUN* pointing out very small faults

nitrate *NOUN* nitrates **1** a chemical compound containing nitrogen **2** potassium or sodium nitrate, used as a fertilizer

nitrogen (ny- tro- jen) *NOUN* a gas that makes up about four-fifths of the air

no *ADJECTIVE* not any ● *We have no money.*

no *ADVERB* **1** used to deny or refuse something ● *Will you come? No.* **2** not at all ● *She is no better.*

No. or **no.** *ABBREVIATION* Nos. or nos. number

noble *ADJECTIVE* nobler, noblest **1** of high social rank; aristocratic **2** having a very good character or qualities ● *a noble king* **3** stately or impressive ● *a noble building*
▷ **nobly** *ADVERB* **nobility** *NOUN*

noble *NOUN* nobles a person of high social rank
▷ **nobleman** *NOUN* **noblewoman** *NOUN*

nobody *PRONOUN* no person; no one

nobody *NOUN* nobodies (informal) an unimportant or unimpressive person; a nonentity

nocturnal *ADJECTIVE* **1** happening at night **2** active at night ● *Badgers are nocturnal animals.*

nod *VERB* nods, nodding, nodded **1** move the head up and down, especially as a way of agreeing with somebody or as a greeting **2** be drowsy
▷ **nod** *NOUN*

noise *NOUN* noises a sound, especially one that is loud or unpleasant
▷ **noisy** *ADJECTIVE* **noisily** *ADVERB* **noiseless** *ADJECTIVE*

nomad *NOUN* nomads a member of a tribe that moves from place to place looking for pasture for their animals
▷ **nomadic** *ADJECTIVE*

no man's land *NOUN* an area that does not belong to anybody, especially the land between opposing armies

nominate *VERB* nominates, nominating, nominated propose someone as a candidate in an election or to be appointed to a post
▷ **nomination** *NOUN* **nominator** *NOUN*

non- *PREFIX* not

noncommissioned officer *NOUN* noncommissioned officers a member of the armed forces, such as a corporal or sergeant, who has not been commissioned as an officer but has been promoted from the ranks of ordinary soldiers

Thesaurus

nobility *NOUN* **1** *actions that showed true nobility* ► honor, dignity, nobleness, uprightness, virtue, worthiness, greatness, integrity, magnanimity, morality **2** *The king had the support of the nobility.* ► aristocracy, gentry, nobles, lords, peerage

noble *ADJECTIVE* **1** *He came from a noble family.* ► aristocratic, high-born, patrician, princely, (informal) blue-blooded AN OPPOSITE IS humble **2** *a noble deed* ► honorable, virtuous, worthy, brave, chivalrous, courageous, gallant, glorious, heroic, magnanimous AN OPPOSITE IS ignoble **3** *a noble building* ► imposing, impressive, magnificent, elegant, grand, majestic, splendid, stately, dignified, distinguished, great AN OPPOSITE IS unimpressive

noble *NOUN* *War was the principal activity of many of the nobles in Edward's reign.* ► aristocrat, nobleman, noblewoman, lord, peer, grandee, lady, peers

nod *VERB* **1** *She nodded to him to go in.* ► signal, gesture, indicate, sign **2** *He nodded his head in agreement.* ► incline, bob, dip, lower

nod off *She nodded off and started to snore.* ► fall asleep, go to sleep, doze off, drop off

nod *NOUN* *He gave us a discreet nod.* ► signal, gesture, cue

noise *NOUN* *The noise from below battered her eardrums.* ► sound, din, clamor, racket, uproar, tumult, commotion, crash, clatter, clash, (more informal) hullabaloo AN OPPOSITE IS silence

noisy *ADJECTIVE* **1** *He loved this noisy, busy city.* ► loud, clamorous, rackety, tumultuous, turbulent, deafening **2** *The plane completed its noisy take-off.* ► loud, deafening, ear-splitting, thunderous **3** *They were disturbed by the noisy argument going on in the next room.* ► loud, vociferous, raucous, rowdy, strident, shouting, shrieking

nonchalant *ADJECTIVE* *Kate leaned back, trying to look nonchalant.* ► unconcerned, detached, relaxed, indifferent, dispassionate, unemotional, unruffled, blasé, calm, casual, cool, (more informal) laid-back AN OPPOSITE IS anxious

A
B
C
D
E
F
G
H
I
J
K
L
M
N
O
P
Q
R
S
T
U
V
W
X
Y
Z

noncommittal ADJECTIVE not committing yourself; not showing what you think

nondescript ADJECTIVE having no special or distinctive qualities and therefore difficult to describe

none PRONOUN **1** not any **2** no one • *None can tell.*

USAGE It is better to use a singular verb (e.g., *None of them is here*), but the plural is not incorrect (e.g., *None of them are here*).

nonentity (non- en- tit- ee) NOUN nonentities an unimportant person

nonexistent ADJECTIVE not existing or unreal

nonfiction NOUN writings that are not fiction; books about real people and things and true events

nonflammable ADJECTIVE not able to be set on fire

USAGE See note at **inflammable**.

nonplussed ADJECTIVE puzzled or confused

nonsense NOUN **1** words put together in a way that does not mean anything **2** stupid ideas or behaviour

▷ **nonsensical** (non- sens- ik- al) ADJECTIVE

nonstop ADJECTIVE, ADVERB **1** not stopping • *They talked nonstop for hours.* **2** not stopping between two main stations • *a nonstop train*

noodles PLURAL NOUN pasta made in narrow strips, used in soups, etc. [from German *Nudel*]

nook NOUN nooks a sheltered corner; a recess

noon NOUN twelve o'clock midday

no one NOUN no person; nobody

noose NOUN nooses a loop in a rope that gets smaller when the rope is pulled

nor CONJUNCTION and not • *She cannot do it; nor can I.*

normal ADJECTIVE **1** usual or ordinary **2** natural and healthy; without a physical or mental illness

▷ **normally** ADVERB **normality** NOUN

Norman NOUN Normans a member of the people of Normandy in northern France, who conquered England in 1066

▷ **Norman** ADJECTIVE

north NOUN **1** the direction to the left of a person who faces east **2** the northern part of a country, city, etc.

north ADJECTIVE, ADVERB toward or in the north

▷ **northerly** ADJECTIVE **northern** ADJECTIVE **northerner** NOUN **northernmost** ADJECTIVE

northeast NOUN, ADJECTIVE, & ADVERB midway between north and east

▷ **northeasterly** ADJECTIVE **northeastern** ADJECTIVE

northward ADJECTIVE, ADVERB toward the north

▷ **northward** ADVERB

Thesaurus

noncommittal ADJECTIVE *He held up a hand in a noncommittal gesture.* ▶ guarded, cautious, wary, discreet, (more informal) cagey

nondescript ADJECTIVE *The town was a nondescript, cheerless place.* ▶ ordinary, undistinguished, commonplace, average, dull, uninspiring OPPOSITES ARE distinctive, remarkable

nonexistent ADJECTIVE *The danger was non-existent.* ▶ imaginary, fictitious, mythical, supposed, unreal, hypothetical, imagined, legendary, made-up AN OPPOSITE IS existing

nonplussed ADJECTIVE *The confusion left us feeling nonplussed.* ▶ surprised, disconcerted, astonished, astounded, bewildered, stunned, flummoxed, stupefied, perplexed, (more informal) thunderstruck

nonsense NOUN **1** *They're talking nonsense.* ▶ rubbish, balderdash, gibberish, claptrap, drivel, gobbledegook, (more informal) rot, (more informal) twaddle **2** *The idea was a complete nonsense.* ▶ absurdity, folly, mistake, inanity

nonsensical ADJECTIVE *The suggestion was nonsensical and shouldn't be taken seriously.* ▶ absurd, ludicrous, meaningless, ridiculous, senseless, unreasonable, incomprehensible, foolish, crazy, laughable, silly, stupid, fatuous, inane, illogical, irrational AN OPPOSITE IS sensible

nonstop ADJECTIVE **1** *nonstop fun and laughter* ▶ continuous, constant, endless, uninterrupted, unending, never-ending, ceaseless

nonstop ADVERB **1** *We worked nonstop to get the job finished.* ▶ continuously, all the time, unceasingly, incessantly, steadily, round the clock

norm NOUN *Society imposes its own norms of behavior.* ▶ standard, principle, yardstick, benchmark, pattern, basis, guide (to)

normal ADJECTIVE **1** *They seem like a perfectly normal couple.* ▶ ordinary, average, typical, run-of-the-mill, standard, conventional, everyday **2** *During the holidays you can borrow books in the normal way.* ▶ usual, customary, standard, regular, routine, habitual, established

normality NOUN *The household returned to something like normality.* ▶ routine, regularity, typicality, usualness

normally ADVERB **1** *Reminders are normally sent out at the beginning of the month.* ▶ usually, ordinarily, customarily, typically AN OPPOSITE IS exceptionally **2** *They just wanted to be able to live normally again.* ▶ as normal, in the normal way

northwest NOUN, ADJECTIVE, & ADVERB midway between north and west
▷ **northwesterly** ADJECTIVE **northwestern** ADJECTIVE

Nos. or **nos.** plural of No. or no.

nose NOUN **noses** 1 the part of the face that is used for breathing and for smelling things 2 the front end or part

nosedive NOUN **nosedives** a steep downward dive, especially of an aircraft
▷ **nosedive** VERB

nostalgia (nos- tal- ja) NOUN sentimental remembering or longing for the past
▷ **nostalgic** ADJECTIVE **nostalgically** ADVERB

nostril NOUN **nostrils** either of the two openings in the nose

nosy ADJECTIVE **nosier, nosiest** inquisitive
▷ **nosily** ADVERB **nosiness** NOUN

not ADVERB used to change the meaning of something to its opposite or absence

notation NOUN **notations** a system of symbols representing numbers, quantities, musical notes, etc.

notch NOUN **notches** a small V-shape cut into a surface

note NOUN **notes** 1 something written down as a reminder or as a comment or explanation 2 a short letter 3 a banknote 4 a single sound in music 5 any of the black or white keys on a piano, etc. (see key 3) 6 a sound or quality that indicates something ● *a note of warning* 7 notice or attention ● *Take note*

note VERB **notes, noting, noted** 1 make a note about something; write down 2 notice or pay attention to ● *Note what we say.*

notebook NOUN **notebooks** a book with blank pages on which to write notes

notepaper NOUN paper for writing letters

nothing NOUN 1 no thing; not anything 2 no amount; nought
for nothing 1 without payment, free 2 without a result

notice NOUN **notices** 1 something written or printed and displayed for people to see 2 attention ● *It escaped my notice.* 3 warning that something is going to happen 4 formal information that you are about to end an agreement or a person's employment, etc. ● *We gave him a month's notice.*

notice VERB **notices, noticing, noticed** see or become aware of something

noticeable ADJECTIVE easily seen or noticed
▷ **noticeably** ADVERB

Thesaurus

nose NOUN 1 *He stood scratching the side of his nose.* ► nostrils, (*technical*) proboscis, snout RELATED ADJECTIVE ► nasal 2 *The nose of a boat appeared at the harbor entrance.* ► prow, bow, front

nose VERB *He nosed the car into a gap in the traffic.* ► ease, inch, edge, move, maneuver

nosy ADJECTIVE *He always wanted to help, but sometimes he seemed too nosy for his own good.* ► inquisitive, prying, intrusive, curious, (*more informal*) snoopy

notable ADJECTIVE 1 *Musicians (with some notable exceptions) are highly practical people.* ► significant, noteworthy, remarkable, important, memorable AN OPPOSITE IS insignificant 2 *a notable American statesman* ► prominent, famous, distinguished, noted, eminent, illustrious OPPOSITES ARE obscure, unknown

note NOUN 1 *Leave me a note before you go.* ► message, communication, letter, memo, line 2 *I'll make a note of her new address.* ► record, entry, reminder 3 *Someone had written notes in the margin.* ► comment, annotation, gloss, remark 4 *a writer of some note* ► importance, distinction, renown, eminence, acclaim

note VERB 1 *Note what the new cafeteria built since our last visit.* ► observe, notice, see, remark 2 *I'll be happy to note your suggestion.* ► consider, heed, bear in mind, make a note

of, take into account 3 *Note the dates in your diary.* ► write down, jot down, enter, record, scribble

notebook NOUN *She wrote the details in a notebook.* ► exercise book, jotter, writing book, diary

noted ADJECTIVE *a noted local celebrity* ► famous, well-known, renowned, notable OPPOSITES ARE obscure, unknown

noteworthy ADJECTIVE *a noteworthy addition to his collection* ► important, significant, notable, remarkable, striking OPPOSITES ARE insignificant, unimportant

notice NOUN 1 *There was a notice pinned on the classroom door.* ► announcement, message, note, information sheet, poster, sticker, sign, placard, warning 2 *Nothing escaped her notice that day.* ► attention, observation, awareness, perception, heed
take no notice of *Take no notice of the shouting.* ► ignore, disregard, pay no attention to, pass over

notice VERB 1 *Did you notice the window was open?* ► observe, perceive, see, spot 2 *I noticed a smell of gas in the kitchen.* ► detect, perceive, note

noticeable ADJECTIVE *a noticeable reduction in the cost* ► perceptible, appreciable, observable, conspicuous, recognizable, distinct, marked, significant, unmistakable AN OPPOSITE IS imperceptible

a
b
c
d
e
f
g
h
i
j
k
l
m
n
o
p
q
r
s
t
u
v
w
x
y
z

A B C D E F G H I J K L M **N** O P Q R S T U V W X Y Z

notion NOUN notions an idea, especially one that is vague or incorrect

notorious ADJECTIVE well-known for something bad
▷ **notoriously** ADVERB **notoriety** (noh- ter- I- it-ee) NOUN

notwithstanding PREPOSITION in spite of

nought (nawt) NOUN **1** the figure 0 **2** nothing

noun NOUN nouns a word that stands for a person, place, or thing. *Common nouns* are words such as *boy, dog, river, sport, table,* which are used of a whole kind of people or things; *proper nouns* are words such as *Charles, Mississippi,* and *Boston* which name a particular person or thing.

nourish VERB nourishes, nourishing, nourished keep a person, animal, or plant alive and well by means of food
▷ **nourishing** ADJECTIVE **nourishment** NOUN

novel NOUN novels a story that fills a whole book

novel ADJECTIVE of a new and unusual kind • *a novel experience* [from Latin *novus* = new]

novelist NOUN novelists a person who writes novels

novelty NOUN novelties **1** newness and originality **2** something new and unusual **3** a cheap toy or ornament

November NOUN the eleventh month of the year [from Latin *novem* = nine, because it was the ninth month of the ancient Roman calendar]

novice NOUN novices **1** a beginner **2** a person preparing to be a monk or nun

now ADVERB **1** at this time **2** by this time **3** immediately • *You must go now.* **4** I wonder, or I am telling you • *Now why didn't I think of that?*
now and again or **now and then** sometimes; occasionally

now CONJUNCTION as a result of or at the same time as something • *Now that you have come, we'll start.*

now NOUN this moment • *They will be at home by now.*

nowadays ADVERB at the present time, as contrasted with years ago

nowhere ADVERB not anywhere

nowhere NOUN no place • *Nowhere is as beautiful as the Rocky Mountains.*

nozzle NOUN nozzles the spout of a hose, pipe, or tube

nuclear ADJECTIVE **1** to do with a nucleus, especially of an atom **2** using the energy that is created by reactions in the nuclei of atoms • *nuclear power* • *nuclear weapons*

nucleus NOUN nuclei **1** the part in the center of something, around which other things are grouped **2** the central part of an atom or of a seed or a biological cell

nude ADJECTIVE not wearing any clothes; naked
▷ **nudity** NOUN

Thesaurus

notify VERB *Parents will be notified of any changes.* ► inform, advise, tell, apprise, let somebody know

notion NOUN **1** *Paul was a dreamer, his head full of wild notions.* ► idea, belief, concept, thought, image, perception, opinion **2** *He had no notion of what her words meant.*
► understanding, idea, knowledge, clue

notional ADJECTIVE *the notional line along the horizon* ► theoretical, hypothetical, conjectural, putative, imaginary

nought NOUN **1** *Her card number has a lot of noughts in it.* ► zero, nil, O **2** *One of the contestants scored a resounding nought.* ► nil, zero, nothing, (more informal) zilch

nourish VERB *They had just enough money to nourish their children.* ► feed, provide for, support, sustain, maintain

nourishing ADJECTIVE *a nourishing diet* ► nutritious, wholesome, sustaining, healthy, nutritive, beneficial, health-giving

nourishment NOUN *the nourishment that elderly people require* ► sustenance, nutriment, nutrition, diet, food, subsistence, goodness

novel ADJECTIVE *a novel idea for its time* ► new, original, innovative, unconventional, unfamiliar, unusual, fresh, imaginative, different, singular, surprising, uncommon
OPPOSITES ARE familiar, common, hackneyed

novelty NOUN **1** *the beauty and novelty of the poetry* ► freshness, originality, unfamiliarity, unconventionality, imaginativeness, newness **2** *a little shop selling sweets and novelties*
► knick-knack, trinket, souvenir, bauble, curiosity, gimmick

now ADVERB **1** *You need to decide now.*
► immediately, straight away, here and now, on the spot, without delay **2** *The box office is closed now.* ► at present, at the moment, at the minute, currently

nub NOUN *Money is the nub of the problem.*
► crux, essence, central point, core, gist

nucleus NOUN *These three chapters form the nucleus of the description.* ► heart, core, center, kernel

nude ADJECTIVE *Nude bathing is forbidden.*
► naked, unclothed, undressed, uncovered, bare

nudge VERB nudges, nudging, nudged **1** poke a person gently with your elbow **2** push slightly or gradually
▷ **nudge** NOUN

nugget NOUN nuggets **1** a rough lump of gold or platinum found in the earth **2** a small but useful fact

nuisance NOUN nuisances an annoying person or thing

numb ADJECTIVE unable to feel or move
▷ **numbly** ADVERB **numbness** NOUN

number NOUN numbers **1** a symbol or word indicating how many; a numeral or figure **2** a numeral given to a thing to identify it • *a telephone number* **3** a quantity of people or things • *the number of people present* **4** one issue of a magazine or newspaper **5** a song or piece of music
USAGE Note that *a number of*, meaning "several," should be followed by a plural verb: *A number of problems remain.*

number VERB numbers, numbering, numbered **1** mark with numbers **2** count **3** amount to • *The crowd numbered 10,000.*

numeral NOUN numerals a symbol that represents a certain number; a figure

numerate (new- mer- at) ADJECTIVE having a good basic knowledge of mathematics
▷ **numeracy** NOUN

numerator NOUN numerators the number above the line in a fraction, showing how many parts are to be taken, e.g., 2 in $\frac{2}{3}$
COMPARE **denominator**

numerical (new- merri- kal) ADJECTIVE to do with or consisting of numbers • *in numerical order*
▷ **numerically** ADVERB

numerous ADJECTIVE many

nun NOUN nuns a member of a community of women who live according to the rules of a religious organization COMPARE **monk**

nunnery NOUN nunneries a convent

nurse NOUN nurses **1** a person trained to look after people who are ill or injured **2** (*old use*) a woman employed to look after young children

nurse VERB nurses, nursing, nursed **1** look after someone who is ill or injured **2** feed a baby at the breast **3** have a feeling for a long time • *She's been nursing a grudge against him for years.* **4** hold carefully

nursemaid NOUN nursemaids (*old use*) a young woman employed to look after young children

nursery NOUN nurseries **1** a place where young children are looked after or play **2** a place where young plants are grown and are usually for sale

nursery rhyme NOUN nursery rhymes a simple rhyme or song of the kind that young children like

nursery school NOUN nursery schools a school for children below primary school age

nursing home NOUN nursing homes a small hospital or home for invalids

nut NOUN nuts **1** a fruit with a hard shell **2** a kernel **3** a small piece of metal with a hole in the middle, for screwing onto a bolt **4** (*slang*) the head **5** (*slang*) a mad or eccentric person
▷ **nutty** ADJECTIVE

Thesaurus

nudge VERB *Every time he laughed she nudged him in his side.* ► poke, prod, shove, jog, jolt, bump, hit , touch

nuisance NOUN **1** *What a nuisance for you, having to go back into the hospital.*
► inconvenience, annoyance, bother, bore, trial, irritant, irritation, worry, pest, vexation, trouble, (*more informal*) pain **2** *I'm sorry if I'm being a nuisance.* ► pest, bother, trial, burden

numb ADJECTIVE *My hands were numb with cold.*
► dead, frozen, numbed, benumbed, insensitive, unfeeling AN OPPOSITE IS sensitive

numb VERB *Sheer terror had numbed her senses.*
► deaden, paralyze, desensitize, freeze, immobilize, make numb, anaesthetize

number NOUN **1** *The paper had a line of numbers written on it.* ► figure, numeral, integer, digit, unit RELATED ADJECTIVE ► numerical **2** *a large number of children* ► quantity, amount, collection, sum, total, crowd, multitude,

aggregate **3** *The film included a few musical numbers.* ► item, piece, song **4** *the spring number of the magazine* ► issue, edition, publication, impression, printing

number VERB *Visitors to the city this year numbered over ten million.* ► total, add up to, amount to, come to

numeral NOUN *Items over a hundred are written in numerals.* ► figure, digit, integer, number

numerous ADJECTIVE *Numerous reasons have been given to justify the invasion.* ► many, several, a lot of, plenty of, copious, abundant, profuse, multitudinous, diverse, sundry AN OPPOSITE IS few

nurse VERB **1** *She nursed her old father for years.* ► look after, care for, take care of, tend, treat **2** *A woman was nursing a baby.* ► breastfeed, feed, suckle **3** *hopes that have to be nursed until they become reality* ► preserve, sustain, support,

a b c d e f g h i j k l m **n** o p q r s t u v w x y z

A
B
C
D
E
F
G
H
I
J
K
L
M
N
O
P
Q
R
S
T
U
V
W
X
Y
Z

nutcrackers *PLURAL NOUN* pincers for cracking nuts

nutrition (new- trish- on) *NOUN*
1 nourishment **2** the study of what nourishes people
▷ **nutritional** *ADJECTIVE* **nutritionally** *ADVERB*

nutritious (new- trish- us) *ADJECTIVE*
nourishing; giving good nourishment
▷ **nutritiousness** *NOUN*

nutshell *NOUN* **nutshells** the shell of a nut
in a nutshell stated very briefly

nuzzle *VERB* **nuzzles, nuzzling, nuzzled** rub gently with the nose

NW *ABBREVIATION* **1** northwest **2** northwestern

nylon *NOUN* a synthetic, strong, lightweight cloth or fibre

NZ *ABBREVIATION* New Zealand

Thesaurus

cherish, maintain, encourage **4** *They went on nursing their grievance all their lives.* ► harbor, foster, bear

nutritious *ADJECTIVE* *nutritious food*
► nourishing, wholesome, sustaining, healthy, nutritive, beneficial, health-giving

Oo

O *INTERJECTION* oh

oaf *NOUN* oafs a stupid lout

oak *NOUN* oaks a large deciduous tree with seeds called acorns
▷ **oaken** *ADJECTIVE*

oar *NOUN* oars a pole with a flat blade at one end, used for rowing a boat
▷ **oarsman** *NOUN* **oarsmanship** *NOUN*

oasis (oh-**ay**-sis) *NOUN* oases a fertile place in a desert, with a spring or well of water

oath *NOUN* oaths **1** a solemn promise to do something or that something is true, sometimes appealing to God as witness **2** a swear word
on *or* **under oath** having sworn to tell the truth in a court of law

oats *PLURAL NOUN* a cereal used to make food (*oats* for horses, *oatmeal* for people)

obedient *ADJECTIVE* doing what you are told; willing to obey
▷ **obediently** *ADVERB* **obedience** *NOUN*

obey *VERB* obeys, obeying, obeyed do what you are told to do by a person, law, etc.

obituary *NOUN* obituaries an announcement in a newspaper of a person's death, often with a short account of his or her life

object (ob-jikt) *NOUN* objects **1** something that can be seen or touched **2** a purpose or intention **3** a person or thing to which some action or feeling is directed • *She has become an object of pity.* **4** (in grammar) the word or words naming who or what is acted upon by a verb or by a preposition, e.g., *him* in *the dog bit him* and *against him*

object (ob-**jekt**) *VERB* objects, objecting, objected say that you are not in favor of something or do not agree; protest
▷ **objector** *NOUN*

objection *NOUN* objections **1** objecting to something **2** a reason for objecting

objectionable *ADJECTIVE* unpleasant or nasty
▷ **objectionably** *ADVERB*

objective *NOUN* objectives what you are trying to reach or do; an aim

objective *ADJECTIVE* **1** real or actual • *Is there any objective evidence to prove his claims?* **2** not influenced by personal feelings or opinions • *an objective account of the quarrel* COMPARE subjective
▷ **objectively** *ADVERB* **objectivity** *NOUN*

obligation *NOUN* obligations **1** being obliged to do something **2** what you are obliged to do; a duty

Thesaurus

oaf *NOUN* She called him a loud-mouthed oaf.
► lout, fool, dolt, ass, idiot, clod, clot

oath *NOUN* **1** The nobles refused to take the oath of allegiance to the king. ► vow, pledge, promise, affirmation, avowal **2** He uttered a terrible oath.
► swear word, profanity, expletive, imprecation, curse, obscenity

obedient *ADJECTIVE* She was described as a good girl, always obedient. ► dutiful, compliant, deferential, respectful, well-behaved, subservient, submissive, acquiescent, amenable, biddable, tractable AN OPPOSITE IS disobedient

obese *ADJECTIVE* The proportion of obese men has risen to 8 percent. ► fat, overweight, outsize, corpulent, rotund

obey *VERB* **1** I obeyed him without question. ► do what someone says, take orders from, submit to, defer to **2** He was not too good at obeying orders. ► follow, carry out, perform, discharge, execute **3** Her legs wouldn't obey her brain's command to move. ► respond to, respect, abide by

object *NOUN* **1** It's an object I found on the beach.
► article, body, item, thing **2** Research is published regularly with the object of providing the most up-to-date findings. ► objective, purpose, intention, aim, point, target, end, goal, intent

object *VERB* **1** I'll open a window if you don't object. ► mind, protest, demur **2** object to I hope they don't object to us coming. ► oppose, protest against, be against, disapprove of, take exception to

objection *NOUN* The project went ahead despite many objections. ► protest, protestation, challenge, complaint, exception, dissent, disapproval, opposition, remonstration

objectionable *ADJECTIVE* He can be objectionable when he wants to be.There was an objectionable smell in the room. ► unpleasant, offensive, disagreeable, obnoxious, intolerable, unacceptable, nasty, repellent, distasteful

objective *ADJECTIVE* **1** The case lacks objective evidence. ► impartial, unbiased, disinterested, neutral, detached, dispassionate AN OPPOSITE IS subjective **2** a research program based on objective investigation ► factual, scientific, rational

objective *NOUN* The main objective is to build a strong business. ► object, purpose, intention, aim, point, target, end, goal, intent

obligation *NOUN* She believed she had an obligation to help. ► responsibility, duty, liability, commitment, requirement, need

a
b
c
d
e
f
g
h
i
j
k
l
m
n
o
p
q
r
s
t
u
v
w
x
y
z

under an obligation owing gratitude to someone who has helped you

obligatory (ob- lig- a- ter- ee) ADJECTIVE compulsory, not optional

oblige VERB obliges, obliging, obliged **1** force or compel **2** help and please someone • *Can you oblige me with a loan?*
be obliged to someone feel gratitude to a person who has helped you

obliging ADJECTIVE polite and helpful

oblique (ob- leek) ADJECTIVE **1** slanting **2** not saying something straightforwardly • *an oblique reply*
▷ **obliquely** ADVERB

obliterate VERB obliterates, obliterating, obliterated blot out; destroy and remove all traces of something
▷ **obliteration** NOUN

oblong ADJECTIVE rectangular in shape and longer than it is wide
▷ **oblong** NOUN

obnoxious ADJECTIVE very unpleasant; objectionable

oboe NOUN oboes a high-pitched woodwind instrument
▷ **oboist** NOUN

obscene (ob- seen) ADJECTIVE indecent in a very offensive way
▷ **obscenely** ADVERB **obscenity** NOUN

obscure ADJECTIVE **1** difficult to see or to understand; not clear **2** not well-known
▷ **obscurely** ADVERB **obscurity** NOUN

obscure VERB obscures, obscuring, obscured make a thing obscure; darken or conceal
• *Clouds obscured the sun.*

observant ADJECTIVE quick at observing or noticing things
▷ **observantly** ADVERB

observation NOUN observations **1** observing or watching **2** a comment or remark

observatory NOUN observatories a building with telescopes, etc., for observing the stars or weather

observe VERB observes, observing, observed **1** see and notice; watch carefully **2** obey a law **3** keep or celebrate a custom or religious festival etc. **4** make a remark
▷ **observer** NOUN

obsolescent ADJECTIVE becoming obsolete; going out of use or fashion
▷ **obsolescence** NOUN

Thesaurus

---

obligatory ADJECTIVE *Use of seat belts in the back seats is now obligatory.* ► compulsory, mandatory, binding, required, stipulated, unavoidable, de rigueur, imperative, imposed, incumbent, inescapable, official AN OPPOSITE IS optional

oblige VERB *We cannot oblige them to agree, but we can persuade them.* ► force, compel, require, constrain, make

obliged ADJECTIVE *We'd be obliged if you would let us know when you arrive.* ► grateful, indebted, gratified, appreciative, thankful

obliging ADJECTIVE *Richard is an obliging sort of guy.* ► helpful, accommodating, considerate, cooperative, thoughtful, willing, agreeable, civil, courteous, friendly, kind, neighborly, polite OPPOSITES ARE disobliging, unhelpful

obliterate VERB *The explosion might obliterate the entire building.* ► destroy, demolish, wipe out, ruin, wreck, devastate, shatter, blow up

obscene ADJECTIVE *obscene literature*
► pornographic, indecent, improper, immodest, immoral, depraved, salacious, shocking, suggestive

obscenity NOUN **1** *laws against obscenity*
► indecency, immodesty, impurity, impropriety, pornography, licentiousness, grossness, indelicacy **2** *The crime was an obscenity.* ► atrocity, abomination, outrage, enormity, evil **3** *louts uttering obscenities*
► swear word, profanity, curse, expletive

obscure ADJECTIVE *He was suffering from an obscure disease that made his hand shaky.*
► unknown, little-known, unheard-of, mysterious, dubious

obscure VERB **1** *Clouds obscured the sun.* ► hide, conceal, cover, veil, shroud, mask, envelop
2 *Their evidence has merely obscured the issues.*
► confuse, complicate, muddle, obfuscate

observant ADJECTIVE *Her observant eye took in every detail.* ► alert, attentive, vigilant, watchful, perceptive, percipient, eagle-eyed, sharp-eyed, heedful, quick AN OPPOSITE IS inattentive

observation NOUN **1** *He was sent to the hospital for observation.* ► monitoring, scrutiny, examination, inspection, surveillance, attention **2** *Put any further observations on a separate sheet of paper.* ► remark, comment, statement, opinion

observe VERB **1** *She observed her friends over by the bar.* ► notice, see, perceive, discern, spot, descry, behold **2** *James observed that Rachel looked unhappy.* ► remark, comment, mention, note, declare, announce, state **3** *From her window she could observe what was going on in the street.* ► watch, view, survey, regard, monitor, witness, scrutinize

observer NOUN *Brian was merely an observer and took no part in the action.* ► spectator, onlooker, bystander, viewer, watcher, commentator, eye-witness, witness

obsolete ADJECTIVE not used any more; out of date

obstacle NOUN obstacles something that stands in the way or obstructs progress

obstinate ADJECTIVE **1** keeping firmly to your own ideas or ways, even though they may be wrong **2** difficult to overcome or remove • *an obstinate problem*
▷ **obstinately** ADVERB **obstinacy** NOUN

obstreperous (ob-strep-er-us) ADJECTIVE noisy and unruly

obstruct VERB obstructs, obstructing, obstructed stop a person or thing from getting past; hinder
▷ **obstruction** NOUN **obstructive** ADJECTIVE

obtain VERB obtains, obtaining, obtained get or be given something
▷ **obtainable** ADJECTIVE

obtrusive ADJECTIVE unpleasantly noticeable
▷ **obtrusiveness** NOUN

obtuse angle NOUN obtuse angles an angle of more than 90° but less than 180° COMPARE acute angle

obvious ADJECTIVE easy to see or understand
▷ **obviously** ADVERB

occasion NOUN occasions **1** the time when something happens **2** a special event **3** a suitable time; an opportunity
on occasion from time to time

occasional ADJECTIVE **1** happening from time to time but not regularly or frequently **2** for special occasions • *occasional music*
▷ **occasionally** ADVERB

occult ADJECTIVE to do with the supernatural or magic • *occult powers*

Thesaurus

obsess VERB **1** *Thoughts of death obsessed him.*
▶ preoccupy, dominate, haunt, prey on, engross, possess, take a hold on **2** be obsessed with OR by *I was totally obsessed with food and controlling my weight.* ▶ be fixated with OR by, be preoccupied with OR by, (more informal) be hung up on

obsession NOUN *These memories rapidly became an obsession.* ▶ fixation, preoccupation, mania, passion, infatuation, compulsion, addiction

obsessive ADJECTIVE *His jealousy was becoming obsessive.* ▶ compulsive, consuming, all-consuming, dominating, controlling, fanatical, addictive

obsolete ADJECTIVE *The machinery installed in the 1990s had become obsolete.* ▶ out of date, outdated, outmoded, anachronistic, antiquated, extinct, superseded, old-fashioned, passé, disused, dated, primitive OPPOSITES ARE current, up to date

obstacle NOUN *a major obstacle in the peace process* ▶ barrier, hurdle, hindrance, stumbling block, obstruction, drawback, difficulty, impediment, problem, snag, bar, interference

obstinate ADJECTIVE *They were too obstinate to see the advantages of the scheme.* ▶ stubborn, inflexible, intractable, immovable, intransigent, unbending, unyielding, dogged, headstrong OPPOSITES ARE amenable, open-minded

obstruct VERB **1** *The opposite side of the road was obstructed by cars.* ▶ block, jam, clog up, choke up **2** *He was charged with obstructing the course of justice.* ▶ impede, hinder, hamper, frustrate, thwart, hold up, inhibit, retard, interfere with OPPOSITES ARE assist, further

obstruction NOUN *an obstruction to learning*
▶ barrier, hurdle, hindrance, stumbling block, drawback, difficulty, impediment, problem, snag, bar, interference

obstructive ADJECTIVE *He accused her of being deliberately obstructive.* ▶ uncooperative, unhelpful, awkward, difficult, disobliging, stalling OPPOSITES ARE helpful, cooperative

obtain VERB *You will need to obtain the necessary permission.I obtained the books at half price.*
▶ get, acquire, secure, procure, come by, achieve

obvious ADJECTIVE *It's obvious that she's attracted to Bill. He spoke with an obvious French accent.*
▶ clear, plain, evident, self-evident, patent, apparent, glaring, perceptible AN OPPOSITE IS imperceptible

obviously ADVERB *She was obviously very upset.*
▶ clearly, plainly, patently, evidently, discernibly, indubitably, manifestly, unmistakably, without doubt

occasion NOUN **1** *She had spoken to him on several occasions.* ▶ instance, point, time, moment **2** *His eighteenth birthday would be a special occasion.* ▶ event, affair, celebration **3** *I'll mention it if the occasion arises.*
▶ opportunity, chance, opening, right moment **4** *I've never had any occasion to complain.* ▶ reason, cause, grounds, excuse, need, justification, pretext

occasional ADJECTIVE *There were still occasional air raids.* ▶ intermittent, periodic, sporadic, infrequent, irregular, isolated, odd, rare, random

occasionally ADVERB *Tess turned her head occasionally to look at him.* ▶ sometimes, from time to time, now and then, every so often, intermittently, periodically, sporadically, infrequently, irregularly

a
b
c
d
e
f
g
h
i
j
k
l
m
n
o
p
q
r
s
t
u
v
w
x
y
z

A
B
C
D
E
F
G
H
I
J
K
L
M
N
O
P
Q
R
S
T
U
V
W
X
Y
Z

occupation NOUN occupations **1** a person's job or profession **2** something you do to pass your time **3** capturing a country etc. by military force

occupational ADJECTIVE caused by an occupation • *an occupational disease*

occupational therapy NOUN creative work designed to help people to recover from certain illnesses

occupy VERB occupies, occupying, occupied **1** live in a place; inhabit **2** fill a space or position **3** capture a country etc. and place troops there **4** keep somebody busy
▷ **occupier** NOUN

occur VERB occurs, occurring, occurred **1** happen or exist **2** be found; appear • *These plants occur in ponds.* **3** come into a person's mind • *An idea occurred to me.*

ocean NOUN oceans the seas that surround the continents of the earth, especially one of the large named areas of this • *the Pacific Ocean*
▷ **oceanic** ADJECTIVE

o'clock ADVERB by the clock • *Lunch is at one o'clock.*

octagon NOUN octagons a flat shape with eight sides and eight angles
▷ **octagonal** ADJECTIVE

octave NOUN octaves the interval of eight steps between one musical note and the next note of the same name above or below it

October NOUN the tenth month of the year [from Latin *octo* = eight, because it was the eighth month of the ancient Roman calendar]

octopus NOUN octopuses a sea creature with eight long tentacles [from Greek *okto* = eight + *pous* = foot]

oculist NOUN oculists a doctor who treats diseases of the eye

odd ADJECTIVE **1** strange or unusual **2** (said about a number) not able to be divided exactly by 2; not even **3** left over from a pair or set • *I've got one odd sock.* **4** of various kinds; not regular • *odd jobs*
▷ **oddly** ADVERB **oddness** NOUN

oddity NOUN oddities a strange person or thing

oddments PLURAL NOUN scraps or pieces left over from a larger piece or set

odds PLURAL NOUN **1** the chances that a certain thing will happen **2** the proportion of money that you will win if a bet is successful • *When the odds are 10 to 1, you will win $10 if you bet $1.* **odds and ends** oddments

odious (oh-dee-us) ADJECTIVE extremely unpleasant; hateful
▷ **odiously** ADVERB **odiousness** NOUN

Thesaurus

occupant NOUN *The apartment had two occupants at the time.* ► resident, inhabitant, tenant, occupier, lodger, householder

occupation NOUN *Passports no longer specify your occupation.* ► job, profession, work, line of work, walk of life, employment, business **2** *The occupation of the country continued for much longer than predicted.* ► invasion, annexation, seizure, takeover, occupancy, possession **3** *a house built for multiple occupation* ► occupancy, residence, habitation, tenancy, possession, use **4** *Swiming is my favorite leisure occupation.* ► pastime, hobby, interest, activity, diversion

occupy VERB **1** *Colin occupies the top floor.* ► live in, inhabit, be the tenant of, reside in, lodge in, possess, have possession of, own **2** *These problems occupied her mind for several days.* ► absorb, engage, hold, preoccupy, engross, divert **3** *The army occupied the country in the spring.* ► capture, seize, invade, take over, take possession of, overrun, annex, conquer, garrison

occur VERB **1** *We need to know everything that occurred that morning.* ► happen, take place, come about **2** *The disease occurs only in tropical climates.* ► be found, exist, be prevalent, appear, show itself, manifest itself **3** *occur to It occurred to him that she might still be waiting there.It never occurred to us that we'd have to pay extra.* ► cross your mind, enter your head

occurrence NOUN *Bicycle theft has become a common occurrence.* ► event, happening, incident, experience, circumstance, affair, occasion, phenomenon

odd ADJECTIVE **1** *It was an odd thing to do.* ► strange, peculiar, weird, unusual, bizarre, curious, eccentric **2** *His friends thought him quite odd.* ► eccentric, strange, peculiar, abnormal, weird **3** *the odd numbers* ► uneven **4** *Do you have any odd change you could give him?* ► spare, leftover, miscellaneous, sundry, available **5** *She noticed he was wearing odd socks.* ► unmatched, different, unpaired, clashing

oddity NOUN **1** *people remembered chiefly for their oddity* ► strangeness, abnormality, peculiarity, idiosyncrasy, quirkiness **2** *He is regarded as a bit of an oddity.* ► eccentric, crank, misfit, maverick, curiosity, character

oddments PLURAL NOUN *oddments left over from a jumble sale* ► bits and pieces, odds and ends, scraps, fragments, remnants, leftovers, offcuts

odds PLURAL NOUN *The odds are that they have left the country.* ► likelihood, probability, chances USAGE If you use *likelihood* or *probability* you should use a singular verb, e.g., *The likelihood is that they have left the country.*

odious ADJECTIVE *odious methods of dealing with their political opponents* ► hateful, offensive, repulsive, repellent, obnoxious, unpleasant, abhorrent, detestable, abominable

odor NOUN **odors** a smell, especially an unpleasant one
▷ **odorous** ADJECTIVE **odorless** ADJECTIVE

odyssey (od- iss- ee) NOUN **odysseys** a long adventurous journey

o'er PREPOSITION, ADVERB (poetic) over

of PREPOSITION (used to indicate relationships) **1** belonging to • *the mother of the child;* **2** concerning; about • *news of the disaster;* **3** made from • *built of stone;* **4** from • *north of the town*

off PREPOSITION **1** not on; away or down from • *He fell off the ladder* **2** not taking or wanting • *She is off her food* **3** deducted from • *$5 off the price*

off ADVERB **1** away or down from something • *His hat blew off.* **2** not working or happening • *The heating is off.* • *The match is off because of snow.* **3** to the end; completely • *Finish it off.* **4** as regards money or supplies • *How are you off for cash?* **5** behind or at the side of a stage • *There were noises off.* **6** (said about food) beginning to go bad • *The milk was going off.*

offal NOUN the organs of an animal (e.g., liver or kidneys) sold as food

off-color ADJECTIVE slightly unwell

offense NOUN **offenses 1** an illegal action **2** a feeling of annoyance or resentment
give offense hurt someone's feelings
take offense be upset by something said or done

offend VERB **offends, offending, offended 1** cause offense to someone; hurt a person's feelings **2** do wrong or commit a crime
▷ **offender** NOUN

offensive ADJECTIVE **1** causing offense; insulting **2** disgusting • *an offensive smell* **3** used in attacking • *offensive weapons*
▷ **offensively** ADVERB **offensiveness** NOUN

offensive NOUN **offensives** an attack
take the offensive be the first to attack

offer VERB **offers, offering, offered 1** present something so that people can accept it if they want to **2** say that you are willing to do or give something or to pay a certain amount

offer NOUN **offers 1** offering something **2** an amount of money offered **3** a specially reduced price

offhand ADJECTIVE **1** said or done without preparation **2** (said about a remark, etc.) rather casual and rude; curt
▷ **offhanded** ADJECTIVE

office NOUN **offices 1** a room or building used for business; the people who work there **2** a

Thesaurus

off ADJECTIVE **1** *The milk is off.* ► bad, rotten, putrid **2** *The game is now off.* ► postponed, canceled **3** *I think their remarks were a bit off, to put it mildly.* ► unacceptable, objectionable, unsatisfactory, disappointing

offbeat ADJECTIVE *an offbeat humor*
► unconventional, unorthodox, idiosyncratic, strange, weird, bizarre, quirky

off-color ADJECTIVE *He was feeling a bit off-color and decided to stay at home.* ► unwell, poorly, ill, queasy, peaky, nauseous

offense NOUN **1** *The company might even be guilty of a criminal offense.* ► crime, misdemeanor, wrong, wrongdoing, misdeed, fault, transgression **2** *We don't want to cause any offense.* ► annoyance, anger, resentment, indignation, irritation, upset, displeasure, disgust
take offense *She made it clear she had taken offense.* ► be OR feel offended, be upset, be OR feel aggrieved, be OR feel affronted, take umbrage

offend VERB **1** *I didn't mean to offend you.*
► give OR cause offence to, upset, hurt, displease, annoy, affront, insult, anger, irritate, disgust, make angry, outrage, provoke, rile, vex **2** *A large percentage of prisoners released early went on to offend again.*
► break the law, commit a crime, do wrong,

transgress, feel offended ► take offence, be upset, be OR feel aggrieved, be OR feel affronted, take umbrage

offensive ADJECTIVE *The remarks were clearly offensive.* ► insulting, derogatory, depreciatory, disrespectful, abusive, objectionable, provocative, discourteous, insolent, uncivil, rude OPPOSITES ARE complimentary, courteous

offer VERB **1** *Counselors are on hand to offer advice and support.* ► provide, give, extend, make available, put forward, hold out, suggest **2** *Many local people offered to help in the search.* ► volunteer, come forward, present yourself, show willing **3** *The job offers good career prospects.* ► provide, afford, present, hold out, involve, entail

offer NOUN **1** *a business offer* ► bid, proposal, tender, proposition, submission **2** *kind offers of help* ► proposal, proposition, overture

offering NOUN *an offering of a few silver coins*
► contribution, donation, gift, benefaction, present

offhand ADJECTIVE *His manner was most offhand.*
► casual, indifferent, cool, cavalier, brusque, abrupt, aloof, curt, uncooperative, perfunctory OPPOSITES ARE polite, courteous

office NOUN **1** *Her office was just a few blocks away.* ► workplace, place of work, place of

a b c d e f g h i j k l m n o p q r s t u v w x y z

A
B
C
D
E
F
G
H
I
J
K
L
M
N
O
P
Q
R
S
T
U
V
W
X
Y
Z

government department **3** an important job or position

be in office hold an official position

officer NOUN officers **1** a person who is in charge of others, especially in the armed forces **2** an official **3** a member of the police

official ADJECTIVE **1** done or said by someone with authority **2** done as part of your job or position ● *official duties*

▷ **officially** ADVERB

official NOUN officials a person who holds a position of authority

offing NOUN

in the offing likely to happen soon

off-putting ADJECTIVE making you less keen on something; disconcerting

offshoot NOUN offshoots **1** a side shoot on a plant **2** a by-product

offside ADJECTIVE, ADVERB (said about a player in soccer, etc.) in a position where the rules do not allow him or her to play the ball

often ADVERB many times; in many cases

ogre NOUN ogres **1** a cruel giant in fairy tales **2** a terrifying person

oh INTERJECTION an exclamation of pain, surprise, delight, etc., or used for emphasis ● *Oh yes I will!*

ohm NOUN ohms a unit of electrical resistance

oil NOUN oils **1** a thick slippery liquid that will not dissolve in water **2** a kind of petroleum used as fuel **3** oil paint

oil VERB oils, oiling, oiled put oil on something, especially to make it work smoothly

oilfield NOUN an area where oil is found

oil rig NOUN oil rigs a structure with equipment for drilling for oil

oil well NOUN oil wells a hole drilled in the ground or under the sea to get oil

oily ADJECTIVE **1** containing or like oil; covered or soaked with oil **2** behaving in an insincerely polite way

▷ **oiliness** NOUN

ointment NOUN ointments a cream or slippery paste for putting on sore skin and cuts

OK or **okay** ADVERB, ADJECTIVE (*informal*) all right

old ADJECTIVE **1** not new; born or made or existing from a long time ago **2** of a particular age ● *I'm ten years old.* **3** former or original ● *in its old place* **4** (*informal*) used

Thesaurus

business, bureau **2** *The new prime minister took up his office immediately.* ► post, position, appointment, function, task, duty, responsibility, situation

officer NOUN *The trade union had few full-time officers.* ► official, functionary, office-holder, representative, executive, administrator

official ADJECTIVE **1** *There were calls for an official inquiry into the matter.a member of an official organization* ► authorized, accredited, approved, proper, authentic, authenticated, certified, formal **2** *They were dressed for an official function.* ► formal, ceremonial

official NOUN *An official came down to escort us to the president's office.* ► officer, functionary, office-holder, representative, executive, administrator

officious ADJECTIVE *An officious waiter led us to a table in a poky corner.* ► self-important, bumptious, bossy, over-zealous, dictatorial, interfering, meddling, (*more informal*) pushy

off-putting ADJECTIVE *She tried to think of some off-putting remark to make them go away.* ► discouraging, unpleasant, intimidating, unnerving, unsettling, disconcerting, unappealing, unattractive, disagreeable, distasteful

offshoot NOUN *The business has offshoots all over Europe.* ► branch, subsidiary, (*more informal*) spin-off

offspring NOUN **1** *the core of the family: parents and their offspring* ► children, sons and

daughters, progeny, family **2** *Their latest offspring was playing in the garden.* ► child, baby, infant, little one, son, daughter, youngster

often ADVERB *She often asks about you.* ► frequently, regularly, repeatedly, constantly, again and again, many times, time after time

oil VERB *She went to the shed to oil her bike.* ► lubricate, grease

oily ADJECTIVE **1** *oily skin;an oily substance* ► greasy, oleaginous, slimy **2** *an oily manner* ► smooth, unctuous, fawning, ingratiating, obsequious, (*more informal*) smarmy

OK or **okay** ADJECTIVE (*informal*) *Is everything OK now?The film is OK.* ► all right, satisfactory, fine, in order, acceptable, adequate, reasonable

OK or **okay** INTERJECTION (*informal*) *OK, I'll go with you.* ► all right, very well, very good, right you are, right, fine

OK or **okay** NOUN (*informal*) *The manager gave his OK.* ► permission, approval, consent, authorization, agreement, assent

OK or **okay** VERB (*informal*) *Get a parent to okay your proposal.* ► agree to, approve, authorize, consent to, endorse, ratify

old ADJECTIVE **1** *an old man* ► elderly, aged, advanced in years, senile **2** *old buildings* ► antiquated, dilapidated, ramshackle, ruined, historic **3** *old clothes* ► worn, shabby, threadbare, frayed, moth-eaten **4** *in the old*

casually or for emphasis • *good old Mom!*
▷ **oldness** NOUN
[from Old English]

old age NOUN the time when a person is old

Old English NOUN the English language from about 700 to 1150, also called **Anglo-Saxon**

old-fashioned ADJECTIVE of the kind that was usual a long time ago; no longer fashionable

Old Norse NOUN the language spoken by the Vikings, the ancestor of modern Scandinavian languages

olive NOUN olives **1** an evergreen tree with a small bitter fruit **2** this fruit, from which an oil (olive oil) is made **3** a shade of green like an unripe olive

olive branch NOUN olive branches something you do or offer that shows you want to make peace [from a story in the Bible, in which a dove brings Noah an olive branch as a sign that God is no longer angry with the human race]

Olympic Games or **Olympics** PLURAL NOUN a series of international sports contests held every four years in a different part of the world

omega (oh- meg- a) NOUN the last letter of the Greek alphabet, a long o

omelette NOUN omelettes eggs beaten together and cooked in a pan, often with a filling

omen NOUN omens an event regarded as a sign of what is going to happen

ominous ADJECTIVE suggesting that trouble is coming
▷ **ominously** ADVERB

omit VERB omits, omitting, omitted **1** miss something out **2** fail to do something
▷ **omission** NOUN

omnibus NOUN omnibuses **1** a single book, television program, etc., containing several

instalments that were previously published or broadcast separately **2** (old use) a bus

omniscient (om- nish- ent) ADJECTIVE knowing everything
▷ **omniscience** NOUN

omnivorous (om- niv- er- us) ADJECTIVE feeding on all kinds of food COMPARE carnivorous, herbivorous

on PREPOSITION **1** supported by; covering; added or attached to • *the sign on the door* **2** close to; toward • *The army advanced on Paris.* **3** during; at the time of • *on my birthday* **4** by reason of • *Arrest him on suspicion of murder.* **5** concerning • *a book on butterflies* **6** in a state of; using or showing • *The house was on fire.*

on ADVERB **1** so as to be on something • *Put it on* **2** further forward • *Move on* **3** working; in action • *Is the heater on?*
on and off not continually

once ADVERB **1** for one time or on one occasion only • *They came only once.* **2** formerly • *They once lived here.*

once NOUN one time • *Once is enough.*

once CONJUNCTION as soon as • *You can go once I have taken your names.*

oncoming ADJECTIVE approaching; coming towards you • *oncoming traffic*

one ADJECTIVE **1** single **2** individual or united

one NOUN **1** the smallest whole number, 1 **2** a person or thing alone
one another each other

one PRONOUN any person or thing • *I need a pen but I can't find one.* • *One likes to help.*
▷ **oneself** PRONOUN

one-sided ADJECTIVE **1** with one side or person in a contest, conversation etc. being much stronger or doing a lot more than the other • *a one-sided match* **2** showing only one point of view in an unfair way • *This is a very one-sided account of the conflict.*

Thesaurus

days ► past, former, bygone, early, ancient, olden **5** *an old practice* ► long-standing, time-honored, traditional, established, familiar **6** *an old joke* ► hackneyed, stale, tired, overworked

old-fashioned ADJECTIVE *a big old-fashioned bathroom with noisy pipes* ► outdated, out of date, outmoded, antiquated, obsolescent OPPOSITES ARE up to date, modern, fashionable

omit VERB **1** *Someone had omitted her name from the list.* ► leave out, miss out, exclude, ignore, cut, drop, overlook, edit out, eliminate OPPOSITES ARE include, add, insert **2** *I omitted*

to tell you. ► forget, neglect, fail AN OPPOSITE IS remember

once ADVERB *We were good friends once.* ► at one time, in the past, formerly, previously

one-sided ADJECTIVE **1** *a one-sided account of the conflict* ► biased, prejudiced, partisan, partial, preferential, slanted, unfair OPPOSITES ARE impartial, fair **2** *a one-sided argument* ► unequal, uneven, unbalanced AN OPPOSITE IS even

ongoing ADJECTIVE **1** *an ongoing problem with noisy neighbors* ► continuous, continuing, persistent, constant, ceaseless **2** *A road improvement program is ongoing.* ► under way, in progress, developing, progressing, evolving, continuing, current, extant, existing

A
B
C
D
E
F
G
H
I
J
K
L
M
N
O
P
Q
R
S
T
U
V
W
X
Y
Z

onion NOUN **onions** a round vegetable with a strong flavor
▷ **oniony** ADJECTIVE

onlooker NOUN **onlookers** a spectator

only ADJECTIVE being the one person or thing of a kind; sole • *my only wish*
only child a child who has no brothers or sisters

only ADVERB no more than; and that is all
• *There are only three cookies left.*

only CONJUNCTION but then; however • *He makes promises, only he never keeps them.*

onomatopoeia (on- om- at- o- pee- a) NOUN the formation of words that imitate what they stand for, e.g., *cuckoo, plop*
▷ **onomatopoeic** ADJECTIVE

onshore ADJECTIVE from the sea toward the land • *an onshore breeze*

onslaught NOUN **onslaughts** a fierce attack

onto PREPOSITION to a position on

onward ADVERB, ADJECTIVE going forward; further on
▷ **onwards** ADVERB

ooze VERB **oozes, oozing, oozed** 1 flow out slowly; trickle 2 allow something to flow out slowly • *The wound oozed blood.*

ooze NOUN mud at the bottom of a river or sea

opal NOUN **opals** a kind of stone in which small points of shifting color can be seen
▷ **opalescent** ADJECTIVE

opaque (o- payk) ADJECTIVE not able to be seen through; not transparent or translucent

open ADJECTIVE 1 allowing people or things to go in and out; not closed or fastened 2 not covered or blocked up 3 spread out; unfolded 4 not limited or restricted • *an open championship* 5 letting in visitors or customers 6 with wide empty spaces • *open country* 7 honest and frank; not secret or secretive • *Be open about the danger.* 8 willing to listen to other ideas • *an open mind* • *I'm open to suggestions.*
▷ **openness** NOUN
in the open air not inside a house or building

open VERB **opens, opening, opened** 1 make or become open or more open 2 begin
▷ **opener** NOUN

opencast ADJECTIVE (said about a mine) worked by removing layers of earth from the surface, not underground

opening NOUN **openings** 1 a space or gap; a place where something opens 2 the beginning of something 3 an opportunity

openly ADVERB without secrecy

opera NOUN **operas** a drama set to music, with singers acting the story
▷ **operatic** ADJECTIVE

operate VERB **operates, operating, operated** 1 make a machine work 2 be in action; work 3 perform a surgical operation on somebody
▷ **operable** ADJECTIVE

Thesaurus

---

only ADJECTIVE *She is their only child.* ► sole, single, solitary, lone, unique

ooze VERB *Blood oozed from a wound on his arm.* ► seep, leak, issue, exude, escape, flow, dribble

opaque ADJECTIVE *The glass of the bottle was opaque so the contents could not be seen.* ► cloudy, nontransparent, obscure, blurred, misty, dark, hazy, unclear OPPOSITES ARE clear, transparent

open ADJECTIVE 1 *an open door* ► unclosed, ajar, unlocked AN OPPOSITE IS closed 2 *an open box* ► uncovered, unfastened, unsealed, lidless OPPOSITES ARE closed, fastened 3 *open access* ► free, unrestricted, clear, unobstructed, wide, available AN OPPOSITE IS restricted 4 *open country* ► sweeping, rolling, broad, extensive, unenclosed 5 *an open secret* ► plain, evident, overt, obvious, conspicuous, noticeable AN OPPOSITE IS closed 6 *an open question* ► unresolved, unsettled, undecided, debatable, moot AN OPPOSITE IS closed 7 *open about his feelings* ► frank, honest, candid, unreserved, natural OPPOSITES ARE reserved, guarded 8 *a procedure open to abuse* ► vulnerable, subject, susceptible, liable

open VERB 1 *A young woman opened the door.* ► unfasten, unlock, unbolt 2 *He started to open the packet.* ► unwrap, undo, untie, unseal 3 *A new superstore will open next month.* ► start trading 4 *The story opens with a train journey.* ► begin, start, (*more formal*) commence 5 *The chairman then opened the meeting.* ► begin, start, inaugurate, set in motion

opening NOUN 1 *an opening in the wall* ► doorway, gateway, entry, aperture, breach, chink, crack, cleft, hole, fissure 2 *looking for openings in accountancy* ► opportunity, chance, (*more informal*) break

opening ADJECTIVE *the opening line of the poem* ► first, initial, beginning, introductory, inaugural AN OPPOSITE IS final

operate VERB 1 *The alarms had been switched off and were not operating.* ► work, function, run, act, perform, be operative, go 2 *a machine that's difficult to operate* ► work, use, utilize, handle, manage, deal with, drive 3 *X-rays will show whether doctors will need to operate on him.* ► perform surgery, carry out an operation

operating system NOUN operating systems (in computing) the software that controls a computer's basic functions

operation NOUN operations **1** a piece of work or method of working **2** something done to a patient's body to take away or repair a damaged part **3** a planned military activity
▷ **operational** ADJECTIVE
in operation working or in use • When does the new system come into operation?

operator NOUN operators a person who works something, especially a telephone switchboard or exchange

opinion NOUN opinions what you think of something; a belief or judgement

opinion poll NOUN opinion polls an estimate of what people think, made by questioning a sample of them

opium NOUN a drug made from the juice of certain poppies, used in medicine

opponent NOUN opponents a person or group opposing another in a contest or war

opportunist NOUN opportunists a person who is quick to seize opportunities
▷ **opportunism** NOUN

opportunity NOUN opportunities a good chance to do a particular thing

oppose VERB opposes, opposing, opposed **1** argue or fight against; resist **2** contrast
• "Soft" is opposed to "hard."
as opposed to in contrast with
be opposed to be strongly against • We are opposed to parking in the town center.

opposite ADJECTIVE **1** placed on the other or further side; facing • on the opposite side of the road **2** moving away from or toward each other • The trains were traveling in opposite directions. **3** completely different • opposite characters

opposite NOUN opposites an opposite person or thing

opposite PREPOSITION opposite to • They live opposite the school.

opposition NOUN **1** opposing something; resistance **2** the people who oppose something

oppress VERB oppresses, oppressing, oppressed **1** govern or treat somebody cruelly or unjustly **2** weigh somebody down with worry or sadness
▷ **oppression** NOUN **oppressive** ADJECTIVE **oppressor** NOUN

Thesaurus

operation NOUN **1** There are few other business operations the size of ours. ► enterprise, undertaking, procedure, proceeding, process, transaction **2** Military operations have been delayed by the weather. ► campaign, exercise, action, activity, maneuver, movement, effort **3** a committee to ensure the smooth operation of the system ► running, functioning, working, direction, control, management **4** a surgical operation ► biopsy, surgery, transplant

operative ADJECTIVE Perhaps you're right: the operative word is "perhaps." ► key, significant, important, principal, relevant, crucial, effective

opinion NOUN You can have an opinion but you must back it up with facts or reasons. ► belief, judgment, view, point of view, viewpoint, thought, attitude, standpoint, stance, idea, notion, feeling

opponent NOUN **1** He threw the ball at an opponent's head. ► adversary, opposer, rival, antagonist, competitor, contestant, enemy, foe, opposition OPPOSITES ARE ally, partner **2** an opponent of reform ► objector (to), opposer, dissident, dissenter

opportune ADJECTIVE It was an opportune moment to speak out. ► appropriate, suitable, timely, auspicious, convenient, favorable, propitious, advantageous, lucky, right OPPOSITES ARE unsuitable, inconvenient

opportunity NOUN (informal) This was a good opportunity to make some money. ► chance, occasion, possibility, moment, opening, time, (more informal) break

oppose VERB **1** There was a large group of protesters who opposed the plans for a new runway. ► object to, be against, protest against, disapprove of, take exception to OPPOSITES ARE support, defend **2** If you want to go I won't oppose you. ► resist, counter, withstand, take issue with, defy, confront

opposed ADJECTIVE **opposed to** The village was opposed to the scheme for a new hostel. ► against, hostile to, antagonistic to, antipathetic to, unsympathetic to

opposite ADJECTIVE **1** She lived in a house opposite the church. ► facing, across from **2** There is a long mirror on the opposite wall. ► opposing, facing **3** They were brothers who had fought on opposite sides in the civil war. ► rival, opposing, conflicting, contrary, enemy AN OPPOSITE IS allied

opposite NOUN He always says one thing and does the opposite. ► contrary, reverse, other extreme, antithesis, converse AN OPPOSITE IS same

opposition NOUN **1** The suggestion met with fierce opposition. ► resistance, hostility, antagonism, disapproval, scepticism, unfriendliness, competition AN OPPOSITE IS support **2** In the argument she quickly won over the opposition. ► opponents, opposing side, other side

oppress VERB **1** He could not get rid of the gloomy feelings that oppressed him. ► depress, cast down, weigh down, burden, hang over, dispirit **2** a people that had been oppressed by

a
b
c
d
e
f
g
h
i
j
k
l
m
n
o
p
q
r
s
t
u
v
w
x
y
z

opt VERB opts, opting, opted choose
opt out decide not to take part in something

optical ADJECTIVE to do with sight; aiding sight
• *optical instruments*
▷ **optically** ADVERB

optical illusion NOUN optical illusions a deceptive appearance that makes you think you see something that is not really there

optician NOUN opticians a person who tests people's eyesight and makes or sells glasses and contact lenses

optimist NOUN optimists a person who expects that things will turn out well COMPARE pessimist
▷ **optimism** NOUN **optimistic** ADJECTIVE **optimistically** ADVERB

optimum ADJECTIVE best; most favorable
▷ **optimum** NOUN **optimal** ADJECTIVE

option NOUN options **1** the right or power to choose something **2** something chosen or that may be chosen

optional ADJECTIVE that you can choose, not compulsory
▷ **optionally** ADVERB

or CONJUNCTION used to show that there is a choice or an alternative • *Do you want a muffin or a cookie?*

-or SUFFIX forms nouns meaning "a person or thing that does something" (e.g., *tailor, refrigerator*)

oracle NOUN oracles **1** a shrine where the ancient Greeks consulted one of their gods for advice or a prophecy **2** a wise or knowledgeable adviser
▷ **oracular** (or- **ak**- yoo- ler) ADJECTIVE

oral ADJECTIVE **1** spoken, not written **2** to do with or using the mouth
▷ **orally** ADVERB
USAGE Do not confuse with aural.

orange NOUN oranges **1** a round juicy citrus fruit with reddish-yellow peel **2** a reddish-yellow color

orangeade NOUN an orange-flavored drink

orangutan NOUN orangutans a large ape of Borneo and Sumatra

orator NOUN orators a person who is good at making speeches in public
▷ **oratorical** ADJECTIVE **oratory** NOUN

orbit NOUN orbits **1** the curved path taken by something moving around a planet, moon, or star **2** the range of someone's influence or control
▷ **orbital** ADJECTIVE

orbit VERB orbits, orbiting, orbited move in an orbit around something • *The satellite has been orbiting the earth since 1986.*

orchard NOUN orchards a piece of ground planted with fruit trees

orchestra NOUN orchestras a large group of people playing various musical instruments together
▷ **orchestral** ADJECTIVE
[from Greek, = the space where the chorus danced during a play]

Thesaurus

---

successive invaders ► persecute, abuse, maltreat, tyrannize, repress, suppress, subjugate, subdue, keep down

oppressed ADJECTIVE *oppressed minorities in the community* ► persecuted, downtrodden, repressed, abused, maltreated, tyrannized, suppressed AN OPPOSITE IS privileged

oppressive ADJECTIVE **1** *an oppressive dictatorship* ► dictatorial, autocratic, authoritarian, despotic, brutal, cruel, harsh, repressive, tyrannical **2** *oppressive weather* ► humid, muggy, sultry, stuffy, airless, close, hot, stifling, heavy

oppressor NOUN *The angry mob thirsted for the blood of its oppressors.* ► persecutor, intimidator, tormentor, despot, tyrant, autocrat

optimism NOUN *Despite the difficulties he tried to keep up a note of optimism.* ► confidence, hopefulness, hope, positiveness, cheerfulness, good cheer AN OPPOSITE IS pessimism

optimistic ADJECTIVE **1** *I am really optimistic about winning the match tomorrow.* ► cheerful, confident, positive, hopeful, upbeat, sanguine, cheerful, buoyant AN OPPOSITE IS pessimistic **2** *The accounts included an optimistic assessment of the financial outlook.* ► favorable, encouraging, hopeful, upbeat, bright, rosy AN OPPOSITE IS pessimistic

optimum ADJECTIVE *The announcement is timed to have the optimum effect.* ► best, maximum, most favorable, most advantageous, highest, ideal, perfect AN OPPOSITE IS worst

option NOUN *We had little option but to agree.* ► choice, alternative, possibility

optional ADJECTIVE *The exam consists of two compulsory questions and an optional essay.* ► voluntary, discretionary, noncompulsory, elective OPPOSITES ARE compulsory, obligatory

oral ADJECTIVE *Witnesses give oral evidence to the inquiry.* ► spoken, unwritten, verbal, by mouth, said AN OPPOSITE IS written

orbit NOUN **1** *the earth's orbit around the sun* ► course, path, circuit, track, trajectory, rotation, revolution **2** *This question is outside the orbit of the ordinary officials.* ► domain, sphere, range, scope, ambit

orbit VERB *other planets that orbit the sun* ► circle, go around, travel around

orchid NOUN orchids a kind of plant with brightly coloured, often unevenly shaped, flowers

ordain VERB ordains, ordaining, ordained **1** make a person a member of the clergy in the Christian Church • *He was ordained in 2001.* **2** declare or order something by law

ordeal NOUN ordeals a difficult or horrific experience

order NOUN orders **1** a command **2** a request for something to be supplied **3** the way things are arranged • *in alphabetical order* **4** a neat arrangement; a proper arrangement or condition • *in working order* **5** obedience to rules or laws • *law and order* **6** a kind or sort • *She showed courage of the highest order.* **7** a group of monks or nuns who live by certain religious rules
in order that or **in order to** for the purpose of

order VERB orders, ordering, ordered **1** command **2** ask for something to be supplied **3** put something into order; arrange neatly

orderly ADJECTIVE **1** arranged neatly or well; methodical **2** well-behaved and obedient
▷ **orderliness** NOUN

ordinal number NOUN ordinal numbers a number that shows a thing's position in a series, e.g., first, fifth, twentieth, etc. COMPARE cardinal number

ordinary ADJECTIVE normal or usual; not special
▷ **ordinarily** ADVERB
out of the ordinary unusual

ordination NOUN ordinations ordaining or being ordained as a member of the clergy

ore NOUN ores rock with metal or other useful substances in it • *iron ore*

organ NOUN organs **1** a musical instrument from which sounds are produced by air forced through pipes, played by keys and pedals **2** a part of the body with a particular function • *the digestive organs*

organic ADJECTIVE **1** to do with the organs of the body • *organic diseases* **2** to do with or formed from living things • *organic matter* **3** organic food is grown or produced without the use of chemical fertilizers, pesticides, etc. • *organic farming*
▷ **organically** ADVERB

organism NOUN organisms a living thing; an individual animal or plant

organist NOUN organists a person who plays the organ

organization NOUN organizations **1** an organized group of people, such as a business,

Thesaurus

ordeal NOUN *She helped nurse him back to health after his four-year ordeal as a captive.* ► trial, tribulation, suffering, difficulty, test, torture, unpleasant experience, nightmare

order NOUN **1** *He gave the order to charge.* ► command, directive, instruction, direction, decree, edict **2** *It would not be easy to restore order.* ► peace, control, calm, quiet, law and order, discipline, harmony **3** *The plants were put in in a set order.* ► sequence, arrangement, disposition **4** *I've put in an order for a hundred storage boxes.* ► request, requisition, booking, demand, application **5** *the lowest orders in society* ► class, rank, hierarchy **6** *an ancient order of craftsmen* ► association, society, guild, company, lodge, brotherhood, sisterhood **7** *skills of a very high order* ► type, kind, sort, nature, variety, category **out of order 1** *The ticket machine was, as usual, out of order.* ► broken, not working, inoperative **2** *Remarks like that would be ruled out of order.* ► improper, uncalled-for, unacceptable, irregular, unwarranted

order VERB **1** *She ordered them to leave the room.* ► instruct, command, direct, charge, enjoin **2** *I ordered the tickets on the Internet.* ► book, reserve, apply for, requisition **3** *He tried hard to order his thoughts.* ► arrange, organize, sort out, set in order, regulate

orderly ADJECTIVE **1** *The army began an orderly withdrawal.* ► methodical, systematic, ordered, regular, well organized, well regulated AN OPPOSITE IS disorganized **2** *The children were told to form an orderly line.* ► neat, tidy, controlled, well behaved AN OPPOSITE IS disorderly

ordinary ADJECTIVE **1** *just an ordinary day's work* ► usual, normal, typical, habitual, customary OPPOSITES ARE unusual, abnormal **2** *Susan is not like ordinary women.* ► average, normal, typical, conventional OPPOSITES ARE abnormal, unconventional **3** *My life seemed so ordinary; I needed a change.* ► routine, humdrum, run-of-the-mill, dull, routine, unremarkable, uninteresting, unexceptional, unexciting, commonplace OPPOSITES ARE exceptional, unique

organic ADJECTIVE **1** *an organic substance* ► natural, animate, live, living, biological AN OPPOSITE IS inorganic **2** *organic foods* ► natural, additive-free, pesticide-free, non-chemical **3** *society as an organic whole* ► integrated, organized, structured, coherent, systematic, harmonious AN OPPOSITE IS disparate

organization NOUN **1** *Sara is responsible for the organization of trips and visits.* ► planning, administration, coordination, running

a b c d e f g h i j k l m n o p q r s t u v w x y z

charity, government department, etc. **2** the organizing of something
▷ **organizational** ADJECTIVE

organize VERB **organizes, organizing, organized 1** plan and prepare something • *We organized a picnic.* **2** form people into a group to work together **3** put things in order
▷ **organizer** NOUN

orgasm NOUN **orgasms** the climax of sexual excitement

orgy NOUN **orgies 1** a wild party that involves a lot of drinking and sex **2** an extravagant activity • *an orgy of spending*

orient VERB **orients, orienting, oriented 1** place something or face in a certain direction **2** get your bearings • *I'm just trying to orientate myself.*
▷ **orientation** NOUN

oriental ADJECTIVE to do with the countries east of the Mediterranean Sea, especially China and Japan

origami (o- rig- ah- mee) NOUN folding paper into decorative shapes [from Japanese *ori* = fold + *kami* = paper]

origin NOUN **origins 1** the start of something; the point or cause from which something

began **2** a person's family background • *a man of humble origins* **3** the point where two or more axes on a graph meet [from Latin *oriri* = to rise]

original ADJECTIVE **1** existing from the start; earliest • *the original inhabitants* **2** new in its design, etc.; not a copy **3** producing new ideas; inventive
▷ **originally** ADVERB **originality** NOUN

originate VERB **originates, originating, originated 1** cause something to begin; create **2** have its origin • *The quarrel originated in rivalry.*
▷ **origination** NOUN **originator** NOUN

ornament NOUN **ornaments** an object displayed or worn as a decoration
▷ **ornamental** ADJECTIVE

ornament VERB **ornaments, ornamenting, ornamented** decorate something with beautiful things
▷ **ornamentation** NOUN

ornithology NOUN the study of birds
▷ **ornithologist** NOUN **ornithological** ADJECTIVE

orphan NOUN **orphans** a child whose parents are dead

Thesaurus

2 *Organization is an important aspect of essay writing.* ► structure, planning, arrangement, composition **3** *an international organization with branches throughout the world* ► institution, enterprise, operation, company, (*more informal*) outfit, (*more informal*) set-up

organize VERB **1** *The protesters used cell phones and the Internet to organize a demonstration.* ► arrange, coordinate, plan, make arrangements for, assemble, bring together, run **2** *Try to organize your ideas on paper.* ► order, marshal, structure, assemble, develop, coordinate, establish, systematize, put in order, form, shape

organized ADJECTIVE *a well-organized sales promotion* ► systematic, coordinated, efficient, well ordered, well planned, well run, meticulous, methodical, orderly, scientific, structured OPPOSITES ARE disorganized, inefficient

orient VERB **1** *After her father left, she had to orient herself to a new way of life.* ► adapt, adjust, accommodate, familiarize, acclimatize, accustom **2** *orient yourself They looked out for landmarks to orient themselves.* ► get your bearings, get the lie of the land

oriental ADJECTIVE *oriental countries* ► eastern, Far Eastern, Asian, Asiatic

origin NOUN **1** *a discussion of the origin of the universe* ► beginning, start, birth, genesis, dawning, emergence, inception, source

OPPOSITES ARE end, conclusion **2** *a man of Irish origins* ► descent, ancestry, parentage, extraction, family, pedigree, background, stock

original ADJECTIVE **1** *the original inhabitants of North America* ► earliest, first, indigenous, native, aboriginal, initial AN OPPOSITE IS recent **2** *an original idea for a story* ► new, creative, innovative, novel, fresh, unfamiliar, unique, unusual, firsthand, imaginative, inventive, unconventional OPPOSITES ARE unoriginal, commonplace **3** *an original painting by Picasso* ► authentic, genuine, real

originate VERB **1** *Where did the rumor originate?* ► arise, start, begin, emerge, emanate, evolve, be born, crop up **2** *It is not clear who originated the idea.* ► conceive, invent, create, initiate, introduce, inaugurate, discover, inspire, pioneer, be the inventor of, give birth to, institute, launch

ornament NOUN **1** *a plain style of clothing without ornament* ► decoration, adornment, embellishment, trimming, accessory, filigree, frill, frippery, finery, garnish, jewel, tracery **2** *a shelf covered with ornaments* ► trinket, knick-knack, bauble, gewgaw

ornamental ADJECTIVE *an ornamental ceiling* ► decorative, fancy, attractive, ornate, ornamented, showy

ornate ADJECTIVE **1** *an ornate mirror over the fireplace* ► ornamented, decorated, elaborate,

A B C D E F G H I J K L M N O P Q R S T U V W X Y Z

orthodox ADJECTIVE **1** holding beliefs that are correct or generally accepted **2** conventional or normal
▷ **orthodoxy** NOUN

Orthodox Church NOUN the Christian Churches of eastern Europe

orthopedics (orth- o- pee- diks) NOUN the treatment of deformities and injuries to bones and muscles
▷ **orthopedic** ADJECTIVE
[from Greek *orthos* = straight+ *paideia* = rearing of children (because the treatment was originally of children)]

oscillate VERB oscillates, oscillating, oscillated **1** move to and fro like a pendulum; vibrate **2** waver or vary
▷ **oscillation** NOUN **oscillator** NOUN

osmosis NOUN the passing of fluid through a porous partition into another more concentrated fluid

ostentatious ADJECTIVE making a showy display of something to impress people
▷ **ostentatiously** ADVERB **ostentation** NOUN

osteopath NOUN osteopaths a person who treats certain medical conditions, diseases, etc., by manipulating a patient's bones and muscles
▷ **osteopathy** NOUN **osteopathic** ADJECTIVE

ostrich NOUN ostriches a large long-legged African bird that can run very fast but cannot fly. It was said to bury its head in the sand when pursued, in the belief that it cannot then be seen.

other ADJECTIVE **1** different • *some other tune* **2** remaining • *Try the other shoe.* **3** additional • *my other friends* **4** just recent or past • *I saw him the other day.*

other PRONOUN, NOUN others the other person or thing • *Where are the others?*

otherwise ADVERB **1** if things happen differently; if you do not • *Write it down, otherwise you'll forget.* **2** in other ways • *It rained, but otherwise the holiday was good.* **3** differently • *We could not do otherwise.*

otter NOUN otters a fish-eating animal with webbed feet, a flat tail, and thick brown fur, living near water [from Old English]

ought AUXILIARY VERB expressing duty (*We ought to feed them*), rightness or advisability (*You ought to take more exercise*), or probability (*At this speed, we ought to be there by noon*)

oughtn't (*mainly spoken*) ought not

ounce NOUN ounces a unit of weight equal to one sixteenth of a pound (about 28 grams)

our ADJECTIVE belonging to us

ours POSSESSIVE PRONOUN belonging to us • *These seats are ours.*
USAGE It is incorrect to write *our's*.

ourselves PRONOUN we or us and nobody else

oust VERB ousts, ousting, ousted drive a person out from a position or office

out ADVERB **1** away from or not in a particular place or position or state, etc.; not at home **2** into the open; into existence or sight etc. • *The sun came out.* **3** no longer burning or shining **4** in error • *Your estimate was 10% out.* **5** to or at an end; completely • *sold out* • *tired out* **6** without restraint; boldly or loudly • *Speak out!*
be out for or **out to** be seeking or wanting • *They are out to make trouble.*
be out of have no more of something left
out of date 1 old-fashioned **2** not valid any more
out of doors in the open air
out of the way remote
USAGE Use hyphens when *out of date* is used as an adjective before a noun, e.g. *out-of-date information* (but *The information is out of date*).

out and out ADJECTIVE thorough or complete • *an out and out villain*

outboard motor NOUN outboard motors a motor fitted to the outside of a boat's stern

outbreak NOUN outbreaks the start of a disease or war or anger etc.

outburst NOUN outbursts a sudden bursting out of anger or laughter, etc.

Thesaurus

showy AN OPPOSITE IS plain **2** *ornate language* ► elaborate, florid, fancy, grandiose, affected, pretentious

orthodox ADJECTIVE *He has orthodox views on most things.* ► conventional, mainstream, established, conservative, standard, traditional, conformist OPPOSITES ARE unorthodox, unconventional

ostentatious ADJECTIVE *Their ostentatious attempts to look busy fool nobody.* ► showy, pretentious, conspicuous, flamboyant, obtrusive, vulgar, theatrical, overdone AN OPPOSITE IS modest

oust VERB *The president knew that his opponent would never unite to oust him.* ► depose, overthrow, remove, drive out, expel, unseat, defeat

out-and-out ADJECTIVE *an out-and-out success* ► complete, utter, outright, thoroughgoing, downright, absolute, thorough, unmitigated

outbreak NOUN **1** *an outbreak of flu; new outbreaks of violence* ► eruption, upsurge, outburst, epidemic, rash, spate **2** *the outbreak of war* ► start, beginning, onset

outburst NOUN *At this there was a loud outburst of laughter.* ► eruption, burst, explosion, outbreak, surge, spasm

a b c d e f g h i j k l m n **o** p q r s t u v w x y z

A
B
C
D
E
F
G
H
I
J
K
L
M
N
O
P
Q
R
S
T
U
V
W
X
Y
Z

outcast NOUN outcasts a person who has been rejected by family, friends, or society

outcrop NOUN outcrops a piece of rock from a lower level that sticks out on the surface of the ground

outcry NOUN outcries a strong protest

outdo VERB outdoes, outdoing, outdid, outdone do better than another person

outdoors ADVERB in the open air

outer ADJECTIVE outside or external; nearer to the outside
▷ **outermost** ADJECTIVE

outer space NOUN the universe beyond the earth's atmosphere

outfit NOUN outfits **1** a set of clothes worn together **2** a set of equipment **3** (informal) a team or organization

outgrow VERB outgrows, outgrowing, outgrew, outgrown **1** grow out of clothes or habits etc. **2** grow faster or larger than another person or thing

outhouse NOUN outhouses a small building (e.g., a shed or barn) that belongs to a house but is separate from it

outing NOUN outings a journey for pleasure

outlandish ADJECTIVE looking or sounding strange or foreign

outlast VERB outlasts, outlasting, outlasted last longer than something else

outlaw NOUN outlaws a person who is punished by being excluded from legal rights and the protection of the law, especially a robber or bandit

outlay NOUN outlays what is spent on something

outlet NOUN outlets **1** a way for something to get out **2** a way of expressing strong feelings **3** a place from which goods are sold or distributed

outline NOUN outlines **1** a line round the outside of something, showing its boundary or shape **2** a summary

Thesaurus

outcast NOUN a social outcast ► reject, pariah, leper, outsider, exile, outlaw, castaway

outclass VERB She won every game, outclassing every rival. ► surpass, outdo, outstrip, outshine, beat, exceed, eclipse, excel, be better than

outcome NOUN speculation about the outcome of the next election ► result, consequence, conclusion, upshot, issue, conclusion

outcry NOUN an outcry about the state of the railways ► protest, complaint, furore, clamor, tumult

outdated ADJECTIVE an outdated road network ► out-of-date, obsolete, old-fashioned, dated, decrepit, antiquated, ancient

outdo VERB Everyone tried to outdo each other with stories of how exciting their holidays had been. ► surpass, outstrip, outshine, exceed, eclipse, excel, be better than, outclass, beat

outdoor ADJECTIVE an outdoor sport such as archery ► open-air, outside, alfresco

outer ADJECTIVE **1** It was so hot they began to shed their outer clothing. ► outermost, exterior, external, outside, outward, surface, superficial **2** superstores built in the outer areas of cities ► outlying, distant, remote, peripheral, further, suburban AN OPPOSITE IS inner

outfit NOUN **1** a complete photography outfit ► equipment, kit, apparatus, (more informal) gear, (more informal) set-up **2** The weather was still too cold for summer outfits. ► costume, ensemble, suit, dress, clothing, (informal) get-up, (informal) turn-out, (more informal) gear, (more informal) togs

outgoing ADJECTIVE **1** She was in a bright, outgoing mood that day. ► sociable, friendly, amiable, genial, congenial, demonstrative, pleasant, agreeable, kind, kindly, kindhearted, well-disposed, sympathetic, likeable, approachable, receptive **2** the outgoing president ► departing, leaving, retiring, former, ex- AN OPPOSITE IS incoming

outing NOUN family outings to the coast ► trip, excursion, jaunt, expedition, drive, run, ride, joyride

outlandish ADJECTIVE We could dream up all sorts of outlandish ideas. ► weird, strange, extraordinary, odd, queer, eccentric, bizarre, quirky

outlaw NOUN those notorious outlaws Frank and Jesse James ► bandit, brigand, fugitive, desperado, renegade, robber, marauder, criminal, outcast

outlaw VERB The state in effect outlawed political opposition. ► ban, prohibit, bar, forbid, disallow, banish, embargo, condemn, veto

outlet NOUN **1** The boiler has an outlet for fumes. ► vent, duct, channel, opening, orifice, exit, mouth, way out **2** We need a better outlet for complaints. ► channel, process, means **3** retail outlets for these goods ► shop, store, retailer, market

outline NOUN **1** the outline of a low building ► profile, silhouette, shape, form, contour, shadow, figure **2** (informal) He sat down and wrote an outline of his essay. ► summary, sketch, framework, skeleton, plan, draft, rough idea, bare bones

outlook NOUN outlooks **1** a view on which people look out **2** a person's mental attitude to something **3** future prospects • *The outlook is bleak.*

outlying ADJECTIVE far from the centre; remote • *the outlying districts*

outmoded ADJECTIVE out of date

outnumber VERB outnumbers, outnumbering, outnumbered be more numerous than another group

outpatient NOUN outpatients a person who visits a hospital for treatment but does not stay there

outpost NOUN outposts a distant settlement

output NOUN outputs **1** the amount produced **2** the information or results produced by a computer

outrage NOUN outrages **1** something that shocks people by being very wicked or cruel **2** great anger
▷ **outrageous** ADJECTIVE **outrageously** ADVERB

outrage VERB outrages, outraging, outraged shock and anger people greatly

outright ADVERB **1** completely; not gradually • *This drug should be banned outright.* **2** frankly • *We told him this outright.*

outright ADJECTIVE thorough or complete • *an outright fraud*

outrun VERB outruns, outrunning, outran, outrun run faster or further than another

outset NOUN the beginning of something • *from the outset of his career*

outside NOUN outsides the outer side, surface, or part
at the outside at the most • *a mile at the outside*

outside ADJECTIVE **1** on or coming from the outside • *the outside edge* **2** greatest possible • *the outside price* **3** remote or slight • *an outside chance*

outside ADVERB on or to the outside; outdoors • *Leave it outside* • *It's cold outside*

outside PREPOSITION on or to the outside of • *Leave it outside the door.*

outside broadcast NOUN outside broadcasts a broadcast made on location and not in a studio

outsider NOUN outsiders **1** a person who does not belong to a certain group **2** a horse or person thought to have no chance of winning a race or competition

Thesaurus

outlook NOUN **1** *The house has a glorious outlook over the downs.* ► view, vista, prospect, panorama, aspect, vantage point **2** *The sisters were totally different in character and outlook.* ► attitude, way of thinking, standpoint, viewpoint, frame of mind, point of view **3** *Lower interest rates will improve the economic outlook.* ► prospects, expectations, forecast, hopes, future, prognosis, prediction, (*more informal*) lookout

outnumber VERB *On these occasions males usually outnumber females.* ► exceed, be more than, outstrip

out-of-date ADJECTIVE **1** *He handed over an out-of-date passport.* ► expired, lapsed, invalid, void **2** *She was using a machine that was totally out of date.* ► old-fashioned, outdated, obsolete, dated, obsolescent

out-of-the-way ADJECTIVE *out-of-the-way places* ► distant, outlying, faraway, remote, isolated, far-flung, far-off

output NOUN *a marked increase in industrial output* ► production, productivity, product, yield, manufacture

outrage NOUN **1** *I was outraged by the way he spoke to me.* ► anger, indignation, fury, disgust, affront, horror **2** *The country's suffering is an outrage.* ► scandal, disgrace, atrocity, enormity, barbarity, infamy

outrageous ADJECTIVE **1** *an outrageous slur on his character* ► disgraceful, shocking, scandalous, appalling, monstrous, shameful, dreadful, intolerable, wicked, heinous AN OPPOSITE IS mild **2** *We were invited to tell outrageous stories about people we knew.* ► far-fetched, extravagant, preposterous, unlikely, questionable, dubious AN OPPOSITE IS reasonable **3** *If you're not careful about the extras the cost can become outrageous.* ► excessive, exorbitant, extortionate

outright ADJECTIVE *By now it was clear the whole story was an outright fabrication.* ► complete, utter, out-and-out, thoroughgoing, downright, absolute, thorough, unmitigated AN OPPOSITE IS indefinite

outside ADJECTIVE **1** *An outside light will improve security.* ► exterior, external, outer, outdoor, outward AN OPPOSITE IS inside **2** *We must resist all outside interference.* ► external, extraneous, foreign, alien AN OPPOSITE IS inside **3** *There is an outside chance of thunder.* ► slight, remote, slender, slim, faint, negligible

outside NOUN *The outside of the building is covered in ivy.* ► exterior, façade, surface, outer surface, shell, skin AN OPPOSITE IS inside

outsider NOUN *I still felt like an outsider after years of living in the village.* ► stranger, visitor, foreigner, alien, newcomer, incomer, interloper, intruder, immigrant, nonresident, outcast AN OPPOSITE IS insider

a b c d e f g h i j k l m n o p q r s t u v w x y z

A
B
C
D
E
F
G
H
I
J
K
L
M
N
O
P
Q
R
S
T
U
V
W
X
Y
Z

outsize ADJECTIVE much larger than average

outskirts PLURAL NOUN the outer parts or districts, especially of a town

outspoken ADJECTIVE speaking or spoken very frankly

outstanding ADJECTIVE 1 extremely good or distinguished 2 not yet paid or dealt with

outstrip VERB outstrips, outstripping, outstripped 1 run faster or further than another; outrun 2 surpass in achievement or success

outward ADJECTIVE 1 going outwards 2 on the outside
▷ **outwardly** ADVERB **outwards** ADVERB

outwit VERB outwits, outwitting, outwitted deceive somebody by being crafty

ova plural of ovum

oval ADJECTIVE shaped like a 0, rounded and longer than it is broad
▷ **oval** NOUN

ovary NOUN ovaries 1 either of the two organs in which ova or egg cells are produced in a woman's or female animal's body 2 part of the pistil in a plant, from which fruit is formed

oven NOUN ovens a closed space in which things are cooked or heated

over PREPOSITION 1 above 2 more than • *It's over a mile away.* 3 concerning • *They quarrelled over money.* 4 across the top of; on or to the other side of • *They rowed the boat over the lake.* 5 during • *We can talk over dinner.* 6 in superiority or preference to • *their victory over United*

over ADVERB 1 out and down from the top or edge; from an upright position • *He fell over.* 2 so that a different side shows • *Turn it over.* 3 at or to a place; across • *Walk over to our house.* 4 remaining • *There is nothing left over.* 5 all through; thoroughly • *Think it over.* 6 at an end • *The lesson is over.*
over and over many times; repeatedly

over NOUN overs a series of six balls bowled in cricket [from Old English]

overact VERB overacts, overacting, overacted (said about an actor) act in an exaggerated manner

overall ADJECTIVE including everything; total • *the overall cost*

overalls PLURAL NOUN a piece of clothing like a shirt and trousers combined, worn over other clothes to protect them

overarm ADJECTIVE, ADVERB with the arm lifted above shoulder level and coming down in front of the body • *bowling overarm*

overawe VERB overawes, overawing, overawed overcome a person with awe

overbalance VERB overbalances, overbalancing, overbalanced lose balance and fall over

overbearing ADJECTIVE domineering

overblown ADJECTIVE 1 exaggerated or pretentious 2 (said about a flower) too fully open; past its best

overboard ADVERB from in or on a ship into the water • *She jumped overboard.*

overcast ADJECTIVE covered with cloud

overcoat NOUN overcoats a warm outdoor coat

overcome VERB overcomes, overcoming, overcame, overcome 1 win a victory over somebody; defeat 2 have a strong physical or emotional effect on someone and make them helpless • *He was overcome by the fumes.* 3 find a way of dealing with a problem, etc.

Thesaurus

outskirts PLURAL NOUN *a group of buildings on the outskirts of the city* ► outer areas, outlying districts, edge, fringe, suburbs, margin, periphery, purlieus OPPOSITES ARE centre, heart

outspoken ADJECTIVE *some outspoken remarks* ► frank, forthright, candid, direct, blunt, plain-speaking, straightforward, unequivocal OPPOSITES ARE guarded, diplomatic

outstanding ADJECTIVE 1 *She is an outstanding musician.* ► excellent, exceptional, superb, superlative, fine, extraordinary, distinguished, celebrated OPPOSITES ARE mediocre, unexceptional 2 *All outstanding questions will be answered.* ► unresolved, unsettled, remaining, pending

outweigh VERB *The benefits of the plan have to outweigh the costs.* ► exceed, be better than, be greater than, prevail over, override, have the edge on

outwit VERB *The besieged garrison managed to outwit the enemy.* ► outsmart, dupe, fool, hoodwink, hoax, cheat, deceive, trick, (more informal) take in, (more informal) outfox

oval ADJECTIVE *an oval lawn* ► egg-shaped, elliptical, ovoid

overall ADJECTIVE *It was a good overall result.* ► general, all-inclusive, all-embracing, comprehensive, inclusive AN OPPOSITE IS specific

overall ADVERB *Things have improved overall.* ► generally, in general, generally speaking, altogether, all in all, for the most part, on the whole, in the main, on balance, on average

overcome VERB 1 *Neither army was strong enough to overcome the other.* ► defeat, beat, conquer, overpower, vanquish, overwhelm, trounce 2 *It would be be easy to overcome his fear of flying.* ► control, master, get the better of, repress, subdue

overdo VERB overdoes, overdoing, overdid, overdone **1** do something too much **2** cook food for too long

overdose NOUN overdoses too large a dose of a drug

overdraft NOUN overdrafts the amount by which a bank account is overdrawn

overdraw VERB overdraws, overdrawing, overdrew, overdrawn draw more money from a bank account than the amount you have in it

overdue ADJECTIVE late; not paid or arrived, etc., by the proper time

overhaul VERB overhauls, overhauling, overhauled **1** examine something thoroughly and repair it if necessary **2** overtake
▷ **overhaul** NOUN

overhead ADJECTIVE, ADVERB **1** above the level of your head **2** in the sky

overheads PLURAL NOUN the expenses of running a business

overhear VERB overhears, overhearing, overheard hear something accidentally or without the speaker intending you to hear it

overjoyed ADJECTIVE filled with great joy

overlap VERB overlaps, overlapping, overlapped **1** lie across part of something **2** happen partly at the same time
▷ **overlap** NOUN

overlay VERB overlays, overlaying, overlaid cover with a layer; lie on top of something

overload VERB overloads, overloading, overloaded put too great a load on someone or something

overlook VERB overlooks, overlooking, overlooked **1** not notice or consider something **2** deliberately ignore something wrong; not punish an offence **3** have a view over something

overpower VERB overpowers, overpowering, overpowered defeat someone by greater strength or numbers

overpowering ADJECTIVE very strong

overrate VERB overrates, overrating, overrated have too high an opinion of something

override VERB overrides, overriding, overrode, overridden **1** overrule **2** be more important than • *Safety overrides all other considerations.*
▷ **overriding** ADJECTIVE

overrule VERB overrules, overruling, overruled reject a suggestion, etc., by using your authority • *We voted for having a disco but the headteacher overruled the idea.*

overrun VERB overruns, overrunning, overran, overrun **1** spread over and occupy or harm something • *Mice overran the place.* **2** go on for longer than it should • *The broadcast overran by ten minutes.*

oversee VERB oversees, overseeing, oversaw, overseen watch over or supervise people working
▷ **overseer** NOUN

oversight NOUN oversights a mistake made by not noticing something

---

Thesaurus

---

overdo VERB *She spoilt her case by overdoing the emotion.* ► exaggerate, overstate, overplay, overemphasize, overdramatize OPPOSITES ARE underplay, play down

overdue ADJECTIVE **1** *The train is overdue.* ► late, delayed, behind time, tardy, unpunctual, slow AN OPPOSITE IS early **2** *Our phone bill is overdue.* ► unpaid, unsettled, outstanding, owing, in arrears

overeat VERB *The food was so horrible at least there was no danger of them overeating.* ► overindulge, eat too much, be greedy, gorge, guzzle, binge, (*more informal*) stuff yourself, (*more informal*) make a pig of yourself OPPOSITES ARE diet, fast, undereat

overflow VERB *The water tank overflowed, causing damage to the roof.* ► spill over, flow over, pour over, run over, brim over, flood

overjoyed ADJECTIVE *Brian was overjoyed at the birth of his daughter.* ► thrilled, delighted, ecstatic, pleased, excited, happy, glad OPPOSITES ARE dejected, disappointed

overlook VERB **1** *a mistake we are willing to overlook* ► ignore, disregard, take no notice of, pay no attention to, discount, overlook, pass over, let pass, excuse, forget, make light of, brush aside, (*more informal*) turn a blind eye to AN OPPOSITE IS penalize **2** *The house overlooks a car park.* ► look out on, have a view of, look on to, look over, face, front

overpowering ADJECTIVE **1** *an overpowering feeling of sorrow* ► overwhelming, irrepressible, irresistible, uncontrollable, oppressive, intense OPPOSITES ARE slight, weak **2** *The smell was overpowering.* ► stifling, suffocating, nauseating, sickening, pungent AN OPPOSITE IS mild **3** *overpowering evidence of their guilt* ► compelling, irrefutable, undeniable, incontrovertible, conclusive, forceful, powerful, strong OPPOSITES ARE unconvincing, inconclusive

overrule VERB *A higher court overruled the decision.* ► overturn, override, revoke, reverse, cancel, rescind, quash, set aside, countermand OPPOSITES ARE confirm, endorse, allow

oversight NOUN *The delay was caused by oversight.* ► omission, lapse, carelessness, neglect, error

a
b
c
d
e
f
g
h
i
j
k
l
m
n
o
p
q
r
s
t
u
v
w
x
y
z

overtake ➡ own goal

overtake VERB overtakes, overtaking, overtook, overtaken **1** pass a moving vehicle or person, etc. **2** catch up with someone

overthrow VERB overthrows, overthrowing, overthrew, overthrown remove someone from power by force • *They overthrew the king.*

overtime NOUN time spent working outside the normal hours; payment for this

overture NOUN overtures **1** a piece of music written as an introduction to an opera, ballet, etc. **2** a friendly attempt to start a discussion • *They made overtures of peace.*

overturn VERB overturns, overturning, overturned **1** turn over or upside down **2** reverse a legal decision

overwhelm VERB overwhelms, overwhelming, overwhelmed **1** bury or drown beneath a huge mass **2** overcome completely
▷ **overwhelming** ADJECTIVE

ovum (oh- vum) NOUN ova a female cell that can develop into a new individual when it is fertilized [from Latin, = egg]

owe VERB owes, owing, owed **1** have a duty to pay or give something to someone, especially money **2** have something because of the action of another person or thing • *They owed their lives to the pilot's skill.*
owing to because of; caused by
USAGE The use of *owing to* as a preposition meaning "because of" is entirely acceptable, unlike this use of *due to*, which some people object to. See note at **due**.

owl NOUN owls a bird of prey with large eyes, usually flying at night

own ADJECTIVE belonging to yourself or itself
get your own back get revenge
on your own alone

own VERB owns, owning, owned **1** possess; have something as your property **2** acknowledge or admit something • *I own that I made a mistake.*
own up confess; admit guilt

owner NOUN owners the person who owns something
▷ **ownership** NOUN

own goal NOUN own goals a goal scored by a member of a team against their own side

Thesaurus

overtake VERB **1** *Huge trucks were overtaking one another.* ► pass, pull ahead of, go past, overhaul, catch up with **2** *Fruit had overtaken oil as the country's main export.* ► outstrip, exceed, surpass, outdo **3** *Another disaster overtook the family.* ► befall, overwhelm, overpower, strike, hit, afflict, engulf

overthrow VERB *The emperor was finally overthrown by his own guard.* ► depose, oust, remove, drive out, expel, unseat, defeat

overthrow NOUN *the overthrow of the tyrant* ► downfall, defeat, removal, fall, collapse, deposing, ousting, expulsion, unseating

overtone NOUN *The word "compulsory" has threatening overtones.* ► connotation, association, implication, undertone, undercurrent, reverberation, suggestion

overturn VERB **1** *The boat overturned in a squall.* ► capsize, turn over, tip over, keel over, turn turtle, overbalance **2** *Someone had overturned a box of tools over the garage floor.* ► upset, spill, knock over, tip over, topple **3** *The decision was overturned in the Supreme Court.* ► overrule, override, revoke, reverse, cancel, rescind, quash, set aside, countermand

overweight ADJECTIVE *I had put on twenty pounds and was noticeably overweight.* ► fat, obese, corpulent, gross OPPOSITES ARE underweight, undernourished

overwhelm VERB **1** *The home side overwhelmed the visitors in the league game.* ► defeat,

overcome, crush, overpower, rout, trounce, win against, conquer, vanquish, subdue, get the better of, (*more informal*) thrash **2** *Monsoons would soon overwhelm the region.* ► overrun, inundate, submerge, engulf, flood, deluge, bury **3** *She bent her head, overwhelmed by grief.* ► overcome, overpower, strike, crush

overwhelming ADJECTIVE **1** *The campaign received overwhelming support.* ► strong, massive, formidable, sweeping, forceful, powerful **2** *The army suffered another overwhelming defeat.* ► crushing, devastating, great, overpowering

owing ADJECTIVE *There is a small amount of money still owing.* ► due, outstanding, unpaid, payable, owed, unsettled, overdue
owing to *He would not use the lifts, owing to his claustrophobia.* ► because of, as a result of, on account of, as a consequence of, by reason of, thanks to

own VERB *Many more people own their own house.* ► possess, be the owner of, have, hold
own up to *He was waiting for a good moment to own up to the mistake.* ► confess, admit, acknowledge, tell the truth about, (*more informal*) come clean about, (*more informal*) make a clean breast of

owner NOUN **1** *Maintenance of the service road is the responsibility of the properties' owners.* ► possessor, proprietor, freeholder, landlord, landlady **2** *Dog owner should not let their pets soil the pavements.* ► keeper, master, mistress

ox *NOUN* **oxen** a large animal kept for its meat and for pulling carts

oxide *NOUN* **oxides** a compound of oxygen and one other element

oxygen *NOUN* a colorless odorless tasteless gas that exists in the air and is essential for living things

oyster *NOUN* **oysters** a kind of shellfish whose shell sometimes contains a pearl

ozone *NOUN* a form of oxygen with a sharp smell

ozone layer *NOUN* a layer of ozone high in the atmosphere, protecting the earth from harmful amounts of the sun's radiation

Thesaurus

A
B
C
D
E
F
G
H
I
J
K
L
M
N
O
P
Q
R
S
T
U
V
W
X
Y
Z

Pp

p. *ABBREVIATION* **pp.** page

pace *NOUN* **paces** 1 one step in walking, marching, or running 2 speed ● *He set a fast pace.*

pacemaker *NOUN* **pacemakers** 1 a person who sets the pace for another in a race 2 an electrical device to keep the heart beating

pacifist (pas- if- ist) *NOUN* **pacifists** a person who believes that war is always wrong
▷ **pacifism** *NOUN*

pacify *VERB* **pacifies, pacifying, pacified** 1 calm a person down 2 bring peace to a country or to people who are fighting
▷ **pacification** *NOUN*

pack *NOUN* **packs** 1 a bundle or collection of things wrapped or tied together 2 a set of playing cards (usually 52) 3 a bag carried on your back 4 a large amount ● *a pack of lies* 5 a group of hounds or wolves etc. 6 a group of people; a group of Brownies or Cub Scouts

pack *VERB* **packs, packing, packed** 1 put things into a suitcase, bag, or box, etc., in order to move or store them 2 crowd together; fill tightly

pack off (*informal*) send a person away

send a person packing (*informal*) dismiss him or her

package *NOUN* **packages** 1 a parcel or packet 2 a number of things offered or accepted together
▷ **packaging** *NOUN*

packet *NOUN* **packets** a small parcel

pack ice *NOUN* a mass of pieces of ice floating in the sea

pad *NOUN* **pads** 1 a soft thick mass of material, used, e.g., to protect or stuff something 2 a piece of soft material worn to protect your leg in soccer and other games 3 a set of sheets of paper fastened together at one edge 4 the soft fleshy part under an animal's foot or the end of a finger or toe 5 a flat surface from which rockets are launched or where helicopters take off and land

pad *VERB* **pads, padding, padded** put a pad on or in something

pad out make a book, speech, etc., longer than it needs to be

padding *NOUN* material used to pad things

Thesaurus

pace *NOUN* 1 *She moved back a few paces.* ► step, stride 2 *The traffic was moving at a slow pace.* ► speed, rate, velocity, movement, quickness, gait, (*informal*) lick 3 *They quickened their pace to a run.* ► stride, gait, tread, walk, march, speed, progress

pace *VERB* *Richard paced up and down for ages before going in.* ► walk, stride, tread, march

pacify *VERB* *It was too late to pacify her now, and she stormed off.* ► appease, placate, calm, conciliate, mollify, soothe, assuage, propitiate, quieten AN OPPOSITE IS anger

pack *NOUN* 1 *The bookshelves come in a self-assembly pack. A pack of cigarettes lay on the table.* ► package, packet, container, carton, box, parcel, bundle 2 *a group of walkers with packs on their backs* ► backpack, rucksack, knapsack, kitbag 3 *a pack of wolves* ► group, herd, troop 4 *a pack of youths* ► group, crowd, band, gang, set, throng, horde, mob

pack *VERB* 1 *The children helped to pack the hamper.* ► fill, load, stuff, put things in 2 *She decided to pack her belongings and leave.* ► bundle, parcel, wrap, stow, store 3 *On rainy days visitors pack the local museums.* ► throng, crowd into, cram into, squash into, squeeze into, fill, jam

pack in (*informal*) *James has decided to pack in his job.* ► give up, leave, resign from, (*informal*) quit, (*informal*) chuck in

pack up 1 (*informal*) *If you're not having a good time perhaps it's time to pack up.* ► stop, break off, call it a day

package *NOUN* *A strange package arrived by special delivery.* ► parcel, packet, container, consignment

packed *a packed room* ► crowded, full, crammed, jam-packed

packet *NOUN* 1 *a packet of sugar* ► pack, carton, bag, box, container 2 **a packet** (*informal*) *new shoes that cost a packet* ► a fortune, a small fortune, a huge amount, a king's ransom, (*informal*) an arm and a leg

pact *NOUN* *The two countries signed a non-aggression pact.* ► treaty, alliance, agreement, settlement, truce, protocol, understanding

pad *NOUN* 1 *Take a pad to sit on as the seats are hard.* ► cushion, pillow, padding, squab, bolster, wad 2 *She made notes on a small pad.* ► notebook, notepad, jotter, sketchbook

pad *VERB* 1 *You can pad the cushion with plastic foam.* ► stuff, pack, fill, line, upholster 2 *He padded along to the bathroom.* ► walk, creep, tiptoe

pad out *Try not to pad out your letter with irrelevant detail.* ► expand, inflate, fill out, elaborate, lengthen, spin out, stretch out

padding *NOUN* 1 *The sofa burst open and masses of gray padding fell out.* ► stuffing, wadding, filling, cushioning 2 *The story could be much*

paddle[1] VERB **paddles, paddling, paddled** walk about in shallow water
▷ **paddle** NOUN

paddle NOUN **paddles** a short oar with a broad blade; something shaped like this

paddle[2] VERB **paddles, paddling, paddled** move a boat along with a paddle or paddles; row gently

paddock NOUN **paddocks** a small field where horses are kept

padlock NOUN **padlocks** a detachable lock with a metal loop that passes through a ring or chain, etc.
▷ **padlock** VERB

pagan (pay- gan) NOUN **pagans** a person who does not believe in one of the chief religions; a heathen
▷ **pagan** ADJECTIVE
[from Latin *paganus* = country dweller, civilian. In Christian Latin the word was used of anyone who was a civilian in the sense of not being in the "army" of Christ.]

page[1] NOUN **pages** a piece of paper that is part of a book or newspaper, etc.; one side of this

page[2] NOUN **pages 1** a boy or man employed to go on errands or be an attendant **2** a young boy attending a bride at a wedding

pageant NOUN **pageants 1** a play or entertainment about historical events and people **2** a procession of people in costume as an entertainment
▷ **pageantry** NOUN

pagoda (pag- oh- da) NOUN **pagodas** a Buddhist tower, or a Hindu temple shaped like a pyramid, in India and the Far East [via Portuguese from Persian]

paid *past tense of* **pay**
put paid to (*informal*) put an end to someone's activity or hope etc.

pail NOUN **pails** a bucket

pain NOUN **pains 1** an unpleasant feeling caused by injury or disease **2** suffering in the mind
▷ **painful** ADJECTIVE **painfully** ADVERB **painless** ADJECTIVE
take pains make a careful effort with work etc.

painkiller NOUN **painkillers** a medicine or drug that relieves pain

painstaking ADJECTIVE very careful and thorough

paint NOUN **paints** a liquid substance put on something to color it
▷ **paintbox** NOUN **paintbrush** NOUN

paint VERB **paints, painting, painted 1** put paint on something **2** make a picture with paints

Thesaurus

shorter but for all the tedious padding.
► verbiage, verbosity, prolixity, wordiness, (*informal*) waffle

paddle NOUN *You'll need to use the paddle to reach the shore.* ► oar, scull

paddle VERB **1** *We paddled furiously to get to safety.* ► row, scull, pull **2** *You can paddle a long way out at low tide.* ► dabble, wade, splash about

pagan NOUN *pagans who worshipped nature* ► heathen, infidel, nonbeliever, unbeliever
USAGE You should only use *pagan* with reference to people in the past. It is an unfavorable term used by Christians and other believers in God to refer to nonbelievers. It is not an ordinary equivalent to words such as *atheist*, which is a more neutral term for someone who believes there is no God.

pagan ADJECTIVE *pagan festivals* ► heathen, infidel, ungodly, atheistic, godless, idolatrous, irreligious, unchristian
USAGE See the note at the previous entry.

page NOUN **1** *He had written a whole page by the time she returned.* ► side, sheet, folio, leaf **2** *Clare's little brother had been a page at her friend's wedding.* ► pageboy, attendant, train-bearer

pain NOUN **1** *The pain in his tooth was fading.* ► ache, soreness, hurt, tenderness, throb, discomfort **2** *How could anyone be expected to put up with so much pain?* ► suffering, discomfort, agony, affliction **3** *the pain of losing a child* ► grief, sorrow, distress, torment, anguish, misery, trauma **4** (*informal*) *Younger brothers could be a pain at times like this.*
► nuisance, pest, bother, bore, trial, tribulation, inconvenience

pain VERB *It pained him to think of all the trouble they had been through.* ► hurt, sadden, grieve, distress, mortify

painful ADJECTIVE **1** *The knight had a painful wound in his side.* ► sore, hurting, tender, agonizing, excruciating **2** *The journey had been a painful experience.* ► unpleasant, traumatic, disagreeable, bitter, wretched OPPOSITES ARE pleasant, agreeable

paint NOUN *They chose a bright paint for the walls.* ► color, pigment, tint, coloring, stain

paint VERB **1** *Kim couldn't make up her mind whether to paint the room or paper it.* ► color, tint, use paint on, coat with paint, apply paint to, decorate **2** *The article paints a vivid picture of life in rural Wisconsin.* ► describe, depict, portray, present, sketch, outline, delineate

a b c d e f g h i j k l m n o **p** q r s t u v w x y z

A
B
C
D
E
F
G
H
I
J
K
L
M
N
O
P
Q
R
S
T
U
V
W
X
Y
Z

painting NOUN **paintings 1** a painted picture **2** using paints to make a picture

pair NOUN **pairs 1** a set of two things or people; a couple **2** something made of two joined parts • *a pair of scissors*

pair VERB **pairs, pairing, paired** put two things together as a pair
pair off *or* **up** form a couple

pajamas PLURAL NOUN a loose jacket and pants worn in bed [from Persian or Urdu *pay* = leg + *jamah* = clothing]

palace NOUN **palaces** a mansion where a king, queen, or other important person lives

palatable ADJECTIVE tasting pleasant

palate NOUN **palates 1** the roof of your mouth **2** a person's sense of taste

pale ADJECTIVE **1** almost white • *a pale face* **2** not bright in color or light • *pale green* • *the pale moonlight*
▷ **palely** ADVERB **paleness** NOUN

pale NOUN **pales** a boundary
beyond the pale beyond the limits of good taste or behavior, etc.

palindrome NOUN **palindromes** a word or phrase that reads the same backwards as forwards, e.g., *radar* or *Madam, I'm Adam* [from Greek *palindromos* = running back again]

paling NOUN **palings** a fence made of wooden posts or railings; one of its posts

pall (pawl) NOUN **palls 1** a cloth spread over a coffin **2** a dark covering • *A pall of smoke lay over the town.*

pall (pawl) VERB **palls, palling, palled** become uninteresting or boring to someone • *The novelty of the new computer game soon began to pall.*

palliative NOUN **palliatives** something that lessens pain or suffering
▷ **palliative** ADJECTIVE

palm NOUN **palms 1** the inner part of the hand, between the fingers and the wrist **2** a palm tree
palm off deceive a person into accepting something

palm tree NOUN **palm trees** a tropical tree with large leaves and no branches

palpitate VERB **palpitates, palpitating, palpitated 1** (said about the heart) beat hard and quickly **2** (said about a person) quiver with fear or excitement
▷ **palpitation** NOUN

pampas NOUN wide grassy plains in South America

pamper VERB **pampers, pampering, pampered** treat or look after someone very kindly and indulgently

pamphlet NOUN **pamphlets** a leaflet or booklet giving information on a subject [from *Pamphilet*, the name of a long 12th-century poem in Latin]

pan NOUN **pans 1** a wide container with a flat base, used for cooking, etc. **2** something shaped like this **3** the bowl of a lavatory

Thesaurus

painting NOUN *She was eager to buy one of his larger paintings.* ► picture, oil painting, watercolor

pair NOUN **1** *a pair of earrings* ► set, set of two **2** *The guests drank to the happy pair.* ► couple, partners, husband and wife, man and wife **3** *The pair sang, one standing and the other at the piano.* ► couple, duo, two, twosome

pal NOUN (*informal*) *The boys had been pals since primary school.* ► friend, companion, (*informal*) mate, (*informal*) buddy, (*informal*) chum

palace NOUN *A royal palace open to the public* ► official residence, château, mansion, stately home, castle RELATED ADJECTIVE ► palatial

pale ADJECTIVE **1** *He frowned and turned pale.* ► pallid, white, wan, ashen, anaemic, sallow AN OPPOSITE IS flushed **2** *a pale shade of pink* ► light, soft, muted, pastel, faint, weak OPPOSITES ARE dark, strong **3** *a pale light* ► dim, weak, watery, feeble OPPOSITES ARE bright, strong

pally ADJECTIVE *The two men had become quite pally over the years.* ► friendly, close, on good terms, intimate, (*informal*) matey, (*informal*) chummy

palm VERB **palm off** *They palmed off the worst wines on their visitors.* ► foist, fob off, get rid of, dispose of, offload, (*more informal*) unload

paltry ADJECTIVE *All he gave was a paltry five dollars.* ► meager, negligible, pitiful, miserable, modest, scanty, scant, sparse, (*more informal*) measly OPPOSITES ARE generous, extravagant

pamper VERB *His mother tended to pamper him.* ► spoil, indulge, overindulge, cosset, mollycoddle, coddle, humor, pander to

pamphlet NOUN *a pamphlet on bee-keeping* ► leaflet, brochure, booklet, handout, folder, notice

pan NOUN *Fry the mushrooms and onions in a large pan.* ► frying-pan, saucepan, container, vessel, pot

pan VERB (*informal*) *The reviews all panned the film mercilessly.* ► criticize, attack, lambaste, censure, (*informal*) hammer, (*informal*) take apart, (*informal*) knock OPPOSITES ARE praise, commend, recommend

pancake NOUN pancakes a thin round cake of batter fried on both sides

panda NOUN pandas a large bearlike black-and-white animal found in China

pandemonium NOUN uproar and complete confusion [from *Pandemonium*, John Milton's name for the capital of hell in his poem "Paradise Lost," from *pan-* = all + demon]

pane NOUN panes a sheet of glass in a window

panel NOUN panels **1** a long flat piece of wood, metal, etc., that is part of a door, wall, piece of furniture, etc. **2** a flat board with controls or instruments on it **3** a group of people chosen to discuss or decide something
▷ **panelled** ADJECTIVE **panelling** NOUN

pang NOUN pangs a sudden sharp pain

panic NOUN sudden uncontrollable fear
▷ **panic-stricken** ADJECTIVE **panicky** ADJECTIVE

panic VERB panics, panicking, panicked fill or be filled with panic

panorama NOUN panoramas a view or picture of a wide area
▷ **panoramic** ADJECTIVE

pant VERB pants, panting, panted take short quick breaths, usually after running or working hard

panther NOUN panthers a leopard, especially a black one

pantomime NOUN pantomimes **1** a Christmas entertainment, usually based on a fairy tale **2** mime

pantry NOUN pantries a small room for storing food; a larder

pants PLURAL NOUN trousers

paper NOUN papers **1** a substance made in thin sheets from wood, rags, etc., and used for writing or printing or drawing on or for wrapping things **2** a newspaper **3** wallpaper **4** a document **5** a set of examination questions • *a history paper*

paper VERB papers, papering, papered cover a wall or room with wallpaper

paperback NOUN paperbacks a book with a thin flexible cover

papier mâché (pap- yay mash- ay) NOUN paper made into pulp and molded to make models, ornaments, etc.

parable NOUN parables a story told to teach people something, especially one of those told by Jesus Christ

parabola (pa- rab- ol- a) NOUN parabolas a curve like the path of an object thrown into the air and falling down again
▷ **parabolic** ADJECTIVE

parachute NOUN parachutes an umbrella-like device on which people or things can float slowly to the ground from an aircraft
▷ **parachute** VERB **parachutist** NOUN

parade NOUN parades **1** a procession that displays people or things **2** an assembly of troops for inspection, drill, etc.; a ground for this **3** a public square, promenade, or row of shops

parade VERB parades, parading, paraded **1** move in a parade **2** assemble for a parade

Thesaurus

panache NOUN *Julian produced the flowers with all the panache of a successful conjuror.*
► confidence, enthusiasm, flourish, spirit, style, verve, zest

pandemonium NOUN *The meeting ended in pandemonium.* ► chaos, uproar, bedlam, mayhem, confusion, disorder, muddle

pander VERB
pander to *Susan was prepared to pander to some of their foibles, but there were limits.* ► gratify, indulge, satisfy, cater to

panel NOUN **1** *He stared at the control panel, looking for the right switch.* ► console, fascia, board **2** *The case will be decided by a panel of judges.* ► group, team, body, board, council, commission

panic NOUN *They rushed out in panic.* ► alarm, fright, fear, trepidation, consternation, horror, terror, frenzy

panic VERB *There is no need to panic yet.* ► be alarmed, take fright, lose your head, lose your nerve, overreact, (*more informal*) flap

panicky ADJECTIVE *Her voice became breathless and panicky.* ► panic-stricken, alarmed, frantic, hysterical, frightened, overexcited, terror-stricken, unnerved AN OPPOSITE IS calm

pants NOUN *a pair of pants* ► trousers, underpants, briefs, trunks, shorts, (*for men*) (*for women*) panties

paper NOUN **1** *They had to show their papers at the border.* ► document, credentials, identification, authorization, certificate **2** *I'll go and buy a paper.* ► newspaper, daily, broadsheet (= large newspaper), tabloid (= small newspaper), magazine **3** *Her father was writing a paper for a medical journal.* ► article, essay, study, lecture, dissertation, thesis

parade NOUN *a military parade* ► procession, march, cavalcade, spectacle, display, pageant, review, show

parade VERB **1** *The teams will parade through the city.* ► process, troop, march past **2** *He paraded up and down in the corridor.* ► stride, strut, walk **3** *She was eager to parade her knowledge.* ► display, show off, demonstrate, exhibit, make a show of

A
B
C
D
E
F
G
H
I
J
K
L
M
N
O

P

Q
R
S
T
U
V
W
X
Y
Z

paradise NOUN **1** heaven; a heavenly place **2** the Garden of Eden

paradox NOUN paradoxes a statement that seems to contradict itself but is in fact true
▷ **paradoxical** ADJECTIVE **paradoxically** ADVERB

paraffin NOUN a kind of oil used as fuel

paragraph NOUN paragraphs one or more sentences on a single subject, forming a section of a piece of writing and beginning on a new line, usually slightly in from the margin of the page

parallel ADJECTIVE **1** (said about lines, etc.) side by side and the same distance apart from each other for their whole length, like railway lines **2** similar or corresponding • *When gas prices rise, there is a parallel rise in bus fares.*
▷ **parallelism** NOUN

parallel NOUN parallels **1** something similar or corresponding **2** a comparison • *You can draw a parallel between the two situations.* **3** a line that is parallel to another **4** a line of latitude
USAGE Take care with the spelling of this word: one *r*, two *l*s, then one *l*.

parallelogram NOUN parallelograms a quadrilateral with its opposite sides equal and parallel

paralyze VERB paralyzes, paralyzing, paralyzed **1** cause paralysis in a person **2** make something be unable to move • *She was paralysed with fear.*

paralysis NOUN being unable to move, especially because of a disease or an injury to the nerves
▷ **paralytic** (pa- ra- **lit**- ik) ADJECTIVE

paramedic NOUN paramedics a person who is trained to do medical work, especially

emergency first aid, but is not a fully qualified doctor

parameter (pa- **ram**- it- er) NOUN parameters a quantity, quality, or factor that is variable and affects other things by its changes
USAGE Do not confuse with **perimeter**.

paramount ADJECTIVE more important than anything else • *Secrecy is paramount.*

parapet NOUN parapets a low wall along the edge of a balcony, bridge, roof, etc.

paraphernalia NOUN numerous pieces of equipment, belongings, etc.

paraphrase VERB paraphrases, paraphrasing, paraphrased give the meaning of something by using different words
▷ **paraphrase** NOUN

parasite NOUN parasites an animal or plant that lives in or on another, from which it gets its food
▷ **parasitic** ADJECTIVE
[from Greek *parasitos* = guest at a meal]

paratroops PLURAL NOUN troops trained to be dropped from aircraft by parachute
▷ **paratrooper** NOUN

parcel NOUN parcels something wrapped up to be sent by post or carried

parcel VERB parcels, parceling, parceled **1** wrap something up as a parcel **2** divide something into portions • *parcel out the work*
[from old French, related to **particle**]

parched ADJECTIVE very dry or thirsty

parchment NOUN parchments a kind of heavy paper, originally made from animal skins
[from the city of Pergamum, now in Turkey, where parchment was made in ancient times]

pardon NOUN **1** forgiveness **2** the canceling of a punishment • *a free pardon*

Thesaurus

---

paradise NOUN **1** *non-Christian theories about Paradise* ► heaven, Utopia, Eden, Elysium, nirvana **2** *Their holiday had been absolute paradise.* ► bliss, heaven, joy, delight, ecstasy

parallel VERB *Their lives parallel each other in many respects.* ► resemble, match, be similar to, compare with, correspond to

paralyze VERB **1** *The injury paralyzed his right leg for a time.* ► disable, immobilize, cripple, incapacitate, deaden **2** *The country was paralyzed by a wave of strikes.* ► bring to a standstill, bring to a halt, cripple, halt, freeze

paralyzed ADJECTIVE *I had a paralyzed right arm.* ► disabled, handicapped, incapacitated, immobilized, crippled, lame, unusable

paralysis NOUN **1** *a disease that can cause paralysis* ► immobility, incapacity, paraplegia **2** *paralysis of the country's transport system* ► shutdown, immobilization, stopping, standstill

parameter NOUN *It is important to define the parameters for this research.* ► criterion, guideline, framework, limit, boundary

paramount ADJECTIVE *an issue of paramount importance* ► supreme, prime, primary, central, preeminent, highest, cardinal, foremost, utmost

parcel NOUN *a parcel of food* ► package, packet, pack, consignment, bale, bundle, carton

parcel VERB parcel out *Land was parceled out in small plots.* ► divide up, distribute, share out, apportion, portion out, split up

pardon VERB **1** *The king would pardon them if they admitted their guilt.* ► forgive, excuse, absolve, grant a pardon to, reprieve, amnesty, acquit AN OPPOSITE IS punish **2** *These are faults we can forgive and even admire.* ► forgive, excuse, condone

pardon VERB pardons, pardoning, pardoned
1 forgive or excuse somebody **2** cancel a person's punishment
▷ **pardonable** ADJECTIVE **pardonably** ADVERB

pardon INTERJECTION used to mean 'I didn't hear or understand what you said'

parent NOUN parents **1** a father or mother; a living thing that has produced others of its kind **2** a source from which others are derived • *the parent company*
▷ **parenthood** NOUN **parenting** NOUN **parental** (pa- **rent**- al) ADJECTIVE

parenthesis (pa- ren- thi- sis) NOUN parentheses **1** something extra that is inserted in a sentence, usually between brackets or dashes **2** either of the pair of brackets (like these) used to mark off words from the rest of a sentence
▷ **parenthetical** ADJECTIVE

parish NOUN parishes a district with its own church
▷ **parishioner** NOUN
[from Greek *paroikia* = neighbourhood]

park NOUN parks **1** a large garden or recreation ground for public use **2** an area of grassland or woodland belonging to a country house

park VERB parks, parking, parked leave a vehicle somewhere for a time

parliament NOUN parliaments an assembly that makes a country's laws (in the United Kingdom and some other nations)
▷ **parliamentary** ADJECTIVE
[from early French *parlement* = speaking]

parlor NOUN parlors (old use) a sitting room

parody NOUN parodies an amusing imitation of the style of a writer, composer, literary work, etc.

parody VERB parodies, parodying, parodied make or be a parody of a person or thing

parole NOUN the release of a prisoner before the end of his or her sentence on condition of good behaviour • *He was on parole.*
▷ **parole** VERB

paroxysm (pa- roks- izm) NOUN paroxysms a sudden outburst of rage, jealousy, laughter, etc.

parrot NOUN parrots a brightly colored tropical bird that can learn to repeat words etc.

parsley NOUN a plant with crinkled green leaves used to flavour and decorate food

parsnip NOUN parsnips a plant with a pointed pale yellow root used as a vegetable

parson NOUN parsons a member of the clergy, especially a rector or Protestant pastor

part NOUN parts **1** some but not all of a thing or number of things; anything that belongs to something bigger **2** the character played by an actor or actress **3** the words spoken by a character in a play **4** how much a person or thing is involved in something • *She played a huge part in her daughter's success.* **5** one side in an agreement or in a dispute or quarrel
take in good part not be offended at something
take part join in an activity

part VERB parts, parting, parted separate or divide
part with give away or get rid of something

Thesaurus

pardon NOUN *A pardon was offered to the rebels.*
► amnesty, reprieve, release, discharge

parent NOUN *She had an elderly parent to look after.* ► mother or father, guardian

parentage NOUN *a young man of Indian parentage* ► origin, ancestry, lineage, pedigree, extraction, descent, heredity, roots, stock, derivation, blood, ancestors, forebears

park NOUN *The children went off to play in the park.* ► recreation ground, public gardens, playground, parkland

park VERB *She parked the car outside her friend's house.* ► leave, position, station, stop, place

parliament NOUN *The country's parliament dates back to the Middle Ages.* ► legislature, congress, assembly, council, government, senate, conclave, convocation

parody NOUN **1** *He swiveled his hips in a parody of the belly dance.* ► caricature, lampoon, comic imitation, mimicry, mockery, skit, (more informal) take-off, (more informal) spoof, (more informal) send-up **2** *The article was no more than a parody of the truth.* ► travesty, distortion, mockery, caricature

parson NOUN *The parson shook hands outside the church.* ► clergyman, clergywoman, cleric, minister, priest, vicar, preacher

part NOUN **1** *This is only one part of the story.* ► bit, piece, portion, segment, section, episode, chapter, constituent OPPOSITES ARE whole, entirety **2** *A part of the house has been closed off.* ► section, portion **3** *The washing machine has broken and needs a new part.* ► component, element, unit **4** *Deborah would take the lead part in the school play.* ► role, character **5** *Her parents lived in another part of town.* ► region, district, neighborhood, quarter, section, sector **6** *Their part in the affair had not been very distinguished.* ► involvement, role, function, concern, responsibility, contribution (to)

part VERB **1** *They did not want to part on such bad terms.* ► separate, leave, say goodbye, say farewell, break up, go away OPPOSITES ARE

A B C D E F G H I J K L M N O **P** Q R S T U V W X Y Z

part exchange NOUN giving something that you own as part of the price of what you are buying

partial ADJECTIVE **1** not complete or total ● *a partial eclipse* **2** favouring one side more than the other; biased or unfair
▷ **partially** ADVERB **partiality** NOUN
be partial to be fond of something

participate VERB participates, participating, participated take part or have a share in something
▷ **participant** NOUN **participation** NOUN **participator** NOUN

participle NOUN participles a word formed from a verb (e.g., *gone, going; guided, guiding*) and used with an auxiliary verb to form certain tenses (e.g., *It has gone. It is going.*) or the passive (e.g., *We were guided to our seats*), or as an adjective (e.g., *a guided missile; a guiding light*) The past participle (e.g., *gone, guided*). describes a completed action or past condition. The present participle (which ends in *-ing*) describes a continuing action or condition.

particle NOUN particles a very small piece or amount

particular ADJECTIVE **1** of this one and no other; individual ● *This particular stamp is very* rare. **2** special ● *Take particular care of it.* **3** giving something close attention; choosing carefully ● *He is very particular about his clothes.*
▷ **particularly** ADVERB **particularity** NOUN

particular NOUN particulars a detail or single fact ● *Can you give me some particulars of the job?* in particular **1** especially ● *We liked this one in particular.* **2** special ● *We did nothing in particular.*

parting NOUN partings **1** leaving or separation **2** a line where hair is combed away in different directions

partisan NOUN partisans **1** a strong supporter of a party or group etc. **2** a member of an organization resisting the authorities in a conquered country

partition NOUN partitions **1** a thin wall that divides a room or space **2** dividing something, especially a country, into separate parts

partition VERB partitions, partitioning, partitioned **1** divide something into separate parts **2** divide a room or space by means of a partition

partly ADVERB to some extent but not completely

partner NOUN partners **1** one of a pair of people who do something together, such as

---

Thesaurus

---

meet, reunite **2** *The authorities are anxious not to part the children.* ► separate, divide, split
part with *advertising designed to persuade shoppers to part with their money.* ► give up, relinquish, hand over, let go of, give up, forgo, surrender, discard

partial ADJECTIVE **1** *The economic collapse was followed by a partial recovery.* ► incomplete, qualified, limited, restricted, imperfect, unfinished AN OPPOSITE IS complete
be partial to *She had always been partial to ice cream.* ► like, love, enjoy, be fond of, have a fondness for, be keen on, appreciate, (more informal) go for

particle NOUN *There was not a single particle of food left.* ► bit, piece, morsel, scrap, shred, crumb, drop, fragment, grain, iota, jot, sliver, speck

particular ADJECTIVE **1** *The article criticized a particular group of companies.* ► specific, certain, distinct, definite, discrete **2** *This is a matter of particular interest to us.* ► special, exceptional, marked, unusual, uncommon, noteworthy, remarkable **3** *He was not too particular about the methods they used.* ► fussy, discriminating, finicky, fastidious, (more informal) choosy

particulars PLURAL NOUN *A police officer will call to take your particulars.* ► details, facts, information, circumstances

particularly ADVERB *The river trip is particularly enjoyable.* ► especially, exceptionally, remarkably, unusually, distinctly, notably

parting NOUN **1** *It will be an emotional parting.* ► farewell, goodbye, departure, leaving OPPOSITES ARE meeting, reunion **2** *They would tell their son and daughter that evening about their intended parting.* ► separation, breakup, split-up, divorce AN OPPOSITE IS reconciliation

partisan NOUN *The country was swarming with Tito's partisans.* ► supporter, follower, adherent, devotee, champion, guerrilla, fighter

partisan ADJECTIVE *the bitterly partisan nature of the debate* ► biased, one-sided, prejudiced, colored, partial, slanted, factional

partition NOUN **1** *the partition of the country after the war* ► division, dividing, splitting, breaking-up **2** *A partition separated the two parts of a room.* ► screen, panel, divider, barrier, dividing wall

partition VERB *A UN resolution partitioned the country into two states.* ► divide, split, subdivide, separate

partly ADVERB *The work was now partly finished* ► partially, in part, to some extent, up to a point

partner NOUN **1** *Jack had been his business partner for many years.* ► colleague, associate, collaborator, ally, confederate, comrade, dancing or playing a game **2** a person who jointly owns a business with one or more other people **3** the person that someone is married to or is having a sexual relationship with

▷ **partnership** *NOUN*

part of speech *NOUN* parts of speech any of the groups (also called **word classes**) into which words are divided in grammar (noun, pronoun, adjective, verb, adverb, preposition, conjunction, and interjection)

partridge *NOUN* partridges a game bird with brown feathers

part-time *ADJECTIVE, ADVERB* working for only some of the normal hours

▷ **part-timer** *NOUN*

party *NOUN* parties **1** a gathering of people to enjoy themselves • *a birthday party* **2** a group working or traveling together **3** an organized group of people with similar political beliefs • *the Democratic Party* **4** a person who is involved in an action or lawsuit, etc. • *the guilty party*

pass *VERB* passes, passing, passed **1** go past something; go or move in a certain direction **2** move something in a certain direction • *Pass*

the cord through the ring. **3** give or transfer something to another person • *Could you pass the butter?* **4** (in ball games) kick or throw the ball to another player of your own side **5** be successful in a test or examination **6** approve or accept • *They passed a law.* **7** occupy time • *They passed several hours chatting together.* **8** happen • *We heard what passed when they met.* **9** come to an end **10** utter • *Pass a remark.* **11** (in a game, quiz, etc.) let your turn go by or choose not to answer

pass out 1 complete your military training **2** faint

pass *NOUN* passes **1** passing something **2** a success in an examination **3** (in ball games) kicking or throwing the ball to another player of your own side **4** a permit to go in or out of a place **5** a route through a gap in a range of mountains **6** a critical state of affairs • *Things have come to a pretty pass!*

passage *NOUN* passages **1** a way through something; a corridor **2** a journey by sea or air **3** a section of a piece of writing or music **4** passing • *the passage of time*

▷ **passageway** *NOUN*

Thesaurus

---

companion **2** *Staff were encouraged to bring their partners to the party.* ► girlfriend *or* boyfriend, husband *or* wife, spouse, consort, mate

partnership *NOUN* **1** *a business partnership* ► company, firm, corporation, organization, syndicate, alliance, combination, cooperative, affiliation **2** *a partnership between nations* ► cooperation, association, coalition, collaboration

party *NOUN* **1** *a house-warming party* ► celebration, gathering, festivity, function, merrymaking, (*more informal*) get-together, (*more informal*) do **2** *a political party* ► faction, group, grouping, league, alliance, association, cabal, coalition **3** *a search party* ► team, crew, squad, company, group

pass *VERB* **1** *Lots of heavy traffic passed through the village.* ► drive, go, move, stream, progress **2** *She went to pass him the sugar and spilled it.* ► hand, give, deliver **3** *Eventually the storm passed.* ► blow over, go away, fade, fade away, disappear, come to an end **4** *As time passed he gradually forgot her.* ► elapse, go by, advance, progress, tick by

pass away *He passed away in his sleep.* ► die, pass on, lose your life, meet your end, breathe your last, expire

pass off *The meeting passed off without any trouble.* ► happen, take place, go off, occur, turn out

pass out *She must have passed out.* ► faint, lose

consciousness, black out, (*more informal*) flake out

pass over *Perhaps we can pass over these mistakes.* ► disregard, overlook, ignore, forget, take no notice of, pay no attention to, discount

pass up *He was not one to pass up a chance of a free vacation.* ► forgo, reject, refuse, turn down, miss out on

pass *NOUN* **1** *a pass through the mountains* ► route, way, defile, gap, gorge, ravine, canyon **2** *Your pass will get you into all the city's museums.* ► permit, ticket, warrant, authority, authorization, license

passable *ADJECTIVE* **1** *The food was no more than passable.* ► adequate, acceptable, satisfactory, tolerable, moderate, ordinary, sufficient, all right, fair, mediocre, middling, (*more informal*) so-so AN OPPOSITE IS unacceptable **2** *The road is passable again after being closed because of floods.* ► traversable, navigable, open, usable, unblocked, clear AN OPPOSITE IS impassable

passage *NOUN* **1** *the passage of time* ► passing, advance, course, march, progress, progression, moving on **2** *a sea passage* ► crossing, journey, voyage, trip, cruise, sail **3** *a narrow passage leading to the garden* ► corridor, passageway, walkway, thoroughfare, hallway, way through **4** *a passage between the two houses* ► alley, alleyway, path, pathway, way, lane, track **5** *a passage from The Amber Spyglass* ► excerpt, extract, section, episode, scene, paragraph, piece, quotation

a b c d e f g h i j k l m n o **p** q r s t u v w x y z

471

A
B
C
D
E
F
G
H
I
J
K
L
M
N
O
P
Q
R
S
T
U
V
W
X
Y
Z

passenger NOUN passengers a person who is driven or carried in a car, train, ship, or aircraft, etc.

passerby NOUN passersby a person who happens to be going past something

passion NOUN passions 1 strong emotion 2 great enthusiasm
the Passion the sufferings of Jesus Christ at the Crucifixion
[from Latin *passio* = suffering]

passionate ADJECTIVE full of passion
▷ **passionately** ADVERB

passive ADJECTIVE 1 not resisting or fighting against something 2 acted upon and not active 3 (in grammar, said about a form of a verb) used when the subject of the sentence receives the action, e.g., *was hit* in "She was hit on the head." COMPARE active 4 (said about an activity) that you get the effect of because other people are doing it ● *passive smoking*
▷ **passively** ADVERB **passiveness** NOUN **passivity** NOUN

Passover NOUN a Jewish religious festival commemorating the freeing of the Jews from slavery in Egypt [from *pass over*, because according to the Bible, God spared the Jews from the fate that affected the Egyptians]

passport NOUN passports an official document that entitles the person holding it to travel abroad

password NOUN passwords 1 a secret word or phrase used to distinguish friends from enemies 2 a word you need to key in to gain access to certain computer files

past ADJECTIVE of the time gone by ● *during the past week*

past NOUN the time gone by

past PREPOSITION 1 beyond ● *Walk past the school.* 2 after ● *It is past midnight.*
past it (*slang*) too old to be able to do something

paste NOUN pastes 1 a soft, moist, and sticky substance 2 a glue, especially for paper 3 a soft edible mixture ● *tomato paste* 4 a hard glassy substance used to make imitation jewelry

paste VERB pastes, pasting, pasted 1 stick something onto a surface by using paste 2 coat something with paste 3 (*slang*) beat or thrash someone

pastel NOUN pastels 1 a crayon that is like chalk 2 a light delicate color

pasteurize VERB pasteurizes, pasteurizing, pasteurized purify milk by heating and then cooling it [named after Louis Pasteur, a 19th-century French scientist who invented the process]

pastille NOUN pastilles a small flavored candy

pastime NOUN pastimes something you do to make time pass pleasantly; a hobby or game

Thesaurus

passenger NOUN *Passengers were told to get out at the next station.* ► traveller, commuter, voyager, rider

passerby NOUN *Passersby stopped and looked.* ► bystander, onlooker, observer, spectator, watcher, witness, eyewitness

passing ADJECTIVE *a passing feeling of regret* ► brief, temporary, short-lived, transient, momentary, cursory, short

passion NOUN 1 *You could talk about your passion for hang-gliding.* ► fondness, enthusiasm, eagerness, mania, appetite, interest (in), fanaticism, zeal, craving, commitment (to) OPPOSITES ARE indifference (to), apathy 2 *He recalled the passion with which she had kissed him.* ► feeling, ardor, intensity, emotion, fervor, love, longing, craving, desire, excitement, fire, heat AN OPPOSITE IS detachment 3 *He spoke with a fierce passion.* ► emotion, feeling, vehemence, anger, rage, fury, frenzy, paroxysm OPPOSITES ARE coolness, indifference

passionate ADJECTIVE 1 *a passionate appeal for help* ► impassioned, emotional, heartfelt, intense, ardent, fervent, impulsive OPPOSITES ARE half-hearted, cool 2 *a passionate embrace* ► loving, amorous, sensual, (*more informal*)

steamy AN OPPOSITE IS cold 3 *His passionate temperament got the better of him.* ► excitable, hot-blooded, intense, fiery, wild, violent OPPOSITES ARE placid, phlegmatic

passive ADJECTIVE 1 *a passive acceptance of hardship* ► submissive, resigned, compliant, impassive, docile, long-suffering, non-violent, indifferent, patient, unresisting OPPOSITES ARE active, lively 2 *Tim had played a passive role in the affair.* ► inactive, uninvolved, non-participating OPPOSITES ARE active, assertive

past ADJECTIVE *memories of past happiness* ► bygone, former, previous, earlier, ended, finished, gone, (*more informal*) over and done with OPPOSITES ARE present, future

past NOUN *She was trying hard to forget the past.* ► antiquity, days gone by, history, old days, olden days, past times OPPOSITES ARE present, future

paste NOUN 1 *He used paste to fix his photos in an album.* ► glue, gum, adhesive, fixative 2 *Mix the ingredients into a smooth paste.* ► purée, spread, mixture, pulp

paste VERB *She was busy pasting wallpaper.* ► fix, fasten, glue, gum, hang

pastime NOUN *a time when art was a rich man's pastime* ► hobby, activity, recreation,

pastoral ADJECTIVE to do with country life • *a pastoral scene*

pastry NOUN **pastries 1** dough made with flour, fat, and water, rolled flat and baked **2** something made of pastry

pasture NOUN **pastures** land covered with grass, etc., that cattle, sheep, or horses can eat

pasture VERB **pastures, pasturing, pastured** put animals to graze in a pasture

pasty (pas- tee) NOUN **pasties** pastry with a filling of meat and vegetables, baked without a dish to shape it

pasty (pay- stee) ADJECTIVE looking pale and unhealthy

pat VERB **pats, patting, patted** tap gently with the hand open or with something flat

pat NOUN **pats 1** a patting movement or sound **2** a small piece of butter or other soft substance **a pat on the back** praise

patch NOUN **patches 1** a piece of material or metal, etc., put over a hole or damaged place **2** an area that is different from its surroundings **3** a piece of ground • *the cabbage patch* **4** a small area or piece of something • *There are patches of fog.*

patch VERB **patches, patching, patched** put a patch on something
patch up 1 repair something roughly **2** settle an argument

patchwork NOUN needlework in which small pieces of different cloth are sewn edge to edge

patchy ADJECTIVE occurring in patches; uneven
▷ **patchily** ADVERB **patchiness** NOUN

pâté (pat- ay) NOUN **pâtés** paste made of meat or fish

pâté de foie gras (pat- ay der fwah grah) NOUN a rich paste made from goose liver

patent (pat- ent, pay- tent) NOUN **patents** the official right given to an inventor to make or sell his or her invention and to prevent other people from copying it

patent VERB **patents, patenting, patented** get a patent for something

patent ADJECTIVE obvious
▷ **patently** ADVERB

paternal ADJECTIVE **1** to do with a father **2** fatherly
▷ **paternally** ADVERB

paternalistic ADJECTIVE treating people in a paternal way; providing for people's needs but giving them no responsibility
▷ **paternalism** NOUN

paternity NOUN **1** fatherhood **2** being the father of a particular baby

path NOUN **paths 1** a narrow way along which people or animals can walk **2** a line along which a person or thing moves **3** a course of action

pathetic ADJECTIVE **1** making you feel pity or sympathy **2** miserably inadequate or useless • *a pathetic attempt*
▷ **pathetically** ADVERB

Thesaurus

diversion, amusement, entertainment, occupation, game, sport, relaxation

pastoral ADJECTIVE **1** *a pastoral scene of trees and cows* ► rural, rustic, country, outdoor, agrarian, bucolic, farming, idyllic AN OPPOSITE IS urban **2** *the pastoral duties of a vicar's wife* ► ecclesiastical, priestly, parochial, ministerial, caring

pasty ADJECTIVE *a row of people with pasty faces* ► pale, pallid, white, wan, sickly, anaemic, unhealthy OPPOSITES ARE healthy, ruddy

pat VERB *Les leaned forward to pat her hand.* ► tap, touch, dab, stroke, rub, fondle

pat ADJECTIVE *His answers sounded pat, as if he'd rehearsed them.* ► glib, slick, facile, simplistic, smooth, unconvincing, perfunctory, superficial

pat ADVERB **1** *She trotted out her suggestion pat.* ► opportunely, at the right moment, in a timely way
down pat *They have the right language down pat.* ► by heart, by rote, word for word, parrot-fashion

patch NOUN **1** *old jeans covered in patches* ► mend, repair **2** *The family was going through a difficult patch.* ► period, time, spell, phase,

stretch **3** *Harry had a vegetable patch up the road.* ► plot, piece of ground, strip, row, area

patch VERB *He had got someone to patch his jacket at the elbow.* ► mend, repair, reinforce, put a patch on, cover, darn, fix, sew up, stitch up

patchy ADJECTIVE **1** *They drove through stretches of patchy fog.* ► irregular, uneven, sporadic, intermittent, variable, erratic, inconsistent, unpredictable, bitty, changeable AN OPPOSITE IS constant **2** *a piece of patchy grass* ► uneven, speckled, mottled, dappled, multicolored **3** *Their story was patchy and confusing.* ► fragmentary, deficient, variable, limited, inadequate OPPOSITES ARE comprehensive, complete

path NOUN **1** *a path by the train station* ► footpath, pathway, track, alley, lane **2** *His path was blocked by the barricades.* ► way, route, course, passage, progress

pathetic ADJECTIVE **1** *a pathetic wave of the hand* ► pitiful, pitiable, poignant, plaintive, sad, touching, moving, affecting, distressing, heartrending, lamentable, wretched
2 (*informal*) *He added up his pathetic savings.* ► inadequate, paltry, meager, feeble, derisory, miserable, wretched, worthless

a b c d e f g h i j k l m n o **p** q r s t u v w x y z

pathos (pay- thoss) NOUN a quality of making people feel pity or sympathy

patience NOUN **1** being patient **2** a card game for one person

patient ADJECTIVE able to wait or put up with trouble or inconvenience without becoming anxious or angry
▷ **patiently** ADVERB

patient NOUN patients a person who has treatment from a doctor or dentist, etc.

patio NOUN patios a paved area beside a house [from Spanish, = courtyard]

patriarch (pay- tree- ark) NOUN patriarchs **1** the male who is head of a family or tribe **2** a bishop of high rank in the Orthodox Christian churches
▷ **patriarchal** ADJECTIVE

patriot (pay- tree- ot, pat- ree- ot) NOUN patriots a person who loves his or her country and supports it loyally
▷ **patriotic** ADJECTIVE **patriotically** ADVERB **patriotism** NOUN

patrol VERB patrols, patrolling, patrolled walk or travel regularly over an area in order to guard it and see that all is well

patrol NOUN patrols **1** a patrolling group of people, ships, aircraft, etc. **2** a group of Scouts
on patrol patrolling

patron (pay- tron) NOUN patrons **1** someone who supports a person or cause with money or encouragement **2** a regular customer
▷ **patronage** (pat- ron- ij) NOUN

patronize (pat- ron- I'z) VERB patronizes, patronizing, patronized **1** be a regular customer of a particular shop, restaurant, etc. **2** talk to someone in a way that shows you think they are stupid or inferior to you

patter[1] NOUN a series of light tapping sounds

patter VERB patters, pattering, pattered make light tapping sounds ● *Rain pattered on the window panes.*

patter[2] NOUN the quick talk of a comedian, conjuror, salesperson, etc. [originally = recite a prayer: from Latin *pater noster* = Our Father, the first words of a Christian prayer]

pattern NOUN patterns **1** a repeated arrangement of lines, shapes, or colors, etc. **2** a thing to be copied in order to make something ● *a dress pattern* **3** the regular way in which something happens ● *Our French*

Thesaurus

---

patience NOUN **1** *Great care and patience is needed to avoid damaging the plants.*
▶ diligence, perseverance, persistence, self-control, stoicism, endurance, fortitude **2** *Will's behavior was stretching their patience to the limit.*
▶ toleration, forbearance, composure, calmness, restraint, equanimity, resignation

patient ADJECTIVE **1** *She tried to be patient while her husband hunted for the key.* ▶ composed, calm, self-controlled, restrained, forbearing, indulgent, tolerant, lenient, understanding, forbearing, philosophical OPPOSITES ARE impatient, intolerant **2** *The task called for a great deal of patient work.* ▶ diligent, persistent, persevering, tenacious, determined, dogged, resolved, purposeful

patient NOUN *the relation between doctor and patient* ▶ invalid, sick person, sufferer, case

patriotic ADJECTIVE *Many of his patriotic songs have a stirring lilt.* ▶ nationalistic, loyal, flag-waving, (*disapproving*) jingoistic, (*disapproving*) chauvinistic

patrol NOUN **1** *Security guards remain on patrol all night.* ▶ surveillance, watch, guard, duty **2** *A four-man patrol set off through the jungle.*
▶ guard, lookout, party, task force, convoy, detail

patrol VERB *Guards with dogs patrol the estate.*
▶ police, tour, inspect, keep watch on, be on patrol on, go the rounds of

patron NOUN **1** (*informal*) *a patron of the arts*
▶ sponsor, supporter, benefactor, champion, backer, defender **2** *Parking outside the shops is for patrons only.* ▶ client, customer, (*more informal*) regular

patronize VERB **1** *The parents of girls like Sally patronized the little shop.* ▶ do business with, be a customer of, frequent, shop at, buy from, deal with **2** *The nobility patronized music and the arts.* ▶ sponsor, support, finance, back, foster, encourage **3** *She accused them of patronizing her.* ▶ condescend to, talk down to, look down on, put down

patronizing ADJECTIVE *He should learn to adopt a less patronizing tone.* ▶ condescending, supercilious, superior, disdainful, haughty, lofty, paternalistic, snobbish OPPOSITES ARE humble, modest

patter VERB **1** *Rain pattered against the window.*
▶ beat, tap, rattle, clatter, pitter-patter **2** *The children pattered up to their rooms.* ▶ scurry, scamper, scuttle

patter NOUN **1** *the patter of feet* ▶ pattering, pitter-patter, scurrying, scuttling **2** *a salesman's patter* ▶ chatter, babble, line, (*more informal*) spiel

pattern NOUN **1** *patterns drawn in the sand*
▶ design, device, figure, motif, shape, figuration, arrangement, decoration, ornamentation **2** *Their actions might set a pattern* ▶ example, model, standard, guide,

classes follow a set pattern. **4** an excellent example or model
▷ **patterned** *ADJECTIVE*

paunch *NOUN* paunches a large belly

pauper *NOUN* paupers a person who is very poor

pause *NOUN* pauses a temporary stop in speaking or doing something

pause *VERB* pauses, pausing, paused **1** stop speaking or doing something for a short time **2** temporarily interrupt the playing of a CD, videotape, etc.

pave *VERB* paves, paving, paved lay a hard surface on a road or path, etc.
▷ **paving stone** *NOUN*
pave the way prepare for something

pavement *NOUN* pavements a paved path along the side of a street

pavilion *NOUN* pavilions **1** a building for use by players and spectators, etc., especially at a playing field **2** an ornamental building or shelter used for dances, concerts, exhibitions, etc.

paw *NOUN* paws the foot of an animal that has claws

paw *VERB* paws, pawing, pawed touch or scrape something with a hand or foot

pawn *NOUN* pawns **1** the least valuable piece in chess **2** a person whose actions are controlled by somebody else

pawn *VERB* pawns, pawning, pawned leave something with a pawnbroker as security for a loan

pawnbroker *NOUN* pawnbrokers a shopkeeper who lends money to people in return for objects that they leave as security
▷ **pawnshop** *NOUN*

pay *VERB* pays, paying, paid **1** give money in return for goods or services **2** give what is owed • *pay your debts* • *pay the rent* **3** be profitable or worthwhile • *It pays to advertise* **4** give or express • *Try to pay attention* • *It's time we paid them a visit* • *He doesn't often pay people compliments* **5** suffer a penalty **6** let out a rope by loosening it gradually
▷ **payer** *NOUN*
pay off **1** pay in full what you owe **2** be worthwhile or have good results • *All the preparation she did really paid off.*
pay up pay the full amount you owe

pay *NOUN* salary or wages

payable *ADJECTIVE* that must be paid

payment *NOUN* payments **1** paying **2** money paid

pay phone *NOUN* pay phones a public telephone operated by coins or a card

PC *ABBREVIATION* **1** personal computer **2** politically correct

PE *ABBREVIATION* physical education

pea *NOUN* peas the small round green seed of a climbing plant, growing inside a pod and used as a vegetable; the plant bearing these pods

peace *NOUN* **1** a time when there is no war, violence, or disorder **2** quietness and calm

Thesaurus

norm, original, precedent, archetype, criterion, prototype, sample, specimen **3** *The insects have a special behaviour pattern.*
► system, order, method, scheme

pauper *NOUN* *The revolution left the family almost paupers.* ► beggar, bankrupt, insolvent, down and out

pause *VERB* *She paused for a moment before going in.* ► hesitate, wait, stop, delay, halt, waver, hang back, break off, rest, have a pause

pause *NOUN* *There was a short pause while the band regrouped.* ► break, interruption, interval, delay, rest, wait, interlude, intermission, lull, stoppage, respite, stop, suspension, (*more informal*) breather

pave *VERB* *She decided to pave part of the garden to put a table on.* ► cover, concrete, flag, tile, asphalt
pave the way for *Tax cuts paved the way for an economic recovery.* ► prepare for, lay the foundations for, clear the way for, herald, precede

pavement *NOUN* *A parked car was blocking the pavement.* ► footpath, path, walkway, sidewalk

paw *NOUN* *She stroked the cat's paw.* ► foot, pad

pay *NOUN* *Her pay would go up in April.*
► income, earnings, salary, wages, payment, (*more formal*) remuneration, (*more formal*) emolument

pay *VERB* **1** *I'd rather pay more and get a better machine.* ► spend, expend, pay out, part with, (*more informal*) shell out, (*more informal*) dish out **2** *He said he'd pay me for the broken window.* ► reimburse, recompense, refund, repay, pay back **3** *Stella is trying to pay her debts.* ► discharge, settle, pay off, meet, clear, honour **4** *I'll make them pay for this.* ► suffer, make amends, atone, answer **5** *It would pay us to wait until the new model comes out.* ► benefit, profit, be an advantage to

payment *NOUN* **1** *You can settle in six or twelve monthly payments.* ► installment, contribution, remittance **2** *There is a discount for prompt payment.* ► settlement, remittance **3** *You get extra payment for working late.* ► pay, wages, income, remuneration

peace *NOUN* **1** *It's not easy to get any peace in this house.* ► tranquillity, calm, quiet, silence, relaxation, hush OPPOSITES ARE disturbance, noise **2** *The country longed for peace after years*

a b c d e f g h i j k l m n o **p** q r s t u v w x y z

peaceable ADJECTIVE fond of peace; not quarrelsome or warlike
▷ **peaceably** ADVERB

peaceful ADJECTIVE quiet and calm
▷ **peacefully** ADVERB **peacefulness** NOUN

peach NOUN **peaches** **1** a round soft juicy fruit with a pinkish or yellowish skin and a large stone **2** (*informal*) an extremely good thing
• *a peach of a shot*

peacock NOUN **peacocks** a large male bird with a long brightly colored tail that it can spread out like a fan
▷ **peahen** NOUN

peak NOUN **peaks** **1** a pointed top, especially of a mountain **2** the highest or most intense part of something • *Traffic reaches its peak at 5 p.m.* **3** the part of a cap that sticks out in front
▷ **peaked** ADJECTIVE

peak VERB **peaks, peaking, peaked** reach its highest point or value

peal NOUN **peals** **1** the loud ringing of a bell or set of bells **2** a loud burst of thunder or laughter

peal VERB **peals, pealing, pealed** (said about bells) ring loudly

peanut NOUN **peanuts** a small round nut that grows in a pod in the ground

pear NOUN **pears** a juicy fruit that gets narrower near the stalk

pearl NOUN **pearls** a small shiny white ball found in the shells of some oysters and used as a jewel
▷ **pearly** ADJECTIVE

peasant NOUN **peasants** a person who belongs to a farming community, especially in poor areas of the world
▷ **peasantry** NOUN
[from Latin *paganus* = country dweller]

peat NOUN rotted plant material that can be dug out of the ground and used as fuel or in gardening
▷ **peaty** ADJECTIVE
[from Latin *peta*, probably from a Celtic word]

pebble NOUN **pebbles** a small round stone
▷ **pebbly** ADJECTIVE

peck VERB **pecks, pecking, pecked** **1** bite at something quickly with the beak **2** kiss someone lightly on the cheek

peck NOUN **pecks** **1** a quick bite by a bird **2** a light kiss on the cheek

peckish ADJECTIVE (*informal*) hungry

peculiar ADJECTIVE **1** strange or unusual **2** belonging to a particular person, place, or thing; restricted • *This custom is peculiar to this tribe.*
▷ **peculiarly** ADVERB **peculiarity** NOUN

Thesaurus

of civil unrest. ► order, harmony, harmoniousness, nonviolence AN OPPOSITE IS disorder **3** *A peace will be signed and the war ended.* ► armistice, truce, ceasefire, treaty, agreement, concord

peaceable ADJECTIVE *a peaceable nation*
► peace-loving, unwarlike, nonviolent, pacific, peaceful, placid, conciliatory, cooperative, friendly, harmonious OPPOSITES ARE aggressive, warlike, belligerent

peaceful ADJECTIVE **1** *a peaceful part of the country* ► quiet, restful, serene, tranquil, secluded, undisturbed, unruffled, untroubled, calm, still, pleasant, relaxing, balmy OPPOSITES ARE noisy, troubled **2** *The country wants to resolve the dispute in a peaceful manner.* ► calm, cordial, amicable, friendly, orderly **3** *Tanya had a peaceful temperament.* ► serene, calm, placid, amicable, friendly, unruffled, pacific, gentle OPPOSITES ARE turbulent, agitated

peak NOUN **1** *the peaks of the mountains*
► summit, tip, top, crest, pinnacle, crown, point **2** *Ruth had reached the peak of her career.* ► height, highest point, zenith, acme, climax, culmination OPPOSITES ARE nadir, trough

peaked ADJECTIVE *Josh had been looking peaked all morning, and stayed at home.* ► pale, pallid, pasty, unwell, sickly, poorly, queasy, out of sorts

peal NOUN *a peal of bells* ► chime, carillon, ringing, clang

peal VERB *The bells pealed* ► chime, ring, toll, resound, resonate

peasant NOUN **1** *There were rows of peasants picking tomatoes in the fields.* ► countryman, rustic, farmhand **2** (*informal*) *He became angry and called them a bunch of peasants.* ► lout, oaf, bumpkin

peculiar ADJECTIVE **1** *Something peculiar was happening to her computer.* ► strange, odd, unusual, weird, curious, funny, extraordinary, bizarre, abnormal OPPOSITES ARE normal, ordinary **2** *By that stage of the journey we were all feeling a bit peculiar.* ► unwell, ill, sick, poorly, queasy, out of sorts **3** *Norman had his own peculiar way of doing things.* ► special, characteristic, distinctive, individual, particular, singular, unique, idiosyncratic, (*more informal*) wacky, (*more informal*) screwy

peculiarity NOUN **1** *Find out about the peculiarities of the local weather when you go abroad. He had a strange physical peculiarity.*
► oddity, peculiar or special feature, abnormality, foible, idiosyncrasy, quirk, trait, characteristic, eccentricity **2** *We will have to accept the peculiarity of this arrangement.*
► strangeness, abnormality, oddness, oddity, eccentricity, bizarreness

pedal NOUN **pedals** a lever pressed by the foot to operate a bicycle, car, machine, etc., or in certain musical instruments

pedal VERB **pedals, pedaling, pedaled** use a pedal; move or work something, especially a bicycle, by means of pedals

pedantic ADJECTIVE too concerned with minor details or with sticking strictly to formal rules
▷ **pedantically** ADVERB

peddle VERB **peddles, peddling, peddled 1** go from house to house selling goods **2** sell illegal drugs **3** try to get people to accept an idea, way of life, etc.

peddler NOUN **peddlers** a person who goes from house to house selling small things [from Middle English *ped* = a hamper or basket (in which a pedlar carried his goods)]

pedestal NOUN **pedestals** the raised base on which a statue or pillar, etc., stands
put someone on a pedestal admire him or her greatly

pedestrian NOUN **pedestrians** a person who is walking

pedestrian ADJECTIVE ordinary and dull

pedestrian crossing NOUN **pedestrian crossings** a place where pedestrians can cross the road safely

pediatrics (peed- ee- at- riks) NOUN the study of children's diseases
▷ **pediatric** ADJECTIVE **pediatrician** NOUN [from Greek *paidos* = of a child + *iatros* = doctor]

pedigree NOUN **pedigrees** a list of a person's or animal's ancestors, especially to show how well an animal has been bred [from early French *pé de grue* = crane's foot (from the shape made by the lines on a family tree)]

peel NOUN **peels** the skin of certain fruits and vegetables

peel VERB **peels, peeling, peeled 1** remove the peel or covering from something **2** come off in strips or layers **3** lose a covering or skin

peelings PLURAL NOUN strips of skin peeled from potatoes etc.

peep VERB **peeps, peeping, peeped 1** look quickly or secretly **2** look through a narrow opening **3** come slowly or briefly into view
● *The moon peeped out from behind the clouds.*
▷ **peep** NOUN **peephole** NOUN

peer VERB **peers, peering, peered** look at something closely or with difficulty

peer NOUN **peers 1** a noble **2** someone who is equal to another in rank, merit, or age etc.
● *She had no peer.*
▷ **peeress** NOUN **peerage** NOUN

peer group NOUN **peer groups** a group of people of roughly the same age or status

peerless ADJECTIVE without an equal; better than the others

peevish ADJECTIVE irritable

peg NOUN **pegs** a piece of wood or metal or plastic for fastening things together or for hanging things on

peg VERB **pegs, pegging, pegged 1** fix something with pegs **2** keep wages or prices at a fixed level
peg away work diligently; persevere

Pekinese or **Pekingese** NOUN **Pekinese** or **Pekingese** a small kind of dog with short legs, a flat face, and long silky hair [from **Peking**, the old name of Beijing, the capital of China (where the breed came from)]

pelican NOUN **pelicans** a large bird with a pouch in its long beak for storing fish

pellet NOUN **pellets** a tiny ball of metal, food, paper, etc.

Thesaurus

pedantic ADJECTIVE **1** *He has a pedantic style of writing.* ► academic, bookish, formal, humorless, learned, old-fashioned, pompous, scholarly, schoolmasterly, stilted AN OPPOSITE IS informal **2** *a pedantic application of the rules* ► inflexible, precise, strict, over-scrupulous, unimaginative, (*more informal*) nit-picking AN OPPOSITE IS flexible

peek VERB *A face peeked around the doorway.* ► peep, peer, glance, look

peek NOUN *He took a quick peek at the recipe.* ► peep, glance, glimpse, look

peel NOUN *Orange peel lay in a spiral on the table.* ► rind, skin, covering, zest

peel VERB *Jeff peeled an apple.* ► pare, skin, strip

peep VERB *Jane peeped through the keyhole.* ► peek, peer, glance, look

peep NOUN *Have a peep at the baby.* ► peek, glance, glimpse, look

peer VERB *A woman peered at us from a corner of the room.* ► gaze, look, glance, squint, peep, peek

peeved ADJECTIVE *Paula still felt peeved about it.* ► annoyed, irritated, angry, cross, displeased, vexed, infuriated, incensed, enraged, (*more informal*) miffed, (*more informal*) put out AN OPPOSITE IS pleased

peg NOUN *She put her coat on a peg.* ► hook, pin, spike, knob

peg VERB **1** *Make sure you peg the tent to the ground.* ► fasten, fix, secure, attach **2** *Prices will be pegged for six months.* ► fix, hold, hold down, keep down, freeze, control

A
B
C
D
E
F
G
H
I
J
K
L
M
N
O
P
Q
R
S
T
U
V
W
X
Y
Z

pelt VERB **pelts, pelting, pelted 1** throw a lot of things at someone **2** run fast **3** rain very hard

at full pelt as fast as possible

pelt NOUN **pelts** an animal skin, especially with the fur still on it

pen[1] NOUN **pens** an instrument with a point for writing with ink

pen[2] NOUN **pens** an enclosure for cattle, sheep, hens, or other animals

pen VERB **pens, penning, penned** shut animals, etc., into a pen or other enclosed space

penalize VERB **penalizes, penalizing, penalized** punish; give someone a penalty
▷ **penalization** NOUN

penalty NOUN **penalties 1** a punishment **2** a point or advantage given to one side in a game when a member of the other side has broken a rule, e.g., a free kick at goal in soccer

pence PLURAL NOUN SEE **penny**

pencil NOUN **pencils** an instrument for drawing or writing, made of a thin stick of graphite or colored chalk, etc., enclosed in a cylinder of wood or metal

pendant NOUN **pendants** an ornament worn hanging on a cord or chain round the neck

pending PREPOSITION **1** until • *Please take charge, pending his return.* **2** during • *pending these discussions*

pending ADJECTIVE **1** waiting to be decided or settled **2** about to happen

pendulum NOUN **pendulums** a weight hung so that it can swing to and fro, especially in the works of a clock

penetrate VERB **penetrates, penetrating, penetrated** make or find a way through or into something; pierce
▷ **penetration** NOUN **penetrative** ADJECTIVE

penguin NOUN **penguins** an Antarctic seabird that cannot fly but uses its wings as flippers for swimming

penicillin NOUN an antibiotic obtained from mould

peninsula NOUN **peninsulas** a piece of land that is almost surrounded by water
▷ **peninsular** ADJECTIVE
[from Latin *paene* = almost + *insula* = island]

penis (peen- iss) NOUN **penises** the part of the body with which a male urinates and has sexual intercourse

penitence NOUN regret for having done wrong
▷ **penitent** ADJECTIVE **penitently** ADVERB

penknife NOUN **penknives** a small folding knife

pen name NOUN **pen names** a name used by an author instead of his or her real name

penniless ADJECTIVE having no money; very poor

penny NOUN **pennies 1** a U.S. coin worth one-hundredth of a dollar

pen pal NOUN **pen pals** a friend you write to regularly without meeting

pension NOUN **pensions** an income consisting of regular payments made to someone who is retired, widowed, or disabled

pensioner NOUN **pensioners** a person who receives a pension

pentagon NOUN **pentagons** a flat shape with five sides and five angles
▷ **pentagonal** (pent- ag- on- al) ADJECTIVE
the Pentagon a five-sided building in Washington, headquarters of the leaders of the American armed forces
[from Greek *pente* = five + *gonia* = angle]

pentameter NOUN **pentameters** a line of verse with five rhythmic beats [from Greek *pente* = five + *metron* = measure]

Thesaurus

pelt VERB **1** *The boys were pelting each other with snowballs.* ► bombard, shower, attack, assail, batter **2** *It was pelting down outside.* ► pour, teem, rain cats and dogs **3** *The players pelted back to the dressing room.* ► rush, dash, run, hurry, sprint, charge, streak

pen NOUN **1** *sheep in a pen* ► enclosure, compound, paddock, stockade **2** *He wrote it down with a pen.* ► ballpoint, biro, felt-tipped pen, fountain pen

penalty NOUN *a fixed penalty for illegal parking* ► punishment, fine, forfeit AN OPPOSITE IS reward

penetrate VERB **1** *Make sure the screws do not penetrate the top surface of the shelf.* ► pierce, puncture, perforate, bore through, make a

hole in **2** *An advance force penetrated the city's outer defenses.* ► infiltrate, enter, get through, slip through, probe **3** *Damp had penetrated the stonework.* ► impregnate, permeate, pervade, seep into

penetrating ADJECTIVE **1** *She looked away from his penetrating dark eyes.* ► piercing, probing, staring, sharp, keen **2** *The students asked some penetrating questions.* ► perceptive, sharp, acute, intelligent, incisive, profound, searching **3** *The silence was interrupted by a penetrating scream.* ► shrill, piercing, strident, ear-splitting, deafening

penniless ADJECTIVE *Epstein was a penniless student in Paris.* ► poor, impoverished, destitute, poverty-stricken, moneyless, (*more informal*) skint

pentathlon ➡ perennial

pentathlon NOUN pentathlons an athletic contest consisting of five events [from Greek *pente* = five + *athlon* = contest]

Pentecost NOUN **1** the Jewish harvest festival, fifty days after Passover **2** Whit Sunday [from Greek *pentekoste* = fiftieth (day)]

pent-up ADJECTIVE shut in ● *pent-up feelings*

penultimate ADJECTIVE last but one

peony NOUN peonies a plant with large round red, pink, or white flowers

people PLURAL NOUN human beings; persons, especially those belonging to a particular country, area, or group, etc.

people NOUN peoples a community or nation ● *a warlike people* ● *the English-speaking peoples*

pepper NOUN peppers **1** a hot-tasting powder used to flavor food **2** a bright green, red, or yellow vegetable
  ▷ **peppery** ADJECTIVE

pepper VERB peppers, peppering, peppered **1** sprinkle with pepper **2** pelt with many small objects

peppermint NOUN peppermints **1** a kind of mint used for flavoring **2** a sweet flavored with this mint

per PREPOSITION for each ● *The charge is $2 per person.*

perceive VERB perceives, perceiving, perceived see, notice, or understand something

percent ADVERB for or in every hundred ● *three percent (3%)*

percentage NOUN percentages an amount or rate expressed as a proportion of 100

perceptible ADJECTIVE able to be seen or noticed
  ▷ **perceptibly** ADVERB **perceptibility** NOUN

perception NOUN perceptions the ability to see, notice, or understand something

perceptive ADJECTIVE quick to notice or understand things

perch¹ NOUN perches **1** a place where a bird sits or rests **2** a seat high up

perch VERB perches, perching, perched rest or place on a perch

perch² NOUN perch an edible freshwater fish

percolate VERB percolates, percolating, percolated flow through small holes or spaces
  ▷ **percolation** NOUN

percolator NOUN percolators a pot for making coffee, in which boiling water percolates through coffee grounds

percussion NOUN **1** musical instruments (e.g., drums or cymbals) played by being struck or shaken **2** the striking of one thing against another
  ▷ **percussive** ADJECTIVE

perdition NOUN eternal damnation

peregrine NOUN peregrines a kind of falcon

perennial ADJECTIVE lasting for many years; keeping on recurring
  ▷ **perennially** ADVERB

perennial NOUN perennials a plant that lives for many years

Thesaurus

people NOUN **1** *By mid-afternoon many people were hungry. People like to read books like these.* ► persons, individuals, human beings, humans, folk, mortals, humanity, humankind, mankind USAGE Note that *humanity, humankind,* and *mankind* are all singular nouns and you use a singular verb with them, e.g., *Humankind likes to read books like these.* **2** *The government will appeal to the people in a general election.* ► nation, electorate, voters, electors, community **3** *a shopping center that serves the people of the area; a proud and brave people* ► populace, population, citizens, inhabitants, public, society, common people, community, electorate, nation RELATED ADJECTIVES ► ethnic, national **4** *Her people live in Ireland.* ► family, relatives, relations, parents, clan, kith and kin

pep NOUN *The project needed a lot more pep.* ► energy, vigor, vitality, spirit, verve, exuberance, fizz

pep VERB
pep up *He added some herbs to pep up the flavor.* ► liven up, vitalize, enhance, intensify

perceive VERB **1** *Those in the room perceived voices outside.* ► hear, discern, distinguish,

make out, notice, recognize, become aware of **2** *Some animals cannot perceive color.* ► see, discern, distinguish, recognize, observe, identify **3** *I began to perceive her meaning.* ► understand, comprehend, apprehend, grasp, realize, sense, deduce, gather, know **4** *We all perceive the world in different ways.* ► regard, consider, view, judge, deem, think of, look on

perception NOUN **1** *The public's perception of the government's honesty has changed.* ► impression, consciousness, apprehension, sense, view, awareness, cognition, comprehension, understanding, recognition, sensation **2** *She speaks with great perception on these problems.* ► insight, perceptiveness, discernment, understanding, perspicacity, astuteness, shrewdness, intelligence, observation

perceptive ADJECTIVE *A few perceptive questions can liven up the interview.* ► discerning, astute, shrewd, intelligent, insightful, perspicacious OPPOSITES ARE obtuse, inept

perch VERB *A monkey came in and perched on a table.* ► sit, settle, rest, balance, alight

a b c d e f g h i j k l m n o **p** q r s t u v w x y z

479

A
B
C
D
E
F
G
H
I
J
K
L
M
N
O
P
Q
R
S
T
U
V
W
X
Y
Z

perfect (per- fikt) ADJECTIVE **1** so good that it cannot be made any better **2** complete • *a perfect stranger* **3** (in grammar, said about a tense of a verb) showing a completed action, e.g., *He has arrived.*
▷ **perfectly** ADVERB

perfect (per- fekt) VERB **perfects, perfecting, perfected** make a thing perfect
▷ **perfection** NOUN
to perfection perfectly

perfectionist NOUN **perfectionists** a person who is only satisfied if something is done perfectly

perforate VERB **perforates, perforating, perforated 1** make tiny holes in something, especially so that it can be torn off easily **2** pierce
▷ **perforated** ADJECTIVE **perforation** NOUN

perform VERB **performs, performing, performed 1** do something in front of an audience • *The school will perform a play.* **2** do or carry out something • *Surgeons had to perform an emergency operation.*
▷ **performance** NOUN **performer** NOUN

perfume NOUN **perfumes 1** a pleasant smell **2** a liquid for giving something a pleasant smell; scent
▷ **perfume** VERB **perfumery** NOUN
[originally used of pleasant-smelling smoke from something burning: via French from old Italian *parfumare* = to smoke through]

perfunctory ADJECTIVE done without much care or interest • *a perfunctory glance*
▷ **perfunctorily** ADVERB

perhaps ADVERB it may be; possibly

peril NOUN **perils** danger
▷ **perilous** ADJECTIVE **perilously** ADVERB
at your peril at your own risk

Thesaurus

perfect ADJECTIVE (with the stress on *per-*) **1** *It was the start to a perfect day.* ► superb, excellent, superlative, wonderful, marvellous, idyllic, blissful **2** *a secondhand book in perfect condition* ► impeccable, flawless, immaculate, spotless, pristine OPPOSITES ARE imperfect, flawed **3** *a copy so perfect you can't tell it from the original* ► exact, precise, faithful, accurate, true, close AN OPPOSITE IS inaccurate **4** *A digital radio will make a perfect birthday present.* ► ideal, suitable, fitting, apt, appropriate, OPPOSITES ARE unsuitable, inappropriate **5** *He felt a perfect fool. They had never met; they were perfect strangers.* ► complete, absolute, utter, total, entire, thoroughgoing

perfect VERB (with the stress on *-fect*) *He is spending some time perfecting his speech.*
► improve, make perfect, refine, complete, finish, fulfil, realize

perfection NOUN **1** *the perfection of her complexion* ► faultlessness, flawlessness, excellence, beauty, completeness, ideal, wholeness AN OPPOSITE IS imperfection **2** *the perfection of their plans* ► completion, consummation, fulfillment, realization, accomplishment, fruition, achievement

perfectionist NOUN *He was such a perfectionist he wouldn't allow any mistakes.* ► idealist, purist, precisionist, (more informal) stickler

perfectly ADVERB **1** *He brought in a perfectly baked cake.* ► superbly, impeccably, faultlessly, flawlessly, beautifully, excellently **2** *I'm perfectly happy to let them use the house. He can be perfectly horrid at times.* ► absolutely, completely, entirely, totally, utterly **3** *You know perfectly well what I mean.* ► very, quite, full, (more informal) jolly

perform VERB **1** *The two devices perform the same function. She has her duties to perform.*
► fulfil, exercise, carry out, execute, discharge, accomplish, achieve **2** *The company performed the new play in London.* ► present, stage, put on, produce, mount **3** *The speakers perform best at a fairly high volume.* ► function, operate, work, behave

performance NOUN **1** *the performance of their duties* ► execution, carrying out, discharge, accomplishment, fulfillment, completion, implementation **2** *The music received a fine performance.* ► rendition, interpretation, rendering, account **3** *The review praised the new range of cars for their performance.* ► operation, running, functioning, behavior **4** *He made a huge performance of thanking them.* ► fuss, exhibition, act, scene, parade

performer NOUN *The song was sung by the original performers.* ► singer, entertainer, artist, artiste, musician, player, star, actor, actress

perfume NOUN **1** *With a final spray of exotic perfume she left the room.* ► scent, toilet water, eau de cologne **2** *the fresh, sweet perfume of roses* ► smell , scent, fragrance, aroma, odor, whiff

perfunctory ADJECTIVE *They greeted each other with perfunctory grunts.* ► cursory, desultory, fleeting, casual, hurried, offhand, half-hearted, unthinking, mechanical, automatic OPPOSITES ARE enthusiastic, careful

perhaps ADVERB *Perhaps they took the train to New Haven.* ► maybe, possibly, conceivably, feasibly

peril NOUN **1** *the perils of the sea* ► danger, hazard, risk, menace, uncertainty OPPOSITES ARE security, safety
in peril *The climbers found themselves in great peril.* ► in danger, at risk, in jeopardy

perimeter NOUN perimeters **1** the outer edge or boundary of something **2** the distance round the edge

USAGE Do not confuse with **parameter**.

period NOUN periods **1** a length of time **2** the time allowed for a lesson in school **3** the time when a woman menstruates **4** (in punctuation) a full stop

periodic ADJECTIVE occurring at regular intervals
▷ **periodically** ADVERB

periodical NOUN periodicals a magazine published at regular intervals (e.g., monthly)

periodic table NOUN a table in which the chemical elements are arranged in order of increasing atomic number

periscope NOUN periscopes a device with a tube and mirrors with which a person in a trench or submarine etc. can see things that are otherwise out of sight

perish VERB perishes, perishing, perished **1** die; be destroyed **2** rot • *The rubber ring has perished.*
▷ **perishable** ADJECTIVE

perjure VERB perjures, perjuring, perjured perjure yourself commit perjury

perjury NOUN telling a lie while you are on oath to speak the truth

perk VERB perks, perking, perked perk up make or become more cheerful

perk NOUN perks (*informal*) something extra given to a worker • *Free bus travel is one of the perks of the job.*

perky ADJECTIVE lively and cheerful
▷ **perkily** ADVERB

perm or **permanent wave** NOUN permanent waves treatment of the hair to give it long-lasting waves

permafrost NOUN a permanently frozen layer of soil in polar regions

permanent ADJECTIVE lasting for always or for a very long time
▷ **permanently** ADVERB **permanence** NOUN

permeate VERB permeates, permeating, permeated spread into every part of something; pervade • *Smoke had permeated the hall.*
▷ **permeation** NOUN

permissible ADJECTIVE permitted or allowed

permission NOUN the right to do something, given by someone in authority; authorization

permissive ADJECTIVE letting people do what they wish; tolerant or liberal

permit (per- mit) VERB permits, permitting, permitted give permission or consent or a chance to do something; allow

permit (per- mit) NOUN permits written or printed permission to do something or go somewhere

permutation NOUN permutations **1** changing the order of a set of things **2** a changed order • *3, 1, 2 is a permutation of 1, 2, 3*

peroxide NOUN a chemical used for bleaching hair

perpendicular ADJECTIVE upright; at a right angle (90°) to a line or surface

Thesaurus

perimeter NOUN **1** *The airport perimeter is closely guarded.* ► boundary, periphery, confines, edge, fringe, border, margin, borderline, bounds, circumference **2** *The perimeter is about twelve miles.* ► circumference, outer edge

period NOUN **1** *They suffered from several long periods of separation.* ► spell, interval, stretch, term, bout, run, span, phase, session **2** *the Hanoverian period of English history* ► age, era, years, epoch, time **3** *There was a double period of math on Monday.* ► lesson, class, session

perish VERB **1** *Many people perished in the floods.* ► die, be killed, lose your life, pass away **2** *The tires had started to perish.* ► decay, decompose, disintegrate, crumble away, rot

perk NOUN (*informal*) *company cars and other perks* ► benefit, extra, bonus, (*more formal*) perquisite, (*more informal*) plus

perk up VERB *He perked up when he saw Susan coming.* ► cheer up, liven up, brighten, take heart, pick up, bounce back

permanent ADJECTIVE **1** *We are looking for a permanent solution to the problem.* ► continuing,
lasting, durable, fixed, long-term, unchangeable, irreversible, everlasting, perpetual, eternal **2** *Leslie has got his first permanent job.* ► stable, fixed, established, secure, firm

permission NOUN *We will need permission to miss the afternoon classes.* ► authorization, authority, leave, consent, approval, agreement, license, assent, clearance, dispensation, (*more informal*) the go-ahead, (*informal*) the green light

permit VERB **1** *The authorities would not permit release of the documents.* ► allow, authorize, endorse, agree to, consent to, approve of, give permission for, sanction, license, tolerate OPPOSITES ARE prohibit, prevent, ban **2** *His club will permit him to play in the national side.* ► allow, authorize, give an opportunity, make it possible OPPOSITES ARE forbid, prohibit (from)

permit NOUN *The warden asked to see his permit.* ► authorization, licence, pass, warrant, certification, passport, visa, charter

A
B
C
D
E
F
G
H
I
J
K
L
M
N
O
P
Q
R
S
T
U
V
W
X
Y
Z

perpetrate VERB perpetrates, perpetrating, perpetrated commit or be guilty of
• *perpetrate a crime*
▷ perpetration NOUN perpetrator NOUN

perpetual ADJECTIVE lasting for a long time; continual
▷ perpetually ADVERB

perplex VERB perplexes, perplexing, perplexed bewilder or puzzle somebody
▷ perplexity NOUN

persecute VERB persecutes, persecuting, persecuted be continually cruel to somebody, especially because you disagree with his or her beliefs
▷ persecution NOUN persecutor NOUN

persevere VERB perseveres, persevering, persevered go on doing something even though it is difficult
▷ perseverance NOUN

Persian ADJECTIVE to do with Persia, a country in the Middle East now called Iran

Persian NOUN the language of Persia

persist VERB persists, persisting, persisted
1 continue firmly or obstinately • *She persists in breaking the rules.* **2** continue to exist • *The custom persists in some countries.*
▷ persistent ADJECTIVE persistently ADVERB persistence NOUN persistency NOUN

person NOUN people or persons **1** a human being; a man, woman, or child **2** (in grammar) any of the three groups of personal pronouns and forms taken by verbs The first person (= I, me, we, us) refers to the person(s) speaking; the second person (= you) refers to the person(s) spoken to; the third person (= he, him, she, her, it, they, them) refers to the person(s) spoken about
in person being actually present oneself • *She hopes to be there in person.*
[from Latin *persona* = mask used by an actor]

personal ADJECTIVE **1** belonging to, done by, or concerning a particular person • *personal belongings* **2** private • *We have personal business to discuss.* **3** criticizing a person's appearance, character, or private affairs • *making personal remarks*
▷ personally ADVERB
USAGE Do not confuse with **personnel**.

Thesaurus

perpetual ADJECTIVE **1** *The Arctic is in almost perpetual daylight.* ► continuous, everlasting, eternal, nonstop AN OPPOSITE IS temporary **2** *the perpetual evolution of humanity* ► constant, permanent, continuous, ceaseless, eternal, unending, uninterrupted OPPOSITES ARE transitory, temporary **3** *Their perpetual rows upset the children.* ► continual, interminable, incessant, constant, eternal, endless, ceaseless OPPOSITES ARE occasional, intermittent

perplex VERB *a helpline that answers any questions that perplex you* ► baffle, bewilder, puzzle, mystify, confuse, bemuse, disconcert, confound, fox, (more informal) flummox, (more informal) floor

persecute VERB **1** *In Rome, Christians were being persecuted by the Emperor Nero.* ► oppress, victimize, martyr, discriminate against, maltreat, ill-treat, tyrannize **2** *He thought everyone was persecuting him.* ► harass, hound, pester, pursue, bother, plague, torment, intimidate, bully, terrorize

persecution NOUN *victims of political persecution* ► oppression, victimization, discrimination, harassment, maltreatment, martyrdom, tyranny, abuse

perseverance NOUN *The job required perseverance and patience.* ► persistence, tenacity, determination, resolve, doggedness, diligence, dedication, application, commitment, endurance, stamina

persevere VERB *He decided to persevere, in spite of some early failures.* ► persist, continue, keep going, carry on, press on, endure, (more informal) soldier on, (more informal) hang on, (more informal) keep at it, (informal) stick at it, (more informal) plug away OPPOSITES ARE give up, stop

persist VERB **1** *The officer persisted with his questions.* ► persevere, continue, keep going, carry on, press on, endure, (more informal) soldier on, (more informal) hang on, (more informal) keep at it, (informal) stick at it, (more informal) plug away OPPOSITES ARE desist, give up, stop **2** *If the pain persists, you should see a doctor.* ► continue, carry on, keep on, go on, linger, last, remain AN OPPOSITE IS cease **3** *persist in He would persist in interrupting her.* ► keep on, insist on

persistent ADJECTIVE **1** *The company should respond to its more persistent critics.* ► determined, tenacious, persevering, resolute, single-minded **2** *They were interrupted by a persistent knocking at the door.* ► continuing, constant, steady, incessant, endless, nonstop

person NOUN *We must find the person responsible. She was the first person to arrive. There was not a person to be seen.* ► individual, man *or* woman, being, human being, soul, body

personal ADJECTIVE **1** *a story based on the author's personal experiences* ► own, individual, particular, special, exclusive OPPOSITES ARE general, public **2** *The letter was marked "personal."* ► private, confidential, secret

personal computer NOUN personal computers a small computer designed to be used by one person at a time

personality NOUN personalities **1** a person's character • *She has a cheerful personality.* **2** a well-known person • *a TV personality*

personify VERB personifies, personifying, personified represent a quality or idea etc. as a person
▷ **personification** NOUN

personnel NOUN the people employed by a firm or other large organization
USAGE Do not confuse with personal.

perspective NOUN perspectives **1** the impression of depth and space in a picture or scene **2** a person's point of view
in perspective giving a well-balanced view of things

perspire VERB perspires, perspiring, perspired sweat
▷ **perspiration** NOUN

persuade VERB persuades, persuading, persuaded make someone believe or agree to do something
▷ **persuasion** NOUN **persuasive** ADJECTIVE

pert ADJECTIVE cheeky
▷ **pertly** ADVERB **pertness** NOUN

perturb VERB perturbs, perturbing, perturbed worry someone
▷ **perturbation** NOUN

pervade VERB pervades, pervading, pervaded spread all through something
▷ **pervasion** NOUN **pervasive** ADJECTIVE

perverse ADJECTIVE obstinately doing something different from what is reasonable or required
▷ **perversely** ADVERB **perversity** NOUN

pervert (per- vert) VERB perverts, perverting, perverted **1** turn something from the right course of action • *By giving false evidence they perverted the course of justice.* **2** make a person behave wickedly or abnormally
▷ **perversion** NOUN

pervert (per- vert) NOUN perverts a person whose sexual behavior is thought to be unnatural or disgusting

pessimist NOUN pessimists a person who expects that things will turn out badly
COMPARE optimist
▷ **pessimism** NOUN **pessimistic** ADJECTIVE **pessimistically** ADVERB

pest NOUN pests **1** a destructive insect or animal, such as a locust or a mouse **2** a nuisance

---

Thesaurus

---

personality NOUN **1** *He has a warmth of personality and a generous nature.* ► character, nature, disposition, temperament, identity, individuality, (*more informal*) makeup **2** *a television personality* ► celebrity, star, superstar, name

perspective NOUN *Since the war we see history from a different perspective.* ► outlook, viewpoint, point of view, slant, view, angle
in perspective *To put this in perspective, ten percent of buyers admitted to being dissatisfied with what they had bought.* ► in context, in proportion

persuade VERB *Will you be able to persuade Susie to go back to England?* ► prevail on *or* upon, induce, coax, convince, make, entice, influence, pressure, pressurize, tempt, urge, bring round, cajole, inveigle, talk into AN OPPOSITE IS dissuade

persuasion NOUN **1** *I shall need a lot of persuasion to change my mind.* ► persuading, coaxing, coercion, convincing, inducement, exhortation, cajolery, enticement, argument **2** *people with a wide range of political persuasions* ► belief, conviction, view, opinion, faith

persuasive ADJECTIVE *There's a lot of persuasive talk but not much action.* ► convincing, compelling, cogent, sound, valid, plausible, reasonable, forceful, strong, telling, credible, effective, eloquent, influential, logical, watertight OPPOSITES ARE unconvincing, unpersuasive

perverse ADJECTIVE *He has the perverse habit of calling all young girls "madam" and all older women "girls."* ► contrary, wayward, awkward, unreasonable, tiresome, capricious, wilful, obstinate, stubborn, unhelpful, rebellious
OPPOSITES ARE reasonable, obliging

pessimism NOUN *His pessimism prevented him from taking any risks.* ► despondency, fatalism, negativeness, hopelessness, gloom, despair, resignation, unhappiness, cynicism AN OPPOSITE IS optimism

pessimistic ADJECTIVE *Manufacturers are pessimistic about the economic future.*
► negative, fatalistic, gloomy, downbeat, downhearted, unhopeful, defeatist, despairing, despondent, resigned, unhappy, cynical AN OPPOSITE IS optimistic

pest NOUN **1** *Vincent's demands for attention were becoming a pest.* ► nuisance, bother, annoyance, irritation, curse, trial, bore, bane, vexation, (*more informal*) pain, (*more informal*) pain in the neck **2** *the rise in crop pests* ► insect, bug, parasite

a
b
c
d
e
f
g
h
i
j
k
l
m
n
o
p
q
r
s
t
u
v
w
x
y
z

A
B
C
D
E
F
G
H
I
J
K
L
M
N
O
P
Q
R
S
T
U
V
W
X
Y
Z

pester VERB pesters, pestering, pestered keep annoying someone by frequent questions or requests

pesticide NOUN pesticides a substance for killing harmful insects and other pests

pestilence NOUN pestilences a deadly epidemic

pestle (pes- el) NOUN a heavy tool with a rounded end, used for crushing substances in a mortar [from Latin *pinsere* = to pound]

pet NOUN pets **1** a tame animal kept for companionship and pleasure **2** a person treated as a favorite • *a teacher's pet*

pet ADJECTIVE favorite • *my pet subject*

pet VERB pets, petting, petted treat or fondle someone affectionately

petal NOUN petals one of the separate colored outer parts of a flower

peter VERB peters, petering, petered peter out become gradually less and cease to exist

petition NOUN petitions a formal request for something, especially a written one signed by many people

petrify VERB petrifies, petrifying, petrified **1** make someone so terrified that he or she cannot move **2** turn to stone
▷ **petrifaction** NOUN

petroleum NOUN an oil found underground that is refined to make fuel (e.g., petrol or paraffin) or for use in dry-cleaning, etc.

petticoat NOUN petticoats a woman's or girl's dress-length piece of underwear worn under a skirt or dress

petting NOUN affectionate touching or fondling

petty ADJECTIVE pettier, pettiest **1** unimportant or trivial • *petty regulations* **2** mean and small-minded
▷ **pettily** ADVERB **pettiness** NOUN

petty cash NOUN cash kept by an office for small payments

pew NOUN pews a long wooden seat, usually fixed in rows, in a church

pewter NOUN a grey alloy of tin and lead

pH NOUN a measure of the acidity or alkalinity of a solution Pure water has a pH of 7, acids have a pH between 0 and 7, and alkalis have a pH between 7 and 14

phantom NOUN phantoms **1** a ghost **2** something that does not really exist

Pharaoh (fair- oh) NOUN Pharaohs the title of the king of ancient Egypt

pharmacy NOUN pharmacies **1** a shop selling medicines; a dispensary **2** the job of preparing medicines

phase NOUN phases a stage in the progress or development of something

phase VERB phases, phasing, phased do something in stages, not all at once • *a phased withdrawal*

Ph.D. ABBREVIATION Doctor of Philosophy; a university degree awarded to someone who has done advanced research in their subject

pheasant (fez- ant) NOUN pheasants a game bird with a long tail

---

Thesaurus

---

pester NOUN *Claire was nice and didn't pester him with silly questions.* ► badger, harass, annoy, bother, irritate, nag, harry, chivvy, hound, trouble, besiege, (*more informal*) hassle, (*more informal*) bug, (*more informal*) keep on at, (*more informal*) go on at

pet NOUN (*informal*) *They teased him and called him teacher's pet.* ► favorite, darling, treasure

pet ADJECTIVE **1** *Whoever heard of a pet rattlesnake?* ► tame, domestic **2** *The shop was very much his own pet scheme.* ► favorite, cherished, prized, precious, special, personal

pet VERB **1** *Kim sat holding the kitten and petting it.* ► pat, stroke, pamper, caress, cuddle, fondle, kiss, touch **2** *She wouldn't let boys pet her on their first date.* ► fondle, caress, kiss and cuddle

peter out VERB *The traffic began to peter out.* ► dwindle, diminish, decrease, subside, disappear, fall off, die out, wane, shrink

petition NOUN *a petition protesting at the new building plans* ► appeal, list of signatures, application, supplication, entreaty, plea

petty ADJECTIVE **1** *The meeting was called for petty reasons.* ► trivial, minor, trifling, unimportant, insignificant, slight, secondary, paltry **2** *The criticisms were unfair and petty.* ► spiteful, small-minded, vindictive, mean, ungenerous, grudging

petulant ADJECTIVE *He sounded as petulant as an obstinate child.* ► peevish, bad-tempered, irritable, fractious, irascible, fretful, touchy, sullen, snappy, crotchety OPPOSITES ARE good-humored, agreeable

phantom NOUN **1** *a phantom that appeared at night* ► ghost, specter, spirit, apparition, wraith, (*more informal*) spook **2** *He realized that what he had seen had been a phantom of his own mind.* ► hallucination, figment, illusion, delusion, vision **3** *a phantom pregnancy* ► imaginary, imagined, false, unreal

phase NOUN **1** *The final phase of the war* ► stage, part, period, step, chapter **2** *The marriage was going through a difficult phase.* ► period, stage, spell, time, state

phenomenal ADJECTIVE amazing or remarkable
▷ **phenomenally** ADVERB

phenomenon NOUN phenomena an event or fact, especially one that is remarkable
USAGE Note that **phenomena** is a plural. It is incorrect to say "this phenomena" or "these phenomena."

phial NOUN phials a small glass bottle

philanthropy NOUN concern for fellow human beings, especially as shown by kind and generous acts that benefit large numbers of people
▷ **philanthropist** NOUN **philanthropic** ADJECTIVE

philistine (fil- ist- I'n) NOUN philistines a person who dislikes art, poetry, etc.

philosopher NOUN philosophers an expert in philosophy

philosophical ADJECTIVE **1** to do with philosophy **2** calm and not upset after a misfortune or disappointment • *Be philosophical about losing.*
▷ **philosophically** ADVERB

philosophy NOUN philosophies **1** the study of truths about life, morals, etc. **2** a set of ideas or principles or beliefs

phobia (foh- bee- a) NOUN phobias great or abnormal fear of something

phone NOUN phones a telephone

phone VERB phones, phoning, phoned telephone

phone-in NOUN phone-ins a radio or television program in which people telephone the studio and take part in a discussion

phonetic (fon- et- ik) ADJECTIVE **1** to do with speech sounds **2** representing speech sounds
▷ **phonetically** ADVERB

phosphorus NOUN a chemical substance that glows in the dark

photo NOUN photos a photograph

photograph NOUN photographs a picture made by the effect of light or other radiation on film or special paper, using a camera

photograph VERB photographs, photographing, photographed take a photograph of a person or thing
▷ **photographer** NOUN

photography NOUN taking photographs
▷ **photographic** ADJECTIVE

photosynthesis NOUN the process by which green plants use sunlight to turn carbon dioxide and water into complex substances, giving off oxygen

phrase NOUN phrases **1** a group of words that form a unit in a sentence or clause, e.g., *in the garden* in "The Queen was in the garden" **2** a short section of a tune

physical ADJECTIVE **1** to do with the body rather than the mind or feelings **2** to do with things that you can touch or see **3** to do with physics
▷ **physically** ADVERB

Thesaurus

phenomenal ADJECTIVE *Lutyens had a phenomenal memory for detail.* ► remarkable, extraordinary, outstanding, amazing, astonishing, astounding, staggering, sensational, breathtaking OPPOSITES ARE ordinary, run-of-the-mill

philosophical ADJECTIVE **1** *a new approach to old philosophical ideas* ► theoretical, analytical, rational, reasoned, abstract, academic, metaphysical, ideological, intellectual, learned, logical, wise, erudite **2** *He felt in a philosophical mood.* ► thoughtful, reflective, contemplative, meditative, introspective, studious, ruminative **3** *Jane was philosophical about life's problems.* ► calm, composed, collected, resigned, unemotional, unruffled, stoical, self-possessed, patient AN OPPOSITE IS emotional

philosophy NOUN **1** *a student of philosophy* ► thinking, reasoning, metaphysics, wisdom, knowledge, logic **2** *Taylor spent his life promoting his philosophy.* ► convictions, beliefs, ideology, principles, theories, credo, attitudes, viewpoint

phobia NOUN *He has a phobia about noise.* ► aversion (to), dread (of), fear (of) , anxiety, obsession, neurosis, revulsion, dislike (of),

hatred (of), horror, (*more informal*) hang-up, (*more informal*) thing

phone VERB *She tried to phone home on her cell.* ► call, ring, telephone, reach, dial

phony ADJECTIVE *He gave a phony name.* ► false, bogus, sham, fake, made-up, invented, fictitious, assumed, spurious OPPOSITES ARE genuine, authentic

phony NOUN *The lawyer was a phony.* ► impostor, sham, fraud, fake, charlatan, swindler

photograph NOUN *She published her best photographs in a magazine.* ► photo, picture, snapshot, snap, image, print, slide, transparency

photograph VERB *I photographed them as people first and models second.* ► shoot, snap, take a picture of

phrase NOUN *He searched in his mind for the right phrase to describe his feelings.* ► expression, wording, group of words, form of words, construction, idiom

phrase VERB *She thought about how to phrase the question.* ► express, word, put in words, formulate, couch, frame, present

physical ADJECTIVE **1** *It is hard to describe his physical appearance* ► bodily, corporal,

A
B
C
D
E
F
G
H
I
J
K
L
M
N
O
P
Q
R
S
T
U
V
W
X
Y
Z

physical education or **physical training** NOUN exercises and sports done to keep the body healthy

physician NOUN physicians a doctor, especially one who is not a surgeon

physicist (**fiz**- i- sist) NOUN physicists an expert in physics

physics (**fiz**- iks) NOUN the study of the properties of matter and energy (e.g., heat, light, sound, movement) [from Greek *physikos* = natural]

physiotherapy (fiz- ee- o- therra- pee) NOUN the treatment of a disease or weakness by massage, exercises, etc.
▷ **physiotherapist** NOUN

physique (fiz- **eek**) NOUN physiques a person's build

pi NOUN the symbol (p) for the ratio of the circumference of a circle to its diameter The value of pi is approximately 3.14159

pianist NOUN pianists a person who plays the piano

piano NOUN pianos a large musical instrument with a keyboard

piccolo NOUN piccolos a small high-pitched flute

pick VERB picks, picking, picked **1** separate a flower or fruit from its plant • *We picked apples.* **2** choose; select carefully **3** pull bits off or out of something **4** open a lock by using something pointed, not with a key
pick a quarrel deliberately provoke a quarrel with somebody
pick holes in find fault with
pick on single someone out for criticism or unkind treatment
pick someone's pocket steal from it

pick up 1 lift or take up **2** collect **3** take someone into a vehicle **4** manage to hear something **5** get better or recover

pick[1] NOUN **1** choice • *take your pick* **2** the best of a group

pick[2] NOUN picks **1** a pickaxe **2** a plectrum

pickaxe NOUN pickaxes a heavy pointed tool with a long handle, used for breaking up hard ground etc.

picket NOUN pickets **1** a striker or group of strikers who try to persuade other people not to go into a place of work during a strike **2** a pointed post as part of a fence

picket VERB pickets, picketing, picketed stand outside a place of work to try to persuade other people not to go in during a strike

pickle NOUN pickles **1** a strong-tasting food made of pickled vegetables **2** (*informal*) a mess

pickle VERB pickles, pickling, pickled preserve food in vinegar or salt water

pickpocket NOUN pickpockets a thief who steals from people's pockets or bags

pick-up NOUN pick-ups **1** an open truck for carrying small loads **2** the part of a record player that holds the stylus

picnic NOUN picnics a meal eaten in the open air away from home

picnic VERB picnics, picnicking, picnicked have a picnic
▷ **picnicker** NOUN

picture NOUN pictures **1** a representation of a person or thing made by painting, drawing, or photography **2** a film at the cinema **3** how something seems; an impression
in the picture fully informed about something

Thesaurus

corporeal, carnal AN OPPOSITE IS mental **2** *our physical existence* ► earthly, material, mortal, terrestrial, tangible, fleshly, substantial AN OPPOSITE IS spiritual

pick VERB **1** *We spent the afternoon picking fruit.*
► gather, collect, pluck, harvest, garner **2** *He picked a card and held it to his chest. Pick a time and place that suit you.* ► choose, select, take, decide on, opt for, settle on, fix on, single out
pick on *They are always picking on Freddie.*
► victimize, bully, persecute, tease, (*more informal*) get at
pick out *It was difficult to pick anything out in the fog.* ► see, discern, spot, distinguish, make out, recognize, identify
pick up 1 *It was too heavy to pick up.* ► lift, raise, take up, hoist **2** *You can pick up a bargain at the sales.* ► find, discover, obtain, acquire, get hold of, buy, purchase **3** *Lisa*

picked up some Spanish during her stay abroad.
► learn, acquire, absorb, get to know, master
4 *He offered to pick up the children from school.*
► collect, fetch, go to get, call for **5** *The weather began to pick up.* ► improve, recover, get better, brighten **6** *Be careful you don't pick up an infection.* ► catch, contract, get, come down with

pick NOUN **1** *Take your pick.* ► choice, preference, selection, option **2** *the pick of the bunch* ► best, finest, prime, top, cream, choicest, élite

picture NOUN **1** *the famous picture of Bubbles*
► painting, portrait, likeness, portrayal, representation, depiction, profile, image
2 *Kevin wanted to take a picture of them.*
► photograph, snapshot, snap, shot

picture VERB **1** *Charles is pictured on the right receiving his prize.* ► depict, show, portray,

picture VERB pictures, picturing, pictured **1** show in a picture **2** imagine

picturesque ADJECTIVE **1** forming an attractive scene • *a picturesque village* **2** vividly described; expressive • *picturesque language*
▷ **picturesquely** ADVERB

pie NOUN pies a baked dish of meat, fish, or fruit covered with pastry

piece NOUN pieces **1** a part or portion of something; a fragment **2** a separate thing or example • *a fine piece of work* **3** something written, composed, or painted, etc. • *a piece of music* **4** one of the objects used to play a game on a board • *a chess piece* **5** a coin • *a 25-cent piece*

piece VERB pieces, piecing, pieced put pieces together to make something

piecemeal ADJECTIVE, ADVERB done or made one piece at a time

pie chart NOUN pie charts a circle divided into sectors to represent the way in which a quantity is divided up

pier NOUN piers **1** a long structure built out into the sea for people to walk on **2** a pillar supporting a bridge or arch

pierce VERB pierces, piercing, pierced make a hole through something; penetrate

piety NOUN being very religious and devout; piousness

pig NOUN pigs **1** a fat animal with short legs and a blunt snout, kept for its meat

2 (*informal*) someone greedy, dirty, or unpleasant
▷ **piggy** ADJECTIVE, NOUN

pigeon NOUN pigeons a bird with a fat body and a small head

pigeonhole NOUN pigeonholes a small compartment above a desk etc., used for holding letters or papers

piggyback ADVERB carried on somebody else's back or shoulders
▷ **piggyback** NOUN

pig-headed ADJECTIVE obstinate

piglet NOUN piglets a young pig

pigment NOUN pigments a substance that colors something
▷ **pigmented** ADJECTIVE **pigmentation** NOUN

pigsty NOUN pigsties **1** a partly covered pen for pigs **2** a filthy room or house

pigtail NOUN pigtails a plait of hair worn hanging at the sides of the head

pike NOUN pikes **1** a heavy spear **2** pike a large freshwater fish

pile[1] NOUN piles **1** a number of things on top of one another **2** (*informal*) a large quantity; a lot of money **3** (*informal*) a large impressive building

pile VERB piles, piling, piled put things into a pile; make a pile

pile[2] NOUN piles a heavy beam made of metal, concrete, or timber driven into the ground to support something

Thesaurus

illustrate, represent, delineate, outline **2** *I can picture him now, a thin tall figure smoking his pipe.* ► visualize, imagine, call to mind, see in your mind, conceive, envisage, think up

picturesque ADJECTIVE **1** *He had spent the morning painting picturesque views of his master.* ► attractive, pretty, beautiful, charming, pleasant, scenic AN OPPOSITE IS ugly **2** *She was trying to find a more picturesque way to describe it.* ► colorful, graphic, descriptive, expressive, vivid, imaginative, poetic AN OPPOSITE IS prosaic

piece NOUN **1** *a piece of cheese; a piece of stone* ► bit, chunk, lump, hunk, portion, fragment, morsel, particle **2** *a piece of furniture* ► item, article **3** *She wrote a piece for the local newspaper.* ► article, story, feature, essay, account

piece VERB **piece together** *It is difficult to piece the evidence together into a convincing case.* ► assemble, compose, fit together, join together

pied ADJECTIVE ► dappled, flecked, mottled, particolored, piebald, spotted, variegated

pier NOUN **1** *Boats were tied up at the pier.* ► jetty, quay, wharf, dock, landing stage,

breakwater **2** *Immense piers supported a high vault.* ► column, pillar, support, buttress, upright, pile

pierce VERB *a spear that could pierce the thickest armour* ► penetrate, puncture, perforate, make a hole in, probe, enter, transfix, impale

piercing ADJECTIVE **1** *From the wood comes a piercing screech.* ► shrill, sharp, penetrating, shattering, ear-splitting, high-pitched, strident, deafening, loud **2** *a piercing wind* ► freezing, bitter, biting, wintry, stinging **3** *a piercing pain* ► stabbing, intense, excruciating, agonizing, stinging

piety NOUN *a priest respected for his piety* ► devoutness, devotion, piousness, holiness, godliness, saintliness, sanctity, religion, faith AN OPPOSITE IS impiety

pig NOUN **1** (*informal*) *He was always a bit of a pig when it came to food.* ► glutton, guzzler, gourmand **2** *Her husband can be a real pig at times.* ► brute, monster, beast, fiend, animal, demon

pile NOUN **1** *a pile of stones* ► heap, stack, mass, mound, mountain, collection, hoard **2** *We*

A
B
C
D
E
F
G
H
I
J
K
L
M
N
O
P
Q
R
S
T
U
V
W
X
Y
Z

pile³ NOUN a raised surface on fabric, made of upright threads • *a carpet with a thick pile*

pileup NOUN pileups a road accident that involves a number of vehicles

pilfer VERB pilfers, pilfering, pilfered steal small things
▷ **pilferer** NOUN **pilferage** NOUN

pilgrim NOUN pilgrims a person who travels to a holy place for religious reasons
▷ **pilgrimage** NOUN

pill NOUN pills a small solid piece of medicine for swallowing
the pill a contraceptive pill

pillage VERB pillages, pillaging, pillaged carry off goods using force, especially in a war; plunder
▷ **pillage** NOUN

pillar NOUN pillars a tall stone or wooden post

pillar box NOUN pillar boxes a postbox standing in a street

pillion NOUN pillions a seat behind the driver on a motorcycle

pillow NOUN pillows a cushion for a person's head to rest on, especially in bed [from Latin *pulvinus* = cushion]

pillowcase or **pillowslip** NOUN pillowcases or pillowslips a cloth cover for a pillow

pilot NOUN pilots 1 a person who works the controls for flying an aircraft 2 a person qualified to steer a ship in and out of a port or through a difficult stretch of water 3 a guide

pilot VERB pilots, piloting, piloted 1 be pilot of an aircraft or ship 2 guide or steer

pilot ADJECTIVE testing on a small scale how something will work • *a pilot program* [from Greek *pedon* = oar or rudder]

pilot light NOUN pilot lights 1 a small flame that lights a larger burner on a gas cooker, etc. 2 an electric indicator light

pimp NOUN pimps a man who gets clients for prostitutes and lives off their earnings

pimple NOUN pimples a small round raised spot on the skin
▷ **pimply** ADJECTIVE

PIN ABBREVIATION personal identification number; a number used as a person's password so that he or she can use a cash dispenser, computer, etc.

pin NOUN pins 1 a short thin piece of metal with a sharp point and a rounded head, used to fasten pieces of cloth or paper, etc., together 2 a pointed device for fixing or marking something
pins and needles a tingling feeling in the skin

pin VERB pins, pinning, pinned 1 fasten something with a pin or pins 2 make a person or thing unable to move • *He was pinned under the wreckage.* 3 fix blame or responsibility on someone • *They pinned the blame on her sister.*

pincer NOUN pincers the claw of a shellfish such as a lobster

pincers PLURAL NOUN a tool with two parts that are pressed together for gripping and holding things

pinch VERB pinches, pinching, pinched 1 squeeze something tightly or painfully between two things, especially between the finger and thumb 2 *(informal)* steal

pinch NOUN pinches 1 a pinching movement 2 the amount that can be held between the tips of the thumb and forefinger • *a pinch of salt*
at a pinch in time of difficulty; if necessary
feel the pinch suffer from lack of money

Thesaurus

have piles of work to do. ► plenty, a lot, a great deal, *(more informal)* lots, *(more informal)* masses, *(more informal)* heaps

pile VERB 1 *They piled everything into a corner.*
► heap, stack, pack, jam, accumulate, amass, load, mass, store, collect, gather, hoard
pile up *Problems were beginning to pile up.*
► build up, mount up, increase, grow, accumulate

pilfer VERB *People were pilfering bricks from building sites.* ► steal, take, snatch, pinch, filch, *(more informal)* swipe, *(more informal)* nick, *(more informal)* knock off

pillar NOUN *A row of pillars supports the roof.*
► column, pier, support, buttress, upright, pile

pillow NOUN *She rested her head on a pillow.*
► cushion, bolster, headrest, pad

pilot NOUN 1 *the pilot of an aircraft* ► airman or airwoman, *(old-fashioned)* aviator 2 *a harbor pilot* ► navigator, helmsman, steersman, coxswain, guide

pilot ADJECTIVE *a pilot program* ► experimental, trial, test, sample, model

pilot VERB *He piloted the little plane to the island.*
► fly, guide, lead, navigate, steer, direct, drive

pimple NOUN *a face covered in pimples* ► spot, blackhead, swelling, *(more informal)* zit

pin NOUN *The notice was attached by a pin.*
► tack, nail, spike, brad, skewer

pin VERB *She pinned a badge on him.* ► fasten, attach, fix, stick

pinch VERB 1 *She pinched his arm.* ► nip, squeeze, crush, tweak 2 *Someone has pinched my pen.* ► steal, take, pilfer, snatch, filch, *(more*

pincushion NOUN **pincushions** a small pad into which pins are stuck to keep them ready for use

pine NOUN **pines** an evergreen tree with needle-shaped leaves

pine VERB **pines, pining, pined 1** feel an intense longing for somebody or something **2** become weak through longing for somebody or something

pineapple NOUN **pineapples** a large tropical fruit with a tough prickly skin and yellow flesh

ping-pong NOUN table tennis

pinion NOUN **pinions** a bird's wing, especially the outer end

pinion VERB **pinions, pinioning, pinioned 1** clip a bird's wings to prevent it from flying **2** hold or fasten someone's arms or legs in order to prevent them from moving

pink ADJECTIVE pale red
▷ **pinkness** NOUN

pink NOUN **pinks 1** a pink color **2** a garden plant with fragrant flowers, often pink or white

pinnacle NOUN **pinnacles 1** a pointed ornament on a roof **2** a high pointed piece of rock **3** the highest point of something • *It was the pinnacle of her career.*

pinpoint ADJECTIVE exact or precise • *with pinpoint accuracy*

pinpoint VERB **pinpoints, pinpointing, pinpointed** find or identify something precisely

pinstripe NOUN **pinstripes** one of the very narrow stripes that form a pattern in cloth
▷ **pinstriped** ADJECTIVE

pint NOUN **pints** a measure for liquids, equal to one-eighth of a gallon

pinup NOUN **pinups** (*informal*) a picture of an attractive or famous person for pinning on a wall

pioneer NOUN **pioneers** one of the first people to go to a place or do or investigate something
▷ **pioneer** VERB

pious ADJECTIVE very religious; devout
▷ **piously** ADVERB **piousness** NOUN

pip NOUN **pips 1** a small hard seed of an apple, pear, orange, etc. **2** one of the stars on the shoulder of an army officer's uniform **3** a short high-pitched sound • *She heard the six pips of the time signal on the radio.*

pipe NOUN **pipes 1** a tube through which water or gas, etc., can flow from one place to another **2** a short narrow tube with a bowl at one end in which tobacco can burn for smoking **3** a tube forming a musical instrument or part of one
the pipes bagpipes

pipe VERB **pipes, piping, piped 1** send something along pipes **2** transmit music or other sound by wire or cable **3** play music on a pipe or the bagpipes **4** decorate a cake with thin lines of icing, cream, etc.
pipe down (*informal*) be quiet
pipe up begin to say something

pipe dream NOUN **pipe dreams** an impossible wish

pipeline NOUN **pipelines** a pipe for carrying oil or water, etc., a long distance
in the pipeline in the process of being made or organized

piping NOUN **1** pipes; a length of pipe **2** a decorative line of icing, cream, etc., on a cake or other dish **3** a long narrow pipelike fold decorating clothing, upholstery, etc.

piping ADJECTIVE shrill • *a piping voice*
piping hot very hot

pirate NOUN **pirates 1** a person on a ship who attacks and robs other ships at sea **2** someone who produces or publishes or

Thesaurus

informal) swipe, (*more informal*) nick, (*more informal*) knock off

pine VERB *He thinks you were pining from love.*
► languish, wither, fade, droop, sicken
pine for *The Smiths were pining for their home.*
► long for, yearn for, hanker after, miss, crave

pioneer NOUN **1** *pioneers of the American West*
► settler, colonist, colonizer, discoverer, explorer **2** *a pioneer of birth control*
► developer, innovator, originator, pathfinder, groundbreaker

pioneer VERB *a scientist who pioneered genetic fingerprinting* ► develop, introduce, evolve, create, discover, invent, originate, initiate, spearhead

pious ADJECTIVE **1** *His second wife was a remarkably pious woman.* ► religious, devout,

devoted, spiritual, dutiful OPPOSITES ARE impious, irreligious **2** *The remark was no more than a pious platitude.* ► sanctimonious, insincere, self-righteous AN OPPOSITE IS sincere

pipe NOUN *a water pipe* ► duct, channel, tube, conduit, hose, pipeline

pipe VERB **1** *The liquid is piped into containers.*
► channel, funnel, siphon, carry, run **2** *birds piping* ► chirp, cheep, tweet, trill, peep, chirrup, sing
pipe down *informal He got annoyed and told them to pipe down.* ► be quiet, be silent, quieten down, stop talking, hush

pirate NOUN *Pirates attacked the ship.*
► freebooter, marauder, privateer, (*historical*) buccaneer, (*old-fashioned*) corsair

pirouette ➔ pity

broadcasts illegally • *a pirate radio station* • *pirate videos*

▷ **piratical** ADJECTIVE **piracy** NOUN

pirouette (pir- oo- et) NOUN pirouettes a spinning movement of the body made while balanced on the point of the toe or on one foot

▷ **pirouette** VERB

[from French, = spinning top]

pistil NOUN the female organs of a flower

pistol NOUN pistols a small handgun

piston NOUN pistons a disc or cylinder that fits inside a tube in which it moves up and down as part of an engine or pump etc.

pit NOUN pits **1** a deep hole **2** a hollow **3** a coal mine **4** the part of a race circuit where racing cars are refuelled and repaired during a race

pit VERB pits, pitting, pitted **1** make holes or hollows in something • *The ground was pitted with craters.* **2** put somebody in competition with somebody else • *He was pitted against the champion in the final.*

▷ **pitted** ADJECTIVE

pitch[1] NOUN pitches **1** the highness or lowness of a voice or a musical note **2** intensity or strength • *Excitement was at fever pitch.* **3** the steepness of a slope • *the pitch of the roof*

pitch VERB pitches, pitching, pitched **1** throw or fling **2** set up a tent or camp **3** fall heavily • *He pitched forward as the bus braked suddenly.*

4 move up and down on a rough sea **5** set something at a particular level • *They pitched their hopes high.* **6** (said about a bowled ball in cricket) strike the ground

pitch in (*informal*) start working or doing something vigorously

pitch[2] NOUN a black sticky substance rather like tar

pitch-black or **pitch-dark** ADJECTIVES very black or very dark

pitched battle NOUN pitched battles a battle between troops in prepared positions

pitcher NOUN pitchers a large jug

pitchfork NOUN pitchforks a large fork with two prongs, used for lifting hay

pitchfork VERB pitchforks, pitchforking, pitchforked **1** lift something with a pitchfork **2** put a person somewhere suddenly

pitfall NOUN pitfalls an unsuspected danger or difficulty

pitiable ADJECTIVE making you feel pity

pitiful ADJECTIVE **1** making you feel pity **2** very bad or inadequate

▷ **pitifully** ADVERB

pity NOUN **1** the feeling of being sorry because someone is in pain or trouble **2** a cause for regret • *It's a pity that you can't come.*

take pity on feel sorry for someone and help them

pity VERB pities, pitying, pitied feel pity for someone

Thesaurus

pit NOUN **1** *A deep pit had been dug in the ground.* ► hole, ditch, trench, shaft, hollow, depression, trough, cavity, chasm, abyss **2** *increasing pit closures* ► mine, coal mine, colliery, quarry, shaft, working

pitch NOUN **1** *Their voices rose in pitch with the excitement.* ► tone, timbre, key, modulation **2** *His anger reached such a pitch that he became almost violent.* ► level, point, height, degree, intensity **3** *the pitch of the roof* ► steepness, angle, gradient, incline, slope, slant, tilt

pitch VERB **1** *This is where we pitch our tents for the night.* ► put up, raise, fix, erect, set up **2** *She picked up the ball and pitched it into the neighboring garden.* ► throw, fling, toss, hurl, lob, sling, bowl, heave, cast, (*more informal*) bung, (*more informal*) chuck **3** *Several lads pitched into the water.* ► plunge, dive, plummet, drop, topple **4** *The boat was pitching in the storm.* ► lurch, toss, wallow, rock, roll, reel, flounder, dip up and down

pitfall NOUN *Drama producers no longer need to fear the pitfalls of live television.* ► hazard, snag, trap, danger, peril, snare, difficulty, drawback, catch

pitiful ADJECTIVE **1** *She was a pitiful sight, still lying where she had fallen.* ► pathetic, pitiable, sad, sorrowful, wretched, touching, affecting, distressing, heartbreaking, heartrending **2** *He trudged off with the pitiful few pounds he had made that day.* ► meager, negligible, paltry, miserable, modest, scanty, scant, sparse, (*more informal*) mingy, (*more informal*) measly OPPOSITES ARE generous, extravagant

pitiless ADJECTIVE *Dinah did not break under the pitiless criticism.* ► merciless, relentless, ruthless, unrelenting, callous, cruel, hard, heartless, inexorable, unfeeling OPPOSITES ARE merciful, compassionate

pity NOUN **1** *He had never felt pity for anyone in his life.* ► compassion, sympathy, commiseration, tenderness, understanding, feeling, forbearance, mercy, forgiveness, humanity, kindness OPPOSITES ARE indifference, animosity **2 a pity** *It's a pity it was dark and we couldn't see the garden.* ► a shame, unfortunate, a piece of bad luck, a cause for regret

pity VERB *He always pitied people who had to ask for money.* ► feel sorry for, feel pity for, feel for, sympathize with, commiserate with, take pity on

pivot NOUN pivots a point or part on which something turns or balances
▷ **pivotal** ADJECTIVE

pivot VERB pivots, pivoting, pivoted turn or place something to turn on a pivot

pixel (piks- el) NOUN pixels one of the tiny dots on a computer display screen from which the image is formed [short for *picture element*]

pixie NOUN pixies a small fairy; an elf

pizza (peets- a) NOUN pizzas an Italian food that consists of a layer of dough baked with a savory topping [from Italian, = pie]

pizzicato (pits- i- kah- toh) ADJECTIVE, ADVERB plucking the strings of a musical instrument

placard NOUN placards a poster or notice, especially one carried at a demonstration [from early French *plaquier* = to lay flat]

placate VERB placates, placating, placated make someone feel calmer and less angry

place NOUN places **1** a particular part of space, especially where something belongs; an area or position **2** a seat • *Save me a place.* **3** a job; employment **4** a building; a home • *Come around to our place.* **5** a duty or function • *It's not my place to interfere.* **6** a point in a series of things • *In the first place, the date is wrong.*
in place 1 in the right position **2** suitable
in place of instead of

out of place 1 in the wrong position **2** unsuitable

place VERB places, placing, placed put something in a particular place
▷ **placement** NOUN

placid ADJECTIVE calm and peaceful; not easily made anxious or upset
▷ **placidly** ADVERB **placidity** NOUN

plagiarize (play- jee- er- I'z) VERB plagiarizes, plagiarizing, plagiarized take someone else's writings or ideas and use them as if they were your own
▷ **plagiarism** NOUN **plagiarist** NOUN

plague NOUN plagues **1** a dangerous illness that spreads very quickly **2** a large number of pests • *a plague of locusts*

plague VERB plagues, plaguing, plagued pester or annoy • *We've been plagued by wasps all afternoon.*

plain ADJECTIVE **1** simple; not decorated or elaborate **2** not beautiful **3** easy to see or hear or understand **4** frank and straightforward
▷ **plainly** ADVERB **plainness** NOUN

plain NOUN plains a large area of flat country
USAGE Do not confuse with **plane**.

plainclothes NOUN civilian clothes worn instead of a uniform, e.g., by police

Thesaurus

place NOUN **1** *She rose quietly from her place at the table.* ► seat, chair, position, space **2** *They would choose a foreign place for their next holiday.* ► locality, region, resort, city, town, village **3** *Seaview is the ideal place to write and work quietly.* ► locale, location, venue, spot, point **4** *They badly wanted a place of their own.* ► home, house, residence, dwelling, property, flat, apartment, establishment, accommodation **5** *She was offered a place on the company's board.* ► position, post, appointment, situation **6** *I know my place and won't interfere.* ► status, position, station, standing, rank

place VERB **1** *He placed the shopping on the table.* ► put, set, lay, deposit, leave, (more informal) stick, (more informal) dump, (more informal) plonk **2** *The judges placed her second overall.* ► rank, grade, position **3** *The face was familiar but I couldn't quite place it.* ► recognize, identify, remember

plague NOUN **1** *a study of the effects of the plague on two major cities* ► pestilence, blight, epidemic, contagion, infestation, outbreak **2** *a plague of flies* ► infestation, invasion, nuisance, scourge, swarm **3** *the plague of street crime in the area* ► bane, curse, blight, scourge, affliction, cancer

plague VERB **1** *The fears which had menaced her before returned to plague her.* ► afflict, bedevil,

beset, torment, hound, torture, persecute **2** *He was being plagued with questions.* ► pester, badger, harass, trouble, annoy, bother, disturb, irritate, molest, vex, worry, (more informal) nag

plain ADJECTIVE **1** *The forms are written in plain English.* ► clear, simple, straightforward, understandable, intelligible, direct OPPOSITES ARE obscure, unclear **2** *It was plain that someone had been in the house before them.* ► obvious, clear, evident, apparent, manifest **3** *They thought some plain speaking was needed.* ► frank, candid, outspoken, blunt, direct, explicit, unequivocal **4** *The house had a rather plain appearance.* ► unattractive, ordinary, unprepossessing, ugly AN OPPOSITE IS attractive **5** *The room was decorated in a plain style.* ► simple, basic, restrained, unadorned, unembellished, unelaborate, unpretentious OPPOSITES ARE elaborate, fancy

plain NOUN *the movement of wildebeest across the plains of Africa* ► grassland, flatland, prairie, savannah, steppe

plain ADVERB *Many people are just plain scared of making the change.* ► downright, completely, totally, utterly, really, thoroughly, absolutely, simply

a
b
c
d
e
f
g
h
i
j
k
l
m
n
o
p
q
r
s
t
u
v
w
x
y
z

plaintiff NOUN **plaintiffs** the person who brings a complaint against somebody else to a law court COMPARE **defendant**

plaintive ADJECTIVE sounding sad • *a plaintive cry*

plait (plat) VERB **plaits, plaiting, plaited** weave three or more strands of hair or rope to form one length

plait NOUN **plaits** a length of hair or rope that has been plaited

plan NOUN **plans** 1 a way of doing something thought out in advance 2 a drawing showing the arrangement of parts of something 3 a map of a town or district

plan VERB **plans, planning, planned** make a plan for something
▷ **planner** NOUN

plane[1] NOUN **planes** 1 an airplane 2 a tool for making wood smooth by scraping its surface 3 a flat or level surface

plane VERB **planes, planing, planed** smooth wood with a plane

plane ADJECTIVE flat or level • *a plane surface* USAGE Do not confuse with **plain**.

plane[2] NOUN **planes** a tall tree with broad leaves

planet NOUN **planets** one of the bodies that move in an orbit around the sun. The main planets are Mercury, Venus, Earth, Mars, Jupiter, Saturn, Uranus, and Neptune.
▷ **planetary** ADJECTIVE

plank NOUN **planks** a long flat piece of wood

plankton NOUN microscopic plants and animals that float in the sea, lakes, etc.

plant NOUN **plants** 1 a living thing that cannot move, makes its food from chemical substances, and usually has a stem, leaves, and roots 2 a small plant, not a tree or shrub 3 a factory or its equipment 4 (*informal*) something deliberately placed for other people to find, usually to mislead people or cause trouble

plant VERB **plants, planting, planted** 1 put something in soil for growing 2 fix something firmly in place 3 place something where it will be found, usually to mislead people or cause trouble
▷ **planter** NOUN

plantation NOUN **plantations** 1 a large area of land where cotton, tobacco, or tea, etc., is planted 2 a group of planted trees

plaque (plak) NOUN **plaques** 1 a flat piece of metal or porcelain fixed on a wall as an ornament or memorial 2 a filmy substance that forms on teeth and gums, where bacteria can live

plaster NOUN **plasters** 1 a small covering put over the skin around a cut or wound to protect it 2 a mixture of lime, sand, and water, etc., for covering walls and ceilings 3 plaster of Paris, or a cast made of this to hold broken bones in place

plaster VERB **plasters, plastering, plastered** 1 cover a wall, etc., with plaster 2 cover something thickly; daub

plaster of Paris NOUN a white paste used for making molds or for casts around a broken leg or arm

plastic NOUN **plastics** a strong light synthetic substance that can be molded into a permanent shape

Thesaurus

plan NOUN 1 (*informal*) *a plan of the building* ► chart, diagram, map, layout, blueprint, representation 2 *a clever plan for raising money* ► scheme, idea, proposal, project, program, strategy, suggestion, proposition

plan VERB 1 *She began planning tomorrow's journey.* ► organize, arrange, work out, think out, prepare 2 *some tips for anyone planning a new garden* ► design, devise, contrive, sketch out 3 *We plan to go abroad this year.* ► intend, propose, aim, mean, envisage, contemplate, be thinking of USAGE If you use any of the last three synonyms instead of *to go*, you have to say *going* instead of *to go*, e.g., *We envisage going abroad this year.*

plane NOUN 1 *The plane rose gently in the air.* ► airplane, aircraft, jet, airliner, craft 2 *The thought that came to her now was on a more creative plane.* ► level, stage, degree, position

planet NOUN *the population of the planet* ► globe, world, orb

plank NOUN *a plank of wood* ► board, floorboard, beam, timber

plant NOUN 1 **plants** ► greenery, growth, flora, undergrowth, vegetation 2 *industrial plant* ► machinery, machines, equipment, apparatus 3 *a plant of the FBI* ► informer, informant, spy, agent, infiltrator, mole

plant VERB 1 *Plant the seeds in September.* ► sow, bury, set out, put in the ground 2 *Someone had planted the idea in her mind.* ► establish, introduce, fix, put, lodge, impress, instil, imprint

plaster NOUN 1 *He stripped the wall down to the plaster.* ► plasterwork, mortar, stucco 2 *A nurse put a plaster on the cut.* ► dressing, sticking plaster, bandage

plaster VERB *The floor was plastered with mud.* ► cover, daub, coat, smother, smear, spread

plastic ADJECTIVE *They were drinking warm beer from plastic cups.* ► PVC, polystyrene, polyurethane, celluloid

plastic ADJECTIVE **1** made of plastic **2** soft and easy to mold • *Clay is a plastic substance.*
▷ **plasticity** NOUN
[from Greek *plastos* = molded or formed]

plastic surgery NOUN surgery to repair deformed or injured parts of the body
▷ **plastic surgeon** NOUN

plate NOUN **plates 1** an almost flat usually circular object from which food is eaten or served **2** a thin flat sheet of metal, glass, or other hard material **3** an illustration on special paper in a book
▷ **plateful** NOUN

plate VERB **plates, plating, plated 1** coat metal with a thin layer of gold, silver, tin, etc. **2** cover something with sheets of metal

plateau (plat- oh) NOUN **plateaux** (plat- ohz) a flat area of high land

platform NOUN **platforms 1** a flat raised area along the side of a line at a railway station **2** a flat surface above the level of the floor, especially one from which someone speaks to an audience **3** the policies that a political party puts forward

platinum NOUN a valuable silver-colored metal that does not tarnish

platitude NOUN **platitudes** a trite or overused remark
▷ **platitudinous** ADJECTIVE

plausible ADJECTIVE seeming to be honest or worth believing but perhaps deceptive • *a plausible excuse*
▷ **plausibly** ADVERB **plausibility** NOUN

play VERB **plays, playing, played 1** take part in a game, sport, or other amusement **2** make music or sound with a musical instrument, record player, etc. **3** perform a part in a play or film
▷ **player** NOUN

play about or **play around** have fun or be mischievous

play down give people the impression that something is not important

play up (*informal*) tease or annoy someone

play NOUN **plays 1** a story acted on a stage or on radio or television **2** playing or having fun [from Old English]

playful ADJECTIVE **1** wanting to play; full of fun **2** done in fun; not serious
▷ **playfully** ADVERB **playfulness** NOUN

Thesaurus

plate NOUN **1** *She helped herself to a plate of food.* ► dish, platter, dinner plate, plateful, helping, serving, portion, bowl **2** *Someone had removed the plates from the end of the book.* ► illustration, picture, print, photograph, lithograph **3** *There was a brass plate by the front door.* ► plaque, nameplate, sign

platform 1 *A speaker addressed the audience from the platform.* ► dais, rostrum, podium, stand, stage **2** *the Democrats' election platform* ► policy, program, manifesto, plan, party line

plausible ADJECTIVE **1** *He knew he had presented a plausible explanation.* ► credible, reasonable, believable, convincing, persuasive, tenable, likely, feasible, probable, possible, acceptable, conceivable AN OPPOSITE IS implausible **2** *He had the sort of plausible charm that Georgina was wary of.* ► smooth, smooth-talking, glib, specious

play NOUN **1** *a balance between work and play* ► amusement, entertainment, relaxation, recreation, enjoyment, leisure, pleasure, diversion, fun **2** *a play by Shakespeare* ► drama, theatrical work, stage play, tragedy, comedy, production, performance, show **3** *There was some play in the mechanism.* ► movement, freedom of movement, looseness, flexibility, latitude, leeway

play VERB **1** *The children were playing in the garden.* ► amuse yourself, have fun, enjoy yourself, play games, romp, frolic, caper **2** *I enjoy playing indoor sports.* ► take part in,

engage in, participate in, join in, compete in **3** *The two sides play each other next week.* ► compete against, take on, challenge, oppose, vie with **4** *We need someone to play Hamlet.* ► act, perform, portray, act the part of, play the part of, take the role of **5** *He regretted not being able to play a musical instrument.* ► perform on, make music on

play down *The government played down the effect of the tax increases.* ► minimize, make light of, gloss over, underplay OPPOSITES ARE exaggerate, play up

play on *advertising that plays on people's anxieties* ► exploit, take advantage of, make use of, capitalize on, trade on

play up 1 *Some of the children began to play up.* ► misbehave, behave badly, be naughty, cause trouble **2** *The newspapers played up the scandal.* ► emphasize, accentuate, exaggerate, underline, highlight, give prominence to, stress OPPOSITES ARE minimize, play down

player NOUN **1** *The team has bought some new players.* ► team member, sportsman or sportswoman, competitor, contestant **2** *players on stage* ► actor or actress, performer, artist, entertainer **3** *players in an orchestra* ► musician, performer, instrumentalist, soloist, artist

playful ADJECTIVE **1** *She came back from the party in a playful mood.* ► frisky, lively, jolly, spirited **2** *a few playful remarks* ► lighthearted, joking, teasing, jocular, frivolous

a
b
c
d
e
f
g
h
i
j
k
l
m
n
o
p
q
r
s
t
u
v
w
x
y
z

A
B
C
D
E
F
G
H
I
J
K
L
M
N
O
P
Q
R
S
T
U
V
W
X
Y
Z

playground NOUN playgrounds a piece of ground for children to play on

playgroup NOUN playgroups a group of very young children who play together regularly, supervised by adults

playing card NOUN playing cards each of a set of cards (usually 52) used for playing games

playing field NOUN playing fields a field used for outdoor games

playmate NOUN playmates a person you play games with

play-off NOUN play-offs an extra match that is played to decide a draw or tie

plaything NOUN playthings a toy

playwright NOUN playwrights a person who writes plays

plea NOUN pleas **1** a request or appeal • *a plea for mercy* **2** an excuse • *He stayed at home on the plea of a headache.* **3** a formal statement of "guilty" or "not guilty" made in a lawcourt by someone accused of a crime

plead VERB pleads, pleading, pleaded **1** beg someone to do something **2** state formally in a court of law that you are guilty or not guilty of a crime **3** give something as an excuse

• *She didn't come on vacation with us, pleading poverty.*

pleasant ADJECTIVE pleasing; giving pleasure
▷ **pleasantly** ADVERB **pleasantness** NOUN

please VERB pleases, pleasing, pleased **1** make a person feel satisfied or glad **2** (used to make a request or an order polite) • *Please ring the bell.* **3** like; think suitable • *Do as you please.*

pleasure NOUN pleasures **1** a feeling of satisfaction or gladness; enjoyment **2** something that pleases you

plectrum NOUN plectra a small piece of metal or bone, etc., for plucking the strings of a musical instrument

pledge NOUN pledges **1** a solemn promise **2** a thing handed over as security for a loan or contract

pledge VERB pledges, pledging, pledged **1** promise solemnly to do or give something **2** hand something over as security

plenty NOUN quite enough; as much as is needed or wanted

plenty ADVERB (informal) quite or fully • *It's plenty big enough.*

Thesaurus

playground NOUN *a playground behind the school* ► play area, recreation ground, amusement park

playing field NOUN *The train passed a playing field where a game was going on.* ► sports ground, ground, pitch, recreation ground

plea NOUN **1** *a plea for mercy* ► appeal, petition, request, entreaty, supplication, invocation, prayer **2** *His plea was that he had been ill.* ► claim, excuse, defence, justification, pretext

plead VERB *The prisoners pleaded for their lives.* ► beg, implore, entreat, petition, request, solicit, appeal, ask, importune

pleasant ADJECTIVE **1** *It was a pleasant afternoon.* ► enjoyable, pleasing, agreeable, satisfying, delightful, lovely, nice AN OPPOSITE IS unpleasant **2** *The assistants are all very pleasant.* ► friendly, agreeable, congenial, likable, personable, good-humored, nice OPPOSITES ARE unpleasant, disagreeable

please VERB **1** *She did her best to please them.* ► make happy, satisfy, give pleasure to, gladden, gratify, amuse, content, delight, entertain **2** *Do what you please* ► want, like, wish, desire, feel like

pleased ADJECTIVE *We were so pleased to see you.* ► happy, glad, delighted, satisfied, overjoyed, thrilled OPPOSITES ARE displeased, annoyed

pleasing ADJECTIVES *a very pleasing result* ► pleasant, agreeable, gratifying, satisfying, welcome, acceptable

pleasure NOUN **1** *She found great pleasure in fashionable clothes.* ► enjoyment, gratification, happiness, satisfaction, amusement, contentment, fulfillment, delight, comfort, entertainment, gladness, joy, solace **2** *the pleasures that children bring* ► joy, delight, enjoyment

pledge NOUN **1** *a pledge to spend billions on education* ► promise, undertaking, assurance, commitment, guarantee **2** *She gave her rings as a pledge.* ► surety, security, bond, deposit, bail

pledge VERB *They all pledged their loyalty to the king.* ► promise, swear, vow, guarantee, undertake

plentiful ADJECTIVE *a plentiful supply of fruit* ► abundant, copious, ample, liberal, profuse, generous, lavish, rich, bountiful, prolific, inexhaustible OPPOSITES ARE sparse, scarce
be plentiful *The flowers are plentiful at this time of year.* ► abound, proliferate, be abundant, flourish, thrive

plenty NOUN **1** *a time of plenty* ► affluence, prosperity, wealth, opulence, luxury, well-being, comfort **2** *plenty of There is plenty of time before they arrive.* ► a lot of, a great deal of, much, enough, (more informal) lots of, (more informal) heaps of, (more informal) loads of, (more informal) masses of

pliable ADJECTIVE **1** easy to bend; flexible **2** easy to influence or control
▷ **pliability** NOUN

pliers PLURAL NOUN pincers that have jaws with flat surfaces for gripping things

plight NOUN **plights** a difficult or dangerous situation

PLO ABBREVIATION Palestine Liberation Organization

plod VERB **plods, plodding, plodded 1** walk slowly and heavily **2** work slowly but steadily
▷ **plodder** NOUN

plop NOUN **plops** the sound of something dropping into water
▷ **plop** VERB

plot NOUN **plots 1** a secret plan **2** the story in a play, novel, or film **3** a small piece of land

plot VERB **plots, plotting, plotted 1** make a secret plan **2** make a chart or graph of something • *We plotted the ship's route on our map.*

plow NOUN **plows** a farming implement for turning the soil over, in preparation for planting seeds

plow VERB **plows, plowing, plowed 1** turn over soil with a plow **2** go through something with great effort or difficulty • *He plowed through the book.*
▷ **plowman** NOUN
plow back reinvest profits in the business that produced them

pluck VERB **plucks, plucking, plucked 1** pick a flower or fruit **2** pull the feathers off a bird **3** pull something up or out **4** pull a string (e.g., on a guitar) and let it go again
pluck up courage summon up courage and overcome fear

pluck NOUN courage or spirit

plucky ADJECTIVE **pluckier, pluckiest** brave or spirited
▷ **pluckily** ADVERB

plug NOUN **plugs 1** something used to stop up a hole • *a bath plug* **2** a device that fits into a socket to connect wires to a supply of electricity **3** (*informal*) a piece of publicity for something

plug VERB **plugs, plugging, plugged 1** stop up a hole **2** (*informal*) publicize something
plug in put a plug into an electrical socket

Thesaurus

pliable ADJECTIVE **1** *a pliable material* ► flexible, bendable, pliant, supple, plastic, springy, (*more informal*) bendy AN OPPOSITE IS stiff **2** *a pliable mind* ► adaptable, impressionable, responsive, suggestible, compliant, flexible, tractable, biddable, accommodating AN OPPOSITE IS rigid

plight NOUN *the plight of the homeless* ► difficulty, predicament, danger, trouble, extremity, quandary, straits

plod VERB **1** *Mary plodded up the path.* ► trudge, tramp, lumber, stomp **2** *It will take hours to plod through the whole book.* ► plough, wade, trawl, labor, persevere, grind on

plot NOUN **1** *He grew vegetables in a plot behind the house.* ► piece of ground, patch, allotment, smallholding, lot **2** *The novel has a complicated plot.* ► storyline, story, outline, action, thread, scenario, narrative **3** *A plot was revealed against the government.* ► conspiracy, intrigue, plan, scheme, cabal, machination

plot VERB **1** *The president's brother was plotting his downfall.* ► plan, scheme, concoct, devise, hatch **2** *He was accused of plotting against the government.* ► conspire, scheme, intrigue **3** *They plotted their course on the map.* ► chart, mark, map

plow VERB **1** *Farmers plowed the fields.* ► cultivate, till, work, turn over **2** *A van had* plowed into a shop window. ► plunge, crash, career, smash, bulldoze

ploy NOUN *It was just a ploy to get rid of Doreen.* ► ruse, trick, move, device, stratagem, maneuver

pluck NOUN *It must have taken a lot of pluck to walk along a path marked "danger."* ► courage, daring, nerve, audacity, boldness, heroism, (*more informal*) bottle, (*more informal*) grit, (*more informal*) guts

pluck VERB **1** *She began to pluck hairs off her skirt.* ► pick, pull, take off, snatch **2** *He sang and plucked a guitar.* ► pick, twang, strum, finger **3** *The girls stood plucking fruit from the trees.* ► pick, gather, collect, harvest, garner

plucky ADJECTIVE *a plucky young woman's tale of escape* ► brave, courageous, bold, daring, intrepid, valiant, resolute OPPOSITES ARE timid, cowardly

plug NOUN **1** *He put a plug in the top of the bottle.* ► stopper, cork, bung **2** (*informal*) *They put in a plug for their new song.* ► advertisement, piece of publicity, mention, (*informal*) puff, (*informal*) boost

plug VERB **1** *The first thing to do was plug the leak.* ► seal, stop up, block up, close **2** (*informal*) *He wanted to plug the new film.* ► publicize, promote, advertise, mention frequently
plug away *He plugged away at the work he had to do.* ► toil, labor, soldier on, plod on

A
B
C
D
E
F
G
H
I
J
K
L
M
N
O
P
Q
R
S
T
U
V
W
X
Y
Z

plum NOUN **plums** **1** a soft juicy fruit with a pointed pit in the middle **2** a reddish-purple color **3** (*informal*) something very good • *a plum job*

plumb VERB **plumbs, plumbing, plumbed** **1** measure how deep something is **2** get to the bottom of a matter • *We could not plumb the mystery.* **3** fit a room or building with a plumbing system

plumb ADJECTIVE exactly upright; vertical • *The wall was plumb*

plumb ADVERB (*informal*) exactly • *It fell plumb in the middle.*

plumber NOUN **plumbers** a person who fits and mends plumbing

plumbing NOUN **1** the water pipes, water tanks, and drainage pipes in a building **2** the work of a plumber

plumb line NOUN a line with a heavy object tied to it, used for finding a vertical line on an upright surface or for testing the depth of water

plume NOUN **plumes** **1** a large feather **2** something shaped like a feather • *a plume of smoke*

plummet NOUN **plummets** a plumb line or the weight on its end

plummet VERB **plummets, plummeting, plummeted** **1** drop downward quickly **2** decrease rapidly in value • *Prices have plummeted.*

plump ADJECTIVE slightly fat; rounded
▷ **plumpness** NOUN

plump VERB **plumps, plumping, plumped** make something rounded • *plump up a cushion*

plump VERB **plumps, plumping, plumped** **plump for** (*informal*) choose

plunder VERB **plunders, plundering, plundered** rob a person or place using force, especially during a war or riot
▷ **plunderer** NOUN

plunder NOUN **1** plundering **2** goods, etc., that have been plundered

plunge VERB **plunges, plunging, plunged** **1** go or push forcefully into something; dive **2** fall or go downwards suddenly **3** go or force into action, etc. • *They plunged the world into war.*

plunge NOUN **plunges** a sudden fall or dive **take the plunge** start a bold course of action

plural NOUN **plurals** the form of a noun or verb used when it stands for more than one person or thing • *The plural of "child" is "children."* COMPARE **singular**
▷ **plural** ADJECTIVE **plurality** NOUN

plus PREPOSITION with the next number or thing added • *2 plus 2 equals four (2 + 2 = 4)* [from Latin, = more]

plush NOUN a thick velvety cloth used in furnishings
▷ **plushy** ADJECTIVE

plutonium NOUN a radioactive substance used in nuclear weapons and reactors [named after the planet Pluto]

ply NOUN **plies** **1** a thickness or layer of wood or cloth etc. **2** a strand in yarn • *4-ply wool*

ply VERB **plies, plying, plied** **1** use or wield a tool or weapon **2** work at • *Tailors plied their trade.* **3** keep offering • *They plied her with food or with questions.* **4** go regularly • *The boat plies between the two harbors.* **5** drive or wait about looking for custom • *Taxis are allowed to ply for hire.*

plywood NOUN strong thin board made of layers of wood glued together

PM ABBREVIATION Prime Minister

p.m. ABBREVIATION after noon

Thesaurus

plumb ADVERB *The arrow hit the target plumb in the middle.* ► exactly, precisely, dead, (*more informal*) slap

plumb VERB *They seem to have plumbed the depths of despair.* ► penetrate, probe, sound, explore, measure

plummet VERB *A stone came loose and plummeted to the ground.* ► plunge, fall, hurtle, drop, crash, dive

plump ADJECTIVE *a plump little boy* ► chubby, podgy, tubby, fat , dumpy, rotund, round, overweight, stout, portly, pudgy OPPOSITES ARE thin, slim, skinny

plump VERB *Jill plumped down on the sofa and fell asleep.* ► sink, drop, flop, fall, collapse

plump for *I'm going to plump for the vegetarian meal.* ► choose, opt for, go for, pick, decide on

plunder VERB *Pirates plundered towns and villages near the coast.* ► despoil, loot, pillage, raid, ransack, ravage, rifle, rob, sack, steal from

plunder NOUN *The army was bent on plunder and murder.* ► looting, robbery, pillage, pillaging, marauding

plunge VERB **1** *The plane plunged to the ground.* ► dive, plummet, fall, hurtle, drop, crash, dive, swoop, nosedive **2** *I plunged into the lake.* ► dive, leap, jump, throw yourself, hurl yourself **3** *He plunged the knife into the ripe fruit.* ► thrust, force, stab, shove, stick, push **4** *She plunged a hand in the water.* ► dip, immerse, submerge, sink

pneumatic (new- mat- ik) ADJECTIVE filled with or worked by compressed air • *a pneumatic drill*
▷ **pneumatically** ADVERB
[from Greek *pneuma* = wind]

pneumonia (new- moh- nee- a) NOUN a serious illness caused by inflammation of one or both lungs [from Greek *pneumon* = lung]

PO ABBREVIATION **1** Post Office **2** postal order

poach VERB poaches, poaching, poached **1** cook an egg (removed from its shell) in or over boiling water **2** cook fish or fruit, etc., in a small amount of liquid **3** steal game or fish from someone else's land or water **4** take something unfairly • *One club was poaching members from another.*
▷ **poacher** NOUN

pocket NOUN pockets **1** a small bag-shaped part, especially in a piece of clothing **2** a person's supply of money • *The expense is beyond my pocket.* **3** an isolated part or area • *small pockets of rain*
▷ **pocketful** NOUN
be out of pocket have spent more money than you have gained

pocket ADJECTIVE small enough to carry in a pocket • *a pocket calculator*

pocket VERB pockets, pocketing, pocketed put something into a pocket [from old French *pochet* = little pouch]

pocket money NOUN money given to a child to spend as he or she likes

pod NOUN pods a long seed container of the kind found on a pea or bean plant

poem NOUN poems a piece of poetry

poet NOUN poets a person who writes poetry
▷ **poetess** NOUN

poetry NOUN writing arranged in short lines, usually with a particular rhythm and sometimes with rhymes
▷ **poetic** ADJECTIVE **poetical** ADJECTIVE **poetically** ADVERB

poignant (poin- yant) ADJECTIVE very distressing; affecting the feelings • *poignant memories*
▷ **poignancy** NOUN

point NOUN points **1** the narrow or sharp end of something **2** a dot • *the decimal point* **3** a particular place or time • *At this point she was winning.* **4** a detail or characteristic • *He has his good points.* **5** the important or essential idea • *Keep to the point!* **6** purpose or value • *There is no point in hurrying.* **7** an electrical socket **8** a device for changing a train from one track to another

point VERB points, pointing, pointed **1** show where something is, especially by holding out a finger toward it **2** aim or direct • *She pointed her finger at me.* **3** fill in the parts between bricks with mortar or cement
point out draw attention to something

point-blank ADJECTIVE **1** aimed or fired from close to the target **2** direct and straightforward • *a point-blank refusal*

point-blank ADVERB in a point-blank manner • *He refused point-blank.*

Thesaurus

---

poach VERB *The new company was poaching staff from its rivals.* ► steal, purloin, filch, (*more informal*) pinch, (*more informal*) nick

pocket NOUN *There were some pockets of resistance to the new regime.* ► area, patch, centre, cluster

pocket VERB *The management was accused of pocketing all the profits.* ► appropriate, steal, help yourself to, take for yourself

podgy ADJECTIVE (British) *She looked a bit podgy.* ► plump, chubby, tubby, fat , dumpy, rotund, round, overweight, pudgy OPPOSITES ARE thin, slim, skinny

poem NOUN *He read her some of his poems.* ► verse, rhyme, poetry

poet NOUN *She wrote stories and was a poet.* ► writer of verse, rhymester, rhymer, lyricist, versifier, bard

poetic ADJECTIVE *poetic language* ► expressive, lyrical, poetical, emotive, metrical, imaginative AN OPPOSITE IS prosaic

poetry NOUN *a book of poetry* ► poems, verses, rhymes

point NOUN **1** *the point of the needle* ► tip, end, sharp end, spike, extremity **2** *points of light*

► spot, speck, dot, fleck **3** *At this point, the door opened.* ► moment, instant, time, stage **4** *I wish they would get to the point.* ► essence, crux, meaning, thrust **5** *a few points of detail* ► detail, item, issue, factor, consideration, particular, facet, feature **6** *She admitted he had some good points.* ► characteristic, feature, attribute, aspect, peculiarity, side **7** *There didn't seem much point in staying.* ► purpose, reason, object, aim, goal, advantage, benefit **8** *They could get on the train at a point further up the line.* ► place, position, location, spot, site, locality

point VERB **1** point or point to *An official pointed the way. He pointed to a picture on the stairs.* ► indicate, point out, draw attention to, show, signal **2** *She saw the man was pointing a gun at her.* ► aim, direct, level, train **3** *I'll point you in the right direction.* ► direct, guide, lead, steer

point-blank ADJECTIVE **1** *The gun was fired at point-blank range.* ► close **2** *Their request met with a point-blank refusal.* ► blunt, direct, straight, plain, frank, open, explicit, forthright

point-blank ADVERB *She told him point-blank that it was over.* ► bluntly, directly, straight,

a
b
c
d
e
f
g
h
i
j
k
l
m
n
o
p
q
r
s
t
u
v
w
x
y
z

A
B
C
D
E
F
G
H
I
J
K
L
M
N
O
P
Q
R
S
T
U
V
W
X
Y
Z

pointed ADJECTIVE **1** with a point at the end **2** clearly directed at a person • *a pointed remark*
▷ **pointedly** ADVERB

pointer NOUN pointers **1** a stick, rod, or mark, etc., used to point at something **2** a dog that points with its muzzle towards birds that it scents **3** an indication or hint

pointless ADJECTIVE without a point; with no purpose
▷ **pointlessly** ADVERB

poise VERB poises, poising, poised balance

poise NOUN **1** a dignified self-confident manner **2** balance

poison NOUN poisons a substance that can harm or kill a living thing if swallowed or absorbed into the body
▷ **poisonous** ADJECTIVE

poison VERB poisons, poisoning, poisoned **1** give poison to; kill somebody with poison **2** put poison in something **3** corrupt or spoil something • *He poisoned their minds.*
▷ **poisoner** NOUN
[via early French from Latin *potio* = potion]

poke VERB pokes, poking, poked **1** prod or jab **2** push out or forward; stick out **3** search • *I was poking about in the attic.*
poke fun at ridicule

poke NOUN pokes a poking movement; a prod

poker¹ NOUN pokers a stiff metal rod for poking a fire

poker² NOUN a card game in which players bet on who has the best cards

polar ADJECTIVE **1** to do with or near the North Pole or South Pole **2** to do with either pole of a magnet
▷ **polarity** NOUN

polar bear NOUN polar bears a white bear living in Arctic regions

polarize VERB polarizes, polarizing, polarized **1** keep vibrations of light waves, etc., to a single direction **2** divide into two groups of completely opposite extremes of feeling or opinion • *Opinions had polarized.*
▷ **polarization** NOUN

Polaroid camera NOUN Polaroid cameras (*trade mark*) a camera that takes a picture and produces the finished photograph a few seconds later

pole¹ NOUN poles a long slender rounded piece of wood or metal

pole² NOUN poles **1** a point on the earth's surface that is as far north (**North Pole**) or as far south (**South Pole**) as possible **2** either of the ends of a magnet **3** either terminal of an electric cell or battery

pole star NOUN the star above the North Pole

Thesaurus

straight out, frankly, openly, plainly, clearly, forthrightly

pointed ADJECTIVE **1** *He used the pointed end of a stick.* ► sharp, tapered, spiky **2** *Kathleen greeted this pointed remark with a smile.* ► cutting, biting, trenchant, caustic, acerbic, scathing, barbed, sharp, insinuating, hurtful AN OPPOSITE IS bland

pointless ADJECTIVE *The country was being dragged into a pointless military conflict. It was pointless to try to catch them now.* ► futile, senseless, fruitless, useless, needless, vain, aimless, meaningless, unprofitable OPPOSITES ARE useful, valuable

poise NOUN *Claudia admired her poise.* ► composure, calmness, equanimity, aplomb, assurance, self-confidence, self-control, coolness, dignity, elegance, equilibrium

poised ADJECTIVE **1** *Both forces were poised to take the city.* ► prepared, ready, set, waiting, keyed up **2** *She gave a poised performance.* ► assured, self-assured, self-confident, dignified, composed, graceful, elegant

poison NOUN **1** *A gram of the poison is enough to kill a man.* ► toxin, venom **2** *a poison in society* ► blight, contamination, contagion, cancer

poison VERB **1** *to poison someone* ► kill **2** *Chemicals are poisoning the country's rivers.* ► pollute, contaminate, infect, foul, taint

3 *The media were accused of trying to poison people's minds.* ► prejudice, subvert, corrupt, embitter, color, warp, affect, pervert

poisonous ADJECTIVE **1** *a poisonous insect* ► venomous, deadly, virulent **2** *a cloud of poisonous gases* ► toxic, lethal, noxious, fatal, mortal **3** *a poisonous remark* ► malicious, malevolent, hostile, vicious, spiteful, vitriolic

poke VERB *They poked burning sticks at him. He poked her with his elbow.* ► prod, dig, jab, nudge, thrust, stab, shove, stick
poke about or **around** *Someone was poking about in the cupboard.* ► search, rummage, root around
poke fun at *They laughed and poked fun at him.* ► ridicule, mock, make fun of, jeer at
poke out *A hand was poking out of the back window.* ► protrude, stick out, jut out, peek, project

poke NOUN *Amy gave him a poke.* ► prod, dig, jab, nudge, shove

poky ADJECTIVE *a poky room with one chair* ► confined, cramped, tiny, small, uncomfortable, restrictive AN OPPOSITE IS spacious

pole NOUN **1** *The fence was held up by a series of poles.* ► post, pillar, stake, stick, upright, support, shaft, spar **2** *Their opinions are at opposite poles.* ► extreme, extremity, limit

pole vault NOUN an athletic contest in which competitors jump over a high bar with the help of a long flexible pole

police NOUN the people whose job is to catch criminals and make sure that the law is kept
▷ **policeman** NOUN **police officer** NOUN **policewoman** NOUN

police VERB polices, policing, policed keep order in a place by means of police

policy[1] NOUN policies the aims or plan of action of a person or group

policy[2] NOUN policies a document stating the terms of a contract of insurance

polish VERB polishes, polishing, polished **1** make a thing smooth and shiny by rubbing **2** make a thing better by making corrections and alterations
▷ **polisher** NOUN
polish off finish off

polish NOUN polishes **1** a substance used in polishing **2** a shine **3** elegance of manner

polite ADJECTIVE having good manners
▷ **politely** ADVERB **politeness** NOUN

political ADJECTIVE connected with the governing of a country or region
▷ **politically** ADVERB

politician NOUN politicians a person who is involved in politics

politics NOUN political matters; the business of governing a country or region

poll (rhymes with *pole*) NOUN **polls 1** voting or votes at an election **2** an opinion poll **3** (*old use*) the head

poll VERB polls, polling, polled **1** vote at an election **2** receive a stated number of votes in an election
▷ **polling booth** NOUN **polling station** NOUN

pollen NOUN powder produced by flowers, containing male cells for fertilizing other flowers

pollen count NOUN pollen counts a measurement of the amount of pollen in the air, given as a warning for people who are allergic to pollen

pollinate VERB pollinates, pollinating, pollinated fertilize a plant with pollen
▷ **pollination** NOUN

poll tax NOUN poll taxes a tax that every adult has to pay regardless of income

pollute VERB pollutes, polluting, polluted make the air, water, etc., dirty or impure
▷ **pollutant** NOUN **pollution** NOUN

polygamy (pol- ig- a- mee) NOUN having more than one wife at a time
▷ **polygamous** ADJECTIVE **polygamist** NOUN

polygon NOUN polygons a shape with many sides. Hexagons and octagons are polygons
▷ **polygonal** ADJECTIVE

polyhedron NOUN polyhedrons a solid shape with many sides

polytechnic NOUN polytechnics a college giving instruction in many subjects at degree level or below

Thesaurus

poles apart *Our political views are poles apart.*
► completely different, worlds apart, like chalk and cheese, irreconcilable, incompatible

police NOUN *The police soon arrived at the scene.*
► police force, (*more informal*) the law, (*more informal*) the fuzz

police VERB *It would be difficult to police such a large area.* ► control, supervise, watch over, monitor, patrol, keep in order, keep the peace at, provide a police presence at

policeman or **policewoman** NOUN
► police officer, officer, (*more informal*) cop, (*more informal*) copper

policy NOUN **1** *the school's policy on truancy*
► strategy, code of practice, approach (to), procedure **2** *It's always a good policy to read the instructions carefully.* ► practice, habit, custom, rule

polish VERB **1** *I must polish my shoes.* ► shine, brush up, clean, buff up, burnish, brighten, rub down, rub up, wax
polish off *The boys polished off a plate of burgers.*
► finish, eat up

polish up *She sat down to polish up her essay.*
► improve, refine, enhance, brush up

polish NOUN **1** *The table had a lovely bright polish.* ► shine, sheen, gloss, lustre, patina, finish **2** *His years abroad had given him polish.*
► refinement, sophistication, suavity, urbanity, class, finesse, grace, style, elegance

polished ADJECTIVE **1** *a polished table* ► shiny, shining, bright, glossy, gleaming, lustrous, burnished, glassy OPPOSITES ARE dull, tarnished **2** *polished manners* ► refined, sophisticated, suave, urbane, polite, cultured, elegant, gracious, perfected, (*more informal*) posh OPPOSITES ARE rough, crude **3** *a polished performance* ► accomplished, skilful, masterly, expert, flawless, faultless

polite ADJECTIVE *They were too polite to complain.*
► well-mannered, courteous, respectful, civil, well behaved, considerate, cultivated AN OPPOSITE IS rude

poll NOUN **1** *There would have to be a second poll to decide the winner.* ► ballot, vote, election **2** *The store organized a poll to determine views on smoking.* ► survey, opinion poll, sampling, census, plebiscite, referendum

a
b
c
d
e
f
g
h
i
j
k
l
m
n
o
p
q
r
s
t
u
v
w
x
y
z

A
B
C
D
E
F
G
H
I
J
K
L
M
N
O
P
Q
R
S
T
U
V
W
X
Y
Z

polythene NOUN a lightweight plastic used to make bags, wrappings, etc.

pomegranate NOUN pomegranates a tropical fruit with many seeds [from Latin *pomum* = apple + *granatum* = having many seeds]

pomp NOUN the ceremonial splendor that is traditional on important public occasions

pompous ADJECTIVE full of excessive dignity and self-importance
▷ **pompously** ADVERB **pomposity** NOUN

pond NOUN ponds a small lake

ponder VERB ponders, pondering, pondered think deeply and seriously

ponderous ADJECTIVE **1** heavy and awkward **2** laborious and dull • *He writes in a ponderous style.*
▷ **ponderously** ADVERB

pontificate VERB pontificates, pontificating, pontificated give your opinions in a pompous way
▷ **pontification** NOUN

pony NOUN ponies a small horse

ponytail NOUN ponytails a bunch of long hair tied at the back of the head

poodle NOUN poodles a dog with thick curly hair

pool[1] NOUN pools **1** a pond **2** a puddle **3** a swimming pool

pool[2] NOUN pools **1** the fund of money staked in a gambling game **2** a group of things shared by several people **3** a game resembling billiards

the pools gambling based on the results of football matches

pool VERB pools, pooling, pooled put money or things together for sharing

poor ADJECTIVE **1** with very little money or other resources **2** not good; inadequate • *a poor piece of work* **3** unfortunate; deserving pity • *Poor fellow!*
▷ **poorness** NOUN

poorly ADVERB in a poor way • *We've played poorly this season.*

poorly ADJECTIVE rather ill • *You look poorly.*

pop[1] NOUN pops **1** a small explosive sound **2** a fizzy drink

pop VERB pops, popping, popped **1** make a pop **2** (*informal*) go or put quickly • *Pop down to the shop.* • *I'll just pop this pie into the microwave.*

pop[2] NOUN modern popular music

Pope NOUN Popes the leader of the Roman Catholic Church

pop-eyed ADJECTIVE with bulging eyes

poplar NOUN poplars a tall slender tree

poppadom NOUN poppadoms a thin crisp biscuit made of lentil flour, eaten with Indian food

poppy NOUN poppies a plant with large red flowers

popular ADJECTIVE **1** liked or enjoyed by many people **2** believed by many people • *popular opinion* **3** intended for the general public
▷ **popularly** ADVERB **popularity** NOUN

Thesaurus

pompous ADJECTIVE *He sounded so pompous I couldn't help giggling.* ► self-important, grandiose, overbearing, haughty, arrogant, conceited, pretentious, puffed up, condescending, domineering AN OPPOSITE IS modest

ponder VERB ponder or ponder about *It was a good time to ponder the events of the last week.* ► consider, think about, contemplate, reflect on, meditate on, review, mull over

ponderous ADJECTIVE **1** *He spoke in a slow ponderous way.* ► clumsy, awkward, lumbering, cumbersome, ungainly OPPOSITES ARE elegant, graceful

pool NOUN **1** *a pool of water* ► pond, puddle, lake, mere, tarn **2** *a pool of hire cars* ► supply, stock, reserve

poor ADJECTIVE **1** *The program was intended to rehouse poor families.* ► impoverished, poverty-stricken, badly off, impecunious, hard-up, destitute, penniless OPPOSITES ARE rich, wealthy **2** *The workmanship was of poor quality.* ► inferior, substandard, deficient, defective, unsatisfactory, mediocre, second-rate, shoddy

OPPOSITES ARE superior, fine **3** *The poor man had to wait ten hours for a train.* ► unfortunate, unlucky, luckless, wretched, pitiful, unhappy OPPOSITES ARE fortunate, lucky

poorly ADJECTIVE *She began to feel poorly in the taxi home.* ► ill, unwell, sick, out of sorts, off color, indisposed, ailing, peaky, queasy, nauseous

pop NOUN *the pop of an air rifle* ► crack, bang, explosion, burst, snap

pop VERB *Corks were popping everywhere.* ► crack, go bang, explode, go off, burst, snap

poppycock NOUN (*informal*) *They rejected the charges as poppycock.* ► nonsense, garbage, claptrap, gibberish, drivel

popular ADJECTIVE **1** *a popular student* ► well-liked, favored, favorite, liked, admired, accepted **2** *a popular line in women's fashion* ► modish, sought-after, well-known, current, (*more informal*) trendy

popularize VERB **1** *to popularize a new product* ► make popular, bring into vogue or fashion, promote, spread **2** *There are several good books that popularize the subject.* ► simplify, make

populate VERB populates, populating, populated supply with a population; inhabit

population NOUN populations the people who live in a district or country; the total number of these people

porcelain NOUN the finest kind of china

porch NOUN porches a shelter outside the entrance to a building

porcupine NOUN porcupines a small animal covered with long prickles

pore NOUN pores a tiny opening on the skin through which moisture can pass in or out

pore VERB pores, poring, pored
pore over study with close attention • *He was poring over his books.*
USAGE Do not confuse with **pour**.

pork NOUN meat from a pig [from Latin *porcus* = pig]

pornography (porn- og- ra- fee) NOUN obscene pictures or writings
▷ **pornographic** ADJECTIVE

porpoise (por- pus) NOUN porpoises a sea animal rather like a small whale

porridge NOUN a food made by boiling oatmeal to a thick paste [from an old word *pottage* = soup]

port[1] NOUN ports 1 a harbor 2 a city or town with a harbor 3 the left-hand side of a ship

or aircraft when you are facing forward
COMPARE **starboard** [from Latin *portus* = harbour]

port[2] NOUN a strong red Portuguese wine [from the city of Oporto in Portugal]

portable ADJECTIVE able to be carried [from Latin *portare* = carry]

porter[1] NOUN porters a person whose job is to carry luggage or other goods [from Latin *portare* = carry]

porter[2] NOUN porters a person whose job is to look after the entrance to a large building [from Latin *porta* = gate]

porthole NOUN portholes a small window in the side of a ship or aircraft

portion NOUN portions a part or share given to somebody

portion VERB portions, portioning, portioned divide something into portions • *Portion it out.*

portly ADJECTIVE portlier, portliest rather fat
▷ **portliness** NOUN

portrait NOUN portraits 1 a picture of a person or animal 2 a description in words

pose NOUN poses 1 a position or posture of the body, e.g., for a portrait or photograph 2 a way of behaving that someone adopts to give a particular impression

---

Thesaurus

---

accessible, make easy, present in a popular way, universalize

population NOUN *the population of the country*
▶ inhabitants, people, populace, residents, citizens, occupants, community

pore VERB pore over *She was poring over a map of Greece.* ▶ study, peruse, scan, scrutinize, be absorbed in, be engrossed in

port NOUN *A large liner had entered the port.*
▶ harbor, seaport, marina, anchorage, dock , dockyard, haven

portable ADJECTIVE *a portable computer*
▶ transportable, mobile, movable, lightweight, compact, easy to carry, handy, light, manageable, small

porter NOUN 1 *The apartment block had its own porter.* ▶ caretaker, doorkeeper, doorman, janitor, commissionaire, concierge 2 *A porter helped her with her luggage.* ▶ baggage-carrier, baggage-handler, baggage-attendant, bearer, carrier

portion NOUN 1 *a large portion of rice*
▶ helping, serving, plateful, bowlful, share, amount, ration, (*more informal*) dollop 2 *Use the rear portion of the train.* ▶ section, part, segment 3 *Her portion of the inheritance came to several millions.* ▶ share, allocation, quota, division, ration, percentage

portrait NOUN *a portrait of his grandmother*
▶ painting, picture , drawing, portrayal, depiction, representation, image, likeness

portray VERB 1 *The artist portrayed her in profile.* ▶ paint, draw, sketch, depict, show 2 *The novel portrays London life in Victorian England.* ▶ depict, describe, picture, characterize, represent, illustrate, show, delineate, evoke

pose VERB 1 *River levels pose a threat at this time of year.* ▶ present, constitute, create, produce 2 *The article poses a number of important questions.* ▶ raise, put forward, advance, offer, posit, broach, suggest 3 *She posed for a local artist on Saturday afternoons.* ▶ sit, model, be a model 4 *From his manner it was clear he was only posing.* ▶ pretend, put on an act, strike a pose, put on airs, feign, masquerade 5 pose as *He decided to pose as a police officer.*
▶ impersonate, pretend to be, masquerade as, pass yourself off as

pose NOUN 1 *a model in a suggestive pose*
▶ attitude, position 2 *His behavior was only a pose.* ▶ pretence, act, affectation, façade, show, front, masquerade, posture

poser NOUN 1 (*informal*) How to get home in time was a bit of a poser. ▶ problem, difficulty, dilemma, puzzle 2 (*informal*) The bar was full of posers showing off to the girls. ▶ exhibitionist,

A
B
C
D
E
F
G
H
I
J
K
L
M
N
O
P
Q
R
S
T
U
V
W
X
Y
Z

pose VERB poses, posing, posed **1** take up a pose **2** put someone into a pose **3** pretend **4** put forward or present • *It poses several problems for us.*

posh ADJECTIVE (*informal*) **1** very smart; high-class • *a posh restaurant* **2** upper-class • *a posh accent*

position NOUN positions **1** the place where something is or should be **2** the way a person or thing is placed or arranged • *in a sitting position* **3** a situation or condition • *I am in no position to help you.* **4** paid employment; a job
▷ **positional** ADJECTIVE

positive ADJECTIVE **1** definite or certain • *Are you positive you saw him?* • *We have positive proof that he is guilty.* **2** agreeing; saying "yes" • *We received a positive reply.* **3** confident and hopeful **4** showing signs of what is being tested for • *Her pregnancy test was positive.* **5** greater than nought **6** to do with the kind of electric charge that lacks electrons **7** (in grammar, said about an adjective or adverb) in the simple form, not comparative or

superlative • *The positive form is "big," the comparative is "bigger," the superlative is "biggest."*
▷ **positively** ADVERB
USAGE The opposite of senses 1-4 is **negative**.

possess VERB possesses, possessing, possessed **1** have or own something **2** control someone's thoughts or behavior • *I don't know what possessed you to do such a thing!*
▷ **possessor** NOUN

possessed ADJECTIVE seeming to be controlled by strong emotion or an evil spirit • *He fought like a man possessed.*

possession NOUN possessions **1** something you possess or own **2** owning something

possessive ADJECTIVE **1** wanting to possess and keep things for yourself **2** (in grammar) showing that somebody owns something • *a possessive pronoun* (see pronoun)

possibility NOUN possibilities **1** being possible **2** something that may exist or happen etc.

possible ADJECTIVE able to exist, happen, be done, or be used

---

Thesaurus

---

poseur, (*informal*) phony, (*informal*) pseud, (*informal*) show-off

posh ADJECTIVE (*informal*) *The car was parked outside a posh hotel.* ► smart, stylish, high-class, luxury, luxurious, fashionable, elegant, plush, showy, (*informal*) classy, (*informal*) swanky, (*informal*) snazzy, (*informal*) swish

position NOUN **1** *The map shows the position of the house.* ► location, situation, setting, locality, site, point **2** *She rose to a standing position.* ► posture, pose, stance, attitude **3** *His lack of money left him in an awkward position.* ► situation, circumstances, predicament, plight **4** *They well knew their position in society.* ► status, standing, level, role, rank, grade **5** *advertisements for positions in banking* ► job, post, situation, appointment, vacancy **6** *the opposition's position on the war* ► point of view, viewpoint, attitude, policy, stand, standpoint, stance, outlook

position VERB *Chairs had been positioned along the walls.* ► put, arrange, deploy, dispose, locate, place, settle, situate, stand, station

positive ADJECTIVE **1** *I was positive they would come back.* ► certain, sure, convinced, confident, satisfied, assured OPPOSITES ARE uncertain, unsure **2** *The case lacked positive proof.* ► definite, conclusive, categorical, unequivocal, incontrovertible, irrefutable, indisputable, clear, explicit OPPOSITES ARE doubtful, unclear **3** *The criticism was positive.* ► helpful, constructive, practical, useful AN OPPOSITE IS negative **4** *a positive advantage* ► definite, conclusive, clear, unmistakable, emphatic, unequivocal, undeniable AN

OPPOSITE IS vague **5** *a positive attitude* ► optimistic, confident, hopeful, assured AN OPPOSITE IS pessimistic **6** *The journey was a positive nightmare.* ► absolute, utter, complete, sheer, perfect

possess VERB **1** *The family possessed a house in France.* ► own, have, be in possession of **2** *Foreign armies possessed the country* ► seize, occupy, take over, acquire, control, dominate, govern, rule **3** *A strange feeling possessed him.* ► preoccupy, obsess, dominate, haunt, consume

possession NOUN **1** *She came into possession of the fortune.* ► ownership, control, title, tenure, custody **2** possessions *She put her few possessions in the van.* ► belongings, things, property, chattels, effects, assets, goods, bits and pieces

possessive ADJECTIVE *He was very possessive and grew angry when she wanted to leave.* ► proprietorial, overprotective, clinging, domineering, jealous, selfish

possibility NOUN **1** *There was still a possibility they might come.* ► chance, likelihood, probability, prospect, hope, fear **2** *the possibility of starting their own business* ► feasibility, practicality, capability, potentiality **3** *They even considered the possibility of going to war.* ► option, alternative, choice

possible ADJECTIVE **1** *An improvement next year might be possible.* ► feasible, practicable, achievable, attainable, viable, workable AN OPPOSITE IS impossible **2** *There is another possible explanation.* ► conceivable, imaginable,

possibly ADVERB **1** in any way • *I can't possibly do it.* **2** perhaps

post[1] NOUN posts **1** an upright piece of wood, concrete, or metal, etc., set in the ground **2** the starting point or finishing point of a race • *He was left at the post.*

post VERB posts, posting, posted put up a notice or poster, etc., to announce something

post[2] NOUN **1** the collecting and delivering of letters, parcels, etc. **2** these letters and parcels etc.

post VERB posts, posting, posted put a letter or parcel etc. into a postbox for collection **keep me posted** keep me informed

post[3] NOUN posts **1** a position of paid employment; a job **2** the place where someone is on duty • *a sentry post* **3** a place occupied by soldiers, traders, etc.

post VERB posts, posting, posted place someone on duty • *We posted sentries.*

postage NOUN the charge for sending something by post

postage stamp NOUN postage stamps a stamp for sticking on things to be mailed, showing the amount paid

postal ADJECTIVE to do with or by the post

postal order NOUN postal orders a document bought from a post office for sending money by post

postbox NOUN postboxes a box into which letters are put for collection

postcard NOUN postcards a card for sending messages by post without an envelope

poster NOUN posters a large sheet of paper announcing or advertising something, for display in a public place

posterity NOUN future generations of people • *These letters and diaries should be preserved for posterity*

postman NOUN postmen a person who delivers or collects letters, etc.

postmark NOUN postmarks an official mark put on something sent by post to show where and when it was mailed

postmortem NOUN postmortems an examination of a dead body to discover the cause of death

posthumous (poss- tew- mus) ADJECTIVE coming after a person's death • *a posthumous award for bravery*
▷ **posthumously** ADVERB

post office NOUN post offices **1** a building or room where postal business is carried on **2** the national organization responsible for postal services

postpone VERB postpones, postponing, postponed fix a later time for something • *They postponed the meeting for a fortnight.*
▷ **postponement** NOUN

postscript NOUN postscripts something extra added at the end of a letter (after the writer's signature) or at the end of a book

posture NOUN postures a particular position of the body, or the way in which a person stands, sits, or walks

postwar ADJECTIVE happening during the time after a war

pot[1] NOUN pots **1** a deep, usually round, container
go to pot (informal) lose quality; be ruined
take pot luck (informal) take whatever is available

pot VERB pots, potting, potted put into a pot

pot[2] NOUN (informal) cannabis

potassium NOUN a soft silvery-white metal substance that is essential for living things

potato NOUN potatoes a starchy white tuber growing underground, used as a vegetable [via Spanish from a Caribbean word]

Thesaurus

plausible, likely, believable, tenable, credible OPPOSITES ARE unlikely, inconceivable **3** *He is regarded as a possible party leader.* ► potential, prospective, probable, promising, likely OPPOSITES ARE unlikely, improbable

possibly ADVERB **1** *Possibly Jane will be there too.* ► maybe, perhaps, conceivably **2** *Could you possibly bring some food?* ► conceivably, by any chance, at all

post NOUN **1** *a flat roof supported by wooden posts* ► pole, pillar, stake, stick, upright, support, shaft, spar **2** *The post hasn't come yet.* ► mail, letters, delivery **3** *The post will be advertised in the local newspaper.* ► job, position, situation, appointment, vacancy

post VERB **1** *An announcement had been posted on all notice boards.* ► display, pin up, put up,

stick up, advertise, announce **2** *I must go and post a letter.* ► mail, send, dispatch, put in the post, send off, get off

postpone VERB *The game was postponed for a week.* ► put off, defer, delay, put back, adjourn, hold over, suspend, put on ice

posture NOUN *He bent his head forward in a posture of respect.* ► position, stance, pose, attitude, bearing, deportment

posy NOUN *a posy of violets and freesias* ► bouquet, bunch, spray, nosegay, buttonhole, corsage

pot NOUN *a pot of stew* ► pan, saucepan, vessel, casserole, cauldron, stewpot, stockpot, crock, urn

a
b
c
d
e
f
g
h
i
j
k
l
m
n
o
p
q
r
s
t
u
v
w
x
y
z

potentate (poh- ten- tayt) NOUN **potentates** a powerful monarch or ruler

potential (po- ten- shal) ADJECTIVE capable of happening or being used or developed • *a potential winner*
▷ **potentially** ADVERB **potentiality** NOUN

potential NOUN **1** the ability of a person or thing to develop in the future **2** (in science) the voltage between two points

pothole NOUN **potholes 1** a deep natural hole in the ground **2** a hole in a road

potion NOUN **potions** a liquid for drinking as a medicine, etc.

potted ADJECTIVE **1** grown in a pot **2** preserved in a pot • *potted shrimp* **3** shortened or abridged • *a potted account of the story*

potter NOUN **potters** a person who makes pottery

potter VERB **potters, pottering, pottered** work or move about in a leisurely way • *I spent the afternoon pottering around in the garden.*

pottery NOUN **potteries 1** cups, plates, ornaments, etc., made of baked clay **2** the craft of making these things **3** a place where a potter works

pouch NOUN **pouches 1** a small bag **2** a fold of skin in which a kangaroo etc. keeps its young **3** something shaped like a bag

poultry NOUN birds (e.g., chickens, geese, and turkeys) kept for their eggs and meat

pounce VERB **pounces, pouncing, pounced** jump or swoop down quickly on something
▷ **pounce** NOUN

pound[1] NOUN **pounds 1** a unit of money (in Britain = 100 pence) **2** a unit of weight equal to 16 ounces or about 454 grams [from Old English *pund*]

pound[2] NOUN **pounds 1** a place where stray animals are taken **2** a public enclosure for vehicles officially removed [origin unknown]

pound VERB **pounds, pounding, pounded 1** hit something often, especially in order to crush it **2** run or go heavily • *He pounded down the stairs.* **3** thump • *My heart was pounding.* [from Old English *punian*]

pour VERB **pours, pouring, poured 1** flow or make something flow **2** rain heavily • *It poured all day.* **3** come or go in large amounts • *Letters poured in.*
▷ **pourer** NOUN
USAGE Do not confuse with **pore**.

pout VERB **pouts, pouting, pouted** push out your lips when you are annoyed or sulking
▷ **pout** NOUN

poverty NOUN **1** being poor **2** a lack or scarcity • *a poverty of ideas*

powder NOUN **powders 1** a mass of fine dry particles of something **2** a medicine or cosmetic, etc., made as a powder **3** gunpowder
▷ **powdery** ADJECTIVE

powder VERB **powders, powdering, powdered 1** put powder on something **2** make something into powder

power NOUN **powers 1** strength or energy **2** the ability to do something • *the power of speech* **3** political authority or control **4** a powerful country, person, or organization **5** mechanical or electrical energy; the electricity supply • *There was a power failure after the storm.* **6** (in science) the rate of doing work, measured in watts or horsepower **7** (in mathematics) the product of a number multiplied by itself a given number of times • *The third power of 2 = 2 x 2 x 2 = 8*
▷ **powered** ADJECTIVE **powerless** ADJECTIVE

Thesaurus

---

potent ADJECTIVE **1** *a potent drug* ► strong, powerful, pungent, intoxicating **2** *a potent influence* ► strong, powerful, vigorous, compelling, impressive, dominant, overpowering, weighty

pounce VERB **pounce on** *The animal pounced on its prey.* ► jump on, spring on, leap on, swoop on, bound at, lunge at, attack, ambush

pound VERB **1** *Hans pounded his huge fists on the desk and glared.* ► beat, strike, thump, thud, batter, bang, bash **2** **pound on** *He pounded on the gates, shouting wildly.* ► batter, beat, thump, pummel, bang on, strike, hit **3** *Her heart was pounding.* ► throb, pulsate, thump, thud, race **4** *Pound the garlic with a little salt.* ► crush, grind, powder, mash, pulverize

pour VERB **1** *Blood poured from his wound.*

► spill, issue, stream, run, discharge, flow, gush, spout **2** *She poured milk from the jug.* ► serve, tip, decant

poverty NOUN *The region suffered from years of poverty.* ► want, penury, privation, destitution, hardship, shortage, need, necessity AN OPPOSITE IS wealth

powdery ADJECTIVE *a white powdery deposit* ► dusty, sandy, grainy, chalky, crumbly, fine, granular, loose, pulverized

power NOUN **1** *His father had a stroke and lost the power of speech.* ► faculty, property, capability, capacity, ability, competence **2** *Who knows where the real power lies.* ► control, authority, influence, dominance, mastery, domination **3** *The governor has the power to impose a curfew.* ► right, prerogative, authorization, authority **4** *a speech of great*

powerful ADJECTIVE having great power, strength, or influence
▷ **powerfully** ADVERB

power station NOUN power stations a building where electricity is produced

pp. ABBREVIATION pages

practicable ADJECTIVE able to be done
USAGE Do not confuse with **practical**.

practical ADJECTIVE **1** able to do or make useful things • *a practical person* **2** likely to be useful • *a very practical invention* **3** actually doing something, rather than just learning or thinking about it • *She has had practical experience.*
▷ **practicality** NOUN
USAGE Do not confuse with **practicable**.

practical NOUN practicals a lesson or examination in which you actually do or make something rather than reading or writing about it • *a chemistry practical*

practical joke NOUN practical jokes a trick played on somebody

practically ADVERB **1** in a practical way **2** almost • *I've practically finished.*

practice NOUN practices **1** doing something repeatedly in order to become better at it • *Have you done your piano practice?* **2** actually doing something; action, not theory • *It works well in practice.* **3** the professional business of a doctor, dentist, lawyer, etc. **4** a habit or custom • *It is his practice to work until midnight.*
out of practice no longer skillful because you have not practiced recently

practice VERB practices, practicing, practiced **1** do something repeatedly in order to become better at it **2** do something actively or habitually • *Practice what you preach.* **3** work as a doctor, dentist, or lawyer

practiced ADJECTIVE experienced or expert

prairie NOUN prairies a large area of flat grass-covered land

praise VERB praises, praising, praised **1** say that somebody or something is very good **2** honor God in words

praise NOUN words that praise somebody or something
▷ **praiseworthy** ADJECTIVE

Thesaurus

---

power ► force, strength, potency, vigour, intensity, energy AN OPPOSITE IS weakness

powerful ADJECTIVE **1** *a powerful blow* ► violent, hard, strong, forceful AN OPPOSITE IS weak **2** *a powerful ruler* ► dominant, commanding, forceful, strong, vigorous, effective OPPOSITES ARE weak, ineffective **3** *a powerful physique* ► strong, muscular, sturdy, hefty, mighty, solid, burly OPPOSITES ARE weak, puny **4** *a powerful argument* ► strong, convincing, compelling, cogent, overwhelming OPPOSITES ARE weak, unconvincing

powerless 1 *We felt powerless in the face of such determination.* ► impotent, helpless, ineffectual, ineffective, incapable, defenseless, feeble, weak OPPOSITES ARE powerful, strong **2** *The police were powerless to act.* ► unable, incapable (of acting), without power

practicable ADJECTIVE *Such a detailed plan would not be practicable.* ► realistic, feasible, viable, workable, achievable, attainable, possible, sensible, practical OPPOSITES ARE impracticable, impractical

practical ADJECTIVE **1** *You need practical experience of the work before you apply for the job.* ► real, actual, hands-on, empirical, relevant AN OPPOSITE IS theoretical **2** *We can't think of any practical alternatives.* ► workable, feasible, realistic, viable, reasonable, possible, achievable AN OPPOSITE IS impractical **3** *Let's be practical and not try far-fetched ideas.* ► pragmatic, sensible, realistic, down-to-earth, commonsensical, hardheaded AN OPPOSITE IS impractical **4** *a cute little gadget but*

also practical ► handy, functional, useful, serviceable, utilitarian OPPOSITES ARE impractical, useless

practically ADVERB *The place was practically deserted.* ► almost, nearly, virtually, just about, more or less, close to

practice NOUN **1** *It has become a common practice to use robots to disarm devices.* ► custom, procedure, convention, policy, routine, method, system **2** *It takes a lot of practice to play that well.* ► training, rehearsal, preparation, exercise, drill **3** *He was better at the theory than the practice of medicine.* ► application, exercise, use, execution, implementation **4 in practice** *The idea is good but probably won't work in practice.* ► in real life, for real, in reality, in actuality, in effect, in operation

practice VERB **1** *They practiced these pieces for weeks.* ► do exercises, drill, exercise, prepare, rehearse, train, warm up **2** *These customs are still practiced in some parts of the world.* ► follow, carry out, perform, put into practice, observe, apply, engage in

praise VERB **1** *The judge praised her for her bravery.* ► commend, applaud, pay tribute to, express approval of, compliment, congratulate, admire, acclaim, acknowledge, eulogize **2** *They praised God for the good harvest.* ► worship, glorify, honor, exalt, adore

praise NOUN **1** *The firefighters deserve all our praise.* ► approval, acclaim, admiration, commendation, applause, adulation, recognition, tribute **2** *Give praise to God.*

A
B
C
D
E
F
G
H
I
J
K
L
M
N
O
P
Q
R
S
T
U
V
W
X
Y
Z

pram NOUN prams a four-wheeled carriage for a baby, pushed by a person walking

prance VERB prances, prancing, pranced move about in a lively or happy way

prank NOUN pranks a trick played for mischief; a practical joke
▷ **prankster** NOUN

prattle VERB prattles, prattling, prattled chatter like a young child
▷ **prattle** NOUN

prawn NOUN prawns an edible shellfish like a large shrimp

pray VERB prays, praying, prayed **1** talk to God **2** ask earnestly for something **3** (formal) please • Pray be seated.

prayer NOUN prayers praying; words used in praying

pre- PREFIX before (as in prehistoric)

preach VERB preaches, preaching, preached give a religious or moral talk
▷ **preacher** NOUN

precarious (pri- kair- ee- us) ADJECTIVE not very safe or secure
▷ **precariously** ADVERB

precaution NOUN precautions something done to prevent future trouble or danger
▷ **precautionary** ADJECTIVE

precede VERB precedes, preceding, preceded come or go before someone or something else
USAGE Do not confuse with proceed.

precedence (press- i- dens) NOUN the right of someone or something to be first
take precedence have priority

precedent (press- i- dent) NOUN precedents a previous case that is taken as an example to be followed

precinct (pree- sinkt) NOUN precincts **1** the area around a place, especially around a cathedral **2** a part of a town where traffic is not allowed • a shopping precinct

precious ADJECTIVE **1** very valuable **2** greatly loved
▷ **preciousness** NOUN

precious ADVERB (informal) very • We have precious little time.

precipice NOUN precipices a very steep place, such as the face of a cliff

précis (pray- see) NOUN précis (pray- seez) a summary

precise ADJECTIVE exact; clearly stated
▷ **precisely** ADVERB **precision** NOUN

precocious (prik- oh- shus) ADJECTIVE (said about a child) very advanced or developed for his or her age
▷ **precociously** ADVERB **precocity** NOUN

predator (pred- a- ter) NOUN predators an animal that hunts or preys upon others
▷ **predatory** ADJECTIVE

predecessor (pree- dis- ess- er) NOUN predecessors an earlier person or thing, e.g. an ancestor or the former holder of a job

predicate NOUN predicates the part of a sentence that says something about the subject, e.g., "is short" in life is short

predicative (prid- ik- a- tiv) ADJECTIVE forming part of the predicate, e.g., old in • The dog is old. COMPARE attributive
▷ **predicatively** ADVERB

Thesaurus

▶ homage, honor, worship, thanks, thanksgiving, glory, adoration

praiseworthy ADJECTIVE a praiseworthy attempt to put things right ▶ commendable, laudable, admirable, creditable, worthy, estimable, exemplary, deserving, honorable, meritorious OPPOSITES ARE deplorable, blameworthy

prank NOUN It had been a prank that had gone tragically wrong. ▶ escapade, trick, practical joke, game, hoax, stunt, (more informal) lark

pray VERB pray to The village prayed to God for a good harvest. ▶ ask, beg, call upon, entreat, beseech, invoke, supplicate, say prayers to

prayer NOUN The priest murmured some prayers. ▶ invocation, devotion, supplication, entreaty

precaution NOUN As an extra precaution, tell a neighbor when you are going to be away.
▶ safeguard, safety measure, insurance, protection, defence, provision

precious ADJECTIVE **1** a collection of precious

paintings ▶ valuable, priceless, choice, costly, inestimable, rare **2** The ring was her most precious possession. ▶ treasured, cherished, valued, prized, favorite, dearest, beloved **3** This action gained them a few precious minutes. ▶ valuable, priceless, vital

precise ADJECTIVE **1** I don't know the precise time. Here are the precise measurements of the room.
▶ exact, accurate, correct, detailed, definite OPPOSITES ARE imprecise, approximate, rough **2** The train stopped at that precise moment.
▶ exact, particular, specific, actual **3** The workmanship is very precise. ▶ meticulous, careful, exact, detailed, finicky, punctilious, scrupulous AN OPPOSITE IS careless

precisely ADVERB **1** The plane took off at three o'clock precisely. ▶ exactly, on the dot, promptly **2** The house is precisely what we are looking for. ▶ exactly, absolutely, entirely, altogether, in every way

predict VERB predicts, predicting, predicted say what will happen in the future; foretell or prophesy
▷ **predictable** ADJECTIVE **prediction** NOUN **predictor** NOUN

predispose VERB predisposes, predisposing, predisposed make you likely to be in favor of something • *We are predisposed to help them.*
▷ **predisposition** NOUN

predominate VERB predominates, predominating, predominated be the largest or most important or most powerful
▷ **predominant** ADJECTIVE **predominance** NOUN

preeminent ADJECTIVE excelling others; outstanding
▷ **preeminently** ADVERB **preeminence** NOUN

preen VERB preens, preening, preened (said about a bird) smooth its feathers with its beak **preen yourself** smarten your appearance

preface (pref- as) NOUN prefaces an introduction at the beginning of a book or speech
▷ **preface** VERB

prefect NOUN prefects **1** a regional official in France, Japan, and other countries

prefer VERB prefers, preferring, preferred **1** like one person or thing more than another **2** (formal) put forward • *They preferred charges of forgery against him.*
▷ **preference** NOUN

preferable (pref- er- a- bul) ADJECTIVE liked better; more desirable
▷ **preferably** ADVERB

prefix NOUN prefixes a word or syllable joined to the front of a word to change or add to its meaning, as in *disorder, outstretched, unhappy*

pregnant ADJECTIVE having a baby developing in the womb
▷ **pregnancy** NOUN

prehensile ADJECTIVE (said about an animal's foot or tail etc.) able to grasp things

prehistoric ADJECTIVE belonging to very ancient times, before written records of events were made
▷ **prehistory** NOUN

prejudice NOUN prejudices an unfavourable opinion or dislike formed without examining the facts fairly
▷ **prejudiced** ADJECTIVE

preliminary ADJECTIVE coming before an important action or event and preparing for it

prelude NOUN preludes **1** a thing that introduces or leads up to something else **2** a short piece of music, especially one that introduces a longer piece

premature ADJECTIVE too early; coming before the usual or proper time
▷ **prematurely** ADVERB

premeditated ADJECTIVE planned beforehand • *a premeditated crime*

premier NOUN premiers a prime minister or other head of government

première (prem- yair) NOUN premières the first public performance of a play or film

premises PLURAL NOUN a building and its grounds

Thesaurus

predict VERB *The polls predicted a landslide victory.* ► forecast, prophesy, foretell, foresee, divine, forewarn, anticipate, envisage

predictable ADJECTIVE *David's reaction was entirely predictable.* ► foreseeable, to be expected, likely, probable, certain AN OPPOSITE IS unpredictable

prefer VERB **1** *I prefer tea thanks.* ► like better, would rather have, favor, go for, opt for, plump for **2 prefer to** *We'd prefer to travel by car.* ► would rather, would sooner, would like better

preferable ADJECTIVE *Many people find self-catering preferable.* ► advantageous, better, more desirable, more suitable, superior, nicer, advisable, preferred OPPOSITES ARE disadvantageous, undesirable

preference NOUN **1** *Our preference is for winter vacations.* ► liking, choice, inclination, option, partiality, predilection, leaning, wish, fancy **2** *Preference will be given to applicants with a foreign language.* ► precedence, priority, favor, advantage

pregnant ADJECTIVE *It is probably best to cut out alcohol altogether when pregnant.* ► expecting a baby, carrying a child, expectant, (more informal) expecting

prejudice NOUN *They were the victims of widespread prejudice.* ► bigotry, bias, discrimination, partisanship, chauvinism, favoritism, intolerance, racism, sexism AN OPPOSITE IS tolerance

prejudice VERB **1** *He feared the accused's attitude might prejudice the jury.* ► influence, bias, sway, predispose, color **2** *The reports might prejudice his election chances.* ► damage, harm, injure, be detrimental to, adversely affect, undermine

prejudiced ADJECTIVE **1** *Racially prejudiced attitudes are thought to be widespread.* ► biased, discriminatory, chauvinistic, intolerant, partial **2** *The staff seemed prejudiced against the poor.* ► biased, intolerant (of), partial, conditioned

premium NOUN premiums **1** an amount or instalment paid to an insurance company **2** an extra charge or payment **at a premium** in demand but scarce

premonition NOUN premonitions a feeling that something is about to happen, especially something bad

preoccupied ADJECTIVE having your thoughts completely busy with something ▷ **preoccupation** NOUN

prep NOUN (*informal*) homework

preparation NOUN preparations **1** getting something ready **2** something done in order to get ready for an event or activity • *last-minute preparations*

preparatory school NOUN preparatory schools a school that prepares pupils for a higher school

prepare VERB prepares, preparing, prepared get ready; make something ready **be prepared to** be willing to do something

preposition NOUN prepositions a word used with a noun or pronoun to show place,

position, time, or means, e.g., *at* home, *in* the hall, *on* Sunday, *by* train

preposterous ADJECTIVE completely absurd or ridiculous

prep school NOUN prep schools a preparatory school

Presbyterian (prez- bit- eer- ee- an) NOUN Presbyterians a member of a Christian Church governed by elders who are all of equal rank, especially the national Church of Scotland

prescribe VERB prescribes, prescribing, prescribed **1** advise a person to use a particular medicine or treatment **2** say what should be done

prescription NOUN prescriptions **1** a doctor's written order for a medicine **2** the medicine prescribed **3** prescribing

presence NOUN **1** being present in a place • *Your presence is required.* **2** a person's impressive appearance or manner

presence of mind NOUN the ability to act quickly and sensibly in an emergency

present ADJECTIVE **1** in a particular place • *No one else was present.* **2** belonging or referring

---

Thesaurus

---

preoccupied ADJECTIVE **1** *He looked anxious and preoccupied.* ► pensive, thoughtful, lost in thought, absentminded, rapt **2** *preoccupied with Sarah became more and more preoccupied with her child.* ► engrossed in, absorbed in, obsessed with, involved with, taken up with, concerned with, wrapped up in, engaged in, immersed in

preparation NOUN **1** *They devoted the next week to the preparation of plans.* ► devising, drawing up, putting together, development, formulation **2** *More staff were taken on to help with the preparations for the hotel's opening.* ► arrangements, plans, provisions, preliminaries, groundwork

prepare VERB **1** *Students have to prepare their presentations well in advance.* ► draw up, write, compose, construct, put together, get ready, make ready **2** *The cooks have to start preparing the food early each morning.* ► make ready, get ready, make, assemble, cook **3** *We should begin to prepare for the future.* ► plan, make arrangements, make provision *or* provisions, get ready

prepared ADJECTIVE **1** *We are prepared to wait for the right person to be found.* ► willing, ready, disposed, predisposed, inclined, able, set AN OPPOSITE IS unwilling **2** *His solicitor read out a prepared statement.* ► pre-arranged, arranged, agreed, organized

preposterous ADJECTIVE *Anyone who maintained such a preposterous theory would be considered mad.* ► absurd, ridiculous, ludicrous, laughable, incredible, farcical, risible, foolish,

idiotic, (*more informal*) crazy, (*more informal*) daft, (*more informal*) barmy, (*more informal*) zany OPPOSITES ARE reasonable, sensible

prerequisite ADJECTIVE *prerequisite qualifications for entry to college* ► compulsory, indispensable, mandatory, necessary, prescribed, required, requisite, specified, stipulated AN OPPOSITE IS optional

prescribe VERB **1** *The doctor decided to prescribe penicillin.* ► write a prescription for, authorize, advise, recommend **2** *The teachers would prescribe the topics to be dealt with.* ► stipulate, specify, lay down, assign, fix, impose, ordain, dictate

prescription NOUN **1** *Some of these medicines can be bought without a prescription.* ► authorization, order, instruction, direction **2** *She ran to the chemist to fetch her prescription before closing time.* ► medicine, medication, mixture, pills, tablets, drug

presence NOUN **1** *She could not explain the presence of Richard's car outside her house.* ► existence, being there **2** *He requested the presence of a solicitor.* ► attendance, company, appearance, support **3** *She had a strong presence which gave her added authority.* ► aura, air, demeanor, bearing, manner, appearance, charisma **4** *the presence of her family in the area* ► proximity, nearness, closeness, vicinity **5** *They felt some sort of presence in the room* ► spirit, ghost, specter, phantom

present ADJECTIVE (with the stress on *pres-*) **1** *A police officer should be present whenever possible.* ► in attendance, at hand, nearby, attending, to what is happening now; existing now • *the present chairman*

present[1] NOUN present times or events
at present now, for the time being

present[2] NOUN **presents** something given or received without payment; a gift

present (priz- ent) VERB **presents, presenting, presented** **1** give something, especially with a ceremony • *Who is to present the prizes?* **2** introduce someone to another person **3** introduce a radio or television program to an audience **4** put on a play or other entertainment **5** show **6** cause or provide a problem or difficulty
▷ **presentation** NOUN **presenter** NOUN

presently ADVERB **1** soon • *I shall be with you presently.* **2** now • *the person who is presently in charge*

preservative NOUN **preservatives** a substance added to food to preserve it

preserve VERB **preserves, preserving, preserved** keep something safe or in good condition
▷ **preserver** NOUN **preservation** NOUN

preserve NOUN **preserves** **1** jam made with preserved fruit **2** an activity that belongs to a particular person or group

preside VERB **presides, presiding, presided** be in charge of a meeting etc.

president NOUN **presidents** **1** the person in charge of a club, society, or council, etc. **2** the head of a republic
▷ **presidency** NOUN **presidential** ADJECTIVE

press VERB **presses, pressing, pressed** **1** put weight or force steadily on something; squeeze **2** make something by pressing **3** make clothes smooth by ironing them **4** urge; make demands • *They pressed for an increase in wages.*

press NOUN **presses** **1** a device for pressing things • *a trouser press* **2** a machine for printing things **3** a firm that prints or publishes books etc. • *Oxford University Press* **4** newspapers; journalists

pressing ADJECTIVE needing immediate action; urgent • *a pressing need*

pressure NOUN **pressures** **1** continuous pressing **2** the force with which something presses **3** the force of the atmosphere on the earth's surface • *a band of high pressure* **4** an

Thesaurus

available, there *or* here AN OPPOSITE IS absent **2** *The shares are not expected to maintain their present high value.* ► current, present-day, existing, prevailing, contemporary
at present *or* **at the present time** *We have no plans to increase taxes at present.* ► just now, right now, at the moment, at this time, currently

present NOUN (with the stress on *pres-*) **1** *a history of the family from the sixteenth century to the present* ► present day, modern times, today **2** *She let him keep the pen as a present.* ► gift, donation, gratuity, contribution, offering

present VERB (with the stress on *-sent*) **1** *She presented a prize to the winners.* ► hand out, give out, hand over, award, grant, bestow (on) **2** *The committee has presented its report.* ► submit, tender, hand in, offer, proffer, publish **3** *The situation presents some novel features.* ► show, demonstrate, display, exhibit **4** *A compère presented each act.* ► introduce, announce

presently ADVERB **1** *We'll be there presently.* ► shortly, soon, directly, in a while, (*more informal*) in a bit **2** *The family is presently abroad.* ► currently, at present, at the moment, now

preserve VERB **1** *Local action can also preserve wildlife.* ► safeguard, secure, protect, conserve, maintain, sustain, uphold, defend, guard OPPOSITES ARE endanger, neglect **2** *She*

wanted to preserve him from harm. ► protect, defend, guard, safeguard, shield **3** *special containers for preserving fruit* ► conserve, bottle, store, keep, save

preside VERB *We elect a chairman to preside at the meeting.* ► officiate, take charge, be in charge, take the chair
preside over *The finance director presides over the annual budget review.* ► be in charge of, direct, have responsibility for, manage, be in control of

press VERB **1** *She pressed his hand.* ► squeeze, grip, clutch, clinch **2** *He pressed some clothes into a suitcase.* ► squash, stuff, cram, push, squeeze, force **3** *Donna needed time to press her clothes.* ► iron, smooth, smooth out, flatten **4** *The next process is to press the grapes.* ► crush, squeeze, compress, mash, pulp **5** *People pressed round to see what was going on.* ► gather, cluster, crowd, swarm, throng **6** *You must press them to give you an answer.* ► urge, pressure, persuade, compel, plead with, force, insist on
USAGE If you use insist on you say *You must insist on them giving* (or **their giving**) *you an answer.*

pressure NOUN **1** *The pressure on the foundations caused them to crack.* ► force, load, weight, burden, strain, stress **2** *The team is working under severe pressure.* ► stress, strain, difficulty, (*more informal*) hassle **3** *She was under a lot of pressure to accept the offer.* ► constraint,

a b c d e f g h i j k l m n o **p** q r s t u v w x y z

A
B
C
D
E
F
G
H
I
J
K
L
M
N
O
P
Q
R
S
T
U
V
W
X
Y
Z

influence that persuades or compels you to do something

prestige (pres- teej) NOUN good reputation
▷ **prestigious** ADJECTIVE
[from Latin *praestigium* = an illusion, glamour]

presumably ADVERB according to what you may presume

presume VERB presumes, presuming, presumed **1** suppose; assume something to be true • *I presumed that they were dead.*
2 (*formal*) take the liberty of doing something; venture • *May we presume to advise you?*
▷ **presumption** NOUN

presumptuous ADJECTIVE too bold or confident
▷ **presumptuously** ADVERB

presuppose VERB presupposes, presupposing, presupposed suppose or assume something beforehand
▷ **presupposition** NOUN

pretend VERB pretends, pretending, pretended behave as if something is true or real when you know that it is not, either in play or so as to deceive people

pretender NOUN pretenders a person who claims a throne or title

pretense NOUN pretenses an attempt to pretend that something is true
false pretenses pretending to be something that you are not in order to deceive people
• *You've invited me here under false pretenses.*

pretentious ADJECTIVE **1** trying to impress by claiming greater importance or merit than is actually the case **2** showy or ostentatious
▷ **pretentiously** ADVERB **pretentiousness** NOUN

pretext NOUN pretexts a reason put forward to conceal the true reason

pretty ADJECTIVE prettier, prettiest attractive in a delicate way
▷ **prettily** ADVERB **prettiness** NOUN

pretty ADVERB (*informal*) quite • *It's pretty cold.*
[from Old English]

prevent VERB prevents, preventing, prevented **1** stop something from happening **2** stop a person from doing something
▷ **preventable** ADJECTIVE **prevention** NOUN
preventive ADJECTIVE

preview NOUN previews a showing of a film or play, etc., before it is shown to the general public

Thesaurus

coercion, duress, harassment, compulsion, intimidation

prestige NOUN *Achieving an agreement would bring the president added prestige.* ► status, reputation, standing, credit, kudos, renown, esteem, fame, glory, honor, importance

presume VERB **1** *We presume there will be a call-out charge.* ► assume, expect, suppose, imagine, take it, dare say, guess, conjecture, surmise, believe **2** *Don't presume to take charge yourself.* ► venture, dare, have the nerve, have the temerity, have the audacity, be so bold as, go so far as

presumptuous ADJECTIVE *It was presumptuous to make a decision without consulting us.* ► arrogant, audacious, forward, bold, impudent, insolent, bumptious, unwarranted, conceited, impertinent, overconfident, shameless, (*more informal*) pushy, (*more informal*) cheeky

pretend VERB **1** *She pretended to understand, but we were all confused.* ► affect, profess, claim, purport **2** *Let's pretend we're ghosts.* ► imagine, make believe, suppose, play being

pretend ADJECTIVE (*informal*) *He made his room into a pretend cave.* ► imaginary, make-believe, fantasy, fanciful, mythical, pretended

pretense NOUN *Their self-confidence turned out to be just a pretense.* ► make-believe, act, show, display, front, affectation, deception,

posturing, façade, masquerade, charade, subterfuge, falsehood, sham, pose, ruse, bluff, cover, faking, dissembling

pretentious ADJECTIVE *The best food can often be found in smaller, less pretentious restaurants.*
► ostentatious, showy, affected, conspicuous, flashy, grandiose, extravagant OPPOSITES ARE modest, unassuming

pretty ADJECTIVE *a pretty little garden*
► attractive, lovely, good-looking, beautiful, charming, appealing, pleasing, (*more informal*) cute OPPOSITES ARE plain, ugly, hideous

pretty ADVERB (*informal*) *It was a pretty daft thing to do.* ► rather, quite, somewhat, fairly, moderately, (*more informal*) kind of

prevail VERB **1** *attitudes that prevailed in the 1960s* ► exist, hold, obtain, be prevalent, be current **2** *Common sense prevailed in the end.*
► win, win through, triumph, reign, rule, predominate **3** *The Greek army prevailed against all the odds.* ► be victorious, triumph, win

prevail on or **upon** *Can you prevail on her to change her mind?* ► persuade, induce, urge, pressure, pressurize, tempt

prevent VERB **1** *It was too late to prevent the accident.* ► stop, avert, avoid, head off, forestall, frustrate, hinder **2** *I'll try to prevent them from coming in before you're ready.* ► stop, restrain, check, inhibit, block, bar

previous ADJECTIVE coming before this; preceding
▷ **previously** ADVERB

prey (rhymes with *pray*) NOUN an animal that is hunted or killed by another for food

prey VERB preys, preying, preyed
prey on **1** hunt or take as prey **2** cause to worry • *The problem preyed on his mind.*

price NOUN prices **1** the amount of money for which something is bought or sold **2** what must be given or done in order to achieve something

priceless ADJECTIVE **1** very valuable **2** (*informal*) very amusing

prick VERB pricks, pricking, pricked **1** make a tiny hole in something **2** hurt somebody with a pin or needle, etc.
▷ **prick** NOUN
prick up your ears start listening suddenly

prickle NOUN prickles **1** a small thorn **2** a sharp spine on a hedgehog or cactus, etc. **3** a feeling that something is pricking you
▷ **prickly** ADJECTIVE

prickle VERB prickles, prickling, prickled feel or cause a pricking feeling

pride NOUN prides **1** a feeling of deep pleasure or satisfaction when you have done something well **2** something that makes you feel proud **3** dignity or self-respect **4** too high an opinion of yourself **5** a group of lions
pride of place the most important or most honored position

pride VERB prides, priding, prided
pride yourself on be proud of

priest NOUN priests **1** a member of the clergy in certain Christian Churches **2** a person who conducts religious ceremonies in a non-Christian religion
▷ **priestess** NOUN **priesthood** NOUN **priestly** ADJECTIVE

prig NOUN prigs a self-righteous person
▷ **priggish** ADJECTIVE

prim ADJECTIVE primmer, primmest formal and correct in manner; disliking anything rough or rude
▷ **primly** ADVERB **primness** NOUN

Thesaurus

---

previous ADJECTIVE *a review of the previous three years* ► preceding, foregoing, antecedent, last, earlier, former, prior AN OPPOSITE IS following

previously ADVERB *Previously she had worked in a chemist.* ► formerly, earlier, in the past, at one time, before this or that, hitherto

prey NOUN *Lions are often slower than their prey.* ► quarry, victim, game, kill

prey VERB **prey on** *Wild dogs will also prey on cattle.* ► hunt, catch, kill, eat, feed on **2** *The thought kept preying on his mind.* ► trouble, oppress, disturb, distress, haunt, beset, burden, weigh down, worry

price NOUN **1** *The price of your holiday is fully guaranteed.* ► cost, terms, rate, amount, charge (for), outlay (on) **2** *What price should you charge?* ► amount, figure, sum, fee, rate, charge, levy **3** *Isolation was one price of their peaceful existence.* ► consequence, result, penalty, sacrifice, downside

priceless ADJECTIVE **1** *a priceless collection of watercolors; a priceless away goal* ► precious, valuable, irreplaceable, inestimable, treasured, prized, costly **2** (*informal*) *a priceless remark that made them all laugh* ► hilarious, riotous, uproarious, funny, (*more informal*) hysterical

prick VERB **1** *He pricked the lid and put it in the microwave.* ► pierce, puncture, perforate, make a hole in, stab, jab, punch **2** *The smoke made my eyes start to prick.* ► sting, smart, prickle, hurt **3** *His conscience was pricking him.* ► trouble, worry, disturb, distress, oppress, torment, afflict

prickle NOUN **1** *The bush was covered with prickles.* ► thorn, spike, needle, spine, quill, barb **2** *The shuffling sound outside sent a prickle down my spine.* ► tingle, tingling, prickling, chill, thrill

prickle VERB *The grass prickled their legs.* ► sting, prick, tickle

prickly ADJECTIVE **1** *a prickly bush* ► spiky, spiny, thorny, bristly, scratchy, sharp **2** (*informal*) *He's quite a prickly character.* ► irritable, irascible, peevish, testy, edgy, touchy, grumpy, short-tempered, fractious

pride NOUN **1** *Pride prevented him from accepting the offer.* ► conceit, vanity, arrogance, snobbery **2** *She took great pride in her work.* ► satisfaction, pleasure, delight, joy, comfort, sense of achievement **3** *Their victory was a source of great pride to them.* ► self-esteem, self-respect, gratification, honor, dignity

priest NOUN ► clergyman or clergywoman, minister, pastor, vicar, padre RELATED ADJECTIVE ► sacerdotal

priggish ADJECTIVE *She too was in danger of seeming priggish and opinionated.* ► self-righteous, smug, sanctimonious, sententious, prudish, prim, strait-laced, stuffy, starchy

prim ADJECTIVE *She sat behind her desk looking prim.* ► demure, proper, formal, strait-laced, prissy, prudish, starchy, fastidious AN OPPOSITE IS broad-minded

a b c d e f g h i j k l m n o **p** q r s t u v w x y z

primary ADJECTIVE first; most important
COMPARE **secondary**
▷ **primarily** (pry- mer- il- ee) ADVERB

primary color NOUN primary colors one of the colors from which all others can be made by mixing (red, yellow, and blue for paint; red, green, and violet for light)

primary school NOUN primary schools a school for the first stage of a child's education

primate (pry- mayt) NOUN primates **1** an animal of the group that includes human beings, apes, and monkeys **2** an archbishop

prime ADJECTIVE **1** chief; most important • *the prime cause* **2** excellent; first-rate • *prime beef*

prime NOUN the best time or stage of something • *in the prime of life*

prime VERB primes, priming, primed **1** prepare something for use or action **2** put a coat of liquid on something to prepare it for painting **3** equip a person with information

prime minister NOUN prime ministers the leader of a government (in a parliamentary system)

prime number NOUN prime numbers a number (e.g., 2, 3, 5, 7, 11) that can be divided exactly only by itself and one

primeval (pry- mee- val) ADJECTIVE belonging to the earliest times of the world

primitive ADJECTIVE **1** at an early stage of civilization **2** at an early stage of development; not complicated or advanced • *primitive technology*

primrose NOUN primroses a pale yellow flower that blooms in spring [from Latin *prima rosa* = first rose]

prince NOUN princes **1** the son of a king or queen **2** a man or boy in a royal family
▷ **princely** ADJECTIVE

princess NOUN princesses **1** the daughter of a king or queen **2** a woman or girl in a royal family **3** the wife of a prince

principal ADJECTIVE chief; most important
▷ **principally** ADVERB

principal NOUN principals the head of a college or school [from Latin *principalis* = first or chief]
USAGE Do not confuse with **principle**.

principle NOUN principles **1** a general truth, belief, or rule • *She taught me the principles of geometry.* **2** a rule of conduct • *Cheating is against his principles.*
in principle as a general idea, without going into details
on principle because of your principles of behavior
[from Latin *principium* = source]
USAGE Do not confuse with **principal**.

print VERB prints, printing, printed **1** put words or pictures on paper by using a machine **2** write with letters that are not joined together **3** press a mark or design on a surface **4** make a picture from the negative of a photograph

print NOUN prints **1** printed lettering or words **2** a mark made by something pressing on a

Thesaurus

primarily ADVERB *The work is primarily funded by a grant from the government.* ► chiefly, principally, mainly, mostly, predominantly, basically, in the main

primary ADJECTIVE **1** *Their primary aim was to make money.* ► main, chief, principal, key, prime, paramount, overriding, ultimate, supreme **2** *the primary cause of the infection* ► original, initial, first

prime ADJECTIVE **1** *The prime reason for his decision was a wish for change.* ► main, chief, principal, key, primary, paramount, overriding, ultimate, supreme **2** *a hundred acres of prime agricultural land* ► best, choice, select, superior, first-class, high-grade, top-quality

primitive ADJECTIVE **1** *primitive peoples* ► ancient, early, earliest, prehistoric AN OPPOSITE IS developed **2** *primitive tools* ► crude, basic, rudimentary, simple, undeveloped, elementary, rough OPPOSITES ARE sophisticated, advanced

principal ADJECTIVE *Traffic noise is the principal objection to the new road scheme.* ► chief, main, primary, prime, most important, overriding, foremost, fundamental, key, crucial, central, paramount, predominant, basic, essential

principally ADVERB *The place was full of foreigners, principally Canadians.* ► chiefly, mainly, primarily, mostly, predominantly, especially, essentially

principle NOUN **1** *a woman of principle* ► honor, integrity, morality, ideals, conscience, scruples, decency, virtue **2** *a basic principle of physics* ► rule, law, formula, canon, dictum, axiom, tenet
in principle *In principle the idea is a good one.* ► in theory, theoretically, in general, in the main, by and large

principles PLURAL NOUN **1** *They were praised for sticking to their principles.* ► morals, values, morality, standards, moral standards, code of behavior **2** *the first principles of a subject* ► essentials, fundamentals, basics, elements, laws

print VERB **1** *The company logo is printed at the top of each page.* ► mark, stamp, imprint, impress, engrave, reproduce **2** *The books are printed in the Far East.* ► set in print, run off, produce, reproduce, manufacture **3** *The publishers plan to print ten thousand copies of the book.* ► issue, publish, produce **4** *Print your name at the top of the form.* ► write in capital letters *or* large letters surface **3** a printed picture, photograph, or design

in print available from a publisher

out of print no longer available from a publisher

printed circuit NOUN printed circuits an electric circuit made by pressing thin metal strips on to a board

printer NOUN printers **1** a machine that prints on paper from data in a computer **2** someone who prints books or newspapers

printout NOUN printouts information produced in printed form by a computer

priority NOUN priorities **1** being earlier or more important than something else; precedence **2** something considered more important than other things • *Safety is a priority.*

prism (prizm) NOUN prisms **1** a solid shape with ends that are triangles or polygons which are equal and parallel **2** a glass prism that breaks up light into the colors of the rainbow
▷ **prismatic** ADJECTIVE

prison NOUN prisons a place where criminals are kept as a punishment [from early French]

prisoner NOUN prisoners **1** a person kept in prison **2** a captive

private ADJECTIVE **1** belonging to a particular person or group • *private property* **2** confidential • *private talks* **3** quiet and secluded **4** not holding public office • *a private citizen* **5** independent or commercial; not run by the government • *private education* • *a private hospital*
▷ **privately** ADVERB **privacy** (prīv- a- see) NOUN
in private where only particular people can see or hear; not in public

private NOUN privates a soldier of the lowest rank

privatize VERB privatizes, privatizing, privatized transfer the running of a business or industry from the state to private owners
▷ **privatization** NOUN

privilege NOUN privileges a special right or advantage given to one person or group
▷ **privileged** ADJECTIVE

prize NOUN prizes **1** an award given to the winner of a game or competition, etc. **2** something taken from an enemy

prize VERB prizes, prizing, prized value something greatly

pro NOUN pros (*informal*) a professional

probable ADJECTIVE likely to happen or be true
▷ **probably** ADVERB **probability** NOUN

Thesaurus

print NOUN **1** *The print was difficult to read.* ► type, typeface, printing, lettering, letters, characters **2** *There were prints of feet in the sand* ► impression, imprint, mark, indentation, stamp **3** *A print would be less costly than an original painting.* ► reproduction, engraving, lithograph, copy, duplicate, photograph

priority NOUN **1** *Traffic from the right has priority.* ► right of way, precedence **2** *Education will have priority at this year's conference.* ► precedence, preference, first place, first importance, primacy, predominance

prison NOUN *They would spend the next three years in prison.* ► jail, confinement, detention, custody, place of detention, penitentiary

prisoner NOUN *The prisoners staged a demonstration on the prison roof.* ► detainee, convict, captive, hostage, inmate, internee, (*more informal*) jailbird

privacy NOUN *The little room gave her some privacy.* ► seclusion, solitude, tranquillity, peace and quiet, quietness, secrecy, isolation

private ADJECTIVE **1** *He had amassed a huge private fortune.* ► personal, exclusive, individual, special **2** *Private talks were held at the White House.* ► confidential, secret, covert, clandestine OPPOSITES ARE public, open **3** *She*

had her own private thoughts on the matter.
► personal, secret, hidden, intimate **4** *They needed somewhere private to talk.* ► secluded, undisturbed, out of the way, isolated, solitary, quiet, peaceful, tranquil AN OPPOSITE IS busy **5** *John is a very private sort of person.*
► reserved, withdrawn, intimate, reticent, unsocial

privilege NOUN **1** *Full members enjoy special privileges.* ► benefit, entitlement, advantage, prerogative, concession, right **2** *It had been a privilege to meet them.* ► honor, pleasure

privileged ADJECTIVE *He enjoyed a privileged social position.* ► advantaged, affluent, prosperous, wealthy, favored, fortunate, special, superior, élite, powerful OPPOSITES ARE disadvantaged, underprivileged

prize NOUN *Helen won the prize three years in a row.* ► award, reward, trophy, honor, accolade

prize VERB *They prize their freedom above all else.* ► value, appreciate, cherish, esteem, treasure, hold dear, regard, rate, approve of, revere, like

probable ADJECTIVE *Engine failure was the most probable cause of the crash. It is probable that this road was heavily guarded.* ► likely, plausible, credible, feasible, believable, expected, possible, predictable, presumed, (*more informal*) odds-on, (*more informal*) on the cards OPPOSITES ARE improbable, unlikely

A
B
C
D
E
F
G
H
I
J
K
L
M
N
O
P
Q
R
S
T
U
V
W
X
Y
Z

probation NOUN the testing of a person's character and abilities, e.g., to see whether they are suitable for a job they have recently started
▷ **probationary** ADJECTIVE
on probation being supervised by a probation officer instead of being sent to prison

probation officer NOUN probation officers an official who supervises the behavior of a convicted criminal who is not in prison

probe NOUN probes **1** a long thin instrument used to look closely at something such as a wound **2** an unmanned spacecraft used for exploring **3** an investigation

probe VERB probes, probing, probed **1** explore something with a probe **2** investigate

problem NOUN problems **1** something difficult to deal with or understand **2** something that has to be done or answered
▷ **problematic** ADJECTIVE

procedure NOUN procedures an orderly way of doing something

proceed VERB proceeds, proceeding, proceeded **1** go forward or onward

2 continue; go on to do something • *She proceeded to explain the plan.*
USAGE Do not confuse with **precede**.

proceedings PLURAL NOUN **1** things that happen; activities **2** a lawsuit

proceeds PLURAL NOUN the money made from a sale or event

process (pra- sess) NOUN processes a series of actions for making or doing something
in the process of in the course of doing something

process VERB processes, processing, processed put something through a manufacturing or other process • *processed cheese*

procession NOUN processions a number of people or vehicles, etc., moving steadily forward following each other

processor NOUN processors **1** a machine that processes things **2** the part of a computer that controls all its operations

proclaim VERB proclaims, proclaiming, proclaimed announce something officially or publicly
▷ **proclamation** NOUN

Thesaurus

---

probe VERB **1** *The inquiry will probe the circumstances of the accident.* ► investigate, examine, inquire into, look into, scrutinize, analyze, study, go into **2** *Unmanned underwater vehicles probed the ocean depths.* ► sound, plumb, penetrate, explore, feel

probe NOUN **1** *a space probe* ► exploration, expedition **2** *a police probe* ► inquiry, investigation, examination, study, research, scrutiny

problem NOUN **1** *He gave them a page of problems to solve.* ► puzzle, question, riddle, conundrum, enigma, mystery, (*more informal*) brainteaser, (*more informal*) poser **2** *Money was becoming a big problem for them.* ► burden, complication, difficulty, dilemma, dispute, (*informal*) headache, predicament, quandary, setback, snag, trouble, worry

problematic ADJECTIVE *Unraveling this argument can be problematic.* ► difficult, complicated, complex, problematical, intractable, tricky, thorny, knotty, taxing, involved, enigmatic, controversial OPPOSITES ARE straightforward, simple, easy

procedure NOUN *There is a special procedure for dealing with complaints.* ► course of action, process, routine, system, policy, strategy, approach, proceeding

proceed VERB **1** *We still don't know how to proceed.* ► begin, make a start, act, take action, make a move, progress **2** *They turned*

off the main road and proceeded as far as the village. ► advance, continue, progress, make your way, carry on, press on
proceed with *Despite opposition, they decided to proceed with the changes.* ► implement, carry out, go ahead with, put into effect

process NOUN **1** *Sending email attachments is a simple process.* ► operation, procedure, activity, exercise, affair **2** *a new process for producing color pictures* ► system, method, technique, procedure **3** *The learning process continues for many years.* ► progression, course, development, experience, evolution

process VERB **1** *Officials hope to process asylum claims more quickly.* ► deal with, attend to, handle, expedite, treat, see to, sort out **2** *The crude oil is processed at this refinery.* ► refine, convert, make usable, prepare, transform, treat

procession NOUN *A procession passed through the town.* ► parade, march, cavalcade, spectacle, display, pageant, review, show

proclaim VERB **1** *She proclaimed her love for him.* ► declare, announce, profess, make known, affirm, assert, give out, pronounce **2** *The president proclaimed the day a public holiday.* ► decree, declare, pronounce

proclamation NOUN *The queen issues a proclamation dissolving Parliament.* ► decree, edict, order, command, ruling, announcement, declaration

prod VERB prods, prodding, prodded **1** poke **2** stimulate someone into action
▷ **prod** NOUN

prodigal ADJECTIVE wasteful or extravagant
▷ **prodigally** ADVERB **prodigality** NOUN

prodigious ADJECTIVE wonderful or enormous
▷ **prodigiously** ADVERB

prodigy NOUN prodigies **1** a person with wonderful abilities **2** a wonderful thing

produce VERB produces, producing, produced **1** make or create something; bring something into existence **2** bring something out so that it can be seen **3** organize the performance of a play, making of a film, etc. **4** supervise the making of a musical recording
▷ **producer** NOUN

produce (prod- ooss) NOUN things produced, especially by farmers

product NOUN products **1** something produced **2** the result of multiplying two numbers COMPARE quotient

production NOUN productions **1** the process of making or creating something **2** the amount produced • *Oil production increased last year*

productive ADJECTIVE producing a lot of useful things or results
▷ **productivity** NOUN

profanity NOUN profanities words or language that show disrespect for religion

profession NOUN professions **1** an occupation that needs special education or training, such as medicine or law **2** a declaration • *They made professions of loyalty.* [from Latin *professio* = public declaration]

professional ADJECTIVE **1** to do with a profession **2** doing a certain kind of work as a full-time job for payment, not as an amateur • *a professional athlete* **3** done with a high standard of skill
▷ **professional** NOUN **professionally** ADVERB

professor NOUN professors a university lecturer of the highest rank
▷ **professorship** NOUN

profile NOUN profiles **1** a side view of a person's face **2** a short description of a person's character or career
keep a low profile try not to attract attention [from early Italian *profilare* = draw in outline]

Thesaurus

---

prod VERB **1** *The cook grumbled as he prodded the potatoes. He continued to prod her palms with the needle.* ▶ jab, poke, stab, dig, nudge, push **2** *He always needs someone to prod him into action.* ▶ goad, spur, stir, rouse, prompt, urge, stimulate, egg on, incite, provoke

prod NOUN **1** *She gave him a prod that woke him up.* ▶ jab, poke, stab, dig, nudge, shove, push **2** *The phone call was a prod to remind him to put the trash out that night.* ▶ prompt, reminder, stimulus

produce VERB (with the stress on *-duce*) **1** *The remark produced a wave of sniggers through the room.* ▶ cause, give rise to, occasion, provoke, bring about, result in, generate, effect **2** *He had failed to produce an essay for the third week running.* ▶ present, submit, offer, hand in, supply, provide **3** *He put his hand in his pocket and produced his passport.* ▶ show, display, present, bring out, take out **4** *It would be difficult to produce the required output that year.* ▶ yield, supply, deliver, provide **5** *The company produced Hamlet at the Shakespeare Festival.* ▶ stage, mount, present, put on, show

produce NOUN (with the stress on *prod-*) *an increase in organically grown produce* ▶ food, crops, harvest, output, products, commodities, yield, fruit, vegetables

product NOUN **1** *The company will announce its new product at the trade fair.* ▶ commodity, output, production, artifact, produce, end-product, goods, merchandise **2** *The story was the product of a vivid imagination.* ▶ result, consequence, outcome, effect, fruit, upshot

productive ADJECTIVE **1** *He still had years of productive work ahead.* ▶ useful, valuable, worthwhile, constructive, creative, effective, gainful, profitable, profitmaking, rewarding, beneficial, busy OPPOSITES ARE unproductive, fruitless **2** *a productive area of land* ▶ fertile, fruitful, rich, prolific, lush OPPOSITES ARE unproductive, barren

profession NOUN **1** *She was no longer attracted by the teaching profession.* ▶ career, occupation, vocation, line of work, business, calling, employment, work **2** *a profession of loyalty* ▶ declaration, acknowledgment, affirmation, avowal, confession, statement, protestation

professional ADJECTIVE **1** *the study of modern languages as a preparation for professional life* ▶ working, business, executive **2** *the use of professional judgment* ▶ expert, qualified, skilled, trained, competent, efficient, proficient **3** *The plays were recorded in a studio with professional actors.* ▶ paid, salaried, full-time OPPOSITES ARE amateur, voluntary **4** *He was a thoroughly professional journalist.* ▶ conscientious, businesslike, proficient, dutiful, responsible AN OPPOSITE IS unprofessional

profile NOUN **1** *a beautiful woman with a perfect profile* ▶ shape, side view, contour, figure, outline, silhouette **2** *a profile of John F Kennedy* ▶ biography, sketch, portrait, study, account **3** *The company has raised its profile in eastern Europe.* ▶ influence, presence, image

a
b
c
d
e
f
g
h
i
j
k
l
m
n
o
p
q
r
s
t
u
v
w
x
y
z

A B C D E F G H I J K L M N O P Q R S T U V W X Y Z

profit NOUN **profits 1** the extra money obtained by selling something for more than it cost to buy or make **2** an advantage gained by doing something
▷ **profitable** ADJECTIVE **profitably** ADVERB

profit VERB **profits, profiting, profited** gain an advantage or benefit from something

profiteer NOUN **profiteers** a person who makes a great profit unfairly
▷ **profiteering** NOUN

profound ADJECTIVE **1** very deep or intense ● *We take a profound interest in it.* **2** showing considerable knowledge or thought ● *a profound remark*
▷ **profoundly** ADVERB **profundity** NOUN

prognosis (prog- noh- sis) NOUN **prognoses** a forecast or prediction, especially about a disease
▷ **prognostication** NOUN

program NOUN **programs** (in computing) a series of coded instructions for a computer to carry out

program VERB **programs, programming, programmed** put instructions into a computer by means of a program
▷ **programmer** NOUN

program NOUN **programs 1** a list of planned events **2** a leaflet giving details of a play, concert, match, etc. **3** a show, play, or talk etc. on radio or television

progress (prah- gress) NOUN **1** forward movement; an advance **2** a development or improvement
in progress taking place

progress (pro- gress) VERB **progresses, progressing, progressed 1** move forward **2** improve
▷ **progression** NOUN **progressive** ADJECTIVE

prohibit VERB **prohibits, prohibiting, prohibited** forbid or ban ● *Smoking is prohibited.*
▷ **prohibition** NOUN

prohibitive ADJECTIVE **1** prohibiting **2** (said about prices) so high that people will not buy things

project (proj- ekt) NOUN **projects 1** a plan or scheme **2** the task of finding out as much as you can about something and writing about it

project (pro- jekt) VERB **projects, projecting, projected 1** stick out **2** show a picture on a screen **3** give people a particular impression

---

Thesaurus

---

profit NOUN **1** *The company made a modest profit in the last financial year.* ► return, surplus, yield, excess **2** *profits Two percent of profits contribute to the social fund.* ► revenue, income, takings, earnings, proceeds **3** *There would be no profit in continuing.* ► advantage, benefit, value, use, gain, point, purpose

profit VERB **1** *It would profit us to wait for a while.* ► benefit, advantage, be an advantage to, pay, help **2 profit by** or **from** *No one profited from these changes.* ► benefit from, gain advantage from, do well out of

profitable ADJECTIVE *a profitable undertaking* ► moneymaking, profitmaking, remunerative, lucrative, paying, productive, fruitful, gainful, rewarding, advantageous, beneficial, commercial, useful, valuable, worthwhile AN OPPOSITE IS unprofitable

profound ADJECTIVE **1** *I offered my profound sympathy.* ► sincere, deep, heartfelt, intense AN OPPOSITE IS insincere. **2** *a profound disagreement* ► complete, total, utter, absolute, extreme **3** *a profound argument* ► learned, wise, erudite, intelligent, perceptive, penetrating, thoughtful

program NOUN **1** *a varied program of events* ► schedule, agenda, timetable, calendar, listing, plan, order, (more informal) line-up **2** *a television program* ► broadcast, transmission, performance, production, show

progress NOUN (with the stress on *pro-*) **1** *major progress in medical research* ► advance,

development, headway, improvement, movement, progression, breakthrough, (more informal) step forward **2** *The heavy rain made further progress difficult.* ► travel, headway, advance, movement

progress VERB (with the stress on *-gress*) *The plans are progressing slowly.* ► advance, develop, move forward, make progress, make headway, proceed, prosper, mature, improve, (more informal) come on OPPOSITES ARE regress, deteriorate

progressive ADJECTIVE **1** *a progressive improvement in health* ► continuous, continuing, steady, increasing, ongoing, accelerating, growing, escalating OPPOSITES ARE faltering, fluctuating, unsteady **2** *a party leader with progressive ideas* ► liberal, advanced, radical, modern, forward-looking, enlightened, avant-garde, contemporary, enterprising, up-to-date AN OPPOSITE IS conservative

prohibit VERB **1** *a law prohibiting the advertising of tobacco products.* ► forbid, ban, disallow, proscribe, outlaw, make illegal **2** *Her commitments prohibited her from attending the funeral.* ► prevent, preclude, rule out, restrict, impede, obstruct

project NOUN (with the stress on *proj-*) **1** *a project to create more conservation areas* ► scheme, undertaking, plan, proposal, venture, enterprise, idea **2** *They're doing a*

• He likes to project an image of absentminded brilliance.
▷ **projection** NOUN

projectile NOUN projectiles a missile

projector NOUN projectors a machine for showing films or photographs on a screen

prolific ADJECTIVE producing a lot • a prolific author
▷ **prolifically** ADVERB

prologue (proh- log) NOUN prologues an introduction to a poem or play, etc.

prolong VERB prolongs, prolonging, prolonged make a thing longer or make it last for a long time
▷ **prolongation** NOUN

prom NOUN proms (informal) **1** a promenade **2** a promenade concert

promenade (prom- in- ahd) NOUN promenades **1** a place suitable for walking, especially beside the seashore **2** a leisurely walk
▷ **promenade** VERB

promenade concert NOUN promenade concerts a concert where part of the audience may stand or walk around

prominent ADJECTIVE **1** easily seen; conspicuous • The house stood in a prominent position. **2** sticking out **3** important
▷ **prominently** ADVERB **prominence** NOUN

promiscuous ADJECTIVE **1** having many casual sexual relationships **2** indiscriminate
▷ **promiscuously** ADVERB **promiscuity** NOUN

promise NOUN promises **1** a statement that you will definitely do or not do something **2** an indication of future success or good results • His work shows promise.

promise VERB promises, promising, promised make a promise

promote VERB promotes, promoting, promoted **1** move a person to a higher rank or position **2** help the progress of something • He has done much to promote the cause of peace.
▷ **promoter** NOUN **promotion** NOUN

Thesaurus

---

history project. ► assignment, piece of research, piece of work, activity, task

project VERB (with the stress on -ject) **1** Balconies project from the upstairs windows. ► protrude, stand out, stick out, extend, jut out, overhang, bulge **2** The flashlight projected a strong beam. ► cast, throw, throw out, flash, shine **3** You can project the year's income from these monthly figures. ► estimate, reckon, forecast, predict, extrapolate

proliferate VERB The problems proliferated. ► multiply, increase, escalate, build up, mushroom, intensify, snowball, spread

prolific ADJECTIVE **1** a prolific crop of vegetables ► plentiful, abundant, copious, profuse, productive, rich, bountiful, fertile, fruitful AN OPPOSITE IS unproductive **2** a prolific writer ► productive, creative, inventive

prolong VERB She didn't want to prolong the argument. ► lengthen, protract, extend, continue, perpetuate, spin out, draw out, increase, make longer, stretch out OPPOSITES ARE shorten, curtail

prominent ADJECTIVE **1** a prominent member of the government ► important, well known, leading, eminent, distinguished, notable, noteworthy, celebrated

promise VERB **1** He promised to pay for the damage. ► undertake, guarantee, agree, contract **2** He promised she'd be there. ► give your word, say, pledge, swear **3** The bright sky

promised a fine day ► indicate, presage, suggest, signify, augur, predict

promiscuous ADJECTIVE She was promiscuous in her younger days. ► licentious, loose, immoral, dissolute, abandoned, wanton, casual OPPOSITES ARE moral, chaste

promise NOUN **1** You have my promise. ► assurance, word, word of honor, pledge, undertaking, commitment, guarantee, oath, vow **2** a group of pupils showing outstanding promise ► potential, ability, aptitude, talent, capability

promising ADJECTIVE **1** There are promising signs of an improvement. ► encouraging, hopeful, favorable, auspicious, propitious, talented **2** a promising young talent ► budding, gifted, up-and-coming, able

promote VERB **1** She was promoted in the recent executive reshuffle. ► upgrade, move up, give a promotion to, advance, honor **2** He will promote his new novel on the television. ► advertise, publicize, push, sponsor, boost, (more informal) plug **3** an organization promoting equal opportunities ► champion, further, advance, sponsor, encourage, stimulate, foster, nurture, boost

promotion NOUN **1** He is hoping for a promotion next year. ► advancement, upgrading, elevation, preferment, rise **2** the promotion of her new film ► marketing, publicity, advertising, backing, selling, pushing, (more informal) plugging

p

prompt ADJECTIVE **1** without delay • *a prompt reply* **2** punctual
▷ **promptly** ADVERB **promptness** NOUN **promptitude** NOUN

prompt VERB **prompts, prompting, prompted 1** cause or encourage a person to do something **2** remind an actor or speaker of words when he or she has forgotten them
▷ **prompter** NOUN

prone ADJECTIVE
be prone to be likely to do or suffer from something • *He is prone to jealousy*

prong NOUN **prongs** one of the spikes on a fork
▷ **pronged** ADJECTIVE

pronoun NOUN **pronouns** a word used instead of a noun. **Demonstrative pronouns** are *this, that, these, those*; **interrogative pronouns** are *who?, what?, which?*, etc.; **personal pronouns** are *I, me, we, us, thou, thee, you, ye, he, him, she, her, it, they, them*; **possessive pronouns** are *mine, yours, theirs*, etc.; **reflexive pronouns** are *myself, yourself*, etc.; **relative pronouns** are *who, what, which, that*

pronounce VERB **pronounces, pronouncing, pronounced 1** say a sound or word in a particular way • *"Two" and "too" are pronounced* the same. **2** declare something formally • *I now pronounce you man and wife.*

pronounced ADJECTIVE noticeable • *This street has a pronounced slope.*

pronunciation NOUN **pronunciations** the way a word is pronounced
USAGE Note the spelling; this word should not be written or spoken as 'pronounciation'.

proof NOUN **proofs 1** a fact or thing that shows something is true **2** a printed copy of a book or photograph etc. made for checking before other copies are printed

proof ADJECTIVE able to resist something or not be penetrated • *a bulletproof jacket*

prop[1] NOUN **props** a support, especially one made of a long piece of wood or metal

prop VERB **props, propping, propped** support something by leaning it against something else

prop[2] NOUN **props** an object or piece of furniture used on a theatre stage or in a film

propaganda NOUN biased or misleading publicity intended to make people believe something

propel VERB **propels, propelling, propelled** push something forward

---

Thesaurus

---

prompt ADJECTIVE *We hope for a prompt response.* ► quick, swift, rapid, speedy, early, punctual, immediate, expeditious OPPOSITES ARE late, slow

prompt VERB **1** *We are not sure what prompted such an angry outburst.* ► cause, give rise to, bring about, occasion, lead to, produce, bring on, precipitate, trigger, spark off OPPOSITES ARE deter, prevent **2** *A noise prompted her to turn around.* ► cause, lead, induce, stimulate, prod, provoke AN OPPOSITE IS discourage (from) **3** *He forgot what to say and his wife had to prompt him.* ► remind, cue, prod, jog the memory

prone ADJECTIVE **1** *A man was lying prone on the floor* ► face down, on your front, prostrate AN OPPOSITE IS upright **2** *People here are prone to exaggerate.* ► apt, inclined, susceptible, predisposed, disposed, given, liable OPPOSITES ARE resistant, immune

prong NOUN *the prong of a fork* ► point, spike, spur, tine

pronounce VERB **1** *The name is difficult to pronounce.* ► say, enunciate, articulate, sound, speak, utter, get your tongue round **2** *The doctor pronounced me well.* ► declare, proclaim, judge, announce, affirm, assert USAGE If you use *affirm* or *assert* you say *The doctor affirmed or asserted that I was well.*

pronunciation NOUN *The key to pronunciation of long words is often the stress.* ► enunciation, articulation, intonation, accent, diction, elocution, inflection

proof NOUN *If there is a problem, return the goods with proof of purchase.* ► evidence, confirmation, verification, authentication, certification, corroboration, demonstration

prop NOUN **1** *The bridge is supported by steel props.* ► post, strut, upright, support, buttress, bolster **2** *She had become the family's emotional prop.* ► support, mainstay, pillar, anchor, backbone

prop VERB *He propped his bike against the wall.* ► lean, rest, stand

prop up *The old tree was propped up with posts.* ► support, hold up, brace, strengthen, reinforce, shore up, buttress

propagate VERB **1** *They were accused of propagating false reports.* ► spread, transmit, disseminate, pass on, communicate, put about, circulate, proliferate **2** *The plants are propagated in large greenhouses.* ► breed, grow, cultivate, generate **3** *Wild flowers thrive and propagate.* ► reproduce, multiply, proliferate, procreate

propel VERB **1** *He propelled the ball high into the air.* ► throw, toss, fling, hurl, pitch, launch, shoot, kick, punt **2** *The little craft was propelled by a small outboard motor.* ► drive, move, power, impel, set in motion, push

A B C D E F G H I J K L M N O P Q R S T U V W X Y Z

propeller NOUN propellers a device with blades that spin round to drive an aircraft or ship

proper ADJECTIVE **1** suitable or right • *the proper way to hold a bat* **2** respectable • *prim and proper* **3** (*informal*) complete or thorough • *You're a proper nuisance!*
▷ **properly** ADVERB

proper fraction NOUN proper fractions a fraction that is less than 1, with the numerator less than the denominator, e.g., $\frac{1}{2}$

proper noun NOUN proper nouns the name of an individual person or thing, e.g., *Mary, St. Louis, Spain*, usually written with a capital first letter

property NOUN properties **1** a thing or things that belong to somebody **2** a building or someone's land **3** a quality or characteristic • *It has the property of becoming soft when heated.*

prophecy NOUN prophecies **1** a statement that prophesies something **2** the action of prophesying

prophesy VERB prophesies, prophesying, prophesied say what will happen in the future; foretell

prophet NOUN prophets **1** a person who makes prophecies **2** a religious teacher who is believed to be inspired by God
▷ **prophetess** NOUN **prophetic** ADJECTIVE
the Prophet Muhammad, who founded the Muslim faith

proportion NOUN proportions **1** a part or share of a whole thing **2** a ratio **3** the correct relationship in size, amount, or importance between two things • *You've drawn his head out of proportion.*
▷ **proportional** ADJECTIVE **proportionally** ADVERB **proportionate** ADJECTIVE
proportions PLURAL NOUN size • *a ship of large proportions*

proportional representation NOUN a system in which each political party has a number of legislators in proportion to the number of votes for all its candidates

proposal NOUN proposals **1** something that is proposed; a formal suggestion **2** an offer of marriage

propose VERB proposes, proposing, proposed **1** suggest an idea or plan, etc. **2** plan or intend to do something **3** ask a person to marry you

proposition NOUN propositions **1** a suggestion or offer **2** a statement **3** (*informal*) an undertaking or problem • *a difficult proposition*

proprietor NOUN proprietors the owner of a shop or business
▷ **proprietress** NOUN

prosaic ADJECTIVE plain or dull and ordinary
▷ **prosaically** ADVERB

prose NOUN writing or speech that is not in verse

prosecute VERB prosecutes, prosecuting, prosecuted **1** make someone go to a court of

a b c d e f g h i j k l m n o **p** q r s t u v w x y z

Thesaurus

proper ADJECTIVE **1** *It was about time he found a proper job.* ► real, genuine, bona fide **2** *She doesn't think it proper that the children all share a room.* ► right, correct, decent, respectable, decorous **3** *You have to apply through the proper channels.* ► correct, right, appropriate, official, established, usual **4** (*informal*) *He felt a proper fool.* ► complete, utter, perfect, absolute, positive

property NOUN **1** *He left all his property to his nephew.* ► possessions, belongings, assets, worldly goods, wealth, valuables, chattels, effects, fortune **2** *people looking for property to buy abroad* ► buildings, premises, houses, estate **3** *the medicinal properties of garlic* ► quality, attribute, characteristic, power, peculiarity, trait, feature

prophet NOUN *an Old Testament prophet* ► seer, soothsayer, clairvoyant, oracle, forecaster, fortune teller

proportion NOUN **1** *the proportion of girls to boys in a class* ► ratio, balance, relationship, distribution **2** *A large proportion of the country is forested.* ► part, portion, amount, quantity, percentage, section, share, piece, quota

proportions *a building of huge proportions* ► dimensions, measurements, size, magnitude

proposal NOUN *There is a proposal to build a ring road.* ► plan, scheme, proposition, suggestion, project, bid, motion, offer, recommendation

propose VERB **1** *Charles proposed Greece for their next holiday.* ► suggest, put forward, recommend, offer, come up with, submit, ask for, present AN OPPOSITE IS withdraw **2** *How do you propose to find the money?* ► plan, intend, mean, aim, have in mind **3** *Six candidates have been proposed for election.* ► nominate, put up

proposition NOUN **1** *They discussed the proposition that war was inevitable.* ► theory, hypothesis, premiss, notion, idea **2** *a business proposition* ► proposal, plan, scheme, suggestion, project

prosecute VERB *The police are going to prosecute him for dangerous driving.* ► charge, prefer charges against, institute legal proceedings against, bring to trial, take legal proceedings against, indict

law to be tried for a crime **2** continue with something; pursue • *prosecuting their trade*
▷ **prosecution** NOUN **prosecutor** NOUN

prospect NOUN prospects **1** a possibility or expectation of something • *There is no prospect of success.* **2** a wide view

prospect (pro- spekt) VERB prospects, prospecting, prospected explore in search of gold or some other mineral
▷ **prospector** NOUN

prospective ADJECTIVE expected to be or to happen; possible • *prospective customers*

prospectus NOUN prospectuses a booklet describing and advertising a school, business company, etc.

prosperous ADJECTIVE successful or rich
▷ **prosperity** NOUN

prostitute NOUN prostitutes a person who takes part in sexual acts for payment
▷ **prostitution** NOUN

protect VERB protects, protecting, protected keep safe from harm or injury
▷ **protection** NOUN **protective** ADJECTIVE **protector** NOUN

protein NOUN proteins a substance that is found in all living things and is an essential part of the food of animals

protest (proh- test) NOUN protests a statement or action showing that you disapprove of something

protest (pro- test) VERB protests, protesting, protested **1** make a protest **2** declare firmly • *They protested their innocence.*
▷ **protestation** NOUN

Protestant NOUN Protestants a member of any of the western Christian Churches that are separate from the Roman Catholic Church

proton NOUN protons a particle of matter with a positive electric charge

prototype NOUN prototypes the first model of something, from which others are copied or developed

protractor NOUN protractors a device for measuring angles, usually a semicircle marked off in degrees

protrude VERB protrudes, protruding, protruded stick out from a surface

proud ADJECTIVE **1** very pleased with yourself or with someone else who has done well • *We are all so proud of you.* **2** causing pride • *This is a proud moment for us.* **3** full of self-respect and independence • *They were too proud to ask for help.* **4** having too high an opinion of yourself

Thesaurus

prospect NOUN **1** *She went to India with every prospect of a long stay.* ► chance, expectation, likelihood, possibility, probability, promise, hope **2** *There is a magnificent prospect from the penthouse apartment.* ► view, vista, outlook, panorama, landscape, perspective, scene, sight, spectacle **3** prospects *His job prospects were looking good.* ► future, potential, outlook, possibilities, hopes

prosper VERB *The market in cell phones continues to prosper.* ► thrive, do well, flourish, boom, blossom, expand, succeed, progress, make progress

prosperity NOUN *The future prosperity of inner cities depends on how safe they are to live in.* ► success, welfare, wealth, affluence, growth, plenty, profitability

prosperous ADJECTIVE *She took out a dress she had bought in more prosperous times.* ► thriving, prospering, flourishing, affluent, well-off, well-to-do, wealthy, fortunate, successful, booming, buoyant, profitable, rich AN OPPOSITE IS unsuccessful

protect VERB **1** *The men were anxious to protect their women and children. The city fought a war to protect its democracy.* ► defend, safeguard, keep safe, preserve, secure, shield, guard, save **2** *An armed guard protected the convoy.* ► escort, guard, accompany, defend, cover, shield

protection NOUN **1** *They looked for some form of protection from the wind and rain.* ► shelter,

refuge, security, shield **2** *Military strength would be no protection against terrorist activities of that sort.* ► barrier, buffer, screen, bulwark, security, insurance

protective ADJECTIVE **1** *protective clothing* ► protecting, insulating, shielding, sheltering, defensive **2** *Her parents had always been protective towards her.* ► caring, solicitous, watchful, vigilant, jealous, defensive, possessive

protest NOUN (with the stress on pro-) **1** *The violence shown in the program caused a wave of protests.* ► complaint, objection, outcry, protestation, remonstrance, cry of disapproval **2** *There will be a large protest in the town square.* ► demonstration, rally, march, sit-in, (more informal) demo

protest VERB (with the stress on -test) **1** *People protested against the export of animals.* ► demonstrate, object, make a protest, remonstrate, express disapproval (of) **2** *The neighbors protested that the music was too loud.* ► complain, object, grumble, expostulate, fulminate, argue, take exception **3** *He continued to protest his innocence.* ► maintain, insist on, claim, profess, proclaim, assert, contend

proud ADJECTIVE **1** *He's too proud to admit his mistake.* ► conceited, arrogant, vain, big-headed, self-important, full of yourself, presumptuous, boastful OPPOSITES ARE

▷ **proudly** ADVERB
[via Old English from old French *prud* = brave]

prove VERB proves, proving, proved **1** show that something is true **2** turn out • *The forecast proved to be correct.*
▷ **provable** ADJECTIVE

proverb NOUN proverbs a short well-known saying that states a truth, e.g., "Many hands make light work"

proverbial ADJECTIVE **1** referred to in a proverb **2** well known

provide VERB provides, providing, provided **1** make something available; supply **2** prepare for something • *Try to provide for emergencies.*
▷ **provider** NOUN

provided CONJUNCTION on condition • *You can stay provided that you help.*

providing CONJUNCTION provided

province NOUN provinces **1** a section of a country **2** the area of a person's special knowledge or responsibility • *I'm afraid carpentry is not my province.*
▷ **provincial** ADJECTIVE

the provinces the parts of a country outside its capital city

provision NOUN provisions **1** providing something **2** a statement in a document • *the provisions of the treaty*

provisional ADJECTIVE arranged or agreed upon temporarily but possibly to be altered later
▷ **provisionally** ADVERB

provisions PLURAL NOUN supplies of food and drink

provoke VERB provokes, provoking, provoked **1** make a person angry **2** cause or give rise to something • *The joke provoked laughter.*
▷ **provocation** NOUN **provocative** ADJECTIVE

prow NOUN prows the front end of a ship

prowl VERB prowls, prowling, prowled move about quietly or cautiously, like a hunter
▷ **prowl** NOUN **prowler** NOUN

proxy NOUN proxies a person authorized to represent or act for another person • *I will be abroad, so I have arranged to vote by proxy.*

prude NOUN prudes a person who is easily shocked
▷ **prudish** ADJECTIVE **prudery** NOUN

prudent ADJECTIVE careful, not rash or reckless
▷ **prudently** ADVERB **prudence** NOUN **prudential** ADJECTIVE

prune[1] NOUN prunes a dried plum

Thesaurus

modest, unassuming, humble **2** *They are a proud people.* ► noble, dignified, honorable, self-respecting **3** proud of *Anna was so proud of her garden.* ► pleased with, delighted with, thrilled with, satisfied with, happy about, glad about, gratified at, fond of AN OPPOSITE IS ashamed of

prove VERB **1** *The new evidence proves your innocence.* ► confirm, corroborate, demonstrate, establish, substantiate, attest, authenticate, bear out, show to be true, verify AN OPPOSITE IS disprove **2** *The story proved to be true.* ► turn out, happen, be found

proverb NOUN *the old proverb about too many cooks* ► saying, maxim, adage, dictum, byword, catchphrase

provide VERB **1** *The hotel can provide a picnic.* ► supply, furnish, serve, produce, present, contribute, bear out, arrange for **2** provide for *He now made enough money to provide for his family.* ► support, maintain, feed, keep, sustain, provide food for **3** provide for *The agreement provides for arbitration in the case of disputes.* ► allow for, make provision for, stipulate, specify, require, call for, arrange for

provincial ADJECTIVE **1** *the provincial government* ► local, regional, district, territorial **2** *the provincial attitudes of the middle classes* ► unsophisticated, insular, parochial,

suburban, small-town, narrow-minded, dreary, dull

provisional ADJECTIVE *The provisional total is over a million dollars.* ► interim, temporary, tentative, conditional, stopgap OPPOSITES ARE definite, permanent

provisions PLURAL NOUN ► supplies, food and drink, foodstuff, stores, subsistence, rations, groceries, requirements

provocation NOUN *He refused to react despite extreme provocation.* (informal) ► annoyance, goading, aggravation, irritation, harassment, taunting, incitement, inducement, grounds, justification, motivation

provoke VERB **1** *Plans for a new ring road have provoked a lot of interest.* ► arouse, rouse, prompt, cause, kindle, instigate, spark off, stimulate, stir up, (more informal) whip up AN OPPOSITE IS allay **2** *She was provoked into making comments that she later regretted.* ► goad, spur, prick, sting **3** *Better not to provoke him while he's in a good mood.* ► annoy, irritate, anger, incense, offend, tease, taunt

prudent ADJECTIVE **1** *It's not always prudent to speak to strangers.* ► wise, advisable, sensible, shrewd AN OPPOSITE IS unwise **2** *a prudent attitude to money* ► cautious, careful, shrewd, far-sighted, thoughtful, wary

a b c d e f g h i j k l m n o p q r s t u v w x y z

prune ➡ puddle

prune[2] VERB **prunes, pruning, pruned** cut off unwanted parts of a tree or bush

pry VERB **pries, prying, pried** look into or ask about someone else's private business

P.S. ABBREVIATION postscript

psalm (sahm) NOUN **psalms** a religious song, especially one from the Book of Psalms in the Bible
▷ **psalmist** NOUN

pseudonym NOUN **pseudonyms** a false name used by an author

psychiatrist (sy- ky- a- trist) NOUN **psychiatrists** a doctor who treats mental illnesses
▷ **psychiatry** NOUN **psychiatric** ADJECTIVE

psychic (sy- kik) ADJECTIVE **1** supernatural **2** having supernatural powers, especially being able to predict the future **3** to do with the mind or soul
▷ **psychical** ADJECTIVE

psychoanalysis NOUN investigation of a person's mental processes, especially in the treatment of mental illness
▷ **psychoanalyst** NOUN

psychology NOUN the study of the mind and how it works
▷ **psychological** ADJECTIVE **psychologist** NOUN

PT ABBREVIATION physical training

pterodactyl (te- ro- dak- til) NOUN **pterodactyls** an extinct flying reptile

pub NOUN **pubs** a building licensed to serve alcoholic drinks to the public

puberty (pew- ber- tee) NOUN the time when a young person is developing physically into an adult

public ADJECTIVE belonging to or known by everyone, not private
▷ **publicly** ADVERB

public NOUN people in general
in public openly, not in private

publication NOUN **publications** **1** publishing **2** a published book or newspaper, etc.

public house NOUN **public houses** (formal) a pub

publicity NOUN public attention; doing things (e.g. advertising) to draw people's attention to something

public school NOUN **public schools** a school run by a local authority or by the state

publish VERB **publishes, publishing, published 1** have something printed and sold to the public **2** announce something in public
▷ **publisher** NOUN

pucker VERB **puckers, puckering, puckered** wrinkle

pudding NOUN **puddings** **1** a cooked sweet food eaten at the end of a meal

puddle NOUN **puddles** a shallow patch of liquid, especially of rainwater on a road

Thesaurus

pry VERB *I didn't mean to pry, I was just curious.*
▶ delve, interfere, meddle, poke about, nose about, ferret about, be inquisitive, snoop, (informal) stick your nose in

psychic ADJECTIVE *She seemed to have psychic powers and knew exactly what would happen.*
▶ clairvoyant, telepathic, extrasensory, supernatural, mystic, occult, psychical

psychological ADJECTIVE *The effects are mostly psychological.* ▶ mental, subconscious, emotional, subjective, irrational AN OPPOSITE IS physical

public ADJECTIVE **1** *public gardens* ▶ communal, open, free, community, unrestricted AN OPPOSITE IS private **2** *a public figure* ▶ prominent, well known, celebrated, leading, eminent, important, distinguished, notable, famous OPPOSITES ARE unknown, obscure **3** *This is all public knowledge by now.* ▶ general, common, recognized, widely known, open

public NOUN *houses open to the public* ▶ people, the populace, the community, the country, the nation, citizens

publication NOUN **1** *Publication of the report will be in July.* ▶ issuing, appearance,

publishing, printing, production, dissemination **2** *a list of the latest publications* ▶ book, volume, title, work, tome, opus, newspaper, magazine

publicity NOUN **1** *The film was launched in a blaze of publicity.* ▶ attention, media attention, public interest, exposure **2** *Publicity will include television advertising.* ▶ promotion, marketing, advertising, (more informal) hype

publicize VERB *The event is being publicized weeks in advance.* ▶ advertise, make known, announce, report, (more informal) plug OPPOSITES ARE suppress, conceal

publish VERB **1** *A sequel to the story was published last year.* ▶ issue, bring out, produce, print **2** *The letters should be published as soon as possible.* ▶ make public, make known, publicize, disseminate, put out, make available

pucker VERB *She felt her lips pucker and her eyes grow moist.* ▶ wrinkle, screw up, crease, purse, tighten, compress

pudding NOUN *When Steve arrived the others were starting their pudding.* ▶ dessert

puddle NOUN *He woke up to find a puddle of water on his sleeping bag.* ▶ pool, splash, spill

puff NOUN puffs **1** a short blowing of breath, wind, or smoke etc. **2** a soft pad for putting powder on the skin **3** a cake of very light pastry filled with cream

puff VERB puffs, puffing, puffed **1** blow out puffs of smoke etc. **2** breathe with difficulty; pant **3** inflate or swell something ● *He puffed out his chest.*

puffy ADJECTIVE puffed out; swollen
▷ **puffiness** NOUN

pugnacious ADJECTIVE wanting to fight; aggressive
▷ **pugnaciously** ADVERB **pugnacity** NOUN

puke VERB pukes, puking, puked (*informal*) vomit

pull VERB pulls, pulling, pulled **1** make a thing come towards or after you by using force on it **2** move by a driving force ● *The car pulled out into the road.*
▷ **pull** NOUN
pull a face make a strange face
pull in 1 (said about a vehicle) move to the side of the road and stop **2** (said about a train) come to a station and stop
pull somebody's leg tease him or her
pull off achieve something
pull through recover from an illness
pull up (said about a vehicle) stop abruptly
pull yourself together become calm or sensible

pulley NOUN pulleys a wheel with a rope, chain, or belt over it, used for lifting or moving heavy things

pullover NOUN pullovers a knitted piece of clothing for the top half of the body

pulp NOUN **1** the soft moist part of fruit **2** any soft moist mass
▷ **pulpy** ADJECTIVE

pulpit NOUN pulpits a small enclosed platform for the preacher in a church or chapel

pulsate VERB pulsates, pulsating, pulsated expand and contract rhythmically; vibrate
▷ **pulsation** NOUN

pulse[1] NOUN pulses **1** the rhythmical movement of the arteries as blood is pumped through them by the beating of the heart ● *The pulse can be felt in a person's wrists.* **2** a throb

pulse VERB pulses, pulsing, pulsed throb or pulsate

pulse[2] NOUN pulses the edible seed of peas, beans, lentils, etc.

pulverize VERB pulverizes, pulverizing, pulverized crush something into powder
▷ **pulverization** NOUN

puma NOUN pumas a large brown animal of western America; a mountain lion [via Spanish from Quechua (a South American language)]

pump[1] NOUN pumps a device that pushes air or liquid into or out of something, or along pipes

Thesaurus

puff NOUN **1** *a puff of wind* ► gust, blast, breath, rush, draught, flurry **2** *a puff of grey smoke* ► cloud, whiff

puff VERB *He was puffing when he reached the top of the stairs.* ► gasp, pant, wheeze, breathe heavily, blow
puff out *The curtains puffed out in the draught.* ► swell, distend, become inflated, billow, rise

puke VERB *She had eaten something that upset her and went off to puke.* ► vomit, be sick, retch, heave, (*informal*) throw up

pull VERB **1** *She pulled another chair to where she was sitting.* ► drag, draw, tug, heave, (*more informal*) yank **2** *Cars were pulling trailers and caravans.* ► tow, haul, lug, drag, trail **3** *The match will pull huge crowds.* ► attract, draw, bring in, entice, allure, tempt **4** *He had pulled a muscle and was forced to withdraw.* ► strain, sprain, wrench, dislocate **5** *A dentist might need to pull the tooth.* ► extract, take out, remove, pull out
pull apart *Only pull the machine apart if you know how to put it together again.* ► dismantle, take apart, take to pieces, dismember, separate
pull down *A row of houses will be pulled down to*

make space for the new complex. ► demolish, knock down, tear down, bulldoze, dismantle
pull someone's leg *They stopped pulling his leg when they realized he was upset.* ► tease, rag, make fun of, play tricks on
pull off *The gang have pulled off another bank robbery.* ► achieve, accomplish, manage, carry out, bring off, succeed in
pull out *The army will pull out by the end of the year.* ► withdraw, retreat, leave, depart, quit, move out
pull through *She is likely to pull through despite severe injuries.* ► recover, get better, improve, come through, recuperate
pull together *Everyone has to pull together if we are going to succeed.* ► cooperate, work together, work as a team, collaborate

pull NOUN **1** *He gave the handle a pull.* ► tug, jerk, heave, (*more informal*) yank **2** *The beauty of the place exerted quite a pull.* ► attraction, lure, draw, influence, enticement

pulp NOUN *a fruit with a juicy pulp* ► flesh, mash, mush, paste, pap

pulse NOUN *The music lacked a regular pulse.* ► beat, rhythm, throb, oscillation, vibration

pump ➡ pure

A
B
C
D
E
F
G
H
I
J
K
L
M
N
O
P
Q
R
S
T
U
V
W
X
Y
Z

pump VERB pumps, pumping, pumped **1** move air or liquid with a pump **2** (*informal*) question a person to obtain information
pump up inflate

pump² NOUN pumps a woman's dress shoe

pumpkin NOUN pumpkins a very large round fruit with a hard orange skin [from Greek *pepon*, a kind of large melon]

pun NOUN puns a joking use of a word sounding the same as another, e.g. "Deciding where to bury him was a *grave* decision."

punch VERB punches, punching, punched **1** hit someone with your fist **2** make a hole in something

punch¹ NOUN punches **1** a hit with a fist **2** a device for making holes in paper, metal, leather, etc. **3** vigor

punch² NOUN a drink made by mixing wine or spirits and fruit juice in a bowl

punch line NOUN punch lines words that give the climax of a joke or story

punctual ADJECTIVE doing things exactly at the time arranged; not late
▷ **punctually** ADVERB **punctuality** NOUN

punctuate VERB punctuates, punctuating, punctuated **1** put punctuation marks into something **2** put something in at intervals
● *His speech was punctuated with cheers.*

punctuation NOUN marks such as commas, full stops, and brackets put into a piece of writing to make it easier to read

puncture NOUN punctures a small hole made by something sharp, especially in a tire

puncture VERB punctures, puncturing, punctured make a puncture in something

pungent (pun- jent) ADJECTIVE **1** having a strong taste or smell **2** (said about remarks) sharp
▷ **pungently** ADVERB **pungency** NOUN

punish VERB punishes, punishing, punished make a person suffer because he or she has done something wrong
▷ **punishable** ADJECTIVE **punishment** NOUN

punk NOUN punks **1** (also punk rock) a loud aggressive style of rock music **2** a person who likes this music

punt NOUN punts a flat-bottomed boat, usually moved by pushing a pole against the bottom of a river while standing in the punt

punt¹ VERB punts, punting, punted move a punt with a pole

punt² VERB punts, punting, punted kick a football after dropping it from your hands and before it touches the ground

pupa (pew- pa) NOUN pupae a chrysalis

pupil NOUN pupils **1** someone who is being taught by a teacher, especially at school **2** the opening in the centre of the eye

puppet NOUN puppets **1** a kind of doll that can be made to move by fitting it over your hand or working it by strings or wires **2** a person whose actions are controlled by someone else
▷ **puppetry** NOUN

puppy NOUN puppies a young dog

purchase VERB purchases, purchasing, purchased buy
▷ **purchaser** NOUN

purchase NOUN purchases **1** something bought **2** buying **3** a firm hold or grip

pure ADJECTIVE **1** not mixed with anything else
● *pure olive oil* **2** clean or clear ● *pure spring*

Thesaurus

pump VERB *The crew rushed to pump the water out of the boat.* ► drain, draw off, empty, force, drive, raise, siphon
pump up *We'd better pump up the tires.*
► inflate, blow up, fill

pun NOUN ► double meaning, wordplay, play on words

punch VERB **1** *Ken punched him in the stomach.* ► hit , strike, bash, thump, box, sock, clout, jab, poke, prod, beat, cuff, slog **2** *He punched a hole in the wall.* ► pierce, puncture, perforate

punch NOUN *a punch on the nose* ► blow, bash, thump, box, poke

punctual ADJECTIVE *We're expected to be punctual.* ► on time, prompt, in good time, (*more informal*) on the dot OPPOSITES ARE unpunctual, late

puncture NOUN *Her bike had a puncture on the way home.* ► flat tire, burst tire, (*more informal*) flat

puncture VERB *Vandals had punctured her tires.* ► make a hole in, pierce, rupture, let down, deflate

punish VERB *The culprits would be punished.* ► penalize, discipline, correct, chastise, scold, make an example of

punishment NOUN *The punishment has to be reasonable.* ► penalty, discipline, correction, chastisement RELATED ADJECTIVE ► penal

puny ADJECTIVE *He looked small and puny for his age.* ► weak, feeble, frail, sickly, undersized, undernourished, stunted OPPOSITES ARE sturdy, strong

pupil NOUN *She is an able pupil.* ► student, scholar, schoolgirl or schoolboy, learner

pure ADJECTIVE **1** *pure gold* ► unalloyed, unmixed, genuine, natural OPPOSITES ARE impure, adulterated **2** *places where the air is pure* ► clean, fresh, clear, untainted,

524

water **3** free from evil or sin **4** mere; nothing but • *pure nonsense*
▷ **purely** ADVERB **pureness** NOUN **purity** NOUN

purée (pewr- ay) NOUN **purées** fruit or vegetables made into pulp

purge VERB **purges, purging, purged** get rid of unwanted people or things
▷ **purge** NOUN

purify VERB **purifies, purifying, purified** make a thing pure
▷ **purification** NOUN **purifier** NOUN

Puritan NOUN **Puritans** a Protestant in the 16th and 17th centuries who wanted simpler religious ceremonies and strictly moral behavior

purple NOUN a deep reddish-blue color

purpose NOUN **purposes 1** what you intend to do; a plan or aim **2** determination • *walk with purpose*
▷ **purposeful** ADJECTIVE **purposefully** ADVERB
on purpose by intention, not by accident

purr VERB **purrs, purring, purred** make the low murmuring sound that a cat does when it is happy
▷ **purr** NOUN

purse NOUN **purses** a small pouch for carrying money

purse VERB **purses, pursing, pursed**
purse your lips draw them tightly together because you are annoyed or frustrated

pursue VERB **pursues, pursuing, pursued**
1 chase someone in order to catch them
2 continue with something; work at • *We are pursuing our inquiries.*
▷ **pursuer** NOUN

pursuit NOUN **pursuits 1** pursuing **2** a regular activity

pus NOUN a thick yellowish substance produced in inflamed or infected tissue, e.g., in an abscess or boil

push VERB **pushes, pushing, pushed 1** make a thing go away from you by using force on it
2 move yourself by using force • *He pushed in front of me.* **3** try to force someone to do or use something; urge
push off (*informal*) go away

push NOUN **pushes** a pushing movement or effort
at a push if necessary but only with difficulty
get the push (*informal*) be dismissed from a job

pushchair NOUN **pushchairs** a folding chair on wheels, for pushing a young child along

---

Thesaurus

---

unpolluted, uncontaminated OPPOSITES ARE impure, polluted **3** *a pure mind* ► virtuous, moral, chaste, good, innocent, righteous, blameless OPPOSITES ARE immoral, dirty

purely ADVERB *The lights are purely for show.*
► simply, only, solely, entirely, totally, completely, exclusively

purity NOUN **1** *The purity of the water*
► cleanliness, clearness, freshness, naturalness, wholesomeness **2** *the purity of their thoughts*
► virtue, morality, goodness, rightness, uprightness, integrity, honesty

purpose NOUN **1** *They made their purpose clear.*
► intention, motive, justification **2** *I can't see any purpose in doing that.* ► point, advantage, benefit, gain **3** *Their actions show a lot of purpose.* ► determination, resolution, resolve, single-mindedness, tenacity, enthusiasm
on purpose *He says it was an accident but I'm sure he did it on purpose.* ► deliberately, intentionally, purposely, consciously, knowingly

purse NOUN **1** *Keep your foreign money in a separate purse.* ► pouch, wallet, money bag, bag **2** *activities that are paid for out of the public purse* ► fund *or* funds, resources, money, kitty, finances, resources

pursue VERB **1** *I pursued a fox to the end of the lane.* ► chase, go after, run after, follow, track **2** *It was an ambitious objective to pursue.* ► strive for, work towards, aim at, aspire to **3** *She is*

determined to pursue a career in politics.
► follow, undertake, take up, engage in **4** *He pursues a number of interests in his spare time.*
► carry on, maintain, follow, continue, devote yourself to

pursuit NOUN **1** *Police gave up the pursuit when they lost the trail in Houston.* ► chase, hunt, search, tracking **2** *The family enjoy their outdoor pursuits.* ► activity, pastime, diversion, amusement **3** *the pursuit of knowledge*
► search (for), quest (for), striving (for), aim, goal, objective

push VERB **1** *She pushed a chair against the door.*
► shove, thrust, press, propel, nudge AN OPPOSITE IS pull **2** *I pushed a few things into a bag.* ► pack, cram, squash, squeeze, jam, ram, crush, put, insert **3** *He tried to push his way through the crowd.* ► force, thrust, shove, elbow, jostle, shoulder, prod, press **4** *Better not to push them to come if they don't want to.*
► press, pressure, pressurize, put pressure on, urge, persuade, cajole, browbeat, coerce, bully, compel, (*more informal*) lean on **5** *Each software company wants to push its own product.*
► promote, publicize, advertise, popularize, make known, market, (*more informal*) plug
push around *He was fed up with being pushed around.* ► bully, domineer, boss about *or* around, trample on, mistreat
push for *Trade unions are pushing for the repeal*

a
b
c
d
e
f
g
h
i
j
k
l
m
n
o
p
q
r
s
t
u
v
w
x
y
z

pusher NOUN pushers a person who sells illegal drugs

pushy ADJECTIVE unpleasantly self-confident and eager to do things

puss NOUN (informal) a cat

put VERB puts, putting, put 1 move a person or thing to a place or position • Put the lamp on the table. 2 make a person or thing do or experience something or be in a certain condition • Put the light on. • The news put me in a good mood. 3 express in words • She put it tactfully.

be hard put have difficulty in doing something

put off 1 postpone 2 dissuade 3 stop

someone wanting something • The smell puts me off.

put out 1 stop a fire from burning or a light from shining 2 annoy or inconvenience • Our lateness has put her out.

put up 1 construct or build 2 raise 3 give someone a place to sleep • Can you put me up for the night?

put up with endure or tolerate

putt VERB putts, putting, putted hit a golf ball gently towards the hole
▷ putt NOUN putter NOUN putting green NOUN

putty NOUN a soft paste that sets hard, used for fitting the glass into a window frame

Thesaurus

of some of these laws. ► demand, insist on, press for, urge

push off (informal) She was busy and told us to push off. ► go away, leave, be off, run along, depart, (informal) beat it, (informal) scram

push NOUN 1 She felt a push in her back. ► shove, thrust, prod, nudge, jolt, poke, knock 2 The enemy's push was aimed at reaching the coast. ► advance, thrust, drive, offensive, onslaught, assault

pushy ADJECTIVE He needed to appear in control without seeming too pushy. ► assertive, dominating, dominant, aggressive, forceful, officious

put VERB 1 He put the case on the table. They put a guard on the door. ► place, leave, set, deposit, position, stand, settle, station, post 2 I wanted to say something but I wasn't sure how to put it. ► express, word, phrase, formulate, couch 3 The government will put a tax on it. ► impose, inflict, levy, apply (to), assign (to) 4 They put the cost at over a million. ► estimate, reckon, calculate, assess, evaluate, measure, judge 5 We have some ideas to put to you. ► submit, present, propose, advance, offer, suggest

put across The government needs to put its message across clearly. ► communicate, convey, get across, spell out, make clear, express

put aside We have put aside some money. ► save, set aside, put by, keep, keep in reserve, reserve

put away 1 The judge put him away for life. ► jail, imprison, send to prison, lock up, put behind bars, incarcerate, commit 2 Did you see how much food they put away? ► eat, consume, devour

put back 1 I'll put the book back. ► replace, return 2 The meeting has been put back for a week. ► postpone, defer, delay, hold over AN OPPOSITE IS bring forward

put by She wanted to put something by each week

for emergencies. ► save, set aside, keep, earmark

put down 1 I'd better put down some details. ► write down, record, enter, note down, make a note of 2 The army quickly put down the rebellion. ► suppress, crush, quell, quash, defeat 3 He enjoyed putting people down, especially in public. ► criticize, belittle, disparage, humiliate, mortify 4 You can put it down to laziness. ► attribute, ascribe, blame (on)

put forward Stella put forward a new suggestion. ► advance, offer, propose, suggest, present, submit AN OPPOSITE IS withdraw

put in You have to put in a new ink cartridge ► insert, install, fit OPPOSITES ARE remove, take out

put off 1 The noise put her off. ► deter, discourage, disconcert, unnerve, repel, distract, intimidate AN OPPOSITE IS attract 2 We'd better put off a decision. ► postpone, defer, delay, hold over, shelve, reschedule AN OPPOSITE IS bring forward

put on 1 He put on an air of importance. ► assume, affect, simulate, feign, sham 2 The gallery is putting on a special exhibition. ► mount, organize, stage, produce, present

put out 1 Nina was put out by this criticism. ► offend, annoy, anger, irritate, affront, insult 2 I hope it won't put you out if I stay a few days. ► inconvenience, bother, trouble, impose on 3 The government put out an appeal. ► announce, publish, broadcast, circulate

put up 1 He put up a shed in the garden. ► erect, build, construct, assemble OPPOSITES ARE take down, demolish 2 We can put you up for a few days. ► accommodate, house, lodge, take in, give a bed to, shelter 3 They have put up their prices. ► increase, raise, lift, (more informal) bump up

put up with She is not prepared to put up with such behavior. ► tolerate, stand for, accept, bear, take, endure, stomach

puzzle NOUN puzzles **1** a difficult question or problem **2** a game or toy that sets a problem to solve or a difficult task to complete **3** a jigsaw puzzle

puzzle VERB puzzles, puzzling, puzzled **1** give someone a problem so that they have to think hard **2** think patiently about how to solve something
▷ **puzzlement** NOUN

pygmy (pig- mee) NOUN pygmies **1** a very small person or thing **2** a member of certain unusually short peoples in parts of Africa

pylon NOUN pylons a tall framework made of strips of steel, supporting electric cables [from Greek, = monumental gateway, which a modern pylon resembles in shape]

pyramid NOUN pyramids **1** a structure with a square base and with sloping sides that meet in a point at the top **2** an ancient Egyptian tomb shaped like this
▷ **pyramidal** (pir- am- id- al) ADJECTIVE

python NOUN pythons a large snake that kills its prey by coiling around and crushing it [from the name of a large serpent or monster in Greek legend, killed by Apollo]

Thesaurus

puzzle NOUN *It is a hard puzzle to solve.*
► problem, riddle, question, enigma, paradox

puzzle VERB **1** *Mike's angry response puzzled me.*
► confuse, perplex, baffle, mystify, bewilder, disconcert, confound, fox, (*more informal*) flummox

puzzled ADJECTIVE *Freda had a puzzled look on her face.* ► confused, baffled, perplexed, mystified, bewildered, at a loss, nonplussed, (*more informal*) stumped

puzzling ADJECTIVE *There was something puzzling about the shape of the house.* ► confusing, baffling, bewildering, perplexing, mystifying, mysterious, inexplicable, extraordinary
OPPOSITES ARE straightforward, comprehensible

a
b
c
d
e
f
g
h
i
j
k
l
m
n
o
p
q
r
s
t
u
v
w
x
y
z

A
B
C
D
E
F
G
H
I
J
K
L
M
N
O
P
Q
R
S
T
U
V
W
X
Y
Z

Qq

QED *ABBREVIATION* quod erat demonstrandum (Latin, = which was the thing that had to be proved)

quack[1] *VERB* **quacks, quacking, quacked** make the harsh cry of a duck
▷ **quack** *NOUN*
[imitating the sound]

quack[2] *NOUN* **quacks** a person who falsely claims to have medical skill or have remedies to cure diseases [from Dutch *quacken* = to boast]

quadratic equation *NOUN* **quadratic equations** an equation that involves quantities or variables raised to the power of two, but no higher than two

quadrilateral *NOUN* **quadrilaterals** a flat geometric shape with four sides

quadruped *NOUN* **quadrupeds** an animal with four feet

quagmire (kwog)-mire *NOUN* **quagmires** a bog or marsh

quail *NOUN* **quail** or **quails** a bird related to the partridge

quail *VERB* **quails, quailing, quailed** feel or show fear

quaint *ADJECTIVE* attractively odd or old-fashioned
▷ **quaintly** *ADVERB* **quaintness** *NOUN*

quake *VERB* **quakes, quaking, quaked** tremble; shake with fear

Quaker *NOUN* **Quakers** a member of a religious group called the Society of Friends, founded by George Fox in the 17th century [originally an insult, probably from George Fox's saying that people should "tremble at the name of the Lord"]

qualification *NOUN* **qualifications 1** a skill or ability that makes someone suitable for a job **2** an exam that you have passed or a course of study that you have completed **3** something that qualifies a remark or statement

qualify *VERB* **qualifies, qualifying, qualified 1** make or become able to do something through having certain qualities or training, or by passing an exam **2** make a remark or statement less extreme; limit its meaning **3** (in grammar, said about an adjective) add meaning to a noun

quality *NOUN* **qualities 1** how good or bad something is **2** a characteristic; something that is special in a person or thing

qualm (kwahm) *NOUN* **qualms** a misgiving or scruple

quandary *NOUN* **quandaries** a difficult situation where you are uncertain what to do

quantity *NOUN* **quantities 1** how much there is of something; how many things there are of one sort **2** a large amount

quantum leap or **quantum jump** *NOUN* **quantum leaps** or **quantum jumps** a sudden large increase or advance

quarantine *NOUN* keeping a person or animal isolated in case they have a disease which could spread to others [from Italian *quaranta* = forty (because the original period of isolation was 40 days)]

quarrel *NOUN* **quarrels** an angry disagreement

Thesaurus

---

quaint *ADJECTIVE* *a quaint little shop that served teas* ► charming, picturesque, antiquated, strange, sweet, old-world, (*more informal*) twee

qualification *NOUN* **1** *You need a professional qualification in social work.* ► certificate, diploma, degree, training, skill, competence, eligibility, fitness **2** *He agreed without any qualification.* ► reservation, hesitation, restriction, exception, condition, modification

qualified *ADJECTIVE* **1** *His two sons were both qualified doctors.* ► certified, chartered, skilled, trained, professional, graduate, competent AN OPPOSITE IS unqualified **2** *She could only give the idea qualified approval.* ► limited, modified, conditional, cautious, guarded, reserved, restricted, equivocal, halfhearted OPPOSITES ARE unqualified, unconditional

qualify *VERB* **1** *The course qualifies you to teach young children.* ► authorize, permit, allow, entitle, prepare, equip, fit AN OPPOSITE IS disqualify (from) **2** *I may qualify for a discount.* ► be eligible, be entitled (to), be allowed **3** *He qualified his conclusion with a few reservations.* ► moderate, modify, restrict, mitigate, limit

quality *NOUN* **1** *work of a high quality* ► standard, caliber, class, grade, rank, sort, value, condition, excellence **2** *He has many good qualities.* ► characteristic, feature, attribute, point, aspect, peculiarity, property, trait

quantity *NOUN* *A huge quantity of stolen goods was recovered.* ► amount, number, total, volume, lot, portion, proportion, consignment

quarrel *NOUN* *A quarrel developed in which Kemp was struck over the head.* ► argument, disagreement, altercation, difference of opinion, dispute, squabble, clash, tiff, row OPPOSITES ARE agreement, reconciliation

quarrel VERB quarrels, quarrelling, quarrelled have a quarrel
▷ **quarrelsome** ADJECTIVE

quarry[1] NOUN quarries an open place where stone or slate is dug or cut out of the ground

quarry VERB quarries, quarrying, quarried dig or cut from a quarry

quarry[2] NOUN quarries an animal, etc., being hunted or pursued

quart NOUN quarts two pints, a quarter of a gallon

quarter NOUN quarters **1** each of four equal parts into which a thing is or can be divided **2** three months, one-fourth of a year **3** a district or region • *People came from every quarter.*
at close quarters very close together
give no quarter show no mercy

quarter VERB quarters, quartering, quartered **1** divide something into quarters **2** put soldiers, etc., into lodgings

quarterfinal NOUN quarterfinals each of the matches or rounds before a semifinal, in which there are eight contestants or teams

quarters PLURAL NOUN lodgings

quartet NOUN quartets **1** a group of four musicians **2** a piece of music for four musicians **3** a set of four people or things

quartz NOUN a hard mineral, often in crystal form [via German from a Polish dialect word *kwardy* = hard]

quaver VERB quavers, quavering, quavered tremble or quiver

quaver NOUN quavers **1** a quavering sound

quay (kee) NOUN quays a landing place where ships can be tied up for loading and unloading; a wharf
▷ **quayside** NOUN

queasy ADJECTIVE feeling slightly sick
▷ **queasily** ADVERB **queasiness** NOUN

queen NOUN queens **1** a woman who is the ruler of a country through inheriting the position **2** the wife of a king **3** a female bee or ant that produces eggs **4** an important piece in chess **5** a playing card with a picture of a queen on it
▷ **queenly** ADJECTIVE
[from Old English]

queer ADJECTIVE **1** strange or eccentric **2** slightly ill or faint **3** (*informal*) homosexual
▷ **queerly** ADVERB **queerness** NOUN

queer VERB queers, queering, queered queer a person's pitch spoil his or her chances beforehand
[perhaps from German *quer* = perverse]

quell VERB quells, quelling, quelled **1** crush a rebellion **2** stop yourself from feeling fear, anger, etc.; suppress

quench VERB quenches, quenching, quenched **1** satisfy your thirst by drinking **2** put out a fire or flame

query (kweer- ee) NOUN queries **1** a question **2** a question mark

Thesaurus

quarrel VERB **1** *They were always quarrelling.* ► argue, disagree, row, squabble, bicker, fall out, tiff, fight AN OPPOSITE IS agree **2 quarrel with** *I can't quarrel with your version of what happened.* ► disagree with, find fault with, criticize, oppose

quarrelsome ADJECTIVE *He didn't want to stay with such a quarrelsome family.*
► argumentative, contentious, belligerent, disputatious, aggressive, factious, confrontational, ill-tempered AN OPPOSITE IS peaceable

quarter NOUN **1** *a house in the poor quarter of the city* ► district, locality, neighborhood, vicinity, area, region, part, sector **2** *There was help from an unexpected quarter.* ► source, direction, point, location

quash VERB **1** *The Court of Appeals may quash the sentence.* ► overrule, revoke, rescind, overturn, set aside, cancel, retract, repeal, nullify **2** *The rebellion was brutally quashed. The statement failed to quash rumors.* ► put an end to, stamp out, suppress, crush, quell, subdue, overthrow

quaver VERB *She broke off as her voice began to quaver.* ► tremble, quiver, waver, shake, flutter, vibrate, pulsate

quay NOUN *Overlooking the quay was a small hotel.* ► dock, wharf, pier, harbor, jetty, landing-stage, berth

queasy ADJECTIVE *He had been feeling tired and queasy for the past few days.* ► nauseous, bilious, sick, unwell, poorly, queer, out of sorts

queen NOUN *She knew she would be queen one day.* ► ruler, monarch, sovereign, crowned head RELATED ADJECTIVES ► regal, royal

queer ADJECTIVE **1** *There was something queer going on.* ► odd, strange, unusual, weird, peculiar, funny, curious, bizarre, puzzling, mysterious, remarkable OPPOSITES ARE ordinary, normal **2** *I was feeling a bit queer.* ► sick, unwell, poorly, queasy, out of sorts, nauseous, bilious, faint, dizzy

quell VERB *Troops were sent in to quell the rising.* ► suppress, put an end to, stamp out, crush, quash, subdue, overthrow

query NOUN *Please send a stamped addressed envelope with any queries.* ► question, enquiry, problem, doubt, uncertainty

A
B
C
D
E
F
G
H
I
J
K
L
M
N
O
P
Q
R
S
T
U
V
W
X
Y
Z

query VERB queries, querying, queried question whether something is true or correct [from Latin *quaere* = ask]

quest NOUN quests a long search for something ● *the quest for gold*

question NOUN questions **1** a sentence asking something **2** a problem to be discussed or solved ● *Congress debated the question of education.* **3** doubt ● *Whether we shall win is open to question.*
in question being discussed or disputed ● *His honesty is not in question.*
out of the question impossible

question VERB questions, questioning, questioned **1** ask someone questions **2** say that you are doubtful about something
▷ **questioner** NOUN

questionable ADJECTIVE causing doubt; not certainly true or honest or advisable

question mark NOUN question marks the punctuation mark ? placed after a question

questionnaire NOUN questionnaires a written set of questions asked to provide information for a survey

quibble NOUN quibbles a trivial complaint or objection

quibble VERB quibbles, quibbling, quibbled make trivial complaints or objections

quick ADJECTIVE **1** taking only a short time to do something **2** done in a short time **3** able to notice or learn or think quickly **4** (*old use*) alive ● *the quick and the dead*
▷ **quickly** ADVERB **quickness** NOUN

quicksand NOUN quicksands an area of loose wet deep sand that sucks in anything resting or falling on top of it [from **quick** in the old sense "alive" (because the sand moves as if it were alive and "eats" things)]

quiet ADJECTIVE **1** silent ● *Be quiet!* **2** with little sound; not loud or noisy **3** calm and peaceful; without disturbance ● *a quiet life* **4** (said about colors) not bright
▷ **quietly** ADVERB **quietness** NOUN

Thesaurus

---

query VERB *She had to query the wisdom of such a plan.* ► question, doubt, suspect, have doubts about, have reservations about, feel uneasy about, challenge, dispute AN OPPOSITE IS accept

quest NOUN *a quest to find Iron-Age remains* ► expedition, mission, search, hunt, crusade

question NOUN **1** *You haven't answered the question.* ► enquiry, query, problem AN OPPOSITE IS answer **2** *There is the question of all his debts.* ► issue, matter, business, point, subject, problem **3** *There's some question about who will be in charge.* ► uncertainty, doubt, misgiving, argument, reservation, debate, dispute, controversy, objection
out of the question *Sending them more money was out of the question.* ► impossible, inconceivable, unthinkable, unrealistic, not feasible, impractical, (*more informal*) not on OPPOSITES ARE possible, feasible

question VERB **1** *A man is being questioned at the police station.* ► interrogate, interview, crossexamine, investigate, (*more informal*) quiz, (*more informal*) grill, (*more informal*) pump **2** *She never questioned his right to be there.* ► query, doubt, suspect, have doubts about, have reservations about, feel uneasy about, challenge, dispute

questionable ADJECTIVE *All these arguments are highly questionable.* ► debatable, doubtful, dubious, suspect, unreliable, disputable, uncertain, unclear, unprovable, (*more informal*) iffy, (*more informal*) shady OPPOSITES ARE unquestionable, indisputable, acceptable

quibble VERB *He accepted the offer without quibbling.* ► complain, find fault, carp, cavil, object , equivocate, split hairs, nit-pick

quibble NOUN *Her only quibble was about the cost.* ► objection, complaint, reservation, doubt, query, criticism

quick ADJECTIVE **1** *She gave a quick glance at her watch.* ► hasty, brief, cursory, furtive, fleeting, rapid OPPOSITES ARE long, careful **2** *He was always a quick worker.* ► fast, swift, rapid, speedy, lively, sprightly, prompt AN OPPOSITE IS slow **3** *There is no quick solution to the problem.* ► instant, instantaneous, ready, sudden **4** *Kevin wasn't as quick as some of the others in the class.* ► bright, clever, intelligent, gifted, able, sharp, alert, acute, (*more informal*) on the ball AN OPPOSITE IS dull

quicken VERB **1** *The pace quickened.* ► speed up, accelerate, get *or* go faster, hasten, hurry OPPOSITES ARE slow, slow down **2** *The program quickened their interest in archaeology.* ► arouse, rouse, stimulate, excite, revive, galvanize AN OPPOSITE IS dull

quickly ADVERB **1** *She began to walk more quickly.* ► fast, swiftly, rapidly, speedily AN OPPOSITE IS slowly **2** *We quickly realized they had gone.* ► soon, at once, straight away, right away, rapidly, immediately, instantly, directly, suddenly

quiet ADJECTIVE **1** *The house is in a quiet village near the river.* ► peaceful, tranquil, secluded, isolated, calm, restful, pleasant OPPOSITES ARE noisy, busy **2** *He spoke in a quiet voice.* ► soft, low, muted, muffled OPPOSITES ARE loud, raised **3** *Can we have a quiet word together?* ► private, confidential, secret **4** *Fiona's a*

quiet NOUN quietness

quieten VERB quietens, quietening, quietened make or become quiet

quill NOUN quills **1** a large feather **2** a pen made from a large feather **3** one of the spines on a hedgehog

quilt NOUN quilts a padded bedcover [from Latin *culcita* = mattress or cushion]

quintet NOUN quintets **1** a group of five musicians **2** a piece of music for five musicians

quirk NOUN quirks **1** a peculiarity of a person's behaviour **2** a trick of fate
▷ **quirky** ADJECTIVE

quit VERB quits, quitting, quitted or quit **1** leave or abandon **2** (*informal*) stop doing something
▷ **quitter** NOUN

quite ADVERB **1** completely or entirely • *I am quite all right.* **2** somewhat; to some extent • *She is quite a good swimmer.* **3** really • *It's quite a change.*

quits ADJECTIVE even or equal after retaliating or paying someone back • *I think you and I are quits now.*

quiver[1] NOUN quivers a container for arrows

quiver[2] VERB quivers, quivering, quivered tremble
▷ **quiver** NOUN

quiz NOUN quizzes a series of questions, especially as an entertainment or competition

quiz VERB quizzes, quizzing, quizzed (*informal*) question someone closely

quoit (koit) NOUN quoits a ring thrown at a peg in the game of quoits

quota NOUN quotas **1** a fixed share that must be given or received or done **2** a limited amount

quotation NOUN quotations **1** quoting **2** something quoted **3** a statement of the price of goods or services that can be supplied

quotation marks PLURAL NOUN punctuation marks ("and") used to mark a quotation

quote VERB quotes, quoting, quoted **1** repeat words that were first written or spoken by someone else **2** mention something as proof **3** state the price of goods or services that you can supply

quote NOUN quotes a quotation

quotient (kwoh- shent) NOUN quotients the result of dividing one number by another COMPARE **product** [from Latin *quotiens* = how many times?]

Thesaurus

---

lovely, quiet person. ► shy, reserved, private, subdued, taciturn, withdrawn, calm, placid, serene, composed, untroubled, unruffled AN OPPOSITE IS outgoing **5** *It's hard to keep rumors like that quiet.* ► secret, silent, private, confidential, undisclosed AN OPPOSITE IS public

quieten VERB **1** *The audience quietened when the curtain went up.* ► go quiet, fall silent, grow silent, hush, shush, (*more informal*) shut up **2** *He was so excited it was impossible to quieten him.* ► calm, calm down, pacify, mollify, appease, assuage

quirk NOUN *One of his quirks is that he checks things over and over again.* ► peculiarity, oddity, idiosyncrasy, foible, whim, caprice

quit VERB **1** *She's much too determined to quit now.* ► give up, stop, leave, depart, go, cease **2** (*informal*) *It's time you quit smoking.* ► give up, stop, cease, discontinue, drop, (*more informal*) pack in **3** *He decided to quit his job and go abroad.* ► leave, resign from, retire from, renounce, forsake, abandon

quite ADVERB **1** *The two sisters are quite different in appearance.* ► completely, totally, wholly, entirely, utterly **2** *It was quite late by now.*

► rather, fairly, a bit, somewhat, comparatively, relatively, (*more informal*) pretty

quits ADJECTIVE *After four games we called it quits.* ► level, even, square, equal

quiver VERB *The trees quivered in the wind. I sat quivering with fright.* ► shake, tremble, shudder, shiver, quaver, flutter

quiz NOUN *The day ended with a quiz between the two teams.* ► competition, questionnaire, test, examination, questioning

quiz VERB (*informal*) *The police are quizzing a suspect.* ► question, interrogate, interview, crossexamine, investigate

quotation NOUN **1** *a quotation from Shakespeare* ► citation, quote, reference, excerpt, extract, piece, passage **2** *First we need a quotation for the work.* ► estimate, price, quote, figure, tender

quote VERB **1** *She quoted a few lines from a poem.* ► cite, recite, recall, repeat, mention, refer to **2** *The figure the builder quoted was too high.* ► estimate, offer, tender, bid, specify

a
b
c
d
e
f
g
h
i
j
k
l
m
n
o
p
q
r
s
t
u
v
w
x
y
z

A
B
C
D
E
F
G
H
I
J
K
L
M
N
O
P
Q
R
S
T
U
V
W
X
Y
Z

Rr

rabbi (rab- I) NOUN **rabbis** a Jewish religious leader

rabbit NOUN **rabbits** a furry animal with long ears that digs burrows

rabble NOUN **rabbles** a disorderly crowd or mob

rabid (rab- id) ADJECTIVE **1** fanatical • *a rabid tennis fan* **2** suffering from rabies

rabies (ray- beez) NOUN a fatal disease that affects dogs, cats, etc. and can be passed to humans by the bite of an infected animal

race[1] NOUN **races 1** a competition to be the first to reach a particular place or to do something **2** a strong fast current of water • *the tidal race*

race VERB **races, racing, raced 1** compete in a race **2** move very fast
▷ **racer** NOUN
[from Old Norse]

race[2] NOUN **races** a very large group of people thought to have the same ancestors and with physical characteristics (e.g. color of skin and hair, shape of eyes and nose) that differ from those of other groups
▷ **racial** ADJECTIVE
[via French from Italian *razza*]

racehorse NOUN **racehorses** a horse bred or kept for racing

racetrack NOUN **racetracks** a track for horse or vehicle races

racism (ray- sizm) NOUN **1** belief that a particular race of people is better than others **2** discrimination against or hostility towards people of other races
▷ **racist** NOUN

rack[1] NOUN **racks 1** a framework used as a shelf or container **2** a bar or rail with cogs into which the cogs of a gear or wheel, etc., fit **3** an ancient device for torturing people by stretching them

rack VERB **racks, racking, racked** torment • *He was racked with guilt.*
rack your brains think hard in trying to solve a problem

rack[2] NOUN
go to rack and ruin gradually become worse in condition from neglect
[a different spelling of **wreck**]

racket[1] NOUN **rackets** a bat with strings stretched across a frame, used in tennis, badminton, and squash [from Arabic *rahat* = palm of the hand]

racket[2] NOUN **rackets 1** a loud noise; a din **2** (*informal*)a dishonest or illegal business • *a drugs racket* [perhaps imitating the sound of clattering]

racy ADJECTIVE **racier, raciest** lively and slightly shocking in style • *She gave a racy account of her travels.*

radar NOUN a system or apparatus that uses radio waves to show on a screen, the position of objects that cannot be seen because of darkness, fog, distance, etc.

radiant ADJECTIVE **1** radiating light or heat, etc. **2** radiated • *radiant heat* **3** looking very bright and happy
▷ **radiantly** ADVERB **radiance** NOUN

radiate VERB **radiates, radiating, radiated 1** send out light, heat, or other energy in rays **2** give out a strong feeling or quality • *She*

Thesaurus

---

rabble NOUN *He was met by a rabble of angry, noisy youths.* ► crowd, throng, horde, mob, gang, group, herd, swarm

race NOUN **1** *people of many different races* ► ethnic group, nation, people, clan, tribe RELATED ADJECTIVES ► ethnic, racial **2** *Donald won the race easily.* ► contest, competition, chase, heat, event

race VERB **1** *The children were racing each other in the garden.* ► have a race with, run against, compete with, try to beat **2** *She raced towards the house.* ► dash, rush, shoot, sprint, streak, dart, hare, hasten, hurry, run, tear, zoom, career, fly, gallop, move fast **3** *All kinds of thoughts raced through my mind.* ► rush, dart, fly, shoot, zoom

racial ADJECTIVE *laws against racial discrimination* ► ethnic, national, cultural

racism NOUN *the struggle to end racism in all its forms* ► discrimination, racialism, racial hatred,
intolerance, prejudice, xenophobia, bigotry, chauvinism

racist ADJECTIVE *racist attitudes* ► discriminatory, racialist, intolerant, prejudiced, xenophobic, biased, bigoted, chauvinist OPPOSITES ARE tolerant, unbiased

rack NOUN *a vegetable rack; a luggage rack* ► stand, shelf, support, framework, frame

racket NOUN **1** *The machines make a frightful racket.* ► noise, din, commotion, hubbub, clamor, tumult, rumpus, uproar **2** (*informal*) *He was involved in a stolen car racket.* ► swindle, fraud, dodge, fiddle, deception, (*more informal*) con, (*informal*) scam

radiant ADJECTIVE **1** *a radiant moon* ► bright, shining, brilliant OPPOSITES ARE dark, dull **2** *a radiant smile* ► beautiful, glowing, dazzling, sparkling, beaming, joyful, elated, happy OPPOSITES ARE faint, weak *radiated confidence.* **3** spread out from a central point like the spokes of a wheel

radiation NOUN **1** light, heat, or other energy radiated **2** the energy or particles sent out by a radioactive substance **3** the process of radiating

radiator NOUN **radiators 1** a device that gives out heat, especially a metal case that is heated electrically or through which steam or hot water flows **2** a device that cools the engine of a motor vehicle

radical ADJECTIVE **1** basic and thorough • *radical changes* **2** wanting to make great reforms • *a radical politician*
▷ **radically** ADVERB

radical NOUN **radicals** a person who wants to make great reforms

radio NOUN **radios 1** the process of sending and receiving sound or pictures by means of electromagnetic waves **2** an apparatus for receiving sound (a **receiver**) or sending it out (a **transmitter**) in this way **3** sound broadcasting [from Latin *radius* = a spoke or ray]

radioactive ADJECTIVE having atoms that break up spontaneously and send out radiation which produces electrical and chemical effects and penetrates things
▷ **radioactivity** NOUN

radiocarbon dating NOUN the use of a kind of radioactive carbon that decays at a steady rate, to find out how old something is

radio telescope NOUN **radio telescopes** an instrument that can detect radio waves from space

radiotherapy NOUN the use of radioactive substances in treating diseases such as cancer

radish NOUN **radishes** a small hard round red vegetable, eaten raw in salads

radium NOUN a radioactive metal, often used in radiotherapy [from Latin *radius* = a spoke or ray]

radius NOUN **radii** or **radiuses 1** a straight line from the center of a circle or sphere to the circumference; the length of this line **2** a range or distance from a central point • *The school takes pupils living within a radius of ten kilometers.*

radon NOUN a radioactive gas used in radiotherapy

raffle NOUN **raffles** a kind of lottery, usually to raise money for a charity

raffle VERB **raffles, raffling, raffled** offer something as a prize in a raffle

raft NOUN **rafts** a flat floating structure made of wood, etc., used as a boat

rafter NOUN **rafters** any of the long sloping pieces of wood that hold up a roof

rag NOUN **rags 1** an old or torn piece of cloth **2** a piece of ragtime music

rag VERB **rags, ragging, ragged** (*slang*) tease

rage NOUN **rages** great or violent anger
all the rage very popular or fashionable for a time

rage VERB **rages, raging, raged 1** be very angry **2** continue violently or with great force • *A storm was raging.*

ragged ADJECTIVE **1** torn or frayed **2** wearing torn clothes **3** irregular or uneven • *a ragged performance* [from Old Norse *roggvathr* = tufted]

raid NOUN **raids 1** a sudden attack **2** a surprise visit by police, etc., to arrest people or seize illegal goods

raid VERB **raids, raiding, raided** make a raid on a place
▷ **raider** NOUN

Thesaurus

radical ADJECTIVE **1** *a radical course of action* ► fundamental, drastic, thoroughgoing, thorough, comprehensive, sweeping, rigorous, complete, basic AN OPPOSITE IS superficial **2** *a government committed to radical change* ► revolutionary, extreme, extremist, militant OPPOSITES ARE moderate, conservative

raffle NOUN *She won a prize in a raffle.* ► draw, lottery, tombola, sweepstake

rage NOUN **1** *He stormed out of the room in a burst of rage.* ► anger, fury, temper, outrage, passion, pique, exasperation **2** *the rage for portable DVD players* ► craze, vogue, trend, fashion, passion

rage VERB **1** *He raged on for a while about loyalty.* ► fume, storm, seethe, rant, fulminate, be angry **2** *A fierce blizzard raged for days.* ► blow, storm, thunder, rampage

ragged ADJECTIVE **1** *She spent the morning mending ragged clothes.* ► tattered, torn, frayed, threadbare, ripped, shabby, tatty, unkempt, worn out **2** *He drilled his ragged collection of men.* ► disorganized, disordered, disorderly, erratic, irregular, uneven

raid NOUN **1** *Sentries watched out for any air raids.* ► attack, assault, strike, swoop, blitz, foray, sortie, onslaught, invasion **2** *He had killed a guard during a bank raid.* ► robbery, burglary, break-in, holdup, (*more informal*) heist

raid VERB **1** *The army raided towns on the border.* ► pillage, loot, plunder, ransack, maraud, assault, attack, storm, descend on **2** *Burglars raided local jewellers for the second time.* ► rob, hold up, burgle, break into **3** *Police raided homes and offices in the area.* ► search, swoop on

a b c d e f g h i j k l m n o p q **r** s t u v w x y z

rail NOUN **rails 1** a level or sloping bar for hanging things on or forming part of a fence, banisters, etc. **2** a long metal bar forming part of a railway track
by rail on a train
[from old French; related to **rule**]

rail VERB **rails, railing, railed** protest angrily or bitterly [via French from Latin *rugire* = to bellow]

railings PLURAL NOUN a fence made of metal bars

railway NOUN **1** the parallel metal bars that trains travel on **2** **railways** a system of transport using rails

rain NOUN drops of water that fall from the sky
▷ **rainy** ADJECTIVE

rain VERB **rains, raining, rained 1** fall as rain or like rain **2** send down like rain • *They rained blows on him.*

rainbow NOUN **rainbows** an arch of all the colors of the spectrum formed in the sky when the sun shines through rain

rainfall NOUN the amount of rain that falls in a particular place or time

rain forest NOUN **rain forests** a dense tropical forest in an area of very heavy rainfall

raise VERB **raises, raising, raised 1** move something to a higher place or an upright position **2** increase the amount or level of something • *We are trying to raise standards.* **3** collect; manage to obtain • *They raised $100 for charity.* **4** bring up young children or animals • *She had to raise her family alone.* **5** rouse or cause • *He raised a laugh with his*

joke. **6** put forward • *We raised objections.* **7** end a siege [from Old Norse]

raisin NOUN **raisins** a dried grape [from French, = grape]

rake NOUN **rakes** a gardening tool with a row of short spikes fixed to a long handle

rake VERB **rakes, raking, raked 1** gather or smooth with a rake **2** search
rake up 1 collect **2** remind people of an old scandal etc. that would be best forgotten • *Don't rake that up.*

rally NOUN **rallies 1** a large meeting to support something or share an interest **2** a competition to test skill in driving • *the Monte Carlo Rally* **3** a series of strokes in tennis before a point is scored **4** a recovery

rally VERB **rallies, rallying, rallied 1** bring or come together for a united effort • *They rallied support.* • *People rallied round.* **2** revive; recover strength

RAM ABBREVIATION (in computing) random-access memory, with contents that can be retrieved or stored directly without having to read through items already stored

ram NOUN **rams 1** a male sheep **2** a device for ramming things

ram VERB **rams, ramming, rammed** push one thing hard against another

Ramadan NOUN the ninth month of the Muslim year, when Muslims do not eat or drink between dawn and sunset [Arabic, from *ramida* = to be parched]

ramble NOUN **rambles** a long walk in the country

Thesaurus

railings PLURAL NOUN *A notice had been put on the railings.* ▸ fence, paling, barrier

railway NOUN *They were warned not to cross the railway.* ▸ track, line, rails

rain NOUN *The rain had started again.* ▸ rainfall, wet weather, drizzle, shower, downpour, cloudburst, raindrops, rainstorm, squall, deluge, (*more formal*) precipitation

rain VERB *It rained all afternoon.* ▸ pour, bucket, teem, pelt, drizzle, spit

rainy ADJECTIVE *a rainy day* ▸ wet, showery, drizzly, damp AN OPPOSITE IS dry

raise VERB **1** *Ben raised his hand.* ▸ put up, lift **2** *A crane will raise the load to the top of the building.* ▸ lift, hoist **3** *The company was forced to raise its prices.* ▸ increase, put up, push up, lift **4** *She will need to raise her game for the away match.* ▸ improve, enhance, strengthen, heighten, boost, step up, put more life into **5** *We need to raise five thousand dollars.* ▸ collect, get, obtain, gather, net, amass, scrape together, yield, assemble **6** *This good news raised their hopes.* ▸ arouse, rouse, excite,

increase, improve, encourage **7** *She raised three children on her own.* ▸ bring up, provide for, nurture, look after, educate **8** *Charles raised several objections to the idea.* ▸ present, bring up, introduce, advance, put forward, pose, offer **9** *The incident raises questions about rail safety.* ▸ give rise to, occasion, cause, bring about, produce, engender

rally NOUN *an antiwar rally* ▸ demonstration, meeting, protest, march, (*more informal*) demo

rally VERB **1** *The king rallied his troops at the border. They tried to rally support for the election.* ▸ muster, assemble, marshal, amass, gather, round up, organize **2** *Our spirits rallied.* ▸ recover, improve, pick up, get better, look up, perk up

ram VERB *The getaway van rammed a police car.* ▸ hit, strike, smash into, be in collision with, slam into, collide with, crash into

ramble VERB **1** *We spent a week rambling in the countryside.* ▸ walk, roam, trek, tramp, hike, rove, stroll **2** *He was rambling on about his schooldays.* ▸ chatter, blather, prattle, drift,

ramble VERB rambles, rambling, rambled **1** go for a ramble; wander **2** talk or write a lot without keeping to the subject
▷ **rambler** NOUN

ramifications PLURAL NOUN **1** the branches of a structure **2** the many effects of a plan or action

ramp NOUN ramps a slope joining two different levels [from French *ramper* = to climb]

rampage VERB rampages, rampaging, rampaged rush about wildly or destructively
on the rampage rampaging

rampant ADJECTIVE **1** growing or spreading uncontrollably • *Disease was rampant in the poorer districts.* **2** (said about an animal on coats of arms) standing upright on a hind leg • *a lion rampant*

rampart NOUN ramparts a wide bank of earth built as a fortification or a wall on top of this

ramshackle ADJECTIVE badly made and rickety • *a ramshackle hut*

ranch NOUN ranches a large cattle farm in America

rancid ADJECTIVE smelling or tasting unpleasant like stale fat

random NOUN
at random using no particular order or method • *numbers chosen at random*

random ADJECTIVE done or taken at random • *a random sample*

range NOUN ranges **1** a set of different things of the same type • *a wide range of backgrounds* • *a lovely range of colors* **2** the limits between which things exist or are available; an extent

• *the age range 15 to 18* **3** the distance that a gun can shoot, an aircraft can travel, a sound can be heard, etc. **4** a place with targets for shooting practice **5** a line or series of mountains or hills **6** a large open area of grazing land or hunting ground **7** a kitchen fireplace with ovens

range VERB ranges, ranging, ranged **1** exist between two limits; extend • *Prices ranged from $1 to $50.* **2** arrange **3** move over a wide area; wander

ranger NOUN rangers someone who looks after or patrols a park, forest, etc.

rank NOUN ranks **1** a line of people or things **2** a place where taxis stand to await customers **3** a position in a series of different levels • *He holds the rank of sergeant.*

rank VERB ranks, ranking, ranked **1** put things in order according to their rank **2** have a certain rank or place • *She ranks among the greatest novelists.*

rank ADJECTIVE ranker, rankest **1** growing too thickly and coarsely **2** smelling very unpleasant **3** unmistakably bad • *rank injustice*
▷ **rankly** ADVERB **rankness** NOUN

rank and file NOUN the ordinary people or soldiers, not the leaders

ransack VERB ransacks, ransacking, ransacked **1** search thoroughly or roughly **2** rob or pillage a place

ransom NOUN ransoms money that has to be paid for a prisoner to be set free
hold to ransom hold someone captive or in your power and demand a ransom

Thesaurus

run, maunder, (*more informal*) rabbit, (*more informal*) witter

rambling ADJECTIVE **1** *a long rambling speech* ▶ verbose, long-winded, diffuse, disjointed, disconnected, incoherent, roundabout, digressive

ramp NOUN *There's a ramp for wheelchairs.* ▶ slope, incline, gradient, rise, sloping surface

ramshackle ADJECTIVE *a ramshackle old house* ▶ dilapidated, tumbledown, derelict, decrepit, rickety, shaky, unsafe, broken down, ruined, tottering, crumbling AN OPPOSITE IS sturdy

random ADJECTIVE *Her house came up in a random sample of houses in the area.* ▶ indiscriminate, arbitrary, chance, haphazard, casual, unplanned, accidental, unconsidered, unpremeditated, fortuitous, irregular AN OPPOSITE IS systematic

range NOUN **1** *a range of mountains* ▶ chain, row, line, series, string, file **2** *a wide range of food* ▶ variety, assortment, selection, array,

scope, choice, spectrum, extent **3** *an age range between 20 and 30* ▶ span, scope, compass, radius

range VERB **1** *Prices range between $100 and $600.* ▶ extend, vary, differ, fluctuate, reach **2** *Sheep ranged over the hills.* ▶ roam, rove, wander, stray, travel **3** *Pupils are ranged by ability.* ▶ classify, class, categorize, rank, order, group

rank NOUN **1** *She was promoted to the rank of assistant manager.* ▶ level, grade, position, status, standing, station, title, class, degree **2** *a family of rank* ▶ high standing, distinction, importance, nobility, aristocracy **3** *The front rank began to move forward.* ▶ row, line, file, column

rank VERB *He's ranked number two in the world.* ▶ grade, class, categorize, classify, designate, list

ransom NOUN *The ransom was set at four million dollars.* ▶ pay-off, release money, payment, price

A
B
C
D
E
F
G
H
I
J
K
L
M
N
O
P
Q
R
S
T
U
V
W
X
Y
Z

ransom VERB ransoms, ransoming, ransomed **1** free someone by paying a ransom **2** get a ransom for someone

rant VERB rants, ranting, ranted speak loudly and violently [from Dutch ranten = talk nonsense]

rap VERB raps, rapping, rapped **1** knock loudly **2** (informal) reprimand **3** (informal) chat **4** perform rap music

rap NOUN raps **1** a rapping movement or sound **2** (informal) blame or punishment • take the rap **3** (informal) a chat **4** a type of popular music in which words are spoken rhythmically to an instrumental backing

rapacious (ra- pay- shus) ADJECTIVE **1** greedy **2** using threats or force to get everything you can
  ▷ **rapaciously** ADVERB **rapacity** NOUN

rape[1] NOUN rapes the violent act of having sexual intercourse with a person without their consent

rape VERB rapes, raping, raped force someone to have sexual intercourse against their will
  ▷ **rapist** NOUN
[from Latin rapere = take by force]

rape[2] NOUN a plant with bright yellow flowers, grown as food for sheep and for its seed from which oil is obtained [from Latin rapum = turnip (to which it is related)]

rapid ADJECTIVE moving very quickly; swift
  ▷ **rapidly** ADVERB **rapidity** NOUN

rapids PLURAL NOUN part of a river where the water flows very quickly

rapt ADJECTIVE very intent and absorbed
  ▷ **raptly** ADVERB

rapture NOUN very great delight
  ▷ **rapturous** ADJECTIVE **rapturously** ADVERB

rare[1] ADJECTIVE rarer, rarest **1** unusual; not often found or happening **2** (said about air) thin; below normal pressure
  ▷ **rarely** ADVERB **rareness** NOUN **rarity** NOUN

rare[2] ADJECTIVE (said about meat) only lightly cooked; undercooked

rarefied ADJECTIVE **1** (said about air) rare **2** remote from everyday life • the rarefied atmosphere of the university

rascal NOUN rascals a dishonest or mischievous person; a rogue
  ▷ **rascally** ADJECTIVE

rash ADJECTIVE doing something or done without thinking of the possible risks or effects
  ▷ **rashly** ADVERB **rashness** NOUN

rash NOUN rashes **1** an outbreak of spots or patches on the skin **2** a number of (usually unwelcome) events happening in a short time • a rash of accidents

rasp NOUN rasps **1** a file with sharp points on its surface **2** a rough grating sound

rasp VERB rasps, rasping, rasped **1** scrape roughly **2** make a rough grating sound or effect

raspberry NOUN raspberries a small soft red fruit

Rastafarian NOUN Rastafarians a member of a religious group that started in Jamaica

rat NOUN rats **1** an animal like a large mouse **2** (informal) an unpleasant or treacherous person

rate NOUN rates **1** speed • The train traveled at a great rate. **2** a measure of cost, value, etc. • Postage rates went up. **3** quality or standard • first-rate
at any rate anyway

Thesaurus

ransom VERB The kidnappers demanded a million dollars to ransom the girl. ► obtain the release of, release, redeem, liberate, free

rap VERB He rapped on the big oak door. ► knock on, strike, tap, hit

rapid ADJECTIVE They made rapid progress. ► fast, quick, swift, speedy, brisk, lively, smooth, sharp, prompt, headlong OPPOSITES ARE slow, leisurely

rare ADJECTIVE **1** a rare moment of peace
► infrequent, uncommon, scarce, occasional, sporadic, odd, singular OPPOSITES ARE frequent, common **2** a person of rare abilities
► exceptional, remarkable, incomparable, unusual, uncommon, special, abnormal

rascal NOUN **1** One of the rascals had stolen money from the drawer. ► rogue, scoundrel, ne'er-do-well **2** Dad asked, "What's the little rascal been up to?" ► scamp, scalawag, monkey, mischief-maker, wretch, monster

rash ADJECTIVE He regretted making such a rash promise. ► reckless, impulsive, impetuous, foolhardy, hasty, precipitate, imprudent, incautious, injudicious, indiscreet, ill-advised, ill-considered, headstrong, unthinking, heedless, hotheaded, hurried OPPOSITES ARE cautious, considered, prudent

rash NOUN **1** Her skin broke out in a rash.
► spots, eruption, hives **2** a rash of break-ins in the area ► outbreak, spate, series, succession

rate NOUN **1** They were pedalling at a furious rate.
► speed, pace, tempo, velocity, (more informal) lick **2** You can hire a boat for a reasonable daily rate. ► charge, amount, price, cost, payment, fare, fee, figure

rate VERB **1** They do not rate our chances very highly. ► assess, evaluate, appraise, judge, regard, value, count, weigh, estimate, calculate, consider, measure **2** The suggestion only rated a brief mention. ► merit, deserve,

rate VERB rates, rating, rated **1** put a value on something **2** regard as ● *He rated me among his friends*

rates PLURAL NOUN a local tax paid by owners of commercial land and buildings

rather ADVERB **1** slightly or somewhat ● *It's rather dark* **2** preferably or more willingly ● *I would rather not go* **3** more exactly; instead of ● *He is lazy rather than stupid*

rating NOUN ratings **1** the way something is rated **2** a sailor who is not an officer

ratio (ray- shee- oh) NOUN ratios **1** the relationship between two numbers, given by the quotient ● *The ratio of 2 to 10 = 2:10 = $\frac{2}{10}$ = $\frac{1}{5}$* **2** proportion ● *Mix flour and butter in the ratio of two to one* (= two measures of flour to one measure of butter).

ration NOUN rations an amount allowed to one person

ration VERB rations, rationing, rationed share something out in fixed amounts

rational ADJECTIVE **1** reasonable or sane **2** able to reason
▷ **rationally** ADVERB **rationality** NOUN

rationalize VERB rationalizes, rationalizing, rationalized **1** make a thing logical and consistent ● *Attempts to rationalize English spelling have failed.* **2** justify something by inventing a reasonable explanation for it ● *They rationalized their meanness by calling it*

economy. **3** make an industry, etc., more efficient by reorganizing it
▷ **rationalization** NOUN

rations PLURAL NOUN a fixed daily amount of food issued to a soldier, etc.

rattle VERB rattles, rattling, rattled **1** make a series of short sharp hard sounds **2** make a person nervous or flustered
rattle off say or recite rapidly

rattle NOUN rattles **1** a rattling sound **2** a device or baby's toy that rattles

rattlesnake NOUN rattlesnakes a poisonous American snake with a tail that rattles

raucous (raw- kus) ADJECTIVE loud and harsh ● *a raucous voice*

ravages PLURAL NOUN damaging effects ● *the ravages of war*

rave VERB raves, raving, raved **1** talk wildly or angrily or madly **2** talk enthusiastically about something

rave NOUN raves a large party or event with dancing to loud fast electronic music

ravenous ADJECTIVE very hungry
▷ **ravenously** ADVERB

ravine (ra- veen) NOUN ravines a deep narrow gorge or valley

ravishing ADJECTIVE very beautiful

raw ADJECTIVE **1** not cooked **2** in the natural state; not yet processed ● *raw materials* **3** without experience ● *raw recruits* **4** with the

Thesaurus

warrant, be worthy of **3** (*informal*) *I don't rate this stuff like you do.* ► think much of, think highly of, admire, value, enjoy

rather ADVERB **1** *It sounds rather difficult.* ► fairly, somewhat, quite, slightly, moderately, relatively, (*more informal*) pretty **2** *I'd rather leave it until the weekend.* ► sooner, preferably

ratio NOUN *The ratio of men to women has changed.* ► proportion, balance, relationship, correlation, correspondence

ration NOUN *They decided not to increase their daily ration of fat.* ► allowance, allocation, quota, share, measure, helping, portion
rations *The expedition might soon run out of rations.* ► supplies, provisions, stores, food, necessaries, necessities

ration VERB *Fuel is strictly rationed in wartime.* ► control, limit, restrict, conserve, allocate, allot, apportion

rational ADJECTIVE **1** *Feelings are so high it's difficult to have a rational discussion.* ► reasoned, logical, sensible, coherent, cogent, reasonable, balanced, sane, intelligent, judicious, lucid, normal OPPOSITES

ARE irrational, illogical **2** *In the last year of his life he was often barely rational.* ► lucid, coherent, sane, intelligible, in your right mind

rattle VERB **1** *He rattled the coins in his purse.* ► jangle, clink, clunk **2** *A row of trucks rattled along the track.* ► clatter, jolt, shake, bounce **3** *The wind rattled at the doors and windows* ► shake, batter, beat **4** *This news had rattled her badly.* ► disconcert, disturb, unnerve, fluster, shake, discomfit, (*more informal*) throw
rattle off *He rattled off the words he had learned.* ► recite, run through, reel off, repeat, list

rattle NOUN *the rattle of pans in the kitchen* ► clatter, clattering, clank, clanking

raucous ADJECTIVE *the raucous clamor of alarm bells* ► harsh, shrill, strident, jarring, grating, noisy, loud, rough

rave VERB **1** *He was raving and swearing at them.* ► rage, rant, shout, roar, bellow, storm **2** *Everyone raved about the food that day.* ► praise, idolize, be ecstatic about, go into raptures over

rave ADJECTIVE *The film got a rave review.* ► enthusiastic, rapturous, glowing, ecstatic, wonderful

raw ADJECTIVE **1** *She ate a piece of raw onion.* ► uncooked, fresh **2** *the high cost of raw*

a
b
c
d
e
f
g
h
i
j
k
l
m
n
o
p
q
r
s
t
u
v
w
x
y
z

A
B
C
D
E
F
G
H
I
J
K
L
M
N
O
P
Q
R
S
T
U
V
W
X
Y
Z

skin removed • *a raw wound* **5** cold and damp • *a raw morning*
▷ **rawness** NOUN
a raw deal (*informal*) unfair treatment

raw material NOUN raw materials natural substances used in industry • *rich in iron ore, coal, and other raw materials*

ray NOUN rays **1** a thin line of light, heat, or other radiation **2** each of a set of lines or parts extending from a center **3** a slight trace of something • *a ray of hope*

raze VERB razes, razing, razed destroy a building or town completely • *The fort was razed to the ground.*

razor NOUN razors a device with a very sharp blade, especially one used for shaving

re- PREFIX **1** again (as in *rebuild*) **2** back again, to an earlier condition (as in *reopen*) **3** in return; to each other (as in *react*) **4** against (as in *rebel*) **5** away or down (as in *recede*)

reach VERB reaches, reaching, reached **1** go as far as; arrive at a place or thing **2** stretch out your hand to get or touch something **3** succeed in achieving something • *The cheetah can reach a speed of 70 m.p.h.* • *Have you reached a decision?*
▷ **reachable** ADJECTIVE

reach NOUN reaches **1** the distance a person or thing can reach **2** a distance you can easily travel • *We live within reach of the sea.* **3** a straight stretch of a river or canal [from Old English]

react VERB reacts, reacting, reacted **1** respond to something; have a reaction **2** (in science) undergo a chemical change

reaction NOUN reactions **1** an effect or feeling, etc., produced in one person or thing by another **2** (in science) a chemical change caused when substances act upon each other

reactionary ADJECTIVE opposed to progress or reform

reactor NOUN reactors an apparatus for producing nuclear power in a controlled way

read VERB reads, reading, read (red) **1** look at something written or printed and understand it or say it aloud **2** (in computing) copy, search, or extract data **3** indicate or register • *The thermometer reads 20° Celsius.*
▷ **readable** ADJECTIVE

reader NOUN readers **1** a person who reads **2** a book that helps you learn to read

readily (red- il- ee) ADVERB **1** willingly **2** easily; without any difficulty

---

Thesaurus

---

materials ▶ natural, untreated, unprocessed, basic **3** *His skin had become raw.* ▶ sore, inflamed, red, tender **4** *You could sense the raw passion.* ▶ strong, intense, powerful, fervent, unrestrained **5** *They walked against the raw wind.* ▶ cold, bitter, biting, freezing, piercing, chilly

ray NOUN **1** *A ray of light shone through the branches.* ▶ beam, shaft, stream, streak, finger, glint, glimmer **2** *There was one ray of hope left.* ▶ glimmer, flicker, gleam, spark, trace, sign, hint, indication

reach VERB **1** *After a while the walkers reached a village.* ▶ arrive at, get to, come to, go as far as, (*more informal*) end up at, (*more informal*) make it to **2** *The government has not reached any of its major targets yet.* ▶ achieve, attain, succeed in, (*more informal*) hit, (*more informal*) make **3** *I can't reach the switch.* ▶ get hold of, grasp, get your hand to, take, touch **4** *You can reach me on my cell phone.* ▶ contact, get in touch with, communicate with

reach out *She reached out her hand.* ▶ stretch out, stick out, hold out, put out, extend, raise

reach NOUN **1** *The station is within easy reach.* ▶ distance, range, compass, scope **2** *The fugitives were now beyond the reach of the law.*

▶ jurisdiction, authority, control, sway, command **3** *Aim at achievements that are within your reach.* ▶ capabilities, abilities, capacity

react VERB *Zoe wondered how he would react if she told him everything.* ▶ respond, reply, answer, behave, take it, act

reaction NOUN *His reaction had puzzled her.* ▶ response, manner of response, reply, answer, rejoinder, retort, behavior

read VERB **1** *He sat on the sofa, reading the papers.* ▶ peruse, study, scan, skim, glance at, pore over, dip into **2** *She promised to read them a story.* ▶ read out, tell, say aloud, recite **3** *The writing is not hard to read.* ▶ decipher, make out, make sense of, understand, decode

readable ADJECTIVE **1** *a readable book* ▶ enjoyable, entertaining, interesting, well written, compulsive, gripping OPPOSITES ARE boring, unreadable **2** *readable handwriting* ▶ legible, clear, decipherable, understandable, neat, plain AN OPPOSITE IS illegible

readily ADVERB **1** *Janet readily agreed.* ▶ willingly, gladly, happily, unhesitatingly, promptly, eagerly, freely, voluntarily AN OPPOSITE IS reluctantly **2** *The town is readily reached from the shore.* ▶ easily, quickly, without difficulty

reading NOUN readings **1** reading books **2** the figure shown on a meter, gauge, or other instrument **3** a gathering of people at which something is read aloud • *a poetry reading*

ready ADJECTIVE readier, readiest able or willing to do something or be used immediately; prepared
▷ **readiness** NOUN
at the ready ready for use or action

ready ADVERB beforehand • *This meat is ready cooked*
▷ **ready-made** ADJECTIVE

real ADJECTIVE **1** existing or true; not imaginary **2** genuine; not an imitation • *real pearls* **3** (said about food or drink) regarded as superior because it is produced by traditional methods • *real ale*

realism NOUN seeing or showing things as they really are
▷ **realist** NOUN

realistic ADJECTIVE **1** true to life; showing things as they really are **2** sensible and practical about what is possible
▷ **realistically** ADVERB

reality NOUN realities **1** what is real • *You must face reality.* **2** something real • *Her worst fears had become a reality.*

realize VERB realizes, realizing, realized **1** be fully aware of something; accept something as true **2** make a hope or plan, etc., happen • *She realized her ambition to become a racing driver.* **3** obtain money in exchange for something by selling it
▷ **realization** NOUN

really ADVERB **1** truly or in fact **2** very • *She's really clever.*

realm (relm) NOUN realms **1** a kingdom **2** an area of knowledge, interest, etc. • *in the realms of science*

reams PLURAL NOUN a large quantity of writing

reap VERB reaps, reaping, reaped **1** cut down and gather corn when it is ripe **2** obtain as the result of something done • *They reaped great benefit from their training.*
▷ **reaper** NOUN

rear NOUN the back part

rear ADJECTIVE placed at the rear

Thesaurus

reading NOUN **1** *He gave the letters a hurried reading.* ▶ study, perusal, scrutiny, scan, browse, glance, look through **2** *This is our reading of the evidence.* ▶ interpretation, understanding, construal

ready ADJECTIVE **1** *We are ready to leave. He wasn't ready for the answer he got.* ▶ prepared, set, primed, (more informal) psyched up **2** *They were more than ready to take us to the station.* ▶ willing, prepared, happy, pleased, eager, keen, agreeable, disposed **3** *Everything was ready to start the game.* ▶ prepared, in place **4** ready to *By the time she got home she was ready to collapse.* ▶ about to, close to, likely to, on the point of, on the verge of, on the brink of **5** *He has a ready answer to all criticisms.* ▶ prompt, quick, immediate, telling, perceptive, sharp, astute

real ADJECTIVE **1** *Is that real cream?* ▶ genuine, natural, authentic, bona fide, (German) echt OPPOSITES ARE false, artificial **2** *Some viewers treat characters in soaps as if they were real people.* ▶ actual, physical, existing, unimaginary OPPOSITES ARE imaginary, made-up **3** *"Carl" is not his real name.* ▶ true, actual, proper AN OPPOSITE IS assumed **4** *She began to feel real remorse for what had happened.* ▶ sincere, genuine, honest, heartfelt AN OPPOSITE IS insincere **5** (informal) *I felt like a real idiot.* ▶ complete, utter, absolute, total, (informal) right, (informal) proper

realistic ADJECTIVE **1** *The film was meant to be a realistic portrayal of the events.* ▶ authentic,
truthful, true to life, faithful, lifelike, natural, genuine, convincing, recognizable, representational, graphic OPPOSITES ARE fictional, imaginary **2** *To stand any chance the plan has to be realistic.* ▶ practical, sensible, pragmatic, reasonable, commonsensical OPPOSITES ARE impractical, idealistic **3** *Wage rises have to be realistic.* ▶ reasonable, moderate, acceptable, adequate, fair, justifiable OPPOSITES ARE unrealistic, excessive

reality NOUN *He sometimes finds it hard to distinguish reality from fantasy.* ▶ truth, fact, actuality, certainty, the real world AN OPPOSITE IS fantasy

realize VERB **1** *I realized it was going to be difficult.* ▶ understand, grasp, register, comprehend, appreciate, recognize, accept, (more informal) twig **2** *They will realize their life's ambition at last.* ▶ achieve, accomplish, fulfill, attain, bring about, bring off, complete **3** *The picture could realize thousands at auction.* ▶ fetch, sell for, be sold for, earn, bring in, produce

realm NOUN **1** *the defense of the realm* ▶ kingdom, monarchy, state, empire, principality **2** *the realm of scientific research* ▶ sphere, domain, field, area, activity, department

rear NOUN **1** *There is a door at the rear of the house.* ▶ back, back part, other end, other side **2** *We went to the rear of the line.* ▶ end, tail, back **3** *He gave the horse a slap on the rear.* ▶ bottom, backside, behind, rump, buttocks

a
b
c
d
e
f
g
h
i
j
k
l
m
n
o
p
q
r
s
t
u
v
w
x
y
z

rear VERB rears, rearing, reared **1** bring up young children or animals **2** rise up; raise itself on hind legs • *The horse reared in fright.* **3** (said of a building) appear very large or high

rearguard NOUN rearguards troops protecting the rear of an army

fight a rearguard action go on defending or resisting something even though you are losing

rearrange VERB rearranges, rearranging, rearranged arrange in a different way or order
▷ **rearrangement** NOUN

reason NOUN reasons **1** a cause or explanation of something **2** reasoning; common sense • *You must listen to reason.*
USAGE Do not use the phrase *the reason is* with the word **because** (which means the same thing). Correct usage is *We cannot come. The reason is that we both have flu* (not "The reason is because ...").

reason VERB reasons, reasoning, reasoned **1** use your ability to think and draw conclusions **2** try to persuade someone by giving reasons • *We reasoned with the rebels.*

reasonable ADJECTIVE **1** ready to use or listen to reason; sensible or logical **2** fair or moderate; not expensive • *reasonable prices* **3** acceptable or fairly good • *a reasonable standard of living*
▷ **reasonably** ADVERB

reassure VERB reassures, reassuring, reassured restore someone's confidence by removing doubts and fears
▷ **reassurance** NOUN

rebel (rib- el) VERB rebels, rebelling, rebelled refuse to obey someone in authority, especially the government; fight against the rulers of your own country

rebel (reb- el) NOUN rebels someone who rebels against the government, or against accepted standards of behavior [from *re-* = again + Latin *bellum* = war (originally referring to a defeated enemy who began to fight again)]

rebellion NOUN rebellions organized armed resistance to the government; a revolt
▷ **rebellious** ADJECTIVE

reboot VERB reboots, rebooting, rebooted switch a computer off and then on again

Thesaurus

rear ADJECTIVE *The animal had hurt one of its rear legs.* ► back, hind, hindmost, rearmost AN OPPOSITE IS front

rear VERB *I was born and reared in New York.* ► bring up, raise, educate, care for, nurture

reason NOUN **1** *Money was his main reason for changing jobs.* ► cause, ground *or* grounds, justification, excuse, pretext, case, motive, explanation, apology, argument, incentive, occasion, rationale **2** *arguments based on reason rather than emotion* ► reasoning, logic, sense, rationality, intellect, judgment, common sense **3** *She was terrified of losing her reason.* ► sanity, mind, mental faculties, senses, wits, (more *informal*) marbles RELATED ADJECTIVE
► rational

reason VERB **1** *John reasoned that it was too late to reach home in time now.* ► calculate, conclude, come to the conclusion, work out, deduce, judge, consider, infer **2** *Her husband tried to reason with her.* ► persuade, talk round, bring round, prevail on, debate with, argue with, remonstrate with, discuss with

reasonable ADJECTIVE **1** *Any reasonable person would have to agree with you.* ► sensible, rational, logical, fair-minded OPPOSITES ARE unreasonable, irrational **2** *It was a reasonable explanation.* ► logical, cogent, convincing, compelling, sound, credible, plausible, viable OPPOSITES ARE unreasonable, illogical **3** *They charge a reasonable fee for this service.* ► modest,

moderate, acceptable, tolerable OPPOSITES ARE unreasonable, excessive

reasoning NOUN *I couldn't follow his reasoning.* ► thinking, logic, train of thought, rationality, rationale, argumentation, arguments, hypothesis, interpretation

reassure VERB *Danny tried hard to reassure us.* ► comfort, calm, hearten, support, encourage, assure, bolster up, inspirit, give confidence to OPPOSITES ARE unnerve, disconcert

rebel NOUN (with the stress on *reb-*) *The rebels took control of the region.* ► revolutionary, insurgent, revolutionist, guerrilla, dissenter, malcontent, mutineer, renegade

rebel ADJECTIVE (with the stress on *reb-*) *Rebel forces captured the town.* ► insurgent, revolutionary, rebellious, mutinous

rebel VERB (with the stress on *-bel*) *The people of the south rebelled.* ► revolt, mutiny, riot, rise up, mount a rebellion

rebellion NOUN *Troops were sent in to crush the rebellion.* ► uprising, revolt, rising, insurrection, insurgency, sedition, mutiny, insubordination, resistance, revolution

rebellious ADJECTIVE **1** *rebellious troops* ► mutinous, insurgent, rebel, rebelling, mutinying, subversive **2** *rebellious staff* ► defiant, insubordinate, unruly, ungovernable, unmanageable, uncontrollable, recalcitrant, obstreperous

A B C D E F G H I J K L M N O P Q R S T U V W X Y Z

rebound VERB **rebounds, rebounding, rebounded** bounce back after hitting something
▷ **rebound** NOUN

rebuff NOUN **rebuffs** an unkind refusal; a snub
▷ **rebuff** VERB
[from re- = again + Italian buffo = a gust]

rebuke VERB **rebukes, rebuking, rebuked** speak severely to a person who has done wrong
▷ **rebuke** NOUN

recalcitrant ADJECTIVE disobedient or uncooperative
▷ **recalcitrance** NOUN
[from Latin recalcitrare = to kick back]

recall VERB **recalls, recalling, recalled** 1 bring back into the mind; remember 2 ask a person to come back 3 ask for something to be returned
▷ **recall** NOUN

recapitulate VERB **recapitulates, recapitulating, recapitulated** state again the main points of what has been said
▷ **recapitulation** NOUN

recapture VERB **recaptures, recapturing, recaptured** 1 capture again 2 bring or get back a mood or feeling
▷ **recapture** NOUN

recede VERB **recedes, receding, receded** go back from a certain point • The floods have receded.

receipt (ris- eet) NOUN **receipts** 1 a written statement that money has been paid or something has been received 2 receiving something [via early French from Latin recipire = to receive]

receive VERB **receives, receiving, received** 1 take or get something that is given or sent to you 2 experience something • He received injuries to his face and hands. 3 greet someone who comes

receiver NOUN **receivers** 1 a person or thing that receives something 2 a person who buys and sells stolen goods 3 an official who takes charge of a bankrupt person's property 4 a radio or television set that receives broadcasts 5 the part of a telephone that receives the sound and is held to a person's ear

recent ADJECTIVE happening or made or done a short time ago
▷ **recently** ADVERB

reception NOUN **receptions** 1 the way a person or thing is received 2 a formal party to receive guests • a wedding reception 3 a place in a hotel or office, etc., where visitors are received and registered 4 the quality of television or radio signals

receptionist NOUN **receptionists** a person whose job is to greet and deal with visitors, clients, patients, etc.

receptive ADJECTIVE quick or willing to receive ideas etc.

recess NOUN **recesses** 1 a small space set back in a wall 2 a time when work or business is stopped for a while

recession NOUN **recessions** 1 a reduction in a country's trade or prosperity 2 receding from a point

recharge VERB **recharges, recharging, recharged** refill or reload something, especially put an electric charge into a used battery

recipe (ress- ip- ee) NOUN **recipes** instructions for preparing or cooking food

Thesaurus

rebound VERB 1 The ball rebounded off the wall.
► bounce, bounce back, ricochet, recoil, boomerang 2 His devious tactics rebounded on him. ► backfire, misfire, recoil, boomerang, come back

recall VERB She could not recall what he had said.
► remember, recollect, call to mind, think, cast your mind back to AN OPPOSITE IS forget

receipt NOUN 1 Make sure you keep the receipt.
► sales slip, proof of purchase, bill, ticket, counterfoil, stub 2 Receipt of your tickets is guaranteed within three working days.
► delivery, arrival, receiving
receipts receipts from the sale of council houses
► income, proceeds, revenue, earnings, profits, takings, gains

receive VERB 1 He received an award for gallantry. ► be given, earn, get, accept, collect, obtain, gain, take, acquire, be sent OPPOSITES

ARE give, present 2 He received some minor injuries in the accident. ► sustain, suffer, experience, undergo, bear AN OPPOSITE IS inflict 3 She received the news in complete silence. ► hear, listen to, respond to, react to, take, greet

recent ADJECTIVE Recent events have caused them to change their minds. ► new, current, fresh, latest, present-day, up-to-date, contemporary, modern, novel OPPOSITES ARE old, earlier

reception NOUN 1 We got a friendly reception. ► greeting, welcome 2 A reception will be held at the local hotel. ► party, function, gathering, celebration, get-together, social event, (more informal) do

recipe NOUN 1 She would try out her new soufflé recipe. ► method, procedure, directions, instructions 2 The measures might prove to be a recipe for disaster. ► prescription, formula, procedure, likely cause (of)

A
B
C
D
E
F
G
H
I
J
K
L
M
N
O
P
Q
R
S
T
U
V
W
X
Y
Z

reciprocal (ris- ip- rok- al) ADJECTIVE given and received; mutual • *reciprocal help*
▷ **reciprocally** ADVERB **reciprocity** NOUN

reciprocal NOUN reciprocals a reversed fraction, • $\frac{3}{2}$ is the reciprocal of $\frac{2}{3}$

recital NOUN recitals **1** reciting something **2** a musical entertainment given by one performer or group

recite VERB recites, reciting, recited say a poem, etc., aloud from memory
▷ **recitation** NOUN

reckless ADJECTIVE rash; ignoring risk or danger
▷ **recklessly** ADVERB **recklessness** NOUN

reckon VERB reckons, reckoning, reckoned **1** calculate or count up **2** have as an opinion; feel confident • *I reckon we shall win.* reckon with think about or deal with • *We didn't reckon with the train strike when we planned our journey.*

reclaim VERB reclaims, reclaiming, reclaimed **1** claim or get something back **2** make a thing usable again • *reclaimed land*
▷ **reclamation** NOUN

recognize VERB recognizes, recognizing, recognized **1** know who someone is or what something is because you have seen that person or thing before **2** realize • *She recognized the truth of what he was saying.* **3** accept something as genuine, welcome, or lawful, etc. • *Nine countries recognized the island's new government.*
▷ **recognition** NOUN **recognizable** ADJECTIVE

recoil VERB recoils, recoiling, recoiled **1** move back suddenly in shock or disgust **2** (said about a gun) jerk backwards when it is fired

recollect VERB recollects, recollecting, recollected remember
▷ **recollection** NOUN

recommend VERB recommends, recommending, recommended say that a person or thing would be good or suitable for a particular job or purpose
▷ **recommendation** NOUN

reconcile VERB reconciles, reconciling, reconciled **1** make people who have quarrelled become friendly again **2** persuade a person to put up with something • *New frames reconciled him to wearing glasses.* **3** make

---

Thesaurus

recital NOUN **1** *She gave her first piano recital at the age of eight.* ► concert, public performance, program **2** *a recital of poems* ► recitation, rendering, saying aloud, delivery, narration

recite VERB **1** *She announced that she would recite a poem.* ► say aloud, read out, deliver, perform, declaim **2** *It would take too long to recite all the events of the week.* ► list, enumerate, detail, recount, relate, repeat, run through, reel off, specify

reckless ADJECTIVE *For such a mild man he could be amazingly reckless behind the wheel of a car.* ► rash, careless, heedless, mindless, thoughtless, negligent, foolhardy, daredevil

reckon VERB **1** *They reckoned the cost at about three thousand dollars.* ► assess, estimate, calculate, work out, figure out, gauge, evaluate, count, add up, compute, total **2** (*informal*) *I reckon she likes him.* ► think, believe, suspect, consider, dare say, have an idea, fancy, guess **3** *These animals are reckoned the most dangerous.* ► consider, regard as, deem, judge, count
reckon on *We didn't reckon on such stiff opposition.* ► expect, foresee, plan for, bargain for, figure on

reckoning NOUN *By my reckoning we should make a small profit.* ► calculation, estimation, estimate, judgement, evaluation

reclaim VERB **1** *You can reclaim your traveling expenses.* ► get back, claim back, recover, (*more informal*) put in for **2** *an area of land reclaimed from the sea* ► recover, restore, save, make usable, regenerate

recognize VERB **1** *I didn't recognize him in his suit.* ► identify, place, know, remember, recall, call to mind, put a name to **2** *They recognize his abilities without liking his work very much.* ► acknowledge, admit, accept, concede, grant, allow, appreciate, confess, realize **3** *The qualification is not recognized in Britain.* ► approve, acknowledge, accept, accredit, admit, endorse, support

recoil VERB **1** *She recoiled instinctively as he put his hand out.* ► flinch, draw back, shy away, jerk back, start, wince, shrink back **2** *Their deception will recoil on them.* ► rebound, backfire, misfire, boomerang, come back

recollect VERB *I don't recollect any such promise.* ► remember, recall, call to mind, think, cast your mind back to AN OPPOSITE IS forget

recollection NOUN *She had no recollection of what happened.* ► memory, remembrance, recall, impression

recommend VERB **1** *His doctor recommended surgery.* ► advise, counsel, propose, advocate, suggest, urge, prescribe **2** *This book is recommended by teachers.* ► approve of, advocate, endorse, commend, suggest, praise, speak well of, vouch for, (*more informal*) plug

recommendation NOUN **1** *The governors accepted the main recommendation of the committee.* ► advice, counsel, guidance, proposal, suggestion **2** *She supported him with her personal recommendation.* ► commendation, endorsement, advocacy, testimonial, reference, blessing

things agree • *I cannot reconcile what you say with what you do.*
▷ **reconciliation** NOUN

recondition VERB **reconditions, reconditioning, reconditioned** overhaul and repair

reconnaissance (rik- on- i- suns) NOUN an exploration of an area, especially in order to gather information about it for military purposes

reconstruct VERB **reconstructs, reconstructing, reconstructed** 1 construct or build something again 2 create or act past events again • *Police reconstructed the robbery.*
▷ **reconstruction** NOUN

record (rek- ord) NOUN **records** 1 information kept in a permanent form, e.g., written or printed 2 a disc on which sound has been recorded 3 the best performance in a sport, etc., or the most remarkable event of its kind • *He holds the record for the high jump.* 4 facts known about a person's past life or career, etc. • *She has a good school record.*

record (rik- ord) VERB **records, recording, recorded** 1 put something down in writing or other permanent form 2 store sounds or scenes (e.g., television pictures) on a disc or magnetic tape, etc., so that you can play or show them later

recorder NOUN **recorders** 1 a kind of flute held downward from the player's mouth 2 a person or thing that records something

recover VERB **recovers, recovering, recovered** 1 get something back again after losing it; regain 2 get well again after being ill or weak
▷ **recovery** NOUN

recreation NOUN **recreations** 1 refreshing or entertaining yourself with an enjoyable activity 2 a game or hobby, etc., that is an enjoyable pastime
▷ **recreational** ADJECTIVE

recruit NOUN **recruits** 1 a person who has just joined the armed forces 2 a new member of a society, company, or other group

recruit VERB **recruits, recruiting, recruited** enlist recruits
▷ **recruitment** NOUN

rectangle NOUN **rectangles** a shape with four sides and four right angles
▷ **rectangular** ADJECTIVE

rector NOUN **rectors** a member of the clergy in charge of a parish

rectum NOUN **rectums** the last part of the large intestine, ending at the anus

recuperate VERB **recuperates, recuperating, recuperated** get better after an illness
▷ **recuperation** NOUN

Thesaurus

reconnoiter VERB *Helicopters reconnoitered the area ahead of ground troops.* ► survey, patrol, scout, spy out, explore, investigate, scan, examine, gather intelligence about, inspect

reconstruct VERB 1 *They will have to reconstruct a large part of the building.* ► rebuild, renovate, restore, reassemble AN OPPOSITE IS demolish 2 *Police will reconstruct the incident using actors.* ► recreate, reenact

record NOUN(with the stress on *rec-*) 1 *You should keep a record of everything they say.* ► account, report, note, log 2 *records There are more historical records for these years.* ► documents, archives, evidence, accounts, documentation, annals 3 *She stayed in listening to records.* ► CD, disc, compact disc, album, recording, LP 4 *There is not a single mistake to tarnish his record.* ► background, career, CV 5 *The new time was a world record.* ► best performance, fastest time

record VERB(with the stress on *-cord*) 1 *He recorded everything he heard in a notebook.* ► note, register, enter, put down, set down, write down, transcribe, log, minute 2 *They wanted to record the song and send it in.* ► tape, tape-record, make a recording of, video, preserve, keep

recover VERB 1 *She was recovering from a mild stroke.* ► recuperate, convalesce, get better,

improve, heal, mend, rally, revive, pull around or through, (more informal) be on the mend 2 *Police say they have recovered some of the stolen property.* ► trace, find, get back, track down, retrieve, reclaim, recoup, repossess, salvage

recovery NOUN 1 *Her recovery is proving slow.* ► recuperation, convalescence, return to health, improvement, healing, cure 2 *The economy is showing signs of recovery.* ► improvement, revival, upturn, picking up 3 *A reward will be paid on recovery of the stolen paintings.* ► retrieval, repossession, restoration, recapture, reclamation, salvaging

recreation NOUN *a study of the use of the countryside for recreation* ► relaxation, amusement, diversion, enjoyment, pleasure, leisure, entertainment, fun, play, games, pastime

recruit NOUN 1 *The army is trying to attract more recruits.* ► initiate, new member, conscript 2 *Many recruits to the industry turn out to be unsuitable.* ► new entrant, trainee, apprentice, novice, new member, newcomer

recruit VERB 1 *The services recruit a high proportion of graduates.* ► enlist, enroll, draft, conscript 2 *The company provides training for the staff it has recruited.* ► hire, employ, enroll, engage, take on, advertise for OPPOSITES ARE dismiss, lay off, make redundant

A
B
C
D
E
F
G
H
I
J
K
L
M
N
O
P
Q

R

S
T
U
V
W
X
Y
Z

recur VERB recurs, recurring, recurred happen again; keep on happening
▷ **recurrent** ADJECTIVE **recurrence** NOUN

recurring decimal NOUN recurring decimals (in mathematics) a decimal fraction in which a digit or group of digits is repeated indefinitely, e.g., 0.666 ...

recycle VERB recycles, recycling, recycled convert waste material into a form in which it can be reused

red ADJECTIVE redder, reddest **1** of the color of blood or a color rather like this **2** to do with communists; favoring communism
▷ **redness** NOUN

red NOUN **1** red color **2** a communist
in the red in debt (because debts were entered in red in account books)
see red become suddenly angry

redden VERB reddens, reddening, reddened make or become red

redeem VERB redeems, redeeming, redeemed **1** buy something back or pay off a debt **2** save a person from damnation • *Christians believe that Christ redeemed sinners.* **3** make up for faults • *His one redeeming feature is his kindness.*
▷ **redeemer** NOUN **redemption** NOUN

red-handed ADJECTIVE
catch red-handed catch while actually committing a crime

red herring NOUN red herrings something that draws attention away from the main subject; a misleading clue

red-hot ADJECTIVE very hot; so hot that it has turned red

red tape NOUN use of too many rules and forms in official business

reduce VERB reduces, reducing, reduced **1** make or become smaller or less **2** force someone into a condition or situation • *She was reduced to tears.*
▷ **reduction** NOUN

redundant ADJECTIVE no longer needed, especially for a particular job
▷ **redundancy** NOUN

reecho VERB reechoes, reechoing, reechoed echo; go on echoing

reed NOUN reeds **1** a tall plant that grows in water or marshy ground **2** a thin strip that vibrates to make the sound in a clarinet, saxophone, oboe, etc.

reef NOUN reefs a ridge of rock, coral, or sand, especially one near the surface of the sea

reek VERB reeks, reeking, reeked smell strongly or unpleasantly
▷ **reek** NOUN

reel NOUN reels **1** a round device on which cotton, thread, film, etc., is wound **2** a lively Scottish dance

reel VERB reels, reeling, reeled **1** wind something on to or off a reel **2** stagger

---

Thesaurus

---

recur VERB *The problem is certain to recur if we don't do something about it.* ► return, happen again, reappear, come again, be repeated, persist

recycle VERB *The department is advising customers on how to recycle their waste.* ► reuse, reprocess, reclaim, recover, salvage, use again

red ADJECTIVE **1** *She wore a red dress.* ► scarlet, vermilion, ruby, crimson, cherry, claret, maroon, flame-colored **2** *He was red in the face with embarrassment.* ► flushed, blushing, flaming, ruddy, florid, glowing, inflamed, rosy, rubicund **3** *The chemicals in the water made his eyes red.* ► bloodshot, inflamed, swollen, sore

redeem VERB **1** *Freddie had to redeem his oboe from the pawnbroker's.* ► reclaim, retrieve, recover, repossess, buy back **2** *You can redeem your voucher at any branch of the store.* ► exchange, cash in, exchange for cash, return, trade in
redeem yourself *He failed the first test but redeemed himself in the second.* ► vindicate, absolve

reduce VERB **1** *The goal is to reduce carbon emissions by 20 percent.* ► lessen, lower,

decrease, bring down, curtail, moderate OPPOSITES ARE increase, enlarge **2** *The novel has been greatly reduced in the television adaptation.* ► shorten, abridge, condense AN OPPOSITE IS expand **3** *The father's gambling debts reduced the family to poverty.* ► drive, force, bring to the point of

reduction NOUN **1** *a reduction in pollution* ► decrease, drop, fall, lessening, lowering, diminution AN OPPOSITE IS increase **2** *a series of price reductions* ► cut, discount, (more informal) slash AN OPPOSITE IS increase

redundant ADJECTIVE *There are three redundant churches in the area.* ► unnecessary, unwanted, superfluous, surplus, excessive, too many AN OPPOSITE IS necessary
make someone redundant *They plan to make twenty members of the workforce redundant just before Christmas.* ► lay off, dismiss, sack, discharge

reel VERB *A woman reeled towards him clutching a half-eaten burger.* ► stagger, stumble, sway, totter, lurch, swerve
reel from *When the worst happens you reel from it and the shock is enormous.* ► be shaken by, be shocked by, be stunned by, be staggered by, be aghast at

3 feel giddy or confused • *I am still reeling from the shock.*

reel off say something quickly

refer VERB refers, referring, referred pass a problem, etc., to someone else • *My doctor referred me to a specialist.*

▷ **referral** NOUN

refer to 1 mention or speak about • *I wasn't referring to you.* **2** look in a book, etc., for information • *We referred to our dictionary.*

referee NOUN referees someone appointed to see that people keep to the rules of a game

reference NOUN references **1** referring to something • *There was no reference to recent events.* **2** a direction to a book or page or file, etc., where information can be found **3** a letter from a previous employer describing someone's abilities and qualities

in or with reference to concerning or about

reference book NOUN reference books a book (such as a dictionary or encyclopedia) that gives information systematically

referendum NOUN referendums or referenda a vote on a particular question by all the people of a country [from Latin, = something to be referred]

refill VERB refills, refilling, refilled fill again

refill NOUN refills a container holding a substance which is used to refill something • *This pen needs a refill.*

refine VERB refines, refining, refined **1** purify **2** improve something, especially by making

small changes [from re- = again + Middle English *fine* = make pure]

refined ADJECTIVE **1** purified **2** having good taste or good manners

refinement NOUN refinements **1** the action of refining **2** being refined **3** something added to improve a thing

refinery NOUN refineries a factory for refining something • *an oil refinery*

reflect VERB reflects, reflecting, reflected **1** send back light, heat, or sound, etc., from a surface **2** form an image of something as a mirror does **3** think something over; consider **4** be a sign of something; be influenced by something • *Prices reflect the cost of producing things.*

▷ **reflection** NOUN **reflective** ADJECTIVE **reflector** NOUN

reflex NOUN reflexes a movement or action done without any conscious thought

reflexive pronoun NOUN reflexive pronouns any of the pronouns myself, herself, himself, etc. (as in "She cut *herself*"), which refer back to the subject of the verb

reflexive verb NOUN reflexive verbs a verb in which the subject and the object are the same person or thing, as in "They *hurt themselves*," "The cat *washed itself*"

reform VERB reforms, reforming, reformed **1** make changes in something in order to

Thesaurus

reel off *He reeled off one joke after another.*
▶ recite, rattle off, fire off, run off

refer VERB **1** *His doctor referred him to a specialist. The manager referred the matter to head office.* ▶ pass, send, transfer, direct, entrust, hand on, send on **2** refer to *The police officer referred to her notes.* ▶ consult, look up, turn to, look in, search in **3** refer to *The third paragraph of the article refers to new publications.* ▶ mention, detail, list, touch on, describe, allude to, cite

referee NOUN **1** *The referee blew his whistle.*
▶ umpire, judge, adjudicator, arbitrator, (more informal) ref

reference NOUN **1** *The title Brave New World is a reference to Shakespeare.* ▶ allusion, quotation (from), citation (from), example (of), illustration (from), instance (of), mention (of) **2** *His teacher had given him a glowing reference.*
▶ testimonial, recommendation, endorsement, backing

with reference to *She spoke to him with reference to his recent conduct.* ▶ about, with regard to, in relation to, a propos of, on the subject of

refined ADJECTIVE **1** *refined sugar* ▶ purified,

pure, processed, clarified, distilled, concentrated **2** *a refined man* ▶ cultivated

reflect VERB **1** *The window reflected their faces staring in.* ▶ mirror, send back, shine back, throw back **2** *The looks on their faces reflected their feelings.* ▶ indicate, show, reproduce, demonstrate, correspond to, echo, exhibit, match, reveal, bear witness to

reflect on *She reflected on the promises she had made to her friends.* ▶ think about, consider, contemplate, meditate on, ponder, brood on, ruminate on, mull over, muse on, reminisce about, (more informal) chew over

reflection NOUN **1** *We could see our reflections in the water.* ▶ image, likeness **2** *The test will provide an accurate reflection of a child's ability.*
▶ indication, demonstration, manifestation, expression, evidence, echo, result **3** *After some reflection, he decided to accept the offer.*
▶ deliberation, consideration, contemplation, thought, thinking, meditation, rumination, pondering, musing

reform VERB **1** *He realized he would have to reform.* ▶ mend your ways, turn over a new leaf, improve, do better **2** *Everyone agrees on*

improve it **2** give up a criminal or immoral lifestyle, or make someone do this
▷ **reformer** NOUN **reformative** ADJECTIVE **reformatory** ADJECTIVE

reform NOUN reforms **1** reforming **2** a change made in order to improve something

reformation NOUN reforming
the Reformation a religious movement in Europe in the 16th century intended to reform certain teachings and practices of the Roman Catholic Church, which resulted in the establishment of the Reformed or Protestant Churches

refract VERB refracts, refracting, refracted bend a ray of light at the point where it enters water or glass, etc., at an angle
▷ **refraction** NOUN **refractor** NOUN **refractive** ADJECTIVE

refrain VERB refrains, refraining, refrained stop yourself from doing something • *Please refrain from talking.*

refrain NOUN refrains the chorus of a song

refresh VERB refreshes, refreshing, refreshed make a tired person feel fresh and strong again
refresh someone's memory remind someone of something by going over previous information

refreshing ADJECTIVE **1** producing new strength • *a refreshing sleep* **2** pleasantly different or unusual • *refreshing honesty*

refreshments PLURAL NOUN drinks and snacks provided at an event

refrigerator NOUN refrigerators an appliance or room in which food is stored at a very low temperature

refuge NOUN refuges a place where a person is safe from pursuit or danger
take refuge go somewhere or do something so that you are protected

refugee NOUN refugees someone who has had to leave their home or country and seek refuge elsewhere, e.g., because of war or persecution or famine

refund VERB refunds, refunding, refunded pay money back

refund NOUN refunds money paid back

refuse (ri- **fewz**) VERB refuses, refusing, refused say that you are unwilling to do or give or accept something
▷ **refusal** NOUN

refuse (**ref**- yooss) NOUN waste material • *Trucks collected the refuse.*

regain VERB regains, regaining, regained **1** get something back after losing it **2** reach a place again

regalia (rig- **ayl**- i- a) PLURAL NOUN the emblems of royalty or rank • *The royal regalia include the crown, scepter, and orb.*

regard VERB regards, regarding, regarded **1** think of in a certain way; consider to be • *We regard the matter as serious.* **2** look or gaze at

Thesaurus

the need to reform the prison system.
► reconstitute, regenerate, remodel, reorganize, revolutionize, purge

reform NOUN the need for reform
► improvement, betterment, change, adjustment, reorganization, (*more informal*) shake-up

refrain VERB refrain from *Please refrain from shouting comments during the speeches.* ► desist from, avoid, do without, forgo, abstain from, eschew, forbear, (*more informal*) quit, (*more informal*) leave off, stop

refresh VERB **1** *A bit of air will refresh us.* ► invigorate, cool, freshen, revive, revitalize, restore, enliven, renew **2** *Revisiting the scene might refresh my memory.* ► prompt, jog, stimulate, remind, prod

refreshing ADJECTIVE **1** *a refreshing drink: a refreshing breeze* ► invigorating, revitalizing, reviving, enlivening, stimulating, bracing, exhilarating, cool, restorative, thirst-quenching, tingling **2** *a refreshing change* ► welcome, stimulating, different, interesting, fresh, new, original

refreshments PLURAL NOUN *You can get some refreshments in the interval.* ► food and drink,

sustenance, snacks, (*more informal*) eats, (*more informal*) nibbles

refuge NOUN **1** *The homeless seek refuge in doorways and under bridges.* ► shelter, protection, safety, sanctuary, security, cover, hideout, hiding place, retreat **2** *The mountains provide a refuge for the freedom fighters.*
► sanctuary, shelter, haven, retreat, hideaway, hideout, hiding place

refusal NOUN **1** *There have been two refusals to the invitation so far.* ► rejection, negative reply, nonacceptance, regrets, no AN OPPOSITE IS acceptance **2** *Her refusal to see him again caused great distress.* ► unwillingness, disinclination, reluctance, aversion

refuse VERB(with the stress on *-fuse*) **1** *He refused several invitations that week.* ► decline, turn down, reject, say no to, rebuff, spurn, baulk at, give a negative reply to AN OPPOSITE IS accept **2** *The local council refused permission for the building to go ahead.* ► withhold, deny, not grant, deprive of AN OPPOSITE IS grant

regard VERB **1** *She regarded them closely for a while.* ► look at, observe, eye, gaze at, stare at, watch, contemplate, scrutinize, view AN OPPOSITE IS disregard **2** *We regard these*

regard ➡ regret

regard NOUN **1** a gaze **2** consideration or heed • *You acted without regard to people's safety.* **3** respect • *We have a great regard for her.* **4** a gaze
with regard to concerning

regarding PREPOSITION concerning • *There are laws regarding drugs.*

regardless ADVERB without considering something • *Do it, regardless of the cost.*

regards PLURAL NOUN kind wishes sent in a message • *Give him my regards.*

regatta NOUN regattas a meeting for boat or yacht races

regenerate VERB regenerates, regenerating, regenerated give new life or strength to something
▷ **regeneration** NOUN

regent NOUN regents a person appointed to rule a country while the monarch is too young or unable to rule

reggae (reg- ay) NOUN a West Indian style of music with a strong beat

regime (ray- *zheem*) NOUN regimes a system of government or organization • *a Fascist regime*

regiment NOUN regiments an army unit, usually divided into battalions or companies
▷ **regimental** ADJECTIVE

region NOUN regions an area; a part of a country or of the world • *in tropical regions*
▷ **regional** ADJECTIVE **regionally** ADVERB
in the region of near • *The cost will be in the region of $100.*

register NOUN registers **1** an official list of things or names, etc. **2** a book in which information about school attendances is recorded **3** the range of a voice or musical instrument

register VERB registers, registering, registered **1** list something in a register **2** indicate; show • *The thermometer registered 100°.* **3** make an impression on someone's mind **4** pay extra for a letter or parcel to be sent with special care
▷ **registration** NOUN

registrar NOUN registrars an office where records are kept

regret NOUN regrets a feeling of sorrow or disappointment about something that has happened or been done
▷ **regretful** ADJECTIVE **regretfully** ADVERB

regret VERB regrets, regretting, regretted feel regret about something
▷ **regrettable** ADJECTIVE **regrettably** ADVERB

Thesaurus

paintings as the best from the 11-14 age group.
► consider, look on, view, judge, rate, deem, reckon, account, esteem, value

regard NOUN **1** *Good planning must have due regard for the costs involved.* ► attention, care, concern, consideration, deference, heed, notice, respect, thought **2** *They have a high regard for your opinions.* ► respect, esteem, appreciation (of), approval (of), estimation (of), admiration, affection

regardless ADVERB **1** *The cliff walk was dangerous, but we carried on regardless.* ► anyway, anyhow, nonetheless, nevertheless, even so, just the same **2** regardless of *Dinghy sailing has something to offer everyone, regardless of age or fitness.* ► irrespective of, without regard to, disregarding, no matter OPPOSITES ARE mindful of, taking account of

regime NOUN **1** *members of the former military regime* ► government, administration, rule, reign, jurisdiction, command **2** *Dieters usually start a new health regime on a Monday.* ► program, plan, system, arrangement, scheme, diet

region NOUN *The family came from the coastal region.* ► district, area, territory, neighborhood, locality, sector, quarter, zone, terrain, land
in the region of *It will cost in the region of five million dollars.* ► about, approximately, roughly, in the neighborhood of

register NOUN *The local authority keeps a register of disabled people.* ► list, official list, directory, record, index, file

register VERB **1** *We wish to register a protest. The car is registered in his wife's name.* ► record, put on record, file, log, list, enter, submit, report **2** *You can still register for a place on the course.* ► enrol, enlist, put your name down, check in, apply, enter **3** *Their faces registered relief.* ► show, display, express, indicate, exhibit, betray, manifest

regret VERB **1** *You may come to regret your decision.* ► be sorry about, repent, rue, deplore **2** *She said how much she regretted her uncle's death.* ► lament, mourn, grieve over, feel sorrow for, be upset about

regret NOUN **1** *Both men expressed regret for their actions.* ► remorse, sorrow, shame, contrition, repentance, guilt **2** *We left our old home with a feeling of regret.* ► sadness, sorrow, unhappiness, disappointment

regretful ADJECTIVE *She was regretful about what had happened.* ► sorry, remorseful, apologetic, repentant, contrite, penitent, ashamed, sorrowful, disappointed, sad OPPOSITES ARE unrepentant, happy

regrettable ADJECTIVE *It was a regrettable thing to say but it was too late to change it.* ► undesirable, unfortunate, unwelcome, ill-advised, inappropriate, unsuitable, distressing,

a b c d e f g h i j k l m n o p q **r** s t u v w x y z

547

regular ➡ rejoice

regular ADJECTIVE **1** always happening or doing something at certain times ● *Try to eat regular meals.* **2** even or symmetrical ● *regular teeth* **3** normal, standard, or correct ● *the regular procedure* **4** belonging to a country's permanent armed forces ● *a regular soldier*
▷ **regularly** ADVERB **regularity** NOUN

regulate VERB regulates, regulating, regulated **1** control, especially by rules **2** make a machine work at a certain speed
▷ **regulator** NOUN

regulation NOUN **1** regulating **2** a rule or law

rehabilitation NOUN restoring a person to a normal life or a building, etc., to a good condition
▷ **rehabilitate** VERB

rehearse VERB rehearses, rehearsing, rehearsed practice something before performing to an audience
▷ **rehearsal** NOUN

reign VERB reigns, reigning, reigned **1** rule a country as king or queen **2** be supreme; be the strongest influence ● *Silence reigned.*

reign NOUN the time when someone reigns

reimburse VERB reimburses, reimbursing, reimbursed repay money that has been spent
● *Your traveling expenses will be reimbursed.*
▷ **reimbursement** NOUN

rein NOUN reins a strap used to guide a horse

reincarnation NOUN being born again into a new body

reindeer NOUN reindeer a kind of deer that lives in Arctic regions

reinforce VERB reinforces, reinforcing, reinforced strengthen by adding extra people or supports etc.

reinforcements PLURAL NOUN extra troops or ships, etc., sent to strengthen a force

reiterate VERB reiterates, reiterating, reiterated say something again or repeatedly
▷ **reiteration** NOUN

reject (ri- jekt) VERB rejects, rejecting, rejected **1** refuse to accept a person or thing **2** throw away or discard
▷ **rejection** NOUN

reject (ree- jekt) NOUN rejects a person or thing that is rejected, especially because of being faulty or poorly made

rejoice VERB rejoices, rejoicing, rejoiced feel or show great joy

Thesaurus

upsetting, lamentable, shameful OPPOSITES ARE fortunate, suitable

regular ADJECTIVE **1** *She had a regular route to work each morning.* ▶ routine, habitual, customary, typical, usual, normal, established **2** *There were regular complaints about the noise.* ▶ frequent, periodic, constant, continual, persistent OPPOSITES ARE rare, occasional **3** *a regular procedure for dealing with enquiries* ▶ systematic, methodical, efficient, well organized, established, approved, conventional AN OPPOSITE IS haphazard

regulate VERB **1** *a body that regulates the trains* ▶ supervise, oversee, monitor, administer, manage, control, (more informal) keep an eye on **2** *The clocks need to be regulated every so often.* ▶ control, manage, adjust, alter, change, moderate

regulation NOUN **1** *A copy of the regulations about working hours is pinned on the notice board.* ▶ rule, ruling, law, order, requirement, procedure, ordnance, statute, decree, edict **2** *the regulation of traffic in the city center* ▶ control, management, supervision, direction, monitoring, overseeing, administration

rehearse VERB *We need to rehearse the last scene a bit more.* ▶ practice, go over or through, run through, try out, prepare, (informal) run over

reign VERB *Victoria reigned for sixty-four years.* ▶ rule, be queen or king, be on the throne,

wear the crown, govern, be in power RELATED ADJECTIVE ▶ regnal

reign NOUN *She had a long and successful reign.* ▶ rule, monarchy, sovereignty

reinforce VERB **1** *Two stone supports reinforce the old wall. These events reinforced all our suspicions.* ▶ strengthen, fortify, support, bolster, buttress, underpin, prop up, hold up, stiffen, toughen, back up, give strength to **2** *Two more legions were sent to reinforce the army on the Rhine.* ▶ strengthen, supplement, increase, augment

reinforcements PLURAL NOUN *The police unit badly needed reinforcements.* ▶ support, back-up, additional help

reject VERB **1** *The union rejected the new offer.* ▶ turn down, refuse, decline, say no to, dismiss, veto AN OPPOSITE IS accept **2** *Although she loved him, in the end she rejected him.* ▶ rebuff, spurn, jilt, repudiate, cast aside, (more informal) dump

rejection NOUN **1** *Their leaders urged rejection of the offer.* ▶ refusal, nonacceptance, dismissal, turning down AN OPPOSITE IS acceptance **2** *Her rejection of Clive hurt him deeply.* ▶ spurning, repudiation, rebuff, shunning, (more informal) dumping

rejoice VERB *Scientists rejoiced at the new discovery.* ▶ celebrate, delight, exult, revel, be happy OPPOSITES ARE lament, be sad

rejuvenate VERB rejuvenates, rejuvenating, rejuvenated make a person seem young again
▷ **rejuvenation** NOUN

relapse VERB relapses, relapsing, relapsed return to a previous condition; become worse after improving
▷ **relapse** NOUN

relate VERB relates, relating, related **1** narrate **2** connect or compare one thing with another **3** understand and get on well with • *Some people cannot relate to animals.*

related ADJECTIVE belonging to the same family

relation NOUN relations **1** a relative **2** the way one thing is related to another

relationship NOUN relationships **1** how people or things are related **2** how people get on with each other **3** an emotional or sexual association between two people

relative NOUN relatives a person who is related to another

relative ADJECTIVE connected or compared with something; compared with the average • *They live in relative comfort.*
▷ **relatively** ADVERB
relative pronoun see pronoun

relax VERB relaxes, relaxing, relaxed **1** stop working; rest **2** become less anxious or worried **3** make a rule, etc., less strict or severe **4** make a limb or muscle less stiff or tense
▷ **relaxation** NOUN

relay (ri- lay) VERB relays, relaying, relayed pass on a message or broadcast

relay (re- lay) NOUN relays **1** a fresh group taking the place of another • *The firemen worked in relays.* **2** a relay race **3** a device for relaying a broadcast

relay race NOUN relay races a race between teams in which each person covers part of the distance

release VERB releases, releasing, released **1** set free or unfasten **2** let a thing fall or fly or go out **3** make a film or record, etc., available to the public

release NOUN releases **1** being released **2** something released, such as a new film or CD **3** a device that unfastens something

relegate VERB relegates, relegating, relegated **1** put into a less important place **2** put a sports team into a lower division of a league
▷ **relegation** NOUN

relent VERB relents, relenting, relented become less severe or more merciful

relentless ADJECTIVE not stopping or relenting; pitiless
▷ **relentlessly** ADVERB

relevant ADJECTIVE connected with what is being discussed or dealt with (The opposite is irrelevant)
▷ **relevance** NOUN

Thesaurus

---

rejoicing NOUN *It was a time for rejoicing.*
► celebration, festivity, jubilation, euphoria, gladness, happiness AN OPPOSITE IS mourning

relate VERB **1** *They have many stories to relate about their adventures abroad.* ► tell, recount, narrate, report, present, describe, recite **2** *Police are relating the two crimes.* ► link, connect, associate, see a connection between **3 relate to** *The questions relate to an incident that took place the previous week.* ► refer to, concern, have to do with, apply to, bear on, pertain to, involve **4 relate to** *They wanted a worker who could communicate with the young and relate to them.* ► identify with, sympathize with, understand, feel for, have a rapport with

relationship NOUN **1** *the relationship between religion and politics* ► connection, relation, link, association, correlation, correspondence, affinity **2** *Her relationship with her stepmother had deteriorated.* ► rapport, friendship, understanding, attachment, closeness

relative ADJECTIVE **1** *Assess the relative importance of each fact.* ► comparative, respective, corresponding **2 relative to** *evidence relative to the incident* ► related to, relevant to, pertinent

to, connected with, germane to, associated with

relative NOUN *She's a relative of mine.*
► relation, member of the same family, (*more formal*) kinsman *or* kinswoman

relax VERB **1** *Yoga helps you to relax.* ► unwind, unbend, ease up, let up, take it easy **2** *She relaxed her grip on the handle.* ► loosen, slacken, loose, let go, weaken, reduce **3** *His presence helped to relax her.* ► calm, calm down, soothe, pacify

relaxation NOUN *a few hours left for relaxation*
► recreation, relaxing, rest, unwinding, enjoyment, loosening up

release VERB **1** *The guerrillas promised to release one hostage.* ► free, liberate, let go OPPOSITES ARE imprison, detain **2** *The names of the victims were released when the families had been informed.* ► make public, make known, publish, reveal, divulge, disclose, publicize, circulate, communicate OPPOSITES ARE withhold, keep secret

relevant ADJECTIVE *Take a note of any relevant information.* ► pertinent, applicable, significant, apposite, material, suitable AN OPPOSITE IS irrelevant

a
b
c
d
e
f
g
h
i
j
k
l
m
n
o
p
q
r
s
t
u
v
w
x
y
z

A
B
C
D
E
F
G
H
I
J
K
L
M
N
O
P
Q

R

S
T
U
V
W
X
Y
Z

reliable ADJECTIVE able to be relied on; trustworthy
▷ **reliably** ADVERB **reliability** NOUN

relic NOUN relics something that has survived from an earlier period of history

relief NOUN reliefs **1** the ending or lessening of pain, trouble, boredom, etc. **2** something that gives relief or help **3** help given to people in need ● *a relief fund for the tsunami victims* **4** a person who takes over a turn of duty when another finishes **5** a method of making a design, etc., that stands out from a surface

relief map NOUN relief maps a map that shows hills and valleys by shading or molding

relieve VERB relieves, relieving, relieved give relief to a person or thing
relieve of take something from a person ● *The thief relieved him of his wallet.*

religion NOUN religions **1** what people believe about God or gods, and how they worship **2** a particular system of beliefs and worship

religious ADJECTIVE **1** to do with religion **2** believing firmly in a religion and taking part in its customs
▷ **religiously** ADVERB

relish NOUN relishes **1** great enjoyment **2** a tasty sauce or pickle that adds flavor to plainer food

relish VERB relishes, relishing, relished enjoy greatly

relive VERB relives, reliving, relived remember something that happened very vividly, as though it was happening again

reluctant ADJECTIVE unwilling or not keen
▷ **reluctantly** ADVERB **reluctance** NOUN

rely VERB relies, relying, relied
rely on 1 trust a person or thing to help or support you **2** be dependent on something ● *Many people rely on this local bus service.*

remain VERB remains, remaining, remained **1** be there after other parts have gone or been dealt with; be left over **2** continue to be in the same place or condition; stay

remainder NOUN **1** the remaining part or people or things **2** the number left after subtraction or division

Thesaurus

reliable ADJECTIVE **1** *The case lacked any reliable evidence.* ► dependable, valid, trustworthy, sound, genuine, authentic AN OPPOSITE IS unreliable **2** *John was his most reliable friend.* ► trustworthy, dependable, faithful, devoted, staunch, constant, true, good

relic NOUN **1** *The book was a relic of her schooldays.* ► survival (from), souvenir, memento, remnant, reminder, token, vestige **2** relics *a saint's relics* ► remains, sacred objects

relief NOUN **1** *It was a relief to find the village after miles of empty countryside.* ► reassurance, consolation, comfort, solace **2** *The medicine offered some relief from the pain.* ► alleviation (of), easing (of), lessening (of), remedy (for), assuagement (of), mitigation (of) AN OPPOSITE IS intensification **3** *He needed a little light relief from his work.* ► respite, diversion, release, recreation, amusement, entertainment **4** *Aircraft brought relief to the beleaguered inhabitants.* ► help, aid, assistance, succour, deliverance

relieve VERB **1** *The pills helped to relieve her headache.* ► alleviate, ease, lessen, assuage, mitigate, diminish **2** *A video might relieve the boredom of the afternoon.* ► reduce, counteract, lighten, dispel **3** *It relieved us to know she was safely home.* ► reassure, comfort, console, soothe, please, gladden **4** *The army sent in supplies to relieve the townspeople.* ► help, aid, support, assist, sustain **5** *Her spell of duty was nearly over and a colleague would soon relieve her.* ► replace, take over from, stand in for

religion NOUN *the country's official religion* ► faith, belief, form of worship

religious ADJECTIVE **1** *religious beliefs; religious music* ► spiritual, sacred, holy, theological AN OPPOSITE IS secular **2** *a religious person* ► devout, pious, reverent, holy, saintly, God-fearing AN OPPOSITE IS irreligious

relish NOUN *He ate his meal with relish.* ► appetite, delight, enjoyment, enthusiasm, gusto, zest OPPOSITES ARE disgust, dislike

relish VERB *He was relishing his moment of triumph.* ► enjoy, delight in, revel in, take pleasure in, savor, appreciate, like, love

reluctant ADJECTIVE *I was reluctant to admit where I had been.* ► unwilling, disinclined, averse, hesitant (about), resistant, opposed, loath OPPOSITES ARE willing, ready, eager

rely VERB *We can rely on them to help us.* ► depend on, count on, trust, have confidence in, (more informal) bank on

remain VERB **1** *He remained in the hospital for several weeks.* ► stay, continue, stop, linger **2** *Even after the revolution the chief of police remained in power.* ► survive, continue, persist, prevail, endure **3** *By the end of the evening only a handful of guests remained.* ► be left, be present, survive, stay around

remainder NOUN **1** *They were excused duties for the remainder of the day.* ► rest, residue, balance **2** *Finish what you can and do the remainder tomorrow.* ► rest, extra, difference, remnant, residue, what is left

remains ➡ remote

remains PLURAL NOUN **1** all that is left over after other parts have been removed or destroyed **2** ancient ruins or objects; relics **3** a dead body

remand VERB remands, remanding, remanded send a prisoner back into custody while further evidence is being gathered
▷ **remand** NOUN
on remand in prison while waiting for a trial

remark NOUN remarks something said; a comment

remark VERB remarks, remarking, remarked **1** make a remark; say **2** notice

remarkable ADJECTIVE unusual or extraordinary
▷ **remarkably** ADVERB

remedial ADJECTIVE **1** helping children who learn slowly **2** helping to cure an illness or deficiency

remedy NOUN remedies something that cures or relieves a disease, etc., or that puts a matter right

remember VERB remembers, remembering, remembered **1** keep something in your mind **2** bring something back into your mind
▷ **remembrance** NOUN

remind VERB reminds, reminding, reminded **1** help or make a person remember something • Remind me to buy some stamps. **2** make a person think of someone or something because of being similar • She reminds me of my history teacher.
▷ **reminder** NOUN

reminisce (rem-in-iss) VERB reminisces, reminiscing, reminisced think or talk about things that you remember
▷ **reminiscence** NOUN **reminiscent** ADJECTIVE

remiss ADJECTIVE negligent; careless about doing what you ought to do

remnant NOUN remnants a part or piece left over from something

remonstrate VERB remonstrates, remonstrating, remonstrated make a protest • We remonstrated with him about his behavior.

remorse NOUN deep regret for having done wrong
▷ **remorseful** ADJECTIVE **remorsefully** ADVERB

remote ADJECTIVE **1** far away or isolated **2** some but very little; unlikely • a remote chance
▷ **remotely** ADVERB **remoteness** NOUN

Thesaurus

remaining ADJECTIVE **1** She wanted to remove any remaining doubts. ► persisting, surviving, lingering, abiding, continuing, residual **2** Melt the remaining butter and brush it over the pastry. ► left over, unused, surplus, extra

remains PLURAL NOUN **1** He ate the remains of his sandwich in one huge mouthful. ► remainder, rest, residue, remnant **2** The saint's remains are in the crypt. ► body, corpse, ashes, relics

remark NOUN We had the usual conversational remarks about the weather. ► comment, observation, thought, utterance, reflection, statement, word, opinion

remark VERB **1** He remarked that it was very quiet in the room. ► comment, observe, mention, note, say, state, declare, reflect **2** We did not remark anything unusual. ► note, mark, notice, observe, heed, see, perceive

remarkable ADJECTIVE **1** They were bubbling with excitement after their remarkable journey. ► extraordinary, amazing, astonishing, memorable, unforgettable, wonderful, marvellous, breathtaking, fantastic, strange, incredible, astounding, startling, staggering, stunning AN OPPOSITE IS ordinary **2** It was certainly a remarkable achievement. ► outstanding, striking, impressive, noteworthy, exceptional, memorable, phenomenal, distinguished

remedy NOUN **1** a flu remedy ► cure, treatment, medicine, medication, relief, antidote **2** He suggested a day out as a remedy for their boredom. ► answer, solution, cure, relief, corrective, palliative

remedy VERB The government will pass a bill to remedy the problem. ► put right, correct, rectify, solve, resolve, fix, deal with, sort out, redress, counteract

remember VERB **1** a lot of facts to remember ► memorize, learn, commit to memory **2** Do you remember my cousin Alice? I can't remember where I put my keys. ► recall, recollect, recognize **3** Remember that she won't be here for several days yet. ► bear in mind, keep in mind, take into account, not forget **4** They sat on the terrace remembering their childhoods. ► reminisce about, recall, recollect, look back on, muse on, be nostalgic about

remind VERB **1** A note on the fridge reminded me to feed the cat. ► prompt, nudge, hint at, tell **2** remind you of something The music reminded me of my holiday. ► make you think of, take you back to

reminder NOUN **1** She forgot about him and needed a reminder to phone. ► prompt, nudge, cue, hint, suggestion **2** The photo was a reminder of a happy time. ► memento, souvenir

remorse NOUN He was filled with remorse for the harm he had done. ► contrition, guilt, shame, sorrow, repentance, penitence, compunction, regret, bad conscience

remote ADJECTIVE **1** The works would be sited at a remote place for safety. ► isolated, outlying,

a b c d e f g h i j k l m n o p q r s t u v w x y z

A
B
C
D
E
F
G
H
I
J
K
L
M
N
O
P
Q
R
S
T
U
V
W
X
Y
Z

remote control NOUN controlling something from a distance, usually by electricity or radio

removal NOUN removing or moving something

remove VERB removes, removing, removed take something away or off

remove NOUN removes a distance or degree away from something • *That is several removes from the truth.*

Renaissance (ren- ay- sans) NOUN the revival of classical styles of art and literature in Europe in the 14th–16th centuries [from French, = new birth]

rename VERB renames, renaming, renamed give a new name to a person or thing

render VERB renders, rendering, rendered **1** cause to become • *This news rendered us speechless.* **2** give or perform something • *The local community was quick to render help to the victims.*

rendezvous (rond- ay- voo) NOUN rendezvous (rond- ay- vooz) **1** a meeting with somebody **2** a place arranged for this [from French, = present yourselves]

renew VERB renews, renewing, renewed **1** restore something to its original condition or replace it with something new **2** begin or make or give again • *We renewed our request.*
▷ **renewal** NOUN

renewable resource NOUN renewable resources a resource (such as power from the sun, wind, or waves) that can never be used up, or which can be renewed

renounce VERB renounces, renouncing, renounced give up or reject
▷ **renunciation** NOUN

renovate VERB renovates, renovating, renovated repair a thing and make it look new
▷ **renovation** NOUN

renowned ADJECTIVE well known or famous

rent[1] NOUN rents a regular payment for the use of something, especially a house that belongs to another person

rent VERB rents, renting, rented have or allow the use of something in return for rent

rent[2] NOUN rents a torn place; a split

reorganize VERB reorganizes, reorganizing, reorganized change the way in which something is organized
▷ **reorganization** NOUN

repair VERB repairs, repairing, repaired put something into good condition after it has been damaged or broken, etc.
▷ **repairable** ADJECTIVE

Thesaurus

secluded, out-of-the-way, distant, faraway, inaccessible, cut-off AN OPPOSITE IS central **2** *There was a remote chance the decision would be overruled.* ► slight, small, slim, slender, faint, unlikely, doubtful, improbable, negligible AN OPPOSITE IS strong **3** *His manner was remote and unfriendly.* ► aloof, detached, distant, withdrawn, reserved, stand-offish, uncommunicative OPPOSITES ARE warm, friendly

removal NOUN **1** *A local company would take care of the removal.* ► relocation, transfer, transportation **2** *The nail took some removal.* ► extraction, withdrawal, taking out, drawing **3** *The king insisted on the prime minister's removal from office.* ► dismissal, expulsion, displacement, elimination, ejection, ousting OPPOSITES ARE restoration, appointment

remove VERB **1** *It took ten minutes to remove the tooth.* ► extract, pull out, take out, withdraw **2** *She decided to remove the last sentence from her letter.* ► delete, erase, expunge, efface, rub out, strike out AN OPPOSITE IS restore (to) **3** *He tidied up the garden and removed some dead branches.* ► cut off, pull off, detach, strip off **4** *Karen went into the bathroom and removed her clothes.* ► take off, peel off, slip out of, shed, cast off AN OPPOSITE IS put on **5** *The more severe penalties had been removed.* ► abolish, get rid of, eliminate, withdraw, do away with,

(*more informal*) axe OPPOSITES ARE impose, restore

render VERB **1** *The blow rendered him unconscious.* ► make, leave, cause to be **2** *People were eager to render assistance.* ► offer, give, provide, tender, furnish, supply **3** *Scholars rendered the Latin original into modern English.* ► translate, transcribe, adapt

renew VERB **1** *It was time to renew her interest in the countryside.* ► refresh, revive, restore, revitalize, resurrect, awaken **2** *I'll have to renew my passport next month.* ► extend, prolong **3** *The interior of the building was completely renewed in the eighteenth century.* ► renovate, restore, rebuild, modernize, refurbish, revamp, reconstruct, redecorate, make over, recondition, overhaul, transform

renovation NOUN *the renovation of an old building* ► improvement, modernization, overhaul, reconditioning, redevelopment, refit, refurbishment, renewal, repair, restoration, transformation, updating

rent VERB **1** *You can rent a car at the airport.* ► hire, lease, charter **2** *They rent out their apartment during the festival.* ► let, lease, sublet

repair VERB *Public money will be spent to repair the damage. He longed to get back with Maggie and repair their broken marriage.* ► mend, fix,

repair NOUN **repairs 1** repairing • *closed for repair* **2** a mended place • *The repair is hardly visible.*
in good repair in good condition; well maintained

repartee NOUN witty replies and remarks

repatriate VERB **repatriates, repatriating, repatriated** send a person back to his or her own country
▷ **repatriation** NOUN

repeal VERB **repeals, repealing, repealed** cancel a law officially
▷ **repeal** NOUN

repeat VERB **repeats, repeating, repeated 1** say or do the same thing again **2** tell another person about something told to you
▷ **repeatedly** ADVERB

repeat NOUN **repeats 1** the action of repeating **2** something that is repeated, especially a television program

repel VERB **repels, repelling, repelled 1** drive back or away • *They fought bravely and repelled the attackers.* **2** push something away from itself by means of a physical force • *One north magnetic pole repels another.* **3** disgust somebody
▷ **repellent** ADJECTIVE, NOUN

repent VERB **repents, repenting, repented** be sorry for what you have done
▷ **repentance** NOUN **repentant** ADJECTIVE

repercussion NOUN **repercussions** a result or reaction produced indirectly by something

repertoire (rep- er- twahr) NOUN a stock of songs or plays, etc., that a person or company knows and can perform

repetition NOUN **repetitions 1** repeating **2** something repeated
▷ **repetitious** ADJECTIVE

repetitive ADJECTIVE full of repetitions
▷ **repetitively** ADVERB

replace VERB **replaces, replacing, replaced 1** put a thing back in its place **2** take the place of another person or thing **3** put a new or different thing in place of something
▷ **replacement** NOUN

replay NOUN **replays 1** a sports match played again after a draw **2** the playing or showing again of a recording
▷ **replay** VERB

replica NOUN **replicas** an exact copy [from Italian]

reply NOUN **replies** something said or written to deal with a question, letter, etc.; an answer

Thesaurus

put right, rectify, overhaul, patch up, renew, renovate

repair NOUN **1** *The engine is in dire need of repair.* ► mending, fixing, overhaul, maintenance, renovation **2** *The building is in good repair.* ► condition, state, shape, fettle

repay VERB **1** *The debt has been completely repaid.* ► pay off, pay back, settle, expunge, extinguish **2** *We must repay your train fare.* ► refund, reimburse, pay back, recompense, compensate, remunerate, settle **3** *He was eager to repay their kindness.* ► reciprocate, return, recompense, requite

repeat VERB **1** *Neither of them had any wish to repeat their experience.* ► have again, do again, redo, reexperience, reproduce, duplicate **2** *The tale became more colorful every time someone repeated it.* ► say again, restate, reiterate, reproduce, recite, relate

repeat NOUN **1** *We are hoping for a repeat of last week's successes.* ► repetition, repeating, recurrence, reiteration, rerun, return **2** *I watched a repeat of the program.* ► replay, rerun, reshowing, rebroadcast, repetition

repel VERB **1** *The invaders were repelled at the border.* ► repulse, drive back, beat back, push back, ward off, parry, put to flight **2** *a device for repelling cats* ► deter, keep away, scare off AN OPPOSITE IS attract **3** *Such selfishness repelled me.* ► revolt, disgust, sicken, offend, nauseate OPPOSITES ARE delight, please

repellent ADJECTIVE *Reviewers found the program repellent.* ► revolting, disgusting, sickening, repulsive, offensive, repugnant, nauseating

repetition NOUN *The authorities do not want to see any repetition of last week's incident.* ► repeat, repeating, recurrence, reiteration, rerun, return, reappearance, duplication

repetitive ADJECTIVE *To him fixing tiles was repetitive and boring.* ► monotonous, tedious, boring, humdrum, mechanical, repetitious, unchanging, unvaried, (more informal) samey AN OPPOSITE IS varied

replace VERB **1** *She replaced the book on the shelf.* ► put back, return, reinstate, restore **2** *He did not need to look far for someone to replace him when he left.* ► succeed, follow, take over from, take the place of, supersede, supplant, be a substitute for, come after **3** *a program to replace dying trees* ► renew, change, provide a substitute for

replacement NOUN *Thomas had lost his phone and bought a replacement.* ► substitute, alternative, successor, surrogate, stand-in

replica NOUN *Katie wore a replica of her sister's dress.* ► copy, duplicate, imitation, reproduction, likeness, double, clone, facsimile, model, reconstruction

reply VERB **1** *She replied that they would just have to wait.* ► answer, respond, retort, counter **2** *reply to He never replies to letters.* ► answer,

a
b
c
d
e
f
g
h
i
j
k
l
m
n
o
p
q
r
s
t
u
v
w
x
y
z

A
B
C
D
E
F
G
H
I
J
K
L
M
N
O
P
Q
R
S
T
U
V
W
X
Y
Z

reply VERB **replies, replying, replied** give a reply to; answer

report VERB **reports, reporting, reported 1** describe something that has happened or that you have done or studied **2** make a complaint or accusation against somebody **3** go and tell somebody that you have arrived or are ready for work

report NOUN **reports 1** a description or account of something **2** a regular statement of how someone has worked or behaved, e.g., at school **3** an explosive sound

reported speech NOUN indirect speech

reporter NOUN **reporters** a person whose job is to collect and report news for a newspaper, radio or television program, etc.

repose NOUN calm, rest, or sleep

repose VERB **reposes, reposing, reposed** rest or lie somewhere

repossess VERB **repossesses, repossessing, repossessed** take something back because it has not been paid for

reprehensible ADJECTIVE extremely bad and deserving blame or rebuke

represent VERB **represents, representing, represented 1** help someone by speaking or doing something on their behalf **2** symbolize

or stand for ● *In Roman numerals, V represents 5.* **3** be an example or equivalent of something **4** show a person or thing in a picture or play etc. **5** describe a person or thing in a particular way
▷ **representation** NOUN

representative NOUN **representatives** a person or thing that represents another or others

representative ADJECTIVE **1** representing others **2** typical of a group

repress VERB **represses, repressing, repressed 1** keep down; control by force **2** restrain or suppress
▷ **repression** NOUN **repressive** ADJECTIVE

reprieve NOUN **reprieves** postponement or cancellation of a punishment, etc., especially the death penalty

reprimand NOUN **reprimands** a rebuke, especially a formal or official one

reprimand VERB **reprimands, reprimanding, reprimanded** give someone a reprimand

reprisal NOUN **reprisals** an act of revenge

reproach VERB **reproaches, reproaching, reproached** tell someone you are upset and disappointed by something he or she has done
▷ **reproach** NOUN **reproachful** ADJECTIVE **reproachfully** ADVERB

Thesaurus

acknowledge, give a reply to, respond to, react to

reply NOUN *My letter called for a reply.* ► answer, response, acknowledgement, reaction, rejoinder, retort

report VERB **1** *She threatened to report him to the police.* ► inform on, make a complaint against **2** *You must report for duty at 9 o'clock.* ► present yourself, arrive, appear, turn up, check in, clock in **3** *The government has reported an increase in exports.* ► announce, proclaim, declare, communicate, notify, relate, recount, note

report NOUN **1** *There is a full report of the incident in today's newspaper.* ► account, description, review, article, announcement, record, statement, story, (*more informal*) write-up **2** *We heard the report of a gun.* ► bang, blast, crack, noise, explosion, detonation, pop

reporter NOUN *A group of reporters waited outside the house.* ► journalist, correspondent, newspaperman or newspaperwoman

represent VERB **1** *The picture represents a winter scene.* ► depict, describe, portray, show, illustrate, delineate, draw, paint, picture, exhibit, enact **2** *Each character in the play represents a particular human quality.*
► embody, stand for, symbolize, typify, personify, epitomize, exemplify **3** *They chose a spokesperson to represent their views.* ► speak for, express, present, be an example of

representation NOUN *a representation of a young woman* ► portrayal, depiction, likeness, image, picture, portrait, resemblance, delineation

representative ADJECTIVE **1** *a representative sample of American society* ► typical, characteristic, average, archetypal, illustrative, normal AN OPPOSITE IS abnormal **2** *The Greeks devised forms of representative government.*
► democratic, elected, elective, popular, chosen

representative NOUN **1** *the queen's representative abroad* ► ambassador, delegate, deputy, consul, diplomat, spokesperson, spokesman or spokeswoman, proxy, stand-in **2** *a sales representative* ► agent, salesperson, salesman or saleswoman, (*informal*) rep

reprimand VERB *They were reprimanded for their bad behavior.* ► rebuke, admonish, reprove, reproach, upbraid, censure, scold, chide, criticize, reprehend, (*more informal*) tell off, (*more informal*) tick off OPPOSITES ARE praise, commend

reprimand NOUN *The police gave them a formal reprimand.* ► rebuke, admonishment, admonition, reproof, scolding, (*more informal*) telling-off, (*more informal*) talking-to

reproachful ADJECTIVE *She gave him a reproachful frown.* ► disapproving, reproving, scornful, accusatory, censorious, critical, withering AN OPPOSITE IS approving

reproduce VERB reproduces, reproducing, reproduced **1** cause to be seen or heard or happen again **2** make a copy of something **3** produce offspring
▷ **reproduction** NOUN **reproductive** ADJECTIVE

reprove VERB reproves, reproving, reproved rebuke or reproach
▷ **reproof** NOUN

reptile NOUN reptiles a cold-blooded animal that has a backbone and very short legs or no legs at all, e.g., a snake, lizard, crocodile, or tortoise [from Latin reptilis = crawling]

republic NOUN republics a country that has a president, especially one who is elected COMPARE **monarchy**
▷ **republican** ADJECTIVE
[from Latin res publica = public affairs]

repudiate VERB repudiates, repudiating, repudiated reject or deny
▷ **repudiation** NOUN

repulsive ADJECTIVE **1** disgusting **2** repelling things (The opposite is attractive)
▷ **repulsively** ADVERB **repulsiveness** NOUN

reputable (rep-yoo-ta-bul) ADJECTIVE having a good reputation; respected
▷ **reputably** ADVERB

reputation NOUN reputations what people say about a person or thing

reputed ADJECTIVE said or thought to be something ● This is reputed to be the best hotel.
▷ **reputedly** ADVERB

request VERB requests, requesting, requested **1** ask for a thing **2** ask a person to do something

request NOUN requests **1** asking for something **2** a thing asked for

require VERB requires, requiring, required **1** need **2** make somebody do something; oblige ● Drivers are required to pass a test.

requirement NOUN requirements what is required; a need

rescue VERB rescues, rescuing, rescued save from danger, harm, etc.; free from captivity
▷ **rescuer** NOUN

Thesaurus

---

reproduce VERB **1** The drawings are reproduced in beautiful color illustrations. ► copy, reprint, duplicate, transcribe, print, simulate, reissue, repeat, photocopy **2** These animals reproduce in large numbers. ► breed, bear young, produce offspring, multiply, propagate, procreate, spawn, increase

reproduction NOUN **1** methods of reproduction in fish ► breeding, propagation, procreation, multiplying **2** The portrait is only a reproduction. ► copy, replica, duplicate, facsimile, imitation, fake, forgery, likeness, print AN OPPOSITE IS original

reproof NOUN He tutted at her in mild reproof. ► reprimand, rebuke, admonishment, admonition, censure AN OPPOSITE IS approval

repudiate VERB **1** He repudiated all the charges made against him. ► dispute, rebuff, reject, deny, disagree with, renounce, refute OPPOSITES ARE accept, acknowledge **2** She did not want to repudiate their agreement. ► disown, go back on, recant, rescind, retract, reverse, revoke

repugnant ADJECTIVE Polygamy may seem repugnant to us. ► abhorrent, repulsive, revolting, repellent, offensive, disgusting, loathsome

repulse VERB **1** The rebels attacked and were repulsed. ► repel, drive back, beat back, push back, ward off, parry, put to flight **2** He showed her affection but was repulsed. ► reject, rebuff, spurn, snub, jilt

repulsive ADJECTIVE His appearance was repulsive. ► revolting, disgusting, repugnant, repellent, loathsome, obnoxious, hideous AN OPPOSITE IS attractive

reputable ADJECTIVE Make sure you get a reputable builder to do the work. ► dependable, reliable, highly regarded, well thought of, tried and trusted, respectable, respected, trustworthy, creditable AN OPPOSITE IS disreputable

reputation NOUN His reputation had been damaged by the affair. ► good name, name, standing, stature, character, esteem, honor, repute, image, prestige

request NOUN Our request for assistance has been accepted. ► appeal, plea, petition, entreaty, application, call, supplication

request VERB **1** We requested immediate help. ► ask for, appeal for, call for, seek, plead for, require, solicit **2** They requested us to stop. ► ask, call on, require, implore, beseech

require VERB **1** One of the victims required immediate surgery. ► need, have to have **2** The situation required extreme care. ► call for, need, necessitate, involve, entail **3** An official required me to show my passport. ► order, instruct, direct, command, oblige, request

requirement NOUN One of the requirements for this work is a quiet place to go and do it. ► need, necessity, essential, requisite, prerequisite, stipulation, condition, proviso

rescue VERB **1** In a few hours someone would come and rescue them. ► set free, free, release, save, liberate, deliver, extricate, ransom **2** I went back to the house to rescue some of my belongings. ► recover, retrieve, salvage, get back, bring away

a b c d e f g h i j k l m n o p q **r** s t u v w x y z

A
B
C
D
E
F
G
H
I
J
K
L
M
N
O
P
Q
R
S
T
U
V
W
X
Y
Z

rescue NOUN **rescues** the action of rescuing

research NOUN careful study or investigation to discover facts or information

research (ri- serch) VERB **researches, researching, researched** do research into something [from early French *recerche* = careful search]

resemblance NOUN **resemblances** likeness or similarity

resemble VERB **resembles, resembling, resembled** be like another person or thing

resent VERB **resents, resenting, resented** feel indignant about or insulted by something
▷ **resentful** ADJECTIVE **resentfully** ADVERB **resentment** NOUN

reservation NOUN **reservations** **1** reserving **2** something reserved • *a hotel reservation* **3** an area of land kept for a special purpose **4** a limit on how far you agree with something • *I believe most of his story, but I have some reservations.*

reserve VERB **reserves, reserving, reserved** **1** keep or order something for a particular person or a special use **2** postpone • *reserve judgement*

reserve NOUN **reserves** **1** a person or thing kept ready to be used if necessary **2** an extra player chosen in case a substitute is needed in a team **3** an area of land kept for a special purpose • *a nature reserve* **4** shyness; being slow to reveal opinions or emotions

reservoir (rez- er- vwar) NOUN **reservoirs** a place where water is stored, especially an artificial lake

residence NOUN **residences** a place where a person lives

resident NOUN **residents** a person living in a particular place
▷ **resident** ADJECTIVE

residential ADJECTIVE **1** containing people's homes • *a residential area* **2** providing accommodation • *a residential course*

Thesaurus

---

rescue NOUN *The news was all about a dramatic sea rescue.* ► saving, rescuing, recovery, release, deliverance, liberation

research NOUN *More research is needed into the causes of violent crime.* ► investigation, experimentation, testing, exploration, inquiry, analysis, searching, study

research VERB *The disease has been widely researched.* ► investigate, study, inquire into, explore, probe, look into

resemblance NOUN *There is a close resemblance between the two accounts.* ► similarity, correspondence, conformity, agreement, comparison, equivalence, likeness OPPOSITES ARE difference, dissimilarity

resemble VERB *The garden resembled a wilderness.* ► look like, be like, remind you of, be similar to, mirror AN OPPOSITE IS differ from

resent VERB *Jack resented his mother's interference.* ► begrudge, take exception to, take umbrage at, object to, be annoyed about, be resentful of, dislike

resentful ADJECTIVE *Her parents' constant complaining left her feeling resentful.* ► aggrieved, indignant, disgruntled, discontented, offended, bitter, hurt, irritated, antagonistic, sour, jealous, (more informal) put out, (more informal) peeved, (more informal) miffed

resentment NOUN *The appointment of an outsider caused intense resentment among the workforce.* ► indignation, discontent, bad feelings, disgruntlement, rancor, antagonism, irritation

reservation NOUN **1** *You will need to make a reservation if you come on a Friday.* ► booking, advance booking, prior arrangement **2** *Some members of the group had reservations about the plan.* ► misgiving, doubt, scepticism, unease, scruple, qualification, hesitation, qualm

reserve VERB **1** *Demand will be high so make sure your newsagent reserves you a copy.* ► keep, put aside, set aside, hold, retain, earmark **2** *Chuck reserved a room at the local hotel.* ► book, secure, arrange for, order

reserve NOUN **1** *Her reserve of money was running out.* ► supply, fund, stock, store, reservoir, hoard, accumulation **2** *a wildlife reserve* ► preserve, reservation, sanctuary, park **3** *His reserve prevented him from joining in the fun.* ► reticence, shyness, diffidence, timidity, restraint, modesty, aloofness AN OPPOSITE IS openness

reserved ADJECTIVE *As a young man he had been rather reserved.* ► shy, reticent, diffident, retiring, unforthcoming, quiet, timid, restrained, distant, aloof OPPOSITES ARE forthcoming, outgoing

reside VERB **reside in** *Most students reside in dormitories during their first year.* ► live in, stay in, have a room in, dwell in, lodge in, settle in, occupy, have as a home, inhabit

residence NOUN *They spent the summer in their country residence.* ► home, house, dwelling, domicile, abode, address, mansion, quarters, habitation

resident NOUN **1** *the residents of Boston* ► inhabitant, citizen, townspeople, denizen, native **2** *The hotel's first duty is to ensure the safety of its residents.* ► guest, boarder, lodger, client, occupant AN OPPOSITE IS nonresident

residue NOUN **residues** what is left over
▷ **residual** ADJECTIVE

resign VERB **resigns, resigning, resigned** give up your job or position
▷ **resignation** NOUN
be resigned or **resign yourself to something** accept that you must put up with it

resist VERB **resists, resisting, resisted** oppose; fight or act against something

resistance NOUN **1** resisting • *The troops came up against armed resistance.* **2** the ability of a substance to hinder the flow of electricity
▷ **resistant** ADJECTIVE

resolute ADJECTIVE showing great determination
▷ **resolutely** ADVERB

resolution NOUN **resolutions 1** being resolute **2** something you have resolved to do • *New Year resolutions* **3** a formal decision made by a committee, etc. **4** the solving of a problem, etc.

resolve VERB **resolves, resolving, resolved 1** decide firmly or formally **2** solve a problem, etc. **3** overcome doubts or disagreements

resolve NOUN **1** something you have decided to do; a resolution **2** great determination

resort VERB **resorts, resorting, resorted** turn to or make use of something • *They resorted to violence.*

resort NOUN **resorts 1** a place where people go for relaxation or holidays **2** resorting • *without resort to cheating*
the last resort something to be tried when everything else has failed

resounding ADJECTIVE **1** loud and echoing **2** very great; outstanding • *a resounding victory*

Thesaurus
---

resign VERB **1** *The manager resigned at the end of the season.* ► leave, stand down, step down, give in your notice, (*informal*) quit, (*more informal*) call it a day, give up **2** *She resigned all her rights in the matter.* ► renounce, relinquish, abandon, surrender, cede, give up, forsake AN OPPOSITE IS take up

resignation NOUN **1** *They faced an uncertain future with resignation.* ► patience, forbearance, tolerance, stoicism, endurance, fortitude, sufferance, acceptance, fatalism **2** *There would be many resignations from the right wing of the party.* ► departure, notice, standing down, retirement, relinquishment

resilient ADJECTIVE **1** *Use a resilient material for harder wear.* ► flexible, supple, pliable, pliant, durable, tough, elastic, springy AN OPPOSITE IS inflexible **2** *She was still young and resilient.* ► adaptable, buoyant, irrepressible, tough, hardy, strong OPPOSITES ARE vulnerable, sensitive

resist VERB **1** *He resisted all our attempts to persuade him.* ► oppose, withstand, stand up to, defy, balk at, fend off, confront, fight OPPOSITES ARE yield to, submit to **2** *a hard varnish that resists wear for years* ► withstand, be proof against, combat, weather, endure, keep out AN OPPOSITE IS succumb to **3** *The temptation was so strong he was unable to resist any longer.* ► hold out, desist, restrain yourself, forbear OPPOSITES ARE yield, give in

resistant ADJECTIVE **1** *a material that is resistant to heat* ► impervious to, proof against, repellent to, immune to, unaffected by AN OPPOSITE IS susceptible to **2 resistant to** *He was always resistant to change.* ► opposed to, averse to, hostile to, suspicious of OPPOSITES ARE receptive to, attracted to

resolute ADJECTIVE *The local people put up a resolute resistance.* ► determined, purposeful, resolved, firm, steadfast, staunch, tenacious, unflinching, undaunted OPPOSITES ARE irresolute, halfhearted, feeble

resolution NOUN **1** *They showed great resolution in the face of danger.* ► determination, resolve, spirit, boldness, courage, firmness, fortitude, commitment, perseverance, doggedness, staunchness, steadfastness, tenacity, will power **2** *The committee passed the resolution by a large majority.* ► motion, proposal, proposition, declaration, decision, judgement **3** *Let's hope financial aid can be a resolution of the country's difficulties.* ► settlement, solution, answer (to)

resolve VERB **1** *It will take months to resolve the matter completely.* ► settle, sort out, work out, solve, put right, straighten out, rectify, deal with **2** *The boys resolved to keep going until dark.* ► determine, decide, make up your mind, take a decision

resolve NOUN *Opposition to his ideas only strengthened his resolve.* ► resolution, determination, firmness of purpose, steadfastness, tenacity OPPOSITES ARE indecision, hesitancy

resort NOUN **1** *Going on strike would be a last resort.* ► option, choice, alternative, course of action, expedient, recourse, refuge **2** *a seaside resort on the south coast* ► tourist spot, retreat, spa

resort VERB **resort to** *I don't want to have to resort to threats.* ► have recourse to, fall back on, make use of, turn to, adopt, utilize, use, sink to, stoop to

resound VERB *Thunder resounded in the hills.* ► resonate, reverberate, ring, echo, boom, vibrate

A
B
C
D
E
F
G
H
I
J
K
L
M
N
O
P
Q
R
S
T
U
V
W
X
Y
Z

resource NOUN **resources** **1** something that can be used; an asset ● *The country's natural resources include coal and oil.* **2** an ability; ingenuity

resourceful ADJECTIVE clever at finding ways of doing things
▷ **resourcefully** ADVERB **resourcefulness** NOUN

respect NOUN **respects** **1** admiration for a person's or thing's good qualities **2** politeness or consideration ● *Have respect for people's feelings.* **3** a detail or aspect ● *In this respect he is like his sister.* **4** reference ● *The rules with respect to bullying are quite clear.*

respect VERB **respects, respecting, respected** have respect for a person or thing

respectable ADJECTIVE **1** having good manners and character, etc. **2** fairly good ● *a respectable score*
▷ **respectably** ADVERB **respectability** NOUN

respectful ADJECTIVE showing respect
▷ **respectfully** ADVERB

respective ADJECTIVE belonging separately to each one of several ● *We went to our respective rooms*

respectively ADVERB in the same order as the people or things already mentioned ● *Ruth and Emma finished first and second*, respectively.

respiration NOUN breathing
▷ **respiratory** ADJECTIVE

respirator NOUN **respirators** **1** a device that fits over a person's nose and mouth to purify air before it is breathed **2** an apparatus for giving artificial respiration

resplendent ADJECTIVE brilliant with color or decorations

respond VERB **responds, responding, responded** **1** reply **2** act in answer to, or because of, something; react

response NOUN **responses** **1** a reply **2** a reaction

responsibility NOUN **responsibilities** **1** being responsible **2** something for which a person is responsible

responsible ADJECTIVE **1** looking after a person or thing and having to take the blame if something goes wrong **2** reliable and trustworthy **3** with important duties ● *a responsible job* **4** causing something ● *His carelessness was responsible for their deaths.*
▷ **responsibly** ADVERB

Thesaurus

resounding ADJECTIVE **1** *His fist hit the table with a resounding thump.* ▶ resonant, vibrant, reverberating, clear, ringing, echoing, booming **2** *The show had been a resounding success.* ▶ decided, emphatic, decisive, thorough, complete, outstanding, tremendous, great

resourceful ADJECTIVE *They were resourceful in using the few materials available.* ▶ imaginative, enterprising, inventive, creative, ingenious, innovative, original, talented, clever AN OPPOSITE IS unimaginative

resources PLURAL NOUN *The business had to survive on limited resources.* ▶ assets, funds, wealth, money, riches, capital, reserves

respect NOUN **1** *He showed the respect due to such a great writer.* ▶ esteem, regard, honor, deference, homage, admiration, awe, reverence, veneration, consideration **2** *The conclusions were correct in every respect.* ▶ aspect, regard, particular, point, characteristic, detail, facet, feature, way

respect VERB **1** *We respected them for their honesty.* ▶ admire, esteem, think well of, appreciate, regard, commend AN OPPOSITE IS despise **2** *She promised to respect her father's wishes.* ▶ comply with, abide by, observe, honor, obey, follow, conform to, adhere to

respectable ADJECTIVE **1** *He came from a respectable family in New England.* ▶ reputable, honorable, respected, upright, worthy, decent

AN OPPOSITE IS disreputable **2** *She found a job and now earns a respectable income.* ▶ decent, reasonable, substantial, considerable, sizeable

respectful ADJECTIVE *Two attendants were standing at a respectful distance.* ▶ deferential, courteous, polite, dutiful, reverential, gracious, civil OPPOSITES ARE disrespectful, rude

respective ADJECTIVE *We handed the horses back to their respective lads.* ▶ separate, individual, own, various, particular, several

respond VERB **respond to** *He responded to each question with a shrug.* ▶ answer, react to, reply to, acknowledge, greet, counter

response NOUN *The comment brought an angry response.* ▶ answer, reply, retort, reaction, rejoinder, riposte, acknowledgement, counter, (more informal) comeback

responsible ADJECTIVE **1** *He is responsible for the day-to-day running of the computer system.* ▶ accountable, answerable, in charge of **2** *Kim was responsible for the damage.* ▶ culpable, guilty, liable **3** *Mr. Jones was one of her most responsible tenants.* ▶ trustworthy, reliable, dependable, conscientious, honest, sensible AN OPPOSITE IS irresponsible **4** *She has a responsible position in a city bank.* ▶ important, powerful, influential, authoritative, executive

responsive ADJECTIVE *Educational institutions must become more responsive to the needs of students.* ▶ alert, alive, aware, impressionable,

rest[1] NOUN **rests 1** a time of sleep or freedom from work as a way of regaining strength **2** a support • *a chin rest* **3** an interval of silence between notes in music

rest VERB **rests, resting, rested 1** have a rest; be still **2** allow to rest • *Sit down and rest your feet.* **3** lean or place something so it is supported; be supported • *Rest the ladder against the wall.* **4** be left without further investigation etc. • *And there the matter rests.*

rest[2] NOUN the rest the remaining part; the others

rest VERB **rests, resting, rested** remain • *Rest assured, it will be a success.*
rest with be left to someone to deal with • *It rests with you to suggest a date.*

restaurant NOUN **restaurants** a place where you can buy a meal and eat it

restful ADJECTIVE giving rest or a feeling of rest

restive ADJECTIVE restless or impatient because of delay, boredom, etc.

restless ADJECTIVE unable to rest or keep still
▷ **restlessly** ADVERB

restore VERB **restores, restoring, restored 1** put something back to its original place or condition **2** clean and repair a work of art or building, etc., so that it looks as good as it did originally
▷ **restoration** NOUN

restrain VERB **restrains, restraining, restrained** hold a person or thing back; keep under control
▷ **restraint** NOUN

restrict VERB **restricts, restricting, restricted** keep within certain limits
▷ **restriction** NOUN **restrictive** ADJECTIVE

result NOUN **results 1** something produced by an action or condition, etc.; an effect or

Thesaurus

interested, open, perceptive, receptive, sympathetic, warmhearted, willing OPPOSITES ARE insensitive, apathetic

rest NOUN **1** *The rest of the group went to visit a gallery.* ► remainder, balance, remains, others **2** *You need a rest, Fran, you look tired.* ► break, breathing space, time off, nap, snooze, respite, pause, (*more informal*) breather **3** *alternating periods of rest and exercise* ► relaxation, leisure, respite, inactivity, ease, calm, tranquillity

rest VERB **1** *She went to rest in her room.* ► relax, take a rest, lie down, ease up, have a sleep, have a nap, have a snooze **2** *Her hand rested on his shoulder.* ► lie, be laid **3** *She rested her bike against the wall.* ► prop, lean, stand, support, place, put **4** *The success of the idea rests on the financial support they can bring in.* ► depend, rely, hang, hinge

restaurant NOUN *She wondered if the restaurant had a sushi bar.* ► eating place, eating house

restful ADJECTIVE *He enjoyed the most restful night he could remember.* ► relaxing, soothing, calm, peaceful, placid, quiet, tranquil, leisurely, untroubled OPPOSITES ARE restless, disturbed

restless ADJECTIVE **1** *My mother was restless, waiting for the family to return.* ► agitated, anxious, edgy, nervous, restive, fidgety, impatient, jittery, jumpy, worried AN OPPOSITE IS relaxed. **2** *a restless night of tossing and turning* ► sleepless, disturbed, troubled, uncomfortable, unsettled, interrupted AN OPPOSITE IS restful

restore VERB **1** *The interim government wished to restore democracy as soon as possible.* ► reinstate, bring back, reinstitute, reinstall, give back, put back, replace, return AN OPPOSITE IS abolish **2** *We must restore the property to its rightful owners.* ► return, give back, hand back, take

back, replace AN OPPOSITE IS retain **3** *The building has been beautifully restored.* ► renovate, repair, rebuild, recondition, reconstruct, refurbish, clean, (*more informal*) do up, renew AN OPPOSITE IS neglect **4** *An operation was needed to restore the girl's sight.* ► bring back, reestablish, rehabilitate, reinstate, reintroduce, revive

restrain VERB **1** *The dogs were restrained by leads.* ► bind, fetter, confine, restrict, tie, shackle **2** *She found it hard to restrain her laughter.* ► control, hold back, suppress, check, curb, prevent OPPOSITES ARE encourage, stimulate **3** *He had to restrain himself from jumping up and looking out of the window.* ► stop, keep, prevent, hold back AN OPPOSITE IS force

restrained ADJECTIVE *He was unusually restrained and conventional.* ► self-controlled, muted, unemotional, undemonstrative, inhibited, quiet, discreet, reserved, reticent, repressed, subdued AN OPPOSITE IS uninhibited

restrict VERB **1** *A busy working life restricted her opportunities to get away.* ► limit, constrain, impede, hinder, hamper, restrain, curtail AN OPPOSITE IS increase **2** *The prisoners were restricted to their cells.* ► confine, restrain, enclose, imprison, keep, shut AN OPPOSITE IS free

restriction NOUN **1** *There is a restriction on the number of places available.* ► limit, limitation, constraint, control, curb, restraint, check **2** *a society that imposes restrictions on personal freedom* ► limitation, reduction, diminution, curtailment, cutback

result NOUN **1** *The water shortage is a result of the hot weather.* ► consequence, effect, outcome, sequel, repercussion, upshot, fruit,

a
b
c
d
e
f
g
h
i
j
k
l
m
n
o
p
q
r
s
t
u
v
w
x
y
z

A B C D E F G H I J K L M N O P Q R S T U V W X Y Z

consequence **2** the score or situation at the end of a game, competition, or race, etc. **3** the answer to a sum or calculation

result VERB results, resulting, resulted **1** happen as a result **2** have a particular result
● *The match resulted in a draw.*
▷ **resultant** ADJECTIVE

resurrect VERB resurrects, resurrecting, resurrected bring back into use or existence
● *It is time to resurrect this old custom.*

resurrection NOUN **1** coming back to life after being dead **2** the revival of something **the Resurrection** in the Christian religion, the resurrection of Jesus Christ three days after his death

resuscitate VERB resuscitates, resuscitating, resuscitated revive a person from unconsciousness or apparent death
▷ **resuscitation** NOUN

retail NOUN selling to the general public
COMPARE **wholesale**
▷ **retailer** NOUN

retain VERB retains, retaining, retained **1** continue to have something; keep in your possession or memory, etc. **2** hold something in place

retaliate VERB retaliates, retaliating, retaliated repay an injury or insult, etc., with

a similar one; attack someone in return for a similar attack
▷ **retaliation** NOUN

reticent (ret- i- sent) ADJECTIVE not telling people what you feel or think; discreet
▷ **reticence** NOUN

retina NOUN retinas a layer of membrane at the back of the eyeball, sensitive to light

retinue NOUN retinues a group of people accompanying an important person

retire VERB retires, retiring, retired **1** give up your regular work when you reach a certain age **2** retreat or withdraw **3** go to bed or to your private room
▷ **retirement** NOUN

retiring ADJECTIVE shy; avoiding company

retort NOUN retorts **1** a quick or witty or angry reply **2** a glass bottle with a long downward bent neck, used in distilling liquids **3** a receptacle used in making steel, etc.

retort VERB retorts, retorting, retorted make a quick, witty, or angry reply

retract VERB retracts, retracting, retracted **1** pull back or in ● *The snail retracts its horns.* **2** withdraw an offer or statement
▷ **retraction** NOUN **retractable** ADJECTIVE

retreat VERB retreats, retreating, retreated go back after being defeated or to avoid danger or difficulty, etc.; withdraw

Thesaurus

issue, product, end-product **2** *the result of a trial* ► verdict, decision, judgment **3** *the result of an exam* ► mark, grade, score, assessment, ranking **4** *the result of a calculation* ► answer, solution

result VERB *What resulted from your interview?*
► arise, come about, culminate, develop, emanate, emerge, ensue, eventuate, follow, happen, issue, occur, proceed, spring, stem, take place, turn out
result in *The accident resulted in serious injuries.*
► end in, cause, involve, bring about, lead to, give rise to, achieve, provoke

resume VERB *It is essential to resume talks to reach an agreement.* ► restart, reopen, recommence, continue, begin again, start again, carry on, proceed with, reconvene

retain VERB **1** *When he retired he retained his shares in the company.* ► keep, hold on to, hang on to, preserve AN OPPOSITE IS surrender **2** *She retained her composure despite much provocation.* ► keep control of, maintain, preserve AN OPPOSITE IS lose **3** *Some students are good at retaining facts from their reading.*
► remember, memorize, keep in mind, learn, recall, recollect AN OPPOSITE IS forget

retaliate VERB *After the attack the Egyptians were powerless to retaliate.* ► fight back, strike

back, hit back, respond, reciprocate, take revenge, get even

retaliation NOUN *The best safeguard is the power to threaten retaliation.* ► reprisal, retribution, revenge, counterattack, vengeance

retire VERB **1** *She retired two years ago after a long career in teaching.* ► stop working, give up work **2** *Jane retired to her room for the evening.*
► withdraw, adjourn, retreat, decamp **3 retire from** *He intended to retire from the Senate before the next election.* ► resign from, withdraw from, give up, leave, quit

retort NOUN *She intended to make a sharp retort.*
► response, answer, reply, riposte, rejoinder, comeback, counter

retort VERB *"It's worth a try, surely," Jenkins retorted.* ► reply, answer, respond, counter, react, snap back

retract VERB **1** *The landing gear is retracted on takeoff.* ► pull in, draw in, pull back **2** *She apologized and retracted the accusations.*
► withdraw, take back, abandon, rescind, reverse, revoke, recant, renounce, cancel, disclaim, disown, repeal, repudiate

retreat NOUN **1** *Before he could say anything I made a hasty retreat.* ► departure, withdrawal, escape, exit, flight **2** *The family had a weekend retreat in the hills.* ► refuge, resort, haven, hideaway, hideout, sanctuary, shelter

retreat NOUN retreats 1 retreating 2 a quiet place to which someone can withdraw

retribution NOUN retributions a deserved punishment

retrieve VERB retrieves, retrieving, retrieved 1 bring or get something back 2 rescue
▷ **retrievable** ADJECTIVE **retrieval** NOUN

retriever NOUN retrievers a kind of dog that is often trained to retrieve game

retrograde ADJECTIVE 1 going backwards 2 becoming less good

retrospect NOUN
in retrospect when you look back at what has happened

retrospective ADJECTIVE 1 looking back on the past 2 applying to the past as well as the future ● *The law could not be made retrospective.*
▷ **retrospection** NOUN

return VERB returns, returning, returned 1 come back or go back 2 bring, give, put, or send back 3 elect to parliament

return NOUN returns 1 returning 2 something returned 3 profit ● *He gets a good return on his savings.* 4 a return ticket

return ticket NOUN return tickets a ticket for a journey to a place and back again

reunion NOUN reunions 1 reuniting 2 a meeting of people who have not met for some time

reunite VERB reunites, reuniting, reunited unite again after being separated

reuse VERB reuses, reusing, reused use something again
▷ **reusable** ADJECTIVE

reuse NOUN using something again

reveal VERB reveals, revealing, revealed let something be seen or known

revel VERB revels, revelling, revelled 1 take great delight in something 2 hold revels
▷ **reveller** NOUN

revelation NOUN revelations 1 revealing 2 something revealed, especially something surprising

revels PLURAL NOUN lively and noisy festivities

revenge NOUN harming somebody in return for harm that they have done to you

revenge VERB revenges, revenging, revenged revenge yourself take vengeance

---

Thesaurus

---

retreat VERB 1 *The army retreated in disarray.*
► withdraw, retire, draw back, fall back, move back, back away, depart, go away, leave, (more informal) run away, (more informal) turn tail AN OPPOSITE IS advance 2 *The tide retreated rapidly.* ► recede, shrink back, go out, ebb, flow back AN OPPOSITE IS come in 3 *The management had to retreat over their modernization plan.* ► back down, climb down, change your mind, backtrack, do a U-turn, withdraw AN OPPOSITE IS persevere

retrieve VERB 1 *She went next door to retrieve her ball.* ► get back, fetch back, bring back, recover, regain, rescue, find, reclaim, repossess, track down, salvage, save, trace 2 *It would not be easy to retrieve such an awkward situation.* ► put right, set right, rectify, remedy, sort out, straighten out, put to rights

return VERB 1 *They returned to Paris the next day.*
► go back, come back, get back, depart (for), set off (for), set out (for) 2 *I'll see you when I return.* ► come back, get back, arrive back, come home, get home, reappear 3 *She had found a stray cat and wanted to return it to its owner.* ► give back, send back, take back, restore, deliver, reunite (with) 4 *Things will soon return to their normal state.* ► go back, be back, revert 5 *After a while the headaches returned.* ► happen again, recur, reappear 6 *Neil came to return the money I had lent him.* ► give back, repay, refund, reimburse 7 *Jenny was eager to repay the favor.* ► reciprocate, repay, requite, recompense

return NOUN 1 *Their return was delayed by bad weather.* ► setting off back, departure 2 *We look forward to your return.* ► arrival, homecoming, reappearance 3 *the country's return to normality after the war* ► reversion, restoration (of), reestablishment (of) 4 *There is every danger of a return of the problem.*
► recurrence, reappearance, repetition 5 *We all want a good return on our investments.*
► income, profit, gain, interest 6 *There was a notice requesting the return of all library books.*
► replacement, bringing back, giving back, restitution

reveal VERB 1 *Kenny revealed the truth at last.*
► admit, confess, impart, divulge, tell, disclose, communicate, expose OPPOSITES ARE hide, conceal 2 *The police were unwilling to reveal the man's whereabouts.* ► disclose, divulge, publicize, broadcast, publish, betray OPPOSITES ARE conceal, keep secret 3 *He removed the cloth to reveal a beautiful bronze statuette.* ► expose, display, exhibit, show, uncover, unveil AN OPPOSITE IS cover

revenge NOUN 1 *The family is seeking revenge for Nino's killing.* ► vengeance, retribution, retaliation, reprisal, satisfaction 2 *They shot Maria's brother out of revenge.* ► vengefulness, vindictiveness, spite, malice, maliciousness, hatred

revenge VERB *He was determined to revenge his brother's ill-treatment.* ► avenge, take revenge for, retaliate for, have satisfaction for, repay, (more informal) get your own back for

A
B
C
D
E
F
G
H
I
J
K
L
M
N
O
P
Q
R
S
T
U
V
W
X
Y
Z

revenue NOUN revenues **1** a country's income from taxes, etc., used for paying public expenses **2** a company's income

reverberate VERB reverberates, reverberating, reverberated resound or re-echo
▷ **reverberation** NOUN

reverence NOUN a feeling of awe and deep or religious respect

Reverend NOUN the title of a member of the clergy • *the Reverend John Smith*
USAGE Do not confuse with reverent.

reverent ADJECTIVE feeling or showing reverence
▷ **reverently** ADVERB
USAGE Do not confuse with Reverend.

reverie (rev- er- ee) NOUN reveries a daydream

reversal NOUN reversals **1** reversing or being reversed **2** a piece of bad luck; a reverse

reverse ADJECTIVE opposite in direction, order, or manner etc.

reverse NOUN reverses **1** the reverse side, order, manner, etc. **2** a piece of misfortune in reverse the opposite way around

reverse VERB reverses, reversing, reversed **1** turn in the opposite direction or order etc.; turn something inside out or upside down **2** move backward **3** cancel a decision or decree
▷ **reversible** ADJECTIVE

reverse gear NOUN a gear that allows a vehicle to be driven backwards

review NOUN reviews **1** an inspection or survey **2** a published description and opinion of a book, film, play, etc.

review VERB reviews, reviewing, reviewed **1** write a review of a book, film, play, etc. **2** reconsider **3** inspect or survey
▷ **reviewer** NOUN
USAGE Do not confuse with revue.

revise VERB revises, revising, revised **1** go over work that you have already done **2** alter or correct something
▷ **revision** NOUN

revive VERB revives, reviving, revived come or bring back to life, strength, activity, or use, etc.
▷ **revival** NOUN

Thesaurus

---

be revenged *He would be revenged on them before the year was out.* ► take revenge on, have revenge on, retaliate against, get even with

revenue NOUN *The government is looking to increase its revenue from taxes on tobacco.*
► income, proceeds, receipts, return, yield, gain, profits, takings, money

reverberation NOUN **1** *The hall had a long reverberation period, making it unsuitable for their music.* ► resonance, resounding, echo, echoing, reechoing, ringing **2** *The scandal had reverberations for years.* ► repercussion, ramification, consequence, result, aftermath

revere VERB *They still revere him as a national hero.* ► respect, honor, esteem, admire, venerate, pay homage to, idolize, exalt, feel reverence for AN OPPOSITE IS despise

reverence NOUN *a deep reverence for their country's heroic past* ► respect, esteem, veneration, awe, homage, admiration, adoration (of), devotion (to), deference (to) OPPOSITES ARE disrespect, contempt

reverent ADJECTIVE *A reverent silence fell on the room.* ► respectful, reverential, deferential, awestruck, awed, solemn, devout, dutiful, pious OPPOSITES ARE irreverent, disrespectful

reverse NOUN **1** *The story turned out to be the reverse of the truth.* ► opposite, contrary, converse, inverse, antithesis **2** *Last year saw a mixture of successes and reverses.* ► failure, misfortune, setback, defeat, reversal, upset

reverse VERB **1** *We can reverse the order of events if you like.* ► turn around, swap around, change around, transpose, invert, alter **2** *He*

reversed the car into a tree. The truck reversed into the opening. ► back, go or drive backwards **3** *The referee refused to reverse his decision.* ► rescind, retract, revoke, undo, countermand, negate, overturn, repeal

review NOUN **1** *a review of the year's achievements* ► survey, report, reappraisal, study, analysis, reassessment, look back (at) **2** *On Saturday the paper has book reviews.* ► criticism, critique, notice, appreciation, (informal) write-up **3** *The research is described in a scientific review.* ► journal, periodical, magazine, publication **4** *a military review* ► inspection, parade, display, demonstration

review VERB **1** *Let's review the situation and decide what to do.* ► consider, survey, assess, evaluate, appraise, weigh up, go over, study, reconsider, reexamine, scrutinize **2** *She reviewed the book on a television arts program.* ► criticize, discuss, assess, evaluate

revise VERB **1** *I am not about to revise my opinion.* ► reconsider, reassess, rethink, change, alter

revival NOUN *a revival of interest in politics* ► resurgence, reawakening, renewal, recovery, restoration, resurrection, upsurge, rebirth, renaissance, return, revitalization AN OPPOSITE IS decline

revive VERB **1** *The man was unconscious but soon revived.* ► regain consciousness, recover, come round, come to, awake **2** *Hot drinks soon revived us.* ► reinvigorate, revitalize, resuscitate, refresh, freshen up, renew, restore, bring back to life

revolt VERB revolts, revolting, revolted **1** rebel **2** disgust somebody

revolt NOUN revolts a rebellion

revolting ADJECTIVE disgusting

revolution NOUN revolutions **1** a rebellion that overthrows the government **2** a complete change **3** revolving or rotation; one complete turn of a wheel, engine, etc.
▷ **revolutionary** ADJECTIVE

revolve VERB revolves, revolving, revolved **1** turn in a circle around a central point **2** have something as the most important element ● *Her life revolves around her work.*

revolver NOUN revolvers a pistol with a revolving mechanism that makes it possible to fire it a number of times without reloading

revue NOUN revues an entertainment consisting of songs, sketches, etc., often about current events
USAGE Do not confuse with **review**.

revulsion NOUN a feeling of disgust

reward NOUN rewards **1** something given in return for something good you have done **2** a sum of money offered for help in catching a criminal or finding lost property

reward VERB rewards, rewarding, rewarded give a reward to someone

rewarding ADJECTIVE giving satisfaction and a feeling of achievement ● *a rewarding job*

rewind VERB rewinds, rewinding, rewound wind a cassette or videotape back to or towards the beginning

rhetorical question NOUN rhetorical questions a question asked for dramatic effect and not intended to get an answer, e.g. "Who cares?" (= nobody cares)

rheumatism NOUN a disease that causes pain and stiffness in joints and muscles
▷ **rheumatic** ADJECTIVE **rheumatoid** ADJECTIVE [from Greek *rheuma*, a substance in the body which was once believed to cause rheumatism]

Thesaurus

revoke VERB *The new regime revoked his passport.* ► cancel, withdraw, rescind, abrogate, invalidate, retract, nullify

revolt VERB **1** *The island revolted against Athenian rule.* ► rebel, rise up, defect, mutiny **2** *Their cruelty revolted us.* ► disgust, sicken, shock, outrage, offend, repel, nauseate

revolt NOUN *a revolt in the Netherlands* ► rebellion, uprising, revolution, defection, mutiny

revolting ADJECTIVE *There was a revolting mess on the floor.* ► disgusting, repulsive, nauseating, offensive, sickening, loathsome, repugnant, unpleasant

revolution NOUN **1** *A revolution brought the democrats to power again.* ► rebellion, revolt, rising, uprising, coup, coup d'état, mutiny, civil war **2** *a revolution of the earth* ► rotation, circuit, cycle, orbit, turn **3** *a revolution in information technology* ► transformation, dramatic change, sea change, shift

revolutionary ADJECTIVE **1** *Revolutionary forces attacked the city.* ► rebel, rebellious, renegade, seditious, subversive, extremist **2** *a revolutionary idea for traffic control* ► original, innovative, innovatory, radical, novel, new, unconventional, progressive, inventive, advanced, experimental, avant-garde, challenging AN OPPOSITE IS conservative

revolve VERB **1** *The ceiling fan began to revolve.* ► turn, go around, rotate, spin, whirl **2** *The moon revolves around the earth.* ► circle, orbit, gyrate **3 revolve around** *Their lives revolved around their dogs.* ► concentrate on, center on, focus on *or* be focused on, be absorbed in, be preoccupied with

revulsion NOUN *a feeling of revulsion against the savagery of these acts* ► disgust, repulsion, abhorrence, repugnance, horror, loathing, nausea, contempt (for)

reward NOUN **1** *a reward for years of loyal service* ► honor, award, remuneration, prize, bonus, return, decoration, medal **2** *The dog's owners have offered a reward for its safe return.* ► recompense, payment, compensation, inducement, present, bounty AN OPPOSITE IS punishment

reward VERB **1** *All three soldiers were rewarded for their bravery.* ► decorate, honor, recognize AN OPPOSITE IS punish **2** *You will be well rewarded for your work.* ► recompense, remunerate, pay, repay, compensate, give a reward to AN OPPOSITE IS punish

rewarding ADJECTIVE *The trip proved to be a rewarding experience.* ► satisfying, worthwhile, pleasing, gratifying, fulfilling, fruitful, valuable OPPOSITES ARE unrewarding, thankless

reword VERB *Do you think you should reword the last sentence?* ► rephrase, recast, rewrite, put another way, express differently, revise, redraft, edit

rhetoric NOUN **1** *a statesman renowned for his rhetoric* ► oratory, eloquence, power of speech **2** *Ignore the rhetoric and there are some interesting things in these speeches.* ► pomposity, bombast, extravagant language, grandiloquence, verbosity, wordiness, exaggeration, hyperbole

rhetorical ADJECTIVE *His manner of speaking tends to be rhetorical.* ► extravagant, grandiloquent, bombastic, oratorical, high-flown, ornate, artificial, pretentious, verbose, wordy, flowery OPPOSITES ARE plain, direct

a
b
c
d
e
f
g
h
i
j
k
l
m
n
o
p
q
r
s
t
u
v
w
x
y
z

rhino NOUN rhino or rhinos (*informal*) a rhinoceros

rhinoceros NOUN rhinoceros or rhinoceroses a large heavy animal with a horn or two horns on its nose [from Greek *rhinos* = of the nose + *keras* = horn]

rhizome NOUN rhizomes a thick underground stem which produces roots and new plants

rhododendron NOUN rhododendrons an evergreen shrub with large trumpet-shaped flowers [from Greek *rhodon* = rose + *dendron* = tree]

rhombus NOUN rhombuses a shape with four equal sides but no right angles, like the diamond on playing cards

rhubarb NOUN a plant with thick reddish stalks that are cooked and eaten as fruit

rhyme NOUN rhymes **1** a similar sound in the endings of words, e.g. *bat/fat/mat* or *batter/fatter/matter* **2** a poem with rhymes **3** a word that rhymes with another

rhyme VERB rhymes, rhyming, rhymed **1** form a rhyme **2** have rhymes

rhythm NOUN rhythms a regular pattern of beats, sounds, or movements
▷ **rhythmic** ADJECTIVE **rhythmical** ADJECTIVE **rhythmically** ADVERB

rib NOUN ribs **1** each of the curved bones round the chest **2** a curved part that looks like a rib or supports something • *the ribs of an umbrella*
▷ **ribbed** ADJECTIVE

ribbon NOUN ribbons **1** a narrow strip of silk or nylon etc. used for decoration or for tying something **2** a long narrow strip of inked material used in a typewriter, etc.

rice NOUN a cereal plant grown in flooded fields in hot countries, or its seeds

rich ADJECTIVE **1** having a lot of money or property; wealthy **2** having a large supply of something • *The country is rich in natural resources.* **3** (said about color, sound, or smell) pleasantly deep or strong **4** (said about food) containing a lot of fat, butter, eggs, etc. **5** expensive or luxurious
▷ **richness** NOUN

richly ADVERB **1** in a rich or luxurious way **2** fully or thoroughly • *This award is richly deserved.*

rickety ADJECTIVE shaky; likely to break or fall down

rickshaw NOUN rickshaws a two-wheeled carriage pulled by one or more people, used in the Far East [from Japanese *jin-riki-sha* = person-power-vehicle]

ricochet (rik- osh- ay) VERB ricochets, ricocheting, ricocheted bounce off something; rebound • *The bullets ricocheted off the wall.*
▷ **ricochet** NOUN
[from French, = the skipping of a flat stone on water]

ricotta NOUN a kind of soft Italian cheese made from sheep's milk [from Italian]

rid VERB rids, ridding, rid make a person or place free from something unwanted • *He rid the town of rats.*
get rid of remove something or throw it away

riddle NOUN riddles a puzzling question, especially as a joke

Thesaurus

rhyme NOUN *She tried to remember the words of the rhyme.* ► poem, verse, ditty, ode, song, jingle

rhythm NOUN **1** *the rhythm of the poem* ► meter, measure, accent, flow **2** *the heavy rhythm of the rock music upstairs* ► beat, throb, pulse

rhythmic ADJECTIVE *the rhythmic beat of the music* ► pulsing, rhythmical, metrical, throbbing, steady, regular, lilting AN OPPOSITE IS irregular

rich ADJECTIVE **1** *Rich people pay higher rates of tax.* ► wealthy, affluent, moneyed, well-to-do, prosperous, opulent, (*more informal*) flush, (*more informal*) loaded OPPOSITES ARE poor, impoverished **2** *a room of rich furnishings* ► sumptuous, opulent, luxurious, ornate, lavish, costly, fine, gorgeous, elaborate, splendid **3** *acres of rich agricultural land* ► fertile, productive, fruitful, lush OPPOSITES ARE infertile, unproductive **4** *a rich output of music dramas* ► plentiful, abundant, copious, prolific, profuse, plenteous, ample, teeming **5** *the rich colors of autumn* ► deep, full, strong, intense, vibrant, vivid, warm AN OPPOSITE IS pale

riches PLURAL NOUN *He spoke dreamily of the riches of Hollywood.* ► wealth, money, affluence, fortune, treasure, assets, means, property

rickety ADJECTIVE *a small wild garden with a rickety greenhouse* ► shaky, unsteady, unstable, wobbly, flimsy, decrepit, ramshackle, dilapidated, broken-down

rid VERB *The builders should rid the house of asbestos and all dangerous substances.* ► clear, free, strip, purge, cleanse
get rid of *Scotland had gotten rid of its usurper.* ► dispose of, expel, remove, eject, evict, throw out, dispense with, (*more informal*) dump

riddle NOUN *The authorities want to solve the riddle of the man's identity.* ► enigma, mystery, puzzle, question, problem, conundrum, (*more informal*) poser

riddle VERB riddles, riddling, riddled pierce with many holes • *The car was riddled with bullets.*

ride VERB rides, riding, rode, ridden **1** sit on a horse, bicycle, etc., and be carried along on it **2** travel in a car, bus, train, etc. **3** float or be supported on something • *The ship rode the waves.*

ride NOUN rides **1** a journey on a horse, bicycle, etc., or in a vehicle **2** a roller coaster, etc., that you ride on at a fair or amusement park

ridge NOUN ridges **1** a long narrow part higher than the rest of something **2** a long narrow range of hills or mountains
▷ **ridged** ADJECTIVE

ridicule VERB ridicules, ridiculing, ridiculed make fun of a person or thing
▷ **ridicule** NOUN

ridiculous ADJECTIVE so silly that it makes people laugh or despise it
▷ **ridiculously** ADVERB

rifle NOUN rifles a long gun with spiral grooves (called **rifling**) inside the barrel that make the bullet spin and so travel more accurately

rifle VERB rifles, rifling, rifled search and rob • *They rifled his desk.*

rift valley NOUN rift valleys a steep-sided valley formed where the land has sunk

rig[1] VERB rigs, rigging, rigged **1** provide a ship with ropes, spars, sails, etc. **2** set something up quickly or out of makeshift materials • *We managed to rig up a shelter for the night.*
rig out provide with clothes or equipment

rig NOUN rigs **1** a framework supporting the machinery for drilling an oil well **2** the way a ship's masts and sails etc. are arranged **3** (*informal*) an outfit of clothes [probably from a Scandinavian language]

rig[2] VERB rigs, rigging, rigged arrange the result of an election or contest dishonestly [origin unknown]

rigging NOUN the ropes, etc., that support a ship's mast and sails

right ADJECTIVE **1** on or towards the east if you think of yourself as facing north **2** correct; true • *the right answer* **3** morally good; fair or just • *Is it right to cheat?* **4** (said about political groups) conservative; not in favor of socialist reforms
▷ **right-hand** ADJECTIVE **rightly** ADVERB **rightness** NOUN

right ADVERB **1** on or towards the right-hand side • *Turn right here.* **2** straight • *Go right on.* **3** completely • *Turn right round.* **4** exactly • *right in the middle* **5** correctly or appropriately • *Did I do that right?*
right away immediately

Thesaurus

riddle VERB **1** *The gunman riddled the door with holes.* ► perforate, puncture, pepper, pierce **2** *Her body was riddled with arthritis.* ► overrun, infest, permeate, pervade, cripple

ride VERB **1** *I'm learning to ride a horse.* ► control, handle, manage, sit on **2** *She rode through the town on a bicycle.* ► travel, pedal, drive, steer, progress

ride NOUN *The house is a short ride from the city center.* ► journey, trip, drive, run, jaunt, outing, (*more informal*) spin

ridicule NOUN *We will be open to ridicule if we get things wrong.* ► derision, mockery, scorn, contempt, taunting, jeering, banter, teasing

ridicule VERB *I did not ridicule him as the others did.* ► deride, mock, make fun of, laugh at, jeer at, sneer at, scoff at, humiliate, taunt

ridiculous ADJECTIVE *It was ridiculous to feel so worried.* ► absurd, preposterous, ludicrous, senseless, silly, stupid, unreasonable, nonsensical, incredible, irrational, insane, mad

rife ADJECTIVE *Terror and torture were rife then.* ► widespread, common, prevalent, general, universal, endemic, abundant

rift NOUN **1** *a rift in the ice* ► crack, fault, flaw, fracture, split, break, fissure **2** *a rift between the two leaders* ► breach, division, disagreement, difference of opinion, falling-out, estrangement, schism, alienation

rig NOUN **1** *He was wearing the rig of an army captain.* ► uniform, dress, outfit, livery **2** *She was busy setting up the recording rig for the afternoon.* ► equipment, apparatus, machinery, gear, system, kit, tackle

rig VERB *They were accused of rigging the election.* ► manipulate, falsify, tamper with, interfere with, gerrymander, influence

right ADJECTIVE **1** *What is the right thing to do? Are you sure he's the right person for the job?* ► proper, appropriate, suitable, fitting, ideal OPPOSITES ARE wrong, unsuitable **2** *She gave the right answer.* ► correct, accurate, exact, precise, true, actual, real, apposite, appropriate, apt, factual, genuine, proper OPPOSITES ARE wrong, incorrect **3** *It's not right for them to be treated in this way.* ► fair, just, equitable, lawful, ethical, honourable, moral AN OPPOSITE IS unjust

right NOUN **1** *Everyone should have the right to say what they believe.* ► entitlement, prerogative, freedom, liberty, privilege (of saying), facility **2** *We believe we have right on our side.* ► justice, virtue, fairness, goodness, legality, integrity, morality, honesty

right VERB *We will do our best to right the situation.* ► remedy, rectify, put right, set right, redress, repair, resolve, correct, sort out, make amends for

A
B
C
D
E
F
G
H
I
J
K
L
M
N
O
P
Q

right NOUN rights **1** the right-hand side or part etc. **2** what is morally good or fair or just **3** something that people are allowed to do or have • *People over 18 have the right to vote in elections.*

right VERB rights, righting, righted **1** make a thing right or upright • *They righted the boat.* **2** put right • *The fault might right itself.*

right angle NOUN an angle of 90°

rightful ADJECTIVE deserved or proper • *in her rightful place*
▷ **rightfully** ADVERB

right hand NOUN right hands the hand that most people use more than the left, on the right side of the body

right-handed ADJECTIVE using the right hand in preference to the left hand

right of way NOUN rights of way **1** a public path across private land **2** the right of one vehicle to pass or cross a junction, etc., before another

rigid ADJECTIVE **1** stiff or firm; not bending • *a rigid support* **2** strict • *rigid rules*
▷ **rigidly** ADVERB **rigidity** NOUN

rigmarole NOUN rigmaroles **1** a long rambling statement **2** a complicated procedure

rigorous ADJECTIVE **1** strict or severe **2** careful and thorough
▷ **rigorously** ADVERB

rim NOUN rims the outer edge of a cup, wheel, or other round object

rind NOUN the tough skin on bacon, cheese, or fruit

ring NOUN rings **1** a circle **2** a thin circular piece of metal worn on a finger **3** the space where a circus performs **4** a square area in which a boxing match or wrestling match takes place

ring[1] VERB rings, ringing put a ring around something; encircle

ring[2] VERB rings, ringing, rang, rung **1** cause a bell to sound **2** make a loud clear sound like that of a bell **3** be filled with sound • *The hall rang with cheers* **4** telephone • *Please ring me tomorrow.*
▷ **ringer** NOUN

ring NOUN rings the act or sound of ringing **give someone a ring** (*informal*) telephone someone

ringleader NOUN ringleaders a person who leads others in rebellion, mischief, crime, etc.

ringmaster NOUN ringmasters the person in charge of a performance in a circus ring

rink NOUN rinks a place made for skating

rinse VERB rinses, rinsing, rinsed **1** wash something lightly **2** wash in clean water to remove soap

rinse NOUN rinses **1** rinsing **2** a liquid for coloring the hair

riot NOUN riots wild or violent behavior by a crowd of people
run riot behave or spread in an unruly or uncontrolled way

Thesaurus

R
S
T
U
V
W
X
Y
Z

rightful ADJECTIVE **1** *The car was returned to its rightful owner.* ▶ lawful, legal, legitimate, genuine, approved, authorized, proper, real, true, valid AN OPPOSITE IS wrongful **2** *He felt he had been denied his rightful place in the company.* ▶ deserved, due, merited, earned, proper, fitting, just, right

rigid ADJECTIVE **1** *It's best to keep your lunch in a rigid container.* ▶ stiff, hard, firm, inflexible **2** *He had not yet established a rigid routine for his work.* ▶ fixed, set, firm, definite, unvarying, hard-and-fast **3** *She had a reputation as a rigid disciplinarian.* ▶ strict, stern, severe, harsh, uncompromising, unyielding AN OPPOSITE IS flexible

rigorous ADJECTIVE **1** *a rigorous attention to detail* ▶ meticulous, thorough, careful, scrupulous, painstaking, conscientious, diligent, fastidious, stringent OPPOSITES ARE lax, careless **2** *a rigorous climate* ▶ harsh, severe, inclement, extreme, inhospitable, unfriendly, unpleasant AN OPPOSITE IS mild

rile VERB (*informal*) *His companions seemed determined to rile him.* ▶ irritate, annoy, anger, enrage, exasperate, incense, upset, peeve, vex,

(*more informal*) needle, (*more informal*) bug, (*more informal*) rub up the wrong way

rim NOUN *They stared over the rim of the crater.* ▶ brim, edge, lip, border, brink, verge, circumference

rind NOUN *the rind of a lemon* ▶ peel, skin, husk, crust, outer layer

ring NOUN **1** *A ring of fire would protect her.* ▶ circle, loop, round, circuit, halo **2** *a spy ring* ▶ network, organization, syndicate, association, gang, group, cell, cartel **3** *a ring of spectators* ▶ circle, band, group, crowd, throng **4** *a circus ring* ▶ arena, enclosure RELATED ADJECTIVE ▶ annular

ring VERB **1** *Riot police ringed the area.* ▶ surround, circle, encircle, confine, enclose, encompass, form a ring round **2** *Church bells rang all morning.* ▶ peal, chime, toll, clang, resound, jangle, reverberate **3** *I'll ring you tomorrow evening.* ▶ phone, call, telephone, ring up, (*informal*) give a buzz

rinse VERB *Campers were rinsing their plates in the stream.* ▶ wash, wash out, swill, bathe, clean, sluice

riot NOUN *The authorities were reluctant to make arrests for fear of sparking a riot.* ▶ uproar,

riot VERB riots, rioting, rioted take part in a riot

riotous ADJECTIVE **1** disorderly or unruly **2** boisterous • *riotous laughter*

R.I.P. ABBREVIATION may he or she (or they) rest in peace

rip VERB rips, ripping, ripped **1** tear roughly **2** rush

rip off (*informal*) swindle or charge too much

rip NOUN a torn place

ripe ADJECTIVE riper, ripest **1** ready to be harvested or eaten **2** ready and suitable • *The time is ripe for revolution.*
▷ **ripeness** NOUN
a ripe old age a great age

ripen VERB ripens, ripening, ripened make or become ripe

rip-off NOUN rip-offs (*informal*) a swindle or excessive charge

ripple NOUN ripples a small wave or series of waves

ripple VERB ripples, rippling, rippled form ripples

rise VERB rises, rising, rose, risen **1** go upward **2** increase • *Prices are expected to rise.* **3** get up from lying, sitting, or kneeling **4** get out of bed **5** rebel • *They rose in revolt against the tyrant.* **6** (said about bread or cake, etc.) swell up by the action of yeast **7** (said about a river) begin its course **8** (said about the wind) begin to blow more strongly

rise NOUN rises **1** the action of rising; an upward movement **2** an increase in amount, etc., or in wages **3** an upward slope
give rise to cause

rising NOUN risings a revolt

risk NOUN risks a chance of danger or loss

risk VERB risks, risking, risked **1** take the chance of damaging or losing something • *They were risking their lives.* **2** accept the risk of something unpleasant happening • *He risks injury.*

risky ADJECTIVE riskier, riskiest full of risk

ritual NOUN rituals the series of actions used in a religious or other ceremony
▷ **ritual** ADJECTIVE **ritually** ADVERB

rival NOUN rivals a person or thing that competes with another or tries to do the same thing
▷ **rivalry** NOUN
[from Latin *rivalis* = someone using the same stream (from *rivus* = stream)]

Thesaurus

insurrection, uprising, rising, tumult, commotion, brawl, street fight, fracas

riot VERB *The crowd rioted and pulled down the gates.* ► rampage, run riot, create a riot, run amok, go berserk, revolt, rise up, mutiny, rebel

riotous ADJECTIVE *a riotous party* ► wild, lively, boisterous, roisterous, loud, noisy, uproarious, rollicking OPPOSITES ARE orderly, restrained

rip VERB *She read the note and ripped it into little pieces. The travelers ripped a way through the foliage.* ► tear, slash, cut, rend, gash

ripe ADJECTIVE **1** *a ripe melon* ► mature, ripened, tender, juicy OPPOSITES ARE unripe, green **2** *an area ripe for development* ► ready, suitable, fit AN OPPOSITE IS unsuitable

ripen VERB *The apples need time to ripen.* ► become ripe, mature, develop, mellow

rise VERB **1** *The little plane rose into the air.* ► ascend, go up, fly up, climb OPPOSITES ARE fall, descend **2** *The castle walls rose above us.* ► tower, soar, loom, reach up **3** *Incomes have risen by an average 3 percent.* ► increase, grow, go up, get higher, escalate **4** *She rose from her chair.* ► stand up, get up, jump up, leap up

rise NOUN **1** *We walked up the rise to the castle.* ► slope, incline, elevation, ascent, hill, ramp, bank **2** *another rise in interest rates* ► increase, jump, leap, upturn

risk NOUN **1** *She faced the risk of being stopped by the police.* ► chance, likelihood, possibility, danger **2** *Travelling at such a high speed involved risk.* ► hazard, peril, danger, speculation, uncertainty, gamble

risk VERB **1** *He didn't want to risk leaving her alone.* ► chance, dare, venture **2** *She risked everything to meet him again.* ► endanger, jeopardize, put at risk, put in peril, chance, imperil, hazard

risky ADJECTIVE **1** *Any project involving rockets is always risky.* ► dangerous, hazardous, unsafe, perilous, (*more informal*) dodgy AN OPPOSITE IS safe **2** *Farming is a risky business.* ► precarious, uncertain, chancy, touch-and-go AN OPPOSITE IS secure

ritual NOUN **1** *a religious ritual* ► ceremony, rite, ceremonial, observance, service, liturgy **2** *The Sunday outing had become something of a ritual.* ► custom, tradition, habit, formality

rival NOUN *Leo was his main rival for the job.* ► competitor, adversary, challenger, opponent, contender, contestant

rival ADJECTIVE *A rival supermarket has opened.* ► competing, competitive, opposing

rival VERB *Few countries rival Greece for its beauty.* ► compete with, contend with, compare with, equal, match, be as good as, emulate, vie with

rivalry NOUN *There was growing rivalry between the two teams.* ► competitiveness, competition, contention, opposition, conflict, antagonism AN OPPOSITE IS cooperation

A
B
C
D
E
F
G
H
I
J
K
L
M
N
O
P
Q
R
S
T
U
V
W
X
Y
Z

river NOUN rivers a large stream of water flowing in a natural channel

rivet NOUN rivets a strong nail or bolt for holding pieces of metal together. The end opposite the head is flattened to form another head when it is in place.

rivet VERB rivets, riveting, riveted **1** fasten with rivets **2** hold firmly • He stood riveted to the spot. **3** fascinate • The concert was riveting.
▷ **riveter** NOUN

road NOUN roads **1** a level way with a hard surface made for traffic to travel on **2** a way or course • the road to success [from Old English]

roadblock NOUN roadblocks a barrier across a road, set up by the police or army to stop and check vehicles

road rage NOUN violent or aggressive behavior by a driver towards other drivers

roadworthy ADJECTIVE safe to be used on roads

roam VERB roams, roaming, roamed wander
▷ **roam** NOUN

roar NOUN roars a loud deep sound like that made by a lion

roar VERB roars, roaring, roared **1** make a roar **2** laugh loudly
do a roaring trade do very good business

roast VERB roasts, roasting, roasted **1** cook meat etc. in an oven or by exposing it to heat **2** make or be very hot

roast ADJECTIVE roasted • roast beef

roast NOUN roasts **1** meat for roasting **2** roast meat [from early French]

rob VERB robs, robbing, robbed take or steal from somebody • He robbed me of my watch.
▷ **robber** NOUN **robbery** NOUN

robe NOUN robes a long loose garment

robin NOUN robins a small brown bird with a red breast [from early French, = Robert]

robot NOUN robots **1** a machine that looks or acts like a person **2** a machine operated by remote control
▷ **robotic** ADJECTIVE
[from Czech robota = forced labour]

robust ADJECTIVE strong and vigorous
▷ **robustly** ADVERB **robustness** NOUN

rock NOUN rocks **1** a large stone or boulder **2** the hard part of the earth's crust, under the soil

rock VERB rocks, rocking, rocked **1** move gently backward and forward while supported on something **2** shake violently • The earthquake rocked the city.

rock NOUN **1** a rocking movement **2** rock music

rock and roll or **rock 'n' roll** NOUN a kind of popular dance music with a strong beat, originating in the 1950s

rock-bottom ADJECTIVE at the lowest level
• rock-bottom prices

Thesaurus

---

river NOUN a trip down the river ► stream, waterway, watercourse, brook, rivulet, creek

road NOUN a busy road ► roadway, route, way, highway, motorway, street, avenue, boulevard

roadworthy ADJECTIVE a roadworthy vehicle ► safe, usable

roam VERB People like to roam over the hills. ► wander, rove, ramble, stroll, amble, walk, meander, travel, stray, range

roar NOUN the roars of the crowd ► yell, shout, clamor, bellow, howl

roar VERB **1** Bill roared at them to stop. ► bellow, yell, shout, bawl, clamor, shriek **2** A motorbike roared past. ► speed, zoom, whizz, flash **3** He had the audience roaring. ► guffaw, howl, hoot, (more informal) split your sides, (more informal) kill yourself laughing

rob VERB **1** The gang had robbed banks all over the southeast. ► burgle, hold up, steal from, break into, raid, loot, rifle **2** She was attacked and robbed on her way home that evening. ► mug, steal from, hold up **3** They thought they had been robbed of their victory. ► deprive, cheat, defraud, swindle

robber NOUN Robbers attacked the travellers on the road north. ► thief, brigand, bandit, raider, highwayman, marauder USAGE You can also use burglar and housebreaker for robbers who steal from buildings, and mugger for robbers who attack people in the street.

robbery NOUN a wave of robberies and other crimes ► burglary, theft, thieving, stealing, housebreaking, shoplifting, pilfering, hold-up, mugging, (more informal) stick-up

robot NOUN ► automaton, computerized machine, automated machine, android

robust ADJECTIVE **1** a man with a robust physique ► strong, vigorous, hardy, muscular, powerful, rugged, athletic, brawny, healthy, sound **2** The tools will need to be very robust. ► sturdy, durable, strong, tough, serviceable AN OPPOSITE IS fragile

rock NOUN **1** a castle high up on a rock ► cliff, crag, outcrop **2** Rocks were strewn across the road. ► boulder, stone

rock VERB **1** The woman rocked gently in her chair. ► sway, swing, move gently **2** The ship rocked in the storm. ► toss, lurch, sway, pitch, plunge, roll **3** News of the disaster rocked the nation. ► stun, shake, stagger, astound, astonish, startle, dumbfound

rockery NOUN rockeries a mound or bank in a garden, where plants are made to grow between large rocks

rocket NOUN rockets 1 a firework that shoots high into the air 2 a structure that flies by expelling burning gases, used to send up a missile or a spacecraft

rocket VERB rockets, rocketing, rocketed move quickly upwards or away

rocking horse NOUN rocking horses a model of a horse that can be rocked by a child sitting on it

rock music NOUN popular music with a heavy beat

rocky[1] ADJECTIVE rockier, rockiest 1 like rock 2 full of rocks

rocky[2] ADJECTIVE rockier, rockiest unsteady
▷ **rockiness** NOUN

rod NOUN rods 1 a long thin stick or bar 2 a stick with a line attached for fishing

rodent NOUN rodents an animal that has large front teeth for gnawing things. Rats, mice, and squirrels are rodents.

rodeo (roh- di- oh) NOUN rodeos a display of cowboys' skill in riding, controlling horses, etc.

roe[1] NOUN a mass of eggs or reproductive cells in a fish's body

roe[2] NOUN roes or roe a kind of small deer of Europe and Asia. The male is called a **roebuck**

rogue NOUN rogues 1 a dishonest person 2 a mischievous person
▷ **roguery** NOUN

role NOUN roles 1 a performer's part in a play or film, etc. 2 someone's or something's purpose or function • the role of computers in education

role model NOUN role models a person admired by others as an example of how to behave

roll VERB rolls, rolling, rolled 1 move along by turning over and over, like a ball or wheel 2 form something into the shape of a cylinder or ball 3 flatten something by rolling a rounded object over it 4 rock from side to side 5 pass steadily • The years rolled on. 6 make a long vibrating sound • The thunder rolled.

roll NOUN rolls 1 a cylinder made by rolling something up 2 a small individual portion of bread baked in a rounded shape 3 an official list of names 4 a long vibrating sound • a drum roll

roll call NOUN roll calls the calling of a list of names to check that everyone is present

roller NOUN rollers 1 a cylinder for rolling over things, or on which something is wound 2 a long swelling sea wave

Rollerblade NOUN Rollerblades (trade mark) a boot like an ice-skating boot, with a line of wheels in place of the skate, for rolling smoothly on hard ground
▷ **rollerblading** NOUN

roller coaster NOUN roller coasters a type of railway used for amusement at fairgrounds, etc., with a series of alternate steep descents and ascents

roller skate NOUN roller skates a framework with wheels, fitted under a shoe so that the wearer can roll smoothly over the ground
▷ **roller-skating** NOUN

rolling pin NOUN a heavy cylinder for rolling over pastry to flatten it

ROM ABBREVIATION (in computing) read-only memory, a type of memory with contents that can be searched or copied but not changed

Thesaurus

rocket VERB Prices have rocketed under this government. ► shoot up, soar, escalate, spiral, increase rapidly, (more informal) go through the roof

rocky ADJECTIVE 1 a rocky hillside ► stony, rock-strewn, craggy, shingly, pebbly, rugged 2 The table is rocky. ► unsteady, shaky, wobbly, rickety, tottery 3 The marriage had become decidedly rocky. ► precarious, difficult, problematic, unstable

rod NOUN 1 an iron rod ► bar, pole, baton, staff, shaft, scepter 2 He was beaten with a rod. ► cane, switch

rogue NOUN In the story, everyone is either a fool or a rogue. ► villain, scoundrel, rascal, good-for-nothing, reprobate, crook

role NOUN 1 The director took a small role in the film. ► part, character, portrayal 2 He spoke in his role of government adviser. ► capacity, function, position, office, post, job

roll NOUN 1 a roll of film ► reel, spool, cylinder, drum, scroll 2 an electoral roll ► register, list, record, index, catalogue, schedule, inventory

roll VERB 1 The can rolled into the gutter. The huge wheels began to roll. ► rotate, revolve, turn, spin, whirl, gyrate 2 She rolled the paper into a ball. ► wind, fold, coil, twist, curl, screw 3 The ship began to roll. ► rock, sway, lurch, pitch, toss, reel 4 He was in the kitchen, rolling pastry. ► smooth, flatten, level, even out 5 Thunder rolled in the distance. ► rumble, boom, resound, reverberate, thunder

roll up (informal) He rolled up with some friends just as we were leaving. ► arrive, appear, come, show your face, (informal) turn up, (informal) show up

A
B
C
D
E
F
G
H
I
J
K
L
M
N
O
P
Q
R
S
T
U
V
W
X
Y
Z

Roman ADJECTIVE to do with ancient or modern Rome or its people
▷ **Roman** NOUN

Roman alphabet NOUN the alphabet used by the ancient Romans, in which most European languages are written

Roman Catholic ADJECTIVE belonging to or to do with the Christian Church that has the Pope as its leader

Roman Catholic NOUN Roman Catholics a member of this Church

romance (ro- manss) NOUN romances **1** tender feelings, experiences, and qualities connected with love **2** a love story **3** a love affair **4** an imaginative story about the adventures of heroes • *a romance of King Arthur's court*

Roman numerals PLURAL NOUN letters that represent numbers (I = 1, V = 5, X = 10, etc.), used by the ancient Romans COMPARE **arabic numerals**

romantic ADJECTIVE **1** to do with love or romance **2** sentimental or idealistic; not realistic or practical
▷ **romantically** ADVERB

romp VERB romps, romping, romped play in a lively way
▷ **romp** NOUN

roof NOUN roofs **1** the part that covers the top of a building, shelter, or vehicle **2** the top inside surface of something • *the roof of the mouth*

rook[1] NOUN rooks a black crow that nests in large groups

rook VERB rooks, rooking, rooked (*informal*) swindle; charge people an unnecessarily high price

rook[2] NOUN rooks a chess piece shaped like a castle

room NOUN rooms **1** a part of a building with its own walls and ceiling **2** enough space • *Is there room for me?*
▷ **roomful** NOUN

roost VERB roosts, roosting, roosted (said about birds) perch or settle for sleep

roost NOUN roosts a place where birds roost

root NOUN roots **1** that part of a plant that grows under the ground and absorbs water and nourishment from the soil **2** a source or basis • *The love of money is the root of all evil.* **3** a number in relation to the number it produces when multiplied by itself • *9 is the square root of 81 (9 x 9 = 81)*
take root 1 grow roots **2** become established

root[1] VERB roots, rooting, rooted **1** take root; cause something to take root **2** fix firmly • *Fear rooted us to the spot.*
root out get rid of something

root[2] VERB roots, rooting, rooted **1** (said about an animal) turn up ground in search of food **2** rummage; find something by doing this • *I've managed to root out some facts and figures.*

rope NOUN ropes a strong thick cord made of twisted strands of fiber
show someone the ropes show him or her how to do something

rope VERB ropes, roping, roped fasten with a rope
rope in persuade a person to take part in something

Thesaurus

---

romance NOUN **1** *a historical romance* ► love story, romantic novel, fantasy **2** *the romance of travel* ► glamor, excitement, adventure, fascination, mystique **3** *Romance was in the air.* ► love, passion, ardor **4** *They were having a wild romance.* ► love affair, relationship, attachment

romantic ADJECTIVE **1** *He was handsome and romantic.* ► amorous, passionate, loving, tenderhearted, affectionate **2** *romantic stories set in the Far East* ► imaginary, fanciful, sentimental, (*more informal*) soppy **3** *a pretty village in a romantic landscape* ► idyllic, picturesque, fairy-tale **4** *Their notions about life were highly romantic.* ► idealistic, idealized, starry-eyed, unrealistic, visionary, utopian, fanciful, dreamy

romp VERB *The children romped in the garden.* ► cavort, caper, leap about, run about, skip about, bound, frisk, frolic, gambol

room NOUN **1** *There wasn't enough room for a bed.* ► space, capacity, volume **2** *We need more room to live our own lives.* ► freedom, latitude, leeway, allowance, elbow room **3** *There's always room for improvement.* ► scope, capacity, margin, opportunity

roomy ADJECTIVE *The apartment was bright and roomy.* ► spacious, capacious, large, sizable, extensive, commodious, voluminous OPPOSITES ARE cramped, poky

root NOUN **1** *The plant had long stringy roots.* ► tuber, radicle, rhizome, rootlet **2** *Money is the root of the problem.* ► source, origin, cause, basis, starting point, seed, germ

root VERB **root out** *The magistrates were determined to root out corruption.* ► discover, unearth, dig out, ferret out, remove, eliminate, extirpate

rope NOUN *A rope attached the boat to the quayside.* ► cable, cord, line, halyard, hawser, lanyard

rose NOUN roses **1** a shrub that has showy flowers, often with thorny stems **2** a deep pink color **3** a nozzle with many holes, e.g., on a watering can or hosepipe

rose past tense of rise

Rosh Hashanah or **Rosh Hashana** NOUN the Jewish New Year

roster NOUN rosters a list showing people's turns to be on duty, etc.

rosy ADJECTIVE rosier, rosiest **1** deep pink **2** hopeful or cheerful • a rosy future
▷ **rosiness** NOUN

rot VERB rots, rotting, rotted go soft or bad and become useless; decay

rot NOUN **1** rotting or decay **2** (informal) nonsense

rota (roh- ta) NOUN rotas a list of people to do things or of things to be done in turn

rotate VERB rotates, rotating, rotated **1** go around like a wheel; revolve **2** arrange or happen in a series; take turns at doing something
▷ **rotation** NOUN **rotary** ADJECTIVE **rotatory** ADJECTIVE

rote NOUN
by rote from memory or by routine, without full understanding of the meaning • We used to learn French songs by rote.

rotor NOUN rotors a rotating part of a machine or helicopter

rotten ADJECTIVE **1** rotted • rotten apples **2** (informal) very bad or unpleasant • rotten weather
▷ **rottenness** NOUN

rouge (roozh) NOUN a reddish cosmetic for coloring the cheeks
▷ **rouge** VERB

rough ADJECTIVE rougher, roughest **1** not smooth; uneven **2** not gentle or careful; violent • a rough push **3** not exact • a rough guess **4** (said about weather or the sea) wild and stormy
▷ **roughly** ADVERB **roughness** NOUN

rough VERB roughs, roughing, roughed rough it do without ordinary comforts rough out draw or plan something roughly rough up (slang) treat a person violently

roughen VERB roughens, roughening, roughened make or become rough

round ADJECTIVE **1** shaped like a circle or ball or cylinder; curved **2** full or complete • a round dozen **3** returning to the start • a round trip
▷ **roundness** NOUN
in round figures approximately, without giving exact units

round NOUN rounds **1** a series of visits made by a doctor, postman, etc. **2** one section or

Thesaurus

rot NOUN **1** The surveyor found traces of rot in the roof timbers. ► decay, decomposition, mold, mildew, dry rot, wet rot **2** (informal) You're talking rot ► nonsense, rubbish, gibberish, drivel, codswallop, claptrap

rot VERB The floorboards had begun to rot.
► decay, decompose, perish, become rotten, degenerate, deteriorate, crumble, disintegrate

rotate VERB The arms of the windmill were rotating. ► revolve, turn around, go around, move around, spin, gyrate, twirl, swivel, roll

rotten ADJECTIVE **1** Some of the wood looked rotten. ► decayed, decaying, decomposed, crumbling, disintegrating **2** the stench of rotten meat ► moldy, moldering, putrid, decayed, decaying, foul, tainted AN OPPOSITE IS fresh **3** (informal) They had a rotten time. ► unpleasant, disagreeable, terrible, bad OPPOSITES ARE pleasant, good **4** (informal) The builders had done a rotten job. He would make a rotten teacher. ► poor, inferior, inadequate, bad, low-grade, (informal) crummy, (informal) ropy, (informal) lousy OPPOSITES ARE fine, good

rough ADJECTIVE **1** She picked her way over the rough ground. ► bumpy, rugged, uneven, broken, irregular, rocky, stony, coarse, craggy AN OPPOSITE IS even **2** rough skin ► dry, chapped, coarse, hairy, bristly, shaggy, unshaven AN OPPOSITE IS smooth **3** rough treatment; It was pretty rough on your mother. ► harsh, severe, hard, tough, stern **4** a rough sea; the ability to withstand rough weather ► choppy, turbulent, agitated, stormy, tempestuous, violent, wild AN OPPOSITE IS calm **5** a rough voice ► harsh, grating, gruff, rasping, hoarse, husky AN OPPOSITE IS soft **6** She doesn't like rough kids. ► rowdy, boisterous, disorderly, unrestrained AN OPPOSITE IS polite **7** The tower is of rough workmanship. ► amateurish, careless, clumsy, crude, hasty, imperfect, inept, (informal) rough and ready, unfinished, unpolished, unskilful AN OPPOSITE IS skilful **8** This gives you a rough idea of what we mean. ► approximate, imprecise, inexact, estimated, hazy, crude, vague AN OPPOSITE IS exact **9** He went home. He was feeling rough. ► ill, unwell, sick, poorly, out of sorts, queasy, off color, (more informal) lousy OPPOSITES ARE well, fit

roughly ADVERB **1** There were roughly equal numbers of men and women. ► about, around, approximately, nearly, close to **2** Geoffrey pulled his arm roughly away. ► violently, forcefully, forcibly, abruptly

round ADJECTIVE **1** a round window ► spherical, circular, bulbous, curved, cylindrical, globular

A
B
C
D
E
F
G
H
I
J
K
L
M
N
O
P
Q
R
S
T
U
V
W
X
Y
Z

stage in a competition • *Winners go on to the next round.* **3** a shot or volley of shots from a gun; ammunition for this **4** a whole slice of bread; a sandwich made with two slices of bread **5** a song in which people sing the same words but start at different times **6** a set of drinks bought for all the members of a group

round VERB **rounds, rounding, rounded**
1 make or become round • *The car rounded the corner.*
round off finish something
round up gather people or animals together

roundabout NOUN **roundabouts 1** a road junction where traffic has to pass round a circular structure in the road **2** a circular revolving ride at a fair

roundabout ADJECTIVE indirect; not using the shortest way of going or of saying or doing something • *I heard the news in a roundabout way.*

rounders NOUN a game in which players try to hit a ball and run around a circuit

round-the-clock ADJECTIVE lasting or happening all day and all night

round trip NOUN **round trips** a trip to one or more places and back to where you started

roundup NOUN **roundups 1** a gathering-up of cattle or people • *a police roundup of suspects* **2** a summary • *a roundup of the news*

rouse VERB **rouses, rousing, roused 1** make or become awake **2** cause to become active or excited

rousing ADJECTIVE loud or exciting • *three rousing cheers*

rout VERB **routs, routing, routed** defeat and chase away an enemy
▷ **rout** NOUN

route (root) NOUN **routes** the way taken to get to a place

routine (roo- teen) NOUN **routines** a regular way of doing things
▷ **routinely** ADVERB

rove VERB **roves, roving, roved** roam or wander
▷ **rover** NOUN

row[1] (rhymes with go) NOUN **rows** a line of people or things

row (rhymes with go) VERB **rows, rowing, rowed** make a boat move by using oars
▷ **rower** NOUN **rowing boat** NOUN

row[2] (rhymes with cow) NOUN **rows 1** a loud noise **2** a quarrel

---

Thesaurus

---

2 *a man with a short round figure* ▶ rounded, plump, chubby, rotund, ample, full, fat

round NOUN **1** *the most exciting tie of the second round* ▶ stage, game, series, sequence, contest **2** *an endless round of radio and television interviews* ▶ cycle, series, succession, sequence
round off *We rounded the evening off with some drinks.* ▶ end, finish, complete, conclude, cap, top
round up *His dog, Nell, rounded up 300 sheep.* ▶ herd, drive together, muster, marshal, assemble

roundabout ADJECTIVE *He reached the town square by a roundabout route.* ▶ indirect, circuitous, devious, winding, rambling, meandering, tortuous, twisting, long AN OPPOSITE IS direct

roundabout NOUN **1** *Let's play on the roundabout.* ▶ merry-go-round, carousel **2** *Turn right at the next roundabout.* ▶ traffic circle, rotary

rouse VERB **1** *Next morning he was roused by the clanging of church bells.* ▶ arouse, awaken, wake up **2** *His words roused feelings of sympathy in her.* ▶ arouse, provoke, stir up, trigger, spark off, kindle, cause **3** *He can be violent when he's roused.* ▶ anger, annoy, provoke, incite, inflame, incense, work up

rousing ADJECTIVE *a rousing speech* ▶ stirring, inspiring, moving, stimulating, exciting

rout VERB *They went on to rout the Communist forces.* ▶ crush, defeat, overwhelm, trounce, thrash, put to flight, drive off, (more informal) hammer

route NOUN *This route is direct but gets tedious in the later stages.* ▶ way, road, course, direction, path, passage, itinerary, journey

routine NOUN **1** *Their evening routine never varied.* ▶ procedure, pattern, way, method, course of action, practice, system, custom, drill, habit **2** *I've been practicing a new dance routine.* ▶ act, performance, program, number, turn

routine ADJECTIVE *It is now a fairly routine operation done under local anesthetic.* ▶ standard, normal, ordinary, everyday, run-of-the-mill

row NOUN (rhymes with crow) *a row of small plants* ▶ line, string, chain, series, sequence, cordon, file

row (rhymes with cow) (British) **1** *She and Paul had had a row.* ▶ quarrel, argument, squabble, fight, scrap, altercation, disagreement, dispute, (more informal) slanging match AN OPPOSITE IS reconciliation **2** *The crowd was making a dreadful row.* ▶ noise, racket, rumpus, tumult, din, disturbance, uproar, commotion

rowdy ADJECTIVE rowdier, rowdiest noisy and disorderly
▷ **rowdiness** NOUN

royal ADJECTIVE to do with a king or queen
▷ **royally** ADVERB
[via early French from Latin *regalis*]

royalty NOUN **1** being royal **2** a royal person or people ● *in the presence of royalty* **3** royalties a payment made to an author or composer, etc. for each copy of a work sold or for each performance

RSVP ABBREVIATION répondez s'il vous plaît [French, = please reply]

rub VERB rubs, rubbing, rubbed move something backwards and forwards while pressing it on something else
▷ **rub** NOUN
rub out remove something by rubbing

rubber NOUN rubbers **1** a strong elastic substance used for making tires, balls, hoses, etc. **2** a piece of rubber for rubbing out pencil or ink marks
▷ **rubbery** ADJECTIVE

rubbish NOUN **1** things that are worthless or not wanted **2** nonsense

rubble NOUN broken pieces of brick or stone

rubella (roo- bel- la) NOUN an infectious disease that causes a red rash, which can damage a baby if the mother catches it early in pregnancy [from Latin *rubellus* = reddish]

ruble (roo- bul) NOUN rubles the unit of money in Russia

ruby NOUN rubies a red jewel [from Latin *rubeus* = red]

rucksack NOUN rucksacks a bag on straps for carrying on the back [from German *Rücken* = back + *Sack* = bag, sack]

rudder NOUN rudders a hinged upright piece at the back of a ship or aircraft, used for steering

ruddy ADJECTIVE ruddier, ruddiest red and healthy-looking ● *a ruddy complexion*

rude ADJECTIVE ruder, rudest **1** impolite **2** indecent or improper **3** roughly made; crude ● *a rude shelter* **4** vigorous and hearty ● *in rude health*
▷ **rudely** ADVERB **rudeness** NOUN

rudimentary ADJECTIVE **1** to do with rudiments; elementary **2** not fully developed ● *Penguins have rudimentary wings.*

rudiments (rood- i- ments) PLURAL NOUN the basic principles of a subject ● *She taught me the rudiments of chemistry.*

ruff NOUN ruffs **1** a starched pleated frill worn around the neck in the 16th century **2** a collar-like ring of feathers or fur around a bird's or animal's neck

ruffian NOUN ruffians a violent lawless person
▷ **ruffianly** ADJECTIVE

Thesaurus

rowdy ADJECTIVE *a bunch of rowdy men* ► unruly, disorderly, riotous, noisy, badly behaved, rough, wild, disruptive, boisterous OPPOSITES ARE quiet, peaceful

royal ADJECTIVE **1** *the royal family* ► regal, imperial, kingly, princely, queenly, majestic, stately **2** *We received a royal welcome.* ► magnificent, splendid, excellent, fine

rub VERB **1** *John rubbed the back of his leg.* ► stroke, knead, massage, caress, smooth **2** *She rubbed lotion on the children's backs.* ► apply (to), smear, smooth, spread, put on **3** *His new shoes were rubbing dreadfully.* ► chafe, pinch, abrade, graze, scrape, hurt **4** *Stella rubbed the table with polish.* ► polish, buff, shine, wipe
rub out *Someone had rubbed out his name.* ► erase, remove, delete, efface, expunge, blot out

rubbish NOUN (British) **1** *Household rubbish is collected on Wednesdays.* ► refuse, waste, garbage, debris, junk, leavings, litter, trash **2** *They are talking rubbish.* ► nonsense, balderdash, gibberish, claptrap, drivel, gobbledegook, (more informal) rot, (more informal) twaddle

rubble NOUN *Often he had to clear away piles of rubble before he could continue.* ► debris, ruins, remains, wreckage, fragments

rude NOUN **1** *He was sometimes rude, but always honest.* ► impolite, discourteous, disrespectful, impertinent, impudent, insolent, ill-mannered, ill-bred, uncivil, offensive, abusive OPPOSITES ARE polite, civil **2** *a rude joke* ► vulgar, coarse, dirty, smutty, filthy AN OPPOSITE IS clean

rudeness NOUN *"You," she called, with uncharacteristic rudeness.* ► discourtesy, disrespect, impoliteness, bad manners, incivility, impertinence, impudence, insolence, churlishness, cheek

rudimentary ADJECTIVE **1** *You'll need a rudimentary knowledge of first aid.* ► simple, basic, elementary, primitive, fundamental, crude AN OPPOSITE IS advanced **2** *The pelycosaurs tended to develop rudimentary teeth.* ► incomplete, embryonic, primitive **3** *a rudimentary language course* ► introductory, basic, elementary, preliminary, initial

ruffian NOUN *A group of ruffians assaulted a university student on his way home.* ► thug, hoodlum, hooligan, lout, rogue, scoundrel, brute, bully, villain, mugger, (more informal) tough, (more informal) yob

a
b
c
d
e
f
g
h
i
j
k
l
m
n
o
p
q
r
s
t
u
v
w
x
y
z

A B C D E F G H I J K L M N O P Q **R** S T U V W X Y Z

ruffle VERB ruffles, ruffling, ruffled **1** disturb the smoothness of a thing **2** upset or annoy someone

ruffle NOUN ruffles a gathered ornamental frill

rug NOUN rugs **1** a thick mat for the floor **2** a piece of thick fabric used as a blanket

rugby NOUN a kind of game using an oval ball that players may carry or kick [named after Rugby School in Warwickshire, where it was first played]

rugged ADJECTIVE **1** having an uneven surface or outline; craggy **2** sturdy

ruin NOUN ruins **1** severe damage or destruction to something **2** a building that has fallen down

ruin VERB ruins, ruining, ruined damage or destroy a thing so severely that it is useless ▷ **ruination** NOUN

ruinous ADJECTIVE **1** causing ruin **2** in ruins; ruined

rule NOUN rules **1** something that people have to obey **2** ruling; governing • *under French rule* **3** a carpenter's ruler **as a rule** usually; more often than not

rule VERB rules, ruling, ruled **1** govern or reign **2** make a decision • *The referee ruled that it was a foul.* **3** draw a straight line with a ruler or other straight edge [from early French]

ruler NOUN rulers **1** a person who governs **2** a strip of wood, metal, or plastic with straight edges, used for measuring and drawing straight lines

ruling NOUN rulings a judgment

rum NOUN a strong alcoholic drink made from sugar or molasses

Thesaurus

ruffle VERB **1** *A light wind ruffled the leaves of the trees.* ► stir, agitate, ripple, disturb **2** *Isobel took off her scarf and ruffled her hair.* ► rumple, tousle, run your fingers through, dishevel, mess up AN OPPOSITE IS smooth **3** *Don't let their stupid remarks ruffle you.* ► annoy, upset, unsettle, disconcert, fluster, irritate, vex, worry, (more informal) nettle, (more informal) rattle AN OPPOSITE IS calm

rug NOUN **1** *The children sat on a rug on the floor.* ► mat, runner, matting **2** *She was wrapped in a rug to keep out the cold.* ► blanket, coverlet, throw

rugged ADJECTIVE **1** *a Spanish village nestling in rugged hills* ► rough, uneven, rocky, craggy, stark, bumpy, jagged, irregular OPPOSITES ARE smooth, gentle **2** *The only softness about his rugged face was in his lips.* ► strong, sturdy, rough, tough, robust, hardy, burly, husky, muscular, weather-beaten

ruin NOUN **1** *They now face financial ruin.* ► bankruptcy, insolvency, failure, breakdown, collapse, downfall, ruination, undoing **2** *It was the ruin of all their hopes.* ► destruction, disintegration, devastation, overthrow, failure, undoing, ruination **3** *The house is a sad ruin in a beautiful location.* ► remnant, shell, group of remains **4 ruins** *They explored the ruins of the castle.* ► remains, rubble, debris, wreckage

ruin VERB **1** *Once again the rain has ruined what promised to be a good contest.* ► spoil, wreck, destroy, shatter, blight, wreak havoc on, torpedo, (more informal) mess up OPPOSITES ARE save, rescue **2** *He would be ruined if he had to pay.* ► bankrupt, impoverish, financially cripple

ruined ADJECTIVE *the gateway to a ruined fortress* ► derelict, dilapidated, ramshackle, ruined, tumbledown, crumbling

ruinous ADJECTIVE **1** *activity that has a ruinous effect on the environment* ► disastrous, catastrophic, devastating, calamitous, destructive, cataclysmic, dire, fatal **2** *They found the building in a ruinous condition.* ► ruined, dilapidated, derelict

rule NOUN **1** *the rules governing procedures in case of fire* ► regulation, law, code, convention, precept, principle, routine, practice, custom **2** *British rule had ended in 1947.* ► jurisdiction, control, administration, sovereignty, mastery, command, domination, dominion, authority, government, supremacy, sway **3** *The normal rule is to apply for tickets by letter.* ► procedure, practice, protocol, form, custom, convention

rule VERB **1** *How could a city-state like Rome rule an empire?* ► govern, administer, manage, run, control, direct, command, dominate, lead, reign over **2** *The king's successor ruled for less than a year.* ► reign, be ruler, be in power, be monarch **3** *The judge ruled that the defendant should be awarded the costs of the case.* ► decree, order, direct, pronounce, resolve, decide, determine, adjudicate, determine, find, judge **rule out** *We cannot rule out suicide as a cause of death.* ► exclude, discount, reject, eliminate, dismiss, preclude, disregard

ruler NOUN *a much-respected ruler* ► leader, sovereign, overlord, governor, dynast, monarch, president (of a republic), head of state

ruling NOUN *A ruling came from the president himself.* ► decision, pronouncement, resolution, decree, judgment, adjudication, order, command, instruction

rumble VERB rumbles, rumbling, rumbled make a deep heavy continuous sound like thunder
▷ **rumble** NOUN

ruminant ADJECTIVE ruminating

ruminant NOUN ruminants an animal that chews the cud (see cud)

ruminate VERB ruminates, ruminating, ruminated 1 chew the cud 2 meditate or ponder
▷ **rumination** NOUN **ruminative** ADJECTIVE

rummage VERB rummages, rummaging, rummaged turn things over or move them about while looking for something
▷ **rummage** NOUN

rumor NOUN rumors information that spreads to a lot of people but may not be true

rumor VERB
be rumored be spread as a rumor
[from Latin *rumor* = noise]

rump NOUN rumps the hind part of an animal

rumple VERB rumples, rumpling, rumpled crumple; make a thing untidy

rump steak NOUN rump steaks a piece of meat from the rump of a cow

rumpus NOUN rumpuses (*informal*) an uproar; an angry protest

run VERB runs, running, ran, run 1 move with quick steps so that both or all feet leave the ground at each stride 2 go or travel; flow • *Tears ran down his cheeks.* 3 produce a flow of liquid • *Run some water into it.* 4 work or function • *The engine was running smoothly.* 5 manage or organize • *She runs a corner shop.* 6 compete in a contest • *He ran for president.* 7 extend • *A fence runs round the estate.* 8 go or take in a vehicle • *I'll run you to the station.*
run a risk take a chance
run away leave a place secretly or quickly
run down 1 run over **2** stop gradually; decline **3** (*informal*) say unkind or unfair things about someone
run into 1 collide with **2** happen to meet
run out 1 have used up your stock of something
run over knock down or crush with a moving vehicle
run through examine or rehearse

run NOUN runs **1** the action of running; a time spent running • *I went for a run.* **2** a point scored in baseball or other game **3** a continuous series of events, etc. • *She had a run of good luck.* **4** an enclosure for animals • *a chicken run* **5** a series of damaged stitches in a pair of tights or stockings **6** a track • *a ski run*
on the run running away, especially from the police
[from Old English]

Thesaurus

rumble VERB *Thunder rumbled in the distance.*
► boom, reverberate, resound, echo

rumor NOUN **1** *A rumor had started that the company would close.* ► report, story, piece of gossip, whisper **2** *The suggestion was only rumor.* ► gossip, hearsay, talk, tittle-tattle

rumpus NOUN *A terrible rumpus was going on outside.* ► commotion, uproar, racket, tumult, hullabaloo, hubbub, fracas, furore, upheaval, agitation, excitement

run VERB **1** *We ran across the field.* ► sprint, race, jog, tear, dash, rush, hasten, speed, streak, bolt, scamper, scoot **2** *The buses don't run on Sundays.* ► operate, function, go, provide a service **3** *The car has been running erratically.* ► function, perform, work, behave **4** *His car was stolen because he had left the engine running.* ► operate, tick over, go **5** *Water ran down the wall.* ► stream, trickle, flow, flood, pour, spill, gush, cascade, dribble, leak **6** *She was running a small business in town.* ► manage, be in charge of, direct, control, administer, conduct, supervise, govern, look after, maintain, rule **7** *He could no longer afford to run a car.* ► maintain, keep, own, use, drive **8** *She ran me back to my house.* ► drive, take, bring, ferry, give a lift to **9** *It is important to run exhaustive tests.* ► carry out, perform, complete, do, fulfil **10** *A sharp pain ran up her arm.* ► pass, move, shoot, travel, go **11** *The road runs north.* ► extend, reach, stretch, go, continue

run across *I ran across your sister in Paris.* ► meet, encounter, come across, run into, chance on

run after *Jill ran after him with his keys.* ► chase, pursue, follow

run away *He threw down his weapon and ran away.* ► escape, flee, bolt, abscond, (*more informal*) make off

run down 1 *A dog ran into the road and he was run down.* ► run over, knock over, hit, struck **2** (*informal*) *She didn't want to run him down in public.* ► criticize, denigrate, disparage, belittle, find fault with

run into *Did you run into any of your friends?* ► meet, encounter, come across, run across, chance on

run out *My subscription runs out in December.* ► expire, terminate, end, come to an end, cease, dry up

run NOUN **1** *a run across the park* ► jog, dash, sprint, spurt, trot, gallop, canter, race **2** *a run in the car* ► drive, ride, trip, excursion, journey, (*more informal*) spin **3** *a run of bad luck* ► sequence, stretch, series, chain, course **4** *a chicken run* ► enclosure, compound, coop, pen

a b c d e f g h i j k l m n o p q **r** s t u v w x y z

A
B
C
D
E
F
G
H
I
J
K
L
M
N
O
P
Q
R
S
T
U
V
W
X
Y
Z

runaway NOUN runaways someone who has run away

runaway ADJECTIVE **1** having run away or out of control **2** won easily • *a runaway victory*

run-down ADJECTIVE **1** tired and in bad health **2** in bad condition; dilapidated

rung NOUN rungs one of the crossbars on a ladder

rung *past participle of* ring²

runner NOUN runners **1** a person or animal that runs, especially in a race **2** a stem that grows away from a plant and roots itself **3** a groove, rod, or roller for a thing to move on; each of the long strips under a sledge **4** a long narrow strip of carpet or covering

runner bean NOUN runner beans a kind of climbing bean with long green pods which are eaten

runner-up NOUN runners-up someone who comes second in a competition

running *present participle of* run
in the running competing and with a chance of winning

running ADJECTIVE continuous or consecutive; without an interval • *It rained for four days running.*

runny ADJECTIVE runnier, runniest **1** flowing like liquid • *runny sauce* **2** producing a flow of liquid • *a runny nose*

runway NOUN runways a long hard surface on which aircraft take off and land

rural ADJECTIVE to do with or belonging to the countryside

ruse NOUN ruses a deception or trick

rush VERB rushes, rushing, rushed **1** move or do something quickly **2** make someone hurry **3** attack or capture by dashing forward suddenly

rush¹ NOUN rushes **1** a hurry **2** a sudden movement towards something **3** a sudden great demand for something

rush² NOUN rushes a plant with a thin stem that grows in marshy places

rush hour NOUN rush hours the time when traffic is busiest

rusk NOUN rusks a kind of hard, dry biscuit, especially for feeding babies

rust NOUN **1** a red or brown substance that forms on iron or steel exposed to damp and corrodes it **2** a reddish-brown color

rust VERB rusts, rusting, rusted make or become rusty

rustic ADJECTIVE **1** rural **2** made of rough timber or branches • *a rustic bridge*

rustle VERB rustles, rustling, rustled **1** make a sound like paper being crumpled **2** steal horses or cattle • *cattle rustling*
▷ **rustle** NOUN **rustler** NOUN
rustle up (*informal*) produce • *rustle up a meal*

rusty ADJECTIVE rustier, rustiest **1** coated with rust **2** weakened by lack of use or practice • *My French is a bit rusty.*
▷ **rustiness** NOUN

rut NOUN ruts **1** a deep track made by wheels in soft ground **2** a settled and usually dull way of life • *We are getting into a rut.*
▷ **rutted** ADJECTIVE

Thesaurus

runaway NOUN *a safe house for young runaways*
► fugitive, escapee, refugee, absconder

runner NOUN **1** *There are seven runners in the next race.* ► competitor, entrant, participant, athlete **2** *The commanding officer sent a runner to headquarters.* ► courier, messenger

running NOUN **1** *A private company has taken over the running of the school.* ► administration, management, direction, controlling, supervision **2** *These measures will ensure the smooth running of the organization.* ► operation, working, functioning

runny ADJECTIVE *a runny mixture of egg and milk*
► watery, thin, fluid, liquid, free-flowing
OPPOSITES ARE solid, viscous

rural ADJECTIVE *The majority lived in rural communities outside the city.* ► country, rustic, pastoral, agricultural, agrarian, countrified AN OPPOSITE IS urban

rush VERB *She rushed into the garden.* ► hurry, hasten, dash, run, sprint, race, tear, streak, bolt OPPOSITES ARE dawdle, saunter

rush NOUN **1** *a frantic rush to put out the flames*
► hurry, haste, dash, race, scramble **2** *It stopped the rush of water for a time.* ► flood, gush, spate, cataract **3** *There was a sudden rush for the doors.* ► charge, stampede, surge (toward)

rust VERB *a special coating to prevent the iron from rusting* ► corrode, become rusty, oxidize, crumble away, decay, rot

rustic ADJECTIVE **1** *a house in rustic surroundings*
► rural, country, pastoral, agricultural, agrarian, countrified AN OPPOSITE IS urban **2** *She sat down on a rustic wooden seat.* ► plain, simple, crude, rough, artless, unsophisticated

rusty ADJECTIVE **1** *Nothing causes more blisters than using a rusty trowel.* ► corroded, rusted, oxidized, rotten, tarnished, discolored **2** *My French is a little rusty.* ► unpracticed, neglected, below par, deficient, weak, unused, (*more informal*) creaky

ruthless *ADJECTIVE* pitiless, merciless, or cruel
▷ **ruthlessly** *ADVERB* **ruthlessness** *NOUN*
[from Middle English *ruth* = pity]

rye *NOUN* a cereal used to make bread, biscuits, etc.

Thesaurus

ruthless 1 *a ruthless dictator* ➤ merciless, pitiless, brutal, cruel, callous, unfeeling, heartless, vicious, violent, ferocious, fierce AN OPPOSITE IS compassionate **2** *He carried out his instructions with ruthless efficiency.* ➤ relentless, unrelenting, inexorable, unremitting, intense, implacable

Ss

S. ABBREVIATION **1** south **2** southern

sabbath NOUN sabbaths a weekly day for rest and prayer, Saturday for Jews, Sunday for Christians [from Hebrew *shabat* = rest]

sabotage NOUN deliberate damage or disruption to hinder an enemy, employer, etc.
▷ **sabotage** VERB **saboteur** NOUN
[from French *saboter* = make a noise with *sabots* (= wooden clogs)]

saccharin (sak- er- in) NOUN a very sweet substance used as a substitute for sugar

sack NOUN sacks a large bag made of strong material
▷ **sacking** NOUN
the sack (*informal*) dismissal from a job ● *He got the sack.*

sack[1] VERB sacks, sacking, sacked (*informal*) dismiss someone from a job [via Old English and Latin from Greek *sakkos*]

sack[2] VERB sacks, sacking, sacked (*old use*) plunder a captured town in a violent destructive way
▷ **sack** NOUN
[from French *mettre à sac* = put (booty) in a sack]

sacrament NOUN sacraments an important Christian religious ceremony such as baptism or Holy Communion

sacred ADJECTIVE holy; to do with God or a god

sacrifice NOUN sacrifices **1** an offering to a god of a killed animal or other special thing **2** giving up a thing you value, so that something good may happen **3** a thing sacrificed
▷ **sacrificial** ADJECTIVE

sacrifice VERB sacrifices, sacrificing, sacrificed offer something or give it up as a sacrifice

sacrilege (sak- ril- ij) NOUN disrespect or damage to something people regard as sacred
▷ **sacrilegious** ADJECTIVE

sad ADJECTIVE sadder, saddest unhappy; showing or causing sorrow
▷ **sadly** ADVERB **sadness** NOUN
[from Old English]

Thesaurus

sabotage NOUN *The crash was probably caused by engine failure and not sabotage.* ► wilful damage, deliberate destruction, vandalism, wrecking, disruption, treachery

sabotage VERB **1** *A gang had sabotaged the cash machines in the shopping mall.* ► wreck, deliberately damage, destroy, disable, put out of action, cripple, vandalize **2** *Are you telling me he deliberately set out to sabotage your work?* ► wreck, ruin, spoil, thwart, undermine, disrupt

sack NOUN **1** *The flour was in an open sack on the floor.* ► bag, pack, pouch **2** *When she complained she promptly got the sack.* ► notice, dismissal, discharge, your cards, (*more informal*) the boot

sack VERB **1** *Unbelievably, he sacked his son-in-law and replaced him with Trevor.* ► dismiss, give notice to, get rid of, lay someone off, let someone go, (*more informal*) fire, (*more informal*) kick out **2** *The invaders sacked the town.* ► destroy, raid, loot, plunder, pillage, ravage

sacred ADJECTIVE **1** *The new pope was enthroned in the most sacred place in the basilica.* ► holy, blessed, consecrated, sanctified, hallowed, dedicated, venerated AN OPPOSITE IS unconsecrated **2** *The recital mixed operatic arias with traditional sacred melodies.* ► religious, spiritual, devotional, ecclesiastical AN OPPOSITE IS secular

sacrifice NOUN **1** *The festival involved a sacrifice of a ram and seven lambs.* ► offering, ritual slaughter, votive offering, oblation **2** *The building was rebuilt with some sacrifice of its earlier features.* ► loss, abandonment, discarding, rejection, surrender, giving up, yielding, renunciation, renouncing

sacrifice VERB **1** *They have sacrificed their principles and lost their good name; a memorial to the bomber crews who sacrificed their lives in the war* ► give up, forfeit, relinquish, surrender, forgo, go without **2** *The goat had been sacrificed at the shrine.* ► offer up, kill, slaughter, immolate

sacrilege NOUN *Wearing armor in a holy place was sacrilege.* ► blasphemy, desecration, impiety, profanity, irreverence, disrespect, ungodliness OPPOSITES ARE piety, respect

sad ADJECTIVE **1** *Everyone was sad to be leaving. He looked at her sad face.* ► unhappy, sorrowful, dejected, downcast, despondent, downhearted, depressed, miserable, glum, in low spirits **2** *I told my brother and sister the sad news. The story is sadder than we realized.* ► distressing, upsetting, depressing, grave, tragic, unfortunate, regrettable, serious, heartrending **3** *This sad state of affairs does not have to continue.* ► sorry, wretched, unfortunate, regrettable, shameful, disgraceful **4** (*informal*) *They live in a sad little house.* ► pathetic, pitiful, inadequate

sadden VERB saddens, saddening, saddened make a person sad

saddle NOUN saddles **1** a seat for putting on the back of a horse or other animal **2** the seat of a bicycle **3** a ridge of high land between two peaks

saddle VERB saddles, saddling, saddled put a saddle on a horse, etc.
saddle someone with burden someone with a task or problem

sadist (say- dist) NOUN sadists a person who enjoys hurting or humiliating other people
▷ **sadism** NOUN **sadistic** ADJECTIVE
[named after an 18th-century French novelist, the Marquis de Sade, noted for the cruelties in his stories]

safari NOUN safaris an expedition to see or hunt wild animals [from Arabic *safar* = a journey]

safari park NOUN safari parks a park where wild animals are kept in large enclosures to be seen by visitors

safe ADJECTIVE **1** not in danger **2** not dangerous
• *a safe speed*
▷ **safely** ADVERB **safeness** NOUN **safety** NOUN

safe NOUN safes a strong cupboard or box in which valuables can be locked safely

safeguard NOUN safeguards a protection

safe sex NOUN sexual activity using a condom or other precautions to prevent the spread of infection

safety pin NOUN safety pins a U-shaped pin with a clip fastening over the point

sag VERB sags, sagging, sagged hang or go down in the middle from its own weight or because something heavy is pressing on it
▷ **sag** NOUN

saga (sah- ga) NOUN sagas a long story with many episodes or adventures

sage[1] NOUN a kind of herb used in cooking and formerly used in medicine

sage ADJECTIVE wise
▷ **sagely** ADVERB

sage[2] NOUN sages a wise and respected person

sago NOUN a starchy white food used to make puddings

said *past tense* of say

sail NOUN sails **1** a large piece of strong cloth attached to a mast, etc., to catch the wind and make a ship or boat move **2** a short voyage **3** an arm of a windmill
set sail start on a voyage in a ship

sail VERB sails, sailing, sailed **1** travel in a ship or boat **2** start a voyage • *We sail at noon.* **3** control a ship or boat **4** move quickly and smoothly
▷ **sailing ship** NOUN

sailboard NOUN sailboards a flat board with a mast and sail, used in windsurfing

sailor NOUN sailors a person who sails; a member of a ship's crew or of a navy

saint NOUN saints a holy or very good person
▷ **saintly** ADJECTIVE **saintliness** NOUN

Thesaurus

sadden VERB *That brief reminder of her husband saddened her.* ▶ dispirit, distress, upset, grieve, dishearten AN OPPOSITE IS cheer up

sadistic ADJECTIVE *a sadistic killer* ▶ callous, cruel, brutal, brutish, pitiless, cold-blooded, ruthless, merciless, vile

sadness NOUN *She could not hide her sadness.* ▶ unhappiness, sorrow, dejection, misery, melancholy, low spirits, depression, regret

safe ADJECTIVE **1** *The building was safe from attack.* ▶ secure, protected, guarded, invulnerable, impregnable **2** *The missing children were all safe.* ▶ unharmed, unhurt, uninjured, out of danger **3** *She is a safe driver. Better safe than sorry.* ▶ prudent, cautious, circumspect, attentive **4** *He's a safe person to be with.* ▶ trustworthy, reliable, responsible, sensible, levelheaded, upright **5** *a medicine that is safe for young children* ▶ harmless, innocuous, proven

safeguard NOUN *Burglar alarms are an additional safeguard.* ▶ protection, defense, guard, shield, precaution, security, assurance

safeguard VERB *The charter safeguards your human rights.* ▶ protect, preserve, defend, secure, look after, shield, guard

safety NOUN **1** *The safety of passengers is paramount.* ▶ security, protection, welfare, well-being AN OPPOSITE IS danger **2** *The refugees looked for a place of safety.* ▶ refuge, shelter, sanctuary, protection

safety belt NOUN ▶ safety harness, seat belt

sag VERB **1** *The ceiling sags in the middle.* ▶ hang down, sink, slump, dip, droop, fall **2** *His spirits were beginning to sag.* ▶ falter, fade, weaken, wilt, shrivel

saga NOUN *They longed to tell the saga of their day's adventures.* ▶ tale, story, catalog, rigmarole

sail VERB **1** *John loves sailing his boat.* ▶ pilot, navigate, skipper, steer, captain **2** *We had a vacation sailing in the Mediterranean.* ▶ cruise, voyage, boat, yacht, go sailing, navigate **3** *The ferry sails at midday.* ▶ put to sea, set sail, leave harbor, weigh anchor

sailor NOUN *He did not make a very good sailor.* ▶ seaman, seafarer, mariner, boatman, yachtsman *or* yachtswoman

saintly ADJECTIVE *a saintly priest* ▶ holy, godly, pious, devout, spiritual, God-fearing, blessed, virtuous AN OPPOSITE IS unholy

a b c d e f g h i j k l m n o p q r **s** t u v w x y z

sake NOUN
for the sake of so as to help or please a person, get a thing, etc.
for someone's sake so as to help or please them • *Don't go to any trouble for my sake.*

salad NOUN salads a mixture of vegetables eaten raw or cold

salary NOUN salaries a regular wage, usually for a year's work, paid in monthly installments
▷ **salaried** ADJECTIVE

sale NOUN sales **1** selling **2** a time when things are sold at reduced prices
for sale or on sale available to be bought

salient (say- lee- ent) ADJECTIVE most important or noticeable • *the salient features of the plan*

saliva NOUN the natural liquid in a person's or animal's mouth
▷ **salivary** ADJECTIVE

sallow ADJECTIVE (said about the skin) slightly yellow
▷ **sallowness** NOUN

salmon (sam- on) NOUN salmon a large edible fish with pink flesh

salon NOUN salons **1** a large elegant room **2** a room or shop where a hairdresser, etc., receives customers

saloon NOUN saloons a pub or bar

salt NOUN salts **1** sodium chloride, the white substance that gives sea water its taste and is used for flavoring food **2** a chemical compound of a metal and an acid
▷ **salty** ADJECTIVE

salt VERB salts, salting, salted flavor or preserve food with salt

salt cellar NOUN salt cellars a small dish or perforated pot holding salt for use at meals

salute VERB salutes, saluting, saluted **1** raise your right hand to your forehead as a sign of respect **2** greet **3** say that you respect or admire something • *We salute this achievement.*

salute NOUN salutes **1** the act of saluting **2** the firing of guns as a sign of greeting or respect

salvage VERB salvages, salvaging, salvaged save or rescue something such as a damaged ship's cargo so that it can be used again
▷ **salvage** NOUN

salvation NOUN **1** saving from loss or damage, etc. **2** (in Christian teaching) saving the soul from sin and its consequences

same ADJECTIVE **1** of one kind, exactly alike or equal **2** not changing; not different
▷ **sameness** NOUN

samosa NOUN samosas a triangular, thin pastry case filled with spicy meat or vegetables, fried and eaten as a snack

sample NOUN samples a small amount that shows what something is like; a specimen

sample VERB samples, sampling, sampled **1** take a sample of something **2** try part of something

sanatorium NOUN sanatoriums or sanatoria a hospital for treating long-term diseases or people recovering from diseases

sanctimonious ADJECTIVE making a show of being virtuous or pious

sanction NOUN sanctions **1** action taken against a nation that is considered to have

---

Thesaurus

sake NOUN **for the sake of** *He did it for the sake of his family.* ► for the good of, in the interests of, for the benefit of, for the advantage of, on behalf of

sale NOUN *laws to control the sale of drugs* ► selling, marketing, trading (in), dealing (in), traffic (in), disposal AN OPPOSITE IS purchase

salty ADJECTIVE *a thick salty paste used for flavoring* ► salt, salted, piquant, saline, briny, tangy, spicy OPPOSITES ARE fresh, bland

salute VERB **1** *You call me "sir" but you don't salute me, OK?* ► greet, acknowledge, hail, address, welcome **2** *I salute them for having the courage to admit their mistakes.* ► pay tribute to, acknowledge, celebrate, recognize, honor

salute NOUN *He gave a quick salute.* ► greeting, acknowledgment, salutation, wave

same ADJECTIVE **1** *Is that the same person?* ► actual, identical, selfsame **2** **the same** *The witnesses' versions were all essentially the same.* ► similar, identical, alike, comparable, equivalent, matching, indistinguishable OPPOSITES ARE different, unalike **3** **the same**

The timetable tends to remain the same from year to year. ► unchanged, constant, unvarying, identical **4** *Let's celebrate again on the same day next year.* ► corresponding, analogous

sample NOUN **1** *Finalists will submit samples of their photographic work.* ► specimen, example, representative piece, selection, demonstration, illustration, indication, instance, model, pattern **2** *The survey was based on a sample of a thousand voters.* ► cross section, sampling

sample VERB *Guests will sample some of the great wines of the world with their dinner.* ► try out, try, test, check out, inspect, taste

sanctimonious ADJECTIVE *What happened to all the sanctimonious talk about putting his family first?* ► self-righteous, holier-than-thou, smug, superior, moralizing, priggish, mealy-mouthed, pious, unctuous AN OPPOSITE IS modest

sanctions PLURAL NOUN *The UN will vote on whether to lift the sanctions.* ► restrictions, penalties, embargo, boycott, prohibition broken an international law, etc. ● *Sanctions against that country include refusing to trade with it.* **2** a penalty for disobeying a law **3** permission or authorization

sanction VERB **sanctions, sanctioning, sanctioned** permit or authorize

sanctity NOUN being sacred; holiness

sanctuary NOUN **sanctuaries 1** a safe place; a refuge **2** an area where wildlife is protected ● *a bird sanctuary* **3** a sacred place; the part of a church where the altar stands

sand NOUN the tiny particles that cover the ground in deserts, seashores, etc.

sand VERB **sands, sanding, sanded** smooth or polish with sandpaper or some other rough material
▷ **sander** NOUN

sandal NOUN **sandals** a lightweight shoe with straps over the foot
▷ **sandalled** ADJECTIVE

sandpaper NOUN strong paper coated with sand or a similar substance, rubbed on rough surfaces to make them smooth

sandwich NOUN **sandwiches** two or more slices of bread with jam, meat, or cheese, etc., between them

sandwich VERB **sandwiches, sandwiching, sandwiched** put a thing between two other things [named after the Earl of Sandwich (1718–1792), who invented them so that he could eat while gambling]

sandy ADJECTIVE **1** like sand **2** covered with sand **3** yellowish-red ● *sandy hair*
▷ **sandiness** NOUN

sane ADJECTIVE **1** having a healthy mind; not mad **2** sensible
▷ **sanely** ADVERB **sanity** NOUN

sanitary ADJECTIVE **1** free from germs and dirt; hygienic **2** to do with sanitation

sanitary napkin NOUN **sanitary towels** an absorbent pad worn by women during menstruation

sanitation NOUN arrangements for drainage and the disposal of sewage

sanity NOUN being sane

Sanskrit NOUN an ancient language of India

sap NOUN the liquid inside a plant, carrying food to all its parts

sap VERB **saps, sapping, sapped** take away a person's strength gradually

sapling NOUN **saplings** a young tree

sapphire NOUN **sapphires** a bright blue jewel

sarcastic ADJECTIVE saying amusing or contemptuous things that hurt someone's feelings
▷ **sarcastically** ADVERB **sarcasm** NOUN

sardine NOUN **sardines** a small sea fish, usually sold in tins, packed tightly in oil

sari NOUN **saris** a length of cloth worn wrapped round the body as a dress, especially by Indian women and girls [from Hindi]

sash NOUN **sashes** a strip of cloth worn round the waist or over one shoulder [from Arabic *shash* = turban]

satchel NOUN **satchels** a bag worn on the shoulder or the back [from Latin *saccellus* = little sack]

satellite NOUN **satellites 1** a spacecraft put in orbit round a planet to collect information or transmit communications signals **2** a moon moving in an orbit around a planet **3** a country that is under the influence of a more powerful country

satellite dish NOUN **satellite dishes** a bowl-shaped aerial for receiving broadcasting signals transmitted by satellite

satin NOUN a silky material that is shiny on one side
▷ **satiny** ADJECTIVE
[from an Arabic word = 'from Tsinkiang', a town in China]

satire NOUN **satires 1** using humor or exaggeration to criticize people in authority

---

Thesaurus

---

sanctuary NOUN *an escape route provided by sanctuary north of the border* ▶ protection, refuge, asylum, safety, security, shelter

sand NOUN *The children played on the sand for hours.* ▶ beach, sands, shore, seaside, strand

sane ADJECTIVE *Humor was what helped keep them sane.* ▶ rational, lucid, normal, balanced, reasonable, sensible, (*informal*) compos mentis, levelheaded, sound, stable AN OPPOSITE IS mad

sanity NOUN *He was not sure enough of his own sanity to take these risks.* ▶ reason, senses, rationality, balance of mind, mental health, lucidity

sap VERB *a fever that sapped his strength and depressed his mind* ▶ drain, exhaust, deplete, erode, bleed, wear away

sarcasm NOUN *She spoke with more than a hint of sarcasm in her voice.* ▶ ridicule, derision, mockery, irony, scorn, scoffing

sarcastic ADJECTIVE *If bosses are sarcastic, try not to react.* ▶ sardonic, ironic, derisive, scornful, scathing, scoffing, sneering, withering

sash NOUN *She wore a girlish blue sash round her waist.* ▶ girdle, belt, band, waistband, cummerbund

satire NOUN *a smutty satire about marriage* ▶ parody, lampoon, burlesque, caricature, invective, irony, mockery, (*more informal*)

2 a play or sketch that does this
▷ **satirical** ADJECTIVE **satirically** ADVERB **satirist** NOUN **satirize** VERB

satisfaction NOUN **1** satisfying a need or want **2** a feeling of pleasure arising from having what you need or want **3** something that satisfies a desire, etc.

satisfactory ADJECTIVE good enough; sufficient
▷ **satisfactorily** ADVERB

satisfy VERB **satisfies, satisfying, satisfied**
1 give someone what they need or want
2 make someone feel certain; convince • *The police are satisfied that the death was accidental.*
3 fulfill • *You have satisfied all our requirements.*

saturate VERB **saturates, saturating, saturated**
1 make a thing very wet **2** make something take in as much as possible of a substance or goods etc.
▷ **saturation** NOUN

Saturday NOUN the day of the week following Friday [from Old English *Saeternesdaeg* = day of Saturn, a Roman god]

sauce NOUN **sauces** **1** a thick liquid served with food to add flavor **2** (*informal*) being impudent [from Latin *salsus* = salted]

saucepan NOUN **saucepans** a metal cooking pan with a handle at the side

saucer NOUN **saucers** a small shallow object on which a cup is placed [from early French *saussier* = container for sauce]

saucy ADJECTIVE **saucier, sauciest** impudent
▷ **saucily** ADVERB **sauciness** NOUN

sauna NOUN **saunas** a room or compartment filled with steam, used as a kind of bath [from Finnish]

saunter VERB **saunters, sauntering, sauntered** walk slowly and casually
▷ **saunter** NOUN

sausage NOUN **sausages** a tube of skin or plastic stuffed with minced meat and other filling [from early French; related to **sauce**]

savage ADJECTIVE wild and fierce; cruel
▷ **savagely** ADVERB **savageness** NOUN **savagery** NOUN

savage NOUN **savages** **1** a savage person
2 (*old use*) a member of a people thought of as primitive or uncivilized

savage VERB **savages, savaging, savaged** attack by biting or wounding • *The sheep had been savaged by a dog.*

save VERB **saves, saving, saved** **1** keep safe; free a person or thing from danger or harm

---

Thesaurus

---

spoof, (*more informal*) send-up, (*more informal*) take-off

satirical ADJECTIVE *a satirical cartoon series.*
► ironical, irreverent, mocking, critical, disparaging, disrespectful, sarcastic

satirize VERB *an attempt to satirize films and filmmakers* ► mock, parody, ridicule, caricature, burlesque, criticize, deride, lampoon, travesty, make fun of, (*more informal*) send up, (*more informal*) take off

satisfaction NOUN **1** *This year, she thought with satisfaction, she was well-prepared. Job satisfaction tends to be high.* ► contentment, comfort, happiness, pleasure, pride, self-satisfaction, sense of achievement, enjoyment, fulfillment, gratification AN OPPOSITE IS dissatisfaction
2 *They may have to turn to the courts for satisfaction.* ► settlement, reparation, compensation, recompense, reparation, amends, justice, redress

satisfactory ADJECTIVE *There was no satisfactory method of dealing with trivial complaints.*
► adequate, acceptable, satisfying, suitable, reasonable, tolerable, fair, passable, sufficient, (*more informal*) all right, (*informal*) up to scratch AN OPPOSITE IS unsatisfactory

satisfy VERB **1** *There are not enough terminals to satisfy demand.* ► fulfill, gratify, answer, meet, fill, service, provide for AN OPPOSITE IS

frustrate **2** *Neither place had fully satisfied him.*
► content, make happy AN OPPOSITE IS dissatisfy

saturate VERB *Heavy rainfall had saturated the ground. The Colombian cartel saturated the market with cocaine.* ► soak, drench, impregnate, permeate, suffuse, steep, wet

saturated ADJECTIVE **1** *Saturated soil lacks air.*
► soaked, sodden, waterlogged, steeped (in)
2 *Her clothes had become saturated in the downpour.* ► soaked, soaking wet, sopping, drenched, wringing

saucy ADJECTIVE **1** *saucy postcards* ► titillating, suggestive, rude, lewd **2** *a saucy child*
► impudent, insolent, impertinent, disrespectful, pert, brazen, cocky, presumptuous OPPOSITES ARE polite, respectful

savage ADJECTIVE **1** *savage peoples of the past*
► primitive, uncivilized, barbarian, uncultivated, uneducated AN OPPOSITE IS civilized **2** *Savage dogs roamed the streets.*
► fierce, wild, ferocious, vicious, untamed AN OPPOSITE IS tame **3** *a savage assault* ► fierce, ferocious, brutal, cruel, sadistic AN OPPOSITE IS humane **4** *The speech was a savage attack.*
► fierce, scathing, vitriolic, harsh, blistering, searing

save VERB **1** *They wanted to save money for a vacation.* ► put by, set aside, store up, conserve, reserve, retain, scrape together,

2 keep something, especially money, so that it can be used later **3** avoid wasting something • *This will save time.* **4** (in computing) keep data by storing it in the computer's memory or on a disk **5** (in sports) prevent an opponent from scoring
▷ **save** NOUN **saver** NOUN

savings PLURAL NOUN money saved

savior NOUN saviors a person who saves someone
the or **our Saviour** (in Christianity) Jesus Christ

savory ADJECTIVE **1** tasty but not sweet **2** having an appetizing taste or smell

saw NOUN saws a tool with a zigzag edge for cutting wood or metal etc.

saw[1] VERB **saws, sawing, sawed, sawn 1** cut something with a saw **2** move to and fro as a saw does [from Old English]

saw[2] past tense of **see**

sawdust NOUN powder that comes from wood cut by a saw

saxophone NOUN saxophones a brass wind instrument with a reed in the mouthpiece
▷ **saxophonist** NOUN
[named after a 19th-century Belgian instrument maker, Adolphe Sax, who invented it]

say VERB **says, saying, said 1** speak or express something in words **2** give an opinion

say NOUN the power to decide something • *I have no say in the matter.*

saying NOUN sayings a well-known phrase or proverb or other statement

scab NOUN scabs a hard crust that forms over a cut or graze while it is healing
▷ **scabby** ADJECTIVE
[from Old Norse]

scaffold NOUN scaffolds a platform on which criminals are executed

scaffolding NOUN a structure of poles or tubes and planks making platforms for workers to stand on while building or repairing a house etc.

scald VERB **scalds, scalding, scalded 1** burn yourself with very hot liquid or steam **2** heat milk until it is nearly boiling **3** clean pans, etc., with boiling water
▷ **scald** NOUN

scale[1] NOUN scales **1** a series of units, degrees, or qualities etc. for measuring something **2** a series of musical notes going up or down in a fixed pattern **3** proportion or ratio • *The scale of this map is one centimeter to the kilometer.* **4** the relative size or importance of something • *They organize parties on a large scale.*
to scale with the parts in the same proportions as those of an original • *The architect's plans were drawn to scale.*

scale VERB **scales, scaling, scaled** climb • *She scaled the ladder.*
scale down or **up** reduce or increase at a fixed rate, or in proportion to something else [from Latin *scala* = ladder]

scale[2] NOUN scales **1** each of the thin overlapping parts on the outside of fish, snakes, etc.; a thin flake or part like this **2** a hard substance formed in a kettle or boiler by hard water, or on teeth
▷ **scaly** ADJECTIVE

scale VERB **scales, scaling, scaled** remove scales or scale from something [from old French; related to **scales**]

scale model NOUN scale models a model of something, made to scale

Thesaurus

(*more informal*) **stash away** OPPOSITES ARE waste, squander **2** *Try to save gas during the fuel crisis.* ► economize on, cut back on, be sparing with, use wisely AN OPPOSITE IS waste **3** *The crew managed to save all the passengers after an emergency landing.* ► rescue, free, release, liberate, recover, retrieve, salvage, set free **4** *A bit of help would have saved me from exhausting myself.* ► prevent, preserve, protect, safeguard, defend, guard, shield

saving NOUN *a saving of 20% on the regular price*
► reduction, cut, discount
savings *With all his savings gone he could not afford to work for nothing.* ► nest egg, funds, reserves, resources

savory ADJECTIVE *Sun-dried tomatoes give a pizza a savory taste.* ► piquant, spicy, appetizing, mouth-watering, delectable, delicious, luscious

say VERB **1** *She could not say his name.* ► speak, utter, voice, articulate, enunciate **2** *"It's snowing," he said* ► observe, remark, declare,

state, announce, answer, reply, respond **3** *Hugh says he didn't do it.* ► maintain, claim, assert, insist, contend **4** *He lit a candle and said a prayer.* ► recite, utter, speak **5** *What are you trying to say?* ► express, put into words, communicate, make known **6** *We cannot say what might happen.* ► guess, foretell, imagine, judge, estimate

saying NOUN *You know the saying about too many cooks?* ► proverb, adage, maxim, dictum, aphorism

scale NOUN **1** *people at different ends of the social scale* ► hierarchy, ladder, spectrum, ranking, sequence, progression **2** *the scale of a map* ► proportion, ratio, measure, relative size **3** *the scale of the tragedy* ► extent, size, scope, magnitude, degree, range

scale VERB *The intruders had to scale a 10-foot fence.* ► climb, ascend, clamber up, scramble up, shin up, go up, go over, mount

a
b
c
d
e
f
g
h
i
j
k
l
m
n
o
p
q
r
s
t
u
v
w
x
y
z

A
B
C
D
E
F
G
H
I
J
K
L
M
N
O
P
Q
R
S
T
U
V
W
X
Y
Z

scales PLURAL NOUN a device for weighing things [from Old Norse *skal* = bowl]

scalp NOUN scalps the skin on the top of the head

scamp NOUN scamps a rascal

scamper VERB scampers, scampering, scampered run quickly, lightly, or playfully
▷ **scamper** NOUN

scan VERB scans, scanning, scanned **1** look at every part of something **2** glance at something **3** count the beats of a line of poetry; be correct in rhythm ● *This line doesn't scan.* **4** sweep a radar or electronic beam over an area to examine it or in search of something **5** (in computing) use a scanner to convert printed text or pictures into digital form for storing in a computer

scan NOUN scans **1** scanning **2** an examination using a scanner ● *a brain scan*

scandal NOUN scandals **1** something shameful or disgraceful **2** gossip about people's faults and wrongdoings
▷ **scandalous** ADJECTIVE
[from Greek *skandalon* = stumbling block]

scandalize VERB scandalizes, scandalizing, scandalized shock a person by something considered shameful or disgraceful

scanner NOUN scanners **1** a machine that examines things by means of light or other rays **2** a machine that converts printed text, pictures, etc. into a form that can be stored in a computer

scant ADJECTIVE barely enough or adequate ● *We paid scant attention.*

scanty ADJECTIVE scantier, scantiest small in amount or extent; meagre ● *a scanty harvest*
▷ **scantily** ADVERB **scantiness** NOUN

scapegoat NOUN scapegoats a person who is made to bear the blame or punishment for what others have done [from *escape* and *goat*, after the goat which the ancient Jews allowed to escape into the desert after the priest had symbolically laid the people's sins upon it]

scar NOUN scars **1** the mark left by a cut or burn, etc., after it has healed **2** a lasting bad effect left by an unpleasant experience

scar VERB scars, scarring, scarred make a scar or scars on skin etc.

scarce ADJECTIVE scarcer, scarcest **1** not enough to supply people **2** rare
▷ **scarcity** NOUN
make yourself scarce (*informal*) go away; keep out of the way

scarcely ADVERB only just; only with difficulty ● *She could scarcely walk.*

Thesaurus

---

scamp NOUN *He was an idle young scamp in those days.* ▶ rascal, scallywag, devil, monkey, imp

scamper VERB *Sam scampered off and waited at the gate.* ▶ scurry, scuttle, dash, dart, scoot, run, rush, hasten, hurry
scamper about *Dogs scampered about the churchyard.* ▶ gambol, frisk, frolic, run about, romp

scan VERB **1** *We scanned the trees and caught sight of a magpie.* ▶ study, examine, regard, view, watch, gaze at, look at, scrutinize, survey, search, stare at **2** *Mungo scanned the books to see what Vic might like.* ▶ skim, glance through, flick through, have a look at

scandal NOUN **1** *The tabloids loved reporting scandal.* ▶ gossip, rumor, aspersions, notoriety, sensation, slander, calumny **2** *The college had been involved in a drug scandal.* ▶ wrongdoing, affair, business **3** *It's a scandal that the hospital has to close.* ▶ disgrace, outrage, injustice, affront, insult, shame

scandalize VERB *behavior that scandalized polite society* ▶ shock, outrage, horrify, disgust, appal, sicken, insult

scandalous ADJECTIVE **1** *This is a scandalous way to treat people who have risked their lives for the sake of their country.* ▶ shameful, disgraceful, shocking, outrageous, monstrous, appalling, wicked **2** *This was scandalous behavior and the palace gave her a firm warning.* ▶ discreditable,

disreputable, improper, shameful **3** *The scandalous rumors had been quickly forgotten.* ▶ scurrilous, malicious, libellous, slanderous, defamatory

scanty ADJECTIVE **1** *a conclusion based on scanty evidence* ▶ meagre, sparse, scant, paltry, minimal, negligible, pitiful, miserable, modest, (*more informal*) mingy, (*more informal*) measly AN OPPOSITE IS plentiful **2** *They looked bored and cold in their scanty dresses.* ▶ skimpy, revealing, insubstantial, short, thin

scar NOUN *a scar on his left cheek* ▶ mark, injury, wound , disfigurement, blemish, cicatrix

scar VERB **1** *The wound scarred his face.* ▶ disfigure, mark, leave a scar on, deface, brand, damage, spoil **2** *He was scarred for life by his mother's early death.* ▶ traumatize, disturb, distress, upset, damage

scarce ADJECTIVE (*informal*) *When money became scarce, he tried to go on welfare.* ▶ sparse, meagre, in short supply, hard to find, hard to come by, scanty, at a premium, rare, lacking, deficient AN OPPOSITE IS plentiful

scarcely ADVERB *There was scarcely enough to go around.* ▶ barely, hardly, only just

scarcity NOUN *a scarcity of good job opportunities* ▶ shortage, dearth, deficiency, want, paucity, inadequacy, insufficiency, lack OPPOSITES ARE abundance, surplus

scare VERB scares, scaring, scared frighten

scare NOUN scares **1** a fright **2** a sudden widespread sense of alarm about something • *a bomb scare* [from Old Norse]

scarecrow NOUN scarecrows a figure of a person dressed in old clothes, set up to frighten birds away from crops

scarf NOUN scarves a strip of material worn around the neck or head

scarlet ADJECTIVE, NOUN bright red

scary ADJECTIVE (*informal*) frightening

scathing (skay*th*- ing) ADJECTIVE severely criticizing a person or thing

scatter VERB scatters, scattering, scattered **1** throw or send or move in various directions **2** run or leave quickly in all directions

scavenge VERB scavenges, scavenging, scavenged **1** search for useful things amongst rubbish **2** (said about a bird or animal) search for decaying flesh as food
▷ **scavenger** NOUN

scene NOUN scenes **1** the place where something has happened • *the scene of the crime* **2** a part of a play or film **3** a view as seen by a spectator **4** an angry or noisy outburst • *He made a scene about the money.* **5** stage scenery **6** an area of activity • *the local music scene*

scenery NOUN **1** the natural features of a landscape **2** things put on a stage to make it look like a place

scent NOUN scents **1** a pleasant smell **2** a liquid perfume **3** an animal's smell that other animals can detect
▷ **scented** ADJECTIVE

scepter (sep)-ter NOUN scepters a rod carried by a king or queen as a symbol of power

schedule (sked- yool) NOUN schedules a program or timetable of planned events or work

schematic (skee- mat- ik) ADJECTIVE in the form of a diagram or chart

scheme NOUN schemes a plan of action

Thesaurus

scare VERB **1** *I didn't mean to scare you. I just wanted to talk.* ► alarm, startle, shake, unnerve, dismay, shock AN OPPOSITE IS calm **2** *The bogeyman could not scare him any more.* ► frighten, intimidate, terrorize, threaten, make afraid, menace, panic, bully, cow AN OPPOSITE IS reassure

scare NOUN *Finding the door unlocked gave her a scare.* ► fright, shock, start, turn, jolt, alarm

scared ADJECTIVE *Many of us are too scared to go out alone.* ► frightened, afraid, fearful, anxious, alarmed, terrified, panic-stricken

scary ADJECTIVE *It's not so scary now with all these people around.* ► frightening, scaring, alarming, eerie, spooky, creepy, terrifying, chilling, spine-chilling, intimidating

scathing ADJECTIVE *There followed a scathing attack on the government for its lack of action.* ► critical, scornful, cutting, withering, caustic, vitriolic, devastating, harsh AN OPPOSITE IS complimentary

scatter VERB **1** *The crowd quickly scattered.* ► disperse, break up, disband, separate, disintegrate, go off in all directions **2** *She scattered breadcrumbs across the path.* ► strew, sprinkle, spread, throw, fling, toss, shower AN OPPOSITE IS gather

scatterbrained ADJECTIVE *She was scatterbrained about such things and left everything to Tod.* ► absentminded, disorganized, forgetful, dreamy, featherbrained, muddled, empty-headed, unsystematic, vague, (*more informal*) scatty

scene NOUN **1** *Police were called to the scene of the accident.* ► location, site, place, position, point, spot, setting, locale, locality, whereabouts **2** *a beautiful scene by the lake* ► view, vista, outlook, prospect, panorama, landscape, picture, tableau, sight, spectacle **3** ► backdrop, scenery, set, stage **4** *The last scene of the novel is set in France.* ► part, section, episode, sequence **5** *He lost his money and there was a scene at the checkout.* ► fuss, commotion, disturbance, outburst, contretemps, exhibition, argument, quarrel, drama, (*more informal*) to-do

scenery NOUN *They stopped to admire the scenery.* ► landscape, terrain, panorama, scene, vista, outlook, surroundings

scenic ADJECTIVE *There is a scenic route through the mountains.* ► picturesque, panoramic, pretty, pleasing, attractive, beautiful, lovely, spectacular, striking

scent NOUN **1** *The scent of rose water hung in the air.* ► smell , odor, perfume, fragrance, aroma, redolence **2** *a bottle of scent* ► perfume, toilet water, lavender water, cologne **3** *The dogs picked up the scent.* ► trail, track

scepticism NOUN *Others expressed scepticism about using this method.* ► distrust, mistrust, disbelief, suspicion, doubt, incredulity, lack of confidence, cynicism AN OPPOSITE IS confidence

schedule NOUN *There was hardly any spare time in her busy schedule. I will organize a schedule of visits.* ► timetable, agenda, program, scheme, calendar, diary, list, plan

scheme NOUN *a scheme to steal the jewels* ► plot, conspiracy, intrigue, secret plan, ruse, ploy, (*more informal*) racket, (*more informal*) scam **3** *a bright color scheme* ► design, arrangement, pattern, layout

a b c d e f g h i j k l m n o p q r **s** t u v w x y z

A
B
C
D
E
F
G
H
I
J
K
L
M
N
O
P
Q
R

S

T
U
V
W
X
Y
Z

scheme VERB schemes, scheming, schemed make plans; plot
▷ **schemer** NOUN

scholar NOUN scholars 1 a person who has studied a subject thoroughly 2 a person who has been awarded a scholarship
▷ **scholarly** ADJECTIVE

scholarship NOUN scholarships 1 a grant of money given to someone to help to pay for his or her education 2 scholars' knowledge or methods; advanced study

school[1] NOUN schools 1 a place where teaching is done, especially of pupils aged 5–18 2 the pupils in a school 3 the time when teaching takes place in a school ● School begins at 9 a.m. 4 a group of people who have the same beliefs or style of work, etc.

school VERB schools, schooling, schooled teach or train ● She was schooling her horse for the competition. [from Greek skhole]

school[2] NOUN schools a shoal of fish or whales, etc. [from early German or Dutch schole = a troop]

schoolchild NOUN schoolchildren a child who goes to school
▷ **schoolboy** NOUN **schoolgirl** NOUN

schooling NOUN 1 training 2 education, especially in a school

schoolteacher NOUN schoolteachers a person who teaches in a school

science NOUN the study of the physical world by means of observation and experiment [from Latin scientia = knowledge]

science fiction NOUN stories about imaginary scientific discoveries or space travel and life on other planets

science park NOUN science parks an area set up for industries using science or for organizations doing scientific research

scientific ADJECTIVE 1 to do with science or scientists 2 studying things systematically and testing ideas carefully
▷ **scientifically** ADVERB

scientist NOUN scientists 1 an expert in science 2 someone who uses scientific methods

scintillating ADJECTIVE 1 shining brightly; sparkling 2 very lively and witty

scissors PLURAL NOUN a cutting instrument used with one hand, with two blades pivoted so that they can close against each other

scoff VERB scoffs, scoffing, scoffed 1 jeer; speak contemptuously 2 (informal) eat greedily
▷ **scoffer** NOUN

scold VERB scolds, scolding, scolded speak angrily; tell someone off
▷ **scolding** NOUN

scone (skon, skohn) NOUN scones a soft flat cake, usually eaten with butter

scoop NOUN scoops 1 a kind of deep spoon for serving ice cream, etc. 2 a deep shovel for lifting grain, sugar, etc. 3 a scooping movement 4 an important piece of news published by only one newspaper

---

Thesaurus

---

scheme VERB The emperor's wife schemed to exercise power through her son. ▶ plot, intrigue, connive, conspire, collude, plan

scholar NOUN a leading classical scholar ▶ academic, authority, expert, savant, intellectual, intellect, man or woman of letters

scholarly ADJECTIVE a serious, scholarly woman ▶ intellectual, learned, erudite, academic, lettered, knowledgeable

scholarship NOUN 1 a music scholarship worth $2,000 a year ▶ award, grant, bursary, exhibition 2 a person of great scholarship ▶ learning, erudition, knowledge, wisdom, academic achievement, intellectual attainment

school NOUN Have you asked them what makes a good school? ▶ college, academy, educational institution, centre of learning, institute

schooling NOUN the last two years of schooling ▶ education, instruction, tuition, teaching, training, coaching

science NOUN the science of forensic medicine ▶ technology, discipline, field, technique, art

scientific ADJECTIVE 1 scientific research ▶ science-based, technical, technological 2 Our methods are not scientific enough. ▶ systematic, methodical, analytical, organized, precise, rigorous, thorough, regulated

scientist NOUN the accusation that scientists are "playing God" ▶ researcher, scientific expert, technologist

scoff VERB scoff at 1 Experts are inclined to scoff at such theories. ▶ mock, ridicule, sneer at, jeer at, scorn, deride, make fun of, poke fun at 2 (informal) You feel guilty when you scoff a sherry trifle. ▶ eat up, guzzle, gobble up, wolf, wolf down, devour, (more informal) tuck into, (more informal) polish off

scold VERB Busy young mothers scolded their children. ▶ reprimand, rebuke, admonish, reprove, reproach, upbraid, censure, chide, criticize, reprehend, (more informal) tell off, (more informal) tick off OPPOSITES ARE praise, commend

scoop VERB 1 scoop out They would scoop out holes in the sand. ▶ gouge, dig, scrape,

scoop _VERB_ scoops, scooping, scooped lift or hollow something out with a scoop

scoot _VERB_ scoots, scooting, scooted **1** propel a bicycle or scooter by sitting or standing on it and pushing it along with one foot **2** (_informal_) run or go away quickly

scooter _NOUN_ scooters **1** a kind of motorcycle with small wheels **2** a board with wheels and a long handle, which you ride on by scooting

scope _NOUN_ **1** opportunity or possibility for something. ● _There is scope for improvement._ **2** the range or extent of a subject

scorch _VERB_ scorches, scorching, scorched make something go brown by burning it slightly

scorched-earth policy _NOUN_ the burning of crops and destruction of anything that might be useful to an opposing army

score _NOUN_ scores or, in sense 2, score **1** the number of points or goals made in a game; a result **2** (_old use_) twenty ● _"Three score years and ten" means 3 x 20 + 10 = 70 years._ **3** written or printed music
on that score for that reason, because of that ● _You needn't worry on that score._

score _VERB_ scores, scoring, scored **1** get a point or goal in a game **2** keep a count of the score **3** mark with lines or cuts **4** write out a musical score
▷ **scorer** _NOUN_
[from Old Norse]

scores _PLURAL NOUN_ many; a large number

scorn _NOUN_ contempt
▷ **scornful** _ADJECTIVE_ **scornfully** _ADVERB_

scorn _VERB_ scorns, scorning, scorned **1** treat someone with contempt **2** refuse something scornfully

scorpion _NOUN_ scorpions an animal that looks like a tiny lobster, with a poisonous sting

Scot _NOUN_ Scots a person who comes from Scotland

scotch _NOUN_ whisky made in Scotland

scotch _VERB_ scotches, scotching, scotched put an end to an idea or rumor, etc.

scot-free _ADJECTIVE_ without harm or punishment

Scots _ADJECTIVE_ from or belonging to Scotland
USAGE See note at **Scottish**.

Scottish _ADJECTIVE_ to do with or belonging to Scotland
USAGE **Scottish** is the most widely used word for describing things to do with Scotland: _Scottish education, Scottish mountains._ **Scots** is less common and is mainly used to describe people: _a Scots girl._ **Scotch** is only used in fixed expressions like _Scotch terrier_, a breed of terrier with rough hair.

scoundrel _NOUN_ scoundrels a wicked or dishonest person

scour¹ _VERB_ scours, scouring, scoured **1** rub something until it is clean and bright **2** clear a channel or pipe by the force of water flowing through it
▷ **scourer** _NOUN_

Thesaurus

---

excavate, hollow, cut **2 scoop out** _Scoop out the flesh of the pineapple halves._ ► remove, take out, scrape out, spoon out, extract **3 scoop up** _She scooped up her things and left hurriedly._ ► pick up, gather up, grab, collect

scope _NOUN_ **1** _issues that are beyond the scope of the inquiry_ ► extent, limit, range, competence, terms of reference, remit, ambit, capacity, compass, sphere, reach **2** _There is plenty of scope for new ideas._ ► opportunity, chance, latitude, leeway, freedom, room, space

scorch _VERB_ _Some of the walls had been scorched by fire._ ► burn, singe, char, blacken

score _NOUN_ **1** _The final score did not reflect the balance of the game._ ► result, tally, total, mark, number of points **2** _They had a score to settle._ ► debt, grievance

score _VERB_ **1** _a move that scored double points_ ► earn, win, gain, achieve, make, (_more informal_) chalk up **2** _A pattern had been scored in the surface._ ► cut, engrave, incise, mark, gouge, scratch, scrape, slash

scorn _NOUN_ _She treated that remark with the scorn it deserved._ ► contempt, disdain, derision,

disparagement, ridicule, mockery AN OPPOSITE IS admiration

scorn _VERB_ _Their haircuts are severe and they scorn make-up._ ► deride, despise, scoff at, ridicule, mock, spurn, look down on, dismiss AN OPPOSITE IS admire

scornful _ADJECTIVE_ _Richard was prepared to put up with the scornful disapproval of Eve and Ted._ ► contemptuous, derisive, disdainful, supercilious, scathing, disparaging, mocking, scoffing, sneering, withering OPPOSITES ARE admiring, respectful

scotch _VERB_ _Hopes of trying a first kiss were scotched when she fell asleep the moment she got into the car._ ► end, bring to an end, put paid to, frustrate, shatter, wreck, destroy, scupper

scot-free _ADJECTIVE_ _You wouldn't want to see the real villains getting off scot-free._ ► unpunished, unscathed, unharmed, unhurt, safe

scoundrel _NOUN_ _It wasn't her fault she had a scoundrel for a grandson._ ► rascal, rogue, ruffian, ne'er-do-well, good-for-nothing, villain, knave, scallywag, scamp

scour _VERB_ **1** _They were made to scrub kitchen floors and scour out pans._ ► scrub, clean, scrape,

A
B
C
D
E
F
G
H
I
J
K
L
M
N
O
P
Q
R
S
T
U
V
W
X
Y
Z

scour² VERB scours, scouring, scoured search thoroughly

scourge (skerj) NOUN scourges 1 a whip for flogging people 2 something that inflicts suffering or punishment

Scout NOUN Scouts a member of the Boy Scouts or Girl Scouts

scout NOUN scouts someone sent out to collect information

scout VERB scouts, scouting, scouted 1 act as a scout 2 search an area thoroughly

scowl NOUN scowls a bad-tempered frown

scowl VERB scowls, scowling, scowled make a scowl

scrabble VERB scrabbles, scrabbling, scrabbled 1 scratch or claw at something with the hands or feet 2 grope or struggle to get something

scraggy ADJECTIVE thin and bony

scramble VERB scrambles, scrambling, scrambled 1 move quickly and awkwardly 2 struggle to do or get something 3 (said about aircraft or their crew) hurry and take off quickly 4 cook eggs by mixing them up and heating them in a pan 5 mix things together 6 alter a radio or telephone signal so that it cannot be used without a decoding device
▷ **scrambler** NOUN

scramble NOUN scrambles 1 a climb or walk over rough ground 2 a struggle to do or get something 3 a motorcycle race over rough ground

scrap¹ NOUN scraps 1 a small piece 2 trash; waste material, especially metal that is suitable for reprocessing

scrap VERB scraps, scrapping, scrapped get rid of something that is useless or unwanted

scrap² NOUN scraps (informal) a fight

scrap VERB scraps, scrapping, scrapped (informal) fight

scrape VERB scrapes, scraping, scraped 1 clean or smooth or damage something by passing something hard over it 2 make a harsh sound by rubbing against a rough or hard surface 3 remove by scraping • *Scrape the mud off your shoes.* 4 get something by great effort or care • *They scraped together enough money for a vacation.*
▷ **scraper** NOUN
scrape through only just succeed, pass an exam, etc.

scrape NOUN scrapes 1 a scraping movement or sound 2 a mark, etc., made by scraping 3 (informal) an awkward situation caused by mischief or foolishness

Thesaurus

wash, buff up, burnish, polish, rub 2 *Rita scoured the junk shops for secondhand pieces to fill the rooms.* ► ransack, rummage through, search, comb, forage through, hunt through

scourge NOUN *High interests were the scourge of those years.* ► affliction, bane, curse, misfortune, torment

scout NOUN *Scouts came back with information about the enemy positions.* ► lookout, outrider, advance guard, spy

scout VERB **scout about** or **around** *I asked Claire to scout around to find him a place to stay.* ► look about, reconnoitre, search, explore, hunt, investigate, cast about, get information

scowl VERB *She scowled at him and told him to go away.* ► glower, frown, glare, grimace

scrabble VERB *She scrabbled about in her pockets until she found her glasses.* ► rummage, grope, root, fumble, claw, dig

scraggy ADJECTIVE *She kept out of the way of her sister's scraggy old cat.* ► scrawny, skinny, thin, lanky, gaunt, lean, bony, emaciated, underfed OPPOSITES ARE plump, fat

scram VERB (informal) *Scram or I'll call the police.* ► go away, leave, get going, get moving, (informal) beat it, (informal) shove off, (informal) clear out

scramble NOUN *Getting there in time proved quite a scramble.* ► struggle, rush, hustle, dash

scramble VERB 1 *I scrambled down the slope toward the car. Daniel scrambled to his feet and left the room.* ► clamber, climb, crawl, scrabble, move awkwardly 2 *She saw the two men scramble for the fallen gun.* ► scuffle, struggle, tussle, fight, jostle 3 *They quickly scrambled into the plane.* ► dash, hasten, hurry, run, rush

scrap NOUN 1 *There were a few scraps of food on the table.* ► bit, piece, morsel, particle, crumb, speck, fragment, mouthful 2 *Not a scrap of evidence could be found.* ► shred, speck, iota, jot, ounce, trace 3 *a truck loaded with scrap* ► junk, refuse, rubbish, salvage, waste, litter, odds and ends 4 *He wanted to avoid a scrap with Kevin.* ► fight, quarrel, disagreement, tussle, brawl

scrap VERB 1 *Local residents want the road plan to be scrapped.* ► abandon, cancel, discard, (informal) ditch, drop, give up, jettison, throw away, write off 2 *The younger children are always scrapping.* ► fight, quarrel, argue, brawl

scrape VERB 1 *Elaine had scraped her skin against the wall.* ► graze, scratch, scuff, abrade, bark, lacerate 2 *He scraped his boots before going inside.* ► scrub, scour, rub, clean
scrape together *We scraped enough money together to get home* ► collect, amass, rake together, dredge up

scrappy ADJECTIVE **1** made of scraps or bits or disconnected things **2** carelessly done
▷ **scrappiness** NOUN

scratch VERB scratches, scratching, scratched **1** mark or cut the surface of a thing with something sharp **2** rub the skin with fingernails or claws because it itches **3** withdraw from a race or competition

scratch NOUN scratches **1** a mark made by scratching **2** the action of scratching
▷ **scratchy** ADJECTIVE
start from scratch start from the beginning or with nothing prepared
up to scratch up to the proper standard

scrawl NOUN scrawls untidy handwriting

scrawl VERB scrawls, scrawling, scrawled write in a scrawl

scrawny ADJECTIVE scraggy

scream NOUN screams **1** a loud cry of pain, fear, anger, or excitement **2** a loud piercing sound **3** (informal) a very amusing person or thing

scream VERB screams, screaming, screamed make a scream

screech NOUN screeches a harsh high-pitched scream or sound
▷ **screech** VERB

screen NOUN screens **1** a special surface for displaying films, television pictures, or computer data **2** a movable panel used to hide, protect, or divide something **3** a vehicle's windscreen

screen VERB screens, screening, screened **1** protect, hide, or divide with a screen **2** show a movie or television pictures on a screen **3** carry out tests on someone to find out if they have a disease **4** check whether a person is suitable for a job

screenplay NOUN screenplays the script of a movie, with instructions to the actors etc.

screw NOUN screws **1** a metal pin with a spiral ridge (the thread) around it, holding things together by being twisted in **2** a twisting movement **3** something twisted **4** a propeller, especially for a ship or motor boat

screw VERB screws, screwing, screwed **1** fasten with a screw or screws **2** fit or turn something by twisting

screwdriver NOUN screwdrivers a tool for turning screws

scribble VERB scribbles, scribbling, scribbled **1** write quickly or untidily or carelessly **2** make meaningless marks
▷ **scribble** NOUN

script NOUN scripts **1** handwriting **2** the text of a play, film, broadcast talk, etc.

scripture NOUN scriptures **1** sacred writings **2** (in Christianity) the Bible

scroll NOUN scrolls **1** a roll of paper or parchment used for writing on **2** a spiral design

Thesaurus

scrape NOUN Try not to get into any scrapes ▶ predicament, difficulty, tight spot, mischief, trouble

scrappy ADJECTIVE The game turned out to be a scrappy affair. ▶ disorganized, disjointed, uneven, slipshod, unsatisfactory AN OPPOSITE IS well-organized

scratch VERB **1** Be careful not to scratch the table top. ▶ scrape, mark, score, gash, cut, damage the surface of, gouge **2** The thorns were scratching his legs. ▶ graze, chafe, prick, cut, lacerate

scratch NOUN **1** There were scratches in the paintwork. ▶ gash, groove, line, mark, scoring, scrape **2** He had a long scratch down one side of his face. ▶ graze, laceration, wound , cut
up to scratch The work was not up to scratch. ▶ satisfactory, adequate, acceptable, good enough, passable, all right

scream VERB She screamed at them to stop. ▶ yell, shriek, shout, bawl, screech, roar, howl, wail

scream NOUN He let out a scream of pain. ▶ yell, shriek, shout, screech, roar, howl, wail

screen NOUN **1** a computer with a 17-inch screen ▶ monitor, display, VDU or visual display unit

2 A screen divided the room in two. ▶ partition, divider, curtain, blind

screen VERB **1** A low hedge screened the dustbins. ▶ hide, conceal, mask, shield, shelter **2** Staff are regularly screened in the interests of security. ▶ vet, scrutinize, examine, investigate

screw VERB **1** She screwed the lid on the jar. ▶ fasten, tighten, twist, turn **2** James screwed the piece of paper into a tight ball. ▶ twist, wind, wring **3** The last thing to do was screw the boards back down. ▶ fix, fasten, secure **4** (informal) He was not going to let them screw him for money like that again. ▶ cheat, swindle, defraud, pressurize, extort, squeeze USAGE If you use extort or squeeze you have to say (for example) He was not going to let them extort money from him like that again.

scribble VERB He quickly scribbled a shopping list. ▶ scrawl, dash off, jot down, write

scribe NOUN He would need to get a scribe to write his letter for him. ▶ copyist, clerk, transcriber, amanuensis, scrivener, secretary

script NOUN **1** The note had been written in an elegant script. ▶ handwriting, hand, autograph **2** The film was spoilt by a poor script. ▶ screenplay, text, dialogue

a b c d e f g h i j k l m n o p q r **s** t u v w x y z

A
B
C
D
E
F
G
H
I
J
K
L
M
N
O
P
Q
R

S

T
U
V
W
X
Y
Z

scroll VERB scrolls, scrolling, scrolled move the display on a computer screen up or down to see what comes before or after it

scrounge VERB scrounges, scrounging, scrounged get something without paying for it
▷ **scrounger** NOUN

scrub VERB scrubs, scrubbing, scrubbed 1 rub with a hard brush, especially to clean something 2 (informal) cancel
▷ **scrub** NOUN

scrub NOUN 1 low trees and bushes 2 land covered with these

scruff NOUN the back of the neck

scruffy ADJECTIVE shabby and untidy
▷ **scruffily** ADVERB **scruffiness** NOUN

scrum NOUN scrums 1 (also scrummage) a group of players from each side in rugby football who push against each other and try to kick back the ball when it is thrown between them 2 a crowd pushing against each other

scruple NOUN scruples a feeling of doubt or hesitation when your conscience tells you that an action would be wrong

scruple VERB scruples, scrupling, scrupled have scruples • He would not scruple to betray us. [from Latin scrupum, literally = rough pebble]

scrupulous ADJECTIVE 1 very careful and conscientious 2 strictly honest or honorable
▷ **scrupulously** ADVERB

scrutinize VERB scrutinizes, scrutinizing, scrutinized look at something carefully
▷ **scrutiny** NOUN

scuba diving NOUN swimming underwater using a tank of air strapped to your back [from the initials of self-contained underwater breathing apparatus]

scuff VERB scuffs, scuffing, scuffed 1 drag your feet while walking 2 scrape with your foot; mark or damage something by doing this

scuffle NOUN scuffles a confused fight or struggle

scuffle VERB scuffles, scuffling, scuffled take part in a scuffle [probably from a Scandinavian language]

scullery NOUN sculleries a room where dishes etc. are washed up

sculptor NOUN sculptors a person who makes sculptures
▷ **sculpt** VERB

sculpture NOUN sculptures 1 making shapes by carving wood or stone or casting metal 2 a shape made in this way
▷ **sculpture** VERB

scum NOUN 1 froth or dirt on top of a liquid 2 worthless people

scuttle NOUN scuttles a bucket or container for coal in a house

scuttle[1] VERB scuttles, scuttling, scuttled scurry; hurry away

scuttle[2] VERB scuttles, scuttling, scuttled sink a ship deliberately by letting water into it

scythe NOUN scythes a tool with a long curved blade for cutting grass or corn

scythe VERB scythes, scything, scythed cut with a scythe

SE ABBREVIATION 1 southeast 2 southeastern

Thesaurus

scrounge VERB Street urchins scrounged money from the tourists. ► beg, cadge, sponge

scrounger NOUN He was neither a scrounger nor a misfit. ► cadger, sponger, parasite

scrub VERB 1 She decided to scrub the bathroom floor. ► scour, wash, clean, rub, brush 2 (informal) If interest rates went up again they would have to scrub their vacation. ► cancel, scrap, go without, do without, call off, drop, abandon, (informal) ditch

scruffy ADJECTIVE 1 He had worn scruffy jeans and a T-shirt to his breakfast. ► shabby, worn, ragged, worn-out, dirty AN OPPOSITE IS smart 2 He was standing in a bar, scruffy and long-haired. ► unkempt, untidy, dishevelled, ungroomed, messy, bedraggled AN OPPOSITE IS tidy

scrupulous ADJECTIVE 1 The story had been written with a scrupulous attention to historical accuracy. ► conscientious, diligent, fastidious, meticulous, minute, painstaking, precise, punctilious, rigorous, strict, systematic,

thorough 2 The accounts will be reviewed by the most scrupulous auditor. ► honest, honorable, upright, upstanding, principled, right-minded, fair-minded, ethical AN OPPOSITE IS unscrupulous

scuff VERB The toe was scuffed and the shoes would need fixing. ► scrape, scratch, rub, graze, brush

scuffle NOUN There was a scuffle and the sound of people running. ► fight, fracas, brawl, struggle, tussle, scrap, rumpus, commotion, argument

scuffle VERB Three teenage boys were scuffling and messing around. ► fight, brawl, struggle, tussle, scrap, come to blows

sculpture NOUN a marble sculpture of Venus ► carving, figure, statue, effigy, image USAGE A small sculpture is called a statuette. A bust is a sculpture of the top part of a person.

scum NOUN The water had a thick scum on it. ► froth, foam, film, impurities

scurry VERB Officials scurried about. ► scamper, scuttle, dash, dart, rush, hurry

sea NOUN **seas** **1** the salt water that covers most of the earth's surface; a part of this **2** a large lake • *the Sea of Galilee* **3** a large area of something • *a sea of faces*
at sea 1 on the sea **2** not knowing what to do

sea anemone NOUN **sea anemones** a sea creature with short tentacles around its mouth

seaboard NOUN **seaboards** a coastline or coastal region

seafaring ADJECTIVE, NOUN working or travelling on the sea
▷ **seafarer** NOUN

seafood NOUN fish or shellfish from the sea eaten as food

seagull NOUN **seagulls** a seabird with long wings

seal[1] NOUN **seals** a sea mammal with thick fur or bristles, that breeds on land [from Old English]

seal[2] NOUN **seals** **1** a piece of metal with an engraved design for pressing on a soft substance to leave an impression **2** an impression made on a piece of wax **3** something designed to close an opening and prevent air or liquid, etc., from getting in or out **4** a confirmation or guarantee • *a seal of approval*

seal VERB **seals**, **sealing**, **sealed** **1** close something by sticking two parts together **2** close securely; stop up **3** press a seal on something **4** settle or decide • *His fate was sealed.*
seal off prevent people getting to an area [from early French; related to **sign**]

sea level NOUN the level of the sea halfway between high and low tide

sealing wax NOUN a substance that is soft when heated but hardens when cooled, used

for sealing documents or for marking with a seal

sea lion NOUN **sea lions** a kind of large seal that lives in the Pacific Ocean

seam NOUN **seams** **1** the line where two edges of cloth or wood etc. join **2** a layer of coal in the ground

seamanship NOUN skill in seafaring

seamy ADJECTIVE
seamy side the less attractive side or part • *Police see a lot of the seamy side of life* [originally, the "wrong" side of a piece of sewing, where the rough edges of the seams show]

sear VERB **sears**, **searing**, **seared** scorch or burn the surface of something

search VERB **searches**, **searching**, **searched** look very hard or carefully in order to find something
▷ **search** NOUN **searcher** NOUN

search engine NOUN **search engines** (in computing) a program that searches for data, especially on the Internet

searchlight NOUN **searchlights** a light with a strong beam that can be turned in any direction

search party NOUN **search parties** a group of people organized to search for a missing person or thing

search warrant NOUN **search warrants** an official document giving the police permission to search private property

seasick ADJECTIVE sick because of the movement of a ship
▷ **seasickness** NOUN

seaside NOUN a place by the sea where people go for holidays

season NOUN **seasons** **1** each of the four main parts of the year (spring, summer, autumn,

---

Thesaurus

---

sea ADJECTIVE *sea creatures; a sea voyage; a sea port*
► aquatic, marine, maritime, nautical, naval, oceangoing, oceanic, saltwater, seafaring, seagoing

sea NOUN **1** *They caught sight of the sea in the distance.* ► water, ocean, waves RELATED ADJECTIVES ► marine, maritime, nautical, naval **2** *sea creatures* ► aquatic, marine, seafaring, ocean, salt **3** *a sea of friendly faces* ► mass, host, multitude, profusion

seal NOUN *the queen's seal* ► emblem, crest, insignia, symbol, stamp

seal VERB **1** *She folded the letter and sealed the envelope.* ► stick down, close, fasten, secure **2** *He filled the jar and sealed it.* ► stop up, close, plug, stopper **3** *He held out a hand to seal the agreement.* ► confirm, clinch, complete, secure, (more informal) sew up

seal off *Police sealed off the city center.*

search VERB **1** *We searched for clues.* ► explore, ferret about, hunt, look, nose about, poke about, prospect, pry, seek **2** *Security staff will search passengers and their luggage.* ► check, examine, investigate, scrutinize, inspect, (more informal) frisk **3** *I searched the house for my keys.* ► scour, comb, ransack, rummage through, forage through, hunt through

search NOUN *We began our search for a place to eat.* ► hunt, quest, exploration, investigation, look, check

seaside NOUN *a trip to the seaside* ► coast, beach, seashore, shore RELATED ADJECTIVE ► littoral

season NOUN *The holiday season lasts until October these days.* ► period, time of year, time, phase and winter) **2** the time of year when something happens • *the football season* **in season** available and ready for eating • *Strawberries are in season in the summer.*

season VERB **seasons, seasoning, seasoned 1** give extra flavor to food by adding salt, pepper, or other strong-tasting substances **2** dry and treat timber, etc., to make it ready for use

seasonable ADJECTIVE suitable for the season • *Hot weather is seasonable in summer.*
▷ **seasonably** ADVERB
USAGE Do not confuse with **seasonal**.

seasonal ADJECTIVE **1** for or to do with a season **2** happening in a particular season • *Fruit-picking is seasonal work.*
▷ **seasonally** ADVERB
USAGE Do not confuse with **seasonable**.

seasoning NOUN **seasonings** a substance used to season food

season ticket NOUN **season tickets** a ticket that can be used as often as you like throughout a period of time

seat NOUN **seats 1** a thing made or used for sitting on **2** the right to be a member of a council, committee, legislature, etc. • *She won the seat ten years ago.* **3** the buttocks; the part of a skirt or pants covering these **4** the place where something is based or located • *Washington, D.C., is the seat of the government.*

seat VERB **seats, seating, seated 1** place in or on a seat **2** have seats for • *The theater seats 3,000 people.*

seat belt NOUN **seat belts** a strap to hold a person securely in a seat

seating NOUN **1** the seats in a place • *seating for 400* **2** the arrangement of seats • *a seating plan*

sea urchin NOUN **sea urchins** a sea animal with a round shell covered in sharp spikes

seaweed NOUN a plant or plants that grow in the sea

seaworthy ADJECTIVE (said about a ship) fit for a sea voyage
▷ **seaworthiness** NOUN

secateurs PLURAL NOUN clippers held in the hand for pruning plants

secluded ADJECTIVE quiet or sheltered from view • *a secluded beach*
▷ **seclusion** NOUN

second[1] ADJECTIVE **1** next after the first **2** another • *a second chance* **3** less good • *second quality*
▷ **secondly** ADVERB
have second thoughts wonder whether a decision you have made was the right one

second NOUN **seconds 1** a person or thing that is second **2** an attendant of a fighter in a boxing match, duel, etc. **3** a thing that is not of the best quality, often sold cheaply **4** one-sixtieth of a minute of time or of a degree used in measuring angles

second[1] VERB **seconds, seconding, seconded 1** assist someone **2** support a proposal, motion, etc.
▷ **seconder** NOUN

second[2] British (sik- ond) VERB **seconds, seconding, seconded** transfer a person temporarily to another job or department etc.
▷ **secondment** NOUN

secondary ADJECTIVE **1** coming after or from something **2** less important **3** (said about education etc.) for children of more than about 11 years old • *a secondary school*
COMPARE **primary**

Thesaurus

---

season VERB **1** *herbs for seasoning fish* ► flavor, spice, salt, add seasoning to **2** *The wood should be well seasoned.* ► mature, age, temper, condition

seat NOUN **1** *There were not enough seats for everyone to sit on.* ► chair, bench, stool, pew, place **2** *The capital city is not always the seat of government.* ► center, headquarters, location, site, base, nucleus, heart, hub **3** *a country seat in England* ► residence, ancestral, mansion, abode, stately home

seat VERB **1** *She seated her guests around a large oval table.* ► place, position, put, settle **2** *The smaller cinema seats thirty.* ► accommodate, hold, take, have seats for, sit

secede VERB **secede from** *The Southern states seceded from the Union.* ► withdraw from, separate from, break away from, leave, quit, split with

second ADJECTIVE **1** *There won't be a second chance.* ► another, further, additional, repeated, alternative, extra **2** *We keep a second set of data in another building.* ► spare, extra, alternative, backup

second NOUN **1** *They were only gone for a second.* ► moment, instant, bit, flash, (more informal) jiffy, (more informal) tick **2** *Chris was acting as his second.* ► assistant, attendant, supporter, right-hand man or woman, helper

secondary ADJECTIVE **1** *issues that are regarded as secondary* ► subsidiary, subordinate, minor, lesser, lower, inferior, second-rate **2** *A secondary action was started in support of the main attack.* ► ancillary, auxiliary, supplementary, supportive, reinforcing, extra, second, reserve

secondhand ADJECTIVE **1** bought or used after someone else has owned it **2** selling used goods • *a secondhand shop*

second nature NOUN behavior that has become automatic or a habit • *Lying is second nature to him.*

second-rate ADJECTIVE inferior; not very good

secret ADJECTIVE **1** that must not be told or shown to other people **2** not known by everybody **3** working secretly
▷ **secretly** ADVERB **secrecy** NOUN

secret NOUN **secrets** something secret

secretary (sek- rit- e- ree) NOUN **secretaries** **1** a person whose job is to help with letters, answer the telephone, and make business arrangements for a person or organization **2** the chief assistant of a government minister or ambassador
▷ **secretarial** ADJECTIVE
[from Latin *secretarius* = an officer or servant allowed to know his employer's secrets]

secrete (sik- reet) VERB **secretes**, **secreting**, **secreted** **1** hide something **2** produce a substance in the body • *Saliva is secreted in the mouth.*
▷ **secretion** NOUN

secretive (seek- rit- iv) ADJECTIVE liking or trying to keep things secret
▷ **secretively** ADVERB **secretiveness** NOUN

secret service NOUN a government department responsible for espionage

sect NOUN **sects** a group of people whose beliefs differ from others in the same religion

section NOUN **sections** **1** a part of something **2** a cross-section

sector NOUN **sectors** **1** one part of an area **2** a part of something • *the private sector of industry* **3** (in mathematics) a section of a circle between two lines drawn from its center to its circumference

secular ADJECTIVE to do with worldly affairs, not spiritual or religious matters

secure ADJECTIVE **1** safe, especially against attack **2** certain not to slip or fail **3** reliable
▷ **securely** ADVERB

secure VERB **secures**, **securing**, **secured** **1** make a thing secure **2** fasten something firmly **3** obtain • *We secured two tickets for the show.*

security NOUN **securities** **1** being secure; safety **2** precautions against theft or spying, etc. **3** something given as a guarantee that a promise will be kept or a debt repaid **4** investments such as stocks and shares

sedate ADJECTIVE calm and dignified
▷ **sedately** ADVERB **sedateness** NOUN

sedate VERB **sedates**, **sedating**, **sedated** give a sedative to
▷ **sedation** NOUN

Thesaurus

---

secondhand ADJECTIVE **1** *a secondhand car*
► used, pre-owned, old AN OPPOSITE IS new **2** *She was relying on secondhand information.*
► indirect, secondary, derivative AN OPPOSITE IS personal.

second-rate ADJECTIVE *a second-rate camp entertainer* ► second-class, second-best, substandard, mediocre, middling, ordinary, below par, commonplace, indifferent, inferior, low-grade

secret ADJECTIVE **1** *secret information*
► confidential, classified, restricted, (*more informal*) hush-hush AN OPPOSITE IS public **2** *They met at a secret location.* ► private, secluded, hidden, isolated, remote, unknown, undisclosed OPPOSITES ARE public, well-known **3** *a secret operation* ► clandestine, covert, undercover, surreptitious AN OPPOSITE IS overt

secretary NOUN *She called in her secretary to take notes of the meeting.* ► assistant, personal assistant or PA, clerk, typist

secretive ADJECTIVE *He was being very secretive about his intentions.* ► uncommunicative, unforthcoming, reticent, tight-lipped, cagey, close, withdrawn AN OPPOSITE IS communicative

section NOUN **1** *You must complete every section of the application form.* ► part, division, portion, paragraph **2** *the reference section of your local library* ► department, part, division

secular ADJECTIVE *secular music; a secular ceremony* ► nonreligious, temporal, worldly, earthly, civil, lay OPPOSITES ARE sacred, religious

secure ADJECTIVE **1** *Check that all doors and windows are secure.* ► locked, sealed, closed tight, impregnable, invulnerable OPPOSITES ARE insecure, vulnerable **2** *We felt secure indoors during the storm.* ► protected, safe, unharmed, unhurt, unscathed OPPOSITES ARE exposed, in danger **3** *The ladder needs to be made secure.* ► stable, steady, firm, fast, fixed, immovable OPPOSITES ARE insecure, unsteady

secure VERB **1** *Secure the front door when you leave.* ► fasten, close, lock, shut, seal, bolt **2** *a charter that secures the rights of the individual*
► ensure, assure, guarantee, protect, confirm **3** *Jenny secured a senior post in the company.*
► obtain, acquire, gain, get, be given

security NOUN **1** *The first priority is the security of passengers.* ► safety, protection, care, guarding, freedom from harm AN OPPOSITE IS vulnerability **2** *The president's visit called for unprecedented levels of security.* ► safety measures, safeguards, protection, surveillance

sedate ADJECTIVE **1** *The procession moved forward at a sedate pace.* ► steady, unhurried, deliberate, gentle, easygoing, comfortable, slow OPPOSITES ARE brisk, lively **2** *They enjoyed*

A
B
C
D
E
F
G
H
I
J
K
L
M
N
O
P
Q
R
S
T
U
V
W
X
Y
Z

sedative (sed-a-tiv) NOUN **sedatives** a medicine that makes a person calm

sedentary (sed-en-ter-ee) ADJECTIVE done sitting down • *sedentary work*

Seder (say)-der NOUN **Seders** (in Judaism) a ritual and a ceremonial meal to mark the beginning of Passover

sedge NOUN a grasslike plant growing in marshes or near water

sediment NOUN fine particles of solid matter that float in liquid or sink to the bottom of it

sedimentary ADJECTIVE formed from particles that have settled on a surface • *sedimentary rocks*

sedition NOUN speeches or actions intended to make people rebel against the authority of the State
▷ **seditious** ADJECTIVE

seduce VERB **seduces, seducing, seduced** **1** persuade a person to have sexual intercourse **2** attract or lead astray by offering temptations
▷ **seducer** NOUN **seduction** NOUN **seductive** ADJECTIVE

see VERB **sees, seeing, saw, seen 1** perceive with the eyes **2** meet or visit somebody • *See a doctor about your cough.* **3** understand • *She saw what I meant.* **4** imagine • *Can you see yourself as a teacher?* **5** consider • *I will see what can be done.* **6** make sure • *See that the windows are shut.* **7** discover • *See who is at the door.* **8** escort • *See her to the door.*

see through not be deceived by something
see to attend to

seed NOUN **seeds** or **seed 1** a fertilized part of a plant, capable of growing into a new plant **2** (*old use*) descendants **3** a seeded player

seed VERB **seeds, seeding, seeded 1** plant or sprinkle seeds in something **2** name the best players and arrange for them not to play against each other in the early rounds of a tournament

seedling NOUN **seedlings** a very young plant growing from a seed

seedy ADJECTIVE **seedier, seediest 1** full of seeds **2** shabby and disreputable
▷ **seediness** NOUN

seeing CONJUNCTION considering • *Seeing that we have all finished, let's go.*

seek VERB **seeks, seeking, sought 1** search for **2** try to do or obtain something • *to seek fame*

seem VERB **seems, seeming, seemed** give the impression of being something • *She seems worried about her work.*
▷ **seemingly** ADVERB

Thesaurus

---

their *sedate suburban life and didn't dream about the bright lights.* ► calm, staid, prim, sober, seemly, demure, dignified, serene

sedentary ADJECTIVE *People with sedentary lifestyles need to exercise.* ► seated, sitting, desk-bound, immobile, inactive AN OPPOSITE IS active

seductive ADJECTIVE **1** *Lori gave him one of her most seductive smiles.* ► sexy, alluring, captivating, ravishing, bewitching, appealing, attractive, enticing, irresistible, provocative, tempting OPPOSITES ARE repulsive, repellent **2** *the seductive warmth of a coal fire* ► attractive, appealing, enticing, comforting

see VERB **1** *She saw Eve waiting for her. Did you see who got into the car with him?* ► discern, perceive, glimpse, make out, pick out, recognize, identify, distinguish RELATED ADJECTIVE ► visible **2** *She could see how difficult it might be.* ► understand, follow, know, comprehend, realize, recognize, take in, grasp, appreciate, fathom **3** *I can see trouble ahead.* ► foresee, envisage, picture, visualize, predict, imagine, anticipate, conceive **4** *We'll see what we can do.* ► consider, think about, reflect on, weigh, decide, investigate **5** *They are going to see the game on Saturday.* ► watch, attend, be a spectator at **6** *Is she still seeing Stephen?* ► go out with, be dating, meet, visit **7** *Keith offered to see her home.* ► escort, accompany, take, conduct **8** *Stuart went to see the doctor about his leg.* ► visit, consult, confer with, talk to, speak to **9** *I saw an old friend in town.* ► encounter, meet by chance, run into, run across, chance on, (*more informal*) bump into **10** *I must go and see what the dog is up to.* ► find out, discover, ascertain, establish

see to *Will you see to the repairs?* ► attend to, deal with, take care of, look after, sort out, organize, manage

seed NOUN **1** *The male provides the seed to fertilize the female egg.* ► sperm, semen, seminal fluid **2** *The birds feed on insects, seed, and shoots.* ► grains **3** *The fruit was full of seeds.* ► pip, stone **4** *The conflict was the seed for all future troubles.* ► source, origin, cause, basis RELATED ADJECTIVE ► seminal

seedy ADJECTIVE *a seedy hotel on the seafront* ► sleazy, squalid, shabby, rundown, sordid, seamy, rough

seek VERB **1** *The fleet sailed south to seek the enemy.* ► look for, search for, pursue, follow, try to find, hunt **2** *They will need to seek advice from a lawyer.* ► call on, ask for, get **3** *Spain is seeking the extradition of the suspects.* ► request, solicit, try to obtain **4** *We seek to please our customers.* ► try, attempt, endeavour, strive, aspire

seem VERB *The woman seemed too afraid to speak.* ► appear, look, sound, give the impression of being

seemly ADJECTIVE (old use) (said about behavior, etc.) proper or suitable
▷ **seemliness** NOUN
[from an old sense of seem = be suitable]

seep VERB seeps, seeping, seeped ooze slowly out or through something
▷ **seepage** NOUN

seesaw NOUN seesaws a plank balanced in the middle so that two people can sit, one on each end, and make it go up and down

seethe VERB seethes, seething, seethed **1** bubble and surge like water boiling **2** be very angry or excited

segment NOUN segments a part that is cut off or separates naturally from other parts • the segments of an orange
▷ **segmented** ADJECTIVE

segregate VERB segregates, segregating, segregated **1** separate people of different religions, races, etc. **2** isolate a person or thing
▷ **segregation** NOUN

seismic (sy- zmik) ADJECTIVE to do with earthquakes or other vibrations of the earth

seize VERB seizes, seizing, seized **1** take hold of a person or thing suddenly or forcibly **2** take possession of something by force or by legal authority • Customs officers seized a lot of smuggled goods. **3** take eagerly • Seize your chance! **4** have a sudden effect on • Panic seized us.

seize up become jammed, especially because of friction or overheating

seizure NOUN seizures **1** seizing **2** a sudden fit, as in epilepsy or a heart attack

seldom ADVERB rarely; not often

select VERB selects, selecting, selected choose a person or thing
▷ **selector** NOUN

select ADJECTIVE **1** carefully chosen • a select group **2** (said about a club, etc.) choosing its members carefully; exclusive

selection NOUN selections **1** selecting; being selected **2** a person or thing selected **3** a group selected from a larger group **4** a range of goods from which to choose

self NOUN selves **1** a person as an individual **2** a person's particular nature • She has recovered and is her old self again. **3** a person's own advantage • He always puts self first.

self-assured ADJECTIVE confident

self-centered ADJECTIVE selfish

self-confident ADJECTIVE confident of your own abilities

self-conscious ADJECTIVE embarrassed or unnatural because you know that people are watching you

self-contained ADJECTIVE (said about accommodation) complete in itself; containing all the necessary facilities

Thesaurus

seep VERB Smoke seeped into the auditorium.
► leak, ooze, escape, exude, flow, trickle, dribble

seething ADJECTIVE Rose was seething about what had happened. ► fuming, furious, angry, livid, infuriated, incensed, outraged

segregate VERB The school agreed to segregate them for swimming lessons. ► separate, isolate, keep apart, set apart, put apart, exclude, cut off

segregation NOUN **1** Racial segregation has been outlawed. ► apartheid, discrimination, separation **2** the segregation of smokers and nonsmokers in public places ► isolation, separation, keeping apart

seize VERB **1** He seized the remote and turned up the volume. ► grab, snatch, take hold of OPPOSITES ARE release, let go of **2** Rebels have seized an outpost in the jungle. ► capture, take, take possession of, take over, overrun OPPOSITES ARE abandon, relinquish **3** Customs officers seized a large cache of drugs.
► confiscate, appropriate, impound OPPOSITES ARE return, give back **4** Bandits seized his wife and children. ► kidnap, abduct, take prisoner, capture, (more informal) snatch OPPOSITES ARE release, let go

seldom ADVERB She was seldom away from home for long. ► rarely, not often, hardly ever, infrequently AN OPPOSITE IS often

select VERB The committee met to select a chairperson. ► choose, pick, appoint, name, elect, vote for, nominate, decide on

selection NOUN **1** There's a wide selection of food to choose from. ► range, variety, assortment **2** Mike put a coin in the machine and made his selection. ► choice, pick, option

selective ADJECTIVE She's very selective in her reading. ► discerning, discriminating, particular, careful, (more informal) choosy AN OPPOSITE IS indiscriminate

self-confident ADJECTIVE In a self-confident mood, Franco pressed ahead with this plans.
► self-assured, self-possessed, sure of yourself, confident, positive, assertive, assured, poised AN OPPOSITE IS diffident

self-conscious ADJECTIVE He felt self-conscious about having to borrow money from his father.
► embarrassed, bashful, diffident, uneasy, awkward, uncomfortable, unnatural, coy, shy, ill at ease, nervous OPPOSITES ARE natural, confident

a b c d e f g h i j k l m n o p q r s t u v w x y z

self-control NOUN the ability to control your own behavior
▷ **self-controlled** ADJECTIVE

self-denial NOUN deliberately going without things you would like to have

self-determination NOUN a country's right to rule itself and to choose its own method of government

self-employed ADJECTIVE working independently, not for an employer

self-esteem NOUN your own opinion of yourself and your own worth

self-evident ADJECTIVE obvious and not needing proof or explanation

self-important ADJECTIVE pompous

selfish ADJECTIVE doing what you want and not thinking of other people; keeping things for yourself
▷ **selfishly** ADVERB **selfishness** NOUN

selfless ADJECTIVE unselfish

self-made ADJECTIVE rich or successful because of your own efforts

self-pity NOUN too much sorrow and pity for yourself and your own problems

self-possessed ADJECTIVE calm and dignified

self-rising ADJECTIVE (said about flour) making cakes rise without needing to have baking powder, etc., added

self-respect NOUN your own proper respect for yourself

self-righteous ADJECTIVE smugly sure that you are behaving virtuously

self-service ADJECTIVE where customers help themselves to things and pay a cashier for what they have taken

self-sufficient ADJECTIVE able to produce or provide what you need without help from others

self-supporting ADJECTIVE earning enough to keep yourself without needing money from others

sell VERB sells, selling, sold **1** exchange something for money **2** be on sale at a certain price ● *It sells for $5.99.*
▷ **seller** NOUN

sell out 1 sell all your stock of something **2** (*informal*) betray someone **3** abandon your principles for reasons of convenience because it suits you

sell NOUN
hard sell putting pressure on someone to buy something
sell-by date a mark on the packaging of food showing the date by which it must be sold
soft sell selling by gentle persuasion

sellout NOUN sellouts an entertainment, sporting event, etc., for which all the tickets have been sold

selves plural of self

semaphore NOUN a system of signaling by holding flags out with your arms in positions that indicate letters of the alphabet

semen (seem- en) NOUN a white liquid produced by males and containing sperm

semibreve NOUN semibreves the longest musical note normally used (𝅝), lasting four times as long as a quarter note

semicircle NOUN semicircles half a circle
▷ **semicircular** ADJECTIVE

semicolon NOUN semicolons a punctuation mark (;) used to mark a break that is more than that marked by a comma

semiconductor NOUN semiconductors a substance that can conduct electricity but not as well as most metals do

semidetached ADJECTIVE (said about a house) joined to another house on one side

Thesaurus

self-control NOUN *He lost self-control and shouted at her.* ► composure, restraint, self-discipline, calmness, coolness, self-command

selfish ADJECTIVE *People are seen as being more selfish and less tolerant.* ► self-centered, egocentric, inconsiderate, self-absorbed, self-obsessed OPPOSITES ARE unselfish, considerate, generous, selfless

selfishness NOUN *They were motivated by greed and selfishness.* ► egotism, self-obsession, self-interest, thoughtlessness, meanness OPPOSITES ARE unselfishness, generosity

selfless ADJECTIVE *He made a selfless sacrifice for his country.* ► generous, magnanimous, unselfish

self-respect NOUN *Under the new president, the country prospered and recovered its self-respect.* ► pride, dignity, self-confidence, self-esteem

self-righteous ADJECTIVE *He called her a stuck-up, self-righteous "Miss Perfect."* ► sanctimonious, holier-than-thou, priggish, smug, self-satisfied, moralizing, unctuous

self-satisfied ADJECTIVE *Hilary relaxed and gave a little self-satisfied smile.* ► smug, complacent, self-congratulatory

sell VERB **1** *The corner shop sells basic provisions.* ► stock, trade in, deal in, retail, handle, peddle **2** *They are having problems selling their house.* ► dispose of, put on the market, (more formal) vend

seller NOUN *sellers of household goods* ► supplier, trader (in), dealer (in), vendor, retailer, stockist, purveyor

semifinal NOUN semifinals a match or round whose winner will take part in the final

seminar NOUN seminars a meeting for advanced discussion and research on a subject

semiquaver NOUN semiquavers a sixteenth note in music (♪), equal in length to one quarter of a quarter note

Semitic (sim- it- ik) ADJECTIVE to do with the Semites, the group of people that includes the Jews and Arabs
  ▷ **Semite** (see- my't) NOUN

semitone NOUN semitones half a tone in music

semolina NOUN hard round grains of wheat used to make milk puddings and pasta

senate NOUN senates 1 the governing council in ancient Rome 2 the upper house of the parliament of the United States, France, and certain other countries
  ▷ **senator** NOUN

send VERB sends, sending, sent 1 make a person or thing go or be taken somewhere 2 cause to become • The noise is sending me to the roof.
  ▷ **sender** NOUN
send for order a person or thing to come or be brought to you
send up (informal) make fun of something by imitating it

senile (seen- I'll) ADJECTIVE weak or confused and forgetful because of old age
  ▷ **senility** NOUN

senior ADJECTIVE 1 older than someone else 2 higher in rank 3 for older children • a senior high school
  ▷ **seniority** NOUN

senior NOUN seniors 1 a person who is older or higher in rank than you are • He is my senior. 2 a member of a senior school

senior citizen NOUN senior citizens an elderly person, especially a pensioner

sensation NOUN sensations 1 a feeling • a sensation of warmth 2 a very excited condition; something causing this • The news caused a great sensation.

sensational ADJECTIVE 1 causing great excitement, interest, or shock 2 (informal) very good; wonderful
  ▷ **sensationally** ADVERB

sense NOUN senses 1 the ability to see, hear, smell, touch, or taste things 2 the ability to feel or appreciate something • a sense of guilt • a sense of humor 3 the power to think or make wise decisions • Hasn't he got the sense to come in out of the rain? 4 meaning • The word "run" has many senses.
make sense 1 have a meaning 2 be a sensible idea

sense VERB senses, sensing, sensed 1 feel; get an impression • I sensed that she did not like me. 2 detect something • This device senses radioactivity.

senseless ADJECTIVE 1 stupid; not showing good sense 2 unconscious

Thesaurus

send VERB 1 I'll send you a letter. ► dispatch, post, mail, convey, forward 2 She sent John a message. ► transmit, fax, e-mail, wire 3 The space program will be sending a satellite into orbit. ► launch, propel, shoot, direct, fire 4 It's the sort of remark that sends you mad. ► make, drive, cause to be
send for They decided to send for the police. ► call, fetch, summon, ask to come

senile ADJECTIVE Her husband was becoming senile and difficult to cope with. ► old, aged, doddering, infirm, feeble, decrepit AN OPPOSITE IS in his or her prime

senior ADJECTIVE 1 a senior pupil ► older, elder 2 a senior official ► high-ranking, superior, chief OPPOSITES ARE junior, subordinate

sensation NOUN 1 She felt a sensation of floating. ► feeling, sense, awareness, impression 2 The affair caused a sensation. ► commotion, excitement, stir, furor, outrage, scandal, surprise, thrill

sensational ADJECTIVE 1 a sensational murder trial ► shocking, horrifying, lurid, scandalous, thrilling, blood-curdling, breathtaking, exciting, hair-raising 2 Her singing was

sensational. ► amazing, extraordinary, remarkable, wonderful, fabulous, fantastic, magnificent, great, marvelous, spectacular, superb

sense NOUN 1 She has a strong sense of rhythm. ► sensation, feeling, perception 2 He felt a sense of guilt. ► awareness, feeling, sensation, perception 3 They had the sense to get out in time. ► wisdom, common sense, intelligence, wit, shrewdness 4 I couldn't see the sense of leaving then. ► point, purpose, advantage, benefit 5 I didn't grasp the sense of their message. ► meaning, significance, substance, implication, import, drift, gist, point
make sense of It's hard to make sense of these remarks. ► understand, grasp, comprehend

sense VERB We sensed that they didn't trust us. ► discern, feel, suspect, perceive, realize, get the impression, appreciate, guess, notice, be aware, detect

senseless ADJECTIVE 1 It was a senseless crime. ► pointless, futile, needless, aimless, absurd, nonsensical, foolish, stupid 2 They found him in the morning, senseless but alive. ► unconscious, comatose, stunned, out cold

a b c d e f g h i j k l m n o p q r **s** t u v w x y z

A
B
C
D
E
F
G
H
I
J
K
L
M
N
O
P
Q
R
S
T
U
V
W
X
Y
Z

senses PLURAL NOUN sanity • *He is out of his senses.*

sensible ADJECTIVE wise; having or showing good sense
▷ **sensibly** ADVERB

sensitive ADJECTIVE **1** affected by something • *Photographic paper is sensitive to light.* **2** receiving impressions quickly and easily • *sensitive fingers* **3** easily hurt or offended • *She is very sensitive about her age.* **4** considerate about other people's feelings **5** needing to be dealt with tactfully • *a sensitive subject*
▷ **sensitively** ADVERB **sensitivity** NOUN

sensor NOUN sensors a device or instrument for detecting a physical property such as light, heat, or sound

sentence NOUN sentences **1** a group of words that express a complete thought and form a statement, question, exclamation, or command **2** the punishment announced to a convicted person in a lawcourt

sentence VERB sentences, sentencing, sentenced give someone a sentence in a lawcourt • *The judge sentenced him to a year in prison.* [from Latin *sententia* = opinion]

sententious ADJECTIVE giving moral advice in a pompous way

sentiment NOUN sentiments **1** an opinion **2** sentimentality

sentimental ADJECTIVE showing or arousing tenderness or romantic feeling or foolish emotion
▷ **sentimentally** ADVERB **sentimentality** NOUN

sentinel NOUN sentinels a guard or sentry

sentry NOUN sentries a soldier guarding something

separate ADJECTIVE **1** not joined to anything **2** not shared
▷ **separately** ADVERB

separate VERB separates, separating, separated **1** make or keep separate; divide

---

Thesaurus

---

sensible ADJECTIVE **1** *Joanna was sensible enough to listen. Everyone agreed that this was a sensible decision.* ▸ prudent, thoughtful, farsighted, shrewd, wise, judicious, intelligent, pragmatic, responsible, realistic, rational, levelheaded OPPOSITES ARE foolish, unwise **2** *She liked to wear sensible clothes.* ▸ practical, functional, comfortable, useful, (*informal*) no-nonsense OPPOSITES ARE impractical, fashionable

sensitive ADJECTIVE **1** *The human eye is very sensitive to green.* ▸ responsive, reactive, susceptible, affected (by), conscious (of) AN OPPOSITE IS insensitive **2** *The problem needs sensitive handling.* ▸ tactful, thoughtful, considerate, sympathetic, understanding, perceptive OPPOSITES ARE insensitive, tactless **3** *She's a very sensitive girl, so take care what you say.* ▸ emotional, easily offended, easily upset, volatile, thin-skinned, touchy AN OPPOSITE IS thick-skinned **4** *Take care in the sun if you have a fair sensitive skin.* ▸ delicate, soft, tender, fragile, fine OPPOSITES ARE tough, resilient **5** *The court ruling comes at a sensitive time for the government.* ▸ awkward, tricky, controversial, delicate AN OPPOSITE IS uncontroversial

sentence NOUN **1** *The judge will decide on a sentence next week.* ▸ judgment, ruling, decision, verdict **2** *Her husband is serving a three-year sentence for robbery.* ▸ prison term, (*more informal*) stretch

sentence VERB *The men will be sentenced at a later date.* ▸ pass judgment on, pronounce sentence on, punish

sentiment NOUN **1** *I agree with the sentiments expressed in your letter.* ▸ view, opinion, belief, thought, attitude, idea, judgment **2** *There's*

not much room for sentiment in this kind of business. ▸ sentimentality, emotionalism, finer feelings, sensibility, softheartedness, mawkishness

sentimental ADJECTIVE **1** *The family held a sentimental attachment to their old home.* ▸ nostalgic, emotional, affectionate, tender, romantic, softhearted **2** *a sentimental story about separated twins* ▸ maudlin, mawkish, overemotional, sickly, saccharine, syrupy, indulgent, gushing, corny, (*more informal*) soppy, (*more informal*) mushy, (*more informal*) treacly OPPOSITES ARE unsentimental, realistic

sentry NOUN *A sentry was on duty at the gate.* ▸ guard, sentinel, lookout, watchman, patrol, picket

separable ADJECTIVE *The components are separable and can be replaced individually. Teaching and research are not completely separable activities.* ▸ separate, distinct, detachable, divisible, removable, distinguishable

separate ADJECTIVE **1** *The guards took care to keep the two groups separate.* ▸ apart, segregated, cut off, divided, divorced, fenced off, isolated OPPOSITES ARE together, united **2** *You may prefer to have the kitchen separate from the dining area. The reports may have been referring to two separate events.* ▸ distinct, detached, different, discrete, unattached (to), unconnected (to) AN OPPOSITE IS joined

separate VERB **1** *They were arguing so fiercely it was difficult to separate them. The war separated us for many years.* ▸ divide, part, break up, split up, segregate AN OPPOSITE IS unite **2** *Only a short distance separated them.* ▸ divide, come between AN OPPOSITE IS unite **3** *We*

2 become separate **3** stop living together as a married couple
▷ **separation** NOUN **separator** NOUN

September NOUN the ninth month of the year [from Latin *septem* = seven, because it was the seventh month of the ancient Roman calendar]

septic ADJECTIVE infected with harmful bacteria that cause pus to form

sepulcher (sep- ul- ker) NOUN **sepulchers** a tomb

sequel NOUN **sequels 1** a book or film, etc., that continues the story of an earlier one **2** something that follows or results from an earlier event

sequence NOUN **sequences 1** the following of one thing after another; the order in which things happen **2** a series of things

seraph NOUN **seraphim** or **seraphs** a kind of angel

serenade NOUN **serenades** a song or tune of a kind played by a man under his lover's window

serenade VERB **serenades, serenading, serenaded** sing or play a serenade to someone

serene ADJECTIVE calm and cheerful
▷ **serenely** ADVERB **serenity** NOUN

serf NOUN **serfs** a farm laborer who worked for a landowner in the Middle Ages, and who was not allowed to leave
▷ **serfdom** NOUN

sergeant (sar- jent) NOUN **sergeants** a soldier or policeman who is in charge of others

sergeant major NOUN **sergeant majors** a soldier who is one rank higher than a sergeant

serial NOUN **serials** a story or film, etc., that is presented in separate parts
USAGE Do not confuse with cereal.

serial killer NOUN **serial killers** a person who commits a series of murders

serial number NOUN **serial numbers** a number put onto an object, usually by the manufacturers, to distinguish it from other identical objects

series NOUN **series 1** a number of things following or connected with each other **2** a number of games or matches between the same competitors **3** a number of separate radio or television programs with the same characters or on the same subject

serious ADJECTIVE **1** solemn and thoughtful; not smiling **2** sincere; not casual or lighthearted • *a serious talk* • *a serious attempt*

Thesaurus

separated at the station and I went home. ► part company, go different ways, split up AN OPPOSITE IS meet **4** *The path separated and went up the hill.* ► diverge, fork, branch off AN OPPOSITE IS merge **5** *Separate the yolks of the eggs from the whites.* ► extract, remove, isolate, abstract, filter out AN OPPOSITE IS mix **6** *When his parents separated he lived with his mother.* ► split up, break up, divorce, part, become estranged, part company **7 separate from** *She separated herself from the company and formed her own business.* ► withdraw from, break away from, leave, quit, dissociate yourself from AN OPPOSITE IS join

separation NOUN **1** *the separation of church and state* ► division, splitting, dissociation, severance, detachment, disconnection, parting, isolation, removal, segregation, cutting off OPPOSITES ARE merging, unification **2** *The separation of the prince and princess has been formally announced.* (informal) ► breakup, split, parting, rift, estrangement AN OPPOSITE IS marriage

septic ADJECTIVE *One of her toes looked septic.* ► infected, poisoned, putrefying, festering, putrid, inflamed, purulent, suppurating

sequel NOUN **1** *The immediate sequel was a riot in the capital.* ► consequence, result, outcome, upshot **2** *a sequel to Daphne du Maurier's*

Rebecca. ► continuation, (*more informal*) follow-up

sequence NOUN **1** *A similar sequence of events occurred in the Baltic States.* ► succession, order, course, progression, series, chain, cycle **2** *Here is a short sequence from her new film.* ► excerpt, scene, clip, extract, section, episode

serene ADJECTIVE *Her eyes lit up, and a serene smile spread across her face.* ► calm, composed, contented, untroubled, unruffled, placid, tranquil, peaceful, imperturbable, quiet AN OPPOSITE IS agitated

series NOUN **1** *Guerrillas carried out a series of kidnappings.* ► succession, sequence, string, chain, wave, spate, rash, outbreak, run **2** *Filming has started on a six-part drama series.* ► serial, run of programs

serious ADJECTIVE **1** *She wore a serious expression.* ► solemn, grave, earnest, thoughtful, pensive, somber, unsmiling, grim, dour OPPOSITES ARE jovial, cheerful **2** *A serious disagreement arose between them.* ► important, significant, momentous, critical, urgent, weighty, crucial, grave OPPOSITES ARE unimportant, frivolous **3** *She suffered serious injuries when she fell from her horse; robbery, assault, theft, and other serious crimes* ► severe, critical, bad, acute, shocking, terrible, appalling, dreadful, grave, grievous AN OPPOSITE IS trivial **4** *He said he was only interested in serious literature.*

a b c d e f g h i j k l m n o p q r **s** t u v w x y z

A B C D E F G H I J K L M N O P Q R S T U V W X Y Z

3 causing anxiety, not trivial • *a serious accident*

▷ **seriously** ADVERB **seriousness** NOUN

sermon NOUN sermons a talk given by a preacher, especially as part of a religious service

serpent NOUN serpents a snake

serried ADJECTIVE arranged in rows close together • *serried ranks of troops*

servant NOUN servants a person whose job is to work or serve in someone else's house

serve VERB serves, serving, served **1** work for a person or organization or country, etc. **2** sell things to people in a shop **3** give out food to people at a meal **4** spend time in something; undergo • *He has served a prison sentence.* **5** be suitable for something • *This will serve our purpose.* **6** start play in tennis, etc., by hitting the ball

▷ **server** NOUN

it serves you right you deserve it

serve NOUN serves a service in tennis, etc.

service NOUN services **1** working for a person or organization or country etc. **2** something that helps people or supplies what they want • *a bus service* **3** the army, navy, or air force • *the armed services* **4** a religious ceremony **5** providing people with goods, food, etc. • *The service at the restaurant was slow.* **6** a set

of dishes and plates for a meal • *a dinner service* **7** the servicing of a vehicle or machine, etc. **8** the action of serving in tennis etc.

service VERB services, servicing, serviced **1** repair or keep a vehicle or machine, etc., in working order **2** supply with services

serviceable ADJECTIVE usable; suitable for ordinary use or wear

service station NOUN service stations a place beside a major road where motorists can stop for fuel, light meals, etc.

serving NOUN servings a helping of food

session NOUN sessions **1** a meeting or series of meetings • *The vice president will open the next session of the Senate.* **2** a time spent doing one thing • *a recording session*

set VERB sets, setting, set **1** put or fix• *Set the vase on the table.* • *They've set a date for the wedding.* **2** make ready to work • *I'd better set the alarm.* **3** make or become firm or hard• *Leave the jelly to set.* **4** give someone a task• *This sets us a problem.* **5** put into a condition• *Set them free.* **6** go down below the horizon• *The sun was setting.*

set about 1 start doing something **2** (*informal*) attack somebody

set off 1 begin a journey **2** start something happening **3** cause something to explode

---

Thesaurus

▶ profound, intellectual, scholarly, learned, highbrow, (*more informal*) heavy **5** *Are you serious about leaving?* ▶ sincere, in earnest, genuine, committed, wholehearted AN OPPOSITE IS uncommitted

seriously ADVERB **1** *He looked at her seriously, frowning deeply.* ▶ solemnly, earnestly, thoughtfully, sternly, dourly **2** *The baby was seriously ill in hospital.* ▶ severely, critically, badly, acutely, gravely **3** *Do you seriously expect me to believe you?* ▶ really, actually, honestly

servant NOUN *A servant appeared, carrying a tray.* ▶ attendant, retainer, domestic, valet, butler, maid, menial, helper, (*more informal*) flunky

serve VERB **1** *They served their masters well.* ▶ attend, assist, look after, minister to, work for **2** *He claimed to use his business skills to serve the public interest.* ▶ further, advance, benefit, advantage, support **3** *The book served as a useful guide to the city's attractions. a slogan that would serve for the whole range of products* ▶ function, be adequate, be useful **4** *a tool that serves a special purpose* ▶ fulfil, answer, perform, satisfy, complete, discharge **5** *At that point he went in to serve the food.* ▶ give out, dish up, distribute, provide **6** *Molly spent the summer serving in a local shop.* ▶ assist, be an assistant, sell **7** serve on *He had served on the*

committee for ten years. ▶ work on, be a member of, sit on, contribute to

service NOUN **1** *The contract lists the terms of service.* ▶ employment, work, business, labor, duty **2** *They have done us quite a service.* ▶ favor, benefit, assistance, kindness, good turn **3** *products that will give years of service* ▶ use, usage, utility **4** *She took the car in for a service.* ▶ overhaul, maintenance check **5** *a church service* ▶ ceremony, worship, ritual, rite, observance

service VERB *A local garage services their car.* ▶ overhaul, maintain, repair, check, mend

serving NOUN *a large serving of pasta* ▶ portion, helping, plateful, plate, share, amount, ration, (*more informal*) dollop

session NOUN **1** *The council held its first session in October.* ▶ meeting, sitting, assembly, conference, discussion, hearing **2** *More practice sessions were needed.* ▶ period, time, spell, bout

set NOUN **1** *There was a set of keys on the table. The government will announce a set of new proposals on human rights.* ▶ collection, group , series, batch, bunch, assortment, array **2** *She belonged to a fashionable Hollywood set.* ▶ circle, clique, group, crowd, coterie, company **3** *a television set* ▶ apparatus, receiver **4** *a chemistry set* ▶ kit, outfit, apparatus **5** *The production* set out **1** begin a journey **2** display or make known

set sail begin a voyage

set to **1** begin doing something vigorously **2** begin fighting or arguing

set up **1** place in position **2** arrange or establish • *set up house* **3** cause or start • *set up a dinner*

set NOUN sets **1** a group of people or things that belong together **2** a radio or television receiver **3** (in mathematics) a collection of things that have a common property **4** the way something is placed • *the set of his jaw* **5** the scenery or stage for a play or film **6** a group of games in a tennis match **7** a badger's burrow

set ADJECTIVE **1** fixed or arranged in advance • *a set time* **2** ready or prepared to do something

set on determined about doing something

setback NOUN setbacks something that stops progress or slows it down

settee NOUN settees a long soft seat with a back and arms

setter NOUN setters a dog of a long-haired breed that can be trained to stand rigid when it scents game

setting NOUN settings **1** the way or place in which something is set **2** music for the words of a song, etc. **3** a set of cutlery or dishes for one person at a meal

settle VERB settles, settling, settled **1** arrange; decide or solve something • *That settles the problem.* **2** make or become calm or comfortable or orderly; stop being restless • *Stop yelling and settle down!* **3** go and live somewhere • *They settled in Canada.* **4** sink; come to rest on something • *Dust had settled on his books.* **5** pay a bill or debt

settlement NOUN settlements **1** settling something **2** the way something is settled **3** a small number of people or houses established in a new area

Thesaurus

boasted a spectacular set and lavish costumes.
► staging, setting, scenery, stage furniture

set VERB **1** *She set the bags on a bench in the porch.* ► put, place, deposit, position, stand, leave, settle, station, post **2** *We should set a date for the next meeting.* ► fix, decide on, agree on, establish, choose, select, name, arrange, schedule **3** *She set the alarm for five the next morning.* ► adjust, regulate, program, synchronize **4** *The sun was setting.* ► go down, sink, subside, vanish, disappear **5** *Leave the Jello in the fridge to set.* ► harden, solidify, thicken, stiffen, gel

set about 1 *He set about the task with gusto.* ► begin, start, make a start on, get down to, embark on, tackle **2** *The boxer set about his opponent.* ► attack, assault, assail, fall on, lay into

set aside 1 *Daphne set aside money each month toward her vacation.* ► save, put by, keep, earmark **2** *The decision was set aside in the Appeals Court.* ► overrule, overturn, reverse, revoke, quash, annul

set off or **out** *We set off early for the airport.* ► set out, start out, leave, depart

set out *He set out his collection of coins.* ► lay out, arrange, display, exhibit, present

set up 1 *A statue will be set up in the main square.* ► erect, put up, raise, construct **2** *The company plans to set up a branch in New York.* ► establish, found, start, institute **3** *Her secretary set up a meeting for the following week.* ► organize, arrange, fix, schedule

setback NOUN *He had survived a whole series of setbacks.* ► difficulty, problem, hitch, delay, holdup, obstacle, reverse, snag, blow, upset, disappointment, complication, misfortune,

(more informal) glitch, (more informal) hiccup
OPPOSITES ARE advance, breakthrough

setting NOUN **1** *a relaxing retreat in a quiet setting* ► surroundings, location, position, site, background, environment, locale **2** *diamonds in a silver setting* ► mounting, mount, fixture, surround **3** *a drama in a historical setting* ► backdrop, context, (French) mise en scène, scene, set

settle VERB **1** *Further talks will be held today in an attempt to settle the dispute.* ► resolve, conclude, clear up, put an end to, find a solution to, reach an agreement about **2** *The lawyers will settle their affairs.* ► arrange, organize, sort out, put in order, order, complete **3** *We can settle the bill in the morning.* ► pay, square, clear **4** *Jack settled into an armchair by the fire.* ► sink, fall, drop, subside **5** *A bird settled on a branch.* ► land, alight, descend **6** *He needed something to settle his nerves.* ► calm, soothe, compose, pacify, quell
AN OPPOSITE IS agitate

settle down *Why can't you settle down?* ► calm down, quieten down, be quiet, be still, relax

settle down to *Rachel wanted her to settle down to something.* ► get down to, apply yourself to, concentrate on, focus on

settle for *Sam wasn't a man to settle for a dull life.* ► agree to, accept, acquiesce in, compromise on

settle in *After the war the family settled in Delaware.* ► set up home, make your home, move to, establish yourself in

settle on *It was high time they settled on a date for the wedding.* ► decide, choose, fix, agree on, name, arrange, organize, schedule

settlement NOUN **1** *a legal settlement* ► agreement, deal, arrangement, treaty,

A
B
C
D
E
F
G
H
I
J
K
L
M
N
O
P
Q
R
S
T
U
V
W
X
Y
Z

settler NOUN **settlers** one of the first people to settle in a new country

setup NOUN (informal) the way something is organized or arranged

seven NOUN, ADJECTIVE **sevens** the number 7
▷ **seventh** ADJECTIVE, NOUN

seventeen NOUN, ADJECTIVE the number 17
▷ **seventeenth** ADJECTIVE, NOUN

seventy NOUN, ADJECTIVE **seventies** the number 70
▷ **seventieth** ADJECTIVE, NOUN

several ADJECTIVE, NOUN more than two but not many

severe ADJECTIVE **1** strict; not gentle or kind **2** intense or forceful • *severe gales* **3** very plain • *a severe style of dress*
▷ **severely** ADVERB **severity** NOUN

sew VERB **sews, sewing, sewed, sewn** or **sewed 1** join things together by using a needle and thread **2** work with a needle and thread or with a sewing machine
USAGE Do not confuse with **sow**.

sewage (soo- ij) NOUN liquid waste matter carried away in drains

sewer (soo- er) NOUN **sewers** a large underground drain for carrying away sewage

sewing machine NOUN **sewing machines** a machine for sewing things

sex NOUN **sexes 1** each of the two groups (*male* and *female*) into which living things are placed according to their functions in the process of reproduction **2** the instinct that causes members of the two sexes to be attracted to one another **3** sexual intercourse

sexism NOUN discrimination against people of a particular sex, especially women
▷ **sexist** ADJECTIVE, NOUN

sexual ADJECTIVE **1** to do with sex or the sexes **2** (said about reproduction) happening by the fusion of male and female cells
▷ **sexually** ADVERB **sexuality** NOUN

sexual intercourse NOUN an intimate act between two people, in which the man puts his penis into the woman's vagina, to express love, for pleasure, or to conceive a child

sexy ADJECTIVE **sexier, sexiest** (informal) **1** sexually attractive **2** concerned with sex

---

Thesaurus

---

contract **2** *The dispute is no nearer settlement.* ► resolution, solution, sorting out, settling **3** *an Iron Age settlement near the modern trunk road* ► community, colony, encampment, commune, town, village

setup NOUN *a modern communications setup; a new constitutional set-up for the EU* ► system, arrangement, framework, organization, business, operation

sever VERB **1** *The arm had been severed at the shoulder.* ► cut off , cut, chop off, hack off, shear off, slice off, separate, amputate, disconnect, remove **2** *Henry VIII severed his relationship with the Church of Rome.* ► break off, cut off, terminate, disconnect, cease

several ADJECTIVE **1** *The cable is split into several strands. He had admitted the murder several times.* ► a number of, many, some, a few **2** *There are several ways of looking at the problem.* ► various, miscellaneous, a number of, sundry, assorted

severe ADJECTIVE **1** *The region faced a severe threat of mass starvation. Wreckage covered the road, causing severe traffic disruption.* ► serious, acute, grave, extreme, critical, dire, grievous AN OPPOSITE IS minor **2** *Many birds were found injured or dead after the severe weather.* ► harsh, hard, extreme, turbulent, stormy AN OPPOSITE IS mild **3** *Oliver developed a severe stomach ulcer. The pains could be severe and disruptive.* ► acute, intense, painful, excruciating AN OPPOSITE IS slight **4** *The expedition will be a severe test of their stamina.* ► demanding, hard, formidable, difficult, onerous, burdensome OPPOSITES ARE

simple, easy **5** *She did not expect the criticism to be so severe.* ► fierce, harsh, sharp, scathing, caustic AN OPPOSITE IS mild **6** *More severe penalties were needed for hit-and-run drivers. They deplored the imposition of such severe censorship.* ► strict, harsh, draconian, ruthless AN OPPOSITE IS mild **7** *It was described as neoclassical architecture in a severe style.* ► plain, simple, spare, stark, unadorned OPPOSITES ARE ornate, elaborate

sew VERB *His aunt sewed the patch on his sleeve.* ► stitch, tack, attach, fasten OPPOSITES ARE unpick, remove
sew up *You need to sew up the hole in your sleeve.* ► darn, stitch, mend, patch, repair

sex NOUN **1** *The disease affects children of both sexes.* ► gender **2** *There is nothing wrong in asking questions about sex.* ► the facts of life, sexual activity, reproduction, sexual reproduction **3** *Unsafe sex in this age group was increasing.* ► sexual intercourse, intercourse, making love, lovemaking, sexual relations
have sex *Derek said they'd been having sex.* ► have sexual intercourse, make love, go to bed together, (more informal) go all the way

sexual ADJECTIVE **1** *A bit of petting had been the only sexual activity.* ► erotic, physical, sensual, carnal, sexy **2** *A diagram of the sexual organs might help.* ► reproductive, procreative, genital

sexy ADJECTIVE **1** *"You're young," he said coolly, "beautiful, sexy, and intelligent."* ► sexually attractive, desirable, seductive, sensual **2** *Louise stripped to her sexy lace underwear.*

SF ABBREVIATION science fiction

shabby ADJECTIVE shabbier, shabbiest **1** in a poor or worn-out condition; dilapidated **2** poorly dressed **3** unfair or dishonorable • *a shabby trick*
▷ shabbily ADVERB shabbiness NOUN

shack NOUN shacks a roughly built hut

shackle NOUN shackles an iron ring for fastening a prisoner's wrist or ankle to something

shackle VERB shackles, shackling, shackled put shackles on a prisoner

shade NOUN shades **1** slight darkness produced where something blocks the sun's light **2** a device that reduces or shuts out bright light **3** a color; how light or dark a color is **4** a slight difference • *The word had several shades of meaning.* **5** (poetical) a ghost

shade VERB shades, shading, shaded **1** shelter something from bright light **2** make part of a drawing darker than the rest **3** move gradually from one state or quality to another • *evening shading into night*

shadow NOUN shadows **1** the dark shape that falls on a surface when something is between the surface and a light **2** an area of shade **3** a slight trace • *a shadow of doubt*
▷ shadowy ADJECTIVE

shadow VERB shadows, shadowing, shadowed **1** cast a shadow on something **2** follow a person secretly

shady ADJECTIVE shadier, shadiest **1** giving shade • *a shady tree* **2** in the shade • *a shady place* **3** (informal) not completely honest; disreputable • *a shady deal*

shaft NOUN shafts **1** a long slender rod or straight part • *the shaft of an arrow* **2** a ray of light **3** a deep narrow hole • *a mine shaft*

shaggy ADJECTIVE shaggier, shaggiest **1** having long rough hair or fiber **2** rough, thick, and untidy • *shaggy hair*

Thesaurus

▶ titillating, erotic, suggestive, salacious, lewd, racy, sexually explicit, (more informal) steamy

shabby ADJECTIVE **1** *Florrie straightened the lapel of her shabby coat.* ▶ worn, scruffy, ragged, tattered **2** *She went into a shabby coffee bar in the center of town.* ▶ run-down, scruffy, dilapidated, seedy, dingy, dirty, poky, tatty **3** *He hated resorting to such shabby lying.* ▶ shameful, mean, cheap, contemptible, despicable, rotten

shack NOUN *a shack in the woods* ▶ hut, cabin, shanty, shed, hovel

shade NOUN **1** *They spend most of the day lying in the shade.* ▶ shadow, shelter, cover **2** *The shades of evening drew on.* ▶ darkness, twilight, gloominess, dimness, obscurity, shadow **3** *She pulled the shade down over the window.* ▶ blind, screen, curtain, awning, canopy **4** *a mass-produced shirt in a harsh shade of blue* ▶ hue, tinge, tint, tone, color **5** *There was a shade of distrust in her voice.* ▶ hint, trace, dash, suggestion, suspicion, tone, nuance **6** *All shades of opinion were represented.* ▶ variety, variation, form, nuance, subtlety **7** *a shade Silvio laughed a shade too heartily.* ▶ a little, a bit, a touch, rather, (more informal) a tad

shade VERB **1** *A tall fence shaded most of the garden.* ▶ overshadow, cast a shadow over, screen, shield, shroud, veil, conceal, obscure, mask, protect **2** *You can shade the background with a dark pencil.* ▶ color in, darken, block in

shadow NOUN **1** *He lingered in the shadow of the corridor outside the room.* ▶ shade, darkness, dimness, semi-darkness, gloom **2** *She saw a shadow on the wall.* ▶ silhouette, outline, shape, profile, contour **3** *There's not a shadow of doubt that they were there at the time of the crime.* ▶ trace, slightest bit, scrap, shred, crumb, ounce, particle, iota, jot **4** *There was a shadow of a smile across her face.* ▶ hint, flicker, suspicion, trace, suggestion, sign

shadow VERB *He continued to shadow the van until forced to return.* ▶ follow, trail, track, stalk, pursue

shadowy ADJECTIVE **1** *They made out a shadowy form in front of them.* ▶ indistinct, hazy, vague, blurred, blurry, nebulous, unsubstantial, indeterminate, indistinguishable, unrecognizable **2** *She let herself out into the shadowy hall.* ▶ dark, shady, shaded

shady ADJECTIVE **1** *Mrs. Halliday took Dot down a shady footpath.* ▶ shaded, shadowy, sheltered, dark, shrouded, sunless OPPOSITES ARE sunny, bright **2** *Blake had been authorized to do shady deals with Russian intelligence.* ▶ dubious, suspect, suspicious, disreputable, unethical, dishonest, untrustworthy, (more informal) fishy, (more informal) shifty AN OPPOSITE IS honest

shaft NOUN **1** *a wooden shaft* ▶ pole, rod, stick, staff, shank, post **2** *The shaft of a pickaxe lay on the ground.* ▶ handle, stem, stock **3** *The first shaft of light broke through the window.* ▶ ray, beam, gleam, bar, finger **4** *a shaft in a mine* ▶ passage, mineshaft, tunnel, duct

shaggy ADJECTIVE *The dog had a shaggy coat. The big shaggy head turned to look at me.* ▶ hairy, bushy, thick, woolly, fleecy, unkempt, dishevelled, unshorn, hirsute OPPOSITES ARE smooth, sleek

A
B
C
D
E
F
G
H
I
J
K
L
M
N
O
P
Q
R
S
T
U
V
W
X
Y
Z

shake VERB shakes, shaking, shook, shaken
1 move quickly up and down or from side to side **2** shock or upset • *The news shook us.*
3 tremble; be unsteady • *His voice was shaking.*
▷ **shaker** NOUN
shake hands clasp a person's right hand with yours in greeting or parting or as a sign of agreement

shake NOUN shakes shaking; a shaking movement
▷ **shaky** ADJECTIVE **shakily** ADVERB
in two shakes very soon

shall AUXILIARY VERB **1** used with I and we to refer to the future • *I shall arrive tomorrow*
2 used with I and we in questions when making a suggestion or offer or asking for advice • *Shall I shut the door?* **3** (old-fashioned use) used with words other than I and we in promises or to express determination • *Trust me, you shall have a party.*

shallow ADJECTIVE shallower, shallowest **1** not deep • *shallow water* **2** not capable of deep feelings • *a shallow character*
▷ **shallowness** NOUN

sham NOUN shams something that is not genuine; a pretence
▷ **sham** ADJECTIVE

sham VERB shams, shamming, shammed pretend

shamble VERB shambles, shambling, shambled walk or run in a lazy or awkward way

shame NOUN **1** a feeling of great sorrow or guilt because you have done wrong **2** dishonor or disgrace **3** something you regret; a pity • *It's a shame that it rained.*
▷ **shameful** ADJECTIVE **shamefully** ADVERB

shame VERB shames, shaming, shamed make a person feel ashamed

shameless ADJECTIVE not feeling or looking ashamed
▷ **shamelessly** ADVERB

Thesaurus

shake VERB **1** *The whole building seemed to shake. We were shaking with fear.* ► tremble, quiver, shudder, shiver, convulse, judder, heave, wobble **2** *The wind shook the window frame.* ► rattle, vibrate **3** *She shook her umbrella at an approaching taxi.* ► wave, waggle, wag, brandish, flourish, jiggle **4** *The news shook them.* ► shock, startle, unnerve, unsettle, upset, alarm, distress, disturb, frighten, perturb
shake something off *Bobby finally shook off his flu and was able to play again.* ► get over, recover from, get rid of, (more informal) see the back of
shake someone off *He looked around to see if he had shaken off his pursuer.* ► escape, elude, get away from, leave behind, give someone the slip

shaky ADJECTIVE **1** *They sat at a shaky table.* ► unsteady, flimsy, wobbly, rickety, rocky, weak, frail, ramshackle **2** *She let out a deep, shaky breath.* ► trembling, shaking, faltering, quivering **3** *His voice was shaky with emotion.* ► faltering, nervous, quavering, tremulous, unsteady AN OPPOSITE IS steady **4** *He had to admit it was a shaky alibi, but he got away with it.* ► precarious, uncertain, unpromising, doubtful, unsound

shallow ADJECTIVE **1** *I do not agree with that shallow view of the situation.* ► superficial, facile, oversimplified, simplistic, narrow, flimsy, lightweight, surface OPPOSITES ARE profound, deep

sham NOUN *The lad's appearance and manner could be a sham.* ► pretence, act, fake, fraud, fiction, lie AN OPPOSITE IS real thing

sham ADJECTIVE *She felt trapped in a sham marriage.* ► false, fake, bogus, pretended, simulated, imitation AN OPPOSITE IS genuine

sham VERB *He wasn't shamming, he was obviously injured.* ► pretend, fake, dissemble

shambles NOUN (informal) *The room was a shambles. The loans program had degenerated into a shambles.* ► mess, muddle, chaos, confusion, disorder

shame NOUN **1** *He couldn't face the shame of being found out.* ► humiliation, opprobrium, dishonor, disgrace, stigma, remorse, guilt, embarrassment, ignominy, mortification, degradation, discredit OPPOSITES ARE honor, pride **2** *a shame It's a shame he didn't stick to chess instead of cards.* ► a pity, unfortunate, a piece of bad luck, a cause for regret OPPOSITES ARE fortunate, lucky

shame VERB **1** *He had been shamed in public.* ► humiliate, mortify, humble, chasten, embarrass, (more informal) show up **2** *You have shamed your family name. He would have shamed an angel with his table manners.* ► disgrace, dishonor, discredit, degrade, taint, tarnish OPPOSITES ARE honor, do credit to

shameful ADJECTIVE *The scheme had been a shameful waste of money.* ► disgraceful, deplorable, contemptible, outrageous, reprehensible, scandalous, unworthy, wicked, vile AN OPPOSITE IS honorable

shameless ADJECTIVE **1** *People said he was a shameless sponger.* ► brazen, bold, audacious, forward, incorrigible, abandoned OPPOSITES ARE reticent, bashful **2** *They knew it was a shameless lie.* ► flagrant, blatant, barefaced, unashamed, overt

shampoo NOUN shampoos **1** a liquid substance for washing the hair **2** a substance for cleaning a carpet, etc., or washing a car **3** a wash with shampoo • *a shampoo and set*

shampoo VERB shampoos, shampooing, shampooed wash or clean with a shampoo [originally = to massage: from Hindi *champo* = press]

shan't (*mainly spoken*) shall not

shanty[1] NOUN shanties a shack [from Canadian French]

shanty[2] NOUN shanties a sailors' song with a chorus [probably from French *chanter* = sing]

shanty town NOUN shanty towns a settlement consisting of shacks

shape NOUN shapes **1** a thing's outline; the appearance an outline produces **2** proper form or condition • *Get it into shape.* **3** the general form or condition of something • *the shape of British industry*

shape VERB shapes, shaping, shaped **1** make into a particular shape • *The plan is shaping up nicely.* [from Old English]

shapeless ADJECTIVE having no definite shape

shapely ADJECTIVE shapelier, shapeliest having an attractive shape

share NOUN shares **1** a part given to one person or thing out of something that is being divided **2** each of the equal parts forming a business company's capital, giving the person who holds it the right to receive a portion (a **dividend**) of the company's profits

share VERB shares, sharing, shared **1** give portions of something to two or more people **2** have or use or experience something jointly with others • *She shared a house with me.*

shark NOUN sharks a large sea fish with sharp teeth

sharp ADJECTIVE **1** with an edge or point that can cut or make holes **2** quick at noticing or learning things • *sharp eyes* **3** steep or pointed; not gradual • *a sharp bend* **4** forceful or severe • *a sharp frost* **5** distinct; loud and shrill • *a sharp cry* **6** slightly sour **7** (in music) one semitone higher than the natural note • *C sharp*

▷ **sharply** ADVERB **sharpness** NOUN

sharp ADVERB **1** sharply • *Turn sharp right here.* **2** punctually • *I'll see you at six o'clock sharp.* **3** (in music) above the correct pitch • *You were singing sharp.*

sharp NOUN sharps (in music) a note one semitone higher than the natural note; the sign (#) that indicates this

---

Thesaurus

---

shape NOUN **1** *The shape of their bodies changes with astonishing speed.* ► form, figure, configuration, physique, outline, profile, silhouette, pattern **2** *For his age he was in pretty good shape.* ► condition, health, state, trim, fettle, (*more informal*) nick

shape VERB *She shaped the clay into a tall pot. A number of factors have shaped their ideas.* ► form, fashion, mold, cast, make, sculpt

shapeless ADJECTIVE **1** *This shapeless mass was my dinner.* ► amorphous, formless, indeterminate, irregular, nebulous, undefined, unformed, vague AN OPPOSITE IS defined. **2** *Gladys removed a shapeless cardigan and hung it over the chair.* ► baggy, saggy, sagging, unshapely, formless, dumpy AN OPPOSITE IS shapely

shapely ADJECTIVE *advertisements full of shapely hips and pretty faces* ► well-proportioned, elegant, graceful, attractive, trim AN OPPOSITE IS shapeless

share NOUN *We will get a share of the profits.* ► portion, part, division, quota, allocation, allowance

share VERB **1** *Member countries will have to share the costs.* ► divide, split, deal out, distribute, ration out, share out, apportion, allocate, allot, go halves with **2** *She had to share a room with two other people.* ► use jointly, live in

3 *share in It is important for everyone to share in the decision-making process.* ► be involved in, take part in, participate in, join in, cooperate in

sharp ADJECTIVE **1** *A sharp knife is essential.* ► keen-edged, keen, pointed, spiky AN OPPOSITE IS blunt **2** *Kittens can strike out with their sharp claws.* ► pointed, jagged, cutting **3** *She felt a sharp pain in her arm.* ► acute, piercing, intense, fierce, stabbing, severe OPPOSITES ARE gentle, mild **4** *a cheese with a sharp flavor* ► strong, piquant, pungent, bitter OPPOSITES ARE mild, mellow **5** *There was a sharp cry from outside. There was a series of sharp raps on the door.* ► loud, piercing, shrill, high-pitched AN OPPOSITE IS soft **6** *A sharp wind blew outside.* ► cold, chilly, bitter, keen, brisk, biting, cutting OPPOSITES ARE gentle, warm **7** *If he disapproves there will be frowns and sharp words.* ► harsh, bitter, cutting, scathing, caustic, acerbic, tart **8** *She adjusted the focus to make the image sharper.* ► distinct, clear, crisp OPPOSITES ARE blurred, indistinct **9** *There could be a sharp drop in prices.* ► abrupt, rapid, steep, sudden AN OPPOSITE IS gradual **10** *His sharp eyes spotted something moving.* ► keen, perceptive, observant, keen-sighted, acute AN OPPOSITE IS weak **11** *He had a quick wit and a sharp mind.* ► perceptive, incisive, discerning, percipient OPPOSITES ARE dull, slow

A
B
C
D
E
F
G
H
I
J
K
L
M
N
O
P
Q
R
S
T
U
V
W
X
Y
Z

sharpen VERB sharpens, sharpening, sharpened make or become sharp
▷ **sharpener** NOUN

sharp practice NOUN dishonest or barely honest dealings in business

shatter VERB shatters, shattering, shattered **1** break violently into small pieces **2** destroy • *It shattered our hopes.* **3** upset greatly • *We were shattered by the news.*

shave VERB shaves, shaving, shaved **1** scrape growing hair off the skin with a razor **2** cut or scrape a thin slice off something
▷ **shaven** ADJECTIVE **shaver** NOUN

shave NOUN shaves the act of shaving the face **close shave** (*informal*) a narrow escape

shavings PLURAL NOUN thin strips shaved off a piece of wood or metal

shawl NOUN shawls a large piece of material worn round the shoulders or head or wrapped round a baby [from Persian or Urdu]

she PRONOUN the female person or animal being talked about

sheaf NOUN sheaves **1** a bundle of cornstalks tied together **2** a bundle of arrows, papers, etc., held together

shear VERB shears, shearing, sheared or, in sense 1, shorn **1** cut or trim; cut the wool off a sheep **2** break because of a sideways or twisting force • *One of the bolts sheared off.*
▷ **shearer** NOUN
USAGE Do not confuse with **sheer**.

shears PLURAL NOUN a cutting tool shaped like a very large pair of scissors and worked with both hands

sheath NOUN sheaths **1** a cover for the blade of a knife or sword etc. **2** a close-fitting cover **3** a condom

shed NOUN sheds a simply made building used for storing things or sheltering animals, or as a workshop

shed VERB sheds, shedding, shed **1** let something fall or flow • *The tree shed its leaves.* **2** give off • *The candle shed soft light on the table.* **3** get rid of • *The company has shed 200 workers.*

sheen NOUN a shine or gloss

sheep NOUN sheep an animal that eats grass and has a thick fleecy coat, kept in flocks for its wool and its meat [from Old English]

sheepdog NOUN sheepdogs a dog trained to guard and herd sheep

sheepish ADJECTIVE **1** bashful **2** embarrassed or shamefaced
▷ **sheepishly** ADVERB **sheepishness** NOUN

sheer ADJECTIVE **1** complete or thorough • *sheer stupidity* **2** vertical, with almost no slope • *a sheer drop* **3** (said about material) very thin; transparent

sheer VERB sheers, sheering, sheered swerve; move sharply away
USAGE Do not confuse with **shear**.

sheet NOUN sheets **1** a large piece of lightweight material used on a bed to sleep under **2** a whole flat piece of paper, glass, or metal **3** a wide area of water, ice, flame, etc.

sheikh (shayk, sheek) NOUN sheikhs the leader of an Arab tribe or village

Thesaurus

sharpen VERB *You will need to sharpen the knife.*
► make sharp, whet, hone, grind, strop, file
AN OPPOSITE IS blunt

shatter VERB **1** *The blast was loud enough to shatter windows. The glass shattered like an eggshell.* ► break, smash, blow out, splinter, crack **2** *The silence was shattered by a warning shout from the alley.* ► destroy, wreck, ruin, dash, overturn, upset

shattered ADJECTIVE **1** *She seemed shattered by the refusal.* ► upset, devastated, stunned, shocked, staggered, distraught **2** *By the time he reached home he felt shattered.* ► exhausted, tired out, worn out, weary, fatigued, (*more informal*) dead tired, (*more informal*) played out, (*more informal*) washed out

shave VERB *His shot shaved the near post.*
► brush, graze, touch, glance off
shave off *Michael shaved off his moustache.*
► cut off, snip off, crop

shed NOUN *Marion kept her rabbits in a garden shed.* ► hut, shack, shelter, storehouse, lean-to, outhouse, potting shed

shed VERB **1** *A truck had shed its load on the inside lane.* ► spill, throw off, drop, scatter, cast off, discard, let fall, shower **2** *We went indoors and shed our coats.* ► take off, discard, peel off, slip out of

sheen NOUN *Using the right polish will give the surface a delicate sheen.* ► shine, gloss, luster, brightness, gleam, patina, burnish, polish

sheer ADJECTIVE **1** *It was sheer chance that Beverley had been to the same hotel. The offense was an act of sheer desperation.* ► utter, complete, absolute, total, pure, unmitigated, unqualified, out-and-out **2** *A few yards ahead was a sheer drop.* ► precipitous, vertical, abrupt, perpendicular **3** *Sheer fabrics look great in a bathroom setting.* ► diaphanous, fine, gauzy, flimsy, see-through, transparent, thin

sheet NOUN **1** *a sheet of paper* ► piece, leaf, page, folio **2** *a sheet of ice* ► layer, film, covering, strip, expanse, surface **3** *a sheet of glass* ► pane, panel, place

shelf NOUN shelves **1** a flat piece of wood, metal, or glass, etc., fixed to a wall or in a piece of furniture so that things can be placed on it **2** a flat level surface that sticks out; a ledge

shell NOUN shells **1** the hard outer covering of an egg, nut, etc., or of an animal such as a snail, crab, or tortoise **2** the walls or framework of a building, ship, etc. **3** a metal case filled with explosive, fired from a large gun

shell VERB shells, shelling, shelled **1** take something out of its shell **2** fire explosive shells at something
shell out (informal) pay out money

shellfish NOUN shellfish a sea animal that has a shell

shelter NOUN shelters **1** something that protects people from rain, wind, danger, etc. ● The bus stop has a shelter beside it. **2** protection ● The villagers sought shelter from the storm.

shelter VERB shelters, sheltering, sheltered **1** provide with shelter **2** protect **3** find a shelter ● They sheltered under the trees.

shelve VERB shelves, shelving, shelved **1** put things on a shelf or shelves **2** fit a wall or cupboard, etc., with shelves **3** postpone or reject a plan, etc. **4** slope ● The bed of the river shelves steeply.

shepherd NOUN shepherds a person whose job is to look after sheep

shepherd VERB shepherds, shepherding, shepherded guide or direct people

sheriff NOUN sheriffs the chief law officer of a county, whose duties vary in different countries

sherry NOUN sherries a kind of strong wine

Shetland pony NOUN Shetland ponies a kind of small, strong, shaggy pony, originally from the Shetland Isles

shield NOUN shields **1** a large piece of metal, wood, etc., carried to protect the body **2** a model of a triangular shield used as a trophy **3** a protection

shield VERB shields, shielding, shielded protect from harm or from being discovered

shift VERB shifts, shifting, shifted **1** move or cause to move **2** (said about an opinion or situation) change slightly
shift for yourself manage without help; rely on your own efforts

shift NOUN shifts **1** a change of position or condition, etc. **2** a group of workers who start work as another group finishes; the time when they work ● the night shift **3** a straight dress with no waist

shifty ADJECTIVE evasive, not straightforward; untrustworthy
▷ **shiftily** ADVERB **shiftiness** NOUN

Thesaurus

shelf NOUN She put the vase back on the shelf.
► ledge, mantelpiece, sill, rack

shell NOUN **1** an insect that has no hard shell to protect it ► pod, casing, case, crust, husk, hull **2** All that was left of the building was its shell.
► skeleton, frame, framework, hull

shelter NOUN **1** Their house provided shelter for countless escapees. ► protection, refuge, sanctuary, safety, cover, haven, lee, asylum **2** We set up a shelter against the wind. ► shield, screen, barrier, cover **3** She ran a shelter for the homeless. ► sanctuary, refuge, haven, safe haven, retreat

shelter VERB **1** The hut sheltered us from the storm. ► protect, keep safe, shield, cover, safeguard, screen, guard **2** The walkers sheltered in doorways. ► take shelter, take refuge, seek protection, take cover **3** His family took it in turns to shelter him. ► harbor, accommodate, give shelter to, hide

sheltered ADJECTIVE **1** a sheltered spot behind the sand dunes ► protected, enclosed, screened, shielded, covered, calm, quiet, windless AN OPPOSITE IS exposed. **2** She had led a sheltered life. ► secluded, withdrawn, cloistered, reclusive, isolated, unadventurous, unexciting AN OPPOSITE IS adventurous

shelve VERB The plans had to be shelved for the time being. ► postpone, defer, put off, put to one side, suspend, abandon, (more informal) put on ice, (more informal) put on the back burner OPPOSITES ARE implement, revive

shield NOUN One coating will afford the metal a shield against corrosion. ► protection, safeguard, guard, screen, shelter, barrier, defence, bulwark

shield VERB She tried to shield her eyes from the glare of the sun. ► protect, shade, screen, cover, defend, guard, keep safe, safeguard, shelter

shift VERB **1** Les shifted the furniture to make more space. ► move, rearrange, reposition, relocate, adjust, transfer, switch round, haul, lug **2** It wouldn't be easy to shift all that dirt. ► remove, dislodge, budge **3** Their opinions had shifted somewhat. ► change, alter, modify, vary, fluctuate

shift NOUN **1** constant shifts in public opinion ► change, alteration, variation, fluctuation **2** His mother was working on the night shift.
► period, stint, stretch

shifty ADJECTIVE She had seen that shifty look before. ► untrustworthy, dishonest, deceitful, furtive, underhand, shady, wily, scheming, dubious AN OPPOSITE IS straightforward

shilling NOUN shillings a former British coin, equal to 5 pence

shimmer VERB shimmers, shimmering, shimmered shine with a quivering light • *The sea shimmered in the moonlight.*
▷ shimmer NOUN

shin NOUN shins the front of the leg between the knee and the ankle

shin VERB shins, shinning, shinned climb by using the arms and legs, not on a ladder

shine VERB shines, shining, shone or, in sense 4, shined **1** give out or reflect light; be bright **2** be excellent • *He doesn't shine in math.* **3** aim a light • *Shine your torch on it.* **4** polish • *Have you shined your shoes?*

shingle NOUN pebbles on a beach

shingles NOUN a disease caused by the chicken pox virus, producing a painful rash

shiny ADJECTIVE shinier, shiniest shining or glossy

ship NOUN ships a large boat, especially one that goes to sea

ship VERB ships, shipping, shipped transport goods, etc., especially by ship

-ship SUFFIX forms nouns meaning condition (e.g., *friendship, hardship*), position (e.g., *chairmanship*), or skill (e.g., *seamanship*)

shipping NOUN **1** ships • *Britain's shipping* **2** transporting goods by ship

shipshape ADJECTIVE in good order; tidy

shipwreck NOUN shipwrecks **1** the wrecking of a ship by storm or accident **2** a wrecked ship
▷ shipwrecked ADJECTIVE

shipyard NOUN shipyards a place where ships are built or repaired

shire NOUN shires a county
the Shires the country areas of (especially central) England, away from the cities

shirk VERB shirks, shirking, shirked avoid a duty or work, etc., selfishly or unfairly
▷ shirker NOUN
[probably from German *Schurke* = scoundrel]

shirt NOUN shirts a piece of clothing for the top half of the body, made of light material and with a collar and sleeves
in your shirtsleeves not wearing a jacket over your shirt

shiver VERB shivers, shivering, shivered tremble with cold or fear
▷ shiver NOUN shivery ADJECTIVE

shoal[1] NOUN shoals a large number of fish swimming together

shoal[2] NOUN shoals **1** a shallow place **2** an underwater sandbank

shock[1] NOUN shocks **1** a sudden unpleasant surprise **2** great weakness caused by pain or injury etc. **3** the effect of a violent shake or knock **4** an effect caused by electric current passing through the body

shock VERB shocks, shocking, shocked **1** give someone a shock; surprise or upset a person greatly **2** seem very improper or scandalous to a person

shock[2] NOUN shocks a bushy mass of hair

Thesaurus

shimmer VERB *The lights shimmered on the surface of the water.* ► glimmer, glint, gleam, glow, glisten, glitter, sparkle, shine, flash

shine VERB **1** *The sun shone through the windows.* ► beam, gleam, glow, glisten, glint, sparkle, flash **2** *He had forgotten to shine his shoes.* ► polish, brush, buff, brighten **3** *There was one thing they all shone at.* ► excel, stand out, be outstanding

shine NOUN *a shine on the furniture* ► polish, sheen, luster, patina, burnish, gleam

shining ADJECTIVE **1** *a knight in shining armor* ► gleaming, brilliant, radiant, glittering, glowing, luminous, shiny, sparkling **2** *a shining example* ► conspicuous, outstanding, splendid, eminent, glorious, praiseworthy, resplendent

shiny ADJECTIVE *He liked her shiny black boots.* ► bright, glossy, gleaming, shining, glistening, polished, burnished, lustrous OPPOSITES ARE dull, matte

ship NOUN *Another very big wave hit the ship.* ► vessel, craft, boat, liner, steamer

ship VERB *Twenty flamingoes were shipped from Tanzania to Atlanta.* ► send, consign, transport, post, mail

shipment NOUN *There's a grain shipment due out tomorrow.* ► load, cargo, consignment, freight, vanload, truckload, boatload, (*more formal*) lading

shirk VERB *We've got responsibilities, and we can't shirk them.* ► dodge, duck, evade, avoid, shun, get out of, shrink from, neglect

shiver VERB *Maria stood at the door shivering.* ► tremble, quiver, shake, shudder, palpitate, flutter

shock NOUN **1** *the shock of an explosion* ► blow, vibration, impact, collision, concussion, jolt **2** *The news came as a shock.* ► blow, upset, surprise, bombshell, bolt from the blue **3** *The state of the room always gave her a shock.* ► surprise, fright, scare, jolt, start, (*more informal*) turn **4** *She was in a state of shock for several days.* ► trauma, distress

shock VERB *The brutal attack shocked the whole community.* ► horrify, appal, stun, stagger,

shocking *ADJECTIVE* **1** causing indignation or disgust **2** (*informal*) very bad • *shocking weather*

shock wave *NOUN* shock waves a sharp change in pressure in the air around an explosion or an object moving very quickly

shoddy *ADJECTIVE* shoddier, shoddiest of poor quality; badly made or done • *shoddy work*
▷ **shoddily** *ADVERB* **shoddiness** *NOUN*

shoe *NOUN* shoes **1** a strong covering for the foot **2** a horseshoe **3** something shaped or used like a shoe
be in somebody's shoes be in his or her situation

shoe *VERB* shoes, shoeing, shod fit with a shoe or shoes

shoelace *NOUN* shoelaces a cord for lacing up and fastening a shoe

shoot *VERB* shoots, shooting, shot **1** fire a gun or missile, etc. **2** hurt or kill by shooting **3** move or send very quickly • *The car shot past us.* **4** kick or hit a ball at a goal **5** (said about a plant) put out buds or shoots **6** slide the bolt of a door into or out of its fastening **7** film or photograph something • *The film was shot in Africa.*

shoot *NOUN* shoots **1** a young branch or new growth of a plant **2** an expedition for shooting animals

shooting star *NOUN* shooting stars a meteor

shop *NOUN* shops **1** a building or room where goods or services are on sale to the public **2** a workshop **3** talk that is about your own work or job • *She is always talking shop.*

shop *VERB* shops, shopping, shopped go and buy things at shops
▷ **shopper** *NOUN*
shop around compare goods and prices in several shops before buying

shop floor *NOUN* **1** the workers in a factory, not the managers **2** the place where they work

shopkeeper *NOUN* shopkeepers a person who owns or manages a shop

shoplifter *NOUN* shoplifters a person who steals goods from a shop after entering as a customer
▷ **shoplifting** *NOUN*

shopping *NOUN* **1** buying goods in shops **2** the goods bought

shore *NOUN* shores the land along the edge of a sea or of a lake [from early German or Dutch *schore*]

shore *VERB* shores, shoring, shored prop something up with a piece of wood, etc. [from early German or Dutch *schoren*]

shorn *past participle of* shear

short *ADJECTIVE* **1** not long; occupying a small distance or time • *a short walk* **2** not tall • *a short person* **3** not enough; not having enough of something • *Water is short in hot weather.* • *We are short of water.* **4** bad-tempered or curt **5** (said about pastry) rich and crumbly because it contains a lot of fat
▷ **shortness** *NOUN*
for short as an abbreviation • *Raymond is called "Ray" for short.*
short for an abbreviation of • *"Ray" is short for Raymond.*

a
b
c
d
e
f
g
h
i
j
k
l
m
n
o
p
q
r
s
t
u
v
w
x
y
z

Thesaurus

---

alarm, outrage, dismay, scandalize, repel, offend, disgust, sicken, revolt

shocking *ADJECTIVE* **1** *Next day they heard the whole shocking story.* ► horrifying, horrific, appalling, alarming, distressing, terrible, dreadful, awful, frightening, upsetting **2** *Their language was quite shocking.* ► offensive, disgusting, outrageous

shoddy *ADJECTIVE* **1** *the shoddy state of our national services* ► inferior, poor-quality, second-rate, cheap, trashy, (*more informal*) tacky AN OPPOSITE IS well-made **2** *The workmanship was noticably shoddy.* ► careless, slapdash, slipshod, sloppy OPPOSITES ARE painstaking, careful

shoot *VERB* **1** *The gunman had been daring the police to shoot him.* ► hit, kill, gun down, snipe at, pick off **2** *A motorcycle shot past.* ► race, dash, zoom, career, fly, rush, streak, hare **3** *They plan to shoot the outdoor scenes on location in Africa.* ► film, make, capture

shop *NOUN* *His father opened a shop in the town.* ► store, retail store, outlet, emporium

shopping *NOUN* *She put her shopping in the back of the car.* ► goods, purchases

shore *NOUN* *They stopped for a picnic near the shore.* ► seashore, beach, sands, coast, foreshore, seaboard, shingle, bank, strand
RELATED ADJECTIVE ► littoral

short *ADJECTIVE* **1** *a short piece of string* ► small, little AN OPPOSITE IS long **2** *a short person* ► small, little, petite, squat, stocky, diminutive AN OPPOSITE IS tall **3** *a short account of the voyage* ► brief, concise, succinct, pithy OPPOSITES ARE long, elaborate, lengthy **4** *Take a short look at this.* ► brief, cursory, fleeting, momentary OPPOSITES ARE prolonged, lengthy **5** *Supplies were short.* ► low, meager, scant, deficient, inadequate, insufficient OPPOSITES ARE plentiful, abundant **6** *She was rather short with me.* ► curt, abrupt, sharp, blunt, brusque, snappy, impatient OPPOSITES ARE courteous, patient

A
B
C
D
E
F
G
H
I
J
K
L
M
N
O
P
Q
R
S
T
U
V
W
X
Y
Z

short of without going to the length of • *I'll do anything to help, short of breaking the law.*

short ADVERB suddenly • *She stopped short.*

shortage NOUN shortages lack or scarcity of something; insufficiency

shortbread NOUN a rich sweet biscuit, made with butter

short circuit NOUN short circuits a fault in an electrical circuit in which current flows along a shorter route than the normal one
▷ **short-circuit** VERB

shortcoming NOUN shortcomings a fault or failure to reach a good standard

short cut NOUN short cuts a route or method that is quicker than the usual one

shorten VERB shortens, shortening, shortened make or become shorter

shorthand NOUN a set of special signs for writing words down as quickly as people say them

shorthanded ADJECTIVE not having enough workers or helpers

shortly ADVERB 1 in a short time; soon • *They will arrive shortly.* 2 in a few words 3 curtly

shorts PLURAL NOUN pants with legs that do not reach to the knee

shortsighted ADJECTIVE 1 unable to see things clearly when they are further away 2 lacking imagination or foresight

short-tempered ADJECTIVE easily becoming angry

short wave NOUN a radio wave of a wavelength between 10 and 100 meters and a frequency of about 3 to 30 megahertz

shot past tense of shoot

shot NOUN shots 1 the firing of a gun or missile, etc.; the sound of this 2 something fired from a gun; lead pellets for firing from small guns 3 a person judged by skill in

shooting • *He's a good shot.* 4 a heavy metal ball thrown as a sport 5 a stroke in tennis, cricket, billiards, etc. 6 a photograph; a filmed scene 7 (*informal*) an attempt • *Have a shot at the crossword.* 8 an injection of a drug or vaccine

shot ADJECTIVE (said about fabric) woven so that different colors show at different angles • *shot silk*

should AUXILIARY VERB 1 used for saying what someone ought to do • *You should have told me.* 2 used for saying what someone expects • *They should be here by ten o'clock.* 3 used for saying what might happen • *If you should happen to see him, tell him to come.* 4 used with I and we to make a polite statement (*I should like to come*) or in a conditional clause (*If they had supported us we should have won*)
USAGE In sense 4, although should is strictly correct, many people nowadays use would and this is not regarded as wrong.

shoulder NOUN shoulders 1 the part of the body between the neck and the arm, foreleg, or wing 2 a side that juts out • *the shoulder of the bottle*

shoulder VERB shoulders, shouldering, shouldered 1 take something on your shoulder or shoulders 2 push with your shoulder 3 accept responsibility or blame

shoulder blade NOUN shoulder blades either of the two large flat bones at the top of your back

shouldn't (*mainly spoken*) should not

shout NOUN shouts a loud cry or call

shout VERB shouts, shouting, shouted give a shout; speak or call loudly

shove VERB shoves, shoving, shoved push roughly
▷ **shove** NOUN

shove off (*informal*) go away

Thesaurus

---

shortage NOUN *a shortage of water* ► scarcity, sparseness, dearth, deficiency, insufficiency, lack, want, paucity, shortfall AN OPPOSITE IS abundance

shortcoming NOUN *He was well aware of his own shortcomings.* ► defect, failing, fault, imperfection, weakness, drawback, foible, vice AN OPPOSITE IS strength

shorten VERB *The composer shortened the work for a concert performance.* ► cut down, reduce, condense, compress, cut, trim, abridge OPPOSITES ARE lengthen, expand

shortly ADVERB *A note arrived shortly afterward.* ► soon, presently, directly, before long, by and by

shortsighted ADJECTIVE *The media tend to be shortsighted when dealing with the arts.*

► narrow-minded, narrow, improvident, intolerant, conservative, illiberal, insular, parochial, small-minded

shot NOUN 1 *A shot rang out.* ► report, bang, blast, explosion 2 *This is a shot of us on the beach.* ► photo, photograph, snap, snapshot 3 *He managed a winning shot.* ► stroke, hit, strike, throw 4 (*informal*) *He wanted a shot at driving the car.* ► attempt, try, go, (*informal*) bash

shout VERB *"Come on," she shouted.* ► cry, call, yell, exclaim, shriek, scream, bawl

shove VERB 1 *She shoved the boy into the back of the van.* ► push, thrust, drive, propel, force 2 *Several large men shoved past them.* ► push, barge, elbow, jostle, hustle, shoulder, crowd

shovel NOUN shovels a tool like a spade with the sides turned up, used for lifting coal, earth, snow, etc.

shovel VERB shovels, shoveling, shoveled **1** move or clear with a shovel **2** scoop or push roughly • He was shoveling food into his mouth

show VERB shows, showing, showed, shown **1** allow or cause something to be seen • Show me your new bike. **2** make a person understand; demonstrate • Show me how to use it. **3** guide • Show him in. **4** treat in a certain way • She showed us much kindness. **5** be visible • That scratch won't show. **6** prove your ability to someone • We'll show them!

show off **1** show something proudly **2** try to impress people

show up **1** make or be clearly visible; reveal a fault, etc. **2** (informal) arrive

show NOUN shows **1** a display or exhibition • a flower show **2** an entertainment **3** (informal) something that happens or is done • He runs the whole show.

showdown NOUN showdowns a final test or confrontation

shower NOUN showers **1** a brief fall of rain or snow **2** a lot of small things coming or falling like rain • a shower of stones **3** a device or cabinet for spraying water to wash a person's body; a wash in this

shower VERB showers, showering, showered **1** fall or send things in a shower **2** wash under a shower

showman NOUN showmen **1** a person who presents entertainments **2** someone who is good at attracting attention
▷ **showmanship** NOUN

show-off NOUN show-offs (informal) a person who tries to impress people boastfully

showpiece NOUN showpieces a fine example of something for people to see and admire

showy ADJECTIVE showier, showiest likely to attract attention; brightly or highly decorated
▷ **showily** ADVERB **showiness** NOUN

shrapnel NOUN pieces of metal scattered from an exploding shell

shred NOUN shreds **1** a tiny piece torn or cut off something **2** a small amount • There is not a shred of evidence.

shred VERB shreds, shredding, shredded cut into shreds
▷ **shredder** NOUN

shrew NOUN shrews **1** a small mouselike animal **2** (old use) a bad-tempered woman who is constantly scolding people
▷ **shrewish** ADJECTIVE

shrewd ADJECTIVE having common sense and good judgement; clever
▷ **shrewdly** ADVERB **shrewdness** NOUN

shriek NOUN shrieks a shrill cry or scream

shriek VERB shrieks, shrieking, shrieked give a shriek

shrill ADJECTIVE sounding very high and piercing
▷ **shrilly** ADVERB **shrillness** NOUN

Thesaurus

show NOUN **1** Thousands came to watch the show. ► entertainment, performance, production, presentation, spectacle, pageant **2** They had to put on a show of strength. ► display, exhibition, demonstration, appearance, impression, facade, pretence, illusion, affectation

show VERB **1** Shall I show you how to do it? ► demonstrate, explain, point out, clarify **2** There's a hole in the sleeve but it won't show. ► be visible, be seen, be obvious, appear **3** This shows you what you can achieve with limited resources. ► demonstrate, reveal, illustrate, prove, exemplify **4** They are showing his watercolors at the local gallery. ► exhibit, display **5** Flora began to show her impatience. ► reveal, manifest, convey, indicate, communicate, expose **6** A girl showed them to their seats. ► escort, accompany, take, conduct, walk

shower NOUN **1** a shower of rain ► fall, drizzle, downpour **2** a shower of compliments ► spate, wave, flood, rush, volley, barrage, torrent, flurry

shower VERB **1** A passing car showered mud over the pavement. ► spray, spatter, splash, sprinkle, rain **2** The awards committee showered praise on the winners. ► lavish, pour, heap, load

show-off NOUN a show-off with a big flashy car ► exhibitionist, boaster, poser, bragger, egotist

showy ADJECTIVE showy fake jewelry ► ostentatious, pretentious, gaudy, flashy, flamboyant, conspicuous, garish, tawdry, (more informal) tacky OPPOSITES ARE sober, restrained

shred NOUN Not a shred of evidence could be found. ► scrap, speck, iota, jot, ounce, trace shreds The dress had been torn to shreds. ► tatters, ribbons, rags, strips

shrewd ADJECTIVE a shrewd politician; a shrewd sense of timing ► astute, sharp, acute, canny, prudent, clever, intelligent, quick-witted, perceptive, discerning, crafty, wily AN OPPOSITE IS stupid

shriek VERB The audience shrieked with laughter. "Come and see, quick!" Mary shrieked. ► scream, screech, squeal, roar, howl, bellow, yell

shrill ADJECTIVE "That's not true!" she protested in a shrill voice. ► piercing, penetrating, high-

A
B
C
D
E
F
G
H
I
J
K
L
M
N
O
P
Q
R
S
T
U
V
W
X
Y
Z

shrimp NOUN shrimps a small shellfish, pink when boiled

shrine NOUN shrines an altar, chapel, or other sacred place

shrink VERB shrinks, shrinking, shrank, shrunk **1** make or become smaller **2** move back to avoid something **3** avoid doing something because of fear, conscience, embarrassment, etc.
▷ **shrinkage** NOUN **shrunken** ADJECTIVE

shrivel VERB shrivels, shriveling, shriveled make or become dry and wrinkled

shroud NOUN shrouds **1** a cloth in which a dead body is wrapped **2** each of a set of ropes supporting a ship's mast

Shrove Tuesday NOUN the day before Ash Wednesday

shrub NOUN shrubs a plant smaller than a tree; a bush
▷ **shrubby** ADJECTIVE

shrubbery NOUN shrubberies an area planted with shrubs

shrug VERB shrugs, shrugging, shrugged raise your shoulders as a sign that you do not care, do not know, etc.
▷ **shrug** NOUN
shrug something off treat it as unimportant

shudder VERB shudders, shuddering, shuddered **1** shiver violently with horror, fear, or cold **2** make a strong shaking movement
▷ **shudder** NOUN

shuffle VERB shuffles, shuffling, shuffled **1** walk without lifting the feet from the ground **2** slide playing cards over each other to get them into random order **3** shift or rearrange
▷ **shuffle** NOUN

shun VERB shuns, shunning, shunned avoid; deliberately keep away from something

shunt VERB shunts, shunting, shunted **1** move a train or wagons on to another track **2** divert to a less important place or position
▷ **shunt** NOUN **shunter** NOUN

shut VERB shuts, shutting, shut **1** move a door, lid, or cover etc. so that it blocks an opening; make or become closed **2** bring or fold parts together ● *Shut the book.*
shut down 1 stop something working **2** stop business
shut up 1 shut securely **2** (*informal*) stop talking or making a noise

shutter NOUN shutters **1** a panel or screen that can be closed over a window **2** the device in a camera that opens and closes to let light fall on the film
▷ **shuttered** ADJECTIVE

shuttle NOUN shuttles **1** a holder carrying the weft thread across a loom in weaving **2** a

Thesaurus

pitched, screaming, sharp, strident, screechy
OPPOSITES ARE soft, gentle

shrink VERB **1** *Your sweater has shrunk in the wash* ▶ become smaller, contract, dwindle, shrivel, wither AN OPPOSITE IS expand **2** *The woman shrank in alarm.* ▶ draw back, cower, cringe, flinch, hang back, back off, recoil

shrivel VERB *The plants were shriveling in the heat.* ▶ shrink, wilt, wither, droop, become parched, dehydrate, dry up, wrinkle

shroud NOUN *a shroud of mist over the sea; the outfit operates behind a shroud of secrecy.* ▶ covering, blanket, mantle, pall, veil

shroud VERB *A mist shrouded the seafront.* ▶ cover, envelop, wrap, blanket, cloak, enshroud, hide, mask, conceal, screen, swathe, veil

shrug VERB **shrug off** *She shrugged off suggestions that she had been unfair.* ▶ dismiss, disregard, ignore, take no notice of, pay no notice of, set aside

shudder VERB *She still shuddered at the thought of what had happened.* ▶ quiver, shake, shiver, tremble, be horrified, convulse, quake, squirm

shudder NOUN *Another mighty shudder passed through the ship.* ▶ tremor, spasm, convulsion, trembling, tremble, quiver

shuffle VERB **1** *He shuffled over to the fireplace.* ▶ shamble, hobble, scuffle, stumble, teeter, totter **2** *She shuffled the cards and began dealing.* ▶ mix, mix up, jumble, rearrange, reorganize

shun VERB *The group shunned all forms of publicity.* ▶ avoid, shy away from, stay clear of, evade, steer clear of, keep away from

shut VERB *I'll shut the window.* ▶ close, fasten, latch, lock, push to, bolt, seal, secure
shut down *They will have to shut down the operation in South Africa.* ▶ close down, discontinue, terminate, cease, suspend
OPPOSITES ARE open up, activate
shut in or **up** *She closed the door to shut the dogs in.* ▶ keep in, confine, detain, enclose, imprison, incarcerate
shut off *They had been shut off without food for two days.* ▶ cut off, isolate, separate, segregate
shut out 1 *He shut them out of the house by mistake.* ▶ lock out, keep out, exclude AN OPPOSITE IS let in **2** *She tried to shut out those bad memories.* ▶ exclude, keep out, suppress, forget AN OPPOSITE IS recall

train, bus, or aircraft that makes frequent short journeys between two points

shuttle VERB shuttles, shuttling, shuttled
move, travel, or send backwards and forwards

shy ADJECTIVE shier, shiest afraid to meet or talk to other people; timid
▷ **shyly** ADVERB **shyness** NOUN

shy VERB shies, shying, shied jump or move suddenly in alarm

SI NOUN an internationally recognized system of metric units of measurement, including the meter and kilogram

Siamese cat NOUN Siamese cats a cat with short pale fur with darker face, ears, tail, and feet

Siamese twins PLURAL NOUN twins who are born with their bodies joined together

sick ADJECTIVE **1** ill; physically or mentally unwell **2** vomiting or likely to vomit ● *I feel sick.* **3** distressed or disgusted **4** making fun of death, disability, or misfortune in an unpleasant way
sick of tired of

sicken VERB sickens, sickening, sickened **1** begin to be ill **2** make or become distressed or disgusted ● *Vandalism sickens us all.*
▷ **sickening** ADJECTIVE

sickle NOUN sickles a tool with a narrow curved blade, used for cutting corn, etc.

sickly ADJECTIVE **1** often ill; unhealthy **2** making people feel sick ● *a sickly smell* **3** weak ● *a sickly smile*

sickness NOUN sicknesses **1** illness **2** a disease **3** vomiting

side NOUN sides **1** a surface, especially one joining the top and bottom of something **2** a line that forms part of the boundary of a triangle, square, etc. **3** either of the two halves into which something can be divided by a line down its center **4** the part near the edge and away from the center **5** the place or region next to a person or thing ● *He stood at my side.* **6** one aspect or view of something ● *Study all sides of the problem.* **7** one of two groups or teams, etc., who oppose each other
on the side as a sideline
side by side next to each other
take sides support one person or group in a dispute or disagreement and not the other

side VERB sides, siding, sided
side with take a person's side in an argument

side effect NOUN side effects an effect, especially an unpleasant one, that a medicine has on you as well as the effect intended

sidelight NOUN sidelights **1** a light at the side of a vehicle or ship **2** light from one side

sideline NOUN sidelines **1** something done in addition to your main work or activity **2** each of the lines on the two long sides of a sports pitch

sidelong ADJECTIVE toward one side; sideways ● *a sidelong glance*

sidetrack VERB sidetracks, sidetracking, sidetracked take someone's attention away from the main subject or problem

sideways ADVERB, ADJECTIVE **1** to or from one side ● *Move it sideways.* **2** with one side facing forward ● *We sat sideways in the bus.*

Thesaurus

---

shy ADJECTIVE *He was too shy to say his name.*
► coy, reserved, diffident, bashful, sheepish, inhibited, embarrassed, modest, self-conscious, hesitant, timid, retiring OPPOSITES ARE assertive, forward, bold, confident

sick ADJECTIVE **1** *He had been sick and had to stay at home.* ► ill, unwell, poorly, out of sorts, off color, indisposed, ailing, peaky, queasy, nauseous **2** *be sick of We are all sick of having to wait so long.* ► be fed up with, be tired of, be weary of, have had enough of

sicken VERB *It sickened us to see so much waste.* ► make someone sick, disgust, revolt, nauseate, repel, put off

sickening ADJECTIVE *The stench of burned fuel oil is sickening. There was a sickening sound of tearing metal.* ► nauseating, revolting, disgusting, offensive, repulsive, repellent, appalling

sickly ADJECTIVE **1** *He was a sickly child with a bad chest.* ► unhealthy, poorly, sick, ill, infirm, frail, feeble, weak **2** *She had a sickly complexion.* ► pale, wan, pasty, sallow, pallid, ashen **3** *The walls were painted a sickly green.* ► insipid, pale, wan

sickness NOUN **1** *She was away because of sickness.* ► illness, disease, ailment, disorder **2** *The spells of sickness lasted four or five days.* ► nausea, queasiness, vomiting, biliousness

side NOUN **1** *The box has an address label on one side.* ► surface, face, facet, elevation, flank **2** *A hut stood by the side of the lake.* ► edge, border, verge, boundary, margin, fringe, brink, limit, perimeter, rim **3** *He was driving over the limit on the wrong side of the road.* ► half, part, lane **4** *I could see both sides in the argument.* ► point of view, aspect, perspective, standpoint, opinion, stance, angle, view, viewpoint, slant **5** *The family had backed the winning side in the civil war.* ► faction, camp, army, team **6** *The home side was one player short.* ► team, squad, lineup RELATED ADJECTIVE ► lateral

side VERB side with *They didn't know which team to side with.* ► support, favor, prefer, take the side of, agree with

A
B
C
D
E
F
G
H
I
J
K
L
M
N
O
P
Q
R
S
T
U
V
W
X
Y
Z

siding NOUN sidings a short railway line by the side of a main line

siege NOUN sieges the surrounding of a place in order to capture it or force someone to surrender
lay siege to begin a siege of a place

sieve (siv) NOUN sieves a device made of mesh or perforated metal or plastic, used to separate the smaller or soft parts of something from the larger or hard parts

sieve VERB sieves, sieving, sieved put something through a sieve

sift VERB sifts, sifting, sifted 1 sieve 2 examine and analyze facts or evidence, etc. carefully
▷ sifter NOUN

sigh NOUN sighs a sound made by breathing out heavily when you are sad, tired, relieved, etc.

sigh VERB sighs, sighing, sighed make a sigh

sight NOUN sights 1 the ability to see 2 a thing that can be seen or is worth seeing
• Our garden is a lovely sight in May.
3 something ugly or ridiculous to look at
• What a sight you are in those clothes! 4 a device looked through to help aim a gun or telescope, etc.
at sight or on sight as soon as a person or thing has been seen
catch sight of to see or glimpse for a moment

in sight 1 visible 2 clearly near • Victory was in sight.
USAGE Do not confuse with site.

sight VERB sights, sighting, sighted 1 see or observe something 2 aim a gun or telescope, etc. [from Old English]

sighted ADJECTIVE able to see; not blind

sight-reading NOUN playing or singing music at sight, without preparation

sightseeing NOUN visiting interesting places in a town, etc.
▷ sightseer NOUN

sign NOUN signs 1 something that shows that a thing exists • There are signs of decay. 2 a mark, device, or notice, etc., that gives a special meaning • a road sign 3 an action or movement giving information or a command etc. 4 any of the twelve divisions of the zodiac, represented by a symbol

sign VERB signs, signing, signed 1 make a sign or signal 2 write your signature on something; accept a contract etc. by doing this 3 use signing
sign on 1 accept a job etc. by signing a contract 2 sign a form to say that you are unemployed and want to claim benefit

signal NOUN signals 1 a device, gesture, or sound, etc., that gives information or a command 2 a message made up of such

---

Thesaurus

sieve NOUN Use a sieve to strain the fruit.
► strainer, sifter, colander, filter, riddle, screen

sieve VERB Sieve the mixture into a bowl.
► strain, sift, filter, riddle, screen

sift VERB 1 Sift the flour over the eggs and milk.
► sieve, strain, filter, riddle, screen 2 sift through Police have been sifting through piles of evidence. ► examine, inspect, sort out, analyze, scrutinize, investigate, review

sigh VERB 1 She sighed with relief. ► breathe out, exhale 2 "Not again," he sighed. ► moan, complain, lament, grumble

sight NOUN 1 His sight was failing. ► eyesight, vision, seeing, visual perception RELATED ADJECTIVES ► visual, optic or optical 2 The enemy was almost in sight. ► range, view, field of vision 3 In the early afternoon they had their first sight of land. ► view, glimpse, appearance, look (at), glance (at) 4 Thousands of visitors enjoy the sights every year. ► place of interest, landmark 5 The fireworks were an impressive sight. ► spectacle, display, show, exhibition, showpiece, scene

sight VERB A plane sighted the survivors. ► spot, discern, make out, glimpse, notice, observe, perceive, distinguish, recognize, see, behold

sign NOUN 1 There are no signs yet of a change in the weather. ► indication, intimation, hint, warning, forewarning, promise, threat, omen, pointer, portent, presage, augury 2 He gave the sign to begin. ► signal, cue, gesture , nod 3 There were signs of a much earlier occupation at the site. ► trace, vestige, clue, proof, reminder 4 Cards are sent as a sign of affection. ► token, marker, manifestation, symptom 5 We'll have to put a sign in the window. ► notice, placard, poster, publicity, signboard, advertisement 6 The walls were daubed with signs and pictures. ► symbol, mark, device, emblem, insignia, badge, logo, cipher, trademark

sign VERB 1 She signed her name at the bottom of the page. ► autograph, inscribe, write, initial, endorse
sign up 1 The brothers all signed up in the army. ► enlist, enrol, register, join 2 The company has signed up many more clerical staff. ► enrol, enlist, recruit, engage, take on, hire

signal NOUN 1 The captain gave the signal to move forward. ► sign, gesture, wave, prompt, cue, nod, (more informal) go-ahead 2 The city mob took Edward's flight as the signal for an orgy of destruction. ► cue, prompt, occasion, excuse, stimulus things **3** a sequence of electrical impulses or radio waves

signal VERB signals, signaling, signaled make a signal to somebody
▷ **signaler** NOUN
USAGE Do not use this word in mistake for *single* in the phrase *to single out*.

signal box NOUN signal boxes a building from which railway signals, points, etc., are controlled

signature NOUN signatures **1** a person's name written by himself or herself **2** (in music) a set of sharps and flats after the clef in a score, showing the key the music is written in (the **key signature**), or the sign, often a fraction such as (the **time signature**), showing the number of beats in the bar and their rhythm

signature tune NOUN signature tunes a special tune always used to announce a particular programme, performer, etc.

significant ADJECTIVE **1** having a meaning; full of meaning **2** important • *a significant event*
▷ **significantly** ADVERB **significance** NOUN

signing or **sign language** NOUN a way of communicating by using movements of the arms and hands, used mainly by and for deaf people

signpost NOUN signposts a sign at a road junction, etc., showing the names and distances of places down each road

Sikh (seek) NOUN Sikhs a member of a religion founded in northern India, believing in one God and accepting some Hindu and some Islamic beliefs
▷ **Sikhism** NOUN

silence NOUN silences absence of sound or speaking
in silence without speaking or making a sound

silence VERB silences, silencing, silenced make a person or thing silent

silencer NOUN silencers a device for reducing the sound made by a gun or a vehicle's exhaust system

silent ADJECTIVE **1** without any sound **2** not speaking
▷ **silently** ADVERB

silhouette (sil- oo- et) NOUN silhouettes a dark shadow seen against a light background
▷ **silhouette** VERB

silicon NOUN a substance found in many rocks, used in making transistors, chips for microprocessors, etc.

silk NOUN silks **1** a fine soft thread or cloth made from the fiber produced by silkworm caterpillars for making their cocoons **2** a length of silk thread used for embroidery
▷ **silken** ADJECTIVE **silky** ADJECTIVE

silly ADJECTIVE sillier, silliest foolish or unwise
▷ **silliness** NOUN

Thesaurus

signal VERB **1** *A police officer signaled to him to stop.* ► gesture, indicate, motion, sign, wave, beckon, communicate, flag, gesticulate, give a signal **2** *The pointed gun signaled his intentions very clearly.* ► indicate, express, reveal, announce, proclaim, declare, show

significance NOUN *He thought hard about the significance of her remarks.* ► importance, import, force, purport, implication, meaning, relevance, sense, point, signification, message
AN OPPOSITE IS insignificance

significant ADJECTIVE **1** *The tests produced some significant results.* ► meaningful, revealing, informative, important, indicative, expressive, (*more informal*) telltale **2** *The measures would have a significant effect on prices.*
► considerable, important, noteworthy, serious, sizable, remarkable, influential, big
AN OPPOSITE IS insignificant

signify VERB **1** *Red signifies danger.* ► mean, denote, symbolize, represent, indicate, stand for, imply **2** *Signify your agreement by signing your name at the bottom of the letter.* ► indicate, express, show, declare

silence NOUN **1** *There was silence for a time, while they thought.* ► quiet, quietness, stillness, tranquillity, peace, peacefulness, calm, hush
AN OPPOSITE IS noise **2** *The criticism reduced him*

to silence. ► speechlessness, dumbness, muteness, reticence, taciturnity, uncommunicativeness OPPOSITES ARE speech, verbosity

silence VERB **1** *The menace in his voice silenced them.* ► quieten, keep quiet, make silent, suppress, muzzle, shut up, gag **2** *A special muffler helps to silence exhaust noise* ► deaden, muffle, mute

silent ADJECTIVE **1** *George was silent until they reached the car park.* ► speechless, quiet, unspeaking, voiceless, dumb, mute, taciturn, reticent **2** *It was totally silent in the kitchen.*
► quiet, hushed, peaceful, tranquil, noiseless, soundless

silhouette NOUN *I made out the long silhouette of a tall man.* ► outline, profile, contour, shape, figure, form, features

silky ADJECTIVE *She ran her fingers through her dark silky hair.* ► smooth, soft, sleek, velvety, glossy, fine, satiny

silly ADJECTIVE **1** *"I'm not quite as silly as you think," she said.* ► stupid, foolish, crazy, mad, (*more informal*) daft **2** *People often do silly things.* ► foolish, unwise, stupid, imprudent, rash, reckless, foolhardy, senseless, idiotic, (*more informal*) daft

a
b
c
d
e
f
g
h
i
j
k
l
m
n
o
p
q
r
s
t
u
v
w
x
y
z

A
B
C
D
E
F
G
H
I
J
K
L
M
N
O
P
Q
R
S
T
U
V
W
X
Y
Z

silt NOUN sediment laid down by a river or sea, etc.

silt VERB silts, silting, silted
silt up block or clog or become blocked with silt

silver NOUN **1** a shiny white precious metal **2** the color of silver **3** coins or objects made of silver or silver-colored metal **4** a silver medal, usually given as second prize
▷ **silver** ADJECTIVE **silvery** ADJECTIVE

silver VERB silvers, silvering, silvered make or become silvery

silver wedding NOUN silver weddings a couple's 25th wedding anniversary

similar ADJECTIVE **1** nearly the same as another person or thing; of the same kind **2** (in mathematics) having the same shape but not the same size • *similar triangles*
▷ **similarly** ADVERB **similarity** NOUN

simile (sim- il- ee) NOUN similes a comparison of one thing with another (e.g., *He is as strong as a horse* or *We ran like the wind.*)

simmer VERB simmers, simmering, simmered boil very gently
simmer down calm down

simper VERB simpers, simpering, simpered smile in a silly affected way
▷ **simper** NOUN

simple ADJECTIVE simpler, simplest **1** easy • *a simple question* **2** not complicated or elaborate

3 plain, not showy • *a simple cottage* **4** without much sense or intelligence **5** not of high rank; ordinary • *a simple countryman*
▷ **simplicity** NOUN

simpleminded ADJECTIVE not having much intelligence

simplify VERB simplifies, simplifying, simplified make a thing simple or easy to understand
▷ **simplification** NOUN

simply ADVERB **1** in a simple way • *Explain it simply.* **2** without doubt; completely • *It's simply marvelous.* **3** only or merely • *It's simply a question of time.*

simulator NOUN simulators a machine or device for simulating actual conditions or events, often used for training • *a flight simulator*

simultaneous (sim- ul- tay- nee- us) ADJECTIVE happening at the same time
▷ **simultaneously** ADVERB

sin NOUN sins **1** the breaking of a religious or moral law **2** a very bad action

sin VERB sins, sinning, sinned commit a sin
▷ **sinner** NOUN

since CONJUNCTION **1** from the time when • *Where have you been since I last saw you?* **2** because • *Since we have missed the bus we must walk home.*

Thesaurus

---

simian ADJECTIVE ► monkeylike

similar ADJECTIVE **1** *The boys are similar in appearance.* ► alike, identical, indistinguishable, close, like, the same OPPOSITES ARE dissimilar, different **2** *hills and similar features*
► comparable, analogous, equivalent
3 *similar to Her views are similar to my own.*
► like, comparable to, close to OPPOSITES ARE unlike, dissimilar to, different from

similarity NOUN *There is a startling similarity between them.* ► resemblance, likeness, affinity, closeness, correspondence, congruity, similitude, sameness, uniformity AN OPPOSITE IS difference

simple ADJECTIVE **1** *a simple method of fixing up shelving* ► straightforward, easy, uncomplicated, elementary, undemanding OPPOSITES ARE complicated, difficult **2** *The forms are written in simple language.* ► clear, plain, straightforward, unambiguous, direct **3** *They led simple, honest lives. He is a simple sort of guy.* ► unpretentious, unsophisticated, ordinary, unassuming, innocent, artless

simplicity NOUN **1** *The solution was amazing for its simplicity.* ► straightforwardness, simpleness, ease AN OPPOSITE IS difficulty **2** *The house appealed because of the simplicity of its style.*

► plainness, unpretentiousness, restraint, purity, austerity AN OPPOSITE IS ornateness

simplify VERB *The rules are difficult to apply and need to be simplified.* ► make simple, clarify, disentangle, streamline AN OPPOSITE IS complicate

simply ADVERB **1** *It was simply impossible to tell the difference.* ► wholly, absolutely, completely, utterly **2** *She did it simply because we asked her to.* ► merely, just, purely, solely, only **3** *It is important to dress simply and avoid flamboyance.* ► plainly, soberly, without fuss, without frills, with restraint **4** *He writes simply and effectively.* ► clearly, plainly, straightforwardly, intelligibly **5** *They lived simply.* ► modestly, unpretentiously, naturally, quietly

simultaneous ADJECTIVE *There were three simultaneous bomb attacks in the city.* ► concurrent, coinciding, synchronized, synchronous, contemporaneous, parallel

sin NOUN **1** *It was a sin against their gods.* ► offense, wrong, transgression, evil, iniquity **2** *a powerful sermon on the dangers of sin* ► wickedness, wrongdoing, sinfulness, immorality, evil AN OPPOSITE IS virtue

sin VERB *He confessed he had sinned and incurred the wrath of his God.* ► do wrong, be guilty of sin, transgress, err, go astray, offend

since PREPOSITION from a certain time • *She has been here since Christmas.*

since ADVERB between then and now • *He ran away and hasn't been seen since.*

sincere ADJECTIVE without pretense; truly felt or meant • *my sincere thanks*
▷ **sincerely** ADVERB **sincerity** NOUN
Yours sincerely SEE **yours**

sine NOUN **sines** (in a right-angled triangle) the ratio of the length of a side opposite one of the acute angles to the length of the hypotenuse COMPARE **cosine**

sinew NOUN **sinews** strong tissue that connects a muscle to a bone
▷ **sinewy** ADJECTIVE

sinful ADJECTIVE 1 guilty of sin 2 wicked
▷ **sinfully** ADVERB **sinfulness** NOUN

sing VERB **sings, singing, sang, sung** 1 make musical sounds with the voice 2 perform a song
▷ **singer** NOUN

singe (sinj) VERB **singes, singeing, singed** burn something slightly

single ADJECTIVE 1 one only; not double or multiple 2 suitable for one person • *single beds* 3 separate • *We sold every single thing.* 4 not married 5 for the journey to a place but not back again • *a single ticket*
▷ **singly** ADVERB

single NOUN **singles** 1 a single person or thing 2 a single ticket 3 a record with one short piece of music on each side

single VERB **singles, singling, singled**

single out pick out or distinguish from other people or things

single file NOUN in single file in a line, one behind the other

single-handed ADJECTIVE without help

single-minded ADJECTIVE with your mind set on one purpose only

singsong ADJECTIVE having a monotonous tone or rhythm • *a singsong voice*

singular NOUN **singulars** the form of a noun or verb used when it stands for only one person or thing • *The singular is "man," the plural is "men."*

singular ADJECTIVE 1 to do with the singular 2 uncommon or extraordinary • *a woman of singular courage*
▷ **singularly** ADVERB **singularity** NOUN

sinister ADJECTIVE 1 looking evil or harmful 2 wicked • *a sinister motive* [from Latin, = on the left (which was thought to be unlucky)]

sink VERB **sinks, sinking, sank, sunk** 1 go or cause to go under the surface or to the bottom of the sea, etc. • *The ship sank.* • *They sank the ship.* 2 go or fall slowly downward • *He sank to his knees.* 3 push something sharp deeply into something soft • *The dog sank its teeth into my leg.* 4 dig or drill • *They sank a well.* 5 invest money in something
sink in become understood

sink NOUN **sinks** a fixed basin with a drainpipe and usually a tap or taps to supply water

sip VERB **sips, sipping, sipped** drink in small mouthfuls
▷ **sip** NOUN

Thesaurus

---

sincere ADJECTIVE 1 *Their praise was completely sincere.* ► heartfelt, honest, candid, genuine, truthful, wholehearted, open AN OPPOSITE IS insincere 2 *Jane is a very sincere person.*
► honest, genuine, truthful, straightforward, ingenuous, artless

sincerity NOUN *I trust the sincerity of their intentions.* ► honesty, genuineness, integrity, openness, straightforwardness, trustworthiness, truthfulness

sinful ADJECTIVE *Such behavior was sinful.*
► wicked, wrong, evil, iniquitous, unrighteous, ungodly AN OPPOSITE IS virtuous

sing VERB *To cheer herself up she began to sing.*
► chant, croon, hum, intone, trill

single ADJECTIVE 1 *All the chocolates were gone apart from a single orange cream.* ► solitary, lone, sole, isolated AN OPPOSITE IS plural. 2 *He had remained single all his life.* ► unattached, unmarried, a bachelor, unwedded AN OPPOSITE IS married 3 *She listened to every single word.* ► individual, particular

single VERB **single out** *It would be invidious to single out any individual for praise.* ► pick out, choose, select, fix on, separate out

singular ADJECTIVE *They acted with singular determination.* ► extraordinary, remarkable, exceptional, uncommon, unusual, conspicuous, notable

sinister *His words had a sinister undertone.*
► menacing, threatening, ominous, disturbing, alarming, disquieting, malevolent, baleful, (*more informal*) scary, (*more informal*) creepy

sink VERB 1 *The sun sank below the horizon.*
► descend, dip, fall, drop, disappear, vanish AN OPPOSITE IS rise 2 *Their hopes began to sink.*
► dwindle, fade, flag, fail, weaken, lessen, subside, collapse AN OPPOSITE IS revive 3 *The ship sank with the loss of many lives.* ► founder, go under, submerge, capsize OPPOSITES ARE rise, float

sip VERB *She sat sipping tea.* ► drink slowly, taste, sample, (*more informal*) slurp

sip NOUN *He took another sip of his beer.*
► mouthful, drink, drop, taste, (*more informal*) slurp

a
b
c
d
e
f
g
h
i
j
k
l
m
n
o
p
q
r
s
t
u
v
w
x
y
z

A
B
C
D
E
F
G
H
I
J
K
L
M
N
O
P
Q
R
S
T
U
V
W
X
Y
Z

siphon NOUN siphons **1** a pipe or tube in the form of an upside-down U, arranged so that liquid is forced up it and down to a lower level **2** a bottle containing soda water which is released through a tube

siphon VERB siphons, siphoning, siphoned flow or draw out through a siphon

sir NOUN **1** a word used when speaking politely to a man • *Please, sir, may I go?* **2** Sir the title given to a knight or baronet • *Sir John Moore*

siren NOUN sirens **1** a device that makes a long loud sound as a signal **2** a dangerously attractive woman [named after the Sirens in Greek legend, women who by their sweet singing lured seafarers to shipwreck on the rocks]

sissy NOUN sissies (*informal*) a timid or cowardly person [from *sis*, a shortening of *sister*]

sister NOUN sisters **1** a daughter of the same parents as another person **2** a woman who is a fellow member of an association, etc. **3** a nun
▷ **sisterly** ADJECTIVE
[from Old English]

sister-in-law NOUN sisters-in-law **1** the sister of a married person's husband or wife **2** the wife of a person's brother

sit VERB sits, sitting, sat **1** rest with your body supported on the buttocks; occupy a seat • *We were sitting in the front row.* **2** seat; cause someone to sit **3** (said about birds) perch; stay on the nest to hatch eggs **4** be a candidate for an examination **5** be situated; stay **6** (said about Congress or a court, etc.) be assembled for business

sitcom NOUN sitcoms (*informal*) a radio or television comedy based on characters

reacting to unusual or comic situations [short for *situation comedy*]

site NOUN sites the place where something happens or happened or is built, etc. • *a camping site* [from Latin *situs* = position] USAGE Do not confuse with **sight**.

sit-in NOUN sit-ins a protest in which people sit down or occupy a public place and refuse to move

sitter NOUN sitters a person who looks after children, pets, or a house while the owners are away

sitting NOUN sittings the time when people are served a meal or when an official body of people does business

sitting room NOUN sitting rooms a room with comfortable chairs for sitting in

situation NOUN situations **1** a position, with its surroundings **2** a state of affairs at a certain time • *The police faced a difficult situation.* **3** a job

six NOUN, ADJECTIVE sixes the number 6
▷ **sixth** ADJECTIVE, NOUN
at sixes and sevens in disorder or disagreement

sixteen NOUN, ADJECTIVE the number 16
▷ **sixteenth** ADJECTIVE, NOUN

sixth sense NOUN the ability to know something by instinct rather than by using any of the five senses; intuition

sixty NOUN, ADJECTIVE sixties the number 60
▷ **sixtieth** ADJECTIVE, NOUN

sizable ADJECTIVE large or fairly large

size NOUN sizes **1** the measurements or extent of something **2** any of the series of standard measurements in which certain things are made • *a size eight shoe*

Thesaurus

sister NOUN ► sibling RELATED ADJECTIVE
► sororal

sit VERB **1** *Julian sat in an armchair.* ► settle, perch, flop, ensconce yourself **2** *The hall sat about a hundred people.* ► seat, accommodate, have seats for, hold, take, has room for **3** *Parliament sits again in a week's time.* ► meet, assemble, convene, gather, be in session **4** *She sits her exams this year.* ► take, go in for, be a candidate in

site NOUN *the site for the new hospital* ► location, situation, setting, spot, plot, locality, ground

site VERB *Bus stops are sited at intervals of no more than half a mile.* ► position, place, situate, locate, erect, station, install

sitting NOUN *a sitting of Congress* ► session, assembly, meeting, period

sitting room NOUN ► living room, drawing room, lounge, front room, reception room

situated ADJECTIVE *a market situated near the highway* ► located, positioned, sited, built, placed, established

situation NOUN **1** *new houses in a pleasant situation* ► locality, location, position, setting, site, spot, place **2** *Their financial situation had improved significantly.* ► circumstances, position, state, state of affairs, condition, plight, predicament USAGE You use *plight* and *predicament* about bad situations. **3** *She applied for a situation with an estate agent.*
► job, position, post, employment

sizable ADJECTIVE *A sizable reward is being offered.*
► large, substantial, considerable, significant, decent, generous, worthwhile, (*more informal*) tidy

size NOUN **1** *the vast size of the main bedroom*
► dimensions, proportions, scale, magnitude,

size VERB sizes, sizing, sized arrange things according to their size
size up 1 estimate the size of something **2** form an opinion or judgement about a person or thing

sizzle VERB sizzles, sizzling, sizzled make a crackling or hissing sound

skate NOUN skates **1** a boot with a steel blade attached to the sole, used for sliding smoothly over ice **2** a roller skate

skate VERB skates, skating, skated move on skates
▷ **skater** NOUN

skateboard NOUN skateboards a small board with wheels, used for standing and riding on as a sport
▷ **skateboarder, skateboarding** NOUNS

skein NOUN skeins a coil of yarn or thread

skeleton NOUN skeletons **1** the framework of bones of the body **2** the shell or other hard part of a crab etc. **3** a framework, e.g., of a building
▷ **skeletal** ADJECTIVE
[from Greek *skeletos* = dried-up]

skeptical (skep- tik- al) ADJECTIVE inclined to question things; not believing easily
▷ **sceptically** ADVERB **scepticism** NOUN

sketch NOUN sketches **1** a rough drawing or painting **2** a short account of something **3** a short amusing play

sketch VERB sketches, sketching, sketched make a sketch

sketchy ADJECTIVE rough and not detailed or careful

skewer NOUN skewers a long pin pushed through meat to hold it together while it is being cooked
▷ **skewer** VERB

ski (skee) NOUN skis each of a pair of long narrow strips of wood, metal, or plastic fixed under the feet for moving quickly over snow

ski VERB skies, skiing, skied travel on skis
▷ **skier** NOUN
[from Norwegian]

skid VERB skids, skidding, skidded slide accidentally

skid NOUN skids **1** a skidding movement **2** a runner on a helicopter, for use in landing
[probably from Old Norse *skith* = ski]

ski jump NOUN ski jumps a steep slope with a sharp drop where it levels out at the bottom, for skiers to jump off as a sport

skillful ADJECTIVE having or showing great skill
▷ **skilfully** ADVERB

skill NOUN skills the ability to do something well
▷ **skilled** ADJECTIVE
[from Old Norse]

skim VERB skims, skimming, skimmed **1** remove something from the surface of a liquid; take the cream off milk **2** move quickly over a surface or through the air **3** read something quickly [from early French *escume* = scum]

Thesaurus

---

area, volume **2** *the size of the job* ► scale, extent, scope, range, immensity

sizzle VERB *Food sizzled in the pan.* ► crackle, frizzle, hiss, sputter

skeleton NOUN **1** *the skeleton of a building* ► framework, frame, bones, structure **2** *a skeleton of the plan* ► outline, draft, abstract, blueprint, sketch

skeptical ADJECTIVE *He was initially sceptical about her abilities but soon changed his mind.* ► dubious, doubtful, distrustful, mistrustful, disbelieving, incredulous, suspicious, uncertain, unconvinced, unsure, cynical AN OPPOSITE IS confident

sketch NOUN **1** *She drew a sketch of the scene.* ► drawing, outline, picture , diagram, plan **2** *a biographical sketch* ► description, portrait, profile, cameo **3** *a brief sketch of the main events* ► outline, summary, synopsis, rundown **4** *a comic sketch from the television series* ► scene, skit, turn, routine, number

sketch VERB *He decided to sketch the garden instead of taking a photograph.* ► draw, make a drawing of, portray, depict, rough out, represent
sketch out *We will sketch out our plan.*

► outline, describe, summarize, rough out, draft, give the gist of

sketchy ADJECTIVE *The information was too sketchy to act on.* ► incomplete, imperfect, perfunctory, bitty, scrappy, skimpy, meagre, rough, vague, imprecise, scanty OPPOSITES ARE detailed, comprehensive

skillful ADJECTIVE *a skillful negotiator; a skillful use of the materials* ► expert, skilled, able, capable, accomplished, proficient, adroit, deft, talented, clever, masterly, consummate AN OPPOSITE IS incompetent

skill NOUN *work that needs a lot of skill* ► expertise, ability, skillfulness, aptitude, adeptness, dexterity, competence, talent AN OPPOSITE IS incompetence

skilled ADJECTIVE *a skilled engineer* ► experienced, trained, qualified, skilful, proficient, accomplished, expert, practiced, versed OPPOSITES ARE unskilled, inexperienced

skim VERB **1** *The boat skim across the water.* ► glide, skate, plane, slide, float, coast **2** *skim through* *He skimmed through a picture book.* ► scan, skip through, flick through, look through, riffle through, read quickly

a b c d e f g h i j k l m n o p q r **s** t u v w x y z

skimp VERB **skimps, skimping, skimped** supply or use less than is needed • *Don't skimp on the food.*

skimpy ADJECTIVE **skimpier, skimpiest** scanty or too small

skin NOUN **skins 1** the flexible outer covering of a person's or animal's body **2** an outer layer or covering, e.g., of a fruit **3** a skinlike film formed on the surface of a liquid

skin VERB **skins, skinning, skinned** take the skin off something

skinny ADJECTIVE **skinnier, skinniest** very thin

skip VERB **skips, skipping, skipped 1** move along lightly, especially by hopping on each foot in turn **2** jump with a skipping rope **3** go quickly from one subject to another **4** miss something out • *You can skip chapter six.*

skip NOUN **skips** a skipping movement [probably from Scandinavian]

skipping rope NOUN **skipping ropes** a rope, usually with a handle at each end, that is swung over your head and under your feet as you jump

skirt NOUN **skirts 1** a piece of clothing for a woman or girl that hangs down from the waist **2** the part of a dress below the waist

skirt VERB **skirts, skirting, skirted** go around the edge of something

skittish ADJECTIVE frisky; lively and excitable

skulk VERB **skulks, skulking, skulked** loiter stealthily

skull NOUN **skulls** the framework of bones of the head

skunk NOUN **skunks** a North American animal with black and white fur that can spray a bad-smelling fluid [from a Native American word]

sky NOUN **skies** the space above the earth, appearing blue in daylight on fine days [from Old Norse]

skylight NOUN **skylights** a window in a roof

skyline NOUN **skylines** the outline of buildings, etc., against the sky

skyscraper NOUN **skyscrapers** a very tall building

slab NOUN **slabs** a thick flat piece

slack ADJECTIVE **1** not pulled tight **2** not busy; not working hard
▷ **slackly** ADVERB **slackness** NOUN

slack VERB **slacks, slacking, slacked** avoid work; be lazy
▷ **slacker** NOUN

slacken VERB **slackens, slackening, slackened** make or become slack

slacks PLURAL NOUN trousers for informal occasions

slag NOUN waste material separated from metal in smelting

slag heap NOUN **slag heaps** a mound of waste matter from a mine, etc.

slain *past participle* of **slay**

slake VERB **slakes, slaking, slaked** quench • *slake your thirst*

slam VERB **slams, slamming, slammed 1** shut loudly **2** hit violently
▷ **slam** NOUN

Thesaurus

skimp VERB *Despite the low price you won't skimp on comfort here.* ► stint on, be frugal with, economize on, cut corners on

skimpy ADJECTIVE *I'd rather have my clothes too long than looking skimpy.* ► scanty, short, flimsy, low-cut

skin NOUN **1** *The animal has a tough skin.* ► hide, pelt **2** *the skin of an apple* ► peel, rind, outside

skin VERB *She skinned three tomatoes.* ► peel, pare, strip

skinny ADJECTIVE *We have to find skinny people to try our designs on.* ► thin, scrawny, scraggy, lean, lanky, spindly, emaciated

skip VERB **1** *Cathy skipped along the path.*
► prance, trip, frisk **2** *We can skip these details.*
► pass over, ignore, omit, leave out, miss out, dispense with, forget **3** *We skipped school to go on the demo.* ► miss, be absent from, play truant from, absent yourself from, cut

sky NOUN *Suddenly the whole sky around them was filled with birds.* ► heavens, atmosphere, blue yonder RELATED ADJECTIVE ► celestial

slab NOUN *slabs of rock cut from the quarries*
► block, piece, tablet, chunk, hunk, lump, slice

slack ADJECTIVE **1** *The rope suddenly went slack.*
► limp, loose AN OPPOSITE IS tight **2** *A slack defense let in several goals.* ► disorganized, negligent, careless, undisciplined, inattentive, lax, lazy, listless, easygoing OPPOSITES ARE alert, diligent. **3** *Business tends to be slack just after Christmas.* ► sluggish, slow, quiet, inactive, slow-moving, depressed OPPOSITES ARE brisk, busy

slack VERB *This was no time for slacking.* ► idle, shirk, be lazy, (*more informal*) skive

slacken VERB **1** *The boat lurched as he slackened his grip on the wheel.* ► loosen, relax, release, ease off AN OPPOSITE IS tighten **2** *The rain might just have slackened by now.* ► decrease, ease, lessen, abate, lower, moderate, reduce, slow down

slacker NOUN *There was no room for slackers.*
► layabout, idler, shirker, loafer, malingerer, sluggard

slam VERB **1** *He stormed out and slammed the door.* ► bang, shut, fling shut, crash

slander NOUN **slanders** a spoken statement that damages a person's reputation and is untrue COMPARE **libel**
▷ **slanderous** ADJECTIVE

slander VERB **slanders, slandering, slandered** make a slander against someone
▷ **slanderer** NOUN

slang NOUN words that are used very informally to add vividness or humor to what is said, especially those used only by a particular group of people • *teenage slang*
▷ **slangy** ADJECTIVE

slant VERB **slants, slanting, slanted 1** slope **2** present news or information, etc., from a particular point of view

slap VERB **slaps, slapping, slapped 1** hit with the palm of the hand or with something flat **2** put forcefully or carelessly • *We slapped paint on the walls.*
▷ **slap** NOUN

slapdash ADJECTIVE hasty and careless

slapstick NOUN comedy with people hitting each other, falling over, etc.

slash VERB **slashes, slashing, slashed 1** make large cuts in something **2** cut or strike with a long sweeping movement **3** reduce greatly • *Prices were slashed.*

slash NOUN **slashes 1** a slashing cut **2** a slanting line (/) used in writing and printing

slate NOUN **slates 1** a kind of grey rock that is easily split into flat plates **2** a piece of this rock used in covering a roof or (formerly) for writing on
▷ **slaty** ADJECTIVE

slate VERB **slates, slating, slated 1** cover a roof with slates **2** (*informal*) criticize severely

slaughter VERB **slaughters, slaughtering, slaughtered 1** kill an animal for food **2** kill people or animals ruthlessly or in great numbers
▷ **slaughter** NOUN

slaughterhouse NOUN **slaughterhouses** a place where animals are killed for food

slave NOUN **slaves** a person who is owned by another and obliged to work for him or her without being paid
▷ **slavery** NOUN

slave VERB **slaves, slaving, slaved** work very hard [from Latin *sclavus* = captive]

slavish ADJECTIVE **1** like a slave **2** showing no independence or originality

Thesaurus

slander NOUN *He'd sue me for slander if I made the accusations publicly.* ► defamation, misrepresentation, calumny, libel, slur, aspersion, malicious gossip, scandalmongering OPPOSITES ARE compliment, praise

slander VERB *She discovered that her friend had been slandering her behind her back.* ► defame, libel, smear, vilify, besmirch

slanderous ADJECTIVE *The truth can often be slanderous if you put it in a certain way.* ► defamatory, libelous, disparaging, pejorative, scurrilous, malicious, abusive

slant NOUN **1** *The floor seemed to be on a slant.* ► slope, angle, incline, diagonal, gradient, list, rake, ramp, pitch, tilt **2** *The Youth Theater brings a new slant to Christmas shows.* ► point of view, viewpoint, standpoint, angle, perspective, emphasis, bias

slant VERB **1** *The handwriting slants to the right. Joe slanted his gaze towards the door.* ► tilt, lean, slope, incline, be at an angle, be skewed **2** *He slanted his version of the story to avoid awkward admissions.* ► bias, distort, twist, warp, weight, color, prejudice

slanting ADJECTIVE *The slanting sunlight cast long shadows.* ► oblique, sloping, angled, inclined, diagonal, listing, raked, askew, skewed, slantwise, tilted OPPOSITES ARE straight, level

slap VERB **1** *Anne was at the end of her patience and wanted to slap him.* ► smack, strike, hit, whack, spank **2** *She had slapped a parking ticket on his Mercedes.* ► fling, throw, toss, hurl

3 *Slap some varnish on to seal the surface.* ► daub, plaster, spread, apply

slap NOUN *He heard the sound of a slap from the next room.* ► smack, whack, blow, thump

slash VERB **1** *Someone had slashed the tires.* ► cut, slit, gash, rip, tear, knife **2** *Prices will be slashed out of the high season.* ► reduce, cut, drop

slash NOUN *He had a deep slash across his arm.* ► cut, gash, laceration, wound, injury

slate VERB (*informal*) *The critics all slated the production, though they liked the music.* ► criticize, pillory, lambaste, revile, (*informal*) pan

slaughter NOUN *The senseless slaughter of dolphins takes place merely to catch a few extra tuna.* ► massacre, carnage, killing, butchery, murder, bloodshed

slaughter VERB *A whole legion was ambushed and slaughtered.* ► massacre, butcher, kill, annihilate, eliminate, murder, slay

slave NOUN *Most of the work was done by slaves at that time.* ► serf, thrall, vassal, drudge, servant RELATED ADJECTIVE ► servile

slave VERB *That's all the thanks you get for slaving over a hot stove all morning.* ► toil, labor, grind, sweat, work, drudge, exert yourself, work your fingers to the bone, (*more informal*) work your socks off OPPOSITES ARE relax, skive

slavery NOUN *They were being sent back to torture, slavery, and death.* ► bondage, enslavement, servitude, captivity, serfdom AN OPPOSITE IS freedom

a
b
c
d
e
f
g
h
i
j
k
l
m
n
o
p
q
r
s
t
u
v
w
x
y
z

A
B
C
D
E
F
G
H
I
J
K
L
M
N
O
P
Q
R
S
T
U
V
W
X
Y
Z

slay VERB slays, slaying, slew, slain (*poetical*) kill

sled NOUN sleds a vehicle for traveling over snow, with strips of metal or wood instead of wheels
▷ **sledding** NOUN

sledgehammer NOUN sledgehammers a very large heavy hammer

sleek ADJECTIVE smooth and shiny

sleep NOUN the condition or time of rest in which the eyes are closed, the body relaxed, and the mind unconscious
go to sleep (said about part of the body) become numb
put to sleep kill an animal painlessly, e.g., with an injection of a drug

sleep VERB sleeps, sleeping, slept have a sleep
sleep with have sexual intercourse with [from Old English]

sleeper NOUN sleepers 1 someone who is asleep 2 each of the wooden or concrete beams on which the rails of a railway rest 3 a railway car with beds or berths for passengers to sleep in; a place in this

sleepwalker NOUN sleepwalkers a person who walks about while asleep
▷ **sleepwalking** NOUN

sleepy ADJECTIVE feeling a need or wish to sleep
▷ **sleepily** ADVERB **sleepiness** NOUN

sleet NOUN a mixture of rain and snow or hail

sleeve NOUN sleeves 1 the part of a piece of clothing that covers the arm 2 the cover of a record
up your sleeve hidden but ready for you to use

sleight (sounds like *slight*) NOUN
sleight of hand skill in using the hands to do conjuring tricks, etc.

slender ADJECTIVE 1 slim and graceful 2 slight or small ● *a slender chance*
▷ **slenderness** NOUN

sleuth (slooth) NOUN sleuths a detective [from Old Norse *sloth* = a track or trail]

slew past tense of slay

slice NOUN slices 1 a thin piece cut off something 2 a portion

slice VERB slices, slicing, sliced 1 cut into slices 2 cut from a larger piece ● *Slice the top off the egg.* 3 cut cleanly ● *The knife sliced through the apple.*

slick ADJECTIVE 1 done or doing things quickly and cleverly 2 slippery

slick NOUN slicks 1 a large patch of oil floating on water 2 a slippery place

slide VERB slides, sliding, slid 1 move or cause to move smoothly on a surface 2 move quietly or secretly ● *The thief slid behind a bush.*

slide NOUN slides 1 a sliding movement 2 a smooth surface or structure on which people or things can slide 3 a photograph that can be projected on a screen 4 a small glass plate on which things are placed to be examined

Thesaurus

slay VERB *Thousands of men and women were slain in the reprisals.* ► kill, slaughter, massacre, butcher, murder, put to death, exterminate, annihilate, cut down, (*informal*) finish off

sleazy ADJECTIVE *a sleazy little cafe on the edge of town* ► dirty, squalid, shabby, run-down, sordid, seamy, rough

sleek ADJECTIVE 1 *She combed her sleek dark hair.* ► silky, glossy, shiny, smooth, brushed, soft, velvety, well-groomed AN OPPOSITE IS dull 2 *a sleek sports car* ► streamlined, graceful, elegant, aerodynamic 3 *a group of sleek young men in smart suits* ► stylish, well-groomed, prosperous AN OPPOSITE IS unkempt

sleep NOUN *She often had a sleep in the afternoon.* ► snooze, nap, rest, doze, catnap, siesta, (*more informal*) kip, (*more informal*) forty winks

sleep VERB *He had slept for about an hour.* ► snooze, doze, rest, slumber, (*more informal*) kip, (*more informal*) drop off, (*more informal*) nod off, (*more informal*) doze down

sleepy ADJECTIVE 1 *I wasn't sleepy, so I decided to walk around for a bit.* ► drowsy, somnolent, lethargic, weary, tired, torpid, sluggish, soporific, heavy-eyed, (*informal*) dopey, ready

to sleep AN OPPOSITE IS awake 2 *a sleepy little town near the border* ► quiet, peaceful, tranquil, inactive, dull, unexciting OPPOSITES ARE lively, busy

slender ADJECTIVE 1 *a slender youth with dark hair* ► slim, lean, slight, thin, graceful, svelte AN OPPOSITE IS fat 2 *a slender thread* ► fine, fragile, tenuous, feeble AN OPPOSITE IS strong 3 *slender hopes* ► faint, slim, remote, flimsy 4 *a verdict based on slender evidence* ► meager, scanty, flimsy, tenuous, inadequate AN OPPOSITE IS adequate

slice NOUN *a slice of bread* ► piece, sliver (=thin slice), chunk (= thick slice), hunk (= thick slice), tranche, slab

slice VERB *She sliced the cheese into thin pieces.* ► cut, cut up, chop, carve, divide

slick ADJECTIVE *a slick marketing campaign* ► smooth, efficient, smart, polished, streamlined, skilful, professional AN OPPOSITE IS inept

slide VERB *The spoon slid across the table.* ► glide, slither, skim, skid, slip

slight ADJECTIVE 1 *There was a slight problem with this plan.* ► small, modest, tiny, imperceptible, insignificant, negligible, slim, minor, trivial under a microscope **5** a fastener to keep hair tidy

slight *ADJECTIVE* very small; not serious or important
▷ **slightly** *ADVERB* **slightness** *NOUN*

slim *ADJECTIVE* **slimmer, slimmest 1** thin and graceful **2** small; hardly enough • *a slim chance*
▷ **slimness** *NOUN*

slim *VERB* **slims, slimming, slimmed** make yourself thinner, especially by dieting
▷ **slimmer** *NOUN*

slime *NOUN* unpleasant wet slippery stuff
▷ **slimy** *ADJECTIVE* **sliminess** *NOUN*

sling *NOUN* **slings 1** a loop or band placed around something to support or lift it • *He had his arm in a sling.* **2** a looped strap used to throw a stone, etc.

sling *VERB* **slings, slinging, slung 1** hang or support something so that it hangs loosely **2** (*informal*) throw carelessly

slink *VERB* **slinks, slinking, slunk** move in a stealthy or guilty way
▷ **slinky** *ADJECTIVE*

slip *VERB* **slips, slipping, slipped 1** slide accidentally; lose your balance by sliding **2** move or put quickly and quietly • *Slip it in your pocket.* • *We slipped away from the party.* **3** escape from • *The dog slipped out of its leash. It slipped my memory.*
slip up make a mistake

slip *NOUN* **slips 1** an accidental slide or fall **2** a mistake **3** a small piece of paper **4** a petticoat **5** a pillowcase
give someone the slip escape or avoid someone skilfully

slipper *NOUN* **slippers** a soft comfortable shoe to wear indoors

slippery *ADJECTIVE* smooth or wet so that it is difficult to stand on or hold
▷ **slipperiness** *NOUN*

slipshod *ADJECTIVE* careless; not systematic

slipstream *NOUN* **slipstreams** a current of air driven backward as an aircraft or vehicle is propelled forward

slit *NOUN* **slits** a narrow straight cut or opening

slit *VERB* **slits, slitting, slit** make a slit or slits in something

slither *VERB* **slithers, slithering, slithered** slip or slide unsteadily

sliver (sliv- er) *NOUN* **slivers** a thin strip of wood or glass etc.

slog *VERB* **slogs, slogging, slogged 1** hit hard **2** work or walk hard and steadily
▷ **slog** *NOUN* **slogger** *NOUN*

slogan *NOUN* **slogans** a phrase used to advertise something or to sum up the aims of a campaign etc. • *Their slogan was "Ban the bomb!"* [from Scottish Gaelic *sluagh-ghairm* = battle-cry]

slope *VERB* **slopes, sloping, sloped** lie or turn at an angle; slant
slope off (*informal*) go away

Thesaurus

---

2 *her slight figure* ► slim, slender, delicate, dainty, graceful, petite, svelte AN OPPOSITE IS big

slightly *ADVERB* *The new models are slightly bigger. He was slightly taken aback by this.* ► a little, a bit, rather, somewhat, a shade, moderately AN OPPOSITE IS very

slim *ADJECTIVE* **1** *She is tall, slim, and dignified.* ► slender, lean, slight, thin, graceful, svelte **2** *a slim chance of winning* ► faint, slender, remote, flimsy

slimy *ADJECTIVE* *He slid helplessly down the slimy walls.* ► slithery, slippery, sticky, oozy, greasy

sling *VERB* *He slung his coat on a chair.* ► throw, hurl, toss, fling, cast, pitch, heave

slink *VERB* *He slunk round to the back of the house.* ► creep, sneak, slip, steal, edge, sidle

slip *VERB* **1** *People were slipping on the icy ground.* ► slide, slither, fall, trip, stumble **2** *He got up and slipped quietly out of the door.* ► creep, sneak, slink, steal, edge, sidle **3** *He slipped some money into his pocket.* ► put, tuck, stick, shove, stuff

slip *NOUN* **1** *a slip of paper* ► piece, scrap, chit, sheet **2** *Did you mean to write "yes" or was that a slip?* ► mistake, error, gaffe, lapse, blunder

slippery *ADJECTIVE* **1** *The floor was wet and slippery.* ► slithery, greasy, slimy, slippy **2** *a slippery character* ► devious, unreliable, dishonest, crafty, cunning

slit *NOUN* **1** *He peeped through a slit in a fence.* ► opening, chink, gap, crack, aperture, slot **2** *She made a slit in the side of the box.* ► cut, incision, gash, tear, slash

slit *VERB* *Henry looked for a knife to slit open his letter.* ► cut, tear, rip, slice

slog *NOUN* (*informal*) *The work was a year's hard slog.* ► toil, labor, struggle, work, (*informal*) grind

slope *NOUN* **1** *A flat roof must have a slope for drainage.* ► incline, gradient, slant, angle, pitch **2** *They had their picnic on a grassy slope.* ► hillock, hill, bank, rise

slope *VERB* *The garden slopes gently away from the house.* ► slant, fall or rise, fall away, shelve, bank, incline

a
b
c
d
e
f
g
h
i
j
k
l
m
n
o
p
q
r
s
t
u
v
w
x
y
z

A B C D E F G H I J K L M N O P Q R S T U V W X Y Z

slope NOUN slopes **1** a sloping surface **2** the amount by which something slopes

sloppy ADJECTIVE sloppier, sloppiest **1** liquid and splashing easily **2** careless or slipshod • *sloppy work* **3** weakly sentimental • *a sloppy story*
▷ **sloppily** ADVERB **sloppiness** NOUN

slot NOUN slots a narrow opening to put things in
▷ **slotted** ADJECTIVE

slot VERB slots, slotting, slotted put something into a place where it fits

sloth (rhymes with *both*) NOUN sloths **1** laziness **2** a South American animal that lives in trees and moves very slowly
▷ **slothful** ADJECTIVE

slot machine NOUN slot machines a machine worked by putting a coin in the slot

slouch VERB slouches, slouching, slouched stand, sit, or move in a lazy awkward way, not with an upright posture
▷ **slouch** NOUN

slovenly (slov-en-lee) ADJECTIVE careless or untidy
▷ **slovenliness** NOUN

slow ADJECTIVE **1** not quick; taking more time than is usual **2** showing a time earlier than the correct time • *Your watch is slow.* **3** not clever; not able to understand quickly or easily
▷ **slowly** ADVERB **slowness** NOUN

slow ADVERB slowly • *Go slow.*

slow VERB slows, slowing, slowed go more slowly; cause to go more slowly • *The storm slowed us down.*

slowworm NOUN slowworms a small European legless lizard that looks like a snake and gives birth to live young

sludge NOUN thick mud

slug NOUN slugs **1** a small slimy animal like a snail without a shell **2** a pellet for firing from a gun

sluggish ADJECTIVE slow-moving; not alert or lively

sluice gate NOUN sluice gates a sliding barrier for controlling a flow of water

slum NOUN slums an area of dirty overcrowded houses

slumber VERB slumbers, slumbering, slumbered sleep
▷ **slumber** NOUN **slumberer** NOUN **slumberous** or **slumbrous** ADJECTIVE

slump VERB slumps, slumping, slumped fall heavily or suddenly

slump NOUN slumps a sudden great fall in prices or trade

slur VERB slurs, slurring, slurred **1** pronounce words indistinctly by running the sounds together **2** mark with a slur in music

slur NOUN slurs **1** a slurred sound **2** something that harms a person's reputation **3** (in music) a curved line placed over notes to show that they are to be sung or played smoothly without a break

Thesaurus

sloppy ADJECTIVE **1** *The cement mixture was much too sloppy.* ► liquid, runny, slushy, watery, messy, wet AN OPPOSITE IS solid **2** *sloppy work* ► careless, slovenly, slapdash, slipshod AN OPPOSITE IS careful

slosh VERB **1** *Michael threatened to slosh anyone else who said anything.* ► hit, strike, bash **2** *Water was sloshing around.* ► splash, slop, spill, splatter

slot NOUN **1** *She put another coin in the slot and waited.* ► slit, chink, aperture, opening **2** *a weekly radio slot for listeners' comments* ► spot, time, place, space

slovenly ADJECTIVE **1** *He was criticized for his slovenly appearance.* ► untidy, scruffy, messy, disheveled AN OPPOSITE IS careful **2** *The work is slovenly and needs to be redone.* ► careless, slapdash, slipshod, untidy, thoughtless

slow ADJECTIVE **1** *They walked on at a slow pace.* ► leisurely, unhurried, measured, moderate, steady, deliberate, plodding **2** *It was slow work.* ► lengthy, prolonged, protracted, tedious **3** *He could be extremely slow at times.* ► obtuse, stupid, slow-witted, dim, (more informal) dense

slow VERB *The huge vehicle slowed to a halt.* ► decelerate, go slower, slow down, reduce speed, brake OPPOSITES ARE accelerate, speed up

sluggish ADJECTIVE *He woke up feeling sluggish after a sleepless night.* ► lethargic, lifeless, listless, torpid, unresponsive, dull, idle, lazy, slothful OPPOSITES ARE lively, vigorous

slump VERB **1** *House values have slumped in the last few months.* ► decline, drop, fall off, collapse, plummet, plunge, sink, worsen OPPOSITES ARE soar, rise **2** *Joanna slumped into a chair.* ► flop, slouch, collapse, loll, droop, sag **3** *He slumped to the ground, clutching his leg.* ► fall, sink, collapse, drop

slump NOUN *a financial crisis and a slump in world trade* ► decline, depression, downturn, collapse, drop, fall, tumble, crash, trough AN OPPOSITE IS boom

slur NOUN *This is a slur on one of our great national heroes.* ► insult, slight, slander, libel, defamation

slurp VERB slurps, slurping, slurped eat or drink with a loud sucking sound
▷ **slurp** NOUN

slush NOUN partly melted snow on the ground
▷ **slushy** ADJECTIVE

sly ADJECTIVE slier, sliest **1** unpleasantly cunning or secret **2** mischievous and knowing • *a sly smile*
▷ **slyly** ADVERB **slyness** NOUN

smack¹ NOUN smacks **1** a slap **2** a loud sharp sound • *It hit the wall with a smack.* **3** (*informal*) a loud kiss

smack¹ VERB smacks, smacking, smacked **1** slap **2** smash into
smack your lips close and then part them noisily in enjoyment

smack ADVERB (*informal*) forcefully or directly • *The ball went smack through the window.*

smack² NOUN smacks a slight flavor of something; a trace

smack² VERB smacks, smacking, smacked have a slight flavor or trace • *His manner smacks of conceit.*

small ADJECTIVE **1** not large; less than the usual size **2** not important or significant
▷ **smallness** NOUN
the small of the back the lower part of a person's back, where the spine curves in

smallholding NOUN smallholdings a small area of land used for farming
▷ **smallholder** NOUN

small hours PLURAL NOUN the early hours of the morning, after midnight

small-minded ADJECTIVE selfish; petty

smallpox NOUN a serious contagious disease that causes a fever and produces spots that leave scars on the skin

smarmy ADJECTIVE (*informal*) trying to win someone's favour by being friendly in an insincere or exaggerated way

smart ADJECTIVE **1** neat and elegant; dressed well **2** clever **3** forceful; brisk • *She ran at a smart pace.*
▷ **smartly** ADVERB **smartness** NOUN

smart card NOUN smart cards a card like a credit card, which stores information or enables you to use a cash machine, etc.

smarten VERB smartens, smartening, smartened make or become smarter

smash VERB smashes, smashing, smashed **1** break noisily into pieces **2** hit or move with great force **3** destroy or defeat completely

smash NOUN smashes **1** the action or sound of smashing **2** a collision between vehicles

smash hit NOUN smash hits (*informal*) a very successful song, show, etc.

smashing ADJECTIVE (*informal*) excellent or beautiful
▷ **smasher** NOUN

Thesaurus

sly ADJECTIVE *The master was a devious, sly man.*
► cunning, crafty, clever, wily, foxy, canny, knowing, shifty, sneaky, furtive, scheming, conniving

smack VERB *She smacked the dog.* ► slap, strike, hit, whack, spank

smack NOUN *It was a hard smack.* ► slap, clout, whack, blow, thump

small ADJECTIVE **1** *A small packet lay on the mat.*
► little, tiny, minute, compact, baby, diminutive, minuscule AN OPPOSITE IS large **2** *His mother was a small woman.* ► short, little, slight, petite OPPOSITES ARE big, large, tall **3** *We will need to make some small changes.*
► minor, trivial, trifling, insignificant, unimportant, negligible OPPOSITES ARE major, substantial **4** *They wanted to complain about the small portions.* ► meager, inadequate, paltry, insufficient OPPOSITES ARE large, generous, ample

small-minded ADJECTIVE *a lot of small-minded chauvinists* ► narrow-minded, intolerant, narrow, bigoted, conservative, illiberal, insular, parochial, short-sighted OPPOSITES ARE broad-minded, open-minded, tolerant

smarmy ADJECTIVE *His manner was over-polite and smarmy.* ► smooth, oily, unctuous, obsequious, fawning

smart ADJECTIVE **1** *He looked smart in his new suit.*
► elegant, well dressed, stylish, spruce, trim, chic, fashionable AN OPPOSITE IS scruffy **2** *Jenny had always been the smart member of the family.* ► clever, bright, intelligent, sharp, shrewd, astute AN OPPOSITE IS stupid **3** *They would stay in a smart hotel and eat out every night.* ► fashionable, high-class, exclusive, fancy, (*more informal*) posh AN OPPOSITE IS low-class **4** *They set off at a smart pace.* ► brisk, fast, quick, lively, spirited AN OPPOSITE IS slow

smart VERB *The smoke made her eyes smart.*
► sting, tingle, prickle, prick, hurt

smarten VERB **1** smarten up *The house had been smartened up before it was put on the market.*
► refurbish, renovate, do up, improve, redecorate **2** smarten yourself up *Eleanor went to smarten herself up for dinner.* ► dress, spruce yourself up, freshen yourself up, make yourself smart

smash VERB **1** *He dropped the glass and smashed it.* ► break, shatter, crack **2** smash into *A car had smashed into the lamppost.* ► crash into, collide with, smack into, bash into, thump into, hit

smashing ADJECTIVE *They had a smashing time.*
► marvelous, excellent, wonderful, splendid, lovely, delightful, (*more informal*) terrific

a b c d e f g h i j k l m n o p q r **s** t u v w x y z

smear VERB smears, smearing, smeared **1** rub something greasy or sticky or dirty on a surface **2** try to damage someone's reputation
▷ **smeary** ADJECTIVE

smear NOUN smears **1** smearing; something smeared **2** material smeared on a slide to be examined under a microscope **3** a false accusation **4** a smear test

smear test NOUN smear tests the taking and examination of a sample of the cervix lining, to check for faulty cells which may cause cancer

smell VERB smells, smelling, smelt or smelled **1** be aware of something by means of the sense organs of the nose • *I can smell smoke.* **2** give out a smell

smell NOUN smells **1** something you can smell; a quality in something that makes people able to smell it **2** an unpleasant quality of this kind **3** the ability to smell things
▷ **smelly** ADJECTIVE

smile NOUN smiles an expression on the face that shows pleasure or amusement, with the lips stretched and turning upwards at the ends

smile VERB smiles, smiling, smiled give a smile

smirk NOUN smirks a self-satisfied smile

smirk VERB smirks, smirking, smirked give a smirk

smite VERB smites, smiting, smote, smitten (*old use*) hit hard

smith NOUN smiths **1** a person who makes things out of metal **2** a blacksmith

smithereens PLURAL NOUN small fragments [from Irish]

smock NOUN smocks **1** an overall shaped like a very long shirt **2** a loose top with the upper part gathered into stitched pleats

smog NOUN a mixture of smoke and fog

smoke NOUN **1** the mixture of gas and solid particles given off by a burning substance **2** a period of smoking tobacco • *He wanted a smoke.*
▷ **smoky** ADJECTIVE

smoke VERB smokes, smoking, smoked **1** give out smoke **2** have a lighted cigarette, cigar, or pipe between your lips and draw its smoke into your mouth; do this as a habit **3** preserve meat or fish by treating it with smoke
• *smoked haddock*
▷ **smoker** NOUN

smoke screen NOUN smoke screens **1** a mass of smoke used to hide the movement of troops **2** something that conceals what is happening

smolder VERB smolders, smoldering, smoldered **1** burn slowly without a flame **2** feel an emotion strongly without showing it • *He was smoldering with jealousy.*

smooth ADJECTIVE **1** having a surface without any lumps, wrinkles, roughness, etc. **2** moving without bumps or jolts etc. **3** not harsh • *a smooth flavor* **4** without problems or difficulties
▷ **smoothly** ADVERB **smoothness** NOUN

Thesaurus

---

smear VERB **1** *He smeared grease on the bearings.* ► daub, spread, wipe, plaster, rub, dab, smudge **2** *The canvas was smeared with paint.* ► cover, coat, rub, streak **3** *The newspapers tried to smear his reputation.* ► sully, besmirch, tarnish, blacken, defame, malign, vilify

smear NOUN **1** *a smear of paint* ► streak, smudge, daub, mark **2** *smears about them in the press* ► slander, libel, defamation, imputation, false report

smell NOUN **1** *the fresh smells of spring* ► fragrance, scent, perfume, aroma **2** *a smell of cooking* ► aroma, odor **3** *a bad smell* ► odor, stench, stink, reek RELATED ADJECTIVE ► olfactory

smell VERB **1** *Smell the flowers.* ► scent, sniff **2** (*informal*) *The milk was starting to smell.* ► stink, whiff, reek

smelly ADJECTIVE *The room was damp and smelly.* ► smelling, stinking, malodorous, reeking, foul, putrid, (*more informal*) pongy

smile VERB *Jo smiled at her.* ► beam, grin, simper, smirk, leer USAGE Note that *smirk* and *leer* are unpleasant expressions.

smoke VERB **1** *The fire was smoking.* ► smoulder, emit smoke, fume, reek **2** *He was smoking a cigar.* ► puff on, draw on, inhale

smooth ADJECTIVE **1** *a smooth road* ► even, level, flat, horizontal OPPOSITES ARE uneven, rough **2** *a smooth surface* ► shiny, polished, glossy, silky AN OPPOSITE IS dull **3** *a smooth sea* ► calm, still, tranquil, placid, serene, glassy AN OPPOSITE IS rough **4** *a smooth talker* ► suave, articulate, glib, slick, smarmy, plausible, persuasive AN OPPOSITE IS awkward **5** *the smooth running of the engine* ► regular, steady, rhythmic, flowing, fluent OPPOSITES ARE irregular, jerky **6** *a smooth operation* ► straightforward, efficient, well-run, trouble-free, untroubled OPPOSITES ARE troubled, fraught

smooth VERB **1** *He took his clothes out of the bag and smoothed them before putting them away.* ► flatten, press, iron **2** *Use sandpaper to smooth the surface.* ► plane, sand, polish, level **3** *Extra support would smooth their progress.* ► ease, facilitate, help, assist, expedite

smooth VERB smooths, smoothing, smoothed make a thing smooth

smote past tense of smite

smother VERB smothers, smothering, smothered **1** suffocate **2** put out a fire by covering it **3** cover thickly • *The buns were smothered in sugar.* **4** restrain or conceal • *She smothered a smile.*

smudge NOUN smudges a dirty mark made by rubbing something
▷ **smudgy** ADJECTIVE

smudge VERB smudges, smudging, smudged make a smudge on something; become smudged

smug ADJECTIVE self-satisfied; too pleased with your own good fortune or abilities
▷ **smugly** ADVERB **smugness** NOUN

smuggle VERB smuggles, smuggling, smuggled bring something into a country, etc., secretly or illegally
▷ **smuggler** NOUN

snack NOUN snacks **1** a small meal **2** food eaten between meals

snag NOUN snags **1** an unexpected difficulty **2** a sharp or jagged part sticking out from something **3** a tear in material that has been caught on something sharp

snail NOUN snails a small animal with a soft body and a shell

snake NOUN snakes a reptile with a long narrow body and no legs
▷ **snaky** ADJECTIVE

snap VERB snaps, snapping, snapped **1** break suddenly or with a sharp sound **2** bite suddenly or quickly **3** say something quickly and angrily **4** take something or move quickly **5** take a snapshot of something
snap your fingers make a sharp snapping sound with your thumb and a finger

snap NOUN snaps **1** the action or sound of snapping **2** a snapshot

snappy ADJECTIVE **1** snapping at people **2** quick and lively
▷ **snappily** ADVERB

snapshot NOUN snapshots an informal photograph

snare NOUN snares **1** a trap for catching birds or animals **2** something that attracts someone but is a trap or a danger

snare VERB snares, snaring, snared catch in a snare

snarl VERB snarls, snarling, snarled **1** growl angrily **2** speak in a bad-tempered way
▷ **snarl** NOUN
[imitating the sound]

snatch VERB snatches, snatching, snatched seize; take quickly, eagerly, or by force

snatch NOUN snatches **1** snatching **2** a short and incomplete part of a song, conversation, etc.

Thesaurus

---

smother VERB **1** *He tried to smother the flames with his coat.* ► put out, extinguish, snuff out, damp down, dampen, douse **2** *A young mother was accused of smothering her baby.* ► suffocate, stifle, asphyxiate, strangle, choke

smudge NOUN *His thumb left a smudge on the paper.* ► smear, mark, stain, blot, streak

smudge VERB **1** *Her hand slipped and she smudged the writing.* ► blur, smear, streak **2** *The wall was smudged with heavy drops of rain.* ► mark, stain, blot, dirty

smug ADJECTIVE *He tried not to look smug when the results were announced.* ► self-satisfied, conceited, superior, self-righteous, complacent, priggish AN OPPOSITE IS humble

smutty ADJECTIVE *They had been telling each other smutty jokes.* ► dirty, rude, filthy, crude, indecent, coarse, obscene

snack NOUN *They had a quick snack before leaving.* ► bite, bite to eat, light meal, refreshments, (more informal) nibble

snag NOUN *The snag was that nobody wanted to make the first move.* ► disadvantage, catch, hitch, obstacle, problem, setback, complication, hindrance, difficulty, (informal) stumbling-block

snap VERB **1** *The rope snapped and the trailer slipped backwards.* ► break, split, separate **2** *The dogs were snapping at them.* ► snarl, growl, bark, bite **3** *"I wasn't there," Ginny snapped.* ► retort, bark, snarl, say angrily, rejoin **4** *After years of suffering she finally snapped.* ► crack, lose control, go to pieces, (more informal) lose your cool, (more informal) freak out

snap NOUN **1** *He closed the case with a snap.* ► click, crack **2** *There is often a cold snap just after Christmas.* ► spell, period, interval, stretch **3** *She showed us her holiday snaps.* ► photo, photograph, picture, image

snap ADJECTIVE *a snap decision* ► instant, on-the-spot, off-the-cuff, abrupt

snappy ADJECTIVE **1** *We need a snappy answer.* ► quick, prompt, brisk **2** *a snappy dresser* ► smart, stylish, fashionable, chic, (more informal) trendy **3** *The campaign needs a slogan that's snappy.* ► pithy, crisp, memorable

snarl VERB *"Leave me alone," he snarled.* ► growl, snap, bark, say angrily

snatch VERB *Thieves had snatched her handbag near the station.* ► steal, seize, grab, take, grasp, pluck, wrench away, wrest away

A
B
C
D
E
F
G
H
I
J
K
L
M
N
O
P
Q
R
S
T
U
V
W
X
Y
Z

sneak VERB sneaks, sneaking, sneaked **1** move quietly and secretly **2** (*informal*) take secretly ● *He sneaked a cookie from the tin.* **3** (*informal*) tell tales

sneak NOUN sneaks (*informal*) a telltale

sneaky ADJECTIVE dishonest or deceitful
▷ **sneakily** ADVERB **sneakiness** NOUN

sneer VERB sneers, sneering, sneered speak or behave in a scornful way
▷ **sneer** NOUN

sneeze VERB sneezes, sneezing, sneezed send out air suddenly and uncontrollably through the nose and mouth in order to get rid of something irritating the nostrils
▷ **sneeze** NOUN
[from Old English *fneosan*, imitating the sound]

sniff VERB sniffs, sniffing, sniffed **1** make a sound by drawing in air through the nose **2** smell something
▷ **sniff** NOUN **sniffer** NOUN

sniffle VERB sniffles, sniffling, sniffled **1** sniff slightly **2** keep on sniffing
▷ **sniffle** NOUN

snigger VERB sniggers, sniggering, sniggered giggle slyly
▷ **snigger** NOUN

snip VERB snips, snipping, snipped cut with scissors or shears in small quick cuts
▷ **snip** NOUN

snipe VERB snipes, sniping, sniped **1** shoot at people from a hiding place **2** attack someone with critical remarks
▷ **sniper** NOUN

snippet NOUN snippets a small piece of news, information, etc.

snivel VERB snivels, snivelling, snivelled cry or complain in a whining way

snob NOUN snobs a person who despises those who have not got wealth, power, or particular tastes or interests
▷ **snobbery** NOUN **snobbish** ADJECTIVE

snoop VERB snoops, snooping, snooped pry; ask or look around secretly
▷ **snooper** NOUN

snooze NOUN snoozes (*informal*) a short sleep
▷ **snooze** VERB

snore VERB snores, snoring, snored breathe very noisily while sleeping
▷ **snore** NOUN

snort VERB snorts, snorting, snorted make a rough sound by breathing forcefully through the nose
▷ **snort** NOUN

snout NOUN snouts an animal's projecting nose and jaws

snow NOUN frozen drops of water that fall from the sky in small white flakes

snow VERB snows, snowing, snowed come down as snow

Thesaurus

sneak VERB **1** *The boys sneaked in when nobody was around.* ► creep, steal, slink, slip, sidle

sneaking ADJECTIVE **1** *She has a sneaking fondness for Turkish delight.* ► secret, private, hidden, concealed, inward, unexpressed **2** *Claudia had a sneaking feeling that Myra could be right.* ► nagging, niggling, lingering, lurking

sneaky ADJECTIVE (*informal*) *a sneaky trick* ► sly, cunning, crafty, clever, wily, foxy, canny, knowing, shifty, sneaky, furtive, scheming, conniving OPPOSITES ARE honest, open

sneer VERB *sneer at It is easy to sneer at their first efforts.* ► scoff at, mock, scorn, ridicule, deride, jeer at, laugh at, look down on

snide ADJECTIVE *His snide remarks became irritating.* ► disparaging, deprecating, sarcastic, scornful, sneering, spiteful, mocking, nasty AN OPPOSITE IS complimentary

snigger VERB *They might snigger at him behind his back.* ► snicker, giggle, laugh, titter, chuckle, sneer

snip VERB **1** *She snipped the ends off the stalks.* ► cut, clip, trim, crop, chop, dock **2** *The inspector snipped our tickets.* ► clip, nick, notch, snick

snippet NOUN *snippets of information* ► piece, scrap, bit, morsel, fragment, particle, shred, snatch

snivel VERB *If you get caught, don't snivel about the consequences.* ► complain, grizzle, moan, grouse, whine, make a fuss, (*more informal*) whinge

snobbery NOUN *Forget the snobbery and mystique that is associated with choosing wine.* ► snobbishness, snootiness, arrogance, affectation, pretension, superciliousness

snobbish ADJECTIVE *She dislikes the snobbish and materialistic attitudes of many people.* ► snooty, snobby, pretentious, superior, condescending, (*more informal*) stuck up AN OPPOSITE IS unpretentious

snoop VERB *You shouldn't snoop into our affairs.* ► pry, meddle (in *or* with), nose, sneak, (*informal*) stick your nose (in *or* into)

snooze VERB (*informal*) *There he was snoozing by the fire.* ► sleep, doze, rest, nap, take a nap, catnap

be snowed under be overwhelmed with a mass of letters or work etc.

snowball NOUN snowballs a ball of snow pressed together for throwing

snowball VERB snowballs, snowballing, snowballed grow quickly in size or intensity

snowdrop NOUN snowdrops a small white flower that blooms in early spring

snowdrift NOUN snowdrifts a large heap or bank of snow piled up by the wind

snowflake NOUN snowflakes a flake of snow

snowshoe NOUN snowshoes a frame rather like a tennis racket for walking on soft snow

snowstorm NOUN snowstorms a storm in which snow falls

snub VERB snubs, snubbing, snubbed treat in a scornful or unfriendly way

snub NOUN snubs scornful or unfriendly treatment

snub-nosed ADJECTIVE having a short turned-up nose

snuff NOUN powdered tobacco for taking into the nose by sniffing

snuff VERB snuffs, snuffing, snuffed put out a candle by covering or pinching the flame
▷ **snuffer** NOUN

snuffle VERB snuffles, snuffling, snuffled sniff in a noisy way
▷ **snuffle** NOUN

snug ADJECTIVE snugger, snuggest **1** cosy **2** fitting closely
▷ **snugly** ADVERB **snugness** NOUN

snuggle VERB snuggles, snuggling, snuggled curl up in a warm comfortable place

so ADVERB **1** in this way; to such an extent • Why are you so cross? **2** very • Baseball is so boring. **3** also • I was wrong but so were you.
and so on and other similar things

or so or about that number
so far up to now
so long! (informal) goodbye
so what? (informal) that is not important

so CONJUNCTION for that reason • They threw me out, so I came here.

soak VERB soaks, soaking, soaked make a person or thing very wet
▷ **soak** NOUN
soak up take in a liquid in the way that a sponge does

soap NOUN soaps **1** a substance used with water for washing and cleaning things **2** a soap opera
▷ **soapy** ADJECTIVE

soap opera NOUN soap operas a television serial about the everyday lives of a group of people [originally sponsored by soap manufacturers]

soar VERB soars, soaring, soared **1** rise high in the air **2** increase by a lot • Prices are soaring.

sob VERB sobs, sobbing, sobbed make a gasping sound when crying
▷ **sob** NOUN
[probably from early Dutch]

sober ADJECTIVE **1** not drunk **2** serious and calm **3** (said about color) not bright or showy
▷ **soberly** ADVERB **sobriety** (so- bry- it- ee) NOUN

sober VERB sobers, sobering, sobered make or become sober

so-called ADJECTIVE named in what may be the wrong way • This so-called gentleman slammed the door.

soccer NOUN a game played between two teams using a round ball; the object is to propel the ball into a goal

sociable ADJECTIVE liking to be with other people; friendly
▷ **sociably** ADVERB **sociability** NOUN

Thesaurus

snub VERB They snubbed the hosts by leaving the party early. ► insult, affront, offend, rebuff, reject, scorn, (more informal) put down

snug ADJECTIVE **1** The cottage was warm and snug. ► cosy, comfortable, homely, cheerful, welcome, reassuring, (more informal) comfy OPPOSITES ARE forbidding, unwelcoming **2** She wore a snug long dress. ► close-fitting, tight, figure-hugging

soak VERB **1** You need to soak the beans overnight in liquid. ► immerse, steep, wet, submerge **2** Days of rain had soaked the ground. ► drench, saturate, swamp, inundate
soak into Ink had soaked into the paper. ► permeate, penetrate, saturate
soak up A sponge soaks up water. ► absorb, take up, draw up, suck up

soaking ADJECTIVES By the time they returned their clothes were soaking. ► drenched, soaked, wet

through, dripping, wringing, sodden, sopping AN OPPOSITE IS dry

soar VERB **1** Birds soared overhead. ► climb, ascend, wing, glide, drift **2** Prices have continued to soar. ► rise, escalate, rocket

sob VERB He turned his face to the wall and began to sob. ► weep, cry, shed tears, blubber, snivel

sober ADJECTIVE **1** Matt craved a drink but knew he had to stay sober. ► temperate, abstemious, not drunk AN OPPOSITE IS drunk **2** After sober reflection I decided to stay the way I was. ► serious, thoughtful, calm, levelheaded, sensible, somber, grave, earnest, down-to-earth, commonsensical AN OPPOSITE IS lighthearted **3** She dressed in a sober style. ► subdued, somber, austere, severe, staid AN OPPOSITE IS flamboyant

sociable ADJECTIVE She had been a lively, bright, and sociable girl before the accident. ► friendly,

a
b
c
d
e
f
g
h
i
j
k
l
m
n
o
p
q
r
s
t
u
v
w
x
y
z

A
B
C
D
E
F
G
H
I
J
K
L
M
N
O
P
Q
R
S
T
U
V
W
X
Y
Z

social ADJECTIVE **1** living in a community, not alone • *Bees are social insects.* **2** to do with life in a community • *social science* **3** concerned with people's welfare • *a social worker* **4** helping people to meet each other • *a social club* **5** sociable
▷ **socially** ADVERB
[from Latin *sociare* = unite, associate]

socialism NOUN a political system where wealth is shared equally between people, and the main industries and trade, etc., are controlled by the government COMPARE capitalism

socialist NOUN socialists a person who believes in socialism

social security NOUN money and other assistance provided by the government for those in need through being unemployed, ill, disabled, or elderly

social services PLURAL NOUN welfare services provided by the government, including schools, hospitals, and pensions

society NOUN societies **1** a community; people living together in a group or nation • *We live in a multiracial society.* **2** a group of people organized for a particular purpose • *the school dramatic society* **3** company or companionship • *We enjoy the society of our friends.*

sock NOUN socks a piece of clothing that covers your foot and the lower part of your leg [from Old English]

socket NOUN sockets **1** a hollow into which something fits • *a tooth socket* **2** a device into which an electric plug or bulb is put to make a connection

soda water NOUN water made fizzy with carbon dioxide, used in drinks

sodden ADJECTIVE made very wet

sodium NOUN a soft white metal

sodium bicarbonate NOUN a soluble white powder used in fire extinguishers and fizzy drinks, and to make cakes rise

sofa NOUN sofas a long soft seat with a back and arms [from Arabic *suffa* = long stone bench]

soft ADJECTIVE **1** not hard or firm; easily pressed **2** smooth, not rough or stiff **3** gentle; not loud **4** (said about drugs) not likely to be addictive
▷ **softly** ADVERB **softness** NOUN

soft drink NOUN soft drinks a cold drink that is not alcoholic

soften VERB softens, softening, softened make or become soft or softer
▷ **softener** NOUN

software NOUN (in computing) programs and data, which are not part of the machinery of a computer COMPARE hardware

soggy ADJECTIVE soggier, soggiest very wet and heavy • *soggy ground* [from a dialect word *sog* = swamp]

Thesaurus

outgoing, companionable, convivial, gregarious, clubbable, cordial, affable, amicable OPPOSITES ARE unsociable, unfriendly

social ADJECTIVE **1** *Ants are social creatures.* ► gregarious, organized, civilized, collaborative AN OPPOSITE IS solitary **2** *a range of cultural and social interests* ► communal, community, public, group AN OPPOSITE IS individual

social NOUN *The club has a social every month.* ► party, gathering, function

society NOUN **1** *In our society, men historically have occupied the positions of power.* ► civilization, nation, culture, community **2** *We must remember our position in society.* ► the community, the population, the public **3** *They enjoy the society of their friends.* ► company, fellowship, friendship, companionship, camaraderie **4** *He joined a local history society.* ► association, club, group, organization, circle, fraternity

soft ADJECTIVE **1** *a soft pillow* ► supple, pliable, springy, yielding, flexible, malleable, squashy AN OPPOSITE IS hard **2** *soft ground* ► squelchy,

swampy, marshy, boggy, heavy AN OPPOSITE IS firm **3** *soft music* ► gentle, soothing, melodious AN OPPOSITE IS harsh **4** *a soft voice* ► quiet, low, faint, muted, subdued AN OPPOSITE IS loud **5** *soft colors* ► pale, pastel, muted, subtle OPPOSITES ARE bright, lurid **6** *a soft fabric* ► velvety, silky, smooth, downy, fleecy **7** *Some teachers are too soft with their pupils.* ► lenient, easygoing, indulgent, permissive, forbearing OPPOSITES ARE strict, severe

soften VERB **1** *Lower interest rates might soften the effect of the tax increases.* ► moderate, temper, alleviate, ease, relieve, assuage AN OPPOSITE IS intensify **2** *The butter softened in the warmth of the kitchen.* ► melt, liquefy, go soft AN OPPOSITE IS harden

softhearted ADJECTIVE *You were always too soft-hearted to tell them what you thought.* ► kind, kindhearted, gentle, easygoing, generous, charitable

soggy ADJECTIVE *a pile of soggy clothes* ► sodden, sopping, saturated, soaked, drenched, wet through AN OPPOSITE IS dry

soil NOUN soils **1** the loose earth in which plants grow **2** territory • *on British soil* [from early French]

solar panel NOUN solar panels a panel designed to catch the sun's rays and use their energy for heating or to make electricity

solar power NOUN electricity or other forms of power derived from the sun's rays

solar system NOUN the sun and the planets that revolve round it

soldier NOUN soldiers a member of an army

sole NOUN soles **1** the bottom surface of a foot or shoe **2** a flat edible sea fish

sole VERB soles, soling, soled put a sole on a shoe

sole ADJECTIVE single; only • *She was the sole survivor.*
▷ **solely** ADVERB

solemn ADJECTIVE **1** not smiling or cheerful **2** dignified or formal
▷ **solemnly** ADVERB **solemnity** NOUN

solicit VERB solicits, soliciting, solicited ask for or try to obtain • *I've been soliciting opinions from rail users.*

solicitor NOUN solicitors a lawyer who advises clients, prepares legal documents, etc.

solid ADJECTIVE **1** not hollow; with no space inside **2** keeping its shape; not liquid or gas **3** continuous • *for two solid hours* **4** firm or

strongly made; not flimsy • *a solid foundation* **5** showing solidarity; unanimous
▷ **solidly** ADVERB **solidity** NOUN

solid NOUN solids **1** a solid thing **2** a shape that has three dimensions (length, width, and height or depth)

solids PLURAL NOUN solid food; food that is not liquid • *Is your baby eating solids yet?*

soliloquy (sol- **il**- ok- wee) NOUN soliloquies a speech in which a person speaks his or her thoughts aloud when alone or without addressing anyone
▷ **soliloquize** VERB
[from Latin *solus* = alone + *loqui* = speak]

solitary ADJECTIVE **1** alone, without companions **2** single • *a solitary example*

solitary confinement NOUN a form of punishment in which a prisoner is kept alone in a cell and not allowed to talk to others

solo NOUN solos something sung, played, danced, or done by one person
▷ **solo** ADJECTIVE, ADVERB **soloist** NOUN

soluble ADJECTIVE **1** able to be dissolved **2** able to be solved
▷ **solubility** NOUN

solution NOUN solutions **1** a liquid in which something is dissolved **2** the answer to a problem or puzzle

solve VERB solves, solving, solved find the answer to a problem or puzzle [from Latin *solvere* = unfasten]

Thesaurus

soil NOUN **1** *The tiny eggs can also be picked up in garden soil.* ► earth, loam, ground, humus, topsoil **2** *English troops withdrew from Scottish soil.* ► territory, land, space, jurisdiction

soil VERB *Try not to soil your clothes.* ► dirty, make dirty, stain, tarnish, contaminate, defile, pollute

soldier NOUN *The town was surrounded by enemy soldiers.* ► serviceman or servicewoman, fighting man or woman, trooper RELATED ADJECTIVE ► military

sole ADJECTIVE *The sole intention is to raise money.* ► one, only, single, solitary, exclusive, singular, individual, unique

solemn ADJECTIVE **1** *He was tall with a thin, solemn face.* ► serious, earnest, somber, staid, sober, thoughtful, reverential, glum, grave, grim AN OPPOSITE IS cheerful **2** *The ceremony was a solemn occasion.* ► dignified, formal, grand, stately, majestic, impressive, pompous, awe-inspiring, ceremonious, imposing AN OPPOSITE IS frivolous

solid ADJECTIVE **1** *The floor was of solid concrete. The metal below him was quite solid.* ► hard, firm, dense, rigid, fixed, unyielding OPPOSITES ARE liquid, gaseous, hollow **2** *a solid sort of person* ► dependable, reliable, trustworthy,

honest, upright, levelheaded OPPOSITES ARE unreliable, dishonest **3** *The police needed solid evidence.* ► real, genuine, substantial **4** *a ring of solid gold* ► pure, genuine, unalloyed AN OPPOSITE IS alloyed **5** *He can expect solid support from a third of the delegates.* ► firm, united, unanimous AN OPPOSITE IS divided

solidify VERB *As the liquid cools it rapidly solidifies.* ► harden, set, thicken, stiffen, congeal, clot, coagulate AN OPPOSITE IS liquefy

solitary ADJECTIVE **1** *He leads a solitary existence.* ► lonely, unsociable, friendless, isolated, cloistered, companionless AN OPPOSITE IS sociable **2** *a solitary survivor* ► single, sole, one, only **3** *a few solitary villages dotted on the landscape* ► isolated, out-of-the-way, remote, secluded, hidden, sequestered, unfrequented, desolate

solution NOUN **1** *There is no easy solution to the problem.* ► answer, resolution, key, solving (of), explanation (of) **2** *a solution of ammonia in water* ► mixture, mix, blend, compound

solve VERB *This will solve our immediate problem.* ► resolve, answer, settle, sort out, put right, deal with

A
B
C
D
E
F
G
H
I
J
K
L
M
N
O
P
Q
R
S
T
U
V
W
X
Y
Z

solvent ADJECTIVE **1** having enough money to pay all your debts **2** able to dissolve another substance
▷ **solvency** NOUN

solvent NOUN solvents a liquid used for dissolving something

somber ADJECTIVE dark and gloomy

some ADJECTIVE **1** a few; a little • *some apples* • *some money* **2** an unknown person or thing • *Some fool left the door open.* **3** about • *We waited some 20 minutes.*
sometime at some point in time • *You must come around for a meal sometime.*

some PRONOUN a certain number or amount that is less than the whole • *Some of them were late.*

somebody PRONOUN **1** some person **2** an important or impressive person

somehow ADVERB in some way

someone PRONOUN somebody

somersault NOUN somersaults a movement in which you turn head over heels before landing on your feet
▷ **somersault** VERB
[from Latin *supra* = above + *saltus* = a leap]

something NOUN some thing; a thing which you cannot or do not want to name
something like 1 rather like • *It's something like a rabbit.* **2** approximately • *It cost something like $10.*

sometimes ADVERB at some times but not always • *We sometimes walk to school.*

somewhat ADVERB to some extent • *He was somewhat annoyed.*

somewhere ADVERB in or to some place

son NOUN sons a boy or man who is someone's child

sonata NOUN sonatas a piece of music for one instrument or two, in several movements

song NOUN songs **1** a tune for singing **2** singing • *He burst into song.*
a song and dance (*informal*) a great fuss
for a song bought or sold very cheaply

sonic boom NOUN sonic booms a loud noise caused by the shock wave of an aircraft traveling faster than the speed of sound

son-in-law NOUN sons-in-law a daughter's husband

sonnet NOUN sonnets a kind of poem with 14 lines [from Italian *sonetto* = a little sound]

soon ADVERB **1** in a short time from now **2** not long after something
as soon as willingly • *I'd just as soon stay here.*
as soon as at the moment that
sooner or later at some time in the future

soot NOUN the black powder left by smoke in a chimney or on a building, etc.
▷ **sooty** ADJECTIVE

soothe VERB soothes, soothing, soothed **1** calm or comfort **2** ease pain or distress
▷ **soothingly** ADVERB

sop VERB sops, sopping, sopped
sop up soak up liquid like a sponge

sophisticated ADJECTIVE **1** having refined tastes or experienced about the world **2** complicated • *a sophisticated machine*
▷ **sophistication** NOUN

sopping ADJECTIVE very wet; drenched

soppy ADJECTIVE **1** very wet **2** (*informal*) sentimental in a silly way

soprano NOUN sopranos a woman, girl, or boy with a high singing voice

sorcerer NOUN sorcerers a person who can perform magic
▷ **sorceress** NOUN **sorcery** NOUN

Thesaurus

somber ADJECTIVE **1** *somber colors* ► dark, dull, sober, drab, dreary, gloomy AN OPPOSITE IS cheerful **2** *His face bore a somber expression.* ► solemn, thoughtful, reverential, glum, grave

sometimes ADVERB *He sometimes seems preoccupied.* ► occasionally, from time to time, at times, now and then, now and again

song NOUN *She sang an old song.* ► air, strain, melody, tune, number

soon ADVERB *We'll be there soon.* ► shortly, presently, quickly, before long, in a while, in a moment *or* minute

soothe VERB *She patted him gently to soothe him.* ► calm, comfort, console, pacify, mollify, settle, subdue, quiet, still OPPOSITES ARE agitate, disturb

soothing ADJECTIVE **1** *a soothing ointment* ► palliative, comforting, emollient, balmy,

healing, mild **2** *soothing words* ► calming, relaxing, restful, gentle, peaceful, pleasant

sophisticated ADJECTIVE **1** *sophisticated techniques for crime detection* ► advanced, developed, complex, elaborate **2** *a sophisticated person* ► urbane, worldly, experienced, cultivated, refined

soppy ADJECTIVE (*informal*) **1** *a soppy story* ► sentimental, mawkish, maudlin, sugary, corny **2** *a soppy child* ► silly, feeble, soft, foolish

sorcerer *or* **sorceress** NOUN *Come and see the sorcerer's workshop.* ► wizard *or* witch, magician, conjuror, enchanter *or* enchantress, warlock, witch doctor

sorcery NOUN *She was charged with sorcery by his successor, Richard III, and made to do public penance.* ► magic *or* black magic, charms, witchcraft, wizardry, conjuring, magic, voodoo

sordid ADJECTIVE **1** dirty and nasty **2** dishonorable; selfish and mercenary • *sordid motives*
▷ **sordidly** ADVERB **sordidness** NOUN

sore ADJECTIVE **1** painful or smarting **2** (*informal*) annoyed or offended **3** serious or distressing • *in sore need*
▷ **soreness** NOUN

sore NOUN **sores** a sore place

sorrow NOUN **sorrows 1** unhappiness or regret caused by loss or disappointment **2** something that causes this
▷ **sorrowful** ADJECTIVE **sorrowfully** ADVERB

sorry ADJECTIVE **sorrier, sorriest 1** feeling regret • *I'm sorry I forgot your birthday.* **2** feeling pity or sympathy **3** wretched • *His clothes were in a sorry state.*

sort NOUN **sorts** a group of things or people that are similar; a kind or variety
out of sorts slightly unwell or depressed
sort of (*informal*) rather; to some extent • *I sort of expected it.*
USAGE Correct use is *this sort of thing* or *these sorts of things* (not 'these sort of things').

sort VERB **sorts, sorting, sorted** arrange things in groups according to their size, kind, etc.
▷ **sorter** NOUN
sort out 1 deal with and solve a problem or difficulty **2** (*informal*) deal with and punish someone

sortie NOUN **sorties 1** an attack by troops coming out of a besieged place **2** an attacking expedition by a military aircraft [from French *sortir* = go out]

SOS NOUN **SOSs** an urgent appeal for help [the international Morse code signal of extreme distress, chosen because it is easy to recognize, but often said to stand for "Save Our Souls"]

sought *past tense* of seek

soul NOUN **souls 1** the invisible part of a person that is believed to go on living after the body has died **2** a person's mind and emotions etc. **3** a person • *There isn't a soul around.* **4** a kind of popular music that originated in gospel music

sound NOUN **sounds 1** vibrations that travel through the air and can be detected by the ear; the sensation they produce **2** sound reproduced in a film etc. **3** a mental impression • *We don't like the sound of his plans.*

sound[1] VERB **sounds, sounding, sounded 1** produce or cause to produce a sound **2** give an impression when heard • *He sounds angry.* **3** test by noting the sounds heard • *A doctor sounds a patient's lungs with a stethoscope.* [from Latin *sonus*]

sound[2] VERB **sounds, sounding, sounded** test the depth of water beneath a ship
sound out try to find out what a person thinks or feels about something
[from Latin *sub* = under + *unda* = a wave]

Thesaurus

sore ADJECTIVE **1** *a sore arm* ► painful, hurting, aching, smarting, tender, stinging, burning, injured, wounded **2** (*informal*) *They were sore at us for leaving them like that.* ► annoyed, angry, upset, aggrieved, peeved (with), (*more informal*) miffed (with)

sore NOUN *There were sores all down his leg.*
► swelling, inflammation, abscess, laceration, contusion, lesion, boil, carbuncle, ulcer

sorrow NOUN **1** *The loss caused him great sorrow.*
► sadness, unhappiness, regret, misery, grief, distress, anguish, heartbreak, tribulation AN OPPOSITE IS joy **2** *He related all the sorrows of his life.* ► trouble, difficulty, affliction, problem

sorrowful ADJECTIVE *She gave a sorrowful smile.*
► sad, unhappy, dejected, miserable, despondent, disconsolate OPPOSITES ARE happy, cheerful

sorry ADJECTIVE **1** *He called his parents to say he was sorry for what he had done.* ► apologetic, ashamed (of), penitent, regretful, remorseful, repentant, conscience-stricken, contrite **2** *He felt rather sorry for his father.* ► sympathetic, compassionate, full of pity, pitying, understanding **3** *The house was in a sorry state*

► pitiful, pitiable, wretched, unfortunate, pathetic, dismal

sort NOUN **1** *What sort of films do you like to see?*
► type, kind, variety, category, class, genre, style, nature

sort VERB *The eggs are sorted by size and color.*
► class, grade, group, categorize, classify, divide
sort out *It took a long time to sort out the difficulties.* ► resolve, settle, put right, deal with

soul NOUN **1** *the immortality of the soul* ► psyche, spirit, inner being **2** (*informal*) *The poor soul had to wait for hours to be seen.* ► person, individual, creature

sound NOUN *They could hear the sound of traffic in the street.* ► noise, din, hubbub, racket, tone RELATED ADJECTIVES ► aural, acoustic, sonic

sound VERB **1** *A signal sounded.* ► be heard, become audible, resound, resonate, reverberate, make a noise **2** *Opening a door or window will sound the alarm.* ► set off, operate, blast **3** *He sounded angry.* ► seem, appear, give the impression of being **4** *You can sound the depth of a river with a pole.* ► measure, gauge, plumb, determine, probe, test, try

A
B
C
D
E
F
G
H
I
J
K
L
M
N
O
P
Q
R
S
T
U
V
W
X
Y
Z

sound ADJECTIVE **1** in good condition; not damaged **2** healthy; not diseased **3** reasonable or correct • *His ideas are sound.* **4** reliable or secure • *a sound investment* **5** thorough or deep • *a sound sleep*
▷ **soundly** ADVERB **soundness** NOUN
[from Old English *gesund* = healthy]

sound barrier NOUN the resistance of the air to objects moving at speeds near the speed of sound

sound bite NOUN sound bites a short piece taken from a speech or statement because it has a special interest

sound effects PLURAL NOUN sounds produced artificially to make a play, film, etc., seem more realistic

sound track NOUN sound tracks the sound that goes with a cinema film

soup NOUN soups liquid food made from stewed bones, meat, fish, vegetables, etc.
in the soup (*informal*) in trouble
[from early French *soupe* = broth poured on bread, from Latin *suppa*]

sour ADJECTIVE **1** tasting sharp like unripe fruit **2** stale and unpleasant, not fresh • *sour milk* **3** bad-tempered
▷ **sourly** ADVERB **sourness** NOUN

source NOUN sources **1** the place from which something comes **2** the starting point of a river

sour grapes PLURAL NOUN pretending that something you want is no good because you know you cannot have it

south NOUN **1** the direction to the right of a person who faces east **2** the southern part of a country, city, etc.

south ADJECTIVE, ADVERB towards or in the south
▷ **southerly** (su*th*- er- lee) ADJECTIVE **southern** ADJECTIVE **southerner** NOUN **southernmost** ADJECTIVE

southeast NOUN, ADJECTIVE, & ADVERB midway between south and east
▷ **southeasterly** ADJECTIVE **southeastern** ADJECTIVE

southward ADJECTIVE, ADVERB towards the south
▷ **southwards** ADVERB

southwest NOUN, ADJECTIVE, & ADVERB midway between south and west
▷ **southwesterly** ADJECTIVE **southwestern** ADJECTIVE

souvenir (soo- ven- eer) NOUN souvenirs something that you keep to remind you of a person, place, or event

sovereign NOUN sovereigns **1** a king or queen who is the ruler of a country; a monarch **2** an old British gold coin, originally worth £1

sow (rhymes with *go*) VERB sows, sowing, sowed, sown or sowed **1** put seeds into the ground so that they will grow into plants **2** cause feelings or ideas to develop • *Her words sowed doubt in my mind.*
▷ **sower** NOUN
[from Old English *sawan*]
USAGE Do not confuse with sew.

sow (rhymes with *cow*) NOUN sows a female pig
[from Old English *sugu*]

soy sauce or **soya sauce** NOUN a Chinese or Japanese sauce made from fermented soya beans [from Chinese words meaning "salted beans" and "oil"]

space NOUN spaces **1** the whole area outside the earth, where the stars and planets are **2** an area or volume • *This table takes too much space.* **3** an empty area; a gap **4** an interval of time • *within the space of an hour*

space VERB spaces, spacing, spaced arrange things with spaces between • *Space them out.*

spacecraft NOUN spacecraft a vehicle for traveling in outer space

Thesaurus

sound out *The survey will sound out public opinion.* ► canvass, measure, gauge, test, investigate

sound ADJECTIVE **1** *sound advice* ► valid, well-founded, reasonable, dependable AN OPPOSITE IS unsound **2** *The foundations seem sound.* ► firm, sturdy, solid, well built, substantial, stable AN OPPOSITE IS unsafe **3** *a sound investment* ► wise, judicious, well chosen AN OPPOSITE IS unwise **4** *She fell into a sound sleep.* ► deep, prolonged, unbroken, uninterrupted OPPOSITES ARE light, shallow

sour ADJECTIVE **1** *a sour taste* ► sharp, acid, tart, bitter **2** *a sour look* ► embittered, resentful, peevish, acrimonious, disagreeable

source NOUN **1** *the source of the problem* ► origin, originator, initiator, author, cause, fount, root, derivation, starting point **2** *the source of the river* ► spring, origin, head, beginning, start

sow VERB *Sow the seeds in parallel rows.* ► plant, scatter, spread, distribute, put in the ground

space NOUN **1** *A minibus would have space for ten people.* ► room, capacity, accommodation, seating, seats, volume **2** *The city has very few green spaces left.* ► area, stretch, expanse **3** *There are spaces between the houses.* ► gap, interval, opening, aperture

spaceship NOUN spaceships a spacecraft, especially one carrying people

space shuttle NOUN space shuttles a spacecraft for repeated use to and from outer space

space station NOUN space stations a satellite that orbits the earth and is used as a base by scientists and astronauts

spacious ADJECTIVE providing a lot of space; roomy
▷ spaciousness NOUN

spade¹ NOUN spades a tool with a long handle and a wide blade for digging

spade² NOUN spades a playing card with black shapes like upside-down hearts on it, each with a short stem

spaghetti NOUN pasta made in long thin sticks [from Italian, = little strings]

span NOUN spans **1** the length from end to end or across something **2** the part between two uprights of an arch or bridge **3** the length of a period of time **4** the distance from the tip of the thumb to the tip of the little finger when the hand is spread out

span VERB spans, spanning, spanned reach from one side or end to the other ● A bridge spans the river.

spaniel NOUN spaniels a kind of dog with long ears and silky fur [from early French espaigneul = Spanish (because the dog originally came from Spain)]

spank VERB spanks, spanking, spanked smack a person several times on the backside as a punishment

spanner NOUN spanners a tool for gripping and turning the nut on a bolt, etc. [from German spannen = tighten]

spar NOUN spars a strong pole used for a mast or boom etc. on a ship [from Old Norse]

spar VERB spars, sparring, sparred **1** practise boxing **2** quarrel or argue [from Old English]

spare VERB spares, sparing, spared **1** afford to give something or do without it ● Can you spare a moment? **2** be merciful toward someone; not hurt or harm a person or thing **3** avoid making a person suffer something ● Spare me the details. **4** use or treat economically ● No expense will be spared.
to spare left over without being needed ● We arrived with five minutes to spare.

spare ADJECTIVE **1** not used but kept ready in case it is needed; extra ● a spare wheel **2** thin; lean
▷ sparely ADVERB spareness NOUN
go spare (slang) become very annoyed

spare time NOUN time not needed for work

sparing (spair- ing) ADJECTIVE careful or economical; not wasteful
▷ sparingly ADVERB

spark NOUN sparks **1** a tiny glowing particle **2** a flash produced electrically **3** a trace ● a spark of hope

spark VERB sparks, sparking, sparked give off a spark or sparks

sparkle VERB sparkles, sparkling, sparkled **1** shine with tiny flashes of light **2** show brilliant wit or liveliness
▷ sparkle NOUN

sparkler NOUN sparklers a handheld firework that gives off sparks

Thesaurus

spacious ADJECTIVE A spacious hallway leads to the living rooms. ► roomy, sizable, ample, capacious, commodious, extensive, generous, large, big OPPOSITES ARE cramped, poky

span VERB An old iron bridge spans the river. ► cross, straddle, bridge, pass over, reach over, stretch over, extend across, traverse, arch over

spank VERB She warned him that next time she would spank him. ► smack, slap, chastise, give someone a spanking

spare VERB **1** We can't spare all that money. ► afford, manage, part with, do without **2** The captors would not spare any of the hostages. ► pardon, show mercy to, let off, be lenient with, leave unharmed or unhurt

spare ADJECTIVE **1** Our neighbors have a spare set of house keys. ► extra, additional, supplementary, alternative, backup **2** Do you have any spare paper? ► surplus, leftover, odd, unwanted, superfluous, unused, unnecessary **3** a spare figure ► slender, slim, lean, slight,

thin AN OPPOSITE IS fat

go spare (informal) They'll go spare if they find out. ► lose your temper, be or become angry, go wild, (informal) hit the roof, (informal) go bananas, (informal) go ballistic

spark NOUN a spark of light ► flash, gleam, glint, flicker, sparkle, twinkle

spark VERB The comments sparked a furious row. ► cause, give rise to, bring about, occasion, set off, stir up, provoke, stimulate, precipitate

sparkle VERB Lights sparkled in the distance. ► glitter, glint, glisten, glimmer, twinkle, gleam, shimmer

sparkling ADJECTIVE **1** sparkling jewelry ► glittering, glinting, glistening, twinkling, flashing, scintillating, brilliant, shining, shiny AN OPPOSITE IS dull **2** a sparkling drink ► effervescent, fizzy, bubbly, bubbling, aerated, carbonated, foaming OPPOSITES ARE still, flat

a
b
c
d
e
f
g
h
i
j
k
l
m
n
o
p
q
r
s
t
u
v
w
x
y
z

spark plug NOUN spark plugs a device that makes a spark to ignite the fuel in an engine

sparrow NOUN sparrows a small brown bird

sparse ADJECTIVE thinly scattered; not numerous • *a sparse population*
▷ **sparsely** ADVERB **sparseness** NOUN

spasm NOUN spasms **1** a sudden involuntary movement of a muscle **2** a sudden brief spell of activity etc. [from Greek *spasmos*, from *span* = to pull]

spasmodic ADJECTIVE happening or done at irregular intervals
▷ **spasmodically** ADVERB

spastic NOUN spastics (*offensive*) a person suffering from spasms of the muscles and jerky movements, especially caused by cerebral palsy

spat past tense of spit

spate NOUN spates a sudden flood or rush

spatter VERB spatters, spattering, spattered **1** scatter in small drops **2** splash • *spattered with mud*
▷ **spatter** NOUN

spawn NOUN **1** the eggs of fish, frogs, toads, or shellfish **2** the threadlike matter from which fungi grow

spawn VERB spawns, spawning, spawned **1** produce spawn **2** be produced from spawn **3** produce something in great quantities

speak VERB speaks, speaking, spoke, spoken **1** say something; talk **2** be able to talk in a foreign language • *Do you speak French?*
speak up 1 speak more loudly **2** give your opinion

speaker NOUN speakers **1** a person who is speaking **2** someone who makes a speech **3** a loudspeaker
the Speaker the person who controls the debates in the House of Representatives or a similar assembly

spear NOUN spears a weapon for throwing or stabbing, with a long shaft and a pointed tip

special ADJECTIVE **1** not ordinary or usual; exceptional • *a special occasion;* • *Take special care of it* **2** meant for a particular person or purpose • *You need a special tool for this job.*

special effects PLURAL NOUN illusions created for movies or television by using props, trick photography, or computer images

specialist NOUN specialists an expert in one subject • *a skin specialist*

speciality NOUN specialities **1** something in which a person specializes **2** a special product, especially a food

specialize VERB specializes, specializing, specialized give particular attention or study to one subject or thing • *She specialized in biology.*
▷ **specialization** NOUN

special needs PLURAL NOUN educational needs resulting from special reasons such as learning difficulties or physical disability

species (spee-shiz) NOUN species a group of animals or plants that are very similar

specific ADJECTIVE definite or precise; of or for a particular thing • *The money was given for a specific purpose.*
▷ **specifically** ADVERB

specific gravity NOUN the weight of something as compared with the same volume of water or air

Thesaurus

sparse ADJECTIVE *an area of sparse vegetation*
▶ meagre, sparse, scarce, scant, paltry, minimal, negligible AN OPPOSITE IS dense

spartan ADJECTIVE *They led a spartan life.*
▶ austere, harsh, frugal, ascetic, arduous, stringent, strict, stern OPPOSITES ARE luxurious, opulent

spasm NOUN **1** *a spasm of coughing* ▶ fit, attack, outbreak, eruption, seizure **2** *a muscular spasm* ▶ convulsion, contraction, twitch

spasmodic ADJECTIVE *The night was interrupted by spasmodic gunfire.* ▶ intermittent, fitful, sporadic, occasional, irregular, erratic OPPOSITES ARE regular, continuous

spate NOUN *a spate of burglaries* ▶ series, succession, run, string, outbreak, wave AN OPPOSITE IS trickle

speak VERB **1** *She left before anyone could speak. He refused to speak about the incident.* ▶ talk, say anything, converse, communicate **2** *We must speak the truth.* ▶ tell, utter, express, declare,

voice **3** *The chairman spoke for an hour.*
▶ declaim, lecture, give a speech, hold forth **4** *speak to She promised to speak to them soon. He did not speak to her for six months after that.*
▶ communicate with, say something or anything, converse with, contact

special ADJECTIVE **1** *a special occasion*
▶ important, exceptional, significant, particular, remarkable, extraordinary **2** *a perfume with a special smell* ▶ distinct, distinctive, characteristic, peculiar, unique, exclusive

specific ADJECTIVE *There is no specific evidence to support the allegations.* ▶ definite, particular, explicit, precise, special, clear-cut, detailed, exact AN OPPOSITE IS general

specify VERB *He would not specify the source of his information.* ▶ name, identify, state, mention, spell out, indicate, designate, detail, be specific about

specimen NOUN specimens **1** a sample **2** an example • *a fine specimen of an oak tree*

speck NOUN specks a small spot or particle

speckle NOUN speckles a small spot or mark
▷ **speckled** ADJECTIVE

spectacle NOUN spectacles **1** an impressive sight or display **2** a ridiculous sight

spectacles PLURAL NOUN a pair of glasses
▷ **spectacled** ADJECTIVE

spectacular ADJECTIVE impressive or striking

spectator NOUN spectators a person who watches a game, show, incident, etc. [from Latin *spectare* = to look at]

specter NOUN specters a ghost
▷ **spectral** ADJECTIVE

spectrum NOUN spectra **1** the bands of colors seen in a rainbow **2** a wide range of things, ideas, etc.

speculate VERB speculates, speculating, speculated **1** form opinions without having any definite evidence **2** invest in stocks, property, etc., in the hope of making a profit but with the risk of loss
▷ **speculation** NOUN **speculator** NOUN **speculative** ADJECTIVE

sped *past tense* of speed

speech NOUN speeches **1** the action or power of speaking **2** a talk to an audience **3** a group of lines spoken by a character in a play

speechless ADJECTIVE unable to speak because of great emotion

speed NOUN speeds **1** a measure of the time in which something moves or happens **2** quickness or swiftness
at speed quickly

speed VERB speeds, speeding, sped (in sense 3 speeded) **1** go quickly • *The train sped by.* **2** make or become quicker • *This will speed things up.* **3** drive faster than the legal limit

speed camera NOUN speed cameras a camera by the side of a road which automatically photographs any vehicle which is going too fast

speed limit NOUN speed limits the maximum speed at which vehicles may legally travel on a particular road

speedometer NOUN speedometers a device in a vehicle, showing its speed

speedy ADJECTIVE speedier, speediest quick or swift
▷ **speedily** ADVERB

Thesaurus

specimen NOUN *They asked for a specimen of his handwriting.* ► sample, illustration, example, demonstration, instance, model, pattern, copy

speck NOUN *a speck of dust* ► particle, bit, fleck, grain, speckle, spot, trace, dot

speckled ADJECTIVE *a speckled brown egg* ► flecked, speckly, spotted, freckly, freckled, mottled

spectacle NOUN **1** *The parade proved quite a spectacle.* ► display, show, performance, pageant, extravaganza, exhibition **2** *The group did look quite an odd spectacle.* ► sight, scene, vision, picture **3** *I think we're making a spectacle of ourselves.* ► exhibition, laughing stock, fool

spectacular ADJECTIVE *a spectacular display* ► magnificent, splendid, impressive, sensational, dazzling, showy, stunning, outstanding

spectator NOUN *Spectators lined the streets.* ► onlooker, watcher, viewer, observer, bystander

speculate VERB **1** *His colleagues tended to speculate about his private life.* ► conjecture, theorize, wonder, hypothesize, make guesses, meditate, reflect, muse **2** *People have been speculating on the stock exchange.* ► gamble, venture, hazard

speculative ADJECTIVE **1** *Their conclusions are merely speculative.* ► conjectural, theoretical, hypothetical, notional, tentative **2** *a series of speculative investments* ► risky, hazardous, unpredictable, unsafe, unsound

speech NOUN **1** *the power of speech* ► speaking, talking, verbal communication RELATED ADJECTIVES ► oral, phonetic **2** *His speech was slurred.* ► diction, articulation, enunciation, utterance, elocution, delivery **3** *an after-dinner speech* ► talk, address, lecture, oration, discourse

speechless ADJECTIVE *She was speechless with rage.* ► dumbfounded, dumbstruck, thunderstruck, aghast, tongue-tied OPPOSITES ARE talkative, verbose

speed NOUN **1** *It's important to check your speed on this piece of road.* ► velocity, pace, rate, tempo **2** *They completed the work with amazing speed.* ► rapidity, swiftness, alacrity, celerity, quickness, expeditiousness, promptness, fleetness, dispatch

speed VERB **1** *We sped back home* ► hurry, hasten, rush, dash, chase, hurtle, hustle, move quickly, (*more informal*) belt OPPOSITES ARE go slowly, amble **2** *He was over the limit and speeding.* ► break the speed limit, go or drive too fast
speed up *He called to them to speed up.* ► hurry up, go faster, increase speed, get a move on, quicken, accelerate

A
B
C
D
E
F
G
H
I
J
K
L
M
N
O
P
Q
R
S
T
U
V
W
X
Y
Z

spell[1] NOUN **spells** a saying or action, etc., supposed to have magical power [from Old English *spel* = speech, story]

spell[2] NOUN **spells** 1 a period of time 2 a period spent doing a certain task or activity, etc. [from Old English *spelian* = take someone's place, take over a task]

spell VERB **spells, spelling, spelled** 1 put letters in the right order to make a word or words 2 (said about letters) form a word • *C-A-T spells "cat."* 3 have as a result • *Wet weather spells ruin for crops.*
▷ **speller** NOUN
[from early French]

spellbound ADJECTIVE entranced as if by a magic spell

spend VERB **spends, spending, spent** 1 use money to pay for things 2 use up • *Don't spend too much time on it.* 3 pass time • *We spent a holiday in Spain.*

sperm NOUN **sperms** or **sperm** the male cell that fuses with an ovum to fertilize it [from Greek *sperma* = seed]

sphere NOUN **spheres** 1 a perfectly round solid shape; the shape of a ball 2 a field of action or interest, etc. • *That country is in Russia's sphere of influence.*
▷ **spherical** ADJECTIVE

sphinx NOUN **sphinxes** a stone statue with the body of a lion and a human head, especially the huge one (almost 5,000 years old) in Egypt [named after the Sphinx in Greek mythology, a winged creature with a woman's head and a lion's body]

spice NOUN **spices** 1 a strong-tasting substance used to flavor food, often made from dried parts of plants 2 something that adds interest or excitement • *Variety is the spice of life.*
▷ **spicy** ADJECTIVE

spick and span ADJECTIVE neat and clean [*span* is from Old Norse; *spick* is probably from early Dutch]

spider NOUN **spiders** a small animal with eight legs that spins webs to catch insects on which it feeds [from Old English *spithra* = spinner]

spike NOUN **spikes** a pointed piece of metal; a sharp point
▷ **spiky** ADJECTIVE

spill VERB **spills, spilling, spilled** 1 let something fall out of a container • *Try not to spill your drink.* 2 become spilled • *The coins came spilling out.*
▷ **spillage** NOUN

spin VERB **spins, spinning, spun** 1 turn around and around quickly 2 make raw wool or cotton into threads by pulling and twisting its fibers 3 (said about a spider or silkworm)

Thesaurus

speedy ADJECTIVE *We got a speedy response.*
▶ quick, rapid, swift, fast, prompt, immediate, brisk

spell NOUN 1 *a magic spell* ▶ incantation, charm, magic formula, bewitchment, sorcery, witchcraft, conjuration, conjuring, enchantment 2 *She cast her spell on all around her.* ▶ allure, charm, magic, fascination, influence, glamour 3 *a spell of dry weather* ▶ period, interval, stretch, run, patch, turn, stint

spell VERB *Lack of rain has spelt disaster for the natural life of the region.* ▶ mean, lead to, result in, signal, signify, presage, herald, foretell, indicate, suggest

spell out *Let me spell out what I plan to do.*
▶ explain, elucidate, clarify, make plain, set out, specify, detail

spellbound ADJECTIVE *The audience was spellbound by the performance.* ▶ enthralled, entranced, captivated, enchanted, transfixed, mesmerized, gripped, bewitched, charmed, fascinated, hypnotized, transported

spend VERB 1 *You needn't spend more than $50 on it.* ▶ pay, pay out, expend, disburse, fritter, squander, (more informal) fork out, (more informal) shell out 2 *They spent all their time arguing.* ▶ pass, occupy, fill, while away

spendthrift NOUN *He was a spendthrift and lived luxuriously.* ▶ big spender, profligate, prodigal, wastrel, squanderer OPPOSITES ARE miser, scrooge, skinflint

sphere NOUN 1 *A glass sphere hung from the ceiling.* ▶ ball, globe, orb, spheroid, globule 2 *She has a lot of experience in this sphere* ▶ domain, field, milieu, area, department, scope, subject, province, range, territory

spice NOUN 1 *Add some spices to liven up your dish.* ▶ herb, seasoning, flavoring 2 *The risk of getting caught added spice to the adventure.*
▶ excitement, interest, zest, color

spiel NOUN (*informal*) *He gave the usual spiel about raising standards.* ▶ speech, monologue, rigmarole, patter, line

spike NOUN *She tore her dress on a spike.*
▶ prong, point, barb, stake, skewer, spit

spike VERB *He spiked another pea with his fork.*
▶ pierce, spear, skewer, impale

spill VERB 1 *Keith slipped and spilled his drink.*
▶ knock over, tip over, upset, slop, overturn, splash about 2 *Water spilled over the top of the bath.* ▶ overflow, flow, brim, run, pour 3 *A truck had spilled its load.* ▶ shed, tip, scatter, discharge, drop 4 *People spilled into the streets.*
▶ stream, pour, surge, swarm, throng

make a web or cocoon out of threads from its body

spin a yarn tell a story

spin out make something last as long as possible

spinach NOUN a vegetable with dark green leaves [via early French from Persian]

spinal cord NOUN spinal cords the thick cord of nerves enclosed in the spine, that carries impulses to and from the brain

spindly ADJECTIVE thin and long or tall

spin doctor NOUN spin doctors a person who works for a political party and publishes information in a way that shows it in the best possible light

spine NOUN spines 1 the line of bones down the middle of the back 2 a thorn or prickle 3 the back part of a book where the pages are joined together

spineless ADJECTIVE 1 without a backbone 2 lacking in determination or strength of character

spin-off NOUN spin-offs something extra produced while making something else

spinster NOUN spinsters a woman who has not married [The original meaning was "someone who spins"; many unmarried women used to earn their living by spinning, which could be done at home.]

spiny ADJECTIVE covered with spines; prickly

spiral ADJECTIVE going around a central point and becoming gradually closer to it or further from it; twisting continually around a central line or cylinder, etc.

▷ **spirally** ADVERB

spiral NOUN spirals a spiral line or course

spiral VERB spirals, spiraling, spiraled 1 move in a spiral 2 increase or decrease continuously and quickly ● *Prices are spiralling* [from Greek *speira* = winding]

spire NOUN spires a tall pointed part on top of a church tower

spirit NOUN spirits 1 the soul 2 a person's mood or mind and feelings ● *He was in good spirits.* 3 a ghost or a supernatural being 4 courage or liveliness ● *She answered with spirit.* 5 a kind of quality in something ● *the romantic spirit of the book* 6 a strong distilled alcoholic drink

spirit VERB spirits, spiriting, spirited carry off quickly and secretly ● *They spirited her away.*

spirit level NOUN spirit levels a device consisting of a tube of liquid with an air bubble in it, used to find out whether something is level

spiritual ADJECTIVE 1 to do with the human soul; not physical 2 to do with religion
▷ **spiritually** ADVERB **spirituality** NOUN

spiritual NOUN spirituals a religious folk song, originally sung by black Christians in America

spiritualism NOUN the belief that the spirits of dead people communicate with living people
▷ **spiritualist** NOUN

spit VERB spits, spitting, spat or spit 1 send out drops of liquid etc. forcibly from the mouth ● *He spat at me.* 2 fall lightly ● *It's spitting with rain.*

Thesaurus

spin VERB 1 *A wheel spins on an axle.* ► rotate, revolve, gyrate, turn, whirl, twirl 2 *My head was spinning.* ► reel, swim, whirl, go round

spindle NOUN *The yarn is spun on a spindle.* ► axle, rod, shaft

spine NOUN 1 *The posture puts an unnecessary stress on the spine.* ► backbone, spinal column, vertebrae 2 *the spines of a hedgehog* ► needle, quill, spike, bristle, point

spiral ADJECTIVE *a spiral column of smoke* ► coiled, curling, winging, corkscrew, turning

spiral NOUN *a spiral of smoke* ► coil, twist, whorl, corkscrew, screw

spiral VERB 1 *Costs continued to spiral.* ► soar, rise, mount, escalate, shoot up 2 *Feelings of anger and jealousy can spiral violently out of control.* ► deteriorate, decline, degenerate, worsen, nosedive

spirit NOUN 1 *a philosophy of reconciling the body and the spirit* ► soul, psyche, inner self, inner being 2 *They went about their task with a good deal of spirit.* ► enthusiasm, vigor, energy, vivacity, ardor, zest, keenness, eagerness,

liveliness, animation, resolution 3 *There is a legend of spirits haunting the place.* ► ghost, specter, phantom, apparition, wraith, shadow 4 *We need to approach this challenge with a positive spirit.* ► attitude, frame of mind, outlook 5 *My spirit was dampened by these setbacks.* ► mood, morale, temperament, disposition, humor 6 *an action that breaks the spirit of the law if not the letter* ► substance, essence, true meaning

spirited ADJECTIVE *The team gave a spirited performance; an attractive and spirited young person* ► lively, vivacious, vibrant, animated, energetic, high-spirited, vigorous, dynamic, sparkling, vital OPPOSITES ARE timid, lifeless

spiritual ADJECTIVE 1 *a spiritual existence* ► nonmaterial, incorporeal, unworldly, otherworldly, metaphysical OPPOSITES ARE physical, material 2 *spiritual music* ► religious, sacred, holy, divine, devotional

spit VERB *Don't spit in public.* ► expectorate, hawk

spit out *He spat out a lemon pip.* ► eject, spew

a b c d e f g h i j k l m n o p q r s t u v w x y z

A
B
C
D
E
F
G
H
I
J
K
L
M
N

spit[1] _NOUN_ saliva

spit[2] _NOUN_ spits **1** a long thin metal spike put through meat or vegetables to hold them together while they are being roasted **2** a narrow strip of land sticking out into the sea

spite _NOUN_ a desire to hurt or annoy somebody
▷ **spiteful** _ADJECTIVE_ **spitefully** _ADVERB_ **spitefulness** _NOUN_
in spite of not being prevented by ● _We went out in spite of the rain._

spitting image _NOUN_ an exact likeness

splash _VERB_ splashes, splashing, splashed **1** make liquid fly about in drops **2** (said about liquid) fly about in drops **3** make wet by splashing ● _The bus splashed us._

splash _NOUN_ splashes **1** the action or sound or mark of splashing **2** a bright patch of color or light
make a splash attract a lot of attention

splay _VERB_ splays, splaying, splayed spread or slope apart

splendid _ADJECTIVE_ **1** magnificent; full of splendor **2** excellent
▷ **splendidly** _ADVERB_

splendor _NOUN_ a brilliant display or appearance

splint _NOUN_ splints a straight piece of wood or metal, etc., tied to a broken arm or leg to hold it firm

splinter _NOUN_ splinters a thin sharp piece of wood, glass, stone, etc., broken off a larger piece

splinter _VERB_ splinters, splintering, splintered break into splinters

split _VERB_ splits, splitting, split **1** break apart, especially along the length of something **2** divide something into parts
split up 1 end a marriage or other relationship **2** go in different directions

split _NOUN_ splits **1** the splitting or dividing of something **2** a place where something has split **3** an acrobatic position in which the legs are stretched widely in opposite directions

split second _NOUN_ a very brief moment of time; an instant

splutter _VERB_ splutters, spluttering, spluttered **1** make a quick series of spitting sounds **2** speak quickly but not clearly
▷ **splutter** _NOUN_
[imitating the sound]

Thesaurus

O
P
Q
R
S
T
U
V
W
X
Y
Z

spit _NOUN_ _He wiped the spit from his face._
► spittle, saliva, dribble, sputum

spite _NOUN_ _He publicly criticized her out of spite._
► malice, maliciousness, spitefulness, animosity, vindictiveness, rancor, ill will, ill feeling, resentment, malevolence

spiteful _ADJECTIVE_ _The speech contained many spiteful remarks._ ► malicious, malevolent, ill-natured, hostile, hurtful, vicious, venomous, wounding, unkind, snide, cruel, nasty

splash _VERB_ **1** _A passing van splashed water over us._ ► splatter, spray, shower, spatter, slosh, slop, sprinkle, squirt, wash **2** _Children splashed about in the water._ ► paddle, wade, dabble, wallow, slosh **3** _The newspapers splashed the story across their front pages._ ► blazon, display, spread, flaunt, trumpet, plaster, publicize

splash _NOUN_ **1** _a splash of color_ ► spot, patch, splodge, speck, burst, touch, dash **2** _The scandal made quite a splash._ ► effect, impact, display

splendid _ADJECTIVE_ **1** _The roses can be enjoyed in a splendid park setting._ ► magnificent, impressive, imposing, noble, glorious, spectacular, gorgeous, sumptuous **2** _He is a splendid police officer._ ► distinguished, outstanding, remarkable, exceptional, celebrated, acclaimed **3** _He had clearly had a splendid day out._ ► wonderful, marvelous, excellent, lovely, delightful

splendor _NOUN_ _the classical splendor of the viceroy's palace_ ► magnificence, grandeur,

sumptuousness, brilliance, resplendence, majesty, richness, pomp, spectacle, stateliness

splice _VERB_ _The cables were spliced in mid-ocean._
► join, unite, connect, interweave, mesh, entwine

splinter _NOUN_ _a splinter of wood; small splinters of glass_ ► sliver, chip, flake, shard, fragment, shaving, shiver

splinter _VERB_ _She had a voice that could splinter a glass._ ► shatter, shiver, crack, fracture, chip, smash, split

split _NOUN_ **1** _There was a large split in the rock._
► crack, fissure, crevice, breach, break, cleft **2** _His T-shirt was stained and had a split in the side._ ► tear, rip, cut, slash, slit **3** _The policy might produce a split in the party._ ► division, schism, rift, breach AN OPPOSITE IS union **4** _After the split with her partner she moved to London._ ► breakup, separation (from), parting, estrangement (from)

split _VERB_ **1** _The child had pulled the curtain and split it._ ► tear, rip, slash, slit **2** _He split the log with an axe._ ► chop, cut, hew, break, cleave **3** _They worked out a system for splitting the proceeds._ ► divide, share, distribute, allocate, apportion **4** _Further on the paths split._ ► fork, divide, diverge, branch AN OPPOSITE IS merge **5** _The proposal would split the Party._ ► divide, disunite

split up _Her parents had split up when she was small._ ► separate, break up, part, divorce

a
b
c
d
e
f
g
h
i
j
k
l
m
n
o
p
q
r
s
t
u
v
w
x
y
z

spoil VERB spoils, spoiling, spoiled **1** damage something and make it useless or unsatisfactory **2** make someone selfish by always letting them have what they want

spoke[1] NOUN spokes each of the bars or rods that go from the center of a wheel to its rim

spoke[2] past tense of speak

spokesperson NOUN spokespersons a person who speaks on behalf of a group of people
▷ **spokesman** NOUN **spokeswoman** NOUN

sponge NOUN sponges **1** a sea creature with a soft porous body **2** the skeleton of this creature, or a piece of a similar substance, used for washing or padding things **3** a soft lightweight cake or pudding
▷ **spongy** ADJECTIVE

sponge VERB sponges, sponging, sponged **1** wipe or wash something with a sponge **2** (informal) get money or food off other people without giving anything in return, ● He's always sponging off his friends.
▷ **sponger** NOUN

sponsor NOUN sponsors **1** a person or organization that provides money for an arts or sports event or for a broadcast in return for advertising **2** someone who gives money to a charity in return for something achieved by another person
▷ **sponsorship** NOUN

sponsor VERB sponsors, sponsoring, sponsored be a sponsor for a person or thing [from Latin sponsum = promised]

spontaneous (spon- tay- nee- us) ADJECTIVE happening or done naturally; not forced or suggested by someone else
▷ **spontaneously** ADVERB **spontaneity** NOUN

spool NOUN spools a rod or cylinder on which something is wound

spoon NOUN spoons a small device with a rounded bowl on a handle, used for lifting things to the mouth or for stirring or measuring things
▷ **spoonful** NOUN **spoonfuls**

spoonerism NOUN spoonerisms an accidental exchange of the initial letters of two words, e.g., by saying a boiled sprat instead of a spoiled brat [named after Canon Spooner (1844–1930), who made mistakes of this kind]

spore NOUN spores a tiny reproductive cell of a plant such as a fungus or fern

sport NOUN sports **1** an athletic activity; a game or pastime, especially outdoors **2** games of this kind ● Do you like sports? **3** (informal) a person who behaves fairly and generously ● Thanks for being such a good sport.

sporting chance NOUN a reasonable chance of success

sports car NOUN sports cars an open low-built fast car

sportsman NOUN sportsmen **1** a man who takes part in sport **2** a person who shows sportsmanship

sportsmanship NOUN behaving fairly and generously to rivals

sportswoman NOUN sportswomen **1** a woman who takes part in sport **2** a woman who shows sportsmanship

spot NOUN spots **1** a small round mark **2** a pimple **3** a small amount ● We had a spot of trouble. **4** a place **5** a drop ● a few spots of rain

Thesaurus

spoil VERB **1** She stayed off the beach because she didn't want to spoil her shoes. ► damage, harm, mar, hurt, blemish, disfigure, deface OPPOSITES ARE improve, enhance **2** An emergency at a time like this could spoil everything. ► ruin, wreck, upset, mess up, destroy, undo, scupper, sabotage, scotch AN OPPOSITE IS further **3** She decided to spoil herself with a vintage champagne. ► indulge, pamper, cosset AN OPPOSITE IS neglect

sponge VERB **1** He asked his nephew to sponge the windows. ► wash, clean, swab, mop, rinse, swill, wipe **2 sponge off** He didn't want to be sponging off his parents any longer. ► live off, impose on, cadge from, scrounge from

spongy ADJECTIVE The material was light and spongy. ► soft, springy, squashy, cushioned, absorbent, porous OPPOSITES ARE solid, hard

spontaneous ADJECTIVE **1** The March Revolution was a spontaneous uprising. ► unplanned, unpremeditated, unprepared, unrehearsed, voluntary, impromptu, impulsive,

unconstrained, unforced AN OPPOSITE IS premeditated **2** The verdict was announced to cheers and spontaneous applause. ► involuntary, automatic, natural, reflex, instinctive **3** She always seems to friendly and spontaneous. ► natural, uninhibited, unaffected, open, genuine AN OPPOSITE IS inhibited

spooky ADJECTIVE I bet this place is really spooky late at night. ► eerie, sinister, creepy, frightening, ghostly, weird, (more informal) scary

sport NOUN **1** They showed a lot of interest in sport. ► games, competitive games, physical recreation, physical exercise

sporting ADJECTIVE It was sporting of them to pay the bill. ► generous, considerate, decent, sportsmanlike AN OPPOSITE IS unsporting

sporty ADJECTIVE They look sporty in their jogging suits. ► athletic, fit, healthy, energetic

spot NOUN **1** There was a dirty spot in the middle of the carpet. ► stain, mark, smudge, blotch, smear **2** He had a small spot on the side of his

A
B
C
D
E
F
G
H
I
J
K
L
M
N
O
P
Q
R
S
T
U
V
W
X
Y
Z

on the spot without delay or change of place; under pressure to take action • *This really puts him on the spot!*

spot on (*informal*) exactly right or accurate

spot VERB spots, spotting, spotted **1** mark with spots **2** (*informal*) notice or recognize • *We spotted her in the crowd.* **3** watch for and take note of • *trainspotting*
▷ **spotter** NOUN

spotlight NOUN spotlights **1** a strong light that can shine on one small area **2** public attention • *Celebrities are used to being in the spotlight.*

spotty ADJECTIVE marked with spots

spouse NOUN spouses a person's husband or wife

spout NOUN spouts **1** a pipe or similar opening from which liquid can pour **2** a jet of liquid

spout VERB spouts, spouting, spouted **1** come or send out as a jet of liquid **2** (*informal*) speak for a long time

sprain VERB sprains, spraining, sprained injure a joint by twisting it
▷ **sprain** NOUN

sprawl VERB sprawls, sprawling, sprawled **1** sit or lie with the arms and legs spread out loosely **2** spread out loosely or untidily
▷ **sprawl** NOUN

spray VERB sprays, spraying, sprayed scatter tiny drops of liquid over something

spray[1] NOUN sprays **1** tiny drops of liquid sent through the air **2** a device for spraying liquid **3** a liquid for spraying • *fly spray*

spray[2] NOUN sprays **1** a single shoot with its leaves and flowers **2** a small bunch of flowers

spread VERB spreads, spreading, spread **1** open or stretch something out to its full size • *The bird spread its wings.* **2** make something cover a surface • *We spread jam on the bread.* **3** become longer or wider • *The stain was spreading.* **4** make or become more widely known or felt or distributed, etc. • *We spread the news* • *The story quickly spread around the village.*

spread NOUN spreads **1** the action or result of spreading **2** a thing's breadth or extent **3** a paste for spreading on bread **4** (*informal*) a large or grand meal

Thesaurus

nose. ► pimple, freckle, mole, blemish **3** *a bright fabric with small spots* ► dot, speck, fleck **4** *We stopped at a quiet spot near the sea.* ► place, position, location, locality, setting, site **5** *Money problems left them in a bit of a spot.* ► predicament, difficulty, plight, mess, corner, trouble, awkward situation, quandary, dilemma, (*more informal*) jam, (*more informal*) fix

spot VERB **1** *My apron was spotted with splashes of grease.* ► stain, mark, smudge, spatter, speckle, streak, blot, discolor, fleck, mottle **2** *She spotted Jack weeding in the garden.* ► notice, observe, glimpse, spy, see, make out, discern, detect

spotless ADJECTIVE **1** *He was wearing his spotless white shirt.* ► unmarked, perfectly clean, immaculate, gleaming **2** *They had a spotless reputation for fair dealing.* ► unblemished, unsullied, untarnished, blameless, faultless, pure, immaculate, irreproachable, pure, (*more informal*) whiter than white

spotty ADJECTIVE *a spotty face* ► pimply, pimpled, potmarked, spotted, blotchy, freckled

spout NOUN *Water poured from the spout.* ► nozzle, outlet, jet, sprinkler

spout VERB **1** *Molten lava was spouting from the crater.* ► spurt, gush, spew, pour, stream, shoot, surge, discharge, issue **2** *He spouted endlessly about how much better life used to be.*

► hold forth, sound off, go on, pontificate, declaim, (*more informal*) mouth off, (*more informal*) rabbit on

sprain VERB SEE wound VERB

sprawl VERB **1** *He sprawled on a huge armchair.* ► stretch out, lounge, recline, slump, slouch, flop **2** *The woods sprawled across the hillside.* ► spread, stretch, straggle, be scattered

spray NOUN **1** *a fine spray of water* ► shower, sprinkling, fountain, splash, mist **2** *a spray of flowers* ► bouquet, bunch, posy, nosegay, garland **3** *a paint spray* ► aerosol, atomizer, spray gun, sprinkler

spray VERB **1** *A sprinkler was spraying water over the grass.* ► sprinkle, spread, shower, disperse, diffuse **2** *Water sprayed into the air.* ► spout, gush, spurt, shoot

spread NOUN **1** *the spread of civilization* ► expansion, extension, growth, proliferation, diffusion, advance **2** *a vast spread of open country* ► stretch, expanse, extent, sweep, span **3** (*informal*) *There was a good spread on the table.* ► meal, feast

spread VERB **1** *He sat back and spread his arms.* ► extend, stretch **2** *I found a map and spread it on the table.* ► open out, unfurl, unroll, display **3** *She spread seeds along the edge of the flower bed.* ► scatter, strew, diffuse **4** *new ways of spreading information* ► diffuse, communicate, propagate, broadcast, transmit, circulate, advertise **5** *These feelings of resentment were beginning to spread.* ► grow, increase, proliferate, escalate, develop, broaden

spread-eagled ADJECTIVE with arms and legs stretched out • *He lay spread-eagled on the bed* [A *spread eagle* was originally a picture of an eagle with legs and wings stretched out, used as an emblem in heraldry.]

spreadsheet NOUN **spreadsheets** (in computing) a program for handling information, especially figures, displayed in a table

spree NOUN **sprees** something you do with a lot of freedom and enjoyment • *a shopping spree*

sprig NOUN **sprigs** a small branch; a shoot [from early German]

sprightly ADJECTIVE **sprightlier, sprightliest** lively and full of energy

spring VERB **springs, springing, sprang, sprung** **1** jump; move quickly or suddenly • *He sprang to his feet.* **2** originate or develop • *The trouble has sprung from carelessness.* • *Weeds have started to spring up.* **3** present or produce suddenly • *They sprang a surprise on us.*

spring NOUN **springs** **1** a springy coil or bent piece of metal **2** a springing movement **3** a place where water comes up naturally from the ground **4** the season when most plants begin to grow [from Old English]

springboard NOUN **springboards** a springy board from which people jump in diving and gymnastics

spring-clean VERB **spring-cleans, spring-cleaning, spring-cleaned** clean a house thoroughly in springtime

springy ADJECTIVE **springier, springiest** able to spring back easily after being bent or

squeezed
▷ **springiness** NOUN

sprinkle VERB **sprinkles, sprinkling, sprinkled** make tiny drops or pieces fall on something
▷ **sprinkler** NOUN

sprint VERB **sprints, sprinting, sprinted** run very fast for a short distance
▷ **sprint** NOUN **sprinter** NOUN [from Old Norse]

sprout VERB **sprouts, sprouting, sprouted** start to grow; put out shoots

sprout NOUN **sprouts** **1** a shoot of a plant **2** a Brussels sprout

spruce NOUN **spruces** a kind of fir tree

spruce ADJECTIVE neat and trim; smart

spruce VERB **spruces, sprucing, spruced** smarten • *Spruce yourself up.*

spry ADJECTIVE **sprier, spriest** active, nimble, and lively

spur NOUN **spurs** **1** a sharp device worn on the heel of a rider's boot to urge a horse to go faster **2** a stimulus or incentive **3** a ridge that sticks out from a mountain
on the spur of the moment on an impulse; without planning

spur VERB **spurs, spurring, spurred** urge on; encourage

spurious ADJECTIVE not genuine

spurn VERB **spurns, spurning, spurned** reject scornfully

spurt VERB **spurts, spurting, spurted** **1** gush out **2** increase your speed suddenly

spurt NOUN **spurts** **1** a sudden gush **2** a sudden increase in speed or effort

Thesaurus

sprightly ADJECTIVE *He's very sprightly for his age.* ► lively, active, spry, agile, nimble, spirited, vivacious, vigorous OPPOSITES ARE doddering, lethargic

spring NOUN **1** *With a sudden spring he was out of the door.* ► leap, jump, bound, vault **2** *The cushion had lost its spring.* ► bounce, springiness, resilience, elasticity, flexibility

spring VERB **1** *Steve sprang to his feet.* ► leap, jump, bound, bounce **2** *Some of these ideas spring from earlier research.* ► originate, derive, arise, develop, come
spring up *New hotels are springing up all along the coast.* ► appear, develop, emerge, shoot up

springy ADJECTIVE **1** *The floor felt springy under their feet.* ► elastic, stretchy, pliable, resilient, spongy, supple, bendy, flexible AN OPPOSITE IS rigid **2** *He walked on with a springy step.* ► jaunty, bouncy, buoyant, lively, light

sprinkle VERB **1** *He sprinkled sugar over his cereal.* ► scatter, strew, shower **2** *Sprinkle the grass with seed.* ► dust, powder, pepper

sprint VERB *She sprinted up the road.* ► run, dash, tear, shoot, dart, (more informal) belt

sprout VERB *The seeds began to sprout.* ► grow, germinate, shoot up, spring up, bud, develop, emerge

spur NOUN *Music can become a spur to our imaginations.* ► stimulus, incentive, impetus, encouragement, enticement, filip
on the spur of the moment *He decided to go with her on the spur of the moment.* ► on impulse, impulsively, impetuously, spontaneously, all of a sudden

spur VERB *The boy's frantic calls spurred her to action.* ► stimulate, encourage, drive, prompt, goad, incite

spurt VERB *Blood spurted from his finger and he swore.* ► squirt, gush, shoot, stream, pour, spew, erupt, surge

a
b
c
d
e
f
g
h
i
j
k
l
m
n
o
p
q
r
s
t
u
v
w
x
y
z

A
B
C
D
E
F
G
H
I
J
K
L
M
N
O
P
Q
R
S
T
U
V
W
X
Y
Z

spy NOUN **spies** someone who works secretly for one country, person, etc., to find out things about another

spy VERB **spies, spying, spied** **1** be a spy **2** keep watch secretly • *Have you been spying on me?* **3** see or notice • *She spied a house in the distance.* [from early French *espier* = catch sight of]

squabble VERB **squabbles, squabbling, squabbled** quarrel or bicker
▷ **squabble** NOUN

squad NOUN **squads** a small group of people working or being trained together

squadron NOUN **squadrons** part of an army, navy, or air force

squalid ADJECTIVE dirty and unpleasant
▷ **squalidly** ADVERB **squalor** NOUN

squall NOUN **squalls** **1** a sudden storm or gust of wind **2** a baby's loud cry

squall VERB **squalls, squalling, squalled** (said about a baby) cry loudly

squander VERB **squanders, squandering, squandered** spend money or time, etc., wastefully

square NOUN **squares** **1** a flat shape with four equal sides and four right angles **2** an area surrounded by buildings • *Herald Square* **3** the result of multiplying a number by itself• *9 is the square of 3 (9 = 3 x 3)*

square ADJECTIVE **1** having the shape of a square **2** forming a right angle • *The desk has square corners.* **3** equal or even • *The teams are all square with six points each.*
▷ **squarely** ADVERB **squareness** NOUN

square foot, square meter, *etc* the area of a surface with sides that are one foot or one meter, etc., long

square VERB **squares, squaring, squared** **1** make a thing square **2** multiply a number by itself • *5 squared is 25* **3** match; make or be consistent • *His story doesn't square with yours.* **4** settle or pay

square deal NOUN a deal that is honest and fair

square meal NOUN **square meals** a good satisfying meal

square root NOUN **square roots** the number that gives a particular number if it is multiplied by itself • *3 is the square root of 9 (3 x 3 = 9)*

squash VERB **squashes, squashing, squashed** **1** press something so that it becomes flat or out of shape **2** force into a small space; pack tightly **3** suppress or quash

squash NOUN **squashes** **1** a crowded condition **2** a game played with rackets and a soft ball in a special indoor court

squat VERB **squats, squatting, squatted** **1** sit on your heels; crouch **2** live in an unoccupied building without permission
▷ **squat** NOUN **squatter** NOUN

squat ADJECTIVE short and fat

Thesaurus

---

spy NOUN *He had never thought of himself as a traitor, or a spy.* ► secret agent, undercover agent, double agent, (*more informal*) plant, (*more informal*) mole

spy VERB **1** spy on *She sent you to spy on me.* ► snoop on, keep an eye on, watch, shadow, trail **2** *We heard a rustle and spied a baby adder slithering away.* ► notice, observe, glimpse, spot, see, make out, discern, detect

squabble VERB *Every evening a crowd gathered to squabble over politics.* ► argue, quarrel, bicker, wrangle, dispute, clash, fight

squalid ADJECTIVE **1** *a depressing mixture of cheap housing and squalid surroundings* ► dirty, filthy, grimy, grubby, sordid, seedy, dingy AN OPPOSITE IS clean **2** *squalid attempts to rig the election* ► improper, shameful, sordid, dishonest, corrupt AN OPPOSITE IS honorable

squander VERB *The girl he married squandered every penny of his.* ► waste, misspend, fritter away, dissipate, (*more informal*) blow AN OPPOSITE IS save

square ADJECTIVE **1** *They sat at a square table.* ► rectangular, right-angled, quadrilateral **2** *The sides were still square at full time.* ► level, even, neck and neck **3** *All they wanted was a square deal.* ► fair, honest, just, equitable, genuine, above-board, (*more informal*) on-the-level

square NOUN **1** *They arranged to meet in the town square.* ► piazza, plaza **2** (*informal*) *He must have seemed such a square to them.* ► old fogy, conservative, traditionalist, conformist, conventional person, (*informal*) stick-in-the-mud

square VERB **1** *He went in to square his bill.* ► settle, pay, clear, discharge **2** *He needed to square a few things with his dad.* ► resolve, settle, sort out, clear up, put right, remedy, reconcile **3** *These facts don't quite square with the accepted version of what happened.* ► agree, tally, accord, harmonize

squash VERB **1** *Someone had squashed the flowers in the garden.* ► crush, flatten, press, mangle, trample on, compress **2** *He squashed a few things into his case.* ► stuff, force, cram, ram, pack **3** *The uprising was ruthlessly squashed.* ► suppress, quash, quell, put down **4** *He meanly squashed them in front of everyone.* ► humiliate, humble, show up, put down, mortify, snub

squat VERB *The children squatted on the floor to listen.* ► crouch, stoop, sit

squawk VERB squawks, squawking, squawked
make a loud harsh cry
▷ **squawk** NOUN

squeak VERB squeaks, squeaking, squeaked
make a short high-pitched cry or sound
▷ **squeak** NOUN **squeaky** ADJECTIVE **squeakily**
ADVERB

squeal VERB squeals, squealing, squealed
make a long shrill cry or sound
▷ **squeal** NOUN

squeamish ADJECTIVE easily disgusted or
shocked
▷ **squeamishness** NOUN

squeeze VERB squeezes, squeezing, squeezed
1 press something from opposite sides,
especially to get liquid out of it **2** force into
or through a place • *We squeezed through a gap
in the hedge.*
▷ **squeezer** NOUN

squeeze NOUN squeezes **1** the action of
squeezing **2** a drop of liquid squeezed out
• *Add a squeeze of lemon.* **3** a time when
money is difficult to get or borrow

squelch VERB squelches, squelching,
squelched make a sound like someone
treading in thick mud
▷ **squelch** NOUN

squid NOUN squids a sea animal with eight
short tentacles and two long ones

squint VERB squints, squinting, squinted **1** be
cross-eyed **2** peer; look with half-shut eyes at
something
▷ **squint** NOUN

squire NOUN squires **1** the man who owns
most of the land in a country parish or district
2 a young nobleman in the Middle Ages who
served a knight

squirm VERB squirms, squirming, squirmed
wriggle about, especially when you feel
embarrassed

squirrel NOUN squirrels a small animal with a
bushy tail and red or grey fur, living in trees
[via early French from Greek *skia* = shade +
oura = tail]

squirt VERB squirts, squirting, squirted send or
come out in a jet of liquid
▷ **squirt** NOUN

St. or **St** ABBREVIATION **1** Saint **2** Street

stab VERB stabs, stabbing, stabbed pierce or
wound with something sharp

stab NOUN stabs **1** the action of stabbing **2** a
sudden sharp pain • *She felt a stab of fear.*
3 (*informal*) an attempt • *I'll have a stab at it.*

stability NOUN being stable

stable ADJECTIVE **1** steady and firmly fixed
2 not likely to change or end suddenly • *a
stable relationship* **3** sensible and dependable
▷ **stably** ADVERB

stable NOUN stables a building where horses
are kept

Thesaurus

squawk VERB *A bird squawked overhead.*
▶ screech, shriek, squeal, cry, call

squeak VERB **1** *The door squeaked.* ▶ creak,
grate, rasp **2** *The bird squeaked in its cage.*
▶ chirp, peep, cheep

squeal VERB *She squealed with pain.* ▶ cry, yell,
yelp, screech, scream, shriek

squeamish ADJECTIVE *Her father had always been
squeamish about changing diapers.* ▶ queasy,
nauseated, fastidious, finicky, fussy, choosy,
particular, prim, prissy

squeeze VERB **1** *Katherine squeezed her
daughter's hand affectionately.* ▶ clasp, press,
grip, hug, squash, wring, compress, crush,
embrace, enfold **2** *She put her arm around him
and squeezed him.* ▶ hug, embrace, cuddle,
hold, clasp **3** *They squeezed the audience into a
room that was obviously too small. She squeezed
herself into a bright red minidress.* ▶ cram, push,
ram, shove, stuff, thrust, crowd, wedge **4** *Two
elderly Americans squeezed past her chair.* ▶ push,
force your way **5** *The government seems
determined to squeeze as much money out of the
motorist as it can.* ▶ wring, wrest, extort,
extract, force, milk

squeeze NOUN **1** *He gave her hand a squeeze.*
▶ press, pinch, grip, grasp, clasp **2** *Three of us
in the back of the car was quite a squeeze.*
▶ crush, jam, huddle, crowd

squirt VERB **1** *The first bite made jam squirt down
my chin.* ▶ spurt, shoot, gush, spout, spray,
erupt, surge **2** *She squirted me with water.*
▶ splash, spray, shower, spatter, splatter,
sprinkle

stab NOUN **1** *He got a stab in the leg.* ▶ wound,
wounding, blow, jab, cut, prick, thrust **2** *She
felt a brief stab of pain.* ▶ twinge, pang, sting,
throb, spasm **3** (*informal*) *I'll have a stab at it.*
▶ try, go, attempt, (*informal*) bash, (*informal*)
shot

stab VERB **1** *One of the gang stabbed him in the
arm.* ▶ knife, spear, pierce, jab, stick, thrust,
wound **2** *She stabbed at the ground with a
spade.* ▶ thrust, jab, prod, lunge, poke

stable ADJECTIVE **1** *Make sure the equipment is
stable.* ▶ steady, firm, secure, balanced, fixed,
solid OPPOSITES ARE unstable, flimsy **2** *Their
power and authority depend on a stable regime.*
▶ well-founded, well-established, secure, firm,
enduring, durable, lasting, sound, strong
OPPOSITES ARE unstable, changeable

a
b
c
d
e
f
g
h
i
j
k
l
m
n
o
p
q
r
s
t
u
v
w
x
y
z

stable VERB stables, stabling, stabled put or keep in a stable

stack NOUN stacks **1** a neat pile **2** a haystack **3** (*informal*) a large amount • *I have a stack of work to do.* **4** a single tall chimney; a group of small chimneys

stack VERB stacks, stacking, stacked pile things up [from Old Norse]

stadium NOUN stadiums a sports ground surrounded by seats for spectators [via Latin from Greek *stadion*]

staff NOUN staffs or, in sense 4, staves **1** the people who work in an office, shop, etc. **2** the teachers in a school or college **3** a stick or pole used as a weapon or support or as a symbol of authority **4** a set of five horizontal lines on which music is written

staff VERB staffs, staffing, staffed provide with a staff of people • *The center is staffed by volunteers.*

stag NOUN stags a male deer

stage NOUN stages **1** a platform for performances in a theater or hall **2** a point or part of a process, journey, etc. • *Now for the final stage.*

the stage the profession of acting or working in the theater

stage VERB stages, staging, staged **1** present a performance on a stage **2** organize • *We decided to stage a protest.*

stagecoach NOUN stagecoaches a horse-drawn coach that formerly ran regularly from one point to another along the same route

stage manager NOUN stage managers the person in charge of the scenery, lighting, sound, etc. in a theatre during a performance

stagger VERB staggers, staggering, staggered **1** walk unsteadily **2** amaze or shock deeply • *We were staggered at the price.* **3** arrange things so that they do not all happen together • *Please stagger your holidays so that there is always someone here.*
▷ **stagger** NOUN

stagnant ADJECTIVE **1** not flowing **2** not active or developing • *business is stagnant*

stain NOUN stains **1** a dirty mark on something **2** a blemish on someone's character or past record **3** a liquid used for staining things

stain VERB stains, staining, stained **1** make a stain on something **2** color with a liquid that sinks into the surface [from an old word *distain* = dye]

stained glass NOUN pieces of colored glass held together in a lead framework to make a picture or pattern

stainless steel NOUN steel that does not rust easily

stair NOUN stairs each of the fixed steps in a series that lead from one level or floor to another in a building

staircase NOUN staircases a set of stairs

stake NOUN stakes **1** a thick pointed stick to be driven into the ground **2** the post to which people used to be tied for execution by being burnt alive **3** an amount of money bet on something **4** an investment that gives a person a share or interest in a business, etc.
at stake being risked

Thesaurus

---

stack NOUN **1** *The publisher had a stack of unsold copies on his hands.* ► heap, pile, mound, mass, load, accumulation, stockpile, mountain **2** *a stack of hay* ► rick, stook, haycock

stack VERB *The boxes were stacked on desks and tables.* ► pile, heap, load, mass, assemble, collect, accumulate, build up, gather

staff NOUN **1** *We have extra staff on duty over the busy period.* ► personnel, assistants, employees, workers, workforce, crew, officers, team **2** *Magistrates carried a staff as a sign of their authority.* ► cane, crosier, pole, rod, sceptre, stave, stick

stage NOUN **1** *They faced the long last stage of their journey.* ► part, section, phase, portion, stretch, lap **2** *The treaty marks a new stage in relations between the two countries.* ► point, phase, step, juncture

stage VERB **1** *They even staged an opera.* ► mount, put on, present, perform, arrange **2** *Workers staged a two-hour strike on November 5.* ► organize, mount, set up, go through with

stagger VERB **1** *He staggered up the stairs to bed.* ► totter, stumble, lurch, reel, sway, falter, walk unsteadily, waver, wobble **2** *Rory was staggered by his answer.* ► astonish, amaze, astound, surprise, dumbfound, flabbergast, shock, startle, stun, stupefy

stain NOUN **1** *Her eyes alighted on a milk stain on the tablecloth.* ► mark, spot, smear, blemish, smudge, blot, blotch, discoloration **2** *It was not seen as a stain on their character.* ► blemish, taint, blot, slur, disgrace, discredit

stain VERB **1** *Sweat had stained his shirt.* ► discolor, mark, blemish, dirty, sully, spoil, blacken **2** *There is a product that will stain and varnish in one go.* ► dye, color, tinge, tint, paint

stake NOUN **1** *The soldier had been speared with a wooden stake.* ► pole, post, spike, stave, stick, paling, pile **2** *The multinational has bought a 40% stake in the company.* ► share, interest, involvement **3** *If you win, you get your stake back plus ten times its value.* ► bet, pledge, wager

stake VERB **stakes, staking, staked** **1** fasten, support, or mark out with stakes **2** bet or risk money, etc., on an event
stake a claim claim or obtain a right to something

stalactite NOUN **stalactites** a stony spike hanging like an icicle from a cave roof [from Greek *stalaktos* = dripping]
USAGE See note at **stalagmite**.

stalagmite NOUN **stalagmites** a stony spike standing like a pillar on the floor of a cave [from Greek *stalagma* = a drop]
USAGE Remember that a **stalagmite** stands up from the ground, while a **stalactite** hangs down from the ceiling.

stale ADJECTIVE **1** not fresh **2** bored and not having any good ideas
▷ **staleness** NOUN

stalemate NOUN **1** a drawn position in chess when a player cannot make a move without putting his or her king in check **2** a deadlock; a situation in which neither side in an argument will give way

stalk NOUN **stalks** a stem of a plant, etc.

stalk VERB **stalks, stalking, stalked** **1** track or hunt stealthily **2** walk in a stiff or dignified way

stall NOUN **stalls** **1** a table or counter from which things are sold **2** a place for one animal in a stable or shed

stall VERB **stalls, stalling, stalled** **1** delay things or avoid giving an answer to give yourself more time **2** stop suddenly from lack of power • *The car engine stalled.* **3** put an animal into a stall

stallion NOUN **stallions** a male horse

stalls PLURAL NOUN the seats in the lowest level of a theatre

stalwart ADJECTIVE strong and faithful • *my stalwart supporters*

stamen NOUN **stamens** the part of a flower bearing pollen [from Latin, = thread]

stamina NOUN strength and ability to endure hard effort over a long time [from Latin, plural of **stamen** (referring to the threads of life spun by the Fates, three mythological godesses who were believed to determine each person's birth and death)]

stammer VERB **stammers, stammering, stammered** keep repeating the same syllables when you speak
▷ **stammer** NOUN

stamp NOUN **stamps** **1** a small piece of gummed paper with a special design on it; a postage stamp **2** a small device for pressing words or marks on something; the words or marks made by this **3** a distinctive characteristic • *His story bears the stamp of truth.*

stamp VERB **stamps, stamping, stamped** **1** bang your foot heavily on the ground **2** walk with loud heavy steps **3** stick a postage stamp on a letter or packet **4** press a mark or design, etc., on something
stamp out **1** put out a fire by stamping **2** stop something • *We have stamped out bullying.*

stampede NOUN **stampedes** a sudden rush by animals or people
▷ **stampede** VERB
[from Spanish *estampida* = crash, uproar]

Thesaurus

stale ADJECTIVE **1** *You can make the pudding with stale bread and milk.* ▶ dry, hard, old, musty, moldy **2** *The war had already become stale news.* ▶ worn out, jaded, hackneyed, out-of-date, uninteresting, unoriginal, overused AN OPPOSITE IS fresh

stalemate NOUN *The negotiations ended in a stalemate.* ▶ deadlock, impasse, standstill

stalk NOUN the stalk of a plant ▶ stem, shoot, branch, trunk, twig

stalk VERB **1** *The cat began to stalk her through the long grass.* ▶ track, trail, hunt, pursue, shadow, tail, follow **2** *He rose and stalked out of the door.* ▶ stride, strut, march, flounce, sweep

stall NOUN *The school will have a stall at the fair.* ▶ stand, booth, kiosk

stall VERB *He clearly believed she was only stalling.* ▶ procrastinate, prevaricate, temporize, play for time, delay, hang back

stamp NOUN **1** *The license needs an official stamp to be valid.* ▶ mark, seal, brand, imprint **2** *She*
left *her stamp on history as an inspired visionary.* ▶ mark, impression **3** *The new head was of a different stamp from her predecessor.* ▶ type, kind, sort, brand, character

stamp VERB **1** *"Bad girl," she said and stamped her foot.* ▶ strike, bring down, thump **2** *Sir George had stamped his authority firmly on the subject.* ▶ imprint, mark, print, brand, engrave, impress
stamp on *Ellie moved forward and stamped on the creature.* ▶ tread on, crush, trample
stamp out *The police are trying to stamp out racism.* ▶ eliminate, eradicate, extinguish, end, put an end to, suppress

stampede NOUN *In the stampede that follows, the young elephants can easily get trampled.* ▶ charge, rush, dash, rout, panic

stampede VERB *The audience panicked and stampeded for the exit.* ▶ dash, bolt, charge, rush, flee

a
b
c
d
e
f
g
h
i
j
k
l
m
n
o
p
q
r
s
t
u
v
w
x
y
z

A
B
C
D
E
F
G
H
I
J
K
L
M
N
O
P
Q
R
S
T
U
V
W
X
Y
Z

stand VERB **stands, standing, stood 1** be on your feet without moving • *We were standing at the back of the hall.* **2** rise to your feet • *Please all stand now.* **3** set or be upright; place • *We stood the vase on the table.* **4** stay the same • *My offer still stands.* **5** be a candidate for election • *She stood for the Senate.* **6** tolerate or endure • *I can't stand that noise.*

it stands to reason it is reasonable or obvious
stand by be ready for action
stand for 1 represent • *"U.S." stands for "United States."* **2** tolerate
stand in for take someone's place
stand out be clear or obvious
stand up for support or defend
stand up to 1 resist bravely **2** stay in good condition in spite of prolonged use

stand NOUN **stands 1** something made for putting things on • *a music stand* **2** a stall where things are sold or displayed **3** a grandstand **4** a stationary condition or position • *He took his stand near the door.* **5** resistance to attack • *The time has come to make a stand.*

standard NOUN **standards 1** how good something is • *a high standard of work* **2** a thing used to measure or judge something

else **3** a special flag • *the royal standard* **4** an upright support

standard ADJECTIVE **1** of the usual or average quality or kind **2** regarded as the best and widely used • *the standard book on spiders*

standby NOUN
on standby ready to be used if needed

stand-in NOUN **stand-ins** a deputy or substitute

standing order NOUN **standing orders** an instruction to a bank to make regular payments, or to a trader to supply something regularly

standoffish ADJECTIVE cold and formal; not friendly

standpoint NOUN **standpoints** a point of view

standstill NOUN a stop; an end to movement or activity

staple NOUN **staples 1** a small piece of metal pushed through papers and clenched to fasten them together **2** a U-shaped nail
▷ **staple** VERB **stapler** NOUN

staple ADJECTIVE main or usual • *Rice is their staple food.*
▷ **staple** NOUN

star NOUN **stars 1** a large mass of burning gas that is seen as a speck of light in the sky at

---

Thesaurus

stand VERB **1** *The choir stood for the final chorus.* ▶ rise, get to your feet, get up **2** *A house once stood on this spot.* ▶ be situated, be located, be sited, exist, sit, be **3** *She stood the packet on the table.* ▶ put, place, set, deposit, position, situate, station, locate, (*more informal*) plonk **4** *The offer still stands.* ▶ remain in force, remain valid, be unchanged, stay, continue **5** *Her heart could not stand the strain.* ▶ withstand, endure, handle, cope with **6** *I can't stand noise.* ▶ bear, abide, endure, tolerate, put up with, suffer, (*more informal*) stick, (*more informal*) stomach, (*more informal*) wear

stand by *He was determined to stand by his friends.* ▶ support, defend, stand or stick up for, be faithful to, be loyal to, adhere to, stay with, stick to OPPOSITES ARE betray, let down
stand down *He would have to accept responsibility and stand down.* ▶ resign, step down, retire, (*more informal*) quit
stand for *What do the initials stand for?* ▶ mean, represent, signify, denote, indicate, symbolize, be a sign for
stand in for *She stood in for the lead singer who was unwell.* ▶ replace, substitute for, take over from, be a substitute for, deputize for, cover for, understudy
stand out *He stands out in that suit.* ▶ be prominent, be obvious, catch the eye, show, stick out

stand up for *It is important to stand up for our principles.* ▶ support, defend, champion, stand or stick by, be faithful to, be loyal to, adhere to, stay with, stick to AN OPPOSITE IS betray
stand up to *The little band stood up bravely to the attack.* ▶ resist, withstand, confront, face up to, defy, oppose OPPOSITES ARE give in to, succumb to

stand NOUN **1** *a large vase on a stand* ▶ base, pedestal, support, tripod, trivet, rack **2** *a newspaper stand* ▶ stall, booth, kiosk **3** *They are taking a bold stand.* ▶ attitude, stance, viewpoint, position, policy, posture

standard ADJECTIVE *The fee is subject to tax at the standard rate. The council said the letter was part of their standard procedure.* ▶ normal, usual, typical, customary, conventional

standard NOUN **1** *The standard of music-making can be very high indeed.* ▶ quality, level, caliber, grade, excellence **2** *a standard of behaviour* ▶ norm, principle, yardstick, criterion, benchmark, example **3** *Next day at dawn they raised the regimental standard for the last time.* ▶ flag, banner, pennant, colors, ensign

standing NOUN *The superintendent has to be a medical practitioner of high standing.* ▶ reputation, distinction, status, repute, rank, stature, seniority, eminence

star NOUN **1** *a sky full of stars* ▶ celestial body, heavenly body RELATED ADJECTIVES ▶ astral, night **2** a shape with points or rays sticking out from it; an asterisk **3** an object or mark of this shape showing rank or quality • *a five-star hotel* **4** a famous performer; one of the chief performers in a play, film, or show

star VERB **stars, starring, starred 1** be one of the main performers in a film or show **2** have someone as a main performer **3** mark with an asterisk or star symbol

starboard NOUN the right-hand side of a ship or aircraft when you are facing forward COMPARE **port** [from Old English *steor* = paddle for steering (usually mounted on the right-hand side), + **board**]

starch NOUN **starches 1** a white carbohydrate in bread, potatoes, etc. **2** this or a similar substance used to stiffen clothes
▷ **starchy** ADJECTIVE

starch VERB **starches, starching, starched** stiffen with starch

stare VERB **stares, staring, stared** look at something intensely
▷ **stare** NOUN

starfish NOUN **starfish** or **starfishes** a sea animal shaped like a star with five points

stark ADJECTIVE **1** complete or unmistakable • *stark nonsense* **2** desolate and bare • *the*

stark lunar landscape
▷ **starkly** ADVERB **starkness** NOUN

stark ADVERB completely • *stark naked*

starling NOUN **starlings** a noisy black bird with speckled feathers

starry ADJECTIVE full of stars

starry-eyed ADJECTIVE made happy by foolish dreams or unrealistic hopes

start VERB **starts, starting, started 1** begin or cause to begin **2** make an engine or machine begin running, • *I'll start the car.* **3** begin a journey **4** make a sudden movement because of pain or surprise
▷ **starter** NOUN

start NOUN **starts 1** the beginning; the place where a race starts **2** an advantage that someone starts with • *We gave the young ones ten minutes' start.* **3** a sudden movement

startle VERB **startles, startling, startled** surprise or alarm someone

starve VERB **starves, starving, starved 1** suffer or die from lack of food; cause to do this **2** deprive someone of something they need, • *She was starved of love.*
▷ **starvation** NOUN

starving ADJECTIVE (*informal*) very hungry

Thesaurus

stellar **2** *She was an international star by the age of nineteen.* ► celebrity, famous person, public figure, big name, idol

stare VERB **1** *She seemed stunned and sat staring in front of her.* ► gaze, gape, glare, goggle, look fixedly, peer

stare at *Simon was staring at him.* ► gaze at, eye, scrutinize, study, watch, contemplate, examine

stark ADJECTIVE **1** *Those who survived had the stark choice of submitting or fleeing into exile.* ► grim, blunt, harsh, plain, bald **2** *Their barracks are a stark contrast to the brightness elsewhere.*
► absolute, complete, utter, total, sheer

start VERB **1** *The film starts at 8:00 PM.* ► begin, (*more formal*) commence **2** *She wants to start a reading group.* ► set up, establish, found, launch, begin, institute, originate, activate, create, embark on, inaugurate, initiate, instigate, introduce, open AN OPPOSITE IS finish **3** *The bus was ready to start.* ► depart, leave, move off, set off, set out, (*more informal*) get going AN OPPOSITE IS stop **4** *We'd better start if we are going to finish in time.* ► make a start, begin, (*more informal*) get going, (*more informal*) get cracking **5** *A crash in the kitchen made us start.* ► jump, recoil, flinch, spring up, blench, jerk, twitch, wince

start out *They would have to start out before breakfast.* ► set off, set out, set forth, make a

start, depart, leave, (*more informal*) get going, (*more informal*) hit the road

start NOUN **1** *It was the start of a long process.* ► beginning, outset, inception, birth, dawn, initiation, inauguration OPPOSITES ARE end, conclusion **2** *A good education gives you a start in life.* ► advantage, opportunity, encouragement, helping hand **3** *This was the start of all our problems.* ► origin, cause, source, starting point OPPOSITES ARE end, culmination **4** *The doorbell rang, giving me a start* ► shock, jump, surprise

startle VERB *Some caterpillars manage to startle their attackers by raising themselves up like small snakes.* ► alarm, frighten, scare, surprise, give you a start, take by surprise, catch unawares, make you start, shake, shock AN OPPOSITE IS calm

startling ADJECTIVE *It was startling to see hundreds of people toiling up and down the hill. The letter contained some startling news.*
► surprising, astonishing, amazing, staggering, disconcerting, unsettling

starvation NOUN *The civil war left most of the population facing starvation.* ► hunger, malnutrition, undernourishment, malnourishment, deprivation, famine

starve VERB *Many starved in the famine.* ► die of starvation, go hungry, go without, perish

starving ADJECTIVE **1** *She devoted her energies to helping the starving children of the world.*

a
b
c
d
e
f
g
h
i
j
k
l
m
n
o
p
q
r
s
t
u
v
w
x
y
z

A
B
C
D
E
F
G
H
I
J
K
L
M
N
O
P
Q
R
S
T
U
V
W
X
Y
Z

state NOUN **states** **1** the quality of a person's or thing's characteristics or circumstances; condition **2** an organized community under one government (*the state of Israel*) or forming part of a republic (*the 50 states of the USA*) **3** a country's government • *Help for the earthquake victims was provided by the state.* **4** a grand style • *She arrived in state* **5** (*informal*) an excited or upset condition • *Don't get into a state about the robbery.*

state VERB **states, stating, stated** express something in spoken or written words

stately ADJECTIVE **statelier, stateliest** dignified, imposing, or grand
▷ **stateliness** NOUN

statement NOUN **statements** **1** words stating something **2** a formal account of facts • *The witness made a statement to the police.* **3** a written report of a financial account • *a bank statement*

state school NOUN **state schools** a school that is funded by the government

statesman NOUN **statesmen** a person, especially a man, who is important or skilled in governing a country
▷ **statesmanship** NOUN **stateswoman** NOUN

static ADJECTIVE not moving or changing

static electricity NOUN electricity that is present in something, not flowing as current

station NOUN **stations** **1** a stopping place for trains, buses, etc., with platforms and buildings for passengers and goods **2** a building equipped for people who serve the public or for certain activities • *the police station* **3** a broadcasting company with its own frequency **4** a place where a person or thing stands or is stationed; a position [from Latin *statio* = a stand, standing]

stationary ADJECTIVE not moving • *The car was stationary when the van hit it.*
USAGE Do not confuse with **stationery**.

stationery NOUN paper, envelopes, and other articles used in writing or typing
USAGE Do not confuse with **stationary**.

statistician (stat- is- **tish**- an) NOUN **statisticians** an expert in statistics

statistics NOUN **1** the study of information based on the numbers of things **2** facts obtained from studying statistics

statue NOUN **statues** a model made of stone or metal, etc., to look like a person or animal

statuette NOUN **statuettes** a small statue

stature NOUN **1** the natural height of the body **2** greatness gained by ability or achievement

status (**stay**- tus) NOUN **statuses** **1** a person's or thing's position or rank in relation to others **2** high rank or prestige

statute NOUN **statutes** a law passed by a legislature
▷ **statutory** ADJECTIVE

staunch ADJECTIVE firm and loyal • *our staunch supporters*
▷ **staunchly** ADVERB

Thesaurus

▶ starved, underfed, undernourished, emaciated **2** *Let's go and eat, I'm starving.*
▶ very hungry, famished, ravenous

state NOUN **1** *The closure reflects the state of the town's economy.* ▶ condition, situation, shape, circumstances, predicament, position, health **2** *a sovereign state* ▶ country, nation, land, (*more formal*) polity
in a state *Try not to get in a state.* ▶ agitated, flustered, anxious, panicky, frenzied, (*more informal*) uptight

state VERB *In the speech she stated her company's objectives.* ▶ declare, express, communicate, voice, utter, tell, say, affirm, make known, reveal, disclose, divulge

stately ADJECTIVE *a stately procession through the town* ▶ dignified, majestic, ceremonious, grand, splendid, imposing, noble

statement NOUN *The president issued a brief statement.* ▶ announcement, declaration, account, report, communication, utterance

static ADJECTIVE **1** *a static display of work and photographs* ▶ stationary, immobile, motionless, fixed, still, unmoving AN OPPOSITE IS mobile **2** *Prices have remained static for several years.* ▶ unchanged, steady, stable, constant, invariable, stagnant AN OPPOSITE IS variable

station NOUN **1** *a nuclear power station in Armenia; a research station funded by the EU* ▶ establishment, facility, base, depot, post, plant, headquarters, office **2** *a radio station* ▶ channel, transmitter, wavelength, company **3** *It's one of the busiest railway stations in the world.* ▶ stopping place, terminus, halt, platform **4** *a grand station in life* ▶ standing, status, position, rank, situation, calling

station VERB *She used to date John when he was stationed in Berlin.* ▶ post, base, assign (to), deploy, locate, establish

stationary ADJECTIVE *One moment we were stationary, the next moving forward smoothly.* ▶ still, at a standstill, motionless, standing, immobile, at rest, halted, static AN OPPOSITE IS moving

statistics NOUN *a comprehensive volume of facts, records, and statistics* ▶ data, figures, information, numbers

statue NOUN *a bronze statue of a Roman emperor* ▶ figure, sculpture, effigy, carving, bronze

stave VERB **staves, staving, staved** or **stove** dent or break a hole in something ● *The collision stove in the front of the ship.*
stave off keep something away ● *We staved off the disaster.*

stave NOUN **staves** a set of five horizontal lines on which music is written

stay VERB **stays, staying, stayed 1** continue to be in the same place or condition; remain **2** spend time in a place as a visitor **3** satisfy temporarily ● *We stayed our hunger with a sandwich.* **4** pause **5** show endurance in a race or task
stay put (*informal*) remain in place

stay NOUN **stays** a time spent somewhere ● *We made a short stay in Rome.* **2** a postponement ● *a stay of execution*

stead NOUN
in a person's or **thing's stead** instead of this person or thing
stand a person in good stead be very useful to him or her

steadfast ADJECTIVE firm and not changing ● *a steadfast refusal*

steady ADJECTIVE **steadier, steadiest 1** not shaking or moving; firm **2** regular; continuing the same ● *a steady pace*
▷ **steadily** ADVERB **steadiness** NOUN

steak NOUN **steaks** a thick slice of meat (especially beef) or fish [from Old Norse]

steal VERB **steals, stealing, stole, stolen 1** take and keep something that does not belong to you; take secretly or dishonestly **2** move secretly or without being noticed ● *He stole out of the room.*

stealthy (stelth- ee) ADJECTIVE **stealthier, stealthiest** quiet and secret, so as not to be noticed
▷ **stealth** NOUN **stealthily** ADVERB **stealthiness** NOUN

steam NOUN **1** the gas or vapor that comes from boiling water; this used to drive machinery **2** energy ● *He ran out of steam.*
▷ **steamy** ADJECTIVE

steam VERB **steams, steaming, steamed 1** give off steam **2** move by the power of steam ● *The ship steamed down the river.* **3** cook or treat by steam ● *a steamed pudding*
steam up be covered with mist or condensation

steam engine NOUN **steam engines** an engine driven by steam

steamroller NOUN **steamrollers** a heavy vehicle with a large roller used to flatten surfaces when making roads [so called because the first ones were powered by steam]

steed NOUN **steeds** (*old or poetical use*) a horse [from Old English]

steel NOUN **steels 1** a strong metal made from iron and carbon **2** a steel rod for sharpening knives

steel VERB **steels, steeling, steeled**

Thesaurus

stay VERB **1** *The officer told him to stay where he was.* ► wait, remain, continue, (*more informal*) hang on OPPOSITES ARE leave, depart **2** *It was vital to stay calm.* ► remain, keep, continue, carry on being **3** *He said it would be better to stay in a hotel.* ► live, lodge, reside, settle, board, dwell, be accommodated, be a guest, be housed, sojourn, stop, visit

stay NOUN **1** *I had several suitcases, in preparation for a long stay.* ► visit, stop, stopover, break, holiday, sojourn

steady ADJECTIVE **1** *The ladder doesn't look steady.* ► secure, stable, settled, fixed, balanced, fast, firm, solid, safe AN OPPOSITE IS unsteady. **2** *The Middle East has provided him with a steady stream of work.* ► continuous, regular, constant, even, reliable, uninterrupted, consistent, dependable, ceaseless, nonstop AN OPPOSITE IS intermittent **3** *Talk in a firm voice without shouting.* ► regular, even, invariable, rhythmic, smooth, uniform **4** *He didn't then have a steady girlfriend.* ► regular, habitual, settled, established, devoted, faithful, loyal, serious, steadfast

steady VERB **1** *Alec steadied himself as the ground shook again.* ► stabilize, balance, brace, make

steady, secure **2** *I needed something to steady my nerves.* ► calm, soothe, settle, quieten, quell, control

steal VERB **1** *He rushed in to help when a mugger tried to steal a fan's camera. He had been caught stealing from a friend.* ► thieve, pilfer, purloin, appropriate, rob, run off with, (*more informal*) filch, (*more informal*) pinch, (*more informal*) nick, (*more informal*) swipe (*more informal*) **2** *I stole quietly out of the room.* ► creep, slink, sneak, move stealthily, tiptoe **3** *Carson stole sideways glances at his passenger.* ► snatch, sneak, take

stealing NOUN *They were convicted of stealing.* ► theft, thieving, robbery, burglary, pilfering, shoplifting

stealthy ADJECTIVE *a lot of stealthy movement from one room to another* ► furtive, secretive, covert, secret, surreptitious, sneaking, sly, slinky, clandestine AN OPPOSITE IS blatant

steam NOUN *The kitchen was full of steam.* ► vapor, condensation, moisture, haze, mist

steamy ADJECTIVE **1** *The windows were steamy.* ► misty, cloudy, hazy **2** *the hot steamy jungle* ► humid, muggy, sticky, close, sultry, sweaty, damp, moist

A B C D E F G H I J K L M N O P Q R **S** T U V W X Y Z

steel yourself find courage to face something difficult

steely ADJECTIVE **1** like or to do with steel **2** cold, hard, and severe • *a steely glare*

steep ADJECTIVE **1** sloping very sharply, not gradually **2** (*informal*) unreasonably high • *a steep price*
▷ **steeply** ADVERB **steepness** NOUN
[from Old English]

steep VERB **steeps, steeping, steeped** soak thoroughly; saturate
be steeped in be completely filled or familiar with something. • *The story is steeped in mystery.*
[probably from a Scandinavian language]

steepen VERB **steepens, steepening, steepened** make or become steeper

steeple NOUN **steeples** a church tower with a spire on top

steer VERB **steers, steering, steered** make a car, ship, or bicycle, etc., go in the direction you want; guide
▷ **steersman** NOUN
steer clear of take care to avoid

steering wheel NOUN **steering wheels** a wheel for steering a car, boat, etc.

stem NOUN **stems 1** the main central part of a tree, shrub, or plant **2** a thin part on which a leaf, flower, or fruit is supported **3** a thin upright part, e.g., the thin part of a wineglass between the bowl and the foot **4** the main part of a verb or other word, to which endings are attached **5** the front part of a ship • *from stem to stern*

stem[1] VERB **stems, stemming, stemmed**
stem from arise from; have as its source
[from Old English]

stem[2] VERB **stems, stemming, stemmed** stop the flow of something [from Old Norse]

stench NOUN **stenches** a very unpleasant smell

stencil NOUN **stencils** a piece of card, metal, or plastic with pieces cut out of it, used to produce a picture or design etc.

step NOUN **steps 1** a movement made by lifting the foot and setting it down **2** the sound of a person putting down their foot when walking or running **3** a level surface for placing the foot on in climbing up or down **4** each of a series of things done in some process or action • *The first step is to find somewhere to practice.*
in step 1 stepping in time with others in marching or dancing **2** in agreement
watch your step be careful

step VERB **steps, stepping, stepped** tread or walk
step in intervene
step on it (*informal*) hurry
step up increase something

stepfather NOUN **stepfathers** a man who is married to your mother but is not your natural father

stepladder NOUN **stepladders** a folding ladder with flat treads

stepmother NOUN **stepmothers** a woman who is married to your father but is not your natural mother

stepping stone NOUN **stepping stones 1** each of a line of stones put into a shallow stream so that people can walk across **2** a way of achieving something, or a stage in achieving it • *good exam results can be a stepping stone to a career*

stereo NOUN **stereos 1** stereophonic sound or recording **2** a stereophonic CD player, record player, etc.

stereophonic ADJECTIVE using sound that comes from two different directions to give a natural effect

stereotype NOUN **stereotypes** a fixed idea or image of a person or thing • *The stereotype of a*

Thesaurus

---

steep ADJECTIVE **1** *steep cliffs overlooking the sea*
▶ precipitous, sheer, abrupt, perpendicular, vertical, sudden, sharp AN OPPOSITE IS gentle **2** *The costs seem rather steep.* ▶ expensive, dear, costly, exorbitant, extortionate, (*more informal*) pricey, (*more informal*) stiff OPPOSITES ARE reasonable, moderate

steer VERB *She steered the huge vehicle into the garage.* ▶ direct, drive, guide, navigate, control, pilot
steer clear of *The rickety old barn was a place to steer clear of.* ▶ avoid, keep away from, give a wide berth to

step NOUN **1** *She took a step backward.* ▶ pace, stride, footstep **2** *Anyone seeking political asylum is taking a major step.* ▶ decision, move,

action, course, measure **3** *This was a good first step toward retaining her title.* ▶ phase, stage, action, measure, maneuver **4** *an important step toward achieving peace* ▶ advance, movement, progress, progression **5** *steps I climbed the steps and knocked on the door.*
▶ stairs, staircase

step VERB *I stepped over several mounds of brick and rubble.* ▶ tread, put your foot, walk , stamp, trample
step down *The chairperson would step down at the next election.* ▶ resign, stand down, retire, (*more informal*) quit
step up *The army stepped up the attack.*
▶ intensify, increase, escalate, augment, boost

hero is one who is tall, strong, brave, and good-looking.

▷ **stereotypical** *ADJECTIVE*

sterile *ADJECTIVE* **1** not fertile; barren **2** free from germs

▷ **sterility** *NOUN*

sterilize *VERB* **sterilizes, sterilizing, sterilized** **1** make a thing free from germs, e.g., by heating it **2** make a person or animal unable to reproduce

▷ **sterilization** *NOUN* **sterilizer** *NOUN*

sterling *NOUN* British money

sterling *ADJECTIVE* **1** genuine ● *sterling silver* **2** excellent; of great worth ● *her sterling qualities*

stern *ADJECTIVE* strict and severe, not lenient or kindly

▷ **sternly** *ADVERB* **sternness** *NOUN*

stern *NOUN* **sterns** the back part of a ship

stew *VERB* **stews, stewing, stewed** cook slowly in liquid

stew *NOUN* **stews** a dish of stewed food, especially meat and vegetables

in a stew (*informal*) very worried or agitated

steward *NOUN* **stewards** **1** a man whose job is to look after the passengers on a ship or aircraft **2** an official who keeps order or looks after the arrangements at a large public event

stewardess *NOUN* **stewardesses** a woman whose job is to look after the passengers on a ship or aircraft

stick *NOUN* **sticks** **1** a long thin piece of wood **2** a walking stick **3** the implement used to hit the ball in hockey, polo, etc. **4** a long thin piece of something ● *a stick of rock*

stick *VERB* **sticks, sticking, stuck** **1** push a thing into something ● *Stick a pin in it.* **2** fix or be fixed by glue or as if by this ● *Stick stamps on the parcel.* **3** become fixed and unable to move ● *The drawer keeps sticking.* **4** (*informal*) endure or tolerate ● *I can't stick that noise!*

stick out **1** come or push out from a surface; stand out from the surrounding area **2** be very noticeable

stick to **1** remain faithful to a friend or promise etc. **2** keep to and not alter ● *He stuck to his story.*

stick together **1** stay together **2** support each other

stick up for (*informal*) stand up for

be stuck with (*informal*) be unable to avoid something unwelcome

stickler *NOUN* **sticklers** a person who insists on something ● *a stickler for punctuality*

sticky *ADJECTIVE* **stickier, stickiest** **1** able or likely to stick to things **2** (said about weather) hot and humid, causing perspiration

Thesaurus

sterile *ADJECTIVE* **1** *sterile soil* ► infertile, barren, unproductive, arid, dry, lifeless AN OPPOSITE IS fertile **2** *a sterile bandage* ► sterilized, antiseptic, aseptic, clean, disinfected, germ-free, hygienic, uninfected AN OPPOSITE IS unsterilized **3** *a sterile discussion* ► fruitless, unfruitful, pointless, unprofitable, useless, abortive, hopeless AN OPPOSITE IS fruitful

sterilize *VERB* **1** *The room should be clean but you don't have to sterilize everything.* ► disinfect, fumigate, decontaminate, make sterile, pasteurize, purify, clean, cleanse OPPOSITES ARE contaminate, infect **2** *In the poorest families both husband and wife have been sterilized.* ► make infertile, give a hysterectomy *or* vasectomy to

stern *ADJECTIVE* **1** *Their father looked stern for a while, but soon went to them.* ► severe, strict, harsh, grim, grave, serious, austere, authoritarian, dour OPPOSITES ARE genial, kindly **2** *Stern measures were needed.* ► strict, severe, stringent, rigorous, harsh, drastic, tough OPPOSITES ARE lenient, lax

stew *NOUN* *stew for dinner* ► casserole, ragout, goulash, hash

stick *NOUN* **1** *a pile of dry sticks* ► twig, branch, stalk ● *She threatened him with a stick.* ► rod, cane

stick *VERB* **1** *Iris stuck her fork in the earth.* ► poke, prod, dig, jab, stab, thrust **2** *He stuck a message on her computer screen.* ► affix, attach, fasten, fix, glue, paste, pin **3** *The plastic seats stuck to her skin.* ► adhere, cling, bond, fuse **4** (*informal*) *I've got some stewed fruit I stuck in the freezer.* ► put, place, leave, deposit, drop, (*informal*) bung, (*informal*) dump **5** *The wheels stuck in the soft mud.* ► become trapped, jam **6** *A particular memory stuck in his mind.* ► remain, linger, persist, stay **7** (*informal*) *I couldn't stick it any longer.* ► tolerate, put up with

stick at (*informal*) *If you want to learn a language, you'll have to stick at it.* ► persevere with, persist with, keep at, work hard at

stick out *He had his hands on his hips and his chin stuck out.* ► jut out, protrude, project

stick to *She advises her staff to stick to six basic safety guidelines.* ► abide by, adhere to, keep, hold to, fulfil

stick up *The monument sticks up above the trees.* ► rise, stand out, loom, tower

stick up for *I was born here and I try to stick up for my country.* ► support, defend, stand up for

sticky *ADJECTIVE* **1** *She tied up the package with sticky tape.* ► adhesive, gummed, self-adhesive, glued **2** *There was a patch of sticky fluid on the carpet.* ► gluey, tacky, gummy, treacly, (more*

a
b
c
d
e
f
g
h
i
j
k
l
m
n
o
p
q
r
s
t
u
v
w
x
y
z

A
B
C
D
E
F
G
H
I
J
K
L
M
N
O
P
Q
R
S
T
U
V
W
X
Y
Z

3 (*informal*) difficult or awkward • *a sticky situation*
▷ **stickily** ADVERB **stickiness** NOUN
come to a sticky end (*informal*) die or end in a painful or unpleasant way

stiff ADJECTIVE **1** not bending or moving or changing its shape easily **2** not fluid; hard to stir • *a stiff dough* **3** difficult • *a stiff examination* **4** formal in manner; not friendly **5** severe or strong • *a stiff breeze*
▷ **stiffly** ADVERB **stiffness** NOUN

stiffen VERB **stiffens, stiffening, stiffened** make or become stiff
▷ **stiffener** NOUN

stifle VERB **stifles, stifling, stifled 1** suffocate **2** suppress • *She stifled a yawn.*

stigma NOUN **stigmas 1** a mark of disgrace **2** part of a flower's pistil that receives the pollen [from Greek]

stile NOUN **stiles** an arrangement of steps or bars for people to climb over a fence

stiletto heel NOUN **stiletto heels** a high pointed shoe heel

still ADJECTIVE **1** not moving • *still water* **2** silent **3** not fizzy
▷ **stillness** NOUN

still ADVERB **1** without moving • *Stand still.* **2** up to this or that time • *He was still there.*

3 in a greater amount or degree • *You can do still better.* **4** nevertheless • *They've lost. Still, they tried, and that was good.*

stillborn ADJECTIVE born dead

still life NOUN **still lifes** a painting of lifeless things such as ornaments and fruit

stilted ADJECTIVE stiffly formal

stilts PLURAL NOUN a pair of poles with supports for the feet so that the user can walk high above the ground

stimulate VERB **stimulates, stimulating, stimulated 1** make someone excited or enthusiastic **2** cause or arouse • *The program has stimulated a lot of interest in her work.*
▷ **stimulant** NOUN **stimulation** NOUN

sting NOUN **stings 1** a sharp-pointed part of an animal or plant, often containing a poison, that can cause a wound **2** a painful wound caused by this part

sting VERB **stings, stinging, stung 1** wound or hurt with a sting **2** feel a sharp pain **3** make someone feel upset or hurt • *I was stung by this criticism.* **4** (*slang*) cheat a person by overcharging; extort money from someone

stingy (stin-jee) ADJECTIVE **stingier, stingiest** mean, not generous; giving or given in small amounts
▷ **stingily** ADVERB **stinginess** NOUN

Thesaurus

informal) gooey AN OPPOSITE IS dry **3** *It was a hot sticky afternoon.* ▶ humid, muggy, sultry, clammy, close OPPOSITES ARE fresh, cool

stiff ADJECTIVE **1** *You'll need a sheet of stiff cardboard.* ▶ rigid, firm, hard OPPOSITES ARE limp, flexible **2** *Make a stiff paste.* ▶ thick, firm, semi-solid, viscous **3** *Her muscles were stiff. I was so stiff it was difficult to climb upstairs.* ▶ achy, aching, arthritic, painful, immovable, rheumatic, taut, tight AN OPPOSITE IS supple **4** *a long stiff climb up the hillside* ▶ arduous, strenuous, difficult, tough, exacting, hard, tiring AN OPPOSITE IS easy **5** *We will face some stiff competition later this year.* ▶ strong, powerful, severe **6** *His manner was stiff and aloof.* ▶ formal, reserved, unfriendly, cool, awkward AN OPPOSITE IS relaxed **7** *The judge handed out stiff sentences.* ▶ harsh, severe, punitive, strict, hard, swingeing AN OPPOSITE IS lenient **8** *A stiff breeze made it hard going.* ▶ fresh, strong, brisk AN OPPOSITE IS gentle **9** *They all needed a stiff drink.* ▶ strong, potent, alcoholic AN OPPOSITE IS weak

stifle VERB **1** *The heat can stifle you.* ▶ suffocate, choke, smother **2** *Margaret stifled a cough. The policy has stifled realistic thinking.* ▶ suppress, check, smother, restrain, muffle, curb

still ADJECTIVE **1** *Paul stood still and looked around.* ▶ motionless, immobile, stationary, unmoving, static, inert, lifeless AN OPPOSITE IS

moving **2** *The evening was warm and still.* ▶ quiet, calm, silent, soundless, noiseless, wind-free OPPOSITES ARE windy, stormy

stimulate VERB **1** *The literature course stimulated their interest in modern fiction.* ▶ trigger, activate, kindle, rouse, arouse, stir, increase, enhance AN OPPOSITE IS discourage **2** *The right words from you might stimulate them to keep trying.* ▶ encourage, prompt, motivate, inspire, provoke

stimulating ADJECTIVE *a stimulating lecture by Professor Smithers* ▶ thought-provoking, interesting, entertaining, challenging, exciting, rousing, stirring, exhilarating, inspiring, invigorating, provoking OPPOSITES ARE boring, dull

stimulus NOUN *Cash is the best stimulus to economic development in the region.* ▶ spur, stimulant, encouragement, incentive, inducement, impetus, fillip AN OPPOSITE IS deterrent

sting NOUN **1** *an ointment to soothe a wasp sting* ▶ bite, prick, wound **2** *He felt the sting of the wound still.* ▶ smarting, stinging, pain, burn, pricking

sting VERB **1** *an insect that stings.* ▶ bite, nip, prick **2** *The salt water began to sting.* ▶ smart, tingle, hurt, burn

stingy ADJECTIVE *Derek was notoriously stingy.* ▶ mean, miserly, niggardly, penny-pinching,

stink NOUN stinks **1** an unpleasant smell **2** (*informal*) an unpleasant fuss or protest

stink VERB stinks, stinking, stank or stunk have an unpleasant smell

stint NOUN stints **1** a fixed amount of work to be done **2** limitation of a supply or effort • *They gave help without stint.*

stint VERB stints, stinting, stinted be sparing; restrict to a small amount • *Don't stint on the cream.*

stir VERB stirs, stirring, stirred **1** mix a liquid or soft mixture by moving a spoon, etc., around and around in it **2** move slightly; start to move **3** excite or stimulate • *They stirred up trouble.*

stir NOUN **1** the action of stirring **2** a disturbance; excitement • *The news caused a stir.*

stir-fry VERB stir-fries, stir-frying, stir-fried cook by frying quickly over a high heat while stirring and tossing
▷ stir-fry NOUN

stirrup NOUN stirrups a metal part that hangs from each side of a horse's saddle, for a rider to put his or her foot in

stitch NOUN stitches **1** a loop of thread made in sewing or knitting **2** a method of arranging the threads • *cross stitch* **3** a sudden sharp pain in the side of the body, caused by running

stitch VERB stitches, stitching, stitched sew or fasten with stitches

stoat NOUN stoats a kind of weasel

stock NOUN stocks **1** a number of things kept ready to be sold or used **2** livestock **3** a line of ancestors • *a man of Irish stock* **4** a number of shares in a company's capital **5** liquid made by stewing meat, fish, or vegetables, used for making soup, etc. **6** the main stem of a tree or plant **7** the base, holder, or handle of an implement, weapon, etc. **8** a garden flower with a sweet smell **9** a kind of cravat

stock VERB stocks, stocking, stocked **1** keep goods in stock **2** provide a place with a stock of something
stock up buy a supply of goods, etc.

stockade NOUN stockades a fence made of stakes

stockbroker NOUN stockbrokers a broker who deals in stocks and shares

stock exchange NOUN stock exchanges a country's central place for buying and selling stocks and shares

stocking NOUN stockings a piece of clothing covering the foot and part or all of the leg

stock market NOUN stock markets **1** a stock exchange **2** the buying and selling of stocks and shares

stockpile NOUN stockpiles a large stock of things kept in reserve
▷ stockpile VERB

stocks PLURAL NOUN a wooden structure in which people used to be locked as a public punishment

stock-still ADJECTIVE quite still

stocktaking NOUN the counting, listing, and checking of the amount of stock held by a shop or business

stocky ADJECTIVE stockier, stockiest short and solidly built • *a stocky man*

stodgy ADJECTIVE stodgier, stodgiest **1** (said about food) heavy and filling **2** dull and boring • *a stodgy book*
▷ stodginess NOUN

Thesaurus

parsimonious, (*more informal*) tight-fisted AN OPPOSITE IS generous

stink VERB **1** *The room stank of smoke.* ► reek, smell, (*more informal*) pong

stink NOUN *The stink hits you as soon as you open the door.* ► stench, reek, foul smell, odor, (*more informal*) pong, (*more informal*) niff

stint NOUN *A three-month stint on night duty* ► spell, stretch, period, term, turn, shift, run, session

stir NOUN *The arrival of the car caused quite a stir.* ► commotion, fuss, excitement, disturbance, sensation, to-do

stir VERB **1** *Use a wooden spoon to stir the mixture.* ► mix, blend, beat, agitate, whisk, fold in **2** *Mary stirred in her sleep.* ► quiver, tremble, twitch, move slightly **3** *A gentle breeze stirred.* ► rustle, shake, flutter **4** *a thought to stir our imaginations* ► kindle, rouse, arouse, stimulate, excite, inspire, trigger, activate

stir up *These remarks stirred up considerable anger.* ► whip up, work up, rouse, arouse, trigger, spark off, provoke

stitch VERB *He stitched a patch on his jeans.* ► sew, tack, darn, mend, repair

stock NOUN **1** *a stock of fuel; a stock of jokes* ► supply, store, hoard, reserve, quantity, cache, fund **2** *During winter the stock is kept in sheds.* ► livestock, farm animals, cattle, beasts **3** *The shop will be closed for a day to review its stock.* ► merchandise, goods, wares, commodities, **4** *He is descended from Italian stock.* ► descent, ancestry, origins, parentage, pedigree, heritage

stodgy ADJECTIVE **1** *a rich stodgy sauce* ► starchy, indigestible, heavy, lumpy, soggy, solid, filling AN OPPOSITE IS light **2** *a stodgy story about his childhood* ► boring, dull, tedious, turgid, unexciting, unimaginative, uninteresting, stuffy OPPOSITES ARE lively, exciting

a
b
c
d
e
f
g
h
i
j
k
l
m
n
o
p
q
r
s
t
u
v
w
x
y
z

A
B
C
D
E
F
G
H
I
J
K
L
M
N
O
P
Q
R
S
T
U
V
W
X
Y
Z

stoical (stoh- ik- al) ADJECTIVE bearing pain or difficulties, etc., calmly without complaining
▷ **stoically** ADVERB **stoicism** NOUN

stoke VERB stokes, stoking, stoked put fuel in a furnace or on a fire
▷ **stoker** NOUN

stole past tense of steal

stolid ADJECTIVE not showing much emotion or excitement
▷ **stolidly** ADVERB **stolidity** NOUN

stomach NOUN stomachs 1 the part of the body where food starts to be digested 2 the abdomen

stomach VERB stomachs, stomaching, stomached endure or tolerate

stone NOUN stones 1 a piece of rock 2 stones or rock as material, e.g., for building 3 a jewel 4 the hard case around the kernel of plums, cherries, etc. 5 a unit of weight equal to 14 pounds (635 kg) ● She weighs 8 stone.

stone VERB stones, stoning, stoned 1 throw stones at somebody 2 remove the stones from fruit [from Old English]

Stone Age NOUN the earliest period of human history, when tools and weapons were made of stone

stone-cold ADJECTIVE extremely cold

stone-deaf ADJECTIVE completely deaf

stony ADJECTIVE 1 full of stones 2 like stone; hard 3 unfriendly and not answering ● a stony silence

stool NOUN stools 1 a movable seat without arms or a back 2 a footstool 3 a lump of feces

stoop VERB stoops, stooping, stooped 1 bend your body forward and down 2 lower yourself ● He would not stoop to cheating.
▷ **stoop** NOUN

stop VERB stops, stopping, stopped 1 bring or come to an end; no longer do something 2 be no longer moving or working ● A car stopped in front of us. 3 prevent or obstruct something 4 stay for a short time 5 fill a hole

stop NOUN stops 1 stopping; a pause or end 2 a place where a bus or train regularly stops 3 a punctuation mark, especially a full stop 4 a lever or knob that controls pitch in a wind instrument or allows organ pipes to sound

stopcock NOUN stopcocks a valve controlling the flow of liquid or gas in a pipe

stopgap NOUN stopgaps a temporary substitute

stoppage NOUN stoppages 1 an interruption in the work of a factory, etc. 2 a blockage 3 an amount taken off someone's wages

stopper NOUN stoppers a plug for closing a bottle etc.

stopwatch NOUN stopwatches a watch that can be started and stopped when you wish, used for timing races, etc.

store NOUN stores 1 a supply of things kept for future use 2 a place where things are kept until they are needed 3 a shop, especially a large one
in store 1 being stored 2 going to happen ● There's a surprise in store for you.
set store by something value it greatly

store VERB stores, storing, stored keep things until they are needed
▷ **storage** NOUN

Thesaurus

stomach NOUN I was hungry and my stomach started to rumble. ► gut, belly, abdomen, (more informal) tummy RELATED ADJECTIVE ► gastric

stone NOUN 1 A gang threw stones. ► rock, pebble, boulder 2 a ring with a bright red stone ► gem, gemstone, jewel 3 A memorial stone stood by the grave. ► gravestone, headstone, tombstone, tablet

stony ADJECTIVE 1 a stony path ► rocky, pebbly, rough, shingly 2 a stony silence ► unfriendly, cold, chilly, frosty, icy, hostile, stern, severe, unfeeling, heartless AN OPPOSITE IS friendly

stoop VERB 1 Fred stooped to pick up the dog. ► crouch, bend, kneel, lean, squat, bow, duck 2 I would never stoop to accepting such an idea. ► lower yourself, sink, descend, condescend, deign

stop VERB 1 measures taken to stop tax fraud ► check, prevent, thwart, frustrate, reduce, put and end to, put a stop to OPPOSITES ARE start, encourage 2 He wanted to stop smoking. ► give up, discontinue, cease, desist from,

refrain from, quit OPPOSITES ARE begin, start, resume 3 The bus stopped near the corner. ► halt, come to a stop, come to a halt, pull up, draw up, pull in, come to rest 4 He tried to stop her from leaving the house. ► prevent, intercept, hinder, obstruct, bar 5 a special dressing to stop the escape of blood ► stem, staunch, check, restrict, block, arrest

stop NOUN 1 Business came to a stop for the day. ► halt, end, finish, standstill, conclusion, stoppage, cessation 2 They had a short stop at the rest area. ► break, pause, stopover, rest

store NOUN 1 a store of food ► supply, stock, hoard, reserve, quantity, cache, fund 2 the coal store ► storeroom, storehouse, repository, depository 3 a clothing store ► shop, outlet, retail business, retailers, supermarket, mart

store VERB a place to store food for the winter ► stow, keep, save, put aside, hoard, accumulate, amass, lay by, deposit, (more informal) stash

storehouse NOUN storehouses a building for storing goods

stork NOUN storks a large bird with long legs and a long beak

storm NOUN storms **1** a very strong wind usually with rain, snow, etc. **2** a violent attack or outburst • *a storm of protest*
▷ **stormy** ADJECTIVE
a storm in a teacup a great fuss over something unimportant

storm VERB storms, storming, stormed **1** move or behave violently or angrily • *He stormed out of the room.* **2** suddenly attack and capture a place • *They stormed the castle.*

story NOUN stories **1** an account of a real or imaginary event **2** the plot of a play or novel etc. **3** (*informal*) a lie • *Don't tell stories!* [from Latin *historia* = history] **4** one floor of a building

stout ADJECTIVE **1** rather fat **2** thick and strong **3** brave and determined • *a stout defender of human rights*
▷ **stoutly** ADVERB **stoutness** NOUN

stove NOUN stoves **1** a device containing an oven or ovens **2** a device for heating a room

stove past tense of stave

stow VERB stows, stowing, stowed pack or store something away
▷ **stowage** NOUN
stow away hide on a ship or aircraft so as to travel without paying **stowaway** NOUN

straddle VERB straddles, straddling, straddled have a position across or astride something

straggle VERB straggles, straggling, straggled **1** grow or spread in an untidy way **2** lag behind; wander on your own
▷ **straggler** NOUN **straggly** ADJECTIVE

straight ADJECTIVE **1** going continuously in one direction; not curving or bending **2** level or upright • *Is the picture straight?* **3** tidy; in proper order **4** honest and frank • *a straight answer*
▷ **straightness** NOUN

straight ADVERB **1** in a straight line or manner **2** directly; without delay • *Go straight home.*
straight away immediately
USAGE Do not confuse with strait.

straighten VERB straightens, straightening, straightened make or become straight

straightforward ADJECTIVE **1** easy, not complicated **2** honest and frank

Thesaurus

storm NOUN **1** *A storm blew up out at sea.*
► tempest, gale, squall, hurricane, typhoon, deluge **2** *a storm of protest* ► outburst, outcry, uproar, clamor, commotion, furore

storm VERB **1** *Police decided to storm the building.*
► attack, assault, rush, charge **2** *He stormed out in a rage.* ► march, stomp, stalk, flounce

stormy ADJECTIVE **1** *The weather was wet and stormy.* ► blustery, squally, tempestuous, turbulent, gusty, wild AN OPPOSITE IS calm

story NOUN **1** *the dramatic story of a rescue at sea; What happened that night turned out to be a long story.* ► tale, account, narrative, history, yarn, (*more informal*) spiel **2** *a novel with a gripping story* ► plot, storyline, scenario **3** *She read the newspaper stories.* ► news item, report, feature, piece

stout ADJECTIVE **1** *You'll need a stout pair of boots.*
► sturdy, strong, substantial, robust, solid, thick, tough, reliable, sound AN OPPOSITE IS flimsy **2** *The small stout man marched on ahead.*
► fat, plump, stocky, portly, beefy, bulky, burly, chubby, heavy, tubby, well-built OPPOSITES ARE thin, slender **3** *The defenders put up a stout resistance.* ► brave, courageous, determined, spirited, valiant, strong, forceful, staunch, resolute, firm AN OPPOSITE IS feeble

stow VERB *He left her to stow the shopping in the fridge.* ► store, load, put, stack, (*more informal*) stuff, (*more informal*) stash

straight ADJECTIVE **1** *They were driving along a straight stretch of road* ► direct, smooth,
undeviating, unswerving OPPOSITES ARE winding, crooked **2** *I'll make the room straight for our visitors.* ► tidy, neat, orderly, shipshape, organized, right AN OPPOSITE IS untidy **3** *They have staged something of a comeback with three straight victories.* ► consecutive, continuous, unbroken, uninterrupted, nonstop **4** *John is a straight character and very much his own man. I'll give you a straight answer if I can.* ► honest, direct, frank, straightforward AN OPPOSITE IS evasive

straight ADVERB *We would be walking straight into a trap. She looked straight into his face.*
► directly, squarely, plumb, (*more informal*) slap bang
straight away *He went to see her straight away when he got the news.* ► at once, directly, immediately, instantly, now, without delay

straighten VERB *Rick straightened his tie.*
► adjust, arrange, put straight, neaten, order
straighten out *It will take a while to straighten out all the confusion.* ► sort out, put right, settle, disentangle, make straight, clear up, tidy, unbend, untwist

straightforward ADJECTIVE *It is hard to resist one straightforward conclusion. They seem straightforward enough.* ► blunt, candid, direct, easy, forthright, frank, genuine, honest, intelligible, lucid, open, plain, simple, sincere, straight, truthful, uncomplicated AN OPPOSITE IS devious

A
B
C
D
E
F
G
H
I
J
K
L
M
N
O
P
Q
R
S
T
U
V
W
X
Y
Z

strain VERB **strains, straining, strained 1** injure or weaken something by stretching or working it too hard **2** stretch tightly **3** make a great effort **4** put something through a sieve or filter to separate liquid from solid matter

strain[1] NOUN **strains 1** straining; the force of straining **2** an injury caused by straining **3** something that uses up strength, patience, resources, etc. **4** exhaustion **5** a part of a tune

strain[2] NOUN **strains 1** a breed or variety of animals, plants, etc.; a line of descent **2** an inherited characteristic • *There's an artistic strain in the family.*

strait NOUN **straits** a narrow stretch of water connecting two seas
USAGE Do not confuse with **straight**.

straits PLURAL NOUN **1** a strait • *the Straits of Dover* **2** a difficult condition • *We were in dire straits when we lost our money.*

strand NOUN **strands 1** each of the threads or wires, etc., twisted together to form a rope, yarn, or cable **2** a single thread or hair **3** one idea or theme of several in a story

strand VERB **strands, stranding, stranded** be stranded **1** (said about a boat) run onto sand or rocks in shallow water **2** be left in a difficult or helpless position • *We were stranded when our car broke down.*

strange ADJECTIVE **1** unusual or surprising **2** not known or seen or experienced before
▷ **strangely** ADVERB **strangeness** NOUN

stranger NOUN **strangers** a person you do not know, or who is in a place they do not know

strangle VERB **strangles, strangling, strangled 1** kill by squeezing the throat to prevent breathing **2** restrict something so that it does not develop
▷ **strangler** NOUN

strap NOUN **straps** a flat strip of leather or cloth etc. for fastening things or holding them in place

strap VERB **straps, strapping, strapped** fasten with a strap or straps; bind

strapping ADJECTIVE tall and healthy-looking • *a strapping lad*

strata (strah- ta, stray- ta) PLURAL NOUN layers or levels, especially of rock

strategy NOUN **strategies 1** a plan or policy to achieve something • *our economic strategy* **2** the planning of a war or campaign COMPARE **tactics** [from Greek *strategos* = a general]

stratosphere NOUN a layer of the atmosphere between about 10 and 60 kilometers above the earth's surface

straw NOUN **straws 1** dry cut stalks of corn **2** a narrow tube for drinking through [from Old English]

Thesaurus

strain VERB **1** *The dog strained at its leash.* ► tug, pull, stretch, haul, tighten **2** *Martha strained to hear but heard only faint sounds.* ► strive, struggle, make an effort, endeavor, exert yourself, attempt, try **3** *Try not to strain yourself.* ► weaken, wear out, exhaust, tire out, weary **4** *She had strained a muscle in the last race.* ► pull, sprain, twist, wrench, rick, damage, hurt, injure **5** *Strain the liquid to remove impurities.* ► sieve, sift, filter, separate

strain NOUN *the strain of doing jobs for which they are unsuited* ► stress, pressure, tension, worry, anxiety, burden, difficulty, effort

strained ADJECTIVE *the strained relations between Russia and Japan; the dark gaze was intent on her strained face.* ► tense, awkward, uneasy, fraught, uncomfortable, troubled AN OPPOSITE IS relaxed

strand NOUN *Sibyl frowned, absentmindedly twirling a strand of hair round her fingers.* ► fiber, filament, string, thread, wire

stranded ADJECTIVE **1** *marks left by jellyfish stranded on the beach* ► grounded, run aground, marooned, beached **2** *The waiting rooms were filled with stranded passengers.* ► helpless, abandoned, deserted, forsaken, lost

strange ADJECTIVE **1** *I heard a strange noise outside.* ► odd, unusual, weird, peculiar, curious, funny, extraordinary, unexplained AN OPPOSITE IS ordinary **2** *They wear strange clothes.* ► weird, eccentric, bizarre, unconventional, idiosyncratic, (more informal) oddball, (more informal) wacky AN OPPOSITE IS normal **3** *He found it hard to get to sleep in a strange house.* ► unfamiliar, unknown, new, alien AN OPPOSITE IS familiar **4** *She began to feel a little strange and went to the bathroom.* ► unwell, ill, sick, poorly, indisposed, (more informal) funny AN OPPOSITE IS well

stranger NOUN *They were strangers in the town.* ► newcomer, outsider, visitor, alien, foreigner, guest

strangle VERB **1** *The bird had been strangled by the wire fence.* ► throttle, asphyxiate, choke, suffocate, strangulate **2** *She strangled a cry of alarm.* ► suppress, smother, stifle, restrain, choke back

strap NOUN *The package was tied with straps.* ► thong, tie, belt, cord

strap VERB *He strapped the bag to his bicycle.* ► fasten, secure, tie, bind, lash

strawberry NOUN strawberries a small red juicy fruit, with its seeds on the outside

stray VERB strays, straying, strayed leave a group or proper place and wander; get lost

stray ADJECTIVE that has become lost or separated • *a stray cat* • *a stray sock*
▷ **stray** NOUN

streak NOUN streaks **1** a long thin line or mark **2** a trace • *a streak of cruelty* **3** a spell of success, luck, etc. • *on a winning streak*
▷ **streaky** ADJECTIVE

streak VERB streaks, streaking, streaked **1** mark with streaks **2** move very quickly **3** run naked in a public place for fun or to get attention
▷ **streaker** NOUN

stream NOUN streams **1** water flowing in a channel; a brook or small river **2** a flow of liquid or of things or people **3** a group in which children of similar ability are placed in a school

stream VERB streams, streaming, streamed **1** move in or like a stream **2** produce a stream of liquid **3** arrange schoolchildren in streams according to their ability

streamline VERB streamlines, streamlining, streamlined **1** give something a smooth shape that helps it to move easily through air or water **2** organize something so that it works more efficiently
▷ **streamlined** ADJECTIVE

street NOUN streets a road with houses beside it in a city or village [via Old English from Latin *strata via* = paved way]

strength NOUN strengths **1** how strong a person or thing is; being strong **2** an ability or good quality • *Patience is your great strength.*

strengthen VERB strengthens, strengthening, strengthened make or become stronger

stress NOUN stresses **1** a force that acts on something, e.g., by pressing, pulling, or twisting it; strain **2** emphasis, especially the extra force with which you pronounce part of a word or phrase **3** distress caused by having too many problems or too much to do

stress VERB stresses, stressing, stressed **1** emphasize a point or idea • *I must stress the importance of arriving on time.* **2** pronounce part of a word or phrase with extra emphasis **3** cause stress to someone

Thesaurus

stray VERB **1** *The aircraft had strayed into unauthorized airspace.* ► wander, drift, roam, meander **2** *We are rather straying from the main point.* ► digress, diverge, drift, wander, deviate, be sidetracked

streak NOUN **1** *His hair had several streaks of white.* ► strip, stripe, vein, band, line, smear, stain **2** *She admits to having a competitive streak in her.* ► element, trace, component

streak VERB **1** *Their dirty faces were streaked with tears.* ► stain, smear, smudge, daub **2** *Huge trucks streaked past him.* ► hurtle, rush, speed, tear, flash, zoom, whistle

streaky ADJECTIVE *The windows were streaky from the rain.* ► smeary, smudged, streaked, lined, stripy, veined

stream NOUN **1** *a mountain stream* ► brook, burn, beck, rill, river, rivulet, watercourse, channel **2** *a stream of water* ► jet, flow, rush, gush, surge, spurt, spout

stream VERB *Rain streamed through the hole.* ► flow, pour, gush, surge, spurt, flood

street NOUN *The streets are deserted at this time of night.* ► road, avenue, boulevard, thoroughfare

strength NOUN **1** *Physical strength is important.* ► power, brawn, muscle, toughness, sturdiness, robustness, vigor, might AN OPPOSITE IS weakness **2** *She has enormous strength of character.* ► courage, firmness, resolution, spirit, commitment AN OPPOSITE IS feebleness

strengthen VERB **1** *The exercises will help strengthen your back.* ► build up, fortify, toughen, make stronger, harden, tone up AN OPPOSITE IS weaken **2** *Stone supports strengthen the massive walls.* ► bolster, reinforce, support, brace, buttress, prop up **3** *The police want to strengthen their links with the local communities.* ► consolidate, reinforce, substantiate, bolster, fortify, enhance, back up, increase, invigorate AN OPPOSITE IS undermine

strenuous ADJECTIVE **1** *Success was the result of three years' strenuous work.* ► hard, tough, demanding, arduous, taxing, grueling, exhausting **2** *He has made strenuous efforts to get to know the area.* ► vigorous, determined, resolute, energetic, active, forceful

stress NOUN **1** *She was obviously under a lot of stress.* ► anxiety, difficulty, hardship, pressure, strain, tension, trauma, worry **2** *We need to lay greater stress on accuracy.* ► accent, beat, emphasis, importance, weight

stress VERB *I stressed the importance of a balanced diet.* ► accentuate, assert, emphasize, insist on, lay stress on, put the stress on, repeat, underline

stressful ADJECTIVE *She'd had an extremely stressful day.* ► anxious, difficult, tense, traumatic, worrying AN OPPOSITE IS easy

a
b
c
d
e
f
g
h
i
j
k
l
m
n
o
p
q
r
s
t
u
v
w
x
y
z

stretch ➡ stringy

stretch VERB stretches, stretching, stretched **1** pull something or be pulled so that it becomes longer or wider or larger **2** extend or be continuous • *The wall stretches around the estate.* **3** push out your arms and legs as far as you can **4** make use of all your ability or intelligence • *This course should really stretch you.*
stretch out lie down with your arms and legs at full length
stretch NOUN stretches **1** the action of stretching **2** a continuous period of time or area of land or water
stretcher NOUN stretchers a framework for carrying a sick or injured person
strict ADJECTIVE **1** demanding obedience and good behaviour • *a strict teacher* **2** complete or exact • *in strict confidence* • *the strict truth*
▷ **strictly** ADVERB **strictness** NOUN
stride VERB strides, striding, strode, stridden walk with long steps
stride NOUN strides **1** a long step when walking or running **2** progress
get into your stride settle into a fast and steady pace of working
take something in your stride manage or deal with something without difficulty
strife NOUN conflict; fighting or quarrelling
strike VERB strikes, striking, struck **1** hit **2** attack suddenly • *Plague struck the village.* **3** make an impression on someone's mind • *She strikes me as truthful.* **4** light a match by rubbing it against a rough surface **5** refuse to

work as a protest against pay or conditions **6** produce by pressing or stamping something • *They are striking some special coins.* **7** sound • *The clock struck ten.* **8** find gold or oil, etc., by digging or drilling **9** go in a certain direction • *We struck north through the forest.*
strike off or **out** cross out
strike up 1 begin playing or singing **2** start a friendship or conversation
strike NOUN strikes **1** a hit **2** an attack • *an air strike* **3** refusing to work as a way of making a protest **4** a sudden discovery of gold or oil, etc.
on strike (said about workers) striking
striking ADJECTIVE attractive or impressive
▷ **strikingly** ADVERB
string NOUN strings **1** thin cord made of twisted threads, used to fasten or tie things; a piece of this or similar material **2** a piece of wire or cord, etc., stretched and vibrated to produce sounds in a musical instrument **3** a line or series of things • *a string of cars*
string VERB strings, stringing, strung **1** fit or fasten with string **2** thread on a string **3** remove the tough fiber from beans
string along mislead someone over a period of time
string out 1 spread out in a line **2** cause something to last a long time
strings PLURAL NOUN musical instruments with strings
stringy ADJECTIVE **1** like string **2** containing tough fibers

---

Thesaurus

stretch NOUN **1** *a five-hour stretch on duty* ► spell, stint, period, run, term, time **2** *a fine stretch of moorland* ► expanse, sweep, spread, tract, area
stretch VERB **1** *He stretched the rubber until it snapped.* ► pull, strain, tighten, extend, lengthen AN OPPOSITE IS compress **2** *The road stretched into the distance.* ► extend, continue, spread **3** *stretch to My money won't stretch to a two-week vacation.* ► be enough for, cover, reach to
stretch out *She stretched out on a couch.* ► recline, lean back, lie down, sprawl, relax
strict ADJECTIVE **1** *Their parents could be too strict at times.* ► severe, stern, harsh, authoritarian, rigid, austere AN OPPOSITE IS lenient **2** *strict controls on public spending* ► stringent, rigorous, rigid, severe, tough, extreme AN OPPOSITE IS liberal **3** *a strict interpretation of the rule* ► exact, precise, scrupulous, rigid, rigorous AN OPPOSITE IS loose
strident ADJECTIVE *a strident voice* ► harsh, shrill, jarring, grating, raucous, rasping, screeching, loud OPPOSITES ARE soft, quiet

strike NOUN *The dispute ended in a prolonged strike.* ► stoppage, withdrawal of labor, industrial action, work-to-rule, walkout
strike VERB **1** *I struck my head on the low ceiling.* ► hit, knock, bump, smack, thump **2** *The commandos struck without warning.* ► attack, raid, pounce **3** *The two sides struck a deal at the last moment.* ► agree, agree on, reach, endorse, settle on, sign **4** *(informal) The workforce threatened to strike.* ► down tools, stop work, come out, take industrial action, withdraw your labor
striking ADJECTIVE *She has a striking resemblance to her sister.* ► noticeable, conspicuous, outstanding, prominent, distinctive, impressive, memorable, obvious, stunning, telling, unmistakable AN OPPOSITE IS inconspicuous
string NOUN **1** *a piece of string* ► twine, cord, line, rope **2** *a string of vehicles* ► row, succession, series, file, line, procession, queue **3** *a string of misfortunes* ► sequence, series, chain, progression
string VERB *Lights had been strung across the road.* ► hang, link, thread, connect, join, line up

strip VERB strips, stripping, stripped **1** take a covering or layer off something **2** undress **3** deprive a person of something

strip[1] NOUN the distinctive clothes worn by a sports team while playing

strip[2] NOUN strips a long narrow piece or area

strip cartoon NOUN strip cartoons a series of drawings telling a story

stripe NOUN stripes **1** a long narrow band of color **2** a strip of cloth worn on the sleeve of a uniform to show the wearer's rank
▷ **striped** ADJECTIVE **stripy** ADJECTIVE

striptease NOUN stripteases an entertainment in which a person slowly undresses

strive VERB strives, striving, strove, striven **1** try hard to do something **2** carry on a conflict

stroke NOUN strokes **1** a hit **2** a movement; a style of swimming **3** an action or effort • *a stroke of genius* **4** the sound made by a clock striking **5** a sudden illness that often causes paralysis

stroke VERB strokes, stroking, stroked move your hand gently along something
▷ **stroke** NOUN

stroll VERB strolls, strolling, strolled walk in a leisurely way
▷ **stroll** NOUN **stroller** NOUN

strong ADJECTIVE **1** having great power, energy, or effect **2** not easy to break, damage, or defeat **3** great in intensity • *strong feelings* **4** having a lot of flavor or smell **5** having a certain number of members • *an army 5,000 strong*
▷ **strongly** ADVERB
be going strong be making good progress

stronghold NOUN strongholds **1** a fortified place **2** an area where many people live or think in a particular way • *a Republican stronghold*

strove *past tense* of strive

structure NOUN structures **1** something that has been constructed or built **2** the way something is constructed or organized
▷ **structural** ADJECTIVE **structurally** ADVERB

struggle VERB struggles, struggling, struggled **1** move your arms, legs, etc., in trying to get free **2** make strong efforts to do something **3** try to overcome an opponent or a problem, etc.

struggle NOUN struggles the action of struggling; a hard fight or great effort

---

Thesaurus

---

strip NOUN **1** *a strip of paper; a narrow strip of land* ► slip, band, ribbon, belt, sliver, narrow piece, stripe, swathe, lath, line, shred, slat **2** *The team were sporting a new strip.* ► outfit, kit

strip VERB **1** *He stripped and climbed into the shower.* ► undress, take off your clothes, remove your clothes, (more informal) peel off **2** *Thieves had completely stripped the house.* ► empty, clear out, ransack, loot, pillage, burgle
strip down *Mechanics were busy stripping down the engine.* ► dismantle, take to pieces, take apart, disassemble
strip off *First you must strip off the old paint.* ► peel off, remove, take off, scrape off, flake off

stripe NOUN *sweatpants with a stripe down the side* ► line, strip, band, bar, flash

stroke NOUN **1** *a swift stroke of the axe* ► blow, swipe, hit, knock **2** *a stroke of genius* ► feat, accomplishment, achievement, attainment **3** *She gave the cat a gentle stroke.* ► pat, rub, caress

stroke VERB *You can stroke the dog if you like.* ► pat, caress, fondle, touch, brush, pass your hand over, pet

stroll VERB *They strolled together around the grounds.* ► saunter, amble, wander, meander, ramble, dawdle

stroll NOUN *There was time for a stroll in the woods.* ► saunter, amble, ramble, walk, turn

strong ADJECTIVE **1** *a strong lad of nineteen* ► tough, muscular, powerful, brawny, well built, strapping, burly OPPOSITES ARE weak, puny **2** *The door needs a strong lock* ► robust, sturdy, firm, durable, sound, secure AN OPPOSITE IS weak **3** *She had a strong interest in what they were doing.* ► eager, deep, dedicated, passionate, fervent, zealous AN OPPOSITE IS feeble **4** *a cup of strong coffee* ► highly flavored, pungent, piquant AN OPPOSITE IS weak **5** *We have a strong case to make.* ► forceful, persuasive, convincing, cogent, effective OPPOSITES ARE weak, unconvincing

structure NOUN *a tall structure of five stories* ► construction, edifice, building, erection, pile

struggle VERB **1** *We struggled to get free.* ► strive, strain, toil, try, work hard, endeavor, exert yourself, labor, wrestle, make an effort, move violently, wriggle about, writhe about **2** *They had to struggle with a determined enemy.* ► fight, contend, battle, grapple, wrestle, vie **3** *She struggled over the wet rocks.* ► scramble, flounder, stumble, labor

struggle NOUN **1** *It was a struggle to finish the work in time.* ► effort, challenge, difficulty, endeavour, exertion, labor, problem **2** *The police arrested the gang without a struggle.* ► fight, scuffle, brawl, fracas, affray

a b c d e f g h i j k l m n o p q r **s** t u v w x y z

A
B
C
D
E
F
G
H
I
J
K
L
M
N
O
P
Q
R
S
T
U
V
W
X
Y
Z

strum VERB strums, strumming, strummed sound a guitar by running your fingers across its strings

strut VERB struts, strutting, strutted walk proudly or stiffly

strut NOUN struts 1 a bar of wood or metal strengthening a framework 2 a strutting walk

stub NOUN stubs 1 a short stump left when the rest has been used or worn down 2 a counterfoil of a check, ticket, etc.

stub VERB stubs, stubbing, stubbed bump your toe painfully

stub out put out a cigarette by pressing it against something hard

stubble NOUN 1 the short stalks of corn left in the ground after the harvest is cut 2 short hairs growing after shaving

stubborn ADJECTIVE 1 determined not to change your ideas or ways; obstinate 2 difficult to remove or deal with • *stubborn stains*
  ▷ **stubbornly** ADVERB **stubbornness** NOUN

stubby ADJECTIVE short and thick

stuck-up ADJECTIVE (informal) conceited or snobbish

stud NOUN studs 1 a small curved lump or knob 2 a device like a button on a stalk, used to fasten a detachable collar to a shirt

student NOUN students a person who studies a subject, especially at a college or university

studio NOUN studios 1 the room where a painter or photographer, etc., works 2 a place where films are made 3 a room from which radio or television broadcasts are made or recorded

studious ADJECTIVE keen on studying; studying hard
  ▷ **studiously** ADVERB **studiousness** NOUN

study VERB studies, studying, studied 1 spend time learning about something 2 look at something carefully

study NOUN studies 1 the process of studying 2 a subject studied; a piece of research 3 a room used for studying or writing 4 a piece of music for playing as an exercise 5 a drawing done for practice or in preparation for another work

stuff NOUN 1 a substance or material 2 things • *Leave your stuff outside.*

stuff VERB stuffs, stuffing, stuffed 1 fill tightly 2 fill with stuffing 3 push a thing into something • *He stuffed the notebook into his pocket.* 4 (informal) eat greedily

stuffing NOUN 1 material used to fill the inside of something; padding 2 a savory mixture put into meat or poultry, etc., before cooking

---

Thesaurus

---

stub NOUN 1 *a cigarette stub* ▶ butt, end 2 *the stub of a ticket* ▶ counterfoil, slip

stubborn ADJECTIVE *He was too stubborn to admit he was wrong.* ▶ obstinate, obdurate, strong-willed, headstrong, willful, pig-headed OPPOSITES ARE compliant, yielding

stuck ADJECTIVE 1 *The door was stuck and wouldn't open.* ▶ jammed, fixed, fast, immovable 2 *He admitted he was stuck and needed help.*
  ▶ baffled, beaten, at a loss, bewildered, (more informal) stumped

stuck-up ADJECTIVE *a bunch of stuck-up businessmen* ▶ arrogant, conceited, snobbish, snobby, haughty, supercilious, overweening, (more informal) snooty, (more informal) uppish

student NOUN 1 *a student at the university* ▶ undergraduate, postgraduate, scholar 2 *a student at the local school* ▶ pupil, schoolboy or schoolgirl, schoolchild, scholar 3 *a nursing student* ▶ learner, novice, trainee

studied ADJECTIVE *He spoke with studied politeness.* ▶ deliberate, intentional, considered, calculated, affected, thoughtful

studio NOUN *the artist's studio* ▶ workroom, workshop, atelier

studious ADJECTIVE *a studious young pupil* ▶ scholarly, serious-minded, hardworking, diligent, industrious, thoughtful, intellectual, academic, bookish, brainy, earnest

study NOUN 1 *two years of study in college* ▶ learning, education, schooling, reading, academic work, (informal) cramming 2 *a study of the causes of conflict* ▶ investigation (into), inquiry (into), survey, examination, research (into) 3 *The study deals with all aspects of the subject.* ▶ essay, article, report, review

study VERB 1 *She studied the information carefully.* ▶ examine, analyze, survey, consider, investigate, inspect, scrutinize, look into, peruse 2 *They both wanted to study languages.* ▶ learn, work at, be taught, read 3 *Alan had studied hard at school.* ▶ work, apply yourself

stuff NOUN 1 *There was some wet stuff on the floor.* ▶ matter, substance 2 *The skirt was made of a tough lightweight stuff.* ▶ material, fabric, cloth, textile 3 *I'll put all my stuff in a suitcase.*
  ▶ belongings, effects, possessions, things, (more informal) gear

stuff VERB 1 *I stuffed everything in a drawer.* ▶ pack, push, cram, ram, shove, squeeze, force, jam 2 *Use foam to stuff the cushions.* ▶ fill, pad, pack

stuff yourself *They had been stuffing themselves all day and were no longer hungry.* ▶ gorge, guzzle, cram, overindulge, eat

stuffy _ADJECTIVE_ **stuffier, stuffiest 1** badly ventilated; without fresh air **2** with blocked breathing passages • _a stuffy nose_ **3** formal and boring
▷ **stuffily** _ADVERB_ **stuffiness** _NOUN_

stumble _VERB_ **stumbles, stumbling, stumbled 1** trip and lose your balance **2** speak or do something hesitantly or uncertainly
▷ **stumble** _NOUN_
stumble across or **on** find accidentally

stumbling block _NOUN_ **stumbling blocks** an obstacle; something that causes difficulty

stump _NOUN_ **stumps 1** the bottom of a tree trunk left in the ground when the rest has fallen or been cut down **2** something left when the main part is cut off or worn down

stump _VERB_ **stumps, stumping, stumped** be too difficult or puzzling for somebody• _The last question stumped everyone._
stump up (_informal_) produce the money to pay for something

stumpy _ADJECTIVE_ short and thick
▷ **stumpiness** _NOUN_

stun _VERB_ **stuns, stunning, stunned 1** knock a person unconscious **2** daze or shock • _She was stunned by the news._

stunt _VERB_ prevent a thing from growing or developing normally • _a stunted tree_ [from a dialect word meaning "foolish" or "stubborn"]

stunt _NOUN_ **stunts** something unusual or difficult done as a performance or part of a film, or to attract attention [originally American: origin unknown]

stupendous _ADJECTIVE_ amazing or tremendous
▷ **stupendously** _ADVERB_

stupid _ADJECTIVE_ **1** not clever or thoughtful **2** without reason or common sense
▷ **stupidly** _ADVERB_ **stupidity** _NOUN_

sturdy _ADJECTIVE_ **sturdier, sturdiest** strong and vigorous or solid
▷ **sturdily** _ADVERB_ **sturdiness** _NOUN_

stutter _VERB_ **stutters, stuttering, stuttered** stammer
▷ **stutter** _NOUN_

style _NOUN_ **styles 1** the way something is done, made, said, or written **2** fashion or elegance
▷ **stylistic** _ADJECTIVE_

Thesaurus

stuffy _ADJECTIVE_ **1** _a stuffy atmosphere_ ► airless, close, muggy, sultry, musty, stifling, oppressive, unventilated AN OPPOSITE IS airy **2** _a stuffy lecture on citizenship_ ► staid, prim, straitlaced, pompous, conventional, dull, boring AN OPPOSITE IS informal

stumble _VERB_ **1** _She stumbled on a loose paving stone._ ► trip, tumble, lose your balance, totter **2** _He stumbled back to his house._ ► stagger, totter, lumber, lurch, blunder, bumble, hobble **3** _The speaker stumbled through the rest of the speech._ ► stammer, stutter, falter, flounder, hesitate

stump _VERB_ _One of the questions stumped us._ ► baffle, puzzle, perplex, mystify, bewilder, outwit, confound, confuse, defeat, (_more informal_) flummox

stun _VERB_ **1** _A hard blow had stunned him._ ► daze, knock out, knock senseless, make unconscious **2** _The election results stunned everyone._ ► amaze, astonish, astound, stagger, stupefy, shock, dumbfound, flabbergast, bewilder, confound

stunning _ADJECTIVE_ **1** _a stunning victory_ ► remarkable, sensational, spectacular, extraordinary, staggering, incredible **2** _She looked stunning in a red dress._ ► beautiful, dazzling, gorgeous, ravishing, sensational, lovely AN OPPOSITE IS unattractive

stunt _NOUN_ _a circus stunt_ ► trick, exploit, feat, turn, performance

stupendous _ADJECTIVE_ _a stupendous achievement_ ► amazing, astounding, astonishing, extraordinary, remarkable, wonderful, staggering, breathtaking, (_more informal_) mind-boggling AN OPPOSITE IS ordinary

stupid _ADJECTIVE_ **1** _They are not as stupid as they seem._ ► foolish, silly, foolhardy, unintelligent, dim-witted, half-witted, empty-headed, vacuous, dim, dumb, thick OPPOSITES ARE intelligent, wise **2** _It was a stupid thing to do._ ► foolish, silly, unwise, senseless, mindless, idiotic, crass, absurd, ridiculous, ludicrous AN OPPOSITE IS sensible

stupidity _NOUN_ _Their stupidity had been breathtaking._ ► foolishness, folly, silliness, irresponsibility, ineptitude, idiocy OPPOSITES ARE wisdom, intelligence

sturdy _ADJECTIVE_ **1** _a sturdy and handsome young man_ ► strapping, strong, big, brawny, well-built, muscular AN OPPOSITE IS weak **2** _He packed a sturdy pair of shoes for the walk._ ► stout, strong, substantial, robust, solid, thick, tough, reliable, sound AN OPPOSITE IS flimsy

style _NOUN_ **1** _an old-fashioned style of writing_ ► manner, technique, mode, method, fashion, tone, way **2** _the latest styles in the fashion magazines_ ► design, pattern, fashion, mode, vogue, cut, taste **3** _She always dresses with style._ ► elegance, refinement, flair, panache, stylishness, smartness, sophistication, refinement, taste

A
B
C
D
E
F
G
H
I
J
K
L
M
N
O
P
Q
R
S
T
U
V
W
X
Y
Z

stylish ADJECTIVE in a fashionable style

subconscious ADJECTIVE to do with mental processes of which we are not fully aware but which influence our actions
▷ **subconscious** NOUN

subdivide VERB subdivides, subdividing, subdivided divide again or into smaller parts
▷ **subdivision** NOUN

subdue VERB subdues, subduing, subdued **1** overcome or bring under control **2** make quieter or gentler
▷ **subdued** ADJECTIVE

subject NOUN subjects **1** the person or thing being talked or written about or dealt with **2** something that is studied **3** (in grammar) the word or words naming who or what does the action of a verb, e.g., "the book" in ● The book fell off the table. **4** someone who is ruled by a monarch or government

subject ADJECTIVE ruled by a monarch or government; not independent
subject to **1** having to obey **2** liable to ● Trains are subject to delays during fog. **3** depending upon ● Our decision is subject to your approval.

subject (sub-jekt) VERB subjects, subjecting, subjected **1** make a person or thing undergo something ● They subjected him to torture. **2** bring a country under your control
▷ **subjection** NOUN
[from Latin subicere = bring under, include under a heading]

subjective ADJECTIVE **1** existing in a person's mind and not produced by things outside it **2** depending on a person's own taste or opinions COMPARE objective

subjunctive NOUN subjunctives the form of a verb used to indicate what is imagined or wished or possible There are only a few cases where it is commonly used in English, e.g. "were" in "if I were you"

sublime ADJECTIVE **1** noble or impressive **2** extreme; not caring about the consequences ● with sublime carelessness

submarine ADJECTIVE under the sea ● We laid a submarine cable.

submarine NOUN submarines a ship that can travel under water

submerge VERB submerges, submerging, submerged go under or put under water
▷ **submergence** NOUN **submersion** NOUN

submit VERB submits, submitting, submitted **1** let someone have authority over you; surrender **2** put forward for consideration,

---

Thesaurus

---

stylish ADJECTIVE stylish clothes ► chic, fashionable, modish, trendy, snappy, elegant, smart, (more informal) snazzy OPPOSITES ARE unfashionable, dowdy

subdue VERB **1** The army quickly subdued all opposition. ► overcome, defeat, quell, suppress, crush, overpower **2** It was difficult to subdue their excitement. ► restrain, suppress, check, curb, repress, hold back, keep under, quieten

subdued ADJECTIVE **1** Sylvie was in a subdued mood. ► sombre, downcast, restrained, serious, silent, sober, solemn, depressed, grave, reflective, thoughtful AN OPPOSITE IS lively **2** They spoke in subdued tones. ► hushed, muted, quiet, soft, low, faint, calm AN OPPOSITE IS loud

subject NOUN **1** a British subject ► citizen, national, passport-holder **2** a subject for discussion ► theme, topic, affair, business, issue, matter, point, question **3** a subject of study ► discipline, field, branch, course, area

subject ADJECTIVE **1** subject nations ► subjugated, dependent, subservient, tributary AN OPPOSITE IS independent **2** The trains are subject to constant delays. ► liable, prone, disposed, vulnerable **3** subject to The decision is subject to approval by the board.

► dependent on, contingent on, conditional on

subjective ADJECTIVE It is difficult to build a theory on such subjective criteria. ► biased, prejudiced, personal, individual, intuitive, idiosyncratic OPPOSITES ARE objective, unbiased

submerge VERB **1** The utter darkness submerged them. ► inundate, overwhelm, immerse, engulf, inundate, flood, swamp, cover, drown **2** Submerge the vegetables in cold water. ► immerse, dip, plunge, dunk **3** The submarine had no time to submerge. ► dive, go down

submission NOUN **1** Complete submission was common among women in the nineteenth century. ► compliance, submissiveness, acquiescence, passivity, docility, meekness **2** The enemy's submission was only a matter of time. ► surrender, capitulation, defeat **3** There was an alternative submission that the money had been paid under duress. ► contention, claim, proposal, argument, suggestion, theory

submissive ADJECTIVE Be polite, but not submissive. ► acquiescent, compliant, servile, deferential, ingratiating, subservient, docile, uncomplaining, humble, meek, passive OPPOSITES ARE domineering, assertive

submit VERB **1** She had only submitted under duress. ► give in, yield, accede, back down,

testing, etc. • *Submit your plans to the committee*
▷ **submission** NOUN

subnormal ADJECTIVE below normal

subordinate ADJECTIVE **1** less important **2** lower in rank

subordinate NOUN subordinates a person working under someone's authority or control

subordinate VERB subordinates, subordinating, subordinated treat as being less important than another person or thing
▷ **subordination** NOUN

subordinate clause NOUN subordinate clauses a clause which adds details to the main clause of the sentence, but cannot be used as a sentence by itself

subplot NOUN subplots a secondary plot in a play etc.

subscribe VERB subscribes, subscribing, subscribed **1** pay regularly in order to be a member of a society, receive a periodical, have the use of a telephone, etc. **2** contribute money to a project or charity etc. **3** apply to take part in something• *The course is already fully subscribed.* **4** say that you agree • *We cannot subscribe to this theory.*
▷ **subscriber** NOUN **subscription** NOUN

subsequent ADJECTIVE coming after in time or order; later
▷ **subsequently** ADVERB

subside VERB subsides, subsiding, subsided **1** sink into the ground **2** become quieter or less intense • *Her fear subsided.*
▷ **subsidence** NOUN

subsidiary ADJECTIVE **1** less important; secondary **2** (said about a business) controlled by another • *a subsidiary company*
▷ **subsidiary** NOUN

subsidize VERB subsidizes, subsidizing, subsidized pay a subsidy to a person or firm etc.

subsidy NOUN subsidies money paid to an industry etc. that needs help, or to keep down the price at which its goods etc. are sold to the public

subsoil NOUN soil lying just below the surface layer

substance NOUN substances **1** matter of a particular kind **2** the main or essential part of something • *We agree with the substance of your report but not with its details.*

substantial ADJECTIVE **1** of great size, value, or importance • *a substantial sum of money* **2** solidly built • *substantial houses*
▷ **substantially** ADVERB

substitute NOUN substitutes a person or thing that acts or is used instead of another

substitute VERB substitutes, substituting, substituted put or use a person or thing as a substitute
▷ **substitution** NOUN

Thesaurus

surrender, capitulate, relent, succumb, comply, (*more informal*) knuckle under **2** *The union agreed to submit their disagreement to arbitration.* ► present, offer, tender, put forward, suggest, propose

submit to *We refuse to submit to political pressure. Applicants have to submit to a full medical examination.* ► accept, agree to, succumb to, undergo, tolerate, endure, comply with, conform to, defer to, bow to, keep to, obey

subordinate ADJECTIVE *It would not be easy to accept a subordinate role.* ► inferior, lower, lesser, secondary, subservient, subsidiary, minor, junior

subordinate NOUN *There stood the manager with her three subordinates.* ► assistant, junior, inferior, dependant, employee, (*more informal*) underling AN OPPOSITE IS superior

subscribe VERB **subscribe to 1** *There are so many good causes to subscribe to.* ► contribute to, support, donate to, give to **2** *How many magazines do they subscribe to?* ► buy regularly, pay a subscription to, take, read **3** *I don't subscribe to that view at all.* ► agree with, accept, endorse, support, approve of, believe in, advocate, give your blessing to

subside VERB **1** *We'd better wait for the storm to subside.* ► abate, diminish, moderate, slacken, die down, quieten, ease up, let up AN OPPOSITE IS intensify **2** *The flood waters had begun to subside.* ► recede, fall back, ebb **3** *Paul subsided into a chair.* ► collapse, sink, settle, drop AN OPPOSITE IS rise

substance NOUN **1** *a strange sticky substance* ► material, matter, stuff, chemical **2** *The substance of the story is not hard to follow.* ► essence, gist, theme, meaning, content, subject matter **3** *We may wonder how much substance there was in many of the accusations.* ► meaning, force, weight, significance

substantial ADJECTIVE **1** *a substantial building* ► strong, sturdy, hefty, solid, well-made, durable, sound AN OPPOSITE IS flimsy **2** *If you make substantial improvements to your home they might increase its value.* ► significant, sizable, worthwhile, big, considerable, generous, large AN OPPOSITE IS trivial

substitute ADJECTIVE *a substitute teacher* ► acting, replacement, deputy, relief, reserve, standby, surrogate, temporary

substitute NOUN **1** *There is no substitute for practical experience.* ► replacement, alternative (to) **2** *Nurses can often be effective substitutes for*

a
b
c
d
e
f
g
h
i
j
k
l
m
n
o
p
q
r
s
t
u
v
w
x
y
z

A
B
C
D
E
F
G
H
I
J
K
L
M
N
O
P
Q
R
S
T
U
V
W
X
Y
Z

subterranean ADJECTIVE underground

subtitle NOUN **subtitles 1** a secondary or additional title **2** words shown on the screen during a film, e.g., to translate a foreign language

subtle (sut- el) ADJECTIVE **1** faint or delicate ● *a subtle perfume* **2** slight and difficult to detect or describe ● *a subtle distinction* **3** ingenious; not immediately obvious ● *a subtle joke*
▷ **subtly** ADVERB **subtlety** NOUN

subtract VERB **subtracts, subtracting, subtracted** deduct; take away a part, quantity, or number from a greater one
▷ **subtraction** NOUN

suburb NOUN **suburbs** a district with houses that is outside the central part of a city
▷ **suburban** ADJECTIVE

subway NOUN **subways** an underground passage for pedestrians

succeed VERB **succeeds, succeeding, succeeded 1** do or get what you wanted or intended **2** come after another person or thing; become the next king or queen ● *She succeeded to the throne.* ● *Edward VII succeeded Queen Victoria.*

success NOUN **successes 1** doing or getting what you wanted or intended **2** a person or thing that does well ● *The show was a great success.*

successful ADJECTIVE having success; being a success
▷ **successfully** ADVERB

succession NOUN **successions 1** a series of people or things **2** the process of following in order **3** succeeding to the throne; the right of doing this
in succession one after another

successive ADJECTIVE following one after another ● *on five successive days*
▷ **successively** ADVERB

succumb (suk- um) VERB **succumbs, succumbing, succumbed** give way to something overpowering

such ADJECTIVE **1** of the same kind; similar ● *Cakes, cookies, and all such foods are fattening.* **2** of the kind described ● *There's no such person.* **3** so great or intense ● *It gave me such a fright!*
such as for example

such-and-such ADJECTIVE particular but not now named ● *He promises to come at such-and-such a time but is always late.*

Thesaurus

doctors. ► alternative, replacement, stand-in, proxy, surrogate

substitute VERB **1** *You can substitute yogurt for cream cheese in this recipe.* ► change, exchange, interchange, swop, switch, replace USAGE If you use *replace*, you have to say *You can replace cream cheese with yogurt.* **2** *Maggie agreed to substitute for her boss for few days.* ► deputize, stand in, act as a substitute

subtle ADJECTIVE **1** *Add a subtle yet striking change to your hair.* ► mild, slight, faint, delicate, elusive, unobtrusive **2** *a subtle hint* ► gentle, tactful, indirect, understated AN OPPOSITE IS tactless **3** *subtle colors* ► muted, subdued, delicate, faint, pale AN OPPOSITE IS lurid **4** *a subtle distinction* ► fine, nice, precise, tenuous AN OPPOSITE IS crude

subtract VERB *Half a pint of skimmed milk supplies 100 calories, which must be subtracted from your daily total.* ► deduct, take away, remove, debit AN OPPOSITE IS add

suburban ADJECTIVE *The couple disappeared from their suburban house about two weeks ago.*
► residential, outlying, provincial, outer

succeed VERB **1** *For some people, happiness is to compete and succeed no matter how.* ► be successful, do well, prosper, thrive, flourish, triumph, be victorious, accomplish your objective, (more informal) get on, (more informal) make it **2** *The plan might still succeed.*

► be effective, produce results, work, (more informal) catch on AN OPPOSITE IS fail **3** *Kim's ambition to succeed Roh as president* ► replace, take the place of, take over, supersede, come after, follow AN OPPOSITE IS precede

success NOUN **1** *The criteria for judging success would not be the same for all pupils.*
► accomplishment, achievement, attainment, fame, prosperity AN OPPOSITE IS failure **2** *Links with industry are essential for the success of the program.* ► effectiveness, successful outcome, completion OPPOSITES ARE failure, collapse **3** (informal) *Her first novel was an instant success.* ► triumph, hit, sensation, victory, (more informal) winner OPPOSITES ARE failure, disaster **4** *This performance alone might well have made him a success.* ► celebrity, star, big name, household name, sensation

successful ADJECTIVE **1** *Blazer, the successful menswear chain* ► flourishing, prosperous, thriving, effective, profitable, fruitful, lucrative, productive, profit-making OPPOSITES ARE unsuccessful, unprofitable **2** *He had been a successful prizefighter at the time. This wooden airplane was one of the most successful aircraft of all time.* ► victorious, triumphant, winning, effective OPPOSITES ARE unsuccessful, ineffective

succession NOUN *He drifted into a succession of menial jobs.* ► sequence, series, string, chain, run, line, cycle, course, progression

suck VERB **sucks, sucking, sucked** **1** take in liquid or air through the mouth with the lips almost closed **2** squeeze something in your mouth by using your tongue • *sucking a candy* **3** draw in • *The canoe was sucked into the whirlpool.*
▷ **suck** NOUN
suck up to (*informal*) flatter someone in the hope of winning their favor

sucker NOUN **suckers** **1** an organ or device that can stick to a surface by suction **2** a shoot coming up from a root or underground stem **3** (*informal*) a person who is easily deceived

suckle VERB **suckles, suckling, suckled** feed on milk at the mother's breast or udder

suction NOUN **1** sucking **2** producing a vacuum so that things are sucked into the empty space • *Vacuum cleaners work by suction.*

sudden ADJECTIVE happening or done quickly or without warning
▷ **suddenly** ADVERB **suddenness** NOUN

suds PLURAL NOUN froth on soapy water

sue VERB **sues, suing, sued** start a lawsuit to claim money from somebody

suet NOUN hard fat from cattle and sheep, used in cooking

suffer VERB **suffers, suffering, suffered** **1** feel pain or sadness **2** experience something bad • *The house suffered some damage.* • *She suffers from hay fever.* **3** be badly affected • *She's not sleeping and her work is suffering.* **4** (*old use*) allow or tolerate
▷ **sufferer** NOUN **suffering** NOUN

suffice VERB **suffices, sufficing, sufficed** be enough for someone's needs

sufficient ADJECTIVE enough
▷ **sufficiently** ADVERB **sufficiency** NOUN

suffix NOUN **suffixes** a letter or set of letters joined to the end of a word to make another word (e.g., in forge*ful*, lion*ess*, rust*y*) or a form of a verb (e.g., sing*ing*, wait*ed*)

suffocate VERB **suffocates, suffocating, suffocated** **1** make it difficult or impossible for someone to breathe **2** suffer or die because breathing is prevented
▷ **suffocation** NOUN

sugar NOUN a sweet food obtained from the juices of various plants, such as sugar cane or sugar beet
▷ **sugar** VERB **sugary** ADJECTIVE
[via early French from Arabic]

suggest VERB **suggests, suggesting, suggested** **1** put forward an idea or plan for someone to consider **2** cause an idea or possibility to come into the mind
▷ **suggestion** NOUN **suggestive** ADJECTIVE

suicide NOUN **suicides** **1** killing yourself deliberately • *He committed suicide.* **2** a person who deliberately kills himself or herself
▷ **suicidal** ADJECTIVE

suit NOUN **suits** **1** a matching jacket and pants, or a jacket and skirt, that are meant to be worn together **2** a set of clothing for a particular activity • *a diving suit* **3** any of the four sets of cards (clubs, hearts, diamonds, and spades) in a pack of playing cards **4** a lawsuit
USAGE Do not confuse with **suite**.

suit VERB **suits, suiting, suited** **1** be suitable or convenient for a person or thing **2** make a person look attractive

Thesaurus

suck VERB **1** *The boys sat sucking their drinks.*
▶ sip, sup, slurp, drink **2** *Extra roads can suck people away from buses and trains.* ▶ draw, entice, attract, pull
suck up *He fetched a cloth to suck up the water.*
▶ soak up, absorb, draw up, pull up
suck up to (*informal*) *They suck up to him, hanging on his every word.* ▶ flatter, grovel to, kowtow to, behave obsequiously towards

sudden ADJECTIVE **1** *Lydia emitted a sudden giggle. a sudden increase in student numbers*
▶ unexpected, startling, abrupt, sharp, unforeseen, unlooked for, impulsive, quick, rash OPPOSITES ARE expected, gradual

suffer VERB **1** *She loved him too much to see him suffer.* ▶ feel pain, hurt, be in pain, be in distress **2** *England suffered a humiliating defeat.*
▶ undergo, experience, meet with, receive, be subjected to, sustain, encounter **3** *Dustin's relationship with Anne did suffer.* ▶ deteriorate, decline, be damaged, be impaired

suffering NOUN *Damage and suffering are inflicted on the population.* ▶ hardship, distress, misery, anguish, pain, unhappiness, sorrow, grief

sugary ADJECTIVE *a rather sugary Broadway musical* ▶ sentimental, cloying, mawkish, sickly, saccharine, (*more informal*) soppy

suggest VERB **1** *Connie suggested an outing to the lake.* ▶ propose, recommend, advise, propound, put forward, raise, advocate, moot, move **2** *The evidence suggests we could be right.*
▶ imply, indicate, hint, intimate, mean, signal

suggestion NOUN **1** *We have a few suggestions to consider.* ▶ proposal, proposition, recommendation, idea, plan **2** *There has been no suggestion of dishonesty.* ▶ hint, trace, suspicion, sign, implication, insinuation

suit NOUN *He wore a dark suit with a cream shirt.*
▶ outfit, set of clothes, ensemble, clothing

suit VERB **1** *credit terms to suit all pockets*
▶ accommodate, be suitable for, please, satisfy, gratify, fit **2** *Black doesn't really suit me.*
▶ look attractive on, look right on, become, flatter

a
b
c
d
e
f
g
h
i
j
k
l
m
n
o
p
q
r
s
t
u
v
w
x
y
z

A
B
C
D
E
F
G
H
I
J
K
L
M
N
O
P
Q
R
S
T
U
V
W
X
Y
Z

suitable ADJECTIVE satisfactory or right for a particular person, purpose, or occasion, etc.
▷ **suitably** ADVERB **suitability** NOUN

suitcase NOUN suitcases a rectangular container for carrying clothes, usually with a hinged lid and a handle

suite (rhymes with *sweet*) NOUN **suites 1** a set of furniture **2** a set of rooms **3** a set of short pieces of music
USAGE Do not confuse with **suit**.

sulk VERB sulks, sulking, sulked be silent and bad-tempered because you are not pleased
▷ **sulks** PLURAL NOUN **sulky** ADJECTIVE **sulkily** ADVERB **sulkiness** NOUN

sullen ADJECTIVE sulking and gloomy
▷ **sullenly** ADVERB **sullenness** NOUN

sulphur NOUN a yellow chemical used in industry and in medicine
▷ **sulphurous** ADJECTIVE

sultry ADJECTIVE **1** hot and humid • *sultry weather* **2** suggesting passion or sexual desire • *her sultry smile*
▷ **sultriness** NOUN

sum NOUN sums **1** a total **2** a problem in arithmetic **3** an amount of money

sum VERB sums, summing, summed
sum up give a summary at the end of a talk, etc.

summarize VERB summarizes, summarizing, summarized make or give a summary of something

summary NOUN summaries a statement of the main points of something said or written

summary ADJECTIVE **1** brief **2** done or given hastily, without delay • *summary punishment*
▷ **summarily** ADVERB

summer NOUN summers the warm season between spring and autumn
▷ **summery** ADJECTIVE

summerhouse NOUN summerhouses a small building providing shade in a garden or park

summit NOUN summits **1** the top of a mountain or hill **2** a meeting between the leaders of powerful countries • *a summit conference*

summon VERB summons, summoning, summoned **1** order someone to come or appear **2** call people together • *A meeting of the governors was quickly summoned.*
summon up gather together your strength in order to do something • *She summoned up all her courage and knocked on the door.*

sumptuous ADJECTIVE splendid and expensive-looking
▷ **sumptuously** ADVERB

sun NOUN suns **1** the star around which the earth travels **2** light and warmth from the sun • *Go and sit in the sun.* **3** any star in the universe round which planets travel

sun VERB suns, sunning, sunned
sun yourself sit or lie in the sunshine

sunbathe VERB sunbathes, sunbathing, sunbathed expose your body to the sun, especially to get a tan

sunbeam NOUN sunbeams a ray of sun

sunburn NOUN redness of the skin caused by too much exposure to the sun
▷ **sunburned** ADJECTIVE

sundae (sun- day) NOUN sundaes a mixture of ice cream and fruit, nuts, cream, etc.

Sunday NOUN the first day of the week, observed by Christians as a day of rest and

---

Thesaurus

---

suitable ADJECTIVE **1** *Would tomorrow afternoon be a suitable time?* ► convenient, appropriate, fitting, acceptable, satisfactory, apposite AN OPPOSITE IS unsuitable **2** *a film that is considered suitable for all age groups*
► appropriate (to), suited (to), right, relevant (to)

sulk VERB *Dave was sulking in his room.* ► mope, brood, be sullen, pout

sulky ADJECTIVE *A row of sulky faces greeted him.*
► sullen, surly, moody, morose, glum, moping, pouting, disgruntled AN OPPOSITE IS cheerful

sum NOUN **1** *a large sum of money* ► amount, quantity **2** *a sum you can do in your head*
► calculation, problem **3** *These books were the sum of her life's work.* ► total, entirety, totality, sum total, whole, aggregate

summarize VERB *The ideas can be summarized very easily.* ► sum up, outline, review, precis

summary NOUN **1** *There is a summary of the*

main arguments at the end of the article.
► resumé, review, summing-up, summation, outline, recapitulation, abstract, digest **2** *a summary of a story* ► synopsis, precis, abridgement

summit NOUN *This year thirty-two people reached the summit of Everest.* ► top, peak, crest, crown, apex, pinnacle OPPOSITES ARE foot, bottom

summon VERB **1** *Coleman was summoned to Washington for a final briefing.* ► send for, call, order, command, demand, invite **2** *The lawyers then summoned a meeting.* ► convene, assemble, convoke, gather together, call, announce

sun NOUN *Enjoy the sun while you can.* ► sunlight, sunshine RELATED ADJECTIVE ► solar

sunbathe VERB *Jill was sunbathing on the beach.*
► sun yourself, bask, get a tan

sunburned ADJECTIVE *His neck and shoulders were sunburnt.* ► burned, inflamed, peeling, red, blistered AN OPPOSITE IS pale worship [from Old English *sunnandaeg* = day of the sun]

sundial NOUN sundials a device that shows the time by a shadow on a dial

sundry ADJECTIVE various or several
all and sundry everyone

sunglasses PLURAL NOUN dark glasses to protect your eyes from strong sunlight

sunken ADJECTIVE sunk deeply into a surface
• *Their cheeks were pale and sunken.*

sunlamp NOUN sunlamps a lamp which uses ultraviolet light to give people an artificial tan

sunlight NOUN light from the sun
▷ sunlit ADJECTIVE

sunny ADJECTIVE sunnier, sunniest **1** full of sunshine **2** cheerful • *She was in a sunny mood.*
▷ sunnily ADVERB

sunrise NOUN sunrises the rising of the sun; dawn

sunset NOUN sunsets the setting of the sun

sunshade NOUN sunshades a parasol or other device to protect people from the sun

sunshine NOUN sunlight with no cloud between the sun and the earth

sunstroke NOUN illness caused by being in the sun too long

suntan NOUN suntans a brown color of the skin caused by the sun
▷ suntanned ADJECTIVE

super ADJECTIVE (*informal*) excellent or superb

superb ADJECTIVE magnificent or excellent
▷ superbly ADVERB

superficial ADJECTIVE **1** on the surface • *a superficial cut* **2** not deep or thorough • *a superficial knowledge of French*
▷ superficially ADVERB superficiality NOUN

superfluous ADJECTIVE more than is needed
▷ superfluity NOUN

superhuman ADJECTIVE **1** beyond ordinary human ability • *their superhuman strength* **2** higher than human; divine

superimpose VERB superimposes, superimposing, superimposed place a thing on top of something else
▷ superimposition NOUN

superintend VERB superintends, superintending, superintended supervise

superintendent NOUN superintendents **1** a supervisor **2** a police officer above the rank of inspector

superior ADJECTIVE **1** higher in position or rank • *She is your superior officer.* **2** better than another person or thing **3** showing conceit
▷ superiority NOUN

Thesaurus

sunny ADJECTIVE **1** *It will be a day of sunny spells and showers.* ► bright, clear, fine, cloudless, summery, sunlit AN OPPOSITE IS dull **2** *There was rage beneath the sunny smile.* ► cheerful, happy, joyful, joyous, smiling, beaming, bright, jolly OPPOSITES ARE miserable, gloomy

sunrise NOUN *A farmer's day begins at sunrise.*
► dawn, daybreak, daylight, crack of dawn

sunset NOUN *Walk along the beach at sunset.*
► dusk, twilight, sundown, evening, close of day, half-light, (*literary*) gloaming

super ADJECTIVE *There is a super kitchen with a traditional tiled stove.* ► excellent, superb, superlative, first-class, first-rate, marvelous, magnificent, wonderful, splendid, fine, remarkable, (*more informal*) brilliant, (*more informal*) fantastic, (*more informal*) terrific, (*more informal*) awesome

superb ADJECTIVE *The large bay has a superb backdrop of mountains.* ► excellent, superlative, marvellous, magnificent, wonderful, splendid, fine, remarkable, (*more informal*) fantastic, (*more informal*) awesome

superficial ADJECTIVE **1** *He sustained superficial injuries which soon disappeared. Time spent on repairing superficial damage is well worthwhile.*
► surface, exterior, external, slight, moderate OPPOSITES ARE severe, deep **2** *These similarities are purely superficial.* ► apparent, cosmetic,
slight, shallow, specious OPPOSITES ARE significant, meaningful **3** *At a superficial level these categories appear to be the same.* ► shallow, surface AN OPPOSITE IS deep **4** *It was no more than a superficial examination of the subject.*
► cursory, casual, perfunctory, desultory, hurried, lightweight OPPOSITES ARE thorough, rigorous

superfluous ADJECTIVE **1** *Superfluous material can be trimmed from around the edges.* ► excess, surplus, spare, redundant, unwanted **2** *This is so obvious that at first sight it might seem superfluous to state it.* ► unnecessary, needless, pointless, gratuitous, redundant

superior ADJECTIVE **1** *Lewis watched, aware of his superior status.* ► senior, higher, higher-level, higher-ranking, greater, more important OPPOSITES ARE inferior, lower **2** *Superior rooms are all recently renovated. The Americans have superior technology.* ► first-class, first-rate, high-quality, top-quality, better, exclusive, choice, fine, select, surpassing OPPOSITES ARE inferior, low-quality **3** *He found her cold and superior.*
► haughty, arrogant, disdainful, condescending, patronizing, supercilious, self-important, stuck-up, (*informal*) snooty, (*informal*) hoity-toity OPPOSITES ARE modest, approachable

a b c d e f g h i j k l m n o p q r **s** t u v w x y z

superior NOUN superiors a person who is higher in position or rank than someone else

superlative ADJECTIVE of the highest degree or quality • *superlative skill*
▷ **superlatively** ADVERB

superlative NOUN superlatives the form of an adjective or adverb that expresses "most"
• *The superlative of "great" is "greatest."* COMPARE positive, comparative

supermarket NOUN supermarkets a large self-service shop that sells food and other goods

supermodel NOUN supermodels a very successful and famous fashion model

supernatural ADJECTIVE not belonging to the natural world or having a natural explanation
• *supernatural beings such as ghosts*

superpower NOUN superpowers one of the most powerful nations of the world, such as the U.S.

supersede VERB supersedes, superseding, superseded take the place of something

supersonic ADJECTIVE faster than the speed of sound

superstition NOUN superstitions a belief or action that is not based on reason or

evidence, e.g., the belief that it is unlucky to walk under a ladder
▷ **superstitious** ADJECTIVE

supervise VERB supervises, supervising, supervised be in charge of a person or thing and inspect what is done
▷ **supervision** NOUN **supervisor** NOUN **supervisory** ADJECTIVE

supper NOUN suppers a meal eaten in the evening

supple ADJECTIVE bending easily; flexible
▷ **supplely** ADVERB **suppleness** NOUN

supplement NOUN supplements **1** something added as an extra **2** an extra section added to a book or newspaper • *the color supplement*
▷ **supplementary** ADJECTIVE

supplement VERB supplements, supplementing, supplemented add to something • *She supplements her pocket money by working on Saturdays.*

supply VERB supplies, supplying, supplied give or sell or provide what is needed or wanted
▷ **supplier** NOUN

supply NOUN supplies **1** an amount of something that is available for use when needed **2** the action of supplying something

support VERB supports, supporting, supported **1** keep a person or thing from falling or

Thesaurus

superiority *The professional troops soon proved their technical superiority over the poorly trained local forces.* ► advantage, supremacy, dominance, predominance, ascendancy, pre-eminence, edge, lead AN OPPOSITE IS inferiority

supersede VERB *Steel began to supersede iron in the 1880s.* ► replace, supplant, take the place of, displace, oust, succeed

superstition NOUN *the old superstition that seagulls were the souls of dead sailors* ► myth, superstitious belief, delusion, illusion, old wives' tale

superstitious ADJECTIVE **1** *a haze of superstitious beliefs and practices* ► irrational, mythical, traditional, unfounded, unprovable, groundless, illusory OPPOSITES ARE rational, factual, scientific **2** *I'm not superstitious like some people I could mention.* ► credulous, gullible AN OPPOSITE IS skeptical

supervise VERB *People are needed during the summer to supervise children and organize activities.* ► oversee, watch over, superintend, be in charge of, be responsible for, direct, manage

supervision NOUN *These tasks should be carried out under the supervision of a senior member of staff.* ► oversight, surveillance, control, direction, care, charge, oversight, management

supervisor NOUN *The housewife is her own supervisor.* ► manager, director, overseer, superintendent, controller, boss

supplement NOUN **1** *A supplement is payable for rooms with a sea view.* ► surcharge, additional payment, excess **2** *the newspaper's new travel supplement* ► insert, pull-out, addendum, addition

supplement VERB *the need to supplement the family income* ► augment, increase, boost, enlarge, swell, add to, top up, complement, reinforce

supply NOUN *As a breeder, I give one week's supply of food with each puppy.* ► stock, store, quantity, amount, stockpile, reserve
supplies *Many people use their cars to buy a whole week's supplies.* ► provisions, stores, rations, materials, shopping, food, necessities

supply VERB **1** *studios set up to supply cheaply-made films* ► produce, provide, purvey, sell, contribute **2** *The reservoir supplies water to an area of about five hundred square miles.* ► serve, provide, furnish **3** *They were unable to supply us with what we needed.* ► equip, provide, furnish **4** *A supermarket that supplies all your needs.* ► provide, fulfill, fill

support NOUN **1** *The group offers emotional support to members in times of stress.* ► encouragement, solace, comfort, succour, relief, strength, friendship, protection **2** *The*

sinking; hold something up **2** give strength, help, or encouragement to someone • *Support your local team.* **3** provide with the necessities of life • *She has two children to support.*
▷ **supporter** NOUN **supportive** ADJECTIVE

support NOUN **supports 1** the action of supporting **2** a person or thing that supports

suppose VERB **supposes, supposing, supposed 1** think that something is likely to happen or be true **2** assume; consider as a suggestion • *Suppose the world were flat.*
▷ **supposedly** ADVERB **supposition** NOUN
be supposed to be expected to do something; have as a duty

suppress VERB **suppresses, suppressing, suppressed 1** put an end to something

forcibly or by authority • *Troops suppressed the rebellion.* **2** keep something from being known or seen • *They suppressed the truth.*
▷ **suppression** NOUN **suppressor** NOUN

supreme ADJECTIVE **1** most important or highest in rank **2** greatest • *supreme courage*
▷ **supremely** ADVERB **supremacy** NOUN

sure ADJECTIVE **1** completely confident that you are right; feeling no doubt **2** certain to happen or do something • *Our team is sure to win.* **3** reliable; undoubtedly true
▷ **sureness** NOUN
for sure definitely
make sure 1 find out exactly **2** make something happen or be true • *Make sure the door is locked.*

Thesaurus

Arts Council eventually withdrew all financial support. ► backing, funding, funds, aid, subsidy, donations, money **3** *The shelf was resting on three supports.* ► prop, brace, bracket, pillar, foundation

support VERB **1** *The walls were too weak to support the weight of the roof. He supported the old man over to his bed.* ► carry, bear, sustain, hold up, prop up, provide a support for, underpin **2** *She was determined to support Alice during these difficult weeks.* ► comfort, be a support to, sustain, encourage, hearten, console, fortify, reassure, succour AN OPPOSITE IS abandon **3** *His land was not fertile enough to support his family.* ► maintain, nourish, provide for, sustain, feed, keep AN OPPOSITE IS neglect **4** *The company supports research into the causes of back pain.* ► sponsor, subsidize, fund, patronize, contribute to, encourage AN OPPOSITE IS discourage **5** *They both support some sort of fees. The Socialist party agreed to support the bill. There is no evidence to support such a notion.* ► advocate, endorse, promote, substantiate, uphold, agree with, argue for, confirm, corroborate, defend, justify AN OPPOSITE IS oppose

supporter NOUN **1** *The perpetrators were unlikely to be genuine political supporters.* ► enthusiast, follower, devotee, fan **2** *The United States became an important supporter of the project.* ► champion, advocate, adherent, defender, seconder, upholder, apologist (for) **3** *the party's supporters in business* ► backer, adherent, ally, sponsor, henchman

supportive ADJECTIVE *Alan and Ian were the most supportive friends in her life.*
► encouraging, helpful, caring, concerned, reassuring, sympathetic, understanding, protective, interested, kind, loyal, positive OPPOSITES ARE unhelpful, discouraging

suppose VERB **1** *I suppose it would be nice for you to earn a little pin money.* ► assume, expect, guess, infer, dare say, presume, imagine,

fancy, surmise, suspect, think, conclude, conjecture, judge **2** *just suppose I saw her again* ► imagine, pretend, hypothesize, fancy, assume

supposed ADJECTIVE *Where is this supposed cousin of yours?* ► alleged, assumed, presumed, rumored, reputed, imagined, conjectural, hypothetical, reported, putative
be supposed to *You are supposed to read the whole book.* ► be meant to, be expected to, be required to, be obliged to, have to, need to, ought to

supposition NOUN *Terry had gone to bed happy in the supposition that he would get revenge.*
► belief, assumption, presumption, notion, suspicion, expectation, conjecture, idea, hunch, feeling

suppress VERB **1** *The National Guard was established to suppress antigovernment demonstrations.* ► quash, quell, crush, subdue, overcome, overthrow, conquer, put an end to, put down, stamp out, stop **2** *She had been advised to suppress all critical remarks. McGuire made a conscious effort to suppress his emotions.* ► conceal, hide , restrain, stifle, repress, control, contain, hold back, smother, silence, cover up, bottle up, choke back

sure ADJECTIVE **1** *I'm sure Dan will be perfectly safe.* ► certain, convinced, confident, positive, assured, definite, persuaded, satisfied, decided, resolute OPPOSITES ARE doubtful, uncertain **2** *He's sure to ask us what we were doing.* ► bound, certain, likely, destined, compelled, obliged, required AN OPPOSITE IS unlikely **3** *He left in the sure knowledge that he would be returning. He was pacing the floor, a sure sign of anxiety.* ► clear, undoubted, indisputable, inescapable, undeniable, undisputed, guaranteed, convincing, precise, proven, inevitable, accurate, true OPPOSITES ARE uncertain, doubtful, unsure **4** *James was always a sure friend.* ► dependable, steadfast, steady, reliable, faithful, firm, solid, trusty,

surely ADVERB **1** in a sure or certain way **2** I feel sure • *Surely we met last year.*

surf NOUN the white foam of waves breaking on a rock or shore

surf VERB surfs, surfing, surfed **1** go surfing **2** browse through the Internet

surface NOUN surfaces **1** the outside of something **2** any of the sides of an object, especially the top part **3** an outward appearance • *On the surface he was a kindly man.*

surfboard NOUN surfboards a board used in surfing

surfeit (ser- fit) NOUN too much of something
▷ **surfeited** ADJECTIVE

surfing NOUN balancing yourself on a board that is carried to the shore on the waves
▷ **surfer** NOUN

surf riding NOUN surfing
▷ **surf rider** NOUN

surge VERB surges, surging, surged **1** move forward or upward like waves **2** increase suddenly and powerfully
▷ **surge** NOUN

surgeon NOUN surgeons a doctor who treats disease or injury by removing or repairing the affected parts of the body

surgery NOUN surgeries **1** the work of a surgeon **2** the place where a doctor or dentist regularly gives advice and treatment to patients
▷ **surgical** ADJECTIVE **surgically** ADVERB

surly ADJECTIVE surlier, surliest bad-tempered and unfriendly
▷ **surliness** NOUN

surname NOUN surnames the name held by all members of a family

surpass VERB surpasses, surpassing, surpassed do or be better than all others; excel

surplus NOUN surpluses an amount left over after spending or using all that was needed
▷ **surplus** ADJECTIVE

surprise NOUN surprises **1** something unexpected **2** the feeling caused by something that was not expected
take someone by surprise happen to someone unexpectedly

surprise VERB surprises, surprising, surprised **1** be a surprise; make someone feel surprise **2** come upon or attack somebody unexpectedly
▷ **surprisingly** ADVERB

surrender VERB surrenders, surrendering, surrendered **1** stop fighting and give yourself up to an enemy **2** hand something over to

---

Thesaurus

---

trustworthy, effective, loyal, safe, secure, unfailing, unswerving OPPOSITES ARE fickle, unreliable.

surf VERB *surfing the Internet* ▸ browse, explore, search, probe, research, survey, scrutinize

surface NOUN **1** *The surface of the door had become rotten.* ▸ outside, exterior, facade, veneer, covering, face AN OPPOSITE IS inside **2** *A cube has six surfaces.* ▸ face, side, facet, plane

surface VERB *A submarine surfaced in the bay. A new idea had surfaced* ▸ come up, rise, appear, emerge, materialize, come to light, (*informal*) pop up AN OPPOSITE IS dive

surge NOUN **1** *a surge of water* ▸ gush, rush, sweep, flow, wave **2** *a surge of excitement* ▸ outburst, upsurge, outpouring, rush, gush, increase, onrush

surge VERB **1** *Water surged into people's houses.* ▸ gush, rush, stream, flow, swirl, roll **2** *The crowd surged forward* ▸ rush, sweep, push, stampede

surplus NOUN *a fruit surplus* ▸ excess, surfeit, glut, superfluity, oversupply, oversufficiency, superabundance, profusion

surprise NOUN **1** *Alice looked at him in surprise.* ▸ amazement, astonishment, incredulity, wonder, alarm, consternation, bewilderment,

dismay **2** *This might come as a surprise to you.* ▸ shock, revelation, bolt from the blue, (*more informal*) bombshell, (*more informal*) eye-opener

surprise VERB **1** *Here's a piece of information that will surprise you.* ▸ astonish, amaze, astound, shock, stupefy, dumbfound, stagger, disconcert, flabbergast, nonplus, take your breath away, take aback, (*more informal*) bowl over **2** *He surprised an intruder, who ran off.* ▸ discover, take unawares, take by surprise, come upon, catch out, catch in the act, catch red-handed, detect

surprised ADJECTIVE *I was surprised to see Lisa sitting up in bed reading.* ▸ astonished, amazed, astounded, dumbfounded, flabbergasted, nonplussed, shocked, speechless, staggered, disconcerted, incredulous, startled, stunned, taken aback, taken by surprise, thunderstruck

surprising ADJECTIVE *They completed the task with surprising speed.* ▸ astonishing, amazing, astounding, unexpected, extraordinary, remarkable, incredible, staggering, startling, stunning OPPOSITES ARE predictable, unsurprising

surrender VERB **1** *The rebels surrendered after months of fierce fighting.* ▸ capitulate, submit, yield, succumb, give up, resign, (*more informal*)

another person, especially when compelled to do so
▷ **surrender** NOUN

surreptitious (su- rep- tish- us) ADJECTIVE stealthy
▷ **surreptitiously** ADVERB

surrogate mother NOUN surrogate mothers a woman who agrees to conceive and give birth to a baby for a woman who cannot do so herself, using a fertilized egg of the other woman or sperm from the other woman's partner

surround VERB surrounds, surrounding, surrounded come or be all around a person or thing • *Police surrounded the building.*

surroundings PLURAL NOUN the conditions or area around a person or thing

survey (ser- vay) NOUN surveys **1** a general look at something **2** an inspection of an area, building, etc.

survey (ser- vay) VERB surveys, surveying, surveyed make a survey of something; inspect
▷ **surveyor** NOUN

survival NOUN survivals **1** surviving; the likelihood of surviving **2** something that has survived from an earlier time

survive VERB survives, surviving, survived **1** stay alive; continue to exist **2** remain alive after an accident or disaster • *Only two people survived the crash.* **3** continue living after someone has died
▷ **survivor** NOUN

susceptible (sus- ept- ib- ul) ADJECTIVE likely to be affected by something • *She is susceptible to colds.*
▷ **susceptibility** NOUN

suspect (sus- pekt) VERB suspects, suspecting, suspected **1** think that a person is not to be trusted or has committed a crime; distrust **2** have a feeling that something is likely or possible

suspect (sus- pekt) NOUN suspects a person who is suspected of a crime, etc.
▷ **suspect** ADJECTIVE

suspend VERB suspends, suspending, suspended **1** hang something up **2** postpone; stop something temporarily **3** remove a person from a job or position for a time **4** keep something from falling or sinking in air or liquid, • *Particles are suspended in the fluid.*

Thesaurus

throw in the towel **2** *We are being asked to surrender personal freedoms in the national interest.* ▶ relinquish, give up, forgo, cede, abandon, renounce, waive

surround VERB **1** *The garden surrounds the ruins of a fourteenth-century castle.* ▶ encircle, ring, skirt, encompass **2** *Anabelle found herself surrounded by angry faces.* ▶ besiege, beset, engulf, girdle, hedge in, hem in

surroundings NOUN *The hotel is set in the beautiful surroundings of a country park.* ▶ environment, location, setting, vicinity, neighbourhood, background, ambience, milieu

surveillance NOUN *Police surveillance prevented us from contacting your sister-in-law.* ▶ check, observation, scrutiny, supervision, vigilance, watch

survey NOUN **1** *In our main survey, people were asked where they would go for a loan.* ▶ poll, investigation, appraisal, inquiry, census, count, evaluation, study, assessment, examination, inspection, scrutiny, (technical) triangulation **2** *a survey of recent work on the subject* ▶ review, overview, synopsis, summary **3** *Be sure to get a survey of the house before making an offer.* ▶ inspection, assessment, appraisal, examination, valuation

survey VERB **1** *Those who wish can survey the scene from a panoramic tower.* ▶ observe, view, look at, look over **2** *The artist stood back to survey his work.* ▶ examine, inspect, study,

scrutinize, consider, review **3** *Engineers arrived to survey the area.* ▶ do a survey of, reconnoitre, plot, map out, plan out, measure, (technical) triangulate

survive VERB **1** *They had enough water to survive until help came.* ▶ remain alive, live, last, carry on, keep going, sustain yourself, continue, endure AN OPPOSITE IS perish **2** *Some of the workers' cottages still survive.* ▶ remain, exist **3** *Six people survived the crash.* ▶ withstand, come through, live through, weather AN OPPOSITE IS succumb to **4** *She is survived by her husband and three sons.* ▶ outlast, outlive

susceptible ADJECTIVE *Network cables are susceptible to electrical interference.* ▶ vulnerable, prone, liable, subject, sensitive, inclined, predisposed OPPOSITES ARE resistant, immune

suspect ADJECTIVE *Two suspect packages stood by the door.* ▶ suspicious, doubtful, dubious, questionable, (more informal) fishy

suspect VERB **1** *The plan's only going to be successful if they don't suspect anything.* ▶ distrust, mistrust, call into question, have doubts about, doubt **2** *I suspect another visit may not be possible.* ▶ expect, surmise, presume, assume, imagine, dare say, think, fancy, guess, infer, conclude, conjecture, judge

suspend VERB **1** *Long sacks were suspended from hooks on the wall.* ▶ hang, sling, swing, dangle, drape **2** *The stock exchange decided to suspend trading.* ▶ adjourn, discontinue, interrupt, break off, postpone, put off, defer, delay

A
B
C
D
E
F
G
H
I
J
K
L
M
N
O
P
Q
R
S
T
U
V
W
X
Y
Z

suspender NOUN suspenders a fastener to hold up a sock or stocking by its top

suspense NOUN an anxious or uncertain feeling while waiting for something to happen or become known

suspension NOUN **1** suspending **2** the springs etc. in a vehicle that lessen the effect of rough road surfaces **3** a liquid containing small pieces of solid material which do not dissolve

suspicion NOUN suspicions **1** suspecting or being suspected; distrust **2** a slight belief

suspicious ADJECTIVE feeling or causing suspicion
▷ **suspiciously** ADVERB

sustain VERB sustains, sustaining, sustained **1** keep someone alive **2** keep something happening **3** undergo or suffer • *We sustained another defeat.* **4** support or uphold
▷ **sustainable** ADJECTIVE

SW ABBREVIATION **1** southwest **2** southwestern

swab (swob) NOUN swabs **1** a mop or pad for cleaning or wiping something; a small pad for cleaning a wound **2** a specimen of fluid from the body taken on a swab for testing

swab VERB swabs, swabbing, swabbed clean or wipe with a swab

swagger VERB swaggers, swaggering, swaggered walk or behave in a conceited way; strut
▷ **swagger** NOUN

swallow VERB swallows, swallowing, swallowed **1** make something go down your throat **2** believe something that ought not to be believed
▷ **swallow** NOUN

swallow up take in and cover; engulf • *She was swallowed up in the crowd.*
[from Old English *swelgan*]

swallow NOUN swallows a small bird with a forked tail and pointed wings [from Old English *swealwe*]

swamp NOUN swamps a marsh
▷ **swampy** ADJECTIVE

swamp VERB swamps, swamping, swamped **1** flood **2** overwhelm with a great mass or number of things

swan NOUN swans a large white water bird with a long neck

swank VERB swanks, swanking, swanked (*informal*) boast or swagger; show off

swank NOUN (*informal*) showing yourself or your possessions off in a conceited way

swan song NOUN swan songs a person's last performance or work

swap VERB swaps, swapping, swapped (*informal*) exchange one thing for another
▷ **swap** NOUN
[formerly = seal a bargain by slapping each other's hands; imitating the sound]

Thesaurus

3 *Two directors were suspended for a year.*
► exclude, debar, remove, dismiss, expel

suspense NOUN *There is an art to building up suspense.* ► tension, uncertainty, doubt, anticipation, expectation, expectancy, excitement, apprehension, drama

suspicion NOUN **1** *The KGB did not need proof; suspicion was more than enough.* ► intuition, conjecture, speculation, supposition, belief, caution, wariness **2** *As we drank our coffee I outlined my suspicions about Martinez.*
► misgiving, doubt, qualm, uncertainty, reservation **3** *A suspicion of a grin appeared on her face.* ► trace, hint, glimmer, shadow, suggestion, tinge, touch

suspicious ADJECTIVE **1** *It was clear that he was increasingly suspicious of his visitor.* ► doubtful, distrustful, mistrustful, unsure, sceptical, apprehensive, wary, chary, disbelieving, incredulous, unconvinced (about), uneasy (about) OPPOSITES ARE trusting, credulous **2** *He's a highly suspicious character and we haven't spoken for years. At first the police treated the case as a suspicious death.* ► questionable, suspect, dubious, disreputable, unreliable, untrustworthy, peculiar, irregular, (*more informal*) fishy, (*more informal*) shady OPPOSITES ARE straightforward, innocent

sustain VERB **1** *The country would have to sustain a large population.* ► maintain, keep, continue, preserve, provide for, nurture **2** *She had some bread and cheese to sustain her.* ► nourish, feed **3** *They were sustained by these happy memories.*
► comfort, support, encourage, succor, hearten, (*more informal*) buck up **4** *It was doubtful whether the structure could sustain the increased weight.* ► support, bear, carry

swallow VERB **1** *He was finding it hard to swallow food.* ► eat, drink, consume, devour, gulp down, guzzle **2** *I was a little surprised when they swallowed my story.* ► accept, believe, (*more informal*) buy

swallow up *The darkness swallowed them up.*
► engulf, enfold, envelop, absorb, enclose

swamp NOUN *The rains had turned the fields into a huge swamp.* ► marsh, bog, quagmire, mire, fen, marshland, morass, wetland, slough

swamp VERB **1** *A tidal wave swamped the coastal regions.* ► flood, inundate, overwhelm, engulf, drench, saturate, submerge, waterlog **2** *Journalists had swamped the unfortunate village.* ► overrun, overwhelm, inundate, besiege, beset

swap VERB *Helen swapped her Spanish stamps for some Belgian ones she didn't have.* ► exchange, barter, bargain, switch

swarm NOUN swarms a large number of insects or birds, etc., flying or moving about together

swarm VERB swarms, swarming, swarmed **1** gather or move in a swarm **2** be crowded with people, etc. ● *The town is swarming with tourists in the summer.*

swarthy ADJECTIVE having a dark complexion
▷ **swarthiness** NOUN

swastika NOUN swastikas an ancient symbol formed by a cross with its ends bent at right angles, adopted by the Nazis as their sign [from Sanskrit *svasti* = well-being, luck]

swat VERB swats, swatting, swatted hit or crush a fly, etc.
▷ **swatter** NOUN

swathe (swayth) VERB swathes, swathing, swathed wrap in layers of bandages, paper, or clothes

swathe NOUN swathes a broad strip or area ● *vast swathes of countryside*

sway VERB sways, swaying, swayed **1** move or swing gently from side to side **2** influence ● *His speech swayed the crowd.*
▷ **sway** NOUN

swear VERB swears, swearing, swore, sworn **1** make a solemn promise ● *She swore to tell the truth.* **2** make a person take an oath ● *We swore him to secrecy.* **3** use curses or coarse

words in anger or surprise etc.
swear by have great confidence in something

sweat (swet) NOUN moisture given off by the body through the pores of the skin; perspiration
▷ **sweaty** ADJECTIVE

sweat VERB sweats, sweating, sweated give off sweat; perspire

sweater NOUN sweaters a jersey or pullover

sweatshirt NOUN sweatshirts a thick cotton jersey worn for sports or casual wear

sweep VERB sweeps, sweeping, swept **1** clean or clear with a broom or brush, etc. **2** move or remove quickly ● *The floods swept away the bridge.* **3** go smoothly and quickly ● *She swept out of the room.* **4** spread quickly over an area ● *A new craze is sweeping the country.*
▷ **sweeper** NOUN

sweep NOUN sweeps **1** the process of sweeping ● *Give this room a good sweep.* **2** a sweeping movement **3** a chimney sweep **4** a sweepstake

sweeping ADJECTIVE general or wide-ranging ● *He made sweeping changes.*

sweet ADJECTIVE **1** tasting as if it contains sugar; not bitter **2** very pleasant ● *a sweet smell* **3** charming or delightful
▷ **sweetly** ADVERB **sweetness** NOUN
a sweet tooth a liking for sweet things

Thesaurus

swarm NOUN *There were swarms of police everywhere.* ▶ crowd, horde, mass, throng, multitude, host

swarm VERB *Reporters were swarming all over the place.* ▶ crowd, throng, flock, mass, cluster, congregate
be swarming with *The beaches were swarming with tourists.* ▶ be overrun with, be crawling with, be teeming, be full of, be infested with, be invaded by, abound in

sway VERB **1** *The branches swayed in the breeze.* ▶ swing, bend, rock, wave, lurch, lean from side to side, move to and fro, oscillate **2** *Many people are swayed by what they read in the newspapers.* ▶ influence, persuade, affect, govern **3** *She would not sway in her resolve to go through with it.* ▶ fluctuate, waver, swerve, vacillate, hesitate, veer, divert, go off course

swear VERB **1** *He swore he had told the truth.* ▶ vow, pledge, promise, give your word, affirm, attest, declare, state on oath, take an oath, testify **2** *She spilled her drink and swore.* ▶ blaspheme, curse, use bad language

swearword NOUN *In those days you never heard a swearword on television.* ▶ expletive, obscenity, profanity, curse, oath, four-letter word
swearwords ▶ bad language, foul language, profanity, swearing

sweat VERB *He had begun to sweat in the heat.* ▶ perspire, swelter, exude

sweat NOUN **1** *By now he was drenched in sweat.* ▶ perspiration, moisture, dampness **2** (*informal*) *We were in a sweat to get away.* ▶ panic, fluster, state of agitation, state of anxiety **3** (*informal*) *Taking all the children home had been quite a sweat.* ▶ chore, task, labor, ordeal

sweaty ADJECTIVE *He shook Karl's sweaty hand.* ▶ sweating, perspiring, sticky, clammy, damp, moist

sweep VERB **1** *It was time to sweep the kitchen floor.* ▶ brush, clean, scrub, wipe, hoover **2** *Another bus swept past them.* ▶ sail, glide, streak, tear, hurtle, whizz

sweet ADJECTIVE **1** *The tea was too sweet.* ▶ sweetened, sugary, saccharine, honeyed, cloying **2** *the sweet perfume of roses* ▶ fragrant, aromatic, sweet-smelling, balmy, scented **3** *She sang a sweet song.* ▶ melodious, lyrical, mellifluous, sweet-toned **4** *Life can be sweet.* ▶ pleasant, pleasing, enjoyable, satisfying, delightful, agreeable **5** *the sweet air of the mountains* ▶ fresh, pure, wholesome, clear, clean **6** *a sweet little baby* ▶ cute, pretty, delightful **7** *Dora has a sweet nature.* ▶ loving, appealing, affectionate, adorable, lovely, charming

a b c d e f g h i j k l m n o p q r **s** t u v w x y z

sweet NOUN sweets **1** a small shaped piece of sweet food made with sugar, chocolate, etc. **2** the sweet course in a meal **3** a beloved person

sweeten VERB sweetens, sweetening, sweetened make or become sweet
▷ **sweetener** NOUN

sweetheart NOUN sweethearts a person you love very much

swell VERB swells, swelling, swelled, swollen or swelled **1** make or become larger • *My ankle was starting to swell.* **2** increase in amount, volume, or force

swell NOUN swells **1** the process of swelling **2** the rise and fall of the sea's surface

swelling NOUN swellings a swollen place

swerve VERB swerves, swerving, swerved turn to one side suddenly
▷ **swerve** NOUN

swift ADJECTIVE quick or rapid
▷ **swiftly** ADVERB **swiftness** NOUN

swift NOUN swifts a small bird rather like a swallow

swill VERB swills, swilling, swilled pour water over or through something; wash or rinse

swim VERB swims, swimming, swam, swum **1** move the body through the water; be in the water for pleasure **2** cross by swimming • *She swam the Channel.* **3** float **4** be covered with or full of liquid • *Our eyes were swimming with tears.* **5** feel dizzy • *His head swam.*
▷ **swimmer** NOUN

swim NOUN swims the action of swimming • *We went for a swim.*
▷ **swimsuit** NOUN

swimming bath NOUN swimming baths a public swimming pool

swimming pool NOUN swimming pools an artificial pool for swimming in

swindle VERB swindles, swindling, swindled cheat a person in business, etc.
▷ **swindle** NOUN **swindler** NOUN
[from German *Schwindler* = a fool, a cheat]

swine NOUN swine **1** a pig **2** (*informal*) a very unpleasant person

swing VERB swings, swinging, swung **1** move back and forth while hanging **2** move or turn in a curve • *The door swung open.* **3** change from one opinion or mood etc. to another

swing NOUN swings **1** a swinging movement **2** a seat hung on chains or ropes, etc., so that it can be moved backward and forward **3** the amount by which votes or opinions, etc., change from one side to another **4** a kind of jazz music
in full swing at the height of activity

swipe VERB swipes, swiping, swiped **1** hit with a swinging blow **2** (*informal*) steal something **3** pass a credit card through an

Thesaurus

sweeten VERB **1** *You may need to sweeten the juice a little.* ► make sweeter, sugar **2** *She was furious and he had no idea how to sweeten her.* ► mollify, pacify, calm, soothe, appease, mellow

swell VERB **1** *He could almost feel his stomach swelling.* ► expand, dilate, distend, enlarge, bloat, bulge, balloon, inflate, puff up, billow OPPOSITES ARE contract, shrink **2** *The droning in her head swelled and faded.* ► intensify, increase, heighten, surge **3** *The population swelled with immigration after the war.*
► increase, enlarge, expand, grow *or* get bigger, build up, extend OPPOSITES ARE decrease, decline

swell NOUN *a heavy swell in the Channel* ► surge, roll, billow, undulation

swerve VERB *The car swerved to avoid a squirrel.*
► turn aside, deviate, swing, weave, change direction, veer, take avoiding action

swift ADJECTIVE **1** *Her letter brought a swift reply.*
► quick, rapid, prompt, immediate, instant, speedy, fast, instantaneous, punctual AN OPPOSITE IS slow **2** *They all made swift progress.*
► rapid, quick, speedy, fast, brisk, lively

swindle VERB *The company had been swindled out of a large sum of money.* ► cheat, defraud, trick, fleece, dupe, deceive, (*more informal*) con, (*more informal*) diddle, (*more informal*) do, (*more informal*) bamboozle

swindle NOUN *an insurance swindle* ► fraud, fiddle, racket, deception, sham, (*more informal*) con

swindler NOUN *Thousands of pensioners had fallen victim to the swindlers.* ► fraudster, confidence trickster, confidence man, trickster, imposter, cheat, charlatan, (*more informal*) con man

swing VERB **1** *The inn sign swung in the wind.*
► sway, flap, dangle, hang loose, rock, swivel, oscillate, turn, wave around **2** *The van swung across the carriageway.* ► swerve, veer, turn aside, deviate, weave **3** *Public opinion was swinging in favor of the war.* ► fluctuate, shift, change, waver, move, alter, oscillate

swing NOUN **1** *a huge swing in public opinion*
► shift, fluctuation, movement, change, oscillation, variation **2** *a swing of the pendulum*
► oscillation

swipe VERB **1** *He threatened to swiped at her with the towel.* ► hit, strike **2** (*informal*) *Someone swiped my pen.* ► steal, take, filch, snatch, (*informal*) nick, (*informal*) pinch

electronic reading device when making a payment
▷ **swipe** NOUN

swirl VERB swirls, swirling, swirled move around quickly in circles
▷ **swirl** NOUN
[probably from early German or Dutch]

swish VERB swishes, swishing, swished move with a hissing sound
▷ **swish** NOUN

Swiss roll NOUN Swiss rolls a thin sponge cake spread with jam or cream and rolled up

switch NOUN switches **1** a device that is pressed or turned to start or stop something working, especially by electricity **2** a change of opinion, policy, or methods **3** a mechanism for moving the points on a railway track **4** a flexible rod or whip

switch VERB switches, switching, switched **1** turn something on or off by means of a switch **2** change or replace something

switchback NOUN switchbacks a railway at a fair, with steep slopes up and down alternately

switchboard NOUN switchboards a panel with switches, etc., for making telephone connections or operating electric circuits

swivel VERB swivels, swivelling, swivelled turn round

swivel NOUN swivels a device joining two things so that one can revolve without turning the other

swollen past participle of swell

swoon VERB swoons, swooning, swooned (old use or poetical) faint
▷ **swoon** NOUN

swoop VERB swoops, swooping, swooped **1** come down with a rushing movement **2** make a sudden attack or raid
▷ **swoop** NOUN

sword (sord) NOUN swords a weapon with a long pointed blade fixed in a handle or hilt
▷ **swordsman** NOUN

swordfish NOUN swordfish a large sea fish with a long swordlike upper jaw

sworn ADJECTIVE **1** given under oath, • sworn testimony **2** determined to remain so • They are sworn enemies.

sycamore NOUN sycamores a tall tree with winged seeds, often grown for its timber

syllable NOUN syllables a word or part of a word that has one vowel sound when you say it • "Cat" has one syllable, "el-e-phant" has three syllables.
▷ **syllabic** ADJECTIVE

syllabus NOUN syllabuses a summary of the things to be studied by a class or for an examination, etc. [via Latin from Greek sittuba = label The tt was misread in Latin as ll]

symbol NOUN symbols **1** a thing used as a sign • The crescent is a symbol of Islam. **2** a mark or sign with a special meaning (e.g. +, -, and x, in mathematics)
USAGE Do not confuse with **cymbal**.

symbolic ADJECTIVE acting as a symbol of something; representing something
▷ **symbolical** ADJECTIVE **symbolically** ADVERB

symbolize VERB symbolizes, symbolizing, symbolized make or be a symbol of something

symmetrical ADJECTIVE able to be divided into two halves which are exactly the same but the opposite way around
▷ **symmetrically** ADVERB **symmetry** NOUN

Thesaurus

swipe NOUN She took a playful swipe at his face.
▶ blow, strike, swing, slap, smack, clout, hit

switch NOUN Whitlock activated the switch on the dashboard. ▶ button, control, key, lever, handle

switch VERB She managed to switch places so she was sitting next to Neil. ▶ change, swap, exchange, replace, shift, substitute

switch on or **off** The user must not switch off the computer before this option is chosen. ▶ turn on or off, put on or off, activate or deactivate, power up or down

swollen ADJECTIVE I climbed the ladder despite my swollen foot. ▶ inflamed, distended, bloated, enlarged, puffed up, puffy, tumescent
OPPOSITES ARE shrunken, shrivelled

swoop VERB Wagtails swooped across my path.
▶ dive, sweep, plunge, plummet, drop, descend, fly down, lunge

swoop on Fifty police officers swooped on a group of farm buildings. ▶ descend on, pounce on, raid, besiege, search

sword NOUN James had armed himself with a sword. ▶ blade, foil, rapier, sabre, broadsword, cutlass, scimitar

symbol NOUN **1** Snakes were seen as symbols of sexuality. ▶ emblem, token, sign, image, figure, representation, mark **2** Too many symbols make the timetable difficult to use if you are in a hurry. ▶ sign, character, hieroglyph **3** The Red Cross symbol was painted on the roof of the vehicle. ▶ logo, badge, mark, crest, insignia

A
B
C
D
E
F
G
H
I
J
K
L
M
N
O
P
Q
R
S
T
U
V
W
X
Y
Z

sympathize VERB sympathizes, sympathizing, sympathized show or feel sympathy
▷ **sympathizer** NOUN

sympathy NOUN sympathies **1** the sharing or understanding of other people's feelings, opinions, etc. **2** a feeling of pity or tenderness toward someone who is hurt, sad, or in trouble
▷ **sympathetic** ADJECTIVE **sympathetically** ADVERB

symphony NOUN symphonies a long piece of music for an orchestra
▷ **symphonic** ADJECTIVE

symptom NOUN symptoms a sign that a disease or condition exists ● *Red spots are a symptom of measles.*
▷ **symptomatic** ADJECTIVE

synagogue (sin- a- gog) NOUN synagogues a place where Jews meet for worship

syndicate NOUN syndicates **1** a group of people or firms who work together in business **2** a group of people who buy something together, or who gamble together, sharing the cost and any gains

syndrome NOUN syndromes a set of signs that are characteristic of a condition, especially of a disease

synonym (sin- o- nim) NOUN synonyms a word that means the same or almost the same as another word ● *"Large" and "great" are synonyms of "big."*
▷ **synonymous** (sin- on- im- us) ADJECTIVE

syntax (sin- taks) NOUN the way words are arranged to make phrases or sentences
▷ **syntactic** ADJECTIVE **syntactically** ADVERB

synthesizer NOUN synthesizers an electronic musical instrument that can make a large variety of sounds

synthetic ADJECTIVE artificially made; not natural
▷ **synthetically** ADVERB

syringe NOUN syringes a device for sucking in a liquid and squirting it out [from Greek *syrinx* = pipe, tube]

syrup NOUN a thick sweet liquid
▷ **syrupy** ADJECTIVE
[from Arabic *sharab* = a drink]

system NOUN systems **1** a set of parts, things, or ideas that are organized to work together **2** a way of doing something ● *a new system of training motorcyclists*

systematic ADJECTIVE methodical; carefully planned
▷ **systematically** ADVERB

Thesaurus

sympathetic ADJECTIVE **1** *She managed a sympathetic smile.* ► commiserating, comforting, supportive, understanding, appreciative, consoling, caring, compassionate, considerate, tender OPPOSITES ARE unsympathetic, unfeeling **2** *sympathetic to All the parents felt very sympathetic to what their daughters were going through.* ► understanding of, appreciative of, concerned about, well-disposed toward **3** *sympathetic to Some of the republics seem to have been sympathetic to this idea.* ► in favor of, in sympathy with, in agreement with, supportive of, receptive to

sympathize VERB **sympathize with 1** *We sympathize with the views of the people living in the area.* ► understand, agree with, approve of, support, commend, appreciate **2** *Many trade unionists instinctively sympathized with the plight of the miners.* ► commiserate with, show sympathy for, be sympathetic toward, be sorry for, identify with, empathize with, feel for, side with, pity

sympathy NOUN *Friends expressed sympathy for those who died or were injured. Don't waste your sympathy on them.* ► commiseration, pity, compassion, condolences, feeling, fellow-feeling, tenderness, understanding, consideration, empathy

symptom NOUN **1** *Several patients suffered from symptoms such as nausea and vomiting.* ► manifestation, indicator, indication, feature **2** *The first symptom of a frozen waste pipe is that the water won't flow out.* ► sign, evidence, indication, warning, testimony

synthetic ADJECTIVE *The whole pitch has been replaced by a synthetic surface.* ► artificial, imitation, manufactured, simulated, substitute, manmade, unnatural, concocted, mock, ersatz, fabricated, fake OPPOSITES ARE natural, real, genuine

system NOUN **1** *a reform of the criminal justice system* ► organization, structure, framework, network, institution, (*informal*) set-up **2** *a system for recording accidents at work* ► procedure, process, routine, scheme, arrangement, means (of), method, methodology, plan, structure, set of rules **3** *a system of government that commands the confidence of all the people* ► philosophy, regime, science, constitution, principles

systematic ADJECTIVE *Citizenship should be taught in every school in a systematic way.* ► methodical, ordered, orderly, organized, structured, planned, systematized, coherent, scientific, logical AN OPPOSITE IS unsystematic

Tt

tab NOUN tabs a small flap or strip that sticks out

tabby NOUN tabbies a grey or brown cat with dark stripes

table NOUN tables **1** a piece of furniture with a flat top supported on legs **2** a list of facts or figures arranged in order **3** a list of the results of multiplying a number by other numbers • *multiplication tables*

tablecloth NOUN tablecloths a cloth for covering a table, especially at meals

tablespoon NOUN tablespoons a large spoon for serving food
▷ **tablespoonful** NOUN

tablet NOUN tablets **1** a pill **2** a solid piece of soap **3** a flat piece of stone or wood, etc., with words carved or written on it

table tennis NOUN a game played on a table divided by a net, over which you hit a small ball with bats

taboo ADJECTIVE not to be done or used or talked about
▷ **taboo** NOUN
[from Tongan (South Pacific) *tabu* = sacred]

tack[1] NOUN tacks **1** a short nail with a flat top **2** a tacking stitch **3** (in sailing) the direction taken when tacking **4** a course of action or policy • *I think we need to change tack.*

tack VERB tacks, tacking, tacked **1** nail something down with tacks **2** fasten material together with long stitches **3** sail a zigzag course to take advantage of what wind there is
tack on (*informal*) add an extra thing

tack[2] NOUN harness, saddles, etc.

tackle VERB tackles, tackling, tackled **1** try to do something that needs doing **2** try to get the ball from someone else in a game of football or hockey **3** talk to someone about a difficult or awkward matter

tackle NOUN tackles **1** equipment, especially for fishing **2** a set of ropes and pulleys **3** tackling someone in football or hockey

tacky ADJECTIVE sticky, not quite dry • *The paint is still tacky.*
▷ **tackiness** NOUN

tact NOUN skill in not offending people
▷ **tactful** ADJECTIVE **tactfully** ADVERB **tactless** ADJECTIVE **tactlessly** ADVERB

tactics NOUN **1** the method of arranging troops, etc., skillfully for a battle **2** the

---

Thesaurus

table NOUN **1** *He put the glasses on the table.*
► dining table, kitchen table, worktop, working surface, coffee table **2** *The table on page three shows monthly rainfall in the region.*
► chart, diagram, graph, list

tablet NOUN **1** *There is a stone tablet over the doorway.* ► plaque, slab, plate, sign **2** *She rang reception and asked for another tablet of soap.*
► bar, piece, block, chunk, slab **3** *He went to his room and took a headache tablet.* ► pill, capsule, caplet

taboo NOUN *There is a taboo against doing business on the sabbath.* ► ban, prohibition, proscription, veto, restriction, anathema

taboo ADJECTIVE *Politics were a taboo subject at the dinner table.* ► forbidden, prohibited, banned, proscribed, unacceptable, disapproved of, unmentionable

tack NOUN **1** *The carpet was held down with a row of tacks.* ► pin, drawing pin, nail, tin tack **2**

tack VERB **1** *He tacked a photo to the notice board.*
► pin, nail, fix **2** *She tacked the hem and tried it on for length.* ► stitch, sew
tack on *A few maps and plans are tacked on at the back of the book.* ► attach, add, append

tackle NOUN **1** *He wanted to buy new fishing tackle.* ► gear, equipment, apparatus, implements, kit, outfit, paraphernalia, rig, tools **2** *The referee penalized him for a late tackle.*
► challenge, interception, attack, block

tackle VERB **1** *The government is determined to tackle the issue of tax avoidance.* ► deal with, grapple with, address yourself to, confront, cope with, face up to, sort out, handle, manage, attend to, combat, set about, undertake **2** *An opposing player tackled him near the touchline.* ► challenge, intercept, stop, confront, attack, take on **3** *Lettie decided to tackle him directly about her pay.* ► confront, approach, challenge, address

tacky ADJECTIVE **1** *The paint was still tacky.*
► sticky, wet, gluey AN OPPOSITE IS dry **2** *tacky quizzes and game shows* ► vulgar, coarse, crude, tawdry, garish, trashy AN OPPOSITE IS tasteful

tact NOUN *A police officer told her the news with great tact.* ► discretion, consideration, sensitivity, tactfulness, delicacy, diplomacy, thoughtfulness, understanding OPPOSITES ARE indiscretion, tactlessness

tactful ADJECTIVE *Molly gave them a tactful reminder about the rent.* ► discreet, judicious, considerate, polite, delicate, diplomatic, sensitive, thoughtful OPPOSITES ARE tactless, indiscreet

tactless ADJECTIVE *She was plainly upset by his tactless remark.* ► indiscreet, insensitive, thoughtless, unthinking, indelicate, clumsy OPPOSITES ARE tactful, discreet

A
B
C
D
E
F
G
H
I
J
K
L
M
N
O
P
Q
R
S
T
U
V
W
X
Y
Z

methods you use to achieve something or gain an advantage
▷ **tactical** ADJECTIVE **tactically** ADVERB **tactician** NOUN
[from Greek *taktika* = things arranged]
USAGE *Strategy* is a general plan for a whole campaign; *tactics* is for one part of this.

tadpole NOUN **tadpoles** a young frog or toad that has developed from the egg and lives entirely in water

tag[1] NOUN **tags** **1** a label tied on or stuck into something **2** a metal or plastic point at the end of a shoelace

tag VERB **tags**, **tagging**, **tagged** **1** label something with a tag **2** add as an extra thing • *A postscript was tagged on to her letter.* **3** (*informal*) go with other people • *Her sister tagged along.*

tag[2] NOUN a game in which one person chases the others

tail NOUN **tails** **1** the part that sticks out from the rear end of the body of a bird, fish, or animal **2** the part at the end or rear of something **3** the side of a coin opposite the head • *Heads or tails?*

tail VERB **tails**, **tailing**, **tailed** **1** remove stalks, etc., from fruit • *top and tail berries* **2** (*informal*) follow someone closely

tail off become fewer, smaller, or slighter, etc.; cease gradually

tailor NOUN **tailors** a person who makes men's clothes

taint NOUN **taints** a small amount of decay, pollution, or a bad quality that spoils something

taint VERB **taints**, **tainting**, **tainted** give something a taint

take VERB **takes**, **taking**, **took**, **taken** **1** get something into your hands or possession or control etc.• *Take this cup.* **2** carry or convey • *Take this parcel to the post.* **3** make use of • *Shall we take a taxi?* **4** indulge in or undertake • *You need to take a holiday.* **5** perform or deal with • *When do you take your music exam?* **6** study or teach a subject• *Who do you take for math?* **7** make an effort • *Thanks for taking the trouble to see me.* **8** experience a feeling • *Don't take offense.* **9** accept or endure • *I'll take a risk.* **10** require • *It takes a strong man to lift this.* **11** write down• *take notes* **12** make a photograph **13** subtract• *take 4 from 10* **14** assume • *I take it that you agree.*
▷ **taker** NOUN

take after have traits similar to a parent, etc.
take in deceive somebody
take leave of say goodbye to

Thesaurus

---

tag VERB *Each bottle was tagged with a different colored label.* ► label, mark, identify, ticket
tag on *A note was tagged on at the end of the letter.* ► add, attach, append, tack on
tag along *Sometimes he let me tag along.* ► follow, go along, accompany

tail NOUN *They waited at the tail of the queue.* ► back, end, rear, extremity, tail end

tail VERB *A squad of reporters had tailed him for five years.* ► follow, shadow, stalk, pursue, track, trail

tail off *Her words tailed off at the expression in his eyes.* ► fade, wane, ebb, peter out, drop away, subside, dwindle, decline, decrease, lessen, reduce, slacken

taint NOUN *free from the taint of corruption* ► stain, smear, hint, trace, blight, contamination

taint VERB **1** *an area tainted by pollution* ► contaminate, pollute, poison, soil, adulterate, dirty, infect **2** *These unhappy events tainted their reputation for ever.* ► tarnish, stain, sully, besmirch, blacken, dishonour, smear, ruin, slander

take VERB **1** *Many prisoners were taken.* ► catch, seize, capture, take captive, arrest **2** *He took her hand gently.* ► clasp, clutch, grasp, grab, grip, take hold of, lay hold of **3** *Someone had taken his car.* ► steal, remove, make off with,

appropriate, (*more informal*) pinch, (*more informal*) nick, (*more informal*) filch, (*more informal*) swipe **4** *Take ten percent from the total.* ► subtract, deduct, knock off, discount **5** *It takes a long time to recover from an illness like this.* ► need, require, call for, necessitate **6** *The pain was more than he could take.* ► bear, put up with, endure, tolerate, suffer, stomach **7** *I'll take you home.* ► accompany, drive, bring, convey, conduct, escort, guide, transport, carry
be taken with *Tanya was rather taken with the idea.* ► be interested in, be attracted by, be captivated by, be fascinated by, be delighted by, be enchanted by
take aback *This suggestion took us aback.* ► surprise, astonish, astound
take apart *a cot that can be easily taken apart* ► dismantle, take to pieces, disassemble
take back *I took back everything I had said.* ► withdraw, retract, disown, recant, repudiate, deny
take down *A police officer took down the details.* ► write down, note, jot down, record
take in **1** *a confidence trick that took everyone in* ► fool, deceive, mislead, dupe, trick, hoodwink, cheat **2** *It was too much information to take in at once.* ► understand, comprehend, grasp, absorb, assimilate, digest **3** *a cruise that takes in the main Greek islands* ► include, incorporate, encompass, comprise, cover

take off (said about an aircraft) leave the ground and become airborne

take on 1 begin to employ someone **2** play or fight against someone **3** (*informal*) show that you are upset

take over take control

take place happen or occur

take up 1 start something **2** occupy space or time etc. **3** accept an offer
[from Old Norse]

takeout NOUN a cooked meal for customers to take away

tale NOUN tales a story [from Old English]

talent NOUN talents a special or very great ability
▷ **talented** ADJECTIVE
[from Greek *talanton* = sum of money. The meaning in English is based on the use of the word in a parable in the New Testament (Matthew 25:14-30), in which a man gives his servants "talents" of money to put to good use.]

talk VERB **talks, talking, talked** speak; have a conversation
▷ **talker** NOUN

talk NOUN **talks 1** a conversation or discussion **2** an informal lecture

talkative ADJECTIVE talking a lot

tall ADJECTIVE **1** higher than the average ● *a tall tree* **2** measured from the bottom to the top ● *It is 10 meters tall.*
▷ **tallness** NOUN

tall tale NOUN **tall tales** (*informal*) a story that is hard to believe

tally VERB **tallies, tallying, tallied** correspond or agree with something else ● *Does your list tally with mine?*

talon NOUN **talons** a strong claw

tambourine NOUN **tambourines** a circular musical instrument with metal discs round it, tapped or shaken to make it jingle

Thesaurus

take it *I take it you want to stay.* ► assume, infer, deduce

take off 1 *I took off my shoes before going in.* ► remove, shed, throw off, discard **2** *a plan that might never take off* ► succeed, do well, catch on **3** *The man took off at a run.* ► run off, run away, leave, escape, depart, disappear

take on *She took on more responsibilities that year.* ► accept, assume, undertake, acquire, shoulder

take up 1 *She took up painting in her forties.* ► engage in, practice, become interested in **2** *a cupboard that takes up a lot of space* ► occupy, absorb, use up, fill

takeoff NOUN **1** *The flight was bumpy for a while after take-off.* ► lift-off, departure, ascent **2** *The sketch is a take-off of the American president.* ► parody, imitation, pastiche, satire, lampoon

tale NOUN *a tale about dragons and heroes* ► story, narrative, narration, history, account, yarn

talent NOUN *a talent for playing the violin* ► gift, aptitude, ability, accomplishment, flair, genius, skill, capacity, expertise, knack, prowess

talented ADJECTIVE *a talented young player* ► gifted, able, accomplished, skilful, skilled, artistic, brilliant, clever, distinguished, expert
OPPOSITES ARE inept, unskilful

talk VERB **1** *I was talking to a friend.* ► speak, chat, converse (with) **2** *They were talking complete rubbish.* ► speak, utter, express, articulate, communicate **3** *They looked for a quiet spot to talk.* ► have a talk, have a chat, converse, confer, speak to one another, communicate with one another **4** *He refused to talk.* ► give information, confess, admit anything **5** *People were beginning to talk.* ► gossip, spread rumors, make remarks, pass comments

talk of *She talked of leaving and settling abroad.* ► speak about, mention, refer to

talk to *He talked to an eager audience.* ► speak to, address, lecture

talk NOUN **1** *too much talk and not enough action* ► conversation, speaking, chatter, discussion, dialogue, (*more informal*) yakking **2** *There was talk of an affair.* ► rumor, gossip (about), (*more informal*) tittle-tattle **3** *a talk in the village hall* ► lecture, address, speech, presentation, discourse **4** *talks* *Peace talks will resume next week.* ► negotiations, discussions, consultations

talkative ADJECTIVE *He had chanced on an unusually talkative taxi driver.* ► chatty, loquacious, garrulous, voluble, effusive, vocal, communicative, forthcoming, articulate
OPPOSITES ARE taciturn, unforthcoming

talking-to NOUN (*informal*) *He was given a severe talking-to and told not to come back.* ► reprimand, lecture, scolding, (*informal*) telling-off, (*informal*) dressing-down

tall ADJECTIVE **1** *a tall man* ► large, big **2** *a tall building* ► high, lofty, towering, soaring, elevated

tally NOUN *a final tally of twenty goals scored during the season* ► total, count, reckoning, account

tally VERB *Her explanation did not tally with the evidence before their eyes.* ► agree, accord, correspond (with to), concur, fit

a
b
c
d
e
f
g
h
i
j
k
l
m
n
o
p
q
r
s
t
u
v
w
x
y
z

A
B
C
D
E
F
G
H
I
J
K
L
M
N
O
P
Q
R
S
T
U
V
W
X
Y
Z

tame ADJECTIVE **1** (said about animals) gentle and not afraid of people; not wild or dangerous **2** not exciting; dull
▷ **tamely** ADVERB **tameness** NOUN

tame VERB **tames, taming, tamed** make an animal become tame
▷ **tamer** NOUN

tamper VERB **tampers, tampering, tampered** meddle or interfere with something

tampon NOUN **tampons** a plug of soft material that a woman puts into her vagina to absorb the blood during her menstrual period

tan NOUN **tans 1** a light brown color **2** a brown color in skin that has been exposed to sun

tan VERB **tans, tanning, tanned 1** make or become brown by exposing skin to the sun **2** make an animal's skin into leather by treating it with chemicals

tandem NOUN **tandems** a bicycle for two riders, one behind the other
in tandem one behind another; together [Latin, = at length]

tang NOUN **tangs** a strong flavor or smell

tangent NOUN **tangents** a straight line that touches the outside of a curve or circle

go off at a tangent move away suddenly from a subject or line of thought being considered

tangerine NOUN **tangerines** a kind of small orange

tangle VERB **tangles, tangling, tangled** make or become twisted into a confused mass
▷ **tangle** NOUN

tango NOUN **tangos** a ballroom dance with gliding steps

tank NOUN **tanks 1** a large container for a liquid or gas **2** a heavy armored vehicle used in war

tankard NOUN **tankards** a large mug for drinking beer from, usually made of silver or pewter

tanker NOUN **tankers 1** a large ship for carrying oil **2** a large lorry for carrying liquid

tantalize VERB **tantalizes, tantalizing, tantalized** tease or torment a person by showing him or her something good but keeping it out of reach

tantrum NOUN **tantrums** an outburst of bad temper

Thesaurus

tame ADJECTIVE **1** *The animal was so tame that it shinned up his leg and dived into a deep pocket.*
► domesticated, gentle, manageable, disciplined, trained, meek, obedient, safe, subdued, submissive, tractable AN OPPOSITE IS wild **2** *Aren't you Joe's tame reporter?*
► cooperative, willing, amenable, biddable AN OPPOSITE IS uncooperative **3** *It turned out to be a tame evening after all.* ► dull, tedious, boring, unexciting, uninteresting, humdrum, bland, feeble, flat, lifeless, uninspiring, unadventurous AN OPPOSITE IS exciting

tame VERB **1** *Wild rabbits can be tamed in captivity.* ► domesticate, break in, train, discipline, house-train, master **2** *She made strenuous efforts to tame her behavior.* ► control, subdue, curb, conquer, master, moderate, mitigate, quell, repress, subjugate, suppress, temper

tamper VERB
tamper with *A student was able to enter the cockpit of an empty aircraft and tamper with the controls.* ► interfere with, meddle with, tinker with, alter, change, adjust, play about with, fiddle about with, make adjustments to

tan ADJECTIVE *a tan overcoat* ► light brown, pale brown, tawny

tangible ADJECTIVE *The experiment brought no tangible results.* ► definite, solid, substantial, concrete, actual, real, material, positive, discernible AN OPPOSITE IS intangible

tangle NOUN *a tangle of wires and cables* ► mass, muddle, jumble, confusion, maze, jungle, knot, twist

tangle VERB **1** *She had managed to tangle her hair.* ► entangle, knot, twist, ravel OPPOSITES ARE untangle, disentangle **2** *A dolphin had become tangled in the net.* ► trap, ensnare, entrap, catch, enmesh **3** *Better not to tangle with people like that.* ► become involved with, come into conflict with, confront, quarrel with, cross swords with

tangled ADJECTIVE **1** *Later they emigrated, but could never escape their tangled past.*
► complicated, complex, confused, convoluted, involved, entangled, intricate AN OPPOSITE IS straightforward **2** *an undergrowth of tangled bushes and trees* ► knotted, matted, convoluted, dishevelled, tousled, unkempt, untidy AN OPPOSITE IS tidy

tangy ADJECTIVE *Citrus adds a tangy taste to all sorts of savory dishes.* ► sharp, pungent, piquant, appetizing, spicy, strong, tart, fresh, refreshing OPPOSITES ARE insipid, bland

tank NOUN **1** *a hot water tank* ► container, cistern, reservoir, basin **2** *a tank of fish*
► aquarium, bowl

tantrum NOUN *He threw a tantrum and rolled on the floor, kicking and screaming.* ► fit of rage, fit of temper, scene, outburst, (more informal) paddy, (more informal) wobbly

tap[1] NOUN taps a device for letting out liquid or gas in a controlled flow

tap VERB taps, tapping, tapped 1 take liquid out of something, especially through a tap 2 obtain supplies or information, etc., from a source 3 fix a device to a telephone line so that you can overhear conversations on it

tap[2] NOUN taps a quick light hit; the sound of this

tap VERB taps, tapping, tapped hit a person or thing quickly and lightly

tape NOUN tapes 1 a narrow strip of cloth, paper, plastic, etc. 2 a narrow plastic strip coated with a magnetic substance and used for making recordings 3 a tape recording 4 a tape measure

tape VERB tapes, taping, taped 1 fix, cover, or surround something with tape 2 record something on magnetic tape
get or have something taped (slang) know or understand it; be able to deal with it

tape measure NOUN tape measures a long strip marked in centimeters or inches for measuring things

taper VERB tapers, tapering, tapered 1 make or become thinner toward one end 2 make or become gradually less

tape recorder NOUN tape recorders a machine for recording music or sound on magnetic tape and playing it back
▷ **tape recording** NOUN

tapestry NOUN tapestries a piece of strong cloth with pictures or patterns woven or embroidered on it

tapeworm NOUN tapeworms a long flat worm that can live as a parasite in the intestines of people and animals

tar NOUN a thick black liquid made from coal or wood, etc., and used in making roads

target NOUN targets something aimed at; a thing that someone tries to hit or reach

tariff NOUN tariffs a list of prices or charges

tarmac NOUN an area surfaced with a mixture of tar and broken stone (called **tarmacadam**), especially on an airfield

tarnish VERB tarnishes, tarnishing, tarnished 1 make or become less shiny • The silver had tarnished. 2 spoil or blemish • The scandal tarnished his reputation.
▷ **tarnish** NOUN

tarpaulin NOUN tarpaulins a large sheet of waterproof canvas

tarry (tar- ee) ADJECTIVE covered with or like tar

tarry (ta- ree) VERB tarries, tarrying, tarried (old use) stay for a while longer; linger

tart NOUN tarts an open pastry case with a sweet filling

tart ADJECTIVE 1 sour 2 sharp in manner • a tart reply
▷ **tartly** ADVERB **tartness** NOUN

tartan NOUN a pattern with colored stripes crossing each other, especially one that is used by a Scottish clan

tartar[1] NOUN tartars a person who is fierce or difficult to deal with

tartar[2] NOUN tartars a hard chalky deposit that forms on teeth

task NOUN tasks a piece of work to be done
take a person to task rebuke him or her

tassel NOUN tassels a bundle of threads tied together at the top and used to decorate something
▷ **tasselled** ADJECTIVE

taste VERB tastes, tasting, tasted 1 take a small amount of food or drink to try its flavor 2 be able to perceive flavors 3 have a certain flavor

Thesaurus

tap NOUN 1 a water tap ► faucet, valve 2 There was a tap at the window. ► knock, rap, knocking, touch

tap VERB 1 She tapped on the door. ► knock, rap, strike 2 I leaned forward to tap her shoulder. ► pat, touch, poke, nudge

tape NOUN 1 The parcel was bound with tape. ► band, binding, strip, braid, ribbon 2 They listened to music on tapes. ► cassette, tape recording

tape VERB I'll tape up the parcel. ► bind, tie, seal

taper VERB 1 The leaves taper to a point. ► narrow, thin, become narrower 2 Their enthusiasm soon tapered off. ► decrease, lessen, dwindle, wane, diminish, die down, peter out

target NOUN 1 a target of $100,000 ► goal, objective, aim, ambition, end, intention 2 the

target of attacks ► victim, butt, object, quarry, prey

tart ADJECTIVE 1 the tart taste of cooked apples ► sharp, sour, acid, tangy, piquant, pungent OPPOSITES ARE sweet, bland 2 He regretted his rather tart response. ► acerbic, sharp, biting, cutting, caustic, scathing

task NOUN Finishing the book in time proved a daunting task. ► job, undertaking, enterprise, exercise, chore, duty, charge, burden, labor, work, mission, requirement
take to task He took his advisers to task for misleading him. ► criticize, rebuke, reproach, reprove, upbraid, censure, admonish

taste NOUN 1 I don't much like the taste of raisins. ► flavor, savor, character 2 Would you like a

a
b
c
d
e
f
g
h
i
j
k
l
m
n
o
p
q
r
s
t
u
v
w
x
y
z

A
B
C
D
E
F
G
H
I
J
K
L
M
N
O
P
Q
R
S
T
U
V
W
X
Y
Z

taste NOUN **tastes** **1** the feeling caused in the tongue by something placed on it **2** the ability to taste things **3** the ability to enjoy beautiful things or to choose what is suitable • *She shows good taste in her choice of clothes.* **4** a liking • *I've developed quite a taste for skiing.* **5** a very small amount of food or drink

tasteful ADJECTIVE showing good taste
▷ **tastefully** ADVERB **tastefulness** NOUN

tasteless ADJECTIVE **1** having no flavor **2** showing poor taste
▷ **tastelessly** ADVERB **tastelessness** NOUN

tasty ADJECTIVE **tastier, tastiest** having a strong pleasant taste

tattered ADJECTIVE badly torn; ragged

tatters PLURAL NOUN rags; badly torn pieces **in tatters** torn to pieces • *My coat was in tatters.*

tattoo[1] VERB **tattoos, tattooing, tattooed** mark a person's skin permanently with a picture or pattern by using a needle and dye

tattoo NOUN **tattoos** a tattooed picture or pattern [from a Polynesian (South Pacific) language]

tattoo[2] NOUN **tattoos** **1** a drumming or tapping sound **2** an entertainment consisting of military music, marching, etc. [from Dutch *taptoe* = close the tap of a cask]

taunt VERB **taunts, taunting, taunted** jeer at or insult someone
▷ **taunt** NOUN

taut ADJECTIVE stretched tightly
▷ **tautly** ADVERB **tautness** NOUN

tautology NOUN **tautologies** saying the same thing in different words, e.g., *You can get*

the book free for nothing (where *free* and *for nothing* mean the same)

tavern NOUN **taverns** (old use) an inn or public house

tawny ADJECTIVE brownish-yellow

tax NOUN **taxes** **1** money that people or business firms have to pay to the government, to be used for public purposes **2** a strain or burden • *The long walk was a tax on his strength.*

tax VERB **taxes, taxing, taxed** **1** put a tax on something **2** charge someone a tax **3** pay the tax on something • *I have taxed the car up to June.* **4** put a strain or burden on a person or thing • *This will tax your strength.* **5** accuse • *I taxed him with leaving the door open.*
▷ **taxable** ADJECTIVE **taxation** NOUN

taxi NOUN **taxis** a car that carries passengers for payment, usually with a meter to record the fare to be paid
▷ **taxicab** NOUN

taxi VERB **taxies, taxiing, taxied** (said about an aircraft) move along the ground or water, especially before or after flying

tea NOUN **teas** **1** a drink made by pouring hot water on the dried leaves of an evergreen shrub **2** these dried leaves **3** a drink made with the leaves of other plants • *camomile tea* **4** a meal in the afternoon or early evening
▷ **teacup** NOUN **tea leaf** NOUN **teatime** NOUN [via Dutch from Chinese]

tea bag NOUN **tea bags** a small bag holding about a teaspoonful of tea

teach VERB **teaches, teaching, taught** **1** give a person knowledge or skill; train **2** give lessons, especially in a particular subject

Thesaurus

taste of my pudding? ► mouthful, bite, morsel, nibble, bit, piece, sample **3** *a millionaire with a taste for travel* ► liking, appreciation, fondness, desire, inclination, preference **4** *Hilary is a person of taste. The decoration was done with taste.* ► judgment, discernment, discretion, discrimination, perception, refinement, sensitivity, style

taste VERB *Anna tasted her drink and smiled.* ► sample, test, try, sip, check

tasteful ADJECTIVE *a plain and tasteful decor* ► discriminating, refined, restrained, sensitive, smart, stylish, well-judged, elegant, fashionable, in good taste, judicious, fastidious, proper AN OPPOSITE IS tasteless

tasteless ADJECTIVE **1** *The vegetables were overcooked and tasteless.* ► flavorless, bland, insipid, weak, watery, characterless, mild, uninteresting AN OPPOSITE IS tasty **2** *a tasteless remark* ► crude, indelicate, uncouth, vulgar, tactless, crass, injudicious, unseemly OPPOSITES ARE tasteful, delicate

tasty ADJECTIVE *a tasty meal* ► delicious, appetizing, luscious, mouth-watering, (more informal) yummy, (more informal) scrumptious

taunt VERB *People taunted him about his marriage.* ► tease, torment, jeer at, mock, ridicule, bait

taut ADJECTIVE *The rope should be taut.* ► tight, tense, firm, rigid, stretched AN OPPOSITE IS slack

tax NOUN *The new government immediately imposed a tax on imports.* ► duty, tariff, charge, imposition, levy RELATED ADJECTIVE ► fiscal

tax VERB **1** *It seems unfair to many people to tax pensions.* ► impose a tax on, levy a tax on **2** *The long walk taxed them severely.* ► tire, strain, exhaust, burden, make heavy demands on

teach VERB **1** *He taught me to swim in the holidays.* ► instruct, train, coach **2** *She teaches children with special needs.* ► educate, tutor, instruct, coach

3 show someone what to do or avoid • *That will teach you not to meddle!*

teacher NOUN **teachers** a person who teaches others, especially in a school

team NOUN **teams 1** a set of players forming one side in certain games and sports **2** a set of people working together **3** two or more animals harnessed to pull a vehicle or a plough etc.

teapot NOUN **teapots** a pot with a lid and a handle, for making and pouring tea

tear[1] (teer) NOUN **tears** a drop of the water that comes from the eyes when a person cries
▷ **teardrop** NOUN
in tears crying

tear (tair) VERB **tears, tearing, tore, torn 1** pull something apart, away, or into pieces **2** become torn • *Newspaper tears easily.* **3** (*informal*) run or travel hurriedly

tear[2] NOUN **tears** a split made by tearing

tear gas NOUN a gas that makes people's eyes water painfully

tease VERB **teases, teasing, teased 1** amuse yourself by deliberately annoying or making fun of someone **2** pick threads apart into separate strands

tease NOUN **teases** a person who often teases others

teaspoon NOUN **teaspoons** a small spoon for stirring tea, etc.
▷ **teaspoonful** NOUN

tea towel NOUN **tea towels** a cloth for drying washed dishes, cutlery, etc.

technical ADJECTIVE **1** to do with technology **2** to do with a particular subject and its methods • *the technical terms of chemistry*

3 using language that only experts can understand
▷ **technically** ADVERB

technical college NOUN **technical colleges** a college where technical subjects are taught

technicality NOUN **technicalities 1** being technical **2** a technical word, phrase, or detail

technician NOUN **technicians** a person whose job is to look after scientific equipment and do practical work in a laboratory

technique NOUN **techniques** the method of doing something skilfully

technology NOUN **technologies** the study of machinery, engineering, and how things work
▷ **technological** ADJECTIVE **technologist** NOUN

teddy bear NOUN **teddy bears** a soft furry toy bear

tedious ADJECTIVE annoyingly slow or long; boring
▷ **tediously** ADVERB **tediousness** NOUN **tedium** NOUN

tee NOUN **tees 1** the flat area from which golfers strike the ball at the start of play for each hole **2** a small piece of wood or plastic on which a golf ball is placed for being struck

teem VERB **teems, teeming, teemed** be full of something • *The river was teeming with fish.*

teenage ADJECTIVE to do with teenagers

teenager NOUN **teenagers** a person in his or her teens

teens PLURAL NOUN the time of life between 13 and 19 years of age

teething NOUN (said about a baby) having its first teeth beginning to grow through the gums

---

Thesaurus

---

teacher NOUN *He had been a teacher all his working life.* ► educator, tutor, instructor, schoolteacher, schoolmaster schoolmistress, pedagogue, academic RELATED ADJECTIVE
► pedagogic pedagogical

team NOUN **1** *the local baseball team* ► squad, side, line-up **2** *the show's production team* ► group, crew, company, body, gang

team VERB **team up** *She teamed up with her fellow artists for a joint exhibition.* ► join forces, collaborate, cooperate, get together, band together, work together, combine, unite

tear NOUN USAGE rhymes with *fear* *There was a tear in his eyes.* ► teardrop, droplet
tears *She was so upset she was close to tears.*
► crying, weeping, sobbing, blubbering

tear VERB (rhymes with *bear*) **1** *Take care you don't tear your clothes.* ► rip, slit, snag, split **2** *She tore the packet open.* ► rip, pull **3** *He tore the book from my hands.* ► snatch, grab, seize,

wrench, wrest **4** (*informal*) *James tore round to the shop.* ► rush, hurry, race, speed, shoot, bolt AN OPPOSITE IS stroll

tear NOUN (rhymes with *bear*) *There's a tear in my jeans.* ► rip, hole, split, slit, rent, gash

tearful ADJECTIVE **1** *Glenda was tearful.* ► in tears, crying, weeping, close to tears, upset OPPOSITES ARE cheerful, happy **2** *a tearful farewell* ► emotional, distressing, upsetting, sorrowful, sad, heartbreaking

tease VERB *His friends teased him about his hair.* ► make fun of, poke fun at, laugh at, mock, taunt, provoke, torment

tedious ADJECTIVE *The work is tedious and time-consuming.* ► dull, boring, monotonous, uninteresting, dreary, humdrum, laborious, irksome, tiresome, unexciting, wearisome OPPOSITES ARE interesting, exciting

teem VERB **teem with** *The pond teemed with fish.* ► be full of, abound in, seethe with, swarm with, be infested with, be crawling with

teetotal ➡ temperamental

teetotal ADJECTIVE never drinking alcohol
▷ **teetotaller** NOUN

telecommunications PLURAL NOUN
communications over a long distance, e.g., by
telephone, telegraph, radio, or television

telegram NOUN telegrams a message sent by
telegraph

telegraph NOUN a way of sending messages by
using electric current along wires or by radio
▷ **telegraphic** ADJECTIVE **telegraphy** NOUN

telepathy (til- ep- ath- ee) NOUN
communication of thoughts from one person's
mind to another without speaking, writing, or
gestures
▷ **telepathic** ADJECTIVE

telephone NOUN telephones a device or
system using electric wires or radio, etc., to
enable one person to speak to another who is
some distance away

telephone VERB telephones, telephoning,
telephoned speak to a person on the
telephone

telescope NOUN telescopes an instrument
using lenses to magnify distant objects
▷ **telescopic** ADJECTIVE

telescope VERB telescopes, telescoping,
telescoped **1** make or become shorter by
sliding overlapping sections into each other
2 compress or condense something so that it
takes less space or time [from Greek tele- = far
+ skopein = look at]

televise VERB televises, televising, televised to
show a programme on television

television NOUN televisions **1** a system using
radio waves to reproduce a view of scenes,
events, or plays, etc., on a screen **2** an

apparatus for receiving these pictures
3 televised programmes [from Greek tele- = far
+ vision]

tell VERB tells, telling, told **1** make a thing
known to someone, especially by words
2 speak • Tell the truth. **3** order • Tell them to
wait. **4** reveal a secret • Promise you won't tell.
5 decide or distinguish • Can you tell the
difference between butter and margarine?
6 produce an effect • The strain began to tell on
him.
all told in all, all together • There are ten of
them, all told.
tell off (informal) reprimand
tell tales report something wrong or bad that
someone has done

telling ADJECTIVE having a strong effect or
meaning • It was a telling reply.

telltale ADJECTIVE revealing or indicating
something • There was a telltale spot of jam on
his chin.

temper NOUN tempers **1** a person's mood
• He is in a good temper. **2** an angry mood
• She was in a temper.
lose your temper become angry

temper VERB tempers, tempering, tempered
1 harden or strengthen metal, etc., by heating
and cooling it **2** moderate or soften the
effects of something • Justice needs to be
tempered with mercy.

temperament NOUN temperaments a
person's nature as shown in the way he or she
usually behaves • a nervous temperament

temperamental ADJECTIVE **1** likely to become
excitable or moody suddenly **2** to do with a
person's temperament
▷ **temperamentally** ADVERB

Thesaurus

tell VERB **1** Tell me what happened. ► inform,
advise, notify (of), let know, acquaint (with)
2 She told us there would be another train in an
hour. ► assure, promise, advise, inform **3** I'll
tell you a secret. ► disclose, reveal, confess,
admit **4** He became more and more excited as he
told his story. ► recount, narrate, relate,
describe, communicate, speak **5** Colin told us
to leave. ► order, instruct, command, direct,
call on **6** It's not easy to tell them apart.
► distinguish, differentiate, identify,
recognize, discern
tell off (informal) He told them off for being late.
► reprimand, scold, rebuke, upbraid, censure,
berate, (informal) tick off

telling ADJECTIVE The argument is expressed in a
few telling phrases. ► revealing, forceful,
striking, persuasive, potent, compelling,
effective AN OPPOSITE IS insignificant

telling-off NOUN (informal) They were lucky to

escape with a mild telling-off. ► reprimand,
scolding, rebuke, caution, admonishment,
(informal) ticking-off

temper NOUN **1** He walked out in a temper.
► rage, fury, fit of rage, passion, tantrum
2 Jenny's temper flared. ► anger, fury, rage,
annoyance, irritation, irritability, petulance
3 Both children had a calm temper.
► temperament, disposition, nature,
character, personality
lose your temper Diana was capable of losing
her temper. ► become angry, fly into a rage,
lose control, blow up, go berserk, (more
informal) go mad, (more informal) go crazy,
(more informal) go bananas, (more informal) fly
off the handle, (more informal) go through the
roof, (more informal) have a fit, (more informal)
see red

temperamental ADJECTIVE **1** The new king
proved to be a temperamental despot. ► moody,
excitable, emotional, volatile, unpredictable,

temperate ADJECTIVE neither extremely hot nor extremely cold • *Britain has a temperate climate.*

temperature NOUN **temperatures 1** how hot or cold a person or thing is **2** an abnormally high temperature of the body

tempest NOUN **tempests** a violent storm

template NOUN **templates** a thin sheet of shaped metal, plastic, etc., used as a guide for cutting or shaping things

temple[1] NOUN **temples** a building where a god is worshipped [from Latin *templum* = consecrated place]

temple[2] NOUN **temples** the part of the head between the forehead and the ear [from Latin *tempora* = sides of the head]

tempo NOUN **tempos** or **tempi** the speed or rhythm of something, especially of a piece of music [Italian, from Latin *tempus* = time]

temporary ADJECTIVE lasting for a limited time only; not permanent
▷ **temporarily** ADVERB

tempt VERB **tempts, tempting, tempted** try to persuade or attract someone, especially into doing something wrong or unwise
▷ **temptation** NOUN **tempter** NOUN **temptress** NOUN

ten NOUN, ADJECTIVE **tens** the number 10

tenacious (ten- ay- shus) ADJECTIVE **1** holding or clinging firmly to something **2** obstinate and persistent
▷ **tenaciously** ADVERB **tenacity** NOUN

tenant NOUN **tenants** a person who rents a house, building, or land etc. from a landlord
▷ **tenancy** NOUN

tend[1] VERB **tends, tending, tended** be inclined or likely to do something • *Prices tend to rise.*

tend[2] VERB **tends, tending, tended** look after • *Shepherds were tending their sheep.*

tendency NOUN **tendencies** the way a person or thing is likely to behave • *She has a tendency to be lazy.*

tender[1] ADJECTIVE **1** easy to chew; not tough or hard **2** easily hurt or damaged; sensitive or delicate • *tender plants* **3** (said about a part of the body) painful when touched **4** gentle and loving • *a tender smile*
▷ **tenderly** ADVERB **tenderness** NOUN

tender[2] VERB **tenders, tendering, tendered** offer something formally • *He tendered his resignation.*

tender NOUN **tenders** a formal offer to supply goods or carry out work at a stated price • *The council asked for tenders to build a school.*
legal tender kinds of money that are legal for making payments

Thesaurus

high-strung, sensitive, capricious, mercurial, touchy, neurotic OPPOSITES ARE placid, phlegmatic **2** *He had a strong temperamental dislike of all conflict.* ► natural, inherent, innate, inborn, characteristic, congenital, constitutional

temporary ADJECTIVE *The restrictions on imports were a temporary measure only.* ► short-term, interim, provisional, stop-gap, short-lived, transitory, momentary, transient, ephemeral AN OPPOSITE IS permanent

tempt VERB *Window displays tempt shoppers into their stores.* ► entice, lure, allure, attract, persuade, coax, woo, inveigle, seduce OPPOSITES ARE deter, repel, discourage

temptation NOUN **1** *She had to resist the temptation to call him from her cell phone.* ► urge, desire, impulse, inclination **2** *I could see the dangers in the temptations of life in New York.* ► attraction, appeal, lure, pull, fascination, seduction, allurement, draw, enticement

tempting ADJECTIVE *It was a tempting package, and I bought the whole deal.* ► attractive, enticing, appealing, beguiling, tantalizing, irresistible

tenable ADJECTIVE *This theory is disproved by modern science and is no longer tenable.* ► credible, defensible, plausible, reasonable,

sensible, viable, sound, feasible, justifiable, arguable, legitimate, logical, rational OPPOSITES ARE untenable, indefensible

tend VERB **1** *She spends many hours in the garden tending her flowers.* ► look after, attend to, manage, take care of, care for, cultivate, mind **2** *Nurses tend the sick and wounded in the field hospitals.* ► look after, attend to, care for, minister to, treat, nurse **3 tend to** *At this time of year, our appetites tend to favor rich desserts.* ► be inclined to, be apt to, be liable to, have a tendency to, be disposed to

tendency NOUN *John has a tendency to put his foot in it.* ► propensity, proclivity, readiness, susceptibility, predilection, predisposition, disposition, inclination, liability, partiality, penchant, trend

tender ADJECTIVE **1** *She liked him tender, gentle like this.* ► kind, caring, compassionate, considerate, humane, affectionate, sensitive, warmhearted OPPOSITES ARE hardhearted, callous, uncaring **2** *He pressed a tender loving kiss on her fingertips.* ► fond, loving, affectionate **3** *In my tender preteen years, I hadn't yet learned to be critical.* ► young, youthful, early, callow, immature, green, inexperienced, impressionable OPPOSITES ARE advanced, mature **4** *Alan's voice cut into the*

a b c d e f g h i j k l m n o p q r **s** **t** u v w x y z

A
B
C
D
E
F
G
H
I
J
K
L
M
N
O
P
Q
R
S
T
U
V
W
X
Y
Z

tendril NOUN **tendrils** **1** a threadlike part by which a climbing plant clings to a support **2** a thin curl of hair, etc.

tennis NOUN a game played with rackets and a ball on a court with a net across the middle

tenor NOUN **tenors** **1** a male singer with a high voice **2** the general meaning or drift of something • *What was the tenor of her speech?*

tenpin bowling NOUN a game in which players try to knock over ten pins set up at the end of a track by rolling hard balls down it

tense NOUN **tenses** the form of a verb that shows when something happens, e.g., he *came* (**past tense**), he *comes* or *is coming* (**present tense**), he *will come* (**future tense**)

tense ADJECTIVE **1** tightly stretched **2** nervous or worried and unable to relax **3** making people tense • *a tense moment*
▷ **tensely** ADVERB **tenseness** NOUN

tense VERB **tenses, tensing, tensed** make or become tense

tension NOUN **tensions** **1** how tightly stretched a rope or wire is **2** a feeling of anxiety or nervousness about something that is just about to happen **3** voltage • *high-tension cables*

tent NOUN **tents** a shelter made of canvas or other material

tentacle NOUN **tentacles** a long flexible part of the body of certain animals (e.g., snails or octopuses), used for feeling or grasping things or for moving

tentative ADJECTIVE cautious; trying something out • *a tentative suggestion*
▷ **tentatively** ADVERB

tenth ADJECTIVE, NOUN next after the ninth

tenuous ADJECTIVE very slight or thin • *tenuous threads* • *a tenuous connection*

tepid ADJECTIVE only slightly warm; lukewarm • *tepid water*

term NOUN **terms** **1** the period of weeks when a school or college is open **2** a definite period • *a term of imprisonment* **3** a word or expression • *technical terms*

term VERB **terms, terming, termed** name; call something by a certain term • *This music is termed jazz.*

terminal NOUN **terminals** **1** the place where something ends; a terminus **2** a building where air passengers arrive or depart **3** a place where a wire is connected in an electric circuit or battery, etc. **4** a monitor and keyboard used for putting data into a computer, or for receiving it

terminal ADJECTIVE **1** to do with or at the end or boundary of something **2** (said of a disease) leading to death
▷ **terminally** ADVERB

terminate VERB **terminates, terminating, terminated** end; stop finally
▷ **termination** NOUN

terminology NOUN **terminologies** the technical terms of a subject
▷ **terminological** ADJECTIVE

terminus NOUN **termini** or **terminuses** the last station on a railway or bus route

termite NOUN **termites** a small insect that is very destructive to timber

terms PLURAL NOUN **1** a relationship between people • *They remained on friendly terms.* **2** conditions offered or accepted • *peace terms*

Thesaurus

tender little scene coldly. This is one of the author's most tender passages. ► romantic, touching, moving, poignant **5** *Cook the rice in boiling salted water until tender.* ► soft, succulent, juicy, fleshy OPPOSITES ARE hard, tough **6** *He lifted her up with tender care, holding her head to his cheek.* ► gentle, fond, loving **7** *Her ankle felt tender.* ► sore, painful, sensitive, inflamed, raw

tense ADJECTIVE **1** *The muscles in his neck were tense.* ► taut, tight, strained, stretched AN OPPOSITE IS slack **2** *Angela was feeling tense and nervy.* ► anxious, nervous, edgy, on edge, strained, stressed, agitated, apprehensive, jittery, fidgety, ill at ease, jumpy, (*more informal*) uptight OPPOSITES ARE calm, relaxed **3** *There was a tense atmosphere in the room.* ► fraught, uncomfortable, strained, charged AN OPPOSITE IS relaxed

tension NOUN **1** *the tension of the ropes* ► tightness, tautness, strain, stretching AN OPPOSITE IS slackness **2** *The tension was unbearable.* ► stress, strain, anxiety, suspense,

apprehension, excitement, nervousness, unease, worry AN OPPOSITE IS relaxation.

tentative ADJECTIVE **1** *This conclusion can only be tentative.* ► provisional, unconfirmed, cautious, diffident, doubtful, halfhearted **2** *a few tentative steps* ► hesitant, indecisive, indefinite, nervous, timid, uncertain AN OPPOSITE IS decisive

tenuous ADJECTIVE *a tenuous argument* ► slight, insubstantial, flimsy, thin , weak, unconvincing AN OPPOSITE IS strong

term NOUN **1** *a technical term* ► word, expression, name, designation **2** *a five-year term of office* ► period, duration, interval, spell, session

terminal ADJECTIVE *a terminal illness* ► incurable, untreatable, inoperable, fatal, mortal, lethal, deadly

terms PLURAL NOUN **1** *She was on good terms with all her staff.* ► relations, standing, footing **2** *The two kings came to terms.* ► agreement, understanding, deal **3** *The terms of the contract* come to terms with become reconciled to a difficulty or unwelcome situation

terrace NOUN terraces 1 a level area on a slope or hillside 2 a paved area beside a house 3 a row of houses joined together 4 a series of steps for spectators at a sports ground
▷ **terraced** ADJECTIVE

terrestrial ADJECTIVE to do with the earth or land

terrible ADJECTIVE very bad; awful
▷ **terribly** ADVERB

terrier NOUN terriers a kind of small lively dog

terrific ADJECTIVE (informal) 1 very great • a terrific storm 2 excellent
▷ **terrifically** ADVERB

terrify VERB terrifies, terrifying, terrified fill someone with terror

territory NOUN territories an area of land, especially one that belongs to a country or person
▷ **territorial** ADJECTIVE

terror NOUN terrors 1 very great fear 2 a terrifying person or thing

terrorist NOUN terrorists a person who uses violence for political purposes
▷ **terrorism** NOUN

terrorize VERB terrorizes, terrorizing, terrorized fill someone with terror; frighten someone by threatening them
▷ **terrorization** NOUN

test NOUN tests 1 a short examination 2 a way of discovering the qualities, abilities, or presence of a person or thing • a test for radioactivity 3 a test match

test VERB tests, testing, tested carry out a test on a person or thing
▷ **tester** NOUN

testament NOUN testaments 1 a written statement 2 either of the two main parts of the Bible, the Old Testament or the New Testament

testicle NOUN testicles either of the two glands where semen is produced

Thesaurus

prevented this. ► conditions, provisos, stipulations, specifications 4 The hotel offers good terms out of season. ► rates, prices, tariff, charges

terrestrial ADJECTIVE one of the factors that give rise to intelligent terrestrial life ► earthly, worldly, mundane, earthbound, ordinary OPPOSITES ARE heavenly, extraterrestrial USAGE Mundane has the special meaning "ordinary." Also, be careful how you use the opposite word heavenly, which has a common second meaning, "wonderful."

terrible ADJECTIVE 1 I had a terrible fall which left me with two broken legs. ► dreadful, frightful, horrible, awful, fearful, ghastly, hideous, shocking, frightening, terrifying 2 There was a terrible smell in the kitchen. ► disgusting, nasty, unpleasant, dreadful, horrible

terribly ADVERB 1 This is terribly important. ► very, extremely, exceptionally, exceedingly, dreadfully, awfully 2 In the next game they played dreadfully. ► badly, atrociously, awfully, appallingly, dismally

terrific ADJECTIVE 1 We heard a terrific thud. ► tremendous, huge, mighty, massive, colossal, enormous, gigantic 2 The novel provides the basis for a terrific movie. ► excellent, wonderful, marvelous, outstanding, magnificent, superb, splendid, first-class, first-rate

terrified ADJECTIVE She gave them a terrified glance, and then bolted. ► petrified, frightened, scared, alarmed, terror-stricken, horror-stricken, panic-stricken

terrify VERB The prospect of all that responsibility terrified him. ► frighten, petrify, scare, horrify, appal, dismay, shock, unnerve

terrifying ADJECTIVE Water was pouring in with terrifying speed. ► frightening, horrifying, petrifying, dreadful, hair-raising, blood-curdling, spine-chilling, appalling, unnerving, (more informal) scary

territory NOUN 1 France sought to locate the launching site on French territory. ► land, country, terrain, ground 2 a Dutch territory in the East ► domain, state, dependency, dominion, colony, possession

terror NOUN Men were driven to do these things by hunger and terror. ► fear, extreme fear, alarm, fright, horror, panic, shock, trepidation

terrorize VERB In the 1820s, Romney Marsh was openly terrorized by armed gangs of smugglers. ► threaten, intimidate, torment, tyrannize, menace, persecute, victimize, oppress, terrify, frighten

test NOUN 1 They will have to pass a test to continue to be paid for the work. ► exam, examination, appraisal, assessment, evaluation 2 We'll be conducting a series of scientific tests. ► trial, experiment, study, evaluation, investigation, analysis, probe

test VERB 1 Psychologists have developed experiments to test their ideas. ► check, appraise, evaluate, validate, examine, analyse, assess, study, screen, try out 2 Here's a chance to test your skills. ► try out, put to the test, explore, trial 3 These demands tested his patience to breaking point. ► strain, tax, put a strain on, stretch, make demands on, sap, drain

a
b
c
d
e
f
g
h
i
j
k
l
m
n
o
p
q
r
s
t
u
v
w
x
y
z

testify VERB testifies, testifying, testified **1** give evidence; swear that something is true **2** be evidence or proof of something [from Latin *testis* = witness]

testimonial NOUN testimonials **1** a letter describing someone's abilities, character, etc. **2** a gift presented to someone as a mark of respect

testosterone (test- ost- er- ohn) NOUN a male sex hormone

test tube NOUN test tubes a tube of thin glass with one end closed, used for experiments in chemistry, etc.

tether VERB tethers, tethering, tethered tie an animal so that it cannot move far

tether NOUN tethers a rope for tethering an animal
at the end of your tether unable to endure something any more

tetrahedron NOUN tetrahedrons a solid with four triangular sides (i.e. a pyramid with a triangular base)

text NOUN texts **1** the words of something written or printed **2** a sentence from the Bible used as the subject of a sermon etc.

textbook NOUN textbooks a book that teaches you about a subject

text message NOUN text messages a written message sent on a cell phone

texture NOUN textures the way that the surface of something feels

than CONJUNCTION compared with another person or thing ● *His brother is taller than he is* or *taller than him.*

thank VERB thanks, thanking, thanked tell someone that you are grateful to him or her **thank you** an expression of thanks

thankful ADJECTIVE grateful

thankfully ADVERB **1** in a grateful way **2** fortunately ● *Thankfully, John remembered to bring some money.*

thankless ADJECTIVE not likely to win thanks from people ● *a thankless task*

thanks PLURAL NOUN **1** statements of gratitude **2** (*informal*) thank you **thanks to** as a result of; because of ● *Thanks to your help, we succeeded.*

that ADJECTIVE, PRONOUN those the one there ● *That book is mine.* ● *Whose is that?*

that ADVERB to such an extent ● *I'll come that far but no further.*

that RELATIVE PRONOUN which, who, or whom ● *This is the record that I wanted.* ● *We liked the people that we met on holiday.*

that CONJUNCTION used to introduce a wish, reason, result, etc. ● *I hope that you are well* ● *The puzzle was so hard that no one could solve it.*

thatch NOUN straw or reeds used to make a roof

thatch VERB thatches, thatching, thatched make a roof with thatch
▷ **thatcher** NOUN

Thesaurus

testify VERB **1** *I may be called on to testify in court.* ► give evidence, be a witness, go into the dock **2** *He testified that he had not been present at the time of the incident.* ► swear, state on oath, attest, declare, affirm, give evidence **3** *The latest finds testify to the great wealth of the city in antiquity.* ► confirm, attest to, demonstrate, substantiate

testy ADJECTIVE *I would get very testy if things weren't exactly right.* ► irritable, bad-tempered, irascible, grumpy, grouchy, touchy, tetchy, crotchety, cantankerous, peevish, fractious, cross, (*more informal*) stroppy, (*more informal*) shirty AN OPPOSITE IS good-humored

text NOUN **1** *Supplying material on disk saves having to retype the text.* ► words, wording, content **2** *a literary text* ► piece of writing, work, book, textbook **3** *a text from the Bible* ► passage, extract, reading, quotation

texture NOUN *The dough should have a soft spongy texture.* ► consistency, composition, quality, feel, constitution, structure, touch

thank VERB **1** *I want to thank all those people who*
have supported us over the years. ► acknowledge, express thanks to, show or express gratitude to, express appreciation of, recognize **2** *He only had himself to thank for the mess he was in.* ► blame, hold responsible

thankful ADJECTIVE *She was thankful for the moonlight, without which she would never have found her way.* ► grateful, appreciative (of), pleased (about), relieved (about), happy (about) OPPOSITES ARE disappointed, ungrateful USAGE Note that *thankful* and *thankless* are not opposites: *thankful* is normally used about a person, whereas *thankless* is used about an activity.

thankless ADJECTIVE *The United States inherited Britain's thankless task of maintaining stability in the region.* ► unenviable, unappreciated, unrecognized, unrewarding, fruitless OPPOSITES ARE worthwhile, rewarding USAGE See the note at thankful.

thanks NOUN *Julia smiled her thanks and then turned to accept David's invitation.* ► gratitude, appreciation, acknowledgement, recognition, thanksgiving

thaw VERB thaws, thawing, thawed melt; stop being frozen

thaw NOUN thaws a period of warm weather that thaws ice and snow [from Old English]

the ADJECTIVE (called the *definite article*) a particular one; that or those

theater NOUN theaters **1** a building where plays, etc., are performed to an audience **2** the writing, acting, and producing of plays **3** a special room where surgical operations are done • *the operating theater* [from Greek *theatron* = place for seeing things]

theatrical ADJECTIVE **1** to do with plays or acting **2** (said about a person's behavior) exaggerated and done for showy effect
▷ **theatrically** ADVERB

thee PRONOUN (*old use*) you (referring to one person and used as the object of a verb or after a preposition)

theft NOUN thefts stealing

their ADJECTIVE **1** belonging to them • *Their coats are over there.* **2** belonging to a person • *Somebody has left their coat on the bus.* [from Old Norse]
USAGE Do not confuse with **there** or **they're**.

theirs POSSESSIVE PRONOUN belonging to them • *These coats are theirs.*
USAGE It is incorrect to write *their's*.

them PRONOUN the form of **they** used as the object of a verb or after a preposition • *We saw them.*

theme NOUN themes **1** the subject about which a person speaks, writes, or thinks **2** a melody

themselves PRONOUN they or them and nobody else

then ADVERB **1** at that time • *We were younger then.* **2** after that; next • *Make the tea, then pour it out.* **3** in that case • *If this is yours, then this must be mine.*

theology NOUN the study of religion
▷ **theological** ADJECTIVE **theologian** NOUN [from Greek *theos* = a god]

theorem NOUN theorems a mathematical statement that can be proved by reasoning

theoretical ADJECTIVE based on theory not on practice or experience
▷ **theoretically** ADVERB

theory NOUN theories **1** an idea or set of ideas put forward to explain something • *Darwin's theory of evolution* **2** the principles of a subject rather than its practice
in theory according to what should happen rather than what may in fact happen

therapy NOUN therapies a way of treating a physical or mental illness, especially without using surgery or medicines
▷ **therapeutic** ADJECTIVE

there ADVERB **1** in or to that place, etc. **2** used to call attention to something (*There's a good boy!*) or to introduce a sentence where the verb comes before its subject (*There was plenty to eat.*)
USAGE Do not confuse with **their** or **they're**.

thereabouts ADVERB near there

therefore ADVERB for that reason

Thesaurus

thaw VERB *The snow was beginning to thaw.*
► melt, unfreeze, soften, liquefy, defrost AN OPPOSITE IS freeze

theater NOUN **1** *This is a work that needs to be heard in a theater.* ► playhouse, auditorium **2** *What made you take up the theater?* ► acting, drama, theatricals, performing

theatrical ADJECTIVE **1** *She wanted a theatrical career.* ► dramatic, acting, stage, thespian **2** *"My dear," cried Ruby making a theatrical gesture.* ► affected, exaggerated, ostentatious, melodramatic, showy, stagy, stilted, unnatural AN OPPOSITE IS natural. USAGE In the first meaning, be careful how you use *dramatic*, which has a common second meaning "sudden and exciting."

theft NOUN *a report of the theft of jewels from a hotel room* ► robbery, stealing, thieving, pilfering, burglary

theme NOUN **1** *Public services have become the dominant theme of domestic politics.* ► topic, issue, subject, concern, question, matter **2** *The*

theme is played by the orchestra and then picked up by the soloist. ► melody, motif, subject, tune, air

theoretical ADJECTIVE **1** *theoretical physics* ► conceptual, pure, abstract, academic OPPOSITES ARE practical, applied **2** *a theoretical possibility* ► hypothetical, notional, conjectural, suppositional, speculative, postulated OPPOSITES ARE concrete, actual, real

theory NOUN **1** *His theories are based on observations and experiments.* ► argument, assumption, belief, conjecture, explanation, guess, hypothesis, idea, notion, speculation, supposition, surmise, thesis, view **2** *the theory of quantum physics* ► laws, principles, rules, science AN OPPOSITE IS practice

therefore ADVERB *This is only a story and therefore you shouldn't believe a word of it.*
► consequently, accordingly, for this or that reason, as a result, as a consequence, so, thus, hence

a
b
c
d
e
f
g
h
i
j
k
l
m
n
o
p
q
r
s
t
u
v
w
x
y
z

thermodynamics ➡ thin

thermodynamics NOUN the science dealing with the relation between heat and other forms of energy

thermometer NOUN thermometers a device for measuring temperature

thermostat NOUN thermostats a piece of equipment that automatically keeps the temperature of a room or piece of equipment steady
▷ **thermostatic** ADJECTIVE **thermostatically** ADVERB

thesaurus (thi- sor- us) NOUN thesauruses or thesauri a kind of dictionary containing sets of words grouped according to their meaning [from Greek *thesauros* = storehouse, treasury]

these plural of this

they PRONOUN **1** the people or things being talked about **2** people in general • *They say the show is a great success.* **3** he or she; a person • *I am never angry with anyone unless they deserve it.*

they're (*mainly spoken*) they are
USAGE Do not confuse with their or there.

thick ADJECTIVE **1** measuring a lot between opposite surfaces **2** measuring from one side to the other • *The wall is ten centimeters thick.*

3 (said about a line) broad, not fine
4 crowded with things; dense • *a thick forest*
• thick fog **5** fairly stiff, not flowing easily
• *thick cream* **6** (*informal*) stupid
▷ **thickly** ADVERB **thickness** NOUN

thicken VERB thickens, thickening, thickened make or become thicker

thicket NOUN thickets a number of shrubs and small trees etc. growing close together

thief NOUN thieves a person who steals things
▷ **thievish** ADJECTIVE **thievery** NOUN **thieving** NOUN

thigh NOUN thighs the part of the leg between the hip and the knee

thimble NOUN thimbles a small metal or plastic cap worn on the end of the finger to push the needle in sewing

thin VERB thins, thinning, thinned make or become less thick
▷ **thinner** NOUN
thin out make or become less dense or crowded

thin ADJECTIVE thinner, thinnest **1** not thick; not fat **2** feeble • *a thin excuse*
▷ **thinly** ADVERB **thinness** NOUN

Thesaurus

thesis NOUN **1** *The facts do not bear out his thesis.* ► theory, hypothesis, argument, premise or premiss, proposition, idea **2** *Her research was presented in her PhD thesis.* ► dissertation, monograph, paper, treatise

thick ADJECTIVE **1** *He was stuffing a thick wad of bills into his jacket pocket. The thick felt curtains were closely fastened.* ► fat, chunky, broad, wide, hefty, bulky, solid, stout, sturdy, substantial AN OPPOSITE IS thin **2** *The lava deposit was no more than a few meters thick. He was a good-looking man with a head of thick black hair.* ► deep, heavy **3** *The collision occurred in thick fog. The path wound through thick oak and pine forests.* ► dense, solid, impenetrable OPPOSITES ARE sparse, clear, open **4** *The shallow water was thick with paddling children.* ► crowded, filled, packed, swarming, teeming, covered **5** *Beat the mixture into a thick smooth paste.* ► stiff, heavy, concentrated, condensed, clotted, coagulated, viscous OPPOSITES ARE thin, watery **6** (*informal*) *"Some of these counselors are so thick," said the woman.* ► stupid, foolish, dull, slow, dim-witted, brainless OPPOSITES ARE clever, bright

thicken VERB *Put a little flour in to thicken the sauce.* ► stiffen, concentrate, condense, reduce, set AN OPPOSITE IS thin out

thickness NOUN **1** *You can use paper of similar thickness.* ► breadth, width, bulk **2** *The thickness of the smoke made it impossible to see.* ► density, denseness, murkiness **3** *Great*

thicknesses of pumice and ash had piled up on the slopes of Vesuvius. ► layer, coating, stratum, seam

thick-skinned ADJECTIVE *He was too thick-skinned to notice the insult.* ► insensitive, unfeeling, hardened, tough, (*informal*) hard-boiled OPPOSITES ARE sensitive, thin-skinned

thief NOUN *The 28-old thief was arrested when he returned to collect his dog.* ► robber, burglar, housebreaker, shoplifter, pilferer, bandit

thieving NOUN *a life of thieving* ► theft, robbery, stealing, pilfering, burglary

thin VERB *Thin the paint with water before use.* ► dilute, water down, weaken
thin out *The crowds began to thin out.* ► decrease, diminish, dwindle, disperse, scatter

thin ADJECTIVE **1** *Frankie was small and thin for his age. He wore a silk shirt with a scarf tucked in around his thin neck.* ► slim, slender, lean, slight, skinny AN OPPOSITE IS fat **2** *She was clad only in a thin nightgown. Thermal underwear keeps you warm by trapping a thin layer of air in its fibres.* ► fine, delicate, light, filmy, flimsy, diaphanous, insubstantial, wispy OPPOSITES ARE thick, heavy **3** *When the paint is nearly dry, apply another thin coat.* ► light, runny, watery, dilute, flowing, fluid OPPOSITES ARE thick, heavy **4** *a thin spread of butter* ► sparse, meagre, scanty, scarce AN OPPOSITE IS thick **5** *The soft thin mist gave a mysterious air to the scene.* ► light, rarefied AN OPPOSITE IS dense

692

thine ADJECTIVE, POSSESSIVE PRONOUN (old use) yours (referring to one person)

thing NOUN **things** an object; something which can be seen, touched, thought about, etc.

think VERB **thinks, thinking, thought 1** use your mind; form connected ideas **2** have an idea or opinion • Do you think we have enough time?
▷ **think** NOUN **thinker** NOUN

third ADJECTIVE next after the second
▷ **thirdly** ADVERB

third NOUN **thirds 1** the third person or thing **2** one of three equal parts of something

Third World NOUN the poorer countries of Asia, Africa, and South America, also called "developing countries"

thirst NOUN **1** a feeling of dryness in the mouth and throat, causing a desire to drink **2** a strong desire • a thirst for adventure
▷ **thirsty** ADJECTIVE **thirstily** ADVERB

thirteen NOUN, ADJECTIVE the number 13
▷ **thirteenth** NOUN, ADJECTIVE

thirty NOUN, ADJECTIVE **thirties** the number 30
▷ **thirtieth** ADJECTIVE, NOUN

this ADJECTIVE, PRONOUN **these** the one here • This house is ours. • Whose is this?

this ADVERB to such an extent • I'm surprised he got this far.

thistle NOUN **thistles** a prickly wild plant with purple, white, or yellow flowers

thong NOUN **thongs** a narrow strip of leather etc. used for fastening things

thorn NOUN **thorns 1** a small pointed growth on the stem of a plant **2** a thorny tree or shrub

thorny ADJECTIVE **thornier, thorniest 1** having many thorns; prickly **2** difficult • a thorny problem

thorough ADJECTIVE **1** done or doing things carefully and in detail **2** complete in every way • a thorough mess
▷ **thoroughly** ADVERB **thoroughness** NOUN

Thesaurus

6 "Get on with it," said a thin, peevish voice.
► weak, faint, feeble OPPOSITES ARE strong, loud **7** a thin excuse ► feeble, tenuous, unconvincing, implausible AN OPPOSITE IS convincing

thing NOUN **1** The cupboard was full of weird things. ► object, item, artifact, article, body, device, entity, implement **2** A strange thing happened today. ► event, occurrence, incident, eventuality, happening, phenomenon, affair, circumstance, deed **3** He didn't have a single thing to add. ► idea, point, statement, thought, concept, detail, fact, factor **4** There's a thing we have to do. ► job, task, deed, act, action **5** (informal) He's got this thing about wasps. ► obsession, preoccupation, phobia, fear (of), terror (of), dislike (of), (informal) hang-up

things 1 Susan put her things in the back of the car. ► belongings, possessions, baggage, clothing, luggage, equipment, (more informal) gear, (more informal) stuff **2** Things improved once I had a job. ► circumstances, conditions, life

think VERB **1** Do you think Molly will come? We thought Rose must have gone home. ► believe, expect, imagine, consider, surmise, conclude **2** Jennifer thought hard for a few moments.
► concentrate, ponder, contemplate, deliberate, cogitate, reflect, muse

think about It was time to start thinking about the future. ► consider, contemplate, weigh up, deliberate about

think of He thought of all the good times they had had together. ► recall, remember, recollect, call to mind

think over Think over what we have said.
► consider, reflect on, muse on, ponder, mull over, (more informal) chew over

think to be She was thought to be worthy of high office. ► consider, deem, judge, hold, reckon

think up We tried to think up a convincing excuse.
► concoct, invent, contrive, devise

thin-skinned ADJECTIVE He is thin-skinned and hates criticism. ► sensitive, touchy, defensive, paranoid AN OPPOSITE IS insensitive

thirst NOUN **1** We needed a drink to quench our raging thirst. ► dehydration, thirstiness, dryness **2** their thirst for knowledge ► appetite, hunger, longing, love (of), yearning, craving, hankering, desire, eagerness, passion

thirst VERB **thirst for** They thirsted for power.
► be thirsty for, crave, strive after, long for, have a thirst for, hunger after, yearn for

thirsty ADJECTIVE **1** The boys were hot and thirsty after their run. ► dehydrated, dry, parched, (more informal) gasping (for a drink), (more informal) panting **2** They were thirsty for adventure. ► eager, hungry, yearning, greedy, itching, longing, avid

thorny ADJECTIVE **1** They had to scramble through thorny undergrowth. ► prickly, bristly, sharp, spiky, spiny, scratchy, barbed **2** the thorny question of who would pay ► tricky, difficult, problematic, awkward, delicate

thorough ADJECTIVE **1** a thorough inquiry
► rigorous, exhaustive, thoroughgoing, detailed, in-depth AN OPPOSITE IS superficial. **2** He was slow but very thorough. ► meticulous, scrupulous, conscientious, assiduous, methodical, diligent **3** He's being a thorough

a b c d e f g h i j k l m n o p q r s **t** u v w x y z

thoroughbred ADJECTIVE bred of pure or pedigree stock
▷ **thoroughbred** NOUN

thoroughfare NOUN thoroughfares a public road or path that is open at both ends

those plural of that

thou PRONOUN (old use) you (referring to one person)

though CONJUNCTION in spite of the fact that; even if ● *We can try phoning her, though she's probably left by now.*

though ADVERB however ● *She's right, though.*

thought NOUN thoughts **1** something that you think; an idea or opinion **2** the process of thinking ● *She was deep in thought.*

thought past tense of think

thoughtful ADJECTIVE **1** thinking a lot **2** showing thought for other people's needs; considerate
▷ **thoughtfully** ADVERB **thoughtfulness** NOUN

thoughtless ADJECTIVE **1** careless; not thinking of what may happen **2** inconsiderate
▷ **thoughtlessly** ADVERB **thoughtlessness** NOUN

thousand NOUN, ADJECTIVE thousands the number 1,000
▷ **thousandth** ADJECTIVE, NOUN

thrash VERB thrashes, thrashing, thrashed **1** beat someone with a stick or whip; keep hitting very hard **2** defeat someone thoroughly **3** move violently ● *The crocodile thrashed its tail.*
thrash something out discuss a matter thoroughly

thread NOUN threads **1** a thin length of any substance **2** a length of spun cotton, wool, or nylon, etc., used for making cloth or in sewing or knitting **3** the spiral ridge around a screw **4** a theme or idea running through a story, argument, etc. ● *I'm afraid I've lost the thread.*

thread VERB threads, threading, threaded **1** put a thread through the eye of a needle **2** pass a strip of film, etc., through or around something **3** put beads on a thread

threadbare ADJECTIVE (said about cloth) with the surface worn away so that the threads show

threat NOUN threats **1** a warning that you will punish, hurt, or harm a person or thing **2** a sign of something undesirable **3** a person or thing causing danger

threaten VERB threatens, threatening, threatened **1** make threats against someone **2** be a threat or danger to a person or thing

Thesaurus

nuisance. ► utter, complete, downright, absolute, perfect, thoroughgoing, total

thought NOUN **1** *She appeared to be lost in thought. It only needs a moment's thought.*
► thinking, contemplation, deliberation, meditation, reflection, pondering, regard, consideration, introspection **2** *I had a sudden thought.* ► idea, notion, belief, concept, conception, perception, conjecture, conviction, opinion **3** *We've given up all thought of extending the project.* ► hope, expectation, intention, aspiration, aim, plan, purpose, design, objective **4** *They seem to have no thought for others.* ► consideration, sympathy, regard, concern, caring, understanding, compassion

thoughtful ADJECTIVE **1** *The thoughtful look on his face did not change.* ► pensive, reflective, contemplative, introspective, absorbed, preoccupied OPPOSITES ARE blank, vacant **2** *Members of the audience added thoughtful comments after the lecture.* ► profound, studious, intelligent, scrupulous, thorough, diligent, meticulous AN OPPOSITE IS superficial **3** *It was thoughtful of you to visit.* ► considerate, kind, caring, attentive, helpful, concerned, friendly, good-natured, unselfish AN OPPOSITE IS thoughtless

thoughtless ADJECTIVE **1** *She realized it was thoughtless of her to rush off like that.*

► inconsiderate, insensitive, unthinking, unkind, unfeeling, uncaring AN OPPOSITE IS considerate **2** *One thoughtless remark can prompt a feeling of depression.* ► unthinking, careless, unmindful, injudicious, ill-considered, unwise, rash AN OPPOSITE IS thoughtful

thrash VERB **1** *The boy was thrashed by his exasperated mother.* ► punish, beat, whip, flog, spank, cane, strap, birch **2** *She thrashed her arms, attempting to swim towards him.* ► jerk, toss, flail **3** (informal) *They were thrashed by six points in the final.* ► defeat, beat, trounce, overwhelm

thread NOUN **1** *He sewed it up with a needle and thread in his girlfriend's flat.* ► cotton, yarn, fiber, strand, twine **2** *I lost the thread of the argument.* ► train of thought, line of thought, drift, tenor, continuity, course, direction, theme

threadbare ADJECTIVE *He inched his way along the threadbare strip of carpet.* ► worn, frayed, ragged, shabby, tattered, tatty

threat NOUN **1** *We got bomb threats against our building.* ► warning, ultimatum, menace **2** *It is a brutal regime that poses a threat to world peace.* ► danger, risk, hazard, menace

threaten VERB **1** *When they came in they threatened us.* ► intimidate, menace, make threats against, browbeat, bully, terrorize, frighten, pressurize **2** *The freedom fighters threatened reprisals. A mass of rain clouds*

three *NOUN, ADJECTIVE* **threes** the number 3

three-dimensional *ADJECTIVE* having three dimensions (length, width, and height or depth)

threshold *NOUN* **thresholds** **1** a slab of stone or board, etc., forming the bottom of a doorway; the entrance **2** the point at which something begins to happen or change • *We are on the threshold of a great discovery.*

thrift *NOUN* **1** careful spending or management of money or resources **2** a plant with pink flowers
▷ **thrifty** *ADJECTIVE* **thriftily** *ADVERB*

thrill *NOUN* **thrills** a feeling of excitement

thrill *VERB* **thrills, thrilling, thrilled** have or give a feeling of excitement
▷ **thrilling** *ADJECTIVE*

thriller *NOUN* **thrillers** an exciting story, play, or film, usually about crime

thrive *VERB* **thrives, thriving, thrived** grow strongly; prosper or be successful [from Old Norse, = grasp, get hold of]

throat *NOUN* **throats** **1** the tube in the neck that takes food and drink down into the body **2** the front of the neck [from Old English]

throb *VERB* **throbs, throbbing, throbbed** beat or vibrate with a strong rhythm • *My head throbbed with pain.*
▷ **throb** *NOUN*

thrombosis *NOUN* the formation of a clot of blood in the body

throne *NOUN* **thrones** **1** a special chair for a king, queen, or bishop at ceremonies **2** the position of being king or queen • *the heir to the throne*

throng *NOUN* **throngs** a crowd of people

throng *VERB* **throngs, thronging, thronged** crowd • *People thronged the streets.*

throttle *NOUN* **throttles** a device that controls the flow of fuel to an engine; an accelerator

throttle *VERB* **throttles, throttling, throttled** strangle
throttle back or **down** reduce the speed of an engine by partially closing the throttle

through *PREPOSITION* **1** from one end or side to the other end or side of • *Climb through the window.* **2** by means of; because of • *We lost it through carelessness.* **3** at the end of; having finished successfully • *He is through with his exam.*

through *ADVERB* **1** through something • *We squeezed through.* **2** with a telephone connection made • *I'll put you through to the president.* **3** finished • *Wait till I'm through with these papers.*

through *ADJECTIVE* **1** going through something • *no through road* **2** going all the way to a destination • *a through train*

throughout *PREPOSITION, ADVERB* all the way through; from beginning to end

Thesaurus

threatened a dramatic change in the weather.
► warn of, forebode, foreshadow, forewarn of, give warning of, portend, presage, indicate **3** *Dumping waste here will threaten the safety and well-being of the region.* ► endanger, imperil, jeopardize, put at risk

threatening *ADJECTIVE* *The dog was baring its teeth in threatening snarls.* ► ominous, menacing, sinister, forbidding, grim, minatory, stern, unfriendly AN OPPOSITE IS comforting

thrill *NOUN* *Just to work with him was a thrill.* ► adventure, excitement, sensation, pleasure, tingle, tremor, (*more informal*) buzz, (*more informal*) kick

thrill *VERB* *She knew he was hers and it thrilled her.* ► excite, delight, rouse, stimulate, exhilarate, stir, electrify, titillate AN OPPOSITE IS bore

thrilling *ADJECTIVE* *a thrilling boat ride to the base of Niagara falls* ► exciting, electrifying, riveting, gripping, thrilling, sensational, spectacular, stimulating, (*more informal*) hair-raising OPPOSITES ARE unexciting, boring

thrive *VERB* *Plants often thrive when the same species are massed together. Two-year-olds thrive on attention.* ► flourish, burgeon, grow, prosper,

succeed, be vigorous, develop strongly, do well OPPOSITES ARE decline, wither

thriving *ADJECTIVE* *By Tudor times distilling was a thriving industry in Scotland.* ► flourishing, growing, prosperous, booming, burgeoning, vigorous, developing, expanding, successful, healthy, affluent, lively, profitable OPPOSITES ARE failing, dying

throaty *ADJECTIVE* *Lucinda's smile gave way to a throaty laugh.* ► gruff, guttural, deep, hoarse, husky, croaky, gravelly, rasping, rough, thick

throb *NOUN* *the annoying dull throb of a neighbor's stereo* ► beat, rhythm, pulsation, pounding, thud, thump, thrum, vibration

throb *VERB* *A vein started to throb in his forehead.* ► pound, pulsate, pulse, beat, thump, palpitate

throng *NOUN* *Vehicles mingled with the throng of foot passengers.* ► crowd, mass, horde, mob, crush

throng *VERB* *Tourists thronged the streets and canals.* ► pack, cram, fill, press into, squeeze into

throttle *VERB* *You're lucky Lewis didn't throttle you.* ► strangle, choke, stifle, smother, suffocate, asphyxiate

a
b
c
d
e
f
g
h
i
j
k
l
m
n
o
p
q
r
s
t
u
v
w
x
y
z

throw VERB throws, throwing, threw, thrown
1 send a person or thing through the air
2 put something in a place carelessly or hastily
3 move part of your body quickly • *He threw his head back and laughed.* **4** put someone in a certain condition etc. • *It threw us into confusion.* **5** confuse or upset • *Your question threw me.* **6** move a switch or lever in order to operate it **7** shape a pot on a potter's wheel **8** hold a party
▷ **throw** NOUN **thrower** NOUN
throw away 1 get rid of something because it is useless or unwanted **2** waste • *You threw away an opportunity.*
throw up (*informal*) vomit

thrush NOUN thrushes a songbird with a speckled breast

thrust VERB thrusts, thrusting, thrust push hard
▷ **thrust** NOUN

thud VERB thuds, thudding, thudded make the dull sound of a heavy knock or fall
▷ **thud** NOUN

thug NOUN thugs a rough and violent person
▷ **thuggery** NOUN

thumb NOUN thumbs the short thick finger set apart from the other four
be under a person's thumb be completely under his or her influence

thump VERB thumps, thumping, thumped
1 hit or knock something heavily **2** punch
▷ **thump** NOUN

thunder NOUN **1** the loud noise that is heard with lightning **2** a similar noise • *a thunder of applause*
▷ **thunderous** ADJECTIVE **thunderstorm** NOUN **thundery** ADJECTIVE

thunder VERB thunders, thundering, thundered **1** sound with thunder **2** make a noise like thunder; speak loudly

thunderbolt NOUN thunderbolts a lightning flash thought of as a destructive missile

Thursday NOUN the day of the week following Wednesday [from Old English *thuresdaeg* = day of thunder, named after Thor, the Norse god of thunder]

thus ADVERB **1** in this way • *Hold the wheel thus.* **2** therefore

thwart VERB thwarts, thwarting, thwarted frustrate; prevent someone from achieving something

Thesaurus

throw VERB **1** *They asked her to throw their ball back.* ► toss, fling, hurl, pitch, lob, cast, (*more informal*) chuck, (*more informal*) sling **2** *He threw a quick glance at them.* ► direct, cast, send, shoot, dart **3** *The horse threw its rider.* ► unseat, dislodge, upset, bring down **4** *The torch threw a beam of light across the passage.* ► cast, project, send, emit, radiate
throw away *He cleared out his room and threw lots of stuff away.* ► discard, throw out, dispose of, get rid of, (*more informal*) ditch
throw off *He hoped he had thrown off his pursuers.* ► shake off, escape, elude, give the slip to, get away from
throw out *He tried to get in the house but was thrown out. The government might be thrown out at the next election.* ► eject, expel, remove, force out, oust, get rid of
throw up *He was tempted to throw up his job and go abroad.* ► abandon, relinquish, give up, (*more informal*) quit, (*more informal*) chuck in
throw NOUN *With one mighty throw the ball went over the fence.* ► heave, fling, toss, lob, pitch

thrust VERB **1** *He thrust a mug of tea into my hands.* ► push, shove, force, press, stick, poke **2** *His attacker thrust at him with a knife.* ► lunge, jab, prod, stab, plunge, poke, stick
thrust NOUN *He gave the door a firm thrust.* ► shove, push, prod, poke **2** *I strongly support the thrust of your argument.* ► gist, substance, drift, burden, force

thud VERB *Heavy footsteps thudded across the front porch.* ► thump, clump, stomp, crash
thud NOUN *He was hammering on the door, thud after thud.* ► thump, bang, rap, clunk, clonk, crash

thug NOUN (*informal*) *A fight broke out between two armies of thugs.* ► ruffian, hoodlum, tough, bully

thumb VERB *She thumbed through her notes.* ► browse, flick, flip, leaf, riffle, scan

thump NOUN **1** *He sat down with a painful thump on the floor.* ► thud, bang, clunk, clonk, crash **2** *The heavy thump of acid house music was everywhere.* ► beat, rhythm, pulsation, pounding, throb, thud, thrum, vibration
thump VERB *The woman thumped the table with her fist.* ► bang, hit, strike, pound, beat, rap, batter, wallop, knock

thunder NOUN *Her musings were interrupted by the thunder of hooves.* ► rumble, rumbling, boom, booming, roar, roaring, thud, thump, ringing
thunder VERB *Fighter aircraft thundered overhead.* ► roar, boom, rumble, blast

thunderous ADJECTIVE *The speech was greeted by thunderous applause and standing ovations.* ► deafening, tumultuous, resounding, loud, booming

thwart VERB *He stayed in power as long as he could, just to thwart his main rival.* ► frustrate, hinder, impede, foil, obstruct, prevent, stand in the way of, stop OPPOSITES ARE help, further

A B C D E F G H I J K L M N O P Q R S **T** U V W X Y Z

thy ADJECTIVE (old use) your (referring to one person)

tiara (tee- ar- a) NOUN tiaras a woman's jewelled crescent-shaped ornament worn like a crown

tic NOUN tics an unintentional twitch of a muscle, especially of the face

tick[1] NOUN ticks 1 a mark (usually) put by something to show that it is correct or has been checked 2 a regular clicking sound, especially that made by a clock or watch 3 (informal) a moment • I won't be a tick.

tick VERB ticks, ticking, ticked 1 put a tick by something 2 make the sound of a tick **tick off** (informal) reprimand someone

tick[2] NOUN ticks a bloodsucking insect

ticket NOUN tickets 1 a printed piece of paper or card that allows a person to travel on a bus or train, see a show, etc. 2 a label showing a thing's price

tickle VERB tickles, tickling, tickled 1 touch a person's skin lightly in order to produce a slight tingling feeling and laughter 2 (said about a part of the body) have a slight tingling or itching feeling 3 amuse or please somebody

ticklish ADJECTIVE 1 likely to laugh or wriggle when tickled 2 awkward or difficult • a ticklish situation

tidal wave NOUN tidal waves a huge sea wave

tidbit NOUN tidbits a nice little piece of something, e.g., of food, gossip, or information

tide NOUN tides 1 the regular rise and fall in the level of the sea which usually happens twice a day 2 (old use) a time or season • Christmas-tide

tide VERB tides, tiding, tided **tide a person over** provide him or her with what is needed, for a short time

tidy ADJECTIVE tidier, tidiest 1 with everything in its right place; neat and orderly 2 (informal) fairly large • It costs a tidy sum.
▷ **tidily** ADVERB **tidiness** NOUN

tidy VERB tidies, tidying, tidied make a place tidy

tie VERB ties, tying, tied 1 fasten something with string, ribbon, etc. 2 arrange something into a knot or bow 3 make the same score as another competitor **be tied up** be busy

tie NOUN ties 1 a strip of material worn passing under the collar of a shirt and knotted in front 2 a result when two or more competitors have equal scores 3 one of the matches in a competition 4 a close connection or bond • the ties of friendship

Thesaurus

tick NOUN 1 Put a tick in the box marked 'no'.
► mark, stroke, dash, line 2 They heard the tick of a clock. ► ticking, clicking
in a tick (informal) I'll be back in a tick. ► in a moment, in a minute, in a second, in a trice, very soon, very shortly, (informal) in a jiffy

tick VERB 1 It was so quiet I could hear my watch ticking. ► click, make a tick, beat 2 Tick the box against your preferred method of payment.
► mark, check off, indicate
tick off (informal) She ticked off the children for making a noise. ► tell off, scold, reprimand, admonish, rebuke

ticket NOUN 1 a ticket to the game ► pass, permit, token, voucher, coupon 2 a price ticket ► label, tag, sticker, marker, slip, tab

tickle VERB 1 He tickled her toes until she gurgled happily. ► touch, stroke, pet 2 The little story tickled us. ► amuse, entertain, delight, cheer

ticklish ADJECTIVE 1 "It's lucky I'm not ticklish," she squealed. ► giggly, wriggly, sensitive 2 He had the ticklish problem of explaining where he had been all night. ► tricky, awkward, delicate, thorny, difficult, hazardous, risky, touchy, (more informal) dodgy

tide NOUN The tide of opinion was turning against the government. ► trend, tendency, current, course, drift, movement

tidy ADJECTIVE 1 Each desk should be tidy and have a place card. ► neat, orderly, uncluttered, shipshape, smart, spick and span OPPOSITES ARE untidy, messy 2 He tried to be tidy in his new apartment. ► methodical, meticulous, organized, systematic, house-proud OPPOSITES ARE untidy, disorganized 3 (informal) All those books will cost a tidy sum. ► sizeable, considerable, substantial, appreciable, large, (informal) hefty

tidy VERB The girls started to wash up and tidy.
► clean up, put in order, set straight, arrange, smarten, spruce up, neaten, straighten OPPOSITES ARE untidy, muddle

tie VERB 1 The dog was tied to a lamppost.
► fasten, secure, attach, tether, bind, hitch AN OPPOSITE IS untie 2 Her new job tied her to the office. ► restrict, limit, confine, restrain 3 The home side tied its next game. ► draw, finish level
tie up 1 He tied up the boat at the jetty.
► moor, tether, fasten, attach 2 We were keen to tie up the deal. ► complete, finalize, conclude, settle 3 **be tied up** The manager is still tied up I'm afraid. ► be busy, be occupied, be engaged

tie NOUN Family ties are important. ► bond, connection, link, attachment, relationship, association

a
b
c
d
e
f
g
h
i
j
k
l
m
n
o
p
q
r
s
t
u
v
w
x
y
z

A
B
C
D
E
F
G
H
I
J
K
L
M
N
O
P
Q
R
S
T
U
V
W
X
Y
Z

tier (teer) NOUN **tiers** each of a series of rows or levels etc. placed one above the other
▷ **tiered** ADJECTIVE

tiff NOUN **tiffs** a slight quarrel

tiger NOUN **tigers** a large wild animal of the cat family, with yellow and black stripes [from Greek *tigris*]

tight ADJECTIVE **1** fitting very closely **2** firmly fastened **3** fully stretched; tense **4** in short supply • *Money is tight at the moment.* **5** stingy • *He is very tight with his money.* **6** severe or strict • *tight security* **7** (*slang*) drunk
▷ **tightly** ADVERB **tightness** NOUN

tighten VERB **tightens, tightening, tightened** make or become tighter

tightrope NOUN **tightropes** a tightly stretched rope high above the ground, on which acrobats perform

tights PLURAL NOUN a piece of clothing that fits tightly over the feet, legs, and lower part of the body

tile NOUN **tiles** a thin square piece of baked clay or other hard material, used in rows for covering roofs, walls, or floors
▷ **tiled** ADJECTIVE

till PREPOSITION, CONJUNCTION until [from Old English *til* = to]
USAGE It is better to use **until** rather than **till** when the word stands first in a sentence (e.g.

Until last year we had never been abroad.) or when you are speaking or writing formally.

till NOUN **tills** a drawer or box for money in a shop; a cash register [origin unknown]

tilt VERB **tilts, tilting, tilted** move into a sloping position

tilt NOUN a sloping position
at full tilt at full speed or force

timber NOUN **timbers 1** wood for building or making things **2** a wooden beam

time NOUN **times 1** all the years of the past, present, and future; the continuous existence of the universe **2** a particular point or portion of time **3** an occasion • *the first time I saw him* **4** a period suitable or available for something • *Is there time for a cup of tea?* **5** a system of measuring time • *Greenwich Mean Time* **6** (in music) rhythm depending on the number and stress of beats in the bar **7** (**times**) multiplied by • *Five times three is 15 (5 × 3 = 15).*
at times or **from time to time** sometimes; occasionally
in time 1 not late **2** eventually
on time punctual

time VERB **times, timing, timed 1** measure how long something takes **2** arrange when something is to happen
▷ **timer** NOUN
[from Old English]

timeless ADJECTIVE not affected by the passage of time; eternal

Thesaurus

tight ADJECTIVE **1** *The rope was pulled tight.*
▶ taut, stretched, rigid, stiff, tense OPPOSITES ARE slack, loose **2** *Her grip was tight.* ▶ firm, fast, secure, clenched AN OPPOSITE IS relaxed **3** *The joint was completely tight.* ▶ sealed, airtight, impervious AN OPPOSITE IS leaking **4** *The bed had to fit into a tight space.* ▶ small, compact, constricted, snug, poky **5** *He can be very tight with his money.* ▶ mean, stingy, niggardly, miserly, parsimonious, (*more informal*) tightfisted, (*more informal*) penny-pinching AN OPPOSITE IS generous **6** *There is tight security at the airport.* ▶ strict, stringent, rigorous, severe, tough, scrupulous AN OPPOSITE IS lax

tighten VERB **1** *Jane tightened her grip on the rail.* ▶ strengthen, squeeze, tense, stiffen, increase OPPOSITES ARE loosen, relax **2** *You need to tighten your shoelaces.* ▶ make tight, pull tighter, tauten, stretch AN OPPOSITE IS slacken **3** *Tighten all screws when the chair is assembled.* ▶ make tighter, screw up, give another turn to AN OPPOSITE IS loosen
tighten up *Security will be tightened up during the peak season.* ▶ increase, heighten, strengthen, intensify, escalate

tightfisted ADJECTIVE *We were too tightfisted to pay the toll.* ▶ mean, stingy, niggardly, miserly, parsimonious, (*more informal*) penny-pinching

tilt VERB *He tilted his hat to one side. The wall tilted alarmingly.* ▶ lean, slant, slope, tip, angle

tilt NOUN *The tray was on a tilt.* ▶ slant, slope, incline, angle
at full tilt *They ran at full tilt down the bank.* ▶ headlong, pell-mell, at full speed, at full pelt, at a gallop, fast

timber NOUN *Houses built of timber and mud would be very damp.* ▶ wood, planks, planking, beams, laths, boarding, boards, logs, lumber, trees

time NOUN **1** *in the time of Queen Mary* ▶ age, era, period, generation **2** *He lived here for a time.* ▶ while, period, spell **3** *It took a long time to fix the problem.* ▶ while, interval, duration, **4** *When is the best time to come? I didn't know what to do at that time.* ▶ moment, point, juncture, stage, date, occasion RELATED ADJECTIVES ▶ temporal, chronic, chronological

time VERB **1** *She had timed her arrival for half an hour before the party was due to start.* ▶ regulate, choose, fix, set, schedule **2** *The nurse timed ten minutes.* ▶ measure, count

timely ADJECTIVE happening at a suitable or useful time • *a timely warning*

timetable NOUN timetables a list showing the times when things will happen, e.g., when buses or trains will arrive and depart, or when school lessons will take place

timid ADJECTIVE easily frightened
▷ **timidly** ADVERB **timidity** NOUN

timing NOUN 1 the choice of time to do something 2 the time when something happens

timpani PLURAL NOUN kettledrums

tin NOUN tins 1 a silvery-white metal 2 a metal container for food

tinge VERB tinges, tingeing, tinged 1 color something slightly 2 add a slight amount of another feeling • *Our relief was tinged with sadness.*
▷ **tinge** NOUN

tingle VERB tingles, tingling, tingled have a slight pricking or stinging feeling
▷ **tingle** NOUN

tinker VERB tinkers, tinkering, tinkered work at something casually, trying to improve or mend it

tinkle VERB tinkles, tinkling, tinkled make a gentle ringing sound
▷ **tinkle** NOUN

tinny ADJECTIVE 1 like tin 2 (said about a sound) unpleasantly thin and high-pitched

tinsel NOUN strips of glittering material used for decoration

tint NOUN tints a shade of color, especially a pale one

tint VERB tints, tinting, tinted color something slightly

tiny ADJECTIVE tinier, tiniest very small

tip[1] NOUN tips the part right at the top or end of something

tip VERB tips, tipping, tipped put a tip on something

tip[2] NOUN tips 1 a small present of money given to someone who has helped you 2 a small but useful piece of advice; a hint

tip VERB tips, tipping, tipped 1 give a person a tip 2 name someone as a likely winner • *Which team would you tip to win the championship?*
▷ **tipper** NOUN
tip off give a warning or special information about something

tip[3] VERB tips, tipping, tipped 1 tilt or topple 2 empty rubbish somewhere
tip NOUN tips 1 the action of tipping something 2 a place where rubbish etc. is tipped

---

Thesaurus

---

timely ADJECTIVE *The incident was a timely reminder of how dangerous these waters had become.* ► opportune, fitting, suitable, appropriate, apt, prompt

timetable NOUN *They established a timetable for elections and political reform.* ► schedule, agenda, program, calendar, diary, roster, rota

timid ADJECTIVE *Elaine handed him her bag with a timid smile.* ► shy, diffident, bashful, modest, timorous, fainthearted, weak, fearful OPPOSITES ARE bold, brazen

tinge NOUN 1 *The light took on a green tinge.* ► tint, shade, hue, color 2 *There was a tinge of amusement on his face.* ► trace, touch, note, suggestion, flavor, streak

tingle NOUN 1 *There was a strange tingle in her fingers.* ► prickling, stinging, tickle, tickling, itch, itching, pins and needles 2 *Melissa felt a tingle of excitement.* ► quiver, tremor, thrill, sensation, shiver

tingle VERB *His shoes were so tight they made his feet tingle.* ► itch, prickle, sting, tickle

tinker VERB *He saw Nathan tinkering with his bike.* ► fiddle, play, meddle, tamper, dabble, trifle, interfere, (more informal) mess about, (more informal) play about

tint NOUN *smooth glossy paper with a yellowish tint* ► tinge, shade, hue, color

tiny ADJECTIVE 1 *We've got a tiny pond in the front garden.* ► minute, miniature, diminutive, midget, mini, very small, (more informal) teeny, (more informal) titchy AN OPPOSITE IS huge 2 *These manmade gases are present in the atmosphere only tiny amounts.* ► minute, insignificant, negligible, paltry, meager

tip NOUN 1 *He ran the tip of his finger along the handlebar. The tip of the arrow couldn't be far into the tree.* ► end, point, extremity, sharp end, nib 2 *The tip of a mountain was visible above the clouds.* ► summit, peak, pinnacle, top, apex, cap, crown, head 3 *He paid his bill, left a good tip, and walked home.* ► gratuity, gift 4 *My tip is to go for really good-quality ski pants.* ► hint, suggestion, advice, clue, information, warning

tip VERB 1 *He tipped his head back to look. The van was tipping to one side.* ► lean, incline, list, slant, slope, tilt, keel over 2 *She tipped the fish into the sink and began to clean them.* ► empty, dump, pour out, spill, unload 3 *He decided to tip the driver after all.* ► give a tip to, remunerate, reward
tip over *A whale is capable of tipping over a small boat.* ► overturn, capsize, topple, turn over, upset, knock over

tip-off NOUN (informal) *The police received a tip-off about a shipment of cocaine.* ► alert, clue, prompt, piece of information

a b c d e f g h i j k l m n o p q r s **t** u v w x y z

A
B
C
D
E
F
G
H
I
J
K
L
M
N
O
P
Q
R
S
T
U
V
W
X
Y
Z

tipsy *ADJECTIVE* slightly drunk

tiptoe *VERB* tiptoes, tiptoeing, tiptoed walk on your toes very quietly or carefully
on tiptoe walking or standing on your toes

tire *NOUN* tires a covering of rubber fitted around a wheel to make it grip the road and run more smoothly

tire *VERB* tires, tiring, tired make or become tired
▷ **tiring** *ADJECTIVE*

tired *ADJECTIVE* feeling that you need to sleep or rest
be tired of have had enough of something and feel impatient or bored with it

tireless *ADJECTIVE* having a lot of energy; not tiring easily

tiresome *ADJECTIVE* annoying

tissue *NOUN* tissues 1 tissue paper 2 a paper handkerchief 3 the substance forming any part of the body of an animal or plant • *bone tissue*

tissue paper *NOUN* very thin soft paper used for wrapping and packing things

tit[1] *NOUN* tits a kind of small bird

tit[2] *NOUN*
tit for tat something equal given in return; retaliation

titillate *VERB* titillates, titillating, titillated stimulate or excite you pleasantly
▷ **titillation** *NOUN*

title *NOUN* titles 1 the name of a book, film, song, etc. 2 a word used to show a person's rank or position, e.g., *Dr.*, *Mrs.* 3 a championship in sport • *the world heavyweight title* 4 a legal right to something

titter *VERB* titters, tittering, tittered giggle
▷ **titter** *NOUN*

to *PREPOSITION* This word is used to show 1 direction or arrival at a position (*We walked to school; he rose to power*), 2 limit (*from noon to two o'clock*), 3 comparison (*We won by six goals to three*), 4 receiving or being affected by something (*Give it to me; be kind to animals*) Also used before a verb to form an infinitive (*I want to see him*) or to show purpose, etc. (*He does that to annoy us*), or alone when the verb is understood (*We meant to go but forgot to*)

to *ADVERB* 1 to or in the proper or closed position or condition • *Push the door to.* 2 into a state of activity • *We set to and cleaned the kitchen.*
to and fro backwards and forwards

toad *NOUN* toads a frog-like animal that lives mainly on land

toadstool *NOUN* toadstools a fungus (usually poisonous) with a round top on a stalk

toast *VERB* toasts, toasting, toasted 1 heat bread, etc., to make it brown and crisp 2 warm something in front of a fire, etc. 3 drink in honor of someone

toast *NOUN* toasts 1 toasted bread 2 the call to drink in honor of someone; the person honored in this way

tobacco *NOUN* the dried leaves of certain plants prepared for smoking in cigarettes, cigars, or pipes or for making snuff [via Spanish from a Central American language]

toboggan *NOUN* toboggans a small sledge used for sliding downhill
▷ **tobogganing** *NOUN*
[via Canadian French from a Native American language]

today *NOUN* this present day • *Today is Monday.*

today *ADVERB* on this day • *Have you seen him today?*

Thesaurus

---

tire *VERB* *The long walk tired us.* ► exhaust, fatigue, weary, tire out, wear out, drain
OPPOSITES ARE refresh, invigorate

tired *ADJECTIVE* 1 *He was tired from his hectic battle with the goblins.* ► exhausted, fatigued, wearied, worn out OPPOSITES ARE energetic, refreshed 2 *tired old debates about nature and nurture* ► stale, hackneyed, overworked, banal OPPOSITES ARE fresh, new
tired of *They grew tired of waiting.* ► bored with, fed up with, sick of, impatient with

tireless *ADJECTIVE* *a tireless campaigner on behalf of chimpanzees in the wild* ► vigorous, energetic, determined, unflagging, untiring, indefatigable, persistent, zealous, diligent, sedulous, unceasing AN OPPOSITE IS lazy USAGE Note that *tireless* and *tiresome* are not opposites.

tiresome *ADJECTIVE* *Richard was back from work after a tiresome day.* ► irritating, annoying,

wearisome, troublesome, trying, irksome, bothersome, vexing, distracting, exasperating OPPOSITES ARE stimulating, exciting USAGE See the note at *tireless*.

tiring *ADJECTIVE* *Day care can be tiring.* ► exhausting, exacting, taxing, wearying, fatiguing, demanding, difficult, hard AN OPPOSITE IS refreshing

title *NOUN* 1 *The title of the picture was printed underneath.* ► caption, heading, name 2 *Specify the title you want to be known by.* ► form of address, designation, appellation, rank, status, office, position 3 *He sought to prove his title to the land.* ► right, entitlement, claim, ownership (of), tenure (of)

toast *VERB* 1 *They toasted bread by the fire.* ► grill, brown, heat, warm 2 *The guests then toasted their host.* ► drink a toast to, drink the health of, raise your glass to, salute, honor

toddler *NOUN* **toddlers** a young child who has only recently learnt to walk
▷ **toddle** *VERB*

to-do *NOUN* **to-dos** a fuss or commotion

toe *NOUN* **toes** **1** any of the separate parts (five in humans) at the end of each foot **2** the part of a shoe or sock etc. that covers the toes
● on your toes alert

toffee *NOUN* **toffees** a sticky candy made from heated butter and sugar

together *ADVERB* with another person or thing; with each other ● *They went to the party together.*

toil *VERB* **toils, toiling, toiled 1** work hard **2** move slowly and with difficulty
▷ **toiler** *NOUN*

toil *NOUN* hard work

toilet *NOUN* **toilets** **1** a bowllike object, connected by pipes to a drain, which you use to get rid of urine and feces **2** a room containing a toilet **3** the process of washing, dressing, and tidying yourself

token *NOUN* **tokens** **1** a piece of metal or plastic that can be used instead of money **2** a voucher or coupon that can be exchanged for goods **3** a sign or signal of something ● *a token of our friendship*

tolerable *ADJECTIVE* able to be tolerated
▷ **tolerably** *ADVERB*

tolerant *ADJECTIVE* willing to accept or tolerate other people's behavior and opinions even if you do not agree with them
▷ **tolerantly** *ADVERB* **tolerance** *NOUN*

tolerate *VERB* **tolerates, tolerating, tolerated 1** allow something even if you do not approve of it **2** bear or put up with something unpleasant
▷ **toleration** *NOUN*

toll (rhymes with *hole*) *NOUN* **tolls 1** a charge made for using a road, bridge, etc. **2** loss or damage caused ● *The death toll in the earthquake is rising.*

toll (rhymes with *hole*) *VERB* **tolls, tolling, tolled** ring a bell slowly
▷ **toll** *NOUN*

tom *NOUN* **toms** a male cat
▷ **tomcat** *NOUN*

tomato *NOUN* **tomatoes** a soft around red fruit eaten as a vegetable [via French, Spanish, or

Thesaurus

together *ADVERB* **1** *They were all speaking together.* ► simultaneously, at the same time, at once, collectively, concurrently, in chorus, in unison, jointly OPPOSITES ARE independently, separately **2** *Naim and I work together.*
► jointly, with each other, in concert, side by side OPPOSITES ARE separately, alone
3 *Nothing happened for days together.* ► in a row, in succession, continuously, consecutively

toil *NOUN* *years of hardship and toil* ► work , labor, donkey work, slaving, drudgery, effort, exertion, industry

toil *VERB* *The team needed to toil all day.* ► work, labor, slave, sweat, struggle, (*more informal*) slog, (*more informal*) grind away

toilet *NOUN* **1** *There is a toilet on the first floor.*
► lavatory, WC, convenience, facilities, privy, (*more informal*) john **2** *She was taking ages over her toilet.* ► washing, bathing

token *NOUN* **1** *Saladin's ring was sent as a token of good faith.* ► symbol, sign, mark, expression, testimony, evidence, indication, proof, reminder **2** *He had her name tattoed on his arm as a token of their love.* ► memento, souvenir, record, keepsake **3** *a book token* ► voucher, coupon, counter

token *ADJECTIVE* **1** *She did the work for a token fee.*
► nominal, minimal, trivial, slight AN OPPOSITE IS substantial **2** *The garrison offered only token resistance.* ► perfunctory, insignificant, superficial, symbolic AN OPPOSITE IS considerable

tolerable *ADJECTIVE* **1** *The pain was barely tolerable.* ► bearable, acceptable, endurable, sufferable, supportable AN OPPOSITE IS intolerable **2** *He was fond of music and had a tolerable voice.* ► adequate, passable, middling, ordinary, satisfactory, fair, mediocre, indifferent

tolerance *NOUN* *He has always preached tolerance for people of whatever religion.*
► toleration, forbearance, sufferance, acceptance, open-mindedness, broad-mindedness, liberalism, understanding, permissiveness

tolerant *ADJECTIVE* *He's a tolerant chap who didn't seem to mind if I got it wrong.*
► understanding, open-minded, long-suffering, forbearing, sympathetic, fair, magnanimous, charitable OPPOSITES ARE intolerant, unsympathetic

tolerate *VERB* **1** *At work she will not tolerate interference.* ► put up with, bear, endure, stand, abide, stomach, suffer, take, (*more informal*) stick **2** *This sort of behavior is difficult to tolerate.* ► accept, condone, countenance, admit, brook, make allowances for, permit, sanction

toll *NOUN* **1** *a road toll* ► charge, fee, levy, tariff, payment, duty, tax **2** *the death toll from the accident* ► count, tally, total, reckoning

toll *VERB* *We heard a bell toll.* ► ring, peal, chime, sound

a b c d e f g h i j k l m n o p q r s **t** u v w x y z

Portuguese from Nahuatl (a Central American language)]

tomb (toom) NOUN **tombs** a place where someone is buried; a monument built over this

tomboy NOUN **tomboys** a girl who enjoys rough noisy games etc.

tombstone NOUN **tombstones** a memorial stone set up over a grave

tomorrow NOUN, ADVERB the day after today

ton NOUN **tons** **1** a unit of weight equal to 2,240 pounds or about 1,016 kilograms **2** a large amount • *There's tons of room.* **3** (*slang*) a speed of 100 miles per hour

tone NOUN **tones** **1** a sound in music or of the voice **2** each of the five larger intervals between notes in a musical scale (the smaller intervals are semitones) **3** a shade of a color **4** the quality or character of something • *a cheerful tone*
▷ **tonal** ADJECTIVE **tonally** ADVERB

tone VERB **tones, toning, toned** **1** give a particular tone or quality to something **2** be harmonious in color
tone down make a thing quieter or less bright or less harsh
[from Greek *tonos* = tension]

tongs PLURAL NOUN a tool with two arms joined at one end, used to pick up or hold things

tongue NOUN **tongues** **1** the long soft muscular part that moves about inside the mouth **2** a language **3** the leather flap on a shoe or boot underneath the laces **4** a pointed flame [from Old English]

tongue-tied ADJECTIVE too shy to speak

tonic NOUN **tonics** **1** a medicine that makes a person healthier or stronger **2** anything that makes a person more energetic or cheerful **3** a fizzy mineral water with a bitter taste, often mixed with gin **4** a keynote in music
▷ **tonic** ADJECTIVE

tonight NOUN, ADVERB this evening or night

tonne NOUN **tonnes** a metric ton (1,000 kilograms)

too ADVERB **1** also • *Take the others, too.* **2** more than is wanted or allowed etc. • *That's too much sugar for me.*

tool NOUN **tools** **1** a device that helps you to do a particular job • *A saw is a tool for cutting wood or metal.* **2** a thing used for a particular purpose • *An encyclopedia is a useful study tool.*

tooth NOUN **teeth** **1** one of the hard white bony parts that are rooted in the gums, used for biting and chewing things **2** one of a row of sharp parts • *the teeth of a saw*
▷ **toothache** NOUN **toothbrush** NOUN **toothed** ADJECTIVE
fight tooth and nail fight very fiercely

toothpaste NOUN **toothpastes** a paste for cleaning your teeth

top[1] NOUN **tops** **1** the highest part of something **2** the upper surface **3** the covering or stopper of a bottle, jar, etc. **4** a piece of clothing for the upper part of the body
on top of in addition to something

top ADJECTIVE highest • *at top speed*

Thesaurus

---

tomb NOUN *the tomb of Ramesses II* ► burial chamber, burial place, sepulchre, grave, catacomb, crypt, mausoleum RELATED ADJECTIVE ► sepulchral

tone NOUN **1** *He objected to the arrogant tone of the letter.* ► manner, mood, spirit, attitude, tenor, quality **2** *She called out in an angry tone of voice.* ► expression, timber, quality, sound, modulation, intonation **3** *emulsion paint with a rosy tone* ► tint, tinge, hue, shade, blush, colour

tone VERB **tone with** *The pastel shades of the wallpaper tone beautifully with the light wood of the furniture.* ► harmonize with, coordinate with, match, go well with, suit
tone down *He was unwilling to tone down his criticisms of the management.* ► moderate, modify, temper, mitigate, soften, restrain, dampen, subdue, play down AN OPPOSITE IS intensify

tongue NOUN *He spoke in a foreign tongue.* ► language, vernacular, idiom, talk, speech, utterance

tongue-tied ADJECTIVE *He is often tongue-tied in company.* ► lost for words, inarticulate, dumbstruck, speechless, mute, silent

tool NOUN **1** *a set of garden tools* ► implement, utensil, device, gadget, appliance, contraption **2** *The tabloid press became a tool of the government.* ► dupe, pawn, puppet, creature, stooge, minion, (*more informal*) poodle

top NOUN **1** *The top of the mountain was still covered in snow.* ► summit, peak, pinnacle, tip, apex, cap, crown, head AN OPPOSITE IS foot **2** *The top of the jar was stuck.* ► lid, cap, cover, covering AN OPPOSITE IS bottom

top ADJECTIVE **1** *an office on the top floor* ► highest, topmost, uppermost, upper OPPOSITES ARE bottom, lowest **2** *some of the world's top golf professionals* ► leading, finest, foremost, principal, chief, preeminent, prime **3** *the top Paris restaurants* ► best, prime, superior, leading, foremost, finest AN OPPOSITE IS inferior

top VERB **1** *The cake can be topped with chopped nuts.* ► cover, cap, decorate, finish off,

top VERB **tops, topping, topped 1** put a top on something **2** be at the top of something • *She tops the list* **3** remove the top of something

top up fill up something that is half empty • *top up your glass*

top² NOUN **tops** a toy that can be made to spin on its point

top hat NOUN **top hats** a man's tall stiff black or grey hat worn with formal clothes

top-heavy ADJECTIVE too heavy at the top and likely to overbalance

topic NOUN **topics** a subject to write, learn, or talk about

topical ADJECTIVE connected with things that are happening now • *a topical film*
▷ **topically** ADVERB **topicality** NOUN

topmost ADJECTIVE highest

topple VERB **topples, toppling, toppled 1** fall over; totter and fall **2** make something fall; overthrow

top secret ADJECTIVE extremely secret • *top secret information*

topsy-turvy ADVERB, ADJECTIVE upside down; muddled

torch NOUN **torches** a stick with burning material on the end, used as a light

torment VERB **torments, tormenting, tormented 1** make someone suffer greatly **2** tease; keep annoying someone
▷ **tormentor** NOUN

torment NOUN **torments** great suffering

tornado (tor- nay- doh) NOUN **tornadoes** a violent storm or whirlwind

torpedo NOUN **torpedoes** a long tube-shaped missile that can be fired under water to destroy ships

torrent NOUN **torrents 1** a rushing stream; a great flow **2** a heavy downpour of rain
▷ **torrential** ADJECTIVE

torso NOUN **torsos** the trunk of the human body

tortoise NOUN **tortoises** a slow-moving animal with a shell over its body

tortoiseshell (tort- as- shell) NOUN **tortoiseshells 1** the mottled brown and yellow shell of certain turtles, used for making combs, etc. **2** a cat or butterfly with mottled brown coloring

torture VERB **tortures, torturing, tortured** make a person feel great pain or worry
▷ **torture** NOUN **torturer** NOUN

Tory NOUN **Tories** a Conservative
▷ **Tory** ADJECTIVE

toss VERB **tosses, tossing, tossed 1** throw something, especially up into the air **2** spin a coin to decide something according to which side of it is upward after it falls **3** move restlessly or unevenly from side to side
▷ **toss** NOUN

Thesaurus

garnish, crown **2** *Sales are expected to top the million mark.* ► exceed, beat, be higher than, outdo, surpass, better, cap, excel

topic NOUN *An article on this topic appeared last month.* ► subject, theme, issue, matter, question

topical ADJECTIVE *Choose a news item of topical interest each week.* ► current, contemporary, recent, up-to-date, up-to-the-minute, newsworthy

topple VERB **1** *The heavy winds toppled several pylons, causing power cuts.* ► knock down, overturn, tip over, throw down, upset **2** *She saw a man topple sideways into the gutter. If kangaroos had no tails, they would topple over.* ► fall, overbalance, tumble **3** *A party revolt had toppled the conservative leadership.* ► bring down, overthrow, oust, unseat, depose

topsy-turvy ADJECTIVE *The carts lay in a topsy-turvy heap at the bottom of the hill. My emotions are all topsy-turvy.* ► disordered, confused, mixed up, muddled, jumbled, untidy, higgledy-piggledy OPPOSITES ARE ordered, neat

torment VERB **1** *The urge to express her feelings tormented her. Sometimes, he was tormented by jealousy.* ► afflict, torture, distress, persecute,

plague, bedevil, bother, be a torment to, pain, vex **2** *Marjory loved tormenting her younger brother.* ► tease, bait, pester, harass, annoy, bully, victimize

torrent NOUN **1** *The sky opened and a heavy torrent fell down.* ► downpour, deluge, flood, shower, flow AN OPPOSITE IS trickle **2** *These points are lost to the reader in a torrent of words.* ► cascade, gush, rush, outburst, spate, stream, tide

torture NOUN **1** *Human rights groups claimed that torture of prisoners had taken place.* ► maltreatment, persecution, cruelty, torment, humiliation, degradation, inquisition **2** *The rest of the journey was torture.* ► agony, torment, misery, affliction

torture VERB **1** *They were out to torture their victims.* ► persecute, inflict pain on, inflict suffering on, be cruel to, degrade, humiliate, hurt, torment **2** *I was having thoughts that tortured me.* ► afflict, torment, distress, persecute, plague, bedevil, bother, be a torment to, pain, vex

toss VERB **1** *He tossed a ball high in the air.* ► throw, fling, hurl, cast, pitch, heave **2** *The boat was tossing about in shallow water.* ► lurch, pitch, reel, rock, roll, bob, shake, wallow,

A
B
C
D
E
F
G
H
I
J
K
L
M
N
O
P
Q
R
S
T
U
V
W
X
Y
Z

toss-up NOUN toss-ups **1** the tossing of a coin **2** an even chance

tot NOUN tots **1** a small child **2** (informal) a small amount of spirits • a tot of rum

total ADJECTIVE **1** including everything • the total amount **2** complete • total darkness
▷ **totally** ADVERB

total NOUN totals the amount you get by adding everything together

total VERB totals, totaling, totaled **1** add up the total **2** amount to something • The cost of the damage totalled $500.

totalitarian ADJECTIVE using a form of government where people are not allowed to form rival political parties

totem pole NOUN totem poles a pole carved or painted by Native Americans with the symbols (totems) of their tribes or families

totter VERB totters, tottering, tottered walk unsteadily; wobble
▷ **tottery** ADJECTIVE

touch VERB touches, touching, touched **1** put your hand or fingers, etc., on something lightly **2** be or come together so that there is no space between **3** come into contact with something or hit it gently **4** move or meddle with something **5** reach • The thermometer

touched 30° Celsius. **6** affect someone's feelings, e.g., by making them feel sympathy • The sad story touched our hearts.

touch and go an uncertain situation

touch down 1 (said about an aircraft) land

touch on discuss a subject briefly

touch up improve something by making small additions or changes

touch NOUN touches **1** the action of touching **2** the ability to feel things by touching them **3** a small amount; a small thing done • the finishing touches **4** a special skill or style of workmanship • She hasn't lost her touch. **5** communication with someone • We lost touch with him

touching ADJECTIVE causing you to have kindly feelings such as pity or sympathy

touchstone NOUN touchstones a test by which the quality of something is judged

touchy ADJECTIVE touchier, touchiest easily offended
▷ **touchily** ADVERB **touchiness** NOUN

tough ADJECTIVE **1** strong; difficult to break or damage **2** difficult to chew **3** able to stand hardship; not easily hurt **4** firm or severe **5** difficult • a tough decision
▷ **toughly** ADVERB **toughness** NOUN

Thesaurus

welter, writhe **3** Marion tossed restlessly in bed.
► twist and turn, move restlessly, flail, thrash about, wriggle, fidget

toss NOUN a toss of a coin ► flip, fling, throw, jerk, heave

tot VERB tot up He was totting up some figures.
► add up, calculate, count, total, find the total of, reckon up, totalize, work out

total ADJECTIVE **1** The total volume of sales reached five million. ► complete, comprehensive, entire, full, gross, overall, whole **2** A senior fire official said it was total carnage. ► sheer, utter, absolute, downright, thorough, unmitigated, unqualified, perfect, out-and-out

total NOUN The airport will handle a total of a million passengers in the week before Christmas.
► sum, totality, aggregate, amount, whole

total VERB The cash bag totaled $1,200. ► amount to, come to, add up to, make, reach

total up Total up your scores. ► add up, calculate, count, tot up, find the total of, reckon up, totalize, work out

touch VERB **1** She touched his arm and he turned.
► pat, brush, contact, feel, rub, stroke, tap, caress, dab **2** Their sorrow touched him.
► move, affect, concern, disturb, influence, inspire, stir, upset **3** Their speed touched 100 m.p.h. ► reach, rise to, attain **4** (informal) Nothing could touch them for good value.
► equal, match, compare with, rival, come up to, parallel

touch on The program touched on recent concerns.
► refer to, deal with, mention, treat, raise, cover

touch up The room had been touched up and given a new carpet. ► improve, repaint, renovate, refurbish, redecorate

touch NOUN **1** Animals communicate by touch.
► feeling, touching, contact **2** She jumped under his touch. ► pat, stroke, tap, caress, contact, dab **3** Funny speeches need a bubbly, light touch. ► manner, style, technique, flair, knack, feel, sensitivity **4** There was a touch of genius in the way he talked that night. ► hint, suggestion, suspicion, tinge, trace **5** A gift of flowers can be a nice touch. ► feature, detail, extra **6** He and Carol kept in touch. ► contact, communication, correspondence RELATED ADJECTIVE ► tactile

touched ADJECTIVE I was touched by their generosity. ► moved, affected, impressed, stirred, responsive (to)

touching ADJECTIVE She was beautiful, her face crossed by a touching sadness. ► moving, affecting, poignant, emotional, tender

touchy ADJECTIVE Like most tired children she was touchy and uncooperative. ► irritable, bad-tempered, irascible, grumpy, grouchy, testy, tetchy, crotchety, cantankerous, peevish, fractious, cross AN OPPOSITE IS good-humored

tough ADJECTIVE **1** It was my first outing in my tough new boots. ► strong, stout, durable,

toughen VERB toughens, toughening, toughened make or become tough

tour NOUN tours a journey visiting several places

tour VERB tours, touring, toured make a tour

tourism NOUN the industry of organizing holidays and visits to places of interest

tourist NOUN tourists a person who makes a tour or visits a place for pleasure

tournament NOUN tournaments a series of games or contests

tow (rhymes with go) VERB tows, towing, towed pull something along behind you
▷ **tow** NOUN
on tow being towed

toward PREPOSITION towards

towards PREPOSITION **1** in the direction of • *She walked towards the sea.* **2** in relation to; regarding • *He behaved kindly towards his children.* **3** as a contribution to • *Put the money toward a new bicycle.* **4** near • *towards four o'clock*

towel NOUN towels a piece of absorbent cloth for drying things

tower NOUN towers a tall narrow building

tower VERB towers, towering, towered be very high; be taller than others • *Skyscrapers towered over the city.*

town NOUN towns a place with many houses, shops, offices, and other buildings

town hall NOUN town halls a building with offices for the local council and usually a hall for public events

towpath NOUN towpaths a path beside a canal or river, originally for use when a horse was towing a barge, etc.

toxic ADJECTIVE poisonous; caused by poison
▷ **toxicity** NOUN

toy NOUN toys a thing to play with

toy ADJECTIVE **1** made as a toy **2** (said about a dog) of a very small breed • *a toy poodle*

toy VERB toys, toying, toyed
toy with handle a thing or consider an idea casually

trace NOUN traces **1** a mark left by a person or thing; a sign • *There was no trace of the thief.* **2** a very small amount

Thesaurus

hard-wearing, indestructible, lasting, unbreakable, well-made OPPOSITES ARE flimsy, delicate **2** *He is tall with a tough physique.* (*informal*) ► sturdy, muscular, strong, beefy, brawny, burly, hardy, robust, stalwart AN OPPOSITE IS weak **3** *They proved to be tough rivals. She's a tough, single-minded woman.* ► determined, tenacious, unyielding, resilient, resolute, resistant, stiff, stubborn AN OPPOSITE IS weak. **4** *The meat was overcooked and tough.* ► chewy, leathery, gristly, rubbery, hard, uneatable AN OPPOSITE IS tender **5** *There was a tough climb ahead.* ► difficult, arduous, strenuous, exacting, exhausting, grueling, stiff, hard, laborious AN OPPOSITE IS easy **6** *They had some tough questions to answer.* ► difficult, baffling, intractable, puzzling, perplexing, (*more informal*) thorny, (*more informal*) knotty AN OPPOSITE IS easy

toughen VERB *ways of toughening wood* ► harden, strengthen, make tougher, reinforce AN OPPOSITE IS weaken

tour NOUN *a tour around the castles of southern Bavaria* ► journey, expedition, trip, ride, drive, outing, excursion

tour VERB *The town is well situated for touring the area.* ► travel around, visit, explore, sightsee, go round, make a tour of

tourist NOUN *Tribal dances are performed for the tourists.* ► sightseer, holidaymaker, visitor, tripper, traveller

tournament NOUN *He was due to take part in a celebrity golf tournament.* ► competition, contest, championship, match, meeting, series

tow VERB *The rope seemed too slender to tow the forty-foot barge.* ► pull, drag, tug, draw, haul, transport, trail

tower NOUN *We passed two abbeys, one with a tower and one without.* ► steeple, turret, column, pillar, belfry

tower VERB *Clouds towered on every side. He stood up, and he towered above her.* ► loom, rear, rise, dominate, stand out, stick up, ascend

towering ADJECTIVE *towering crags and cliffs* ► tall, high, lofty, soaring, mighty, colossal, gigantic, imposing

town NOUN *The family moved to an industrial town.* ► conurbation, urban area, borough, city, municipality, settlement RELATED ADJECTIVE ► urban, civic, municipal

toxic ADJECTIVE *You have two minutes to get out before the heat and toxic fumes overcome you.* ► poisonous, noxious, lethal, deadly, dangerous, harmful OPPOSITES ARE harmless, safe

toy ADJECTIVE *giant toy animals* ► model, imitation, make-believe, simulation, (*more informal*) pretend

toy NOUN *The children can bring their favorite toy.* ► plaything, game, doll

toy VERB **toy with 1** *She picked up her fork and toyed with her food.* ► play with, fiddle with, fidget with, tinker with, peck at, pick at **2** *He toyed with the idea of walking to the station to meet her.* ► think about, play with, consider

trace NOUN **1** *"No," he said with a trace of irritation.* ► hint, touch, suggestion, suspicion

A
B
C
D
E
F
G
H
I
J
K
L
M
N
O
P
Q
R
S
T
U
V
W
X
Y
Z

trace VERB **traces, tracing, traced 1** copy a picture or map etc. by drawing over it on transparent paper **2** follow the traces of a person or thing; find • *The police have been trying to trace her.*
▷ **tracer** NOUN

tracery NOUN a decorative pattern of holes in stone, e.g. in a church window

track NOUN **tracks 1** a mark or marks left by a moving person or thing **2** a rough path made by being used **3** a road or area of ground specially prepared for racing **4** a set of rails for trains or trams, etc. **5** one of the songs or pieces of music on a CD, tape, etc. **6** a continuous band around the wheels of a tank or tractor, etc.
keep or **lose track of** keep or fail to keep yourself informed about where something is or what someone is doing

track VERB **tracks, tracking, tracked 1** follow the tracks left by a person or animal **2** follow or observe something as it moves
▷ **tracker** NOUN
track down find a person or thing by searching

tract[1] NOUN **tracts 1** an area of land **2** a series of connected parts along which something passes • *the digestive tract* [from Latin *tractus* = drawing, draught]

tract[2] NOUN **tracts** a pamphlet containing a short essay, especially about religion or politics [via Old English from Latin]

tractor NOUN **tractors** a motor vehicle for pulling farm machinery or other heavy loads

trade NOUN **trades 1** buying, selling, or exchanging goods **2** business of a particular kind; the people working in this **3** an occupation, especially a skilled craft

trade VERB **trades, trading, traded** buy, sell, or exchange things
▷ **trader** NOUN
trade in give a thing as part of the payment for something new • *He traded in his motorcycle for a car.*

trademark NOUN **trademarks** a firm's registered symbol or name used to distinguish its goods, etc., from those of other firms

tradesman NOUN **tradesmen** a person employed in trade, especially one who sells or delivers goods

trade union NOUN **trade unions** a group of workers organized to help and protect workers in their own trade or industry

tradition NOUN **traditions 1** the passing down of beliefs or customs etc. from one generation to another **2** something passed on in this way
▷ **traditional** ADJECTIVE **traditionally** ADVERB

traffic NOUN **1** vehicles, ships, or aircraft moving along a route **2** trading, especially when it is illegal or wrong • *drug traffic*

traffic lights PLURAL NOUN colored lights used as a signal to traffic at road junctions etc.

Thesaurus

---

2 *The animal had left no trace.* ► trail, track, mark, sign, indication **3** *The investigators could find no trace of blood.* ► sign, remnant, remains, vestige

trace VERB **1** *Police are trying to trace the owner of the car.* ► track down, find, discover, uncover, unearth, detect **2** *It would be best to trace the map from an atlas.* ► copy, draw, outline, mark out, sketch, make a copy of

track NOUN **1** *An animal had left clear tracks.* ► trace, trail, mark, scent, spoor, footmark, footprint **2** *a track across the fields* ► path, way, pathway, footpath, route, lane, trail **3** *a racing track* ► course, circuit, racetrack **4** *Passengers were seen walking along the tracks.* ► rail, line

track VERB *He tracked a bear all day.* ► follow, trail, pursue, stalk, chase, hunt, dog, shadow, trace
track down *It took years to track everyone down.* ► discover, trace, find, detect, recover, retrieve

trade NOUN **1** *international trade* ► commerce, buying and selling, dealing, trading, traffic, transactions, barter, business, marketing
RELATED ADJECTIVE ► mercantile **2** *He wanted*

to be trained in a trade. ► craft, occupation, job, career, profession, calling, pursuit, line of work

trade VERB **1** *The family traded in diamonds.* ► deal, traffic, buy and sell, do business **2** *She traded her old car for a new model.* ► exchange, part-exchange, barter, swap, switch

trader NOUNS *local high-street traders* ► dealer, merchant, retailer, tradesman, shopkeeper, stockist, supplier, vendor

tradition NOUN *the old tradition of first-footing* ► custom, practice, convention, institution, observance, habit, routine

traditional ADJECTIVE **1** *a traditional white wedding* ► conventional, customary, established, accustomed, familiar, time-honored, typical, orthodox, regular, usual AN OPPOSITE IS unconventional **2** *traditional beliefs* ► popular, folk, oral, unwritten, historical OPPOSITES ARE modern, contemporary

traffic NOUN **1** *Road traffic is not allowed in the park.* ► vehicles, cars, transport **2** *goods traffic* ► transport, transportation, movement **3** *illegal traffic in antiquities* ► trade, trading, dealing, commerce, peddling

tragedy NOUN **tragedies 1** a play with unhappy events or a sad ending **2** a very sad or distressing event [from Greek *tragos* = goat + *oide* = song The connection with goats is not known]

tragic ADJECTIVE **1** very sad or distressing **2** to do with tragedies • *a great tragic actor*
▷ **tragically** ADVERB

trail NOUN **trails 1** a track, scent, or other sign left where something has passed **2** a path or track made through the countryside or a forest

trail VERB **trails, trailing, trailed 1** follow the trail of something; track **2** drag or be dragged along behind; lag behind **3** follow someone more slowly or wearily **4** hang down or float loosely **5** become fainter • *Her voice trailed away.*

trailer NOUN **trailers 1** a truck or other container pulled along by a vehicle **2** a short piece from a film or television program, shown in advance to advertise it

train NOUN **trains 1** a railway engine pulling a line of cars or trucks that are linked together **2** a number of people or animals moving in a line • *a camel train* **3** a series of things • *a train of events* **4** part of a long dress or robe that trails on the ground at the back

train VERB **trains, training, trained 1** give a person instruction or practice so that they become skilled **2** practice, especially for a sporting event • *She was training for the race.* **3** make something grow in a particular direction • *We'd like to train roses up the walls.* **4** aim a gun or camera etc.

trainer NOUN **trainers** (British) **1** a person who trains people or animals **2** a soft rubber-soled shoe of the kind worn for running or by athletes, etc., while exercising

traitor NOUN **traitors** a person who betrays his or her country or friends
▷ **traitorous** ADJECTIVE

tram NOUN **trams** a public passenger vehicle running on rails in the road

tramp NOUN **tramps 1** a person without a home or job who walks from place to place **2** a long walk **3** the sound of heavy footsteps

tramp VERB **tramps, tramping, tramped 1** walk with heavy footsteps **2** walk for a long distance

trample VERB **tramples, trampling, trampled** tread heavily on something; crush something by treading on it

trampoline NOUN **trampolines** a large piece of canvas joined to a frame by springs, used by gymnasts for jumping on

---

Thesaurus

---

tragedy NOUN *the tragedy of their son's death*
► disaster, calamity, catastrophe, affliction, blow, misfortune, misadventure

tragic ADJECTIVE **1** *a tragic accident* ► disastrous, catastrophic, calamitous, dreadful, fatal, appalling, terrible, unfortunate AN OPPOSITE IS fortunate **2** *a tragic expression on her face* ► sad, sorrowful, woeful, wretched, distressed, grief-stricken, hurt, pathetic, piteous, pitiful AN OPPOSITE IS comic

trail NOUN **1** *The fox followed the trail of its prey.* ► track, footprints, mark, scent, signs, spoor, traces **2** *a nature trail* ► path, pathway, route, track, road **3** *They left a trail of clues.* ► series, string, stream, chain, line

trail VERB **1** *The car was trailing a large caravan.* ► draw, haul, drag, pull, tow **2** *His feet were trailing in the water.* ► dangle, hang **3** *She suspected someone was trailing her.* ► follow, pursue, shadow, stalk, track, trace, tail, chase **4** *The smaller children were trailing behind.* ► straggle, linger, lag, fall behind, dawdle, dally

train NOUN **1** *a strange train of events* ► chain, series, sequence, succession **2** *The minister had a train of attendants.* ► entourage, retinue, cortège, following, suite

train VERB **1** *Now she had three assistants to train.* ► teach, instruct, tutor, coach, educate,

prepare **2** *The team was training hard.* ► practise, exercise, prepare yourself, get fit, (more informal) work out **3** *The guns were trained on a position in the hills.* ► aim (at), point (at), direct (at), level (at)

trainer NOUN *a fitness trainer* ► instructor, coach, teacher, tutor, mentor

training NOUN *Next week he would report for training.* ► exercise, exercises, physical exercise, fitness routine, (more informal) working out

traitor NOUN *Thousands of students denounced Kim as a traitor.* ► betrayer, defector, deserter, double-crosser, apostate, blackleg, turncoat, collaborator, informer, quisling, renegade

tramp NOUN **1** *the ritual tramp across the swamp* ► trek, trudge, march, walk, (more informal) slog **2** *He remembered an old tramp he used to see by the station.* ► beggar, vagrant, homeless person, destitute person, (more informal) dosser, (more informal) down and out

tramp VERB *We tramped across the wet grass and bracken.* ► trudge, trek, traipse, hike, march, plod, stride, toil

trample VERB *trample on Her dog had trampled on his tulips.* ► tread on, stamp on, walk over, crush, flatten, squash

a
b
c
d
e
f
g
h
i
j
k
l
m
n
o
p
q
r
s
t
u
v
w
x
y
z

A
B
C
D
E
F
G
H
I
J
K
L
M
N
O
P
Q
R
S
T
U
V
W
X
Y
Z

trance NOUN trances a dreamy or unconscious state rather like sleep

tranquil ADJECTIVE calm and quiet
▷ **tranquilly** ADVERB **tranquillity** NOUN

tranquilizer NOUN tranquilizers a medicine used to make a person feel calm

transatlantic ADJECTIVE across or on the other side of the Atlantic Ocean

transcript NOUN transcripts a written copy

transfer VERB transfers, transferring, transferred **1** move a person or thing to another place **2** hand over
▷ **transferable** ADJECTIVE **transference** NOUN

transfer NOUN transfers **1** the transferring of a person or thing **2** a picture or design that can be transferred onto another surface

transfigure VERB transfigures, transfiguring, transfigured change the appearance of something greatly
▷ **transfiguration** NOUN

transfix VERB transfixes, transfixing, transfixed **1** make a person or animal unable to move because of fear or surprise etc. **2** pierce and fix with something pointed

transform VERB transforms, transforming, transformed change the form or appearance or character of a person or thing
▷ **transformation** NOUN

transformer NOUN transformers a device used to change the voltage of an electric current

transfusion NOUN transfusions putting blood taken from one person into another person's body
▷ **transfuse** VERB

transistor NOUN transistors **1** a tiny semiconductor device that controls a flow of electricity **2** (also transistor radio) a portable radio that uses transistors
▷ **transistorized** ADJECTIVE

transit NOUN the process of traveling from one place to another ● *The goods were damaged in transit.*

transition NOUN transitions the process of changing from one condition or form, etc., to another
▷ **transitional** ADJECTIVE

transitive ADJECTIVE (said about a verb) used with a direct object after it, e.g., *change* in *change your shoes* (but not in *change into dry shoes*) COMPARE **intransitive**
▷ **transitively** ADVERB

translate VERB translates, translating, translated put something into another language
▷ **translatable** ADJECTIVE **translation** NOUN **translator** NOUN

transliterate VERB transliterates, transliterating, transliterated write a word in the letters of a different alphabet or language
▷ **transliteration** NOUN

translucent (tranz- **loo-** sent) ADJECTIVE allowing some light to shine through but not transparent

transmission NOUN transmissions **1** transmitting something **2** a broadcast **3** the gears by which power is transmitted from the engine to the wheels of a vehicle

transmit VERB transmits, transmitting, transmitted **1** send or pass on from one

---

Thesaurus

---

trance NOUN *She was lost in a trance.* ► daze, dream, hypnotic state, reverie, day-dream, ecstasy, spell

tranquil ADJECTIVE **1** *the tranquil and pretty hamlet of Springfield* ► peaceful, quiet, calm, restful, placid, serene, still, undisturbed, unruffled OPPOSITES ARE noisy, busy **2** *He felt relaxed and tranquil.* ► calm, placid, sedate, sober, unemotional, unexcited, untroubled, collected, composed, dispassionate, (*more informal*) laid-back AN OPPOSITE IS excited

transfer VERB *The books will be transferred to the central library.* ► move, remove, shift, relocate, take over, take across, convey, transmit

transfer NOUN *the transfer of rights to the new owner* ► change, changeover, shift, shifting, handover, transferral, transmission

transform VERB *The new owners transformed the property into a lovely family house.* ► convert, change, alter, develop, renovate, reorganize, (*more formal*) metamorphose

transformation NOUN *There was a transformation in her attitude.* ► change, conversion, alteration, improvement, revolution, transfiguration, transition, (*more formal*) metamorphosis, (*more informal*) turn-about

translate VERB *a poem by Goethe translated into English* ► render, convert, interpret, express, paraphrase, transcribe

translation NOUN *an English translation of the Iliad* ► version, rendering, transcription, interpretation, gloss, paraphrase

transmission NOUN *The program was scheduled for transmission after 9 o'clock.* ► broadcast, relaying, diffusion, dissemination, sending out

transmit VERB **1** *The broadcast will be transmitted next Saturday.* ► broadcast, relay, send out **2** *Short-wave radios are used to transmit messages.* ► communicate, convey, dispatch, disseminate, emit, pass on AN OPPOSITE IS receive

person or place to another **2** send out a signal or broadcast etc.
▷ **transmitter** NOUN

transmute VERB transmutes, transmuting, transmuted change something from one form or substance into another
▷ **transmutation** NOUN

transparent ADJECTIVE able to be seen through

transplant VERB transplants, transplanting, transplanted **1** remove a plant and put it to grow somewhere else **2** transfer a part of the body to another person or animal
▷ **transplantation** NOUN

transplant NOUN transplants **1** the process of transplanting **2** something transplanted

transport VERB transports, transporting, transported take a person, animal, or thing from one place to another
▷ **transportation** NOUN **transporter** NOUN

transport NOUN the process or means of transporting people, animals, or things ● *The city has a good system of public transport.*

transpose VERB transposes, transposing, transposed **1** change the position or order of something **2** put a piece of music into a different key
▷ **transposition** NOUN

trap NOUN traps **1** a device for catching and holding animals **2** a plan or trick for capturing, detecting, or cheating someone **3** a two-wheeled carriage pulled by a horse **4** a bend in a pipe, filled with water to prevent gases from rising up from a drain

trap VERB traps, trapping, trapped **1** catch or hold a person or animal in a trap **2** prevent someone from escaping ● *The driver was trapped in the wreckage.*
▷ **trapper** NOUN

trapdoor NOUN trapdoors a door in a floor, ceiling, or roof

trapeze NOUN trapezes a bar hanging from two ropes as a swing for acrobats

trapezium NOUN trapeziums or trapezia a quadrilateral in which two opposite sides are parallel and the other two are not

trash NOUN rubbish or nonsense
▷ **trashy** ADJECTIVE

trauma (traw- ma) NOUN traumas a shock that produces a lasting effect on a person's mind
▷ **traumatic** ADJECTIVE **traumatize** VERB

travel VERB travels, traveling, traveled move from place to place
▷ **travel** NOUN

traveler NOUN travelers **1** a person who is travelling or who often travels **2** a gypsy, or a person who does not settle in one place

traveler's check NOUN traveler's checks a check for a fixed amount of money that is sold by banks and that can be exchanged for money in foreign countries

trawl VERB trawls, trawling, trawled fish by dragging a large net along the seabed

trawler NOUN trawlers a boat used in trawling

tray NOUN trays **1** a flat piece of wood, metal, or plastic, usually with raised edges, for carrying cups, plates, food, etc. **2** an open container for holding letters etc. in an office

---

Thesaurus

---

transparent ADJECTIVE *a transparent fabric*
► see-through, translucent, diaphanous, clear, sheer, filmy, gauzy, limpid, pellucid

transport VERB (with the stress on -*port*) *The larger components will be transported by rail.*
► take, carry, convey, ship, transfer, bring, fetch, haul, move, shift

transport NOUN (with the stress on *trans*-) *The village has limited access to public transport.*
► conveyance, haulage, shipping, transportation

trap NOUN **1** *Some kinds of animal traps are illegal.* ► snare, noose, net, gin **2** *The cavalry rode straight into a trap* ► ambush, lure, decoy, ambuscade **3** *The last question might be a trap.*
► trick, ploy, deception, artifice

trap VERB **1** *They had to find a way of trapping the fox before it did any more damage.* ► snare, capture, catch, ensnare, entrap, corner **2** *The question was designed to trap them.* ► trick, deceive, fool, dupe

trash NOUN **1** *The cleaners shake out your carpets and empty your trash.* ► garbage, rubbish,

waste, refuse, litter **2** *He despised himself for having to write such trash.* ► nonsense, drivel, rubbish, gibberish, junk

trash VERB *He went to a phone box but it had been trashed.* ► vandalize, wreck, ruin, destroy

trashy ADJECTIVE (*informal*) *a trashy horror movie from the sixties* ► inferior, poor-quality, second-rate, worthless

traumatic ADJECTIVE *She talked about her traumatic divorce from Ronnie.* ► distressing, stressful, disturbing, shocking, upsetting, hurtful, painful AN OPPOSITE IS soothing

travel NOUN *When he retired he had much more time for travel.* ► traveling, touring, tourism, journeying, sightseeing, excursions, globetrotting

travel VERB *With this ticket you can travel as many miles as you wish.* ► journey, go, ramble, wander, rove, tour, move, proceed, progress

traveler NOUN **1** *refreshments for the weary traveler* ► voyager, passenger, tourist, tripper, holidaymaker, sightseer **2** *ground set aside for travelers' camps* ► gypsy, itinerant, nomad

treacherous ➡ treaty

treacherous ADJECTIVE **1** betraying someone; disloyal **2** dangerous or unreliable ● *It's snowing and the roads are treacherous.*
▷ **treacherously** ADVERB **treachery** NOUN

treacle NOUN a thick sticky liquid produced when sugar is purified
▷ **treacly** ADJECTIVE
[originally = ointment for an animal bite; from Greek *therion* = wild or poisonous animal]

tread VERB **treads, treading, trod, trodden** walk or put your foot on something

tread NOUN **treads 1** a sound or way of walking **2** the top surface of a stair; the part you put your foot on **3** the part of a tire that touches the ground

treadmill NOUN **treadmills 1** a wide mill wheel turned by the weight of people or animals treading on steps fixed round its edge **2** monotonous routine work

treason NOUN betraying your country
▷ **treasonable** ADJECTIVE **treasonous** ADJECTIVE

treasure NOUN **treasures 1** a store of precious metals or jewels **2** a precious thing or person

treasure VERB **treasures, treasuring, treasured** value greatly something that you have

treasurer NOUN **treasurers** a person in charge of the money of a club, society, etc.

treasury NOUN **treasuries** a place where money and valuables are kept
the Treasury the government department in charge of a country's income

treat VERB **treats, treating, treated 1** behave in a certain way towards a person or thing **2** deal with a subject etc. **3** give medical care in order to cure a person or animal **4** put something through a chemical or other process ● *The fabric has been treated to make it waterproof.* **5** pay for someone else's food, drink, or entertainment ● *I'll treat you to an ice cream.*

treat NOUN **treats 1** something special that gives pleasure **2** the process of treating someone to food, drink, or entertainment [from Latin *tractare* = to handle or manage]

treatment NOUN **treatments 1** the process or manner of dealing with a person, animal, or thing **2** medical care

treaty NOUN **treaties** a formal agreement between two or more countries

---

Thesaurus

treacherous ADJECTIVE **1** *She did not believe him capable of such treacherous behavior.*
► traitorous, disloyal, deceitful, faithless, false, unfaithful, perfidious, double-dealing, duplicitous AN OPPOSITE IS loyal **2** *There was a mile of deep treacherous water separating him from the mainland.* ► dangerous, hazardous, perilous, unsafe, unreliable, deceptive, misleading, risky, shifting, unpredictable, unstable OPPOSITES ARE safe, reliable

treachery NOUN *His resignation from the party would be seen as an act of treachery.* ► betrayal, disloyalty, infidelity, perfidy, treason, dishonesty, double-dealing, duplicity, faithlessness, untrustworthiness AN OPPOSITE IS loyalty

tread VERB *There is erosion along the route and walkers should tread carefully.* ► step, walk, proceed, pace, stride
tread on *His father accidentally trod on a model boat he'd been making.* ► step on, walk on, trample, crush, squash, stamp on

treason NOUN *In July 1540 he was beheaded for treason.* ► treachery, betrayal, sedition, rebellion, mutiny OPPOSITES ARE loyalty, allegiance

treasure NOUN **1** *The treasure sank to the bottom of the sea, along with the ship that held it.* ► hoard, cache, jewels, riches, fortune, gold, treasure trove, valuables, wealth **2** *Rosie was a treasure who had brought happiness to the house.* ► gem, paragon, angel, prize, star

treasure VERB *It's a very special photo and we'll treasure it for ever.* ► prize, value, cherish, esteem, guard, keep safe, adore, appreciate, love

treat NOUN **1** *Add some prawns to the dish for a special treat.* ► indulgence, extravagance **2** *She would give the children a birthday treat next year.* ► celebration, surprise, entertainment, outing **3** *The ballet is a treat to the eye.* ► pleasure, delight, joy, thrill

treat VERB **1** *They didn't treat her badly, but she was made to feel a nuisance.* ► behave toward, deal with, look after, care for, use, serve, attend to **2** *The lectures treat all broad aspects of the subject.* ► deal with, discuss, cover, consider, tackle **3** *attempts to treat illness by radiation* ► cure, heal, medicate, dress, tend **4** *People tend to treat the videos as entertainment rather than information.* ► regard, consider, view **5** *If you like, I'll treat you to a movie.* ► give, pay for, provide for, entertain

treatment NOUN **1** *She found it difficult to accept his treatment of her.* ► care, handling, management, behavior (toward), conduct (towards), dealing (with), use **2** *He was responding well to the treatment.* ► therapy, medical care, medication, nursing, healing **3** *The book's treatment of this topic is extremely thorough.* ► coverage, handling, explanation, analysis, discussion

treaty NOUN *The two countries signed a treaty of mutual support.* ► agreement, settlement, pact, deal, entente, alliance, compact,

treble ADJECTIVE three times as much or as many

treble NOUN **trebles** **1** a treble amount **2** a person with a high-pitched or soprano voice

treble VERB **trebles, trebling, trebled** make or become three times as much or as many [from early French; related to **triple**]

tree NOUN **trees** a tall plant with a single very thick hard stem or trunk that is usually without branches for some distance above the ground [from Old English]

trek NOUN **treks** a long walk or journey

trek VERB **treks, trekking, trekked** go on a long walk or journey [from South African Dutch *trekken* = to pull, to travel]

trellis NOUN **trellises** a framework with crossing bars of wood or metal, etc., to support climbing plants

tremble VERB **trembles, trembling, trembled** shake gently, especially with fear
▷ **tremble** NOUN

tremendous ADJECTIVE **1** very large; huge **2** excellent
▷ **tremendously** ADVERB

tremor NOUN **tremors** **1** a shaking or trembling movement **2** a slight earthquake

trench NOUN **trenches** **1** a long narrow hole cut in the ground **2** a ditch dug by troops to protect them from enemy fire

trench VERB dig a trench or trenches

trend NOUN **trends** the general direction in which something is going

trendy ADJECTIVE (*informal*) fashionable; following the latest trends
▷ **trendily** ADVERB **trendiness** NOUN

trespass VERB **trespasses, trespassing, trespassed** **1** go on someone's land or property unlawfully **2** (*old use*) do wrong; sin
▷ **trespasser** NOUN

trespass NOUN **trespasses** (*old use*) wrongdoing; sin

tress NOUN **tresses** a lock of hair

trestle NOUN **trestles** each of a set of supports on which a board is rested to form a table
▷ **trestle table** NOUN

trial NOUN **trials** **1** the process of examining the evidence in a lawcourt to decide whether a person is guilty of a crime **2** testing a thing to see how good it is **3** a test of qualities or ability **4** an annoying person or thing; a hardship
on trial **1** being tried in a lawcourt **2** being tested
trial and error trying out different methods of doing something until you find one that works

triangle NOUN **triangles** **1** a flat shape with three sides and three angles **2** a percussion instrument made from a metal rod bent into a triangle
▷ **triangular** ADJECTIVE

tribe NOUN **tribes** **1** a group of families living in one area as a community, ruled by a chief **2** a set of people
▷ **tribal** ADJECTIVE **tribally** ADVERB **tribesman** NOUN **tribeswoman** NOUN

tribunal (try- bew- nal) NOUN **tribunals** a committee appointed to hear evidence and give judgments when there is a dispute

tributary NOUN **tributaries** a river or stream that flows into a larger one or into a lake

Thesaurus

concordat, convention, protocol, understanding

trek NOUN *a long trek through the hills* ► journey, trip, expedition, march, hike, slog, tramp, trudge, walk

trek VERB *They've trekked all over the Greek mainland.* ► hike, tramp, march, journey, walk, slog

tremble VERB **1** *His hands were trembling.* ► shake, shiver, quake, quaver, quiver **2** *Heavy traffic outside makes the ornaments tremble.* ► vibrate, shake, wobble, shudder, waver

tremendous ADJECTIVE **1** *It had been a tremendous achievement.* ► great, wonderful, marvellous, stylish, stupendous, extraordinary, considerable, significant, immense OPPOSITES ARE insignificant, trivial **2** *There was a tremendous crash.* ► terrible, terrific, frightful, awful, fearful, fearsome, alarming, appalling, frightening, horrifying, shocking OPPOSITES ARE faint, slight

trend NOUN **1** *a downward trend in unemployment* ► tendency, movement, shift, bias, leaning, direction, inclination **2** *the latest trend in rock music* ► fashion, vogue, craze, rage, mode, style, fad, way

trendy ADJECTIVE (*informal*) *trendy clothes* ► fashionable, stylish, up-to-date, contemporary, latest, modern, (*more informal*) cool, (*more informal*) in AN OPPOSITE IS unfashionable

trial NOUN **1** *The trial will last about a month.* ► lawsuit, court case, hearing, tribunal, proceedings, examination **2** *The latest model is undergoing trials.* ► test, testing, experiment, pilot, try-out **3** *Such a long meeting was a real trial.* ► ordeal, problem, tribulation, difficulty, trouble, burden, worry, affliction, hardship **4** *Joan can be a trial at times.* ► nuisance, pest, bother, (*more informal*) pain

tribe NOUN *nomadic tribes* ► people, race, nation, group, horde, stock, clan

a
b
c
d
e
f
g
h
i
j
k
l
m
n
o
p
q
r
s
t
u
v
w
x
y
z

A
B
C
D
E
F
G
H
I
J
K
L
M
N
O
P
Q
R
S
T
U
V
W
X
Y
Z

tribute NOUN tributes **1** something said, done, or given to show respect or admiration **2** payment that one country or ruler was formerly obliged to pay to a more powerful one

trice NOUN (old use)
in a trice in a moment
[from early Dutch *trisen* = to pull quickly, to tug]

trick NOUN tricks **1** a crafty or deceitful action; a practical joke • *Let's play a trick on Jo.* **2** a skilful action, especially one done for entertainment • *magic tricks* **3** the cards picked up by the winner after one round of a card game such as whist

trick VERB tricks, tricking, tricked **1** deceive or cheat someone by a trick **2** decorate • *The building was tricked out with little flags.*

trickery NOUN the use of tricks; deception

trickle VERB trickles, trickling, trickled flow or move slowly
▷ trickle NOUN

tricky ADJECTIVE trickier, trickiest **1** difficult; needing skill • *a tricky job* **2** cunning or deceitful
▷ trickiness NOUN

tricycle NOUN tricycles a vehicle like a bicycle but with three wheels

trifle NOUN trifles **1** a pudding made of sponge cake covered in custard, fruit, cream, etc. **2** a very small amount **3** something that has very little importance or value

trifle VERB trifles, trifling, trifled treat a person or thing without seriousness or respect • *She is not a woman to be trifled with.*

trifling ADJECTIVE small in value or importance

trigger NOUN triggers a lever that is pulled to fire a gun

trigger VERB triggers, triggering, triggered trigger off start something happening

trigonometry (trig- on- **om**- it- ree) NOUN the calculation of distances and angles by using triangles

trill VERB trills, trilling, trilled make a quivering musical sound
▷ trill NOUN

trillion NOUN trillions **1** a million million

trim ADJECTIVE neat and orderly
▷ trimly ADVERB trimness NOUN

trim VERB trims, trimming, trimmed **1** cut the edges or unwanted parts off something

Thesaurus

tribute NOUN **1** *Tributes came in from friends and colleagues.* ► praise, accolade, eulogy, testimonial, appreciation, commendation, recognition, compliment, panegyric **2** *Their eventual success was a tribute to their courage and determination.* ► testimony, evidence (of), proof (of) **3** *The city had to pay an annual tribute to the king.* ► tax, payment, levy, duty, contribution
pay tribute to *She paid tribute to her staff for their hard work.* ► praise, commend, applaud, celebrate, honor, pay homage to, respect

trick NOUN **1** *He entertained the children with conjuring tricks* ► feat, stunt, illusion, magic **2** *He saw through every trick she used.* ► ruse, scheme, stratagem, deceit, deception, subterfuge, maneuver, ploy, pretence, fraud, wile, cheat, (more informal) con **3** *My favorite trick was to hide above everyone and jump on them. Who else would play a trick like that on me?* ► joke, practical joke, prank, stunt **4** *The essential trick is to think backwards and write forwards.* ► knack, secret, skill, device, dodge, technique, art, craft, expertise, gimmick, (informal) know-how

trick VERB *He was furious with himself for being tricked so easily.* ► fool, deceive, cheat, dupe, hoodwink, swindle, trap, outwit, hoax, bluff, mislead, catch out, defraud, (informal) con, (informal) bamboozle

trickery NOUN *The excuses he makes sound like the old trickery.* ► deception, pretence,

cheating, chicanery, deceit, mischief, dishonesty, bluffing, fraud, (informal) monkey business, (informal) shenanigans

trickle VERB *Sweat trickled down his sides despite the cold.* ► drip, dribble, seep, ooze, leak, flow slowly, percolate, run OPPOSITES ARE pour, gush

trickle NOUN *She saw a trickle of blood flow over her fingers.* ► dribble, seepage, thin stream OPPOSITES ARE flood, gush

trickster NOUN *I shall reveal you for the sly trickster that you are.* ► cheat, swindler, fraud, fraudster, impostor, charlatan, deceiver, dissembler

tricky ADJECTIVE **1** *Tony was a tricky individual.* ► cunning, crafty, wily, artful **2** *Tricky negotiations were taking place.* ► difficult, complicated, awkward, delicate, sensitive

trifle NOUN *It cost a mere trifle.* ► small amount, next to nothing, pittance, (more informal) peanuts
a trifle *He looked a trifle embarrassed.* ► a little, a bit, somewhat, a touch, a spot

trifling ADJECTIVE *We shouldn't bother them with such a trifling matter.* ► trivial, unimportant, insignificant, inconsequential, minor, petty

trim VERB **1** *He had trimmed his hair and beard.* ► cut, crop, clip, tidy, shape, shear **2** *The governor will have either to increase taxes or trim his budget.* ► reduce, cut, prune, scale down **3** *The silk curtains were trimmed with gold.* ► decorate, embellish

2 decorate a hat or piece of clothing by adding lace, ribbons, etc. **3** arrange sails to suit the wind

trim NOUN trims **1** cutting or trimming • *Your beard needs a trim.* **2** lace, ribbons, etc., used to decorate something
in good trim in good condition; fit

Trinity NOUN God regarded as three persons (Father, Son, and Holy Spirit)

trinket NOUN trinkets a small ornament or piece of jewellery

trio NOUN trios **1** a group of three people or things **2** a group of three musicians or singers **3** a piece of music for three musicians

trip VERB trips, tripping, tripped **1** catch your foot on something and fall; make someone do this **2** move with quick light steps **3** operate a switch
trip up 1 stumble **2** make a mistake **3** cause a person to stumble or make a mistake

trip NOUN trips **1** a journey or outing **2** the action of tripping; a stumble **3** (*informal*) hallucinations caused by taking a drug

tripe NOUN **1** part of an ox's stomach used as food **2** (*slang*) nonsense

triple ADJECTIVE **1** consisting of three parts **2** involving three people or groups • *a triple alliance* **3** three times as much or as many
▷ **triply** ADVERB

triple VERB triples, tripling, tripled make or become three times as much or as many

triplet NOUN triplets each of three children or animals born to the same mother at one time

triplicate NOUN
in triplicate as three identical copies

tripod (try- pod) NOUN tripods a stand with three legs, e.g., to support a camera

trite (rhymes with *kite*) ADJECTIVE worn out by constant repetition; unoriginal • *a few trite remarks*

triumph NOUN triumphs **1** a great success or victory; a feeling of joy at this **2** a celebration of a victory
▷ **triumphal** ADJECTIVE **triumphant** ADJECTIVE **triumphantly** ADVERB

triumph VERB triumphs, triumphing, triumphed **1** be successful or victorious **2** rejoice in success or victory

trivia PLURAL NOUN unimportant details or pieces of information

trivial ADJECTIVE small in value or importance
▷ **trivially** ADVERB **triviality** NOUN

troll (rhymes with *hole*) NOUN trolls (in Scandinavian mythology) a supernatural being, either a giant or a friendly but mischievous dwarf [originally = witch: from Old Norse]

trolley NOUN trolleys **1** a small table on wheels or castors **2** a small cart or truck **3** a basket on wheels, used in supermarkets

trombone NOUN trombones a large brass musical instrument with a sliding tube

troop NOUN troops **1** an organized group of soldiers, Scouts, etc. **2** a number of people moving along together
USAGE Do not confuse with **troupe**.

troop VERB troops, trooping, trooped move along as a group or in large numbers • *They all trooped in.* [from Latin *troppus* = herd]

Thesaurus

trim ADJECTIVE **1** *a housing estate with trim gardens* ► neat, tidy, orderly, smart, spruce, well-groomed, well-kept AN OPPOSITE IS untidy **2** *Pants help to accentuate a trim figure.* ► slim, slender, lean

trip VERB **1** *Angela tripped along in her red sweater.* ► run, skip, walk **2** *She tripped over the step and cut her knee.* ► stumble, totter, tumble, catch your foot, fall, stagger

trip NOUN *He met the Czar during a trip to Russia in 1908.* ► journey, visit, voyage, excursion, expedition, holiday, jaunt, outing, tour

trite ADJECTIVE *However trite it may sound, there is joy to be found in a spring day.* ► banal, commonplace, ordinary, hackneyed, clichéd, stale

triumph NOUN **1** *He was a key figure in the party's election triumph.* ► victory, win, conquest, (*informal*) walkover AN OPPOSITE IS defeat **2** *She smiled in triumph.* ► celebration, joy, exultation, jubilation, elation **3** *The visit to Wales had been a triumph.* ► success,

accomplishment, achievement, master stroke, (*more informal*) hit

triumph VERB **triumph over** *He had triumphed over disease and misfortune.* ► overcome, defeat, conquer, prevail over, succeed against, be victorious over, win over

triumphant ADJECTIVE **1** *The communists emerged triumphant from the revolution.* ► successful, victorious, dominant, conquering, winning AN OPPOSITE IS unsuccessful **2** *He gave her a knowing, triumphant look.* ► exultant, jubilant, boastful, joyful, elated, gleeful, gloating, immodest, proud OPPOSITES ARE modest, humble

trivial ADJECTIVE *The offense was regarded as trivial.* ► insignificant, unimportant, inconsequential, minor, trifling, incidental OPPOSITES ARE important, significant

troop NOUN *A troop of tourists crossed the square.* ► group, party, band, body, company

troop VERB *Rod looked up as Sara and the others trooped in.* ► march, file, flock, parade, straggle

A
B
C
D
E
F
G
H
I
J
K
L
M
N
O
P
Q
R
S
T
U
V
W
X
Y
Z

trooper NOUN **troopers** a soldier in the cavalry or in an armoured unit

troops PLURAL NOUN armed forces

trophy NOUN **trophies** 1 a cup, etc., given as a prize for winning a competition 2 something taken in war or hunting as a souvenir of success

tropic NOUN **tropics** a line of latitude about 23° north of the equator (**Tropic of Cancer**) or 23° south of the equator (**Tropic of Capricorn**) **the tropics** the hot regions between these two latitudes

tropical ADJECTIVE to do with the tropics • *tropical fish*

trot VERB **trots, trotting, trotted** 1 (said about a horse) run, going faster than when walking but more slowly than when cantering 2 run gently with short steps
trot out (*informal*) produce or repeat • *He trotted out the usual excuses.*

trot NOUN a trotting run
on the trot (*informal*) one after the other without a break • *She worked for ten days on the trot.*

trouble NOUN **troubles** 1 difficulty, inconvenience, or distress 2 a cause of any of these
take trouble take great care in doing something

trouble VERB **troubles, troubling, troubled** 1 cause trouble to someone 2 give yourself trouble or inconvenience, etc. • *Nobody troubled to ask if he needed help.*

troublesome ADJECTIVE causing trouble or annoyance

trough (trof) NOUN **troughs** 1 a long narrow open container, especially one holding water or food for animals 2 a channel for liquid 3 the low part between two waves or ridges 4 a long region of low air pressure

troupe (rhymes with *troop*) NOUN **troupes** a company of actors or other performers
USAGE Do not confuse with **troop**.

trousers PLURAL NOUN a piece of clothing worn over the lower half of the body, with a separate part for each leg [from Irish or Scottish Gaelic]

trout NOUN **trout** a freshwater fish that is caught as a sport and for food

trowel NOUN **trowels** 1 a small garden tool with a curved blade for lifting plants or scooping things 2 a small tool with a flat blade for spreading mortar etc. [from Latin *trulla* = scoop]

truant NOUN **truants** a child who stays away from school without permission
▷ **truancy** NOUN

Thesaurus

trophy NOUN 1 *trophies of war* ► souvenir, memento, reward, spoils, booty, loot 2 *a sports trophy* ► award, cup, medal, prize

tropical ADJECTIVE *tropical areas such as East Africa* ► equatorial, hot, humid, sultry, torrid

trot VERB *Danny trotted into the house.* ► run, scurry, scamper, scuttle, hurry

trouble NOUN 1 *See what trouble you've caused.* ► difficulty, bother, problems, inconvenience, distress, anxiety 2 *He recounted his troubles and asked for advice.* ► problem, misfortune, difficulty, tribulation, trial, affliction, suffering, hardship 3 *We took some trouble to help them.* ► care, effort, bother, exertion, pains 4 *I hope I wasn't a trouble to you.* ► nuisance, bother, irritation 5 *The trouble with these machines is the lack of spare parts.* ► problem, difficulty, disadvantage, weakness, failing OPPOSITES ARE advantage, benefit 6 *There was crowd trouble after the match.* ► disturbance, disorder, unrest, conflict, fighting, violence OPPOSITES ARE order, peace 7 *She suffered from back trouble.* ► ailment, disorder, complaint, illness, disability

trouble VERB 1 *Something was troubling him.* ► bother, worry, distress, concern, pain, vex, torment, upset 2 *I'm very sorry to trouble you.* ► disturb, interrupt, bother, inconvenience

troubled ADJECTIVE 1 *Tara looked troubled.* ► anxious, worried, bothered, concerned, disturbed, perturbed, uneasy, unhappy, vexed, restless OPPOSITES ARE untroubled, peaceful 2 *We live in troubled times.* ► difficult, unsettled, uncertain

troublemaker NOUN *She was branded a troublemaker for complaining about a colleague who harassed her.* ► mischief-maker, agitator, rabble-rouser, ringleader, wrongdoer

troublesome ADJECTIVE 1 *Craig was recovering from a troublesome knee injury.* ► annoying, irritating, irksome, tiresome, trying, bothersome, vexing, distressing, inconvenient, upsetting OPPOSITES ARE trouble-free, harmless 2 *The younger boy was being particularly troublesome.* ► badly behaved, naughty, unruly, disobedient, disorderly, uncooperative, rowdy

trousers NOUN *He was wearing a pair of pale trousers.* ► pants, slacks

truancy NOUN *We are determined to crack down on truancy.* ► absenteeism, malingering, shirking, (more informal) skiving AN OPPOSITE IS attendance

truant NOUN *I was a truant from a detention center.* ► absentee, nonattender, runaway, malingerer, shirker, (more informal) skiver

play truant be a truant
[from early French, = criminal]

truce *NOUN* truces an agreement to stop fighting for a while

truck[1] *NOUN* trucks **1** a large vehicle used to transport heavy loads **2** an open container on wheels; an open railway wagon **3** an axle with wheels attached, fitted under a skateboard

trudge *VERB* trudges, trudging, trudged walk slowly and heavily

true *ADJECTIVE* truer, truest **1** representing what has really happened or exists ● *a true story* **2** genuine or proper; not false ● *He was the true heir.* **3** accurate **4** loyal or faithful ● *Be true to your friends.*
▷ **trueness** *NOUN*
come true actually happen as hoped or predicted

truffle *NOUN* truffles **1** a soft sweet made with chocolate **2** a fungus that grows underground and is valued as food because of its rich flavor

truly *ADVERB* **1** truthfully **2** sincerely or genuinely ● *We are truly grateful.* **3** accurately **4** loyally or faithfully
Yours truly see yours

trump *NOUN* trumps a playing card of a suit that ranks above the others for one game

trump *VERB* trumps, trumping, trumped beat a card by playing a trump
trump up invent an excuse or an accusation etc.

trumpet *NOUN* trumpets **1** a metal wind instrument with a narrow tube that widens near the end **2** something shaped like this

trumpet *VERB* trumpets, trumpeting, trumpeted **1** blow a trumpet **2** (said about an elephant) make a loud sound with its trunk **3** shout or announce something loudly
▷ **trumpeter** *NOUN*

truncheon *NOUN* truncheons a short thick stick carried as a weapon, especially by police

trundle *VERB* trundles, trundling, trundled roll along heavily ● *He was trundling a wheelbarrow.* ● *A bus trundled up.*

trunk *NOUN* trunks **1** the main stem of a tree **2** an elephant's long flexible nose **3** a large box with a hinged lid for transporting or storing clothes, etc. **4** the human body except for the head, arms, and legs

trunk road *NOUN* trunk roads an important main road

trunks *PLURAL NOUN* shorts worn by men and boys for swimming, boxing, etc.

truss *NOUN* trusses **1** a framework of beams or bars supporting a roof or bridge **2** a bundle of hay, etc.

truss *VERB* trusses, trussing, trussed **1** tie up a person or thing securely **2** support a roof or bridge etc. with trusses

trust *VERB* trusts, trusting, trusted **1** believe that a person or thing is good, truthful, or strong **2** let a person have or use something in the belief that they will behave responsibly

Thesaurus

play truant *52 percent admitted to playing truant for the odd lesson now and then.* ► be absent, stay away, desert, malinger

truce *NOUN* *The enemy broke the truce and resumed the war.* ► cease-fire, armistice, moratorium, pact, peace, suspension of hostilities, treaty

truck *NOUN* *The truck was skidding all over the highway.* ► heavy goods vehicle, juggernaut

true *ADJECTIVE* **1** *The story turned out to be true.* ► correct, right, accurate, factual, authentic, confirmed, proper, veracious, veritable OPPOSITES ARE untrue, false **2** *The document was certified as a true copy.* ► exact, faithful, genuine, real, actual AN OPPOSITE IS false **3** *Anne, true friend though she was, would never give in to him.* ► loyal, faithful, devoted, firm, constant, sincere, steady, trustworthy, dependable, honest, honorable OPPOSITES ARE false, unfaithful **4** *He was acting under the authority of the property's true owner.* ► legal, legitimate, rightful, authorized, valid **5** *Such studies do not give a true reflection of people's needs.* ► accurate, precise, exact, perfect, unerring AN OPPOSITE IS inaccurate

truly *ADVERB* **1** *a truly remarkable woman* ► really, absolutely, extremely, very **2** *I'm truly glad for you.* ► sincerely, genuinely, honestly **3** *Tell us truly what you think.* ► truthfully, frankly, candidly, honestly

trumpet *NOUN* *a part for solo trumpet* ► bugle, clarion, cornet
blow your own trumpet *He was blowing his own trumpet and promoting his new show.* ► boast, brag, sing your own praises, congratulate yourself, show off, swank

trunk *NOUN* **1** *A squirrel leapt on a branch and ran up the trunk.* ► stem, bole, stock **2** *A slit in his shirt revealed his powerful trunk.* ► torso, frame, body **3** *He locked the trunk and stored it in a shed.* ► chest, case, coffer, box, crate, suitcase

trust *VERB* **1** *He doesn't trust me not to do it again.* ► believe in, have confidence in, have faith in, rely on, be sure of, bank on, count on, depend on **2** *We trust they will be here soon.* ► hope, expect, presume, suppose, assume, imagine, surmise AN OPPOSITE IS doubt

trust *NOUN* **1** *I am grateful to you for your trust.* ► confidence, faith, belief, reliance, certainty,

a b c d e f g h i j k l m n o p q r s **t** u v w x y z

- *Don't trust him with your CD player!* **3** hope
- *I trust that you are well.*

trust NOUN **trusts 1** the belief that a person or thing can be trusted **2** responsibility; being trusted • *Being a prefect is a position of trust.* **3** a legal arrangement in which money is entrusted to a person with instructions about how to use it
▷ **trustful** ADJECTIVE **trustfully** ADVERB

trustworthy ADJECTIVE able to be trusted; reliable

trusty ADJECTIVE (old use) trustworthy or reliable • *my trusty sword*

truth NOUN **truths 1** something that is true **2** the quality of being true

truthful ADJECTIVE **1** telling the truth • *a truthful boy* **2** true • *a truthful account of what happened*
▷ **truthfully** ADVERB **truthfulness** NOUN

try VERB **tries, trying, tried 1** make an effort to do something; attempt **2** test something by using or doing it • *Try sleeping on your back.* **3** examine the evidence in a court to decide whether a person is guilty of a crime **4** be a strain on • *You are trying my patience.*
try on put on clothes etc. to see if they fit
try out use something to see if it works

try NOUN **tries 1** an attempt

trying ADJECTIVE putting a strain on someone's patience; annoying

T-shirt or **tee shirt** NOUN T-shirts or tee-shirts a short-sleeved casual shirt

tub NOUN **tubs** a round open container holding liquid, ice cream, soil for plants, etc.

tubby ADJECTIVE **tubbier, tubbiest** short and fat
▷ **tubbiness** NOUN

tube NOUN **tubes 1** a long hollow piece of metal, plastic, rubber, glass, etc., especially for liquids or air etc. to pass along **2** a container made of flexible material with a screw cap • *a tube of toothpaste* **3** the underground railway in London

tuber NOUN **tubers** a short thick rounded root (e.g. of a dahlia) or underground stem (e.g. of a potato) that produces buds from which new plants will grow

tuberculosis NOUN a disease of people and animals, producing small swellings in the parts affected by it, especially in the lungs
▷ **tubercular** ADJECTIVE

tuck VERB **tucks, tucking, tucked 1** push a loose edge inwards so that it is hidden or held in place **2** put something away in a small space • *Tuck this in your pocket.*
tuck in (informal) eat heartily
tuck someone in or **up** make someone comfortable in bed by folding the edges of the bedclothes tightly

tuck NOUN **tucks 1** a flat fold stitched in a piece of clothing

---

Thesaurus

---

credence **2** *She enjoyed a position of trust in the city.* ► responsibility, obligation

trusting ADJECTIVE *The trouble with me is I'm too trusting.* ► trustful, credulous, gullible, unquestioning, unsuspecting, ingenuous, innocent OPPOSITES ARE suspicious, cynical

trustworthy ADJECTIVE *Harriet was always trustworthy and hardworking.* ► reliable, dependable, responsible, honest, upright, steadfast OPPOSITES ARE untrustworthy, deceitful

truth NOUN **1** *He doubted the truth of some of these statements.* ► veracity, accuracy, validity, truthfulness, correctness, candor, honesty, authenticity, reliability AN OPPOSITE IS falseness **2** *Elizabeth had been telling the truth.* ► fact facts, reality, actuality **3** *an acknowledged truth* ► fact, axiom, maxim, certitude, truism AN OPPOSITE IS lie

truthful ADJECTIVE **1** *Clive had been less than truthful.* ► honest, sincere, candid, frank, reliable, straight, forthright, credible, straightforward, trustworthy, veracious **2** *The truthful answer has to be "no".* ► proper, right, accurate, correct, true, valid AN OPPOSITE IS dishonest

try VERB **1** *Always try to respond positively.* ► aim, attempt, endeavor, essay, exert yourself, make

an effort, strain, strive, struggle, venture **2** *Why not try another school?* (informal) ► check out, evaluate, examine, experiment with, investigate, test, try out, undertake

try NOUN *I'll have another try.* ► attempt, endeavor, effort, experiment, test, trial, (more informal) bash, (more informal) go, (more informal) shot

trying ADJECTIVE **1** *This could be quite a trying evening.* ► difficult, stressful, taxing, frustrating, troublesome, vexatious **2** *Clare can be very trying.* ► annoying, irritating, tiresome, exasperating, infuriating

tub NOUN **1** *Corbett bathed in the guest house's one and only tub.* ► bath, bathtub **2** *a plastic tub of sandwiches* ► pot, barrel, drum, cask, keg, vat

tubby ADJECTIVE (informal) *A short tubby man was waiting at the front door.* ► chubby, plump, fat , dumpy, rotund, round, overweight, stout, portly, pudgy OPPOSITES ARE thin, slim, skinny

tuck VERB *He tucked his shirt into his jeans.* ► push, ease, insert, stuff, shove, cram
tuck into *We tucked into plates of fish and chips.* ► eat up, consume, devour, gobble up, wolf down

tug VERB tugs, tugging, tugged **1** pull something hard or suddenly **2** tow a ship

tug NOUN tugs **1** a hard or sudden pull **2** a small powerful boat used for towing others

tug of war NOUN a contest between two teams pulling a rope from opposite ends

tuition NOUN teaching, especially when given to one person or a small group

tulip NOUN tulips a large cup-shaped flower on a tall stem growing from a bulb [from Persian *dulband* = turban (because the flowers are this shape)]

tumble VERB tumbles, tumbling, tumbled **1** fall or roll over suddenly or clumsily **2** move or push quickly and carelessly
▷ **tumble** NOUN
tumble to (*informal*) realize what something means

tumbler NOUN tumblers **1** a drinking glass with no stem or handle **2** a part of a lock that is lifted when a key is turned to open it **3** an acrobat

tummy NOUN tummies (*informal*) the stomach

tumor (tew- mer) NOUN tumors an abnormal lump growing on or in the body

tumult (tew- mult) NOUN an uproar; a state of noisy confusion and agitation
▷ **tumultuous** ADJECTIVE

tune NOUN tunes a short piece of music; a pleasant series of musical notes
▷ **tuneful** ADJECTIVE **tunefully** ADVERB
in tune at the correct musical pitch

tune VERB tunes, tuning, tuned **1** put a musical instrument in tune **2** adjust a radio or television set to receive a certain channel **3** adjust an engine so that it runs smoothly
▷ **tuner** NOUN
tune up (said about an orchestra) bring the instruments to the correct pitch

tunic NOUN tunics **1** a jacket worn as part of a uniform **2** a piece of clothing reaching from the shoulders to the hips or knees

tunnel NOUN tunnels an underground passage

tunnel VERB tunnels, tunneling, tunneled make a tunnel [from early French *tonel* = barrel]

turban NOUN turbans a covering for the head made by wrapping a strip of cloth around a cap

turbine NOUN turbines a machine or motor driven by a flow of water, steam, or gas

turbulence NOUN violent and uneven movement of air or water • *We experienced turbulence during the flight.*

turbulent ADJECTIVE **1** moving violently and unevenly • *turbulent seas* **2** involving much change and disagreement or violence • *a turbulent period of history*
▷ **turbulently** ADVERB

turf NOUN turfs **1** short grass and the earth around its roots **2** a piece of this cut from the ground
the turf horse racing

turkey NOUN turkeys a large bird raised for its meat

turmoil NOUN wild confusion or agitation • *Her mind was in turmoil.*

turn VERB turns, turning, turned **1** move around; move to a new direction **2** change in appearance etc.; become • *He turned pale.*

Thesaurus

tug VERB **1** *Lee tugged the rope.* ► pull, heave, drag, draw, haul, lug, tow **2** *tug at A little boy tugged at her skirt.* ► jerk, pluck, twitch, wrench, yank

tumble VERB **1** *He let out a yell as he tumbled into the water.* ► topple, collapse, pitch, stumble, plummet, drop, fall, flop, trip up **2** *Most of the audience then tumbled out of the room.* ► hurry, rush, pile, scramble

tumult NOUN *His voice could not be heard above the tumult.* ► noise, din, commotion, hubbub, clamor, racket, rumpus, uproar

tumultuous ADJECTIVE *John Knox returned to a tumultuous welcome.* ► loud, excited, uproarious, boisterous, unrestrained, deafening, passionate, tempestuous, hectic, turbulent, wild AN OPPOSITE IS restrained

tune NOUN *She sang a tune to the baby.* ► melody, song, air, strain, theme

tuneful ADJECTIVE *She spoke in a quiet, tuneful voice.* ► musical, melodious, mellifluous, pleasant, sweet, rhythmical, catchy OPPOSITES ARE tuneless, discordant

tunnel NOUN *a tunnel under the river* ► underpass, passage, passageway, subway, shaft, gallery

tunnel VERB *A dog had tunneled under the fence.* ► burrow, dig, excavate, mine, penetrate

turbulent ADJECTIVE **1** *Her turbulent feelings got the better of her.* ► passionate, excited, violent, volatile, seething, unrestrained **2** *an increasingly turbulent part of the world* ► unstable, unsettled, troubled, restless, explosive, anarchic AN OPPOSITE IS peaceful **3** *The ship was in turbulent waters.* ► rough, stormy, tempestuous, choppy, violent, wild AN OPPOSITE IS calm

turmoil NOUN (*informal*) *Her mind was in state of turmoil.* ► confusion, chaos, disorder, upheaval, turbulence, agitation, disruption, disturbance, mayhem, unrest, upset OPPOSITES ARE calm, peace

turn VERB **1** *The big wheel started to turn.* ► go round, revolve, rotate, whirl, roll **2** *The gates turned on a set of massive hinges.* ► swivel,

a
b
c
d
e
f
g
h
i
j
k
l
m
n
o
p
q
r
s
t
u
v
w
x
y
z

3 make something change • *You can turn milk into butter.* **4** move a switch or tap to control something • *Turn that radio off.* **5** pass a certain time • *It has turned midnight.* **6** shape something on a lathe

turn down 1 fold down **2** reduce the flow or sound of something **3** reject • *We offered her a job but she turned it down.*

turn out 1 send out **2** empty something, especially to search or clean it **3** happen **4** prove to be • *The visitor turned out to be my uncle.*

turn up 1 appear or arrive **2** increase the flow or sound of something

turn NOUN **turns 1** the action of turning; a turning movement **2** a change; the point where something turns **3** an opportunity or duty, etc., that comes to each person in succession • *It's your turn to wash up.* **4** a short performance in an entertainment **5** (*informal*) an attack of illness; a nervous shock • *It gave me a nasty turn.*

a good turn a helpful action

in turn in succession; one after another

turning NOUN **turnings** a place where one road meets another, forming a corner

turnip NOUN **turnips** a plant with a large round white root used as a vegetable

turnout NOUN **turnouts** the number of people who attend a meeting, vote at an election, etc. • *Despite the rain, there was a pretty good turnout.*

turnover NOUN **turnovers 1** the amount of money received by a firm selling things **2** the rate at which goods are sold or workers leave and are replaced **3** a small pie made by folding pastry over fruit, jam, etc.

turnstile NOUN **turnstiles** a revolving gate that lets one person in at a time

turntable NOUN **turntables** a circular revolving platform or support, e.g., for the record in a record player

turquoise NOUN **turquoises 1** a sky-blue or greenish-blue color **2** a blue jewel

Thesaurus

hinge **3** *She turned to return home.* ► change direction, change course, turn around **4** *The van turned the corner and disappeared.* ► go around, negotiate, take **5** *The path turned to the right.* ► bend, curve, twist, loop, snake **6** *Ellie turned pale.* ► become, go, grow **7** *The house will be turned into luxury apartments.* ► convert, adapt, transform, modify, change, rebuild **8** *The milk had turned.* ► go sour, curdle **9** *turn to She turned to her neighbour for help.* ► resort to, appeal to, approach, have recourse to, apply to

turn away *Reporters were turned away from the house.* ► send away, dismiss, rebuff, reject AN OPPOSITE IS admit (to)

turn down *The panel turned down her application.* ► reject, refuse, decline, dismiss, spurn AN OPPOSITE IS approve

turn in 1 *I decided to turn in early.* ► go to bed, retire **2** *He was ordered to turn in his passport* ► hand in, hand over, surrender, submit

turn off 1 *They had to turn off the highway.* ► leave, branch off, deviate from AN OPPOSITE IS join **2** *She turned off the lights and left the building.* ► switch off, turn out, put out, extinguish OPPOSITES ARE turn on, switch on **3** *The violence in the film turned many people off.* ► deter, put off, discourage, disconcert, unnerve, repel, distract OPPOSITES ARE appeal to, attract

turn on 1 *She turned on the radio.* ► switch on, put on AN OPPOSITE IS turn off **2** *Rick always turned her on.* ► excite, arouse, stimulate, titillate AN OPPOSITE IS turn off

turn out 1 *Her father might well turn her out of*

the house. ► throw out, expel, evict, eject, drive out OPPOSITES ARE admit (to), welcome (to) **2** *It was a relief that things turned out so well.* ► occur, happen, evolve, develop, end up, come out, work out **3** *Don't forget to turn out the light.* ► switch off, turn off, put out, extinguish OPPOSITES ARE turn on, switch on

turn over 1 *The car skidded and turned over.* ► overturn, roll over, keel over, capsize **2** *I've been turning it over in my mind.* ► consider, ponder, deliberate, think about, weigh up, mull over, chew over

turn up 1 *Several guests failed to turn up.* ► arrive, appear, put in an appearance **2** *A gardener in Syria has turned up a hoard of ancient coins.* ► discover, unearth, uncover, bring to light, dig up, find **3** *The voices are inaudible unless you turn the sound up.* ► increase, raise, amplify

turn NOUN **1** *hot water at the turn of a tap* ► twist, spin, twirl, whirl, rotation, revolution, circle, cycle **2** *The car came to a turn in the road.* ► bend, corner, curve, angle, deviation, hairpin bend, junction, loop, twist **3** *an unexpected turn of events* ► reversal, shift, change of direction, turning point **4** *It's your turn to speak.* ► chance, opportunity, occasion, time, stint, spell **5** *She was trying to do James a good turn.* ► favor, support **6** *a comic turn in a concert* ► act, performance, show **7** *His sudden appearance gave her quite a turn.* ► shock, start, surprise, fright, scare, jolt

in turn *The Eastern capital in turn influenced the culture of Venice.* ► in succession, successively

turning NOUN *Take the second turning on the right.* ► turn-off, turn, exit

turret NOUN turrets **1** a small tower on a castle or other building **2** a revolving structure containing a gun
▷ **turreted** ADJECTIVE

turtle NOUN turtles a sea animal that looks like a tortoise
turn turtle capsize

turtle dove NOUN turtle doves a wild dove

tusk NOUN tusks a long pointed tooth that sticks out from the mouth of an elephant, walrus, etc.

tussle NOUN tussles a struggle or conflict over something

tussock NOUN tussocks a tuft or clump of grass

tutor NOUN tutors **1** a private teacher, especially of one pupil or a small group **2** a teacher of students in a college or university

TV ABBREVIATION television

twain NOUN, ADJECTIVE (old use) two

twang VERB twangs, twanging, twanged make a sharp sound like that of a wire when plucked
▷ **twang** NOUN

tweak VERB tweaks, tweaking, tweaked pinch and twist or pull something sharply
▷ **tweak** NOUN

tweed NOUN thick woolen twill, often woven of mixed colors

tweet NOUN tweets the chirping sound made by a small bird
▷ **tweet** VERB

tweezers PLURAL NOUN small pincers for picking up or pulling very small things

twelve NOUN, ADJECTIVE twelves the number 12
▷ **twelfth** ADJECTIVE, NOUN

twenty NOUN, ADJECTIVE twenties the number 20
▷ **twentieth** ADJECTIVE, NOUN

twice ADVERB **1** two times; on two occasions **2** double the amount

twiddle VERB twiddles, twiddling, twiddled turn something round or over and over in an idle way ● He tried twiddling the knob on the radio.
▷ **twiddle** NOUN **twiddly** ADJECTIVE
twiddle your thumbs have nothing to do

twig NOUN twigs a small shoot on a branch or stem of a tree or shrub

twilight NOUN dim light from the sky just after sunset or just before sunrise

twin NOUN twins **1** either of two children or animals born to the same mother at one time **2** either of two things that are exactly alike

twin VERB twins, twinning, twinned **1** put things together as a pair **2** if a town is twinned with a town in a different country, the two towns exchange visits and organize cultural events together

twine VERB twines, twining, twined twist or wind together or round something

twinge NOUN twinges a sudden pain or unpleasant feeling

twinkle VERB twinkles, twinkling, twinkled shine with tiny flashes of light; sparkle
▷ **twinkle** NOUN

twirl VERB twirls, twirling, twirled twist quickly
▷ **twirl** NOUN

twist VERB twists, twisting, twisted **1** turn the ends of something in opposite directions **2** turn around or from side to side ● The road twisted through the hills. **3** bend something out of its proper shape **4** pass threads or strands

Thesaurus

tussle NOUN His glasses were broken in the tussle.
► fight, scuffle, fracas, brawl, struggle, scrap, rumpus, commotion, argument

tussle NOUN Some of the crowd tussled with police.
► fight, scuffle, brawl, struggle, scrap, come to blows

tweak VERB She tweaked Peter's ear. ► twist, pinch, nip, pull, squeeze

twiddle VERB Link your fingers in your lap so you're not tempted to twiddle them. ► fiddle with, fidget with, twirl, twist

twin ADJECTIVE twin towers on the French pattern
► identical, matching, balancing, corresponding, duplicate, paired, similar, symmetrical, indistinguishable

twin NOUN Fiona drove her own car, the twin of Harry's. ► double, duplicate, clone, match, (more informal) lookalike

twinge NOUN **1** I was getting sharp twinges in one knee. ► pain, stab, spasm **2** She felt a twinge of sadness. ► pang, prick, qualm

twinkle VERB I could see Beverly Hills twinkling in the distance. ► glimmer, glitter, glint, glow, shine, flash, glisten, gleam, sparkle, shimmer

twinkle NOUN the twinkle of a thousand lights
► sparkle, glimmer, glitter, glint, glow, shimmer

twirl VERB **1** They twirled around the room arm in arm. ► spin, turn, twist, whirl, wheel, gyrate, pirouette, revolve, rotate **2** He twirled his empty glass in his hands. ► twiddle, twist, play with

twist VERB **1** Huge girders had been twisted in the explosion. ► crush, buckle, mangle, misshape, deform **2** He twisted a strand of her hair around his fingers. ► coil, curl, wind, entwine, twine **3** Twist the cork slowly as you pull it. ► turn, screw, revolve **4** She fell off her bike and twisted her ankle. ► sprain, wrench, rick **5** He accused the newspaper of twisting his words. ► distort, change, alter, misrepresent, garble, contort, pervert

around something or around each other
5 distort the meaning of something • *You're twisting my words.*
▷ **twister** NOUN

twist NOUN **twists** a twisting movement or action
▷ **twisty** ADJECTIVE

twitch VERB **twitches, twitching, twitched** move or pull with a slight jerk
▷ **twitch** NOUN

twitter VERB **twitters, twittering, twittered** make quick chirping sounds
▷ **twitter** NOUN

two NOUN, ADJECTIVE **twos** the number 2
be in two minds be undecided about something

two-faced ADJECTIVE insincere or deceitful

tycoon NOUN **tycoons** a rich and influential business person [from Japanese *taikun* = great prince]

tying present participle of **tie**

type NOUN **types** **1** a kind or sort **2** letters or figures, etc., designed for use in printing

type VERB **types, typing, typed** write something by using a typewriter
▷ **typist** NOUN

typewriter NOUN **typewriters** a machine with keys that are pressed to print letters or figures etc. on a piece of paper
▷ **typewritten** ADJECTIVE

typhoon NOUN **typhoons** a violent hurricane in the western Pacific or East Asian seas [from Chinese *tai fung* = great wind]

typical ADJECTIVE **1** having the usual characteristics or qualities of a particular type of person or thing • *a typical school playground* **2** usual in a particular person or thing • *He worked with typical carefulness.*
▷ **typically** ADVERB

tyranny (tirran- ee) NOUN **tyrannies** **1** government by a tyrant **2** the way a tyrant behaves towards people
▷ **tyrannical** ADJECTIVE **tyrannous** ADJECTIVE

tyrant (ty- rant) NOUN **tyrants** a person who rules cruelly and unjustly; someone who insists on being obeyed [from Greek *tyrannos* = ruler with full power]

Thesaurus

---

twist NOUN **1** *Give the lid a firm twist.* ► turn, screw, jerk, spin **2** *a twist in the rope* ► coil, curl, loop, kink, tangle, knot **3** *a twist in the road* ► bend, turn, zigzag **4** *There was an unexpected twist to the story.* ► development, surprise, quirk, oddity

twisted ADJECTIVE **1** *A mass of twisted metal barred the way.* ► crumpled, buckled, crushed, mangled, distorted, misshapen, deformed, warped **2** *It seemed to be the product of a twisted mind* ► perverted, depraved, warped, deviant, corrupt

twit NOUN (*informal*) *You're an ignorant little twit.* ► fool, idiot, clot, ass, halfwit, dimwit, blockhead, dunderhead, nincompoop

twitch NOUN *She suppressed an involuntary twitch of her lip.* ► spasm, jerk, tremor, tic, blink, convulsion, flutter, jump

twitch VERB *The bushes twitched again.* ► start, tremble, jerk, jump, fidget, flutter

two-faced ADJECTIVE *I consider you have been a two-faced liar.* ► deceitful, insincere, double-dealing, dishonest, duplicitous, hypocritical OPPOSITES ARE sincere, honest

tycoon NOUN *a newspaper advertisement sponsored by an oil tycoon* ► magnate, mogul, industrialist, baron, supremo, big businessman

type NOUN **1** *This type of injury could happen to any player at any time.* ► kind, sort, category, class, form, variety, classification, description, designation, genre, group, species **2** *Footnotes are printed in small type.* ► print, characters, typeface, font, letters

typhoon NOUN *aid for victims of the typhoon* ► cyclone, tornado, hurricane, whirlwind

typical ADJECTIVE **1** *Decorative carving is a typical feature of late Gothic architecture.*
► characteristic, distinctive, particular, representative, special OPPOSITES ARE untypical, uncharacteristic **2** *It had been a fairly typical week.* ► average, ordinary, normal, usual, conventional, orthodox, predictable, standard, unsurprising OPPOSITES ARE untypical, unusual USAGE There is a slight difference in meaning between *untypical* and *atypical*: *untypical* means "not typical, unusual," whereas *atypical* means "not belonging to this type."

typify VERB *The village typifies the beauty of the Lake District.* ► epitomize, exemplify, characterize, embody, represent

tyrannical ADJECTIVE *His father is portrayed as a stern, tyrannical disciplinarian.* ► authoritarian, autocratic, despotic, dictatorial, domineering, oppressive, overbearing, cruel, brutal, harsh, imperious, ruthless, severe, tyrannous, unjust OPPOSITES ARE liberal, tolerant, easygoing

tyrannize VERB *He tyrannized his family.*
► dominate, domineer over, oppress, bully, intimidate

tyranny NOUN *the injustice, cruelty, and tyranny in the world* ► despotism, autocracy, dictatorship, oppression

tyrant NOUN *She was a tyrant to the girls.*
► despot, autocrat, dictator, oppressor, slave-driver

Uu

ubiquitous (yoo- **bik**- wit- us) ADJECTIVE found everywhere • *Cell phones are ubiquitous these days.*
▷ **ubiquity** NOUN

udder NOUN **udders** the baglike part of a cow, ewe, female goat, etc., from which milk is taken

ugly ADJECTIVE **uglier, ugliest** **1** unpleasant to look at; not beautiful **2** hostile and threatening • *The crowd was in an ugly mood.*
▷ **ugliness** NOUN
[from Old Norse *uggligr* = frightening]

UK ABBREVIATION United Kingdom

ulcer NOUN **ulcers** a sore on the inside or outside of the body
▷ **ulcerated** ADJECTIVE **ulceration** NOUN

ulterior ADJECTIVE beyond what is obvious or stated • *an ulterior motive*

ultimate ADJECTIVE furthest in a series of things; final • *Our ultimate destination is Chicago.*
▷ **ultimately** ADVERB
[from Latin *ultimus* = last]

ultimatum (ul- tim- **ay**- tum) NOUN **ultimatums** a final demand or statement that unless something is done by a certain time action will be taken or war will be declared

ultramarine NOUN a deep bright blue [from Latin *ultra mare* = beyond the sea (because it was originally imported "across the sea" from the East)]

ultrasound NOUN sound of a frequency beyond the range of human hearing, used in medical examinations

ultraviolet ADJECTIVE (said about light rays) beyond the violet end of the spectrum and so not visible to the human eye

umbilical cord NOUN **umbilical cords** the tube through which a baby receives nourishment before it is born, connecting its body with the mother's womb

umbrella NOUN **umbrellas** **1** a circular piece of material stretched over a folding frame with a central stick used as a handle, or a central pole, which you open to protect yourself from rain or sun **2** a general protection [from Italian *ombrella* = a little shade]

umpire NOUN **umpires** a referee in baseball, tennis, and some other games

umpire VERB **umpires, umpiring, umpired** act as an umpire

UN ABBREVIATION United Nations

un- PREFIX **1** not (as in *uncertain*) **2** (before a verb) reversing the action (as in *unlock* = release from being locked) *Many words beginning with this prefix are not listed here if their meaning is obvious.*

unable ADJECTIVE not able to do something

unaccountable ADJECTIVE **1** unable to be explained • *For some unaccountable reason I completely forgot your birthday.* **2** not accountable for what you do
▷ **unaccountably** ADVERB

unanimous (yoo- **nan**- im- us) ADJECTIVE with everyone agreeing • *a unanimous decision*
▷ **unanimously** ADVERB **unanimity** (yoo- nan- im- it- ee) NOUN
[from Latin *unus* = one + *animus* = mind]

Thesaurus

ugly ADJECTIVE **1** *He may be ugly, but at least he writes good songs.* ▶ unattractive, unsightly, deformed, repulsive, hideous, plain, grisly, unpleasant, monstrous AN OPPOSITE IS attractive **2** *an ugly iron bedstead* ▶ unsightly, hideous, inelegant, tasteless, unattractive, unpleasant, displeasing, inartistic, plain AN OPPOSITE IS beautiful **3** *There were a number of ugly scenes behind the goalposts.* ▶ angry, dangerous, threatening, ominous, unpleasant, sinister, unfriendly, forbidding, hostile, menacing AN OPPOSITE IS pleasant

ultimate ADJECTIVE *the decline and ultimate disappearance of the city-state* ▶ eventual, final, consequent

ultimately ADVERB *Perhaps these problems will ultimately prove too great.* ▶ eventually, finally, in the end, in the long run, in time

umbrage NOUN
take umbrage *He amused them without taking umbrage when they laughed at him.* ▶ take offense, take exception, be offended, be annoyed, be aggrieved, be insulted, bridle

umpire NOUN *They all abided by the umpire's decision.* ▶ referee, adjudicator, arbiter, judge, linesman, arbitrator, moderator, (*more informal*) ref

umpteen ADJECTIVE (*informal*) *He had to tell the story umpteen times.* ▶ many, numerous, plenty of, countless, innumerable

unacceptable ADJECTIVE *Public opinion has rejected this strategy as shortsighted and unacceptable.* ▶ intolerable, unsatisfactory, inadmissible, inappropriate, unsuitable, inadequate OPPOSITES ARE acceptable, satisfactory

unaided ADJECTIVE *by your own unaided efforts* ▶ single-handed, alone, by yourself, without help, independently

unanimous ADJECTIVE *The resulting decision was unanimous.* ▶ united, harmonious, of one mind

a
b
c
d
e
f
g
h
i
j
k
l
m
n
o
p
q
r
s
t
u
v
w
x
y
z

unassuming ADJECTIVE modest; not arrogant or pretentious

unavoidable ADJECTIVE not able to be avoided

unawares ADVERB unexpectedly; without warning • *His question caught me unawares.*

unbearable ADJECTIVE not able to be endured
▷ **unbearably** ADVERB

unbeaten ADJECTIVE not defeated or surpassed

unbecoming ADJECTIVE **1** not making a person look attractive **2** not suitable or fitting

unbelievable ADJECTIVE not able to be believed; incredible
▷ **unbelievably** ADVERB

unbend VERB unbends, unbending, unbent **1** change from a bent position; straighten up **2** relax and become friendly

unblock VERB unblocks, unblocking, unblocked remove an obstruction from something

unborn ADJECTIVE not yet born

unbroken ADJECTIVE not broken or interrupted

uncalled-for ADJECTIVE not justified or necessary • *Such rudeness was quite uncalled for.*

uncanny ADJECTIVE **uncannier, uncanniest** strange or mysterious • *an uncanny coincidence*
▷ **uncannily** ADVERB **uncanniness** NOUN

uncertain ADJECTIVE **1** not known certainly **2** not sure about something **3** not reliable
• *His aim is rather uncertain.*
▷ **uncertainly** ADVERB **uncertainty** NOUN
in no uncertain terms clearly and forcefully

uncharitable ADJECTIVE making unkind judgements of people or actions
▷ **uncharitably** ADVERB

Thesaurus

unarmed ADJECTIVE *Troops shot at unarmed civilians.* ► defenseless, undefended, weaponless, unprotected, unmindful, exposed, vulnerable AN OPPOSITE IS armed

unassuming ADJECTIVE *Sparks was an unassuming and kindly man.* ► modest, retiring, humble, self-effacing, unobtrusive

unavoidable ADJECTIVE *Job losses are unavoidable.* ► inevitable, inescapable, certain, necessary, obligatory, mandatory OPPOSITES ARE avoidable, unnecessary

unaware ADJECTIVE *They seemed to be unaware of everything that had happened.* ► ignorant, oblivious, unconscious, unmindful, heedless OPPOSITES ARE aware, conscious

unbalanced ADJECTIVE **1** *We must not give an unbalanced picture.* ► unfair, unjust, biased, one-sided, partial, partisan OPPOSITES ARE balanced, fair **2** *She said her husband had become unbalanced and capable of doing crazy things.* ► unstable, disturbed, deranged, demented, crazy, insane

unbearable ADJECTIVE *The pain was unbearable.* ► unendurable, intolerable, excruciating, agonizing, insufferable, unmanageable OPPOSITES ARE bearable, tolerable

unbeatable ADJECTIVE **1** *When in good form the side is unbeatable.* ► invincible, unassailable, indestructible, indomitable, unconquerable, matchless, supreme **2** *As a flavor enhancer, lemon is unbeatable.* ► incomparable, unrivalled, unsurpassed, matchless, supreme

unbelievable ADJECTIVE **1** *You may find the story bizarre, even unbelievable.* ► incredible, improbable, implausible, far-fetched, unconvincing, preposterous **2** *He acted with unbelievable recklessness.* ► incredible, unimaginable, inconceivable, unthinkable

unbiased ADJECTIVE *Every effort is made to obtain an unbiased opinion.* ► impartial, objective, dispassionate, neutral, independent OPPOSITES ARE biased, partial

unbroken ADJECTIVE **1** *an unbroken night's sleep* ► continuous, uninterrupted, constant **2** *a world record that remains unbroken* ► unbeaten, unsurpassed, unequalled, unrivalled

uncalled-for ADJECTIVE *Such strict rules are totally uncalled-for.* ► unnecessary, gratuitous, needless, inappropriate, unwarranted, unjustified, unreasonable, unwelcome OPPOSITES ARE opportune, appropriate

uncanny ADJECTIVE **1** *The silence was uncanny.* ► eerie, unnatural, weird, creepy, unreal, ghostly, unaccountable AN OPPOSITE IS normal

uncertain ADJECTIVE **1** *The side effects of the treatment are uncertain.* ► unknown, unclear, indefinite, undetermined, unforeseeable, unresolved, undecided, inconclusive, ambiguous, imprecise, indeterminate, speculative OPPOSITES ARE known, definite **2** *I was uncertain what to say.* ► unsure, undecided, doubtful, unconvinced (about), ambivalent (about), dubious (about), hazy (about), wavering (about), in two minds (about) **3** *Workers in the industry face an uncertain future.* ► changeable, variable, erratic, unpredictable, unreliable, precarious AN OPPOSITE IS certain

uncertainty NOUN **1** *He tried to disguise his uncertainty.* ► doubt, misgiving, apprehension, qualm, hesitation, scruple OPPOSITES ARE certainty, positiveness **2** *Some degree of uncertainty is bound to ensue.*
► unpredictability, unreliability, changeability, risk, danger OPPOSITES ARE certainty, assurance

uncivilized ADJECTIVE not civilized; not having much culture

uncle NOUN uncles the brother of your father or mother; your aunt's husband

uncomfortable ADJECTIVE not comfortable
▷ **uncomfortably** ADVERB

uncommon ADJECTIVE not common; unusual

uncompromising (un- **komp**- rom- I- zing) ADJECTIVE not allowing a compromise; inflexible

unconcerned ADJECTIVE not caring about something; not worried

unconditional ADJECTIVE without any conditions; absolute • *unconditional surrender*
▷ **unconditionally** ADVERB

unconscious ADJECTIVE **1** not conscious **2** not aware of things
▷ **unconsciously** ADVERB **unconsciousness** NOUN

uncouth (un- **kooth**) ADJECTIVE rude and rough in manner

uncover VERB uncovers, uncovering, uncovered **1** remove the covering from something **2** reveal or expose • *They uncovered a plot to kill the king.*

undecided ADJECTIVE **1** not yet settled; not certain **2** not having made up your mind yet

undeniable ADJECTIVE impossible to deny; undoubtedly true
▷ **undeniably** ADVERB

Thesaurus

uncivilized ADJECTIVE *I am sorry to see such uncivilized behavior.* ► uncouth, primitive, barbaric, rough, boorish, antisocial, barbaric, barbarous, uncultured, uneducated, unenlightened, unsophisticated, wild OPPOSITES ARE civilized, respectable

unclear ADJECTIVE **1** *The answers are all very unclear.* ► vague, obscure, ambiguous, equivocal, puzzling, opaque, cryptic, hazy, imprecise OPPOSITES ARE clear, straightforward, unambiguous **2** *It was unclear whether the move was backed by the government.* ► uncertain, debatable, unsure, unsettled, doubtful, dubious OPPOSITES ARE clear, obvious

uncomfortable ADJECTIVE **1** *The lecture room had uncomfortable plastic chairs.* ► hard, cramped, restrictive, stiff, tight, ill-fitting, tight-fitting, lumpy AN OPPOSITE IS comfortable **2** *Carrying the bike over your shoulder is uncomfortable in the extreme.* ► painful, disagreeable, excruciating, inconvenient **3** *British workers felt uncomfortable about the slogans common in Japanese factories.* ► uneasy, embarrassed, awkward, troubled, worried, distressed, nervous, restless

uncommon ADJECTIVE *Two or three nights without sleep were not uncommon.* ► unusual, infrequent, rare, exceptional, abnormal OPPOSITES ARE common, usual

unconditional ADJECTIVE *All four offered their unconditional support.* ► unqualified, unrestricted, unlimited, unreserved, unquestioning, total, outright, absolute, complete AN OPPOSITE IS conditional

unconnected ADJECTIVE *The two events were unconnected. She has since died from causes unconnected with the incident.* ► unrelated (to), distinct (from), irrelevant (to), independent, discrete, disparate

unconscious ADJECTIVE **1** *My mother was still unconscious in hospital.* ► concussed, knocked out, insensible, senseless, comatose **2** *unconscious of He ranted on, unconscious of the danger.* ► unaware of, heedless, ignorant

of, disregardful of, disregarding, ignoring, impervious to **3** *He carries with him an unconscious guilt for his little sister's death.* ► subconscious, repressed, suppressed, involuntary, latent, subliminal, instinctive

unconventional ADJECTIVE *A wide range of colors can be used to create unconventional patterns.* ► unusual, unorthodox, unfamiliar, innovative, original, experimental, individual OPPOSITES ARE conventional, orthodox

unconvincing ADJECTIVE *They found that an unconvincing explanation. She put on a smile, but it was unconvincing.* ► dubious, doubtful, implausible, incredible, strained, forced, feeble, weak

uncooperative ADJECTIVE *The lawyers were proving to be uncooperative.* ► unhelpful, disobliging, awkward, obstructive, unaccommodating, inflexible, unwilling AN OPPOSITE IS cooperative

uncouth ADJECTIVE *They were rough uncouth men with the air of outcasts.* ► coarse, rude, ill-mannered, uncivilized, unrefined AN OPPOSITE IS refined

uncover VERB **1** *The earth had to be scraped away to uncover a trap door.* ► reveal, disclose, expose, lay bare, exhibit, show, strip, unmask, unveil, unwrap OPPOSITES ARE cover, conceal **2** *The intention was to uncover the causes of human social behavior.* ► detect, discover, locate, unearth, expose, make known, come across, make public, dig up OPPOSITES ARE conceal, cover up

undecided ADJECTIVE **1** *The question of where to hold the trial remained undecided.* ► uncertain, unresolved, undetermined, unsettled, unclear, indefinite OPPOSITES ARE decided, settled **2** *She stood undecided in the rain, wanting to find Simon but not daring to step inside.* ► hesitant, wavering, indecisive, unsure, uncertain, dithering, in two minds AN OPPOSITE IS certain

undeniable ADJECTIVE *The undeniable fact is that chlorine is building up in the atmosphere.* ► indisputable, irrefutable, unquestionable,

a
b
c
d
e
f
g
h
i
j
k
l
m
n
o
p
q
r
s
t
u
v
w
x
y
z

under ➡ understand

under PREPOSITION **1** below or beneath • *Hide it under the desk.* **2** less than • *under 5 years old* **3** governed or controlled by • *The country prospered under his rule.* **4** in the process of; undergoing • *The road is under repair.* **5** using • *He writes under the name of Lewis Carroll.* **6** according to the rules of • *This is permitted under our agreement.*
under way in motion or in progress

under ADVERB in or to a lower place or level or condition • *Slowly the diver went under.*

under ADJECTIVE lower • *the under layers*

undercarriage NOUN undercarriages an aircraft's landing wheels and their supports

undercover ADJECTIVE done or doing things secretly • *an undercover agent*

undercurrent NOUN undercurrents **1** a current that is below the surface or below another current **2** an underlying feeling or influence • *an undercurrent of fear*

undercut VERB undercuts, undercutting, undercut sell something for a lower price than someone else sells it

underdone ADJECTIVE not thoroughly done; undercooked

underestimate VERB underestimates, underestimating, underestimated make too low an estimate of a person or thing

undergo VERB undergoes, undergoing, underwent, undergone experience or endure something; be subjected to • *The new aircraft underwent intensive tests.*

undergraduate NOUN undergraduates a student at a university who has not yet taken a degree

underground ADJECTIVE, ADVERB **1** under the ground **2** done or working in secret

underground NOUN a train or car that runs through tunnels under the ground

undergrowth NOUN bushes and other plants growing close together, especially under trees

underhand ADJECTIVE done or doing things in a sly or secret way

underline VERB underlines, underlining, underlined **1** draw a line under a word, etc. **2** emphasize something

underlying ADJECTIVE **1** forming the basis or explanation of something • *the underlying causes of the trouble* **2** lying under something • *the underlying rocks*

undermine VERB undermines, undermining, undermined weaken something gradually

underneath PREPOSITION, ADVERB below or beneath

underpants PLURAL NOUN a piece of men's underwear covering the lower part of the body, worn under trousers

underprivileged ADJECTIVE having less than the normal standard of living or rights in a community

understand VERB understands, understanding, understood **1** know what something means or how it works or why it exists **2** know and tolerate a person's ways **3** have been told • *I understand that you would like to speak to me.* **4** take something for

Thesaurus

incontrovertible, undoubted, proven, certain OPPOSITES ARE questionable, debatable

undercover ADJECTIVE *Undercover agents are suspected of the assassination.* ► secret, covert, clandestine, underground, surreptitious, hidden, furtive

underestimate VERB **1** *Radiation fallout was underestimated by 40 times.* ► misjudge, miscalculate, set too low OPPOSITES ARE overestimate, exaggerate **2** *Sara puzzled him; he had underestimated her.* ► underrate, undervalue, misjudge, belittle, disparage, minimize, dismiss OPPOSITES ARE overestimate, overrate

undergo VERB *He may have to undergo more surgery.* ► experience, endure, go through, submit to, be subjected to, put up with, face, bear, suffer, withstand

underground ADJECTIVE **1** *the waters of an underground river* ► subterranean, buried, sunken AN OPPOSITE IS surface **2** *The two main underground opposition groups have decided to unite.* ► secret, clandestine, covert, surreptitious, undercover, unofficial

underline VERB *The killings underlined the need for political talks to resume.* ► emphasize, highlight, stress, accentuate, point up OPPOSITES ARE minimize, play down

undermine VERB *He denied that the change would undermine local democracy.* ► weaken, subvert, threaten, compromise, enfeeble, sap, wear away, destroy, ruin OPPOSITES ARE support, enhance, boost

underprivileged ADJECTIVE *Many children from underprivileged families have been able to join youth clubs.* ► needy, deprived, disadvantaged, impoverished, destitute, poor OPPOSITES ARE privileged, wealthy

underrate VERB *Most of us have a tendency to underrate our own skills.* ► underestimate, undervalue, belittle, disparage, minimize, dismiss, misjudge OPPOSITES ARE overrate, exaggerate

understand VERB **1** *They were unusually quiet, and I could not understand why. He began to understand the story in its full horror.* ► comprehend, grasp, perceive, discern, apprehend, fathom, follow, take in **2** *Do they*

granted • *Your expenses will be paid, that's understood*
▷ **understandable** ADJECTIVE **understandably** ADVERB
understanding NOUN **1** the power to understand or think; intelligence **2** sympathy or tolerance **3** agreement in opinion or feeling • *a better understanding between nations*
understatement NOUN understatements an incomplete or very restrained statement of facts or truth • *To say they disagreed is an understatement: they had a violent quarrel.*
understudy NOUN understudies an actor who learns a part in order to be able to play it if the usual performer is ill or absent
undertake VERB undertakes, undertaking, undertook, undertaken **1** agree or promise to do something **2** take on a task or responsibility
undertaker NOUN undertakers a person whose job is to arrange funerals and burials or cremations

undertone NOUN undertones **1** a low or quiet tone • *They spoke in undertones.* **2** an underlying quality or feeling, etc. • *His letter has a threatening undertone.*
underwear NOUN clothes worn next to the skin, under indoor clothing
underweight ADJECTIVE not heavy enough
underwent past tense of undergo
underworld NOUN **1** the people who are regularly involved in crime **2** (in myths and legends) the place for the spirits of the dead, under the earth
undeveloped ADJECTIVE not yet developed
undo VERB undoes, undoing, undid, undone **1** unfasten or unwrap **2** cancel the effect of something • *He has undone all our careful work.*
undoing NOUN
be someone's undoing be the cause of their ruin or failure

Thesaurus

not understand how much people like me love Morrissey? ► appreciate, realize, recognize, acknowledge **3** *We understand that the university doesn't have a science park.* ► believe, think, suppose, conclude, surmise, fancy
understanding NOUN **1** *Coins can contribute to our understanding of the past.* ► knowledge, comprehension, perception, grasp AN OPPOSITE IS ignorance **2** *We should look on them with deep understanding.* ► compassion, sympathy, feeling, consideration AN OPPOSITE IS indifference **3** *My understanding was that there is a three-year guarantee.* ► belief, perception, conviction, notion, idea, conclusion **4** *She is a woman of acute understanding.* ► intelligence, intellect, intuition, discernment, judgement **5** *The various groups had come to an understanding.* ► agreement, arrangement, deal, settlement, pact, treaty, entente
understate VERB *The level of complaints received may well understate the scale of the problem.* ► play down, underplay, minimize, belittle, make light of, soft-pedal OPPOSITES ARE overstate, exaggerate
undertake VERB **1** *He undertook to guarantee her son's safety.* ► agree, promise, guarantee, pledge, consent **2** *Some students undertake an industrial placement in their third year.* ► begin, commence, embark on, take on, take up, engage in, take responsibility for, manage, handle
undertaking NOUN **1** *Finding a suitable site is a difficult undertaking.* ► enterprise, venture, project, operation, endeavor, business, task, affair, scheme **2** *Booksellers agreed to sign an undertaking not to sell the book.* ► agreement, commitment, pledge, assurance

undervalue VERB *He seemed to undervalue his own work.* ► underestimate, underrate, misjudge, belittle, disparage, minimize, dismiss OPPOSITES ARE overestimate, overrate
underwater ADJECTIVE *Underwater sonar equipment was used to test for the presence of Nessie.* ► undersea, subaquatic, submarine, submerged, immersed
undesirable ADJECTIVE **1** *These undesirable side effects cannot be disregarded.* ► unpleasant, unwelcome, unwanted, disagreeable OPPOSITES ARE desirable, pleasant **2** *Adam had allowed some undesirable people access to the place.* ► nasty, repellent, objectionable, disagreeable, distasteful OPPOSITES ARE pleasant, agreeable
undivided ADJECTIVE *Be prepared to give your undivided attention and listen carefully.* ► complete, unqualified, unreserved, unbroken, full, total, whole, absolute OPPOSITES ARE divided, partial
undo VERB **1** *She hardly had time to undo her safety belt and get out of the car.* ► unfasten, release, untie, unbutton, unlock, unhitch, loosen OPPOSITES ARE fasten, tie up **2** *Human error undid years of endeavor in a few seconds.* ► undermine, subvert, overturn, nullify, scupper, sabotage **3** *A higher court might undo this decision.* ► reverse, overturn, revoke, overrule, disallow, rescind, annul
undoing NOUN *At this point fear was his undoing.* ► ruin, downfall, ruination, destruction, overthrow, weakness, failing
undoubtedly ADVERB *There will undoubtedly be things you do well already.* ► definitely, doubtless, indubitably, certainly, of course,

A
B
C
D
E
F
G
H
I
J
K
L
M
N
O
P
Q
R
S
U
V
W
X
Y
Z

undress VERB undresses, undressing, undressed take your clothes off

undue ADJECTIVE excessive; too great
▷ **unduly** ADVERB

undulate VERB undulates, undulating, undulated move like a wave or waves; have a wavy appearance
▷ **undulation** NOUN

undying ADJECTIVE everlasting

unearth VERB unearths, unearthing, unearthed **1** dig something up; uncover something by digging **2** find something by searching

unearthly ADJECTIVE **1** unnatural; strange and frightening **2** (informal) very early or

inconvenient • We had to get up at an unearthly hour.

uneasy ADJECTIVE **1** worried or anxious **2** uncomfortable
▷ **uneasily** ADVERB **uneasiness** NOUN

unemployed ADJECTIVE without a job
▷ **unemployment** NOUN

unequal ADJECTIVE **1** not equal in amount, size, or value **2** not giving the same opportunities to everyone • an unequal society
▷ **unequaled** ADJECTIVE **unequally** ADVERB

unerring (un- er- ing) ADJECTIVE making no mistake • unerring accuracy

uneven ADJECTIVE **1** not level or regular **2** not equally balanced • an uneven contest
▷ **unevenly** ADVERB **unevenness** NOUN

Thesaurus

---

surely, undeniably, unquestionably AN OPPOSITE IS possibly

undress VERB The patient has to undress slowly and carefully. ► take off your clothes, strip, disrobe, (more informal) peel off AN OPPOSITE IS dress

undressed ADJECTIVE She was half undressed when the doorbell rang. ► naked, unclothed, disrobed, nude, stripped, bare

undue ADJECTIVE If people are under undue stress, they make mistakes. ► excessive, extreme, unwarranted, unreasonable, disproportionate, unnecessary OPPOSITES ARE due, appropriate

unduly ADVERB Perhaps you think me unduly harsh to express these things so openly.
► excessively, unreasonably, inordinately, immoderately, unnecessarily

unearth VERB They have done all they can to unearth the truth. ► uncover, detect, discover, expose, make known, make public, dig up OPPOSITES ARE conceal, cover up

unearthly ADJECTIVE **1** She was a lady of unearthly beauty. ► eerie, uncanny, strange, supernatural, otherworldly, weird OPPOSITES ARE ordinary, mundane **2** (informal) I had a job that involved getting up at an unearthly hour.
► unreasonable, abnormal, unusual, (informal) ungodly OPPOSITES ARE reasonable, comfortable

uneasy ADJECTIVE **1** The uneasy peace lasted a few months. ► precarious, insecure, unsettled AN OPPOSITE IS comfortable **2** Moore was uneasy about the coat. ► anxious, nervous, apprehensive, troubled, worried, concerned, fearful, jittery AN OPPOSITE IS confident **3** There was an uneasy atmosphere in the room. ► tense, awkward, fraught, strained, edgy, uncomfortable

uneducated ADJECTIVE The superstition was by no means confined to uneducated people. ► ill-educated, untaught, ignorant, ill-informed,

uninformed, uncultured, unsophisticated OPPOSITES ARE educated, learned

unemployed ADJECTIVE I don't know what his job is; is he unemployed at the moment? ► out of work, jobless, on the dole, not working, redundant OPPOSITES ARE employed, working, in work

unending ADJECTIVE Her work seemed to be unending. ► endless, interminable, never-ending, everlasting, unceasing, incessant

unenthusiastic ADJECTIVE He was distinctly unenthusiastic about the idea. ► indifferent, apathetic, halfhearted, lukewarm

unenviable ADJECTIVE The job of being a project leader is an unenviable one. ► unpleasant, disagreeable, undesirable, unwelcome, thankless

unequal ADJECTIVE **1** The chair had four legs of unequal length. ► different, differing, varying, uneven, dissimilar, disparate AN OPPOSITE IS equal **2** the unequal distribution of power and resources in society ► unfair, unjust, inequitable, disproportionate OPPOSITES ARE fair, equitable **3** Should I give up the unequal struggle? ► unbalanced, uneven, unfair, ill-matched, one-sided OPPOSITES ARE equal, well-balanced **4** unequal to Melanie felt unequal to the task she had been given.
► inadequate for, incapable of, unqualified for, not up to, (more informal) not cut out for

unequaled ADJECTIVE The tour provides evidence of unequaled richness. ► incomparable, unmatched, unparalleled, unrivalled, unsurpassed, inimitable, supreme, surpassing, matchless, peerless

uneven ADJECTIVE **1** Be careful when wheeling a cart over uneven ground. ► bumpy, rough, rutted, undulating, bent, broken, crooked, irregular, jagged, jerky, pitted, wavy AN OPPOSITE IS smooth **2** The demand for electricity is uneven throughout the day. ► inconsistent, variable, spasmodic, unpredictable, varying,

unfair ➡ unfounded

unfair ADJECTIVE not fair; unjust
▷ **unfairly** ADVERB **unfairness** NOUN

unfaithful ADJECTIVE not faithful; disloyal

unfamiliar ADJECTIVE not familiar
▷ **unfamiliarity** NOUN

unfasten VERB unfastens, unfastening,
unfastened open the fastenings of something

unfavorable ADJECTIVE not favorable
▷ **unfavorably** ADVERB

unfeeling ADJECTIVE not caring about other
people's feelings; unsympathetic

unfit ADJECTIVE **1** unsuitable **2** not in perfect
health from lack of exercise

unfold VERB unfolds, unfolding, unfolded
1 open; spread out **2** make or become known
slowly • *as the story unfolds*

unfortunate ADJECTIVE **1** unlucky
2 unsuitable or regrettable • *an unfortunate
remark*
▷ **unfortunately** ADVERB

unfounded ADJECTIVE not based on facts

Thesaurus

erratic, fitful, fluctuating AN OPPOSITE IS
consistent. **3** *Uneven steps led down to a rocky
cove.* ► irregular, unsteady, lopsided,
unbalanced **4** *He soon gave up the uneven
contest.* ► unequal, unfair, ill-matched, one-
sided, unbalanced AN OPPOSITE IS balanced

unexpected ADJECTIVE *An unexpected error had
occurred.* ► unforeseen, accidental,
unpredictable, chance, fortuitous, sudden,
surprising, unhoped for, unlooked for,
unplanned, unusual OPPOSITES ARE expected,
predictable

unfair ADJECTIVE **1** *It was so unfair that she could
never see him.* ► unjust, unreasonable,
inequitable OPPOSITES ARE fair, just **2** *It
seemed to James an unfair remark. He claims I
have unfair advantages.* ► undeserved,
unwarranted, uncalled-for, unreasonable,
unjustified, unwarranted OPPOSITES ARE fair,
justified **3** *The law was placing an unfair burden
on small businesses.* ► unreasonable,
discriminatory OPPOSITES ARE reasonable,
legitimate **4** *The rules relating to unfair play
need to be tightened up.* ► illegal, unsporting,
dishonorable, illegitimate OPPOSITES ARE fair,
honorable

unfaithful ADJECTIVE *He could not deny that he
had been an unfaithful husband.* ► adulterous,
disloyal, untrustworthy, deceitful, duplicitous,
faithless OPPOSITES ARE faithful, loyal

unfamiliar ADJECTIVE *An unfamiliar smell was
drifting from the house.* ► strange, unusual,
curious, novel, different

unfashionable ADJECTIVE *Now that they were
unfashionable, maybe it would be OK to get a
personal organizer.* ► old-fashioned, outmoded,
out of date, passé, obsolete OPPOSITES ARE
fashionable, trendy

unfavorable ADJECTIVE **1** *A new head would face
unfavorable comparison with his predecessor.*
► critical, hostile, unfriendly, adverse,
negative, uncomplimentary, unsympathetic
OPPOSITES ARE favorable, positive **2** *A high cost
of living and unfavorable exchange rates ate into
their holiday funds.* ► bad, adverse,
unsatisfactory, undesirable, unenviable
OPPOSITES ARE favorable, advantageous

unfeeling ADJECTIVE *He smiled, but it was a cool,
unfeeling smile.* ► insensitive, heartless, hard-
hearted, callous, uncaring OPPOSITES ARE
sensitive, sympathetic

unfinished ADJECTIVE *The work remained
unfinished on his death.* ► incomplete,
uncompleted, imperfect, rough, sketchy,
unpolished AN OPPOSITE IS complete

unfit ADJECTIVE **1** *The house was rapidly becoming
unfit for habitation. They were unfit to pass
judgment on modern architecture.* ► unsuited, ill-
equipped, inadequate, unsatisfactory, useless,
incapable (of) **2** *Kevin was also unfit, leaving the
defense weakened.* ► out of condition, out of
shape, unhealthy, feeble OPPOSITES ARE fit,
healthy

unfold VERB **1** *Mick unfolded the space blanket.*
► open out, spread out, straighten out, unfurl
AN OPPOSITE IS fold up **2** *Come and see history
unfold before your eyes.* ► happen, evolve,
develop, take place, progress, emerge

unforeseen ADJECTIVE *Many of the long-term
results were unforeseen.* ► unexpected,
unpredicted, unthought of, surprising,
unanticipated OPPOSITES ARE foreseen,
predictable

unforgettable ADJECTIVE *The recreation park
will provide hours of fun and an unforgettable
experience.* ► memorable, striking, noteworthy,
remarkable, impressive, distinctive OPPOSITES
ARE forgettable, unexceptional

unforgivable ADJECTIVE *Losing your temper with
him was unforgivable.* ► inexcusable,
reprehensible, shameful, unjustifiable,
unpardonable, unwarrantable AN OPPOSITE IS
forgivable

unfortunate ADJECTIVE **1** *Some of these
unfortunate prisoners were later found to be
innocent.* ► unlucky, hapless, wretched, poor,
unhappy, ill-fated, luckless **2** *The incident led to
the most unfortunate disagreement between the
Allies.* ► disastrous, disadvantageous,
unwelcome, inopportune, harmful,
regrettable, lamentable, deplorable **3** *He said
it would be unfortunate if one year's results were
regarded as typical.* ► regrettable,
inappropriate, unsuitable

a b c d e f g h i j k l m n o p q r s t **u** v w x y z

A
B
C
D
E
F
G
H
I
J
K
L
M
N
O
P
Q
R
S
T
U
V
W
X
Y
Z

unfriendly ADJECTIVE not friendly
▷ **unfriendliness** NOUN

unfurl VERB unfurls, unfurling, unfurled unroll; spread out • *They unfurled a large flag.*

ungainly ADJECTIVE awkward-looking or clumsy
▷ **ungainliness** NOUN

ungodly ADJECTIVE **1** not giving reverence to God; not religious **2** (*informal*) outrageous; very inconvenient • *She woke me at an ungodly hour.*
▷ **ungodliness** NOUN

unguarded ADJECTIVE **1** not guarded **2** without thought or caution; indiscreet • *He said this in an unguarded moment.*

unhappy ADJECTIVE **1** not happy; sad **2** unfortunate or unsuitable • *an unhappy coincidence*
▷ **unhappily** ADVERB **unhappiness** NOUN

unhealthy ADJECTIVE not healthy
▷ **unhealthiness** NOUN

unheard of ADJECTIVE never known or done before; extraordinary

unhinge VERB unhinges, unhinging, unhinged cause a person's mind to become unbalanced

unicorn NOUN unicorns (in legends) an animal that is like a horse with one long straight horn growing from its forehead

uniform NOUN uniforms special clothes showing that the wearer is a member of a certain organization, school, etc.

uniform ADJECTIVE always the same; not varying • *The desks are of uniform size.*
▷ **uniformly** ADVERB **uniformity** NOUN

unilateral ADJECTIVE done by one person or group or country, etc. • *a unilateral decision*

Thesaurus

unfriendly ADJECTIVE *He glowered back in an unfriendly manner.* ► hostile, aggressive, disagreeable, unpleasant, antagonistic, unsociable, standoffish, aloof OPPOSITES ARE friendly, amiable

ungainly ADJECTIVE *A kangaroo must use a lot of energy in its lopsided and ungainly walk.*
► awkward, clumsy, ungraceful, graceless, inelegant OPPOSITES ARE elegant, graceful

ungrateful ADJECTIVE *I'm going to seem so ungrateful if I refuse the offer.* ► unappreciative, unthankful, ungracious, ill-mannered, selfish OPPOSITES ARE grateful, thankful

unhappy ADJECTIVE **1** *Her absence made Thomas unhappy.* ► sad, sorrowful, melancholy, miserable, dejected, despondent, dispirited, depressed OPPOSITES ARE happy, pleased **2** *One person at least had benefited from these unhappy events.* ► unlucky, unfortunate, luckless, ill-fated AN OPPOSITE IS fortunate **3** *Clearly it has been an unhappy compromise.* ► inappropriate, unsuitable, inapt, unsatisfactory, unfortunate OPPOSITES ARE happy, satisfactory **4** *Graham was very unhappy with his performance.* ► dissatisfied, disappointed, displeased, discontented

unharmed ADJECTIVE *Almost all the population seem to have escaped unharmed.* ► safe, safe and sound, uninjured, unhurt, unscathed, intact OPPOSITES ARE harmed, injured

unhealthy ADJECTIVE **1** *He was looking tired and unhealthy.* ► sickly, ill-looking, ailing, unwell, poorly, frail, weak OPPOSITES ARE healthy, well **2** *They lived in an unhealthy environment.*
► insalubrious, dirty, insanitary, polluted, unhygienic, unwholesome OPPOSITES ARE healthy, salubrious **3** *As a nurse I knew it was unhealthy to be so overweight.* ► harmful, unnatural, deleterious AN OPPOSITE IS healthy

unheard of ADJECTIVE *It was unheard of in those days for anyone to get so much money.*
► unprecedented, inconceivable, unimaginable, exceptional, extraordinary, unusual, uncommon AN OPPOSITE IS common

unhelpful ADJECTIVE *The bank teller had been unhelpful.* ► uncooperative, disobliging, inconsiderate, uncivil, unwilling, negative, slow OPPOSITES ARE helpful, obliging

unidentified ADJECTIVE *An unidentified vandal drew a moustache on the portrait.* ► unknown, unnamed, nameless, unrecognized, unspecified, anonymous, incognito, unfamiliar OPPOSITES ARE identified, known, named

uniform ADJECTIVE *A thermostat will maintain a uniform temperature.* ► regular, consistent, unvarying, homogeneous, identical, indistinguishable, similar, single OPPOSITES ARE varying, inconsistent

uniform NOUN *He had never worn a uniform in his life.* ► outfit, livery, regalia, costume

unify VERB *He was concerned to unify the country.*
► unite, integrate, harmonize, bring together, combine, consolidate, amalgamate, bind, fuse, join, merge, weld together OPPOSITES ARE divide, separate, split

unimaginable ADJECTIVE *He was motivated by the promise of unimaginable rewards.*
► inconceivable, unbelievable, incredible, unthinkable, unheard of, untold, mind-boggling

unimaginative ADJECTIVE *The drawings were flat and unimaginative.* ► boring, dull, uninspired, uncreative, uninventive, uninteresting, unexciting, unoriginal, pedestrian, prosaic, stale, trite, banal, derivative, ordinary OPPOSITES ARE imaginative, creative

unimportant ADJECTIVE *The size of the power supply is unimportant.* ► insignificant,

uninhabitable ADJECTIVE unfit to live in

union NOUN unions **1** the joining of things together; uniting **2** a trade union

Union Jack NOUN Union Jacks the flag of the United Kingdom

unique (yoo- neek) ADJECTIVE being the only one of its kind ● *This jewel is unique.*
▷ **uniquely** ADVERB
[from French, from Latin *unicus* = one and only]

unison NOUN
in unison **1** with all sounding or singing the same tune, etc., together, or speaking in chorus **2** in agreement

unit NOUN units **1** an amount used as a standard in measuring or counting things ● *Centimeters are units of length.* **2** a group, device, piece of furniture, etc., regarded as a single thing but forming part of a larger group or whole ● *an army unit* ● *a sink unit*

3 (in mathematics) any whole number less than 10

unite VERB unites, uniting, united join together; make or become one thing

unity NOUN **1** being united; being in agreement **2** something whole that is made up of parts **3** (in mathematics) the number one

universal ADJECTIVE to do with or including or done by everyone or everything
▷ **universally** ADVERB

universe NOUN everything that exists, including the earth and living things and all the stars and planets

university NOUN universities a place where people go to study at an advanced level after leaving school [from Latin *universitas*, literally = the universe, and later = a community of teachers and students]

unjust ADJECTIVE not fair or just

Thesaurus

inconsequential, immaterial, irrelevant, trivial, trifling, minor, of no account, of no consequence AN OPPOSITE IS important

uninhabited ADJECTIVE *The center of the island is vast and uninhabited.* ► empty, unoccupied, unpeopled, unsettled, deserted, depopulated, deserted, uncolonized, vacant AN OPPOSITE IS inhabited

unintelligible ADJECTIVE *The conversation was unintelligible to Gina.* ► incomprehensible, incoherent, unfathomable, baffling, perplexing, obscure, cryptic, opaque, mysterious, confusing, inscrutable, enigmatic OPPOSITES ARE intelligible, comprehensible

unintentional ADJECTIVE *Sometimes the harassment may be unintentional.* ► unintended, inadvertent, accidental, involuntary, unconscious, unplanned, unwitting, fortuitous AN OPPOSITE IS intentional

uninterrupted ADJECTIVE *A few extra hours of uninterrupted sleep can remedy the situation.* ► continuous, unbroken, undisturbed, constant, sustained, consecutive OPPOSITES ARE interrupted, intermittent, broken

union NOUN **1** *A union was formed to fight the war with Persia.* ► alliance, coalition, league, federation, confederation, confederacy **2** *The company was formed from the union of three smaller firms.* ► merger, merging, amalgamation, fusion, combination, unification, uniting, joining

unique ADJECTIVE **1** *Each file has a unique name.* ► distinctive, special, individual, peculiar, single, singular, (*more informal*) one-off AN OPPOSITE IS common **2** *The production was a unique opportunity to hear the music in its original form.* ► remarkable, outstanding, incomparable, extraordinary, unparalleled,

unprecedented, unusual AN OPPOSITE IS unremarkable

unit NOUN *The family is a fundamental unit of society.* ► component, constituent, element, entity, item, portion, section, segment

unite VERB **1** *They tried to unite the population in a common war effort against the English.* ► unify, integrate, combine, bring together, bind, join AN OPPOSITE IS divide **2** *Police and politicians united to solve the problem.* ► combine, join forces, cooperate, collaborate **3** *Mother and son were united after the war.* ► bring together, join

united ADJECTIVE *the potential power of a united Germany* ► unified, integrated, merged, amalgamated, combined AN OPPOSITE IS disunited
be united *They were united on this one issue.*
► agree, be in agreement, be in accord, be unanimous, be of the same mind, have the same opinion OPPOSITES ARE be disunited, disagree

unity NOUN **1** *Creating national unity is a fundamental task for our people.* ► agreement, harmony, accord, consensus, concord OPPOSITES ARE discord, disagreement **2** *the issue of government unity* ► union, unification, federation OPPOSITES ARE division, disunity

universal ADJECTIVE *A sudden fall in house prices is a universal fear.* ► common, general, ubiquitous, widespread, worldwide, global, all-embracing, all-round OPPOSITES ARE restricted, local

unjust ADJECTIVE **1** *She was still reeling from her unjust dismissal.* ► unfair, unjustified, undeserved, unmerited, unreasonable, unwarranted, unlawful, wrong, wrongful, indefensible, inequitable OPPOSITES ARE just,

A
B
C
D
E
F
G
H
I
J
K
L
M
N
O
P
Q
R
S
T
U
V
W
X
Y
Z

unkempt ADJECTIVE looking untidy or neglected [from *un-* = not + an old word *kempt* = combed]

unkind ADJECTIVE not kind
▷ **unkindly** ADVERB **unkindness** NOUN

unleaded ADJECTIVE (said about gasoline) without added lead

unleash VERB unleashes, unleashing, unleashed **1** set a dog free from a leash **2** let a strong feeling or force be released

unless CONJUNCTION except when; if ... not • *We cannot go unless we are invited.*

unlike PREPOSITION not like • *Unlike me, she enjoys baseball.*

unlike ADJECTIVE not alike; different • *The two children are very unlike*

unlikely ADJECTIVE unlikelier, unlikeliest not likely to happen or be true

unlimited ADJECTIVE not limited; very great or very many

unload VERB unloads, unloading, unloaded remove the load of things carried by a ship, aircraft, vehicle, etc.

unlock VERB unlocks, unlocking, unlocked open something by undoing a lock

unlucky ADJECTIVE not lucky; having or bringing bad luck
▷ **unluckily** ADVERB

unmask VERB unmasks, unmasking, unmasked **1** remove a person's mask **2** reveal what a person or thing really is

unmentionable ADJECTIVE too bad or embarrassing to be spoken of

unmistakable ADJECTIVE not able to be mistaken for another person or thing
▷ **unmistakably** ADVERB

unmitigated ADJECTIVE absolute • *an unmitigated disaster*

unnatural ADJECTIVE not natural or normal
▷ **unnaturally** ADVERB

Thesaurus

justified **2** *The report was widely criticized for being unjust.* ▸ unfair, biased, one-sided, partial, partisan, prejudiced, bigoted OPPOSITES ARE just, fair, balanced

unkind ADJECTIVE *He says unkind things that cause her pain.* ▸ cruel, thoughtless, unfeeling, callous, uncharitable, unpleasant, inconsiderate, unfriendly, malicious, malevolent, spiteful, harsh OPPOSITES ARE kind, considerate

unknown ADJECTIVE **1** *Some of the civilians were transferred to unknown destinations. For some unknown reason, the blinds were always drawn. The date of their marriage is unknown.*
▸ unspecified, unidentified, unnamed, undisclosed, mysterious, strange, unrecognized, anonymous, nameless AN OPPOSITE IS named **2** *Lowell began a search for this unknown planet.* ▸ undiscovered, unfamiliar, unexplored, unmapped, uncharted, alien, foreign AN OPPOSITE IS familiar **3** *The part was taken by the then unknown Maria.* ▸ unheard of, obscure, little known, undistinguished, lowly, inconsequential, insignificant, unimportant AN OPPOSITE IS famous

unlikely ADJECTIVE **1** *It is unlikely that they will attend, being so busy.* ▸ doubtful, improbable, dubious AN OPPOSITE IS likely **2** *They would hardly believe such an unlikely explanation.*
▸ implausible, improbable, far-fetched, incredible, suspect, suspicious, dubious, questionable, unbelievable, unconvincing AN OPPOSITE IS likely

unlimited ADJECTIVE **1** *The president emphasized that the U.S. did not have unlimited funds.*
▸ limitless, inexhaustible, infinite, unbounded, boundless, bottomless OPPOSITES

ARE limited, finite **2** *All parts carry a 12-month unlimited mileage warranty.* ▸ unrestricted, unqualified, unconditional, open, unhindered, clear OPPOSITES ARE limited, restricted

unload VERB **1** *Unload the box of essential items first.* ▸ remove, take off, offload, drop off, unpack, discharge AN OPPOSITE IS load **2** *About thirty men would be needed to unload the ship.* ▸ unpack, empty, unburden

unlock VERB *He took the keys from his pocket and unlocked the boot.* ▸ open, release, unfasten, undo OPPOSITES ARE lock, fasten

unlucky ADJECTIVE **1** *You could be ruined as a result of some unlucky accident.* ▸ chance, untimely, unfortunate, unintended, disastrous, dreadful, tragic, calamitous, unwelcome OPPOSITES ARE lucky, timely, fortunate **2** *Miss Hill was unlucky not to get a medal. Phil was again unlucky with injuries.*
▸ unfortunate, hapless, luckless, unhappy, unsuccessful, wretched OPPOSITES ARE lucky, fortunate **3** *The 13th proved to be unlucky for one American skier.* ▸ inauspicious, ominous, unfavorable, jinxed, cursed, ill-fated, ill-omened, ill-starred OPPOSITES ARE lucky, auspicious

unmistakable ADJECTIVE *Then came the unmistakable sound of a gun shot.* ▸ distinct, distinctive, clear, plain, obvious, unambiguous, telltale OPPOSITES ARE uncertain, unclear

unnatural ADJECTIVE **1** *It was an unnatural crime: was the man mad? He was uneasy in this unnatural silence.* ▸ abnormal, unusual, uncanny, weird, bizarre, strange, odd, unaccountable, inexplicable, extraordinary AN OPPOSITE IS normal **2** *Her voice sounded unnatural.* ▸ affected, self-conscious, mannered, stilted, theatrical, unspontaneous,

unnecessary ADJECTIVE not necessary; more than is necessary

unorthodox ADJECTIVE not generally accepted
• an unorthodox method

unpack VERB unpacks, unpacking, unpacked take things out of a suitcase, bag, box, etc.

unpaid ADJECTIVE 1 not yet paid • an unpaid bill 2 not receiving payment for work you do

unpick VERB unpicks, unpicking, unpicked undo the stitching of something

unpleasant ADJECTIVE not pleasant
▷ unpleasantly ADVERB unpleasantness NOUN

unpopular ADJECTIVE not popular

unprecedented (un- press- id- en- tid) ADJECTIVE that has never happened before

unprepared ADJECTIVE not prepared beforehand; not ready or equipped

unprintable ADJECTIVE too rude or indecent to be printed

unprofessional ADJECTIVE not professional; not worthy of a member of a profession

unqualified ADJECTIVE 1 not officially qualified to do something 2 not limited • We gave it our unqualified approval.

unravel VERB unravels, unravelling, unravelled 1 disentangle 2 undo something that is knitted 3 investigate and solve a mystery etc.

unready ADJECTIVE not ready; hesitating USAGE In the title of the English king Ethelred the Unready the word means "lacking good advice or wisdom."

unreal ADJECTIVE not real; existing in the imagination only
▷ unreality NOUN

Thesaurus

feigned, (more informal) put on OPPOSITES ARE natural, normal 3 The white fur looked unnatural. ► artificial, fabricated, imitation, manmade, manufactured, simulated, synthetic OPPOSITES ARE natural, genuine

unnecessary ADJECTIVE 1 Let's not take any unnecessary risks. ► inessential, nonessential, needless, uncalled-for, unjustified, unneeded, unwanted, excessive, extra OPPOSITES ARE necessary, essential 2 A deposit is unnecessary with this order. ► superfluous, dispensable, redundant OPPOSITES ARE necessary, obligatory

unofficial ADJECTIVE 1 She acted as an unofficial bank, cashing checks for customers. ► informal, casual, private, personal, unauthorized OPPOSITES ARE official, formal 2 Unofficial figures put the dead and wounded at over 300. ► unconfirmed, unauthenticated, unsubstantiated OPPOSITES ARE official, confirmed

unpaid ADJECTIVE 1 There were unpaid bills spread all over the table. ► outstanding, overdue, unsettled, owing, due OPPOSITES ARE paid, settled 2 Some staff also did unpaid charity work. ► voluntary, unremunerative OPPOSITES ARE paid, professional

unpleasant ADJECTIVE 1 It reminded him of an earlier unpleasant experience. ► disagreeable, distressing, distasteful, nasty, horrible, horrid, uncomfortable OPPOSITES ARE pleasant, agreeable 2 They were the most unpleasant people I had ever met. ► unlikable, disagreeable, objectionable, unattractive, unfriendly, obnoxious, repugnant, repulsive, revolting, repellent, ill-natured OPPOSITES ARE friendly, agreeable 3 substances that give rise to unpleasant odors ► repulsive, revolting, unappealing OPPOSITES ARE pleasant, appealing

unpopular ADJECTIVE 1 The tax proved deeply unpopular and was later abolished. ► hated, disliked, detested, unwelcome, unwanted, rejected, despised AN OPPOSITE IS popular 2 He was unpopular at school. ► disliked, friendless, unliked, shunned

unpredictable ADJECTIVE 1 The weather is unpredictable in the hills. ► changeable, variable, erratic, uncertain, unreliable, unforeseeable, unexpected AN OPPOSITE IS predictable 2 She was unpredictable and likely to say anything. ► unreliable, fickle, erratic, volatile, capricious, moody, unstable AN OPPOSITE IS predictable

unqualified ADJECTIVE 1 Too many nursing lectures are given by unqualified lecturers. ► untrained, inexperienced, incapable, incompetent, unsuitable, ineligible OPPOSITES ARE qualified, competent 2 The experiment was an unqualified success. ► absolute, unreserved, complete, outright, total, utter, unmitigated OPPOSITES ARE qualified, partial

unravel VERB 1 He cut the climbing rope and started to unravel its strands. ► disentangle, untangle, unwind, untwist, undo, separate AN OPPOSITE IS entangle 2 the sequence of events that archaeologists attempt to unravel ► resolve, sort out, solve, puzzle out, interpret, explain, elucidate, clarify

unreal ADJECTIVE It is a curiously unreal state of affairs. ► false, artificial, fake, sham, illusory, imaginary OPPOSITES ARE real, genuine

unrealistic ADJECTIVE It would be unrealistic to think of removing road congestion entirely. ► impractical, unreasonable, unworkable, fanciful, impracticable, over-ambitious, idealistic, impossible OPPOSITES ARE realistic, practical, pragmatic

a b c d e f g h i j k l m n o p q r s t **u** v w x y z

A
B
C
D
E
F
G
H
I
J
K
L
M
N
O
P
Q
R
S
T
U
V
W
X
Y
Z

unreasonable ADJECTIVE **1** not reasonable **2** excessive or unjust
▷ **unreasonably** ADVERB

unrelieved ADJECTIVE without anything to vary it • *unrelieved gloom*

unreserved ADJECTIVE **1** not reserved **2** without restriction; complete • *unreserved loyalty*
▷ **unreservedly** ADVERB

unrest NOUN trouble or rioting caused because people are dissatisfied

unroll VERB unrolls, unrolling, unrolled open something that has been rolled up

unruly ADJECTIVE difficult to control; disorderly
▷ **unruliness** NOUN

unsavory ADJECTIVE unpleasant or disgusting

unscrew VERB unscrews, unscrewing, unscrewed unfasten something by twisting it or loosening screws

unscrupulous ADJECTIVE having no scruples about wrongdoing

unseemly ADJECTIVE not proper or suitable; indecent

unseen ADJECTIVE not seen; invisible

unseen NOUN unseens a passage for translation without previous preparation

---

Thesaurus

---

unreasonable ADJECTIVE **1** *I knew I was being unreasonable.* ► unfair, unjust, unhelpful, uncooperative, obstructive OPPOSITES ARE reasonable, helpful, fair **2** *It was unreasonable of him to expect her to know the answer.* ► irrational, illogical, perverse, unwarranted, absurd OPPOSITES ARE reasonable, sensible **3** *They were making unreasonable demands.* ► excessive, immoderate, exorbitant, extortionate OPPOSITES ARE reasonable, moderate

unrecognizable ADJECTIVE *He's unrecognizable as the boy we once knew.* ► unidentifiable, unknowable, changed (from), altered (from) AN OPPOSITE IS recognizable

unrelated ADJECTIVE **1** *Two men had been charged after the match in unrelated incidents.* ► separate, distinct, unconnected **2** *He was assigned to a menial post unrelated to his abilities.* ► irrelevant, unconnected (with), dissimilar

unrelenting ADJECTIVE *Success came through unrelenting hard work.* ► constant, continuous, relentless, remorseless, persistent, unremitting, unflagging, merciless, ruthless AN OPPOSITE IS intermittent

unreliable ADJECTIVE **1** *The official figures are unreliable for gauging levels of unemployment.* ► inaccurate, misleading, deceptive, suspect, false, implausible, unconvincing OPPOSITES ARE reliable, accurate **2** *The more he defended himself, the more unreliable he sounded.* ► untrustworthy, irresponsible, undependable, changeable, inconsistent, unpredictable, unsound, unstable, fallible, fickle OPPOSITES ARE reliable, dependable

unrivaled ADJECTIVE *From the hotel you look out on unrivaled views of Venice.* ► incomparable, unequalled, unmatched, unparalleled, unsurpassed, inimitable, supreme, surpassing, matchless, peerless

unruffled ADJECTIVE *Matthew's unruffled manner had evidently soothed them.* ► calm, composed, collected, self-possessed, cool, poised, unperturbed, unflustered, unbothered, untroubled, (*more informal*) unflappable, (*more informal*) laid-back OPPOSITES ARE excited, anxious, upset

unruly ADJECTIVE *A military unit had been stoned by a hungry and unruly mob.* ► disorderly, rowdy, wild, rebellious, disruptive, undisciplined, disobedient, boisterous, rough OPPOSITES ARE orderly, disciplined

unsafe ADJECTIVE **1** *They agreed it would be unsafe to try to get a message to Boston.* ► dangerous, risky, hazardous, precarious, insecure OPPOSITES ARE safe, harmless *The verdicts were unsafe because they were based entirely on confessions.* ► unreliable, unsound, insecure, doubtful, unstable OPPOSITES ARE safe, reliable, secure

unsatisfactory ADJECTIVE *It was an unsatisfactory conclusion to an otherwise useful visit.* ► disappointing, dissatisfying, unacceptable, unhappy, displeasing, inadequate, unworthy, poor, unsatisfying AN OPPOSITE IS satisfactory

unscathed ADJECTIVE *Richard walked away unscathed from the wreckage of his car.* ► unharmed, unhurt, uninjured, safe, intact OPPOSITES ARE injured, hurt

unscrupulous ADJECTIVE *He showed himself to be a cunning and unscrupulous politician.* ► dishonest, dishonorable, unprincipled, unethical, immoral, improper, self-interested, shameless OPPOSITES ARE honest, principled

unseen ADJECTIVE *The magician made the box disappear as though by unseen hands.* ► hidden, concealed, invisible, unnoticed, obscured, imperceptible OPPOSITES ARE visible, seen

unselfish ADJECTIVE *They were motivated by entirely unselfish motives.* ► kind, selfless, thoughtful, altruistic, disinterested, magnanimous, charitable, considerate, caring, generous, humanitarian, philanthropic AN OPPOSITE IS selfish

unsettled ➡ unthinking

unsettled ADJECTIVE **1** not settled or calm **2** (said about weather) likely to change

unshakable ADJECTIVE not able to be shaken; firm

unshaven ADJECTIVE (said about a man) not recently shaved

unsightly ADJECTIVE not pleasant to look at; ugly
▷ **unsightliness** NOUN

unskilled ADJECTIVE not having or not needing special skill or training

unsolicited ADJECTIVE not asked for
● *unsolicited advice*

unsound ADJECTIVE **1** nor reliable or firm **2** not healthy

unspeakable ADJECTIVE too bad to be described; very objectionable

unstable ADJECTIVE not stable; likely to change or become unbalanced

unstuck ADJECTIVE
come unstuck 1 cease to stick **2** (*informal*) fail or go wrong

unsure ADJECTIVE not sure or confident

unthinkable ADJECTIVE too bad or too unlikely to be worth considering

unthinking ADJECTIVE thoughtless

Thesaurus

unsettled ADJECTIVE **1** *Unsettled weather makes a long painting session impossible.* ► changeable, variable, changing, unreliable, unpredictable, unsteady OPPOSITES ARE settled, calm **2** *He looked anxious and unsettled.* ► disturbed, upset, troubled, agitated, restless, uneasy, flustered OPPOSITES ARE settled, composed

unsociable ADJECTIVE *He was grumpy and unsociable.* ► unfriendly, aloof, distant, taciturn, reclusive, uncommunicative, uncongenial OPPOSITES ARE sociable, friendly

unsound ADJECTIVE **1** *Many of the older buildings were structurally unsound.* ► unsafe, unstable, unsteady, flimsy, weak OPPOSITES ARE sound, strong **2** *These arguments are obviously unsound.* ► untenable, flawed, erroneous, defective, ill-founded, fallacious OPPOSITES ARE sound, cogent

unspeakable ADJECTIVE *The gang was guilty of the most unspeakable acts.* ► indescribable, awful, dreadful, appalling, repellent, frightful, unutterable, inexpressible, monstrous

unstable ADJECTIVE **1** *The buildings are highly unstable.* ► unsteady, shaky, rickety, wobbly, flimsy, insecure, unsafe, precarious **2** *an emotionally unstable young student named Karl* ► unbalanced, disturbed, insecure, deranged, demented **3** *The country has a history of unstable government.* ► unreliable, changeable, erratic, unsettled, volatile

unsteady ADJECTIVE **1** *She balanced her cup on an unsteady iron table. He smelled of alcohol and was unsteady on his feet.* ► shaky, rickety, unstable, wobbly, insecure, unsafe, precarious OPPOSITES ARE steady, firm **2** *She took a deep unsteady breath.* ► irregular, uneven, changeable, erratic, inconstant, intermittent, variable OPPOSITES ARE steady, regular **3** *He read by the unsteady light of a candle.*
► flickering, fluctuating, wavering, quavering, quivering, trembling, tremulous AN OPPOSITE IS steady

unsuccessful ADJECTIVE *He was the leader of an unsuccessful military coup against the previous government.* ► failed, abortive, fruitless, futile, ill-fated, vain, ineffective, ineffectual, unproductive, unsatisfactory, useless OPPOSITES ARE successful, effective

unsuitable ADJECTIVE *I think the proposed new site is unsuitable.* ► inappropriate, unsuited, ill-suited, inapt, unsatisfactory, unfitting, unfit, out of keeping, ill-chosen, ill-judged, mistaken, inapposite OPPOSITES ARE suitable, appropriate

unsure ADJECTIVE *I was unsure of my welcome when I visited the cottage the next afternoon.* ► uncertain, doubtful, dubious, sceptical, suspicious, mistrustful, distrustful AN OPPOSITE IS confident
unsure of yourself *She was still a little unsure of herself in formal society.* ► unconfident, hesitant, diffident, timid, timorous OPPOSITES ARE sure of yourself, self-confident

unsympathetic ADJECTIVE **1** *The planning authority showed an unsympathetic attitude to applications for new homes.* ► uncaring, unconcerned, unresponsive, indifferent, insensitive, unfeeling, hostile, antagonistic AN OPPOSITE IS sympathetic **2 unsympathetic to** *The new assembly was quite unsympathetic to these views.* ► opposed to, hostile to, unconcerned about, antagonistic towards, ill-disposed towards OPPOSITES ARE sympathetic to, understanding of

unsystematic ADJECTIVE *Their use of data was unsystematic.* ► disorganized, unmethodical, disorderly, haphazard, muddled, jumbled, unstructured, indiscriminate, inconsistent AN OPPOSITE IS systematic

unthinkable ADJECTIVE *In a free society such a ban would be unthinkable.* ► inconceivable, unimaginable, unbelievable, undreamed of, incredible, absurd, preposterous, implausible OPPOSITES ARE conceivable, plausible

a b c d e f g h i j k l m n o p q r s t **u** v w x y z

untidy ADJECTIVE untidier, untidiest not tidy
  ▷ **untidily** ADVERB **untidiness** NOUN

untie VERB unties, untying, untied undo
something that has been tied

until PREPOSITION, CONJUNCTION up to a particular
time or event [from an Old Norse word *und* =
as far as, added to *till*]
  USAGE See the note on till[1].

untold ADJECTIVE 1 not told 2 too much or too
many to be counted • *untold wealth*

untruth NOUN untruths an untrue statement;
a lie
  ▷ **untruthful** ADJECTIVE **untruthfully** ADVERB

unused ADJECTIVE 1 (un-yoozd) not yet used
  • *an unused stamp* 2 (un-yoost) not
accustomed • *He is unused to eating meat.*

unusual ADJECTIVE not usual; strange or
exceptional
  ▷ **unusually** ADVERB

unveil VERB unveils, unveiling, unveiled
1 remove a veil or covering from something
2 reveal

unwarranted ADJECTIVE not justified; uncalled
for

unwell ADJECTIVE not in good health

unwholesome ADJECTIVE not wholesome

unwieldy ADJECTIVE awkward to move or
control because of its size, shape, or weight
  ▷ **unwieldiness** NOUN

unwind VERB unwinds, unwinding, unwound
1 unroll 2 (*informal*) relax after a time of
work or strain

unwise ADJECTIVE not wise; foolish
  ▷ **unwisely** ADVERB

unworthy ADJECTIVE not worthy or deserving

unwrap VERB unwraps, unwrapping,
unwrapped open something that is wrapped

Thesaurus

---

untidy ADJECTIVE 1 *He staggered out of his untidy
bedroom. The handwriting was untidy.*
  ▶ disorganized, messy, cluttered, muddled,
disordered, chaotic OPPOSITES ARE tidy,
orderly 2 *Her hair looked untidy.* ▶ dishevelled,
scruffy, bedraggled, uncombed, ungroomed,
unkempt, rumpled, shabby, tangled, tousled,
uncared for OPPOSITES ARE tidy, neat

untie VERB *She began to untie the string around
the box.* ▶ undo, loosen, unfasten, unknot,
release, unbind, disentangle, free, untether
AN OPPOSITE IS tie up

untrue ADJECTIVE *The claims were completely
untrue.* ▶ wrong, false, inaccurate, erroneous,
incorrect, mistaken, unfounded, fallacious
OPPOSITES ARE true, correct

unusual ADJECTIVE 1 *The town had electric
lighting, unusual in those days.* ▶ uncommon,
rare, unfamiliar OPPOSITES ARE usual, common
2 *It was an unusual story.* ▶ strange, odd,
curious, weird, queer, bizarre, peculiar,
exceptional, unconventional OPPOSITES ARE
normal, conventional 3 *Vera was a woman of
unusual quality.* ▶ remarkable, exceptional,
extraordinary, untypical AN OPPOSITE IS typical

unwanted ADJECTIVE 1 *Lila kept guard dogs to
ward off unwanted visitors.* ▶ unwelcome,
undesirable, undesired, unsolicited, uninvited,
rejected OPPOSITES ARE welcome, wanted,
desirable 2 *The ants will bring dead ants and
unwanted garbage from their nests.*
  ▶ superfluous, discarded, redundant, unused
OPPOSITES ARE needed, useful, wanted

unwary ADJECTIVE *Deep potholes can bring down
an unwary rider and his horse.* ▶ careless,
unthinking, inattentive, absent-minded,
thoughtless, unguarded, incautious OPPOSITES
ARE wary, attentive

unwelcome ADJECTIVE 1 *As she went downstairs,
an unwelcome voice reached her ears.*
  ▶ disagreeable, unacceptable, undesirable,
unwanted AN OPPOSITE IS welcome 2 *He had
been made to feel unwelcome.* ▶ unwanted,
unpopular, excluded, spurned, uninvited

unwell ADJECTIVE *She told the ambulance service
she was feeling unwell.* ▶ ill, sick, poorly,
indisposed, out of sorts, under the weather
OPPOSITES ARE well, in good health

unwieldy ADJECTIVE *He would also need to
transport some unwieldy equipment.* ▶ awkward,
cumbersome, clumsy, bulky, unmanageable,
ungainly, heavy, massive OPPOSITES ARE
manageable, handy

unwilling ADJECTIVE 1 *He called together his
group of unwilling helpers.* ▶ unenthusiastic,
grudging, reluctant, uncooperative, half-
hearted, hesitant OPPOSITES ARE willing, keen
2 *A spokesman was unwilling to give a precise
date.* ▶ reluctant, disinclined, averse, loath
OPPOSITES ARE willing, ready

unwind VERB 1 *Kitty unwound balls of pink and
blue yarn.* ▶ unroll, unreel, unravel, untwist,
undo, uncoil, untwine 2 *He found the farm a
place to unwind and let himself go.* ▶ relax, ease
up, loosen up

unwise ADJECTIVE *You would be unwise to ignore
the warning signs.* ▶ foolish, stupid, silly, ill-
advised, crazy, mad, insane, (*more informal*)
daft OPPOSITES ARE wise, sensible

unworthy ADJECTIVE 1 *His was an unworthy
remark.* ▶ shameful, discreditable,
dishonorable, undeserving, unsuitable,
despicable, disreputable, ignoble,
inappropriate AN OPPOSITE IS worthy 2 *Such
claims are unworthy of consideration.*
  ▶ undeserving, unfit (for), ineligible (for)
OPPOSITES ARE worthy, deserving

A B C D E F G H I J K L M N O P Q R S T U V W X Y Z

up ADVERB **1** to or in a higher place or position or level ● *Prices have gone up.* **2** so as to be upright ● *Stand up* **3** out of bed ● *It's time to get up.* **4** completely ● *Eat up your carrots.* **5** finished ● *Your time is up.* **6** (*informal*) happening ● *Something is up.*

up against 1 close to **2** (*informal*) faced with difficulties, dangers, etc.

ups and downs alternate good and bad luck

up to 1 until **2** busy with or doing something ● *What are you up to?* **3** capable of ● *I don't think I'm up to it.* **4** needed from ● *It's up to us to help her.*

up to date 1 modern or fashionable **2** giving recent information, etc.

USAGE Use hyphens when this is used as an adjective before a noun, e.g. *up-to-date information* (but *The information is up to date*).

up PREPOSITION upward through or along or into ● *Water came up the pipes.* [from Old English]

upbringing NOUN the way someone is trained during childhood

update VERB updates, updating, updated bring a thing up to date
▷ **update** NOUN

upgrade VERB upgrades, upgrading, upgraded improve a machine by installing new or better parts in it
▷ **upgrade** NOUN

upheaval NOUN upheavals a sudden violent change or disturbance

uphill ADVERB up a slope

uphill ADJECTIVE **1** going up a slope **2** difficult ● *It was an uphill struggle.*

uphold VERB upholds, upholding, upheld support or maintain a decision or belief etc.

upholster VERB upholsters, upholstering, upholstered put a soft padded covering on furniture
▷ **upholstery** NOUN

upkeep NOUN keeping something in good condition; the cost of this

uplifting ADJECTIVE making you feel more cheerful

upon PREPOSITION on

upper ADJECTIVE higher in place or rank, etc.

upper class NOUN upper classes the highest class in society, especially the aristocracy
▷ **upper-class** ADJECTIVE

uppermost ADJECTIVE highest

uppermost ADVERB on or to the top or the highest place ● *Keep the painted side uppermost.*

upright ADJECTIVE **1** vertical or erect **2** strictly honest or honourable

upright NOUN uprights a post or rod etc. placed upright, especially as a support

uprising NOUN uprisings a rebellion or revolt

uproar NOUN an outburst of noise or excitement or anger

uproot VERB uproots, uprooting, uprooted **1** remove a plant and its roots from the ground **2** make someone leave the place where he or she has lived for a long time

upset VERB upsets, upsetting, upset **1** overturn; knock something over **2** make a person unhappy or distressed **3** disturb the normal working of something; disrupt ● *This has really upset my plans.*

Thesaurus

update VERB *You should continually update your information.* ► review, amend, upgrade, bring up to date, correct, revise, modernize

upgrade VERB *You can upgrade our system free of charge.* ► improve, enhance, update, make better, renovate, expand

upheaval NOUN *Further changes could be made without major upheaval.* ► disruption, commotion, disturbance, confusion, disorder, turmoil

uphill ADJECTIVE *We are all facing an uphill struggle.* ► hard, arduous, strenuous, taxing, tough, difficult, exhausting, grueling, laborious, stiff AN OPPOSITE IS easy

upper ADJECTIVE *There are elevators to the upper floors of the building.* ► higher, upstairs, raised, elevated, superior

upright ADJECTIVE **1** *Crude figures are incised on upright stones.* ► perpendicular, vertical, erect **2** *upright people with a strong sense of family pride* ► honorable, honest, respectable, reputable, righteous, upstanding, moral,

principled, virtuous, trustworthy OPPOSITES ARE dishonorable, corrupt

uprising NOUN *The uprising was soon suppressed by the army.* ► rebellion, revolt, rising, insurrection, insurgence, revolution, mutiny USAGE You use *mutiny* about members of the armed forces.

uproar NOUN **1** *There was an uproar when the council refused to hear the delegation.* ► outcry, clamour, protest, furor, rumpus **2** *They found the place in uproar.* ► turmoil, confusion, disorder, pandemonium, mayhem, commotion

uproot VERB **1** *He always imagined himself as some great monster uprooting trees.* ► pull up, tear up, rip out, root out, weed out, remove, destroy, (*more formal*) extirpate AN OPPOSITE IS plant **2** *Building a dam would uproot over a million people.* ► displace, disrupt, remove

upset VERB **1** *I would never want to upset anyone.* ► distress, trouble, agitate, disturb, unsettle, disquiet, disconcert, unnerve, dismay, grieve, perturb, fluster, confuse OPPOSITES ARE reassure, put at ease **2** *Grazing sheep is prohibited so as not to upset the natural balance.*

a
b
c
d
e
f
g
h
i
j
k
l
m
n
o
p
q
r
s
t
u
v
w
x
y
z

A
B
C
D
E
F
G
H
I
J
K
L
M
N
O
P
Q
R
S
T
U
V
W
X
Y
Z

upset ADJECTIVE **1** unhappy or distressed **2** slightly ill • *an upset stomach*

upset NOUN upsets **1** a slight illness • *a stomach upset* **2** an unexpected result or setback • *There has been a major upset in the quarter-finals.*

upshot NOUN upshots the eventual outcome

upside-down ADVERB, ADJECTIVE **1** with the upper part underneath instead of on top **2** in great disorder; very untidy • *Everything had been turned upside-down.*

upstairs ADVERB, ADJECTIVE to or on a higher floor

upstart NOUN upstarts a person who has risen suddenly to a high position, especially one who then behaves arrogantly

uptake NOUN
quick on the uptake quick to understand
slow on the uptake slow to understand

uptight ADJECTIVE (*informal*) tense and nervous or annoyed

upward ADJECTIVE, ADVERB going towards what is higher
▷ **upwards** ADVERB

uranium NOUN a heavy radioactive grey metal used as a source of nuclear energy [named after the planet Uranus]

urban ADJECTIVE to do with a town or city [from Latin *urbis* = of a city]

urchin NOUN urchins **1** a poorly dressed or mischievous boy **2** a sea urchin [via early French from Latin *hericius* = hedgehog]

urge VERB urges, urging, urged **1** try to persuade a person to do something **2** drive people or animals onward **3** recommend or advise

urge NOUN urges a strong desire or wish

urgent ADJECTIVE needing to be done or dealt with immediately
▷ **urgently** ADVERB **urgency** NOUN

urinate (yoor- in- ayt) VERB urinates, urinating, urinated pass urine out of your body
▷ **urination** NOUN

urine (yoor- in) NOUN waste liquid that collects in the bladder and is passed out of the body
▷ **urinary** ADJECTIVE

urn NOUN urns **1** a large metal container with a tap, in which water is heated **2** a container shaped like a vase, usually with a foot, especially a container for holding the ashes of a cremated person

---

Thesaurus

► disrupt, disturb, interfere with, affect, throw out, ruin OPPOSITES ARE maintain, restore **3** *He upset a pot of soup.* ► tip over, knock over, spill, overturn

upset NOUN *The youngsters put the upset behind them.* ► distress, worry, trouble, upheaval, bother, anxiety

upset ADJECTIVE **1** *She was upset about missing all the excitement.* ► distressed, dismayed, disturbed, troubled, unsettled, disconcerted, worried, anxious, grieved **2** *He called to say he had an upset stomach.* ► queasy, disordered

upside-down ADJECTIVE **1** *I could read the writing upside-down on his desk.* ► the wrong way up, inverted, topsy-turvy, upturned OPPOSITES ARE upright, the right way up **2** *Somebody broke in and turned the place upside-down. It is traumatic having one's life turned upside-down like this.* ► into disarray, into chaos, into a muddle, untidy, chaotic AN OPPOSITE IS tidy

uptight ADJECTIVE (*informal*) *When Ian gets uptight it can affect his game.* ► tense, anxious, nervous, edgy, on edge, strained, stressed, agitated, apprehensive, jittery, fidgety, ill at ease, jumpy OPPOSITES ARE calm, relaxed

up-to-date ADJECTIVE **1** *None of the disks contained up-to-date programs.* ► current, latest, recent, new, modern, present-day, advanced AN OPPOSITE IS out-of-date **2** *Use the Internet to*

keep yourself up to date on this topic. ► informed (about), in touch (with), conversant (with), (*more informal*) up to speed AN OPPOSITE IS uninformed

urban ADJECTIVE *greenfield sites on the edge of urban areas* ► built-up, town, city, densely populated, metropolitan, suburban, municipal

urge VERB **1** *We would urge people to be aware and alert with fireworks.* ► encourage, entreat, exhort, advise, counsel, appeal to, entreat, beg, press, plead with, beseech, implore, recommend OPPOSITES ARE deter, discourage **2** *The working group urged caution in implementing any changes.* ► advise, recommend, counsel, advocate, suggest **3** *He urged his crew on through the mountainous waves.* ► drive, spur, press, force, compel, impel, propel, push

urge NOUN *The urge to give him a hug was almost impossible to resist.* ► desire, wish, need, impulse, inclination, eagerness, compulsion, craving, fancy, instinct, longing, yearning, (*more informal*) itch, (*more informal*) yen

urgent ADJECTIVE **1** *The buildings are in urgent need of renovation.* ► immediate, pressing, acute, grave, dire, desperate, critical, serious, essential, drastic, extreme, instant, top-priority **2** *He was roused from sleep by the urgent calls of his mother.* ► insistent, persistent, earnest, determined, eager, pleading AN OPPOSITE IS casual

U.S. _ABBREVIATION_ United States

us _PRONOUN_ the form of **we** used when it is the object of a verb or after a preposition

U.S.A. _ABBREVIATION_ United States of America

use (yooz) _VERB_ **uses, using, used** perform an action or job with something • _Use soap for washing._
▷ **user** NOUN

used to 1 was or were in the habit of doing • _We used to go by train._ **2** accustomed to or familiar with • _I'm used to his strange behavior._

use up use all of something

use (yooss) _NOUN_ **uses 1** the action of using something; being used • _the use of computers in schools_ **2** the purpose for which something is used • _Can you find a use for this crate?_ **3** the quality of being useful • _These scissors are no use at all._ [via early French from Latin _uti_]

used _ADJECTIVE_ not new; second-hand • _used cars_

useful _ADJECTIVE_ able to be used a lot or to do something that needs doing
▷ **usefully** ADVERB **usefulness** NOUN

useless _ADJECTIVE_ not useful; producing no effect • _Their efforts were useless._
▷ **uselessly** ADVERB **uselessness** NOUN

user-friendly _ADJECTIVE_ designed to be easy to use

usher _NOUN_ **ushers** a person who shows people to their seats in a cinema, theater, or church

usher _VERB_ **ushers, ushering, ushered** lead someone in or out; escort someone as an usher [via early French from Latin _ostiarius_ = doorkeeper]

usherette _NOUN_ **usherettes** a woman who shows people to their seats in a cinema or theater

usual _ADJECTIVE_ such as happens or is done or used always or most of the time
▷ **usually** ADVERB

utensil (yoo- ten- sil) _NOUN_ **utensils** a tool, device, or container, especially one for use in the house • _cooking utensils_

Thesaurus

usable _ADJECTIVE_ **1** _a thousand square meters of usable floor space_ ► functional, working, available, practical, serviceable, fit for use, functioning, operating, operational AN OPPOSITE IS unusable. **2** _The ticket is usable at all the country's museums and galleries._ ► valid, acceptable, current AN OPPOSITE IS invalid

use NOUN **1** _What's the use of arguing?_ ► point, advantage, purpose, benefit, value, sense, usefulness, reason (for) **2** _There isn't much use for mechanical calculators any more._ ► need, call, demand, necessity, reason, justification **3** _There was trial and error in the use of video equipment._ ► utilization, employment, operation, application, usage **4** _People have to make the best use of their time._ ► application, utilization, employment, exercise

use VERB **1** _They use the garden like an extra room._ ► utilize, make use of, employ, avail yourself of, put to use **2** _He learned to use a word processor._ ► work, operate, utilize, handle, manage, make use of **3** _You will need to use all your judgment._ ► exercise, apply, employ, draw on, make use of, implement **4** _How much milk did you use?_ ► use up, consume, exhaust, waste

to use up _By now Billy had used up all his money._ ► spend, get through, exhaust, deplete, squander, consume USAGE You use _squander_ when you are talking about wasting something or using it extravagantly. You use _consume_ when you are talking about food.

used to _He was used to being woken up in the middle of the night._ ► accustomed to, familiar with, in the habit of, no stranger to

used _ADJECTIVE_ _They always bought used cars._ ► secondhand, pre-owned, nearly new, old OPPOSITES ARE unused, new

useful _ADJECTIVE_ **1** _These specialists can offer useful advice and practical support._ ► helpful, beneficial, worthwhile, valuable, profitable, advantageous, positive, constructive, good, invaluable OPPOSITES ARE useless. **2** _This is a useful tool for working in tight spaces._ ► handy, practical, convenient, effective, efficient, powerful, productive, utilitarian OPPOSITES ARE useless, awkward **3** _They had some useful players._ ► skilful, talented, competent, capable, proficient, effective, successful OPPOSITES ARE useless, incompetent

useless _ADJECTIVE_ **1** _I'm full of useless bits of knowledge like that. Further inquiries would be useless._ ► worthless, pointless, futile, fruitless, vain, hopeless, unavailing, unprofitable, unsuccessful OPPOSITES ARE useful, helpful, practical **2** _It was a useless suggestion._ ► impractical, unusable, unworkable, ineffective, hopeless, (more informal) dud OPPOSITES ARE useful, positive **3** _She's useless at spelling._ ► bad, inept, no good, incompetent, ineffective, untalented, incapable (of) OPPOSITES ARE useful, competent

usual _ADJECTIVE_ _Today he didn't take his usual route home._ ► normal, customary, habitual, regular, routine, typical, familiar, accustomed, conventional, traditional, standard, orthodox OPPOSITES ARE unusual, exceptional

usually _ADVERB_ _Usually he lingered by the stream to throw in stones._ ► normally, generally, habitually, as a rule, customarily, routinely, regularly, often OPPOSITES ARE exceptionally, seldom, rarely

a
b
c
d
e
f
g
h
i
j
k
l
m
n
o
p
q
r
s
t
u
v
w
x
y
z

A
B
C
D
E
F
G
H
I
J
K
L
M
N
O
P
Q
R
S
T
U
V
W
X
Y
Z

utilitarian ADJECTIVE designed to be useful rather than decorative or luxurious; practical

utility NOUN utilities **1** usefulness **2** an organization that supplies water, gas, electricity, etc., to the community

utilize VERB utilizes, utilizing, utilized use; find a use for something
▷ **utilization** NOUN

utmost ADJECTIVE extreme or greatest • *Look after it with the utmost care.*
▷ **utmost** NOUN
do your utmost do the most that you are able to

Utopia (yoo- **toh**- pee- a) NOUN Utopias an imaginary place or state of things where

everything is perfect
▷ **Utopian** ADJECTIVE

utter VERB utters, uttering, uttered say or speak; make a sound with your mouth
▷ **utterance** NOUN
[from early Dutch]

utter ADJECTIVE complete or absolute • *utter misery*
▷ **utterly** ADVERB
[from Old English *uttra* = outer]

uttermost ADJECTIVE, NOUN utmost

U-turn NOUN U-turns **1** a U-shaped turn made in a vehicle so that it then travels in the opposite direction **2** a complete change of policy

---
Thesaurus
---

utter ADJECTIVE *Amy stared at him in utter disbelief.* ► absolute, complete, total, sheer, positive, thorough, outright, downright, out-and-out, unmitigated

utter VERB *They were all too stunned to utter a word.* ► say, speak, express, voice, articulate, enunciate

utterly ADVERB *The whole exercise seems utterly pointless.* ► absolutely, completely, totally, perfectly, quite, unquestionably, unreservedly

U-turn NOUN *It had been the most dramatic U-turn of her political career.* ► change of mind, reversal of policy, volte-face, about-face, about-turn, shift

Vv

vacant ADJECTIVE **1** empty; not filled or occupied • *a vacant seat* • *a vacant post* **2** without expression; blank • *a vacant stare*
▷ **vacantly** ADVERB **vacancy** NOUN
[from Latin *vacans* = being empty]

vacation (vak-**ay**-shun) NOUN vacations **1** a respite, or a time of respite from something **2** vacating a place etc.

vaccinate (vak-sin-ayt) VERB vaccinates, vaccinating, vaccinated inoculate someone with a vaccine
▷ **vaccination** NOUN

vaccine (vak-seen) NOUN vaccines a substance used to give someone immunity against a disease [from Latin *vacca* = cow (because serum from cows was used to protect people from the disease smallpox)]

vacuum NOUN vacuums **1** a completely empty space; a space without any air in it **2** (*informal*) a vacuum cleaner

vacuum VERB vacuums, vacuuming, vacuumed to clean a floor with a vacuum cleaner

vacuum cleaner NOUN vacuum cleaners an electrical device that sucks up dust and dirt etc.

vagabond NOUN vagabonds a person with no settled home or regular work; a vagrant

vagina (va-**jy**-na) NOUN vaginas the passage that leads from the vulva to the womb

vagrant (**vay**-grant) NOUN vagrants a person with no settled home or regular work; a tramp
▷ **vagrancy** NOUN

vague ADJECTIVE **1** not definite or clear **2** not thinking clearly or precisely
▷ **vaguely** ADVERB **vagueness** NOUN

vain ADJECTIVE **1** conceited, especially about your appearance **2** useless • *They made vain attempts to save her.*
▷ **vainly** ADVERB
in vain with no result; uselessly
USAGE Do not confuse with vane or vein.

valency NOUN valencies (in science) the power of an atom to combine with other atoms, measured by the number of hydrogen atoms it is capable of combining with

valentine NOUN valentines **1** a card sent on St. Valentine's day (February 14) to someone you are fond of **2** the person you send this card to

valiant ADJECTIVE brave or courageous
▷ **valiantly** ADVERB

valid ADJECTIVE **1** legally able to be used or accepted • *a valid passport* **2** (said about reasoning) sound and logical
▷ **validity** NOUN

valley NOUN valleys **1** a long low area between hills **2** an area through which a river flows • *the Nile valley*

Thesaurus

vacant ADJECTIVE **1** *There is a plan to build offices on a vacant site in the city center.* ▶ unused, unoccupied, unfilled, empty, bare, blank, clear, free, available AN OPPOSITE IS occupied **2** *Guns and ammunition were found in a planned search of a vacant house.* ▶ empty, unoccupied, deserted AN OPPOSITE IS occupied **3** *She maintained a vacant expression.* ▶ blank, expressionless, deadpan, absent-minded, vacuous, abstracted, inattentive, dreamy, far away OPPOSITES ARE attentive, alert

vacate VERB *They must vacate the premises by the end of the month.* ▶ leave, evacuate, quit, withdraw from, abandon, depart from, give up AN OPPOSITE IS occupy

vacation NOUN *Although I'm officially on vacation, I'm actually working.* ▶ leave, time off

vague ADJECTIVE **1** *He was full of vague promises.* ▶ indefinite, imprecise, inexact, unspecific, ill-defined, generalized OPPOSITES ARE specific, definite **2** *Vague shapes could be made out in the distance.* ▶ hazy, unclear, indistinct, indefinite, blurred OPPOSITES ARE distinct, clear **3** *He always seemed vague about money.* ▶ uncertain, unclear, unsure, confused, indecisive, uninformed OPPOSITES ARE certain, informed

4 *Our plans are fairly vague at this stage.* ▶ unsettled, uncertain, inexact, open, unsure, indefinite OPPOSITES ARE firm, definite

vain ADJECTIVE **1** *They are vain and ostentatious by nature.* ▶ conceited, arrogant, self-satisfied, self-important, boastful, egotistical AN OPPOSITE IS modest **2** *Dr. Neil made vain attempts to stop the bleeding.* ▶ unsuccessful, ineffective, futile, abortive, fruitless, unavailing OPPOSITES ARE successful, effective

valid ADJECTIVE **1** *This may be a valid conclusion.* ▶ legitimate, reasonable, rational, sound, cogent, convincing, acceptable OPPOSITES ARE invalid, spurious **2** *Make sure you have a valid passport and a visa if necessary.* ▶ current, up-to-date, legal, certified, approved, authorized, official, suitable, bona fide, genuine AN OPPOSITE IS invalid

valley NOUN *Pupils will be taught in the school across the valley.* ▶ dale, glen, dell, vale, hollow, gorge, gulch

valor NOUN *The medals are awarded for acts of valor.* ▶ bravery, courage, daring, gallantry, heroism AN OPPOSITE IS cowardice

valuable ➡ variable

A B C D E F G H I J K L M N O P Q R S T U **V** W X Y Z

valuable ADJECTIVE worth a lot of money; of great value
▷ **valuably** ADVERB

valuables PLURAL NOUN valuable things

value NOUN values **1** the amount of money, etc., that is considered to be the equivalent of something, or for which it can be exchanged **2** how useful or important something is • *They learned the value of regular exercise.* **3** (in mathematics) the number or quantity represented by a figure, etc. • *What is the value of x?*

value VERB values, valuing, valued **1** think that something is valuable **2** estimate the value of a thing
▷ **valuation** NOUN **valuer** NOUN

valve NOUN valves **1** a device for controlling the flow of gas or liquid through a pipe or tube **2** a structure in the heart or in a blood vessel allowing blood to flow in one direction only **3** a device that controls the flow of electricity in old televisions, radios, etc. **4** each piece of the shell of oysters etc.
▷ **valvular** ADJECTIVE

vampire NOUN vampires a dead creature that is supposed to leave its grave at night and suck blood from living people [from Hungarian *vampir*, perhaps from a Turkish word *uber* = witch]

van NOUN vans **1** a covered vehicle for carrying goods

vandal NOUN vandals a person who deliberately breaks or damages things, especially public property

▷ **vandalism** NOUN
[named after the Vandals, a Germanic people who invaded the Roman Empire in the 5th century, destroying many books and works of art]

vandalize VERB vandalizes, vandalizing, vandalized damage things as a vandal

vane NOUN vanes **1** a weathervane **2** the blade of a propeller, sail of a windmill, or other device that acts on or is moved by wind or water [from Old English]
USAGE Do not confuse with **vain** or **vein**.

vanilla NOUN a flavoring obtained from the pods of a tropical plant [from Spanish *vainilla* = little pod]

vanish VERB vanishes, vanishing, vanished disappear completely

vanity NOUN conceit; being vain

vanquish VERB vanquishes, vanquishing, vanquished defeat thoroughly

vantage point NOUN vantage points a place from which you have a good view of scenery or something interesting [from Middle English *vantage* = advantage]

vaporize VERB vaporizes, vaporizing, vaporized change or be changed into vapor
▷ **vaporization** NOUN **vaporizer** NOUN

vapor NOUN vapors a visible gas to which some substances can be converted by heat; steam or mist

variable ADJECTIVE likely to vary; changeable
▷ **variably** ADVERB **variability** NOUN

Thesaurus

valuable ADJECTIVE **1** *You need separate insurance cover for the more valuable jewelry.* ► costly, high-priced, expensive, precious, priceless, dear OPPOSITES ARE valueless, worthless **2** *The work provided them with valuable experience.* ► helpful, beneficial, advantageous, constructive, invaluable, positive, profitable, useful, valued, worthwhile, good AN OPPOSITE IS worthless USAGE Note that *invaluable* is not an opposite of *valuable*, but means "too great to be valued," i.e. "extremely valuable," as in *an invaluable member of the team.*

value NOUN **1** *Houses in the area have practically doubled in value.* ► price, cost, worth, market value **2** *The value of regular exercise cannot be overestimated.* ► importance, merit, benefit, advantage, significance, usefulness, use

value VERB **1** *The vineyard is valued at $160 million.* ► assess, evaluate, price, cost, estimate the value of, (more informal) put a figure on **2** *His honesty endeared him to many who valued his wise advice.* ► appreciate, prize, rate highly, esteem, hold in high regard, have a high opinion of, set store by OPPOSITES ARE neglect, disregard

values PLURAL NOUN *Each generation has its special values.* ► principles, standards, morality, morals, moral code, code of behavior

vanish VERB **1** *Maria had vanished into the garden.* ► disappear, leave, withdraw, clear off OPPOSITES ARE appear, reappear **2** *All thoughts of her vanished in the excitement.* ► evaporate, melt away, dissolve, end, come to an end, dwindle, fade, go away, disperse, pass OPPOSITES ARE materialize, endure

vanity NOUN *A divorce would hit her vanity and her pocket.* ► pride, self-regard, self-admiration, conceit, arrogance, egoism AN OPPOSITE IS modesty

vapor NOUN *His breath formed a vapor on the air.* ► mist, haze, fog, smoke, steam, fumes, gas, miasma

variable ADJECTIVE *The photos are of variable quality.* ► changing, varying, changeable, fluctuating, irregular, inconsistent, unpredictable, vacillating, unstable, unsteady, temperamental OPPOSITES ARE constant, uniform

740

variable ➡ vehement

variable NOUN variables something that varies or can vary; a variable quantity

variant ADJECTIVE differing from something
• *"Gipsy" is a variant spelling of "gypsy."*
▷ **variant** NOUN

variation NOUN variations **1** varying; the amount by which something varies **2** a different form of something

varied ADJECTIVE of different sorts; full of variety

variegated (vair- ig- ay- tid) ADJECTIVE with patches of different colors
▷ **variegation** NOUN

variety NOUN varieties **1** a quantity of different kinds of things **2** the quality of not always being the same; variation **3** a particular kind of something • *There are several varieties of spaniel.* **4** an entertainment that includes short performances of various kinds

various ADJECTIVE **1** of several kinds; unlike one another • *for various reasons* **2** several • *We met various people.*
▷ **variously** ADVERB

varnish NOUN varnishes a liquid that dries to form a hard, shiny, clear coating

varnish VERB varnishes, varnishing, varnished coat something with varnish

vary VERB varies, varying, varied **1** make or become different; change **2** be different

vase NOUN vases an open, usually tall, container used for holding cut flowers or as an ornament

vast ADJECTIVE very great, especially in area • *a vast expanse of water*
▷ **vastly** ADVERB **vastness** NOUN

VAT ABBREVIATION value added tax; a tax on goods and services

vat NOUN vats a very large container for holding liquid

vault VERB vaults, vaulting, vaulted jump over something, especially while supporting yourself on your hands or with the help of a pole

vault NOUN vaults **1** a vaulting jump **2** an arched roof **3** an underground room used to store things **4** a room for storing money or valuables **5** a burial chamber

vaulted ADJECTIVE having an arched roof

vaunt VERB vaunts, vaunting, vaunted (*old use or poetical*) boast
▷ **vaunt** NOUN

VCR ABBREVIATION video cassette recorder

VDU ABBREVIATION visual display unit

veal NOUN calf's flesh used as food

vector NOUN vectors (in mathematics) a quantity that has size and direction, such as velocity (which is speed in a certain direction)
▷ **vectorial** ADJECTIVE
[from Latin, = carrier, traveller]

veer VERB veers, veering, veered change direction; swerve

vegetable NOUN vegetables a plant that can be used as food [from Latin *vegetare* = enliven, animate]

vegetarian NOUN vegetarians a person who does not eat meat
▷ **vegetarianism** NOUN

vegetation NOUN **1** plants that are growing **2** vegetating

vehement (vee- im- ent) ADJECTIVE showing strong feeling • *a vehement refusal*
▷ **vehemently** ADVERB **vehemence** NOUN

Thesaurus

variation NOUN **1** *There was considerable regional variation in these findings.* ► diversity, deviation, diversification, disparity, inequality, difference, discrepancy **2** *Prices are subject to variation.* ► change, alteration, adjustment, modification

varied ADJECTIVE *There is a varied choice of restaurants and tavernas.* ► diverse, assorted, wide-ranging, miscellaneous, mixed, sundry, motley, (*more formal*) heterogeneous

variety NOUN **1** *It is hard work, but the variety makes it stimulating.* ► diversity, variation, diversification, change, many-sidedness, unpredictability **2** *one-day courses on a variety of themes* ► assortment, array, miscellany, mixture, multiplicity, range, collection, medley **3** *The list offers sixteen varieties of chocolate.* ► kind, sort, type, form, brand, category, class, strain, make, species, breed

various ADJECTIVE **1** *The job can be done in various ways.* ► different, differing, diverse,

distinct, varying, varied, assorted, dissimilar, miscellaneous AN OPPOSITE IS similar **2** *An uneasy truce existed between the various political parties.* ► numerous, many, several, innumerable, countless, multifarious, sundry

vary VERB **1** *Prices vary enormously for group holidays.* ► differ, fluctuate, range, change, shift, go up and down, (*more formal*) oscillate OPPOSITES ARE static, be fixed **2** *The routine never varies.* ► change, alter, differ, deviate, diverge, fluctuate **3** *You can vary the size of your pictures.* ► alter, adapt, adjust, modify, diversify AN OPPOSITE IS fix

vast ADJECTIVE **1** *The birds fly over vast distances.* ► huge, great, extensive, enormous, immense, colossal, tremendous OPPOSITES ARE small, short **2** *The vast majority of patients are elderly.* ► great, huge, large

vehement ADJECTIVE *We are quite vehement in our pursuit of safety procedures. Opposition to the whale hunt drew vehement criticism from the*

741

A
B
C
D
E
F
G
H
I
J
K
L
M
N
O
P
Q
R
S
T
U

V

W
X
Y
Z

vehicle NOUN vehicles a means of transporting people or goods, especially on land

veil NOUN veils a piece of thin material worn to cover the face or head
take the veil become a nun

veil VERB veils, veiling, veiled **1** cover something with a veil **2** partially conceal something • *veiled threats*

vein NOUN veins **1** any of the tubes that carry blood from all parts of the body to the heart COMPARE artery **2** a line or streak on a leaf, rock, insect's wing, etc. **3** a long deposit of mineral or ore in the middle of a rock **4** a mood or manner • *She spoke in a serious vein.*
USAGE Do not confuse with vain or vane.

velocity NOUN velocities speed in a given direction

velvet NOUN a woven material with very short soft furry fibers on one side
▷ **velvety** ADJECTIVE

vendetta NOUN vendettas a long-lasting bitter quarrel; a feud [from Italian, from Latin *vindicta* = vengeance]

vending machine NOUN vending machines a slot machine from which you can obtain drinks, chocolate, cigarettes, etc.

veneer NOUN veneers **1** a thin layer of good wood covering the surface of a cheaper wood in furniture, etc. **2** an outward show of some good quality • *a veneer of politeness*

venerable ADJECTIVE worthy of respect or honor, especially because of great age

venerate VERB venerates, venerating, venerated honor with great respect or reverence
▷ **veneration** NOUN

venereal disease NOUN venereal diseases a disease passed on by sexual intercourse

vengeance NOUN revenge
with a vengeance with great intensity

venison NOUN deer's flesh as food

Venn diagram NOUN Venn diagrams (in mathematics) a diagram in which circles are used to show the relationships between different sets of things

venom NOUN **1** the poisonous fluid produced by snakes, scorpions, etc. **2** strong bitterness or spitefulness
▷ **venomous** ADJECTIVE

vent NOUN vents an opening in something, especially to let out smoke or gas etc.
give vent to express your feelings openly

vent VERB vents, venting, vented **1** make a vent in something **2** give vent to feelings

ventilate VERB ventilates, ventilating, ventilated let air move freely in and out of a room etc.
▷ **ventilation** NOUN **ventilator** NOUN

ventriloquist NOUN ventriloquists an entertainer who makes his or her voice sound as if it comes from another source
▷ **ventriloquism** NOUN
[from Latin *venter* = abdomen + *loqui* = speak]

venture NOUN ventures something you decide to do that is risky

venture VERB ventures, venturing, ventured dare or be bold enough to do or say something or to go somewhere • *We ventured out into the snow.*

venturesome ADJECTIVE ready to take risks; daring

veracity (ver- **as**- it- ee) NOUN truth
▷ **veracious** (ver- **ay**- shus) ADJECTIVE

Thesaurus

islanders. ▶ fierce, passionate, forceful, impassioned, intense, ardent, eager, fervent, vigorous, violent, enthusiastic, animated, excited, heated, strong, powerful, urgent OPPOSITES ARE mild, apathetic

vehicle NOUN *Vehicles are not allowed in the town center.* ▶ motor vehicle, car, automobile, wheeled transport

vengeance NOUN *He swore vengeance when he was banished four years ago.* ▶ revenge, retribution, retaliation, reprisal

vengeful ADJECTIVE *He felt vengeful towards his attackers.* ▶ revengeful, unforgiving, spiteful, bitter, avenging, vindictive, rancorous AN OPPOSITE IS forgiving

venom NOUN **1** *Snake venom is usually clear yellow.* ▶ poison, toxin **2** *She was told to leave with such venom she recoiled.* ▶ malice, malevolence, rancor, ill-will, acrimony, animosity, bitterness, vitriol, virulence, hatred

venomous ADJECTIVE **1** *The only mammals with venomous bites are certain moles and shrews.*
▶ poisonous, toxic, noxious, deadly AN OPPOSITE IS harmless **2** *He wrote a venomous criticism of their work.* ▶ vicious, spiteful, malicious, malevolent, vindictive, baleful, vitriolic, rancorous AN OPPOSITE IS friendly

venture NOUN *This new venture holds great promise for the future.* ▶ enterprise, undertaking, project, scheme, endeavor, operation, adventure

venture VERB **1** *Harry ventured an opinion.*
▶ put forward, suggest, offer, dare, risk, chance **2** *We venture to ask you for your permission.* ▶ dare, presume, be so bold as to **3** *When darkness came he ventured out.*
▶ journey, set forth, proceed, dare to go, risk going

veranda NOUN **verandas** a terrace with a roof along the side of a house [via Hindi from Portuguese *varanda* = railing, balcony]

verb NOUN **verbs** a word that shows what a person or thing is doing, e.g., *bring, came, sing, were* [from Latin *verbum* = word]

verbal ADJECTIVE **1** to do with or in words; spoken, not written • *a verbal statement* **2** to do with verbs
▷ **verbally** ADVERB

verdict NOUN **verdicts** a judgment or decision made after considering something, especially that made by a jury

verge NOUN **verges** a strip of grass along the edge of a road or path
on the verge of very nearly doing something
• *I was on the verge of tears.*

verge VERB **verges, verging, verged**
verge on border on something; be close to something • *This puzzle verges on the impossible.*

veritable ADJECTIVE real; rightly named • *a veritable villain*
▷ **veritably** ADVERB

vermin PLURAL NOUN animals or insects that damage crops or food or carry disease, such as rats and fleas
▷ **verminous** ADJECTIVE

vernacular (ver- **nak**- yoo- ler) NOUN **vernaculars** the language of a country or district, as distinct from an official or formal language

versatile ADJECTIVE able to do or be used for many different things
▷ **versatility** NOUN

verse NOUN **verses 1** writing arranged in short lines, usually with a particular rhythm and often with rhymes; poetry **2** a group of lines forming a unit in a poem or song **3** each of the short numbered sections of a chapter in the Bible [via Old English from Latin *versus* = a line of writing]

version NOUN **versions 1** a particular person's account of something that happened **2** a translation • *modern versions of the Bible* **3** a special or different form of something • *the latest version of this car*

versus PREPOSITION against; competing with
• *The final was Germany versus Brazil.*

vertebra NOUN **vertebrae** each of the bones that form the backbone

vertebrate NOUN **vertebrates** an animal that has a backbone (The opposite is **invertebrate**)

vertical ADJECTIVE at right angles to something horizontal; upright
▷ **vertically** ADVERB

vertigo NOUN a feeling of dizziness and loss of balance, especially when you are very high up

verve NOUN enthusiasm and liveliness

very ADVERB **1** to a great amount or intensity; extremely • *It was very cold.* **2** (used to emphasize something) • *on the very next day* • *the very last drop*

Thesaurus

verbal ADJECTIVE *A verbal exchange was recorded between two people.* ▶ spoken, oral, word-of-mouth, unwritten AN OPPOSITE IS written

verbose ADJECTIVE *Parts of the speech were repetitive and verbose.* ▶ wordy, loquacious, diffuse, effusive, garrulous, talkative, long-winded, rambling AN OPPOSITE IS succinct

verdict NOUN *The verdict was suicide, but many people thought he was murdered.* ▶ judgment, decision, finding, ruling, adjudication, assessment, conclusion, opinion

verge NOUN **1** *Cars were parked on the grass verge.* ▶ edge, bank, kerb, margin, border, roadside, shoulder, side, wayside **2** *The country was on the verge of bankruptcy.* ▶ brink, point, threshold

verge VERB verge on *By this time the urgency verged on desperation.* ▶ border on, tend toward, approach, come close to

verify VERB *There was no one around to verify what happened.* ▶ prove, support, confirm, substantiate, establish, uphold, show the truth of, validate, authenticate, corroborate, check out, ascertain AN OPPOSITE IS refute

versatile ADJECTIVE **1** *She was a gifted and versatile teacher.* ▶ adaptable, many-sided, all-around, flexible, resourceful, talented, skilful **2** *The property offers spacious and versatile accommodation.* ▶ flexible, adaptable, modifiable, all-purpose AN OPPOSITE IS restricted

verse NOUN *a story written in verse* ▶ rhyme, lines, lyrics, metre, stanza

version NOUN **1** *Would you like to tell us your version of the story?* ▶ account, record, explanation, interpretation, rendering **2** *a new version of the machine* ▶ form, type, model, design

vertical ADJECTIVE **1** *Pull the lever back to its vertical position.* ▶ upright, perpendicular, standing, erect AN OPPOSITE IS horizontal **2** *The passageway ended with a vertical drop into darkness.* ▶ sheer, steep, precipitous

very ADVERB *He felt very ashamed.* ▶ extremely, highly, deeply, exceedingly, acutely, truly, (more informal) terribly AN OPPOSITE IS slightly

very ADJECTIVE **1** *The key on the floor was the very one he had lost the week before. Those were her very words.* ▶ actual, same, selfsame, identical, exact, precise **2** *The very thought of it made him tremble.* ▶ mere, sheer, simple

a b c d e f g h i j k l m n o p q r s t u **v** w x y z

A
B
C
D
E
F
G
H
I
J
K
L
M
N
O
P
Q
R
S
T
U
V
W
X
Y
Z

very ADJECTIVE **1** exact or actual • *It's the very thing we need.* **2** extreme • *at the very end*

vessel NOUN **vessels 1** a ship or boat **2** a container, especially for liquid **3** a tube carrying blood or other liquid in the body of an animal or plant

vest NOUN **vests** an article of clothing covering the trunk of the body

vest VERB **vests, vesting, vested 1** give something as a right • *The power to make laws is vested in Congress.* **2** (old use) clothe

vested interest NOUN **vested interests** a strong reason for wanting something to happen, usually because you will benefit from it

vet NOUN **vets** a person trained to give medical and surgical treatment to animals

vet VERB **vets, vetting, vetted** make a careful check of a person or thing, especially of someone's background before employing them

veteran NOUN **veterans** a person who has long experience, especially in the armed forces

veterinary (vet- rin- ree) ADJECTIVE to do with the medical and surgical treatment of animals • *a veterinary surgeon*

veto (vee- toh) NOUN **vetoes 1** a refusal to let something happen **2** the right to prohibit something

veto VERB **vetoes, vetoing, vetoed** refuse or prohibit something [from Latin, = I forbid]

vex VERB **vexes, vexing, vexed** annoy; cause somebody worry
▷ **vexation** NOUN **vexatious** ADJECTIVE

VHF ABBREVIATION very high frequency

via (vy- a) PREPOSITION through; by way of • *The train goes from New York to Washington via Philadelphia.* [from Latin, = by way of]

viable ADJECTIVE able to work or exist successfully • *a viable plan*
▷ **viability** NOUN

viaduct NOUN **viaducts** a long bridge, usually with many arches, carrying a road or railway over a valley or low ground [from Latin *via* = road + *ducere* = to lead]

vibrant ADJECTIVE full of energy; lively

vibrate VERB **vibrates, vibrating, vibrated 1** shake very quickly back and forth **2** make a throbbing sound
▷ **vibration** NOUN

vicar NOUN **vicars** a member of the Church of England clergy who is in charge of a parish

Thesaurus

vessel NOUN **1** *Pour the liquid into a sterile vessel.* ► container, receptacle, flask, bottle, jar, jug, holder **2** *Small vessels were bobbing about in the harbor.* ► craft, boat, ship USAGE Note that *craft* can be singular or plural (e.g. *a small craft was bobbing about* or *small craft were bobbing about*).

vet VERB *Peter vetted all the outfits and knew exactly what would suit Tara.* ► inspect, examine, screen, assess, evaluate, appraise, scrutinize, investigate, check out

veteran ADJECTIVE *He handled it all like a veteran superstar.* ► established, seasoned, mature, hardened, master, expert

veto NOUN *He had in effect acquired a right of veto over all sales of land.* ► rejection, refusal, embargo, prohibition, ban, (more informal) thumbs down AN OPPOSITE IS approval

veto VERB *The government had vetoed the proposal in late July.* ► reject, turn down, overrule, rule out, throw out, disallow, refuse, dismiss, ban, bar, blackball, forbid, prohibit, say no to, vote against AN OPPOSITE IS approve

vex VERB *His remarks had vexed her deeply.* ► annoy, irritate, displease, anger, infuriate, enrage, exasperate, incense, madden, aggravate, nettle, antagonize, inflame, make angry, (more informal) needle, (more informal)

rile, (more informal) bug, (more informal) rub up the wrong way OPPOSITES ARE please, gratify

vexed ADJECTIVE **1** *She was still vexed with me for bringing Frankie.* ► annoyed, irritated, angry, cross, displeased, peeved, infuriated, incensed, enraged, (more informal) miffed, (more informal) put out AN OPPOSITE IS pleased **2** *The note was about the vexed question of sexism.* ► controversial, difficult, contentious, disputed, thorny, knotty

vibrant ADJECTIVE **1** *Green plants provide splashes of vibrant color.* ► bright, vivid, brilliant, intense, striking OPPOSITES ARE dull, pale **2** *She made the most of her cheerful and vibrant personality.* ► vivacious, spirited, dynamic, alert, alive, energetic, electric OPPOSITES ARE restrained, reserved

vibrate VERB **1** *The room was vibrating from the sounds of rock music.* ► reverberate, throb, pulsate, resonate, resound, thud, ring, boom **2** *The machinery began to vibrate alarmingly.* ► tremble, shake, shudder, quiver, oscillate, rattle, shiver, wobble, quake

vibration NOUN *The special smoke detector produces vibration as well as flashing light.* ► reverberation, oscillation, pulsation, throbbing, trembling, quivering, rattling, shaking, shivering, shuddering, tremor, wobbling

vice[1] NOUN **vices** **1** evil or wickedness **2** an evil or bad habit; a bad fault

vice[2] NOUN **vices** a device for gripping something and holding it firmly while you work on it

vice versa ADVERB the other way around
• *Which do you prefer-blue spots on a yellow background or vice versa?* [from Latin, = the position being turned around]

vicinity NOUN the area near or around a place
• *Is there a newsagent in the vicinity?* [from Latin *vicinus* = neighboring, a neighbor]

vicious ADJECTIVE **1** cruel and aggressive **2** severe or violent
▷ **viciously** ADVERB **viciousness** NOUN

vicious circle NOUN **vicious circles** a situation in which a problem produces an effect which in turn makes the problem worse

victim NOUN **victims** someone who is injured, killed, robbed, etc.

victimize VERB **victimizes, victimizing, victimized** single someone out for cruel or unfair treatment
▷ **victimization** NOUN

victor NOUN **victors** the winner

Victorian ADJECTIVE belonging to the time of Queen Victoria (1837–1901)
▷ **Victorian** NOUN

victory NOUN **victories** success won against an opponent in a battle, contest, or game
▷ **victorious** ADJECTIVE

video NOUN **videos** **1** the recording on tape of pictures and sound **2** a video recorder or cassette **3** a television program or a film recorded on a video cassette

video VERB **videos, videoing, videoed** record something on videotape [from Latin, = I see]

video cassette recorder NOUN **video cassette recorders** a device for recording television programmes on videotape and for playing video cassettes

videotape NOUN **videotapes** magnetic tape suitable for recording television programs

vie VERB **vies, vying, vied** compete; carry on a rivalry • *vying with each other*

view NOUN **views** **1** what can be seen from one place, e.g., beautiful scenery **2** sight; range of vision • *The ship sailed into view.* **3** an opinion • *She has strong views about politics.*
in view of because of
on view displayed for inspection
with a view to with the hope or intention of

Thesaurus

---

vice NOUN **1** *They are determined to put an end to vice and prostitution.* ▶ immorality, depravity, corruption, wickedness, wrongdoing, degeneracy, evil-doing, evil, sin, (*more formal*) venality, (*more formal*) iniquity AN OPPOSITE IS virtue **2** *Cowardice isn't the worst vice.* ▶ failing, fault, weakness, shortcoming, bad habit, blemish, defect, deficiency, imperfection OPPOSITES ARE virtue, strength

vicinity NOUN *There are several castles and abbeys in the vicinity.* ▶ neighborhood, area, district, locality, region, locale, environs, outskirts, proximity

vicious ADJECTIVE **1** *He was finally captured in the vicious street fighting in Berlin in 1945.* ▶ brutal, savage, fierce, ferocious, wild, barbaric OPPOSITES ARE gentle, humane **2** *He hadn't the vicious streak that showed in his brother.* ▶ cruel, malicious, spiteful, malevolent, vindictive, sadistic, brutish, callous, heartless, cold-blooded, aggressive, pitiless, ruthless, merciless, inhuman, vile OPPOSITES ARE kind, benevolent

victim NOUN **1** *It's thought she was the victim of a random attack by a thief. He is the third victim of this tough new policy.* ▶ target, casualty, sufferer, injury, fatality, scapegoat USAGE You use *fatality* about someone who has died as a result of an incident. **2** *At their feet, a white-clad sacrificial victim, was the body.* ▶ offering, martyr, prey, sacrifice

victimize VERB *The company had been victimizing workers for reporting safety concerns.* ▶ discriminate against, persecute, intimidate, oppress, mistreat, harass, treat unfairly, bully, terrorize, torment, (*more informal*) pick on

victorious ADJECTIVE *He emerged victorious in the second round of voting.* ▶ triumphant, successful, first, top, winning, leading, prevailing, undefeated, unbeaten OPPOSITES ARE defeated, unsuccessful

victory NOUN *Her well-deserved victory in this year's Olympics was a boost for the American team.* ▶ win, success, triumph, conquest, knockout, mastery, superiority, achievement, (*more informal*) walkover AN OPPOSITE IS defeat

view NOUN **1** *From the top floor you get a magnificent view across the city.* ▶ outlook, prospect, panorama, perspective, vista, scene, aspect, picture, landscape, scenery, spectacle **2** *She caught a brief view of her top half in the mirror.* ▶ look, sight, glance, peek, vision **3** *Luke came into view.* ▶ sight, vision, range of vision, perspective **4** *He declined to give any official view of the situation.* ▶ opinion, viewpoint, point of view, belief, judgement, notion, perception, idea, thought, attitude, conviction
in view of *In view of the length of time since the incident, no action was taken.* ▶ because of, on account of, considering, as a result of, as a consequence of, owing to, due to

A
B
C
D
E
F
G
H
I
J
K
L
M
N
O
P
Q
R
S
T
U
V
W
X
Y
Z

view VERB views, viewing, viewed **1** look at something **2** consider or regard • *He viewed us with suspicion.*
▷ **viewer** NOUN

viewpoint NOUN viewpoints an opinion or point of view

vigorous ADJECTIVE full of strength and energy
▷ **vigorously** ADVERB

Viking NOUN Vikings a Scandinavian trader and pirate in the 8th–10th centuries [from Old Norse]

vile ADJECTIVE **1** extremely disgusting **2** very bad or wicked
▷ **vilely** ADVERB **vileness** NOUN

villa NOUN villas a house, especially a vacation home abroad [from Latin, = country house]

village NOUN villages a group of houses and other buildings in a country district, smaller than a town and usually having a church
▷ **villager** NOUN
[from early French; related to **villa**]

villain NOUN villains a wicked person or a criminal
▷ **villainous** ADJECTIVE **villainy** NOUN

vindicate VERB vindicates, vindicating, vindicated **1** clear a person of blame or suspicion **2** prove something to be true or worthwhile
▷ **vindication** NOUN

vine NOUN vines a climbing or trailing plant whose fruit is the grape

vinegar NOUN a sour liquid used to flavor food or in pickling

vintage NOUN vintages **1** the harvest of a season's grapes; the wine made from this **2** the period from which something comes

vintage car NOUN vintage cars an old car, a classic

viola (vee- oh- la) NOUN violas a musical instrument like a violin but slightly larger and with a lower pitch

violate VERB violates, violating, violated **1** break a promise, law, or treaty, etc. **2** treat a person or place with disrespect and violence
▷ **violation** NOUN **violator** NOUN

Thesaurus

---

view VERB **1** *He set out at ten and viewed as many houses as possible. A drop from a pond, viewed through a microscope, swarms with tiny organisms.* ► look at, inspect, survey, examine, observe, behold, eye, scan, gaze at, stare at **2** *She viewed him with dislike.* ► regard, contemplate, consider, perceive, behold **3** *Some of the guests were viewing a television programme.* ► watch, look at, see

vigilant ADJECTIVE *Everyone should be vigilant and report anything of a suspicious nature.* ► watchful, observant, alert, attentive, awake, on the lookout, on your guard, on the watch, sharp-eyed, eagle-eyed, careful, wide-awake, (*more informal*) on your toes AN OPPOSITE IS negligent

vigorous ADJECTIVE **1** *Regular vigorous exercise can help to reduce blood pressure.* ► strenuous, energetic, animated, brisk, full-blooded AN OPPOSITE IS feeble **2** *The child is strong and vigorous.* ► healthy, in good health, energetic, vivacious, active, lively, lusty, virile, vital **3** *He made a vigorous case for controlling the money supply.* ► strong, spirited, forceful, effective, robust, energetic, dynamic, active

vigor NOUN **1** *Jeffrey supported his wife's cause with vigor.* ► energy, force, forcefulness, spirit, vitality, gusto, verve, animation, dynamism **2** *He recovered from the illness with renewed vigor.* ► energy, fitness, vitality, stamina, robustness, life, strength, health, resilience, potency

vile ADJECTIVE **1** *It's ironic that such a fine building should house so vile an organization.* ► wicked, evil, foul, contemptible, despicable,

obnoxious, shameful, abhorrent, repellent, loathsome AN OPPOSITE IS pleasant **2** *I drank three cups of vile, greyish coffee.* ► nasty, horrible, foul, unpleasant, disgusting, revolting, repulsive, repellent, dreadful, terrible AN OPPOSITE IS pleasant **3** *The vile weather had emptied the streets.* ► unpleasant, bad, foul, disagreeable, inclement AN OPPOSITE IS fine

villain NOUN *Did not two of history's greatest villains come from beautiful surroundings?* ► wrongdoer, evildoer, rogue, scoundrel, criminal, reprobate, (*more formal*) malefactor, (*more formal*) miscreant

vindicate VERB **1** *He left claiming that history would vindicate him.* ► clear, exonerate, absolve, acquit, excuse, endorse, support, rehabilitate OPPOSITES ARE blame, censure **2** *She was desperate to vindicate her decision to be an artist.* ► justify, uphold, defend, sustain, maintain, assert AN OPPOSITE IS compromise

violate VERB **1** *Uses of these weapons against civilian targets violate international law.* ► breach, break, contravene, infringe, transgress, flout, defy, disobey, disregard, ignore AN OPPOSITE IS comply with **2** *Several of the royal tombs had been violated.* ► desecrate, defile, vandalize, deface **3** *I did not like having my privacy violated.* ► invade, disturb, encroach on, interfere with, abuse AN OPPOSITE IS respect **4** *He set out to trap and violate women.* ► rape, abuse, indecently assault, sexually assault, molest, interfere with

746

violence NOUN **1** physical force that does harm or damage **2** strength or intensity ● *the violence of the storm*
▷ **violent** ADJECTIVE **violently** ADVERB

violet NOUN **violets 1** a small plant with purple or blue flowers **2** purple

violin NOUN **violins** a musical instrument with four strings, played with a bow
▷ **violinist** NOUN
[from Italian *violino* = small viola]

viper NOUN **vipers** a small poisonous snake

virgin NOUN **virgins** a person, especially a girl or woman, who has never had sexual intercourse
▷ **virginal** ADJECTIVE **virginity** NOUN

virgin ADJECTIVE not yet touched or used
● *virgin snow*

virtual ADJECTIVE being something in effect though not strictly in fact ● *His silence was a virtual admission of guilt.*

virtually ADVERB nearly or almost

virtual reality NOUN a computer image or environment that is so realistic it appears to be real

virtue NOUN **virtues 1** moral goodness, or a particular form of this ● *Honesty is a virtue.* **2** a good quality or advantage ● *Jamie's plan has the virtue of simplicity.*
▷ **virtuous** ADJECTIVE **virtuously** ADVERB
by virtue of because of

virtuoso (ver- tew- oh- soh) NOUN **virtuosos** or **virtuosi** a person with outstanding skill, especially in singing or playing music
▷ **virtuosity** NOUN
[from Italian, = skilful]

virus NOUN **viruses 1** a very tiny living thing, smaller than a bacterium, that can cause disease **2** a disease caused by a virus **3** a hidden set of instructions in a computer program that is designed to destroy data

visa (vee- za) NOUN **visas** an official mark put on someone's passport by officials of a foreign country to show that the holder has permission to enter that country

viscount (vy- kownt) NOUN **viscounts** a nobleman ranking below an earl and above a baron
▷ **viscountess** NOUN

visibility NOUN the distance you can see clearly ● *Visibility is down to 20 meters.*

visible ADJECTIVE able to be seen or noticed
● *The ship was visible on the horizon.*
▷ **visibly** ADVERB
USAGE Do not confuse with **visual**.

vision NOUN **visions 1** the ability to see; sight **2** something seen in a person's imagination or in a dream **3** foresight and wisdom in planning things **4** a person or thing that is beautiful to see

visionary ADJECTIVE extremely imaginative or fanciful

Thesaurus

violation NOUN *the violation of human rights throughout the world* ► contravention, breach, infringement, flouting, defiance, transgression, offence (against)

violence NOUN **1** *A whole generation had been brought up in violence.* ► brutality, brute force, savagery, cruelty, barbarity, destructiveness **2** *The violence of the blow made him reel.* ► force, forcefulness, strength, power, might, ferocity

violent ADJECTIVE **1** *There were violent clashes between police and demonstrators.* ► brutal, vicious, rough, aggressive, forceful AN OPPOSITE IS mild **2** *Too often violent criminals do not get sent to prison as they should.* ► rough, brutal, wild, fierce, vicious, aggressive, bloodthirsty, headstrong AN OPPOSITE IS gentle **3** *He felt a rush of violent jealousy.* ► intense, extreme, acute, forceful, devastating AN OPPOSITE IS weak

virtually ADVERB *Once on, paint is virtually impossible to remove.* ► effectively, in effect, practically, as good as, almost

virtue NOUN **1** *the virtue of a simple life* ► goodness, righteousness, virtuousness, rectitude, integrity, honesty, dignity, uprightness, worthiness, decency, morality,

honor, nobility, principle, rectitude AN OPPOSITE IS iniquity **2** *I can see no virtue in such an arrangement.* ► merit, advantage, benefit, point AN OPPOSITE IS disadvantage **3** *Punctuality is not one of her virtues.* ► strength, quality, good point, redeeming feature OPPOSITES ARE failing, weakness

virtuous ADJECTIVE *Sam's virtuous and superior tone was beginning to irritate him.* ► moral, righteous, upright, worthy, honorable, exemplary, high-minded, right-minded, high-principled OPPOSITES ARE wicked, sinful

visible ADJECTIVE *There is no visible pattern in the paper. Kim received the news without any visible signs of emotion.* ► noticeable, perceptible, discernible, obvious, apparent, conspicuous, recognizable, evident, manifest, clear, detectable, distinct AN OPPOSITE IS invisible

vision NOUN **1** *Symptoms include blurred vision and sensitivity to bright lights.* ► eyesight, sight, seeing **2** *The Great Society remained more a vision than a reality.* ► ideal, fantasy, apparition, illusion, mirage, phantasm, daydream, delusion, ghost, hallucination, phantom, specter **3** *The plan made sense but lacked vision.* ► foresight, farsightedness, insight, imagination

A
B
C
D
E
F
G
H
I
J
K
L
M
N
O
P
Q
R
S
T
U
V
W
X
Y
Z

visionary NOUN visionaries a person with extremely imaginative ideas and plans

visit VERB visits, visiting, visited 1 go to see a person or place 2 stay somewhere for a while
▷ **visitor** NOUN

visit NOUN visits 1 going to see a person or place 2 a short stay somewhere

vista NOUN vistas a pleasing view [from Italian, = view]

visual ADJECTIVE to do with or used in seeing; to do with sight
▷ **visually** ADVERB
USAGE Do not confuse with **visible**.

visual aid NOUN visual aids a picture, slide, film, etc. used as an aid in teaching

visual display unit NOUN visual display units a device that looks like a television screen and displays data being received from a computer or fed into it

visualize VERB visualizes, visualizing, visualized form a mental picture of something
▷ **visualization** NOUN

vital ADJECTIVE 1 connected with life; necessary for life to continue • *vital functions such as breathing* 2 essential; very important
▷ **vitally** ADVERB

vitality NOUN liveliness or energy

vitamin (vit- a- min vy- ta- min) NOUN vitamins any of a number of substances that are present in various foods and are essential to keep people and animals healthy

vivacious (viv- ay- shus) ADJECTIVE happy and lively
▷ **vivaciously** ADVERB **vivacity** NOUN

vivid ADJECTIVE 1 bright and strong or clear • *vivid colors* • *a vivid description* 2 active and lively • *her vivid imagination*
▷ **vividly** ADVERB **vividness** NOUN

vivisection NOUN doing surgical experiments on live animals

vixen NOUN vixens a female fox [from Old English]

vocabulary NOUN vocabularies 1 all the words used in a particular subject or language, or that an individual person uses 2 a list of words with their meanings

vocal cords PLURAL NOUN two straplike membranes in the throat that can be made to vibrate and produce sounds

vocalist NOUN vocalists a singer, especially in a pop group

vocation NOUN vocations 1 a person's job or occupation 2 a strong desire to do a particular kind of work, or a feeling of being called by God to do something

vocational ADJECTIVE teaching you the skills you need for a particular job or profession • *vocational training*

vodka NOUN vodkas a strong alcoholic drink very popular in Russia

vogue NOUN vogues the current fashion • *Very short hair for women seems to be the vogue.*
in vogue in fashion • *Striped dresses are definitely in vogue.*

Thesaurus

visit NOUN 1 *Mrs. Carr paid her final visit to the place.* ► call, stay 2 *It was their first visit to Rome.* ► trip, outing, excursion, day out

visit VERB 1 *He was ten years old when he first started visiting the old woman.* ► call on, come to see, make a visit to, pay a call on, stay with, descend on, (*more informal*) drop in on, go to see, (*more informal*) look up 2 *The chairman of the airline recently visited Moscow.* ► travel to, make a trip to, spend time in, stay in

visitor NOUN 1 *Edward was a frequent and welcome visitor.* ► guest, caller 2 *The site will attract visitors during the festival.* ► tourist, sightseer, tripper, globetrotter

visualize VERB *I like to visualize the mood of the song and take it from there.* ► picture, imagine, envisage, conceive, dream up

vital ADJECTIVE 1 *It's vital to keep momentum going. The college is expected to play a vital role in promoting these languages.* ► essential, crucial, fundamental, imperative, important, necessary, indispensable OPPOSITES ARE unimportant, inessential 2 *He was a vital force in pop music.* ► dynamic, lively, energetic, vibrant, vigorous, vivacious, life-giving,

invigorating, exuberant, sparkling, spirited, animated, sprightly, zestful AN OPPOSITE IS lifeless

vitality NOUN *For all her vitality, Faye was only five feet four inches tall.* ► energy, vivacity, vigour, spirit, gusto, verve, dynamism, exuberance, zest, (*more informal*) go AN OPPOSITE IS lethargy

vivid ADJECTIVE 1 *a bouquet with four vivid blue flowers* ► bright, brilliant, colorful, vibrant, showy, striking, gaudy AN OPPOSITE IS dull 2 *Wilson's autobiography gives a vivid account of his experiences.* ► clear, graphic, dramatic, lively, powerful, evocative, lucid, memorable, imaginative, lifelike, realistic AN OPPOSITE IS lifeless

vocal ADJECTIVE 1 *animals capable of vocal sounds* ► voiced, spoken, oral, said, articulated 2 *The students were becoming the most vocal critics of reform.* ► outspoken, vociferous, forthright, plainspoken, candid

vogue NOUN *Small-scale farming is enjoying a new vogue.* ► fashion, mode, trend, style, craze, rage, taste

voice NOUN **voices 1** sounds formed by the vocal cords and uttered by the mouth, especially in speaking, singing, etc. **2** the ability to speak or sing • *She has lost her voice.* **3** someone expressing a particular opinion about something • *Emma's the only dissenting voice.* **4** the right to express an opinion or desire • *I have no voice in this matter.* [via early French *vois* from Latin *vox*]

void ADJECTIVE **1** empty **2** having no legal validity

void NOUN **voids** an empty space or hole

volatile (vol- a- tyl) ADJECTIVE **1** evaporating quickly • *a volatile liquid* **2** changing quickly from one mood or interest to another
▷ **volatility** NOUN

volcano NOUN **volcanoes** a mountain or hill with an opening at the top from which lava, ashes, and hot gases from below the earth's crust are or have been thrown out
▷ **volcanic** ADJECTIVE

vole NOUN **voles** a small animal like a mouse [from Norwegian *vollmus* = field mouse]

volley NOUN **volleys 1** a number of bullets or shells etc. fired at the same time **2** hitting back the ball in tennis, etc., before it touches the ground

volley VERB **volleys, volleying, volleyed** send or hit something in a volley or volleys

volt NOUN **volts** a unit for measuring electric force

voltage NOUN **voltages** electric force measured in volts

volume NOUN **volumes 1** the amount of space filled by something **2** an amount or quantity • *The volume of work has increased.* **3** the

strength or power of sound **4** a book, especially one of a set [from Latin *volumen* = a roll (because ancient books were made in the form of rolled parchment)]

voluntary ADJECTIVE **1** done or doing something willingly, not because you are forced to do it **2** unpaid • *voluntary work*
▷ **voluntarily** ADVERB

voluntary NOUN **voluntaries** an organ solo, often improvised, played before or after a church service

volunteer VERB **volunteers, volunteering, volunteered** give or offer something of your own accord, without being asked or forced to

volunteer NOUN **volunteers** a person who volunteers to do something, e.g., to serve in the armed forces

vomit VERB **vomits, vomiting, vomited** bring up food from the stomach and out through the mouth; be sick
▷ **vomit** NOUN

voodoo NOUN a form of witchcraft and magical rites, especially in the West Indies [from a West African language]

vote VERB **votes, voting, voted** show which person or thing you prefer by putting up your hand, making a mark on a paper, etc.
▷ **voter** NOUN

vote NOUN **votes 1** the action of voting **2** the right to vote

vouch VERB **vouches, vouching, vouched vouch for** guarantee that something is true or certain • *I will vouch for his honesty.*

voucher NOUN **vouchers** a piece of paper that can be exchanged for certain goods or services; a receipt

Thesaurus

in vogue *Suddenly it was in vogue to have an all-over tan.* ► fashionable, in fashion, stylish, modish, smart, chic, (*more informal*) trendy, (*more informal*) all the rage, (*more informal*) cool, (*more informal*) hip

voice NOUN **1** *There was no emotion in his voice.* ► speaking, speech, utterance, tone, inflection **2** *They were able to have a voice in choosing the chairman.* ► opinion, view, say, input, vote

voluntary ADJECTIVE **1** *Voluntary work tends to carry higher prestige than paid work.* ► optional, unpaid, willing AN OPPOSITE IS paid **2** *The pay cuts will be voluntary.* ► optional, discretionary, unforced OPPOSITES ARE obligatory, compulsory **3** *Her decision had been a voluntary act.* ► deliberate, conscious, intentional, intended, willful AN OPPOSITE IS involuntary USAGE Note that *involuntary* is an opposite of *voluntary* only in the third meaning.

volunteer VERB *Having promised his help, he had better volunteer at least.* ► offer your

services, present yourself, step forward, make an offer, propose yourself, show willing

vomit VERB *He rushed towards the bathroom before the urge to vomit overcame him.* ► be sick, regurgitate, retch, heave, bring up, spew up, (*more informal*) throw up, (*more informal*) puke

vote NOUN *People suspected the vote of being rigged.* ► ballot, poll, election, plebiscite, referendum, show of hands

vote VERB **1** *Less than a third of the electorate voted in the last election.* ► cast a vote, go to the polls, ballot **2** *I vote we play another round.* ► suggest, propose, recommend, move
vote for *You may vote for one candidate only.* ► choose, pick, select, opt for, nominate

vouch VERB **vouch for** *I can vouch for the accuracy of these figures.* ► guarantee, verify, affirm, attest to, testify to, corroborate, endorse, confirm, support, speak for

voucher NOUN *You get a wallet of vouchers to pay for the various parts of your trip.* ► coupon, ticket, token, certificate

vow NOUN vows a solemn promise, especially to God or a saint

vow VERB vows, vowing, vowed make a vow

vowel NOUN vowels any of the letters *a, e, i, o, u,* and sometimes *y,* which represent sounds in which breath comes out freely COMPARE consonant

voyage NOUN voyages a long journey on water or in space

voyage VERB voyages, voyaging, voyaged make a voyage
▷ **voyager** NOUN

vulgar ADJECTIVE rude; without good manners
▷ **vulgarly** ADVERB **vulgarity** NOUN
[from Latin *vulgus* = the common or ordinary people]

vulnerable ADJECTIVE able to be hurt or harmed or attacked
▷ **vulnerability** NOUN
[from Latin *vulnus* = wound]

vulture NOUN vultures a large bird that feeds on dead animals

vulva NOUN vulvas the outer parts of the female genitals

vying present participle of vie

Thesaurus

---

vow NOUN *The monks take a vow of silence.*
▶ pledge, oath, promise, commitment, avowal, assurance, guarantee, undertaking, word of honor

vow VERB *She vowed to do better.* ▶ promise, pledge, swear, take an oath, give an assurance, give your word, guarantee

voyage NOUN *The voyage lasted two weeks.*
▶ journey, passage, crossing, trip, expedition, excursion

vulgar ADJECTIVE **1** *She sent him a postcard with a vulgar picture on the back.* ▶ rude, indecent, lewd, suggestive, racy, risqué **2** *The decor was new and vulgar.* ▶ tasteless, gaudy, garish,

tawdry, flashy, (*more informal*) tacky **3** *He was a bit too vulgar for her taste. It was considered vulgar to smoke in public.* ▶ ill-mannered, unrefined, unseemly, impolite, indecorous, coarse, ill-bred

vulnerable ADJECTIVE **1** *We are most vulnerable when we are asleep.* ▶ defenseless, exposed, unguarded, unprotected, at risk, weak, wide open AN OPPOSITE IS invulnerable
2 vulnerable to *More people are vulnerable to age discrimination.* ▶ in danger of, at risk of, exposed to, open to, liable to, prone to, susceptible to AN OPPOSITE IS immune to

Ww

W. ABBREVIATION **1** west **2** western

wad (wod) NOUN **wads** a pad or bundle of soft material or banknotes, papers, etc. [from Dutch]

waddle VERB **waddles, waddling, waddled** walk with short steps, swaying from side to side, as a duck does
▷ **waddle** NOUN

wade VERB **wades, wading, waded** walk through water or mud, etc.
▷ **wader** NOUN
[from Old English]

wafer NOUN **wafers** a kind of thin cracker [from early French]

waffle[1] (wof- el) NOUN **waffles** a small cake made of batter and eaten hot [from Dutch]

waffle[2] (wof- el) NOUN (informal) vague wordy talk or writing
▷ **waffle** VERB
[from a dialect word waff = to bark or yelp]

waft (woft) VERB **wafts, wafting, wafted** carry or float gently through the air or over water [originally = escort a ship: from early German or Dutch]

wag VERB **wags, wagging, wagged** move quickly back and forth • a dog wagging its tail
▷ **wag** NOUN
[from Old English]

wag NOUN **wags** a person who makes jokes [from an old word waghalter = someone likely to be hanged]

wage NOUN or **wages** PLURAL NOUN a regular payment to someone in return for his or her work

wage VERB **wages, waging, waged** carry on a war or campaign

wager (way- jer) NOUN **wagers** a bet
▷ **wager** VERB

waggle VERB **waggles, waggling, waggled** move quickly back and forth
▷ **waggle** NOUN

wagon NOUN **wagons 1** a cart with four wheels, pulled by a horse or an ox **2** an open railway car, e.g., for coal

waif NOUN **waifs** a homeless and helpless person, especially a child

wail VERB **wails, wailing, wailed** make a long sad cry
▷ **wail** NOUN

wainscot or **wainscoting** NOUN wooden paneling on the wall of a room near the floor

waist NOUN **waists** the narrow part in the middle of your body
USAGE Do not confuse with **waste**.

waistcoat NOUN **waistcoats** a short close-fitting jacket without sleeves, worn over a shirt and under a jacket; a vest

waistline NOUN **waistlines** the amount you measure around your waist, which indicates how fat or thin you are

wait VERB **waits, waiting, waited 1** stay somewhere or postpone an action until something happens; pause **2** be left to be dealt with later • This question must wait until next week. **3** wait on people
wait on 1 hand food and drink to people at a meal **2** be an attendant to someone

wait NOUN an act or time of waiting • We had a long wait for the train.

Thesaurus

wad NOUN **1** He took a wad of bills from his pocket and began to count them. ► bundle, roll, pad, (more informal) wodge **2** I needed a wad of cotton. ► lump, mass, chunk, hunk

wadding NOUN sleeping bags insulated with wadding ► padding, lining, packing, filling, stuffing

waffle NOUN (informal) My panic reduced the interview to waffle. ► blather, prattle, nonsense, verbosity, wordiness, evasiveness, padding, prevarication

waffle VERB (informal) She waffled on for a while about things that didn't matter. ► blather, prattle, ramble, babble, chatter on, gabble

wag VERB **1** The dog's tail began to wag frantically. ► shake, swing, wave, waggle **2** "You see what I mean," Eleanor said, wagging her finger. ► wave, shake, waggle, brandish

wage VERB The country lacks any means to wage war. ► carry on, conduct, engage in, fight, undertake

wages PLURAL NOUN He was pleased to be earning regular wages at last. ► earnings, income, pay , recompense

wail VERB He was tearing at his hair and wailing "Why me?" ► howl, bawl, weep, moan, sob, shriek, whimper, snivel, cry, lament, yowl

wail NOUN Tom let out a wail. ► howl, bawl, moan, sob, shriek, cry, whimper, yowl

wait NOUN The photos were ready after a short wait. ► interval, pause, delay, holdup, break, hiatus, halt, hesitation, rest, stay

wait VERB She left the room and waited outside. I can't wait for you any longer. ► remain, rest, linger, stay, stop, halt, delay, mark time, stand by, hold back, pause, hesitate, (old-fashioned) tarry, (more informal) hang about AN OPPOSITE IS proceed

a
b
c
d
e
f
g
h
i
j
k
l
m
n
o
p
q
r
s
t
u
v
w
x
y
z

A
B
C
D
E
F
G
H
I
J
K
L
M
N
O
P
Q
R
S
T
U
V
W
X
Y
Z

waiter NOUN waiters a man who serves people with food and drink in a restaurant

waiting list NOUN waiting lists a list of people waiting for something to become available

waiting room NOUN waiting rooms a room provided for people who are waiting for something

waitress NOUN waitresses a woman who serves people with food and drink in a restaurant

wake VERB wakes, waking, woke, woken **1** stop sleeping • *I woke when I heard the bell.* **2** make someone stop sleeping • *You have woken the baby.*

wake[1] NOUN wakes (in Ireland) a party held after a funeral [from Old English]

wake[2] NOUN wakes **1** the track left on the water by a moving ship **2** currents of air left behind a moving aircraft
in the wake of following or coming after [probably from an Old Norse word = opening in the ice (made by a ship)]

wakeful ADJECTIVE unable to sleep

waken VERB wakens, wakening, wakened wake

walk VERB walks, walking, walked move along on your feet at an ordinary speed
▷ **walker** NOUN

walk NOUN walks **1** a journey on foot **2** the manner of walking **3** a path or route for walking

walking stick NOUN walking sticks a stick used as a support while walking

walk of life NOUN walks of life a person's occupation or social position

walkover NOUN walkovers an easy victory

wall NOUN walls **1** a continuous upright structure, usually made of brick, stone, or wood, forming one of the sides of a building or room or supporting something or enclosing an area **2** the outside part of something • *the stomach wall*

wall VERB walls, walling, walled enclose or block something with a wall • *a walled garden*

wallet NOUN wallets a small flat folding case for holding cash, credit cards, documents, etc.

wallflower NOUN wallflowers a garden plant with fragrant flowers, blooming in spring

wallop VERB wallops, walloping, walloped (*informal*) hit or beat someone
▷ **wallop** NOUN

wallow VERB wallows, wallowing, wallowed **1** roll around in water, mud, etc. **2** get great pleasure by being surrounded by something • *a week wallowing in luxury*
▷ **wallow** NOUN
[from Old English]

wallpaper NOUN wallpapers paper used to cover the inside walls of rooms

walnut NOUN walnuts **1** an edible nut with a wrinkled surface **2** the wood from the tree that bears this nut, used for making furniture

walrus NOUN walruses a large Arctic sea animal with two long tusks [probably from an Old Norse word = horse-whale]

waltz NOUN waltzes a dance with three beats to a bar

Thesaurus

wake VERB **1** *Sara woke to find Rodney's arm around her. When I woke up I was in the back of a car.* ► awake, awaken, waken, become conscious, come around, stir, get up, rise **2** *Be careful not to wake the baby.* ► waken, rouse, disturb, stir, awaken, arouse
wake up to *The country finally woke up to the electronic age.* ► become aware of, appreciate, comprehend, realize
USAGE See the note at **awake** VERB

walk NOUN **1** *Go for short walks near your home.* ► stroll, ramble, saunter, march, hike, tramp, trek **2** *There is a pretty walk around the cathedral.* ► path, pathway, walkway, lane, alley, footway, promenade **3** *He observed her elegant walk.* ► gait, tread, carriage, stride
walk of life *There are cheats in every walk of life.* ► sphere, class, field, calling, profession, activity

walk VERB **1** *She decided to save her bus fare and walk to work.* ► go on foot, travel on foot, be a pedestrian **2** *They walked together along the sands, and talked.* ► stroll, amble, saunter,

stride, pace, trudge, proceed, promenade **3** *I'll walk the children home.* ► accompany, escort, take, see, show

walk all over (*informal*) *You don't want to let the cops walk all over you.* ► take advantage of, make use of, exploit, impose on, manipulate

walk away or **off with** (*informal*) *Someone had walked off with his wallet.* ► steal, pilfer, purloin, filch, take

walk out on (*informal*) *He had just walked out on his girlfriend.* ► leave, abandon, desert, run out on, (*informal*) jilt

wall NOUN *There was a bulletin board on the wall.* ► partition, screen, room divider *The east wall of the castle had been breached.* ► fortification, rampart, barricade, palisade, barrier, bulwark, stockade RELATED ADJECTIVE ► mural

wallet NOUN *The wallet contained some money.* ► purse, notecase, pouch, pocketbook

wallop VERB *She walloped his back with her hand.* ► thump, hit, strike, pound, beat, bang, rap, batter, knock

waltz VERB **waltzes, waltzing, waltzed** dance a waltz

wand NOUN **wands** a thin rod, especially one used by a magician

wander VERB **wanders, wandering, wandered** **1** go about without trying to reach a particular place **2** leave the right path or direction; stray **3** be distracted or digress ● *He let his attention wander.*
▷ **wanderer** NOUN

wane VERB **wanes, waning, waned** **1** (said about the moon) show a bright area that becomes gradually smaller after being full (The opposite is wax) **2** become less, smaller, or weaker ● *His popularity waned.*

wangle VERB **wangles, wangling, wangled** (*informal*) get or arrange something by trickery or clever planning ● *He's managed to wangle himself a trip to Paris.*
▷ **wangle** NOUN

want VERB **wants, wanting, wanted** **1** wish to have something **2** need ● *Your hair wants cutting.* **3** be without something; lack

want NOUN **wants** **1** a wish to have something **2** lack or need of something [from Old Norse]

wanted ADJECTIVE (said about a suspected criminal) that the police wish to find or arrest

war NOUN **wars** **1** fighting between nations or groups, especially using armed forces **2** a serious struggle or effort against crime, disease, poverty, etc.
at war taking part in a war
war crime a crime committed during a war that breaks the international rules of war

warble VERB **warbles, warbling, warbled** sing with a trilling sound, as some birds do
▷ **warble** NOUN

ward NOUN **wards** **1** a room with beds for patients in a hospital **2** a child looked after by a guardian **3** an area electing a lawyer to represent it

ward VERB **wards, warding, warded**
ward off keep something away

warden NOUN **wardens** an official who is in charge of a prison, etc., or who supervises something

wardrobe NOUN **wardrobes** **1** a detached closet to hang clothes in **2** a stock of clothes or costumes

warhead NOUN **warheads** the head of a missile or torpedo, etc., containing explosives

warlike ADJECTIVE **1** fond of making war **2** threatening war

warm ADJECTIVE **1** fairly hot; not cold or cool **2** keeping the body warm ● *a warm coat*

Thesaurus

wand NOUN *No magic wand can solve these problems.* ► baton, stick, rod, staff, sceptre

wander VERB **1** *We spent the day wandering around the old town.* ► ramble, roam, meander, range, rove, stray, walk, wind **2** *She had wandered away from the main group.* ► stray, deviate, digress, drift, veer **3** **wander off** *I've told you not to wander off like that.* ► go away, drift off, leave, get lost

want NOUN **1** *The client always has wants and feelings.* ► demand, desire, need, requirement, wish **2** *The bridge is decaying for want of repair.* ► absence, lack, need

want VERB **1** *A clever alien wants to steal the spaceship.* ► wish, desire, hope, long **2** *That is exactly what he wanted.* ► wish for, desire, long for, yearn for, hanker after, crave, covet, fancy, hunger for, thirst for **3** **want to** (*informal*) *You want to keep an eye on them.* ► need to, ought to, should

war NOUN **1** *During the war he joined the police force. They had been badly affected by the chaos of war.* ► conflict, fighting, hostilities, struggle, warfare, action, military action, strife RELATED ADJECTIVES ► martial, belligerent **2** *a war against drugs* ► campaign, crusade, battle, fight, struggle

ward VERB
ward off **1** *Garlands of garlic are worn to ward off evil spirits.* ► fend off, drive away, beat off,

repel, avert, stave off, thwart, turn aside, repulse **2** *He brought up his arm to ward off the blow.* ► deflect, parry, block, check

wardrobe NOUN **1** *Large areas of wardrobe doors can look plain.* ► cupboard, clothes cupboard, closet, cabinet **2** *Her mother organized her wedding and her wardrobe.* ► clothes, outfit, attire

warfare NOUN *thirty years of continuous warfare* ► fighting, hostilities, war, conflict, combat, bloodshed, action, battle, arms RELATED ADJECTIVES ► martial, belligerent

warlike ADJECTIVE *Tethlis was another warlike ruler.* ► belligerent, aggressive, warmongering, warring, combative, pugnacious AN OPPOSITE IS peaceable

warm ADJECTIVE **1** *She strolled in warm winter sunshine toward San Marco. The sun was already warm on their backs.* ► hot, balmy, summery, sultry, sunny, temperate, tropical, warmish AN OPPOSITE IS cold **2** *the warm waters of the western Mediterranean* ► heated, lukewarm, tepid **3** *She was dressed in warm clothes.* ► thick, cozy, woolly, thermal, winter **4** *He gave them a warm welcome.* ► friendly, cordial, amiable, enthusiastic, affable, genial, affectionate, loving, sympathetic, warmhearted, pleasant OPPOSITES ARE cool, unfriendly

a
b
c
d
e
f
g
h
i
j
k
l
m
n
o
p
q
r
s
t
u
v
w
x
y
z

A B C D E F G H I J K L M N O P Q R S T U V **W** X Y Z

3 friendly or enthusiastic • *a warm welcome* **4** close to the right answer, or to something hidden • *You're getting warm now.*
▷ **warmly** ADVERB **warmness** NOUN **warmth** NOUN

warm VERB **warms, warming, warmed** make or become warm

warm-blooded ADJECTIVE having blood that remains warm permanently

warn VERB **warns, warning, warned** tell someone about a danger or difficulty that may affect them, or about what they should do • *I warned you to take your boots.*
▷ **warning** NOUN
warn off tell someone to keep away or to avoid a thing

warp (worp) VERB **warps, warping, warped 1** bend or twist out of shape, e.g., by dampness **2** distort a person's ideas, judgment, etc. • *Jealousy warped his mind.*

warrant NOUN **warrants** a document that authorizes a person to do something (e.g., to search a place) or to receive something

warrant VERB **warrants, warranting, warranted 1** justify • *Nothing can warrant such rudeness.* **2** guarantee

warren NOUN **warrens 1** a piece of ground where there are many burrows in which

rabbits live and breed **2** a building or place with many winding passages

warrior NOUN **warriors** a person who fights in battle; a soldier

warship NOUN **warships** a ship used in war

wart NOUN **warts** a small hard lump on the skin, caused by a virus

wary (wair- ee) ADJECTIVE cautious; looking carefully for possible danger or difficulty
▷ **warily** ADVERB **wariness** NOUN

wash VERB **washes, washing, washed 1** clean something with water or other liquid **2** suitable for washing • *Cotton washes easily.* **3** flow against or over something • *Waves washed over the deck.* **4** carry along by a moving liquid • *A wave washed him overboard.* **5** (*informal*) be accepted or believed • *That excuse won't wash.*
be washed out (*informal*) (said about an event) be abandoned because of rain
wash up wash dishes and cutlery, etc., after use

wash NOUN **washes 1** the action of washing **2** clothes, etc., being washed **3** the disturbed water behind a moving ship **4** a thin coating of color

washable ADJECTIVE able to be washed without becoming damaged

---

Thesaurus

---

warm VERB **1** *She was in the kitchen warming some soup.* ▸ heat (up), reheat, thaw OPPOSITES ARE cool, chill **2** *warm to Anne was by now warming to her theme.* ▸ take to, become enthusiastic about, get on with, feel attracted by

warmhearted ADJECTIVE *She is a generous, warmhearted person.* ▸ kind, caring, good, kindhearted, kindly, considerate, sympathetic, thoughtful, obliging, tender-hearted, benevolent OPPOSITES ARE unkind, unfriendly

warmth NOUN **1** *Despite the warmth of the fire, Isabel began to shiver.* ▸ heat, warmness, comfort AN OPPOSITE IS coldness **2** *The warmth of their welcome took them by surprise.* ▸ friendliness, cordiality, geniality, enthusiasm AN OPPOSITE IS hostility

warn VERB *The manufacturers had failed to warn doctors of the possible side effects.* ▸ advise, alert, notify, inform, caution, remind, forewarn, give a warning about, (*more informal*) tip off

warning NOUN **1** *The changes were announced without warning.* ▸ notice, advance notice, forewarning, hint, indication, omen, premonition, presage, sign, signal, threat, augury, (*informal*) tip-off **2** *The remarks were a warning of what might be in store.* ▸ omen, sign, signal, presage, portent, premonition, foreboding, prediction, token **3** *The warning in his voice was clear.* ▸ caution, reservation,

caveat, doubt **4** *England received its third and final warning.* ▸ caution, reprimand, admonition

warrior NOUN *a mighty warrior* ▸ fighter, soldier, fighting man, combatant

wary ADJECTIVE *She had been wary of making known her name.* ▸ cautious, chary, careful, circumspect, suspicious, apprehensive, vigilant (about), watchful (about), alert (to), distrustful, heedful OPPOSITES ARE unwary, heedless

wash NOUN **1** *I said the dog needed a wash.* ▸ bath, shower, rinse, shampoo **2** *They give all the cars a wash each morning.* ▸ clean, shampoo, hosing-down

wash VERB **1** *She took a couple of minutes to wash her face and comb her hair. Wash all fruit and vegetables thoroughly before use.* ▸ clean, cleanse, rinse, scrub, shampoo, mop, sluice, swill, wipe OPPOSITES ARE dirty, soil **2** *It was time to wash the dog.* ▸ soap down, sponge down, swab down, hose down **3** *He found the soap and began to wash.* ▸ bath, bathe, shower **4** *She washed, dried, and ironed the clothes.* ▸ launder, clean, scrub, rinse, sponge
wash your hands of something *They cannot wash their hands of social problems.* ▸ disown, renounce, have nothing to do with, disclaim, reject, abandon AN OPPOSITE IS embrace

way NOUN **ways 1** how something is done; a method or style **2** a manner • *She spoke in a kindly way* **3** a line of communication between places, e.g., a path or road **4** a route or direction **5** a distance to be travelled • *Is it a long way away?* **6** a respect • *It's a good idea in some ways.* **7** a condition or state • *Things were in a bad way.*

get or **have your own way** make people let you do what you want

give way 1 collapse **2** let somebody else move first **3** yield

in the way forming an obstacle or hindrance

no way (*informal*) that is impossible!

under way see under

waylay VERB **waylays, waylaying, waylaid** lie in wait for a person or people, especially in order to talk to them or rob them

wayside NOUN

fall by the wayside fail to continue doing something

wayward ADJECTIVE disobedient; willfully doing what you want

we PRONOUN a word used by a person to refer to himself or herself and another or others

weak ADJECTIVE **1** having little power, energy, or effect **2** easy to break, damage, or defeat **3** not great in intensity
▷ **weakness** NOUN

weaken VERB **weakens, weakening, weakened** make or become weaker

weakling NOUN **weaklings** a weak person or animal

wealth NOUN **1** a lot of money or property; riches **2** a large quantity • *The book has a wealth of illustrations.*

Thesaurus

---

wavy ADJECTIVE *She ran her hand through her wavy hair.* ► curly, curling, curving, rippling, sinuous, undulating, winding, zigzag AN OPPOSITE IS straight

way NOUN **1** *His engine overheated on the way home.* ► road, route, journey, direction **2** *There was a long way to go.* ► distance, length, measurement **3** *It was the best way of dealing with the problem.* ► method, means, manner, approach, mode, procedure, process, avenue, course, system, technique, mechanism **4** *He knew he had to change his ways.* ► habit, practice, routine, custom, fashion, style, tradition **5** *The arts benefit society in several ways.* ► respect, particular, aspect, circumstances, detail, feature

way-out ADJECTIVE (*informal*) *He introduced some way-out visual ideas that no one had tried before.* ► unconventional, offbeat, eccentric, quirky, bizarre, weird, odd, (*informal*) wacky

weak ADJECTIVE **1** *The bridge was weak as a result of metal fatigue.* ► unsafe, unsound, fragile, unsteady, rickety, shaky, flimsy, decrepit, substandard AN OPPOSITE IS strong **2** *He was still too weak to get up by himself.* ► frail, feeble, poorly, ill, infirm, sickly, debilitated, helpless, delicate, enervated, exhausted, listless, puny AN OPPOSITE IS strong **3** *A weak man, when provoked, is often more dangerous than a violent one.* ► timid, timorous, irresolute, spineless, ineffectual, pusillanimous, cowardly, fearful, impotent, indecisive, ineffective OPPOSITES ARE strong, brave **4** *His mistakes had put him in a weak position.* ► vulnerable, exposed, defenceless, unguarded, unprotected OPPOSITES ARE strong, powerful **5** *The weak joke fell hollowly.* ► feeble, lame, unconvincing,

unsatisfactory **6** *She sipped the sweet, weak tea and began to feel better.* ► watery, diluted, watered down, insipid, bland, thin, tasteless AN OPPOSITE IS strong **7** *The light was becoming weak.* ► dim, pale, faint, feeble OPPOSITES ARE strong, bright

weaken VERB **1** *Their purpose was to weaken the unions' power.* ► reduce, sap, enfeeble, erode, impair, lessen, diminish, lower, debilitate, destroy, emasculate, enervate, make weaker, ruin, soften, undermine OPPOSITES ARE strengthen, boost **2** *Our resolve had weakened.* ► dwindle, ebb, fade, flag, wane, abate, become weaker, decline, decrease, give way OPPOSITES ARE strengthen, increase, intensify

weakness NOUN **1** *There is an obvious weakness in your argument.* ► fault, flaw, defect, imperfection, weak point, blemish, error, failing, mistake, shortcoming OPPOSITES ARE strength, strong point **2** *The economy is showing signs of weakness.* ► fragility, frailty, flimsiness, inadequacy, softness **3** *Her illness left her with a permanent physical weakness.* ► infirmity, debility, feebleness, illness, impotence, lassitude, vulnerability OPPOSITES ARE strength, vigor **4** *He has a weakness for chocolate cake.* ► liking, fondness, inclination, penchant, predilection, (*more informal*) soft spot

wealth NOUN **1** *We want to see wealth passed down from generation to generation.* ► affluence, assets, opulence, property, prosperity, capital, fortune, money, possessions, riches AN OPPOSITE IS poverty **2** *You realize the wealth of information inside the government.* ► abundance, profusion, plethora, store, plenty

a
b
c
d
e
f
g
h
i
j
k
l
m
n
o
p
q
r
s
t
u
w
x
y
z

A
B
C
D
E
F
G
H
I
J
K
L
M
N
O
P
Q
R
S
T
U
V
W
X
Y
Z

wealthy ADJECTIVE **wealthier, wealthiest** having wealth; rich
  ▷ **wealthiness** NOUN

wean VERB **weans, weaning, weaned** make a baby take food other than its mother's milk
wean off make someone give up a habit, etc., gradually

weapon NOUN **weapons** something used to harm or kill people in a battle or fight
  ▷ **weaponry** NOUN

wear VERB **wears, wearing, wore, worn**
1 have clothes, jewelry, etc. on your body **2** have a certain look on your face • *She wore a frown.* **3** damage something by rubbing or using it often; become damaged in this way • *The carpet has worn thin.* **4** last while in use • *It has worn well.*
  ▷ **wearable** ADJECTIVE **wearer** NOUN
wear off 1 be removed by wear or use **2** become less intense
wear on pass gradually • *The night wore on.*
wear out 1 use or be used until it becomes weak or useless **2** exhaust

wear NOUN **1** what you wear; clothes • *evening wear* **2** (also **wear and tear**)gradual damage done by rubbing or using something

weary ADJECTIVE **wearier, weariest 1** tired **2** tiring • *It's weary work.*
  ▷ **wearily** ADVERB **weariness** NOUN

weary VERB **wearies, wearying, wearied** make or become weary

weasel NOUN **weasels** a small fierce animal with a slender body and reddish-brown fur

weather NOUN the rain, snow, wind, sunshine, etc., at a particular time or place
under the weather feeling ill or depressed

weather VERB **weathers, weathering, weathered 1** expose something to the effects of the weather **2** come through something successfully • *The ship weathered the storm.*

weathercock or **weathervane** NOUN **weathercocks** or **weathervanes** a pointer, often shaped like a cockerel, that turns in the wind and shows from which direction it is blowing

weave VERB **weaves, weaving, wove, woven**
1 make material or baskets, etc., by crossing threads or strips under and over each other **2** put a story together • *She wove a thrilling tale.* **3** (past tense & past participle **weaved**) twist and turn • *He weaved through the traffic.*
  ▷ **weaver** NOUN

Thesaurus

wealthy ADJECTIVE *Her mother was a very wealthy woman.* ► rich, affluent, prosperous, well-off, well-to-do, moneyed, comfortable, (*more informal*) flush, (*more informal*) loaded OPPOSITES ARE poor, impoverished

wear VERB **1** *Did you have to wear any special kind of clothing? Ruth wore a pale lavender cotton dress. He often wore dark glasses to hide the bags under his eyes.* ► dress in, be dressed in, clothe yourself in, put on, have on, present yourself in, wrap up in, don **2** *He wore his usual benign expression.* ► show, assume, present, exhibit **3** *Years of passing footsteps had badly worn the carpet.* ► damage, fray, scuff, mark, weaken **4** *The tires have worn well.* ► last, endure, survive, hold up, (*more informal*) stand the test of time
wear away *Most of the grass had been worn away by the spectators.* ► rub away, erode, grind down, abrade, corrode, eat away
wear off *The effect of the tranquilizers was wearing off.* ► fade, subside, dwindle, reduce, lessen, diminish, peter out, disappear
wear out 1 *His shoes wear out twice as fast when he's working.* ► become worn, deteriorate, become damaged, become scuffed **2** *They cheered until their lungs were worn out.* ► exhaust, fatigue, tire out

wear NOUN **1** *Repairs were made necessary by heavy wear.* ► use, service, utility, wearing **2** *The brakes showed signs of wear.* ► damage,

deterioration, friction, erosion, wear and tear **3** *The guests were dressed in formal wear.* ► dress, clothes, clothing, costume, outfit

wearing ADJECTIVE *The care of others can be a wearing business.* ► tiring, exhausting, tiresome, fatiguing, wearying, wearisome, trying, taxing AN OPPOSITE IS refreshing

weary ADJECTIVE *I have been too sad and too weary to write anything.* ► tired, exhausted, fatigued, wearied, worn out, sapped, drained, spent, (*more informal*) knackered

weather NOUN *She was tempted to use the weather as an excuse to postpone her visit. All farmers are exposed to the vagaries of the weather.* ► climate, the elements, meteorological conditions, atmospheric conditions
under the weather *She felt under the weather and went to rest.* ► unwell, poorly, indisposed, out of sorts, ill, sick OPPOSITES ARE well, in good health RELATED ADJECTIVE
► meteorological

weave VERB **1** *The design had been woven into the carpet.* ► intertwine, interweave, knit, plait, sew, entwine, interlace **2** *Victorian novelists weave romances round great houses. She wove a spell over him, so that he slept forever and never grew old.* ► create, compose, make, plot, put together **3** *He dragged himself out of bed and weaved his way to the bathroom.* ► thread, wind, work, dodge, zigzag

weave NOUN **weaves** a style of weaving • *a loose weave*

web NOUN **webs** 1 a cobweb 2 a network **the Web** the World Wide Web [from Old English *webb* = a piece of woven cloth]

webbed or **web-footed** ADJECTIVE having toes joined by pieces of skin, as ducks and frogs do

web site NOUN **web sites** a place on the Internet where you can get information about a subject, company, etc.

wed VERB **weds, wedding, wedded** 1 marry 2 unite two different things

wedding NOUN **weddings** the ceremony when a man and woman get married

wedge NOUN **wedges** 1 a piece of wood or metal, etc., that is thick at one end and thin at the other It is pushed between things to force them apart or prevent something from moving 2 a wedge-shaped thing

wedge VERB **wedges, wedging, wedged** 1 keep something in place with a wedge 2 pack tightly together • *Ten of us were wedged in the car.*

Wednesday NOUN the day of the week following Tuesday [from Old English *Wodnesdaeg* = day of Woden or Odin, the chief Norse god]

weed NOUN **weeds** a wild plant that grows where it is not wanted

weed VERB **weeds, weeding, weeded** remove weeds from the ground

weedy ADJECTIVE **weedier, weediest** 1 full of weeds 2 thin and weak

week NOUN **weeks** a period of seven days, especially from Sunday to the following Saturday

weekday NOUN **weekdays** a day other than Saturday or Sunday

weekend NOUN **weekends** Saturday and Sunday

weekly ADJECTIVE, ADVERB happening or done once a week

weep VERB **weeps, weeping, wept** 1 shed tears; cry 2 ooze moisture in drops
▷ **weep** NOUN **weepy** ADJECTIVE

weeping ADJECTIVE (said about a tree) having drooping branches • *a weeping willow*

weigh VERB **weighs, weighing, weighed** 1 measure the weight of something 2 have a certain weight • *What do you weigh?* 3 be important or have influence • *Her evidence weighed with the jury.*
weigh anchor raise the anchor and start a voyage
weigh down 1 keep something down by its weight 2 depress or trouble somebody
weigh up estimate or assess something

weight NOUN **weights** 1 how heavy something is; the amount that something weighs 2 a piece of metal of known weight,

Thesaurus

web NOUN 1 *The webs are built to a definite pattern.* ► mesh, net, netting, network, crisscross, lattice 2 *Their lives were caught up in a web of deception.* ► network, nexus, maze, complex

wedding NOUN *The wedding went ahead with two hundred guests.* ► marriage, marriage ceremony, nuptials, union RELATED ADJECTIVE ► nuptial, bridal

wedge NOUN 1 *He put a huge wedge of gleaming chocolate pudding on her plate.* ► slice, segment, triangle, chunk, lump 2 *The window was held open with a wedge.* ► chock, block, door stop

wedge VERB *She wedged the string bag between her feet and took out a book. The children were wedged so tightly that it was difficult to move.* ► squeeze, jam, cram, push, force, thrust, stick, push, fasten, (more informal) shove

weedy ADJECTIVE 1 *I walked up through the weedy garden.* ► untidy, unweeded, overgrown, unkempt, wild, rank 2 (informal) *He was short and physically weedy.* ► weak, puny, feeble, frail

weep VERB *I began to weep, burying my face in my hands.* ► cry, sob, shed tears, whimper, blubber, snivel, wail

weigh VERB 1 *The man weighed some vegetables and put them in a bag.* ► measure the weight of, measure out, put on the scales 2 *I weigh the same now as when I married.* ► have a weight of, tip the scales at 3 **weigh** or **weigh up** *These were considerations that she weighed carefully. I weighed up my chances and decided to go.* ► consider, evaluate, assess, examine, think about, give thought to, ponder, study, mull over, meditate on 4 *Two other matters weigh in their favor.* ► be important, count, have weight

weigh down 1 *No one wants to be weighed down with heavy gear.* ► burden, weight, saddle, load, overload 2 *She walked to her room, mentally weighed down by her thoughts.* ► depress, oppress, trouble, bother, beset, afflict, prey on

weight NOUN 1 *The supports could no longer sustain the weight of the bridge, and it collapsed.* ► heaviness, load, burden, mass, pressure, strain 2 *The president has attached a lot of weight to the scheme.* ► importance, seriousness, significance, authority, emphasis, gravity, substance

a
b
c
d
e
f
g
h
i
j
k
l
m
n
o
p
q
r
s
t
u
w
x
y
z

especially one used on scales to weigh things **3** a heavy object **4** importance or influence
▷ **weighty** ADJECTIVE **weightless** ADJECTIVE

weight VERB **weights, weighting, weighted** put a weight on something

weir (weer) NOUN **weirs** a small dam across a river or canal to control the flow of water

weird ADJECTIVE very strange; uncanny
▷ **weirdly** ADVERB **weirdness** NOUN
USAGE When spelling this word, note that the '*e*' comes before the '*i*', not the other way around.

welcome NOUN **welcomes** a greeting or reception, especially a kindly one

welcome ADJECTIVE **1** that you are glad to receive or see ● *a welcome gift* **2** allowed or invited to do or take something ● *You are welcome to come.*

welcome VERB **welcomes, welcoming, welcomed 1** show that you are pleased when a person or thing arrives **2** be glad to receive or hear of something ● *We welcome this decision.*

weld VERB **welds, welding, welded 1** join pieces of metal or plastic by heating and pressing or hammering them together **2** unite people or things into a whole

welfare NOUN people's health, happiness, and comfort

welfare state NOUN a system in which a country's government provides money to pay for health care, social services, benefits, etc.

well NOUN **wells 1** a deep hole dug to bring up water or oil from underground **2** a deep space, e.g. containing a staircase

well VERB **wells, welling, welled** rise or flow up
● *Tears welled up in our eyes.*

well ADVERB **better, best 1** in a good or suitable way ● *She swims well.* **2** thoroughly ● *Polish it well.* **3** probably or reasonably ● *This may well be our last chance.*
well off 1 fairly rich **2** in a good situation

well ADJECTIVE **1** in good health ● *He is not well.* **2** satisfactory ● *All is well.*

well-being NOUN good health, happiness, and comfort

Thesaurus

weight VERB **1** *Driftwood can be sealed and weighted in the same way.* ► weigh down, make heavy, ballast, hold down, keep down, load **2** *The odds were weighted against them.* ► bias, load, slant, balance

weighty ADJECTIVE **1** *A pile of books can be very weighty.* ► heavy, bulky, cumbersome, massive, clumsy **2** *The weighty question, what is happiness?* ► serious, important, significant, momentous, far-reaching, consequential **3** *It is a weighty responsibility to be given.* ► demanding, onerous, exacting, taxing, troublesome

weird ADJECTIVE **1** *Some pretty weird things seemed to be happening.* ► uncanny, eerie, unearthly, unnatural, ghostly, mysterious, scary, supernatural, unaccountable, (*more informal*) spooky, (*more informal*) creepy OPPOSITES ARE normal, ordinary **2** *They wouldn't make those weird garden ornaments if they'd ever seen a real gnome. The fridge made some really weird noises yesterday.* ► strange, peculiar, bizarre, grotesque, odd, curious, eccentric, outlandish, queer, unusual, abnormal, quirky, unconventional, (*more informal*) wacky, (*more informal*) freaky, (*more informal*) way-out AN OPPOSITE IS conventional

welcome ADJECTIVE *We've received some welcome news.* ► pleasant, pleasing, gratifying, encouraging, good, nice OPPOSITES ARE unwelcome, disappointing

welcome NOUN *Go to the visitors' center, where you can be sure of a warm welcome.* ► reception, greeting, hospitality

welcome VERB **1** *Sophie welcomed her warmly and pulled out a chair.* ► greet, receive, hail, meet **2** *His colleagues welcomed his cheerfulness.* ► appreciate, approve of, delight in, like, want, accept

welfare NOUN *the safety and welfare of people at work* ► well-being, good, security, prosperity, comfort, benefit, happiness, health, interests

well ADJECTIVE *Mary was looking well.* ► healthy, in good health, fit, fine, sound, strong, thriving, flourishing, hearty, lively, robust, vigorous

well ADVERB **1** *They behaved well.* ► satisfactorily, correctly, nicely, properly AN OPPOSITE IS badly **2** *She sings well.* ► ably, skillfully, expertly OPPOSITES ARE badly, poorly **3** *Mix the ingredients well.* ► thoroughly, fully, completely, rigorously AN OPPOSITE IS lightly **4** *You have been working well.* ► carefully, diligently, conscientiously, attentively OPPOSITES ARE badly, poorly **5** *He has made enough money to live well.* ► comfortably, in comfort, prosperously

well VERB *The tears welled in her eyes.* ► flow, stream, spring, course, surge, flood, gush, rise, run, trickle

well-behaved ADJECTIVE *You will have to be quiet and well-behaved.* ► well-mannered, polite, obedient, respectful, courteous, cooperative, good, dutiful, nice AN OPPOSITE IS naughty

well-being NOUN *The medical staff are responsible for the well-being of the patients.*

well-known ADJECTIVE known to many people

well-mannered ADJECTIVE having good manners

well-meaning ADJECTIVE having good intentions

well-read ADJECTIVE having read a lot of good books

well-to-do ADJECTIVE fairly rich

weren't (*mainly spoken*) were not

werewolf NOUN werewolves (in legends and stories) a person who sometimes changes into a wolf [from Old English *wer* = man + **wolf**]

west NOUN **1** the direction where the sun sets, opposite east **2** the western part of a country, city, etc.

west ADJECTIVE **1** situated in the west ● *the west coast* **2** coming from the west ● *a west wind*

west ADVERB towards the west ● *We sailed west.*

westerly ADJECTIVE to or from the west

western ADJECTIVE of or in the west

Western NOUN Westerns a film or story about cowboys or American Indians in the American West during the 19th and early 20th centuries

westward ADJECTIVE, ADVERB toward the west
▷ **westwards** ADVERB

wet ADJECTIVE wetter, wettest **1** soaked or covered in water or other liquid **2** not yet dry ● *wet paint* **3** rainy ● *wet weather*
▷ **wetly** ADVERB **wetness** NOUN

wet VERB wets, wetting, wet or wetted make a thing wet

whale NOUN whales a very large sea animal
a whale of a (*informal*) very good or great
● *We had a whale of a time.*

whaling NOUN hunting whales

what ADJECTIVE used to ask the amount or kind of something (*What kind of bike have you got?*) or to say how strange or great a person or thing is (*What a fool you are!*)

what PRONOUN **1** what thing or things ● *What did you say?* **2** the thing that ● *This is what you must do.*
what's what (*informal*) which things are important or useful

whatever PRONOUN **1** anything or everything
● *Do whatever you like.* **2** no matter what
● *Keep calm, whatever happens.*

whatever ADJECTIVE of any kind or amount
● *Take whatever books you need.* ● *There is no doubt whatever.*

wheat NOUN a cereal plant from which flour is made
▷ **wheaten** ADJECTIVE

wheedle VERB wheedles, wheedling, wheedled persuade by coaxing or flattering

wheel VERB wheels, wheeling, wheeled
1 push a bicycle or trolley, etc., along on its wheels **2** move in a curve or circle; change direction and face another way ● *He wheeled around in astonishment.*

wheel NOUN wheels **1** a round device that turns on a shaft that passes through its center

Thesaurus

► welfare, good, security, prosperity, comfort, benefit, happiness, health, interests

well-dressed ADJECTIVE *A well-dressed young woman came in.* ► smart, stylish, elegant, fashionable, well-groomed, chic, trim

well-known ADJECTIVE **1** *They played well-known types such as the domineering wife and the henpecked husband.* ► familiar, widely known, popular, common, typical **2** *She came from a well-known Boston family.* ► famous, notable, prominent, leading, distinguished, eminent

well-off ADJECTIVE *dream gardens of well-off homeowners* ► rich, wealthy, well-to-do, affluent, moneyed, prosperous, opulent AN OPPOSITE IS poor

wet ADJECTIVE **1** *Her jacket was soaking and clung to her like a wet towel.* ► damp, soaked, saturated, drenched, moistened, sopping, dripping AN OPPOSITE IS dry **2** *The mowers could not be used because the ground was too wet.* ► waterlogged, sodden, boggy, soggy, spongy, swampy, squelchy OPPOSITES ARE dry, firm **3** *They were unlucky enough to meet wet weather at harvest time.* ► rainy, raining, drizzly, showery, pouring, humid, misty OPPOSITES ARE dry, fine **4** *The paint was still*

wet. ► runny, sticky, tacky OPPOSITES ARE dry, set **5** (*informal*) *Some of the trainees seemed a bit wet.* ► feeble, weak, silly, soft, (*informal*) weedy, (*informal*) wimpish OPPOSITES ARE tough, strong

wet NOUN *The front wheels were prone to locking in the wet.* ► rain, dampness, wet weather, damp weather, drizzle

wet VERB *There is no need to wet your hair first.* ► dampen, damp, douse, drench, soak, spray, sprinkle, water, steep, irrigate, moisten, saturate AN OPPOSITE IS dry

whack VERB *I saw him take a stick and whack his dog.* ► hit, strike, smack, slap, thump, (*more informal*) slug

whack NOUN *She gave him a hefty whack across his shoulders.* ► blow, hit, slap, punch, thump, knock, smack

wheel VERB **1** *He grabbed a trolley and began to wheel the luggage away.* ► push, trundle, roll **2** *A flock of birds wheeled above them.* ► circle, gyrate, turn, orbit
wheel around *Elinor wheeled around, a look of horror on her face.* ► turn, swing around, change direction, swerve, veer

a b c d e f g h i j k l m n o p q r s t u v **w** x y z

2 a horizontal revolving disc on which clay is made into a pot

wheelbarrow NOUN **wheelbarrows** a small cart with one wheel at the front and legs at the back, pushed by handles

wheelchair NOUN **wheelchairs** a chair on wheels for a person who cannot walk

wheeze VERB **wheezes, wheezing, wheezed** make a hoarse whistling sound as you breathe
▷ **wheeze** NOUN **wheezy** ADJECTIVE

when ADVERB at what time; at which time
• When can you come to tea?

when CONJUNCTION **1** at the time that • The bird flew away when I moved. **2** although; considering that • Why do you smoke when you know it's dangerous?

whence ADVERB from where; from which

whenever CONJUNCTION at whatever time; every time • Whenever I see it, I smile

where ADVERB in or to what place or that place
• Where did you put it? Leave it where it is.

whereabouts ADVERB in or near what place
• Whereabouts are you going?

whereabouts PLURAL NOUN the place where something is • Do you know the whereabouts of my radio?

whereas CONJUNCTION but in contrast • Some people enjoy sport, whereas others hate it.

whereupon CONJUNCTION after which; and then

wherever ADVERB in or to whatever place

whet VERB **whets, whetting, whetted**
whet your appetite stimulate it
USAGE Do not confuse with **wet**.

whether CONJUNCTION as one possibility; if • I don't know whether to believe her or not.

which ADJECTIVE what particular • Which way did he go?

which PRONOUN **1** what person or thing • Which is your desk? **2** the person or thing referred to
• The film, which is a western, will be shown on Saturday.

whichever PRONOUN, ADJECTIVE no matter which; any which • Take whichever you like.

whiff NOUN **whiffs** a puff or slight smell of smoke, gas, etc.

while CONJUNCTION **1** during the time that; as long as • Whistle while you work. **2** although; but • She is dark, while her sister is fair.

while NOUN a period of time • a long while

while VERB **whiles, whiling, whiled**
while away pass time • We whiled away the afternoon on the river.

whim NOUN **whims** a sudden wish to do or have something

whimper VERB **whimpers, whimpering, whimpered** cry or whine softly
▷ **whimper** NOUN

whimsical ADJECTIVE quaint and playful
▷ **whimsically** ADVERB **whimsicality** NOUN

whine VERB **whines, whining, whined 1** make a long high miserable cry or a shrill sound **2** complain in a petty or feeble way
▷ **whine** NOUN

whip NOUN **whips 1** a cord or strip of leather fixed to a handle and used for hitting people or animals **2** an official of a political party in Parliament

whip VERB **whips, whipping, whipped 1** hit a person or animal with a whip **2** beat cream until it becomes thick **3** move or take something suddenly • He whipped out his pen. **4** (informal) steal something
whip up stir up people's feelings, etc. • She whipped up support for her plans.

Thesaurus

whereabouts NOUN Despite inquiries, his whereabouts remain unknown. ► location, position, situation, vicinity, address, site

whiff NOUN **1** He caught a whiff of expensive perfume. ► scent, aroma, smell , breath, puff, odor USAGE You normally use odor when you mean an unpleasant smell. **2** At the slightest whiff of trouble he takes to his bed. ► hint, trace, suggestion, suspicion, intimation

whim NOUN It was silly to waste a whole morning on a foolish whim. ► impulse, notion, urge, fancy, caprice, desire, quirk

whimper VERB He began to whimper with fear. ► snivel, wail, moan, cry, groan, weep, (more informal) grizzle

whimper NOUN The dog made off with a whimper. ► whine, cry, snivel

whine NOUN There was a whine from the engines. ► drone, whimper, hum

whine VERB **1** Mosquitoes whined in my ears. ► drone, hum **2** (informal) I'm sick of him whining to me about you. ► grumble, complain, carp, grouch, moan, beef, (informal) whinge

whip NOUN He threatened to use a whip on any intruders. ► lash, scourge, cat, cat-o'-nine-tails, horsewhip, riding-crop, switch

whip VERB **1** He whipped the boys and sent them away. ► thrash, beat, flog, lash, scourge **2** Why can you whip cream but not milk? ► whisk, beat, stir vigorously **3** (informal) She whipped a piece of paper out of her pocket. ► pull, whisk, pluck, tug, take **4** (informal) I can always whip around to the corner shop. ► dash, hurry, shoot, run, sprint, rush, race, tear

whirl VERB whirls, whirling, whirled turn or spin very quickly
▷ **whirl** NOUN

whirlpool NOUN whirlpools a whirling current of water

whirlwind NOUN whirlwinds a strong wind that whirls around a central point

whirr VERB whirrs, whirring, whirred make a continuous buzzing sound
▷ **whirr** NOUN

whisk VERB whisks, whisking, whisked
1 move or brush something away quickly and lightly • *A waiter whisked away our plates.*
2 beat eggs, etc., until they are frothy

whisk NOUN whisks **1** a kitchen tool used for whisking things **2** a whisking movement [from Old Norse]

whisker NOUN whiskers **1** a hair of those growing on a man's face, forming a beard or moustache if not shaved off **2** a long bristle growing near the mouth of a cat, etc.
▷ **whiskery** ADJECTIVE

whisky NOUN whiskies a strong alcoholic drink [from Scottish Gaelic *uisge beatha* = water of life]

whisper VERB whispers, whispering, whispered **1** speak very softly **2** talk secretly
▷ **whisper** NOUN

whist NOUN a card game usually for four people

whistle VERB whistles, whistling, whistled make a shrill or musical sound, especially by blowing through your lips
▷ **whistler** NOUN

whistle NOUN whistles **1** a whistling sound **2** a device that makes a shrill sound when air or steam is blown through it

white NOUN whites **1** the very lightest color, like snow or salt **2** the transparent substance (**albumen**) around the yolk of an egg, which turns white when it is cooked **3** a person with a light-colored skin

white ADJECTIVE **1** of the color white **2** (said of a person) having light-colored skin **3** very pale from the effects of illness or fear, etc. **4** (said about coffee) with milk
▷ **whiteness** NOUN

white elephant NOUN white elephants a useless possession, especially one that is expensive to keep

white-hot ADJECTIVE extremely hot; so hot that heated metal looks white

white lie NOUN white lies a harmless or trivial lie that you tell in order to avoid hurting someone's feelings

whiten VERB whitens, whitening, whitened make or become whiter

whitewash NOUN **1** a white liquid containing lime or powdered chalk, used for painting walls and ceilings, etc. **2** concealing mistakes or other unpleasant facts so that someone will not be punished
▷ **whitewash** VERB

whither ADVERB (old use) to what place
USAGE Do not confuse with **wither**.

whittle VERB whittles, whittling, whittled **1** shape wood by trimming thin slices off the surface **2** reduce something by removing various things from it • *We need to whittle down the cost.*

whizz or **whiz** VERB whizzes, whizzing, whizzed **1** move very quickly **2** sound like something rushing through the air

who PRONOUN which person or people; the particular person or people • *This is the boy who stole the apples.*

whoever PRONOUN **1** any or every person who **2** no matter who

whole ADJECTIVE **1** complete **2** not injured or broken

whole NOUN **1** the full amount **2** a complete thing
on the whole considering everything; mainly

Thesaurus

whirl NOUN **1** *His mind was in a whirl and he was worried.* ► daze, spin, muddle, stupor, state of confusion **2** (*informal*) *The only way to find out was to give it a whirl.* ► try, test, (*informal*) shot, (*informal*) bash

whirl VERB *The dancers appear to whirl around with their hands on their hips.* ► circle, gyrate, twirl, spin, rotate, pirouette, reel, revolve, swivel, turn, twist, wheel

whisk VERB **1** *Whisk the sugar and eggs together.* ► beat, mix, stir, whip **2** *You will be whisked off to a studio for a photo session.* ► rush, speed, hurry, sweep, shoot, hurtle **3** *He whisked a blanket off the nearest trolley.* ► pull, pluck, tug, take, (*more informal*) whip

whisper VERB *Anne whispered something in his ear.* ► murmur, breathe, mutter, mumble AN OPPOSITE IS shout

whisper NOUN **1** *He spoke in a whisper.* ► murmur, mutter, undertone, hushed voice **2** *I heard a whisper that he's left the country.* ► rumor, report, piece of gossip, piece of hearsay

white ADJECTIVE **1** *He rested his fingers on the white keys.* ► ivory, snowy, chalky, pale , snow-white, cream **2** *Her face was white with fear.* ► pale, pallid, ashen, colorless, bloodless

whole ADJECTIVE **1** *I don't have time to read the whole book.* ► entire, complete, full, total, full-length, unabridged, uncut, unexpurgated

whole food ➡ widen

whole food NOUN food that is free of additives and has been processed as little as possible

wholehearted ADJECTIVE without doubts or reservations • *You have my wholehearted support.*

wholemeal ADJECTIVE made from the whole grain of wheat

whole number NOUN whole numbers a number without fractions

wholesale NOUN selling goods in large quantities to be resold by others COMPARE retail
▷ **wholesaler** NOUN

wholesale ADJECTIVE, ADVERB **1** on a large scale; including everybody or everything • *wholesale destruction* **2** in the wholesale trade

wholesome ADJECTIVE good for health; healthy • *wholesome food*
▷ **wholesomeness** NOUN

wholly ADVERB completely or entirely

whom PRONOUN the form of **who** used when it is the object of a verb or comes after a preposition, as in • *the boy whom I saw* or *to whom we spoke*

whoop (woop) NOUN whoops a loud cry of excitement
▷ **whoop** VERB

whooping cough (hoop- ing) NOUN an infectious disease that causes spasms of coughing and gasping for breath

whopper NOUN whoppers (slang) something very large

whopping ADJECTIVE (slang) very large or remarkable • *a whopping lie*

who's (mainly spoken) who is; who has
USAGE Do not confuse with **whose**.

whose PRONOUN belonging to what person or people; of whom; of which • *Whose house is that?*
USAGE Do not confuse with **who's**.

why ADVERB for what reason or purpose; the particular reason on account of which • *This is why I came.*

wick NOUN wicks **1** the string that goes through the middle of a candle and is lit **2** the strip of material that you light in a lamp or heater, etc., that uses oil

wicked ADJECTIVE **1** morally bad or cruel **2** mischievous • *a wicked smile* **3** (informal) very good
▷ **wickedly** ADVERB **wickedness** NOUN

wide ADJECTIVE **1** measuring a lot from side to side; not narrow **2** measuring from side to side • *The cloth is one meter wide.* **3** covering a great range • *a wide knowledge of birds* **4** fully open • *eyes wide with excitement* **5** missing the target • *The shot was wide of the mark.*
▷ **widely** ADVERB **wideness** NOUN

wide ADVERB **1** to the full extent; far apart • *Open wide.* **2** missing the target • *The shot went wide.* **3** over a large area • *She traveled far and wide.*

widen VERB widens, widening, widened make or become wider

Thesaurus

OPPOSITES ARE incomplete, partial **2** *The archaeologists uncovered a Greek vase that turned out to be whole.* ▶ intact, in one piece, unbroken, undamaged, unharmed, unscathed, perfect OPPOSITES ARE broken, fragmentary

wholehearted ADJECTIVE *You have our wholehearted support.* ▶ total, complete, unreserved, unqualified, committed, absolute, outright, utter OPPOSITES ARE halfhearted, partial

whopping ADJECTIVE *The bill came to a whopping $500.* ▶ huge, enormous, gigantic, mammoth, immense, massive, colossal

wicked ADJECTIVE **1** *a wicked person a wicked act* ▶ evil, bad, sinful, base, immoral, corrupt, depraved, heinous, iniquitous OPPOSITES ARE moral, good, upright **2** *It was wicked of you to say such things.* ▶ naughty, wrong, nasty, mischievous, unkind OPPOSITES ARE good, kind **3** *There was a wicked gleam in his eye.*
▶ mischievous, playful, rascally, impish, devilish, cheeky **4** (informal) *He makes a wicked fruit salad.* ▶ excellent, marvellous, wonderful, superb AN OPPOSITE IS lousy

wickedness NOUN *the sheer wickedness of their plan* ▶ evil , enormity, iniquity, vileness, baseness, foulness, heinousness, immorality, infamy, sinfulness, villainy, turpitude, wrong, wrongdoing AN OPPOSITE IS goodness

wide ADJECTIVE **1** *The river was fast and wide. Players are spread over a wide area.* ▶ broad, expansive, extensive, vast, large, spacious, spread out, outspread AN OPPOSITE IS narrow **2** *There is a wide choice of dinner menu. The programs reach a wide audience.* ▶ extensive, comprehensive, wide-ranging, inclusive, all-embracing, broad, ample, universal OPPOSITES ARE narrow, limited **3** *Wide-legged pants became fashionable again.* ▶ baggy, loose, full, flared OPPOSITES ARE narrow, tight **4** *The shot went wide.* ▶ off course, off target, off the mark AN OPPOSITE IS on target

wide ADVERB *Her eyes opened wide.* ▶ fully, completely

widen VERB **1** *There are plans to widen parts of the highway.* ▶ broaden, make wider, expand, enlarge, extend, open out, spread, stretch AN OPPOSITE IS narrow **2** *Her smile widened.*
▶ broaden, become wider, spread AN

widespread ADJECTIVE existing in many places or over a wide area • *a widespread belief*

widow NOUN widows a woman whose husband has died

widowed ADJECTIVE made a widow or widower

widower NOUN widowers a man whose wife has died

width NOUN widths how wide something is; wideness

wield VERB wields, wielding, wielded **1** hold and use a weapon or tool • *wielding a sword* **2** have and use power or influence

wife NOUN wives the woman to whom a man is married [from Old English *wif* = woman]

wig NOUN wigs a covering for the head, made of real or artificial hair

wiggle VERB wiggles, wiggling, wiggled move from side to side

wigwam NOUN wigwams a tent formerly used by Native Americans, made by fastening skins or mats over poles

wild ADJECTIVE **1** living or growing in its natural state, not looked after by people **2** not cultivated • *a wild landscape* **3** not civilized • *the Wild West* **4** not controlled; very violent or excited **5** very foolish or unreasonable • *You do have wild ideas.*
▷ **wildly** ADVERB **wildness** NOUN

wilderness NOUN wildernesses a wild uncultivated area; a desert

wildfire NOUN
spread like wildfire (said about rumors etc.) spread very fast

wildlife NOUN wild animals in their natural setting

willful ADJECTIVE **1** obstinately determined to do what you want • *a willful child* **2** deliberate • *willful murder*
▷ **willfully** ADVERB **willfulness** NOUN

Thesaurus

OPPOSITE IS narrow **3** *They must widen the scope of the inquiry.* ► expand, extend, broaden, enlarge, increase OPPOSITES ARE narrow, restrict, limit

widespread ADJECTIVE **1** *These incidents provoked widespread protest.* ► general, extensive, universal, wholesale, far-reaching, global AN OPPOSITE IS uncommon **2** *Death and disease were widespread in these years.* ► rife, prevalent, endemic, pervasive, common

width NOUN *Two white lines should be drawn across the width of the road.* ► breadth, span, girth, diameter

wife NOUN *His new wife is from Paris.* ► spouse, partner, (*more formal*) consort, (*more informal*) woman, (*more informal*) mate, (*more informal*) better half

wiggle VERB *He removed his shoes and wiggled his toes.* ► wriggle, waggle, jiggle

wild ADJECTIVE **1** *He began attacking me like a wild animal.* ► fierce, feral, ferocious, untamed, undomesticated AN OPPOSITE IS tame **2** *There are many wild flowers that can be legally picked.* ► natural, uncultivated, indigenous AN OPPOSITE IS cultivated **3** *Even seemingly wild ideas may be aired at this point.* ► crazy, ridiculous, madcap, absurd, foolish, silly, outrageous, extravagant, impractical, rash, foolhardy OPPOSITES ARE sensible, practical **4** *A wild urge rose up inside her to tell everything.* ► reckless, rash, intense, extreme OPPOSITES ARE gentle, mild **5** *My father liked these wild people.* ► primitive, savage, barbarous, uncivilized, uncultured AN OPPOSITE IS civilized **6** *She said she was sorry for her wild behavior.* ► unruly, rowdy, violent, disorderly, uncontrolled, unrestrained, undisciplined,

unconstrained, unbridled OPPOSITES ARE calm, restrained **7** *The parties involve loud music and wild dancing.* ► lively, flamboyant, boisterous, exuberant, animated AN OPPOSITE IS restrained **8** *Don't plan to go out in really wild weather.* ► rough, stormy, tempestuous, blustery, foul, inclement AN OPPOSITE IS calm **9** *the beautiful wild scenery of the Southwest* ► rugged, rough, desolate, uncultivated, unpopulated, barren **10** *His team-mates were wild with joy.* ► excited, ecstatic, delirious, frantic, frenzied **11** *Without knowing the answer I decided to risk a wild guess.* ► arbitrary, random, haphazard, hit-or-miss AN OPPOSITE IS considered **12** (*informal*) *Being disturbed at this time made him wild.* ► furious, angry, enraged, irate, cross, livid, (*more informal*) hopping mad AN OPPOSITE IS pleased **13 wild about** (*informal*) *I'm not wild about the music.* ► keen on, enthusiastic about, (*informal*) mad about, (*informal*) crazy about

willful ADJECTIVE **1** *He was charged with willful damage and assault.* ► deliberate, intentional, premeditated, intended, planned, calculated, conscious, voluntary AN OPPOSITE IS accidental **2** *She checked her willful and impulsive self.* ► headstrong, self-willed, strong-willed, obstinate, stubborn, perverse, determined, dogged, intransigent, obdurate AN OPPOSITE IS amenable

will NOUN **1** *Corruption exists when politicians have lost the will to enforce the law.* ► determination, resolve, resolution, intention, purpose, aim, desire, inclination, volition, willpower, wish **2** *I don't think it's the will of the people.* ► desire, wish, choice,

a
b
c
d
e
f
g
h
i
j
k
l
m
n
o
p
q
r
s
t
u
v
w
x
y
z

will AUXILIARY VERB used to express the future tense, questions, or promises • *They will arrive soon.* • *Will you shut the door?* • *I will get my revenge.* [from Old English]
USAGE See the entry for **shall**.

will NOUN **wills 1** the mental power to decide and control what you do **2** a desire; a chosen decision • *I wrote the letter against my will.* **3** determination to do something • *They set to work with a will.* **4** a written statement of how a person's possessions are to be disposed of after his or her death
at will whenever you like • *You can come and go at will.*

will VERB **wills, willing, willed** use your will power; influence something by doing this • *I was willing you to win!* [from Old English *willa*]

willing ADJECTIVE ready and happy to do what is wanted
▷ **willingly** ADVERB **willingness** NOUN

willow NOUN **willows** a tree or shrub with flexible branches, usually growing near water

willpower NOUN strength of mind to control what you do

willy-nilly ADVERB whether you want to or not

wilt VERB **wilts, wilting, wilted** lose freshness or strength

wily (wy- lee) ADJECTIVE cunning or crafty
▷ **wiliness** NOUN

win VERB **wins, winning, won 1** defeat your opponents in a battle, game, or contest **2** get or achieve something by a victory or by using effort or skill, etc. • *She won the prize.*
win over gain someone's favor or support
• *By the end he had won over the audience.*

win NOUN **wins** a victory

wince VERB **winces, wincing, winced** make a slight movement because of pain or embarrassment etc.

wind[1] (rhymes with *tinned*) NOUN **winds 1** a current of air **2** gas in the stomach or intestines that makes you feel uncomfortable **3** breath used for a purpose, e.g., for running or speaking **4** the wind instruments of an orchestra
get or **have the wind up** (*informal*) feel frightened
get wind of hear a rumor of something

wind VERB **winds, winding, winded** put a person out of breath • *The climb had winded us.*

wind[2] (rhymes with *find*) VERB **winds, winding, wound 1** go or turn something in twists, curves, or circles **2** make a clock or watch work by tightening its spring
▷ **winder** NOUN

Thesaurus

preference **3** *She had died without making a will.* ► testament, last wishes

will VERB **1** *He willed them not to panic.*
► encourage, inspire, influence, wish **2** *She willed her money equally to all her nephews and nieces.* ► bequeath, leave, pass on

willing ADJECTIVE **1** *Let us know if you are willing to make cakes or prepare sandwiches.*
► prepared, ready, disposed, agreeable, eager, inclined, content, pleased, (*more informal*) game OPPOSITES ARE unwilling, reluctant, disinclined **2** *You'd be surprised what can be achieved by willing hands eager to do good deeds.* ► enthusiastic, helpful, obliging, cooperative, amenable, compliant, consenting OPPOSITES ARE unwilling, unhelpful

wilt VERB **1** *The flowers had begun to wilt.*
► droop, fade, shrivel, wither, become limp, flop, languish, sag OPPOSITES ARE thrive, revive, perk up **2** *Their joy soon wilted.* ► fail, flag, wane, dwindle, evaporate, weaken, diminish, sink AN OPPOSITE IS grow

wily ADJECTIVE *He was constantly in danger of being outwitted by his wily opponents.* ► clever, crafty, shrewd, artful, astute, cunning, devious, guileful, knowing, scheming, shifty, foxy, sly, underhand AN OPPOSITE IS naive

win VERB **1** *She had a good chance of winning.*
► be victorious, be the winner, succeed,

triumph, come first, finish first, prevail, conquer, overcome AN OPPOSITE IS lose **2** *Next year they would win first prize.* ► achieve, receive, acquire, (*more informal*) carry off, (*more informal*) come away with, (*more informal*) pick up, (*more informal*) walk away with **3** *Charles II managed to win the support of the Scots.* ► gain, secure, obtain, earn, deserve, get

win NOUN *His win ended eleven years of domination of the championship.* ► victory, triumph, success, conquest AN OPPOSITE IS defeat

wind NOUN (rhymes with *pinned*) *She shivered in the chill wind.* ► breeze, air current, gust, blast, puff, breath, draught, gale, squall

wind VERB (rhymes with *mind*) **1** *He wound the cord tightly.* ► coil, loop, twist, twine, curl, curve, furl, turn, roll **2** *The Saigon River begins to wind like a serpent.* ► twist, snake, bend, curve, meander, ramble, twist and turn, zigzag
wind up (*informal*) *We could wind up paying the whole lot.* ► end up, finish up, land up, find yourself
wind someone up (*informal*) *I'm sure he's just doing it to wind me up.* ► tease, annoy, disconcert, trick

A B C D E F G H I J K L M N O P Q R S T U V **W** X Y Z

wind up 1 make a clock or watch work by tightening its spring **2** close a business **3** (*informal*) end up in a place or condition • *He wound up in jail.*

windfall NOUN **windfalls 1** a piece of unexpected good luck, especially a sum of money **2** a fruit blown off a tree by the wind

wind instrument NOUN **wind instruments** a musical instrument played by blowing, e.g., a trumpet

windmill NOUN **windmills** a mill worked by the wind turning its sails

window NOUN **windows 1** an opening in a wall or roof, etc., to let in light and often air, usually filled with glass **2** the glass in this opening **3** (in computing) an area on a VDU screen used for a particular purpose [from Old Norse *vind* = wind, air + *auga* = eye]

windpipe NOUN **windpipes** the tube by which air passes from the throat to the lungs

windscreen NOUN **windscreens** the window at the front of a motor vehicle

windsurfing NOUN surfing on a board that has a sail fixed to it
▷ **windsurfer** NOUN

windy ADJECTIVE with much wind • *It's windy outside.*

wine NOUN **wines 1** an alcoholic drink made from grapes or other plants **2** a dark red color

wing NOUN **wings 1** one of the pair of parts used by a bird, bat, or insect for flying **2** one of the pair of long flat parts that stick out from the side of an airplane and support it while it flies **3** a part of a large building that extends from the main part **4** the part of a motor vehicle's body above a wheel **5** a player whose place is at one of the far ends of the forward line in football or hockey, etc. **6** a section of a political party, with more extreme opinions than the others

on the wing flying
take wing fly away
under your wing under your protection
the wings the sides of a theater stage out of sight of the audience

wing VERB **wings, winging, winged 1** fly; travel by means of wings • *The bird winged its way home.* **2** wound a bird in the wing or a person in the arm

winged ADJECTIVE having wings

wink VERB **winks, winking, winked 1** close and open your eye quickly, especially as a signal to someone **2** (said about a light) flicker or twinkle

wink NOUN **winks 1** the action of winking **2** a very short period of sleep • *I didn't sleep a wink.*

winkle VERB **winkles, winkling, winkled winkle out** extract or obtain something with difficulty • *I managed to winkle out some information.*

winner NOUN **winners 1** a person or animal etc. that wins **2** something very successful • *Her latest book is a winner.*

winnings PLURAL NOUN money won

winter NOUN **winters** the coldest season of the year, between autumn and spring
▷ **wintry** ADJECTIVE

wipe VERB **wipes, wiping, wiped** dry or clean something by rubbing it
▷ **wipe** NOUN
wipe out 1 cancel • *wipe out the debt* **2** destroy something completely

wiper NOUN **wipers** a device for wiping something, especially on a vehicle's windscreen

wire NOUN **wires 1** a strand or thin flexible rod of metal **2** a piece of wire used to carry electric current **3** a fence, etc., made from wire **4** a telegram

Thesaurus

windy ADJECTIVE **1** *It was too cold and windy to sit and wait.* ► blowy, breezy, blustery, gusty, squally, boisterous, draughty, stormy AN OPPOSITE IS calm

wing NOUN **1** *The maternity ward is in the north wing of the hospital.* ► section, annex, end, extension **2** *the military wing of the organization* ► section, faction, branch, group

wink VERB *The red light winked.* ► flash, gleam, flicker, sparkle, twinkle

wink NOUN *Then, in a wink, it all turned to dust.* ► instant, moment, second, flash

winner NOUN *The points system produces an overall winner.* ► victor, champion, conqueror, first, prizewinner AN OPPOSITE IS loser

winning ADJECTIVE **1** *For the fourth time she was on the winning side.* ► victorious, successful,

triumphant, champion, conquering, prevailing, leading, top-scoring AN OPPOSITE IS losing **2** *The show lacks a really winning song.* ► appealing, attractive, fetching, charming, engaging

winnings NOUN *She used part of her winnings to buy a new house.* ► prize money, gains, money AN OPPOSITE IS losses

wintry ADJECTIVE *He opened a window, letting in damp wintry air.* ► chilly, frosty, cold, bleak, freezing, icy, biting, snowy

wipe VERB *She wiped the table with a damp cloth. Nathan wiped the crumbs from his mouth.* ► rub, brush, clean, mop, sponge, swab, wash

wipe out *Two hurricanes almost wiped out the flourishing egg industry.* ► destroy, obliterate, annihilate, eradicate, exterminate, demolish

a b c d e f g h i j k l m n o p q r s t u v **w** x y z

A
B
C
D
E
F
G
H
I
J
K
L
M
N
O
P
Q
R
S
T
U
V
W
X
Y
Z

wire VERB wires, wiring, wired **1** fasten or strengthen something with wire **2** fit or connect something with wires to carry electric current

wireless NOUN wirelesses (old use) a radio

wiring NOUN the system of wires carrying electricity in a building or in a device

wiry ADJECTIVE **1** like wire **2** lean and strong

wisdom NOUN **1** being wise **2** wise sayings or writings

wisdom tooth NOUN wisdom teeth a molar tooth that may grow at the back of the jaw of a person aged about 20 or more

wise ADJECTIVE knowing or understanding many things, and making good judgments
▷ **wisely** ADVERB

wish VERB wishes, wishing, wished **1** feel or say that you would like to have or do something or would like something to happen **2** say that you hope someone will get something • Wish me luck!

wish NOUN wishes **1** something you wish for; a desire **2** the action of wishing • Make a wish when you blow out the candles.

wishbone NOUN wishbones a forked bone between the neck and breast of a chicken or other bird

wishful thinking NOUN believing something because you want it to be true rather than because it is likely

wisp NOUN wisps **1** a few strands of hair or bits of straw etc. **2** a small streak of smoke or cloud, etc.
▷ **wispy** ADJECTIVE

wistful ADJECTIVE sadly longing for something
▷ **wistfully** ADVERB **wistfulness** NOUN

wit NOUN wits **1** intelligence or cleverness • Use your wits. **2** a clever kind of humor **3** a witty person
at your wits' end not knowing what to do
keep your wits about you stay alert

witch NOUN witches a person, especially a woman, who uses magic to do things

witchcraft NOUN the use of magic, especially for evil purposes

witch hunt NOUN witch hunts a campaign to find and punish people who hold views that are considered to be unacceptable or dangerous

with PREPOSITION used to indicate **1** being in the company or care of (Come with me), **2** having (a man with a beard), **3** using (Hit it with a hammer), **4** because of (shaking with laughter), **5** feeling or showing (We heard it with pleasure), **6** towards or concerning (I was angry with him), **7** in opposition to; against (Don't argue with your father), **8** being separated from (We had to part with it)

withdraw VERB withdraws, withdrawing, withdrew, withdrawn **1** take back or away; remove • She withdrew money from the bank.

Thesaurus

---

wisdom NOUN He would persuade them of the wisdom of adopting this course. ► sense, prudence, common sense, good sense, intelligence, judgement, astuteness, sagacity, discernment, insight, reason

wise ADJECTIVE **1** Wise parents are able to give support and advice. ► sensible, prudent, shrewd, perceptive, intelligent, sagacious, sage, clever, astute, informed, judicious, discerning, enlightened OPPOSITES ARE unwise, foolish **2** The action they took seemed wise and reasonable. ► sensible, prudent, advisable, appropriate, proper, fair, just, right, sound OPPOSITES ARE unwise, foolish, ill-advised

wish NOUN **1** It was her parents' dearest wish that she should be happy. ► desire, ambition, objective, want, longing, inclination, aim, aspiration, craving, fancy, hankering, hope, yearning **2** He had no wish to appear impolite. ► desire, inclination **3** We will respect your wishes. ► request, bidding, direction, will, order

wish VERB If guests wish to eat out there are several restaurants in the village. ► want, hope

wish for I wish for a really good night's sleep. ► desire, want, long for, yearn for, crave, fancy, hanker after

wit NOUN **1** The speech was improved by moments of great wit. ► humor, wittiness, banter, repartee, drollery, badinage, facetiousness, ingenuity, comedy, jokes **2** Jack was regarded as the club wit. ► joker, comedian, wag, comic, humorist, jester **3** She was a woman of great wit and wisdom. ► intelligence, shrewdness, wisdom, cleverness, sense, understanding

witch NOUN **1** She must look for the witch's hat. ► sorceress, enchantress **2** What are you talking about, you stupid witch? ► hag, crone, harpy

withdraw VERB **1** She withdrew the photo abruptly and returned it to the folder. ► take back, remove, snatch **2** All the objections were eventually withdrawn. ► retract, rescind, revoke, take back, cancel, remove, disclaim, renounce, take away AN OPPOSITE IS introduce **3** The rebels were forced to withdraw into the hills. ► retreat, retire, draw back, move back, fall back AN OPPOSITE IS advance **4** One of the representatives decided to withdraw from future discussions. ► pull out, back out, drop out,

2 go away from a place or people • *The troops withdrew from the frontier.*

withdrawal NOUN **withdrawals 1** taking something out, especially money from a bank **2** the process of stopping taking addictive drugs • *withdrawal symptoms*

withdrawn ADJECTIVE very shy or reserved

wither VERB **withers, withering, withered 1** shrivel or wilt **2** make something shrivel or wilt

USAGE Do not confuse with **whither**.

withering ADJECTIVE scornful or sarcastic • *a withering remark*

withhold VERB **withholds, withholding, withheld** refuse to give or allow information or permission

within PREPOSITION, ADVERB inside; not beyond something

without PREPOSITION **1** not having • *without food* **2** free from • *without fear* **3** (old use) outside • *without the city wall*

without ADVERB (old use) outside • *We looked at the house from within and without.*

withstand VERB **withstands, withstanding, withstood** endure something successfully; resist

witness NOUN **witnesses 1** a person who sees or hears something happen • *There were no witnesses to the accident.* **2** a person who gives evidence in a lawcourt

witness VERB **witnesses, witnessing, witnessed 1** be a witness of something • *Did anyone witness the accident?* **2** sign a document to confirm that it is genuine

witticism NOUN **witticisms** a witty remark

witty ADJECTIVE **wittier, wittiest** clever and amusing; full of wit
▷ **wittily** ADVERB **wittiness** NOUN

wizard NOUN **wizards 1** a male witch; a magician **2** a person with amazing abilities
▷ **wizardry** NOUN

wobble VERB **wobbles, wobbling, wobbled** move unsteadily from side to side; shake slightly
▷ **wobble** NOUN **wobbly** ADJECTIVE

woe NOUN **woes 1** sorrow **2** misfortune
▷ **woeful** ADJECTIVE **woefully** ADVERB

woebegone ADJECTIVE looking unhappy

wok NOUN **woks** a Chinese cooking pan shaped like a large bowl [from Chinese]

wolf NOUN **wolves** a fierce wild animal of the dog family, often hunting in packs

wolf VERB **wolfs, wolfing, wolfed** eat something greedily

woman NOUN **women** a grown-up female human being
▷ **womanhood** NOUN
[from Old English]

womanly ADJECTIVE having qualities that are thought to be typical of women

womb (woom) NOUN **wombs** the hollow organ in a female's body where babies develop before they are born

women's lib or **women**'s liberation NOUN the freedom of women to have the same rights, opportunities, and status as men

Thesaurus

secede, (more informal) cry off AN OPPOSITE IS enter

wither VERB *The flowers had withered in the strong sun.* ► wilt, droop, become limp, dehydrate, dry up, sag, shrivel, waste away, flag, flop AN OPPOSITE IS thrive

withhold VERB *He had deliberately withheld the fact that he couldn't sail.* ► suppress, repress, conceal, hide, hold back, keep back, keep secret, retain

withstand VERB *The boat must be strong enough to withstand the roughest weather.* ► resist, endure, hold out against, last out against, bear up against, stand up to, survive, tolerate, brave, cope with AN OPPOSITE IS succumb to

witness NOUN *The only witness was the office cleaner.* ► observer, bystander, onlooker, spectator, eyewitness, watcher

witness VERB *He said he has witnessed several instances of police brutality.* ► see, observe, be present at, be a witness to, notice, view, watch, attend, behold, look on

witty ADJECTIVE *Dolly is witty and entertaining.* ► humorous, amusing, funny, quick-witted, sharp-witted, waggish, droll, comic, facetious, sparkling AN OPPOSITE IS dull

wizard NOUN **1** *We were still under the wizard's spell.* ► magician, sorcerer, enchanter, warlock **2** *He's an absolute wizard with engines.* ► expert, genius, adept, master, (more informal) star

wobble VERB **1** *She reached out and caught it without so much as wobbling.* ► shake, sway, teeter, totter, be unsteady, oscillate, quake **2** *Once more the glass wobbled.* ► tremble, shake, quiver, vibrate, rock

wobbly ADJECTIVE **1** *The table had a wobbly leg.* ► unsteady, loose, rickety, rocky, unstable, shaky, insecure, unbalanced, unsafe AN OPPOSITE IS steady **2** *He felt wobbly and had to sit down.* ► giddy, dizzy, faint, groggy, unsteady

woman NOUN *The car pulled up and a woman got out.* ► female, lady, girl RELATED ADJECTIVES ► female, feminine

wonder NOUN wonders **1** a feeling of surprise and admiration or curiosity **2** something that causes this feeling; a marvel
no wonder it is not surprising

wonder VERB wonders, wondering, wondered **1** feel that you want to know; try to decide ● *We are still wondering what to do next.* **2** feel wonder

wonderful ADJECTIVE marvelous or excellent
▷ **wonderfully** ADVERB

won't (*mainly spoken*) will not

woo VERB woos, wooing, wooed (*old use*) **1** court a woman **2** seek someone's favor or support
▷ **wooer** NOUN

wood NOUN woods **1** the substance of which trees are made **2** many trees growing close together

wooded ADJECTIVE covered with growing trees

wooden ADJECTIVE **1** made of wood **2** stiff and showing no expression or liveliness
▷ **woodenly** ADVERB

woodlouse NOUN woodlice a small crawling creature with seven pairs of legs, living in rotten wood or damp soil, etc.

woodpecker NOUN woodpeckers a bird that taps tree trunks with its beak to find insects

woodwind NOUN wind instruments that are usually made of wood, e.g., the clarinet and oboe

woodwork NOUN **1** making things out of wood **2** things made out of wood

woodworm NOUN woodworms the larva of a kind of beetle that bores into wood; the damage done by this

woody ADJECTIVE **1** like wood; consisting of wood **2** full of trees

wool NOUN wools **1** the thick soft hair of sheep and goats, etc. **2** thread or cloth made from this

woolen ADJECTIVE made of wool

woolly ADJECTIVE **1** covered with wool or wool-like hair **2** like wool; woollen **3** not thinking clearly; vague or confused ● *woolly ideas*
▷ **woolliness** NOUN

word NOUN words **1** a set of sounds or letters that has a meaning, and when written or printed has no spaces between the letters **2** a brief conversation ● *Can I have a word with you?* **3** a promise ● *He kept his word.* **4** a command or spoken signal ● *Run when I give the word.* **5** a message; information ● *We sent word of our safe arrival.*
have words quarrel
word for word in exactly the same words

word VERB words, wording, worded express something in words ● *Word the question carefully.*

word class NOUN word classes any of the groups (also called **parts of speech**) into which

Thesaurus

wonder NOUN **1** *We were speechless with wonder.* ► awe, admiration, amazement, wonderment, astonishment, fascination, respect, reverence, surprise **2** *a wonder of nature* ► marvel, miracle, sensation, spectacle, prodigy **3** *It's a wonder there were no casualties.* ► marvel, miracle, extraordinary thing

wonder VERB *I was beginning to wonder if they would ever come.* ► ponder, speculate, ask yourself, be curious about, reflect on
wonder at *We wondered at such bravery.* ► marvel at, admire, be amazed by, feel wonder at, stand in awe of

wonderful ADJECTIVE *We had a wonderful time.* ► excellent, marvelous, fantastic, splendid, lovely, delightful, (*more informal*) terrific OPPOSITES ARE awful, dreadful

wood NOUN **1** *There is a nature trail through the wood.* ► forest, woodland, woods, trees, coppice, copse, thicket, grove, spinney RELATED ADJECTIVE ► sylvan **2** *a little cabin made from wood* ► timber, planks, planking, lumber RELATED ADJECTIVE ► ligneous

wooded ADJECTIVE *a wooded valley* ► tree-covered, forested, afforested, woody, timbered, (*poetic*) sylvan

wooden ADJECTIVE **1** *wooden furniture* ► timber, wood **2** *The acting and production were wooden.* ► stiff, unnatural, stilted, lifeless, leaden, deadpan, emotionless, unemotional, expressionless, awkward, clumsy, graceless AN OPPOSITE IS lively

woolly ADJECTIVE **1** *a woolly hat* ► woolen, wool, fleecy **2** *a sheep's woolly coat* ► fleecy, furry, downy, fuzzy, hairy, shaggy, soft **3** *woolly thinking* ► vague, ill-defined, unfocused, unclear, imprecise, confused, muddled, blurry, hazy, foggy

word NOUN **1** *She wanted to find another word for "chuckle."* ► expression, term, locution RELATED ADJECTIVES ► verbal, lexical **2** *Have you had any word from the hospital?* ► news, information, communication, report, comment, advice **3** *I'll have a word with them in private.* ► talk, conversation, chat, discussion, consultation, exchange of views, tête-à-tête USAGE Note that *tête-à-tête* is normally used about a personal conversation between two people. **4** *I gave her my word.* ► promise, guarantee, pledge, assurance, word of honor, oath

word VERB *The book has advice on how to word your CV.* ► phrase, express, construct, formulate, frame, couch, write, say, put words are divided in grammar (noun, pronoun, adjective, verb, adverb, preposition, conjunction, and interjection)

wording NOUN the way something is worded

word of honor NOUN a solemn promise

word perfect ADJECTIVE having memorized every word perfectly ● He was word perfect at the rehearsal.

word processor NOUN word processors a type of computer or program used for editing and printing letters and documents

wordy ADJECTIVE using too many words; not concise

wore past tense of wear

work NOUN works **1** something you have to do that needs effort or energy ● Digging is hard work. **2** a job; employment **3** something produced by work ● The teacher marked our work. **4** (in science) the result of applying a force to move an object **5** a piece of writing, painting, music, etc. ● the works of William Shakespeare
at work working
out of work having no work; unable to find paid employment

work VERB works, working, worked **1** do work **2** have a job; be employed ● She works in a bank **3** act or operate correctly or successfully ● Is the lift working? **4** make something act; operate ● Can you work the lift? **5** shape or press etc. ● Work the mixture into a paste. **6** gradually move into a particular position or state ● The screw had worked loose.
work out **1** find an answer by thinking or calculating **2** have a particular result
work up make people become excited; arouse

workable ADJECTIVE that can be used or will work

worker NOUN workers **1** a person who works **2** a member of the working class **3** a bee or ant etc. that does the work in a hive or colony but does not produce eggs

workforce NOUN workforces the number of people who work in a particular factory, industry, country, etc.

working class NOUN working classes people who work for wages, especially in manual or industrial work

Thesaurus

wording NOUN The wording of the contract was unclear. ▶ phrasing, phraseology, language, choice of words, mode of expression, terminology, style, diction

wordy ADJECTIVE a wordy essay; a wordy speaker ▶ long-winded, verbose, diffuse, rambling, repetitious, protracted, prolix, garrulous, loquacious, talkative OPPOSITES ARE brief , succinct USAGE You would normally use the last three synonyms about a person.

work NOUN **1** The plastering will be several days' work. ▶ labor, effort, exertion, toil, industry **2** Stella's looking for work abroad.
▶ employment, a job, an occupation, a career, business **3** He had finished all his work by lunchtime. ▶ tasks, jobs, assignments, projects, commissions **4** He has written a new work for mixed choir. ▶ composition, piece, opus, oeuvre, production **5** It is a fine literary work. ▶ creation, achievement, accomplishment

work VERB **1** Some staff were still working at nine in the evening. ▶ labor, toil, exert yourself, be at your desk, slave, (more informal) keep at it AN OPPOSITE IS rest **2** Margaret works in a bank. ▶ have a job, be employed, earn a living **3** The dishwasher was working again, thank goodness. ▶ function, operate, perform, run, in working order, (more informal) behave AN OPPOSITE IS break down **4** He showed me how to work the coffee machine. ▶ operate, use, manipulate **5** The plan had worked. ▶ succeed, be successful, work out, take effect, (more informal) pay off, (more informal) do the trick

AN OPPOSITE IS fail **6** farmers who work the land ▶ cultivate, till, dig, farm **7** You can work miracles with the right ingredients. ▶ achieve, accomplish, produce, perform, bring about, cause, (more informal) pull off **8** Work the mixture into a thick dough. ▶ knead, form, mold, mix, blend, stir, shape

work out **1** The idea should work out. ▶ succeed, be successful, work, (more informal) pay off, (more informal) do the trick AN OPPOSITE IS fail **2** Things didn't quite work out as expected. ▶ turn out, occur, happen, evolve, develop, end up, come out

work out at The cost worked out at over a million dollars. ▶ amount to, add up to, come to, total, reach

work something out **1** Let's work out a plan. ▶ devise, draw up, formulate, prepare, put together **2** I can't work out the answer. ▶ calculate, determine, reckon up, resolve, solve **3** We're trying to work out what all this means. ▶ understand, comprehend, make sense of, puzzle out, figure out, clear up

work up It's hard to work up any enthusiasm. ▶ raise, rouse, generate, stimulate, stir up

worker NOUN **1** A strike by clerical workers brought the system to a standstill. ▶ employee, member of staff, operative, working person **2** She was a tireless worker for the party. ▶ laborer, campaigner, supporter

working ADJECTIVE **1** extra support for working mothers ▶ employed, in work, salaried, waged AN OPPOSITE IS unemployed **2** a working model of a steam engine ▶ functioning, operational,

workman NOUN **workmen** a man employed to do manual labor

workmanship NOUN a person's skill in working; the result of this

work of art NOUN **works of art** a fine picture, building, etc.

workout NOUN **workouts** a session of physical exercise or training

works PLURAL NOUN **1** the moving parts of a machine **2** a factory or industrial site

workshop NOUN **workshops** a place where things are made or mended

world NOUN **worlds** **1** the earth with all its countries and peoples **2** all the people on the earth; everyone • *He felt that the world was against him.* **3** a planet • *creatures from another world* **4** everything to do with a certain subject or activity • *the world of sport* **5** a very great amount • *It will do him a world of good.*

worldwide ADJECTIVE & ADVERB over the whole world

World Wide Web NOUN an international information system that connects related sites and documents which can be accessed using the Internet

worm NOUN **worms** **1** a small animal with a long thin soft body **2** (*informal*) an unpleasant person
▷ **wormy** ADJECTIVE

worm VERB **worms, worming, wormed** move along by wriggling or crawling
worm out gradually get someone to tell you something by constantly and cleverly questioning them • *We eventually managed to worm the truth out of them.*

worn past participle of **wear**

worn-out ADJECTIVE **1** exhausted **2** damaged by too much use

worried ADJECTIVE feeling or showing worry

worry VERB **worries, worrying, worried** **1** be troublesome to someone; make a person feel slightly afraid **2** feel anxious **3** hold something in the teeth and shake it • *The dog was worrying a rat.*
▷ **worrier** NOUN

worry NOUN **worries** **1** the condition of worrying; being uneasy **2** something that makes a person worry

worse ADJECTIVE, ADVERB more bad or more badly; less good or less well
worse off less fortunate or well off

Thesaurus

operating, running, usable, going, in use, in working order AN OPPOSITE IS nonfunctioning

workmanship NOUN *The quality of workmanship is of a high standard.*
▶ craftsmanship, artistry, handiwork, technique, expertise, skill

works NOUN **1** *Visitors can explore the glass works and blacksmith's shop.* ▶ factory, workshop, foundry, plant **2** *The works of the clock needed cleaning.* ▶ mechanism, movement, action, parts, machinery, insides

world NOUN **1** *The university has links with academic institutions around the world.* ▶ earth, globe, planet **2** *Representatives came from the world of high finance.* ▶ sphere, domain, field, area, realm, circle, milieu **3** *The world knows that these people need help.* ▶ everyone, everybody, people, humankind, humanity

worldly ADJECTIVE **1** *He had no ambitions for worldly power.* ▶ earthly, terrestrial, temporal, physical, material, materialistic, mundane, avaricious, greedy, selfish AN OPPOSITE IS spiritual **2** *She was worldly enough to understand what was going on.* ▶ sophisticated, experienced, worldly-wise, knowing AN OPPOSITE IS naive

worn ADJECTIVE *His coat was old and worn.*
▶ shabby, threadbare, tattered, frayed, worn out, moth-eaten, ragged, scruffy, (*more informal*) tatty AN OPPOSITE IS smart
worn out *By the time they got home they were all worn out.* ▶ exhausted, tired out, weary, fatigued, shattered, (*more informal*) dead tired, (*more informal*) played out, (*more informal*) washed out

worried ADJECTIVE **1** *She had a worried look on her face. You seem worried about something.*
▶ anxious, troubled, disturbed, uneasy, distraught, apprehensive, bothered, tense, strained, nervous **2** *I was worried that our money would run out.* ▶ afraid, fearful, concerned, frightened, scared

worry VERB **1** *Try not to worry Dad while he's working.* ▶ bother, pester, disturb, annoy **2** *I was trying not to worry.* ▶ be anxious, be troubled, be disturbed, fret, panic AN OPPOSITE IS be unconcerned **3** *Something was worrying her.* ▶ trouble, bother, disturb, distress, upset, concern

worry NOUN **1** *I was too affected by worry to concentrate on the work.* ▶ anxiety, agitation, apprehension, unease, distress, fear, misgiving, tension **2** *Each day seems to bring another worry.* ▶ problem, difficulty, trouble, concern, care, burden, misgiving

worrying ADJECTIVE *There was a worrying smell of gas.* ▶ alarming, disturbing, worrisome, disquieting, distressing, perturbing, troublesome AN OPPOSITE IS reassuring

worsen VERB **1** *Development of the site would worsen traffic problems.* ▶ aggravate, exacerbate, make worse, intensify, magnify, increase AN OPPOSITE IS improve **2** *The*

worship ➡ wrap

worship VERB worships, worshipping, worshipped **1** give praise or respect to God or a god **2** love or respect a person or thing greatly
▷ **worshipper** NOUN

worship NOUN worships **1** worshipping; religious ceremonies **2** a title of respect for a mayor or certain magistrates ● *His Worship the Mayor*

worst ADJECTIVE, ADVERB most bad or most badly; least good or least well

worth ADJECTIVE **1** having a certain value ● *This stamp is worth $100.* **2** deserving something; good or important enough for something ● *That book is worth reading.*

worth NOUN **1** value or usefulness **2** the amount that a certain sum will buy ● *a dollar's worth of stamps*

worthwhile ADJECTIVE important or good enough to deserve the time or effort needed ● *a worthwhile job*

worthy ADJECTIVE having great merit; deserving respect or support ● *a worthy cause*
▷ **worthiness** NOUN

worthy of deserving ● *This charity is worthy of your support.*

would AUXILIARY VERB **1** used as the past tense of **will**[1] (*We said we would do it.*), in questions (*Would you like to come?*) and in polite requests (*Would you come in, please?*) **2** used instead of **should** with I and we and the verbs **like**, **prefer** be glad, etc. (e.g., *I would like to come. We would be glad to help.*) **3** used of something to be expected (*That's just what he would do!*)
USAGE For sense 2, see the note on should 4.

would-be ADJECTIVE wanting or pretending to be ● *a would-be comedian*

wouldn't (*mainly spoken*) would not

wound (woond) NOUN wounds **1** an injury done by a cut, stab, or hit **2** an injury to a person's feelings

wound VERB wounds, wounding, wounded **1** cause a wound to a person or animal **2** hurt a person's feelings ● *She was wounded by these remarks.*

wound (wownd) *past tense of* **wind**[2]

wrap VERB wraps, wrapping, wrapped put paper or cloth, etc., around something as a covering
wrap up put on warm clothes

Thesaurus

economic situation was beginning to worsen.
► get *or* become worse, deteriorate, decline, degenerate, weaken, slide OPPOSITES ARE improve, recover

worship NOUN *Christianity forbade the worship of these deities.* ► adoration, veneration, reverence (for), adulation, exaltation, devotion (to), idolatry

worship VERB *They worshipped the sun as the giver of life.* ► revere, reverence, venerate, glorify, exalt, laud, pray to **2** *a materialistic society that worships consumer goods* ► idolize, revere, adore, dote on, be devoted to, look up to, love AN OPPOSITE IS despise

worth NOUN **1** *She knows her own worth.* ► value, merit, excellence, worthiness, quality, calibre, talents, strengths **2** *He was forced to sell the car for a fraction of its true worth.* ► value, cost, selling price

worthless ADJECTIVE **1** *The certificate turned out to be worthless.* ► valueless, of no value AN OPPOSITE IS valuable **2** *Their advice proved worthless.* ► useless, futile, ineffective, ineffectual, pointless OPPOSITES ARE useful, worthwhile*She regarded him as a worthless slob.* ► good-for-nothing, useless, contemptible, despicable, miserable, wretched, vile, (*more informal*) no-good AN OPPOSITE IS worthy

worthwhile ADJECTIVE **1** *I've never done anything worthwhile like writing a book.* ► useful, valuable, worthy, meaningful, significant, positive, productive, important,

invaluable OPPOSITES ARE worthless, useless **2** *It might be worthwhile to join a local archaeology society.* ► advantageous, beneficial, helpful, useful, profitable, rewarding OPPOSITES ARE pointless, useless

worthy ADJECTIVE **1** *Our support extends to worthy causes around the country.* ► worthwhile, praiseworthy, deserving, creditable, honorable, reputable, commendable, respectable, admirable OPPOSITES ARE unworthy, disreputable **2** *a worthy member of society* ► virtuous, honorable, honest, upright, moral, decent OPPOSITES ARE unworthy, disreputable **3** *worthy of The site yielded pottery worthy of study and publication.* ► deserving, meriting, warranting, good enough for

wound NOUN **1** *There was a deep wound in the animal's forehead.* ► injury, scar, gash, cut, abrasion, disfigurement, hurt **2** *She survived these wounds inflicted by fate.* ► blow, insult, trauma, slight, affront, hurt

wound VERB *He was trying to rescue a colleague who had been wounded.* ► injure, hurt, harm, maim, disable, damage, disfigure

wrap VERB **1** *She wrapped a rug around her legs.* ► fold, swathe, wind, pack, place **2** *Harry wrapped himself in a towel.* ► cover, swathe, envelop, sheathe, enfold **3** *I'll wrap the sandwiches in foil.* ► cover, pack, fold, enclose

A
B
C
D
E
F
G
H
I
J
K
L
M
N
O
P
Q
R
S
T
U
V
W
X
Y
Z

wrapper NOUN **wrappers** a piece of paper, etc., wrapped around something

wrapping NOUN **wrapping** paper or other material for wrapping things in

wreath (reeth) NOUN **wreaths 1** flowers or leaves fastened into a circle • *wreaths of holly* **2** a curving line of mist or smoke

wreathe (reeth) VERB **wreathes, wreathing, wreathed 1** surround or decorate something with a wreath **2** cover • *Their faces were wreathed in smiles.* **3** move in a curve • *Smoke wreathed upwards.*

wreck VERB **wrecks, wrecking, wrecked** damage or ruin something so badly that it cannot be used again

wreck NOUN **wrecks 1** a wrecked ship or building or car, etc. **2** a person who is in a very bad state • *a nervous wreck* **3** the wrecking of something

wreckage NOUN the pieces of a wreck

wren NOUN **wrens** a very small brown bird

wrench VERB **wrenches, wrenching, wrenched** twist or pull something violently

wrench NOUN **wrenches 1** a wrenching movement **2** pain caused by parting • *Leaving home was a great wrench.* **3** an adjustable tool rather like a spanner, used for gripping and turning bolts, nuts, etc.

wrestle VERB **wrestles, wrestling, wrestled 1** take part in a fight in which opponents grapple with each other and try to throw each other to the ground **2** struggle with a problem, etc.
▷ **wrestle** NOUN **wrestler** NOUN

wretch NOUN **wretches 1** a person who is very unhappy or who you pity **2** a person who is disliked

wretched ADJECTIVE **1** miserable or unhappy **2** of bad quality **3** not satisfactory; causing a nuisance • *This wretched car won't start.*
▷ **wretchedly** ADVERB **wretchedness** NOUN

wriggle VERB **wriggles, wriggling, wriggled** move with short twisting movements
▷ **wriggle** NOUN **wriggly** ADJECTIVE
wriggle out of avoid work or blame etc. cunningly

wring VERB **wrings, wringing, wrung 1** twist and squeeze a wet thing to get water out of it **2** squeeze something firmly or forcibly **3** get something by a great effort • *We wrung a promise out of him.*
▷ **wring** NOUN
wringing wet so wet that water can be squeezed out of it

wrinkle NOUN **wrinkles 1** a small furrow or ridge in the skin **2** a small crease in something

---

Thesaurus

wrapper NOUN *The chocolate bar had "extra value" printed on its wrapper.* ► wrapping, cover, packaging

wreck NOUN **1** *The wreck of an ancient gallery was discovered off Sicily.* ► wreckage, shipwreck, remains, hulk, skeleton **2** *It was the wreck of all their hopes.* ► ruin, destruction, undoing, demolition, devastation, overthrow, termination

wreck VERB **1** *The ship had been wrecked in a storm.* ► shipwreck, sink, destroy, break up **2** *He had wrecked his car when it skidded off the road.* ► crash, smash, demolish, shatter, crumple, crush, (*more informal*) write off **3** *A freak virus wrecked their holiday plans.* ► ruin, spoil, disrupt, undo, dash, put an end to

wreckage NOUN **1** *One person had to be cut from the wreckage by firemen.* ► wreck, debris, rubble, remains, ruin **2** *Wreckage from the aircraft was scattered for miles.* ► debris, fragments, remains, detritus, pieces, relics

wrench NOUN **1** *With a wrench he tore himself free.* ► jerk, jolt, pull, tug, twist, (*informal*) yank **2** *It was a wrench leaving the children behind with Polly.* ► trauma, painful experience

wrench VERB *Charlotte heard her wrench the door open.* ► pull, jerk, tug, force, prise, lever, wrest, (*informal*) yank

wretch NOUN **1** *He was a lonely, miserable wretch.* ► poor creature, down and out, beggar, pauper **2** *He had been mugged by some wretches in the park.* ► scoundrel, rogue, villain, rascal, delinquent

wretched ADJECTIVE **1** *She had seldom felt so tired or so wretched.* ► miserable, unhappy, sad, despondent, melancholy, cast down, unwell, poorly **2** *The weather was wretched all week. The family had to endure wretched living conditions.* ► atrocious, appalling, dreadful, dismal, bleak

wriggle VERB **1** *He wriggled further back on the bed till he was leaning up against the wall.* ► twist, writhe, squirm, waggle, wiggle, worm
wriggle out of *He tried to wriggle out of work, as usual.* ► avoid, shirk, dodge, evade, escape from

wring VERB **1** *He went to the sink to wring out the socks.* ► squeeze, twist, compress, crush, press **2** *They managed to wring more money out of the government.* ► extract, coerce, force, wrest, exact, extort **3** *The look on his face wrung her heart.* ► stab, tear, pierce, distress, pain, hurt

wrinkle NOUN *Despite being carefully ironed the shirt was full of wrinkles. The wrinkles on her neck moved when she swallowed.* ► crease, fold, pucker, crinkle, ridge, furrow, dimple, gather, line, pleat

washbasin NOUN washbasins a small sink for washing your hands, etc.

washer NOUN washers **1** a small ring of rubber or metal, etc., placed between two surfaces (e.g. under a bolt or screw) to fit them tightly together **2** a washing machine

washing NOUN clothes, etc., that need washing or have just been washed

washing machine NOUN washing machines a machine for washing clothes, etc.

wasn't (mainly spoken) was not

wasp NOUN wasps a stinging insect with black and yellow stripes around its body

wastage NOUN loss of something by waste

waste VERB wastes, wasting, wasted **1** use something in an extravagant way or without getting enough results **2** fail to use something • You are wasting a good opportunity. **3** become gradually weaker or thinner from lack of nourishment

waste ADJECTIVE **1** left over or thrown away because it is not wanted **2** not used; not usable • waste land
lay waste destroy the crops and buildings etc. of an area

waste NOUN wastes **1** wasting a thing, not using it well • a waste of time **2** things that

are not wanted or not used **3** an area of waste land • the wastes of the Sahara Desert
▷ **wasteful** ADJECTIVE **wastefully** ADVERB **wastefulness** NOUN
USAGE Do not confuse with **waist**.

watch VERB watches, watching, watched **1** look at a person or thing for some time **2** be on guard or ready for something to happen • Watch for the traffic lights to change. **3** pay careful attention to something • Watch where you put your feet. **4** take care of something • His job is to watch the sheep.
▷ **watcher** NOUN

watch NOUN watches **1** a device like a small clock, usually worn on the wrist **2** the action of watching **3** a turn of being on duty in a ship

watchful ADJECTIVE watching closely; alert
▷ **watchfully** ADVERB **watchfulness** NOUN

watchman NOUN watchmen a person employed to look after an empty building, etc., especially at night

watchtower NOUN watchtowers a tall tower used as an observation post

water NOUN waters **1** a colorless liquid that is a compound of hydrogen and oxygen **2** a lake or sea **3** the tide • at high water
pass water urinate

Thesaurus

washing NOUN Even the washing hanging from the windows seemed to be fluttering a welcome.
► laundry, clothes, wash

waste VERB He didn't want to waste money on a taxi fare. ► squander, fritter away, misspend, misuse, throw away, lavish, consume, exhaust, dissipate, use wastefully, use up AN OPPOSITE IS conserve
waste away Many people wasted away from disease and malnutrition. ► wither, become emaciated, become weaker, decline, pine, weaken AN OPPOSITE IS thrive

waste ADJECTIVE **1** Energy savings are achieved by recycling waste materials. ► unwanted, discarded, superfluous, unused, extra **2** There was a patch of waste ground for them to play on. ► bare, wild, empty, overgrown, barren, derelict, undeveloped, run-down, uncared for, uncultivated

waste NOUN **1** Sewage and industrial waste still enter the oceans. ► refuse, debris, effluent, garbage, dross, detritus, trash, junk, rubbish, litter, scraps **2** The trip had been a waste of time and money. ► squandering, misuse, frittering away, misspending, dissipation

wasteful ADJECTIVE a wasteful use of resources
► extravagant, prodigal, profligate,

spendthrift, lavish, reckless, thriftless, excessive, improvident, imprudent, uneconomical, needless AN OPPOSITE IS economical

watch NOUN **1** David checked the time by his new watch. ► wristwatch, pocket watch, timepiece, chronometer, clock, timer **2** One of us should keep watch at the back of the house. ► guard, vigil, lookout, surveillance, heed
on the watch Be on the watch for jellyfish.
► alert, vigilant, attentive

watch VERB **1** She watched him as he cleaned the room. ► look at, observe, keep your eyes on, contemplate, eye, gaze at, survey, heed, regard, see, stare at, take notice of, view, pay attention to, concentrate on, attend to, mark, note **2** We need someone to watch the children for a few hours. ► look after, mind, supervise, keep an eye on, keep watch on, care for, tend, guard, protect, safeguard, shield
watch out Watch out for snakes. ► look out for, be alert, be vigilant, be attentive, (more informal) keep an eye open for

water NOUN **1** a glass of water ► drinking water, tap water, mineral water **2** a picnic by the water ► river, lake, sea, ocean, loch, pond, pool RELATED ADJECTIVES ► aquatic, hydraulic

a
b
c
d
e
f
g
h
i
j
k
l
m
n
o
p
q
r
s
t
u
v
w
x
y
z

A
B
C
D
E
F
G
H
I
J
K
L
M
N
O
P
Q
R
S
T
U
V
W
X
Y
Z

water VERB waters, watering, watered
1 sprinkle or supply something with water
2 produce tears or saliva • *It makes my mouth water.*
water down dilute

watercolor NOUN watercolors **1** paint made with pigment and water (not oil) **2** a painting done with this kind of paint

waterfall NOUN waterfalls a place where a river or stream flows over the edge of a cliff or large rock

waterlogged ADJECTIVE completely soaked or swamped in water

waterproof ADJECTIVE that keeps out water
• *a waterproof jacket*
▷ **waterproof** VERB

waterskiing NOUN the sport of skimming over the surface of water on a pair of flat boards (**waterskis**) while being towed by a motor boat

watertight ADJECTIVE **1** made or fastened so that water cannot get in or out **2** so carefully put together that it cannot be changed or set aside or proved to be untrue • *a watertight excuse*

waterworks PLURAL NOUN a place with pumping machinery, etc., for supplying water to a district

watery ADJECTIVE **1** like water **2** full of water **3** containing too much water

watt NOUN watts a unit of electric power

wave NOUN waves **1** a ridge moving along the surface of the sea etc. or breaking on the shore **2** a curling piece of hair **3** (in science) the wave-like movement by which heat, light, sound, or electricity etc. travels **4** the action of waving

wave VERB waves, waving, waved **1** move your hand back and forth as a greeting or signal, etc. **2** move loosely back and forth or up and down **3** make a thing wavy **4** be wavy

wavelength NOUN wavelengths the size of a sound wave or electromagnetic wave

waver VERB wavers, wavering, wavered **1** be unsteady; move unsteadily **2** hesitate; be uncertain

wavy ADJECTIVE full of waves or curves
▷ **wavily** ADVERB **waviness** NOUN

wax NOUN waxes **1** a soft substance that melts easily, used to make candles, crayons, and polish **2** beeswax
▷ **waxy** ADJECTIVE

wax¹ VERB waxes, waxing, waxed coat or polish something with wax

wax² VERB waxes, waxing, waxed **1** (said about the moon) show a bright area that becomes gradually larger (The opposite is **wane**) **2** become stronger or more important

waxwork NOUN waxworks a model of a person, etc., made in wax

Thesaurus

water VERB *She went out to water the plants.*
▶ sprinkle, wet, moisten, dampen, hose, soak, douse, drench, flood, irrigate, souse
water something down *He asked her to water down his drink.* ▶ dilute, add water to, weaken, thin **2** *The proposals had to be watered down to stand any chance of success.*
▶ moderate, tone down, soften, mitigate, temper, mellow, weaken

waterfall NOUN *They looked down from the top of the waterfall.* ▶ cascade, cataract, shower, torrent, falls, rapids, chute

waterproof ADJECTIVE *a waterproof jacket*
▶ water-repellent, water-resistant, weatherproof, watertight, damp-proof, impermeable, impervious

watertight ADJECTIVE **1** *Use a watertight container.* ▶ sealed, hermetic, sound, waterproof AN OPPOSITE IS leaky **2** *a watertight excuse* ▶ foolproof, unassailable, flawless, conclusive, perfect AN OPPOSITE IS flawed

watery ADJECTIVE **1** *a bowl of watery soup* ▶ runny, sloppy, thin, watered down, weak, insipid, liquid, tasteless, (*more informal*) wishy-washy **2** *His eyes looked watery.* ▶ damp, moist, tear-filled, tearful, wet

wave NOUN **1** *Surfers were riding the waves.*
▶ breaker, roller, billow, crest, ridge, surf, white horse **2** *A wave of panic seemed to grip the crowd.* ▶ surge, upsurge, outbreak, current, flood, rash, sweep, stream, swell **3** *She gave a wave of her hand as he sped past.* ▶ gesture, shake, signal, flourish, gesticulation **4** *Her hair flowed in long waves.* ▶ curl, twist, kink

wave VERB **1** *Jill waved at us to go over.*
▶ beckon, gesture, signal, motion, indicate **2** *He waved his umbrella at them.* ▶ shake, brandish, flourish, waggle, wiggle, wag **3** *A flag waved in the breeze.* ▶ flap, flutter, ripple, quiver, move back and forth
wave aside *All these objections were waved aside.*
▶ dismiss, reject, disregard, ignore, discount, brush aside, shrug off

wavelength NOUN *Tune your radio to the right wavelength.* ▶ channel, station, waveband

waver VERB **1** *Her voice began to waver and she looked faint.* ▶ tremble, falter, quaver, quiver, become unsteady, change, quake, shake, shiver, shudder, sway, teeter, totter, wobble **2** *He could see I was wavering.* ▶ hesitate, be undecided, be indecisive, dither, equivocate, vacillate **3** *the wavering light from the candle* ▶ flicker, quiver, tremble, glimmer

wrinkle VERB **wrinkles, wrinkling, wrinkled** make wrinkles in something; form wrinkles

wrist NOUN **wrists** the joint that connects the hand and arm

wristwatch NOUN **wristwatches** a watch for wearing on the wrist

write VERB **writes, writing, wrote, written** **1** put letters or words, etc., on paper or another surface **2** be the author or composer of something **3** send a letter to somebody **4** (in computing) enter data into a computer memory
▷ **writer** NOUN
write off think something is lost or useless
write up write an account of something

writhe VERB **writhes, writhing, writhed** **1** twist your body because of pain **2** wriggle **3** suffer because of great shame

writing NOUN **writings** something you write; the way you write

wrong ADJECTIVE **1** incorrect; not true • *the wrong answer* **2** not fair or morally right • *It is wrong to cheat.* **3** not working properly • *There's something wrong with the engine.*
▷ **wrongly** ADVERB **wrongness** NOUN

wrong ADVERB wrongly • *You guessed wrong*

wrong NOUN **wrongs** something morally wrong; an injustice
in the wrong having done or said something wrong

wrong VERB **wrongs, wronging, wronged** do wrong to someone; treat a person unfairly

wry ADJECTIVE **wryer, wryest 1** slightly mocking or sarcastic • *a wry smile* **2** twisted or bent out of shape COMPARE **awry**
▷ **wryly** ADVERB **wryness** NOUN

Thesaurus

wrinkle VERB *You have to wrinkle your nose to break the spell.* ► crease, crinkle, pucker up, crumple, fold, furrow, ridge, rumple AN OPPOSITE IS smooth

wrinkled ADJECTIVE *His hands were white and very wrinkled.* ► creased, wrinkly, crinkly, crumpled, furrowed, shrivelled, lined, pleated, ridged, rumpled, wavy, wizened

write VERB **1** *He wrote the details in a notebook.* ► write down, jot down, take down, put down, record, transcribe, make a note of, note down, scribble, register **2** *After a while she stopped writing to him.* ► communicate (with), send letters, keep in touch **3** *The music was written one summer at the lakeside retreat.* ► compose, create, set down, compile, pen, draft
write off *He wrote off for a free voucher.* ► apply, send off, send away
write something off 1 *The government wrote off millions of dollars in unpaid taxes.* ► disregard, cancel, delete, annul **2** (informal)

writer NOUN *one of the great writers of the 20th century* ► author, novelist, dramatist, essayist, wordsmith

writhe VERB *I tossed and writhed on the hard bed.* ► wriggle, squirm, thrash about, toss, flail, struggle, twist, contort

writing NOUN **1** *Her writing is neater than mine.* ► handwriting, penmanship, calligraphy, script, letters, longhand, scribble, scrawl **2** *She took up writing in old age.* ► composition, literature, letters
writings *His political views are clearly reflected in his writings.* ► literary texts, literature, texts, works

wrong ADJECTIVE **1** *It was wrong to take the books without asking.* ► bad, dishonest, blameworthy, reprehensible, sinful, wicked AN OPPOSITE IS right **2** *The law lays down limits and it is wrong to exceed them.* ► unlawful, illegal, criminal, delinquent OPPOSITES ARE lawful, legal **3** *She knew she had given a wrong answer. The visitor pressed the wrong buzzer.* ► incorrect, erroneous, inaccurate, mistaken OPPOSITES ARE correct, right **4** *I must have said something wrong.* ► inappropriate, unsuitable, inapt, ill-advised, ill-judged, unfitting AN OPPOSITE IS appropriate **5** *There's something wrong with the equipment.* ► faulty, defective, amiss, broken down, out of order, unusable AN OPPOSITE IS right

wrong NOUN **1** *He had done many wrongs that needed putting right.* ► misdeed, bad deed, offense, crime, injury, injustice AN OPPOSITE IS good deed **2** *We know the difference between right and wrong.* ► immorality, badness, sinfulness, wickedness, evil OPPOSITES ARE goodness, virtue

wrong VERB *She was determined to forget the man who had wronged her.* ► mistreat, abuse, be unfair to, maltreat, ill-treat, treat unfairly, cheat, do an injustice to, harm, hurt, misrepresent, traduce

wrongful ADJECTIVE *She is claiming damages for wrongful dismissal.* ► unjust, unfair, unlawful, unjustified, unwarranted, undeserved, unreasonable, uncalled-for OPPOSITES ARE rightful, fair

wry ADJECTIVE **1** *Robbie sipped his drink and pulled a wry face.* ► twisted, distorted, contorted, crooked, uneven, bent **2** *Lawrence allowed himself a wry smile.* ► mocking, sardonic, derisive, dry, ironic, droll

a
b
c
d
e
f
g
h
i
j
k
l
m
n
o
p
q
r
s
t
u
v
w
x
y
z

775

Xmas NOUN (*informal*) Christmas

X-ray NOUN X-rays a photograph or examination of the inside of something, especially a part of the body, made by a kind of radiation (called X-rays) that can penetrate solid things

X-ray VERB X-rays, X-raying, X-rayed make an X-ray of something

xylophone (zy- lo- fohn) NOUN xylophones a musical instrument made of wooden bars that you hit with small hammers [from Greek *xylon* = wood + *phone* = sound]

Thesaurus

xenophobia NOUN *Feelings of xenophobia can so easily be whipped up.* ► nationalism, jingoism, racism

xenophobic ADJECTIVE *the triumphs of xenophobic right-wing parties* ► nationalistic, jingoistic, racist

A
B
C
D
E
F
G
H
I
J
K
L
M
N
O
P
Q
R
S
T
U
V
W
X
Y
Z

Yy

yacht (yot) NOUN **yachts 1** a sailing boat used for racing or cruising **2** a private ship
▷ **yachting** NOUN **yachtsman** NOUN **yachtswoman** NOUN
[from Dutch *jaghtschip* = fast pirate ship]

yak NOUN **yaks** an ox with long hair, found in central Asia [from Tibetan]

yank VERB **yanks, yanking, yanked** (*informal*) pull something strongly and suddenly
▷ **yank** NOUN

Yankee NOUN **Yankees** (*informal*) an American, especially of the northern U.S.

yap VERB **yaps, yapping, yapped** bark shrilly
▷ **yap** NOUN

yard[1] NOUN **yards 1** a measure of length, 36 inches or about 91 centimeters **2** a long pole stretched out from a mast to support a sail
[from Old English *gerd*]

yard[2] NOUN **yards** an enclosed area beside a building or used for a certain kind of work
● a timber *yard* [from Old English *geard*]

yarn NOUN **yarns 1** thread spun by twisting fibers together, used in knitting, etc.
2 (*informal*) a tale or story

yawn VERB **yawns, yawning, yawned 1** open the mouth wide and breathe in deeply when feeling sleepy or bored **2** form a wide opening ● *A pit yawned in front of us.*
▷ **yawn** NOUN

ye PRONOUN (old use) you (referring to two or more people)

year NOUN **years 1** the time the earth takes to go right around the sun, about 365 days **2** the time from January 1 to December 31;

any period of twelve months **3** a group of students of roughly the same age
▷ **yearly** ADJECTIVE, ADVERB

yearn VERB **yearns, yearning, yearned** long for something

yeast NOUN a substance that causes alcohol and carbon dioxide to form as it develops, used in making beer and wine and in baking bread, etc.

yell VERB **yells, yelling, yelled** give a loud cry; shout
▷ **yell** NOUN

yellow NOUN **yellows** the color of buttercups and ripe lemons

yellow ADJECTIVE **1** of yellow color **2** (*informal*) cowardly
▷ **yellowness** NOUN

yellow pages PLURAL NOUN a special telephone directory giving addresses and telephone numbers of businesses, arranged according to what services they provide

yelp VERB **yelps, yelping, yelped** give a shrill bark or cry
▷ **yelp** NOUN

yen[1] NOUN **yen** a unit of money in Japan [from Japanese *en* = round]

yen[2] NOUN **yens** a longing for something [from Chinese]

yes ADVERB used to agree to or accept something or as an answer meaning "I am here"

yesterday NOUN, ADVERB the day before today

yet ADVERB **1** up to this time; by this time ● *The post hasn't come yet.* **2** eventually ● *I'll get even with him yet!* **3** in addition; even ● *She became yet more excited.*

yet CONJUNCTION nevertheless ● *It is strange, yet it is true.*

yew NOUN **yews** an evergreen tree with dark green needlelike leaves and red berries

Thesaurus

yank VERB (*informal*) *He yanked the door open and stumbled inside.* ▶ pull, force, jerk, tug, wrench, prise, wrest

yap VERB *A dog yapped frantically somewhere inside.* ▶ yelp, bark, woof

yard NOUN *A pony stood in the middle of the yard.* ▶ court, courtyard, enclosure, quadrangle, (*more informal*) quad

yardstick NOUN *They regard the family as the yardstick to measure values by.* ▶ standard, criterion, benchmark, gauge, guideline, measure

yarn NOUN **1** *This is a lovely soft yarn.* ▶ thread, wool, fiber, strand, twine **2** (*informal*) *He rang with a yarn about problems at his hotel.* ▶ story, tale, rigmarole, anecdote, narrative

yearn VERB *They yearned to be home.* ▶ long, crave, pine, desire, hanker, wish

yearning NOUN *She had always had a yearning to play the piano.* ▶ longing, desire, craving, hankering, wish, (*more informal*) yen

yell VERB *He yelled at them to stop.* ▶ shout, cry out, call, shriek, scream, bawl, exclaim

yell NOUN *She gave a yell of pain.* ▶ cry, shriek, scream, screech

yelp VERB *He yelped with delight.* ▶ squeal, squawk, shriek, scream, howl, yell

yelp NOUN *The dog let out a yelp.* ▶ yap, bark, woof

a
b
c
d
e
f
g
h
i
j
k
l
m
n
o
p
q
r
s
t
u
v
w
x
y
z

yield VERB yields, yielding, yielded **1** give in or surrender **2** agree to do what is asked or ordered; give way ● *He yielded to persuasion.* **3** produce as a crop or as profit, etc.

yoga (yoh- ga) NOUN a Hindu system of meditation and self-control; a system of physical exercises based on this

yogurt (yog- ert) NOUN milk thickened by the action of certain bacteria, giving it a sharp taste [from Turkish]

yoke NOUN yokes **1** a curved piece of wood put across the necks of animals pulling a cart or plow, etc. **2** a shaped piece of wood fitted across a person's shoulders, with a pail or load hung at each end **3** a close-fitting upper part of a piece of clothing, from which the rest hangs

yoke VERB yokes, yoking, yoked harness or join things by means of a yoke [from Old English]
USAGE Do not confuse with **yolk**.

yolk (rhymes with *coke*) NOUN yolks the round yellow part inside an egg
USAGE Do not confuse with **yoke**.

yonder ADJECTIVE, ADVERB over there

you PRONOUN **1** the person or people being spoken to ● *Who are you?* **2** anyone or everyone; one ● *You can't tell what will happen next.*

young ADJECTIVE having lived or existed for only a short time; not old

youngster NOUN youngsters a young person; a child

your ADJECTIVE belonging to you
USAGE Do not confuse with **you're**.

you're (*mainly spoken*) you are
USAGE Do not confuse with **your**.

yours POSSESSIVE PRONOUN belonging to you
Yours faithfully, Yours sincerely ways of ending a letter before you sign it (*Yours faithfully* is more formal than *Yours sincerely*)
USAGE It is incorrect to write *your's*.

yourself PRONOUN yourselves you and nobody else

youth NOUN youths **1** being young; the time when you are young **2** a young man **3** young people
▷ **youthful** ADJECTIVE **youthfulness** NOUN

youth hostel NOUN youth hostels a place where young people can stay cheaply when they are hiking or on vacation

yo-yo NOUN yo-yos a round wooden or plastic toy that moves up and down on a string that you hold [probably from a language spoken in the Philippines]

Yule NOUN (*old use*) the Christmas festival, also called **Yuletide** [originally the name of a pagan festival: from Old English or Old Norse]

Thesaurus

---

yield VERB **1** *The contest continues until one side yields.* ► surrender, succumb, capitulate, submit, give in, give way, concede defeat, (*more informal*) cave in, (*informal*) throw in the towel **2** *The allotment yields a fine crop of root vegetables.* ► produce, grow, bear, supply **3** *an investment yielding a high interest* ► earn, generate, provide, return, pay, attract

yield NOUN **1** *The farm has produced a good yield.* ► crop, harvest, produce, product **2** *I'm looking for a savings bond with a high yield.* ► return, interest, earnings, income, profit

young ADJECTIVE **1** *She enjoyed working with young people.* ► youthful, juvenile, teenage, adolescent OPPOSITES ARE old, elderly **2** *They seem young for their age.* ► immature, childish, babyish AN OPPOSITE IS mature

young NOUN **1** *Parents have an instinct to protect their young.* ► offspring, family, progeny, brood, issue, litter **2 the young** *They enjoyed talking to the young.* ► young people, youths, youngsters, juveniles, minors RELATED ADJECTIVE ► juvenile

youth NOUN **1** *She had spent most of her youth abroad.* ► early life, early years, teenage years, adolescence, boyhood girlhood, childhood, infancy, (*informal*) teens **2** *a group of youths* ► young person, teenager, youngster, adolescent, boy girl, juvenile, (*more informal*) kid, (*more informal*) lad

youthful ADJECTIVE **1** *They sang before a youthful audience.* ► young **2** *He had a youthful appearance.* ► young-looking, fresh, lively, sprightly, vigorous, well-preserved

A B C D E F G H I J K L M N O P Q R S T U V W X Y Z